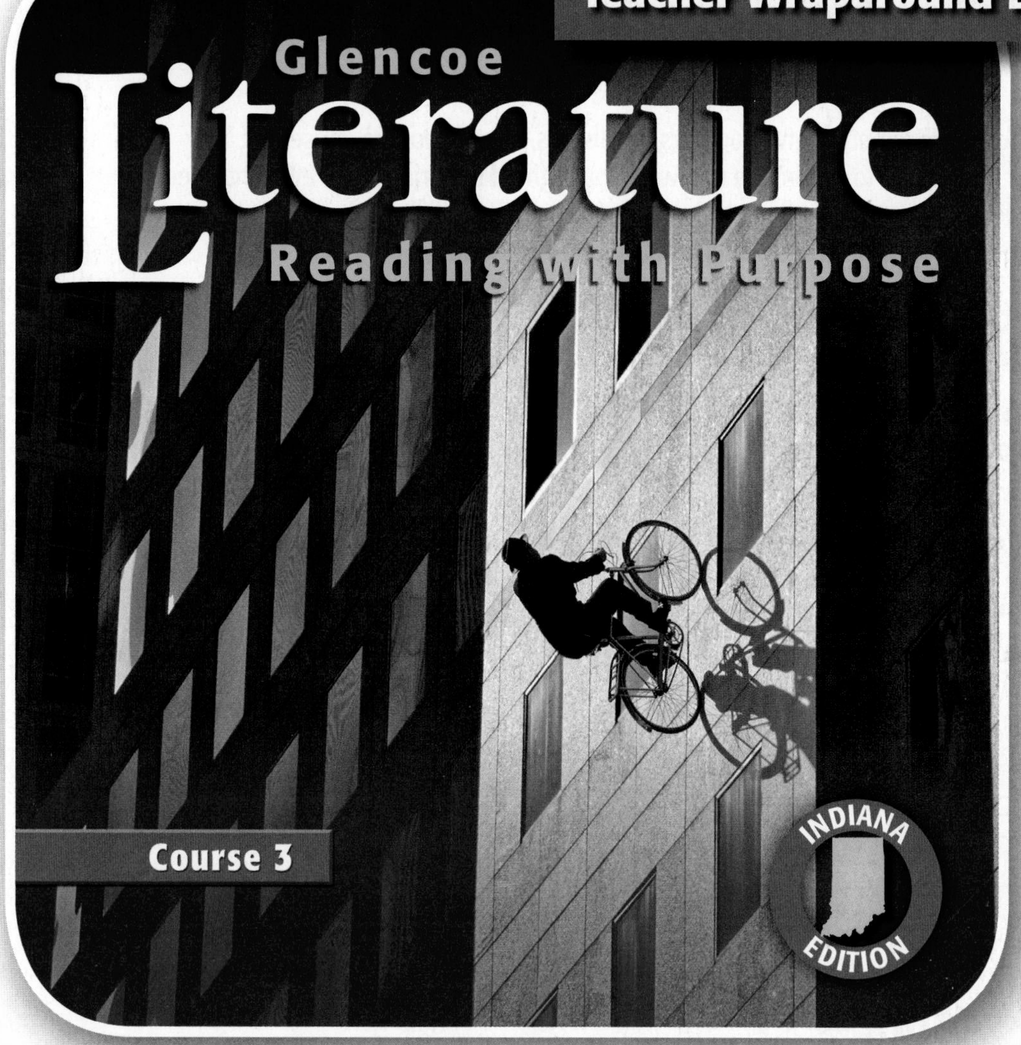

Program Consultants

Jeffrey D. Wilhelm, Ph.D.
Douglas Fisher, Ph.D.
Kathleen A. Hinchman, Ph.D.
David O'Brien, Ph.D.
Taffy Raphael, Ph.D.
Cynthia Hynd Shanahan, Ed.D.

Glencoe

New York, New York Columbus, Ohio Chicago, Illinois Woodland Hills, California

Acknowledgments

Grateful acknowledgment is given authors, publishers, photographers, museums, and agents for permission to reprint the following copyrighted material. Every effort has been made to determine copyright owners. In case of any omissions, the Publisher will be pleased to make suitable acknowledgments in future editions.

Acknowledgments continued on page R80.

Image Credits: T5 Indianapolis Motor Speedway, T6 Andre Jenny/ImageState, T7 Getty Images, T76 SuperStock

The McGraw·Hill Companies

Send all inquiries to:
Glencoe/McGraw-Hill
8787 Orion Place
Columbus, OH 43240-4027

ISBN-13 (student edition): 978-0-07-876430-1
ISBN-10 (student edition): 0-07-876430-0
ISBN-13 (teacher wraparound edition): 978-0-07-876433-2
ISBN-10 (teacher wraparound edition): 0-07-876433-5

Printed in the United States of America.

2 3 4 5 6 7 8 9 079/111 13 12 11 10 09 08 07

Program Consultants

Senior Program Consultants

Jeffrey D. Wilhelm, Ph.D. Jeffrey Wilhelm is Professor of English Education at Boise State University and Director of the Boise State Writing Project. He specializes in reading and adolescent literacy and does research on ways to engage readers and writers. A middle and high school teacher for thirteen years, Wilhelm is author or co-author of eleven books, including the award-winning works *You Gotta BE the Book* and *Reading Don't Fix No Chevys.*

Douglas Fisher, Ph.D. Douglas Fisher is Assistant Professor of Teacher Education and Director of Professional Development at San Diego State University. He is also Director of the award-winning City Heights Educational Pilot, a project for improving urban adolescent literacy. Fisher has published many articles on reading and literacy and has co-authored *Improving Adolescent Literacy: Strategies that Work.*

Program Consultants

Kathleen A. Hinchman, Ph.D. Kathleen Hinchman is Associate Professor and Chair in the Reading and Language Arts Department of Syracuse University. A former middle school English and reading teacher, Hinchman researches social perspectives toward literacy. She is co-author of three books on reading and literacy, including *Principled Practices of a Literate America: A Framework for Literacy and Learning in the Upper Grades.*

David G. O'Brien, Ph.D. David O'Brien is Professor of Literacy Education at the University of Minnesota and a former classroom teacher. O'Brien's research explores reading in content areas as well as ways to motivate learners to engage in school-based literacy tasks. He is conducting studies on the use of technology-based literacy, using computers and related technology.

Taffy Raphael, Ph.D. Taffy Raphael is Professor of Literacy Education at the University of Illinois at Chicago (UIC). She does literacy research on upper elementary and middle school students and has co-authored several books including *Book Club: A Literature-Based Curriculum* and *Book Club for Middle School.* She has received the International Reading Association (IRA) Outstanding Educator Award and is in the IRA Hall of Fame.

Cynthia Hynd Shanahan, Ed.D. Cynthia Hynd Shanahan is Professor in the Reading, Writing, and Literacy program at the University of Illinois at Chicago (UIC). She is also a consultant with the Center for Literacy at UIC. Hynd Shanahan has been a classroom teacher and has taught reading instruction to elementary-level through college-level teachers. She has authored a chapter in the book *Engaged Reading,* edited by John T. Guthrie and Donna Alverman.

Advisory Board

Special Consultants

FOLDABLES **Dinah Zike, Ed.D.** Dinah Zike was a classroom teacher and a consultant for many years before she began to develop Foldables™–a variety of easily created graphic organizers. Zike has written and developed more than 150 supplemental books and materials used in classrooms worldwide. Her *Big Book of Books and Activities* won the Teacher's Choice Award.

Mary A. Avalos, Ph.D. Mary Avalos is Assistant Professor and Director of the TESOL Graduate Program at the University of Miami, Coral Gables, Florida. Her contributions to TESOL books include "No Two Learners Are Alike: Readers with Linguistic and Cultural Differences," in *Reading Assessment and Instruction for All Learners,* by J. S. Schrum (ed.). Avalos is a frequent presenter at reading and TESOL conferences.

Glencoe National Reading and Language Arts Advisory Council

Wanda J. Blanchett, Ph.D.
Associate Dean for Academic Affairs and Associate Professor of Exceptional Education School of Education
University of Wisconsin-Milwaukee
Milwaukee, Wisconsin

William G. Brozo, Ph.D.
Professor of Literacy
Graduate School of Education, College of Education and Human Development
George Mason University
Fairfax, Virginia

Nancy Drew, Ed.D.
LaPointe Educational Consultants
Corpus Christi, Texas

Susan Floria-Ruane Ed.D.
Professor, College of Education
Michigan State University
Lansing, Michigan

Nancy Frey, Ph.D.
Associate Professor of Literacy in Teacher Education
School of Teacher Education
San Diego State University
San Diego, California

Kimberly Lawless, Ph.D.
Associate Professor
Curriculum, Instruction and Evaluation
College of Education
University of Illinois at Chicago
Chicago, Illinois

Sharon Fontenot O'Neal, Ph.D.
Associate Professor
Texas State University
San Marcos, Texas

William Ray, M.A.
Lincoln-Sudbury Regional High School
Sudbury, Massachusetts

Victoria Gentry Ridgeway, Ph.D.
Associate Professor
Reading Education
Clemson University
Clemson, South Carolina

Janet Saito-Furukawa, M.Ed.
Literacy Coach
Washington Irving Middle School
Los Angeles, California

Bonnie Valdes, M.Ed.
Independent Reading Consultant
CRISS Master Trainer
Largo, Florida

Indiana Teacher Reviewers

Angie Bitner-Weston
Seventh Grade Teacher, Language Arts
NorthWood Middle School
Wakarusa, Indiana

Heather Bontratger
Sixth Grade Teacher, Language Arts
NorthWood Middle School
Wakarusa, Indiana

Kristin Cramer
Seventh Grade Teacher, Language Arts
NorthWood Middle School
Wakarusa, Indiana

Alaina DePrez
Seventh Grade Literature and Language Arts Teacher
Doe Creek Middle School
New Palestine, Indiana

Fred Fox
Sixth Grade Teacher, Language Arts
Doe Creek Middle School
New Palestine, Indiana

Dina Koble
Eighth Grade Teacher, Language Arts
NorthWood Middle School
Wakarusa, Indiana

Carla Newcomer
Sixth Grade Teacher, Language Arts
NorthWood Middle School
Wakarusa, Indiana

Madelyn Russell
Eighth Grade Teacher, Literature
Thompkins Middle School
Evansville, Indiana

Brenda G. Scheidler
Supervisor of Language Arts/Reading
Evansville-Vanderburgh School Corporation
Evansville, Indiana

Indianapolis Motor Speedway

Teacher Wraparound Edition Overview

INDIANA EDITION

Research-Based Classroom Solution

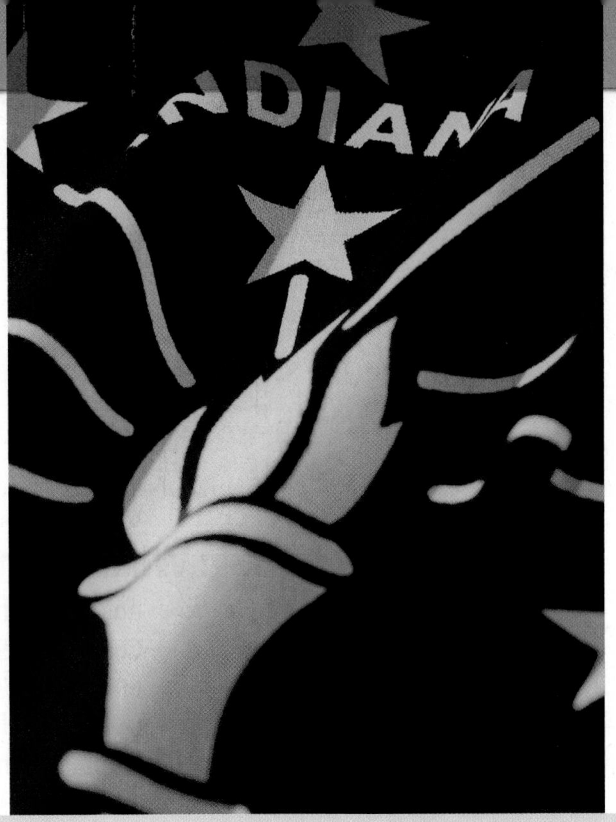

Instructional Planning

The Indiana Student Edition

Book Overview

Reference Section

Contents

UNIT 1

Reading: What's in It for You? 1

Genre Focus: Autobiography and Biography

Reading Skills Focus
Connecting
Setting a Purpose for Reading
Activating Prior Knowledge
Identifying Author's Purpose

Literary Elements
Description
Point of View
Tone
Cultural Reference

Vocabulary Skills
Context Clues

Grammar
Nouns
Pronouns
Verbs

UNIT 2

Genre Focus: Folktales

Reading Skills Focus
Analyzing
Making Inferences
Predicting
Comparing and Contrasting

Literary Elements
Protagonist/Antagonist
Plot
Conflict
Theme

Vocabulary Skills
Vocabulary Building

Grammar
Adjectives and Adverbs
Other Parts of Speech

UNIT 3

Genre Focus: Informational Articles

Reading Skills Focus
Previewing
Skimming and Scanning
Understanding Text Structures
Identifying Main Idea and Supporting Details

Text Elements
Tone
Evidence
Irony
Photographs

Vocabulary Skills
Multiple-Meaning Words
Word References

Grammar
Sentences

UNIT 4

What Do You Do When You Don't Know What to Do?

Genre Focus: Poetry

Reading Skills Focus
Connecting
Evaluating
Interpreting
Monitoring Comprehension

Literary Elements
Free Verse
Figurative Language: Metaphor and Simile
Alliteration
Rhyme

Vocabulary Skills
Compound Nouns
Compound Adjectives
Word Choice

Grammar
Subject-Verb Agreement

UNIT 5

How Do You Stay True to Yourself? 542

Genre Focus: Short Stories

Reading Skills Focus
Analyzing
Questioning
Predicting
Making Inferences

Literary Elements
Characterization
Plot
Theme
Setting

Vocabulary Skills
Structural Analysis

Grammar
Sentences
Sentence Structure

UNIT 6

How Do You Keep from Giving Up When Bad Things Happen?

Genre Focus: Drama

Reading Skills Focus
Drawing Conclusions
Interpreting
Paraphrasing and Summarizing
Visualizing

Literary Elements
Act and Scene
Dialogue and Monologue
Stage Directions
Mood

Vocabulary Skills
Structural Analysis (Greek, Latin, and Anglo-Saxon word parts)

Grammar
Commas
Semicolons

UNIT 7

What's Worth Fighting For? What's Not? . . 922

Genre Focus: Persuasive Writing

Reading Skills Focus
Distinguishing Fact from Opinion
Questioning
Reviewing
Clarifying

Literary Elements
Persuasive Appeals
Author's Bias
Faulty Reasoning

Vocabulary Skills
Denotation
Connotation
Semantic Slanting

Grammar
Punctuation

READING WORKSHOP 2

READING WORKSHOP 3

WRITING WORKSHOP PART 2

READING WORKSHOP 4

READING ACROSS TEXTS WORKSHOP

UNIT 8

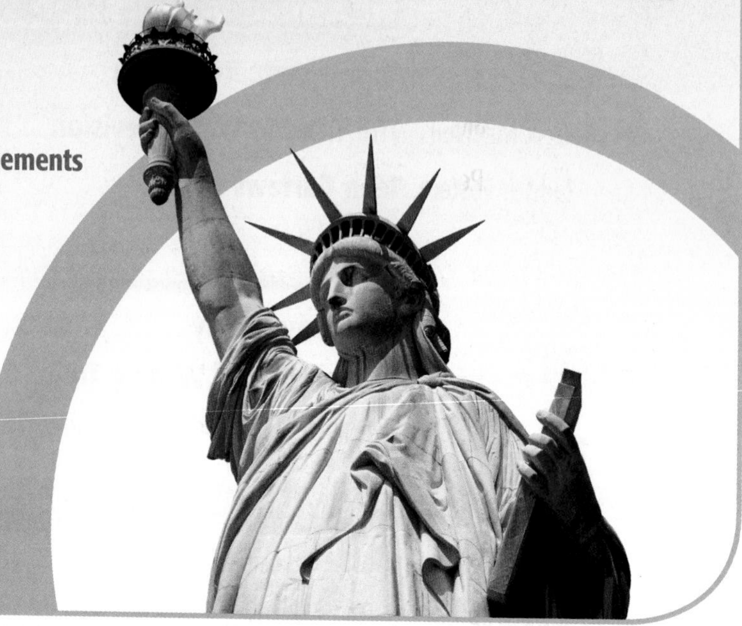

Genre Focus: Historical Text

Reading Skills Focus
Analyzing
Understanding Cause and Effect
Identifying Main Idea and Supporting Details
Identifying Author's Purpose

Vocabulary Skills
Word Origins
Impact of Historical Events on Language

Literary and Text Elements
Chronological Order
Style
Cultural Reference
Metaphor

Grammar
Spelling
Capitalization

Selections by Genre

Fiction

Poetry

Drama

Folktales

Graphic Stories

Personal Essays

Biography, Autobiography, Memoirs, Letters

Informational Texts

Historical Documents

Functional Text

Skills Features

READING SKILLS

Reading Workshops

Reading Across Texts

LITERATURE SKILLS

Literary and Text Elements

Genre Focus

Comparing Literature

VOCABULARY SKILLS

English Language Coach

WRITING SKILLS

Writing Products

Writing Traits

GRAMMAR SKILLS

LISTENING, SPEAKING, AND VIEWING

Philosophy Statement

By Jeffrey D. Wilhelm, Ph.D.

The middle school series, *Reading with Purpose,* is a unique and powerful program designed to engage your students in reading a variety of texts. The program is an integrated, inquiry-oriented approach based on the latest research in motivation, general and literacy education, and cognitive science.

Motivation

Motivating students is the greatest challenge facing teachers today, particularly when it comes to reading and writing. The seminal research of John Guthrie (2002), my own research on adolescent boys and literacy development (Smith and Wilhelm, 2002, 2006), and various national reports and reviews (e.g., Hidi and Harackiewicz, 2000) confirm this challenge. (Editor's note: Wilhelm's research won the NCTE Russell Award for Distinguished Research in English Education.)

When Michael Smith and I undertook our study on the literacy habits of adolescent and teenage males, we found that before students would engage with a literary text, they had to understand the purpose for reading such a text. Students are also more inclined to engage with a text if they are assured to receive the necessary assistance to successfully comprehend the material. The research of Czikszentmihalyi (1990), Gee (2003), and others indicate *Reading with Purpose* is designed first and foremost to meet these motivational prerequisites for engagement and learning.

Inquiry

Inquiry is the most powerful instructional tool to engage students' interest in reading and discovery. George Hillocks (see, e.g., 1995, 1999) famously argued that all reading and writing are forms of inquiry, and therefore most effectively taught and learned through an inquiry process. In our own research (Smith and Wilhelm, 2002, 2006), we found that inquiry met all the conditions of "flow" sought by our student informants.

Essential Questions

An inquiry-oriented program has many positive effects. First, it organizes instruction around an "essential question" (also known as a big, or guiding question). This question must be personally relevant and socially significant to the student. The question must connect students to problems they confront in both the textual material and their own lives.

An essential question makes learning "matter" as students relate to and form individual answers to the question. Inquiry-based learning also provides what is known as "curricular coherence" and "curricular integration" (Jacobs, 1989; Wiggins and McTighe, 2003; see Applebee, Burroughs, Stevens, 2000, and Caskey, 2006 for nice reviews of the importance of coherence and integration to learning).

Curricular coherence is achieved by focusing both conceptual and procedural instruction around the essential question. *Reading with Purpose* presents stories, poems, and informational texts all in the same unit. Although the genres in a particular workshop may vary, every selection is unified by the essential question. By reading selections chosen in service to an essential question, students are exposed to different perspectives they may consider when formulating their own views on a central theme.

Big Understandings

Students using an inquiry approach are more likely to read with purpose and motivation. Students learn major conceptual understandings to apply both to their lives and future reading and writing. The work of John Dewey and Ralph Tyler in the 1930s and 40s (e.g., Tyler, 1949) demonstrates that students quickly forget material presented in information-driven instruction. The hands-on inquiry approach results in central understandings much more likely to be remembered and transferred to new situations.

Strategic Reading and Writing

Curricular integration also includes problem solving, speaking, and listening skills. Inquiry-based learning connects those skills to the student's reading and writing assignments. This approach allows many skills to be taught under one unifying theme—the essential question. Many researchers, including myself (see Wilhelm, Baker, and Dube-Hackett, 2001) have explored how reading and writing are two sides of the same coin. For example, writing a narrative requires the same conventions, declarative knowledge and strategic knowledge as reading a narrative: what a writer must "code" into a narrative or argument, must also be "decoded" and interpreted by the reader of that text. Simply put, teaching the reading and writing techniques of particular genre structures simultaneously makes learning more efficient.

Contextualized Skill and Strategy Development

Reading with Purpose pays special attention to the development of a student "tool box" through the context of unit inquiries. The "tool box" is a concept promoted by socio-cultural psychology and current cognitive science (e.g., Wertsch, 1998). Each unit works step-by-step and activity-by-activity to develop conceptual and strategic tools that are important to exploring, discussing, writing about, and ultimately understanding the knowledge base related to the essential question. Students are given explicit knowledge of and repeated practice with the strategies that are necessary to read and write texts to explore and understand the question. Since particular genres are often particularly powerful for addressing certain topics, *Reading with Purpose* focuses on particular genres in each unit. In this way, strategies are developed to meet a purpose in a meaningful context. The work on "situated cognition" (see Brown, Collins, DuGuid, 1989) shows that "situations co-produce knowledge." With a meaningful purpose, students are motivated to read, develop strategic knowledge, and learn which concepts to concentrate on and remember.

Differentiated Instruction

All classroom teachers understand that their students bring different interests, needs, and abilities to class. It is absolutely necessary to differentiate instruction to meet students in their various "zones of proximal development," the motivational or cognitive zones in which students become motivated to do something that they would not attempt on their own (Wilhelm, 2006).

Differentiated instruction allows students to read texts that are geared to their interests and abilities. Teachers have the flexibility to engage students in particular strategies, work individually or in small groups, and still be part of the common classroom project of pursuing the essential question. With inquiry-based learning, differences become assets and resources; those who read different texts and learn skills at varying levels offer unique contributions to the group's understanding (Wilhelm, 2006). That is why *Reading with Purpose* includes popular culture resources, selections of young adult literature, and canonical texts that can be used with individual students or small groups. We have also recommended various selections and activities to pursue with different students in order to maximize the power of differentiation.

Works Cited

Applebee, A. N., Burroughs, R., and Stevens, A. S. 2000. "Shaping Conversations: A Study of Continuity and Coherence in High School Literature Curricula." *Research in the Teaching of English,* 34: 396–429.

Brown, J., Collins, A., and DuGuid, P. 1989. "Situated Cognition and the Culture of Learning." *Educational Researcher,* 18, 32–42.

Caskey, M. 2006. "The Evidence for Core Curriculum—Past and Present." *Middle School Journal,* (47)3, 48-54.

Csikszentmihalyi, Mihalyi. 1990 *Flow: The psychology of optimal experience.* New York: Harper and Row

Gee, James. 2003. *What Video Games Have to Teach Us About Learning and Literacy.* New York: Palgrave Macmillan.

Guthrie, J. 2002. "Classroom contexts for engaged reading: An Overview." http://www.cori.umd.edu/Research/Papers/Classroom.htm.

Hidi, S., & Harackiewicz, J. M. 2000. "Motivating the academically unmotivated: A critical issue for the 21st century." *Review of Educational Research,* 70, 151-180.

Hillocks, G. 1995. *Teaching Writing as Reflective Practice.* New York: Teachers College Press.

Hillocks, G. 1999. *Ways of Teaching/Ways of Learning* New York: Teachers College Press.

Jacobs, Heidi Hayes. 1989. *Interdisciplinary Curriculum: Design and Implementation.* Washington DC: ASCD.

Smith, Michael W. and Wilhelm, Jeffrey D. 2006. *Going with the Flow: How to engage boys (and girls) in their literacy learning.* Portsmouth, NH: Heinemann.

Smith, Michael W. and Wilhelm, Jeffrey D. 2002. *Reading Don't Fix No Chevys: Literacy in the lives of young men.* Portsmouth, NH: Heinemann.

Tyler, R. 1949. *Basic principles of curriculum and instruction.* Chicago: University of Chicago Press.

Wertsch, J. 1998. *Mind as action.* New York: Oxford University Press.

Wiggins, Grant and McTighe, Jay. 2003. *Understanding by Design.* Washington DC: ASCD.

Wilhelm, J. D., Baker, T. and Dube-Hackett, J. 2001. *Strategic Reading.* Portsmouth, NH: Heinemann.

Wilhelm, Jeffrey D. 2006. *Inquiring Minds Learn to Read and Write: Inquiry, Questioning and Discussion Strategies to Improve Reading and Writing.* New York: Scholastic.

The *Reading Next* Report

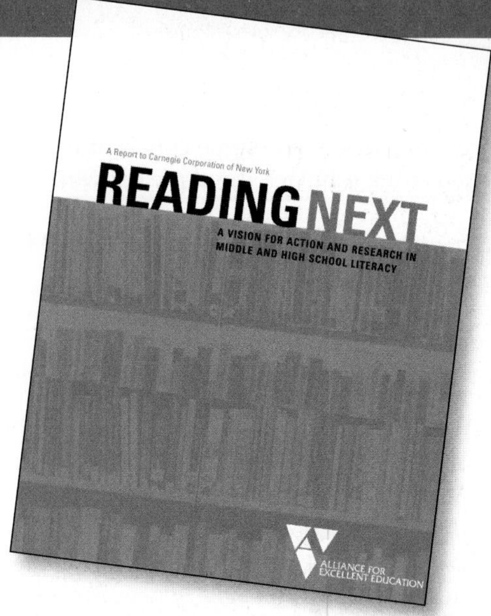

What Is It?

In 2004, the Carnegie Corporation released *Reading Next—A Vision for Action and Research in Middle and High School Literacy: A Report from Carnegie Corporation of New York.* Authored by Harvard researchers Gina Biancarosa and Dr. Catherine Snow, and published by Alliance for Excellent Education in Washington, D.C., the report responds to the growing literacy crisis among middle and high school students.

The statistics bear out the severity of the problem. In the United States today, more than 8 million students in grades 4–12 lack the ability to read proficiently (U.S. DOE, 2003). Every day, more than 3,000 students drop out of high school (Alliance for Excellent Education, 2003)—largely because they lack the literacy skills to keep up (Kamil, 2003; Snow and Biancarosa, 2003). Only 70 percent of high school students graduate on time, and fewer than 60 percent of all African American and Latino students get their diplomas (Greene, 2002). Clearly, these numbers paint a picture of a system in crisis.

The driving force behind the *Reading Next* report is simple. Students who lack literacy skills face serious disadvantages in almost every aspect of their lives—at school, at work, and in the community. Research indicates that most middle and high school readers can decode. Many of these readers, however, are unable to conceptualize what they read or to connect new words and ideas to those they already know. Unable to comprehend the various texts they encounter, these students quickly fall behind.

The *Reading Next* report draws attention to this problem and seeks to dispel the outdated notion that struggling and reluctant middle and high school readers are unable to benefit from literacy instruction. Instead, the report asserts, these students can and *do* benefit—significantly—from literacy instruction. Educators and other interested parties should then work hard to develop effective literacy programs for struggling middle and high school students.

Why Is It Important?

The report identifies fifteen characteristics of an effective literacy program. The first nine characteristics, or recommendations, are instructional—ideas and activities that teachers can implement. The remaining six are infrastructural—ideas and activities that can be realized at the school-wide level, or in the student's home or community.

According to the report, effective literacy programs for struggling readers share the following **instructional** components:

1. **Direct, explicit comprehension instruction,** or teaching core reading strategies.
2. **Effective instructional principles embedded in content,** or teaching students to use reading skills in all content areas.
3. **Motivation and self-directed learning,** or motivating students to read (now *and* after graduation), and to become independent, lifelong learners.
4. **Text-based collaborative learning,** or teaching students to interact with one another vis-à-vis using a variety of texts.
5. **Strategic tutoring,** or giving students intense, individualized instruction when necessary.
6. **Diverse texts,** or using texts whose genre, topic, and level of difficulty vary.
7. **Intensive writing,** or offering instruction that relates to the writing tasks students will perform at the high school level and beyond.
8. **A technology component,** or using technology as a tool for and topic of literacy instruction.
9. **Ongoing formative assessment of students,** or conducting frequent, informal assessments of student progress under current instructional practices.

The report also notes that effective literacy programs share the following **infrastructural** components:

10. **Extended time for literacy,** or offering two to four hours of interdisciplinary (cross-classroom and cross-content area) literacy instruction per day.
11. **Professional development,** or offering long-term and ongoing support for teachers.
12. **Ongoing summative assessment of students and programs,** or evaluating students and educators in order to build accountability and improve systems.

13. **Teacher teams,** or forming interdisciplinary groups that discuss and are accountable for students' progress.
14. **Leadership,** or the execution of program goals by teachers and principals who understand their students and their reading and writing curriculum.
15. **A comprehensive and coordinated literacy program,** or the formation of a literacy program that draws strength from various disciplines, departments, and community organizations.

Reading with Purpose and the *Reading Next* Report

The *Reading Next* report recommends nine instructional improvements, and the *Reading with Purpose* program equips teachers to implement all of them—when, where, and how they choose. Developed with these improvements in mind, this program helps teachers help students in the ways that matter most.

The *Reading Next* Report recommends:	*Reading with Purpose* features:
direct, explicit comprehension instruction	**Genre Focus:** highlights 4 reading skills and 4 literary elements **Reading Workshops: Skill Lesson**–explicit instruction on one reading skill **Reading Selections**–vocabulary instruction and review, side notes that provide explicit reading skill instruction and practice
effective instructional principles embedded in content	**Reading, Writing, Comparing Literature and Reading Across Texts Workshops:** inquiry-based instruction using the Workshop approach; teach-model-practice-assess mode of instruction
motivation and self-directed learning	**Big Questions:** Inquiry-based instruction **Unit Challenges:** choice of activities **Learner's Notebooks and Foldables:** record individual's thoughts and learning
text-based collaborative learning	**Workshop Approach:** emphasis on collaboration **Partner Talk, Think-Pair-Share, Small-Group Discussion, and Whole-Class Discussion:** activities that emphasize collaboration **Unit Challenge:** includes a suggested group activity
strategic tutoring	**Partner Talk and Think-Pair-Share:** students work one-on-one with one another, and/or with an instructor **Reading and Writing Workshops:** opportunity to work in small mentoring groups
diverse texts	**Genre Focus:** one per unit **Diverse reading selections:** fiction, nonfiction, informational text **Reading on Your Own:** suggested readings at the end of each unit
intensive writing	**Writing Workshop:** a two-part writing project in every unit; teaches students to write within the focus genre **Reading Workshops:** students encounter numerous writing activities, including the **Write to Learn** prompt
a technology component	Examples include **glencoe.online,** the **Student Works CD-ROM,** and the **Skills Arcade CD-ROM**
ongoing formative assessment of students	**After You Read:** assessment and skills review following each reading selection **Skills and Strategies Assessment:** unit-ending test practice **Ancillary Assessment materials: Selection Quick Checks, Assessment by Objectives, Examview Pro Assessment Suite, Selection** and **Unit Assessments**

Inquiry-Based Instruction

By Jeffrey D. Wilhelm, Ph.D.

As educators, we often fail to establish the relevance of what we teach. For example, the boys in my *Reading Don't Fix No Chevys* study (Smith and Wilhelm, 2002) felt that what they learned in school was completely separate from, and not useful in, "real" life. In short, they wanted the type of education that MIT physicist Jerrold Zaccharias championed—one that raises, as Zaccharias put it, "questions worth arguing about."

How, then, do we use "hands-on/minds-on" modes of instruction to help students ask and answer worthwhile questions? The research is in, and it points toward inquiry. Shown to improve student engagement, attitude, achievement, and learning in a variety of areas, inquiry approaches eclipse other modes of simple information transmission—and best help students do the work that matters.

What Is Inquiry?

Inquiry is the problem-oriented exploration of questions that drive and organize disciplines. Through inquiry, students learn essential concepts and strategies for applying those concepts in the real world. They engage the same problems and questions that real practitioners of a given discipline engage, and therefore learn to think, read, and write like experts in that area.

Discovering information is part of true inquiry, *but it is only the first step.* Inquirers must then interpret that information and shape it into knowledge. Human beings want to make meanings, not just receive them—or, as James Britton famously remarked, "Being told is the opposite of finding out."

To this end, research shows that inquiry approaches—active, discussion-based, and supported by a purposeful curriculum—focus on HOW to do something, and WHY to do it (Applebee, 1996; Hillocks, 1995, 1999, 2002; Applebee, Langer, Nystrand, and Gamoran, 2003; Nystrand, 1997). However, teacher-centered approaches—often lecture, memorization, and test-based—focus simply on WHAT to do (see, e.g., Rogoff, Matusov, White, 1996).

Literacy researcher George Hillocks argues that reading and writing are forms of inquiry and are best taught, and learned, in that context. His research findings support that argument. According to Hillocks, inquiry approaches had the most powerful effects on student engagement, learning, and achievement (see Hillocks, 1995, 1999, 2002).

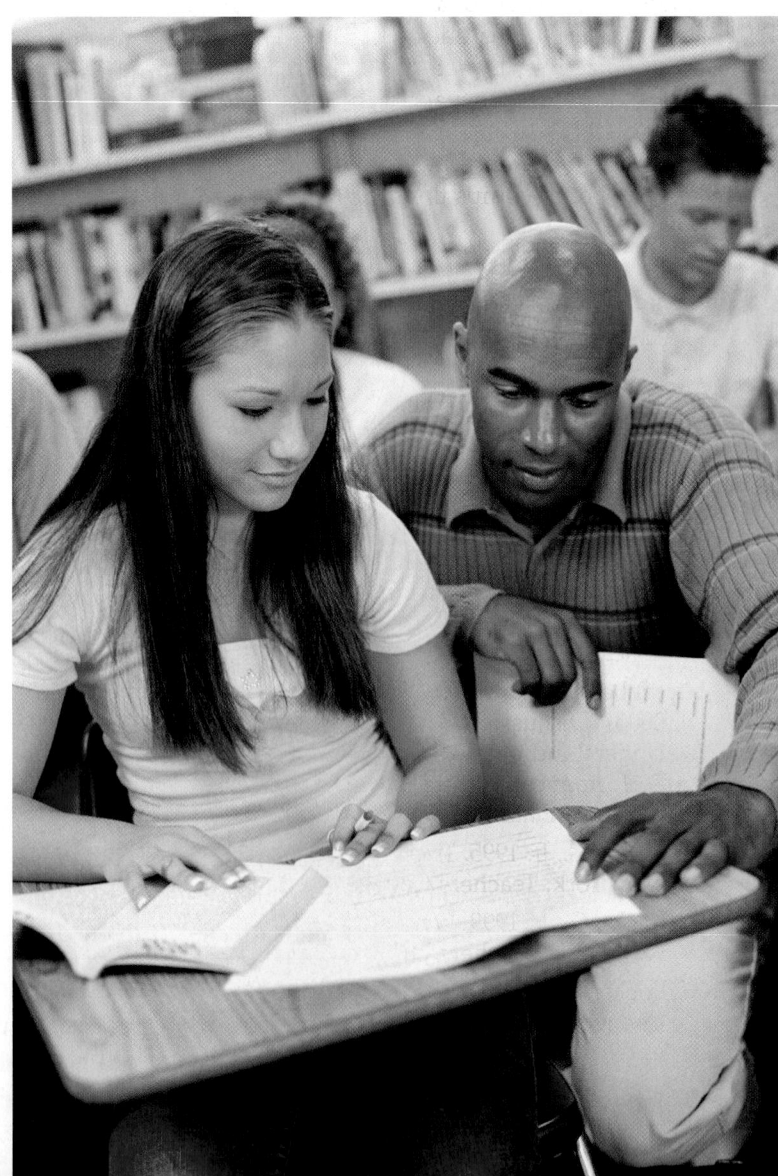

How Is Inquiry Applied in *Reading with Purpose*?

Motivation My research (Smith and Wilhelm, 2002, 2006; Wilhelm and Friedemann, 1998) has shown that the inquiry approach, organized around essential questions, increases student engagement. Because it is organized around Big Questions, the instruction in *Reading with Purpose* makes learning matter to students in very immediate ways.

Meaningful Context In *Reading with Purpose,* the reading, writing, and language activities are organized around real issues that students face in their own lives. When students practice a skill or create a writing product, they are also learning to ask and think through important real-life questions.

Schema Theory Modern cognitive science explains that people learn by either assimilating new data into existing patterns, or "schema," or by changing schema to accommodate new data. In *Reading with Purpose,* units are organized so that students develop their schema text by text and activity by activity. Doing this allows students to build their schema about the inquiry question and to develop key reading and writing tools. This gives students a coherent learning experience, where each activity better equips them for the next.

Curricular Coherence and Integration Inquiry teaching uses what Applebee, Burroughs, and Stevens (2000) call an *integrated* curriculum, or a curriculum that helps students build a set of skills that they apply with increasing sophistication across a range of activities. The integrated curriculum helps students achieve a range of objectives (Wiggins and McTighe, 1998). For example, students address the socially significant Big Question as developing readers and writers. They also encounter grammar in the context of the literary selections—and their own writing—so that the lessons they learn are situated and meaningful. In *Reading with Purpose,* reading and writing are integrated as forms of inquiry taught in an inquiring context. Use this exciting approach and watch your students begin to ask—and answer—the questions that matter most.

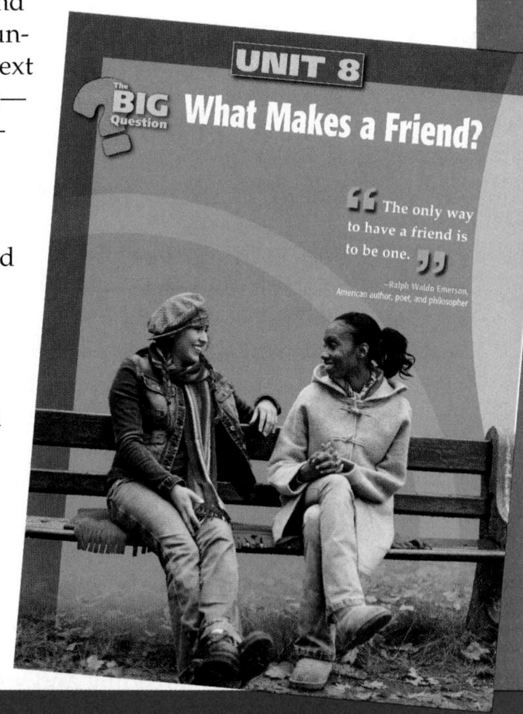

Applebee, A. N., Burroughs, R., and Stevens, A.S. 2000. "Shaping Conversation: A Study of Continuity and Coherence in High School Literature Curricula." *Research in the Teaching of English,* 34: 396–429.

Applebee, A.N. 1996. *Curriculum as conversation: Transforming traditions of teaching and learning.* Chicago: University of Chicago Press.

Applebee, A., Langer, J., Nystrand, M. and Gamoran, A. 2003. "Discussion-Based Approaches to Developing Understanding: Classroom Instruction and Student Performance in Middle and High School English." *American Educational Research Journal,* Fall.

Hillocks, G., Jr. 1995. *Teaching Writing as Reflective Practice.* New York: Teachers College Press.

Hillocks, G., Jr. 1999. *Ways of Thinking, Ways of Teaching.* New York: Teachers College Press.

Hillocks, G., Jr. 2002. *The Testing Trap.* New York: Teachers College Press.

Smith, M. W., and Wilhelm. J. 2002. *Reading Don't Fix No Chevys: Literacy in the Lives of Young Men.* Portsmouth, NH: Heinemann.

Smith, M. W. and Wilhelm, J. 2006. *Going with the Flow: Making literacy learning in school more like life.* Portsmouth, NH: Heinemann.

Soder, R. 1999. "When Words Find Their Meaning: Renewal versus Reform." *Phi Delta Kappan.* April, 568–570.

Wiggins, G., and McTighe, J. 1998. *Understanding by Design.* Alexandria, VA: ASCD.

Wilhelm, J. 2003. *Reading IS Seeing.* New York: Scholastic.

Wilhelm, J., and Friedemann, P. 1998. *Hyperlearning: Where Inquiry, Projects and Technology Meet.* York, ME: Stenhouse.

Research-Based Classroom Solutions

The Workshop Approach

By Douglas Fisher, Ph.D.

While there are a number of ways to provide this instruction, the reading and writing workshops are particularly effective, and therefore hold promise for all students (e.g., Fletcher & Portalupi, 2001; Serafini, 2001).

A Workshop Defined

Workshops are about collaboration and creation. In the classroom, the workshop is a philosophy; it is also a way to organize instructional time. For example, reading and writing workshops provide time for students to respond to texts they have read and to write about their ideas (Atwell, 1987; Calkins, 1986). These workshops also allow students to assume more responsibility for literacy tasks and to become independent learners. In this way, the workshop model provides a context for students to build skills and perfect their craft.

The Evidence Base

As Lausé (2004) noted, the implementation of a workshop approach to teaching reading and writing inspires students to become lifelong readers. According to Lausé's data, it creates faster, more competent readers; it also creates students who enjoy reading (and do read) more.

Taylor and Nesheim (2000/2001) used the workshop model to engage their "high-risk" students in literacy instruction. As they note, the "readers' workshop project prompted students to engage as readers and to experiment with new views of reading" (p. 317). Similarly, Williams (2001) noted that "a workshop format and strategy instruction helped struggling middle school readers connect with books, the teacher, and one another" (p. 588).

The workshop model has also been shown to improve writing achievement (Fisher & Frey, 2003), the use of multiple forms of media (Labbo, 2004), performance on tests (Shelton & Fu, 2004; Santman, 2002), problem solving skills (Christensen, 1990), and the expectations of teachers (Graves, 2004).

A Guiding Philosophy

Simply telling students what they should know will not ensure that they read better and read more. As teachers, we must model, scaffold, guide, and support learning. Current research suggests that the "gradual release of responsibility" model is an effective way to organize instruction (Fisher & Frey, 2003; Pearson & Fielding, 1991). In this model, the teacher moves from assuming "all the

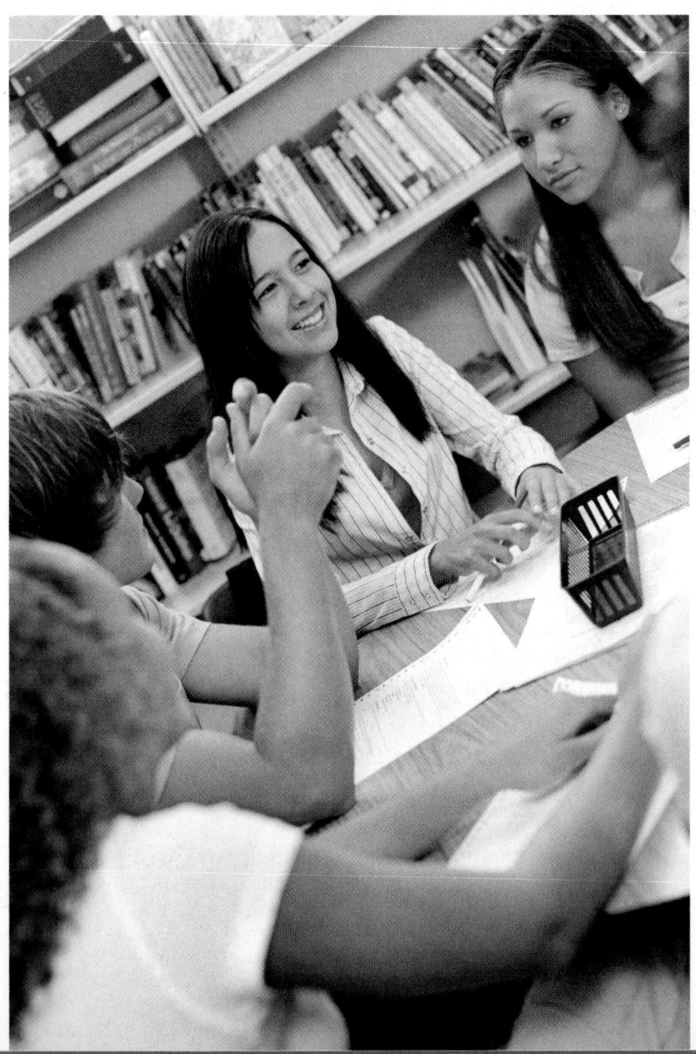

responsibility for performing a task . . . to a situation in which the students assume all of the responsibility" (Duke & Pearson, 2002, p. 211). This gradual release may occur over a day, a week, or a term. In *Reading with Purpose,* reading workshops are designed to encourage this gradual release of responsibility.

Components of the Workshop

To facilitate the gradual release of responsibility, the workshop moves students through phases of extensive teacher support and guided instruction, allowing them to become more independent learners. This model includes the following components:

- **A focus lesson** allows teachers to model a skill, strategy, or writing technique. Some strategies include read and think alouds, shared reading and writing activities, and language-based approaches. In *Reading with Purpose,* every Reading Workshop begins with a Skill Lesson that introduces that unit's reading skill.
- **Guided instruction** gives students an opportunity to practice the skills, strategies, and techniques introduced during the focus lesson under the teacher's close supervision. It provides a scaffold between teacher modeling and student independence. Some strategies include guided reading, guided writing, writing models, and choral reading. In *Reading with Purpose,* reading selections are accompanied by notes that guide students' use of the unit's skills while they read.
- **Collaborative learning** encourages peer work to help students become more competent readers and writers. It also allows students to assist and coach one another. Some strategies include learning centers, paired reading, and reciprocal teaching. In *Reading with Purpose,* Partner Talk activities occur throughout the book.
- **Independent reading and writing** provides time for students to apply skills and strategies practiced during focus lessons, guided instruction, and collaborative learning to their own reading and writing. Independent learning need not be completed in solitary silence; it should, however, give each student a chance to apply new skills and strategies to his or her own work. Teachers may also use this time to conference with students individually. In *Reading with Purpose,* each unit ends with suggested readings to help students further explore the Big Question on their own.

Works Cited

Atwell, N. 1987. *In the middle: Writing, reading, and learning with adolescents.* Portsmouth, NH: Heinemann.

Calkins, L. M. 1986. *The art of teaching writing.* Portsmouth, NH: Heinemann.

Christensen, A. W. 1990. "Problem solving our way through writers' workshop." *The Reading Teacher,* 44, 357–358.

Duke, N. K., & Pearson, P. D. 2002. "Effective practices for developing reading comprehension." In A. Farstrup & J. Samuels (Eds.), *What research has to say about reading instruction* (3rd ed.). Newark, DE: International Reading Association.

Fisher, D., & Frey, N. 2003. "Writing instruction for struggling adolescent readers: A gradual release model." *Journal of Adolescent and Adult Literacy,* 46, 396–405.

Fletcher, R., & Portalupi, J. 2001. *Writing workshop: The essential guide.* Portsmouth, NH: Heinemann.

Frey, N., & Fisher, D. 2006. *Language arts workshop: Purposeful reading and writing instruction.* Upper Saddle River, NJ: Merrill Education.

Graves, D. 2004. "What I've learned from teachers of writing." *Language Arts,* 82(2), 88–94.

Labbo, L. D. 2004. "From writing workshop to multimedia workshop." *Language Arts,* 82(2), 119.

Lausé, J. 2004. "Using reading workshop to inspire lifelong readers." *English Journal, 93*(5), 24–30.

Pearson, P. D., & Fielding, L. 1991. "Comprehension instruction." In R. Barr, M. L. Kamil, P. Mosenthal, & P. D. Pearson (Eds.) *Handbook of reading research* (Vol. II), (pp. 815–860). Mahwah, NJ: Erlbaum.

Santman, D. 2002. "Teaching to the test? Test preparation in the reading workshop." *Language Arts,* 79(3), 203–211.

Serafini, F. 2001. *The reading workshop: Creating space for readers.* Portsmouth, NH: Heinemann.

Shelton, N. R., & Fu, D. 2004. "Creating space for teaching writing and for test preparation." *Language Arts,* 82(2), 120–128.

Taylor, S. V., & Nesheim. D. W. 2000/2001. "Making literacy real for 'high-risk' adolescent emerging readers: An innovative application of readers' workshop." *Journal of Adolescent & Adult Literacy,* 44, 308–318.

Williams, M. 2001. "Making connections: A workshop for adolescents who struggle with reading." *Journal of Adolescent & Adult Literacy,* 44, 588–602.

Differentiated Instruction

By Douglas Fisher, Ph.D.

Today's classroom contains students from a variety of backgrounds and with a variety of learning styles, strengths, and challenges. With careful planning, you can address the needs of all students in the literature classroom, using ***Glencoe Literature: Reading with Purpose.*** The basis for this planning is differentiated learning.

Differentiated Instruction Is a Key to Access

To differentiate instruction, teachers must acknowledge students' differences in background knowledge, current reading, writing, and English language skills, learning styles and preferences, interests, and needs, and they must react accordingly. There are a number of general guidelines for differentiating instruction:

- **Link assessment with instruction.** Assessments should occur before, during, and after instruction to ensure that the curriculum is aligned with what students do and do not know. Using assessments in this way allows you to plan instruction for whole groups, small groups, and individual students.
- **Clarify key concepts and generalizations.** Students need to know what is essential and how this information can be used in their future learning. In addition, students need to develop a sense of the **Big Questions,** which focus on life issues students need to think about in each unit in ***Reading with Purpose.***
- **Emphasize critical and creative thinking.** The content, process, and products used or assigned in the classroom should require that students think about what they are learning. While some students may require support, additional motivation, varied tasks, materials, or equipment, the overall focus on critical and creative thinking allows for all students to participate in the lesson.
- **Include teacher- and student-selected tasks.** A differentiated classroom includes both teacher- and student-selected activities and tasks. At some points in the lesson, the teacher must provide instruction and assign learning activities. In other parts of the lesson, students should be provided choices in how they engage with the content. This balance increases motivation, engagement, and learning.

Supporting Individual Students

The vast majority of students will thrive in a classroom based on differentiated instruction. However, wise teachers recognize that no single option will work for all students and that there may be students who require unique systems of support to be successful.

Tips for Instruction

The following tips for instruction can support your efforts to help all students reach their maximum potential.

- Survey students to discover their individual differences. Use interest inventories of their unique talents so you can encourage contributions in the classroom.
- Be a model for respecting others. Adolescents crave social acceptance. The student with learning differences is especially sensitive to correction and criticism, particularly when it comes from a teacher. Your behavior will set the tone for how students treat one another.
- Expand opportunities for success. Provide a variety of instructional activities that reinforce skills and concepts.
- Establish measurable objectives and decide how you can best help students who meet them.
- Celebrate successes, and make note of and praise "work in progress."
- Keep it simple. Point out problem areas if doing so can help a student effect change. Avoid overwhelming students with too many goals at one time.
- Assign cooperative group projects that challenge all students to contribute to solving a problem or creating a product.

How Do I Reach Students with Learning Disabilities?

- Provide support and structure. Clearly specify rules, assignments, and responsibilities.
- Practice skills frequently. Use games and drills to help maintain student interest.
- Incorporate many modalities into the learning process. Provide opportunities to say, hear, write, read, and act out important concepts and information.
- Link new skills and concepts to those already mastered.

- If possible, allow students to record answers on audiotape.
- Allow extra time to complete assessments and assignments.
- Let students demonstrate proficiency with alternative presentations, including oral reports, role plays, art projects, and musical presentations.
- Provide outlines, notes, or tape recordings of lecture material.
- Pair students with peer helpers, and provide class time for pair interaction.

How Do I Reach English Language Learners?

- Remember, students' ability to speak English does not reflect their academic abilities.
- Try to incorporate the students' cultural experience into your instruction. The help of a bilingual aide may be effective.
- Avoid any references in your instruction that could be construed as cultural stereotypes.
- Preteach important vocabulary and concepts.
- Encourage students to preview text before they begin reading, noting headings.
- Remind students not to ignore graphic organizers, photographs, and maps since there is much information in these visuals.
- Use artifacts and photographs whenever possible to build background knowledge and understanding. An example of this would be coins in a foreign currency or a raw cotton ball to reinforce its importance in history.

How Do I Reach Gifted Students?

- Make arrangements for students to take selected subjects early and to work on independent projects.
- Ask "what if" questions to develop high-level thinking skills. Establish an environment safe for risk taking in your classroom.
- Emphasize concepts, theories, ideas, relationships, and generalizations about the content.
- Promote interest in the past by inviting students to make connections to the present.
- Let students express themselves in alternate ways such as creative writing, acting, debates, simulations, drawing, or music.
- Provide students with a catalog of helpful resources, listing such things as agencies that provide free and inexpensive materials, appropriate community services and programs, and community experts who might be called upon to speak to your students.
- Assign extension projects that allow students to solve real-life problems related to their communities.

References

Fisher, D. 2005. "The missing link: Standards, assessment, and instruction." *Voices from the Middle*, 13(2), 8–11.

McTighe, J., Seif, E., Wiggins, G. 2004. "You can teach for meaning." *Educational Leadership*, 62(1), 26–30.

Pfaum, S. W., & Bishop, P. A. 2004. "Student perceptions of reading engagement: Learning from the Learners." *Journal of Adolescent and Adult Literacy*, 48(3), 202–213.

Tomlinson, C. A., & McTighe, J. 2006. *Integrating differentiated instructions & understanding by design: Connecting content and kids.* Alexandria, VA: Association for Supervision and Curriculum Development.

Question Answer Relationship (QAR)

by Taffy Raphael, Ph.D.

What Is It?

QAR provides a framework that offers teachers a straightforward approach for reading comprehension instruction. QAR can serve as a reasonable starting point for addressing four problems that stand in the way of moving all students to high levels of literacy:

- a shared language to make visible the processes underlying reading and listening comprehension
- a framework for organizing questioning activities and comprehension instruction
- accessible and straightforward reform for literacy instruction oriented toward higher level thinking
- preparing students for high-stakes testing without undermining a strong focus on higher level thinking

Two decades ago, research showed that QAR could reliably improve students' comprehension (Raphael & McKinney, 1983; Raphael & Pearson, 1985; Raphael & Wonnacott, 1985). In the two decades since, literacy educators in a broad range of settings have demonstrated its practical value and shared their experiences in professional journals (e.g., Mesmer & Hutchins, 2002), textbooks (e.g., Leu & Kinzer, 2003; Reutzel & Cooper, 2004; Roe, Smith, & Burns, 2005; Vacca et al., 2003), and on the World Wide Web (e.g., gallery.carnegiefoundation.org/yhutchinson and www.smsd.org/schools/diemer/).

Why Is It Important?

Promoting high levels of literacy for all children is a core responsibility for today's teachers. With increasing accountability at the district, state, and national levels, teachers are often judged on the basis of how well their students perform on mandated, high-stakes tests.

But what does it mean to achieve high levels of literacy? Recent national panels and current reviews detailing what it means to comprehend text help inform us about current policies and future trends (e.g., Pressley, 2002; Snow, 2002; Sweet & Snow, 2003). For example, the RAND report (Snow), commissioned by the U.S. Department of Education, identifies literacy proficiency as reached when a reader can read a variety of materials with ease and interest, can read for varying purposes, and can read with comprehension even when the material is neither easy to understand nor intrinsically interesting. Proficient readers are capable of acquiring new knowledge and understanding new concepts, are capable of applying textual information appropriately, and are capable of being engaged in the reading process and reflecting on what is being read. This same view is reflected in the current National Assessment of Educational Progress (NAEP; Donahue, Daane, & Grigg, 2003), the only federally funded large-scale testing program in the United States, and the framework for the NAEP 2009 reading assessment (National Assessment Governing Board, 2004) pushes the definition for proficiency even further. For example, students will be expected to read comfortably across genres within fiction, nonfiction, procedural texts, and poetry. They will be required to successfully answer questions, 70 to 80 percent of which call for the integration, interpretation, critique, and evaluation of texts read independently.

Traditional questions that simply require readers to locate and recall information will constitute only a third to a fourth of the questions that students will face. Over half of the higher level questions will require students to provide a short or extended written response rather than simply to select from multiple-choice options. To be judged as proficient in reading fiction, students must demonstrate that they can think deeply about, and write in response to, questions that address themes, lessons, elements of plot, and multiple points of view. The kind of strategic knowledge assessed on national and state tests, now and in the future, is central to the achievement of high levels of literacy.

How Do I Do It?

The vocabulary of QAR—**In the Book, In My Head, Right There, Think & Search, Author & Me,** and **On My Own**—gives teachers and students a language for talking about the largely invisible processes that constitute listening and reading comprehension across grades and subject areas.

Teachers know the value of modeling and thinking aloud to make visible the thought processes involved in higher levels of thinking, but it can be frustrating trying to convey complex ideas without a shared vocabulary. Thus, QAR first and foremost provides teachers and students with a much-needed common language. Introduce students to the basic principle underlying QAR: that generating and answering questions draws on two core sources of information. These sources are the texts that we read and our background knowledge and experiences; or, in the language of QAR, information that is **In the Book** or **In My Head,** respectively.

Teachers should use QAR language as they emphasize the importance of both sources of information. Furthermore, teachers should use QAR language to help students learn to use strategies effectively. For example, explain how skimming or scanning might lead to details for an **In the Book** QAR (a typical locate/recall strategy) or how using clues from the title and chapter headings can point to relevant background knowledge for answering an **In My Head** QAR (a relatively simple interpret/integrate/infer task).

Introduce students to the language of QAR by analyzing the differences between questions with answer sources in the book and those where the answer source is students' own heads. Shorter texts work quite effectively for characterizing basic differences between these two information sources, but as students become more experienced with QARs, this simple distinction is not sufficient to capture the range of strategies used to answer and generate questions related to text. Build on **In the Book** and **In My Head** by introducing the four core QARs. Once students are confidently and accurately identifying **In the Book** QARs, introduce its subcategories, **Right There** and **Think & Search.** Similarly, when students are confident and accurate with **In My Head** QARs, introduce its subcategories; **Author & Me** and **On My Own** (see chart below for definitions of each).

Readers functioning at high levels of literacy use strategies in combination and apply different approaches to strategic thinking, depending on the genre or difficulty of the texts. Understanding how strategies interrelate can be quite abstract for students faced with the need to apply several strategies, as well as quite demanding for teachers in terms of providing effective instruction. QAR provides a framework that students can use to link strategies at appropriate points in the reading cycle. Understanding and control of strategies learned helps readers engage in the high levels of literacy for which they are accountable in their day-to-day classroom literacy activities and in high-stakes assessments at the district, state, and national levels.

In the Book	In My Head
Right There The answer is in one place in the text. Words from the question and words that answer the question are often in the same sentence. **Sample Comprehension Strategies:** *Skimming and Scanning* *Note-taking* *Context Clues*	**On My Own** The answer is not in the text. Readers need to use their own ideas and experiences to answer the question. **Sample Comprehension Strategies:** *Activating Prior Knowledge* *Connecting*
Think & Search The answer is in the text. Readers need to put together different parts of the text to find the answer. The answer can be within a paragraph, across paragraphs, or even across chapters and books. **Sample Comprehension Strategies:** *Summarizing* *Compare and Contrast* *Making Simple Inferences* *Clarifying* *Figurative Language*	**Author & Me** The answer is not in the text. To answer the question, readers need to think about how the text and what they already know fit together. **Sample Comprehension Strategies:** *Predicting* *Visualizing* *Making Simple and Complex Inferences* *Distinguishing Fact and Opinion* *Making Text-to-Self Connections*

English Language Learners

by Mary A. Avalos, Ph.D.

English language learners (ELLs) are a growing population in our schools. During the 2000–2001 academic year, more than 4.5 million English language learners were enrolled in U.S. public schools (McREL, 2003). The growth of culturally and linguistically diverse populations is expected to continue into this century. Immigrants come to the United States for various reasons—some to escape political or economic oppression, others to seek higher paying wages or provide a higher standard of living for their families. Although shifting demographics have a greater impact on certain regions of the United States, all teachers should be prepared to teach all students.

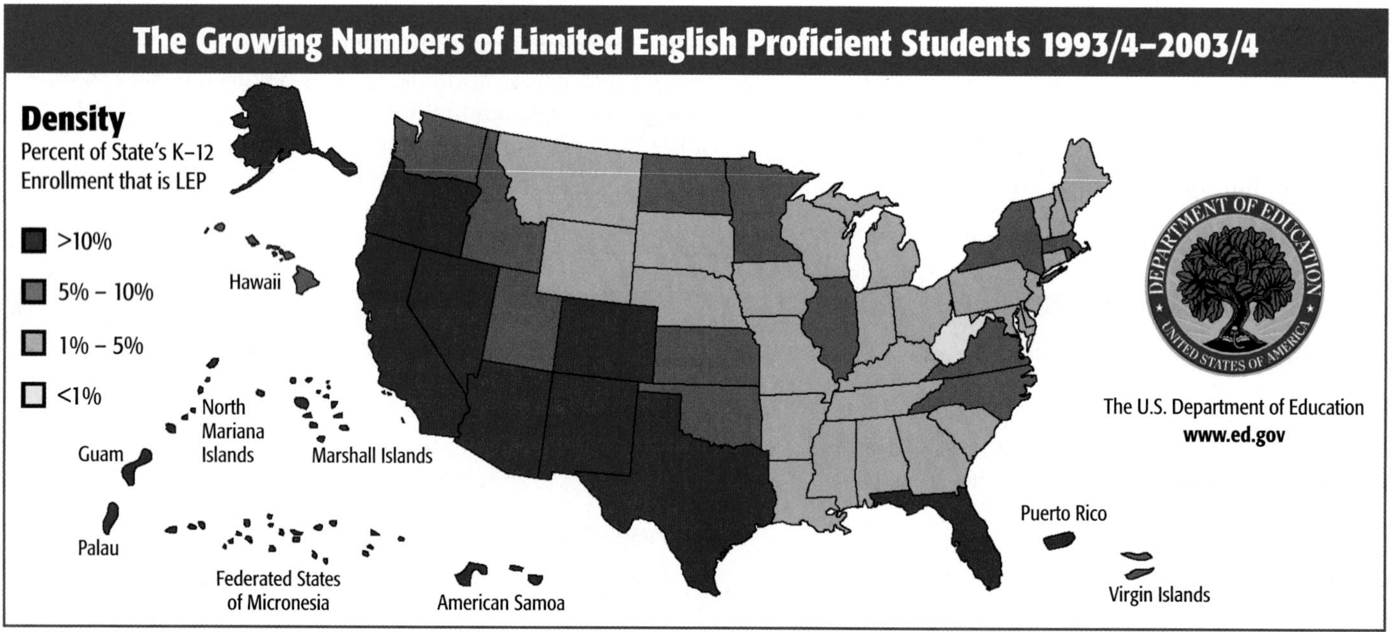

Meeting the Challenge

There are challenges specific to teaching English language learners as they must learn content while learning to read, write, and speak a new language simultaneously. English language learners' literacy proficiency in their first language, or **L1,** will impact their literacy acquisition of a second language, or **L2.** (Au, 1993; Cummins, 2003; Hudelson, 1984; Snow, 1990), particularly if the L1 is similar to the L2.

English language learners make an easier transition between L1 and L2 if both languages share a similar writing system.

Writing System	Example
Alphabetic	English, French, Spanish, Italian
Syllabic	Cherokee
Logographic	Chinese

To provide effective instruction, build upon what English language learners know about language and literacy knowledge. Also consider English language learners' cultural differences, such as celebration and mourning rituals, child-rearing practices, and favorite foods. Try to incorporate the students' cultural experience into your teaching.

Gauging Levels of Language Proficiency

A common misconception exists that once English language learners are able to converse using everyday language, they are ready to proceed to mainstream instruction with little to no support. In reality, there are three levels of language proficiency as labeled by Cummins (2003).

Level of Language Proficiency	Example
Basic Interpersonal Conversation Skills (BICS)	ability to talk about daily activities, make requests, and retell a personal story or event.
Discrete Language Skills	knowledge of phonological awareness, grammar rules, or conventions of writing in the learner's first language
Cognitive Academic Language Proficiency (CALP)	the ability to read and understand technical or subject area texts with low frequency words of Latin or Greek origin

By learning about language acquisition processes, teachers can better meet the needs of English language learners.

Several instructional features of *Glencoe Literature: Reading with Purpose* help English language learners develop higher levels of language proficiency. Note the following examples:

1. Analyzing the reading selections to facilitate comprehension of low frequency vocabulary, as well as identified vocabulary words for study.
2. Prompting students to activate prior knowledge before/while reading to make connections between the reader and the text.
3. Integrating literary elements throughout the selections to provide meaningful prompts in context.
4. Setting objectives to ensure that all students receive high quality, standards-based instruction.
5. Contextualizing writing, grammar, and spelling instruction throughout the program.

All of these aids increase teacher awareness of text- and reader-based features as they are instructing English language learners. This approach to instruction, in turn, better meets the unique needs of English language learners as they learn content and language together.

Works Cited

Au, K. H. 1993. *Literacy instruction in multicultural settings.* Orlando, FL: Harcourt Brace College Publishers.

Cummins, J. 2003. "Reading and the bilingual student: Fact and friction." In G. G. Garcia's (Ed.) *English learners: Reaching the highest level of English literacy.* Newark, DE: International Reading Association.

Hudelson, S. 1984. "Kan yu ret an rayt en ingles: Children become literate in English as a second language." *TESOL Quarterly,* 18, 221–238.

McREL. Fall, 2003. "English language learners and the No Child Left Behind Act." *Changing Schools: A Newsletter from the Central Region Educational Laboratory. Aurora, CO: Mid-continent Research for Education* and Learning. Retrieved from the Internet on February 17, 2006: http://www.mcrel.org/PDF/ChangingSchools/5032NL_CSfall2003.pdf#search='percentage%20of%20English%20language%20learners%20in%20U.S.%20schools

Snow, C. E. 1990. "Rationales for native language instruction in the education of language minority children: Evidence from research." In A. Padilla, H. Fairchild, & C. Valadez (Eds.), *Bilingual education: Issues and strategies,* pp. 60–74. Newbury Park, CA: Sage.

Research-Based Classroom Solutions

Digital Technology

by David G. O'Brien, Ph.D.

Students' Digital Lives

By cultivating an awareness of the issues below, teachers can help students connect the literacy practices they learn in school to their busy lives outside the classroom.

- **New Literacies** In the digital age, many students are fluent in new languages, or literacies—for example, those of instant messaging, text messaging, and blogging.
- **Increased Media Use** Kids and teens spend an average of six hours per day using media (Kaiser Family Foundation, 2005).
- **Internet as Reference Text** An increasing number of young people use the Internet as their primary reference text for everything, including school assignments.
- **Closing the Gap** The digital divide—long cited in the argument against technology-based learning in schools—is slowly closing. More students from all socioeconomic levels are gaining access to technology at home and in the community.

Using Technology to Teach

New technologies—and the media they make available—appeal to a variety of learners. These technologies can help motivate students to engage in reading, writing, and the use of other literacies, including traditional, school-based literacies and multiple texts (O'Brien, 2001, 2003). As you incorporate technology into your classroom, use the tips below.

Connect print text to digital text. Look for Web sites that support kids' reading. An emerging body of research shows that engagement with online texts can motivate struggling readers to read print texts as well (O'Brien, 2001; 2003, in press).

- In *Reading with Purpose,* the Literature Online feature encourages readers to research topics and authors by linking to a provided Web site. These sorts of intertextual links help motivate struggling, disengaged readers who are often tired of typical textbook formats—even when those books are interesting and accessible. For example, a selection in *Reading with Purpose* on skateboarder Tony Hawk (Unit 2's *Tony Hawk: Chairman of the Board*) can be augmented by using print and media texts from Tony Hawk's official Web site.

Connect print to other print media. Texts from popular genres (e.g., cartoons, illustrations, and graphic novels) motivate all learners. They also provide struggling learners, or those learners who lose attention easily when presented with traditional formats, a way to access and understand the lesson.

- In *Reading with Purpose,* cartoons are used to introduce reading skills, highlighting those skills' relevance in new and emerging literacies. Students can also engage the wide variety of reading selections culled from the literature most familiar to them—Web sites, magazines, graphic novels, and cartoons.

Utilize other digital resources to enhance reading. As educators, we want to connect digital texts to traditional ones; we do not, however, want to replace all print texts with digital ones. To foster this connection, though, we must be aware that digital media use is on the rise among middle school students. Also, we cannot ignore the extent to which digital media motivates and engages struggling readers, or readers who have disengaged from more typical reading tasks in school.

- *Reading with Purpose* offers an array of digital products that help students relate to what they read and acquire more skills. One such product is Skill Level Up!™, a computer game that helps students practice and master reading skills in a context with which many are probably familiar. Another product, StudentWorks, gives students a digitized work center wherein they can access many *Reading with Purpose* resources. Finally, the Web site glencoe.com provides a wealth of resources for digitally savvy students to use and enjoy.

Works Cited

Beach, R. 2000. "Critical Issues: Reading and responding to literature at the level of activity." *Journal of Literacy Research,* 32 (2), 237–251.

Beach, R. & O'Brien, D. (in press). "Teaching popular culture texts in the classroom." In D. Leu, J. Coiro, M. Knobel, & C. Lankshear (Eds.). *Handbook of research on new literacies.* Mahwah, NJ: Lawrence Erlbaum Associates.

Kaiser Family Foundation. March, 2005. "Generation M: Media in the Lives of 8–18 Year-olds."

O'Brien, D. G. 2001. "At-risk adolescents: Redefining competence through the multiliteracies of intermediality, visual arts, and representation." *Reading Online,* 4(11). Available http://www.readingonline.org/newliteracies/lit_index.asp?HREF=/newliteracies/obrien/index.html

O'Brien, D. G. 2003. "Juxtaposing traditional and intermedial literacies to redefine the competence of struggling adolescents." *Reading Online,* 6(7). Available: http://www.readingonline.org/newliteracies/lit_index.asp?HREF=obrien2/

O'Brien, D. G. (in press). "Struggling Adolescents' Engagement in Multimediating: Countering the Institutional Construction of Incompetence." In D. E. Alvermann, S. F. Phelps, D. R. Waff, K. A. Hinchman, & D. W. Moore (Eds) (2nd Ed.). *Reconceptualizing the literacies in adolescents' lives.* Mahwah, NJ: Erlbaum Associates.

Rushkoff, D. 1999. *Playing the future: What we can learn from digital kids.* New York: Riverhead.

Sefton-Green, J. (1998). "Introduction: Being Young in the Digital Age." In J. Sefton-Green (Ed.), *Digital Diversions: Youth Culture in the Age of Multimedia* (pp. 1–20). London: UCL Press Limited.

Project CRISS

By Carol M. Santa, Ph.D.

CRISS stands for CReating Independence through Student-owned Strategies. It is a staff development program that I created in collaboration with middle and high school teachers in Kalispell, Montana.

The CRISS Philosophy

Project CRISS is more than a collection of learning strategies. Its underlying power rests not on the individual strategies, but on the teaching philosophy behind them. This philosophy integrates work from cognitive psychology, social learning theory, and neurological research about how the brain learns. It incorporates these overlapping principles:

Background knowledge and purposeful reading are powerful determinants of reading comprehension.

Readers are far more likely to learn new information when they have some previous knowledge before they read or listen.

More Than Simply Reading We warn students not to simply begin reading. We also remind them to preview the assignment and think about their goals for reading. We ask students, *"What might you already know about the topic? What questions do you have about the topic?"*

KWLH One proven CRISS strategy for helping students activate prior knowledge is to develop a **KWHL** chart (**K**now, **W**ant to learn, **L**earned, **H**ow to learn more). Students can work together to generate a KWHL chart based on the model below. They can generate questions about what they want to learn, and then, after completing the reading assignment, they can list the new information they have learned and how they can learn more.

K	W	L	H
What I **KNOW**	What I **WANT** to find out	What I **LEARNED**	**HOW** I can learn more

Reading Goals *"Don't ignore your purposes for reading. Take time to think about them before delving into your reading."* We also suggest ways to make sure your students have clear goals for their reading. Each selection preview in *Glencoe Literature: Reading with Purpose* lists reading strategies and sets reading purposes.

Good readers have an intuitive understanding of the author's craft.

When students know how authors craft their writing, they can more readily understand and remember what they read. Good readers will analyze the author's style of presentation as they read. They might ask themselves, "What is this author doing to help me learn key concepts? How does the writer lead me from one idea to the next?"

Effective learners are actively involved when they listen and read.

We learn best when we act on the information presented. We can do this by using a variety of organizing activities that require us to write, talk, and transform the information we are absorbing.

Students need many opportunities to talk with one another about what they are learning.

We focus on how to get students to lead their own discussions about a topic. We want them to understand that it is their discussing, their oral grappling with meaning that leads to deeper understanding.

Competent readers know several ways to organize information for learning.

We show students different ways to organize information. They can take notes, underline selectively, develop concept maps, and summarize ideas in charts.

Students deserve opportunities to write about what they are learning.

Writing lets us figure out what we know and what we still need to know. The Writing Workshops in *Glencoe Literature: Reading with Purpose* guide students to explore various topics and communicate the information and impressions they have discovered.

Teaching involves explanation and modeling.

Students learn to think strategically when we use these processes as part of our instruction. Our demonstrations are especially critical for struggling readers. Most have never been taught how to learn. We have to show them how.

Take Center Stage When you introduce a new strategy, take center stage: show, tell, model, demonstrate, and explain the skill and how it is used by effective readers. As students learn to use the strategy, gradually release responsibility to them.

Systematic Approach Project CRISS is a valuable basis for instruction. It provides a systematic approach for using what we now know about teaching and learning. The following chart lists questions we need to continually ask ourselves while we are teaching. Use this chart to monitor your efforts to incorporate CRISS principles into your teaching.

CRISS Principles	The CRISS Philosophy	Yes	No	Somewhat
Background knowledge	• Did I assist students in thinking about what they already knew about the topic before beginning the unit? • Did I develop necessary concepts before students read?			
Purpose setting	• Did my students have a clear purpose about what they were going to learn before beginning the lesson?			
Author's craft	• Can my students use the author's style of presentation to facilitate their understanding?			
Active involvement	• Were my students engaged in the topic? • Did I help students become actively involved in their learning?			
Discussion	• Did my students have opportunities to talk about what they were learning?			
Organization	• Did my students organize information in a variety of ways?			
Writing	• Did my students write about what they were learning?			
Teacher modeling	• Did I do enough teacher modeling of learning strategies so that students could begin doing them on their own?			

Jamestown Education: Support for All Readers

For over 35 years, Jamestown Education has made its primary focus helping all readers become better readers. The Jamestown programs shown here are based on the latest research in adolescent literacy and on over 35 years of experience reaching adolescent readers. Each of these programs can help you build a comprehensive and well-coordinated literary program.

Jamestown Literature: An Adapted Reader

- Grade levels 6–10
- Reading Levels 3–8
- Instructional Support:
  This series provides grade-specific collections of literature adapted to lower reading levels. Providing struggling readers with alternative versions of canon literature offers an additional opportunity to differentiate instruction. Look for references to *Jamestown Literature: An Adapted Reader* in the Teacher Wraparound Edition. These mean you can find the same selection in both *Glencoe Literature: Reading with Purpose* and *Jamestown Literature.*

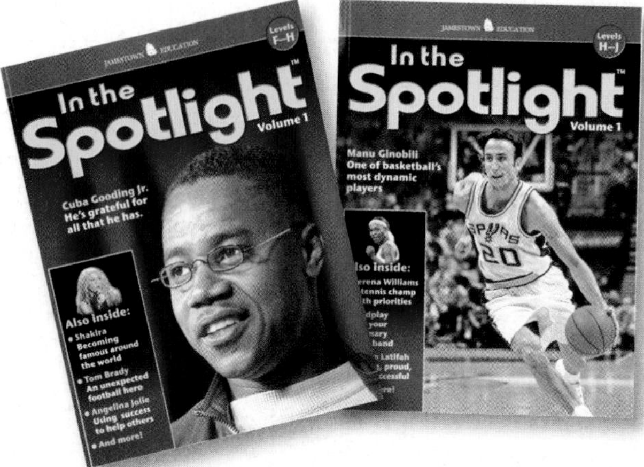

In the Spotlight™

- Reading Levels 2–10
- Instructional Support:
  This eight-book series will provide your students with engaging and motivating biographies to read while building their reading skills and vocabulary development. In each graduated unit, students are guided before, during, and after reading, with comprehension, skill, and vocabulary reinforcement, as well as writing exercises.

Timed Readings, Timed Readings Plus, Timed Readings in Literature

- Reading Levels 1–13+
- Instructional Support:
  Each series (ten books in each) will help your students increase both reading rate and comprehension. The fiction and nonfiction passages of uniform length are designed for systematic classroom practice to improve reading rate and comprehension of text.

Reading Fluency

- Reading Levels 1–10
- Instructional Support:
  This seven-book series will help your students read smoothly, accurately, and expressively. Students work in pairs to provide immediate feedback and self-assessment. Author Camille Blachowicz states that "the ability to read fluently is highly correlated with many other measures of reading competence."

Jamestown Reading Improvement

- Reading Levels 4–10
- Instructional Support:
  Authored by renowned reading expert Edward Fry, this eight-book series focuses on helping build your students' comprehension, vocabulary, and study skills. Repeated practice with targeted exercises ensures mastery of valuable reading skills.

Critical Reading Series

- Reading Levels 2–8
- Instructional Support:
  This 27-book high interest series, written at three reading spans, encourages your reluctant readers to build a love for nonfiction while focusing on critical reading skills. Topics ranging from *Fateful Journeys* to *Weird Science* to *Heroes* draw students in, while giving students ample opportunities to master important skills found on both state and national tests.

Jamestown's Reading Navigator

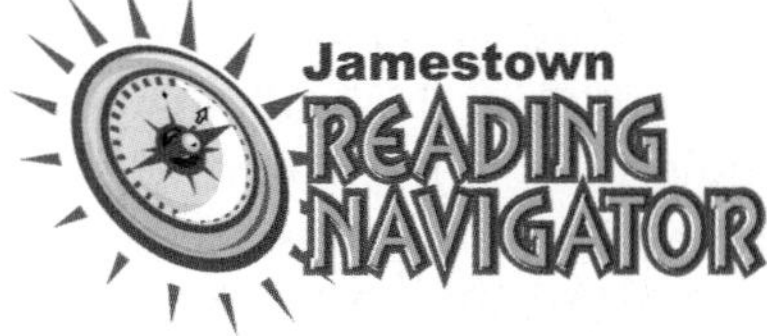

Jamestown Reading Navigator is an online and print-based intervention program built upon the latest research in adolescent literary, *Reading Next.* Here are the key objectives of the online version, available to students 24 hours a day from anywhere they can connect to the Web.

- Increase student achievement through direct, explicit instruction in comprehension strategies and modeling of good reading practices.
- Motivate and engage reluctant readers with a student-directed, self-paced learning environment enriched with interactive activities and media.
- Provide built in formative and summative assessment to help teachers track student progress and make instructional decisions.

Teaching Students from Impoverished Backgrounds

by Ruby K. Payne, Ph.D.

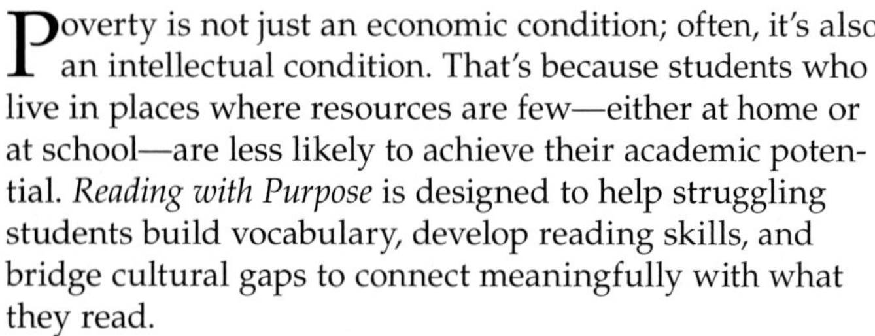

Poverty is not just an economic condition; often, it's also an intellectual condition. That's because students who live in places where resources are few—either at home or at school—are less likely to achieve their academic potential. *Reading with Purpose* is designed to help struggling students build vocabulary, develop reading skills, and bridge cultural gaps to connect meaningfully with what they read.

Many of the students to whom this series is geared lack adequate vocabulary skills. Research indicates that a child whose caregivers are welfare-dependent hears about 10 million words in a given two-year time frame. Within that same time frame, however, a child whose caregivers are educated professionals hears about 30 million words (Betty Hart and Todd Risley). This research also shows that a three-year-old from a professional household has a larger vocabulary than an adult from a welfare-dependent one.

Lev Vygotsky's research tells us that vocabulary is stored and used vis-à-vis schema, or networks of thoughts. That is, we make sense of new ideas in relationship to old ones and are more likely to remember words and concepts that are proximal to the things we know and care about. Margaret McKeown's work shows that vocabulary is best learned in a non-threatening environment, a few words at a time. This is important, as Maria Montano-Harmon's work tells us that the longer children exist in poverty, the less "formal" diction and syntax they know.

Built upon this and other research, *Reading with Purpose* equips kids to learn new words organically and at a moderate pace. Vocabulary exercises are not *just* exercises; instead, vocabulary activities extend and deepen students' knowledge of what they are already reading. In this way, these books invite students to use and expand their own schema, one [manageable] step at a time.

Research also shows that many students from impoverished backgrounds lack the ability to think critically about what they read. They don't know how to set a purpose for reading or how to evaluate, draw conclusions about, or summarize the work they're assigned. Many struggle to form and understand questions. Question-making is an important cognitive skill, as it allows us to assess our knowledge (or lack thereof). It is also a reading skill, though, as questioning facilitates connection to and comprehension of the texts that we encounter.

Reading with Purpose teaches students how to ask the questions that matter. It also gives students focused instruction in other reading skills they need. In that vein, this series' Reading, Comparing Literature, and Reading Across Texts Workshops encourage students to become confident, inquisitive, and independent learners by allowing them to practice—and master—proven strategies.

Other research indicates that, for many students from impoverished backgrounds, there exists a significant gap between the culture of home and the culture of school. For example, if a student's home culture is not print-rich, or values oral traditions over written ones, he or she may struggle in school. If a student's home culture is reactive—but his or her classroom culture is proactive—then he or she may struggle in school. Finally, if a student's home culture says that asking questions or discussing ideas openly is rude or disrespectful, then he or she may (and probably will) struggle in school.

This series demonstrates sensitivity toward these and other cultural differences. It utilizes work by men and women of varying ages, races, and ethnicities. The Unit Challenge feature encourages students to begin each unit with an end project in mind; this strategy helps unfocused students become proactive, productive learners. The Analyzing Cartoons feature appeals to visual learners, as do the graphic story selections. The Reading on Your Own feature gives an eager reader the place to begin his or her own reading adventure.

In the United States today, 13 million children live in poverty. Most of them live in urban areas. As educators, we must strive to reach these learners before it is too late. *Reading with Purpose* seeks to do just that, providing these students with the tools they need for learning success.

Guide to Text Readability

Throughout the teacher materials in your **Teacher Wraparound Edition,** you will encounter DRP readability measures assigned to the reading selections in *Reading with Purpose.* You will also find readability scores based on the Lexile Framework® for Reading and the Dale-Chall Readability Formula. You can use these scores to select reading materials that are suitable for your entire class, or individual students.

Degrees of Reading Power® (DRP)

DRP values indicate the readability of prose text. The higher the value, the more difficult the text. The scale ranges from 1 to 100; commonly encountered English text tends to fall somewhere between 25 and 85. Although middle school texts have an average difficulty of 56 and high school texts have an average difficulty of 62, no single readability level is appropriate for each grade level. Rather, a typical classroom has materials with a range of readability levels available for use—some intended for less-proficient readers, some for average readers, and some for stronger readers. The following chart shows the average DRP readability range for materials widely available for use at each grade. Some materials you might use, however, will certainly fall outside the range for your particular grade.

Grade	DRP Readability Ranges
6	51–61
7	52–62
8	53–64
9	53–65
10	51–68
11	56–67
12	57–68

The Lexile® Framework

A lexile measure assigned to a text is the specific number that describes the reading demands of the text. The typical Lexile Scale ranges from 200 to 1700 Lexiles. As with the DRP measures, there is not a direct translation from a specific Lexile measure to a specific grade level. Within any classroom, there will be a range of readers and a range of materials to be read. The levels shown on the following chart indicate the approximate range of Lexile scores for 50 percent of the materials found in a typical grade-level classroom. For example, the middle half of the instructional materials typically found in a sixth-grade classroom range in difficulty from about 850L to 1050L.

Grade	Text Measures (from Lexile Framework Map)
6	850L to 1050L
7	950L to 1075L
8	1000L to 1100L
9	1050L to 1150L
10	1100L to 1200L
11 and 12	1100L to 1300L

Dale-Chall Readability Formula

The Dale-Chall Formula is based on the average sentence length and the number of unfamiliar words in a passage. The idea behind this formula is that readers typically find it easier to read, process, and recall a passage if the words and sentences are familiar and grade appropriate. The Dale-Chall Formula assesses the difficulty of a passage by computing two different values from the text. The first measure is the average number of words per sentence. The second measure is the percentage of words in the passage not found on the grade appropriate Dale Word List. The following chart shows the average Dale-Chall readability scores for grades 5 through 12.

Grade	DRP Readability Ranges
5–6	5.0 to 5.9
7–8	6.0 to 6.9
9–10	7.0 to 7.9
11–12	8.0 to 8.9

* Degrees of Reading Power, DRP, and TASA are registered trademarks of Touchstone Applied Science Associates, Inc. (TASA). Lexile is a registered trademark of MetaMetrics, Inc.

Scope and Sequence

The following charts provide an overview of the scope and sequence for *Reading with Purpose,* Grade 8. A more detailed Skills Scope and Sequence can be found on the interleaf pages preceding each unit.

○ = focused instruction

● = review

Skills	UNIT 1	UNIT 2	UNIT 3	UNIT 4	UNIT 5	UNIT 6	UNIT 7	UNIT 8
Reading Skills								
Activate prior knowledge	○							
Analyze		○			○	●		○
Clarify							○	
Compare and contrast		○		●		●		
Connect	○	●	●	○	●	●		
Distinguish fact and opinion							○	
Draw conclusions						○		
Evaluate				○				
Identify author's purpose	○							○
Identify main ideas and supporting details			○					○
Infer		○	●		○			
Interpret				○	●	○		
Monitor comprehension				○	●			
Paraphrase and summarize						○		
Predict		○	●		○		●	
Preview			○					
Question					○		○	
Review							○	
Set a purpose for reading	○	●						
Skim and scan			○					
Understand cause and effect								○
Use text features			○					
Visualize						○		●

○ = focused instruction ● = review

Skills	UNIT 1	UNIT 2	UNIT 3	UNIT 4	UNIT 5	UNIT 6	UNIT 7	UNIT 8
Literary Elements								
Art, scene, and stage directions						○		
Characterization					○			
Conflict		○		○				●
Cultural reference	○							○
Description	○		●				○	
Dialogue/monologue						○		○
Figurative language				○		○		○
Foreshadowing			○					
Humor			○					
Imagery			○		○			○
Irony			○			●		
Lyrics				○				
Mood and tone	○		○		○	○		
Plot		○			○		○	
Point of view	○							○
Protagonist and antagonist		○						
Repetition				○				
Rhyme, rhythm, and meter				○				
Sequence	○	○						
Setting		○			○	○		
Sound devices			○	○		○		
Style		○						○
Symbolism			○					
Theme		○			○			○
Text Elements								
Author's bias and credibility			○				○	○
Chronological order								○
Persuasive appeal							○	
Photos and illustrations			○					
Quotations					○			
Titles and heads	○							

○ = focused instruction ● = review

Skills	UNIT 1	UNIT 2	UNIT 3	UNIT 4	UNIT 5	UNIT 6	UNIT 7	UNIT 8
Literary Genres								
Biography	○	●		●	●	●	●	●
Drama						○		
Folktales		○						
Historical documents				●				○
Informational media	●	●	○	●	●	●	●	●
Persuasive writing							○	
Poetry	●	●	●	○	●	●		●
Short story	●	●	●		○	●	●	●
Vocabulary Skills								
Compound words				○				
Context clues	○							
Denotation/editorial connotation							○	
Historical influences on English						○		○
Multiple-meaning words			○					
Semantic slanting							○	
Structural analysis					○			
Structural analysis: Anglo-Saxon						○		
Structural analysis: Greek						○		
Structural analysis: Latin						○		
Synonyms and antonyms		○						
Word choice				○				
Word references			○					
Writing Skills • Writing Products								
Autobiographical narrative	○							
Dramatic scene						○		
Folktale		○						
Letter								○
Persuasive essay							○	
Poem			○					
Research report		○						
Short story				○				

○ = focused instruction   ● = review

Skills	UNIT 1	UNIT 2	UNIT 3	UNIT 4	UNIT 5	UNIT 6	UNIT 7	UNIT 8
Writing Skills • Writing Process								
Drafting	○	●	●	●	●	●	●	●
Editing	○	●	●	●	●	●	●	●
Presenting/publishing	○	●	●	●	●	●	●	●
Prewriting	○	●	●	●	●	●	●	●
Proofreading	○	●	●	●	●	●	●	●
Revising	○	●	●	●	●	●	●	●
Writing Skills • Writing Traits								
Conventions			○					
Ideas		○						
Organization					○			
Presentation								○
Sentence fluency and variety							○	
Voice	○					○		
Word Choice				○				
Writing Skills • Grammar								
Clauses and phrases		○	○		○			
Parts of speech	○	○						
Punctuation			○		○	○	○	
Sentences			○		○			
Subject-verb agreement				○				
Listening, Speaking, and Viewing								
Active listening and group discussion	○	●	●	●	○	●	●	●
Interviewing		●						○
Oral presentations	●	●	○	●	●		●	
Oral reading				○		○	●	
Persuasive techniques		●				●	○	
Storytelling		○						
Using visuals	●	●	●	●	●	●	●	●
Viewing art	●	●	●	●	●	●	●	●
Viewing cartoons	●	●	●	●	●	●	●	●
Viewing photographs	●	●	●	●	●	●	●	●

Teacher Edition Walk-Through

To Teachers:

Welcome to the Teacher Wraparound Edition of *Glencoe Literature: Reading with Purpose.* We have created this teacher edition based on input from experienced teachers and educational consultants. Teaching suggestions, additional resources, and leveled activities for differentiated instruction are all labeled and "wrapped" around the student text for your convenience.

Planning the Unit

Planning pages appear at the beginning of each unit.

Unit Preview Tells you about the Big Question and genre focus found in the unit

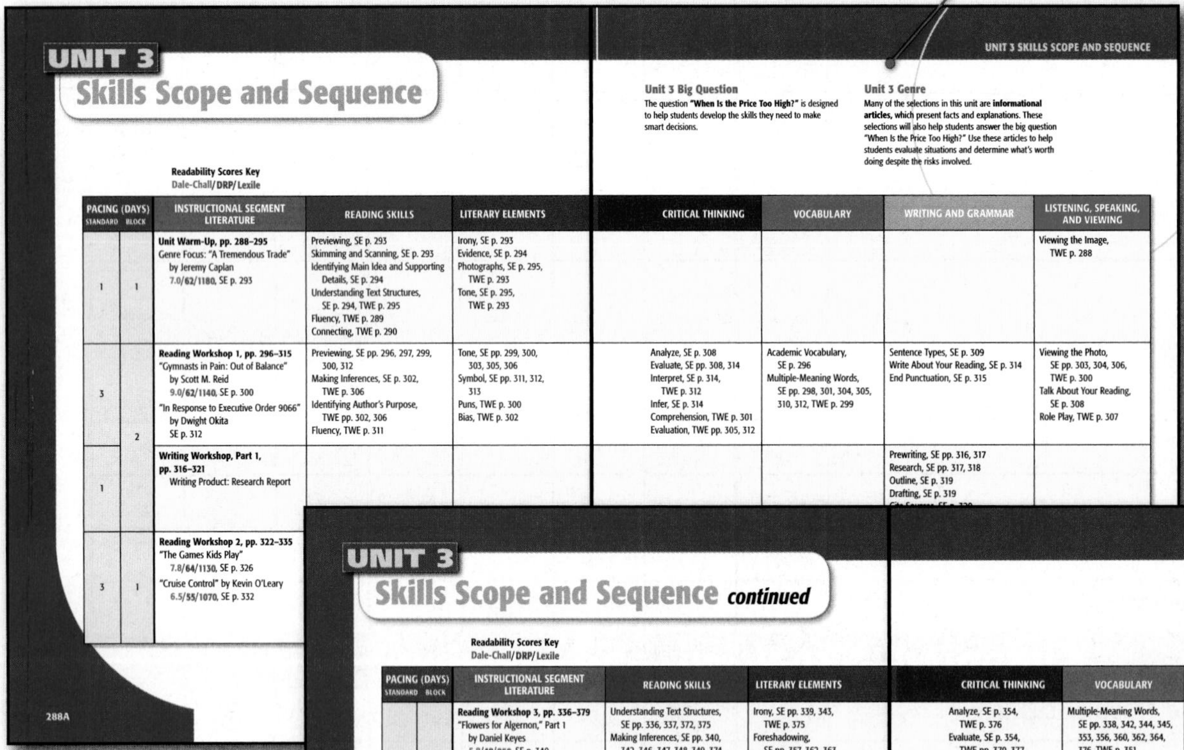

UNIT 3

Skills Scope and Sequence

UNIT 3 SKILLS SCOPE AND SEQUENCE

Unit 3 Big Question

The question **"When Is the Price Too High?"** is designed to help students develop the skills they need to make smart decisions.

Unit 3 Genre

Many of the selections in this unit are **informational articles,** which present facts and explanations. These selections will also help students answer the big question "When Is the Price Too High?" Use these articles to help students evaluate situations and determine what's worth doing despite the risks involved.

Readability Scores Key
Dale-Chall/**DRP**/**Lexile**

PACING (DAYS) STANDARD	BLOCK	INSTRUCTIONAL SEGMENT LITERATURE	READING SKILLS	LITERARY ELEMENTS	CRITICAL THINKING	VOCABULARY	WRITING AND GRAMMAR	LISTENING, SPEAKING, AND VIEWING
1	1	**Unit Warm-Up, pp. 288–295** Genre Focus: "A Tremendous Trade" by Jeremy Caplan 7.0/62/1180, SE p. 293	Previewing, SE p. 293 Skimming and Scanning, SE p. 293 Identifying Main Idea and Supporting Details, SE p. 294 Understanding Text Structures, SE p. 294, TWE p. 295 Fluency, TWE p. 289 Connecting, TWE p. 290	Irony, SE p. 293 Evidence, SE p. 294 Photographs, SE p. 295, TWE p. 293 Tone, SE p. 295, TWE p. 293				Viewing the Image, TWE p. 288
3	2	**Reading Workshop 1, pp. 296–315** "Gymnasts in Pain: Out of Balance" by Scott M. Reid 9.0/62/1140, SE p. 300 "In Response to Executive Order 9066" by Dwight Okita SE p. 312	Previewing, SE pp. 296, 297, 299, 300, 312 Making Inferences, SE p. 302, TWE p. 306 Identifying Author's Purpose, TWE pp. 302, 306 Fluency, TWE p. 311	Tone, SE pp. 299, 300, 303, 305, 306 Symbol, SE pp. 311, 312, 313 Puns, TWE p. 300 Bias, TWE p. 302	Analyze, SE p. 308 Evaluate, SE pp. 308, 314 Interpret, SE p. 314, TWE p. 312 Infer, SE p. 314 Comprehension, TWE p. 301 Evaluation, TWE pp. 305, 312	Academic Vocabulary, SE p. 296 Multiple-Meaning Words, SE pp. 298, 301, 304, 305, 310, 312, TWE p. 299	Sentence Types, SE p. 309 Write About Your Reading, SE p. 314 End Punctuation, SE p. 315	Viewing the Photo, SE pp. 303, 304, 306, TWE p. 300 Talk About Your Reading, SE p. 308 Role Play, TWE p. 307
1		**Writing Workshop, Part 1, pp. 316–321** Writing Product: Research Report					Prewriting, SE pp. 316, 317 Research, SE pp. 317, 318 Outline, SE p. 319 Drafting, SE p. 319	
3	1	**Reading Workshop 2, pp. 322–335** "The Games Kids Play" 7.8/64/1130, SE p. 326 "Cruise Control" by Kevin O'Leary 6.5/55/1070, SE p. 332						

288A

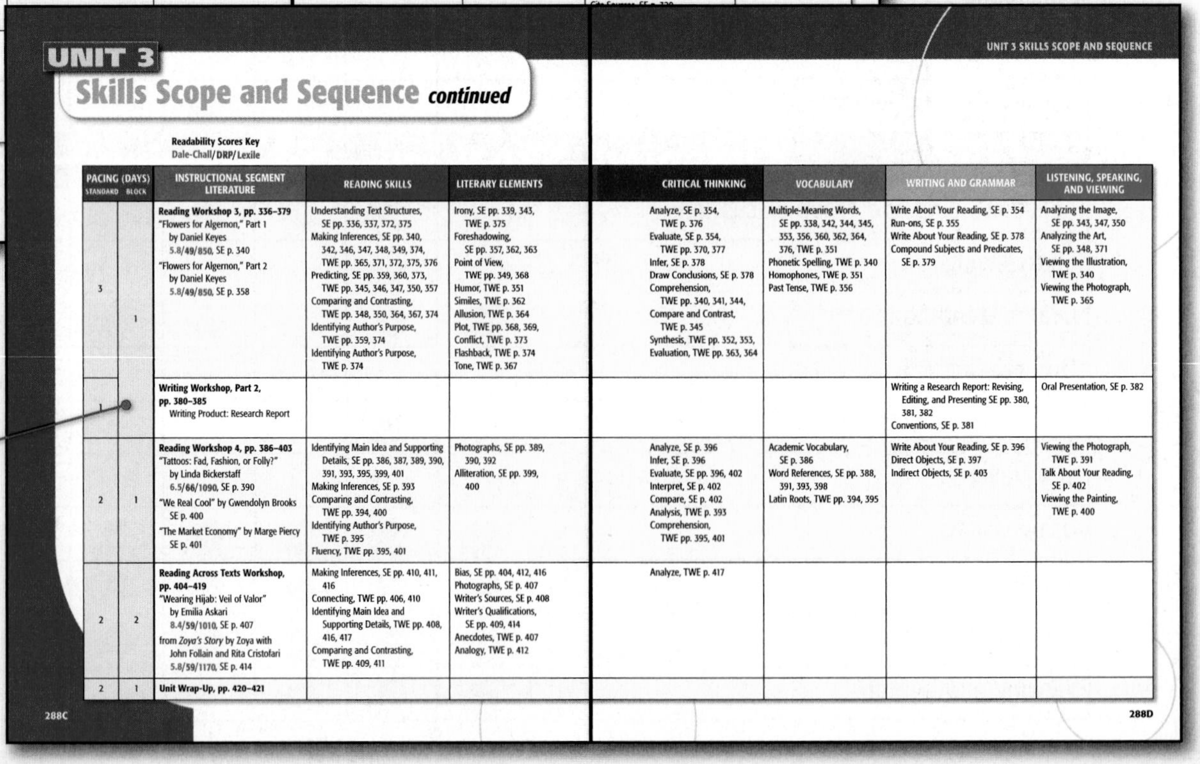

UNIT 3

Skills Scope and Sequence ***continued***

UNIT 3 SKILLS SCOPE AND SEQUENCE

Readability Scores Key
Dale-Chall/**DRP**/**Lexile**

PACING (DAYS) STANDARD	BLOCK	INSTRUCTIONAL SEGMENT LITERATURE	READING SKILLS	LITERARY ELEMENTS	CRITICAL THINKING	VOCABULARY	WRITING AND GRAMMAR	LISTENING, SPEAKING, AND VIEWING
3	1	**Reading Workshop 3, pp. 336–379** "Flowers for Algernon," Part 1 by Daniel Keyes 5.8/49/850, SE p. 340 "Flowers for Algernon," Part 2 by Daniel Keyes 5.8/49/850, SE p. 358	Understanding Text Structures, SE pp. 336, 337, 372, 375 Making Inferences, SE pp. 340, 342, 346, 347, 348, 349, 374, TWE pp. 365, 371, 372, 375, 376 Predicting, SE pp. 359, 360, 373, TWE pp. 345, 346, 347, 350, 357 Comparing and Contrasting, TWE pp. 348, 350, 364, 367, 374 Identifying Author's Purpose, TWE pp. 359, 374 Identifying Author's Purpose, TWE p. 374	Irony, SE pp. 339, 343, TWE p. 375 Foreshadowing, SE pp. 357, 362, 363 Point of View, TWE pp. 349, 368 Humor, TWE p. 351 Similes, TWE p. 362 Allusion, TWE p. 364 Plot, TWE pp. 368, 369, Conflict, TWE p. 373 Flashback, TWE p. 374 Tone, TWE p. 367	Analyze, SE p. 354, TWE p. 376 Evaluate, SE p. 354, TWE pp. 370, 377 Infer, SE p. 378 Draw Conclusions, SE p. 378 Comprehension, TWE pp. 340, 341, 344, Compare and Contrast, TWE p. 345 Synthesis, TWE pp. 352, 353, Evaluation, TWE pp. 363, 364	Multiple-Meaning Words, SE pp. 338, 342, 344, 345, 353, 356, 360, 362, 364, 376, TWE p. 351 Phonetic Spelling, TWE p. 340 Homophones, TWE p. 351 Past Tense, TWE p. 356	Write About Your Reading, SE p. 354 Run-ons, SE p. 355 Write About Your Reading, SE p. 378 Compound Subjects and Predicates, SE p. 379	Analyzing the Image, SE pp. 343, 347, 350 Analyzing the Art, SE pp. 348, 371 Viewing the Illustration, TWE p. 340 Viewing the Photograph, TWE p. 365
1		**Writing Workshop, Part 2, pp. 380–385** Writing Product: Research Report					Writing a Research Report: Revising, Editing, and Presenting SE pp. 380, 381, 382 Conventions, SE p. 381	Oral Presentation, SE p. 382
2	1	**Reading Workshop 4, pp. 386–403** "Tattoos: Fad, Fashion, or Folly?" by Linda Bickerstaff 6.5/66/1090, SE p. 390 "We Real Cool" by Gwendolyn Brooks SE p. 400 "The Market Economy" by Marge Piercy SE p. 401	Identifying Main Idea and Supporting Details, SE pp. 386, 387, 389, 390, 391, 393, 395, 399, 401 Making Inferences, SE p. 393 Comparing and Contrasting, TWE pp. 394, 400 Identifying Author's Purpose, TWE p. 395 Fluency, TWE pp. 395, 401	Photographs, SE pp. 389, 390, 392 Alliteration, SE pp. 399, 400	Analyze, SE p. 396 Infer, SE p. 396 Evaluate, SE pp. 396, 402 Interpret, SE p. 402 Compare, SE p. 402 Analysis, TWE p. 393 Comprehension, TWE pp. 395, 401	Academic Vocabulary, SE p. 386 Word References, SE pp. 388, 391, 393, 398 Latin Roots, TWE pp. 394, 395	Write About Your Reading, SE p. 396 Direct Objects, SE p. 397 Indirect Objects, SE p. 403	Viewing the Photograph, TWE p. 391 Talk About Your Reading, SE p. 402 Viewing the Painting, TWE p. 400
2	2	**Reading Across Texts Workshop, pp. 404–419** "Wearing Hijab: Veil of Valor" by Emilia Askari 8.4/59/1010, SE p. 407 from *Zoya's Story* by Zoya with John Follain and Rita Cristofari 5.8/59/1170, SE p. 414	Making Inferences, SE pp. 410, 411, 416 Connecting, TWE pp. 406, 410 Identifying Main Idea and Supporting Details, TWE pp. 408, 416, 417 Comparing and Contrasting, TWE pp. 409, 411	Bias, SE pp. 404, 412, 416 Photographs, SE p. 407 Writer's Sources, SE p. 408 Writer's Qualifications, SE pp. 409, 414 Anecdotes, TWE p. 407 Analogy, TWE p. 412	Analyze, TWE p. 417			
2	1	**Unit Wrap-Up, pp. 420–421**						

288C

288D

Pacing Chart Specifies skills to each selection and provides time management suggestions for teaching the unit

Teaching the Unit

Reading Preview Background about the skills and selections taught in the unit and how to use the material to help students answer the Big Question

Objectives Lists the main teaching goals of the unit

BQ Focus Some text about the connections and importance of the unit Big Question

INTRODUCING UNIT 3

Key Unit Objectives

- Answer the Big Question
- Apply the unit's key reading skills to informational articles
- Analyze the literary elements of informational articles
- Write a research report

BIG Question

Why Is It Important?
Addressing this Big Question encourages students to weigh costs and benefits when they make a decision.

Viewing the Image
Surfer Bethany Hamilton was 13 when she lost her arm in a shark attack. She began surfing again only a month after the attack and continues to win awards for her skills. **Ask:** How do you think Bethany would respond to the quote on this page? What might she value? Why do you think surfing is worth the risks for her? *(Possible response: Bethany values surfing, athletics, being in the ocean, and competing. It might be worth the risks because she loves it so much.)* OL

UNIT 3

The BIG Question

When Is the Price Too High?

"What you risk reveals what you value."
—Jeanette Winterson, contemporary British novelist

LOOKING AHEAD

The skill lessons and readings in this unit will help you develop your own answer to the Big Question.

289

INTRODUCING UNIT 3

About the Reading
Each selection in this unit provides insights that can help students address the question, "When is the price too high?" As students read, they will consider how people weigh the costs and benefits of their decisions and develop criteria for weighing their own decisions.

About the Skills
The skills taught in this unit have been selected because they are particularly helpful when reading the featured genre—informational articles. Each reading selection provides students with opportunities to practice and develop these skills.

NCLB No Child Left Behind

The goals of the NCLB act include a strong emphasis on reading informational articles. The reading skills featured in this unit are particularly helpful for improving comprehension of informational texts. Make sure students understand the importance of practicing the skills and using them when they read and take tests.

Unit Skills

Reading Skills
- Previewing, p. 296
- Skimming and Scanning, p. 322
- Understanding Text Structures, p. 336
- Identifying Main Idea and Supporting Details, p. 386

Vocabulary
- Multiple-Meaning Words, p. 298
- Word References, p. 388

BIG Question When is the price too high?
Genre Focus: Informational Articles

Literary and Text Elements
- Tone, p. 299
- Evidence, p. 325
- Irony, p. 339
- Photographs, p. 389

Writing Skills/Grammar
- Research Report, pp. 316, 380
- Simple Sentences, p. 321
- Conventions, p. 381

288

Reading Fluency

Practicing Pronunciation Tell students that if they are reading informational articles on new subjects, they may come across new and unfamiliar words. To improve fluency, help students sound out any unfamiliar words they encounter in the informational articles and other selections in this unit. Have students work with partners to practice reading aloud. Encourage them to stop when they come across a new word, work together with their partner to determine pronunciation, and then return to the beginning of the sentence and continue reading smoothly without hesitation. EL BL

Indiana English/Language Arts Academic Standards
TWE: *Reading Fluency* 8.1

289

Quick Skill Reference Convenient page reference of unit skills

NCLB Provides suggestions for meeting No Child Left Behind requirements

Understanding the Brackets and Letters

Letters The letters on the reduced student edition page identify the type of skill or activity. See the key below to learn about the different types of skills and activities.

Brackets Brackets on the reduced student edition page correspond to teaching the skills and activities. The brackets show you exactly where to teach the skills and activities for each workshop.

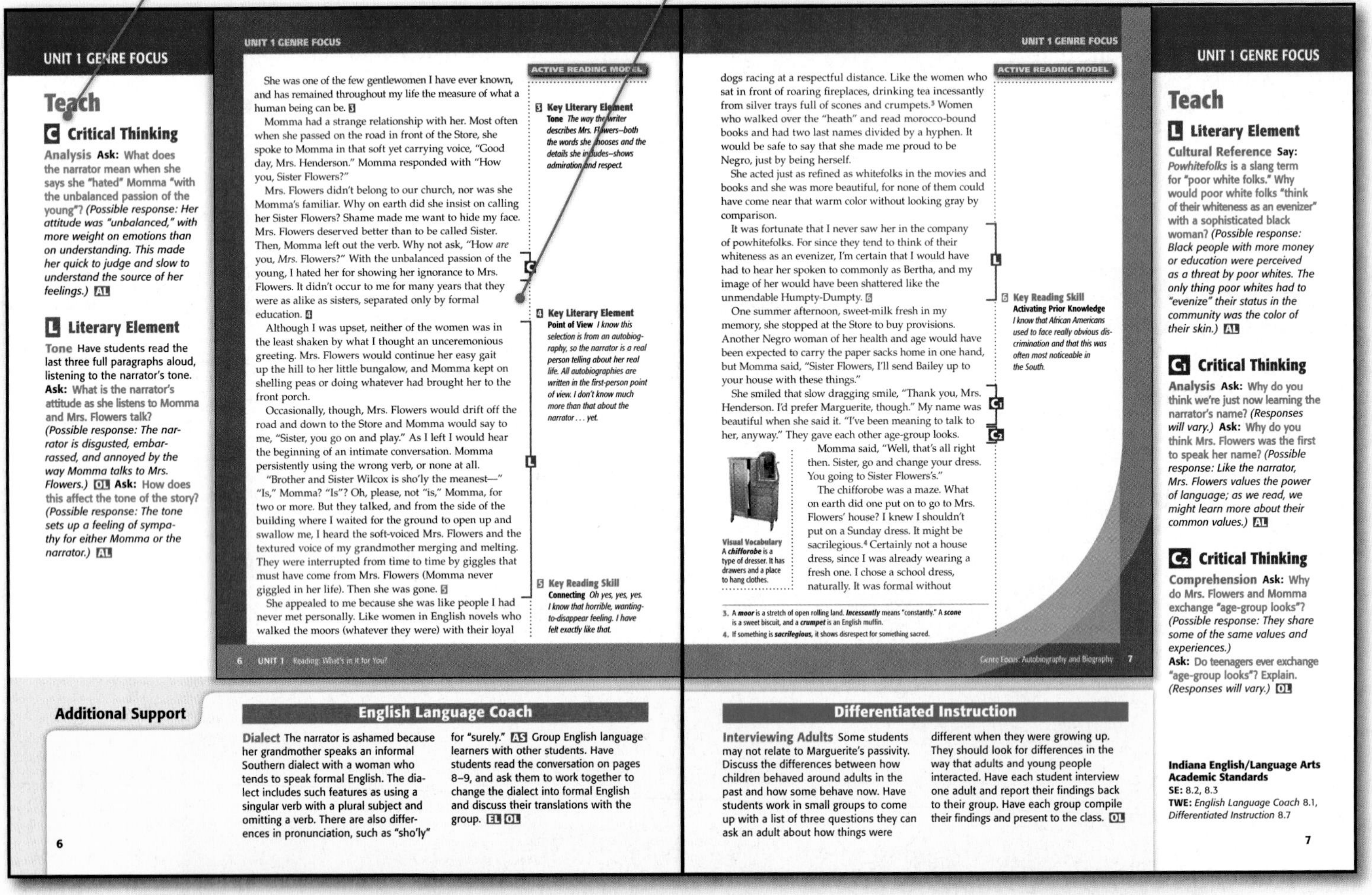

UNIT 1 GENRE FOCUS

Teach

C Critical Thinking

Analysis Ask: What does the narrator mean when she says she "hated" Momma "with the unbalanced passion of the young"? *(Possible response: Her attitude was "unbalanced," with more weight on emotions than on understanding. This made her quick to judge and slow to understand the source of her feelings.)* AL

L Literary Element

Tone Have students read the last three full paragraphs aloud, listening to the narrator's tone. **Ask:** What is the narrator's attitude as she listens to Momma and Mrs. Flowers talk? *(Possible response: The narrator is disgusted, embarrassed, and annoyed by the way Momma talks to Mrs. Flowers.)* OL **Ask:** How does this affect the tone of the story? *(Possible response: The tone sets up a feeling of sympathy for either Momma or the narrator.)* AL

UNIT 1 GENRE FOCUS

ACTIVE READING MODEL

She was one of the few gentlewomen I have ever known, and has remained throughout my life the measure of what a human being can be. 3

Momma had a strange relationship with her. Most often when she passed on the road in front of the Store, she spoke to Momma in that soft yet carrying voice, "Good day, Mrs. Henderson." Momma responded with "How you, Sister Flowers?"

Mrs. Flowers didn't belong to our church, nor was she Momma's familiar. Why on earth did she insist on calling her Sister Flowers? Shame made me want to hide my face. Mrs. Flowers deserved better than to be called Sister. Then, Momma left out the verb. Why not ask, "How *are* you, *Mrs.* Flowers?" With the unbalanced passion of the young, I hated her for showing her ignorance to Mrs. Flowers. It didn't occur to me for many years that they were as alike as sisters, separated only by formal education. 4 [C]

Although I was upset, neither of the women was in the least shaken by what I thought an unceremonious greeting. Mrs. Flowers would continue her easy gait up the hill to her little bungalow, and Momma kept on shelling peas or doing whatever had brought her to the front porch.

Occasionally, though, Mrs. Flowers would drift off the road and down to the Store and Momma would say to me, "Sister, you go on and play." As I left I would hear the beginning of an intimate conversation. Momma persistently using the wrong verb, or none at all. [L]

"Brother and Sister Wilcox is sho'ly the meanest—" "Is," Momma? "Is"? Oh, please, not "is," Momma, for two or more. But they talked, and from the side of the building where I waited for the ground to open up and swallow me, I heard the soft-voiced Mrs. Flowers and the textured voice of my grandmother merging and melting. They were interrupted from time to time by giggles that must have come from Mrs. Flowers (Momma never giggled in her life). Then she was gone. 5

She appealed to me because she was like people I had never met personally. Like women in English novels who walked the moors (whatever they were) with their loyal

3 Key Literary Element
Tone *The way the writer describes Mrs. Flowers—both the words she chooses and the details she includes—shows admiration and respect.*

4 Key Literary Element
Point of View *I know this selection is from an autobiography, so the narrator is a real person telling about her real life. All autobiographies are written in the first-person point of view. I don't know much more than that about the narrator . . . yet.*

5 Key Reading Skill
Connecting *Oh yes, yes, yes. I know that horrible, wanting-to-disappear feeling. I have felt exactly like that.*

6 UNIT 1 Reading: What's in it for You?

UNIT 1 GENRE FOCUS

ACTIVE READING MODEL

dogs racing at a respectful distance. Like the women who sat in front of roaring fireplaces, drinking tea incessantly from silver trays full of scones and crumpets.[3] Women who walked over the "heath" and read morocco-bound books and had two last names divided by a hyphen. It would be safe to say that she made me proud to be Negro, just by being herself.

She acted just as refined as whitefolks in the movies and books and she was more beautiful, for none of them could have come near that warm color without looking gray by comparison.

It was fortunate that I never saw her in the company of powhitefolks. For since they tend to think of their whiteness as an evenizer, I'm certain that I would have had to hear her spoken to commonly as Bertha, and my image of her would have been shattered like the unmendable Humpty-Dumpty. 6 [L]

One summer afternoon, sweet-milk fresh in my memory, she stopped at the Store to buy provisions. Another Negro woman of her health and age would have been expected to carry the paper sacks home in one hand, but Momma said, "Sister Flowers, I'll send Bailey up to your house with these things."

She smiled that slow dragging smile, "Thank you, Mrs. Henderson. I'd prefer Marguerite, though." My name was beautiful when she said it. [C1] "I've been meaning to talk to her, anyway." They gave each other age-group looks. [C2]

Momma said, "Well, that's all right then. Sister, go and change your dress. You going to Sister Flowers's."

The chifforobe was a maze. What on earth did one put on to go to Mrs. Flowers' house? I knew I shouldn't put on a Sunday dress. It might be sacrilegious.[4] Certainly not a house dress, since I was already wearing a fresh one. I chose a school dress, naturally. It was formal without

Visual Vocabulary
A ***chifforobe*** is a type of dresser. It has drawers and a place to hang clothes.

3. A ***moor*** is a stretch of open rolling land. ***Incessantly*** means "constantly." A ***scone*** is a sweet biscuit, and a ***crumpet*** is an English muffin.
4. If something is ***sacrilegious***, it shows disrespect for something sacred.

6 Key Reading Skill
Activating Prior Knowledge *I know that African Americans used to face really obvious discrimination and that this was often most noticeable in the South.*

Genre Focus: Autobiography and Biography 7

UNIT 1 GENRE FOCUS

Teach

L Literary Element

Cultural Reference Say: *Powhitefolks* is a slang term for "poor white folks." Why would poor white folks "think of their whiteness as an evenizer" with a sophisticated black woman? *(Possible response: Black people with more money or education were perceived as a threat by poor whites. The only thing poor whites had to "evenize" their status in the community was the color of their skin.)* AL

C1 Critical Thinking

Analysis Ask: Why do you think we're just now learning the narrator's name? *(Responses will vary.)* **Ask:** Why do you think Mrs. Flowers was the first to speak her name? *(Possible response: Like the narrator, Mrs. Flowers values the power of language; as we read, we might learn more about their common values.)* AL

C2 Critical Thinking

Comprehension Ask: Why do Mrs. Flowers and Momma exchange "age-group looks"? *(Possible response: They share some of the same values and experiences.)*
Ask: Do teenagers ever exchange "age-group looks"? Explain. *(Responses will vary.)* OL

Additional Support

English Language Coach

Dialect The narrator is ashamed because her grandmother speaks an informal Southern dialect with a woman who tends to speak formal English. The dialect includes such features as using a singular verb with a plural subject and omitting a verb. There are also differences in pronunciation, such as "sho'ly" for "surely." AS Group English language learners with other students. Have students read the conversation on pages 8–9, and ask them to work together to change the dialect into formal English and discuss their translations with the group. EL OL

6

Differentiated Instruction

Interviewing Adults Some students may not relate to Marguerite's passivity. Discuss the differences between how children behaved around adults in the past and how some behave now. Have students work in small groups to come up with a list of three questions they can ask an adult about how things were different when they were growing up. They should look for differences in the way that adults and young people interacted. Have each student interview one adult and report their findings back to their group. Have each group compile their findings and present to the class. OL

Indiana English/Language Arts Academic Standards
SE: 8.2, 8.3
TWE: *English Language Coach* 8.1, *Differentiated Instruction* 8.7

7

Teacher Wraparound Edition Key

R Reading Skill These activities help you teach reading skills and vocabulary.

V Vocabulary These activities help students comprehend words and incorporate into reading.

C Critical Thinking These strategies help students apply and extend what they have learned.

BQ BIG Question These activities and questions prompt students to prepare to answer the Big Question.

E Text Element These activities help students recognize and understand the use of text elements.

W Writing These activities provide writing opportunities to help students practice writing and comprehend text.

L Literary Element These activities and questions help students comprehend selections and learn more about each genre.

LSV Listening, Speaking, Viewing These activities help students practice listening, speaking, and viewing skills.

EL English Language Coach These skills help English language learners as well as students who need additional reading support.

Activity Leveling

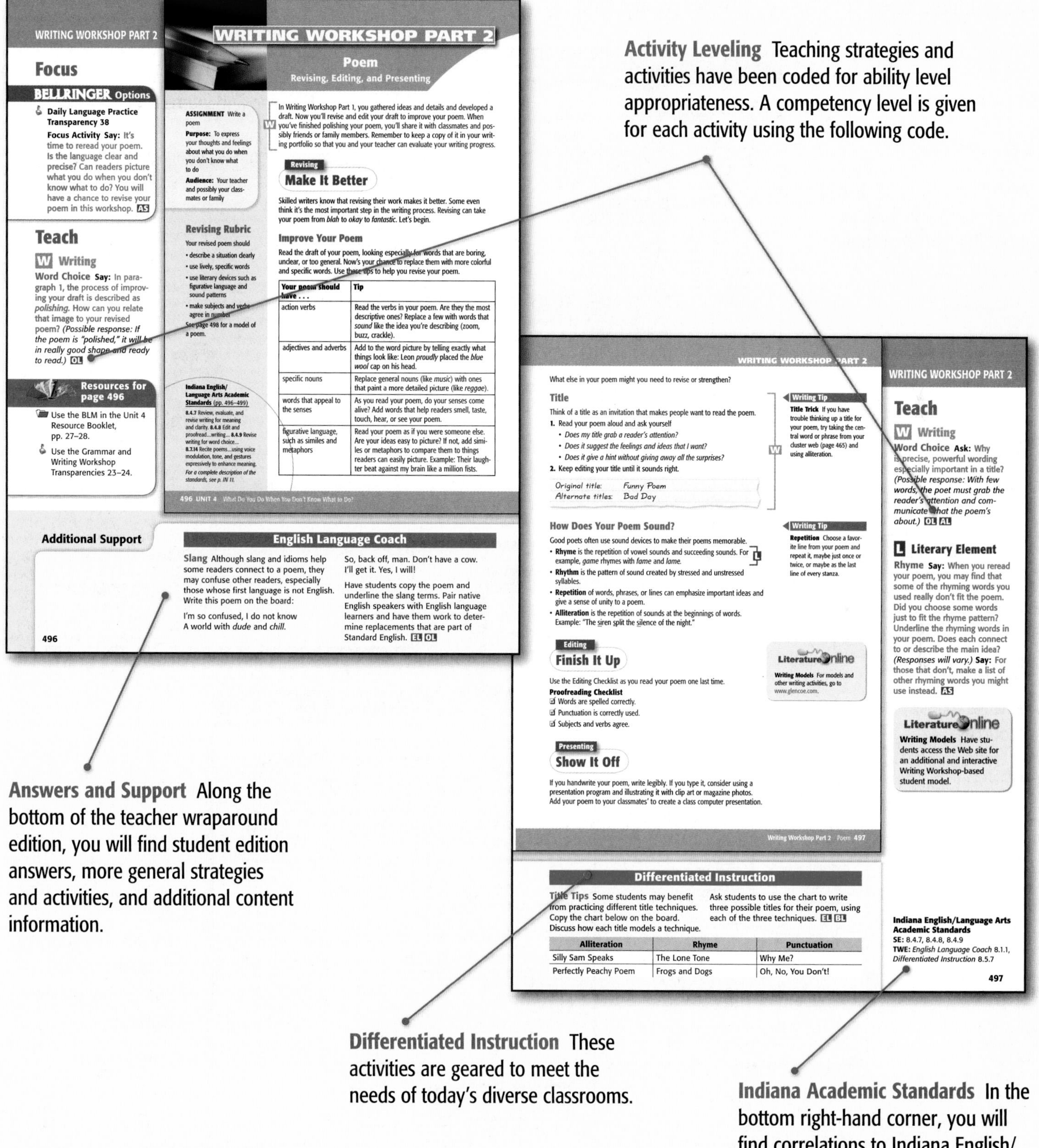

Activity Leveling Teaching strategies and activities have been coded for ability level appropriateness. A competency level is given for each activity using the following code.

Answers and Support Along the bottom of the teacher wraparound edition, you will find student edition answers, more general strategies and activities, and additional content information.

Differentiated Instruction These activities are geared to meet the needs of today's diverse classrooms.

Indiana Academic Standards In the bottom right-hand corner, you will find correlations to Indiana English/ Language Arts Academic Standards.

Workshop Structure

The instructions in each workshop in *Reading with Purpose* is presented in a structured lesson plan: Focus, Teach, Assess, and Close.

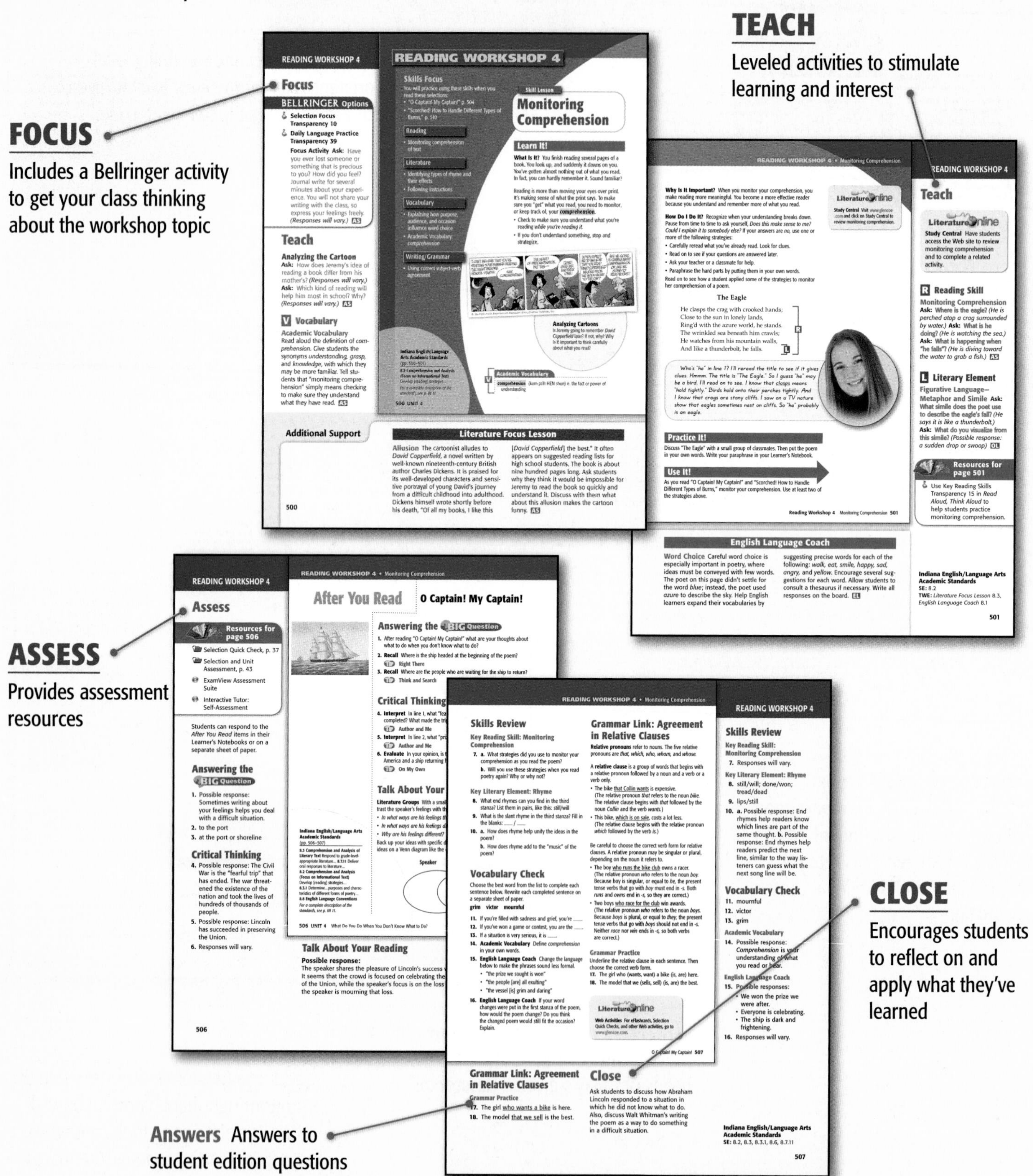
FOCUS
Includes a Bellringer activity to get your class thinking about the workshop topic
TEACH
Leveled activities to stimulate learning and interest
ASSESS
Provides assessment resources
CLOSE
Encourages students to reflect on and apply what they've learned
Answers Answers to student edition questions

Resources and Support

For every unit the teacher wraparound edition includes a page of additional teaching resources and online support for both you and your students.

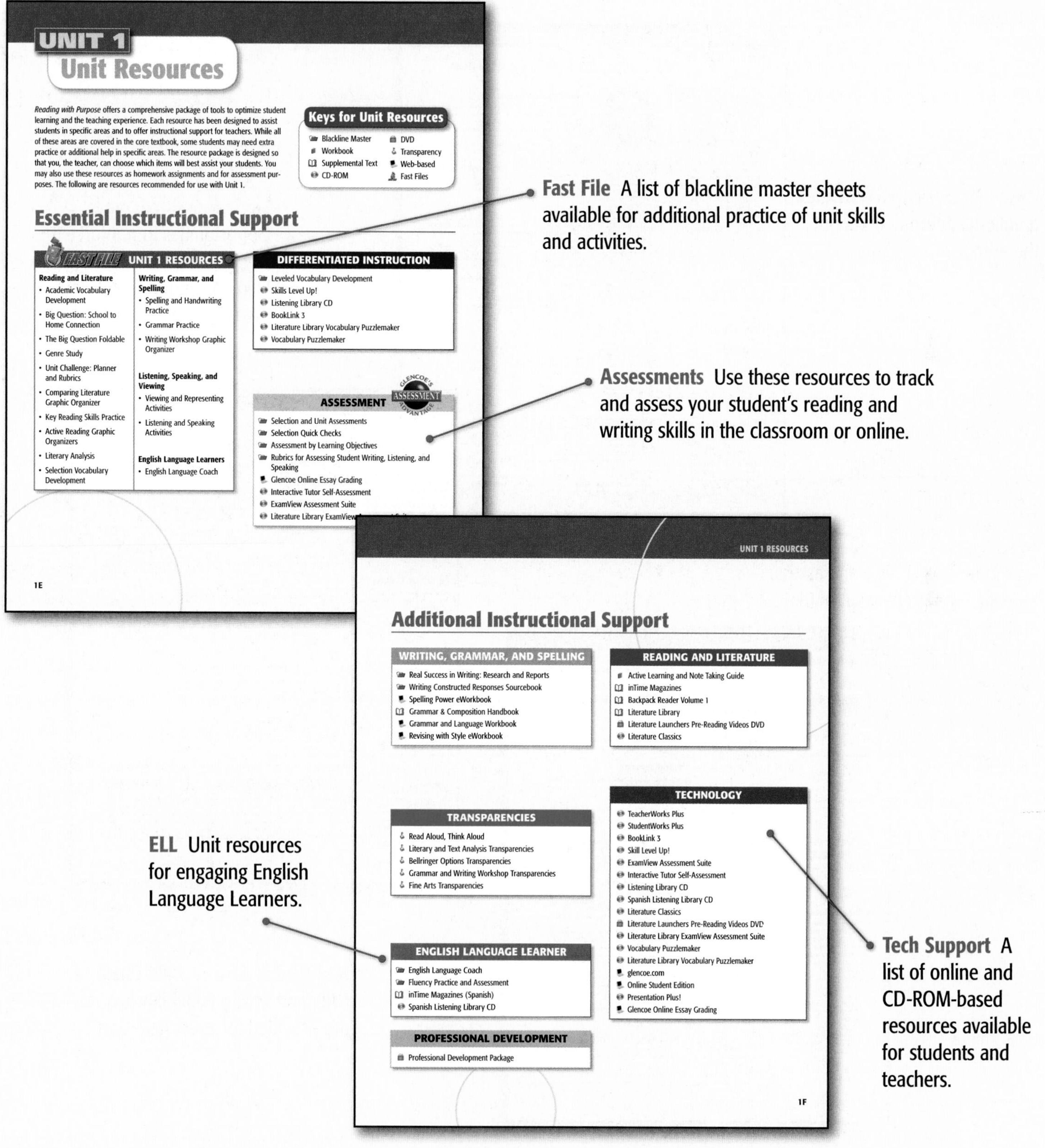

UNIT 1

Unit Resources

Reading with Purpose offers a comprehensive package of tools to optimize student learning and the teaching experience. Each resource has been designed to assist students in specific areas and to offer instructional support for teachers. While all of these areas are covered in the core textbook, some students may need extra practice or additional help in specific areas. The resource package is designed so that you, the teacher, can choose which items will best assist your students. You may also use these resources as homework assignments and for assessment purposes. The following are resources recommended for use with Unit 1.

Keys for Unit Resources

- Blackline Master
- Workbook
- Supplemental Text
- CD-ROM
- DVD
- Transparency
- Web-based
- Fast Files

Essential Instructional Support

FAST FILE UNIT 1 RESOURCES

Reading and Literature
- Academic Vocabulary Development
- Big Question: School to Home Connection
- The Big Question Foldable
- Genre Study
- Unit Challenge: Planner and Rubrics
- Comparing Literature Graphic Organizer
- Key Reading Skills Practice
- Active Reading Graphic Organizers
- Literary Analysis
- Selection Vocabulary Development

Writing, Grammar, and Spelling
- Spelling and Handwriting Practice
- Grammar Practice
- Writing Workshop Graphic Organizer

Listening, Speaking, and Viewing
- Viewing and Representing Activities
- Listening and Speaking Activities

English Language Learners
- English Language Coach

DIFFERENTIATED INSTRUCTION
- Leveled Vocabulary Development
- Skills Level Up!
- Listening Library CD
- BookLink 3
- Literature Library Vocabulary Puzzlemaker
- Vocabulary Puzzlemaker

ASSESSMENT (Glencoe's Assessment Advantage)
- Selection and Unit Assessments
- Selection Quick Checks
- Assessment by Learning Objectives
- Rubrics for Assessing Student Writing, Listening, and Speaking
- Glencoe Online Essay Grading
- Interactive Tutor Self-Assessment
- ExamView Assessment Suite
- Literature Library ExamView

1E

UNIT 1 RESOURCES

Additional Instructional Support

WRITING, GRAMMAR, AND SPELLING
- Real Success in Writing: Research and Reports
- Writing Constructed Responses Sourcebook
- Spelling Power eWorkbook
- Grammar & Composition Handbook
- Grammar and Language Workbook
- Revising with Style eWorkbook

READING AND LITERATURE
- Active Learning and Note Taking Guide
- inTime Magazines
- Backpack Reader Volume 1
- Literature Library
- Literature Launchers Pre-Reading Videos DVD
- Literature Classics

TRANSPARENCIES
- Read Aloud, Think Aloud
- Literary and Text Analysis Transparencies
- Bellringer Options Transparencies
- Grammar and Writing Workshop Transparencies
- Fine Arts Transparencies

TECHNOLOGY
- TeacherWorks Plus
- StudentWorks Plus
- BookLink 3
- Skill Level Up!
- ExamView Assessment Suite
- Interactive Tutor Self-Assessment
- Listening Library CD
- Spanish Listening Library CD
- Literature Classics
- Literature Launchers Pre-Reading Videos DVD
- Literature Library ExamView Assessment Suite
- Vocabulary Puzzlemaker
- Literature Library Vocabulary Puzzlemaker
- glencoe.com
- Online Student Edition
- Presentation Plus!
- Glencoe Online Essay Grading

ENGLISH LANGUAGE LEARNER
- English Language Coach
- Fluency Practice and Assessment
- inTime Magazines (Spanish)
- Spanish Listening Library CD

PROFESSIONAL DEVELOPMENT
- Professional Development Package

1F

Fast File A list of blackline master sheets available for additional practice of unit skills and activities.

Assessments Use these resources to track and assess your student's reading and writing skills in the classroom or online.

ELL Unit resources for engaging English Language Learners.

Tech Support A list of online and CD-ROM-based resources available for students and teachers.

Teaching the Selection

Each selection in the student edition is preceded by a "Before Your Read" page that prepares students for the vocabulary and themes of the selection. Reading selections are followed by an "After Your Read" where students can respond and connect to the selection.

Author Information Provides additional information about the author or selection.

Skills Reinforcement Opportunities to reinforce the key Reading Skills and Literary Elements found throughout the selection.

Resource Guide Directs you to additional Glencoe material developed to enhance and assess students' comprehension of the selection.

Readability Scores Dale-Chall, DRP, and Lexile readability scores are provided for every selection.

Teaching Informational Text

The wide range of informational texts and functional documents in *Glencoe Literature: Reading with Purpose* broadens student reading to include more than poetry, stories, and plays.

InTime Articles from the **TIME** family of magazines deliver insight and facts on timely issues and topics related to the Big Question.

READING WORKSHOP 1

Teach

R Reading Skill

Analyzing Say: Read the text next to the title of the article. After you read this statement, what questions do you have that you hope the article will answer? *(Possible responses: Will the man and his daughter survive? Will they reach their destination safely? What are the harsh conditions of the mountains like?)* **Ask:** Do these questions motivate you to read the rest of the article? *(Responses will vary.)* OL

EL Language Coach

Vocabulary Building: Collections of Synonyms
Say: If you are not certain of a word's meaning, it can be helpful to use a synonym to check your guess. Substitute a synonym for the word, and see whether the sentence still makes sense. For example, what word might you substitute for *perilous* in the first paragraph? *(Possible response: dangerous)* EL BL OL

Readability Scores
Dale-Chall: 5.8
DRP: 65
Lexile: 1210

READING WORKSHOP 1

TIME

A Father's Daring TREK

A Tibetan man takes his 6-year-old daughter on a dangerous journey through the world's highest, harshest mountains to give her a better life. R

By JULIE K.L. DAM

After a weeklong march in the bitter, piercing cold and thin air of the Himalayan Mountains, the Tibetan father Kelsang and his daughter, Yangdol (not their real names), thought they had reached freedom. From the top of Nangapa La, a pass on the southern border of Chinese-occupied Tibet, a peaceful life in **exile** seemed only steps away. Their perilous journey was only half over, though, because the trip down the pass would be just as difficult as the way up. Still the courageous father and daughter struggled on, determined to reach their goal. EL 1

For Tibetans, the trek[1] to freedom is filled with hardships, both physical and emotional. Many make the heart-wrenching decision to become refugees, people who are forced to leave their country of birth because of political or religious **persecution** or war. In 1951, Tibet lost its independence when Chinese troops invaded Lhasa, the Tibetan capital. The

1 Key Reading Skill
Analyzing What does the writer do to interest you in reading the rest of the article? Think about
- the description of the trek
- the people involved
- the reason for the trek

1. A *trek* is a long, often difficult journey.

Vocabulary
exile (EG zyl) *n.* the state of living away from one's home country
persecution (pur suh KYOO shun) *n.* constant cruel or harmful treatment

172 UNIT 2 Which Is More Important, the Journey or the Destination?

Additional Support

Reading in the Real World

Citizenship As students read about the Tibetan refugees in "A Father's Daring Trek," they may wish to learn more about refugees. According to the United States Immigration and Nationality Act, a refugee is a person who flees his or her country to escape persecution "on account of race, religion, nationality, membership in a particular social group, or political opinion." Have students look online or at the library for information about refugees who have come to the United States. Ask students to share their findings with the class. AL

172

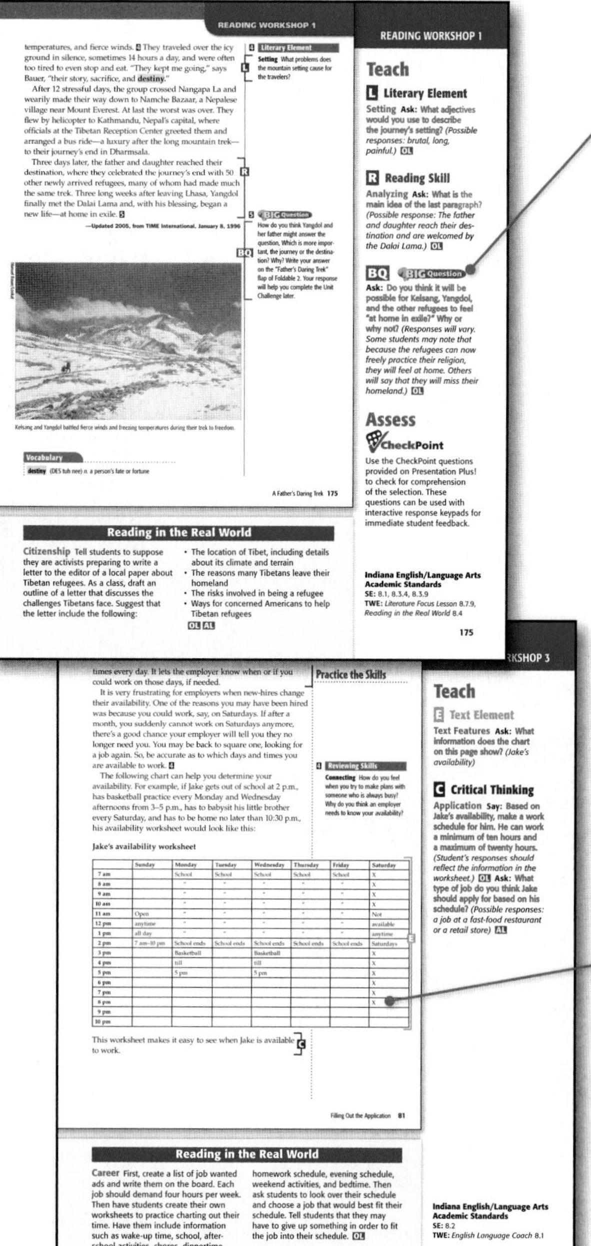

READING WORKSHOP 1

temperatures, and fierce winds. 4 They traveled over the icy ground in silence, sometimes 14 hours a day, and were often too tired to even stop and eat. "They kept me going," says Bauer, "their story, sacrifice, and **destiny**." L

After 12 stressful days, the group crossed Nangapa La and wearily made their way down to Namche Bazaar, a Nepalese village near Mount Everest. At last the worst was over. They flew by helicopter to Kathmandu, Nepal's capital, where officials at the Tibetan Reception Center greeted them and arranged a bus ride—a luxury after the long mountain trek—to their journey's end in Dharmsala.

Three days later, the father and daughter reached their destination, where they celebrated the journey's end with 50 other newly arrived refugees, many of whom had made much the same trek. Three long weeks after leaving Lhasa, Yangdol finally met the Dalai Lama and, with his blessing, began a new life—at home in exile. R 5

—Updated 2005, from TIME International, January 8, 1996

4 Literary Element
Setting What problems does the mountain setting cause for the travelers?

5 BIG Question
How do you think Yangdol and her father might answer the question, Which is more important, the journey or the destination? Why? Write your answer on the "Father's Daring Trek" flap of Foldable 2. Your response will help you complete the Unit Challenge later. BQ

Kelsang and Yangdol battled fierce winds and freezing temperatures during their trek to freedom.

Vocabulary
destiny (DES tuh nee) *n.* a person's fate or fortune

A Father's Daring Trek 175

Reading in the Real World

Citizenship Tell students to suppose they are activists preparing to write a letter to the editor of a local paper about Tibetan refugees. As a class, draft an outline of a letter that discusses the challenges Tibetans face. Suggest that the letter include the following:
- The location of Tibet, including details about its climate and terrain
- The reasons many Tibetans leave their homeland
- The risks involved in being a refugee
- Ways for concerned Americans to help Tibetan refugees

OL AL

READING WORKSHOP 1

Teach

L Literary Element

Setting Ask: What adjectives would you use to describe the journey's setting? *(Possible responses: brutal, long, painful.)* OL

R Reading Skill

Analyzing Ask: What is the main idea of the last paragraph? *(Possible response: The father and daughter reach their destination and are welcomed by the Dalai Lama.)* OL

BQ BIG Question

Ask: Do you think it will be possible for Kelsang, Yangdol, and the other refugees to feel "at home in exile?" Why or why not? *(Responses will vary. Some students may note that because the refugees can now freely practice their religion, they will feel at home. Others will say that they will miss their homeland.)* OL

Assess

CheckPoint

Use the CheckPoint questions provided on Presentation Plus! to check for comprehension of the selection. These questions can be used with interactive response keypads for immediate student feedback.

Indiana English/Language Arts Academic Standards
SE: 8.1, 8.3.4, 8.3.9
TWE: *Literature Focus Lesson* 8.7.9, *Reading in the Real World* 8.4

175

times every day. It lets the employer know when or if you could work on those days, if needed.

It is very frustrating for employers when new-hires change their availability. One of the reasons you may have been hired was because you could work, say, on Saturdays. If after a month, you suddenly cannot work on Saturdays anymore, there's a good chance your employer will tell you they no longer need you. You may be back to square one, looking for a job again. So, be accurate as to which days and times you are available to work. 4

The following chart can help you determine your availability. For example, if Jake gets out of school at 2 p.m., has basketball practice every Monday and Wednesday afternoons from 3–5 p.m., has to babysit his little brother every Saturday, and has to be home no later than 10:30 p.m., his availability worksheet would look like this:

Practice the Skills

4 Reviewing Skills
Connecting How do you feel when you try to make plans with someone who is always busy? Why do you think an employer needs to know your availability?

Jake's availability worksheet

	Sunday	Monday	Tuesday	Wednesday	Thursday	Friday	Saturday
7 am		School	School	School	School	School	X
8 am		"	"	"	"	"	X
9 am		"	"	"	"	"	X
10 am		"	"	"	"	"	X
11 am	Open	"	"	"	"	"	Not
12 pm	anytime	"	"	"	"	"	available
1 pm	all day	"	"	"	"	"	anytime
2 pm	7 am–10 pm	School ends	School ends	School ends	School ends	School ends	Saturdays
3 pm		Basketball		Basketball			X
4 pm		till		till			X
5 pm		5 pm		5 pm			X
6 pm							X
7 pm							X
8 pm							X
9 pm							
10 pm							

This worksheet makes it easy to see when Jake is available to work. C

Filling Out the Application 81

Reading in the Real World

Career First, create a list of job wanted ads and write them on the board. Each job should demand four hours per week. Then have students create their own worksheets to practice charting out their time. Have them include information such as wake-up time, school, after-school activities, chores, dinnertime, homework schedule, evening schedule, weekend activities, and bedtime. Then ask students to look over their schedule and choose a job that would best fit their schedule. Tell students that they may have to give up something in order to fit the job into their schedule. OL

READING WORKSHOP 3

Teach

E Text Element

Text Features Ask: What information does the chart on this page show? *(Jake's availability)*

C Critical Thinking

Application Say: Based on Jake's availability, make a work schedule for him. He can work a minimum of ten hours and a maximum of twenty hours. *(Student's responses should reflect the information in the worksheet.)* OL **Ask:** What type of job do you think Jake should apply for based on his schedule? *(Possible responses: a job at a fast-food restaurant or a retail store)* AL

Indiana English/Language Arts Academic Standards
SE: 8.2
TWE: *English Language Coach* 8.1

81

BQ Connection Teaching suggestions for helping students connect the article to the unit Big Question.

Functional Documents *Reading with Purpose* fulfills state standards requirements for reading and comprehending functional documents that students encounter outside the classroom.

Classroom Resources

Unit Resources

Fast Files Booklets

These blackline master booklets provide all the teaching materials you need to reinforce the content in each unit of *Glencoe Literature: Reading with Purpose.* Worksheets in each booklet focus on the following:

- Unit Warm-Up
- The Big Question Foldables
- The Big Question: Home-School Connection (English and Spanish versions)
- Unit Challenge: Planner and Rubrics
- Literary Analysis
- Genre Study
- Active Reading Graphic Organizers
- Comparing Literature Graphic Organizers
- Spelling and Handwriting Practice
- Academic Vocabulary Development
- Selection Vocabulary Development
- English Language Coach
- Grammar Practice
- Writing Workshop Graphic Organizers
- Key Reading Skills Practice
- Viewing and Representing Activities
- Listening and Speaking Activities

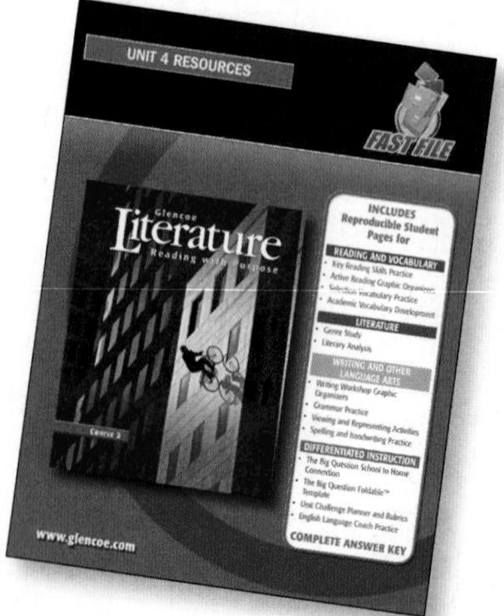

Literature and Reading

Active Learning and Note Taking Guides

This set of consumable workbooks provides structured outline support for students to use before, during, and after reading, helping them focus on key concepts and information. Activities include interactive exercises on literary elements and vocabulary for writing about literature. To meet the needs of all your students, the workbooks are offered in four versions:

- **Active Learning and Note Taking Guide (Grade-Level)**
- **Active Learning and Note Taking Guide: Enriched**
- **Active Learning and Note Taking Guide: Adapted**
- **Active Learning and Note Taking Guide: ELL**

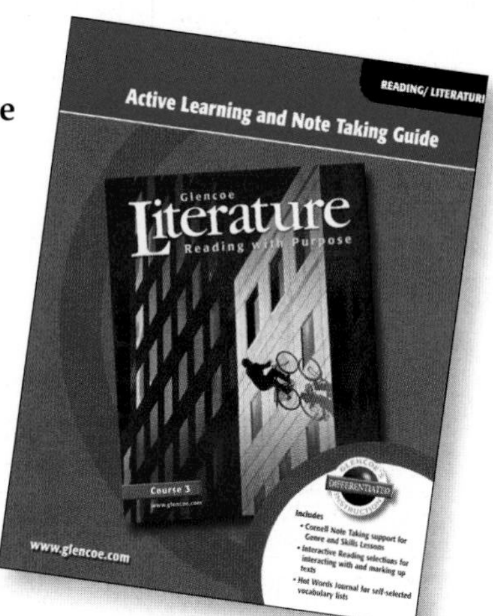

Glencoe Literature Library

This collection of 120 hardcover books helps you encourage your students to read independently. Choose from novels, novellas, plays, and nonfiction. Each book includes related readings from a broad range of genres. Support your teaching with these technology products:

- **Literature Library ExamView Suite Assessment CD-ROM** allows you to create customized tests for all the literary works included in the Literature Library collection.
- **Literature Library Vocabulary Puzzlemaker CD** helps you and your students create word puzzles based on vocabulary selected from the Literature Library collection.

Glencoe Backpack Reader

These portable collections of stories, poems, essays, and plays offer students additional reading for skills practice and personal enjoyment. The leveled selections promote gradual release of responsibility and increase students' confidence in reading and literature.

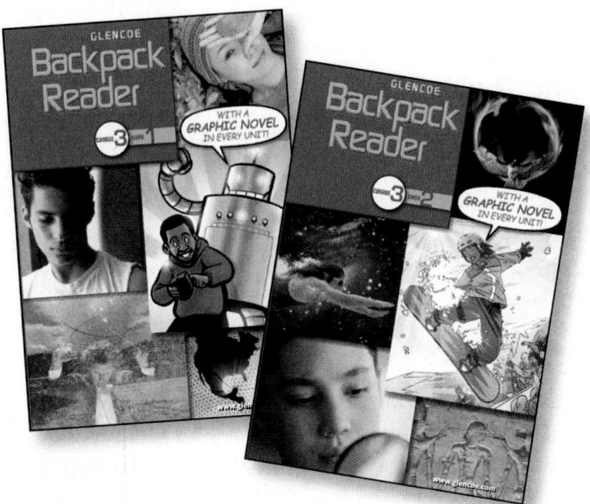

inTIME magazine

These high-interest collections of articles drawn from issues of *TIME* magazine and other Time, Inc., publications help students develop readings strategies to interact with informational text. The *inTIME* magazines are available in both English and Spanish and include teacher guides.

Literature Launchers: Prereading Videos/DVD

These short, lively video segments on DVD introduce each unit in *Glencoe Literature: Reading with Purpose.*

Literature Classics CD

This software brings more than 1,100 additional literature selections—accessible by author, title, date, genre, and big idea—to your classroom. Genre Focus Lesson Plans and blackline masters are also provided.

Writing

Real Success in Writing: Research and Reports

These blackline masters reinforce and extend the coverage of research presented in the student edition.

Writing Constructed Responses Sourcebook

This sourcebook with blackline masters help students respond effectively to short essay questions.

Differentiated Instruction

Leveled Vocabulary Development

These blackline masters provide practice on selection vocabulary words. The booklet is offered in four versions:

- **Leveled Vocabulary Development: (Grade Level)**
- **Leveled Vocabulary Development: Enriched**
- **Leveled Vocabulary Development: Adapted**
- **Leveled Vocabulary Development: English Language Learner**

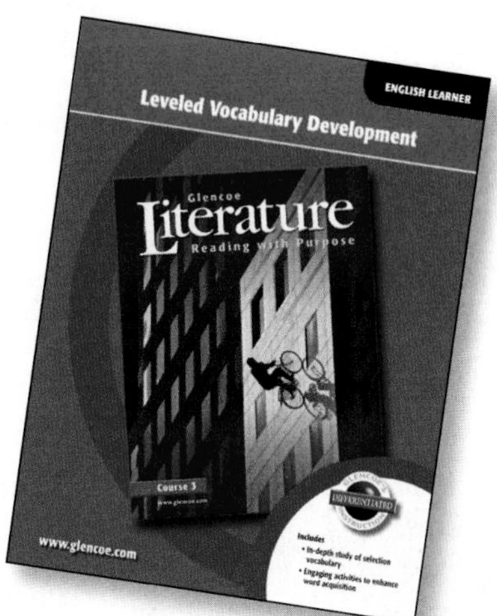

Vocabulary Puzzlemaker

This software lets you or your students create word puzzles based on selection vocabulary.

Listening Library Audio CD-ROM (English and Spanish)

This audio collection offers engaging readings of selections in English and Spanish.

Skill Level Up!™: A Language Arts Game

This CD-ROM game motivates students to practice and master language arts skills covered in *Glencoe Literature: Reading with Purpose* and frequently assessed on standardized tests. Students have fun and you receive valuable skills-based performance data by individual or class.

Glencoe BookLink 3 CD-ROM

Use the *Glencoe BookLink 3* CD-ROM, a database of more than 26,700 titles, to create customized reading lists for your students. Search for award-winning titles and for books on several state-recommended reading lists.

Assessment

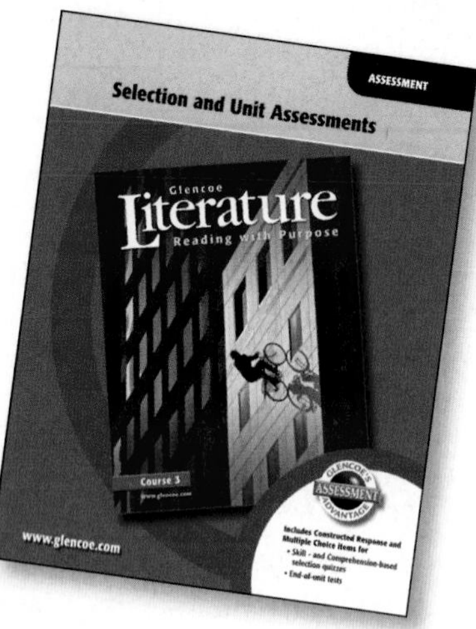

Selection and Unit Assessments

This assessment tool contains comprehensive tests and answer keys for all selections and units.

Selection Quick Check

These short-answer questions serve as a quick way to assess students' basic comprehension of a selection. (Spanish and English)

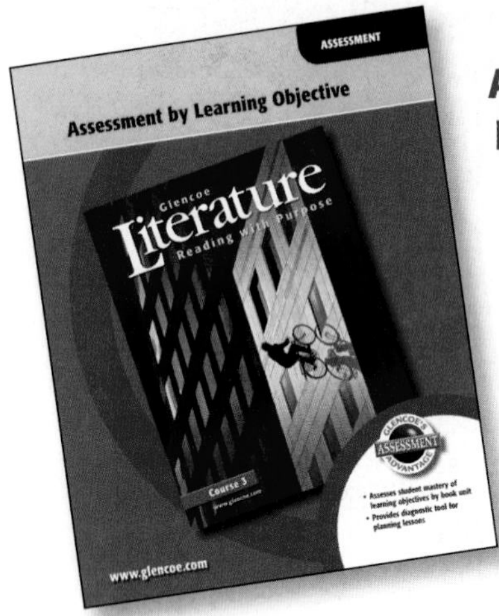

Assessment by Learning Objective

These booklets help you assess learning objectives related to reading strategy, literary element, genre, or literary period or movement.

Rubrics for Assessing Student Writing, Listening, and Speaking

This booklet provides you with rubrics to use fo all Writing Workshop products as well as for key listening and speaking activities.

Standardized Test Preparation and Practice

Contains exercises and activities that get students ready for standardized exams

Technology Resources

StudentWorks™ Plus CD-ROM

StudentWorks™ Plus contains the Student Edition (PDF) with selection audio; student workbooks (PDF); Student Presentation Builder (provides Unit-based multimedia projects, PowerPoint tutorial and PowerPoint presentation template); Daily Assignments and Grade Log allows students to organize their assignments and track their own progress.

Online Student Edition (MHLN)

Showcasing the interactive versions of McGraw-Hill textbooks, mhln.com offers the same content as the printed text, with multimedia-enhanced content. Games, interactivities, and other items are correlated directly to each page.

TeacherWorks™ Plus CD-ROM

TeacherWorks™ Plus contains a suite of easy-to-use and effective tools designed to help you manage daily activities, access all textbook materials, and utilize resources on the Internet. Included are daily lesson plans and a block schedule guide.

ExamViewPro® Assessment Suite

With the Test Generator you can quickly create customized unit- or selection-based assessments in a snap! Use the unit exams or the selection-specific exams provided in both English and Spanish on this CD-ROM, or create your own questions.

Presentation Plus! CD-ROM

This multimedia application enables teachers to present dynamic lessons for every unit and selection in Glencoe Literature. The PowerPoint multimedia presentations can be edited and customized for teacher lesson planning.

Skill Level Up!™: A Language Arts Game

This CD-ROM game motivates students to practice and master language arts skills covered in *Glencoe Literature: Reading with Purpose* and frequently assessed on standardized tests. Students have fun and you receive valuable skills-based performance data by individual or class.

Vocabulary Puzzlemaker

This software lets you or your students create word puzzles based on selection vocabulary.

Literature Classics CD-ROM

This software brings more than 1,100 additional literature selections—accessible by author, title, date, genre, and big idea—to your classroom. Genre Focus Lesson Plans and blackline masters are also provided.

Literature Library ExamView Assessment Suite CD-ROM

This software allows you to create customized tests for all the literary works included in the *Literature Library* collection.

Literature Library Vocabulary Puzzlemaker CD-ROM

This software helps you and your students create word puzzles based on vocabulary selected from the Literature Library collection.

Literature Launchers: Prereading Videos/DVD

These short, lively video segments on DVD introduce each unit in *Glencoe Literature: Reading with Purpose.*

Listening Library Audio CD-ROM (English and Spanish)

This audio collection offers engaging readings of selections in English and Spanish.

Glencoe BookLink 3 CD-ROM

Use the *Glencoe BookLink 3* CD-ROM, a database of more than 26,700 titles, to create customized reading lists for your students. Search for award-winning titles and for books on several state-recommended reading lists.

Glencoe Online Essay Grading

Improve student writing and save time with Glencoe's Online Essay Grading, powered by SkillWriter™. Glencoe's Online Essay Grading will score your students' writing assignments and provide individualized feedback automatically.

Transparencies

- **Read Aloud, Think Aloud** modeling active reading.
- **Bellringer Options Transparencies** include warm-up exercises to engage student interest or provide a quick review of previously taught activities.
- **Literary Analysis Transparencies** help reinforce or reteach literary elements that are the focus of each lesson.
- **Grammar and Writing Workshop Transparencies** help reinforce the skills taught in the grammar and writing workshops in the student edition.
- **Fine Art Transparencies** enhance a strong humanities approach to literature and helps students analyze visual representations of literary concepts and characters/excellent source of writing prompts.

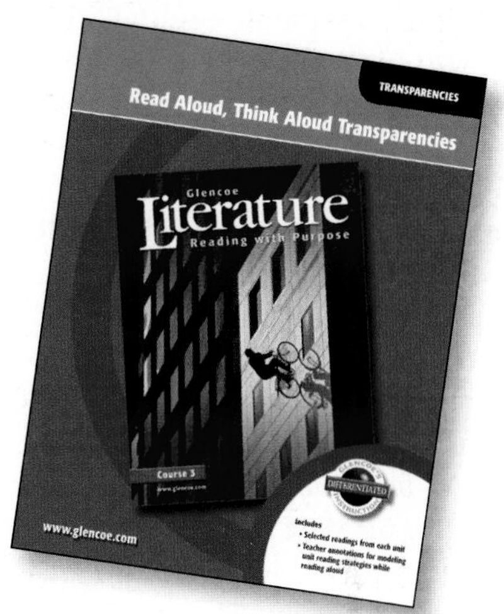

Internet Resources (www.glencoe.com)

For online resources that support the instruction in *Glencoe Literature: Reading with Purpose,* students and teachers can visit our Web site at **www.glencoe.com**. Students will find additional learning, practice, and assessment opportunities.

Glencoe Resources for Independent Reading

Glencoe Literature Library

This collection of hardcover books includes full-length novels, novellas, plays, and works of nonfiction. Each *Glencoe Literature Library* volume consists of a least one complete extended-length reading accompanied by several related readings from a broad range of genres, such as short stories, poems, essays, or informational articles. In addition, a separate **Study Guide** for each *Glencoe Literature Library* book provides teaching notes and reproducible activity pages for students. Students may also find these activity pages on the **Glencoe Web site http://www.glencoe.com.**

Across Five Aprils by Irene Hunt **DRP 59**
The Adventures of Tom Sawyer by Mark Twain **DRP 55**
Anne Frank Remembered: The Story of the Woman Who Helped to Hide the Frank Family by Miep Gies and Alison Leslie Gold **DRP 57**
Bearstone by Will Hobbs **DRP 51**
Bridge to Terabithia by Katherine Paterson **DRP 50**
The Call of the Wild by Jack London **DRP 62**
Cezanne Pinto by Mary Stoltz **DRP 54**
A Christmas Carol by Charles Dickens **DRP 60**
The Clay Marble by Minfong Ho **DRP 49**
Dandelion Wine by Ray Bradbury **DRP 56**
Dogsong by Gary Paulsen **DRP 51**
Dragonwings by Laurence Yep **DRP 54**
The Friends by Rosa Guy **DRP 51**
A Gathering of Days: A New England Girl's Journal 1830–1832 by Joan W. Blos **DRP 56**
The Glory Field by Walter Dean Myers **DRP 51**
Hatchet by Gary Paulsen **DRP 54**
High Elk's Treasure by Virginia Driving Hawk Sneve
Homecoming by Cynthia Voigt **DRP 48**
The House of Dies Drear by Virginia Hamilton **DRP 49**
I, Juan de Pareja by Elizabeth Borton de Treviño **DRP 58**
Island of the Blue Dolphins by Scott O'Dell **DRP 53**
Jacob Have I Loved by Katherine Paterson **DRP 52**
Johnny Tremain by Esther Forbes **DRP 55**
Journey to Jo'burg by Beverly Naidoo **DRP 50**
Julie of the Wolves by Jean Craighead George **DRP 55**
Letters from a Slave Girl by Mary E. Lyons **DRP 51**
Letters from Rifka by Karen Hesse **DRP 49**
Little Women by Louisa May Alcott **DRP 60**
Lupita Mañana by Patricia Beatty **DRP 53**
Missing May by Cynthia Rylant **DRP 53**
Mrs. Frisby and the Rats of NIMH by Robert O'Brien **DRP 52**
Number the Stars by Lois Lowry **DRP 52**
The Pigman by Paul Zindel **DRP 55**
Shabanu: Daughter of the Wind by Suzanne Fisher Staples **DRP 54**
Shiloh by Phyllis Reynolds Naylor **DRP 50**
The Slave Dancer by Paula Fox **DRP 55**
So Far from the Bamboo Grove by Yoko Kawashima Watkins **DRP 50**
Sounder by William H. Armstrong **DRP 53, CRL 9**
The Summer of the Swans by Betsy Byars **DRP 50**
Taking Sides by Gary Soto **DRP 52**
There's a Girl in My Hammerlock by Jerry Spinelli **DRP 46**
Treasure Island by Robert Louis Stevenson **DRP 56**
The True Confessions of Charlotte Doyle by Avi **DRP 52**
Tuck Everlasting by Natalie Babbitt **DRP 56**
The View from Saturday by E.L. Konigsburg **DRP 53**
Walk Two Moons by Sharon Creech **DRP 49**
Where the Red Fern Grows by Wilson Rawls **DRP 47**
Winter Thunder and *The Christmas of the Phonograph Records* by Mari Sandoz
The Witch of Blackbird Pond by Elizabeth George Speare **DRP 57**
A Wrinkle in Time by Madeleine L'Engle **DRP 51**

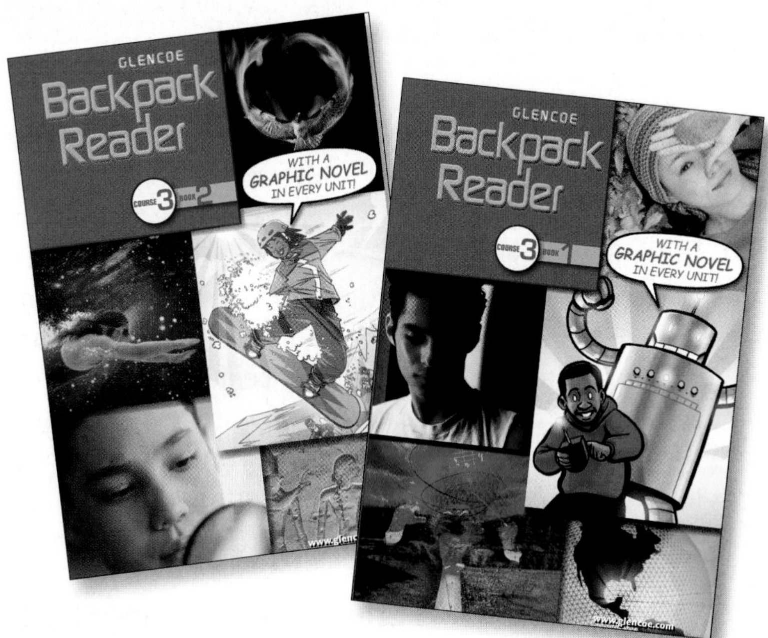

Glencoe Backpack Reader

These portable collections of stories, poems, essays, and plays offer students additional reading for skills practice and personal enjoyment. The selections promote gradual release reading and increase students' confidence in reading and literature. Find teacher resources for Backpack Reader on Teacher Works Plus or glencoe.com.

inTIME magazine

This lively collection of articles drawn from issues of TIME helps students develop the skills they need to interact with informational text in a meaningful way. Each of the news stories, feature articles, reviews, profiles, and essays in the magazines connects to an author, reading selection, or Big Question in ***Glencoe Literature: Reading with Purpose.*** The magazines are availaboe in both English and Spanish editions. In addition, a separate **Teacher Guide,** including lessons and reproducible student worksheets designed to develop students' reading and critical thinking skills, accompanies each magazine.

The Indiana Student Edition

Welcome to the Indiana edition of *Glencoe Literature: Reading with Purpose.* We have written this text with several goals in mind. First, we want you to succeed in this course. We also want you to succeed in your practice of the Indiana English/Language Arts Academic Standards and on the ISTEP+ test. To help you, we have provided lessons for the Academic Standards, which tell you what you are expected to learn throughout the school year. We have also included ISTEP+ test practice at the end of every unit so that you can prepare for the state test. As you read the selections in this book and work through questions and activities, you will become a better reader, a better test-taker, and a more successful student!

Covers the Indiana Grade 8 English/Language Arts Academic Standards

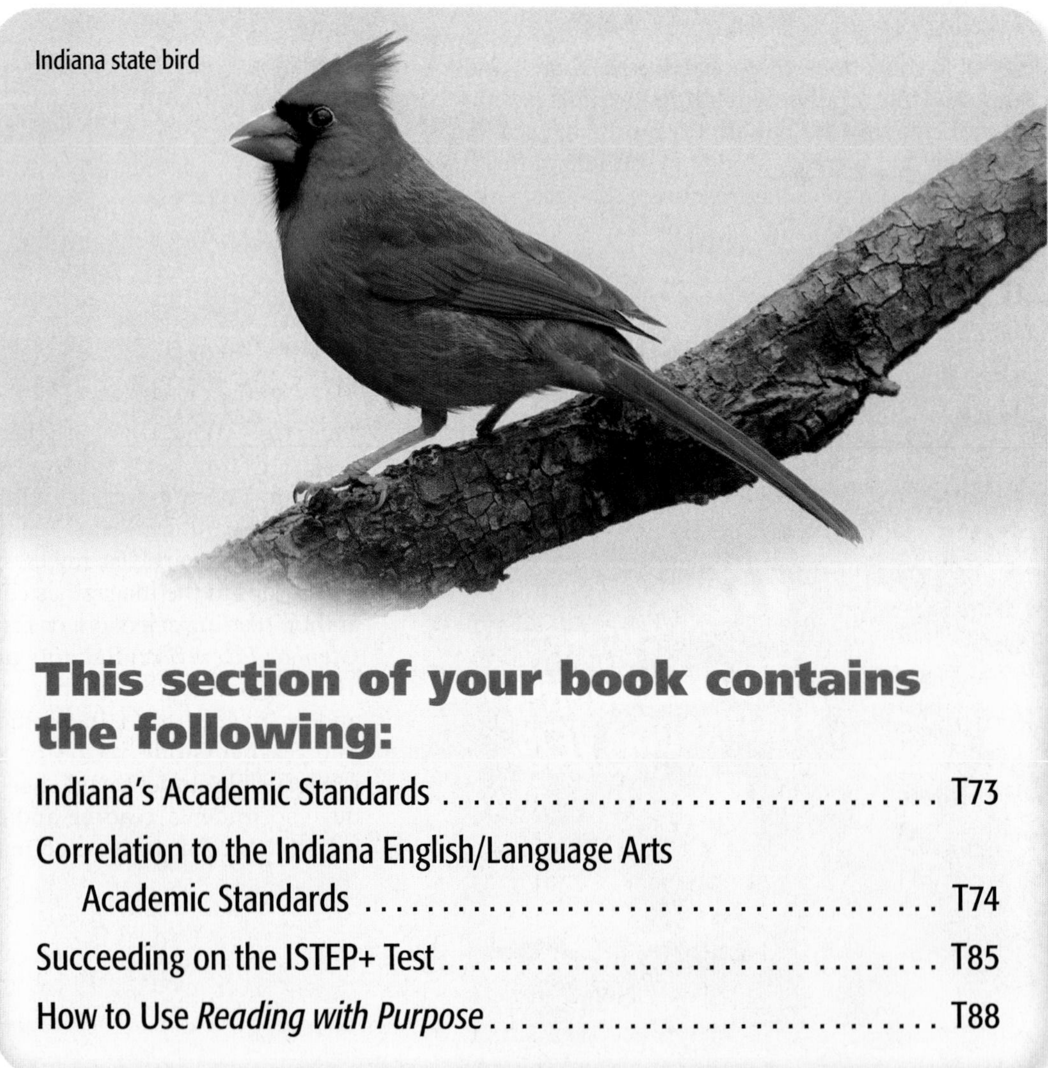

Indiana state bird

This section of your book contains the following:

Indiana Academic Standards

An Introduction to the Indiana English/Language Arts Academic Standards

The standards describe a connected body of linguistic understandings and competencies and are a comprehensive foundation that all students should learn. They describe the knowledge and skills that students should acquire from Kindergarten through high school.

Standard 1: READING: Word Recognition, Fluency, and Vocabulary Development
Word recognition involves the understanding of the basic features of words: word parts, patterns, relationships, and origins. Students use phonics, context clues, and a growing knowledge of English and other languages to determine the meaning of words and become fluent readers.

Standard 2: READING: Comprehension and Analysis (Focus on Informational Text)
Comprehension involves understanding grade-level-appropriate material. Students develop strategies such as asking questions; making predictions; and identifying and analyzing structure, organization, perspective, and purpose. After Grade 5, the focus is on informational texts.

Standard 3: READING: Comprehension and Analysis of Literary Text
Response to grade-level-appropriate literature includes identifying story elements such as character, theme, plot, and setting, and making connections and comparisons across texts. Literary response enhances students' understanding of history, culture, and the social sciences.

Standard 4: WRITING: Processes and Features
The writing process includes prewriting, drafting, editing, and revising. Students progress through these stages to write clear, coherent, and focused paragraphs and essays.

Standard 5: WRITING: Applications
Through the exploration of different types of writing and the characteristics of each, students become proficient at narrative (stories), expository (informational), descriptive (sensory), persuasive (emotional appeal), argumentative (logical defense), and technical writing. Writing demonstrates an awareness of the audience (intended reader) and purpose for writing.

Standard 6: WRITING: English Language Conventions
Conventions include the grade-level-appropriate mechanics of writing, such as penmanship, spelling, grammar, capitalization, punctuation, sentence structure, and manuscript form.

Standard 7: LISTENING AND SPEAKING: Skills, Strategies, and Applications
Response to oral communication includes careful listening and evaluation of content. Speaking skills, such as phrasing, pitch, and tone are developed in conjunction with such strategies as narration, exposition, description, and persuasion and are applied to students' delivery of oral presentations.

Correlation to the Indiana ELA Academic Standards

Reading

INDIANA ACADEMIC STANDARDS	COURSE 3
8.1 Reading: Word Recognition, Fluency, and Vocabulary Development	
8.1.1 Analyze idioms and comparisons—such as analogies, metaphors, and similes—to infer the literal and figurative meanings of phrases. • Idioms: expressions that cannot be understood just by knowing the meanings of the words in the expression, such as *to be an old hand at something or to get one's feet wet.* • Analogies: comparisons of the similar aspects of two different things • Metaphors: implied comparisons, such as *The stars were brilliant diamonds in the night* • Similes: comparisons that use *like* or *as*, such as *The stars were like a million diamonds in the sky.*	Genre Focus: Key Literary Element: Figurative Language 446 Key Literary Element: Simile and Metaphor 471, 472, 473, etc. Key Literary Element: Literal and Figurative Language 849, 890, 893, etc.
8.1.2 Understand the influence of historical events on English word meaning and vocabulary expansion. Example: Recognize how the early influences of Spanish explorers in North America expanded American English vocabulary, adding words such as *tornado, tomato,* and *patio.*	English Language Coach: Historical Influences on English 764, 892, 1062, etc.
8.1.3 Verify the meaning of a word in its context, even when its meaning is not directly stated, through the use of definition, restatement, example, comparison, or contrast. Example: Understand the meaning of *pickle* in a sentence, such as *The pickle was an important part of metal working.* Use a dictionary to help clarify the use of the word *pickle* in this context.	English Language Coach: Context Clues 16, 44, 54, etc.
8.2 Reading: Comprehension and Analysis (Focus on Informational Text)	
8.2.1 Compare and contrast the features and elements of consumer materials to gain meaning from documents. Example: Compare examples of a variety of instructional or technical manuals, such as those for a computer, hair appliance, camera, or electronic game, brought to class by different students. Describe what features make certain instructions easier than others to understand and follow.	Text Element: Instructions 509, 510, 515

Reading: Comprehension and Analysis (Focus on Informational Text) (continued)

INDIANA ACADEMIC STANDARDS	COURSE 3
8.2.2 Analyze text that uses proposition (statement of argument) and support patterns. Example: Read and analyze the organization of the "pro" and the "con" editorials on a topic of interest in *USA Today*. In each, decide if the argument is simply and clearly stated. Decide if there are at least three major points in support of the argument, with the strongest argument given first.	Genre Focus: Key Reading Skill: Distinguishing Fact from Opinion 926–929 Genre Focus: Key Text Element: Persuasive Appeal 926–929 Genre Focus: Key Text Element: Author's Bias 926–929 Genre Focus: Key Text Element: Faulty Reasoning 926–929 Key Reading Skill: Distinguishing Fact from Opinion 929, 930, 933, etc. Key Text Element: Persuasive Appeal 929, 932, 939 Key Text Element: Author's Bias 975, 979, 981, etc. Key Text Element: Faulty Reasoning 995, 996, 999 Reading Across Texts Workshop 1018–1033
8.2.3 Find similarities and differences between texts in the treatment, amount of coverage, or organization of ideas. Example: Read articles on the same current topic in magazines, such as *Time* and *Newsweek*, and editorials in national or local newspapers. Compare and contrast the texts in how they present the issue.	Reading Across Texts Workshop 404–419 Reading Across Texts Workshop 1152–1167 Reading Across Texts Workshop 1018–1033
8.2.4 Compare the original text to a summary to determine whether the summary accurately describes the main ideas, includes the important details, and conveys the underlying meaning. Example: After writing summaries or creating graphic organizers on an informational text read for class, exchange the summary or organizer with another student. Evaluate this classmate's summary, based on how well the student describes the most important elements of the text.	Key Reading Skill: Summarizing 849, 850, 859, etc.
8.2.5 Use information from a variety of consumer and public documents to explain a situation or decision and to solve a problem. Example: Decide which is the most practical and economical wireless telephone to purchase by reading articles, brochures, Web pages, and other consumer sources, such as *Consumer Reports*.	Listening, Speaking, and Viewing:Understanding Persuasive Techniques 995

Reading: Comprehension and Analysis (Focus on Informational Text) (continued)

INDIANA ACADEMIC STANDARDS	COURSE 3
8.2.6 Evaluate the logic, internal consistency, and structural patterns of text. Example: Read *The Brooklyn Bridge: They Said It Couldn't Be Built* by Judith St. George and evaluate the techniques and the effectiveness of the development of the main idea of the book.	Genre Focus: Key Reading Skill: Understanding Text Structures 292, 294 Genre Focus: Key Reading Skill: Identifying the Main Idea and Supporting Details 292, 294 Key Reading Skill: Understanding Text Structures 336–337, 341, 350, etc. Key Reading Skill: Identifying the Main Idea and Supporting Details 386–387, 389, 390, etc.
8.2.7 Analyze the structure, format, and purpose of informational materials (such as textbooks, newspapers, instructional or technical manuals, and public documents).	Text Element: Expository Writing 336, 337, 863, 867
8.2.8 Understand and explain the use of simple equipment by following directions in a technical manual.	**TEACHER EDITION:** Reading in the Real World 86
8.2.9 Make reasonable statements and draw conclusions about a text, supporting them with accurate examples.	Key Reading Skill: Making Inferences 189, 193, 199, 203, 647, 651, etc. Key Reading Skill: Drawing Conclusions 732, 733, 763 Reviewing Skills: Making Inferences 347, 397, 410, 823
8.3 Reading: Comprehension and Analysis of Literary Text	
8.3.1 Determine and articulate the relationship between the purposes and characteristics of different forms of poetry (including ballads, lyrics, couplets, epics, elegies, odes, and sonnets). • Ballad: a poem that tells a story • Lyric: words set to music • Couplet: two successive lines of verse that rhyme • Epic: a long poem that describes heroic deeds or adventures • Elegy: a mournful poem for the dead • Ode: a poem of praise • Sonnet: a rhymed poem of 14 lines Example: Describe the different forms of poetry. Compare poems such as John Ciardi's "Elegy for Jog," Pablo Neruda's "Odes to Common Things," and Edgar Allan Poe's sonnet "To Science."	Genre Focus: Poetry 446–447 Literary Element: Narrative Poetry 185, 186, 190, etc. Talk About Your Reading 454 Writing Tip: Purpose and Audience 465 Literary Element: Lyrics 477–481
8.3.2 Evaluate the structural elements of the plot, such as subplots, parallel episodes, and climax; the plot's development; and the way in which conflicts are (or are not) addressed and resolved. Example: Read a book, such as *Holes* by Louis Sachar, and discuss how the plot is developed, including the climax and its resolution and how different subplots are incorporated into the story.	Genre Focus: Key Literary Element: Plot 150, 158, 159 Genre Focus: Key Literary Element: Conflict 155 Key Literary Element: Plot 195, 197, 198, etc. Key Literary Element: Conflict 207, 209, 213, etc. Reviewing Elements: Conflict 830

Reading: Comprehension and Analysis of Literary Text (continued)

INDIANA ACADEMIC STANDARDS	COURSE 3
8.3.3 Compare and contrast the motivations and reactions of literary characters from different historical eras confronting either similar situations and conflicts or similar hypothetical situations. Example: Compare books that deal with the theme of the impact of war, both on those who fight in the battles and those who remain at home. Books on this theme include books on the Civil War period, such as *Bull Run* by Paul Fleischman, books on World War I, such as *After the Dancing Days* by Margaret Rostkowski, or about the Vietnam War, such as *Park's Quest* by Katherine Patterson.	Genre Focus: Key Literary Element: Conflict 150, 155 Key Literary Element: Conflict 207, 209, 312, etc. How to Compare Literature: Theme 256–257, 260, 262, etc.
8.3.4 Analyze the importance of the setting to the mood, tone, and meaning of the text. Example: Discuss the importance of the setting, including the place, the time period, and the customs, to books, such as *Friendly Persuasion* by Jessamyn West or *Stranded* by Ben Mikaelsen.	Literary Element: Setting 171, 177, 881, 883, etc. Genre Focus: Key Literary Element: Setting 546, 551 Key Literary Element: Setting 637, 638, 640, etc.
8.3.5 Identify and analyze recurring themes (such as good versus evil) that appear frequently across traditional and contemporary works. Example: Explore the theme that heroism demands unusual courage and risk-taking. Read fiction and biographies, such as Rod Serling's television play *Requiem for a Heavyweight* and David Remnick's *King of the World: Muhammed Ali and the Rise of an American Hero*, to identify what both real and imaginary heroes have done.	Genre Focus: Key Literary Element: Theme 150, 159 Key Literary Element: Theme 241, 244, 247, 607, 613, 617, etc. How to Compare Literature: Theme 256, 260, 262, etc. Text Element: Theme and Topic 1089, 1093, etc.
8.3.6 Identify significant literary devices, such as metaphor, symbolism, dialect or quotations, and irony, which define a writer's style and use those elements to interpret the work. • Metaphor: an implied comparison in which a word or phrase is used in place of another, such as *He was drowning in money*. • Symbolism: the use of an object to represent something else; for example, a dove might symbolize peace • Dialect: the vocabulary, grammar, and pronunciation used by people in different regions • Irony: the use of words to express the opposite of the literal meaning of the words, often to be humorous Example: Read several short stories by Mark Twain and discuss his use of dialect in his stories. Watch Alan Jay Lerner and Frederick Loewe's musical *My Fair Lady*, an adaptation of Bernard Shaw's *Pygmalion*, and discuss how the musical presents dialect and how this dialect is important to the conflict in the story.	Literary Element: Style 219, 221, etc. Genre Focus: Key Literary Element: Figurative Language: Metaphor and Simile 446, 447 Key Literary Element: Figurative Language (Metaphor and Simile) 471, 472, 473, etc. Genre Focus: Key Literary Element: Irony 292, 293 English Language Coach: Dialect 470, 472, 476, etc. Key Literary Element: Irony 339, 343, 347, etc.

Reading: Comprehension and Analysis of Literary Text (continued)

INDIANA ACADEMIC STANDARDS	COURSE 3
8.3.7 Analyze a work of literature, showing how it reflects the heritage, traditions, attitudes, and beliefs of its author. Example: Read a short biography of Edgar Allan Poe, Jack London, Shirley Jackson, Helen Keller, or Maya Angelou. Analyze how the author's experiences can be used to interpret his or her writings.	Genre Focus: Key Literary Element: Cultural Reference 4, 12, 1056, 1057, etc. Key Literary Element: Cultural Reference 107, 108, 110, 1097, 1100, 1101, etc. Build Background 17, 31, 45, etc.
8.3.8 Contrast points of view–such as first person, third person, third person limited and third person omniscient, and subjective and objective–in narrative text and explain how they affect the overall theme of the work. • First person: the narrator tells the story from the "I" perspective. • Third person: the narrator tells the story from an outside perspective. • Limited narration: the narrator does not know all thoughts of all characters. • Omniscient narration: the narrator knows all thoughts of all characters. • Subjective: the point of view involves a personal perspective. • Objective: the point of view is from a distanced, informational perspective, as in a news report.	**STUDENT EDITION:** Key Literary Element: Point of View 45, 49, 53 **TEACHER EDITION:** Literature Focus Lesson 349, 427, 670
8.3.9 Analyze the relevance of setting (places, times, customs) to mood, tone, and meaning of text.	Literary Element: Setting 171, 175, 176, 881, 889 Key Literary Element: Setting 637, 643, 644, 651
Writing	
8.4 Writing: Processes and Features	
8.4.1 Discuss ideas for writing, keep a list or notebook of ideas, and use graphic organizers to plan writing.	Writing Workshop: Prewriting 38, 178, 316, etc. Applying Good Writing Traits: Ideas 179
8.4.2 Create compositions that have a clear message, a coherent thesis (a statement of position on the topic), and end with a clear and well-supported conclusion.	Writing Workshop: Research Report 316–321, 380–384 Writing Workshop: Persuasive Essay 952–955, 992–997
8.4.3 Support theses or conclusions with analogies (comparisons), paraphrases, quotations, opinions from experts, and similar devices.	Writing Workshop: Research Report 316–321, 380–384 Writing Workshop: Persuasive Essay 952–955, 992–997
8.4.4 Plan and conduct multiple-step information searches using computer networks.	Writing Workshop: Choose a Topic and Focus Your Ideas 317 Writing Workshop: Research Your Topic 317
8.4.5 Achieve an effective balance between researched information and original ideas.	Writing Workshop: Research Report 316–321, 380–384

Writing: Processes and Features (continued)

INDIANA ACADEMIC STANDARDS	COURSE 3
8.4.6 Use a computer to create documents by using word-processing skills and publishing programs; develop simple databases and spreadsheets to manage information and prepare reports.	Using a Computer for Writing R27 Writing Workshop: Presenting: Show It Off 497, 630 Writing Workshop: Writing Tip 1129
8.4.7 Review, evaluate, and revise writing for meaning and clarity.	Writing Workshop: Revising 92, 234, 380, etc.
8.4.8 Edit and proofread one's own writing, as well as that of others, using an editing checklist or set of rules, with specific examples of corrections of frequent errors.	Writing Workshop: Editing 93, 235, 381, etc.
8.4.9 Revise writing for word choice; appropriate organization; consistent point of view; and transitions among paragraphs, passages, and ideas.	Writing Workshop: Revising 92, 234, 380, etc.
8.4.10 Create an organizational structure that balances all aspects of the composition and uses effective transitions between sentences to unify important ideas.	Writing Workshop: Research Report 319 Writing Workshop: Applying Good Writing Traits 629 Writing Workshop: Persuasive Essay 992, 993 Writing Workshop: Letter 1128
8.4.11 Identify topics; ask and evaluate questions; and develop ideas leading to inquiry, investigation, and research.	Writing Workshop: Research Report 316, 317
8.5 Writing: Applications (Different Types of Writing and Their Characteristics)	
8.5.1 Write biographies, autobiographies, and short stories that: • tell about and incident, event, or situation, using well-chosen details. • reveal the significance of, or the writer's attitude about, the subject. • use narrative and descriptive strategies, including relevant dialogue, specific action, physical description, background description, and comparison or contrast of characters. Example: Write an autobiographical account of one of your most memorable first days of school. Describe the day and its importance clearly enough so the reader can see and feel the day from your perspective.	Writing Workshop: Autobiographical Sketch 38–40, 92–95 Writing Workshop: Short Story 580–583, 628–633 Unit Wrap-Up: Unit Challenge: Group Activity 420 After You Read: Write About Your Reading 1118

Writing: Applications (continued)

INDIANA ACADEMIC STANDARDS	COURSE 3
8.5.2 Write responses to literature that: • demonstrate careful reading and insight into interpretations. • connect response to the writer's techniques and to specific textual references. • make supported inferences about the effects of a literary work on its audience. • support judgments through references to the text, other works, other authors, or to personal knowledge. Example: After reading *The Giver* by Lois Lowry, write a final chapter to the book, describing what happens to the main character after the point where Lowry ends the book. Then, plan a class presentation explaining the new ending and how it is supported by the rest of the book.	After You Read: Write About Your Reading 28, 52, 104, 168, 176, 192, 216, 246, 328, 354, 396, 462, 480, 578, 650, 822, 844, 1092, 1126, 1142
8.5.3 Write or deliver a research report that has been developed using a systematic research process (defines the topic, gathers information, determines credibility, reports findings) and that: • uses information from a variety of sources (books, technology, multimedia) and documents sources independently by using a consistent format for citations. • demonstrates that information that has been gathered has been summarized and that the topic has been refined through this process. • demonstrates that sources have been evaluated for accuracy, bias, and credibility. • organizes information by categorizing and sequencing, and demonstrates the distinction between one's own ideas from the ideas of others, and includes a bibliography (Works Cited). Example: Research the topic of the benefits and drawbacks of public transportation. Conduct research to learn why some experts argue that we should use more public transportation. Survey parents and friends to find out how often they use public transportation for school, business, or pleasure travel. Summarize the findings and write a report on the pros and cons of public transportation.	Writing Workshop: Research Report 316–321, 380–385 After You Read: Write About Your Reading 396, 578

Writing: Applications (continued)

INDIANA ACADEMIC STANDARDS	COURSE 3
8.5.4 Write persuasive compositions that: • include a well-defined thesis that makes a clear and knowledgeable appeal. • present detailed evidence, examples, and reasoning to support effective arguments and emotional appeals. • provide details, reasons, and examples, arranging them effectively by anticipating and answering reader concerns and counterarguments. Example: Using the research completed on public transportation, write a persuasive letter to the mayor on why the community should or should not invest more resources into public transportation.	Writing Workshop: Persuasive Essay 952–955, 992–997 Unit Wrap-Up: Solo Activity: Propose a Change 1035 After You Read: Write About Your Reading 52, 74, 328, 396, 578
8.5.5 Write technical documents that: • identify the sequence of activities needed to design a system, operate a tool, or explain the bylaws of an organization's constitution or guidelines. • include all the factors and variables that need to be considered. • use formatting techniques, including headings and changing the fonts (typeface) to aid comprehension. Example: Write a report of a science experiment that was conducted in class, describing both the process and the scientific conclusions. Describe the steps clearly, using precise scientific vocabulary, so that another reader could follow exactly what the experiment involved and could understand the reasoning behind the conclusion. Add graphics and text design to make the content clearer and easier to follow.	After You Read: Write About Your Reading 514
8.5.6 Write using precise word choices to make writing interesting and exact. Example: Write stories, reports, articles, and letters using a variety of word choices. (Use *adequately* instead of *enough*. Use *encyclopedia* or *mystery novel* instead of *book*.)	Applying Good Writing Traits: Word Choice 466
8.5.7 Write for different purposes and to a specific audience or person, adjusting tone and style as necessary. Example: Write a letter to the editor in response to an opinion column in your school or community newspaper.	Writing Workshop 38–41, 92–94, 178–181, 234–236, 316–321, 380–384, etc. After You Read: Write About Your Reading 52, 74, 104, etc. Unit Wrap-Up: Solo Activity: Write a Poem 911 Unit Wrap-Up: Solo Activity: Propose a Change 1035

Writing: Applications (continued)

INDIANA ACADEMIC STANDARDS	COURSE 3
8.6 Writing: English Language Conventions	
8.6.1 Use correct and varied sentence types (simple, compound, complex, and compound–complex) and sentence openings to present a lively and effective personal style.	Applying Good Writing Traits: Voice 40 Grammar Link 583 Applying Good Writing Traits: Word Choice 869 Applying Good Writing Traits: Sentence Fluency 994
8.6.2 Identify and use parallelism (use consistent elements of grammar when compiling a list) in all writing to present items in a series and items juxtaposed for emphasis. • Correct: *Students having difficulty and needing help should stay after class.* • Incorrect: *Students having difficulty and who need help should stay after class.*	This standard is covered in the teacher's edition.
8.6.3 Use subordination, coordination, noun phrases that function as adjectives (*These gestures–acts of friendship–were noticed but not appreciated.*), and other devices to indicate clearly the relationship between ideas.	Grammar Link 579, 619, 627
8.6.4 Edit written manuscripts to ensure that correct grammar is used.	Writing Workshop: Editing 93, 235, 381, etc.
8.6.5 Use correct punctuation.	Grammar Link 315, 593, 603, 763, 789, 793, 823, 845, 859, 867, 879, 889, 941, 951, 965, 975, 985, 991, 1005
8.6.6 Use correct capitalization.	Grammar Link 1095, 1111, 1127
8.6.7 Use correct spelling conventions.	Spelling R43–R44 Writing Workshop: Editing Checklist 93, 381, 497, 630, 1129 Writing Workshop: Writing Tip: Spelling 235, 381, 630 Writing Workshop: Editing and Proofreading 868
8.6.8 Identify and use infinitives (the word *to* followed by the base form of a verb, such as *to understand* or *to learn*) and participles (made by adding *-ing, -d, -ed, -n, -en, or -t* to the base form of the verb, such as *dreaming, chosen, built,* and *grown*).	Grammar Link: Clauses and Phrases as Parts of Speech 579 Grammar Link: Irregular Verbs 1085 Grammar Link: Verbals 1139
Listening and Speaking	
8.7 Listening and Speaking: Skills, Strategies, and Applications	
8.7.1 Paraphrase (restate) a speaker's purpose and point of view and ask questions concerning the speaker's content, delivery, and attitude toward the subject.	Listening, Speaking, and Viewing: Active Listening 94 After You Read: Talk About Your Reading: Class Debate 308

Listening and Speaking: Skills, Strategies, and Applications (continued)

INDIANA ACADEMIC STANDARDS	COURSE 3
8.7.2 Match the message, vocabulary, voice modulation (changes in tone), expression, and tone to the audience and purpose.	Listening, Speaking, and Viewing: Storytelling 237 Listening, Speaking, and Viewing: Oral Presentation 382 Listening, Speaking, and Viewing: Reading Poetry Aloud 499
8.7.3 Outline the organization of a speech, including an introduction; transitions, previews, and summaries; a logically developed body; and an effective conclusion.	Listening, Speaking, and Viewing: Oral Presentation 382
8.7.4 Use precise language, action verbs, sensory details, appropriate and colorful modifiers (describing words, such as adverbs and adjectives), and the active (*I recommend that you write drafts.*) rather than the passive voice (*The writing of drafts is recommended.*) in ways that enliven oral presentations.	Listening, Speaking, and Viewing: Storytelling 237 Listening, Speaking, and Viewing: Oral Presentation 382 Listening, Speaking, and Viewing: Reading Poetry Aloud 499
8.7.5 Use appropriate grammar, word choice, enunciation (clear speech), and pace (timing) during formal presentations.	Listening, Speaking, and Viewing: Storytelling 237 Listening, Speaking, and Viewing: Oral Presentation 382 Listening, Speaking, and Viewing: Reading Poetry Aloud 499
8.7.6 Use audience feedback, including both verbal and nonverbal cues, to reconsider and modify the organizational structure and/or to rearrange words and sentences for clarification of meaning.	Listening, Speaking, and Viewing: Reading Poetry Aloud 499
8.7.7 Analyze oral interpretations of literature, including language choice and delivery, and the effect of the interpretations on the listener.	Listening, Speaking, and Viewing: Reading Poetry Aloud 499
8.7.8 Evaluate the credibility of a speaker, including whether the speaker has hidden agendas or presents slanted or biased material.	Genre Focus: Key Literary Element: Author's Bias 926 Key Literary Element: Author's Bias 979, 981, 982, etc. English Language Coach: Semantic Slanting 979, 980, 985, etc. Listening, Speaking, and Viewing: Understanding Persuasive Techniques 995
8.7.9 Interpret and evaluate the various ways in which visual image makers (such as graphic artists, illustrators, and news photographers) communicate information and affect impressions and opinions.	Genre Focus: Key Literary and Text Elements: Photographs 292 Key Text Element: Photographs 389, 390, 392, etc.

Listening and Speaking: Skills, Strategies, and Applications (continued)

INDIANA ACADEMIC STANDARDS	COURSE 3
8.7.10 Deliver narrative (story) presentations, such as biographical or autobiographical information that: • relate a clear incident, event, or situation, using well-chosen details. • reveal the significance of the incident, event, or situation. • use narrative and descriptive strategies to support the presentation, including relevant dialogue, specific action, physical description, background description, and comparison or contrast of characters.	Writing Workshop: Autobiographical Sketch: Presenting 93 Listening, Speaking, and Viewing: Dramatizing Literature 871
8.7.11 Deliver oral responses to literature that: • interpret reading and provide insight. • connect personal responses to the writer's techniques and to specific textual references. • make supported inferences about the effects of a literary work on its audience. • support judgments through references to the text, other works, other authors, or personal knowledge.	After You Read: Talk About Your Reading 36, 114, 308, 402, 488, 984
8.7.12 Deliver research presentations that: • define a thesis (a position on the topic). • research important ideas, concepts, and direct quotations from significant information sources and paraphrase and summarize important perspectives on the topic. • use a variety of research sources and distinguish the nature and value of each. • present information on charts, maps, and graphs.	Listening, Speaking, and Viewing: Oral Presentation 382 After You Read: Talk About Your Reading 36
8.7.13 Deliver persuasive presentations that: • include a well-defined thesis (position on the topic). • differentiate fact from opinion and support arguments with detailed evidence, examples, reasoning, and persuasive language. • anticipate and effectively answer listener concerns and counterarguments through the inclusion and arrangement of details, reasons, examples, and other elements. • maintain a reasonable tone.	Writing Workshop: Persuasive Essay 993
8.7.14 Recite poems (of four to six stanzas), sections of speeches, or dramatic soliloquies (sections of plays in which characters speak out loud to themselves) using voice modulation, tone, and gestures expressively to enhance the meaning.	Listening, Speaking, and Viewing: Reading Poetry Aloud 499

Succeeding on the ISTEP+ Test

Glencoe Literature: Reading with Purpose provides standardized test practice at the end of every unit. These tests are like the ones you will take during Grade 8. By practicing these tests now, you will be even better prepared to master the standards covered on the ISTEP+ test.

You will find some tips on the following pages that will help you become a better test-taker.

TIP Always read the test directions carefully before beginning any section of a test. The directions will tell you what you are expected to do in each part of the test.

TIP Read initially for the "big picture." Read carefully, but don't try to memorize details at this time. If you don't understand a particular word, keep reading. The meaning may become clear from the context of later sentences.

UNIT 5 SKILLS AND STRATEGIES ASSESSMENT

ISTEP+ Test Practice

Directions:

In this excerpt from a story about a boy's Sioux heritage, the boy confronts his mixed feelings about his grandfather. Read the excerpt carefully. Then, answer questions 1 through 7.

from The Medicine Bag

By Virginia Driving Hawk Sneve

We always had some authentic Sioux article to show our listeners. One year Cheryl had new moccasins that Grandpa had made. On another visit he gave me a small, round, flat, rawhide drum which was decorated with a painting of a warrior riding a horse. He taught me a real Sioux chant[1] to sing while I beat the drum with a leather-covered stick that had a feather on the end. Man, that really made an impression.

We never showed our friends Grandpa's picture. Not that we were ashamed of him, but because we knew that the glamorous tales we told didn't go with the real thing. Our friends would have laughed at the picture, because Grandpa wasn't tall and stately like TV Indians. His hair wasn't in braids, but hung in stringy, gray strands on his neck and he was old. He was our great-grandfather, and he didn't live in a tipi,[2] but all by himself in a part log, part tar-paper shack on the Rosebud Reservation in South Dakota. So when Grandpa came to visit us, I was so ashamed and embarrassed I could've died.

There are a lot of yippy poodles and other fancy little dogs in our neighborhood, but they usually barked singly at the mailman from the safety of their own yards. Now it sounded as if a whole pack of mutts were barking together in one place.

I got up and walked to the curb to see what the commotion was. About a block away I saw a crowd of little kids yelling, with the dogs yipping and growling around someone who was walking down the middle of the street.

I watched the group as it slowly came closer and saw that in the center of the strange procession was a man wearing a tall black hat. He'd pause now and then to peer at something in his hand and then at the houses on either side of the street. I felt cold and hot at the same time as I recognized the man.

[1] **chant:** a short, simple melody in which a number of syllables or words are sung to the same note.
[2] **tipi:** a cone-shaped tent, usually of animal skins, used especially by the Plains Indians. In the Sioux language, *tipi* is a combination of *ti*, "to dwell," and *pi*, "for use."

702 UNIT 5 How Do You Stay True to Yourself?

TIP **If there are fewer than 10 questions,** you may wish to read quickly through them before you begin reading the selection. This will alert you to important things to look for while you read.

TIP **When a quotation from the selection has been provided** to you in the question, you generally can answer from the quotation alone. You do not need to spend time going back to the selection to find it.

TIP **Pay attention to capitalized words in the question itself.** These are often words such as "mainly" or "most likely." They will help you decide between two answers that may both appear at first to be correct.

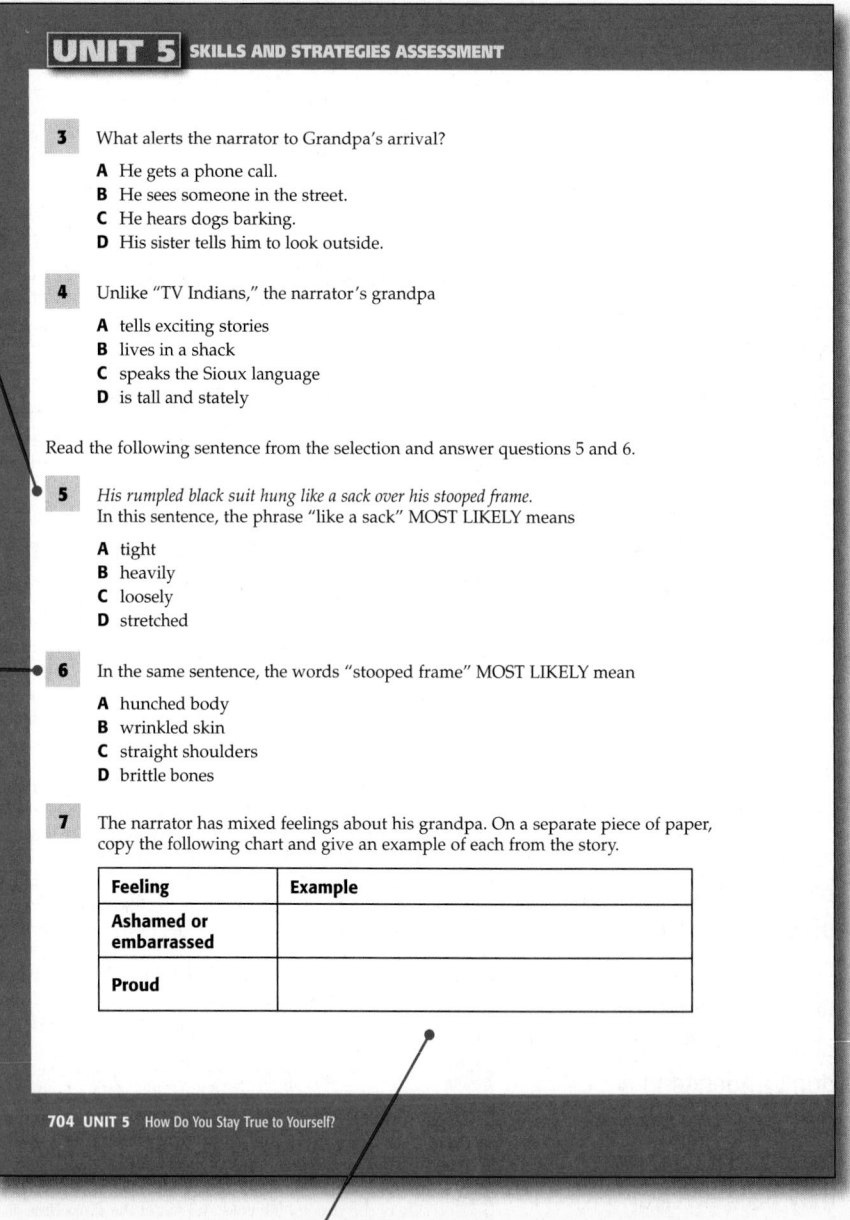

UNIT 5 SKILLS AND STRATEGIES ASSESSMENT

3 What alerts the narrator to Grandpa's arrival?

A He gets a phone call.
B He sees someone in the street.
C He hears dogs barking.
D His sister tells him to look outside.

4 Unlike "TV Indians," the narrator's grandpa

A tells exciting stories
B lives in a shack
C speaks the Sioux language
D is tall and stately

Read the following sentence from the selection and answer questions 5 and 6.

5 *His rumpled black suit hung like a sack over his stooped frame.*
In this sentence, the phrase "like a sack" MOST LIKELY means

A tight
B heavily
C loosely
D stretched

6 In the same sentence, the words "stooped frame" MOST LIKELY mean

A hunched body
B wrinkled skin
C straight shoulders
D brittle bones

7 The narrator has mixed feelings about his grandpa. On a separate piece of paper, copy the following chart and give an example of each from the story.

Feeling	Example
Ashamed or embarrassed	
Proud	

704 UNIT 5 How Do You Stay True to Yourself?

TIP **When a question is asking about specific details** from the selection, go back to the story to find examples before you formulate your answer.

TIP When you have completed a section of the test and if you still have time, go back and review your choices. If you are sure you made a mistake in one of your choices, then change it to the correct answer. If you are not sure, then you are probably better off staying with your first response and not changing your initial answer.

TIP **Read through the answer options and eliminate the obvious.** Then compare what is left before making your choice.

TIP **For questions on language conventions, make sure you understand the question and then read the answer choices slowly and carefully.** As you read, focus specifically on the language convention being tested. For example, if the question asks you to identify the sentence with correct capitalization, you should read each sentence, looking for errors in capitalization.

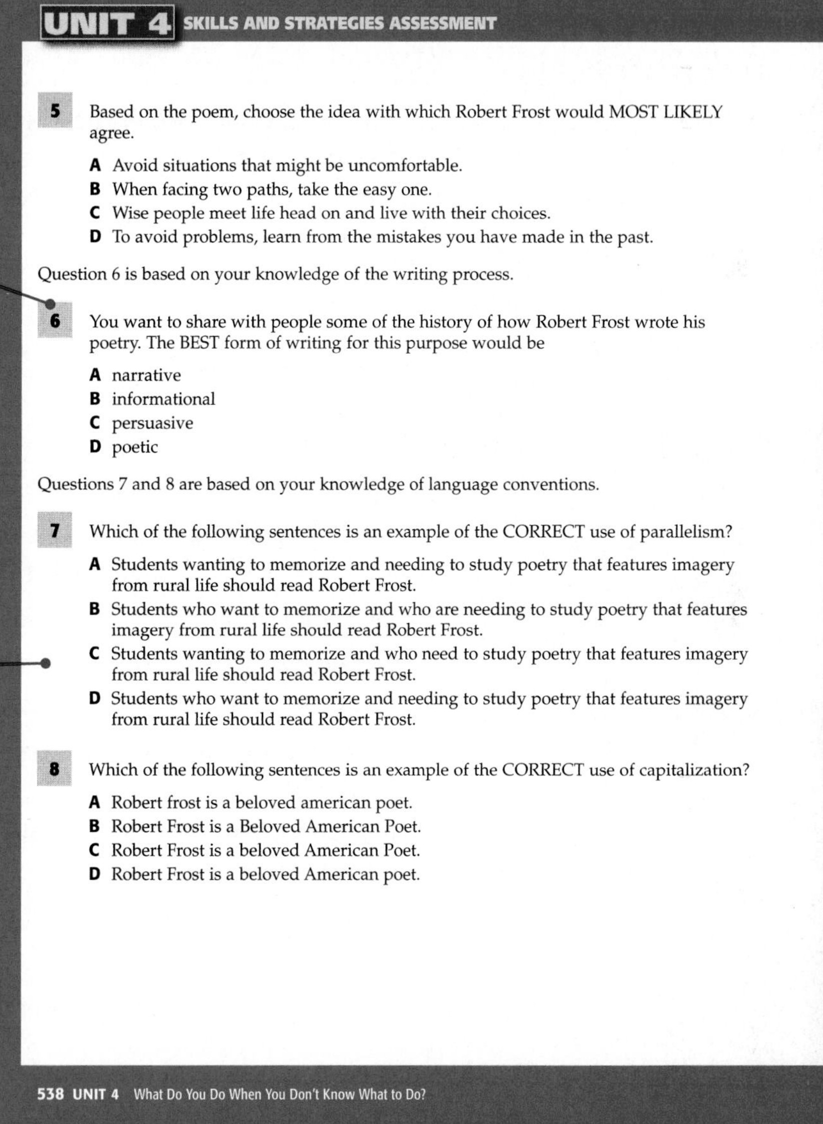

UNIT 4 SKILLS AND STRATEGIES ASSESSMENT

5 Based on the poem, choose the idea with which Robert Frost would MOST LIKELY agree.

- **A** Avoid situations that might be uncomfortable.
- **B** When facing two paths, take the easy one.
- **C** Wise people meet life head on and live with their choices.
- **D** To avoid problems, learn from the mistakes you have made in the past.

Question 6 is based on your knowledge of the writing process.

6 You want to share with people some of the history of how Robert Frost wrote his poetry. The BEST form of writing for this purpose would be

- **A** narrative
- **B** informational
- **C** persuasive
- **D** poetic

Questions 7 and 8 are based on your knowledge of language conventions.

7 Which of the following sentences is an example of the CORRECT use of parallelism?

- **A** Students wanting to memorize and needing to study poetry that features imagery from rural life should read Robert Frost.
- **B** Students who want to memorize and who are needing to study poetry that features imagery from rural life should read Robert Frost.
- **C** Students wanting to memorize and who need to study poetry that features imagery from rural life should read Robert Frost.
- **D** Students who want to memorize and needing to study poetry that features imagery from rural life should read Robert Frost.

8 Which of the following sentences is an example of the CORRECT use of capitalization?

- **A** Robert frost is a beloved american poet.
- **B** Robert Frost is a Beloved American Poet.
- **C** Robert Frost is a beloved American Poet.
- **D** Robert Frost is a beloved American poet.

538 UNIT 4 What Do You Do When You Don't Know What to Do?

How to Use *Reading with Purpose*

Consultant's Note

People read for enjoyment, to help themselves think, to solve problems, and to get work done. Their reading is often organized around "inquiry" questions. These questions help them explore how what they learn can help make a difference in the real world.

–Jeff Wilhelm

Wouldn't you like to read better–and understand more? That's what ***Reading with Purpose*** is all about. This book will help you bridge the gap between a writer's meaning and your understanding.

The next few pages will show you some of the ways ***Reading with Purpose*** can help you read, think, and write better.

What's in It for You?

Every unit in ***Reading with Purpose*** is built around a **Big Question,** a question that you will want to think about, talk about, maybe even argue about, and finally answer. The unit's reading selections will help you come up with your answers.

Organization

Each unit contains:

- A **Unit Warm-Up** that introduces the unit's Big Question
- Four **Reading Workshops,** each one containing reading selections that will help you think about the Big Question
  - **Literature** such as short stories, poems, plays, and biographies
  - **Informational texts** such as nonfiction, newspaper and magazine articles, reference books, and manuals
  - **Functional documents** such as signs, schedules, labels, and instructions
- A two-part **Writing Workshop** to help you put your ideas about the Big Question into writing
- A **Comparing Workshop** that will give you a chance to compare different pieces of writing
- A **Unit Wrap-Up** where you'll answer the Big Question

Reading and Thinking

Here are some of the ways ***Reading with Purpose*** will help you develop your reading and thinking skills.

Skills and Strategies The skills you need to become a better reader are related to the Indiana English/Language Arts Academic Standards.

Consultant's Note

Standards tell what you are expected to do or learn—the learning objectives. They help teachers plan lessons and select reading and writing tasks. In addition, standards ensure that the content taught at one school will be similar to the content at other schools in the state. The standards also help you figure out what will be on tests. Standards help you figure out what you need to learn to do well in school!

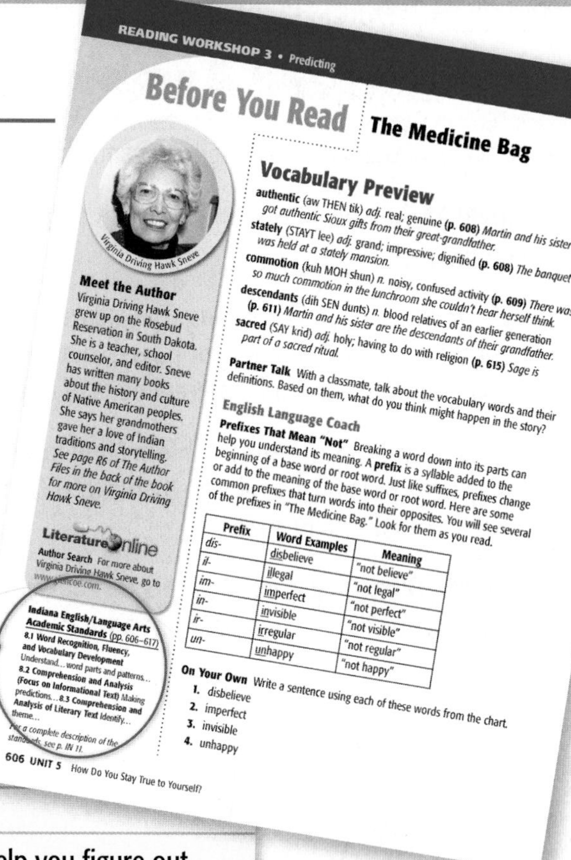

READING WORKSHOP 3 • Predicting

Before You Read **The Medicine Bag**

Virginia Driving Hawk Sneve

Meet the Author

Virginia Driving Hawk Sneve grew up on the Rosebud Reservation in South Dakota. She is a teacher, school counselor, and editor. Sneve has written many books about the history and culture of Native American peoples. She says her grandmothers gave her a love of Indian traditions and storytelling. *See page R6 of The Author Files in the back of the book for more on Virginia Driving Hawk Sneve.*

Literature Online

Author Search For more about Virginia Driving Hawk Sneve, go to www.glencoe.com.

Indiana English/Language Arts Academic Standards (pp. 606–617)

8.1 Word Recognition, Fluency, and Vocabulary Development Understand... word parts and patterns... **8.2 Comprehension and Analysis (Focus on Informational Text)** Making predictions... **8.3 Comprehension and Analysis of Literary Text** Identify... theme...

For a complete description of the standards, see p. IN 11.

Vocabulary Preview

authentic (aw THEN tik) *adj.* real; genuine **(p. 608)** *Martin and his sister got authentic Sioux gifts from their great-grandfather.*

stately (STAYT lee) *adj.* grand; impressive; dignified **(p. 608)** *The banquet was held at a stately mansion.*

commotion (kuh MOH shun) *n.* noisy, confused activity **(p. 609)** *There was so much commotion in the lunchroom she couldn't hear herself think.*

descendants (dih SEN dunts) *n.* blood relatives of an earlier generation **(p. 611)** *Martin and his sister are the descendants of their grandfather.*

sacred (SAY krid) *adj.* holy; having to do with religion **(p. 615)** *Sage is part of a sacred ritual.*

Partner Talk With a classmate, talk about the vocabulary words and their definitions. Based on them, what do you think might happen in the story?

English Language Coach

Prefixes That Mean "Not" Breaking a word down into its parts can help you understand its meaning. A **prefix** is a syllable added to the beginning of a base word or root word. Just like suffixes, prefixes change or add to the meaning of the base word or root word. Here are some common prefixes that turn words into their opposites. You will see several of the prefixes in "The Medicine Bag." Look for them as you read.

Prefix	Word Examples	Meaning
dis-	disbelieve	"not believe"
il-	illegal	"not legal"
im-	imperfect	"not perfect"
in-	invisible	"not visible"
ir-	irregular	"not regular"
un-	unhappy	"not happy"

On Your Own Write a sentence using each of these words from the chart.

1. disbelieve
2. imperfect
3. invisible
4. unhappy

606 UNIT 5 How Do You Stay True to Yourself?

READING WORKSHOP 1

was. He had thick, wavy hair and muscles like Sylvester Stallone. He could surf, he could water-ski on bare feet, he could free-dive to eighty feet and stay down for close to three minutes. He was once stranded on French Frigate Shoals for thirty days with a couple of Filipino fishermen. And except for one, gaping character flaw, he was everything I, at thirteen, wanted to be.

His flaw, though, was a big one, and I didn't understand it until I was much older. But once I figured it out, I could see why I never knew him, either.

It simply wasn't possible.

He wouldn't allow it.

He was a loner and a crusher of **self-esteem**—mine, and my sisters', and eventually my mother's. But for a few years in my life, John was king. He was lean and strong, and he looked like a movie star. In my eyes he could do no wrong. 3 My sisters never saw it that way, but I sure did. I liked him. I was floating on top of the world when Mom said she was going to marry him.

We lived on Oahu at the time. John worked at the Hawaiian Village Hotel in Waikiki, running the water-ski operation. He was then, and had always been, a man of the sea. His skin was a deep red-brown, colored by a lifetime in the sun. And when he moved, it was in a smooth, slow, don't-bother-me kind of way. Most of the time a Marlboro hung from his half-parted lips, his eyes squinting through the smoke like Clint Eastwood's. He could have been the star of *Sea Hunt*, or *Rawhide*, or even *Cliffhanger*, if he wanted to. He had that same kind of raw, manly presence. 4

We moved from Oahu to the Big Island soon after Mom and John were married. We traveled by boat—a thirty-eight-foot deep-sea charter fishing boat that made me sicker than I'd ever been in my life. My sisters took a plane. But Mom and I made the two-day trip with John and his new fully rigged haole sampan, gliding over glassy seas in the lee[2] of the islands and

Visual Vocabulary A ***sampan*** is a boat with a flat bottom. It usually has two oars, or paddles, to make the boat go forward.

2. The ***lee*** is the side of the island that is not being hit by wind.

Vocabulary

self-esteem (self es TEEM) *n.* confidence and satisfaction in oneself

Practice the Skills

3 **Key Reading Skill**

Connecting Is there anyone you know who "can do no wrong"? Do you feel the same way about this person as the author feels about John?

4 **Key Literary Element**

Description There are a lot of descriptive details that appeal to the sense of sight in this paragraph. Which details help you picture what John looks like?

20 UNIT 1 Reading: What's in It for you?

Kevin R. Morris/CORBIS

Margin Notes These notes will help you with a difficult passage, point out an important development, model a skill, or ask a question to get you thinking about what you are reading.

Question and Answer Relationship

Four types of questions are used on standardized tests:

1. **Right There Questions** The answer is "right there" on the page.
2. **Think and Search Questions** The answers to these questions are on the page (or pages), but you'll need to use information from different parts of the text.
3. **Author and Me Questions** Information from the text may help, but you'll put it together with your own ideas to answer a question.
4. **On My Own Questions** Answers do not come from the text. You'll base your answer on what you know.

Knowing how to deal with such questions can help improve your test scores. At the end of most Workshops is a set of questions. In the first two units, each question is followed by a tip to help you answer. For example:

- What promise does Victor make to himself about this school year?

  TIP **Right There** You will find the answer in the story.

Vocabulary

Vocabulary words may be difficult or new to you, but they're useful words.

Vocabulary Preview Vocabulary words are introduced on the Before You Read page. Each word is followed by its pronunciation, its part of speech, a definition, and a sample sentence.

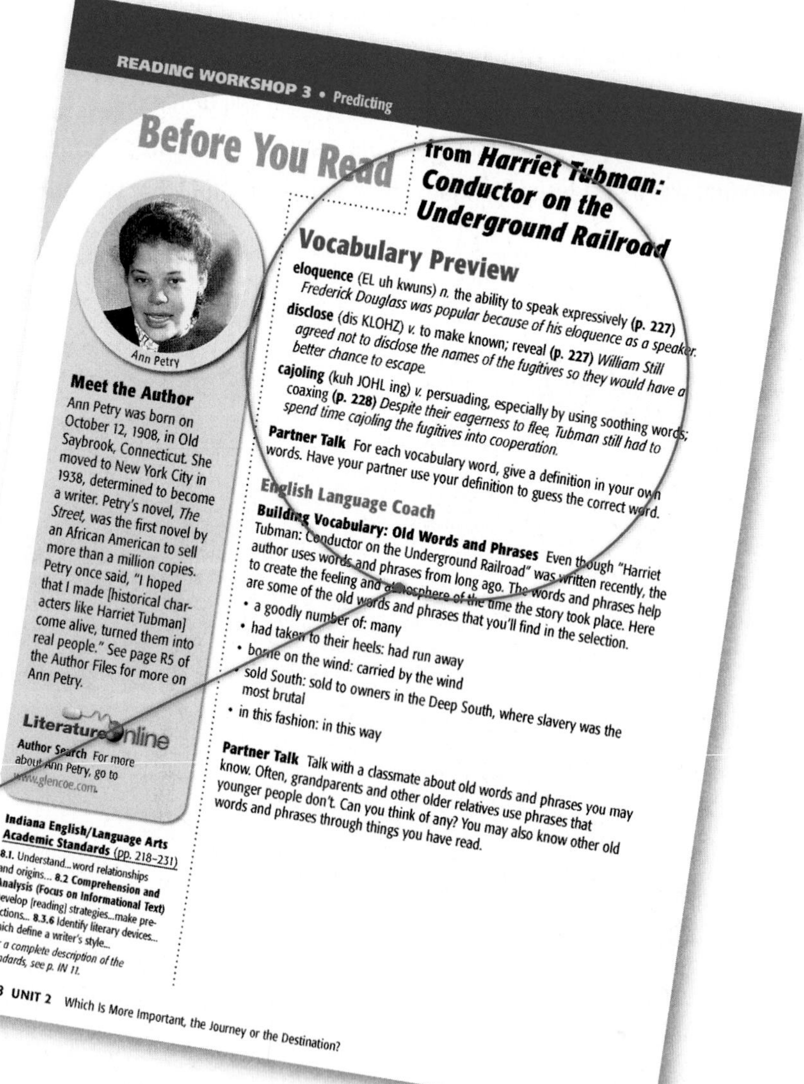

READING WORKSHOP 3 • Predicting

Before You Read

from *Harriet Tubman: Conductor on the Underground Railroad*

Ann Petry

Meet the Author
Ann Petry was born on October 12, 1908, in Old Saybrook, Connecticut. She moved to New York City in 1938, determined to become a writer. Petry's novel, *The Street*, was the first novel by an African American to sell more than a million copies. Petry once said, "I hoped that I made [historical characters like Harriet Tubman] come alive, turned them into real people." See page R5 of the Author Files for more on Ann Petry.

Literature Online
Author Search For more about Ann Petry, go to www.glencoe.com.

Indiana English/Language Arts Academic Standards (pp. 218–231)
8.1. Understand...word relationships and origins... **8.2 Comprehension and Analysis (Focus on Informational Text)** Develop [reading] strategies...make predictions... **8.3.6** Identify literary devices... which define a writer's style...
For a complete description of the standards, see p. IN 11.

Vocabulary Preview

eloquence (EL uh kwuns) *n.* the ability to speak expressively **(p. 227)** *Frederick Douglass was popular because of his eloquence as a speaker.*

disclose (dis KLOHZ) *v.* to make known; reveal **(p. 227)** *William Still agreed not to disclose the names of the fugitives so they would have a better chance to escape.*

cajoling (kuh JOHL ing) *v.* persuading, especially by using soothing words; coaxing **(p. 228)** *Despite their eagerness to flee, Tubman still had to spend time cajoling the fugitives into cooperation.*

Partner Talk For each vocabulary word, give a definition in your own words. Have your partner use your definition to guess the correct word.

English Language Coach

Building Vocabulary: Old Words and Phrases Even though "Harriet Tubman: Conductor on the Underground Railroad" was written recently, the author uses words and phrases from long ago. The words and phrases help to create the feeling and atmosphere of the time the story took place. Here are some of the old words and phrases that you'll find in the selection.

- a goodly number of: many
- had taken to their heels: had run away
- borne on the wind: carried by the wind
- sold South: sold to owners in the Deep South, where slavery was the most brutal
- in this fashion: in this way

Partner Talk Talk with a classmate about old words and phrases you may know. Often, grandparents and other older relatives use phrases that younger people don't. Can you think of any? You may also know other old words and phrases through things you have read.

218 UNIT 2 Which Is More Important, the Journey or the Destination?

READING WORKSHOP 3

The elder[2] daughter said quickly: 'I shall go, of course, since I am the elder.'

'Very well,' replied the man. 'I shall call all my friends and bid the drummers lead you to your husband's home.'

'Indeed you will not,' said the girl haughtily. 'When I go to the home of my husband, I shall go alone.'

Now in that part of Africa it was unheard of for a bride to go to her wedding without a host of friends and relations all singing and dancing for joy. So the father was astonished when his daughter said she would go alone, even though he knew she had been proud and headstrong from childhood.

'But, my daughter,' he **pleaded**, 'no woman ever goes alone to her marriage. It is not the custom.' 2

'Then I shall start a new custom,' said the girl. 'Unless I go alone, I shall not go at all.'

At last the father, realizing that no amount of persuasion would **induce** the girl to change her mind, agreed to her going alone, and early the next morning she set out. He took her across the river and pointed out the way, then returned home unhappily. 3

The girl began her journey without looking back and after a little while she met a mouse on the path. It stood up on its hind-legs, and rubbing its two front paws together, asked politely:

'Would you like me to show you the way to the chief's village?'

The girl scarcely stopped walking and almost trod on the mouse as she replied:

'Get out of my sight! I want no help from you.'

Then she continued on her way while the mouse screeched after her:

'Bad luck to you!'

2. ***Elder*** means older.

Vocabulary

induce (in DOOS) *v.* convince to do something; influence

Practice the Skills

2 **English Language Coach**

Classification Charts The word **pleaded** describes how the father's voice sounds when he talks to his daughter. If you don't know what the word means, use context clues to figure out the definition. Add the word and definition to the classification chart you made earlier.

3 **Key Literary Element**

Conflict The unhappy father has an internal conflict. What external conflict with his daughter caused him to feel unhappy?

Homeward Bound, 2004. Tilly Willis. Oil on canvas. Private Collection.

Analyzing the Painting How does this painting help you visualize the story's setting?

The Snake Chief 209

Vocabulary The word is in **bold** type when it first appears in the reading selection.

Vocabulary The word with its pronunciation, part of speech, and definition appear at the bottom of the same page.

English Language Coach These notes help students whose first language is not English. For example, they help explain multiple-meaning words and also idioms—phrases that mean something other than what their individual words mean.

Footnotes Selection footnote explains words or phrases that you may not know to help you understand the story.

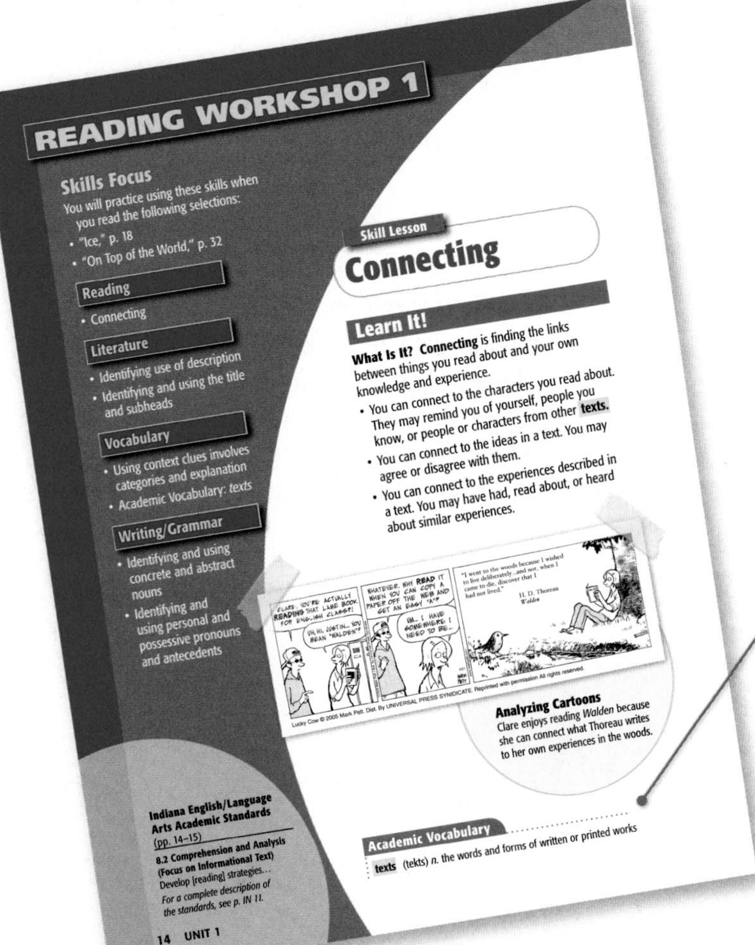

READING WORKSHOP 1

Skills Focus

You will practice using these skills when you read the following selections:

- "Ice," p. 18
- "On Top of the World," p. 32

Reading

- Connecting

Literature

- Identifying use of description
- Identifying and using the title and subheads

Vocabulary

- Using context clues involves categories and explanation
- Academic Vocabulary: texts

Writing/Grammar

- Identifying and using concrete and abstract nouns
- Identifying and using personal and possessive pronouns and antecedents

Indiana English/Language Arts Academic Standards
(pp. 14–15)

8.2 Comprehension and Analysis (Focus on Informational Text) Develop [reading] strategies...

For a complete description of the standards, see p. IN 11.

Skill Lesson

Connecting

Learn It!

What Is It? Connecting is finding the links between things you read about and your own knowledge and experience.

- You can connect to the characters you read about. They may remind you of yourself, people you know, or people or characters from other **texts.**
- You can connect to the ideas in a text. You may agree or disagree with them.
- You can connect to the experiences described in a text. You may have had, read about, or heard about similar experiences.

Lucky Cow © 2005 Mark Pett. Dist. By UNIVERSAL PRESS SYNDICATE. Reprinted with permission All rights reserved.

Analyzing Cartoons
Clare enjoys reading *Walden* because she can connect what Thoreau writes to her own experiences in the woods.

Academic Vocabulary

texts (tekts) *n.* the words and forms of written or printed works

14 UNIT 1

Academic Vocabulary These are words you come across in your school work—in science, math, or social studies books as well as this book. The academic words are treated the same as regular vocabulary words.

Organizing Information

Foldables For every unit, you'll be shown how to make a ***Foldable*** that will help you keep track of your thoughts about the Big Question. See page T94 for more about Foldables.

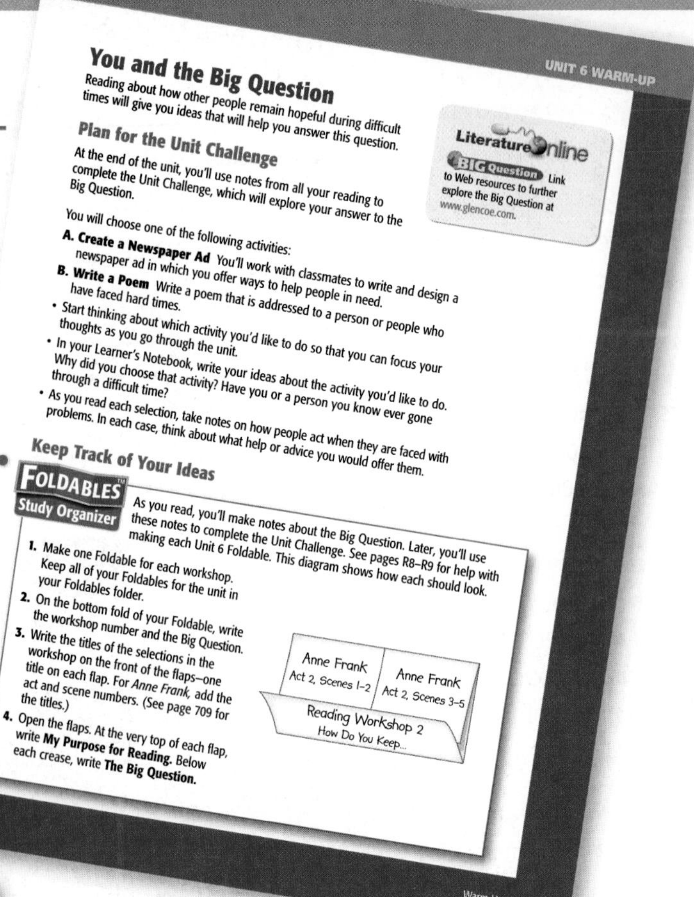
UNIT 6 WARM-UP

You and the Big Question

Reading about how other people remain hopeful during difficult times will give you ideas that will help you answer this question.

Literature Online — BIG Question Link to Web resources to further explore the Big Question at www.glencoe.com.

Plan for the Unit Challenge

At the end of the unit, you'll use notes from all your reading to complete the Unit Challenge, which will explore your answer to the Big Question.

You will choose one of the following activities:

A. Create a Newspaper Ad You'll work with classmates to write and design a newspaper ad in which you offer ways to help people in need.

B. Write a Poem Write a poem that is addressed to a person or people who have faced hard times.

- Start thinking about which activity you'd like to do so that you can focus your thoughts as you go through the unit.
- In your Learner's Notebook, write your ideas about the activity you'd like to do. Why did you choose that activity? Have you or a person you know ever gone through a difficult time?
- As you read each selection, take notes on how people act when they are faced with problems. In each case, think about what help or advice you would offer them.

Keep Track of Your Ideas

FOLDABLES Study Organizer As you read, you'll make notes about the Big Question. Later, you'll use these notes to complete the Unit Challenge. See pages R8–R9 for help with making each Unit 6 Foldable. This diagram shows how each should look.

1. Make one Foldable for each workshop. Keep all of your Foldables for the unit in your Foldables folder.
2. On the bottom fold of your Foldable, write the workshop number and the Big Question.
3. Write the titles of the selections in the workshop on the front of the flaps—one title on each flap. For *Anne Frank,* add the act and scene numbers. (See page 709 for the titles.)
4. Open the flaps. At the very top of each flap, write **My Purpose for Reading.** Below each crease, write **The Big Question.**

Warm-Up 711

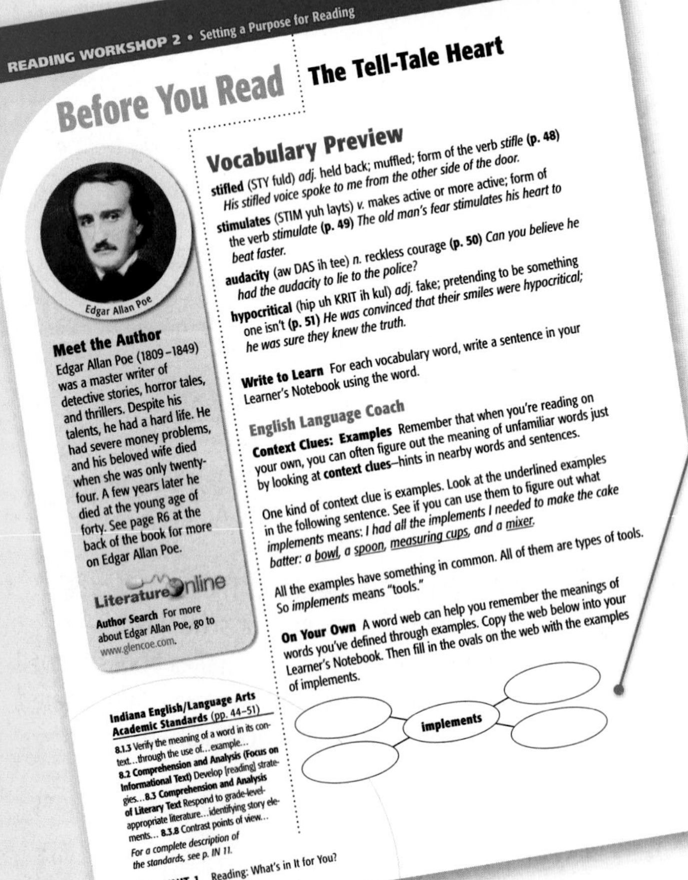
READING WORKSHOP 2 • Setting a Purpose for Reading

Before You Read — The Tell-Tale Heart

Edgar Allan Poe

Meet the Author
Edgar Allan Poe (1809–1849) was a master writer of detective stories, horror tales, and thrillers. Despite his talents, he had a hard life. He had severe money problems, and his beloved wife died when she was only twenty-four. A few years later he died at the young age of forty. See page R6 at the back of the book for more on Edgar Allan Poe.

Literature Online — **Author Search** For more about Edgar Allan Poe, go to www.glencoe.com.

Vocabulary Preview

stifled (STY fuld) *adj.* held back; muffled; form of the verb *stifle* **(p. 48)** *His stifled voice spoke to me from the other side of the door.*

stimulates (STIM yuh layts) *v.* makes active or more active; form of the verb *stimulate* **(p. 49)** *The old man's fear stimulates his heart to beat faster.*

audacity (aw DAS ih tee) *n.* reckless courage **(p. 50)** *Can you believe he had the audacity to lie to the police?*

hypocritical (hip uh KRIT ih kul) *adj.* fake; pretending to be something one isn't **(p. 51)** *He was convinced that their smiles were hypocritical; he was sure they knew the truth.*

Write to Learn For each vocabulary word, write a sentence in your Learner's Notebook using the word.

English Language Coach

Context Clues: Examples Remember that when you're reading on your own, you can often figure out the meaning of unfamiliar words just by looking at **context clues**—hints in nearby words and sentences.

One kind of context clue is examples. Look at the underlined examples in the following sentence. See if you can use them to figure out what *implements* means: *I had all the implements I needed to make the cake batter: a bowl, a spoon, measuring cups, and a mixer.*

All the examples have something in common. All of them are types of tools. So *implements* means "tools."

On Your Own A word web can help you remember the meanings of words you've defined through examples. Copy the web below into your Learner's Notebook. Then fill in the ovals on the web with the examples of implements.

Indiana English/Language Arts Academic Standards (pp. 44–51)
8.1.3 Verify the meaning of a word in its context…through the use of…example… **8.2 Comprehension and Analysis (Focus on Informational Text)** Develop [reading] strategies… **8.3 Comprehension and Analysis of Literary Text** Respond to grade-level-appropriate literature…identifying story elements… **8.3.8** Contrast points of view…
For a complete description of the standards, see p. IN 11.

44 UNIT 1 Reading: What's in It for You?

Graphic Organizers In ***Reading with Purpose,*** you will use different kinds of graphic organizers to help you arrange information. These graphic organizers include, among others, Venn Diagrams, Compare and Contrast Charts, Cluster Diagrams, and Chain-of-Events Charts.

Writing

In the selections in ***Reading with Purpose,*** you'll read many examples of excellent writing, and you'll explore what makes those pieces of writing so good.

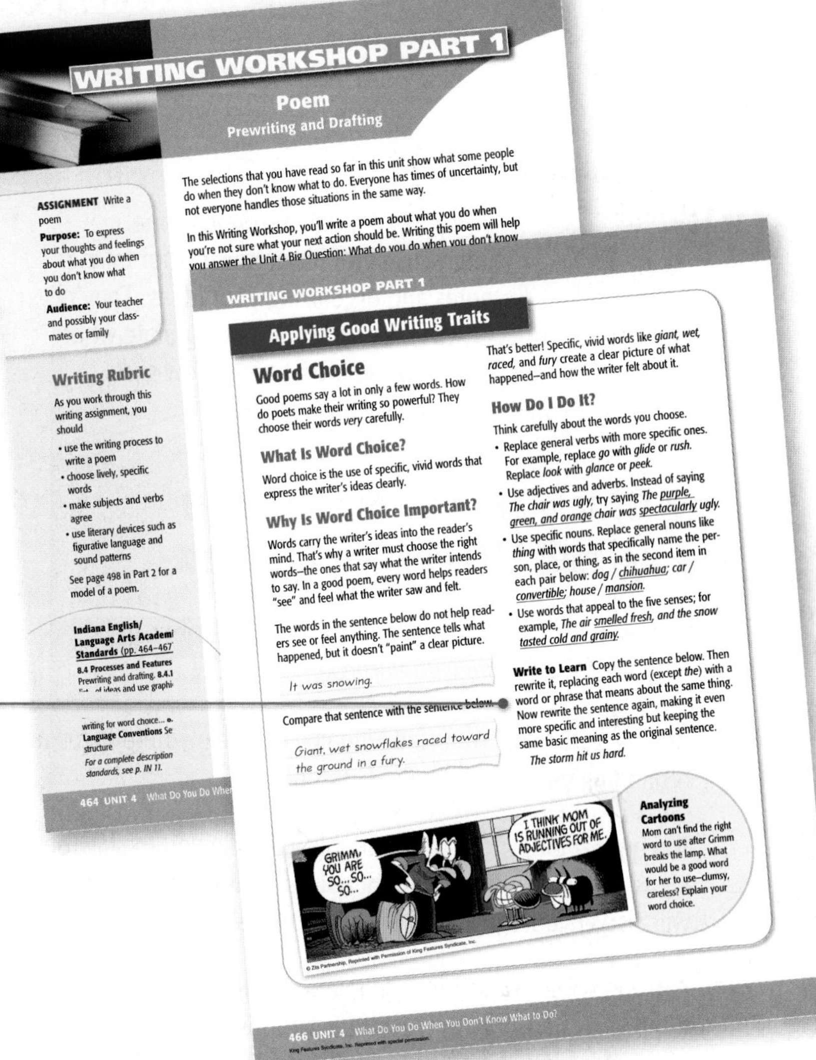

WRITING WORKSHOP PART 1

Poem

Prewriting and Drafting

The selections that you have read so far in this unit show what some people do when they don't know what to do. Everyone has times of uncertainty, but not everyone handles those situations in the same way.

In this Writing Workshop, you'll write a poem about what you do when you're not sure what your next action should be. Writing this poem will help

ASSIGNMENT Write a poem

Purpose: To express your thoughts and feelings about what you do when you don't know what to do

Audience: Your teacher and possibly your classmates or family

Writing Rubric

As you work through this writing assignment, you should

- use the writing process to write a poem
- choose lively, specific words
- make subjects and verbs agree
- use literary devices such as figurative language and sound patterns

See page 498 in Part 2 for a model of a poem.

Indiana English/Language Arts Academic Standards (pp. 464–467)

8.4 Processes and Features Prewriting and drafting, 8.4.1

Language Conventions

For a complete description of standards, see p. IN 11.

464 UNIT 4 What Do You Do When

WRITING WORKSHOP PART 1

Applying Good Writing Traits

Word Choice

Good poems say a lot in only a few words. How do poets make their writing so powerful? They choose their words *very* carefully.

What Is Word Choice?

Word choice is the use of specific, vivid words that express the writer's ideas clearly.

Why Is Word Choice Important?

Words carry the writer's ideas into the reader's mind. That's why a writer must choose the right words—the ones that say what the writer intends to say. In a good poem, every word helps readers "see" and feel what the writer saw and felt.

The words in the sentence below do not help readers see or feel anything. The sentence tells what happened, but it doesn't "paint" a clear picture.

It was snowing.

Compare that sentence with the sentence below.

Giant, wet snowflakes raced toward the ground in a fury.

That's better! Specific, vivid words like *giant, wet, raced,* and *fury* create a clear picture of what happened—and how the writer felt about it.

How Do I Do It?

Think carefully about the words you choose.

- Replace general verbs with more specific ones. For example, replace *go* with *glide* or *rush.* Replace *look* with *glance* or *peek.*
- Use adjectives and adverbs. Instead of saying *The chair was ugly,* try saying *The purple, green, and orange chair was spectacularly ugly.*
- Use specific nouns. Replace general nouns like *thing* with words that specifically name the person, place, or thing, as in the second item in each pair below: *dog / chihuahua; car / convertible; house / mansion.*
- Use words that appeal to the five senses; for example, *The air smelled fresh, and the snow tasted cold and grainy.*

Write to Learn Copy the sentence below. Then rewrite it, replacing each word (except *the*) with a word or phrase that means about the same thing. Now rewrite the sentence again, making it even more specific and interesting but keeping the same basic meaning as the original sentence.

The storm hit us hard.

Analyzing Cartoons Mom can't find the right word to use after Grimm breaks the lamp. What would be a good word for her to use—clumsy, careless? Explain your word choice.

466 UNIT 4 What Do You Do When You Don't Know What to Do?

Writing to Learn As you learn new skills, you will sometimes complete a short writing assignment that will help you practice or think about your new skill.

Test Preparation and Practice

At the end of each unit, you will encounter six pages of ISTEP+ Test Practice. This simulated standardized test will help you become familiar with the content and the format of the state test so that you can succeed in the ISTEP+ testing program.

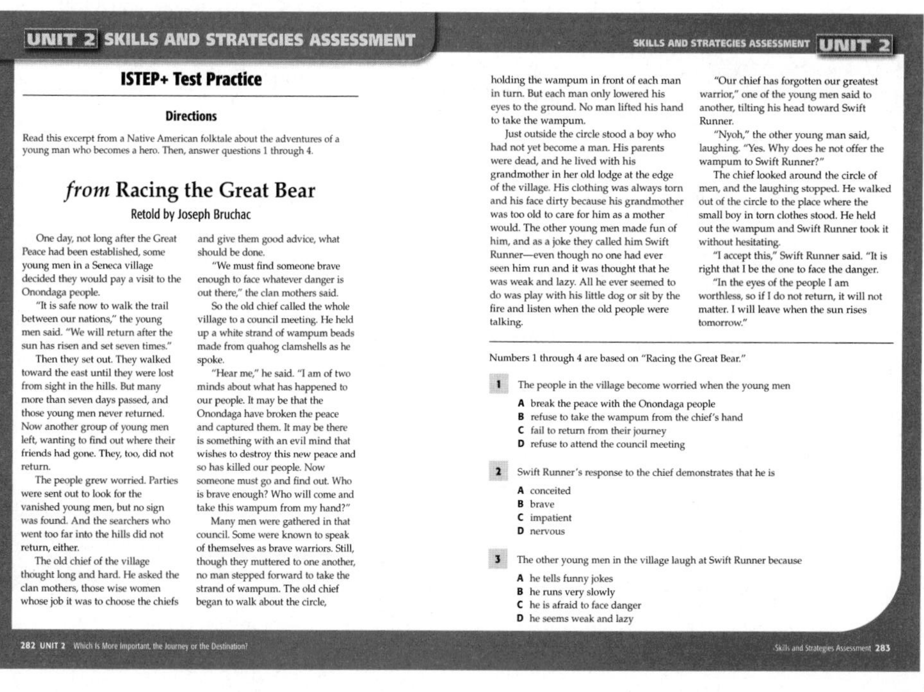

UNIT 2 SKILLS AND STRATEGIES ASSESSMENT

ISTEP+ Test Practice

Directions

Read this excerpt from a Native American folktale about the adventures of a young man who becomes a hero. Then, answer questions 1 through 4.

from Racing the Great Bear

Retold by Joseph Bruchac

One day, not long after the Great Peace had been established, some young men in a Seneca village decided they would pay a visit to the Onondaga people.

"It is safe now to walk the trail between our nations," the young men said. "We will return after the sun has risen and set seven times."

Then they set out. They walked toward the east until they were lost from sight in the hills. But many more than seven days passed, and those young men never returned. Now another group of young men left, wanting to find out where their friends had gone. They, too, did not return.

The people grew worried. Parties were sent out to look for the vanished young men, but no sign was found. And the searchers who went too far into the hills did not return, either.

The old chief of the village thought long and hard. He asked the clan mothers, those wise women whose job it was to choose the chiefs and give them good advice, what should be done.

"We must find someone brave enough to face whatever danger is out there," the clan mothers said.

So the old chief called the whole village to a council meeting. He held up a white strand of wampum beads made from quahog clamshells as he spoke.

"Hear me," he said. "I am of two minds about what has happened to our people. It may be that the Onondaga have broken the peace and captured them. It may be there is something with an evil mind that wishes to destroy this new peace and so has killed our people. Now someone must go and find out. Who is brave enough? Who will come and take this wampum from my hand?"

Many men were gathered in that council. Some were known to speak of themselves as brave warriors. Still, though they muttered to one another, no man stepped forward to take the strand of wampum. The old chief began to walk about the circle, holding the wampum in front of each man in turn. But each man only lowered his eyes to the ground. No man lifted his hand to take the wampum.

Just outside the circle stood a boy who had not yet become a man. His parents were dead, and he lived with his grandmother in her old lodge at the edge of the village. His clothing was always torn and his face dirty because his grandmother was too old to care for him as a mother would. The other young men made fun of him, and as a joke they called him Swift Runner—even though no one had ever seen him run and it was thought that he was weak and lazy. All he ever seemed to do was play with his little dog or sit by the fire and listen when the old people were talking.

"Our chief has forgotten our greatest warrior," one of the young men said to another, tilting his head toward Swift Runner.

"Nyoh," the other young man said, laughing. "Yes. Why does he not offer the wampum to Swift Runner?"

The chief looked around the circle of men, and the laughing stopped. He walked out of the circle to the place where the small boy in torn clothes stood. He held out the wampum and Swift Runner took it without hesitating.

"I accept this," Swift Runner said. "It is right that I be the one to face the danger.

"In the eyes of the people I am worthless, so if I do not return, it will not matter. I will leave when the sun rises tomorrow."

Numbers 1 through 4 are based on "Racing the Great Bear."

1 The people in the village become worried when the young men

A break the peace with the Onondaga people
B refuse to take the wampum from the chief's hand
C fail to return from their journey
D refuse to attend the council meeting

2 Swift Runner's response to the chief demonstrates that he is

A conceited
B brave
C impatient
D nervous

3 The other young men in the village laugh at Swift Runner because

A he tells funny jokes
B he runs very slowly
C he is afraid to face danger
D he seems weak and lazy

282 UNIT 2 Which Is More Important, the Journey or the Destination?

SKILLS AND STRATEGIES ASSESSMENT UNIT 2

Skills and Strategies Assessment 283

Foldables™

by Dinah Zike, Ed.D., Creator of Foldables™

Foldables™ are three-dimensional interactive graphic organizers for taking notes and organizing your ideas. They're also fun! You will fold paper, cut tabs, write, and manipulate what you have made in order to organize information; review skills, concepts, and strategies; and assess your learning.

Using Dinah Zike's Foldables in Reading and Literature Classes

Use Foldables before, during, and after reading selections in *Glencoe Literature: Reading with Purpose.*

- **Before you read:** Your unit Foldable will help you to focus on your purpose for reading by reminding you about the Big Question.
- **During reading:** Your unit Foldable will help you to stay focused and engaged. You will track key ideas and your thoughts about each selection and how it helps you answer the Big Question. It will also encourage you to use higher level thinking skills in approaching text.
- **After reading:** Your unit Foldable will help you to review your thoughts from your reading and to analyze, interpret, and evaluate various aspects of the Big Question. Your Foldable notes will also help you with your unit challenge. They also stimulate rich group discussions and inquiry.

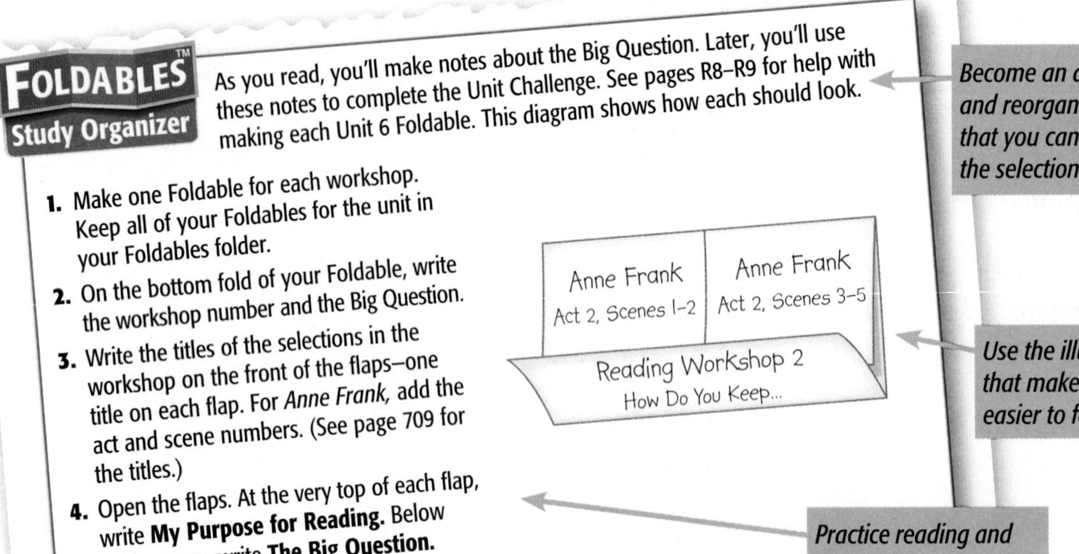
FOLDABLES™
Study Organizer
As you read, you'll make notes about the Big Question. Later, you'll use these notes to complete the Unit Challenge. See pages R8–R9 for help with making each Unit 6 Foldable. This diagram shows how each should look.
1. Make one Foldable for each workshop. Keep all of your Foldables for the unit in your Foldables folder.
2. On the bottom fold of your Foldable, write the workshop number and the Big Question.
3. Write the titles of the selections in the workshop on the front of the flaps—one title on each flap. For *Anne Frank*, add the act and scene numbers. (See page 709 for the titles.)
4. Open the flaps. At the very top of each flap, write **My Purpose for Reading.** Below each crease, write **The Big Question.**
Anne Frank
Act 2, Scenes 1–2
Anne Frank
Act 2, Scenes 3–5
Reading Workshop 2
How Do You Keep...

Become an active reader, track and reorganize information so that you can better understand the selection.

Use the illustrations that make the directions easier to follow.

Practice reading and following step-by-step directions.

Scavenger Hunt

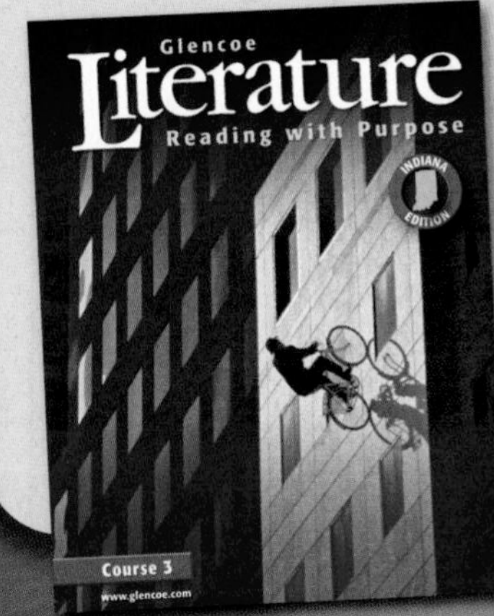

Reading with Purpose has a lot of information, excitement, and entertainment. This Scavenger Hunt will help you explore the book. You'll learn how to find what you need quickly. There are ten questions in your scavenger hunt. All the answers are in this book. Write your answers in your Learner's Notebook.

1. How many units are there in the book?
2. How many types of Workshops are in a unit and what are their names?
3. What is the genre focus of Unit 6?
4. How many short stories are in Unit 3?
5. Where can you find a list of all the poems in this book?
6. What's the fastest way to find a particular short story in the book?
7. Where in this book can you quickly find the correct pronunciation of the word *maneuvers?*
8. Where could you most quickly find the difference between a simile and a metaphor?
9. Where can you look for the answer to a question about grammar?
10. Name two places in the book where you can find biographical information about a writer.

After you answer all the questions, meet with a small group to compare answers.

READING HANDBOOK

You don't read a news article the way you read a novel. You read a news article mainly for information; you read a novel mainly for fun. To get the most out of your reading, you need to choose the right reading strategy to fit the reason you're reading. This handbook focuses on skills and strategies that can help you understand what you read.

Identifying Words and Building Vocabulary

What do you do when you come across a word you don't know as you read? Do you skip over the word and keep reading? If you're reading for fun or entertainment, you might. And that's just fine. But if you're reading for information, an unfamiliar word may get in the way of your understanding. When that happens, try the following strategies to figure out how to say the word and what it means. These strategies will help you better understand what you read. They will also help you increase the vocabulary you use in everyday speaking and reading.

Reading Unfamiliar Words

Sounding the Word Out

One way to figure out how to say a new word is to sound it out, syllable by syllable. Look carefully at the word's beginning, middle, and ending. Inside the new word, do you see a word you already know how to pronounce? What vowels are in the syllables? Use the following tips when sounding out new words.

▶ Ask Yourself

- What letters make up the beginning sound or beginning syllable of the word?

  Example: In the word *coagulate*, *co-* rhymes with *so.*

- What sounds do the letters in the middle part of the word make?

  Example: In the word *coagulate*, the syllable *ag* has the same sound as the *ag* in bag, and the syllable *u* is pronounced like the letter *u.*

- What letters make up the ending sound or syllable?

  Example: In the word *coagulate, late* is a familiar word you already know how to pronounce.

- Now try pronouncing the whole word: *co ag u late.*

Using Word Parts

Looking closely at the parts of a word is another way to learn it. By studying word parts—the root or base word, prefixes, and suffixes—you may discover more than just how to pronounce a word. You may also find clues to the word's meaning.

- **Roots and Base Words** The main part of a word is called its **root.** When the root is a complete word, it may be called the **base word.** Many roots in English come from an old form of English called Anglo-Saxon. You probably know many of these roots already. For example, *endearing* and *remarkable* have the familiar words *dear* and *mark* as their roots. Other roots come from Greek and Latin.

You may not be as familiar with them. For example, the word *spectator* contains the Latin root *spec,* which means "to look at." You can see that meaning in the word *spectator*, "one who looks."

When you come across a new word, check whether you recognize its root or base word. It can help you pronounce the word and figure out its meaning.

- **Prefixes** A prefix is a word part that can be added to the beginning of a root or base word to change the word's meaning. For example,

  the prefix *semi-* means "half" or "partial," so *semicircle* means "half a circle"

  un- means "not," so *unhappy* means "not happy"

- **Suffixes** A suffix is a word part that can be added to the end of a root or base word to change the word's meaning. Adding a suffix to a word can also change that word from one part of speech to another. For example,

  the word *joy* (which is a noun) becomes an adjective when the suffix *-ful* (meaning "full of") is added. *Joyful* means "full of joy"

Determining a Word's Meaning

Using Syntax

Languages have rules and patterns for the way words are arranged in sentences. The way a sentence is organized is called the **syntax** of the sentence. If English is your first language, you have known this pattern since you started talking in sentences. If you're learning English now, you may find the syntax is different from the patterns you know in your first language.

In a simple sentence in English, someone or something (the **subject**) does something (the **predicate** or **verb**) to or with another person or thing (the **object**).

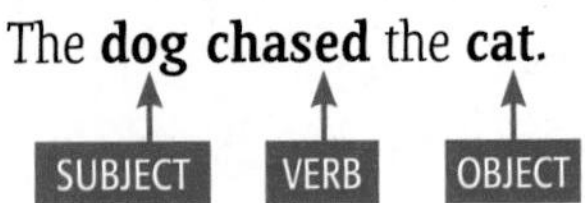

Sometimes adjectives, adverbs, and phrases are added to spice up the sentence.

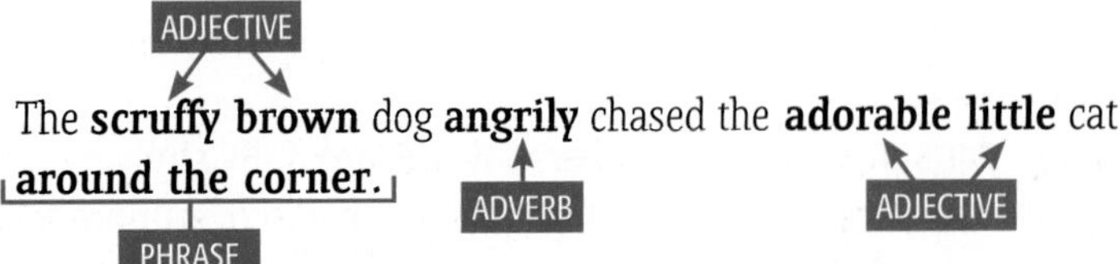

▶ Check It Out

Knowing about syntax can help you figure out the meaning of an unfamiliar word. Just look at how syntax can help you figure out the following nonsense sentence.

The blizzy kwarkles sminched the flerky broogs.

Your experience with English syntax tells you that the action word, or verb, in this sentence is *sminched.*

Who did the *sminching?* The *kwarkles*.

What kind of *kwarkles* were they? *Blizzy.*

Whom did they *sminch?* The *broogs*.

What kind of *broogs* were they? *Flerky.*

Even though you don't know the meaning of the words in the nonsense sentence, you can make some sense of the entire sentence by studying its syntax.

Using Context Clues

You can often figure out the meaning of an unfamiliar word by looking at its context (the words and sentences that surround it).

▶ Do It!

To learn new words as you read, follow these steps for using context clues.

1. Look before and after the unfamiliar word for
   - a definition or a synonym (another word that means the same as the unfamiliar word)

     Some outdoor plants need to be **insulated,** or shielded, against cold weather.
   - a general topic associated with the word

     The painter brushed **primer** on the walls before the first coat of paint.
   - a clue to what the word is similar to or different from

     Like a spinning top, the dancer **pirouetted** gracefully.
   - an action or a description that has something to do with the word

     The cook used a **spatula** to flip the pancakes.
2. Connect what you already know with what the author has written.
3. Predict a possible meaning.
4. Use the meaning in the sentence.
5. Try again if your guess does not make sense.

Using Reference Materials

Dictionaries and other reference sources can help you learn new words. Check out these reference sources:

- A **dictionary** gives the pronunciation and the meaning or meanings of a word. Some dictionaries also give other forms of words, their parts of speech, and synonyms. You might also find the historical background of a word, such as its Greek, Latin, or Anglo-Saxon origins.

- A **glossary** is a word list that appears at the end of a book or other written work. It includes only words that are in that work. Like dictionaries, glossaries have the pronunciation and definitions of words. However, the definitions in a glossary give just enough information to help you understand the words as they are used in that work.
- A **thesaurus** lists groups of words that have the same, or almost the same, meaning. Words with similar meanings are called **synonyms.** Seeing the synonyms of words can help you build your vocabulary.

Understanding Denotation and Connotation

Words can have two types of meaning.

Denotation is the literal meaning, the meaning you find in dictionaries.

Connotation is a meaning or feeling that people connect with the word.

For example, you may say that flowers have a *fragrance* but that garbage has a *stench.* Both words mean "smell," but *fragrance* has a pleasant connotation, while *stench* has a very unpleasant one. As you read, it's important to think about the connotation of a word to completely understand what a writer is saying.

Recognizing Word Meanings Across Subjects

Have you ever learned a new word in one class and then noticed it in your reading for other subjects? The word may not mean exactly the same thing in each class. But you can use what you know about the word's meaning to help you understand what it means in a different subject area.

Look at the following example from three subjects:

Social Studies: One major **product** manufactured in the South is cotton cloth. (something manufactured by a company)

Math: After you multiply those two numbers, explain how you arrived at the **product.** (the result of multiplying two numbers)

Science: One **product** of photosynthesis is oxygen. (the result of a chemical reaction)

In all three subject areas, a product is the result of something.

▶ Practice It!

1. Write each word below in your Learner's Notebook. Then underline the familiar word or root inside it. (Notice that the end of the familiar word or root may change in spelling a little when a suffix is added to it.)
   - **a.** configuration
   - **b.** contemporary
   - **c.** reformation
   - **d.** perspective
   - **e.** invaluable
2. Try to pronounce each of the words. Then check your pronunciation against the pronunciation given in the Glossary at the back of this book.
3. The following sentences can all be completed by the same word or form of the word. Use context clues to find the missing word. Write the word in your Learner's Notebook.
   - **a.** I took the ___ to the photo shop to have a large print made.
   - **b.** Protons are positive; electrons are ___.
   - **c.** You always think ___; can't you think positively for a change?

Reading Fluently

Reading fluently is reading easily. When you read fluently, your brain recognizes each word so you can read without skipping or tripping over words. If you're a fluent reader, you can concentrate on the ideas in your reading because you don't have to worry about what each word means or how to say it.

To develop reading fluency . . .

- **Read often!** The more, the better. Reading often will help you develop a good sight vocabulary–the ability to quickly recognize words.
- **Practice reading aloud.** Believe it or not, reading aloud does help you become a better silent reader.
  - Begin by reading aloud a short, interesting passage that is easy for you.
  - Reread the same passage aloud at least three times or until your reading sounds smooth. Make your reading sound like you are speaking to a friend.
  - Then move on to a longer passage or a slightly more difficult one.

▶ Practice It!

Practice reading the paragraph under the next heading. After you think you can read it fluently–without errors or unnecessary pauses–read it aloud to a partner. Ask your partner to comment on your fluency.

Reading for a Reason

Why are you reading that paperback mystery? What do you hope to get from your science textbook? And are you going to read either of these books in the same way that you read a restaurant menu?

The point is, you read for different reasons. The reason you're reading something helps you decide on the reading strategies you use with a text. In other words, how you read will depend on why you're reading.

Knowing Your Reason for Reading

In school and in life, you'll have many reasons for reading, and those reasons will lead you to a wide range of materials. For example,

- **To learn and understand new information,** you might read news magazines, textbooks, news on the Internet, books about your favorite pastime, encyclopedia articles, primary and secondary sources for a school report, instructions on how to use a calling card, or directions for a standardized test.
- **To find specific information,** you might look at the daily newspaper's sports section for the score of last night's game, a notice on where to register for a field trip, weather reports, bank statements, or television listings.
- **To be entertained,** you might read your favorite magazine, e-mails or letters from friends, the Sunday comics, or even novels, short stories, plays, or poems!

Adjusting How Fast You Read

How quickly or how carefully you should read a text depends on your purpose for reading it. Think about your purpose and choose a strategy that works best. Try out these strategies:

- **Scanning** means quickly running your eyes over the material, looking for **key words** or **phrases** that point to the information you're looking for. Scan when you need to find a particular piece or type of information. For example, you might scan a newspaper for movie show times or an encyclopedia article for facts to include in a research report.
- **Skimming** means quickly reading a piece of writing to **find its main idea** or to **get a general overview** of it. For example, you might skim the sports section of the daily newspaper to find out how your favorite teams are doing. Or you might skim a chapter in your science book to prepare for a test.
- **Careful reading** involves **reading slowly and paying attention** with a purpose in mind. Read carefully when you're learning new concepts, following complicated directions, or preparing to explain information to someone else. You definitely should read carefully when you're studying a textbook to prepare for class.

But you might also use this strategy when you're reading a mystery story and don't want to miss any details. Below are some tips you can use to help you read more carefully.

- **Take breaks** when you need them. There's no point in reading when you're sleepy. And if you're reading on the computer, give your eyes a break about every fifteen minutes by focusing on something more distant than your monitor screen.
- **Take notes** as you read. Write in your book if it's OK or use a notebook or sticky notes on the pages. Your notes may be just words or phrases that will jog your memory when you need to review. If you use a notebook, write page numbers from the book in the margin of your notes. That way you can quickly find the original material later if you need it.
- **Make graphic organizers** to help you organize the information from your reading. These can sort out ideas, clear up difficult passages, and help you remember important points. For example, **webs** can show a main idea and supporting details. A **flowchart** can help you keep track of events in a sequence. A **Venn diagram,** made up of overlapping circles, can help you organize how two characters, ideas, or events are alike and different.

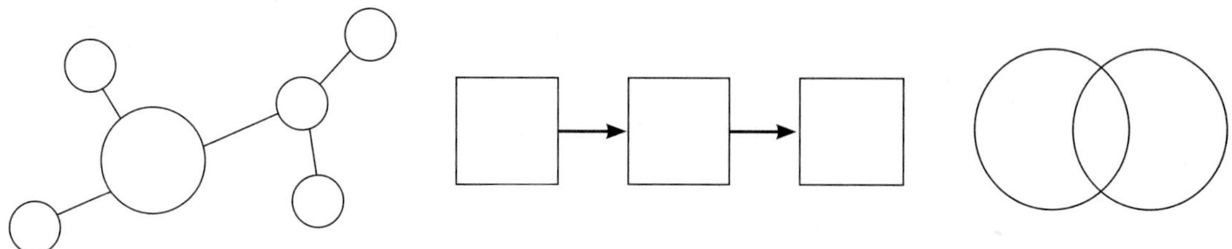

- **Review material** before stopping. Even a short review will help you remember what you've read. Try rereading difficult passages. They will be much easier to understand the second time.

▶ Practice It!

1. In your Learner's Notebook, write whether you would **skim, scan,** or **read carefully** in each of the following cases.
   - **a.** a short story for your English class
   - **b.** the school newspaper for your team's score in last week's game
   - **c.** reviewing a chapter for tomorrow's social studies test
   - **d.** a science book to find if it has information about nuclear waste
   - **e.** to decide which stories and articles to read in a magazine

Becoming Engaged

In reading, *engagement* means relating to what you're reading in a way that makes it meaningful to you. It means finding links between the text and your own life. As you begin to read something, be ready to become engaged with the text. Then as you read, react to the text and relate it to your own experience. Your reading will be much more interesting, and you'll find it easier to understand and remember what you read.

Connect

You will become more involved with your reading and remember events, characters, and ideas better if you relate what you're reading to your own life. **Connecting** is finding the links between what you read and your own experience.

▶ Ask Yourself

- Have I been to places similar to the **setting** described by this writer?
- What **experiences** have I had that compare or contrast with what I am reading?
- What **opinions** do I already have about this topic?
- What **characters** from life or literature remind me of the characters or narrator in the selection?

Respond

Enjoy what you read and make it your own by **responding** to what's going on in the text. Think about and express what you like or don't like, what you find boring or interesting. What surprises you, entertains you, scares you, makes you angry, makes you sad, or makes you laugh out loud? The relationship between you and what you're reading is personal, so react in a personal way.

Understanding What You Read

Reading without understanding is like trying to drive a car on an empty gas tank. You can go through all the motions, but you won't get anywhere! Skilled readers adopt a number of strategies before, during, and after reading to make sure they understand what they read.

Previewing

If you were making a preview for a movie, you would want to let your audience know what the movie is like. When you **preview** a piece of writing, you're treating yourself like that movie audience. You're trying to get an idea about that piece of writing. If you know what to expect before reading, you will have an easier time understanding ideas and relationships. Follow these steps to preview your reading assignments.

▶ Do It!

1. **Look** at the title and any illustrations that are included.
2. **Read** the headings, subheadings, and anything in bold letters.
3. **Skim** over the passage to see how it is organized. Is it divided into many parts? Is it a long poem or short story? Don't forget to look at the graphics–pictures, maps, or diagrams.
4. **Set a purpose** for your reading. Are you reading to learn something new? Are you reading to find specific information?

Activating Prior Knowledge

Believe it or not, you already know quite a bit about what you're going to read. You don't know the plot or the information, of course, but keep in mind that you bring knowledge and unique personal experience to a selection. Drawing on your own background is called **activating prior knowledge,** and it can help you create meaning in what you read. Ask yourself, What do I already know about this topic? What do I know about related topics?

Predicting

You don't need a crystal ball to make **predictions** when you read. The predictions don't even have to be accurate! What's important is that you get involved in your reading from the moment you turn to page one. Take educated guesses before and during your reading about what might happen in the story. Follow these steps:

1. Use your prior knowledge and the information you gathered in your preview to predict what you will learn or what might happen in a selection. Will the hero ever get home? Did the butler do it?
2. As you read on, you may find that your prediction was way off base. Don't worry. Just adjust your predictions and go on reading.
3. Afterwards check to see how accurate your predictions were. You don't have to keep score. By getting yourself involved in a narrative, you always end up a winner.

Visualizing

Creating pictures in your mind as you read—called **visualizing**—is a powerful aid to understanding. As you read, set up a movie theater in your imagination.

- Imagine what a character looks like.
- Picture the setting—city streets, the desert, or the surface of the moon.
- Picture the steps in a process or the evidence that an author wants you to consider. If you can visualize what you read, selections will be more vivid, and you'll recall them better later on.

Identifying Sequence

When you discover the logical order of events or ideas, you are **identifying sequence.** Look for clues and signal words that will help you find the way information is organized.

Are you reading a story that takes place in chronological, or time, order? Do you need to understand step-by-step directions? Are you reading a persuasive speech with the reasons listed in order of importance? You'll understand and remember the information better when you know the organization the author has used.

Determining the Main Idea

When you look for the **main idea** of a selection, you look for the most important idea. The examples, reasons, or details that further explain the main idea are called supporting details.

Some main ideas are clearly stated within a passage–often in the first sentence of a paragraph, or sometimes in the last sentence of a passage.

Other times, an author doesn't directly state the main idea but provides details that help readers figure out what the main idea is.

▶ Ask Yourself

- What is each sentence about?
- Is there one sentence that tells about the whole passage or that is more important than the others?
- What main idea do the supporting details point out?

Questioning

Keep up a conversation with yourself as you read by **asking questions** about the text. Feel free to question anything!

- Ask about the importance of the information you're reading.
- Ask how one event relates to another or why a character acts a certain way.
- Ask yourself if you understand what you just read.
- As you answer your own questions, you're making sure that you understand what's going on.

Clarifying

Clear up, or **clarify,** confusing or difficult passages as you read. When you realize you don't understand something, try these techniques to help you clarify the ideas.

- Reread the confusing parts slowly and carefully.
- Diagram relationships between ideas.
- Look up unfamiliar words.
- Simply "talk out" the part to yourself.

Then read the passage once more. The second time through is often much easier and more informative.

Reviewing

You probably **review** in school every day in one class or another. You review what you learned the day before so the ideas stick in your mind. Reviewing when you read does the same thing.

Take time now and then to pause and review what you've read. Think about the main ideas and reorganize them for yourself so you can recall them later. Filling in study aids such as graphic organizers, notes, or outlines can help you review.

Monitoring Your Comprehension

Who's checking up on you when you read? You are! There's no teacher standing by to ask questions or to make sure that you're paying attention. As a reader, you are both the teacher and the student. It's up to you to make sure you accomplish a reader's most important task: understanding the material. As you read, check your understanding by using the following strategies.

- **Summarize** what you read by pausing from time to time and telling yourself the main ideas of what you've just read. When you **summarize,** include only the main ideas of a selection and only the useful supporting details. Answer the questions *Who? What? Where? When? Why?* and *How?* Summarizing tests your comprehension by encouraging you to clarify key points in your own words.
- **Paraphrase** Sometimes you read something that you "sort of" understand, but not quite. Use **paraphrasing** as a test to see whether you really got the point. Paraphrasing is retelling something in your own words. So shut the book and try putting what you've just read into your own words. If you can't explain it clearly, you should probably have another look at the text.

▶ Practice It!

Here are some strategies good readers use to understand a text. In your Learner's Notebook, tell which strategy is shown by each statement below.

connect	respond	predict	monitor comprehension
visualize	question	clarify	preview

1. I'm sure the doctor's going to be the main character in this story.
2. Why would this smart character make a dumb remark like that?
3. This woman reminds me of my mother when she's really mad.
4. This is a difficult passage. I'd better read it again and also look up the word malefactor in the dictionary.
5. Let's see if I've got this plot straight. So far, Greg's crazy about Donna, but she's hooked on Jesse, who seems interested in Sheila, who is Greg's date for the dance. And Dana's out to mess up everybody.

Thinking Critically About Your Reading

You've engaged with the text and used helpful reading strategies to understand what you've read. But is that all there is to it? Not always. Sometimes it's important to think more deeply about what you've read so that you can get the most out of what the author says. These critical thinking skills will help you go beyond what the words say and get at the important messages of your reading.

Interpreting

When you listen to your best friend talk, you don't just hear the words he or she says. You also watch your friend, listen to the tone of voice, and use what you already know about that person to put meaning to the words. In doing so, you are making meaning from what your friend says by using what you understand. You are **interpreting** what your friend says.

Readers do the same thing when they interpret as they read. Interpreting is more than just understanding the facts or story line you read. It's asking yourself, What's the writer really saying here? and then using what you know about the world to help answer that question. When you interpret as you read, you come to a much better understanding of the work.

Inferring

You may not realize it, but you **infer,** or make inferences, every day. Here's an example:

> You run to the bus stop a little later than usual. There's no one there. "I've missed the bus," you say to yourself. You may be wrong, but that's the way our minds work. We look at the evidence (you're late; no one's there) and come to a conclusion (you've missed the bus).

When you read, you go through exactly the same process because writers don't always directly state what they want you to understand. By providing clues and interesting details, they suggest certain information. Whenever you combine those clues with your own background and knowledge, you are making an inference.

Drawing Conclusions

Skillful readers are always **drawing conclusions,** or figuring out much more than an author says directly. The process is a little like a detective solving a mystery. You combine information and evidence that the author provides to come up with a statement about the topic, about a character, or about anything else in the work. Drawing conclusions helps you find connections between ideas and events and helps you have a better understanding of what you're reading.

Analyzing

Analyzing, or looking at separate parts of something to understand the entire piece, is a way to think critically about written work.

- In analyzing **fiction,** for example, you might look at the characters' values, events in the plot, and the author's style to figure out the story's theme.
- In analyzing persuasive **nonfiction,** you might look at the writer's reasons to see if they actually support the main point of the argument.
- In analyzing **informational text,** you might look at how the ideas are organized to see what's most important.

Distinguishing Fact from Opinion

Distinguishing between fact and opinion is one of the most important reading skills you can learn.

A **fact** is a statement that can be proved with supporting information.

An **opinion,** on the other hand, is what a writer believes on the basis of his or her personal viewpoint. An opinion is something that cannot be proved.

As you examine information, always ask yourself, Is this a fact or an opinion?

Don't think that opinions are always bad. Very often they are just what you want. You read editorials and essays for their authors' opinions. Reviews of movies and CDs can help you decide whether to spend your time and money on something. It's when opinions are based on faulty reasoning or prejudice or when they are stated as facts that they become troublesome.

For example, look at the following examples of fact and opinion.

Fact: California produces fruits and other agricultural products.

Opinion: California is a wonderful place for a vacation.

You could prove that fruits and other agricultural products are grown in California. It's a fact. However, not everyone might agree that California is a great vacation site. That's someone's opinion.

Evaluating

When you form an opinion or make a judgment about something you're reading, you are **evaluating.**

If you're reading **informational texts** or something on the Internet, it's important to evaluate how qualified the author is to write about the topic and how reliable the information that's presented is. Ask yourself whether

- the author seems biased.
- the information is one-sided.
- the argument presented is logical.

If you're reading **fiction,** evaluate the author's style or ask yourself questions such as

- Is this character interesting or dull?
- Are the events in the plot believable or realistic?
- Does the author's message make sense?

Synthesizing

When you **synthesize,** you combine ideas (maybe even from different sources) to come up with something new. It may be a new understanding of an important idea or a new way of combining and presenting information.

Many readers enjoy taking ideas from their reading and combining them with what they already know to come to new understandings. For example, you might

1. Read a manual on coaching soccer

2. Combine what you learn from that reading with your own experiences playing soccer

3. Add what you know about coaches you've had

=

4. Come up with a winning plan for coaching your sister's soccer team this spring.

Understanding Text Structure

Writers organize each piece of their writing in a specific way for a specific purpose. That pattern of organization is called **text structure.** When you know the text structure of a selection, you'll find it easier to locate and recall an author's ideas. Here are four ways that writers organize text, along with some signal words and phrases containing clues to help you identify their methods.

Comparison and Contrast

Comparison-and-contrast structure shows the similarities and differences between people, things, and ideas. When writers use comparison-and-contrast structure, often they want to show you how things that seem alike are different or how things that seem different are alike.

- **Signal words and phrases:** similarly, more, less, on the one hand, on the other hand, in contrast to, but, however

  Example: That day had been the best and worst of her life. **On the one hand,** the tornado had destroyed her home. **On the other hand,** she and her family were safe. Her face was full of cuts and bruises, **but** she smiled at the little girl on her lap.

Cause and Effect

Just about everything that happens in life is the cause or the effect of some other event or action. Sometimes what happens is pretty minor: You don't look when you're pouring milk (cause); you spill milk on the table (effect). Sometimes it's a little more serious: You don't look at your math book before the big test (cause); you mess up on the test (effect).

Writers use **cause-and-effect** structure to explore the reasons for something happening and to examine the results of previous events. A scientist might explain why the rain falls. A sports writer might explain why a team is doing badly. A historian might tell us why an empire rose and fell. Cause-and-effect structure is all about explaining things.

- **Signal words and phrases:** so, because, as a result, therefore, for the following reasons

  Example: The blizzard raged for twelve hours. **Because** of the heavy snow, the streets were clogged within an hour of being plowed. **As a result,** the city was at a standstill. Of course, we had no school that day, **so** we went sledding!

Problem and Solution

How did scientists overcome the difficulty of getting a person to the moon? How can our team win the pennant this year? How will I brush my teeth when I've forgotten my toothpaste? These questions may be very different in importance, but they have one thing in common: each identifies a problem and asks how to solve it. **Problems and solutions** are part of what makes life interesting.

By organizing their texts around that important question-word *how,* writers state the problem and suggest a solution. Sometimes they suggest many solutions. Of course, it's for you to decide if they're right.

- **Signal words and phrases:** how, help, problem, obstruction, overcome, difficulty, need, attempt, have to, must

  Example: A major **difficulty** in learning to drive a car with a standard shift is starting on hills. Students **need** to practice starting slowly and smoothly on a level surface before they graduate to slopes. Observing an experienced driver perform the maneuver will also **help.**

Sequence

Consider these requests: Tell us what happened at the picnic. Describe your favorite CD cover. Identify the causes of the Civil War. Three very different instructions, aren't they? Well, yes and no. They are certainly about different subjects. But they all involve **sequence,** the order in which thoughts are arranged. Take a look at three common forms of sequencing.

- **Chronological order** refers to the order in which events take place. First you wake up; next you have breakfast; then you go to school. Those events don't make much sense in any other order. Whether you are explaining how to wash the car, giving directions to a friend's house, or telling your favorite joke, the world would be a confusing place if people didn't organize their ideas in chronological order. Look for signal words such as *first, next, then, later,* and *finally.*
- **Spatial order** describes the order of things in space. For example, take a look at this description of an ice cream sundae:

  At the bottom of the dish are two scoops of vanilla. The scoops are covered with fudge and topped with whipped cream and a cherry.

  Your eyes follow the sundae from the bottom to the top. Spatial order is important in descriptive writing because it helps you as a reader to see an image the way the author does. Signal words include *above, below, behind, left, right,* and *next to.*
- **Order of importance** is going from most important to least important or the other way around. For example, a typical news article has a most-to-least-important structure. Readers who don't have the time to read the entire article can at least learn the main idea by reading the first few paragraphs. Signal words include *principal, central, important,* and *fundamental.*

Reading for Research

An important part of doing research is knowing how to get information from a wide variety of sources. The following skills will help you when you have a research assignment for a class or when you want information about a topic outside of school.

Reading Text Features

Researching a topic is not only about asking questions. It's about finding answers. Textbooks, references, magazines, and other sources provide a variety of **text features** to help you find those answers quickly and efficiently.

- **Tables of contents** Look at the table of contents first to see whether a resource offers information you need.
- **Indexes** An index is an alphabetical listing of significant topics covered in a book. It is found in the back of a book.
- **Headings and subheadings** Headings often tell you what information is going to follow in the text you're reading. Subheadings allow you to narrow your search for information even further.
- **Graphic features** Photos, diagrams, maps, charts, graphs, and other graphic features can communicate large amounts of information at a glance. They usually include captions that explain what they show.

Interpreting Graphic Aids

When you're researching a topic, be sure to read and interpret the graphic aids you find. **Graphic aids** explain information visually. When reading graphic aids, read the title first to see if you're likely to find information you want.

- **Reading a map** Maps are flat representations of land. A **compass rose** shows you directions–north, south, east, and west. A **legend,** or **key,** explains the map's symbols. A **scale** shows you how distances shown on the map relate to the actual distances.
- **Reading a graph** A graph shows you how two or more things relate. Graphs can use circles, dots, bars, or lines. For example, on the weather part of a TV newscast you might see a weather graph that predicts how the temperatures for the next five days will rise or fall.
- **Reading a table** A table groups numbers or facts and puts them into categories so you can compare what is in each category. The facts are organized in rows and columns. Find the row that has the category you're looking for. Then read across to the column that has the information you need.

Organizing Information

When researching a topic, you can't stop after you've read your sources of information. You also have to make sense of that information, organize it, and put it all together in ways that will help you explain it to someone else. Here are some ways of doing just that.

- **Record** information from your research and keep track of your resources on note cards.
- **Summarize** information before you write it on a note card. That way you'll have the main ideas in your own words.
- **Outline** ideas so you can see how subtopics and supporting information will fit under a main idea.
- **Make a table or graph** to compare items or categories of information.

UNIT 1

Skills Scope and Sequence

Readability Scores Key
Dale-Chall/**DRP**/Lexile

PACING (DAYS) STANDARD	BLOCK	INSTRUCTIONAL SEGMENT LITERATURE	READING SKILLS	LITERARY ELEMENTS
1	1	**Unit Warm-Up, pp. 1–13** Genre Focus: from *I Know Why the Caged Bird Sings* by Maya Angelou 4.6/**54**/910, SE p. 5	Fluency, TWE p. 1 Setting a Purpose for Reading, SE pp. 5, 11 Connecting, SE pp. 5, 6, 9, 10, TWE pp. 8, 13 Activating Prior Knowledge, SE p. 7 Identifying Author's Purpose, SE p. 13	Tone, SE pp. 6, 8, TWE pp. 9, 10 Point of View, SE p. 6, TWE p. 13 Description, SE p. 11, TWE p. 4 Cultural Reference, SE p. 12, TWE p. 7
3	2	**Reading Workshop 1, pp. 14–37** "Ice" by Graham Salisbury 6.2/**52**/770, SE p. 18 "On Top of the World" by Martha Pickerill 6.4/**60**/1050, SE p. 32	Connecting, SE pp. 14, 15, 17, 18, 19, 20, 23, 24, 26, 27, 31, 33 Fluency, SE pp. 15, 19	Description, SE pp. 17, 20, 21, 22, 25, Titles and Subheads, SE pp. 31, 32, 34, TWE p. 30 Sequence, TWE p. 23
1		**Writing Workshop, Part 1, pp. 38–41** Writing Product: Autobiographical Sketch		Description, TWE p. 38 Sequence, TWE p. 39
3	1	**Reading Workshop 2, pp. 42–61** "The Tell-Tale Heart" by Edgar Allan Poe 5.0/**54**/860, SE p. 46 from *The Book of Rock Stars* by Kathleen Krull 7.6/**64**/1130, SE p. 56	Setting a Purpose for Reading, SE pp. 42, 43, 45, 46, 55, 56, 58 Fluency, TWE pp. 43, 48 Connecting, TWE pp. 47, 57	Point of View, SE pp. 45, 46, 47, 49, 55, 57

Unit 1 Big Question

The question **"Reading: What's in It for You?"** is designed to help students recognize the rewards of reading and the many ways it can benefit their lives.

Unit 1 Genre

Many of the selections in this unit are **biographies,** which inform, entertain, and enlighten students. These selections will also help students answer the big question "Reading: What's in It for You?" Use these selections to help students understand how reading can be beneficial and enjoyable.

CRITICAL THINKING	VOCABULARY	WRITING AND GRAMMAR	LISTENING, SPEAKING, AND VIEWING
Analysis, TWE pp. 6, 7, 10, 11, 12, 13 Comprehension, TWE pp. 7, 12	Dialect, TWE p. 6		Viewing the Image, TWE p. 2 Analyzing the Painting, SE pp. 5, 8, 10
Infer, SE pp. 28, 36 Interpret, SE pp. 28, 36 Apply, SE p. 28 Evaluate, SE p. 36, TWE p. 16 Analysis, TWE pp. 18, 19, 21, 25, 31, 34, 35 Comprehension, TWE pp. 22, 26, 33, 34 Evaluation, TWE p. 24	Academic Vocabulary, SE p. 14 Context Clues, SE pp. 16, 21, 23, 30, 33 Diagrams, SE p. 21 Suffixes, TWE p. 32	Write About Your Reading, SE p. 28 Concrete and Abstract Nouns, SE p. 29 Personal and Possessive Pronouns and Antecedents, SE p. 37	Viewing the Photo, SE pp. 19, 21, 25, 26, 33, 34, 35 Talk About Your Reading, SE p. 36
		Prewriting, SE p. 38 Plan, SE p. 39 Drafting, SE p. 40 Applying Good Writing Traits: Voice, SE p. 40 Verbs, SE p. 41	
Infer, SE pp. 52, 60 Classify, SE p. 52 Evaluate, SE p. 52 Interpret, SE p. 60 Analyze, TWE p. 44 Analysis, TWE pp. 46, 47, 49, 50, 51, 57, 58, 59 Evaluate, TWE p. 54 Application, TWE p. 55 Compare and Contrast, TWE p. 57	Context Clues, SE pp. 44, 48, 50, 54, 56 Affixes, TWE p. 49 Synonyms and Antonyms, TWE p. 54	Write About Your Reading, SE p. 52 Common and Proper Nouns, SE p. 53 Noun Plurals, SE p. 61	Viewing the Art, SE p. 49 Viewing the Photo, TWE p. 58

Skills Scope and Sequence *continued*

Readability Scores Key
Dale-Chall/DRP/Lexile

PACING (DAYS) STANDARD	BLOCK	INSTRUCTIONAL SEGMENT LITERATURE	READING SKILLS	LITERARY ELEMENTS
3	1	**Reading Workshop 3, pp. 62–91** "The March of the Mill Children" by Judith Pinkerton Josephson 6.2/58/940, SE p. 66 "Filling Out the Application" by Cindy Pervola and Debby Hobgood 8.4/58/930, SE p. 78 "Exploring Careers" 9.3/62/1010, SE p. 86	Activating Prior Knowledge, SE pp. 62, 63, 65, 66, 68, 72, 77, 78, 80, 83, 84, 86, 87 Connecting, SE pp. 81, 83, 88, TWE pp. 70, 72 Fluency, TWE pp. 72, 83, 89 Setting a Purpose for Reading, SE p. 85	Tone, SE pp. 65, 67, 70, 71, TWE p. 66 Text Features, SE pp. 77, 79, 86 Titles and Subheads, SE p. 86
1		**Writing Workshop, Part 2, pp. 92–95** Writing Product: Autobiographical Sketch	Fluency, TWE p. 95	Sequence, TWE p. 93 Description, TWE p. 95
2	1	**Reading Workshop 4, pp. 96–115** from *Akiko in the Forbidden Foothills of Gozmaturk* by Mark Crilley SE p. 100 "Being Japanese American" by Yoshiko Uchida 6.4/58/1120, SE p. 108	Identifying Author's Purpose, SE pp. 96, 97, 99, 100, 107, 111 Setting a Purpose for Reading, TWE p. 99 Connecting, TWE pp. 108, 109	Sequence, SE pp. 99, 102, 103 Cultural Reference, SE pp. 107, 108, 110, 113 Tone, TWE pp. 101, 102, 109 Foreshadowing, TWE p. 106
2	2	**Comparing Literature Workshop, pp. 116–131** from *A Gift of Laughter* by Allan Sherman 4.8/48/600, SE p. 119 "A Family Thing" by Jerry Spinelli 6.5/57/950, SE p. 124 "Knoxville, Tennessee" by Nikki Giovanni SE p. 129	Connecting, SE p. 127, TWE pp. 117, 118, 119 Identifying Author's Purpose, TWE p. 120 Setting a Purpose for Reading, TWE p. 129	Tone, SE pp. 116, 117, 119, 120, 121, 122, 124, 126, 128, 129 Flashbacks, TWE p. 120 Description, TWE p. 127
2	1	**Unit Wrap-Up, pp. 132–133**		

CRITICAL THINKING	VOCABULARY	WRITING AND GRAMMAR	LISTENING, SPEAKING, AND VIEWING
Compare and Contrast, SE p. 74 Evaluate, SE pp. 74, 90 Apply, SE p. 90 Infer, SE p. 90 Evaluation, TWE pp. 66, 78, 79, 80, 82 Comprehension, TWE pp. 67, 71, 80, 82, 87 Application, TWE p. 81 Analysis, TWE pp. 84, 88, 89	Academic Vocabulary, SE p. 62 Context Clues, SE pp. 64, 69, 76, 82, TWE pp. 68, 80 Synonyms, TWE p. 63 Prefixes and Suffixes, TWE p. 86	Write About Your Reading, SE p. 74 Reflexive and Intensive Pronouns, SE p. 75 Indefinite Pronouns and Agreement, SE p. 91	Viewing the Photo, SE pp. 67, 69, 72, 83, 84 Viewing the Image, SE p. 87 Talk About Your Reading, SE p. 90
		Writing an Autobiographical Sketch: Revising, Editing, and Presenting SE pp. 92, 93 Voice, TWE pp. 93, 95	Active Listening, SE p. 94 Oral Presentation, TWE p. 94
Infer, SE p. 104, TWE p. 98 Evaluate, SE p. 104 Compare and Contrast, SE pp. 114, TWE p. 112 Analyze, SE p. 114, TWE p. 102 Analysis, TWE pp. 102, 103, 110 Comprehension, TWE pp. 110, 111 Evaluation, TWE p. 111	Context Clues, SE pp. 98, 100, 101, 106, 109, 112 Academic Vocabulary, SE pp. 98, 99 Dialect, TWE p. 101 Verb Tenses, TWE p. 111	Write About Your Reading, SE p. 104 Pronouns as Subjects and Objects, SE p. 105 Pronouns as Objects of Prepositions, SE p. 115	Viewing the Photo, SE pp. 110, 111, TWE p. 108 Viewing the Image, SE p. 112 Talk About Your Reading, SE p. 114
Draw Conclusions, SE p. 131 Interpret, SE p. 131 Analyze, SE p. 131 Comprehension, TWE pp. 120, 125, 127, 128 Analysis, TWE pp. 122, 126	Context Clue, SE pp. 118, 121, 123, 125, 127 Synonyms, TWE p. 119 Verb Tenses, TWE p. 121 Plural Possessives, TWE p. 125	Taking notes and using them to make a diagram that compares the tone in two texts, SE p. 131	Analyzing the Photo, SE pp. 120, 126, 127, Viewing the Photo, TWE p. 124

UNIT 1
Unit Resources

Reading with Purpose offers a comprehensive package of tools to optimize student learning and the teaching experience. Each resource has been designed to assist students in specific areas and to offer instructional support for teachers. While all of these areas are covered in the core textbook, some students may need extra practice or additional help in specific areas. The resource package is designed so that you, the teacher, can choose which items will best assist your students. You may also use these resources as homework assignments and for assessment purposes. The following are resources recommended for use with Unit 1.

Keys for Unit Resources

- Blackline Master
- Workbook
- Supplemental Text
- CD-ROM
- DVD
- Transparency
- Web-based
- Fast File

Essential Instructional Support

FAST FILE UNIT 1 RESOURCES

Reading and Literature
- Academic Vocabulary Review
- Big Question: School to Home
- The Big Question Foldable
- Unit Challenge: Planner and Rubrics
- Comparing Literature Graphic Organizer
- Key Reading Skills
- Active Reading Graphic Organizers
- Literary Analysis
- Unit Vocabulary Review

Writing, Grammar, and Spelling
- Spelling and Handwriting Practice
- Grammar Practice
- Writing Workshop Graphic Organizer

Listening, Speaking, and Viewing
- Viewing and Representing
- Listening and Speaking

English Language Learners
- English Language Coach Review

DIFFERENTIATED INSTRUCTION

- Leveled Vocabulary Development
- Skill Level Up!™ A Language Arts Game
- Listening Library CD
- BookLink 3
- Literature Library Vocabulary Puzzlemaker
- Vocabulary Puzzlemaker

ASSESSMENT

GLENCOE'S ASSESSMENT ADVANTAGE

- Selection and Unit Assessments
- Selection Quick Checks
- Assessment by Learning Objectives
- Rubrics for Assessing Student Writing, Listening, and Speaking
- Glencoe Online Essay Grader
- Interactive Tutor: Self-Assessment
- ExamView Assessment Suite
- Literature Library ExamView Assessment Suite

Additional Instructional Support

WRITING, GRAMMAR, AND SPELLING

- Real Success in Writing: Research and Reports
- Writing Constructed Responses
- Spelling Power eWorkbook
- Grammar & Composition Handbook
- Grammar and Language Workbook
- Revising with Style eWorkbook

READING AND LITERATURE

- Active Learning and Note Taking Guide
- inTime Magazines
- Backpack Reader Volume 1
- Literature Library
- Literature Launchers Pre-Reading Videos DVD
- Literature Classics

TRANSPARENCIES

- Read Aloud, Think Aloud Transparencies
- Literary and Text Analysis Transparencies
- Bellringer Options Transparencies
- Grammar and Writing Workshop Transparencies
- Fine Art Transparencies

TECHNOLOGY

- TeacherWorks Plus™
- StudentWorks Plus™
- BookLink 3
- Skill Level Up!™ A Language Arts Game
- ExamView Assessment Suite
- Interactive Tutor: Self-Assessment
- Listening Library CD
- Spanish Listening Library CD
- Literature Classics
- Literature Launchers Pre-Reading Videos DVD
- Literature Library ExamView Assessment Suite
- Vocabulary Puzzlemaker
- Literature Library Vocabulary Puzzlemaker
- glencoe.com
- Online Student Edition
- Presentation Plus!
- Glencoe Online Essay Grader

ENGLISH LANGUAGE LEARNER

- English Language Coach
- Fluency Practice and Assessment
- inTime Magazines (Spanish)
- Spanish Listening Library CD

PROFESSIONAL DEVELOPMENT

- Professional Development Package

Additional Glencoe Resources

Dinah Zike's Foldables

Foldables are three-dimensional, interactive graphic organizers that help students practice basic writing skills, review key vocabulary terms, and answer Big Questions. Every unit contains a foldable activity. You can find the pattern and directions for the Unit 1 Foldable in the Unit 1 Resources Fast Files booklet. You can use the foldables as they are presented or modify them to suit the needs of your students. More information about foldables for Unit 1 can be found on page R8.

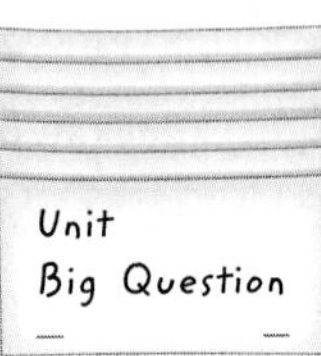

Glencoe Literature Library

This collection of hardcover books includes full-length novels, novellas, plays, and works of nonfiction. Each volume consists of at least one complete extended-length reading accompanied by several related readings from a broad range of genres. A separate Study Guide for each Glencoe Literature Library book provides teaching notes and reproducible activity pages for students.

Glencoe Literature Library titles that complement this unit include:

The Autobiography of Miss Jane Pittman, by Ernest J. Gaines
Barrio Boy, by Ernesto Galarza
Letters from a Slave Girl, by Mary E. Lyons

For a wealth of online resources that support the instruction in Unit 1 of *Glencoe Literature: Reading with Purpose,* students and teachers can visit our Web site at www.glencoe.com. Students will find additional learning, practice, and assessment opportunities such as these, which are noted in the student text:

- **Big Question Overview**
- **Study Central**
- **Author Search**
- **Writing Models**
- **Interactive Literary Elements Handbook**
- **Web Activities**

Teachers will find planning and instructional tools that include the following:

- **Book Lesson Plans**
- **Teacher Forum**
- **Professional Development**
- **Web Activities Lesson Plans (with answers to student activities)**

Go to www.glencoe.com to see the entire selection of Reading with Purpose online resources.

GLENCOE BOOKLINK

Use the Glencoe BookLink 3 CD-ROM, a database of more than 26,700 titles, to *create customized reading lists* for your students.

- Search for award-winning titles, (e.g., Newbery Award winners, Coretta Scott King Award winners, and Caldecott Medal winners) and for books on several state-recommended reading lists.
- Find Degrees of Reading Power™ (DRP) and Lexile™ readability scores for all selections.
- Organize reading lists by students' reading level, author, genre, theme, or area of interest.
- Get a brief summary of each selection.

You can find recommended leveled readings for this unit with Reading on Your Own (see page 138).

Glencoe's **Presentation Plus!**, a multimedia teaching tool, lets you present dynamic lessons that will engage your students. Using Microsoft PowerPoint,® you can customize the presentations to create your own personalized lessons. Use **CheckPoint** questions with interactive response keypads to get immediate student feedback during lessons, to increase student participation, and to assess student comprehension.

A lively collection of articles drawn from issues of the TIME family of magazines helps students develop the skills they need to interact with informational text in a meaningful way. Each of the news stories, feature articles, reviews, profiles, and essays in the magazine connect to an author, work, or theme in *Glencoe Literature: Reading with Purpose.* Articles for Unit 1 are found in Volume A. See the *inTIME* Teacher's Guide for specific connections to each unit and for reproducible student worksheets designed to develop students' reading and critical thinking skills.

Literature Launchers

Set the scene with Glencoe's Literature Launchers, engaging video segments that introduce each unit's genre focus. Each video brings the genre to life, relating it to your students' worlds.

Insert the Glencoe Literature Launchers Pre-Reading Videos DVD into your DVD player. Select the Unit 1 Launcher from the menu to introduce the genre and Big Question for this unit.

Online Essay Grader

Use Glencoe's Online Essay Grader to score your students' writing and to provide individualized feedback to each student automatically.

You and your students can visit www.glencoe.com to link to the essay grader. *Students* can enter their essays and receive feedback on demand. *You* can manage demographic data, assign tests and generate individual student and aggregated reports. The essay grader can help you

- Save time with automatic scoring and individualized feedback.
- Supplement in-class writing instruction using guided writing practice.
- Get reports for individual students or for special populations.
- Track student improvement over time.

REAL Success: Reading Excellence at All Levels

Glencoe now provides all of your students with the tools they need to become better, more enthusiastic readers. The REAL Success suite of reading and language arts products encourages reading excellence by meeting the needs of students at all levels. Glencoe products that can be used in conjunction with Unit 1 include the following:

- Jamestown Literature: An Adapted Reader
- Jamestown *Reading Fluency*
- Jamestown *Critical Reading Series, In the Line of Duty*
- *Vocabulary Builder*
- *The Glencoe Reader, Course 3*

To order these products, call Glencoe at 1-800-USA-READ.

Teacher Wraparound Edition Key

Level Appropriate Code

AS = Activities for all students

AL = Activities for students working above grade level

OL = Activities for students working at grade level

BL = Activities for students working below grade level

EL = Activities for English language learners

Teacher Wraparound Prompts

R **Reading Skill** These activities help you teach reading comprehension skills.

V **Vocabulary** These activities help students comprehend words and incorporate them into their reading and writing.

C **Critical Thinking** These strategies help students apply and extend what they have learned.

BQ **BIG Question** These activities and questions prompt students to prepare to answer the Big Question.

W **Writing** These activities provide writing opportunities to help students practice writing and comprehend text.

L **Literary Element** These activities and questions help students comprehend selections and learn more about each genre.

E **Text Element** These activities help students comprehend text elements.

LSV **Listening, Speaking, Viewing** These activities help students practice listening, speaking, and viewing skills.

EL **English Language Coach** These skills help English language learners as well as students who need additional reading support.

UNIT 1

Professional Development Center

Douglas Fisher

From An Author:

Preparing Students to Read Biographies

Tap into prior knowledge. Quick writes are frequently used in English classrooms at the introduction of a new reading to tap into prior knowledge and reader-related experiences, as well as to initiate a reading/writing connection. The choice of text is crucial, too. Reading multicultural literature can build confidence in fledgling second-language readers and writers. When students relate to good literature on a personal level, they discover a purpose for reading and response, and begin to find their writer's voice. Before reading *The Circuit: Stories From the Life of a Migrant Child* by Francisco Jimenez (1997), the students in Rita ElWardi's ESL class participated in a number of anticipatory activities focused on thought-provoking questions related to a quick write designed to accomplish these objectives.

Make personal connections. In order to establish a personal connection with the character and the central conflict in the story, students were asked to write about a moment they remembered well; a moment when they had to say good-bye. Because English language learners needed structured support in writing, Ms. ElWardi created a list of guiding questions to help even the most reluctant writers begin to recount such an experience. She reminded her students that these questions are there to provoke thought and should not all be answered. To introduce this activity, she recounted an unforgettable moment when she also had to leave a place and a group of friends. Using the questions as her guide, she modeled how these questions could structure a response. Her questions included:

- Where and when did this take place?
- Who was with you and why?
- Why did you have to leave this place or say good-bye to this person?

Teacher to Teacher

My students can be very one-sided in their observations. So, when introducing the Big Question "Reading: What's in It for You?" I have all the students stand on their chairs, and I ask, "How does the room look to you?" Next, I'll have a few students sit on the floor in a corner and ask, "How does the room look to you now?" We discuss how the classroom—a place where they sit every day and largely take for granted—can offer a different perspective. To reinforce the idea, I read the children's picture book *True Story of the Three Little Pigs,* which is told from the point of view of the Big Bad Wolf. We discuss how the book illustrates the fact that when the perspective changes, the story changes.

Lee A. Felts
J.P. Elder Middle School
Fort Worth, Texas

Teacher Chat Room

Using Biographies

How do I make biographies interesting to middle schoolers?

Author Doug Fisher says students need to feel some type of connection to biographical subjects in order to want to read about the subject. To help students connect to subjects, try these strategies:

- Help students recall facts they know about the subjects (activating prior knowledge)
- Choose biographies of people students already know
- Choose biographies based around subjects students already know (some students may not know who Carlos Santana is but they may know something about guitar music)
- Choose biographies that share details from the person's life as a teenager. Students love reading and hearing stories about how life was when someone was their age.

If the subject of the biography is foreign to students, how can I get them interested in the person?

Author Jeff Wilhelm says that in order to help students connect to foreign subjects, you need to dig into the story and find things that students already know. This is often referred to as building background. For instance, most students are probably not very familiar with the Industrial Revolution setting of "March of the Mill Children." The Build Background section helps to explain what was going on at the time to prepare students to read the biographical story of Mother Jones.

What language and structures do writers of biographies use, and how can readers use these elements to inform their own writing?

Author Cyndie Shanahan Hyde says writers often use time order, point of view, and narration to convey their stories in biographies. In this unit, we point out literary elements and help students learn to identify them and think about how they influence the story. In the Writing Workshops and in the assessment section after each selection, students will have a chance to practice writing using some of the elements they've read.

Key Unit Objectives

- Answer the Big Question
- Analyze the literary elements of autobiography and biography
- Apply strategies for reading autobiography and biography
- Write an autobiographical narrative

BIG Question

Why Is It Important?

Addressing this Big Question helps students see the importance of reading and motivates them to develop their reading skills.

Viewing the Illustration

Ask: What does the illustration and quote suggest about reading? *(Possible responses: A wealth of information can be found through reading; Reading can satisfy curiosity.)* **Ask:** How do the image and quote connect to the Big Question? *(Possible response: Reading is one way to fulfill curiosity.)* OL

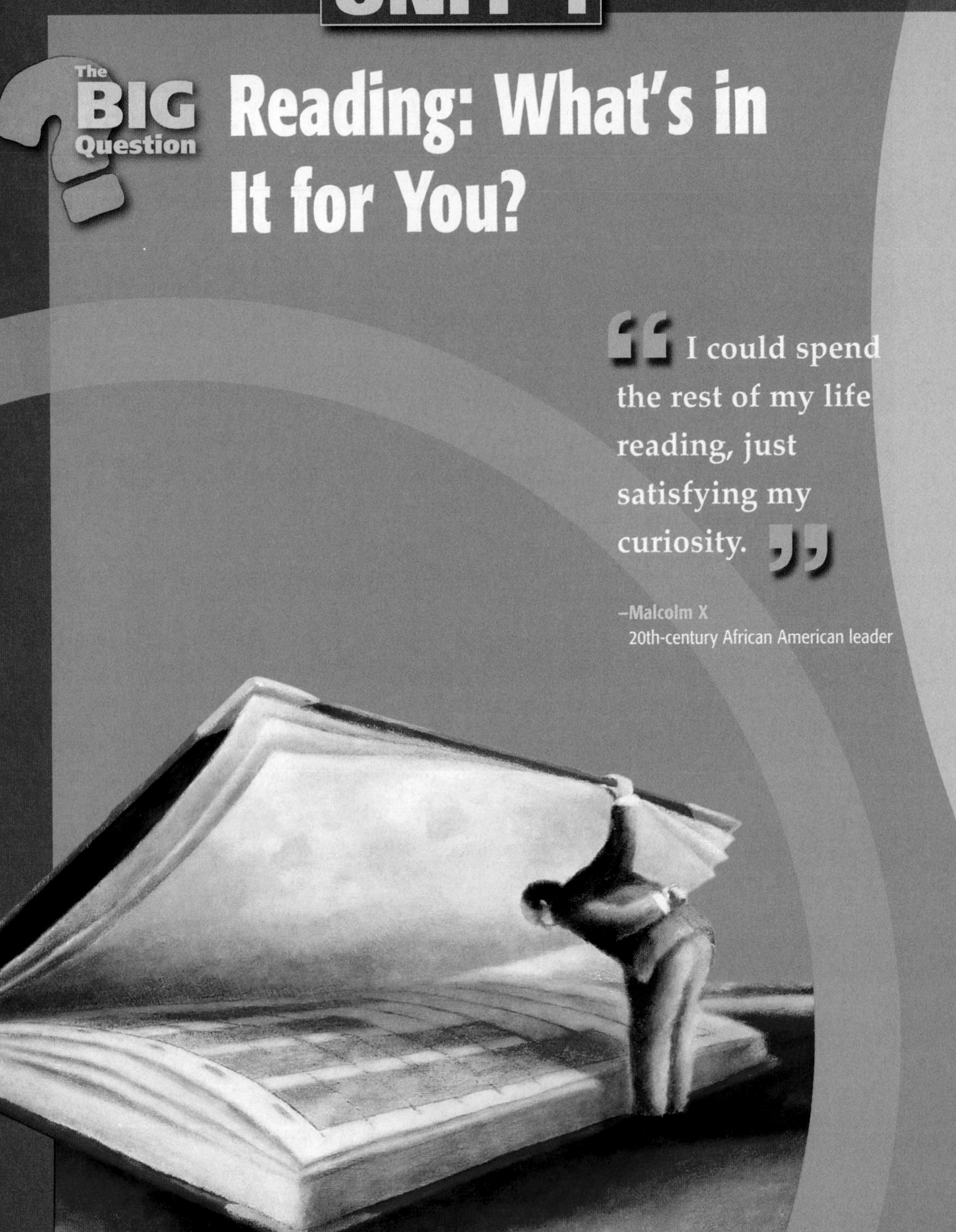

UNIT 1
The BIG Question
Reading: What's in It for You?
"I could spend the rest of my life reading, just satisfying my curiosity."
–Malcolm X
20th-century African American leader

Unit Skills

BIG Question Reading: What's in it for you?
Genre Focus: Autobiography and Biography

Reading Skills

- Connecting, p. 14
- Setting a Purpose for Reading, p. 42
- Activating Prior Knowledge, p. 62
- Identifying Author's Purpose, p. 96

Vocabulary

- Context Clues, p. 16

Literary Elements

- Description, p. 17
- Point of View, p. 45
- Tone, p. 65
- Cultural Reference, p. 107

Writing Skills/Grammar

- Autobiographical Sketch, pp. 38, 92
- Voice, p. 40
- Verbs, p. 41

LOOKING AHEAD

The skill lessons and readings in this unit will help you develop your own answer to the Big Question.

1

Reading Fluency

Peer Reading In order to develop fluency, students should hear good models, practice with properly leveled materials, and evaluate their own progress. One way to help students develop fluency is to pair them and have them read orally to one another from an appropriate text. The listener should keep a record of miscues and errors for the other person. After individual practice, they can repeat the activity until fluency improves. **EL** **BL**

About the Reading

Each selection in this unit helps students think about the role that reading plays in their lives. This unit asks them to probe the concept by considering experiences through the eyes of other people. Students will read autobiographies and biographies and examine how this genre affects them by learning from the tribulations, mistakes, and successes of others. The ultimate goal is to apply this knowledge to their lives.

About the Skills

The skills taught in this unit have been selected because they are particularly helpful when reading the featured genre—autobiography and biography. Each selection provides students with opportunities to practice and develop these skills.

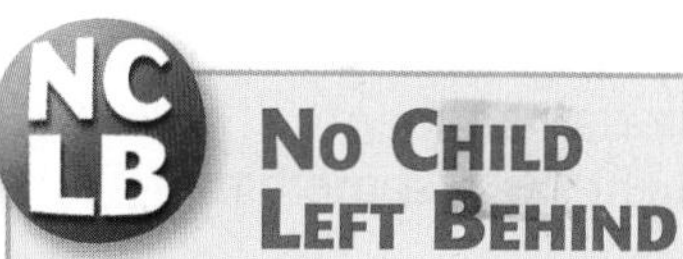

The No Child Left Behind Act was created to help guarantee that all teachers use a research-based approach to teaching reading. The goal of NCLB is that all students become successful readers and also develop a love of books and learning. As you go through this unit, encourage students to read other selections by the authors they liked best so they can further their experience as active readers.

Indiana English/Language Arts Academic Standards
TWE: *Reading Fluency* 8.7

Focus

BELLRINGER Options

- **Literature Launcher: Pre-Reading Videos**
- **Daily Language Practice Transparency 1**

Focus Activity Write on the board: What if you went to another planet and everything was written in a language that you couldn't read? Write about the challenges you would have trying to read a language you didn't understand. *(Responses will vary.)* AS

Teach

R Reading Skill

Connecting To help students connect their experiences to the Big Question, ask them to name things they have read that

- inspired their imagination
- entertained them
- taught them something OL

BQ BIG Question

- Have students discuss what Hector and Oksana get out of reading. OL
- Have them discuss their own reasons for reading, and consider who they have more in common with, Oksana or Hector. AL

UNIT 1 WARM-UP

Connecting to The BIG Question Reading: What's in It for You?

Reading can take you new places and teach you new things. It can make you laugh out loud. It can send a shiver down your spine. It can widen your world and make you glad to be alive. Do you need adventure? Advice? Information? You can find these things—and more—by reading. R

Real Kids and the Big Question

HECTOR belongs to a bike club. He even races a few times a year. Hector never misses a biking event because his local newspaper always has the information he needs. Hector reads. What's in it for him? BQ

OKSANA loves stories. She likes being caught up in lives and problems that are different from her own. She loves mysteries that make her think and suspense stories that keep her turning the pages. She loves any story that seems real to her. Oksana reads. What's in it for her?

Warm-Up Activity

Think about the reasons that you read. Do you read to learn new things or just to have fun? Maybe you read to escape your daily life and experience new adventures. What's in it for you? Write your answers in your Learner's Notebook.

Additional Support

Reading in the Real World

Citizenship Have students leaf through a newspaper and find a section they like (the comics and games pages are excluded). Challenge them to read that section each day and bring in their favorite clipping at the end of the week to write an "editorial," or response to the clipping. OL Alternately, at the end of each week, have students work in groups and photocopy all group members' clippings and pass them out to each member of the group. Have students read each clipping and pick one for group discussion. Before discussion, have each student write three points they'd like to discuss about the clipping. AL

You and the Big Question

There are lots of reasons to read. In this unit you will explore some of those reasons. You will also think about your own reasons for reading to discover what is—or can be—in it for you. BQ

Literature Online

BIG Question

Link to Web resources to further explore the Big Question at www.glencoe.com.

Plan for the Unit Challenge

At the end of the unit, you'll use notes from all your reading to complete the Unit Challenge.

You'll choose one of the following activities:

A. Write a Reading Plan Design a reading plan to help you learn about and do the things in your life that you want to do.

B. Reading Chart Create a reading chart to figure out what you read and why.

- Start thinking about which activity you'd like to do so that you can focus your thoughts as you go through the unit.
- In your Learner's Notebook, write your thoughts about the activity you'd like to do.
- Each time you make notes about the Big Question, think about how your ideas will help you with the Unit Challenge activity you chose.

Keep Track of Your Ideas

As you read, you'll make notes about the Big Question. Later, you'll use these notes to complete the Unit Challenge. See pages R8–R9 for help with making Foldable 1. This diagram shows how it should look.

1. Use this Foldable for all the selections in this unit. On the front cover, write the unit number and the Big Question.
2. Turn the page. Across the top, write the selection title. To the left of the crease, write **My Purpose for Reading.** To the right of the crease, write **the Big Question.**
3. Repeat step 2 until you have all the titles in your Foldable. (See page 1 for the titles.)

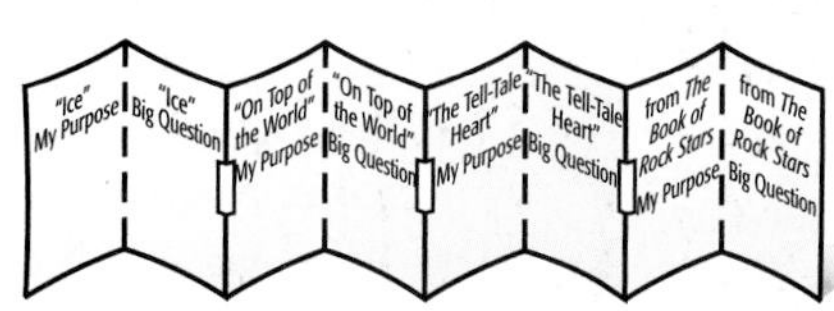

Teach

BQ 

In their Learner's Notebooks, have students answer the Big Question. OL

For each selection they read, students will enter notes about how that selection applies to the Big Question. For details about using Dinah Zike's Foldables, see pages R8–R9.

Assess/Close

Have students discuss why they think it is important to understand what reading has to offer. Begin by touching on these discussion points: reading to study for a test, reading instructions, reading for entertainment, reading to learn, or reading directions.

Resources for page 3

- Use the Unit Challenge Planner BLM in the Unit 1 Resource Booklet, p. 36.
- Use the Foldable BLM in the Unit 1 Resource Booklet, p. 7.

Differentiated Instruction

Flow Charts and Diagrams Draw these graphics on the board:

Plot Diagram: Pie Chart: Bar Graphs:

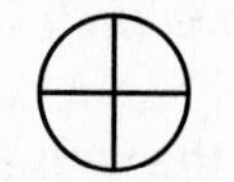
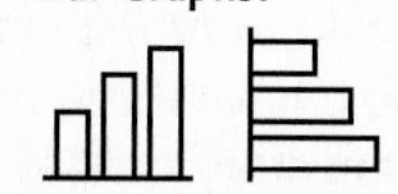

Explain that graphs, charts, and diagrams organize and share information visually.

Ask students to look at each graphic and think about which classes they have seen each graphic in. OL Ask students to discuss what information each graphic might communicate, and ask them to design their own graphic for reading autobiography and biography. AL

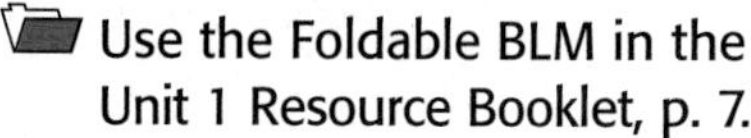

Indiana English/Language Arts Academic Standards

TWE: *Reading in the Real World* 8.5.7, *Differentiated Instruction* 8.2

Focus

BELLRINGER Options

- **Selection Focus Transparency 1**
- **Daily Language Practice Transparency 2**

Focus Activity Say: Think about a time when someone told you a personal story about something that happened to them. What makes such stories interesting? *(Possible response: The storyteller's behavior may be funny, suspenseful, or creepy.)* AS

Teach

R Reading Skill

Why Read Autobiography and Biography? Ask: Who are some real people you may want to read about? *(Possible responses: famous leaders, musicians, athletes, heroes)* AS **Ask:** What could you learn from their experiences? *(Responses will vary.)* OL

UNIT 1 GENRE FOCUS: AUTOBIOGRAPHY AND BIOGRAPHY

Skills Focus

- How to read autobiography and biography

Skills Model

You will see how to use the key reading skills and literary elements as you read

- **from *I Know Why the Caged Bird Sings,*** p. 5

Autobiographies and biographies are types of nonfiction. When a person writes a story about his or her own life, it is called an **autobiography.** When an author writes about another person's life, it is called a **biography.** Reading autobiographies and biographies is a great way to learn about other people.

Why Read Autobiography and Biography?

R Reading about the lives of real people can be fun as well as informative. You can learn about the following things:

- real people and their contributions to the world
- real problems people have faced and ways those people solved them

How to Read Autobiography and Biography

Key Reading Skills

These key reading skills are especially useful tools for reading and understanding autobiographies and biographies. The skills are modeled in the Active Reading Model on pages 5–13; you'll learn more about them later.

- **Connecting** Make connections between what you are reading and your own life, the world around you, or other selections that you have read. (See Reading Workshop 1.)
- **Setting a purpose for reading** Before you read, decide what you hope to get out of a piece of writing. (See Reading Workshop 2.)
- **Activating prior knowledge** Recall what you already know about the people, places, or events in a text. (See Reading Workshop 3.)
- **Identifying author's purpose** Think about why the author wrote the selection. (See Reading Workshop 4.)

Key Literary Elements

Recognizing and thinking about the following literary elements will help you understand more fully what the writer is telling you.

- **Description:** vivid details that enliven writing (See "Ice.")
- **Point of view:** the way the story is "seen" by the narrator and told to the reader (See *The Book of Rock Stars.*)
- **Tone:** the attitude of the writer toward his or her subject (See "March of the Mill Children.")
- **Cultural reference:** mention of a value, belief, custom, or something else important to a particular community (See "Being Japanese American.")

Indiana English/Language Arts Academic Standards
(pp. 4–13)

8.2 Comprehension and Analysis (Focus on Informational Text) Develop [reading] strategies... identifying...purpose.
8.3 Comprehension and Analysis of Literary Text

For a complete description of the standards, see p. IN 11.

Additional Support

Literature Focus Lesson

Description After students have reviewed the definitions for the Literary Elements in this unit, tell them to think about what *description* is and how it can make autobiographies and biographies clearer and easier to understand. Tell students that authors often use descriptions, or imagery, that appeal to the five senses. BL Instruct students to make a chart listing each of the senses (sound, smell, sight, touch, and taste). As they read from *I Know Why the Caged Bird Sings,* have them write each description in the story next to the sense it appeals to on their charts. OL

The notes in the side columns model how to use the skills and elements you read about on page 4.

from I KNOW WHY THE CAGED BIRD SINGS

by Maya Angelou

Autobiography and Biography
ACTIVE READING MODEL

1 Key Reading Skill
Setting a Purpose for Reading *I'd like to know more about Mrs. Flowers, and I want to find out what effect she'll have on the narrator.*

R1

2 Key Reading Skill
Connecting *I've known people like Mrs. Flowers—people I respected so much that it made me happy if they smiled at me.*

R2

Mrs. Bertha Flowers was the aristocrat of Black Stamps. She had the grace of control to appear warm in the coldest weather, and on the Arkansas summer days it seemed she had a private breeze which swirled around, cooling her. She was thin without the taut look of wiry people, and her printed voile[1] dresses and flowered hats were as right for her as denim overalls for a farmer. She was our side's answer to the richest white woman in town. 1

Her skin was a rich black that would have peeled like a plum if snagged, but then no one would have thought of getting close enough to Mrs. Flowers to ruffle her dress, let alone snag her skin. She didn't encourage familiarity. She wore gloves too.

I don't think I ever saw Mrs. Flowers laugh, but she smiled often. A slow widening of her thin black lips to show even, small white teeth, then the slow effortless closing. When she chose to smile on me, I always wanted to thank her. The action was so graceful and inclusively benign.[2] 2

Analyzing the Painting How does this image capture Mrs. Flowers' grace and style?

1. ***Voile*** (voyl) is a light cotton fabric.
2. Here ***benign*** (bih NYN) means "kind."

Teach

R1 Reading Skill

Setting a Purpose for Reading **Ask:** Why would you want to read more about Mrs. Flowers? What interests you about her relationship with the narrator? *(Responses will vary.)* OL

R2 Reading Skill

Connecting **Say:** Take a moment to picture Mrs. Flowers in your mind. What does she look like? *(Possible responses: She is thin but healthy. She dresses in a formal, proper, and elegant way.)* **Ask:** Does she remind you of anyone? Explain. *(Responses will vary.)* **Ask:** How does that person make you feel? *(Responses will vary.)* AS

Readability Scores
Dale-Chall: 4.6
DRP: 54
Lexile: 910

Differentiated Instruction

Research the Author Direct students to use the Internet and library to find out more about Maya Angelou's life and work. Challenge them to find other works by Angelou and read one, or part of one. Some students may enjoy her poetry, while others may find her novels more to their liking. BL Have students present what they learned about Angelou and her life story, as well as about the work she does today. OL

Indiana English/Language Arts Academic Standards
SE: 8.2, 8.3
TWE: *Literature Focus Lesson* 8.3; *Differentiated Instruction* 8.3, 8.7.12

Teach

C Critical Thinking

Analysis Ask: What does the narrator mean when she says she "hated" Momma "with the unbalanced passion of the young"? *(Possible response: Her attitude was "unbalanced," with more weight on emotions than on understanding. This made her quick to judge and slow to understand the source of her feelings.)* **AL**

L Literary Element

Tone Have students read the last three full paragraphs aloud, listening to the narrator's tone. **Ask:** What is the narrator's attitude as she listens to Momma and Mrs. Flowers talk? *(Possible response: The narrator is disgusted, embarrassed, and annoyed by the way Momma talks to Mrs. Flowers.)* **OL** **Ask:** How does this affect the tone of the story? *(Possible response: The tone sets up a feeling of sympathy for either Momma or the narrator.)* **AL**

She was one of the few gentlewomen I have ever known, and has remained throughout my life the measure of what a human being can be. **3**

Momma had a strange relationship with her. Most often when she passed on the road in front of the Store, she spoke to Momma in that soft yet carrying voice, "Good day, Mrs. Henderson." Momma responded with "How you, Sister Flowers?"

Mrs. Flowers didn't belong to our church, nor was she Momma's familiar. Why on earth did she insist on calling her Sister Flowers? Shame made me want to hide my face. Mrs. Flowers deserved better than to be called Sister. Then, Momma left out the verb. Why not ask, "How *are* you, *Mrs.* Flowers?" With the unbalanced passion of the young, I hated her for showing her ignorance to Mrs. Flowers. It didn't occur to me for many years that they were as alike as sisters, separated only by formal education. **4** **C**

Although I was upset, neither of the women was in the least shaken by what I thought an unceremonious greeting. Mrs. Flowers would continue her easy gait up the hill to her little bungalow, and Momma kept on shelling peas or doing whatever had brought her to the front porch.

Occasionally, though, Mrs. Flowers would drift off the road and down to the Store and Momma would say to me, "Sister, you go on and play." As I left I would hear the beginning of an intimate conversation. Momma persistently using the wrong verb, or none at all.

"Brother and Sister Wilcox is sho'ly the meanest—" "Is," Momma? "Is"? Oh, please, not "is," Momma, for two or more. But they talked, and from the side of the building where I waited for the ground to open up and swallow me, I heard the soft-voiced Mrs. Flowers and the textured voice of my grandmother merging and melting. They were interrupted from time to time by giggles that must have come from Mrs. Flowers (Momma never giggled in her life). Then she was gone. **5** **L**

She appealed to me because she was like people I had never met personally. Like women in English novels who walked the moors (whatever they were) with their loyal

ACTIVE READING MODEL

3 Key Literary Element
Tone *The way the writer describes Mrs. Flowers—both the words she chooses and the details she includes—shows admiration and respect.*

4 Key Literary Element
Point of View *I know this selection is from an autobiography, so the narrator is a real person telling about her real life. All autobiographies are written in the first-person point of view. I don't know much more than that about the narrator . . . yet.*

5 Key Reading Skill
Connecting *Oh yes, yes, yes. I know that horrible, wanting-to-disappear feeling. I have felt exactly like that.*

Additional Support

English Language Coach

Dialect The narrator is ashamed because her grandmother speaks an informal Southern dialect with a woman who tends to speak formal English. The dialect includes such features as using a singular verb with a plural subject and omitting a verb. There are also differences in pronunciation, such as "sho'ly" for "surely." **AS** Group English language learners with other students. Have students read the conversation on pages 8–9, and ask them to work together to change the dialect into formal English and discuss their translations with the group. **EL** **OL**

ACTIVE READING MODEL

dogs racing at a respectful distance. Like the women who sat in front of roaring fireplaces, drinking tea incessantly from silver trays full of scones and crumpets.[3] Women who walked over the "heath" and read morocco-bound books and had two last names divided by a hyphen. It would be safe to say that she made me proud to be Negro, just by being herself.

She acted just as refined as whitefolks in the movies and books and she was more beautiful, for none of them could have come near that warm color without looking gray by comparison.

It was fortunate that I never saw her in the company of powhitefolks. For since they tend to think of their whiteness as an evenizer, I'm certain that I would have had to hear her spoken to commonly as Bertha, and my image of her would have been shattered like the unmendable Humpty-Dumpty. 6 L

One summer afternoon, sweet-milk fresh in my memory, she stopped at the Store to buy provisions. Another Negro woman of her health and age would have been expected to carry the paper sacks home in one hand, but Momma said, "Sister Flowers, I'll send Bailey up to your house with these things."

She smiled that slow dragging smile, "Thank you, Mrs. Henderson. I'd prefer Marguerite, though." My name was beautiful when she said it. "I've been meaning to talk to her, anyway." They gave each other age-group looks. C1 C2

Momma said, "Well, that's all right then. Sister, go and change your dress. You going to Sister Flowers's."

The chifforobe was a maze. What on earth did one put on to go to Mrs. Flowers' house? I knew I shouldn't put on a Sunday dress. It might be sacrilegious.[4] Certainly not a house dress, since I was already wearing a fresh one. I chose a school dress, naturally. It was formal without

6 Key Reading Skill
Activating Prior Knowledge
I know that African Americans used to face really obvious discrimination and that this was often most noticeable in the South.

Visual Vocabulary
A ***chifforobe*** is a type of dresser. It has drawers and a place to hang clothes.

3. A ***moor*** is a stretch of open rolling land. ***Incessantly*** means "constantly." A ***scone*** is a sweet biscuit, and a ***crumpet*** is an English muffin.
4. If something is ***sacrilegious,*** it shows disrespect for something sacred.

Differentiated Instruction

Interviewing Adults Some students may not relate to Marguerite's passivity. Discuss the differences between how children behaved around adults in the past and how some behave now. Have students work in small groups to come up with a list of three questions they can ask an adult about how things were different when they were growing up. They should look for differences in the way that adults and young people interacted. Have each student interview one adult and report their findings back to their group. Have each group compile their findings and present to the class. OL

Teach

L Literary Element

Cultural Reference **Say:** *Powhitefolks* is a slang term for "poor white folks." Why would poor white folks "think of their whiteness as an evenizer" with a sophisticated black woman? *(Possible response: Black people with more money or education were perceived as a threat by poor whites. The only thing poor whites had to "evenize" their status in the community was the color of their skin.)* AL

C1 Critical Thinking

Analysis **Ask:** Why do you think we're just now learning the narrator's name? *(Responses will vary.)* **Ask:** Why do you think Mrs. Flowers was the first to speak her name? *(Possible response: Like the narrator, Mrs. Flowers values the power of language; as we read, we might learn more about their common values.)* AL

C2 Critical Thinking

Comprehension **Ask:** Why do Mrs. Flowers and Momma exchange "age-group looks"? *(Possible response: They share some of the same values and experiences.)*
Ask: Do teenagers ever exchange "age-group looks"? Explain. *(Responses will vary.)* OL

Indiana English/Language Arts Academic Standards
SE: 8.2, 8.3
TWE: *English Language Coach* 8.1, *Differentiated Instruction* 8.7

Teach

Viewing the Art

Say: Look at the expression on the girl's face. What do you think she's feeling? *(Responses will vary.)* **AS**

R Reading Skill

Connecting **Say:** Think about how Marguerite feels about Mrs. Flowers. Have you ever had the chance to spend time with someone you admired? Now ask yourself how you would feel if you were asked to help Mrs. Flowers. *(Possible responses: excitement, nervousness, embarrassment, hesitation)* **AS** **Ask:** Based on your connections to Marguerite, what do you think she meant when she said she "trusted" herself back into the Store? *(Possible responses: She had to trust her choice in clothing; she had to get up enough nerve to go back into the Store.)* **OL**

UNIT 1 GENRE FOCUS

ACTIVE READING MODEL

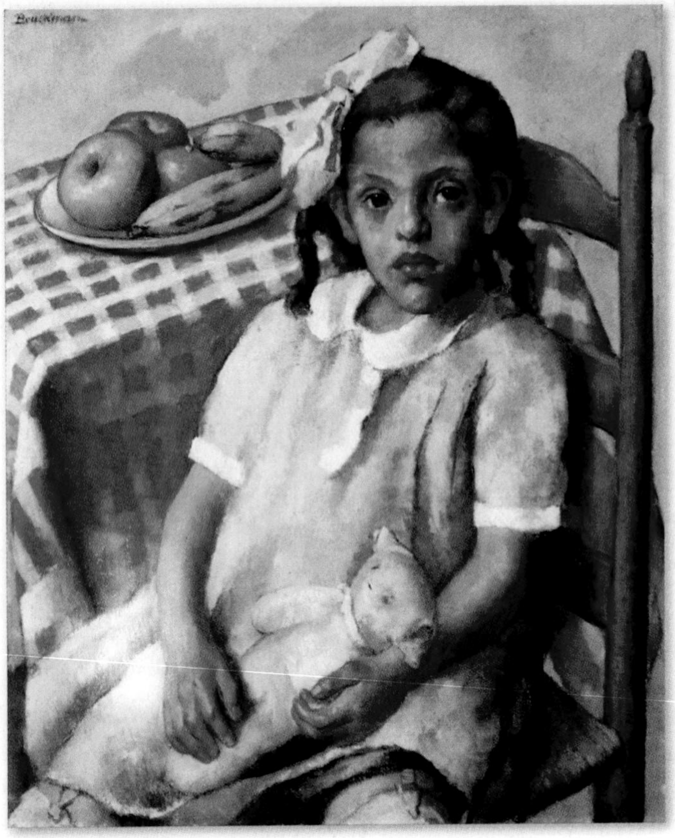

Somewhere in America, ca. 1933–34. Robert Brackman. Oil on canvas, 30 1/8 x 25 1/8 in. Smithsonian American Art Museum, Washington, D.C.

Analyzing the Painting What hopes and dreams might the girl in this painting share with Marguerite?

suggesting that going to Mrs. Flowers' house was equivalent to attending church.

I trusted myself back into the Store. **R**

"Now, don't you look nice." I had chosen the right thing, for once. **7**

"Mrs. Henderson, you make most of the children's clothes, don't you?"

"Yes, ma'am. Sure do. Store-bought clothes ain't hardly worth the thread it take to stitch them."

"I'll say you do a lovely job, though, so neat. That dress looks professional."

Momma was enjoying the seldom-received compliments. Since everyone we knew (except Mrs. Flowers, of course) could sew competently, praise was rarely handed out for the commonly practiced craft.

7 Key Literary Element

Tone *I can tell that the tone is complimentary because the narrator says, "I had chosen the right thing, for once."*

Additional Support

Reading in the Real World

Career Marguerite's grandmother was a talented seamstress. She also ran her own store. Have students talk about people they know who work for themselves. What kinds of jobs do they do? Are they successful? Have students talk about the pros and cons of working for yourself. **OL** Then have them discuss the pros and cons of being a black woman working for yourself in the segregated South (around the 1930s). **AL**

ACTIVE READING MODEL

"I try, with the help of the Lord, Sister Flowers, to finish the inside just like I does the outside. Come here, Sister."

I had buttoned up the collar and tied the belt, apronlike, in back. Momma told me to turn around. With one hand she pulled the strings and the belt fell free at both sides of my waist. Then her large hands were at my neck, opening the button loops. I was terrified. What was happening?

"Take it off, Sister." She had her hands on the hem of the dress.

"I don't need to see the inside, Mrs. Henderson, I can tell . . ." But the dress was over my head and my arms were stuck in the sleeves. Momma said, "That'll do. See here, Sister Flowers, I French-seams around the armholes." Through the cloth film, I saw the shadow approach. "That makes it last longer. Children these days would bust out of sheet-metal clothes. They so rough." **R**

"That is a very good job, Mrs. Henderson. You should be proud. You can put your dress back on, Marguerite."

"No ma'am. Pride is a sin. And 'cording to the Good Book, it goeth before a fall."

"That's right. So the Bible says. It's a good thing to keep in mind."

I wouldn't look at either of them. Momma hadn't thought that taking off my dress in front of Mrs. Flowers would kill me stone dead. If I had refused, she would have thought I was trying to be "womanish" and might have remembered St. Louis. Mrs. Flowers had known that I would be embarrassed and that was even worse. I picked up the groceries and went out to wait in the hot sunshine. It would be fitting if I got a sunstroke and died before they came outside. Just dropped dead on the slanting porch. 8 **L**

There was a little path beside the rocky road, and Mrs. Flowers walked in front swinging her arms and picking her way over the stones.

She said, without turning her head, to me, "I hear you're doing very good school work, Marguerite, but that it's all written. The teachers report that they have trouble getting you to talk in class." We passed the triangular farm on our left and the path widened to allow us to walk together. I hung back in the separate unasked and unanswerable questions.

8 Key Reading Skill

Connecting *I've been embarrassed by my mom like this before—it's the worst feeling in the world. It makes you feel as if you're five years old!*

UNIT 1 GENRE FOCUS

Teach

R Reading Skill

Connecting **Ask:** Has an adult ever embarrassed you in front of someone you admired? *(Responses will vary.)* **AS**

Say: Notice how Mrs. Flowers responds when Momma begins to disrobe Marguerite. Do you think Mrs. Flowers sympathizes with, or understands and relates to, Marguerite? Explain. *(Possible responses: Mrs. Flowers has an interest in Marguerite; She seems to see something special in Marguerite that Marguerite doesn't even see.)* **AL**

L Literary Element

Tone **Say:** Think about what you said earlier about the tone of this selection. Has the tone changed or remained the same? *(Possible response: The tone is still the same; the narrator is still embarrassed by Momma.)* **OL**

Differentiated Instruction

Script Writing Have students work with a partner to read aloud and role-play the conversation between Momma and Mrs. Flowers on pages 8–9. (starting with "Now, don't you . . ." and ending with "That's right. So the Bible . . ."). First, have them write the conversation out like a script and then read through it. Have them read through it a second time but reverse the roles with their partner. **OL** Give students the option to do their skits in front of the class, gesturing and reading with expression. **AL**

Indiana English/Language Arts Academic Standards

SE: 8.2, 8.3

TWE: *Reading in the Real World* 8.7, *Differentiated Instruction* 8.7.2

Teach

C Critical Thinking

Analysis Ask: What similarities and differences do you notice between Mrs. Flowers and Marguerite? *(Possible responses: They both seem to love language, although Mrs. Flowers expresses herself out loud and Marguerite keeps her thoughts to herself. Marguerite is shy and self-conscious; Mrs. Flowers is confident and composed.)* OL

L Literary Element

Tone Say: Remember that *tone* is the attitude of the writer toward her subject. Marguerite's tone is very complimentary and respectful toward Mrs. Flowers. What examples of her tone do you find on this page? *(Possible responses: She memorized part of Mrs. Flowers's statement. She planned to think about what Mrs. Flowers said.)* OL

ACTIVE READING MODEL

Analyzing the Photo How does this image help you create a mental picture of Stamps, Arkansas?

"Come and walk along with me, Marguerite." I couldn't have refused even if I wanted to. She pronounced my name so nicely. Or more correctly, she spoke each word with such clarity that I was certain a foreigner who didn't understand English could have understood her.

"Now no one is going to make you talk—possibly no one can. But bear in mind, language is man's way of communicating with his fellow man and it is language alone which separates him from the lower animals." That was a totally new idea to me, and I would need time to think about it. 9

9 Key Reading Skill

Connecting *I can relate to that. Sometimes my teacher says things that are new to me, and I don't quite get them until later.*

"Your grandmother says you read a lot. Every chance you get. That's good, but not good enough. Words mean more than what is set down on paper. It takes the human voice to infuse them with the shades of deeper meaning."

I memorized the part about the human voice infusing words. It seemed so valid and poetic.

She said she was going to give me some books and that I not only must read them, I must read them aloud. She suggested that I try to make a sentence sound in as many different ways as possible.

"I'll accept no excuse if you return a book to me that has been badly handled." My imagination boggled at the punishment I would deserve if in fact I did abuse a book of Mrs. Flowers'. Death would be too kind and brief.

Additional Support

Reading in the Real World

Career Maya Angelou grew up to be a poet, autobiographer, professor, and well-respected speaker. Have students pick one of those professions (writer, teacher, or speaker) and write a letter to someone in that field. The purpose of the letter should be to examine how that person got into his or her field and what education was needed. (Suggestions for each profession: Writer: newspaper columnist, fiction writer, graphic novelist. Teacher: someone at school. Speaker: politician, professional speaker.) OL

ACTIVE READING MODEL

The odors in the house surprised me. Somehow I had never connected Mrs. Flowers with food or eating or any other common experience of common people. There must have been an outhouse, too, but my mind never recorded it.

The sweet scent of vanilla had met us as she opened the door.

"I made tea cookies this morning. You see, I had planned to invite you for cookies and lemonade so we could have this little chat. The lemonade is in the icebox." 10

It followed that Mrs. Flowers would have ice on an ordinary day, when most families in our town bought ice late on Saturdays only a few times during the summer to be used in the wooden ice-cream freezers. C

She took the bags from me and disappeared through the kitchen door. I looked around the room that I had never in my wildest fantasies imagined I would see. Browned photographs leered or threatened from the walls and the white, freshly done curtains pushed against themselves and against the wind. I wanted to gobble up the room entire and take it to Bailey, who would help me analyze and enjoy it. L

"Have a seat, Marguerite. Over there by the table." She carried a platter covered with a tea towel. Although she warned that she hadn't tried her hand at baking sweets for some time, I was certain that like everything else about her the cookies would be perfect.

They were flat round wafers, slightly browned on the edges and butter-yellow in the center. With the cold lemonade they were sufficient for childhood's lifelong diet. Remembering my manners, I took nice little lady-like bites off the edges. She said she had made them expressly for me and that she had a few in the kitchen that I could take home to my brother. So I jammed one whole cake in my mouth and the rough crumbs scratched the insides of my jaws, and if I hadn't had to swallow, it would have been a dream come true. 11

As I ate she began the first of what we later called "my lessons in living." She said that I must always be intolerant of ignorance but understanding of illiteracy. That some people unable to go to school were more

10 Key Reading Skill

Setting a Purpose for Reading *It looks as if Mrs. Flowers has gone out of her way to talk to Marguerite. I wonder what she wants to tell her. I wonder how Marguerite will respond.*

11 Key Literary Element

Description *This description helps me picture what's happening. I can just see the wafers and feel the scratching of the rough crumbs.*

Teach

C Critical Thinking

Analysis Say: An icebox was a "box" that kept food cold. It was not electric. Instead, people put ice in it to keep the food cold. As the story mentions, most people put new ice in the box only a few times during the summer. Why do you think Mrs. Flowers had ice during the week, or an "ordinary" day? *(Possible response: She could afford to buy it more often than others.)* OL

L Literary Element

Description Have students carefully read the description of Marguerite's first impression of the room. **Ask:** What is one description that appeals to the sense of smell? *("sweet scent of vanilla")* **Ask:** What about the sense of sight? *("Browned photographs" hanging on the walls; fresh curtains)* OL **Ask:** How can the description of the curtains also appeal to the sense of hearing? *(Possible response: A window must have been opened; the curtains "pushed against themselves and against the wind." There must have been the sound of a slight wind, brushing gently through the curtains.)* AL

Differentiated Instruction

Writing & Researching Poetry

Marguerite admires and respects Mrs. Flowers. It's as if Marguerite has the chance to interact with the type of woman she might like to become. Tell students to imagine what it would be like if they could sit down and have a conversation with the adult version of themselves. What "lessons in living" would that adult version tell each student? In the form of a poem, have students write ten short "lessons in living." OL Have students research Maya Angelou's poetry to write their poems in a similar tone. AL

Indiana English/Language Arts Academic Standards

SE: 8.2, 8.3

TWE: *Reading in the Real World* 8.5.7, *Differentiated Instruction* 8.5.7

Teach

C1 Critical Thinking

Comprehension Say: In your own words, explain Marguerite's first "lesson in living." *(Possible response: Don't tolerate ignorance, but try to sympathize with those who lack a formal education because experience can be a good teacher.)* **OL**

C2 Critical Thinking

Analysis Ask: What does the narrator mean when she says she knew from listening to preachers that Mrs. Flowers was coming to the end of her reading even though she had not understood a single word? *(Possible response: She is used to hearing the passionate rise and fall of a preacher's voice and knows by sound the signals that end a sermon.)* **AL**

ACTIVE READING MODEL

educated and even more intelligent than college professors. She encouraged me to listen carefully to what country people called mother wit. That in those homely sayings was couched[5] the collective wisdom of generations. C1

When I finished the cookies she brushed off the table and brought a thick, small book from the bookcase. I had read *A Tale of Two Cities*[6] and found it up to my standards as a romantic novel. She opened the first page and I heard poetry for the first time in my life.

"It was the best of times and the worst of times . . ." 12 Her voice slid in and curved down through and over the words. She was nearly singing. I wanted to look at the pages. Were they the same that I had read? Or were there notes, music, lined on the pages, as in a hymn book? Her sounds began cascading gently. I knew from listening to a thousand preachers that she was nearing the end of her reading, and I hadn't really heard, heard to understand, a single word. C2

12 Key Literary Element
Cultural Reference A Tale of Two Cities *is a very well-known English novel. The quotation "It was the best of times and the worst of times . . ." is one of the most famous lines in English literature. The fact that Mrs. Flowers knows the novel shows that she is an educated woman who is aware of life beyond the small town of Stamps.*

"How do you like that?"

It occurred to me that she expected a response. The sweet vanilla flavor was still on my tongue and her reading was a wonder in my ears. I had to speak.

I said, "Yes, ma'am." It was the least I could do, but it was the most also.

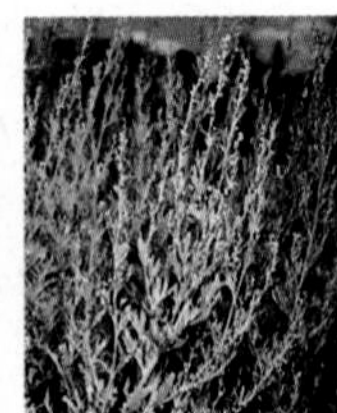

Visual Vocabulary
Wormwood is a sweet-smelling plant, but the word is often used to refer to something unpleasant.

"There's one more thing. Take this book of poems and memorize one for me. Next time you pay me a visit, I want you to recite."

I have tried often to search behind the sophistication of years for the enchantment I so easily found in those gifts. The essence escapes but its aura[7] remains. To be allowed, no, invited, into the private lives of strangers, and to share their joys and fears, was a chance to exchange the Southern bitter wormwood

5. Here, ***homely*** means "ordinary." ***Couch,*** as a verb, means "to say."
6. ***A Tale of Two Cities*** is a novel by Charles Dickens that describes English people who get caught up in the French Revolution.
7. The ***essence*** of a thing is its most basic nature. An ***aura*** (OR uh) is the feeling or mood that surrounds a person, thing, or experience.

Additional Support

Differentiated Instruction

Comparing Lyrics and Poetry The narrator compares Mrs. Flowers's poetic voice to a song, "Her voice slid in and curved down through and over the words. She was nearly singing . . . were there notes, music, lined on the pages, as in a hymn book?" Throughout history, poets have referred to the poetic voice as "singing." Have students bring in lyrics to their favorite (appropriate) song and read the song to the class. Discuss: How is the song like a poem? What lessons can be learned from it? How does the student relate to that song? **AS**

ACTIVE READING MODEL

for a cup of mead with Beowulf or a hot cup of tea and milk with Oliver Twist.[8] When I said aloud, "It is a far, far better thing that I do, than I have ever done . . ." tears of love filled my eyes at my selflessness.

On that first day, I ran down the hill and into the road (few cars ever came along it) and had the good sense to stop running before I reached the Store. **R**

I was liked, and what a difference it made. I was respected not as Mrs. Henderson's grandchild or Bailey's sister but for just being Marguerite Johnson.

Childhood's logic never asks to be proved (all conclusions are absolute). I didn't question why Mrs. Flowers had singled me out for attention, nor did it occur to me that Momma might have asked her to give me a little talking to. All I cared about was that she had made tea cookies for *me* and read to *me* from her favorite book. It was enough to prove that she liked me. 13 **C**

13 Key Reading Skill
Identifying Author's Purpose *Angelou seems to want readers to know about a special person who made a difference in her life by believing in her and helping her believe in herself.*

8. ***Beowulf*** and ***Oliver Twist*** are famous characters from English literature.

Small-Group Discussion Talk with classmates about the relationship between Mrs. Flowers and Marguerite.

- How do you know that reading is important to Mrs. Flowers?
- What does Mrs. Flowers want to show or tell Marguerite about the value of reading good books aloud?

Write to Learn How does listening to Mrs. Flowers read affect Marguerite? What does Marguerite discover about the power of words? Use details from the selection to explain your answer. Think about your own experiences. When was the last time you felt excited or impressed by something you read?

Study Central Visit www.glencoe.com and click on Study Central to review autobiography and biography.

UNIT 1 GENRE FOCUS

Teach

R Reading Skill

Connecting Ask: Why does Marguerite run down the hill? *(Possible response: She runs for sheer joy.)* **Ask:** Why does Marguerite feel so special? *(Possible response: Mrs. Flowers liked her for who she was and not her connection to anyone else.)* **OL**

C Critical Thinking

Analysis Say: The narrator says that Momma might have asked Mrs. Flowers to tutor her. How do you think Marguerite would have responded if she thought that Mrs. Flowers was just doing a favor for Momma? *(Possible response: She might not have felt so special or cared for; She might not have been as receptive to Mrs. Flowers's ideas.)* **OL**

Literature Online

Study Central Have students access the Web site to review autobiography and biography and to complete a related activity.

Literature Focus Lesson

Point of View At the end of the excerpt, Marguerite never questions why Mrs. Flowers may have singled her out. Have students write a "journal entry" from Mrs. Flowers's point of view. In the entry, have Mrs. Flowers explain what her first day with Marguerite was like and why she initiated this new friendship. Did Mrs. Flowers decide to do this on her own? Did Momma ask Mrs. Flowers to give Marguerite a "little talking to"? Did Momma know in advance that Mrs. Flowers planned to begin sharing "lessons in living" with Marguerite? **OL**

Indiana English/Language Arts Academic Standards
SE: 8.2, 8.3
TWE: *Differentiated Instruction* 8.3.1, *Literature Focus Lesson* 8.5.7

Connecting

Teaching Students to Connect

Why Is It Important?

- There are many kinds of connections: self to world, self to text, world to text, text to text, connections within the text.
- Seeing simple and complex implied relationships is essential to understanding an implied main idea or theme.
- Connecting to the reading helps to pique student interest and enhances comprehension.

How to Help Students Get It

- Before, during, and after reading, have students recall events, situations, and emotions they have experienced that can help them connect to the reading.
- Remind students to recall selections they have read, movies they have seen, or other sources that would help them connect the world to the text. Students do not always have to personally experience an event to make a connection. They often "experience" many events through people they know or through situations they have read about or viewed through other media.

Reading to Answer the Big Question

Ice by Graham Salisbury
The narrator of this story tries hard, too hard, to impress his stepfather. John is handsome, athletic, a good fisherman, the strong and silent type; everything his thirteen-year-old stepson wants to be. Eventually the narrator learns that it's not worth fighting to impress someone else. If you are going to fight, it should be to prove something to yourself. Strangely, he doesn't learn this lesson from something his stepfather does or tells him. He learns the lesson from a block of ice.

On Top of the World from TIME by Martha Pickerell
More than fifty years ago, Edmund Hillary led the first team to successfully reach the top of Mount Everest. This article from TIME outlines the naming of the mountain and some of its more recent successful climbs. Sir Hillary is famous for attaining Everest's summit, but says he would rather be remembered for his humanitarian work in Nepal.

Workshop Resources

Pacing (days) Standard	Block	Lesson	Student Materials	Teacher Resources
1	1/2	Key Skill Lesson: Connecting	Key Reading Skills Practice English Language Coach Review, p. 42	Bellringer Options Transparencies – Daily Language Practice 3 Read Aloud, Think Aloud Transparencies – Key Reading Skills 5 Presentation Plus!
1	1	"Ice"	Glencoe Online Unit Vocabulary Review, p. 40 Academic Vocabulary Review, p. 44 English Language Coach Active Reading Graphic Organizer, p. 11 Literary Analysis, p. 10 StudentWorks Plus™ Online Student Edition Literature Classics Selection and Unit Assessments, p. 1	Literary and Text Analysis Transparencies 11 Puzzlemaker Skill Level Up!™ A Language Arts Game BookLink 3 Assessment by Learning Objective (Diagnostic and Formative) Interactive Tutor: Self-Assessment TeacherWorks Plus™
1		"On Top of the World"	Glencoe Online Unit Vocabulary Review Academic Vocabulary Review English Language Coach Active Reading Graphic Organizer StudentWorks Plus™ Online Student Edition Literature Classics Selection and Unit Assessments, p. 2	Literary and Text Analysis Transparencies 55 Puzzlemaker Skill Level Up!™ A Language Arts Game BookLink 3 Assessment by Learning Objective (Diagnostic and Formative) Interactive Tutor: Self-Assessment TeacherWorks Plus™

Keys for Unit Resource

- Blackline Master
- Workbook
- Supplemental Text
- CD-ROM
- DVD
- Transparency
- Web-based
- Fast File

Level Appropriate Code

AS = Activities for all students

AL = Activities for students working above grade level

OL = Activities for students working at grade level

BL = Activities for students working below grade level

EL = Activities for English language learners

Focus

BELLRINGER Options

Daily Language Practice Transparency 3
Focus Activity Say: Look at the cartoon at the bottom of this page. Write a paragraph explaining why you sometimes prefer to be alone and what you do in those moments. *(Responses will vary.)* OL

Teach

R Reading Skill

Connecting Ask: Have you ever read something and thought, "I know exactly how that person feels. I felt that way when . . ."? *(Responses will vary.)* BL **Ask:** How did connecting your experience to the text help you understand the selection better? *(Possible response: I was better able to identify with the person so I understood the entire story better.)* OL

V Vocabulary

Academic Vocabulary
Say: Read the definition of *texts*. What are some texts that you have read? *(Possible responses: Books, magazines, Internet pages)* AS

READING WORKSHOP 1

Skills Focus

You will practice using these skills when you read the following selections:

- "Ice," p. 18
- "On Top of the World," p. 32

Reading

- Connecting

Literature

- Identifying use of description
- Identifying and using the title and subheads

Vocabulary

- Using context clues involves categories and explanation
- Academic Vocabulary: *texts*

Writing/Grammar

- Identifying and using concrete and abstract nouns
- Identifying and using personal and possessive pronouns and antecedents

Skill Lesson

Connecting

Learn It!

What Is It? Connecting is finding the links between things you read about and your own knowledge and experience.

- You can connect to the characters you read about. They may remind you of yourself, people you know, or people or characters from other **texts.** R
- You can connect to the ideas in a text. You may agree or disagree with them.
- You can connect to the experiences described in a text. You may have had, read about, or heard about similar experiences.

Analyzing Cartoons
Clare enjoys reading *Walden* because she can connect what Thoreau writes to her own experiences in the woods.

Indiana English/Language Arts Academic Standards (pp. 14–15)
8.2 Comprehension and Analysis (Focus on Informational Text) Develop [reading] strategies...
For a complete description of the standards, see p. IN 11.

V **Academic Vocabulary**
texts (tekts) *n.* the words and forms of written or printed works

Additional Support

Differentiated Instruction

Analyzing the Cartoon Read aloud the cartoon's quotation from *Walden.* Have students discuss how the quotation answers the question about why someone would actually read a book instead of just "copy a paper off the Web and get an easy 'A.'" OL Alternately, challenge students to write about what one of the following passages from *Walden* means to them: "As if you could kill time without injuring eternity." "If a man does not keep pace with his companions perhaps it is because he hears a different drummer." "To be awake is to be alive." AL

Why Is It Important? You'll become more involved with your reading and remember characters, ideas, and events better if you relate what you're reading to your own life.

Study Central Visit www.glencoe.com and click on Study Central to review connecting.

How Do I Do It? As you read, ask yourself questions like these:

- *Do I know anyone who acts or feels like these characters?*
- *Am I familiar with these ideas? Do I agree or disagree with them?*
- *What experiences from life or books are like the ones in this text?*

Below is a connection a student made to this passage from *I Know Why the Caged Bird Sings.*

> Occasionally . . . Mrs. Flowers would drift off the road and down to the Store and Momma would say to me, "Sister, you go on and play." As I left, I would hear the beginning of an intimate conversation. . . . [T]hey talked, and from the side of the building where I waited for the ground to open up and swallow me, I heard the soft-voiced Mrs. Flowers and the textured voice of my grandmother merging and melting.

I can relate to what the narrator is saying about being asked to go play. When my sister and I were really little, my parents always told us to go outside and play when they wanted to have a grown-up conversation.

Practice It!

These are some of the topics you will read about in the selections:

- a fourteen-year-old boy who is trying to gain his stepfather's approval
- the desire to do something that is extremely difficult and dangerous

In your Learner's Notebook, make a list of experiences, ideas, and people or characters you can connect to these topics.

R

Use It!

As you read, connect to "Ice" and "On Top of the World" by using your list of ideas.

Teach

Study Central Have students access the Web site to review connecting and to complete a related activity.

R Reading Skill

Connecting Have students read the two topics in the *Practice It!* section. Ask several volunteers to name any stories they have read or movies they have seen with similar topics. Write their responses on the board. Direct students to think about how they connected to the movies and stories listed on the board. **Ask:** How might you be able to connect to the two stories in this workshop? *(Responses will vary.)* OL

Resources for page 15

Use Key Reading Skills Transparency 5 in *Read Aloud, Think Aloud* to help students practice connecting.

Reading Fluency

Rereading and Listening To practice reading fluency, students may benefit from hearing and rereading short passages, such as the one from *I Know Why the Caged Bird Sings* on this page. First, ask students to read the passage to themselves. They should remember the passage from the Genre Focus lesson in this unit. Then ask volunteers to take turns reading the passage aloud to the class. Remind students to pause when they see commas and stop after periods. Encourage them to read dialect in a voice that reflects the character. Hearing the passage several times should help students read it more fluently. EL BL

Indiana English/Language Arts Academic Standards
SE: 8.2
TWE: *Differentiated Instruction* 8.3, 8.5.7; *Reading Fluency* 8.7

Teach

More About the Author

Graham Salisbury writes mostly fiction. He says, "To me, exploring fictional themes, situations, and lives is a quietly exhilarating experience. There are times when completely unexpected happenings take place as my fingertips walk the keyboard, things that make me laugh or get all choked up." Salisbury's books often show kids growing and learning through the choices they make.

V Vocabulary

Matching Say: On your own, create a matching exercise for the vocabulary words. In one column, write the list of vocabulary words. In the second column, write the definitions in your own words; make sure the definitions are not in the same row as the words they define. Exchange papers with a partner, and match each word with its definition. OL

Before You Read Ice

Graham Salisbury

Meet the Author

Graham Salisbury grew up in Hawaii. He has worked on boats and taught in an elementary school. He even had a rock 'n' roll band. He has written many short stories and novels for kids. Today Salisbury lives in Oregon with his family. See page R6 of the Author Files in the back of the book for more on Graham Salisbury.

Author Search For more about Graham Salisbury, go to www.glencoe.com.

Indiana English/Language Arts Academic Standards (pp. 16–27)

8.1 Word Recognition, Fluency, and Vocabulary Development Use…context clues…to determine the meaning of words… **8.2 Comprehension and Analysis (Focus on Informational Text)** Develop [reading] strategies… **8.3.6** Identify…literary devices…which define a writer's style…

For a complete description of the standards, see p. IN 11.

Vocabulary Preview

minority (muh NOR uh tee) *n.* a smaller group **(p. 18)** *He was in the minority at school because unlike most kids, his ancestors were not from Hawaii.*

self-esteem (self es TEEM) *n.* confidence and satisfaction in oneself **(p. 20)** *He had low self-esteem because his stepfather constantly put him down.*

oblivious (uh BLIV ee us) *adj.* not aware **(p. 21)** *The boy's mother was so busy that she was oblivious to the boy's problems.*

relentlessly (ruh LENT lis lee) *adv.* without pity or mercy **(p. 21)** *John relentlessly ignored and scorned Graham.*

void (voyd) *n.* empty space **(p. 22)** *John thought Graham was brainless and had a void between his ears.*

On My Own Choose three vocabulary words. Use the words in a paragraph.

English Language Coach

Context Clues: Characteristics When you see a new word while reading, try to define it by using **context clues**—hints in nearby words and sentences. One kind of context clue involves characteristics, or details that tell you what something does, is made of, or looks like. The sentence below contains characteristics of a kelpie. Use them to figure out what a kelpie is. Then read the chart to see if you were right.

- The kelpie barked, wagged its tail, and brought us its favorite rubber ball.

Word	Characteristics	Definition
kelpie	barked, wagged tail, brought rubber ball	a type of dog

Partner Work With a classmate, find the characteristics of a *laceration* in the sentence below. Make a chart like the one shown, and complete it by filling in the characteristics and defining *laceration*. Then look the word up in a dictionary to see if you're right.

- The accident victim was bleeding heavily from a four-inch laceration caused by broken glass.

Additional Support

Author Search To expand students' appreciation of Graham Salisbury, have them access the Web site for additional information and resources.

Literature Focus Lesson

Autobiography As students read this autobiography, have them think about why the writer chose to write about this experience with his stepfather. Ask students to think about how *time* affects the telling of an autobiography. Write the following questions on the board and ask students to answer them as they read the selection.

- How might his story have been different if the author had written it the day it happened?
- Can we trust the author's memory? Do you think he got all the facts right after all this time?
- Do you think that getting the facts right is important to writing autobiography? Explain. OL

Skills Preview

Key Reading Skill: Connecting

"Ice" is about a boy's relationship with his stepfather. As you read, use these tips to connect to the story, and ask yourself the following questions:

- Think about adults in your life whom you admire. *Is your relationship similar to or different from the author's relationship with his stepfather?*
- Think about a time when you wanted someone's approval. *Why was it important to you?*

R

Write to Learn In your Learner's Notebook, explain whose approval you wanted and why.

Key Literary Element: Description

If you like to know what a character looks like or how he or she figures out he or she is in danger, you can thank the writer's **description**. Description tells you what things look, sound, and feel like. A writer describes smells and tastes that make the story or poem come alive. Almost everything in a story besides the characters' thoughts and words involves some description.

When you're reading, your imagination is more important than when you're watching television or a movie. A good description lets you see people and things you're reading about in your mind. But do your part. If the writer says that the character smells a charcoal grill, remember a time when you smelled a grill. If the writer says a balloon is the color of a red tulip, think of how red a tulip is.

L

The selection you are about to read is filled with description. As you read, ask yourself,

- *Which details are especially vivid and original?*
- *How do these details help me imagine what a person, place, or thing is like?*

Interactive Literary Elements Handbook
To review or learn more about the literary elements, go to www.glencoe.com.

Get Ready to Read

Connect to the Reading

Have you ever stubbornly tried to prove a point? For example, the boy in this story tries to carry ice with his bare hands, just to show how tough he can be.

Partner Talk With your partner, discuss times when you or another person tried too hard to prove something. Did the person finally give in? What was the outcome?

Build Background

The author grew up in Hawaii, a chain of islands located in the Central Pacific Ocean. Hawaii became a state in the United States in 1959. People from many different cultures live in Hawaii. More than half the population is Asian.

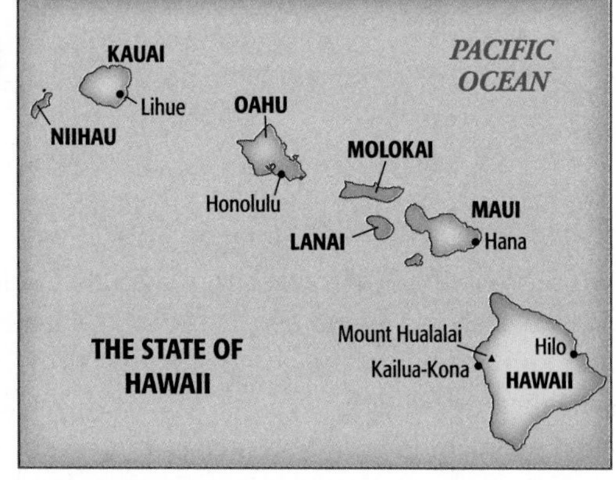

Set Purposes for Reading

BIG Question Read "Ice" to learn what a boy finds out about himself when he spends the summer working with his stepfather.

Set Your Own Purpose What else would you like to learn from the selection to help you answer the Big Question? Write your own purpose on the "Ice" page of Foldable 1.

Keep Moving

Use these skills as you read "Ice."

Teach

R Reading Skill

Connecting Say: Make a list of three adults you admire. Next to each name write two reasons why you admire that adult. BL **Say:** Now use your reasons to write a brief description of one adult on your list. Explain why you admire that person, and detail your relationship with him or her. OL

L Literary Element

Description Say: As you write your description of an adult you admire, add sensory imagery. Write down three details that appeal to the senses; add those details to your description. OL

Interactive Literary Elements Handbook Have students access the Web site to improve their understanding of description.

Differentiated Instruction

Researching Hawaii Have students work in groups of three or four to compile reports about Hawaii. Instruct the groups to make sure that each member researches and reports on a different aspect of Hawaii, like history, foods, language, culture, climate, population diversity, agriculture, or economy. OL Allow students to present their group project to the entire class. Tell them to prepare and use handouts in their presentation. AL

Indiana English/Language Arts Academic Standards
SE: 8.1, 8.2, 8.3.6
TWE: *Literature Focus Lesson* 8.3; *Differentiated Instruction* 8.5.3, 8.7.12

Teach

V Vocabulary

Phonetic Spellings **Say:** Look at the words "shahkbait" and "cock-a-roach." Why do you think the author spells the words like this? *(Possible response: He wants to help the reader hear how the words were spoken.)* OL **Ask:** How does this present dialect without using dialogue, or conversation? *(Possible response: The words are misspelled on purpose. They are written as they would sound in conversation, rather than the way they would look in a dictionary.)* AL

C Critical Thinking

Analysis **Ask:** Why do you think the author tells about his Hawaiian roots? *(Possible response: He points out that his heritage is Hawaiian; he is not an "outsider," but looked like one because he was in the racial minority.)* OL
Ask: How do you feel about the author's attitude toward racism? Are racist remarks different when they come from friends? Explain. *(Responses will vary.)* AL

Readability Scores
Dale-Chall: 6.2
DRP: 52
Lexile: 770

READING WORKSHOP 1

by Graham Salisbury

I got into my share of fights as a kid. I was short. And white. People called me shrimp, shahkbait, mongoose, pipsqueak, runt, hanakuso, half-pint, cock-a-roach, zit, and a lot of other more gross and disgusting things. That was okay when it was coming from my friends. I was a haole[1] boy. A **minority.** Fair game. My roots in the Hawaiian Islands went back to 1820, which meant exactly zero. But I was one of the boys. They liked me and I liked them. Race wasn't an issue. But coolness was, and I was cool enough. **1** I could take whatever they dished out. I knew they were just doing their job. Besides, I called them worse things back. And we all laughed about it.

But sometimes boys who weren't my friends called me things I didn't want to be called.

1. ***Haole*** (HOW lee) is the Hawaiian term for a white person.

Vocabulary

minority (muh NOR uh tee) *n.* a smaller group

Practice the Skills

V

C

1 Key Reading Skill

Connecting Is it important at your school to be "cool" in order to fit in? Explain.

Additional Support

Differentiated Instruction

Interviewing The author says that his friends called him names, he was a "minority," and he was "cool." Have students interview a partner about their experiences as teens with regards to "fitting in." First, have them write interview questions for their partners. Give students time in class to conduct their interviews. Your more advanced students may want to work individually to think of questions. AL Students who need more help can work with partners to come up with interview questions. Direct students who need more guidance to use the five *W's* and *How.* OL Hold a class discussion about student experiences with trying to fit in. AS

Bok! Nobody was calling me a sissy. *Bok! Bok!* **2**

I even fractured my finger once, throwing a punch that missed and hit the school bus window. Hurt like fire for days, and I was sorry I'd gotten into that fight. **L**

Even so, I believed it was good to be a fighter. It was healthy. Got stuff out of my system. I still believe it's good. But I've long since learned that you don't have to fight with your fists to be a fighter. In fact, it's better not to. **C**

My problem was I never asked myself what *kind* of fighter I was. I never even thought about it, and I should have. But for much of my youth, thinking wasn't a primary character trait. I just did it—whatever it was—then paid the price. I should have thought about *why* I got into fights. Was I fighting for myself, or was I just trying to prove something to someone else? There's a difference, you know. A big difference. I learned that the hard way, mostly by fighting stupid fights. **R**

But I learned it best from a block of ice.

I had three fathers, none of whom I knew.

My real father was a fighter pilot in the U.S. Navy. Lt. Commander Henry Forester Graham, VBF 83, USS *Essex*. He went down with his plane on my first birthday. The exact day. April eleventh. He was only twenty-seven years old. I never knew him, except through letters my mother received from his fellow officers after his death, letters which mostly said: "I only hope the boy grows up to be half the man Hank Graham was."

A year or so later my mother married another navy man, Guy Salisbury, who adopted me. He lived with us eight years, fathered my three sisters, then died of cancer at the age of thirty-three. He was a "sweetheart and a fine, fine man, just like your father was," my aunt told me. He was also a busy man, and I hardly ever saw him.

I didn't know him either, but at least I can remember what he looked like.

Two or three years after that my mother married again. A beachboy. A man named John, who was ten years younger than she

Practice the Skills

2 Key Reading Skill

Connecting Think about a time you were in a fight, either with fists or words. Did the argument feel as important after the fight as it did during the fight? Would you do it again?

Analyzing the Photo F6F fighter planes prepare for takeoff on the USS *Essex* in 1945. How does this photo help you visualize the selection's time period?

Teach

L Literary Element

Description Ask: To which of the five senses does the description of punching the school bus window appeal? *(the senses of touch and sound)* **Say:** Restate the description, appealing to the sense of sight. *(Possible response: My finger was all swollen and turned a grayish blue.)* **OL**

C Critical Thinking

Analysis Ask: What other ways are there to fight than with your fists? *(Possible responses: with words, actions, or silence)* **Ask:** Do you think fighting is ever a good thing? Explain. *(Responses will vary.)* **OL**

R Reading Skill

Connecting Say: The author says he never thought about *why* he was fighting. By connecting your own experiences, answer his question, "Was I fighting for myself, or was I just trying to prove something to someone else?" *(Responses will vary.)* **AL**

Reading Fluency

Read Aloud One way to build reading skills is to practice reading aloud with a partner; a reader can "hear" any mistakes he or she makes. Have students pair up and practice reading this page aloud. Partners should alternate reading each paragraph (so that the partner not reading is following along). Tell students to stop and reread anything that doesn't make sense to them. Instruct them to pause for commas and in between sentences. Instruct them to stress italicized words and to raise their voice for sentences with question marks. Encourage students to read the selection smoothly and with natural speech. **EL** **OL**

Indiana English/Language Arts Academic Standards
SE: 8.2, 8.3.6
TWE: *Differentiated Instruction* 8.7, *Reading Fluency* 8.7

Teach

R Reading Skill

Connecting **Ask:** What is it like to admire someone that your friends or family members don't think is so great? *(Responses will vary.)* OL

L Literary Element

Description **Say:** The author says that the boat trip made him sicker than he'd "ever been" in his life. How does this simple statement appeal to most of the five senses? *(Possible response: Most people can relate to being sick and understand that the senses are affected. You look discolored, there is a sour smell and taste in your mouth, and your skin feels clammy to the touch.)* OL

was. He had thick, wavy hair and muscles like Sylvester Stallone. He could surf, he could water-ski on bare feet, he could free-dive to eighty feet and stay down for close to three minutes. He was once stranded on French Frigate Shoals for thirty days with a couple of Filipino fishermen. And except for one, gaping character flaw, he was everything I, at thirteen, wanted to be.

His flaw, though, was a big one, and I didn't understand it until I was much older. But once I figured it out, I could see why I never knew him, either.

It simply wasn't possible.

He wouldn't allow it.

He was a loner and a crusher of **self-esteem**—mine, and my sisters', and eventually my mother's. But for a few years in my life, John was king. He was lean and strong, and he looked like a movie star. In my eyes he could do no wrong. 3 R My sisters never saw it that way, but I sure did. I liked him. I was floating on top of the world when Mom said she was going to marry him.

We lived on Oahu at the time. John worked at the Hawaiian Village Hotel in Waikiki, running the water-ski operation. He was then, and had always been, a man of the sea. His skin was a deep red-brown, colored by a lifetime in the sun. And when he moved, it was in a smooth, slow, don't-bother-me kind of way. Most of the time a Marlboro hung from his half-parted lips, his eyes squinting through the smoke like Clint Eastwood's. He could have been the star of *Sea Hunt*, or *Rawhide*, or even *Cliffhanger*, if he wanted to. He had that same kind of raw, manly presence. 4

We moved from Oahu to the Big Island soon after Mom and John were married. We traveled by boat—a thirty-eight-foot deep-sea charter fishing boat that made me sicker than I'd ever been in my life. L My sisters took a plane. But Mom and I made the two-day trip with John and his new fully rigged haole sampan, gliding over glassy seas in the lee[2] of the islands and

Visual Vocabulary
A ***sampan*** is a boat with a flat bottom. It usually has two oars, or paddles, to make the boat go forward.

2. The ***lee*** is the side of the island that is not being hit by wind.

Vocabulary

self-esteem (self es TEEM) *n.* confidence and satisfaction in oneself

Practice the Skills

3 Key Reading Skill

Connecting Is there anyone you know who "can do no wrong"? Do you feel the same way about this person as the author feels about John?

4 Key Literary Element

Description There are a lot of descriptive details that appeal to the sense of sight in this paragraph. Which details help you picture what John looks like?

Additional Support

Differentiated Instruction

Mapping Using a map can help students get a better idea of how significant a move from Oahu to the Big Island would really be. Have students use an atlas to find a state map of Hawaii. Tell them to measure the distance between Waikiki and Kailua-Kona/Mount Hualalai to calculate the mileage. Point out that a boat or a plane is required to travel from Waikiki and Kailua-Kona. Discuss how this type of move might have affected the author. Ask students how often they think the author got to see his old friends. OL

READING WORKSHOP 1

battering through the channels between them, channels that threw the boat around like a cork in a hurricane. John was in heaven. My mother was **oblivious,** a newlywed caught up in the Big Bopper singing "Chantilly Lace" on the boat's radio. I was sickly green, dehydrated, and barely human.

Two days later we cruised into Kailua-Kona in the calm lee of Mount Hualalai. There, in the shade of groves of coconut trees that lined the shore, was my new home, a serene, turquoise-bayed fishing village where John was going to be a charter-boat skipper. The sun was more brilliant there than in any other place I'd ever been. It made the glassy water in the harbor sparkle. And it warmed the vast, mysterious ocean that **relentlessly** hissed along the shoreline, an ocean that reached out and put its arms around you, called you closer, like the sirens in *The Odyssey.*[3] You could have called it paradise, because it just about was. And there I stood on the pier, the heir apparent to all of John's great wealth of maritime[4] knowledge. **5**

C Day after day I followed him around, watching, mimicking. I walked like John. I scowled like John. I made John remarks to my sisters, terse and scornful and sarcastic. I carried my T-shirt hanging from the back pocket of my shorts and squinted into the sun like I'd been on the ocean all my life.

At home, John did a multitude[5] of secret things in the garage. But mostly he made **lures** out of fiberglass resin. **6** Plugs, he called them. Tubular-shaped things about the size of the cardboard center of a roll of toilet paper. He'd put plastic eyes and pearl inlays into his mold. Then, when they'd dried, he'd fit them with flashy plastic and rubber skirts that

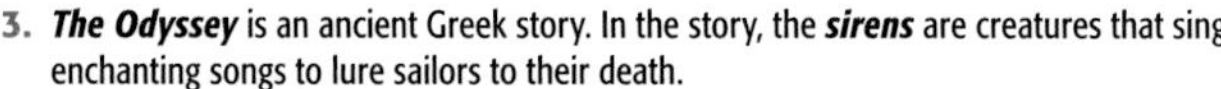

3. ***The Odyssey*** is an ancient Greek story. In the story, the ***sirens*** are creatures that sing enchanting songs to lure sailors to their death.
4. ***Maritime*** means "having to do with the sea."
5. A ***multitude*** means "a great number."

Vocabulary

oblivious (uh BLIV ee us) *adj.* not aware

relentlessly (ruh LENT lis lee) *adv.* without pity or mercy

Analyzing the Photo Craftspeople at the Rapala Normark Group factory in Finland still paint fishing lures by hand. How does this image help you better understand John's hobby?

Practice the Skills

5 Key Literary Element

Description Which details in this paragraph help you picture what the ocean looks like?

6 English Language Coach

Context Clues: Characteristics Find the context clues that help you understand the meaning of **lures.** Look for characteristics of *lures* in the sentences that follow the word. Then define it.

English Language Coach

Geography Terms Have students draw an island with a lee, a channel, a shoreline, and a pier. Direct them to add labels to each of these parts of the picture.
Ask for volunteers who are familiar with boats and/or fishing to share any stories they have about their experiences. **OL**
Have students take it a step further by using the Internet to find an actual map of Hawaii (The Big Island), mark the Kona coast (which includes Kailua-Kona), and create their own "travel brochure." Have them research to find additional facts to place in the margin of their brochure, and use quotes from the story describing the beauty of Hawaii and its waters. **AL**

Teach

Viewing the Photo

Say: John's fishing lures were even bigger than the ones pictured here, "about the size of the cardboard center of a roll of toilet paper." If the bait is that big, imagine the size of the fish he must have been trying to catch. How might this contribute even more to the author's admiration of John? Think about the qualities the author admires in John. *(Possible responses: To catch a fish that big, John must be strong. The author admires all of the qualities that make John seem a strong, handsome, and tough "man of the sea.")* **OL**

C Critical Thinking

Analysis **Ask:** Why might the author be so attracted to John's personality and welcome the thought of being the "heir apparent to all of John's great wealth of maritime knowledge"? *(Possible responses: Because he is John's only stepson, he assumes John will teach him everything he knows about fishing and sea life. He has been without a father figure for a long time and craves that relationship.)* **AL**

Indiana English/Language Arts Academic Standards
SE: 8.1, 8.2, 8.3.6
TWE: *Differentiated Instruction* 8.2; *English Language Coach* 8.2, 8.5.7

Teach

L Literary Element

Description **Ask:** How would you describe a cat watching a dove peck around in the grass? *(Possible response: A cat watches every movement a dove makes and stays still and silent hoping the dove will not notice.)* **OL**

C Critical Thinking

Comprehension **Ask:** Why does the author think his mother asked John to let him work on his boat? *(Possible response: He thinks she might see him as weak and stupid, and she hopes spending time with John would help him.)* **BL** **Ask:** What are some other reasons she may have wanted John to take her son with him? *(Possible response: She hoped that John would grow to love her son if they spent time doing something that John loved–fishing.)* **OL** **Ask:** What does the author's comment suggest about his relationship with his mother? *(Possible response: He doesn't really know how she feels, but he fears she might not think highly of him. She doesn't seem to realize exactly how dismissive John is of Graham.)* **AL**

READING WORKSHOP 1

wiggled in the water. Finally he'd drill a hole down the center and thread through a wire leader and a hook big enough to handle a thousand-pound marlin. He made plugs in every color combination he could think of, trying to find the prize among them, the one that would *work*, the one that would catch the Big Fish.

On a technical level, I was privy[6] to none of this. I could only watch from a distance, could not touch anything, could not even ask a question. The one time I did, his answer was vague and totally useless. Fishermen, it seemed, guarded their secrets even from the ignorant.

Still, I watched him, like a cat watches a dove peck around in the grass. **7**

My mother practically begged him to let me work as his deck hand. John scowled and told her I was too small. He needed someone with muscle, and brains. But Mom persisted. Maybe she was worried that John was right and hoped that a summer on the boat would shape me up.

In the end, her wish was granted. I got the job. I was a deck hand on a deep-sea charter fishing boat, the youngest and smallest in the Kona fleet. All the other skippers and their first-rate deck hands were kind and supportive, always smiled and waved at me from the decks of their boats. One of them even told me I looked like a miniature Tarzan, which I loved to hear, because John looked like Tarzan.

The major part of my job, I soon found out, took place between getting up in the morning and heading out to sea three hours later. Then, for the next eight hours, I did little more than go for a boat ride . . . unless we caught a fish. Then I sat at the wheel and tried to keep the angler's line behind the boat. I was a spectator. Because that's when the muscle came in, and the brains . . . which, of course, I didn't have. John reminded me of the **void** between my ears almost daily, in all sorts of unspoken ways.

But who cared? I was working. On a boat. We caught *big* fish—up to a thousand pounds, sometimes. And we took out famous people, like Red Skelton, Spencer Tracy, and a football

6. When you are ***privy*** to something, you know something that is hidden to others.

Vocabulary

void (voyd) *n.* empty space

Practice the Skills

7 Key Literary Element

Description Here, the author uses a comparison to help you "see" how carefully he watched his stepfather. Picture a cat watching a bird. That's how closely the boy watched John.

Additional Support

Differentiated Instruction

Learning Styles The author learns by watching John. Have students work in groups to talk about the way they learn: (1) **verbally**—through language, (2) with **logic**—math, for instance, (3) through **music**, (4) **visually**, (5) **bodily**—"hands-on" learning, (6) **interpersonally**—or in a group, with others, (7) **intrapersonally**—or by themselves, with a deep understanding of themselves, or (8) through **nature** (plants, minerals, biology). Some questions for group discussion include: How do you learn how to do something? What classes do you excel in? What are your hobbies? **OL** After discussion, have students present to the whole class the way they like to learn, in that style. **AL**

player named Paul Hornung, the biggest human being I'd ever seen in my life. How many other fourteen-year-old boys could say that? 8

I was to work an entire summer with John. That was the deal Mom had made for me. The first week I did nothing but handle the wharf lines, tying and untying the boat at the pier. Then I got to sponge the salt from the seats and windows at the beginning and end of each day. That, I began to realize, was all I was going to get. John was accommodating my mother, not training a deck hand. R

Wanting to prove that I was good enough, and hoping to gain a small shot of approval from John, I dreamed up a set of duties for myself. I figured I could start by doing more to get the boat ready in the mornings.

I studied John's routine until it was as clear as the resin in his prize lures: the night before, check the two-gallon bucket of water in the freezer in the garage; get up at five in the morning and take the bucket out of the freezer and work the ice out, then put the ice on a burlap bag on the back seat of the Jeep; refill the bucket and put it back in the freezer; take a couple of six-packs of Coke and Budweiser from the storage closet and set them next to the ice; unscrew the five-horse Evinrude outboard engine from its sawhorse stand and throw it in the Jeep, too; drive to the harbor in silence; take the ice out of the Jeep and put it on your hand, like a waiter carrying a tray of dishes; grab the outboard with the other hand and walk slowly down to the skiff; set the outboard on the back of the **skiff**, fire it up, and buzz on out into the harbor to get the boat. 9

This was what John did, day after day. It seemed simple enough. I could do all of that. All he'd have to do was have a first cup of coffee from his corroding silver Thermos.

I asked him if I could take over the job of the ice and the outboard.

John studied me a moment, smoke drifting off the end of his cigarette. Then he shrugged, and said, "I don't care." That's all he had to say about it, nothing more, nothing less.

Yes! I thought. I'll do it just like he did it. When I get that down, he'll ask me to do more. He'll see that I can be a good deck hand, that I have muscles and brains. EL

Practice the Skills

8 Key Reading Skill

Connecting Can you connect to how the author feels here? Does he mind having little to do? Why?

9 English Language Coach

Context Clues: Characteristics What is a **skiff**? Look for characteristics of a *skiff* in the paragraph; then define the word.

Literature Focus Lesson

Sequence Explain to students that understanding the sequence of actions in selections can help improve their comprehension. Have students work together to make a sequence chart showing the steps in John's morning routine. BL After they have completed their charts, have students create a storyboard with captions showing each step John takes to prepare for his fishing trip. Some students may want to act out the steps to show what Graham was planning to imitate. OL

READING WORKSHOP 1

Teach

R Reading Skill

Connecting Say: The author points out that John didn't seem to want him onboard and was just "accommodating" his mother. Has anyone ever done something for you just to appease someone else? How do you think that must make Graham feel? *(Responses will vary.)* OL

EL Language Coach

Context Clues English language learners may not understand the expression "get that down." Have them find context clues from the paragraph to figure out its meaning. Instruct students to find other phrases in the story that they may not understand and to write them in their Learner's Notebooks. For each phrase they write, have them add a context clue next to it. If there are no context clues, have students discuss the meaning of new phrases with partners. EL

Indiana English/Language Arts Academic Standards

SE: 8.1, 8.2, 8.3.6

TWE: *Literature Focus Lesson* 8.2

Teach

L Literary Element

Description **Ask:** What onomatopoeic words appeal to sound on this page? *(Responses should include* boom *and* popped.*)* OL Have students say the words aloud so they can hear the sounds the words make. BL

C Critical Thinking

Evaluation Point out this sentence in the fifth paragraph: "John hadn't told me that, and I hadn't noticed." **Ask:** Why do you think John did not tell the author about leaving drop-space? *(Possible responses: John believes people should figure things out on their own. John might want to see the author fail in order to discourage him.)* OL

R Reading Skill

Connecting **Ask:** Have you ever wanted to please someone as much as the author wants to please John? What did it feel like? What lessons did you learn from trying so hard to make someone else happy? *(Responses will vary.)* OL **Ask:** How do you think it must feel to fall short of the expectations you put on yourself under these circumstances? *(Responses will vary.)* AL

That night, I checked to be sure the water in the bucket was freezing up. Even got the drinks and put them in the garage near the outboard. Easy. No sweat.

John banged on my bedroom door at five the next morning, just like always. Boom! One time. That's all. No words. I heard it or I didn't. If I didn't, he'd leave me behind without a second thought. I got up instantly, a habit I developed then, and cling to even to this day.

I couldn't get the ice out of the bucket. I kicked it, I twisted it, I pounded it on the ground, I swore at it, but it wouldn't budge. John suddenly appeared at my side and pushed me out of the way. Without saying a word, he took an ice pick and chiseled an inch of ice off the top, all the way around, leaving a space between the lip of the bucket and the block of ice. Then he turned the bucket over and dropped it on the ground. L

The ice popped out. 10

You needed to leave a drop-space around the top of the bucket. Simple. Part of where the brains came in. John hadn't told me that, and I hadn't noticed. He picked up the ice and put it in the Jeep. Then the Evinrude and the drinks. When we got to the pier, he took both the ice and the engine down to the skiff himself. R C

The next day I did it right, got the ice out of the bucket and put it in the Jeep. Then the outboard engine. It was heavy. I wasn't sure I could carry both of them at the same time.

On the way to the pier, I decided I would only take the ice, at least until I could do that much without screwing up. I told that to John when we got there. He shook his head and grabbed the engine and started walking toward the skiff. No words had passed his lips since the night before, when he told me to do the ice right this time.

I took the ice off the back seat and, as John always did, raised it to my shoulder on the palm of my hand. I started following him, walking slowly, in the don't-bother-me way, which I had mastered. It wasn't far, maybe thirty or forty yards. When we got about halfway, my hand started feeling like it was on fire. It froze so badly it burned. I had to switch hands. I ended up carrying the ice cradled between both arms, nestled against my chest. When we got to the skiff, I dropped the ice down onto the floorboards and jammed my

Practice the Skills

10 Key Reading Skill

Connecting Think of a time when you had trouble doing a task that an adult did very easily. How did you feel? How do you think the author felt?

Additional Support

Reading in the Real World

Career Charter boats are popular in tourist areas on the water. Have students research ways to get the training and experience needed to run a charter boat. Have them work in groups to list several questions a person would need to answer before running his or her own charter boat. *(Possible responses: Where are some of the most popular beaches in which such a business could thrive? How much does it cost to buy and run the boat? How much should I charge people per ride? How many passengers are likely to be on board each time I go out? Is there a peak season? How long is the off-season?)* OL Have them design a flyer for their own charter boat trip using answers to their questions as a guide. AL

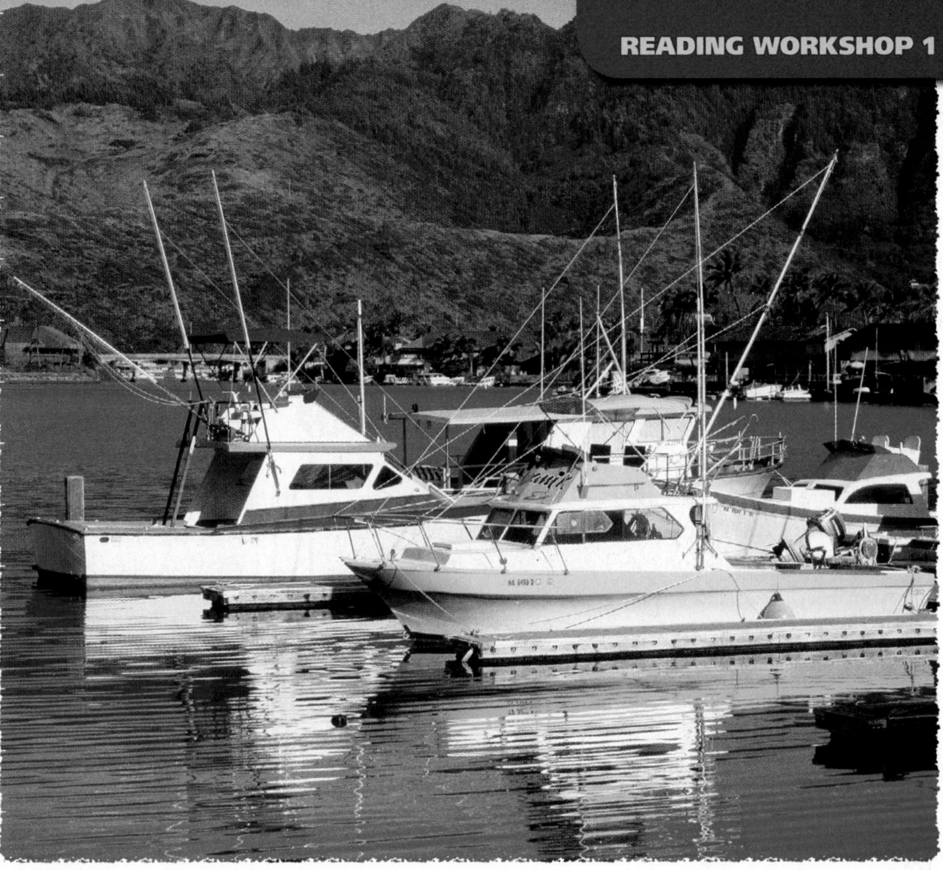

Analyzing the Photo Deep sea charter fishing boats idle in an Oahu harbor. What does this image suggest about the selection's setting?

hands into the warm ocean, and let them sting until I could move my fingers again.

John fired up the outboard and started out into the harbor to the boat, silent and sullen[7] as a flat tire. **11**

I spent the next eight hours being angry at myself, wondering how I was ever going to carry that blasted ice *and* the outboard from the Jeep to the skiff at the same time.

The ice was just too cold to carry in one hand that far, at John's impossibly slow pace. I didn't know how he could do it, except that his hands were thick and leathery from fishing all his life. Mine were lily-white and as soft as raw fish meat. **C** Once, the ice burned me so badly that I had to set it down on the hood of a truck . . . just for a second . . . while I buried my hands in my armpits.

John stopped, and looked back at me, and said, "Tsk . . ."

7. Someone who is ***sullen*** is in a silent, bad mood.

Practice the Skills

11 Key Literary Element

Description Here, the author uses a comparison to help you picture how John looked. What two things are being compared?

READING WORKSHOP 1

Teach

Viewing the Photo

Ask: What do you think it must be like to be on a boat of this size with John all day? Would you get bored, like the author, if John didn't give you enough work to do? Explain. *(Responses will vary.)* **OL**

C Critical Thinking

Analysis Say: Think about the way the author compares his hands with John's. What other comparisons can you draw between their personalities? What differences? *(Possible responses: Similarities: Both love the sea, both try to be tough, and both have an idea of what it means to be manly. Differences: Unlike John, the author is younger and weaker and not used to hard work.)* **OL**

Differentiated Instruction

Interactive Demonstration Before class, use a tape measure to figure out how far thirty to forty yards is in an area of your school—perhaps from one end of the hallway to another. (Or maybe take the class outside and measure this distance.) Bring a large bag of ice and have students carry a few ice cubes in their bare hands for the measured distance. Have students drop the ice if their hands get too cold. Leave buckets along the way if you are doing this activity inside so the floor does not get wet and slippery. Afterward have students discuss how it must feel to carry a few pounds of ice that distance. **AS**

Indiana English/Language Arts Academic Standards

SE: 8.2, 8.3.6

TWE: *Reading in the Real World* 8.4.11, *Differentiated Instruction* 8.2

Teach

C Critical Thinking

Comprehension Ask: How long did the author struggle with the ice in his hands before he put on the glove? *(a couple of weeks)* **BL** **Ask:** What does the author think John will say about him wearing a glove? *(Possible response: He'll call him a "sissy.")* **Ask:** What does the author learn about John when he does not respond to the glove? *(Possible response: He learns that John does not care how the ice gets to the boat, only that it does.)* **OL** **Ask:** What does the author learn about himself from this incident? *(Possible response: that he was overly concerned with impressing John and being like him)* Why does the author call carrying the ice with his bare hands a "self-imposed manly goal"? *(Possible response: because it defines a specific idea of what it means to be "manly" or "macho")* **AL**

Viewing the Photo

Say: Why do you think it's important for people who catch fish to be in good shape? *(Responses will vary.)* **AS**

READING WORKSHOP 1

And I knew I was losing ground.

After a couple of weeks of murdering my screaming hands, I came up with a solution. I put a canvas fish glove on . . . *then* carried the stupid ice. It worked. So simple, and well worth the scorn I figured John would pour all over me for being so sissy as to have to put on a glove.

But he didn't say a word about it.

Not one word.

In fact, I don't think he even noticed. I was trying so hard to be like him, trying to live up to this self-imposed manly goal of carrying ice with my bare hand, when the reality of it all suddenly hit me—*who cared?* **12**

Certainly not John. He didn't give a rat's you-know-what how I carried the ice, just as long as I got it to the boat.

Only I cared.

Why?

Because I didn't know any better. Because I was fighting for the wrong reason. I was being watched. Right? I was being

Practice the Skills

12 **Key Reading Skill**

Connecting Imagine how it feels to try hard to impress someone who doesn't even notice your efforts. How do you think the author felt?

Analyzing the Photo Today, many Hawaiians still make their living from the sea. Why might commercial fishing be challenging for a young boy?

Additional Support

Literature Focus Lesson

Character Webs At this point in the story, students have a lot of information about the way John and the author act in different situations. Have students make character webs, sketches, or charts showing the different actions of each character and what that action tells them about the person. Have students consider similarities and differences between the two, and have them use quotes from the story describing John and the author. Students may want to draw a portrait of how they picture John and the author for the character webs. **OL**

watched by John, and all the other fishermen, and all their ace deck hands, and all the kids on shore who were rubbing their hands together to have my job if I couldn't do it. I had to live up to the code, the image, the machismo.[8] I *had* no choice in the matter. Right? **13**

Wasn't that right?

Carrying ice taught me a great lesson, though I didn't truly understand it until years later. But there it was, right in front of me, and I didn't see it. I *still* tried to carry the ice bare-handed a couple of times, and *still* failed. And I still felt as if I'd never live up to John's expectations.

I kicked myself around for a long time before I finally realized that John didn't *have* any expectations. He didn't seem to care much what I did, one way or the other.

Today, I thank John for letting me work on his boat. And I thank him for being the way he was. I learned a lot simply by being there. He truly was a wealth of knowledge. But most of all, I learned about how hard I tried, even into later years, to please *others* rather than myself, always searching for that elusive[9] outside approval. Long, hard, bumbling years dragged by before I finally understood how foolish, if not impossible, that search was. **EL**

Jeeze. To think back. How I would do all manner of stupid things in order to be accepted, to be seen as manly. Nobody was calling *me* a sissy, confonnit. **BQ**

And nobody's calling *you* one, either. Right?

You're going with the bare hand. Grit it out until your fingers fall off.

Good. I understand that. You're a fighter. You gotta do what you gotta do.

But just one thing. Are you doing it for you? Or are you doing it for someone else? It's an important question. **14** ❍

8. ***Machismo*** (mah CHEEZ moh) is behavior that is meant to show how manly someone is.

9. When something is ***elusive*** (ee LOO siv), it is hard to catch.

Practice the Skills

13 **Key Reading Skill**

Connecting Do you agree with the author? Have you ever felt as if you had no choice in doing something? Explain.

14 **BIG Question**

Did you enjoy reading this selection? Why or why not? Write your answer on the "Ice" page of Foldable 1. Your response will help you complete the Unit Challenge later.

Differentiated Instruction

Small Group Discussion Divide the class into small groups and assign students roles (such as group facilitator, note taker, and reporter). Assign each group a different question for discussion, and have them report their results to the class: (1) What lessons did the author learn and how? (2) Do you think the lessons the author learned are valuable? Explain. (3) What can you learn from this autobiography? **OL** (4) How do our ideas of what it means to be a man affect boys growing up? (5) Why is it important to do things for yourself instead of always doing them to please other people? (6) It's good to do things for yourself, but are there ever times when it's okay to do things for others? **AL**

READING WORKSHOP 1

Teach

EL Language Coach

Context Clues Have students add two expressions to their Learner's Notebooks: "wealth of knowledge" and "years dragged by." Ask for volunteers to explain these phrases. Then have students write their own explanations in their Learner's Notebooks. **EL** **BL**

BQ **BIG Question**

Say: This story is about learning how to have confidence in yourself without worrying about the opinions of others. Can reading this story help you learn this lesson? *(Responses will vary. Students may say it helps because they can relate to the situation and people. Other students may say it only helps a little because they have to put the ideas into practice and sometimes people need to experience things in order to learn lessons.)* **AS**

Assess

CheckPoint

Use the CheckPoint questions provided on Presentation Plus! to check for comprehension of the selection. These questions can be used with interactive response keypads for immediate student feedback.

Indiana English/Language Arts Academic Standards

SE: 8.2

TWE: *Literature Focus Lesson* 8.3, *Differentiated Instruction* 8.3

Assess

Resources for page 28

- Selection Quick Check, p. 1
- Selection and Unit Assessment, p. 1
- ExamView Assessment Suite
- Interactive Tutor: Self-Assessment

Students can respond to the *After You Read* items in their Learner's Notebooks or on a separate sheet of paper.

Answering the

1. Possible response: It is important not to worry about what others think.
2. His father died on his first birthday.
3. His second father died of cancer when the author was about ten years old.

Critical Thinking

4. Possible response: The author wanted a "father" who would be proud of him; he admired and respected John.
5. Possible responses: it helped him learn not to try to get approval from others. The author now sees that John was cruel, but as a boy he thought there was something wrong with himself.
6. Possible response: The author fought with other kids, and worked hard to gain approval from others. I learned that I should not fight for someone else's approval.

After You Read

Ice

Answering the BIG Question

1. What did you get out of reading "Ice"? Explain.
2. **Recall** Why doesn't the author remember what his first (biological) father was like?
   TIP **Right There** The answer is in the selection.
3. **Recall** What happened to the author's second father?
   TIP **Right There** The answer is in the selection.

Critical Thinking

4. **Infer** Why do you think the author wanted to impress John?
   TIP **Think and Search** You will find this information in the text but not all in one place.
5. **Interpret** Now that the author is an adult, how does he feel about the way his stepfather treated him?
   TIP **Author and Me** You will find clues in the text, but you must also use the information in your head.
6. **Apply** How did the author deal with his problems? What, if anything, have you learned about dealing with problems in the future? Explain.
   TIP **Author and Me** You will find clues in the text, but you must also use the information in your head.

Write About Your Reading

Written Response Near the beginning of the selection, the author says, "Was I fighting for myself, or was I just trying to prove something to someone else? There's a big difference, you know. A big difference. I learned that the hard way, mostly by fighting stupid fights. But I learned it best from a block of ice."

In a few paragraphs explain what lesson the author learned from a block of ice and how the block of ice taught him that lesson. Back up your ideas with details from the selection.

Indiana English/Language Arts Academic Standards
(pp. 28–29)

8.3 Comprehension and Analysis of Literary Text Respond to grade-level-appropriate literature... **8.5.2** Write responses to literature...
8.2 Comprehension and Analysis (Focus on Informational Text) Develop [reading] strategies... **8.3.6** Identify... literary devices... which define a writer's style...
8.6 English Language Conventions
For a complete description of the standards, see p. IN 11.

Write About Your Reading

Possible responses:
From the block of ice, Graham learned that John was not really paying attention to him. All of his effort was lost on John. John did not really care one way or the other what Graham did or how he did it—as long as it got done. He may even have been indifferent. Graham also learned that he could not win John's approval. Later in life, Graham applied this lesson to dealing with all people. He learned that you can't force someone to like you, and it is foolish to try for the wrong reasons.

Skills Review

Key Reading Skill: Connecting

7. What part of the selection was easiest to connect to something else you have read—the setting, the people, or the author's experiences?

Key Literary Element: Description

8. Find examples in "Ice" of descriptive details that appeal to each of the following senses: sight, sound, and touch. Put your examples on a chart like the one pictured below. Also include the page number of each example on your chart.

Sense	Example	Page No.
sight		
sound		
touch		

Vocabulary Check

For each vocabulary word below, write a clue on an index card or a sheet of paper to hint at its definition. Shuffle the cards and give them to a partner. Have him or her guess which word goes with each clue.

9. minority
10. self-esteem
11. oblivious
12. relentlessly
13. void
14. **Academic Vocabulary** List three **texts** you have studied this month.
15. **English Language Coach** The sentence below contains characteristics of a *jacamar*. List the characteristics; then define what a *jacamar* is.
    - The jacamar spread its shiny green wings and flew over the forest in search of insects.

    Look up *jacamar* in the dictionary to see if you're right.

Grammar Link: Concrete and Abstract Nouns

Nouns are words that name people, places, things, feelings, or ideas. Nouns can be concrete or abstract.

Concrete nouns name things that you can see or touch. *Tree* and *shoe* are examples of concrete nouns.

Abstract nouns name ideas, qualities, and feelings—things you cannot see or touch. *Friendship, satisfaction,* and *freedom* are abstract nouns.

- Waves crashed against the boat as it headed for shore; the captain urged the crew to fight off fear and maintain hope that they would survive.

The nouns *waves, boat, shore, captain,* and *crew* are concrete. The nouns *fear* and *hope* are abstract.

Grammar Practice

Copy each sentence. Underline all the concrete nouns. Circle all the abstract nouns.

16. The civilians admired the soldier's courage.
17. The young man showed great maturity.
18. She wanted to make peace with her sister.
19. The doctor talked with the patient about good health.
20. The book was filled with wisdom.

Writing Application Review your Write About Your Reading activity. List five concrete nouns and two abstract nouns you used.

Web Activities For eFlashcards, Selection Quick Checks, and other Web activities, go to www.glencoe.com.

Skills Review

Key Reading Skill: Connecting

7. Responses will vary.

Key Literary Element: Description

8. A sample chart is given.

Sense	Example	Page No.
sight	He had thick, wavy hair and muscles like Sylvester Stallone	20
sound	People called me shrimp, shahkbait, mongoose, pipsqueak . . .	18
touch	my hand started feeling like it was on fire	24

Vocabulary Check

9. there are less of us
10. pride
11. out of touch
12. never stopping
13. nothing

Academic Vocabulary

14. Possible responses: newspapers, magazines, books, comic books

English Language Coach

15. **Characteristics:** has shiny green wings, flies, looks for insects; **Definition:** a large flying insect or a bird that lives in a forest and eats insects.

Close

Ask students to summarize what they learned from reading "Ice" to answer the Big Question.

Indiana English/Language Arts Academic Standards
SE: 8.1, 8.2, 8.3, 8.3.6, 8.5.2, 8.6

Grammar Link: Concrete and Abstract Nouns

Grammar Practice

16. **underline**: civilians; **circle**: courage
17. **underline**: man; **circle**: maturity
18. **underline**: she, sister; **circle**: peace
19. **underline**: doctor, patient; **circle**: health
20. **underline**: book; **circle**: wisdom

Literature Online

Web Activities Have students access the Web site for interactive activities that will help them assess their understanding of the selection.

Teach

More About the Author

Martha Pickerill knew she wanted to become a writer when she was in sixth grade. She had written a limerick that her teacher both gently criticized and used to encourage her to become a writer. She studied journalism in college. Today, Pickerill says that some of the things she enjoys about her job are traveling and meeting different people.

V Vocabulary

Story Sentences Have a few volunteers read their stories aloud. Then divide the blackboard into sections for each of the vocabulary words. Begin with the word *feat*. Tell students to write the sentence from their story that uses *feat* on the part of the board labeled *feat*. Continue with the rest of the vocabulary words. In this way, students will be able to see several different sentences for each word. Direct them to choose two sentences for each word and write them in their Learner's Notebooks. **AS**

Before You Read | On Top of the World

Meet the Author

Martha Pickerill is the managing editor of *Time for Kids*. She has been writing for more than 18 years. She writes mostly nonfiction articles and has worked for the Children's Television Workshop.

Author Search For more about Martha Pickerill, go to www.glencoe.com.

Vocabulary Preview

feat (feet) *n.* remarkable action **(p. 32)** *Climbing the world's highest mountain is an amazing feat.*

trekked (trekd) *v.* walked or hiked a long distance; form of the verb *trek* **(p. 35)** *They trekked the many miles from Nepal to Tibet.*

expeditions (ek spuh DISH unz) *n.* groups that take trips for specific purposes **(p. 35)** *Many people who wanted to climb Mount Everest joined expeditions led by Sherpas.*

V **Write to Learn** Work with a partner to write a one-paragraph story about a person who has an adventure. Use the vocabulary words above in your paragraph. Your story can be funny or serious. You decide.

English Language Coach

Context Clues: Explanatory Words and Phrases Sometimes authors will include an explanatory word or phrase to help you understand what an unfamiliar word means. Explanatory words and phrases are usually set off with certain marks of punctuation. Look at the chart below.

Punctuation	Example
pair of dashes	The people believed that genii—**friendly spirits who watch over places**—protected their village.
pair of commas	Down**, the fluffy feathers of geese and ducks,** is used to stuff pillows.
pair of parentheses	The frog's skin contains toxins **(poisons).**
pair of commas with *or*	The story's theme**, or main idea,** is that love conquers all.
pair of commas with *called*	These basic units of rhythm**, called feet,** make up a poem's meter.

On Your Own Use the explanatory words and phrases in the chart to define the following words: *genii, down, toxins, theme,* and *feet.* Write your definitions in your Learner's Notebook.

Indiana English/Language Arts Academic Standards (pp. 30–35)

8.1.3 Verify the meaning of a word in its context…through the use of definition, restatement, example, comparison, or contrast. **8.2 Comprehension and Analysis (Focus on Informational Text)** Develop [reading] strategies…

For a complete description of the standards, see p. IN 11.

Additional Support

Author Search To expand students' appreciation of Martha Pickerill, have them access the Web site for additional information and resources.

Literature Focus Lesson

Titles and Subheads Magazine articles are especially helpful tools to use to teach students about titles and subheads. Have students pick an article from one of their favorite magazines and photocopy it. Instruct them to go through the article and circle the title and subheads. **BL** Next to each subhead, have students write in the margin of the photocopied article a brief summary of how the subhead explains that section of the text. **OL**

Skills Preview

Key Reading Skill: Connecting

Imagine that you're about to climb the tallest mountain in the world. The weather will be very cold. What supplies and equipment will you bring on your journey and why?

Whole Class Discussion As a class, brainstorm a list of items you will take with you on your climb. You will have to carry whatever you bring. So make sure you pack only the most essential things.

Text Element: Title and Subheads

The **title,** or name, of a selection fulfills one or more of these purposes: (1) to let readers know what, in general, the selection will be about; (2) to capture readers' attention so that they want to read on; and (3) to introduce the main, or most important, idea in the selection.

Nonfiction selections may also contain **subheads**—titles that preview the content of each section of the article. Always read and think about the title and subheads of a selection. These elements contain helpful information that can make it easier for you to understand the selection. As you read "On Top of the World," ask yourself these questions:

- *What topic does the title say the selection will be about?*
- *From the subheads, what things about the topic will be discussed?*

Partner Talk The title "On Top of the World" is a **pun**—a phrase with a double meaning. With a classmate, see if you can figure out what the two meanings are. Why do you think the author used a pun in the title?

Interactive Literary Elements Handbook
To review or learn more about the literary elements, go to www.glencoe.com.

Get Ready to Read

Connect to the Reading

R You will read about two people who faced an enormous challenge. What's the greatest challenge you've ever faced? What made it so challenging? How did you feel when you first faced the challenge? What finally happened and how did you feel about it?

Write to Learn In your Learner's Notebook, answer the questions above.

Build Background

About a half century ago, Edmund Hillary and Tenzing Norgay became the first people to climb to the top of Mount Everest, the tallest mountain in the world. Mount Everest is in the Himalayas, a mountain range on the border of Nepal and Tibet, China.

C In interviews, Hillary has said that he was often frightened during the difficult climb—especially when he fell into a large crack in the ice—but that he kept on because "this is part of the challenge."

- Find Nepal and China on the map on the next page. Mount Everest is in the mountain range on the border of these two countries.
- Today's hikers use equipment and clothing that did not exist in 1953, when Hillary and Norgay made their climb. Most of what today's climbers use is strong or warm but light to carry. For example, hikers now wear fabrics that are warmer and thinner than the many layers of wool worn by Hillary and Norgay.

Set Purposes for Reading

BIG Question Read to find out what it's like to hike to the top of the world's highest mountain.

Set Your Own Purpose What else would you like to learn from the selection to help you answer the Big Question? Write your own purpose on the "On Top of the World" page of Foldable 1.

Keep Moving

Use these skills as you read "On Top of the World."

Teach

R Reading Skill

Connecting **Ask:** What are some things you think you would need to do to prepare to climb the tallest mountain? *(Possible responses: get a lot of rest, get in good shape, buy the right equipment)* AS

C Critical Thinking

Analysis **Ask:** Why would it be difficult to climb a mountain while wearing layers and layers of wool? *(Possible responses: Wool would be heavy to wear and heavy to carry if you wanted to take it off. It is also hard to move around, especially trying to maneuver the ropes and other tools for steep mountain climbing, while wearing bulky layers.)* OL

Interactive Literary Elements Handbook Have students access the Web site to improve their understanding of titles and subtitles.

Differentiated Instruction

Career Research Tell students that titles, or headlines, of newspaper or magazine articles are often written last. Writers rarely write headlines for their own stories; usually the editor makes the decision about the title or headline. Ask students to consider why the headline or title is written after the story is completed. *(Possible responses: The story may change as the writer writes it; It's best to read it all before determining what its title will be.)* OL Now have students research the roles of writers and editors. Have them research the differences between a writer and an editor, and what skills are needed to perform each job effectively. AL

Indiana English/Language Arts Academic Standards
SE: 8.1.3, 8.2
TWE: *Literature Focus Lesson* 8.2.1, 8.2.7

Teach

E Text Element

Titles and Subheads Say: Read the title of the article and think about its multiple meanings. What is the meaning of this phrase in casual speech: "I was on top of the world"? *(Possible response: to be very happy or excited)* **Ask:** What is the likely meaning of the title as it relates to the story? *(Possible response: the highest point in the world—climbing Mount Everest)* **Ask:** How can the story use both meanings? *(Possible response: It can describe climbing the highest point and being very excited about it.)* OL

V Vocabulary

Suffixes Say: The suffixes *-or* and *-er* are often added to verbs to make a noun that means "a person who ________." What is a surveyor? *(a person who surveys, or measures, the land)* OL **Say:** Think of other *-er* and *-or* words and identify the verb, or action the person does. *(Possible responses: instructor, dancer, writer, teacher, swimmer, sailor)* BL OL

Readability Scores
Dale-Chall: 6.4
DRP: 60
Lexile: 1050

READING WORKSHOP 1

TIME

On TOP of the WORLD E

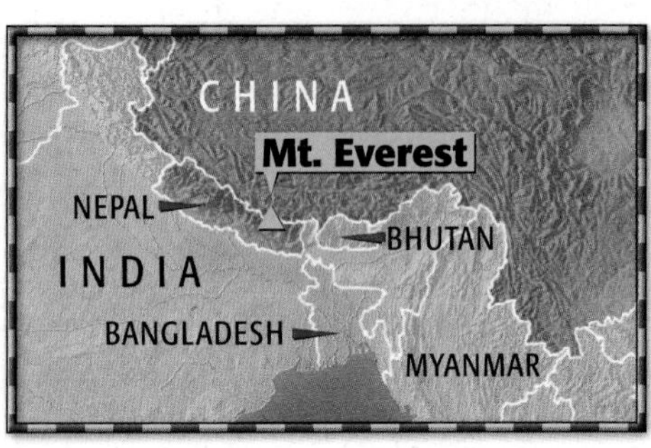

TIME For Kids

It has been more than 50 years since two adventurers first climbed Mount Everest.

By MARTHA PICKERILL

On May 29, 1953, Edmund Hillary and his mountain-climbing companion, Tenzing Norgay, got a glimpse of Asia that no other human had ever enjoyed. They became the first to look down from the dizzying height of the world's tallest mountain, Mount Everest, while standing upon its snowy top. But it wasn't a time for celebrating.

"I didn't leap or throw my hands in the air or something," Hillary recalled in an interview. "We were tired, of course." But finally in May 2003, the long-delayed celebration took place. Hillary, who lives in New Zealand, joined his friends and fans in Kathmandu, Nepal, to honor the 50th anniversary of his towering **feat.**

The Quest for the Top 1

Sir George Everest, a British surveyor who mapped India and part of the Himalayan range, probably never saw the big mountain. But his colleagues,[1] who measured the peak and declared it the world's tallest in 1852, wanted to honor Everest's work by naming it after him. The 29,035-foot-tall mountain straddles the border of Nepal and the Tibet region of China. V

1. ***Colleagues*** are people who work in the same profession

Vocabulary

feat (feet) *n.* remarkable action

1 Text Element

Titles and Subheads Reread the subhead. A *quest* is a difficult journey to reach a goal. What difficult journey do you think this section will be about?

Additional Support

Reading in the Real World

College A cartographer is a person who makes maps. Today, cartographers use satellite images and computers to help them with their work. Instruct students to consider ways cartographers would have made maps *before* satellite technology and computers. AL A cartographer needs to have a strong background in geography and usually needs a college degree. Have students research cartography to find out what type of degree is required and which other subjects cartographers study. Ask students to find two colleges in their state that offer a degree in cartography. OL

READING WORKSHOP 1

Climbing to Mount Everest's summit became an irresistible goal for many adventurers. But people risked their lives to get to the top. Has the challenge been worth the serious risk? When a reporter asked George Mallory, a British mountaineer, why he wanted to climb Everest, he famously replied, "Because it is there." Mallory's final attempt in 1924 to climb to the top of Mount Everest ended in his death. At least 175 climbers are known to have died on Everest since 1920. Nearly 1,200 others have made it to the top. 2

One Mean Mountain

Anyone who has climbed Everest can tell you that humans are not meant to hang around 5.5 miles above sea level. The ice, snow, freezing wind, deep ice cracks, called **crevasses,** and lack of oxygen are constant threats to climbers' safety and health. Because of the thin air, most climbers breathe from oxygen tanks. Some climbers have lost toes, ears, and fingers to frostbite.[2] All of these factors force climbers who do reach the top to turn around and scramble back down as quickly as possible. 3

2 **Key Reading Skill**

Connecting Would you like to climb Mount Everest? Do you think climbing it is worth the risk? Why or why not?

3 **English Language Coach**

Context Clues What are **crevasses?** Use the explanatory phrase in the sentence to figure out the meaning of this word.

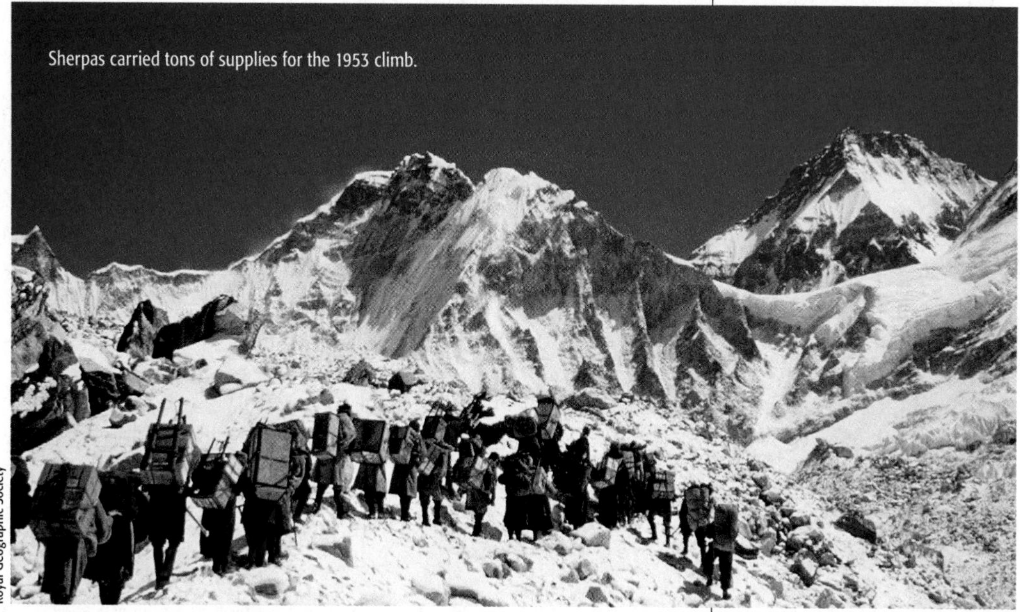

Sherpas carried tons of supplies for the 1953 climb.

Royal Geographic Society

2. ***Frostbite*** happens when a part of the body becomes so cold that the blood cannot circulate. Usually frostbite happens to fingers, toes, and ears.

Teach

C Critical Thinking

Comprehension Say: George Mallory wanted to climb Mount Everest "because it is there." In what other ways do humans defy seemingly impossible odds by conquering nature? *(Possible responses: traveling to outer space, going to the bottom of the ocean, flying)* **OL** **Ask:** Why do you think some people are driven toward these types of challenges? *(Responses will vary.)* **AL**

Viewing the Photo

Say: Everyone in the photograph is on foot. If it was possible to travel long distances up Everest in a vehicle, do you think climbers would be as intrigued with the challenge? Explain. *(Possible response: Probably not—part of the challenge is the climb.)* **OL**

Differentiated Instruction

Research Project People seek adventure in many ways, not just mountain climbing. Have students brainstorm other adventures people might try, such as sky diving, racing cars, riding bulls, etc. **BL** Then have each student research a person who has performed an adventurous feat or set a record. **OL** After students have completed their research, have them write a fact-based biography about their person and their feat. Instruct students to use their research to add details such as dates, locations, and people. **AL**

Indiana English/Language Arts Academic Standards

SE: 8.1.3, 8.2

TWE: *Reading in the Real World* 8.4.4, *Differentiated Instruction* 8.5.1

Teach

C1 Critical Thinking

Analysis **Say:** The selection says that Mount Everest "is much less a mystery now" than it was in 1953. What is the cause of this change? *(Possible response: People have climbed it from fifteen different routes, and there is equipment to make this task easier.)* OL

C2 Critical Thinking

Comprehension **Ask:** How does the article show that climbing Mount Everest is still dangerous regardless of the modern technology and clothing? *(Possible response: The article says that eight climbers died in one night in 1996.)* OL

Viewing the Photo

Say: How do you think it was possible for Hillary and Norgay to reach the top without the advanced equipment and thermal fabrics pictured in the photograph? *(Responses will vary.)* AL

"You cannot conquer Everest. It's not possible," says Norgay's son Jamling, who has climbed Everest with Hillary's son, Peter. "Everest will give you a chance to stand on the top for a few minutes, and that's it."

It's Still There 4

The mountain is much less a mystery now than when Hillary and Norgay reached its peak in 1953. People have approached climbing it from all sides and have succeeded in getting to its top by 15 different routes. Satellite phones and other equipment keep adventurers in touch with the world below. Special clothes made for climbing are now made of high-tech thermal fabrics. Hillary and Norgay had only layers of wool and cotton and a simple cotton tent to keep them warm. They didn't have any high-tech equipment as safety nets. C1

Some modern climbers who are inexperienced pay a lot of money to have professional guides take them to the top. But even with guides, the climb can be risky. In 1996, tragedy struck. On one of the mountain's busiest days, a storm blew in, and eight climbers died in a single night. C2

4 Text Element

Title and Subheads From the subhead and the other parts of the article that you've read, what do you think the section "It's Still There" will be about?

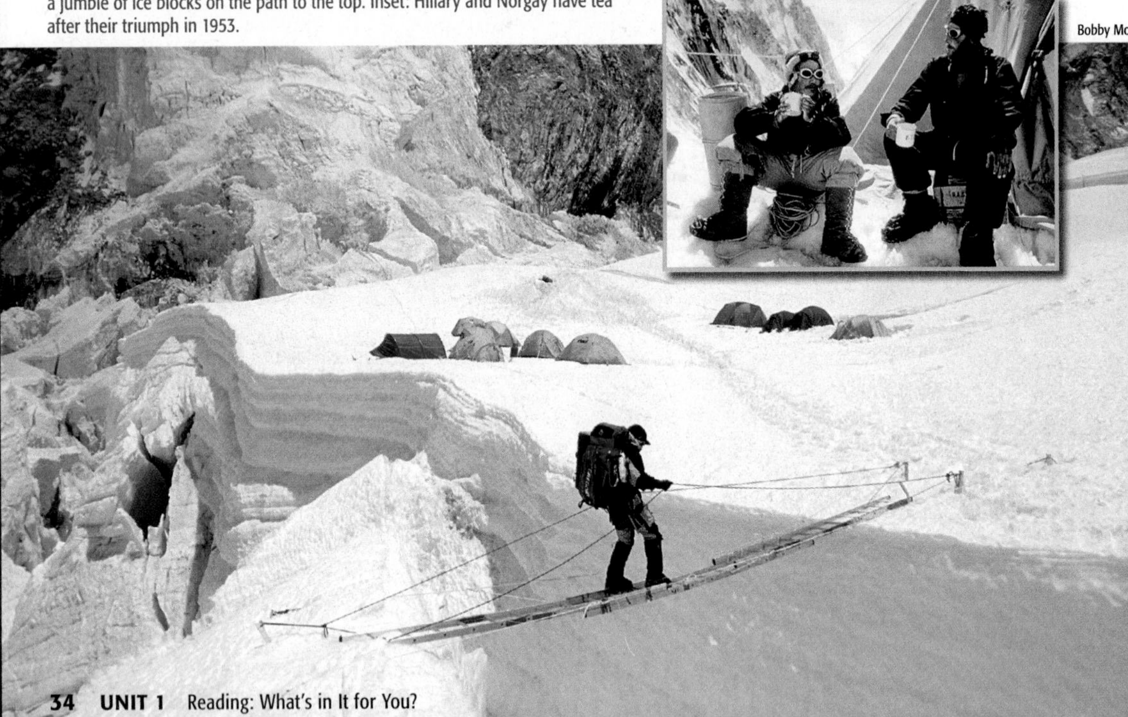

Climber Heidi Howkins uses a ladder to cross a crevasse in the Khumbu Ice Fall, a jumble of ice blocks on the path to the top. Inset: Hillary and Norgay have tea after their triumph in 1953.

Royal Geographic Society

Bobby Model

Additional Support

Reading in the Real World

Citizenship Have groups of students each choose a sport, but make sure no two groups work on the same sport. Instruct the groups to research how technology has changed the way the sport is played. Encourage groups to make several different diagrams of how technology has changed the sport (with each student responsible for a different diagram). Suggestions for charts might be: a chart comparing the sport in the past to the present; a diagram with pictures of the improvements and an explanation of them; a Venn diagram showing how the sport is the same/different; a ranking chart listing the technological advances in order of significance. OL

Hillary continued a life of achievement. After being knighted by Queen Elizabeth II, Sir Edmund Hillary led a team across Antarctica to the South Pole and climbed many mountains. He has worked for decades to build desperately needed schools and hospitals for Norgay's people, the Sherpas of Nepal. "That's how I'd like to be remembered," says Hillary. "Not for Everest but for the work I did and the cooperation I had with my Sherpa friends." 5 C

—Updated 2005, from *TIME For Kids*, May 9, 2003

5 BIG Question

What did you learn about Mount Everest from reading this article? What did you learn about people who set difficult goals for themselves? Write your answer on the "On Top of the World" page of Foldable 1. Your response will help you complete the Unit Challenge later. BQ

The Mountain's Keepers

Tenzing Norgay, who died in 1986, was a Sherpa. The Sherpas are one of about 30 ethnic groups[3] in Nepal. Sherpas, who are mainly farmers and herders, are believed to have **trekked** to Nepal from Tibet about 500 years ago.

Because many live in the Khumbu Valley at the foot of Everest, Sherpas work as porters and guides for outsiders who come to climb the mountain. On big **expeditions,** Sherpas may go ahead of official climbers to carry tons of gear to the few camps along the way. It's hard to imagine that many foreigners would have made it up Everest without help from Sherpas, who are used to working at high altitudes.

Sherpas follow the Buddhist religion, which holds deep respect for nature as a core belief. They call the mountain *Sagarmatha,* which means "goddess mother of the world."

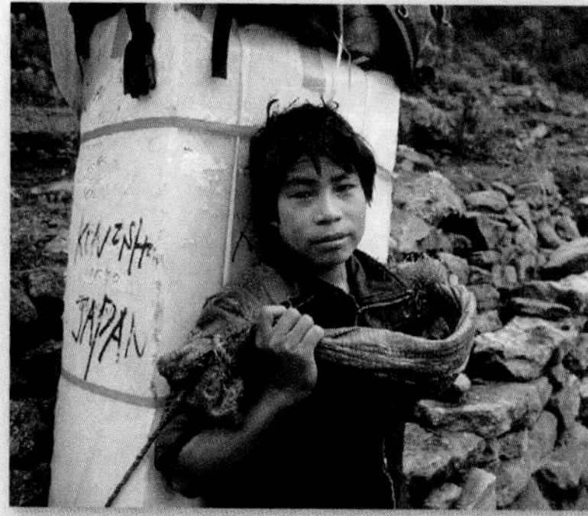

This Sherpa boy carried a heavy load in 1999.

3. ***Ethnic groups*** are groups of people that share a language, customs, and social ideas.

Vocabulary

trekked (trekd) *v.* walked or hiked a long distance

expeditions (ek spuh DISH unz) *n.* groups that take trips for specific purposes

Teach

C Critical Thinking

Analysis Say: Hillary says he wants to be known for helping the Sherpas of Nepal rather than for climbing Mount Everest. Do you think he will be known more for his helpful work or his challenging feat? Explain. *(Responses will vary.)* OL

BQ BIG Question

Ask: Why do you think people read texts like "On Top of the World"? What do you think people get from them? *(Answers will vary.)* OL

Viewing the Photo

Ask: How do you think Sherpas made it possible for people to reach the top of Mount Everest? *(Responses will vary.)* AS

Assess

Use the CheckPoint questions provided on Presentation Plus! to check for comprehension of the selection. These questions can be used with interactive response keypads for immediate student feedback.

Literature Focus Lesson

Lyrics and Poetry Many songs have been written that express the ideas of respecting nature or caring for other people. Have students think of at least two songs with lyrics that could be used as Hillary's "life song." Instruct them to choose one of the songs, print out its lyrics for the class, play the song on CD or MP3, and tell why they chose the song. OL

Challenge students to write their own song or poem expressing the importance of respect for nature. Allow them to present it to the class. AL

Indiana English/Language Arts Academic Standards

SE: 8.2

TWE: *Reading in the Real World* 8.5; *Literature Focus Lesson* 8.3, 8.5.7

Assess

Resources for page 36

- Selection Quick Check, p. 2
- Selection and Unit Assessment, p. 2
- ExamView Assessment Suite
- Interactive Tutor: Self-Assessment

Students can respond to the *After You Read* items in their Learner's Notebooks or on a separate sheet of paper.

Answering the

1. Responses will vary. Students who were not entertained may say they learned a lot from the article.
2. Mount Everest is located in Nepal.
3. Students should name three of these dangers: ice, snow, freezing wind, ice crevasses, lack of oxygen, and temperatures so low that people get frostbite.

Critical Thinking

4. Responses will vary.
5. Possible response: When you conquer something you are in charge of it, you master it. People cannot master a mountain; they still face danger when they climb it.
6. Possible response: Hillary is more concerned about people than his own accomplishments. He wants to be known for how he helped others, not what he did for himself.

After You Read

On Top of the World

Answering the BIG Question

1. Were you entertained by the article? Explain. If you were not entertained, explain what you got out of reading it.
2. **Recall** Where is Mount Everest located?

   TIP **Right There** The answer is in the article.
3. **List** What are some of the dangers people who climb Mount Everest must face? List at least three.

   TIP **Right There** The answer is in the article.

Critical Thinking

4. **Evaluate** Do you think George Mallory had a good reason for climbing the mountain? Why or why not?

   TIP **Author and Me** You will find clues in the text, but you must also use the information in your head.
5. **Interpret** Jamling Norgay has said, "you cannot conquer Everest." What do you think he meant?

   TIP **Author and Me** You will find clues in the text, but you must also use the information in your head.
6. **Infer** Edmund Hillary has said he wishes to be remembered for his friendship with the Sherpas rather than for climbing Mount Everest. What does this wish tell you about Hillary as a person?

   TIP **On My Own** Use your knowledge of people to answer.

Talk About Your Reading

Oral Report Imagine that you're writing a short biography of Hillary. With a small group of classmates, brainstorm a list of at least ten questions you feel you would need to answer about Hillary's life in order to write the biography. They could be questions you would like to ask Hillary in an interview or questions you might answer yourself by doing research on the Internet or in the library. Follow up by doing the research. Present your findings in an oral report to your class.

Indiana English/Language Arts Academic Standards (pp. 36–37)

8.3 Comprehension and Analysis of Literary Text Respond to grade-level-appropriate literature... **8.7.12** Deliver research presentations... **8.2 Comprehension and Analysis (Focus on Informational Text)** Develop [reading] strategies... **8.1.3** Verify the meaning of a word in its context... through the use of definition, restatement, example, comparison, or contrast. **8.6 English Language Conventions**

For a complete description of the standards, see p. IN 11.

Talk About Your Reading

Sample questions:

How did your family feel about you leaving to climb Mount Everest?
How did you train for the climb?
What scared you most when you realized you had reached the top?
Did you ever have any doubts about your decision to try to climb?
When did you first dream of climbing Mount Everest?
Do you think it is easier for climbers today?
What advice would you give to people who want to climb Mount Everest?

Skills Review

Key Reading Skill: Connecting

7. What are some reasons that you have for trying new or difficult activities? How do these reasons help you relate to this story?

Text Element: Title and Subheads

8. Did the subheads help you preview the content of the article? Explain why or why not.

Vocabulary Check

Play a game with a group of three. Follow these steps:

- Write the words below on note cards.
- Turn the cards face down.
- On your turn, choose one card.
- Make up a sentence using the word on that card. Each sentence has to be different from the other ones that used the same word. Keep playing until you have all gone twice.

9. feat
10. trekked
11. expeditions

English Language Coach Each of the following sentences contains an underlined word that may be unfamiliar to you. Copy the sentences. Then circle the explanatory word or phrase that defines the underlined word.

12. Volcanoes are formed when magma, hot liquid rock beneath the earth's surface, breaks through a weak spot in the earth's crust.

13. Daal bhaat (rice with lentil beans) is a common meal for the Sherpas.

14. Yaks—large, shaggy animals that are similar to buffalo and oxen—are native to central Asia.

15. Roving bands of robbers, called dacoits, terrorized the countryside of India.

Grammar Link: Personal and Possessive Pronouns and Antecedents

Pronouns take the place of nouns.	
Personal pronouns refer to people or things	*I, me, you, he, she, him, her, it, we, us, they, them*
Possessive pronouns show ownership	*my, mine, our, ours, you, yours, his, her, hers, its, their, theirs, whose*

The words in dark type below are personal pronouns. The underlined words are possessive pronouns.

- When **I** slipped on ice, **she** put down her book to help **me** get on my feet. Then our friends came to find **us.**

An **antecedent** (an tuh SEE dunt) is the noun that a pronoun refers to. A pronoun must refer clearly to its antecedent.

Cheryl Lynn and Tabitha went to her house.
antecedent *antecedent* *pronoun*

In the example above, the antecedent for *her* is unclear. Did the girls go to Cheryl Lynn's house or Tabitha's house? To fix the unclear pronoun reference, you can replace the pronoun with a noun.

- Cheryl Lynn and Tabitha went to Tabitha's house.

Grammar Practice

Circle the personal pronouns in the sentences below. Underline the possessive pronouns. Correct the sentence if the antecedent of a pronoun is unclear.

16. Juanita likes to tease her friends when she's in a bad mood.

17. I hit a branch with my head, and it broke off.

18. "Whose car is in front of your house?" he asked.

Literature Online

Web Activities For eFlashcards, Selection Quick Checks, and other Web activities, go to www.glencoe.com.

Skills Review

Key Reading Skill: Connecting

7. Answers will vary.

Text Element: Titles and Subheads

8. Possible response: The subheads helped me to see how the article was organized and what types of information I would read.

Vocabulary Check

9.–11. Students' sentences should use the words correctly.

English Language Coach

12. hot liquid rock beneath the Earth's surface
13. rice with lentil beans
14. large, shaggy animals that are similar to buffalo and oxen
15. roving bands of robbers

Close

Ask students what they learned from "On Top of the World" to answer the Big Question.

Literature Online

Web Activities Have students access the Web site for interactive activities that will help them assess their understanding of the selection.

Grammar Link: Personal and Possessive Pronouns and Antecedents

Grammar Practice

16. **circle**: she's; **underline**: her; do not need to change sentence

17. **circle**: I, it; **underline**: my; **new sentence**: The tree branch broke off after my head hit it.

18. **circle**: he; **underline**: whose, your; do not need to change sentence

Indiana English/Language Arts Academic Standards
SE: 8.1.3, 8.2, 8.3, 8.6, 8.7.12

Autobiographical Sketch

Teaching Students to Write an Autobiographical Sketch

Why Is It Important?

- Autobiography provides students with practice writing in the first person point of view.
- Students will enjoy writing about something they really know: their own lives.
- Writing in their own voices will help students hone their understanding of tone and word choice.
- Students will learn to develop voice by utilizing the first person point of view.
- Practicing narrative structure will help students organize their writing in a logical way.
- Writing about reading will help students think about answers to the Big Question: What's in it for you?

How to Help Students Get It

- Remind students to use the language that comes naturally to them; this will help them develop their writing 'voice.'
- Encourage students to start small. Since the finished product entails only one scene, the more tightly focused their scope, the easier revision will be.
- Visual learners may find a graphic organizer especially useful in determining their plot outline or sequence of events. Others may want to pick another sense to help tie together their scene. For example, ask: "Is there a certain sound or song that makes this memory vivid to you? What did the item you were reading feel like?"
- Remind the class to use "I" and "me" in their writing, and to talk about a personal experience of their own.
- The revised sketch will include vivid details, so readers feel like they don't need to ask further questions to understand the story.
- If students do not have room in the margins of their first draft or feel uncomfortable "marking up" their writing, sticky notes might help them comment more freely on their own work. If possible, make sticky notes available to students so that they can attach their comments to first drafts, before making clean copies of their revisions.
- Ask: "Did you include a beginning, middle, and end?"
- Encourage students to use different kinds of sense words to engage the reader and provide detail: "smelled like . . ." "saw . . ." "I could taste . . ." "I could hear . . "
- Ask: "Could a friend identify you as the person in this story without seeing who wrote it?"

Writing Trait	Student Checklist
Ideas: the message or the theme and the details that develop it	• Does the title suggest the theme of the composition? • Does the composition focus on a single narrow topic? • Is the thesis, or main idea, clearly stated? • Do well-chosen details elaborate the main idea?
Organization: the arrangement of main points and supporting details	• Are the beginning, middle, and end clearly linked? • Is the order of ideas easy to follow? • Does the introduction capture readers' attention? • Do sentences and paragraphs flow from one to the next in a way that makes sense? • Does the conclusion wrap up the composition?
Unit Focus **Voice:** a writer's unique way of using tone and style	• Does the writing sound interesting when read aloud? • Does the writing show what the writer thinks about the topic? • Does the writing sound like the writer—or does it sound like the writer is imitating someone else?
Word Choice: the vocabulary a writer uses to convey meaning	• Does the writer use lively verbs to show action? • Does the writer use vivid words to create word pictures in the readers' minds? • Does the writer use precise words to explain his or her ideas simply and clearly?
Sentence Fluency: the smooth rhythm and flow of sentences that vary in length and style	• Do sentences vary in length and structure? • Do transition words and phrases show connections between ideas and sentences? • Does parallelism help balance and unify related ideas?
Conventions: correct spelling, grammar, usage, and mechanics	• Are all words spelled correctly? • Are all proper nouns—as well as the first word of every sentence—capitalized? • Is the composition free of sentence fragments? • Is the composition free of run-on sentences? • Are punctuation marks—such as apostrophes, commas, and end marks—inserted in the right places?
Presentation: the way words and design elements look on a page	Appearance matters, so encourage students to make their compositions inviting to read. Handwritten papers should be neat and legible. If a word processor is used, the text should be double spaced and the font should be readable. Encourage students to also use other design elements—such as boldfaced headings, bulleted lists, pictures, and charts—to make their papers attractive and inviting.

Workshop Resources

Pacing (Days) Standard	Block	Lesson	Student Materials	Teacher Resources
1	1/2	Writing Workshop Part 1: Prewriting and Drafting	Writing Workshop Graphic Organizer, p. 15 Grammar Practice, p. 16 Spelling and Handwriting Practice, p. 46 Grammar and Composition Handbook, p. 97 Real Success in Writing: Research and Reports	TeacherWorks Plus™ Presentation Plus! Rubrics for Assessing Student Writing, Listening, and Speaking, p. 12 Grammar and Writing Workshop Transparencies 13–14
2	1	Writing Workshop Part 2: Editing, Revising, and Presenting	Interactive Grammar and Language Workbook Grammar and Composition Handbook, p. 97 Real Success in Writing: Research and Reports Listening and Speaking, p. 28 Viewing and Representing, p. 29	Grammar and Writing Workshop Transparencies 17–18 Interactive Grammar and Language Workbook Rubrics for Assessing Student Writing, Listening, and Speaking, p. 12

Focus

BELLRINGER Options

Daily Language Practice Transparency
Focus Activity Tell students about a book you read that had a meaningful impact on your life. **Say:** In this Writing Workshop, you will write about a time when reading changed your outlook on life. OL

Teach

L Literary Element

Description **Say:** Describe these images using as many senses as possible: a pie cooling on a windowsill; a fish out of water, flopping on the floor of a boat; a daisy growing through the crack of a busy sidewalk. *(Responses will vary.)* OL

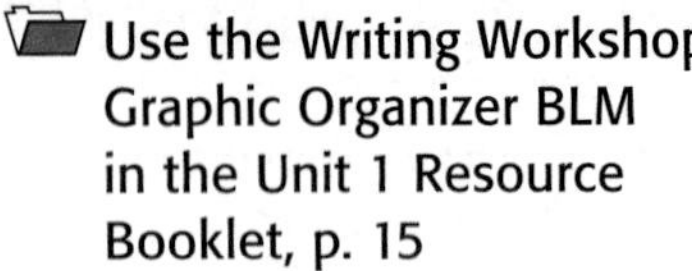

Resources for page 38

Use the Writing Workshop Graphic Organizer BLM in the Unit 1 Resource Booklet, p. 15

Use the Grammar and Writing Workshop Transparencies 13–14

WRITING WORKSHOP PART 1

Autobiographical Sketch

Prewriting and Drafting

ASSIGNMENT Write an autobiographical sketch

Purpose: To describe an experience you've had that shaped your feelings about reading

Audience: Your teacher and your classmates

Writing Rubric

As you work through this writing assignment, you should follow these guidelines:

- develop a sequence of events
- use first-person point of view
- use well-chosen descriptions and details
- develop your writing voice

For a model of an autobiographical sketch, see page 95.

Indiana English/ Language Arts Academic Standards (pp. 38–41)

8.4 Processes and Features prewriting, drafting... **8.5.1** Write... autobiographies... **8.6 English Language Conventions**

For a complete description of the standards, see p. IN 11.

Have you ever found yourself thinking about a special time or event in your life? Could you picture your surroundings in detail, remember the people who were there with you, and relive the feelings you had?

If you wrote this memory down, it could be the beginning of an autobiographical sketch. When a person writes the story of his or her life, it's called an autobiography. A sketch is a short scene that describes only the key details. So if you write an autobiographical sketch you describe one "scene," or event, in your life. L

In this Writing Workshop you'll write an autobiographical sketch about a meaningful event in your life that involved reading. You'll explore how reading changed your outlook and share that experience with others.

Prewriting

Get Ready to Write

What do the following things have in common: stories, cereal boxes, street signs, schoolbooks, notes from friends? They're all things you've read, of course. Think about the different reading experiences you've had.

Gather Ideas and Choose a Topic

In your Learner's Notebook, write about the kinds of reading experiences you've had in your life. Here are some examples to get you started:

- being read to before going to bed at night
- reading your favorite magazine at the newsstand
- reading short stories or books assigned in school
- reading a postcard from traveling friends or family
- reading instructions on how to play a new video game

After you've thought of as many examples as possible, choose an experience from your list. Pick one that you think is interesting and important—one that helped shape how you feel about reading. (Don't worry about choosing the "perfect" experience. If your choice doesn't work out, you can change it later.)

Additional Support

Literature Focus Lesson

Autobiography Hand each student a note card. On one side have them summarize an adventure from their past; on the other side have them write one reason they might want to write about it. Collect the note cards, mix them up, and read them aloud to the class. Have students discuss the different genres and tone each story could be written in. *(a light story, a serious essay, an eerie play)* Help students see that autobiographical sketches come in all different types, depending upon the story and the writer. OL

Develop Your Ideas

Once you've chosen an experience to write about, recall specific details about your experience. These details are important because they will help your readers to understand how you felt at the time. If you have trouble coming up with details, think about the experience in terms of your five senses: sight, sound, taste, touch, and smell.

1. In your Learner's Notebook, jot down as many specific details about your topic as you can remember. W1
2. Make sure that your list includes when and where the experience happened and who else, if anyone, was there.
3. Ask yourself how the experience made you feel. How do you feel about it now?

If you don't have enough details or can't recall how you felt at the time, now is a good time to pick a different reading experience.

Literature Online

Writing Models For models and other writing activities, go to www.glencoe.com.

Make a Plan

After you've developed your ideas, decide what order you want to put them in, or how to **sequence** your sketch.

- You can describe the experience in **chronological order**—the order in which things actually happened. Start at the beginning of your experience and end by telling how it influenced how you feel about reading now—or how you hope to feel in the future.
- You may want to describe your experience in a **flashback**—an interruption in chronological order to describe the past. For example, you might begin by describing how you feel about reading now. Then you could flash back to the past experience that shaped your feelings. You could end by returning to the present.

To help organize your sketch, fill in a map like the one below.

Writing Tip

W2 **Prewriting** Think about interesting ways to begin your autobiographical sketch. You may begin with a question, a dialogue, or a sentence that uses strong action verbs. These are good ways to capture your readers' attention.

When and Where Experience Occurred	Beginning	Middle	End
a friend's party and my bedroom **People Involved** me, a few of my classmates, and my social studies teacher	I come home from a party after having an awful time because people ignored me.	I read a couple of scenes in my Spanish book that I can relate to.	The characters in the book give me hope for the future.

WRITING WORKSHOP PART 1

Teach

W1 Writing

Prewriting Tell students to write *Who, What, Where, When, Why,* and *How* in their Learner's Notebooks. Instruct them to try to answer each of these six questions as they write their sketch. OL

W2 Writing

Prewriting **Say:** The first sentence introduces your sketch to the reader, so make it interesting, humorous, eerie, strange—something to pull the reader in. It will set the tone for your sketch. Once you have an idea for your sketch, practice writing a good first sentence. Come up with three different first sentences, trade with a partner, and discuss which sentence sounds the best. OL

Literature Online

Writing Models Have students access the Web site for an additional and interactive Writing Workshop-based student model.

Differentiated Instruction

Sequence Have students work with partners to try telling their stories with different sequence techniques. Direct students to write about five main events on separate index cards. Tell students to arrange the events sequentially, or in the order the events happened, and use the cards to tell the story in this order to their partners. OL Alternately, have students rearrange the cards and tell the story using flashbacks. Students can rearrange the cards another time and try telling the story again in a different order. AL

Indiana English/Language Arts Academic Standards
SE: 8.4, 8.5.1
TWE: *Literature Focus Lesson* 8.3, *Differentiated Instruction* 8.4

Teach

W Writing

Voice Say: Sometimes a conversational voice, or way of telling a story, helps the reader relate. Writing an autobiographical sketch does not mean giving up your own voice. Can you hear how the narrator kept her voice in this passage from *I Know Why the Caged Bird Sings*? **Read:** "I wouldn't look at either of them. Momma hadn't thought that taking off my dress in front of Mrs. Flowers would kill me stone dead . . . It would be fitting if I got a sunstroke and died before they came outside. Just dropped dead on the slanting porch." **Say:** Describe the narrator's voice. *(Possible response: shy, nervous, a bit dramatic, and comical in her extreme embarrassment)* **Say:** Get your ideas down using your tone and style. Then when you go back and fix the grammar and punctuation, you can make sure to keep parts of the essay that sound like you. OL

Drafting

Start Writing!

Sometimes the hardest part of writing a first draft is getting down the first few words. You don't have to worry, though. You've already done that by writing notes and filling in a story map!

Get It on Paper

Begin writing about your experience. Use your story map as a guide, but feel free to make changes as you go along. You are telling a story that happened to you, so use first-person point of view. Refer to yourself as *I* and *me.* Describe the other people in your story. Tell what they looked like, how they acted, and what they said.

Writing Tip

Conclusion Don't stop writing when you run out of ideas. Give your sketch a strong ending by telling what the experience meant to you.

Applying Good Writing Traits

Voice

One of the best parts about reading a story is discovering the writer's personality from the way he or she sounds on paper.

What is Voice?

When you speak, you don't sound like anyone else—your voice is yours alone. You want to have a one-of-a-kind voice when you write too.

Why Is Voice Important in My Writing?

Using a strong, individual voice in your writing will get your ideas and feelings across to the reader and make your writing more interesting.

How Do I Do It?

- Don't be afraid to show who you really are! Write with personality, as if you are telling close friends about your experience.
- Choose words that show what you really believe and feel.
- Vary the way that you structure sentences. Every sentence in your autobiographical sketch should not start with "I."
- Include details that will help your readers picture in their minds the events in your text.

W **Write to Learn** Here's how you can strengthen the voice in your draft:

1. After you have written your first draft, read your sketch aloud.
2. Make changes when your writing doesn't sound like you.
3. Keep making changes through the rest of the sketch until you feel that your voice is consistent throughout.

Additional Support

Reading in the Real World

Career Some writers spend their entire lives writing biographies, factual stories about other people. They might write about historical figures or famous people who are still alive. If they are lucky, they have the chance to interview the person they're writing about. Write a brief biography about someone in your life that you admire or find interesting. Start by coming up with a list of *Who, What, Where, When, Why,* and *How* questions probing into their past and present. Use those questions to start your interview. Summarizing someone's life is part of the challenge of writing a biography, so try to keep the biography no longer than one page. AL

Grammar Link

Verbs

Verbs are words that show action or a state of being.

What Are the Different Types of Verbs?

Action verbs show action.

- My sister plays on the basketball team.
- The bells ring in the church.

Many action verbs are obvious and easy to spot, but some are not. To find an action verb, look for what something or someone *does*.

Netty reads to her sister Sara. Sara listens carefully. The baby, Patty, bangs on a pot and Sara jumps. Netty closes the book and smiles at Patty.

Some action verbs might be less obvious. Some action verbs show what someone or something is *thinking* or *feeling*.

Netty loves her sisters. She cares about both of them very much. But she wants a brother, too.

Linking verbs show a state of being. They connect a person, place, or thing with a word that *describes* it or *tells what it is*. The most common linking verb is the verb *to be*. Some forms of the *to be* verb are:

is, am, are, was, were, been

- The car is shiny.

  The verb *is* links *car* to *shiny*. *Shiny* describes *the car*.

- The athletes in the gym were all gymnasts.

  The verb *were* links *athletes* to *gymnasts*. *Gymnasts* names the kind of *athletes*.

Other Linking Verbs

Other common linking verbs are:

seem, look, feel, become, appear, grow, turn, taste, feel, smell, sound

- Milk turns sour out of the refrigerator.

  The verb *turns* links *milk* and *sour*. *Sour* describes the *milk*.

- After the show, Marita seemed sad.

  The verb *seemed* links *Marita* to *sad*. *Sad* describes *Marita*.

Writing Application Look back at your autobiographical sketch draft. Check that you correctly used action and linking verbs. Fix any errors that you find.

Looking Ahead

There's another part to this Writing Workshop. Keep the writing you did here. In the next part you'll learn how to turn your first draft into a great autobiographical sketch!

Differentiated Instruction

Storyboard Using their autobiography as a reference point, have students make a storyboard. Demonstrate for students how to make a storyboard to show the plot development of a story. Give students a large poster board to work with. Encourage students to make illustrations for each part of the story, rather than using words. They can use simple pictures, draw cartoons, or even make elaborate drawings. However, they must make sure that the pictures show how the plot moves along. AS

Teach

W Writing

Using Verbs in Writing
Remind students that a verb shows action or a state of being. Have students make up their own sentences using the linking verbs listed on page 41. Write several of these sentences on the board. Then have students come up with sentences using action verbs, and write some of these on the board. Guide students to understand the difference between these two types of verbs. BL

Assess

Have students exchange their drafts with a partner and critique each other's work. Tell students to look to see if their partners have written their sketches with a sequence that makes sense to the reader. After a few minutes, tell students to assess their partner's comments, make any needed revisions, and save their drafts for later use.

Indiana English/Language Arts Academic Standards
SE: 8.5.1, 8.6
TWE: *Reading in the Real World* 8.5.1, *Differentiated Instruction* 8.4

READING WORKSHOP 2

Setting a Purpose for Reading

Teaching Students to Set a Purpose for Reading

Why Is It Important?

- Reading is more interesting and more likely to be recalled when there is a clear purpose.
- It provides a focus for the reader and allows the reader to monitor that he/she is getting what is needed from the reading.
- Good readers read for a variety of reasons, and they know *why* they're reading a specific piece.

How to Help Students Get It

- A purpose can be set by the reader or by someone else. For students who are purposeless readers, they need support to learn about setting purpose.
- Show students the help wanted ads. Ask them why they might read these ads. Then show students the sports page. Ask them why they might read this section of the paper. Proceed through the newspaper generating different purposes for different parts.
- Ask students to make a list of things that they'd like to know more about—an interest inventory. For one of the items on this list, ask them to write a purpose statement. Help students find independent reading materials related to their topic and purpose.
- Discuss the importance of setting a purpose for reading and revisit the title of this book. Predict with students that they will learn a lot about setting a purpose for reading as they learn with this text.

Reading to Answer the Big Question

The Tell-Tale Heart by Edgar Allan Poe
The narrator of this spooky tale describes his plan to murder an old man, and how he carries it out. Just when it seems that he will get away with his crime undetected, he hears the beating of the murdered man's heart. Convinced that the interrogating policemen are toying with him and that they hear the heartbeat too, the narrator, in a frenzied confession, points to the place where the old man lies buried.

from *The Book of Rock Stars* by Kathleen Krull
These one-page biographies of influential rock 'n' roll musicians Bob Marley and Carlos Santana are likely to increase young readers' interest in the music, the men, and in research and reading.

Workshop Resources

Pacing (Days) Standard	Pacing (Days) Block	Lesson	Student Materials	Teacher Resources
1	1/2	Key Skill Lesson: Setting a Purpose for Reading	Key Reading Skills Practice, p. 17 English Language Coach Review, p. 42	Bellringer Options Transparencies – Daily Language Practice 5 – Selection Focus 2 Read Aloud, Think Aloud Transparencies – Key Reading Skills 22 Presentation Plus!
1	1	"The Tell-Tale Heart"	Glencoe Online Unit Vocabulary Review, p. 40 Academic Vocabulary Review, p. 44 English Language Coach Active Reading Graphic Organizer, p. 19 Literary Analysis, p. 18 StudentWorks Plus™ Online Student Edition Literature Classics Selection and Unit Assessments, p. 3	Literary and Text Analysis Transparencies 39 Puzzlemaker Skill Level Up!™ A Language Arts Game BookLink 3 Assessment by Learning Objective (Diagnostic and Formative) Interactive Tutor: Self-Assessment TeacherWorks Plus™
1		from *The Book of Rock Stars*	Glencoe Online Unit Vocabulary Review, p. 40 Academic Vocabulary Review, p. 44 English Language Coach Active Reading Graphic Organizer, p. 21 Literary Analysis, p. 18 StudentWorks Plus™ Online Student Edition Literature Classics Selection and Unit Assessments, p. 4	Literary and Text Analysis Transparencies 39 Puzzlemaker Skill Level Up!™ A Language Arts Game BookLink 3 Assessment by Learning Objective (Diagnostic and Formative) Interactive Tutor: Self-Assessment TeacherWorks Plus™

Keys for Unit Resource

- Blackline Master
- Workbook
- Supplemental Text
- CD-ROM
- DVD
- Transparency
- Web-based
- Fast File

Level Appropriate Code

AS = Activities for all students
AL = Activities for students working above grade level
OL = Activities for students working at grade level
BL = Activities for students working below grade level
EL = Activities for English language learners

Focus

BELLRINGER Options

- **Selection Focus Transparency 2**
- **Daily Language Practice Transparency 5**

Focus Activity Say: Think about why you read your history textbook; then think about why you might read a poem. Compare and contrast your purposes for reading a history textbook and a poem. *(Responses will vary.)* OL

Teach

R Reading Skill

Setting a Purpose for Reading Say: You have a purpose for many of the things you do. Why do you play sports? *(Possible responses: to have fun, to stay in shape)* **Ask:** Why do you do your homework? *(Possible responses: to get good grades, to learn, to stay out of trouble)* **Ask:** Why do you go to the mall? *(Possible responses: to be with friends, to meet people, to go shopping)* **Say:** Having a purpose for why you do these things is the same as setting a purpose for reading. Your purpose gives you a reason for doing the things that you do. OL

READING WORKSHOP 2

Skills Focus

You will practice using these skills when you read the following selections:

- "The Tell-Tale Heart," p. 46
- from *The Book of Rock Stars*, p. 56

Reading

- Setting a purpose for reading

Literature

- Identifying and analyzing the effects of narrative point of view

Vocabulary

- Using examples, synonyms, and antonyms to find the meaning of words
- Academic Vocabulary: *strategy*

Writing/Grammar

- Identifying and using common and proper nouns
- Correctly forming noun plurals

Indiana English/Language Arts Academic Standards
(pp. 42–43)

8.2 Comprehension and Analysis (Focus on Informational Text) Develop [reading] strategies...

For a complete description of the standards, see p. IN 11.

Skill Lesson

Setting a Purpose for Reading

Learn It!

R **What Is It?** Why are you reading that paperback mystery? What do you hope to get from your science textbook? The point is, you read for different reasons. You may read a mystery for entertainment or escape and a science text for knowledge. **Setting a purpose for reading** is deciding why you are reading. Here are some common purposes:

- to be entertained–for a good scare or a good laugh
- to learn and understand new information
- to find out more about a person you admire
- to explore an interest

Analyzing Cartoons
What purpose could you set for reading about people who lived a hundred years ago? What would you like to know about their lives?

Additional Support

Differentiated Instruction

Creating a Timeline After students have talked about the cartoon, emphasize that people read history for several different purposes. Some read historical works to find out how to deal with today's problems. These works teach us how *not* to repeat the mistakes of the past. Ask students to choose a time in history or an event that most interests them, and make a timeline of events leading up to and after that event. *(Examples: Civil War, Revolutionary War, civil rights movement, women's rights movement, colonial period)* OL Once they choose their topic and complete their timeline, have them write about what we can learn from that event today. AL

Why Is It Important? Setting a purpose for reading helps you choose a reading **strategy.** If you're reading a mystery story, for example, you'll probably want to look for clues to solve the mystery. If you want to find the answer to a science question, you can read quickly to look for key words.

How Do I Do It? One way to set a purpose for reading is to read the title of the work. You can also look for subheads and pictures. You might even read the first paragraph or two. Then think about why you want to read. Are you curious about the main character? Do you want to answer a question? Here's how a student set a purpose for reading *I Know Why the Caged Bird Sings*. He began by reading the first paragraph:

R

> Mrs. Bertha Flowers was the aristocrat of Black Stamps. She had the grace and control to appear warm in the coldest weather, and on the Arkansas summer days it seemed she had a private breeze which swirled around, cooling her. She was thin without the taut look of wiry people, and her printed voile dresses and flowered hats were as right for her as denim overalls for a farmer. . . .

Mrs. Flowers sounds pretty interesting. The person describing her obviously admires her. I'd like to find out more about Mrs. Flowers as I read.

Literature Online

Study Central Visit www.glencoe.com and click on Study Central to review setting a purpose for reading.

Practice It!

In your Learner's Notebook, write a purpose for reading each of these:

- a short story about a man who has just committed a murder
- a biography of a famous musician
- want ads in the newspaper

Use It!

When you read the titles and the first few paragraphs of the selections in this workshop, list in your Learner's Notebook your purposes for reading. You can have more than one purpose for reading. As you read, set more purposes for reading and add them to your list.

Academic Vocabulary

strategy (STRAT uh jee) *n.* a careful method or plan

Teach

Literature Online

Study Central Have students access the Web site to review setting a purpose for reading and to complete a related activity.

R Reading Skill

Setting a Purpose for Reading **Say:** There are different purposes for reading different texts. What are some different purposes for reading the various textbooks you have for each class? *(Possible responses: math: to solve problems with numbers; science: to learn fact-based information about the natural world; history: to be informed about the past; English: to be informed and possibly entertained)* **Ask:** What other texts do you read and why do you read them? *(Responses will vary.)* OL

Resources for page 43

- Use Key Reading Skills Transparency 22 in *Read Aloud, Think Aloud* to help students practice setting a purpose for reading.

Reading Fluency

Pausing for Commas and Periods Photocopy the above excerpt from *I Know Why the Caged Bird Sings* and hand it out to the class. Instruct students to read through the passage silently at their desks. Ask them to put a forward slash over each comma and two forward slashes over any punctuation ending a sentence, as such: . . . *she had a private breeze which swirled around/ cooling her//* Have students circle any words they do not know and look them up, writing the definitions in the margin. Finally, allow students to read the excerpt aloud—instruct them to pause at the slashes (which serve as flags). EL BL

Indiana English/Language Arts Academic Standards
SE: 8.2
TWE: *Differentiated Instruction* 8.5.3, *Reading Fluency* 8.7

Teach

More About the Author

Edgar Allan Poe is most known for his horror stories and poetry. He did not finish college. However, while he was a student, he published his first book of poetry. He was only eighteen years old at the time. Today, there are so few of these books in print that one copy recently sold for $200,000—quite a sum when you consider that Poe entered a short story in a contest to win $100 in 1831. Poe continued writing both short stories and poetry throughout his life.

V Vocabulary

Building Vocabulary

Say: Words can be changed by adding a suffix. The adjective *stifled* comes from what verb? *(stifle)* BL **Ask:** What noun was changed to create the adjective *hypocritical*? *(hypocrite)* OL

Before You Read: The Tell-Tale Heart

Meet the Author

Edgar Allan Poe (1809–1849) was a master writer of detective stories, horror tales, and thrillers. Despite his talents, he had a hard life. He had severe money problems, and his beloved wife died when she was only twenty-four. A few years later he died at the young age of forty. See page R6 at the back of the book for more on Edgar Allan Poe.

Author Search For more about Edgar Allan Poe, go to www.glencoe.com.

Indiana English/Language Arts Academic Standards (pp. 44–51)

8.1.3 Verify the meaning of a word in its context…through the use of…example… **8.2 Comprehension and Analysis (Focus on Informational Text)** Develop [reading] strategies… **8.3 Comprehension and Analysis of Literary Text** Respond to grade-level-appropriate literature…identifying story elements… **8.3.8** Contrast points of view…

For a complete description of the standards, see p. IN 11.

Vocabulary Preview

V

stifled (STY fuld) *adj.* held back; muffled; form of the verb *stifle* **(p. 48)** *His stifled voice spoke to me from the other side of the door.*

stimulates (STIM yuh layts) *v.* makes active or more active; form of the verb *stimulate* **(p. 49)** *The old man's fear stimulates his heart to beat faster.*

audacity (aw DAS ih tee) *n.* reckless courage **(p. 50)** *Can you believe he had the audacity to lie to the police?*

hypocritical (hip uh KRIT ih kul) *adj.* fake; pretending to be something one isn't **(p. 51)** *He was convinced that their smiles were hypocritical; he was sure they knew the truth.*

Write to Learn For each vocabulary word, write a sentence in your Learner's Notebook using the word.

English Language Coach

Context Clues: Examples Remember that when you're reading on your own, you can often figure out the meaning of unfamiliar words just by looking at **context clues**—hints in nearby words and sentences.

One kind of context clue is examples. Look at the underlined examples in the following sentence. See if you can use them to figure out what *implements* means: *I had all the implements I needed to make the cake batter: a bowl, a spoon, measuring cups, and a mixer.*

All the examples have something in common. All of them are types of tools. So *implements* means "tools."

On Your Own A word web can help you remember the meanings of words you've defined through examples. Copy the web below into your Learner's Notebook. Then fill in the ovals on the web with the examples of implements.

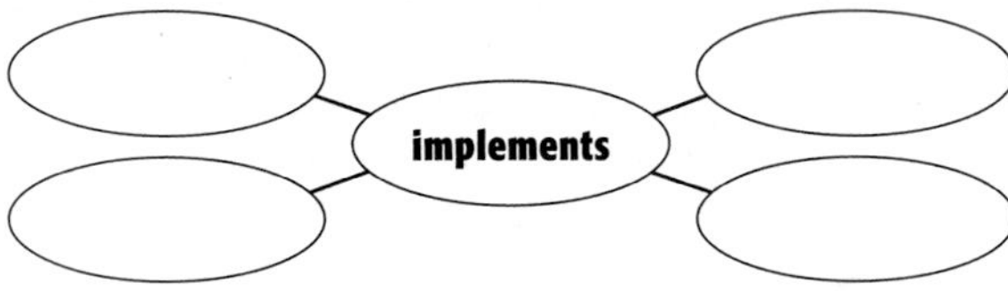

Additional Support

Author Search To expand students' appreciation of Edgar Allan Poe, have them access the Web site for more information and resources.

Literature Focus Lesson

Author's Purpose Discuss an author's purpose in writing a suspense story, such as to entertain or scare. Point out that readers who choose this genre want to be frightened or to enjoy a good mystery. Explain that suspense stories and thrillers use common situations and symbols, such as darkness and murders. Have students list other common symbols or situations they have found in mysteries. *(Possible responses: missing items, detectives)* BL As students read "The Tell-Tale Heart," have them point out symbols and situations that are common in other mysteries. OL

Skills Preview

Key Reading Skill: Setting a Purpose for Reading

You may feel the only reason to read is that a teacher told you to. But it's possible to set a purpose to *enjoy* what you read. "The Tell-Tale Heart" is a thriller, or a story with a great deal of mystery and suspense. You can read a thriller to enjoy the excitement of it, much in the same way that you would enjoy a movie that is a thriller.

Write to Learn In your Learner's Notebook, list the names of at least three things you regularly read. They could be everyday things like TV guides, street signs, and newspapers, or more specialized things like science books, poetry, and novels. Next to each item on your list, jot down your purpose for reading it.

Key Literary Element: Point of View in Fiction

Every story has a storyteller, or **narrator.** The perspective from which the narrator tells the story is the **point of view.** In the **first-person point of view,** the narrator is a character in the story who refers to himself or herself as "I" or "me." The first-person narrator takes part in what happens and describes the events from his or her perspective. When a first-person narrator tells the story, you may feel as though he or she is talking directly to you. **L**

In the **third-person point of view,** the narrator is not a character in the story and does not take part in events. He or she stands apart from the action and describes what is happening. When a third-person narrator tells the story, you may feel a sense of distance from the action.

To identify point of view, ask yourself, *Who is telling this story? Is he or she a character in the story (first-person) or a nameless voice (third-person)?*

On Your Own Read the first paragraph of "The Tell-Tale Heart." What is the point of view?

Get Ready to Read

Connect to the Reading

In your opinion, do most people see themselves as others see them? Explain.

Write to Learn In your Learner's Notebook, jot down your opinion. Back it up with a short example or two that supports your opinion.

Build Background

A superstition (soo per STIH shun) is a belief that is rooted in fear and fantasy rather than reason and evidence. One such superstition is the curse of the Evil Eye. According to this superstition, some people have the power to harm others just by looking at them. Who are these special people? The answer varies from culture to culture. In Mediterranean cultures–those in countries bordering the Mediterranean Sea–many people who believe in the Evil Eye say that blue-eyed individuals are the ones to fear. Other cultures have different ideas. In fact, in some cultures in the Middle East the color blue is believed to protect people from the Evil Eye.

Set Purposes for Reading

Read "The Tell-Tale Heart" to find out why a man commits a murder and whether he gets away with it without being punished.

Set Your Own Purpose What else would you like to learn from the selection to help you answer the Big Question? Write your own purpose on "The Tell-Tale Heart" page of Foldable 1.

Literature Online

Interactive Literary Elements Handbook
To review or learn more about the literary elements, go to www.glencoe.com.

Keep Moving

Use these skills as you read "The Tell-Tale Heart."

Teach

L Literary Element

Point of View **Say:** Think of one advantage and one disadvantage of reading a story told in first-person point of view. *(Possible response: You feel more involved when the narrator is in the story and telling it directly to you; however, you only get one side of the story.)* **Say:** Now think of one advantage and one disadvantage of reading a story told in third-person point of view. *(Possible response: You may get a fairer story when the narrator is not included in the story, but the story may not feel as personal.)* **OL**

Interactive Literary Elements Handbook Have students access the Web site to improve their understanding of point of view.

Differentiated Instruction

Identifying Suspenseful Music

Most, if not all, horror movies use music to help build suspense. Instruct students to watch different movies and note what type of music is played during suspenseful scenes. Have them report back to the class. **OL**

Encourage students to pick three songs they might use for a sound track if they were filming their own thriller movie. Instruct them to write what kind of scene each song would be played in. **AL**

Indiana English/Language Arts Academic Standards
SE: 8.1.3, 8.2, 8.3, 8.3.8
TWE: *Literature Focus Lesson* 8.3

Teach

L Literary Element

Point of View in Fiction
Say: Remember that when the narrator is telling the story from the first-person point of view the reader usually feels as if the narrator is talking directly to him or her. How does the narrator make you feel like he's talking to you? *(Possible responses: He says things like: "I can tell you the whole story" and "You should have seen how wisely I proceeded.")* OL

C Critical Thinking

Analysis **Ask:** According to the narrator, why did he decide to kill the old man? *(The old man had an eerie pale blue eye.)* BL **Ask:** What do you think of the narrator based on his reasons for wanting to kill the old man? *(Possible response: He might be crazy; wanting to kill someone for having an unusual eye is an odd reaction.)* OL

Readability Scores
Dale-Chall: 5.0
DRP: 54
Lexile: 860

The Tell-Tale Heart

by Edgar Allan Poe

True!—nervous—very, very dreadfully nervous I had been and am; but why *will* you say that I am mad? **1** The disease had sharpened my senses—not destroyed—not dulled them. Above all was the sense of hearing acute. I heard all things in the heaven and in the earth. I heard many things in hell. How, then, am I mad? Hearken![1] and observe how healthily—how calmly I can tell you the whole story. **2**

It is impossible to say how first the idea entered my brain; but once conceived,[2] it haunted me day and night. Object there was none. Passion there was none. I loved the old man. He had never wronged me. He had never given me insult. For his gold I had no desire. I think it was his eye! yes, it was this! One of his eyes resembled that of a vulture—a pale blue eye, with a film over it. Whenever it fell upon me, my blood ran cold; and so by degrees—very gradually—I made up my mind to take the life of the old man, and thus rid myself of the eye for ever.

Now this is the point. You fancy me mad. Madmen know nothing. But you should have seen *me*. You should have seen how wisely I proceeded—with what caution—with what foresight—with what dissimulation I went to work![3] I was

1. When the narrator says "***Hearken,***" he is asking the reader to listen.
2. Here, ***conceived*** means "thought of."
3. ***Foresight*** means "care or preparation for the future." ***Dissimulation*** means "the hiding or disguising of one's true feelings and intentions."

Practice the Skills

1 Key Literary Element

Point of View The narrator refers to himself as "I." What is the point of view?

2 Key Reading Skill

Setting a Purpose The narrator insists that he's not crazy and that he can calmly tell his story. So your purpose for reading might be to see whether the narrator really is in his right mind or what story he has to tell.

Additional Support

Leveled Reading An adapted version of this selection (3rd grade readability) is available on page 2 of **Jamestown Literature: An Adapted Reader** for Grade 8.

Reading Fluency

Memorizing a Speech Monologues are often used in plays. It is easy to imagine this story as a monologue—a speech in which the narrator speaks to an audience out loud. Have students take turns reading the first paragraph on this page aloud. AS

Challenge your more verbal students to memorize part (or all) of this paragraph and recite it to the class. Instruct them to mimic the mad rambling speech and possible gestures they imagine a speaker like this would employ. AL never kinder to the old man than during the whole week before I killed him. And every night, about midnight, I turned the latch of his door and opened it—oh, so gently! And then, when I had made an opening sufficient for my head, I put in a dark lantern, all closed, closed, so that no light shone out, and then I thrust in my head. Oh, you would have laughed to see how cunningly[4] I thrust it in! **3** I moved it slowly—very, very slowly, so that I might not disturb the old man's sleep. It took me an hour to place my whole head within the opening so far that I could see him as he lay upon his bed. Ha!—would a madman have been so wise as this? And then, when my head was well in the room, I undid the lantern cautiously—oh, so cautiously—cautiously (for the hinges creaked)—I undid it just so much that a single thin ray fell upon the vulture eye. And this I did for seven long nights—every night just at midnight—but I found the eye always closed; and so it was impossible to do the work; for it was not the old man who vexed[5] me, but his Evil Eye. And every morning, when the day broke, I went boldly into the chamber, and spoke courageously to him, calling him by name in a hearty tone, and inquiring how he had passed the night. So you see he would have been a very profound[6] old man, indeed, to suspect that every night, just at twelve, I looked in upon him while he slept.

Upon the eighth night I was more than usually cautious in opening the door. A watch's minute hand moves more quickly than did mine. Never before that night, had I *felt* the extent of my own powers—of my sagacity.[7] I could scarcely contain my feelings of triumph. To think that there I was, opening the door, little by little, and he not even to dream of my secret deeds or thoughts. I fairly chuckled at the idea; and perhaps he heard me; for he moved on the bed suddenly, as if startled. Now you may think that I drew back—but no. His room was as black as pitch with the thick darkness, (for the shutters were close fastened, through fear of robbers,) and so I knew that he could not see the opening of the door, and I kept pushing it on steadily, steadily. **4**

4. ***Cunningly*** means "cleverly."
5. Another way of saying ***vexed*** is "annoyed" or "made angry."
6. Here, ***profound*** means "very thoughtful and wise."
7. ***Sagacity*** (suh GAS uh tee) is wisdom and judgment.

Practice the Skills

3 Key Literary Element

Point of View Notice how Poe makes it seem as if the narrator is talking directly to you. This draws you into the story.

4 Key Literary Element

Point of View Though you are "seeing" what happened from the narrator's perspective, you don't have to agree with him. He talks about his *sagacity*, or wisdom. Would you call his actions wise? Why or why not?

Differentiated Instruction

Research Have students do some research about when they think the story takes place. Instruct them to complete a "Then and Now" comparison chart, citing the major differences between the time the story takes place and now. Have them research when Poe wrote the story to get some clues. Some clues students should notice are: the narrator uses a lantern to see at night; today we have electricity; the language is different from how we speak today; the police response is different. **OL** **AL**

Teach

R Reading Skill

Review Connecting Say: Think of a time you tried to do something quietly to keep from being noticed or heard, such as opening a candy wrapper in a quiet room. Did you feel like everyone could hear even the quietest sound? How slowly did you move? *(Students will probably say they felt like each little sound was very loud, and they moved incredibly slowly.)* **Ask:** How does this help you picture the narrator's movements at the door? *(Possible response: I can see him barely moving, just as I would do if I did not want to be heard.)* **OL**

C Critical Thinking

Analysis Say: As you are reading, think about the narrator's relationship with the old man. We know that the narrator has access to his house; they must know each other. What kind of relationship do you think the narrator has with the old man? *(Possible responses: He's a caretaker, a relative, a friend, or a neighbor.)* **OL**

Indiana English/Language Arts Academic Standards
SE: 8.2, 8.3
TWE: *Reading Fluency* 8.7.14, *Differentiated Instruction* 8.5.7

Teach

L Literary Element

Point of View in Fiction

Say: The narrator thinks he understands everything the old man is thinking and every gesture he makes—almost as if he can read his mind. How would this story be different if it were told from the old man's point of view? *(Responses will vary.)* OL

EL Language Coach

Context Clues **Say:** Look at the word *stealthily.* Oftentimes the context of a story can help us define unfamiliar words. Based on what is already happening in this story, what do you think the word *stealthily* means? *(slowly, deliberately, secretly)* **Ask:** What helps you define *stealthily*? *(Possible response: The narrator is cautious; he is plotting to kill a man in his sleep so he must be quiet and slow.)* OL

I had my head in, and was about to open the lantern, when my thumb slipped upon the tin fastening, and the old man sprang up in the bed, crying out—"Who's there?"

I kept quite still and said nothing. For a whole hour I did not move a muscle, and in the meantime I did not hear him lie down. He was still sitting up in the bed, listening;—just as I have done, night after night, hearkening to the death watches[8] in the wall.

Presently I heard a slight groan, and I knew it was the groan of mortal terror. It was not a groan of pain or of grief—oh, no!—it was the low **stifled** sound that arises from the bottom of the soul when overcharged with awe. I knew the sound well. Many a night, just at midnight, when all the world slept, it has welled up from my own bosom, deepening, with its dreadful echo, the terrors that distracted me. I say I knew it well. I knew what the old man felt, and pitied him, although I chuckled at heart. I knew that he had been lying awake ever since the first slight noise, when he had turned in the bed. His fears had been ever since growing upon him. He had been trying to fancy them causeless, but could not. He had been saying to himself—"It is nothing but the wind in the chimney—it is only a mouse crossing the floor," or "it is merely a cricket which has made a single chirp." Yes, he has been trying to comfort himself with these **suppositions**: but he had found all in vain. *All in vain;* because Death, in approaching him, had stalked with his black shadow before him, and enveloped[9] the victim. 5 And it was the mournful influence of the unperceived shadow that caused him to feel—although he neither saw nor heard—to *feel* the presence of my head within the room. L

When I had waited a long time, very patiently, without hearing him lie down, I resolved to open a little—a very, very little crevice in the lantern. So I opened it—you cannot imagine how stealthily, stealthily—until, at length, a single dim ray, like the thread of the spider, shot from out the crevice and fell upon the vulture eye. EL

8. ***Death watches*** are beetles that bore into wood, especially of old houses and furniture. Some people believe that the insects' ticking sounds warn that death is approaching.

9. Here, ***enveloped*** means "surrounded."

Vocabulary

stifled (STY fuld) *adj.* held back; muffled

Practice the Skills

5 English Language Coach

Context Clues: Examples
What are **suppositions?** Reread the third paragraph on this page to find the three examples of *suppositions* that the old man makes. Using the examples and the rest of the context, define *suppositions.*

Additional Support

Reading Fluency

Different Voices The narrator tells the story with many different emotions in his voice: tension, suspense, fear, anger, and even sadness. Put students in groups and instruct them to go through this page and decide which sentences convey these emotions. Next, assign each student a different emotion to read—they should read aloud and reflect that emotion in their voice. OL Have each group present their own reading of the page to the entire class. AL

It was open—wide, wide open—and I grew furious as I gazed upon it. I saw it with perfect distinctness—all a dull blue, with a hideous veil over it that chilled the very marrow in my bones; but I could see nothing else of the old man's face or person: for I had directed the ray as if by instinct, precisely upon the damned spot.

And now have I not told you that what you mistake for madness is but overacuteness of the senses?—now, I say, there came to my ears a low, dull, quick sound, such as a watch makes when enveloped in cotton. I knew *that* sound well, too. It was the beating of the old man's heart. It increased my fury, as the beating of a drum **stimulates** the soldier into courage. **L**

But even yet I refrained and kept still. I scarcely breathed. I held the lantern motionless. I tried how steadily I could maintain the ray upon the eye. Meantime the hellish tattoo[10] of the heart increased. It grew quicker and quicker, and louder and louder every instant. The old man's terror *must* have been extreme! It grew louder, I say, louder every moment!—do you mark me well? I have told you that I am nervous: so I am. And now at the dead hour of the night, amid the dreadful silence of that old house, so strange a noise as this excited me to uncontrollable terror. Yet, for some minutes longer I refrained and stood still. But the beating grew louder, louder! I thought the heart must burst. And now a new anxiety seized me—the sound would be heard by a neighbor! The old man's hour had come! **C** With a loud yell, I threw open the lantern and leaped into the room. He shrieked once—once only. In an instant I dragged him to the floor, and pulled the heavy bed over him. I then smiled gaily, to find the deed so far done. 6 But, for many minutes, the heart beat on with a muffled sound. This, however, did not vex me; it would not be heard through the wall. At length it ceased. The old

10. The heart was making a drumming or rapping sound. (This ***tattoo*** comes from a Dutch word; the other *tattoo*, a design on the skin, comes from the language of Tahiti, a Pacific island.)

Vocabulary

stimulates (STIM yuh layts) *v.* makes active or more active

Practice the Skills

6 **Key Literary Element**

Point of View The narrator smiles gaily after the killing. What does this tell you about him?

Analyzing the Art How does this picture illustrate the mood of "The Tell-Tale Heart"?

Teach

L Literary Element

Point of View in Fiction
Ask: How reliable do you think the narrator is? *(Possible response: He might not be very reliable because he seems crazy.)* BL **Ask:** Do you think the narrator can really hear the old man's heartbeat because he has "overacuteness of the senses," or is it something else? Explain. *(Possible responses: He could be imagining the heartbeat because he is in a frenzy, or it could be the narrator's heartbeat.)* OL

C Critical Thinking

Analysis Ask: Why do you think the heartbeat is described so vividly? *(Possible responses: It builds suspense, creates tension, and helps us understand the frenzy in the narrator's head.)* AS

Viewing the Art

Ask: What other pictures could be used to illustrate the mood of this story? *(Possible responses: an old house, a bedroom, a lantern in a doorway)* AS

English Language Coach

Affixes Prefixes and suffixes can be used to change a word's meaning. Write the prefix *un-* and the suffix *-less* on the board. Ask students what the prefix and suffix mean *(un-* means "not" and *-less* means "without"). Have students look through the story for words with these affixes and make a list of them *(motionless, uncontrollable)*. Show students how to break a word down to its root word and its prefix and/or suffix to figure out its meaning. Then have students break down the words on their list and use the affixes to figure out what the words mean. Students may look for these affixes throughout the selection. EL BL

Indiana English/Language Arts Academic Standards
SE: 8.1.3, 8.3, 8.3.8
TWE: *Reading Fluency* 8.7.2, *English Language Coach* 8.1

READING WORKSHOP 2

Teach

C Critical Thinking

Analysis Ask: How does the narrator try to convince you he is not mad? *(By reassuring the reader that a madman would not take "wise precautions" like cutting up and hiding the body.)* **Ask:** How do you feel about his state of mind? *(Responses will vary.)* OL **Ask:** Why do you think the narrator insists he is not crazy and wants you to believe him so desperately? *(Responses will vary.)* AL

R Reading Skill

Setting a Purpose for Reading Say: At this point in the story, the reader knows how the narrator killed his victim and what he did with the body. What else can you learn by reading the rest of the story? *(Possible response: if the narrator gets away with murder, and if so, how?)* OL

man was dead. I removed the bed and examined the corpse. Yes, he was stone, stone dead. I placed my hand upon the heart and held it there many minutes. There was no pulsation. He was stone dead. His eye would trouble me no more.

If still you think me mad, you will think so no longer when I describe the wise precautions I took for the concealment of the body. The night waned, and I worked hastily, but in silence. First of all I **dismembered** the corpse. I cut off the head and the arms and the legs. 7 C

I then took up three planks from the flooring of the chamber, and deposited all between the scantlings.[11] I then replaced the boards so cleverly, so cunningly, that no human eye—not even *his*—could have detected anything wrong. There was nothing to wash out—no stain of any kind—no blood-spot whatever. I had been too wary for that. A tub had caught all—ha! ha! R

When I had made an end of these labors, it was four o'clock—still dark as midnight. As the bell sounded the hour, there came a knocking at the street door. I went down to open it with a light heart—for what had I *now* to fear? There entered three men, who introduced themselves, with perfect suavity,[12] as officers of the police. A shriek had been heard by a neighbor during the night; suspicion of foul play had been aroused; information had been lodged at the police office, and they (the officers) had been deputed[13] to search the **premises.** 8

I smiled—for *what* had I to fear? I bade the gentlemen welcome. The shriek, I said, was my own in a dream. The old man, I mentioned, was absent in the country. I took my visitors all over the house. I bade them search—search *well.* I led them, at length, to *his* chamber. I showed them his treasures, secure, undisturbed. In the enthusiasm of my confidence, I brought chairs into the room, and desired them *here* to rest from their fatigues, while I myself, in the wild **audacity** of my perfect triumph, placed my own seat upon the very spot beneath which reposed the corpse of the victim.

11. The ***scantlings*** are the boards that hold up the floor planks.
12. ***Suavity*** (SWOV uh tee) is a smooth, polite, gracious manner.
13. The officers were assigned a duty, or ***deputed,*** by a superior.

Vocabulary

audacity (aw DAS ih tee) *n.* reckless courage

Practice the Skills

7 English Language Coach

Context Clues: Examples Do you know the meaning of the word **dismembered?** There are context clues in the sentence immediately following the word.

8 English Language Coach

Context Clues: Examples What does **premises** mean in this context? Read on for an example. Then define the word.

Additional Support

Differentiated Instruction

Writing New Endings Students who watch crime shows on TV are familiar with the kinds of tools that investigators use today, including DNA and fingerprinting. Explain that none of these tools were available when this story was written. Have students make up their own version of this story, as if it happened today, telling how the narrator would get caught or not. OL

The officers were satisfied. My *manner* had convinced them. I was singularly at ease. They sat, and while I answered cheerily, they chatted of familiar things. But, ere long, I felt myself getting pale and wished them gone. My head ached, and I fancied a ringing in my ears: but still they sat and still chatted. The ringing became more distinct—it continued and became more distinct: I talked more freely to get rid of the feeling: but it continued and gained definitiveness—until, at length, I found that the noise was *not* within my ears.

No doubt I now grew *very* pale—but I talked more fluently,[14] and with a heightened voice. Yet the sound increased—and what could I do? It was *a low, dull, quick sound—much such a sound as a watch makes when enveloped in cotton.* I gasped for breath—and yet the officers heard it not. I talked more quickly—more vehemently; but the noise steadily increased. I arose and argued about trifles, in a high key and with violent gesticulations;[15] but the noise steadily increased. Why *would* they not be gone? I paced the floor to and fro with heavy strides, as if excited to fury by the observations of the men—but the noise steadily increased. Oh God! what *could* I do? I foamed—I raved—I swore! I swung the chair upon which I had been sitting, and grated it upon the boards, but the noise arose over all and continually increased. It grew louder—louder—*louder!* And still the men chatted pleasantly, and smiled. Was it possible they heard not? Almighty God!—no, no! They heard!—they suspected!—they *knew!*—they were making a mockery of my horror!—this I thought, and this I think. But anything was better than this agony! Anything was more tolerable than this derision![16] I could bear those **hypocritical** smiles no longer! I felt that I must scream or die!—and now—again!—hark! louder! louder! louder! *louder!*— **C**

"Villains!" I shrieked, "dissemble[17] no more! I admit the deed!—tear up the planks!—here, here!—it is the beating of his hideous heart!" **9** ○

14. To speak ***fluently*** is to do so smoothly and effortlessly.
15. ***Trifles*** are unimportant things. Bold, expressive gestures are ***gesticulations***.
16. To make a ***mockery*** of a thing is to make it seem stupid or worthless. ***Derision*** is ridicule.
17. Here, ***dissemble*** means "to disguise one's true thoughts or feelings; act in an insincere way."

Vocabulary

hypocritical (hip uh KRIT ih kul) *adj.* fake; pretending to be something one isn't

Practice the Skills

9 **BIG Question**

BQ Would you recommend this story to others? Why or why not? Write your answer on "The Tell-Tale Heart" page of Foldable 1. Your response will help you complete the Unit Challenge later.

Reading in the Real World

Careers Have students find out what job training is required to become a detective who investigates murders. Have students brainstorm about the kind of reading and writing a detective might be required to do. *(Possible responses: taking notes at a crime scene; reading, understanding, and memorizing laws; interviewing suspects; reading over police reports to understand a crime; writing detailed police reports of their own)* Using their brainstorm list, instruct them to come up with some questions they would ask a detective in an interview. If possible, have a detective visit the classroom and answer students' questions about the job. **AS**

Teach

C Critical Thinking

Analysis **Ask:** Do you think the police really heard the heart beating? *(Possible response: No, the man is dead.)* **Ask:** How do you think the narrator hears the heartbeat of a dead man? *(Possible responses: He is crazed with guilt. His mind is playing tricks on him.)* **OL** **Ask:** Can you connect the ending of the story to the title? *(Possible responses: Because of his guilt and insanity, hearing the imagined beating of a heart makes the narrator tell his tale to the police.)* **AL**

BQ BIG Question

Ask: After reading this selection, how would you answer the Big Question? *(Responses will vary.)* **AS**

Assess

CheckPoint

Use the CheckPoint questions provided on Presentation Plus! to check for comprehension of the selection. These questions can be used with interactive response keypads for immediate student feedback.

Indiana English/Language Arts Academic Standards
SE: 8.1.3, 8.3
TWE: *Differentiated Instruction* 8.5.1, *Reading in the Real World* 8.5.7

Assess

Resources for page 52

- Selection Quick Check, p. 3
- Selection and Unit Assessment, p. 3
- ExamView Assessment Suite
- Interactive Tutor: Self-Assessment

Students can respond to the *After You Read* items in their Learner's Notebooks or on a separate sheet of paper.

Answering the

1. Responses will vary.
2. He did not like his eye.
3. He smothered the man with his mattress.

Critical Thinking

4. Possible responses: I think it was the clock or the narrator's heart. He was very nervous so his heart was probably beating quickly and loudly. He may have imagined the noise altogether.
5. Possible response: The story describes a murder and drags out the details (making it suspenseful). It also has a madman and other eerie elements.
6. Possible response: It is a good title because a heart-beat gives the man away, forcing him to tell his tale.

After You Read

The Tell-Tale Heart

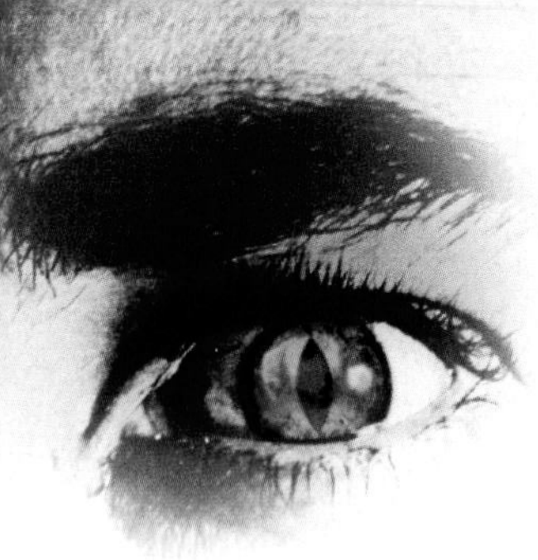

Answering the BIG Question

1. What parts of this story, if any, did you enjoy? Why?
2. **Recall** Why did the narrat ill the old man?
   TIP Right There The answer is found in the story.
3. **Summarize** Sum up how the narrator killed the old man.
   TIP Right There The answer is found in the story.

Critical Thinking

4. **Infer** What is making the "ticking" noise at the end of the story?
   TIP Author and Me You will find clues in the text, but you must also use the information in your head.
5. **Classify** Use evidence from the story to explain why it is called a thriller.
   TIP Think and Search The answer is in the text, but the details are not in one place.
6. **Evaluate** Do you think "The Tell-Tale Heart" is a good title for the story? Explain, using details from the story to support your opinion.
   TIP Author and Me You will find clues in the text, but you must also use the information in your head.

Write About Your Reading

Law Brief Imagine that the narrator is going to trial for the murder of the old man. With a small group of classmates, discuss whether you think the narrator should be held responsible for his actions:

- Is he innocent because he is not in his right mind and therefore unable to tell right from wrong?
- Or is he guilty because he is as perfectly sane as he insists?
- Build a case either for or against the narrator. Use specific evidence from the story to support your opinions.
- Then write a paragraph defending the narrator or sentencing him. Give convincing reasons for your defense or condemnation.

Indiana English/Language Arts Academic Standards
(pp. 52–53)

8.3 Comprehension and Analysis of Literary Text Respond to grade-level-appropriate literature…identifying story elements…**8.3.8** Contrast points of view… **8.5.4** Write persuasive compositions… **8.1.3** Verify the meaning of a word in its context…through the use of…example… **8.6 English Language Conventions**

For a complete description of the standards, see p. IN 11.

Write About Your Reading

Possible responses:

1) This man is guilty and should stand trial. He planned the murder and worked at it for several days. He possessed enough sense to dispose of the body in an attempt to hide evidence. He has admitted committing the crime and might kill again if set free.
2) This man is clearly insane. Who else would describe things the way that he does? He speaks frantically, imagines noises, and hops from one emotion to the next in a matter of seconds. He actually thought an eye was going to attack him.

Skills Review

Key Reading Skill: Setting a Purpose for Reading

7. Review your purposes for reading this story. Did you get what you wanted out of reading it? Explain your thoughts.

Key Literary Element: Point of View in Fiction

8. How would the story change if it were told in the first-person point of view by one of the police officers?

Vocabulary Check

Fill in the blanks with the correct vocabulary word.

stifled stimulates audacity hypocritical

9. Jogging ______ your heart and helps it grow stronger.

10. Monique had the ______ to talk back to the teacher.

11. Mona is so ______; she insists that I be on time, but she's always late.

12. I found my cat when I heard a ______ meow coming from inside the coat closet.

English Language Coach Write these sentences on a separate sheet of paper. Circle the examples in each sentence that help you figure out the meaning of the underlined word.

13. The thief was guilty of <u>dissimulation</u> when he pretended to be the old woman's friend and when he told her he was putting her retirement checks in the bank.

14. She took several <u>precautions</u> before leaving for vacation, including asking the police to check on her house, installing new locks on the front and back doors, and putting timers on several lamps.

15. Academic Vocabulary If your teacher asks you to choose a reading **strategy,** what is he or she asking you to do?

Grammar Link: Common and Proper Nouns

Nouns are words that name people, places, things, feelings, or ideas.

A **common noun** refers to *any* person, place, thing, or idea. A common noun is not capitalized unless it begins a sentence.

- Three students visited a museum.

  (The nouns *students* and *museum* do not refer to specific students or a specific museum. They are common nouns and are therefore not capitalized.)

A **proper noun** refers to a *specific* person, place, thing, or idea. Proper nouns are always capitalized.

- Ed, Alicia, and Al visited Harris Museum.

  (The nouns *Ed, Alicia,* and *Al* refer to specific students; the noun *Harris Museum* refers to a specific museum. The nouns are capitalized because they are proper nouns.)

Grammar Practice

There are five capitalization mistakes in the following paragraph. Copy the paragraph on a separate sheet of paper and fix the mistakes.

When my family and I visited Chicago last year, we went to Lincoln Park zoo. It is next to a beautiful park near lake Michigan. I hadn't been to a Zoo in years, so I had forgotten how much fun it can be to watch the animals. I especially liked watching the Monkeys play. I also enjoyed eating lunch at one of the outdoor Cafés.

Writing Application Check the nouns in the brief you wrote. Fix any capitalization errors.

Web Activities For eFlashcards, Selection Quick Checks, and other Web activities, go to www.glencoe.com.

Grammar Link: Common and Proper Nouns

Grammar Practice

When my family and I visited Chicago last year, we went to Lincoln Park Zoo. It is next to a beautiful park near Lake Michigan. I hadn't been to a zoo in years, so I had forgotten how much fun it can be to watch the animals. I especially liked watching the monkeys play. I also enjoyed eating lunch at one of the outdoor cafés.

Skills Review

Key Reading Skill: Setting a Purpose for Reading

7. Responses will vary.

Key Literary Element: Point of View in Fiction

8. Possible response: We would get to hear about the killer's behavior from a sane and reliable narrator.

Vocabulary Check

9. stimulates

10. audacity

11. hypocritical

12. stifled

English Language Coach

13. when he pretended to be the old woman's friend and when he told her he was putting her retirement checks in the bank

14. asking the police to check on her house, installing new locks on the front and back doors, and putting timers on several lamps

Academic Vocabulary

15. Possible response: The teacher is asking you to read with a purpose and follow a method for understanding what you read.

Close

Ask students to summarize what they learned from reading "The Tell-Tale Heart" to answer the Big Question.

Indiana English/Language Arts Academic Standards

SE: 8.1.3, 8.3, 8.3.8, 8.5.4, 8.6

Teach

More About the Author

Kathleen Krull lives in San Diego, California, and works at home as a writer. She has a background in music and even taught piano lessons when she was a teenager. Krull enjoys writing biographies because she likes finding out about other people. She likes to include as many details as she can in her biographies and tries not to gloss over the bad stuff. She says, "I want to write biographies for kids living in the real world. I know readers have to survive all kinds of hurts and traumas; my way of helping is to dramatize how people in the past have done it."

V Vocabulary

Synonyms and Antonyms Have students read the vocabulary words and think of a synonym and antonym for each word. *(**oppressed:** synonym: held down, antonym: freed; **premature:** synonym: early, antonym: late; **compassion:** synonym: love, antonym: hatred)* OL

Before You Read

from *The Book of Rock Stars*

Meet the Author

Kathleen Krull has been interested in reading for most of her life. In fact, when she was only fifteen, she worked at a library. She has said that she spent so much time reading she didn't get her work done and got fired! Krull has written series of books about presidents, artists, and women. See page R3 of the Author Files in the back of the book for more on Kathleen Krull.

Author Search For more about Kathleen Krull, go to www.glencoe.com.

Indiana English/Language Arts Academic Standards
(pp. 54–59)

8.1.3 Verify the meaning of a word in its context…through the use of…comparison or contrast. **8.2 Comprehension and Analysis (Focus on Informational Text)** Develop [reading] strategies…identifying and analyzing…perspective…

For a complete description of the standards, see p. IN 11.

Vocabulary Preview

V

oppressed (uh PRESD) *adj.* held down; held back; kept from making progress; form of the verb *oppress* **(p. 56)** *The oppressed people of Jamaica had little power to change their situation and improve their lives.*

premature (pree muh CHUR) *adj.* early; before the right time **(p. 57)** *At the age of thirty-six, he was too young to die; his death was premature.*

compassion (kum PASH un) *n.* the feeling of sorrow or pity caused by someone else's misfortunes; sympathy **(p. 59)** *Carlos Santana has compassion for the needy and helps charitable organizations.*

Partner Work Make flash cards. Write each of the vocabulary words on a separate card or sheet of paper. On the other side of the card or paper, write the meaning of the word. Use the flash cards to test a classmate's knowledge of the definitions of each word.

English Language Coach

Context Clues: Contrast Sometimes a context clue can show you what a word does *not* mean. That can be just as helpful.
*I decided to give up being **desolate** all the time and be happy instead.*

The contrasting word "happy" tells you that desolate means "unhappy." The words are antonyms. But sometimes, the contrasting clue is a word or phrase that is not an exact antonym.
*I was tired of the same old places and faces; I wanted something **exotic**.*

The contrasting phrase "same old" tells you that **exotic** means new and different.

On Your Own The chart below contains one word from the selection you are about to read. It also contains a contrasting clue to help you figure out the word's definition. Copy the chart and complete it by filling in the word's definition.

Word	Contrasting Clue	Definition
rural	big city	

Additional Support

Author Search To expand students' appreciation of Kathleen Krull, have them access the Web site for additional information and resources.

Literature Focus Lesson

Biography Remind students that a biography is a story that tells what happened to a person but is written by someone else. Many biographies are written by people who never even met the subject. Many of them are even written after the subject dies. As such, there are many questions to consider when reading a biography. Read these questions to students and have them add some of their own: How did the author get this information? What are his or her sources? Why did the author choose to write about this person? Does the author want to make a point or does the author admire this person? OL

Skills Preview

Key Reading Skill: Setting a Purpose for Reading

The selection you are about to read consists of two short biographies of rock stars. In a biography an author tells someone else's life story. Think about the purposes that people might have for reading biographies.

Whole Class Discussion With your class, brainstorm a list of purposes for reading biographies.

Key Literary Element: Point of View in Nonfiction

L **Point of view** in nonfiction is the perspective from which a factual story is told. In the **first-person point of view,** an author refers to himself or herself as "I" or "me" and describes actual events that he or she took part in or observed. Autobiographies and memoirs are two kinds of nonfiction told in the first person.

In the **third-person point of view,** the author does not refer to himself or herself. He or she is a nameless voice describing events, facts, or ideas. Biographies and newspaper reports are two of the many kinds of nonfiction told in the third person.

To identify the point of view of a nonfiction selection, ask yourself the following question:

- *Does the author refer to himself or herself as "I" or "me" (first-person), or is the author a nameless voice (third-person)?*

Write to Learn In your Learner's notebook, write a few sentences about yourself in the first-person. Then rewrite the sentences in the third-person.

Interactive Literary Elements Handbook
To review or learn more about the literary elements, go to www.glencoe.com.

Get Ready to Read

Connect to the Reading

C What do you know about Bob Marley, reggae, Carlos Santana, and Latin-based rock? What would you like to know about these musicians and their music?

Write to Learn In your Learner's Notebook, write a list of questions you would like to ask these musicians.

Build Background

The following list of facts will help you understand the biographies you are about to read. Read the list carefully, and refer to it as you read.

- Jamaica is the third largest Caribbean island. It has a population of more than 2.7 million.
- The majority of Jamaicans are of African descent, but there are also small, well-established Indian, Chinese, Arab, and European communities.
- B. B. King plays the blues. John Lee Hooker and T-Bone Walker also were blues musicians.
- Woodstock was a rock concert held in New York state in 1969. The concert lasted three days and featured 31 bands. Around 500,000 people gathered.

Set Purposes for Reading

BIG Question Read to find out about the lives of two famous musicians.

Set Your Own Purpose What else would you like to learn from the selection to help you answer the Big Question? Write your own purpose on the *The Book of Rock Stars* page of Foldable 1.

Keep Moving

Use these skills as you read from *The Book of Rock Stars*.

Teach

L Literary Element

Point of View in Nonfiction **Ask:** Can you think of an example when an author might use first-person when writing a biography? *(Possible response: An author who knew or spent time with the subject of the biography might want to share stories of things they did together, in which case the author would say, "I" or "me.")* OL

C Critical Thinking

Application **Say:** Think about some musicians whose music you enjoy. What questions would you ask them if you were writing their biographies? *(Responses will vary.)* OL

Interactive Literary Elements Handbook Have students access the Web site to improve their understanding of point of view.

Reading in the Real World

Career Tell students that music has always been important to people. Have students choose different musicians to research and report on to the class. Encourage them to bring in a recording of music by the musician they researched to play for the class. OL

Have students take it a step further by researching artists who influenced that musician and learn about those influences. Tell students to make a compare/contrast chart between the musician and one of his or her influences. AL

Indiana English/Language Arts Academic Standards
SE: 8.1.3, 8.2
TWE: *Literature Focus Lesson* 8.3, *Reading in the Real World* 8.7.10

Teach

R Reading Skill

Setting a Purpose for Reading **Say:** Look at the birth and death dates next to Bob Marley's name. How old was he when he died? *(thirty-six)* BL **Say:** That's a young age to die. Based on this information, what might be one purpose for reading his biography? *(Possible responses: to see why he died so young, to learn about what he accomplished in such a short life)* OL

Readability Scores
Dale-Chall: 7.6
DRP: 64
Lexile: 1130

from The Book of Rock Stars

by Kathleen Krull

Bob Marley (b. 1945–d. 1981) R

Few rock stars have national holidays in their honor. On the beautiful but poor Caribbean island of Jamaica, February 6 is National Bob Marley Day. 1

He was born into **rural** poverty and left home at fourteen to pursue music in the big city of Kingston. 2 Three years later, he recorded his first single, called "Judge Not." With a catchy Jamaican rock beat—reggae—his fierce songs gave voice to the day-to-day struggles of **oppressed** people.

He teamed up with childhood friends and fellow singers to form a dynamic new reggae band, the Wailers. Members included Bunny Livingstone and Peter Tosh, as well as Rita Anderson, whom he later married. Marley was the hypnotic[1] lead singer, and audiences couldn't stop dancing. The music was infused[2] with devout spirituality, social commentary, and

1. ***Hypnotic*** means "in a way that holds the complete attention of someone."
2. Here, ***infused*** means "filled with."

Vocabulary

oppressed (uh PRESD) *adj.* held down; held back; kept from making progress

Practice the Skills

1 Key Reading Skill

Setting a Purpose for Reading Here's a possible purpose for reading. You can read to find out why there is a national holiday named after Bob Marley.

2 English Language Coach

Context Clues: Contrast What does **rural** mean? Find the contrasting phrase in the sentence.

Additional Support

English Language Coach

Build Background Students may find it helpful to see pictures of rural Jamaica as it looked in the 1950s when Marley was a young boy. Encourage them to go to the library and look for archived photos from that time period. (They can also use the Internet but should be careful to look for historical photos.) Alternately, have them look up pictures of Bob Marley, his family, and his surroundings. Have them look up pictures of his band members and of Kingston. AS Have students use the Internet to find the lyrics to the song "Judge Not" and write about why the song may have been so popular during that time. AL encouragement to rebel. Plus it was pure fun. With tunes like "Stir It Up" and "No Woman, No Cry," Bob Marley and the Wailers could do no wrong in Jamaica. 3

When their song "I Shot the Sheriff" became a hit for Eric Clapton, reggae went global. As the first Third World[3] superstar, Marley introduced Jamaican music to the world and laid the groundwork for much to follow.

Pulsing hits flowed—"Jamming," "Waiting in Vain," "One Love/People Get Ready," and "Is This Love?" They were wildly popular, not just in Jamaica, but also Africa, Great Britain, and Scandinavia. Yet the band made so little in royalties[4] that Marley once worked in a factory for a year to support his family.

His last haircut was in 1968. After that his hair stayed in dreadlocks, as part of the Rastafari faith, the Jamaican religion that was the keystone of his life.

As famous a rock star as Marley was outside Jamaica, those at home saw him as almost godlike. On political and religious issues, ordinary Jamaicans hung on his every word. He became such a national hero that some in power even took him as a threat. In 1976 he was wounded in an assassination attempt and had to leave Jamaica for his safety. C

Five years later, while jogging in New York's Central Park, he collapsed. Doctors discovered that he had advanced cancer. He released his final album, *Uprising*, and died at age thirty-six. Fans went into shock at the **premature** loss of the freedom-fighting entertainer. R

3. The ***Third World*** consists of (relatively) poor, developing countries.

4. Many artists and writers are paid ***royalties.*** These are fees paid to the artist each time his or her work is sold or used.

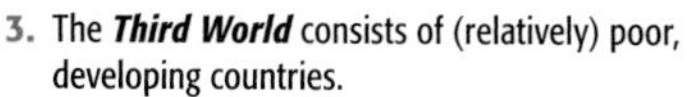

premature (pree muh CHUR) *adj.* early; before the right time

Bob Marley wrote songs about politics, religion, and people's need to be free. He also introduced reggae music to the rest of the world.

Practice the Skills

3 Key Literary Element

Point of View The author is not writing her own life story; she is writing the story of Bob Marley's life. What is the point of view: first-person or third-person?

Teach

C Critical Thinking

Analysis Ask: What other forms of expression—besides music—are good ways to make a political statement? *(Possible responses: art, writing)* **Ask:** What way do you think is the best way? *(Responses will vary.)* **OL**

R Reading Skill

Review Connecting Ask: Can you think of a time someone famous died and it affected you this powerfully? *(Responses will vary.)* **AS** Based on your experiences, describe how Marley's fans must have felt. *(Responses will vary.)* **OL**

Differentiated Instruction

Compare and Contrast Divide students into small groups and have them choose three or four genres of music, including reggae, to compare. Groups should begin by brainstorming characteristics of each of the genres they chose. Instruct the groups to make charts listing the characteristics. Then have them write one or two paragraphs telling how the genres are alike and how they are different. **OL** Have students discuss which genre lends itself best to making political statements. **AL**

Indiana English/Language Arts Academic Standards
SE: 8.1.3, 8.2
TWE: *English Language Coach* 8.4.4, *Differentiated Instruction* 8.5.7

Teach

C Critical Thinking

Analysis Say: Carlos Santana's father tried to teach him to play the violin, but Carlos chose to play the guitar. Although he chose a different instrument, do you think Carlos was influenced by his father? Explain. *(Possible response: Yes, he probably learned to enjoy music from his father.)* **OL**

Viewing the Photo

Ask: If you could write your own caption for this photograph of Carlos Santana, what would it say? *(Responses will vary.)* **AS**

R Reading Skill

Setting a Purpose for Reading Ask: What other purposes do you have for reading about Carlos Santana? *(Responses will vary.)* **AS**

READING WORKSHOP 2

In 1999 Carlos Santana released the album *Supernatural* and made one of the greatest comebacks in rock history.

Carlos Santana (b. 1947)

Carlos Santana came from a Mexican village so tiny it had no running water or electricity. **4** His father, a traditional mariachi violinist, tried to teach him violin, but Carlos preferred guitar, especially the style of American greats B. B. King, John Lee Hooker, and T-Bone Walker. By age eleven, when his family moved to the border town of Tijuana, people were paying to see him playing in nightclubs. **C** **R**

Later, in San Francisco, he worked full-time as a restaurant dishwasher—playing guitar as a street musician during his off time. With some help from Jerry Garcia,[5] he formed a band. He was shy and not really the leader type, but the local musicians' union required paperwork that designated a leader. So he wrote down his name, Santana, which became the band's name.

5. ***Jerry Garcia*** was the leader of the Grateful Dead, an influential rock band.

Practice the Skills

4 Key Reading Skill

Setting a Purpose for Reading Though Carlos Santana was poor as a child, he later became a very successful musician. A possible purpose for reading about him is to see how he managed to become a success.

Additional Support

Differentiated Instruction

History Tell students that Woodstock was an outdoor concert held in 1969 on a farm in Bethel, New York. At that time, 450,000 people was the largest crowd to attend a music concert. In addition, the concert lasted for three days. Help students see that Woodstock still stands as a symbol of the 1960s and early 1970s—years that were marked by the civil rights movement, Vietnam War protests, and an overall idealism and political activism among young adults. Hold a class discussion on the role of music today as it relates to politics and social activism. **AL**

At age twenty-two, when he played for half a million people at the Woodstock festival, the group didn't even have an album yet. They knocked the audience out with "Soul Sacrifice," written just for the event. It was a whole new, Latin-based rock sound featuring an Afro-Cuban beat, mixing congas and timbales with Carlos's spicy lead guitar. Soon after they appeared on *The Ed Sullivan Show,* and surged onto radio with "Oye Como Va," "Evil Ways," "Jingo," "Black Magic Woman," "Everybody's Everything," and "No One to Depend On."

Visual Vocabulary
Congas are tall, single-headed drums played with the hands. They originated in Africa.

In 1973, influenced by Hinduism, he changed his name to Devadip (meaning "the light of the lamp of God") Carlos Santana. He released several albums with specifically spiritual themes, and always his music had humanitarian messages about peace, joy, acceptance, **compassion,** and understanding. Later he converted to Christianity.

The group earned devotion and steady sales with its soulful, heartfelt concerts, but had no radio hits after 1982. Musicians came and went, Carlos always zooming in the lead.

Then, in 1999, Santana made what is considered the greatest comeback in rock history. The album *Supernatural* sold more than ten million—by far the group's best-selling release—and won eight Grammy Awards, including best rock album of the year. C

Famous all over again, Santana continues to support a wide range of causes, including United Farm Workers, Amnesty International, Doctors Without Borders, Rainforest Action Network, and the American Indian College Fund. 5 ❍

Vocabulary

compassion (kum PASH un) *n.* the feeling of sorrow or pity caused by someone else's misfortunes; sympathy

Practice the Skills

5 **BIG Question**

What are the most interesting pieces of information you learned from these biographies? If you haven't already listened to Bob Marley and Carlos Santana's music, are you interested now? Why or why not? Write your answer on *The Book of Rock Stars* page of Foldable 1. Your response will help you complete the Unit Challenge later. BQ

Reading in the Real World

Citizenship Santana has been very successful as a musician. He has also done a great deal to help people all over the globe. Tell students to choose one of the organizations that he supports from the list at the end of the article. Instruct students to make a poster encouraging other people to get involved with this organization. Have students use the Internet to learn more about the organization so they can include specific information on their posters. OL

Teach

C Critical Thinking

Analysis Say: Some other famous musicians who played on Santana's album *Supernatural* are Dave Matthews, Lauryn Hill, Rob Thomas, and Cee-Lo. Has anyone ever listened to them? What can you share about them, and what might they have in common with Carlos Santana? *(Responses will vary.)* OL

BQ BIG Question

Ask: Which of these two musicians did you most enjoy reading about? What did you get from reading his biography? *(Responses will vary.)* OL

Assess

Use the CheckPoint questions provided on Presentation Plus! to check for comprehension of the selection. These questions can be used with interactive response keypads for immediate student feedback.

Indiana English/Language Arts Academic Standards
SE: 8.2
TWE: *Reading in the Real World* 8.4.4

Assess

Resources for page 60

- Selection Quick Check, p. 4
- Selection and Unit Assessment, p. 5
- ExamView Assessment Suite
- Interactive Tutor: Self-Assessment

Students can respond to the *After You Read* items in their Learner's Notebooks or on a separate sheet of paper.

Answering the

1. Responses will vary.
2. He was wounded when someone tried to kill him, so he left Jamaica to live where he would be safer.
3. He liked the guitar.
4. The local musicians' union said the band had to name a leader. Santana wrote in his name and that became the name of the band.

Critical Thinking

5. Possible response: He wrote songs about people dealing with religious or spiritual issues, such as worshipping God, life after death, love, and so on.
6. Possible responses: Fame can bring problems when people think they own you because you are a public figure. Everyone knows who you are and you have no privacy. This also means you become an easy target.

After You Read

from *The Book of Rock Stars*

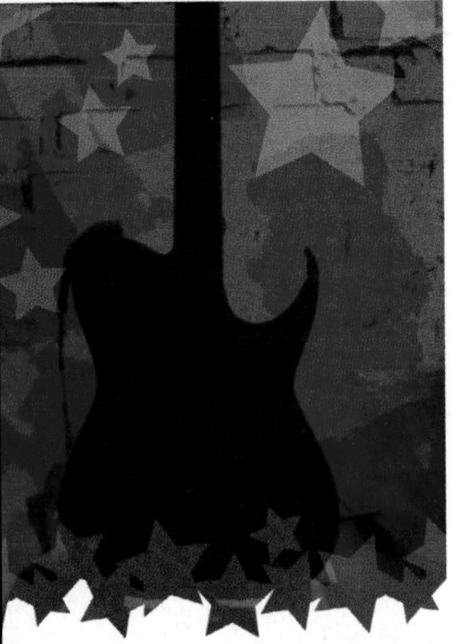

Answering the BIG Question

1. Did you enjoy reading about Bob Marley and Carlos Santana? Why or why not?
2. **Recall** Why did Bob Marley leave Jamaica?
   TIP Right There The answer is in the biography.
3. **Recall** What instrument did Carlos Santana like to play as a child?
   TIP Right There The answer is in the biography.
4. **Summarize** Sum up the story of how the band Santana got its name.
   TIP Right There The answer is in the biography.

Critical Thinking

5. **Interpret** The author says on page 59 that Santana made albums with "spiritual themes." What do you think that phrase means?
   TIP Author and Me There are clues in the biography, but you must also use the ideas in your head.
6. **Infer** Think about the reason that Bob Marley left Jamaica. What does this reason show about the downside of fame?
   TIP Author and Me You will find clues in the text, but you must also use the information in your head.

Talk About Your Reading

Small Group Comparison and Contrast In a small group, compare and contrast the childhoods of Bob Marley and Carlos Santana. Use the following questions to guide your discussion:

- In what ways were Marley's and Santana's childhoods alike?
- In what ways were their childhoods different?
- What, if anything, do you think their childhoods had to do with the music they played? Explain.
- What did you learn from comparing and contrasting?

Indiana English/Language Arts Academic Standards (pp. 60–61)

8.3 Comprehension and Analysis of Literary Text Respond to grade-level-appropriate literature... **8.7.11** Deliver oral responses to [text]... **8.2 Comprehension and Analysis (Focus on Informational Text)** Develop [reading] strategies... identifying and analyzing... perspective... **8.1.3** Verify the meaning of a word in its context... through the use of... comparison or contrast. **8.6 English Language Conventions**

For a complete description of the standards, see p. IN 11.

Talk About Your Reading

Sample responses:

Both of these men were poor as children. They also began playing music professionally when they were quite young—Marley at fourteen and Santana at eleven. They grew up in different parts of the world, with different racial and cultural experiences. The struggles they had growing up made them play the kind of music they did, music about hard times and surviving. Their music shows the kind of life they each lived, including the things they experienced. I learned that comparing and contrasting helps me to think about differences and similarities in a direct way.

Skills Review

Key Reading Skill: Setting a Purpose for Reading

7. What purpose did you set for reading biographies? How did it help you as you read?

Key Literary Element: Point of View in Nonfiction

8. Imagine that the life story of Carlos Santana that you just read was written in the first-person by Santana himself. In what ways do you think the story might change? Why?

Vocabulary Check

For each vocabulary word, write a sentence using the word. Leave a blank space where the word belongs. Trade your sentences with a partner. Fill in the blanks in each other's sentences.

9. oppressed
10. premature
11. compassion

English Language Coach Copy the following sentences on a separate sheet of paper. Circle the contrasting word or phrase in each sentence that helps define the underlined word. Then define the word.

12. The hot sun was so enervating that I jumped into the pool to get some energy.
13. The twins are so different: whereas Jack is volatile, Jake is laid back and even-tempered.

Grammar Link: Noun Plurals

A **singular noun** refers to one person, place, or thing. A **plural noun** refers to more than one person, place, or thing. To form the plural of most nouns, add an *-s* ending. There are four exceptions to the rule:

A. To form the plural of a noun that ends in a consonant + *y*, change the *y* to *i* and add *-es*.

Singular: one city **Plural:** two cities

B. To form the plural of most nouns that end in a consonant + *o*, add *-es*.

Singular: a hero **Plural:** many heroes

C. To form the plural of a noun that ends in *-s, -sh, -ch, -x,* or *-z,* add an *-es* ending.

Singular: that brush **Plural:** those brushes

D. **Irregular nouns** are nouns that do not form the plural with an *-s* ending. If you are not sure how to spell the plural of an irregular noun, check a dictionary.

Singular: one man **Plural:** several men

Grammar Practice

Each of the following sentences has a plural noun. Some of the plural nouns are correctly spelled. Others are not. Copy the sentences on another sheet of paper and fix any misspelled plurals.

14. The two attorneys formed a partnership.
15. Radioes are on sale this weekend.
16. Several deer were hit by cars last summer.
17. Please store the box's in the basement.
18. Why did the women complain to the manager?

Web Activities For eFlashcards, Selection Quick Checks, and other Web activities, go to www.glencoe.com.

Skills Review

Key Reading Skill: Setting a Purpose for Reading

7. Possible responses: to learn, to be entertained.

Key Literary Element: Point of View in Nonfiction

8. Possible response: We might learn more details (both positive and negative) about his childhood and his life. This narrator wrote with a tone as if he or she idolized Santana—we don't learn about his flaws.

Vocabulary Check

9.–11. Responses will vary.

English Language Coach

12. **circle:** energy; stealing one's strength
13. **circle:** laid back and even-tempered; quick to anger

Close

Ask students what they got out of reading about Bob Marley and Carlos Santana.

Literature Online

Web Activities Have students access the Web site for interactive activities that will help them assess their understanding of the selection.

Grammar Link: Noun Plurals

Grammar Practice

14. no misspelled plurals
15. Radios are on sale this weekend.
16. no misspelled plurals
17. Please store the boxes in the basement.
18. no misspelled plurals

Indiana English/Language Arts Academic Standards
SE: 8.1.3, 8.2, 8.3, 8.6, 8.7.11

Activating Prior Knowledge

Teaching Students to Activate Prior Knowledge

Why Is It Important?

- Teaching students to activate prior knowledge helps them use their experience and knowledge to better understand a selection.
- Research has proven that activating prior knowledge increases comprehension.
- Students who activate prior knowledge are better readers.

How to Help Students Get It

- Emphasize that reading is an interactive process: the author and the reader both participate.
- Reading is interactive when you take your experiences and knowledge and combine them with the words in the text to produce meaning.
- Emphasizing that your students have unique experiences and knowledge helps them feel empowered when reading selections.
- Regardless of how foreign the subject may seem to students, helping them activate prior knowledge on even minor points in the selection can give them the confidence and interest they need to gain meaning from a selection.

Reading to Answer the Big Question

The March of the Mill Children by Judith Pinkerton Josephson
In 1903 100,000 mill workers were on strike in Pennsylvania. At the time, despite the state's law prohibiting children under the age of thirteen from working, many of those mill workers were little children. Mother Jones took up the cause of the laboring youngsters, saying that the luxuries of the wealthy in America were purchased with the youth and bodies of American children. Mother Jones led 300 people, children who worked in the mills and their parents, on a march to President Roosevelt's seaside home on Long Island. Although she was unable to attain an audience with the President, Mother Jones made an impression on the national media. Because she loved children, she took action on their behalf.

Filling Out the Application by Cindy Pervola and Debby Hobgood
Step-by-step instructions for young job-seekers on how to fill out a job application that makes the best impression possible. It encourages students to tell the truth, while emphasizing the positive points. Included also are an explanation of questions asked on job applications and a sample job availability worksheet.

Exploring Careers by the US Department of Labor
This excerpt from the Occupational Outlook Handbook published by the Department of Labor gives information on three interesting career paths, including job duties, expected salary, and the training and education needed to enter the field. The careers listed are TV, video, motion picture camera operators and editors; firefighters; and EMTs and paramedics.

Workshop Resources

Pacing (Days) Standard	Block	Lesson	Student Materials	Teacher Resources
1	1/2	Key Skill Lesson: Activating Prior Knowledge	Key Reading Skills Practice, p. 22 English Language Coach Review, p. 42	Bellringer Options Transparencies – Daily Language Practice 6 Read Aloud, Think Aloud Transparencies – Key Reading Skills 1 – Read Aloud, Think Aloud, 1–11 Presentation Plus!
1	1	"The March of the Mill Children"	Glencoe Online Unit Vocabulary Review, p. 40 Academic Vocabulary Review, p. 44 English Language Coach Active Reading Graphic Organizer, p. 24 Literary Analysis, p. 23 StudentWorks Plus™ Online Student Edition Literature Classics Selection and Unit Assessments, p. 5	Literary and Text Analysis Transparencies 56 Puzzlemaker Skill Level Up!™ A Language Arts Game BookLink 3 Assessment by Learning Objective (Diagnostic and Formative) Interactive Tutor: Self-Assessment TeacherWorks Plus™
1		"Filling Out the Application" and "Exploring Careers"	Glencoe Online Unit Vocabulary Review, p. 40 Academic Vocabulary Review, p. 44 English Language Coach Active Reading Graphic Organizer, p. 26 StudentWorks Plus™ Online Student Edition Literature Classics Selection and Unit Assessments , p. 6	Literary and Text Analysis Transparencies 53 Puzzlemaker Skill Level Up!™ A Language Arts Game BookLink 3 Assessment by Learning Objective (Diagnostic and Formative) Interactive Tutor: Self-Assessment TeacherWorks Plus™

Keys for Unit Resource

- Blackline Master
- Workbook
- Supplemental Text
- CD-ROM
- DVD
- Transparency
- Web-based
- Fast File

Level Appropriate Code

AS = Activities for all students
AL = Activities for students working above grade level
OL = Activities for students working at grade level
BL = Activities for students working below grade level
EL = Activities for English language learners

Focus

BELLRINGER Options

Daily Language Practice Transparency 6
Focus Activity Say: Think about childhood. What is special about being a child? List five positive things about being a child. *(Responses will vary.)* OL

Teach

R Reading Skill

Activating Prior Knowledge
Say: We use the skill of activating prior knowledge in many different ways. What are some ways you use this skill when dealing with your friends? *(Possible response: I know what days my friends are busy with other activities, so I don't try to get together with them on those days.)* OL

V Vocabulary

Academic Vocabulary Have a volunteer read the definition of *prior* at the bottom of page 62. **Ask:** What is prior experience? Prior plans? *(earlier experience, earlier plans)* OL

READING WORKSHOP 3

Skills Focus

You will practice using the following skills when you read these selections:

- "The March of the Mill Children," p. 66
- "Filling Out the Application," p. 78
- "Exploring Careers," p. 86

Reading

- Activating prior knowledge

Literature

- Identifying tone
- Identifying and using text features

Vocabulary

- Using word categories and direct definitions to find word meanings
- Academic Vocabulary: *prior*

Writing/Grammar

- Identifying and using reflexive and intensive pronouns
- Identifying and using indefinite pronouns

Indiana English/Language Arts Academic Standards
(pp. 62–63)

8.2 Comprehension and Analysis (Focus on Informational Text) Develop [reading] strategies...

For a complete description of the standards, see p. IN 11.

Skill Lesson

Activating Prior Knowledge

Learn It!

R **What Is It? Activating prior knowledge** means using what you already know. When you read, you bring your own life experiences and knowledge with you. You use this prior knowledge to help you better understand what you read.

- To *activate* something is to make it active, to get it going so it can be useful.
- Your prior *knowledge* is what you already know about a topic.
- *Activating prior knowledge* is using what you already know about a topic to help you understand new ideas.

Analyzing Cartoons
Jeremy is shocked to find how high his phone bill is. How does he activate prior knowledge to understand why the bill is so high?

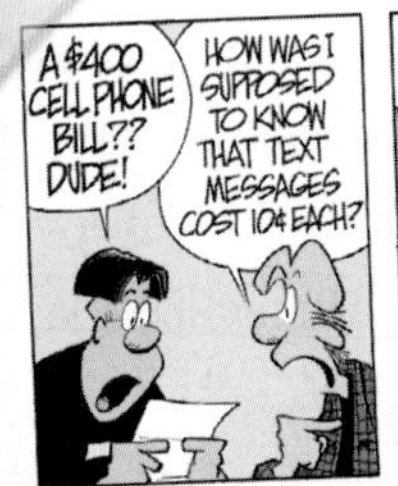

V **Academic Vocabulary**

prior (PRY ur) *adj.* earlier; coming before

Additional Support

Reading in the Real World

Career Tell students that the comic strip on this page was created by cartoonists Jim Borgman and Jerry Scott. Tell interested students to research careers in either the illustration or writing of comic books, graphic novels, or comic strips. Some questions they could start with are: What companies publish graphic novels? What kind of education do you need to be a comic book writer or illustrator? Are there contests for art or stories in this field? AS

Why Is It Important? Activating prior knowledge helps you understand the meanings of certain words and ideas. For example, if you've used a computer before, you might understand why a character who is having trouble moving the *cursor* with her *mouse* is frustrated. R

Study Central Visit www.glencoe.com and click on Study Central to review activating prior knowledge.

How Do I Do It? Before you read, look at the title and quickly look for headlines and pictures. Ask yourself, *What do I already know about this topic?* As you read, look for new information and details that you can connect with your prior knowledge. Here is how a student activated her prior knowledge to understand part of the article "On Top of the World."

> On May 29, 1953, Edmund Hillary and his mountain-climbing companion, Tenzing Norgay . . . became the first to look down from the dizzying height of the world's tallest mountain, Mount Everest, while standing upon its snowy top.

I saw a show about Mount Everest on a cable TV science channel. The main thing I remember is how bad the weather can get near the top of Everest. It's really cold and windy. Snowstorms can strike with little warning.

Practice It!

Make a three-column chart in your Learner's Notebook. Label the columns **Topics, Prior Knowledge,** and **New Information.** List the topics below in the **Topics** column. Fill in the second column with one or two things you know about each topic. Fill in the third column as you read.

- protest marches
- children in the workforce in the United States
- filling out a job application
- jobs in TV, firefighting, and emergency medicine

Use It!

As you read, keep your chart beside you. When you find information to relate to your prior knowledge, note it on your chart.

English Language Coach

Synonyms Have students make a synonym chart for any words that are new or unfamiliar to them. The chart here shows some examples of words they might write and the synonyms for those words. EL BL

New Word	Synonyms
topic	subject, idea, main point
information	facts, details
companion	friend, teammate

Teach

Study Central Have students access the Web site to review activating prior knowledge and to complete a related activity.

R Reading Skill

Activating Prior Knowledge

Say: Look at the *Why Is It Important?* section. Why is activating prior knowledge important? *(It helps you understand the meanings of words and ideas.)* OL

Resources for page 63

Use Key Reading Skills Transparency 1 in *Read Aloud, Think Aloud* to help students practice activating prior knowledge.

Indiana English/Language Arts Academic Standards
SE: 8.2
TWE: *English Language Coach* 8.1

Teach

More About the Author

Judith Pinkerton Josephson cohosts a radio show called *Grammar Patrol* about grammar. She and her cohost, Edith Fine, answer questions about proper English usage and grammar. Together these two women have also written ten grammar books for children ages ten and up. The books teach grammar rules through popular cartoons.

V Vocabulary

Using Vocabulary Words

Say: To help cement new vocabulary words in your memory, use the words right away. Write a paragraph that includes each of the vocabulary words for this selection. The paragraph does not have to make perfect sense, but each word should be used correctly. *(Responses will vary.)* AS

Before You Read

The March of the Mill Children

Meet the Author

Judith Pinkerton Josephson was inspired by her children to write poetry. This led to other writing for magazines, newspapers, and books. Josephson has taught writing to children and adults. She has coauthored grammar books, and she appears on radio shows to answer grammar questions.

Author Search For more about Judith Pinkerton Josephson, go to www.glencoe.com.

Indiana English/Language Arts Academic Standards (pp. 64–73)

8.1 Word Recognition, Fluency, and Vocabulary Development Use…context clues…to determine the meaning of words…**8.2 Comprehension and Analysis (Focus on Informational Text)** Develop [reading] strategies…**8.3.6** Identify significant literary devices…which define a writer's style…

For a complete description of the standards, see p. IN 11.

Vocabulary Preview

V

treacherous (TRECH ur us) *adj.* dangerous; not reliable, not trustworthy **(p. 66)** *That treacherous piece of machinery is unsafe for small children to use.*

mutilated (MYOO tih lay tid) *adj.* damaged in a way that cannot be repaired **(p. 68)** *The copy machine jammed and the paper was mutilated.*

dormitory (DOR mih tor ee) *n.* a building with rooms for people to sleep in **(p. 70)** *The workers lived together in a dormitory that was located next to the factory.*

Small Group Work With two other students, make up a short story using the vocabulary words. Have each person contribute a sentence to the story. Use a vocabulary word in every sentence.

English Language Coach

Context Clues: Category Sometimes you can get an idea of what an unfamiliar word means by thinking about the category of items it belongs to. A **category** is a group of people, places, or things that have something in common. In the sentence below, the word *feverfew* may be unfamiliar to you. See if you can figure out what it refers to by thinking about the other, more familiar items it is grouped with. They are all in the same category.

- The prairie had Indian grass, clover, ragweed, goldenrod, and feverfew.

Feverfew is grouped with other plants. You can tell it is a plant, even though you don't know what kind of plant.

On Your Own Use category context clues to get an idea of what the underlined word in each sentence means. Then define the underlined word as well as you can.

- In the room were a bed, a dresser, night tables, and an armoire.
- The new zoo is home to gorillas, chimpanzees, orangutans, and gibbons.
- The X-ray showed that my wisdom teeth and molars are okay, but there is a cavity in each of the lower right bicuspids.
- Though they may be unfashionable, oxfords are more comfortable than high-heeled boots, ankle-strap heels, or loafers.

Additional Support

Differentiated Instruction

Categorizing Context Clues Guide students as they create word walls for the words in the *On Your Own* section. First have them write each category context clue and the underlined word on separate index cards. *(The first sentence would have cards saying "bed," "dresser," "night tables," and "armoire.")* Then direct students to write a category title on another index card. *(For the first sentence, the card could say "bedroom furniture.")* Once students have done this for all the sentences, tell them to tape each of their cards in a column on the wall under the appropriate category heading for that card. AS

Skills Preview

Key Reading Skill: Activating Prior Knowledge

"The March of the Mill Children" is about child workers at the turn of the 20th century. Recall what you know about this topic.

Whole Class Discussion List facts and ideas you know about child labor, workers' rights, or the labor movement. Briefly discuss each item you list.

Key Literary Element: Tone

"That's a beautiful coat you're wearing" can be a compliment or a cutting remark. It all depends on your tone of voice when you say it. If you mean what you say, your positive attitude will show in your tone of voice, and you'll sound enthusiastic. But if you actually hate the coat and want the person to know it, your negative attitude will show in your sarcastic tone of voice. Just as tone of voice reveals a speaker's attitude, so the tone of a piece of writing reveals the author's attitude toward his or her subject. To tell the tone of a piece of writing, look at the words the author uses. Are they filled with admiration? Sarcasm? Anger? Laughter? "Listen" when you read to "hear" the author's tone. Ask yourself this question:

- *What attitude is reflected in the words the author chose to use?*

L

Partner Talk Describe the tone of each item below.

- Robin Hood was a true hero. He helped countless people by getting money, food, and other items from the rich and giving them to the needy.
- Robin Hood was nothing but a thief. He stole the treasures of good, upright citizens and gave the items to lazy good-for-nothings.

Interactive Literary Elements Handbook
To review or learn more about the literary elements, go to www.glencoe.com.

Get Ready to Read

Connect to the Reading

What do you think is the best part of being a kid? As you read, think about what the children described in the selection missed out on because they had to work.

Whole Class Discussion Brainstorm with your class a list of reasons children should or should not work. How old should someone be to get a job?

Build Background

The selection you are about to read describes the work of Mary Harris Jones, better known as Mother Jones. Born in Ireland in 1837, Jones and her family immigrated to Canada when she was a girl. When she was in her twenties, Jones moved to the United States, married, and began raising a family. Two tragedies changed the course of her life. In 1867 her husband and four children died in a yellow fever epidemic, and in 1871 she lost her home and all her possessions in the Great Chicago Fire. Forced to support herself, she began working and came into contact with the labor movement. She spent most of the rest of her long life fighting for workers' rights.

Set Purposes for Reading

BIG Question Read "The March of the Mill Children" to learn what life was like for children who worked in mills and marched with Mother Jones in the early 1900s.

Set Your Own Purpose What else would you like to learn from the selection to help you answer the Big Question? Write your own purpose on "The March of the Mill Children" page of Foldable 1.

Keep Moving

Use these skills as you read the following selection.

Reading in the Real World

Citizenship Mother Jones was a political activist. She tried to make the general public aware of a problem, and then she worked to get the government to make changes to fix that problem. Have students make a list of past and present political activists. Lists might include Martin Luther King Jr. and Coretta Scott King, Ghandi, and Bono. Then have students write and give a short speech telling how important activists are in a free society, even if the activists' ideas are not popular. OL

Teach

L Literary Element

Tone While students cannot hear the writer's voice, they can use the text to understand the writer's tone. Help students see this in practice by having partners write this sentence in their notes: "That is a beautiful coat you are wearing." Then assign partners different tones, such as serious, sarcastic, bitter, or timid. Tell the partners to write one or more than one sentence that will reveal the tone. Give students an opportunity to read their sentences to the class. OL

Interactive Literary Elements Handbook Have students access the Web site to improve their understanding of tone.

Indiana English/Language Arts Academic Standards
SE: 8.1, 8.2, 8.3.6
TWE: *Differentiated Instruction* 8.1, *Reading in the Real World* 8.7

Teach

R Reading Skill

Activating Prior Knowledge
Ask: Did you activate any other prior knowledge to understand the beginning of this article? Explain. *(Possible response: I thought about what I knew about the textile industry and I know that there were a lot of large machines in factories.)* AL

C Critical Thinking

Evaluation Say: The people on strike were willing to give up some of their pay in order to work fewer hours. These workers were very poor. Do you think it was a good idea for them to work less for less pay? Why do you think they were willing to give up some of their wages to work fewer hours? *(Possible response: Yes, it was a good idea to work less for less pay because they were so tired from the long hours of work that they couldn't even do anything with the small amount of extra money.)* OL

Readability Scores
Dale-Chall: 6.2
DRP: 58
Lexile: 940

The March of the Mill Children

by Judith Pinkerton Josephson

"I love children," Mother Jones once told a reporter. In countless shacks and shanties across the country, she had tied the shoes of children, wiped their noses, hugged them when they cried, scrambled to find food for them, fought for their rights. By the turn of the century, almost two million children under the age of sixteen worked in mills, factories, and mines. Images of the child workers Mother Jones had seen stayed with her—the torn, bleeding fingers of the breaker boys, the mill children living on coffee and stale bread. 1

In June 1903, Mother Jones went to Philadelphia, Pennsylvania—the heart of a vast textile industry.[1] About one hundred thousand workers from six hundred different mills were on strike[2] there. The strikers wanted their workweek cut from sixty to fifty-five hours, even if it meant lower wages. About a sixth of the strikers were children under sixteen. R C

Nationwide, eighty thousand children worked in the textile industry. In the South, Mother Jones had seen how dangerous their jobs were. Barefooted little girls and boys reached their tiny hands into the **treacherous** machinery to repair snapped

1. The ***textile industry*** includes all the businesses that make and use yarn and fabrics.
2. When workers go on ***strike,*** they stop working to protest unfair working conditions.

Vocabulary

treacherous (TRECH ur us) *adj.* dangerous; not reliable; not trustworthy

Practice the Skills

1 Key Reading Skill

Activating Prior Knowledge How did your class discussion of child labor help prepare you for the introduction to this selection?

Additional Support

Literature Focus Lesson

Tone Students may have difficulty determining the tone of this selection. To help students identify tone, read the first paragraph aloud to them expressively. Write the word *sympathetic* on one side of the board. On the other side of the board, write the word *causes.* Ask students to tell you which words show that Mother Jones was sympathetic. List the answers students give under "sympathetic." Explain that this is the overall tone of the paragraph. Then ask the students to identify the causes of Mother Jones's sympathy, and list their answers under "causes." OL threads or crawled underneath the machinery to oil it. At textile union headquarters, Mother Jones met more of these mill children. Their bodies were bone-thin, with hollow chests. Their shoulders were rounded from long hours spent hunched over the workbenches. Even worse, she saw "some with their hands off, some with the thumb missing, some with their fingers off at the knuckles"—victims of mill accidents. **2**

Pennsylvania, like many other states, had laws that said children under thirteen could not work. But parents often lied about a child's age. Poor families either put their children to work in the mills or starved. Mill owners looked the other way, because child labor was cheap. **C**

Mother Jones asked various newspaper publishers why they didn't write about child labor in Pennsylvania. The publishers told her they couldn't, since owners of the mills also owned stock in their newspapers.[3] "Well, I've got stock in these little children," she said, "and I'll arrange a little publicity." **L**

Mother Jones, now seventy-three, gathered a large group of mill children and their parents. She led them on a one-mile march from Philadelphia's Independence Square to its courthouse lawn. Mother Jones and a few children climbed up on a platform in front of a huge crowd. She held one boy's arm up high so the crowd could see

Practice the Skills

2 **Key Literary Element**

Tone The author says the children are "bone-thin, with hollow chests." These words show the sympathy and concern she feels for them. The tone might be called compassionate and concerned.

Analyzing the Photo Children work in the spinning room of a South Carolina cotton mill in 1903. What does this picture reveal about working conditions there?

3. People who own ***stock*** in a company own part of the company. Because the mill owners were part owners of the newspapers, they could tell the papers what to print.

Teach

C Critical Thinking

Comprehension **Say:** Explain how and why both the parents and the mill owners broke the law. *(Possible responses: Parents sent their children to work in the mills because they were so poor that if they didn't have the money the children made, their families would starve. The mill owners also broke the laws by hiring child workers. They hired children because they didn't have to pay them as much as they would have to pay adults.)* **OL**

L Literary Element

Tone **Ask:** What is Mother Jones's tone when she tells the newspapers that she has "stock in these little children"? *(Possible responses: anger, outrage, disgust, determination)* **OL**

Differentiated Instruction

Mapping the March Have students work in groups to study a map of Philadelphia, looking for the streets and landmarks from Independence Square to the courthouse. **BL** Challenge students to try to figure out which route Mother Jones took. One person in the group can make a sketch or a drawing or give step-by-step directions showing which streets he or she thinks Mother Jones took. Other students can research the different landmarks on the route, with each student choosing a different landmark and giving interesting information about that landmark. Caution students to write only about landmarks that would have been around in 1903, during Mother Jones's march. **AL**

Indiana English/Language Arts Academic Standards

SE: 8.2, 8.3.6

TWE: *Literature Focus Lesson* 8.3, *Differentiated Instruction* 8.4.4

Teach

EL Language Coach

Context Clues Help students see how context clues can help them figure out the meaning of metaphors. **Say:** The mansions were not literally built on broken bones and other body parts. What does Mother Jones mean by this? *(Possible response: The children had suffered with broken bones and other injuries when they worked in the factories. The children's work made the factory owners so wealthy they could buy mansions.)* OL

R Reading Skill

Activating Prior Knowledge Have students think about what they already know about the time period of the early 1900s and how difficult the trip might have been at that time. **Ask:** Why did the children walk the whole way? *(Possible response: It would have been very expensive to buy each child a train ticket or stagecoach ticket, and most people didn't own cars then.)* OL

his **mutilated** hand. "Philadelphia's mansions were built on the broken bones, the quivering hearts,[4] and drooping heads of these children," she said. She lifted another child in her arms so the crowd could see how thin he was. EL

Mother Jones looked directly at the city officials standing at the open windows across the street. "Some day the workers will take possession of your city hall, and when we do, no child will be sacrificed on the altar of profit."[5] Unmoved, the officials quickly closed their windows.

Local newspapers and some New York newspapers covered the event. How, Mother Jones wondered, could she draw national attention to the evils of child labor? Philadelphia's famous Liberty Bell, currently on a national tour and drawing huge crowds, gave her an idea. She and the textile union leaders would stage their own tour. They would march the mill children all the way to the president of the United States—Theodore Roosevelt. Mother Jones wanted the president to get Congress to pass a law that would take children out of the mills, mines, and factories, and put them in school. 3 R

When Mother Jones asked parents for permission to take their children with her, many hesitated. The march from Philadelphia to Sagamore Hill—the president's seaside mansion on Long Island near New York City—would cover 125 miles. It would be a difficult journey. But finally, the parents agreed. Many decided to come along on the march. Other striking men and women offered their help, too.

On July 7, 1903, nearly three hundred men, women, and children—followed by four wagons with supplies—began the long march. Newspapers carried daily reports of the march, calling the group "Mother Jones's Industrial Army," or "Mother Jones's Crusaders." The army was led by a fife-and-drum corps[6] of three children dressed in Revolutionary War uniforms. Mother Jones wore her familiar, lace-fringed black dress. The marchers sang and carried flags, banners, and L

4. When something is ***quivering,*** it is shaking. Mother Jones is describing the children as being really scared.

5. In a religious ***sacrifice,*** an animal is killed on an ***altar.*** Mother Jones is saying that she will not allow children to be harmed, or sacrificed, just so that people can make a lot of money.

6. This ***fife-and-drum corps*** was a small marching band that played drums and flutes.

Vocabulary

mutilated (MYOO tih lay tid) *adj.* damaged in a way that cannot be repaired

Practice the Skills

3 Key Reading Skill

Activating Prior Knowledge Have you seen other protest marches in movies or on TV? How does your knowledge of them help you understand the march described here?

Additional Support

Reading in the Real World

Citizenship Point out to students that there are many different ways to work for a cause one believes in. One can contribute money, one can make speeches, or one can act. Ask them to identify causes today (local, national, and/or international) that people contribute their time and/or money to. Have students look in magazines, in newspapers, or on the Internet for information about a cause that interests them. If possible, encourage students to work on a project that involves direct action on their part. AL

READING WORKSHOP 3

placards that read "We Want to Go to School!" "We Want Time to Play." "Prosperity Is Here, Where Is Ours?" "55 Hours or Nothing." "We Only Ask for Justice." "More School, Less Hospitals." 4

The temperature rose into the nineties. The roads were dusty, the children's shoes full of holes. Many of the young girls returned home. Some of the marchers walked only as far as the outskirts of Philadelphia. For the hundred or so marchers who remained, this trip was an adventure in spite of the heat. They bathed and swam in brooks and rivers. Each of them carried a knapsack with a knife, fork, tin cup, and plate inside. Mother Jones took a huge pot for cooking meals on the way. Mother Jones also took along costumes, makeup, and jewelry so the children could stop in towns along the route and put on plays about the struggles of textile workers. The fife-and-drum corps gave concerts and passed the hat.

Practice the Skills

L

4 **English Language Coach**

Context Clues: Category Look at the words that come before **placards.** What do you think a *placard* is?

Analyzing the Photo Mother Jones's march from Philadelphia to New York began on July 7, 1903. Can you draw any conclusions about Mother Jones from her posture and facial expression in this photo?

Teach

L Literary Element

Tone Say: People usually commit to such a march because they are fed up with being treated unjustly and they want to bring about change. How do their actions, banners, and placards express a tone of frustration and insistence? *(Possible responses: Their actions, banners, and placards show they seriously desire change. They are furious with how they have been treated and they will no longer sit back and take it.)* AL

Viewing the Photo

Remind students that this picture was taken during the summer. Instruct students to compare and contrast the way the people are dressed in the photo to the way people dress today. *(Students should note that the women all wore long dresses and more formal clothing. Both the men and women wore hats. Today women wear pants, shorts, or dresses and do not wear long dresses for everyday occasions. Today few people wear hats, and people generally dress more casually.)* OL

Differentiated Instruction

Creating Slogans Explain to students that slogans are brief phrases used to get people's attention. Slogans are often used in campaigns, advertising, and announcements. Ask students to reread the slogans written on the placards. As a class, discuss the meaning of each slogan and whether or not the students think the slogan is effective. BL Then invite students to create their own slogans for this cause. They may draw them on placards and post them throughout your classroom. OL

Indiana English/Language Arts Academic Standards

SE: 8.1, 8.2

TWE: *Differentiated Instruction* 8.3, 8.5

Teach

L Literary Element

Tone **Ask:** What seems to be the writer's attitude about Mother Jones, and how does this affect the tone of this section? *(Possible response: The writer seems to respect Mother Jones and wants to defend her actions. This makes the tone both supportive and defensive.)* OL

R Reading Skill

Review Connecting Have students think about different items they could carry that weigh about seventy-five pounds and consider how difficult it would be for a young child to carry such a heavy item. If possible, bring in a bathroom scale. Have students weigh books on the scale to see how many would equal that weight. AS

READING WORKSHOP 3

People listened and donated money. Farmers met the marchers with wagonloads of fruits, vegetables, and clothes. Railroad engineers stopped their trains and gave them free rides. Hotel owners served free meals.

On July 10, the marchers camped across the Delaware River from Trenton, New Jersey. They had traveled about forty miles in three days. At first, police told the group they couldn't enter the city. Trenton mill owners didn't want any trouble. But Mother Jones invited the policemen to stay for lunch. The children gathered around the cooking pot with their tin plates and cups. The policemen smiled, talked kindly to them, then allowed them to cross the bridge into Trenton. There Mother Jones spoke to a crowd of five thousand people. That night, the policemen's wives took the children into their homes, fed them, and packed them lunches for the next day's march.

By now, many of the children were growing weak. More returned home. Some adults on the march grumbled that Mother Jones just wanted people to notice *her.* They complained to reporters that Mother Jones often stayed in hotels while the marchers camped in hot, soggy tents filled with whining mosquitoes. **5** Sometimes Mother Jones did stay in hotels, because she went ahead of the marchers to arrange for lodging and food in upcoming towns and to get publicity for the march. **L**

As the remaining marchers pushed on to Princeton, New Jersey, a thunderstorm struck. Mother Jones and her army camped on the grounds of former President Grover Cleveland's estate. The Clevelands were away, and the caretaker let Mother Jones use the big, cool barn for a **dormitory.**

Mother Jones got permission from the mayor of Princeton to speak opposite the campus of Princeton University. Her topic: higher education. She spoke to a large crowd of professors, students, and residents. Pointing to one ten-year-old boy, James Ashworth, she said, "Here's a textbook on economics." The boy's body was stooped from carrying seventy-five-pound bundles of yarn. "He gets three dollars a week and his sister, who is fourteen, gets six dollars. They work in a carpet factory ten hours a day while the children **R**

Vocabulary

dormitory (DOR mih tor ee) *n.* a building with rooms for people to sleep in

Practice the Skills

5 Key Literary Element

Tone What is the tone of the first few sentences of this paragraph? Think about the following words, which appear in the paragraph. Then describe the tone.

- "grumbled"
- "complained"
- "hot, soggy tents"
- "whining mosquitoes"

Additional Support

Reading in the Real World

College In 1903 fewer people went to college than today. Still, even back then, people with a college education had much better job opportunities. It would have been impossible for children working in factories, mills, and mines to attend college because they hadn't even attended grammar or high school. Today a college education is even more critical in opening up job opportunities. Have students brainstorm a list of reasons to go to college, including job opportunities. OL of the rich are getting their higher education." Her piercing glance swept over the students in the crowd.

Mother Jones talked about children who could not read or write because they spent ten hours a day in Pennsylvania's silk mills. Those who hired these child workers used "the hands and feet of little children so they might buy automobiles for their wives and police dogs for their daughters to talk French to." She accused the mill owners of taking "babies almost from the cradle." **6**

The next night, the marchers slept on the banks of the Delaware River. In every town, Mother Jones drew on what she did best—speaking—to gather support for her cause. One reporter wrote, "Mother Jones makes other speakers sound like tin cans."

Battling heat, rain, and swarms of mosquitoes at night, the marchers arrived in Elizabeth. Socialist party members helped house and feed the weary adults and children. The next morning, two businessmen gave Mother Jones her first car ride. She was delighted with this new "contraption."[7]

On July 15, Mother Jones wrote a letter to President Roosevelt. She told him how these poor mill children lived, appealed to him as a father, and asked him to meet with her and the children. President Roosevelt did not answer Mother Jones's letter. Instead, he assigned secret service officers to watch her. They thought she might be a threat to the president. That made her furious.

On July 24, after more than two weeks on the road, the marchers reached New York City. By now, just twenty marchers remained. One of them was Eddie Dunphy, a child whose job was to sit on a high stool eleven hours a day handing thread to another worker. For this he was paid three dollars a week. Mother Jones talked about Eddie and about Gussie Rangnew, a child who packed stockings in a factory. She too worked eleven hours a day for pennies.

7. A ***contraption*** is a mechanical device.

Practice the Skills

6 Key Literary Element

Tone How would you describe Mother Jones's tone? Which words and phrases help you identify this tone?

Differentiated Instruction

Calculating Wages Students may not understand the value of the $3 a week salary that mill workers received. Tell students that the monthly rent for a two-room apartment ranged from $4 to $7 a month. Ask students to figure out what percentage of that $3 a week salary went to pay rent. Then have students learn the minimum wage for your state and calculate how much a worker earns in a forty-hour week. Have them look in the newspaper for the monthly rent for a studio or one-bedroom apartment. Guide students as they figure out what percentage of a minimum wage salary would pay the rent today. Ask students if they think today's minimum wage workers are any better off than the child workers of the past. **AL**

Teach

C Critical Thinking

Comprehension Ask: What does Mother Jones say are the mill owners' real reasons for hiring children? What do the children sacrifice to work in the factories and mills? *(Possible response: Factory and mill owners want to get rich. The children sacrifice their health and their chance to get an education.)* **OL**

EL Language Coach

Context Clues Ask: What context clues help you figure out the meaning of *banks* in this sentence? *(slept, Delaware River)* What are some other meanings for the word *bank*? *(Possible response: a building or an institution that holds people's money; a small container that people use to hold money; to place trust in someone or something)* **EL**

R Reading Skill

Activating Prior Knowledge

Ask: What do you know about the secret service from watching television shows or reading books? *(Possible response: They protect the president.)* Why do you think the secret service thought Mother Jones might hurt the president? *(Possible response: Sometimes people think that those who protest against government officials might harm or hurt them.)* **OL**

Indiana English/Language Arts Academic Standards

SE: 8.3.6

TWE: *Differentiated Instruction* 8.2

Teach

R Reading Skill

Review Connecting **Ask:** How does it feel to visit an amusement park or play in an ocean, a lake, or a swimming pool? How do you think these children felt about being able to play freely? How does this contrast with their work in the factories and mills? *(Possible responses: Amusement parks are a lot of fun, and I feel free and relaxed when I play in water. The children probably had an incredible sense of freedom and relaxation. They most likely never felt these feelings working in the factories or mills. They couldn't relax because they had to work.)* OL

Viewing the Photo

Ask: How does this picture help to show the dangers that children faced while working in factories? *(Possible response: The children are not even wearing shoes, and if they slip on the machinery, they could be seriously injured.)* **Ask:** How might someone think this picture shows factory life as "not that bad"? *(Possible response: The picture does not show a child who is hurt, and it does not show anyone mistreating the children who are working.)* OL

At one meeting, a crowd of thirty thousand gathered. "We are quietly marching toward the president's home," she told the people. "I believe he can do something for these children, although the press declares he cannot."

One man wanted the children to have some fun while they were in New York City. Frank Bostick owned the wild animal show at Coney Island, an amusement park and resort. He invited the mill children to spend a day at the park. The children swam in the ocean and played along the beach. R

When Frank Bostick's wild animal show ended that night, he let Mother Jones speak to the crowd that had attended. To add drama, she had some of the children crawl inside the empty cages. The smells of sawdust and animals hung in the air. But instead of lions and tigers, the cages held children. The children gripped the iron bars and solemnly stared out at the crowd while Mother Jones spoke. 7

Practice the Skills

7 Key Reading Skill

Activating Prior Knowledge
Have you ever seen an animal in a cage? How did it make you feel about the animal? Use your experience to understand why Mother Jones asked the children to crawl into the cages. What effect did she hope it would have on the crowd?

Analyzing the Photo Not tall enough to operate these looms from the ground, two young boys climb the machines to do their jobs. What do you notice about the boy in the foreground? Why might this job be particularly risky for him?

Additional Support

Reading Fluency

Reading Dialogue Mother Jones's dialogue in this story can help students practice reading fluency. Have students find the dialogue on each page. Ask them to read the dialogue to themselves and to determine the tone Mother Jones uses when she speaks. Then have students read the passage in the same tone Mother Jones probably used when she spoke the words. EL BL

"We want President Roosevelt to hear the wail of the children who never have a chance to go to school, but work eleven and twelve hours a day in the textile mills of Pennsylvania," she said, "who weave the carpets that he and you walk upon; and the lace curtains in your windows, and the clothes of the people." L1

She continued, "In Georgia where children work day and night in the cotton mills they have just passed a bill to protect songbirds. What about the little children from whom all song is gone?" After Mother Jones finished speaking, the crowd sat in stunned silence. In the distance, a lone lion roared.

The grueling walk had taken almost three weeks. Mother Jones had written the president twice with no answer. On July 29, she took three young boys to Sagamore Hill, where the president was staying. But the secret service stopped them at the mansion's gates. The president would not see them.

The group returned to New York City. Discouraged, Mother Jones reported her failure to the newspapers. Most of the marchers decided to return home. She stayed on briefly with the three children. Once more, she wrote President Roosevelt: "The child of today is the man or woman of tomorrow. . . . I have with me three children who have walked one hundred miles. . . . If you decide to see these children, I will bring them before you at any time you may set."

The president's secretary replied that the president felt that child labor was a problem for individual states to solve. "He is a brave guy when he wants to take a gun out and fight other grown people," said Mother Jones in disgust, "but when those children went to him, he could not see them." L2

In early August, Mother Jones finally took the last three children home. Soon after, the textile workers gave up and ended their strike. Adults and children went back to work, their working conditions unchanged.

Though she had not met with the president, Mother Jones had drawn the attention of the nation to the problem of child labor. She became even more of a national figure. Within a few years, Pennsylvania, New York, New Jersey, and other states did pass tougher child labor laws. The federal government finally passed a child labor law (part of the Fair Labor Standards Act) in 1938—thirty-five years after the march of the mill children. 8 ❍

Practice the Skills

8 BIG Question

BQ Was it interesting to learn about Mother Jones and the mill children? Explain. Write your answer on "The March of the Mill Children" page of Foldable 1. Your response will help you complete the Unit Challenge later.

Teach

L1 Literary Element

Tone Have several students read Mother Jones's lines from these paragraphs. **Ask:** What is Mother Jones's tone here? *(angry and determined)* OL

L2 Literary Element

Tone **Say:** Again, Mother Jones shows her anger. What statement does she make that has a sarcastic tone? *("He is a brave guy.")* OL

BQ BIG Question

Ask: What can you learn from reading about people like Mother Jones? *(Students may say that it is important to stand up for your beliefs even if it seems that no one else cares. Sometimes it takes a long time to bring about big changes, but someone has to start the process.)* OL

Assess

Use the CheckPoint questions provided on Presentation Plus! to check for comprehension of the selection. These questions can be used with interactive response keypads for immediate student feedback.

Differentiated Instruction

Critical Thinking Lead students in a discussion about the idea that Mother Jones alludes to when she talks about the law in Georgia that protects songbirds. The idea goes something like this: "We are more concerned about protecting nature than we are about protecting or caring for people." Have students give reasons why they agree or disagree with this thinking. OL Ask students why they think the state of Georgia passed a law protecting songbirds but did not pass a law protecting children from working in the mills. AL

Indiana English/Language Arts Academic Standards
SE: 8.2
TWE: *Reading Fluency* 8.7, *Differentiated Instruction* 8.7.2

READING WORKSHOP 3

Assess

Resources for page 74

- Selection Quick Check, p. 5
- Selection and Unit Assessment, p. 5
- ExamView Assessment Suite
- Interactive Tutor: Self-Assessment

Students can respond to the *After You Read* items in their Learner's Notebooks or on a separate sheet of paper.

Answering the BIG Question

1. Possible responses: (1) In the early 1900s, many children worked in the textile industry. (2) Children who worked in factories and mills were not able to get an education, and many suffered from poor health. (3) Mother Jones led a march to protest child labor.
2. Parents sometimes broke the law because their families needed the money.
3. Possible response: Mother Jones and an army of children marched to raise awareness. She then took her protestors to visit the president to ask him to change child labor laws.

Critical Thinking

4. Possible response: Today there are both child labor laws and laws making the workplace safe in the United States.
5. Responses will vary.
6. Responses will vary.

After You Read

The March of the Mill Children

Answering the BIG Question

1. What did you get out of reading "The March of the Mill Children"? List at least three facts about Mother Jones, the labor movement, or child labor that you learned by reading the selection.
2. **Recall** Child labor laws of Mother Jones's time banned children under the age of thirteen from working. Why did parents sometimes break these laws and allow their children to work?
   TIP **Right There** The answer is in the text.
3. **Summarize** In a sentence or two, sum up the actions that Mother Jones took to protest child labor.
   TIP **Think and Search** The answer is in the text but not in one place.

Critical Thinking

4. **Compare and Contrast** How are working conditions different today from what they were in Mother Jones's day?
   TIP **Author and Me** You will find the answer in the text, but you must also use your own knowledge.
5. **Evaluate** Do you think Mother Jones should have put children in animal cages? Explain your answer.
   TIP **On My Own** You must use your own knowledge and experience to answer the question.
6. **Evaluate** Do you think the march was a failure or a success? Why?
   TIP **Author and Me** You will find the answer in the text, but you must also use your own knowledge.

Write About Your Reading

Persuasive Poster Mother Jones believed in a cause; she wanted child labor to end. What cause do you believe in? Create a poster asking people to march to support a cause. Include an appropriate picture. Make sure your poster has the following information:

- the name of the cause
- the ways in which the march will help the cause
- the time and location to meet before the start of the march
- the route of the march–where the march will start and finish

Indiana English/Language Arts Academic Standards (pp. 74–75)

8.3 Comprehension and Analysis of Literary Text Respond to grade-level-appropriate literature... **8.5.7** Write for different purposes... **8.2 Comprehension and Analysis (Focus on Informational Text)** Develop [reading] strategies... **8.3.6** Identify significant literary devices...which define a writer's style... **8.1 Word Recognition, Fluency, and Vocabulary Development** Use...context clues...to determine the meaning of words... **8.6 English Language Conventions**

For a complete description of the standards, see p. IN 11.

Write About Your Reading

Student posters should name the cause and persuade people to join the march. To do this, students will need to explain the cause and its purpose. For example, they could write "Save the Park" and then tell which park needs to be saved and why. (Is it polluted? Is it about to be sold for development?) The posters should also make clear how to join the march, the starting time and place of the march, and the route of the march.

Skills Review

Key Reading Skill: Activating Prior Knowledge

7. What did you already know about child labor before you read the selection? How did this information help you understand the selection?

Key Literary Element: Tone

8. How would you describe the overall tone of "The March of the Mill Children"? Quote sentences from the selection to support your answer.

Vocabulary Check

Fill in the blank with the correct vocabulary word.

treacherous **mutilated** **dormitory**

9. Over one hundred students sleep in the ______ at my brother's college.

10. The sharp turn in the road is a ______ place to stop and change a tire.

11. The child's ______ hand horrified the crowd.

12. Academic Vocabulary What **prior** knowledge of child labor conditions made Mother Jones decide to go on her march?

13. English Language Coach Copy the following sentence. Circle the context clues you can use to infer the meaning of the underlined word.

There were outbreaks of the flu, yellow fever, chicken pox, and diphtheria.

Web Activities For eFlashcards, Selection Quick Checks, and other Web activities, go to www.glencoe.com.

Grammar Link: Reflexive and Intensive Pronouns

Reflexive and Intensive Pronouns	
Singular	**Plural**
myself, yourself, himself, herself, itself	ourselves, yourselves, themselves

Reflexive pronouns serve a special purpose. All pronouns refer back to another noun or pronoun, but we use reflexive pronouns when a pronoun that is *not possessive* refers back to the subject. Instead of "I pinched me," we say "I pinched myself." The pinched one *reflects* the pincher, so we use a reflexive pronoun.

- The machine stopped itself.
- Maria bought herself flowers.

Intensive pronouns have the same form as reflexive pronouns, but their purpose is to emphasize the subject.

- The principal herself introduced the speaker.

(The intensive pronoun *herself* emphasizes that it was not just anyone who did the introduction. It was the principal.)

Look Out! These are not standard words: *theirselves, hisself.* Never use them.

Grammar Practice

Copy each sentence. Circle the correct pronoun.

14. Jake (himself, hisself) sent (her, herself) the letter.

15. They gave us the gift (themselves, theirselves).

16. I (my, myself) would rather trade with (her, herself).

17. Juan and (I, myself) went to the movies.

18. I reminded my little brother to wash (himself, hisself) before going to bed.

19. I got (me, myself) a new pair of boots yesterday.

20. Sara told her guests to help (themselves, theirselves) to chips and soda.

Writing Application Look back at your Write About Your Reading activity. Check to make sure that you used all pronouns correctly.

Skills Review

Key Reading Skill: Activating Prior Knowledge

7. Responses will vary.

Key Literary Element: Tone

8. Possible responses: The overall tone conveys admiration for Mother Jones. Some sentences that show this are: "In countless shacks and shanties . . . she had . . . wiped their noses, hugged them . . . fought for their rights." "She became even more of a national figure."

Vocabulary Check

9. dormitory

10. treacherous

11. mutilated

Academic Vocabulary

12. Possible response: The children were being seriously injured, and even killed, on the job. She also knew that factories and mills were hiring children even though the law said they were too young to work.

English Language Coach

13. Students should circle this phrase: "outbreaks of the flu, yellow fever, chicken pox."

Close

Ask students to summarize how they would answer the Big Question after reading "The March of the Mill Children."

Grammar Link: Reflexive and Intensive Pronouns

Grammar Practice

14. himself, her

15. themselves

16. myself, her

17. I

18. himself

19. myself

20. themselves

LiteratureOnline

Web Activities Have students access the Web site for interactive activities that will help them assess their understanding of the selection.

Indiana English/Language Arts Academic Standards
SE: 8.1, 8.2, 8.3, 8.3.6, 8.5.7, 8.6

Teach

More About the Author

Debby Hobgood is a regional recruiter for a retail chain; she's responsible for recruitment of more than five hundred young people a year. The cowriter of the book, Cindy Pervola, has a master's degree in written communications. The two writers say they wrote *How to Get a Job If You're a Teenager* to give teen job-seekers a guide catered specifically to their needs.

EL Language Coach

Context Clues: Direct Definitions Point out to students that writers do not always boldface a word that they define in a text. After students complete *Partner Talk*, hold a class discussion about the different ways that authors mark words for definition and how to know if a word is being defined even if it isn't marked by a different typeface. EL OL

Before You Read

Filling Out the Application *and* Exploring Careers

Meet the Authors

Debby Hobgood and Cindy Pervola wrote "Filling Out the Application" as part of their book *How To Get A Job If You're A Teenager.* Hobgood has years of experience hiring young people for various companies. Pervola is a freelance writer and a counselor who works with teens.

The second selection, "Exploring Careers," comes from the *Young Person's Occupational Outlook Handbook,* published by JIST Works. It is based on information from the United States Department of Labor.

Author Search For more about Debby Hobgood and Cindy Pervola, go to www.glencoe.com.

Indiana English/Language Arts Academic Standards (pp. 76–89)

8.1.3 Verify the meaning of a word in its context... through the use of definition... **8.2 Comprehension and Analysis (Focus on Informational Text)** Develop [reading] strategies... **8.2.6** Evaluate the structural patterns of text.

For a complete description of the standards, see p. IN 11.

Vocabulary Preview

prone (prohn) *adj.* likely to act or be a certain way **(p. 78)** *John never studies vocabulary, so he is prone to making spelling errors.*

residences (REH zuh den suz) *n.* places where one lives **(p. 79)** *Junette lives with her mother during the week and her father on the weekend; she has two residences.*

Partner Work With a classmate, write a paragraph in which you correctly use the vocabulary words.

English Language Coach

Context Clues: Direct Definitions In articles that contain technical language that is specific to a particular field, authors sometimes define words for you directly. These words may be highlighted in boldface, or darker, type. Suppose, for example, you run across the following passage in a manual for Internet users. To signal that *bulletin board system* will be defined, the authors put it in boldface and then define it.

Internet Users' Handbook

A **bulletin board system** is an Internet function that allows users to carry on discussions, upload and download files, and post announcements without users being online at the same time.

EL **Partner Talk** With a classmate, quickly look over a chapter from a textbook you use for another class. Then answer the following questions:

- How many words are directly defined for you?
- Are these words in boldface type, or is a different type of signal used to indicate defined words?
- If a different type of signal is used, what is it?

Additional Support

Author Search To expand students' appreciation of Debby Hobgood and Cindy Pervola, have them access the Web site for more information and resources.

Differentiated Instruction

Mapping Minimum Wage The U.S. Department of Labor has a huge task—to keep workplaces safe, protect workers from discrimination, and regulate minimum wage. Have students visit the Department of Labor's Web site to find the answers to the following questions: About how many states have the same minimum wage as the federal rate? Which places have minimum wages that are less than the federal minimum? What is the minimum wage in our state? Then have students name three states that have minimum wages that are higher than the federal minimum. OL

Skills Preview

Key Reading Skill: Activating Prior Knowledge

Before you read the selections, look at each title. Think about what you already know about these topics:

- ways to look for a job
- guidelines for filling out a job application
- the work of television and movie camera operators and editors
- the work of firefighters, emergency medical technicians, and paramedics

Whole Class Discussion As a class, discuss what jobs you might like to hold in the future and how you would apply for them. Talk about what you'd like to learn from the selections.

Text Element: Text Features

Text features are visual clues that help readers find and understand information. Common text features include the following elements:

- titles and subheads
- graphic aids such as charts and graphs
- visual aids such as maps and photographs
- numbered or bulleted lists
- boldface type and italic type

E

The selections you are about to read contain many of these text features. As you read, look for text features and ask yourself, *How does this feature help me find or understand the information in this article?*

Partner Work With a classmate, look over the selection that begins on the next page. In your Learner's Notebook, list all the text features used in the selection.

Interactive Literary Elements Handbook
To review or learn more about the literary elements, go to www.glencoe.com.

Get Ready to Read

Connect to the Reading

What kinds of application forms have you filled out during the past few years? An application for a library card? An application to take part in a school activity? Something else? Think about the forms.

Whole Class Discussion Together as a class, list the kinds of application forms that you have had experience filling out. What parts of each application, if any, did you find tricky to complete? Why?

Build Background

R

- Most employers require a person interested in working for them to fill out a job application. This form gives the employer personal and work information about the job applicant. Employers use this information to decide whether to interview the applicant.
- Minimum wage is an hourly rate of pay that is set by the federal government. In 2005 the minimum wage was $5.15 per hour. All companies have to pay at least this amount to their employees.
- Many laws protect children in the workplace. The legal age to get a job in most states is between 14 and 16 years of age. Some states require a person who is under 18 years of age to get a work permit.

Set Purposes for Reading

BIG Question Read to learn how to fill out a job application correctly and to learn about various careers.

Set Your Own Purpose What else would you like to learn from the selection to help you answer the Big Question? Write your own purpose on the "Filling Out the Application" and "Exploring Careers" page of Foldable 1.

Keep Moving

Use these skills as you read "Filling Out the Application" and "Exploring Careers."

Teach

E Text Element

Text Features **Ask:** What are the different subheads on this page, and how do they help you as you read? *(Possible responses: Skills Preview, Get Ready to Read, Whole Class Discussion. Students may say the subheads help them as they read because they show them what to expect before they begin reading.)* OL

R Reading Skill

Activating Prior Knowledge
Ask: What do you already know about job applications, minimum wage, and work permits? *(Possible response: My brother had to get a work permit before he could start working at the grocery store.)* OL

Interactive Literary Elements Handbook Have students access the Web site to improve their understanding of text features.

Literature Focus Lesson

Text Features Review the different elements described under *Text Element: Text Features.* Have students discuss where they have encountered these elements. *(Possible responses: Titles and subheads are common in magazine articles; charts and graphs are found in many magazine articles; maps and photographs are found in newspaper articles.)* If possible, bring in several pamphlets and magazines for students to leaf through. Allow students to identify the text features they find and tell how they are helpful to them as readers. BL OL

Indiana English/Language Arts Academic Standards
SE: 8.1.3, 8.2, 8.2.6
TWE: *Differentiated Instruction* 8.4.4, *Literature Focus Lesson* 8.2

Teach

R Reading Skill

Activating Prior Knowledge
Ask: Have you ever filled out an application for anything, such as a library card? What were some of the questions you were asked? *(Responses will vary.)* BL

C Critical Thinking

Evaluation Ask: What do you think about the advice on this page? Which information is most helpful? Which information is not very helpful? Explain. *(Responses will vary.)* OL

V Vocabulary

Using Vocabulary Words
Say: Name two things you are prone to do. *(Responses will vary.)* EL BL **Say:** Now write two sentences about the two things you are prone to do. *(Responses will vary.)* OL

Readability Scores
Dale-Chall: 8.4
DRP: 58
Lexile: 930

READING WORKSHOP 3

INFORMATIONAL TEXT
REFERENCE BOOK
How to Get a Job If You're a Teenager

Filling Out the Application

by Cindy Pervola and Debby Hobgood

The two most important things to keep in mind when filling out an application are to be **honest** and to fill it out **completely.** An application is a legal document, and you could get fired for lying on your application. 1

Employers do not like to see any blank spaces on applications they receive. Every bit of information you can give them about yourself is extremely helpful, so do not leave any questions unanswered.

Complete the application in pen with black or blue ink and get a dictionary or use a spell checker to avoid misspelling. Print neatly and take your time. A sloppy application with words crossed out or misspelled turns off an employer right away, and your application will end up at the bottom of the stack. (You might even ask for two applications if you're **prone** to making mistakes.)

The following is a guide to filling out a typical application. Every application is a little different but all the basic information is the same.

Practice the Skills

1 **Key Reading Skill**

C R **Activating Prior Knowledge** How might remembering applications you've filled out be helpful in understanding this selection?

Vocabulary

prone (prohn) *adj.* likely to act or be a certain way V

Additional Support

Reading in the Real World

Career Bring in several different job applications from fast-food chains, grocery stores, retail stores, or camps. You most likely will be able to download some from the Internet. Have students evaluate the applications to see how they are similar and how they are different. Ask students to point out the things that are different or seem tricky on any of the applications. OL Have students share why they think certain questions are asked on some applications and not on others. AL

READING WORKSHOP 3

Date: Write today's date. **2**

Name: Your full name as it appears on your birth certificate or driver's license. If you go by a nickname, you can put your nickname in parenthesis. For example, you can write, Jacob (Jake) Williams, if you wish to be called Jake.

Social Security Number: If you do not have a social security number, you can find out how to apply for one by calling 1-800-772-1213. You can also look in the phone book for Social Security under "United States Government" for an office close to you. Do not apply for a job until you have a Social Security Number.

- **SSN:** abbreviation for Social Security Number.

Address: Employers want your current address. For example, if you are in college, use your college address. Use your permanent address (or home address) for your tax information. **C**

Telephone number: Write in your home telephone number. Be sure to include a second number if you have two **residences.** For instance, if your parents are divorced and you spend time with both of them, write in both telephone numbers.

- **applicant:** person applying for a job.

Under 18? The employer wants to know if you will need a work permit. If you are over 18, you don't need a work permit. If you're under 18, you might need one, but it varies with each state. A work permit tells the employer how many hours a day and a week you are allowed to work. Your high school will issue your work permit or tell you how to get one.

Are you a U.S. citizen? If you are not a U.S. citizen, the employer will need to see your alien card when you are hired.

Practice the Skills

2 Text Element

E **Text Features** Why do you think the authors put the word *date* in darker type?

Vocabulary

residences (REH zuh den suz) *n.* places where one lives

Teach

E Text Element

Text Features Ask: How do the different subheads help you read this page? *(Possible response: By glancing at the boldfaced type, you get a better idea of the kind of information that's required on an application.)* **OL**

C Critical Thinking

Evaluation Ask: Do you think employers have a right to demand the information requested on this page? *(Possible responses: Yes, your employer should know your name, phone number, and address so you can be contacted, or someone in your family can be contacted, in case of an emergency. The employer has a right to know if you are a U.S. citizen or have an alien card because it's against the law for someone who isn't a U.S. citizen to work in the United States without one.)* **OL**

Differentiated Instruction

Make a Poster Most students have a limited understanding of what social security really is. Explain that the Social Security Administration helps people if they become disabled and when they retire. It also provides benefits to the spouses and children of a worker who dies. Have students make a poster advertising these three benefits that the Social Security Administration provides. If students need more information for their posters, they can visit www.ssa.gov. For a kid-friendly page, they can visit www.ssa.gov/kids/kids.htm. **OL AL**

Indiana English/Language Arts Academic Standards
SE: 8.2, 8.2.6
TWE: *Reading in the Real World* 8.2, *Differentiated Instruction* 8.4.4

Teach

C1 Critical Thinking

Evaluation **Say:** Read what Maria wrote when asked about her desired salary. What do you think about her reasons for wanting more than the minimum wage? *(Responses will vary.)* **Ask:** What would your response have been to her if you were the hiring manager? *(Responses will vary.)* OL

C2 Critical Thinking

Comprehension **Ask:** In which section of the application would you write when you could begin working? *(on the "Date available to start work" line)* **Ask:** Where would you write that you could not work during the day on weekdays? *(in the "Availability" section)* BL **Ask:** If you know you cannot work on certain days, do you think it is wise to put that information on your application. Why or why not? *(Responses will vary.)* AS

READING WORKSHOP 3

- **alien:** a person who is from another country.

Position applied for (or desired): They want to know if you are applying for a sales position, stock person, waiter/waitress, bus person, dishwasher, etc. If you are interested in anything that they have open, it's okay to put "any position available."

Full time, part time, seasonal: They want to know how many hours a week you would prefer to work. Full-time is usually 30–40 hours a week and part time is usually 0–30 hours per week. This will vary with each company. Seasonal refers to temporary work for under 90 days during a certain time of year, usually summer and winter holiday. 3

Salary desired (or rate of pay requested): Put "minimum wage" if this is your first job. If you have worked before, put the rate of pay when you left your last job. If you feel you were underpaid at your last job or you need extra pay because you will need to use public transportation or have other expenses, add 5%–10% more per hour. Also, be sure you're ready to tell them why you feel you deserve that amount.

"I asked for $1 over minimum wage because I had to take the bus. I live about 45 minutes away but I needed full-time work for the summer and I said I could work any day of the week as long as the buses were running. They needed somebody with experience that could work any time, so they gave me more than minimum wage, but not as much as I requested."
—Maria, age 18. C1

Date available to start work: If you can start working tomorrow, write that date. If you're applying for a seasonal job, put in the date when you can start working. For example, if you are applying for a summer job but don't get out of school for three weeks, write in the date after the last day of school when you can actually begin working. Be specific. C2

Availability: Here, the employer wants to know specifically when you can work each day of the week. It doesn't necessarily mean that you will be scheduled to work at those

Practice the Skills

3 Key Reading Skill

Activating Prior Knowledge
Think of jobs that are seasonal. What jobs depend on the weather? What jobs last only through a holiday season, such as December?

Additional Support

English Language Coach

Context Clues Use the concept of *minimum wage* to help students better understand the words *minimum* and *maximum*. Draw a vertical line on the board. Write the word *minimum* at the bottom of the line and *maximum* at the top of the line. Have students practice using the words to describe different things. Here are some model questions: What is the maximum score you can get on a test? *(The maximum score you can usually get on a test is 100.)* You have to write at least three papers this year. What is the minimum number of papers you have to write? *(I have to write a minimum of three papers.)* EL times every day. It lets the employer know when or if you could work on those days, if needed.

It is very frustrating for employers when new-hires change their availability. One of the reasons you may have been hired was because you could work, say, on Saturdays. If after a month, you suddenly cannot work on Saturdays anymore, there's a good chance your employer will tell you they no longer need you. You may be back to square one, looking for a job again. So, be accurate as to which days and times you are available to work. 4

The following chart can help you determine your availability. For example, if Jake gets out of school at 2 p.m., has basketball practice every Monday and Wednesday afternoons from 3–5 p.m., has to babysit his little brother every Saturday, and has to be home no later than 10:30 p.m., his availability worksheet would look like this:

Jake's availability worksheet

	Sunday	Monday	Tuesday	Wednesday	Thursday	Friday	Saturday
7 am		School	School	School	School	School	X
8 am		"	"	"	"	"	X
9 am		"	"	"	"	"	X
10 am		"	"	"	"	"	X
11 am	Open	"	"	"	"	"	Not
12 pm	anytime	"	"	"	"	"	available
1 pm	all day	"	"	"	"	"	anytime
2 pm	7 am–10 pm	School ends	School ends	School ends	School ends	School ends	Saturdays
3 pm		Basketball		Basketball			X
4 pm		till		till			X
5 pm		5 pm		5 pm			X
6 pm							X
7 pm							X
8 pm							X
9 pm							
10 pm							

This worksheet makes it easy to see when Jake is available to work. C

Practice the Skills

4 Reviewing Skills

Connecting How do you feel when you try to make plans with someone who is always busy? Why do you think an employer needs to know your availability?

Reading in the Real World

Career First, create a list of job wanted ads and write them on the board. Each job should demand four hours per week. Then have students create their own worksheets to practice charting out their time. Have them include information such as wake-up time, school, after-school activities, chores, dinnertime, homework schedule, evening schedule, weekend activities, and bedtime. Then ask students to look over their schedule and choose a job that would best fit their schedule. Tell students that they may have to give up something in order to fit the job into their schedule. OL

Teach

E Text Element

Text Features Ask: What information does the chart on this page show? *(Jake's availability)*

C Critical Thinking

Application Say: Based on Jake's availability, make a work schedule for him. He can work a minimum of ten hours and a maximum of twenty hours. *(Student's responses should reflect the information in the worksheet.)* OL **Ask:** What type of job do you think Jake should apply for based on his schedule? *(Possible responses: a job at a fast-food restaurant or a retail store)* AL

Indiana English/Language Arts Academic Standards
SE: 8.2
TWE: *English Language Coach* 8.1

Teach

E Text Element

Text Features **Ask:** What sorts of text features appear on this page? *(a chart, boldfaced type, italic type)* OL

C1 Critical Thinking

Comprehension **Ask:** On which day or days could Jake begin work at 3? *(Sunday, Tuesday, Thursday, and Friday)* **Ask:** On which day or days is Jake unavailable to work? *(Saturday)* BL

R Reading Skill

Review Connecting Tell students to consider jobs they have done for neighbors or family members. If they accepted the responsibility of doing something and agreed upon a rate of pay, they performed a job. **Ask:** What are some jobs you have done that might not fall into the more formal category described here? *(Possible responses: I mow lawns for two of my neighbors every week. I babysit my cousins once a month.)* OL

READING WORKSHOP 3

On the application, Jake's availability would look like this (N/A means not available):

C1

Sunday	Monday	Tuesday	Wednesday	Thursday	Friday	Saturday
anytime	6–10	3–10	6–10	3–10	3–10	N/A

"I had to give up basketball to get my job at the computer store. I couldn't do it all. I think I made the right choice."
—Shane, age 17.

Work experience: List the jobs you have had in the past, beginning with your most recent position. Fill this out **completely.** You might need to make some phone calls or look in the phone book to get the information. You will need to know the date you started and ended those jobs, your supervisors' names, the addresses and telephone numbers of the places of business, your job title and duties, your starting and ending salary and the reason for leaving. 5 R

Good Idea Don't forget jobs like babysitting, yard work, odd jobs, volunteer work and community service in this section. All that counts as work experience, too.

Dos and Don'ts . . .

There may be a section titled 'reason for leaving.' Do **not** leave this section blank. Be honest about why you left your last job and always try to turn it into something positive.

- **terminated:** to be let go from or fired from a job.

Do write: "I was **terminated** because I was late too often, but I have learned from this experience and now I make sure I'm at work five minutes before I'm scheduled to work." 6
Don't write: "I got fired because I was late all the time."

Do write: "I want to work for a company that works as a team." C2
Don't write: "I didn't get along with my boss."

Do write: "I'm looking for a company with better opportunities."
Don't write: "I need more money."

Do write: "I needed more hours and they were only able to give me 10 hours a week."
Don't write: "I quit."

Practice the Skills

5 Key Reading Skill

Activating Prior Knowledge What kinds of jobs have you had or work have you done for others? What information about these experiences would you add to a job application?

6 English Language Coach

Context Clues: Direct Definition What does **terminated** mean? Look at the definition above the word to understand its meaning. Then define it.

Additional Support

Differentiated Instruction

Mapping Time Have students study Jake's availability worksheet and think about any other ways they could show different pieces of information from the worksheet. For example, they might make a circle graph showing how much of Jake's time is spent in school, how much is spent at basketball, how much is spent babysitting, and how much is free time. Have students create a graphic display of their own time schedule. OL

Do write: "I had a hard time getting to work but I am now applying to businesses within walking distance from my house."
Don't write: "Transportation problem."

Do write: "I had too many conflicts with school. I have learned to manage my time better and now I only work on weekends."
Don't write: "Left because of school."

Do write: "I had some family (or personal) problems that are now resolved."
Don't write: "Family problems." or "Personal problems." 7

May we contact your current employer? If you are working and you do not want your current employer to know you are looking for another job, put "no." But if the reason you are leaving is that you need more hours or better pay, you might want to let your current employer know that. Maybe they cannot give you any more hours or they won't be able to give you a raise for another six months. If that's the case, they'll probably understand your desire to look for another job and appreciate that you let them know you are leaving. It will give them time to look for a replacement for you.

"I was scared to tell my boss I was giving my two week notice. I thought he'd get mad. He didn't though. He asked if I was tired of taking orders and if I wanted to try making pizzas, instead. I got a raise, too."
—Michelle, age 17.

References: A reference is an adult, other than a relative, who knows you well and can say what kind of worker you are. A reference is not a friend, a relative or previous employer that

Practice the Skills

C2

7 Reviewing Skill

Connecting Have you ever had to quit a job? How could you explain your reason for quitting in a positive way?

Analyzing the Photo Why might the young man in this photograph make a good impression on a potential employer?

Teach

Viewing the Photo

Guide students in a discussion about the importance of first impressions and dressing well. **Ask:** What does dressing well for an interview tell the employer about you? *(Possible response: It says that I am neat and professional. It also shows that I respect the employer.)* **Ask:** Do you think you should dress well for an interview even if the job has no dress code? Why? *(Possible response: Yes, because it shows that I take the job seriously enough to dress for the interview.)* OL

C2 Critical Thinking

Evaluation Ask: If you were a hiring manager, which of the reasons for leaving would make you most likely to hire someone? Explain. *(Responses will vary.)* AL

Reading Fluency

Build Fluency One way to help students develop fluency is to pair them and have them read orally to one another. Have partners echo read this page aloud. One student reads the text under a subhead, and the partner reads the text under the next subhead. Model how to read the subheads, showing how you pause after the subhead before going on to the next sentence. BL

Indiana English/Language Arts Academic Standards
SE: 8.1.3, 8.2
TWE: *Reading Fluency* 8.7

Teach

C Critical Thinking

Analysis Ask: Why do you think it is important to list all of the schools you've attended as well as additional training you've received? *(Possible response: This shows the amount of knowledge you may have to use on a certain job.)* OL

Viewing the Photo

Ask: What else does the woman do besides make eye contact? *(She shakes hands with the person interviewing her.)* BL

E Text Element

Text Features Ask: What subhead could you put above the paragraph that begins "Have you ever been convicted of a crime?" *(Possible responses: Other Questions; Criminal Record)* OL

READING WORKSHOP 3

you have already listed on the application. It can be an adult friend of the family, a teacher, a coach, a neighbor or religious leader. You will need to call and ask if you can use them as a reference on your job application before you name them, though. A good reference can get you the job, so it is a good idea to be careful who you ask.

"I put a friend of my Mom's down as a reference, but I didn't let her know. When they called her, she told them she had never heard of me. She couldn't think of any adults she knew named Monica. She felt really bad after she realized they were asking about me. I won't do that again."
—Monica, age 18.

Analyzing the Photo The woman in this photograph smiles and makes eye contact with her interviewer. How do these actions show that she is confident?

Education: Be specific and fill this out completely. List your high school(s) and college(s) with their addresses and the number of years you have completed. Make sure you include any additional training, such as computer classes, first aid training, swimming instruction, foreign language, etc. C

Have you ever been convicted of a crime?[1] It might also say "Have you ever been convicted of a felony?" They are asking if you have been convicted of more serious crimes here, such as murder, assault, battery or rape. This does not refer to parking tickets or other minor traffic offenses. E

The open-ended question: This is a question that cannot be answered with a "yes" or "no." It is usually the last question on the application before your signature and will be worded in different ways: 8

- List any additional information you would like us to consider.
- Detail outstanding features of your last job.

8 Key Reading Skill

Activating Prior Knowledge
Think of an open-ended question you've answered recently for school. (Hint: Look at the *Big Questions* and the *responding* questions.) Can you think of any others, either from this book or another subject?

1. To be ***convicted*** of a crime is to be found guilty.

Additional Support

Reading in the Real World

Career Have students act out asking for a job application (or a few, if they want extra copies). Students should take turns role-playing the manager, a worker, and the person asking for the application. Remind students that they will most likely have to ask a worker for the manager before they can ask for an application. BL

- Why do you want to work for our company?
- What strengths would you bring to our company?
- Indicate any skills or experience which you believe reflect on your capability to perform . . .
- List any hobbies or special interests you have.
- Applicant comments.

They are all looking for the same thing. **They want to know something about you.** They want you to tell them something about yourself that will make them want to hire you. (They will also be looking to see if you can write a complete sentence.) Be truthful, enthusiastic, positive and brag about yourself. Tell them what you are and not what you aren't. Tell them what you have accomplished. Think of words that best describe you and use those, but be honest about yourself. Remember that the employer will probably check your references.

"When I applied at the grocery store, I wrote that I was a hard worker and dependable. I also wrote that I had handled money in my last job and dealt with customers. I think I got the job because I said I was dependable. People call in sick here all the time." —*Eric, age 16.* R

When You're Done

Once you have completed the application and signed it, you may then take it back to the employer, following the same dress code you did when you obtained the application. The employer might want to do the interview when you return the application, so be prepared. 9 ❍ BQ

Practice the Skills

9 **BIG Question**

What have you learned from this article that will help you apply for a job with confidence? Write your answer on the "Filling Out the Application" page of Foldable 1. Your response will help you complete the Unit Challenge later.

Teach

R Reading Skill

Review Setting a Purpose for Reading **Ask:** Why would you want to read about other people's experiences with filling out applications and getting jobs? *(Possible response: This can help me know what to expect, plan ahead, and then do well enough to get the job.)* OL

BQ BIG Question

Ask: How is reading important in getting a job? *(Possible response: It is important because you have to be able to read the application and fill it out.)* OL

Assess

CheckPoint

Use the CheckPoint questions provided on Presentation Plus! to check for comprehension of the selection. These questions can be used with interactive response keypads for immediate student feedback.

Differentiated Instruction

Description Guide the class as they brainstorm a list of characteristics that an employer would value. *(punctuality, dependability, team player, hard worker, leadership qualities, sincerity, willingness to go above and beyond the call of duty)* Divide the class into small groups. Challenge students to choose one characteristic from the list that describes themselves. Ask students to write about how they've displayed this characteristic in a real situation. For example, they may write about a time when they volunteered to stay after school to help a teacher set up for an event. This would be an example of willingness to go above and beyond the call of duty. OL

Indiana English/Language Arts Academic Standards
SE: 8.2
TWE: *Reading in the Real World* 8.7, *Differentiated Instruction* 8.5.7

Teach

R Reading Skill

Activating Prior Knowledge
Ask: What do you know about filmmaking? *(Responses will vary.)* **Ask:** How much film do you think is typically shot for a movie? *(hundreds of hours)* **Ask:** How do you think the film editors decide which scenes to include and which to cut? *(Possible response: They think about which scenes make the movie better and which ones are not good, or at least are not needed.)* OL

E Text Element

Titles and Subheads **Ask:** What are the three subheads on this page? *(On the Job, Subjects to Study, and Discover More)* BL

Readability Scores
Dale-Chall: 9.3
DRP: 62
Lexile: 1010

READING WORKSHOP 3

INFORMATIONAL TEXT HANDBOOK
Young Person's Occupational Outlook Handbook

Exploring Careers

Television, Video & Motion Picture Camera Operators & Editors

On the Job 10

Camera operators work behind the scenes on TV shows, documentaries,[1] motion pictures, and industrial films.

Visual Vocabulary
Scaffolding is a raised wooden frame on which workers sit or stand when doing things at heights above the ground.

They shoot the film you see on screen, sometimes from high up on scaffolding or flat on their bellies on the ground. They may work long, irregular hours in places all over the world. Film editors look at the hundreds of hours worth of film shot for a project and decide which scenes to include and which to cut. R

Subjects to Study

English, journalism, photography, art, creative writing, business, accounting 11

Discover More

Use a digital camcorder to make your own movie. These cameras let you load your movie onto a computer and then alter the images in countless ways. Give your leading lady green hair, drop in a few aliens, and you've got the ultimate in science fiction!

1. ***Documentaries*** are videos or films about real people and events.

Practice the Skills

10 Text Element
E **Text Features** How might the red subheads help you find information in the selection?

11 Key Reading Skill
Activating Prior Knowledge What do you already know about the subjects listed under "Subjects to Study"? How could studying these subjects help a camera operator do his or her job?

Additional Support

Reading in the Real World

Career Explain to students that camera operators must often learn to use complicated tools and equipment. Bring to class a camcorder and its instruction manual (or borrow one from your school's media technology center). Have student pairs practice reading the manual and following its instructions. Students should be able to turn the camcorder on and off and use its basic features.

Related Jobs

Artists and related workers, broadcast and sound engineering technicians and radio operators, designers, photographers C1

Something Extra

For a good view of what's possible in filmmaking today, rent the movie *Forrest Gump.* Among other tricks, the filmmakers spliced and altered vintage film to show their hero, Tom Hanks, shaking hands with John F. Kennedy, more than 30 years after Kennedy's death.

Education & Training

Short-term OJT to voc/tech[2] training C2

Earnings

$$$$

Job Outlook

Average increase[3]

Analyzing the Image A career in film editing requires technical and creative know-how. How might the men here use both types of skills?

Firefighting Occupations 12

On the Job

Firefighters protect people from the dangers of fires. They must stay physically fit and strong. At the scene of a fire, they rescue victims, perform emergency medical aid, and operate and maintain equipment. During their shifts, firefighters live at the fire station. Most work 50 hours a week or more. Forest firefighters may parachute into a fire area to put out fires and dig a fire line. Firefighting is one of the most dangerous jobs in the U.S. economy.

Subjects to Study

Physical science, chemistry, driver's education, physical education

12 Key Reading Skill

Activating Prior Knowledge
List some facts that you already know about firefighters.

2. ***OJT*** is short for on-the-job training; ***voc/tech,*** vocational/technical.
3. ***Average increase*** means that this field should grow at an average rate.

READING WORKSHOP 3

Teach

C1 Critical Thinking

Comprehension Ask: What are some jobs related to camera operators and editors? *(artists, broadcast and sound engineering technicians, radio operators, designers, photographers)* **Ask:** Why do you think these jobs are related? *(Possible response: These are other people who work in the television, video, and motion picture industries.)* OL

C2 Critical Thinking

Comprehension Ask: What does OJT mean? *(on-the-job training)* **Ask:** What does voc/tech stand for? *(vocational/technical)* **Ask:** What text feature helped you to answer these questions? *(the footnotes)* BL

Reading in the Real World

Career Have students create a photo montage for an occupation in which they are interested. Students can print out pictures from Web sites and copy pictures they find in different magazines or books. Direct students to try to find photos that show all the different things someone in their chosen occupation might do as part of his or her job. Have students write a caption for each photo. OL

Indiana English/Language Arts Academic Standards
SE: 8.2, 8.2.6
TWE: *Reading in the Real World* (p. 86) 8.2.8

Teach

E Text Element

Text Features Say: Identify the text features that appear on this page, and explain how they help you understand what you're reading. *(Possible responses: The occupation title is a subhead in large boldfaced type. Under the subheads are different categories that pertain to the job, such as education, earnings, and related jobs. These categories are in smaller boldfaced type. These subheadings break up the text so the information doesn't seem so overwhelming. There is also a photograph that helps me to visualize the danger firefighters must face. The footnotes explain new information.)* OL

C Critical Thinking

Analysis Say: Look at the dollar signs under the title "Earnings." Usually one dollar sign means a little money and five means a lot of money. Why do you think that firefighters are paid so well? *(Firefighting is a very dangerous job.)* **Ask:** Do you think the high pay is worth the risks? *(Responses will vary.)* OL

READING WORKSHOP 3

Discover More

Tour the fire station in your neighborhood or at your local airport. Ask the firefighters about their jobs, the training they receive, and the risks of the job.

Related Jobs

Emergency medical technicians and paramedics, police and detectives

Something Extra

Firefighters who battle wildfires are a special breed. During the hot, dry months of late summer, they travel from state to state, helping local firefighters battle forest fires. They may jump from airplanes into a fire zone to dig fire lines. If a fire travels too quickly and they get trapped, they drop to the ground and cover themselves with a special fireproofed tent. They wait until the fire has passed over them, get up, and keep on fighting the flames. 13

Education & Training

Voc/tech training

Earnings

$$$$–$$$$$

Job Outlook

Average increase

Firefighters may have to run—or jump!—into fires like this one. They risk their lives to help other people.

Practice the Skills

13 Reviewing Skills

Connecting When you think of firefighters, what images come to mind? Did reading this description of the job change how you think about firefighting as a career? Explain.

Emergency Medical Technicians & Paramedics

On the Job

Emergency medical technicians (EMTs) and paramedics drive ambulances and give emergency medical care. They determine a patient's medical condition at the scene, stabilize[4]

4. When an EMT ***stabilizes*** a patient, he or she makes sure that the patient is well enough to travel in an ambulance.

Additional Support

Differentiated Instruction

Research Have students do some research to learn how forest fires actually help nature. They can find out how forest fires are part of the natural cycle of forests and how quickly a forest floor begins to regrow after a fire. Challenge students to find out how government officials decide where and when to set forest fires in order to protect the areas where people live. AL the patient, then drive him or her to the hospital. They work outdoors in all kinds of weather, and the work can be very stressful. Some patients may become violent, and EMTs may be exposed to diseases. They work for fire departments, hospitals, and private ambulance services.

Subjects to Study

Driver's education, health, biology, chemistry, anatomy, English, foreign languages **C**

Discover More

Check with the Red Cross in your area to register for a first-aid or CPR course. You can learn how to save another person's life and be helpful in different kinds of emergencies.

Related Jobs

Air traffic controllers, firefighting occupations, physician assistants, police and detectives, registered nurses

Something Extra

What's a typical day like for an EMT? There is no such thing! Because EMTs respond to emergencies, their jobs are never the same from day to day. They might be the first on the scene of a car accident in the morning, revive a heart attack victim at lunch, and deliver a baby in a taxicab by dinner. **BQ** EMTs must be able to remain calm in any situation—because they never know what's around the next corner.

Education & Training

Voc/tech training

Earnings

$$$

Job Outlook

Above-average increase 14 ❍

Practice the Skills

14 **BIG Question**

What did you learn about careers that you didn't know before you read this article? Write your answer on the "Filling Out the Application" and "Exploring Careers" page of Foldable 1. Your response will help you complete the Unit Challenge later.

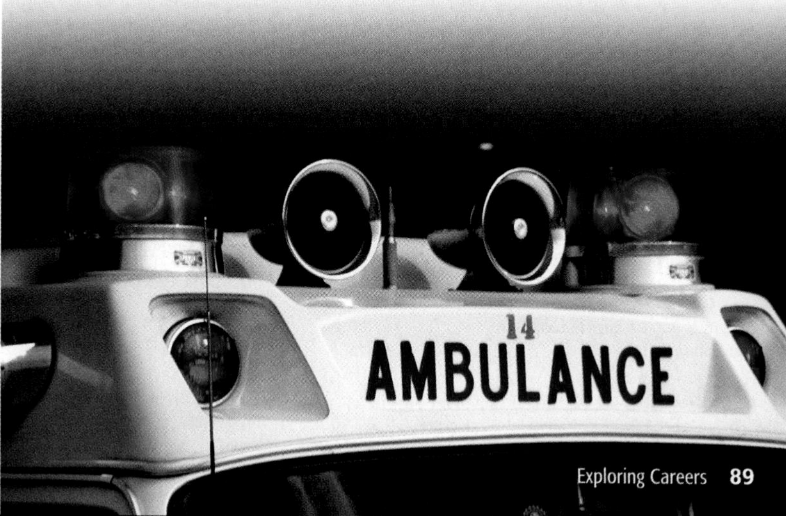

Reading in the Real World

Career Have an EMT or another medical professional visit your class and talk about his or her job. Have students prepare several questions to ask the visitor before he or she comes. Review the questions with the students to ensure appropriateness, clarity, and importance. Try to send the questions to the speaker before the visit, so he or she will know what is of particular interest to your students. **OL**

Teach

C Critical Thinking

Analysis **Ask:** Why do you think each of the subjects is important for a firefighter to study? *(Possible responses: driver's education–to be a good driver in stressful situations or when it is hard to see; health and anatomy–to help sick or injured people; biology and chemistry–to know how different chemicals affect people and other living creatures as well as which chemicals may make a fire worse; foreign languages–to be able to speak to people in trouble who do not speak English well; English–to be able to read, write, and communicate)* **OL**

BQ BIG Question

Ask: How did this article help you learn more about different careers? *(Possible response: It showed the different types of things I need to study if I want to do any of these jobs.)* **OL**

Assess

CheckPoint

Use the CheckPoint questions provided on Presentation Plus! to check for comprehension of the selection. These questions can be used with interactive response keypads for immediate student feedback.

Indiana English/Language Arts Academic Standards

SE: 8.2

TWE: *Text Element* 8.2.7, *Reading in the Real World* 8.5.7

Assess

Resources for page 90

- Selection Quick Check, p. 6
- Selection and Unit Assessment, p. 6
- ExamView Assessment Suite
- Interactive Tutor: Self-Assessment

Students can respond to the *After You Read* items in their Learner's Notebooks or on a separate sheet of paper.

Answering the

1. Possible response: I learned about the different kinds of information requested on an application. I learned about education requirements for different jobs.
2. Possible responses: a coach, a teacher, a neighbor, or a religious leader.
3. An open-ended question is one that cannot be answered with a yes or no.

Critical Thinking

4. Responses will vary.
5. Responses will vary.
6. Possible responses: A television camera operator could use accounting to help him or her stay within a project's budget. A firefighter could use chemistry to help him or her know how a chemical will react with fire. A paramedic could use foreign languages to help him or her understand someone hurt or in trouble who does not speak English.

After You Read

Filling Out the Application *and* Exploring Careers

Answering the

1. How can you use what you learned from reading "Filling Out the Application" to help yourself get a job? How can you use what you learned from "Exploring Careers" to decide what career you want?
2. **Recall** Who would be a good reference to list on a job application?
   TIP Right There The answer is found in the text.
3. **Recall** Describe what an "open-ended question" is.
   TIP Right There The answer is found in the text.

Critical Thinking

4. **Apply** Are you interested in any of the careers described in "Exploring Careers"? Why? If your answer is no, describe a career that you are interested in.
   TIP On My Own Answer from your own ideas or experience.
5. **Evaluate** Do you feel ready to apply for a job after reading the selections? What more would you like to know?
   TIP Author and Me The answer is in the text, but you must also use your own knowledge.
6. **Infer** Why would a television camera operator need to study accounting? Why would a firefighter need to study chemistry? Why would a paramedic want to study foreign languages?
   TIP Author and Me The answer is in the text, but you must also use your own knowledge.

Talk About Your Reading

Interview Imagine that you could apply for your dream job. Tell your partner what the job is, and have him or her interview you for the position. Then switch roles and interview your partner. Use questions that could be found on a job application. Ask and answer at least five questions.

Indiana English/Language Arts Academic Standards
(pp. 90–91)

8.3 Comprehension and Analysis of Literary Text Respond to grade-level-appropriate literature [text]... **8.7 Listening and Speaking** [Develop] speaking skills... **8.2 Comprehension and Analysis (Focus on Informational Text)** Develop [reading] strategies... **8.2.6** Evaluate the... structural patterns of text. **8.6 English Language Conventions**...

For a complete description of the standards, see p. IN 11.

Talk About Your Reading

Sample questions:
What was your last job?
Why should I hire you for this job?
How much are you looking to be paid?
What is your work experience?
What is your availability?
Can you work late in the evening?
Can you work early in the morning when we first open?

Skills Review

Key Reading Skill: Activating Prior Knowledge

7. List two things you already knew about job applications and two things you already knew about the careers described in "Exploring Careers." How did your prior knowledge help you understand the new information you learned?

Text Element: Text Features

8. Which text features did you find the most helpful when you were reading the selection? Why?

Reviewing Skills: Connecting

9. Think of the people you know who have interesting careers. After reading "Exploring Careers," what questions would you ask them about their jobs?

Vocabulary Check

Write *true* if the sentence is true or *false* if it is false.

10. If someone is prone to making grammar mistakes, he or she almost never makes any grammar errors when writing.

11. A family with many residences has more than one home.

12. **English Language Coach** Figure out the meaning of the underlined word by using contrast clues. Write your definition for the word.

The crowd at the basketball game fell silent as Jill shot a three-pointer with less than a second to go. But, as the ball swished through the hoop, pandemonium broke out among the crowd.

Web Activities For eFlashcards, Selection Quick Checks, and other Web activities, go to www.glencoe.com.

Grammar Link: Indefinite Pronouns and Agreement

An **indefinite pronoun** does *not* refer to a particular person, place, thing, or idea. Use indefinite pronouns to speak in general terms.

Examples of Singular Indefinite Pronouns

- Is anyone going to the library today?
- Is everybody here?

Examples of Plural Indefinite Pronouns

- Both were mistaken.
- Few have climbed Mount Everest to its top.

Examples of Indefinite Pronouns That Can Be Singular or Plural

- Is some left?
- Most are on the shelf, but some are on the table.

Look Out! Do not use plural pronouns to refer to singular indefinite pronouns. Pronouns must agree in number with their antecedents.

Wrong: Nobody remembered to bring their book. (The pronouns do not agree in number. *Nobody* is singular; *their* is plural.)

Right: Nobody remembered to bring his or her book. (Note that the pronouns agree in number. *Nobody* is singular and so are *his* and *her.*)

Grammar Practice

Copy the following paragraph on a separate sheet of paper. Find and fix the three agreement errors.

I judge people by their behavior, not by their clothes, grades, or anything else. If somebody is kind and friendly, I usually like them. On the other hand, if a person is mean to me, I avoid them. Nobody wants their feelings hurt, and I am no exception.

Skills Review

Key Reading Skill: Activating Prior Knowledge

7. Responses will vary, but students should explain how their prior knowledge helped them as they read the articles.

Text Element: Text Features

8. Possible response: The subheads in the second article were very helpful. They showed me what each paragraph or group of paragraphs would be about.

Reviewing Skills: Connecting

9. Possible response: I would ask about the kinds of classes I should take and how much education is needed.

Vocabulary Check

10. false

11. true

English Language Coach

12. Possible response: *Pandemonium* means that there was a lot of noise and confusion.

Close

Ask students to tell how the Big Question helped them as they read "Filling Out the Application" and "Exploring Careers."

Grammar Link: Indefinite Pronouns and Agreement

Grammar Practice

Sentence 2: "them" should be him or her;

Sentence 3: "them" should be him or her;

Sentence 4: "their" should be his or her

Literature Online

Web Activities Have students access the Web site for interactive activities that will help them assess their understanding of the selections.

Indiana English/Language Arts Academic Standards

SE: 8.2, 8.2.6, 8.3, 8.6, 8.7

Focus

BELLRINGER Options

Daily Language Practice Transparency 7
Focus Activity Ask: What is the most challenging part of writing your autobiographical sketch? *(Responses will vary.)* OL

Teach

W Writing

Revising Review the elements listed in the *Revising Rubric*.

- **Say:** *Clear focus* means the reader knows what your sketch is about.
- **Ask:** Did you add details and descriptions that make the story more interesting?
- **Say:** Remember *point of view* is who is telling the story.
- **Ask:** Can a reader easily follow the story?
- **Ask:** Does your story sound like you? OL

Resources for page 92

- Use the BLM in the Unit 1 Resource Booklet, p. 28–29
- Use the Grammar and Writing Workshop Transparencies 17–18

WRITING WORKSHOP PART 2

Autobiographical Sketch

Revising, Editing, and Presenting

ASSIGNMENT Write an autobiographical sketch

Purpose: To describe an experience you've had that shaped your feelings about reading

Audience: Your teacher and your classmates

You're off to a great start with your first draft! Now think about how to improve, edit, and present your sketch. Keep a copy of the final draft in a writing portfolio so you and your teacher can evaluate your writing progress.

Revising

Make It Better

Here are some things that you can do to make your first draft into something you'll be proud to share with someone else.

- Read your draft and write notes about things you want to change. Then go through the draft again, checking for items in the Revising Rubric.
- Remember to include vivid details in your sketch. Providing the "specifics" of a story helps make it memorable to readers.
- Make changes as you go. If you're not sure of the exact words to write, make notes to yourself so you can go back and make the changes later. Don't get stuck on one trouble spot—keep making progress.

Revising Rubric

Your revised sketch should have these elements:

- a clear focus
- interesting details and descriptions
- a clear point of view
- a logical organization
- a strong voice

W

needs more details | *I got home from the party and started reading.*

Consider the Audience

Remember that your main audience is your teacher and classmates.

- What do you want to tell them about your reading experience?
- How can you help them understand what you want to say about reading?

I want my teacher and classmates to know that I've always liked relating to the characters in books.

Indiana English/Language Arts Academic Standards (pp. 92–95)

8.4.7 Review, evaluate, and revise writing for meaning and clarity. **8.4.8** Edit and proofread...writing... **8.5.1** Write...autobiographies... **8.7.1** Paraphrase...a speaker's purpose...and ask questions...

For a complete description of the standards, see p. IN 11.

Additional Support

English Language Coach

Writing a Second Draft Encourage English language learners to write an extra draft of their paper. Suggest that students set aside their essays before making this second revision. Then encourage them to read their essays aloud to listen for words and phrases that sound awkward or confusing. They can also ask you or another adult who is fluent in English to review their work and help them identify any grammatical errors in usage, punctuation, and spelling. If students are having difficulty relating certain experiences or ideas, suggest they recount the information aloud to an adult who can then write the information down for them. EL BL

Check the Voice

Ask yourself these questions as you reread your draft.

- *Have I chosen an experience that I feel strongly about?*
- *Is the language lively?*
  Is the sentence structure varied?
- *Does my sketch express my unique point of view?*
- *How do I feel about the details and descriptions I've written? Did I include enough details and descriptions for the reader to understand my experience?*

Writing Models For models and other writing activities, go to www.glencoe.com.

Check the Sequence

Make sure the reader can follow the events in your sketch. Have you used sequence signal words like *first, next, then*? If the events have moved forward or backward in time, are the time shifts clear to the reader?

Editing

Finish It Up

For your final copy, read your autobiographical sketch aloud and use the Editing Checklist to help you spot errors. Use the proofreading symbols in the chart on page R19 to mark needed corrections.

Editing Checklist

- ☑ Proper nouns are correctly capitalized.
- ☑ Pronouns are in the correct form and agree with their antecedents.
- ☑ All sentences end with a punctuation mark.
- ☑ All words are correctly spelled.

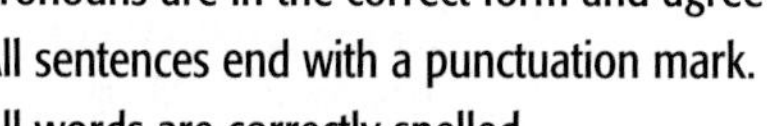

W2

Writing Tip

Spelling Carefully check your work for words that sound the same but have different meanings, such as *too, to, two; their, they're, there; you're, your; its, it's; which, witch.* These are called **homophones.** Look for other words that you sometimes mix up. Make sure you use the correct spelling for the word you want.

Presenting

Show It Off

Make a clean final copy of your sketch. Read it to a small group of your classmates. Listen to them read their sketches. Then discuss any common ideas about reading that came up. Also talk about any surprising feelings about reading that people in the class might have expressed.

Writing Tip

Handwriting Make your final draft easy to read. Use your best handwriting. Make each letter and punctuation mark clear for the reader.

Teach

W1 Writing

Sequence Remind students of these sequence words: *first, second, third, next, finally, last, before, after, yesterday,* and *tomorrow.* BL

W2 Writing

Editing **Ask:** What are proper nouns? *(the names of people or places)* **Ask:** What is an antecedent? *(the word that a pronoun refers to)* BL OL

Literature Online

Writing Models Have students access the Web site for an additional and interactive Writing Workshop-based student model.

Literature Focus Lesson

Voice Emphasize the importance of voice in writing. Ask students to check the voice of their writing by reading it aloud to friends or family members. Instruct them to note any parts of the work that seem odd to them, that "do not feel right" or "do not sound like them." These are the parts of their writing that they will need to revisit. Encourage students to use precise words that communicate exactly what they want to say. Suggest they use a thesaurus, a synonym finder, a dictionary, or word processing software that contains an electronic dictionary. BL OL

Indiana English/Language Arts Academic Standards
SE: 8.4.7, 8.4.8, 8.5.1
TWE: *English Language Coach* 8.4.7, *Literature Focus Lesson* 8.4.9

Teach

LSV1 Listening, Speaking, and Viewing

Active Listening Help students understand why this is such an important skill to develop. Divide the class into small groups. Have the groups give each member a chance to tell about a time when they stopped listening and it got them into trouble. OL

LSV2 Listening, Speaking, and Viewing

Active Listening Say: In order to make your writing better you cannot be defensive when classmates talk about your work. Don't try to prove that your classmates are wrong. Think of your classmates as your audience. Listen to what they have to say about your writing. You may even want to ask them how they think you can make your writing better. OL

WRITING WORKSHOP PART 2

Listening, Speaking, and Viewing

Active Listening

Many times we listen to what people are saying, but we don't focus only on listening to them. Sometimes we are thinking about what we want to say next. Or sometimes our minds wander to something else entirely. Active listening helps us to focus on what the speaker is saying.

What Is Active Listening?

Active listening is a way of being involved as a listener. You listen carefully to what the speaker says. Then you tell the speaker what you heard. LSV1

Why Is Active Listening Important?

To make your autobiographical sketch as good as it can be, you need feedback from others. When they share their thoughts about your writing, you need to listen carefully. Active listening will help you do many things, including these:

- understand what they are saying about your writing
- learn how they see your work
- get ideas about how to make your writing better

LSV2

How Do I Do It?

When someone talks to you, listen to what he or she is saying. Do not think about what you want to say next. Don't try to immediately come up with answers to the person's questions. Don't let your mind wander.

When the person is done talking, tell him or her what you heard. Here are some phrases to get you started.

- So what I think you're saying is ______.
- What I heard you say was ______.

Small Group Discussion With two or three other students, talk about your autobiographical sketch and the benefits you got from reading it. The rest of the group should practice active listening. When you are done, each person should tell the group what he or she thinks you just said. Then have another person in the group speak. Now it's your turn to practice active listening. Take turns until everyone has a chance to be the speaker.

Analyzing Cartoons
What advice would you give Baldo on how to be a better listener?

Additional Support

Differentiated Instruction

Oral Presentation There is always interaction between speakers and their audience—the more positive that interaction, the better the experience. Have students work in groups to compose a list of guidelines for making a good oral presentation. Their suggestions might include:

- Speak on a subject of interest to the audience.
- Look at the audience, making occasional eye contact.
- Speak naturally.
- Add meaning to your words with facial expressions and gestures.

Make copies of the lists, or post them where students can review the guidelines before making their presentation. AS

Writer's Model

Comfort from a Book

Reading has always helped lift my spirits whenever I've felt sad. For example, there was the time I got home from a party at my friend Lisa's and felt really down. I went straight to my room and fell onto the bed. I felt more lonely than usual and wanted to forget about what happened that night. My Spanish book was on my small bedside table. I picked it up and opened it to the Escena de la Vida (Scene from Life), which we had been assigned to read over the weekend. In the scene, Estela was alone in her room, listening to a love song, while her "friends" were getting ready to go to a party without her. That's not too different from being at a party where your "friends" ignore you. That's what happened at Lisa's party. That's why I was feeling so sad.

I wanted to find out more about Estela, so I turned to the Escena de la Vida in the next chapter. Estela wasn't in that scene, but a guy named Ricardo was calling his English teacher "The Witch." He said he was sick of her jokes.

The teacher who told jokes reminded me of my social studies teacher, Ms. Carne. People call her a witch because she yells so much, but they think she's really funny, too. When she was a teenager on crutches, she must have had plenty of lonely times like Estela and me, but now she has a husband, a good job, and, most important, a positive, no-nonsense attitude. I can deal with being like Estela now if I can be like Ms. Carne when I grow up.

I've always known books could show me that other people have the same problems I do. Now I know reading can also remind me that someday my life will be better.

W1

W2

Active Writing Model

The writer makes it clear that the events happened in the past. Here and throughout the sketch, the writer's use of time order makes it easy to follow the order of events.

Details and descriptions help the readers share the writer's experience.

The writer uses first-person point of view throughout the sketch.

The writer's attitude toward the events comes through in the sketch.

The sketch maintains a clear focus from the beginning to the end. Notice how the conclusion sums up the main idea of the sketch.

Teach

W1 Writing

Voice Say: Look for aspects of the story that show the writer's voice. What are some statements that show the writer is a student or teenager? *(Possible response: "which we had been assigned to read over the weekend")* **OL**

W2 Writing

Description Ask: What are some details that the writer uses in this sketch? *(Possible responses: The students call the teacher a witch. The writer's teacher uses crutches and has a positive attitude.)* **OL**

Assess

Have students exchange their papers and use the *Revising Rubric* on page 92 and the *Editing Checklist* on page 93 to critique each other's work. Have students make last-minute changes to their work and then add their stories to the class binder.

Reading Fluency

Reading and Writing Some students might find that it helps them to analyze their drafts better if they read them aloud. Allow these students to pair partners for this oral reading. Students should take turns reading their own drafts to their partners and then discuss the content, including voice. Encourage students to use the *Revising Rubric* from page 92 and the *Editing Checklist* from page 93 as a guideline for discussing their drafts. **OL**

Indiana English/Language Arts Academic Standards

SE: 8.7.1

TWE: *Differentiated Instruction* 8.7, *Reading Fluency* 8.7.6

Identifying Author's Purpose

Teaching Students to Identify Author's Purpose

Why Is It Important?

- Students will learn that an author's purpose for writing is affected by his or her perspective and experience.
- An author's purpose is not always clearly stated; identifying it will help students understand the point of the selection.
- Identifying an author's purpose will help students understand how the writer wants them to respond after they read the selection.

How to Help Students Get It

- Remind students that an author's purpose is his or her reason for writing about a topic.
- Tell students that they can look for clues in the text, such as the author's word choices and how he or she organized the writing, to help them identify the author's purpose.
- Students may also benefit from re-reading the author's background to get a better sense of his or her purpose.

Reading to Answer the Big Question

from *Akiko in the Forbidden Foothills of Gozmaturk* by Mark Crilley
Spuckler's friend has been kidnapped by a dragon. The gang must rescue Mr. Beeba, but it's going to take more than threatening words to subdue the beast. After Spuckler's failed rescue attempt, Poog succeeds by trying something less aggressive. Everyone agrees that a little coordination beforehand could save time, and face, for Spuckler. Mr. Beeba is glad to have escaped, and the gang is glad to have him back unharmed.

Being Japanese American by Yoshiko Uchida
This collection of anecdotes focuses on the difference between the narrator's view of herself as being an American girl, and the view others take of her as Japanese. She describes events in her life that highlighted these traits, and concludes that she is both—Japanese American.

Workshop Resources

Pacing (Days) Standard	Block	Lesson	Student Materials	Teacher Resources
1	1/2	Key Skill Lesson: Author's Purpose and Perspective	Key Reading Skills Practice, p. 30 English Language Coach Review, p. 42	Bellringer Options Transparencies – Daily Language Practice 8 Read Aloud, Think Aloud Transparencies – Key Reading Skills 10 Presentation Plus!
1	1	from *Akiko in the Forbidden Foothills of Gozmaturk*	Glencoe Online Unit Vocabulary Review, p. 40 Academic Vocabulary Review, p. 44 English Language Coach Active Reading Graphic Organizer, p. 31 StudentWorks Plus™ Online Student Edition Literature Classics Selection and Unit Assessments, p. 7	Literary and Text Analysis Transparencies 44 Puzzlemaker Skill Level Up!™ A Language Arts Game BookLink 3 Assessment by Learning Objective (Diagnostic and Formative) Interactive Tutor: Self-Assessment TeacherWorks Plus™
1		"Being Japanese American"	Glencoe Online Unit Vocabulary Review, p. 40 Academic Vocabulary Review, p. 44 English Language Coach Active Reading Graphic Organizer, p. 34 Literary Analysis, p. 33 StudentWorks Plus™ Online Student Edition Literature Classics Selection and Unit Assessments, p. 8	Literary and Text Analysis Transparencies 10 Puzzlemaker Skill Level Up!™ A Language Arts Game BookLink 3 Assessment by Learning Objective (Diagnostic and Formative) Interactive Tutor: Self-Assessment TeacherWorks Plus™

Keys for Unit Resource

- Blackline Master
- Workbook
- Supplemental Text
- CD-ROM
- DVD
- Transparency
- Web-based
- Fast File

Level Appropriate Code

AS = Activities for all students
AL = Activities for students working above grade level
OL = Activities for students working at grade level
BL = Activities for students working below grade level
EL = Activities for English language learners

Focus

BELLRINGER Options

Daily Language Practice Transparency 8
Focus Activity Write the phrases "melting pot" and "salad bowl" on the board. Have students discuss which of these phrases best describes America and why. *(Responses will vary.)* AS

Teach

R Reading Skill

Identifying Author's Purpose **Ask:** What is another example of a piece that is written to entertain? *(a movie, a novel)* **Ask:** How can a writer entertain people? *(by making a piece funny, suspenseful, or interesting)* **Ask:** What are advertisements trying to persuade people to do? *(to buy something)* **Say:** Give an example of something you have read that has at least two of these purposes. *(Possible response: I read an ad in a magazine that was very funny and also tried to persuade me to buy something.)* OL AL

READING WORKSHOP 4

Skills Focus

You will practice using these skills when you read the following selections:

- from *Akiko in the Forbidden Foothills of Gozmaturk,* p. 100
- "Being Japanese American," p. 108

Reading

- Identifying author's purpose

Literature

- Identifying cultural references
- Identifying and analyzing sequence

Vocabulary

- Using visual and general context clues
- Academic Vocabulary: *visual, sequence*

Writing/Grammar

- Using the correct pronoun case

Skill Lesson

Identifying Author's Purpose

Learn It!

What Is It? The **author's purpose** is the reason that he or she wrote the text–his or her aim, or goal, for writing. Four common purposes are as follows:

- to entertain, such as with a comic strip, a short story, or a funny letter
- to persuade, such as with a commercial or a letter to the editor of a newspaper
- to inform, such as with a brochure that explains how to live a healthy lifestyle
- to express a feeling, such as with a love poem

Analyzing Cartoons
The reader enjoys Allende's work even if it is "made up." Allende is a fiction writer. What might be her purpose in writing a novel?

Indiana English/Language Arts Academic Standards (pp. 96–97)

8.2 Comprehension and Analysis (Focus on Informational Text)
Develop [reading] strategies...identifying and analyzing...purpose.

For a complete description of the standards, see p. IN 11.

Additional Support

Differentiated Instruction

Using the Library Have the class go to the library. Assign different groups of students to different sections of the library, such as nonfiction, autobiographies, periodicals, and fiction. Direct each group to find at least two examples of texts from their genre for each of the purposes listed on page 96. Ask the groups to report their findings to the class. In this way, students can see how writers can use any of the genres to achieve these goals. For example, even nonfiction books can have purposes other than "to inform." OL

Why Is It Important? When you know why an author wrote something, you can better understand and evaluate what you are reading.

How Do I Do It? To figure out the author's purpose, look at several things. Is the text fiction or nonfiction? Most fiction entertains or gives the reader insight into human life. Nonfiction often informs or persuades by using strong word choices and emotional appeals. Also, look to see if the text was written for a particular occasion or audience.

Study Central Visit www.glencoe.com and click on Study Central to review identifying the author's purpose.

Here's how a student described Maya Angelou's purpose in writing *I Know Why the Caged Bird Sings.* Read the passage from Angelou's work, below.

> She appealed to me because she was like people I had never met personally. Like women in English novels who walked the moors (whatever they were) with their loyal dogs racing at a respectful distance. Like the women who sat in front of roaring fireplaces, drinking tea incessantly from silver trays full of scones and crumpets. . . . It would be safe to say that she made me proud to be Negro, just by being herself.

I think Maya Angelou's purpose in this passage might be to entertain readers with her memories of Mrs. Flowers.

Practice It!

Every kind of writing has a purpose. In your Learner's Notebook, copy these two columns. Then draw lines from one column to another, matching the kind of writing to its most likely purpose.

kind of writing	purpose
article about a forest fire	to provide information about events
job application	to provide information about a person
advertisement	to express a feeling
patriotic song	to persuade someone to buy something

Use It!

As you read *Akiko* and "Being Japanese American," look for clues that will help you identify each author's purpose. Add these to your Learner's Notebook. Read each piece with that purpose in mind.

Literature Focus Lesson

Author's Purpose Direct students to think about activities that they do and the reasons they do them. Explain that this is similar to an author's purpose—it is the reason an author writes. Students can make a list of the things they do in a typical week and the reasons they do them. Of course the list of purposes, or reasons, will not be the same as the four author purposes, but students will see the connection between action and purpose. **AL**

Teach

Study Central Have students access the Web site to improve their understanding of identifying author's purpose and to complete a related activity.

R Reading Skill

Identifying Author's Purpose

Say: Look at the *How Do I Do It?* section. How would a speech at a pep rally have a different purpose than a speech before student council members? Name some possible characteristics of each speech that would reveal its purpose. *(Possible responses: The purpose of a speech at a pep rally is to rouse the crowd and get them excited. This speech would be cheerful, positive, rowdy, and upbeat. The purpose of a speech before student council members would be to discuss or change student policy. This speech would be serious, earnest, and informative.)* **OL**

Resources for page 97

Use Key Reading Skills Transparency 10 in *Read Aloud, Think Aloud* to help students practice identifying author's purpose.

Indiana English/Language Arts Academic Standards
SE: 8.2
TWE: *Differentiated Instruction* 8.2, *Literature Focus Lesson* 8.2

Teach

More About the Author

After Mark Crilley graduated from college, he taught English in Taiwan and Japan. In 1992, when he was in Japan, he began writing his comic books about Akiko. Since that time, Crilley has written novelized versions of some of these comic books. He continues to write more comic books (and novelized versions) in the Akiko series, as well as books in his newer series about Billy Clikk. Crilley lives with his family in Michigan.

EL Language Coach

Visual Context Clues Ask: What are some examples of visual context clues? *(pictures of characters' expressions, characters' actions, setting, and made-up words)* BL OL

Before You Read

from *Akiko in the Forbidden Foothills of Gozmaturk*

Mark Crilley

Meet the Author

Mark Crilley began drawing at a young age. After college, he worked in Japan, where he invented the character Akiko. Since then, he has published more than 50 issues of the *Akiko* comic book series. He writes that "somewhere underneath all the silly drawings and slapstick humor lies a gentle reminder of the little 4th grader within us all . . . ."

Author Search For more about Mark Crilley, go to www.glencoe.com.

Indiana English/Language Arts Academic Standards (pp. 98–103)

8.1 Word Recognition, Fluency, and Vocabulary Development Use…context clues…to determine the meaning of words…**8.2 Comprehension and Analysis (Focus on Informational Text)** Develop [reading] strategies…identifying and analyzing…purpose. **8.3.2** Evaluate the structural elements of the plot…

For a complete description of the standards, see p. IN 11.

Vocabulary Preview

wretched (RECH id) *adj.* very unpleasant or uncomfortable; terrible **(p. 103)** *The gooey, wretched stuff stuck to everything and everyone.*

coordinate (koh OR duh nayt) *v.* to make (things) work together smoothly **(p. 103)** *To avoid extra work, they decided to coordinate their efforts.*

Write to Learn Write a short paragraph using both vocabulary words.

English Language Coach

Context Clues: Visual Context Clues Usually, when you look for context clues to the meaning of a word, you look at the sentences and words around it. In a graphic novel, you have pictures that are **visual context clues**. The expressions on the characters' faces are clues. Suppose a character looks very sad and is saying, "I'm miserable." That's a very strong clue to the meaning of *miserable* (very sad). The characters' actions are clues. Suppose two characters are fighting. One says, "You will never triumph!" That's a clue to the meaning of *triumph* (win).

EL

The setting of the story can contain clues, too. Suppose a character is looking at a very tall mountain and says, "It's too high to scale." That's a clue to the meaning of *scale* (climb). Or perhaps the characters are walking through a dark forest. The branches of the trees reach out like claws. There are eyes looking out from the darkness. One of the characters says, "What an eerie place!" You can be pretty sure that *eerie* has something to do with being weird and scary.

Visual clues can be very important in a graphic novel or cartoon. Often writers use words they make up, especially for noises. As you're reading the selection from *Akiko in the Forbidden Foothills of Gozmaturk,* look at the visual clues to identify the actions that go with words such as *skraw* and *shrlup*.

Partner Talk Without looking at the story, write meanings for *skraw* and *shrlup* in your Learner's Notebook. Don't try to write dictionary-style definitions. Instead, say each word aloud; then write a few notes about what the sound of the word suggests to you.

Academic Vocabulary

visual (VIZH wul) *adj.* able to be viewed or seen

Additional Support

Author Search To expand students' appreciation of Mark Crilley, have them access the Web site for additional information and resources.

English Language Coach

Build Background: Graphic Stories The unique thing about graphic stories is that the writer uses pictures to tell most of the story. The dialogue in a graphic story does not use quotation marks and the denotations of "he/she said." Instead a reader knows who is speaking by looking at the bubble and seeing which character it is attached to. In many graphic stories, there are events or actions that are not pictured. The reader must infer what happened by looking at the next frame and using logical reasoning. EL

Skills Preview

Key Reading Skill: Identifying Author's Purpose

How can you tell Mark Crilley's purpose in *Akiko*? Use the following tips.

- Look at the pictures. Think about the mood, or feeling, they create and the story they tell.
- Think about the genre, or type of writing, of *Akiko* and the usual purpose of that genre.

On Your Own As you read *Akiko*, think particularly about the intended audience.

Literary Element: Sequence

A **sequence** is a regular order or arrangement. Text sequences commonly used to organize writing are as follows:

- **chronological order**–time order. This is often used in biographies and nonfiction, where it's important to know the order in which events actually happened.
- **spatial order**–the order within a certain space, such as left to right, top to bottom, foreground to background, and clockwise. Spatial order is best for describing people and places and giving directions.
- **order of importance**–going from most to least important or from least to most important. This form of sequence is often used in nonfiction.

L

Partner Talk What sequence would you expect in a graphic story? Talk it over with a partner.

Interactive Literary Elements Handbook To review or learn more about the literary elements, go to www.glencoe.com.

Academic Vocabulary

sequence (SEE kwens) *n.* a regular order or arrangement in time, space, or importance

Get Ready to Read

Connect to the Reading

Your best friend has been kidnapped by a dragon! Yoiks! It will destroy your friend if you don't pay a ransom. Gadzooks! Do you reply "What's in it for me?" Of course not! Think about stories you've read or seen in which one character rescues another.

Write to Learn In *Akiko*, one of the characters is captured by a dragon. Jot down what you think that character's friends will do. Use your imagination!

Build Background

The selection you are about to read is from *Akiko in the Forbidden Foothills of Gozmaturk,* one of many graphic novels featuring Akiko and her friends. (The main characters live on the planet Smoo, but their adventures take them many places.) Here is a list of the main characters and a description of each:

- Akiko (the girl with pigtails)
- Spuckler Boach (the guy with spiky hair)
- Mr. Beeba (the bald creature with glasses)
- Gax (the one with the long neck)
- Poog (the floating head)

You'll read only the ending of this adventure, but all you need to know is that a dragon has captured Mr. Beeba, and his pals are trying to rescue him.

Set Purposes for Reading

BIG Question Read this story to learn how a group of friends tries to save one of their own, without worrying about reward or danger.

R

Set Your Own Purpose What would you like to learn from the story to help you answer the Big Question? Write your own purpose on the *Akiko* page of Foldable 1.

Keep Moving

Use these skills as you read the following selection.

Teach

L Literary Element

Sequence Ask students to write a brief paragraph about something, using one of the sequences here. Then ask for volunteers to read their paragraphs to the class. Allow other students to guess the type of sequence used. OL AL

R Reading Skill

Review Setting a Purpose for Reading **Ask:** Why do you want to read this adventure? State your reason as a purpose for reading. *(Answers will vary.)* BL OL

Interactive Literary Elements Handbook Have students access the Web site to improve their understanding of sequence.

Literature Focus Lesson

Sequence Some students may have difficulty differentiating between the three different sequential orders listed on this page. To help students understand these orders, ask them to write a short paragraph story, using one of the sequencing orders. Next, have them write the same story twice, using the other two sequential orders. Afterward, have students exchange papers with partners. Partners should read the stories and label the three paragraphs as chronological order, spatial order, and order of importance. OL AL

Indiana English/Language Arts Academic Standards

SE: 8.1, 8.2, 8.3.2

TWE: *English Language Coach* 8.2.6, *Literature Focus Lesson* 8.2.6

Teach

L Literary Element

Sequence Ask: Describe the sequence of events on this page. Which pattern of organization is used on this page? *(First, Spuckler Boach and Akiko find large footprints. Spuckler Boach then gets a knife from Gax. Afterward, all three enter the cave. This is chronological order.)* BL OL

R Reading Skill

Identifying Author's Purpose
Say: Spuckler Boach is holding a small knife in order to go and fight a very large creature. What is the author's purpose here? *(to entertain, or make the reader laugh)* BL OL

READING WORKSHOP 4

from Akiko in the Forbidden Foothills of Gozmaturk

by Mark Crilley

Practice the Skills

1 Key Reading Skill

Identifying Author's Purpose Notice the odd markings on the stones. Although we don't know what they represent, they're fun to look at. This may hint at Crilley's purpose.

2 English Language Coach

Context Clues The way Gax speaks (or sounds) looks different from the way the others speak. What are two differences?

Additional Support

Differentiated Instruction

Creating Thought Bubbles Have students redraw the last picture frame, adding thought bubbles for Gax and Akiko. Students should be creative in writing the thoughts of each of these characters. Then ask students to explain how they created a bubble that showed the characters were only thinking these things and not speaking them aloud. *(Possible responses: dashed lines, circles, or other markers)* OL

READING WORKSHOP 4

Practice the Skills

L1

L2

3 **English Language Coach**

Context Clues Look at the visual context clues for *skraw* and *shrlup.* Do you think Crilley invented good words for the actions they represent?

Teach

L1 Literary Element

Review Tone Ask: What is Spuckler Boach's tone? *(Possible response: He is bossy, sarcastic, and self-confident.)* **Ask:** Why do you think he takes on this tone? *(Possible response: He wants to save his friend, and he doesn't want to reveal fear or insecurity.)* OL AL

L2 Literary Element

Review Tone Ask: What tone does the dragon's sounds "SKRAW" and "SHRLUP" reveal? *(Possible response: These words show that the dragon is not threatened by Spuckler Boach and that he is strong and fierce.)* OL

English Language Coach

Dialect Sometimes a writer writes the dialogue as it sounds when the speaker says it. For example, in the first frame on this page, Spuckler Boach says, "Ya might wanna hang back a little." The writer could have written the correct words, "You might want to hang back a little." Have students study the rest of the dialogue on the page and rewrite it in its more formal form. Tell students to think about whether or not the dialect makes this story more realistic. OL

Indiana English/Language Arts Academic Standards
SE: 8.1, 8.2
TWE: *Differentiated Instruction* 8.5, *English Language Coach* 8.3

Teach

L1 Literary Element

Sequence **Ask:** Why do you think this cartoon is written in chronological order? *(Possible response: It's easier to follow the story when the events are told in the order that they happen.)* OL

L2 Literary Element

Review Tone **Ask:** Do you think the tone of Mr. Beeba's lines is angry, enthusiastic, or sarcastic? *(sarcastic)* OL

C Critical Thinking

Analysis **Ask:** Why do you think Mr. Beeba refers to the music as the heavenly choir? *(Possible response: He thinks they are about to die.)* **Ask:** Who is really singing? *(Poog)* BL **Ask:** Why is the bubble with the comment "it's Poog" not attached to a speaker? *(Possible response: The person who is speaking is not in this frame of the cartoon; it's a continuation of what Buckler said in the previous frame.)* OL

Practice the Skills

4 Literary Element

Sequence Which of the patterns of organization described on page 99 is used in this selection?

Additional Support

Literature Focus Lesson

Author's Purpose Explain that comic writers often use exaggeration for comic effect. Ask students to identify at least two ways Crilley uses exaggeration and explain his purpose for using exaggeration. Have students review several cartoons from a newspaper. Students should note which cartoons rely on exaggeration. Ask them to identify the ways the cartoonists have used exaggeration for comic effect and to make a point. OL AL

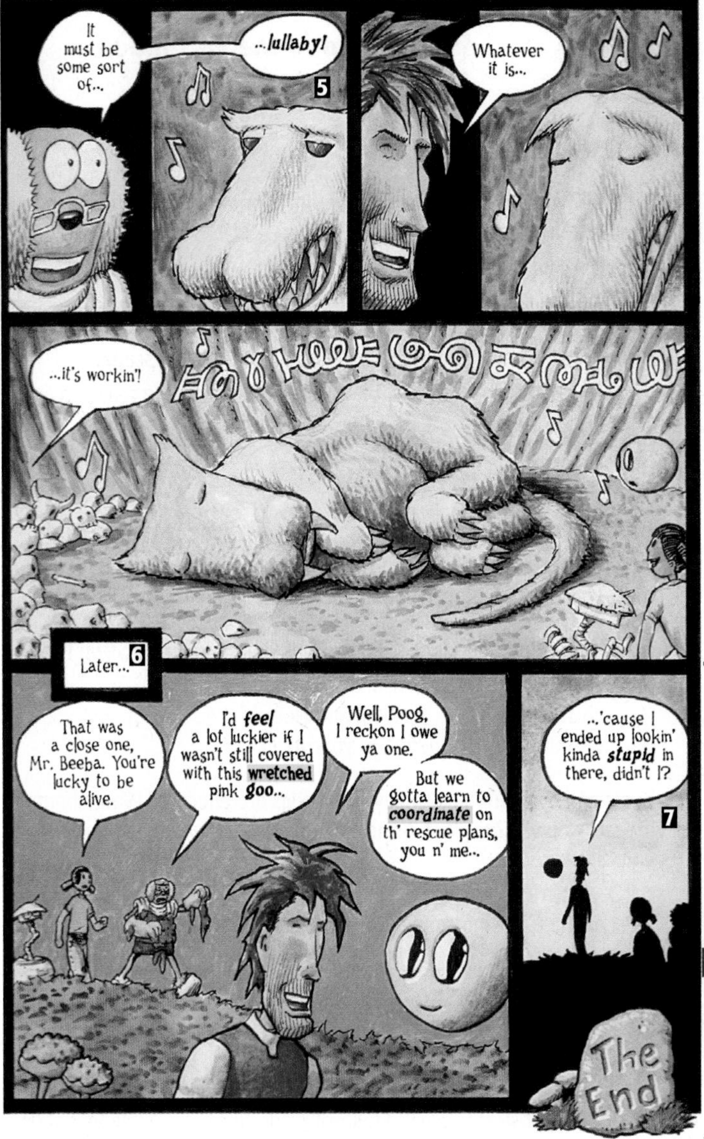

Practice the Skills

5 Literary Element

Sequence It's the sequence of what happens to the dragon that tells Mr. Beeba what kind of song Poog is singing.

6 Literary Element

Sequence Chronological order is often signaled by words such as *later, after, then,* and, of course, *The End.*

7 BIG Question

C BQ What did you get out of reading *Akiko?* Write your answer on the *Akiko* page of Foldable 1. Your response will help you complete the Unit Challenge later.

Vocabulary

wretched (RECH id) *adj.* very unpleasant or uncomfortable; terrible

coordinate (koh OR duh nayt) *v.* to make (things) work together smoothly

READING WORKSHOP 4

Teach

C Critical Thinking

Analysis Say: You can look at the characters' actions and listen to their words to learn about their personalities. What do Spuckler Boach's last words tell you about him? *(Possible response: He was just in a life-threatening situation, and all he cares about is how he looked. He is grateful to Poog, but he's also a bit conceited.)* AL

BQ BIG Question

Ask: How did the illustrations enhance your reading? How would this story have been different had there not been any pictures? *(Responses will vary.)* OL

Assess

CheckPoint

Use the CheckPoint questions provided on Presentation Plus! to check for comprehension of the selection. These questions can be used with interactive response keypads for immediate student feedback.

Reading in the Real World

Career Have students make a list of different careers in which people rescue others. Then ask them to focus on one career and write a paragraph explaining why teamwork is important in that job. Students having difficulty explaining aspects of teamwork may want to write about a rescue they witnessed in real life or on the news. Ask them to describe how people worked together to successfully perform the rescue. AS

Indiana English/Language Arts Academic Standards

SE: 8.3.2

TWE: *Literature Focus Lesson* 8.3, *Reading in the Real World* 8.5.7

Assess

Resources for page 104

- Selection Quick Check, p. 7
- Selection and Unit Assessment, p. 7
- ExamView Assessment Suite
- Interactive Tutor: Self-Assessment

Students can respond to the *After You Read* items in their Learner's Notebooks or on a separate sheet of paper.

Answering the BIG Question

1. Possible response: When I read a graphic story, I get a visual idea of how the writer imagines the characters look.
2. Possible response: Gax is a robot or an alien. From the picture, I can see that he is not human.
3. Poog sings lullaby music until the dragon falls asleep. Then Akiko unties Spuckler and Mr. Beeba and they all walk out of the cave.

Critical Thinking

4. Possible response: Spuckler sees that the creature has big footprints and infers that the creature must be large.
5. Possible response: Spuckler is probably reckless and likes to be the hero or center of attention. He is also bossy.
6. Possible response: Yes, I can see the characters' expressions instead of just reading about them.

After You Read

from *Akiko in the Forbidden Foothills of Gozmaturk*

Answering the BIG Question

1. What do you get out of reading graphic stories that you might not get from reading a novel?
2. **Recall** What is Gax? How can you tell?
   TIP Right There You will find this information in the selection.
3. **Recall** How does Poog help Spuckler and Mr. Beeba escape?
   TIP Right There You will find this information in the selection.

Critical Thinking

4. **Infer** Why does Spuckler want a weapon when he enters the cave?
   TIP Author and Me You will find clues in the selection, but you must also use the information in your head.
5. **Infer** Based on Spuckler's actions, what kind of person do you think he is? How might he act during other adventures?
   TIP Author and Me You will find clues in the selection, but you must also use the information in your head.
6. **Evaluate** Do you think Crilley's drawings are effective? What about the story he tells? Explain, using examples from *Akiko* to support your answer.
   TIP Author and Me You will find clues in the selection, but you must also use the information in your head.

Write About Your Reading

Postcard Pretend you are Akiko. Write a postcard to your friends on your home planet, describing your adventure with the dragon. Draw a picture for the front of the postcard. Use the following questions as a guide to writing your message for the back of the card.

- What happened when you entered the cave?
- How did you feel when the dragon tied up Spuckler?
- How did you help your friends in the cave?
- How did you escape?
- Where are you off to next?

Indiana English/Language Arts Academic Standards
(pp. 104–105)

8.3 Comprehension and Analysis of Literary Text Respond to grade-level-appropriate literature... **8.5.7** Write for different purposes... **8.2 Comprehension and Analysis (Focus on Informational Text)** Develop [reading] strategies... identifying and analyzing... purpose. **8.3.2** Evaluate the structural elements of the plot... **8.6 English Language Conventions**

For a complete description of the standards, see p. IN 11.

Write About Your Reading

Postcards should be written from Akiko's viewpoint, as an observer of most of the action who unties her friends at the end. Postcards should tell what she and Buckler saw before entering the cave, how Buckler spoke to the dragon, how the dragon attacked Buckler, how Poog made lullaby music, how the dragon went to sleep, and how Akiko freed her friends. Akiko may even tell how she felt after all this, when Buckler acted as if she'd had nothing to do with the rescue at all. The postcard should also mention the next adventure she will go on.

Skills Review

Key Reading Skill: Identifying Author's Purpose

7. What do you think was the most important purpose Crilley had in creating the *Akiko* stories?

Explain your answer.

Literary Element: Sequence

8. What is the main form of sequence Crilley uses in his graphic story?
9. What happens before Spuckler, Akiko, Poog, and Gax enter the cave?
10. What happens after Poog begins to sing?
11. Look at the second-to-last drawing on page 103. Which form of sequence would be best for identifying the characters in this drawing?
    - chronological order
    - spatial order
    - order of importance

Vocabulary Check

12. List three nouns that the word *wretched* might describe.
13. Think of a group of people who would need to **coordinate** their actions. Write two or three sentences explaining why. Be sure to use the word *coordinate* in at least one sentence.
14. **Academic Vocabulary** Which of the following would be a **visual** aid:

    a spoken description or a photo?
15. **English Language Coach** Look at the pictures containing the words *skraw* and *shrlup*. Using visual context clues from the selection, rewrite the meaning for each word.

Grammar Link: Pronouns as Subjects and Objects

A **subject pronoun** is used as the subject of a sentence. The subject of a sentence is who or what the sentence is about.

An **object pronoun** is a pronoun that receives the action expressed by the verb in the sentence.

	Subject Pronouns	Object Pronouns
Singular	I, you, he, she, it	me, you, her, him, it
Plural	we, you, they	us, you, them

To figure out when to use a subject or object pronoun, get rid of the extra person (or people) in a sentence.

- ~~Maurice~~, ~~Phil~~, ~~and~~ (him? he?) agreed.
- They spoke to ~~Bianca and~~ (I? me?).

You would never say "Him agreed," so you should use "he" in the first example. You would never say "They spoke to I," so you should use "me" in the second example.

Grammar Practice

Rewrite each sentence, using the correct pronoun in parentheses.

16. My friends and (I, me) like mystery novels.
17. Tina, Ashley, or (she, her) will ask Mrs. Hill.
18. Please give Sandy and (I, me) a chance.
19. Guess what happened to Paul and (I, me)!
20. (Me and my brother, My brother and I) went shopping.

Writing Application Review the postcard you wrote for the Write About Your Reading activity. Make sure you correctly used subject and object pronouns. Fix any mistakes.

Web Activities For eFlashcards, Selection Quick Checks, and other Web activities, go to www.glencoe.com.

Skills Review

Key Reading Skill: Identifying Author's Purpose

7. Responses will vary. Most students will say his primary purpose was to entertain.

Literary Element: Sequence

8. chronological
9. Mr. Beeba is captured by the dragon.
10. The dragon falls asleep.
11. Possible response: The best way to identify the characters in this drawing is spatial order, from left to right, right to left, front to back, or back to front.

Vocabulary Check

12. Responses will vary.
13. Responses will vary.

Academic Vocabulary

14. a photo

English Language Coach

15. Possible answers: Skraw is the sound of an animal spitting out some sort of sticky goo. Shrlup is the sound of someone being tied up tightly in goo.

Close

Ask students to summarize how they would answer the Big Question after reading "Akiko in the Forbidden Foothills of Gozmaturk."

Grammar Link: Pronouns as Subjects and Objects

Grammar Practice

16. I
17. she
18. me
19. me
20. My brother and I

Literature Online

Web Activities Have students access the Web site for interactive activities that will help them assess their understanding of the selection.

Indiana English/Language Arts Academic Standards

SE: 8.2, 8.3, 8.3.2, 8.5.7, 8.6

Teach

More About the Author

Yoshiko Uchida went to the University of California at Berkeley. During her senior year, she was sent to an internment camp for Japanese American citizens. Years later, Uchida wrote a fictional book about an eleven-year-old girl's experience at this camp. This book, *Journey to Topaz*, may be of great interest to your students.

EL Language Coach

General Context Clues **Ask:** What is the difference between a general context clue and an example context clue? *(Possible response: An example context clue is a familiar word or phrase that shows what the unfamiliar word means. A general context clue is the overall text surrounding the unfamiliar word.)* **OL**

Before You Read | Being Japanese American

Meet the Author

Yoshiko Uchida was born in 1921, in Alameda, California. During World War II, Uchida and her family were sent to an internment camp for Japanese American citizens. Uchida taught while in the camp and learned to love education. When she was released, she went on to write many books about Japanese American culture. Uchida died in 1992. See page R7 of the Author Files for more on Yoshiko Uchida.

Author Search For more about Yoshiko Uchida, go to www.glencoe.com.

Indiana English/Language Arts Academic Standards (pp. 106–113)

8.1 Word Recognition, Fluency, and Vocabulary Development Use…context clues…to determine the meaning of words…**8.2 Comprehension and Analysis (Focus on Informational Text)** Develop [reading] strategies…identifying and analyzing…purpose. **8.3.7** Analyze a work of literature, showing how it reflects the heritage, tradition…of its author.

For a complete description of the standards, see p. IN 11.

Vocabulary Preview

corresponded (kor uh SPON did) *v.* wrote letters to one another; form of the verb *correspond* **(p. 109)** *Yuri and Ko corresponded with their families while they were away at college.*

relish (REL ish) *n.* enjoyment or delight **(p. 109)** *Casey smiled as he played his favorite sport with much relish.*

humiliated (hyoo MIL ee ayt ud) *adj.* embarrassed; ashamed **(p. 110)** *Jonah felt humiliated when other kids made fun of him.*

Write to Learn Make a fill-in-the-blank worksheet. List each vocabulary word at the top of a sheet of paper. Then write a sentence for each vocabulary word. Leave a blank where the vocabulary word should go. Trade worksheets with a partner and try to complete each other's sentences.

English Language Coach

EL

General Context Clues You've used all of the following kinds of clues: characteristics, explanatory words, examples, synonyms and antonyms, category, direct definition, and visual. But sometimes there are **general context clues** that don't fit into one of these types. They may require you to look at more than one sentence and make inferences. Look at this example.

- *It is not clear whether the dinosaurs cooperated in hunting, as wolves or lions do. They may have mobbed their quarry or just gathered around after one of them made a kill.*

It's pretty easy to figure out what *quarry* means. It's what the dinosaurs hunted. You must make some inferences, but they are not difficult.

Use the following tips for using context:

- Look before, at, and after the unfamiliar word for a general topic or action associated with the word.
- Connect what you know with what the author has written.
- Predict a possible meaning, and apply it in a sentence.
- Try again if your guess did not make any sense.

Partner Talk Get the front page of a newspaper. With a partner, search for a word that neither of you know the meaning of. Then try to figure out the meaning from the context. Talk it out together. Then look the word up in a dictionary to see if you were right.

Additional Support

Author Search To expand students' appreciation of Yoshiko Uchida, have them access the Web site for more information and resources.

Literature Focus Lesson

Foreshadowing When a writer uses foreshadowing, he or she gives the reader clues about what is going to happen later in the story. Sometimes the foreshadowing is obvious, and the reader cannot miss the clue. Other times, the writer is subtle about it. As students read this story, they may find that Yoshiko Uchida gives a clue about what will happen later in the story. Challenge them to find the foreshadowing clue as they read "Being Japanese American." *("Still, I didn't truly realize how different I was until the summer I was eleven" on page 109.)* **AL**

Skills Preview

Key Reading Skill: Identifying Author's Purpose

As you read "Being Japanese American," think about everything you just read about Yoshiko Uchida. Use this information to identify what her purpose might be for writing this text.

Partner Talk Think of something that has happened in your life that you would like to write a story about. Talk with a partner about what happened and determine what the purpose of sharing your story should be.

Key Literary Element: Cultural Reference

A **reference** is a mention of a character, place, or situation from another work of art or literature, or from history. A **cultural reference** is a mention of a value, belief, tradition, or custom practiced in a certain culture. For example, you may read about a powwow in a Native American story. A powwow is a Native American cultural event where traditional dancing, drumming, and chanting are performed. Such cultural events are unique to Native Americans, and you most likely won't be reading about them in Japanese, Chinese, or Russian stories.

To identify cultural references, look for ideas or customs that are not practiced worldwide. When you read about events or beliefs, think about whether they are part of your culture or specific to another culture.

Small Group Work Imagine that a new student from another country is joining your class. In a small group, make a list of American customs to teach the new student about the culture.

Interactive Literary Elements Handbook
To review or learn more about the literary elements, go to www.glencoe.com.

Get Ready to Read

Connect to the Reading

Think about your family background. What are your roots, or heritage, and customs?

Whole Class Discussion Americans come from families with many different backgrounds. What do you think is good about this? Why is it hard sometimes? Talk about these questions with your class.

Build Background

This selection describes growing up in Berkeley, California, as a second generation Japanese American, or *Nisei*.

- During World War II, the United States fought against Japan.
- Many Japanese Americans living on the West Coast were imprisoned during World War II in crowded, badly built internment camps in the desert, mainly because they "looked like the enemy."

Set Purposes for Reading

BIG Question Read to find out how a young Japanese American girl struggles to accept and understand her heritage.

Set Your Own Purpose What would you like to learn about being Japanese American by reading this selection? Write your own purpose on the "Being Japanese American" page of Foldable 1.

Keep Moving

Use these skills as you read "Being Japanese American."

Teach

L Literary Element

Cultural Reference Ask: What are some examples of cultural references you have read in other books or seen in movies? *(Responses will vary.)* OL

EL Language Coach

Context Clue Ask: What is a Nisei? *(a second generation Japanese American)* **Ask:** How did you figure out what this word means? *(The definition is before the word.)* BL

Interactive Literary Elements Handbook Have students access the Web site to improve their understanding of cultural references.

Differentiated Instruction

Research and Present Have students work in small groups to research the Japanese American internment during World War II. Each group should prepare a three- to five-minute oral presentation on one item of interest. Suggest that groups use visual aids, such as photographs or charts, to enhance their presentations. Some students may want to focus on the physical setup of the camps (cramped living space, bathroom facilities, dining arrangements); some on the daily life and activities; some on what happened to the homes, personal belongings, and businesses of people in the camps; and some on how individuals survived. OL

Indiana English/Language Arts Academic Standards
SE: 8.1, 8.2, 8.3.7
TWE: *Literature Focus Lesson* 8.3, *Differentiated Instruction* 8.7.12

Teach

Viewing the Photo

Say: What is taking place in this photo? What ideas does it bring to mind? *(Possible response: This is a montage of an American flag and young Japanese American girls saying the Pledge of Allegiance. It calls to mind patriotism and allegiance.)* **AS**

R Reading Skill

Review Connecting Say: Many people feel a sense of pride and patriotism when they recite the Pledge of Allegiance. Have you ever felt this way or read about or watched someone else who felt this way? *(Responses will vary.)* **Say:** Use these feelings to connect to Uchida's American pride. **OL**

Readability Scores
Dale-Chall: 6.4
DRP: 58
Lexile: 1120

READING WORKSHOP 4

Being Japanese American

by Yoshiko Uchida

Superstitions were not the only Japanese things in my life. A lot more of me was Japanese than I realized, whether I liked it or not.

I was born in California, recited the Pledge of Allegiance to the flag each morning at school, and loved my country as much as any other American—maybe even more. **1** **R**

Still, there was a large part of me that was Japanese simply because Mama and Papa had passed on to me so much of their own Japanese spirit and soul. Their own values of loyalty, honor, self-discipline, love, and respect for one's parents, teachers, and superiors were all very much a part of me.

There was also my name, which teachers couldn't seem to pronounce properly even when I shortened my first name to Yoshi. And there was my Japanese face, which closed more and more doors to me as I grew older.

Practice the Skills

1 Key Literary Element

Cultural Reference The Pledge of Allegiance is a custom practiced in many schools across the country. By reciting the Pledge of Allegiance daily, Uchida shows her loyalty and involvement in American culture.

Additional Support

Reading in the Real World

Citizenship Share some history of the Pledge of Allegiance. It was first written in 1892 to celebrate Columbus Day. Write the original words on the board: *I pledge allegiance to my Flag, and to the Republic for which it stands: one Nation indivisible, With Liberty and Justice for all.* In 1923 it was changed to say "the flag of the United States" instead of "my Flag." A year later the words "of America" were added. During World War II, most schools were saying it each day. In 1943 the Supreme Court ruled that children could not be forced to say the pledge. Over ten years later, President Eisenhower added the phrase "under God." Have students write a paragraph telling what they think of the Pledge of Allegiance. **OL** **AL**

How wonderful it would be, I used to think, if I had blond hair and blue eyes like Marian and Solveig. Or a name like Mary Anne Brown or Betty Johnson. **R**

If only I didn't have to ask such questions as, "Can we come swim in your pool? We're Japanese." Or when we were looking for a house, "Will the neighbors object if we move in next door?" Or when I went for my first professional haircut, "Do you cut Japanese hair?" **L**

Still, I didn't truly realize how different I was until the summer I was eleven. Although Papa usually went on business trips alone, bringing back such gifts as silver pins for Mama or charm bracelets for Keiko and me, that summer he was able to take us along, thanks to a railroad pass.

We took the train, stopping at the Grand Canyon, Houston, New Orleans, Washington, D.C., New York, Boston, Niagara Falls, and on the way home, Chicago, to see the World's Fair.

Crossing the Mississippi River was a major event, as our train rolled onto a **barge** and sailed slowly over that grand body of water. **2** We all got off the train for a closer look, and I was so impressed with the river's majesty, I felt impelled[1] to make some kind of connection with it. Finally, I leaned over the barge rail and spit so a part of me would be in the river forever.

For my mother, the high point of the trip was a visit to the small village of Cornwall, Connecticut. There she had her first meeting with the two white American pen pals with whom she had **corresponded** since her days at Doshisha University. She also visited one of her former missionary teachers, Louise DeForest, who had retired there. And it was there I met a young girl my age, named Cathy Sellew. We became good friends, corresponded for many years, and met again as adults when I needed a home and a friend.

Everyone in the village greeted us warmly, and my father was asked to say a few words to the children of the Summer Vacation Church School—which he did with great **relish.**

1. Here, to feel ***impelled*** means to feel a strong urge to make a connection.

Vocabulary

corresponded (kor uh SPON did) *v.* wrote letters to one another

relish (REL ish) *n.* enjoyment or delight

Practice the Skills

2 English Language Coach

General Context Clues You can use context clues to figure out the meaning of **barge.** The train uses one to cross a river. Also, notice the word *sailed.* You know that boats sail. What do you think a *barge* is?

Teach

R Reading Skill

Review Connecting Ask: Have you ever wished you looked more like someone else? How did you think it would make your life better? Use your experience to explain how Uchida must have felt. *(Responses will vary.)* **BL** **OL**

L Literary Element

Review Tone Ask: What tone do you think the author used when she asked these questions? *(embarrassed and maybe even slightly ashamed)* **BL**

Differentiated Instruction

Designing a Travel Brochure Explain to students that tourism is a large industry. Many people travel to other states or countries to see how people in different cultures live, to experience different climates, food, or scenery, or to simply relax. Many workers make up the tourist industry, such as travel agents, hotel and restaurant workers, tour guides, museum workers, entertainment directors, and various transportation attendants. Tell students to design the vacation of their dreams and list all of the different persons in the tourism industry that would be responsible for making their trip successful. Students may search online for the department of tourism for the state or country of their choice to get ideas. **OL**

Indiana English/Language Arts Academic Standards

SE: 8.1, 8.3.7

TWE: *Reading in the Real World* 8.5.7, *Differentiated Instruction* 8.4.4

Teach

C1 Critical Thinking

Comprehension Ask: Why is the woman surprised that Uchida speaks English so beautifully? *(Possible response: She looks at her face and outward appearance and assumes that she speaks only Japanese or with a heavy accent.)* OL

L Literary Element

Cultural Reference Say: Name other ways people of various cultures show respect when greeting each other. *(Possible response: handshakes, kisses, hugs)* EL OL

C2 Critical Thinking

Analysis Ask: Why is Uchida so upset by her mother's bowing and the situation at the post office? *(Possible response: Uchida does not want to be different in any way. When her mother bows, for example, she shows that the family is different. The situation at the post office is another reminder to her that she is different.)* OL

READING WORKSHOP 4

Analyzing the Photo Yoshiko Uchida, second from the left, is ten years old here. Her parents, grandmother, and older sister are also pictured. What does this photo suggest about Uchida's family?

Most of the villagers had never before met a Japanese American. One smiling woman shook my hand and said, "My, but you speak English so beautifully." She had meant to compliment me, but I was so astonished, I didn't know what to say. I realized she had seen only my outer self—my Japanese face—and addressed me as a foreigner. I knew then that I would always be different, even though I wanted so badly to be like my white American friends. C1

I hated having Mama stop on the street and greet a friend with a series of bows as was customary in Japan. "Come on, Mama," I would say impatiently tugging at her sleeve. I felt as though everyone was staring at us. **3** L

I was **humiliated** when the post office called us one Sunday requesting that we pick up immediately a package of rotting food. Actually, it was just some pungent[2] pickled *daikon* (long white radish), sent by a friend who knew Papa loved eating it with rice and hot tea. But the man at the post office thrust it at us at arm's length, as though it were a piece of stinking garbage. C2

2. When something is ***pungent***, it has a very strong smell.

Vocabulary

humiliated (hyoo MIL ee ayt ud) *adj.* embarrassed; ashamed

Practice the Skills

3 Key Literary Element

Cultural Reference In Japan, bowing is the traditional way to greet someone. Bows signify respect and are used both when meeting and parting. How does Uchida react to her mother's bowing? Who is more Americanized, Uchida or her mother?

Additional Support

Literature Focus Lesson

Written Expression Direct students to think of how they would feel if they had been Uchida when she met the villager in Connecticut. Tell students to write an editorial or another piece in which they express their feelings. Remind students to give their audience the background information and tell them what they should do when they meet people for the first time. (For example, they might write, "Make sure that you do not look just at the outside person." Or they might write, "Don't assume that all Americans look the same.") OL AL

Keiko and I absolutely refused when Mama wanted us to learn how to read and write Japanese. We wanted to be *Americans,* not Japanese! C1

"Wouldn't it be nice to write to your grandmother in Japanese?" she asked.

"It's easier if you write her, Mama," we said.

"Don't you want to be able to read those nice storybooks from Japan?"

We didn't. Not really. We liked having Mama read them to us. We read our own favorites in English.

I loved going to the South Berkeley branch of the public library, where I would head for the children's corner. There I looked for the books with stars on their spines, which meant they were mysteries. I read such books as Augusta H. Seaman's *The Boarded Up House* and *The Mystery of the Old Violin.* I also liked Hugh Lofting's *Dr. Doolittle* books, and loved Louisa May Alcott's *Little Women* and *Little Men.* Other favorites were Anna Sewell's *Black Beauty* and Frances Hodgson Burnett's *The Secret Garden.* C2

Learning Japanese, Keiko and I felt, would only make us seem more different from our white classmates. So Mama didn't force us to go to Japanese Language School after regular school, as many of our Nisei (second-generation Japanese) friends did. 4

We finally agreed, however, to let her teach us Japanese during summer vacations when she also taught us how to embroider. We loved learning how to make daisies and rosebuds on pillowcases, but we certainly didn't make it easy for Mama to teach us Japanese. Keiko and I grumbled endlessly as we tried to learn how to read and write the complicated Japanese characters,[3] and by the time each summer rolled around, we had forgotten most of what we had learned the year before.

Practice the Skills

4 Key Reading Skill

Identifying Author's Purpose
The author wanted to be more like her white classmates than her *Nisei* friends. Remember that the author is a *Nisei.* What does this tell you about her purpose for writing this selection?

Analyzing the Photo This picture of Yoshiko and Keiko was taken in Berkeley, California. Does this photo help you understand their relationship? Explain.

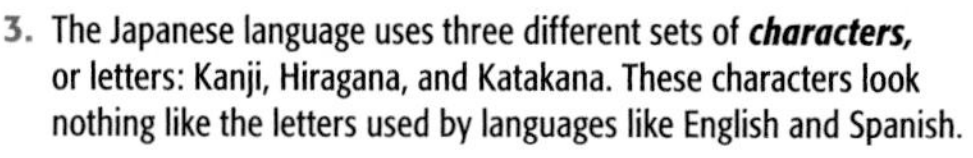

3. The Japanese language uses three different sets of ***characters,*** or letters: Kanji, Hiragana, and Katakana. These characters look nothing like the letters used by languages like English and Spanish.

English Language Coach

Verb Tenses Draw a three-column chart on the board and label the columns: *present, past,* and *future.* Ask students to copy the chart on a sheet of paper. Have students make a list of seven verbs from this page of the story, and have them write the present, past, and future tense of each verb in the chart. On the side of the chart, ask them to draw an illustration of at least two of the verbs. Below the chart, have them write one sentence for each verb, choosing only one of the tenses of that verb. EL BL OL

Teach

C1 Critical Thinking

Evaluation Say: The girls want "to be Americans, not Japanese." Do you think that by refusing to speak Japanese the girls were making other people consider them "more American"? *(Possible response: No, you can speak many different languages and still be considered American.)* OL AL

C2 Critical Thinking

Comprehension Ask: What is the reason that Uchida and her sister do not go to Japanese Language School? *(Possible response: They do not want to seem any more different than they already do.)* OL AL

Indiana English/Language Arts Academic Standards
SE: 8.2, 8.3.7
TWE: *Literature Focus Lesson* 8.5.7, *English Language Coach* 8.1

Teach

L Literary Element

Identifying Author's Purpose **Say:** Uchida points out that even though she and her sister refused to attend Japanese Language School, they still managed to learn many Japanese words. Also, she gives details of how she was influenced by some aspects of Japanese culture. What is Uchida's purpose in emphasizing these details? *(Possible response: Even though Uchida saw herself as American, her life was heavily influenced by Japanese language and culture. She's making a point that being American doesn't mean you can practice only American traditions—you can practice traditions from other cultures and still be considered American.)* OL

EL Language Coach

General Context Clues After students have used context clues to define *hybrid*, have them look up the word in dictionaries. Ask them to compare their definitions to the dictionaries' definitions. EL BL

READING WORKSHOP 4

Still, we managed to learn a lot of Japanese by osmosis. Our parents spoke Japanese to each other and to us, although we usually answered in English, sprinkling in a few Japanese words here and there.

Then there were many Japanese phrases we used every day. We always said, "*Itadaki masu*," before each meal, and "*Gochiso sama*" afterward to thank Mama for preparing the food. The first thing we called out when we came home from school was "*Tadaima*! I'm home!"

The Japanese names Mama gave to the tools and implements around the house were the sounds they made. The vacuum cleaner was the *buhn-buhn*. The carpet sweeper was the *goro-goro*. Mama's little sewing scissors with the silver bell tied to it was the *chirin-chirin*.

Keiko and I often talked in a strange **hybrid** language. 5 "It's your turn to do the *goro-goro* today." Or, "Mama said to *buhn-buhn* the living room." And anytime Mama asked us to fetch the *chirin-chirin*, we knew exactly what she meant.

Every night when we were little, Keiko and I would climb into bed and wait for Mama to come sit between our two beds and read a Japanese story to us. I first heard such wonderful folktales as "The Old Man Who Made the Flowers Bloom" and "The Tongue-Cut Sparrow" from her.

Although Papa loved to sing American folk songs, he and Mama taught us many Japanese songs that still float through my memory today. Their prayers, too, were always in Japanese—Papa's grace before meals (nice and short) and Mama's prayers at bedtime (not so short). So when it came to praying, I always did it in Japanese, even after I grew up.

We always celebrated Doll's Festival Day[4] on March 3, as all girls did in Japan, displaying special dolls for the occasion. Mama would open the big brown trunk in the basement and bring up dozens of tiny wooden boxes containing her Japanese doll collection. These

Practice the Skills

5 English Language Coach

General Context Clues The author uses examples of phrases that use a **hybrid** language. The phrases use both English and Japanese words. What do you think *hybrid* means? EL

On Doll's Festival Day, Japanese girls dress dolls like this one in ceremonial kimonos. Why are traditions like this one important? What traditions do you celebrate?

4. ***Doll's Festival Day*** is a holiday in Japan to pray for the growth and happiness of all young girls. On this day, girls display dolls in their homes and dedicate peach blossoms to them.

Additional Support

Literature Focus Lesson

Folktales Help students find copies of the two Japanese folktales mentioned in the story: "The Old Man Who Made the Flowers Bloom" and "The Tongue-Cut Sparrow." Students can also find other Japanese folktales. Have students either read a short section of their folktale aloud to the class or give the class a brief summary of their folktale. Direct students to report on how these folktales are similar to and/or different from the American folktales that they know. OL AL were not dolls to be played with, but to be treasured carefully and viewed only once a year.

A formal festival doll set consisted of an emperor and empress presiding over their court of musicians, guards, ladies-in-waiting, and so forth down to the lowliest member of the imperial court. 6

But Mama's collection was different. She did have an emperor and empress, but the rest were tiny dolls or toys that had caught her fancy. There were good-luck charms on ivory rings, round-bottomed *daruma* dolls that always sprang up when pushed down, miniature tea sets and kitchen utensils, dolls that were characters from folktales or dolls she'd dressed herself as a child, balls made of colored silk thread, small clay bells from old temples, folk toy animals that brought good luck, and anything else Mama wanted to include. It was all sort of a pleasant, Mama-like jumble laid out on a table covered with a festive red felt cloth. L

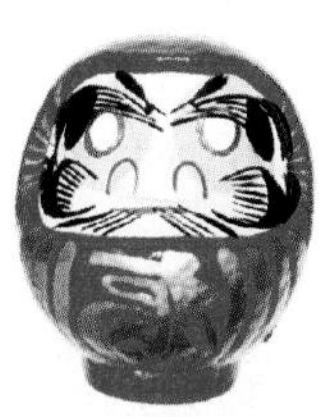

Visual Vocabulary ***Daruma dolls*** are round dolls with red-painted bodies and white faces.

"Bring out your own dolls, too," she would tell us. "We don't want them to feel left out."

So Keiko and I would bring out our white baby dolls with brown hair and green glass eyes and place them around the table as well.

Until I was much older and wiser, the Japanese dolls didn't mean much to me. Mama seemed to enjoy them more than Keiko or I did, and she would often have friends to tea to share her pleasure in their yearly appearance.

As for me, it was my white baby doll and my Patsy doll that I loved, even though they didn't look anything like me. I suppose it was because I always thought of myself as being an American. I just didn't realize how much of me was Japanese as well. 7 ❍ BQ

Practice the Skills

6 Key Literary Element

Cultural Reference What Japanese holiday is celebrated in the last two paragraphs? What aspects make it a uniquely Japanese holiday?

7 BIG Question

What did you learn about being Japanese American from reading this selection? Write your answer on the "Being Japanese American" page of Foldable 1. Your response will help you complete the Unit Challenge later.

Teach

L Literary Element

Cultural Reference Read the first line of the second complete paragraph aloud to the class: "But Mama's collection was different." Talk about how this collection had some American influences, such as Yoshiko and Keiko's white baby dolls. **Ask:** How can this collection symbolize Yoshiko as a Japanese American? *(Possible response: Yoshiko is influenced and shaped by two cultures.)* AL

BQ BIG Question

Ask: What does Yoshiko say she didn't realize about herself? *(She did not realize how much of her was Japanese as well as American.)* **Ask:** How does reading this selection help you answer the Big Question? *(Responses will vary.)* AS

Assess

Use the CheckPoint questions provided on Presentation Plus! to check for comprehension of the selection. These questions can be used with interactive response keypads for immediate student feedback.

Differentiated Instruction

Identifying Your Own Cultural References Have students think about a tradition or custom from their own culture. Suggest that students write a short essay that includes cultural references. Encourage English language learners to write about a custom or tradition practiced in their native country. In their essays, students should address the following points: how and when the tradition or custom is practiced; what the tradition or custom means to them; what it means to family or friends; whether or not they plan to continue practicing this custom or tradition and possibly pass it on to future generations. AS

Indiana English/Language Arts Academic Standards
SE: 8.1, 8.3.7
TWE: *Literature Focus Lesson* 8.7.11, *Differentiated Instruction* 8.5.7

Assess

Resources for page 114

- Selection Quick Check, p. 8
- Selection and Unit Assessment, p. 8
- ExamView Assessment Suite
- Interactive Tutor: Self-Assessment

Students can respond to the *After You Read* items in their Learner's Notebooks or on a separate sheet of paper.

Answering the

1. Responses will vary.
2. eleven
3. Possible responses: When she got her hair cut or wanted to swim in a friend's pool. She felt different when she was traveling with her family and someone was amazed that she spoke English so well. She felt uncomfortable when her mother bowed instead of just saying, "hello."

Critical Thinking

4. Possible response: They did not go to Japanese Language School; this made them different. They were similar in that they spoke some Japanese and had Japanese parents, habits, and traditions.
5. Possible response: She realized that others did not see her as "American."
6. Possible response: She came to appreciate the doll festival as a part of her heritage.

After You Read

Being Japanese American

Answering the BIG Question

1. What have you learned about being an American after reading this selection?
2. **Recall** How old was the author when she first realized she was "different"?

   TIP **Right There** You will find the answer in the text.
3. **Summarize** The author wrote about some of the difficulties she faced being Japanese American. Summarize the situations she described where she felt different for being Japanese American.

   TIP **Think and Search** You will find the answer in the text, but you will need to search for it.

Critical Thinking

4. **Compare and Contrast** The author and her sister did not want to be like other *Nisei.* How were they different from other *Nisei?* How were they the same?

   TIP **Author and Me** Use information from the text plus your own knowledge.
5. **Analyze** Think about what happened when Yoshiko went to Connecticut. What did Yoshiko learn about the way other people saw her?

   TIP **Author and Me** Use information from the text plus your own knowledge.
6. **Analyze** How did Yoshiko's feelings about the Japanese dolls change as she got older?

   TIP **Author and Me** Use information from the text plus your own knowledge.

Talk About Your Reading

List of Details In the first paragraph Uchida directly states the main, or most important, idea of the selection: "A lot more of me was Japanese than I realized, whether I liked it or not." With a small group of classmates, list at least five specific details that Uchida gives to support the main idea. Then share your list with the rest of the class.

Indiana English/Language Arts Academic Standards (pp. 114–115)

8.3 Comprehension and Analysis of Literary Text Respond to grade-level-appropriate literature... **8.7 Listening and Speaking** Speaking skills... are developed... **8.2 Comprehension and Analysis (Focus on Informational Text)** Develop [reading] strategies... identifying and analyzing... purpose. **8.3.7** Analyze a work of literature, showing how it reflects the heritage, tradition... of its author. **8.6 English Language Conventions**

For a complete description of the standards, see p. IN 11.

Talk About Your Reading

Sample details:

Yoshiko "looked" Japanese, and when she was in Connecticut, a stranger thought this meant she was not American at all.

Yoshiko and her sister spoke some Japanese at home, even if they used just a few Japanese words.

Yoshiko's family had Japanese traditions and habits, such as bowing and the doll festival.

Yoshiko's parents taught her Japanese songs.

Yoshiko's teachers had trouble pronouncing her Japanese name.

Skills Review

Key Reading Skill: Identifying Author's Purpose

7. Now that you have read the selection, why do you think Yoshiko Uchida wrote the text?

Key Literary Element: Cultural Reference

8. Give four examples of how members of the Uchida family still practice Japanese customs or traditions, even though they live in the United States.

9. What are Japanese "characters," and why does Uchida resist learning them?

Reviewing Skills: Activating Prior Knowledge

10. How does the author's experiences in the story remind you of experiences you know about or have read about second generation Americans?

Vocabulary Check

Choose the best word from the list to complete each sentence below. Rewrite each sentence with the correct word in place.

corresponded **relish** **humiliated**

11. He ate his wife's delicious cooking with great ______.

12. Sometimes Yoshiko felt ______ because of her family background.

13. The American children ______ with their friends who lived in Japan.

14. **English Language Coach** In your Learner's Notebook, write a sentence using a general context clue for the following words you learned while reading "Being Japanese American."

barge **osmosis** **astonished** **hybrid**

Grammar Link: Pronouns as Objects of Prepositions

A **preposition** is a word that relates a noun or a pronoun to another word in a sentence. Examples of prepositions are *about, across, against, before, during, into, off, on, to, through, under,* and *with.* When a pronoun is the object of a preposition, use an object pronoun.

- Joel gave the computer to *her.*
- Hamal went before *me.*

Use the object pronoun *whom* after a preposition.

- To *whom* did you give the folder?
- The person with *whom* I'm going is Terrence.

Be careful when a preposition has a compound object with both a noun and a pronoun. It still takes an object pronoun.

- Alex will apologize to the teacher and *me.*
- Can you come to the movie with Joe and *us?*

Look out! Never use the pronoun *I* after the preposition to.

Grammar Practice

Copy each sentence. Underline each preposition. Then circle the correct form of the pronoun in parentheses.

15. To (who, whom) should Yoshiko send the package?

16. Oh, you arrived at class before (I, me).

17. This gift is from your grandmother and (we, us).

18. Give it to Marie and (I, me).

Writing Application Look back at your Write About Your Reading activity. Did you use pronouns as objects of prepositions correctly? Fix any mistakes.

Web Activities For eFlashcards, Selection Quick Checks, and other Web activities, go to www.glencoe.com.

Skills Review

Key Reading Skill: Identifying Author's Purpose

7. Responses will vary.

Key Literary Element: Cultural Reference

8. Students may choose any four of these examples: they bow when greeting people, celebrate the doll festival, tell Japanese folktales, sing Japanese songs, pray in Japanese, and eat Japanese food.

9. Japanese characters are the letters used for writing in Japanese. Uchida resists learning them because she does not want to be different from other Americans.

Reviewing Skills: Activating Prior Knowledge

10. Responses will vary.

Vocabulary Check

11. relish

12. humiliated

13. corresponded

English Language Coach

14. Responses will vary.

Close

Ask students to summarize how reading "Being Japanese American" helped them answer the Big Question.

Grammar Link: Pronouns as Objects of Prepositions

Grammar Practice

15. **underline**: to; **circle**: whom

16. **underline**: before; **circle**: me

17. **underline**: from; **circle**: us

18. **underline**: to; **circle**: me

Literature Online

Web Activities Have students access the Web site for interactive activities that will help them assess their understanding of the selection.

Indiana English/Language Arts Academic Standards

SE: 8.2, 8.3, 8.3.7, 8.6, 8.7

Comparing Literature: Tone

Teaching Students to Compare Tone

Why Is It Important?

- Identifying the tone in selections is important for understanding authors' themes, writing styles, and viewpoints. When students understand subtleties such as tone, they can handle more difficult texts and more complex ideas.
- Fathoming and comparing tone in texts will help students develop insight into life and human nature. Students will internalize truths and ideas more fully when their feelings, as well as their intellect, are engaged by a text.
- Authors often use tone for specific instructive or aesthetic purposes. Students must be able to recognize the tone in order to fully understand what the author wants to communicate.

How to Help Students Get It

- Read aloud several short selections, each with a distinctly different tone, such as: enthusiastic, humorous, threatening, inspiring, or challenging. Work as a class or in small groups to identify the tone of each selection. Then ask students to select or search for other selections that reflect the same tones.
- For students who have trouble recognizing subtleties in language or written text, provide graphic selections to help them learn to identify and compare tone. Instruct them to use visual clues such as settings or the expressions on people's faces to distinguish and compare differences.
- Have students listen to audio selections in which the tone is enhanced by the expression in the reader's voice, background music, or other auditory clues. Then have the students read the same selections, reminding them to use those clues to enhance their perception of the tone.

Reading to Answer the Big Question

from *A Gift of Laughter* by Allan Sherman
Allan's son Robbie interrupts an important discussion to present his dad with a drawing. After yelling at his son for interrupting, Allan is reminded of a similar incident in his life, when he learned the importance of gifts from a child.

A Family Thing by Jerry Spinelli
We see many different views of 'family' in this autobiographical story. Spinelli describes home-cooked meals eaten in the kitchen with many aunts and uncles, reunion picnics, and softball games. Christmas is described as "a Bible thing . . . a wrapped-presents thing . . . most of all . . . a family thing." He shows us that presents aren't just the objects themselves, but the love and family feeling that go along with them.

Knoxville, Tennessee by Nikki Giovanni
This poem describes the delights of family and being home. In the summer, the garden is producing and the weather is fine. One feels "warm/all the time."

Workshop Resources

Pacing (Days) Standard	Pacing (Days) Block	Lesson	Student Materials	Teacher Resources
1	2	Comparing Literature: Tone	English Language Coach Review, p. 42	Bellringer Options Transparencies – Daily Language Practice 9 Presentation Plus!
1		from *A Gift of Laughter*	Glencoe Online Unit Vocabulary Review, p. 40 Academic Vocabulary Review, p. 44 English Language Coach Comparing Literature Graphic Organizer, p. 35 StudentWorks Plus™ Online Student Edition Literature Classics	Puzzlemaker Skill Level Up!™ A Language Arts Game BookLink 3 Assessment by Learning Objective (Diagnostic and Formative) Interactive Tutor: Self-Assessment TeacherWorks Plus™ ExamView Assessment Suite
1		"A Family Thing" and "Knoxville, Tennessee"	Glencoe Online Unit Vocabulary Review, p. 40 Academic Vocabulary Review, p. 44 English Language Coach Comparing Literature Graphic Organizer, p. 35 StudentWorks Plus™ Online Student Edition Literature Classics	Puzzlemaker Skill Level Up!™ A Language Arts Game BookLink 3 Assessment by Learning Objective (Diagnostic and Formative) Interactive Tutor: Self-Assessment TeacherWorks Plus™ ExamView Assessment Suite

Keys for Unit Resource

- Blackline Master
- Workbook
- Supplemental Text
- CD-ROM
- DVD
- Transparency
- Web-based
- Fast File

Level Appropriate Code

AS = Activities for all students
AL = Activities for students working above grade level
OL = Activities for students working at grade level
BL = Activities for students working below grade level
EL = Activities for English language learners

Focus

BELLRINGER Options

Daily Language Practice Transparency 9

Focus Activity Have students silently think of two friends that they could compare. Tell students not to name the friends but to give a comparison statement, such as "One friend is quieter than the other." OL

Teach

L Literary Element

Tone **Say:** Let's think of different tones that these stories and poem might have, such as happy, angry, or sad. What are some ways a writer can show each of these tones? *(Possible responses: A writer can show a happy tone by telling funny stories or having characters who see things from a positive point of view; a writer can show anger by describing a situation that made him or her mad; a writer can show a sad tone by having characters mourn.)* Write student responses on the board in a two-column chart with the headings *Tone* and *How a Writer Shows This Tone.* OL AL

COMPARING LITERATURE WORKSHOP

from *A Gift of Laughter*

by Allan Sherman

& A Family Thing

by Jerry Spinelli

& KNOXVILLE, TENNESSEE

by Nikki Giovanni

What You'll Learn

- How to compare three pieces of literature
- How to identify tone

What You'll Read

- from *A Gift of Laughter*, p. 119
- "A Family Thing," p. 124
- "Knoxville, Tennessee," p. 129

Point of Comparison

- Tone

Purpose

- To compare the tone of two personal essays and a poem
- Academic Vocabulary: *analyze*

Indiana English/ Language Arts Academic Standards (pp. 116–117)

8.3.7 Analyze... literature, showing how it reflects the... attitudes... of its author.

For a complete description of the standards, see p. IN 11.

Have you ever wanted to taste a new food? You probably asked, "What does it taste like?" In other words, you wanted to know how it was similar to or different from something you've tried before. Making comparisons helps you understand new things and relate to new people.

How to Compare Literature: Tone

Before you compare anything–friends, food, or things you read–you need to choose a point of comparison. In this workshop, your point of comparison is tone.

Tone is the writer's attitude toward a subject as shown in the language he or she uses. Tone can be serious or lighthearted; it can be funny, scary, or even sarcastic.

As you read, use the tips below to find and understand the tone in a selection from *A Gift of Laughter,* and in "A Family Thing" and "Knoxville, Tennessee."

L
- Look at the words the author uses.
  Are they strong words that describe emotions, such as joy, anger, sadness, or love?
- Look at what the characters do.
  Do they laugh, scream, smile, or cry?
- Look at the details the author includes.
  Do they influence the way you feel about the topic? How?

After you read, compare the tone of the three selections.

Additional Support

Literature Focus Lesson

Comparing Tone Help students see that comparing the tone of two pieces of literature is very different from comparing the story, or content, of those pieces. For example, two stories can be about the same type of sad topic and yet have very different tones. In one story, characters may find joy in the midst of sorrow, and the story will have a joyous, cheerful tone. And in another story, characters may be overcome with grief, and the tone would be sad and sorrowful.

Tell students to think about
- how the characters from the different stories might react in similar situations
- the overall emotional feel or attitude of each story OL AL

Get Ready to Compare

As you read, use a chart like the one below for help in identifying tone. Copy three of these charts in your Learner's Notebook–one for each selection. As you look for tone, pay attention to the words and details the author uses. Notice the feelings you have as you respond to the words and details.

Title (from *A Gift of Laughter*)	My Response	Author's Attitude (Tone)
Words		
Details		
Actions or Events		

Making Your Comparison

Look at this selection from *A Gift of Laughter* on page 119. Then use the steps below to understand the tone.

"Robbie, *please!*" I said. Then I appealed to my wife. "Can't we have just five minutes around here without kids screaming?" R

Step 1: Look at how the narrator speaks to–or about–other characters.

- *How does the narrator speak to Robbie? How does he speak to his wife? Does he seem calm or flustered? How can you tell?*

Step 2: Look at the action the author includes.

- *The narrator requests five minutes "without kids screaming." What does this tell you about his attitude toward what's happening around him?*

Step 3: Look at punctuation marks and italics that show strong feeling.

- *The narrator says, "Robbie,* please!*" Does it seem as if he is shouting? If he is, what tone does this create?*

As you read the selections in this workshop, you will use these steps and others to compare the tone of the readings. You can also use the steps to analyze the tone in other selections.

Teach

R Reading Skill

Review Connecting Say: This line of dialogue–"Can't we have just five minutes around here without kids screaming?"–may be something you have heard adults say around you. How is that adult usually feeling when he or she says something like this? *(Possible response: upset about too much noise or feeling a need to be alone and have some quiet)* BL OL

Assess/Close

Have students think about the two friends they compared in the Bellringer activity. Direct students to write a brief paragraph comparing these two friends in terms of their attitudes, or tones, about something they feel strongly about.

Resources for page 117

Use the Comparing Literature Graphic Organizer BLM in the Unit 1 Resource Booklet, p. 35.

Reading in the Real World

College Have students choose two different colleges to compare. Direct them to make a chart comparing the two schools and then write a simple comparison. Have students share their comparisons in a small group. Students should compare the following: size of school, location, academic programs, extracurricular activities, athletics, and tuition. OL

Indiana English/Language Arts Academic Standards

SE: 8.3.7

TWE: *Literature Focus Lesson* 8.3, *Reading in the Real World* 8.4

Teach

More About the Author

Allan Sherman wrote scripts for actors such as Jackie Gleason. He created and produced the television game show *I've Got a Secret.* Sherman went on to write for (and produce) *The Tonight Show Starring Steve Allen.* At the same time, Sherman wrote music and released his own albums.

R Reading Skill

Review Connecting Allow volunteers to discuss their responses to the Connect to the Reading question. They may also tell how they tried to make things right again. OL

Author Search To expand students' appreciation of Allan Sherman, have them access the Web site for additional information and resources.

Before You Read from *A Gift of Laughter*

Meet the Author

Allan Sherman was born in Chicago in 1924. He is well known for his funny songs. His most famous song is "Hello Muddah, Hello Faddah." It's about a boy at summer camp. In 1965 he published his autobiography, *A Gift of Laughter.* He died in 1973 at age 48.

Author Search For more about Allan Sherman, go to www.glencoe.com.

Indiana English/Language Arts Academic Standards
(pp. 118–122)

8.1 Word Recognition, Fluency, and Vocabulary Development Use... context clues... to determine the meaning of words... **8.3 Comprehension and Analysis of Literary Text** Respond to grade-level-appropriate literature...

For a complete description of the standards, see p. IN 11.

Vocabulary Preview

appealed (uh PEELD) *v.* made a serious request **(p. 119)** *Ramone appealed to his teacher for a higher grade.*

bewilderment (bih WIL dur munt) *n.* confusion **(p. 119)** *Maria looked at her messy math notes with bewilderment.*

English Language Coach

Context Clue Review As you worked through Unit 1, you practiced using different kinds of context clues. They include looking for word characteristics, explanatory words and phrases, examples, synonyms, antonyms, and word categories. In this workshop you will practice applying some of these clues. Look at the sentences below, from "A Family Thing." What does *tend* mean, and how can you tell?

- *During the growing months, every day after work, he went to . . .* ***tend*** *his vegetables. [A]s he put hoe to earth, he sometimes reflected . . . .*

In this context, *tend* means "take care of." The context clue is "put hoe to earth." It gives an example of tending.

Get Ready to Read

Connect to the Reading

R Recall a time when you were short-tempered with someone you care about. How did you feel afterward?

Build Background

- In this selection, Sherman recalls an event from his past.
- Sherman's grandmother has a thick Yiddish accent. Yiddish is a language that comes from German and Hebrew. It also borrows words from Slavic and Romance languages and from English. Yiddish developed in Europe hundreds of years ago.

Set Purposes for Reading

BIG Question Read to find out what lesson Allan Sherman learns from his grandmother and how he applies the lesson.

Set Your Own Purpose What else would you like to learn from the selection to help you answer the Big Question? Write your own purpose on the *Gift of Laughter* page of Foldable 1.

Additional Support

Literature Focus Lesson

Anecdote An anecdote is a short story that tells about one single, interesting event. Anecdotes are usually biographical and will reveal some aspect of a person's character. As students read this story, they can think about what this anecdote tells them about the writer. Have students write their own anecdotes about an interesting event they've experienced. Invite students to volunteer to read their anecdotes to the class. OL

from *A Gift of Laughter*

by Allan Sherman

"DaddydaddyDADDY!" That's how it came out—one long, excited word. He started yelling it at the top of the stairs, and by the time he bounded into the living room he really had it going good. I'd been talking to his mother about a money problem, and it stopped me mid-sentence.

"Robbie, *please*!" I said. Then I **appealed** to my wife. "Can't we have just five minutes around here without kids screaming?"

Robbie had been holding something behind his back. Now he swung it around for me to see. "Daddy, *look*!"

It was a picture, drawn in the messy crayon of a seven-year-old. It showed a weird-looking creature with one ear three times as big as the other, one green eye and one red; the head was pear-shaped, and the face needed a shave. **R**

I turned on my son. "Is *that* what you interrupted me for? Couldn't you wait? I'm talking to your mother about something *important*!" **1**

His face clouded up. His eyes filled with **bewilderment,** rage, then tears. "Awright!" he screamed, and threw the picture to the floor. "But it's *your* birthday Saturday!" Then he ran upstairs. **L**

Practice the Skills

1 Comparing Literature

Tone What is Sherman's attitude here? How can you tell? Make notes on your chart to tell what you know about Sherman so far.

Vocabulary

appealed (uh PEELD) *v.* made a serious request

bewilderment (bih WIL dur munt) *n.* confusion

Teach

R Reading Skill

Review Connecting Ask: Have you ever created something special for someone? What did you expect from them when you gave your creation to them? Based on your experiences, how do you think Robbie felt when his dad reacted to his drawing? *(Possible response: I expected the person to be happy and grateful for my gift; I think Robbie is probably very hurt and angry.)* **OL**

L Literary Element

Tone Ask: What is Sherman's tone at the bottom of this page? How has it changed from the beginning of the story? *(Possible response: He is now hurt and angry. At the beginning of the story, Sherman was excited and happy.)* **OL**

Readability Scores

Dale-Chall: 4.8
DRP: 48
Lexile: 600

English Language Coach

Synonyms Read aloud this phrase: "he bounded into the living room." The author could have written, "he ran, jumping into the living room." In this case, *bounded* is the better word choice because it evokes a certain image. Explain that good writers choose synonyms for variety and to express precise meaning.

Most synonyms have slightly different shades of meaning. Challenge students to explain subtle differences between the following pairs of synonyms and to use each in a sentence: *screaming/screeching; bewilderment/confusion; rage/anger.* **EL** **OL**

Indiana English/Language Arts Academic Standards

SE: 8.1, 8.3

TWE: *Literature Focus Lesson* 8.5.1, *English Language Coach* 8.1

Teach

R Reading Skill

Review Identifying Author's Purpose **Say:** The author begins to connect this event to something that happened to him a long time ago. Why do you think he is going to tell a story about his childhood? *(Possible responses: to explain how he got to be this type of parent; to show that he now understood how his son felt)* OL AL

C Critical Thinking

Comprehension **Ask:** What did Sherman pay for the football? *(Possible response: He got punched in the face and had to give Gudgie his new sled and all his marbles.)* **Ask:** Do you think a new sled would cost the same as a football that needed air? *(Possible response: probably not)* **Ask:** Why would Sherman be willing to trade the sled for it? *(Possible response: He wanted to give his grandmother what she needed.)* OL

I looked at the picture on the floor. At the bottom, in Robbie's careful printing, were some words I hadn't noticed: MY DAD by Robert Sherman.

Just then Robbie slammed the door of his room. But I heard a different door, a door I once slammed— 25 years ago—in my grandmother's house in Chicago. R

It was the day I heard my grandmother say she needed a *football*. I heard her tell my mother there was going to be a party tonight for the whole family, and she had to have a football, for after supper.

I couldn't imagine *why* Grandmother needed a football. I was sure she wasn't going to play the game with my aunts and uncles.

She had been in America only a few years, and still spoke with a deep Yiddish accent. But Grandma wanted a football, and a football was something in *my* department. If I could get one, I'd be important, a contributor to the party. I slipped out the door. C

There were only three footballs in the neighborhood, and they belonged to older kids. Homer Spicer wasn't home. Eddie Polonsky wouldn't sell or rent, at any price.

The last possibility was a tough kid we called Gudgie. It was just as I'd feared. Gudgie punched me in the nose. Then he said he would trade me his old football for my new sled, plus all the marbles I owned.

I filled Gudgie's football with air at the gas station. Then I sneaked it into the house and shined it with shoe polish. When I finished, it was a football worthy of Grandmother's party. All the aunts and uncles would be proud. When nobody was looking I put it on the dining-room table. Then I waited in my room for Grandma to notice it. 2

But it was Mother who noticed it. "Allan!" she shouted.

I ran to the dining room.

Analyzing the Photo Can a photographer express a tone, or attitude, in a picture? Can you describe the photographer's tone in this picture? Explain.

Practice the Skills

2 Comparing Literature

Tone Here Sherman is talking about himself as a child. What words and phrases show you that, as a kid, Allan was eager to please his family? Record your answers on your chart.

Additional Support

Literature Focus Lesson

Flashbacks A flashback is an interruption in the sequence of a piece of writing to describe a scene that happened at an earlier time. Skillful writers sometimes use flashbacks to give background information to readers so they can better understand what is happening at the present time. For example, a character in a story may meet someone he or she knew years earlier. A flashback to that earlier time could tell the reader about the relationship between the two characters. OL

"You know your grandmother's giving a party tonight. Why can't you put your things where they belong?"

"It's not mine," I protested.

"Then give it back to whoever it belongs to. Get it out of here!"

"But it's for Grandma! She said she needed a football for the party." I was holding back the tears.

Mother burst into laughter. "A *football* for the party! Don't you understand your own grandma?" Then, between peals of laughter, Mother explained: "Not football. Fruit bowl! Grandma needs a fruit bowl for the party." **3**

I was starting to cry, so I ran to my room and slammed the door. The worst part of crying was trying to stop. I can still feel it—the shuddering, my breath coming in little, **staccato** jerks. **4** And each sputtery breath brought back the pain, the frustration, the unwanted feeling that had made me cry in the first place. I was still trying to stop crying when the aunts and uncles arrived. I heard their voices (sounding very far away), and the clink-clink of Grandma's good china, and now and then an explosion of laughter.

After dinner, Mother came in. "Allan," she said, "come with me. I want you to see something." I followed her into the living room.

Grandma was walking around the room like a queen, holding out to each of the aunts and uncles the biggest, most magnificent cut-glass bowl I'd ever seen. There were grapes and bananas in it, red apples, figs and tangerines. And in the center of the bowl, all shiny and brown, was Gudgie's football. **R**

Just then my Uncle Sol offered Grandma a compliment.[1]

"Esther," he said, "that's a beautiful *football*. Real *cott gless*."

Grandma looked at Uncle Sol with great superiority. "Sol," she said, "listen close, you'll learn something. This *cott gless* is called a *frutt boll*, not a *football*. This in the middle, *this* is a *football*."

Uncle Sol was impressed. "Very smot,"[2] he said. "Very nice. But, Esther, now tell me something. How come you got a *football* in your *frutt boll*?" He pronounced them both very carefully. **L**

"Because," Grandma said, "today mine Allan brought me a nice present, this football. It's beautiful, no?"

1. A ***compliment*** is an expression of admiration or respect.
2. The author is writing the words so that you can hear how they sound. Uncle Sol is saying the word *smart.* With his accent, it sounds like ***smot.***

Practice the Skills

3 Comparing Literature

Tone The tone changes at this point. How would you describe Mother's tone? Why?

4 English Language Coach

Context Clue Review The writer uses the word **staccato** to describe his breath. Look at the context clues in the sentence: *shuddering, little,* and *jerks.* What do you think *staccato* means?

Teach

R Reading Skill

Review Activating Prior Knowledge **Ask:** From reading about how grandmothers usually act toward their grandchildren, or seeing this relationship portrayed in movies or on television, how do you expect them to act? *(Possible response: They are usually kind toward their grandchildren and appreciate everything they do.)* **Ask:** How does Sherman's grandmother represent the stereotypical grandmother? *(Possible response: She actually puts his football in her fruit bowl.)* **OL**

L Literary Element

Tone **Say:** Compare the tone that Grandma uses with Uncle Sol when she explains the pronunciation of the words to her tone when she explains why she has a football in the bowl. *(At first she has a matter-of-fact tone, just explaining how something should be; she still has a teaching tone in the next part, but she also shows her pride in her grandchild.)* **AL**

English Language Coach

Verb Tenses Work with students to identify the use of past tense in this selection. Explain that when writing about events that occurred in the past, writers must be sure that all the verbs they use are in the past tense. Students should understand that there is no shift in tense unless there is a shift in the time of the story.

Have students each write a paragraph about something interesting they did yesterday. Remind them to use the past tense for verbs that describe past actions. Partners can check each other's paragraphs for consistency in verb tense. **EL** **BL** **OL**

Indiana English/Language Arts Academic Standards

SE: 8.1, 8.3

TWE: *Literature Focus Lesson* 8.3, *English Language Coach* 8.6

Teach

C Critical Thinking

Analysis **Ask:** Do you think the relationship between Sherman and his son will change after this? *(Responses will vary. Students may think that Sherman will appreciate his son more.)* OL

Have students discuss how their answers to the Big Question have changed after reading this selection. OL

Assess

CheckPoint

Use the CheckPoint questions provided on Presentation Plus! to check for comprehension of the selection. These questions can be used with interactive response keypads for immediate student feedback.

Before Uncle Sol could answer, Grandma continued, "It's beautiful, yess—because from a child is beautiful, anything." 5

. . . *From a child is beautiful, anything.*

I picked up Robbie's picture from the floor. It wasn't bad, at that. One of my ears *is* a little bigger than the other. And usually, when Robbie sees me at the end of the day, I *do* need a shave.

I went up to his room. "Hi, Rob," I said.

His breath was shuddering, and his nose was running. He was packing a cardboard box, as he always does when he Leaves Home. I held up the picture. "Say, I've been looking this over. It's very good."

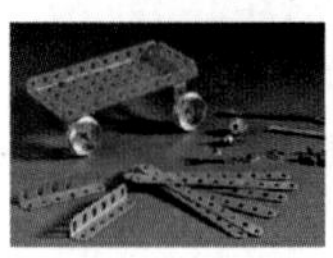

Visual Vocabulary
An ***erector set*** is a building toy made of small parts.

"I don't care," he said. He threw a comic book into the box and some Erector-set pieces. "Tear it up if you want to. I can't draw, anyhow."

He put on his cap and jacket, picked up the box and walked right past me. I followed him with the picture in my hand. 6

When he got to the front door, he just stood there, his hand on the knob, the way he always does. I suppose he thinks of the same things I used to, whenever I Left Home. You stand there by the door, and pray *they* won't let you go, because you have no place to go, and if *they* don't want you, who does?

I got my coat and joined him. "Come on," I said. "I'm going with you." And I took him by the hand. C

He looked up at me, very scared. "Where we going?"

"The shopping center is open tonight," I said. "We're going to buy a frame for this picture. It's a beautiful picture. We'll hang it in the living room. After we get the frame we're going to have an ice-cream soda and I'll tell you about something." BQ

"About what?"

"Well, you remember that old football your great-grandma keeps in the cut-glass bowl on her dining-room table?"

"Yes."

"Well, I'm going to tell you how she got it." 7 ❍

Practice the Skills

5 Comparing Literature

Tone Sherman's grandma says his present is beautiful. How does this make him feel? What words and phrases tell you that this is a positive memory for him? Explain your answers on your chart.

6 Comparing Literature

Tone What words and phrases does Sherman use to show that his attitude—and his tone—toward Robbie has changed? On your chart, make notes about the tone here.

7 BIG Question

Sherman learned that every child's gift is valuable. What did you learn from reading this selection? Write your answer on the *Gift of Laughter* page of Foldable 1. Your response will help you complete the Unit Challenge later.

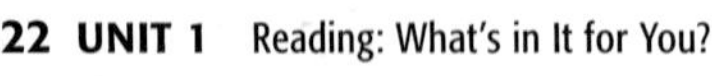

Additional Support

Differentiated Instruction

Writing Endings Have students write one of the following extensions to this story:

- a dialogue between Robbie and his father, showing what they say to each other as they drink their ice-cream sodas
- a letter that Robbie wrote while sitting in his room and planning to run away
- a letter from Sherman to Robbie teaching him about how to be a good father OL

Before You Read

A Family Thing *and* Knoxville, Tennessee

Meet the Authors

Jerry Spinelli

Jerry Spinelli was born in Norristown, Pennsylvania, in 1941. He has written more than 20 books. "A Family Thing" is a chapter from his autobiography *Knots in My Yo-yo String.*

Nikki Giovanni was born in Knoxville, Tennessee, in 1943. She grew up in Ohio but spent many summers in Tennessee. Giovanni has written more than 24 books. She is committed to fighting for civil rights and equality.

Author Search For more about Jerry Spinelli and Nikki Giovanni, go to www.glencoe.com.

Indiana English/Language Arts Academic Standards
(pp. 123–129)

8.1 Word Recognition, Fluency, and Vocabulary Development Use… context clues…to determine the meaning of words… **8.3 Literary Response and Analysis** Respond to grade-level-appropriate literature…

For a complete description of the standards, see p. IN 11.

Vocabulary Preview

procedure (pro SEE jur) *n.* series of steps taken to do something **(p. 124)** *The students followed a safety procedure when the fire alarm went off.*

recollections (rek uh LEK shunz) *n.* memories **(p. 125)** *Arnie's grandfather shared his recollections of the past.*

eclipsed (ee KLIPSD) *v.* made to seem unimportant; form of the verb *eclipse* **(p. 127)** *The team won the state championship and eclipsed its earlier losses.*

English Language Coach

Context Clue Review As you read, find the words below in "A Family Thing." Use context clues to understand their meanings. Remember to read the whole paragraph—and not just the sentence—as you hunt for context clues.

- triptych
- gauge

Get Ready to Read

Connect to the Reading

The authors of these selections write about places they love. Is there a place you love to go? Why is it meaningful to you? Write your answer in your Learner's Notebook.

Build Background

- The essay talks about holidays in the Spinelli household.
- The poem describes summers in Knoxville, Tennessee.
- Both the essay and the poem describe childhood memories.

Set Purposes for Reading

BIG Question Read "A Family Thing" and "Knoxville, Tennessee" to find out what the authors remember about the great family, food, and friends they had growing up.

Set Your Own Purpose What else would you like to learn from the story and poem to help you answer the Big Question? Write your own purpose on the "A Family Thing" and "Knoxville, Tennessee" page of Foldable 1.

COMPARING LITERATURE

Teach

More About the Author

When Jerry Spinelli was just sixteen years old, one of his poems was published in a local newspaper. Students may be surprised to learn that Spinelli was not a big reader when he was a young boy. He says that he only read sports pages and cereal boxes. Now Spinelli writes books for young adults.

Nikki Giovanni teaches writing at Virginia Tech. She has written several volumes of poetry and has made a few CDs of her readings. In fact, Giovanni's CD *The Nikki Giovanni Poetry Collection* was a finalist for a Grammy Award in 2003. Giovanni has written several books of poetry for children.

Literature Online

Author Search To expand students' appreciation of Jerry Spinelli and Nikki Giovanni, have them access the Web site for additional information and resources.

Differentiated Instruction

Picture It Have students create pictures to show images of the places they love to go. Tell students to include pictures that show different things that make the place special. For example, if they love going to visit a certain relative, they can include pictures of the people they like seeing there as well as pictures showing some of the things they do together. **OL**

Indiana English/Language Arts Academic Standards
SE: 8.1, 8.3
TWE: *Differentiated Instruction* (p. 122) 8.5.1

Teach

Viewing the Photo

Ask: How does this photograph help you determine what this story is going to be about? *(Possible response: The older pictures make me think that this story is going to be about memories and family members.)* **AS**

L Literary Element

Tone Ask: What words helped you determine the tone for this part of the story? *(Responses will vary.)* **OL**

Readability Scores
Dale-Chall: 6.5
DRP: 57
Lexile: 950

A Family Thing

by Jerry Spinelli

On the night of May 16, 1936, my mother and father got married. This was three years after Lou Spinelli, nicknamed Poppy, had spotted pretty, dark-haired Lorna Bigler on the dance floor at the Orioles Lodge and said to his friend Babe Richards, "See that girl. That's who I'm going to marry." On the night of their wedding, they were on another dance floor, at the Little Ritz, a nightspot on Route 202 north of town. They were broke, so this was all the honeymoon they would have. **1**

At one point during the evening an announcement was made: A contest would determine the prettiest lady in attendance. My mother doesn't recall the contest **procedure,** only the result. The winner was the new Mrs. Lou Spinelli. Her prize was a gift certificate to have her portrait done at the Davis Photography Studio. **L**

Four and a half years later, on February 1, 1941, I was born. My brother, Bill, came along four and a half years after that, on July 29, 1945. My mother's wedding-day prize, the framed

Vocabulary

procedure (pro SEE jur) *n.* series of steps taken to do something

Practice the Skills

1 Comparing Literature

Tone The author, Jerry Spinelli, begins with a story about his parents. Look at the words Spinelli has chosen and the details he includes. What's the tone of this part of the essay? Write your answer on your chart.

Additional Support

Reading in the Real World

Careers Have students do some research to learn about photographers, especially wedding photographers. Challenge students to interview different photographers in your school or community. Students should try to find out

- how the photographers get most of their work
- if they specialize in one type of photography or do all different types
- how technology has changed their work over the years (examples of technology are digital photography and videography on either video or CD-ROM) **OL** **AL**

portrait from Davis Studio, stands today on her bedroom dresser, the center of a **triptych** flanked by photo portraits of toddlers Bill and me. **2**

Mothers can get short-changed by memory. My **recollections,** for example, begin somewhere in my third year. By then some of my best experiences with my mother, some three years' worth of constant daily interaction, were already over. When my mind's recorder finally turned on, it was moments with my father that made the more memorable impressions: trips to high school ball games, backyard baseball, setting up the Christmas crèche. My mother's attentions continued, of course, but they tended to be less obvious, less noticed. They were the background of my life, the everyday care and support that at last came into full recognition when I acquired a family of my own. **EL**

Visual Vocabulary
A ***crèche*** (kresh) is a representation of Jesus's birth in a stable.

The marriage of Louis Anthony Spinelli and Lorna Mae Bigler brought together two heritages: Italian (my father) and Pennsylvania Dutch (my mother).

When I think of my Italian side, I think first of Sundays after church. The four of us would walk—or after 1954, when we got our first car, ride—the four blocks from First Presbyterian to my grandparents' home at 226 Chestnut. It was a row house with porches front and back and a rose arbor and dark polished furniture that made the living and dining rooms feel gloomy to me. The kitchen was where the light and the people and the food were. **C**

Around the kitchen table sat aunts and uncles and cousins and, always at the head, my grandfather, Alessandro "Alex" Spinelli. In front of him was a small glass pitcher of red wine. Before each meal, including breakfast of cold spaghetti, he drew the wine from his own barrel in the cellar. He was bald and he did not speak English very well and his breath always smelled of garlic and he smoked thin black wicked stogies and his fingers were as thick as sausages. He had labored many years for the Pennsylvania Department of Highways. Later the Borough of Norristown employed him as a street

Vocabulary

recollections (rek uh LEK shunz) *n.* memories

Practice the Skills

2 **English Language Coach**

Context Clue Review What is a **triptych?** Use context clues to write a definition. (Hint: How many pictures are on the dresser?)

Teach

EL Language Coach

Context Clues Explain to students that *flanked* means "to be placed on both sides of." This is a context clue that will help them understand *triptych.* **AL**

C Critical Thinking

Comprehension Ask: What does Spinelli recall about going to his grandparent's house on Sundays? *(He remembers how their home is dark except for the kitchen, where the light, food, and people were.)*
Say: Give four details about his grandfather, Alessandro "Alex" Spinelli. *(Possible response: He always sat at the head of the table, and before each meal he drew wine from his own barrel in the cellar. He was bald and did not speak English very well.)* **OL**

English Language Coach

Plural Possessives A common error when making a plural word into a possessive is to put the apostrophe before the plural *s.* Note the correctly written example on this page—grandparents' home. With plurals not ending in *s,* the opposite mistake is often made. Since these plurals do not end in *s,* the writer mistakenly writes *s'.* For example, a writer might mistakenly write *childrens'* instead of *children's.* Write the following examples on the board without apostrophes and have students copy them, placing apostrophes to form possessives: children's money, people's rights, countries' taxes, diplomats' briefcases. **EL** **OL**

Indiana English/Language Arts Academic Standards
SE: 8.1, 8.3
TWE: *Reading in the Real World* 8.7.9, *English Language Coach* 8.6.5

Teach

R Reading Skill

Review Activating Prior Knowledge **Say:** Think about what you know about travel on steamships from Europe to America. Why is it so impressive to Spinelli that his grandfather made this trip alone as a teenager? *(Possible response: Students will likely know that this trip took many weeks, maybe four to six weeks, and many people got seasick along the way. Being a young man, all alone, meant that Spinelli's grandfather had no one to look out for him along the way.)* OL

C Critical Thinking

Analysis **Ask:** Based on this paragraph, what do you think Spinelli feels about his grandfather? *(Possible response: Spinelli looked up to his grandfather and wanted to be like him.)* OL

sweeper. Sometimes, riding my bike, I would see him with other old men, pushing a broom along a curb.

That was his job. His love was the "farm," a small patch of vacant land that he rented in the East End. During the growing months, every day after work, he went to the farm to tend his vegetables. I like to think that, as he put hoe to earth, he sometimes reflected on what to me was the remarkable central fact of his life:

"He came over on a boat all by himself when he was only fourteen years old."

That's how I say it, even now, when describing my grandfather's coming to this country. He was an orphan in Italy. He worked in the olive groves around Naples. An aunt arranged for relatives to meet him in New York, handed him a one-way ticket on a steamship, and off he went, across the Atlantic Ocean, a black-haired teenager, alone, *solo.* R

Fifty years later I, a nine-year-old American-born boy, sat at his kitchen table, eating the roast chicken with my fingers because that's how he did it, trying to imagine the bald old man at the head of the table with black hair. C

The first course was always salad, as simple as salad gets: lettuce with oil and vinegar. Then came the chicken, then spaghetti and meatballs. My grandmother often made her own spaghetti, rolling out the dough and slicing it into strands with a device that reminded me of a harp. She would spend a whole day nursing the gravy at the stove. (To many Italians, spaghetti sauce is "gravy.") The dessert was often hot chestnuts, roasted on a second stove in the cellar. 3

As with the Spinellis, a table stands in the center of my memory of the maternal relatives. In this case the table is not in a kitchen but on a sloping lawn under a huge oak tree. Made of planks laid over sawhorses, the table is very long and

Analyzing the Photo How does this image capture the "feel" of Spinelli's hometown?

Practice the Skills

3 Comparing Literature

Tone Describe Spinelli's attitude toward the people and food he remembers. Write your answers on your chart.

Additional Support

Reading in the Real World

Citizenship Spinelli's grandfather was an immigrant who came from Italy. Have students think about reasons that people might want to immigrate to the United States. Then challenge groups of students to create a survey that asks questions about immigration—they may choose to ask questions about why people immigrate, questions about people's feelings about immigration, or some other topic. However, their surveys should try to address one aspect of immigration and give about five questions. Then have students survey a person they know who has immigrated to the United States. Groups can evaluate the data from their surveys and report their findings to the class. OL AL is crowded with pickled eggs and cold cuts and potato salad and three-bean salad and lemon meringue pie and dozens of other goodies. The place is my Aunt Isabel and Uncle Ted's home in Phoenixville, Pennsylvania, about ten miles from Norristown. The occasion is the annual family reunion. **L**

In my early years the reunion was, after Christmas, the biggest event on my calendar. It was the only time I got to see Aunt Lizzie and her gang from Highspire, some eighty miles away. Even their names seemed different. There was a Willard and a Juanita and a second cousin exotically named Kendra. **4**

One year there was even more excitement than usual: Uncle Elwood and Aunt Kay drove in from Michigan. I kept staring at my Midwestern cousins Bruce, Janey, and Suzie. They might as well have come from Mars. Alas for Aunt Margaret and Uncle Chet and their kids Cindy, George, JoAnne, and Patty, there was no magic of distance. They lived on Chain Street in Norristown, a mere block and a half from 802 George. I barely noticed them.

As a once-a-year event, the reunion became a **gauge** by which to measure my progress, both physical and social. **5** On the tennis court-size side yard, the uncles always got up a game of softball for the kids. I began as a tiny, grunting fumbler, swinging in vain at the slowest underhand tosses with a bat as big as I was. By the age of ten or eleven, I was clipping the grass with sharp grounders; then line drives to the garage; then, as a seasoned teenage shortstop, long flies into the strawberry patch beyond the trees. But by then the family reunion was no longer number two on my calendar. It had been **eclipsed** by such happenings as school dances and miniature golf with my friends. The year came when I felt myself too big to participate in the softball game. In college, some years, I did not even attend the reunion. **C**

But home—home is a reunion daily. And I never felt too big for Christmas. Christmas was a Bible thing, of course, and a school-vacation thing and a wrapped-presents thing and a homemade-

Vocabulary

eclipsed (ee KLIPSD) *v.* made to seem unimportant

Practice the Skills

4 Reviewing Skills

Connecting Think about your favorite memory. How would you describe it to someone else? What details would you use to show how you feel about the people, places, and things you're describing?

5 English Language Coach

Context Clue Review What is a **gauge**? Use context clues to write a definition. (Hint: Spinelli says he uses the *gauge* "to measure.")

Analyzing the Photo What does Spinelli remember about the way his grandmother made spaghetti? How are his memories of food and family related?

Teach

L Literary Element

Review Description Ask: What senses do these descriptions appeal to most? *(sense of taste and sight)* BL

C Critical Thinking

Comprehension Ask: How do the family reunion softball games serve as a gauge to measure Spinelli's progress? *(Possible response: When Spinelli was really young, he couldn't hit the ball—he swung the bat in vain. Then when he was a little older, he began to hit "sharp grounders." He continued hitting the ball farther and farther each year until he felt too old for the softball games and no longer played.)* OL

English Language Coach

Softball Terminology Explain to students that softball is a game that was invented in the United States but is now played in many different countries throughout the world. Some students will not be familiar with the softball terminology Spinelli uses on this page. Explain the following definitions:

- **grounder:** a hit ball that rolls or bounces on the ground, usually in the infield
- **line drive:** a hit ball that goes in a low, fast line
- **long fly:** a hit ball that flies high and deep into the outfield BL

Indiana English/Language Arts Academic Standards

SE: 8.1, 8.3

TWE: *Reading in the Real World* 8.7, *English Language Coach* 8.1

Teach

C Critical Thinking

Comprehension: Say: Spinelli says that his parents gave him and his brother a lot of gifts at Christmastime and did not spend much on themselves. What is the effect of this later in Spinelli's life? *(Possible response: He realizes that his parents gave him selfless love.)* OL

BQ BIG Question

Ask: What did you learn about Spinelli's ideas about family from this selection? *(Possible response: Spinelli felt loved by both of his parents and has fond memories of spending time with his father's and mother's families, mostly around special meals and holidays. Family is important to him, and he thinks it is valuable.)* OL

Assess

CheckPoint

Use the CheckPoint questions provided on Presentation Plus! to check for comprehension of the selection. These questions can be used with interactive response keypads for immediate student feedback.

cookies thing—but most of all, as I look back, it was a family thing.

My parents spent almost nothing on themselves. They bought only the clothes they needed. It was a big deal to treat themselves to a milkshake. They never went to the movies. And yet, for all they gave my brother and me, you'd have thought they were rich. My Christmas gifts came in piles. From Lincoln Logs to the inevitable walnut in the toe of my red felt stocking, I accepted the presents strictly as the objects they appeared to be. Only years later did I realize the truth: the gift was my parents' selfless love. **6** **C**

Analyzing the Photo What does this photograph tell you about the way the Spinellis celebrated Christmas?

One Christmas morning it bounced lightly off my chest as I came down the stairs, and I looked to see my first football wobbling at my feet. Another year it waited for me in the kitchen. I had unwrapped the last present from under the tree, and my father said, "Well, I guess that's it. Looks like you did pretty good this year." And then someone asked me to go to the kitchen for something, and there it was, in front of the sink: a spanking-new cream and green whitewall-tired Roadmaster bicycle. Love leaning on a kickstand. **7** ○

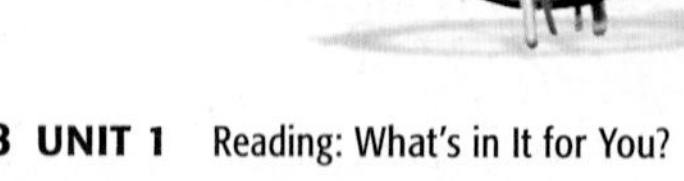

Practice the Skills

6 Comparing Literature

Tone What words and phrases does Spinelli use in this paragraph to show that he loves and respects his parents? What tone do the words and phrases create? Write your answers on your chart.

7 BIG Question **BQ**

What emotions did you feel as you read "A Family Thing"? Did reading about Spinelli's family cause you to think about your own? Write your answer on the "A Family Thing" page of Foldable 1. Your response will help you complete the Unit Challenge later.

Additional Support

Differentiated Instruction

Researching Traditions Invite students to research different holiday traditions and report back to the class. You may choose to have each student report on a different country and its holiday traditions, or you may allow students to choose a specific holiday or country and report on that. Combine students' findings in a holiday traditions book. OL

KNOXVILLE, TENNESSEE

by Nikki Giovanni

A Chat in the Road, 1991. Anna Belle Lee Washington. Oil on canvas, 20 x 30 in.

I always like summer
best
you can eat fresh corn
from daddy's garden
and okra*
and greens*
and cabbage*
and lots of
barbecue
and buttermilk
and homemade ice-cream
at the church picnic
and listen to
gospel music
outside
at the church
homecoming **1**
and go to the mountains with
your grandmother
and go barefooted
and be warm
all the time
not only when you go to bed
and sleep **2** ❍

5, 6, 7 ***Okra, greens,*** and ***cabbage*** are all vegetables commonly eaten in the South.

Practice the Skills

1 Comparing Literature

Tone What is the speaker's attitude toward summer and summer foods? What words and phrases tell you so? Put them on your chart.

2 BIG Question

BQ What did you learn from reading "Knoxville, Tennessee"? Did the poem make you think about the place you come from in a new way? Explain. Write your answers on the "Knoxville, Tennessee" page of Foldable 1.

Teach

R Reading Skill

Review Setting a Purpose for Reading **Say:** You already know that this poem will be about one of the writer's childhood experiences. What might you want to get out of reading this poem? *(Possible responses: I can learn more about the poet and her childhood in Tennessee. I can find out if her experience was one that most people experience or if it was unique to her and that time and place.)* OL

BQ BIG Question

Ask: How can reading a poem about someone else's childhood be meaningful for a reader? *(Possible response: It can show how we all have the same feelings, hopes, and dreams, or it can help us to think about how other people experience the world.)* OL

Assess

CheckPoint

Use the CheckPoint questions provided on Presentation Plus! to check for comprehension of the selection. These questions can be used with interactive response keypads for immediate student feedback.

Literature Focus Lesson

Sensory Imagery Prompt students to brainstorm a vivid memory from their childhood. Instruct them to fill in this sentence: *My memory is about* ____. Next, have them make a bullet-pointed list of the details of their memory with simple, yet descriptive, imagery (as in Giovanni's poem). Remind them to use language that appeals to the senses. Now have them remove the phrase *"My memory is about"* from the sentence. The remainder will serve as the first line of their poem. Beneath the opening line, instruct them to rewrite the bullet-pointed list in the form of a poem. OL

Indiana English/Language Arts Academic Standards
SE: 8.3
TWE: *Literature Focus Lesson* 8.4

Assess

Resources for page 130

- Selection Quick Check, pp. 9–10
- ExamView Assessment Suite
- Interactive Tutor: Self-Assessment

Students can respond to the *After You Read* items in their Learner's Notebooks or on a separate sheet of paper.

Vocabulary Check

from A Gift of Laughter and "A Family Thing"

1. cross out the word *denied*
2. cross out the word *manual*
3. cross out the phrase *fell behind*
4. cross out the word *excitement*
5. cross out the word *songs*
6. Possible response: When Kip broke his ankle, he fell behind at school and his classmates eclipsed him academically.
7. correct
8. Possible response: Feeling bewilderment about the material, Mario had difficulty completing his French homework.
9. correct
10. Possible response: Calvin appealed, or asked, for more working hours.

English Language Coach

11. Solo; alone; by himself.

After You Read

from *A Gift of Laughter* & **A Family Thing** & **KNOXVILLE, TENNESSEE**

Vocabulary Check

In your Learner's Notebook, copy 1–10 below. For 1–5, cross out the word or phrase that does not belong with the others.

from *A Gift of Laughter* and **A Family Thing**

appealed procedure eclipsed bewilderment recollections

1. requested, appealed, asked for, denied
2. procedure, process, manual, method
3. eclipsed, moved beyond, outran, fell behind
4. confusion, astonishment, excitement, bewilderment
5. memories, thoughts, recollections, songs

Look at 6–10. If the boldfaced word is used correctly in the sentence, write *correct* above it. If not, rewrite the sentence using the boldfaced word correctly.

6. When Kip broke his ankle, he fell behind at school and **eclipsed** his classmates academically.
7. Following standard **procedure,** the paramedics responded to the call.
8. Feeling **bewilderment** about the material, Mario finished his French homework with ease.
9. Starla's grandparents loved to share their **recollections** of the past.
10. Calvin **appealed** for fewer working hours because he needed the money.
11. **English Language Coach** Read the following sentence from "A Family Thing." Use context clues to figure out what *solo* means; then define it.

    An aunt . . . handed him a one-way ticket on a steamship, and off he went, across the Atlantic Ocean, a black-haired teenager, alone, ***solo.***

Indiana English/Language Arts Academic Standards
(pp. 130–131)

8.3.7 Analyze. . . literature, showing how it reflects the. . . attitudes. . . of its author.

For a complete description of the standards, see p. IN 11.

Reading/Critical Thinking

from *A Gift of Laughter*

12. **Recall** Why did Robbie pack his bags and try to leave home?
   TIP Right There The answer is in the text.

13. **Draw Conclusions** What lesson did Sherman learn from his grandmother?
   TIP Think and Search The answer is in the text, but the details are not in one place.

14. **Interpret** What did Grandma mean when she said, "From a child is beautiful, anything"?
   TIP Author and Me You will find clues in the text, but you must also use your ideas.

A Family Thing and KNOXVILLE, TENNESSEE

15. **Summarize** Summarize Spinelli's main idea in "A Family Thing."
   TIP Think and Search The answer is in the text, but the details are not in one place.

16. **Analyze** What did Spinelli's family mean to him when he was a child? What do you think his family means to him now?
   TIP Author and Me You will find clues in the text, but you must also use your ideas.

17. **Interpret** What might the speaker in "Knoxville, Tennessee" mean when she says that summer is a time to "be warm / all the time / not only when you go to bed / and sleep"?
   TIP Author and Me You will find clues in the text, but you must also use your ideas.

Writing: Compare the Literature

Use Your Notes

Follow these steps to compare the tones of the selection from *A Gift of Laughter* and "A Family Thing" and "Knoxville, Tennessee."

Step 1: Study the chart you made for each selection. Did you notice similar dialogue, descriptions, or events in any of the selections? Circle those details on your charts.

Step 2: Look at the notes you made in the "Writer's Attitude" column. Did you note any similarities among the three selections? Underline those details on your charts.

Step 3: Look at the notes you made in the "My Response" column. Do your responses to the selections have anything in common? Draw a box around those details on your charts.

Step 4: Look over all the similarities you just found. Use your notes and your own ideas to write responses to the questions below.

Get It on Paper

Remember that **tone** is a writer's attitude toward the subject he or she is writing about. Tone can be positive, negative, sentimental, playful, funny, or serious, among other things.

How are the tones of the selections alike? How are they different? Copy and complete these statements on a separate sheet of paper. Use the details from your comparison charts in your answers.

18. The tone of "Knoxville, Tennessee" is ______. These details support my statement: ______.
19. The tone of "A Family Thing" is ______. These details support my statement: ______.
20. The tone of *A Gift of Laughter* is ______. These details support my statement: ______.
21. "Knoxville, Tennessee," "A Family Thing," and *A Gift of Laughter* share a ______ tone. They share these similarities: ______.

Reading/Critical Thinking

from *A Gift of Laughter*

12. Possible response: Robbie was upset because his dad did not like the gift that he had made for him.
13. Possible response: Sherman realized that when his child made something for him, it was special, and he needed to appreciate it the way that his grandmother had appreciated the football .
14. Possible response: His grandmother meant that a gift from a child is always special.

"A Family Thing" and "Knoxville, Tennessee"

15. Possible response: Spinelli's main idea is that his family loved him and he enjoyed being with them.
16. Possible response: When Spinelli was a child, he enjoyed being with his family. He went through a time when he skipped some of the family reunions, but he always wanted to be with them at Christmas. Now his family means even more to him because he realizes how much they love him.
17. Possible response: She means that summer is a time when you are warm all the time physically as well as emotionally.

Writing: Compare the Literature

Get It on Paper

18–21. Responses will vary. Students should support their answers with details from the selection.

Close

Ask students which of the three selections helped them best answer the Big Question and why.

Indiana English/Language Arts Academic Standards
SE: 8.3.7

The Unit Challenge

Focus

BELLRINGER Options

Daily Language Practice Transparency 10
Focus Activity Say: Think about the stories we read in this unit. Which story did you get the most from reading and why? *(Responses will vary.)* AS

Teach

Group Activity: Write a Reading Plan

- You may select the note-taker or ask for a volunteer.
- Each group member should create at least one separate web diagram.
- Each group member should write his or her own list and make sure to write neatly so that others can read it.

Assess/Close

Group Activity

Ask: How can you use the lists and diagrams to help you get the most out of your reading? *(Responses will vary. Suggest that students write their answers in their Learner's Notebooks.)* OL

Answering The BIG Question: Reading: What's in It for You?

As you read the selections, you have been thinking about people's reasons for reading. Now use what you've learned to do the Unit Challenge.

The Unit Challenge

Follow the directions for the activity you've chosen.

A. Group Activity: Write a Reading Plan

With your group, you are going to make a Reading Plan for your own life. The plan will help you figure out what you can read to help you develop your interests and reach your goals. If you don't read a lot now, don't worry! This activity will help you think about how to read—with a sense of purpose—the things that relate to you.

1. **Brainstorm** Work with your group to make a list of goals you'd like to achieve. (Choose one person to be the note-taker for the group.) Do you want to go to college? What do you want to be when you grow up? Maybe you have a favorite hobby, such as drawing or playing music, and you dream of turning that hobby into a career someday.

2. **Create Diagrams** Review the notes you made on your Foldable, and think about how reading can help you reach these goals. For example, some books might show you how to do something, like make a sculpture or draw a still-life. Other books might tell you about people who share your interests. Use web diagrams to show the different things you might read. Make a separate web for each of the goals you listed in Step 1. Look at this example:

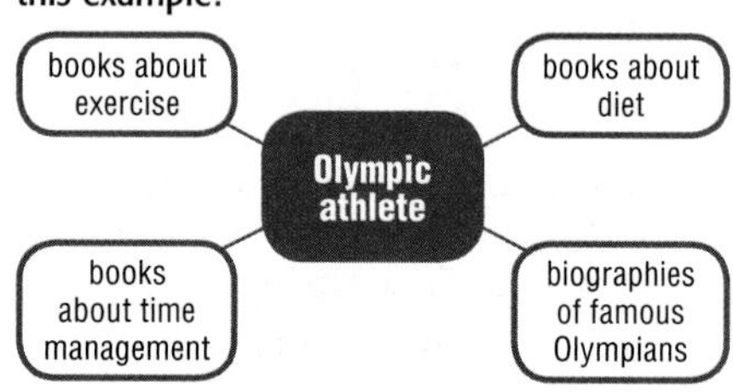

3. **Make Lists** Talk with your group about how reading can help you meet your goals and learn about interesting things. Think about the word webs you just made. Use the lists below to develop your reading plans.

   Goal or Dream ______

What else do I need to know?	Where can I find out?
1. ______	1. ______
2. ______	2. ______

4. **Put It All Together** Staple together the lists and diagrams your group just made. If you can, make copies for everyone in the group. Display one copy for the class.

B. Solo Activity: Create a Reading Chart

The selections in this unit have helped you think about why you read. Now it's time to make a chart that will help you answer the Big Question. If you don't read a lot, use this activity to think about what you might like to read and why.

1. **What Do You Like to Read?** Maybe you like to read comic books, emails, and text messages from friends. Maybe you like to read books, magazines, and newspapers. Think about what you enjoy reading. What do you read often? List and explain your answers.

2. **Create a Chart** Draw a chart like the one on this page. Use the list you just made to fill it in. If there's something you've been meaning to read but haven't, write that down too. Think about why you read the things you listed.

   Maybe you read for reasons like these:
   - to find out what happened
   - to learn the facts for a test
   - for fun

   Think about what you got from reading each selection in Unit 1. Use the notes you made on your Foldable to help you.

   Maybe you gained benefits like these from reading the things on your chart.
   - learned to do something new
   - continued a friendship
   - had fun thinking about a far-off place

3. **Present Your Chart** In a small group, take turns presenting your charts. Tell group members what you read, and what you "got" from reading. Remember that not everything you read grabs your interest–sometimes you just read to get information you need. Use one or two examples from the chart to help explain why you read different things.

4. **Plan for the Future** Reading is like exercise for your brain. It helps keeps your mind in good shape. What do you want to read in the future to keep your mind in shape? Think about your hobbies, interests, and goals. With a partner, discuss topics that you'd like to know more about. Then, use your discussion to help your partner make a reading list of his or her own.

What I Read	Why I Read It	What I "Got" from Reading It
e-mails from my best friend	to find out what she did last weekend	exciting news from a person I care about

Big Question Link to Web resources to further explore the Big Question at www.glencoe.com.

Teach

Solo Activity: Create a Reading Chart

- Have students think about things they like to read and name them in general terms (such as email, short stories, or "magazine articles about nature and animals") and specifics (such as "letters from my aunt" and "articles about Yellowstone National Park").
- Have students use their charts to help them as they speak to their groups. They can refer to different items on the chart to help them realize some of the different reasons they read.
- Instruct students to create their reading plans and reading lists in their Learner's Notebooks.
- Encourage students to challenge themselves to read a certain amount each week or each month. For example, they might try to read one short story a week or one novel a month.

Assess/Close

Solo Activity

Encourage students to study their charts and write what they have learned about how reading can help them. **AS**

Literature Online

Big Question Have students access the Web site for English and Spanish summaries and annotated links to related Web resources.

Focus

Vocabulary Preview

List the following words on the board:

- consequence
- deprivation
- silhouette
- spectacle
- toxic
- unsanitary

Review their definitions before students begin reading.

Build Background

Kate Montgomery wrote this letter while working with the Peace Corps in Kenya.

- The Peace Corps sends people to work in developing countries, mostly teaching in schools.
- Usually Peace Corps workers are in remote villages that may not have telephones, running water, or electricity.

Teach

L Literary Element

Tone Say: Kate says that she and her husband are "full-time housewives." What is the tone in this paragraph? *(Possible response: She is trying to be funny by using this word but goes on to describe their chores.)* OL

Readability Scores

Dale-Chall: 6.3
DRP: 58
Lexile: 1150

UNIT 1

Your Turn: Read and Apply Skills

Meet the Authors

Kate Montgomery grew up in Rhode Island. She went to Yale and Columbia University. She met Hilary Liftin at college. After college Montgomery went to Kenya with the Peace Corps. She and Liftin wrote letters back and forth to each other. This selection is a letter she wrote from Kenya.

Author Search For more about Hilary Liftin and Kate Montgomery, go to www.glencoe.com.

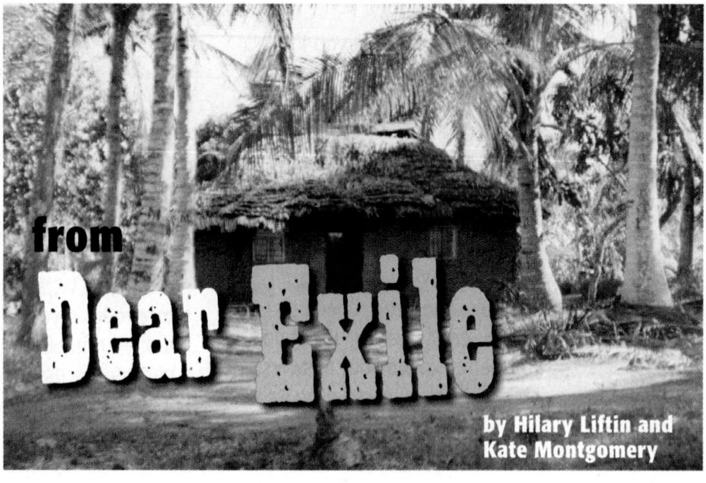

from
Dear Exile
by Hilary Liftin and Kate Montgomery

Dear Hilary,

For the time being, Kenya has totally kicked both of our butts. Now we are full-time housewives, in a big way. Every day we have to go to market (most food spoils overnight), get water by bicycle, and sweep the red dust out of our house. Every day we cook over charcoal fires, burn the trash, bury the compost, pour our tea-colored water through a coffee filter to get out the chunks, boil it (yes, start the fire again), put it through a filter, and sometimes wash our clothes. Then perhaps a nice flour and water meal and a sponge bath by candlelight, and we try to sleep through the shrieks of the bush babies.[1] And now to be teaching too (well, not yet). (As Dave said, the term ends in April, so school probably has to start sometime before that, right?)

We finally met some of our students-to-be this week, and it got us more excited to start teaching because chatting with them was so much fun. They were really shy at first, but

1. A ***bush baby*** is a small African animal, somewhat like a monkey, that lives in trees.

Additional Support

Author Search To expand students' appreciation of Kate Montgomery, have them access the Web site for more information and resources.

Literature Focus Lesson

Summary In this letter, Kate Montgomery describes her daily life living in Kenya as a Peace Corps volunteer. She and her husband, Dave, both took positions there as teachers. She uses a dry sense of humor to share the details of their everyday adventure living in a country that doesn't have a lot of the comforts most people in the United States are used to having. This letter informs about the culture of Kenya and points out the privilege of the American way of life. OL when we spoke to them in Kiswahili[2] and were willing to make fools of ourselves doing it, they started to laugh and ask us questions. One boy wanted to know how many cows Dave had traded to marry me. I think he seriously damaged my credibility as a teacher by saying I was free. The kids thought it was very funny. Later, while having tea, Mr. Mbogo, the Islamic studies teacher, asked us if it was really true. When David confirmed it, Mr. Mbogo raised his hands to the sky and said, "Oh God, take me to America, where the women are free!" Anyway, we're hoping classes will begin in earnest next week.

About your vision of me having a face-off with a big spider in a mud hut: I don't live in a mud hut. It's made of concrete. (But there is usually a lot of mud in it tracked in by goats and chickens. The door doesn't close very well.) Upon seeing a spider I mostly walk away and assume she'll be gone by the time I come back. The house feels like home now, although because it's so big mostly the rooms are empty.

Already, Ramisi is starting to look different to me. At first I could only see the fallen down, ghost-town decay of the place. Then yesterday while coming back from market, I noticed that on some of the houses, the stoops were washed, the clotheslines taut, and the dirt around the front was packed down and its edges neatened. I thought, How clean! Some parts of Ramisi seem downright bright.

As for food, yesterday when I saw a shriveled up carrot for sale in the market I dove on it excitedly. We pick rocks out of the rice like we are supposed to but never get them all, and it would increase your nightmares of losing your teeth. On the bright side, we can now add coconut milk to our short but growing list of ingredients. The other night we decided to make coconut rice. We had the coconut, a hammer, and a deadly, deer-gutting knife we got as a wedding present. I was holding the knife and the coconut while Dave tried to pound it open and hold the tin dish under it to catch the juice. There were a lot of hands and instruments and noise going on, and not a lot of coconut juice. To make it all that much more embarrassing, there were about twenty neighborhood kids staring at us from our doorway (as always since we're such a spectacle),[3] probably thinking we were trying to do a magic trick. To make conversation I said, Hey kids, I can't get the coconut open. Cute little Ali dashed off, and I figured I had scared him, but he soon came back bringing one of our neighbor women whom we hadn't met. She was carrying a huge double-edged sword and looked very determined. I was thinking, Sure, we're having a little trouble here, but you don't have to kill us for it. (Then I thought, Yes, maybe that would be best.) She walked right in, helped herself to our tortured coconut, and with one blow cracked it in half. It was a Wonder Woman moment. Dave is very excited that we will be buying such a manly kitchen instrument. Unfortunately, all the coconut juice went onto the floor when she did it, but who's going to argue with a woman with a *panga*?[4] (This incident has evolved into a friendship, and Mama Abdu has

2. ***Kiswahili*** is the language the people speak in Ramisi.

3. A ***spectacle*** is a strange sight.

4. A ***Panga*** is a large, swordlike knife.

Teach

C Critical Thinking

Comprehension Ask: How do they eventually open the coconut, and what happens to the juice? *(A neighbor woman, Mama Abdu, comes with a sword and cracks it open. The juice spills onto the floor.)* Is there anything positive about this experience? *(Yes, Kate and Dave become friends with Mama Abdu.)* **BL**

L Literary Element

Sequence Point out that up to now, Kate has not told anything in chronological order. **Ask:** Why does Kate use chronological sequence now? *(She is telling a story about what happened, and it makes the most sense in chronological order.)* **OL**

R Reading Skill

Identifying Author's Purpose
Ask: Why do you think the writer tells this story? *(Possible responses: She wants to share a funny story with her friend. The writer's purpose is both to inform and to entertain.)* **OL**

Reading in the Real World

Careers The Peace Corps was developed to promote world peace and friendship. Peace Corps volunteers travel to other countries to help people build better lives for themselves and their children. Have students create a brochure about a country and region where Peace Corps volunteers live and work. Students may gather information by logging on to their Web site at www.peacecorps.gov. Student brochures should include the following information:

- brief history of a country and region
- photo or illustration of the region
- list of specific jobs Peace Corps volunteers do in that region

Indiana English/Language Arts Academic Standards
TWE: *Reading in the Real World* 8.4

Teach

R Reading Skill

Connecting Explain that an infomercial is a commercial that is usually about a half-hour long and shows the many different ways a person can use the product that is being sold. Have students think of some infomercials they have seen. **Ask:** Is Kate being serious about this being an infomercial? *(No, she is being funny.)* **Ask:** What does she mean? *(Possible response: She means that she did not realize there were so many ways she could use flour.)* OL AL

EL Language Coach

General Context Clues
Ask: What do you think *Habari* and *Jambo* mean? *(hello or good-bye)* **Ask:** How does the context help you figure this out? *(Possible response: Kate and her husband are sitting outside and people yell this to them as they pass by on their bicycles.)* OL

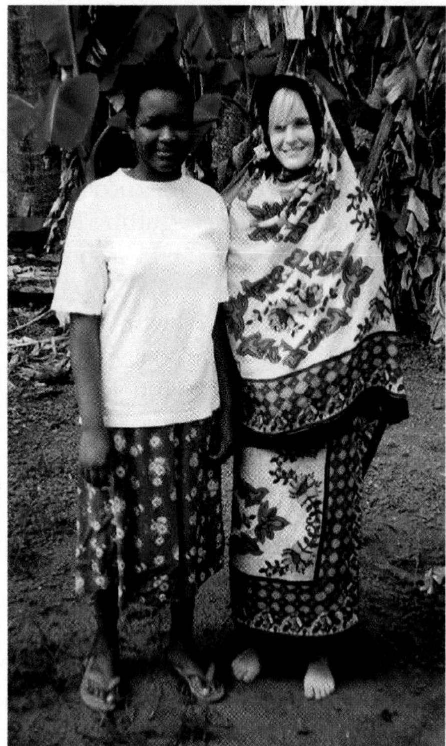

Kate and a friend pose for a quick photo. The brightly colored cloth garment Kate wears is called a *khanga*.

since taught me many cooking tricks, like that coconut milk isn't the whitish water in the center of the nut, it's made from the meat. Who knew!)

It's amazing the different meals Mama Abdu taught me to cook out of just flour and water (and some lard): a hot, liquidy, Cream of Wheat thing for breakfast called *uji*, a lump like Play-Doh for lunch called *ugali*, and a flattened fried patty for dinner, called *chapati*. I felt like I was watching an infomercial for flour. R

Last night Dave and I sat on our back stoop and watched the sunset. Yes, we sort of have a wasteland in the backyard, but in the not-so-distant distance, beyond the burnt ground, is some greenery—trees and palmy things, and there's a palm tree right by the house, so we saw the pink and orange sunset, the silhouette[5] of a coconut palm, and a bright planet overhead. We were just sitting there by the charcoal fire, and occasionally a monkey or a jungle chicken would squawk or a sheep would wander over and nose through our compost. Then we had ourselves some warm, flat Coke, and Dave fried up some *chapati*, which he is very good at cooking, and we munched in the toxic[6] incense of mosquito-repellant smoke. Now and then a child running by would yell, "*Habari*, Daudi! *Jambo*, Katie!" Or a man returning from the next-door village would stop and chat with us about the day. We were thinking—hey, this is pretty okay. EL

But I don't think you need to prepare for us living here permanently. I miss you all too much, and it's too much work. Still, I am learning how to do things for the first time, with help from our neighbors, who teach us how to do everything because it's never done the way you might think (the Lesson of the Coconut). I can't just go to the store and get Scotch tape to fix things. If I need to make two items stick together, I have to figure out how to do that with whatever is around—spit, dirt, melted garbage, whatever. My students use thorns as pins to hold their papers together—when they want to hold their papers together. It's nice not to feel the

5. A ***silhouette*** is the dark outline of something against a light background. In this case, they could see the dark outline of the coconut palm against the bright sunset.
6. ***Toxic*** means "poisonous."

Additional Support

Differentiated Instruction

Creating Infomercials Have groups of students plan their own infomercial about an ingredient that is used in many foods they eat. Students can plan their infomercial, deciding which person will do what in the presentation. Then have them present their infomercial to the class. If possible, allow students to bring in foods as props. If not, students will have to pantomime the things they are doing with the foods. Tell students to prepare for about a ten-minute presentation. OL

Analyzing the Photo Taking a midday break, Kate and some of her new neighbors pause for a photo. Living in Ramisi, what does Kate realize about the place she calls her "American world"?

slightest need for plastic wrap. Yes, Hilary, I know plastic wrap prevents a lot of very unsanitary[7] things from happening. But since a person doesn't die right away from eating food that hasn't been wrapped in plastic (usually), and because thorns seem to work rather well as paper fasteners (when you don't accidentally run your fingers over the corners of your students' papers, leaving a messy dribble of blood), it gives one a feeling of independence.

Of course, I can walk through a magical doorway any second I choose and be back in my American world of OfficeMax and plastic popper-pins-that-tell-you-when-the-turkey's-done-roasting. So my feeling of independence is really not from deprivation[8] but actually from privilege and wealth. I can feel lighter, relieved of the load of a life of luxury. Poor American me. This is how I make myself sick in my free time—by making sure I realize that I'm lucky to have those things that I'm happy not to have.

Still unable to carry anything of consequence[9] atop my head,

Kate

Analyzing the Photo Study this picture of one of Kate's students. From the photo, what can you tell about this student's personality?

7. If something is ***unsanitary,*** it is unclean.
8. ***Deprivation*** is the condition of not having things you need.
9. Something of ***consequence*** is something large or important.

YOUR TURN

Teach

L Literary Element

Cultural Reference Ask: How is the reference to plastic wrap a reference to Hilary and Kate's American culture? *(Possible response: Kate is describing the way that she used to be able to wrap up her food and the way that she had access to all different "everyday items" in America that are not considered "everyday items" where she is now.)* OL

BQ BIG Question

Ask: How has reading made a difference in Kate's life? *(Possible response: Reading enabled Kate to become a teacher with the Peace Corps. Reading also enables her to write letters to her friend and keep their friendship going across a huge distance.)* OL

Assess

Use the CheckPoint questions provided on Presentation Plus! to check for comprehension of the selection. These questions can be used with interactive response keypads for immediate student feedback.

Differentiated Instruction

Essay: Writing About Conveniences Have students brainstorm a list of modern conveniences they most appreciate. Next to each product, they should write how the product makes their life easier. Then have them choose one product they feel they cannot live without, and ask them to write a brief essay about the product. Students can research the invention of that product, tell how it helps them in their ordinary life, and explain why it is so important to them. *(Answers will vary.)* OL

Indiana English/Language Arts Academic Standards
TWE: *Differentiated Instruction* 8.7.2, *Differentiated Instruction* 8.5.7

Tips for Independent Reading

Suggest that students set aside a certain time for reading each day, such as after dinner or before going to bed. They can try reading some of the books shown here, related to the Big Question, or look for others in the local library.

Fiction

Tell students that reading fiction can be a great form of entertainment as well as very educational. Share with students some of your favorite works of fiction.

Ask students to share an example of a fictional book or story they have read and enjoyed. Then ask them what they think they might have learned from reading the piece of fiction.

UNIT 1

Reading on Your Own

To read more about the Big Question, choose one of these books from your school or local library. Work on your reading skills by choosing books that are challenging to you.

Fiction

A Separate Peace
by John Knowles

Gene is quiet, studious, and lonely. Finny is outgoing, athletic, and a daredevil. In the summer of 1942, the boys are roommates at a boarding school in New Hampshire. This is the story of their friendship and the tragic accident that changes their lives forever.

The Adventures of Huckleberry Finn
by Mark Twain

To escape his cruel father, thirteen-year-old Huckleberry Finn fakes his own death and runs away. With Jim, a runaway enslaved person, Huck travels on a raft down the Mississippi River. On shore they run into thieves, feuding families, and swindlers who kidnap Jim. To rescue him, Huck needs the help of his friend Tom Sawyer.

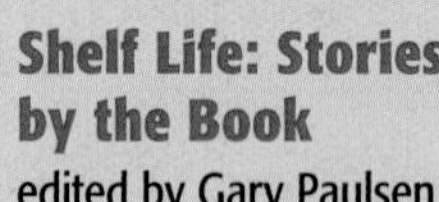

M. C. Higgins, the Great
by Virginia Hamilton

Sarah's Mountain has been home to fifteen-year-old Mayo Cornelius Higgins's family ever since his great-grandmother escaped from enslavement and settled there. Now their home is threatened by a pile of rubble from a mine. When two strangers arrive and offer a solution to the problem, M. C. learns about the importance of making good choices.

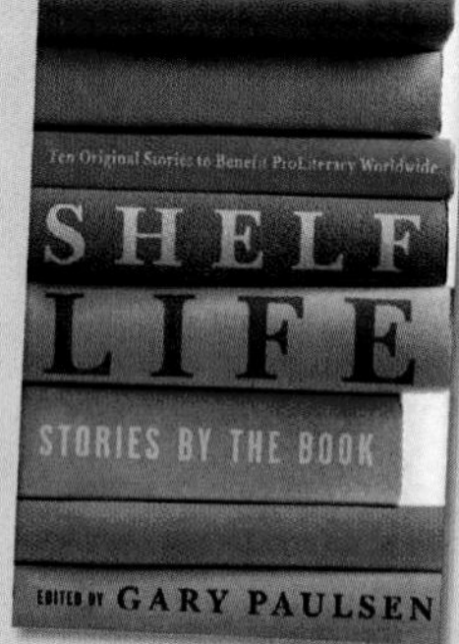

Shelf Life: Stories by the Book
edited by Gary Paulsen

A homeless teenager, a girl who has been brought up on Mars, and an eighth grader with a learning disability are among the characters featured in these ten short stories about how books can change lives. Authors who contributed to this collection include Joan Bauer, M.T. Anderson, and Margaret Peterson Haddix.

Additional Support

Differentiated Instruction

Use the Glencoe BookLink CD-ROM to create customized reading lists to help students answer the Big Question. Suggestions for Unit 1:

Grade 4: *Albert Einstein: Young Thinker* by Marie Hammontree
Grade 5: *When I Was Your Age* by Amy Ehrlich
Grade 6: *Steven Spielberg* by D.L. Mabery
Grade 7: *Sky Pioneer: A Photobiography of Amelia Earhart* by Corinne Szabo
Grade 8: *Extraordinary American Indians* by Susan Avery and Linda Skinner

Nonfiction

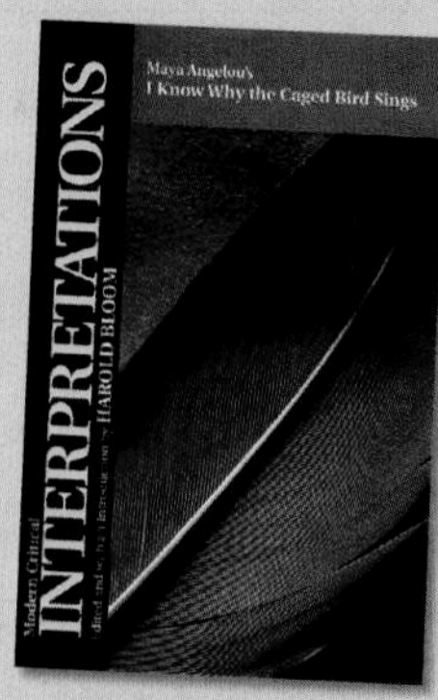

I Know Why the Caged Bird Sings
by Maya Angelou

Maya Angelou is a well-known and highly respected writer of poetry and memoir. In this autobiography Angelou tells about her childhood in the deep South. She writes about her real experiences, even though many of them were painful. She also writes about some of the people who helped her along the way. (A selection from *I Know Why the Caged Bird Sings* is in the Genre Focus of Unit 1.)

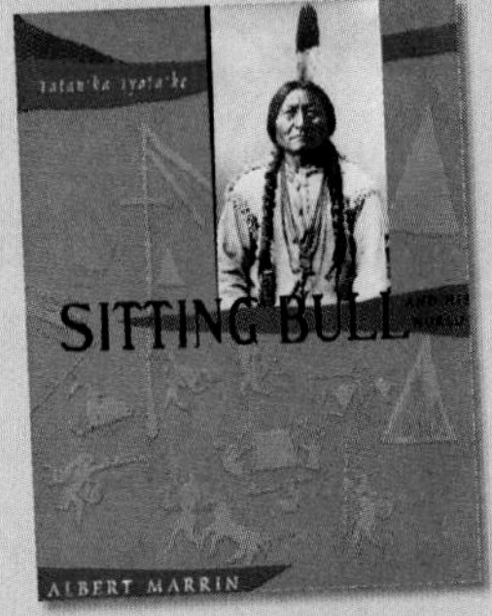

Sitting Bull and His World
by Albert Marrin

This biography of a distinguished Native American describes not only the life and times of this influential leader but also the customs and beliefs that made him who he was. Sitting Bull's youth, his development into a brave and wise man, and his tragic death are all presented, along with helpful explanations of the culture of the Plains Indians.

Open Your Eyes: Extraordinary Experiences in Faraway Places
edited by Jill Davis

This collection of autobiographical stories reveals how being exposed to other cultures can change a young person's life. Ten writers describe their experiences in places as different as a boarding school in England and a small shop in Tokyo. In one of the two stories set in the United States, Piper Dellums writes about the foreign-exchange student who comes to live in her home and is shocked to discover that the African American Dellums are her host and not the household servants.

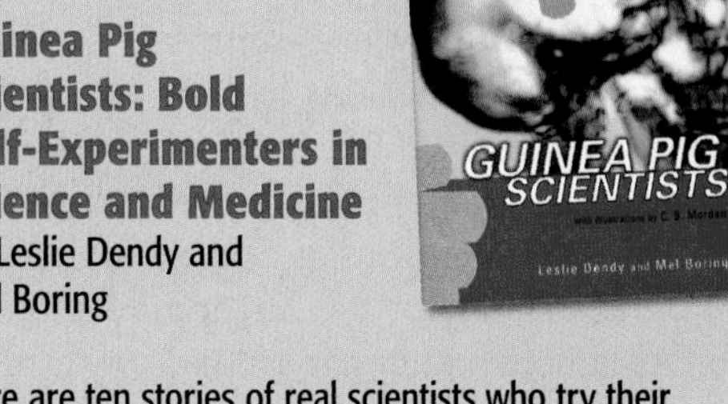

Guinea Pig Scientists: Bold Self-Experimenters in Science and Medicine
by Leslie Dendy and Mel Boring

Here are ten stories of real scientists who try their experiments on themselves. Their explorations of such things as digestion, deadly diseases, and safety gear are brave, often dangerous, and sometimes shocking. Each chapter ends with a description of what is learned from the scientist's work and what is now known about the subject.

READING ON YOUR OWN

Nonfiction
Share with students that the books on this page are all nonfiction books. They will give detailed accounts of the lives of the subjects.

Autobiographies and Biographies
Ask: Can you tell if these books are autobiographies or biographies by reading the title, viewing the cover, and knowing the author? *(Possible response: Yes. If the name of the subject is also the name of the author, the book is an autobiography.)* OL

About the Subjects
Invite students to share any information they know about the subjects on this page.
Ask: What would you expect to learn from reading these autobiographies and biographies? *(Response will vary.)* OL

Test-Taking Tips

TIP Remind students of the general strategy for multiple-choice questions:

- First, answer each question for which you know the answer.
- If you're not certain about the answer to a question, skip it for now.
- When you've answered all the questions you're sure about, return to the ones you're not sure about.
- For each of those, eliminate any answers that you know are wrong.
- If eliminating wrong answers reveals the right answer, fine. Move on.
- If eliminating wrong answers still leaves a choice, make your best guess.

ISTEP+ Test Practice

Directions:

Read this selection carefully. Then, answer questions 1 through 5.

from *The Book of Rock Stars,* By Kathleen Krull

Bob Marley (b. 1945–1981)

Few rock stars have national holidays in their honor. On the beautiful but poor Caribbean island of Jamaica, February 6 is National Bob Marley Day.

He was born into rural poverty and left home at fourteen to pursue music in the big city of Kingston. Three years later, he recorded his first single, called "Judge Not." With a catchy Jamaican rock beat—reggae—his fierce songs gave voice to the day-to-day struggles of oppressed people.

He teamed up with childhood friends and fellow singers to form a dynamic new reggae band, the Wailers. Members included Bunny Livingstone and Peter Tosh, as well as Rita Anderson, whom he later married. Marley was the hypnotic lead singer, and audiences couldn't stop dancing. The music was infused with devout spirituality, social commentary, and encouragement to rebel. Plus it was pure fun. With tunes like "Stir It Up" and "No Woman, No Cry," Bob Marley and the Wailers could do no wrong in Jamaica.

When their song "I Shot the Sheriff" became a hit for Eric Clapton, reggae went global. As the first Third World superstar, Marley introduced Jamaican music to the world and laid the groundwork for much to follow.

Pulsing hits flowed—"Jamming," "Waiting in Vain," "One Love/People Get Ready," and "Is This Love?" They were wildly popular, not just in Jamaica, but also in Africa, Great Britain, and Scandinavia. Yet the band made so little in royalties that Marley once worked in a factory for a year to support his family.

His last haircut was in 1968. After that his hair stayed in dreadlocks, as part of the Rastafari faith, the Jamaican religion that was the keystone of his life.

As famous a rock star as Marley was outside Jamaica, those at home saw him as almost godlike. On political and religious issues, ordinary Jamaicans hung on his every word. He became such a national hero that some in power even took him as a threat. In 1976 he was wounded in an assassination attempt and had to leave Jamaica for his safety.

Five years later, while jogging in New York's Central Park, he collapsed. Doctors discovered that he had advanced cancer. He released his final album, *Uprising*, and died at age thirty-six. Fans went into shock at the premature loss of the freedom-fighting entertainer.

1 Information in the selection is presented as a

A survey of opinions
B summary of ideas
C series of events
D sequence of song titles

2 Read the following sentence from the selection.

As the first Third World superstar, Marley introduced Jamaican music to the world and laid the groundwork for much to follow.

As it is used in the sentence, "laid the groundwork" MOST LIKELY means

A presented the facts
B created a conflict
C made a suggestion
D established the foundation

3 Although Bob Marley's music commented on social issues, it was also

A fun
B traditional
C repetitive
D comical

4 In Jamaica, Bob Marley was not only a rock star but also

A a religious leader
B a national hero
C a wealthy landowner
D a politician

Use your understanding of the writing process to answer Question 5.

5 Which of the following sentences is written MOST clearly?

A Reading comic books, we both like.
B We both enjoy reading comic books.
C To read comic books is something we both like.
D Something we both like is to read comic books.

UNIT 1 ASSESSMENT

Answers:

1. C
2. D
3. A
4. B
5. B

Resources for pages 140–145

Use these resources to review, assess, or reteach the chapter: Active Learning and Note-Taking Guide, ExamView Pro, and Differentiated Instruction Tool Software.

Test-Taking Tips

TIP Tell students that they can often find the tone of a passage by imagining that the writer is speaking aloud to them. The overall impression they get of the writer's attitude while he or she is speaking corresponds to the tone.

TIP Tell students that, in the ISTEP+ tests, they will often see questions for which they have to *write out* a response rather than just choose a correct answer. Before they start writing, students should make sure that they understand the question. Suggest that students reread the question to be sure that they know exactly what the answer should include.

Answers:

6. A

Directions:

Read this passage about the childhood of an author's father. Then, answer questions 6 through 11.

from *Ornaments* Ross's Angel

By Patricia C. and Fredrick McKissack Jr.

When Grandmother Melinda was 18 years old, she married Daniel Ripley and the couple moved to Chicago. Ross Ripley, my father, was the youngest of their three children. His sister, Grace, was the oldest, and his brother, Thomas, was next.

The November Ross turned seven, Franklin Delano Roosevelt was elected president of the United States, and his daddy died. Times were hard, but Melinda knew they would be harder if she stayed in Chicago. Widowed and poor, she packed up her family and moved back to Thomasville, Tennessee. Grandmother Melinda's folks were still living then, and they welcomed their daughter and three grandchildren into the ancestral home.

By the following year, Melinda had met and married her second husband, Charles Bevels. He was a robust man with large hands and broad shoulders. He had a voice as large as his body, and when he laughed the chandelier tingled in the dining room. Everybody called him Big Dad; everybody was charmed by his warmth and generosity. All except Ross.

"He's not my daddy," Ross said defiantly. "And he'll never be my Daddy."

Nobody knew how much Ross was hurting inside. He missed his father, but he was unable to express his feelings. Instead, he chose not to talk much, because he had developed a stutter. Adding to his problems, Ross was clumsy and slow to smile. Beside his brother and sister, who had sunny dispositions, he became a gray child who would just blend into the scenery. That's where he stayed, thinking nobody really cared.

---

6 In this passage, a **conflict** is developing

- **A** around Ross's feelings about his father and "Big Dad"
- **B** between Ross and his mother
- **C** between Ross and the children who make fun of him
- **D** among the crowded family members

7 What is the author's main purpose in this passage?

A to show how brave Ross's mother is
B to explain how Ross's father died
C to show how Ross is reacting to his father's death
D to explain why Ross's mother was poor

8 The tone of this passage is best described as

A defiant toward "Big Dad"
B making fun of Ross
C sympathetic toward Ross
D remorseful about Ross's father

9 The description of "Big Dad" in the third paragraph shows

A why Ross doesn't like "Big Dad"
B why "Big Dad" married Ross's mother
C why most people like "Big Dad"
D why "Big Dad" is so funny

10 Based on this passage, Ross doesn't like "Big Dad" because

A "Big Dad" is mean to Ross
B "Big Dad" likes Ross's brother and sister more
C Ross is worried about his mother
D Ross misses his father

11 On a seperate piece of paper, copy the chart below and identify one of the problems Ross struggles with in the passage. Then explain how that problem affects Ross.

Ross's problem	How it affects him

Answers:

7. C
8. C
9. C
10. D
11. See bottom channel for solution.

Question 11

Student responses will vary. Typical correct responses would include one item from the left column and an associated item from the right column.

Ross's problem	How it affects him
• Ross misses his father and doesn't know how to express his loss.	• Ross becomes withdrawn.
• Ross feels that he is being disloyal to his father if he likes "Big Dad."	• Ross refuses to accept "Big Dad" as his stepfather.
• Other relevant text-based response	• Other relevant text-based response

Test-Taking Tips

TIP Tell students that when they begin to answer questions they should refer back to the passage to find clues and evidence for their answers. Students are never asked to make an inference or draw a conclusion without adequate evidence in the text.

Directions:

Read this article about author Larry Woiwode. Then answer questions 12 through 16.

Meet Author Larry Woiwode

In his classroom at the University of North Dakota, author and professor Larry Woiwode passes along his lifetime of experience to another generation of writers. It is a fitting venue for Woiwode, whose fiction reflects his family's long history in North Dakota. Five generations of his family had lived on the state's western plains, and the writer and his work have close ties to the area.

In a discussion about regional writing, Woiwode said, "The more you enter your particular region, the area in which you live, or the place in which your characters are set, the more you must be accurate." This accuracy gives his own writing a strong sense of place and character that brings his stories to life.

North Dakota to New York...and Back

Woiwode was born in Carrington, North Dakota, on October 30, 1941. He spent his early childhood in the nearby town of Sykeston, where his parents were both schoolteachers and his father was also superintendent. When Woiwode was nine, his father uprooted the family and moved them to Illinois. A year after moving, his mother died from kidney problems and the tragedy deeply affected the young Woiwode. At the age of eighteen he began attending the University of Illinois and first published his fiction while he was still a student there. Woiwode soon left Illinois and moved to New York City, determined to succeed as either a writer or an actor.

In New York, Woiwode was mentored by the fiction editor of the *New Yorker* magazine, William Maxwell. Maxwell had been famous for helping develop other great authors—such as John Updike and J. D. Salinger—and in the 1960s he helped Woiwode establish himself as one of the premier young writers of his generation. After publishing several stories and poems in the *New Yorker* and other major magazines, Woiwode published his acclaimed first novel, *What I'm Going to Do, I Think,* in 1969. His writing has received numerous awards over the years, and in 1995 he received the Award of Merit Medal from the American Academy of Arts and Letters. Woiwode eventually moved back to North Dakota and now teaches at the university in Grand Forks.

12 Based on this article, moving to New York was good for Woiwode's career because

A he met his mentor in New York
B William Maxwell introduced him to John Updike and J. D. Salinger in New York
C New York was a big city with a broad audience
D he wasn't getting noticed in North Dakota

13 The opening paragraph is MAINLY intended to

A explain why Woiwode became a professor
B provide Woiwode's family history
C show how Woiwode became a writer
D reveal Woiwode's connection to North Dakota

14 When Woiwode left for New York, what was MOST LIKELY the reason for the confidence he had that he would succeed as a writer?

A He had received the Award of Merit Medal.
B Both his parents were schoolteachers.
C William Maxwell had been mentoring him.
D He had already been published.

15 Read these sentences from the passage.

It is a fitting venue for Woiwode, whose fiction reflects his family's long history in North Dakota. Five generations of his family had lived on the state's western plains, and the writer and his work have close ties to the area.

In this sentence, the word *venue* MOST LIKELY means

A place
B profession
C attitude
D philosophy

16 Based on his quote in the article, with which of these statements would Woiwode MOST LIKELY agree?

A In regional writing, setting is more important than character.
B It is more difficult to be accurate when writing about a region.
C Accuracy is important when you write in depth about a place.
D An accurate setting is important for character development.

Answers:

12. A
13. D
14. D
15. A
16. C

UNIT 2

Skills Scope and Sequence

Readability Scores Key
Dale-Chall/DRP/Lexile

PACING (DAYS) STANDARD	BLOCK	INSTRUCTIONAL SEGMENT LITERATURE	READING SKILLS	LITERARY ELEMENTS
1	1	**Unit Warm-Up, pp. 146–159** Genre Focus: "Racing the Great Bear" retold by Joseph Bruchac **4.3/58/760**, SE p. 151	Fluency, TWE pp. 147, 156, 167 Analyzing, SE p. 151, TWE p. 155 Making Inferences, SE p. 152, TWE pp. 157, 158 Predicting, SE pp. 152, 156, 157, TWE p. 153 Connecting, TWE p. 152 Comparing and Contrasting, SE p. 153, TWE p. 154 Fluency, TWE p. 156	Protagonist and Antagonist, SE p. 154, TWE pp. 156, 159 Conflict, SE p. 155, TWE pp. 150, 156 Plot, SE pp. 158, 159 Theme, SE p. 159
3	2	**Reading Workshop 1, pp. 160–177** "The People Could Fly" told by Virginia Hamilton **5.1/46/480**, SE p. 164 "A Father's Daring Trek" by Julie K.L. Dam **5.8/65/1210**, SE p. 172	Fluency, TWE p. 167 Connecting, TWE p. 171 Analyzing, SE pp. 160, 161, 163, 164, 165, 166, 171, 172, 173, 177	Protagonist and Antagonist, SE pp. 163, 166, TWE p. 164 Setting, SE pp. 171, 175
1		**Writing Workshop, Part 1, pp. 178–181** Writing Product: Folktale		Conflict, TWE p. 178 Dialogue, TWE p. 180
3	1	**Reading Workshop 2, pp. 182–203** "Paul Revere's Ride" by Henry Wadsworth Longfellow SE p. 186 "The Oxcart" by Eric Kimmel **6.1/50/610**, SE p. 196	Making Inferences, SE pp. 182, 183, 185, 187, 188, 189, 195, 197, 199, 200 Fluency, TWE pp. 189, 199	Narrative Poetry, SE pp. 185, 186, 190 Rhyme Scheme, TWE p. 185 Mood, TWE p. 191 Plot, SE pp. 195, 197, 198, 199, 201, TWE p. 196

Unit 2 Big Question

The question **"Which is more important, the journey or the destination?"** is designed to help students examine the importance of journeys—both literal and metaphorical—and understand the ways in which "getting there" can sometimes be more important than "being there."

Unit 2 Genre

Many of the selections in this unit are folktales. These selections will help students answer the big question "Which is more important, the journey or the destination?"

CRITICAL THINKING	VOCABULARY	WRITING AND GRAMMAR	LISTENING, SPEAKING, AND VIEWING
Comprehension, TWE p. 151 Analyze, TWE p. 158 Application, TWE p. 170	Idiomatic Expressions, TWE p. 151 Figurative Language, TWE p. 151 Time-order Words, TWE p. 154		Listening and Speaking, TWE pp. 149, 156
Infer, SE pp. 168, 176 Interpret, SE p. 168 Evaluate, SE p. 176	Academic Vocabulary, SE pp. 160, 169 Synonyms and Antonyms, SE pp. 162, 167, 170, TWE p. 172	Adjectives, SE p. 169 Adverbs, SE p. 177	Listening and Speaking, TWE p. 167 Viewing Photos, TWE p. 174 Viewing the Photo, TWE pp. 173, 174
	Synonyms, TWE p. 178	Applying Good Writing Traits: Ideas, SE pp. 178, 179 Plan, SE p. 179 Drafting, SE p. 180 Modifying Phrases and Clauses, SE p. 181 Subordinating Conjunctions, TWE p. 181	
Comprehension, TWE p. 189 Evaluate, SE p. 192, TWE pp. 191, 195 Interpret, SE p. 192 Evaluate, SE pp. 192, 202 Application, TWE p. 194 Analyze, SE p. 202, TWE p. 200 Apply, SE p. 202	Key words, SE p. 184 Roots, TWE p. 184 Compound Words, SE p. 194	Write About Your Reading, SE p. 192 Comparative and Superlative, SE p. 193 Articles and Demonstrative Adjectives, SE p. 203	Viewing the Illustration, TWE p. 190 Viewing the Photo, SE p. 198 Viewing the Painting, SE pp. 200, 201 Talk About Your Reading, SE p. 202

UNIT 2

Skills Scope and Sequence *continued*

Readability Scores Key
Dale-Chall/ **DRP**/ Lexile

PACING (DAYS) STANDARD	BLOCK	INSTRUCTIONAL SEGMENT LITERATURE	READING SKILLS	LITERARY ELEMENTS
3	3	**Reading Workshop 3, pp. 204–233** "The Snake Chief" retold by Kathleen Arnott 4.6/**52**/1030, SE p. 208 from *Harriet Tubman: Conductor on the Underground Railroad* by Ann Petry 5.8/**57**/1050, SE p. 220	Predicting, SE pp. 204, 205, 207, 208, 210, 211, 212, 214, 219, 220, 222, 223, 225, 226, 228, 230 Fluency, TWE pp. 209, 225 Review Making Inferences, TWE pp. 213, 221, 224, 226, 229 Connecting, SE p. 224	Conflict, SE pp. 207, 209, 213 Symbols, TWE p. 215 Style, SE pp. 219, 221, 224, 227, 228, 231, TWE p. 219, 230 Repetition, TWE p. 229
2		**Writing Workshop, Part 2, pp. 234–237** Writing Product: Folktale		Dialogue, TWE p. 236 Setting, TWE p. 236 Style, TWE p. 234
3	1	**Reading Workshop 4, pp. 238–255** "Icarus and Daedelus" by Josephine Preston Peabody 5.9/**57**/1100, SE p. 242 "A Dose of Medicine" by Charlotte Foltz Jones 10.3/**62**/960, SE p. 250	Comparing and Contrasting, SE pp. 238, 239, 241, 242, 243, 245, 249, 250, 252, 253 Fluency, TWE p. 243 Predicting, SE pp. 243, 247 Determining Main Idea, TWE p. 248	Theme, SE pp. 241, 244 Metaphor and Simile, TWE p. 245 Chronological Order, SE pp. 249, 251
3	2	**Comparing Literature Workshop, pp. 256–275** "Kamau's Finish" by Muthoni Muchemi 6.3/**49**/730, SE p. 259 "The Bunion Derby" by Leone Castell Anderson 7.0/**56**/920, SE p. 268	Fluency, TWE p. 261 Connecting, SE pp. 261, 268, 272 Making Inferences, TWE pp. 270, 272 Fluency, TWE p. 271	Connecting, SE pp. 261, 268, 272 Making Inferences, TWE pp. 270, 272
4	2	**Unit Wrap-Up, pp. 276–287**		

CRITICAL THINKING	VOCABULARY	WRITING AND GRAMMAR	LISTENING, SPEAKING, AND VIEWING
Analyze, SE, p. 216, TWE pp. 206, 213, 214 Comprehension, TWE pp. 207, 208, 222 Infer, SE pp. 216, 232 Evaluate, TWE p. 227 Synthesize, TWE p. 229 Interpret, SE p. 232	Academic Vocabulary, SE p. 204 Building Vocabulary SE pp. 206, 209, 211, 218, 222 Old words, TWE p. 211, 220	Write About Your Reading, SE p. 216 Double Negatives, SE p. 217 Misplaced and dangling modifiers, SE p. 233	Listening and Speaking, TWE pp. 212, 221 Viewing the Photo, TWE pp. 215, 225, 230 Talk About Your Reading, SE p. 232
		Writing a Folktale: Revising, Editing, and Presenting SE pp. 234, 235 Partner Review, TWE p. 235	Listening, Speaking, and Viewing: Storytelling, SE p. 237
Interpret, TWE p. 240 Infer, SE pp. 246, 254 Interpret, SE p. 246 Evaluate, SE pp. 246, 254 Comprehension, TWE p. 252	Academic Vocabulary, SE p. 238 Building Vocabulary, SE pp. 240, 242, 248, 251 Context Clues, TWE p. 241	Write About Your Reading, SE p. 246 Prepositions, SE p. 247 Interjections, SE p. 255	Viewing the Painting, SE p. 244 Viewing the Illustration, SE pp. 251, 252, 253 Talk About Your Reading, SE p. 254
Analyze, SE p. 275, TWE pp. 259, 263 Comprehension, TWE pp. 263, 271 Evaluation, TWE pp. 264, 265, SE p. 275 Infer, SE p. 275	Academic Vocabulary, SE p. 256 Synonyms and Antonyms, SE pp. 258, 259, 264, 267, 272 Idiomatic Expressions, TWE p. 269 Fluency with Numbers, TWE p. 273	Researching and Writing, TWE p. 272 Taking Notes and using them to make a diagram that compares the theme in two pieces of literature, SE p. 275	Analyzing the Photo, SE pp. 260, 269, TWE p. 268

UNIT 2

Unit Resources

Reading with Purpose offers a comprehensive package of tools to optimize student learning and the teaching experience. Each resource has been designed to assist students in specific areas and to offer instructional support for teachers. While all of these areas are covered in the core textbook, some students may need extra practice or additional help in specific areas. The resource package is designed so that you, the teacher, can choose which items will best assist your students. You may also use these resources as homework assignments and for assessment purposes. The following are resources recommended for use with Unit 2.

Keys for Unit Resources

- Blackline Master
- Workbook
- Supplemental Text
- CD-ROM
- DVD
- Transparency
- Web-based
- Fast File

Essential Instructional Support

FAST FILE UNIT 2 RESOURCES

Reading and Literature

- Academic Vocabulary Review
- Big Question: School to Home
- The Big Question Foldable
- Unit Challenge: Planner and Rubrics
- Comparing Literature Graphic Organizer
- Key Reading Skills
- Active Reading Graphic Organizers
- Literary Analysis
- Unit Vocabulary Review

Writing, Grammar, and Spelling

- Spelling and Handwriting Practice
- Grammar Practice
- Writing Workshop Graphic Organizer

Listening, Speaking, and Viewing

- Viewing and Representing
- Listening and Speaking

English Language Learners

- English Language Coach Review

DIFFERENTIATED INSTRUCTION

- Leveled Vocabulary Development
- Skill Level Up!™ A Language Arts Game
- Listening Library CD
- BookLink 3
- Literature Library Vocabulary Puzzlemaker
- Vocabulary Puzzlemaker

ASSESSMENT

- Selection and Unit Assessments
- Selection Quick Checks
- Assessment by Learning Objectives
- Rubrics for Assessing Student Writing, Listening, and Speaking
- Glencoe Online Essay Grader
- Interactive Tutor: Self-Assessment
- ExamView Assessment Suite
- Literature Library ExamView Assessment Suite

Additional Instructional Support

WRITING, GRAMMAR, AND SPELLING

- Real Success in Writing: Research and Reports
- Writing Constructed Responses
- Spelling Power eWorkbook
- Grammar & Composition Handbook
- Grammar and Language Workbook
- Revising with Style eWorkbook

READING AND LITERATURE

- Active Learning and Note Taking Guide
- inTime Magazines
- Backpack Reader Volume 1
- Literature Library
- Literature Launchers Pre-Reading Videos DVD
- Literature Classics

TRANSPARENCIES

- Read Aloud, Think Aloud Transparencies
- Literary and Text Analysis Transparencies
- Bellringer Options Transparencies
- Grammar and Writing Workshop Transparencies
- Fine Art Transparencies

TECHNOLOGY

- TeacherWorks Plus™
- StudentWorks Plus™
- BookLink 3
- Skill Level Up!™ A Language Arts Game
- ExamView Assessment Suite
- Interactive Tutor: Self-Assessment
- Listening Library CD
- Spanish Listening Library CD
- Literature Classics
- Literature Launchers Pre-Reading Videos DVD
- Literature Library ExamView Assessment Suite
- Vocabulary Puzzlemaker
- Literature Library Vocabulary Puzzlemaker
- glencoe.com
- Online Student Edition
- Presentation Plus!
- Glencoe Online Essay Grader

ENGLISH LANGUAGE LEARNER

- English Language Coach
- Fluency Practice and Assessment
- inTime Magazines (Spanish)
- Spanish Listening Library CD

PROFESSIONAL DEVELOPMENT

- Professional Development Package

Additional Glencoe Resources

Dinah Zike's Foldables

Foldables are three-dimensional, interactive graphic organizers that help students practice basic writing skills, review key vocabulary terms, and answer Big Questions. Every unit contains a foldable activity. You can find the pattern and directions for the Unit 2 Foldable in the Unit 2 Resources Fast Files booklet. You can use the foldables as they are presented or modify them to suit the needs of your students. More information about foldables for Unit 2 can be found on page R8.

Glencoe Literature Library

This collection of hardcover books includes full-length novels, novellas, plays, and works of nonfiction. Each volume consists of at least one complete extended-length reading accompanied by several related readings from a broad range of genres. A separate Study Guide for each Glencoe Literature Library book provides teaching notes and reproducible activity pages for students.

Glencoe Literature Library titles that complement this unit include:

A Christmas Carol, by Charles Dickens
Dogsong, by Gary Paulsen
A Girl Named Disaster, by Nancy Farmer

For a wealth of online resources that support the instruction in Unit 2 of *Glencoe Literature: Reading with Purpose,* students and teachers can visit our Web site at www.glencoe.com. Students will find additional learning, practice, and assessment opportunities such as these, which are noted in the student text:

- **Big Question Overview**
- **Study Central**
- **Author Search**
- **Writing Models**
- **Interactive Literary Elements Handbook**
- **Web Activities**

Teachers will find planning and instructional tools that include the following:

- **Book Lesson Plans**
- **Teacher Forum**
- **Professional Development**
- **Web Activities Lesson Plans (with answers to student activities)**

Go to www.glencoe.com to see the entire selection of Reading with Purpose online resources.

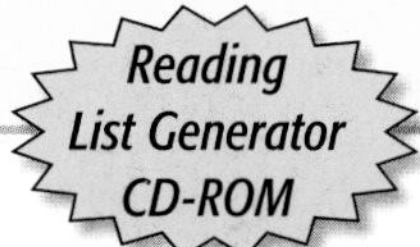

GLENCOE BOOKLINK

Use the Glencoe BookLink 3 CD-ROM, a database of more than 26,700 titles, to *create customized reading lists* for your students.

- Search for award-winning titles, (e.g., Newbery Award winners, Coretta Scott King Award winners, and Caldecott Medal winners) and for books on several state-recommended reading lists.
- Find Degrees of Reading Power™ (DRP) and Lexile™ readability scores for all selections.
- Organize reading lists by students' reading level, author, genre, theme, or area of interest.
- Get a brief summary of each selection.

You can find recommended leveled readings for this unit with Reading on Your Own (see page 280).

Glencoe's **Presentation Plus!**, a multimedia teaching tool, lets you present dynamic lessons that will engage your students. Using Microsoft PowerPoint,® you can customize the presentations to create your own personalized lessons. Use **CheckPoint** questions with interactive response keypads to get immediate student feedback during lessons, to increase student participation, and to assess student comprehension.

A lively collection of articles drawn from issues of the TIME family of magazines helps students develop the skills they need to interact with informational text in a meaningful way. Each of the news stories, feature articles, reviews, profiles, and essays in the magazine connect to an author, work, or theme in *Glencoe Literature: Reading with Purpose.* Articles for Unit 2 are found in Volume A. See the *inTIME* Teacher's Guide for specific connections to each unit and for reproducible student worksheets designed to develop students' reading and critical thinking skills.

Literature Launchers

Set the scene with Glencoe's Literature Launchers, engaging video segments that introduce each unit's genre focus. Each video brings the genre to life, relating it to your students' worlds.

Insert the Glencoe Literature Launchers Pre-Reading Videos DVD into your DVD player. Select the Unit 2 Launcher from the menu to introduce the genre and Big Question for this unit.

Online Essay Grader

Use Glencoe's Online Essay Grader to score your students' writing and to provide individualized feedback to each student automatically.

You and your students can visit www.glencoe.com to link to the essay grader. *Students* can enter their essays and receive feedback on demand. *You* can manage demographic data, assign tests and generate individual student and aggregated reports. The essay grader can help you

- Save time with automatic scoring and individualized feedback.
- Supplement in-class writing instruction using guided writing practice.
- Get reports for individual students or for special populations.
- Track student improvement over time.

REAL Success: Reading Excellence at All Levels

Glencoe now provides all of your students with the tools they need to become better, more enthusiastic readers. The REAL Success suite of reading and language arts products encourages reading excellence by meeting the needs of students at all levels. Glencoe products that can be used in conjunction with Unit 2 include the following:

- Jamestown Literature: An Adapted Reader
- Jamestown *Reading Fluency*
- Jamestown *Critical Reading Series, In the Line of Duty*
- *Vocabulary Builder*
- *The Glencoe Reader, Course 3*

To order these products, call Glencoe at 1-800-USA-READ.

Teacher Wraparound Edition Key

Level Appropriate Code

AS = Activities for all students
AL = Activities for students working above grade level
OL = Activities for students working at grade level
BL = Activities for students working below grade level
EL = Activities for English language learners

Teacher Wraparound Prompts

R **Reading Skill** These activities help you teach reading and comprehension skills.

V **Vocabulary** These activities help students comprehend words and incorporate them into their reading and writing.

C **Critical Thinking** These strategies help students apply and extend what they have learned.

BQ **BIG Question** These activities and questions prompt students to prepare to answer the Big Question.

W **Writing** These activities provide writing opportunities to help students practice writing and comprehend text.

L **Literary Element** These activities and questions help students comprehend selections and learn more about each genre.

E **Text Element** These activities help students comprehend text elements.

LSV **Listening, Speaking, Viewing** These activities help students practice listening, speaking, and viewing skills.

EL **English Language Coach** These skills help English language learners as well as students who need additional reading support.

Professional Development Center

Kathleen Hinchman

From an Author:

Preparing Students to Read Myths and Legends

Start with students' known stories. Talk with students about myths and legends they know. These might include myths about teachers, such as those that suggest teachers like to be mean, or that teachers never go to the bathroom. You can also talk with students about urban legends, such as rumors that get passed around the Internet about certain celebrities or computer viruses. Students may know myths or legends that are specific to their community or cultural background, such as the lessons in the African Kwaku Anansi myths, or the Anglo American legend telling how Johnny Appleseed spread apple trees across the land.

Explain literary definitions. A myth is a fictitious story about a supernatural being or force that explains some aspect of nature or of early human history. A legend is also a fictitious story, often passed from generation to generation, but is usually regarded as historical. Telling such stories gave people within a culture a chance to pass along information in a memorable way that would remind the group of what was considered important. Both the journeys and the destinations were important in these stories, reminding people of ways to act and of worthwhile goals.

Activate background knowledge. Students can learn most quickly about myths, legends, and their differences by inventing such stories of their own. Consider phenomena known to the students about which myths can be constructed, such as why the sun rises in the east or why dogs walk around in a circle before lying down. Invite students to work in pairs or groups to invent a myth to explain these or other phenomena, noting that myths should include such features as action by a supernatural being and explanation for something they see every day. Students might also be invited to create their own new legends or myths.

Teacher to Teacher

Cynthia Castillo
Nautilus Middle School
Miami, Florida

I introduce the Big Question "Which is more important, the journey or the destination?" with a short lesson on Greek mythology that focuses on the different qualities possessed by the deities in the Greek pantheon. For example, Athena, the goddess of wisdom, was represented by an owl, the symbol for wisdom. Following class discussion, students choose various teachers and staff people to be "school gods and goddesses" by designating a special quality to each along with a representative symbol. For example, a student may designate a teacher the "god of detention" with a watch and chain as his symbol. Each student then draws a picture of the chosen god or goddess and his or her symbol and writes an essay that supports the illustration.

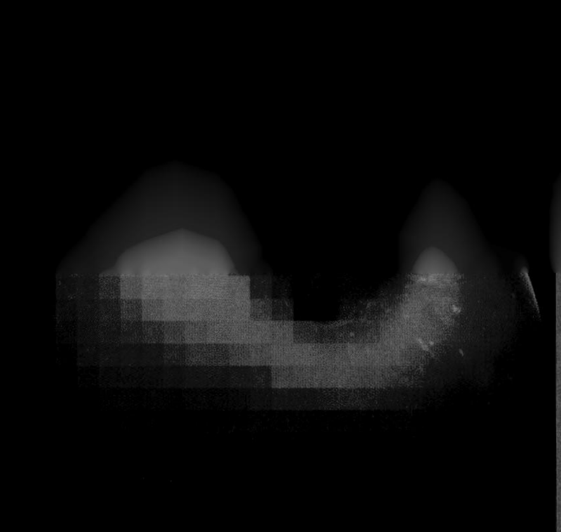

Reading Myths and Legends

Why is it important to understand myths and legends?

Both the journeys and the destinations in these stories tell a great deal about the cultures within which they are found. People as varied as the ancient Greeks, Romans, Africans, and Native Americans used their myths to explain different aspects of relationships and nature, telling us what was important to the people who lived in these societies. Interestingly, different versions of the same story can sometimes be found in many different cultures. The Sasquatch (Bigfoot) story, for instance, is part of Native American, African American, and Scandinavian culture. Cinderella tales can be found in Chinese, European, and Native American cultures.

Why do similar stories appear in cultures that seem very different from one another?

It is in our nature to want to explain the world we observe every day. It also makes sense to figure out ways to get along with one another. Many cultures needed Sasquatch stories to keep their young from wandering off into the woods. Cinderella tales remind us that physical beauty is not as important as how one acts toward others.

How do we know the myths and legends of people who lived long ago?

Myths and legends existed long before printing presses and the Internet made it easier to pass along our explanations for why the world works as it does. In the past, people memorized and told stories to their young people, passing lessons across generations. The stories were usually structured with a strong, simple story line containing a simple problem that needed a solution. Continuing this tradition even today, the best storytellers figure out ways to organize their wording so that it is dramatic and memorable. You might invite storytellers to your school to share their stories with students, or invite your students to organize a storytelling festival of their own to share and learn stories that represent the cultural backgrounds in your classroom.

UNIT 2

The BIG Question: Which Is More Important, the Journey or the Destination?

> A journey of a thousand miles begins with a single step.
>
> —Lao Tzu
> 6th-century B.C. Chinese philosopher

Key Unit Objectives

- Answer the Big Question
- Identify, understand, and apply the key reading skills for reading folktales
- Identify, understand, and apply key literary elements of folktales
- Write folktales

Why Is It Important?

Answering this Big Question helps students examine the importance of journeys—both literal and metaphorical—and understand the ways in which "getting there" can sometimes be more important than "being there."

Viewing the Photo/Illustration

Ask: How might Lao Tzu's quotation help someone feeling overwhelmed by the idea of a long journey or a hard road ahead? *(Possible response: The quote might help someone because it emphasizes that one simple step is all that's needed to begin a long journey.)* **OL**

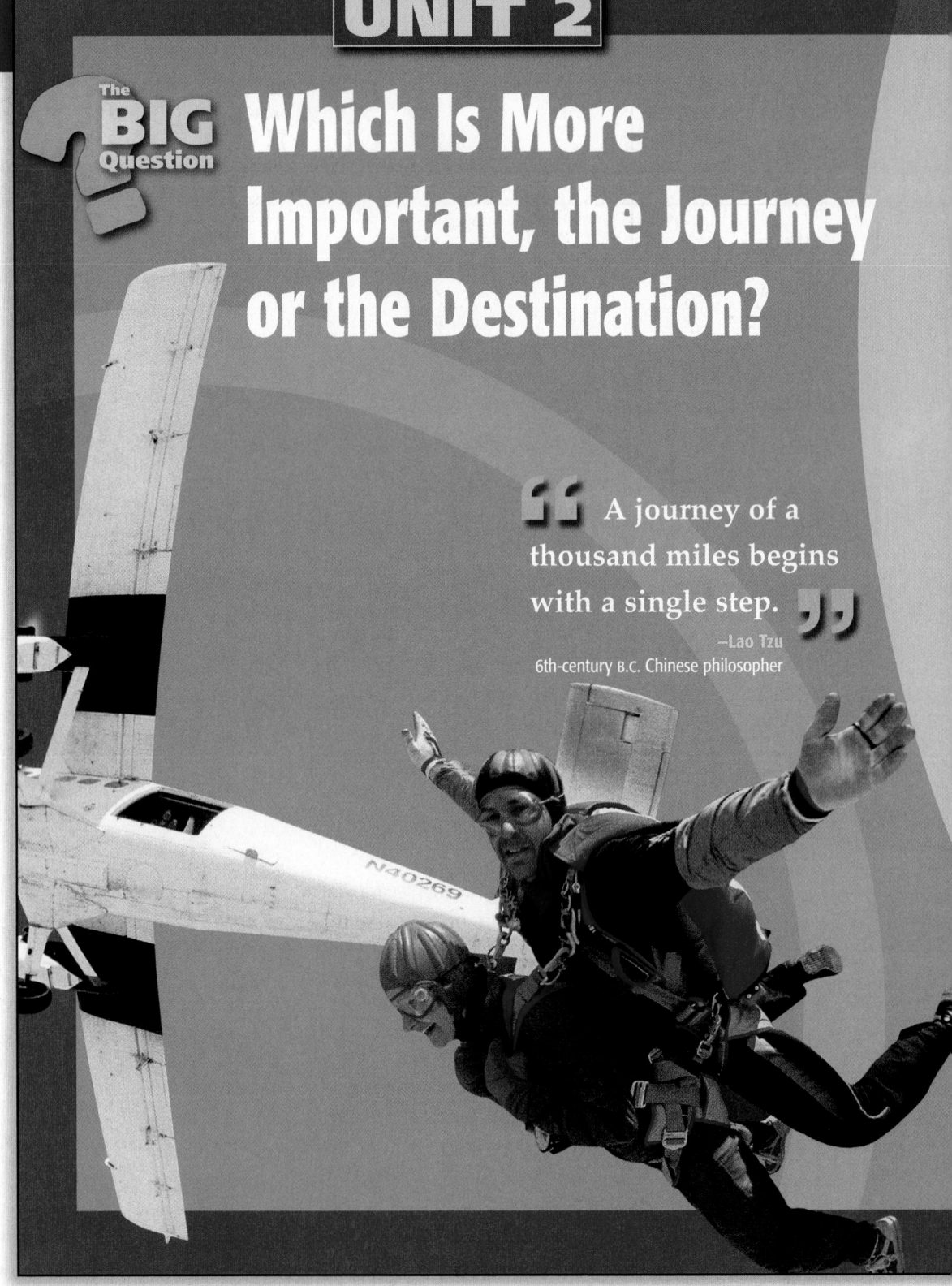

Unit Skills

BIG Question Which is more important, the journey or the destination?

Genre Focus: Folktales

Reading Skills

- Analyzing, p. 160
- Making Inferences, p. 182
- Predicting, p. 204
- Comparing and Contrasting, p. 238

Writing Skills/Grammar

- Modifying Phrases and Clauses, p. 181
- Misplaced and Dangling Modifiers, p. 233

Literary Elements

- Protagonist and Antagonist, p. 163
- Plot, p. 195
- Conflict, p. 207
- Theme, p. 241

Vocabulary

- Synonyms and Antonyms, p. 162
- Compound Words, p. 194

LOOKING AHEAD

The skill lessons and readings in this unit will help you develop your own answer to the Big Question.

About the Reading

Each selection in this unit provides insights that can help students address the question, "Which is more important, the journey or the destination?" Students read about the journeys of real and imagined people and consider how they might answer the Big Question.

About the Skills

The skills taught in this unit have been selected because they are particularly helpful when reading the featured genre—folktales. Each reading selection provides students with opportunities to practice and develop these skills.

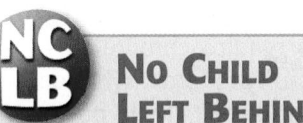

No Child Left Behind

The goals of the NCLB act include a strong emphasis on reading comprehension. Educators have found that "instruction in comprehension can help students understand what they read, remember what they read, and communicate with others about what they read." Help students improve their comprehension by encouraging them to stop frequently and ask themselves questions about what they've read.

Reading Fluency

Build Fluency To develop fluency, students should evaluate their own progress. Encourage students to practice reading aloud with a partner. Have students note when they have to reread a particular section, when they stumble over a difficult word, and when they need help pronouncing a word. Encourage partners to provide each other with constructive feedback and to help each other with the pronunciation and meaning of unfamiliar words. **EL** **BL**

Indiana English/Language Arts Academic Standards
TWE: *Reading Fluency* 8.1

Focus

BELLRINGER Options

- **Literature Launcher: Pre-Reading DVD**
- **Daily Language Practice Transparency 11**

Focus Activity Write on the Board: Have you ever had a great time on a journey? Tell about your experience. *(Responses will vary.)* AS

Teach

BQ BIG Question

- Have students read the profiles and look at the pictures of Julie, Lelia, and Takeshi. To check reading comprehension, ask students: What do Julie and Lelia like to do? What does Takeshi enjoy?
- Have students answer one of the two questions in the profiles. Ask volunteers to share their ideas with the class. OL

UNIT 2 WARM-UP

Connecting to

Which Is More Important, the Journey or the Destination?

It's important to have a destination, or a place where you want to go. But there is much more to life than just reaching your destination. Sometimes your efforts along the way are just as important as the end result. In this unit, you'll read about different people and their journeys.

Real Kids and the Big Question

JULIE and her friend Lelia walk home together every day after school. As they walk, they laugh, talk, and share secrets. Although there's a bus that stops near the girls' homes, they would rather walk home from school. Why do you think Julie and Lelia prefer the journey of walking home?

BQ

TAKESHI loves to ride his bike. He rides it to school every day and to the park on weekends. Most times, Takeshi likes riding to specific places. Other times, he enjoys riding just for fun, with no destination in mind. What do you think Takeshi would say is more important, the journey or the destination?

Warm-Up Activity

On your own, choose one of the questions above and answer it in a few sentences in your Learner's Notebook.

Additional Support

Reading in the Real World

Citizenship Invite an individual in your community who has gone on a major journey to speak to the class. Examples of major journeys include immigrating to the United States, traveling to a foreign country, and moving to another state. Encourage students to make a list of questions to ask the person about his or her journey, including the mode of transportation and details that took place along the way. Be sure to have students ask the person how he or she feels about the Big Question. AS

You and the Big Question

Reading about other people's journeys will help you think about and compare the importance of journeys and destinations. BQ

Literature Online

BIG Question Link to Web resources to further explore the Big Question at www.glencoe.com.

Plan for the Unit Challenge

At the end of the unit, you'll use notes from all your reading to complete the Unit Challenge. You'll choose one of the following activities:

A. Trial TV You'll work with classmates to hold a made-for-TV trial in which you try to convince a jury that either journeys or destinations are more important.

B. Interview Interview a family member, neighbor, or friend about a journey that he or she made, and decide which part of it was most important.

- Start thinking about which activity you'd like to do so that you can narrow your focus as you read each selection. Do you usually enjoy working as part of a group or team? Do you like to act, role play, or perform in front of an audience of classmates? If your answer to these questions is "yes," then you would probably prefer to do Activity A, Trial TV. On the other hand, if you usually prefer working with just one other person, then Activity B may be more your style.
- In your Learner's Notebook, write your thoughts about the activity you'd like to do.
- Each time you make notes about the Big Question, think about how your ideas will help you with the Unit Challenge activity you chose.

Keep Track of Your Ideas

As you read, you'll make notes about the Big Question. Later, you'll use these notes to complete the Unit Challenge. See pages R8–R9 for help with making Foldable 2. This diagram shows how it should look.

1. Use this Foldable for all of the selections in this unit. Label the front flap with the unit number and the Big Question. Label the bottom of each flap below with a title, beginning with "The People Could Fly." (See page 147 for the titles.)
2. Open each flap. Near the top of each flap, write **My Purpose for Reading.**
3. Below each crease, write **The Big Question.**

Unit 2
Which Is More Important, the Journey or the Destination?

Title	Title
Title	Title
Title	Title
Title	Title
Title	Title

Differentiated Instruction

Writing a Script Students with good verbal and speaking skills may like to write a short script about either Julie and Lelia or Takeshi. The script should answer the profile question using the voice of one or more of the three kids. For example, Julie's script might begin, "I love to walk home every day with my friend, Lelia." The script would then follow the two girls as they walk home, talking about their life and sharing details about their day. Have a few students take turns playing the part of one of the real kids, reading the script aloud for the class. OL AL

Teach

Big Question Have students access the Web site for English and Spanish summaries and annotated links to related web resources.

BQ 

Have students write about the Big Question in their Learner's Notebooks. OL

FOLDABLES™ Study Organizer

For each selection they read, students will enter notes about how that selection applies to the Big Question. For details about using Dinah Zike's Foldables™, see pages R8–R9.

Assess/Close

Ask students to think about why a journey might be as important as a destination.

Resources for page 149

- Use the Unit Challenge Planner BLM in the Unit 2 Resource Booklet, p. 36
- Use the Foldable BLM in the Unit 2 Resource Booklet, p. 7

Indiana English/Language Arts Academic Standards

TWE: *Reading in the Real World* 8.7.1, *Differentiated Instruction* 8.4

Focus

BELLRINGER Options

- **Selection Focus 3**
- **Daily Language Practice Transparency 12**

Focus Activity Say: Some stories were told aloud for many generations before they were written down. Do you think stories that were not written down stayed the same over time? Explain. *(Students may say the main ideas and themes stayed the same but story details changed.)* OL

Teach

R Reading Skill

How to Read Folktales

Ask: How might you use each reading skill when reading a folktale? *(Possible responses: **Analyzing:** I can analyze the main character's actions to determine what he or she needs to do to overcome a problem. **Making Inferences:** I can use what characters say and do to make inferences about them. **Predicting:** I can make informed guesses about the lesson a tale might be teaching. **Comparing and Contrasting:** I can compare and contrast the characters in a folktale.)* OL

UNIT 2 GENRE FOCUS: FOLKTALES

Skills Focus

- Key skills for reading folktales
- Key literary elements of folktales

Skills Model

You will see how to use the key reading skills and elements as you read

- ***Racing the Great Bear,*** p. 151

Folktales are stories that have been told from one generation to the next before being written down. Aside from being entertaining, many of the tales also teach a lesson in life or express the beliefs of a group of people. In this unit, you'll read these and other kinds of folktales:

- **Legends**–stories about heroes and extraordinary events. The deeds and events in legends are usually based on fact but become exaggerated as generations of storytellers add to the stories
- **Cautionary Tales**–stories in which people are punished for breaking society's rules or misbehaving
- **Myths**–ancient stories about gods, goddesses, or other supernatural beings and their influence on people and nature

Why Read Folktales?

Throughout history, people have told stories to explain who they are, where they come from, and why things happen. Folktales can help you understand human society, connect the past and present, and pass on cultural ideals.

How to Read Folktales

Literature Online

Study Central Visit www.glencoe.com and click on Study Central to review folktales.

Key Reading Skills

These reading skills are especially useful tools for reading and understanding folktales. You'll see these skills modeled in the Active Reading Model on pages 151–159, and you'll learn more about them later in this unit.

- **Analyzing** Identify the elements of a selection and their relationship to each other. (See Reading Workshop 1.)
- **Making Inferences** Use clues to figure out the meaning of ideas that are not directly stated. (See Reading Workshop 2.)
- **Predicting** Guess what will happen next in a tale, based on what you know and have read. (See Reading Workshop 3.)
- **Comparing and Contrasting** See how things are alike and different. (See Reading Workshop 4.)

R

Key Literary Elements

Recognizing and thinking about the following literary elements will help you understand more fully what the author is telling you.

- **Protagonist and Antagonist:** the main character and the person or force that stands in the way of his or her happiness (See "The People Could Fly.")
- **Plot:** events and the order in which they are arranged (See "The Oxcart.")
- **Conflict:** a struggle between opposing forces (See "The Snake Chief.")
- **Theme:** a story's main idea or life lesson (See "Icarus and Daedalus.")

Indiana English/Language Arts Academic Standards (pp. 150–159)

8.2 Comprehension and Analysis (Focus on Informational Text) Develop [reading] strategies... **8.3 Comprehension and Analysis of Literary Text** Respond to grade-level-appropriate literature... **8.3.2** Evaluate the structural elements of plot... **8.3.5** Identify and analyze recurring themes...

For a complete description of the standards, see p. IN 11.

Additional Support

Study Central Have students access the Web site to review folktales and to complete a related activity.

Literature Focus Lesson

Conflict Explain to students that folktales can involve both *external* (outer) *conflicts* and *internal* (inner) *conflicts*. An external conflict may involve a protagonist's struggle against another person or a force of nature. An internal conflict is a protagonist's struggle within his or her mind, such as a struggle to make an important decision or overcome a personal weakness. List the titles of some stories students have read and ask them to list the external conflicts faced by the main characters. OL Challenge students to name the main character's inner conflict, if any exists. To help students get started, ask, "What decision does the main character have to make?" AL

Racing THE GREAT BEAR

retold by
Joseph Bruchac

The notes in the side columns model how to use the skills and elements you read about on page 150.

Folktale

ACTIVE READING MODEL

NE ONENDJI. Hear my story, which happened long ago. For many generations, the five nations of the Haudenosaunee, the People of the Longhouse, had been at war with one another. No one could say how the wars began, but each time a man of one nation was killed, his relatives sought revenge in the blood feud,[1] and so the fighting continued. Then the Creator took pity on his people and sent a messenger of peace. **1**

1 Key Reading Skill

Analyzing *I know from the first few sentences that this story takes place a long time ago and that it is about Native Americans. I know that many Native American tales entertain and teach lessons, so I'll be on the lookout for the theme.*

The Peacemaker traveled from nation to nation, convincing the people of the Five Nations—the Mohawk, the Oneida, the Onondaga, the Cayuga, and the Seneca[2]—that it was wrong for brothers to kill one another. It was not easy, but finally the nations agreed and the Great Peace began. Most welcomed that peace, though there were some beings with bad hearts who wished to see the return of war.

One day, not long after the Great Peace had been established, some young men in a Seneca village decided they would pay a visit to the Onondaga people.

"It is safe now to walk the trail between our nations," the young men said. "We will return after the sun has risen and set seven times."

Then they set out. They walked toward the east until they were lost from

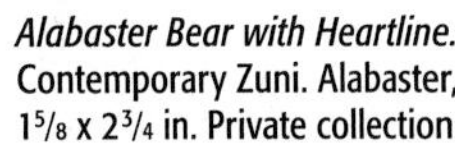

Alabaster Bear with Heartline. Contemporary Zuni. Alabaster, 1⅝ x 2¾ in. Private collection.

1. A ***feud*** is a long, bitter quarrel between two individuals or groups.
2. ***Oneida*** (oh NY duh), ***Onondaga*** (aw nun DAW guh), ***Cayuga*** (ky OO guh), ***Seneca*** (SEN uh kuh)

Teach

C Critical Thinking

Comprehension Say: What do you learn about the plot from the first paragraph? *(Possible response: For many generations, five nations of Native Americans have been at war. Then, the Creator takes pity on the people and sends a messenger of peace.)* BL OL

EL Language Coach

Figurative Language Say: Writers often use figurative language to make descriptions more meaningful. In this selection, the narrator says that there were some beings with "bad hearts" who "wished to see the return of war." What is the meaning of "bad hearts" here? *(Possible response: Here, having a bad heart means to be an evil or unkind person.)* EL BL

Readability Scores
Dale-Chall: 4.3
DRP: 49
Lexile: 760

English Language Coach

Idiomatic Expressions Point out to students that idiomatic expressions are phrases that mean something other than their literal meaning. Learning idiomatic expressions will help students master English. Give students the following idioms from the story, and help them tell what they mean:

- *lost from sight* (pages 151–152)
- *grew worried* (page 152)
- *am of two minds* (page 152)
- *to face the danger* (page 153)

Have students point out other idiomatic expressions in the story and write definitions of them in their Learner's Notebook. EL

Indiana English/Language Arts Academic Standards
SE: 8.2, 8.3, 8.3.2, 8.3.5
TWE: *Literature Focus Lesson* 8.3.2, *English Language Coach* 8.1.1

Teach

R1 Reading Skill

Making Inferences Say: The narrator says the young men who left the nation never returned and the second group of men who went to look for the first group also never returned. Look back at the title of this selection. What might be the reason these men have not returned? *(Possible response: The men have been hurt or killed by a great bear.)* OL

R2 Reading Skill

Review Connecting Say: The chief asks for a brave volunteer to take the wampum and to find out what has happened to the missing men. Have you ever been in a situation in which you or someone you know volunteered to do something challenging? What was the experience like? What was the final outcome? *(Responses will vary.)* **Say:** Use your responses to connect to how the men felt. OL

sight in the hills. But many more than seven days passed, and those young men never returned. Now another group of young men left, wanting to find out where their friends had gone. They, too, did not return. 2

The people grew worried. Parties were sent out to look for the vanished young men, but no sign was found. And the searchers who went too far into the hills did not return, either.

The old chief of the village thought long and hard. He asked the clan[3] mothers, those wise women whose job it was to choose the chiefs and give them good advice, what should be done.

"We must find someone brave enough to face whatever danger is out there," the clan mothers said.

So the old chief called the whole village to a council meeting. He held up a white strand of wampum beads made from quahog[4] clamshells as he spoke.

"Hear me," he said. "I am of two minds about what has happened to our people. It may be that the Onondaga have broken the peace and captured them. It may be there is something with an evil mind that wishes to destroy this new peace and so has killed our people. Now someone must go and find out. Who is brave enough? Who will come and take this wampum from my hand?"

R2 Many men were gathered in that council. Some were known to speak of themselves as brave warriors. Still, though they muttered to one another, no man stepped forward to take the strand of wampum. The old chief began to walk about the circle, holding the wampum in front of each man in turn. But each man only lowered his eyes to the ground. No man lifted his hand to take the wampum. 3

ACTIVE READING MODEL

2 Key Reading Skill

R1 **Making Inferences** *The author does not say for sure, but I think that something bad must have happened to the young men. Otherwise, they would have returned by now.*

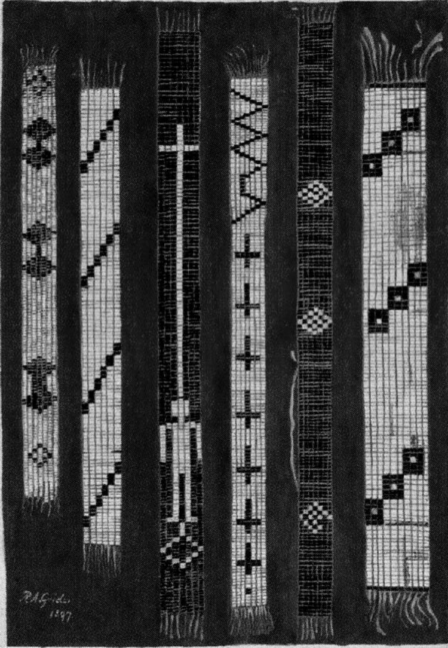

Iroquois Wampum Belts. Rufus Grider. Newberry Library, Chicago.

Wampum is a string of white shell beads. Some Native Americans used wampum as a form of money, and it was also used in tribal rituals and to record history.

3 Key Reading Skill

Predicting *I think that the person who goes after the young men will find that something evil has taken them. Most citizens of the Five Nations want peace, so the Onondaga are probably not behind the young men's disappearance.*

3. A ***clan*** is group of families who descend from a common ancestor.

4. The ***quahog*** (KOH hawg) is a type of clam found on the Atlantic coast of North America.

Additional Support

Leveled Reading An adapted version of this selection (3rd grade readability) is available on page 174 of **Jamestown Literature: An Adapted Reader** for Grade 8.

Differentiated Instruction

The Iroquois Confederacy and the UN The Iroquois Confederacy was formed in 1600 with the goal of promoting "peace, civil authority, righteousness, and the great law." Fifty Chiefs, knows as Sachems, administered the Confederacy. Have one group of students conduct research about the Confederacy, its decision making process, and its influence on history. Then have another group of students conduct research about another peace organization, the United Nations. Have students create a chart in which they compare and contrast the fundamental principles of the two peace organizations. Encourage students to present their findings to the class. AL

ACTIVE READING MODEL

Just outside the circle stood a boy who had not yet become a man. His parents were dead, and he lived with his grandmother in her old lodge at the edge of the village. His clothing was always torn and his face dirty because his grandmother was too old to care for him as a mother would. The other young men made fun of him, and as a joke they called him Swift Runner—even though no one had ever seen him run and it was thought that he was weak and lazy. All he ever seemed to do was play with his little dog or sit by the fire and listen when the old people were talking. R1

"Our chief has forgotten our greatest warrior," one of the young men said to another, tilting his head toward Swift Runner.

"Nyoh," the other young man said, laughing. "Yes. Why does he not offer the wampum to Swift Runner?" R2

The chief looked around the circle of men, and the laughing stopped. He walked out of the circle to the place where the small boy in torn clothes stood. He held out the wampum and Swift Runner took it without hesitating. 4

"I accept this," Swift Runner said. "It is right that I be the one to face the danger.

In the eyes of the people I am worthless, so if I do not return, it will not matter. I will leave when the sun rises tomorrow."

When Swift Runner arrived home at his grandmother's lodge, the old woman was waiting for him.

"Grandson," she said, "I know what you have done. The people of this village no longer remember, but your father was a great warrior. Our family is a family that has power."

Then she reached up into the rafters and took down a heavy bow. It was blackened with smoke and seemed so thick that no man could bend it.

"If you can string this bow, Grandson," the old woman said, "you are ready to face whatever waits for you on the trail."

4 Key Reading Skill

Comparing and Contrasting

This boy is different from the others. He seems braver because he takes the wampum instead of looking at the ground, but he also seems weaker because he is small.

Northeast Woodlands Pottery Vessel. Iroquois. 27 cm.

Reading in the Real World

Citizenship In this Native American folktale, Swift Runner undergoes a rite of passage to prove himself to his community and become an adult. In modern society, young adults often go through rites of passage on their path to adulthood. Have students research some of the rituals in which young adults participate and have them find out what things are required to complete those rituals. Common examples include getting a driver's license, graduating from high school, and registering to vote. Examples of some cultural rites include bar and bat mitzvahs and quinceañeras. Have students learn more about these rites of passage and report on them to the class. OL

Teach

R1 Reading Skill

Predicting **Ask:** How might the boy's attention to his dog and his respect for old people be useful to the boy during his adventure? *(Possible response: Dogs can be useful in tracking and in protecting people. By listening to older people, the boy can learn useful advice for when he encounters a conflict.)* AL

R2 Reading Skill

Comparing and Contrasting **Ask:** How does the way the other young men think of Swift Runner contrast with what you learn about him on this page? *(Possible reponse: They think he is weak and lazy, but the reader learns he is willing to face danger.)* OL

Indiana English/Language Arts Academic Standards

SE: 8.2, 8.3

TWE: *Differentiated Instruction* 8.2.1, *Reading in the Real World* 8.2

Teach

L Literary Element

Protagonist and Antagonist

Ask: What evidence is there that Swift Runner will be a strong protagonist and meet the challenges ahead of him? *(Possible responses: He is able to string the bow; he volunteers for a dangerous task; he comes from a brave and powerful family; he has something to prove to the rest of his community.)* OL

R Reading Skill

Comparing and Contrasting

Say: Think about the size of Swift Runner's dog. How are Swift Runner and his dog alike? *(Both are small and considered weak or insignificant.)* BL

Ask: How does the dog's size contrast with its importance? *(Possible response: Although the dog is small, it still can detect danger with its sharp sense of sight and smell.)* OL

Swift Runner took the bow. It was as thick as a man's wrist, but he bent it with ease and strung it.

"Wah-hah!" said his grandmother. "You are the one I knew you would grow up to be. Now you must sleep. At dawn we will make you ready for your journey." 5

It was not easy for Swift Runner to sleep, but when he woke the next morning, he felt strong and clearheaded. His grandmother was sitting by the fire with a cap in her hand.

"This was your grandfather's cap," she said. "I have sewed four hummingbird feathers on it. It will make your feet more swift."

Swift Runner took the cap and placed it on his head.

His grandmother held up four pairs of moccasins.

"Carry these tied to your waist. When one pair wears out, throw them aside and put on the next pair."

Swift Runner took the moccasins and tied them to his belt.

Next his grandmother picked up a small pouch. "In this pouch is cornmeal mixed with maple sugar," she said. "It is the only food you will need as you travel. It will give you strength when you eat it each evening."

Swift Runner took the pouch and hung it from his belt by the moccasins.

"The last thing I must give you," said the old woman, "is this advice. Pay close attention to your little dog. You have treated him well and so he is your great friend. He is small, but his eyes and nose are keen.[5] Keep him always in front of you. He will warn you of danger before it can strike you."

R Then Swift Runner set out on his journey. His little dog stayed ahead of him, sniffing the air and sniffing the ground. By the time the sun was in the middle of the sky, they were far from the

5. Something that is ***keen*** is highly sensitive or sharp.

ACTIVE READING MODEL

5 Key Literary Element

Protagonist and Antagonist

The tale is now focusing on Swift Runner. He must be the main character, or protagonist. I wonder whom the antagonist will turn out to be? L

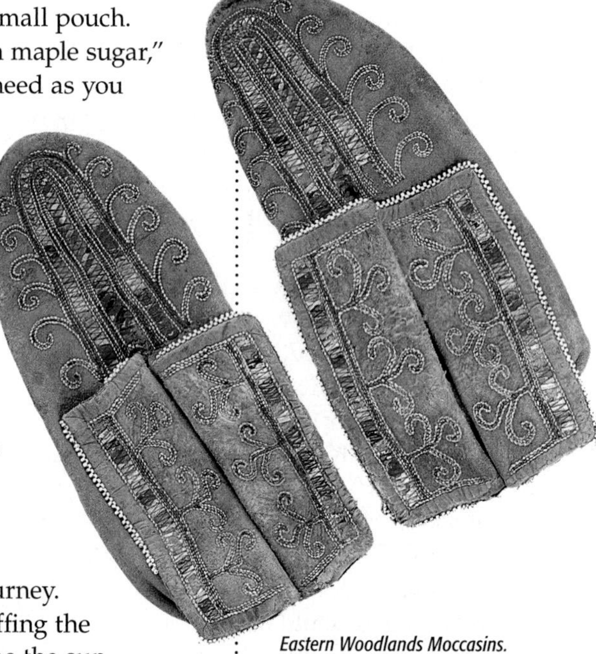

Eastern Woodlands Moccasins. Iroquois. Hide, dyed quills, beads, length: 10 in.

Additional Support

English Language Coach

Time-Order Words Help English language learners understand the order of events by having them note words that indicate time and sequence. First, review time-order words such as *first, last, then,* and *now*. Then discuss other related words and phrases that show the passage of time, such as *the next morning* and *in the middle of the night*. Have English language learners read through the folktale, jotting down time-order words and phrases they notice in the story. After they have recorded these words and phrases, ask students to create a timeline of Swift Runner's activities, noting the major challenges and dangers he faces in the story. EL

ACTIVE READING MODEL

village. The trail passed through deep woods, and it seemed to the boy as if something was following them among the trees. But he could see nothing in the thick brush.

The trail curved toward the left, and the boy felt even more the presence of something watching. Suddenly his little dog ran into the brush at the side of the trail, barking loudly. There were the sounds of tree limbs breaking and heavy feet running. Then out of the forest came a Nyagwahe, a monster bear. Its great teeth were as long as a man's arm. It was twice as tall as a moose. Close at its heels was Swift Runner's little dog.

"I see you," Swift Runner shouted. "I am after you. You cannot escape me."

Swift Runner had learned those words by listening to the stories the old people told. They were the very words a monster bear speaks when it attacks, words that terrify anyone who hears them. On hearing those words, the great bear turned and fled from the boy. **R**

"You cannot escape me," Swift Runner shouted again. Then he ran after the bear.

The Nyagwahe turned toward the east, with Swift Runner and his dog close behind. It left the trail and plowed through the thick forest, breaking down great trees and leaving a path of destruction like that of a whirlwind. It ran up the tallest hills and down through the swamps, but the boy and the dog stayed at its heels. They ran past a great cave in the rocks. All around the cave were the bones of people the bear had caught and eaten.

"My relatives," Swift Runner called as he passed the cave, "I will not forget you. I am after the one who killed you. He will not escape me." 6 **L**

Throughout the day, the boy and his dog chased the great bear, growing closer bit by bit. At last, as the sun began to set, Swift Runner stopped at the head of a small valley and called his small dog to him.

"We will rest here for the night," the boy said. He took

Beaded Pouch. Iroquois. Velvet, metal, beads, cloth, length: 6 1/2 in.

6 Key Literary Element

Conflict *It looks as if trouble is ahead. There's a conflict brewing between Swift Runner and the monster bear, Nyagwahe. If that turns out to be true, then Nyagwahe is the antagonist, and Swift Runner is the protagonist.*

Differentiated Instruction

History of Seneca Indians The Seneca Nation of Indians is one of the six tribes of the Iroquois Confederacy. Have students research the history of the Seneca Indians, and create a brochure that includes the following information:

- Tribal history
- Official language
- Myths and legends
- Leaders and chiefs
- Food and dress

Students should include pictures and illustrations in their brochures. **OL**

Teach

R Reading Skill

Analyzing Ask: What does Swift Runner's reaction to Nyagwahe, the monster bear, show about his personality? *(Possible response: It shows that he is not afraid; he is very brave and determined.)* **OL** **Ask:** What has prepared him to have the confidence and bravery that he shows at this point? *(Possible response: He has listened to the stories that the old people have told, and he has learned how brave warriors behave.)* **AL**

L Literary Element

Conflict Ask: What are Swift Runner's reasons for chasing after Nyagwahe? *(Possible response: He wants to prove himself to his community; he wants revenge for the deaths of his relatives.)* **OL** **Ask:** How has Swift Runner prepared to meet this conflict? *(Possible response: Swift Runner's grandmother has armed him with a bow for protection and given him moccasins; Swift Runner's dog can detect when the bear is near.)* **AL**

Indiana English/Language Arts Academic Standards

SE: 8.3.2

TWE: *English Language Coach* 8.1, *Differentiated Instruction* 8.2

Teach

L1 Literary Element

Protagonist and Antagonist **Ask:** How might being able to take human form help the Nyagwahe capture the other men? *(Possible response: It could have tricked them into thinking it was human and then killed them.)* OL

L2 Literary Element

Conflict **Ask:** What external conflicts does Swift Runner face on his journey? *(Possible responses: the danger of the Nyagwahe, worn shoes, and spoiled food.)* OL

UNIT 2 GENRE FOCUS

ACTIVE READING MODEL

off his first pair of moccasins, whose soles were worn away to nothing. He threw them aside and put on a new pair. Swift Runner made a fire and sat beside it with his dog. Then he took out the pouch of cornmeal and maple sugar, sharing his food with his dog.

"Nothing will harm us," Swift Runner said. "Nothing can come close to our fire." He lay down and slept.

In the middle of the night, he was awakened by the growling of his dog. He sat up with his back to the fire and looked into the darkness. There, just outside the circle of light made by the flames, stood a dark figure that looked like a tall man. Its eyes glowed green.

"I am Nyagwahe," said the figure. "This is my human shape. Why do you pursue[6] me?" L1

"You cannot escape me," Swift Runner said. "I chase you because you killed my people. I will not stop until I catch you and kill you." 7

The figure faded back into the darkness.

"You cannot escape me," Swift Runner said again. Then he patted his small dog and went to sleep.

As soon as the first light of the new day appeared, Swift Runner rose. He and his small dog took the trail. It was easy to follow the monster's path, for trees were uprooted and the earth torn by its great paws. They ran all through the morning. When the sun was in the middle of the sky, they reached the head of another valley. At the other end they saw the great bear running toward the east. Swift Runner pulled off his second pair of moccasins, whose soles were worn away to nothing. He put on his third pair and began to run again.

All through that day, they kept the Nyagwahe in sight, drawing closer bit by bit. When the sun began to set, Swift Runner stopped to make camp. He took off the third pair of moccasins, whose soles were worn away to nothing, and put on the last pair. L2

"Tomorrow," he said to his small dog, "we will catch the monster and kill it." He reached for his pouch of cornmeal and maple sugar, but when he opened it, he found it filled with worms. The magic of the Nyagwahe

7 Key Reading Skill

Predicting *From what I've seen of Swift Runner's personality, I think he'll keep this promise. I predict he won't stop until he catches Nyagwahe.*

6. ***Pursue*** means to chase after something.

Additional Support

Reading Fluency

Dramatizing the Scene Have small groups of students use the dialogue in the text to act out Swift Runner's encounters with the Nyagwahe. In addition to assigning students to read the parts of Swift Runner and the Nyagwahe, choose one or more students to narrate the text that appears between the lines of dialogue. Have students practice reading their lines aloud. Students should vary their tone and volume to reflect the proper mood or emotion of the dialogue. OL

Encourage students to discuss techniques for adding feeling to the simple language. Photocopy pages for students, and have them write suggestions in the margin, describing how to deliver their lines. AL

ACTIVE READING MODEL

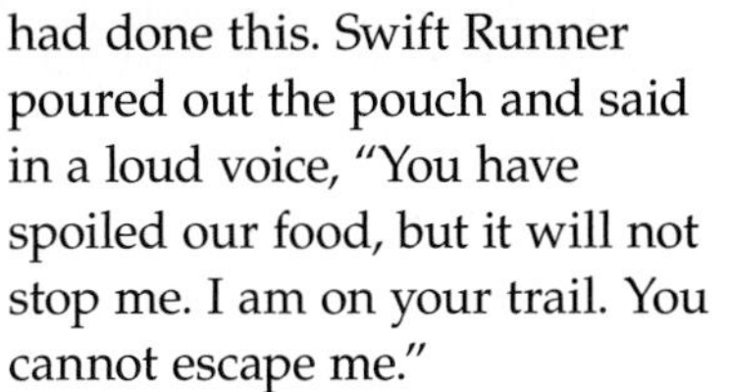

had done this. Swift Runner poured out the pouch and said in a loud voice, "You have spoiled our food, but it will not stop me. I am on your trail. You cannot escape me."

That night, once again, he was awakened by the growling of his dog. A dark figure stood just outside the circle of light.

It looked smaller than the night before, and the glow of its eyes was weak.

"I am Nyagwahe," the dark figure said. "Why do you pursue me?"

"You cannot escape me," Swift Runner said. "I am on your trail. You killed my people. You threatened the Great Peace. I will not rest until I catch you."

"Hear me," said the Nyagwahe. "I see your power is greater than mine. Do not kill me. When you catch me, take my great teeth. They are my power, and you can use them for healing. Spare my life and I will go far to the north and never again bother the People of the Longhouse." 8 R1

"You cannot escape me," Swift Runner said. "I am on your trail."

The dark figure faded back into the darkness, and Swift Runner sat for a long time, looking into the night.

At the first light of day, the boy and his dog took the trail. They had not gone far when they saw the Nyagwahe ahead of them. Its sides puffed in and out as it ran. The trail was beside a big lake with many alder trees close to the water. As the great bear ran past, the leaves were torn from the trees. Fast as the bear went, the boy and his dog came closer, bit by bit. At last, when the sun was in the middle of the sky, the giant bear could run no longer. It fell heavily to the earth, panting so hard that it stirred up clouds of dust.

Swift Runner unslung his grandfather's bow and notched an arrow to the sinewy[7] string.

Bear Claw Necklace. Native American. Bear claws, metal beads, otter or fisher tail, length: 57 1/2 in.

8 Key Reading Skill
Predicting *I'm not sure whether Swift Runner will let Nyagwahe go. It seems to me he wants to prove himself as a warrior, so I predict he won't.* R2

7. Something that is ***sinewy*** is tough and strong.

Teach

R1 Reading Skill

Making Inferences Ask: On the basis of what he tells Swift Runner, what can you infer about the Nyagwahe? *(Possible response: The Nyagwahe is very clever. Now that it's becoming weaker, Nyagwahe is trying to make a deal with Swift Runner.)* **OL**

R2 Reading Skill

Predicting Say: To predict whether Swift Runner will let the Nyagwahe go, think about the things that he values. Which do you think is more important to Swift Runner, having the power to heal or killing the beast that took the lives of his relatives? *(Responses will vary.)* **BL** **Ask:** If you were Swift Runner, would you spare the Nyagwahe? Explain your answer. *(Responses will vary.)* **OL**

Literature Focus Lesson

Fables Most students will be somewhat familiar with the concept of talking animals in stories. Tell students that talking animals frequently appear in fables, which often teach a moral or lesson. Mention that when reading a story in which animals talk, readers must willingly suspend their disbelief to better appreciate the overall message. Ask students to recall fables they have read that included talking animals. **OL**

Indiana English/Language Arts Academic Standards
SE: 8.2
TWE: *Reading Fluency* 8.7.2, *Literature Focus Lesson* 8.3

Teach

R Reading Skill

Making Inferences **Ask:** Why do you think that Swift Runner does not kill the bear? *(Possible response: Swift Runner sees that he can protect his people without killing the bear.)* OL **Ask:** What can you infer about Swift Runner's character from his behavior? *(Possible response: Swift Runner must be a fair and compassionate person because he avoids killing when it is not necessary.)* AL

L Literary Element

Plot **Say:** The monster bear grows smaller as it walks away. What does the Nyagwahe's decreasing size suggest about its power? *(Possible response: The Nyagwahe has lost its strength and will no longer be able to harm Swift Runner's people.)* **Ask:** Why does the Nyagwahe do what Swift Runner says? *(Possible response: The bear knows that it has been defeated, and its source of power—the teeth—have been removed.)* OL

Analyzing the Photo A giant grizzly bares its teeth in a ferocious roar. Does this picture capture the Nyagwahe's enormous size and strength? Why or why not?

"Shoot for my heart," said the Nyagwahe. "Aim well. If you cannot kill me with one arrow, I will take your life."

"No," Swift Runner said. "I have listened to the stories of my elders. Your only weak spot is the sole of your foot. Hold up your foot and I will kill you."

R The great bear shook with fear. "You have defeated me," it pleaded. "Spare my life and I will leave forever."

"You must give me your great teeth," Swift Runner said. "Then you must leave and never bother the People of the Longhouse again."

"I shall do as you say," said the Nyagwahe. "Take my great teeth."

L Swift Runner lowered his bow. He stepped forward and pulled out the great bear's teeth. It rose to its feet and walked to the north, growing smaller as it went. It went over the hill and was gone. 9

Carrying the teeth of the Nyagwahe over his shoulder, Swift Runner turned back to the west, his dog at his side. He walked for three moons before he reached the place where the bones of his people were piled in front of the

ACTIVE READING MODEL

9 Key Literary Element
Plot *This is an important time in the story. The conflict between Swift Runner and Nyagwahe reaches its peak, so this is the climax of the plot.*

Additional Support

Differentiated Instruction

Retelling the Story Ask students to think about why the Nyagwahe might have attacked the Senecas. Have students work in groups to retell the folktale from the Nyagwahe's point of view. Encourage students to think about the great bear's feelings and motivations. Why would it want to kill the Native Americans, especially when all that they want is peace? What does the Nyagwahe do after it loses its power? Suggest that students describe what the monster bear thinks and feels during its encounters with Swift Runner and provide information that only the Nyagwahe would know. Have students write their ideas and share their retellings with the rest of the class. AL

ACTIVE READING MODEL

monster's empty cave. He collected those bones and walked around them four times. "Now," he said, "I must do something to make my people wake up." He went to a big hickory tree and began to push it over so that it would fall on the pile of bones.

"My people," he shouted, "get up quickly or this tree will land on you."

The bones of the people who had been killed all came together and jumped up, alive again and covered with flesh. They were filled with joy and gathered around Swift Runner.

"Great one," they said, "who are you?"

"I am Swift Runner," he said.

"How can that be?" one of the men said. "Swift Runner is a skinny little boy. You are a tall, strong man."

Swift Runner looked at himself and saw that it was so. He was taller than the tallest man, and his little dog was bigger than a wolf. **L**

"I am Swift Runner," he said. "I was that boy and I am the man you see before you."

Then Swift Runner led his people back to the village. He carried with him the teeth of the Nyagwahe, and those who saw what he carried rejoiced. The trails were safe again, and the Great Peace would not be broken. **10** Swift Runner went to his grandmother's lodge and embraced her.

"Grandson," she said, "you are now the man I knew you would grow up to be. Remember to use your power to help the people."

So it was that Swift Runner ran with the great bear and won the race. Throughout his long life, he used the teeth of the Nyagwahe to heal the sick, and he worked always to keep the Great Peace.

Da neho. I am finished. **11** ❍

10 Key Literary Element
Plot *The action is winding down. The conflict is over, Swift Runner has met his goals, and peace is restored. This must be the falling action of the plot.*

11 Key Literary Element
Theme *After analyzing the characters and events in the story, I see a pattern. Swift Runner helps his village by getting rid of Nyagwahe. Then he also helps his relatives by bringing them back to life. Finally, his grandmother tells him he must always help the people, and he does. So a theme of the story must be that helping others can make you a true hero.*

Small Group Discussion With two or three other students, talk about a time that you have predicted the outcome of a TV show or movie. Share how you made inferences that led to your prediction.

Write to Learn In your Learner's Notebook, write the name of someone you think is a modern-day hero. What are some things this person has done that make him or her a hero? How is he or she like a hero in a folktale? Write your answers in your Learner's Notebook.

UNIT 2 GENRE FOCUS

Teach

L Literary Element

Protagonist Ask: What happens to Swift Runner's physical size over the course of the story? *(Swift Runner grows from a little boy to a large, powerful man.)* **BL** How does this compare with what happened to the bear? *(Possible response: While the bear decreased in size as it lost power, Swift Runner increased in size as his power and understanding grew.)* **OL**

BQ BIG Question

Ask: How do you think Swift Runner would answer the question, "Which is more important, the journey or the destination?" Explain your response. *(Responses will vary. Students might think Swift Runner would believe the journey is more important because during his journey, he got to prove his strength and courage to his community.)* **AS**

Reading in the Real World

Citizenship Tell students that many cultures have a tradition of oral storytelling and that many families have stories they share every year at family gatherings. Have students explore the stories of their own families by asking their parents, guardians, grandparents, aunts, or uncles to share a story from their family, perhaps an intriguing tale about an ancestor or a funny story from their childhood. Invite students to share the story with the class. **OL**

Indiana English/Language Arts Academic Standards
SE: 8.3.2, 8.3.5
TWE: *Differentiated Instruction* 8.7.11, *Reading in the Real World* 8.7

Analyzing

Teaching Students to Analyze

Why Is It Important?

- Analyzing helps students look critically at a piece of writing. This ability will allow students to get more out of any text, and reading becomes more meaningful.
- Analyzing a text enables students to discover its theme, its message, and the author's purpose in writing it.
- Taking apart a text to understand its separate parts can help students understand the whole text, as well as the processes of critical thinking.

How to Help Students Get It

- Tell students not to take a selection at face value, but to question each and every element that catches their attention, asking "Why was that choice made? Why was that included? Why not something else?"
- Point out such aspects of the selection as character, setting, plot, and dialogue. For nonfiction, focus on the organization, and the main ideas. How do the pieces fit together?

Reading to Answer the Big Question

The People Could Fly told by Virginia Hamilton
According to this folktale, African people could once fly, but when they were enslaved, many lost their wings and forgot that they could fly. A few people, like Toby, did not forget about his power to fly; he also helps a young mother and her baby escape a beating by reminding the mother of her power.

A Father's Daring Trek from TIME by Julie K.L. Dam
Many people in Chinese-occupied Tibet flee to India in search of a better life in exile. This TIME article includes the account of a photographer who accompanied a Tibetan man and his six-year-old daughter on the arduous and dangerous journey through the world's highest, harshest mountains.

Workshop Resources

Pacing (Days) Standard	Block	Lesson	Student Materials	Teacher Resources
1	1/2	Key Skill Lesson: Analyzing	Key Reading Skills Practice, p. 9 English Language Coach Review, p. 42	Bellringer Options Transparencies –Daily Language Practice 13 –Selection Focus 4 Read Aloud, Think Aloud Transparencies –Key Reading Skills 2 Presentation Plus!
1	1	"The People Could Fly"	Glencoe Online Unit Vocabulary Review, p. 40 Academic Vocabulary Review, p. 43 English Language Coach Active Reading Graphic Organizer, p. 11 Literary Analysis, p. 10 StudentWorks Plus™ Online Student Edition Literature Classics Selection and Unit Assessments, p. 13	Literary and Text Analysis Transparencies 41 Puzzlemaker Skill Level Up!™ A Language Arts Game BookLink 3 Assessment by Learning Objective (Diagnostic and Formative) Interactive Tutor: Self-Assessment TeacherWorks Plus™
1		"A Father's Daring Trek"	Glencoe Online Unit Vocabulary Review, p. 40 Academic Vocabulary Review, p. 43 English Language Coach Active Reading Graphic Organizer, p. 13 StudentWorks Plus™ Online Student Edition Literature Classics Selection and Unit Assessments, p. 14	Literary and Text Analysis Transparencies 45 Puzzlemaker Skill Level Up!™ A Language Arts Game BookLink 3 Assessment by Learning Objective (Diagnostic and Formative) Interactive Tutor: Self-Assessment TeacherWorks Plus™

Keys for Unit Resource

- Blackline Master
- Workbook
- Supplemental Text
- CD-ROM
- DVD
- Transparency
- Web-based
- Fast File

Level Appropriate Code

AS = Activities for all students
AL = Activities for students working above grade level
OL = Activities for students working at grade level
BL = Activities for students working below grade level
EL = Activities for English language learners

Focus

BELLRINGER Options

- **Selection Focus Transparencies 4**
- **Daily Language Practice Transparency 13**

Focus Activity Say: You will read about people who made journeys in search of a better life. How might it feel to have to make such a journey? *(Responses will vary. Students might mention having feelings of fear, hope, and excitement.)* AS

Teach

R Reading Skill

Analyzing Ask: In addition to plot, conflict, and theme, what other elements of a fiction selection might you analyze to better understand a story? *(Possible responses: characters, tone, style, and voice)* AL

V Vocabulary

Academic Vocabulary
Say: Look at the definition for *analyzing* at the bottom of the page. What are some synonyms for *analyzing*? *(Possible responses: examining, studying, investigating, evaluating)* AS

READING WORKSHOP 1

Skills Focus

You will practice these skills when you read the following selections:
"The People Could Fly," p. 164
"A Father's Daring Trek," p. 172

Reading

- Analyzing content and structure

Literature

- Identifying protagonists and antagonists
- Understanding how setting can influence plot

Vocabulary

- Using techniques for building vocabulary
- Academic Vocabulary: *analyzing*

Writing/Grammar

- Using adjectives and adverbs correctly

Indiana English/Language Arts Academic Standards (pp. 160–161)

8.2 Comprehension and Analysis (Focus on Informational Text) Develop [reading] strategies...

For a complete description of the standards, see p. IN 11.

Skill Lesson

Analyzing

Learn It!

R **What Is It? Analyzing** is looking at the separate parts of a selection and thinking how they work together to express ideas. Just as you might take apart a watch to see how it works, so you can take apart a story or article to see what makes it "tick." When you analyze a story, you might look at parts, or elements, like these:

- plot
- conflict
- theme

When you analyze an article, you might think about these elements:

- main ideas
- reasons, examples, descriptions
- organization

Analyzing Cartoons
The bear analyzes his relationship with food by considering his feelings about his sandwich.

V **Academic Vocabulary**

analyzing (AN uh ly zing) *n.* examining by separating into parts and identifying relationships between the parts

Additional Support

Reading in the Real World

College Explain to students that in college, they will be asked to analyze everything from literary passages to scientific articles. To help students develop analyzing strategies that can be applied to different types of text, generate with them a list of common text elements. For example, in addition to plot, conflict, and theme, students may think about characterization and setting when analyzing literary text. In nonfiction text, students may think about main ideas, supporting evidence, examples, organization, illustrations, and style. As you name each element, discuss what it means and how it contributes to a text as a whole. AL

Why Is It Important? Analyzing helps you look carefully at a piece of writing. You'll understand it better, because you know the parts it is made of and the ways that the parts fit together.

How Do I Do It? First, decide what you want to analyze; then separate it into parts. Think about what each part is saying. Then see how the parts fit together to convey an overall idea. To see how this works, read the passage below. Then read to see how a student analyzed the conflict described in the passage.

The stars and moon hid behind the clouds. Still the man walked on, his fingers grasping the handle of his silver sword. He knew he might need it at any moment. Suddenly, a streak of lightning flashed across the sky. In that instant, he saw it. It was waiting for him in the darkness. He held his breath and drew his sword.

R

Everything in the passage tells me a dangerous conflict, or struggle, is about to take place. The darkness and flash of lightning create a sense of danger, and so do the man's thoughts and actions. He holds onto his sword as he walks, so he must feel threatened by someone or something. Then he sees "it." I'm not sure what "it" is—maybe a monster?—but I am sure the man thinks that "it" is about to attack him, because he draws his sword.

Study Central Visit www.glencoe.com and click on Study Central to review analyzing.

Practice It!

Think about a story you have recently read or a movie you have recently seen. Answer these questions.

- Who is the most important character in the story?
- What problem or challenge does that character face?
- How does the character solve the problem or overcome the challenge?
- What is the main message, or theme, of the story?

Use It!

As you read the selections, think about how you might analyze what they mean.

Teach

Study Central Have students access the Web site to review analyzing and to complete a related activity.

R Reading Skill

Analyzing **Say:** Analyzing what you read is like putting together a jigsaw puzzle. You need to put all the separate pieces together to see the full picture. Similarly, the different elements of a story or selection come together to help you better understand the selection. What elements of the selection in the *How Do I Do It?* section lead you to think that "it" is an enemy? *(Responses will vary. Students should point out that the character had to draw his sword and that he holds his breath as if expecting danger.)* **OL**

Resources for page 161

Use Key Reading Skills Transparency 2 in *Read Aloud, Think Aloud* to help students practice Analyzing.

Literature Focus Lesson

Theme The theme of a story is different from its topic. The theme is a message about life that the author conveys using the characters, the action, and the conflict. The theme is usually expressed as a sentence. On the other hand, the topic is the subject of the story; it is usually expressed in one or two words (for example, the topic of "The People Could Fly" is slavery). Tell students that stories may have more than one theme and that readers might see different themes in the same story. After students have read the selections, ask them to tell what they think the themes are. **OL**

Indiana English/Language Arts Academic Standards

SE: 8.2

TWE: *Reading in the Real World* 8.2, *Literature Focus Lesson* 8.3

Teach

More About the Author

A talent for storytelling ran in Virginia Hamilton's family. Her grandfather had escaped from slavery as a child by crossing the Ohio River to freedom. Hamilton said that every year, he used to tell his children, "I'm going to tell you how I escaped from slavery so slavery will never happen to you." Hamilton's mother and father were both talented storytellers who taught Hamilton about her cultural heritage. She has kept this tradition alive, sharing stories of the African American experience with her many admiring readers.

EL Language Coach

Vocabulary Building: Synonyms and Antonyms

Say: One way to remember the difference between a synonym and an antonym is to remember that *synonym* starts with the same letter as the word *same*. *Synonyms* are words that have the *same* meanings, while *antonyms* have opposite meanings. EL

Before You Read: The People Could Fly

Meet the Author

Many of Virginia Hamilton's award-winning books celebrate her African American ancestry and culture. She once said, "In the background of much of my writing is the dream of freedom tantalizingly out of reach." This dream is the source of many folktales, including "The People Could Fly." See page R2 of the Author Files in the back of the book for more on Virginia Hamilton.

Author Search For more about Virginia Hamilton, go to www.glencoe.com.

Indiana English/Language Arts Academic Standards (pp. 162–167)

8.1 Word Recognition, Fluency, and Vocabulary Development Understand...word relationships...
8.2 Comprehension and Analysis (Focus on Informational Text) Develop [reading] strategies...**8.3.2** Evaluate the structural elements of plot...

For a complete description of the standards, see p. IN 11.

Vocabulary Preview

scorned (skornd) *adj.* looked down upon by someone **(p. 164)** *The scorned people longed for justice.*

snarled (snarld) *v.* made tangled or knotted; form of the verb *snarl* **(p. 166)** *The rope snarled around the young girl's ankle.*

English Language Coach

EL

Vocabulary Building: Synonyms and Antonyms Every time you study the vocabulary words in a lesson, you're working on building your vocabulary. But how can you remember all the vocabulary words you study?

One way is to link "new" words with "old" ones you already know. Pair an unfamiliar word with a synonym—a word or phrase that means about the same thing—or an antonym, a word or phrase that means the opposite. Suppose, for example, that you want to remember the word *perplexing* (per PLEKS ing), which means "puzzling" or "confusing." Make a synonym-antonym chart like the one below to help yourself remember the word.

Word	Synonym	Antonym
perplexing	confusing	clear

With a Partner Get together with a classmate, and use a dictionary to look up the underlined words below. Make a synonym-antonym chart for the words.

- The stubborn child was very **exasperating.**
- The **towering** office building had 50 floors.
- That **arrogant** woman thinks she knows more than anybody else.

Word	Synonym	Antonym
exasperating		
towering		
arrogant		

Additional Support

Author Search To expand students' appreciation of Virginia Hamilton, have them access the Web site for additional information and resources.

English Language Coach

Build Background Tell students that versions of some folktales appear in many different cultures. For example, there may be as many as 1,500 versions of the Cinderella story. In one Vietnamese telling, a beautiful girl named Tam is killed by her wicked stepmother. Tam comes back to life as a nightingale and eventually finds happiness and love. Have students of different cultures share any Cinderella tales they know, in addition to other culturally specific folktales that may be unfamiliar to most students. As a class, discuss themes or characteristics of these folktales that are shared across cultures. EL

Skills Preview

Key Reading Skill: Analyzing

As you read "The People Could Fly," you'll analyze ways it is like other folktales you've read. Before you read, spend a few minutes thinking about the tales.

Whole Class Discussion Brainstorm a list of folktales, like "Little Red Riding Hood," "Cinderella," and "Hansel and Gretel." Then discuss the following questions:

- Which tales have characters with magical powers?
- Which tales have at least one character who is very evil and one who is very good?
- In which tales do the good characters win out over the evil ones?
- What do your answers tell you about folktales?

R

Key Literary Element: Protagonist and Antagonist

The main character in a narrative, or story, is known as the **protagonist** (pro TAG oh nist). In traditional stories, like folktales, the protagonist is often a completely good person–someone you like or look up to, identify with, and hope will win in the end. In modern stories, the protagonist is often good *and* bad. Like real people, he or she may have faults and weaknesses.

The **antagonist** (an TAG oh nist) is the person, group of people, or force that stands in the way of the protagonist's happiness. The force might be bad luck or a force of nature. For example, a blinding snowstorm can be the antagonist in a story if the storm keeps the main character from reaching the safety of his or her home. To find the protagonist and antagonist in a story, ask yourself, *Who is this mainly about? Who or what is working against him or her?*

L

Interactive Literary Elements Handbook
To review or learn more about the literary elements, go to www.glencoe.com.

Get Ready to Read

Connect to the Reading

Imagine that you could fly on your own like a bird. When might you use your special ability and why?

Write to Learn In your Learner's Notebook, describe a situation in which you would want to fly and explain why.

Build Background

This story takes place on a plantation in North America during slavery times.

- The practice of kidnapping Africans and bringing them to North America as slaves began in 1619. Slavery was allowed to continue in parts of the United States until the end of the Civil War in 1865.
- "The People Could Fly" can be classified as a legend–a folktale about amazing people and events that are loosely based on fact. In the early 1800s a group of enslaved West Africans rose up against the slave agents that were carrying them from one part of Georgia to another by boat. The agents were killed; the enslaved people were never found. Local slave owners believed that the West Africans drowned themselves to escape bondage. But the enslaved people on their plantations had a very different explanation of what happened. That explanation is preserved in "The People Could Fly."

Set Purposes for Reading

BIG Question Read "The People Could Fly" to learn how some enslaved people were able to make an unusual journey toward freedom.

Set Your Own Purpose What else would you like to learn from the story to help yourself answer the Big Question? Write your own purpose on the "People Could Fly" flap of Foldable 2.

Keep Moving

Use these skills as you read the following selection.

Teach

R Reading Skill

Analyzing Say: Remember that folktales tell you about human society and cultural ideals, or values. What cultural values have you learned about in the folktales you have read? *(Responses will vary. Students might note that many cultures value honesty, kindness, and generosity.)* AL

L Literary Element

Protagonist and Antagonist
Say: Who is the protagonist in your favorite book or movie? Who or what is the antagonist? *(Responses will vary.)* AS
Ask: Is the protagonist mostly good, or does he or she possess some negative characteristics? Give examples to support your answer. *(Responses will vary.)* OL

Literature Online

Interactive Literary Elements Handbook Have students access the Web site to improve their understanding of protagonist and antagonist.

Literature Focus Lesson

African American Folklore Explain that folklore includes the traditional beliefs, customs, stories, songs, and dances of a culture, generally handed down orally through generations. Africans who were enslaved in North America developed a folklore tradition of singing songs and telling stories. They were forbidden to learn to read or write in English or to speak their own languages, so they began this new tradition. Their songs expressed their pain and hope. Have students look online to find a song (or spiritual) sung by African American slaves. What is the topic of the song? What does it tell about life during this time? OL

Indiana English/Language Arts Academic Standards
SE: 8.1, 8.2
TWE: *English Language Coach* 8.3, *Literature Focus Lesson* 8.3.1

Teach

R Reading Skill

Analyzing Ask: How are the characters in this story special? *(They can fly.)* **Ask:** What happened when these special people were captured? *(They lost the ability to fly because they couldn't take their wings with them.)* **BL**

L Literary Element

Protagonist and Antagonist

Say: The narrator calls the Master "a hard lump of clay." To what else does the narrator compare the Master to show that the Master is the antagonist? *(Possible response: The narrator calls him "a hard, glinty coal," "a hard rock pile," and says he "wouldn't be moved.")* **OL** **Ask:** What do these comparisons tell you about the Master? *(Possible response: He is cruel and feels no mercy or compassion toward his slaves.)* **AL**

Readability Scores

Dale-Chall: 5.1

DRP: 46

Lexile: 480

The People Could Fly

told by Virginia Hamilton

They say the people could fly. Say that long ago in Africa, some of the people knew magic. And they would walk up on the air like climbin up on a gate. And they flew like blackbirds over the fields. Black, shiny wings flappin against the blue up there. **R**

Then, many of the people were captured for Slavery. The ones that could fly shed their wings. They couldn't take their wings across the water on the slave ships. Too crowded, don't you know. **1**

The folks were full of misery, then. Got sick with the up and down of the sea. So they forgot about flyin when they could no longer breathe the sweet scent of Africa.

Say the people who could fly kept their power, although they shed their wings. They kept their secret magic in the land of slavery. They looked the same as the other people from Africa who had been coming over, who had dark skin. Say you couldn't tell anymore one who could fly from one who couldn't.

One such who could was an old man, call him Toby. And standin tall, yet afraid, was a young woman who once had wings. Call her Sarah. Now Sarah carried a babe tied to her back. She trembled to be so hard worked and **scorned.**

The slaves labored in the fields from sunup to sundown. The owner of the slaves callin himself their Master. Say he was a hard lump of clay. A hard, glinty coal. A hard rock pile, wouldn't be moved. His Overseer[1] on horseback pointed out the slaves who were slowin down. So the one called **L**

1. In times of slavery, the ***overseer*** directed the field workers.

Vocabulary

scorned (skornd) *adj.* looked down upon by someone

Practice the Skills

1 Key Reading Skill

Analyzing The narrator uses dialect, or nonstandard English (like "climbin" and "flappin"), and conversational phrases. How do you think this would help a reader understand and enjoy this story?

Additional Support

Leveled Reading An adapted version of this selection (4th grade readability) is available on page 202 of **Jamestown Literature: An Adapted Reader** for Grade 8.

Reading in the Real World

Career Tell students that some people make a living telling stories. Professional storytellers go to schools, libraries, bookstores, and special events and tell stories to children and adults. They use their voices and sometimes body language to help bring the stories to life.

Have students do research to find out what it takes to become a professional storyteller: What skills would be necessary for this career? How might you get practice telling stories to a crowd? **OL**

Driver cracked his whip over the slow ones to make them move faster. That whip was a slice-open cut of pain. So they did move faster. Had to.

Sarah hoed and chopped the row as the babe on her back slept.

Say the child grew hungry. That babe started up bawling too loud. Sarah couldn't stop to feed it. Couldn't stop to soothe and quiet it down. She let it cry. She didn't want to. She had no heart to croon[2] to it.

"Keep that thing quiet," called the Overseer. He pointed his finger at the babe. The woman scrunched low. The Driver cracked his whip across the babe anyhow. The babe hollered like any hurt child, and the woman fell to the earth. **2**

The old man that was there, Toby, came and helped her to her feet.

"I must go soon," she told him.

"Soon," he said.

Sarah couldn't stand up straight any longer. She was too weak. The sun burned her face. The babe cried and cried, "Pity me, oh, pity me," say it sounded like. Sarah was so sad and starvin, she sat down in the row. **3**

2. To ***croon*** is to sing or hum in a low, soft tone.

Practice the Skills

2 Key Literary Element

Protagonist and Antagonist The Overseer and Driver whip a baby. That's about as mean as people can get. One or both of them must be the antagonist. **L**

3 Key Reading Skill

Analyzing Think about the Overseer and Driver, their actions, and their effects on Sarah and her baby. What do those pieces of information say about slavery?

The People Could Fly, 1985. Leo & Diana Dillon. Pastel and watercolor. Private collection.

Differentiated Instruction

Connecting Music to Text Have students use the Internet to look up the lyrics of the African American spiritual, "Nobody Knows the Trouble I've Seen." Have students discuss connections between the words of the song and "The People Could Fly." Ask students how the lyrics "Sometimes I'm up, / Sometimes I'm down" and "Sometimes I'm almost to the ground" match ideas in the story. **AS** Ask students to compare and contrast the theme of these lyrics with a modern-day song from the African American culture, such as gospel or hip-hop. **OL**

READING WORKSHOP 1

Teach

L Literary Element

Protagonist and Antagonist

Ask: What do the Overseer's words and actions tell you about how he views the enslaved people? How does this behavior help show that the Overseer is an antagonist? *(Possible responses: He views the slaves as "things," not human beings. He has no sympathy or mercy for them. He whips the baby. He is working against the main characters, which is what an antagonist would do.)* **OL**

Viewing the Art

Ask: What do you think is happening in the artwork? How does the artwork relate to the story? *(Responses may include: the people are flying; they used to be able to fly before they were in slavery.)* **OL**

Indiana English/Language Arts Academic Standards

SE: 8.2, 8.3.2

TWE: *Reading in the Real World* 8.7.12, *Differentiated Instruction* 8.3.1

Teach

L Literary Element

Protagonist and Antagonist Write *Sarah* and *Toby* on the board. **Ask:** Which details from the story show that Sarah is the protagonist? *(Possible responses: Sarah is a good person who works hard and tries to take care of her baby. Readers want her to find safety and escape the cruel Overseer.)* **Ask:** Which details show that Toby is the protagonist? *(Possible responses: Toby is kind and goodhearted. He is able to fly and helps Sarah and others fly.)* **OL** As students list details, write them on the board. Have students add to the list as they finish the story. **AS**

C Critical Thinking

Comprehension Say: The narrator says that Toby spoke the magic words "so quickly, they sounded like whispers and sighs." Why do you think Toby spoke softly? *(Possible response: Toby spoke quietly so that the Overseer would not hear him and stop Sarah's escape. Possibly, he wanted to prevent the Overseer from learning the magic words.)* **OL** **Ask:** What happens when the Overseer hears Toby speak the magic words? *(He orders others to try to capture Toby.)* **BL**

"Get up, you black cow," called the Overseer. He pointed his hand, and the Driver's whip **snarled** around Sarah's legs. Her sack dress tore into rags. Her legs bled onto the earth. She couldn't get up.

Toby was there where there was no one to help her and the babe.

"Now, before it's too late," panted Sarah. "Now, Father!"

"Yes, Daughter, the time is come," Toby answered. "Go, as you know how to go!"

He raised his arms, holding them out to her. *"Kum . . . yali, kum buba tambe,"* and more magic words, said so quickly, they sounded like whispers and sighs. **4**

The young woman lifted one foot on the air. Then the other. She flew clumsily at first, with the child now held tightly in her arms. Then she felt the magic, the African mystery. Say she rose just as free as a bird. As light as a feather.

The Overseer rode after her, hollerin. Sarah flew over the fences. She flew over the woods. Tall trees could not snag her. Nor could the Overseer. She flew like an eagle now, until she was gone from sight. No one dared speak about it. Couldn't believe it. But it was, because they that was there saw that it was. **5**

Say the next day was dead hot in the fields. A young man slave fell from the heat. The Driver come and whipped him. Toby come over and spoke words to the fallen one. The words of ancient Africa once heard are never remembered completely. The young man forgot them as soon as he heard them. They went way inside him. He got up and rolled over on the air. He rode it awhile. And he flew away.

Another and another fell from the heat. Toby was there. He cried out to the fallen and reached his arms out to them. *"Kum kunka yali, kum . . . tambe!"* Whispers and sighs. And they too rose on the air. They rode the hot breezes. The ones flyin were black and shinin sticks, wheelin above the head of the Overseer. They crossed the rows, the fields, the fences, the streams, and were away.

"Seize the old man!" cried the Overseer. "I heard him say the magic *words.* Seize him!"

Vocabulary

snarled (snarld) *v.* made tangled or knotted

Practice the Skills

4 Key Literary Element

Protagonist and Antagonist Who do you think the main character, or protagonist, is: Sarah or Toby? (You could argue either way.)

5 Key Reading Skill

Analyzing How is this part of the tale similar to other folktales you know? Think about

- the way Sarah escapes
- the kind of person Sarah is
- the kind of people the Driver and Overseer are

Additional Support

Reading Fluency

Readers' Theatre Organize students in small groups. Have each group choose up to four paragraphs from the story to read aloud to the class. Each person in the group should read the words of a different character, and one person should read the narration. Encourage students to read with expression and to add gestures. Allow groups to practice reading their selections before they present to the class. After each group has shared, discuss as a class how hearing the story aloud may have changed their understanding of it. **OL**

The one callin himself Master come runnin. The Driver got his whip ready to curl around old Toby and tie him up. The slaveowner took his hip gun from its place. He meant to kill old, black Toby.

But Toby just laughed. Say he threw back his head and said, "Hee, hee! Don't you know who I am? Don't you know some of us in this field?" He said it to their faces. "We are ones who fly!" **L**

And he sighed the **ancient** words that were a dark promise. **6** He said them all around to the others in the field under the whip, *". . . buba yali . . . buba tambe. . . ."*

There was a great outcryin. The bent backs straighted up. Old and young who were called slaves and could fly joined hands. Say like they would ring-sing. But they didn't shuffle in a circle. They didn't sing. They rose on the air. They flew in a flock that was black against the heavenly blue. Black crows or black shadows. It didn't matter, they went so high. Way above the plantation, way over the slavery land. Say they flew away to *Free-dom.* **BQ**

And the old man, old Toby, flew behind them, takin care of them. He wasn't cryin. He wasn't laughin. He was the seer.[3] His gaze fell on the plantation where the slaves who could not fly waited. **C**

"Take us with you!" Their looks spoke it but they were afraid to shout it. Toby couldn't take them with him. Hadn't the time to teach them to fly. They must wait for a chance to run.

"Goodie-bye!" The old man called Toby spoke to them, poor souls! And he was flyin gone.

So they say. The Overseer told it. The one called Master said it was a lie, a trick of the light. The Driver kept his mouth shut.

The slaves who could not fly told about the people who could fly to their children. When they were free. When they sat close before the fire in the free land, they told it. They did so love firelight and *Free-dom,* and tellin. **BQ**

They say that the children of the ones who could not fly told their children. And now, me, I have told it to you. **7** ❍

3. A ***seer*** is a prophet or someone who is unusually wise.

Alexander Chandler, 1955. Andrew Wyeth. Drybrush, 21 1/4 x 14 1/2 in. Private collection. Photograph courtesy of the Wyeth collection. © Andrew Wyeth.

Analyzing the Painting Study the expression and pose of the man in this painting. What personal qualities might he have in common with Toby?

Practice the Skills

6 English Language Coach

Vocabulary Building: Synonyms and Antonyms What does **ancient** mean? In your Learner's Notebook, make a synonym-antonym chart for the word.

7 BIG Question

Where is Toby going? What do you think is more important—the journey he is taking or his destination? Why? Write your answer on the "People Could Fly" flap of Foldable 2. Your response will help you complete the Unit Challenge later.

Teach

L Literary Element

Protagonist and Antagonist
Ask: What can you tell about Toby from his reaction to the Master and the Driver? *(You can tell he is brave.)* OL

C Critical Thinking

Comprehension Say: The narrator calls Toby a "seer." What do you think is the difference between a seer and an average person? *(A seer is wise, can understand things most people can't.)* OL

BQ BIG Question

Say: Note that Hamilton italicizes and hyphenates the word *freedom* to set it apart. How is freedom different from what you might think of as a "destination"? *(Possible response: Freedom isn't a place, but rather a state of being.)* OL

Assess

CheckPoint

Use the CheckPoint questions provided on Presentation Plus! to check for comprehension of the selection. These questions can be used with interactive response keypads for immediate student feedback.

Differentiated Instruction

Illustrating the Story Have students who enjoy drawing or painting illustrate this story. Encourage them to read the paragraph on page 167 that begins "There was a great outcryin." Have students use the details presented in this and other paragraphs to create an illustration that captures both the tone and the theme of the story. Tell students that their illustrations do not have to be realistic—they can use colors, shapes, and lines to create an abstract image that captures the essence of the story. Encourage students to share their illustrations with the class. OL

Indiana English/Language Arts Academic Standards
SE: 8.1, 8.2, 8.3.2
TWE: *Reading Fluency* 8.7, *Differentiated Instruction* 8.7.9

Assess

Resources for page 168

- Selection Quick Check, p. 11
- Selection and Unit Assessment, p. 13
- ExamView Assessment Suite
- Interactive Tutor: Self-Assessment

Students can respond to the *After You Read* items in their Learner's Notebooks or on a separate sheet of paper.

Answering the

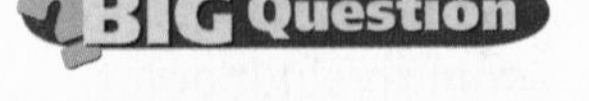

1. The enslaved people's journey leads them to freedom.
2. The people didn't have room on the slave ships for their wings; they forgot about their flying power after leaving Africa.
3. Enslaved Africans could no longer remember how to fly. One day, Toby, an old man who remembers how to fly, speaks the magic words that remind the enslaved people how to fly, and they escape.

Critical Thinking

4. Possible response: Sarah needs to remember she can fly before the words will work.
5. Possible response: The words touched a deep part of the young man's memory.
6. Possible response: The story may have given the enslaved people hope that they would eventually be free.

After You Read

The People Could Fly

Answering the BIG Question

1. What is the importance of the journey the enslaved people take in this story?
2. **Recall** Why didn't the people in the story have wings?
   TIP **Right There** You will find this information in the story.
3. **Summarize** In a few sentences, sum up what happens in the story.
   TIP **Think and Search** The answer is in the story, but it is not all in one place.

Critical Thinking

4. **Infer** Why does Toby speak the magic words when he does?
   TIP **Author and Me** You will find clues in the story, but you must also use the information in your head.
5. **Interpret** When Toby speaks the words of Africa, the words go "way inside" a young enslaved man. What do you think this means?
   TIP **Author and Me** You will find clues in the story, but you must also use the information in your head.
6. **Infer** What message do you think this story may have had for enslaved people who heard it? Why?
   TIP **Author and Me** You will find clues in the story, but you must also use the information in your head.

Write About Your Reading

Story Sequel A sequel (SEE kwul) picks up where a story ends and adds new scenes and actions to it. Use your imagination to write a short sequel to "The People Could Fly." In your sequel, describe the journey Sarah and her baby took and the place they finally landed.

Try to make your sequel sound like the original folktale. For example, you might drop the letter *-g* from the endings of -ing words. And you might use conversational phrases like "don't you know" and "so they say."

Indiana English/Language Arts Academic Standards
(pp. 168–169)

8.3 Comprehension and Analysis of Literary Text Respond to grade-level-appropriate literature... **8.5.2** Write responses to literature...
8.2 Comprehension and Analysis (Focus on Informational Text) Develop [reading] strategies...
8.6 English Language Conventions
For a complete description of the standards, see p. IN 11.

Write About Your Reading

Possible Response:
So they say Sarah came back with her baby. They say she had been flyin for months, thinkin about all the slaves who couldn't remember the magic deep inside. Don't you know the *Free-dom* meant nothin to her if others weren't goin there with her? They say Sarah sang the magic words to those slaves who forgot how to fly, just like Toby did for her. Sarah helped many more slaves remember their inside magic. They flew to *Free-dom* with her that day and landed in a place far away in Canada, where they lived the rest of their days.

Skills Review

Key Reading Skill: Analyzing

7. The following elements are often found in folktales. Which elements are in "The People Could Fly"? Support your answer with examples from the story.
   - at least one character with magical powers
   - at least one character who is very good and one who is very evil
   - good characters who win out over evil ones
8. How did reading "The People Could Fly" add to your understanding of folktales and legends? Use details from the story to support your answer.

Key Literary Element: Protagonist and Antagonist

9. Is the antagonist in the story the Overseer, the Driver, the Master, or slavery itself? Give reasons for your answer.
10. While reading the story, you were asked to identify the protagonist. Now that you've read the story, who do you think the protagonist is—Sarah or Toby? Support your opinion with evidence from the story.

Vocabulary Check

Answer *true* or *false* to each statement. Rewrite each false statement to make it true.

11. A person who is **scorned** is someone whom others appreciate.
12. If your hair is **snarled,** it's full of knots.
13. **Academic Vocabulary** If your teacher asks you to analyze a story, what is he or she asking you to do?
14. **English Language Coach** Look up the word *freedom* in a thesaurus. Then make a synonym-antonym chart for the word *freedom*. List as many synonyms and antonyms for the word *freedom* as you can.

Grammar Link: Adjectives

Adjectives are words that describe, or modify, nouns and pronouns. Adjectives describe by answering one of these questions:

- *What kind?* *happy* man, *stormy* weather
- *How many?* *five* chairs, *several* months
- *How much?* *more* work, *less* rain
- *Which one?* *this* page, *that* day

Adjectives add specific detail to general ideas. Compare the sentences below. Which is better?

- The dogs chased the cats.
- Those enormous stray dogs chased five terrified cats.

The adjectives *those, enormous, stray, five,* and *terrified* make the second sentence clearer and more vivid than the first.

Grammar Practice

Copy the following sentences. Underline all the adjectives. For help in finding the adjectives, answer the questions in parentheses.

15. I like story problems. *(What kind of problems?)*
16. Did you do those equations yourself? *(Which equations?)*
17. My math teacher gave us ten problems to do. *(What kind of teacher? How many problems?)*
18. I prefer less homework. *(How much homework?)*
19. I need more free time. *(How much time? What kind of time?)*
20. I have many hours of homework. *(How many hours?)*

Writing Application Review the sequel you wrote for the Write About Your Reading activity. Add three adjectives to make your writing more vivid.

Web Activities For eFlashcards, Selection Quick Checks, and other Web activities, go to www.glencoe.com.

Skills Review

Key Reading Skill: Analyzing

7. Possible response: Toby, Sarah, and the other enslaved people who can fly have magical powers. Toby is very good; the slaveowner is very evil. Toby wins out over the evil slaveowner by freeing many slaves.
8. Possible response: I realized that folktales helped people through horrible times.

Key Literary Element: Protagonist and Antagonist

9. Possible response: The antagonist is slavery. Slavery, or lack of freedom, was what the enslaved people were escaping from, more than from the Overseer.
10. Responses may vary. Students believe Toby is the real protagonist because he helps many people escape.

Vocabulary Check

11. False. A scorned person is despised by others.
12. True

Academic Vocabulary

13. He or she is asking me to think about the story elements and how they fit together.

English Language Coach

14. Responses will vary.

Grammar Link: Adjectives

Grammar Practice

15. I like story problems.
16. Did you do those equations yourself?
17. My math teacher gave us ten problems to do.
18. I prefer less homework.
19. I need more free time.
20. I have many hours of homework.

Close

Ask students to summarize what they learned about the Big Question from the story.

Indiana English/Language Arts Academic Standards
SE: 8.2, 8.3, 8.5.2, 8.6

Teach

More About the Author

Julie K. L. Dam has recently published a novel called *Some Like it Haute*, which reveals Dam's lighter side of writing. The novel focuses on fashion and is inspired by Dam's weblog with the same title. (A weblog is a personal Web site that provides updated news or journal entries.)

EL Language Coach

Vocabulary Building: Collections of Synonyms

Say: Often, synonyms will have slightly different meanings. What is the difference between someone who is *elated* and someone who is *happy*? *(Possible response: Someone who is elated is probably more excited than someone who is happy.)* **Say:** As you look for synonyms for *nice,* try to find adjectives that provide specific descriptions. EL

Before You Read A Father's Daring Trek

Meet the Author

Julie K. L. Dam is a reporter and feature writer for publications such as *Time* and *People* magazines. She has written on a wide variety of topics, from celebrity interviews to theater reviews. She has also written a novel about a fashion-loving American girl who visits Paris, France, during Fashion Week.

Author Search For more about Julie K. L. Dam, go to www.glencoe.com.

Vocabulary Preview

exile (EG zyl) *n.* the state of living away from one's home country **(p. 172)** *The father and daughter chose to live in exile because life in their country was so hard.*

persecution (pur suh KYOO shun) *n.* constant cruel or harmful treatment **(p. 172)** *The Tibetan people suffered terrible persecution.*

destiny (DES tuh nee) *n.* a person's fate or fortune **(p. 175)** It was *Yangdol's destiny to live a good life in India.*

Sentence Challenge Write a sentence for each vocabulary word.

English Language Coach

Vocabulary Building: Collections of Synonyms Do you find yourself using the same words over and over? Use a thesaurus (thih SOR us)—a collection of synonyms—to find other words that mean about the same thing. Whether in book or electronic form, thesauruses are easy to use. Suppose that you want to find a synonym for the word *happy.* If you're using a thesaurus in book form, look up *happy* just as you would if you were using a dictionary. If you're using an online thesaurus, enter the word *happy* in the search box. Either way, you'll get an entry that looks something like this:

Main Word: happy
Part of Speech: adjective
Synonyms: pleased, joyous, glad, contented

To help yourself remember all the synonyms, put them on a word web like the one below:

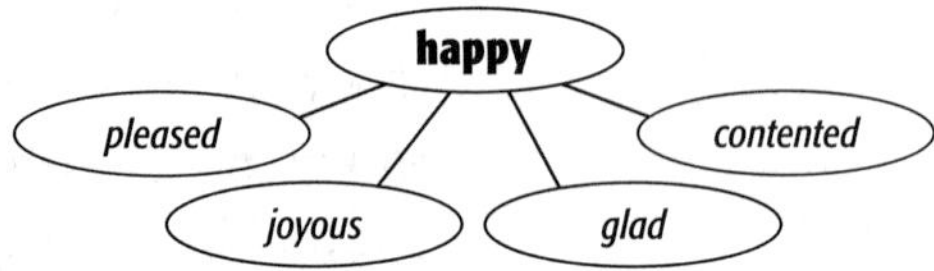

Partner Work With a classmate, look up the word *nice* in a thesaurus. Together, make a word web of synonyms that could be used in place of *nice* in this sentence: The weather was nice today.

Indiana English/Language Arts Academic Standards (pp. 170–175)

8.1 Word Recognition, Fluency, and Vocabulary Development Understand...word relationships... **8.2 Comprehension and Analysis (Focus on Informational Text)** Develop [reading] strategies...identify and analyze structure, organization... **8.3.2** Analyze the importance of setting... **8.3.9** Analyze the relevance of setting...

For a complete description of the standards, see p. IN 11.

Additional Support

Author Search To expand students' appreciation of Julie K. L. Dam, have them access the Web site for additional information and resources.

Literature Focus Lesson

Photo Essay Swiss photographer Manuel Bauer persuaded the Tibetan refugees featured in "A Father's Daring Trek" to let him accompany them and take photographs of their trek. The article's photographs help readers better understand the dangers Kelsang and Yangdol face. Sometimes, stories such as this are told almost entirely in photos.

A photo-essay is a collection of photos arranged to tell a story or to explore a theme. Ask students to think about a journey that they have taken. Have them list five images they would include in a photo-essay about their journey. Ask students to write short captions for each image. AS

Skills Preview

Key Reading Skill: Analyzing

As you read "A Father's Daring Trek," you'll analyze the parts of a magazine article and the order in which they appear. Think about articles you've read before. Most of them follow this pattern:

1. An **attention-getting device,** or interesting opener that makes you want to read on
2. **Main point or points,** a preview of the most important general ideas in the article
3. **Background,** or basic information you need to know about a topic to understand it. Not all topics require background information
4. **Details** that explain main point(s)
5. A **conclusion,** or ending, that wraps up the main point(s) in an interesting or inspiring way

Partner Talk Imagine that you're writing an article about one of the topics below. What would be an interesting way to begin your article? With a classmate come up with an idea or two.

- a game one of your school teams won in overtime
- a how-to-do-it article on a popular hobby
- an article about a new fad or fashion

Literary Element: Setting

The **setting** is the world of the story. Its details tell about the characters. The kind of house a character lives in tells you a great deal about that character. The part of the world a character lives in can tell you about his or her cultural beliefs and customs. Setting may even be a source of conflict for the characters. L

Whole Class Discussion Discuss conflicts you think might occur in these settings:

- an 1800s pioneer trail across Native American country
- a space station on Mars during the 24th century

Get Ready to Read

Connect to the Reading

R Imagine that it's winter in a cold part of the world. You're about to go on a long journey on foot through high mountains. What problems do you think you might face? Brainstorm a list of possible dangers.

Think-Pair-Share Pair up with a classmate and share your lists. Did you write down the same dangers or different ones? Combine your lists.

Build Background

- The article you are about to read takes place in Tibet, a region in southwest China and one of the world's highest places. For that reason, Tibet has been called "The Roof of the World."
- The Himalaya Mountains in southern Tibet are home to Mt. Everest, the world's tallest mountain.
- In general, the higher one climbs in the Himalayas, the harsher the weather conditions become. Winds of 50 to 60 miles an hour are common, as are below-zero temperatures.

Set Purposes for Reading

BIG Question Read "A Father's Daring Trek" to learn about a father and daughter who make a dangerous journey in hopes of beginning a better life.

Set Your Own Purpose What else would you like to learn from the story to help yourself answer the Big Question? Write your own purpose on the "Father's Daring Trek" flap of Foldable 2.

Interactive Literary Elements Handbook
To review or learn more about the literary elements, go to www.glencoe.com.

Keep Moving

Use these skills as you read the following selection.

Differentiated Instruction

Build Background: Maps Share with students a map of China and its surrounding countries. Show students Tibet's location and size in relation to China. Discuss how the different sizes of the two nations affect the balance of power between them. If possible, find a map that clearly shows the extensive mountains in the region so that students can better visualize the terrain the Tibetan refugees must cross. OL AL

Teach

L Literary Element

Setting Say: This article is about a journey, so the details of the setting are very important to understanding what happens. In your Learner's Notebook, write the following headings across the top of a page: "Starting Point," "Middle of the Trek," "Destination." As you read "A Father's Daring Trek," note the details of the setting that fit each heading. *(Responses will vary.)* OL

R Reading Skill

Review Connecting Say: Reread your notes about the dangers you might expect to encounter on a winter journey. Now list some adjectives you would use to describe a winter journey. As you read the selection, compare your adjectives to the ones the author uses. *(Responses will vary.)* OL

Interactive Literary Elements Handbook Have students access the Web site to improve their understanding of setting.

Indiana English/Language Arts Academic Standards
SE: 8.1, 8.3.4, 8.3.9
TWE: *Literature Focus Lesson* 8.7.9, *Differentiated Instruction* 8.2

Teach

R Reading Skill

Analyzing **Say:** Read the text next to the title of the article. After you read this statement, what questions do you have that you hope the article will answer? *(Possible responses: Will the man and his daughter survive? Will they reach their destination safely? What are the harsh conditions of the mountains like?)* **Ask:** Do these questions motivate you to read the rest of the article? *(Responses will vary.)* OL

EL Language Coach

Vocabulary Building: Collections of Synonyms
Say: If you are not certain of a word's meaning, it can be helpful to use a synonym to check your guess. Substitute a synonym for the word, and see whether the sentence still makes sense. For example, what word might you substitute for *perilous* in the first paragraph? *(Possible response: dangerous)* EL BL OL

Readability Scores
Dale-Chall: 5.8
DRP: 65
Lexile: 1210

READING WORKSHOP 1

TIME

A Father's Daring TREK

A Tibetan man takes his 6-year-old daughter on a dangerous journey through the world's highest, harshest mountains to give her a better life. R

By JULIE K.L. DAM

After a weeklong march in the bitter, piercing cold and thin air of the Himalayan Mountains, the Tibetan father Kelsang and his daughter, Yangdol (not their real names), thought they had reached freedom. From the top of Nangapa La, a pass on the southern border of Chinese-occupied Tibet, a peaceful life in **exile** EL seemed only steps away. Their perilous journey was only half over, though, because the trip down the pass would be just as difficult as the way up. Still the courageous father and daughter struggled on, determined to reach their goal. 1

For Tibetans, the trek[1] to freedom is filled with hardships, both physical and emotional. Many make the heart-wrenching decision to become refugees, people who are forced to leave their country of birth because of political or religious **persecution** or war. In 1951, Tibet lost its independence when Chinese troops invaded Lhasa, the Tibetan capital. The

1 Key Reading Skill

Analyzing What does the writer do to interest you in reading the rest of the article? Think about
- the description of the trek
- the people involved
- the reason for the trek

1. A ***trek*** is a long, often difficult journey.

Vocabulary

exile (EG zyl) *n.* the state of living away from one's home country

persecution (pur suh KYOO shun) *n.* constant cruel or harmful treatment

Additional Support

Reading in the Real World

Citizenship As students read about the Tibetan refugees in "A Father's Daring Trek," they may wish to learn more about refugees. According to the United States Immigration and Nationality Act, a refugee is a person who flees his or her country to escape persecution "on account of race, religion, nationality, membership in a particular social group, or political opinion." Have students look online or at the library for information about refugees who have come to the United States. Ask students to share their findings with the class. AL

Chinese government claimed the region as part of its territory. During the 1950s, Tibetans protested Chinese rule and fought for independence. In 1959, the Dalai Lama, the Tibetan spiritual leader, set up a government-in-exile in Dharmsala, a hill town in northern India, and the Tibetans who could escape began to gather to him.

To this day, Tibet's culture has suffered under Chinese rule. China doesn't allow Tibetans to practice their religion, Tibetan Buddhism, and much of Tibetan culture has been lost. Many Tibetans have been imprisoned, tortured, or killed for standing up for their beliefs. Each year, thousands of Tibetan families choose to escape to Dharmsala. Once Tibetans like Kelsang and Yangdol decide that life as a refugee in India would be better than life under Chinese rule, they begin the demanding journey across the Himalayan Mountains, into neighboring Nepal, and—finally—to Dharmsala. 2

2 Key Reading Skill

R **Analyzing** Why does the writer give the reader background information? How does it improve your understanding of the story?

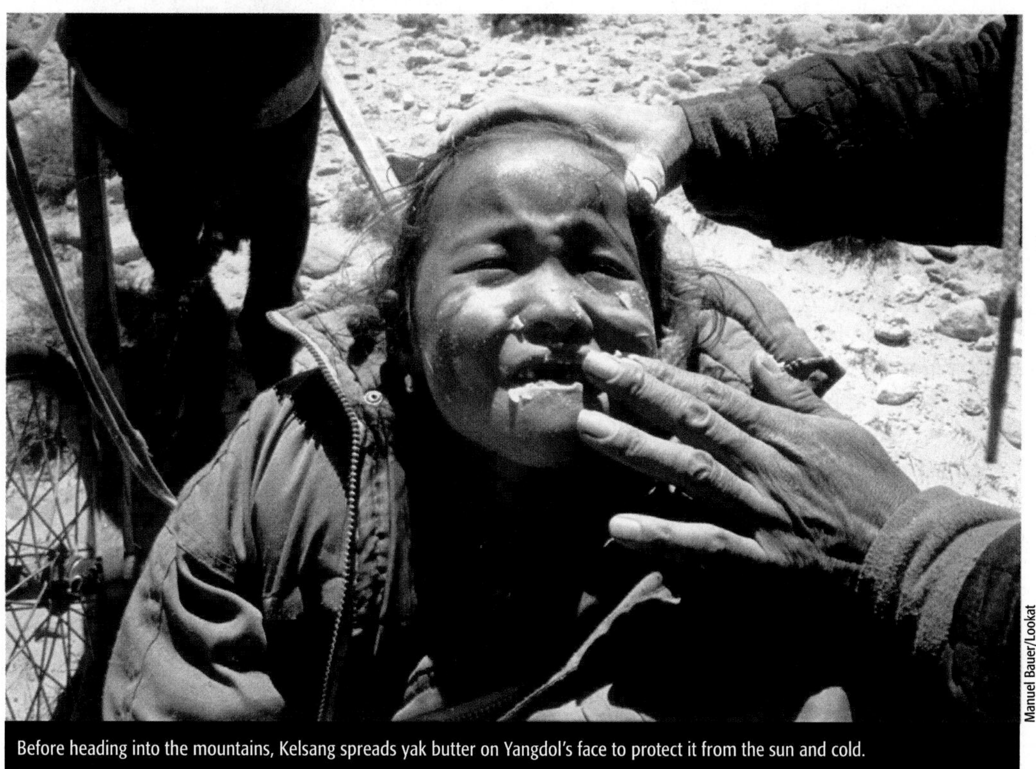

Manuel Bauer/Lookat

Before heading into the mountains, Kelsang spreads yak butter on Yangdol's face to protect it from the sun and cold.

Teach

R Reading Skill

Analyzing **Ask:** After reading the background information about China and Tibet, how would you describe the relationship between these two nations? Which nation holds more power? *(China has control in Tibet and therefore greater power.)* **BL** **Ask:** How does knowing this help you understand the story? *(Students may say that knowing this helps them understand why people might choose to flee Tibet.)* **OL**

Viewing the Photo

Say: Photographers carefully select images that give viewers more information about an event, a situation, or an individual. What information does this photo convey? *(Possible response: This photo shows that people must be prepared for the harsh conditions in the mountains.)* **OL**

Differentiated Instruction

Building More Background Share the following facts about Buddhism:

- Buddhism was founded 2,500 years ago by an Indian Prince named Siddharta Gautama, otherwise known as Buddha.
- Buddhism is the fourth largest religion in the world.
- Buddhism is practiced predominantly in China, Japan, Korea, and Southeast Asia.
- Buddhists believe in reincarnation—the idea that the soul is reborn in many forms.

Instruct students to use library and Internet resources to find three additional pieces of information about Buddhism. **OL** **AL**

Indiana English/Language Arts Academic Standards

SE: 8.2

TWE: *Reading in the Real World* 8.2.5, *Differentiated Instruction* 8.2.5

Teach

Viewing the Photo

Say: Unlike the close-up shot of Yangdol on page 173, this photograph includes details of the landscape and shows both Yangdol and her father. How does this photograph help convey the difficulties that Kelsang and Yangdol face on their journey? *(Possible response: The steep, rocky hillside makes Yangdol and Kelsang seem cold and small in comparison to the terrain.)* **AL**

EL Language Coach

Vocabulary Building: Collections of Synonyms

Say: Look up some synonyms for *achingly.* *(Possible response: painfully, excruciating)* **Ask:** What do these synonyms tell you about the trip? *(Possible response: It is painful as well as long.)* **EL**

Manuel Bauer/Lookat

The mountain wind is so strong that Kelsang and Yangdol have to lie flat on the ground until it dies down.

When Swiss photographer Manuel Bauer first met Kelsang, the 46-year-old father had decided to take his daughter to live in Dharmsala. The father knew the trek across the mountains would be <u>**challenging**</u>, but he believed life in Dharmsala—even as an exile far from home—would be better for him and his child. **3**

The photographer persuaded Kelsang to let him join the father and daughter on their trip across the mountains. The three arranged a ride on the back of a truck and quietly left Lhasa one winter morning. However, their journey was soon delayed by snowstorms. Six days later, they got a lift to Tingri, Tibet, and began the achingly long march on foot across the Himalayas.

The determined threesome hiked higher and higher up the mountains, battling frostbite,[2] dehydration,[3] frigid

3 English Language Coach

Vocabulary Building: Collections of Synonyms

What are some synonyms for the word <u>**challenging**</u>? Jot them down on a word web in your Learner's Notebook.

2. ***Frostbite*** is a serious condition that occurs when a part of the body becomes too cold.

3. People suffer ***dehydration*** when they do not have enough water.

Additional Support

Literature Focus Lesson

Text Features: Photographs Manuel Bauer's photographs might interest students in photojournalism. Explain that photojournalists present news and important issues primarily through photographs, relying less on written copy. Invite the school librarian to share photos of recent or historical events. Discuss the ways a photograph can tell a story. Challenge students interested in photojournalism to collect photographs from newspapers, newsmagazines, and Web sites, and have students identify what makes certain photos compelling. Encourage students to take pictures of events at school and in their community. **AS**

READING WORKSHOP 1

temperatures, and fierce winds. 4 They traveled over the icy ground in silence, sometimes 14 hours a day, and were often too tired to even stop and eat. "They kept me going," says Bauer, "their story, sacrifice, and **destiny**." L

After 12 stressful days, the group crossed Nangapa La and wearily made their way down to Namche Bazaar, a Nepalese village near Mount Everest. At last the worst was over. They flew by helicopter to Kathmandu, Nepal's capital, where officials at the Tibetan Reception Center greeted them and arranged a bus ride—a luxury after the long mountain trek—to their journey's end in Dharmsala.

Three days later, the father and daughter reached their destination, where they celebrated the journey's end with 50 other newly arrived refugees, many of whom had made much the same trek. Three long weeks after leaving Lhasa, Yangdol finally met the Dalai Lama and, with his blessing, began a new life—at home in exile. 5 R

—Updated 2005, from TIME International, January 8, 1996

4 Literary Element

Setting What problems does the mountain setting cause for the travelers?

5 BIG Question

How do you think Yangdol and her father might answer the question, Which is more important, the journey or the destination? Why? Write your answer on the "Father's Daring Trek" flap of Foldable 2. Your response will help you complete the Unit Challenge later. BQ

Kelsang and Yangdol battled fierce winds and freezing temperatures during their trek to freedom.

Vocabulary

destiny (DES tuh nee) *n.* a person's fate or fortune

Teach

L Literary Element

Setting **Ask:** What adjectives would you use to describe the journey's setting? *(Possible responses: brutal, long, painful.)* OL

R Reading Skill

Analyzing **Ask:** What is the main idea of the last paragraph? *(Possible response: The father and daughter reach their destination and are welcomed by the Dalai Lama.)* OL

BQ BIG Question

Ask: Do you think it will be possible for Kelsang, Yangdol, and the other refugees to feel "at home in exile?" Why or why not? *(Responses will vary. Some students may note that because the refugees can now freely practice their religion, they will feel at home. Others will say that they will miss their homeland.)* OL

Assess

Use the CheckPoint questions provided on Presentation Plus! to check for comprehension of the selection. These questions can be used with interactive response keypads for immediate student feedback.

Reading in the Real World

Citizenship Tell students to suppose they are activists preparing to write a letter to the editor of a local paper about Tibetan refugees. As a class, draft an outline of a letter that discusses the challenges Tibetans face. Suggest that the letter include the following:

- The location of Tibet, including details about its climate and terrain
- The reasons many Tibetans leave their homeland
- The risks involved in being a refugee
- Ways for concerned Americans to help Tibetan refugees

OL AL

Indiana English/Language Arts Academic Standards

SE: 8.1, 8.3.4, 8.3.9

TWE: *Literature Focus Lesson* 8.7.9, *Reading in the Real World* 8.4

Assess

Resources for page 176

- Selection Quick Check, p. 12
- Selection and Unit Assessment, p. 14
- ExamView Assessment Suite
- Interactive Tutor: Self-Assessment

Students can respond to the *After You Read* items in their Learner's Notebooks or on a separate sheet of paper.

Answering the BIG Question

1. Possible response: People may discover they are physically and emotionally stronger than they thought.
2. In 1951 the Chinese army invaded Tibet, claiming the territory for China. Under Chinese rule, Tibetan culture and religion have been repressed. The Dalai Lama set up a new government in India, and many Tibetans have escaped there.
3. They face bitter cold, frostbite, dehydration, and exhaustion.

Critical Thinking

4. Possible response: The photographer wanted to make the world aware of their difficult journey.
5. Possible response: Tibetans escape to a place where they can live as they wish and practice their religion.
6. Responses will vary.

After You Read

A Father's Daring Trek

Manuel Bauer/Lookat

Answering the BIG Question

1. What do you think people can learn about themselves by taking a difficult journey, such as the one in "A Father's Daring Trek"?
2. **Summarize** What events happened in Tibet that caused people to want to leave?

   TIP **Right There** The answer is in one place in the article.
3. **Recall** What dangers do Yangdol and her father face as they walk through the mountains?

   TIP **Think and Search** You will find this information in the article, but not all in one place.

Critical Thinking

4. **Infer** Why do you think Manuel Bauer joined Yangdol and her father on their journey?

   TIP **Author and Me** You will find clues in the selection, but you must also use the information in your head.
5. **Infer** Why is the journey to Dharmsala so important for Tibetan refugees?

   TIP **Author and Me** You will find clues in the selection, but you must also use the information in your head.
6. **Evaluate** Would you recommend this article to other eighth graders? Why or why not? Use specific examples from the article to support your opinion.

   TIP **On My Own** Answer from your own knowledge.

Write About Your Reading

Postcard Pretend that you have just completed a journey from Tibet to Dharmsala with a group of Tibetan refugees. Write a postcard to your parents that describes

- who you were with
- what you saw on your journey
- what difficulties you faced
- how you felt at the end of the journey

To write your postcard, use facts and details from the article, but also use your imagination.

Indiana English/Language Arts Academic Standards (pp. 176–177)

8.3 Comprehension and Analysis of Literary Text Respond to grade-level appropriate literature... **8.5.1** Write biographies, autobiographies, and short stories... **8.2 Comprehension and Analysis (Focus on Informational Text)** Develop [reading] strategies...identify and analyze structure, organization... **8.3.2** Analyze the importance of setting... **8.3.9** Analyze the relevance of setting... **8.6 English Language Conventions**

For a complete description of the standards, see p. IN 11.

Write About Your Reading

Possible response:

Dear Mom and Dad,

I have just arrived in Dharmsala. For the last two weeks we've been hiking in the extreme cold of the Himalaya Mountains. One night, it was so cold that Kelsang, the father of a six-year-old, woke up with frostbite on his toes. Luckily, we made it to a village where a doctor helped him. I am so relieved and thankful to be at the end of our trip. My Tibetan friends' drive to pursue religious freedom has greatly inspired me.

Skills Review

Key Reading Skill: Analyzing

7. Copy the map below; then analyze "A Father's Daring Trek." Fill in each box on the map with a short summary of the content of the article. The first boxes are filled in to help you start.

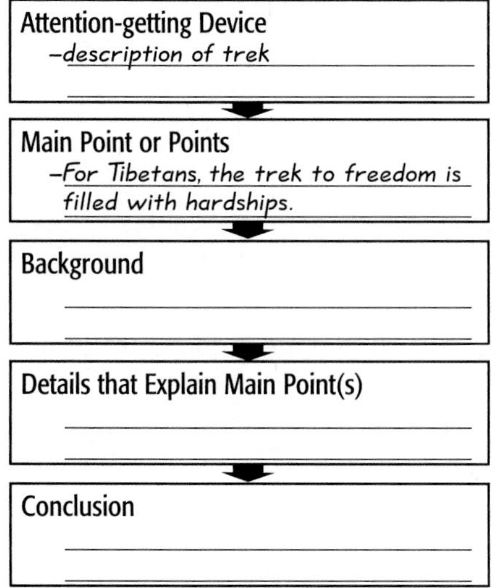

Attention-getting Device
–description of trek
Main Point or Points
–For Tibetans, the trek to freedom is filled with hardships.
Background
Details that Explain Main Point(s)
Conclusion

Literary Element: Setting

8. How are time and place sources of conflict for the father and daughter in the article?

Vocabulary Check

Each sentence below contains an underlined word. Use what you know about these words to tell whether each sentence is true or false. If a sentence is false, rewrite it to make it true.

9. People in exile live in their home country.

10. A person's destiny is the same as a person's fate.

11. Persecution makes people feel welcome in their home country.

12. **English Language Coach** Look back at the thesaurus entry for *happy* on page 170. Choose three of the synonyms, and use each one in a sentence that describes how the father and daughter feel once they reach freedom.

Grammar Link: Adverbs

Adverbs answer these questions: How? When? How often? Where? How much?

He speaks quickly.	How?	quickly
I studied yesterday.	When?	yesterday
She visits weekly.	How often?	weekly
He works there.	Where?	there
I am too busy.	How much?	too much

Adverbs can help you make your writing clearer and livelier. Compare the following two sentences. Which is clearer?

- Nadia said to her little sister, "Go to bed!"
- Yesterday Nadia angrily said to her little sister, "Go to bed NOW!"

The second sentence is clearer because the adverbs *yesterday, angrily,* and *now* tell you when and how actions occurred.

Grammar Practice

Copy the following sentences. Underline the adverbs. For help in finding the adverbs, answer the questions in parentheses.

13. Dad hurriedly left without his jacket. *(How did Dad leave?)*

14. It was too cold outside to be without a jacket. *("How much" cold was it?)*

15. I quickly ran after him to give him his jacket. *(How did you run?)*

Writing Application Look back at the postcard you wrote for the Write About Your Reading activity. Find two sentences in which you describe something that happened. Add an adverb to each sentence to tell *how* or *when* the event happened.

LiteratureOnline
Interactive Literary Elements Handbook
To review or learn more about the literary elements, go to www.glencoe.com.

Skills Review

Key Reading Skill: Analyzing

7. *Background:* The Chinese government persecutes Tibetans for practicing Buddhism, forcing Tibetans into exile. *Details That Explain Main Points:* Possible death for staying under Chinese rule, bitter cold, fierce winds, dehydration. *Conclusion:* Father and daughter made it to Dharmsala with fifty other refugees, met the Dalai Lama, and began a new life.

Literary Element: Setting

8. Possible response: Because the Chinese government now rules over Tibet, Tibetans are forced to obey Chinese law or leave. Because Tibet is in one of the coldest and highest places in the world, it is difficult to leave.

Vocabulary Check

9. False—People in exile have left their home countries.

10. True

11. False—Persecution makes people feel unwelcome.

12. Possible responses: Reaching Dharmsala was a *joyous* event. The Tibetans were *pleased* to see the Dalai Lama. Yangdol and her father are now *contented.*

Grammar Link: Adverbs

Grammar Practice

13. Possible response: hurriedly

14. Possible response: too

15. Possible response: quickly

Close

Ask students to tell how this story of a difficult journey affected their answer to the Big Question.

Indiana English/Language Arts Academic Standards
SE: 8.2, 8.3, 8.3.4, 8.3.9, 8.5.1, 8.6

Folktale

Teaching Students to Write a Folktale

Why Is It Important?

- Folktales are traditionally a way of disseminating shared values throughout a community. Students who write their own folktales will be more aware of the values being prioritized in American society.
- The imaginative nature of the writing will encourage students to think outside the character roles that may initially come to them.
- Students will find that writing a tale with a specific moral or theme helps them identify the main idea or thesis of other materials they read.
- Creating a folktale will help students master the distinction between a folktale and a short fictional story.
- Writing about a protagonist who has a goal and goes on a journey to accomplish the goal will help students think about answering the Big Question: Which is more important, the journey or the destination?
- "Publishing" their folktales in the library, a literary magazine, or a class binder will foster a sense of involvement and community.

How to Help Students Get It

- Encourage students to read ahead, or read a folktale in the textbook not scheduled for class time. Increased exposure to the genre will help them by providing a model of the folktale elements.
- Remind students that their protagonist should embody at least one positive character trait, and all of the protagonist's actions should reflect that.
- Give students examples of folktales that have parallels in many cultures, such as Cinderella.
- Students having difficulty generating a theme can refer to the Index of Skills to be directed to other selections in which "theme" is highlighted. This will help to clarify the concept.
- Before students revise their drafts, ask them to ensure that their folktales include all the necessary elements: a main character who does good deeds and has special (or magical) powers, an evil antagonist, and a storyline that ends with good overcoming evil.
- Students struggling with ideas may find it easier to make the theme explicit at the end of their tale, as in the familiar format of Aesop's fables.
- Review with the students the types of revision they have done on previous writing assignments. Remind them that as their portfolios grow, so do their skill sets.

Writing Trait	Student Checklist
Unit Focus **Ideas:** the message or the theme and the details that develop it	• Does the title suggest the theme of the composition? • Does the composition focus on a single narrow topic? • Is the thesis, or main idea, clearly stated? • Do well-chosen details elaborate the main idea?
Organization	The arrangement of main points and supporting details
Voice	A writer's unique way of using tone and style
Word Choice	The vocabulary a writer uses to convey meaning
Sentence Fluency	The smooth rhythm and flow of sentences that vary in length and style
Conventions	Correct spelling, grammar, usage, and mechanics
Presentation	The way words and design elements look on a page

Workshop Resources

Pacing (Days) Standard	Block	Lesson	Student Materials	Teacher Resources
1	1/2	Writing Workshop Part 1: Prewriting and Drafting	Writing Workshop Graphic Organizer, p. 14 Grammar Practice, p. 15 Spelling and Handwriting Practice, p. 45 Grammar and Composition Handbook, pp. 195, 198 Real Success in Writing: Research and Reports	TeacherWorks Plus™ Presentation Plus! Rubrics for Assessing Student Writing, Listening, and Speaking, p. 22 Grammar and Writing Workshop Transparencies 1–2
2	1	Writing Workshop Part 2: Editing, Revising, and Presenting	Interactive Grammar and Language Workbook Grammar and Composition Handbook, pp. 195, 198 Real Success in Writing: Research and Reports Listening and Speaking, p. 28 Viewing and Representing, p. 29	Grammar and Writing Workshop Transparencies 19–20 Interactive Grammar and Language Workbook Rubrics for Assessing Student Writing, Listening, and Speaking, p. 22

Focus

BELLRINGER Options

Daily Language Practice Transparency 14
Focus Activity Say: Briefly summarize an important journey you've taken, such as visiting family members, or changing from a clumsy basketball player to a skilled athlete. How might you use this journey in your folktale?*(Responses will vary.)* OL

Teach

L Literary Element

Conflict Say: The difficulties faced by your main character are the conflict in the story. Describe a possible conflict for your folktale. *(Review both external and internal conflicts with students.)* OL

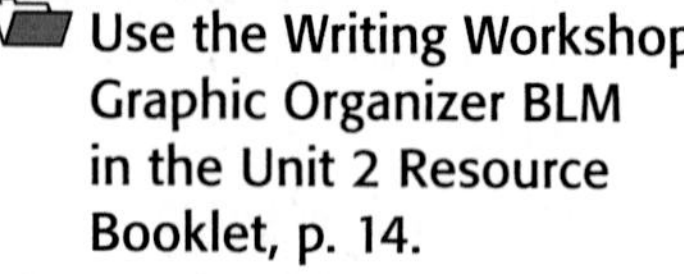

Resources for page 178

- Use the Writing Workshop Graphic Organizer BLM in the Unit 2 Resource Booklet, p. 14.
- Use the Grammar and Writing Workshop Transparencies 1-2

WRITING WORKSHOP PART 1

Folktale

Prewriting and Drafting

ASSIGNMENT Write an entertaining folktale

Purpose: To create a folktale about a character who takes a journey

Audience: Your teacher and your classmates

Writing Rubric

As you work through this writing assignment, you should

- Write in the style of a folktale
- Develop a main character who has the qualities of a folktale protagonist
- Make a point or teach a lesson through your story

See page 236 in Part 2 for a model of a folktale.

Folktales are traditional stories handed down from generation to generation. Most folktales have these basic ingredients:

- a main character (protagonist) who does good deeds and has special, perhaps even magical, powers
- an evil antagonist (which can be a person or a force of nature, like a storm)
- a storyline that ends with good overcoming evil

Many folktales also contain a journey, or quest, for something precious. (Think, for example, of the enslaved people who journey for freedom in "The People Could Fly.") Your folktale will also be about a journey. Writing the folktale will help you think about the Unit 2 Big Question: Which is more important, the journey or the destination?

Prewriting

Get Ready to Write

Before you start writing, think about your main character, the journey he or she will take, and the reason for the journey. Will your main character be young or old? Male or female? Magical or just talented?

L You've probably read and seen many stories about characters that go on a journey in search of something precious. Remember the Greek myth about Jason and his journey to find golden fleece? How about Dorothy, the Tin Man, Cowardly Lion, and Scarecrow in *The Wonderful Wizard of Oz?* They, too, took a long and hard journey in quest of precious things. What journey will your character take? What will the character search for?

Partner Talk Discuss with a classmate the ideas you have so far for a main character and a journey. Jot down notes from your discussion, and use the notes as you work on your story.

Indiana English/ Language Arts Academic Standards (pp. 178–181)

8.4 Processes and Features Prewriting and drafting.
8.5.1 Write...short stories...
8.6 English Language Conventions
For a complete description of the standards, see p. IN 11.

Additional Support

English Language Coach

Vocabulary Building: Collections of Synonyms Encourage students to use synonyms to accurately describe their main characters. Have them complete a synonym chart like the following. Then, have them use a dictionary to determine which synonym best describes their character. AS

Word	pretty	old
Synonym 1		
Synonym 2		

Make a Plan

A story map can help you arrange your ideas into a plan.

Characters	Who is the main character? What's special (or even magical) about him or her? Who (or what) is the antagonist, or bad guy?
Reason for Journey	Why does the main character go on a journey?
Major Events of Journey	What difficulties does he or she face during the journey?
Outcome of Journey	How does the main character overcome the difficulties?
Point, or Central Message, of the Tale	What point, or lesson about life, do you want readers to get from your folktale?

Writing Models For models and other writing activities, go to www.glencoe.com.

Applying Good Writing Traits

Ideas

Without ideas, you'd have nothing to write about or even to think about. Your brain would be a blank as you rode the bus or walked the dog. The good news is that you have dozens of ideas every day.

What Are Ideas?

In this case ideas are your thoughts about your folktale and the things it should include. You've already come up with some ideas about your main character, your antagonist, and the journey.

The main idea of any story is its message, or theme. The theme is not the subject of a story; it is the story's meaning. For example, you might say the main idea of "Little Red Riding Hood" is to be suspicious of "people" who act like something they're not. W1

Why Are Ideas Important?

Readers find fresh, original ideas entertaining and fun. What's more, a central idea that says something important and true about people will probably stay with readers for a long time to come.

How Do I Come Up with Ideas?

- Read other folktales. Notice the basic elements they share with yours.
- Talk over the assignment and your thoughts with classmates, friends, or family. Bounce ideas off each other.
- Pay attention to the people you see, experiences you have, and situations you observe. A particular person, a bit of conversation, or an ordinary event might spark ideas that you can use in your folktale or in other writing assignments.
- Keep story ideas in the back of your mind as you go through the day. Jot down ideas as they come to you. W2

Differentiated Instruction

Story Map If students are struggling with writing fiction, return to the autobiographical journeys that they shared during the Bellringer activity. Instruct students to complete story maps for these journeys. Help students find points at which they can exaggerate events, introduce animal characters, add magical elements, or change the way events happened. Point out that the focus of this assignment is to convey a theme, not to retell events exactly as they happened. BL

Teach

Writing Models Have students access the Web site for an additional and interactive Writing Workshop-based student model.

W1 Writing

Ideas Have students identify the protagonist, the antagonist, the journey or quest, the conflict, and the theme in the folktales they've read in this unit. Then suggest that students borrow from these traditional tales for their own folktales. OL

W2 Writing

Brainstorming If students are having a hard time coming up with ideas, have them hold a brainstorming session with a partner. They might make a chart labeled "Main Character," "Plot Ideas," "Themes," and note ideas in each column. Remind them that they can use a journey from their own lives as a springboard. EL BL

Indiana English/Language Arts Academic Standards
SE: 8.4
TWE: *English Language Coach* 8.1, *Differentiated Instruction* 8.4.1

Teach

W Writing

Dialogue **Say:** In addition to describing each character's appearance and actions, allow your characters to speak by including dialogue. Dialogue can advance the plot and illustrate character traits. For example, if you need to change the scene, you might have a character say, "Let's go to the park." If you need to show that a character is a thief, you might have the character whisper, "Grab that apple from the cart while I ask the vendor a question." Review the rules for punctuating dialogue. OL

Assess

Have student partners exchange drafts and critique each other's work. Ask students to determine whether the partner included all the elements of a folktale. Then, tell each student to assess his or her partner's feedback, make any needed revisions, and save the revised draft for later use.

WRITING WORKSHOP PART 1

Drafting

Start Writing!

Now it's time to start writing your folktale. Grab a pencil or pen and some blank paper or head to the computer.

Get It on Paper

- Start by describing who your main character is and what he or she is doing. Use the map as a writing guide, but don't let it get in the way of new ideas.
- Let your writing flow. Don't worry about correct spelling or punctuation.
- After fifteen minutes or so, read what you've written. If you have more ideas, keep going.
- Think about what you like and what you don't like about your folktale so far. Make notes about those things you want to change.

Writing Tip

Talk It Out If you're having trouble getting started, tell someone about your story. Talking about it can rev up your creativity.

Develop Your Ideas

Here are some things that experienced writers do to go from general ideas to a lively and interesting story.

Use specific details. Pick just the right details to help your readers picture the characters and events in your folktale. Describe how people and things look, sound, smell, taste, and touch.

The queen waved a wand made of coral with a shell at its tip.

Writing Tip

Picture Your People Think about how your characters look and sound. The better you know them, the more real they'll seem to your readers. W

Develop a main point. Make sure all parts of your tale add to the central message. For example, if the message is that courage is rewarded, the main character should act bravely.

Unafraid, Finny ran into the ocean and swam underwater, farther and farther from shore.

Additional Support

Literature Focus Lesson

Folktales A particular benefit of reading folktales is learning about the cultures in which the tales originated. Folktales demonstrate both universal and culturally specific values, beliefs, and themes. Lead students in a discussion of the values and beliefs shared by their own cultures. **Ask:** What values and beliefs are important to your family and community? How might you express these values or beliefs in your folktale? OL

WRITING WORKSHOP PART 1

Grammar Link

Modifying Phrases and Clauses

You've identified one-word adjectives like *tall* and *happy*, and you've found one-word adverbs like *quickly* and *yesterday*. Now learn about adjectives and adverbs that are more than one word.

What Are Modifying Phrases and Clauses?

A **modifying phrase or clause** is a group of words that describes another word in a sentence. The phrase or clause works the same as one-word adjectives and adverbs do.

An **adjective phrase or clause** is a group of words that modifies a noun or a pronoun.

- The kids at the front of the bus are noisy. *(Which kids? the kids at the front of bus)*
- I like buses that are air-conditioned. *(What kinds of buses? buses that are air-conditioned)*

An adverb phrase or clause may modify an action verb, an adjective, or another adverb.

- I caught the bus before it left. *(When did you catch it? before it left)*
- We enter through the front door. *(Where do you enter? through the front door)*
- We exit the bus in a hurry. *(How do you exit? In a hurry)*

Why Are Modifying Phrases and Clauses Important?

Modifying clauses and phrases make a piece of writing more interesting and specific. The details they provide help paint a word picture in the reader's mind. Compare the following sentences.

No modifiers: Look at it.

Adjective modifiers: Look at the red maple tree.

Modifying adjective clause: Look at the red maple tree that is growing next to the shed.

The last sentence, with both one-word adjectives and an adjective clause, is clear and descriptive.

How Do I Use Modifying Phrases and Clauses?

Use an adjective phrase or clause to add detail to a noun or a pronoun. The adjective phrase or clause usually comes *after* the word it describes.

- The drivers behind the bus were impatient.

Sometimes, however, you can place an adjective phrase *before* the noun or pronoun it modifies.

- Sweaty and breathless, he caught the bus.

To use an adverb phrase or clause, describe a verb with a group of words. The adverb phrase or clause may come before *or* after the word it describes.

- After dinner, Anya does her homework.
- Anya does her homework after dinner.

Writing Application Carefully reread the draft of your folktale. Look for any sentences that are dull or unclear. Try adding a modifying phrase or clause to improve the sentences.

Keep Moving

Part 2 of this Writing Workshop is coming up later. Keep the writing you did here, and in Part 2 you'll learn how to improve it.

Teach

Grammar Link

Subordinating Conjunctions

Write on the board: *after, although, as, because, before, if, since, though, unless, until, when, where, while* **Say:** These are subordinating conjunctions. A conjunction is a word that joins single words or groups of words. Adverb clauses are often introduced by subordinating conjunctions. A subordinating conjunction joins a subordinate (less important) idea or clause to a main clause: *I read a book while I was waiting for you.* The subordinating conjunction "while" tells you when. OL

Differentiated Instruction

Modifying Phrases and Clauses

Tell students to add modifying phrases or clauses to the following sentences.

1. The students were tired. (Tell *why* they were tired.) *(The students were tired because they'd run three miles.)*
2. She rang the doorbell. (Tell *which* doorbell she rang.) *(She rang the doorbell of the house on the corner.)*
3. Bob mops the floor. (Tell *when* he mops the floor.) *(After he washes the dishes, Bob mops the floor.)* OL

Indiana English/Language Arts Academic Standards
SE: 8.5.1, 8.6
TWE: *Literature Focus Lesson* 8.3.7, *Differentiated Instruction* 8.4.9

Making Inferences

Teaching Students to Make Inferences

Why Is It Important?

- Inferences depend on seeing connections that are not articulated.
- Most writers do not tell everything a character thinks; readers need to make inferences to fully comprehend what is being communicated.
- Students who make inferences successfully are better able to understand characters and identify themes.

How to Help Students Get It

- Tell students to always pay attention to everything a writer tells them through a character's actions as well as words.
- Help students notice descriptions, dialogue, events, and relationships.
- Encourage students to ask themselves: "Why does the author tell me this? What does this mean about this character or situation?"
- To build their confidence in making inferences while reading, remind students that they already make many inferences in everyday life. (This workshop provides several examples.)

Reading to Answer the Big Question

Paul Revere's Ride by Henry Wadsworth Longfellow
This famous narrative poem celebrates the historic journey of Paul Revere, who rode from Boston to Lexington, Massachusetts, to warn American revolutionaries that British troops were on the move.

The Oxcart by Eric A. Kimmel
This folktale takes place in Japan in an era when there are very strict rules for social behavior. Although only highborn women are allowed to use oxcarts, three samurai decide to secretly ride in one to avoid walking to a distant festival. The journey turns out to be miserable and the tough samurai decide that they would rather face slow death by torture than ever repeat what is an everyday experience for gentlewomen.

Workshop Resources

Pacing (Days) Standard	Block	Lesson	Student Materials	Teacher Resources
1	1/2	Key Skill Lesson: Making Inferences	Key Reading Skills Practice, p. 16 English Language Coach Review, p. 42	Bellringer Options Transparencies –Daily Language Practice 15 –Selection Focus 5 Read Aloud, Think Aloud Transparencies –Key Reading Skills 13 –Read Aloud, Think Aloud 12–17 Presentation Plus!
1	1	"Paul Revere's Ride"	Literary Analysis Transparencies Glencoe Online Unit Vocabulary Review, p. 40 Academic Vocabulary Review, p. 43 English Language Coach Active Reading Graphic Organizer, p. 17 StudentWorks Plus™ Online Student Edition Literature Classics Selection and Unit Assessments, p. 15	Puzzlemaker Skill Level Up!™ A Language Arts Game BookLink 3 Assessment by Learning Objective (Diagnostic and Formative) Interactive Tutor: Self-Assessment TeacherWorks Plus™
1		"The Oxcart"	Glencoe Online Unit Vocabulary Review, p. 40 Academic Vocabulary Review, p. 43 English Language Coach Active Reading Graphic Organizer, p. 20 Literary Analysis, p. 19 StudentWorks Plus™ Online Student Edition Literature Classics Selection and Unit Assessments, p. 16	Literary and Text Analysis Transparencies 37 Puzzlemaker Skill Level Up!™ A Language Arts Game BookLink 3 Assessment by Learning Objective (Diagnostic and Formative) Interactive Tutor: Self-Assessment TeacherWorks Plus™

Keys for Unit Resource

- Blackline Master
- Workbook
- Supplemental Text
- CD-ROM
- DVD
- Transparency
- Web-based
- Fast File

Level Appropriate Code

AS = Activities for all students
AL = Activities for students working above grade level
OL = Activities for students working at grade level
BL = Activities for students working below grade level
EL = Activities for English language learners

Focus

BELLRINGER Options

- **Selection Focus Transparencies 5**
- **Daily Language Practice Transparency 15**

Focus Activity Say: One classmate is making good progress on her math worksheet. She moves from one problem to the next, focused and working at a good pace. Another classmate scratches her head and keeps erasing her work. If you had a question about a math problem on the worksheet, which classmate would you approach for help? Why? *(Possible response: I would ask the person who seems to be completing the worksheet confidently.)* AS

Teach

R Reading Skill

Making Inferences

Say: Making inferences involves looking for evidence and combining it with what you know already. How might a person's body language give you clues as to how he or she is feeling? *(Responses will vary.)* AL

READING WORKSHOP 2

Skills Focus

You will practice these skills when you read the following selections:

- "Paul Revere's Ride," p. 186
- "The Oxcart," p. 196

Reading

- Making inferences

Literature

- Understanding and analyzing narrative poetry
- Identifying the parts of a plot

Vocabulary

- Building vocabulary with key words
- Recognizing and using compound words to expand vocabulary
- Academic Vocabulary: *inferring*

Writing/Grammar

- Using comparative and superlative adjectives and adverbs
- Using articles and demonstratives

Indiana English/Language Arts Academic Standards (pp. 182–183)

8.2 Comprehension and Analysis (Focus on Informational Text) Develop [reading] strategies...

For a complete description of the standards, see p. IN 11.

Skill Lesson

Making Inferences

Learn It!

R

What Is It? Inferring is using your knowledge and experience to figure out something that is not written or stated.

- When you make an inference, you act like a detective, using clues to make guesses about what might be true.
- For example, if you are watching a TV show and you see a character shaking and biting his nails, you might infer that he is nervous.

Analyzing Cartoons
What does the boy infer from the look on his mother's face?

Academic Vocabulary

inferring (in FUR ing) *n.* using reason and experience to make an educated guess

Additional Support

English Language Coach

Building Background The comic strip "Zits" is created by writer Jerry Scott and artist Jim Borgman. The strip chronicles the interactions of a teenager and his parents. Scott says that he and Borgman have "a great affection for this period of life—and a respect for the teenage journey." English language learners may not know that *zits* is a slang term for *pimples*, a common problem among teenagers. EL As a class, discuss other common teenage experiences that occur across cultures. AS Ask students whether they believe that the term *journey* is a good way of describing the experiences of adolescence and the teenage years. OL

Why Is It Important? In life, we never know everything we'd like to know about people and situations. So we make inferences about them. We decide what to think by making educated guesses based on what we do know. **R** In literature, no author tells you *everything* you'd like to know. You make inferences based on what the author *does* say—and on your own experiences.

Literature Online

Study Central Visit www.glencoe.com and click on Study Central to review making inferences.

How Do I Do It? As you read, look for clues. Combine these with what you know from your own experience. Then make an educated guess.

Read the following passage from a story. Then read to see how a student made an inference to answer the question, "How does Kathy feel?"

A crowd gathered around Mrs. Kurstings' door almost the moment she posted the list. Brandi peeked around the door of an empty classroom, scanning the crowd for Kathy's face. Kathy had worked so hard to be a cheerleader. If she didn't make the squad, well . . . . Brandi didn't even want to think about it. Just then, Brandi spotted her friend walking slowly away from Mrs. Kurstings' door. Kathy's shoulders were slumped, and her eyes were on the floor.

I think Kathy feels disappointed. She must not have made the squad. The clues are in the way she walks. Based on experience, I know that people get excited when they are chosen to be cheerleaders. Kathy seems sad rather than excited.

Practice It!

How does Brandi feel about Kathy? Reread the passage; then make inferences about their relationship. Support your inferences with specific clues from the passage.

Use It!

Use the skill as you read "Paul Revere's Ride" and "The Oxcart."

Teach

Study Central Have students access the Web site to review making inferences and to complete a related activity.

R Reading Skill

Making Inferences

Say: Look at the *Why Is It Important?* section. Why do people need to make inferences? *(Possible response: People may need to make inferences because they cannot get information in any other way.)* **OL** **Say:** Think about a time when you had to make an inference while reading. What information did you already have? What information did you need to infer? *(Responses will vary.)* **AL**

Resources for page 183

Use Key Reading Skills Transparency 13 in *Read Aloud, Think Aloud* to help students practice making inferences.

Reading in the Real World

Citizenship Those who work as community architects, civil engineers, and town planners must anticipate the needs of many people, from small children to senior citizens. Ask a community planner or volunteer to visit the class. Have students interview the worker to learn how the city or town makes inferences about the need for schools, parks, and other community establishments and services. Have students ask how community workers gather their facts and what pieces of information they must infer from their research. Ask students to summarize their interviews, highlighting the types of inferences that community workers must make. **AL**

Indiana English/Language Arts Academic Standards

SE: 8.2

TWE: *English Language Coach* 8.7, *Reading in the Real World* 8.7.1

Teach

More About the Author

Henry Wadsworth Longfellow's lineage gave the author a unique sense of American history. His father, Stephen Longfellow, was a member of the Eighteenth Congress of the United States. His mother, Zilpah Wadsworth, descended from a family that had arrived on the *Mayflower,* the ship that brought the Pilgrims to America in 1620.

V Vocabulary

Roots Say: Sometimes the root of a vocabulary word can give you a key word that will help you remember the meaning of the vocabulary word. For example, the word *defiance* comes from *defy,* which means "to refuse to obey." How does the definition of *defy* fit within the definition of *defiance? (Possible response: If you defy someone, you refuse to obey that person. Defiance is the act of refusing to obey.)* OL

Before You Read Paul Revere's Ride

Meet the Author

Henry Wadsworth Longfellow was a teacher and poet who lived from 1807 until 1882. He published his first poem when he was 13 years old. Some of his poems help shape what Americans think of their nation and their past. See page R4 of the Author Files for more on Henry Wadsworth Longfellow.

Author Search For more about Henry Wadsworth Longfellow, go to www.glencoe.com.

Indiana English/Language Arts Academic Standards (pp. 184–191)

8.1 Word Recognition, Fluency, and Vocabulary Development Understand... word parts, patterns, and relationships... **8.2 Comprehension and Analysis (Focus on Informational Text)** Develop [reading] strategies... **8.3.1** Determine and articulate relationships between purpose and characteristics of different forms of poetry.

For a complete description of the standards, see p. IN 11.

Vocabulary Preview

stealthy (STEL thee) *adj.* slow and secretive to avoid being seen and heard **(p. 187)** *Paul's friend had to be stealthy to avoid being heard.*

somber (SOM bur) *adj.* dark and gloomy **(p. 187)** *The atmosphere at the Old North Church was somber as the men prepared to fight.*

lingers (LING urz) *v.* waits or is slow in leaving; form of the verb *linger* **(p. 189)** *Paul decided to linger and watch for a second light.*

emerge (ih MURJ) *v.* to come out into view **(p. 191)** *Paul Revere's friend watched the British ships emerge from the darkness.*

V **defiance** (dih FY uns) *n.* the act of challenging authority **(p. 191)** *The war began with defiance of British rule.*

Partner Talk Answer the following questions with a classmate.

- Which is more stealthy: a burglar or a salesperson?
- Which is somber: a funeral or a party?
- Who lingers at a party: people who are bored or people who are having fun?
- At dawn does the sun emerge from the dark or fade into it?
- Which act is an example of defiance: breaking rules or obeying them?

English Language Coach

Old Words A lot of great literature was written long ago. However, language changes over time. Some words that people knew one hundred years ago are no longer used.

When you come across an unfamiliar word in a story or poem that was written long ago, look first to see if there's a footnote. That's where old or unusual words are often defined. There might be information in a glossary at the end of the book. If not, you can use a dictionary to find the definition of the word. Here are some words you will see in *Paul Revere's Ride*.

- belfry: a tower where a bell hangs
- man-of-war: battleship
- grenadier: a soldier who threw hand grenades
- steed: a horse with a lot of spirit
- meeting-house: town hall
- musket: a gun with a long barrel that shot a lead ball

Partner Work With a classmate, talk about old words you have learned in your reading.

Additional Support

Author Search To expand students' appreciation of Henry Wadsworth Longfellow, have them access the Web site for additional information and resources.

Differentiated Instruction

Using a Chart A narrative poem combines the storytelling aspects of prose with rhyme, rhythm, and other poetic devices. As they read "Paul Revere's Ride," ask students to keep track of the narrative elements of the poem by using a chart like the one shown. Ask students to list the important events of the plot, as well as setting and characters. OL

	Events	Setting	Characters
Stanza			

Skills Preview

Key Reading Skill: Making Inferences

R An author doesn't always tell you why people do what they do or what the consequences of a person's actions will be. As you read "Paul Revere's Ride," think about why Paul Revere and his friend put themselves in danger to warn the colonists of the approach of the British soldiers. What were their motivations?

Write to Learn In your Learner's Notebook write a few sentences about what might have motivated Revere and his friends to take such a risk.

Literary Element: Narrative Poetry

Narrative poetry tells a story in verse. Like all stories, narrative poems have setting, characters, and conflict. Unlike other stories, a narrative poem contains rhythm, rhyme, and other sound devices. These "musical" elements add to the beauty of the language, support the storyline, and make the poem more memorable. As you read "Paul Revere's Ride," ask yourself these questions:

- *When and where does the story take place?*
- *Who is the protagonist, or main character?*
- *What is the protagonist's goal? What antagonist stands in the way?*
- *Does the protagonist reach his or her goal? Why or why not?*

Small Group Discussion With a group of classmates, recite a school cheer that you know. Together, rewrite the cheer in your own words. Do not use rhythm or rhyme. Read aloud each version of the cheer. Then answer the following questions:

- Which version is more stirring and why?
- Which version is easier to remember and why?

Interactive Literary Elements Handbook
To review or learn more about the literary elements, go to www.glencoe.com.

Get Ready to Read

Connect to the Reading

Paul Revere's fellow colonists were counting on him to warn them when British soldiers marched toward their villages. Think of a time when other people counted on you to do an important job.

Write to Learn In a few sentences describe the job and your feelings about doing it.

Build Background

- "Paul Revere's Ride" celebrates the patriotism of Paul Revere (1735–1818), a colonist who supported American independence from Great Britain. On April 18, 1775, Revere rode from Boston to Lexington, Massachusetts, to warn local leaders that British soldiers were preparing to advance. He was arrested before he could reach his final destination.
- Revere was not the only colonist who rode through the countryside sounding the alert that day. He is the best remembered, however, because of the popularity of "Paul Revere's Ride."
- "Paul Revere's Ride" was published in 1861, when the nation was headed toward civil war. In those dark days, some Americans looked to the past for heroes that both Northerners and Southerners could be proud of. Revere was just such a man.

Set Purposes for Reading

BIG Question Read the poem "Paul Revere's Ride" to find out what happened on the night that Paul Revere made his famous ride.

Set Your Own Purpose What else would you like to learn from the poem to help you answer the Big Question? Write your own purpose on the "Paul Revere's Ride" flap of Foldable 2.

Keep Moving

Use these skills as you read the following selection.

Teach

R Reading Skill

Making Inferences

Say: Think about the meanings of words such as *independence, rights,* and *revolution*—words used by the patriots of colonial America. What can you infer about the values of the patriots based on these words? *(Possible responses: These words indicate that the patriots valued personal freedom and human rights, and wanted change.)* AL

Interactive Literary Elements Handbook Have students access the Web site to improve their understanding of narrative poetry.

Literature Focus Lesson

Rhyme Scheme Have students examine the rhyme scheme, or pattern, of Longfellow's poem. Tell them to use a different letter of the alphabet for each word with a different end sound. For example, the first stanza follows the rhyme scheme *aabba cdcd eefff.* Organize the students in groups, and have each group mark the rhyme scheme of a particular stanza. Have students compare the rhyme schemes of each stanza and discuss the differences. OL As a class, discuss whether students think the rhyme scheme is effective. Ask students to explain how the rhymes help keep the story moving forward. AL

Indiana English/Language Arts Academic Standards
SE: 8.1, 8.3.1
TWE: *Differentiated Instruction* 8.3.1, *Literature Focus Lesson* 8.3.1

Teach

L Literary Element

Narrative Poetry Ask: In what way is Longfellow's beginning similar to that of a story told in prose? *(Possible responses: The speaker announces that he will tell a story and invites children to listen.)* **OL** **Ask:** In what way is the opening of this poetic narrative different from a story told in prose? *(Possible response: The rhythm gives special emphasis to end words, such as* hear *and* Revere.*)* **AL**

R Reading Skill

Making Inferences

Say: Revere is rowing silently at night. What can you infer from his actions? *(Possible response: Revere is trying to move soundlessly. He does not want his presence known.)* **OL** **Ask:** From the information in the passage, who or what do you think Revere fears most as he rows to the Charlestown shore? *(Possible response: Someone on the British ship* Somerset *might detect Revere's boat.)* **AL**

READING WORKSHOP 2

Paul Revere's Ride

by Henry Wadsworth Longfellow

Listen, my children, and you shall hear
Of the midnight ride of Paul Revere,
On the eighteenth of April, in Seventy-five;[1]
Hardly a man is now alive
Who remembers that famous day and year.
He said to his friend, "If the British march
By land or sea from the town to-night,
Hang a lantern aloft in the belfry arch
Of the North Church tower as a signal light,—
One, if by land, and two, if by sea;
And I on the opposite shore will be,
Ready to ride and spread the alarm
Through every Middlesex[2] village and farm,
For the country folk to be up and to arm." **1**

Then he said, "Good night!" and with muffled oar
Silently rowed to the Charlestown shore,
Just as the moon rose over the bay,
Where swinging wide at her moorings[3] lay
The Somerset, British man-of-war;

1. ***Seventy-five*** refers to 1775, the year of Paul Revere's ride.
2. The county of ***Middlesex,*** Massachusetts, includes the town of Concord, where the first shots of the Revolutionary War were fired on April 19, 1775.
3. The place where a ship is docked is called its ***moorings.***

Practice the Skills

1 Literary Element

Narrative Poetry In the first lines of the poem, Longfellow sets the scene by describing the time (April 18, 1775), the place (Middlesex county), and the basic storyline.

Additional Support

Differentiated Instruction

Comparing Sources Read this excerpt from a letter in which Paul Revere describes his famous ride. Have students identify which parts of Longfellow's account agree or disagree with Revere's letter.

I returned at Night thro Charlestown; there I agreed with a Col. Conant, and some other Gentlemen, that if the British went out by Water, we would shew [show] two Lanthorns [lanterns] in the North Church Steeple; and if by Land, one, as a Signal. . . . I . . . went to the North part of the Town, Where I had kept a Boat; two friends rowed me across Charles River, a little to the eastward where the Somerset Man of War lay. **AL**

A phantom ship, with each mast and spar
Across the moon like a prison bar,
And a huge black hulk, that was magnified
By its own reflection in the tide.

Meanwhile, his friend, through alley and street,
Wanders and watches with eager ears,
Till in the silence around him he hears
The muster of men at the barrack door,
The sound of arms, and the tramp of feet,
And the measured tread of the grenadiers,[4]
Marching down to their boats on the shore.

Then he climbed the tower of the Old North Church,
By the wooden stairs, with **stealthy** tread, R
To the belfry-chamber overhead,
And startled the pigeons from their perch
On the **somber** rafters, that round him made
Masses and moving shapes of shade,—
By the trembling ladder, steep and tall,
To the highest window in the wall,
Where he paused to listen and look down
A moment on the roofs of the town,
And the moonlight flowing over all. 2

Beneath, in the churchyard, lay the dead,
In their night-encampment on the hill,
Wrapped in silence so deep and still
That he could hear, like a sentinel's[5] tread, C
The watchful night-wind, as it went
Creeping along from tent to tent,
And seeming to whisper, "All is well!"

4. The ***measured tread*** is a steady march or walk. In the British army, ***grenadiers*** (greh nuh DEERZ) were foot soldiers.

5. A ***sentinel*** (SENT nul) is a guard.

Vocabulary

stealthy (STEL thee) *adj.* slow and secretive to avoid being seen and heard

somber (SOM bur) *adj.* dark and gloomy

Practice the Skills

2 Key Reading Skill

Making Inferences How do you think Revere's friend feels as he climbs the tower? Think about these clues:

- his stealthy walk
- the startled pigeons
- the somber rafters
- the trembling ladder

READING WORKSHOP 2

Teach

R Reading Skill

Making Inferences

Say: What do you think might happen to Revere's friend if he is caught? *(Possible response: The British would probably punish Revere's friend for his actions.)* **OL** **Ask:** When he signed the Declaration of Independence, Benjamin Franklin said, "We must all hang together, or assuredly we shall all hang separately." From Franklin's statement, what inference can you make about the dangers that Revere and his friends faced? *(Possible response: Revere and his friends might be killed for their work in supporting the rebellion.)* **AL**

C Critical Thinking

Comprehension **Ask:** What is being described in this stanza? *(a churchyard cemetery)* **Ask:** Who or what seems to whisper to Revere, "All is well"? *(the night wind)* **OL**

English Language Coach

Old Words: Military Terms Students may not be familiar with the military terms used in the poem, especially the historical terms used during the time of the Revolution. Write the following words on the board, and help students determine their meanings.

- man-of-war *(an armed sailing ship)*
- barrack *(a large building or buildings used to house soldiers)*
- red-coats *(British soldiers)*
- musket-ball *(the bullet of a musket, a long-barreled gun used by British and American soldiers during the Revolution)* **AS**

Indiana English/Language Arts Academic Standards

SE: 8.2, 8.3.1

TWE: *Differentiated Instruction* 8.3, *English Language Coach* 8.1

Teach

R1 Reading Skill

Making Inferences **Say:** The person in the belfry (bell tower) is supposed to alert Revere as to whether the British will come by land or by sea. How well do you think the person in the belfry can see? *(Possible response: The night is dark, and the person might have trouble seeing troops or boats that are moving quietly.)* AL

R2 Reading Skill

Making Inferences
Ask: What is Paul Revere doing as he waits for the signal? *(He is pacing and waiting to mount his horse.)* **Ask:** Why do you think Paul Revere feels impatient at this moment? *(Possible response: He wants to begin his mission.)* OL

READING WORKSHOP 2

Paul Revere's Midnight Ride. Artist unknown.
Analyzing the Painting In what ways does this painting capture the drama of Paul Revere's late-night ride?

A moment only he feels the spell
Of the place and the hour, and the secret dread
Of the lonely belfry and the dead;
For suddenly all his thoughts are bent
On a shadowy something far away,
Where the river widens to meet the bay,—
A line of black that bends and floats
On the rising tide, like a bridge of boats. 3

Meanwhile, impatient to mount and ride,
Booted and spurred, with a heavy stride
On the opposite shore walked Paul Revere.

Practice the Skills

3 Key Reading Skill

Making Inferences What do you think is the "line of black that floats and bends"? Think about why Revere's friend is in the tower and what he is looking for.

Additional Support

Differentiated Instruction

Writing Poetry As he awaits the signal from the North Church, Paul Revere probably feels both nervous and excited. Ask students to think about when they have felt this combination of feelings. For example, a player might feel this way before the start of an important sports competition. A student who has done a great deal of studying might feel this way before taking a test. Ask students to write a six- to eight-line poem about how they feel at these critical moments. Invite volunteers to share their poems with the class. OL AL

Now he patted his horse's side,
Now gazed at the landscape far and near,
Then, impetuous, stamped the earth,
And turned and tightened his saddlegirth;[6]
But mostly he watched with eager search
The belfry-tower of the Old North Church,
As it rose above the graves on the hill,
Lonely and spectral[7] and somber and still.
And lo! as he looks, on the belfry's height
A glimmer, and then a gleam of light!
He springs to the saddle, the bridle he turns,
But **lingers** and gazes, till full on his sight
A second lamp in the belfry burns!

A hurry of hoofs in a village street,
A shape in the moonlight, a bulk in the dark,
And beneath, from the pebbles, in passing, a spark
Struck out by a steed flying fearless and fleet:[8]
That was all! And yet, through the gloom and the light,
The fate of a nation was riding that night; **4** C2
And the spark struck out by that steed, in his flight,
Kindled the land into flame with its heat.

He has left the village and mounted the steep,[9]
And beneath him, tranquil and broad and deep,
Is the Mystic,[10] meeting the ocean tides;
And under the alders[11] that skirt its edge,
Now soft on the sand, now loud on the ledge,
Is heard the tramp of his steed as he rides.

6. Here ***impetuous*** means "acting suddenly." When Revere ***tightened his saddlegirth,*** he checked the belt that holds the saddle on a horse.
7. Something ***spectral*** is ghost-like.
8. Here, ***fleet*** means "very fast."
9. As a noun, ***steep*** means "a steep slope."
10. The ***Mystic*** is a short river that flows into Boston Harbor.
11. ***Alders*** are trees in the birch family.

Vocabulary

lingers (LING urz) *v.* waits or is slow in leaving

Practice the Skills

4 Key Reading Skill

Making Inferences Why does the nation's fate, or future, depend on Paul Revere? Think about what Revere saw in the belfry-tower of the church, what his friend saw and heard, and why Revere rides out of town in such a hurry.

Teach

C1 Critical Thinking

Analysis Say: Although Paul Revere is impatient to begin his journey, he lingers after he first sees the lantern in the belfry. What does *linger* mean? Why is Revere's lingering important? *(Possible response: To linger means "to wait or to be slow in leaving." If Paul Revere had ridden off immediately, he might not have seen his friend raise a second lantern in the belfry.)* **AL**

C2 Critical Thinking

Comprehension Ask: What is the meaning of line 78? *(Possible response: Revere's ride would determine the nation's destiny. Alerting the colonists that the British were coming meant that they would have time to prepare a counterattack.)* **Ask:** If Paul Revere's ride had failed, how might our country's government be different today? *(This country might still be a colony of England.)* **OL**

Reading Fluency

Reading Poetry Help students develop fluency by asking them to read aloud a favorite section of the poem. Allow time for students to practice reading their selections before asking them to read aloud to the class. Remind students that when reading a poem, they should be guided by the rhythm and rhyme scheme. By changing the pace and volume of their reading, students can create drama and excitement as they read. Remind students to use punctuation, not the end of the line, to tell them when to pause. **EL** **BL** **OL**

Indiana English/Language Arts Academic Standards
SE: 8.2.9
TWE: *Reading Skill* 8.2.9, *Differentiated Instruction* 8.5, *Reading Fluency* 8.7.14

Teach

Viewing the Art

Ask: What part of the story does this painting depict? *(It depicts Paul Revere riding through the night.)* **BL** **Ask:** How does the painter show that the ride occurred at night? *(Possible response: The painter lights up the area where Revere is riding and the church; he also shows lights in a home; the rest of the painting is dark.)* **OL**

L Literary Element

Narrative Poetry **Say:** Paul Revere faces more than one antagonist, a person or force that works against him. What obstacles—people or forces—does Revere face on his ride? *(Possible response: He must ride quickly in the dark, so both time and the darkness of night are working against Revere. He must also avoid the British, another antagonist.)* **AL**

Midnight Ride of Paul Revere, 1931. Grant Wood. Oil on composition board, 30 x 40 in. The Metropolitan Museum of Art, NY.

It was twelve by the village clock,
When he crossed the bridge into Medford town.
He heard the crowing of the cock,
And the barking of the farmer's dog,
And felt the damp of the river fog,
That rises after the sun goes down.

It was one by the village clock,
When he galloped into Lexington.
He saw the gilded[12] weathercock
Swim in the moonlight as he passed,
And the meeting-house windows, blank and bare,
Gaze at him with a spectral glare,
As if they already stood aghast
At the bloody work they would look upon. **5**

12. A ***gilded*** object has, or seems to have, a thin coating of gold.

Practice the Skills

5 Literary Element

Narrative Poetry Paul Revere is the protagonist of the story. What is his goal, or mission? What antagonist might keep him from reaching it? **L**

Additional Support

Reading in the Real World

Citizenship Paul Revere's ride shows how a community long ago warned citizens of potential danger. Have students learn more about the warning systems used in their own community to alert people to dangers such as floods, tornadoes, hurricanes, or other natural disasters. They can visit the Red Cross Web site to learn safety precautions they can take during a natural disaster. Ask them to share the information with their families. **AS**

It was two by the village clock,
When he came to the bridge in Concord town.
He heard the bleating of the flock,
And the twitter of birds among the trees,
And felt the breath of the morning breeze
Blowing over the meadows brown.
And one was safe and asleep in his bed
Who at the bridge would be first to fall,
Who that day would be lying dead,
Pierced by a British musket-ball. 6

You know the rest. In the books you have read,
How the British Regulars[13] fired and fled,—
How the farmers gave them ball for ball,
From behind each fence and farm-yard wall,
Chasing the red-coats down the lane,
Then crossing the fields to **emerge** again
Under the trees at the turn of the road,
And only pausing to fire and load.

So through the night rode Paul Revere;
And so through the night went his cry of alarm
To every Middlesex village and farm,—
A cry of **defiance** and not of fear,
A voice in the darkness, a knock at the door,
And a word that shall echo forevermore!
For, borne on the night-wind of the Past,
Through all our history, to the last,
In the hour of darkness and peril[14] and need,
The people will waken and listen to hear
The hurrying hoof-beats of that steed,
And the midnight message of Paul Revere. 7 ❍

13. ***Regulars*** are soldiers and officers belonging to a permanent professional army. ***Irregulars*** are those who are drafted for a short time.

14. ***Peril*** means "danger."

Vocabulary

emerge (ih MURJ) *v.* to come out into view

defiance (dih FY uns) *n.* the act of challenging authority

Practice the Skills

6 **English Language Coach**

Old Words If you don't remember what a musket is, look back at the English Language Coach on page 184. Does the context also help you understand what a musket-ball is?

7 **BIG Question**

BQ

Which do you think was more important: Paul Revere's destination or the journey he took to reach it? Why? Write your answer on the "Paul Revere's Ride" flap of Foldable 2. Your response will help you complete the Unit Challenge later.

READING WORKSHOP 2

Teach

C Critical Thinking

Evaluation Say: Do you think this story would have been as exciting if it had been written in prose? Why or why not? *(Possible response: It would not have been as exciting. The poet's use of repetition, rhythm, and rhyme added to the thrill of the story.)* OL

BQ BIG Question

Say: The poet says "You know the rest" and briefly describes what happens after the ride. Do you think the poet feels Revere's journey or the destination was more important? *(Possible response: He felt the journey was more important. He takes many pages to describe it and only one brief stanza to describe what happened later.)* AL

Assess

Use the CheckPoint questions provided on Presentation Plus! to check for comprehension of the selection. These questions can be used with interactive response keypads for immediate student feedback.

Literature Focus Lesson

Mood Mood is the emotional quality or atmosphere of a story or poem. The mood of a poem affects how the reader feels as he or she reads the poem. Writers create mood with the details they give and the words they choose. Longfellow creates a dramatic mood through word choices that color the description and details in his poem.

Ask students to describe the mood set by phrases such as "a phantom ship," "the secret dread," and "hour of darkness and peril and need." Discuss Longfellow's reasons for creating this mood. Have students look back over the poem to find other details, words, or phrases that help create the mood. OL

Indiana English/Language Arts Academic Standards

SE: 8.1, 8.3.1

TWE: *Reading in the Real World* 8.2, *Literature Focus Lesson* 8.3.4

Assess

Resources for page 192

- Selection Quick Check, p. 13
- Selection and Unit Assessment, p. 15
- ExamView Assessment Suite
- Interactive Tutor: Self-Assessment

Students can respond to the *After You Read* items in their Learner's Notebooks or on a separate sheet of paper.

Answering the BIG Question

1. Possible response: Revere's journey symbolized the colonists' willingness to fight for their freedom.
2. One lamp meant that the British troops would come by land. Two lamps meant that the troops were traveling by sea.
3. Paul Revere was alerted that British troops were arriving. He rode from Boston to Concord to alert colonists to prepare to fight the British.

Critical Thinking

4. Possible response: The "land" is the American colonies. The land is "kindled into flame" as the colonists embrace the ideals of liberty and prepare to fight the British.
5. Possible response: The fictional elements enhance the poem's emotional impact in a way that the presentation of facts cannot.

After You Read

Paul Revere's Ride

Answering the BIG Question

1. Why do you think Paul Revere's journey through the countryside helped make him an American legend?
2. **Recall** In the secret code Revere and his friend use, what is the meaning of the two lanterns hanging in the church tower?

   TIP **Right There** The answer is in one place in the poem.
3. **Summarize** In a few sentences sum up the story of Revere's ride as it is described in the poem.

   TIP **Think and Search** The answer is in the poem, but it is not all in one place.

Critical Thinking

4. **Interpret** Lines 79–80 say that "the spark struck out by [Revere's horse], in his flight, / Kindled the land into flame with its heat." What "land" is the poem referring to? How was it "kindled into flame"?

   TIP **Author and Me** Draw on your knowledge of American history and think about the poem.
5. **Evaluate** The poem says that Revere rode into Concord. In reality, he was arrested before he could get there. Do you think the poem would be improved if it were completely factual, rather than a mix of fact and fiction?

   TIP **Author and Me** Think about the poem and formulate your own opinion about it.

Write About Your Reading

Diary Entry Scan the poem for things that Paul Revere sees and hears. Write your examples in a copy of the chart below.

Sights	Sounds

Pretend that you are Paul Revere. Use information in your chart to write a diary entry dated April 19, 1775, that describes the events of the previous night. Explain how you feel about the night's events and what lies ahead.

Indiana English/Language Arts Academic Standards (pp. 192–193)

8.3 Comprehension and Analysis of Literary Text Respond to grade-level-appropriate literature... **8.5.2** Write responses to literature... **8.2 Comprehension and Analysis (Focus on Informational Text)** Develop [reading] strategies... **8.2.9** Make reasonable statements and draw conclusions... **8.3.1** Determine and articulate relationship between purpose and characteristics of different forms of poetry. **8.6 English Language Conventions**

For a complete description of the standards, see p. IN 11.

Write About Your Reading

Possible responses:

Sights	Sounds
Lanterns in North Church, British ships, gilded weathercock, village clocks, meeting house	British soldiers marching, wind in churchyard, horse's hooves, a cock crowing, a dog barking, flocks bleating

April 19, 1775

It was dark as could be on my ride last night. Strange, but as I rode from one town to another, warning villagers of the British advance, it seemed that I could hear everything in the darkness. I heard dogs, horses, chickens, sheep, birds—everything seemed to be urging me forward, helping me ride faster and faster! I only hope that we are ready to fight for our liberty.

Skills Review

Key Reading Skill: Making Inferences

6. In the first two lines of the poem, an adult asks a group of children to listen as he tells the tale of Revere's ride. How do these lines help set up the idea that Paul Revere is an American legend?
7. What do you think Longfellow wanted Americans to think of Paul Revere? Use details from the poem to support your opinion.

Literary Element: Narrative Poetry

8. Read aloud lines 73–86 and listen to the rhythm, or beat, of the poem. Try to picture the actions that are described. Why is it fitting that the actions are described in a regular pattern of rhythm?
9. What are the rhyming words in the first stanza (lines 1–14)? Copy the chart below. Then, in the bottom row, fill in the word or words that rhyme with each word above.

hear	-five	march	to-night	sea	alarm

Vocabulary Check

Write an antonym for each vocabulary word below. An antonym has the opposite meaning of a word. You may use a thesaurus to help you.

10. stealthy ___
11. somber ___
12. linger ___
13. emerge ___
14. defiance ___

15. **Academic Vocabulary** Imagine that a friend asks you what *inferring* means. Define the word and give an example that shows what it means.
16. **English Language Coach** Choose an old word from the poem and use it in a sentence.

Web Activities For eFlashcards, Selection Quick Checks, and other Web activities, go to www.glencoe.com.

Grammar Link: Comparative and Superlative

- The **comparative forms** of adjectives and adverbs are used to compare one person, place, thing, or action with another. The **superlative forms** are used to compare one person, place, thing, or action with more than one other.
- To form the comparative, add *-er* to the end of adjectives or adverbs of one syllable and to some with two syllables. To form the **superlative,** add *-est.*
- Carrie is older than Heba. (One person's age is compared to another person's.)
- Lou is the oldest of the eight children. (One person's age is compared to several others'.)

Use the word *more* or *less* to form the comparative of adjectives or adverbs of two syllables or more. Use the word *most* or *least* to form the superlative.

- Donna is the most musical of all the kids. (The word *most* is used instead of an *-est* ending because *musical* has three syllables.)
- Teddy runs the least gracefully. (The word *least* is used instead of an *-est* ending because *gracefully* has three syllables.)

Look out! Never use the ending *-er* or *-est* and *more* or *most, less* or *least* at the same time.
Wrong: He is the most smartest person I know.
Right: He is the smartest person I know.

Grammar Practice

On a separate piece of paper, write the comparative and superlative forms of each of these words: *loud, big, popular,* and *talented.*

Writing Application Look back at the diary entry you wrote for the Write About Your Reading activity. Check any comparatives and superlatives you used to make sure you formed them correctly.

Skills Review

Key Reading Skill: Making Inferences

6. Possible response: The opening lines create a sense that the story is important and should be told to every generation.
7. Possible response: Longfellow wanted Americans to think of Paul Revere as heroic.

Literary Element: Narrative Poetry

8. Possible response: The rhythm fits the action because it echoes the beat of a horse's hooves.

9.

hear	Revere, year
-five	alive
march	arch
to-night	light
sea	be
alarm	farm, arm

Vocabulary Check

Possible responses:

10. loud; obvious
11. lighthearted
12. rush; flee
13. disappear; hide
14. acceptance

Academic Vocabulary

15. Inferring means using what you know to make an educated guess about something you don't know. Examples will vary.

English Language Coach

16. Responses will vary.

Grammar Link: Comparative and Superlative

Grammar Practice

loud, louder, loudest
big, bigger, biggest
popular, more popular, most popular
talented, more talented, most talented

Close

Ask students to consider whether the title of Longfellow's poem emphasizes Revere's destination or his journey.

Indiana English/Language Arts Academic Standards
SE: 8.2, 8.2.9, 8.3, 8.3.1, 8.5.2, 8.6

Teach

More About the Author

Eric A. Kimmel grew up in a diverse Brooklyn neighborhood. He spoke Yiddish, and his neighbors spoke Armenian, Italian, Chinese, and Spanish. His Ukrainian grandmother spoke five languages. Hearing these diverse voices tell many different stories sparked Kimmel's love of storytelling.

EL Language Coach

Building Vocabulary: Compound Words **Say:** Sometimes you can figure out a compound word's meaning by looking at the two words that form it. Other times, you'll need to use a dictionary to determine the meaning. For instance, you cannot guess the meaning of *outskirts* just by knowing what *out* and *skirts* mean. Look up this word. What does *outskirts* mean? *(Possible response: It means the outer edge of a place.)* EL

Before You Read The Oxcart

Eric A. Kimmel

Meet the Author

"The Oxcart" is a folktale that was told for hundreds of years before it was written down. Everyone who told it gave a slightly different version, so in a way the story has many authors. The person responsible for writing this version of the story is Eric A. Kimmel. He is well known for his stories about cultures from all over the world. See page R3 of the Author Files in the back of the book for more on Eric Kimmel.

Author Search For more about Eric A. Kimmel, go to www.glencoe.com.

Indiana English/Language Arts Academic Standards (pp. 194–201)

8.1 Word Recognition, Fluency, and Vocabulary Development Understand...word parts and patterns... **8.2 Comprehension and Analysis (Focus on Informational Text)** Develop [reading] strategies... **8.3.2** Evaluate the structural elements of plot...

For a complete description of the standards, see p. IN 11.

Vocabulary Preview

procession (proh SEH shun) *n.* a group of individuals walking forward together in a ceremony **(p. 197)** *People stopped to watch the procession of soldiers go by.*

elegant (EL lih gunt) *adj.* beautiful and tasteful **(p. 198)** *The queen had an elegant coach drawn by four horses.*

lurching (LURCH ing) *v.* rolling or swaying in a jerky motion; form of the verb *lurch* **(p. 199)** *The small boat was crazily lurching in the rough water of the bay.*

distinguished (dis TING gwisht) *adj.* well-known for excellence and honor **(p. 201)** *The governor was a distinguished member of the community.*

Partner Talk Answer the questions with a classmate. Give reasons for your answers.

- Which is a procession: bridesmaids walking down an aisle or people crossing the street?
- Which is likely to be elegant: a fast-food meal or a wedding feast?
- Which is a lurching object: a ship at sea during a storm or an airplane parked on a runway?
- Who is more distinguished: an infamous criminal or an award-winning scientist?

English Language Coach

Building Vocabulary: Compound Words Expand your vocabulary with **compound words**—words made up of two or more words. Divide a compound into the words of which it is made, think about what each word means, and use the meanings to understand other compounds. For example, if you know that a *high-level* official is one who has reached the upper ranks of his or her profession, you might guess that *highborn* (high + born) means "born into the upper (higher) class."

On Your Own Add the word *high* to the beginning of each of the following words to form a compound word. Then use each compound correctly in a sentence.

- **-energy**
- **-spirited**
- **-powered**

Additional Support

Author Search To expand students' appreciation of Eric A. Kimmel, have them access the Web site for additional information and resources.

Literature Focus Lesson

Folktale Stories such as "The Oxcart" capture everyday details about a culture or a people. Have students learn more about the folktales of their own culture. Emphasize that folktales may be preserved and passed on orally, or they may be written down. If possible, ask students to interview older members of their community who are familiar with an oral folklore tradition. Students may also use research tools to find folklore collections from around the world, such as the Grimm brothers' collection of German folktales. AS

Skills Preview

Key Reading Skill: Making Inferences

"The Oxcart" is about three samurai who go on a journey. As you read, be on the lookout for clues that tell what society expected of samurai and of noblewomen. You may find clues in

- what the samurai and the women say
- what they do
- how others respond to them

Whole Class Discussion Preview the art in the selection. What inferences can you make about life in Japan in the days of the samurai?

Key Literary Element: Plot

Every story, novel, and play has a **plot**–a sequence of events that are set into motion by a conflict, or problem. Many plots follow this pattern:

1. **Exposition (eks puh ZIH shun):** description or dialogue that introduces the characters, the setting, and the situation
2. **Rising action:** events that complicate the situation by introducing a conflict
3. **Climax:** the moment of highest tension in the conflict, when a character takes decisive action or makes an important decision
4. **Falling action:** as the action winds down, the effects of the action or decision are revealed
5. **Resolution (rez uh LOO shun):** the final outcome of the conflict is described, and loose ends are tied up

Small Group Discussion Analyze the plot of a story, a TV show, or a movie you know. Discuss what happens during each of the five stages of plot.

Interactive Literary Elements Handbook
To review or learn more about the literary elements, go to www.glencoe.com.

Get Ready to Read

Connect to the Reading

Have you ever tried to take an easy way out of a situation and discovered that it wasn't so easy after all?

Write to Learn In a few sentences summarize what the situation was, what you did to try to get out of it, and what you learned from the experience.

Build Background

- "The Oxcart" takes place in Japan hundreds of years ago, when there were very strict rules about how people should behave. At that time, it was impossible to rise out of the working class. If a noble disgraced himself, he could be thrown out of his house and have everything taken from him by the ruler. People who were rich and powerful were expected to live up to the rules of their social level. No one had any pity for those who broke the rules and fell down the social ladder.
- "The Oxcart" can be classified as a **cautionary tale**–a story in which people are punished for breaking society's rules or misbehaving. Though the punishment in cautionary tales is usually harsh and heavy-handed, the punishment in "The Oxcart" is definitely light-hearted.

Set Purposes for Reading

BIG Question Read "The Oxcart" to find out what happens to the three samurai on their journey and what lesson they learn in the end.

Set Your Own Purpose What else would you like to learn from the story to help you answer the Big Question? Write your own purpose on the "Oxcart" flap of Foldable 2.

Keep Moving

Use these skills and strategies as you read the following selection.

English Language Coach

Compound Words Have students combine the words listed below to complete the following sentences.

cart	sun	sea
sick	ox	shine

1. The passenger had a terrible voyage because he became ______ during the storm. *(seasick)*
2. We took off our warm jackets as soon as we stepped out into the warm ______. *(sunshine)*
3. The goods were too heavy to carry, so the merchants loaded them into an ______. *(oxcart)* EL

Teach

L Literary Element

Plot Ask: Why do you think the exposition usually comes at the beginning of a story? *(Possible response: because it tells the reader where the story happens, who the characters are, and what the situation is)* OL **Ask:** When is the conflict usually introduced in a story? *(during the rising action)* BL

C Critical Thinking

Evaluation Say: Read the *Build Background* section. How is the setting of this story different from the United States today? *(Possible responses: Some people can move into a different social class today. Government officials aren't allowed to take people's possessions from them without due cause.)* OL

Interactive Literary Elements Handbook Have students access the Web site to improve their understanding of plot.

Indiana English/Language Arts Academic Standards
SE: 8.1, 8.2, 8.3.2
TWE: *Literature Focus Lesson* 8.3.7, *English Language Coach* 8.1

Teach

L Literary Element

Plot Ask: What do you learn in the exposition of this story? *(Possible response: You learn about the strict rules of this culture, the uncomfortable oxcarts that are ridden only by women, and the three samurai who try to cut corners.)* AL

EL Language Coach

Compound Words Say: The word *outstanding* is a compound word. What two words make up this compound word? *(out* and *standing)* **Ask:** Can you guess its meaning from these words, or do you need to look it up? *(Some students might think of the phrase "to stand out" and guess* outstanding *means "exceptional.")* EL BL

Readability Scores
Dale-Chall: 6.1
DRP: 50
Lexile: 610

READING WORKSHOP 2

From the Illustrations to 100 poems by 100 poets. Katsushika Hokusai (1760–1849). Japan.

The Oxcart

by Eric A. Kimmel

Old Japan had strict rules governing how people of all classes should behave. Highborn women were not allowed to have any contact with commoners. They could travel only in two-wheeled oxcarts. Small windows and heavy curtains hid the passengers from unwelcome stares. Although these carts were beautifully furnished and decorated, they were cramped, poorly ventilated, and extremely uncomfortable to ride in. The oxcarts were reserved for women. No male samurai could ride in one. If he did and was caught, he faced severe punishment, possibly even the loss of his samurai status. The three samurai in this story tried to cut corners. They learned a well-deserved lesson. 1

The governor of Settsu had three outstanding samurai[1] in his service. Their names were Taira no Hidemichi, Taira no Suetake, and Sakata no Kintoki. Once in late fall, when the time of the Kamo festival was approaching, the three samurai

1. A ***samurai*** was a member of the Japanese military class, just below powerful nobles in importance. Samurai were expected to fight bravely and lead perfect lives.

Practice the Skills

1 Reviewing Skills

Setting a Purpose for Reading The author gives background information to help readers understand the folktale. What can you expect to learn from reading this story? Write your answer in your Learner's Notebook.

Additional Support

Reading in the Real World

Citizenship Have students use resource materials to learn more about the samurai code of bravery and honor, or *bushido.* Have students compare the samurai concepts of loyalty and honor with their own ideas of good citizenship. Ask students to create a Venn diagram to illustrate their comparison. OL wanted to go to Murasakino to watch the **procession**. 2 They looked forward to seeing the beautiful shrines[2] pulled through the streets on wagons while the great *taiko* drums filled the air with their pounding rhythm.

"How will we get to Murasakino?" Hidemichi asked.

"We'll ride our horses," Suetake suggested.

"That's not a good idea," said Kintoki. "The streets in Murasakino are going to be crowded. Our horses are trained for war. Once they find themselves in the middle of those crowds, they'll think they're on a battlefield. They'll start kicking and plunging. Someone's bound to get hurt, and it will be our fault. The governor will be very angry with us."

"Then we'll walk," said Hidemichi.

"Three samurai walking along on foot, like common peasants? We'd be disgraced," Suetake replied.

"We could cover our faces so no one would know who we are," Kintoki suggested.

Hidemichi argued against that idea. "The city guards would take us for bandits. We'd end up in jail, and the governor would have to get us out. Even if we could go by foot, it's a long walk to Murasakino and back. I don't want to do it."

"Neither do we," Kintoki and Suetake agreed. C1

"If we can't walk or ride, how will we get there?" Suetake asked.

"I have an idea," Kintoki said. "We'll go in an oxcart." 3

"What? A farmer's wagon?"

"No! I mean the kind of closed oxcart that the wives and daughters of highborn nobles ride in."

"Is that a good idea?" Hidemichi asked. "Samurai are warriors. We aren't allowed to ride in carts or wagons. If anyone sees us, we'll be disgraced." C2

"Nobody will see us," Kintoki assured him. "These oxcarts are completely enclosed. The windows are covered with heavy curtains so no one can see inside." 4

2. In this case, a ***shrine*** is a case or a box for sacred objects.

Vocabulary

procession (proh SEH shun) *n.* a group of individuals walking forward together in a ceremony

Practice the Skills

2 Key Literary Element

Plot Here, in the exposition, the three main characters and the setting are introduced.

3 Key Literary Element

Plot The exposition continues as the situation is introduced. Here is the situation in a nutshell: The samurai want to go to a festival, but the streets will be too crowded for them to ride their horses. They decide to ride in an oxcart instead.

4 Key Reading Skill

Making Inferences What can you infer about the lives of upper-class women in old Japan? Think about these clues:

- The women do not ride on horseback; they ride in carts and wagons.
- The windows of the carts and wagons are covered so no one can look in.
- The covers also prevent the women from looking out the windows.

READING WORKSHOP 2

Teach

C1 Critical Thinking

Comprehension Ask: Why does Suetake object to walking? *(Possible response: He fears they'll be disgraced for walking like common peasants.)* Why does Hidemichi object to riding in an oxcart? *(Possible response: He fears that someone will see the samurai and that they will be disgraced.)* OL

C2 Critical Thinking

Analysis Ask: Do you think the decision to ride in the oxcart is characteristic of a samurai? *(Responses will vary. Students may say no, samurai are warriors and they are not used to taking the easy way out. They also would not want to risk losing their samurai status.)* OL

Differentiated Instruction

Draw a Diagram Ask students to list the different types of people who are mentioned in the story, including peasants, bandits, samurai, city guards, noblewomen, and governors. Then have the class work together to create a pyramid chart that illustrates people's position in society, building from who was considered the least important to the most important. Students should use context clues from the story to determine people's places in the chart. Discuss why it makes sense to represent the members of Old Japan's highest classes at the top of the pyramid. OL Challenge students to expand their charts by reading more about medieval Japanese society. AL

Indiana English/Language Arts Academic Standards

SE: 8.2, 8.3.2

TWE: *Reading in the Real World* 8.4.5, *Differentiated Instruction* 8.2

Teach

EL Language Coach

Compound Words Ask: Why is calling Suetake a "seasick traveler" a good way of describing how he looks and feels? *(Possible response: This description is effective because it makes clear that the motion of the cart makes Suetake sick. It also reveals that Suetake has an upset stomach.)* OL

Viewing the Photo

Ask: What does the armor worn by the samurai in the photo tell about the way they fought? *(Possible response: The samurai are holding swords. Their heads and bodies seem to be protected with sturdy armor, which must have been designed to ward off blows by swords or other weapons.)* OL

Ask: What about their armor and weapons suggests that the samurai have a high social status? *(Possible response: Their armor and weapons are elaborately decorated. The armor seems as much for show as for battle. Only members of a high social class could afford such armor.)* AL

READING WORKSHOP 2

"How will we get one?" Suetake asked. "Three samurai can't hire an oxcart without the whole town learning about it."

"I've thought of that already," said Kintoki. "My sister is lady-in-waiting[3] to the governor's wife. The governor has plenty of oxcarts. Some are hardly ever used. My sister can arrange for us to borrow one. We'll walk along beside it on the way through town, pretending we're an escort.[4] When no one is looking, we'll get in and ride all the way to Murasakino. Our servant, Akira, will lead the ox while we travel in comfort."

The plan worked perfectly—except for one unforeseen difficulty. The three samurai had never traveled in an oxcart. Although the vehicle looked **elegant,** it had no springs. Every bump in the road bounced them around like grains of rice pounded in a mortar. And there were many, many bumps, holes, and gullies along the way to Murasakino.

They had hardly gone a mile when Suetake turned pale. **5** "I feel sick. I think I'm going to throw up," he said. "Hurry! Open the door! Let me out!"

Kintoki and Hidemichi grabbed him. "You can't go out! The road is full of people. If they see us riding in this oxcart, we'll be in trouble!"

"I can't help it!" Suetake moaned. "You have to let me out. I'm going to be—"

Poor Suetake threw up all over the oxcart. Like a <u>seasick</u> traveler, he couldn't stop EL

Japanese samurai warriors, c. 1880. R.P. Kingston.

Analyzing the Photo How does this photograph capture the nobility of the Japanese samurai?

3. A ***lady-in-waiting*** was a noblewoman who was a servant to an even more rich and powerful woman, often a queen.

4. An ***escort*** is one who accompanies another person on a journey.

Vocabulary

elegant (EL lih gunt) *adj.* beautiful and tasteful

Practice the Skills

5 Key Literary Element

Plot Which stage of the plot begins here? Hint: The situation is complicated by a conflict–the bumpy ride makes Suetake sick.

Additional Support

English Language Coach

Build Background Students may not be familiar with *samurai* warriors. The Japanese warriors known as samurai came to power in twelfth-century Japan. They were known for their military skills and prided themselves on their bravery and ability to tolerate physical stress. Despite this emphasis on discipline and honor, refined rituals such as the tea ceremony and the art of bonsai and floral arranging also emerged from the samurai culture. The samurai class disappeared in the 1870s, when feudalism was abolished in Japan. Share this information with students. AS Ask students to choose an aspect of samurai culture they find intriguing and gather more information about it. AL

READING WORKSHOP 2

vomiting, even when his stomach was empty. 6 He lay helpless on the floor, moaning and coughing.

Hidemichi turned pale. "What a terrible stench! Open the curtains, Kintoki, or I'll be sick, too!"

"I can't open the curtains! No one must see us in here!" said Kintoki.

"Then I am going to be sick with Suetake!" Hidemichi clutched his stomach and threw up, too. Within minutes, Kintoki joined him. The three samurai lay in a heap, vomiting on each other, groaning in misery.

The people on the road to Murasakino heard terrible groans coming from the oxcart. "What is going on in there?" they asked Akira, the samurais' servant. "It sounds as if someone is dying. Open the door! The people inside need help."

L "Don't touch that door!" Akira blurted out. He could not allow his masters to be discovered riding in a women's oxcart. "The governor's aunt is inside. She was suddenly stricken with a terrible disease. Oozing sores broke out all over her body. The doctors can't help her. She is going to the temple in Murasakino to pray for a cure. No one must go near that cart. She might have the plague."[5] 7

Needless to say, no one approached the cart again. The opposite happened. People on the road ran away when they saw the oxcart coming. It continued on to Murasakino, **lurching** back and forth on the bumpy road, with the three miserable samurai tumbling around inside it. 8

At last the cart stopped. "Masters, we are here. We've reached the outskirts of Murasakino," Akira whispered. He waited for a reply but heard nothing. Finally he said, "I'm going to find a pasture for the ox. Then I'm going to watch the procession. Come quickly. It will be starting soon." R

Akira unhitched the ox and led it away. When he returned hours later, he found the oxcart door still shut, with no sign that his masters had ever emerged. Fearing they might be dead, Akira opened the door and peeped inside.

He saw the three samurai lying in a heap, too weak to stand or even groan. Akira lifted them out of the cart, one by one.

5. The ***plague*** is an infectious, deadly disease.

Vocabulary

lurching (LURCH ing) *v.* rolling or swaying in a jerky motion

Practice the Skills

6 English Language Coach

Compound Words What two words are in the compound word **seasick?** What does *seasick* mean?

7 Key Literary Element

Plot When people hear groans coming from the oxcart, the conflict intensifies. Is this the climax of the plot? Who takes decisive action to protect the samurai, and what action does he take?

8 Key Reading Skill

Making Inferences The samurai feel terrible, but they do not get out of the cart. Why are they so stubborn about not being seen riding in the oxcart?

Teach

L Literary Element

Plot Ask: At the moment of greatest tension, which character saves the day? How? *(Possible response: Akira, the servant, thinks of a lie that prevents people from opening the door of the oxcart and discovering the samurai.)* OL

R Reading Skill

Making Inferences Say: From the samurai's behavior, what can you infer about the importance of shame and honor in Japanese culture? *(Possible response: The samurai will do anything to avoid dishonoring themselves. Undergoing the punishment of riding in the oxcart in a heap of vomit is preferable to receiving help and being shamed.)* AL

Reading Fluency

Reading Exclamations The author indicates the characters' dire circumstances by punctuating their complaints with exclamations, such as "What a terrible stench!" Discuss with students the difference that exclamation points make in emphasis and emotion. In addition, tell them that exclamation points help the author show the humor of a ridiculous situation. Ask students to practice reading aloud a section of the text until they can indicate the emphasis and humor shown by the author's punctuation. EL BL

Indiana English/Language Arts Academic Standards

SE: 8.1, 8.2, 8.2.9, 8.3.2

TWE: *Reading Skill* 8.2.9, *English Language Coach* 8.2, *Reading Fluency* 8.6.5

Teach

R Reading Skill

Making Inferences Ask: What does the characters' body language as they walk back to Settsu tell you about how they feel? *(Possible response: They walk slowly and clutch their stomachs, indicating that they still feel uncomfortable, disappointed, and sick.)* OL

L Literary Element

Plot Say: Think back to the exposition that began the story. The author says that the samurai "learn a well-deserved lesson" when they try to "cut corners." In your own words, state the lesson that the samurai learn. *(Possible response: The samurai have learned that taking the easy way often doesn't pay.)* OL

READING WORKSHOP 2

"Ashida" from *Sixty-nine Stations on the Kisokaido Highway,* c. 1838. Ando or Utagawa Hiroshige. Woodblock color print. Brooklyn Museum of Art, New York. Frank L. Babbott Fund.

Analyzing the Painting What aspect of the samurai's journey to Murasakino does this picture depict?

"Masters, I am so sorry. I did not know you were so ill. Have you been here the whole time? Didn't you go to the festival?"

"How could we?" Kintoki answered. "We were so sick we could hardly lift our heads."

"How stupid we were to ride in that cart!" Suetake exclaimed.

Hidemichi agreed. "We suffered for nothing. We missed the whole festival."

Akira ran to an inn down the road. He returned with hot water, new clothes, and a kettle of hot soup. The samurai felt better after cleaning themselves and eating.

"Let's go home," Kintoki said, disgusted.

"Not in that cart," said Hidemichi and Suetake. "We'll walk beside it. We'll pretend we're an escort."

The three samurai walked all the way back to Settsu. It took a long time to get there. They walked slowly, holding their stomachs, dragging their swords in the dust. 9 R

Kintoki's sister was waiting for them. "Where have you been? I was expecting you hours ago. Why do you look so pale? Why does the cart smell so bad?"

"You're lucky we brought it back at all. This cart should be burned!" Kintoki told her.

"The horrid vehicle nearly killed us!" Hidemichi added.

"I'd rather face slow death by torture than ride in an oxcart again!" said Suetake.

Practice the Skills

9 Key Reading Skill

Making Inferences From this description of how the samurai are walking, what can you infer about how they feel?

Additional Support

Reading in the Real World

Citizenship Read aloud this excerpt from *Code of the Samurai: A Modern Translation of the Bushido Shoshinsu.* Have students discuss what two duties are important to the samurai.

". . . if you realize that the life that is here today is not certain on the morrow, then when you take your orders from your employer, and when you look in on your parents, you will have the sense that this may be that last time, so you cannot fail to become truly attentive to your employer and your parents. This is why I say you also fulfill the paths of loyalty and familial duty when you keep death in mind." AL

Kintoki's sister began to laugh. "You samurai are always telling your wives and sisters how tough you are! You only went to Murasakino. **10** One short ride in an oxcart and you come back looking like corpses. We women are tougher than you! We ride in these carts all the time. Ha, ha, ha!" **R**

Kintoki, Suetake, and Hidemichi slunk away without a word.

The three samurai had long, **distinguished** careers. Kintoki climbed the walls of an enemy castle and opened the gate, all by himself. Suetake stood alone in the middle of a bridge and fought off an attacking army. Hidemichi, after losing his sword, pulled an enemy general off his horse and captured him with his bare hands. But brave as they were, not one of the three ever went near an oxcart again. **11**

"A samurai does not fear death," they would say. "But some things are worse than death. An oxcart is one of them." **12** ○

Vocabulary

distinguished (dis TING gwisht) *adj.* well-known for excellence and honor

Mount Fuji viewed from the province of Hara in Suruga, 1860. Hiroshige II. Colour woodcut. Victoria and Albert Museum, London.

Analyzing the Painting Does this image capture the fun and festivity of the procession to Murasakino? Why or why not?

Practice the Skills

10 Key Literary Element

Plot The action is winding down, and the outcome of the conflict is becoming clear. The women think it's funny that the "tough" samurai got sick in the oxcart. At this point, what stage of the plot is the story in?

11 Key Literary Element

Plot The plot is now in the final stage—resolution. What is the final outcome of the conflict?

12 BIG Question

The samurai go on to be brave men, but they never go in an oxcart again. What do you think their journey taught them about themselves? Write your answer on the "Oxcart" flap of Foldable 2. Your response will help you complete the Unit Challenge later. **BQ**

READING WORKSHOP 2

Teach

R Reading Skill

Making Inferences Ask: Why do you think the three men slunk away? *(Possible response: They were embarrassed that they could not ride in the oxcart without getting sick and that the women were teasing them.)* **OL**

BQ BIG Question

Say: A familiar saying claims that you cannot understand another person until you walk a mile in that person's shoes. What do you think the samurai understand about Japanese women after traveling in their oxcart? *(Possible response: The samurai probably understand that the oxcart is not a luxury for the women. Being confined in such a place can be inconvenient, uncomfortable, and even unhealthy.)* **OL**

Assess

CheckPoint

Use the CheckPoint questions provided on Presentation Plus! to check for comprehension of the selection. These questions can be used with interactive response keypads for immediate student feedback.

Differentiated Instruction

Analyzing Japanese Art Japanese artists over the past three centuries have shared many common traits. Many painted with watercolor or ink. They painted on very fine paper or silk, often creating screens out of multiple layers of paper and a final layer of silk. These screens could be moved, so they often depicted different times of year and were replaced to match the season. Japanese artists were less concerned with depicting objects exactly as they saw them and more concerned with capturing the "soul" of the object. Have students interested in art mimic the style of art presented on pages 196, 200, and 201. Encourage students to share their paintings with the class. **OL**

Indiana English/Language Arts Academic Standards

SE: 8.2, 8.3.2

TWE: *Reading in the Real World* 8.2, *Differentiated Instruction* 8.7.9

Assess

Resources for page 202

- Selection Quick Check, p. 14
- Selection and Unit Assessment, p. 16
- ExamView Assessment Suite
- Interactive Tutor: Self-Assessment

Students can respond to the *After You Read* items in their Learner's Notebooks or on a separate sheet of paper.

Answering the BIG Question

1. Possible response: The journey is more important because it teaches the samurai a lesson.
2. They couldn't ride their horses safely into the crowd, and they didn't want to walk because the destination was far away.
3. Responses will vary.

Critical Thinking

4. Possible response: They get very sick, but must remain inside the cart anyway. They are also shamed when Kintoki's sister laughs at them.
5. Possible response: The samurai's illness is a fitting punishment for their pride and laziness.
6. Possible response: The situation is funny because brave samurai cannot endure the transportation designed for "delicate" noblewomen.

After You Read

The Oxcart

Answering the BIG Question

1. Was the samurai's destination an important part of the story? Why or why not?
2. **Recall** Why did the samurai decide to ride in an oxcart?
   TIP **Right There** You will find this information in the story.
3. **Summarize** In a few sentences sum up what happens in the story.
   TIP **Think and Search** You will find the answer in the story but not all in one place.

Critical Thinking

4 **Analyze** How are the samurai punished for breaking the rules of their society?
   TIP **Author and Me** To answer the question, combine your understanding of the story with your own knowledge and experience.
5. **Evaluate** In your opinion, does the samurai's punishment fit the "crime" the samurai committed? Explain why or why not.
   TIP **Author and Me** To answer the question, combine your understanding of the story with your own knowledge and experience.
6. **Infer** Why would people think it was funny for the samurai to be sick?
   TIP **Author and Me** To answer the question, combine your understanding of the story with your own knowledge and experience.

Talk About Your Reading

Interview Get together with another student and pretend one of you is a journalist and the other one is one of the samurai in the story. The journalist should interview the samurai about his ride in the oxcart and things he learned from the experience. Be sure to ask *Who, What, When, Where, How,* and *Why* questions. Here are some examples:

- Who were your traveling companions on your journey?
- What was the purpose of your journey?
- Where did you journey?

Jot down your questions and answers in your Learner's Notebook.

Indiana English/Language Arts Academic Standards
(pp. 202–203)

8.3 Comprehension and Analysis of Literary Text Respond to grade-level-appropriate literature... **8.7.11 Listening and Speaking** Deliver oral responses to literature... **8.3.2** Evaluate the structural elements of plot... **8.2 Comprehension and Analysis (Focus on Informational Text)** Develop [reading] strategies... **8.2.9** Make reasonable statements and draw conclusions... **8.6 English Language Conventions**

For a complete description of the standards, see p. IN 11.

Talk About Your Reading

Sample interview:

Journalist: Who were your traveling companions?
Hidemichi: Suetake and Kintoki.
Journalist: Where were you going?
Hidemichi: To the fair.
Journalist: What was the ride like?
Hidemichi: It was terrible. We all got very sick and had to stay, enclosed, in our own vomit.
Journalist: What did you learn from the experience?
Hidemichi: We learned not to break the rules. We also learned that noblewomen are much stronger than they look!

Skills Review

Key Reading Skill: Making Inferences

7. What did society in Old Japan expect of samurai? Write two rules that explain how samurai were supposed to behave. Support each rule with an example or other evidence from the story.

Key Literary Element: Plot

8. The pyramid diagram below shows the relationship among the parts of a plot. Copy the diagram and complete it by taking notes on what happens in each part of the story's plot.

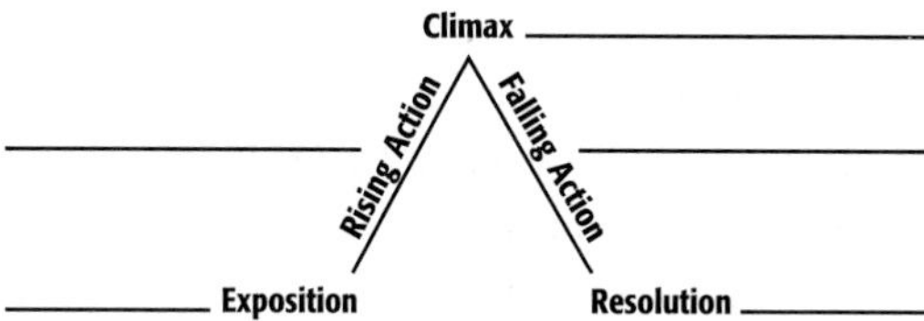

Reviewing Skills: Setting a Purpose for Reading

9. Read your Learner's Notebook notes about what you expected to learn from reading the story. Did you learn what you expected to learn? Explain.

Vocabulary Check

Answer *true* or *false* to each statement.

10. Soldiers marching in formation are an example of a **procession.**
11. A **lurching** rollercoaster car would jerk from side to side.
12. **Elegant** clothes are ugly and in bad taste.
13. A person who is **distinguished** is looked down upon by others.
14. **English Language Coach** While reading "The Oxcart," you analyzed the compound word *seasick*. Now apply what you learned. Define each of the following similar compound words:

• heartsick • carsick

Grammar Link: Articles and Demonstrative Adjectives

The adjectives *a, an,* and *the* are **articles.** Use the **definite article** *the* when writing about a specific person, place, thing, feeling or idea. Use the **indefinite articles** *a* and *an* with general nouns.

- **General:** I want to buy a book. *(Any book will do.)*
- **Specific:** The book I want is at the mall. *(The speaker wants a particular book.)*

Watch Out! Do not confuse *a* and *an*. The word *an* goes with a noun that begins with a vowel sound. *A* goes with a noun that begins with a consonant sound.

- an egg • an hour (silent *h*) • a cottage

Demonstrative adjectives describe nouns by answering the question *which one*? or *which ones*?

Use the demonstratives *this* and *these* to refer to nearby people, places, and things. *This* is singular. *These* is plural. Use the demonstratives *that* and *those* to refer to people, places, and things that are farther away. *That* is singular. *Those* is plural.

Near: Do this one. / These bugs are cute.
Far away: I saw that movie. / I met those girls.

Grammar Practice

Copy the words below on another sheet of paper. Add an article or demonstrative adjective in front of each word. Use a different article or demonstrative adjective for each.

- **ant**
- **months**
- **honor**
- **idea**

Web Activities For eFlashcards, Selection Quick Checks, and other Web activities, go to www.glencoe.com.

Vocabulary Check

10. True
11. True
12. False
13. False

English Language Coach

14. heartsick: sick at heart, or perhaps brokenhearted

    carsick: made sick by the motion of a car

Grammar Link: Articles and Demonstrative Adjectives

Grammar Practice

Possible responses:

the ant	an honor
those months	this idea

Skills Review

Key Reading Skill: Making Inferences

7. Possible response: Society expected samurai to be brave (the three samurai fought their enemies). Samurai were to behave differently from commoners. (They couldn't walk among common peasants).

Key Literary Element: Plot

8. **Exposition:** The samurai want to go to the festival.

   Rising Action: The samurai choose to travel in an oxcart.

   Climax: Though the samurai get ill, they cannot leave the oxcart.

   Falling Action: The samurai's servant helps them, and the samurai walk back home. They are teased for their weakness.

   Resolution: The samurai lead honorable lives, but they never again ride in an oxcart.

Reviewing Skills: Setting a Purpose for Reading

9. Responses will vary.

Close

Ask students to think about uncomfortable journeys and what they can teach us about ourselves. Ask: If we always travel in comfort, are we likely to learn as much? Have students to explain their answers.

Indiana English/Language Arts Academic Standards
SE: 8.2, 8.2.9, 8.3, 8.3.2, 8.6, 8.7.11

Predicting

Teaching Students to Predict

Why Is It Important?

- Predicting outcomes is one of the many kinds of inferences good readers make.
- Students who are actively engaged in the text will find it helpful to stop and make predictions. Checking their predictions against the selection will help their reading and thinking skills and maintain their interest in the text.
- Making predictions and checking them against further reading will confirm a student's understanding of the text or alert the student to areas that need to be reexamined.

How to Help Students Get It

- Begin by activating prior knowledge. Some predictions can be made before viewing the body of the text, based on text features such as title, headers, or graphics.
- As students read, prompt them to predict what happens next, and ask what they base the predictions on. Later, have them adjust their predictions as further information is revealed.

Reading to Answer the Big Question

The Snake Chief retold by Kathleen Arnott
This South African folktale chronicles the journeys of two sisters, each of whom travels to another village to wed the chief. The first sister rejects the advice of her father and everyone she meets along the way; her arrogance brings her to a bad end. The second sister humbly accepts all of the wisdom offered; she successfully completes the journey and breaks an evil spell on the chief, enabling him to marry her.

from *Harriet Tubman: Conductor on the Underground Railroad*
by Ann Petry
In this account of one of Harriet Tubman's many journeys north on the Underground Railway, she and her eleven companions must walk from Maryland to Canada in the coldest part of winter. Tubman encourages the group by telling stories of successful journeys. With Harriet's leadership and the help of friends, they finally arrive and learn to survive in Canada.

Workshop Resources

Pacing (Days) Standard	Block	Lesson	Student Materials	Teacher Resources
1	1/2	Key Skill Lesson: Predicting	Key Reading Skills Practice, p. 22 English Language Coach Review, p. 42	Bellringer Options Transparencies –Daily Language Practice 16 Read Aloud, Think Aloud Transparencies –Key Reading Skills 17 Presentation Plus!
1	1	"The Snake Chief"	Glencoe Online Unit Vocabulary Review, p. 40 Academic Vocabulary Review, p. 43 English Language Coach Active Reading Graphic Organizer, p. 24 Literary Analysis, p. 23 StudentWorks Plus™ Online Student Edition Literature Classics Selection and Unit Assessments, p. 17	Literary and Text Analysis Transparencies 9 Puzzlemaker Skill Level Up!™ A Language Arts Game BookLink 3 Assessment by Learning Objective (Diagnostic and Formative) Interactive Tutor: Self-Assessment TeacherWorks Plus™
1		from *Harriet Tubman: Conductor on the Underground Railroad*	Glencoe Online Unit Vocabulary Review, p. 40 Academic Vocabulary Review, p. 43 English Language Coach Active Reading Graphic Organizer, p. 26 StudentWorks Plus™ Online Student Edition Literature Classics Selection and Unit Assessments, p. 18	Bellringer Options Transparencies –Selection Focus 6 Literary and Text Analysis Transparencies 50 Puzzlemaker Skill Level Up!™ A Language Arts Game BookLink 3 Assessment by Learning Objective (Diagnostic and Formative) Interactive Tutor: Self-Assessment TeacherWorks Plus™

Keys for Unit Resource

- Blackline Master
- Workbook
- Supplemental Text
- CD-ROM
- DVD
- Transparency
- Web-based
- Fast File

Level Appropriate Code

AS = Activities for all students
AL = Activities for students working above grade level
OL = Activities for students working at grade level
BL = Activities for students working below grade level
EL = Activities for English language learners

Focus

BELLRINGER Options

- Selection Focus Transparencies 6
- Daily Language Practice Transparency 16

Focus Activity **Say:** Do you think that being a good person is generally rewarded in life? Why or why not? *(Responses will vary.)* AS

Teach

R Reading Skill

Predicting **Say:** Think of a time you made a prediction that turned out to be correct. For example, maybe you correctly predicted the final score at the last school football game. What information did you use to help you make your prediction? *(Responses will vary.)* OL

V Vocabulary

Academic Vocabulary **Say:** Look at the word *predicting* at the bottom of the page. Notice that it has the prefix *pre-*, which means "before." How does this prefix help you understand the meaning of the word? *(Possible response: Predicting means making a guess about something before it happens.)* AL

READING WORKSHOP 3

Skills Focus

You will practice using these skills when you read the following selections:

- "The Snake Chief," p. 208
- from *Harriet Tubman: Conductor on the Underground Railroad* p. 220

Reading

- Predicting

Literature

- Identifying and analyzing conflicts
- Analyzing author's style

Vocabulary

- Classifying words to expand vocabulary
- Academic Vocabulary: *predicting*

Writing/Grammar

- Identifying and correcting double negatives
- Identifying and correcting dangling and misplaced modifiers

Indiana English/Language Arts Academic Standards (pp. 204–205)

8.2 Comprehension and Analysis (Focus on Informational Text) Develop [reading] strategies...making predictions...

For a complete description of the standards, see p. IN 11.

Skill Lesson

Predicting

Learn It!

What Is It? **Predicting** is making an educated guess about what will happen. You make predictions every day. For example, if you say that a ballplayer will win the game with a home run in the ninth inning, you are predicting, or guessing beforehand, how the game will end.

R To predict when you're reading a story, you think about the events and details you've read about so far. Then you use them as clues to guess what might happen next. Once you make a prediction, you read on to see if you guessed right or whether the author surprises you.

To make good predictions:

- Pay attention to the details in the story.
- Use what you already know.

Analyzing Cartoons
What clues in Thomas's baby picture lead you to predict that he may become a circus performer?

Academic Vocabulary

V **predicting** (pree DIKT ing) *n.* using clues to guess what will happen

Additional Support

English Language Coach

Building Cultural Background
Explain to students that the woman in the cartoon notes that Thomas is eighteen because in the United States, eighteen years (not months) is commonly considered the age of adulthood. When people turn eighteen, they generally assume certain responsibilities of adulthood (such as voting), as well as the consequences of adult behavior (such as being tried as an adult in a court). However, the age at which people are considered adults varies in different countries. For example, the voting age is eighteen in the United States, Australia, and China, twenty in Cameroon, and twenty-one in Fiji. Ask students to name the age of adulthood in their countries of origin. EL

Why Is It Important? Predicting gives you a reason to read and helps you get involved in your reading. For example, when you first start reading a story, you might predict what will happen next. The fun part is reading on to see whether your prediction comes true! As you read, adjust or change your predictions if they don't fit what you learn.

Study Central Visit www.glencoe.com and click on Study Central to review predicting.

How Do I Do It? Think about the characteristics of the genre you're reading. For example, if you're reading a folktale, think about the kinds of characters, conflicts, and plots you usually find in folktales. Also look for patterns, or repeated ideas, as you read. The patterns and the genre characteristics are clues that will help you make good predictions. To see how a student made predictions using clues, read the model below. R

Once upon a time a beautiful maiden named Grace lived near a forest. Every day she walked through the woods to see the creatures and smell the flowers. She knew every animal and plant so well they were like family. Then one day a mysterious new plant appeared. Grace was strangely drawn to its velvety black flowers and blood-red thorns. She wanted to bring some flowers home, but she was afraid. The plant smelled so strange!

"Once upon a time" tells me this is a folktale. It also tells me this is the beginning of the tale. That's when the characters, setting, and situation are usually introduced. Since the mysterious plant is described at the beginning, it must have something to do with the situation. I predict that Grace will pick the flowers and that something bad will happen as a result. I think something bad will happen because if it didn't there wouldn't be any conflict.

Practice It!

Do you agree with the student's prediction? If so, predict what bad thing will happen in the folktale. If not, predict what will happen instead. Give reasons for your prediction.

Use It!

As you read "The Snake Chief" and from *Harriet Tubman*, make predictions about what will happen.

Teach

Study Central Have students access the Web site to review predicting and to complete a related activity.

R Reading Skill

Predicting Say: The endings of folktales can be easy to predict because there are similar patterns that show up in many folktales and legends. What are some patterns you've found so far in the stories in this unit? *(Possible response: Evil is punished, and good is rewarded.)* OL

Resources for page 205

- Use Key Reading Skills Transparency 17 in *Read Aloud, Think Aloud* to help students practice predicting.

Reading in the Real World

Career Give students the following list of careers and ask them how they involve making predictions:

- Meteorologists—Use data and prior knowledge to predict weather patterns.
- Designers—Predict trends in fashion and living styles.
- Business owners—Use sales data to predict their quarterly or yearly profits.
- Economists—Study a variety of factors to predict short-term and long-term economic trends. OL

Indiana English/Language Arts Academic Standards
SE: 8.2
TWE: *English Language Coach* 8.2, *Reading in the Real World* 8.2

Teach

More About the Author

Kathleen Arnott is part of a literary movement aimed at popularizing African folktales. Her husband, David W. Arnott, is an expert in African folklore. Together, they have worked to collect and retell African folktales.

V Vocabulary

See, Say, Write **Say:** One useful way to learn new vocabulary words is the "see, say, write" method. When you see an unfamiliar vocabulary word, follow these three steps: 1) look at the word; 2) say the word aloud; 3) write the word. After you perform the steps several times, add the definition of the word. EL BL

Before You Read

The Snake Chief

Meet the Author

Kathleen Arnott was born in England in 1914. She taught elementary school in Beckingham, Kent, England, and later in Nigeria. Arnott first started writing fiction for African children when she discovered that her students and other children in local schools had no Nigerian storybooks. When she returned to England, Arnott continued to write, alternating between writing more fiction for African children and retelling African folktales for British and American children.

Author Search For more about Kathleen Arnott, go to www.glencoe.com.

Indiana English/Language Arts Academic Standards (pp. 206–215)

8.1 Word Recognition, Fluency, and Vocabulary Development Determine the meaning of words... **8.2 Comprehension and Analysis (Focus on Informational Text)** Develop [reading] strategies...making predictions... **8.3.2** Evaluate...the way in which conflicts are addressed and resolved.

For a complete description of the standards, see p. IN 11.

Vocabulary Preview

induce (in DOOS) *v.* convince to do something; influence **(p. 209)** *Even a high salary would not induce the lazy man to work.*

quavered (KWAY vurd) *v.* spoke in a shaky or trembling voice; form of the verb *quaver* **(p. 211)** *"I feel ill," the old woman quavered.*

incompetence (in KOM puh tuns) *n.* lack of ability or skill **(p. 212)** *Her failure to make good bread was a sign of her incompetence.*

reluctantly (ree LUK tunt lee) *adv.* against one's wishes **(p. 213)** *She reluctantly agreed to marry, although she thought she was too young.*

V

Write to Learn In your Learner's Notebook, write a definition in your own words for each of the vocabulary words.

English Language Coach

Building Vocabulary: Classification Charts A useful way to build your vocabulary is to make classification charts. These charts can help you remember words and their definitions by putting words that belong together into groups. For example, you might group *quavered* with other words that describe how voices may sound. All the words on the chart below are from "The Snake Chief."

Descriptions of Voices	
quavered	spoke in a shaky or trembling voice
screeched	cried out in a high, piercing voice
hissed	spat out words in an angry voice

As the different definitions show, the words are *not* synonyms, because they have different meanings. Yet they belong together because they all are ways of using your voice.

Partner Work Copy the classification chart on another sheet of paper. With a classmate, add two or three other words that describe how someone's voice might sound.

Additional Support

Author Search To expand students' appreciation of Kathleen Arnott, have them access the Web site for additional information and resources.

Literature Focus Lesson

Folktales In many folktales, one or more characters offer advice that the main character chooses to ignore. That character's failure to follow the advice usually results in a discovery or a lesson learned. Ask students to note what advice the characters in "The Snake Chief" get. Who chooses to ignore the advice? Who doesn't? What lesson is learned as a result of a character's failure to follow advice? OL

Skills Preview

Key Reading Skill: Predicting

"The Snake Chief" is a folktale about two sisters. One of them is stubborn, conceited, and rude. The other is gentle, courteous, and kind. Think about what you have learned about folktales and the characters in them. What do you think might happen to each sister?

Whole Class Discussion As a class, predict what will happen to each sister and why.

Key Literary Element: Conflict

Conflict is a struggle between opposing forces in a story or play.

- **External conflict** occurs when a main character, or protagonist, clashes with an outside force, or antagonist. The force might be another character, society, fate, or a natural event, such as a tornado. L
- An **internal conflict** is a psychological or emotional struggle that takes place within a character. External conflicts often cause internal conflicts. For example, a character who continually argues with his parents (external conflict) may wonder if he's doing the right thing (internal conflict).
- To find the conflicts in "The Snake Chief," ask yourself questions like these: *With whom or what do the characters clash? Does this struggle cause psychological or emotional upset? If so, how?*

Write to Learn Classify the conflicts listed below. Which are external? Internal? Why? Jot down your thoughts in your Learner's Notebook.

- playing an opposing baseball team
- making a tough decision
- wanting to spend your money or to save it
- battling a storm while on a boat at sea

Interactive Literary Elements Handbook
To review or learn more about the literary elements, go to www.glencoe.com.

Get Ready to Read

Connect to the Reading

Think about a time when people tried to give you good advice, but you refused to take it.

Write to Learn In a few sentences sum up what the situation was, whose advice you ignored, and how the situation turned out.

Build Background

"The Snake Chief" is a folktale that was first told by the Xhosa (KO suh), a group of South African tribes.

Traditionally, the typical Xhosa village was close knit. Relatives lived in the same small, circular hut or built huts near each other. The cooking areas were outside the huts, making it easy and natural to share food. Cooking over open fires in cast-iron pots, Xhosa women welcomed their neighbors to sample their cooking. The Xhosa believed that it was important for people to cooperate, share, and help one another. C

Storytelling was an important part of Xhosa life. Through stories, older members of the village taught the kids what their history was, what the Xhosa community valued most in life, and how to behave in ways that were true to Xhosa values. As you read "The Snake Chief," think about the values the story might have taught to kids.

Set Purposes for Reading

BIG Question Read "The Snake Chief" to find out what journeys lie ahead for two sisters—and where their journeys will take them.

Set Your Own Purpose What else would you like to learn from the story to help you answer the Big Question? Write your own purpose on the "Snake Chief" flap of Foldable 2.

Keep Moving

Use these skills as you read the following selection.

Teach

L Literary Element

Conflict **Ask:** What are some typical examples of external conflicts that teenagers face? *(Possible responses: pressure from friends about dating and other social habits; disagreements with parents about curfews; academic and athletic competition)* **Ask:** What are some typical examples of internal conflicts that teenagers face? *(Possible responses: wanting to be independent, low self-esteem)* AS

C Critical Thinking

Comprehension **Ask:** According to the Build Background note, for what three reasons did older Xhosa villagers tell stories? *(to teach kids history, values, and good behavior)* BL

Interactive Literary Elements Handbook Have students access the Web site to improve their understanding of conflict.

Reading in the Real World

Citizenship Have students brainstorm ways in which the local community offers to help teenagers cope with both external and internal conflicts. If students do not come up with these ideas on their own, discuss the availability of guidance counselors, teen centers, support groups, telephone hotlines, and other resources that may be available in your community. Finally, have students suggest additional actions they can take to help their peers cope with typical external and internal conflicts. OL

Indiana English/Language Arts Academic Standards
SE: 8.1, 8.2, 8.3.2
TWE: *Literature Focus Lesson* 8.3, *Reading in the Real World* 8.2

Teach

R1 Reading Skill

Predicting **Ask:** From reading the title, what is one prediction that you can make about the chief? *(Students may suggest that the chief is an actual snake, or a snakelike person, mean and conniving.)* OL

C Critical Thinking

Comprehension **Ask:** What do you learn about women and marriage in the father's village? *(Women marry at a particular age. They do not choose their own husbands.)* OL

R2 Reading Skill

Predicting **Ask:** From reading the first page, what can you predict about the conflict in this story? *(Possible answer: There will be a conflict between the father and his daughters.)* OL

Readability Scores
Dale-Chall: 4.6
DRP: 52
Lexile: 1030

READING WORKSHOP 3

The Snake Chief

retold by Kathleen Arnott

There were once two sisters who lived in a village beside a river. When they were old enough to be married, their father looked around for suitors,[1] but alas, none came, so he decided he must visit other villages and let it be known that he had two daughters ready to be wed.

One day, he took his small canoe and crossed the big river. Then he walked along a path until he came to a village. It appeared to be a happy place and the people greeted him kindly.

'Welcome!' they cried 'What news have you brought?'

'I have no news of importance,' he replied. 'Have you?'

'Our chief is looking for a wife,' the people replied, 'otherwise nothing we can think of is worth repeating.' 1

Now the man had found out what he wanted to know, and he told the people that he would send a wife for the chief the next day.

He re-crossed the river and went to his house, smiling contentedly. When his daughters came back from their work in the fields he called them and said:

'At last I have found a man who is worthy to be the husband of one of my daughters. The chief in the village across the water is looking for a wife. Which of you shall I send?'

Practice the Skills

1 Key Reading Skill

Predicting Think about what you've read about the father and his daughters. What do you think will happen next?

1. ***Suitors*** are men who wish to marry.

Additional Support

Differentiated Instruction

Research Project and Group Discussion Tell students that throughout history, and in some cultures today, parents chose the person their children would marry. Have students look online to see which cultures still have arranged marriages. Then ask students to form groups and discuss what this might be like. What might be the benefits and disadvantages of arranged marriages? Have students present the ideas to the class. OL

The elder[2] daughter said quickly: 'I shall go, of course, since I am the elder.'

'Very well,' replied the man. 'I shall call all my friends and bid the drummers lead you to your husband's home.'

'Indeed you will not,' said the girl haughtily. 'When I go to the home of my husband, I shall go alone.'

Now in that part of Africa it was unheard of for a bride to go to her wedding without a host of friends and relations all singing and dancing for joy. So the father was astonished when his daughter said she would go alone, even though he knew she had been proud and headstrong from childhood.

'But, my daughter,' he **pleaded**, 'no woman ever goes alone to her marriage. It is not the custom.' **2** EL

'Then I shall start a new custom,' said the girl. 'Unless I go alone, I shall not go at all.'

At last the father, realizing that no amount of persuasion would **induce** the girl to change her mind, agreed to her going alone, and early the next morning she set out. He took her across the river and pointed out the way, then returned home unhappily. **3** L

The girl began her journey without looking back and after a little while she met a mouse on the path. It stood up on its hind-legs, and rubbing its two front paws together, asked politely:

'Would you like me to show you the way to the chief's village?'

The girl scarcely stopped walking and almost trod on the mouse as she replied:

'Get out of my sight! I want no help from you.'

Then she continued on her way while the mouse screeched after her:

'Bad luck to you!'

Homeward Bound, 2004. Tilly Willis. Oil on canvas. Private Collection.

Analyzing the Painting How does this painting help you visualize the story's setting?

2. ***Elder*** means older.

Vocabulary

induce (in DOOS) *v.* convince to do something; influence

Practice the Skills

2 English Language Coach

Classification Charts The word **pleaded** describes how the father's voice sounds when he talks to his daughter. If you don't know what the word means, use context clues to figure out the definition or look it up. Add the word and definition to the classification chart you made earlier.

3 Key Literary Element

Conflict The unhappy father has an internal conflict. What external conflict with his daughter causes him to feel unhappy?

Teach

EL Language Coach

Context Clues Help students learn how to use context clues to determine meaning.
Ask: How do you think the father feels when he learns that his daughter does not wish to follow the African custom? *(Students may say that he feels upset, disappointed, or even desperate.)* **Ask:** On the basis of your answer, what do you think *pleaded* means? *(begged or appealed)* OL

L Literary Element

Conflict **Say:** Simply being unhappy is not an internal conflict. An internal conflict is a struggle that takes place between two forces inside a character's mind. What is the father's internal conflict? *(Possible response: The father wants his daughter to be happy, but he also wants her to follow tradition. He must decide whether to allow her to ignore tradition and travel to the village alone.)* OL

Reading Fluency

Build Fluency Have students find a quiet place to practice reading the text on this page aloud. Encourage students to identify words and phrases that are unfamiliar and practice saying them aloud until they know them well. After they have read through the text several times, have students begin changing their tone of voice when reading the dialogue. As students grow more confident, encourage them to use different voices for the elder daughter, the father, and the mouse. EL BL

Indiana English/Language Arts Academic Standards
SE: 8.1, 8.2, 8.3.2
TWE: *Differentiated Instruction* 8.4.4, *Reading Fluency* 8.7.5

Teach

R Reading Skill

Predicting Say: The author gives a major clue about what will happen to the sister. Think about what the mouse, the frog, and the boy all say to the girl. What can you predict will happen to her? Why will it happen? *(Possible response: She will have bad luck because she has been mean to all three of them.)* OL

L Literary Element

Conflict Ask: What causes all of the conflicts the girl has on her journey? *(her meanness and arrogance)* BL Based on this fact, how do you think she will treat the old woman? *(Possible response: She'll treat her with disrespect. She probably won't follow her advice.)* OL

A little further on the girl met a frog, sitting on a stone at the side of the path.

'Would you like me to show you the way?' he croaked.

'Don't you speak to me!' answered the girl, tipping the frog off the stone with her foot. 'I am going to be a chief's wife and am far too important to have anything to do with a mere frog.'

'Bad luck to you then,' croaked the frog, as he picked himself up from where he had fallen and jumped off into the bush.

Soon after this the girl began to feel tired and she sat down under a tree to rest. In the distance she could hear goats bleating[3] and presently a herd of them passed by, driven by a little boy.

'Greetings, sister,' he said politely. 'Are you going on a long journey?'

'What business is that of yours?' demanded the girl.

'I thought you might be carrying food with you,' replied the boy, 'and I hoped you might give me something to eat for I am so hungry.' 4

'I have no food,' said the girl, 'and even if I had I should not dream of giving any to you.'

The boy looked disappointed and hurried after his goats, turning back to say over his shoulder:

'Bad luck to you then.'

Presently the girl got to her feet and continued her journey. Suddenly she found herself face to face with a very old woman.

'Greetings, my daughter,' she said to the girl. 'Let me give you some advice.

'You will come to some trees which will laugh at you, but do not laugh back at them.

'You will find a bag of thick, curdled[4] milk, but do not on any account drink it.

'You will meet a man who carries his head under his arm, but you must not drink water if he offers you any.'

3. ***Bleating*** is a sound that goats make, similar to whining or crying.

4. ***Curdled milk*** is similar to yogurt.

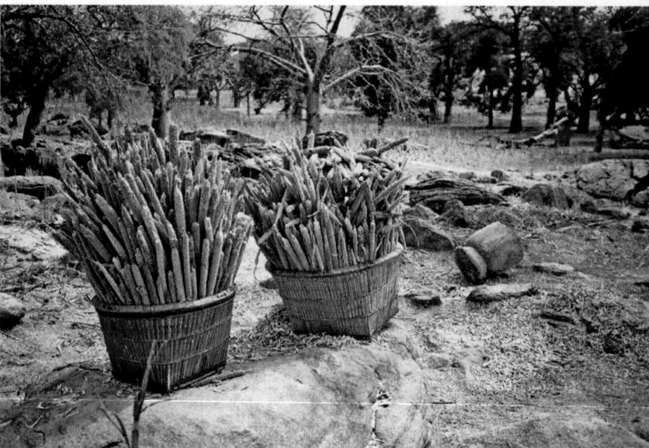

Analyzing the Photo These hand-woven baskets contain millet, a staple food for many African people. What aspect(s) of village life might this image represent?

Practice the Skills

4 Key Reading Skill

Predicting Do you think the daughter will share her food with the hungry boy? Think about

- how she treated her father
- how she treated the mouse
- how she treated the frog

Additional Support

Differentiated Instruction

Advice Column Have students choose a character in the story and write a letter to a newspaper from that character's perspective, asking for advice. For example, students may choose to write a letter from the father, asking for advice about how to handle his internal conflict about his elder daughter. Then, have students exchange letters and compose responses in the style of an advice columnist. Bring in a copy of the advice column from your local newspaper to use as a model, and encourage students to think of creative or humorous ways to sign and address their letters. OL

'Be quiet, you ugly old thing!' exclaimed the girl, pushing the old woman aside. 'If I want any advice from you, I'll ask for it.'

'You will have bad luck if you don't listen to me,' **quavered** the old woman, but the girl took no notice and went on her way.

Sure enough she soon came to a clump of trees which began to laugh loudly as she approached them.

'Stop laughing at me,' she **commanded**, and when they did not, she laughed noisily at them in return as she passed them by. **5** EL

A little further on, she saw a bag made from a whole goatskin, lying at her feet. On picking it up, she discovered it was full of curdled milk and since this was something she was particularly fond of, she drank it with relish, exclaiming:

'How lucky I found this! I was getting so thirsty with such a long journey.'

Then she threw the bag into the bush and continued on her way. As she walked through a shady grove, she was a little taken aback at the strange sight of a man coming towards her, carrying his head under one arm. The eyes in the head looked at her and the mouth spoke:

'Would you like some water to drink, my daughter?' it said, and the hand that was not carrying the head held out a calabash[5] of water to the girl. **6**

She was not really thirsty but decided to taste the water and see whether it was sweet, so she took a sip, found it delicious and drank the whole calabash full. Then she continued, without a word of thanks to the strange creature.

As she turned the next bend in the path, she saw in the distance the village she was seeking and knew that her journey was almost over. She had to cross a small stream and found a girl bending there, filling her water-pot.

She was about to pass on when the village girl greeted her and asked:

'Where are you going, pray?'

With scarcely a glance at her questioner she replied:

5. A *calabash* is a dried gourd that is used as a container.

Vocabulary

quavered (KWAY vurd) *v.* spoke in a shaky or trembling voice

Practice the Skills

5 English Language Coach

Classification Charts How do you think a voice sounds when it has **commanded** something? Add the word to your classification chart.

6 Key Reading Skill

Predicting Do you think the daughter will go against the old woman's advice and drink the water? Think about

- whether she followed her father's advice
- how she treated the old woman
- whether she followed the other advice the old woman gave her

R

Teach

EL Language Coach

Context Clues Ask: How would you describe the elder daughter's personality? ***(bossy, rude, and aggressive)*** **Ask:** What tone do you think she uses when she says, "Stop laughing at me"? ***(Students may say that she says it loudly and aggressively.)*** **Ask:** On the basis of your answers, what do you think *commanded* means? ***(Possible responses: gave an order; spoke in a strong or powerful way)*** EL BL

R Reading Skill

Predicting Say: The daughter has been mean to everyone she has encountered. How do you think she will behave when she meets her potential husband? Explain your prediction. ***(Some students might think the daughter will be mean to him, too. Others might believe she will be nice to her potential husband because she wants him to marry her.)*** OL

English Language Coach

Old Words Tell students that "Where are you going, pray?" is an example of antiquated, or outdated, language. Explain that the word "pray" is associated with asking or requesting because prayer is partly about seeking help. Although people no longer speak this way, the word *pray* used to be included in questions, as it is in the village girl's question. Be sure to explain that the word "pray" does not add to or change the meaning of the sentence. The village girl is simply asking, "Where are you going?" AS

Indiana English/Language Arts Academic Standards
SE: 8.1, 8.2
TWE: *Differentiated Instruction* 8.5, *English Language Coach* 8.1.2

Teach

R Reading Skill

Predicting Say: Remember that folktales often end in a predictable way. However, some folktales do not follow the expected pattern. Explain whether you think the daughter's expectations will come true and why. *(Possible response: The daughter has not treated others well. She will have bad luck and will not marry the chief.)* AL

L Literary Element

Conflict Ask: Why do you think the daughter does not take the time to grind the corn properly? How do you think this will add to the conflict in the story? *(Students may say that she is impatient. There will be some consequence to the daughter's not grinding the corn properly.)* AL

'I am going to that village to marry a chief. You have no right to speak to me, for I am older than you and far more important.'

Now the younger girl was the chief's sister, but she did not boast about this. She merely said:

'Let me give you some advice. Do not enter the village from this side. It is unlucky to do so. Go right round past those tall trees and enter it on the far side.'

The girl took no notice at all but just walked on to the nearest entrance with her head in the air. When she arrived, the women crowded round her to find out who she was and what she wanted.

'I have come to marry your chief,' she explained. 'Get away, and let me rest.' 7

'How can you be a bride if you come alone?' they asked. 'Where is the bridal procession, and are there no drummers with you?'

The girl did not answer, but she sat down in the shade of a hut to rest her aching legs.

Presently some of the older women came over to her.

'If you are to be the wife of our chief,' they said, 'then you must prepare his supper, as all good wives do.'

The girl realized that this was true, so she asked:

'And from where shall I get the millet to cook my husband's supper?'

They gave her some millet and told her to grind it, showing her where the grinding-stones were, but unlike most women, she only ground the corn for a very short time, so that the flour was coarse and gritty. Then she made some bread, and when the other women saw it, they went away together and laughed at her **incompetence.**

Visual Vocabulary
Millet is a grass that produces seeds that can be eaten or crushed into flour.

As the sun set, a mighty wind blew up. The roof of the hut shook and shivered and the girl crouched against the mud walls in fear. But worse was to come. A huge snake with five heads suddenly appeared, and coiling itself up at the door of the hut, told her to bring it the supper she had cooked.

Vocabulary

incompetence (in KOM puh tuns) *n.* lack of ability or skill

Practice the Skills

7 Key Reading Skill

Predicting The daughter assumes she will become the chief's wife. Do you think she will? Why or why not?

Additional Support

Differentiated Instruction

Acting Out Expressions Have students reread the paragraph in which the daughter walks "with her head in the air." Invite a volunteer to demonstrate this in front of the class and then discuss what attitude it conveys. Encourage students to look up the meanings of other expressions that involve facial features, such as "turning your nose up," "having your nose in a book," and "keeping an eye on your valuables." For each expression, have students act out the movement in a small group and discuss the implied meaning of the expression. EL BL

Analyzing the Photo In the story, members of a community keep old traditions alive. How might the people in this photo be doing the same thing?

'Did you not know that I am the chief?' asked the snake, as it began to eat the bread. Then it uttered a fearful scream, spat the food from its mouth and hissed:

'This supper is so badly cooked, I refuse to have you for a wife! So I shall slay you!' and with a mighty blow from his tail, he killed her. 8

When the news of her death at last reached her father, he still had not found a husband for his younger daughter, whose name was Mpunzanyana. R1

'Let me go to this chief,' she begged him. 'I am sure I could please him if I tried.'

Rather **reluctantly** the father called together all his relations and friends and asked them to make up a bridal procession for his second daughter. They were all delighted and went away to put on their best clothes, while the father summoned the musicians and drummers who were to lead the way. R2

They set off early in the morning, and crossing the big river, they sang joyfully as they went. They began the long journey along the same little path that the eldest daughter had taken not so long ago, and presently they met a mouse.

'Shall I tell you how to get there?' it asked of Mpunzanyana, as she stopped to avoid treading on it.

Vocabulary

reluctantly (ree LUK tunt lee) *adv.* against one's wishes

Practice the Skills

8 Key Literary Element

Conflict What kind of conflict has just taken place between the chief and the daughter—internal or external? Explain.

READING WORKSHOP 3

Teach

R1 Reading Skill

Review Making Inferences
Ask: Why do you think the second daughter asks to meet the chief? *(Responses will vary. Students may suggest that she wants to restore honor to her family and village and make up for her sister's mistakes.)* AL

R2 Reading Skill

Predicting **Say:** The second daughter starts out her journey with her fellow villagers surrounding her, as tradition calls for. What can you predict about her journey based on this fact? *(Possible response: It will be easier and more pleasant than the older daughter's journey.)* OL

Literature Focus Lesson

Author's Purpose Remind students that many authors have a specific purpose in mind when telling a story. As students learned in the Build Background section on page 207, Xhosa villagers had three purposes for telling stories to children:

- to teach them history
- to teach them village values
- to teach them how to behave properly

Have students form groups to discuss which of the three—history, values, or behavior—kids would learn from hearing this story. Encourage students to share their findings with the class. BL OL

Indiana English/Language Arts Academic Standards
SE: 8.2, 8.3.2
TWE: *Differentiated Instruction* 8.1.1, *Literature Focus Lesson* 8.3.7

Teach

R Reading Skill

Predicting Ask: So far, how has Mpunzanyana behaved differently from her sister? *(Mpunzanyana treats the animals and people she meets on her journey with respect and follows their advice.)* **BL**
Ask: What can you predict about her journey from her behavior? *(You can predict her journey will end successfully.)* **OL**

C Critical Thinking

Analysis Ask: If stories like this one were meant to teach the values of Xhosa community, how might Xhosa villagers believe you can avoid conflict? *(Possible response: by being polite, by following others' advice and by being part of the community instead of going it alone)* **AL**

READING WORKSHOP 3

'Thank you very much,' she replied, and listened courteously as the tiny animal told them which path to take.

On they went until they came to a deep valley and found a very old woman sitting beside a tree. The ugly old creature rose shakily to her feet to stand before the girl. Then she said:

'When you come to a place where two paths meet, you must take the little one, not the big one as that is unlucky.'

'Thank you for telling me, grannie,' Mpunzanyana answered. 'I will do as you say and take the little path.'

They journeyed on and on, meeting no one for some time, until suddenly a coney[6] stood on the path in front of them all. Stretching up its head, it looked at the girl and said:

'You are nearly there! But let me give you some advice. Soon you will meet a young girl carrying water from the stream. Mind you speak politely to her.

'When you get to the village they will give you millet to grind for the chief's supper. Make sure you do it properly.

'And finally, when you see your husband, do not be afraid. I beg you, have no fear, or at least, do not show it.' **9**

'Thank you for your advice, little coney,' said the girl. 'I will try to remember it all and do as you say.'

Sure enough, as they turned the last bend in the path, they caught sight of the village, and coming up from the stream they overtook a young girl carrying a pot of water on her head. It was the chief's sister, and she asked:

'Where are you bound for?'

'We are going to this village where I hope to be the chief's bride,' answered Mpunzanyana.

'Let me lead you to the chief's hut,' said the younger girl, 'and do not be afraid when you see him.'

Mpunzanyana followed the girl, and the bridal party followed Mpunzanyana, so that all the people came out of their huts to see what the joyful noise was about. They welcomed the visitors politely and gave them food to eat. Then the chief's mother brought millet to Mpunzanyana and said:

'If you are to be the wife of our chief, then you must prepare his supper, as all good wives do.'

So the girl set to work and ground the millet as finely as she could, then made it into light, delicious bread.

6. A ***coney*** is a type of rabbit.

Practice the Skills

9 Key Reading Skill

R

Predicting There is a pattern in the way the daughter treats animals and people. Based on this pattern, do you think the daughter will follow the coney's advice? Explain.

Additional Support

Differentiated Instruction

Storytelling Traditional African stories were first told orally. Each storyteller had the ability to change elements of the story, including the names of characters and the types of conflicts that they encountered. For example, in this version of the folktale, the snake chief has five heads. Encourage students to consider what they would change about the story if they were to retell it. In particular, have students brainstorm other tests of character as alternatives to baking bread for the snake chief. **AL**

As the sun set, a strong wind arose which shook the house and when Mpunzanyana heard the people saying: 'Here comes our chief,' she began to tremble. Then she remembered what she had been told and even when one of the poles which supported the roof fell to the ground, she did not run outside in a panic but stood quietly waiting for her husband to come home.

She almost cried out when she saw the huge snake, but when it asked her for food, she gave it the bread she had cooked and it ate it with obvious enjoyment.

'This bread is delicious,' said the snake. 'Will you be my wife?'

For one moment, Mpunzanyana was struck dumb, but she smiled bravely when she thought of all the advice she had had, and replied:

'Yes, O chief, I will marry you.'

At her words, the shining snake-skin fell from the chief and he rose up, a tall, handsome man.

'By your brave words, you have broken the spell,' he explained.

That night a feast was begun in the chief's village which lasted for twenty days. Oxen were slaughtered, beer was brewed and all the time the sound of music and drumming made the people's hearts glad.

So Mpunzanyana became the wife of a rich and splendid chief, and in course of time they had many sons, while the village prospered under her husband's wise rule. 10 ❍

Practice the Skills

10 BIG Question

BQ Which daughter do you think learned more from her journey—the older daughter or the younger? Explain. Write your answer on the "Snake Chief" flap of Foldable 2. Your response will help you complete the Unit Challenge later.

Analyzing the Photo How does this photo help you understand the difficulty of Mpunzanyana's task?

Teach

BQ 

Ask: What lesson does the first daughter's journey teach? *(Possible response: It is wise to accept help from others.)* OL

Viewing the Photo

Ask: Is this how you visualize the grinding of millet? Compare and contrast your ideas with the picture. *(Responses will vary.)* OL

Assess

CheckPoint

Use the CheckPoint questions provided on Presentation Plus! to check for comprehension of the selection. These questions can be used with interactive response keypads for immediate student feedback.

Literature Focus Lesson

Symbols In many Western cultures, the snake or serpent is a symbol of evil. This idea is present in the Biblical story of the Garden of Eden, in which a serpent represents Satan and is responsible for bringing temptation into the world. In African culture, the serpent is a symbol of royalty. Although the chief is under a spell, the villagers allow the chief to remain in command in his snake form. It is only when Mpunzanyana agrees to marry the snake chief that his human form is restored. Ask students to find another story that uses symbols for either evil or royalty. Have students share with the class how the symbols are used in the stories they find. OL

Indiana English/Language Arts Academic Standards

SE: 8.2

TWE: *Differentiated Instruction* 8.7.7, *Literature Focus Lesson* 8.3.6

Assess

Resources for page 216

- Selection Quick Check, p. 15
- Selection and Unit Assessment, p. 17
- ExamView Assessment Suite
- Interactive Tutor: Self-Assessment

Students can respond to the *After You Read* items in their Learner's Notebooks or on a separate sheet of paper.

Answering the

1. Responses will vary. Students may suggest that both the journey and the destination are equally important. The second daughter learns to listen to advice during her journey, so she is rewarded when she reaches her destination.
2. She sets out to marry the chief of a neighboring village.
3. The elder daughter is rude and proud. She refuses any help.

Critical Thinking

4. Responses will vary. Students may say that the elder daughter's greatest flaw is her pride.
5. Posssible response: The chief may want to know whether his potential wife is a good cook. This suggests that women in Xhosa society cook and do other household chores.

After You Read | The Snake Chief

Answering the BIG Question

1. How do you think "The Snake Chief" answers the Big Question, "Which is more important, the journey or the destination?" Explain.
2. **Recall** Why does the elder sister set out on a journey?
   TIP **Right There** The answer is in the story.
3. **Summarize** How does the elder sister respond to those who try to help her?
   TIP **Think and Search** The answer is in the story, but it is not all in one place.

Critical Thinking

4. **Analyze** What is the elder sister's greatest weakness or flaw?
   TIP **Author and Me** To answer, think about the story and draw on your knowledge of people.
5. **Infer** Why might a chief want his future wife to first prepare a meal for him? What does this suggest about the role of women in Xhosa society?
   TIP **Author and Me** To answer, think about the story and your prior knowledge.

Write About Your Reading

RAFT Assignment Use the RAFT system to write about "The Snake Chief." A **RAFT** assignment provides four details:

- **R** is for your *role* as a writer—who or what you must pretend to be as you write.
- **A** stands for your *audience*—the person or group who will read what you write.
- **F** means *format*—the form for your writing, such as a letter or a speech.
- **T** means *topic*—what your writing should be about.

Role: the snake chief
Audience: the snake chief's future children
Format: narrative
Topic: Explain how you felt when you first met the person who would become your wife and how you felt about her older sister.

Indiana English/Language Arts Academic Standards (pp. 216–217)

8.3 Comprehension and Analysis of Literary Text Respond to grade-level-appropriate literature... **8.5.7** Write for different purposes... **8.2 Comprehension and Analysis (Focus on Informational Text)** Develop [reading] strategies...making predictions... **8.3.2** Evaluate...the way in which conflicts are addressed and resolved. **8.6 English Language Conventions**

For a complete description of the standards, see p. IN 11.

Write About Your Reading

Possible response:

I am writing this so that you will have a record of what I have learned in this world. Long before you were born, your mother's older sister lost her life because she refused to honor the traditions and advice of those who came before her. Thankfully, this trait was not passed on to your wonderful mother. Your mother knows the value of village traditions. My hope is that you, too, will honor the past as a way of protecting the future.
Your father, the Snake Chief

Skills Review

Key Lesson Skill: Predicting

6. Which of your predictions were right? Which were wrong? For each wrong prediction, figure out why you guessed wrong.

Key Literary Element: Conflict

7. The older daughter has external conflicts with several characters. Look back at the story, and make a list of all the people and animals with whom she clashes.
8. Do you think the older daughter's conflicts with other characters cause internal conflicts for her? Explain, using evidence from the story to back up your opinion.

Vocabulary Check

Choose the best word from the list to complete each sentence below. On a separate piece of paper, rewrite each sentence with the correct word in place.

incompetence
reluctantly
induce
quavered

9. Her ___ as a cook was clear when the Snake Chief spat out her bread.
10. ___, the father agreed to let his younger daughter make the dangerous journey.
11. No amount of persuasion could ___ her to follow the customs of the village.
12. "What was that sound?" the frightened child ___.
13. **Academic Vocabulary** Describe a time when you used *predicting* outside of school. Was your prediction right or wrong?
14. **English Language Coach** Review your classification chart. Choose four words, and use each one in a sentence.

Grammar Link: Double Negatives

Negative words express the idea of "no." Examples of negative words include *not, never, nobody, none, nothing,* and *nowhere.* Two negative words used together in the same sentence create an error called a *double negative.* Avoid using two negative words in the same sentence.

Incorrect: Mpunzanyana didn't have no fear when she faced the snake chief.

Correct: Mpunzanyana didn't have any fear when she faced the snake chief.

Correct: Mpunzanyana had no fear when she faced the snake chief.

Double negatives can make your writing awkward and confusing. Only one negative word is necessary to convey a negative meaning. Correct a sentence that has a double negative by removing one of the negative words or by replacing one of the negative words with an affirmative word, such as *always, anybody, all, any, someone, something,* and *some.*

Grammar Practice

Each sentence below contains a double negative. Underline the word or words in parentheses that best complete each sentence.

15. I didn't see (nothing, anything) that I wanted to buy.
16. I can't find my shoes (nowhere, anywhere).
17. We never have (no, any) good food around here.

Writing Application Look back at the RAFT assignment you wrote. Make sure that you haven't used any double negatives.

Web Activities For eFlashcards, Selection Quick Checks, and other Web activities, go to www.glencoe.com.

READING WORKSHOP 3

Skills Review

Key Lesson Skill: Predicting

6. Responses will vary. Students may have correctly predicted that the elder daughter would have bad luck. They may not have predicted that the younger daughter would marry the Snake Chief because he seemed so evil.

Key Literary Element: Conflict

7. Possible response: Her external conflicts are with her father, the mouse, the frog, the boy, the old woman, the chief's sister, the women in the village, and the chief.
8. Possible response: The elder daughter's external conflicts do not cause internal conflicts because she never questions her own behavior.

Close

Ask students to summarize what they learned from the folktale to answer the Big Question.

Web Activities Have students access the Web site for interactive activities that will help them assess their understanding of the selection.

Vocabulary Check

9. incompetence
10. Reluctantly
11. induce
12. quavered

Academic Vocabulary

13. Responses will vary.

English Language Coach

14. Check students' responses.

Grammar Link: Double Negatives

Grammar Practice

15. anything
16. anywhere
17. any

Indiana English/Language Arts Academic Standards
SE: 8.2, 8.3, 8.3.2, 8.5.7, 8.6

Teach

More About the Author

As a writer, Ann Petry strove to highlight the legacy of black men and women in American history. She said, "Remember for what a long, long time black people have been in this country, have been a part of America: a sturdy, indestructible, wonderful part of America, woven into its heart and into its soul."

V Vocabulary

Quick Pick Have students answer these questions to test their understanding of the vocabulary words. **Ask:** Does someone who has eloquence speak well or stammer? *(speak well)* **Ask:** Does cajoling involve teasing or convincing? *(convincing)* **Ask:** If you disclose a secret, do you keep it or tell it? *(tell it)* OL

Before You Read

from *Harriet Tubman: Conductor on the Underground Railroad*

Ann Petry

Meet the Author

Ann Petry was born on October 12, 1908, in Old Saybrook, Connecticut. She moved to New York City in 1938, determined to become a writer. Petry's novel, *The Street,* was the first novel by an African American to sell more than a million copies. Petry once said, "I hoped that I made [historical characters like Harriet Tubman] come alive, turned them into real people." See page R5 of the Author Files for more on Ann Petry.

Author Search For more about Ann Petry, go to www.glencoe.com.

Indiana English/Language Arts Academic Standards (pp. 218–231)

8.1. Understand...word relationships and origins... **8.2 Comprehension and Analysis (Focus on Informational Text)** Develop [reading] strategies...make predictions... **8.3.6** Identify literary devices... which define a writer's style...

For a complete description of the standards, see p. IN 11.

Vocabulary Preview

V

eloquence (EL uh kwuns) *n.* the ability to speak expressively **(p. 227)** *Frederick Douglass was popular because of his eloquence as a speaker.*

disclose (dis KLOHZ) *v.* to make known; reveal **(p. 227)** *William Still agreed not to disclose the names of the fugitives so they would have a better chance to escape.*

cajoling (kuh JOHL ing) *v.* persuading, especially by using soothing words; coaxing **(p. 228)** *Despite their eagerness to flee, Tubman still had to spend time cajoling the fugitives into cooperation.*

Partner Talk For each vocabulary word, give a definition in your own words. Have your partner use your definition to guess the correct word.

English Language Coach

Building Vocabulary: Old Words and Phrases Even though "Harriet Tubman: Conductor on the Underground Railroad" was written recently, the author uses words and phrases from long ago. The words and phrases help to create the feeling and atmosphere of the time the story took place. Here are some of the old words and phrases that you'll find in the selection.

- a goodly number of: many
- had taken to their heels: had run away
- borne on the wind: carried by the wind
- sold South: sold to owners in the Deep South, where slavery was the most brutal
- in this fashion: in this way

Partner Talk Talk with a classmate about old words and phrases you may know. Often, grandparents and other older relatives use phrases that younger people don't. Can you think of any? You may also know other old words and phrases through things you have read.

Additional Support

Author Search To expand students' appreciation of Ann Petry, have them access the Web site for additional information and resources.

Differentiated Instruction

Writing Activity According to Ann Petry, Harriet Tubman discovered that "freedom meant more than the right to change jobs at will, more than the right to keep the money that one earned." Invite students to write several sentences that begin with the words "Freedom is . . ." Provide students with models such as the following: "Freedom is walking down the street without having to look over your shoulder." Have students transfer their best sentences to a freedom banner you can display in your classroom. OL

Skills Preview

Key Reading Skill: Predicting

The selection you are about to read tells the true story of Harriet Tubman and her role in the underground railroad. Think about other nonfiction stories you have read about people from the past. Recall what you already know about the Underground Railroad. R

Whole Class Discussion As a class, predict what kinds of facts and details you'll find in the selection.

Literary Element: Style

Style is the distinctive way an author writes. Elements of style include word choice, sentence type and length, "sound devices" like repetition, and description. To analyze an author's style, ask yourself questions like these: L

- *Does the author mainly use short, simple words or longer, more difficult words?*
- *Does the author mainly use short, simple sentences or longer, complex ones?*
- *Does the author use repetition or other sound devices?*
- *Does the author use descriptive language?*

Partner Talk With a classmate, use the questions above to compare the style of the two passages below.

- It was cold. Very cold. At 20 degrees below zero, breathing is hard. The ice on a man's mustache grows thicker with every breath.
- How cold it was! Every time the man drew in his breath, icy needles pierced his lungs. When he exhaled, small icy clouds formed. Each breath left its frosty mark as drops of ice on his mustache.

Interactive Literary Elements Handbook
To review or learn more about the literary elements, go to www.glencoe.com.

Get Ready to Read

Connect to the Reading

Recall a time when you were a member of a group. If the group's task was difficult, there probably were times when the group members wanted to give up.

- How did you react when people stopped trying?
- Did you get angry or frustrated?
- Did you find ways to persuade them not to give up?

Write to Learn Write a few sentences about your experiences working in a group.

Build Background

The Underground Railroad wasn't really a railroad, and it wasn't really underground. It was a secret series of travel routes, hiding places, and safe houses where people who were against slavery helped hide people who had escaped from slavery on their way north.

- The people who guided the runaways along the Underground Railroad were called "conductors."
- Most enslaved people hid during the day and traveled during the night to avoid being caught.

Set Purposes for Reading

BIG Question Read the selection from *Harriet Tubman: Conductor on the Underground Railroad* to find out about the long and difficult journey that Harriet Tubman took to bring a group of escapees to freedom.

Set Your Own Purpose What else would you like to learn from the selection to help you answer the Big Question? Write your own purpose on the "Harriet Tubman" flap of Foldable 2.

Keep Moving

Use these skills as you read the following selection.

Teach

R Reading Skill

Predicting Say: Remember to use prior knowledge, or information that you already know, to make predictions. What do you know about how some enslaved people escaped from slavery? *(Students may note that some people escaped alone at night. Others escaped in groups with help from the Underground Railroad.)* AS

L Literary Element

Style Say: Create a chart in your Learner's Notebook to help you keep track of Ann Petry's style in this selection. As you read, fill in the chart with specific examples. Label the columns "Interesting Word Choices and Sentences," "Sound Devices," and "Description." OL

Interactive Literary Elements Handbook Have students access the Web site to improve their understanding of style.

Literature Focus Lesson

Style One way to reinforce the concept of style is to contrast several short pieces of writing. For example, read an excerpt from a document such as an apartment lease or a loan offer. Discuss the use of lengthy sentences and content-specific vocabulary. Contrast the first document with an informal article from a magazine and a piece of nonfiction. Discuss the differences in how the pieces of writing sound. Encourage students to make observations about the effectiveness of the styles in the given selections. OL

Indiana English/Language Arts Academic Standards
SE: 8.1, 8.2, 8.3.6
TWE: *Differentiated Instruction* 8.5.6, *Literature Focus Lesson* 8.3

Teach

L Literary Element

Style **Say:** Petry chooses to begin her story by describing a mysterious man named Moses. She uses words like *fantastic* and *unbelievable* to describe him. What is the effect of these word choices? *(Possible response: It makes Moses sound like a mystical figure who may not even exist.)* AL

EL Language Coach

Old Words **Say:** Use a dictionary to find definitions for the words *plantation, master,* and *overseer.* Remember that this selection is about slavery. Look for definitions that make sense in this context. *(Possible responses:* ***plantation:*** *large farm for growing crops where enslaved laborers worked;* ***master:*** *person who owned the plantation and had power or authority over the people who were enslaved;* ***overseer:*** *person who looked over and directed the work of the people who were enslaved)* EL BL

Readability Scores

Dale-Chall: 5.8

DRP: 57

Lexile: 1050

from HARRIET TUBMAN: *Conductor on the Underground Railroad*

by Ann Petry

Harriet Tubman, 1945. William H. Johnson. Oil on paperboard, 29³/₈ x 23³/₈ in. National Museum of American Art, Washington, DC.

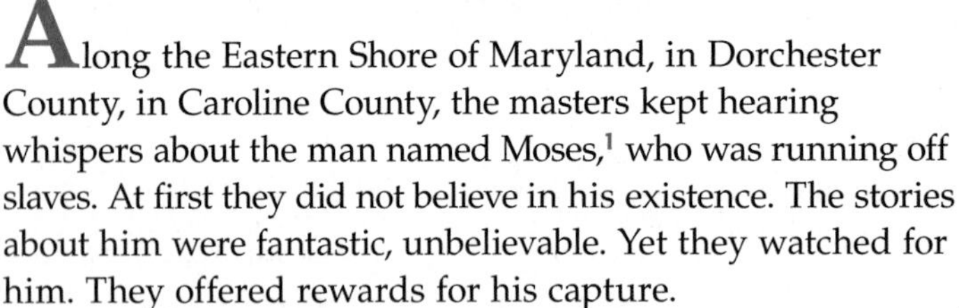

Along the Eastern Shore of Maryland, in Dorchester County, in Caroline County, the masters kept hearing whispers about the man named Moses,[1] who was running off slaves. At first they did not believe in his existence. The stories about him were fantastic, unbelievable. Yet they watched for him. They offered rewards for his capture. L

They never saw him. Now and then they heard whispered rumors to the effect that he was in the neighborhood. The woods were searched. The roads were watched. There was never anything to indicate his whereabouts. But a few days afterward, a goodly number of slaves would be gone from the plantation. Neither the master nor the overseer had heard or seen anything unusual in the quarter.[2] Sometimes one or the other would vaguely remember having heard a whippoorwill call somewhere in the woods, close by, late at night. Though it was the wrong season for whippoorwills. 1 EL

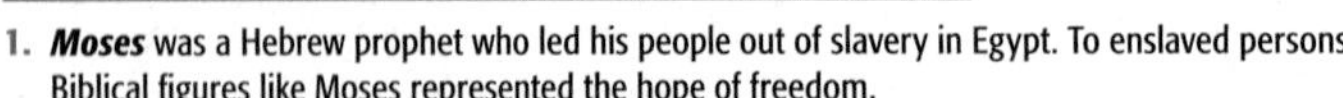

1. ***Moses*** was a Hebrew prophet who led his people out of slavery in Egypt. To enslaved persons, Biblical figures like Moses represented the hope of freedom.
2. Here, ***quarter*** refers to the area in which the enslaved people lived on a farm or plantation.

Practice the Skills

1 Key Reading Skill

Predicting In the context of the story, who do you think Moses will turn out to be? Use these clues to make your prediction:

- The first paragraph says that Moses is someone "who was running off slaves."
- The second paragraph says, "They never saw him."

Additional Support

Differentiated Instruction

Mapping Activity Obtain a map of the eastern United States and Canada. Have students find the following locations: eastern shore of Maryland; Wilmington, Delaware; Philadelphia, Pennsylvania; Burlington, New Jersey; Syracuse, New York; Rochester, New York; and St. Catharines, Ontario. Use thumbtacks to pinpoint the locations. As students study the map, tell them to imagine traveling this route by foot and brainstorm what problems the landscape may have presented for Tubman and her group. AS

Sometimes the masters thought they had heard the cry of a hoot owl, repeated, and would remember having thought that the intervals between the low moaning cry were wrong, that it had been repeated four times in succession instead of three. There was never anything more than that to suggest that all was not well in the quarter. Yet when morning came, they invariably discovered that a group of the finest slaves had taken to their heels.

Unfortunately, the discovery was almost always made on a Sunday. Thus a whole day was lost before the machinery of pursuit could be set in motion. The posters offering rewards for the fugitives could not be printed until Monday. The men who made a living hunting for runaway slaves were out of reach, off in the woods with their dogs and their guns, in pursuit of four-footed game, or they were in camp meetings[3] saying their prayers with their wives and families beside them.

Visual Vocabulary The ***whippoorwill,*** a North American bird, is active mainly at night; its name imitates the sound of its call.

Harriet Tubman could have told them that there was far more involved in this matter of running off slaves than signaling the would-be runaways by imitating the call of a whippoorwill, or a hoot owl, far more involved than a matter of waiting for a clear night when the North Star was visible. **2**

In December, 1851, when she started out with the band of fugitives that she planned to take to Canada, she had been in the vicinity of the plantation for days, planning the trip, carefully selecting the slaves that she would take with her. **L**

She had announced her arrival in the quarter by singing the forbidden spiritual[4]—"Go down, Moses, 'way down to Egypt Land"—singing it softly outside the door of a slave cabin, late at night. The husky voice was beautiful even when it was barely more than a murmur borne[5] on the wind.

Once she had made her presence known, word of her coming spread from cabin to cabin. The slaves whispered to

3. ***Camp meetings*** are religious meetings held in a tent or outdoors.

4. Many African American ***spirituals*** like "Go Down Moses," had secret references to the Underground Railroad. Certain songs were forbidden for fear that they might inspire enslaved people to escape or rebel. **R**

5. ***Borne*** is the past participle of *to bear* and, here, means "carried."

Practice the Skills

2 Literary Element

Style Ann Petry uses long sentences in the second and third paragraphs on this page. Are lengthy sentences part of her writing style? To find out, look for other long sentences as you continue reading.

Differentiated Instruction

Researching Lyrics Make use of the resources in the audiovisual department of a local library to obtain an audio copy of the spiritual "Go Down, Moses" to play for students. Use the lyrics to the song to review the story of the Hebrew exodus from Egypt and to discuss the parallels to the story of the Underground Railroad. Encourage students to compare figures in the two stories. For example, ask, "How was Harriet Tubman like Moses?" and "Who was the Pharaoh in Harriet Tubman's story?" **OL**

Teach

L Literary Element

Style **Say:** Writers often change the length of their sentences for effect. Why might long sentences be appropriate for describing how the process of pursuit slowed down on Sundays? *(Possible response: Long sentences slow down your reading speed. They mimic the difficulty of the journey.)* **OL**

R Reading Skill

Review Making Inferences
Ask: Why do you think masters might have feared that spirituals would inspire people to escape or rebel? *(Possible response: The spirituals might give people hope. Hearing about other enslaved people who escaped might inspire people to believe they, too, could escape.)* **AL**

Indiana English/Language Arts Academic Standards
SE: 8.2, 8.3.6
TWE: *Differentiated Instruction* 8.2, *Differentiated Instruction* 8.3.1

Teach

R Reading Skill

Review Making Inferences
Ask: Why do you think the people who were enslaved used code words to talk about Tubman's visits? *(Possible response: If anyone discovered her true identity, she would have been caught.)* OL

C Critical Thinking

Comprehension **Ask:** Who are Thomas Sims, Jerry, and Shadrach? *(They are fugitive slaves.)* BL **Ask:** Why does Petry mention them? What does she want to emphasize in this paragraph? *(Possible response: She mentions them as examples of people who were returned to slavery as a result of the Fugitive Slave Law. She wants to emphasize the danger faced by Tubman and the escaped enslaved people.)* AL

READING WORKSHOP 3

Visual Vocabulary
Ashcake is a cornmeal bread that's baked among the ashes at the back of a fireplace.

each other, ear to mouth, mouth to ear, "Moses is here." "Moses has come." "Get ready. Moses is back again." The ones who had agreed to go North with her put ashcake and salt herring in an old bandanna, hastily tied it into a bundle, and then waited patiently for the signal that meant it was time to start. 3

There were eleven in this party, including one of her brothers and his wife. It was the largest group that she had ever conducted, but she was determined that more and more slaves should know what freedom was like. R

She had to take them all the way to Canada. The Fugitive Slave Law[6] was no longer a great many incomprehensible words written down on the country's lawbooks. The new law had become a reality. It was Thomas Sims, a boy, picked up on the streets of Boston at night and shipped back to Georgia. It was Jerry and Shadrach, arrested and jailed with no warning. C

She had never been in Canada. The route beyond Philadelphia was strange to her. But she could not let the runaways who accompanied her know this. As they walked along she told them stories of her own first **flight**, she kept painting vivid word pictures of what it would be like to be free.

But there were so many of them this time. She knew moments of doubt when she was half-afraid, and kept looking back over her shoulder, imagining that she heard the sound of pursuit. They would certainly be pursued. Eleven of them. Eleven thousand dollars' worth of flesh and bone and muscle that belonged to Maryland planters. If they were caught, the eleven runaways would be whipped and sold South, but she—she would probably be hanged. 4

They tried to sleep during the day but they never could wholly relax into sleep. She could tell by the positions they assumed, by their restless movements. And they walked at night. Their progress was slow. It took them three nights of walking to reach the first stop. She had told them about the place where they would stay, promising warmth and good

6. The 1850 ***Fugitive Slave Law*** allowed owners to get back escaped slaves, even if the slaves had reached free states.

Practice the Skills

3 Key Reading Skill

Predicting Here, you learn that "Moses" was a code name for Harriet Tubman. Did you correctly predict who Moses would turn out to be?

4 English Language Coach

Old Words and Phrases Do you remember the meaning of the phrase "sold South"? If not, look back on page 218.

Additional Support

Reading in the Real World

College Students who plan to attend college should become adept at research. Have students research the Fugitive Slave Act:

- What did it require courts, police, and private citizens to do?
- What were the consequences for people who failed to do so?
- Did fugitives have a right to a jury trial?
- How did the act fuel the abolitionist (antislavery) movement?

Have students share their findings with the class. AL

Underground Railroad, c. 1945. William H. Johnson. Oil on paperboard, 33 3/8 x 36 3/8 in. National Museum of American Art, Washington, DC.

food, holding these things out to them as an incentive to keep going.

When she knocked on the door of a farmhouse, a place where she and her parties of runaways had always been welcome, always been given shelter and plenty to eat, there was no answer. She knocked again, softly. A voice from within said, "Who is it?" There was fear in the voice.

She knew instantly from the sound of the voice that there was something wrong. She said, "A friend with friends," the password on the Underground Railroad. **5**

R The door opened, slowly. The man who stood in the doorway looked at her coldly, looked with unconcealed astonishment and fear at the eleven disheveled runaways who were standing near her. Then he shouted, "Too many, too many. It's not safe. My place was searched last week. It's not safe!" and slammed the door in her face.

L She turned away from the house, frowning. She had promised her passengers food and rest and warmth, and instead of that, there would be hunger and cold and more walking over the frozen ground. Somehow she would have to instill courage into these eleven people, most of them

Practice the Skills

5 Key Reading Skill

Predicting After reading this paragraph, what do you think might happen to Tubman and the fugitives?

Differentiated Instruction

Research Activity The National Park Service maintains an online registry of historic places. Take students on a virtual tour of safe houses on the Underground Railroad by visiting the Web site, *Aboard the Underground Railroad: A National Register Travel Itinerary*, and clicking on the list of sites. **BL**

Lead students in a discussion about why people would have been willing to provide safe houses for fugitives. What character traits did such an act require? **OL**

READING WORKSHOP 3

Teach

R Reading Skill

Predicting Ask: Based on what you've read thus far, what problems can you predict the fugitives might face during the rest of their journey? *(Possible response: They might face hunger, they might continue to be refused housing, they might be caught and sent back to the South.)* **OL**

L Literary Element

Style Ask: What does Petry mean when she says Tubman had to feed the people "on hope and bright dreams of freedom"? *(Possible response: She means she'll have to convince them to keep going based on promises of a better life rather than on the food she had promised them.)* **OL** **Ask:** What type of language is the author using here? *(figurative language)* **AL**

Indiana English/Language Arts Academic Standards

SE: 8.1, 8.2

TWE: *Reading in the Real World* 8.2.5, *Differentiated Instruction* 8.4.4

Teach

R Reading Skill

Review Making Inferences
Ask: What do you think gave the fugitives strength to keep going when they were tired and hungry? *(Possible responses: the danger of being caught; the hope of reaching free territory)* OL

L Literary Element

Style Ask: What words does Petry use to describe Thomas Garrett's appearance? What is the effect of her word choice? *(Possible response: Her use of words such as "soft, almost like a baby's," "kindest eyes she had ever seen," "a big man and strong," "never used his strength to hurt anyone" indicate he is strong but gentle and an admirable person.)* OL

strangers, would have to feed them on hope and bright dreams of freedom instead of the fried pork and corn bread and milk she had promised them.

They stumbled along behind her, half-dead for sleep, and she urged them on, though she was as tired and as discouraged as they were. She had never been in Canada but she kept painting wondrous word pictures of what it would be like. She managed to dispel[7] their fear of pursuit, so that they would not become hysterical, panic-stricken. Then she had to bring some of the fear back, so that they would stay awake and keep walking though they drooped with sleep. R

Yet during the day, when they lay down deep in a thicket, they never really slept, because if a twig snapped or the wind sighed in the branches of a pine tree, they jumped to their feet, afraid of their own shadows, shivering and shaking. It was very cold, but they dared not make fires because someone would see the smoke and wonder about it. 6

She kept thinking, eleven of them. Eleven thousand dollars' worth of slaves. And she had to take them all the way to Canada. Sometimes she told them about Thomas Garrett, in Wilmington. She said he was their friend even though he did not know them. He was the friend of all fugitives. He called them God's poor. He was a Quaker and his speech was a little different from that of other people. His clothing was different, too. He wore the wide-brimmed hat that the Quakers wear.

She said that he had thick white hair, soft, almost like a baby's, and the kindest eyes she had ever seen. He was a big man and strong, but he had never used his strength to harm anyone, always to help people. He would give all of them a new pair of shoes. Everybody. He always did. Once they reached his house in Wilmington, they would be safe. He would see to it that they were. 7

She described the house where he lived, told them about the store where he sold shoes. She said he kept a pail of milk and a loaf of bread in the drawer of his desk so that he would have food ready at hand for any of God's poor who should suddenly appear before him, fainting with hunger. There was a hidden room in the store. A whole wall swung open, and behind it was a room where he could hide fugitives. On the wall there were shelves filled with small boxes—boxes of L

7. To ***dispel*** something is to make it go away or disappear.

Practice the Skills

6 Reviewing Skills

Connecting Think of a time when you were so frightened or anxious that you couldn't sleep. How did you feel the next morning? Now think about what it must have been like for the fugitives to stay awake for the long night walks, often with little rest.

7 Literary Element

Style Ann Petry uses a lot of description in this paragraph. Is description part of her style? Read on to see.

Additional Support

Reading in the Real World

Citizenship The Quakers, also known as the Society of Friends, are a Christian group that believes that humans are inherently good. The Quakers have always been advocates of nonviolence and social reform. Many were part of the abolitionist movement in the 1800s. Some Quakers migrated west because they refused to live in a culture that permitted slavery. Until the late 1880s, the Quakers used a form of English known as plain speech, in which they used such terms as *thee* instead of *you*. Plain speech was meant to deny the existence of social classes by referring to everyone as equals. Have students research where Quakers live today and what their culture is like. OL shoes—so that you would never guess that the wall actually opened.

While she talked, she kept watching them. They did not believe her. She could tell by their expressions. They were thinking, New shoes, Thomas Garrett, Quaker, Wilmington—what foolishness was this? Who knew if she told the truth? Where was she taking them anyway? 8

That night they reached the next stop—a farm that belonged to a German. She made the runaways take shelter behind trees at the edge of the fields before she knocked at the door. She hesitated before she approached the door, thinking, suppose that he, too, should refuse shelter, suppose— Then she thought, Lord, I'm going to hold steady on to You and You've got to see me through—and knocked softly.

She heard the familiar guttural[8] voice say, "Who's there?"

She answered quickly, "A friend with friends."

He opened the door and greeted her warmly. "How many this time?" he asked.

"Eleven," she said and waited, doubting, wondering.

He said, "Good. Bring them in."

He and his wife fed them in the lamp-lit kitchen, their faces glowing, as they offered food and more food, urging

Practice the Skills

8 **Key Reading Skill**

Predicting Notice how Tubman describes Thomas Garrett and his house to the fugitives. They do not seem to believe her. Do you? Predict whether Tubman's story is true or just meant to motivate the people to keep walking.

In this undated photo, Harriet Tubman *(left)* poses with some of the people she helped escape from slavery.

Analyzing the Photo How might these individuals be similar to those in the selection?

8. A ***guttural*** (GUT ur ul) voice has a rough, harsh sound.

Reading Fluency

Reading Dialogue Remind students that the text in quotation marks on this page is dialogue, words spoken by the people in the story. Point out to students that Petry gives specific directions about how the dialogue on this page should sound. Direct students to use verbal cues from the text as they read the dialogue aloud. For example, discuss and model how a "guttural voice" might sound. EL BL

Teach

R Reading Skill

Predicting **Ask:** Based on what Harriet Tubman and the fugitives have faced on their journey so far, what do you predict will happen to them at the next stop? *(Some students may say that the group has already experienced a lot of trouble, and that it will probably continue. Others may say that Tubman has been successful leading fugitives in the past, so the next stop might be a positive experience for the group.)* AS

Viewing the Photo

Ask: What can you tell about the lives of the people from their expressions and body language in this photo? *(Possible response: Because of their body language, you may think that their lives have been difficult and painful.)* OL

Indiana English/Language Arts Academic Standards

SE: 8.2, 8.3.6

TWE: *Reading in the Real World* 8.2.5, *Reading Fluency* 8.7

Teach

R1 Reading Skill

Predicting **Ask:** Why might a member of the group rebel or refuse to go on? *(Possible response: The fugitives are exhausted and may be doubtful about reaching freedom; one of them may decide it's better to go back than to face uncertainty.)* **OL** **Ask:** What could happen if one of the fugitives left the group and set out alone? *(Possible response: Without Tubman's guidance, he or she would probably be discovered. He or she might also be forced to give away the location of the rest of the group.)* **AL**

R2 Reading Skill

Review Making Inferences
Ask: Why does Tubman tell stories? *(Possible response: She hopes that by telling stories about people who escaped from slavery, the fugitives will find hope and the courage to go on.)* **OL**

them to eat, saying there was plenty for everybody, have more milk, have more bread, have more meat.

They spent the night in the warm kitchen. They really slept, all that night and until dusk the next day. When they left, it was with reluctance. They had all been warm and safe and well-fed. It was hard to exchange the security offered by that clean warm kitchen for the darkness and the cold of a December night.

Harriet had found it hard to leave the warmth and friendliness, too. But she urged them on. For a while, as they walked, they seemed to carry in them a measure of contentment; some of the serenity and the cleanliness of that big warm kitchen lingered on inside them. But as they walked farther and farther away from the warmth and the light, the cold and the darkness entered into them. They fell silent, sullen, suspicious. She waited for the moment when some one of them would turn mutinous.[9] It did not happen that night. **9**

Two nights later she was aware that the feet behind her were moving slower and slower. She heard the irritability in their voices, knew that soon someone would refuse to go on. **R1**

She started talking about William Still and the Philadelphia Vigilance Committee. No one commented. No one asked any questions. She told them the story of William and Ellen Craft and how they escaped from Georgia. Ellen was so fair that she looked as though she were white, and so she dressed up in a man's clothing and she looked like a wealthy young planter. Her husband, William, who was dark, played the role of her slave. Thus they traveled from Macon, Georgia, to Philadelphia, riding on the trains, staying at the finest hotels. **R2** Ellen pretended to be very ill—her right arm was in a sling, and her right hand was bandaged, because she was supposed to have rheumatism. Thus she avoided having to sign the register at the hotels for she could not read or write. They finally arrived safely in Philadelphia, and then went on to Boston.

No one said anything. Not one of them seemed to have heard her.

Practice the Skills

9 Key Reading Skill

Predicting Tubman expects one of the fugitives to "turn mutinous," but nothing happens that night. After reading this paragraph, predict what might happen later in the selection.

9. To turn ***mutinous*** (MYOO tun us) means to become openly rebellious.

Additional Support

Reading in the Real World

Citizenship The National Underground Railroad Freedom Center opened on August 23, 2004. Situated on the banks of the Ohio River in Cincinnati, Ohio, the Freedom Center is dedicated to educating the public about issues of freedom in the past, present, and future. Invite students to visit the Freedom Center's Web site (www.freedomcenter.org) to learn more about the center and its goals. **AL**

She told them about Frederick Douglass, the most famous of the escaped slaves, of his **eloquence**, of his magnificent appearance. Then she told them of her own first vain effort at running away, evoking[10] the memory of that miserable life she had led as a child, reliving it for a moment in the telling.

But they had been tired too long, hungry too long, afraid too long, footsore too long. One of them suddenly cried out in despair, "Let me go back. It is better to be a slave than to suffer like this in order to be free."

She carried a gun with her on these trips. She had never used it—except as a threat. Now as she aimed it, she experienced a feeling of guilt, remembering that time, years ago, when she had prayed for the death of Edward Brodas, the Master, and then not too long afterward had heard that great wailing cry that came from the throats of the field hands, and knew from the sound that the Master was dead.

One of the runaways said, again, "Let me go back. Let me go back," and stood still, and then turned around and said, over his shoulder, "I am going back."

L She lifted the gun, aimed it at the despairing slave. She said, "Go on with us or die." The husky low-pitched voice was grim. **10**

He hesitated for a moment and then he joined the others. They started walking again. She tried to explain to them why none of them could go back to the plantation. If a runaway returned, he would turn traitor, the master and the overseer would force him to turn traitor. The returned slave would **disclose** the stopping places, the hiding places, the cornstacks they had used with the full knowledge of the owner of the farm, the name of the German farmer who had fed them and sheltered them. These people who had risked their own security to help runaways would be ruined, fined, imprisoned.

BQ She said, "We got to go free or die. And freedom's not bought with dust." **11**

10. Tubman is ***evoking,*** or calling up, this memory.

Vocabulary

eloquence (EL uh kwuns) *n.* the ability to speak expressively

disclose (dis KLOHZ) *v.* to make known; reveal

Practice the Skills

10 Literary Element

Style What are a few of the descriptive words that Petry uses on this page? Would you say that description is part of her writing style? Explain.

11 BIG Question

Judging from this quotation, which do you think Harriet Tubman feels is more important, the journey or the destination? Write your answer on the "Harriet Tubman" flap of Foldable 2.

Differentiated Instruction

Frederick Douglass Ask volunteers to read aloud each of the quotations below from Frederick Douglass. Then encourage students to state what each quotation means and discuss whether they agree.

"If there is no struggle, there is no progress."

"The thing worse than rebellion is the thing that causes rebellion."

"People might not get all they work for in this world, but they must certainly work for all they get." **AL**

Teach

L Literary Element

Style Ask: How does Petry describe Tubman's voice? *(It is "husky," "low-pitched," and "grim.")* **BL Ask:** What is the effect of this description? *(Possible response: It makes Tubman sound determined and intimidating.)* **OL**

BQ BIG Question

Ask: According to Tubman, what are the two options for herself and the group? *(Go free or die.)* **BL Ask:** In her mind, is there really a choice? Explain. *(Possible response: No; Tubman considers freedom to be the only option.)* **OL**

Indiana English/Language Arts Academic Standards

SE: 8.2, 8.3.6

TWE: *Reading in the Real World* 8.4.4, *Differentiated Instruction* 8.7

Teach

EL Language Coach

Old Words and Phrases
Ask: What is the meaning of the phrase *curious fits of sleep*? *(unexplained spells of dizziness or unconsciousness)* How does the use of this phrase effect the feeling and atmosphere of the story? *(Responses will vary.)* OL

R Reading Skill

Predicting Ask: What do you predict will happen based on the runaways' actions when Tubman falls asleep? *(Possible response: I predict they will arrive at their journey safely because they trust Tubman and do as she says.)* AL

READING WORKSHOP 3

This time she told them about the long agony of the Middle Passage[11] on the old slave ships, about the black horror of the holds, about the chains and the whips. **12** They too knew these stories. But she wanted to remind them of the long hard way they had come, about the long hard way they had yet to go. She told them about Thomas Sims, the boy picked up on the streets of Boston and sent back to Georgia. She said when they got him back to Savannah, got him in prison there, they whipped him until a doctor who was standing by watching said, "You will kill him if you strike him again!" His master said, "Let him die!"

Thus she forced them to go on. Sometimes she thought she had become nothing but a voice speaking in the darkness, **cajoling**, urging, threatening. Sometimes she told them things to make them laugh, sometimes she sang to them, and heard the eleven voices behind her blending softly with hers, and then she knew that for the moment all was well with them.

EL

She gave the impression of being a short, muscular, indomitable[12] woman who could never be defeated. Yet at any moment she was liable to be seized by one of those curious fits of sleep,[13] which might last for a few minutes or for hours.

R

Even on this trip, she suddenly fell asleep in the woods. The runaways, ragged, dirty, hungry, cold, did not steal the gun as they might have, and set off by themselves, or turn back. They sat on the ground near her and waited patiently until she awakened. They had come to trust her implicitly,[14] totally. They, too, had come to believe her repeated statement, "We got to go free or die." She was leading them into freedom, and so they waited until she was ready to go on. **13**

11. The ***Middle Passage*** was the sea route followed by slave traders between Africa and the Americas.
12. ***Indomitable*** (in DAHM it uh bul) means "cannot be conquered," or "unbeatable."
13. Tubman's ***curious fits of sleep*** were occasional unexplained spells of dizziness or unconsciousness.
14. To trust ***implicitly*** (im PLIS it lee) is to have complete faith, with no question, doubt, or hesitation.

Vocabulary

cajoling (kuh JOHL ing) *v.* persuading, especially by using soothing words; coaxing

Practice the Skills

12 Literary Element

Style In this sentence Petry repeats the word *about*. Repetition helps unify the ideas in the sentence and create rhythm in the prose. Is repetition part of Petry's style? To find out, look for repeated words and phrases as you continue reading.

13 Key Reading Skill

Predicting Use the information in this paragraph to predict whether Harriet Tubman will succeed in bringing the fugitive slaves to freedom. Explain your answer.

Additional Support

English Language Coach

Building Background European slave traders captured Africans and transported them to the Americas on slave ships containing layers of platforms below the deck to hold many slaves. The slaves were chained to the platforms for two or three months. This period of travel became known as the Middle Passage. The slaves were fed an inadequate diet of rice, yams, or beans. The conditions below deck were dirty, and many did not survive the passage. It was not uncommon for a ship to reach port with as few as half the slaves alive. Have students explain why Tubman might have shared stories about the Middle Passage. *(Possible response: to show the runaways that their ancestors had endured far worse.)* OL

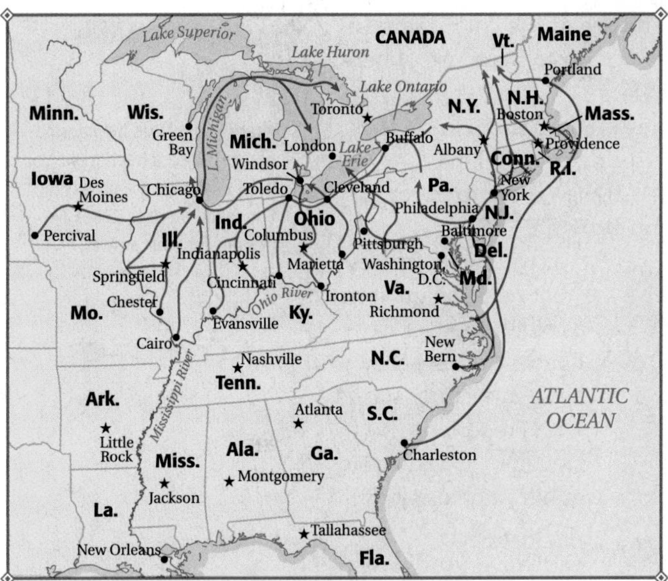

Underground Railroad routes traveled by people escaping slavery during the 1800s.

Finally, they reached Thomas Garrett's house in Wilmington, Delaware. Just as Harriet had promised, Garret gave them all new shoes, and provided carriages to take them on to the next stop.

By slow stages they reached Philadelphia, where William Still hastily recorded their names, and the plantations **whence** they had come, and something of the life they had led in slavery. **14** Then he carefully hid what he had written, for fear it might be discovered. In 1872 he published this record in book form and called it *The Underground Railroad.* In the foreword to his book he said: "While I knew the danger of keeping strict records, and while I did not then dream that in my day slavery would be blotted out, or that the time would come when I could publish these records, it used to afford me great satisfaction to take them down, fresh from the lips of fugitives on the way to freedom, and to preserve them as they had given them." **R** **C**

William Still, who was familiar with all the station stops on the Underground Railroad, supplied Harriet with money and sent her and her eleven fugitives on to Burlington, New Jersey.

Harriet felt safer now, though there were danger spots ahead. But the biggest part of her job was over. As they went farther and farther north, it grew colder; she was aware of

Practice the Skills

14 English Language Coach

Can you figure out the meaning of the old word **whence** in the second line of this paragraph? If not, look it up in the dictionary.

READING WORKSHOP 3

Teach

R Reading Skill

Review Making Inferences
Ask: Why do you think William Still kept records of the enslaved people who reached Philadelphia? *(Responses will vary. Some students may say that Still kept records for the sake of history.)* **OL**

C Critical Thinking

Synthesis Say: Many people were willing to help Tubman and the runaways on their journey. Why do you think they were willing to risk jail to help them? *(Possible response: They believed strongly in the antislavery cause and wanted to help as many people as possible.)* **OL**

Literature Focus Lesson

Repetition Repetition is often used in poetry, just as Petry uses it in this prose selection. When a word or group of words is repeated at the beginning of successive phrases or sentences, it is called *anaphora* (ah NA for uh). Like other forms of repetition, anaphora can make language sound grand or important.

For example, the following lines by Walt Whitman demonstrate anaphora:

"Out of the cradle endlessly rocking,/ Out of the mocking-bird's throat, the musical shuttle,/Out of the Ninth-month midnight . . ."

Have students find instances of repetition and anaphora in Petry's story. **AL**

Indiana English/Language Arts Academic Standards
SE: 8.1, 8.2
TWE: *English Language Coach* 8.2, *Literature Focus Lesson* 8.3.1

Teach

Viewing the Photo

Say: When Frederick Douglass met John Brown, he noted, "though a white gentleman, [Brown] is in sympathy a black man, and as deeply interested in our cause, as though his own soul had been pierced with the iron of slavery." What can you tell about him from this photograph? *(Possible response: He looks fiercely determined.)* BL

EL Language Coach

Old Words and Phrases

Ask: What is the meaning of the phrase *fastidious in either direction* as it is used in this passage? *(difficult to please or satisfy with just any type of food or shelter)* In what ways did the fugitives show they were not fastidious? Give examples from the text. *(Possible responses: They were content with plain food. They didn't mind sleeping on the floor or on straw in the barn.)* OL

READING WORKSHOP 3

the wind on the Jersey ferry and aware of the cold damp in New York. From New York they went on to Syracuse, where the temperature was even lower. 15

In Syracuse she met the Reverend J. W. Loguen, known as "Jarm" Loguen. This was the beginning of a lifelong friendship. Both Harriet and Jarm Loguen were to become friends and supporters of Old John Brown.

John Brown, pictured here, was a leader of the American antislavery movement. In 1859 he led an unsuccessful raid of a federal weapons storehouse in Virginia, hoping to inspire a slave rebellion.

From Syracuse they went north again, into a colder, snowier city—Rochester. Here they almost certainly stayed with Frederick Douglass, for he wrote in his autobiography:

"On one occasion I had eleven fugitives at the same time under my roof, and it was necessary for them to remain with me until I could collect sufficient money to get them to Canada. It was the largest number I ever had at any one time, and I had some difficulty in providing so many with food and shelter, but, as may well be imagined, they were not very fastidious[15] in either direction, and were well content with very plain food, and a strip of carpet on the floor for a bed, or a place on the straw in the barnloft." EL

Late in December, 1851, Harriet arrived in St. Catharines, Canada West (now Ontario), with the eleven fugitives. It had taken almost a month to complete this journey; most of the time had been spent getting out of Maryland.

That first winter in St. Catharines was a terrible one. Canada was a strange frozen land, snow everywhere, ice everywhere, and a bone-biting cold the like of which none of

15. If the fugitive slaves had been ***fastidious*** (fas TIH dee us), they would have been difficult to please or satisfy.

Practice the Skills

15 Key Reading Skill

Predicting Does the information in this paragraph make you want to change the prediction you made on page 228? Give reasons for your answer.

Additional Support

Differentiated Instruction

Journal Entry About her escape from slavery, Harriet Tubman once said, "I had crossed the line. I was free; but there was no one to welcome me to the land of freedom. I was a stranger in a strange land." Lead students in a discussion about why Tubman felt that she was a "stranger in a strange land." Then ask students to write a brief journal entry describing a time when they felt out of place, or like a stranger in a strange land. OL them had ever experienced before. Harriet rented a small frame house in the town and set to work to make a home. The fugitives boarded with her. They worked in the forests, felling trees, and so did she. Sometimes she took other jobs, cooking or cleaning house for people in the town. She cheered on these newly arrived fugitives, working herself, finding work for them, finding food for them, praying for them, sometimes begging for them.

Often she found herself thinking of the beauty of Maryland, the mellowness of the soil, the richness of the plant life there. The climate itself made for an ease of living that could never be duplicated in this bleak, barren countryside. **16**

In spite of the severe cold, the hard work, she came to love St. Catharines, and the other towns and cities in Canada where black men lived. She discovered that freedom meant more than the right to change jobs at will, more than the right to keep the money that one earned. It was the right to vote and to sit on juries. It was the right to be elected to office. In Canada there were black men who were county officials and members of school boards. St. Catharines had a large colony of ex-slaves, and they owned their own homes, kept them neat and clean and in good repair. They lived in whatever part of town they chose and sent their children to the schools.

When spring came she decided that she would make this small Canadian city her home—as much as any place could be said to be home to a woman who traveled from Canada to the Eastern Shore of Maryland as often as she did.

In the spring of 1852, she went back to Cape May, New Jersey. She spent the summer there, cooking in a hotel. That fall she returned, as usual, to Dorchester County, and brought out nine more slaves, conducting them all the way to St. Catharines, in Canada West, to the bone-biting cold, the snow-covered forests—and freedom.

She continued to live in this fashion, spending the winter in Canada, and the spring and summer working in Cape May, New Jersey, or in Philadelphia. She made two trips a year into slave territory, one in the fall and another in the spring. She now had a definite crystallized[16] purpose, and in carrying it out, her life fell into a pattern which remained unchanged for the next six years. **17** ❍

16. Here, ***crystallized*** (KRIS tuh lyzd) means "having a clear, specific form."

Practice the Skills

16 **Literary Element**

L **Style** On this page Petry uses a lot of descriptive words. In your opinion, which descriptions are the most original? Which are the most effective?

17 **BIG Question**

BQ What did you learn from reading about the journey Tubman and the fugitives took? Write your answer on the "Harriet Tubman" flap of Foldable 2. Your response will help you complete the Unit Challenge later.

Reading in the Real World

Citizenship Oprah Winfrey has said, "I am where I am because of the bridges that I crossed. Sojourner Truth was a bridge. Harriet Tubman was a bridge. Ida B. Wells was a bridge. Madame C. J. Walker was a bridge. Fannie Lou Hamer was a bridge." Explain that all of the women Winfrey mentions were strong African Americans who lived admirable lives. Have students draw a bridge with themselves as a baby on one side and a current photograph on the other. Encourage students to populate their bridge with people who helped them become who they are today. Students should annotate their drawings with explanations of each person's contribution. **OL**

Teach

L Literary Element

Style **Ask:** What words does Petry use to describe Canada? *(Possible responses: "strange, frozen land, snow everywhere, ice everywhere," "bone-biting cold," "bleak, barren countryside")* **Ask:** What are some words that Petry uses to describe Maryland? *(Possible responses: "mellowness of the soil," "richness of the plant life," "ease of living")* **BL** **Ask:** Why does Petry contrast the coldness of Canada with the beauty of Maryland? *(Responses will vary. Students may suggest that Petry wants to show what the fugitive enslaved people were willing to endure for freedom.)* **AL**

BQ BIG Question

Ask: What did Tubman teach the eleven fugitives during the journey? *(Possible response: Tubman taught the eleven fugitives about the rewards of sacrifice and perseverance.)* **OL**

Assess

Use the CheckPoint questions provided on Presentation Plus! to check for comprehension of the selection. These questions can be used with interactive response keypads for immediate student feedback.

Indiana English/Language Arts Academic Standards
SE: 8.2, 8.3.6
TWE: *Differentiated Instruction* 8.5, *Reading in the Real World* 8.7.9

Assess

Resources for page 232

- Selection Quick Check, p. 16
- Selection and Unit Assessment, p. 18
- ExamView Assessment Suite
- Interactive Tutor: Self-Assessment

Students can respond to the *After You Read* items in their Learner's Notebooks or on a separate sheet of paper.

Answering the

1. Responses will vary. Students may say that the value of the journey rested on reaching the destination.
2. Even in northern states, slave owners could reclaim the fugitives. The Fugitive Slave Act was not valid in Canada.
3. The conductors and fugitives were breaking the law. The success of the Underground Railroad depended on secrecy.

Critical Thinking

4. Students may say that because Tubman escaped from slavery, she felt driven to help others do the same.
5. Possible response: If the runaways left Tubman, they wouldn't know where to go. They needed her help to escape.
6. Possible response: Tubman saw only two options: freedom or death. Returning to dust, or dying, eliminated the possibility of reaching freedom.

After You Read

from *Harriet Tubman: Conductor on the Underground Railroad*

Answering the BIG Question

1. After reading the selection from *Harriet Tubman: Conductor on the Underground Railroad,* which do you think was more important, the fugitives' destination or the journey they took to get there? Explain.
2. **Recall** Why does Tubman have to take the fugitives all the way to Canada rather than just to a northern state?

   TIP **Right There** The answer is in one place in the text.
3. **Summarize** Why was it so important that the Underground Railroad be kept a secret?

   TIP **Think and Search** The answer is in the text, but it is not all in one place.

Critical Thinking

4. **Infer** What do you think motivated Tubman to risk her own life to help others? Use details from the selection to support your ideas.

   TIP **Author and Me** To answer the question, apply your understanding of what Tubman was like.
5. **Infer** When Tubman fell asleep, none of the fugitives left, even though they were doubtful of where she was taking them. Why do you think they remained with Tubman?

   TIP **Author and Me** To answer the question, combine your understanding of the text with your understanding of human nature.
6. **Interpret** What did Tubman mean when she said, "We got to go free or die. And freedom's not bought with dust"?

   TIP **Author and Me** Think about the text and about Tubman's experiences.

Talk About Your Reading

Role Play Imagine that you are the German farmer who allowed the eleven fugitives to eat and sleep in your house. A friend has recently written you a letter, telling you to stop helping people who were enslaved escape to freedom because you are taking too much of a risk. How would you respond to your friend's concerns? With a partner or small group, explain why you have chosen to risk your own safety to help others escape and how you feel about your choice.

Indiana English/Language Arts Academic Standards (pp. 232–233)

8.3 Comprehension and Analysis of Literary Text Respond to grade-level appropriate literature... **8.7.11** Deliver oral responses to [texts]... **8.2 Comprehension and Analysis (Focus on Informational Text)** Develop [reading] strategies...make predictions... **8.3.6** Identify literary devices...which define a writer's style... **8.6 English Language Conventions**

For a complete description of the standards, see p. IN 11.

Talk About Your Reading

Possible response:

I am helping the fugitives despite the risk to my safety because I strongly believe slavery is wrong. I am more than willing to risk my life to help people free themselves from the terrible conditions in which they live. Thank you for caring about me, but I am doing what I believe is best.

Skills Review

Key Reading Skill: Predicting

7. Review the predictions you made with your class before reading. State whether your predictions were accurate and explain why.

Literary Element: Style

8. What is Petry's writing style like? Use the questions on page 219 to analyze her style. Then write a few sentences that describe her style.

Reviewing Skills: Connecting

9. Were there any feelings or thoughts in the story that you could connect to? Have you ever felt tired or afraid? Have you ever accomplished something you weren't sure you could? Explain.

Vocabulary Check

Match the words in Column A with the correct definition in Column B.

Column A	Column B
10. disclose ___	(a) to make known
11. cajoling ___	(b) ability to speak well
12. eloquence ___	(c) persuading

13. Academic Vocabulary What does *predicting* mean? Define it in your own words.

14. English Language Coach Does the following sentence use the underlined phrase correctly? If you need to, go back to the ELC on page 218. People escaping from slavery dreaded the thought of being sold South.

Web Activities For eFlashcards, Selection Quick Checks, and other Web activities, go to www.glencoe.com.

Grammar Link: Misplaced and Dangling Modifiers

Adjectives and adverbs should point clearly to the words they modify. A **misplaced modifier** describes, or modifies, the wrong word or group of words. Misplaced modifiers are a problem because they can cause readers to misunderstand the meaning of sentences.

- Sam went home to eat lunch on his skates. (It sounds as if Sam ate *on his skates!*)

To fix a misplaced modifier, bring the modifier closer to the word it describes.

- Sam went home on his skates to eat lunch. (The phrase "on his skates" tells how Sam went home. By moving the phrase closer to "went home," the writer fixed the misplaced modifier.)

A **dangling modifier** makes it unclear *who* is doing *what* in a sentence. To correct a dangling modifier, add a clear subject for the modifier to describe.

Wrong: Wiggling, Mom held my little brother. (Is Mom wiggling? Is the little brother wiggling?)

Right: Mom held my little brother, who was wiggling.

Grammar Practice

On a separate sheet of paper, copy each pair of sentences below. For each pair, underline the correct placement or form of modifier.

15. I went to the field to play hockey on my bike./ I went to the field on my bike to play hockey.

16. Running in circles, Ivanna watched the dog./ Ivanna watched the dog running in circles.

17. While walking to school, a thunderstorm struck the neighborhood. / A thunderstorm struck the neighborhood while I was walking to school.

18. After reading the review, I think the movie seems unappealing. / After reading the review, the movie seems unappealing.

Skills Review

Key Reading Skill: Predicting

7. Responses will vary.

Literary Element: Style

8. Possible description of style: Petry uses repetition, imagery, and descriptive language to bring her subject to life.

Reviewing Skills: Connecting

9. Possible response: Thinking about times when I felt tired and scared helped me imagine what the runaways felt.

Vocabulary Check

10. (a) to make known

11. (c) persuading

12. (b) ability to speak well

Academic Vocabulary

13. *Predicting* means "using clues to guess what will happen."

English Language Coach

14. Correct.

Close

Ask students to summarize what they learned about the Big Question from the story.

Grammar Link: Misplaced and Dangling Modifiers

Grammar Practice

15. I went to the field on my bike to play hockey.

16. Ivanna watched the dog running in circles.

17. A thunderstorm struck the neighborhood while I was walking to school.

18. After reading the review, I think the movie seems unappealing.

Web Activities Have students access the Web site for interactive activities that will help them assess their understanding of the selection.

Indiana English/Language Arts Academic Standards

SE: 8.2, 8.3, 8.3.6, 8.6, 8.7.11

Focus

BELLRINGER Options

Daily Language Practice Transparency 17
Focus Activity Say: Talk about the process of writing a folktale. Which elements are easy, and which are challenging? Explain. *(Responses will vary.)* **OL**

Teach

W Writing

Color Coding Say: Assign a different color for each of the following elements: protagonist, antagonist, plot or journey, conflict, and theme. This will help you determine which elements need additional work. **OL**

Resources for page 234

Use the BLM in the Unit 2 Resource Booklet, pp. 28–29.

Use the Grammar and Writing Workshop Transparencies 19–20

WRITING WORKSHOP PART 2

Folktale

Revising, Editing, and Presenting

ASSIGNMENT Write an entertaining folktale

Purpose: To create a folktale about a character who takes a journey

Audience: Your teacher and your classmates

Revising Rubric

Your revised folktale should have

- The major elements of a folktale
- A major character who is trying to do good
- A central message
- Correct spelling, grammar, and punctuation

See page 236 for a model of a folktale.

Indiana English/Language Arts Academic Standards (pp. 234–237)

8.5.1 Write...short stories... **8.4.7** Review, evaluate, and revise writing... **8.4.8** Edit and proofread writing... **8.7.6** Use audience feedback to...modify...structure...

For a complete description of the standards, see p. IN 11.

In Writing Workshop 1, you drafted an original folktale about a character on a journey. Now it's time to make changes. You can add a new story event, leave out something you don't like, add a new character (good or evil!), or change the ending. You'll also keep a copy in a writing portfolio so that you and your teacher can evaluate your writing progress over time.

Revising

Make It Better

When story writers revise, they ask themselves, "Does my story make sense?" To make sure your story will be clear to readers, ask yourself these questions:

- Is it clear what my characters are like? Will readers recognize my protagonist, or main character, as a good person? Will they recognize the antagonist as a bad person? Put a checkmark next to any words or phrases that show good or evil actions.
- Is it clear why my character went on a journey? Did I explain that early in the story? Put a checkmark next to the paragraph that tells why the journey was necessary. **W**
- Is it clear what difficulties my main character faced and overcame during the journey? Did I make sure the character's personality traits or special powers helped him or her solve those problems? Put a checkmark next to each paragraph that shows the character overcoming an obstacle.
- Is the outcome of the journey clear? Will readers understand what happened to the main character and why? Put a checkmark next to the paragraph that tells the journey's result.
- Did various parts of the story add to the main idea? Put a checkmark next to any detail that helps support the central message.

If you're missing any checkmarks, you may need to revise parts of your folktale. Make sure that your story describes events in the order that they happen. Include story events that support the message and help move the story toward a satisfying ending.

Additional Support

Reading Fluency

Reading Aloud and Revising
Remind students that many folktales were passed on orally from generation to generation, so they should have a style that sounds like natural speech, with a smooth flow and an interesting rhythm. Once students are happy with the content of their stories, have them read their folktales aloud to check how they sound. Encourage students to read their tales to a partner and have the partner point out times when the writing seems stiff or unnatural. **AS**

Editing and Proofreading

Trade Papers

1. After you have revised your draft, trade it with a partner. Ask your partner to underline any sentences in your draft that he or she finds confusing. Circle any spelling or punctuation mistakes. Pay close attention to your use of adjectives and adverbs.
   - Did you use adjectives and adverbs well?
   - Did you use the correct forms for comparative and superlative adjectives?
   - Are there any double negatives in the draft?
2. Ask your partner to return your draft, and look at what he or she has circled on your paper. Use a dictionary, the Grammar Links in this book, or Glencoe's *Grammar and Composition Handbook* to see how to fix your spelling and grammar mistakes.
3. Look at the underlined parts of your story. Ask your partner why he or she found these parts confusing. Brainstorm ways to make these details clearer.
4. When you're finished editing and proofreading, read your folktale aloud to your partner or just to yourself. If there's any place where you stumble as you read, you may need to revise that section a little bit more.
5. Make sure the title of your folktale fits the story and will attract readers' attention.
6. Take one last quick look through your folktale before you hand it in. Ask yourself, *Is this as good as I can make it? Did I miss anything?*

W

Writing Tip

Spelling When you proofread, double-check your spelling. Sometimes words that sound the same are spelled differently, but a computer spellchecker may not catch these mistakes.

Publishing and Presenting

Show It Off

Consider sending your folktale out for other people to read.

- You and your classmates might put together a collection of all the folktales your class has written. Bind your stories in a three-ring binder or post them on a school bulletin board.
- Your class might give copies of your folktales to your school library or the children's room of your community library so that other readers can enjoy them.
- You might send your folktale to an appropriate print or online magazine. For instructions on how to do so, check the Web sites of magazines you like, or ask a librarian for help. Make sure the magazine you choose publishes folktales.

Writing Tip

Publishing and Presenting When you have edited and proofread your folktale, rewrite it or enter it on a computer that has a wordprocessing program. Make your paper as neat as possible.

Writing Models For models and other writing activities, go to www.glencoe.com.

Differentiated Instruction

Class Anthology Encourage students to create a class anthology of folktales organized by theme. Computer-savvy students might create a class Web site with a home page that includes an intriguing title, an illustration, and a list of links to stories with similar themes. Alternatively, students could collect their stories in a folder, and use dividers to separate stories by theme. Assign students different tasks, such as creating a Table of Contents, drawing or finding illustrations, organizing the stories thematically, and coming up with a title for the anthology. OL

Teach

W Writing

Partner Review Say: Provide your partner with constructive, helpful feedback. For each confusing sentence you underline, use the margin to explain why the sentence is confusing. Be as specific as possible. A comment such as "This sentence is confusing" doesn't help your partner know what to fix. Instead, ask a specific question, such as "What obstacles does your protagonist face?" You can also offer a suggestion, such as "Add details to clarify what your characters are like." OL

Literature Online

Writing Models Have students access the Web site for an additional and interactive Writing Workshop-based student model.

Indiana English/Language Arts Academic Standards
SE: 8.4.7, 8.4.8, 8.5.1, 8.7.6
TWE: *Reading Fluency* 8.4.9, *Differentiated Instruction* 8.4.6

Teach

W1 Writing

Evaluating Dialogue Say: Read the dialogue in the story aloud. Do you think the writer does a good job of creating dialogue? Why or why not? *(Possible response: I think the writer does a good job because the dialogue sounds like real speech.)* **OL**

W2 Writing

Using Adjectives Say: Compare and contrast the following sentences: *She waved a wand. She waved a coral wand tipped with a shell. (Students will note that the addition of adjectives helps the reader visualize the wand.)* **OL**

Active Writing Model

Like many main characters in folktales, Finny has a special talent. She can hold her breath underwater for hours at a time.

Finny is a good person. She goes on a dangerous journey to help her parents.

The evil Sea Queen is the antagonist. Finny saves the day by offering her gifts.

The central message is that goodness and courage are rewarded. Finny was selfless and brave enough to make the journey to help her parents, and the Sea Queen granted her request.

Writer's Model

Finny Thinks Fast

Long ago a girl lived along the seacoast. She was called Finny because she could swim like a fish and hold her breath for hours. Finny's parents carved beautiful bowls. The bowls were so beautiful the wicked Sea Queen wanted them all for herself. One night she turned Finny's parents into stone and took their bowls.

The next morning Finny ran into the ocean and swam deep underwater. She had to find the Sea Queen. "Oh, Sea Queen, where are you?" she cried.

Suddenly a creature that was half human, half fish swam up to her. "It's a long journey to the palace," he said. He took her hand, and they swam farther into the depths. Mile after mile, they swam. Just when Finny's lungs were about to burst, she saw the palace. It was a giant seashell guarded by sharks! "I must leave you here," the creature said.

W1

"Please, sharks, do not hurt me," Finny cried. "I have to help my parents! The Sea Queen has cast a spell on them!"

The sharks felt sorry for her. "We will take you to her," they said.

They swam into the giant seashell and up to the Sea Queen's throne. Finny said, "I beg you to lift the spell from my parents!"

"Why should I?" asked the Sea Queen.

Finny thought fast. "If you make my parents well, they can carve more bowls. Every year on this day, we'll leave them on the shore for you."

The queen lovingly ran her fingers over one of the bowls she had stolen. "All right," she said. She waved a coral wand tipped with a shell. "You'll find your parents back to normal when you return." W2

The Sea Queen kept her word, and they all lived happily ever after.

Additional Support

Literature Focus Lesson

Setting Encourage students to describe the setting of their folktales. Point out that the reader learns little about the setting in "Finny Thinks Fast." The writer notes that the story takes place on a seacoast and in the ocean, but leaves many of the remaining details for the reader to supply. Is the ocean cold or warm? Are there other magical creatures in the sea? What plant life exists? Such details would help the reader understand the degree of danger involved in Finny's journey. Encourage students to review their folktales for details that depict the setting. **AL**

Listening, Speaking, and Viewing

Storytelling

Long before books, radio, movies, or TV, people entertained each other by telling stories. Storytelling is almost as old as humankind itself.

What Is Storytelling?

A storyteller presents a story to listeners rather than readers. Many stories were never written down. Instead they were passed along by word of mouth. Each person told a story a little differently, changing details to suit his or her style and audience. As a result, the story changed over time.

Why Is Storytelling Important?

Stories can be both entertaining and educational. Storytelling provides people with a way to preserve and pass along their history, beliefs, and culture. In the time of slavery, the folktale that's now called "The People Could Fly" was an entertainment, but it also gave enslaved people hope and a sense of pride in their African roots.

Storytelling also provides older people with a way to teach younger people how to behave. In the folktale "The Snake Chief," the selfish and headstrong daughter is punished, and the kind and obedient daughter is rewarded.

How Do I Tell a Story?

Like all kinds of public speaking, storytelling becomes easier with practice. Here are some basic steps you can follow to get you started.

Step 1: Know Your Story Unless you are experienced at making up stories on the spot, your first step should be to learn your story. Do not try to memorize it word for word. Your goal should be to *tell* a story, not *recite* it. Read your story several times until you know the storyline well.

Step 2: Rehearse Alone Practice telling your story without an audience. Don't be afraid to act parts out! In general, the more you liven up your storytelling, the more your audience will enjoy it. Use your voice and your body to make the story come alive.

- Speak clearly and with expression. Vary the speed of your voice and the pitch (high or low) to show different emotions and characters.
- Remember that pauses can be powerful. Pausing after an important point can give it emphasis.
- Use facial expressions, gestures, and movements to support dialogue and action.

Step 3: Rehearse with an Audience Practice telling your story to an audience of family members, classmates, or friends. Apply the guidelines in the bulleted list above. Also practice making eye contact with audience members. Do not look above their heads or at their feet. Briefly make eye contact with different people at different times.

Step 4: Ask for Feedback Ask your rehearsal audience to evaluate your storytelling. Here's a checklist you can use.

- Could you hear me clearly?
- Did I speak too quickly or too slowly?
- Did I vary my expression enough to help you picture each character in the story?
- Did I pause for emphasis?
- Did I use appropriate facial expressions?
- Did I use gestures effectively?
- What could I do to improve my storytelling?

Use audience feedback to improve how you tell your story. Then practice some more.

Tell Your Tales Work with a few classmates to practice telling your folktale. Do not *read* your story; practice *telling* it. Ask your classmates to use the checklist above to give you feedback on your storytelling. Give them feedback on their stories too. When you all feel ready, tell your stories to the whole class.

Teach

W Writing

Preparing for Storytelling Write the following emotions on the board. Have students tell how they would use their voice or body language to convey the following emotions when telling a story. Ask volunteers for a demonstration.

Sorrow: *(I would use a low tone of voice and a sad facial expression. I would slouch my shoulders.)*

Joy: *(I would use a high tone of voice and I would smile.)*

Anger: *(I would use a loud voice and furrow my brow. I might shake my fists.)* OL

Assess/Close

Discuss with students the effects of body, voice, and facial expression on storytelling. How do these elements help the speaker communicate a message? How do these elements affect the audience?

Differentiated Instruction

Storytelling Models Make use of your school or local library to obtain audio or video recordings of storytellers. You might also consult local arts councils for directories of storytellers who practice in your area. If possible, invite a local storyteller to perform for your class. Provide students with several storytelling models. Then lead students in identifying the techniques of each storyteller. List these techniques on the board. Ask students which techniques are most effective and why. Remind students to use these same techniques as they present their folktales. OL

Indiana English/Language Arts Academic Standards
SE: 8.7.6
TWE: *Literature Focus Lesson* 8.3.4, *Differentiated Instruction* 8.7

Comparing and Contrasting

Teaching Students to Compare and Contrast

Why Is It Important?

- Comparing and contrasting helps writers relate to and influence readers.
- Comparing and contrasting helps readers find and understand the argument in a selection.
- Students who are able to see similarities and differences in events, people, and ideas in a text are better able to construct meaning from a selection.

How to Help Students Get It

- Ask students to look carefully at the descriptions and other details an author includes in a selection.
- Have students look for clue words that signal that the author is comparing or contrasting items, such as *both, same, alike, also,* and *similarly,* or *unlike, but, although, yet,* and *instead.*
- Invite students to think about why a writer might compare or contrast things or people. Is there a larger purpose or idea the author may wish to convey?
- Tell students that sometimes there are no signal words to indicate comparison or contrast. In those instances, students must use descriptive details to infer similarities or differences between items.

Reading to Answer the Big Question

Icarus and Daedalus by Josephine Preston Peabody
An ancient Greek myth relates the tragic tale of the master architect Daedalus and his son Icarus who are imprisoned on the island of Crete. Daedalus builds wings to help them fly away. On the journey Icarus ignores his father's warning to stay away from the sun and falls to his death when his wings are melted by its heat. Daedalus is filled with grief and never again attempts to fly.

A Dose of Medicine by Charlotte Foltz Jones
Scientific and medical advancements come as a result of long journeys of experimentation and study. Students will learn about several of the people who contributed to the development of anesthesia—from phony professors demonstrating laughing gas to dentists searching for ways to help deaden the pain of tooth removal. They will also learn how Louis Pasteur's efforts to cure ailing chickens led to his development of human vaccines.

Workshop Resources

Pacing (Days) Standard	Block	Lesson	Student Materials	Teacher Resources
1	1/2	Key Skill Lesson: Comparing and Contrasting	Key Reading Skills Practice, p. 30 English Language Coach Review, p. 42	Bellringer Options Transparencies –Daily Language Practice 18 Read Aloud, Think Aloud Transparencies –Key Reading Skills 4 –Read Aloud, Think Aloud 18–20 Presentation Plus!
1	1	"Icarus and Daedalus"	Glencoe Online Unit Vocabulary Review, p. 40 Academic Vocabulary Review, p. 43 English Language Coach Active Reading Graphic Organizer, p. 32 Literary Analysis, p. 31 StudentWorks Plus™ Online Student Edition Literature Classics Selection and Unit Assessments, p. 19	Literary and Text Analysis Transparencies 54 Puzzlemaker Skill Level Up!™ A Language Arts Game BookLink 3 Assessment by Learning Objective (Diagnostic and Formative) Interactive Tutor: Self-Assessment TeacherWorks Plus™
1		"A Dose of Medicine"	Glencoe Online Unit Vocabulary Review, p. 40 Academic Vocabulary Review, p. 43 English Language Coach Active Reading Graphic Organizer, p. 34 StudentWorks Plus™ Online Student Edition Literature Classics Selection and Unit Assessments, p. 20	Puzzlemaker Skill Level Up!™ A Language Arts Game BookLink 3 Assessment by Learning Objective (Diagnostic and Formative) Interactive Tutor: Self-Assessment TeacherWorks Plus™

Keys for Unit Resource

- Blackline Master
- Workbook
- Supplemental Text
- CD-ROM
- DVD
- Transparency
- Web-based
- Fast File

Level Appropriate Code

- **AS** = Activities for all students
- **AL** = Activities for students working above grade level
- **OL** = Activities for students working at grade level
- **BL** = Activities for students working below grade level
- **EL** = Activities for English language learners

Focus

BELLRINGER Options

Daily Language Practice Transparency 18
Focus Activity Say: Name two things that are similar about you and your best friend. Name two things that are different. *(Responses will vary.)* AS

Teach

R Reading Skill

Comparing and Contrasting

Say: You compare when you say, "This is the same as that." You contrast when you say, "This is different than that." What qualities might a group of friends compare and contrast when making plans for a Saturday evening activity? *(Possible response: Friends might compare the costs and locations of different activities and which activity is more enjoyable.)* OL

V Vocabulary

Academic Vocabulary

Say: Look at the definition at the bottom of page 238. What are some synonyms for *similar*? *(Responses will vary. Students should use a thesaurus if needed.)* AS

READING WORKSHOP 4

Skills Focus

You will practice using these skills when you read the following selections:

- "Icarus and Daedalus," p. 242
- "A Dose of Medicine," p. 250

Reading

- Comparing and contrasting within and across texts

Literature

- Identifying the theme

Vocabulary

- Using systematic methods to build vocabulary
- Academic Vocabulary: *similar*

Writing/Grammar

- Identifying and using prepositional phases
- Identifying and using interjections

Skill Lesson

Comparing and Contrasting

Learn It!

R **What Is It?** When you **compare,** you notice how two things are **similar**, or alike. When you **contrast,** you notice how they are different. For example, if you want to buy a new bike, being able to compare and contrast features, price, and quality will help you get the best bike for the best price. Comparing the ingredients on the label of a snack can help you pick the healthiest snack. Comparing and contrasting is also useful when you read:

- You can compare and contrast characters, settings, and events within a selection.
- You can also compare and contrast characters, plots, and themes across different reading selections.
- You can even compare how authors organize and present information in reading selections.

Analyzing Cartoons
One character compares bike riding to studying and reaching a goal. Can you compare the lipstick case to a problem you might face while studying?

Indiana English/Language Arts Academic Standards (pp. 238–239)

8.3 Comprehension and Analysis of Literary Text Make connections and comparisons across texts...

For a complete description of the standards, see p. IN 11.

V **Academic Vocabulary**

similar (SIM uh lur) *adj.* alike, but not exactly the same

Additional Support

English Language Coach

Building Background Hector Cantú and Carlos Castellanos created the comic strip "Baldo" in 2000. Its main character is a teenager named Baldo Bermudez. It is the first nationally syndicated strip to feature a Hispanic family. The creators base their strip on their own experiences. Castellanos says, "What we try to do is depict Hispanics in a very real way." Discuss why a comic strip that is printed in many magazines might be an effective way to present different cultural perspectives. Ask students why it is important that newspapers, magazines, television, and other types of media portray different cultures in a realistic way. EL OL

Why Is It Important? As your reading takes you across a variety of sources, it is helpful to compare and contrast the similarities and differences within and among your reading selections. That way you'll gain a better understanding of all the material you've read. You'll also learn to read more critically and get more out of each selection.

Study Central Visit www.glencoe.com and click on Study Central to review comparing and contrasting.

How Do I Do It? As you read a selection, think about the characters' thoughts, words, and actions. Ask yourself, *In what ways are the characters alike and different?* As you read more than one selection, ask yourself what was included in one selection that might have been left out of another and why might that be.

Here's how a student compared and contrasted main characters in "The Snake Chief" and "Icarus and Daedalus."

The older sister in "The Snake Chief" is stubborn and self-centered, and she refuses to take good advice. In "Icarus and Daedalus," Icarus has some of the same faults. Though he is not stubborn and self-centered like the older sister, he is similar in that he does not follow his father's advice. In both stories, not following the advice of other people causes serious problems for the characters. **R**

Practice It!

Make a list of your favorite after-school activities and hobbies, and have a partner do the same. Then compare your lists. Which activities are alike? Which are different? What can you learn about each other by comparing and contrasting the activities you like to do?

Use It!

As you read "Icarus and Daedalus" and "A Dose of Medicine," look for ways that the characters' thoughts, words, and actions are alike and different. Also notice how each story is told and what details are given. Write your notes in your Learner's Notebook.

Teach

Study Central Have students access the Web site to review comparing and contrasting and to complete a related activity.

R Reading Skill

Comparing and Contrasting

Say: Look at the *How Do I Do It?* section. What elements from the stories does the writer use to compare and contrast Icarus and the older sister? *(Possible response: The writer compares the behavior, the personalities, and the values of Icarus and the older sister.)* OL

Resources for page 239

Use Key Reading Skills Transparency 4 in *Read Aloud, Think Aloud* to help students practice comparing and contrasting.

Reading in the Real World

College In college, students will be asked to think critically about the world around them. One way to do this is to compare and contrast media depictions of an event. Challenge students to find two brief news articles about the same current event. Ask students to compare and contrast the way the two articles treat their subject. Students should note whether the articles contain different information and whether the authors have the same opinion on the subject. Encourage students to consider whether they agree with one text more than the other and why. AL

Indiana English/Language Arts Academic Standards
SE: 8.3
TWE: *English Language Coach* 8.7.9, *Reading in the Real World* 8.2.3

Teach

More About the Author

Josephine Preston Peabody adapted classical myths for children in a book called *Old Greek Folk-Stories Told Anew.* Her book was written as a supplement to collections of children's stories previously published by the novelist Nathaniel Hawthorne. Peabody is also known for her plays. In 1910, her play *The Piper,* a retelling of the Pied Piper of Hamelin legend, won a prestigious play competition in England.

V Vocabulary

Building Vocabulary

Say: You may find that different strategies are more effective for one word than another. For example, a synonym collection might work well for the word *veered.* Synonyms include *swerved, turned,* and *bent.* When learning new vocabulary, choose a strategy that works well for you and that fits the word or words you are studying. EL BL

Before You Read | Icarus and Daedalus

Josephine Preston Peabody

Meet the Author

Josephine Preston Peabody was born in Brooklyn, New York, in 1874 and died in Cambridge, Massachusetts, in 1922. She published her first poem when she was fourteen years old. Six years later, the publication of her poems in magazines helped her attend Radcliffe College. See page R5 of the Author Files in the back of the book for more on Josephine Preston Peabody.

Author Search For more about Josephine Preston Peabody, go to www.glencoe.com.

Indiana English/Language Arts Academic Standards (pp. 240–245)

8.1 Word Recognition, Fluency, and Vocabulary Development Determine the meaning of words... **8.3 Comprehension and Analysis of Literary Text** Identify story elements such as...theme...make connections and comparisons across texts...

For a complete description of the standards, see p. IN 11.

Vocabulary Preview

veered (veerd) *v.* suddenly changed direction; form of the verb *veer* **(p. 242)** *The young boy veered off course and headed off the sidewalk.*

wavered (WAY vurd) *v.* swayed unsteadily; form of the verb *waver* **(p. 243)** *The first time he tried to fly, Daedalus wavered a bit before he was able to steady himself.*

rash (rash) *adj.* reckless; done without thought or concern **(p. 243)** *Icarus was young and inexperienced and therefore made many rash decisions that worried his father.*

quench (kwench) *v.* to satisfy a need **(p. 244)** *He flew as high as he could in an attempt to quench his need to reach the sun.*

V

Write to Learn In your Learner's Notebook, write a sentence for each of the vocabulary words above.

English Language Coach

Building Vocabulary: Parts of Speech One way to build your vocabulary is to build on the words you already know. When you're reading, you may see a word that looks familiar. Often, you can use the meaning of the word you already know to help you figure out the new word.

In "Icarus and Daedulus," one of the words you'll find is *cunning.* Cunning means "clever and skillful." But another word in the story is *cunningly.* You can tell from the way the word is used in the sentence that it is an adverb. It describes the way something was done. So you know right away that it means "in a clever and skillful way."

Another sentence in the story is "he gathered a store of feathers." You know that *store* can be a verb that means "to put away for later use." *Store* in this sentence is a noun, and it makes sense that it means "a supply of things put away for future use."

Partner Work With another student, come up with a list of adjectives. Then see whether you can turn them into adverbs by adding *-ly.* After you do, try using them in sentences.

Additional Support

Author Search To expand students' appreciation of Josephine Preston Peabody, have them access the Web site for additional information and resources.

Literature Focus Lesson

Mythology Myths of ancient Greece both entertain the reader and illustrate values held by Greek culture. Many people in ancient Greece believed the stories to be true, and they were thought to embody timeless truths. After your students read "Icarus and Daedalus," discuss as a class what the story reveals about Greek values and morals. **Ask:** What timeless truth does the story convey? Can you think of other stories that convey similar truths? *(Students should name stories that teach children to listen to their parents.)* OL

Skills Preview

Key Reading Skill: Comparing and Contrasting

As you read "Icarus and Daedalus," look for ways in which Icarus and Daedalus are alike and different.

Write to Learn Use a Venn diagram like the one below to record similarities and differences between Icarus and Daedalus as you read.

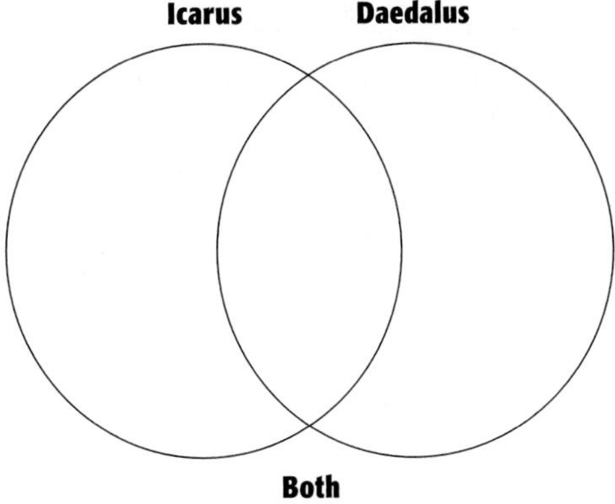

Key Literary Element: Theme

L A **theme** is the main message of a literary work. Most themes are "lessons in life"–things that characters learn from the conflicts they experience. In a **directly stated theme,** the author sums up the lesson in a general statement, such as "Slow but steady wins the race," the moral at the end of the fable "The Tortoise and the Hare." Most literary works have **implied themes**–lessons in life that are hinted at rather than stated. To find an implied theme, think about the central conflict, or the problem the main character struggles to overcome. Ask yourself what he or she learns from the experience. That lesson is a theme of the work.

Whole Class Discussion Think of a story or movie in which a reckless young person does not heed warnings about avoiding danger. What was the theme of the work? Put it in your own words.

Get Ready to Read

Connect to the Reading

C Have you ever wanted something so badly that you went about getting it in a reckless way? Have you ever wished that you could "do it over" so that the outcome would be different?

Write to Learn Write a few sentences about a time when you or someone you know would have liked to relive a situation in order to change it.

Build Background

"Icarus and Daedalus" is an ancient Greek myth that has been retold many times over the centuries. The story is set "once upon a time" in Greece when, supposedly, humans and gods lived on the island of Crete. A **myth** is an ancient story about gods, goddesses, or other supernatural beings and their influence on people and nature. When people in myths overstep their bounds and try to act like supernatural beings, they usually learn a hard lesson in life.

Set Purposes for Reading

Read "Icarus and Daedalus" to learn what happens to a boy on a dangerous mythological journey when he doesn't behave with caution.

Set Your Own Purpose What else would you like to learn from the story to help you answer the Big Question? Write your own purpose on the "Icarus and Daedalus" flap of Foldable 2.

Literature Online

Interactive Literary Elements Handbook
To review or learn more about the literary elements, go to www.glencoe.com.

Keep Moving

Use these skills as you read the following selections.

READING WORKSHOP 4

Teach

L Literary Element

Theme Say: Remember that a story's theme is different from its topic. Think of the last story you read. What was the topic, or subject of the story? What was its theme? *(Responses will vary.)* OL

C Critical Thinking

Application Say: Think about the situation you or a friend would like to relive. How do you think lessons from this experience will influence you in the future? *(Responses will vary.)* AS

Interactive Literary Elements Handbook Have students access the Web site to improve their understanding of theme.

English Language Coach

Context Clues Write the vocabulary words on the board. Read each of the sentences, and ask students to choose the correct word to complete each sentence. Advise students to listen for context clues to help them complete the sentences correctly.

veered *wavered* *quench*

1. Judy ran straight ahead, but Ting _______ from one side of the path to the other. *(veered)*
2. Though he drank a lot of water, he could not _______ his thirst. *(quench)*
3. The waitperson could hold three dinner plates steadily, but her tray _______ when a fourth was added. *(wavered)* EL

Indiana English/Language Arts Academic Standards
SE: 8.1, 8.3
TWE: *Literature Focus Lesson* 8.3, *English Language Coach* 8.1

Teach

R1 Reading Skill

Comparing and Contrasting
Have students find the word *cunning* in a dictionary.
Say: How does Daedalus's cunning make him different from other people? *(Possible response: Daedalus is much more clever than other people. His intelligence almost matches that of the gods.)* OL

R2 Reading Skill

Comparing and Contrasting
Say: Reread the last paragraph on this page. How does the author contrast the main characters' situation with that of the sea gulls? *(Possible response: The author writes that the gulls had the ability to fly free while Daedalus and his son were still captives on the island.)* **Ask:** Does this contrast help you understand what's occurring in the story? *(Responses will vary.)* OL

Readability Scores
Dale-Chall: 5.9
DRP: 57
Lexile: 1100

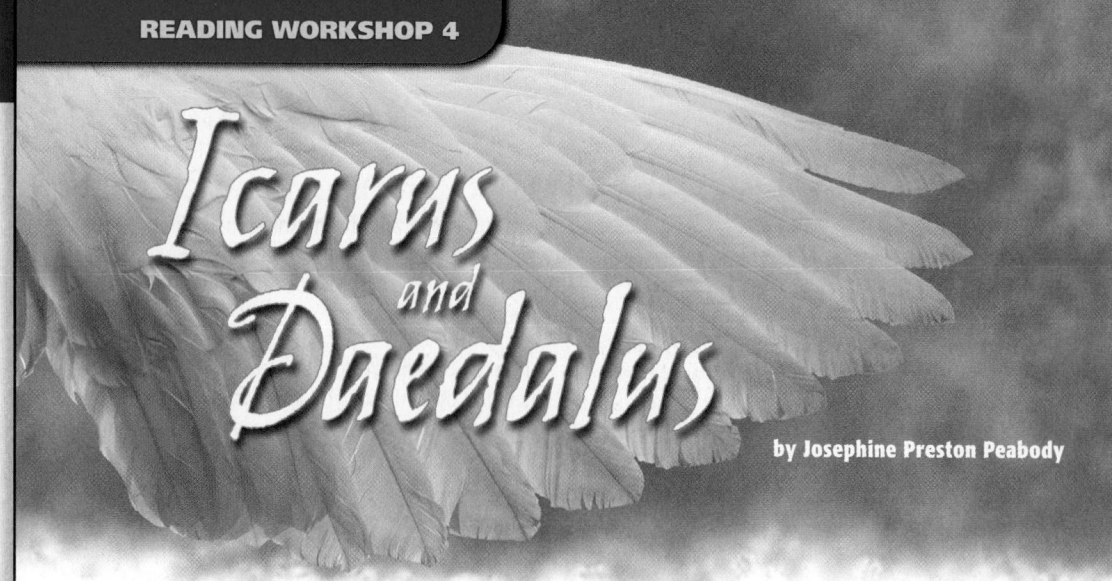

READING WORKSHOP 4

Icarus and Daedalus

by Josephine Preston Peabody

Among all those mortals[1] who grew so wise that they learned the secrets of the gods, none was more cunning[2] than Daedalus.[3] **1**

He once built, for King Minos of Crete, a wonderful Labyrinth of winding ways so cunningly tangled up and twisted around that, once inside, you could never find your way out again without a magic clue. But the king's favor **veered** with the wind, and one day he had his master architect imprisoned in a tower. Daedalus managed to escape from his cell; but it seemed impossible to leave the island, since every ship that came or went was well guarded by order of the king.

Visual Vocabulary
The ***Labyrinth*** was a huge maze in which a complicated, twisted path enclosed by high walls made it nearly impossible for people to find their way out.

At length, watching the sea gulls in the air—the only creatures that were sure of liberty—he thought of a plan for himself and his young son Icarus,[4] who was captive with him.

1. Humans are ***mortals***, which means that they die. Greek gods were believed to be immortal.
2. ***Cunning*** (KUH ning) means "clever and skillful."
3. ***Daedalus*** (DED uh lus)
4. ***Icarus*** (IK uh rus)

Vocabulary

veered (veerd) *v.* suddenly changed direction

Practice the Skills

1 Key Reading Skill

Comparing and Contrasting When you contrast, you show how two things are different. The author contrasts Daedalus to other mortals in the first paragraph. How is Daedalus different?

Additional Support

Leveled Reading An adapted version of this selection (4th grade readability) is available on page 192 of **Jamestown Literature: An Adapted Reader** for Grade 8.

Differentiated Instruction

Illustrating Daedalus is famous for the creation of the Labyrinth of Crete. According to legend, the king of Crete kept the Minotaur, a ferocious beast that was half man and half bull, in the Labyrinth. Every year, fourteen youths were sent into the Labyrinth, where they were eaten by the Minotaur. The hero Theseus finally slays the Minotaur and finds his way out of the Labyrinth by following a magical ball of yarn. Ask students to draw their own versions of the Labyrinth. Have them trace their original drawing and indicate the solution on the copy. Let students attempt to solve one another's labyrinths. AS

Little by little, he gathered a store of feathers great and small. He fastened these together with thread, molded them in with wax, and so fashioned[5] two great wings like those of a bird. When they were done, Daedalus fitted them to his own shoulders, and after one or two efforts, he found that by waving his arms he could winnow the air and cleave[6] it, as a swimmer does the sea. He held himself aloft, **wavered** this way and that with the wind, and at last, like a great fledgling,[7] he learned to fly.

Without delay, he fell to work on a pair of wings for the boy Icarus, and taught him carefully how to use them, bidding him beware of **rash** adventures among the stars. "Remember," said the father, "never to fly very low or very high, for the fogs about the earth would weigh you down, but the blaze of the sun will surely melt your feathers apart if you go too near."

For Icarus, these cautions went in at one ear and out by the other. Who could remember to be careful when he was to fly for the first time? Are birds careful? Not they! And not an idea remained in the boy's head but the one joy of escape. **2** **L**

The day came, and the fair wind that was to set them free. The father bird put on his wings, and, while the light urged them to be gone, he waited to see that all was well with Icarus, for the two could not fly hand in hand. Up they rose, the boy after his father. The hateful ground of Crete sank beneath them; and the country folk, who caught a glimpse of them when they were high above the treetops, took it for a vision of the gods—Apollo, perhaps, with Cupid[8] after him. **3**

At first there was a terror in the joy. The wide vacancy of the air dazed them—a glance downward made their brains reel. But when a great wind filled their wings, and Icarus felt **R**

5. Here, ***fashioned*** means "made" or "constructed."
6. ***Winnow*** and ***cleave*** both mean "to separate or divide."
7. A ***fledging*** is a young bird that has recently grown the feathers it needs to fly.
8. In mythology, ***Apollo*** is the god of the sun, and ***Cupid*** is the god of love.

Vocabulary

wavered (WAY vurd) *v.* swayed unsteadily

rash (rash) *adj.* reckless; done without thought or concern

Practice the Skills

2 Key Reading Skill

Comparing and Contrasting Compare and contrast Icarus's and Daedalus's attitude toward flight. Which one of them is cautious? Which one seems more reckless? How do you know? Remember to include these ideas on your Venn diagram.

3 Reviewing Skills

Predicting What do you think will happen to Icarus? To Daedalus? Think about what usually happens in myths to people who try to act like gods.

Teach

L Literary Element

Theme **Ask:** What evidence in the passage leads you to think that Icarus might not listen to his father's advice? *(His father's cautions went in one ear and out the other.)* **Ask:** In your own words, how would you describe Icarus? *(Responses will vary. Students may say that Icarus is young, carefree, excited, and reckless.)* **OL**

R Reading Skill

Review Predicting **Ask:** What character traits of Daedalus and Icarus help you predict how their journey might turn out? *(Possible response: Daedalus is smart and careful. He will probably make his invention work correctly. Icarus is too excitable to follow directions and too young to take care of himself. He will not have the discipline to fly safely and carefully.)* **OL**

Reading Fluency

Pronouncing Proper Nouns

Students may not be familiar with the proper nouns used for people and places in the story. Direct students to the pronunciations of *Daedalus* and *Icarus* at the bottom of page 242. Allow them time to use dictionaries to find the pronunciations of other proper nouns such as *Minos, Crete, Apollo, Cupid, Icaria,* and *Sicily.* Have students practice saying the proper nouns aloud until they can read the words in their contexts without hesitation. **AS**

Indiana English/Language Arts Academic Standards

SE: 8.2, 8.3

TWE: *Differentiated Instruction* 8.7.9, *Reading Fluency* 8.1

Teach

L Literary Element

Theme **Ask:** What makes Icarus forget his father's warning? *(Possible responses: Icarus is enthusiastic and energetic. He is excited by the possibilities that lie before him and eager to challenge himself by flying.)* OL **Ask:** Do you think the response Icarus has to flying is understandable? How would you feel in that situation? *(Responses will vary. Students may feel that his response is entirely understandable, or they may say that they would be more frightened in his place.)* AS

Viewing the Art

Ask: Does this painting present the joy of Icarus's flight? *(Responses will vary.)* AL

READING WORKSHOP 4

himself sustained, like a halcyon-bird[9] in the hollow of a wave, like a child uplifted by his mother, he forgot everything in the world but joy. He forgot Crete and the other islands that he had passed over: he saw but **vaguely** that winged thing in the distance before him that was his father Daedalus. He longed for one draft[10] of flight to **quench** the thirst of his captivity: he stretched out his arms to the sky and made toward the highest heavens. 4 5

Alas for him! Warmer and warmer grew the air. Those arms, that had seemed to uphold him, relaxed. His wings wavered, drooped. He fluttered his young hands vainly—he was falling—and in that terror he remembered. The heat of the sun had melted the wax from his wings; the feathers were falling, one by one, like snowflakes; and there was none to help.

Mountains in the Fog. Cindy Kassab.

Analyzing the Painting Does this painting help you understand how Icarus felt as he flew over Crete? Explain your answer.

9. Here, ***sustained*** means "to be kept from sinking or falling." The ***halcyon-bird***, or kingfisher, glides slowly and smoothly near the water's surface as it hunts for fish.

10. Here, ***draft*** means "taste."

Vocabulary

quench (kwench) *v.* to satisfy a need

Practice the Skills

4 Key Literary Element

Theme Icarus seems to be forgetting his father's warning. Be on the lookout for the lesson in life that Icarus learns from this mistake. It is a theme of the story.

5 English Language Coach

Building Vocabulary: Parts of Speech If you know that the word *vague* means "unclear," what does *vaguely* mean in this paragraph?

Additional Support

Differentiated Instruction

Studying a Painting and a Poem A painting by the artist Brueghel, entitled *The Fall of Icarus*, depicts people going about their everyday lives as Icarus falls from the sky. W. H. Auden wrote a poem about the painting, "Musée des Beaux Arts," commenting on how people were indifferent to the event. Have students find the painting and poem online. Tell students to read the poem and study the painting. Then ask them to state the theme of the painting and poem. AL

The Fall of Icarus, 1975. Marc Chagall. Private collection.

Analyzing the Painting How does this painting illustrate the action described in the paragraph below?

He fell like a leaf tossed down the wind, down, down, with one cry that overtook Daedalus far away. When he returned, and sought high and low for the poor boy, he saw nothing but the bird-like feathers afloat on the water, and he knew that Icarus was drowned. 6

The nearest island he named Icaria, in memory of the child; but he, in heavy grief, went to the temple of Apollo in Sicily, and there hung up his wings as an offering. Never again did he attempt to fly. 7 ❍

Practice the Skills

6 **Key Reading Skill**

Comparing and Contrasting What similarities can you find between the flight of Icarus and the flight of Daedalus? What is the main difference in the outcome of their flights?

7 **BIG Question**

BQ What is the destination of Icarus and Daedalus? What prevents them both from reaching it? Write your answer on the "Icarus and Daedalus" flap of Foldable 2. Your response will help you complete the Unit Challenge later.

READING WORKSHOP 4

Teach

L Literary Element

Theme Say: What does Icarus most likely "remember" during his fall? *(His father's warning.)* OL **Ask:** What might be one theme of this story? *(Possible response: Listen to your parents.)* AL

BQ

Say: What do you think influenced Icarus to be so reckless on his journey? *(Possible responses: His desire to experience freedom after being in captivity; his youth.)* OL

Assess

CheckPoint

Use the CheckPoint questions provided on Presentation Plus! to check for comprehension of the selection. These questions can be used with interactive response keypads for immediate student feedback.

Literature Focus Lesson

Metaphor and Simile Remind students that metaphors and similes are literary forms of comparison in which two things, unlike in most ways, have something in common. Similes use the words *like* or *as*. Metaphors do not. Discuss this metaphor and simile:

- He longed for one draft of flight to quench the thirst of his captivity.

Ask: *How might flying after being a captive be like quenching thirst?*

- He fell like a leaf tossed down the wind. . . .

Ask: *What two things are being compared in this simile? How are they alike?* AL

Indiana English/Language Arts Academic Standards

SE: 8.1, 8.3

TWE: *Differentiated Instruction* 8.3, *Literature Focus Lesson* 8.1.1

Assess

Resources for page 246

- Selection Quick Check, p. 17
- Selection and Unit Assessment, p. 19
- ExamView Assessment Suite
- Interactive Tutor: Self-Assessment

Students can respond to the *After You Read* items in their Learner's Notebooks or on a separate sheet of paper.

Answering the BIG Question

1. Possible response: The destination was more important to Daedalus because he wanted to escape. The journey was more important to Icarus because he wanted to enjoy flying.
2. King Minos imprisons them in a tower.
3. Daedalus tells his son, "Remember never to fly very low or very high, for the fogs about the earth would weigh you down, but the blaze of the sun will surely melt your feathers apart if you go too near."

Critical Thinking

4. Possible response: The people assume that only gods can fly.
5. Possible response: Icarus feels so safe, comfortable, and happy when he is in flight that he forgets his father's warnings.
6. Responses will vary.

After You Read

Icarus and Daedalus

Answering the BIG Question

1. What do you think was more important to Daedalus, the journey or the destination? What do you think was more important to Icarus? Why?
2. **Recall** What does King Minos do to keep Daedalus and Icarus from escaping Crete?

   TIP **Right There** The answer is in one place in the story.
3. **Quote** What warning does Daedalus give his son about flying? Copy it word for word from the story.

   TIP **Right There** The warning is in one place in the story.

Critical Thinking

4. **Infer** Why do the people of Crete think that Daedalus and Icarus are gods when they see the father and son flying overhead?

   TIP **Author and Me** Use your understanding of the myth and of the beliefs of people long ago.
5. **Interpret** In your own words, tell what the following sentence means: "Icarus felt himself sustained, like a halcyon-bird in the hollow of a wave, like a child uplifted by his mother, he forgot everything in the world but joy." (pages 243–244).

   TIP **Author and Me** To answer the question, use the footnotes and your understanding of how Icarus feels.
6. **Evaluate** Do you think Daedalus is a concerned father? Do you think he feels responsible for what happens to his son? Why or why not?

   TIP **On My Own**

Write About Your Reading

Newspaper Article Imagine that you have been assigned to write a news story about Daedalus, Icarus, and their flight to freedom. Write a short news report about what happened. Make sure you answer the following questions in your story:

- *What* happened?
- *Who* was involved?
- *When* did it happen?
- *Where* did it happen?
- *Why* did it happen?
- *How* did it happen?

Indiana English/Language Arts Academic Standards (pp. 246–247)

8.3 Comprehension and Analysis of Literary Text Respond to grade-level-appropriate literature...identify story elements such as...theme... make connections and comparisons...
8.5.7 Write for different purposes...
8.6 English Language Conventions
For a complete description of the standards, see p. IN 11.

Write About Your Reading

Possible response:
Today the *Sicily Times* learned that Daedalus, the famous inventor from Crete, flew here to freedom. Daedalus and his son, Icarus, had been imprisoned on Crete by King Minos. Daedalus created wings that enabled him and his son to fly. Unfortunately, Icarus was drowned during their flight to freedom when extreme heat caused the wings to melt and sent Icarus crashing into the sea.

Skills Review

Key Reading Skill: Comparing and Contrasting

7. How were Daedalus and Icarus alike and how were they different? Use the notes you made on your Venn diagram to help you answer the question.

Key Literary Element: Theme

8. Think about the theme of the story. Write the theme in one sentence in your own words.

9. How might the theme of "Icarus and Daedalus" apply to life today? Give an example of a situation that could happen in today's world, and explain how the theme might apply to it.

Reviewing Skills: Predicting

10. Did you predict what would happen to Daedalus and Icarus? Did you get close? Did knowing about myths help you? Explain.

Vocabulary Check

Match the words below to their definitions.

11. veered — a. to satisfy
12. rash — b. without caution
13. quench — c. became unsteady
14. wavered — d. changed direction

15. Academic Vocabulary What is a synonym for *similar?*

16. English Language Coach Building Vocabulary: Parts of Speech See if you can figure out the meaning of *fueled* used as a verb in the following sentence. Use your knowledge of the meaning of *fuel* as a noun and any context clues in the sentence.

- The story of Daedalus and Icarus was so interesting to me that it **fueled** my imagination.

Grammar Link: Prepositions

A **preposition** connects a noun or pronoun to another word in a sentence. Some common prepositions are *above, after, as, at, before, behind, during, for, from, inside, in, near, over, since, under,* and *with.* In the sentence below, the preposition *on* shows the relationship between *bus* and *boy.*

- The boy on the bus looks happy.

A **prepositional phrase** is a group of words that begins with a preposition and ends with a noun or pronoun, called the **object of the preposition.**

- Jamilla ran [beside his best friend].
  (The prepositional phrase in brackets begins with the preposition beside *and ends with the noun* friend.*)*
- Jamilla ran [beside him].
  (The prepositional phrase in brackets begins with the preposition beside *and ends with the pronoun* him.*)*

Compound prepositions consist of more than one word. Some compound prepositions are *along with, because of, in front of, instead of,* and *on top of.*

- Yoshi stood in front of his locker.

Grammar Practice

Copy the prepositional phrase in each sentence.

17. The athletes raced to the finish line.
18. Carlita jumped into the pool.
19. Can I come along with you?
20. The books on the table are mine.

Writing Application Review your news story. Make sure you used prepositions correctly.

Web Activities For eFlashcards, Selection Quick Checks, and other Web activities, go to www.glencoe.com.

Skills Review

Key Reading Skill: Comparing and Contrasting

7. Responses will vary.

Key Literary Element: Theme

8. Possible response: Great gifts can be a danger to young people who do not follow the advice of elders.

9. Possible response: The theme applies to life today because parents give advice to their children. Children may think their parents' advice is too cautious, but parents often base their advice on experiences.

Reviewing Skills: Predicting

10. Possible response: Knowing that people's pride and desire to have powers of the gods often fail helped me guess that something bad would happen to someone.

Vocabulary Check

11. d.
12. b.
13. a.
14. c.

Academic Vocabulary

15. alike

English Language Coach

16. Possible response: energized

Grammar Link: Prepositions

Grammar Practice

17. to the finish line
18. into the pool
19. with you
20. on the table

Close

Ask students to summarize what they learned from the story about the need to balance enjoyment of the journey with a focus on the destination.

Indiana English/Language Arts Academic Standards
SE: 8.1, 8.3, 8.5.7, 8.6

Teach

More About the Author

Charlotte Foltz Jones writes books enjoyed by young adults, but she affirms that she writes these books for herself. "When I sit down to write, I don't think in terms that I am writing for children. I write for myself—maybe for the part of me that never grew up, the part that still wonders and looks about in amazement."

EL Language Coach

Building Vocabulary Say: As you make a personalized list of key terms for "A Dose of Medicine," pay attention to how the words are used in sentences. As you note the definitions of unfamiliar words, copy the sentences in which the words appear. To check your understanding of an unfamiliar word, try to use it in an original sentence of your own. EL

Before You Read A Dose of Medicine

Meet the Author

Charlotte Foltz Jones was born in 1945. She has written many science books for young readers to try to make the subject interesting for young people. Aside from *Mistakes That Worked,* she has written *Accidents May Happen* and *Fingerprints and Funny Bones: How Real-Life Crimes are Solved.* See page R3 of the Author Files in the back of the book for more information on Charlotte Foltz Jones.

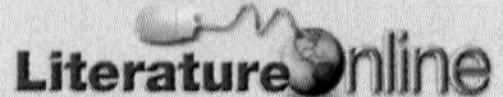

Author Search For more about Charlotte Foltz Jones, go to www.glencoe.com.

Indiana English/Language Arts Academic Standards (pp. 248–253)

8.1 Word Recognition, Fluency, and Vocabulary Development Determine the meaning of words... **8.3 Comprehension and Analysis of Literary Text** Make connections and comparisons across texts... **8.2 Comprehension and Analysis (Focus on Informational Text)** Identify and analyze structure and organization...

For a complete description of the standards, see p. IN 11.

Vocabulary Preview

prospect (PRAH spekt) *n.* that which is expected **(p. 250)** *The prospect of having a tooth pulled is usually very unpleasant.*

hilarious (hih LAR ee us) *adj.* very funny **(p. 251)** *Everything seemed hilarious to the comedians.*

deaden (DEH dun) *v.* to make weak or dull **(p. 251)** *The shot will deaden the pain in my tooth.*

consciousness (KON shus nus) *n.* the state of being fully awake or alert **(p. 251)** *The injury to his head knocked him flat and made him lose consciousness.*

publicized (PUB lih syzd) *v.* made the public aware of something; form of the verb *publicize* **(p. 252)** *People knew about the doctor's discovery after it was publicized in the morning paper.*

Small Group Work With a small group of classmates, write a paragraph with sentences that include each of the vocabulary words above.

English Language Coach

Building Vocabulary: Preview List The selection "A Dose of Medicine" contains words and phrases from science and medicine that may be unfamiliar to you. As you learned in Reading Workshop 3, you can make it easier to understand selections with unfamiliar vocabulary by creating your own personalized list of key terms.

On Your Own Quickly look over "A Dose of Medicine" before you read it. As you look, jot down at least three key terms that are new to you. Use context clues, a dictionary, footnotes, or other aids to define the words on your list. Keep the list nearby when you read the selection, and add other terms to your list if you need to. Here's a sample to help you get started. EL

1. nitrous oxide (page 250): laughing gas
2. cholera (page 252): deadly disease
3. contracted (page 252): caught
4. organism (page 252): living thing

Additional Support

Author Search To expand students' appreciation of Charlotte Foltz Jones, have them access the Web site for additional information and resources.

Literature Focus Lesson

Nonfiction Tell students that unlike many of the selections in this unit, "A Dose of Medicine" is nonfiction. Nonfiction texts provide readers with factual information. They include main ideas—the most important ideas in a selection—that are backed up with supporting details. AS Have students note the most important ideas in "A Dose of Medicine." Ask them to give one supporting detail for each main idea in the passage. OL

Skills Preview

Key Reading Skill: Comparing and Contrasting

Before you read the selection, think about how advances in science and medicine have improved our lives.

Write to Learn List some of the discoveries that have been made in your lifetime. Next to each discovery, tell how the discovery has made your life different.

Text Element: Chronological Order

When an author presents events in the order in which they actually happened, he or she is using **chronological order,** or time order.

E
- This sequence is useful for nonfiction narratives such as biographies and autobiographies, history articles, and newspaper stories.
- Chronological order is also often used in fictional narratives, such as short stories and novels.

To help readers understand what happened first, next, and so on, authors may include **time-order signal words,** which are transitions that tell when something happened.

Whole Class Discussion As a class, brainstorm a list of time-order transition words and phrases. Try to list at least ten different words. The following examples will help you get started.

- then
- later
- after
- before
- yesterday
- today

Interactive Literary Elements Handbook
To review or learn more about the literary elements, go to www.glencoe.com.

Get Ready to Read

Connect to the Reading

How do you feel about going to the doctor to get a shot or a vaccination? Think about your experiences getting shots.

Write to Learn In your Learner's Notebook jot down a few sentences describing how you feel about shots and why.

Build Background

Until Louis Pasteur discovered that a bacteria caused cholera, that disease and others killed thousands of people each year.

- Between the 1840s and 1860s, many major cities experienced severe outbreaks of cholera. Immigrants traveling to America on unsanitary and crowded boats brought cholera to the cities in which they settled.
- In 1849 678 people died from cholera in Chicago. About half of these deaths happened between July 25 and August 28. Though Pasteur had not yet completed his work, people in Chicago thought that there had to be a relationship between dirty drinking water and the spread of cholera. After an 1854 outbreak killed 1,424 people, pipes were built into Lake Michigan to bring fresh water to the city. This system reduced the amount of drinking water people got from buckets and wells and greatly cut the number of cholera deaths in the coming years. R

Set Purposes for Reading

BIG Question Read "A Dose of Medicine" to find out how both Dr. Wells and Louis Pasteur worked hard to discover ways to make peoples' lives better.

Set Your Own Purpose What else would you like to learn from the selection to help you answer the Big Question? Write your own purpose on the "Dose of Medicine" flap of Foldable 2.

Keep Moving

Use these skills as you read the following selections.

Teach

E Text Element

Chronological Order

Ask: Why is it important to know the chronological order, or time order, of events? *(Possible response: Knowing the order of events helps readers understand what happened and why and how events unfolded.)* OL

R Reading Skill

Comparing and Contrasting

Ask: What was life like in Chicago before pipes bringing fresh water were built, and afterwards? *(Possible response: Life before was dangerous; many people got cholera and died. Life afterwards was less dangerous. The number of cholera deaths decreased.)* OL

Interactive Literary Elements Handbook Have students access the Web site to improve their understanding of chronological order.

English Language Coach

Build Background Many medical terms are fairly new to the English language. The term *vaccination*, for example, was first used in the late eighteenth and early nineteenth centuries by British scientist Edward Jenner. Jenner used the term to describe the technique he had developed for preventing smallpox, a terrible disease that was especially deadly in women and children. Jenner injected people with a harmless virus called cowpox. This virus prevented people from getting sick from the more dangerous smallpox virus. *Vaccination* comes from *vacca*, the Latin word for *cow.* AS Have students explain why Jenner might have used the word *vaccination.* AL

Indiana English/Language Arts Academic Standards
SE: 8.1, 8.2, 8.3
TWE: *Literature Focus Lesson* 8.2.4, *English Language Coach* 8.1

Teach

C Critical Thinking

Evaluation **Say:** Read the quote by Martin H. Fisher. What do you think he means? *(Responses will vary.)* OL **Ask:** How well do you think this quote applies to a story about medicine? Explain your answer. *(Responses will vary.)* AL

Viewing the Illustration

Say: Look at the illustration at the top of the page. How would you describe the people in this image? *(Possible response: The man holding the string looks sort of evil or crazy. The man in the chair looks like he's very uncomfortable and in a lot of pain.)* AS **Ask:** Do you think this image accurately depicts what it was like to have a tooth pulled a few centuries ago? *(Responses will vary. Some may say the image looks very exaggerated. Others may say that it seems to fit the description in the first two paragraphs of the selection.)* OL

Readability Scores
Dale-Chall: 10.3
DRP: 62
Lexile: 960

A Dose of Medicine

Tooth Extraction Caricature, 1773. John Collier.

by Charlotte Foltz Jones

"All the world is a laboratory to the inquiring mind."
—Martin H. Fischer

ETHER AND NITROUS OXIDE

Do you need to have a tooth pulled, an appendix removed, or a cut stitched up? A couple of centuries ago surgery was a pretty grim **prospect.**

If you couldn't stand the pain (and who could?), there were several options. You could be:

frozen,
beaten senseless,
asphyxiated,[1]
pumped full of alcohol,
or given a piece of wood to bite down on. **1**

But in the 1800s things changed.

New gases had been discovered—ether and nitrous oxide, which was called laughing gas because it made people who inhaled it sing, laugh, act silly, or fight. At first these two gases were mainly used for entertainment at parties called ether frolics or laughing gas parties.

1. To be ***asphyxiated*** (as FIK see ayt id) means to be deprived of oxygen.

Vocabulary

prospect (PRAH spekt) *n.* that which is expected

Practice the Skills

1 Key Reading Skill

Comparing and Contrasting
Contrast the pain-relieving methods used before the discovery of modern pain medicine to what is used today. How are they different?

Additional Support

Reading in the Real World

Citizenship Instruct students to conduct interviews with elderly members of their community. Alternatively, have students prepare questions for a medical historian who can visit the class. Guide students to prepare questions about health care practices of the past. Suggest that students ask about diseases that people may have considered very dangerous a few decades ago but that pose little threat today. Invite students to share their findings with the class. OL

Also, so-called professors traveled from town to town giving public lectures. They administered ether or nitrous oxide to a volunteer, and that person's **hilarious** behavior made the audience laugh. **2**

At one of these **demonstrations** an accident occurred. In 1844 in Hartford, Connecticut, a "professor" named Colton asked for someone to inhale nitrous oxide. **3** Samuel Cooley volunteered, but he soon became violent, tripped, and fell. When he went back to his seat, someone noticed that Cooley was bleeding from his fall.

Horace Wells, a dentist, had come to the demonstration with Cooley. He realized that Cooley felt no pain from his fall, and he reasoned that the gas might **deaden** patients' pain while he performed dental work.

Wells began testing the gases. He breathed some nitrous oxide and had a fellow dentist pull one of his teeth. The procedure went so well that Wells decided to give a demonstration at a university. He was probably excited and eager to prove the success of the gas. After giving a patient some gas, Wells began to remove the patient's tooth. The gas had not taken effect, and the patient screamed out in pain. The audience of students hissed and drove Wells away in disgrace.

Wells, however, still felt confident that the gas would be effective, and he continued to use it in his practice.

Another dentist, William T. G. Morton, learned of Wells's use of nitrous oxide. He tried some on his patients. Then his partner, Charles T. Jackson, suggested using ether. So Morton extracted[2] a tooth from a patient on September 30, 1846, using ether.

Still another physician, Dr. Crawford W. Long of Jefferson, Georgia, said he had seen a slave lose **consciousness**—yet breathe normally—after

2. ***Extracted*** (eks TRAKT id) means "pulled out."

Vocabulary

hilarious (hih LAR ee us) *adj.* very funny

deaden (DEH dun) *v.* to make weak or dull

consciousness (KON shus nus) *n.* the state of being fully awake or alert

Practice the Skills

R1

2 Text Element

Chronological Order Notice the time-order clues that the author gives you at the beginning of this article. She states when the events began (the 1800s) and includes the time-order signal words *at first.*

3 English Language Coach

Building Vocabulary: Preview List Did you put the word **demonstrations** on your preview list? Can you tell from the context what it means, or do you need to look it up?

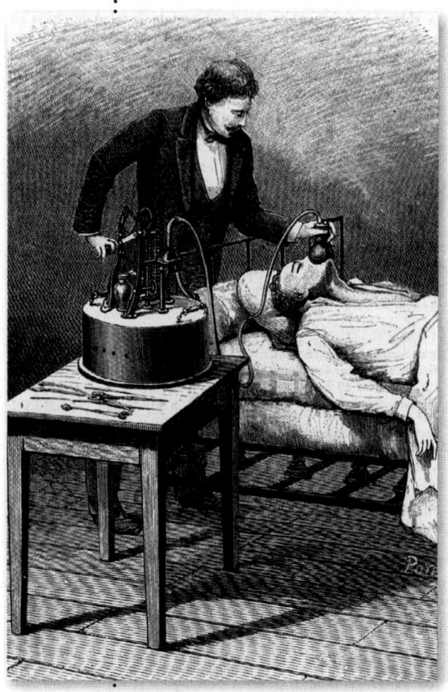

Illustration in *La Nature,* March 21, 1885.

Analyzing the Painting How does this scene compare to a modern-day doctor's office?

Teach

R1 Reading Skill

Comparing and Contrasting
Ask: How do the "lectures" given by "professors" in the passage compare to lectures professors normally give? *(Possible response: The lectures in the passage were actually just a form of entertainment. Real professors give information at lectures.)* **OL**

R2 Reading Skill

Comparing and Contrasting
Point out that when new drugs are introduced today, they must go through rigorous testing in laboratories and get government approval before they can be given to patients.
Ask: How does this process compare to the events described on this page? *(Possible response: The dentists tried out nitrous oxide and ether in their offices on patients. They didn't get government approval to use or experiment with the drugs.)* **OL**

Viewing the Illustration

Say: Look at the clothing that the surgeon wears in the illustration. How does his clothing differ from what a surgeon would wear today? *(Possible response: Surgeons wear hospital uniforms or scrubs that they can discard after surgery.)* **OL**

Differentiated Instruction

Creating an Advertisement Tell students to imagine they work for an advertising agency that has been hired by Horace Wells, who has just discovered the effects of ether and nitrous oxide. Wells wants to encourage patients to visit his clinic and experience these wonderful new numbing agents. Have students create an advertisement for Wells that explains the benefits of these drugs and persuades readers to visit his dental office. Encourage students to find or create an illustration to include on the advertisement. **BL** **OL**

Indiana English/Language Arts Academic Standards
SE: 8.1, 8.2, 8.3
TWE: *Reading in the Real World* 8.7, 8.4.11; *Differentiated Instruction* 8.4

Teach

R Reading Skill

Comparing and Contrasting **Say:** "Professor" Colton demonstrated nitrous oxide before Horace Wells used the gas. In what way was Wells's use more significant than Colton's? *(Possible response: Colton used the gas for entertainment, while Wells recognized its anesthetic properties and applied them to dentistry.)* **OL** **Ask:** Do you think it was fair for the American Dental Association and the American Medical Association to credit Horace Wells with the invention of anesthesia? Why or why not? *(Possible response: Yes, it was fair because Wells recognized its usefulness.)* **AL**

E Text Element

Chronological Order **Ask:** Which happened first, Dr. Long used ether on a patient or Louis Pasteur battled chicken cholera? *(Long used ether on a patient)* **BL**

C Critical Thinking

Comprehension **Ask:** Why does Pasteur expect the chickens to get sick and die? *(because he fed them deadly cholera germs)* **BL** **OL**

READING WORKSHOP 4

inhaling ether. Long claimed that on March 30, 1842, he used ether as an anesthesia[3] while removing a tumor from a patient's neck. He continued using ether on patients but never **publicized** his discovery.

So four doctors claimed to have first used ether or nitrous oxide to dull pain. The U.S. Congress offered $100,000 to the person who discovered anesthesia. But since it could not decide who should receive the award, Congress never paid the money.

The American Dental Association and the American Medical Association finally decided that Horace Wells was the discoverer of anesthesia in the United States. 4

INOCULATION[4]

Louis Pasteur was one of the most brilliant chemists of the nineteenth century. In 1880 he helped the French chicken industry battle chicken cholera. It was a terrible disease. Chickens that contracted it soon had drooping wings, feathers standing on end, and tottery legs. A chicken would stagger around until it collapsed, flutter its wings, and die.

Pasteur grew the organism that caused the cholera and stored the germs in bottles. One day he fed some of the germs to a few chickens. He expected them to get sick and die. The chickens acted a little sickly for a while, but then they recovered. C

Curly-Haired Cockerel, c. 1767-1776. Hand colored engraving. Private collection, The Stapleton Collection/ Bridgeman Art Library.

3. Here, ***anesthesia*** (an uh STEE zhuh) is a substance that causes a loss of feeling in order to numb or block pain.

4. ***Inoculation*** (ih nawk yoo LAY shun) is the process of injecting the body with medicine to prevent disease.

Vocabulary

publicized (PUB lih syzd) *v.* made the public aware of something

Practice the Skills

4 Key Reading Skill

Comparing and Contrasting Notice that the author explains how four different doctors tried to use ether or nitrous oxide to deaden pain. Compare and contrast the different techniques that the four doctors used. R

Additional Support

Reading in the Real World

Career Tell students that medical scientists research human diseases in order to improve people's health. They may conduct their own studies of diseases to find their causes or use the results of other studies to help them develop cures for diseases. Medical scientists have either a PhD in science or a medical degree (MD), so this field requires a lot of schooling. Have interested students learn more about the field of medical science. **AL**

Practice the Skills

Analyzing the Art What does this picture tell you about the nature of scientific research in Pasteur's time?

The germs had been growing for about six weeks, and Pasteur figured they must be stale. So he fed a fresh crop of the germs to the same birds.

Nothing happened.

Pasteur fed some of the same fresh crop of germs to a different set of chickens. All of those birds got sick and died, as he had expected. 5

Pasteur had discovered by accident that the "old" crop of germs had somehow changed. They no longer caused serious disease, and they protected the chickens from getting the disease later, even when the chickens were exposed to fresh germs. R

Pasteur quickly realized that the same thing would happen with bacteria[5] affecting humans, and in 1881 he developed the anticholera vaccine.[6] 6 ❍

5. ***Bacteria*** (bak TEER ee uh) are tiny one-celled organisms. Some bacteria help digest food, while others cause diseases.
6. A ***vaccine*** (vak SEEN) is medicine given to people or animals to protect them from a specific disease.

5 **Key Reading Skill**

Comparing and Contrasting How was Pasteur's approach different from that of the dentists and doctors who experimented with anesthesia?

6 **BIG Question**

BQ What lessons about the methods of scientific discovery can we learn from this selection? Explain. Write your answer on the "Dose of Medicine" flap of Foldable 2. Your response will help you complete the Unit Challenge later.

READING WORKSHOP 4

Teach

R Reading Skill

Comparing and Contrasting

Ask: How was Pasteur's approach to the cholera problem similar to a scientist's approach to research today? *(Possible response: Pasteur developed a hypothesis—that the stale germs protected the chickens from developing the disease later—and tested that hypothesis. Scientists today use experiments to test their hypotheses.)* AL

BQ BIG Question

Ask: Why is patience an important part of the "journey" scientists take? *(Possible response: Scientists must be patient and watch changes that occur over time. They cannot rush an experiment because that could alter the accuracy of the results.)* OL

Assess

CheckPoint

Use the CheckPoint questions provided on Presentation Plus! to check for comprehension of the selection. These questions can be used with interactive response keypads for immediate student feedback.

Differentiated Instruction

Pasteurization Louis Pasteur invented a process called pasteurization, in which a food is heated to destroy disease-causing microorganisms. Pasteurization is still used today. Have students interested in science find out what pasteurization involves by answering these questions:

- What happens during pasteurization?
- Why is it necessary?
- What might happen to food that is not pasteurized?

AL

Indiana English/Language Arts Academic Standards
SE: 8.2
TWE: *Reading in the Real World* 8.2.5, *Differentiated Instruction* 8.2.5

Assess

Resources for page 254

- Selection Quick Check, p. 18
- Selection and Unit Assessment, p. 20
- ExamView Assessment Suite
- Interactive Tutor: Self-Assessment

Students can respond to the *After You Read* items in their Learner's Notebooks or on a separate sheet of paper.

Answering the BIG Question

1. Possible response: The discoveries are more important because the discoveries help people directly.
2. Pasteur thought the chickens would get sick. Instead, they survived.
3. Anesthesia dulled pain and caused patients to lose consciousness during painful dental work and surgery.

Critical Thinking

4. Possible response: People probably respected Pasteur greatly after he developed the anticholera vaccine.
5. Possible response: Wells made the greatest contribution because he discovered its use.
6. Possible response: The author seems to understand that many discoveries are made accidentally and that accidents can often be blessings in disguise.

After You Read | A Dose of Medicine

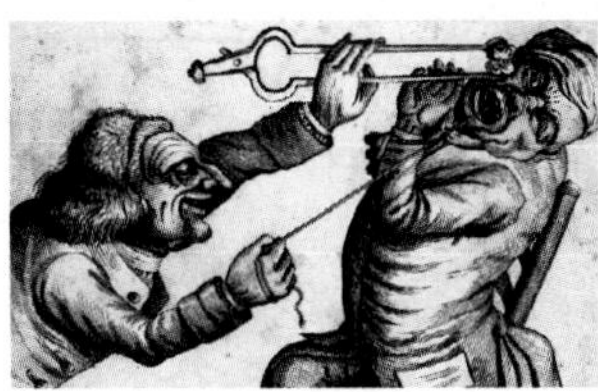

Answering the BIG Question

1. What is more important—the journeys that scientists take toward making discoveries or the discoveries themselves? Explain.
2. **Recall** What happened when Louis Pasteur first fed the cholera germs to chickens?
   TIP **Right There** The answer is in the selection.
3. **Summarize** How did the use of anesthesia help dental patients?
   TIP **Think and Search** The answer is in the selection, but it is not all in one place.

Critical Thinking

4. **Infer** What do you think people thought of Louis Pasteur?
   TIP **Author and Me** Use your understanding of the selection and of people.
5. **Evaluate** Which of the four doctors do you think made the biggest contribution to the development of anesthesia? Explain your answer.
   TIP **Author and Me** Use your own judgment.
6. **Infer** How does the author feel about the "mistakes" scientists make?
   TIP **Author and Me** Use your understanding of the selection and your own judgment.

Talk About Your Reading

Round Table Working in a group of six classmates, jot down questions that you might ask each of these people mentioned in the article:

- Horace Wells
- Charles T. Jackson
- Louis Pasteur
- William T. G. Morton
- Crawford W. Long

Write questions that can be answered only by reading "A Dose of Medicine." For example, you might ask Wells, "How did you figure out that nitrous oxide would deaden pain?" When you have at least one question for each person, assign roles to group members—the five people listed plus a "host." Then hold a roundtable discussion, with the host asking the questions and group members answering them in character.

Indiana English/Language Arts Academic Standards (pp. 254–255)

8.3 Comprehension and Analysis of Literary Text Respond to grade-level-appropriate literature...make connections and comparisons across texts... **8.7.11** Deliver oral responses to literature... **8.2 Comprehension and Analysis (Focus on Informational Text)** Develop [reading] strategies... identify and analyze structure and organization... **8.6 English Language Conventions**

For a complete description of the standards, see p. IN 11.

Talk About Your Reading

Possible questions are provided. Students should use information in the passage to answer the questions.

Horace Wells: How did you feel after the demonstration at the university?

William T. G. Morgan: Why did you use nitrous oxide on your patients?

Charles T. Jackson: What did you suggest Morgan use on his patients and why?

Dr. Crawford W. Long: What led you to use ether as an anesthesia?

Louis Pasteur: How did you develop the anticholera vaccine?

Skills Review

Key Reading Skill: Comparing and Contrasting

7. Compare a visit to the dentist today with a visit to the dentist in the 1800s. Use information from the selection and information from your own personal experience.
8. Think about the ways Pasteur and Wells went about their experiments. How were their methods alike? How were they different? Explain.

Text Element: Chronological Order

9. What are some time-order signal words that the author uses in the article? List at least three.
10. Make a time line that begins with 1842 and ends with 1846. On your time line, list in chronological order the major events that led to the discovery of anesthesia.

Vocabulary Check

Rewrite each sentence on a separate sheet of paper, using the correct vocabulary word.

prospect publicized consciousness hilarious deaden

11. The ___ antics of people who used nitrous oxide made people who were watching them laugh.
12. One way doctors tried to ___ pain was to knock their patients out.
13. The discovery of a new vaccine is usually well ___.
14. Anesthesia allowed patients to have surgery without losing ___.
15. In the early 1800s, the ___ of recovery from major surgery was not very good.
16. **English Language Coach** Choose any three words from your personalized preview list, and use them correctly in a paragraph.

Grammar Link: Interjections

An **interjection** is a word or group of words that expresses emotion or attracts attention. It has no grammatical connection to the rest of the sentence, so it is set off by an exclamation point or a comma.

An interjection that expresses strong emotion may stand alone. Though not a sentence, it begins with a capital letter and ends with an exclamation point.

- Ouch! You are stepping on my foot!
- Good grief! I'm going to sit somewhere else.

An interjection that expresses mild emotion is set off from the sentence with commas.

- No, I'm not hungry.
- Well, maybe I am hungrier than I thought I was.

Some Common Interjections		
aha	hey	oops
yikes	hooray	ouch
good grief	my	well
great	no	wow
ha	oh	yes

Grammar Practice

On a separate sheet of paper, copy each sentence below. Underline the interjections.

17. I took the test, and, oh, it was hard.
18. Well! It's about time you showed up.
19. Yes, I would love some more carrots.
20. Oh, no, here we go again!

Web Activities For eFlashcards, Selection Quick Checks, and other Web activities, go to www.glencoe.com.

Skills Review

Key Reading Skill: Comparing and Contrasting

7. Responses will vary.
8. Possible response: Both Pasteur and Wells relied on observation, and both made mistakes. Pasteur's approach relied more on laboratory work and animals, while Wells conducted his experiments on humans.

Text Element: Chronological Order

9. *at first, then,* and *finally*
10. Time lines should include the following entries:

    1842: Crawford Long performs surgery using anesthesia.

    1844: Samuel Cooley experiences the effects of pain numbing at a demonstration of nitrous oxide.

    1846: T. G. Morton uses nitrous oxide and ether to numb his patients during teeth extraction.

Close

Ask students to discuss whether important discoveries can be made without research "accidents."

Vocabulary Check

11. hilarious
12. deaden
13. publicized
14. consciousness
15. prospect

English Language Coach

16. Responses will vary.

Grammar Link: Interjections

Grammar Practice

17. I took the test, and oh, it was hard.
18. Well! It's about time you showed up.
19. Yes, I would love some more carrots.
20. Oh, no, here we go again!

Indiana English/Language Arts Academic Standards
SE: 8.2, 8.3, 8.6, 8.7.11

Comparing Literature: Theme

Teaching Students to Compare Themes

Why Is It Important?

- Students need to learn the importance of identifying the theme in all texts.
- Students need to understand how a variety of texts in different genres can have similar themes.
- When students understand how to identify the theme in selections, they are better able to comprehend the text and are often more eager to read.

How to Help Students Get It

- Analyze the title. Sometimes it tells a good deal about the theme.
- Pay attention to patterns, symbols, moods, or other literary devices. Often these lead to the theme.
- Ask yourself: "What are the details and particulars in the story? What greater meaning might they have?"

Reading to Answer the Big Question

Kamau's Finish by Muthoni Muchemi
It is very important to Kamau that Baba, his father, see him win a race on Sports Day at his school in Nairobi, Kenya. Mami, his mother, says that achievement is what matters. However, when a rival shoves Kamau, causing him to lose the race, his father is there to show him that finishing the race is more important than winning it.

The Bunion Derby by Leone Castell Anderson
Andy Payne went through five pairs of shoes in a journey across the United States. In 1927 Payne entered the International Trans-Continental Foot Race, hoping the win the $25,000 prize so he could pay off his family's home and convince his girlfriend Vivian to marry him. Payne endured fatigue, illness, and pain but kept "stepping along." He won the race, paid off the mortgage, married Vivian—and had a remarkable experience on the journey.

Workshop Resources

Pacing (Days) Standard	Pacing (Days) Block	Lesson	Student Materials	Teacher Resources
1	1/2	Comparing Literature: Theme	English Language Coach Review, p. 42	Bellringer Options Transparencies –Daily Language Practice 19 Presentation Plus!
1	1	"Kamau's Finish"	Glencoe Online Unit Vocabulary Review, p. 40 Academic Vocabulary Review, p. 43 English Language Coach Comparing Literature Graphic Organizer, p. 35 StudentWorks Plus™ Online Student Edition Literature Classics	Puzzlemaker Skill Level Up!™ A Language Arts Game BookLink 3 Assessment by Learning Objective (Diagnostic and Formative) Interactive Tutor: Self-Assessment TeacherWorks Plus™ ExamView Assessment Suite
1		"The Bunion Derby"	Glencoe Online Unit Vocabulary Review, p. 40 Academic Vocabulary Review, p. 43 English Language Coach Comparing Literature Graphic Organizer, p. 35 StudentWorks Plus™ Online Student Edition Literature Classics	Puzzlemaker Skill Level Up!™ A Language Arts Game BookLink 3 Assessment by Learning Objective (Diagnostic and Formative) Interactive Tutor: Self-Assessment TeacherWorks Plus™ ExamView Assessment Suite

Keys for Unit Resource

- Blackline Master
- Workbook
- Supplemental Text
- CD-ROM
- DVD
- Transparency
- Web-based
- Fast File

Level Appropriate Code

AS = Activities for all students
AL = Activities for students working above grade level
OL = Activities for students working at grade level
BL = Activities for students working below grade level
EL = Activities for English language learners

Focus

BELLRINGER Options

Daily Language Practice Transparency 19

Focus Activity Draw a Venn diagram on the board. **Say:** Think of two movies or TV shows that you like. How are they alike? How are they different? Use the diagram to compare them. The overlapping region will show how the movies or TV shows are alike. *(Responses will vary.)* AS

Teach

L Literary Element

Theme Remind students that although the theme is the main idea or message of a piece of writing, some selections may have more than one theme. **Ask:** What are some life lessons that might be appropriate themes for a story about running? *(Possible response: It is better to finish last honestly than to win by cheating.)* OL

COMPARING LITERATURE WORKSHOP

Kamau's Finish & The Bunion Derby

by Muthoni Muchemi

by Leone Castell Anderson

Skills Focus

You will use these skills as you read and compare the following selections:

- "Kamau's Finish," p. 259
- "The Bunion Derby," p. 268

Reading

- Making connections across texts
- Comparing and contrasting information in different texts

Literature

- Recognizing and analyzing theme

Writing

- Using comparison and contrast to understand author's use of theme

Indiana English/Language Arts Academic Standards (pp. 256–257)

8.3 Comprehension and Analysis of Literary Text Make connections and comparisons across texts...

For a complete description of the standards, see p. IN 11.

Have you ever tried to describe a new song to a friend? Maybe you compared the song to other songs you know. Making comparisons is a great way to understand–and help others understand–new things.

When you compare two pieces of writing, you look at certain elements, or points of comparison, to see how they are similar or different. Points of comparison may be setting, conflict, or other elements that you use to understand what you read.

How to Compare Literature: Theme

In this workshop, your point of comparison is **theme.** Theme is the main idea or message of what you read. A theme is often stated directly, such as "Be honest" or "Respect your elders." But sometimes a theme is not stated directly, and you must figure it out by looking closely at the characters and events. Themes that are not stated directly are **implied** themes.

L As you read "Kamau's Finish" and "The Bunion Derby," you'll notice that the subject of both selections is running. Don't confuse subject with theme. Subject is what the selection is about. Theme is the selection's message, or main idea. As you look for theme, ask yourself

- what problems do the characters in these selections face?
- do they meet their goals?
- how would they answer the Big Question?

Academic Vocabulary

implied (im PLYD) *adj.* expressed indirectly; suggested rather than said plainly

Additional Support

Literature Focus Lesson

Narrator Tell students that the narrator of a fiction or nonfiction story is the person telling what happened. In cases of nonfiction, the narrator is most likely the author. In cases of fiction, the narrator may be a character in the story or someone watching or remembering the story. Remind students of the terms "first person" ("I") and "third person" ("he/she"). Tell students that stories can have first-person or third-person narrators. Have students point out the narrator in "Kamau's Finish" and "The Bunion Derby." Encourage them to consider what details in each story would be different if the story were told by a different narrator. OL

Get Ready to Compare

In your Learner's Notebook, make a chart like the one below. As you read, answer the questions in the chart. If the answer is "yes," put a check mark in the column for that story. Briefly explain your answer in the "Notes" column. If the answer is "no," leave the space blank. After you read, you'll use the checklist and notes to help you compare the theme of "Kamau's Finish" and "The Bunion Derby."

"Kamau's Finish" & "The Bunion Derby"

Does the runner...	Kamau's Finish	The Bunion Derby	Notes
love running?			
want support from family and friends?			
run for a prize?			
face obstacles while racing?			
try his best?			
value winning above everything else?			
win the race?			
learn something?			

Use Your Comparison

Think about this unit's Genre Focus selection, "Racing the Great Bear." What is its theme? The theme is implied in the selection–you must find it by thinking about the characters and events. When you look at *how* Swift Runner accepts the task and faces the great bear, you might answer, "It takes courage, wisdom, and determination to conquer challenges."

As you read the following selections, pay attention to what the characters think and say about the things that happen to them. Look for themes that are stated directly or implied. Compare how the characters in each selection deal with events. Ask yourself the questions below and keep track of your thoughts in the chart you just made.

L

1. Does the narrator or a character directly state the theme?
   - *Are there any messages or lessons stated in a sentence?*
   - *Is there a statement about life or human nature?*
2. Is the theme implied throughout the selection?
   - *Do the events teach a character something valuable?*
   - *Does a character's attitude toward a subject or event hint at a larger message?*

Reading in the Real World

Career Although many people aspire to become professional athletes, relatively few succeed. Fortunately, there are many options open to people interested in a career in athletics. People who are interested in a career in athletics might become:

- a high school or college coach
- an agent
- an umpire or referee
- a physical/sports therapist

Have students interested in one of these careers make a list of qualities that would be important for someone in the field to possess. **OL**

Teach

L Literary Element

Theme Tell students to write these questions in their Learner's Notebook. Encourage students to answer the questions on their own after they've read each selection to help them understand the themes. **OL**

Assess/Close

Ask students to choose one selection other than "Racing the Great Bear" and jot down a sentence or two about what they learned by reading that selection. What is its theme? Is the theme stated directly or is it implied? **AL**

Resources for page 257

Use the Comparing Literature Graphic Organizer BLM in the Unit 2 Resource Booklet, p. 35.

Indiana English/Language Arts Academic Standards

SE: 8.3

TWE: *Literature Focus Lesson* 8.3.8, *Reading in the Real World* 8.4.1

Teach

More About the Author

Muthoni Muchemi's story "Kamau's Finish" appears in a collection of short stories and poems by American and African authors. The selections in this anthology not only provide a unique glimpse of life in various African countries—including Muchemi's homeland, Kenya—but also present the experiences of Americans in Africa and those of Africans in the United States.

EL Language Coach

Using Synonyms **Say:** Use a thesaurus to create a word web of synonyms for the verb *distract*. Include a definition for each synonym because synonym meanings will vary slightly from the definition of the original word. *(Responses will vary, but should demonstrate an understanding of using a thesaurus and creating a word web.)* EL BL

Before You Read | Kamau's Finish

Meet the Author

Muthoni Muchemi lives in Kenya with her husband, four children, and two dogs. She has been published in the United States and Africa. "Kamau's Finish" is based on her childhood memories of school races—races in which her parents encouraged her to run like a famous Kenyan runner.

Author Search For more about Muthoni Muchemi, go to www .glencoe.com.

Indiana English/Language Arts Academic Standards (pp. 258–266)

8.1 Word Recognition, Fluency, and Vocabulary Development Understand...word relationships...
8.3 Comprehension and Analysis of Literary Text Respond to grade-level-appropriate literature...make connections and comparisons across texts...

For a complete description of the standards, see p. IN 11.

Vocabulary Preview

financial (fy NAN chul) *adj.* concerning money **(p. 261)** *Mami worries about her family's financial problems because she has three children to feed.*

distracted (dih STRAK tid) *adj.* losing attention easily **(p. 261)** *Since Kamau is distracted in school, he doesn't get good grades.*

dramatic (druh MA tik) *adj.* showing strong emotion **(p. 266)** *When the runner crossed the finish line, he gave a dramatic cry of relief.*

sheepishly (SHEEP ish lee) *adv.* with embarrassment **(p. 266)** *Kamau smiled sheepishly as the crowd shouted his name.*

English Language Coach

EL **Vocabulary Building: Collections of Synonyms** You can use synonyms to help you understand an unfamiliar word. As you read, look up words and make a word web of synonyms like the one below.

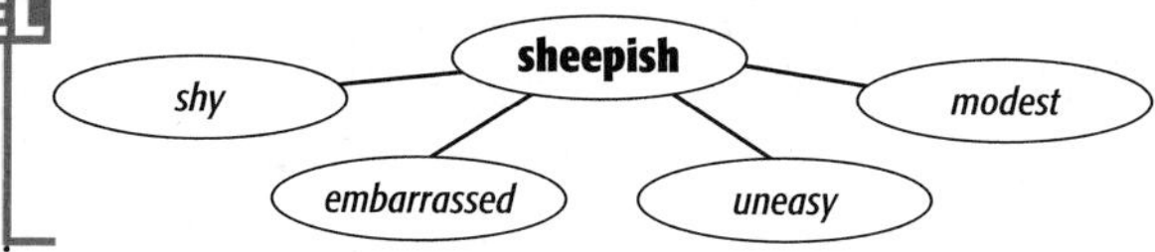

Get Ready to Read

Connect to the Reading

Think about a time when you wanted to prove something about yourself to others. What did you want to prove and why?

Build Background

This story takes place in Nairobi, the capital of Kenya, a country in East Africa. In Kenya, English is the official language used in business and law, and Kiswahili is the common language spoken on the streets and in homes. Two Kiswahili words you'll see, *Baba* and *Mami*, mean father and mother.

Set Purposes for Reading

BIG Question Read to find out what Kamau learns on the way to the finish line.

Set Your Own Purpose What else would you like to learn from the selection to help you answer the Big Question? Write your own purpose on the "Kamau's Finish" Flap of Foldable 2.

Additional Support

Author Search To expand students's appreciation of Muthoni Muchemi, have them access the Web site for additional information and resources.

English Language Coach

Building Vocabulary Remind students that they can make their own preview list of key terms and phrases before reading the selection. Suggest students do the following:

- Scan the text for unfamiliar words.
- List the new words and the page number on which the word is found.
- Find and write the meaning of each word, using a variety of strategies to determine their meaning, including context clues, footnotes, glossaries, and dictionaries.
- Add words to the list as you read. EL BL

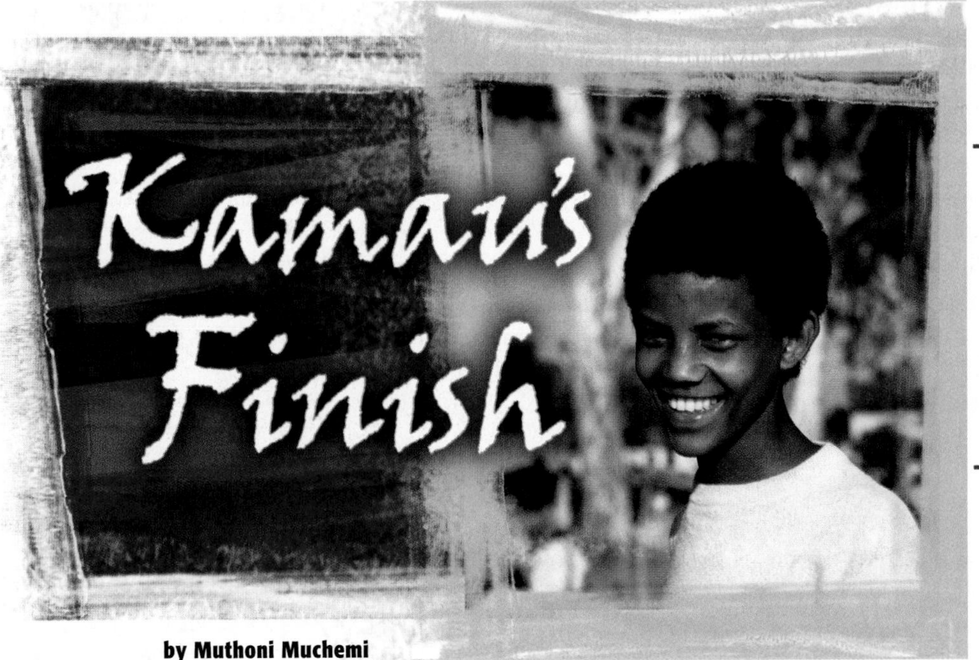

by Muthoni Muchemi

"Wooyay, please with sugarcane juice," I silently pray. "Let me be one of the lucky ones today." Although Kenyatta Primary Academy in Nairobi has almost four hundred students, not many parents have showed up for Sports Day. I don't care about other parents so long as Baba is there for me.

While the headmistress screeches something or other on the squeaky microphone, I scan the group standing on the other side of the track. Baba is not among them. He's tall and big like Meja Rhino the champion wrestler, so you can't miss him. **1**

My team is the Red House, and we're squashed between the Yellow and Blue House teams. Immediately across is the three-step winners' podium.[1] I cross my eyes three times in its direction, shooting lucky *uganga*[2] rays.

But Chris and Daudi pull my T-shirt and break my concentration. I bat their hands away and crouch down. We're

1. A ***podium*** (POH dee um) is a raised structure for giving speeches or receiving awards.
2. ***Uganga*** (yoo GAWNG uh) is a Swahili word that means "magic" or "charms."

Practice the Skills

1 **English Language Coach**

Vocabulary Building Use a dictionary or a thesaurus to look up the verb **screech**. Then make a word web of synonyms.

Teach

L Literary Skill

Theme Explain that in the context of this story, the word *finish* refers to the end of a race. **Ask:** What ideas does the title give you about the theme of this story? *(Responses will vary. Students may say that the theme of this story has to do with finishing a race.)* AL

EL Language Coach

Synonyms Have students identify new vocabulary on this page, such as *scan, squash,* and *crouch*. Tell students to find the words in a dictionary or thesaurus and then write synonyms for each word in their Learner's Notebooks. Suggest that students do the same with other new words as they continue reading the selection. EL BL

Readability Scores
Dale-Chall: 6.3
DRP: 49
Lexile: 730

Literature Focus Lesson

Short Story "Kamau's Finish" is a short story, or brief work of fiction. Remind students that short stories include the following elements. Have students describe the elements in this story:

- setting *(a school in Nairobi, Kenya)*
- characters *(Kamau, Baba, Mami, Njau, Mr. Juma)*
- external conflict *(between Kamau and the other racers)*
- plot *(Kamau wants his father to think he's special so he tries hard to win a race.)* OL

Indiana English/Language Arts Academic Standards
SE: 8.1
TWE: *English Language Coach* 8.4.1, *Literature Focus Lesson* 8.3

Teach

L Literary Element

Theme Ask: What does Kamau seem to want most? How do you know? *(Some students may observe that Kamau's main goal is to win because he prays to be "one of the lucky ones" and shoots lucky magic rays at the winners' podium; others may respond that what Kamau wants most is for Baba to be at the race because Kamau looks for Baba and uses a secret word to pray that he will come.)* OL

Viewing the Photo

Ask: How does the classroom shown in the photo compare with your classroom? What is the same? What is different? *(Responses will vary. Students may note that the students in the picture are all wearing a uniform, which may be different for some students.)* BL OL

sitting on the ground right in front of the track. Mr. Juma, our sports master, let us sit here because we helped him mark the track into lanes with white chalk. Murram[3] dust will fly in our face during the races, but we'll still have the best view.

Suddenly I see a tall figure approaching from a distance and shoot up again. But Baba is half bald, and this man has tight clumps that look like sleeping safari ants scattered about his head.

"Down, Kamau!" barks Mr. Juma.

My race will start in a few minutes. I close my eyes and slowly mouth the secret word. *Ndigidigimazlpixkarumbeta!* Please let Baba be here by the end of this blink. But I open my eyes too soon, way too soon.

Still, I will not lose faith. 2

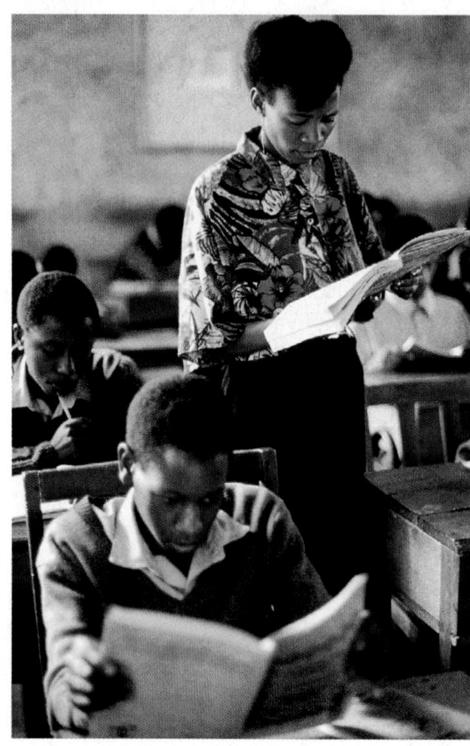

Analyzing the Photo What aspect of the story's setting does this photograph capture?

3. A ***murram*** (MUR um) road is made of hard soil and stones.

Practice the Skills

2 Comparing Literature

L **Theme** Think about what you've learned about Kamau. Is he determined? What does he seem to want most? Begin filling in your chart.

Additional Support

Literature Focus Lesson

Simile Read aloud the sentence that describes the man that Kamau at first mistakes for Baba. Point out that comparing the man's hair to safari ants is a figure of speech known as a *simile*. Similes use the words *like* or *as* to compare two seemingly unlike things. Guide students in identifying examples of similes, such as "pretty as a picture," "roared like a lion," "quiet as a mouse," and so on. AS Have students locate other similes in the selection. OL Ask students to use at least two similes to describe Kamau. AL

Just this morning, I pressed my thumb into the fleshy pad of Baba's thumb. He didn't pull away.

"I have an important business meeting, Kamau, so we'll just have to see." His dark brown eyes seemed full of heavy thoughts.

I pushed my thumb in harder to drill my way into focus. "Please, Baba . . ." **3**

Mami butted in, "Stop pestering your father. Only thinking about yourself. How selfish can you be?" She is hugely pregnant and can scold until your head vibrates. "Your father has to work. Do you think the money we use to educate you is donated by foreign aid?[4] Maybe you think we can feed on saliva like bacteria, or live on yesterday's skin like fleas? You have no idea about the **financial** problems—" **C**

Baba coughed. Mami stopped talking, and for a moment they stared at each other. Mami lashed at me again. "What's that mashing thumbs *uganga* anyway?"

My eight-year-old sister, Wanja, laughed, giving us all a good long look at the mushy stuff in her mouth. Neither of my parents said anything about her bad manners. She had just shown them her report card and, as vomit usual, she was first in her class. Of course, they then asked for mine, and I had to dig it out of the bottom of my bag.

"Kamau needs to concentrate. He is easily **distracted** . . ." Mami had waved the report at Baba. "Didn't I tell you that all this boy does night and day is dream? If they tested a subject called dreaming, Kamau's grades would burst through the ceiling and pierce the cover of the sky!"

Baba had nodded his head in Mami's direction. Did he agree with Mami?

"Kamau's head is full of nonsense!" She'd prodded my head. I let it bob up and down like a rubber ball on a string. "He needs to knuckle down. I want him to succeed. Achievement is what matters. Maybe he dreams he'll be the next president of this country. President Kamau? Heh! **BQ**

4. ***Foreign aid*** is money or other help given from one country to another.

Vocabulary

financial (fy NAN chul) *adj.* concerning money

distracted (dih STRAK tid) *adj.* losing attention easily

Practice the Skills

3 Reviewing Skills

Connecting Kamau admires Baba and wants his attention. Who have you looked up to like Kamau looks up to Baba? Explain your answer in your Learner's Notebook.

Teach

C Critical Thinking

Comprehension **Ask:** What is Mami's reason for scolding Kamau? *(Possible response: She thinks he is pestering his father. She also doesn't think Kamau is aware of their family's financial problems.)* **OL**

BQ BIG Question

Ask: Which does Mami think is more important, the journey or the destination? Explain. *(Possible response: She thinks the destination is more important, because she believes that achievement is more important than effort.)* **OL**

Reading Fluency

Dramatic Reading Have groups of students present a dramatic reading of the scene at Kamau's home on the morning of the race. One student in each group can be Kamau, and the others should take the parts of Baba, Mami, and Njau. Allow sufficient time for students to practice reading their parts aloud smoothly and clearly before presenting their readings to the class. **OL**

Indiana English/Language Arts Academic Standards

SE: 8.3

TWE: *Literature Focus Lesson* 8.1.1, *Reading Fluency* 8.7.10

Teach

R1 Reading Skill

Review Analyzing
Say: Mami seems very critical of Kamau. How can you tell that she cares about him and how he does in the race? *(She packs his special energy lunch for him.)* OL

R2 Reading Skill

Review Predicting **Ask:** Who is usually the fastest runner in the class? *(Kip)* BL Do you predict Kamau will outrun the fastest boy in class during the big race? Explain your prediction. *(Responses will vary.)* OL

Kamau, get serious. Even future kings need to work."

It was no use telling her I try.

My friend Chris once told me his mother said babies in the belly kick. So I squinted and sent mega-*uganga* rays to the baby in Mami's belly to make its legs stronger. She stopped talking and placed a hand over her side.

Maybe my *uganga* rays were too strong.

I held my breath in awe of my powers, but nothing else happened.

Then Njau, my four-year-old brother, had piped up in his high voice, "Baba said effort is what matters."

Baba rumbled, "And problems help us grow." 4

Mami had scrunched her face as though a mountain of firewood pressed her head and waddled off to pack my special energy lunch—sweet potato slices, *maziwa lala*,[5] boiled egg, two carrots, and an orange. R1

I bite into the pad of my thumb. It's tingling. *Ndigidigimazlp-ixkarumbeta!*

"Sit down, Kamau, how many times do I have to tell you?" Mr. Juma's voice rises up and whips me back down.

I glance over at the Yellows and silently chant, "Yellow, yellow, dirty fellow," when my eyes lock with Kip's. He points his index finger and cocks his thumb at me. I duck the imaginary bullet, but he's laughing, trading high-fives with his mates, and doesn't notice. Kip is ten, a year younger than most of my class, and usually the fastest. But twice during R2

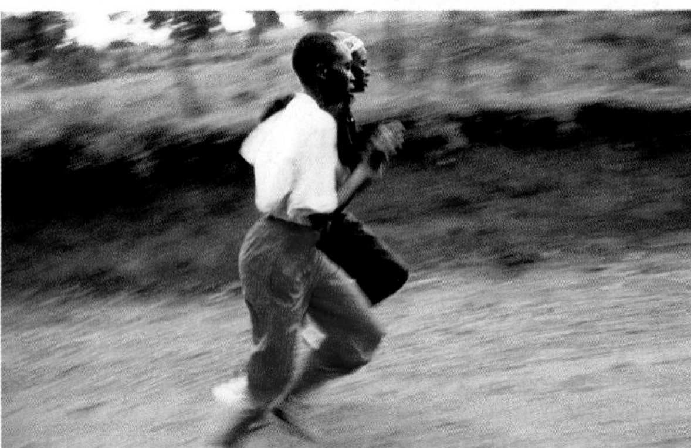

Analyzing the Photo Which line from the story would be a good caption for this photo? Explain your choice.

5. ***Maziwa lala*** (mah ZEE wah lah lah) is a kind of thick milk, similar to yogurt.

Practice the Skills

4 Comparing Literature

Theme Mami says that achievement matters most. But Baba thinks that effort is what matters. Both of these direct statements could be themes. Which one do you think is more important?

Additional Support

English Language Coach

Building Vocabulary Remind students that linking unfamiliar words with words they already know is a good way to build vocabulary. Have students use a dictionary to find at least one synonym and one antonym for *desperately*. *(Possible responses include* urgently *and* casually.*)* Have students create a chart in their Learner's Notebooks and use it to record synonyms and antonyms for other new vocabulary words that they encounter. EL BL practice runs this term, I beat him. He spat at me and sulked off. Everyone else clapped me on the back, even Mr. Juma.

When I told Baba, he said, "Well done, son," and "Good for you."

Now if only Baba would get here, I'd show him how I did it. I'd prove to him that I'm not just a hopeless dreamer. **5**

Our 800-meter race is announced over the screechy microphone. I stare desperately at the parents' side of the track as we file to the starting block. He isn't there.

Three runners from each team stand at attention. Mr. Juma calls for silence.

"Good luck," says Chris in a hoarse voice.

"Same to you," I whisper as we crouch down in starting position.

"On your marks!"

Daudi is in the farthest lane. His lips are moving in silent prayer. Kip calls him *mkiha,* the last carriage of a train. Of course, Kip sees himself as the engine, the one that always gets to its destination first.

I look past Daudi. No sign of Baba, only other parents jostling[6] to get a better view of their sons at the starting line.

Mami said I was selfish to need Baba here today, but I so want to prove to him and Mami that I can be a winner. If he comes just this once, I'll never ask him again.

"Get set!"

I look down at my hands splayed on the ground and feel such a sharp tingling in my thumb that I glance up.

And there he is! My thumb never lies. There is Baba, pushing his way through the throng[7] of parents along the track. There is no mistaking that huge shining head floating above the rest, hurrying in my direction.

Boom! The gun goes off.

I want to burst with happiness. But a blur of bodies has already bolted forward. They have a head start.

I have to concentrate on the race instead of thinking about the miracle of Baba being here. I glue my eyes on the nearest

6. The parents are ***jostling,*** or pushing and shoving lightly, to get a better view.

7. A ***throng*** is a large group.

Practice the Skills

5 Comparing Literature

Theme Kamau wants to prove that he's a winner to Baba. Use this information to continue filling in your chart.

Teach

C1 Critical Thinking

Comprehension Ask: How did Kip react when Kamau beat him during practice runs? *(Kip spat at Kamau and sulked.)* **Ask:** How did everyone else react? *(Mr. Juma and Kamau's teammates congratulated him; Baba said, "Well done, son.")* **BL**

L Literary Element

Theme Say: Think about Mami's and Baba's statements about achievement and effort. Whose side does Kamau appear to be taking? Explain. *(Possible response: Kamau seems to be agreeing with his mother, who believes that achievement matters most.)* **OL**

C2 Critical Thinking

Comprehension Ask: What makes Kamau want to burst with happiness? *(He spots Baba in the crowd.)* **BL**

Differentiated Instruction

Read and Discuss Sports journalism is an exciting career field with job opportunities online and in print, radio, and television. Have students gather in small groups to read and discuss a sports article from a newspaper or magazine. Ask students: Does the writer make you feel as though you were present at the event? If so, how did the reporter accomplish this? **BL** Challenge students to write a sports article that captures the action of an event in which they participated, or Kamau's race. Then have students read their articles aloud. **AL**

Indiana English/Language Arts Academic Standards

SE: 8.3

TWE: *English Language Coach* 8.1; *Differentiated Instruction* 8.2, 8.5

Teach

EL Language Coach

Synonyms Have students start a chart of words that describe running.
Ask: What verbs does Kamau use to describe how he and others run? *(bolt, overtake, pound, tear)* Tell students to use a dictionary to find the definitions of these words and to list the words and definitions in their charts. Encourage students to add other words related to running to their charts as they continue to read about the race. EL

C Critical Thinking

Comprehension Ask: How does Baba's presence affect Kamau's efforts in the race? *(When he thinks he hears Baba cheering him on, he gets "a new energy" and tears ahead of Chris.)* OL

Analyzing the Photo How is the man in this photo similar to or different from the Baba you've imagined?

runner, a blue T-shirt. I concentrate on catching up with him. I run like Ananse[8] the hungry hare on his way to Mr. Elephant's feast. I overtake him.

Concentration, concentration, concentration now begins. To that beat, I run faster. I run in long hard strides that bounce off the ground and pull on the backs of my thighs. My legs feel strong. I set my sights on a yellow back. A surge of warmth **floods** my body as I overtake him. 6

I can tell it's Daudi directly in front of me, because he runs with his head facing the sky. He's already slowing. I pound past him with my eyes locked on Kip's yellow shirt. EL

He's in a cluster, but I know Kip always goes for the flashy sprint finish. I have to catch up with him now if I'm to have a chance. Concentration, concentration, concentration now begins.

Amid all the crowd noises, I think I hear Baba yell, "Run, son!"

A new energy tingles from my feet, up along my legs, loosens my hips, and expands my chest. I tear past Chris, who is panting like a horse. *Uganga* magic is with me! C

8. Known for his tricks, ***Ananse*** (ah NAWN see) is a character found in many African folktales.

Practice the Skills

6 English Language Coach

Vocabulary Building Some synonyms for **floods,** as it is used here, are *rushes through* and *pours through*. Do you think either of them works as well as *floods* to communicate what Kamau is feeling?

Additional Support

Literature Focus Lesson

Repetition Point out that the author uses repetition to help describe the rhythm of Kamau's run. Ask students to tell what words the author repeats on page 264 *(Concentration, concentration, concentration now begins)*. Note that Kamau says he runs faster to this beat.

Have students say the words aloud and ask them to imagine saying them as they run a race. How would saying these words help a runner pace himself or herself? *(The words create a rhythm that a runner could use to keep a fast and steady pace.)* BL

The cluster is breaking up. Kip is racing ahead. My heart hammers in my ribs. I open my mouth wider to take in more air. I'm catching up. I'm in the dispersing cluster. I overtake one, two, three boys.

I'm flying, my feet almost slapping my bottom, half a step behind Kip.

When I win this race, Mami will never scold me again. When I win this race, Wanja will swallow her snickering. Best of all, Baba will look in my eyes to congratulate me. Baba will finally see me. **L1**

Everything feels slow motion. The noise, the people, and the track float away into the great *uganga*-land of dreams. I hear only distant echoes. "Win, win, win!"

I'm neck and neck with Kip, matching him stride for stride. He leans in my direction as though to draw strength from me. The finish-line ribbon flutters red maybe fifty meters ahead.

I'm going to win! I'm going to win! My teammates will carry me on their shoulders, shouting, "Hero! Hero!" When I climb the winner's podium to collect my medal, I won't even punch the air or do a show-off dance. Baba will already know I'm a hero. Baba will— **7**

An unexpected shove jolts me out of my dream and back to the moment. Then I'm wobbling, fighting for control. I fall. **L2**

Unbelievable!

I swallow the grit on my tongue and shake my head to clear the ringing in my ears. I feel confused. Not quite on this earth. My hands are grazed with white track chalk mixed with brown soil and smudges of blood. I shape them into fists and press hard to force the pain away. A blue shirt whizzes by, kicking dust in my face.

While I was in my dream, Kip must have pushed me with his elbow. Mami would be proud of a son like Kip, who knows winning is what matters.

Legs zoom past me in a whir of hot air and dust. I glance toward the side of the track. The crowd probably thinks Kip and I touched accidentally.

A cheer goes up and I realize Kip must have crossed the red ribbon. Kip has won my race. No. Kip has stolen my race. **C**

Practice the Skills

7 **Comparing Literature**

Theme Think about what is most important to Kamau right now. Do you think he agrees with Mami that winning is what matters? Or does he agree with Baba that effort is most important? Look back at your chart and see which questions you can answer.

Teach

L1 Literary Element

Theme Have students continue filling in their comparison charts as they answer the following questions.
Ask: What matters most to Kamau as he catches up with Kip? *(winning the race)* **Ask:** Why does Kamau want so badly to win? *(Possible response: He wants his family members and teammates to see him as a hero.)* **OL**

L2 Literary Element

Theme Ask: What new or unexpected development occurs in the race? *(Kamau falls, and Kip and the other runners rush past him.)* **BL**
Ask: How might this event affect the theme of the story? *(Possible response: Perhaps "achievement matters most" is not the theme of the story.)* **OL**

C Critical Thinking

Evaluation Ask: Do you think Kamau is right when he thinks Kip stole his race? Explain. *(Responses will vary; those who agree will observe that Kamau says that Kip made him fall; those who disagree will note that Kamau was daydreaming about winning when he fell and that there is no proof that Kip made Kamau fall.)* **OL**

Reading in the Real World

Citizenship Baba is a person who inspires others by his faith in them. There is a psychological theory that suggests that a person's performance can be influenced by what persons in authority expect of that person. Have students discuss this idea in small groups and identify and relate situations in which they did better because a teacher, coach, or other authority figure had faith in them and clearly conveyed positive expectations. **OL** Have students brainstorm and develop a list of things authority figures can do to convey positive expectations and help young people succeed. **AL**

Indiana English/Language Arts Academic Standards
SE: 8.1, 8.3
TWE: *Literature Focus Lesson* 8.3.6, *Reading in the Real World* 8.3

Teach

 **Literary Element**

Theme **Ask:** Why is Baba beaming? *(He is proud of his son.)* **Ask:** How might his actions relate to the theme of this selection? *(Possible response: Baba thinks finishing the race is important, even if you come in last.)* **OL**

Ask: Which would Baba say is more important, the journey or the destination? Explain. *(Possible response: Because he favors effort over achievement, Baba would say that the journey is more important.)* **AL**

Assess

Use the CheckPoint questions provided on Presentation Plus! to check for comprehension of the selection. These questions can be used with interactive response keypads for immediate student feedback.

I want to call to Baba that I should have won. Will he believe that Kip tripped me?

Most of the runners are finishing. Daudi rushes past me, his tongue lolling out of his mouth, probably elated not to be the *mkiha* for once.

I look back and see Baba's shiny face. He is running alongside the track, gesturing wildly—up, up, up—pointing to the finish line. But how will getting up help me? I'll pretend my leg is broken. I'll give a **dramatic** cry for help. I'll— **8**

I become aware of the noise, the cheering. They're chanting my name. "KA-MA-UU! KA-MA-UU! KA-MA-UU!" They're shouting for me to finish. I feel like shouting back, "Whatever for? All I'm good for is dreaming."

Then I notice their eyes are not on me, but on my lumbering Baba, who has crossed onto the track behind me. He is wearing a black suit and shiny lizard shoes he bought donkey years ago that usually make me cringe.

My ears buzz, but I think I hear him shout, "Run, son! Get up and run!"

Uncertain, I scramble up and gape at Baba. Sweat streams down his face, and he holds a hand over his chest. Is he having a heart attack?

He can't be. His eyes are shining. I can see every tooth in his mouth.

Baba is beaming! **L**

So I wipe my nose with my wrist and laugh through the tears. It sounds like I am crying. But Baba is beaming.

I keep my eyes on him and trot **sheepishly** alongside to the finish. So much noise, so many people crowding the finish area. Mr. Juma is probably shouting for order.

But I only have ears for Baba. **9** ❍

Vocabulary

dramatic (druh MA tik) *adj.* showing strong emotion

sheepishly (SHEEP ish lee) *adv.* with embarrassment

Practice the Skills

8 Comparing Literature

Theme Kamau doesn't want to finish the race. Why does he feel that it's useless to keep going? Think about Mami's definition of what matters, and how that might influence Kamau.

9  **BQ**

What has Kamau learned about running, and finishing, a race? Finish filling in your chart and write your answer on the "Kamau's Finish" flap of Foldable 2. Your response will help you complete the Unit Challenge later.

Additional Support

Differentiated Instruction

Interview To check for understanding of characters, events, and theme, organize students in pairs to conduct an interview with Kamau after the race. Have one student pose as the interviewer and the other student as Kamau. Pairs should work together to create a script for the interview. Questions and answers should focus on the following topics:

- Kamau's goal in the race
- the relationship between Kamau and his parents
- Kamau's thoughts during the race
- important events in the race
- lessons learned from the race

Allow students to present their interviews to the class. **OL** **AL**

Before You Read: The Bunion Derby

Meet the Author

Leone Castell Anderson has written many stories for young people, including two historical novels titled *Sean's War* and *Sean's Quest*. She lives in an old schoolhouse in Illinois, but she travels the country giving writing workshops for children of all ages.

Author Search For more about Leone Castell Anderson, go to www.glencoe.com.

Indiana English/Language Arts Academic Standards (pp. 267–273)

8.1 Word Recognition, Fluency, and Vocabulary Development Understand...word relationships...
8.3 Comprehension and Analysis of Literary Text Respond to grade-level-appropriate literature...make connections and comparisons across texts...

For a complete description of the standards, see p. IN 11.

Vocabulary Preview

V

furnished (FUR nisht) *v.* supplied; given; form of the verb *furnish* **(p. 270)** *Mr. Pyle furnished the runners with food and water.*

promoter (pruh MOH tur) *n.* a person who organizes and pays the costs of a sporting event **(p. 271)** *The promoter of the race made sure the runners had a place to sleep.*

grimacing (GRIM us ing) *v.* making a face that shows discomfort or disgust; form of the verb *grimace* **(p. 273)** *The runner was grimacing after he twisted his ankle.*

English Language Coach

Vocabulary Building: Synonyms A great way to remember an unfamiliar word is to pair it with a synonym or two. Use a synonym chart like the one below to help you remember unfamiliar words.

Word	Synonym	Synonym
furnish	provide	supply

Get Ready to Read

Connect to the Reading

Think about a goal you've set for yourself. What did you do to reach it?

Build Background

Imagine running more than 26 miles in one day! That's what marathon runners do. Marathoners don't just run for good times, though. They run for personal pride–and money. For example, the winner of the Boston marathon, one of the country's most popular marathons, can expect to win a $100,000 prize.

Set Purposes for Reading

BIG Question Read to find out how Andy Payne, a young man from Oklahoma, ran an amazing race across the United States.

Set Your Own Purpose What else would you like to learn from the selection to help you answer the Big Question? Write your own purpose on the "Bunion Derby" flap of Foldable 2.

Teach

More About the Author

Leone Castell Anderson has had several careers connected with writing and books. She has worked as a copywriter and a librarian and has even owned a bookstore. Anderson has won various prizes for her writing, including the Highlights for Children fiction award. She is a popular speaker at libraries, bookstores, reading clubs, and schools, where she shares her experiences and thoughts about being an author of both children and adult books.

V Vocabulary

Pronunciation The Vocabulary Preview includes the correct pronunciation for each vocabulary word in parentheses. Guide students in pronouncing the words as indicated. Explain that students can also sound out unfamiliar words, syllable by syllable, if no pronunciation is given. EL BL

English Language Coach

Synonyms and Antonyms Help students practice identifying synonyms and antonyms by giving them the following simple words and having them tell which is a synonym and which is an antonym for each word.

- **strong:** powerful, weak
- **miserable:** joyful, unhappy
- **assertive:** shy, confident
- **rapid:** slow, swift
- **generous:** giving, stingy

EL BL OL

Indiana English/Language Arts Academic Standards
SE: 8.1, 8.3
TWE: *Differentiated Instruction* 8.3, English Language Coach 8.1

Teach

Viewing the Photo

Have students compare the photograph on this page with the photograph of the runners on page 262 in "Kamau's Finish." **Ask:** What differences do the photographs suggest between short races and long-distance races? *(Possible response: Runners in short races stay close together; runners in long-distance races run on their own at least part of the time.)* AS

R Reading Skill

Review Predicting

Ask: How does Andy react to the notice about the foot race? *(His heart starts pounding and he imagines what he will do with the winnings.)* BL

Ask: What can you predict will happen based on Andy's reaction? *(Possible response: He will sign up for the race.)* OL

Readability Scores

Dale-Chall: 7.0

DRP: 5.6

Lexile: 920

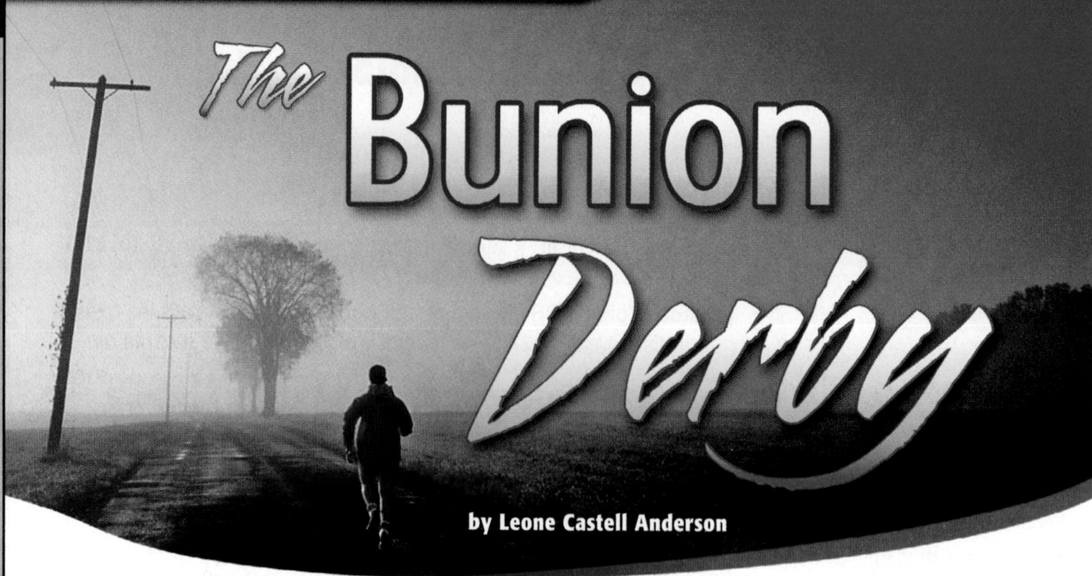

The Bunion Derby

by Leone Castell Anderson

What would your mom say if you wore out a pair of shoes and had to get a new pair every 17 days? Too many shoes?

That's what Andy Payne did, and his mother never scolded him.

Andrew Hartley Payne, who was part Cherokee, grew up on his parents' farm near the town of Foyil, just up the road from Claremore, Oklahoma. From the time he was a kid, he loved to run. He ran the five miles to grade school, practiced running in the fields and hills, and ran the mile at Foyil High School, where he could never be beaten. **1**

After graduation in 1927, he went west to Los Angeles, California, seeking to make his fortune. One day as Andy searched the want ads, he saw a notice about "runners wanted" for an International Trans-Continental Foot Race. His heart pounded as he read on. Runners were to cross the country from Los Angeles to Chicago, on the new Route 66, and then go on to Madison Square Garden in New York City. The winner's prize would be $25,000. **R**

Twenty-five thousand! Andy later told an interviewer, "I knew I was strong and could run. And I just concluded that I would stand as good a chance as any." He dreamed about how he would use the winnings. He'd help pay off the

Practice the Skills

1 Reviewing Skills

Connecting Think about your hobbies—maybe you draw, skateboard, write poetry, or dance. What do you love to do as much as Andy loves to run? In your Learner's Notebook, explain your answer.

Additional Support

Literature Focus Lesson

Nonfiction "The Bunion Derby," by Leone Castell Anderson, is an example of nonfiction, or writing that tells about real-life people, places, and events. Anderson combines facts and sensory details to help readers picture the race and understand what Payne experienced.

Tell students that Payne died in 1977. How might Anderson have gotten the facts and details necessary to write this article? *(Possible response: from history books, friends, articles, and old interviews with Andy.)* OL mortgage on his family's farm. And his fame and fortune would help him convince Vivian Shaddox, his high-school sweetheart, to marry him.

Andy soon learned about the $25 entry fee and the $100 deposit for a return ticket from New York. He didn't let that stop him. Making his way back to Oklahoma, Andy went first to Claremore's chamber of commerce. He asked the members to sponsor[1] him in the race. They hemmed and hawed. They looked at the slender 20-year-old, with his dark wavy hair and his good looks. They weren't sure, they told him.

Andy persisted. He was young, he was strong, he'd been a runner all his life, he'd made records at running, he told them. The chamber finally came through with some of the money. **2**

Andy's father, Andrew Lane Jackson Payne, was more confident. He borrowed enough to cover Andy's entry fee and expenses.

After signing up to enter the race, Andy knew he needed to get back in shape for running. Throughout the winter months, then, he ran. Up and down the rolling hills of southern California he ran. Tom Young, a high-school coach from Los Angeles, spurred him on. Andy felt his legs getting stronger, his wind improving, his staying power returning. He spent three weeks in the training camp at the Ascot Speedway in Los Angeles "for final conditioning[2] for the race," as the runners were required to do.

Now the big day arrived: 4 March 1928. Andy took his place on the track of the Ascot Speedway, his number 43 on his athletic undershirt. He felt the jostling of the other runners as they vied for the best starting positions. Over 240 of them, he'd been told. He saw the crowd . . . thousands of people. He heard their wild cheering.

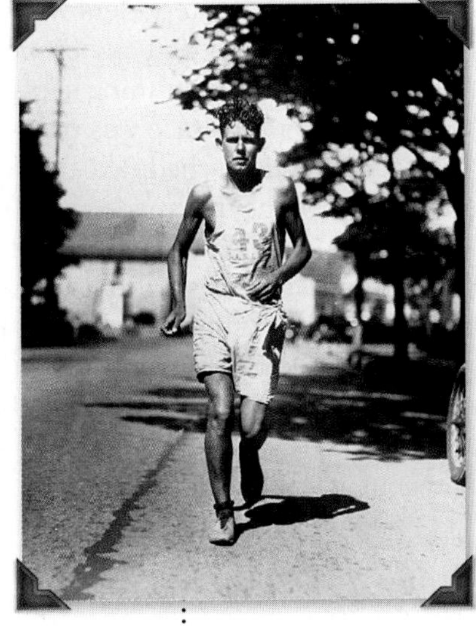

Andy Payne leads the pack in this 1928 photo.

1. A ***chamber of commerce*** is an association that promotes a community. To ***sponsor*** someone means to support his or her effort, usually with money.
2. ***Conditioning*** (kun DIH shun ing) is a kind of training to get in shape.

Practice the Skills

L

2 Comparing Literature

Theme What have you learned about Andy so far? Fill in your chart.

Teach

L Literary Element

Theme Say: Both Kamau and Andy dream about winning their races. How do their dreams about winning differ? *(Possible response: Kamau dreams about what Baba and others will think of him when he wins; Andy dreams about what he will do with the prize money.)* **OL**

Viewing the Photo

Ask: Judging from the photograph of Andy, how would you compare the way runners dressed in the 1920s with the way runners dress today? *(Students may observe that running clothing of the 1920s looks more or less the same as running clothing today but seems less brand-oriented and less high-tech.)* **BL**

English Language Coach

Old Words and Phrases In this selection, some familiar words are used in slightly different or unusual ways. Below are some examples.

- To "hem and haw" is an idiom that means "to hesitate."
- To "cover" an entry fee means to pay it.
- "Wind" can refer to one's breath control.
- "Staying power" refers to the ability to continue and persist
- To "vie for position" means to compete for a good starting place.

Have students note other unfamiliar phrases and use context clues and peer help to determine their meanings. **AS**

Indiana English/Language Arts Academic Standards

SE: 8.3

TWE: *Literature Focus Lesson* 8.3, *English Language Coach* 8.1

Teach

L Literary Element

Theme **Say:** Think about how Andy's technique compares with Kamau's technique. *(Possible response: In order to win, Kamau must run as fast as he can throughout the entire race, but the best way for Andy to win is to keep a steady pace.)* OL

R Reading Skills

Review Making Inferences
Ask: Why do you think the newspaper reporters were calling the race the Bunion Derby? *(Possible response: because so many racers were developing bunions on their feet from the long hours spent running)* OL

Andy waited for the signal from Red Grange, the famous football player known as the Galloping Ghost. He flexed his muscles. He bounced lightly on his canvas sneakers. He took a deep breath. Suddenly a loud boom sounded. Andy sprang forward, sensing the other runners beside and behind him. He was on his way to New York, just 3,422.3 miles away.

On that first day, a cool cloudy one, Andy kept up a steady pace, covering the assigned daily route. He knew his time would be noted. Each day's time would be added to his total. Winning the race depended on having the lowest time over the entire course. 3

As he ran, Andy was aware of his competitors. Some were close to his age. Some were older. Andy stepped along. He knew there were some well-known runners, from places like Germany and Italy and England. And from Canada and the States, too. There were Finns and Greeks and Hopi Indians offering Andy tough competition.

Andy stared at a passing runner. He'd seen some in overalls or BVDs or even a sheet, wearing boots or moccasins.[3] But that last one was running in his bare feet!

Andy knew newspaper reporters were calling the race the Bunion Derby. He'd never had any bunions.[4] But he had taken time to break in his running shoes. He was sure they'd need replacing before the race was over.

He arrived at the first scheduled checkpoint in Puente, California, by noon, having made about six miles an hour, a good average. He enjoyed the first of the meals **furnished** the runners. Later, after exercising to keep in shape, Andy ate a tasty dinner with the other competitors. He soon headed for his cot in the tent housing arranged for them by the organizer of the race, Mr. C. C. Pyle. His personal belongings and blanket, all marked with his number 43, were there. The rule was lights out at 9 P.M., and Andy slept.

3. ***BVD*** is a brand of underwear, and ***moccasins*** (MAWK uh sinz) are soft, leather shoes.
4. ***Bunions*** are swollen areas on the joint of the big toe.

Vocabulary

furnished (FUR nisht) *v.* supplied; given

Practice the Skills

3 Comparing Literature

Theme Andy must keep a steady pace and not tire himself out if he wants to win the race. From what you've read, can you think of a theme for this selection?

Additional Support

Differentiated Instruction

Calculating the Distance To help students appreciate the length of the Transcontinental Foot Race, have them use the distance from Los Angeles to New York—3,422.3 miles—to estimate the number of days it would take to complete it. First, estimate that contestants ran for about 8 hours each day. Then determine the rate at which the contestants ran. A good estimate is 5 mph. This means runners would average about 40 miles per day. Use these figures to arrive at the approximate number of days it would take to run 3,422.3 miles. *(A contestant running at 40 miles per day would need about 86 days to cover the distance—3422.3 divided by 40 = 85.6 days.)* AL

As days went by, Andy struggled along with the others. Heavy rains slashed at his face and soaked his jersey. They made the ground underfoot sticky with mud that pulled at his shoes. He struggled up Cajon Pass, the first of the steep slopes he knew he'd have to climb, and noticed other runners dropping back. As he shuffled across the hot sands of the Mojave Desert, the blazing sun blistered his nose and ears, and the gritty sand wore down the soles of his sneakers. He stumbled through sandstorms with his hands in front of his face. But he just kept "stepping along," as he told reporters later.

Adding to his problems, Andy learned that C. C. Pyle was a pinchpenny **promoter**. The promised "deluxe" food was replaced with a daily tasteless mulligan stew.[5] With Pyle's 35-cent allowance given the runners for each meal, then, Andy bought himself sandwiches and other more passable food in the towns they ran through. The tent housing proved hot, the blankets unwashed. Sometimes the caravan carrying the tents, cots, blankets, and belongings didn't make it to the checkpoints in time. Andy and the other runners were sometimes put up in stables or barns, even chicken houses.

By the time the runners reached northern Arizona, many had begun dropping out from exhaustion, sore feet, sprains, shin splints, and other ailments. Andy himself, his throat sore and running a fever from tonsillitis,[6] was not racing well. But Arthur Newton, the front runner, unable to breathe in the thin air of the high elevation of 6,000 feet, dropped out of the race on the road into Winslow, Arizona. The coordinators announced, "The totals thus far show Andy Payne is in first place." Andy took a deep breath and grinned. But he knew there were miles to go. He replaced his worn-out shoes and kept running. **C** **L** **4**

5. ***Mulligan stew*** is a soup made of meat, vegetables, and broth.
6. ***Tonsillitis*** (tawn sul EYE tus) is an irritation of the tonsils, or part of the throat.

Vocabulary

promoter (pruh MOH tur) *n.* a person who organizes and pays the costs of a sporting event

Practice the Skills

John Salo and Peter Garrizzi run nearly neck and neck in this 1929 photo.

4 Comparing Literature

Theme In "Kamau's Finish," Kamau's main obstacle is another runner. What obstacles does Andy face during his race? Remember to fill in your chart.

Teach

C Critical Thinking

Comprehension **Ask:** How does Andy react to the news that he is the front runner in the race? *(He is pleased.)* **BL** **Ask:** Is he sure that he can win now? Why or why not? *(He is not sure; he knows that he still has a long way to go.)* **OL**

L Literary Element

Review Conflict **Say:** Think back to what you learned about internal and external conflict. Which type of conflict does Andy face most often? Explain. *(Andy most often faces external conflicts such as poor food and shelter, and worn-out shoes.)* **OL** **Ask:** How do Andy's conflicts compare with those that Kamau faces? *(Some students may say that Kamau, too, faces external conflicts, such as Kip. Other students may note that Kamau faces internal conflicts as well, such as wanting Baba's approval and feeling pressure from Mami.)* **AL**

Reading Fluency

Reading Long Sentences Have students work in groups of three to read aloud the text on this page. Each student in the group should select one of the three main paragraphs to practice reading aloud. Model reading the page aloud once for students so that they can hear how the proper flow of sentences. Be sure to emphasize the importance of pausing for commas, especially in longer sentences. After students have practiced in their groups, you may want to have them read to the class. **EL** **BL**

Indiana English/Language Arts Academic Standards
SE: 8.3
TWE: *Differentiated Instruction* 8.2, *Reading Fluency* 8.1

Teach

R Reading Skill

Review Making Inferences
Ask: What do you think motivated the people along the race route to watch the runners and cheer them on? *(Possible responses: curiosity or excitement about the event; admiration for the runners' effort and endurance)* OL

EL Language Coach

Building Vocabulary **Say:** Other runners try to *surpass* Andy's time. What does "surpass" mean? *(to be better or greater; to go beyond the limits of some thing)* BL **Ask:** What are some other things that can be surpassed? *(Possible responses: expectations, goals, beauty)* OL AL

The race went on, across New Mexico and Texas. Sometimes cheering town residents lined the streets as the runners went by. Schools along the route would excuse children from class so they could watch the race, and the kids would sometimes run alongside Andy and the others. Sometimes enthusiastic drivers would try to follow them. A Finnish runner endured broken ribs from a collision with a car, but got up and kept running. Two other runners left the race after similar encounters. But Andy just kept "stepping along."

On 15 April Governor Henry S. Johnston of Andy's home state and a cheering crowd met the race leaders at the fairgrounds in Oklahoma City. Invited to the speaker's stand, Andy said, "Hello, home folks. I'm glad to be back. Hope to see you in New York."

But it was in Claremore, Oklahoma, on 17 April that the biggest and most enthusiastic crowd welcomed Andy, and a squad of cadets from the military academy ran on either side of him. It was the exact halfway point of the race. Andy smiled and greeted everyone, but he kept on running, knowing he had to maintain his time. However, the next day he did take some moments to visit with his family and friends, especially Vivian, when he entered his hometown of Foyil. He assured them he was going to make it—and replaced his shoes with still another pair. 5

Andy was aware of the runners who were trying to match and **surpass** his time. John Salo of New Jersey was close. Salo had adopted one of the dogs who had begun following the runners, naming him Blisters and taking care of him. Another challenger was Phillip Granville, a tall Jamaican from Canada, who changed his strategy of walking to running in an effort to catch Andy. 6

But Andy learned he had a strong rival for first place as the course took the runners across the Midwest. He befriended the bearded Englishman, Peter Gavuzzi, who was two years older and an experienced marathon runner. They often ran side by side. Through a corner of Kansas, across Missouri, and into Illinois they went, until they reached Chicago, the

Practice the Skills

Clouds Over Seligman, September 1, 1947. Andreas Feininger. Silver gelatin photograph.

The race wound through arid Arizona (above), where cumulus clouds billow over a flat, dry landscape.

5 Reviewing Skills

R **Connecting** The people in Andy's hometown cheer him on when he races through. Think about the people who cheer you on. Why is it important to have the support of others as you work toward your goals?

6 English Language Coach

EL **Vocabulary Building** Look up the word **surpass** in a dictionary or a thesaurus. Make a synonym chart to help you remember what the word means.

Additional Support

Differentiated Instruction

Researching and Writing Ask students to choose one of the runners mentioned in the selection (Arthur Newton, John Salo, Phillip Granville, and Peter Gavuzzi) and use the information in the selection to write a fact sheet that tells the runner's name, where he was from, obstacles he encountered in the race, and how he performed. BL

Have students write a journal entry from the runner's point of view, dated the day he completed or dropped out of the race. OL

Invite students to research other runners who participated in the Bunion Derby and write a short biography on one of them. Information is available at www.itvs.org/footrace. AL end of Route 66. They headed for New York, still keeping pace with each other, although Andy knew Peter had a lead over him by several hours.

As they were crossing Indiana, Andy saw his friend **grimacing**, and when he asked what his problem was, Peter told him it was an abscessed[7] tooth. Peter Gavuzzi kept doggedly[8] on until they reached Wauseon, Ohio, when the pain proved too much for him, and he dropped out of the race. Andy reluctantly left his friend behind. But he knew he was now the only front runner.

On 26 May 1928, wearing pair number five of his Bunion Derby shoes, Andy Payne was one of 55 weary runners who arrived at New York's Madison Square Garden track. Over the daily routes, varying in length from 15 to 75 miles, it had taken Andy 573 hours, 4 minutes, and 34 seconds and 84 consecutive days to run the 3,422.3 miles of "C. C. Pyle's First Annual International Trans-Continental Foot Race: Los Angeles to New York City."

Andy Payne was declared the winner of the $25,000 prize. John Salo placed second, with a prize of $10,000. Phillip Granville finished in third place, which paid $5,000. **7**

With a tired smile on his face, Andy the Bunion Derby winner pointed to his feet. "No bunions," he said. **8**

Author's Note

Andy did pay off the mortgage on his family farm and built his folks a new home. He married Vivian in 1929. Six years later, he hung up his racing shoes for good and entered a political race. He was elected clerk of the Supreme Court of Oklahoma in 1934 and served for 38 years. He died at age 69 in 1977.

On 16 May 1992, the Cherokee Heritage Center in Tahlequah, Oklahoma, dedicated a life-sized statue of Andy Payne, honoring him as a notable member of the tribe. ❍

7. If something is ***abscessed*** (AB sest), it is infected.
8. ***Doggedly*** means in a stubborn or determined way.

Vocabulary

grimacing (GRIM us ing) *v.* making a face that shows discomfort or disgust

Practice the Skills

7 Comparing Literature

L **Theme** The theme of this selection is implied. We learn about Andy by his actions. What makes Andy a successful runner? What doesn't he do?

8 BIG Question

BQ Which would Andy Payne say is more important, running his best race or winning the prize? Write your answer on the "Bunion Derby" flap of Foldable 2. Your response will help you complete the Unit Challenge later.

Teach

L Literary Element

Theme **Ask:** How would you describe Andy's attitude toward the obstacles along the way, the other runners, and the race in general? *(Possible response: Andy pushed through the obstacles with determination, he was fair and caring toward the other runners, and he paced himself throughout the race.)* **OL** Have students finish filling in their charts. **AS**

BQ BIG Question

Ask: What did you learn about determination and commitment from Andy Payne's journey? *(Responses will vary)* **OL**

Assess

CheckPoint

Use the CheckPoint questions provided on Presentation Plus! to check for comprehension of the selection. These questions can be used with interactive response keypads for immediate student feedback.

Reading Fluency

Fluency with Numbers Numbers can present a special challenge to students who are learning English. Have students practice reading aloud the paragraph that begins "On 26 May 1928, . . ." Suggest that they read the first date as "the twenty-sixth of May." Then tell students to reread the paragraph several times until they can read all of the numbers correctly and smoothly. Urge students to ask for help if they encounter any problems. **EL**

Indiana English/Language Arts Academic Standards

SE: 8.1, 8.3

TWE: *Differentiated Instruction* 8.5.7, *Reading Fluency* 8.2

Assess

Resources for page 274

- Selection Quick Check, pp. 19–20
- ExamView Assessment Suite
- Interactive Tutor: Self-Assessment

Vocabulary Check

Kamau's Finish

1. dramatic
2. distracted
3. sheepishly
4. financial

The Bunion Derby

5. promoter
6. grimacing
7. furnished

Academic Vocabulary

8. Possible response: An implied theme is the main idea or message of a selection that readers must infer from the actions and experiences of the characters.

English Language Coach

9. Possible response:

Word	Synonym	Synonym
notable	significant	important

Reading/Critical Thinking
Kamau's Finish

10. Possible response: At the beginning of the story, Kamau thinks that winning the race is what matters most. By the end of the story, he sees that there are more important things, such as finishing the race and making Baba proud.
11. Possible response: Kamau wants to prove that he is not a hopeless dreamer but a hero who can achieve something.
12. Possible response: Baba values effort and determination.

The Bunion Derby

13. Possible response: Andy is fair and caring toward his competitors.
14. Possible response: Andy's strategy is to keep running at a steady pace and avoid distractions. Yes, it works.
15. Possible response: Determination, focus, and fairness toward others are useful skills for achieving goals. They are especially good qualities for someone who becomes a clerk of the Supreme Court, such as Andy had.

After You Read

Kamau's Finish & The Bunion Derby

Vocabulary Check

Rewrite the sentences below. Replace the word in parentheses ( ) with the vocabulary word that means about the same thing.

Kamau's Finish

financial distracted sheepishly dramatic

1. The game's score was tied, promising a (thrilling) finale.
2. Waylon tried to think about homework, but he kept getting (sidetracked) watching TV.
3. "I've never flown on an airplane," Gabrielle told her friend (self-consciously).
4. Loretta asked her banker for (money-related) advice.

The Bunion Derby

furnished promoter grimacing

5. Not even the (event coordinator) could believe the boxing match went twelve rounds.
6. The dancer tripped, (wincing), and knew she'd sprained her foot.
7. The chef (supplied) his guests with cake and other desserts.
8. **Academic Vocabulary** What is an **implied** theme?
9. **English Language Coach** In 1992 Andy Payne was honored as a **notable** member of his tribe. What does *notable* mean? Copy the synonym chart below, and use a dictionary or a thesaurus to fill in the chart.

Word	Synonym	Synonym
notable		

Indiana English/Language Arts Academic Standards (pp. 274–275)

8.3 Comprehension and Analysis of Literary Text Respond to grade-level-appropriate literature...make connections and comparisons across texts...

For a complete description of the standards, see p. IN 11.

Reading/Critical Thinking

On a separate sheet of paper, answer the following questions.

Kamau's Finish

10. **Compare** Compare Kamau's attitude about winning at the beginning of the story with his attitude about winning at the end of the story.
    TIP Author and Me
11. **Infer** What does Kamau want to prove to Mami and Baba by winning?
    TIP Think and Search
12. **Analyze** Why is it important to Baba that Kamau finish the race?
    TIP Author and Me

The Bunion Derby

13. **Evaluate** How does Andy treat his competitors?
    TIP Think and Search
14. **Identify** What is Andy's strategy, or plan, for running the race? Does it work?
    TIP Think and Search
15. **Analyze** Do you think Andy's personal characteristics and habits helped him later in his life? Why or why not?
    TIP Think and Search

Writing: Compare the Literature

Use Your Notes

16. Follow these steps to compare the themes in "Kamau's Finish" and "The Bunion Derby."

    Step 1: Look at your completed chart. You probably answered "yes" in both columns for a few questions, which means that Kamau and Andy Payne are alike in some ways. They may also have similar experiences. Circle the questions to which you answered "yes" about both selections.

    Step 2: Reread the notes you made about those questions in your chart. Use those notes to write a few sentences about how both selections are alike. Then write one or two sentences describing how they are different.

    Step 3: Use your chart to identify the themes of the selections. You may find different themes for each selection. Or you may find that one theme works for both selections. (Hint: Think about why Kamua and Andy run and what they learn from competing.)

    Step 4: Make a table like the one below. Label one column "Kamau's Finish" and the other column "The Bunion Derby." Then write the theme or themes of the selections.

"Kamau's Finish"	"The Bunion Derby"
Theme:	Theme:
1:	1:
2:	2:
3:	3:

Step 5: Go back to the selections and look for details that support the theme or themes you've chosen. Look closely at what Kamau, Andy, and other people say and do. Then list at least three details in your chart for each selection.

Get It On Paper

To show your understanding of theme in "Kamau's Finish" and "The Bunion Derby," answer the questions below on a separate sheet of paper.

17. What obstacles do Kamau and Andy Payne face as they run?
18. What do Kamau and Andy Payne hope to achieve by running in a race?
19. What lessons do Kamau and Andy Payne learn about doing their best?

BIG Question

20. What did Kamau and Andy Payne learn about working hard to achieve a goal? What did they learn about winning? How would Kamau and Andy Payne answer the Big Question?

Writing: Compare the Literature

Use Your Notes

16. Completed charts will differ.
    Questions to which the answer is "yes" for both selections:
    - want support from family and friends
    - face obstacles while racing
    - try his best
    - learn something

    Student responses should discuss how the themes of "effort over achievement" and "the importance of determination" relate to "Kamau's Finish" and "The Bunion Derby," respectively.

Get It on Paper

17. Possible response: Kamau's obstacles include facing Kip, difficulty concentrating, and falling down. Andy faces bad weather, worn-out shoes, poor food and lodging, and tonsillitis.
18. Possible response: Kamau hopes to please Baba and prove himself worthy to his family and friends. Andy hopes to win the prize and help his family.
19. Possible response: Kamau learns that trying your best and following through on your efforts is more important than winning. Andy learns that determination pays off.

BIG Question

20. Possible responses: Both Kamau and Andy learn that winning is not always the most important thing. Both would probably say that the journey and the destination are equally important.

Close

Hold a class discussion based on responses to question 20.

Indiana English/Language Arts Academic Standards
SE: 8.3

The Unit Challenge

Focus

BELLRINGER Options

Daily Language Practice Transparency 20
Focus Activity Ask: In the selections, which characters pursue destinations that are similar to goals that you have or have had? Which journey did you find most interesting? Why?

To respond to these questions, students must reflect how selections in the unit relate to the Big Question and to students' own lives. This exercise will prepare students to complete the Unit Challenge group activity or solo activity. AS

Teach

Group Activity: Trial TV

- You may wish to assign teams and tell each team whether it represents "Journey" or "Destination."
- Tell team members to consult their Foldable™ notes to identify selections that support the journey or the destination.
- Set a time limit of two minutes each for the opening arguments of the lawyers. Before the trial, have teammates give feedback to the lawyers about their opening statements.
- Have team members compile a list of questions for each witness.

UNIT 2 WRAP-UP

Answering Which Is More Important, the Journey or the Destination?

You've just read about people who made journeys in pursuit of a destination. Now use what you've learned to do the Unit Challenge.

The Unit Challenge

Choose Activity A or Activity B and follow the directions for that activity.

A. Group Activity: Trial TV

This week's case on Trial TV seeks to answer the question "Is the journey or the destination more important?" Two teams, one representing "Journey" and the other "Destination," will try to convince a panel of peers which is more important, the journey or the destination.

1. **Discuss the Assignment**
   - Form your teams. Assign sides.
   - Together, choose a selection from this unit that you believe clearly shows that either the journey or the destination is more important. To choose your selection, review and discuss the notes you took on your unit Foldables.
   - Once you've chosen your selection, discuss how it supports your side. Look for details that help you argue either that the journey is more important or that the destination is more important.
   - Choose two students from each team to act as lead "lawyers." The lawyers' job is to argue the group's position. Choose another student to represent one of the characters from your selection and act as the "witness."
   - Team members should be prepared to discuss details of the character's journey and destination with emphasis on what was more important.
   - Other class members serve as the jury.

2. **Review Your Notes and Prepare** The lawyers should prepare an opening argument. In your teams, review the notes you took in your Foldable. The "witnesses" from the unit should reread parts of their selections and review notes to back up their testimony. The jury may wish to prepare a list of questions that they need to have answered to come up with a verdict.

3. **Make a Decision** After the cases have been presented, the jury should meet privately to discuss which argument is more convincing. When each jury reaches a final decision, a jury member should announce the answer to the Big Question: Which is more important, the journey or the destination?

4. **Meet as a Class** As a class, discuss whether you agree or disagree with the decision.

Assess/Close

Group Activity

Say: State whether or not the group activity changed your mind about the importance of the journey or the destination. Explain your response. *(Students may write their responses in their Learner's Notebooks or share them orally in class discussion.)* AS

B. Solo Activity: Interview

You'll interview a family member, family friend, or neighbor who has taken a major journey in his or her life. Your purpose is to see which was more important, the journey or the destination.

1. **Prepare** After you have chosen which person you are going to interview, you should prepare for the interview by making a list of questions. Use the notes on your Foldable to help you think of interview questions. For example:
   - What was your destination?
   - When did the journey take place? Why did you decide to take this journey?
   - What happened when you reached your destination?
   - How did you feel at the end of the journey?
   - Which was more important: your destination or the journey to get there?

2. **Interview and Organize** Ask your questions, and write down the person's answers. If possible, record the interview on tape so that you can listen to it later. On a separate sheet of paper, fill in a graphic organizer like the one shown below to record your answers.

Name:
Destination: | Time of Destination: | Outcome:
Journey:
End Result:

3. **Reflect and Write** Look at your chart. Based on the person's answers, write a short paper explaining which was more important, the journey or the destination. Begin your paper with an introductory paragraph. In the paragraph, tell whom you interviewed, when, and why. End the paragraph with a sentence that states what you learned from the interview. The sentence should explain whether the journey or the destination is more important.

   In the next paragraph or two of your paper, give reasons why you believe the journey or destination is more important. Your reasons should be based on the answers you received from the person you interviewed.

   End your paper with a short paragraph describing how you felt about the interview and what, if anything, you would do differently the next time you interview someone.

4. **Review** Look over your paper before you hand it in. Check to make sure that your paper is complete and that your writing is clear. You may want to ask another student to look over your paper to see whether it needs improving. Also check to make sure there aren't any spelling errors or other kinds of mistakes. Then give your paper to your teacher.

Teach

Solo Activity: Interview

- Have each student set up a specific time and place for meeting the selected interviewee. Remind students to be respectful and courteous at all times. Have them send a thank-you note after the interview is completed.
- Have students write out and review their questions before the interview. The interview should start with the most important questions and flow in a logical order.
- Warn students to avoid questions that can be answered with a simple yes or no. Students should focus on asking *who, what, where, when, why,* and *how.*
- Remind students who plan to tape the interview to request the interviewee's permission to do so.
- Suggest that students ask follow-up questions if they need additional information about a particular response.
- Encourage students to note in their Learner's Notebooks their impressions about the interview and any ideas that the interview sparked. Point out that students should do this as soon as possible after the interview.

Assess/Close

Solo Activity

Ask: What new understanding of the Big Question have you gained by interviewing someone on the topic? Explain. *(Responses will vary.)* **AS**

Big Question Have students access the Web site for English and Spanish summaries and annotated links to related Web resources.

Focus

Build Background

The poem tells about the speaker's love of train travel.

- The height of train travel in the United States occurred in 1920, when more than 1.2 billion people traveled by train.
- The boom in train travel was short. Business declined on passenger trains because of the widespread use of cars, buses, and airplanes.
- By 1970, airlines carried 73 percent of all travelers, and railroads carried only 7 percent.

Teach

R Reading Skill

Making Inferences

Ask: How does the speaker of the poem feel about train travel? Explain. *(Possible response: The speaker seems to have had an enjoyable experience on a train. She loves trains so much she's willing to give up friendships to travel on them.)* **AL**

UNIT 2

Your Turn: Read and Apply Skills

Edna St. Vincent Millay

Meet the Author

Throughout her life, Edna St. Vincent Millay was one of the most successful and respected poets in the United States. Millay dreamed of becoming a concert pianist, but her music teacher said that Millay's hands were too small. Millay then threw her energies into writing. She wrote not only poetry, but also plays, and a libretto (lyrics) for an opera. Millay received many awards for her poetry, including the Gold Medal of the Poetry Society and a Pulitzer Prize. See page R4 of the Author Files for more on Edna St. Vincent Millay.

Author Search For more about Edna St. Vincent Millay go to www.glencoe.com.

by Edna St. Vincent Millay

The railroad track is miles away,
And the day is loud with voices speaking,
Yet there isn't a train goes by all day
But I hear its whistle shrieking.

All night there isn't a train goes by,
Though the night is still for sleep and dreaming
But I see its cinders* red on the sky,
And hear its engine steaming.

My heart is warm with the friends I make,
And better friends I'll not be knowing,
Yet there isn't a train I wouldn't take,
No matter where it's going.

7 ***Cinders*** are hot coals without flames.

Additional Support

Author Search To expand students's appreciation of Edna St. Vincent Millay, have them access the Web site for additional information and resources.

Literature Focus Lesson

Summary In this poem, the speaker muses about her love of travel, particularly by train. Although she lives far from the track, she still hears the train "whistle's shrieking" and imagines that she sees the engine's red cinders. In the third stanza, she claims that she does not care where she goes, and that she is willing to travel despite sacrifices to her current and future relationships. **AS**

Teach

Viewing the Photo

Ask: Do you think this photograph makes train travel look like fun? Why or why not? *(Possible response: The photo is dark and there is a lot of dreary smoke coming out of the train. I don't think the photo makes train travel look like fun.)* **AS**

BQ BIG Question

Ask: Which do you think is more important for the speaker in this poem—the journey or the destination? *(Possible response: The journey is more important. In the last line of the poem, the speaker says that the destination is not important.)* **OL**

Differentiated Instruction

Designing Home Pages Have students work in small groups to design the home page of a Web site for tourists wanting to visit a large city, such as New York or Hollywood. If your students do not have access to appropriate technology, they may design the look and content of the home page on paper. The home page should feature interesting information about the city, as well as practical information on traveling there. Students might include details about climate, population, attractions, and recreation. **OL**

Indiana English/Language Arts Academic Standards
TWE: *Differentiated Instruction* 8.4.6

Tips for Independent Reading

Make sure that selected student books for independent reading are appropriate for students' reading level. Although independent reading should help students improve their reading, it should be an enjoyable activity, free from time constraints or assessment.

Fiction

Tell students that reading fictional accounts of journeys can give them new perspectives on the journeys they have taken, as well as help them answer the Big Question.

Ask students to share examples of fictional journeys they have read about, and prompt them to discuss whether the focus was on the journey or the destination.

UNIT 2

Reading on Your Own

To read more about the Big Question, choose one of these books from your school or local library. Work on your reading skills by choosing books that are challenging to you.

Fiction

Banner in the Sky
by James Ramsey Ullman

When Rudi's father dies in his attempt to scale a mountain in the Alps, Rudi decides that he must conquer the peak that killed his father. Read to find out more as the author, an experienced climber, adds detailed information to a tense tale of courage and determination.

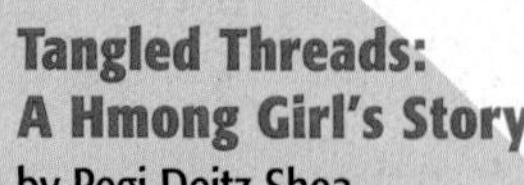

Tangled Threads: A Hmong Girl's Story
by Pegi Deitz Shea

Mai was a young girl when she and her grandmother escaped Laos. After living in a refugee camp for years, they join Mai's uncle in the United States. Life in a new culture can be hard, but Mai welcomes the change. Her grandmother has a harder time getting used to life in the United States.

After the War
by Carol Matas

Ruth is fifteen when she is freed from a Nazi concentration camp and fears that she is the only surviving member of her family. She joins an underground organization to make a dangerous and illegal journey to Palestine. Read to learn how she rediscovers her inner strength and finds reasons for hope along the way.

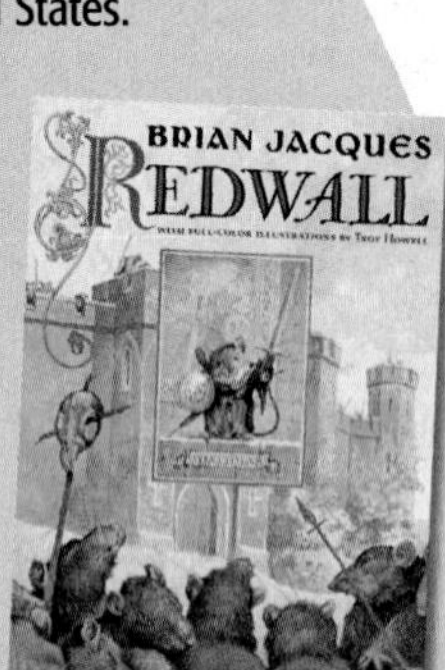

Redwall
by Brian Jacques

The creatures living at Redwall Abbey are a peaceful group until the king of vermin declares war against them. Read about Matthias, an apprentice mouse, who sets out to find a magic sword that can save Redwall. This is the first book in a series of more than ten tales of quests and fights between good and evil.

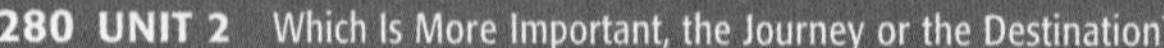

Additional Support

Differentiated Instruction

GLENCOE BOOKLINK Use the Glencoe BookLink CD-ROM to create customized reading lists to help students answer the Big Question. Suggestions for Unit 2:

Grade 4: *A Small Tall Tale from the Far Far North* by Peter Sis
Grade 5: *The Way to Rainy Mountain* by N. Scott Momaday
Grade 6: *Journey to Topaz* by Yoshiko Uchida
Grade 7: *Raymond's Run* by Toni Cade Bambara
Grade 8: *In the Heart of the Sea: The Tragedy of the Whaleship Essex* by Nathaniel Philbrick

Nonfiction

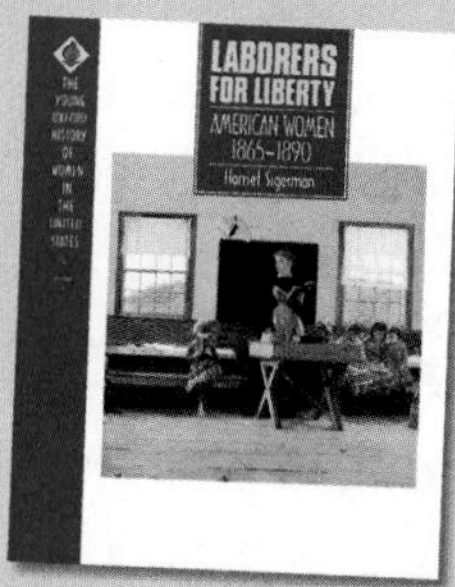

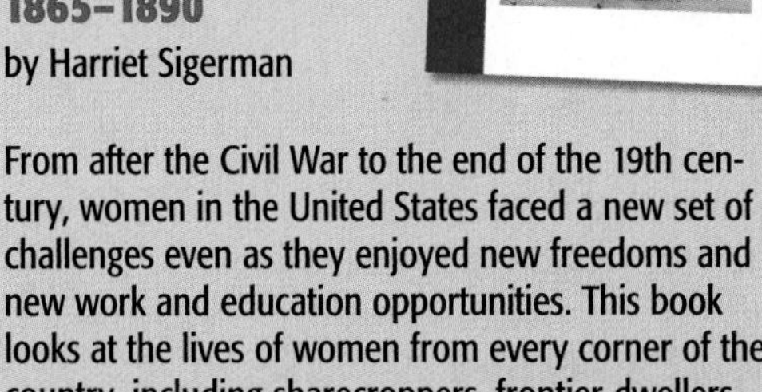

Laborers for Liberty: American Women 1865–1890
by Harriet Sigerman

From after the Civil War to the end of the 19th century, women in the United States faced a new set of challenges even as they enjoyed new freedoms and new work and education opportunities. This book looks at the lives of women from every corner of the country, including sharecroppers, frontier dwellers, and champions of causes, such as getting the right to vote.

Curse of the Pharaohs: My Adventures with Mummies
by Zahi Hawass

Zahi Hawass, head of Egypt's Supreme Council of Antiquities, tells of his adventures and close shaves while searching for pieces of Egypt's ancient civilization. Read to find out whether Hawass experiences the effects of the pharaoh's curse.

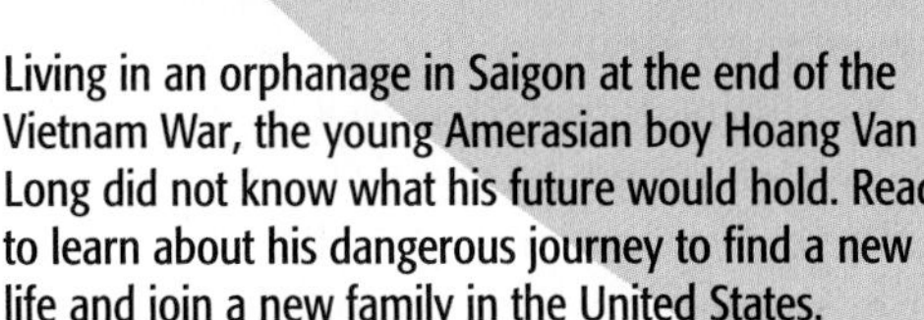

Escape from Saigon: How a Vietnam War Orphan Became an American Boy
by Andrea Warren

Living in an orphanage in Saigon at the end of the Vietnam War, the young Amerasian boy Hoang Van Long did not know what his future would hold. Read to learn about his dangerous journey to find a new life and join a new family in the United States.

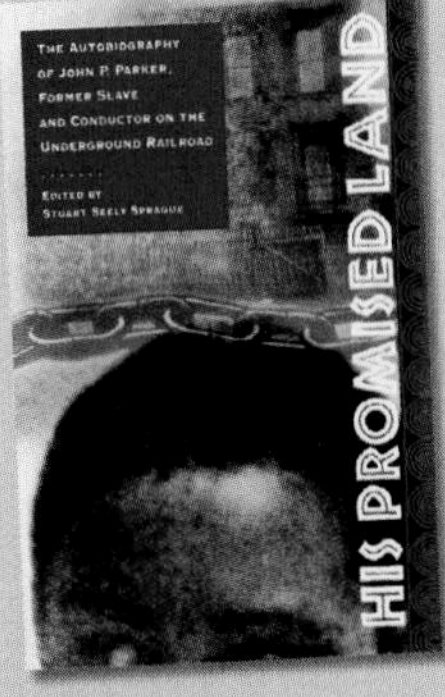

His Promised Land: The Autobiography of John P. Parker, Former Slave and Conductor on the Underground Railroad
edited by Stuart Seely Sprague

John P. Parker is born enslaved, but he purchases his own freedom after teaching himself to read. As a freeman, Parker becomes an important member of the Underground Railroad. Read to learn how Parker risks his life time and again to help hundreds of people who were enslaved escape to freedom.

READING ON YOUR OWN

Nonfiction
Share with students that the books on this page are all nonfiction books. They will give detailed accounts of real people, places, and events.

Period Books
Say: Each of these four books has a main title, which is short and catchy, and a subtitle, which is longer and more descriptive. Look closely at these subtitles. What do most of them seem to have in common? *(Possible response: Three of the four books are about a specific time period, such as the second half of the nineteenth century, the end of the Vietnam War, and the pre-Civil War South.)* **OL**

About the Subjects
Invite students to share information they know about the subjects on this page.
Ask: What is a pharaoh? *(a ruler of ancient Egypt)*
Ask: When was the United States involved in the Vietnam War? *(1965–1973)* **Ask:** What was the Underground Railroad? *(a network of people who helped enslaved persons escape to the North)* **BL** **OL**

Test-Taking Tips

TIP Let students know that sometimes more than one answer will seem correct. When this happens, they should try to eliminate as many answers that are clearly wrong as possible. Then they should choose the answer that seems best or most likely from the remaining answers.

TIP Remind students that making mistakes during test-taking practice is actually helpful. Mistakes are good indicators of what can be improved and avoided on the actual test.

ISTEP+ Test Practice

Directions

Read this excerpt from a Native American folktale about the adventures of a young man who becomes a hero. Then, answer questions 1 through 4.

from Racing the Great Bear

Retold by Joseph Bruchac

One day, not long after the Great Peace had been established, some young men in a Seneca village decided they would pay a visit to the Onondaga people.

"It is safe now to walk the trail between our nations," the young men said. "We will return after the sun has risen and set seven times."

Then they set out. They walked toward the east until they were lost from sight in the hills. But many more than seven days passed, and those young men never returned. Now another group of young men left, wanting to find out where their friends had gone. They, too, did not return.

The people grew worried. Parties were sent out to look for the vanished young men, but no sign was found. And the searchers who went too far into the hills did not return, either.

The old chief of the village thought long and hard. He asked the clan mothers, those wise women whose job it was to choose the chiefs and give them good advice, what should be done.

"We must find someone brave enough to face whatever danger is out there," the clan mothers said.

So the old chief called the whole village to a council meeting. He held up a white strand of wampum beads made from quahog clamshells as he spoke.

"Hear me," he said. "I am of two minds about what has happened to our people. It may be that the Onondaga have broken the peace and captured them. It may be there is something with an evil mind that wishes to destroy this new peace and so has killed our people. Now someone must go and find out. Who is brave enough? Who will come and take this wampum from my hand?"

Many men were gathered in that council. Some were known to speak of themselves as brave warriors. Still, though they muttered to one another, no man stepped forward to take the strand of wampum. The old chief began to walk about the circle, holding the wampum in front of each man in turn. But each man only lowered his eyes to the ground. No man lifted his hand to take the wampum.

Just outside the circle stood a boy who had not yet become a man. His parents were dead, and he lived with his grandmother in her old lodge at the edge of the village. His clothing was always torn and his face dirty because his grandmother was too old to care for him as a mother would. The other young men made fun of him, and as a joke they called him Swift Runner—even though no one had ever seen him run and it was thought that he was weak and lazy. All he ever seemed to do was play with his little dog or sit by the fire and listen when the old people were talking.

"Our chief has forgotten our greatest warrior," one of the young men said to another, tilting his head toward Swift Runner.

"Nyoh," the other young man said, laughing. "Yes. Why does he not offer the wampum to Swift Runner?"

The chief looked around the circle of men, and the laughing stopped. He walked out of the circle to the place where the small boy in torn clothes stood. He held out the wampum and Swift Runner took it without hesitating.

"I accept this," Swift Runner said. "It is right that I be the one to face the danger.

"In the eyes of the people I am worthless, so if I do not return, it will not matter. I will leave when the sun rises tomorrow."

Numbers 1 through 4 are based on "Racing the Great Bear."

1 The people in the village become worried when the young men

A break the peace with the Onondaga people
B refuse to take the wampum from the chief's hand
C fail to return from their journey
D refuse to attend the council meeting

2 Swift Runner's response to the chief demonstrates that he is

A conceited
B brave
C impatient
D nervous

3 The other young men in the village laugh at Swift Runner because

A he tells funny jokes
B he runs very slowly
C he is afraid to face danger
D he seems weak and lazy

UNIT 2 ASSESSMENT

Answers:

1. C
2. B
3. D

Resources for pages 282–287

Use these resources to review, assess, or reteach the chapter: Active Learning and Note-Taking Guide, ExamView Pro, and Differentiated Instruction Tool Software.

Answers:

4. A

Test-Taking Tips

TIP Remind students that it's often helpful to read the questions on a language arts test before they read a passage. That way they will know what to look for as they read.

4 Read this sentence from the story.

> *"Our chief has forgotten our greatest warrior," one of the young men said to another, tilting his head toward Swift Runner.*

Based on the details in the story, choose what the young man MOST LIKELY means.

A Swift Runner is not a warrior.
B Swift Runner is the tribe's greatest warrior.
C Swift Runner is very brave.
D Swift Runner will not accept the wampum.

Directions

Read this excerpt from an African American folktale about a people's magical powers. Then, answer questions 5 through 8.

from The People Could Fly

Told by Virginia Hamilton

They say the people could fly. Say that long ago in Africa, some of the people knew magic. And they would walk up on the air like climbin up on a gate. And they flew like blackbirds over the fields. Black, shiny wings flappin against the blue up there.

Then, many of the people were captured for Slavery. The ones that could fly shed their wings. They couldn't take their wings across the water on the slave ships. Too crowded, don't you know.

The folks were full of misery, then. Got sick with the up and down of the sea. So they forgot about flyin when they could no longer breathe the sweet scent of Africa.

Say the people who could fly kept their power, although they shed their wings. They kept their secret magic in the land of slavery. They looked the same as the other people from Africa who had been coming over, who had dark skin. Say you couldn't tell anymore one who could fly from one who couldn't.

One such who could was an old man, call him Toby. And standin tall, yet afraid, was a young woman who once had wings. Call her Sarah. Now Sarah carried a babe tied to her back. She trembled to be so hard worked and scorned.

The slaves labored in the fields from sunup to sundown. The owner of the slaves callin himself their Master. Say he was a hard lump of clay. A hard, glinty coal. A hard rock pile, wouldn't be moved. His Overseer on horseback pointed out the slaves who were slowin down. So the one called Driver cracked his whip over the slow ones to make them move faster. That whip was a slice-open cut of pain. So they did move faster. Had to.

Sarah hoed and chopped the row as the babe on her back slept.

Say the child grew hungry. That babe started up bawling too loud. Sarah couldn't stop to feed it. Couldn't stop to soothe and quiet it down. She let it cry. She didn't want to. She had no heart to croon to it.

"Keep that thing quiet," called the Overseer. He pointed his finger at the babe. The woman scrunched low. The Driver cracked his whip across the babe anyhow. The babe hollered like any hurt child, and the woman fell to the earth.

The old man that was there, Toby, came and helped her to her feet.

"I must go soon," she told him.

"Soon," he said.

Sarah couldn't stand up straight any longer. She was too weak. The sun burned her face. The babe cried and cried. "Pity me, oh, pity me," say it sounded like. Sarah was so sad and starving, she sat down in the row.

"Get up, you black cow," called the Overseer. He pointed his hand, and the Driver's whip snarled around Sarah's legs. Her sack dress tore into rags. Her legs bled onto the earth. She couldn't get up.

Toby was there where there was no one to help her and the babe.

"Now, before it's too late," panted Sarah. "Now, Father!"

"Yes, Daughter, the time is come," Toby answered. "Go, as you know how to go!"

He raised his arms, holding them out to her. "Kum. . . yali, kum buba tambe," and more magic words said so quickly, they sounded like whispers and sighs.

The young woman lifted one foot on the air, then the other. She flew clumsily at first, with the child now held tightly in her arms. Then she felt the magic, the African mystery. Say she rose just as free as a bird. As light as a feather.

Numbers 5 through 8 are based on "The People Could Fly."

5 The attitude of the narrator toward her characters can BEST be described as

A impatient
B critical
C sympathetic
D surprised

6 Which of the following is a major theme in the story?

A overcoming oppression
B developing friendships
C discovering opportunity
D learning a trade

Answers:

5. C

6. A

Answers:

7. B

8. B

Test-Taking Tips

TIP Remind students to make sure their written responses are clean and legible. After writing a response, students should also check their spelling and punctuation.

TIP Remind students that after they've finished a test, if they still have time left, they should go back and check their answers. They should reread each question and possible answer to make sure they haven't misread or misinterpreted anything.

7 The style of the storytelling can BEST be described as

A humorous
B conversational
C complex
D formal

Use your understanding of the writing process and English language conventions to answer question 8.

8 If these sentences were written in a single paragraph, which sentence would be the topic sentence?

A People fleeing slavery could find shelter and rest at "stations" along the way.
B Many enslaved people escaped to freedom using the Underground Railroad.
C Houses, taverns, and even churches were part of the Underground Railroad.
D Information about escape routes was sometimes communicated through songs.

Directions

Read this Native American folktale. Then, answer questions 9 through 13.

The Sun Snarer

One day while two elder brothers were out hunting in the forest, the youngest went away to hide himself and to mourn because he was not permitted to join them. He had with him his bow and arrows and his beaver-skin robe; but when the Sun rose high in the sky he became tired and laid himself down to weep, covering himself entirely with his robe to keep out the Sun. When the Sun was directly overhead and saw the boy, it sent down a ray which burned spots upon the robe and made it shrink until it exposed the boy. Then the Sun smiled, while the boy wept more violently than before. He felt that he had been cruelly treated both by his brothers and now by the Sun. . . .

The boy then gathered up his bow and arrows, and taking his burnt robe, returned to the wigwam, where he lay down in a dark corner and again wept. . . .

When he awoke, he said to his sister, "My sister, give me a thread; I wish to use it."

Then he started out to where the Sun's path touched the earth. When he reached the place where the Sun was when it burned his robe, the little boy made a noose and stretched it across the path, and when the Sun came to that point the noose caught him around the neck and began to choke him until he almost lost his breath. It became dark and the Sun called out, . . . "Help me, my brothers, and cut this string before it kills me." The Mouse came up and gnawed at the string, but it was difficult work, because the string was hot and deeply embedded in the Sun's neck. After working at the string a good while, however, the Mouse succeeded in cutting it, when the Sun breathed again and the darkness disappeared. If the Mouse had not succeeded, the Sun would have died. Then the boy said to the Sun, "For your cruelty I have punished you; now you may go."

The boy then returned to his sister, satisfied with what he had done.

Numbers 9 through 13 are based on "The Sun Snarer."

9 The word *snarer* in the story's title MOST LIKELY means

A fighter
B trapper
C tricker
D punisher

10 What does the boy do with the string his sister gives him?

A He repairs his robe.
B He catches the Mouse.
C He makes a noose.
D He weaves a basket.

11 When the Sun loses his breath,

A he begins to weep
B the world becomes dark
C his path touches the earth
D the boy's sister smiles

12 Read this sentence from the story.

> *The Mouse came up and gnawed at the string, but it was difficult work, because the string was hot and deeply embedded in the Sun's neck.*

What does *embedded* MOST LIKELY mean in the sentence?

A knotted
B burned
C chewed
D set

13 In the story, the Sun is portrayed with human characteristics. What are TWO examples of these characteristics?

UNIT 2 ASSESSMENT

Answers:

9. C
10. C
11. B
12. D
13. Student responses should indicate that the sun does two of the following:
- smiles
- breathes
- talks
- exhibits fear

UNIT 3

Skills Scope and Sequence

Readability Scores Key
Dale-Chall/DRP/Lexile

PACING (DAYS) STANDARD	BLOCK	INSTRUCTIONAL SEGMENT LITERATURE	READING SKILLS	LITERARY ELEMENTS
1	1	**Unit Warm-Up, pp. 288–295** Genre Focus: "A Tremendous Trade" by Jeremy Caplan **7.0/62/1180**, SE p. 293	Previewing, SE p. 293 Skimming and Scanning, SE p. 293 Identifying Main Idea and Supporting Details, SE p. 294 Understanding Text Structures, SE p. 294, TWE p. 295 Fluency, TWE p. 289 Connecting, TWE p. 290	Irony, SE p. 293 Evidence, SE p. 294 Photographs, SE p. 295, TWE p. 293 Tone, SE p. 295, TWE p. 293
3	2	**Reading Workshop 1, pp. 296–315** "Gymnasts in Pain: Out of Balance" by Scott M. Reid **9.0/62/1140**, SE p. 300 "In Response to Executive Order 9066" by Dwight Okita SE p. 312	Previewing, SE pp. 296, 297, 299, 300, 312 Making Inferences, SE p. 302, TWE p. 306 Identifying Author's Purpose, TWE pp. 302, 306 Fluency, TWE p. 311	Tone, SE pp. 299, 300, 303, 305, 306 Symbol, SE pp. 311, 312, 313 Puns, TWE p. 300 Bias, TWE p. 302
1		**Writing Workshop, Part 1, pp. 316–321** Writing Product: Research Report		Primary and Secondary Sources, TWE p. 317 Writing a Thesis, TWE p. 319
3	1	**Reading Workshop 2, pp. 322–335** "The Games Kids Play" **7.8/64/1130**, SE p. 326 "Cruise Control" by Kevin O'Leary **6.5/55/1070**, SE p. 332	Skimming and Scanning, SE pp. 322, 323, 325, 326, 331, 332 Connecting, SE p. 333 Making Inferences, TWE p. 325	Nonfiction Text Features, TWE p. 322 Evidence, SE pp. 325, 327 Humor, SE pp. 331, 332 Anecdotes, TWE p. 330

Unit 3 Big Question

The question **"When is the price too high?"** is designed to help students develop the skills they need to make smart decisions.

Unit 3 Genre

Many of the selections in this unit are **informational articles,** which present facts and explanations. These selections will also help students answer the big question "When is the price too high?" Use these articles to help students evaluate situations and determine what's worth doing despite the risks involved.

CRITICAL THINKING	VOCABULARY	WRITING AND GRAMMAR	LISTENING, SPEAKING, AND VIEWING
			Viewing the Image, TWE p. 288
Analyze, SE p. 308 Evaluate, SE pp. 308, 314 Interpret, SE p. 314, TWE p. 312 Infer, SE p. 314 Comprehension, TWE p. 301 Evaluation, TWE pp. 305, 312	Academic Vocabulary, SE p. 296 Multiple-Meaning Words, SE pp. 298, 301, 304, 305, 310, 312, TWE p. 299	Sentence Types, SE p. 309 Write About Your Reading, SE p. 314 End Punctuation, SE p. 315	Analyzing the Photo, SE pp. 303, 304, 306, Viewing the Photo, TWE p. 300 Talk About Your Reading, SE p. 308 Role Play, TWE p. 307
		Prewriting, SE pp. 316, 317 Research, SE pp. 317, 318 Outline, SE p. 319 Drafting, SE p. 319 Cite Sources, SE p. 320 Simple Sentences, SE p. 321	
Evaluate, SE pp. 328, 334 Analyze, SE p. 328 Infer, SE p. 334 Apply, SE p. 334, TWE p. 333 Comprehension, TWE pp. 326, 333 Analysis, TWE p. 331 Evaluation, TWE p. 332	Academic Vocabulary, SE p. 322 Multiple-Meaning Words, SE pp. 324, 327, 330, 332 Related Words, TWE p. 324 Word Structure, TWE p. 330	Write About Your Reading, SE p. 328 Fragments That Lack a Subject or a Verb, SE p. 329 Dependent Clauses as Sentence Fragments, SE p. 335	Talk About Your Reading, SE p. 334

UNIT 3
Skills Scope and Sequence *continued*

Readability Scores Key
Dale-Chall/DRP/Lexile

PACING (DAYS) STANDARD	PACING (DAYS) BLOCK	INSTRUCTIONAL SEGMENT LITERATURE	READING SKILLS	LITERARY ELEMENTS
3	3	**Reading Workshop 3, pp. 336–379** "Flowers for Algernon," Part 1 by Daniel Keyes **5.8/49/850**, SE p. 340 "Flowers for Algernon," Part 2 by Daniel Keyes **5.8/49/850**, SE p. 358	Understanding Text Structures, SE pp. 336, 337, 339, 341, 350, 352, 353, 357, 358, 361, 364, 365, 367, 370, 372, 375 Making Inferences, SE pp. 340, 342, 346, 347, 348, 349, 374 Predicting, SE pp. 359, 360, 373, TWE pp. 345, 346, 347, 350, 357 Comparing and Contrasting, TWE pp. 348, 350, 364, 367, 374 Identifying Author's Purpose, TWE pp. 359, 374	Irony, SE pp. 339, 343, 347, 349, 351, 366, TWE p. 375 Foreshadowing, SE pp. 357, 362, 363, 369 Point of View, TWE pp. 349, 368 Humor, TWE p. 351 Similes, TWE p. 362 Plot, TWE pp. 368, 369, 375 Conflict, TWE p. 373 Tone, TWE p. 367
1		**Writing Workshop, Part 2, pp. 380–385** Writing Product: Research Report		
3	1	**Reading Workshop 4, pp. 386–403** "Tattoos: Fad, Fashion, or Folly?" by Linda Bickerstaff **6.5/66/1090**, SE p. 390 "We Real Cool" by Gwendolyn Brooks SE p. 400 "The Market Economy" by Marge Piercy SE p. 401	Identifying Main Idea and Supporting Details, SE pp. 386, 387, 389, 390, 391, 393, 395, 399, 401 Making Inferences, SE p. 393 Comparing and Contrasting, TWE pp. 394, 400 Identifying Author's Purpose, TWE p. 395 Fluency, TWE pp. 395, 401	Photographs, SE pp. 389, 390, 392 Alliteration, SE pp. 399, 400
3	2	**Reading Across Texts Workshop, pp. 404–419** "Wearing Hijab: Veil of Valor" by Emilia Askari **8.4/59/1010**, SE p. 407 from *Zoya's Story* by Zoya with John Follain and Rita Cristofari **5.8/59/1170**, SE p. 414	Making Inferences, SE pp. 410, 411, 416 Connecting, TWE pp. 406, 410 Identifying Main Idea and Supporting Details, TWE pp. 408, 416, 417 Comparing and Contrasting, TWE pp. 409, 411	Bias, SE pp. 404, 412, 416 Photographs, SE p. 407 Writer's Sources, SE p. 408 Writer's Qualifications, SE pp. 409, 414 Description, SE p. 415 Point of View, TWE p. 414 Figurative Language, TWE p. 415
4	2	**Unit Wrap-Up, pp. 420–441**		

CRITICAL THINKING	VOCABULARY	WRITING AND GRAMMAR	LISTENING, SPEAKING, AND VIEWING
Analyze, SE p. 354 Evaluate, SE p. 354 Infer, SE p. 378 Draw Conclusions, SE p. 378 Comprehension, TWE pp. 340, 341, 344, 348, 349, 361, 362, 372, 373, 376 Compare and Contrast, TWE p. 345 Synthesis, TWE pp. 352, 353, 377 Evaluation, TWE pp. 363, 364	Multiple-Meaning Words, SE pp. 338, 342, 344, 345, 353, 356, 360, 362, 364, 376, TWE p. 351 Phonetic Spelling, TWE p. 340 Homophones, TWE p. 351 Past Tense, TWE p. 356	Write About Your Reading, SE p. 354 Run-ons, SE p. 355 Write About Your Reading, SE p. 378 Compound Subjects and Predicates, SE p. 379	Analyzing the Image, SE pp. 343, 347, 350 Analyzing the Art, SE pp. 348, 371 Viewing the Illustration, TWE p. 340 Viewing the Photograph, TWE p. 365
		Revising, Editing, and Presenting SE pp. 380, 381, 382 Applying Good Writing Traits: Conventions, SE p. 381	Oral Presentation, SE p. 382
Analyze, SE p. 396 Infer, SE p. 396 Evaluate, SE pp. 396, 402 Interpret, SE p. 402 Compare, SE p. 402 Analysis, TWE p. 393 Comprehension, TWE pp. 395, 401	Academic Vocabulary, SE p. 386 Word References, SE pp. 388, 391, 393, 398 Latin Roots, TWE pp. 394, 395	Write About Your Reading, SE p. 396 Direct Objects, SE p. 397 Indirect Objects, SE p. 403	Viewing the Photograph, TWE p. 391 Talk About Your Reading, SE p. 402 Viewing the Painting, TWE p. 400
Analyze, TWE p. 417			

UNIT 3

Unit Resources

Reading with Purpose offers a comprehensive package of tools to optimize student learning and the teaching experience. Each resource has been designed to assist students in specific areas and to offer instructional support for teachers. While all of these areas are covered in the core textbook, some students may need extra practice or additional help in specific areas. The resource package is designed so that you, the teacher, can choose which items will best assist your students. You may also use these resources as homework assignments and for assessment purposes. The following are resources recommended for use with Unit 3.

Keys for Unit Resources

- Blackline Master
- Workbook
- Supplemental Text
- CD-ROM
- DVD
- Transparency
- Web-based
- Fast File

Essential Instructional Support

FAST FILE UNIT 3 RESOURCES

Reading and Literature

- Academic Vocabulary Review
- Big Question: School to Home
- The Big Question Foldable
- Unit Challenge: Planner and Rubrics
- Comparing Literature Graphic Organizer
- Key Reading Skills
- Active Reading Graphic Organizers
- Literary Analysis
- Unit Vocabulary Review

Writing, Grammar, and Spelling

- Spelling and Handwriting Practice
- Grammar Practice
- Writing Workshop Graphic Organizer

Listening, Speaking, and Viewing

- Viewing and Representing
- Listening and Speaking

English Language Learners

- English Language Coach Review

DIFFERENTIATED INSTRUCTION

- Leveled Vocabulary Development
- Skill Level Up!™ A Language Arts Game
- Listening Library CD
- BookLink 3
- Literature Library Vocabulary Puzzlemaker
- Vocabulary Puzzlemaker

ASSESSMENT

GLENCOE'S ASSESSMENT ADVANTAGE

- Selection and Unit Assessments
- Selection Quick Checks
- Assessment by Learning Objectives
- Rubrics for Assessing Student Writing, Listening, and Speaking
- Glencoe Online Essay Grader
- Interactive Tutor: Self-Assessment
- ExamView Assessment Suite
- Literature Library ExamView Assessment Suite

Additional Instructional Support

WRITING, GRAMMAR, AND SPELLING

- Real Success in Writing: Research and Reports
- Writing Constructed Responses Sourcebook
- Spelling Power eWorkbook
- Grammar & Composition Handbook
- Grammar and Language Workbook
- Revising with Style eWorkbook

READING AND LITERATURE

- Active Learning and Note Taking Guide
- inTime Magazines
- Backpack Reader Volume 1
- Literature Library
- Literature Launchers Pre-Reading Videos DVD
- Literature Classics

TRANSPARENCIES

- Read Aloud, Think Aloud
- Literary and Text Analysis Transparencies
- Bellringer Options Transparencies
- Grammar and Writing Workshop Transparencies
- Fine Arts Transparencies

TECHNOLOGY

- TeacherWorks Plus
- StudentWorks Plus
- BookLink 3
- Skill Level Up!
- ExamView Assessment Suite
- Interactive Tutor Self-Assessment
- Listening Library CD
- Spanish Listening Library CD
- Literature Classics
- Literature Launchers Pre-Reading Videos DVD
- Literature Library ExamView Assessment Suite
- Vocabulary Puzzlemaker
- Literature Library Vocabulary Puzzlemaker
- glencoe.com
- Online Student Edition
- Presentation Plus!
- Glencoe Online Essay Grading

ENGLISH LANGUAGE LEARNER

- English Language Coach
- Fluency Practice and Assessment
- inTime Magazines (Spanish)
- Spanish Listening Library CD

PROFESSIONAL DEVELOPMENT

- Professional Development Package

Additional Glencoe Resources

Dinah Zike's Foldables

Foldables are three-dimensional, interactive graphic organizers that help students practice basic writing skills, review key vocabulary terms, and answer Big Questions. Every unit contains a foldable activity. You can find the pattern and directions for the Unit 3 Foldable in the Unit 3 Resources Fast Files booklet. You can use the foldables as they are presented or modify them to suit the needs of your students. More information about foldables for Unit 3 can be found on page R9.

For a wealth of online resources that support the instruction in Unit 3 of *Glencoe Literature: Reading with Purpose,* students and teachers can visit our Web site at www.glencoe.com. Students will find additional learning, practice, and assessment opportunities such as these, which are noted in the student text:

- **Big Question Overview**
- **Study Central**
- **Author Search**
- **Writing Models**
- **Interactive Literary Elements Handbook**
- **Web Activities**

Teachers will find planning and instructional tools that include the following:

- **Book Lesson Plans**
- **Teacher Forum**
- **Professional Development**
- **Web Activities Lesson Plans (with answers to student activities)**

Go to www.glencoe.com to see the entire selection of Reading with Purpose online resources.

Glencoe's **Presentation Plus!**, a multimedia teaching tool, lets you present dynamic lessons that will engage your students. Using Microsoft PowerPoint,® you can customize the presentations to create your own personalized lessons. Use **CheckPoint** questions with interactive response keypads to get immediate student feedback during lessons, to increase student participation, and to assess student comprehension.

Glencoe Literature Library

This collection of hardcover books includes full-length novels, novellas, plays, and works of nonfiction. Each volume consists of at least one complete extended-length reading accompanied by several related readings from a broad range of genres. A separate Study Guide for each Glencoe Literature Library book provides teaching notes and reproducible activity pages for students.

Glencoe Literature Library titles that complement this unit include:

Across Five Aprils, by Irene Hunt
The Glory Field, by Walter Dean Myers
Sounder, by William H. Armstrong

GLENCOE BOOKLINK

Use the Glencoe BookLink 3 CD-ROM, a database of more than 26,700 titles, to *create customized reading lists* for your students.

- Search for award-winning titles, (e.g., Newbery Award winners, Coretta Scott King Award winners, and Caldecott Medal winners) and for books on several state-recommended reading lists.
- Find Degrees of Reading Power™ (DRP) and Lexile™ readability scores for all selections.
- Organize reading lists by students' reading level, author, genre, theme, or area of interest.
- Get a brief summary of each selection.

You can find recommended leveled readings for this unit with Reading on Your Own (see page 434).

A lively collection of articles drawn from issues of the TIME family of magazines helps students develop the skills they need to interact with informational text in a meaningful way. Each of the news stories, feature articles, reviews, profiles, and essays in the magazine connect to an author, work, or theme in *Glencoe Literature: Reading with Purpose.* Articles for Unit 3 are found in Volume A. See the *inTIME* Teacher's Guide for specific connections to each unit and for reproducible student worksheets designed to develop students' reading and critical thinking skills.

Literature Launchers

Set the scene with Glencoe's Literature Launchers, engaging video segments that introduce each unit's genre focus. Each video brings the genre to life, relating it to your students' worlds.

Insert the Glencoe Literature Launchers Pre-Reading Videos DVD into your DVD player. Select the Unit 3 Launcher from the menu to introduce the genre and Big Question for this unit.

Online Essay Grader

Use Glencoe's Online Essay Grader to score your students' writing and to provide individualized feedback to each student automatically.

You and your students can visit www.glencoe.com to link to the essay grader. *Students* can enter their essays and receive feedback on demand. *You* can manage demographic data, assign tests and generate individual student and aggregated reports. The essay grader can help you

- Save time with automatic scoring and individualized feedback.
- Supplement in-class writing instruction using guided writing practice.
- Get reports for individual students or for special populations.
- Track student improvement over time.

REAL Success: Reading Excellence at All Levels

Glencoe now provides all of your students with the tools they need to become better, more enthusiastic readers. The REAL Success suite of reading and language arts products encourages reading excellence by meeting the needs of students at all levels. Glencoe products that can be used in conjunction with Unit 3 include the following:

- Jamestown Literature: An Adapted Reader
- Jamestown *Reading Fluency*
- Jamestown *Critical Reading Series, In the Line of Duty*
- *Vocabulary Builder*
- *The Glencoe Reader, Course 3*

To order these products, call Glencoe at 1-800-USA-READ.

Teacher Wraparound Edition Key

Level Appropriate Code

AS = Activities for all students
AL = Activities for students working above grade level
OL = Activities for students working at grade level
BL = Activities for students working below grade level
EL = Activities for English language learners

Teacher Wraparound Prompts

R **Reading Skill** These activities help you teach reading comprehension skills.

V **Vocabulary** These activities help students comprehend words and incorporate them into their reading and writing.

C **Critical Thinking** These strategies help students apply and extend what they have learned.

BQ **BIG Question** These activities and questions prompt students to prepare to answer the Big Question.

W **Writing** These activities provide writing opportunities to help students practice writing and comprehend text.

L **Literary Element** These activities and questions help students comprehend selections and learn more about each genre.

E **Text Element** These activities help students comprehend text elements.

LSV **Listening, Speaking, Viewing** These activities help students practice listening, speaking, and viewing skills.

EL **English Language Coach** These skills help English language learners as well as students who need additional reading support.

UNIT 3

Professional Development Center

Douglas Fisher

From an Author:

Preparing Students to Read Informational Media

Start with an illustration. Students enjoy looking at illustrations and graphics, often in the form of graphic novels and illustrations. Start the class by sharing a current political cartoon or photograph. Invite students to discuss the graphic with a partner: what do they see? What does it mean? This type of partner conversation builds interest in the topic as well as background information about the topic. Describe the ways in which informational media uses illustrations. For example, newspaper and magazine articles often have photographs or illustrations. Ask students to discuss the purposes of photographs and illustrations in informational media. Why are they there? What do they do? How do they help the reader?

Activate background knowledge. Informational media often relates to the current events in our lives. Ask students about the current events being covered in magazines and newspapers. How are those stories being reported? Whose perspective is shared in these types of articles? Preview the selections in this unit by inviting students to skim the table of contents. Ask them to note the types of topics being discussed—gymnasts, video games, tattoos, etc. Ask students what they already know about these topics and what they'd like to know about these topics.

Teacher to Teacher

Ana B. Dominguez
Wester Elementary School
Lubbock, Texas

To reinforce the Big Question "When is the price too high?" I use an economic plan tied into our school's reward system—a special closet from which students purchase gifts with incentive coupons. The plan discourages an attitude of entitlement and encourages responsibility by dividing many of my duties into jobs for students in the classroom. Each student receives a specific job, which involves an interview and a training process. Jobs include computer technologist, librarian, attendance clerk, mail carrier, and accountant. At the end of the week the accountant disperses payment coupons into envelopes that the mail carrier delivers. Students who neglect their jobs don't get paid, which means they have no coupon with which to visit the incentive closet. The system also provides a measure of discipline by exacting fines as penalties.

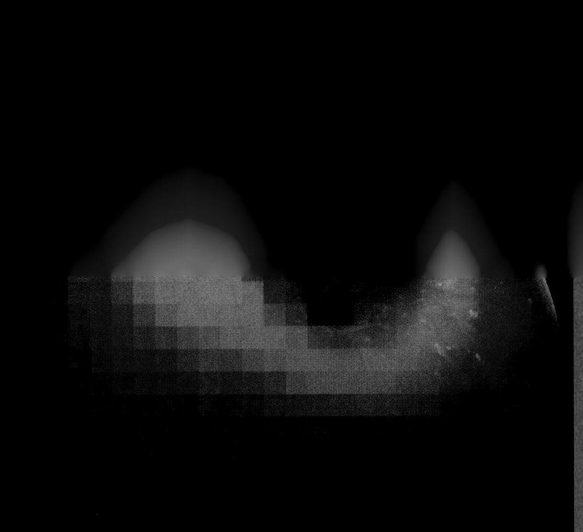

Using Informational Media

What is informational media and why is it important?

This genre focuses on the types of texts used to inform—and teach—people about topics important in their lives. It extends traditional nonfiction texts to include a wide range of media outlets that can provide people with accurate information. Informational media is important as it is one of the primary ways that people receive information in the world. For example, we read newspapers, magazines, and the Internet to find out the answers to our questions and to understand the events of the world. In fact, informational media is one of the most common types of texts adults read. Middle school students need to know how to read for information and how to evaluate the information they read.

Are students interested in informational media?

Very much so. In fact, there is evidence that reluctant readers and many male students prefer informational media and texts. The difficulty with this type of text is the background knowledge that is assumed by some authors. For example, in the selection "Gymnasts in Pain," the author assumes his readers know what gymnasts do. To help students understand this text, which many of them will find fascinating, you may want to focus on key ideas before sharing the text. Building background and frontloading information is always a good idea as it helps students make connections between what they already know and what they will learn.

How are informational media texts organized?

Authors of informational media texts use a number of structures. In many newspaper articles, for example, the key ideas are presented toward the beginning of the article and details are presented in the paragraphs that follow. This is for ease of editing when a paragraph needs to be cut. Magazine articles often use descriptive structures that allow a reader to develop a deeper sense of the content. Of course, all of the informational text structures can be used, including problem/solution, cause/effect, and temporal/sequence. Helping readers understand the structure of the text facilitates their comprehension of the content.

Key Unit Objectives

- Answer the Big Question
- Apply the unit's key reading skills to informational articles
- Analyze the literary elements of informational articles
- Write a research report

Why Is It Important?
Addressing this Big Question encourages students to weigh costs and benefits when they make a decision.

Viewing the Image
Surfer Bethany Hamilton was 13 when she lost her arm in a shark attack. She began surfing again only a month after the attack and continues to win awards for her skills. **Ask:** How do you think Bethany would respond to the quote on this page? What might she value? Why do you think surfing is worth the risks for her? *(Possible response: Bethany values surfing, athletics, being in the ocean, and competing. It might be worth the risks because she loves it so much.)* OL

UNIT 3

The BIG Question

When Is the Price Too High?

> "What you risk reveals what you value."
>
> –Jeanette Winterson, contemporary British novelist

Unit Skills

Reading Skills
- Previewing, p. 296
- Skimming and Scanning, p. 322
- Understanding Text Structures, p. 336
- Identifying Main Idea and Supporting Details, p. 386

Vocabulary
- Multiple-Meaning Words, p. 298
- Word References, p. 388

BIG Question When is the price too high?
Genre Focus: Informational Articles

Literary and Text Elements
- Tone, p. 299
- Evidence, p. 325
- Irony, p. 339
- Photographs, p. 389

Writing Skills/Grammar
- Research Report, pp. 316, 380
- Simple Sentences, p. 321
- Conventions, p. 381

LOOKING AHEAD

The skill lessons and readings in this unit will help you develop your own answer to the Big Question.

About the Reading

Each selection in this unit provides insights that can help students address the question, "When is the price too high?" As students read, they will consider how people weigh the costs and benefits of their decisions and develop criteria for weighing their own decisions.

About the Skills

The skills taught in this unit have been selected because they are particularly helpful when reading the featured genre—informational articles. Each reading selection provides students with opportunities to practice and develop these skills.

No Child Left Behind

The goals of the NCLB act include a strong emphasis on reading informational articles. The reading skills featured in this unit are particularly helpful for improving comprehension of informational texts. Make sure students understand the importance of practicing the skills and using them when they read and take tests.

Reading Fluency

Practicing Pronunciation Tell students that if they are reading informational articles on new subjects, they may come across new and unfamiliar words. To improve fluency, help students sound out any unfamiliar words they encounter in the informational articles and other selections in this unit. Have students work with partners to practice reading aloud. Encourage them to stop when they come across a new word, work together with their partner to determine pronunciation, and then return to the beginning of the sentence and continue reading smoothly without hesitation. EL BL

Indiana English/Language Arts Academic Standards
TWE: *Reading Fluency* 8.1

Focus

BELLRINGER Options

- **Literature Launchers: Pre-Reading Videos**
- **Daily Language Practice Transparency 21**

Focus Activity Say: Sometimes success comes at a high price. For example, movie stars might gain fame, but they might lose their privacy in the process. Do you think losing your privacy would be worth the benefits of fame? Why or why not? *(Responses will vary.)* AS

Teach

R Reading Skill

Review Connecting To help students connect their experiences to the Big Question, ask them to write several sentences in their Learner's Notebooks about a goal they would like to achieve. Provide the following question as a prompt:

- What would you gain by achieving this goal and what would it cost? *(Responses will vary.)* OL

BQ 

- Have students read the profiles and encourage them to answer the questions. *(Responses will vary.)* AS

UNIT 3 WARM-UP

Connecting to The BIG Question When Is the Price Too High?

When is a decision worth its price, when is the price too high, and how do you know? In this unit you'll read about what prices people pay for their decisions and what they think about their decisions later on. R

Real Kids and the Big Question

DORI and Charise have been friends since they were little girls. Dori wants to be friends with a popular group of girls that don't like Charise. Now, Dori has been avoiding Charise. Do you think that becoming part of a popular group is worth the price of friendship? Why or why not? BQ

RAUL likes to play the piano. He spends hours practicing. His friends think he should spend more time with them, just hanging out and having fun. But Raul says he wants to play in an orchestra someday, and he has to practice if he wants to be good. For him practicing the piano is fun. Is what Raul wants to do worth not being with his friends? Why or why not?

Warm-Up Activity

What would you be willing to pay a price to do? Write your answer in your Learner's Notebook. Then give an example of something you wouldn't do because the price would be too high.

Additional Support

Reading in the Real World

Career Point out to students that they will need to weigh costs and benefits when choosing a career. For example, some jobs are stressful and demanding, but they might pay well. On the other hand, some jobs that don't pay well are more fulfilling. Ask students to identify a job they find interesting. Discuss with students the costs and benefits of training for that job. OL Provide resources for exploring careers, such as the *Occupational Outlook Handbook,* which is also available online. AS

You and the Big Question

The question of whether the price is too high comes up in many situations. As you read the selections in this unit, think about how you would answer the Big Question. That will help guide your thinking throughout this unit. BQ

Link to Web resources to further explore the Big Question at www.glencoe.com.

Plan for the Unit Challenge

At the end of the unit, you'll use notes from all your reading to complete the Unit Challenge.

You'll choose one of the following activities:

A. What's the Ending? Write a story with two different endings.

B. Is It Worth It? Create a chart that lists the pros and cons of a decision.

- Start thinking about which activity you'd like to do so that you can focus your thoughts as you go through the unit.
- In your Learner's Notebook write your thoughts about the activity you'd like to do and why.
- Each time you make notes about the Big Question, think about how your ideas will help you with the Unit Challenge activity you chose.

Keep Track of Your Ideas

As you read, you'll make notes about the Big Question. Later, you'll use these notes to complete the Unit Challenge. See pages R8–R9 for help with making each Unit 3 Foldable. This diagram shows how each should look.

1. Make one Foldable for each workshop. Keep all of your Foldables for the unit in your Foldables folder.
2. On the bottom fold of your Foldable, write the workshop number and the Big Question.
3. Write the titles of the selections in the workshop on the front of the flaps—one title on each flap. (See page 289 for the titles.)
4. Open the flaps. At the very top of each flap, write **My Purpose for Reading.** Below each crease, write **The Big Question.**

Teach

BQ 

Have students write a response to the question, "What would make it *not* worth reaching a goal?" *(Responses will vary.)* OL

FOLDABLES™ Study Organizer

For each selection they read, students will enter notes about how that selection applies to the Big Question. For details about using Dinah Zike's Foldables, see pages R8–R9.

Assess/Close

Ask students to share why looking for an answer to the Big Question might be important. You might invite students to share stories about important decisions they've made.

Resources for page 291

- Use the Unit Challenge Planner BLM in the Unit 3 Resource Booklet, p. 37.
- Use the Foldable BLM in the Unit 3 Resource Booklet, p. 7.

Differentiated Instruction

Using a Graphic Organizer Tell students that making a Pros and Cons chart is an excellent way to make an important decision. These charts will clearly present information. As a class, complete a Pros and Cons chart for both Dori and Raul. Then, have students make a recommendation to both Dori and Raul based on the information from the chart. EL BL

Pros (Benefits)	Cons (Costs)

Indiana English/Language Arts Academic Standards
TWE: *Reading in the Real World* 8.2, *Differentiated Instruction* 8.2

Focus

BELLRINGER Options

Daily Language Practice Transparency 22

Focus Activity Ask: When might you read an informational article? *(Possible responses: to find out about something new; to read about world events; to learn what's happening in my community)* OL

Teach

R Reading Skill

How to Read Informational Articles Ask: How do you think each reading skill helps you understand informational articles? *(Possible responses: **Previewing:** Tells you what information will be covered and how it is organized; **Skimming and scanning:** Helps you find information quickly; **Understanding text structures:** Helps you understand how information is organized; **Identifying main idea and supporting details:** Helps you identify important information and the details that support it.)* OL

UNIT 3 GENRE FOCUS: INFORMATIONAL ARTICLES

Skills Focus

- How to read informational articles

Skills Model

You will see how to use the key reading skills and literary elements as you read

- **"A Tremendous Trade,"** p. 293

What Are Informational Articles?

Informational articles present information, facts, and explanations of topics. They are found in textbooks as well as newspapers, magazines, and Web sites.

Why Read Informational Articles?

When you want information about an unfamiliar topic or something you're interested in learning about, you can often find it in informational articles. For example, you can use informational articles to get the latest news, find interesting facts, and learn how to make something.

How to Read Informational Articles

Key Reading Skills

These key reading skills are useful for reading and understanding informational articles. You'll see these skills modeled in the Active Reading Model on pages 293–295, and you'll learn more about them in this unit.

R

- **Previewing** Look over a selection before you read it to see what it is about. (See Reading Workshop 1.)
- **Skimming and scanning** Skim a selection by reading through quickly for a general overview. Scan to find key words and phrases. (See Reading Workshop 2.)
- **Understanding text structures** Look at how the writing is organized. (See Reading Workshop 3.)
- **Identifying main idea and supporting details** Find the most important idea and the details that help support it. (See Reading Workshop 4.)

Key Literary and Text Elements

Recognizing and thinking about the following literary elements will help you understand informational articles better.

- **Tone:** the writer's attitude toward a subject (See "Gymnasts in Pain.")
- **Evidence:** facts, expert opinion, studies, and other types of details used to support an idea or an opinion (See "The Games Kids Play.")
- **Irony:** the difference between what is expected and what actually happens or exists (See "Flowers for Algernon," Part 1.)
- **Photographs:** pictures that explain, clarify, or add more information to an informational article (See "Tattoos: Fad, Fashion, or Folly?")

Indiana English/ Language Arts Academic Standards (pp. 292–295)

8.2 Comprehension and Analysis (Focus on Informational Text) Develop [reading] strategies such as... identifying and analyzing structure, organization, perspective, and purpose. **8.2.2** Analyze text that uses proposition and support patterns. **8.3.6** Identify significant literary devices, such as... irony, which define a writer's style and use [them] to interpret a work.

For a complete description of the standards, see p. IN 11.

Additional Support

Literature Focus Lesson

Informational Articles Explain to students that their purpose for reading most likely affects the way they read informational articles. For example, if readers want a general idea of the day's current events, they might skim a newspaper for basic information. They might not read every word. On the other hand, readers who want to become experts on a subject might read informational articles more carefully, even reading them multiple times. Have students tell when they scan informational articles and when they read them more carefully. OL

The notes in the side columns model how to use the reading skills and literary elements you read about on page 292.

Informational Articles

ACTIVE READING MODEL

TIME

A Tremendous TRADE

A superstar swap had baseball fans buzzing. 1

By JEREMY CAPLAN

In early 2004, the New York Yankees rocked the baseball world by trading two players, second baseman Alfonso Soriano and a minor league player, to get Alex Rodriguez, who is widely considered the game's best player. It was the first time in Major League Baseball history that the current most valuable player had been traded. "I think the coolest thing in the world is being a Yankee and having the opportunity to win consistently," said Rodriguez, whose nickname is A-Rod. His former team, the Texas Rangers, had finished in last place for the last three seasons that A-Rod was with them. 2

A-Rod played shortstop with the Rangers but plays third base for the Yankees because the team already has an all-star shortstop in Derek Jeter. When A-Rod first joined the Yankees, he was the highest paid player in the Major Leagues. His contract with the Yankees will earn him $252 million over 10 years. 3

Timothy A. Clary/AFP/Getty Images

E

$25,200,000

In his first New York press conference, **ALEX RODRIGUEZ** says he feels honored and proud to be a Yankee.

1 Key Reading Skill
Previewing *Glancing at the title and subtitle, I see that the article is about baseball teams trading players. The graphics show how much money the players make. It's amazing how high their salaries are.*

2 Key Reading Skill
Skimming and Scanning *As I skim the article, I see that it names Alex Rodriguez several times. I'm going to scan to find out how much he makes.*

3 Key Literary Element
Irony *It's ironic that the team with the most valuable player ended up as the last-place team for three years. I would expect it to win with such a great player.*

UNIT 3 GENRE FOCUS

Teach

R Reading Skill

Skimming and Scanning
Say: Scan to find out how much money Alex Rodriguez will make. *($252 million over 10 years)* BL
Ask: What is the benefit of scanning for information? *(Possible response: Scanning is faster than reading every word—it helps readers find details quickly.)* OL

L Literary Element

Tone **Ask:** How would you describe the author's tone, or attitude toward the subject, in the title and first paragraph? Which words suggest the tone? *(Possible response: The tone is positive. The author calls the trade "tremendous" and says it "rocked the baseball world.")* OL

E Text Element

Photograph **Say:** Photographs can give you information not provided in the text. What additional information about Rodriguez can you get from his photograph? *(Possible response: He looks very young. The text doesn't mention his youth.)* OL

Reading in the Real World

Citizenship Many people expect baseball players and other athletes to be good role models. Lead a discussion about whether star athletes owe anything to the community in return for their large salaries. Have students work in small groups to write short profiles of athletes who are models of good character or community service. Students might present their information in the form of "model athlete cards" with a picture of the athlete on one side and a description of his or her character traits or community service record on the other. AS

Indiana English/Language Arts Academic Standards
SE: 8.2, 8.2.2, 8.3.6
TWE: *Literature Focus Lesson* 8.2, *Reading in the Real World* 8.2

Teach

R Reading Skill

Identifying Main Ideas and Supporting Details Ask: What is the main idea of the last paragraph on this page? *(Possible response: Workers in all professions, including baseball, earn what people are willing to pay them.)* OL **Say:** Name two details the writer uses to support the main idea. *(Possible responses: Teams earn a lot of money because baseball is popular. Teams pay a lot for good baseball players so that fans will attend games.)* AL

E Text Element

Evidence Ask: What evidence does the writer give that good players attract fans? *(Possible response: He writes that the Yankees sold $2 million in tickets after announcing A-Rod would join the team.)* OL

UNIT 3 GENRE FOCUS

ACTIVE READING MODEL

Many fans celebrated A-Rod's switch to New York, saying that his presence on the team would make baseball more exciting. Other fans say he's overpaid.

You Get What You Pay For

Some people say the league should limit players' salaries. They argue that some salaries are so high that teams with smaller budgets simply cannot afford to compete with richer teams. "We have a spending limit, and the Yankees apparently don't," said John Henry, owner of the rival Boston Red Sox. Henry's attempt to get Rodriguez to play for his team failed. 4

Other people question why baseball players earn so much more than people in other professions who may struggle to make a living. For example, how is it that a baseball player can earn more than 800 times what some teachers earn in one year? 5

It might not seem fair, but in every profession, workers earn whatever people are willing to pay them. Baseball is no exception. Teams compete to offer as much money as they can to players who are among the league's best, like Rodriguez. Because baseball is such a popular sport, watched by ticket-buying fans at stadiums and on television by millions, a team can earn many millions of dollars each season. Teams use much of their earnings to pay their stars' salaries because the best players attract the most fans to games. For example, soon after the Yankees announced that A-Rod would be coming to town, the team sold $2 million worth of tickets. 6

4 **Key Reading Skill**
Identifying Main Idea and Supporting Details *The main idea of this paragraph seems to be that all teams cannot compete for the same players because they don't all have the same amount of money. The quotation from John Henry and the fact that his team couldn't hire A-Rod are details that support the main idea.*

5 **Key Text Element**
Evidence *The author states that a player may make 800 times as much as a teacher. He uses this statistic as evidence that players may be paid too much.*

6 **Key Reading Skill**
Understanding Text Structures *The word* because *shows up twice in this paragraph. I see that this cause-and-effect text structure explains why teams can pay players so much.*

Lou Cappozola/Sports Illustrated

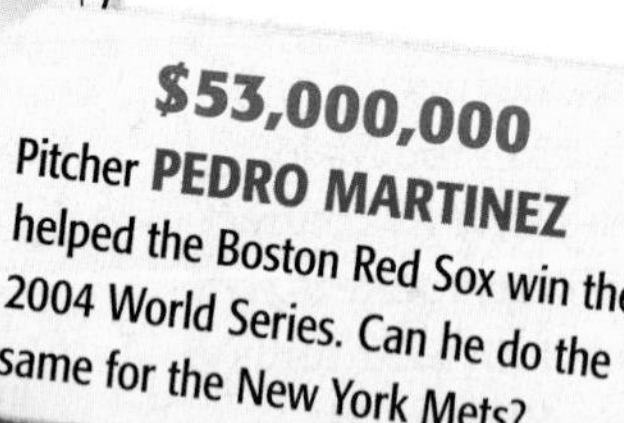

$53,000,000
Pitcher **PEDRO MARTINEZ** helped the Boston Red Sox win the 2004 World Series. Can he do the same for the New York Mets?

294

Additional Support

Differentiated Instruction

Main Idea-Details Chart Work with students to create a main idea-details chart for the first paragraph under "You Get What You Pay For." Then ask them to work alone or with a partner to make a similar chart for the second paragraph. EL BL

Main Idea:
Small teams cannot compete with teams that can pay higher salaries.

Detail:
"We have a spending limit."

Detail:
Red Sox couldn't hire A-Rod.

ACTIVE READING MODEL

Can Money Buy a Winner?

Now that the Yankees have A-Rod, New York fans have high hopes for future success. But Rodriguez alone won't guarantee his new team championships. "If you're a team with more money, you get to hire better players, but it doesn't mean you're going to win," says Andrew Zimbalist, a top sports economist.[1] **R** Injuries, batting slumps, a lack of teamwork, and even bad luck can get in the way.

Even though the baseball world buzzed about the big trade and star players' soaring salaries, A-Rod and his teammates will be expected to catch, throw, and swing their way to success for years to come. After all, when the World Series rolls around each October, it will be skills, not salaries, that count. **L** 7 8

—Updated 2005, from *TIME FOR KIDS*, February 27, 2004

David N. Seelig/Icon SMI

$20,000,000
Boston Red Sox slugger **MANNY RAMIREZ** has averaged more than 40 homers a year over the last seven seasons.

Eric Miller/Reuters

$18,900,000
New York Yankees' captain, sure-handed shortstop **DEREK JETER**, has helped guide the team to the World Series at least four times.

1. An ***economist*** is someone who studies money and the ways things of value are made, bought, and sold.

7 Key Text Element
Photographs *The photos of players on these pages are exciting action shots. They help me understand why baseball players get huge salaries.*

8 Key Literary Element
Tone *The words* buzzed *and* soaring *make me think of action and excitement. I can almost hear the crowd at a game. The writer's tone seems fair and friendly, but he's also excited about baseball.*

Write to Learn Answer the following question in your Learner's Notebook. Imagine that you are going to write a letter to the editor of a sports magazine on the subject of salaries earned by professional athletes. What would you say about the very large amounts of money they earn?

Literature Online

Study Central Visit www.glencoe.com and click on Study Central to review informational articles.

UNIT 3 GENRE FOCUS

Teach

R Reading Skill

Understanding Text Structures **Say:** Writers sometimes use a comparison and contrast text structure to compare two sides of an issue. This author presents arguments for and against the idea that baseball players deserve high salaries. What arguments *for* the idea are presented in the article? *(Possible responses: Big name players bring in more money; "you get what you pay for.")* **Ask:** What arguments against big salaries are presented? *(Possible responses: Smaller teams can't compete, and higher-paid players don't guarantee a championship.)* **OL**

L Literary Element

Tone **Ask:** How can you tell that the writer likes baseball? *(Possible response: He talks about how skills will be important during the World Series, not salaries. He seems interested in the players and their teams.)* **AL**

Literature Online

Study Central Have students access the Web site to review informational articles and to complete a related activity.

Literature Focus Lesson

Tone Write the phrase "That's just great" on the board and ask students to read it aloud with different tones—for example, enthusiastic, sarcastic, and indifferent. Explain that when they read, they cannot actually hear the narrator's tone of voice. However, they can look at the words the writer chooses to infer how the writer feels about a subject. **AS** Ask students how they would describe the writer's tone, or attitude, toward baseball players in this selection. **OL**

Indiana English/Language Arts Academic Standards
SE: 8.2, 8.2.2, 8.3.6
TWE: *Differentiated Instruction* 8.2, *Literature Focus Lesson* 8.3

Previewing

Teaching Students to Preview

Why Is It Important?

- Previewing is one of the first steps good readers do in determining the purpose for their reading. When they look over a piece of text, they can decide why they would read it.
- Previewing helps students focus on the most important parts by drawing attention to the title, headings, graphics, etc.
- Previewing allows students to make connections between what they see in the text and what they already know.

How to Help Students Get It

- Model previewing using something you're reading. You might demonstrate the following steps: (1) read the title, (2) read the headings, (3) look at the visuals, and (4) scan for special terms.
- Remind students about the importance of setting a purpose for their reading and ask them to discuss how previewing can help with setting a purpose.
- Ask students to list questions about a text after they have previewed it. To help students get started, have the class create questions based on the titles of the selections. Over time, students will automatically create questions in their minds when they preview texts and answer those questions as they read.
- Tell students that during a preview, they should make a mental note of how much of the information is new to them. Then they can determine how closely and carefully they need to read or if they will need extra background information.

Reading to Answer the Big Question

Gymnasts in Pain: Out of Balance by Scott M. Reid
Girls in their early and mid-teens who participate in gymnastics often live a dangerous life. Broken bones, surgeries, isolation, and eating disorders are common. This article recounts the experiences of gymnasts who won gold medals and gymnasts who withdrew from the sport.

In Response to Executive Order 9066 by Dwight Okita
This poem is in the form of a letter written by a teenaged girl. She is responding to the forced relocation of Japanese Americans to internment camps during World War II. Her letter reveals that she doesn't understand why she must move or why her best friend has turned against her.

Workshop Resources

Pacing (Days) Standard	Pacing (Days) Block	Lesson	Student Materials	Teacher Resources
1	1	Key Skill Lesson: Previewing	Key Reading Skills Practice, p. 9 English Language Coach Review, p. 43	Bellringer Options Transparencies –Daily Language Practice 23 Read Aloud, Think Aloud Transparencies –Key Reading Skills 18 Presentation Plus!
1	1	"Gymnasts in Pain: Out of Balance"	Glencoe Online Unit Vocabulary Review, p. 41 Academic Vocabulary Review, p. 44 English Language Coach Active Reading Graphic Organizer, p. 11 Literary Analysis, p. 10 StudentWorks Plus™ Online Student Edition Literature Classics Selection and Unit Assessments, p. 25	Literary and Text Analysis Transparencies 56 Puzzlemaker Skill Level Up!™ A Language Arts Game BookLink 3 Assessment by Learning Objective (Diagnostic and Formative) Interactive Tutor: Self-Assessment TeacherWorks Plus™
1		"In Response to Executive Order 9066"	Glencoe Online Unit Vocabulary Review, p. 41 Academic Vocabulary Review, p. 44 English Language Coach Active Reading Graphic Organizer, p. 13 StudentWorks Plus™ Online Student Edition Literature Classics Selection and Unit Assessments, p. 26	Literary and Text Analysis Transparencies 51 Puzzlemaker Skill Level Up!™ A Language Arts Game BookLink 3 Assessment by Learning Objective (Diagnostic and Formative) Interactive Tutor: Self-Assessment TeacherWorks Plus™

Keys for Unit Resource

- Blackline Master
- Workbook
- Supplemental Text
- CD-ROM
- DVD
- Transparency
- Web-based
- Fast File

Level Appropriate Code

AS = Activities for all students
AL = Activities for students working above grade level
OL = Activities for students working at grade level
BL = Activities for students working below grade level
EL = Activities for English language learners

Focus

BELLRINGER Options

Daily Language Practice Transparency 23

Focus Activity Ask: Have you ever worked really hard to achieve a goal? Write about a time you set a goal for yourself and how it felt to accomplish it. *(Responses will vary.)* **AS**

Teach

R Reading Skill

Previewing Say: You know that the prefix *pre-* means "before." How does that help you understand what it means to preview a selection? *(Possible response: Previewing is looking over a selection before you read it.)* **OL**

V Vocabulary

Academic Vocabulary Say: Look at the definition for the word *available* at the bottom of page 296. What are some synonyms for the word *available*? You may use a thesaurus if necessary. *(Possible responses: accessible, reachable, obtainable, there, close by, convenient)* **AS**

READING WORKSHOP 1

Skills Focus

You will practice using these skills when you read the following selections:

- "Gymnasts in Pain: Out of Balance," p. 300
- "In Response to Executive Order 9066," p. 312

Reading

- Previewing to understand texts, their structures, and their purposes

Literature

- Understanding tone

Vocabulary

- Understanding multiple-meaning words in context
- Academic Vocabulary: *available*

Writing/Grammar

- Identifying types of sentences
- Correctly using end marks of punctuation

Skill Lesson

Previewing

Learn It!

R **What Is It? Previewing** is looking over something to see what it's like in order to find out what you can expect from it. You probably preview often without even realizing it. For example, when you rent a movie, you preview it by reading the title and the description on the back of the case. Previewing helps you make good use of **available** information.

Analyzing Cartoons
Peter previews the book and learns, to his dismay, that the text is tiny. What else can you learn about a selection from looking over it before you read?

Indiana English/ Language Arts Academic Standards (pp. 296–297)

8.2 Comprehension and Analysis (Focus on Informational Text) Develop [reading] strategies…

For a complete description of the standards, see p. IN 11.

V **Academic Vocabulary**

available (uh VAY luh bul) *adj.* at hand; easily obtained

Additional Support

Differentiated Instruction

Building Background Explain to students that "The horror, the horror" is one of the most famous lines in literature. They are the dying words of Kurtz, a character in *Heart of Darkness,* a novel that explores the dark side of humanity. The joke in the cartoon is that Peter states these words, indicating he already knows something about the story, but his teacher points out that he says them about every assignment. Have students consider what they already know about the subjects as they preview the article and poem in this workshop. **AS**

Why Is It Important? Previewing a reading selection saves you time by giving you a head start with your reading. Previewing helps you do all these things:

- understand what the text is about
- decide whether you want or need to read it
- plan a strategy for reading the text

R

How Do I Do It? Before you read a selection, follow these steps:

1. Look at the title, headlines, or anything in bold (heavy, dark) letters.
2. Look over pictures, charts, captions, and other text features.
3. Read the first paragraph and the first lines or sentences of other paragraphs. Try to find the most important information.
4. Quickly describe for yourself what the selection is about.
5. Decide whether to read the selection and how you'll read it.

Study Central Visit www.glencoe.com and click on Study Central to review previewing.

Here's what one student learned from previewing "A Tremendous Trade."

1. I can tell from the title, subheads, and graphics that this story is about baseball, money, and winning games.

2. The graphics show how much money some players make.

3. From reading the first lines of several paragraphs, I think the most important part is the section "You Get What You Pay For."

4. This article seems to be about how much money baseball players make and why they can get so much.

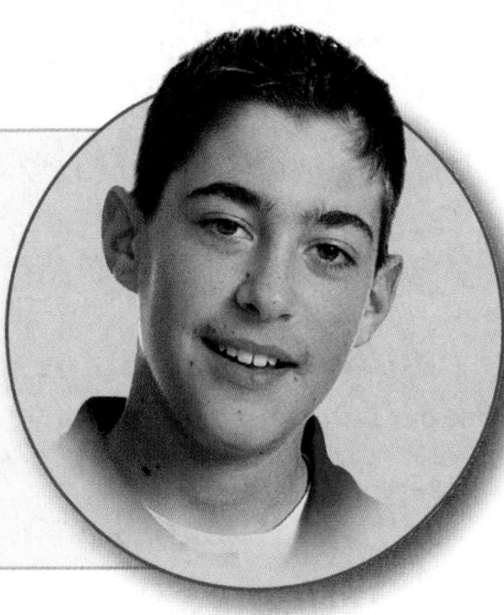

Practice It!

Pretend you haven't already worked through pages 296–297. Go back and preview this skill lesson. Follow steps 1–4 above. Write your preview notes in your Learner's Notebook.

Use It!

Before you read the next two selections, preview them. After you preview each text, write in your Learner's Notebook two things you learned from previewing.

Teach

Study Central Have students access the Web site to review previewing and to complete a related activity.

R Reading Skill

Previewing Ask: What are three benefits of previewing? *(Possible response: It saves time, gives you a head start with your reading, and helps you decide if you want or need to read the selection.)* **OL** **Ask:** How might you preview a magazine to decide what to read? *(Possible response: I'd read the title of the magazine, then I'd look at the table of contents for interesting articles and I'd read the article descriptions to find ones that catch my attention. I might also look over the first paragraph of an article to decide if it is really worth reading.)* **AL**

Resources for page 297

Use Key Reading Skills Transparency 18 in *Read Aloud, Think Aloud* to help students practice previewing.

Reading in the Real World

Career Researchers found that many Americans spend two to three hours reading at work each day. This reading includes memos, forms, and instructions. Tell students to imagine they have a very busy job that requires a lot of reading. Discuss how previewing might help them keep up with reading required on the job. For example, they can preview to:

- determine how long it will take to read an article or complete a form.
- set priorities about which information to read first.
- see what additional information they might need in order to complete forms or to follow instructions. **AS**

Indiana English/Language Arts Academic Standards

SE: 8.2

TWE: *Differentiated Instruction* 8.2, *Reading in the Real World* 8.2

Teach

More About the Author

Scott M. Reid has won five awards for investigative reporting. In addition to problems suffered by elite gymnasts, he has reported on problems with drug testing for U.S. Olympic athletes and Title IX violations by California community colleges. (Title IX prohibits gender discrimination in education, including athletics.) He has also been honored for his articles about the Olympics. Reid has been with the *Orange County Register* since 1996.

V Vocabulary

Vocabulary Questions Reinforce the vocabulary words by having students answer these questions:

1. Are decades periods of ten years or one hundred years? *(ten years)*
2. If you are an elite basketball player, are you new to the sport or very good at the sport? *(very good)*
3. If someone thinks there will be a bad outcome, do they have low expectations or low maneuvers? *(expectations)* EL BL

Before You Read

Gymnasts in Pain: Out of Balance

Meet the Author

Scott M. Reid is a sports reporter for the *Orange County Register* newspaper. Before joining the *Register* in 1996, Reid worked at the *Atlanta Journal Constitution* and at the *Dallas Times Herald.*

Author Search For more about Scott M. Reid, go to www.glencoe.com.

Indiana English/Language Arts Academic Standards
(pp. 298–307)

8.1.3 Verify the meaning of a word in its context... **8.2 Comprehension and Analysis (Focus on Informational Text)** Develop [reading] strategies... **8.3.6** Identify significant literary devices...which define a writer's style...

For a complete description of the standards, see p. IN 11.

Vocabulary Preview

V

expectations (ek spek TAY shunz) *n.* outcomes considered likely to happen **(p. 301)** *People have the same high expectations of gymnasts as they do of other professional athletes.*

maneuvers (muh NOO vurs) *n.* clever or skillful moves or actions **(p. 301)** *Gymnasts must learn a complicated set of maneuvers to compete on gymnastics equipment.*

elite (eh LEET) *adj.* best or most talented **(p. 302)** *The most elite gymnasts compete in the Olympics.*

decades (DEK aydz) *n.* periods of ten years **(p. 306)** *Most gymnasts compete for only a few years of their lives before they retire, but the pain from injury lasts for many decades.*

Partner Talk With a partner write a paragraph about athletes in professional sports. Use all the vocabulary words above in your paragraph.

English Language Coach

Multiple-Meaning Words You already know that words can have many, or multiple, meanings. For example, you probably know the word *pool* as it relates to a swimming pool and even to the game of pool. But what does it mean in the following sentence?

- The students added their money to the *pool* for a new school flag.

You need to know another definition for the word *pool* to understand what the sentence means. A *pool* can be a supply or collection shared by a group. In the sentence above, then, *pool* is the collection of money that students are gathering, not a body of water or a game.

Watch for this word and other multiple-meaning words when you read "Gymnasts in Pain: Out of Balance." Use context clues or a dictionary to figure out what the words mean.

Write to Learn How many different meanings do you know for each word listed below? Write the words and their meanings in your Learner's Notebook. Then look up each word in a dictionary. If you left out definitions, add them.

1. break
2. deal
3. senior
4. tumble

Additional Support

Author Search To expand students' appreciation of Scott M. Reid, have them access the Web site for additional information and resources.

English Language Coach

Multiple-Meaning Words Help students determine the meaning of the word *low* in the following sentence: "Taking that little kid's lunch was a *low* move."

1. Discuss the different meanings of *low.*
2. Replace the word with a blank.
3. Try inserting the different meanings of *low* in the sentence.

In this case, *close to the ground* and *quiet* do not make sense in this sentence, but the words *mean* and *nasty* do make sense. EL BL

Skills Preview

Key Reading Skill: Previewing

Remember that previewing gives you a head start in understanding what you read. To preview, read the title and headings. Examine photographs, charts, and other illustrations, and read their captions. R

Partner Talk What might you learn by previewing an article before you read it closely? Talk it over.

Key Literary Element: Tone

Tone is an author's attitude toward the subject he or she is writing about. Any word that can be used to describe an attitude can also be used to describe a tone. Some examples are *objective, serious, sarcastic, lighthearted, sad,* and *angry.* L

The tone of a selection is shown in the words that the author uses. When you read, look for the emotion behind the words. That emotion reveals the tone.

Here is the way three different people might talk about a job they're doing.

- We have a few problems that we will work out easily.
- It's going to be hard to get through this.
- This job is a real mess.

To identify the tone of "Gymnasts in Pain: Out of Balance," ask yourself these questions:

- *Why did the author choose certain words and details?*
- *What feeling, if any, do these words communicate?*

Partner Work Tell the plot of the story "Goldilocks and the Three Bears" in two different tones. First tell the story as if the narrator is angry with Goldilocks and thinks she's a little jerk. Then tell it with Goldilocks being a very sweet girl.

Interactive Literary Elements Handbook
To review or learn more about the literary elements, go to www.glencoe.com.

Get Ready to Read

Connect to the Reading

Think about a goal that was really important to you. How hard were you willing to work for it? As you read about the gymnasts, think about how their experiences compare to your own.

Write to Learn Describe your experiences with having a goal and the effort it took to reach it.

Build Background

The information in this article comes from a survey the writer did of more than 100 members of the United States women's national gymnastics teams.

- In the sport today, female gymnasts reach their peak before age sixteen, which means they are competing when their bodies are still growing and have less strength than that of an adult.
- More than a half-million kids take part in U.S. school-sponsored gymnastics competitions.
- Every year more than 25,000 children under the age of fifteen are treated in U.S. hospital emergency rooms for injuries related to gymnastics. Most of these injuries are mild to moderate. The most common injuries are sprains, strains, and stress fractures. However, serious injuries also occur.

Set Purposes for Reading

BIG Question Read "Gymnasts in Pain: Out of Balance" to find out what some girls experience as they try to become the best gymnasts in the world. What do they gain? What do they lose?

Set Your Own Purpose What else would you like to learn from this article to help you answer the Big Question? Write your own purpose on the "Gymnasts in Pain" flap of the Foldable for Workshop 1.

Keep Moving

Use these skills as you read "Gymnasts in Pain: Out of Balance."

Teach

R Reading Skill

Previewing Say: Skim the *Build Background* section to find out how many gymnasts the author interviewed. *(more than 100)* BL **Ask:** How does knowing about this research influence the way you will approach reading the article? *(Responses will vary; students may say that the research makes the article seem more credible.)* OL

L Literary Element

Tone Say: The title of this article is "Gymnasts in Pain: Out of Balance." What tone does the title set for the article? *(Possible responses: The title indicates that the article will be critical of the sport; it suggests sympathy for gymnasts.)* AL

Interactive Literary Elements Handbook Have students access the Web site to improve their understanding of tone.

Differentiated Instruction

Investigative Reporting All reporters try to find the important details of a story, such as *Who, What, When, Where, Why,* and *How.* However, investigative reporters often dig deeper. Their stories may take months or years to research. They check public records and conduct in-depth interviews. Like other investigative reporters, Scott M. Reid uncovers wrongdoing because problems and abuses can be corrected only if people know about them. Discuss with students what issues they might look into if they were investigative reporters and how they would go about doing the research. OL

Indiana English/Language Arts Academic Standards
SE: 8.1.3, 8.2, 8.3.6
TWE: *English Language Coach* 8.1

Teach

Viewing the Photo

Say: Alyssa Beckerman was U.S. national champion on balance beam in 2000. What signs can you see that she is competing with injuries? *(Possible response: Both of her wrists are wrapped.)* **OL**

L Literary Element

Tone **Ask:** Why might a disapproving tone be appropriate for this investigative article? *(Possible response: The writer has found many instances of abuse. The tone shows that he does not approve of the abuse, and it helps readers see how serious the problem is.)* **AL**

Readability Scores
Dale-Chall: 9.0
DRP: 62
Lexile: 1140

INFORMATIONAL TEXT
NEWSPAPER
Orange County Register

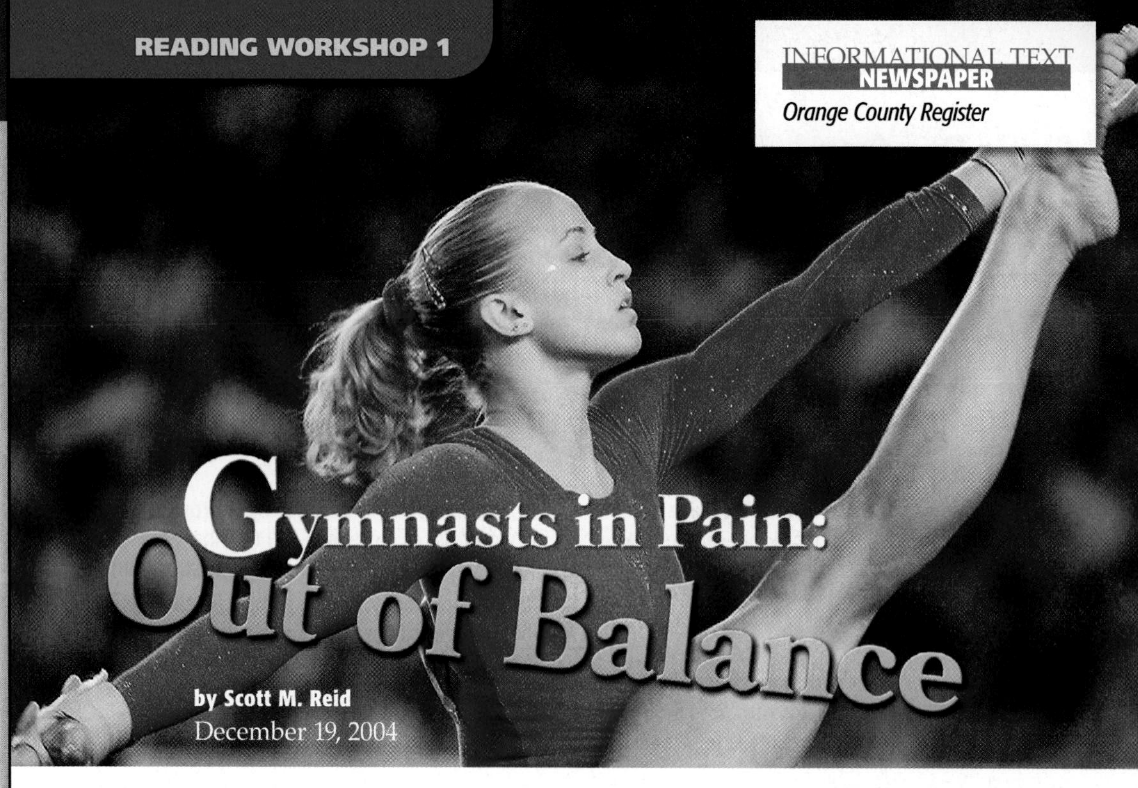

Gymnasts in Pain: Out of Balance

by Scott M. Reid
December 19, 2004

By the time Alyssa Beckerman arrived for a U.S. national team training camp at Bela Karolyi's Texas ranch, three months before the 2000 Olympic Games, she wasn't sure what hurt worse. The year-old break in her wrist that hadn't been allowed to heal? Or her stomach burning from nerves and a daily diet of anti-inflammatory[1] drugs? **1**

The 19-year-old U.S. champion broke her wrist a year earlier, but she continued to compete and train 40 hours a week—pressured, she said, by an often-screaming coach who accused her of faking the injury and driven by her own desire to win Olympic gold.

"That's what you've been dreaming about since you were a little girl," she said.

By the time she retired from international gymnastics later that year, Beckerman had broken nine bones and undergone two surgeries. **2**

1. ***Anti-inflammatory*** (an ty in FLAM uh tor ee) drugs make swelling go down.

Practice the Skills

1 Key Reading Skill

Previewing To preview the article, read the title and subtitle. Look at the pictures and read the headings. Reread the first paragraph. What do you think the main idea of the article is?

2 Key Literary Element

Tone So far, the tone is disapproving. Here are some words and phrases that reveal this tone: **L**

- Alyssa Beckerman says she was "pressured . . . by an often-screaming coach."
- The article says the coach "accused [Beckerman] of faking the injury."

Additional Support

Literature Focus Lesson

Puns A *pun* is a play on words that suggests two or more meanings at the same time. Puns can be humorous, as in the sentence, "Waiter, there is a hare in my rabbit soup!" They can also be serious, as in the subtitle of this piece: "Out of Balance." Have students tell what meanings they know for the word *balance*. Discuss how the *balance beam* is equipment used in gymnastics, while *balance* can mean physical steadiness or refer to people's priorities. Ask students to explain what they think the writer probably means by "Out of Balance." Have them suggest other subtitles for the article. **OL**

The *Orange County Register* interviewed nearly half of the **roughly** 300 women who competed on the U.S. junior or senior national teams from 1982 to 2004. **3** More than 93 percent of the women interviewed suffered broken bones or had injuries that required surgery.

Current and former U.S. national team members—almost all girls in their early and mid-teens—describe a way of life that repeatedly places girls in danger. They train year-round as much as twelve hours a day, often living thousands of miles from home and away from other teens.

Like Beckerman, they do so often with broken bones or torn muscles and almost always without regular, if any, medical care. At the same time, they must deal with pressures and **expectations** similar to those for highly paid pro athletes.

The *Register* also found:

The rate of injuries has almost doubled since 1966 as women train longer and try more daring and dramatic **maneuvers.**

Nine out of every ten gymnasts interviewed said that they had continued to train on injuries that resulted in broken bones or surgery or that they had begun training again without getting a doctor's OK.

The sport's obsession with weight and diet, especially within the U.S. national team program, often has led to eating disorders. U.S. gymnasts competing in the 2001 World Championships said they were provided so little food that family members smuggled snacks into the team hotel by stuffing them inside teddy bears.

Three out of four gymnasts interviewed continue to experience health problems related to gymnastics. **C**

Top gymnastics officials downplayed the *Register's* finding. Robert V. Colarossi, chief executive officer of USA Gymnastics, insisted his sport is no different from any other.

Practice the Skills

3 English Language Coach

Multiple-Meaning Words
Roughly comes from the word *rough*. One meaning of *rough* is "not smooth." Another is "approximately, or about." Which definition of *roughly* makes sense here?

Vocabulary

expectations (ek spek TAY shunz) *n.* outcomes considered likely to happen

maneuvers (muh NOO vurs) *n.* clever or skillful moves or actions

Teach

R Reading Skill

Previewing Say: Think about the things you learned about this article by previewing. Tell two things you learned so far by reading the article. *(Possible response: Ninety-three percent of the women interviewed suffered broken bones or had other injuries; Top gymnasts train year round.)* **Ask:** Does the article cover the topics you thought it would? Why or why not? *(Possible response: I expected information about injuries, but didn't expect so many examples.)* **OL**

C Critical Thinking

Comprehension Ask: What does the writer identify as some of the causes of health problems related to gymnastics? *(Possible responses: longer training, routines that are more difficult, obsession with weight and diet, and lack of adequate medical care)* **OL**

Differentiated Instruction

Graphic Organizer Discuss the different ways to present statistics in graph form. Explain the differences between pie charts, bar graphs, and line graphs. Then ask students to skim this page for statistics. As a class, work with them to make a graph based on one of the statistics, such as a pie chart showing that nine out of ten gymnasts trained with injuries. Then have students work with a partner to make a graph based on the statistics about broken bones given on page 304. Help students determine the best way to provide the information. **AL**

Indiana English/Language Arts Academic Standards
SE: 8.1.3, 8.2, 8.3.6
TWE: *Literature Focus Lesson* 8.1.1, *Differentiated Instruction* 8.2

Teach

R Reading Skill

Review Identifying Author's Purpose **Say:** The author's purpose is to show readers the negative side of gymnastics. How does comparing gymnastics to the National Football League help him fulfill this purpose? *(Possible responses: He can show that while gymnasts look pretty, their sport is as rough as football and their risk of injuries is as high as those of football players.)* AL

L Literary Element

Tone **Ask:** What does the writer compare in the third paragraph of this page? *(He compares the sparkly outfits, smiles, and perfect 10s to the horrible injuries of the young women.)* **Ask:** How does this comparison help the writer develop tone? *(Possible response: By comparing the glamour of the sport to its realities, the writer creates a grim tone.)* OL

"**Elite** athletes in every sport push themselves to the limit," he said. He noted that the 22 years covered in the *Register*'s survey was a time of change in the sport. "It's unfair to draw an analysis over that many years," Colarossi continued. "The kids are doing skills that are more and more difficult. The equipment is getting better but still has a ways to go. The (scoring) is more difficult. In the past the sport was based more on artistry, and now it's based a lot more on skill. The one thing that hasn't changed is gravity. That's the constant."

Colarossi acknowledged gymnastics has "a lot more (physical) impact than other sports." Don Peters, head coach of the 1984 U.S. Olympic team, said he didn't believe the sports injury rates were as high as the *Register* found but said the comparison between gymnastics and the NFL is valid. "We're both contact sports," said Peters, owner of Scats Gymnastics Academy in Huntington Beach. "But in gymnastics we're dealing with very fragile athletes who don't wear protective gear. We're doing really dangerous things. We're flying through the air . . . . I think you have to remember whatever goes up has to come down. And every time something comes down, there's a chance somebody's going to get hurt. Considering everything, I think we do an amazing job." R

Record numbers of Americans tune in every four years to what has become the Summer Olympics' most popular event. But behind the sparkly outfits, smiles and perfect 10's is a sport that has left a generation of young American women bearing physical and emotional scars that many will carry for the rest of their lives. 4 L

Doctors discovered 22 stress fractures[2] on the spine of Olympian Kelly Garrison. Double Olympic medalist Kathy Johnson said she took so many anti-inflammatory drugs to deal with her injuries that she had to wash down the pills with Maalox. Melinda Baimbridge, a U.S. team member in

Practice the Skills

4 Key Literary Element

Tone Think about the image the author is creating here. Is it a clue to the author's tone? Explain.

2. A ***stress fracture*** is a very thin break in a bone, usually from putting too much pressure (stress) on the bone.

Vocabulary

elite (eh LEET) *adj.* best or most talented

Additional Support

Literature Focus Lesson

Bias Point out that bias, or a slanted point of view, is not always negative; in investigative reporting, bias can help convince readers to make changes for the better. For example:

1. **Choice of words:** The headings all suggest a point of view.
2. **Placement of information:** The writer begins and ends the article with details about an injured athlete.
3. **Choice of quotations:** This writer includes quotations from both sides of the issue, but chooses more emotional quotes from gymnasts. AS

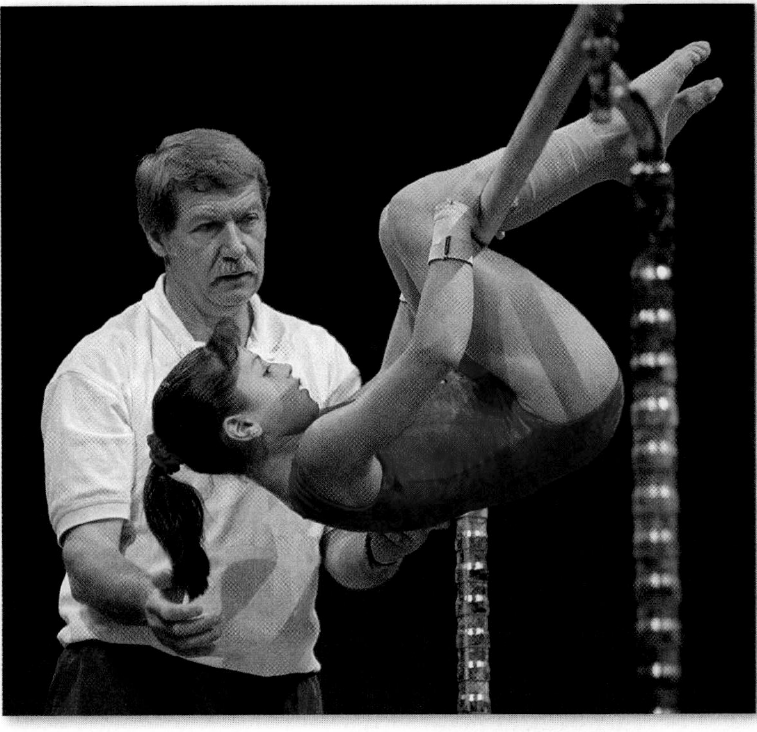

Analyzing the Photo Spotted by her coach Bela Karolyi, Dominique Moceanu practices a difficult move. How does this picture capture the intensity of Karolyi's—and Moceanu's—concentration?

the late 1990s, trained with a fractured back even though her legs turned numb.

"People don't see the real sport," said Sierra Sapunar, a recent U.S. team member. "They see what looks pretty and elegant on the surface, but they don't realize what really goes on. All the nerves and pain and emotion and fear and abuse."

And too often, Johnson said, the sport has forgotten who the gymnasts are. "I think we have to remember," Johnson said, "yes, these are world-class athletes, but they're also little girls." **5**

Demands, injuries rise

American girls are being pushed harder than ever to reach the Olympic dream. As the sport has become more difficult—and dangerous—the demands of training have increased. An estimated 3.4 million girls participate in gymnastics in the United States—many of whom got their start in tumbling classes as toddlers. About 80,000 athletes today are registered with USA Gymnastics.

Practice the Skills

5 **Key Literary Element**

Tone How do the quotations from Sapunar and Johnson affect the tone of this article? Jot down words or phrases that support your answer.

Teach

Viewing the Photo

Ask: How does this photograph support the quotation by Kathy Johnson further down on the page? *(Possible response: Kathy Johnson says these are "world-class athletes, but they're also little girls." The athlete in the photograph looks like a little girl, especially compared to the big coach.)* **OL**

R Reading Skill

Previewing **Say:** Preview the section "Demands, injuries rise." What do you think it will be about? *(Possible response: It will be about how injuries in gymnastics rose as demands for perfection increased.)* **OL**

Reading in the Real World

Citizenship Students who are interested in gymnastics may want to conduct research to find out what it is like to participate in this sport at the amateur level. Remind students that although this article focuses on females, both men and women participate in gymnastics. Have students interview a local student gymnast or coach to find out more about the sport. Have them ask about the requirements, benefits, and disadvantages of gymnastics. Have students report their findings to the class. **OL**

Indiana English/Language Arts Academic Standards
SE: 8.2, 8.3.6
TWE: *Literature Focus Lesson* 8.3.7, *Reading in the Real World* 8.2.5

Teach

C Critical Thinking

Comprehension **Ask:** Did gymnasts who competed for the national team during and before 1994 experience more or fewer injuries requiring surgery than those who competed after 1996? *(Gymnasts competing during or before 1994 experienced fewer injuries requiring surgery than those competing after 1996.)* **Ask:** What does this statistic show? *(Possible response: There is a sharp rise in injuries among elite gymnasts.)* AL

Viewing the Photo

Ask: What evidence in this photograph shows that Carly Patterson has experienced an injury? *(There is a large scar on her elbow.)* **Ask:** How would you feel about competing in a gymnastics competition after experiencing such an injury? *(Responses will vary.)* AS

READING WORKSHOP 1

At the very top of the sport in this country are the 120 women who compete at what is known as the elite level. It is from this group that U.S. national junior and senior teams and, finally, the Olympic team are selected. This deep talent **pool** has provided the foundation for perhaps the most successful period in USA Gymnastics' history. 6

But, along with that success has come a sharp rise in injuries, the *Register* found in its interviews with 122 elite gymnasts. Women whose participation on the U.S. national team ended in 1994 or earlier averaged 2.75 broken bones or injuries that required surgery. Women who competed for the United States after 1996 averaged four such injuries. Overall, more than 68 percent of the gymnasts interviewed by the *Register* said they had needed surgery. 7 C

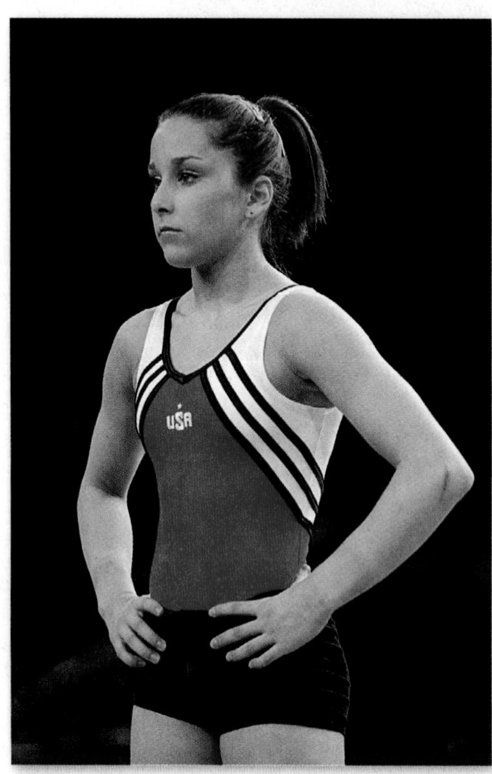

Analyzing the Photo Carly Patterson focuses on her next event at a 2004 competition at Madison Square Garden. How would you describe Patterson's posture and facial expression?

Practice the Skills

6 English Language Coach

Multiple-Meaning Words Think about the definitions for the word **pool** that you learned in the "Before You Read" section. What is the meaning of *pool* as it is used here? How do you know?

7 Reviewing Skills

Fact and Opinion Does this paragraph state facts or the author's opinion? Do these facts support the opinion that seems clear from the author's tone?

Additional Support

English Language Coach

Multiple-Meaning Words Help students apply the three-step multiple-meaning word strategy to answer side note 6:

1. Have students replace the word they want to figure out with a blank.
2. Ask students to think of other words that could fit into the blank and still make sense. In this case, *supply* and *source* make sense.
3. Then ask students what the words that would work have in common. For example, they all suggest that a large number of talented athletes are available. Have students refer to the "Before You Read" section for additional help. EL BL

Visual Vocabulary
The ***uneven bars*** are two horizontal bars set a distance apart from each other and raised off of the floor. A gymnast flips between the bars.

Karolyi, the well-known coach, dismissed the *Register*'s findings. "A **gross** exaggeration," he said. "There are no problems with our sport. We have an action-packed sport, and from time to time people get injured." 8

But Carly Patterson, who won Olympic gold in 2004, acknowledged the risks. "It's a dangerous sport," said Patterson, who competed in the 2003 Worlds with a fractured elbow that would require two screws to hold it together. "It's really tough on your muscles and joints and bones. It's a lot of pounding every day."

How much pounding? Consider this: A gymnast can reach a height of 10 feet on her dismount from the uneven bars. Imagine standing on a basketball rim and jumping onto a mat less than 8 inches thick, several times a day, seven days a week. 9

Coaches in control

At the center of the gymnast's universe is the coach. Too often, athletes said, many coaches push girls too hard even when it's clear that they're hurt.

Michelle Hilse, a U.S. team member in the 1980s, said she was struck in the head by a well-known coach after breaking her hand while training. "He yelled, 'Get out of my face,'" Hilse recalled. "Then he slapped my head and yelled, 'Stop your crying.'"

In 1998, U.S. champion Beckerman, then 17, left her family in New Jersey to train at the Cincinnati Gymnastics Academy. By the next year, her coach had her training as much as 10 hours a day, Beckerman said, while consuming fewer calories than the number recommended for a 2-year-old, 25-pound toddler. Beckerman, in fact, said she was swallowing anti-inflammatory drugs more often than she was eating.

According to Beckerman, when her training shifted to the pre-Olympic camp, her wrist throbbed constantly, and the combination of drugs and nervousness left her in so much stomach pain that she could barely stand.

Similar problems for other gymnasts have been met with yelling, scorn, disbelief, swearing, threats and even physical

Practice the Skills

8 English Language Coach

Multiple-Meaning Words
You probably know that **gross** can refer to something disgusting. But there are other definitions: *adj.* huge, enormous; and *v.* to earn money. What is the meaning of *gross* as it is used here? How do you know?

9 Reviewing Skills

Comparing and Contrasting
Does the comparison the author uses here help make his point?

Literature Focus Lesson

Tone Explain to students that sometimes using a relatively neutral tone rather than an outraged one can be the best way for a writer to convey a point. For example, the details the writer gives about the abusive coaches are outrageous, yet for the most part, the writer presents them in a matter-of-fact tone. Discuss with students how the writer's argument might have been affected if the writer had called the coaches names or said, "All gymnastic coaches are mean and abusive." Ask students to explain whether or not readers would still find his argument credible. OL

Teach

L Literary Element

Tone Say: The writer uses the word *dismissed* instead of *replied to* or *refuted* to describe how the coach responded to the newspaper's findings. How does the word *dismissed* show the writer's tone, or attitude, toward the coach? *(Possible response: The word* dismissed *implies that the coach rejected the findings without even thinking about them. This shows that the writer does not like or respect the coach.)* AL

C1 Critical Thinking

Evaluation Ask: Why does the writer have readers imagine jumping off a basketball rim onto a thin mat? *(Possible response: to help them imagine what the gymnasts go through)* OL **Ask:** Do you think this is an effective comparison? *(Possible response: Yes; made my feet hurt)* BL

C2 Critical Thinking

Evaluation Ask: How well do you think the writer conveys the abuse inflicted by some coaches? Explain your response. *(Possible response: I think the writer does a good job. He gives many examples of coaches refusing to help injured athletes.)* OL AL

Indiana English/Language Arts Academic Standards
SE: 8.1.3, 8.3.6
TWE: *English Language Coach* 8.1.3, *Literature Focus Lesson* 8.3

Teach

R Reading Skill

Review Making Inferences

Ask: What can you infer about the athletes from their decisions not to stop training even though they are in physical and emotional pain? *(Possible responses: They are dedicated to winning; they have been pressured to win; they feel trapped.)* AL

Viewing the Photo

Say: Look at the photograph on this page and think about what you've read about gymnastics coaches in this article. How do the actions of the coach in this photograph compare to the way gymnastics coaches have been described? *(Responses will vary.)* OL

abuse, according to dozens of gymnasts. Sixty percent of the gymnasts interviewed said they were either verbally abused by their coaches when they told them or were afraid to raise the subject with the coaches.

"The first thing they do is accuse you of making it up," said Sheehan Lemley, a U.S. team member in the late 1990s. "That's the last thing I wanted them to think. So you hold it in until it gets really bad, until you can't walk."

Lemley trained so long on an injured ankle that six operations haven't been able to repair it. "I basically ruined my ankle," she said.

Yet many gymnasts said that, even when faced with training for months on a broken bone and the almost daily verbal abuse, they didn't walk away because they had long been trained to accept injuries and pain as the price they had to pay for Olympic glory. 10 R

Analyzing the Photo Coach Bela Karolyi carries injured gymnast Kerri Strug at the 1996 Olympic Games in Atlanta, Georgia. What emotions do you think Strug feels?

Legacy of pain

While a gymnast's career might be brief, her pain often lasts a lifetime. Injuries suffered as teenagers continue to affect many gymnasts **decades** later. Fifty-two percent of retired U.S. team members who spoke to the *Register* have had surgery for injuries related to gymnastics.

"I've been in constant pain since 1985," said Lisa McVay, a U.S. team member in the 1980s who broke her back at age 15. "I live with it daily. I deal with it constantly."

Double Olympic medalist Johnson has had five knee surgeries since winning her medals in 1984. Sunja Knapp, a U.S. team member in the 1980s, fractured her back three times between ages 12 and 14. Today, at 31, she sometimes needs a half-hour to get out of bed in the morning.

Practice the Skills

10 Reviewing Skills

Author's Purpose What do you think the author's purpose was in this article?

Vocabulary

decades (DEK aydz) *n.* periods of ten years

Additional Support

Reading in the Real World

Citizenship This article focuses on the serious disadvantages of elite gymnastics. To help students understand why women might be willing to undergo abuse and physical pain, have students brainstorm some of the benefits of being an elite gymnast. Discuss the following benefits:

- endorsement deals (money)
- fame
- representing the country in the Olympics
- positive attention from fans

Ask students to explain whether or not the benefits outweigh the drawbacks or vice versa. OL

Former Olympian Garrison is facing knee surgery and hip replacement at age 37.

In 1991, Michelle Campi won a silver medal at the World Championships. By 1994, she was training 10 hours a day, six days a week. "I was emotionally tired," she said. "I was exhausted. I was an accident waiting to happen."

The crash came late in a workout while Campi was working on a move on the uneven bars. She lost her grip, fell and landed on her back.

"I don't think she broke anything," Campi recalled her coach telling her mother, Celi Campi, who was in the gym at the time.

"My mother said, 'She needs to take a break. She needs a break,' " Campi continued. "He said, 'No, we'll soak her in an ice bath after practice. She'll be fine.' So he made me climb back up on the bar. It was really painful. I dropped down and had this sensation that I was going to throw up."

Celi Campi finally took her daughter to the emergency room. Campi had fractured her back. Rods had to be inserted to support her spine. None of it seemed to matter to Campi as she lay in a hospital bed that night.

"It was really weird," she said. "Life as I knew it was over. I was lying there in bed, and I wasn't thinking about whether I was going to be able to walk again. I wasn't thinking about what was going to happen to my life—was I going to be crippled? I don't know if relieved is the right word, but I kept thinking, 'At least I don't have to go into the gym tomorrow. I don't have to go back into the gym.' " **11** ○

Practice the Skills

11 BIG Question

Why do you think girls and young women pay such a high price to compete in international gymnastics? After reading this article, do you think the price is too high? Write your answers on the "Gymnasts in Pain" flap of the Foldable for Workshop 1. Your response will help you complete the Unit Challenge later. **BQ**

Analyzing the Photo Gymnast Kathy Johnson competes on the balance beam in the 1984 Olympics.

Teach

R Reading Skill

Review Identifying Author's Purpose **Ask:** Why do you think the writer chose to end the article with stories of gymnasts who are still suffering? *(Possible response: to show that the injuries suffered during the sport affect the women for life; to show that the problem is serious)* OL

BQ BIG Question

Ask: How do you think the author would answer the question: "Do female gymnasts pay too high a price to compete?" What evidence can you find to support your answer? *(Possible response: The author would say the gymnasts pay too high a price. Specific evidence from the text includes statistics, stories about injuries, quotations from gymnasts, and examples of the author's tone.)* OL

Assess

Use the CheckPoint questions provided on Presentation Plus! to check for comprehension of the selection. These questions can be used with interactive response keypads for immediate student feedback.

Differentiated Instruction

Role Play Have students role-play a news broadcast based on this article. Ask them to identify speakers who defend and criticize elite gymnastics. Select students to role-play these speakers, a reporter, and a news anchor. Have students work in groups to prepare and present a newscast that gives a balanced perspective on injuries suffered by gymnasts. OL

Indiana English/Language Arts Academic Standards

SE: 8.2

TWE: *Reading in the Real World* 8.3, *Differentiated Instruction* 8.7

Assess

Resources for page 308

- Selection Quick Check, p. 21
- Selection and Unit Assessment, p. 25
- ExamView Assessment Suite
- Interactive Tutor: Self-Assessment

Students can respond to the *After You Read* items in their Learner's Notebooks or on a separate sheet of paper.

Answering the BIG Question

1. The price is too high because the athletes are often in pain for years.
2. eating disorders
3. Coaches often don't believe athletes who say they are injured; they may also respond with demands to tough it out.

Critical Thinking

4. Possible response: Coaches, parents, and others involved want to make money and see the gymnasts succeed.
5. Possible response: After pushing herself to her limits, Campi was glad not to have to keep training. Responses to the second part of the question will vary.
6. Possible response: The author is highly critical of USA Gymnastics, but does allow its CEO and Bela Karolyi to present their side.

After You Read

Gymnasts in Pain: Out of Balance

Answering the BIG Question

1. The gymnasts in the article suffered pain and damage to their bodies while trying to become the best gymnasts in the world. Do you think the price they and other athletes pay to be the best is too high? Explain.
2. **Recall** Besides physical injuries, what other serious health problems might gymnasts experience?
   TIP **Think and Search**
3. **Summarize** What kind of negative response have some gymnasts received from their coaches after reporting their injuries?
   TIP **Think and Search**

Critical Thinking

4. **Analyze** Why do you think young gymnasts are being pushed so hard to reach the Olympic dream?
   TIP **Author and Me**
5. **Analyze** Why would the gymnast Michelle Campi have felt relief while she was lying in the hospital bed? Have you ever felt the same way about something? Explain.
   TIP **Author and Me**
6. **Evaluate** Do you think the writer presented a fair picture of training for international gymnastic competition? Why or why not? Use specific details from the article to support your opinion.
   TIP **Author and Me**

Talk About Your Reading

Class Debate Divide into two teams and debate the positive and negative sides of training for international gymnastic competition.

- Start with a statement about whether or not you support international gymnastics competition.
- Explain your position.
- Give specific reasons to support your position.
- Respond to at least one point the other team makes.

Indiana English/Language Arts Academic Standards (pp. 308–309)

8.3 Comprehension and Analysis of Literary Text Respond to grade-level-appropriate literature... **8.7.13** Deliver persuasive presentations... **8.2 Comprehension and Analysis (Focus on Informational Text)** Develop [reading] strategies... **8.3.6** Identify significant literary devices... which define a writer's style... **8.6 English Language Conventions**

For a complete description of the standards, see p. IN 11.

Talk About Your Reading

Before students present their debates, review their position statements and the evidence they plan to use. As they debate, use a checklist to evaluate their evidence, presentation skills, and response to the other team.

Skills Review

Key Reading Skill: Previewing

7. What did you do to preview the selection before you read it? Which previewing skill helped you the most to understand the reading? Explain.

Key Literary Element: Tone

8. What does the phrase "out of balance" in the title tell readers about the writer's attitude?
9. What is the overall tone of this article? Support your answer with specific details from the article.

Reviewing Skills: Fact and Opinion

10. The author of this article has very strong opinions about the practices of women's gymnastics. Does he support these opinions with facts? Write a few sentences about what you think the author's opinion is and how he does or does not support them. Be sure to consider the statements of the athletes themselves.

Vocabulary Check

Match each word to its correct definition. Then use each word in a sentence.

11. expectations	**a.** clever or skillful moves or actions
12. elite	**b.** periods of ten years
13. decades	**c.** what someone thinks is likely to happen
14. maneuvers	**d.** best, most skilled

15. **English Language Coach** Write two sentences using a different meaning of the word *pool* in each sentence. Then do the same for the word *gross.*
16. **Academic Vocabulary** If your teacher asks you to find out what kinds of resources are **available** in the neighborhood library, what is he or she asking you to do?

Grammar Link: Sentence Types

A sentence is a group of words that expresses a complete thought. There are four types of sentences.

A **declarative sentence** makes a statement or tells something about the subject of the sentence.

- Sonya is practicing.
- I like popsicles.

An **interrogative sentence** asks a question.

- Did Hanna soak her foot?
- What is your address?

An **imperative sentence** gives a command. In other types of sentences, the subject is stated. In imperative sentences, the subject is the word *you.* However, *you* isn't written down or spoken in commands–it's just "understood" that the subject is *you.* For example, in the sentence *Sit down,* the speaker means *(You) sit down.*

- Pick up your socks now!
- Come back at 3:00.

An **exclamatory sentence** expresses strong feeling.

- We won the competition!
- That book was funny!

Grammar Practice

Copy each sentence below. Then write whether the sentence is *declarative, interrogative, imperative,* or *exclamatory.*

17. Do you like scary movies?
18. Juan skated all afternoon.
19. Stop!
20. I want to go now!

Web Activities For eFlashcards, Selection Quick Checks, and other Web activities, go to www.glencoe.com.

Skills Review

Key Reading Skill: Previewing

7. Possible response: I read the title, subtitles, and first lines of some paragraphs and looked at the photos. They helped determine the passage's topic.

Key Literary Element: Tone

8. The writer is critical of the sport.
9. Possible response: The tone is matter-of-fact but concerned; the author argues that the sport needs to change.

Reviewing Skills: Fact and Opinion

10. Responses will vary.

Vocabulary Check

Possible sentences follow each correct answer.

11. c; My coaches' expectations are high.
12. d; Elite gymnasts' routines are extremely difficult.
13. b; It can take gymnasts decades to heal from a break.
14. a; Maneuvers like backflips on a balance beam are dangerous.

English Language Coach

15. Possible responses: We swim in the pool. American gymnastics has a large pool of talent. The overcooked pasta was gross. That is a gross exaggeration.

Academic Vocabulary

16. To find out *what* resources are on hand in the library

Grammar Link: Sentence Types

Grammar Practice

17. interrogative
18. declarative
19. imperative
20. exclamatory

Close

Have students state whether they would be willing to make the same sacrifices as the elite gymnasts to reach their goals.

Indiana English/Language Arts Academic Standards
SE: 8.2, 8.3, 8.3.6, 8.6, 8.7.13

Teach

More About the Author

Dwight Okita started writing poetry in the first grade because stories were hard for him. He published his first poem that year. Later Okita began writing plays and screenplays as well. "In Response to Executive Order 9066" is one of his most well-known works. Okita's parents didn't talk much about their time in the internment camps, so the poem is based on what he imagines his mother would have done if she had been able to say goodbye to her classmates.

V Vocabulary

Vocabulary File Say: One way to learn and remember the vocabulary words is to keep a vocabulary file. In your Learner's Notebooks, include the pronunciation if you need it, the meaning, and a sentence that gives you an example of how to use each word. This is a good way to file any information that you want to learn and keep. AS

Before You Read

In Response to Executive Order 9066

Meet the Author

Dwight Okita was born in 1958 in Chicago, where he still lives. He started writing poems in first grade and published his first book of poems in 1992. His mother's experience at a relocation camp during World War II inspired Mr. Okita to write "In Response to Executive Order 9066." For more about Dwight Okita, see page R5 of the Author Files in the back of this book.

Author Search For more about Dwight Okita, go to www.glencoe.com.

Indiana English/Language Arts Academic Standards (pp. 310–313)

8.1.3 Verify the meaning of a word in its context... **8.2 Comprehension and Analysis (Focus on Informational Text)** Develop [reading] strategies... **8.3.6** Identify significant literary devices, such as...symbolism...which define a writer's style...

For a complete description of the standards, see p. IN 11.

Vocabulary Preview

V

descent (dih SENT) *n.* lineage; ancestry **(p. 312)** *Many people of Japanese descent live along the west coast of the United States.*

ripened (RYP und) *v.* became ready to eat; form of the verb *ripen* **(p. 313)** *She knew the tomatoes had ripened when they turned completely red.*

Write to Learn With a partner, write a sentence for each word in the Vocabulary Preview.

English Language Coach

Multiple-Meaning Words While reading, you may find that a familiar word has unfamiliar meanings. When this happens, try to figure out the unfamiliar meaning by using context clues. If that doesn't work, use a dictionary to look up all the meanings of the word. Then choose the meaning that makes sense in context. Suppose, for example, that you see the word *mules* used in an unusual way:

- The woman sat on the edge of her bed and slipped into her mules.

You can tell that mules are not animals in the context of the sentence. So what are they? Look below at the sample dictionary entry for the word. Which definition makes the most sense?

mule (myool) *n.* [Middle English, from Old French *mul,* from Latin *mulus*] **1.** a cross between a horse and a donkey **2.** an unusually inflexible or stubborn person **3.** machinery that twists fiber into thread **4.** a slip-on shoe or slipper

Definition 4–a slip-on shoe or slipper–makes the most sense in the context of the sentence.

Partner Talk Discuss the different meanings of each word below. How many meanings for each word can you think of?

1. race
2. recall
3. round
4. run
5. sentence

Additional Support

Author Search To expand students' appreciation of Dwight Okita, have them access the Web site for additional information and resources.

Differentiated Instruction

Finding Primary Sources Several primary sources related to the Japanese American internment are available online, including copies of Executive Order 9066, photographs of the internment camps by Ansel Adams, and court decisions about civil rights and reparations. Encourage students to search the online collections of the Smithsonian Institution and the Japanese American Relocation Digital Archives (JARDA). Have them create a "webliography" of recommended resources about what happened to Japanese Americans during World War II. AL

Skills Preview

Key Reading Skill: Previewing

Before you read the poem, read the Build Background information on this page. Then preview the poem by looking at its title, its shape, and the first two or three lines. Quickly look at the rest of the poem. R

Whole Class Discussion What do you think the poem will be about? Why?

Literary Element: Symbol

A **symbol** is a person, place, or thing that stands for, or represents, something else. Sometimes writers use common symbols, such as a dove to represent peace or the colors red, white, and blue to represent the United States. Other times writers create special symbols for particular stories or poems. Use these tips to find and understand symbols: L

- Look for common symbols you've seen in other selections, such as a rose representing love.
  Do any familiar symbols appear in the selection?
- Notice which objects seem to be especially meaningful to the narrator or a character.
  Is there an object that has special importance to one of the characters?
- Think about qualities, emotions, or ideas that are associated with the meaningful objects.
  What does the object make you think of?

Whole Class Discussion What do you think each of the following objects symbolizes? As a class, discuss your ideas.

wedding ring • American flag • snake

Interactive Literary Elements Handbook
To review or learn more about the literary elements, go to www.glencoe.com.

Get Ready to Read

Connect to the Reading

Recall a time when you were accused of doing something that you didn't do. How did you feel? As you read the poem, imagine how the speaker feels.

Partner Talk Discuss what it's like to be unfairly accused of something. Then talk about why this can happen to a whole group of people. What can be done to prevent it?

Build Background

- As used in the poem's title, the term "executive order" refers to a rule or order issued by the President of the United States. An executive order has the same force and effect as a law that has been passed by Congress.
- In December 1941 Japanese planes attacked the U.S naval base at Pearl Harbor, Hawaii. The United States then declared war on Japan and entered World War II. A wave of fear and prejudice against Japanese Americans swept over the U.S.
- In February 1942 President Franklin D. Roosevelt signed Executive Order 9066. Under that order, Japanese Americans who lived along the West Coast were forced to leave their homes and move to "internment camps," or "relocation centers." More than 100,000 people had to live in these camps until the end of the war.

Set Purposes for Reading

BIG Question Read "In Response to Executive Order 9066" to learn about the sacrifice an American teenager had to make during World War II.

Set Your Own Purpose What else would you like to learn from this poem to help you answer the Big Question? Write your own purpose on the "In Response to Executive Order 9066" flap of the Foldable for Workshop 1.

Keep Moving

Use these skills as you read "In Response to Executive Order 9066."

Teach

R Reading Skill

Previewing Invite students to share what they learned from previewing the poem. OL

L Literary Element

Symbol Once students have identified the ring as a symbol of love, the flag as a symbol of freedom or love of country, and the snake as a symbol of evil, have them identify other objects and tell what they might symbolize in a poem. Responses might include books (symbolizing learning) or expensive cars (symbolizing wealth or luxury). AS

Interactive Literary Elements Handbook Have students access the Web site to improve their understanding of symbol.

Reading Fluency

Build Fluency Hearing good models is an excellent way for students to build fluency. After analyzing the poem, read it aloud, using your tone of voice to convey both the sadness and the hope in the poem. Then have students take turns reading lines from "In Response to Executive Order 9066." Tell them to practice reading the lines smoothly with expression and understanding. Encourage them to use their tone of voice to convey meaning as you did in your reading. EL BL

Indiana English/Language Arts Academic Standards
SE: 8.1.3, 8.2, 8.3.6
TWE: *Differentiated Instruction* 8.4.4, *Reading Fluency* 8.1

Teach

L Literary Element

Review Tone **Ask:** What tone is set by the title "In Response to Executive Order 9066"? *(Possible response: an impersonal or official tone.)* **OL** **Ask:** How does this tone contrast with the rest of the poem? *(Possible response: The rest of the poem has the sweet, sad tone of a letter written by a young girl. It is not official at all.)* **AL**

C Critical Thinking

Evaluation **Ask:** What details make the Japanese American speaker seem like any other fourteen-year-old? *(Possible responses: She doesn't like being different; she has "bad spelling" and her room is "messy"; her favorite food is hot dogs.)* **OL** **Ask:** Why do you think the author includes these details? *(Possible responses: to show that those sent to the internment camps were just like other Americans, not "the Enemy"; to contrast these personal details with the impersonal executive order)* **AL**

In Response to Executive Order 9066 L

All Americans of Japanese **Descent** Must **Report** to Relocation Centers **1**

by Dwight Okita

2 Dear Sirs:

Of course I'll come. I've packed my galoshes*
and three packets of tomato seeds. Denise calls them
love apples. My father says where we're going
they won't grow. **3**

I am a fourteen-year-old girl with bad spelling
and a messy room. If it helps any, I will tell you
I have always felt funny using chopsticks
and my favorite food is hot dogs. **C**
My best friend is a white girl named Denise—
we look at boys together. She sat in front of me
all through grade school because of our names:
O'Connor, Ozawa. I know the back of Denise's head
very well.

I tell her she's going bald. She tells me I copy on tests.
We are best friends.

2. ***Galoshes*** (gah LAH shez) are waterproof covers for shoes that protect them from rain or snow.

Vocabulary

descent (dih SENT) *n.* lineage; ancestry

Practice the Skills

1 English Language Coach

Multiple-Meaning Words What is the correct meaning of the word **report** as it is used in the subtitle?

2 Key Reading Skill

Previewing Look quickly at the structure of the poem. Why do you think the poet wrote in the form of a letter? Explain.

3 Literary Element

Symbol The tomato seeds must be important to the speaker because they're one of only two objects she packs. Also, it's unusual to call tomato seeds "love apples." These clues hint that tomato seeds may be a symbol in the poem.

Additional Support

Literature Focus Lesson

Epistolary Poems The word *epistle* comes from the Latin word for letter. An epistolary poem is a poem written in the form of a letter. Have students tell what words in Okita's poem indicate that it is an epistolary poem. *(Dear Sirs)* Then have a class discussion about who the "dear sirs" in the poem might be. Possible responses may include the people organizing the internment camps or the United States government. Then have students try writing their own epistolary poem to the "Sirs." **AL**

I saw Denise today in Geography class.
She was sitting on the other side of the room.
"You're trying to start a war," she said, "giving secrets
away to the Enemy. Why can't you keep your big
mouth shut?"

I didn't know what to say.
I gave her a packet of tomato seeds
and asked her to plant them for me, told her
when the first tomato **ripened**
she'd miss me. 4 5 ❍

L

Vocabulary

ripened (RYP und) *v.* became ready to eat

Practice the Skills

4 Literary Element

Symbol The speaker asks Denise to plant tomato seeds. Think about all the feelings and ideas that might be associated with planting seeds. What do you think the tomato seeds represent?

5 BIG Question

What does the speaker of the poem lose because of Executive Order 9066? What does Denise lose? Do you think they pay too high a price? Write your answers on the "In Response to Executive Order 9066" flap of the Foldable for Workshop 1. Your response will help you complete the Unit Challenge later. BQ

Teach

L Literary Element

Symbol **Ask:** What do seeds often symbolize? *(Possible responses: new life; hope; great things from small beginnings)*
OL **Ask:** Why might the speaker have chosen tomato seeds as a gift? *(Possible responses: Denise's name for them—love apples—makes them a good symbol of friendship; Denise's hostility could end their friendship, but the speaker responds with a symbol of new beginnings; the speaker still has hope for the future)* **AL**

BQ **BIG Question**

Ask: What price are you willing to pay for your safety? *(Responses will vary. Students may note that taking innocent people from their homes is too high a price to pay for "safety.")* **OL**

Assess

CheckPoint

Use the CheckPoint questions provided on Presentation Plus! to check for comprehension of the selection. These questions can be used with interactive response keypads for immediate student feedback.

Differentiated Instruction

Before and After Charts Draw a two-column chart on the board. Label the first column *Before* and the second column *After*. Ask students to describe what the relationship between Denise and the speaker was like before Executive Order 9066. Write students' suggestions in the first column. Then have students describe how their relationship changed after the order. Record students' answers in the second column. Then have students explain whether or not they think the speaker changed, or Denise changed, and why. **OL**

Indiana English/Language Arts Academic Standards
SE: 8.1.3, 8.2, 8.3.6
TWE: *Literature Focus Lesson* 8.1.2, *Differentiated Instruction* 8.2

Assess

Resources for page 314

- Selection Quick Check, p. 22
- Selection and Unit Assessment, p. 26
- ExamView Assessment Suite
- Interactive Tutor: Self-Assessment

Students can respond to the *After You Read* items in their Learner's Notebooks or on a separate sheet of paper.

Answering the

1. Possible response: Relocation centers don't really make people safe. They are too high a price because they deny people basic human rights.
2. Denise stops feeling friendly toward the speaker because she thinks she's the "Enemy."
3. The speaker asks Denise to plant tomato seeds and remember her when they ripen.

Critical Thinking

4. Possible response: They suggest the family is going to a place that does not nourish plants or people.
5. Possible response: Denise is influenced by adults' fears.
6. Possible response: The choice of a young girl makes it easy to see how hard the order was on innocent people.

After You Read

In Response to Executive Order 9066

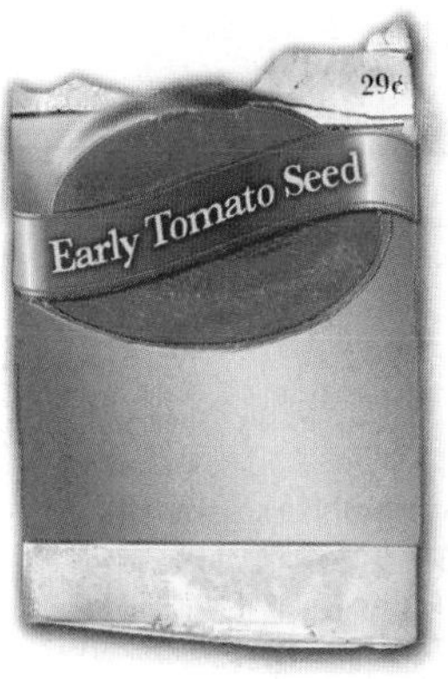

Answering the BIG Question

1. Putting Japanese Americans in relocation centers was intended to make other Americans feel safer. Do you believe in security at any cost, or would you draw the line at relocation centers? Explain.
2. **Recall** How do Denise's feelings toward the speaker change as a result of Executive Order 9066?
   TIP **Think and Search**
3. **Recall** What does the speaker ask Denise to do for her?
   TIP **Right There**

Critical Thinking

4. **Interpret** In lines 3–5 the speaker says love apples won't grow where the family is going. What do you think these lines say about the relocation camp they're going to?
   TIP **Author and Me**
5. **Infer** Why do you think Denise accuses her best friend of trying to start a war? Where do you think she got that idea?
   TIP **Author and Me**
6. **Evaluate** The poet chose to write his poem as a letter written by a young girl. How does that choice affect your understanding of the poem? Do you think it's a good choice? Explain.
   TIP **Author and Me**

Write About Your Reading

Letter Imagine that you are the speaker's friend Denise. Write a letter that apologizes for the way you acted. Explain why you were mean and what you miss about the speaker.

Indiana English/Language Arts Academic Standards (pp. 314–315)

8.3 Comprehension and Analysis of Literary Text Respond to grade-level-appropriate literature... **8.5.7** Write for different purposes... **8.2 Comprehension and Analysis (Focus on Informational Text)** Develop [reading] strategies... **8.3.6** Identify significant literary devices, such as...symbolism...which define a writer's style... **8.1.3** Verify the meaning of a word in its context... **8.6.5** Use correct punctuation.

For a complete description of the standards, see p. IN 11.

Write About Your Reading

Dear Friend,

I miss you very much. I know I seemed angry, but I was foolish and scared. I miss all the fun we used to have together at school. Is life in the camp rough? I've heard some people have to sleep in a room with many other families. I'd really miss my privacy! I'm glad you gave me the packet of seeds. The plants give me a chance to care for something while you are away. I hope I'll get to see you soon.

Love,

Denise

Skills Review

Key Reading Skill: Previewing

7. How did previewing the poem help you understand it? Explain.

Literary Element: Symbol

8. What does Denise call tomatoes? What do you think the speaker wants Denise to realize about their friendship when Denise sees a ripened tomato?

Vocabulary Check

Choose the word that best completes each sentence. Write the sentences on a separate sheet of paper.

descent • ripened

9. My ancestors came from Norway, so I am of Norwegian _______.
10. The fruit _______ because the weather conditions were perfect.
11. **English Language Coach** The sample dictionary entry below shows different meanings for the word *report.* Choose the meaning that makes sense in the subtitle of the poem. Then choose two other meanings. On a separate sheet of paper, write a sentence for each of the different meanings of *report,* for a total of three sentences.

> **report** *v.* [Middle English, from Old French *reportare,* from Latin *re-* + *portare,* to carry] **1.** to relate, as a story **2.** to serve as a messenger **3.** to act as a newspaper reporter **4.** to complain about to authorities **5.** to let one's superiors know of one's arrival, as in soldiers reporting for duty **6.** to announce a problem to the proper authorities, as in reporting an accident or fire

Grammar Link: End Punctuation

When you talk, you change your tone of voice to indicate your emotions and you pause to separate your ideas. When you write, punctuation expresses your emotions and indicates pauses.

Use a question mark (?) to ask a question.

- What are you wearing to the band concert?

Use an exclamation point (!) to express strong feelings. Exclamatory sentences *always* end with an exclamation point.

- We won the championship!

An imperative sentence, or command, may end with an exclamation point or a period. An exclamation point is ordinarily used only when the command expresses strong emotion.

- Please lower your voice. • Look out!

Use a period (.) whenever you don't need a question mark or an explanation point.

- Tired, she decided to go to bed.

Grammar Practice

Copy each sentence below, adding correct punctuation.

12. The hawk flew overhead
13. Hurry up
14. Did you see the rainbow this afternoon
15. I wonder where George went

Web Activities For eFlashcards, Selection Quick Checks, and other Web activities, go to www.glencoe.com.

Skills Review

Key Reading Skill: Previewing

7. Possible response: I asked "Who is Denise?" I learned she is the speaker's friend.

Literary Element: Symbol

8. Possible response: Denise calls tomatoes "love apples." The speaker wants Denise to realize that the two girls love each other and that their friendship will outlast the horrible rumors about Japanese Americans.

Vocabulary Check

9. descent
10. ripened

English Language Coach

11. Possible responses:
    - The soldier had to report for duty (same meaning as title).
    - I am going to report the misuse of school property to the principal today.
    - The scientist will report her findings when she finishes her study.

Close

Ask students to summarize what they learned about the Big Question from "In Response to Executive Order 9066."

Grammar Link: End Punctuation

Grammar Practice

Possible responses:

12. The hawk flew overhead.
13. Hurry up!
14. Did you see the rainbow this afternoon?
15. I wonder where George went.

Indiana English/Language Arts Academic Standards
SE: 8.1.3, 8.2, 8.3, 8.3.6, 8.5.7, 8.6.5

Research Report

Teaching Students to Write a Research Report

Why Is It Important?

- Writing a research report helps students synthesize information, which fosters both comprehension and writing with purpose.
- Doing research builds literacy by ensuring that students make use of different sources and different media.
- Research shows that reading one's own writing—notes, highlighted text, and data—for the purpose of synthesizing it improves one's ability to read critically like a writer and write as critical reader—in other words, getting down the important points and details.
- Knowing that one will write a report following data-gathering improves the inquiry process because it contributes to a clear purpose for doing research.
- Comparing sources on the same material provides an opportunity for students to determine author credibility.

How to Help Students Get It

- Guide students through inquiry components such as brainstorming what they know about a topic; asking questions they want to answer; listing ways they might answer those questions.
- Show and model an information-search strategy involving multiple sources (books, periodicals, reference works, CDs, DVDs, and the Web).
- Encourage students to be very specific in their questions.
- Help students use a comprehensive method of writing to record information and data using note cards, data sheets or databases, word processors, graphic organizers, and diagrams.
- Focus on how to select important information and how to use a variety of sources in writing the report; model various report formats, including print formats and media presentations.
- Show students examples of source cards to help them prepare a bibliography. Remind them that source cards are different from note cards, and that each source is assigned an individual card and identifying number. This number is written on the note cards to show the source of that particular information.
- Review paraphrasing and quoting, giving examples of each and showing how to identify each by punctuation. Also talk about plagiarism and how to prevent it.

Writing Trait	Student Checklist
Ideas	The message or the theme and the details that develop it
Organization	The arrangement of main points and supporting details
Voice	A writer's unique way of using tone and style
Word Choice	The vocabulary a writer uses to convey meaning
Sentence Fluency	The smooth rhythm and flow of sentences that vary in length and style
Unit Focus **Conventions:** correct spelling, grammar, usage, and mechanics	• Are all words spelled correctly? • Are all proper nouns—as well as the first word of every sentence—capitalized? • Is the composition free of sentence fragments? • Is the composition free of run-on sentences? • Are punctuation marks—such as apostrophes, commas, and end marks—inserted in the right places?
Presentation	The way words and design elements look on a page

Workshop Resources

Pacing (Days) Standard	Block	Lesson	Student Materials	Teacher Resources
1	1/2	Writing Workshop Part 1: Prewriting and Drafting	Writing Workshop Graphic Organizer, p. 15 Grammar Practice, p. 16 Spelling and Handwriting Practice, p. 46 Grammar and Composition Handbook, p. 74 Real Success in Writing: Research and Reports	TeacherWorks Plus™ Presentation Plus! Rubrics for Assessing Student Writing, Listening, and Speaking, p. 21 Grammar and Writing Workshop Transparencies 13–14
2	1	Writing Workshop Part 2: Editing, Revising, and Presenting	Interactive Grammar and Language Workbook Grammar and Composition Handbook, p. 74 Real Success in Writing: Research and Reports Listening and Speaking, p. 29 Viewing and Representing, p. 30	Grammar and Writing Workshop Transparencies 21–22 Interactive Grammar and Language Workbook Rubrics for Assessing Student Writing, Listening, and Speaking, p. 21

Focus

BELLRINGER Options

Daily Language Practice Transparency 24
Focus Activity Ask: What are some topics you want to know more about? *(Write responses on the board.)* **Say:** In this workshop, you'll write a research report on a topic that has both positive and negative sides. AS

Teach

W Writing

Choosing a Topic Say: If you're having a hard time coming up with a topic, you might consider these suggestions for finding ideas:
- Skim magazines and journals.
- Watch news shows, or read online newspapers.
- Talk to your friends and family to find out what topics interest them and might also interest you. AS

Resources for page 316

Use the Writing Workshop Graphic Organizer BLM in the Unit 3 Resource Book, p. 15.

Use the Grammar and Writing Workshop Transparencies 13-14

WRITING WORKSHOP PART 1

Research Report

Prewriting and Drafting

ASSIGNMENT Write a research report

Purpose: To research a subject and write a report on what you find

Audience: Your teacher and your classmates

Writing Rubric

As you work through this writing assignment, you should

- write a thesis statement that clearly states what you are reporting
- support your thesis with evidence and details
- effectively organize and present the information
- cite sources correctly
- write an effective introduction and conclusion
- effectively use simple sentences

See pages 383–385 in Part 2 for a model of a research report.

Indiana English/ Language Arts Academic Standards (pp. 316–321)

8.5.3 Write research reports... **8.4 Processes and Features** Prewriting and drafting. **8.4.11** Identify topics. **8.4.10** Create an organizational structure... **8.6 English Language Conventions** **8.6.1** Use varied sentence types.

For a complete description of the standards, see p. IN 11.

In this unit you will research and write about a topic that has positive and negative sides—a person, action, or event that may have good aspects but "costs" a high price. Your research report will present your thoughts about this topic, and you will back up your ideas with factual information from expert sources. Writing a research report will help you think about the Big Question: When is the price too high? As you write your report, refer to the **Writing Handbook,** pp. R17–R27.

Prewriting

Get Ready to Write

Prewriting is an important part of writing a research report. When you prewrite, you explore ideas for topics, choose one, and research information about that topic. The following directions will guide you through the prewriting process.

Gather Ideas

Ask yourself these questions to think of possible ideas to research.
- *What do I want to learn about?*
- *What do I care about?*
- *What have I (or people I know) paid a high price for?*

Work with a partner to brainstorm a list of possible topics. Write your list in your Learner's Notebook. Both of you don't have to write down the same ideas, but one of your partner's ideas may trigger an idea of your own. For example, your partner might suggest the history of baseball, which might W make you think about all the hours your sister puts in training for soccer. That might make you wonder about the trade-offs student athletes make.

Here are some topic ideas to get you started.

- *space exploration—is learning about space worth risking human lives?*
- *violent video games—are they worth the violence they might cause?*
- *global warming—are daily conveniences worth harming our planet?*

Differentiated Instruction

Evaluating Web Sites Remind students that Web sites can include information written by anyone, so not all Web sites contain reliable, accurate information. Help students create a list of questions, such as the following, to help them evaluate Web sites.

1. Who writes or maintains the site?
2. What is the purpose of the site?
3. Are words spelled correctly? Are grammar and usage correct?
4. Does the writer seem to have a bias?
5. When was the site written? (Is it up-to-date?) AS

Choose a Topic and Focus Your Ideas

W1

1. Choose one topic to research.
2. Do some general research to help you focus on a specific aspect, or part, of your topic.

- If your topic is too narrow, you won't be able to find enough information to write your report.
- If your topic is too broad, you'll find too much information, and your report may be too general.

One student decided to report on the history of unfair treatment against Native Americans. This chart shows examples of topics that are too broad, too narrow, and just right.

Too Broad	Still Too Broad	Just Right	Too Narrow	Way Too Narrow
Native Americans	the treatment of Native Americans in the 1800s	how and why the U.S. government relocated the Cherokee people in the 1800s	the Cherokee people and the U.S. Supreme Court	Cherokee Chief John Ross's child-hood

Keep your mind open as you research. The amount and type of information you uncover may lead you to change or reshape your topic.

Research your Topic

Begin your research by writing four or five questions about the topic you've chosen. If you have trouble thinking of questions, ask *who, what, where, when, why,* and *how.* If you were researching the relocation of the Cherokee tribe, you might ask questions like the ones below.

Where did the Cherokees live in the 1800s?
Who or what made them leave their homeland?
What happened when they left?
Who benefited from the Cherokees' leaving?
What effects did the relocation have on the Cherokee people?
Where are the Cherokees today?

Look for answers to your questions in books, magazines, newspapers, and reliable Web sites. Library indexes and databases may be helpful. Depending on your topic, you may want to use primary sources, such as letters or diaries.

Literature Online

Writing Models For models and other writing activities, go to www.glencoe.com.

Writing Tip

Sources Encyclopedias and textbooks are good general reference books for early research. W2

Writing Tip

Evaluating Information
Not all Web sites deserve your trust. Find out who maintains the site you're using. Check facts you find against facts from another, reliable source. If they don't agree, find a third source for comparison.

WRITING WORKSHOP PART 1

Teach

Literature Online

Writing Models Have students access the Web site for an additional and interactive Writing Workshop-based student model.

W1 Writing

Narrowing Your Topic Say: You might consider doing some preliminary research at the library or online to find some aspect of your topic that interests you. Be sure you don't make your topic so narrow that you'll run out of things to say. AS

W2 Writing

Finding Sources Tell students that finding too many sources on their topic may be confusing. Encourage students to find four to six good sources of information for their topic. OL

Literature Focus Lesson

Primary and Secondary Sources
Tell students to use both primary and secondary sources in their research.

- **Primary sources** are first-hand information sources that have not been evaluated or analyzed by someone else. Examples: eyewitness accounts, a letter, and an interview with an expert.
- **Secondary sources** are information sources that have been organized, evaluated, and analyzed by someone else. Examples: an article that includes a witness's comments and most books and magazine articles.

Discuss with students why using primary sources might be important. AS

Indiana English/Language Arts Academic Standards
SE: 8.4, 8.4.11, 8.5.3, 8.6, 8.6.1
TWE: *Differentiated Instruction* 8.2, *Literature Focus Lesson* 8.5.3

Teach

W Writing

Taking Notes To give students practice in taking concise notes, choose a short passage from this unit and ask them to make a note card for it. Afterward, have students compare notes. Then create a note card as a class, working to include all of the important information in as few words as possible. Also check to be sure that any words taken directly from the text are placed in quotation marks. **Say:** To keep track of your notes, you might buy multicolored note cards and use a new color for each source you use. AS

Make Source Cards

In a research report, you must cite, or name, the source of your information. To keep track of your sources, write the author, title, publication information, and location of each source on a separate note card. Give each source card a number, and write it in the upper right corner. These cards will be useful for writing a bibliography.

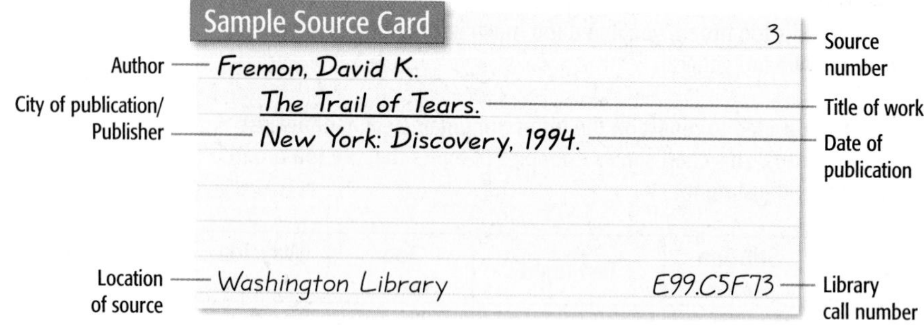

Take Notes

Writing Tip

Taking Notes When you take notes, write important facts and details on separate note cards. It is useful to organize note cards into categories.

As you research, write down useful information on note cards. Keep track of the source of the information.

- At the top of each card, write a key word or phrase that tells you about the information. Also, write the number of the source you used.
- Write only the details and ideas that relate to your topic.
- Be careful to summarize information in your own words.
- Write down a phrase or a quotation only when the words are especially interesting or come from an important source. If you quote directly, copy the words exactly and place them in quotation marks to show that they are not your own words. That will help you avoid making mistakes later.

This sample note card shows information to include.

W

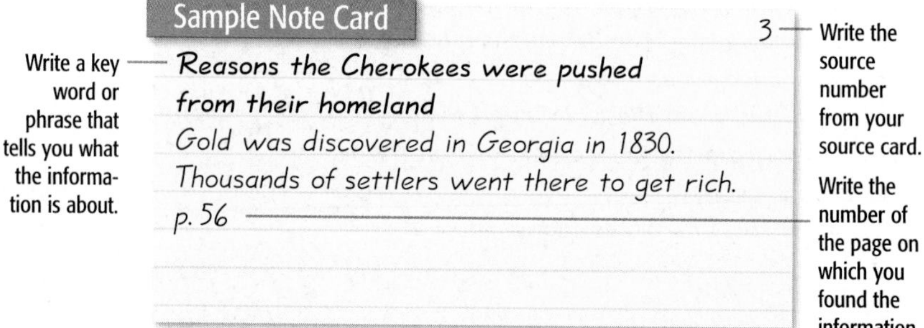

Sample Note Card
3
Write the source number from your source card.
Write a key word or phrase that tells you what the information is about.
Reasons the Cherokees were pushed from their homeland
Gold was discovered in Georgia in 1830.
Thousands of settlers went there to get rich.
p. 56
Write the number of the page on which you found the information.

Additional Support

Differentiated Instruction

Note Taking English language learners and other students may need practice summarizing information. Tell students that to avoid paraphrasing a source too closely, they should look away from the source while taking notes. Have students practice by reading a paragraph from one of their sources and then telling you or a partner the main points of the paragraph in their own words. Encourage students to read, think about what they read, and then write their notes. EL BL

Create an Outline

When you have finished taking notes, sort your note cards and write a rough outline of your paper. (You can revise your outline later.)

1. Group together note cards on similar topics. Use each group as a main topic in your outline. (Main topics are noted on outlines with Roman numerals.)
2. Within each group of note cards, cluster similar note cards into subgroups that support and explain the larger and more general main topic. Use these subgroups as the subtopics in your outline (the capital letters).
3. Organize your piles of note cards in an order that makes sense for your topic.
4. Set aside note cards that don't fit under any heading.

The Trail of Tears

I. Background
   A. Cherokee life in their homeland
   B. White settlers' demand for more land
   C. Treaty of Echota
II. Forced removal
   A. Rounding up the Cherokees
   B. March to Oklahoma
III. Effect on Cherokee life
   A. Life in Oklahoma
   B. Life for Cherokees who escaped the roundup

Writing Tip

Text Structure You may want to organize your report in chronological order or cause-and-effect order. W

Drafting

Start Writing!

With your outline and your note cards by your side, write your first draft. It should have an introduction, a body, and a conclusion.

- The introduction grabs readers' attention, presents the topic, and makes a **thesis statement,** or statement of the paper's main ideas.
- The body supports the thesis with evidence found during research.
- The conclusion summarizes main points and restates the thesis.

Writing Tip

Drafting Many writers like to write the body of the report and then go back and write the introduction and thesis statement. Others like to write a thesis statement and then write the body. Wherever you start, focus on getting your ideas down on paper.

WRITING WORKSHOP PART 1

Teach

W Writing

Text Structure Tell students they can use any of the following ways to organize their ideas, depending on their topic:

- **Chronological:** Arrange information according to when it happened.
- **Cause and Effect:** Arrange items to show how one idea or event led to another.
- **Compare and Contrast:** Arrange information to show similarities and differences. (This type of organization might work well for a paper telling the good and bad sides of a topic.)
- **Order of Importance:** Arrange ideas from most to least or least to most important.

Say: Remember that all the points in your paper should support your thesis. Make sure you haven't included any information that doesn't fit your topic. AS

Literature Focus Lesson

Writing a Thesis If students have difficulty writing a thesis statement, share the following three-step method.

1. Look back at the research questions you wrote. Consider the answers you found during your research.
2. Consider your opinion on the topic. Do the positive aspects outweigh the negative? If so, why? If not, why not?
3. Write a concise statement that tells your central idea.

Share the following sample thesis statement: "Although playing video games can be fun and entertaining, the risks for violence far outweigh the benefits." Have students write a thesis statement using the same format: "Although ______, ______." BL OL

Indiana English/Language Arts Academic Standards

SE: 8.4, 8.4.10, 8.5.3

TWE: *Differentiated Instruction* 8.4, *Literature Focus Lesson* 8.4.2

Teach

W Writing

Citing Sources **Say:** If you're confused about when to cite sources, ask yourself these questions. If you answer "yes" to any of them, you need to cite your source.

- Did I use someone else's exact words?
- Did I summarize a particular idea?
- Did I use information that is not generally known or found in most books on a subject? OL

Cite Your Sources

W In your report, you need to give your readers information about any words, facts, or ideas that are not your own. If you use another writer's ideas or words without citing your source, you are plagiarizing. It is illegal and unethical to plagiarize! Your teacher may tell you how to cite your sources. Here are some guidelines for a common method called parenthetical documentation.

- Give the source in parentheses at the end of the sentence, paragraph, or passage that contains the information.
- For many print sources, you can simply give the author's last name and the page number where you found the information. If you mention the author in the sentence, include only the page number in parentheses at the end of the sentence.
- If the source doesn't give the author's name, give the source's title instead.
- See pages R23–R24 of the **Writing Handbook** or search the Internet for more information on citing sources and creating a Works Cited list.

Writing Tip

Researching *The Reader's Guide to Periodical Literature* can help you find magazine articles on your topic.

The chart below shows two ways to cite works in your research report.

Type	Explanation	Example
Author cited in text	Page number in parentheses	According to Brown . . . (172).
Book with one author	Name of author followed by page number(s)	(Downing 15).

Writing Tip

Text Features Save time by using the title page, table of contents, index, and appendix to judge whether a source will be useful and to find specific information within a book.

Use these examples and models as you make your list of works cited.

Type	Example
Article in a magazine	Johnson, Sally A. "A Beekeeper's Year." *Apiculture* (Sept. 1999): 40–44.
Article in a newspaper	Bertram, Jeffrey. "African Bees: Fact or Myth?" *Orlando Sentinel* 18 Aug. 1999: D2.
Book with one author	Stelley, Diane G. *Beekeeping: An Illustrated Handbook.* Blue Ridge Summit, PA: Tab, 1993.
Web site	Sanford, Malcolm T. "Small Hive Beetle." *Bee Culture* (Feb. 1999). 13 Feb. 2001 <http://www.bee.airoot.com/beeculture/99feb4.html>.

Additional Support

Reading in the Real World

College Tell students that plagiarism is considered a serious offense in college and can lead to failing a course or even to being expelled. Ask students to tell why they think plagiarism is taken so seriously in college. *(Possible responses: College is a place to learn; if you steal other people's ideas, you're not really learning. When you write papers, you're supposed to give your own ideas, not other people's.)* OL AL

WRITING WORKSHOP PART 1

Grammar Link

Simple Sentences

Simple sentences are some of the most important pieces of your paragraphs. They are simple but powerful because they convey your ideas clearly, so that your readers can easily understand you.

What Is a Simple Sentence?

A **simple sentence** has one complete subject and one complete predicate. The **complete subject** tells who or what a sentence is about. The **complete predicate** tells what the subject is, does, or has.

- Arturo and his sister / play basketball.

(Who plays basketball? Arturo and his sister. The complete subject is "Arturo and his sister." What do Arturo and his sister do? They play basketball. The complete predicate is "play basketball.")

Complete Subject	Complete Predicate
Ali	danced.
Ali and Leila	danced.
Ali and Leila	danced and sang.

In the examples, the sentences were made up of nouns and verbs and a few other words. Simple sentences are more interesting when you add elements like modifiers, verb phrases, or prepositional phrases.

Complete Subject	Complete Predicate
Ali	danced joyfully around the room.
Ali and Leila	danced across the stage.
The handsome, charming Ali	danced and sang.

Why Are Simple Sentences Important in My Writing?

Simple sentences are important because they allow you to say what you need to say without a lot of extra words. They also allow you to communicate with a larger audience because they are easier for some people to follow.

How Do I Do It?

- Decide on the subject of your sentence. Which noun or pronoun will you use?
- Decide on what the subject will do or think or feel. Which verb will you use?

Write to Learn Write three or four simple sentences—one about each main point you plan to make in your research report. 

Looking Ahead

Part 2 of this Writing Workshop is coming up later. Keep the writing you did here. In Part 2, you'll learn how to turn it into a clear, well-written research report!

Reading Fluency

Reading and Writing Some students might find that it helps them to analyze their drafts better if they read them aloud. Allow these students to work with partners. Students should take turns reading their own drafts to their partners and then discuss the content, including point of view and chronological order. Encourage students to use the bullet points under Start Writing! on page 319 as a guideline for discussing their drafts. AS

Teach

W1 Writing

Simple Sentences Help students identify complete subjects and predicates. Write these sentences on the board, and have students state the complete subject and the complete predicate. *(The complete subject is underlined once; the complete predicate is underlined twice.)*

1. Chuck and Aaron rode their bikes.
2. The doctors ran into the emergency room.
3. The mother called out to her toddler.
4. Jose and Marie won the art contest.
5. Rick watched the movie and ate a treat. EL BL OL

W2 Writing

Simple Sentences Have students share the simple sentences they wrote for the *Write to Learn* activity with a partner. Have each pair choose the best sentences between them and read them to the class aloud. Emphasize that good writing is most often simple and concise. AS

Assess

Have students exchange their papers with a partner and critique each other's work. After a few minutes, tell students to assess their work, make any needed revisions, and save it for later use.

Indiana English/Language Arts Academic Standards

SE: 8.4, 8.5.3, 8.6, 8.6.1

TWE: *Reading in the Real World* 8.5.3, *Reading Fluency* 8.7.6

Skimming and Scanning

Teaching Students to Skim and Scan

Why Is It Important?

- Skimming and scanning are very useful tools when readers need to find information quickly.
- Skimming includes looking quickly through the selection to get an idea of what it is about.
- Skimming is best used when students need to find out how helpful a document will be; they will not need to read it all if it does not contain the information they are searching for.
- Scanning is glancing over a selection to find specific information, such as a person's full name or an exact date.

How to Help Students Get It

- Tell students that they already use these skills.
- While skimming, students should read headlines, headings, captions, and part of the first paragraph to get an idea of what the piece is about.
- While scanning, students should look for key words that would help them.
- Tell students to know generally what they are looking for before they begin to skim or scan.

Reading to Answer the Big Question

The Games Kids Play

This article addresses the issue of violence in video games played by teenagers. Proponents of the games argue that teens know the difference between fantasy and reality. Opponents argue that playing violent games demeans women and increases aggressive behavior.

Cruise Control by Kevin O'Leary

To encourage better driving by teenagers, some courts issue bumper stickers displaying a phone number that other drivers can call to report bad driving. In this article, teens share their feelings about this practice.

Workshop Resources

Pacing (Days) Standard	Block	Lesson	Student Materials	Teacher Resources
1	1/2	Key Skill Lesson: Skimming and Scanning	Key Reading Skills Practice, p. 17 English Language Coach Review, p. 43	Bellringer Options Transparencies –Daily Language Practice 25 Read Aloud, Think Aloud Transparencies –Key Reading Skills 23 Presentation Plus!
1	1	"The Games Kids Play"	Glencoe Online Unit Vocabulary Review, p. 41 Academic Vocabulary Review, p. 44 English Language Coach Active Reading Graphic Organizer, p. 19 Literary Analysis, p. 18 StudentWorks Plus™ Online Student Edition Literature Classics Selection and Unit Assessments, p. 27	Puzzlemaker Skill Level Up!™ A Language Arts Game BookLink 3 Assessment by Learning Objective (Diagnostic and Formative) Interactive Tutor: Self-Assessment TeacherWorks Plus™
1		"Cruise Control"	Glencoe Online Unit Vocabulary Review, p. 41 Academic Vocabulary Review, p. 44 English Language Coach Active Reading Graphic Organizer, p. 21 StudentWorks Plus™ Online Student Edition Literature Classics Selection and Unit Assessments, p. 28	Literary and Text Analysis Transparencies 22 Puzzlemaker Skill Level Up!™ A Language Arts Game BookLink 3 Assessment by Learning Objective (Diagnostic and Formative) Interactive Tutor: Self-Assessment TeacherWorks Plus™

Keys for Unit Resource

- Blackline Master
- Workbook
- Supplemental Text
- CD-ROM
- DVD
- Transparency
- Web-based
- Fast File

Level Appropriate Code

AS = Activities for all students
AL = Activities for students working above grade level
OL = Activities for students working at grade level
BL = Activities for students working below grade level
EL = Activities for English language learners

Focus

BELLRINGER Options

Daily Language Practice Transparency 25
Focus Activity Ask: Should people your age be allowed to play video games that are rated Mature? Give reasons for your opinion. *(Responses will vary.)* OL

Teach

R Reading Skill

Skimming and Scanning

Ask: How is scanning different from skimming? *(Skimming looks at the whole text to get a general idea of what it's about; scanning looks for one particular piece of information.)* OL

V Vocabulary

Academic Vocabulary

Say: Look at the word *identify* at the bottom of page 322. What are some synonyms for identify? *(Possible responses: name, see, classify, pinpoint)* OL

READING WORKSHOP 2

Skills Focus

You will practice using these skills when you read the following selections:

- "The Games Kids Play," p. 326
- "Cruise Control," p. 332

Reading

- Skimming and scanning

Literature

- Identifying and evaluating text evidence

Vocabulary

- Understanding multiple-meaning words
- Academic Vocabulary: *identify*

Writing/Grammar

- Recognizing and correcting fragments

Skill Lesson

Skimming and Scanning

Learn It!

R

What Is It? Skimming and scanning are two ways to read a text.

- When you **skim** a text, you look it over quickly to get a general idea of what the whole thing is about. (When you previewed text in Reading Workshop 1 of this unit, you were skimming the text.)
- When you **scan** a text, you read it quickly to **identify,** or find, specific information. You also scan to find key words or phrases that point to the information you're looking for.

Analyzing Cartoons
If Peter thinks one page is a lot to read, he'd better learn to skim and scan! How might skimming and scanning help you understand what you read?

Indiana English/ Language Arts Academic Standards (pp. 322–323)

8.2 Comprehension and Analysis (Focus on Informational Text) Develop [reading] strategies…

For a complete description of the standards, see p. IN 11.

Academic Vocabulary

identify (eye DEN tuh fy) *v.* find; recognize

Additional Support

Literature Focus Lesson

Nonfiction Tell students that there are elements of nonfiction that can help them skim and scan more effectively.

- **Summaries** in the Table of Contents or at the beginning of an article tell you what the article will cover.
- **Subtitles** give information about portions of a nonfiction text.
- **Visuals,** such as illustrations and graphics, tell you more about a subject.

Have students look for these elements as they skim and scan the informational articles in this unit. OL

Why Are They Important? Skimming and scanning save you time while helping you read.

- Skimming text tells you quickly what a reading selection is about.
- Scanning helps you quickly find specific information.
- Skimming and scanning also help you remember what you've read.

R

Literature Online

Study Central Visit www.glencoe.com and click on Study Central to review skimming and scanning.

How Do I Do Them?

To skim, follow these steps:

1. Read the title of the selection and quickly look over the entire piece.
2. Read headings, captions, and part of the first paragraph.
3. Look at summaries, lists, subheadings, and illustrations.

To scan, follow these steps:

1. Decide what information you're looking for.
2. Move your eyes quickly over the lines of text, looking for key words or phrases that will help you locate that information.
3. Try not to read; just focus on finding the key words.

Here's what a student learned from skimming and scanning the article "Gymnasts in Pain: Out of Balance" in Reading Workshop 1.

From skimming this article I see right away that it's about girls who suffer injuries from gymnastics training. The photos and heads are about girls with injuries, and each paragraph talks about injuries, pain, and training.

I scanned to find names of gymnasts I admire: Alyssa Beckerman, Kelly Garrison, and my favorite, Carly Patterson.

Practice It!

1. **Skim** the poem "In Response to Executive Order 9066" on pages 312–313. Then write a quick summary of the poem in your Learner's Notebook.
2. **Scan** the Looking Ahead page for Unit 3 (p. 289) to find the skill lesson topic for Reading Workshop 3. Write it in your Learner's Notebook.

Use It!

Before you read the next two selections, skim them to see what they're about. For the After You Read questions, scan the selections to find answers.

Differentiated Instruction

Skimming Ask students to reread the How Do I Do Them? section on page 323. Then model this technique for students by speaking aloud as you skim "A Tremendous Trade" on page 293. Point out the title, the heads, and the illustrations, and make comments on each. Have students take notes in their Learner's Notebooks as you read, highlighting each feature that you skim on the page. Then, invite volunteers to speak aloud as they scan another selection in the book. Have them refer to their notes to help them skim the important features of the selection. EL BL

Teach

Study Central Have students access the Web site to review skimming and scanning and to complete a related activity.

R Reading Skill

Skimming and Scanning

Ask: What is the main benefit of skimming and scanning? *(They save time.)* BL **Ask:** Why might you scan a newspaper? *(Possible response: You might scan a newspaper to find a certain piece of information, such as when a football game will take place or who won an election.)* OL

Resources for page 323

Use Key Reading Skills Transparency 23 in *Read Aloud, Think Aloud* to help students practice skimming and scanning.

Indiana English/Language Arts Academic Standards

SE: 8.2

TWE: *Literature Focus Lesson* 8.2, 8.2.7, *Differentiated Instruction* 8.2

Teach

Did You Know?
The Entertainment Software Rating Board rates over 1,000 games each year. The board considers most games suitable for everyone. According to the ESRB Web site, in 2004, the ratings board gave games the following ratings:
54% received an E (Everyone) rating
33% received a T (Teen) rating
12% received an M (Mature) rating
fewer than 1% received an EC (Early Childhood) rating
fewer than 1% received an AO (Adults Only) rating

V Vocabulary

Related Words **Say:** One way to remember a new vocabulary word is to associate it with a word you already know. For example, a *portrait* is an image that shows what a person looks like. You often see portraits of famous people. One example is the portrait of George Washington on the dollar bill. How are the words *portrait* and *portray* related? *(Possible response: both show what something is like)* OL

Before You Read | The Games Kids Play

Did You Know?
Since the early 1990s, video games receive "safe-to-play" ratings. These ratings let parents and other people know whether the content of a video game is OK for kids. The ratings system was created by the Entertainment Software Rating Board (ESRB), which is part of the Entertainment Software Association (ESA). Here are the three main ESRB ratings:

- **Early Childhood, or EC:** The content of EC video games may be suitable for kids age three and older.
- **Everyone 10+, or E 10+:** The content of E 10+ video games may be suitable for kids age ten and older.
- **Mature, or M:** The content of M video games may be suitable for people age seventeen and older. These games may contain strong language, violence, and other material that people may find objectionable.

Vocabulary Preview

V

gory (GOR ee) *adj.* bloody; involving a lot of bloodshed **(p. 326)** *Some people like to play gory video games that show lots of physical violence.*

clamor (KLAM ur) *v.* to demand something in a noisy way **(p. 326)** *Kids and teenagers clamor for action-packed video games.*

modified (MOD uh fyd) *adj.* changed; altered **(p. 327)** *Sometimes teens play modified video games that are more violent than the original.*

portray (por TRAY) *v.* to show or represent someone or something **(p. 327)** *Many people do not approve of the glamorous way that video games portray gun violence.*

conclusive (kun KLOO siv) *adj.* definite; proven without doubt **(p. 327)** *The researchers thought they found conclusive evidence that the video games were harmful to kids.*

Write to Learn In your Learner's Notebook, rewrite the definition for each vocabulary word in your own words.

English Language Coach

Multiple-Meaning Words It is not unusual for a word to have many meanings. Remember to use the right definition for a word when you look it up in a dictionary. Pick the meaning that makes sense in the context in which you found the word while reading a selection. Below are four definitions for the word *conflict.* Read the definitions.

conflict (KON flikt) *n.* **1.** a military struggle or battle; **2.** a clash between people or ideas; **3.** tension between characters in a story
conflict (kun FLIKT) *v.* to be in disagreement with a person or thing

Partner Talk With a partner, read the following sentences. Then, using the definitions above and context clues in each sentence, decide which definition for **conflict** is correct.

1. My brother and I had a conflict over who would choose the TV show.
2. My ideas about what I should wear to school conflict with my mother's.
3. The conflict between the two countries resulted in many deaths.

Indiana English/Language Arts Academic Standards
(pp. 324–327)

8.1.3 Verify the meaning of a word in its context... **8.2 Comprehension and Analysis (Focus on Informational Text)** Develop [reading] strategies... **8.2.2** Analyze text that uses proposition and support patterns.

For a complete description of the standards, see p. IN 11.

Additional Support

English Language Coach

Multiple-Meaning Words Tell students that sometimes the pronunciation of a word changes depending on whether it is used as a noun or a verb. Ask students to look at the two definitions of *conflict.* Explain that usually nouns are stressed on the first syllable, while verbs are stressed on the last syllable. Have students note that *conflict* follows this principle. Give them a list of words that can be used as nouns and verbs, such as *contrast, object, permit, present,* and *record.* Have them work with a partner to make up sentences using the words correctly. EL BL

Skills Preview

Key Reading Skill: Skimming and Scanning

Before you read "The Games Kids Play," do the following:

- skim the title, subtitle, headings, and illustrations.
- scan the pages to identify, or find, sections that describe the effects of playing video games.

Write to Learn After you skim and scan the article, write down a few notes about what stands out in the article and what you want to learn from it.

Key Text Element: Evidence

To support their ideas and opinions, authors present **evidence**—details that help prove that an idea, position, or opinion is correct. There are many kinds of evidence. They include the following kinds of details:

- **Statistics,** or numbers, such as the number of people who attend baseball games each year or the yearly salary a baseball player makes.
- **Expert opinion,** or the beliefs of a person who has studied a subject carefully or is part of a profession important to the subject. For example, a quotation from the Surgeon General about the effects of smoking would be an expert opinion.
- **Results of studies,** or conclusions based on research. For example, if a university does a study of the effects of violence on kids, the conclusions of that study might be used as evidence.

E

Whole Class Discussion As a class, discuss the kinds of evidence that you find the most convincing.

Interactive Literary Elements Handbook
To review or learn more about the literary elements, go to www.glencoe.com.

Get Ready to Read

Connect to the Reading

Do you ever watch movies or TV shows that have violence in them? Have you played violent video games? How do you think being exposed to violence in entertainment affects you?

Whole Class Discussion As a class, discuss how you react to watching violence in movies, on television, or in video games. Discuss whether you think movies, shows, or games might cause people to be more violent.

Build Background

- The first video games were developed in the 1950s and 1960s. They ran on huge computers.
- In the 1970s coin-operated game machines were built, which led to video arcades—public places where people can play video games. Later, video game equipment was developed that allowed people to play the games in their homes.
- Even early in the history of video games, people worried about the violence in the games. Some studies suggest that people who play violent video games are less upset by real-life violence than people who don't play the games. R

Set Purposes for Reading

BIG Question Read the article "The Games Kids Play" to learn more about the effects of playing violent video games. Then decide whether the price the players and society pay is too high.

Set Your Own Purpose What else would you like to learn from the article to help you answer the Big Question? Write your own purpose on the "Games Kids Play" flap of the Reading Workshop 2 Foldable.

Keep Moving

Use these skills as you read "The Games Kids Play."

Teach

E Text Element

Evidence Ask: What kinds of evidence can authors use to support their opinions? *(Responses should include statistics, expert opinion, and results of studies.)* BL

R Reading Skill

Review Making Inferences

Say: Why might people who play a lot of violent video games, or watch a lot of violence on TV or at the movies, be less sensitive to real-life violence? *(Possible responses: People who see a lot of violence might start to see it as normal. Also, video games and movies often don't show the pain and suffering involved with violence and its long-term effects, so people might forget that violence has terrible consequences.)* AL

CheckPoint

Use the CheckPoint questions provided on Presentation Plus! to check for skimming and scanning skills. These questions can be used with interactive response keypads for immediate student feedback.

Reading in the Real World

College Students who are planning to further their education should have practice using evidence to support their point of view. Have students form small groups. Have each group either support or refute the link between video games and increased violence. Groups should find evidence online or in magazines or journals that supports their point of view. Encourage students to find statistics, expert opinions, and study results. Have students present their findings in a debate. AL

Indiana English/Language Arts Academic Standards
SE: 8.1.3, 8.2, 8.2.2
TWE: *English Language Coach* 8.1.3, *Reading in the Real World* 8.7.13

Teach

C Critical Thinking

Comprehension Ask: Why does the author refer to *Grand Theft Auto: Vice City* as a "gory game"? *(Possible response: It involves violence, breaking the law, and a lot of bloodshed.)* AL

E Text Element

Evidence Ask: In the first paragraph of "Real Life Vice?", what evidence is used to support the idea that violent video games spark violent behavior in those who play them? *(studies done by researchers and an expert opinion by a university professor)* OL

Readability Scores
Dale-Chall: 7.8
DRP: 64
Lexile: 1130

INFORMATIONAL TEXT
MAGAZINE
Current Events

Are mature video games too violent for teens?

PRESS START and you become Tommy Vercetti, an ex-convict with nothing to lose. You race down the streets of Vice City, scoring points by stealing cars, robbing banks, dealing drugs, and killing women. 1

The deadly gun battles and wild car chases are all part of the action of *Grand Theft Auto: Vice City*, one of the hottest video games around. But is the **gory** game harmless fun? C

Some people aren't so sure.

Vice City and a few other popular video games have mature ratings, meaning they might contain violent content, strong language, and nudity. M-rated games are recommended for people seventeen and up.

Even though M-rated games are meant for adults, their popularity often extends all the way down to elementary schools. And as kids and teens **clamor** to play the games, the debate is heating up over whether those kids are old enough to walk the violent streets of Vice City.

Real Life Vice? Researchers say playing M-rated games could spark violent behavior. They say studies have shown E

Vocabulary

gory (GOR ee) *adj.* bloody; involving a lot of bloodshed

clamor (KLAM ur) *v.* to demand something in a noisy way

Practice the Skills

1 **Key Reading Skill**

Skimming and Scanning Before you read this selection, skim the article to get a general idea of what it is about. What do the title, the subtitle, and the first paragraph tell you about the main topic of the article?

Additional Support

Differentiated Instruction

Pros-and-Cons Chart Write on the board the thesis *"Playing M-rated games increases violence."* Then create a two-column chart beneath it. Write the heading *Pro* above the first column and *Con* above the second column. Ask students to find evidence for and against the thesis in the article. Summarize the evidence and add it to the appropriate column. Then have students use the chart to discuss whether or not they think the pros outweigh the cons or vice versa and explain why. OL that people who play violent video games are more aggressive. "It increases the likelihood youngsters are going to react to **conflict** with aggression instead of cooperation," Iowa State University professor Craig Anderson told the *Star Tribune.* **2**

Experts point to Eric Harris as an example. Harris was one of two teens who opened fire in Columbine High School in Littleton, Colorado, in 1999, killing thirteen people before shooting himself. Harris had a **modified** version of *Doom,* an M-rated video game, on his Web site. His version resembled the Columbine shootings—two shooters, unlimited ammunition, and victims who couldn't shoot back. **3**

Some people say games like Vice City should be taken off the shelves because of the way they **portray** women. "I'm really offended that anybody would sell a [game] that has this kind of violence in it, that kicking a woman to death is a game, is fun," father Howard Winkler told the *Olympian.*

Just Fantasy Many parents and teens argue that no normal kid would be transformed by a video game's violence.

They say teens are smart enough to tell the difference between reality and fantasy.

"The guns, the weapons, blowing stuff up—it's just got something you can't do in real life," said 15-year-old Bryce Conley of Springfield, Missouri. "You might go shoot the cops in the game, but I'm not going to go out and shoot a cop in real life," he told newspapers.

The Interactive Digital Software Association[1] says there is no **conclusive** link between video games and violent behavior. They point out that as video games increase in popularity, youth violence in the United States declines.

What do you think? Should teens be allowed to play mature video games? **4** ○

1. The ***Interactive Digital Software Association,*** now called the Entertainment Software Association, works with companies that make and sell video games.

Vocabulary

modified (MOD uh fyd) *adj.* changed; altered

portray (por TRAY) *v.* to show or represent someone or something

conclusive (kun KLOO siv) *adj.* definite; proven without doubt

Practice the Skills

2 English Language Coach

Multiple-Meaning Words Look back at the definitions that you learned in the Before You Read section. What is the correct definition of the word **conflict** as it is used here? Write it in your Learner's Notebook.

3 Key Text Element

Evidence Whose expert opinion does the author quote as evidence that playing violent games may spark violent acts? What example do experts point to as evidence?

4 BIG Question

What do people gain from playing violent video games? What might they lose? What is the possible price society pays for violent video games? Write your answers on the "Games Kids Play" flap of the Reading Workshop 2 Foldable. Your response will help you complete the Unit Challenge later. BQ

Reading in the Real World

Citizenship Ask students to consider whose responsibility it is to keep young children from playing M-rated games: the people who make the games, the stores who sell them, parents, or lawmakers. What—if anything—should our society do to stop young children from playing violent games? Hold a class discussion about this issue. Invite as many students as possible to share their opinions. AS Then have students compile their responses in a pamphlet about the pros and cons of video game playing. OL

Teach

E Text Element

Evidence Ask: How does the example of Eric Harris support the expert opinion? *(Possible response: Eric Harris played violent video games and was also violent.)* OL **Ask:** How might people who disagree with the expert respond to this opinion? *(Possible response: They might say that there's no way to prove that Eric Harris was violent because he played violent video games.)* AL

BQ BIG Question

Ask: How do you think the writer of this article would answer the question, "Is the price of playing violent video games too high?" *(Possible response: The writer might say that if a definite link between violence and violent video games could be proven, the price would be too high.)* OL

Assess

Use the CheckPoint questions provided on Presentation Plus! to check for comprehension of the selection. These questions can be used with interactive response keypads for immediate student feedback.

Indiana English/Language Arts Academic Standards

SE: 8.1.3, 8.2, 8.2.2

TWE: *Differentiated Instruction* 8.2, *Reading in the Real World* 8.3

Assess

Resources for page 328

- Selection Quick Check, p. 23
- Selection and Unit Assessment, p. 27
- ExamView Assessment Suite
- Interactive Tutor: Self-Assessment

Students can respond to the *After You Read* items in their Learner's Notebooks or on a separate sheet of paper.

Answering the BIG Question

1. Possible response: The risk is more important because aggressive behavior can have terrible consequences. There are other ways to be entertained.
2. Playing violent video games reduces cooperation and increases aggression.
3. Arguments against video games: they increase aggression, are played by young children, and are offensive to women. Arguments in favor: players know the games aren't real; violent crimes by youth have declined as more video games are played.

Critical Thinking

4. Possible response: I think they should be eighteen, old enough to tell the difference between reality and fantasy.
5. Possible response: You could add more challenges, such as following a complicated map.
6. Responses will vary.

After You Read

The Games Kids Play

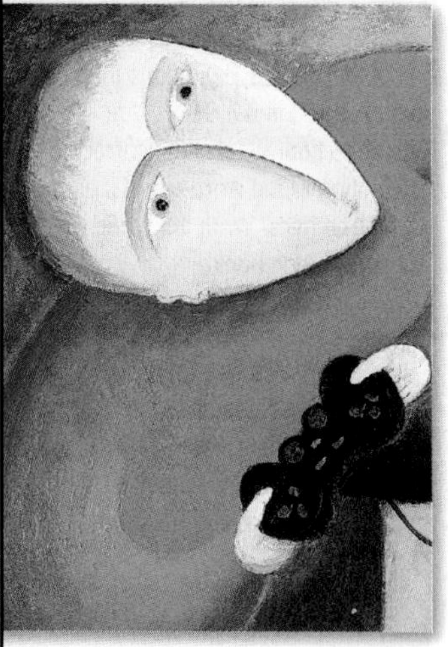

Answering the BIG Question

1. In your opinion, which is more important: a) the enjoyment that young people get from playing violent video games, or b) the risk that these young people might become more aggressive?
2. **Recall** What does the Iowa State University professor say about the effects of M-rated video games on people?
   TIP Right There
3. **Summarize** In the article, what arguments do people make against M-rated video games? What are the arguments in support of the games?
   TIP Think and Search

Critical Thinking

4. **Evaluate** In your opinion, how old should someone be to play M-rated video games with wild car chases and deadly gun battles? Why?
   TIP On My Own
5. **Analyze** How could you remove the violence from a game like *Grand Theft Auto: Vice City* but still keep it exciting? Explain.
   TIP On My Own
6. **Evaluate** If you knew for sure that children who play M-rated video games would become more violent, what advice would you give parents who have children your age?
   TIP On My Own

Write About Your Reading

Write an E-mail Use the RAFT system to write about "The Games Kids Play." The RAFT assignment provides four details:

Role: Write as if you are a parent, grandparent, or other adult.

Audience: You

Format: An e-mail

Topic: M-rated video games. Write what the adult would say to you about playing these games. Use details from the article to support your points.

Indiana English/Language Arts Academic Standards (pp. 328–329)

8.3 Comprehension and Analysis of Literary Text Respond to grade-level-appropriate literature... **8.5.7** Write for different purposes... **8.2 Comprehension and Analysis (Focus on Informational Text)** Develop [reading] strategies... **8.2.2** Analyze text that uses proposition and support patterns. **8.6 English Language Conventions**

For a complete description of the standards, see p. IN 11.

Write About Your Reading

To: nicole@internetcompany.net
Subject: Your birthday present
Hi Nicole-
I know you wanted the latest edition of *Grand Theft Auto.* Here's why I got you a CD player instead. You might have seen the article about video games in the paper. It said that playing violent games can make people less cooperative and more aggressive. That concerns me, so I decided to get you something without any guns or gore. Hope you like it. :)
Love,
Grandma

Skills Review

Key Reading Skill: Skimming and Scanning

7. How did skimming and scanning before you read help you understand the information discussed in "The Games Kids Play"? Explain.

Key Text Element: Evidence

8. What evidence does the Interactive Digital Software Association present to support its opinion that there is no conclusive link between video games and violent behavior?
9. What possible biases might the Digital Software Association have?

Vocabulary Check

Choose the best word from the list to complete each sentence below. Rewrite each sentence with the correct word in place.

gory clamor modified portray conclusive

10. Every year kids ______ for more and more action-filled video games.
11. Some people say that M-rated video games should be banned because of the way the games ______ women.
12. There are many nonviolent video games, but kids seem to like the really ______ ones.
13. The Video Game Association states that there is no ______ evidence that shows video games make kids more aggressive.
14. Some people say that games would be more acceptable if they were ______ to show less violence.
15. **Academic Vocabulary** Which arguments for or against M-rated video games would you **identify** as most reasonable?
16. **English Language Coach** Look up *game* in a dictionary. Write three sentences, each one using a different definition of the word.

Grammar Link: Fragments That Lack a Subject or a Verb

A **fragment** is an incomplete sentence. A sentence may be incomplete because it is missing a subject or because it is missing a verb.

- **Fragment:** Lila and Nathan.
  (What about Lila and Nathan? The verb is missing. To fix the fragment, add a verb.)
- **Complete:** Lila and Nathan have arrived.
- **Fragment:** Sold her scooter.
  (Who or what sold? The subject is missing. To fix the fragment, add a subject.)
- **Complete:** Emily sold her scooter.

Grammar Practice

Copy each item below. Write *subject* next to the item if the subject is missing. Write *verb* if the verb is missing. If the item is a complete sentence, write *C.*

17. Played games for a while.
18. I wanted to see whether I could get to the next level.
19. The loud, pounding sound effects.
20. Levels three and four.
21. Feeling the excitement of the game.
22. I played for several minutes.
23. No one else playing.
24. Everyone else had stopped.

Writing Application Review your Write About Your Reading activity. Check to make sure that you do not have any sentence fragments. Fix any mistakes.

Web Activities For eFlashcards, Selection Quick Checks, and other Web activities, go to www.glencoe.com.

Grammar Link: Fragments That Lack a Subject or a Verb

Grammar Practice

17. subject	21. subject
18. C	22. C
19. verb	23. verb
20. verb	24. C

Close

Hold a class discussion based on students' responses to question 4.

Skills Review

Key Reading Skill: Skimming and Scanning

7. Possible response: Skimming helped me understand that the article would present both sides of the issue of video games and violence.

Key Text Element: Evidence

8. Possible response: As games become more popular, the number of violent acts committed by kids goes down.
9. Possible response: The association wants as many people as possible to buy the games so its members can make more money.

Vocabulary Check

10. clamor
11. portray
12. gory
13. conclusive
14. modified

Academic Vocabulary

15. Possible response: I would identify the argument that fewer violent acts are committed by kids even though more people are playing video games.

English Language Coach

16. Possible responses: The basketball *game* went into overtime. The hunters were looking for big *game*. My little sister was *game* to ski the toughest hill.

Indiana English/Language Arts Academic Standards
SE: 8.2, 8.2.2, 8.3, 8.5.7, 8.6

Teach

Did You Know?
The Web site mentioned in this article, www.tellmy-mom.com, provides tips for safe driving. Included in the tips is a recommendation not to drive while talking on a cell phone. According to SADD (Students Against Destructive Decisions), 62 percent of teens drive while using a cell phone. Studies have shown that teens who drive while on a cell phone have the reaction time of a seventy-year-old driver. Studies have also shown that teens are four times more distracted than adults when using a cell phone while driving

V Vocabulary

Analyzing Word Structure

Say: One way to remember a new vocabulary word is to see if you already know its root. For example, the word *restrictions* is based on the root word *restrict.* If you already know that *to restrict* means "to limit," you can figure out that restrictions are limits. AS

Before You Read

Cruise Control

Did You Know?
More than forty states now have graduated driver licensing. Under this system young drivers must get driving experience before they receive full driving rights. In general, graduated driver licensing consists of these steps:

- **Learner** During this step the young driver cannot drive alone. A fully licensed driver who is at least twenty-one years old must be in the car with the driver.
- **Intermediate** During this step the young driver can drive alone but only during certain hours. Late-night driving is generally banned, and the number of teens who can be in the car with the driver is limited.
- **Full Licensure** During this last step the driver is given full driving privileges.

Statistics show that graduated drivers licensing programs save lives. Though many teenagers dislike the programs, all drivers are safer because of them.

Indiana English/Language Arts Academic Standards (pp. 330–333)

8.1.3 Verify the meaning of a word in its context... **8.2 Comprehension and Analysis (Focus on Informational Text)** Develop [reading] strategies... **8.3.6** Identify significant literary devices...which define a writer's style and use [them] to interpret a work.

For a complete description of the standards, see p. IN 11.

Vocabulary Preview

V

restrictions (ree STRIK shunz) *n.* limits to things one can and can't do **(p. 332)** *Many states are placing driving restrictions on teenagers.*

perceives (pur SEEVZ) *v.* understands something in a particular way; form of the verb *perceive* **(p. 333)** *The father said his daughter will start to drive better if she perceives that someone will report her driving errors.*

Write to Learn Using each vocabulary word correctly, write a few sentences about yourself or someone you know.

English Language Coach

Multiple-Meaning Words Below are definitions for two multiple-meaning words that you will read in "Cruise Control." As you read, watch for these words and use context clues to choose the correct meaning of each word.

trend (trend) *n.* **1.** a general tendency, movement, or direction toward something; **2.** a current fashion or style

trend (trend) *v.* to show a general movement toward something

sentence (SEN tens) *n.* **1.** a group of words with a verb and subject; **2.** a punishment from a court

sentence (SEN tens) *v.* to give a punishment for a crime

Partner Talk With a partner, read these sentences. Talk about which definition of the underlined word makes the most sense in each sentence.

1. Designer sunglasses are the latest trend.
2. "Write a complete sentence using all the vocabulary words," said Ms. Adams.
3. It's always a problem when gas prices trend up.
4. Jake was given a five-year prison sentence for stealing money from the store.
5. The judge will sentence Jake's brother next week.

Additional Support

Literature Focus Lesson

Anecdotes Writers have many choices about the way they present information to their readers. One way to appeal to readers is to include anecdotes, brief accounts or stories about real people. By telling stories about people, writers can present information in a casual, entertaining way. Have students look for anecdotes in "Cruise Control." Have them respond to the following questions.

- What stories does the writer tell?
- Who are the people in the stories?
- How do these stories provide information about driving restrictions?
- Why might they be more interesting to readers than just facts or statistics? OL

Skills Preview

Key Reading Skill: Skimming and Scanning

Before you read "Cruise Control," do these things:

- Scan the selection to get a general idea of what it is about. Look for the title, subtitle, headings, and any photos or illustrations in the selection.
- Skim the paragraphs to get an idea of the topic of the article.
- Plan how you will read this selection. For example, will you read the graphics first or read the text and then check the graphics?

Write to Learn In your Learner's Notebook, write a list of the things you learned by skimming and scanning this article. To get more out of your reading, refer to this list as you read the article.

Literary Element: Humor

Some informational articles use humor to engage readers and make a point. One way that writers create humor is unexpected silly twists of language. Two techniques are hyperbole and puns.

Hyperbole (hy PER buhl ee) is making huge exaggerations about something to emphasize a point—for example, *Her eyes were as big as saucers.*

A **pun** is a play on words—for example, *Joe: "My grammar's not so good." Pete: "Well I hope she feels better soon!"*

As you read the following article, use these tips to recognize the humor.

- Watch for hyperbole, or exaggeration of ideas.
  Notice words that seem out of place, or too strong for the situation being described.
- Look for puns used to bring attention to a point.
  Think about what the writer might be trying to say with the pun.

Partner Talk Express the following idea as a hyperbole: He is very, very tall.

Get Ready to Read

Connect to the Reading

Think about a time you thought about breaking a rule or were caught breaking a rule. Are you more likely to follow the rules if you think you will get caught? Why or why not?

Write to Learn In a few sentences describe a time when you or someone you know got caught breaking rules. What happened? Who caught you? Were there any consequences?

Build Background

C
- Teenage drivers are more likely than older drivers to speed, run red lights, and make illegal turns. Teenagers are also less likely to wear seatbelts.
- Teenagers are four times more likely to be involved in driving accidents than older drivers.
- The risk of a car crash is greatest during the first year a driver has his or her license.

Set Purposes for Reading

BIG Question Read "Cruise Control" to find out how some parents use a creative way to help their teenagers practice better driving habits.

L

Set Your Own Purpose What else would you like to learn from the article to help you answer the Big Question? Write your own purpose on the "Cruise Control" flap of the Reading Workshop 2 Foldable for Unit 3.

Interactive Literary Elements Handbook
To review or learn more about the literary elements, go to www.glencoe.com.

Keep Moving

Use these skills as you read "Cruise Control."

Teach

L Literary Element

Humor Have students identify the following sentences as hyperbole and puns:

- I'm so hungry I could eat a horse! *(hyperbole)*
- I hated my haircut, but now it's growing on me. *(pun)*
- There must have been a thousand people in line for tickets at the mall movie theater. *(hyperbole)* BL OL

C Critical Thinking

Analysis Say: Look at the statistics in the *Build Background* section. Why do you think teens make these mistakes? *(Possible response: Teens are younger and less experienced drivers. Some of them are more irresponsible than adults.)* AL

Interactive Literary Elements Handbook Have students access the Web site to improve their understanding of humor.

Reading in the Real World

Citizenship Encourage students to find out if their state has any special requirements for young drivers, such as graduated licensing programs. You might also invite a traffic officer or driver's education instructor to talk to students and answer their questions about teen drivers and safety. AS Then have students work in small groups to put together pamphlets about safe driving. Encourage them to use the library and the Internet, as well as information gathered from the driver education presentation to do research. Have them present their work to the rest of the class. OL

Indiana English/Language Arts Academic Standards
SE: 8.1.3, 8.2, 8.3.6
TWE: *Literature Focus Lesson* 8.2; *Reading in the Real World* 8.2.5, 8.7.12

Teach

L Literary Element

Humor **Say:** People refer to driving around with no particular destination as "cruising." What is the pun in the title of this article? *(Possible response: Cruise control in a car is a function that allows a driver to keep a set speed. This article is about how parents control teenage "cruising.")* AL

C Critical Thinking

Evaluation **Ask:** Do you think it is effective for the writer of this piece to choose a humorous tone? Why or why not? *(Responses will vary. Some students may say that it captures the attention of a teenage audience while others may say this is a serious topic, and the humorous tone is inappropriate.)* OL AL

Readability Scores
Dale-Chall: 6.5
DRP: 55
Lexile: 1070

INFORMATIONAL TEXT
MAGAZINE
Teen People

CRUISE CONTROL 1

L

New Teen Driving **Restrictions** Put Parents in the Rear Window

by Kevin O'Leary

Anne Rekerdres likes to call it "the everlasting punishment." When the 17-year-old North Dallas senior came home with a speeding ticket in March, her dad, Randy, 47, slapped the back bumper of her beloved '92 red Ford Explorer with a sticker that read: "How's my driving? 1-866-2-TELLMOM." "It was humiliating," says Anne. But there was nothing she could do. "I told her, 'If the sticker comes off,'" recalls Randy, "'there go your keys.'"

Tattletale bumper stickers, which publicize where to call to notify parents about bad driving, are a trend that won't end soon. Besides the Web site on which Anne's dad bought hers, two other services—the San Diego-based Dad's Eyes (877-DADS-EYES) and 800-4-MYTEEN of Arlington, Texas—also allow strangers to play Big Mother. 2 The stickers have even become popular in Texas's municipal court[1] system, where several judges regularly **sentence** speeding teens to six months with the embarrassing banners. 3

1. A ***municipal court*** manages court cases for a city.

Vocabulary

restrictions (ree STRIK shunz) *n.* limits to things one can and can't do

Practice the Skills

1 Key Reading Skill

Skimming and Scanning
Before you read, skim and scan the selection to get an idea of what the article is about. What words and other features tell you what the topic of the article is?

2 Literary Element

Humor: Pun "Big Mother" is a pun referring to the novel *1984* by George Orwell. In that novel, set in the future, Big Brother watches over everything that happens. "Big Brother" came to mean someone who has complete control over people's lives. How does this pun help you understand the author's attitude toward his subject?

3 English Language Coach

Multiple-Meaning Words
Review the definitions you learned for the word *sentence*. What is the meaning of *sentence* as it is used here? Write the meaning in your Learner's Notebook.

Additional Support

Literature Focus Lesson

Pun and Hyperbole Have students work in groups to design other bumper stickers that might encourage teenagers to drive safely. Encourage them to use what they have learned from the article to come up with both serious and funny slogans. Remind them also about the differences they've learned about pun and hyperbole. Then have them pick their favorite slogan and draw a bumper sticker. Post the stickers on a "Driver Safety" wall in the classroom. AS

But do the stickers actually make teens drive more safely? "As long as she **perceives** she can be reported," says Randy, "it works." His attitude is exactly what angers Anne. "What if someone called and said, 'I saw your daughter run a red light,' and I didn't? Who's he going to believe? It's a trust-breaker." 4 ❍

C

You Are So Busted!

"I got a ticket for doing 45 in a 30 zone,[2] and the judge ordered me to have a sticker for six months. My mom thought it was unfair too. I haven't tried to cover it or anything, but it came off when I washed my car. I had to get another one."

–Missy Leavell, 19, Cleburne, Texas

"I always think about the sticker when I'm driving. When [other drivers] do something stupid, sometimes I feel like I want to cut them off, but then I remember the sticker is there, and I stay calm. When I first got it, people were like, 'What's that?' But then it just got old. I don't get teased anymore." 5

–Stephanie Collins, 16, Green Bay, Wis.

2. Here, ***zone*** refers to the speed zone, which was 30 miles per hour. Leavell was driving 15 miles above the limit.

Vocabulary

perceives (pur SEEVZ) *v.* understands something in a particular way

Practice the Skills

4 **Reviewing Skills**

Connecting How do you think it would feel to be driving alone for the first time? Do you think a "How's My Driving" bumper sticker would make you a better driver? Explain.

5 **BIG Question**

Do you think putting bumper stickers on the cars teenagers drive is worth the embarrassment the teens might feel? Explain. Write your answer on the "Cruise Control" flap of the Reading Workshop 2 Foldable for Unit 3.

Teach

C Critical Thinking

Comprehension Ask: What is Randy's reason for putting the sticker on Anne's car? *(He thinks that if she knows she can be reported, she'll drive safely.)* **BL** **Ask:** Does Stephanie Collins's story support or contradict Randy's opinion? *(Possible response: It supports it. Stephanie says when she thinks about doing something foolish, she thinks of the bumper sticker and stops herself.)* **OL**

Assess

Use the CheckPoint questions provided on Presentation Plus! to check for comprehension of the selection. These questions can be used with interactive response keypads for immediate student feedback.

Differentiated Instruction

Creating Advertisements Have students create an advertisement for Dad's Eyes. Tell them the ad should do the following:

- Tell the purpose of the service
- Tell why the service is needed
- Persuade parents to use the service

Tell students to use facts, opinions, and anecdotes from the article, along with a vivid illustration, to convince their readers. Hold a class contest to choose the best ad. **OL**

Indiana English/Language Arts Academic Standards

SE: 8.1.3, 8.2, 8.3.6

TWE: *Literature Focus Lesson* 8.5.7, *Differentiated Instruction* 8.5.7

Assess

Resources for page 334

- Selection Quick Check, p. 24
- Selection and Unit Assessment, p. 28
- ExamView Assessment Suite
- Interactive Tutor: Self-Assessment

Students can respond to the *After You Read* items in their Learner's Notebooks or on a separate sheet of paper.

Answering the BIG Question

1. Possible response: Some would say they were too high a price because they're embarrassing; others would say they're lifesavers.
2. Dad's Eyes and 800-4-MYTEEN

Critical Thinking

3. Possible response: The author thinks they're invasive. He uses the words *tattletale* and *embarrassing* to describe them.
4. Possible response: I think they're a great idea. They make kids stop and think about their actions.
5. Possible response: I would tell because I'd want the driver to know there are consequences for bad decisions.
6. Possible response: These laws are useful because they save lives.

After You Read

Cruise Control

CRUISE CONTROL

Answering the BIG Question

1. Do you think the teens interviewed would say the bumper stickers were too high a price to pay for breaking traffic regulations? Why or why not? Use specific details from the article to support your views.
2. **Recall** Name two places mentioned in the article where parents can get bumper stickers for their teenagers' cars.
   TIP **Right There**

Critical Thinking

3. **Infer** How do you think the author of the article feels about the bumper sticker programs? List words or phrases from the article to support your answer.
   TIP **Author and Me**
4. **Evaluate** How do *you* feel about the bumper sticker program? Use what you learned from reading the article and your own experiences to support your opinion.
   TIP **Author and Me**
5. **Apply** Imagine that you are riding in a car when another car suddenly swerves in front of you and almost causes an accident. The car has a "Tell Mom" or "Dad's Eyes" bumper sticker on it and a telephone number. Would you call the number to report the driver? Why or why not?
   TIP **On My Own**
6. **Evaluate** Many governments protect their citizens by limiting what individuals can do. Examples include laws about the legal driving age and laws against speeding. Do you think these laws are useful? Why or why not?
   TIP **On My Own**

Indiana English/Language Arts Academic Standards
(pp. 334–335)

8.3 Comprehension and Analysis of Literary Text Respond to grade-level-appropriate literature… **8.7.11** Deliver oral responses to literature… **8.2 Comprehension and Analysis (Focus on Informational Text)** Develop [reading] strategies… **8.3.6** Identify significant literary devices… **8.6 English Language Conventions**

For a complete description of the standards, see p. IN 11.

Talk About Your Reading

Small Group Discussion In small groups, talk about other ways to help people become safer drivers. Do you think a bumper sticker program would work well for adults too? Why or why not? Have someone in the group jot down everyone's ideas, then present them to the class.

Talk About Your Reading

If students are having difficulty thinking of ways to help people, offer the following suggestions and have students evaluate their effectiveness:

- ad campaigns
- stricter laws
- more severe punishments for breaking the law

Skills Review

Key Reading Skill: Skimming and Scanning

7. How did skimming and scanning this article help you get more out of reading it?

Literary Element: Humor

8. In the first sentence of this article, Anne Rekerdres calls the bumper stickers "everlasting punishment." Later you learn that these bumper stickers last only a short time, so the word *everlasting* is a huge exaggeration. How does this hyperbole, or exaggeration, add to your understanding of the article?

Reviewing Skills: Connecting

9. After reading "Cruise Control," how do you feel about getting your driver's license? Will you get one as soon as you are old enough? Explain.

Vocabulary Check

Match each vocabulary word with a word or phrase that means the same thing or nearly the same thing. Each word will be used more than once.

restrictions **perceives**

10. controls
11. recognizes
12. sees
13. believes
14. understands
15. limitations
16. realizes
17. rules

English Language Coach

18. The author of the article uses the multiple-meaning word *trend.* Look back at the definitions for *trend* listed on page 330 and write sentences correctly using the definitions.

Grammar Link: Dependent Clauses as Sentence Fragments

As you've learned, a sentence may be a **fragment,** or incomplete, because it is missing a subject or a verb. Another type of fragment is a dependent clause punctuated as if it were a complete sentence. A dependent clause has a subject and a verb, but it does not express a complete thought, so it cannot stand alone as a sentence.

- After we study.

  (What should we do after we study? The sentence has a subject and verb, but it does not express a complete thought.)

To fix the fragment, connect it to an independent clause, or complete thought.

- After we study, **we will watch a movie.**

Grammar Practice

The following paragraph has four fragments. Two are dependent-clause fragments and two are fragments that lack a subject and verb. Copy the paragraph. Then underline and revise the fragments. (There is more than one right way to fix them.)

I am learning to play the drums. I really like it. Pounding on the drums is fun and helps me relax. Though my family sometimes complains about the noise. I try to practice everyday anyway. Also, I meet every Wednesday afternoon with a music teacher. For an hour-long lesson. I plan to try out for the band. When I start high school next year. By then I think I will be able to read music well enough. To play with other musicians.

Web Activities For eFlashcards, Selection Quick Checks, and other Web activities, go to www.glencoe.com.

Skills Review

Key Reading Skill: Skimming and Scanning

7. Possible response: By skimming and scanning, I knew what the topic was before I started to read the article more thoroughly. I had time to consider my opinion before reading to learn more.

Literary Element: Humor

8. Possible response: By including the hyperbole, the writer is saying he understands that Anne is embarrassed by the punishment and thinks it's too severe.

Reviewing Skills: Connecting

9. Possible response: I want my license as soon as I'm old enough, but I'll be sure to drive safely so my parents don't buy one of those stickers.

English Language Coach

18. Possible response: Following a recent trend, the city council proposed a ban on smoking in public places. Playing video games is a trend with young people.

Close

Have students tell what they learned about the Big Question from reading this article.

Vocabulary Check

10. restrictions
11. perceives
12. perceives
13. perceives
14. perceives
15. restrictions
16. perceives
17. restrictions

Grammar Link: Dependent Clauses as Sentence Fragments

The following fragments should be underlined: Revisions will vary.
Though my family sometimes complains about the noise.
For an hour-long lesson.
When I start high school next year.
To play with other musicians.

Indiana English/Language Arts Academic Standards
SE: 8.2, 8.3, 8.3.6, 8.6, 8.7.11

Understanding Text Structures

Teaching Students to Understand Text Structures

Why Is It Important?

- Informational texts have common structures. Understanding these structures helps students predict how a writer will present information.
- Text structures provide readers clues about information and where to find it.
- Text structures are conventions that writers use to help readers. As such, they are conventions that students need to learn to become effective writers.

How to Help Students Get It

- Focus on common text structures and how they can help readers predict the information presented in a text.
- As an example, discuss the difference between a problem-and-solution text structure and a compare-and-contrast structure. Ask students to consider how understanding this difference might help them with comprehending selections and with setting purposes for reading.

Reading to Answer the Big Question

Flowers for Algernon by Daniel Keyes
Mentally handicapped Charlie Gordon participates in an experiment to triple his intelligence. After an operation, Charlie's intelligence increases rapidly to the genius level. At his peak, he observes a decline in a laboratory mouse named Algernon who had the same surgery. Charlie is helpless to stop his own regression.

Workshop Resources

Pacing (Days) Standard	Block	Lesson	Student Materials	Teacher Resources
1	1/2	Key Skill Lesson: Understanding Text Structures	Key Reading Skills Practice, p. 23 English Language Coach Review, p. 43	Bellringer Options Transparencies –Daily Language Practice 26–27 –Selection Focus 7 Read Aloud, Think Aloud Transparencies –Key Reading Skills 29 Presentation Plus!
1	1	from *Flowers for Algernon* (1)	Glencoe Online Unit Vocabulary Review, p. 41 Academic Vocabulary Review, p. 44 English Language Coach Active Reading Graphic Organizer, p. 25 Literary Analysis, p. 24 StudentWorks Plus™ Online Student Edition Literature Classics Selection and Unit Assessments, p. 29	Literary and Text Analysis Transparencies 27 Puzzlemaker Skill Level Up!™ A Language Arts Game BookLink 3 Assessment by Learning Objective (Diagnostic and Formative) Interactive Tutor: Self-Assessment TeacherWorks Plus™
1		from *Flowers for Algernon* (2)	Glencoe Online Unit Vocabulary Review, p. 41 Academic Vocabulary Review, p. 44 English Language Coach Active Reading Graphic Organizer, p. 25 StudentWorks Plus™ Online Student Edition Literature Classics Selection and Unit Assessments, p. 30	Literary and Text Analysis Transparencies 19 Puzzlemaker Skill Level Up!™ A Language Arts Game BookLink 3 Assessment by Learning Objective (Diagnostic and Formative) Interactive Tutor: Self-Assessment TeacherWorks Plus™

Keys for Unit Resource

- Blackline Master
- Workbook
- Supplemental Text
- CD-ROM
- DVD
- Transparency
- Web-based
- Fast File

Level Appropriate Code

- **AS** = Activities for all students
- **AL** = Activities for students working above grade level
- **OL** = Activities for students working at grade level
- **BL** = Activities for students working below grade level
- **EL** = Activities for English language learners

Focus

BELLRINGER Options

- **Selection Focus Transparency 7**
- **Daily Language Practice Transparency 26–27**

Focus Activity

Say: Imagine you could have an operation that would make you smarter than anyone you know. What would be the benefits of getting the operation? What might be the disadvantages? *(Possible benefits: doing well on tests, skipping grades, getting a good job; possible disadvantages: not having the same interests as others, being different)* AS

Teach

R Reading Skill

Understanding Text Structures **Say:** Look at the *What Is It?* section. What does it tell you about text structures in this section? *(Writers use different text structures, or ways of organizing their text, according to what they're writing about. There are four commonly used text structures.)* BL

READING WORKSHOP 3

Skills Focus

You will practice using these skills when you read the following selections:

- "Flowers for Algernon," Part 1, p. 340
- "Flowers for Algernon," Part 2, p. 358

Reading

- Recognizing and understanding text structures

Literature

- Understanding irony
- Analyzing the effects of foreshadowing

Vocabulary

- Understanding multiple-meaning words in context
- Academic Vocabulary: *structure*

Writing/Grammar

- Correcting run-on sentences
- Understanding compound subjects and predicates

Indiana English/Language Arts Academic Standards (pp. 336–337)

8.2 Comprehension and Analysis (Focus on Informational Text) Develop [reading] strategies...
8.2.7 Analyze the structure... of informational materials...

For a complete description of the standards, see p. IN 11.

Skill Lesson

Understanding Text Structures

Learn It!

What Is It? What do you think of when you hear the word **structure?** You probably think of something that you can see, like a house or a bridge. But writing has structure too. Authors organize their writing in a specific way for a specific purpose. These patterns of organization are called **text structures.**

R Here are some common text structures:

- **Comparison and contrast** shows how things are the same and different.
- **Cause and effect** shows how events are related.
- **Problem and solution** describes a problem and offers solutions.
- **Chronological order** presents events in time order.

Analyzing Cartoons
Why isn't this a logical solution? What else could they do to solve their money problem?

Academic Vocabulary

structure (STRUK chur) *n.* the arrangement or organization of parts in a body or system

Additional Support

English Language Coach

Building Background The comic strip *Hägar the Horrible* was created by Richard Brown. His son Chris suggested several gags for the strip and then began drawing it after his father died in 1989. Hägar remains the same character: On the outside, he's a fierce Viking warrior, but on the inside, he's a man who loves his family and his wife Helga's cooking. Today the strip appears in more than 1,900 papers in 13 different languages. Have students tell the problem and solution being discussed in the strip. BL

Why Is It Important? Recognizing, or identifying, the text structure in a reading selection helps you locate the writer's important points and understand how ideas relate to each other.

How Do I Do It? When you read, watch for signal words and phrases that tell you the text structure. Study the lists below.

- **Comparison and contrast:** like, as, however, similarly, on the other hand, but, in contrast
- **Cause and effect:** because, has led to, as a result, so, therefore
- **Problem and solution:** so, need, answer, issue
- **Chronological order:** first, second, then, last, finally, earlier, later

R

Literature Online

Study Central Visit www.glencoe.com and click on Study Central to review using text structures.

Here's how a student figured out the cause-and-effect structure of this paragraph from "Gymnasts in Pain: Out of Balance."

> The sport's obsession with weight and diet, especially within the U.S. national team program, often has led to eating disorders. U.S. gymnasts competing in the 2001 World Championships said they were provided so little food that family members smuggled snacks into the team hotel by stuffing them inside teddy bears.

The phrase "has led to" makes me think what comes before the phrase is a cause and what comes after is the effect. The sport's obsession with weight and diet is the cause of eating disorders (the effect). The paragraph also says the gymnasts get so little food that family members sneak them snacks. That's cause and effect too.

Practice It!

With a partner, decide which text structure is indicated by each of these signal words and phrases.

next • as a result • solve • in contrast

Use It!

As you read "Flowers for Algernon," look for clues that can help you figure out the text structures in the story.

Differentiated Instruction

Time Order Words Write the words *First, Second,* and *Next* on the board. Work with students to develop instructions for a familiar task, such as using the spell checker to check a word processing document. After writing the final step, ask, What word could we use to introduce this step? *(finally, last)* What would happen if someone did the steps out of order? *(Answers will vary.)* EL BL

Teach

Study Central Have students access the Web site to review understanding text structures and to complete a related activity.

R Reading Skill

Understanding Text Structures To help students understand the uses of different text structures, have them name which one a writer might use to:

- tell how two new cars are alike and different *(comparison and contrast)*
- tell a story about what happened over a period of a week *(chronological order)*
- tell the series of events that led to a conflict *(cause and effect)*
- tell possible ways to prevent traffic accidents *(problem and solution)*
- tell the results of a poor diet *(cause and effect)*

OL

Resources for page 337

Use Key Reading Skills Transparency 29 in *Read Aloud, Think Aloud* to help students practice understanding text structures.

Indiana English/Language Arts Academic Standards
SE: 8.2, 8.2.7
TWE: *English Language Coach* 8.3, *Differentiated Instruction* 8.5.5

Teach

More About the Author

As a photographer, editor, teacher, and merchant seaman, Daniel Keyes has met and observed a wide range of people. This experience is reflected in his 1959 short story "Flowers for Algernon," which won the Hugo Award for Science Fiction Achievement the following year. Keyes adapted the work into a best-selling novel, a drama, and a movie, *Charly.* In 2000 he described how he came to write the book in *Algernon, Charlie and I: A Writer's Journey.*

Before You Read

Flowers for Algernon, Part 1

Daniel Keyes

Meet the Author

Daniel Keyes was born in 1927 in New York. In college he studied psychology. He has said that he loves to explore the "complexities of the human mind," and his writing shows his interest in personality and intelligence. Mr. Keyes has won literary awards for "Flowers for Algernon." See page R3 of the Author Files in the back of the book for more on Daniel Keyes.

Literature Online

Author Search For more about Daniel Keyes, go to www.glencoe.com.

Indiana English/Language Arts Academic Standards (pp. 338–353)

8.1.3 Verify the meaning of a word in its context... **8.2 Comprehension and Analysis (Focus on Informational Text)** Develop [reading] strategies such as...identifying and analyzing structure and organization... **8.3.6** Identify significant literary devices, such as...irony, which define a writer's style and use [them] to interpret a work.

For a complete description of the standards, see p. IN 11.

Vocabulary Preview

You probably know most of the words in this part of "Flowers for Algernon," but you might not recognize the spelling. That's because the story is written as if the main character, Charlie, is keeping a diary or journal. Charlie misspells many of the words.

English Language Coach

Multiple-Meaning Words Remember that if you read a word you know but it doesn't make sense in context, the word has multiple meanings.

Look at the two words below. Study the meanings that are given. You'll see these words in "Flowers for Algernon."

Decide which definition makes sense for each word when you see it in context as you read the story.

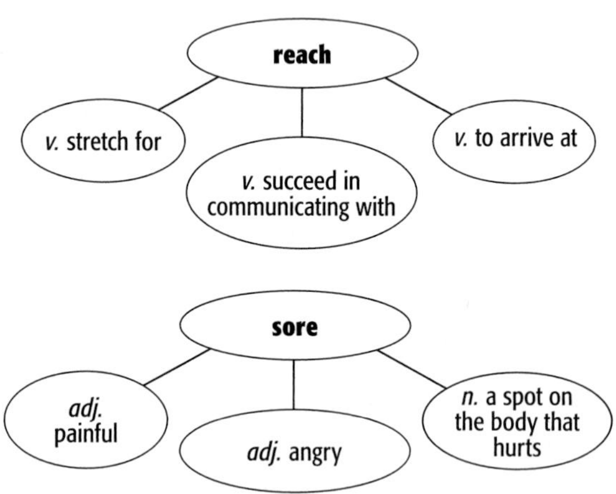

Partner Talk Read these sentences. Work with a partner to decide which meaning given above is the right one for each sentence.

1. I was sore at my older brother because he wouldn't let me play ball with him.
2. I tried to reach the cookies on the top shelf, but I was too short.
3. My arm is sore after throwing so many pitches.
4. Did you reach the student who needed help?

Additional Support

Author Search To expand students' appreciation of Daniel Keyes, have them access the Web site for additional information and resources.

Reading in the Real World

Career Although this story originally appeared in a science fiction magazine, the tests the scientists give Charlie are real. The professionals working with Charlie include:

- neurosurgeons, who study and operate on the brain
- psychiatrists, who study the workings of the mind and prescribe medications
- psychologists, who study behavior, including thoughts, feelings, and learning abilities and often do therapy with clients

Have students who are interested in these fields research one of them and present their findings to the class. AL

Skills Preview

Key Reading Skill: Understanding Text Structures

These signal words and phrases can tell you how the parts of a text are related.

- **Comparison and Contrast:** similarly, on the other hand, in contrast to, but, however
- **Cause and Effect:** so, because, as a result
- **Problem and Solution:** need, issue, solve
- **Chronological Sequence:** first, next, then, later

Think-Pair-Share Write two sentences with signal words that show one of the text structures listed above. Then exchange papers with a partner and see whether he or she can tell what text structure you used.

Key Literary Element: Irony

You probably already know about **verbal irony.** "Nice job," someone says, when they really mean you messed it up. There's a different kind of irony that you will find when you read. It's called **dramatic irony** and it happens when you, as a reader, know something a character doesn't. For example, suppose the narrator has just told you that there's a fire-breathing dragon around the next corner and the main character says, "This looks like a nice safe path." That's dramatic irony.

As you read, use these tips to understand irony.

- Pay attention to a character's thoughts about himself or herself or about a situation.
  Do you have knowledge that he or she doesn't?

Get Ready to Read

Connect to the Reading

Have you ever wished your life would change overnight? What would you wish to change? What would happen if your wish for change really came true?

Write to Learn If you could make one wish to change your life, what would it be? In your Learner's Notebook, describe something you'd like to change and tell how that change would make your life better.

Build Background

- Psychologists study how people behave, think, learn, and feel about things.
- There are many tests to measure human intelligence. The Intelligence Quotient, or IQ, is one such measure.
- In recent years, scientists have come to think that people have "multiple intelligences"—special abilities in language, music, art, and physical coordination, for example.

R

Set Purposes for Reading

Read "Flowers for Algernon" to find out what happens to Charlie Gordon and his dream of growing smart.

Set Your Own Purpose What else would you like to learn from the selection to help you answer the Big Question? Write your own purpose on the "Flowers for Algernon," Part 1, flap of the Reading Workshop 3 Foldable.

Literature Online

Interactive Literary Elements Handbook
To review or learn more about the literary elements, go to www.glencoe.com.

Keep Moving

Use these skills as you read "Flowers for Algernon," Part 1.

Differentiated Instruction

Multiple Intelligences Dr. Howard Gardner identified nine kinds of intelligence: linguistic (verbal and writing skills), logical-mathematical (ability to see numerical patterns), spatial (ability to visualize), bodily-kinesthetic (ability to control movement), musical (ability to produce and appreciate music), interpersonal (people skills), intrapersonal (self-understanding), naturalist (ability to recognize and categorize plants, animals, and natural objects), and existentialist (asking deep questions about life). Explain each intelligence to students and ask them to consider which of the intelligences they think are most prominent in them and why. OL AL

Teach

R Reading Skill

Review Making Inferences

Say: In the past few years, scientists have found that a person's Emotional Intelligence can be as important as his or her IQ. What might an Emotional Intelligence test measure? *(Possible responses: how well you interact with others; your ability to communicate; your ability to react to situations in a healthy way)* AL

Literature Online

Interactive Literary Elements Handbook Have students access the Web site to improve their understanding of irony.

Indiana English/Language Arts Academic Standards
SE: 8.1.3, 8.2, 8.3.6
TWE: *Reading in the Real World* 8.3, *Differentiated Instruction* 8.3

Teach

Viewing the Illustration

Say: The Rorschach test is a psychological test based on what people see in inkblots. Do you see any pictures in the inkblot? *(Responses will vary.)* **Say:** As you read, notice the different ways that Charlie responds to the inkblot test. AS

C Critical Thinking

Comprehension Ask: What do you learn about Charlie from his first progress report? *(Possible responses: He is 37. He just had a birthday. He is not a good speller. He has a doctor who wants to make him smarter in some way. He knows someone named Miss Kinnian.)* BL

R Reading Skill

Review Making Inferences

Ask: What details in Charlie's report make him seem much younger than 37? *(Possible responses: his spelling; his sentence construction)* OL

Readability Scores
Dale-Chall: 5.8
DRP: 49
Lexile: 850

READING WORKSHOP 3

Flowers for Algernon

by Daniel Keyes

progris riport 1–martch 5 1965

Dr. Strauss says I shud rite down what I think and evrey thing that happins to me from now on. I dont know why but he says its importint so they will see if they will use me. I **C** hope they use me. Miss Kinnian says maybe they can make me smart. I want to be smart. My name is Charlie Gordon. I am 37 years old and 2 weeks ago was my birthday. I have nuthing more to rite now so I will close for today. **1**

progris riport 2–martch 6

R I had a test today. I think I faled it. and I think that maybe now they wont use me. What happind is a nice young man was in the room and he had some white cards with ink

Practice the Skills

1 Reviewing Skills

Making Inferences You can learn a lot about Charlie from the way he writes. For instance, you can tell from his spelling and difficulty understanding other people that he finds it hard to do things most other people do easily.

Additional Support

English Language Coach

Phonetic Spelling Tell students that the misspellings and punctuation and capitalization errors in Charlie's reports are intentional. The author wrote this way to reproduce how Charlie thinks and writes. Explain that Charlie spells phonetically, or the way words sound.

Have students point out words that Charlie has spelled phonetically *(Possible responses: shud, rite, happins)*. Tell students that if they have a hard time reading Charlie's writing, they should try reading it aloud. EL BL spillled all over them. He sed Charlie what do you see on this card. I was very skared even tho I had my rabits foot in my pockit because when I was a kid I always faled tests in school and I spillled ink to.

I told him I saw a inkblot. He said yes and it made me feel good. I thot that was all but when I got up to go he stopped me. He said now sit down Charlie we are not thru yet. **Then** I dont remember so good but he wantid me to say what was in the ink. I dint see nuthing in the ink but he said there was picturs there other pepul saw some picturs. I coudnt see any picturs. I reely tryed to see. I held the card close up and then far away. Then I said if I had my glases I coud see better I usally only ware my glases in the movies or TV but I said they are in the closit in the hall. I got them. Then I said let me see that card agen I bet Ill find it now. 2

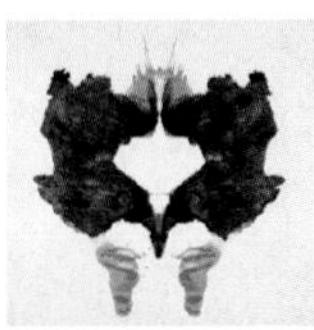

Visual Vocabulary
An ***inkblot*** is an ink mark made by dropping ink on a piece of paper and then folding the paper in half to make an interesting picture.

I tryed hard but I still coudnt find the picturs I only saw the ink. I told him maybe I need new glases. He rote somthing down on a paper and I got skared of faling the test. I told him it was a very nice inkblot with littel points al around the eges. He looked very sad so that wasnt it. I said please let me try agen. Ill get it in a few minits becaus Im not so fast somtimes. Im a slow reeder too in Miss Kinnians class for slow adults but I'm trying very hard.

He gave me a chance with another card that had 2 kinds of ink spillled on it red and blue.

He was very nice and talked slow like Miss Kinnian does and he explaned it to me that it was a *raw shok*.[1] He said pepul see things in the ink. I said show me where. He said think. I told him I think a inkblot but that wasnt rite eather. He said what does it remind you—pretend something. I closd my eyes for a long time to pretend. I told him I pretned a fowntan pen with ink leeking all over a table cloth. Then he got up and went out.

I dont think I passd the *raw shok* test.

1. When Charlie says ***raw shok***, he is talking about the ***Rorschach*** (ROR shok) test, which gathers information about personality and intelligence.

Practice the Skills

2 Key Reading Skill

Understanding Text Structures Notice how many times Charlie uses the word then in this paragraph. What does this tell you about the text structure of the selection?

READING WORKSHOP 3

Teach

R Reading Skill

Review Making Inferences
Ask: What does Charlie do when he can't see any pictures in the inkblots? ***(He goes to get his glasses and keeps trying to get it right.)*** **Ask:** What can you infer about his character from this action? ***(Possible response: He wants to please and works hard to overcome his learning disability.)*** OL

C Critical Thinking

Comprehension **Ask:** What do you learn about Miss Kinnian in this progress report? ***(She is Charlie's teacher. She teaches a reading class for adults with learning disabilities.)*** BL

Differentiated Instruction

Using Images to Understand Text
Direct attention to the Visual Vocabulary information at the top of the page. Tell students that they can use images to help them understand what they read. Help students understand that good readers look at images whenever they are helpful, often moving back and forth between the images and the text. BL Have students tell how the Visual Vocabulary on this page helps them understand the text. *(Possible responses: Knowing what an inkblot looks like helps readers imagine what Charlie is seeing.)* OL

Indiana English/Language Arts Academic Standards
SE: 8.2
TWE: *English Language Coach* 8.1, *Differentiated Instruction* 8.2

Teach

R Reading Skill

Review Making Inferences
Say: Unlike most tests given at school, the kinds of tests Charlie is taking are meant to measure not his knowledge, but rather his intelligence and personality. How do you know that Charlie doesn't understand this? *(Possible response: He keeps referring to failing the tests.)* OL **Ask:** What can you infer about Charlie's previous experiences with tests from his words and actions? *(Possible response: You can infer he did poorly on tests because he talks about getting bad marks and he is nervous about failing them.)* AL

progris report 3–martch 7

Dr Strauss and Dr Nemur say it dont matter about the inkblots. I told them I dint spill the ink on the cards and I coudnt see anything in the ink. They said that maybe they will still use me. I said Miss Kinnian never gave me tests like that one only spelling and reading. They said Miss Kinnian told that I was her bestist pupil in the adult nite scool becaus I tryed the hardist and I reely wantid to lern. They said how come you went to the adult nite scool all by yourself Charlie. How did you find it. I said I askd pepul and sumbody told me where I shud go to lern to read and spell good. They said why did you want to. I told them becaus all my life I wantid to be smart and not dumb. But its very hard to be smart. They said you know it will probly be tempirery. I said yes. Miss Kinnian told me. I dont care if it herts.

Later I had more crazy tests today. The nice lady who gave it me told me the name and I asked her how do you spellit so I can rite it in my progris riport. THEMATIC APPERCEPTION TEST.[2] I dont know the frist 2 words but I know what *test* means. You got to pass it or you get bad marks. This test lookd easy becaus I coud see the picturs. Only this time she dint want me to tell her the picturs. That mixd me up. I said the man yesterday said I shoud tell him what I saw in the ink she said that dont make no difrence. She said make up storys about the pepul in the picturs.

I told her how can you tell storys about pepul you never met. I said why shud I make up lies. I never tell lies any more becaus I always get caut.

She told me this test and the other one the raw-shok was for getting personalty. I laffed so hard. I said how can you get that thing from inkblots and fotos. She got **sore** and put her picturs away. I dont care. It was sily. I gess I faled that test too. 3

Later some men in white coats took me to a difernt part of the hospitil and gave me a game to play. It was like a race with a white mouse. They called the mouse Algernon. Algernon was in a box with a lot of twists and turns like all kinds of walls and they gave me a pencil and a paper with

2. A ***Thematic Apperception*** (thee MAT ik ap ur SEP shun) ***Test*** asks people to look at a few pictures and then make up a story about the pictures.

Practice the Skills

R

3 **English Language Coach**

Multiple-Meaning Words
Which meaning of **sore** makes the most sense here? Write the meaning in your Learner's Notebook.

Additional Support

English Language Coach

Building Background The name Algernon comes from the Old French *als gernons,* meaning "with mustaches," or "whiskered." Keyes came across the name when he was doing homework for a college English class and read a piece by the English poet Algernon Charles Swinburne. Ask students to tell why Algernon is a good name for a mouse. *(Mice have whiskers.)* EL BL lines and lots of boxes. On one side it said START and on the other end it said FINISH. They said it was *amazed*[3] and that Algernon and me had the same *amazed* to do. I dint see how we could have the same *amazed* if Algernon had a box and I had a paper but I dint say nothing. Anyway there wasnt time because the race started.

One of the men had a watch he was trying to hide so I woudnt see it so I tryed not to look and that made me nervus.

Anyway that test made me feel worser than all the others because they did it over 10 times with difernt *amazeds* and Algernon won every time. I dint know that mice were so smart. Maybe thats because Algernon is a white mouse. Maybe white mice are smarter then other mice. L1

progris riport 4–Mar 8

Their going to use me! Im so exited I can hardly write. Dr Nemur and Dr Strauss had a argament about it first. Dr Nemur was in the office when Dr Strauss brot me in. Dr Nemur was worryed about using me but Dr Strauss told him Miss Kinnian rekemmended me the best from all the people who she was teaching. 4 I like Miss Kinnian becaus shes a very smart teacher. And she said Charlie your going to have a second chance. If you volenteer for this experament you mite get smart. They dont know if it will be perminint but theirs a chance. Thats why I said ok even when I was scared because she said it was an operashun. She said dont be scared Charlie you done so much with so little I think you deserv it most of all.

So I got scaird when Dr Nemur and Dr Strauss argud about it. Dr Strauss said I had something that was very good. He said

Practice the Skills

4 Key Literary Element

Irony Charlie is excited that the scientists are going to use him. He thinks of the experiment as a reward for being a good student. Think about what you've learned about Charlie and the doctors so far. What information do you have that Charlie does not have? What's the irony in this passage? L3

Charly, 1967. Selmur Productions. Movie still.

Analyzing the Image What does this scene from the film show you about Charlie's struggle at this point in the story?

3. Charlie says ***amazed,*** but he means "a maze," which is a confusing set of paths that are easy to get lost in.

READING WORKSHOP 3

Teach

L1 Literary Element

Irony **Ask:** How is the mouse beating Charlie an example of irony? *(Readers would expect that a person, even one with pretty low intelligence, could beat a mouse at a game.)* OL

L2 Literary Element

Irony **Say:** Remember that dramatic irony is when readers know something characters in a story do not know. Charlie thinks that Algernon is really smart because he's a white mouse. You know that the mouse is in the lab where the experiments to make Charlie smarter will take place. What might be another reason the mouse is so smart? *(Possible response: The mouse might have had the operation Charlie will have.)* AL

L3 Literary Element

Irony Students should note that the doctors are not rewarding Charlie for being a good student. Rather, they want to conduct an experiment on him. If students have trouble responding to side note 4, ask them to think about whether "use me" has another meaning. *(to take advantage of)* BL OL

Differentiated Instruction

Characterization Chart Draw the following chart on the board. Have students find examples of each type of characterization on pages 340–344. BL OL Have students evaluate the characterization of Charlie. AL

Charlie's Words	Charlie's Thoughts	Charlie's Actions	Others' Words about Him
"Im not so fast . . . but I'm trying very hard"	"All my life I wanted to be smart"	He keeps trying on the inkblot test.	Miss Kinnian says he's motivated.

Indiana English/Language Arts Academic Standards

SE: 8.1.3, 8.2, 8.3.6

TWE: *Reading Skill* 8.2.9, *English Language Coach* 8.1.2, *Differentiated Instruction* 8.3

Teach

Viewing the Photo

Ask: How does this photograph help you visualize the selection? ***(Possible response: It shows an image of a white mouse, and helps me visualize what Algernon probably looked like.)*** **BL**

C Critical Thinking

Comprehension Ask: What is the purpose of the operation? ***(Possible response: The operation will triple his intelligence.)*** **OL**

READING WORKSHOP 3

I had a good *motor-vation.*[4] I never even knew I had that. I felt proud when he said that not every body with an eye-q[5] of 68 had that thing. I dont know what it is or where I got it but he said Algernon had it too. Algernons *motor-vation* is the cheese they put in his box. But it cant be that because I didnt eat any cheese this week.

Then he told Dr Nemur something I dint understand so while they were talking I wrote down some of the words.

He said Dr Nemur I know Charlie is not what you had in mind as the first of your new brede of intelek** (coudnt get the word) superman. But most people of his low ment** are host** and uncoop** they are usualy dull apath** and hard to **reach.** He has a good natcher hes intristed and eager to please. **5**

Dr Nemur said remember he will be the first human beeng ever to have his intelijence trippled by surgicle meens. **C**

Dr Strauss said exakly. Look at how well hes lerned to read and write for his low mentel age its as grate an acheve** as you and I lerning einstines therey of **vity[6] without help. That shows the intenss motorvation. Its comparat** a tremen** achev** I say we use Charlie.

I dint get all the words and they were talking to fast but it sounded like Dr Strauss was on my side and like the other one wasnt.

Then Dr Nemur nodded he said all right maybe your right. We will use Charlie. When he said that I got so exited I jumped up and shook his hand for being so good to me. I told him thank you doc you wont be sorry for giving me a second chance. And I mean it like I told him. After the operashun Im gonna try to be smart. Im gonna try awful hard.

---

4. Charlie means ***motivation*** (moh tih VAY shun). When people have motivation to do something, they feel that they want very much to do it.
5. When Charlie says ***eye-q*** he means IQ, which stands for "intelligence quotient" (KWOH shent). An IQ is the score a person gets on an intelligence test, which is supposed to measure a person's ability to learn.
6. When Charlie says ***einstines therey of **vity,*** he is talking about the theory of relativity developed by the scientist Albert Einstein which changed the way people understand the world.

Practice the Skills

5 English Language Coach

Multiple-Meaning Words
Which meaning of **reach** makes the most sense here? How do you know? Write your answer in your Learner's Notebook.

Additional Support

English Language Coach

Building Background IQ tests were first developed in France to distinguish between average and below average intelligence. Children with below average intelligence were placed in special schools to help them learn. Charlie's IQ score is 68. According to most scales, this means that he has a low intelligence. A score of around 100 indicates average intelligence. Most experts agree that a person's IQ gives only a rough estimate of academic intelligence and doesn't indicate other talents, such as gifts in athletics, music, or art. As students read, have them tell what gifts besides intelligence make Charlie special. **OL**

progris ript 5–Mar 10

Im skared. Lots of people who work here and the nurses and the people who gave me the tests came to bring me candy and wish me luck. I hope I have luck. I got my rabits foot and my lucky penny and my horse shoe. Only a black cat crossed me when I was comming to the hospitil. Dr Strauss says dont be supersitis Charlie this is sience. Anyway Im keeping my rabits foot with me.

R1 I asked Dr Strauss if Ill beat Algernon in the race after the operashun and he said maybe. If the operashun works Ill show that mouse I can be as smart as he is. Maybe smarter. Then Ill be abel to read better and spell the words good and know lots of things and be like other people. I want to be smart like other people. If it works perminint they will make everybody smart all over the wurld.

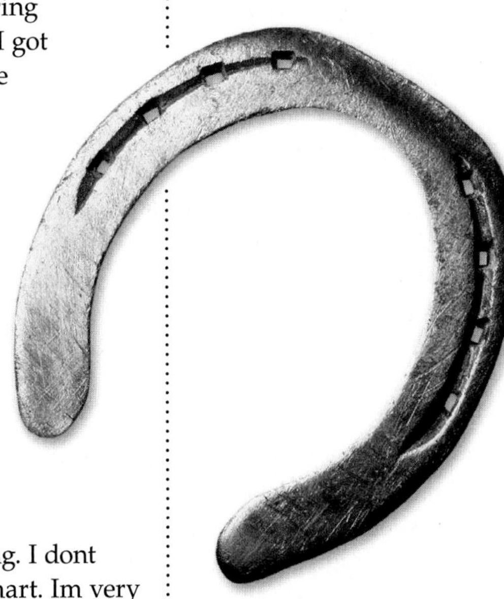

They dint give me anything to eat this morning. I dont know what that eating has to do with getting smart. Im very hungry and Dr Nemur took away my box of candy. That Dr Nemur is a grouch. Dr Strauss says I can have it back after the operashun. You cant eat befor a operashun . . .

Progress Report 6–Mar 15

The operashun dint hurt. He did it while I was sleeping. They took off the bandijis from my eyes and my head today so I can make a PROGRESS REPORT. Dr Nemur who looked at some of my other ones says I spell PROGRESS wrong and he told me how to spell it and REPORT too. I got to try and remember that.

R2 I have a very bad memary for spelling. Dr Strauss says its ok to tell about all the things that happin to me but he says I shoud tell more about what I feel and what I think. When I told him I dont know how to think he said try. All the time when the bandijis were on my eyes I tryed to think. Nothing happened. I dont know what to think about. Maybe if I ask him he will tell me how I can think now that Im suppose to get smart. What do smart people think about. **Fancy** things I suppose. I wish I knew some fancy things alredy. 6

Practice the Skills

6 **English Language Coach**

Multiple-Meaning Words
Look up **fancy** in a dictionary. How many meanings of *fancy* are there? What does it mean in the context of the selection? (Hint: What part of speech is *fancy* in the selection?)

Differentiated Instruction

Comparison and Contrast Chart Authors often use comparison and contrast to develop characters. Have students draw a two-column chart in their Learner's Notebooks and label the first column *Before the Operation* and the second *After the Operation.* Have students complete the first column, describing Charlie's actions, thoughts, words, and beliefs. As students continue reading, have them add details to the second column. To make the activity collaborative, ask students to share their observations and then revise their charts. EL BL

Teach

R1 Reading Skill

Review Predicting **Say:** Charlie hopes that the operation will make him "smart like other people." How do you think the operation will change Charlie's life? *(Possible response: Charlie might be happier because he will understand more. He might have more friends.)* OL

R2 Reading Skill

Review Predicting **Ask:** How quickly do you think Charlie will change? *(Possible answer: He will probably change slowly because he still has trouble thinking.)* OL

Indiana English/Language Arts Academic Standards
SE: 8.1.3
TWE: *English Language Coach* 8.2, *Differentiated Instruction* 8.2.6

Teach

R1 Reading Skill

Review Making Inferences
Ask: Why do you think Keyes doesn't explain the details of Charlie's operation? *(Possible responses: This kind of operation doesn't really exist. He is more interested in the operation's effect on Charlie than on the technical details. He is writing science fiction that explores ideas instead of science fiction that is focused on technology.)* AL

R2 Reading Skill

Review Predicting **Say:** Charlie is probably going to change a lot in the near future. How do you predict these changes will affect his work life? *(Possible responses: His coworkers might appreciate his new intelligence, or they might be intimidated by it.)* OL

Progress Report 7–mar 19

Nothing is happining. I had lots of tests and different kinds of races with Algernon. I hate that mouse. He always beats me. Dr Strauss said I got to play those games. And he said some time I got to take those tests over again. Thse inkblots are stupid. And those pictures are stupid too. I like to draw a picture of a man and a woman but I wont make up lies about people.

I got a headache from trying to think so much. I thot Dr Strauss was my frend but he dont help me. He dont tell me what to think or when Ill get smart. Miss Kinnian dint come to see me. I think writing these progress reports are stupid too. **7**

Progress Report 8–Mar 23

Im going back to work at the factery. They said it was better I shud go back to work but I cant tell anyone what the operashun was for and I have to come to the hospitil for an hour evry night after work. They are gonna pay me mony every month for lerning to be smart.

Im glad Im going back to work because I miss my job and all my frends and all the fun we have there. R2

Dr Strauss says I shud keep writing things down but I dont have to do it every day just when I think of something or something speshul happins. He says dont get discoridged because it takes time and it happins slow. He says it took a long time with Algernon before he got 3 times smarter than he was before. Thats why Algernon beats me all the time because he had that operashun too. That makes me feel better. I coud probly do that *amazed* faster than a reglar mouse. Maybe some day Ill beat Algernon. Boy that would be something. So far Algernon looks like he mite be smart perminent.

Mar 25 (I dont have to write PROGRESS REPORT on top any more just when I hand it in once a week for Dr Nemur to read. I just have to put the date on. That saves time)

We had a lot of fun at the factery today. Joe Carp said hey look where Charlie had his operashun what did they do Charlie put some brains in. I was going to tell him but I remembered Dr Strauss said no. Then Frank Reilly said what

Practice the Skills

7 **Reviewing Skills**

Making Inferences Notice the change in Charlie's personality from earlier in the story. Why do you think he's getting cranky and calling everything "stupid"? R1

Additional Support

Literature Focus Lesson

Science Fiction Science fiction stories imagine how advances in science and technology might affect people's lives. Sometimes what science fiction authors imagine becomes reality. For example, in 1865 Jules Verne's *From the Earth to the Moon* described a flight to the moon launched from Florida. In 1972 the astronauts on Apollo 11 began their journey to the moon at Cape Canaveral, Florida. Ask students if they think people will ever be able to increase their intelligence. If they could, would it be a good thing? Why or why not? *(Answers will vary.)* AS did you do Charlie forget your key and open your door the hard way. That made me laff. Their really my friends and they like me. 8

Sometimes somebody will say hey look at Joe or Frank or George he really pulled a Charlie Gordon. I dont know why they say that but they always laff. This morning Amos Borg who is the 4 man at Donnegans used my name when he shouted at Ernie the office boy. Ernie lost a packige. He said Ernie for godsake what are you trying to be a Charlie Gordon. I dont understand why he said that. I never lost any packiges. 9

Mar 28 Dr Strauss came to my room tonight to see why I dint come in like I was suppose to. I told him I dont like to race with Algernon any more. He said I dont have to for a while but I shud come in. He had a present for me only it wasnt a present but just for lend. I thot it was a little television but it wasnt. He said I got to turn it on when I go to sleep. I said your kidding why shud I turn it on when Im going to sleep. Who ever herd of a thing like that. But he said if I want to get smart I got to do what he says. I told him I dint think I was going to get smart and he put his hand on my sholder and said Charlie you dont know it yet but your getting smarter all the time. You wont notice for a while. I think he was just being nice to make me feel good because I dont look any smarter.

Oh yes I almost forgot. I asked him when I can go back to the class at Miss Kinnians school. He said I wont go their. He said that soon Miss Kinnian will come to the hospitil to start and teach me speshul. I was mad at her for not comming to see me when I got the operashun but I like her so maybe we will be frends again.

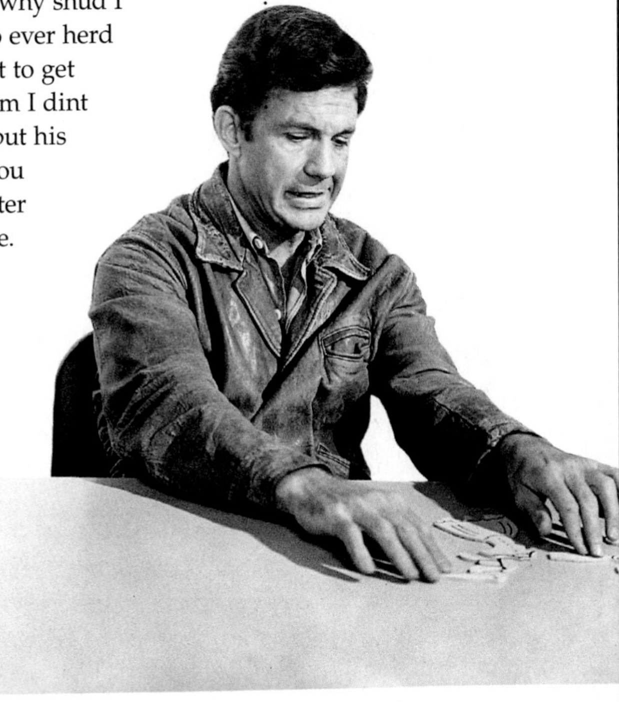

Charly, 1967. Selmur Productions. Movie still.

Analyzing the Image Can you see Charlie's determination in this photograph?

Practice the Skills

R1

8 Key Literary Element

Irony What is the dramatic irony here? (Hint: What are Charlie's thoughts about his friends' behavior? How do his thoughts about his friends differ from yours?)

9 Reviewing Skills

R2

Making Inferences What do you think it means when someone says, "He really pulled a Charlie Gordon"? Support your inference with story details.

Teach

R1 Reading Skill

Review Predicting **Ask:** What will likely happen to Charlie's friendship with Joe and Frank if he gets more intelligent? *(Possible responses: As his intelligence grows, Charlie will realize that his "friends" are mocking his limitations. He will no longer like them, and they will probably not like him, either.)* AL

R2 Reading Skill

Review Making Inferences **Ask:** Why do you think Charlie doesn't like racing Algernon any more? *(Possible responses: He is changing after the operation, and his interests are changing. He is tired of the mouse beating him.)* OL

Differentiated Instruction

Class Discussion In *Algernon, Charlie and I* (2000), Daniel Keyes explains how he developed the story of Charlie. It started with a student who said, "I know this is a dummy class. . . . If I try hard and I get smart by the end of the term, will you put me in a regular class? I want to be smart." The question started Keyes thinking.

Have students discuss why authors might use experiences from their own lives as an inspiration for writing. AL

Indiana English/Language Arts Academic Standards

SE: 8.2.9, 8.3.6

TWE: *Literature Focus Lesson* 8.3, *Differentiated Instruction* 8.3

Teach

C Critical Thinking

Comprehension Ask: What problem does Charlie have? How does Dr. Strauss help Charlie solve it? *(Problem: The sleep machine is too loud. Solution: Dr. Strauss shows Charlie how to turn it down.)* BL

R Reading Skill

Review Comparing and Contrasting Ask: How is Charlie changing? How is he staying the same? *(Possible responses: He is beginning to think for himself and to question authority, such as asking how the sleep machine works. He also mentions looking up words in the dictionary, which he would not have been able to do before. However, he still thinks of himself as "dumb.")* OL

Mar 29 That crazy TV kept me up all night. How can I sleep with something yelling crazy things all night in my ears. And the nutty pictures. Wow. I dont know what it says when Im up so how am I going to know when Im sleeping.

Dr Strauss says its ok. He says my brains are lerning when I sleep and that will help me when Miss Kinnian starts my lessons in the hospitl (only I found out it isnt a hospitil its a labatory). I think its all crazy. If you can get smart when your sleeping why do people go to school. That thing I dont think will work. I use to watch the late show and the late late show on TV all the time and it never made me smart. Maybe you have to sleep while you watch it. **10** C

PROGRESS REPORT 9–April 3

Dr Strauss showed me how to keep the TV turned low so now I can sleep. I dont hear a thing. And I still dont understand what it says. A few times I play it over in the morning to find out what I lerned when I was sleeping and I dont think so. Miss Kinnian says Maybe its another langwidge or something. But most times it sounds american. It talks so fast faster then even Miss Gold who was my teacher in 6 grade and I remember she talked so fast I coudnt understand her.

I told Dr Strauss what good is it to get smart in my sleep. I want to be smart when Im awake. He says its the same thing and I have two minds. Theres the *subconscious*[7] and the *conscious* (thats how you spell it). And one dont tell the other one what its doing. They dont even talk to each other. Thats why I dream. And boy have I been having crazy dreams. Wow. Ever since that night TV. The late late late late late show. R

I forgot to ask him if it was only me or if everybody had those two minds.

(I just looked up the word in the dictionary Dr Strauss gave me. The word is *subconscious. adj. Of the nature of mental operations yet not present in consciousness; as, subconscious conflict of desires.)* Theres more but I still don't know what it means. This isnt a very good dictionary for dumb people like me.

7. A person is not aware of the thoughts and feelings in the ***subconscious*** (sub KON shus) part of his or her mind.

Practice the Skills

10 Reviewing Skills

Making Inferences What has changed about Charlie? (Hint: How does Charlie feel about Dr. Strauss's television idea?)

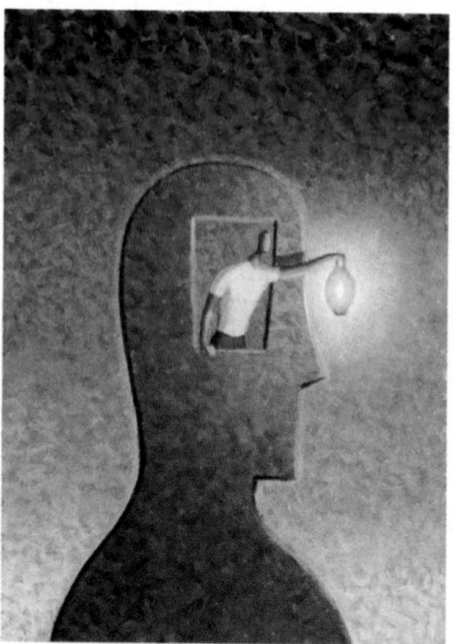

Analyzing the Art How does this image help you understand the idea of a *subconscious* mind?

Additional Support

English Language Coach

Building Background Sigmund Freud, the famous psychologist who invented psychoanalysis, believed that the mind was divided into three parts: the ego (the awake mind), the id, and the superego (the two parts of the subconscious). Freud believed that the subconscious, the part of the mind we are not aware of, controls much of a person's behavior. Have students tell how this theory explains why Dr. Strauss would have Charlie listen to a sleep machine. AL

Anyway the headache is from the party. My frends from the factery Joe Carp and Frank Reilly invited me to go with them to Muggsys Saloon for some drinks. I dont like to drink but they said we will have lots of fun. I had a good time.

Joe Carp said I shoud show the girls how I mop out the toilet in the factory and he got me a mop. I showed them and everyone laffed when I told that Mr Donnegan said I was the best janiter he ever had because I like my job and do it good and never come late or miss a day except for my operashun.

I said Miss Kinnian always said Charlie be proud of your job because you do it good.

Everybody laffed and we had a good time and they gave me lots of drinks and Joe said Charlie is a card when hes potted.[8] I dont know what that means but everybody likes me and we have fun. I cant wait to be smart like my best frends Joe Carp and Frank Reilly. **11**

I dont remember how the party was over but I think I went out to buy a newspaper and coffe for Joe and Frank and when I came back there was no one their. I looked for them all over till late. Then I dont remember so good but I think I got sleepy or sick. A nice cop brot me back home. Thats what my landlady Mrs Flynn says.

But I got a headache and a big lump on my head and black and blue all over. I think maybe I fell but Joe Carp says it was the cop they beat up drunks some times. I don't think so. Miss Kinnian says cops are to help people. Anyway I got a bad headache and Im sick and hurt all over. I dont think Ill drink anymore.

April 6 I beat Algernon! I dint even know I beat him until Burt the tester told me. Then the second time I lost because I got so exited I fell off the chair before I finished. But after that I beat him 8 more times. I must be getting smart to beat a smart mouse like Algernon. But I dont *feel* smarter.

I wanted to race Algernon some more but Burt said thats enough for one day. They let me hold him for a minit. Hes not so bad. Hes soft like a ball of cotton. He blinks and when he opens his eyes their black and pink on the eges.

8. ***Charlie is a card when he's potted*** is a slang way of saying that Charlie is funny when he drinks too much alcohol.

Practice the Skills

11 **Key Literary Element**

Irony This scene is an example of dramatic irony. What do you, the reader, know that Charlie does not know? How does this bit of irony make you feel about Charlie and his situation?

Teach

L Literary Element

Irony **Say:** Explain why each of the following is an example of dramatic irony. What does the reader know that Charlie doesn't?

- Charlie says "everybody likes me and we have fun." ***(The reader knows that Joe and Frank have actually invited Charlie out to make fun of him.)***
- Charlie says "I cant wait to be smart like my best friends Joe Carp and Frank Reilly." ***(The reader knows that Joe and Frank aren't really that smart. The reader also knows they're not good friends to Charlie.)*** OL

C Critical Thinking

Comprehension **Ask:** What evidence does Charlie have that he's getting smarter? ***(He beats Algernon in the game.)*** BL **Ask:** In what ways is he still the same as he was before the operation? ***(Possible responses: He says he doesn't feel smarter. He wants to hold Algernon. His spelling is still bad at times.)*** OL

Literature Focus Lesson

Point of View Remind students that the point of view is the perspective from which a story is told. This story is told from Charlie's perspective. Have students rewrite Charlie's journal entry about the party (from "Anyway the headache is from the party" to "I dont think I'll drink anymore") from another point of view. You might have them work with a partner and assign some pairs to write from the viewpoint of one of Charlie's "friends" and some from an objective viewpoint. Have students explain how writing from a different viewpoint changes the story. OL AL

Indiana English/Language Arts Academic Standards
SE: 8.2, 8.3.6
TWE: *English Language Coach* 8.2, *Literature Focus Lesson* 8.3.8

Teach

Viewing the Photo

Ask: Does the actor in this photograph look like how you imagined Charlie would look? How is he similar? How is he different? *(Responses will vary. Students may note that the actor looks kind, as they'd imagined. They may be surprised by his age because despite the fact that Charlie says he is 37, his thoughts and opinions make him seem very young.)* **OL**

R1 Reading Skill

Review Comparing and Contrasting **Ask:** How are Charlie and Algernon similar? *(Possible responses: They've both had tests to make them intelligent. They're both being studied by scientists.)* **BL**

R2 Reading Skill

Review Predicting **Say:** Charlie has just realized that he's getting smarter. What hints can you find that his intelligence might not last? *(Possible responses: Miss Kinnian is worried about him, and she says the worst that can happen is that Charlie will have his intelligence for "a littel wile.")* **OL** **AL**

READING WORKSHOP 3

Charly, 1967. Selmur Productions. Movie still.
Analyzing the Image How would you describe Charlie's feelings toward Algernon?

R1 I said can I feed him because I felt bad to beat him and I wanted to be nice and make frends. Burt said no Algernon is a very specshul mouse with an operashun like mine, and he was the first of all the animals to stay smart so long. He told me Algernon is so smart that every day he has to solve a test to get his food. Its a thing like a lock on a door that changes every time Algernon goes in to eat so he has to lern something new to get his food. That made me sad because if he coudnt lern he woud be hungry.

I dont think its right to make you pass a test to eat. How woud Dr Nemur like it to have to pass a test every time he wants to eat. I think Ill be frends with Algernon. **12**

R2 ***April 9*** Tonight after work Miss Kinnian was at the laboratory. She looked like she was glad to see me but scared. I told her dont worry Miss Kinnian Im not smart yet and she laffed. She said I have confidence in you Charlie the way you struggled so hard to read and right better than all the others. At werst you will have it for a littel wile and your doing somthing for sience.

Practice the Skills

12 Key Reading Skill

Understanding Text Structures Most selections have more than one text structure. Reread the first two paragraphs on this page. The text structure in these paragraphs is cause and effect. What causes and effects can you find here?

Additional Support

Differentiated Instruction

Cause-and-Effect Chart Draw a cause-and-effect chart on the board showing the first cause-and-effect relationship in the April 6 entry:
Charlie gets excited → He falls off his chair.
Ask students to identify other cause-and-effect relationships.
(Possible responses: Charlie beats Algernon, so he realizes he must be getting smarter. Charlie feels bad about beating Algernon, so he wants to be Algernon's friend. Charlie learns Algernon must pass a test to get food, so he feels sorry for him.) **BL** **OL**

We are reading a very hard book. I never read such a hard book before. Its called *Robinson Crusoe* about a man who gets merooned on a dessert Iland. Hes smart and figers out all kinds of things so he can have a house and food and hes a good swimmer. Only I feel sorry because hes all alone and has no frends. But I think their must be somebody else on the iland because theres a picture with his funny umbrella looking at footprints. I hope he gets a frend and not be lonly. R

April 10 Miss Kinnian teaches me to spell better. She says look at a word and close your eyes and say it over and over until you remember. I have lots of truble with *through* that you say *threw* and *enough* and *tough* that you dont say *enew* and *tew.* You got to say *enuff* and *tuff.* Thats how I use to write it before I started to get smart. Im confused but Miss Kinnian says theres no reason in spelling.

April 14 Finished *Robinson Crusoe.* I want to find out more about what happens to him but Miss Kinnian says thats all there is. *Why*

April 15 Miss Kinnian says Im lerning fast. She read some of the Progress Reports and she looked at me kind of funny. She says Im a fine person and Ill show them all. I asked her why. She said never mind but I shoudnt feel bad if I find out that everybody isnt nice like I think. She said for a person who god gave so little to you done more then a lot of people with brains they never even used. I said all my frends are smart people but there good. They like me and they never did anything that wasnt nice. Then she got something in her eye and she had to run out to the ladys room. 13

April 16 Today, I lerned, the *comma,* this is a comma (,) a period, with a tail, Miss Kinnian, says its importent, because, it makes writing, better, she said, sombeody, could lose, a lot of money, if a comma, isnt, in the, right place, I dont have, any money, and I dont see, how a comma, keeps you, from losing it, L

But she says, everybody, uses commas, so Ill use, them too,

April 17 I used the comma wrong. Its punctuation. Miss Kinnian told me to look up long words in the dictionary to lern to spell them. I said whats the difference if you can read it anyway. She said its part of your education so now on Ill

EL Practice the Skills

13 Key Literary Element

Irony Charlie thinks Miss Kinnian has run out of the room because she got something in her eye. What is the real reason she leaves? (Hint: How do you think she feels about the way Charlie's friends treat him?)

READING WORKSHOP 3

Teach

EL Language Coach

Multiple-Meaning Words

Say: The word *hard* can have the following meanings. Which fits the first sentence on this page?

- very strong
- causing damage
- difficult

(The third definition is correct.) EL

R Reading Skill

Review Making Inferences

Ask: How does the description of Charlie's reaction to *Robinson Crusoe* show how Charlie is changing? *(Possible responses: Charlie is reading harder books; he is able to infer that the footprints Crusoe sees must mean someone else is on the island.)* AL

L Literary Element

Humor **Ask:** What is funny about Charlie's April 16th entry? *(Possible response: He learns about commas, but he doesn't yet understand how to use them, so he puts them everywhere.)* OL

English Language Coach

Spelling Homophones Point out that the spelling words give Charlie difficulty because they are not spelled the way they sound. Point out that homophones are words that sound the same but have different spellings and meanings. Work with students to make a list of homophones that give them trouble (such as *hare* and *hair; bear* and *bare; their, they're, there; weather* and *whether*). Suggest students write a sample sentence for each word to help them remember its meaning. EL BL

Indiana English/Language Arts Academic Standards

SE: 8.2, 8.3.6

TWE: *Differentiated Instruction* 8.2, *English Language Coach* 8.1

Teach

C1 Critical Thinking

Synthesis **Say:** Review what you've learned about the sleeping machine and the subconscious. How might the TV working in his sleep have helped Charlie figure out the punctuation rules? *(Possible response: The machine helped Charlie's subconscious mind learn the punctuation rules, so when he woke up, he was able to understand what he couldn't get the day before.)* **OL**

C2 Critical Thinking

Synthesis **Say:** Think about what you've read about Miss Kinnian. Do you think she cares about Charlie? Why or why not? *(Possible responses: Yes, she cares about Charlie. She recommended him for the operation. She wants him to do well. She is slow and patient with him. No, she submits him for an experiment that might be dangerous; she doesn't visit him in the hospital.)* **AL**

READING WORKSHOP 3

look up all the words Im not sure how to spell. It takes a long time to write that way but I think Im remembering. I only have to look up once and after that I get it right. Anyway thats how come I got the word *punctuation* right. (Its that way in the dictionary). Miss Kinnian says a period is punctuation too, and there are lots of other marks to lern. I told her I thot all the periods had to have tails but she said no.

You got to mix them up, she showed? me" how. to mix! them(up,. and now; I can! mix up all kinds" of punctuation, in! my writing? There, are lots! of rules? to lern; but Im gettin'g them in my head.

One thing I? like about, Dear Miss Kinnian: (thats the way it goes in a business letter if I ever go into business) is she, always gives me' a reason" when—I ask. She's a gen'ius! I wish! I cou'd be smart" like, her;

(Punctuation, is; fun!)

April 18 What a dope I am! I didn't even understand what she was talking about. I read the grammar book last night and it explanes the whole thing. Then I saw it was the same way as Miss Kinnian was trying to tell me, but I didn't get it. I got up in the middle of the night, and the whole thing straightened out in my mind.

Miss Kinnian said that the TV working in my sleep helped out. She said I reached a plateau. Thats like the flat top of a hill. **C1**

After I figgered out how punctuation worked, I read over all my old Progress Reports from the beginning. Boy, did I have crazy spelling and punctuation! I told Miss Kinnian I ought to go over the pages and fix all the mistakes but she said, "No, Charlie, Dr. Nemur wants them just as they are. That's why he let you keep them after they were photostated,[9] to see your own progress. You're coming along fast, Charlie."

That made me feel good. After the lesson I went down and played with Algernon. We don't race any more. **14**

9. Anything that is ***photostated*** (FOH toh stat ud) has been photocopied onto specially treated paper.

Practice the Skills

14 Key Reading Skill

Understanding Text Structures The author organizes the text in time order. How does the text structure help you see how quickly changes are happening to Charlie?

Additional Support

Differentiated Instruction

Making a Time Line To understand the speed at which Charlie is progressing, have students plot key events on a time line: March 15—has operation; April 3—uses a dictionary; April 6—beats Algernon; April 14—finishes *Robinson Crusoe;* April 16—learns about commas; April 17—uses punctuation at random; April 18—realizes his mistake. As students continue reading, periodically ask if an event is important enough to include on the time line. **EL** **BL**

April 20 I feel sick inside. Not sick like for a doctor, but inside my chest it feels empty like getting punched and a heartburn at the same time.

I wasn't going to write about it, but I guess I got to, because it's important. Today was the first time I ever stayed home from work.

Last night Joe Carp and Frank Reilly invited me to a party. There were lots of girls and some men from the factory. I remembered how sick I got last time I drank too much, so I told Joe I didn't want anything to drink. He gave me a plain Coke instead. It tasted funny, but I thought it was just a bad taste in my mouth.

We had a lot of fun for a while. Joe said I should dance with Ellen and she would teach me the steps. I fell a few times and I couldn't understand why because no one else was dancing besides Ellen and me. And all the time I was tripping because somebody's foot was always sticking out. **15**

Then when I got up I saw the look on Joe's face and it gave me a funny feeling in my stomack. "He's a **scream**," one of the girls said. Everybody was laughing. **16**

Frank said, "I ain't laughed so much since we sent him off for the newspaper that night at Muggsy's and ditched him."

"Look at him. His face is red." **R**

"He's blushing. Charlie is blushing."

"Hey, Ellen, what'd you do to Charlie? I never saw him act like that before."

I didn't know what to do or where to turn. Everyone was looking at me and laughing and I felt naked. I wanted to hide myself. I ran out into the street and I threw up. Then I walked home. It's a funny thing I never knew that Joe and Frank and the others liked to have me around all the time to make fun of me. **C**

Now I know what it means when they say "to pull a Charlie Gordon."

I'm ashamed. **17**

Practice the Skills

15 **Key Reading Skill**

Understanding Text Structures Charlie's writing is improving. Look at how he uses signal words for chronological order in the first four paragraphs on this page. What signal words can you find?

16 **English Language Coach**

Multiple-Meaning Words What does **scream** mean here? Write its definition in your Learner's Notebook. Use a dictionary if you need help.

17 **BIG Question**

What price does Charlie pay for getting smarter? Is the price too high? Write your answer on the "Flowers for Algernon," Part 1, flap of the Reading Workshop 3 Foldable. Your response will help you complete the Unit Challenge later. **BQ**

English Language Coach

Building Background Point out that when Charlie realizes his coworkers are making fun of him, he does not get angry at them. Instead, he turns inward and feels "naked" and ashamed. People feel shame when they think that something is wrong with them. People who study childhood development say that children may develop feelings of shame between the ages of eighteen months and four years. Discuss with students how Keyes includes this part of the story to show that Charlie is developing emotionally as well as intellectually. Have them look for other times when Charlie feels shame. **AS**

Teach

R Reading Skill

Review Making Inferences

Ask: Why is Charlie's face red? *(Possible responses: Charlie realizes that he is being made fun of, and he is embarrassed.)* **AL**

C Critical Thinking

Synthesis **Say:** At the beginning of the reports, Charlie said he didn't know how to tell about his feelings. How has Charlie changed? *(Students may say Charlie is now able to describe the devastation of being mocked by his "friends.")* **OL**

BQ BIG Question

Ask: Do you think the price Charlie has paid for his intelligence is too high? Explain. *(Some students may think it's good that Charlie knows Joe and Frank are not good friends. Others may think Charlie was better off not knowing.)* **AS**

Assess

Use the CheckPoint questions provided on Presentation Plus! to check for comprehension of the selection. These questions can be used with interactive response keypads for immediate student feedback.

Indiana English/Language Arts Academic Standards
SE: 8.1.3, 8.2
TWE: *Differentiated Instruction* 8.2, *English Language Coach* 8.3

Assess

Resources for page 354

- Selection Quick Check, p. 25
- Selection and Unit Assessment, p. 29
- ExamView Assessment Suite
- Interactive Tutor: Self-Assessment

Students can respond to the *After You Read* items in their Learner's Notebooks or on a separate sheet of paper.

Answering the

1. Responses will vary. Students will note that Charlie is more intelligent and more independent, but he has lost his trust in his friends and is ashamed of himself.
2. Before his operation, Charlie saw himself as dumb and other people as good and trustworthy.

Critical Thinking

3. Charlie feels ashamed because he realizes his "friends" have been making fun of him all along.
4. Before, Charlie struggled to understand the facts and took everything literally. Now he is thinking critically and asking questions.
5. Responses will vary. Students might address the issues of whether Charlie was harmed by the experiment and whether he could give informed consent.

After You Read

Flowers for Algernon, Part 1

Answering the BIG Question

1. How has Charlie changed since his operation? What has he gained and what has he lost?
2. **Recall** How did Charlie see himself before his operation? How did he feel toward other people?
   TIP Right There

Critical Thinking

3. **Analyze** What makes Charlie feel so ashamed at the end of Part 1?
   TIP Author and Me
4. **Analyze** Charlie ends the April 14 Progress Report with the word *Why.* How does this word show that Charlie's thinking has changed?
   TIP Author and Me
5. **Evaluate** What is your opinion so far about the experiment that Charlie is part of? Do you think it is a good thing or is it too dangerous for human beings? Explain your reasons for your opinion.
   TIP Author and Me

Write About Your Reading

Written Report The author presents "Flowers for Algernon" as a series of progress reports or journal entries written by Charlie. Write a brief report that compares Charlie before the operation with the person he's becoming since the operation. Write in your own voice and style, not in Charlie's. Follow this plan for your report:

- In the first paragraph, describe (a) how Charlie was before the operation and (b) the ways in which he's still the same at the end of Part 1.
- In the second paragraph, explain how Charlie has changed since the operation. Give examples.
- In the third paragraph, tell whether the changes that you noted are good or bad for Charlie. Give details from the story to support your opinion.

Indiana English/ Language Arts Academic Standards (pp. 354–355)

8.3 Comprehension and Analysis of Literary Text Respond to grade-level-appropriate literature… **8.5.2** Write responses to literature… **8.2 Comprehension and Analysis (Focus on Informational Text)** Develop [reading] strategies such as…identifying and analyzing structure and organization… **8.3.6** Identify significant literary devices, such as…irony…**8.6 English Language Conventions**

For a complete description of the standards, see p. IN 11.

Write About Your Reading

Possible response:

Before his operation, Charlie Gordon was kindhearted; he cared about Miss Kinnian and his coworkers.

Charlie is still kind after the operation; he plays with Algernon, for example. After his operation, Charlie becomes more intelligent. His spelling and grammar improve; he begins to ask questions and think abstractly; he learns that people he thought were his friends have been mocking him.

Charlie's progress is not all good for him. Although he is learning to think for himself, he is now "ashamed" of his limitations. He is still kindhearted, but he knows why Miss Kinnian warned him about people.

Skills Review

Key Reading Skill: Understanding Text Structures

6. What is the main text structure of the selection? Why do you think the story is organized this way? Write the answer in your Learner's Notebook.
7. Name at least one other text structure, besides chronological order, that you noticed in Part 1 of the story. In your Learner's Notebook, write down the page number and a description of the passage with that text structure.

Key Literary Element: Irony

8. What example of irony in Part 1 stands out most for you? How does it affect the way you feel about Charlie and other characters?
9. You only have the information Charlie gives you in this story. There is no narrator to tell you anything else. So how do you know the things that Charlie doesn't?

Reviewing Skills: Making Inferences

10. Why do the doctors want Charlie to keep his operation a secret from his coworkers?

Vocabulary Check

11. **English Language Coach** Review the meanings of the words *sore* and *reach* on page 338. In your Learner's Notebook, write a sentence for each word that explains one of its meanings.
12. **Academic Vocabulary** What is a synonym for the word **structure?**

Web Activities For eFlashcards, Selection Quick Checks, and other Web activities, go to www.glencoe.com.

Grammar Link: Run-ons

Never run two or more independent clauses together. This mistake is called a **run-on sentence.**

Wrong: Jeremy has two brothers he is the oldest of the three boys.

There are two kinds of run-ons. In the above example, two independent clauses are jammed together with no conjunction or punctuation to separate the ideas. In a second kind of run-on, only a comma separates the two clauses.

Wrong: Jeremy has two brothers, he is the oldest of the three boys.

One way to fix a run-on is to separate the two ideas by making each one a complete sentence. Just insert the proper end punctuation and capitalization.

Right: Jeremy has two brothers. He is the oldest of the three boys.

You can also separate the two ideas with a comma and coordinating conjunction to make a compound sentence. (Use the conjunction that makes the sentence mean what you want it to mean.)

Right: Jeremy has two brothers, but he is the oldest of the three boys.

Grammar Practice

On another piece of paper, copy these sentences and correct each run-on error.

13. Estela can't wait for spring it is her favorite season.
14. Otto loves to draw, he is very artistic.
15. Juanita missed school today she has a fever.
16. My dog's name is Otis, he likes to jump and chew toys.
17. Carrie went to the store she bought milk, cereal, and eggs.
18. The rain stopped the sun came out.

Writing Application Review your Write About Your Reading activity. Fix any run-on sentences.

Skills Review

Key Reading Skill: Understanding Text Structures

6. chronological order Possible response: This organization allows readers to see how Charlie changes each day.
7. Possible response: The cause-and-effect structure on page 350 explains that Algernon gets food only if he learns something new.

Key Literary Element: Irony

8. Possible response: Charlie thinking his coworkers are his friends. It makes me pity Charlie and dislike his coworkers.
9. Responses will vary.

Reviewing Skills: Making Inferences

10. Possible response: The doctors don't want to make their experiment public until they know if it will be successful.

Vocabulary Check

English Language Coach

11. Answers will vary.

Academic Vocabulary

12. Possible responses: arrangement, format, composition

Grammar Link: Run-ons

Grammar Practice

13. Estela can't wait for spring. It is her favorite season.
14. Otto loves to draw. He is very artistic.
15. Juanita missed school today. She has a fever.
16. My dog's name is Otis. He likes to jump and chew toys.
17. Carrie went to the store. She bought milk, cereal, and eggs.
18. The rain stopped. The sun came out.

Close

Hold a class discussion based on students' responses to question 5. Be sure students explain their decisions.

Indiana English/Language Arts Academic Standards
SE: 8.2, 8.3, 8.3.6, 8.5.2, 8.6

Focus

BELLRINGER Options

Daily Language Practice Transparency 27

Focus Activity Say: At the end of Part 1, Charlie's IQ was becoming average. What do you think will happen if his IQ becomes higher than average? *(Responses will vary.)* OL

Teach

V Vocabulary

Fill in the Blank Write these sentences on the board and have students fill in the blanks with the vocabulary words:

- Residents are upset because the tall new building will _______ their view. *(obscure)*
- I'm a shopaholic because when I go to the mall, I _______ buy something. *(invariably)*
- My scared little puppy _______ whenever the doorbell rang. *(cowered)*
- Knocking people on a certain point on their knees is a _______ that can cause their legs to raise. *(stimulus)*
- The engagement ring was _______ evidence of his love for her. *(tangible)* OL

Before You Read

Flowers for Algernon, Part 2

Vocabulary Preview

tangible (TAN juh bul) *adj.* able to be seen, touched, or felt **(p. 364)** *The doctor wants to see tangible results that he can measure.*

invariably (in VAIR ee uh lee) *adv.* constantly; always **(p. 367)** *Invariably, when a waiter breaks a glass in a restaurant, customers laugh.*

V

cowered (KOW urd) *v.* moved away in fear; form of the verb *cower* **(p. 367)** *The new dishwasher cowered when the owner yelled at him.*

obscure (ub SKYOOR) *v.* to hide **(p. 371)** *The success of the operation cannot obscure the fact that it is not practical.*

stimulus (STIM yoo lus) *n.* something that causes a response **(p. 371)** *Food was the stimulus that caused the mouse to learn.*

Whole Class Discussion As a class, talk about the following questions.

- What are three things that are tangible?
- What invariably happens when you get to school in the morning?
- Why would a person cower?
- What might a used car salesperson seek to obscure?
- What stimulus might cause you to squint?

English Language Coach

Multiple-Meaning Words When you come across a multiple-meaning word, use context clues to figure out which meaning makes sense.

Look at these two words and some of their meanings. You'll see these words in Part 2 of "Flowers for Algernon."

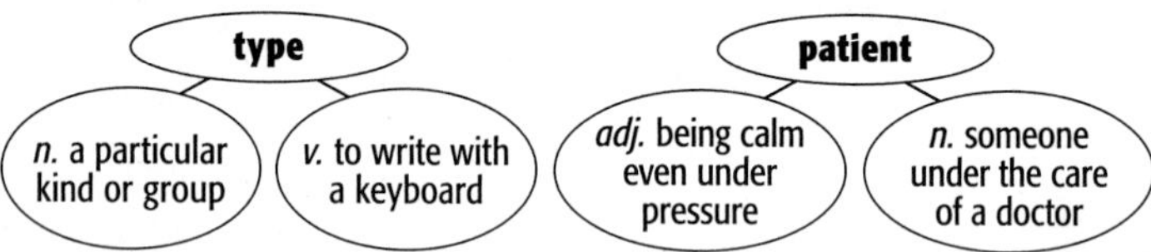
type
n. a particular kind or group
v. to write with a keyboard
patient
adj. being calm even under pressure
n. someone under the care of a doctor

Write to Learn For each word above, write a sentence correctly using one of the meanings of the word.

Indiana English/ Language Arts Academic Standards (pp. 356–377)

8.1.3 Verify the meaning of a word in its context... **8.2 Comprehension and Analysis (Focus on Informational Text)** Develop [reading] strategies such as... identifying and analyzing structure and organization... **8.3.6** Identify significant literary devices... and use [them] to interpret a work.

For a complete description of the standards, see p. IN 11.

Additional Support

English Language Coach

Past Tense Invite students to discuss what has happened in the story up to this point. Guide students in writing a three- to five-sentence group summary of the first part of the story. Explain to students that because they are writing about what has happened so far, they should be consistent in using the past tense of verbs. Have students point out the different past tenses used in the group summary. EL BL

Skills Preview

Key Reading Skill: Understanding Text Structures

When you read Part 2 of the story, look for signal words and phrases that help identify how the writer has organized ideas.

Remember the signal words that show these text structures: cause and effect, comparison and contrast, problem and solution, and chronological order.

Write to Learn Think back to Part 1 of the story. The main text structure for that part is chronological order, but other text structures appear also. In your Learner's Notebook, describe one point in Part 1 in which Charlie uses a different kind of text structure in his own writing.

Literary Element: Foreshadowing

Foreshadowing is the planting of clues to prepare readers for events that will happen later. Foreshadowing can add suspense to a story, get readers involved in a story, and warn them that the story is going to take a different turn. Use these tips to recognize foreshadowing in "Flowers for Algernon." L

- Pay attention to what Charlie and other characters say about future hopes, dreams, and fears.
  What possibilities for the future does the author want you to know about?
- Think about what the characters' actions tell you.
  Do the characters' actions hint at future events?
- When something new happens, think about what you read earlier that warned you this would happen.

Partner Talk Make a list of the statements and actions in Part 1 that might foreshadow what will happen next in the story. Share your list with a classmate and then discuss what you think might happen in Part 2. Write your predictions in your Learner's Notebook.

Get Ready to Read

Connect to the Reading

How would your life change if you woke up ten times smarter than you are now? What would you do with your new intelligence? When you read the rest of the story, compare what you would do with what Charlie Gordon does when he becomes very smart.

Partner Talk With a partner, talk about the changes in Charlie after his operation in Part 1 of the story. Include changes in his abilities to read, write, and think. Then talk about the changes in his feelings toward other people.

Build Background

- Psychologists rate someone who scores 140 or above on an IQ test a genius.
- Some geniuses can see connections between things that are not obvious to other people.
- There is debate over whether people are born geniuses, become geniuses because of their experiences, or both.

Set Purposes for Reading

BIG Question Read Part 2 of "Flowers for Algernon" to find out what happens to Charlie and Algernon and what prices they pay.

Set Your Own Purpose What else would you like to learn from the story to help you answer the Big Question? Write your own purpose on the "Flowers for Algernon," Part 2, flap of the Reading Workshop 3 Foldable.

Interactive Literary Elements Handbook To review or learn more about the literary elements, go to www.glencoe.com.

Keep Moving

Use these skills as you read "Flowers for Algernon," Part 2.

Teach

R Reading Skill

Review Predicting Ask students to share their predictions about what will happen to Charlie and Algernon. AS

L Literary Element

Foreshadowing **Say:** Think about a movie you've seen. How did the filmmaker foreshadow that something scary, exciting, or sad was about to happen? *(Possible responses: by using music or different lighting)* **Ask:** What clues has Keyes given so far about what might happen to Charlie? *(Possible responses: Miss Kinnian has expressed fears that Charlie's intelligence won't last; Charlie has learned his old friends weren't really friends, indicating he may end up lonely.)* OL AL

Interactive Literary Elements Handbook Have students access the Web site to improve their understanding of foreshadowing.

Reading in the Real World

Citizenship Reading "Flowers for Algernon" helped students at Kimball Middle School in Arlington Heights, Illinois, develop empathy for people like Charlie. They decided to collect money for a local home called Little Angels, which helped developmentally disabled children and adults. The students donated money, as well as craft and library supplies to Little Angels. Have students describe some other ways they could help people who are developmentally disabled. AS

Indiana English/Language Arts Academic Standards

SE: 8.1.3, 8.2, 8.3.6

TWE: *English Language Coach* 8.6, *Reading in the Real World* 8.3

Teach

R1 Reading Skill

Review Making Inferences
Ask: Why might Mrs. Flynn be frightened of Charlie? *(Possible response: She doesn't understand why he has changed so much; his depression may scare her.)* BL OL

L Literary Element

Review Irony **Ask:** What is the dramatic irony in Charlie calling himself "dumb" at this point in the story? *(Possible response: The reader knows he is no longer dumb and that it is only by becoming smarter that he can understand why people made fun of him before.)* AL

R2 Reading Skill

Review Making Inferences
Ask: What clues suggest that Charlie is becoming more intelligent than the average person? *(Possible response: He can see a page like a picture, suggesting he is developing a photographic memory, and he is going to learn multiple languages, something most people do not do.)* AL

Flowers for Algernon

by Daniel Keyes

PROGRESS REPORT 11

April 21 Still didn't go into the factory. I told Mrs. Flynn my landlady to call and tell Mr. Donnegan I was sick. Mrs. Flynn looks at me very funny lately like she's scared of me. R1

I think it's a good thing about finding out how everybody laughs at me. I thought about it a lot. It's because I'm so dumb and I don't even know when I'm doing something dumb. People think it's funny when a dumb person can't do things the same way they can. 1 L

Anyway, now I know I'm getting smarter every day. I know punctuation and I can spell good. I like to look up all the hard words in the dictionary and I remember them. I'm reading a lot now, and Miss Kinnian says I read very fast. Sometimes I even understand what I'm reading about, and it stays in my mind. There are times when I can close my eyes and think of a page and it all comes back like a picture.

Besides history, geography, and arithmetic, Miss Kinnian said I should start to learn a few foreign languages. Dr. Strauss gave me some more tapes to play while I sleep. I still don't understand how that conscious and unconscious mind works, but Dr. Strauss says not to worry yet. He asked me to promise that when I start learning college subjects next week I wouldn't read any books on psychology—that is, until he gives me permission. R2

Practice the Skills

1 Key Reading Skill

Understanding Text Structures Charlie begins a new progress report here, but it's only one day after the last entry (in Part 1). What changes do you notice in Charlie from the last report entry to this one?

Additional Support

Literature Focus Lesson

Character After students identify the changes they notice in Charlie's character from April 20 to April 21, work with them to make a Venn diagram. In the left circle, list what Charlie was like on April 20. *(ashamed, upset that people are laughing at him)* In the right circle, list what Charlie was like on April 21. *(realizes he's getting smarter, has decided it's good to know people are laughing at him, is finding new challenges)* Where the circles overlap, list the things that have not changed. *(still wants to make friends, trusts Miss Kinnian, kindhearted, hardworking)* BL

READING WORKSHOP 3

I feel a lot better today, but I guess I'm still a little angry that all the time people were laughing and making fun of me because I wasn't so smart. When I become intelligent like Dr. Strauss says, with three times my I.Q. of 68, then maybe I'll be like everyone else and people will like me and be friendly. **2**

I'm not sure what an I.Q. is. Dr. Nemur said it was something that measured how intelligent you were—like a scale in the drugstore weighs pounds. But Dr. Strauss had a big argument with him and said an I.Q. didn't weigh intelligence at all. He said an I.Q. showed how much intelligence you could get, like the numbers on the outside of a measuring cup. You still had to fill the cup up with stuff. **R1**

Then when I asked Burt, who gives me my intelligence tests and works with Algernon, he said that both of them were wrong (only I had to promise not to tell them he said so). Burt says that the I.Q. measures a lot of different things including some of the things you learned already, and it really isn't any good at all.

So I still don't know what I.Q. is except that mine is going to be over 200 soon. I didn't want to say anything, but I don't see how if they don't know *what* it is, or *where* it is—I don't see how they know *how much* of it you've got.

Dr. Nemur says I have to take a *Rorshach Test* tomorrow. I wonder what *that* is.

April 22 I found out what a *Rorshach* is. It's the test I took before the operation—the one with the inkblots on the pieces of cardboard. The man who gave me the test was the same one. **R2**

I was scared to death of those inkblots. I knew he was going to ask me to find the pictures and I knew I wouldn't be able to. I was thinking to myself, if only there was some way of knowing what kind of pictures were hidden there. Maybe there weren't any pictures at all. Maybe it was just a trick to see if I was dumb enough to look for something that wasn't there. Just thinking about that made me sore at him.

Practice the Skills

2 Reviewing Skills

Predicting Charlie thinks that once he is smarter he'll be like everyone else and people will like him. What do you predict will happen? Why? Read on to see if your prediction matches what happens.

Teach

R1 Reading Skill

Understanding Text Structures **Ask:** What text structure does the author use during the discussion about IQs? *(comparison-contrast)* **OL**

R2 Reading Skill

Review Identifying Author's Purpose **Ask:** Why do you think the author has Charlie recall the first time he took the Rorschach test? *(Possible response: to show how much Charlie's mind has developed and how much of his faith in other people's good intentions has been lost)* **OL** **AL**

Differentiated Instruction

Measuring Intelligence Encourage students to learn more about IQ and the concept of intelligence. Note that in recent years, there has been a great deal of controversy about the validity of such tests. Some people think they do not measure ability because they are culturally biased. Others note that the tests are designed to measure only two types of intelligence: linguistic and logical-mathematical. Have students do research to complete this thesis statement: I think IQ tests are valid/invalid because ________. **AL**

Indiana English/Language Arts Academic Standards
SE: 8.2
TWE: *Literature Focus Lesson* 8.3, *Differentiated Instruction* 8.2

Teach

R Reading Skill

Review Making Inferences
Say: Charlie is stunned when the tester tells him the directions are the same as the first time he took the test. What can you infer about Charlie from his reaction to this information? *(Possible responses: Charlie is now more intelligent, more suspicious, less eager to please, and more independent in his thinking.)* AL

L Literary Element

Foreshadowing Ask: How is Charlie different at work now? *(He is figuring out things that neither his boss nor anyone else at the factory had noticed.)* OL **Ask:** What does this foreshadow about Charlie's work life? *(Possible response: It will no longer make him happy. His coworkers may become jealous of him.)* AL

"All right, Charlie," he said, "you've seen these cards before, remember?"

"Of course I remember."

The way I said it, he knew I was angry, and he looked surprised. "Yes, of course. Now I want you to look at this one. What might this be? What do you see on this card? People see all sorts of things in these inkblots. Tell me what it might be for you—what it makes you think of." **3**

I was shocked. That wasn't what I had expected him to say at all. "You mean there are no pictures hidden in those inkblots?"

He frowned and took off his glasses. "What?"

"Pictures. Hidden in the inkblots. Last time you told me that everyone could see them and you wanted me to find them too."

He explained to me that the last time he had used almost the exact same words he was using now. I didn't believe it, and I still have the suspicion that he misled me at the time just for the fun of it. Unless—I don't know any more—could I have been *that* feeble-minded?[1]

We went through the cards slowly. One of them looked like a pair of bats tugging at something. Another one looked like two men fencing with swords. I imagined all sorts of things. I guess I got carried away. But I didn't trust him any more, and I kept turning them around and even looking on the back to see if there was anything there I was supposed to **catch.** While he was making his notes, I peeked out of the corner of my eye to read it. But it was all in code that looked like this: **4**

WF+A DdF-Ad orig. WF-A SF+obj

The test still doesn't make sense to me. It seems to me that anyone could make up lies about things that they didn't really see. How could he know I wasn't making a fool of him by mentioning things that I didn't really imagine? Maybe I'll understand it when Dr. Strauss lets me read up on psychology. **5**

April 25 I figured out a new way to line up the machines in the factory, and Mr. Donnegan says it will save him ten thousand dollars a year in labor and increased production. He gave me a twenty-five-dollar bonus.

1. Learning and understanding can be very difficult for a ***feeble-minded*** person.

Practice the Skills

3 Reviewing Skills

Predicting How do you think Charlie will react to the inkblots this time? Why? Read on to find out what happens and if your prediction comes true.

4 English Language Coach

Multiple-Meaning Words Look up the verb **catch** in a dictionary and a thesaurus. Decide which meaning of the word matches how it is used in the selection. Then find a synonym that could replace *catch* in the story.

5 Reviewing Skills

Predicting Does Charlie's reaction to the inkblot test match your prediction? Why or why not?

Additional Support

Reading in the Real World

Career The Rorschach test is still given today, although its validity has been challenged. Testers ask people to look at ten inkblots and describe what they see. The inkblots themselves are meaningless. Testers look for patterns in people's responses, for example, do they tend to notice shapes or colors? Do they see animals or people? Although the results are compared to established norms, different testers tend to interpret the results differently.

Have students research careers related to psychology or mental health. OL AL

I wanted to take Joe Carp and Frank Reilly out to lunch to celebrate, but Joe said he had to buy some things for his wife, and Frank said he was meeting his cousin for lunch. I guess it'll take a little time for them to get used to the changes in me. Everybody seems to be frightened of me. When I went over to Amos Borg and tapped him on the shoulder, he jumped up in the air.

People don't talk to me much any more or kid around the way they used to. It makes the job kind of lonely. **6** **L**

April 27 I got up the nerve today to ask Miss Kinnian to have dinner with me tomorrow night to celebrate my bonus.

At first she wasn't sure it was right, but I asked Dr. Strauss and he said it was okay. Dr. Strauss and Dr. Nemur don't seem to be getting along so well. They're arguing all the time. This evening when I came in to ask Dr. Strauss about having dinner with Miss Kinnian, I heard them shouting. Dr. Nemur was saying that it was *his* experiment and *his* research, and Dr. Strauss was shouting back that he contributed just as much, because he found me through Miss Kinnian and he performed the operation. Dr. Strauss said that someday thousands of neurosurgeons[2] might be using his technique all over the world.

Dr. Nemur wanted to publish the results of the experiment at the end of this month. Dr. Strauss wanted to wait a while longer to be sure. Dr. Strauss said that Dr. Nemur was more interested in the Chair of Psychology at Princeton[3] than he was in the experiment. Dr. Nemur said that Dr. Strauss was nothing but an opportunist[4] who was trying to ride to glory on *his* coattails. **7** **C**

When I left afterwards, I found myself trembling. I don't know why for sure, but it was as if I'd seen both men clearly for the first time. I remember hearing Burt say

Visual Vocabulary
Coattails are the back flaps of a man's dress coat. (They are also called simply "tails.")

If you "ride on someone's coattails," you use, or take advantage of, that person's power to gain power for yourself.

2. ***Neurosurgeons*** are doctors who study and operate on the brain.
3. The ***Chair of Psychology*** is the head of a psychology department at a college or university. ***Princeton*** is a famous university in New Jersey.
4. An ***opportunist*** is someone who takes advantage of every opportunity, regardless of consequences.

Practice the Skills

6 **BIG Question**

So far, what has Charlie gained and what has he lost since his operation? Write your answer on the "Flowers for Algernon," Part 2, flap of the Reading Workshop 3 Foldable. Your response will help you complete the Unit Challenge later.

7 **Key Reading Skill**

Understanding Text Structures In this paragraph about the two doctors, the text structure is comparing and contrasting. In your Learner's Notebook, jot down differences between the two doctors.

Teach

L Literary Element

Review Irony **Say:** Charlie hoped that having the operation would help him fit in. How is what actually happens an example of situational irony? *(Possible response: Charlie is just as isolated and lonely as a genius as he was as a learning-disabled person, which is irony because it is not what was expected.)* **OL** **AL**

C Critical Thinking

Comprehension **Say:** Charlie says he feels he is seeing the doctors for the first time. What does he see? *(Possible response: He sees two men who want to get ahead in their field. He sees two regular people, not the geniuses he thought they were.)* **OL** **Ask:** How is the world changing for Charlie as he becomes more intelligent? *(Possible response: He is starting to see things from the perspective of an adult, rather than a child.)* **AL**

Differentiated Instruction

Talking It Through Before students respond to side note number 6, have them list the things Charlie has gained and lost on scrap paper. Then invite them to share their lists with a partner or in small groups. After students have discussed their ideas, have them write their responses to the question on their Foldable "Flowers for Algernon" page. **AS**

Indiana English/Language Arts Academic Standards

SE: 8.1.3, 8.2

TWE: *Reading in the Real World* 8.2; *Differentiated Instruction* 8.3, 8.5.2

Teach

C Critical Thinking

Comprehension Say: Charlie says that every time he sees Miss Kinnian, she grows younger and more lovely. What is really happening? *(Possible response: He is becoming more intelligent and seeing Miss Kinnian from the perspective of a smart adult rather than a less intelligent child.)* **OL**

L Literary Element

Foreshadowing Say: Dr. Strauss thinks it's too soon to publicize the results of Charlie's operation. Who else is concerned that the effects of the operation might not be permanent? How do you know? *(Possible response: Miss Kinnian is wondering if she should have encouraged Charlie to have the operation. She may think the results will not be permanent.)* **OL**

that Dr. Nemur had a shrew[5] of a wife who was pushing him all the time to get things published so that he could become famous. Burt said that the dream of her life was to have a big-shot husband.

Was Dr. Strauss really trying to ride on his coattails?

April 28 I don't understand why I never noticed how beautiful Miss Kinnian really is. She has brown eyes and feathery brown hair that comes to the top of her neck. She's only thirty-four! I think from the beginning I had the feeling that she was an unreachable genius—and very, very old. Now, every time I see her she grows younger and more lovely. **C**

We had dinner and a long talk. When she said that I was coming along so fast that soon I'd be leaving her behind, I laughed.

"It's true, Charlie. You're already a better reader than I am. You can read a whole page at a glance while I can take in only a few lines at a time. And you remember every single thing you read. I'm lucky if I can recall the main thoughts and the general meaning."

"I don't feel intelligent. There are so many things I don't understand."

She took out a cigarette and I lit it for her. "You've got to be a *little* **patient.** You're accomplishing in days and weeks what it takes normal people to do in half a lifetime. That's what makes it so amazing. You're like a giant sponge now, soaking things in. Facts, figures, general knowledge. And soon you'll begin to connect them, too. You'll see how the different branches of learning are related. There are many levels, Charlie, like steps on a giant ladder that take you up higher and higher to see more and more of the world around you. **8**

"I can see only a little bit of that, Charlie, and I won't go much higher than I am now, but you'll keep climbing up and up, and see more and more, and each step will open new worlds that you never even knew existed." She frowned. "I hope . . . I just hope to God—"

"What?"

"Never mind, Charles. I just hope I wasn't wrong to advise you to go into this in the first place." **9** **L**

5. Here, ***shrew*** means "a bad-tempered, nagging woman."

Practice the Skills

8 English Language Coach

Multiple-Meaning Words Use the definitions given earlier to decide which meaning of **patient** makes sense here.

9 Literary Element

Foreshadowing Why do you think Miss Kinnian is worried about getting Charlie involved in the project? What events might this foreshadow?

Additional Support

Literature Focus Lesson

Similes Remind students that similes are comparisons of two unlike things that use the words *like* or *as.* Have students point out the two similes Miss Kinnian uses to explain intelligence to Charlie:

- "You're like a giant sponge now, soaking things in. Facts, figures, general knowledge."
- "There are many levels [of learning] . . . like steps on a giant ladder that take you up higher and higher to see more and more of the world around you."

Have students form small groups to explain each simile: What is being described and compared? What do these comparisons suggest about how Miss Kinnian regards learning? **OL** **AL**

I laughed. "How could that be? It worked, didn't it? Even Algernon is still smart."

We sat there silently for a while and I knew what she was thinking about as she watched me toying with the chain of my rabbit's foot and my keys. I didn't want to think of that possibility any more than elderly people want to think of death. I *knew* that this was only the beginning. I knew what she meant about levels because I'd seen some of them already. The thought of leaving her behind made me sad. **10**

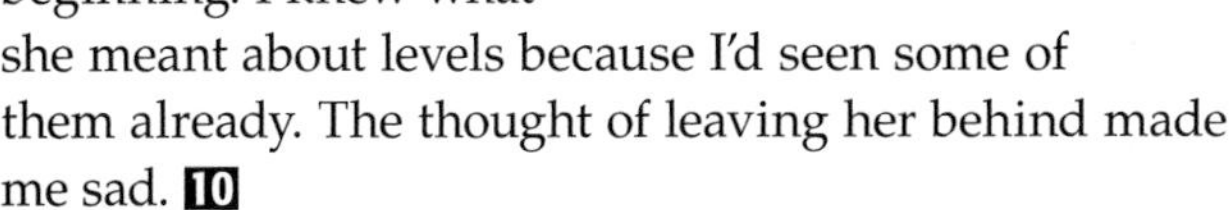

I'm in love with Miss Kinnian.

PROGRESS REPORT 12

April 30 I've quit my job with Donnegan's Plastic Box Company. Mr. Donnegan insisted that it would be better for all concerned if I left. What did I do to make them hate me so?

The first I knew of it was when Mr. Donnegan showed me the petition. Eight hundred and forty names, everyone connected with the factory, except Fanny Girden. Scanning the list quickly, I saw at once that hers was the only missing name. All the rest demanded that I be fired.

Joe Carp and Frank Reilly wouldn't talk to me about it. No one else would either, except Fanny. She was one of the few people I'd known who set her mind to something and believed it no matter what the rest of the world proved, said, or did—and Fanny did not believe that I should have been fired. She had been against the petition on principle and despite the pressure and threats she'd held out.

"Which don't mean to say," she remarked, "that I don't think there's something mighty strange about you, Charlie. Them changes. I don't know. You used to be a good, dependable, ordinary man—not too bright maybe, but honest. Who knows what you done to yourself to get so smart all of a sudden. Like everybody around here's been saying, Charlie, it's not right."

Practice the Skills

10 Literary Element

Foreshadowing What is Charlie worried about? Explain how his concern could be a foreshadowing clue.

READING WORKSHOP 3

Teach

C Critical Thinking

Evaluation Ask: Which do you think is worse: never having superior intelligence or having once had it and losing it? Relate your response to Charlie's life. *(Possible response: When Charlie was learning disabled, he envied people who learned and read easily, but he was otherwise contented with his life. Now that he has gained intelligence, he may also have to experience losing it, which would be like dying. So it seems that it is worse to have intelligence and then lose it than never to have had it.)* OL AL

R Reading Skill

Review Making Inferences

Say: After he leaves the factory, Charlie asks, "What did I do to make them hate me so?" Why do you think his coworkers asked that Charlie be fired? *(Possible response: They are frightened by the changes in Charlie and intimidated by his intelligence.)* OL

Differentiated Instruction

Writing Activity Like many science fiction writers, Keyes began the writing process with a question: "I wonder what would happen if we could increase human intelligence artificially?" Keyes wrote the question in a notebook when he was in college, but forgot about it until an editor asked him to write a short story. Have students write a question they could answer in a science fiction short story. Have students complete the question, "What would happen if ________?" OL AL

Indiana English/Language Arts Academic Standards

SE: 8.1.3, 8.3.6

TWE: *Literature Focus Lesson* 8.1.1, *Differentiated Instruction* 8.3

Teach

C Critical Thinking

Evaluation **Say:** Fannie implies that what has happened to Charlie is evil. Do you agree? *(Responses will vary. Some may feel that intelligence should not be artificially enhanced and that genetic engineering could be dangerous. Others might agree with Charlie, pointing to the potential for good offered by these techniques.)* OL AL

R Reading Skill

Review Comparing and Contrasting **Say:** In the past, Charlie had a hard time understanding people. What does Dr. Strauss's reminder to Charlie tell you about how Charlie has changed? *(Possible response: He is now so smart that he must be careful to speak simply so that others may understand him.)* OL

"But how can you say that, Fanny? What's wrong with a man becoming intelligent and wanting to acquire knowledge and understanding of the world around him?"

She stared down at her work and I turned to leave. Without looking at me, she said: "It was evil when Eve listened to the snake and ate from the tree of knowledge. It was evil when she saw that she was naked. If not for that none of us would ever have to grow old and sick, and die." C

Once again now I have the feeling of shame burning inside me. This intelligence has driven a wedge between me and all the people I once knew and loved. Before, they laughed at me and despised me for my ignorance and dullness; now, they hate me for my knowledge and understanding. What in God's name do they want of me? 11

They've driven me out of the factory. Now I'm more alone than ever before . . .

May 15 Dr. Strauss is very angry at me for not having written any progress reports in two weeks. He's justified because the lab is now paying me a regular salary. I told him I was too busy thinking and reading. When I pointed out that writing was such a slow process that it made me impatient with my poor handwriting, he suggested that I learn to **type.** It's much easier to write now because I can type nearly seventy-five words a minute. Dr. Strauss continually reminds me of the need to speak and write simply so that people will be able to understand me. 12 R

I'll try to review all the things that happened to me during the last two weeks. Algernon and I were presented to the American Psychological Association sitting in convention with the World Psychological Association last Tuesday. We created quite a sensation. Dr. Nemur and Dr. Strauss were proud of us.

I suspect that Dr. Nemur, who is sixty—ten years older than Dr. Strauss—finds it necessary to see **tangible** results of his work. Undoubtedly the result of pressure by Mrs. Nemur.

Contrary to my earlier impressions of him, I realize that Dr. Nemur is not at all a genius. He has a very good mind, but it struggles under the spectre[6] of self-doubt. He wants people to

6. A ***spectre*** is something that haunts or troubles your mind a lot.

Vocabulary

tangible (TAN juh bul) *adj.* able to be seen, touched, or felt

Practice the Skills

11 Key Reading Skill

Understanding Text Structures How does the compare-and-contrast text structure in this passage help you understand what Charlie is going through?

12 English Language Coach

Multiple-Meaning Words The word **type** has several meanings. Which meaning from page 356 makes sense here?

Additional Support

Literature Focus Lesson

Allusion An allusion is a reference to a well-known event, person, or other work of literature. Fanny refers to a biblical story in which Adam and Eve, the first people, eat fruit from the forbidden tree of knowledge and are forced to leave Paradise. After eating the fruit, they become aware of their nakedness and develop shame. Have students tell how Charlie's story is similar:

- Charlie gains knowledge and is driven out of the factory (his "paradise").
- When Charlie learns that his coworkers are mocking him, he says he feels "naked."
- Charlie develops shame as his intelligence grows. AL

Charly, 1967. Selmur Productions. Movie still.

Analyzing the Image How does this photo show that Charlie has changed?

take him for a genius. Therefore, it is important for him to feel that his work is accepted by the world. I believe that Dr. Nemur was afraid of further delay because he worried that someone else might make a discovery along these lines and take the credit from him.

Dr. Strauss on the other hand might be called a genius, although I feel that his areas of knowledge are too limited. He was educated in the tradition of narrow specialization;[7] the broader aspects of background were neglected far more than necessary—even for a neurosurgeon. **13** **R1**

I was shocked to learn that the only ancient languages he could read were Latin, Greek, and Hebrew, and that he knows almost nothing of mathematics beyond the elementary levels of the calculus of variations.[8] When he admitted this to

7. Most people who get a PhD, a type of advanced university degree, are educated ***in the tradition of narrow specialization,*** which means they learn only one subject.
8. ***Calculus*** is a branch of advanced mathematics. The ***calculus of variations*** is even more complicated than simple calculus.

Practice the Skills

13 Key Reading Skill

Understanding Text Structures What is the text structure of this paragraph and the one above it? Look for signal words and phrases. **R2**

Differentiated Instruction

Movie Adaptation The photographs accompanying the story are stills from the film *Charly,* a movie adaptation of *Flowers for Algernon.* The star of the movie, Cliff Robertson, won the 1968 Best Actor Oscar for his performance as Charlie.

Have students form groups to
- tell what changes probably needed to be made to the story to adapt it for film.
- evaluate the film's title. Is it better than the short story title? Why or why not? **AS**

Teach

Viewing the Photo

Say: Look at the photographs of Charlie on pages 343 and 350. Then compare these to his photograph on this page. How has he changed? *(Possible response: In the first two photos, his facial expressions and posture are childlike. In this photo, he looks like a grown man. He has become more mature, but he has also lost his smile and innocence.)* **OL**

R1 Reading Skill

Review Making Inferences

Say: Miss Kinnian told Charlie that he would begin to see how different areas of knowledge were connected. What do his comments about Dr. Strauss suggest? *(Possible response: They suggest Charlie's awareness of how knowledge is connected is now far greater than Dr. Strauss's.)* **OL** **AL**

R2 Reading Skill

Understanding Text Structures Students should see that these paragraphs have a comparison-contrast text structure. Charlie describes Dr. Nemur and then compares him to Dr. Strauss. If students cannot see the structure, **Say:** Charlie uses the words on the other hand. What text structure do these words suggest? *(comparison-contrast)* **OL**

Indiana English/Language Arts Academic Standards

SE: 8.1.3, 8.2

TWE: *Literature Focus Lesson* 8.1.1, *Differentiated Instruction* 8.2

Teach

L Literary Element

Review Irony **Ask:** What is ironic about Charlie giving Dr. Nemur an inferiority complex, or making him feel less intelligent? *(Possible response: Dr. Nemur was responsible for making Charlie smart, so it is unexpected that Charlie would make Dr. Nemur feel inferior.)* AL

BQ 

Ask: Why does Charlie gets angry at Dr. Strauss and at Miss Kinnian? *(He thinks they're making fun of him.)* **Ask:** Charlie has gained intelligence, but according to these experiences, what has he lost? *(Possible response: He has lost his innocent belief that people are kind. He has become suspicious and insecure.)* OL

READING WORKSHOP 3

me, I found myself almost annoyed. It was as if he'd hidden this part of himself in order to deceive me, pretending—as do many people I've discovered—to be what he is not. No one I've ever known is what he appears to be on the surface. **14**

Dr. Nemur appears to be uncomfortable around me. Sometimes when I try to talk to him, he just looks at me strangely and turns away. I was angry at first when Dr. Strauss told me I was giving Dr. Nemur an inferiority complex.[9] I thought he was mocking me and I'm oversensitive at being made fun of. **L**

How was I to know that a highly respected psychoexperimentalist like Nemur was unacquainted with Hindustani[10] and Chinese? It's absurd when you consider the work that is being done in India and China today in the very field of this study.

I asked Dr. Strauss how Nemur could refute[11] Rahajamati's attack on his method and results if Nemur couldn't even read them in the first place. That strange look on Dr. Strauss' face can mean only one of two things. Either he doesn't want to tell Nemur what they're saying in India, or else—and this worries me—Dr. Strauss doesn't know either. I must be careful to speak and write clearly and simply so that people won't laugh.

May 18 I am very disturbed. I saw Miss Kinnian last night for the first time in over a week. I tried to avoid all discussions of intellectual concepts[12] and to keep the conversation on a simple, everyday level, but she just stared at me blankly and asked me what I meant about the mathematical variance equivalent in Dorbermann's *Fifth Concerto*.

When I tried to explain she stopped me and laughed. I guess I got angry, but I suspect I'm approaching her on the wrong level. No matter what I try to discuss with her, I am unable to communicate. I must review Vrostadt's equations on *Levels of Semantic Progression*. I find that I don't communicate with people much any more. Thank God for books and music and things I can think about. I am alone in my apartment at Mrs. Flynn's boardinghouse most of the time and seldom speak to anyone.

9. Someone with an ***inferiority complex*** feels less worthy or valuable than others.
10. ***Hindustani*** (hin dew STAHN ee) is a dialect spoken in India.
11. To ***refute*** the attack would be to prove that the criticism is false or incorrect.
12. ***Intellectual concepts*** are ideas that relate to learning and thinking.

Practice the Skills

14 Reviewing Elements

Irony Before the operation, there were things Charlie didn't know about the people around him. That helped to create dramatic irony. Are there things he doesn't know now?

Additional Support

Literature Focus Lesson

Proverb Write this saying on the board: *Be careful what you wish for because you just might get it.* Ask students to explain in a brief paragraph how this saying applies to Charlie. Encourage students to use evidence from the story, such as Charlie's comment that he now spends most of his time alone, to support their answers. OL

May 20 I would not have noticed the new dishwasher, a boy of about sixteen, at the corner diner where I take my evening meals if not for the incident of the broken dishes.

They crashed to the floor, shattering and sending bits of white china under the tables. The boy stood there, dazed and frightened, holding the empty tray in his hand. The whistles and catcalls from the customers (the cries of "hey, there go the profits!" . . . "*Mazeltov!*"[13] . . . and "well, *he* didn't work here very long . . ." which **invariably** seem to follow the breaking of glass or dishware in a public restaurant) all seemed to confuse him.

When the owner came to see what the excitement was about, the boy **cowered** as if he expected to be struck and threw up his arms as if to ward off the blow.

"All right! All right, you dope," shouted the owner, "don't just stand there! Get the broom and sweep that mess up. A broom . . . a broom, you idiot! It's in the kitchen. Sweep up all the pieces."

The boy saw that he was not going to be punished. His frightened expression disappeared and he smiled and hummed as he came back with the broom to sweep the floor. A few of the rowdier customers kept up the remarks, amusing themselves at his expense.

"Here, sonny, over here there's a nice piece behind you . . ."

"C'mon, do it again . . ."

"He's not so dumb. It's easier to break 'em than to wash 'em . . ."

As his vacant eyes moved across the crowd of amused onlookers, he slowly mirrored their smiles and finally broke into an uncertain grin at the joke which he obviously did not understand.

I felt sick inside as I looked at his dull, vacuous smile, the wide, bright eyes of a child, uncertain but eager to please. They were laughing at him because he was mentally retarded. **15**

And I had been laughing at him too.

Suddenly, I was furious at myself and all those who were smirking at him. I jumped up and shouted, "Shut up! Leave

13. ***Mazeltov*** or ***mazel tov*** (MAH zul tov) means "congratulations" in the Hebrew language.

Vocabulary

invariably (in VAIR ee ub lee) *adv.* constantly; always

cowered (KOW urd) *v.* moved away in fear

Practice the Skills

15 Key Reading Skill

Understanding Text Structures The dishwasher dropping dishes sets off a chain of causes and effects that leads Charlie to this understanding. Quickly scan the May 20 journal entry to find the causes and effects that lead Charlie to this point.

Teach

L Literary Element

Review Tone Ask: What is the owner's tone as he speaks to the dishwasher? *(It is cruel and impatient.)* **Ask:** What is the tone of the crowd? *(It is mocking and unkind.)* OL

R Reading Skill

Review Comparing and Contrasting Ask: What similarities does Charlie see between himself and the dishwasher? *(Possible response: At one time, he too would have tried to play along with the joke instead of realizing that people were mocking him.)* **Ask:** Why does Charlie get angry? *(Possible response: He realizes that he has been laughing at someone who couldn't understand or defend himself.)* OL AL

Differentiated Instruction

Building Background The incident with the dishwasher is based on something that actually happened to the author. When he was in college, he worked at a restaurant. One day, he dropped several glasses and plates. The owner yelled, "What's the matter with you? A college boy and he can't even wait on tables. Clean it up, moron!" Keyes recalled the incident when he was looking for a way to show how many people laugh and feel superior when the mentally challenged make a mistake. Ask students why they think people laugh during such incidents. Do they intend to be cruel? Why or why not? AS

Indiana English/Language Arts Academic Standards

SE: 8.2, 8.3.6

TWE: *Literature Focus Lesson* 8.3, *Differentiated Instruction* 8.3

Teach

L1 Literary Element

Review Irony Ask: Why is Charlie upset when he finds himself sharing the laughter at the dishwasher? *(Possible responses: He is upset to discover he has been making fun of someone the way he used to be mocked and angry that people treat the mentally disabled with such disrespect.)* OL **Say:** Charlie once wanted to be like everyone else. How is his being like everyone else here an example of situational irony? *(Possible response: Charlie expected that being like everyone else would be a good thing. In this situation, being like everyone else means being cruel and making fun of the way he used to be.)* OL AL

L2 Literary Element

Review Plot Ask: How is the incident in the restaurant a turning point for Charlie? *(Possible answer: Charlie has a chance to see himself as others once saw him. It gives him a sense of how far he has come, but he also feels a profound sense of identity with the boy and anger at the people in the restaurant. It inspires him to work to help the mentally challenged.)* AL

READING WORKSHOP 3

him alone! It's not his fault he can't understand! He can't help what he is! But for God's sake . . . he's still a human being!"

The room grew silent. I cursed myself for losing control and creating a scene. I tried not to look at the boy as I paid my check and walked out without touching my food. I felt ashamed for both of us. L1

How strange it is that people of honest feelings and sensibility, who would not take advantage of a man born without arms or legs or eyes—how such people think nothing of abusing a man born with low intelligence. It infuriated me to think that not too long ago I, like this boy, had foolishly played the clown. 16

And I had almost forgotten.

I'd hidden the picture of the old Charlie Gordon from myself because now that I was intelligent it was something that had to be pushed out of my mind. But today in looking at that boy, for the first time I saw what I had been. *I was just like him!*

Only a short time ago, I learned that people laughed at me. Now I can see that unknowingly I joined with them in laughing at myself. That hurts most of all.

I have often reread my progress reports and seen the illiteracy, the childish naiveté,[14] the mind of low intelligence peering from a dark room, through the keyhole, at the dazzling light outside. I see that even in my dullness I knew that I was inferior, and that other people had something I lacked—something denied me. In my mental blindness, I thought that it was somehow connected with the ability to read and write, and I was sure that if I could get those skills I would automatically have intelligence too. L2

Even a feeble-minded man wants to be like other men.

A child may not know how to feed itself, or what to eat, yet it knows of hunger.

This then is what I was like, I never knew. Even with my gift of intellectual awareness, I never really knew.

This day was good for me. Seeing the past more clearly, I have decided to use my knowledge and skills to work in the field of increasing human intelligence levels. Who is better equipped for this work? Who else has lived in both worlds? These are my people. Let me use my gift to do something for them.

14. ***Naiveté*** (nah EVE tay) is innocence, or lack of worldly knowledge and experience.

Practice the Skills

16 **BIG Question**

Charlie realizes that he was once laughed at by others. The pain he feels is a price he has to pay for becoming smarter. Is the price too high? Discuss your answer with a partner. Then write your ideas on the "Flowers for Algernon," Part 2, flap of the Reading Workshop 3 Foldable.

Additional Support

Literature Focus Lesson

Point of View Tell students that the author made several attempts to write the story but was dissatisfied with all of them until he started writing from Charlie's point of view. He finally decided "it had to be first person. . . . in Charlie's mind and through Charlie's eyes all the way." Help students see how it is especially helpful to see the incident with the dishwasher from Charlie's perspective: Charlie is in a unique position to understand the situation because he has experienced both the dishwasher's perspective and the perspective of the crowd. OL

Tomorrow, I will discuss with Dr. Strauss the manner in which I can work in this area. I may be able to help him work out the problems of widespread use of the technique which was used on me. I have several good ideas of my own.

There is so much that might be done with this technique. BQ If I could be made into a genius, what about thousands of others like myself? What fantastic levels might be achieved by using this technique on normal people? On *geniuses?*

There are so many doors to open. I am impatient to begin.

PROGRESS REPORT 13

May 23 It happened today. Algernon bit me. I visited the lab to see him as I do occasionally, and when I took him out of his cage, he snapped at my hand. I put him back and watched him for a while. He was unusually disturbed and vicious. **17**

May 24 Burt, who is in charge of the experimental animals, tells me that Algernon is changing. He is less cooperative; he refuses to run the maze any more; general motivation has decreased. And he hasn't been eating. Everyone is upset about what this may mean.

May 25 They've been feeding Algernon, who now refuses to work the shifting-lock problem. Everyone identifies me with Algernon. In a way we're both the first of our kind. They're all pretending that Algernon's behavior is not necessarily significant for me. But it's hard to hide the fact that some of the other animals who were used in this experiment are showing strange behavior. L

Dr. Strauss and Dr. Nemur have asked me not to come to the lab any more. I know what they're thinking but I can't accept it. I am going ahead with my plans to carry their research forward. With all due respect to both of these fine scientists, I am well aware of their limitations. If there is an answer, I'll have to find it out for myself. Suddenly, time has become very important to me. **18**

May 29 I have been given a lab of my own and permission to go ahead with the research. I'm on to something. Working day and night. I've had a cot moved into the lab. Most of my writing time is spent on the notes which I keep in a separate folder, but from time to time I feel it necessary to put down my moods and my thoughts out of sheer habit.

Practice the Skills

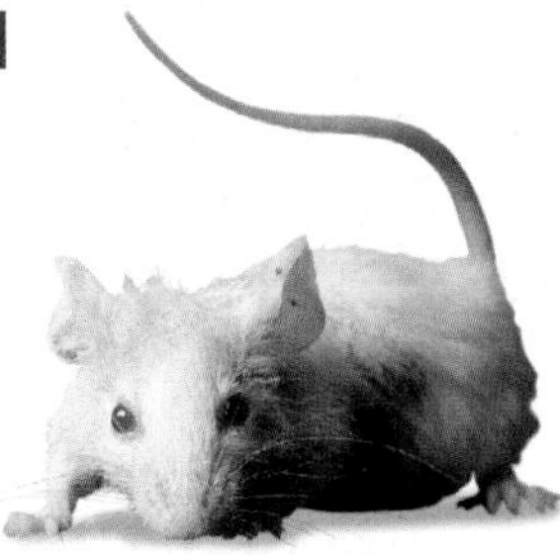

17 Literary Element

Foreshadowing What might this event foreshadow? Remember, Charlie has had the same operation as Algernon.

18 Literary Element

Foreshadowing Why has time all of a sudden become so important to Charlie? What does he feel is going to happen?

Teach

BQ BIG Question

Ask: What evidence do you see that Charlie thinks his intelligence is worth the price he's had to pay for it? *(Possible response: He wants to keep working on the technique. He sees it opening "many doors.")* OL

L Literary Element

Foreshadowing Say: Charlie says that everyone is upset about what the changes in Algernon may mean. What do you think these changes mean? *(Possible response: What is happening to Algernon will probably happen to Charlie.)*
Ask: What evidence do you find that Charlie knows what may happen to him? *(Possible response: He says, "Suddenly, time has become very important to me." This indicates he knows he doesn't have much more time to use his new intelligence.)* OL

Differentiated Instruction

Diagraming Plot Structure This story is praised for its tight narrative. After Charlie is introduced, the rising action begins with his intelligence slowly increasing. The complication is that the effects of the operation are short-lived. The falling action—the decrease of intelligence—parallels the rising action and returns Charlie to his original condition. The changes in Algernon mark the beginning of the falling action. Work with students to diagram the action so far. Ask them to copy the diagram into their Learner's Notebooks and add events to the falling action as they read. AS

Indiana English/Language Arts Academic Standards
SE: 8.3.6
TWE: *Literature Focus Lesson* 8.3, *Differentiated Instruction* 8.3.2

Teach

L Literary Element

Foreshadowing **Ask:** What does Charlie expect will happen to him? How do you know? *(Possible response: He expects his intelligence to decline quickly because of the "sharp regression in Algernon" and the formula he has developed. He realizes that the experiment conducted by Drs. Nemur and Strauss has failed.)* **OL** **Ask:** How would your reaction to the story be different if Charlie didn't realize what was happening to him? *(Responses will vary. Students might feel the story would be less moving if Charlie was unaware of his regression.)* **AL**

READING WORKSHOP 3

I find the *calculus of intelligence* to be a fascinating study. Here is the place for the application of all the knowledge I have acquired. In a sense it's the problem I've been concerned with all my life.

May 31 Dr. Strauss thinks I'm working too hard. Dr. Nemur says I'm trying to cram a lifetime of research and thought into a few weeks. I know I should rest, but I'm driven on by something inside that won't let me stop. I've got to find the reason for the sharp regression[15] in Algernon. I've got to know *if* and *when* it will happen to me. **L**

June 4 **19**

LETTER TO DR. STRAUSS (*copy*)

Dear Dr. Strauss:

Under separate cover I am sending you a copy of my report entitled, "The Algernon-Gordon Effect: A Study of Structure and Function of Increased Intelligence," which I would like to have you read and have published.

As you see, my experiments are completed. I have included in my report all of my formulae, as well as mathematical analysis in the appendix. Of course, these should be verified.

Because of its importance to both you and Dr. Nemur (and need I say to myself, too?) I have checked and rechecked my results a dozen times in the hope of finding an error. I am sorry to say the results must stand. Yet for the sake of science, I am grateful for the little bit that I here add to the knowledge of the function of the human mind and of the laws governing the artificial increase of human intelligence.

I recall your once saying to me that an experimental *failure* or the *disproving* of a theory was as important to the advancement of learning as a success would be. I know now that this is true. I am sorry, however, that my own contribution to the field must rest upon the ashes of the work of two men I regard so highly.

Yours truly,

Charles Gordon
encl.: rept.

15. When something returns to an earlier stage, it shows ***regression*** (ree GREH shun).

Practice the Skills

19 **Key Reading Skill**

Understanding Text Structures The story continues in chronological order. Why do you think the author chose to use chronological order? How does following events in order add to the impact of the story?

Additional Support

Literature Focus Lesson

Point of View Tell students that writers must choose a format that fits their purpose. Once Daniel Keyes had decided to tell the story of Charlie's operation from Charlie's point of view, he had a challenge. How could a mentally disabled man tell a complex story from beginning to end? Keyes decided that Charlie's doctors would ask him to keep a record of his progress. To his knowledge, this approach had never been used in a short story. Have students evaluate this format. What are its benefits? What are its limitations? **AL**

June 5 I must not become emotional. The facts and the results of my experiments are clear, and the more sensational aspects of my own rapid climb cannot **obscure** the fact that the tripling of intelligence by the surgical technique developed by Drs. Strauss and Nemur must be viewed as having little or no practical applicability (at the present time) to the increase of human intelligence. **20**

As I review the records and data on Algernon, I see that although he is still in his physical infancy, he has regressed mentally. Motor activity is impaired; there is a general reduction of glandular activity; there is an accelerated loss of co-ordination.

There are also strong indications of progressive[16] amnesia.

As will be seen by my report, these and other physical and mental deterioration syndromes[17] can be predicted with statistically significant results by the application of my formula.

The surgical **stimulus** to which we were both subjected has resulted in an intensification and acceleration of all mental processes. The unforeseen development, which I have taken the liberty of calling the *Algernon-Gordon Effect,* is the logical extension of the entire intelligence speed-up. The hypothesis[18] here proven may be described simply

16. ***Progressive amnesia*** is a loss of memory that is getting worse.
17. ***Deterioration*** is a worsening, and ***syndromes*** are groups of symptoms that, together, indicate disease. The combined term refers to diseases that result in a lessening of some ability or strength.
18. A ***hypothesis*** is an unproven idea or theory.

Vocabulary

obscure (ub SKYOOR) *v.* to hide

stimulus (STIM yoo lus) *n.* something that causes a response

Conversion. Diana Ong. Computer generated.

Analyzing the Art How might this face show what is happening to Charlie?

20 Reviewing Elements

Style How has Charlie's style of writing changed in the last few entries?

Reading Fluency

Reading Difficult Text Charlie's word choice and sentence structure become more complex as his intelligence increases. Suggest students use these strategies to help them understand his writing:

- looking up hard words
- using context clues to guess meanings
- restating ideas in your own words

Help students summarize the main points of his June 5 report by having them read aloud each paragraph and then stop to write a sentence or two that summarizes the main points. **EL** **BL**

READING WORKSHOP 3

Teach

Viewing the Art

Say: This piece of art depicts a face, but it is not realistic because it has an unusual perspective. It's like looking at a person from two different perspectives at once, or like looking at two different sides of a person. Why is this painting an appropriate illustration for Charlie's story? *(Possible response: Charlie changes so much in the story, he is like two people: the person he was before the operation and the person he was after it.)* **OL**

R Reading Skill

Review Making Inferences

Ask: What language does Charlie use in this report? *(very scientific, complex language)* **Ask:** How might using this kind of language be a coping mechanism for him? *(Possible response: He knows he is losing his intelligence, but instead of becoming upset about it, he is trying to stay detached, or separated from it, as though it were happening to someone else.)* **OL**

Indiana English/Language Arts Academic Standards

SE: 8.2

TWE: *Literature Focus Lesson* 8.2, *Reading Fluency* 8.1

Teach

C1 Critical Thinking

Comprehension Ask: What signs of Charlie's decline do you see? *(Possible responses: He notices he is absent-minded; he is irritable, depressed, and afraid he will lose everything he's learned; he is frustrated when he can no longer understand* Paradise Lost*; he realizes that his brain is undergoing the same changes Algernon's did.)* BL OL

R Reading Skill

Review Making Inferences Ask: How does Charlie react when Algernon dies? *(He cries.)* BL **Ask:** Why do you think he cries? *(Possible responses: He is sad that his friend has died. He is sad that he, too, will lose his intelligence. He may be afraid that he will die, too.)* OL

C2 Critical Thinking

Comprehension Ask: Why does Charlie get angry and throw the book across the room? *(Possible response: He is frustrated because he can no longer understand it.)* BL

in the following terms: Artificially increased intelligence deteriorates at a rate of time directly proportional to the quantity of the increase.

I feel that this, in itself, is an important discovery.

As long as I am able to write, I will continue to record my thoughts in these progress reports. It is one of my few pleasures. However, by all indications, my own mental deterioration will be very rapid. **21**

I have already begun to notice signs of emotional instability and forgetfulness, the first symptoms of the burnout.

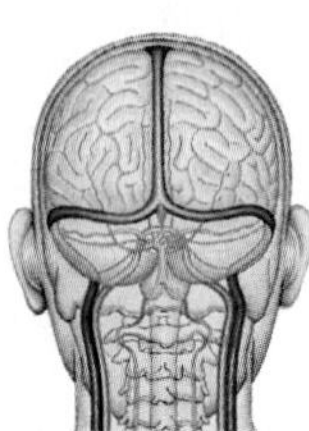

Visual Vocabulary Charlie cuts up Algernon's brain to study it ***(dissection)***. A healthy brain surface would have many irregular folds ***(convolutions)*** and cracks ***(fissures)*** that are long, narrow, and shallow.

June 10 Deterioration progressing. I have become absentminded. Algernon died two days ago. Dissection shows my predictions were right. His brain had decreased in weight and there was a general smoothing out of cerebral convolutions as well as a deepening and broadening of brain fissures.

I guess the same thing is or will soon be happening to me. Now that it's definite, I don't want it to happen.

I put Algernon's body in a cheese box and buried him in the back yard. I cried. R

June 15 Dr. Strauss came to see me again. I wouldn't open the door and I told him to go away. I want to be left to myself. I have become touchy and irritable. I feel the darkness closing in. It's hard to throw off thoughts of suicide. I keep telling myself how important this introspective[19] journal will be.

It's a strange sensation to pick up a book that you've read and enjoyed just a few months ago and discover that you don't remember it. I remembered how great I thought John Milton was, but when I picked up *Paradise Lost* I couldn't understand it at all. I got so angry I threw the book across the room. C2

I've got to try to hold on to some of it. Some of the things I've learned. Oh, God, please don't take it all away.

Practice the Skills

21 Key Reading Skill

Understanding Text Structures How has comparing his situation with Algernon's allowed Charlie to make this prediction?

19. ***Introspective*** means "looking into or examining your own feelings and thoughts."

Additional Support

Differentiated Instruction

Building Background The use of animals in scientific and cosmetic testing is a very controversial subject. Supporters point to scientific advancements and increased product safety; opponents see testing as cruel and unnecessary. Have students write two benefits and two disadvantages of animal testing. Ask them, "If the intelligence experiment had worked, would Algernon's death have been a price worth paying? Why or why not?" OL AL

June 19 Sometimes, at night, I go out for a walk. Last night I couldn't remember where I lived. A policeman took me home. I have the strange feeling that this has all happened to me before—a long time ago. I keep telling myself I'm the only person in the world who can describe what's happening to me.

June 21 Why can't I remember? I've got to fight. I lie in bed for days and I don't know who or where I am. Then it all comes back to me in a flash. Fugues of amnesia. Symptoms of senility[20]—second childhood. I can watch them coming on. It's so cruelly logical. I learned so much and so fast. Now my mind is deteriorating rapidly. I won't let it happen. I'll fight it. I can't help thinking of the boy in the restaurant, the blank expression, the silly smile, the people laughing at him. No—please—not that again . . . **22**

June 22 I'm forgetting things that I learned recently. It seems to be following the classic pattern—the last things learned are the first things forgotten. Or is that the pattern? I'd better look it up again . . .

I reread my paper on the *Algernon-Gordon Effect* and I get the strange feeling that it was written by someone else. There are parts I don't even understand.

Motor activity impaired. I keep tripping over things, and it becomes increasingly difficult to type.

Visual Vocabulary This is an old-style manual ***typewriter.*** People used typewriters before computers were invented.

June 23 I've given up using the typewriter completely. My coordination is bad. I feel that I'm moving slower and slower. Had a terrible shock today. I picked up a copy of an article I used in my research, Krueger's *Uber psychische Ganzheit,* to see if it would help me understand what I had done. First I thought there was something wrong with my eyes. Then I realized I could no longer read German. I tested myself in other languages. All gone.

20. ***Fugues*** (FYOOGS) ***of amnesia*** (am NEE zha) are times when a person seems to be aware of his or her actions but can't recall them later. ***Senility*** refers to the loss of physical and mental abilities that can accompany old age.

Practice the Skills

22 Reviewing Skills

Predicting Do you think Charlie will be able to keep his mind from deteriorating? Why or why not?

Teach

C Critical Thinking

Comprehension Ask: What signs does Charlie have that the effects of the operation are wearing off? *(He can't remember where he lives; he doesn't know who he is or where he is; he is very forgetful; he can't understand things he read and wrote in the past.)* **BL OL**

BQ BIG Question

Say: Charlie's progress reports from June 19 through June 30 show in great detail how Charlie feels as he loses his intelligence. Do you think the price he is paying for his time as a "smart person" is too high? Why or why not? *(Possible response: Yes, the price is too high. He experiences pain and confusion as the effects of the operation wear off.)* **AS**

Literature Focus Lesson

Conflict Remind students that the conflict in a story is the struggle between opposing forces. It can be internal (in the main character's mind) or external (between two characters, between a character and another force, between two forces or ideas). Have students describe the following conflicts and tell which they think is the main conflict in the story:

- between Dr. Nemur and Dr. Strauss
- between Charlie and his coworkers
- between scientific knowledge and ethical treatment of people
- between Charlie and "normal culture" **OL AL**

Indiana English/Language Arts Academic Standards
SE: 8.2
TWE: *Differentiated Instruction* 8.2, *Literature Focus Lesson* 8.3.2

Teach

R1 Reading Skill

Review Identifying Author's Purpose **Say:** Keyes describes Charlie's pain as he loses his intelligence. Do you think he is suggesting Charlie would have been better off without the operation? Why or why not? *(Responses will vary. Possible response: No, Charlie believes that his experience could have value for science, and he doesn't blame the doctors; Yes, Keyes emphasizes how much the process hurts Charlie, showing how painful and lonely it has been.)* **OL** **AL**

R2 Reading Skill

Review Comparing and Contrasting **Say:** Compare Charlie's entry on June 30 to his entry on July 10. How has his language changed? *(On June 30, Charlie uses a simile—"slipping away like sand through my fingers,"—and he still looks up hard words. On July 10, his language is more childlike. He doesn't use much punctuation and decides not to use a dictionary anymore.)* **OL** **Ask:** How has his emotional intelligence changed? *(On June 30, he knows he's feeling angry and how Dr. Strauss feels guilty. By July 10, he says he thinks he's sick, indicating he no longer knows how he feels.)* **AL**

June 30 A week since I dared to write again. It's slipping away like sand through my fingers. Most of the books I have are too hard for me now. I get angry with them because I know that I read and understood them just a few weeks ago.

I keep telling myself I must keep writing these reports so that somebody will know what is happening to me. But it gets harder to form the words and remember spellings. I have to look up even simple words in the dictionary now and it makes me impatient with myself.

Dr. Strauss comes around almost every day, but I told him I wouldn't see or speak to anybody. He feels guilty. They all do. But I don't blame anyone. I knew what might happen. But how it hurts. **23**

July 7 I don't know where the week went. Todays Sunday I know because I can see through my window people going to church. I think I stayed in bed all week but I remember Mrs. Flynn bringing food to me a few times. I keep saying over and over Ive got to do something but then I forget or maybe its just easier not to do what I say Im going to do.

I think of my mother and father a lot these days. I found a picture of them with me taken at a beach. My father has a big ball under his arm and my mother is holding me by the hand. I dont remember them the way they are in the picture. All I remember is my father drunk most of the time and arguing with mom about money.

He never shaved much and he used to scratch my face when he hugged me. My mother said he died but Cousin Miltie said he heard his mom and dad say that my father ran away with another woman. When I asked my mother she slapped my face and said my father was dead. I dont think I ever found out which was true but I don't care much. (He said he was going to take me to see cows on a farm once but he never did. He never kept his promises . . .)

July 10 My landlady Mrs Flynn is very worried about me. She says the way I lay around all day and dont do anything I remind her of her son before she threw him out of the house. She said she doesnt like loafers. If Im sick its one thing, but if Im a loafer thats another thing and she wont have it. I told her I think Im sick.

I try to read a little bit every day, mostly stories, but sometimes I have to read the same thing over and over again

Practice the Skills

R1 **23** **Reviewing Skills**

Making Inferences Why do you think Dr. Strauss and all the others feel guilty?

Additional Support

Literature Focus Lesson

Flashback A flashback is a scene from the past that interrupts the action in a story. Because the format of this story is a type of journal, the author uses Charlie's memory to present a flashback. Have students point out the flashback and tell why Charlie might be thinking about the past *(possible responses follow):*

- Charlie remembers his mother and father.
- His current pain might be reminding him of pain from his past.
- He might be thinking of his childhood because he is becoming childlike again. **AL**

READING WORKSHOP 3

because I dont know what it means. And its hard to write. I know I should look up all the words in the dictionary but its so hard and Im so tired all the time.

Then I got the idea that I would only use the easy words instead of the long hard ones. That saves time. I put flowers on Algernons grave about once a week. Mrs Flynn thinks Im crazy to put flowers on a mouses grave but I told her that Algernon was special.

July 14 Its sunday again. I dont have anything to do to keep me busy now because my television set is broke and I dont have any money to get it fixed. (I think I lost this months check from the lab. I dont remember) **24**

I get awful headaches and asperin doesnt help me much. Mrs Flynn knows Im really sick and she feels very sorry for me. Shes a wonderful woman whenever someone is sick.

July 22 Mrs Flynn called a strange doctor to see me. She was afraid I was going to die. I told the doctor I wasnt too sick and that I only forget sometimes. He asked me did I have any friends or relatives and I said no I dont have any. I told him I had a friend called Algernon once but he was a mouse and we used to run races together. He looked at me kind of funny like he thought I was crazy. **R**

He smiled when I told him I used to be a genius. He talked to me like I was a baby and he winked at Mrs Flynn. I got mad and chased him out because he was making fun of me the way they all used to.

July 24 I have no more money and Mrs Flynn says I got to go to work somewhere and pay the rent because I havent paid for over two months. I dont know any work but the job I used to have at Donnegans Plastic Box Company. I dont want to go back there because they all knew me when I was smart and maybe theyll laugh at me. But I dont know what else to do to get money. **L**

July 25 I was looking at some of my old progress reports and its very funny but I cant read what I wrote. I can make out some of the words but they dont make sense.

Miss Kinnian came to the door but I said go away I dont want to see you. She cried and I cried too but I wouldnt let her in because I didnt want her to laugh at me. I told her I didn't like her any more. I told her I didnt want to be smart any

Practice the Skills

24 Key Reading Skill

Understanding Text Structures What has Charlie done over the past week? Why do you think the author organizes information in chronological order? How does this help you understand the changes that are happening to Charlie?

Teach

R Reading Skill

Review Making Inferences
Ask: How does Charlie behave during the incident with the "strange doctor"? *(He tells the truth and then gets angry when the doctor patronizes him and doesn't believe him.)* **Ask:** What do you learn about Charlie from this incident? *(Possible responses: Charlie is no longer a genius, but he has retained some idea that he should be treated with respect.)* **OL AL**

L Literary Element

Review Irony **Say:** Charlie is losing all the knowledge he gained except the understanding that people once laughed at him. Notice that he repeatedly worries he is being made fun of. Think about the goal of the operation. How is what has happened to him an example of situational irony? *(Possible response: The goal of the operation was to improve Charlie's life. Instead, his life is even more difficult than it was before because he remembers that people make fun of him.)* **AL**

Differentiated Instruction

Creating a Plot Diagram Review the plot structure of the story with students. Draw an inverted *V* on the board. Explain that the left side of the *V* is the rising action, the top is the climax, or turning point, and the right side is the falling action. Have students help you label your plot diagram with these main events of the story:

- **Rising action**—Charlie is selected for surgery; has the operation; beats Algernon; triples his IQ.
- **Climax**—Algernon dies.
- **Falling action**—Charlie realizes he will decline; symptoms start; loses abilities to read and type; goes back to his old job. **AS**

Indiana English/Language Arts Academic Standards
SE: 8.2
TWE: *Literature Focus Lesson* 8.3.2, *Differentiated Instruction* 8.3.2

Teach

R Reading Skill

Review Making Inferences
Ask: How do Charlie's coworkers treat him when he returns to work? *(They are kind to him and tell the new man not to make fun of him.)* BL **Ask:** Why do you think Charlie's coworkers treat him differently now? *(Possible responses: Charlie is no longer a threat to them; they have learned that Charlie is a real person with feelings.)* OL AL

C Critical Thinking

Comprehension Ask: What is the "dumb thing" Charlie does on July 28? *(He forgets he's not in Miss Kinnian's class and sits in his old seat waiting for the lesson to start.)* BL **Ask:** Why does it make Miss Kinnian cry? *(Possible responses: She is upset that the experiment failed. She misses Charlie.)* OL

READING WORKSHOP 3

more. Thats not true. I still love her and I still want to be smart but I had to say that so shed go away. She gave Mrs Flynn money to pay the rent. I dont want that. I got to get a job.

Please . . . please let me not forget how to read and write . . .

July 27 Mr Donnegan was very nice when I came back and asked him for my old job of janitor. First he was very suspicious but I told him what happened to me then he looked very sad and put his hand on my shoulder and said Charlie Gordon you got guts.

Everybody looked at me when I came downstairs and started working in the toilet sweeping it out like I used to. I told myself Charlie if they make fun of you dont get **sore** because you remember their not so smart as you once thot they were. And besides they were once your friends and if they laughed at you that doesnt mean anything because they liked you too. 25

One of the new men who came to work there after I went away made a nasty crack he said hey Charlie I hear your a very smart fella a real quiz kid. Say something intelligent. I felt bad but Joe Carp came over and grabbed him by the shirt and said leave him alone you lousy cracker or Ill break your neck. I didnt expect Joe to take my part so I guess hes really my friend. R

Later Frank Reilly came over and said Charlie if anybody bothers you or trys to take advantage you call me or Joe and we will set em straight. I said thanks Frank and I got choked up so I had to turn around and go into the supply room so he wouldnt see me cry. Its good to have friends.

July 28 I did a dumb thing today I forgot I wasnt in Miss Kinnians class at the adult center any more like I use to be. I went in and sat down in my old seat in the back of the room and she looked at me funny and she said Charles. I dint remember she ever called me that before only Charlie so I said hello Miss Kinnian Im redy for my lesin today only I lost my reader that we was using. She startid to cry and run out of the room and everybody looked at me and I saw they wasnt the same pepul who used to be in my class. C

Then all of a suddin I rememberd some things about the operashun and me getting smart and I said holy smoke I reely pulled a Charlie Gordon that time. I went away before she come back to the room.

Practice the Skills

25 Key Reading Skill

Understanding Text Structures The author uses a comparing and contrasting text structure when Charlie returns to the factory. What is the difference between the way the other workers treat him in the beginning of the story and the way they treat him now?

Additional Support

Literature Focus Lesson

Tragedy In a tragedy, the main character suffers a downfall or death caused by personal weakness, such as pride, or by uncontrollable outside forces. The ancient Greek playwrights who invented tragedy thought the downfall should occur from a great height.

Ask students to explain how this story is a tragedy.

- Charlie suffers a downfall because of outside forces. He loses both his intelligence and his old way of life.
- Charlie falls from a great height. He was once more intelligent than most people. OL AL

Thats why Im going away from New York for good. I dont want to do nothing like that agen. I dont want Miss Kinnian to feel sorry for me. Evry body feels sorry at the factery and I dont want that eather so Im going someplace where nobody knows that Charlie Gordon was once a genus and now he cant even reed a book or rite good.

Im taking a cuple of books along and even if I cant reed them Ill practise hard and maybe I wont forget every thing I lerned. If I try reel hard maybe Ill be a littel bit smarter than I was before the operashun. I got my rabits foot and my luky penny and maybe they will help me.

If you ever reed this Miss Kinnian dont be sorry for me Im glad I got a second chanse to be smart becaus I lerned a lot of things that I never even new were in this world and Im grateful that I saw it all for a littel bit. I dont know why Im dumb agen or what I did wrong maybe its becaus I dint try hard enuff. But if I try and practis very hard maybe Ill get a littl smarter and know what all the words are. I remember a littel bit how nice I had a feeling with the blue book that has the torn cover when I red it. Thats why Im gonna keep trying to get smart so I can have that feeling agen. Its a good feeling to know things and be smart. I wish I had it rite now if I did I would sit down and reed all the time. Anyway I bet Im the first dumb person in the world who ever found out something importent for sience. I remember I did somthing but I dont remember what. So I gess its like I did it for all the dumb pepul like me. **26** **C**

Good-by Miss Kinnian and Dr. Strauss and evreybody. And P.S. please tell Dr Nemur not to be such a grouch when pepul laff at him and he woud have more frends. Its easy to make frends if you let pepul laff at you. Im going to have lots of frends where I go.

P.P.S. Please if you get a chanse put some flowrs on Algernons grave in the bak yard . . . ○

Practice the Skills

26 **BIG Question**

What price did Charlie pay to have the operation? Do you think that he was sorry he had the operation? Why or why not? Write your answers on the "Flowers for Algernon," Part 2, flap of the Reading Workshop 3 Foldable. Your response will help you complete the Unit Challenge later. **BQ**

Teach

C Critical Thinking

Synthesis Ask: Who does Charlie blame for the failure of the experiment? *(He blames himself, saying he may not have tried hard enough.)* **BL** **Say:** Think back to other incidents in the story. How is self-blame a pattern in Charlie's life? *(Possible response: Charlie blames himself when his coworkers are mean to him and when he loses his job. He often talks about having to "try hard" to remember, as though it is his responsibility if the experiment doesn't work.)* **OL** **Ask:** Why do you think someone like Charlie would blame himself if things don't go right? *(Possible response: Other people, such as his parents and coworkers, have always been critical of him.)* **AL**

BQ BIG Question

Before students respond to the Big Question prompt, ask them to reread the paragraph beginning "If you ever reed this . . . ." **AS**

Differentiated Instruction

Discuss the Ending When Keyes submitted this story to a well-known magazine, the editor said the ending was too depressing. He wanted the operation to be a success and Charlie and Miss Kinnian to marry.

Keyes took the story to another editor. He did have to change the ending, but only because the story was over the magazine's 15,000 word limit. He cut a scene in which Miss Kinnian reads Charlie's last report and goes looking for him. Instead, the story ends as it began, in Charlie's own words. Invite students to discuss whether Keyes made the right decision when he refused to give the story a happy ending. **OL**

Indiana English/Language Arts Academic Standards
SE: 8.1.3
TWE: *Literature Focus Lesson* 8.3, *Differentiated Instruction* 8.3

Assess

Resources for page 378

- Selection Quick Check, p. 26
- Selection and Unit Assessment, p. 30
- ExamView Assessment Suite
- Interactive Tutor: Self-Assessment

Students can respond to the *After You Read* items in their Learner's Notebooks or on a separate sheet of paper.

Answering the BIG Question

1. Possible response: No, I would not want to experience that much pain.
2. Possible responses: Charlie beats Algernon and eventually knows more than the scientists. His language becomes more complex, and he has to remind himself to speak simply so people can understand him.
3. Possible responses: He loses his memory and his ability to type. Charlie most fears losing the ability to read and write.

Critical Thinking

4. Possible response: She is distressed by Charlie's deterioration.
5. Possible response: He says that he doesn't want to be pitied, but some may feel that he is preparing for death.

After You Read

Flowers for Algernon, Part 2

Answering the 

1. Knowing what happened to Charlie Gordon, would you pay the price he paid for the experience that he had? Why or why not?
2. **List** How does the author show you that Charlie is becoming smarter? List examples.
   TIP Think and Search
3. **Recall** What are some of the first things that Charlie loses when the experiment starts to fail? What does he fear losing the most?
   TIP Right There

Critical Thinking

4. **Infer** When Charlie goes back to Miss Kinnian's class, why does she start to cry and then run out of the room?
   TIP Author and Me
5. **Draw Conclusions** At the end of the story, why does Charlie decide to move away from New York?
   TIP Author and Me

Write About Your Reading

Cause-and-Effect Chart Even though the main text structure in this story is chronological order, many parts are organized in the cause-and-effect text structure. Copy and complete the following cause-and-effect chart. The first entry is done for you.

Cause	→	Effect
Because Charlie has a strong desire to learn,	→	Miss Kinnian recommends him for the operation.
1. Because Charlie's operation is a success,	→	
2.	→	the factory workers demand that Charlie be fired.
3. Because he loses his job,	→	

Indiana English/Language Arts Academic Standards (pp. 378–379)

8.3 Comprehension and Analysis of Literary Text Respond to grade-level-appropriate literature... **8.5.7** Write for different purposes... **8.2 Comprehension and Analysis (Focus on Informational Text)** Develop [reading] strategies such as...identifying and analyzing structure and organization... **8.3.6** Identify significant literary devices...and use [them] to interpret a work. **8.6 English Language Conventions**

For a complete description of the standards, see p. IN 11.

Write About Your Reading

Possible responses for cause-and-effect chart:

1. He gains intelligence.
2. Because Charlie is smarter than they are,
3. Charlie feels alone and rejected.

Skills Review

Key Reading Skill: Understanding Text Structures

6. Think of four ways that Charlie changed after his operation. Write them in chronological order. Write a paragraph about these changes, using chronological order as the text structure.

Literary Element: Foreshadowing

7. Look over the story and list the clues that foreshadow the failure of the experiment. How would the story have been different if the failure had come as a complete surprise?
8. After Charlie starts to lose his intelligence, the friends who once laughed at him defend him (see the July 27 Progress Report). What earlier event foreshadows their defense of Charlie?

Reviewing Elements: Irony

9. One of the things the reader knows at the end is that Charlie completed an important scientific report on artificially-increased intelligence. Charlie only remembers that he did something. Is this dramatic irony? Explain.

Vocabulary Check

Answer *true* or *false* to the statements below.

10. Apples and oranges are **tangible.**
11. A sudden noise might be a **stimulus** that makes someone jump.
12. If something happens **invariably,** nobody can predict it.
13. If you want to **obscure** something, you should let everyone see it.
14. If a boy **cowered** when his teacher spoke to him, he might have been afraid of her.
15. **English Language Coach** Review the word **type** on page 356. Then write two sentences, each using a different meaning of the word.

Grammar Link: Compound Subjects and Predicates

A **compound subject** is made up of two or more simple subjects that have the same predicate. When the subjects are joined by *and* or by *both . . . and,* the plural form of the verb is used.

- Keisha, Hala, *and* Saba are sisters.

(The subjects Keisha, Hala, and Saba are joined by *and.* The compound subject is *Keisha, Hala,* and *Saba.*)

When two simple subjects are joined by *or, either . . . or,* or *neither . . . nor,* the verb must agree with the simple subject closer to it.

- Neither Keisha nor *Saba* likes country music.
- Neither her sisters nor *Keisha* likes country music.
- Neither Keisha nor her *sisters* like country music.

A **compound predicate** is made up of two or more verbs that have the same subject. They are joined by *and, or, but, both . . . and, either . . . or,* or *neither . . . nor.*

- The rabbit ran quickly and dashed into the hole.

(The verbs *ran* and *dashed* are joined by *and.*)

Grammar Practice

Copy the sentences below on a separate sheet of paper. Underline compound subjects. Circle compound predicates.

16. The monkeys and chimps screech from the tree.
17. Neither he nor I can go.
18. My dad and my uncles were sitting and resting.
19. Aunt Sherry fries or bakes her own potato chips.

Web Activities For eFlashcards, Selection Quick Checks, and other Web activities, go to www.glencoe.com.

Skills Review

Key Reading Skill: Understanding Text Structures

6. Sample paragraph: First Charlie's writing improves. Then, he develops an increased understanding of other people and an ability to see himself as others see him. Next, he becomes more independent and can think for himself. Finally, his feelings for Miss Kinnian change, and he becomes smarter than the doctors who operated on him.

Literary Element: Foreshadowing

7. Possible responses: Dr. Strauss wants to delay publishing. Miss Kinnian hopes it wasn't wrong for her to advise Charlie to participate. Algernon becomes angry and bites Charlie and then dies. Additional responses will vary.
8. Possible response: Charlie's defense of the dishwasher foreshadows his friends' defense of him.

Reviewing Elements: Irony

9. Responses will vary.

Vocabulary Check

10. true
11. true
12. false
13. false
14. true

English Language Coach

15. Possible responses: What *type* of dog is it? I can *type* fast.

Grammar Link: Compound Subjects and Predicates

Grammer Practice

16. The monkeys and chimps screech from the tree.
17. Neither he nor I can go.
18. My dad and my uncles were sitting and resting.
19. Aunt Sherry fries or bakes her own potato chips.

Close

Hold a class discussion about the benefits and disadvantages of Charlie's operation.

Indiana English/Language Arts Academic Standards
SE: 8.2, 8.3, 8.3.6, 8.5.7, 8.6

Focus

BELLRINGER Options

Daily Language Practice Transparency 28

Focus Activity Ask: Why do you think it might be helpful to put your writing away for a few days before revising it? *(Possible response: You can see it fresh. You might see problems you didn't notice before.)* OL

Teach

W Writing

Revising Say: When you revise your writing, check for one element, or strategy, at a time. For example, the first time you read through your report, make sure everything in it is related to your thesis. The second time, check to be sure that you have transitions, such as *first, next,* or *on the other hand,* to help readers follow your thoughts. AS

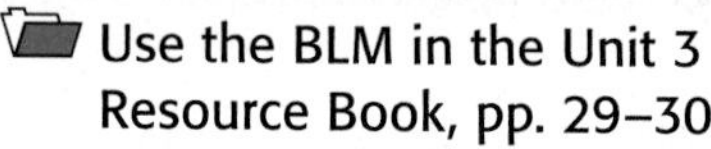

Resources for page 380

Use the BLM in the Unit 3 Resource Book, pp. 29–30.

Use the Grammar and Writing Workshop Transparencies 21–22

WRITING WORKSHOP PART 2

Research Report

Revising, Editing, and Presenting

ASSIGNMENT Write a research report

Purpose: To research a subject and write a report on what you find

Audience: Your teacher and your classmates

Revising Rubric

Your revised research report should have

- a clear thesis statement that states what you are reporting
- evidence and details that support your thesis
- effective organization
- accurately cited sources and a works cited list
- a strong introduction and conclusion
- effective simple sentences

Indiana English/ Language Arts Academic Standards (pp. 380–385)

8.5.3 Write research reports... **8.4.7** Review, evaluate, and revise writing for meaning and clarity. **8.4.8** Edit and proofread... writing... **8.6 English Language Conventions 8.7.12** Deliver [oral] research presentations...

For a complete description of the standards, see p. IN 11.

In Part 2, you'll revise and edit your research report draft. Revising and editing can be hard work, but the hard work pays off in the end. Your final draft will be much easier to read and understand than your first draft. When you're finished, you'll keep a copy of your report in a writing portfolio so that you and your teacher can evaluate your writing progress over time.

Revising

Make It Better

Reread your first draft carefully and ask yourself the questions below. Write your answers in your Learner's Notebook. Then use the suggestions to revise.

Question	Suggestion
Does my introduction grab readers' attention and include a thesis statement?	If not, begin with a surprising statement or question to get readers interested in your topic. Make sure your thesis statement is near the end of your introduction.
Is my thesis, or main idea, clearly stated?	If not, rewrite it until it says exactly what your report is about.
Does each paragraph have a clear main idea supported by details?	If not, rewrite the topic sentence. Add supporting details that relate directly to the topic sentence. Remove details that aren't necessary.
Do I stick to my topic throughout my report?	If not, make sure the topic sentence of each paragraph supports your thesis statement. Delete off-track sentences and paragraphs.
Does my conclusion restate my thesis and say what I think about the topic?	If not, rewrite sentences that summarize your topic. Add one or two sentences that state your final thoughts about your topic.
Have I correctly cited my sources?	If not, review Writing Workshop Part 1 and see the **Writing Handbook** for help.

After you read and comment on your draft, give it to a peer reviewer (a classmate). Have your reviewer read it and answer the questions. His or her comments may be helpful, but you decide what changes to make. See page R18 of the **Writing Handbook** for more on peer reviewers.

Additional Support

Reading in the Real World

Career Tell students that providing constructive criticism is an important part of many jobs, particularly management positions. Explain that reviewing a peer's work requires more than just telling him or her his work is good or bad. Rather, giving constructive criticism means providing specific feedback and suggestions that will help a peer improve. Encourage students to use the suggestions under "Make It Better" to help them provide constructive criticism to their peers. BL OL

Editing

Finish It Up

It's time to get your report ready to share with others. Use the **Editing Checklist** below to help you spot errors.

Writing Models For models and other writing activities, go to www.glencoe.com.

Editing Checklist

- ☑ Verb forms are correct, and verb tenses are consistent.
- ☑ Pronouns agree with antecedents.
- ☑ All sentences are complete, begin with a capital letter, and end with correct punctuation.
- ☑ All words are spelled correctly.
- ☑ All citations and the works cited list are in correct form.

Writing Tip

Spelling If you are using a computer to write your report, you can use the Spell Check feature to check your spelling. But the only way to be completely sure of a word's spelling is to look it up. W2

Applying Good Writing Traits

Conventions

Conventions make your writing easier to read and understand. It can be difficult to master all the writing conventions at once, but don't worry! You probably know more than you think you do.

What Are Conventions?

Conventions are the rules of language: spelling, capitalization, punctuation, grammar and usage, and paragraphing. Formal Standard English–the kind you speak and write in school and most businesses–has many conventions.

Why Are Conventions Important?

When you use conventions, your writing is clearer. Readers can pay attention to your ideas instead of struggling to figure out what you are trying to say. You can bend some rules when you write stories or poems. But when you write formal papers, such as research reports, you must follow the rules of Standard English.

Look at how conventions can affect meaning:

- Did you see that weasel?
- Did you see that, weasel?

The punctuation makes a big difference in the meanings of the sentences. In the first, the speaker is pointing out a weasel to a listener. In the second, the speaker is calling the listener a weasel!

How Do I Use Conventions?

Read your final draft carefully. Be sure to see the words as they appear on the page, not as they're *supposed* to appear. Then read your paper several times and look for one kind of error each time.

1. Check the spellings of difficult words.
2. Check for proper capitalization. Each sentence should start with a capital letter. Proper nouns and proper adjectives should be capitalized.
3. Make sure that each sentence ends with the correct punctuation mark and that commas are in the right places.
4. Fix errors in grammar and usage. Reading your paper aloud may help.
5. Make sure the first line of every paragraph is indented.

Partner Work Follow the steps above to spot and correct errors in conventions. Trade papers with a partner and circle any errors in the paper.

Teach

W1 Writing

Revising When their first drafts are complete, encourage students to review their notes, looking for interesting material they could include. In particular, have them check their notes for expert quotations that would make their reports come alive. AS

W2 Writing

Spelling Say: There are some misspelled words spell check will not catch. Why is this? *(Spell Check will not catch words, such as there, their, and they're, that sound alike but have different meanings. Spell Check cannot tell if these words are spelled incorrectly in context.)* Challenge students to list any homonyms they tend to misuse and find ways to proof for them. *(For example, they could use the find-and-replace feature to search for* weather *and see if they should have used* whether.*)* OL AL

Literature Online

Writing Models Have students access the Web site for an additional and interactive Writing Workshop-based student model.

Differentiated Instruction

Visuals After completing their reports, students might add visuals. Explain that visuals should supplement the information in a report, not just illustrate it. Have students select a maximum of four visuals, enough to add interest but not overwhelm.

- Students can create or copy charts or graphs that support information in the report. These visuals can give readers a lot of information quickly.
- Students can include illustrations that support a point, such as photographs showing how the environment has changed due to global warming.

Encourage students to add captions explaining their visuals. AL

Indiana English/Language Arts Academic Standards

SE: 8.4.7, 8.4.8, 8.5.3, 8.6, 8.7.12

TWE: *Writing* 8.4.10, *Differentiated Instruction* 8.5.3

Teach

LSV1 Listening, Speaking, Viewing

Rate of Speech **Say:** In conversation, people normally speak at a rate of about 125–150 words per minute. When you're nervous, it's easy to speak faster than that. If you find yourself racing through your speech, try to slow your breathing. Also, let yourself vary your rate of speech. Speeding up can build suspense or express anger; slowing down emphasizes important points. AS

LSV2 Listening, Speaking, Viewing

Looking Confident **Say:** Speakers who look confident will gain the confidence of their audience. Follow these tips to appear confident during your presentation:

- Stand up straight.
- Look at your audience as much as possible. Do not read directly from your report. Try to memorize short parts so you can make eye contact frequently.
- Do not turn your back on your audience to show visuals. Instead, stand next to any visuals. AS

WRITING WORKSHOP PART 2

Presenting

Show It Off

Writing Tip

Handwriting Make your final draft easy to read. Use your best handwriting. Make each letter and punctuation mark clear for the reader.

Rewrite or print out a clean copy of your report. Then follow these steps to write a summary and share it with some of your classmates.

1. Reread your report and write down your thesis in one sentence.
2. Write three to four sentences that help you prove and support your thesis.
3. Read your summary to a small group. Then share and explain the most interesting thing you learned from your research.

Listening, Speaking, and Viewing

Oral Presentation

The final step of a research report is sharing what you've learned with others. An oral presentation gives you this opportunity.

What Is an Oral Presentation?

An oral presentation is a formal speech given to a group of people.

Why Is It Important?

An oral presentation gives the speaker a chance to share interesting and important information with others. It also gives listeners a chance to learn about a topic without having to research it.

How Do I Give an Oral Presentation?

When you prepare an oral presentation, you use the writing process to develop the content of your presentation. Your presentation should have a thesis statement that is supported with evidence. It should also have three main parts—an introduction, a body, and a conclusion. The tips below will help you prepare and give a great oral presentation.

- Think about your purpose and audience. Choose your words carefully and explain any terms or ideas that your audience might not know.
- Write your main points on note cards. You will glance at these notes while you are speaking to keep track of where you are in your speech.
- Prepare a visual aid (a graphic) that shows something you are going to talk about. Make sure your visual aid is big enough for your audience to see. You may use a slide projector or PowerPoint presentation, or you may make copies of your graphic and hand them out to your audience.
- Practice and practice again! Give your speech in front of a mirror or a family member. Ask your family member how you can improve your presentation. Make sure your presentation is within the time limit that your teacher assigned.
- Relax! When you give your presentation, try to stay calm. Speak slowly and clearly and make eye contact with your listeners.

Write and Speak to Learn Use the tips above to prepare and give an oral presentation based on your research report. Be sure to organize your ideas and include a visual aid, so your listeners can easily understand your points.

As you listen to other presentations, take notes about what makes a good presentation and how you might improve your own presentation skills.

Additional Support

Differentiated Instruction

Adaptation for Nervous Speakers
Some students may experience a great amount of anxiety about public speaking. If students are too nervous to speak in front of the class, have students deliver their speech to you and one or two of their peers. The small-group environment may help eliminate fears and inspire confidence in nervous speakers. OL

Writer's Model

America's Betrayal and the Trail of Tears

Why would one group of people remove another group from their homeland by force? Could the moved group ever recover? In 1838 Cherokee people living in Georgia were rounded up by federal troops and forced to walk eight hundred miles to land in Oklahoma. The Cherokees call the journey the "Trail Where They Cried." Some historians call it the "Trail of Tears." The events surrounding the Trail of Tears reveal a story of betrayal, unfair treatment, and great sacrifice.

The Cherokees had very old and strong ties to their homeland. Their territory covered a large area, including what is now the state of Georgia. When European explorers arrived during the mid-1500s, the Cherokees were the largest Native American group in North America.

Over time, the white settlers wanted more and more Cherokee land. The Cherokees and the settlers struggled for control. By 1827 the Cherokees had written and adopted a constitution declaring themselves their own nation. White Georgians who felt threatened claimed that the Cherokee Constitution went against the U.S. Constitution. The governor of Georgia asked President John Quincy Adams to support this position, and the state legislature took steps to force the Cherokees from Georgia.

In 1830 the discovery of gold in Georgia drew thousands of settlers who were looking to make their fortunes (Fremon 56). Also, white settlers and Southern cotton planters pressured the tribe to trade their rich land for land in the West. But the Cherokees refused to give in.

The Cherokees asked the U.S. Supreme Court to defend Native Americans' rights in the Southeast. Georgia claimed the right to make laws for the Cherokees. The Cherokees claimed that federal agreements and the U.S. Constitution protected their group as a self-ruling nation. In 1832, the Supreme Court declared that Georgia's

Active Writing Model

Notice how the introductory paragraph grabs your attention. The first two sentences help you connect to the Cherokees' experience. The third sentence tells you the paper's topic, and the final sentence is the thesis statement.

The writer organizes this report in chronological order (time order). The paragraphs move forward in time from the mid-1500s to 1827 and then to 1830. As you read on, the paper will discuss events that occurred throughout the 1830s leading up to the Trail of Tears in 1838.

Teach

C Critical Thinking

Evaluate Say: Use the chart in the "Make It Better" section on page 380 to evaluate the model paper. On your own or with a partner, answer each of the questions in the left column. OL AL

W Writing

Transitions Have students identify the time order words on this page used to help readers follow chronological order. *(during the mid-1500s, over time, by 1827, in 1830, in 1832)* EL BL

Literature Focus Lesson

Research Report Draw the following graphic organizer on the board. After students have read the model, have them help you complete the organizer with details from the report. Remind students to include an introduction (that grabs readers' attention and includes a thesis), a body (that supports the thesis with evidence), and a conclusion (that summarizes main points) in their report.

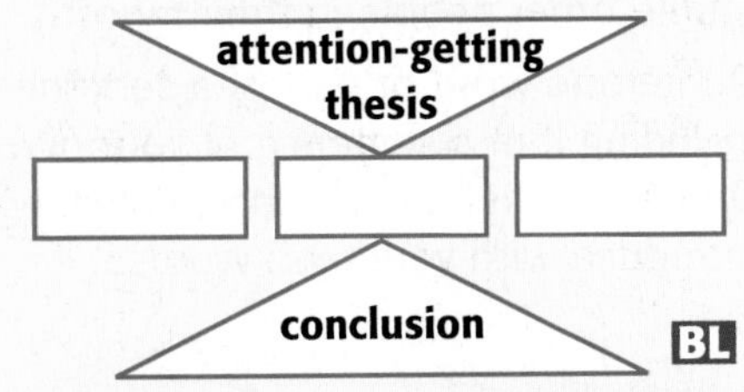

BL

Indiana English/Language Arts Academic Standards
SE: 8.5.3, 8.7.12
TWE: *Differentiated Instruction* 8.7, *Literature Focus Lesson* 8.4.2

Teach

W Writing

Integrating Quotations

Direct attention to the way the quotations are integrated. The first (in the first full paragraph) is a blended quotation; the writer picked the most important words and worked them into a sentence. In the third full paragraph, the writer uses a signal phrase to introduce the author, "Army private John Burnett." AS

WRITING WORKSHOP PART 2

Active Writing Model

actions against the Cherokees were unconstitutional. But President Jackson still sided with Georgia.

While the Supreme Court had been thinking about the Cherokee Nation's claim to its land, Jackson pushed the Indian Removal Act of 1830 through Congress. This act gave the federal government the power to negotiate treaties with Native Americans in the Southwest. The goal of these treaties was to make Native Americans move west. The moving was supposed to be "voluntary and peaceful," but if tribes resisted, Jackson forced them to move ("Indian").

In 1835 the federal government persuaded a small group of Cherokees to sign the Treaty of New Echota, which gave them $5 million to exchange their lands in the East for lands in the West. Most Cherokees did not sign the treaty, so Cherokee law considered it invalid (Bealer 64). Even former president John Quincy Adams, who was not always kind to the Cherokees, said the treaty "brings eternal disgrace upon the country" (Fremon 71). This unfair treaty became the justification for removing the Cherokees from their homeland.

The writer cites sources for two pieces of information: the background about the treaty and the quotation from John Quincy Adams. Both citations have the effect of making readers trust what the writer says.

The principal chief of the Cherokees appealed to the country's leaders one last time. The new president, Martin Van Buren, agreed to let the Cherokees remain on their land for two more years, but then he changed his mind. On May 23, 1838, army troops stormed into Cherokee land, invaded homes, and dragged people from their fields. Thousands of Cherokees were put into stockades to wait for the long march to their new lands ("Trail" screens 1, 3). The forced march began during October and November of 1838. The conditions of the eight-hundred-mile journey were terrible, and more than 4,000 Cherokees died. Army private John Burnett said, "The sufferings of the Cherokees were awful. . . . They had to sleep in the wagons and on the ground without fire. And I have known as many as twenty-two of them to die

The writer uses a quotation to strengthen a point. The quotation also supports the thesis statement.

Additional Support

Differentiated Instruction

Quoting Others Tell students that there are several techniques they can use to quote other people in their report.

- Quote one word or part of a sentence, including it in a sentence of your own.
- Quote a complete sentence, which you introduce with your own words.
- Omit words from a quotation by using ellipses in place of the omitted words.
- Use a quotation of more than four lines by starting a new line and indenting the quote. In this case, you don't need to use quotation marks. AS

Active Writing Model

in one night of pneumonia due to ill treatment, cold, and exposure" ("Trail" screens 1-2).

In Oklahoma, there were more problems. The Cherokees who had opposed the Treaty of New Echota were still angry with those who had signed it. In fact, two of the men who had helped create the treaty were murdered by an anti-treaty group. Also, the new arrivals had to get along with another Native American group who had moved from the East many years earlier. For several years, the new Cherokee land was the scene of violent conflicts.

The Cherokees' claim to their land was respected by many people, including several U.S. senators. The Cherokees placed their trust in the American legal system, but that trust was betrayed. President Jackson's and President Van Buren's administrations used unfair strategies to force the Cherokees from their land. In order to have more land for settlers, the U.S. government crossed the line and paid too high a price—the loss of thousands of Cherokees and a unique culture.

This conclusion restates the writer's thesis. The writer ties up the paper and tells what he or she thinks of the events surrounding the Trail of Tears.

W

Works Cited

Bealer, Alex W. Only the Names Remain. New York: Little, Brown, 1996.

"Brief History of the Trail of Tears." Cherokee Messenger. 1995. The Cherokee Cultural Society of Houston. 11 Nov. 2005 <http://www.powersource.com/cherokee/history.html>.

Fremon, David K. The Trail of Tears. New York: New Discovery, 1994.

"Indian Removal." PBS Online. 11 Nov. 2005 <http://www.pbs.org/wgbh/aia/part4/4h1567.html>.

"The Trail of Tears." Cherokee Publishing. 11 Oct. 2000 <http://www.chota.com/cherokee/trail.html>.

The list of works cited gives all the information that readers need to check the writer's sources: authors, titles, dates, and Web sites. **C**

Teach

C Critical Thinking

Analysis Ask: In addition to checking the writer's sources, what else might a reader use a works cited list for? *(Possible response: to find more information on the topic)* **OL**

W Writing

Works Cited Say: Some sources in the Works Cited list have no author. From the examples given, can you figure out the rule for citing sources when you don't know the author's name? *(Begin with the title.)* **Ask:** How can you tell which titles are long works, such as books, and which are shorter works, such as articles? *(Titles of longer works are italicized; those of shorter works are in quotation marks.)* **AL**

Assess

Have students exchange their papers from the writing activity with a partner and critique each other's work. After a few minutes, tell students to assess their work and make any final revisions.

Reading in the Real World

Citizenship Once students have completed their research reports, have them reconsider the big question, "When is the price too high?" Have students form groups to discuss how their research affected their feelings about the big question. What did they learn about their topic? What decisions did they make about the benefits and costs associated with their topic? After students' group discussions, have them summarize their findings for the class. **OL** **AL**

Indiana English/Language Arts Academic Standards
SE: 8.5.3
TWE: *Differentiated Instruction* 8.6, *Reading in the Real World* 8.7

Identifying Main Idea and Supporting Details

Teaching Students to Identify the Main Idea and Supporting Details

Why Is It Important?

- Understanding the main ideas in a selection helps students comprehend the material better.
- Supporting details help to point readers to the main ideas.
- Readers can use the details they identify to visualize what is happening in the story, which will improve comprehension.
- When students can clearly distinguish main ideas from supporting details, they will also become better writers. They will better understand the need to add ideas that support and enhance their main ideas.

How to Help Students Get It

- Ask students where they might find the key idea of a selection. The main idea is often presented as the topic sentence in informational text, but it's usually not included in a creative attention-getting introduction. It's also rare to have the main idea clearly stated in fiction.
- Ask students to review a text from a previous unit, focusing on the author's use of details. Remembering to notice details will help students learn to incorporate them into their own writing.
- Discuss the types of details that an author can use, including facts, statistics, anecdotes, adjectives, dialogue, and rich descriptions.
- Ask students to use the details from a text to create visual images, which will help them determine main ideas.

Reading to Answer the Big Question

Tattoos: Fad, Fashion, or Folly? by Linda Bickerstaff
This article is a comprehensive overview of tattooing–the history, philosophy, art, and technology. Students will be informed of the repercussions of tattooing and learn of an alternate method that is safe and temporary.

We Real Cool by Gwendolyn Brooks
This eight-stanza poem succinctly sums up the inevitable cost of reckless living.

The Market Economy by Marge Piercy
The speaker of this poem links our modern conveniences to the widespread increase of disease and pollution. Readers are asked to consider the real cost of polyvinyl cups and color TVs.

Workshop Resources

Pacing (Days) Standard	Pacing (Days) Block	Lesson	Student Materials	Teacher Resources
1	1/2	Key Skill Lesson: Identifying Main Idea and Supporting Details	Key Reading Skills Practice, p. 31 English Language Coach Review, p. 43	Bellringer Options Transparencies –Daily Language Practice 29 Read Aloud, Think Aloud Transparencies –Key Reading Skills 6 –Read Aloud, Think Aloud 21–29 Presentation Plus!
1	1	"Tattoos: Fad, Fashion, or Folly?"	Glencoe Online Unit Vocabulary Review, p. 41 Academic Vocabulary Review, p. 44 English Language Coach Active Reading Graphic Organizer, p. 33 Text Analysis, p. 32 StudentWorks Plus™ Online Student Edition Literature Classics Selection and Unit Assessments, p. 31	Puzzlemaker Skill Level Up!™ A Language Arts Game BookLink 3 Assessment by Learning Objective (Diagnostic and Formative) Interactive Tutor: Self-Assessment TeacherWorks Plus™
1		"We Real Cool" "Market Economy"	Glencoe Online Unit Vocabulary Review, p. 41 Academic Vocabulary Review, p. 44 English Language Coach Active Reading Graphic Organizer, p. 35 StudentWorks Plus™ Online Student Edition Literature Classics Selection and Unit Assessments, p. 32	Puzzlemaker Skill Level Up!™ A Language Arts Game BookLink 3 Assessment by Learning Objective (Diagnostic and Formative) Interactive Tutor: Self-Assessment TeacherWorks Plus™

Keys for Unit Resource

- Blackline Master
- Workbook
- Supplemental Text
- CD-ROM
- DVD
- Transparency
- Web-based
- Fast File

Level Appropriate Code

AS = Activities for all students
AL = Activities for students working above grade level
OL = Activities for students working at grade level
BL = Activities for students working below grade level
EL = Activities for English language learners

Focus

BELLRINGER Options

Daily Language Practice Transparency 29
Focus Activity Say: Think of a choice you made recently. What were the positive or negative effects of your choice? *(Responses will vary.)* OL

Teach

R Reading Skill

Identifying Main Idea and Supporting Details Ask: Why might it be important to include supporting details in persuasive writing? In informative writing? *(Possible responses: In persuasive writing, supporting details can convince readers of the writer's opinion. In informative writing, supporting details can provide additional information about a topic.)* AL

READING WORKSHOP 4

Skills Focus

You will practice using these skills when you read the following selections:

- "Tattoos: Fad, Fashion, or Folly?" p. 390
- "We Real Cool," p. 400
- "The market economy," p. 401

Reading

- Identifying main idea and supporting details

Literature

- Understanding graphics and other visual aids
- Understanding and using alliteration

Vocabulary

- Using word references
- Academic Vocabulary: *implied*

Writing/Grammar

- Understanding and using direct objects and indirect objects

Indiana English/Language Arts Academic Standards (pp. 386–387)

8.2 Comprehension and Analysis (Focus on Informational Text)
Develop [reading] strategies…

For a complete description of the standards, see p. IN 11.

Skill Lesson

Identifying Main Idea and Supporting Details

Learn It!

What Is It? The **main idea** is the general point of a selection—the "big idea" that the author wants you to understand and remember.

R Supporting details are the specific details that explain the main idea. They may be examples, descriptions, facts, reasons—any specifics that make the point. The main idea of a selection may be directly stated, or it may be **implied,** or suggested, through details.

Analyzing Cartoons
Jeremy got "the picture," or main idea, about Pierce's weekend. When you identify the main idea, you find the most important thought in what you read or hear. What main idea does Pierce communicate?

Additional Support

English Language Coach

Building Background Jeremy Duncan has been hanging out with his friends since 1997, when "Zits" debuted. The strip is a collaboration between Jim Borgman, who won the 1991 Pulitzer Prize for editorial cartooning, and Jerry Scott, creator of another strip, "Baby Blues." The two have twice won the National Cartoonists Society's top award for "Zits." Originally carried by 200 newspapers, the strip now appears in nearly 1,300. The artists keep it fresh by introducing new characters such as Pierce, whom Scott describes as a "Perforated-American." If possible, provide students with other "Zits" comic strips to read. AS

Why Is It Important? Identifying main idea helps you figure out what's really important in a selection. It also helps you understand and remember what you read.

How Do I Do It? To find the main idea, ask yourself these questions:

- What is this generally about?
- What sentence or sentences state the general point?
- If the general point is not stated, what do the supporting details have in common?

R

Literature Online

Study Central Visit www.glencoe.com and click on Study Central to review identifying main idea and supporting details.

Here is how one student identified the main idea of this passage from the article "A Tremendous Trade."

Now that the Yankees have A-Rod, New York fans have high hopes for future success. But Rodriguez alone won't guarantee his new team championships. "If you're a team with more money, you get to hire better players, but it doesn't mean you're going to win," says Andrew Zimbalist, a top sports economist. Injuries, batting slumps, a lack of teamwork, and even bad luck can get in the way.

I see the writer's point—money can buy good players, but there's no guarantee that a team will do well. The main idea is stated in the quotation. The last sentence gives specific examples of what can get in the way of winning championships. Those are supporting details.

Practice It!

The statements below are about the next selection. Copy them into your Learner's Notebook. Then underline the one that is most likely the main idea. Remember that a main idea is a *big* idea—not a specific detail.

- People from the Stone Age (35,000 to 10,000 B.C.) practiced tattooing.
- Tattooing is not just a passing fad.
- Mummies found in Egypt show that tattooing existed 4,000 years ago.

Use It!

As you read the next selection, write the main idea of each section in your Learner's Notebook. After you've finished reading, use your notes to identify the main idea of the whole article.

Differentiated Instruction

Practicing the Skill Read the following paragraph aloud. Have students tell the main idea (underlined) and two supporting details from the paragraph. Ask, is the main idea stated directly or implied? *My dogs Mollie and Sophie are excellent companions.* <u>I think I should be allowed to take Mollie and Sophie to outdoor restaurants.</u> *They are well-behaved and would sit at my feet without bothering anyone. They would be popular with children, who could pet them while their parents talked. Finally, they could help me make new friends because other dog lovers would approach me to talk about my beautiful dogs.* EL BL

Teach

Literature Online

Study Central Have students access the Web site to review identifying main idea and supporting details and to complete a related activity.

R Reading Skill

Identifying Main Idea and Supporting Details **Ask:** According to the information in the *How Do I Do It?* section, how do you find the main idea? *(You ask what the passage is about and look for sentences that state the main point or for the common elements in the supporting details.)* BL

Resources for page 387

Use Key Reading Skills Transparency 6 in *Read Aloud, Think Aloud* to help students practice identifying the Main Idea and Supporting Details.

Indiana English/Language Arts Academic Standards
SE: 8.2
TWE: *English Language Coach* 8.2, *Differentiated Instruction* 8.2

Teach

More About the Author

When Linda Bickerstaff, M.D., was practicing surgery, she had several patients who wanted tattoos removed. The process of removing tattoos isn't easy. The challenge sparked the surgeon's interest in tattooing. Bickerstaff has written articles about tattoos and other subjects of interest to young people.

EL Language Coach

Word References Ask: Which reference would you use to find a word with a similar meaning? *(a thesaurus)* **Ask:** Which would you use to find out how to pronounce scientific terms? *(a specialized dictionary.)* **Ask:** Which would you use to find the history of a word? *(a general dictionary)* EL BL

Before You Read

Tattoos: Fad, Fashion, or Folly?

Meet the Author

Linda Bickerstaff is a retired surgeon, who found dealing with tattoos in her medical practice to be quite challenging. A regular contributor to *Odyssey: Adventures in Science* and other publications, she writes about health, medical, and teen issues.

Author Search For more about Linda Bickerstaff, go to www.glencoe.com.

Indiana English/Language Arts Academic Standards (pp. 388–395)

8.1 Word Recognition, Fluency, and Vocabulary Development Determine the meaning of words...
8.2 Comprehension and Analysis (Focus on Informational Text) Develop [reading] strategies...

For a complete description of the standards, see p. IN 11.

Vocabulary Preview

migrated (MY gray tud) *v.* moved from one place to another; form of the verb *migrate* **(p. 391)** *When a group of people migrated from one area to another, they held on to their traditions.*

indelible (in DEL ih bul) *adj.* impossible to erase, remove, or blot out **(p. 391)** *Tattoos are made with indelible ink, which leaves a permanent stain.*

compiled (kum PYLD) *v.* collected into a book or list; form of the verb *compile* **(p. 392)** *The student gathered the facts and compiled a book about the history of tattooing.*

Write to Learn Copy the following clues into your Learner's Notebook. Next to each clue, write the vocabulary word it describes.

- Someone who puts together a collection of information has done this.
- This describes something that cannot be removed.
- Someone who has done this has lived in more than one place.

English Language Coach

EL

Word References What should you do when you can't figure out what a word means, you aren't sure how to spell it, or you can't decide which word works best in your writing? Use one of these resources about words!

- A **glossary** will help you understand the vocabulary words in your school books. You'll find glossaries in the backs of many of your textbooks.
- A **general dictionary** gives pronunciations, parts of speech, spellings, and definitions as well as the histories, or origins, of words.
- A **specialized dictionary** or **glossary** gives pronunciations, parts of speech, spellings, and definitions of words used in a specific subject area, such as medicine or automobile mechanics.
- A **thesaurus** gives synonyms and antonyms for words.

Partner Talk Copy the chart below into your Learner's Notebook. With a partner, use a dictionary and thesaurus to complete the chart.

This has...	definitions	synonyms	antonyms	word origins	pronunciations
a dictionary	yes				
a thesaurus			yes		

Additional Support

Author Search To expand students' appreciation of Linda Bickerstaff, have them access the Web site for additional information and resources.

Reading in the Real World

Career Point out that many employers advertise positions for "detail-oriented" people. What are some jobs in which paying attention to detail would be important? *(Possible responses: bookkeeper, engineer, medical assistant)* What are some jobs in which seeing the big picture would be more important? *(CEO, architect, entrepreneur)* OL Ask students which type of job they think they'd be better suited for—a detail-oriented or a big-picture job. Have them explain their response and research specific careers that fit that mold. AL

Skills Preview

Key Reading Skill: Identifying Main Idea and Supporting Details

"Tattoos: Fad, Fashion, or Folly?" has directly stated main ideas. Look for sentences in the first paragraph that sum up the "big ideas" in the article. As you read the rest of the article, pay special attention to the subheads. Each subhead sums up what a section of the article is about. Notice how each section supports the main ideas.

Key Text Element: Photographs

Photographs can add a lot to your reading experience. For example, you might not ever climb Mount Everest, but you can get an idea of what it's like to be on the mountain by looking at a photo of it. To get the most out of a photo, do these things:

- Read the caption–the words printed above, beside, or below the photo.
  Who took the photograph? Where was it shot? What exactly does it show?
- Look closely at the details.
  How do they help you understand the article?
- Think about why this particular photo was included with the selection.
  Does the photograph show something that's described in the article? Does it add information? Or is it just for decoration?

E

Write to Learn Choose an interesting photograph from this textbook. Spend one minute making a list of what you see in the photo. Answer these questions:

- Who or what is in the photo?
- What is happening in the photo?
- When and where was the photo taken?

Interactive Literary Elements Handbook
To review or learn more about the literary elements, go to www.glencoe.com.

Get Ready to Read

Connect to the Reading

Think about tattoos you have seen on people or in pictures. What did you think of the tattoos?

Partner Talk With a partner, discuss possible reasons someone might get a tattoo. List the reasons in your Learner's Notebook. Then add to your list as you read the selection.

Build Background

- Tattoos are designs created on a person's skin. Permanent tattoos are made by inserting dye under the top layer of skin.
- Our skin is made up of a sensitive inner layer and a thin outer layer. When the cells of the outer layer die, they flake off. A tattoo is made by punching a tiny hole and inserting dye into the *inner* layer of skin, underneath the layer that flakes off. That way the color is permanent.
- Archaeologists have long known that ancient peoples practiced the art of tattooing. Archaeologists learn about ancient civilizations by digging into the earth to find the remains of people and evidence of how they lived.

Set Purposes for Reading

BIG Question Read "Tattoos: Fad, Fashion, or Folly?" to learn about some of the hidden dangers that people face when they get tattoos.

Set Your Own Purpose What else would you like to learn from the article to help you answer the Big Question? Write your own purpose on the "Tattoos" flap of the Reading Workshop 4 Foldable for Unit 3.

Keep Moving

Use these skills as you read "Tattoos: Fad, Fashion, or Folly?"

Teach

E Text Element

Photographs Ask: If you were going to write an article about the negative side of tattooing, what photograph would you choose? *(Possible response: a photo showing a faded tattoo or a person getting a tattoo removed)* **Ask:** What photograph would you choose to accompany an article on the positive side of tattooing? *(Possible response: a beautiful tattoo on a happy person)* BL

Interactive Literary Elements Handbook Have students access the Web site to improve their understanding of photographs.

Reading in the Real World

Career Many people see tattoos and body piercing as a form of personal expression. However, dress codes may require employees to have no visible tattoos or piercings. In some cases, jewelry is considered a safety risk because it can get caught in equipment. If employees handle food, piercings can be a health risk. Employers can also insist that an employee's appearance not offend customers. Have students write about whether they think employers should be able to prohibit employees from showing tattoos or body piercing. Why or why not? AS

Indiana English/Language Arts Academic Standards
SE: 8.1, 8.2
TWE: *Reading in the Real World* (p. 388) 8.2, *Reading in the Real World* (p. 389) 8.3

Teach

E Text Element

Photographs **Say:** Look at the title of the article and think of other titles you've seen. How can a photograph add to the presentation of the title? *(Possible responses: It pairs an image with the words and might even make you more interested in reading—or not.)* **Ask:** Why do you think this photograph was chosen for the tattoo title? *(Possible response: It shows a tattoo being given with a needle so you can see the painful process of getting a tattoo.)* OL

R Reading Skill

Identifying Main Idea and Supporting Details
Say: The writer of this article presents her main ideas as questions rather than statements. What might this tell you about her goal for writing the article? *(Possible responses: She wants to find answers to these questions; She wants the reader to ask questions; She is not certain of the answers.)* AL

Readability Scores
Dale-Chall: 6.5
DRP: 66
Lexile: 1090

READING WORKSHOP 4

INFORMATIONAL TEXT
MAGAZINE
Odyssey

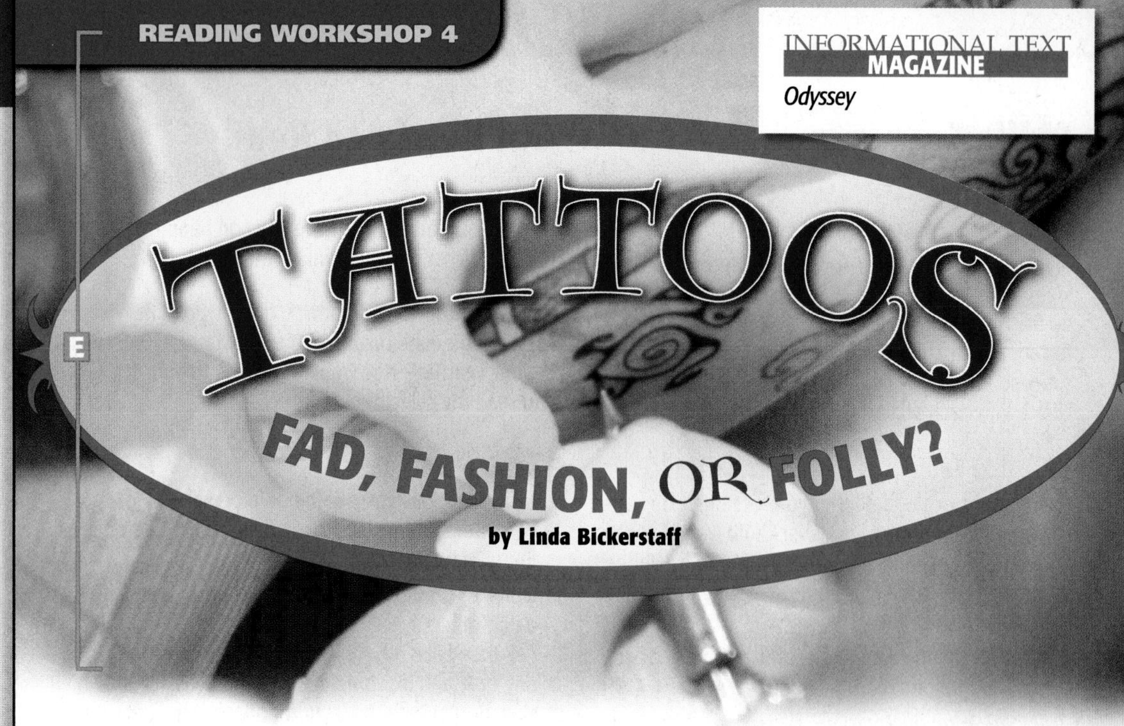

TATTOOS
FAD, FASHION, OR FOLLY?
by Linda Bickerstaff

E

From a tiny butterfly hiding behind a knee to an elaborate, multicolored, geometric design **emblazoning** muscular arms—tattoos are cropping up everywhere. Just take a look at some of the famous tattoo canvases.[1] 1

For instance, professional snowboarder Tara Dakides has a dragon tattooed on her left side and Cat-in-the-Hat adorns her right calf. The three Dixie Chicks have small chick footprints tattooed on their feet, and Whoopi Goldberg sports Woodstock from *Peanuts* on her skin.[2] But it isn't just the famous who sport tattoos. Even some teachers, librarians, and other professionals proudly wear them. Is tattooing a passing fad? Or is it a fashion statement that's here to stay? And then there's the most important question of all: Is getting a tattoo a fashion mistake? 2 R

Tattoo Time Line

Although today's tattooing techniques are high-tech, the practice is ancient. Archaeological evidence from Europe indicates that tattooing was practiced in the Stone Age or upper Paleolithic

1. Here, ***canvases*** refers to the skin on people's bodies.
2. The ***Dixie Chicks*** are a top-selling, all-girl country music group. ***Whoopi Goldberg*** is a comedian and actress. ***Woodstock*** is the name of a bird character in ***Peanuts,*** a popular comic strip that ran in thousands of newspapers from 1950–2000.

Practice the Skills

1 English Language Coach

Word References Use a word reference to look up the meaning of the word *emblazon* in order to understand the meaning of **emblazoning**.

2 Key Reading Skill

Identifying Main Idea and Supporting Details Do these questions give you a sense of what the main idea will be?

Additional Support

Differentiated Instruction

Building Background Tell students that native New Zealanders, Maoris, have used elaborate tattoos, which they call Ta Moko, for many years to signal a person's achievements and his or her place in society. Men often have their entire faces covered in tattoos, while women have their upper lips, chins, or shoulders tattooed. Have students look online or in books to find photographs of Maoris with Ta Moko. Ask them to tell how traditional Maori reasons for tattooing differ from modern American reasons. AL period (35,000 to 10,000 B.C.). In 1991, the body of a hunter, estimated to be 5,300 years old, was discovered in the Austrian Alps. Called the "Iceman," the mummy was so well preserved that the tattoo of a cross on the inside of his knee was still visible. Fifty-seven other simple tattoos were found on his body. Mummies found in Egypt and archaeological discoveries in China, Russia, and Japan indicate that tattooing was widespread there 4,000 years ago. As people **migrated,** they carried the practice of tattooing with them.

The modern history of tattooing and the word "tattoo" date to 1769 when Captain James Cook first saw tattooed South Sea islanders. In the *Endeavor*'s ship log, Captain Cook wrote: "They stain their bodies by indenting or pricking the skin with a small instrument made of bone, cut into short teeth; which indenting they fill up with a dark-blue or black mixture prepared from the smoke [soot] of an oily nut. . . . This operation, which is called by the natives 'tattaw,' leaves an **indelible** mark on the skin. It is usually performed when they are about 10 or 12 years of age, and on different parts of the body." The Tahitian word "tattau," meaning "to mark," is the origin of the modern word, tattoo. **3**

Why Tattoo? R

Why do people as different as the Iceman, President Franklin Delano Roosevelt, and members of the Dixie Chicks get tattoos? The earliest people probably used tattooing as a means of expressing bereavement.[3] When a member of their band died, they slashed themselves with sharp implements and rubbed ashes from a fire into their wounds. Permanent carbon deposits were left under their skin. Professor Konrad Spindler of Innsbruck University in Austria thinks that the Iceman's tattoos were applied to cure pain and other ailments.[4] President Roosevelt's tattoo was a family **crest.** **4** The Dixie Chicks' chick print tattoos reinforce the group's identity and are good publicity.

3. ***Bereavement*** means "deep sadness over death."
4. ***Ailments*** are illnesses or physical problems.

Vocabulary

migrated (MY gray tud) *v.* moved from one place to another

indelible (in DEL ih bul) *adj.* impossible to erase, remove, or blot out

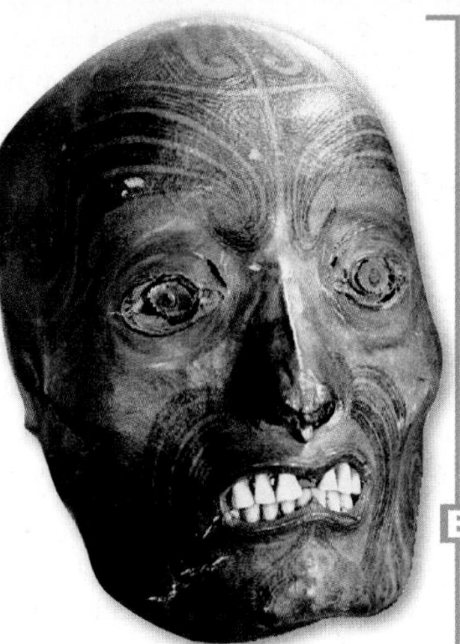

E

Analyzing the Image This mid-19th century Maori skull is covered with shell inlay and inked designs. Why might this tribe have used tattoos?

Practice the Skills

3 Key Reading Skill

Identifying Main Idea and Supporting Details In the section titled "Tattoo Time Line," the author gives examples of different groups of people from long ago who had tattoos. What is the main idea of this section? Where in the section is the main idea directly stated?

4 English Language Coach

Word References What does **crest** mean in this context? Look up the word in a dictionary. Define it in your own words.

READING WORKSHOP 4

Teach

E Text Element

Photographs Say: Maoris are actually native New Zealanders who originated from a number of different tribes. Why might they have used tattoos? *(Possible response: To distinguish their tribal origins from the entire group.)* OL

R Reading Skill

Identifying Main Idea and Supporting Details
Say: Each subhead gives you a clue about the main idea of the paragraphs that follow it. For example, "Tattoo Time Line" suggests that the next paragraphs will discuss tattooing's long history. What clue does the second subhead give you? *(Possible response: The main idea will be about the many reasons people have for getting tattoos.)* OL

Differentiated Instruction

Creating a Tattoo Time Line Point out that the information presented in paragraph form under the subhead "Tattoo Time Line" could also be presented in graphic form. Have students work with a partner to make a time line of the history of tattooing. Ask students:

- What might you use as illustrations? *(Possible answers: ancient tattooing tools, pictures of traditional tattoos, or tattoos found on mummies)*
- How would pictures of what archaeologists have discovered about tattoos help readers? *(Possible answers: show what is being described; provide authentic images)* BL OL

Indiana English/Language Arts Academic Standards
SE: 8.1, 8.2
TWE: *Differentiated Instruction* (p. 390) 8.2, *Differentiated Instruction* (p. 391) 8.2

Teach

R Reading Skill

Identifying Main Idea and Supporting Details
Ask: What is the main idea in the second paragraph on this page? *(Many teens get tattoos to express themselves or to rebel.)* **Ask:** What details support the main idea? *(Possible response: A professor surveyed college students, who said that they got tattoos to express themselves and to feel unique.)* OL

E Text Element

Photographs Ask: Why do you think this photograph was included with the article? *(Possible response: It show traditional tattoos readers might not have seen before.)* AL

READING WORKSHOP 4

Katherine Krcmarik, a graduate art student at the University of Michigan, who recently **compiled** *The History of Tattooing,* says: "The practice of tattooing means different things in different cultures. In early practice, decoration appears to have been the most common motive for tattooing, and that still holds true today." Krcmarik points out that in some cultures tattoos had many purposes: to identify a wearer's rank in society, to mark special events in the wearer's life, to identify a person as belonging to a particular clan or family, or as evidence of a wearer's adventures. 5

In 2002, Myrna L. Armstrong, a professor at Texas Tech University Health Sciences Center, surveyed 520 college students about their interests and attitudes toward tattooing. Ninety-seven of the students had tattoos. When asked why they got a tattoo, the most common answer was, "I just wanted one." Other answers included "To help me express myself" and "To feel unique." Armstrong concluded that for many teens, getting a tattoo is a means of self-expression or a nonviolent form of rebellion. R

Tattooing also has been and continues to be used to mark people as inferior. In ancient Greece, tattooing was used to identify slaves. Romans marked criminals with tattoos. During World War II, one of the ways that Nazis dehumanized[5] prisoners taken to Auschwitz, the largest Nazi concentration camp in Europe, was to tattoo a registration number on the arm of each person. By 1942, most of the people at Auschwitz were Jewish. Most were killed before the war's end. Although only used at Auschwitz, the arm tattoo has become a symbol of the horrors of the Holocaust. E

Today, neo-Nazis, racist skinheads, white supremacists, and others in the "hate" movement use symbols such as swastikas, Nazi "SS" thunderbolts, and ancient runes,[6] tattooed on various parts of their bodies, to instill a sense of fear and insecurity in those around them.

A Tahitian chief wears traditional tattoos in French Polynesia.

5. To ***dehumanize*** is to take away someone's human qualities, personality, or spirit.
6. ***Runes*** are characters of an alphabet used by the Germanic peoples from about the 3rd to the 13th centuries.

Vocabulary

compiled (kum PYLD) *v.* collected into a book or list

Practice the Skills

5 Key Text Element

Photographs How can you connect the text in this paragraph to what you see in the photo on this page? How do you think the man feels about his tattoos?

Additional Support

Reading in the Real World

Citizenship Hold a class discussion on the reasons that people get tattoos. Ask students to give an example that illustrates each reason. Help students to think about the different historical, political, and cultural factors that influence the practice of tattooing. Prompt students to discuss the positive and negative effects of getting a tattoo, and make a chart on the board listing those positives and negatives. OL Using the positive and negative reasons as talking points, divide the class in half and have the two groups debate the issue. Have the students who are for tattoos debate *against* them, and those against tattoos debate *for* them. AL

Acceptance into a "gang" usually requires the initiate[7] to be tattooed with a symbol unique to that gang. Even if not involved in the gang's activities, a member tattooed with its symbol shares the gang's reputation. 6

You Decide

Tattooing is certainly not a fad, as it has been practiced for over 35,000 years. Today, over 40 million Americans (16 percent of the population) **sport** at least one tattoo. According to *U.S. News and World Report,* tattooing was the sixth fastest growing retail venture[8] in the United States in the 1990s. 7 C

So, is a tattoo for you? Getting even a tiny one is a BIG decision to make. Take the Tattoo Test . . . . Perhaps it will help you decide if a tattoo would be fashion or folly for you.

Is a Tattoo for You? Take the Tattoo Test!

Never make an important decision that could affect your health or well-being before weighing all the information. See if you know the straight facts about tattoos. Answer True or False to the following questions:

1. Thomas Alva Edison contributed to the development of the first tattoo machine.
2. Modern tattooing techniques are painless.
3. Once done, a tattoo will remain the same forever.
4. Tattooing is risk-free and available to anyone who can pay for it.
5. It costs more to have a tattoo removed than to get one.

Tattoo Test Answers:

1. **True.** Prior to 1891, tattooing was done by piercing or cutting the skin with a variety of instruments, ranging from sharpened bones to metal awls and needles. The wounds were then rubbed with some type of pigment.[9] Samuel O'Reilly patented the first tattoo machine in 1891. It was a modification of a stencil transfer machine invented by Edison. Today, electrically driven, handheld machines move a needle up and down at a rate of several hundred vibrations per minute, injecting ink about a millimeter deep into the dermis of the skin. EL

7. An ***initiate*** is a new member of a group.
8. A ***venture*** is a new, often risky, business.
9. A ***pigment*** is a substance that gives colors to things.

Practice the Skills

6 **Key Reading Skill**

Identifying Main Idea and Supporting Details
Sometimes people choose to get tattoos. Sometimes people are tattooed against their will by others. These are some of the supporting details in this section. What is the main idea?

7 **English Language Coach**

Word References Here, **sport** is used as a verb. Use a thesaurus to find another word that means about the same thing as *sport.*

Teach

C Critical Thinking

Analysis Ask: What evidence does the author use to support the generalization that tattooing is not a fad? *(Possible responses: She discusses tattooing's long history over 35,000 years and growing popularity —more than 40 million Americans have a tattoo, and it was the sixth-fastest growing business in the 1990s.)* BL OL

EL Language Coach

Word References Say: Inventors patent their inventions so that other people cannot copy and make money from them. What type of word reference would give you more information about patenting? *(a specialized dictionary)* BL

Differentiated Instruction

Conducting a Survey Have students answer the questions in the "Tattoo Test" before they read on. After students have finished, tally the results for each item on the board. Ask these questions:

- Can you see any patterns in the results? *(Responses will vary, depending on the results. Students will probably observe that they know more about some questions than others.)*
- Did taking the test show that you had any mistaken ideas about tattoos? *(Answers will vary.)* OL

Indiana English/Language Arts Academic Standards
SE: 8.1, 8.2
TWE: *Reading in the Real World* 8.2, *Differentiated Instruction* 8.2

Teach

R Reading Skill

Review Comparing and Contrasting Ask: Which of the negative effects of tattooing is the most serious? *(Possible response: The possible risk of diseases being transmitted or of infections.)* BL **Ask:** Which of these effects, if any, would convince you not to get a tattoo? *(Possible response: The fact that the tattoo may fade and change shape would convince me not to get one.)* OL

E Text Element

Photographs Ask: Do you think this photograph adds information to the article or is it mostly just for illustration? *(Possible response: I think it's mostly just for illustration. Most people know what modern tattoos look like.)* OL

2. **False.** Individual pain tolerance, the size and location of a tattoo, and the skill and experience of the tattoo artist influence the amount of pain experienced by an individual.
3. **False.** Tattoo inks are injected into the dermis of the skin so that the design will not be lost due to the sloughing[10] of epidermal cells. Over time, however, the color of pigments may fade—especially if heavily exposed to the sun. Weight gain or loss, pregnancies, and injuries with scar formation at tattoo sites all can change the look of tattoos.
4. **False.** Bacteria from the skin surface may cause infection if carried into the dermis by tattoo needles. In some instances, although less common today, hepatitis B and C as well as syphilis and tuberculosis have been transmitted to tattoo recipients. To date, no documented cases of AIDS have been transmitted by tattooing. Mild to life-threatening allergic reactions to tattoo inks may occur. In most states and Canada, kids under the age of 18 must have parental consent for professional tattooing.
5. **True.** The cost of a small tattoo (less than a square inch) is about $100. The cost of a custom tattoo covering a large area is more than $1,000. The real cost comes, however, with tattoo removal. Dermatologic surgeons use at least three types of high-tech lasers for tattoo removal. Getting rid of even the smallest tattoo can require several treatments, each costing $300 to $400, depending on where you live. Removal of larger tattoos may cost thousands of dollars. Removal is considered cosmetic surgery, so few insurance plans will cover the cost. Tattoo removal is quite painful, has a 5 percent chance of leaving a permanent scar, and may fail to completely obliterate[11] the tattoo. In spite of this, with improvement in results, tattoo removal is in big demand. Several studies have shown that by age 40, over 50 percent of people with tattoos wish they did not have them. Many are seeking to have them removed. 8

Visual Vocabulary The skin is made up of a sensitive inner layer, called the ***dermis,*** and a thin outer layer, called the ***epidermis.***

Practice the Skills

8 **BIG Question** The author describes the different kinds of costs, financial as well as personal, that go with getting tattoos. Do you think these prices are too high? Write your answers on the "Tattoos" flap of the Reading Workshop 4 Foldable. Your response will help you complete the Unit Challenge later.

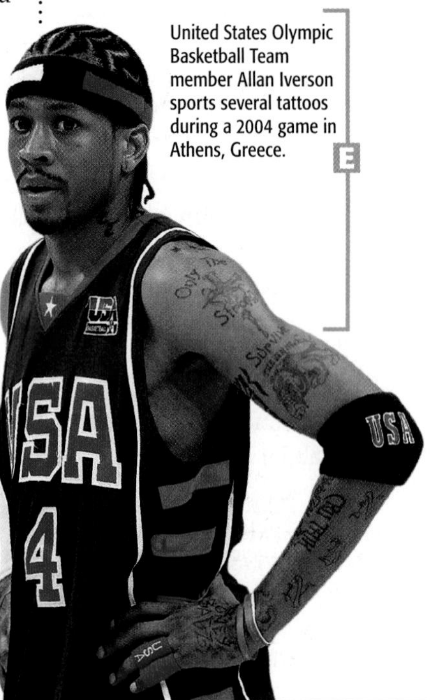

United States Olympic Basketball Team member Allan Iverson sports several tattoos during a 2004 game in Athens, Greece. E

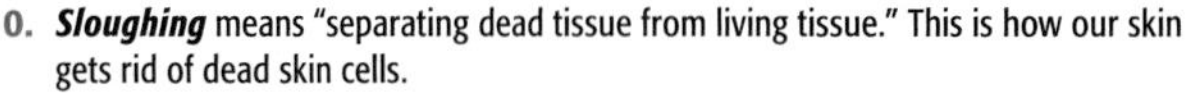

10. ***Sloughing*** means "separating dead tissue from living tissue." This is how our skin gets rid of dead skin cells.
11. To ***obliterate*** something is to remove or destroy it completely.

Additional Support

English Language Coach

Latin Roots Explain that the Latin root *derm* means "skin." Ask students, "If dermis is a layer of the skin, then what does a dermatological surgeon probably specialize in?" (*skin*) Tell students they can use Latin roots to determine the meaning of other unfamiliar words. Give students these roots and have them write two words they know that are made up of each:

- scrib: to write *(describe, scribble, transcribe)*
- ject: to throw *(project, reject, subject)*
- port: to carry *(import, export, report)*

EL

Henna: The Tattoo Temp 10

Do you secretly yearn for just a *tiny* tattoo, but know that your parents would never allow it? Do you think a mouse might look cool tattooed on your ankle, but you aren't really sure? Does the idea of having your skin pierced by needles make you feel faint? If you answered "yes" to these questions, your solution might be a tattooing technique used for many thousands of years in India and other parts of the world—henna tattooing.

Henna is the Arabic name for the shrub *Lawsonia inermis* or *L. alba.* Its leaves are harvested, dried, and then crushed into a powder that is mixed with oil, lemon, and other ingredients to form a paste.

When the paste is applied to skin, reddish-brown pigments from the paste are transferred to the epidermis of the skin. The longer the henna is in contact with the skin, the darker the pigment transfer will be. Henna is usually left on the skin for 6 to 12 hours for the best results, then washed off.

Henna tattooing should really be called henna appliqué or henna painting. Henna tattoos differ from real tattoos in several ways: They are temporary, lasting only a few weeks; they are painless to apply; and they are relatively inexpensive to obtain. They are also an excellent way to get your tattoo without upsetting your parents. R

The cells of the skin that are pigmented by the henna are epidermal cells. Over the course of several weeks, these cells die and are sloughed off the surface of the skin. As this happens, the henna tattoo fades and eventually disappears altogether. Depending on where the tattoo is placed on the body, it may last for one to three weeks.

Pre-prepared, do-it-yourself henna tattoo kits are available commercially. They contain patterns as well as instructions for applying.

Is a henna tattoo for you? Maybe, but be sure to check with Mom and Dad first.

C

CAUTION: Do not buy a kit or use any product containing "black henna." Black henna has a chemical compound called paraphenylenediamine (PPD) that is mixed with classic henna. The purpose of the PPD is to speed up the process of pigment transfer to the skin and to make the tattoo black instead of reddish-brown. PPD causes severe contact dermatitis in many EL people. People who are sensitive to it have a reaction similar to a bad case of poison ivy. They are miserable for many days. ❍

Practice the Skills

10 Key Reading Skill

Identifying Main Idea and Supporting Details The main idea of this section is that henna tattoos can be a safer alternative to permanent tattoos. As you read, watch for the supporting details the author includes.

Differentiated Instruction

Conduct an Interview Have students conduct an interview with a family member, adult friend, or acquaintance who has one or more tattoos. Students might ask the following questions:

- Why did you get your tattoo?
- Has it changed over time?
- Do you ever regret getting it?
- What are the benefits or costs of having a tattoo?

Have students share their findings with the class. Students should note similarities and differences between their interviewee's experience and the experience of the people in the article. AL

Teach

R Reading Skill

Review Identifying Author's Purpose Ask: Why might the writer have included this page at the end of her article? *(Possible response: She might be trying to convince readers to try henna tattoos instead of or before getting a real tattoo. By ending with this, she might hope it will stay in readers' minds.)* AL

C Critical Thinking

Comprehension Ask: Why does the writer include the caution at the end of the article? *(Possible response: The writer wants readers to be aware black henna can cause a bad skin reaction.)* OL

EL Language Coach

Latin Roots Say: If you know that the Latin root *derm* means "skin," what do you think dermatitis is? *(a skin condition)* AL

Assess

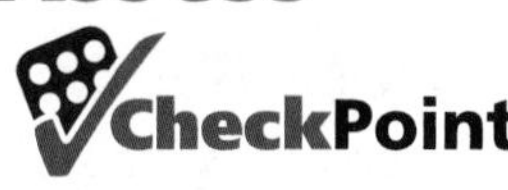

Use the CheckPoint questions provided on Presentation Plus! to check for comprehension of the selection. These questions can be used with interactive response keypads for immediate student feedback.

Indiana English/Language Arts Academic Standards

SE: 8.2

TWE: *English Language Coach* 8.1, *Differentiated Instruction* 8.2

Assess

Resources for page 396

- Selection Quick Check, p. 27
- Selection and Unit Assessment, p. 31
- ExamView Assessment Suite
- Interactive Tutor: Self-Assessment

Students can respond to the *After You Read* items in their Learner's Notebooks or on a separate sheet of paper.

Answering the BIG Question

1. Possible responses: The pain and expense of getting a tattoo, the risk of fading, the danger of infection, and the difficulty of removing tattoos.
2. Since the Stone Age (35,000 to 10,000 B.C.)
3. Skin infections, hepatitis B and C, syphilis, and tuberculosis.

Critical Thinking

4. Possible response: By dressing similarly, such as wearing school athletic jackets or science club t-shirts
5. Possible response: There are many reasons for tattooing and it is common in many cultures, so people are unlikely to stop.
6. Possible response: It swayed me against tattoos. They can be dangerous, and many people who get them change their minds later.

After You Read

Tattoos: Fad, Fashion, or Folly?

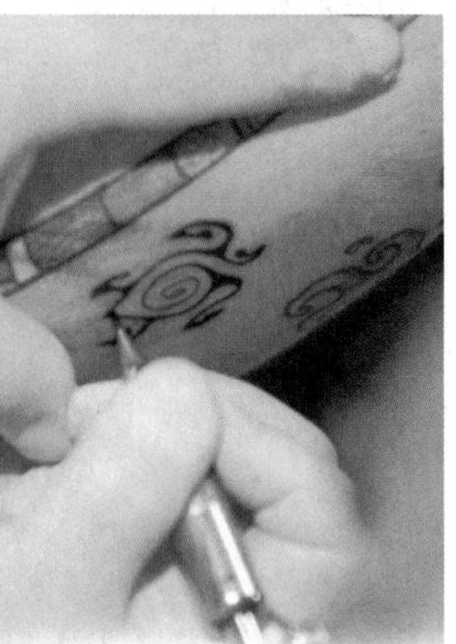

Indiana English/Language Arts Academic Standards (pp. 396–397)

8.3 Comprehension and Analysis of Literary Text Respond to grade-level-appropriate literature... **8.5.7** Write for different purposes... **8.2 Comprehension and Analysis (Focus on Informational Text)** Develop [reading] strategies... **8.2.9** Make reasonable statements and draw conclusions... **8.6 English Language Conventions**

For a complete description of the standards, see p. IN 11.

Answering the BIG Question

1. What are some of the prices that people pay for getting tattoos? Think about the dollar cost of tattoos and also about intangible costs, such as the pain and permanence of tattoos.
2. **Recall** How long has tattooing been around?
   TIP **Right There**
3. **Recall** What physical problems or illnesses are related to getting and living with tattoos?
   TIP **Think and Search**

Critical Thinking

4. **Analyze** Many people get tattoos to decorate their bodies or to identify themselves as part of a group. What other ways do people in your school and community identify themselves as part of a group?
   TIP **On My Own**
5. **Infer** Why do you think tattooing has been around for so long? Do you think people will stop using tattoos some day? Explain your answer.
   TIP **Author and Me**
6. **Evaluate** Did this article sway you to be in favor of tattoos or against them? Explain your response.
   TIP **Author and Me**

Write About Your Reading

Newspaper Article Imagine that there are a lot of students at your school who are thinking about getting tattoos. Write an article for your school newspaper that tells them what you know about tattoos. The article should end with advice.

- Discuss the popularity of tattoos.
- Discuss the possible costs of getting a tattoo.
- End with your own advice to students who want to get a tattoo.

Write About Your Reading

Sample article

"Everybody's getting one," you say, but your parents refuse to let you get a tattoo. Perhaps they think tattoos are a fad. You can tell them that tattoos have been around since the Stone Age. Maybe they think tattoos cost too much. The price of a small tattoo is $100, so they may have a point.

Why not stop fighting with mom and dad? You have all the time in the world to decide whether to get a tattoo, but once it's there, it'll be difficult and expensive to remove. Try a temporary henna tattoo instead. They stay on for a couple of weeks and will give you an idea of how a tattoo might look. Avoid any products with "black henna," which can cause severe allergic reactions.

Skills Review

Key Reading Skill: Identifying Main Idea and Supporting Details

7. What is the author's main idea about tattoos?
8. List three supporting details from the article that support the main idea you wrote for question 7.

Key Text Element: Photographs

9. How could a photo of a henna tattoo be useful if you were deciding whether one is right for you?
10. If you could add a photo to this selection, what would you choose to show readers? Why?

Reviewing Skills: Making Inferences

11. What can you infer about the writer's attitude toward tattoos? Is she in favor of people getting tattoos? Is she against it? Or is she neutral, not caring either way? Use evidence from the article to support your inference.

Vocabulary Check

Choose the best word from the list to complete each sentence below. Rewrite each sentence with the correct word.

migrated • indelible • compiled

12. The birds ______ south to spend the winter months in warmer climates.
13. At the end of the year, Juanita ______ a book of poems written by her classmates.
14. I hope that's not ______ ink. That's one of my favorite sweaters.
15. **English Language Coach** What type of reference book would you use to learn more about *tuberculosis* and *dermatitis?* Explain your choice.
16. **Academic Vocabulary** If a main idea is **implied,** is it stated or only hinted at?

Grammar Link: Direct Objects

A **direct object** is the noun or pronoun in a sentence that receives the action of the verb. In fact, the direct object is located *after* the action verb. You can usually find it by asking *what?* or *whom?* The answer will be the direct object.

- After lunch, Cynthia always eats an apple.

First, find the verb in the sentence: *eats.* Then ask the question "*What* does Cynthia always eat?" The answer is an *apple.* So in this sentence, apple is the direct object.

A sentence may have more than one direct object. This is referred to as a **compound direct object.**

- Jenell helped Ryan and Lee with their project.

First, find the verb in the sentence: *helped.* Then ask the question, "*Whom* did Jenell help?" The answer is *Ryan* and *Lee.* So in this sentence, Ryan and Lee is the compound direct object.

Grammar Practice

Underline the verb and circle the direct object in each of the following sentences.

17. Ramona teaches history.
18. Nan watched the artist paint.
19. Mr. Delmar took the students on a field trip.
20. Victor spent time and money at the mall today.
21. He bought shoes, socks, and a shirt.
22. Victor also bought a new video game.

Web Activities For eFlashcards, Selection Quick Checks, and other Web activities, go to www.glencoe.com.

Skills Review

Key Reading Skill: Identifying Main Idea and Supporting Details

7. Possible response: People should consider the risks and benefits before getting a tattoo.
8. Possible responses: 1) Tattooing can show individuality. 2) Tattooing can be expensive and painful. 3) Removing tattoos is expensive.

Key Text Element: Photographs

9. Possible responses: The photo would help me judge the look of a henna tattoo.
10. Possible response: a photo of a scar from tattoo-removal surgery

Reviewing Skill: Making Inferences

11. Responses will vary. Students may note the writer presents the facts for readers to consider.

Vocabulary Check

12. migrated
13. compiled
14. indelible

English Language Coach

15. Possible response: A scientific dictionary or an encyclopedia, which will have detailed information

Grammar Link: Direct Objects

Grammar Practice

17. Ramona teaches history.
18. Nan watched the artist paint.
19. Mr. Delmar took the students on a field trip.
20. Victor spent time and money at the mall today.
21. He bought shoes, socks, and a shirt.
22. Victor also bought a new video game.

Academic Vocabulary

16. hinted at

Close

Hold a class discussion based on students' responses to question 4.

Indiana English/Language Arts Academic Standards
SE: 8.2, 8.2.9, 8.3, 8.5.7, 8.6

Teach

More About the Authors

Gwendolyn Brooks
Gwendolyn Brooks loved poetry from early childhood and began to write when she was only seven. Her first poem was published when she was thirteen. Many of her poems reflect life on Chicago's South Side. Before her death in 2000, Brooks held poetry workshops for youths in the inner city.

Marge Piercy
Writing poetry is a way of learning to pay attention, according to Marge Piercy, who began writing when she was fifteen. She believes poetry tells the pain and pleasure of people's lives. Piercy wants the readers of her poems to say, "Oh, yes, it was that way for me too."

Before You Read

We Real Cool *and* The market economy

Meet the Authors

Poet Gwendolyn Brooks was the first African American writer to win the Pulitzer Prize. Brooks was born in 1917 in Topeka, Kansas and raised in Chicago, where she died in 2000. See page R1 of the Author Files for more on Gwendolyn Brooks.

Marge Piercy is a poet, novelist, and essayist. Piercy was born in Detroit, Michigan, in 1936. She has published fifteen books of poetry. See page R6 of the Author Files for more on Marge Piercy.

Author Search For more about these poets, go to www.glencoe.com.

Indiana English/Language Arts Academic Standards (pp. 398–401)

8.1 Word Recognition, Fluency, and Vocabulary Development Determine the meaning of words… **8.2 Comprehension and Analysis (Focus on Informational Text)** Develop [reading] strategies… **8.3.6** Identify… literary devices…which define a writer's style and use [them] to interpret a work.

For a complete description of the standards, see p. IN 11.

Vocabulary Preview

Previewing these words and phrases from "We Real Cool" and "The market economy" will help you recognize and understand them when you read the poems.

- The word **lurk** means to hang around trying not to be seen. You might lurk outside your sister's bedroom door to find out her secrets.
- In a **market economy,** the things and services people buy are priced according to what people are willing to pay for them.
- **Polyvinyl cups** and **wash and wear suits** are products made from types of plastic (polyvinyl and polyester fibers). These plastic products are cheaper and easier to care for than similar products made from natural materials, such as glass, cotton, or wool. However, polyvinyl can cause cancer, and the production of plastics causes dangerous pollution.
- **Fine print** is the section of an agreement that describes the risks involved in the agreement. This section is often printed in tiny type, or "fine print."

English Language Coach

Using Word References Dictionaries and glossaries are reference sources that can help you learn the meanings of words. Thesauruses can help you find synonyms and antonyms for words. All these resources are available in print and online. Words are listed in alphabetical order.

Here's how the word *flower* appears in a dictionary. A glossary entry would be similar to this.

> **flower** *n.* [ME *flour*, fr. AF *flur*, *flour*, fr. L *flor-*] **1.** the blossom of a plant. **2.** a flowering plant. **3.** full bloom. **4.** the best or greatest part or time of something.
> *v.* **1.** to form flowers; to bloom. **2.** to come into full development; reach the peak or best time. flowered, flowering

Write to Learn Using a dictionary and a thesaurus, write one definition and one synonym for each word below.

1. conflict
2. test
3. smart
4. vacation
5. cold

Additional Support

Author Search To expand students' appreciation of Gwendolyn Brooks and Marge Piercy, have them access the Web site for additional information and resources.

English Language Coach

Dialect Both Brooks and Piercy use informal English in their poems. Their writing is very similar to the way people speak every day in informal conversations. Brooks's poem has elements of an African American dialect. Dialects, like this one, have their own rules. For example, instead of saying "We are cool," speakers of this dialect might say "We cool." Ask students why poets might want to write the way people actually speak. EL OL

Skills Preview

Key Reading Skill: Identifying Main Idea and Supporting Details

Reading a poem is different from reading an article. The main idea of a poem may not be directly stated as it usually is in an article. Poets often use images and emotions to communicate their main ideas. To determine the main idea of a poem, ask yourself these questions:

- What are the main images and symbols in this poem?
- What emotions do I feel when I read this poem?
- What is the poet saying about the topic?

Partner Talk Discuss your experiences reading poetry with a partner. Do you enjoy reading poetry? How is it different from reading articles or short stories?

R

Literary Element: Alliteration

Alliteration is the repetition of consonant sounds at the beginnings of words. A consonant is any letter of the alphabet except the vowels, *a, e, i, o,* and *u.* Poets use alliteration to create a musical effect, to emphasize meaning, or to draw attention to particular words.

Use these tips to think about alliteration in a poem.

- Read the poem aloud, exaggerating the pronunciation of words.
  Do you hear any repeated consonant sounds?
- How does the alliteration help the poem flow?
  Does the alliteration give you a sense of rhythm? Can you "hear" the speaker saying the words?

Small Group Work Form a group of four students and play this card game.

1. Write these words on separate index cards: *check, shoes, guzzle, put.* Then shuffle the cards.
2. Take turns picking a card and creating a sentence or phrase that repeats the consonant sound that begins the word on your card. For example, if you pick *guzzle,* you might come up with this sentence: *The gross green goblin grows giggles in his garden.* Be as serious or as silly as you like.

Get Ready to Read

Connect to the Reading

When you read the poems "We Real Cool" and "The market economy," think about your hopes for the future and the decisions that lie ahead of you.

Partner Talk With two or three classmates, talk about some of the decisions you will have to make in your future. Which decisions do you think will be easy? Which ones do you think will be harder?

Build Background

- A pool hall is a place where people get together to play pool. Pool is a game played on a table by hitting balls with a long, thin stick into holes at the corners of the table.
- In "We Real Cool," the Golden Shovel is the name of a pool hall.
- Smog is a type of pollution. Smog is caused when the smoke and waste products from factories and automobiles combine with sunlight. The chemical reaction creates a thick, fine dust that looks like yellow fog.

Set Purposes for Reading

Read "We Real Cool" and "The market economy" to learn how the choices people make can put their lives at risk.

Set Your Own Purpose What else would you like to learn from these poems to help you answer the Big Question? Write your own purpose in the Reading Workshop 4 Foldable for Unit 3.

Literature Online

Interactive Literary Elements Handbook
To review or learn more about the literary elements, go to www.glencoe.com.

Keep Moving

Use these skills as you read "We Real Cool" and "The market economy."

Teach

R Reading Skill

Identifying Main Idea and Supporting Details

Ask: How is identifying the main idea in poetry different from identifying the main idea in an informative article? *(Possible response: In poetry, you look at the images and symbols, think about how you feel, and consider what the poet is saying about the topic. In an informative article, you look for sentences that state or infer the main idea.)* AL

Interactive Literary Elements Handbook Have students access the Web site to improve their understanding of alliteration.

Reading in the Real World

College How much does a college degree increase your income? According to the National Center for Education Statistics, earnings increase with education. People who do not finish high school, like the young people in "We Real Cool," earn 30 percent less than those who finish high school. High school graduates earn between 49 and 60 percent less than college graduates. Ask students to name other ways staying in school as long as possible might benefit them. *(Possible responses: To learn to think more critically, to train for a more interesting job)* AS

Indiana English/Language Arts Academic Standards
SE: 8.1, 8.2, 8.3.6
TWE: *English Language Coach* 8.3.6, *Reading in the Real World* 8.2

Teach

Viewing the Illustration

Ask: Does this image look like the kind of place you imagine the poem to take place in? *(Responses will vary.)* **BL**
Ask: What words in the poem match the details in the image? *(Possible responses: Pool Players, Strike straight)* **OL**

R1 Reading Skill

Review Comparing and Contrasting **Ask:** What is the difference between the speakers at the beginning of the poem and at the end of the poem? *(Possible response: At the beginning, the speakers sound tough and in control, but by the end, they have no power to make a future.)* **AL**

R2 Reading Skill

Identifying Main Idea and Supporting Details **Ask:** What is the poet saying about not attending school in this poem? *(She's saying it is a bad idea.)* **AL** **Ask:** What detail supports this main idea? *(The players say they will die soon.)* **OL**

We Real Cool

by Gwendolyn Brooks

THE POOL PLAYERS.
SEVEN AT THE GOLDEN SHOVEL.

We real cool. We
Left school. We

Lurk late. We R1
Strike straight. We

Sing sin. We R2
Thin gin. We

Jazz June. We
Die soon. **1**

Practice the Skills

1 Literary Element

Alliteration There is alliteration in almost every line of this poem. How does it affect the rhythm of the poem?

Additional Support

Differentiated Instruction

Oral Interpretation Share this comment from Gwendolyn Brooks on how her poem should be read aloud: "The 'We'—you're supposed to stop after the 'We.' . . . I say it rather softly because I want to represent their basic uncertainty, which they don't bother to question every day, of course."

Remind students that poets often put much effort into a poem's sound, which can be missed if the work is read silently. Invite several volunteers to read "We Real Cool" aloud. Ask students to comment on the effect of placing emphasis in different places, changing pace, and other interpretative techniques. **AL**

READING WORKSHOP 4

The market economy

by Marge Piercy

Suppose some peddler offered
you can have a color TV
but your baby will be
born with a crooked spine;
you can have polyvinyl cups
and wash and wear
suits but it will cost
you your left lung
rotted with cancer; suppose
somebody offered you
a frozen precooked dinner
every night for ten years
but at the end
your colon dies
and then you do,
slowly and with much pain.

You get a house in the suburbs
but you work in a new plastics
factory and die at fifty-one
when your kidneys turn off.

But where else will you
work? Where else can
you rent but Smog City?
The only houses for sale
are under the yellow sky.
You've been out of work for
a year and they're hiring
at the plastics factory.
Don't read the fine
print, there isn't any. **2** **3** ○

Practice the Skills

2 **Key Reading Skill**

Determining Main Idea and Supporting Details Summarize both poems. What is the main idea of each poem? How are they related?

3 **BIG Question**

In both poems, people choose one way to live and then pay the price. On the Reading Workshop 4 Foldable, write the choices the people make, what they gain, and what they lose in each poem. Then note whether you think the prices they pay are too high or not.

Teach

L Literary Element

Alliteration Ask: What alliteration do you see in the first ten lines? *(can/color; but/baby/born; wash/wear; left lung)* **OL**

C Critical Thinking

Comprehension Ask: What are the benefits of the things offered in the first stanza? *(They are entertaining and convenient.)* **Ask:** What are the costs? *(They can deform children and cause terrible diseases and death.)* **OL**

R Reading Skill

Review Comparing and Contrasting Ask: What future do the people in both poems have? *(Possible response: In both cases, the people face terrible futures where they die young.)* **Ask:** What can they do about the dead ends they face? *(Answers will vary.)* **OL**

Assess

Use the CheckPoint questions provided on Presentation Plus! to check for comprehension of the selections. These questions can be used with interactive response keypads for immediate student feedback.

Reading Fluency

Using an Everyday Tone Piercy says that "The Market Economy" is written in a "short, breathier, more conversational" style than some of her formal poems. Tell students to practice reading the poem aloud, trying to use everyday tone as they read. Remind students to use punctuation and meaning, rather than line breaks, to tell them when to pause reading. **EL** To help them further with fluency, have them rewrite the poem in sentence form (without any of the line breaks). **BL**

Indiana English/Language Arts Academic Standards

SE: 8.1, 8.2, 8.3.6

TWE: *Reading Skill* 8.2.9, *Differentiated Instruction* 8.7.14, *Reading Fluency* 8.7.14

Assess

Resources for page 402

- Selection Quick Check, p. 28
- Selection and Unit Assessment, p. 32
- ExamView Assessment Suite
- Interactive Tutor: Self-Assessment

Students can respond to the *After You Read* items in their Learner's Notebooks or on a separate sheet of paper.

Answering the BIG Question

1. Possible response: The people in both poems made decisions based on short-term benefits, not long-term costs. The people in the second poem don't have many choices.
2. The speakers in "We Real Cool" are young people playing pool at the Golden Shovel.
3. Possible responses: Color TVs, plastic cups, and frozen dinners.

Critical Thinking

4. Possible response: The use of "you" brings me into the poem and makes me feel like the poet is talking about my life.
5. Possible response: The decision to leave school is *not* taking advantage of an opportunity, while the decision to work at the factory is taking advantage of an opportunity that is destructive.
6. Responses will vary.

After You Read

We Real Cool *and* The market economy

Answering the BIG Question

1. Both poems talk about the prices people pay for their decisions. Do you think these people thought about costs before they made their decisions? Explain.
2. **Recall** Who are the "We" in "We Real Cool"?
   TIP **Right There**
3. **Recall** What are some of the conveniences of modern life mentioned in "The market economy"?
   TIP **Right There**

Critical Thinking

4. **Interpret** The speaker of "The market economy" speaks directly to the reader by using "you" and "your." What effect does this have on you as a reader?
   TIP **Author and Me**
5. **Compare** How is the decision to leave school in "We Real Cool" different from the decision to work at a plastics factory in "The market economy"?
   TIP **Author and Me**
6. **Evaluate** The poet who wrote "The market economy" seems to think that in a market economy some people do not have a choice about where they can work and live. Do you think this is true? Why or why not?
   TIP **Author and Me**

Indiana English/Language Arts Academic Standards (pp. 402–403)

8.3 Comprehension and Analysis of Literary Text Respond to grade-level-appropriate literature... **8.7.11** Deliver oral responses to literature...
8.2 Comprehension and Analysis (Focus on Informational Text) Develop [reading] strategies... **8.3.6** Identify... literary devices... which define a writer's style and use [them] to interpret a work.
8.6 English Language Conventions
For a complete description of the standards, see p. IN 11.

Talk About Your Reading

Role Play Imagine you are one of the people referred to in the poem "We Real Cool" or "The market economy." You could be one of the kids hanging out at the pool hall or a person who lives in Smog City. Tell the class about yourself—how old you are, the kind of place where you grew up, what your family is like, what you're interested in—and talk about whether you agree or disagree with the poet's message.

Talk About Your Reading

Possible Response:
I am a fifty-year-old single father. The job in the factory is the best paid job I've ever had. I know the factory is bad for me, but I have four kids to feed, and I need the money. Yes, we eat TV dinners. I don't have time to fix gourmet meals after ten hours at the factory. I worry about my kids' health and my own, but I worry more about paying the bills and living to see next week in our new home.

Skills Review

Key Reading Skill: Identifying Main Idea and Supporting Details

7. What do you think the main idea of "The market economy" is? State it in your own words and explain why you do or don't think it's true.
8. What are some of the images and examples Piercy uses to support the main idea of the poem?

Literary Element: Alliteration

9. Give examples of the alliteration Brooks uses in "We Real Cool." How does alliteration make the poem sound–like a song, a rap, or a riddle? Explain.
10. Give examples of the alliteration Piercy uses in "The market economy." Is it as obvious as in "We Real Cool"? How are the sounds of the two poems different?

Vocabulary Check

Answer the following questions about these words and phrases from "We Real Cool" and "The market economy."

11. In a **market economy,** why is a gold bracelet more expensive than one made of glass beads?
12. Why would people buy **polyvinyl cups** instead of glass ones?
13. If your shirt is **wash and wear,** would it be made of wool?
14. Who would be better at **lurking**–an active, noisy three-year-old child or a burglar?
15. Give an example of a document that is likely to include **fine print.**
16. **English Language Coach** Use a thesaurus to find synonyms for *cost.*

Web Activities For eFlashcards, Selection Quick Checks, and other Web activities, go to www.glencoe.com.

Grammar Link: Indirect Objects

An **indirect object** answers the question *to what? to whom? for what?* or *for whom?* It always comes between the verb and the direct object in a sentence. You will **never** find an *indirect* object in a sentence that doesn't have a *direct* object.

Susan gave Mrs. Monroe a flower.

verb (gave) *indirect object* (Mrs. Monroe) *direct object* (flower)

(Susan gave a flower to *whom?* She gave it to *Selma.*)

A word is an indirect object only if *to* or *for* is **not** stated. If *to* or *for* is there, it's the object of a preposition. These two sentences contain prepositional phrases, not indirect objects:

My cat brought her toy to me.
Mike sent an e-mail to his boss.

Here are the same sentences with indirect objects:

My cat brought me her toy.
Mike sent my boss an e-mail.

Grammar Practice

Copy the following sentences. Underline the indirect object and circle the direct object.

17. The soccer coach gave Michael an award.
18. My brother sent his girlfriend a love letter.
19. Did you give your grandmother her birthday gift yet?
20. Lorenzo threw his dog a treat.
21. When will you tell Sari the truth?
22. Sandi gave the bus driver one dollar and one quarter.
23. After dinner, we wrote Aunt Louisa a letter.
24. Please give James his jacket.
25. Show me your favorite game.
26. My mother baked me a birthday cake.

Skills Review

Key Reading Skill: Identifying Main Idea and Supporting Details

7. Possible response: Modern lifestyles are convenient but deadly.
8. The images she uses include color TVs and birth defects; plastics and cancer; a job working with industrial chemicals that leads to premature death.

Literary Element: Alliteration

9. Responses will vary.
10. Responses will vary.

Vocabulary Check

11. people value gold more than glass
12. they're inexpensive
13. no, wool is not usually washable
14. a burglar
15. a contract

English Language Coach

16. Possible responses: price, expense, loss

Close

Have students summarize what they learned from reading these poems to answer the Big Question.

Grammar Link: Indirect Objects

Grammar Practice

17. The soccer coach gave Michael an award.
18. My brother sent his girlfriend a love letter.
19. Did you give your grandmother her birthday gift yet?
20. Lorenzo threw his dog a treat.
21. When will you tell Sari the truth?
22. Sandi gave the bus driver one dollar and one quarter.
23. After dinner, we wrote Aunt Louisa a letter.
24. Please give James his jacket.
25. Show me your favorite game.
26. My mother baked me a birthday cake.

Indiana English/Language Arts Academic Standards
SE: 8.2, 8.3, 8.3.6, 8.6, 8.7.11

Comparing Literature: Reading for Author's Credibility

Teaching Students to Read for Author's Credibility

Why Is It Important?

- Students need to be able to differentiate between statements and information that are credible and those that are not.
- Knowing when an author is credible will help students choose helpful sources when creating their own documents.

How to Help Students Get It

- Have students look for author's bias.
- Have students look at the writer's sources—those cited and implied.
- Have students think about the author's background and why he or she might be writing about the particular subject.

Reading to Answer the Big Question

Wearing Hijab by Emilia Askari
In this article, three women tell why they choose to follow the Muslim custom of wearing a head cloth called *hijab*. The speakers relate the good and bad experiences they have had since donning the covering.

from **Zoya's Story** by Zoya with John Follain and Rita Cristofari
Zoya's Story is about a real woman who, for her personal safety, is identified as "Zoya." This excerpt recounts a time when she traveled from Pakistan to her homeland, Afghanistan, during the oppressive rule of the Taliban. Forced to temporarily don the *burqa* to hide her face and body, Zoya comes to understand what her countrywomen are forced to endure every day of their lives.

Workshop Resources

Pacing (Days) Standard	Pacing (Days) Block	Lesson	Student Materials	Teacher Resources
1	1	Comparing Literature: Reading for Author's Credibility	English Language Coach Review, p. 43	Bellringer Options Transparencies –Daily Language Practice 30 Presentation Plus!
1	1	"Wearing Hijab"	Glencoe Online Unit Vocabulary Review, p. 41 Academic Vocabulary Review, p. 44 English Language Coach Reading Across Texts Graphic Organizer, p. 36 StudentWorks Plus™ Online Student Edition Literature Classics	Puzzlemaker Skill Level Up!™ A Language Arts Game BookLink 3 Assessment by Learning Objective (Diagnostic and Formative) Interactive Tutor: Self-Assessment TeacherWorks Plus™ ExamView Assessment Suite
1		from *Zoya's Story*	Glencoe Online Unit Vocabulary Review, p. 41 Academic Vocabulary Review, p. 44 English Language Coach Reading Across Texts Graphic Organizer, p. 36 StudentWorks Plus™ Online Student Edition Literature Classics	Puzzlemaker Skill Level Up!™ A Language Arts Game BookLink 3 Assessment by Learning Objective (Diagnostic and Formative) Interactive Tutor: Self-Assessment TeacherWorks Plus™ ExamView Assessment Suite

Keys for Unit Resource

- Blackline Master
- Workbook
- Supplemental Text
- CD-ROM
- DVD
- Transparency
- Web-based
- Fast File

Level Appropriate Code

AS = Activities for all students
AL = Activities for students working above grade level
OL = Activities for students working at grade level
BL = Activities for students working below grade level
EL = Activities for English language learners

Focus

BELLRINGER Options

Daily Language Practice Transparency 30

Focus Activity Ask: Is there anything you choose to wear that tells people who you are, what you believe, or what you enjoy? *(religious icons, band t-shirts, political buttons)* **Ask:** How would it be different if someone forced you to wear this? *(It would say what someone else wanted me to be, think, or like.)* AS

Teach

L1 Literary Element

Writer's Qualifications Ask: How might you find out a writer's qualifications? *(Possible response: by looking online or looking for a short bio at the end of the essay or book)* BL OL

L2 Literary Element

Writer's Sources Ask: How might you find out what sources a writer has used? *(The writer might mention them in the text of an article or book, or there might be a list of sources at the end of the piece.)* OL AL

READING ACROSS TEXTS WORKSHOP

Wearing Hijab: Veil of Valor

by Emilia Askari

from ZOYA'S STORY

by Zoya with John Follain and Rita Cristofari

Skills Focus

You will use these skills as you read and compare the following selections:

- "Wearing Hijab: Veil of Valor," p. 407
- from *Zoya's Story: An Afghan Woman's Struggle for Freedom*, p. 414

Reading

- Read and understand texts representing a variety of authors, subjects, and genres
- Clarify understanding of texts by creating a graphic organizer
- Analyze author's qualifications and sources.

Indiana English/ Language Arts Academic Standards (pp. 404–405)

8.2 Comprehension and Analysis (Focus on Informational Text) Develop [reading] strategies... identifying and analyzing...perspective... **8.2.3** Find similarities and differences between texts...

For a complete description of the standards, see p. IN 11.

In this unit, you've read about the trade-offs people make. You've thought about what can happen when events and experiences cost people and communities too much. But who or what affects how you think and feel about a subject? Many times, writers help you decide when the price is too high.

How to Read Across Texts

When you read across two texts, you look at what subjects the writers discuss and how they communicate their ideas to readers. You think like a detective, asking questions about the writers and their subjects. That way, you learn more about the subject by evaluating how and why each writer writes about it.

As a reader, you need to think about the following questions:

- L1 What are the writer's **qualifications?** Does he or she know about this topic from formal education, research, or personal experience?
- L2 What are the writer's **sources?** Was the writer a witness to the events? If not, does he or she identify where the information came from?

Additional Support

Literature Focus Lesson

Identifying Bias Tell students that there are many ways a writer might show bias for or against a subject. Provide students with the following questions they can ask to detect bias.

- Does the writer use opinion words, such as "I think" or "I believe"?
- Does the writer use strong adjectives to describe something, such as *tragic* or *remarkable*?
- Does the writer include only the opinions of experts or others who agree with his or her point of view?
- Does the writer neglect one point of view or imply it is invalid?

AS

Get Ready to Compare

In your Learner's Notebook, draw a graphic organizer like the one below. Use your organizer to keep track of details about the writers as you read the following selections. Your notes will help you better understand the subject and compare the selections.

Writer	Emilia Askari	Zoya
Writer's Qualifications		
Writer's Sources		

Use Your Comparison

The two selections you will read in this workshop have something in common. They are both about the clothing many Muslim women wear. But the writers explore the issue in very different ways. One writer shares the stories of three women through a newspaper article, while the other writer draws upon her own experience.

As you read, use the information you add to your chart to think about how each writer approaches the issue.

- How does each writer share information and experiences? How does her approach make you think and feel as you read?
- What do you learn from one writer that you don't learn from the other?
- How does each selection make you, the reader, think about the issue in different ways?

Teach

L Literary Element

Writer's Qualifications

Say: One of the writers uses her own experiences to write about wearing clothing Muslim women wear. What might be the advantage of reading a first-hand account, such as this one? *(Possible response: The writer will be able to provide details about the experience.)* **Ask:** What might be a disadvantage? *(Possible responses: The writer's point of view may be biased.)* AL

Assess/Close

Ask students to consider what qualifications a writer should have to write about the clothing Muslim women wear. Who would be good sources of information on this subject? What biases might writers have? *(Possible responses: A writer who has done research or who has worn the clothing would be qualified. Muslim women would be good sources of information. Writers might be biased for or against wearing the traditional clothes.)* OL AL

Resources for page 405

Use the Reading Across Texts Graphic Organizer BLM in the Unit 3 Resource Booklet, p. 36.

Reading in the Real World

Citizenship Tell students that France has a law against wearing conspicuous religious symbols in public schools. Although the law bans large crosses and Jewish skullcaps as well as veils, it has been interpreted as an anti-*hijab* law and several Muslim girls have been expelled for wearing veils to school. Have students write a short paragraph explaining their opinion of this law. Ask student volunteers to read their paragraph aloud. OL AL

Indiana English/Language Arts Academic Standards
SE: 8.2, 8.2.3
TWE: *Literature Focus Lesson* 8.3.7, *Reading in the Real World* 8.2

Teach

Did You Know?

The tradition of wearing veils is not mandated by the Qur'an (the Islamic holy text), but it is based on religious faith. Wearing a veil is not strictly a Muslim tradition. Catholic nuns traditionally wore veils, and there are references to the practice in the Bible.

R Reading Skill

Review Connecting Discuss student responses to the *Connect to the Reading* prompt. Ask students to name some of the benefits and costs of standing up for what they believe in. When might the price be too high? *(Responses will vary.)* AS

Before You Read

Wearing Hijab: Veil of Valor

Emilia Askari

Meet the Author

Emilia Askari is a prize-winning journalist who has covered environmental and public health issues for more than a decade. She lives in the Detroit area and is a former president of the Society of Environmental Journalists. She works for the *Detroit Free Press*.

Author Search For more about Emilia Askari, go to www.glencoe.com.

Indiana English/Language Arts Academic Standards
(pp. 406–412)

8.1.3 Verify the meaning of a word in its context... **8.2 Comprehension and Analysis (Focus on Informational Text)** Develop [reading] strategies... identifying and analyzing... perspective...

For a complete description of the standards, see p. IN 11.

Vocabulary Preview

valor (VAL or) *n.* courage **(p. 407)** *In Arthurian legend, the Knights of the Round Table are known for their valor.*

intercede (in tur SEED) *v.* to try to help settle differences between others **(p. 410)** *The teacher decided to intercede when the vote for class president ended in a tie.*

tolerance (TOL ur uns) *n.* the ability to recognize and respect different beliefs **(p. 410)** *Samir's grandfather was a devout Hindu, but he encouraged the tolerance of other faiths.*

English Language Coach

Multiple-Meaning Words Many words have more than one meaning. To discover the correct meaning of a word, you can look at context clues.

For example, the word *case* can mean:

(a) a container; (b) an occurrence; (c) someone who is being helped or treated by a professional

In "Wearing Hijab: Veil of Valor," you will find the word *case.* Use context clues to decide which meaning of *case* makes sense.

Get Ready to Read

Connect to the Reading

R Have you ever stood up for something you believed in, even though doing so made you unpopular? How did that feel?

Build Background

First published in November 2001, this article is about women who follow the Muslim practice of covering their heads with scarves, called *hijab.* Many Muslim women choose to wear *hijab* as an expression of their faith.

Set Purposes for Reading

BIG Question Read to find out why women decide to wear *hijab* and what it can cost them.

Set Your Own Purpose What else would you like to learn from the selection to help you answer the Big Question? Write your own purpose on your Reading Across Texts Foldable.

Additional Support

Author Search To expand students' appreciation of Emilia Askari, have them access the Web site for additional information and resources.

Differentiated Instruction

Build Background Wearing *hijab* has a long history. A verse from the Qur'an states, "O Prophet! Tell thy wives and thy daughters and the women of the believers to draw their cloaks close [veils] around them. That will be better, so that they may be recognized and not annoyed." Some Muslim women believe that wearing *hijab* allows them to be individuals who are not objectified (seen as objects of beauty or desire) by men. Tell students to read to see why the women in the article wear *hijab.* OL

INFORMATIONAL TEXT
NEWSPAPER
Detroit Free Press

Wearing Hijab: Veil of Valor C

by Emilia Askari

Alya Kazak had been thinking about wearing *hijab,* a scarf that would publicly identify her as Muslim, for a long time.

It was just a rectangle of cloth, plain and black. But it was heavy with symbolism—a reminder of her faith, her modesty, her wish that strangers would be attracted by her personality and not her physical beauty. 1

So what if she worked in a Victoria's Secret selling cosmetics? Sure, there was a conflict there. But the life of an American Muslim is punctuated with cultural clashes. This one didn't seem any bigger than most.

Or did it?

The first day Kazak took up the veil, tears were pouring down her face as she drove toward the Somerset Collection.

She pulled over to the side of the road, daubed her eye makeup and prayed.

Vocabulary

valor (VAL or) *n.* courage

Practice the Skills

1 Reviewing Elements

Photographs How does the photograph above add to the author's description of *hijab*?

Teach

C Critical Thinking

Comprehension Say: You learned in the Vocabulary Preview that *valor* means "courage." What does the title of this article tell you about the writer's opinion of *hijab*? *(She supports wearing the veil and sees doing so as courageous.)* OL

Viewing the Photo

Ask: How do you think the woman pictured feels about wearing *hijab*? *(Possible response: Her smile suggests she is happy about wearing the veil.)* BL

Readability Scores
Dale-Chall: 8.4
DRP: 59
Lexile: 1010

Literature Focus Lesson

Anecdotes An anecdote is a brief story about an incident that is especially funny, interesting, or illustrative. Writers and speakers frequently begin with an anecdote to capture the attention of their audience. Why do you think Askari began with a story instead of with her opinion about *hijab*? *(Responses will vary. Students may suggest that the story is a good way to counter prejudices that readers might have about the custom or that, as a reporter, she wants to remain objective.)* BL OL

Indiana English/Language Arts Academic Standards
SE: 8.1.3, 8.2
TWE: *Differentiated Instruction* 8.2, *Literature Focus Lesson* 8.3

Teach

C Critical Thinking

Comprehension Ask: What evidence does Kazak give that wearing *hijab* has affected her positively? *(She explains that she has more self-esteem and gets more respect when wearing* hijab.*)* BL

L Literary Element

Writer's Qualifications
Ask: Why might it have been important to interview Muslim women when writing this article? *(Possible response: People who are not Muslim might not fully understand the religious tradition of wearing* hijab.*)* **Ask:** Do you think Askari chose her sources well? *(Possible response: Askari chose well; she selected women who know a lot about wearing* hijab *and how it affects their life.)* OL AL

Please make this an easy transition for me. Please make me strong.

Today, about two and a half years later, Kazak is among tens of thousands of Muslim women in Michigan who wear *hijab*—pronounced hee-JAHB—in public. The practice often is misunderstood by non-Muslims, who may associate it with female oppression. But most *hijabis,* as women who wear the scarves are called, say that covering their hair was a personal choice. They credit the veils with improving their relationships with people and God. **2**

Here are the stories of three Muslim females in metro Detroit and their experiences with *hijabs.* They share faith in Islam and believe that publicly identifying themselves as Muslims is more important since Sept. 11.

Wearing *hijab* "clarified for me my identity as a Muslim woman," says Kazak, who left her part-time job at Victoria's Secret when her schedule of Oakland University classes changed. Now that she's graduated, she works full-time as a **case** manager for refugees at ACCESS, the Arab Community Center for Economic and Social Services in Dearborn. **3**

The scarf she wraps around her head each morning has liberated Kazak from the coquettish[1] games other people play, she says. "I notice a different level of respect, and I just love that. Self-esteem . . . I just feel so much better about myself, so much more respectable. I feel my personality come out with my scarf." **C**

She burbles with confidence, happy to demonstrate how she pins the scarf after matching its color to her day's outfit. "It's like a declaration: Hello, I am Muslim," says Kazak, 22. She lives with her parents and sister in Bloomfield Hills, driving to work in a car sporting a vanity license and floor mats emblazoned[2] with her nickname, Princess. **4**

Kazak, who is of Palestinian descent, says taking up the veil was "the most positive decision I have made in my life."

With the world's attention focused on Muslims in the wake of the attacks, Kazak says she feels people staring a bit longer at her veil, giving her a wider berth[3] as she passes them on the street or in the mall. Still, she has been lucky. No one has

1. When people are ***liberated*** (LIH bur ay tid), they are set free. ***Coquettish*** (koh KET ish) means "playful" or "flirtatious."
2. ***Emblazoned*** (em BLAY zund) means "decorated with bold words or colors."
3. ***Giving a wider berth*** means "giving someone a lot of room."

Practice the Skills

2 Reading Across Texts

Writer's Sources The writer does not tell you the source of this information, but newspaper editors usually verify, or check, that the information is correct.

3 English Language Coach

Multiple-Meaning Words Think about the three meanings of **case** on page 406. Now look at the context clues in this sentence. What does *case* mean here?

4 Reading Across Texts

Writer's Qualifications What can you learn from a writer who interviews others? Do you think you can learn more or less from someone who only writes about his or her own experiences? **L**

Additional Support

Differentiated Instruction

Identifying Main Ideas and Supporting Details Ask students to find details to support the idea that women who wear the veil believe it improves "their relationships with people and God." You could have students point out the details in the text or work with them to create a main idea/detail chart. *(Details that students might identify in support include the respect the women feel they receive from others and the freedom to express their personalities [p. 408], pride in standing up for Islam [p. 409], and freedom to excel and be professional [pp. 411–412].)* EL BL OL bothered her because she follows the religion that's also claimed by the killers of thousands of Americans.

Another story

Zaiba Lateef has not been so lucky. Perhaps that's because she is 15 and immersed in a peer culture where teasing and showing off are huge preoccupations.

The first shove came out of nowhere on Sept. 11, hours after the 5,000 or so students in the adjoining campuses of Plymouth-Canton and Salem high schools had watched the twin towers collapse on television.

Lateef, whose parents immigrated to Michigan from India, had just finished her American Literature class.

Then from the crowd of people filling the hallway came a boy's voice hissing an expletive,[4] followed by "terrorist." And someone's shoulder slammed Lateef into the wall of lockers.

"It was such a blackout," Lateef recalls. "I was so confused. I was so scared." She turned to see who had pushed her. But it was impossible to tell. **5**

Three young Arab women dance in a circle at a festival in Dearborn, Michigan.

Lateef has worn *hijab* since she was nine. All girls in fifth grade and up are required to cover their hair at the Crescent School, a private Muslim elementary school in Canton that Lateef attended.

Despite the fact that *hijab* was part of her school uniform, Lateef says she never felt forced to wear it. "It was more like a reward" for being old enough and mature enough, she says.

After the incident in the hallway, some of Lateef's relatives suggested that perhaps it would be best if the slim, analytical girl stopped wearing *hijab* for a while. But Lateef wouldn't hear of it. "I want to keep wearing *hijab* to show people that Islam is a true and beautiful religion," she says. "I'm proud to be a Muslim. This is a time when I need to be strong." **C**

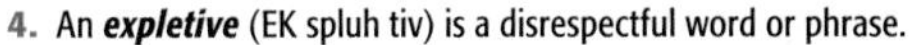

4. An ***expletive*** (EK spluh tiv) is a disrespectful word or phrase.

Practice the Skills

5 Reading Across Texts

Writer's Sources How does the writer (Emilia Askari) know about Kazak's experiences—through education, research, or personal experience? Write your answer in your chart.

Teach

R Reading Skill

Review Comparing and Contrasting **Ask:** How does Lateef's experience contrast with Kazak's? *(Possible response: Lateef was harassed by students who did not understand or respect her tradition, while Kazak has endured nothing worse than stares.)* **OL**

C Critical Thinking

Evaluation **Say:** Some of Lateef's relatives suggested that she stop wearing *hijab.* Do you think that was good advice? Why or why not? *(Possible response: Her relatives wanted to protect her, so it was good advice.)* **AS**

Reading in the Real World

Citizenship Review the way Lateef handled the bullying and discrimination she experienced at school. Have students work in small groups to come up with other suggestions for dealing with bullying.

- What do they think are the best ways for dealing with this problem?
- What methods are ineffective?

Have a representative from each group share the group's findings with the class. **AL**

Indiana English/Language Arts Academic Standards
SE: 8.1.3, 8.2
TWE: *Differentiated Instruction* 8.2, *Reading in the Real World* 8.3

Teach

L Literary Element

Review Description Ask: How does this description of Lateef's reaction help you understand her feelings? *(The description of her reaction shows that the bullying affected her deeply.)* OL

R Reading Skill

Review Connecting Ask: Do you think your school does a good job of teaching cultural tolerance? If not, what could it do better? *(Responses will vary.)* BL

Weeks passed before it happened again. Then, in early October, she was standing in the second floor Spanish hall a few minutes before school was scheduled to start. A heavy shoe kicked her hard in the shin as a boy called out the same insult, laughing.

This time it wasn't as much of a shock. She turned and made a mental note of the boy's face, his green nylon ski jacket, and the bright orange fleece jacket worn by the girl who was with him, laughing. L

Then Lateef says she saw a friend walking down the hall and broke down in tears. "I couldn't even talk," she says. "I couldn't walk. I just kept crying." 6

A week later, she says that she and another friend were walking in a breezeway between two school buildings. A group of boys came up from behind them. One yelled, "Can I have one of those?" He reached for Lateef's *hijab.* Another put an arm around her friend and grabbed at the bun of hair beneath her veil.

Visual Vocabulary
A ***mosque*** is a place of Muslim worship.

Lateef and her friend ran for an open door, choking back tears. She had trouble breathing. She was scared and angry and sad all at once. She leaned against a wall of lockers, caught her breath and went to her next class with a lump in her throat.

At Lateef's mosque, it seemed like everyone was talking of the young girl's troubles. The news eventually reached Haaris Ahmad, executive director of the Council on American Islamic Relations' Michigan office. He decided to **intercede** among the Lateef family, the school, and the families of the boys.

In the end, the boy in the green jacket apologized for kicking Lateef. Lateef forgave him. School officials agreed to enhance their efforts to teach cultural **tolerance,** developing what Ahmad calls a model program for other schools. Among the school's first actions was to encourage all of its students to attend an open house at a nearby mosque for extra credit. R

Vocabulary

intercede (in tur SEED) *v.* to try to help settle differences between others

tolerance (TOL ur uns) *n.* the ability to recognize and respect different beliefs

Practice the Skills

6 Reviewing Skills

Making Inferences Why did Lateef break down in tears?

Additional Support

English Language Coach

Build Background The Council on American-Islamic Relations (CAIR) is a Muslim civil liberties group with thirty-two offices in the United States and Canada. According to the group, its goal is to "enhance the understanding of Islam, encourage dialogue, protect civil liberties, empower American Muslims, and build coalitions that promote justice and mutual understanding." For example, the group provides free materials about the life of the prophet Muhammad and posts editorials about current issues of significance to Muslims. Ask students how a group like this one might be helpful in preventing misunderstandings about Muslim culture. OL

The boy was there with his family. He appeared delighted when a woman wrote his first name in Arabic script, noting that it was the name of an Islamic prophet.

Although wearing *hijab* in public and while praying is encouraged by Islamic teachings, many Muslim women regard the practice as optional. There was a time, perhaps a decade or so ago, when professional, educated women were less likely to wear *hijab* than their Muslim sisters who were less educated or whose lives centered more on the home. **7** **R1**

In fact, some countries with large Muslim populations such as Turkey have tried to discourage or even forbid women from wearing *hijab* in an effort to modernize.

In the last 10 or 15 years, however, it has become less unusual in this country and many others around the world to see women like Dr. Razan Kadry wearing *hijab* as they see patients and consult with other physicians at Detroit Medical Center.

Kadry is a dermatology resident born in Pontiac of Syrian-American parents.

She has no recollection of the exact day, when she was 14, she made the decision to wear *hijab.* But in retrospect,[5] Kadry sees it as a turning point. "I was a very timid person," she says. "I was good in school, but I wasn't stellar." Covering her hair gave her the confidence to excel.

"It opened doors of opportunity," she says. "I was able to focus not so much on my appearance and social things but on what I needed to do at school. My grades shot through the roof. Everything fell into place." **R2**

She wound up skipping three grades and entering Oakland University at 15, then graduated from Wayne State's medical school.

Kadry feels that wearing *hijab* around the hospital makes it easier for her to do her job.

"People deal with me on a much more professional and friendly level because I veil," she explains.

Because she wears *hijab*—perhaps also because she is married and a mother—men treat Kadry, 27, as a comrade, barely noticing her physical appearance.

5. If you think about things ***in retrospect*** (REH troh spekt), you think about the past.

Practice the Skills

7 **Reviewing Skills**

Making Inferences Why might women who worked outside of the home have been less likely to wear *hijab*?

Teach

R1 Reading Skill

Review Making Inferences

Say: The author explains that some Muslim women wear *hijab* and others do not. What can you infer about the practice of Islam from this explanation? *(Possible responses: People practice this religion differently, just as people have different ways of practicing other religions, such as Christianity, Judaism, and Buddhism.)* **OL**

R2 Reading Skill

Review Comparing and Contrasting **Ask:** How does Kadry's reason for wearing *hijab* differ from those of Kazak and Lateef ? *(Possible response: Kazak and Lateef focus on how hijab helps identify them as Muslims. On the other hand, Kadry focuses on how wearing it helped her excel. She says wearing it freed her to be a professional because she no longer had to focus on her appearance.)* **OL** **AL**

Differentiated Instruction

Reversing Expectations Ask students whether they were surprised that some women view the *hijab* as an expression of their freedom. Have students locate places in the article where the author tries to correct misinterpretations of wearing *hijab. (Students might point out the quotations from Kadry, the comment that the custom "is often misunderstood" [page 408], and the way Kazak and Kadry tried to defuse prejudice after 9/11.)* **OL** Discuss how students could use Askari's strategies if they were writing about a topic that is often misunderstood. **AL**

Indiana English/Language Arts Academic Standards

SE: 8.2, 8.2.9

TWE: *English Language Coach* 8.2, *Differentiated Instruction* 8.3.7

Teach

C Critical Thinking

Analysis **Ask:** Do you think Askari is trying to speak for all Muslim women in this article? *(Possible response: No, she has focused on the experience of three Muslim American women living in Detroit.)* **Ask:** In your opinion, is Askari's treatment of *hijab* biased? *(Opinions will depend on whether students think the author equally presented views on the topic.)* OL AL

BQ BIG Question

Before students write in their Foldables, review the reasons each woman chose to wear *hijab.* AS

Assess

Use the CheckPoint questions provided on Presentation Plus! to check for comprehension of the selection. These questions can be used with interactive response keypads for immediate student feedback.

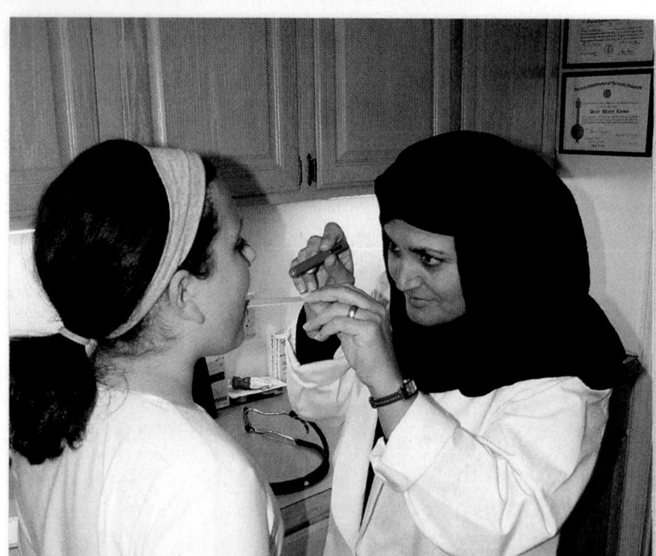

Analyzing the Photo Like the woman in this photo, Kadry practices medicine while wearing *hijab*. How might Kadry's experience as a doctor differ from the experiences of other doctors who don't wear *hijab?*

That camaraderie[6] abruptly faded on Sept. 11 as news of the attacks spread. "For a moment I felt there was a huge wall around me," Kadry says. "Then I started speaking, saying that the people who did this could not have been real Muslims."

The mood changed as everyone realized that she was just as shocked and horrified as they were by the attacks.

Her boss went out of his way to speak with her in private, expressing concern for her safety and suggesting that perhaps she might want to remove her *hijab* until feelings cooled down.

"I told him that was like asking a black person to bleach the color out of their skin," Kadry said. "Now more than ever I have to stay steadfast. I must wear *hijab* and be a better example." 8 9

6. ***Camaraderie*** (kawm RAH dur ee) is another word for "friendship."

Practice the Skills

8 Reviewing Skills

Connecting How do you think you would feel in Kadry's place? Would you be afraid of violence if you wore *hijab?* Would you feel like a coward if you didn't?

9 BIG Question

What price were these three women willing to pay to wear *hijab?* Was that price too high? Write your answer in your Reading Across Texts Foldable.

Additional Support

Literature Focus Lesson

Analogy An analogy is a comparison that is used to make a point. Analogies often compare something familiar to something unfamiliar to make the unfamiliar thing easier to understand. For example, Kadry implies that her *hijab* is as much a part of her as skin color. Ask students, what is something that symbolizes your identity? What comparison could you make to help someone understand its importance? *(Responses will vary.)* OL

Before You Read from *Zoya's Story*

Meet the Author

Because Zoya must hide her true identity to protect her family and friends, two other people helped her write her story. John Follain lives and works in Rome. He writes mostly about the Vatican and the Mafia in Italy. Rita Cristofari has worked as a press officer for the United Nations, Médecins Sans Frontières, and France 2 television.

Author Search For more about these authors, go to www.glencoe.com.

Vocabulary Preview

instinctively (in STINK tiv lee) *adv.* with a natural response **(p. 415)** *When he saw the car coming, Maleek instinctively jumped out of the way.*

perpetrated (PUR pih tray tid) *v.* was responsible for something harmful; form of the verb *perpetrate* **(p. 416)** *The police vowed to catch those who perpetrated the crime.*

English Language Coach

Multiple-Meaning Words *Treatment* is a multiple-meaning word that can mean

(a) a method for helping a person who is ill

(b) the way someone behaves toward you

Watch for the word *treatment* in *Zoya's Story.*

Get Ready to Read

Connect to the Reading

The person in the story you are about to read is treated negatively because she is female. How does it feel to be treated unfairly?

Build Background

- The Taliban (TAL ih ban) is the group that ruled Afghanistan from 1996–2001.
- The Taliban follow a strict form of Islamic law. Under this law, women must cover themselves completely with a *burqa,* a large piece of cloth that covers them from head to toe, including their face and hands.
- This story is told by a woman who was born in Afghanistan but moved away when the Taliban gained control of her country. This selection is about her return to Afghanistan when the Taliban were still in control.

Set Purposes for Reading

BIG Question Read to discover why Zoya returned to Afghanistan and how she felt about wearing a *burqa.*

Set Your Own Purpose What else would you like to learn from the selection to help you answer the Big Question? Write your own purpose on your Reading Across Texts Foldable.

Indiana English/Language Arts Academic Standards (pp. 413–417)

8.1.3 Verify the meaning of a word in its context... **8.2 Comprehension and Analysis (Focus on Informational Text)** Develop [reading] strategies...identifying and analyzing...perspective...

For a complete description of the standards, see p. IN 11.

Teach

More About the Author

Zoya is a member of the Revolutionary Association of the Women of Afghanistan (RAWA), as was her mother. When she was eight, Zoya began carrying secret papers for her mother. Four years later, in 1989, mujahideen soldiers began shelling her hometown. Her parents were killed, and Zoya left Kabul for Pakistan. Now she works with refugees and raises funds for RAWA from international donors.

Literature Online

Author Search To expand students' appreciation of Zoya, John Follain, and Rita Cristofari, have them access the Web site for additional information and resources.

Differentiated Instruction

Building Background When the Taliban came to power, they established a fundamentalist Islamic state, where women were no longer allowed to work and were forced to stay at home unless accompanied by a male relative. In addition, young girls could no longer attend school, and females had restricted access to healthcare. After a rebellion forced them from power in 2001, Hamid Karzai became head of a new constitutional government. In September 2005, the first government elections in thirty years were held in Afghanistan. Discuss with students what it must have been like for women and girls during the Taliban rule. AS

Indiana English/Language Arts Academic Standards

SE: 8.1.3, 8.2

TWE: *Literature Focus Lesson* 8.1.1, *Differentiated Instruction* 8.2

Teach

Viewing the Photo

Ask: What mood is set by the photograph? *(Possible responses: the photograph creates a sense of darkness or sadness because the lighting is gloomy and the women's individual identities are hidden by their garments.)* **OL**

L Literary Element

Writer's Source **Ask:** Who is the writer's source for information in these paragraphs? *(She is her own source.)* **BL** **Ask** By wearing the *burqa* herself, what details can the writer give to help readers understand what it feels like to wear it? *(Possible response: She can tell how difficult it is to move, how the mesh chafes her eyelashes, and how her vision is obscured.)* **OL**

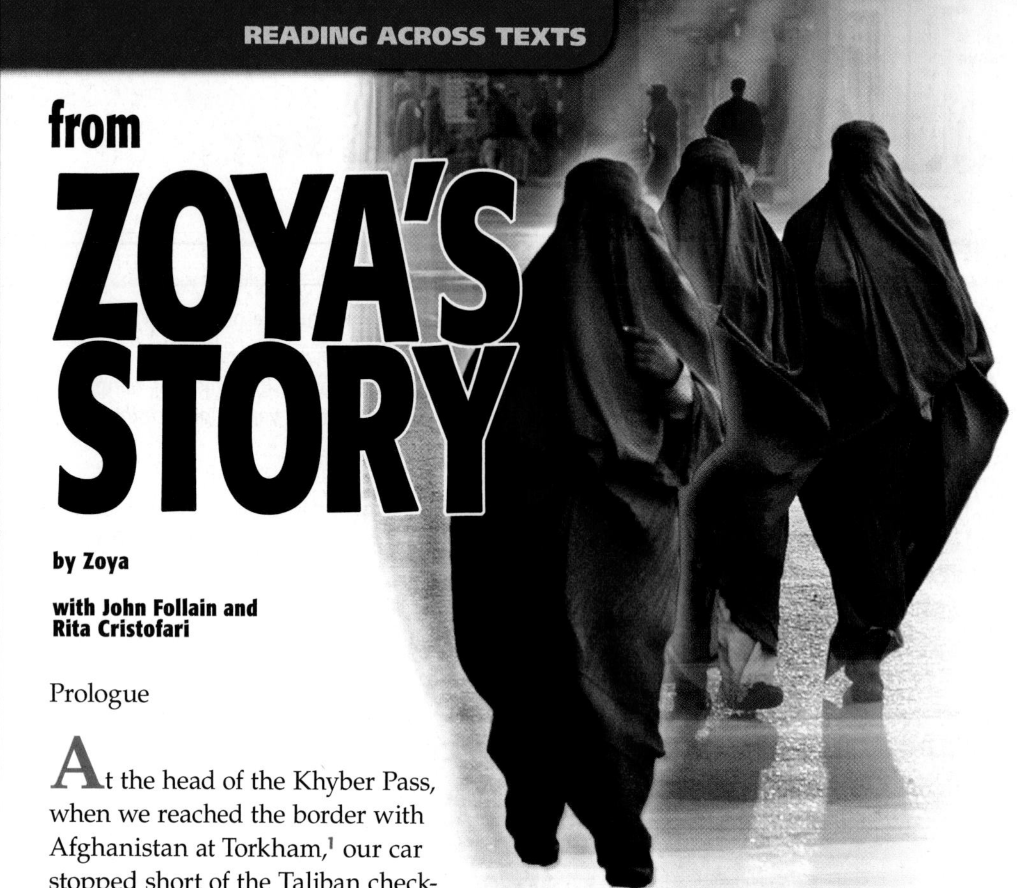

from ZOYA'S STORY

by Zoya

with John Follain and Rita Cristofari

Prologue

At the head of the Khyber Pass, when we reached the border with Afghanistan at Torkham,[1] our car stopped short of the Taliban checkpoint. Before getting out of the car, my friend Abida helped me to put the *burqa* on top of my shirt and trousers and adjusted the fabric until it covered me completely. I felt as if someone had wrapped me in a bag. As best I could in the small mountain of cheap blue polyester, I swung my legs out of the car and got out. **1**

The checkpoint was a hundred yards away, and I stared for a moment at my homeland beyond it. I had been living in exile in Pakistan[2] for five years, and this was my first journey back to Afghanistan. I was looking at its dry and dusty mountains through the bars of a prison cell. The mesh of tiny holes in front of my eyes chafed against my eyelashes. I tried to look up at the sky, but the fabric rubbed against my eyes.

1. The ***Khyber Pass*** is a 33-mile passage that connects Pakistan with ***Afghanistan,*** which is a mountainous country in central Asia. ***Torkham*** is a town on the border between Pakistan and Afghanistan.
2. ***Pakistan*** (PA kih stan) is a country in south Asia that shares borders with India, China, Iran, and Afghanistan.

Practice the Skills

1 Reading Across Texts

Writer's Qualifications How does the writer know about these events? How can you tell?

Additional Support

Literature Focus Lesson

Point of View Remind students that a writer can choose to tell a story from a first-person *(I)*, second-person *(you)*, or third-person *(he, she)* point of view. Ask students to notice the effects of using the first-person point of view to tell this story.

- It makes the story seem very real.
- It helps readers to identify with Zoya.
- It shows that Zoya is writing about her personal experience.
- It makes readers feel close to and care about her story. **OL**

The *burqa* weighed on me like a shroud.[3] I began to sweat in the June sunshine and the beads of moisture on my forehead stuck to the fabric. The little perfume—my small gesture of rebellion—that I had put on earlier at once evaporated. Until a few moments ago, I had breathed easily, **instinctively,** but now I suddenly felt short of air, as if someone had turned off my supply of oxygen. **2**

I followed Javid, who would pretend to be our *mahram,* the male relative without whom the Taliban refused to allow any woman to leave her house, as he set out for the checkpoint. I could see nothing of the people at my side. I could not even see the road under my feet. I thought only of the Taliban edict[4] that my entire body, even my feet and hands, must remain invisible under the *burqa* at all times. I had taken only a few short steps when I tripped and nearly fell down.

When I finally neared the checkpoint, I saw Javid go up to one of the Taliban guards, who was carrying his Kalashnikov rifle slung jauntily over his shoulder. He looked as wild as the Mujahideen, the soldiers who claimed to be fighting a "holy war," whom I had seen as a child: the crazed eyes, the dirty beard, the filthy clothes. I watched him reach to the back of his head, extract what must have been a louse, and squash it between two fingernails with a sharp crack. I remembered what Grandmother had told me about the Mujahideen: "If they come to my house, they won't even need to kill me. I'll die just from seeing their wild faces." **L**

Analyzing the Photo Taliban fighters sit outside of the American embassy in Kabul, Afghanistan, in 2001. How do the men in this picture compare to Zoya's description of Taliban members?

I heard the Taliban ask Javid where he was going, and Javid replied, "These women are with me. They are my daughters. We traveled to Pakistan for some **treatment** because I am sick, and now we are going back home to Kabul." **3** No one asked **EL**

3. A cloth placed over a dead body is called a ***shroud*** (shrowd).
4. An ***edict*** (EE dikt) is a rule or an order.

Vocabulary

instinctively (in STINK tiv lee) *adv.* with a natural response

Practice the Skills

2 Reviewing Elements

Description Which details in this paragraph help you to imagine what it feels like to wear a *burqa*?

3 English Language Coach

Multiple-Meaning Words Look at the two meanings of **treatment** on page 413. Which meaning of *treatment* makes sense here?

Teach

L Literary Element

Review Description Ask: What adjectives does Zoya use to describe the Taliban guard? How do these details show you how she feels about him? *(Students should notice adjectives such as "wild," "crazed," "dirty," "filthy." These negative details show that Zoya clearly doesn't like or respect the guard.)* **BL** **OL**

EL Language Coach

Multiple-Meaning Words
Ask: What word in the sentence gives you a clue about the meaning of *treatment* that makes sense in the sentence? *(The word* sick *gives you a clue that the meaning is "method for helping someone who is ill.")* **BL**

Literature Focus Lesson

Sensory Details and Figurative Language Tell students that to help readers experience a text more fully, writers use sensory details and figurative language.

- **Sensory details** are details based on the five senses (sight, sound, touch, taste, and smell). Have students find examples of the sensory details the writer uses to describe the *burqa.*
- **Figurative language** includes **similes,** which are comparisons that use the words *like* or *as,* and **metaphors,** comparisons between unlike things. What similes or metaphors does the writer use to describe wearing the *burqa*? **AL**

Indiana English/Language Arts Academic Standards
SE: 8.1.3, 8.2
TWE: *Literature Focus Lesson* 8.3, *Literature Focus Lesson* 8.1.1

Teach

C Critical Thinking

Synthesis Ask: Do you think it's appropriate, when discussing brutal crimes such as these, for a writer to show bias? Why or why not? *(Possible response: I do think it's appropriate to show some bias in these cases. Most people will agree with the writer, so it won't affect her credibility.)* OL

R Reading Skill

Review Identifying Main Idea and Supporting Details Ask: Which details in this paragraph support the main idea that the Taliban severely restricts the lives of women? *(The women aren't allowed to speak to the driver, they have to sit at the back, they're not allowed to wear white socks.)* AL

me to show any papers. I had been told that for the Taliban, the *burqa* was the only passport they demanded of a woman. 4

If the Taliban had ordered us to open my bag, he would have found, tied up with string and crammed at the bottom under my few clothes, ten publications of the clandestine[5] association I had joined, the Revolutionary Association of the Women of Afghanistan. They documented, with photographs that made my stomach churn no matter how many times I looked at them, the stonings to death, the public hangings, the amputations performed on men accused of theft, at which teenagers were given the job of displaying the severed limbs to the spectators, the torturing of victims who had fuel poured on them before being set alight, the mass graves the Taliban forces left in their wake. C

These catalogs of the crimes **perpetrated** by the Taliban guard's regime had been compiled on the basis of reports from our members in Kabul. Once they had been smuggled to the city, they would be photocopied thousands of times and distributed to as many people as possible.

But the Taliban made no such request. Shuffling, stumbling, my dignity suffocated, I was allowed through the checkpoint into Afghanistan.

As women, we were not allowed to speak to the driver of a Toyota minibus caked in mud that was waiting to set out for Kabul, so Javid went up to him and asked how much the journey would cost. Then Abida and I climbed in, sitting as far to the back as we could with the other women. We had to wait for a Taliban to jump into the minibus and check that there was nothing suspicious about any of the travelers before we could set off. For him, even a woman wearing white socks would have been suspicious. Under a ridiculous Taliban rule, no one could wear them because white was the color of their flag and they thought it offensive that it should be used to cover such a lowly part of the body as the feet. R

The longer the drive lasted, the tighter the headband on the *burqa* seemed to become, and my head began to ache. The cloth stuck to my damp cheeks, and the hot air that I was

5. A ***clandestine*** (klan DES tin) association is a secret organization.

Vocabulary

perpetrated (PUR pih tray tid) *v.* was responsible for something harmful

Practice the Skills

4 Reviewing Skills

Making Inferences What does the last sentence in this paragraph tell you about how the Taliban view women?

Additional Support

Differentiated Instruction

Building Background Although the Taliban were overthrown in 2001, the Revolutionary Association of the Women of Afghanistan (RAWA) continues its work, sponsoring orphanages and schools and promoting peace and democracy. Among their principles is gender tolerance. The organization believes that "no human being is better than any other because of gender; contrary to the belief of the fundamentalists who treat our women as cattle and represent them as mentally deficient."

breathing out was trapped under my nose. My seat was just above one of the wheels, and the lack of air, the oppressive heat, and the smell of gasoline mixed with the stench of sweat and the unwashed feet of the men in front of us made me feel worse and worse until I thought I would vomit. I felt as if my head would explode.

We had only one bottle of water between us. Every time I tried to lift the cloth and take a sip, I felt the water trickle down my chin and wet my clothes. I managed to take some aspirin that I had brought with me, but I didn't feel any better. I tried to fan myself with a piece of cardboard, but to do so I had to lift the fabric off my face with one hand and fan myself under the *burqa* with the other. I tried to rest my feet on the back of the seat in front of me so as to get some air around my legs. I struggled not to fall sideways as the minibus swung at speed around the hairpin bends, or to imagine what would happen if it toppled from a precipice[6] into the valley below.

I tried to speak to Abida, but we had to be careful what we said, and every time I opened my mouth the sweat-drenched fabric would press against it like a mask. She let me rest my head on her shoulder, although she was as hot as I was.

It was during this journey that I truly came to understand what the *burqa* means. As I stole glances at the women sitting around me, I realized that I no longer thought them backward, which I had as a child. These women were forced to wear the *burqa*. Otherwise they face lashings, or beatings with chains. The Taliban required them to hide their identities as women, to make them feel so ashamed of their sex that they were afraid to show one inch of their bodies. The Taliban did not know the meaning of love. **R**

The mountains, waterfalls, deserts, poor villages, and wrecked Russian tanks that I saw through the *burqa* and the mud-splattered window made little impression on my mind. I could only think ahead to when my trip would end. For the six hours that the journey lasted, we women were never allowed out. The driver stopped only at prayer time, and only the men were allowed to get out of the minibus to pray at the roadside. Javid got out with them and prayed. All I could do was wait. **5** ○

6. A ***precipice*** (PREH sih pis) is the edge of a steep cliff.

Practice the Skills

5 

Zoya faces many dangers, including death, when she returns to Afghanistan. What price would you pay to help others? Write your answer on your Reading Across Texts Foldable. Your response will help you complete the Unit Challenge. **BQ**

Teach

R Reading Skill

Review Identifying Main Idea and Supporting Details **Say:** The author said her ideas about the *burqa* changed. What detail does she give to support this idea? *(Possible response: She no longer looks down on the women wearing* burqas *because she realizes they are forced to wear them.)* **OL**

BQ 

Have students discuss the writer's reasons for returning to Afghanistan. Ask them to identify the risks she took *(beatings or death)* and her motives *(to expose the Taliban and liberate the women they oppress).* **AS**

Assess

CheckPoint

Use the CheckPoint questions provided on Presentation Plus! to check for comprehension of the selection. These questions can be used with interactive response keypads for immediate student feedback.

Literature Focus Lesson

Prologue Remind students that this is just the prologue to *Zoya's Story.* A prologue presents the background that readers need to understand what comes next. Ask students what elements of this prologue would make readers want to know more about the writer's return to her homeland? *(Possible response: The possibility that Zoya might be found out is mentioned in the prologue. This might make readers want to learn more about her story.)* **AS**

Indiana English/Language Arts Academic Standards
SE: 8.2
TWE: *Differentiated Instruction* 8.2, *Literature Focus Lesson* 8.2

Assess

Resources for page 418

- Selection Quick Check, pp. 29-30
- ExamView Assessment Suite
- Interactive Tutor: Self-Assessment

Students can respond to the *After You Read* items in their Learner's Notebooks or on a separate sheet of paper.

Vocabulary Check

Wearing Hijab: Veil of Valor

1. valor
2. intercede
3. tolerance

from ***Zoya's Story***

4. perpetrated
5. instinctively

Academic Vocabulary

6. Possible responses: encyclopedias, text books, approved Web sites.

English Language Coach

7. one's line of ancestors
8. a small insect that lives on warm-blooded animals

After You Read

Wearing Hijab: Veil of Valor & from *Zoya's Story*

Vocabulary Check

For items 1–5, copy the sentences, filling in the blanks with the correct words.

Wearing Hijab: Veil of Valor

intercede tolerance valor

1. Showing great ______, the fireman rushed into the burning house.
2. The school board wanted to ______ between the families and the school.
3. The principal encouraged students to learn about Islam and to show ______ for all religious beliefs.

from ZOYA'S STORY

perpetrated instinctively

4. Finding out who ______ the crime would take a lot of detective work.
5. The young bird ______ flapped its wings as it left the nest and began to fly.

Academic Vocabulary

6. What kinds of **sources** might you use for a history report?

English Language Coach

7. Using context clues and what you know from reading "Wearing Hijab: Veil of Valor," decide which meaning of *descent* makes sense in the sentence below.

   Kazak, who is of Palestinian descent, says taking up the veil was "the most positive decision I have made in my life."
   - a downward slant
   - one's line of ancestors
   - a sudden raid or assault

8. Using context clues and what you know from reading *Zoya's Story*, decide which meaning of *louse* makes sense in the sentence below.

   I watched him reach to the back of his head, extract what must have been a louse, and squash it between two fingernails with a sharp crack.
   - a small insect that lives on warm-blooded animals
   - a mean person

Indiana English/Language Arts Academic Standards (pp. 418–419)

8.1.3 Verify the meaning of a word in its context... **8.2 Comprehension and Analysis (Focus on Informational Text)** Develop [reading] strategies... identifying and analyzing...perspective... **8.2.3** Find similarities and differences between texts...

For a complete description of the standards, see p. IN 11.

Writing: Reading Across Texts

15. Sample chart

Writer	Emilia Askari	Zoya
Writer's Qualifications	Prize-winning journalist	Worked with professional writers, lived the experiences she writes about
Writer's Sources	Interviews with three women who have chosen to wear *hijab*	First-hand experience

Reading/Critical Thinking

On a separate sheet of paper, answer the following questions.

Wearing Hijab: Veil of Valor

9. **Infer** Alya Kazak says that she cried the first day she wore *hijab.* Why might she have been nervous about her decision?
   TIP **Author and Me**

10. **Analyze** Lateef describes three of her conflicts with other students. How do you think these conflicts affected Lateef's determination to wear *hijab?*
    TIP **Author and Me**

11. **Evaluate** Did the author succeed in showing you why these three women wear *hijab?* Explain your answer with examples from the article.
    TIP **Author and Me**

from ZOYA'S STORY

12. **Interpret** Zoya says that she is looking at the "dry and dusty mountains as through the bars of a prison cell." What is Zoya's prison?
    TIP **Right There**

13. **Evaluate** Think about Zoya's reason for returning to Afghanistan. Do you find her courageous? Why or why not?
    TIP **Author and Me**

14. **Evaluate** Do you think Zoya is taking too much of a risk by doing what she believes in? Why or why not?
    TIP **Author and Me**

Writing: Reading Across Texts

Use Your Notes

15. Follow these steps to find similarities and differences between "Wearing Hijab: Veil of Valor" and *Zoya's Story.*

    Step 1: Look at the notes in your chart. Consider each writer's qualifications and sources of information.

    Step 2: In a paragraph, write about how each writer approaches the issue. Explain the similarities and differences among each writer's qualifications and sources.

    Step 3: Jot down a few notes about what each writer shares with readers. How do the women in the selections feel about wearing *hijab* and the *burqa*?

    Step 4: Explain what you learned from reading each selection.

Get It on Paper

To show how you compare the writers of the selections and the experiences of Muslim women, copy the following statements on a separate sheet of paper. Then complete the statements with your own thoughts.

16. In "Wearing Hijab: Veil of Valor," the writer explores the topic of *hijab* by ______.
17. After reading "Wearing Hijab: Veil of Valor," my thoughts about wearing *hijab* are ______.
18. In *Zoya's Story,* the writer explores the topic of the *burqa* by ______.
19. After reading *Zoya's Story,* my thoughts about wearing the *burqa* are ______.

BIG Question

20. The women in each selection pay a price for their beliefs. What do you think they learn about taking risks for things they care about? How do you think they would answer the Big Question?

Reading/Critical Thinking

Wearing Hijab: Veil of Valor

9. Possible response: She might have been worried that people would respond with prejudice.
10. Possible response: Lateef considered the conflicts a test of her Muslim identity and resolved to be strong.
11. Possible response: Yes, the writer presents what the women have gained from wearing *hijab.*

from Zoya's Story

12. Zoya felt imprisoned by the *burqa* she was wearing.
13. Responses will vary.
14. Possible response: Students may feel that the importance of Zoya's cause justifies the risk.

Writing: Reading Across Texts

15. See below for a sample chart and sample paragraph.

Possible responses:

16. presenting the views of three women who choose to wear it.
17. for some Muslim women, it is a positive choice.
18. describing how it makes her feel imprisoned and suffocated.
19. that the Taliban use it to oppress women.

20. Responses will vary.

15. Sample paragraph:
    The women in "Wearing Hajib: Veil of Valor" choose to wear the veil and see it positively. Askari is qualified because she's done research, including interviews with three sources. In *Zoya's Story,* women are forced to wear an uncomfortable veil that restricts movement. Zoya is qualified because she has worn the *burqa*; her source is her own experience. I learned that the veil can be positive when wearing it is a choice and terrible when it is not.

Close

Have students discuss their responses to question 20.

Indiana English/Language Arts Academic Standards
SE: 8.1.3, 8.2, 8.2.3

The Unit Challenge

Focus

BELLRINGER Options

Daily Language Practice Transparency 31
Focus Activity Ask: Think about the people and characters you've read about in this unit. Which ones probably thought the price they paid for what they wanted was reasonable? Which ones probably thought the price was too high?

The discussion will remind students of the selections they've read, which will help them begin the group activity or the solo activity. AS

Teach

Group Activity: What's the Ending?

- Have at least one person take notes as students brainstorm.
- Make sure the group is on step 3 by midway through the class period.
- For the final draft, have someone write or type the story.
- Make each student responsible for reading the story to check it for mistakes.
- Students may choose one group member to read the story aloud, or they can take turns reading portions of the story.

Assess/Close

Group Activity

Ask: Why do you think the class voted on the ending they did? *(Suggest that students write their answers in their Learner's Notebooks.)* OL

UNIT 3 WRAP-UP

Answering The BIG Question: When Is the Price Too High?

You've just read several different selections and you have thought about when the price is too high. Now use what you've learned to do the Unit Challenge.

The Unit Challenge

Choose Activity A or Activity B and follow the directions for that activity.

A. Group Activity: What's the Ending?

Work with your group to write and present a story. In the story, one of the characters must decide if what he or she wants or gets is worth the price it takes to get it. The situation can be either real or imaginary.

1. **Discuss the Assignment** With your group, brainstorm ideas for the story. Don't be afraid to use your imagination. You can use the notes you wrote in your Foldable for ideas, too. Write your ideas in your Learner's Notebook.

2. **Review Your Notes and Make a Decision** Now it's time to choose your story line. Choose the idea you think will be the most fun to write about or the idea that will best illustrate whether or not the goal is worth the price.

3. **Write the Story** After you have chosen a story line, write a draft of the story. Remember it's a draft, so it doesn't have to be perfect. You just want to get your ideas down on paper.
    - Write the title of the story.
    - Describe the character and the situation the character is facing.
    - Then describe the decision the person has to make. Write it as an either-or choice: The person can choose to do *X* or to do *Y*.
    - Write one ending for choice *X* (worth it) and another ending for choice *Y* (not worth it).

4. **Revise and Edit the Story** Make sure each member of the group reviews the draft of the story separately. Each member should take notes about what revisions to make.
    - Make sure the story introduces the character and his or her decision or goal.
    - Make sure the either-or choice is clear and easy to understand.
    - Make sure the consequences of both decisions are clearly illustrated in both endings.
    - Proofread and correct any mistakes in spelling, grammar, and punctuation.

5. **Present the Story** Now you're ready to present your story to the class. At the end of the story, have the class vote on which ending they like best.

B. Solo Activity: Is It Worth It?

Some decisions are easy, but others are difficult. When something is very important to you, it's often hard to make a decision about it. In this activity, you'll use a chart to decide if a decision you have to make is worth the cost or not.

1. **What's Your Decision?** Think of a difficult or important decision such as
   - deciding what group of friends to hang out with
   - choosing how to spend your time after school
   - showing who you really are, even if it shows how you are different from others
   - doing something other people might disapprove of

2. **Draw a Chart** Draw a chart like the one shown below. Then brainstorm the good and bad sides of the decision. Use the notes from your Foldables. Think about the good and the bad sides of the decisions people made in the selections you read.

   Write the good things about your own decision in the **Worth It** column. Write the bad things about the decision in the **Not Worth It** column. List as many things as you can think of.

3. **Is It Worth It?** Look over your chart. When you look at the two columns, which column is more important? Is the decision worth the costs?

4. **Think About Your Chart** Write a paragraph that explains which decision you chose. Be sure to write what you learned from making the chart. How could a chart like the one you made help you make good decisions in the future?

5. **Present Your Decision** Copy your chart onto poster board. Use different colors to highlight the "Worth It" and "Not Worth It" columns. Then write or paste your paragraph below your chart. Hand your poster in to your teacher.

My Decision: I want to hang out with a group of kids my mom doesn't like because they get in trouble a lot.

WORTH IT	NOT WORTH IT
1. I like this group of kids.	My mom will get really mad at me.
2. I have fun with them.	I might get in trouble with them.
3. They are really popular.	My other friends won't like me if I hang out with this other group.

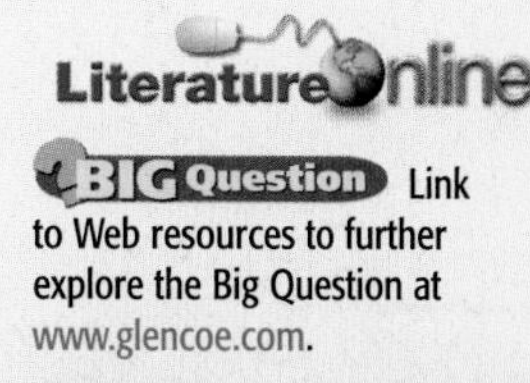

BIG Question Link to Web resources to further explore the Big Question at www.glencoe.com.

Teach

Solo Activity: Is It Worth It?

- As students complete their charts, encourage them to add as many pros and cons as they can.
- Remind students to complete step 3 by midway through the class period to allow time to write a paragraph.
- Have students write a paragraph about their final decision, explaining why they decided it was (or was not) worth it.
- Give students time to complete a final version of their charts to hand in.

Assess/Close

Solo Activity

After students complete their charts, ask them how they could use a similar chart to make decisions in the future. OL

Big Question Have students access the Web site for English and Spanish summaries and annotated links to related Web resources.

Focus

Vocabulary Preview

List the following words on the board:

- constable
- prominent
- provisions
- vicinity
- liberal

Review their definitions before students begin reading.

Build Background

O. Henry's short stories are famous for their surprise twists, but the twist in "The Ransom of Red Chief" is arguably the most famous of all. The short story was made into a television movie in 1998, starring Christopher Lloyd and Haley Joel Osment.

Teach

R Reading Skill

Identifying Main Idea and Supporting Details **Ask:** What have the two men decided to do? *(They've decided to kidnap the child of a banker.)* **Ask:** Why did they choose to kidnap someone in Summit? *(because it has only a police officer and a few lazy dogs)* BL

UNIT 3

Your Turn: Read and Apply Skills

O. Henry

Meet the Author

O. Henry was born William Sidney Porter in 1862 in North Carolina and, as a young man, went through some hard times, including three years in jail. Upon release he moved to New York City and began writing for magazines. In 1884 he took the pen name O. Henry. He soon became America's favorite short story writer. See page R2 of the Author Files for more on O. Henry

Tom Pomplun, who adapted the story, is also an editor and graphic artist. He chose Johnny Ryan to illustrate this story partly because Ryan wants comics to be "fun and crazy and weird and gross."

Author Search For more about O. Henry, go to www.glencoe.com.

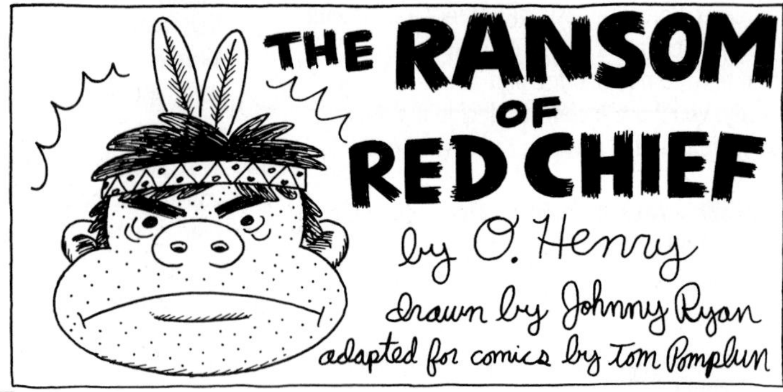

THE RANSOM OF RED CHIEF
by O. Henry
Drawn by Johnny Ryan
adapted for comics by Tom Pomplun

WE WERE DOWN SOUTH, IN ALABAMA- BILL DRISCOLL & MYSELF— WHEN THIS KIDNAPPING IDEA STRUCK US.

R

THERE WAS A TOWN CALLED SUMMIT, WHICH WE KNEW COULDN'T GET AFTER US WITH ANYTHING STRONGER THAN A CONSTABLE & SOME LACKADAISICAL[1] BLOODHOUNDS. SO IT LOOKED GOOD.

WE SELECTED FOR OUR VICTIM THE ONLY CHILD OF A PROMINENT CITIZEN NAMED EBENEZER DORSET, A RESPECTABLE MORTGAGE FANCIER AND FORECLOSER.

THE KID WAS A BOY OF TEN, WITH BAS-RELIEF[2] FRECKLES & FIERY RED HAIR. WE FIGURED THAT EBENEZER WOULD MELT DOWN FOR A RANSOM OF $2000.

1. When someone is ***lackadaisical*** (lak uh DAZE ih kul) he or she is lazy and slow.
2. A ***bas-relief*** (bah rih LEEF) is when something is raised off the surface.

Additional Support

Author Search To expand students' appreciation of O. Henry, have them access the Web site for additional information and resources.

Literature Focus Lesson

Summary Two partners in crime kidnap young Johnny Dorset and hold him for ransom. Johnny, who calls himself Red Chief, enjoys the adventure and doesn't want to go home. Johnny is a rambunctious child who talks incessantly and torments one of the kidnappers nearly beyond endurance. The kidnappers, who had originally planned to request $2,000, mail the boy's father a ransom note, asking for $1,500 in exchange for the boy. The boy's father responds to the ransom note by demanding payment to take the boy back. The kidnappers, demoralized and exhausted, comply with his demand. AS

Teach

L Literary Element

Foreshadowing Ask: What is the first hint that things won't go as smoothly as the men expect? *(Possible response: The boy is throwing rocks at a kitten, which suggests that he is mean and hard to handle, and it is very difficult to get him into the buggy.)* **OL**

R Reading Skill

Review Making Inferences
Ask: What happens in the fourth panel on this page? What clues help you make this inference? *(Possible response: The boy throws a rock and hits Bill in the eye. Clues: the boy is throwing rocks when the men approach him, the line in the fourth panel shows the motion of the rock, and Bill blames the boy, saying, "That will cost the old man an extra five hundred dollars.")* **AL**

Differentiated Instruction

Compare and Contrast Texts An adaptation is a written work that has been recast as another genre; for example, a movie, a play, or a cartoon. Point out that "The Ransom of Red Chief" was originally written as a short story. When stories or novels are adapted, the adaptors often have to change or leave out details.

Ask students to follow the graphic version as you read the beginning of the short story to them. (Widely anthologized, it is also available as an e-text online.) Ask them what differences they find between the two formats. What are the advantages of the graphic format? the original format? **AL**

Indiana English/Language Arts Academic Standards
TWE: *Differentiated Instruction* 8.2

Teach

L Literary Element

Irony **Say:** Remember that situational irony occurs when what happens is the opposite of what you'd expect. What is the situational irony in this part of the story? *(Readers would expect the kidnappers to be in control, but the boy seems to have the upper hand. Instead of being terrified, he is having an adventure.)* OL

R Reading Skill

Review Predicting **Ask:** Based on what you know so far about the child and the kid-nappers, what do you think will happen in this story? *(Possible response: The kidnappers will get sick of the misbehaved kid. The kid will run away when he gets bored.)* BL

Additional Support

English Language Coach

Building Background Students from other countries may not be familiar with the game of Cowboys and Indians. Explain that stories and folklore from the Wild West have spurred the imaginations of children for years. Have students read the middle section of the graphic novel with a partner who can explain the allusions to the Wild West. This will help them distinguish between the kidnap-ping and the games Johnny invents. EL

Literature Focus Lesson

Monologue Tell students that a monologue is a long speech by one character. The boy in this story rambles on in a monologue that reveals his character.

- What do readers learn about the boy from his monologue on page 425? *(He talks constantly, rambles from one topic to the next, and asks endless questions impossible to answer.)*
- Why do you think the author includes this monologue? *(Possible response: to show the boy is a complete nuisance to the kidnappers)* **OL**

Teach

L Literary Element

Humor Say: Remember that hyperbole is exaggeration often used to create humor. How is the child's personality exaggerated for humorous effect? *(He asks a lot of questions, makes a lot of noise, and torments the two men.)* **OL** **Ask:** How would a real child most likely react to the two men? *(Possible response: with fear)* **BL**

R Reading Skill

Review Making Inferences
Ask: Why do you think Bill is screaming? *(Answers will vary, but the narrator's remark that the boy had "terrorized" Bill suggests that he is screaming because of something the boy is doing.)* **OL**

Indiana English/Language Arts Academic Standards
TWE: *English Language Coach* 8.2, *Literature Focus Lesson* 8.3

Teach

L Literary Element

Humor **Say:** The narrator says that Bill's "spirit was broken." How is this an example of hyperbole? *(Possible response: Saying that someone's "spirit was broken" usually implies something tragic has happened to him or her. Here, the phrase is used to describe the effects the little boy's play has on Bill.)* **AL** **Ask:** Why is this situation humorous? *(Possible response: It is humorous because a criminal kidnapper is being tormented by a ten-year-old boy.)* **OL**

R Reading Skill

Review Making Inferences
Say: The narrator says, "I wasn't afraid." Do you think he is telling the truth? Why or why not? *(Possible response: No, I don't think he is telling the truth. He gets up when he remembers the boy was planning on burning him at the stake, and he is careful to place himself out of harm's way.)* **OL**

Additional Support

Literature Focus Lesson

Point of View Point out that humor often depends on the point of view of the author. Discuss with students how the story might be different if it were told from Bill's point of view: If Bill were telling the story, the focus might be on what he suffers. The narrator, however, is able to distance himself from the events, and this objectivity allows readers to laugh at Bill's plight. The narrator also provides reassurance that Bill is made uncomfortable but doesn't suffer any permanent ill effects. **OL** **AL**

3. An ***imp*** is a mischievous, annoying person.
4. To ***dote on*** is to show a lot of attention toward someone.
5. ***Reconnoiter*** (ree kuh NOY tur) means "to look around an area."
6. A ***homebody*** is someone who likes to stay at home.

Teach

C Critical Thinking

Comprehension Ask: Why does Bill start to reconsider the kidnapping plot? *(He wonders if anyone will pay to get the naughty child back.)* **Ask** How does Sam respond to Bill's concern? *(Possible response: He reassures him that the boy's parents will want him back and says he'll go to the mountain to look around.)* **BL**

L Literary Element

Foreshadowing Ask: When Sam goes looking at the mountain top, what hint is provided that the kidnappers' plans are going wrong? *(Possible response: Sam expected a frantic search, but no one is looking for the boy.)* **OL**

Differentiated Instruction

Character Sketch This cartoonist does a good job of imagining how the characters in the story may have looked. Have students interested in art choose one character and draw their own version of how the character might look. Have students use any descriptions in the story, as well as their own imaginations, to aid them. Encourage students to share their drawings with the class. **OL**

Indiana English/Language Arts Academic Standards
TWE: *Literature Focus Lesson* 8.3.8, *Differentiated Instruction* 8.2

Teach

L Literary Element

Irony Ask: How is Sam's threat to the boy an example of situational irony? *(Possible responses: Victims normally want to get away from their kidnappers, but Sam makes the boy behave by threatening to take him home.)* OL

R Reading Skill

Review Making Inferences
Ask: What details suggest that the boy thinks the situation is a game and does not realize the seriousness of the situation? *(He calls Sam "Snake-eye" and wants to play black scout.)* OL

Additional Support

Literature Focus Lesson

Humor Slapstick is a form of humor that gets its effect from wild, even violent, action. When it is used in literature, readers must visualize the action to get the comic effect. Ask students these questions about the physical humor in the story:

- What examples of physical comedy do you find in this story? *(Examples: the boy hitting the kidnapper with a rock and trying to scalp Bill; the boy felling Bill with a slingshot)*
- How does the graphic format help you visualize the physical comedy? *(Possible response: It shows the actions and the effects of the actions, such as Bill's crossed eyes.)* OL

R

L

Teach

R Reading Skill

Review Making Inferences
Ask: What is Bill suggesting in the third panel on this page? *(Possible response: Bill is suggesting he is afraid of what the boy might do.)* **OL** **Ask:** What is the effect of his comment? *(Possible response: His comment is funny because it exaggerates the seriousness of the situation.)* **AL**

L Literary Element

Irony **Ask:** What is the situational irony in the way the boy plays while the kidnappers write the ransom note? *(Possible response: The boy is playing at guarding the cave, the opposite of what a kidnapped person would ordinarily do.)* **OL**

Differentiated Instruction

Casting Call This story includes many humorous physical elements that would make it a great play or movie. Ask students to imagine they are a casting director and have them cast the roles of the four characters in the story. Tell students to write the names of famous actors they think would best play the roles and write a brief explanation of their choices. Have students discuss their choices with the class. **BL**

Indiana English/Language Arts Academic Standards
TWE: *Literature Focus Lesson* 8.3, *Differentiated Instruction* 8.2

Teach

L1 Literary Element

Humor Ask: What is humorous about Bill's request to Sam as he writes the ransom note? *(Bill is willing to reduce the ransom to get rid of the boy.)* OL

EL Language Coach

Multiple-Meaning Words Give students these definitions for the word *terms.*

- limited periods of time
- expressions used to describe something
- conditions

Ask: Which definition fits the meaning of *terms* as it is used in the ransom note? *(The third definition is correct.)* EL

L2 Literary Element

Humor Say: Remember that a pun is the humorous use of a word to suggest more than one meaning. The signature on the note, "Two Desperate Men," is supposed to convince Mr. Dorset that Sam and Bill are willing to take extreme measures if their ransom demand isn't met. How are they really "desperate"? *(Possible responses: They are desperate to get rid of the boy.)* OL

7. ***Treachery*** (TREH chur ee) means "underhanded, tricky behavior."

Additional Support

Literature Focus Lesson

Suspense Suspense is the quality of a story that makes readers eager to find out what will happen next. Writers build suspense by delaying the resolution of a plot, by adding complications, and by suggesting what might happen next. Have students discuss the tactics the author uses in this story to build suspense:

- The author adds complications by making the kidnapped child a nightmare.
- The author suggests things won't go as planned by indicating that no one is looking for the boy.
- The author delays the resolution by having Bill explain how he spent the day with the boy while Sam delivered the note. OL

Teach

Viewing the Illustration

Ask: How does the artist draw Bill to show the way he feels after a day with the boy? *(Possible responses: He draws spirals around Bill's head to indicate he is in pain and exhausted; he draws Bill's hand on his forehead to show he is fed up and maybe has a headache; he draws him slouched over in the fourth panel on this page to show he is tired.)* **OL**

R Reading Skill

Review Predicting **Ask:** How do you think Mr. Dorset will respond to the ransom demand? *(Responses will vary. Students may say that the father will pay the ransom. Others may think he will contact the authorities. Some may anticipate that he will turn the tables on the kidnappers.)* **OL**

English Language Coach

Multiple-Meaning Words Have students choose the appropriate meaning of these multiple-meaning words used in the story: **EL**

"I was to be burned at the stake . . ." (page 426)
- set on fire (correct)
- annoyed

"located the box at the foot of the fencepost . . ." (page 431)
- the lowest part (correct)
- a unit of length

"Just when we should have been clearing fifteen hundred dollars . . ." (page 433)
- freeing from blame
- gaining (correct)

Indiana English/Language Arts Academic Standards
TWE: *Literature Focus Lesson* 8.3, *English Language Coach* 8.1.3

Teach

L1 Literary Element

Irony **Ask:** What is the situational irony in Mr. Dorset's letter? *(Readers would expect Mr. Dorset to be upset and to meet the kidnappers' demands. Instead, he tells them they have to pay him to return the boy.)* OL

L2 Literary Element

Irony **Ask:** What is the situational irony in the kidnappers' response to Mr. Dorset's letter? *(Possible response: Instead of being angry, they think he is being very generous.)* OL

Additional Support

Differentiated Instruction

Plot Diagrams Point out to students that Sam and Bill thought that kidnapping Red Chief would be relatively simple. Draw a line on the board. Write *kidnap boy* at one end, *collect ransom* in the middle, and *escape* at the other end. Tell students that good plots often have complications, or things that make the protagonists' goal difficult or impossible. What complications make it hard for Sam and Bill to reach their goal? Add these to the plot diagram. *(Possible complications include Red Chief's terrorizing of Bill, the boy's reluctance to go home, Mr. Dorset's demand for money to take the boy off their hands.)* EL BL

8. A ***calliope*** (kuh LY uh pee) is an instrument you see at amusement parks; it looks a bit like an organ, but sounds very different.

Teach

R Reading Skill

Review Making Inferences

Ask: Why do you think the boy gets so upset when he realizes the men are going to leave him? *(Possible response: He enjoyed having the men's attention. The text suggests that most people in town can't stand the boy, so he is probably used to being alone.)* **AL**

Reading Fluency

Ask students to choose their favorite scene from this story. Have them practice reading their chosen scene to themselves. Tell them to practice until they can read the scene fluently. **EL** **BL**

Find out what scenes students chose and have them read them in order. You may need to read the scenes students did not choose or you can ask a good reader to fill in. **AS**

Indiana English/Language Arts Academic Standards
TWE: *Differentiated Instruction* 8.3.2

Tips for Independent Reading

Tell students that reading is much more pleasant and rewarding when readers carefully select books with topics or characters that interest them. Explain that all the books on these pages relate to the Big Question. They tell about the risks and benefits of creating a fulfilling life.

Fiction

Tell students that reading fictional accounts of people who have made tough choices can help them decide when the price is too high.

Ask students to share an example of a fictional story they've read that could help them weigh the risks and benefits of choices.

UNIT 3

Reading on Your Own

To read more about the Big Question, choose one of these books from your school or local library. Work on your reading skills by choosing books that are challenging to you.

Fiction

Bud, Not Buddy
by Christopher Paul Curtis

This story is set in the 1930s during the Great Depression. On the run from foster homes, ten-year-old Bud sets out to walk from Flint to Grand Rapids, Michigan, determined to find a musician who he thinks must be his father. Bud takes with him a cardboard suitcase filled with mysteriously labeled rocks, a blanket, a few flyers advertising bands, and his own list of rules.

Nightjohn
by Gary Paulsen

Sarny, an enslaved girl living on the Waller plantation, tells the story of how she learned to read. Even after she is caught and severely punished, Sarny continues to pursue her studies. Her inspiration is Nightjohn, a young man who gives up his freedom and risks torture to teach other enslaved people to read. Based on true events.

A Taste of Salt: A Story of Modern Haiti
by Frances Temple

In a hospital in Haiti, seventeen-year-old Djo tells his story to Jeremie, a young woman who entered a convent school in order to escape the slums. Djo left home at a young age, taught reading to young boys at a shelter, and was then kidnapped and sold into slavery as a sugar cane worker.

Julie of the Wolves
by Jean Craighead George

To escape traditional life in an Inuit village, thirteen-year-old Julie tries to run away to San Francisco, where her pen pal lives. When she becomes lost in the Arctic tundra, a wolf pack takes her in. Julie learns how to survive in the wild and develops an appreciation for her Inuit heritage, but she knows she must eventually leave the wilderness and choose between the old ways and the new.

Additional Support

Differentiated Instruction

Use the Glencoe BookLink CD-ROM to create customized reading lists to help students answer the Big Questions. Suggestions for Unit 3:

Grade 4: *North by Night: A Story of the Underground Railroad* by Katherine Ayres
Grade 5: *Oh, Freedom!* by Casey King and Linda Barrett Osborne
Grade 6: *Women Inventors I* by Jean F. Blashfield
Grade 7: *All Times, All Peoples: A World History of Slavery* by Milton Meltzer
Grade 8: *Spies and Traitors (Fact or Fiction)* by Stewart Ross

Nonfiction

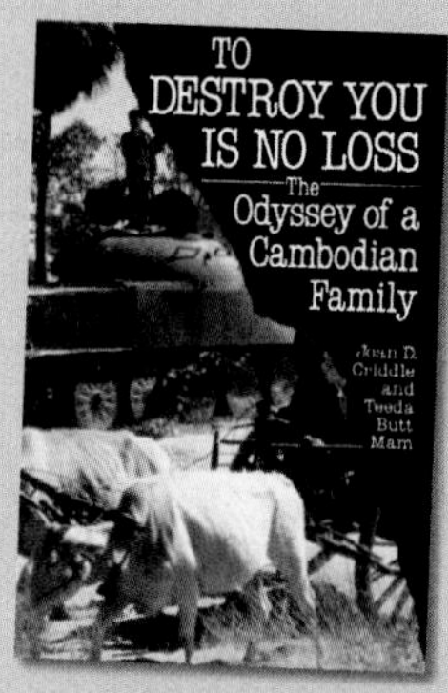

To Destroy You Is No Loss
by Joan Criddle

Told by 15-year-old Teeda, this book recounts the frightening experience of life in Cambodia during the rule of the Khmer Rouge. Teeda and her family are driven out of their home and find a way to survive and make it to the United States.

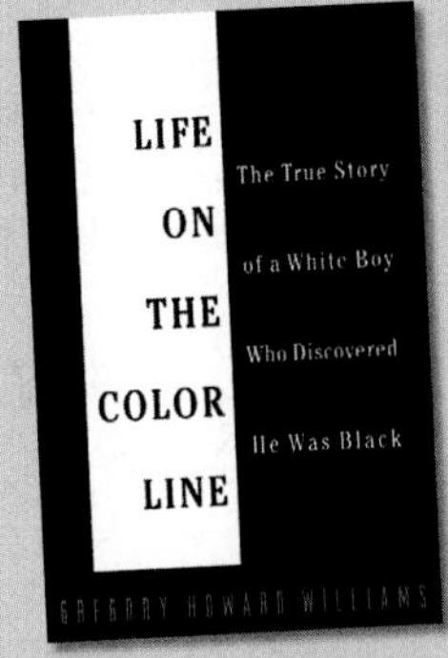

Life on the Color Line
by Gregory Williams

Gregory Williams tells his story about growing up white and finding out his father is African American. When his mother abandons him, Williams learns about his father's side of the family and his African American heritage.

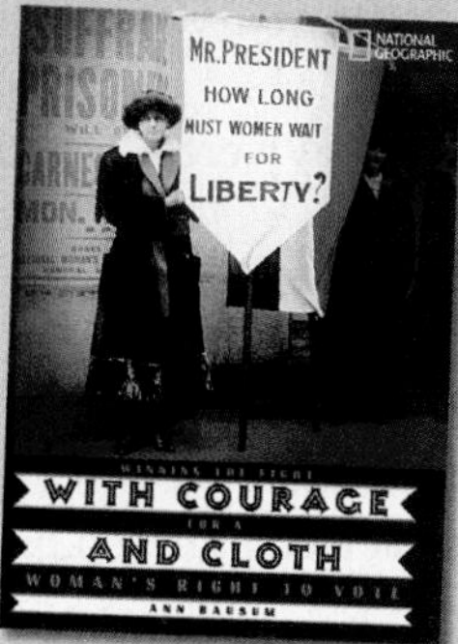

With Courage and Cloth: Winning the Fight for a Woman's Right to Vote
by Ann Bausum

From 1906 to 1920, a new and contentious group of suffragists emerged. Ann Bausum takes a close look at the women of the National Woman's Party and at others who shaped the fight for women's right to vote. Read Bausum's book to learn more about the people—passionate, determined, and utterly fearless—who paid a high price for equality.

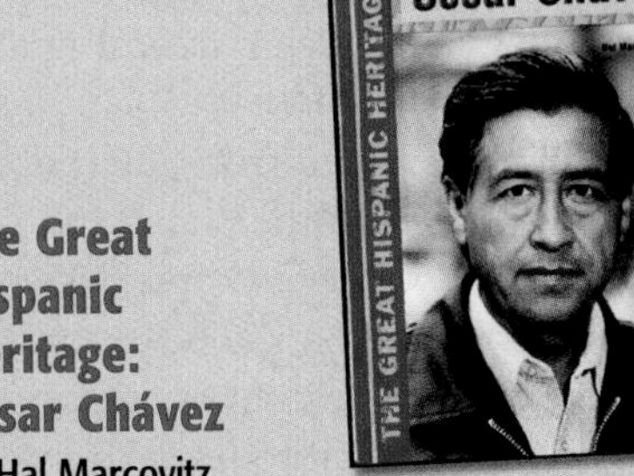

The Great Hispanic Heritage: César Chávez
by Hal Marcovitz

The Great Depression affected many farm families in the Southwest. César Chávez was ten when his family lost their farm in Arizona and left to find jobs in California. As migrant workers, the family moved often from farm to farm across the state. Chávez's experience in the fields led to a lifetime of fighting for the fair treatment of migrant workers.

READING ON YOUR OWN

Nonfiction

Share with students that the nonfiction books on this page all give detailed accounts of the lives of the subjects.

Life Stories

Tell students that the biographies and autobiographies on this page describe choices made by real people. In some cases, the people made choices about their very survival. In others, the people had to weigh the benefits of helping others against a high personal cost.

About the Subjects

You might share these facts about the subjects of these books:

- During the time of the Khmer Rouge, educated people were killed or sent out into the country to perform hard labor, while uneducated, unskilled people were given important positions. Teeda had to learn to hide her education and her city ways in order to survive.
- As the president of a university, Gregory Williams looks back on his difficult childhood in his autobiography.
- Between 1906 and 1920, two groups—the small, radical National Woman's Party led by Alice Paul and the larger, less radical National American Woman Suffrage Movement led by Carie Chapman Catt—worked tirelessly to get women the right to vote.
- César Chávez was a civil rights leader whom Robert F. Kennedy referred to as "one of the heroic figures of our time." His motto in life was "sí se puede" (it can be done).

Test-Taking Tips

TIP Sometimes students may need to combine information from more than one place to find the answer to a question. Remind students to read the questions very carefully so they know exactly what they're looking for.

TIP Remind students that they will never be asked to make an inference or draw a conclusion without adequate evidence. To answer a question that requires an inference or a conclusion, they should refer back to the passage to find clues.

ISTEP+ Test Practice

Directions:

This excerpt is from an article about women's gymnastics training. Read the excerpt carefully. Then, answer questions 1 through 4.

from Gymnasts in Pain: Out of Balance

By Scott M. Reid

By the time Alyssa Beckerman arrived for a U.S. national team training camp at Bela Karolyi's Texas ranch, three months before the 2000 Olympic Games, she wasn't sure what hurt worse. The year-old break in her wrist that hadn't been allowed to heal? Or her stomach burning from nerves and a daily diet of anti-inflammatory drugs?

The 19-year-old U.S. champion broke her wrist a year earlier, but she continued to compete and train 40 hours a week—pressured, she said, by an often-screaming coach who accused her of faking the injury and driven by her own desire to win Olympic gold.

"That's what you've been dreaming about since you were a little girl," she said.

By the time she retired from international gymnastics later that year, Beckerman had broken nine bones and undergone two surgeries.

The *Orange County Register* interviewed nearly half of the roughly 300 women who competed on the U.S. junior or senior national teams from 1982 to 2004. More than 93 percent of the women interviewed suffered broken bones or had injuries that required surgery.

Current and former U.S. national team members—almost all girls in their early and mid-teens—describe a way of life that repeatedly puts the girls in danger. They train year-round as much as twelve hours a day, often living thousands of miles from home and away from other teens.

Like Beckerman, they do so often with broken bones or torn muscles and almost always without regular, if any, medical care. At the same time, they must deal with pressures and expectations similar to those for highly paid pro athletes.

The *Register* also found:

The rate of injuries has almost doubled since 1966 as women train longer and try more daring and dramatic maneuvers.

Nine out of every ten gymnasts interviewed said that they had continued to train on injuries that resulted in broken bones or surgery or that they had begun training again without getting a doctor's OK.

The sport's obsession with weight and diet, especially within the U.S. national team program, often has led to eating disorders. U.S. gymnasts competing in the 2001 World Championships said they were provided so little food that family members smuggled snacks into the team hotel by stuffing them inside teddy bears.

Three out of four gymnasts interviewed continue to experience health problems related to gymnastics.

Questions 1 through 4 are based on the excerpt from "Gymnasts in Pain: Out of Balance."

1 Read the title of the passage.

Gymnasts in Pain: Out of Balance

As it is used here, the phrase "out of balance" MOST LIKELY means

A too much pressure
B prone to falling
C nervous about competing
D complaining too much

2 According to the article, Alyssa Beckerman and other gymnasts

A are not permitted to compete if they are injured
B receive good medical care at the training camps
C often train and compete in spite of injuries
D are discouraged from losing too much weight

3 The sources for most of the information in this excerpt were

A coaches
B judges
C gymnasts
D reporters

4 To support his argument, the writer provides facts and

A presents opposing arguments
B gives his personal opinion
C creates dialogue
D describes one individual's experience

UNIT 3 ASSESSMENT

Answers:

1. A
2. C
3. C
4. D

Resources for pages 436–441

Use these resources to review, assess, or reteach the chapter: Active Learning and Note-Taking Guide, ExamView Pro, and Differentiated Instruction Tool Software.

Test-Taking Tips

TIP When faced with an unfamiliar word or phrase, students should look at the context of the word for help in determining its meaning. There will often be clues just before or just after the unknown word or phrase to help students select the best answer.

TIP Remind students that they *do not need to memorize all of the details* of a story or passage. When students begin to answer questions about the passage, they should look back to the passage to find details, clues, and evidence that will help them identify the right answers.

Directions:

In this excerpt from an article about the history and practice of tattooing, the author discusses henna tattoos. Read the excerpt carefully. Then, answer questions 5 through 8.

from Tattoos: Fad, Fashion, or Folly?
Henna: The Tattoo Temp

By Linda Bickerstaff

Do you secretly yearn for just a *tiny* tattoo, but know that your parents would never allow it? Do you think a mouse might look cool tattooed on your ankle, but you aren't really sure? Does the idea of having your skin pierced by needles make you feel faint? If you answered "yes" to these questions, your solution might be a tattooing technique used for many thousands of years in India and other parts of the world—henna tattooing.

Henna is the Arabic name for the shrub *Lawsonia inermis* or *L. alba*. Its leaves are harvested, dried, and then crushed into powder that is mixed with oil, lemon, and other ingredients to form a paste.

When the paste is applied to the skin, reddish-brown pigments from the paste are transferred to the epidermis of the skin. The longer the henna is in contact with the skin, the darker the pigment transfer will be. Henna is usually left on the skin for 6 to 12 hours for the best results, then washed off.

Henna tattooing should really be called henna appliqué or henna painting. Henna tattoos differ from real tattoos in several ways: They are temporary, lasting only a few weeks; they are painless to apply; and they are relatively inexpensive to obtain. They are also an excellent way to get your tattoo without upsetting your parents.

The cells of the skin that are pigmented by the henna are epidermal cells. Over the course of several weeks, these cells die and are sloughed off the surface of the skin. As this happens, the henna tattoo fades and eventually disappears altogether. Depending on where the tattoo is placed on the body, it may last for one to three weeks.

Pre-prepared, do-it-yourself henna tattoo kits are available commercially. They contain patterns as well as instructions for applying.

Is a henna tattoo for you? Maybe, but be sure to check with Mom and Dad first.

Questions 5 through 8 are based on the excerpt from "Tattoos: Fad, Fashion, or Folly?"

5 What is the MAIN IDEA of this excerpt?

A Henna tattoos can be a good substitute for traditional tattoos.
B Henna tattoos are made by applying a special paste to the skin.
C Henna tattoos are reddish brown in color.
D Henna tattoos can be placed anywhere on the body.

6 According to the article, what should young people do before getting a henna tattoo?

A create special patterns
B learn how to make the henna paste
C read the instructions
D get their parents' permission

7 According to the excerpt, a major advantage of henna tattoos is that they are

A expensive
B dark
C pretty
D temporary

8 Read the following sentence from the excerpt.

Over the course of several weeks, these cells die and are sloughed off the surface of the skin.

What does *sloughed off* MOST LIKELY mean in this context?

A burned off
B scrubbed off
C cast off
D absorbed

Answers:

5. A
6. D
7. D
8. C

Test-Taking Tips

TIP Tell students that when they're answering a multiple-choice question, they should begin by reading the question carefully. Next, they should read each possible response. If necessary, they should reread portions of the passage to look for the answer. Finally, they should choose the best response.

Directions:

Read this article about sea turtles. Then, answer questions 9 through 13.

from Sea Turtles *Diet and Eating Habits*

from the SeaWorld Web site

A. Food preferences and resources

Diet varies with species. Sea turtles may be *carnivorous* (meat eating), *herbivorous* (plant eating), or *omnivorous* (eating both meat and plants). The jaw structure of many species indicates their diet.

1. Green and black sea turtles have finely serrated jaws adapted for a vegetarian diet of sea grasses and algae. In adulthood, they are the only herbivorous sea turtles, but in an aquarium environment all sea turtle species can be maintained on a carnivorous diet.
2. Loggerheads' and ridleys' jaws are adapted for crushing and grinding. Their diet consists primarily of crabs, mollusks, shrimps, jellyfish, and vegetation.
3. A hawksbill has a narrow head with jaws meeting at an acute angle, adapted for getting food from crevices in coral reefs. They eat sponges, tunicates, shrimps, and squid.
4. Leatherbacks have delicate scissorlike jaws that would be damaged by anything other than their normal diet of jellyfish, tunicates, and other soft-bodied animals. The mouth cavity and throat are lined with *papillae* (spinelike projections) pointed backward to help them swallow soft foods.
5. Researchers continue to study the feeding habits of flatbacks. There is evidence that they are opportunistic feeders that eat seaweeds, cuttlefish, and sea cucumbers.

B. Eating habits

Some species change eating habits as they age. For instance, green sea turtles are mainly carnivorous from hatchling until juvenile size; they then progressively shift to a herbivorous diet.

Questions 9 through 13 are based on the excerpt from "Sea Turtles."

9 Which of these statements BEST describes the main idea of number 4 in section A?

A Leatherbacks have delicate scissorlike jaws.
B Leatherbacks are designed to eat soft foods.
C Leatherbacks' jaws would be damaged by eating anything other than soft foods.
D Diet varies with species.

10 This article's type of text structure allows the writer to

A list facts that cover a wide variety of topics
B create a narrative from specific details
C divide a topic into subtopics
D organize details into chronological order

11 Which statement BEST supports the main idea of the article's last paragraph?

A Although young green sea turtles are carnivorous, by adulthood they have become herbivorous.
B All sea turtle hatchlings are carnivorous.
C All sea turtles change eating habits.
D Flatbacks are opportunistic feeders.

12 Choose the word or phrase that is spelled correctly and BEST completes the sentence.

Of all the sea turtles, leatherbacks have the ________________ jaws.

A more delicate
B delicatest
C most delicate
D most delicatest

13 On a separate piece of paper, copy the chart below and complete it by describing the jaws of each kind of sea turtle.

Green	
Hawksbill	
Leatherback	

Answers:

9. B
10. C
11. A
12. C
13. See bottom channel for correct answers.

Question 13

Student responses will vary. A typical correct student response will have at least one detail from each box in the right hand column below.

Green	• Jaws are finely serrated. • Jaws are good for a vegetarian diet.
Hawkbill	• Jaws meet at a sharp angle. • Jaws are good for getting food from crevices.
Leatherback	• Jaws are delicate and scissor-like. • Jaws are good for eating soft animals.

UNIT 4
Skills Scope and Sequence

Readability Scores Key
Dale-Chall/DRP/Lexile

PACING (DAYS) STANDARD	BLOCK	INSTRUCTIONAL SEGMENT LITERATURE	READING SKILLS	LITERARY ELEMENTS
1	1	**Unit Warm-Up, pp. 442–447** Genre Focus: "The Road Not Taken" by Robert Frost SE p. 447	Fluency, TWE p. 443 Connecting, SE p. 447, TWE p. 444 Interpreting, SE p. 447 Monitoring Comprehension, TWE p. 447	Rhyme, SE p. 447 Alliteration, SE p. 447
3	2	**Reading Workshop 1, pp. 448–463** "Wishing Well" by Kate Schmitt p. 452 "Signed, Sealed, Undelivered" by Katharine Weber 5.8/57/970, p. 458	Connecting, SE pp. 448, 449, 451, 453, 457, 459, TWE pp. 460, 461 Fluency, TWE p. 452 Comparing and Contrasting, SE p. 460	Free Verse, SE pp. 451, 453 Examples, SE pp. 457, 459
1		**Writing Workshop, Part 1, pp. 464–467** Writing Product: Poem		Examples, TWE p. 464
3	1	**Reading Workshop 2, pp. 468–481** "Mother to Son" by Langston Hughes SE p. 472 "Harlem" by Langston Hughes SE p. 473 "Sittin' on the Dock of the Bay" by Steve Cropper and Otis Redding SE p. 478	Evaluating, SE pp. 468, 469, 471, 472, 473, 477, 479 Connecting, SE p. 479, TWE p. 477 Fluency, TWE p. 471	Figurative Language–Metaphor and Simile, SE pp. 471, 472, 473, TWE p. 469 Lyrics, SE pp. 477, 479

Unit 4 Big Question

The question **"What Do You Do When You Don't Know What to Do?"** is designed to help students find solutions to problems they face in their everyday lives, including emotional crises, ethical dilemmas, and obstacles to success.

Unit 4 Genre

Many of the selections in this unit are **poetry,** which can illustrate how people have dealt with difficult situations. These selections will also help students answer the big question "What Do You Do When You Don't Know What to Do?" Use these poetry selections to help students develop strategies for coping with adversity.

CRITICAL THINKING	VOCABULARY	WRITING AND GRAMMAR	LISTENING, SPEAKING, AND VIEWING
			Viewing the Art, TWE p. 442
Analyze, SE p. 454 Infer, SE pp. 454, 462 Interpret, SE p. 454 Evaluate, SE p. 462 Comprehension, TWE pp. 458, 461	Compound Nouns, SE pp. 450, 453 Compound Adjectives, SE pp. 456, 458 Academic Vocabulary, SE p. 457 Parts of Speech, TWE p. 456 Compound Words, TWE p. 459	Subject-Verb Agreement, SE p. 455 Subject-Verb Agreement with Noun Subject, SE p. 463 Write About Your Reading, SE p. 462	Viewing the Art, TWE p. 452 Talk About Your Reading, SE p. 454 Viewing the Photo, TWE p. 460
		Prewriting: Ideas and Details, SE p. 464 Purpose and Audience, SE p. 465 Drafting, SE p. 465 Applying Good Writing Traits: Word Choice, SE p. 466, TWE p. 465 Subject-Verb Agreement with Compound Subjects, SE p. 467	
Infer, SE pp. 474, 480 Compare and Contrast, SE p. 474 Apply, SE p. 474 Analyze, SE p. 474, TWE pp. 476, 479 Synthesize, SE p. 474	Academic Vocabulary, SE p. 468 Dialect, SE pp. 470, 472, 476, 479	Write About Your Reading, SE p. 480 Agreement When Subjects Are Separated from Verbs, SE p. 475 Agreement in Inverted Sentences, SE p. 481	Viewing the Painting, SE p. 473 Talk About Your Reading, SE p. 474 Viewing the Photo, TWE p. 478

Skills Scope and Sequence *continued*

Readability Scores Key
Dale-Chall/DRP/Lexile

PACING (DAYS) STANDARD	BLOCK	INSTRUCTIONAL SEGMENT LITERATURE	READING SKILLS	LITERARY ELEMENTS
1	3	**Reading Workshop 3, pp. 482–495** from "To the Democratic National Convention" by Jesse Jackson 4.0/48/620, SE p. 486 "Fable for When There's No Way Out" by May Swenson SE p. 492	Interpreting, SE pp. 482, 483, 485, 486, 487, 491, 492, 493 Fluency, TWE p. 486, 493	Repetition, SE pp. 485, 486, TWE p. 487 Alliteration, SE pp. 491, 492, 493
2		**Writing Workshop, Part 2, pp. 496–499** Writing Product: Poem		Rhyme, Rhythm, Repetition, Alliteration, SE p. 497 Metaphor and Simile, TWE p. 498
3	1	**Reading Workshop 4, pp. 500–515** "O Captain! My Captain!" by Walt Whitman SE p. 504 "Scorched! How to Handle Different Types of Burns" by Stephen Fraser 5.7/58/850, SE p. 510	Monitoring Comprehension, SE pp. 500, 501, 503, 504, 509, 511, TWE pp. 505, 510, 512, 513 Connecting, TWE pp. 503, 511 Fluency, TWE p. 504 Interpreting, TWE p. 509 Evaluating, TWE p. 513	Rhyme, SE pp. 503, 504 Instructions, SE pp. 509, 510, TWE p. 512 Allusion, TWE p. 500 Speaker, TWE p. 502 Metaphor and Simile, TWE p. 501
3	2	**Reading Across Texts Workshop, pp. 516–529** from *Thura's Diary* by Thura Al-Windawi 5.0/51/910, SE p. 519 "Escaping" by Zdenko Slobodnik 6.2/61/1060, SE p. 526	Connecting, SE p. 520, TWE pp. 517, 519, 527 Fluency, TWE p. 519 Evaluating, TWE pp. 523, 524, 527 Monitoring Comprehension, TWE pp. 524, 526 Interpreting, TWE p. 526	Internal and External Conflict, SE pp. 516, 517, 519, 521, 522, 523, 524, 526, 527, TWE p. 520 Plot, TWE p. 518 Personification, TWE p. 520 Figurative Language, TWE p. 527
4	2	**Unit Wrap-Up, pp. 530–541**		

CRITICAL THINKING	VOCABULARY	WRITING AND GRAMMAR	LISTENING, SPEAKING, AND VIEWING
Infer, SE pp. 488, 494 Evaluate, SE pp. 488, 494 Analyze, SE p. 494	Academic Vocabulary, SE p. 482 Word Choice and Audience, SE pp. 484, 486, 487, 490, 493 Use Vocabulary, SE p. 490	Subject-Verb Agreement with Indefinite Pronouns, SE p. 489 Subject-Verb Agreement with Collective Nouns, SE p. 495	Talk About Your Reading, SE p. 488, 494
Connect, TWE p. 498		Writing a Poem: Revising, Editing, and Presenting, SE pp. 496, 497, 498 Word Choice, TWE pp. 496, 497	Reading Poetry Aloud, SE p. 499 Listening to Poetry, TWE p. 499
Interpret, SE p. 506 Evaluate, SE pp. 506, 514 Analyze, TWE pp. 509, 510	Academic Vocabulary, SE p. 500 Word Choice, SE pp. 502, 505, 508, 510, 512, TWE pp. 510, 511, 513 Word Order, TWE p. 505 Specialized Words, TWE p. 511	Write About Your Reading, SE p. 514 Subject-Verb Agreement in Relative Clauses, SE p. 507 With Special Singulars, SE p. 515	Talk About Your Reading, SE p. 506 Viewing the Art, TWE p. 505
Apply, TWE p. 516 Analyze, TWE pp. 519, 525 Comprehension, TWE pp. 521, 522 Synthesis, TWE p. 523	Diction, SE pp. 520, 527, TWE p. 523 Word Choice, TWE p. 526	Taking notes and using them to make a diagram that compares the internal and external conflicts in two texts, SE p. 529	

UNIT 4
Unit Resources

Reading with Purpose offers a comprehensive package of tools to optimize student learning and the teaching experience. Each resource has been designed to assist students in specific areas and to offer instructional support for teachers. While all of these areas are covered in the core textbook, some students may need extra practice or additional help in specific areas. The resource package is designed so that you, the teacher, can choose which items will best assist your students. You may also use these resources as homework assignments and for assessment purposes. The following are resources recommended for use with Unit 4.

Keys for Unit Resources

- Blackline Master
- Workbook
- Supplemental Text
- CD-ROM
- DVD
- Transparency
- Web-based
- Fast Files

Essential Instructional Support

FAST FILE UNIT 4 RESOURCES

Reading and Literature

- Academic Vocabulary Review
- Big Question: School to Home
- The Big Question Foldable
- Unit Challenge: Planner and Rubrics
- Comparing Literature Graphic Organizer
- Key Reading Skills
- Active Reading Graphic Organizers
- Literary Analysis
- Unit Vocabulary Review

Writing, Grammar, and Spelling

- Spelling and Handwriting Practice
- Grammar Practice
- Writing Workshop Graphic Organizer

Listening, Speaking, and Viewing

- Viewing and Representing
- Listening and Speaking

English Language Learners

- English Language Coach Review

DIFFERENTIATED INSTRUCTION

- Leveled Vocabulary Development
- Skill Level Up!™ A Language Arts Game
- Listening Library CD
- BookLink 3
- Literature Library Vocabulary Puzzlemaker
- Vocabulary Puzzlemaker

ASSESSMENT

GLENCOE'S ASSESSMENT ADVANTAGE

- Selection and Unit Assessments
- Selection Quick Checks
- Assessment by Learning Objectives
- Rubrics for Assessing Student Writing, Listening, and Speaking
- Glencoe Online Essay Grader
- Interactive Tutor: Self-Assessment
- ExamView Assessment Suite
- Literature Library ExamView Assessment Suite

Additional Instructional Support

WRITING, GRAMMAR, AND SPELLING

- Real Success in Writing: Research and Reports
- Writing Constructed Responses
- Spelling Power eWorkbook
- Grammar & Composition Handbook
- Grammar and Language Workbook
- Revising with Style eWorkbook

READING AND LITERATURE

- Active Learning and Note Taking Guide
- inTime Magazines
- Backpack Reader Volume 1
- Literature Library
- Literature Launchers Pre-Reading Videos DVD
- Literature Classics

TRANSPARENCIES

- Read Aloud, Think Aloud Transparencies
- Literary and Text Analysis Transparencies
- Bellringer Options Transparencies
- Grammar and Writing Workshop Transparencies
- Fine Art Transparencies

ENGLISH LANGUAGE LEARNER

- English Language Coach
- Fluency Practice and Assessment
- inTime Magazines (Spanish)
- Spanish Listening Library CD

PROFESSIONAL DEVELOPMENT

- Professional Development Package

TECHNOLOGY

- TeacherWorks Plus™
- StudentWorks Plus™
- BookLink 3
- Skill Level Up!™ A Language Arts Game
- ExamView Assessment Suite
- Interactive Tutor: Self-Assessment
- Listening Library CD
- Spanish Listening Library CD
- Literature Classics
- Literature Launchers Pre-Reading Videos DVD
- Literature Library ExamView Assessment Suite
- Vocabulary Puzzlemaker
- Literature Library Vocabulary Puzzlemaker
- glencoe.com
- Online Student Edition
- Presentation Plus!
- Glencoe Online Essay Grader

Additional Glencoe Resources

Dinah Zike's Foldables

Foldables are three-dimensional, interactive graphic organizers that help students practice basic writing skills, review key vocabulary terms, and answer Big Questions. Every unit contains a foldable activity. You can find the pattern and directions for the Unit 4 Foldable in the Unit 4 Resources Fast Files booklet. You can use the foldables as they are presented or modify them to suit the needs of your students. More information about foldables for Unit 4 can be found on pages R8–R9.

Glencoe Literature Library

This collection of hardcover books includes full-length novels, novellas, plays, and works of nonfiction. Each volume consists of at least one complete extended-length reading accompanied by several related readings from a broad range of genres. A separate Study Guide for each Glencoe Literature Library book provides teaching notes and reproducible activity pages for students.

Glencoe Literature Library titles that complement this unit include:

Blizzard!, by Jim Murphy
Dandelion Wine, by Ray Bradbury
Treasure Island, by Robert Louis Stevenson

For a wealth of online resources that support the instruction in Unit 4 of *Glencoe Literature: Reading with Purpose,* students and teachers can visit our Web site at www.glencoe.com. Students will find additional learning, practice, and assessment opportunities such as these, which are noted in the student text:

- **Big Question Overview**
- **Study Central**
- **Author Search**
- **Writing Models**
- **Interactive Literary Elements Handbook**
- **Web Activities**

Teachers will find planning and instructional tools that include the following:

- **Book Lesson Plans**
- **Teacher Forum**
- **Professional Development**
- **Web Activities Lesson Plans (with answers to student activities)**

Go to www.glencoe.com to see the entire selection of Reading with Purpose online resources.

GLENCOE **BOOKLINK**

Use the Glencoe **BookLink 3** CD-ROM, a database of more than 26,700 titles, to *create customized reading lists* for your students.

- Search for award-winning titles, (e.g., Newbery Award winners, Coretta Scott King Award winners, and Caldecott Medal winners) and for books on several state-recommended reading lists.
- Find Degrees of Reading Power™ (DRP) and Lexile™ readability scores for all selections.
- Organize reading lists by students' reading level, author, genre, theme, or area of interest.
- Get a brief summary of each selection.

You can find recommended leveled readings for this unit with Reading on Your Own (see page 534).

Glencoe's **Presentation Plus!**, a multimedia teaching tool, lets you present dynamic lessons that will engage your students. Using Microsoft PowerPoint,® you can customize the presentations to create your own personalized lessons. Use **CheckPoint** questions with interactive response keypads to get immediate student feedback during lessons, to increase student participation, and to assess student comprehension.

A lively collection of articles drawn from issues of the TIME family of magazines helps students develop the skills they need to interact with informational text in a meaningful way. Each of the news stories, feature articles, reviews, profiles, and essays in the magazine connect to an author, work, or theme in *Glencoe Literature: Reading with Purpose.* Articles for Unit 4 are found in Volume A. See the *inTIME* Teacher's Guide for specific connections to each unit and for reproducible student worksheets designed to develop students' reading and critical thinking skills.

Literature Launchers

Set the scene with Glencoe's Literature Launchers, engaging video segments that introduce each unit's genre focus. Each video brings the genre to life, relating it to your students' worlds.

Insert the Glencoe Literature Launchers Pre-Reading Videos DVD into your DVD player. Select the Unit 4 Launcher from the menu to introduce the genre and Big Question for this unit.

Online Essay Grader

Use Glencoe's Online Essay Grader to score your students' writing and to provide individualized feedback to each student automatically.

You and your students can visit www.glencoe.com to link to the essay grader. *Students* can enter their essays and receive feedback on demand. *You* can manage demographic data, assign tests and generate individual student and aggregated reports. The essay grader can help you

- Save time with automatic scoring and individualized feedback.
- Supplement in-class writing instruction using guided writing practice.
- Get reports for individual students or for special populations.
- Track student improvement over time.

REAL Success: Reading Excellence at All Levels

Glencoe now provides all of your students with the tools they need to become better, more enthusiastic readers. The REAL Success suite of reading and language arts products encourages reading excellence by meeting the needs of students at all levels. Glencoe products that can be used in conjunction with Unit 4 include the following:

- Jamestown Literature: An Adapted Reader
- Jamestown *Reading Fluency*
- Jamestown *Critical Reading Series, In the Line of Duty*
- *Vocabulary Builder*
- *The Glencoe Reader, Course 3*

To order these products, call Glencoe at 1-800-USA-READ.

Teacher Wraparound Edition Key

Level Appropriate Code

AS = Activities for all students

AL = Activities for students working above grade level

OL = Activities for students working at grade level

BL = Activities for students working below grade level

EL = Activities for English language learners

Teacher Wraparound Prompts

R **Reading Skill** These activities help you teach reading comprehension skills.

V **Vocabulary** These activities help students comprehend words and incorporate them into their reading and writing.

C **Critical Thinking** These strategies help students apply and extend what they have learned.

BQ **BIG Question** These activities and questions prompt students to prepare to answer the Big Question.

W **Writing** These activities provide writing opportunities to help students practice writing and comprehend text.

L **Literary Element** These activities and questions help students comprehend selections and learn more about each genre.

E **Text Element** These activities help students comprehend text elements.

LSV **Listening, Speaking, Viewing** These activities help students practice listening, speaking, and viewing skills.

EL **English Language Coach** These skills help English language learners as well as students who need additional reading support.

Professional Development Center

From an Author:

Kathleen Hinchman

Preparing Students to Read Poetry

Tap into students' knowledge of the genre. To gain an understanding of what students already know about the genre, teachers can ask students to brainstorm what they already know about poetry, perhaps drawing a web of students' ideas as they speak. Students may remember that sometimes poetry rhymes or has rhythm, that it's a way of expressing feelings, that wording matters, and that there are types of poetry. The web can show relationships among students' ideas about form, function, and word selection. Students can be invited to bring in favorite bits of poetry, perhaps including lyrics to favorite songs, raps, or jump-rope rhymes as they engage in the reading and writing required in this unit.

Make personal connections. Generations of young people have ended up disliking poetry because teachers identified only some poetry interpretations or themes as correct. Instead of being the teacher who perpetuates such antipathy, ask students to share their interpretations first, building small groups, and then, whole class discussions from their ideas. To do this, teachers may find it helpful to invite a group of students to listen to or read from the same poem and to write about the poem—anything they want—for a few minutes after the reading. Invite students to tell one another something about what they wrote, choosing whether or not they actually want to share their quickwrite. This can be followed with a discussion of similarities and differences in students' responses, which can, in turn, lead into a discussion of interpretations—perhaps comparing students' responses to interpretations published in literary criticisms. Seeing how classmates bring prior knowledge to their interpretations of poetry can help students learn to discern themes with increasing acumen.

Teacher to Teacher

Frankie Beard
McKinley Elementary School
South Bend, Indiana

To open the Big Question "What do you do when you don't know what to do?" I bring to class numerous books with pictures that represent hardship. I hand a book to each student and say, "Look at the picture for fifteen seconds and when I say 'pass,' hand it to the person behind you." We keep doing this until each book has returned to the first student to receive it. I collect the books and put them in a central location. I ask students if there is something they have gone through in life that makes it possible for them to identify with a picture in one of these books. I tell students to pick the book with a picture that they relate to and write an essay about it. Then, in small groups, students discuss what they wrote.

Teacher Chat Room

Reading and Writing Poetry

How can I make poetry interesting to middle school students?

Middle grade students will like poetry more when they realize that their favorite lyrics or nursery rhymes are a kind of poetry, that their own first response is grounding for poetic interpretation, and, most importantly, that poetry is a unique, intense way of representing important insights. To help students immerse themselves in different kinds of poetry:

- Bring a wide range of poetry to your classroom. Include the Shel Silverstein poems students will remember from elementary school as well as Robert Frost poems appreciated by older readers.
- Invite students to work in inquiry groups, reading poetry to themselves and each other and finding poetry to share with the class in a daily "read aloud" that ends each day's inquiry.
- Students can bring in examples of poetry they find at home, in song lyrics, and on the Internet in youth poetry collections.
- Maintain an ongoing discussion, noting the reasons individuals find particular poems engaging. Tie this discussion to the study of poetry throughout history, noting variations in use and form represented by Homer, Chaucer, Shakespeare, and more contemporary poets.

How can I help students to understand poetry from different historical periods?

Invite students to team up and engage in brief inquiry about particular time periods during which historical events or issues of gender, race, or class affected the ways in which individuals chose to represent ideas. Students can then read bits of poetry to see what they can discern of its meaning or historical content.

What language and structures do poetry writers use, and how can students use these elements in their own writing?

Teachers should explain that poets use poetic devices to come up with the concise representations that make poetry what it is. Students can learn that writers use such devices to tell the stories in narrative poems or to make points in lyric poems. Teach figurative language and sound devices as they are needed to interpret particular poems, one or two at a time. Post these on a bulletin board or work wall for later reference. Conduct brief mini-lessons during the writing workshops that refer back to examples in poetry that have been read. Invite students to draft bits of poetry using devices taught in these mini-lessons.

Key Unit Objectives

- Analyze the Big Question
- Analyze the literary elements of poetry
- Apply strategies for reading poetry
- Write poetry

BIG Question

Why Is It Important?

Addressing the Big Question helps students consider options and strategies for solving problems that seem unsolvable. Explain how students will benefit from reading about how other people dealt with situations in which they didn't know what to do.

Viewing the Art

Invite students to describe the artwork on this page. Ask them to think about what it suggests and how it makes them feel. Talk about the power of the image of an open door (as opposed to a closed door) and the sun shining brightly. Ask students to describe how the art complements the quote. *(Responses will vary.)* AS

UNIT 4

The BIG Question

What Do You Do When You Don't Know What to Do?

"What you can do or think you can do, begin it. For boldness has magic, power, and genius in it."

—Johann Wolfgang von Goethe, German poet and playwright (1749–1833)

Unit Skills

Reading Skills

- Connecting, p. 448
- Evaluating, p. 468
- Interpreting, p. 483
- Monitoring Comprehension, p. 501

Writing Skills/Grammar

- Word Choice, p. 466
- Subject-Verb Agreement, p. 467

BIG Question What do you do when you don't know what to do?

Genre Focus: Poetry

Literary Elements

- Free Verse, p. 451
- Figurative Language, p. 471
- Alliteration, p. 491
- Rhyme, p. 503

Vocabulary

- Compound Nouns, p. 450
- Compound Adjectives, p. 456

LOOKING AHEAD

The skill lessons and readings in this unit will help you develop your own answer to the Big Question.

UNIT 4 WARM-UP • Connecting to the Big Question

UNIT 4 WRAP-UP • Answering the Big Question

About the Reading

Each selection in this unit provides insights that can help students address the question, "What do you do when you don't know what to do?" Students will have the opportunity to read about how other people dealt with situations that seemed overwhelming and consider strategies for coping with problems that seem too big to handle.

About the Skills

The skills taught in this unit have been selected because they are particularly helpful when reading the featured genre—poetry. Each reading selection provides students with opportunities to practice and develop poetry-reading skills.

No Child Left Behind

NCLB places great emphasis on improving English fluency. Students can improve their reading fluency greatly by reading poetry aloud. Encourage students to read each poetry selection in this unit several times, each time concentrating on a specific area of reading fluency (tone, rate, expression, etc.).

Reading Fluency

Building Fluency In order to develop reading fluency with poetry, encourage students to meet with a partner in a quiet place. Have partners look at the punctuation of the poem. Tell them to read the poem as if it were a sentence. Then have the first student read the first stanza, inserting pauses where there are commas and focusing less on stressing the rhyme. Then have the student's partner read the same stanza. Have partners continue reading the rest of the poem one stanza at a time. Finally, each student should have a turn reading the poem from beginning to end. EL BL

Indiana English/Language Arts Academic Standards
TWE: *Reading Fluency* 8.7.14

Focus

BELLRINGER Options

- Literature Launcher
- Daily Language Practice Transparency 32

Focus Activity Write on the board: When was the last time you weren't sure what to do? Write down what happened in that situation. *(Responses will vary.)* AS

Teach

R Reading Skill

Review Connecting Ask: When might you argue with yourself about what to do? *(Possible response: when there's a video game you'd like to play, but there's also an important test that you need to study for)* **Ask:** What might stop you from discussing your situation with someone else? *(Possible response: You might be embarrassed or get in trouble.)* AS

BQ BIG Question

- Have students read the profiles of Darren and Nicole.
- Have student partners discuss each situation and decide how they'd advise each person to handle it. AS

UNIT 4 WARM-UP

Connecting to The BIG Question What Do You Do When You Don't Know What to Do?

R It's one of the worst feelings in the world. You don't know what to do, and you feel alone and lonely. Whether the issue is large or small, it can make you feel tiny and helpless. So what *do* you do? What *should* you do? In this unit, you'll read about what other people have done when they didn't know what to do. Maybe one of their ideas will give you an idea for a strategy, or plan, of your own.

Real Kids and the Big Question

DARREN doesn't know what to do. A friend of his got into some trouble and told Darren about it. He made Darren promise not to tell anyone. Darren thinks that his friend should tell his parents. Darren wants to help his friend, but he doesn't want to break his promise not to tell anyone. What do you think Darren should do?

BQ

NICOLE is having a rough time understanding math. She is too embarrassed to raise her hand and ask questions. So she just pretends she understands. At night, she almost cries over the math homework because she can't figure out the problems. She doesn't know what to do. What would you advise her to do?

Warm-Up Activity

In a small group, discuss times when you felt you didn't know what to do. How did it make you feel? Talk about what you did to improve the situation. Which solutions worked best?

Additional Support

Reading in the Real World

Career Both Nicole and Darren could benefit from good advice. Many people go to school counselors or private counselors to get advice when they don't know what to do. Have students work in small groups to research the following aspects of a counselor's job: educational requirements, licensure, job duties, job settings, and job opportunities. Assign one aspect to each group. Then ask groups to make charts or write brief reports to share their findings. AL

You and the Big Question

Reading about what other people did when they didn't know what to do will help you think about what you can do when you face a tough problem. **BQ**

Big Question Link to Web resources to further explore the Big Question at www.glencoe.com.

Plan for the Unit Challenge

At the end of the unit, you'll use notes from all your reading to complete the Unit Challenge.

You will choose one of the following activities:

A. Advice Column You'll work with a group to write an advice column. You'll write a letter asking for advice about what to do. Then you'll answer a letter from the perspective of one of the speakers or characters in this unit.

B. Award for Best Supporting Role You'll create an award to honor the person who plays a supporting role in your life by helping you or someone else solve problems.

- Start thinking about which activity you'd like to do so that you can narrow your focus as you read each selection.
- In your Learner's Notebook, write your thoughts about which activity you'd like to do.
- Each time you make notes about the Big Question, think about how your ideas will help you complete the Unit Challenge.

Keep Track of Your Ideas

As you read, you'll make notes about the Big Question. Later, you'll use these notes to complete the Unit Challenge. See pages R8–R9 for help with making Foldable 4. The diagram below shows how it should look.

1. Use this Foldable for all of the selections in this unit. Label the stapled edge with the unit number and the Big Question.
2. Label each flap with a selection title. (See page 443 for the titles.)
3. Open each flap. Near the top of the page, write **My Purpose for Reading.** Below the crease, write **The Big Question.**

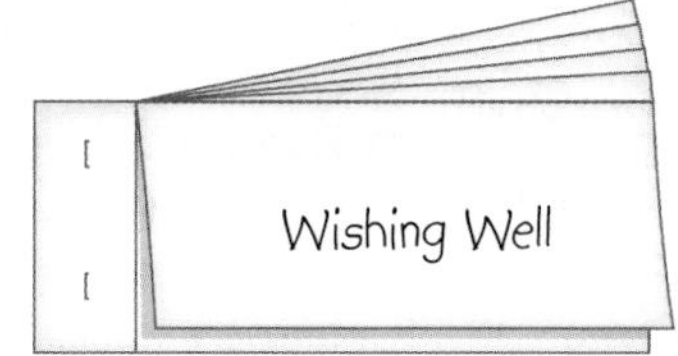

Teach

Big Question Have students access the Web site for English and Spanish summaries and annotated links to related Web resources.

BQ 

Have students write in their Learner's Notebooks one step they might take if they were facing a tough problem. *(Responses will vary.)* **AS**

For each selection they read, students will enter notes about how that selection applies to the Big Question. For details about using Dinah Zike's Foldables, see pages R8–R9.

Assess/Close

Ask students to share their thoughts on why considering the Big Question might help them in the immediate and long-range future.

Resources for page 445

- Use the Unit Challenge Planner BLM in the Unit 4 Resource Booklet p. 35.
- Use the Foldable BLM in the Unit 4 Resource Booklet p. 7.

Indiana English/Language Arts Academic Standards

TWE: *Reading in the Real World* 8.4.4, *Differentiated Instruction* 8.2

Differentiated Instruction

Visual Clues Draw students' attention to the photographs of Darren and Nicole. Discuss how photographs add to the text or make it easier to connect. Ask students to think about how seeing pictures of Darren and Nicole affects their visualizations and interpretations of the pictured students' problems. Seeing pictures of the individuals can provide a way for students to connect Darren's and Nicole's problems to their own experiences and feelings. Encourage students to include magazine photos or brief sketches in their Learner's Notebooks to illustrate their entries about the Big Question. **OL**

Focus

BELLRINGER Options

Daily Language Practice Transparency 33

Focus Activity Say: Think of rhymes you learned as a child or the words of a favorite song. How are both of these forms of poetry? *(Responses will vary.)* OL

Teach

R Reading Skill

How to Read Poetry Say: Poetry often describes how people feel. Why might this help you connect to the poems you read? *(Possible responses: I might realize that the poet and I feel the same way about something. I might recognize my own feelings expressed in a poem.)* **Ask:** How might describing feelings help the poet? *(Possible response: Poetry is one way the poet can work through troubling feelings or even share positive feelings with others.)* OL

UNIT 4 GENRE FOCUS: POETRY

Skills Focus

- Key reading skills for reading poetry
- Key literary elements of poetry

Skills Model

You will see how to use the key reading skills and literary elements as you read

- **"The Road Not Taken,"** p. 447

You know poetry when you see it, even if you really can't explain what it is. **Poetry** looks and sounds different from stories and other kinds of literature. Poetry is organized into lines and stanzas instead of sentences and paragraphs. And in poetry how words sound is often as important as what they mean. In poetry the sounds of words support their meanings.

Why Read Poetry?

R Poetry can help you see everyday things—and life in general—in new ways. It can make you feel less alone when you're lonely. It can inspire you when you're in a rut. It can help you smile when you're sad and work through hard times when the going gets tough. Poetry can also help you sharpen your thinking skills. Like riddles, poems contain clues to meaning that you can understand by thinking in fresh, creative ways.

How to Read Poetry

Key Reading Skills

These reading skills are especially useful tools for reading and understanding poetry. You'll see some of these skills modeled in the Active Reading Model, and you'll learn more about all of them later in this unit.

- **Connecting** Link what you read to events in your own life or to other selections you've read. (See Reading Workshop 1.)
- **Evaluating** Make a judgment or form an opinion about what you read. (See Reading Workshop 2.)
- **Interpreting** Use your own understanding of the world to decide what the events or ideas in a selection mean. (See Reading Workshop 3.)
- **Monitoring Comprehension** Pause from time to time to sum up the main idea and important details. Try putting these ideas into your own words. (See Reading Workshop 4.)

Indiana English/Language Arts Academic Standards (pp. 446–447)

8.3 Comprehension and Analysis of Literary Text Respond to grade-level-appropriate literature...Make connections and comparisons across texts. **8.2 Comprehension and Analysis (Focus on Informational Text)** Develop [reading] strategies... **8.3.1** Determine...purposes and characteristics of different forms of poetry... **8.3.6** Identify significant literary devices, such as metaphor.

For a complete description of the standards, see p. IN 11.

Key Literary Elements

Recognizing and thinking about the following literary elements will help you understand poetry more fully.

- **Free verse:** poetry without regular patterns of rhyme or rhythm (See "Wishing Well.")
- **Figurative language—metaphor and simile:** figures of speech that compare seemingly unlike things (See "Mother to Son" and "Harlem.")
- **Alliteration:** the repetition of consonant sounds at the beginning of words (See "Fable for When There's No Way Out.")
- **Rhyme:** the repetition of sounds, usually at the end of lines (See "O Captain! My Captain!")

Additional Support

Literature Focus Lesson

Poetry Remind students that there are different kinds of poetry. Narrative poems give storytellers a way to preserve or share stories for years to come. Lyric poems allow poets to express feelings and ideas. Many poems are set to music because of their rhyme and beat patterns. Free verse lets a poet share ideas without having to worry about form, punctuation, and other writing mechanics. Ask students to write about a favorite poem. Have them explain how the form adds to their enjoyment of the poem. OL AL

The Road Not Taken

by Robert Frost

The notes in the side column model how to use some of the skills and elements you read about on page 446.

Two roads diverged* in a yellow wood,
And sorry I could not travel both **1**
And be one traveler, long I stood
And looked down one as far as I could
To where it bent in the undergrowth; **2**

Then took the other, as just as fair,
And having perhaps the better claim,
Because it was grassy and wanted wear;
Though as for that the passing there
Had worn them really about the same,

And both that morning equally lay
In leaves no step had trodden* black. **3**
Oh, I kept the first for another day!
Yet knowing how way leads on to way,
I doubted if I should ever come back. **4**

I shall be telling this with a sigh
Somewhere ages and ages hence:
Two roads diverged in a wood, and I—
I took the one less traveled by,
And that has made all the difference.

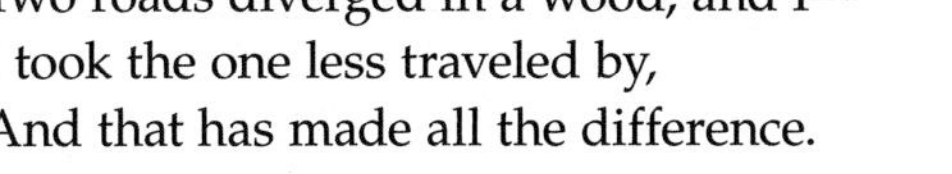

Poetry

ACTIVE READING MODEL

1 Key Reading Skill
Connecting *The speaker has to make a decision. Sometimes I have a hard time making decisions.*

2 Key Literary Element
Rhyme *There seems to be a regular pattern of rhyme. Lines 1, 3, and 4 rhyme; and so do lines 2 and 5.*

3 Key Literary Element
Alliteration *I like the way the "l" sound is repeated in "lay" and "leaves."*

4 Key Reading Skill
Interpreting *This is interesting! The speaker seems to be saying you always think you'll come back to something even when you know you probably won't.*

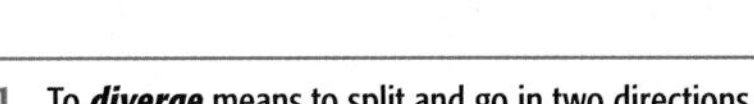

1 To ***diverge*** means to split and go in two directions.
12 ***Trodden*** is the past tense of the old-fashioned verb *to tread.*

Write to Learn In your Learner's Notebook, write a poem about a time when you had to make a difficult decision about something. Include some descriptive details. What might you compare this situation to?

Literature Online

Study Central Visit www.glencoe.com and click on Study Central to review poetry.

UNIT 4 GENRE FOCUS

Teach

R1 Reading Skill

Monitoring Comprehension
Ask: What clue in the first stanza tells readers how difficult the decision was? *(Possible response: The traveler stood a long time before making the decision.)* **OL**

R2 Reading Skill

Interpreting **Ask:** What is the poet suggesting you consider when he writes about the "road less traveled"? *(Possible response: You are free to make choices in life, even if others don't make the same ones.)* **OL** **AL**

Literature Online

Study Central Have students access the Web site to review poetry and to complete a related activity.

English Language Coach

Compound Nouns Frost used the compound noun *undergrowth* in this poem. Like *undergrowth*, many nouns combine the meanings of two words to create a new word. Give students other examples, such as *bellyache, railroad,* and *pancake*. Ask students to list other compound nouns and explain how each smaller word adds to the meaning of the compound word. **EL** **BL**

Indiana English/Language Arts Academic Standards
SE: 8.2, 8.3, 8.3.1, 8.3.6
TWE: *Literature Focus Lesson* 8.3.1, *English Language Coach* 8.1

Connecting

Teaching Students to Connect

Why Is It Important?

- There are many kinds of connections: self to world, self to text, world to text, text to text, connections within the text.
- Seeing simple and complex implied relationships is essential to understanding an implied main idea or theme.
- Connecting to the reading helps to pique student interest and enhances comprehension.

How to Help Students Get It

- Before, during, and after reading, have students recall events, situations, and emotions they have experienced that can help them connect to the reading.
- Remind students to recall selections they have read, movies they have seen, or other sources that would help them connect the world to the text. Students do not always have to personally experience an event to make a connection. They often "experience" many events through people they know or through situations they have read about or viewed through other media.

Reading to Answer the Big Question

Wishing Well by Kate Schmidt
Sleep can't always be taken for granted. In this poem, the speaker lies awake, trying to make sleep come. The image of a wishing well presents an answer: make a wish and relax, waiting for it to come true.

Signed, Sealed, Undelivered by Katharine Weber
This TIME article advocates writing (but not sending) truthful letters that allow the writer to fully express his or her feelings. This method allows the writer to articulate and let go of worrisome issues, without worrying about possible repercussions. When you don't know what to say, how to say it, or who to say it to—write a letter you will never send.

Workshop Resources

Pacing (Days) Standard	Block	Lesson	Student Materials	Teacher Resources
1	1/2	Key Skill Lesson: Connecting	Key Reading Skills Practice, p. 9 English Language Coach Review, p. 41	Bellringer Options Transparencies – Daily Language Practice 34 Read Aloud, Think Aloud Transparencies – Key Reading Skills 5 Presentation Plus!
1	1	"Wishing Well"	Glencoe Online Unit Vocabulary Review, p. 39 Academic Vocabulary Review, p. 43 English Language Coach Active Reading Graphic Organizer, p. 11 Literary Analysis, p. 10 StudentWorks Plus™ Online Student Edition Literature Classics Selection and Unit Assessments, p. 37	Literary and Text Analysis Transparencies 20 Puzzlemaker Skill Level Up!™ A Language Arts Game BookLink 3 Assessment by Learning Objective (Diagnostic and Formative) Interactive Tutor: Self-Assessment TeacherWorks Plus™
1		"Signed, Sealed, Undelivered"	Glencoe Online Unit Vocabulary Review, p. 39 Academic Vocabulary Review, p. 43 English Language Coach Active Reading Graphic Organizer, p. 13 StudentWorks Plus™ Online Student Edition Literature Classics Selection and Unit Assessments, p. 38	Literary and Text Analysis Transparencies 16 Puzzlemaker Skill Level Up!™ A Language Arts Game BookLink 3 Assessment by Learning Objective (Diagnostic and Formative) Interactive Tutor: Self-Assessment TeacherWorks Plus™

Keys for Unit Resource

- Blackline Master
- Workbook
- Supplemental Text
- CD-ROM
- DVD
- Transparency
- Web-based
- Fast File

Level Appropriate Code

- **AS** = Activities for all students
- **AL** = Activities for students working above grade level
- **OL** = Activities for students working at grade level
- **BL** = Activities for students working below grade level
- **EL** = Activities for English language learners

Focus

BELLRINGER Options

Daily Language Practice Transparency 34

Focus Activity Say: Have you ever felt that you needed a change in your life? Why? *(Responses will vary.)* **Say:** List words that describe how you felt that made you want a change. *(Possible responses: bored, frustrated, angry, sad)* AS

Teach

R Reading Skill

Connecting Say: Identify a movie that made you feel like saying, *The same thing happened to me!* or, *I know just how you feel!* Explain why it made you feel that way. *(Responses will vary.)* AS

Analyzing the Cartoon

Say: The cartoon character explains how he learned life lessons by watching horror films. What lesson have you learned from a movie or TV program? *(Responses will vary.)* AS

READING WORKSHOP 1

Skills Focus

You will practice these skills when you read the following selections:

- "Wishing Well," p. 452
- "Signed, Sealed, Undelivered," p. 458

Reading

- Connecting to poems

Literature

- Identifying characteristics of free verse
- Finding and analyzing examples

Vocabulary

- Understanding compound nouns and adjectives
- Academic Vocabulary: *illustrates*

Writing/Grammar

- Understanding how to make subjects and verbs agree

Skill Lesson

Connecting

Learn It!

R **What Is It?** You're watching a movie. During a funny scene, you think, *I know just how that character feels. I've been in the same situation, and I felt the same way.* When you relate a movie to your own life, you're **connecting** with the movie. You can connect what you read to your own life in the same way.

- Compare your experiences to those you read about.
- Think about similarities between different selections you've read.

Analyzing Cartoons

Curtis connects the lessons he's learned from scary movies to his own life. Do you think he understands and likes the movie he's watching better because he connects to it?

Indiana English/ Language Arts Academic Standards (pp. 448–449)

8.3 Comprehension and Analysis of Literary Text Respond to grade-level-appropriate literature...making connections...

For a complete description of the standards, see p. IN 11.

Additional Support

Differentiated Instruction

Building Background Each genre of movie has a different goal. For example, comedies attempt to make an audience laugh. Scary movies attempt to frighten the audience. Drama touches on many human emotions, including anger, sorrow, fear, and love. Discuss with students how, as audience members, we are able to connect to the characters in movies through the feelings their words and actions inspire. Have them describe their favorite movie and write about the emotions they have in response to it. EL BL

Why Is It Important? When you connect with a reading selection, you become more involved in it. It's more interesting to you, and so you get more out of it.

How Do I Do It? As you read, ask yourself

- *Does someone I know remind me of this character?*
- *Have I ever felt this way?*
- *What else have I read or experienced that's similar to this selection?*

Here's how a student connected to part of a poem by A. E. Housman. Read the selection from the poem; then read what the student had to say.

Literature Online

Study Central Visit www.glencoe.com, and click on Study Central to review connecting.

from **Yonder See the Morning Blink**

Oh often have I washed and dressed
And what's to show for all my pain?
Let me lie abed and rest:
Ten thousand times I've done my best
And all's to do again.

I can definitely relate to what the speaker in the poem is saying. It sounds as if the speaker is tired and in a rut. I know how that feels. Some mornings I don't feel like rushing to get dressed or working hard in school all day. I think the speaker wishes he could take a day off. Sometimes I do too.

Practice It!

Below are topics that relate to the selections in this Workshop. What connections can you make with each topic? Jot down some notes in your Learner's Notebook.

- not being able to sleep
- making a wish
- writing a letter to tell someone exactly how you feel

Use It!

As you read "Wishing Well" and "Signed, Sealed, Undelivered," remember the connections you made to the topics. If you make more connections as you read, add to your notes.

Teach

Study Central Have students access the Web site to review connecting and to complete a related activity.

R Reading Skill

Connecting Ask: In the poem, what are the speaker's choices of action? *(to wash and dress or stay in bed)* **OL** **Ask:** Have you ever felt like you didn't want to get up and get ready for your day? *(Students will likely respond that they have felt that way.)* **Ask:** How did you handle the situation? *(Responses will vary.)* **AS**

Resources for page 449

Use Key Reading Skills Transparency 5 in *Read Aloud, Think Aloud* to help students practice connecting.

Reading in the Real World

Citizenship Explain to students that people can express how they feel about a community, state, or world issue by writing letters to the editors of magazines or newspapers. Discuss with students the *do's* and *don'ts* of open letters, such as appropriate topics and language, required identification of the writer, and what constitutes libel and slander. Have students work in pairs to draft a letter to the editor about a school issue that they have an opinion about. Have volunteers give copies of their letters to classmates to read, or have them send their letters to the school newspaper. **OL**

Indiana English/Language Arts Academic Standards
SE: 8.3
TWE: *Differentiated Instruction* 8.3, *Reading in the Real World* 8.5.7

Teach

More About the Author

Kate Schmitt has other talents besides writing poetry. She uses her vivid imagination to create visual artwork that has won both a Rhode Island School of Design Award and a Golden Globe Award. Her artwork includes clocks, books, prints, and paintings. Schmitt currently teaches at the University of Houston and is working on her PhD.

EL Language Coach

Compound Nouns After students define the compound words from the Think-Pair-Share exercise, suggest that they use each of the words in an original sentence. They can record these sentences in their Learner's Notebooks. EL BL

Before You Read | Wishing Well

Meet the Author

Kate Schmitt's poems have been published in many collections. She believes that "by sharing our thoughts and experiences, writers . . . create relationships with readers, make connections between ideas, and illuminate our world." Schmitt is also a bookmaker and a teacher of writing.

Author Search For more about Kate Schmitt, go to www.glencoe.com.

Indiana English/Language Arts Academic Standards (pp. 450–453)

8.1 Word Recognition, Fluency, and Vocabulary Development Use [word parts and]...context clues...to determine the meaning of words... **8.3 Comprehension and Analysis of Literary Text** Respond to grade-level-appropriate literature...making connections... **8.3.1** Determine...purposes and characteristics of different forms of poetry...

For a complete description of the standards, see p. IN 11.

Vocabulary Preview

mesh (mesh) *n.* the weblike pattern of fibers in woven or knitted items **(p. 453)** *Large holes formed in the mesh of the old blanket.*

arc (ark) *n.* a curved line between two points **(p. 453)** *The arc of the fly ball made it easy for the baseball player to catch.*

On Your Own The following words refer to items that have mesh. Use each word in its own sentence that also contains the word *mesh.*

basketball net • knitted scarf

The following words refer to items that can form an arc when they are tossed into the air. Use each word in its own sentence that also contains the word *arc.*

volleyball • crumpled wad of paper

English Language Coach

Compound Nouns A **compound noun** is a combination of two or more words, such as *classroom (class + room)*. When you see an unfamiliar compound that's made up of words you already know, use your knowledge and context clues to figure out the meaning of the compound word. Try it now. See if you can figure out what the compound noun *passerby* means in the following sentence:

- A passerby who was shopping in the neighborhood saw a man running from the bank just after it was robbed.

By dividing *passerby* into the words it is made up of–*passer* and *by*–and thinking about the context, you can tell that *passerby* means "someone passing by, or walking past, a particular place."

EL **Think-Pair-Share** Find the two words in each compound noun below. Then guess what the compound means. Copy the chart in your Learner's Notebook, and write a definition for each compound. Then share your definitions with another student.

Compound Noun	Your Definition
pacesetter	
overcoat	
outgrowth	
paperback	

Additional Support

Author Search To expand students' appreciation of Kate Schmitt, have them access the Web site for additional information and resources.

Literature Focus Lesson

Poetry Explain to students that poetry is filled with sights, sounds, tastes, textures, and smells. These are called sensory descriptions. Have students work in pairs to find poems that appeal to each of the senses. Then have pairs record the descriptive language in each poem and identify the sense to which it appeals. You may then wish to have students make a classroom display in which copies of the poems are categorized according to the senses to which they appeal. OL

Skills Preview

Key Reading Skill: Connecting

As you read a selection, ask yourself questions such as: *Have I ever had the feeling the author describes? Have I ever known anyone like this character? Does this make sense to me?* The best readers ask themselves such questions. You can understand better if you relate what's new in what you're reading to what you've already learned by experience. R

Partner Talk Practice connecting with a partner. Say something you think or feel about a selection in this book. Have your partner say something from his or her own experience that connects to your thoughts or feelings about that selection. Then do it the other way around.

Key Literary Element: Free Verse

Free verse is a type of poetry that is based on the rhythms of spoken language rather than on traditional patterns of rhythm. Free verse may or may not rhyme. As you read the following unrhymed free verse, notice how words are grouped together. Each line groups words together the way a person in a conversation might group them. L

Seeing the plates piled high
with turkey, sweet potatoes,
mashed potatoes,
cranberry relish, green beans,
cornbread, and more,
I'm full
before I've had
a single bite
to eat.

Think about how the rhythm of the lines supports the meaning. The last four lines of the poem force you to pause three times. That slows you down, much as feeling full slows you down. As you read "Wishing Well," ask yourself, *How does the rhythm of the poem help support the meaning?*

Get Ready to Read

Connect to the Reading

Before you read the selection, think about times when you had the following experiences:

- not being able to sleep because of a problem
- hoping that something good will happen
- making a wish

Write to Learn Make a list of wishes you have made and write down whether they came true.

Build Background

The poem you are about to read is about making wishes by throwing a coin into a wishing well. How did this custom begin? In the past, many people believed that wells were sacred places because of the much-needed water they provided. Some people even drank or bathed in the well water in the hopes of having their wishes granted.

Set Purposes for Reading

BIG Question Read "Wishing Well" to see what someone does when she doesn't know what to do.

Set Your Own Purpose What else would you like to learn from the selection to help you answer the Big Question? Write your own purpose on the "Wishing Well" page of Foldable 4.

Interactive Literary Elements Handbook
To review or learn more about the literary elements, go to www.glencoe.com.

Keep Moving

Use these skills as you read the following selection.

Teach

R Reading Skill

Connecting Say: Recall a time when you lay in bed, unable to sleep. What words describe how you felt? *(Possible responses: worried, scared, tired, frustrated)* **Ask:** What thoughts or feelings kept you awake? *(Responses will vary.)* AS

L Literary Element

Free Verse Ask: What aspects of the poem in the *Key Literary Element* section help you identify it as free verse? *(Possible responses: lack of rhyme; differing line lengths; it's all one long sentence)* OL

Interactive Literary Elements Handbook Have students access the Web site to improve their understanding of free verse.

Differentiated Instruction

Sensory Language Explain to students that poets rely heavily on sensory language to express their ideas and emotions. Give students practice in writing their own descriptions using sensory language. Ask students to identify a setting that is familiar to them. Then have them make a chart with the headings *Sight, Smell, Taste, Touch,* and *Hearing.* In each column, students should record a description of their chosen place that appeals to the sense listed in the heading. Invite students to share their descriptions with the class. EL BL

Indiana English/Language Arts Academic Standards
SE: 8.1, 8.3, 8.3.1
TWE: *Literature Focus Lesson* 8.3, *Differentiated Instruction* 8.5.6

Teach

Viewing the Art

Ask: What does this image show? *(pennies falling and drops of water)* **Ask:** What is the title of the poem? *("Wishing Well")* **EL** **BL** **Ask:** Based on the image and the title of the poem, what do you predict the poem will be about? *(Possible response: It will be about making a wish and tossing pennies into a fountain.)* **AS**

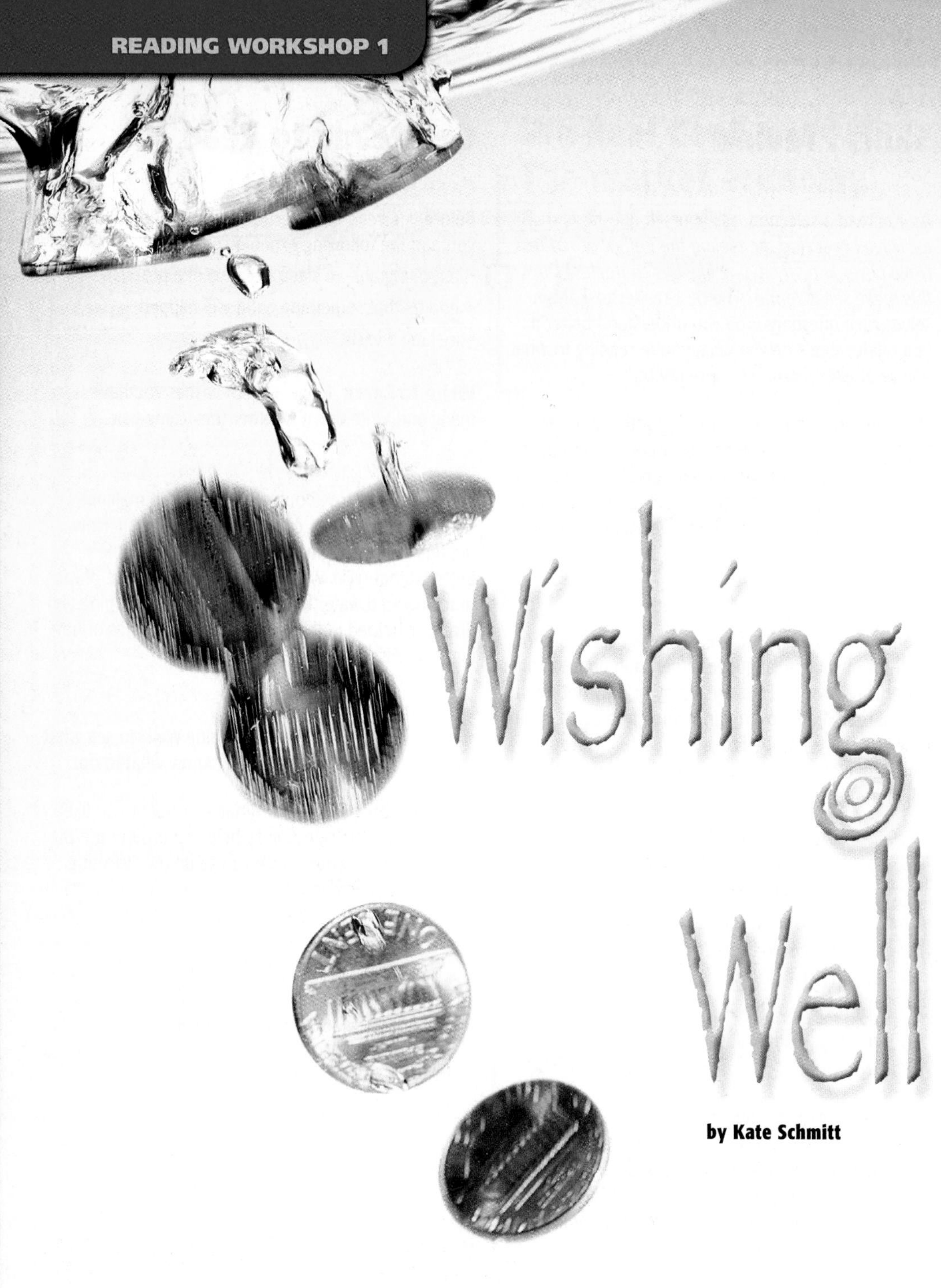

Wishing Well

by Kate Schmitt

Additional Support

Reading Fluency

Clarification Questions Tell students that answering basic questions about a text can help them clarify the text's meaning. Write the following questions on the board. Have students answer them as they read the poem.

- What does the speaker describe in stanza 1? *(her bed)*
- How does it look? *(It is disheveled.)*
- What do you visualize as you read stanza 2? *(Possible response: I imagine a girl with her hood tied so tightly around her face that I can barely see her.)*
- What "things" is the speaker referring to in the last line? *(wishes)* **EL** **BL**

The **mesh** of the blanket tangles
and lumps of comforter*
two-toned flannel* and bedspread
twist and slip. **1**

I haven't slept in a week
so I wear my brown hooded
sweatshirt with the hoodstrings
pulled tightly around my face. **2** **3**

I picture a wishing well
with edges of greening minerals
and coins dull with old water.
I throw my wish in a copper **arc**.

After I've thrown it I lie
unconcerned. These things take time. **4**

EL

BQ

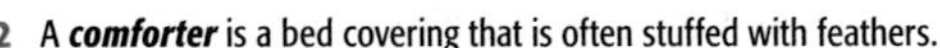

2 A ***comforter*** is a bed covering that is often stuffed with feathers.

3 ***Flannel*** is a kind of warm fabric.

Vocabulary

mesh (mesh) *n.* the weblike pattern of fibers in woven or knitted items

arc (ark) *n.* a curved line between two points

Practice the Skills

1 Key Literary Element

Free Verse Read this stanza aloud. How can you tell that this poem is written in free verse?

R

2 Key Reading Skill

Connecting How would you feel if you didn't sleep for a week?

3 English Language Coach

Compound Nouns Which words in this stanza are compound nouns?

4 BIG Question

According to this poem, what can you do when you can't sleep? How effective do you think this technique is? Why? Write your answer on the "Wishing Well" page of Foldable 4. Your response will help you complete the Unit Challenge later.

READING WORKSHOP 1

Teach

EL Language Coach

Compound Nouns **Ask:** Which word in the first stanza is a compound noun? *(bedspread)* **Ask:** What are the two smaller words that make up this compound word? *(*bed *and* spread*)* **Ask:** What does the word mean? *(It refers to a covering for a bed.)* EL BL

R Reading Skill

Connecting **Ask:** Have you ever gone a long time without sleep? How did you feel? How do you think the author looks and feels? *(Responses will vary.)* AS

BQ BIG Question

Ask: How does the speaker handle a situation in which she doesn't know what to do? *(Possible response: She makes a wish and then relaxes.)* OL

Assess

Use the CheckPoint questions provided on Presentation Plus! to check for comprehension of the selection. These questions can be used with interactive response keypads for immediate student feedback.

Differentiated Instruction

Visual Imagery To picture images described in a poem, some students may benefit from sketching one or more than one picture of them. Write the following poem on the board and ask students to sketch one of the images they visualize.

Hey Diddle Diddle
Hey! diddle, diddle,
The cat and the fiddle,
The cow jumped over the moon;
The little dog laughed
to see such sport,
And the dish ran away with the spoon.
EL BL

Indiana English/Language Arts Academic Standards
SE: 8.1, 8.3, 8.3.1
TWE: *Reading Fluency* 8.3, *Differentiated Instruction* 8.3

Assess

Resources for page 454

- Selection Quick Check, p. 31
- Selection and Unit Assessment, p. 37
- ExamView Assessment Suite
- Interactive Tutor: Self-Assessment

Students can respond to the *After You Read* items in their Learner's Notebooks or on a separate sheet of paper.

Answering the BIG Question

1. Possible response: For those who believe wishes come true, wishing is powerful.
2. one week
3. Responses should include these points: The speaker hasn't slept in a week, hides in a sweatshirt, and visualizes tossing a coin into a wishing well, confident that her problem will be solved.

Critical Thinking

4. Possible response: The tangled bedding suggests that the sleeper is restless.
5. Possible response: The speaker wishes to cover her face, possibly because the speaker doesn't look good or wants to block out the light.
6. Possible response: The penny is sailing through the air. Pennies are made of copper.
7. Responses will vary.

After You Read | Wishing Well

Answering the BIG Question

1. What does "Wishing Well" say about the power of wishing?
2. **Recall** How long has it been since the speaker of the poem has slept?
   TIP **Right There**
3. **Summarize** In your own words, summarize the poem.
   TIP **Think and Search**

Critical Thinking

4. **Analyze** The speaker describes her blankets and bedsheets in detail in the first stanza. How does this description prepare you for the sleeplessness she describes later?
   TIP **Author and Me**
5. **Infer** Why does the speaker pull the hoodstrings of her sweatshirt tightly around her face?
   TIP **Author and Me**
6. **Interpret** In line 12 the speaker says she throws her wish in a "copper arc." What do you think the copper arc is? Explain.
   TIP **Author and Me**
7. **Infer** Why is the speaker "unconcerned" after "throwing" her wish?
   TIP **Author and Me**

Talk About Your Reading

Literature Groups With a small group of classmates, discuss the **structure,** or organization, of the poem. Use the following questions to guide your discussion.

- What is the first stanza mainly about?
- What new idea is the second stanza about?
- Why did the poet begin a new stanza after line 8?
- What is the effect of tying the last two lines together in a stanza?

Indiana English/Language Arts Academic Standards (pp. 454–455)

8.3 Comprehension and Analysis of Literary Text Respond to grade-level-appropriate literature... **8.7.11 Listening and Speaking** Deliver oral responses to literature... **8.3.1** Determine...purposes and characteristics of different forms of poetry... **8.1 Word Recognition, Fluency, and Vocabulary Development** Understand...word parts... **8.6 English Language Conventions**...sentence structure...

For a complete description of the standards, see p. IN 11.

Talk About Your Reading

Possible responses:

- It's a description of messy bedclothes.
- The speaker's sleeplessness is affecting her appearance.
- There is a shift from reality to the speaker's imagination.
- It lets readers know the speaker expects a solution with time.

Skills Review

Key Reading Skill: Connecting

8. How did the activities on pages 450–451 help you connect to this selection? Rank the activities in order of helpfulness, with 1 being the most helpful and 3 the least helpful. Explain your rankings.
   - Connecting to what you already knew about having a problem that keeps you awake at night, hoping that something good would happen, and making a wish
   - Reading the facts in **Build Background**
   - Reading about Kate Schmitt in **Meet the Author**

Key Literary Element: Free Verse

9. You've read several poems in this book that have regular patterns of rhythm and rhyme. Some of those poems might be good as songs or raps. Would this poem work well as a song or rap? Explain your answer.
10. Do you think free verse is a good form for the topic of this poem? Explain your answer.

Vocabulary Check

On a separate piece of paper, write "T" if a sentence is true or "F" if it is false. Rewrite any false sentence to make it true.

11. Mesh is produced by weaving or knitting fibers or metals.
12. An arc is a straight line.
13. **English Language Coach** Divide each of the following compound nouns from "Wishing Well" into the two words it is made of.

    bedspread   sweatshirt   hoodstrings

Grammar Link: Subject-Verb Agreement

Subject-verb agreement is using the verb form that matches, or agrees with, the subject. There are two basic rules to remember when writing the present tense of a verb.

A. If the subject of a sentence is the pronoun *he, she,* or *it,* the verb must end in *-s.*
- He cooks well.
- She cooks even better.
- It cooks quickly.

B. If the subject of a sentence is the pronoun *I, you, we,* or *they,* the verb does not end in *-s.*
- I love cooking.
- You cook well.
- We cook together.
- They cook at home.

Here are the rules in chart form.

Singular Pronoun Subjects	Plural Pronoun Subjects
I run.	*We* run.
You run.	*You* run.
He, she, it runs.	*They* run.

Grammar Practice

In the following sentences, the subject and verb might not agree. Copy the sentences on a separate sheet of paper. If a sentence is correct as is, write "C" after the sentence. If there is an error in the subject-verb agreement, revise the sentence by fixing the verb.

14. He practice the guitar everyday.
15. It sounds great!
16. She love his music.

Web Activities For eFlashcards, Selection Quick Checks, and other Web activities, go to www.glencoe.com.

READING WORKSHOP 1

Skills Review

Key Reading Skill: Connecting

8. Responses will vary.

Key Literary Element: Free Verse

9. Responses will vary.
10. Responses will vary.

Vocabulary Check

11. T
12. F: An arc is a curved line.

English Language Coach

13. bedspread: *bed* and *spread*; sweatshirt: *sweat* and *shirt*; hoodstrings: *hood* and *strings*

Close

Ask students how connecting to this poem helped them address the Big Question.

Grammar Link: Subject-Verb Agreement

Grammar Practice

14. He practices the guitar every day.
15. It sounds great! C
16. She loves his music.

Indiana English/Language Arts Academic Standards

SE: 8.1.3, 8.3, 8.3.1, 8.6, 8.7.11

Teach

More About Letters

The first letters carried by the U.S. Postal Service were communications between the Continental Congress and the units of the Continental Army fighting the British in the American Revolution. It has been said that a postmaster once delivered letters to soldiers on foot because he didn't have enough money to buy a horse.

V Vocabulary

Parts of Speech **Say:** Review the vocabulary words and their definitions. Look at the part of speech of each word. *Neglected* is listed as an adjective. The *–ed* ending allows it to be used as an adjective. Can you also use it as a verb? *(Yes.)* **Say:** Give an example. *(Possible response: I neglected to do my homework.)* **Say:** Adding suffixes often changes a word's part of speech. What is the verb form of *humiliation*? *(humiliate)* OL

Before You Read: Signed, Sealed, Undelivered

Did You Know?

In ancient Egypt, there was a tradition of writing letters to dead relatives. The Egyptians believed that the dead had the power to prevent bad luck. In letters to family members who had recently died, such as husbands, wives, or parents, Egyptians asked for help with problems such as ill health or arguments over property.

Vocabulary Preview

neglected (nih GLEK tud) *adj.* given little attention or respect **(p. 458)** *Writing letters is a neglected form of communication that more people should practice.*

humiliation (hyoo mil ee AY shun) *n.* something that makes a person feel ashamed or foolish **(p. 459)** *Ridiculing her in class is a form of humiliation.*

offensive (uh FEN siv) *adj.* unpleasant or disagreeable, causing anger **(p. 460)** *She wrote an offensive letter expressing her anger, but she knew better than to mail it.*

petty (PEH tee) *adj.* having or displaying a mean, narrow-minded attitude **(p. 461)** *His petty comments were upsetting but not worth fighting over.*

Write to Learn For each word, write a sentence using the word correctly.

English Language Coach

Compound Adjectives A **compound adjective** is a describing word made up of two or more words.

- That well-known actor likes to eat at my dad's restaurant.

  (He is not a *well* actor or a *known actor*. He is a *well-known* actor. The hyphen shows that the words go together.)

- Hector's favorite food is chocolate-chip cookies.

  (They are not *chocolate* cookies or *chip* cookies. They are *chocolate-chip* cookies. The words go together to describe the noun.)

When a compound adjective comes *after* the noun it modifies, it doesn't have a hyphen.

- Hector's favorite cookies are chocolate chip.

There are some other compound adjectives that don't have hyphens. You can recognize them because the words work together to modify the noun. Taking out either one changes the meaning completely

- She is a member of the United States Senate.

On Your Own Copy the following sentences on a separate sheet of paper. Underline the compound adjective in each sentence.

- How many short-sleeved shirts do you own?
- His long-term goal is to run a marathon.
- Ana's little brother likes to watch Saturday morning cartoons.
- My sister is well liked at school.

Indiana English/Language Arts Academic Standards (pp. 456–461)

8.1 Word Recognition, Fluency, and Vocabulary Development Understand...word...patterns and relationships...**8.3 Comprehension and Analysis of Literary Text**...making connections...
8.3.6 Identify significant literary devices...

For a complete description of the standards, see p. IN 11.

Additional Support

Literature Focus Lesson

Personal Essay Tell students that a personal essay expresses a writer's experiences, opinions, and feelings. Personal essay writers often share their own insights about their actions. Personal essays give readers a chance to reflect on their own behavior through the lens of another person's actions and reactions. In the upcoming essay, Katharine Weber shares her experiences with writing letters that she never delivers. Ask students to consider why someone might write a letter and never send it. Allow students to discuss their responses. Ask them if they have ever done the same and why. AS

Skills Preview

Key Reading Skill: Connecting

The title of the article, "Signed, Sealed, Undelivered," refers to letters that do not get sent, so nobody reads them. The writer of this article describes how free she feels when she writes whatever she wants to say without worrying about what people think.

As you read this selection, connect the descriptions and points the writer makes to your own experiences.

Text Element: Examples

An **example** is a specific instance that **illustrates**, or explains, a general statement. Suppose that a writer makes the following statement:

- My brother is messy.

To illustrate what he means, the writer might give examples like these:

- For instance, he throws his dirty socks on the floor, and he leaves banana peels on the kitchen table.

As you read "Signed, Sealed, Undelivered," ask yourself, *What general statements does the author make? What examples does she give to illustrate them?*

Small Group Work With a small group of classmates, take turns adding examples that illustrate the general statements below. Each group member should provide at least one example for each statement.

- Many kinds of music are played on the radio.
- Many sports are played using a ball.

Interactive Literary Elements Handbook
To review or learn more about the literary elements, go to www.glencoe.com.

Academic Vocabulary

illustrates (IL us trayts) *v.* shows clearly through examples

Get Ready to Read

Connect to the Reading

Think about times when you were upset with a friend but didn't feel you could tell him or her. What did you do? Why?

Write to Learn In your Learner's Notebook, write a few sentences about what upset you and what you did.

Build Background

There's a Stevie Wonder song called "Signed, Sealed, Delivered, I'm Yours." In the lyrics, the speaker asks his former girl friend to take him back and regrets "that time I went and said goodbye."

This guy might be in a better situation if he had read the article you're going to read next. It discusses writing letters—that you don't intend to send—to express your angry, upset feelings.

Recent studies have shown that writing about your deepest thoughts and feelings can improve your physical health. Holding in bad feelings causes stress. Expressing them can reduce it.

However, the article warns, keep those letters to yourself. Store them in a safe, private place or, better yet, destroy them. Sending such letters could bring new stress to both you and those you send them to.

Set Purposes for Reading

BIG Question Read "Signed, Sealed, Undelivered" to learn a good technique for dealing with difficult feelings, without bad consequences.

Set Your Own Purpose What else would you like to learn from the selection to help you answer the Big Question? Write your own purpose on the "Signed, Sealed, Undelivered" page of Foldable 4.

Keep Moving

Use these skills as you read the following selection.

Teach

R Reading Skill

Connecting Say: Recall an argument with a friend. Why is it easy to say the "wrong thing" in this kind of situation? *(Possible response: You are angry or hurt and don't take the time to think about what you should do or say.)* AS

E Text Element

Examples Say: What examples would you use to describe a messy person? *(Possible responses: uncombed hair; rumpled clothing; a locker jammed with food wrappers and old papers)* AS

Literature Online

Interactive Literary Elements Handbook Have students access the Web site to improve their understanding of examples.

Differentiated Instruction

Connections Chart Some students may find it easier to make connections with the text if they make a connections chart. Draw this chart on the board. Invite students to use it as they read "Signed, Sealed, Undelivered." EL BL

The text says . . .	I felt/acted this way when . . .
The author wrote an angry letter to a critic.	I wanted to let the drama coach know I felt I deserved a part in the play.

Indiana English/Language Arts Academic Standards
SE: 8.1
TWE: *Literature Focus Lesson* 8.3, *Differentiated Instruction* 8.2

Teach

C Critical Thinking

Comprehension Ask: Why did the author shred the note that she wrote to God? *(Possible responses: She didn't want anyone to read it. She was afraid to actually ask the question.)* OL

EL Language Coach

Compound Adjectives

Say: Compound adjectives with first words ending in *–ly* are not hyphenated. Paragraph 2 contains two compound adjectives that precede the words they modify. Which words are they? *(real-life, deeply felt)* EL BL

Readability Scores
Dale-Chall: 5.8
DRP: 57
Lexile: 970

READING WORKSHOP 1

TIME

Signed, Sealed, Undelivered

Writing a brutally honest letter feels good. But sending it probably isn't a good idea.

By KATHARINE WEBER

The summer I was 7, my 11-year-old brother was at the Mayo Clinic in Rochester, Minnesota, for heart surgery. I was sent to stay with my aunt and uncle in Evanston, Illinois. The day of his operation, I wrote a note to God on a tiny scrap of paper and then instantly shredded it into my cousin's guinea pig's cage. It was a five-word question—"Is he going to die?"—one that I didn't dare ask grown-ups. **1** The guinea pig died later that summer; my brother lived. **C**

Unsent letters are a marvelous and far too **neglected** form of communication, one that I have been practicing for most of my life. Writing letters that will never be read is emotionally satisfying. I am free to express my deepest feelings without holding back. And by not mailing them, I have saved myself the real-life consequences that deeply felt letters can, for better or worse, cause. **EL**

In this age of e-mail and instant messaging, we all know stories about unfortunate messages sent too quickly, too

1 English Language Coach

Compound Adjectives Identify the compound adjective in this sentence.

Vocabulary

neglected (nih GLEK tud) *adj.* given little attention or respect

Additional Support

Literature Focus Lesson

Letters When people write their immediate reactions, opinions, and feelings in a letter, they often use strong and possibly insensitive language. Write the following letter on the board. Invite students to point out needed revisions. AS

To my ex-best friend—
How can you be so stupid? You know I hate bowling, yet you planned a bowling party for my birthday. You probably did it on purpose. Some best friend *you* are!
—Your former best friend

angrily, too carelessly. The typed or handwritten letter (which can be revised for hours) is nearly a thing of the past. Letting an important letter slip and then vanish beyond reach into the belly of a mailbox has been replaced for most of us by watching the blip of the Send icon, clicked almost involuntarily. We think, *Oh, no, did I really say that? Did I really mean that? Did I accidentally hit Reply All?* **2**

When I was in the fifth grade, I wrote a series of despairing letters to my teacher, Mrs. Jacobson. I was convinced that her dislike for me caused her to seek out new forms of **humiliation** on a daily basis. ("Why do you hate me, Mrs. Jacobson? Is it because I finish my assignments before I'm supposed to? Is it because my hair is messy?")

I folded them into tight squares and mailed the first few down the storm drain on my way home from school. But after a classmate named Billy saw me pushing something through the grate and tried to fish it out, I began my collection of unsent letters in a shoe box in my closet. First lesson of unsent letters: Keep them safe.

My secret shoe box of unsent letters filled. There was a shy letter to a boy I liked. There was a pleading letter to a girl who had been unaccountably[1] mean on a field trip. There was a nasty letter to the grouch down the street who would pop out of his house to yell at the neighborhood children. **3**

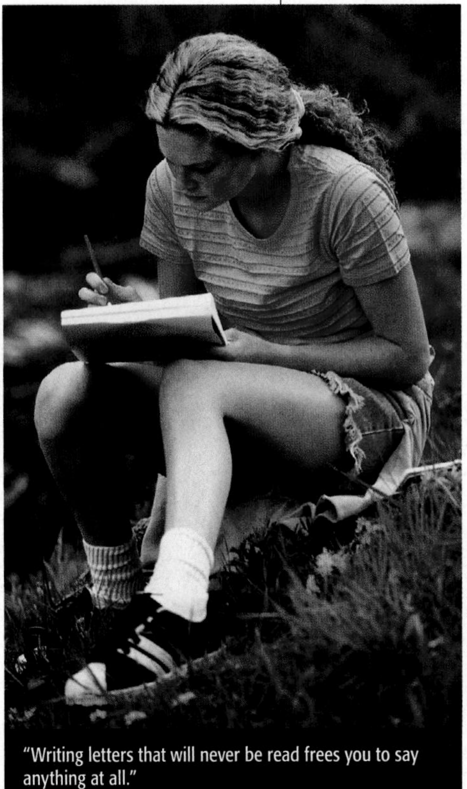

"Writing letters that will never be read frees you to say anything at all."

Steve Mason/Photodisc/Getty Images

1. ***Unaccountably*** means "for no reason."

Vocabulary

humiliation (hyoo mil ee AY shun) *n.* something that makes a person feel ashamed or foolish

2 Key Reading Skill

Connecting Have you ever had this experience when sending an instant message or an e-mail? How did you feel?

3 Text Element

Examples The writer lists examples of the kinds of letters she wrote. How do these examples help you understand what kinds of feelings you can express in unsent letters?

READING WORKSHOP 1

Teach

EL Language Coach

Compound Words Say: The first paragraph on this page has both a compound adjective and a compound noun. What are they? *(handwritten, mailbox)* What do they mean? (Handwritten *means something that is written by hand, not typed. A* mailbox *is a receptacle for mail.)* EL BL

BQ BIG Question

Say: Why might it be difficult to know what to do if you disagree with a teacher? *(Possible response: You might be worried that you'll get a bad grade or get sent to the principal if you react emotionally.)* AS

E Text Element

Examples Say: The writer gives reasons she believes her teacher dislikes her. What are these reasons? *(The author finishes her work before everyone else, and her hair is messy.)* OL **Ask:** Do these reasons make sense? *(Responses will vary.)* AL

Reading in the Real World

Citizenship Explain to students that school citizenship gives them certain rights, including the right to talk with teachers or administrators if they feel they are being treated unfairly. Review with students your policy for dealing with student concerns. Invite the principal to your classroom to discuss school policies regarding student concerns and suggestions. Help students prepare questions before the visit. AS

Indiana English/Language Arts Academic Standards
SE: 8.3, 8.3.6
TWE: *Literature Focus Lesson* 8.5.7

Teach

R Reading Skill

Connecting Ask: When in your life were you glad you stopped yourself from saying or writing something nasty to another person? *(Responses will vary.)* AS

Viewing the Photo

Say: An *antique* is an object made and used many years ago. Why do you think people used seals and wax on letters in the past? *(Possible responses: Envelopes did not have glue or self-sealing strips. Sealing with wax ensured privacy and identified the sender.)* **Ask:** Why might the writer like to use these objects? *(Possible responses: By sealing her letters this way, she makes sure no one will read them. It makes her feel that her letters are more official.)* OL AL

When I left home for college, I took my shoe box with me. Second rule of unsent letters: They should be read only by the person who writes them. Then late in my college years, I decided to start my grown-up life and mailed the entire collection, one letter at a time, into an incinerator chute. And so they vanished from my life.

After having my first novel published in 1995, I once again wrote an unsent letter. A well-known critic[2] gave my novel an unfavorable review. And so I wrote Mr. Famous Literary Critic an angry three-page letter, flinging back at him some remarks he'd made. I was on my way to the mailbox when, fortunately, I thought about the possible consequences of mailing such an **offensive** letter. It had felt good to write it, but what would it feel like to receive it? So I kept it. For no particular reason, I stashed this ugly letter in a beautiful wooden box. 4

4 Reviewing Skills

R Comparing and Contrasting Compare and contrast this example of the writer's adult feelings towards a critic with her childhood feelings about Mrs. Jacobson. How are they the same? Different?

Malcolm Piers/Photographer's Choice/Getty Images

For Katharine Weber, an antique seal and wax add the final comforting touch to a letter she never intends to send.

2. A ***critic*** is a person whose job it is to write an opinion about the strengths and weaknesses of a book, movie, or other work of art.
3. To ***rave*** means to praise with great enthusiasm.

Vocabulary

offensive (uh FEN siv) *adj.* unpleasant or disagreeable, causing anger

petty (PEH tee) *adj.* having or displaying a mean, narrow-minded attitude

Additional Support

English Language Coach

Determining Meaning Students who are below grade level or learning English may benefit from working with students who are at or above grade level. Partner students and ask them to determine the meanings of the following words from the selection: *marvelous, consequences, involuntarily, despairing, storm drain, pleading, grouch, incinerator chute, stashed, haunts.* Encourage students to include any other unfamiliar words in their lists. Provide students with dictionaries in case they are unable to determine meaning through context. AS

Brand X/Punchstock

By writing but not mailing a letter, Weber saves herself the real-life consequences that a deeply felt letter can cause.

In the years since, I have read the letter to the book critic a few times, and each time I have been aware that I was totally correct in every single word I wrote and that it was really a wise move to have kept the letter. Wiser than I could have imagined. Years later, when my third novel was published, the same critic gave it a rave[3] review—the kind of review novelists dream about.

Writing letters that will never be read frees you to say anything at all. You can write to those people whose **petty** meannesses stung you or whose significant cruelties really hurt you. It's open season[4] on expressing as much rage or sadness or wonder as your heart can desire and your sentences can contain. [R] You can write yourself out of a mood or into a mood. You can even reveal your deepest feelings about a troubled relationship that haunts you. [C] You just might find the peace you've been searching for. And you can do it all without having to spend the price of a stamp. **5**

—Updated 2005, from *Real Simple*, May 2004

5 **BIG Question**

What does the writer say about how to deal with difficult relationships? Write your answer on the "Signed, Sealed, Undelivered" page of Foldable 4. Your response will help you complete the Unit Challenge later.

4. The expression ***open season*** usually refers to a period of time when hunting is legally permitted. Here, the writer is saying that an unsent letter gives you total freedom to express your most honest, brutal feelings.

Teach

R Reading Skill

Connecting **Say:** The writer says that letter writing can help you change your mood. Have you had this experience? What other activities help you improve your mood? *(Responses will vary.)* **AS**

C Critical Thinking

Comprehension **Say:** Reread the last three sentences. What do people gain by writing undelivered letters? *(Possible response: peace)* **OL**

Assess

Use the CheckPoint questions provided on Presentation Plus! to check for comprehension of the selection. These questions can be used with interactive response keypads for immediate student feedback.

Reading in the Real World

Career Some students who are interested in art, books, or films might enjoy learning more about the career of a critic. Take students to the library to gather information from print sources or the Internet about a critic's job. Then distribute copies of a review. Ask students to identify the opinions and volunteer how the subject might feel about the review. Then have them write a brief review of a story they have recently read or a movie they have attended. **AL**

Indiana English/Language Arts Academic Standards

SE: 8.3, 8.3.6

TWE: *English Language Coach* 8.1, *Reading in the Real World* 8.5.7

Assess

Resources for page 462

- Selection Quick Check, p. 32
- Selection and Unit Assessment, p. 38
- ExamView Assessment Suite
- Interactive Tutor: Self-Assessment

Students can respond to the *After You Read* items in their Learner's Notebooks or on a separate sheet of paper.

Answering the BIG Question

1. Possible response: Write letters, but don't deliver them.
2. She wrote her first undelivered letter when she was seven and her brother had heart surgery.
3. Keep them safe; Only the writer gets to read the letters.

Critical Thinking

4. Possible response: The critic may have given her a bad review on her third novel in reaction to her previous comments.
5. Responses will vary.

After You Read

Signed, Sealed, Undelivered

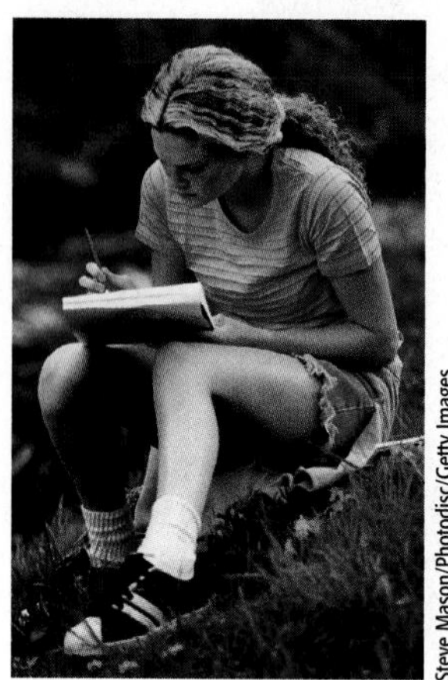

Steve Mason/Photodisc/Getty Images

Answering the BIG Question

1. According to the article "Signed, Sealed, Undelivered," what is one way to deal with fear, anger, or embarrassment?
2. **Recall** When did the writer compose her first undelivered letter?
   TIP **Right There**
3. **List** What are the writer's two rules about undelivered letters?
   TIP **Think and Search**

Critical Thinking

4. **Infer** What might have happened if the writer had mailed her letter to the critic? Explain.
   TIP **Author and Me**
5. **Evaluate** Do you think the writer's ideas about unsent letters are good ones? Explain.
   TIP **On My Own**

Write About Your Reading

Advice Column Imagine that you write an advice column for a school newspaper. Today you received the following letter from a student:

Dear Advisor,

I am a member of one of the sports teams here at school, but you'd never know it. That's because the coach never lets me play. I know I am smaller than most of the other players, but I play hard. I'm really upset because the only thing holding me back is my coach. I am thinking of telling the coach exactly how I feel. Do you think I should?

Signed,
Bench Warmer

Use what you learned from reading "Signed, Sealed, Undelivered." Write a short letter giving advice to "Bench Warmer." In your letter include advice, examples, or other information from the article.

Indiana English/Language Arts Academic Standards (pp. 462–463)

8.3 Comprehension and Analysis of Literary Text Respond to grade-level-appropriate literature...[make] connections...
8.5.7 Write for different purposes...
8.1 Word Recognition, Fluency, and Vocabulary Development Understand...word...patterns and relationships...
8.6 English Language Conventions...sentence structure...
For a complete description of the standards, see p. IN 11.

Write About Your Reading

Possible Response:

Dear Bench Warmer,
I think your best approach is to try to calm down before you do anything. Why not write a letter to your coach explaining how you feel? Then reread your letter as if you were the coach. Would it make your coach give you a chance to play or make him or her angry? Rewrite your letter with your coach's feelings in mind.
Sincerely,
Advisor

Skills Review

Key Reading Skill: Connecting

6. How can you link your experiences to Weber's?

Text Element: Examples

7. At the beginning of paragraph 2, Weber makes the following general statement: "Unsent letters are a marvelous and far too neglected form of communication . . . ." List five specific examples she gives to illustrate that general statement.

Reviewing Skills: Comparing and Contrasting

8. Compare and contrast the author's reason for writing a note to a boy she liked to her reason for writing a letter to a girl who had been mean to her. How were the reasons the same? Different?

Vocabulary Check

Write a sentence to answer each of the following questions.

9. How would you feel if someone made an **offensive** remark to you?
10. What form of **humiliation** might a bully subject someone to?
11. What would you do for a **neglected** puppy if you found one?
12. Would a **petty** comment make you feel happy or irritated?
13. **Academic Vocabulary** Give an **example** of each of the following:
    - music you like
    - sounds you hate
    - people you admire
14. **English Language Coach** Write a few sentences describing a friend or relative. Use at least one compound adjective in each sentence.

Grammar Link: Subject-Verb Agreement with Noun Subjects

In the last Grammar Link, you learned that a present tense verb must end in *-s* to agree with the pronoun subjects *he, she,* and *it.* Not all subjects are in pronoun form, however. How can you tell what verb form to use with a noun subject? "Translate" the noun into the pronoun that could take its place. Then check to make sure that the verb form is correct.

Read the following sentence. The verb in the sentence is *like.* The subject is the noun *Linda.* What pronoun could take the place of *Linda?*

- Linda like to dance.

The pronoun *she* could replace *Linda.* Now check the verb. Notice that it should end in *-s* because the subject *Linda* is equal to *she.* Here is the corrected sentence:

- Linda likes to dance.

Grammar Practice

The subject and verb are underlined in each sentence below. Translate each noun subject into a pronoun. Then check to make sure the verb agrees with the subject. If it doesn't, fix the verb.

15. Linda and her sister take dance lessons.
16. Her sister enjoy modern dance.
17. Linda's brother prefer sports to dance.

Writing Application Reread the letter you wrote for the Write About Your Reading activity. Make sure all subjects and verbs agree. Fix any mistakes.

Web Activities For eFlashcards, Selection Quick Checks, and other Web activities, go to www.glencoe.com.

Skills Review

Key Reading Skill: Connecting

6. Possible response: I can read for events and feelings that I've experienced in my own life.

Text Element: Examples

7. letters to God, her teacher, a boy she liked, a girl who was mean to her, a neighborhood grouch, a book critic

Reviewing Skills: Comparing and Contrasting

8. Possible response: In both cases, she wasn't comfortable sharing her feelings; however, the letter to the boy would have contained positive comments, while the letter to the girl would have been negative or critical.

Vocabulary Check

9.-12. Responses will vary.

Academic Vocabulary

13. Responses will vary.

English Language Coach

14. Responses will vary.

Web Activities Have students access the Web site for interactive activities that will help them assess their understanding of the selection.

Grammar Link: Subject-Verb Agreement with Noun Subjects

Grammar Practice

15. They take dance lessons.
16. She enjoys modern dance.
17. He prefers sports to dance.

Close

Remind students that Weber writes a letter and doesn't send it when she doesn't know what to do. Ask students to compare her actions to what they do in similar situations.

Indiana English/Language Arts Academic Standards
SE: 8.1, 8.3, 8.5.7, 8.6

Poem

Teaching Students to Write a Poem

Why Is It Important?

- Poetry provides a unique opportunity to indulge in play with language.
- Figurative language plays a large role in every communication, written or spoken. Writing a poem will expand students' awareness of the plethora of metaphors in their own verbal lives.
- Students may find it easier to appreciate or analyze poetry after they have created some of their own.
- Revision, the "re-seeing," is especially important to this genre. Each word in a poem must contribute greatly to the whole.
- Poetry can be a place for self-expression—academic or purely personal.
- Students may find that revision of all written work becomes clearer after applying the practice to something personally meaningful, like a "what do I do next?" poem.

How to Help Students Get It

- Review the definitions of verse and stanza with students.
- Ensure that students have plenty of time to freewrite. This important first step in drafting will help them generate ideas, practice expressing themselves in writing, and build confidence in their overall writing skills.
- Share a few of your own favorite "bite-size" poems with the class. You can read them aloud, have students read them, or post them in stations around the classroom.
- Remind students that vivid word choice and figures of speech contribute to the tone of the piece. Ask: "Is your 'what to do' poem happy? sad? funny? scared?"
- Discuss popular clichés and identify them as metaphors and similes. (Examples are "sleep like a baby," "faster than a locomotive".)
- Provide students with access to a thesaurus, in print or online.
- Bring in a short sample of your own favorite poet, and read aloud a section that exemplifies one of the literary concepts applicable to poetry.
- Review the definitions of mood and tone with students.

Writing Trait	Student Checklist
Ideas	the message or the theme and the details that develop it
Organization	the arrangement of main points and supporting details
Voice	a writer's unique way of using tone and style
Unit Focus **Word Choice:** the vocabulary a writer uses to convey meaning	• Does the writer use lively verbs to show action? • Does the writer use vivid words to create word pictures in the readers' minds? • Does the writer use precise words to explain his or her ideas simply and clearly?
Sentence Fluency	the smooth rhythm and flow of sentences that vary in length and style
Conventions	correct spelling, grammar, usage, and mechanics
Presentation	the way words and design elements look on a page

Workshop Resources

Pacing (Days) Standard	Block	Lesson	Student Materials	Teacher Resources
1	1/2	Writing Workshop Part 1: Prewriting and Drafting	Writing Workshop Graphic Organizer, p. 14 Grammar Practice, p. 15 Spelling and Handwriting Practice, p. 45 Grammar and Composition Handbook, p. 223	TeacherWorks Plus™ Presentation Plus! Rubrics for Assessing Student Writing, Listening, and Speaking, p. 24
			Real Success in Writing: Research and Reports	Grammar and Writing Workshop Transparencies 13–14
2	1	Writing Workshop Part 2: Editing, Revising, and Presenting	Interactive Grammar and Language Workbook Grammar and Composition Handbook, p. 223	Grammar and Writing Workshop Transparencies 27–28
			Real Success in Writing: Research and Reports	Interactive Grammar and Language Workbook
			Listening and Speaking, p. 27 Viewing and Representing, p. 28	Rubrics for Assessing Student Writing, Listening, and Speaking, p. 24

Focus

BELLRINGER Options

Daily Language Practice Transparency 35

Focus Activity Say: Summarize an experience in which you were unsure of what to do. *(Responses will vary.)* AS

Teach

E Text Element

Examples Ask: What types of examples would you use to show either a conflict with yourself or another person? *(Possible response: A conflict with yourself would use your thoughts as examples. A conflict with another person would use details from the event as examples.)* AS

Resources for page 464

- Use the Writing Workshop Graphic Organizer BLM in the Unit 4 Resource Booklet, p. 14.
- Use the Grammar and Writing Workshop Transparencies 13-14.

WRITING WORKSHOP PART 1

Poem

Prewriting and Drafting

ASSIGNMENT Write a poem

Purpose: To express your thoughts and feelings about what you do when you don't know what to do

Audience: Your teacher and possibly your classmates or family

Writing Rubric

As you work through this writing assignment, you should

- use the writing process to write a poem
- choose lively, specific words
- make subjects and verbs agree
- use literary devices such as figurative language and sound patterns

See page 498 in Part 2 for a model of a poem.

Indiana English/Language Arts Academic Standards (pp. 464–467)

8.4 Processes and Features Prewriting and drafting. **8.4.1** Keep a list...of ideas and use graphic organizers to plan writing. **8.5.7.** Write for different purposes... **8.4.9** Revise writing for word choice... **8.6 English Language Conventions** Sentence structure

For a complete description of the standards, see p. IN 11.

The selections that you have read so far in this unit show what some people do when they don't know what to do. Everyone has times of uncertainty, but not everyone handles those situations in the same way.

In this Writing Workshop, you'll write a poem about what you do when you're not sure what your next action should be. Writing this poem will help you answer the Unit 4 Big Question: What do you do when you don't know what to do?

Prewriting

Get Ready to Write

E Vivid memories and strong feelings can help you write a good poem. For this writing assignment, be sure to think of a situation that you remember clearly. Your poem can be serious, lighthearted, or anything in between.

Come Up with Ideas

In your Learner's Notebook, make a list of times when you were confused or troubled because you didn't know what to do. Don't worry yet about what experiences will or won't work. Just write.

- *I didn't turn in my science report on time.*
- *My friend wouldn't talk to me*

When your list has three or four good ideas, choose one that you remember clearly and that you want to write about.

Gather Details

You most likely have some general ideas about the situation you chose from your list. Now you need to come up with some specific details to use in your poem. The steps below will help you gather details.

1. Clear your mind and focus only on the situation you will write about. Bring to mind all the feelings and thoughts you had. You may even remember specific sights, sounds, smells, tastes, or feelings connected to the experience. Make notes about these details as they come to mind. You may want to try one of the approaches described on the next page.

Additional Support

English Language Coach

Compound Adjectives Draw two columns on the board. In the first column, write *softness, anger, fear,* and *confusion.* In the second column, write *heart-pounding, baby-fine, brain-numbing,* and *red-hot.* Explain to students that compound adjectives can make feelings come to life. Ask student to give examples of how they would use the words from column 2 to describe those in column 1. Invite students to suggest other compound adjectives for these words and to include these adjectives in their poems. EL BL

- Quickly write what you remember for ten minutes. Don't edit your writing—just let your ideas flow.
- Make a web or cluster map of details. In the middle of a piece of paper, describe the situation and circle it. As you think of details, add them in circles connected to the center circle.

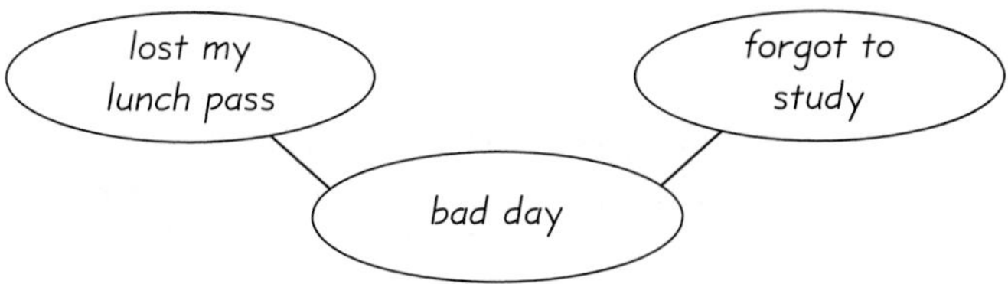

2. When you're finished generating ideas, underline details that you might want to include in your poem. Circle your favorite ideas—the ones you definitely want to use.

Make a Plan

Making a plan will help you start your draft and stay on track as you write. Answer the following questions in your Learner's Notebook.

- *What are the most important ideas I want to express?*
- *How do I want my poem to sound? Sad? Funny? Angry? Calm?*

Last Friday was a really bad day. Everything went wrong, from losing my lunch pass to realizing I hadn't studied for a math test. I want to list what went wrong and the way I felt. The poem will have rhythm—maybe a hip-hop beat—and be funny (I hope!).

Drafting

Start Writing!

There's no right or wrong way to start drafting your poem. Just get something down on paper or computer screen. You can always revise later.

Get It on Paper

Reread your prewriting notes. Use them to start drafting your poem. You can use regular patterns of rhythm and rhyme, or you can write free verse (see page 451). The choice is yours. If words don't come when you sit down to write, set your poem aside. Then try again. Don't be too picky, and don't give up! Just write. Later, you can improve the wording of your poem.

On the next page you'll take a closer look at how to find the right words.

Literature Online

Writing Models For models and other writing activities, go to www.glencoe.com.

Writing Tip

Purpose and Audience Your main purpose is to express your thoughts and feelings in a poem. Another purpose might be to share your thoughts and feelings with a friend or a family member. Think about who will read your poem. You may need to adjust your topic and word choice for your audience.

WRITING WORKSHOP PART 1

Teach

Literature Online

Writing Models Have students access the Web site for an additional and interactive Writing Workshop-based student model.

W Writing

Word Choice Read the following free verse aloud. Tell students to pay attention to the poet's word choice, especially the use of compound adjectives. Ask students to identify words that they feel were effective at expressing meaning or creating a strong visual image. *(Responses will vary.)* AS

Brokenhearted Friday nights
sitting by the phone.
Red-rimmed eyes,
family mustn't see.
Why don't you call, you jerk?
You promised. I believed.
Yet next week will be a carbon-copy duplicate.

What's wrong with me?
You can't see me but I see you.
Your velvet-soft eyes on math.
Why don't they look at me?
You say funny things at lunch.
I'm too far away to hear.
If I wrote my name in neon pink,
Would you know I exist?

Differentiated Instruction

Concept Mapping Some students may more easily recall and organize details about their personal experience if they use a concept map like the one here. Using an invented situation or one from your personal experience, model how to use this map. EL BL

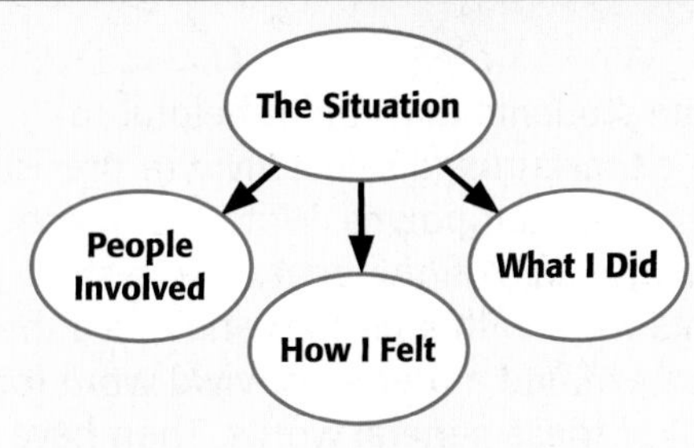

Indiana English/Language Arts Academic Standards
SE: 8.4, 8.4.1, 8.5.7
TWE: *English Language Coach* 8.1, *Differentiated Instruction* 8.4.1

Teach

W Writing

Word Choice Explain to students that a writer's word choice affects every aspect of his or her finished product. The goal in writing poetry is to paint a picture or express a feeling in a precise way. Poetry is more limiting than prose because of its form and length. By choosing precise words to describe, poets can bring a situation or feeling to life. Word choice does not involve only adjectives; students should also focus on precise verbs and nouns. After students review the *How Do I Do It?* section on the student page, have each student write five general sentences, such as "The dog was hungry" or "The day was hot." When students finish, have them trade papers with a partner and rewrite the sentences, using precise words. *(Responses will vary.)* Invite students to share examples of their work. AS

Assess

Have students read the first draft of their poem to a partner. Ask partners to constructively critique each other's writing. After a few minutes, have students assess their own poems, make any needed revisions, and save their revised poems for later use.

Applying Good Writing Traits

Word Choice

Good poems say a lot in only a few words. How do poets make their writing so powerful? They choose their words *very* carefully.

What Is Word Choice?

Word choice is the use of specific, vivid words that express the writer's ideas clearly.

Why Is Word Choice Important?

Words carry the writer's ideas into the reader's mind. That's why a writer must choose the right words—the ones that say what the writer intends to say. In a good poem, every word helps readers "see" and feel what the writer saw and felt.

The words in the sentence below do not help readers see or feel anything. The sentence tells what happened, but it doesn't "paint" a clear picture.

It was snowing.

Compare that sentence with the sentence below.

Giant, wet snowflakes raced toward the ground in a fury.

That's better! Specific, vivid words like *giant, wet, raced,* and *fury* create a clear picture of what happened—and how the writer felt about it.

How Do I Do It?

Think carefully about the words you choose.

- Replace general verbs with more specific ones. For example, replace *go* with *glide* or *rush.* Replace *look* with *glance* or *peek.*
- Use adjectives and adverbs. Instead of saying *The chair was ugly,* try saying *The purple, green, and orange chair was spectacularly ugly.* W
- Use specific nouns. Replace general nouns like *thing* with words that specifically name the person, place, or thing, as in the second item in each pair below: *dog / chihuahua; car / convertible; house / mansion.*
- Use words that appeal to the five senses; for example, *The air smelled fresh, and the snow tasted cold and grainy.*

Write to Learn Copy the sentence below. Then rewrite it, replacing each word (except *the*) with a word or phrase that means about the same thing. Now rewrite the sentence again, making it even more specific and interesting but keeping the same basic meaning as the original sentence.

The storm hit us hard.

Analyzing Cartoons Mom can't find the right word to use after Grimm breaks the lamp. What would be a good word for her to use—clumsy, careless? Explain your word choice.

Additional Support

English Language Coach

Use Word References: Thesaurus Some students may find it helpful to use a thesaurus to select vivid or precise words for their poems. Write *like, pretty, bad,* and *nice* on the board. Have students work with a partner and use a thesaurus to find a precise or vivid word for each of these general words. Then have them write two sentences using two of the words written on the board. Finally, have them replace those two words with synonyms they found in the thesaurus. Discuss with students how using precise words affects the meaning of the sentences. EL BL

Grammar Link

Subject-Verb Agreement with Compound Subjects

What Is It?

Subject-verb agreement is using the verb form that matches, or agrees with, the subject.

Compound subjects are two or more persons, places, or things joined by *and, neither/nor, or,* or *either/or*.

Subjects joined by *and*: Kurt and I like burritos.

Subjects joined by *neither/nor*: Neither the restaurant nor the cafeteria serves enchiladas.

Subjects joined by *or*: Beef or pork goes well with beans.

Why Is It Important?

Many readers (and listeners) notice errors in subject-verb agreement. To be clear and correct, you need to know and follow standard rules of subject-verb agreement.

How Do I Do It?

Find the compound subject, see what word joins the subjects, and then apply the right rule.

1. **Subjects joined by *and*:** If the subjects joined by *and* refer to different people, places, or things, the subject is plural, or equal to *they*.
   - Grammar and spelling count.

     (*Grammar and spelling* are two different things. The compound subject is plural, or equal to *they*, so the verb should not end in *-s*.)

   If the subjects joined by *and* refer to the same person, place, or thing, the compound subject is singular, or equal to *he, she,* or *it*.
   - The winner and new champion speaks three languages!

     (Both *winner* and *new champion* refer to the same person. The compound subject is singular, or equal to *he* or *she*, so the verb must end in *-s*.)
2. **Subjects joined by *neither/nor, or, either/or*:** The verb agrees with the subject that is closer to it.
   - Neither Ellie nor her sisters speak Spanish.

     (*Sisters* is the subject that is closer to the verb. *Sisters* is equal to *they*, so the verb should not end in *-s*.)
   - Neither the sisters nor Ellie speaks Spanish.

     (Now *Ellie* is the subject that is closer to the verb. *Ellie* is equal to *she*, so the verb should end in *-s*.)

Grammar Practice

On a separate sheet of paper, write the compound subject and the correct verb form for each sentence.

1. Mariah and her brother (is, are) throwing an anniversary party for their parents.
2. Neither their mother nor their father (knows, know) about it.
3. Pizza and ice cream (is, are) on the menu.
4. Strawberries and cream (is, are) their favorite flavor of ice cream.
5. You or I (am, is, are) in charge of decorations.

Writing Application Look over the subjects and verbs in your poem. Make sure they all agree.

Looking Ahead

You'll use what you've written and learned in Part 2!

WRITING WORKSHOP PART 1

Grammar Link

Subject-Verb Agreement with Compound Subjects

Review the rules for making compound subjects and verbs agree. Tell students not to be thrown off by intervening prepositional phrases when making their verbs agree with their subjects: for example, The cat and the dogs on the poster *are* very cute. Point out that the word *poster* is the object of the preposition, not the subject of the sentence. The subject is *the cat and the dogs*, so it requires a plural verb. Give students additional examples if they find this concept confusing. **AS**

Grammar Practice

1. Mariah and her brother; are
2. Neither their mother nor their father; knows
3. Pizza and ice cream; are
4. Strawberries and cream; is
5. You or I; am

Differentiated Instruction

Editing and Proofreading Make sure English language learners have a firm grasp on subject-verb agreement with compound subjects and with simple subjects. Then have these students review their writing folders and Learner's Notebooks. Tell students to reread their own writing, looking specifically for subject-verb agreement. When students find errors, they should circle them and write a correction at the side of the paper. Review students' work to make sure they have a solid comprehension of subject-verb agreement. **EL**

Indiana English/Language Arts Academic Standards
SE: 8.4.9, 8.6
TWE: *English Language Coach* 8.5.6; *Differentiated Instruction* 8.4.7, 8.6.4

Evaluating

Teaching Students to Evaluate

Why Is It Important?

- Evaluating is making a judgment or forming an opinion about a text. Students will learn that they can evaluate a character, the author's craft, or the quality of the information in a text.
- Evaluating helps students become wise readers. For example, they can judge whether an author is qualified to speak about a topic or whether the author's points make sense. They can also avoid being misled by what they read.
- Evaluating will also help students make good decisions about situations in their daily lives, such as what to listen to or watch or read next.

How to Help Students Get It

- Is this character realistic and believable? Are the feelings and events in the story or poem realistic and believable?
- Does the author use language, tone, and style that keep you interested in the characters and plot?
- Is this author qualified to write about this subject? Is this author biased? Does this author present opinions as facts?

Reading to Answer the Big Question

Mother to Son by Langston Hughes
A mother describes her life to her son; it has not been an easy life, and sometimes it has been unpleasant. She urges her son to keep going, and never give up, no matter what. Even if you don't know what to do, keep climbing.

Harlem by Langston Hughes
This landmark poem asks "What happens to a dream deferred?" It questions the reader directly, forcing one to consider one's own dreams, and what is being done to further them. How will you keep your dreams from being put off?

Sittin' on the Dock of the Bay by Steve Cropper and Otis Redding
These song lyrics describe a lazy, unconcerned day spent watching the ships come and go. The singer realizes he can't do all the things everybody tells him he should, so instead he will just rest awhile. Rather than do something, he chooses to do nothing.

Workshop Resources

Pacing (Days) Standard	Block	Lesson	Student Materials	Teacher Resources
1	1/2	Key Skill Lesson: Evaluating	Key Reading Skills Practice, p. 16 English Language Coach Review, p. 41	Bellringer Options Transparencies – Daily Language Practice 36 – Selection Focus 9 Read Aloud, Think Aloud Transparencies – Read Aloud, Think Aloud 31–32 – Key Reading Skills 9 Presentation Plus!
1	1	"Mother to Son" "Harlem"	Glencoe Online Unit Vocabulary Review, p. 39 Academic Vocabulary Review, p. 43 English Language Coach Active Reading Graphic Organizer, p. 18 Literary Analysis, p. 17 StudentWorks Plus™ Online Student Edition Literature Classics Selection and Unit Assessments, p. 39	Literary and Text Analysis Transparencies 6 Puzzlemaker Skill Level Up!™ A Language Arts Game BookLink 3 Assessment by Learning Objective (Diagnostic and Formative) Interactive Tutor: Self-Assessment TeacherWorks Plus™
1		"Sittin' on the Dock of the Bay"	Glencoe Online Unit Vocabulary Review, p. 39 Academic Vocabulary Review, p. 43 English Language Coach Active Reading Graphic Organizer, p. 20 StudentWorks Plus™ Online Student Edition Literature Classics Selection and Unit Assessments, p. 40	Literary and Text Analysis Transparencies 29 Puzzlemaker Skill Level Up!™ A Language Arts Game BookLink 3 Assessment by Learning Objective (Diagnostic and Formative) Interactive Tutor: Self-Assessment TeacherWorks Plus™

Keys for Unit Resource

- Blackline Master
- Workbook
- Supplemental Text
- CD-ROM
- DVD
- Transparency
- Web-based
- Fast File

Level Appropriate Code

AS = Activities for all students
AL = Activities for students working above grade level
OL = Activities for students working at grade level
BL = Activities for students working below grade level
EL = Activities for English language learners

Focus

BELLRINGER Options

- **Selection Focus Transparency 9**
- **Daily Language Practice Transparency 36**

Focus Activity Say: Think about a movie that you've seen that you thought was really bad. What made you think so? *(Responses will vary.)* **Say:** Now think of a really good movie. What made it good? *(Responses will vary.)* **Say:** When you determine something is bad or good, you are making an evaluation. AS

Teach

R Reading Skill

Evaluating Ask: What might you evaluate during the school day? *(Possible responses: a book that you've read for class; a classmate's project presentation; the lunch menu)* AS

Analyzing the Cartoon

Say: The cartoon characters prefer the film version of the story to the book. Why? *(Possible response: They prefer it because of its detail. The joke is that the kid does not read any of the details in the book.)* OL

READING WORKSHOP 2

Skills Focus

You will practice these skills when you read the following selections:

- "Mother to Son," p. 472
- "Harlem," p. 473
- "Sittin' on the Dock of the Bay," p. 478

Reading

- Evaluating poems and song lyrics

Literature

- Understanding similes and metaphors
- Understanding song lyrics

Vocabulary

- Learning to recognize dialect and levels of diction
- Academic Vocabulary: *evaluate*

Writing/Grammar

- Understanding subject-verb agreement

Indiana English/ Language Arts Academic Standards (pp. 468–469)

8.3 Comprehension and Analysis of Literary Text Respond to grade-level-appropriate literature...

For a complete description of the standards, see p. IN 11.

Skill Lesson

Evaluating

Learn It!

R **What Is It?** To **evaluate** something is to look at it carefully in order to judge its value, or strengths and weaknesses. Before you buy a new CD, you might listen to some of the songs or discuss them with your friends. That way you can form an opinion about the quality of the CD beforehand. In much the same way, you can evaluate something you read.

For example, you might evaluate

- how believable the characters in a selection are
- whether the way characters speak rings true
- whether an author gives convincing reasons to share his or her opinions

Analyzing Cartoons
The kids in this cartoon evaluate, or make a judgment about, the book they just read. What influenced the opinion they formed?

Academic Vocabulary

evaluate (ih VAL yoo ayt) *v.* form an opinion or make a judgment

Additional Support

Differentiated Instruction

Harlem Renaissance Tell students they will be reading poetry by Langston Hughes, one of the best-known authors of the Harlem Renaissance. The Harlem Renaissance took place in the early 1900s and peaked around 1920 in the Harlem area of New York City. African American authors, singers, and artists emerged with a strong voice to begin what was first called the New Negro Movement. Later it became known as the Harlem Renaissance because it was a rebirth of the art and culture of a particular group of people. Have students research the Harlem Renaissance, and have each student give a brief report on one aspect of the art and literature movement. AL

Why Is It Important? Making judgments and forming your opinions help you get more out of what you read. When you evaluate, you also pay attention to how well the selection was written.

Literature Online

Study Central Visit www.glencoe.com and click on Study Central to review evaluating.

How Do I Do It? Set standards for judgment, called *criteria.* For example, you might use these criteria to judge a poem.

- **Language:** Does the poet use descriptive words and phrases that appeal to your senses? Does the poet use figurative language, such as similes or metaphors? Are these figures of speech fresh and imaginative? L
- **Sound Effects:** Does the poet use rhythm and rhyme well? What other sound effects are in the poem? Are they effective? R
- **Theme and Content:** Did you enjoy the poem? Did it make you think about the subject in a different way? Why or why not?

Here's how a student evaluated part of an Emily Dickinson poem about the first steam-engine trains. Read it and the student's evaluation of it.

from **I Like to See It**

I like to see it lap the miles,
And lick the valleys up,
And stop to feed itself at tanks;
And then, prodigious, step

I like how the poem makes the train seem alive. That makes me see trains in a whole new way. I also like the "music" in the poem. "Step" and "stop" sound good together because they begin and end with the same sounds; and "like," "lap," and "lick" go together because they all start with the sound of "l."

Practice It!

Use the criteria to form your own judgment about the selection from the Emily Dickinson poem.

Use It!

As you read "Mother to Son," "Harlem," and "Sittin' on the Dock of the Bay," use the criteria to evaluate the selections.

Reading in the Real World

Citizenship One of our civic duties as citizens of the United States is to serve on a jury. Members of a jury are asked to evaluate evidence to decide whether a case should go to court or whether someone is guilty of a crime. Jury members receive written and verbal instructions from the court about making fair and honest evaluations. Based on these guidelines and the evidence presented, they make their decision. Have students search the Internet or library for information about serving on a jury and the rules that apply to jury duty. OL AL

Teach

Literature Online

Study Central Have students access the Web site to review evaluating and to complete a related activity.

R Reading Skill

Evaluating Say: Read the *How Do I Do It?* section of the page. Then make your own set of criteria for evaluating poetry. Use the bulleted points mentioned and add others that you think are relevant. *(Responses will vary.)* OL AL

L Literary Element

Figurative Language—Metaphor and Simile Say: The student said that the poem on this page used language that made the train seem alive. What living creature did you picture from the poet's words? *(Students' responses will vary, but will most likely refer to an animal, such as a cat or horse.)* AS

Resources for page 469

- Use Key Reading Skills Transparency 9 in *Read Aloud, Think Aloud* to help students practice evaluating.

Indiana English/Language Arts Academic Standards
SE: 8.3
TWE: *Differentiated Instruction* 8.7.12, *Reading in the Real World* 8.2

Teach

More About the Author

Not all African Americans of the time liked Langston Hughes's poetry. They objected to his use of jazz, the blues, and dialect. Nevertheless, many admired Hughes's ability to translate his own experiences into those all people could understand. His work includes the poetry collections *The Weary Blues* and *Fine Clothes to the Jew,* novels such as *Not Without Laughter* and *The Big Sea,* as well as weekly newspaper columns and a Broadway musical. Hughes is buried in Harlem, whose story he told so well.

EL Language Coach

Dialect **Ask:** Why might reading dialect be difficult for some people? *(Possible response: They may not have heard that particular way of speaking before.)* **Ask:** Why do you think Langston Hughes used dialect in his poetry? *(Possible response: He wanted it to sound real—the way people actually spoke.)* OL

Before You Read

Mother to Son *and* Harlem

Meet the Author

Langston Hughes was born in Joplin, Missouri, in 1902. As a young man, he traveled around the world and held many jobs. He drew on his experiences when he wrote. But it was his experience as an African American that allowed him to create powerful poems, short stories, and plays about African American life. See page R3 of the Author Files for more on Hughes.

Author Resources For more about Langston Hughes, go to www.glencoe.com.

Indiana English/Language Arts Academic Standards (pp. 470–473)

8.3.6 Identify significant literary devices, such as metaphor...and dialect...and use those elements to interpret a work. **8.3 Comprehension and Analysis of Literary Text** Respond to grade-level-appropriate literature... **8.1.1** Analyze idioms and comparisons...to infer literal and figurative meanings...

For a complete description of the standards, see p. IN 11.

Vocabulary Preview

deferred (dih FURD) *adj.* set aside or put off until a later time **(p. 473)** *Because the store didn't allow deferred payments, she had to pay for the new chair right away.*

fester (FES tur) *v.* to rot; to decay **(p. 473)** *Carefully wash and wrap the cut so that it does not fester.*

Write to Learn In your Learner's Notebook, write a sentence for each vocabulary word.

English Language Coach

Dialect Have you ever listened closely to the way people speak in different parts of the country? Or even in different neighborhoods? Even when we all speak English, sometimes the *way* we speak it differs from place to place. These differences make up dialects.

EL A **dialect** is the special form of language spoken by a particular group of people. Dialects sound different from Standard English. To imitate a dialect, writers may drop letters in words (*nothin'* for *nothing*), respell words (*ole* for *old*), or combine words (*don'tcha* for *don't you*). A dialect may suggest where a character comes from, what social group he or she belongs to, and what kind of education he or she has had.

You'll see the following examples of dialect in "Mother to Son." Notice the differences between the dialect and Standard English.

Dialect	Standard English
I'se been a-climbin' on	I've been climbing
And reachin' landin's	And reaching landings

Small Group Talk With a small group of classmates, talk about ways in which people in your part of the country talk. What distinguishes your way of talking from the way people in other parts of the country talk? Try to write a sentence or two in a local dialect.

Additional Support

Author Search To expand students' appreciation of Langston Hughes, have them access the Web site for additional information and resources.

Literature Focus Lesson

Speaker Explain to students that the speaker in a poem is like a narrator in a story. The words of the poem come from the speaker. Direct students' attention to the sample of dialect from "Mother to Son." Ask students to describe the speaker from the lines given. *(Possible responses: The speaker is likely African American and from the South. Given the title, the speaker is likely a mother.)* Tell students to pay attention to the speaker of each poem, and remind them that the speaker cannot always be equated with the author. OL

Skills Preview

Key Reading Skill: Evaluating

R To evaluate poetry, you need criteria–standards by which to judge whether the poem is effective. A list of criteria for judging poetry is on page 469.

Whole-Class Discussion What criteria would you add, subtract, or rewrite? As a class, review the list on page 469. Tailor it to your interests and needs.

Key Literary Element: Figurative Language–Metaphor and Simile

L **Figurative language** is descriptive language that is not to be taken literally. Suppose that a friend says, "That test was a piece of cake." You know that the test was not *actually* a piece of cake. Your friend is using a **metaphor** (MEH tuh for)–a direct comparison between very different things that are similar in some important way. Just as eating a piece of cake is easy, so is taking a test that is not difficult.

If the friend had said, "Taking that test was as easy as eating a piece of cake," she would be using a **simile** (SIM uh lee)–an indirect comparison that contains the word *like* or *as.*

As you read "Mother to Son" and "Harlem," look for metaphors and similes. Ask yourself, *What comparisons are being made? Which are direct? Which contain the words* like *or* as?

Partner Talk With a classmate, analyze the metaphor and simile below. For each, figure out what two things are compared and how they are similar.

Metaphor: Her smile was sunshine.

Simile: It was as cold as a snowman's toes.

Interactive Literary Elements Handbook
To review or learn more about the literary elements, go to www.glencoe.com.

Get Ready to Read

Connect to the Reading

Think about a dream you have for your future or a goal you've set for yourself. Now imagine that you meet with all sorts of problems that make it hard for you to achieve your dream or goal. Will you keep trying? If not, how do you think giving up would affect you? As you read "Mother to Son" and "Harlem," think about what each speaker says about dreams and goals.

Partner Talk With a partner, list qualities you think people must have to reach their goals.

Build Background

- Many of Langston Hughes's poems are about the African American experience in the first half of the 20th century. Though slavery had long been banned, African Americans still did not have the same rights as other U.S. citizens. Hughes addressed this inequality in his poetry. Sometimes he celebrates the strength and beauty of African American life. Other times he expresses frustration over the obstacles African Americans had to overcome.
- Hughes is often associated with Harlem, an African American community in New York City. During the 1920s, Harlem was at the center of African American life in the United States. Hughes gave the title "Harlem" to a poem you'll read. It's also published with the title "Dream Deferred."

Set Purposes for Reading

BIG Question Read the selections "Mother to Son" and "Harlem" to find out the importance of holding fast to your dreams despite obstacles in your path.

Set Your Own Purpose What else would you like to learn from these selections to help you answer the Big Question? Write your own purpose on the "Mother to Son" and "Harlem" page of Foldable 4.

Keep Moving

Use these skills as you read the following selections.

Teach

R Reading Skill

Evaluating **Ask:** Why is it important for you to evaluate what you read? *(Possible response: Evaluating helps you decide if you want to read other selections by the same author.)* OL

L Literary Element

Figurative Language–Metaphor and Simile **Ask:** How do similes and metaphors help readers visualize what the poet is describing? *(Possible response: Similes and metaphors often compare new ideas or images with things that are familiar.)* **Ask:** What simile could you write about someone who is close to you? *(Responses will vary.)* OL

Interactive Literary Elements Handbook Have students access the Web site to improve their understanding of figurative language–metaphor and simile.

Reading Fluency

Build Fluency Because dialect is unique to a region or a group of people, it can be challenging for some readers to pronounce or comprehend. Some students may benefit from reading along silently with a tape. Encourage students to first listen for pronunciation. Suggest that they listen to the tape a second time, if necessary, to clarify their understanding of difficult or unfamiliar words or expressions. Then allow students time to practice reading the dialect aloud on their own. AS

Indiana English/Language Arts Academic Standards
SE: 8.1.1, 8.3.6
TWE: *Literature Focus Lesson* 8.3, *Reading Fluency* 8.2

Teach

L Literary Element

Figurative Language—Metaphor and Simile **Ask:** What metaphor does the poet use to describe times when the speaker was unsure of what she was doing or what would happen next? *(Possible response: He compares not knowing what to do to "goin' in the dark.")* OL AL

R Reading Skill

Evaluating **Ask:** What advice does the mother give her son? *(She tells him to keep going even when times get tough. Never give up.)* **Ask:** Do you think that is good advice? *(Possible response: It is good advice because if a person keeps trying, he or she is likely to succeed.)* OL

BQ BIG Question

Ask: What did the mother decide to do when she didn't know what to do? *(Possible response: She kept going, even when life wasn't easy.)* OL

READING WORKSHOP 2

Mother to Son

by Langston Hughes

Survivor, 1978. Elizabeth Catlett. Linocut, 10 7/8 x 9 7/8 in. Armistad Research Center, Tulane University, New Orleans.

Well, son, I'll tell you:
Life for me ain't been no crystal stair. **1**
It's had tacks in it,
And splinters,
And boards torn up,
And places with no carpet on the floor—
Bare.
But all the time
I'se been a-climbin' on,
And reachin' landin's,
And turnin' corners,
And sometimes goin' in the dark
Where there ain't been no light. **2** L
So, boy, don't you turn back.
Don't you set down on the steps
'Cause you finds it kinder hard. R
Don't you fall now—
For I'se still goin', honey,
I'se still climbin', BQ
And life for me ain't been no crystal stair. **3** ❍

Practice the Skills

1 Key Literary Element

Figurative Language—Metaphor and Simile What is life being compared to? If life were a crystal stair, what would life be like?

2 English Language Coach

Dialect Do you have any trouble understanding the dialect? If so, read it aloud.

3 Key Reading Skill

Evaluating Is the mother's advice to her son believable? Do you think it's something a mother might actually say to her son? Why or why not?

Additional Support

Differentiated Instruction

Visual Imagery Chart To picture a poet's descriptions, some students may benefit from using a chart such as the one below. Using it will help students analyze how the images appeal to the reader's senses. Help students fill in the first rows, and then have them record any other striking descriptions they encounter. EL BL

Image	Sense	Mental Picture
crystal stair	sight	sparkling; pretty; smooth; clear; wonderful
tacks	touch	hurt; *ouch*; stab; bleeding

READING WORKSHOP 2

by Langston Hughes

What happens to a dream **deferred**?

Does it dry up
like a raisin in the sun? **1**
Or **fester** like a sore— **L**
And then run?
Does it stink like rotten meat?
Or crust and sugar over—
like a syrupy sweet?

Maybe it just sags
like a heavy load. **2**

Or does it explode? **3** ❍

Portrait of Langston Hughes, 1902–1967, Poet. Winold Reiss (1886–1953). Pastel on artist board, 76.3 x 54.9 cm. National Portrait Gallery, Washington, DC.

Analyzing the Painting This painting of Langston Hughes shows what he looked like as a young man. How would you describe the mood of the painting? Why?

Vocabulary

deferred (dih FURD) *adj.* set aside or put off until a later time

fester (FES tur) *v.* to rot; to decay

Practice the Skills

1 Key Literary Element

Figurative Language–Metaphor and Simile Reread the first three lines of the poem. What two things are being compared? In what way are they similar?

2 Key Reading Skill

Evaluating In your opinion, does the poem effectively express what it's like to have to set aside your dreams? Explain.

3 BIG Question

Imagine that you don't know what to do with your life. You ask the speakers of "Mother to Son" and "Harlem" for advice. What do you think they would tell you? Write your answer on the "Mother and Son" and "Harlem" page of Foldable 4. Your response will help you answer the Unit Challenge later.

Teach

L Literary Element

Figurative Language–Metaphor and Simile **Ask:** What kind of figurative language does the author use in lines 4–5? *(simile)* **Ask:** How do you know? *(He makes a comparison, using the word like.)* **Ask:** What does he compare with this simile? *(He compares a "dream deferred" to a festering, running sore.)* **OL**

R Reading Skill

Evaluating **Ask:** Which comparison do you think is most effective? *(Responses will vary.)* **Ask:** Why? *(Students should support their responses with examples from the text.)* **OL**

Assess

Use the CheckPoint questions provided on Presentation Plus! to check for comprehension of the selections. These questions can be used with interactive response keypads for immediate student feedback.

Literature Focus Lesson

Literary Allusion Some authors use well-known phrases or characters from literature to describe an idea. Writer Lorraine Hansberry used Hughes's simile—*like a raisin in the sun*—as the title of her play about an African American family struggling to keep dreams alive despite discrimination. Have students obtain a copy of the play to read. You may wish to assign some students different parts to read aloud to the rest of the class. Then ask the entire class to write a short paragraph in their Learner's Notebooks evaluating how the play connects to the poem. **OL** **AL**

Indiana English/Language Arts Academic Standards
SE: 8.1.1, 8.3, 8.3.6
TWE: *Differentiated Instruction* 8.3, *Literature Focus Lesson* 8.3

Assess

Resources for page 474

- Selection Quick Check, p. 33
- Selection and Unit Assessment, p. 39
- ExamView Assessment Suite
- Interactive Tutor: Self-Assessment

Students can respond to the *After You Read* items in their Learner's Notebooks or on a separate sheet of paper.

Answering the BIG Question

1. Responses will vary.
2. Possible response: Keep going, through difficulty and uncertainty.
3. Possible response: A dream can shrivel like a grape dries into a raisin if left in the sun.

Critical Thinking

4. Possible response: She's a survivor who saw tough times *(the bare stair with tacks in it)* but didn't give up *(still goin')*. She loves her son and wants to encourage him *(Don't you set down on the steps, cause you finds it kinder hard)*.
5. Possible response: Both speakers know that obstacles can stand in the way of dreams.
6. Possible response: Keep climbing.
7. Possible response: To emphasize an emotion, possibly anger.
8. Possible response: Don't give up on your dreams or put them off.

Talk About Your Reading

Student responses will vary, although most suggestions for tone will probably focus on negative feelings (anger, hurt, lifelessness, frustration). Possible words to describe tone are *angry, frustrated, discouraged, bitter,* and *sad.*

After You Read

Mother to Son *and* Harlem

Answering the BIG Question

1. After reading "Mother to Son" and "Harlem," do you think you should follow a dream that seems impossible? Explain.
2. **Recall** What advice does the mother give in "Mother to Son"?
   TIP Right There
3. **Restate** In your own words, restate the first three lines of "Harlem."
   TIP On My Own

Critical Thinking

4. **Infer** What is the mother in "Mother to Son" like? Describe her, using evidence from the poem to back up your ideas.
   TIP Author and Me
5. **Compare and Contrast** How are the speakers in each poem alike? How are they different?
   TIP Author and Me
6. **Apply** Think about the mother's advice to her son. If he follows the advice, how will he act when the going gets tough?
   TIP Author and Me
7. **Analyze** Why do you think Hughes put the last line of "Harlem" in italics? How would the poem change if the italics were left out?
   TIP On My Own
8. **Synthesize** What do you think the mother in "Mother to Son" might say to the speaker in "Harlem"? Explain.
   TIP On My Own

Talk About Your Reading

Literature Groups With a small group of students, discuss the tone of "Harlem." If you could hear Langston Hughes read the poem, how do you think his voice would sound? Happy? Sad? Excited? Scared? Sarcastic? Angry? Something else? Take turns reading the poem with different tones of voice. Then decide as a group which tone best fits the poem. Support your opinion with evidence from the poem.

Indiana English/Language Arts Academic Standards (pp. 474–475)

8.3 Comprehension and Analysis of Literary Text Respond to grade-level-appropriate literature... **8.7.7** Analyze oral interpretations of literature... **8.1.1** Analyze idioms and comparisons...to infer literal and figurative meanings... **8.6 English Language Conventions** Sentence structure

For a complete description of the standards, see p. IN 11.

Skills Review

Key Reading Skill: Evaluating

9. Did you enjoy reading "Mother to Son" and "Harlem"? Why or Why not?

10. Did the poems make you look at life in a new way? Explain.

Key Literary Element: Figurative Language–Metaphor and Simile

11. In "Mother to Son," stairs are a metaphor for life. In what way are stairs and life alike?

12. There are five similes in "Harlem." List three of the five things that a "dream deferred" is compared to, and explain what each simile means.

Vocabulary Check

On a separate piece of paper, write "T" if a sentence is true or "F" if it is false. Rewrite any false sentence to make it true.

13. When you defer an action, you do it immediately.

14. When sores fester, they are healed.

15. **Academic Vocabulary** What does it mean to evaluate something you are reading?

16. **English Language Coach** Rewrite lines 15–20 of "Mother to Son" in Standard English. Look at the two versions—your Standard English version and Hughes's version in dialect. Which do you think is better and why?

Web Activities For eFlashcards, Selection Quick Checks, and other Web activities, go to www.glencoe.com.

Grammar Link: Agreement When Subjects Are Separated from Verbs

Subject-verb agreement can be tricky when the subject and verb of a sentence are separated from each other. In cases like this, you may wonder what the real subject of the sentence is. For example, in the sentence below is the subject *one* or *books?*

- One of the books (is, are) missing.

Here's a hint: *Subjects and predicates do not appear in prepositional phrases.* If you mentally leave out the prepositional phrase from the sentence, the real subject becomes easier to find.

One ~~of the books~~ (is, are) missing.
prepositional phrase

Once the prepositional phrase is omitted, it's easy to see that the subject is *one.* Because the subject is *one,* the right verb form is *is.*

Grammar Practice

On a separate piece of paper, copy the sentences below. Cross out the prepositional phrase that separates the subject and verb in each sentence. Underline the subject once and the correct verb form twice.

17. The presents for my grandmother (is, are) on the table in the back of the dining room.

18. One of the gifts (is, are) handmade.

19. The gifts from my sister (has, have) red bows.

20. The cookies on the tray (is, are) for Grandma.

21. The card with all the signatures (is, are) from the whole family.

22. The cupcakes with chocolate icing (tastes, taste) the best.

23. My grandmother's friends in Arizona always (calls, call) her on her birthday.

Grammar Link: Agreement When Subjects Are Separated from Verbs

Grammar Practice

17. The presents ~~for my grandmother~~ are on the table in the back of the dining room.

18. One ~~of the gifts~~ is handmade.

19. The gifts ~~from my sister~~ have red bows.

20. The cookies ~~on the tray~~ are for Grandma.

21. The card ~~with all the signatures~~ is from the whole family.

22. The cupcakes ~~with chocolate icing~~ taste the best.

23. My grandmother's friends ~~in Arizona~~ always call her on her birthday.

Key Reading Skill: Evaluating

9. Responses will vary.

10. Responses will vary.

Key Literary Element: Figurative Language–Metaphor and Simile

11. In both stairs and life, you must take steps to make progress.

12. a raisin; a running sore; rotten meat; a syrupy sweet; a heavy load

Vocabulary Check

13. F: When you defer an action, you put it off until later.

14. F: When sores fester, they need attention.

Academic Vocabulary

15. To evaluate a selection is to judge its value and identify its strengths and weaknesses.

English Language Coach

16. Possible response: Don't sit down on the steps because you find it kind of hard. Don't fall now—for I'm still going, honey, I'm still climbing, and life for me hasn't been a crystal stair. Without the dialect, it's harder to imagine the social and economic background of the mother and her struggle.

Close

Ask students to summarize what they learned from Langston Hughes's poems to answer the Big Question.

Indiana English/Language Arts Academic Standards
SE: 8.1.1, 8.3, 8.3.6, 8.7.7

Teach

More About the Author

Otis Redding's life had its own set of obstacles. He dropped out of high school to join a band so he could help support his family. He often competed in talent shows for a first prize of five dollars. But after winning fifteen times in a row, Redding was no longer allowed to compete. A fan of the Beatles, he listened to their music constantly for inspiration. It was, however, Redding's hard work and songwriting genius that helped him fulfill his dream. Three of his songs alone sold more than 3.5 million records.

EL Language Coach

Dialect Say: Why do you think teens communicate differently with each other than they do with their parents? *(Responses will vary.)* **Ask:** What other family members may have different vocabularies? *(Possible responses: very young children; grandparents; relatives who speak English as a second language)* **OL**

Before You Read

Sittin' on the Dock of the Bay

Otis Redding

Meet the Author

Otis Redding was a talented soul singer. He was born in Dawson, Georgia, in 1941. Redding wrote many of his own songs, but sometimes he collaborated with Steve Cropper of the band Booker T and the MGs. His most famous song, "Sittin' on the Dock of the Bay," which he wrote with Cropper, was recorded three days before he died in a plane crash. He was only 26.

Author Search for more about Otis Redding, go to www.glencoe.com.

Indiana English/Language Arts Academic Standards (pp. 476–479)

8.3.6 Identify significant literary devices, such as...dialect... **8.3 Comprehension and Analysis of Literary Text** Respond to grade-level-appropriate literature...**8.3.1** Determine...purposes and characteristics of different forms of poetry...

For a complete description of the standards, see p. IN 11.

Vocabulary Preview

dock (dok) *n.* a platform where boats land at the edge of a body of water **(p. 479)** *He sat on the dock waiting for the boat to return from the sea.*

roamed (rohmd) *v.* wandered; went from place to place without purpose or direction; form of the verb *roam* **(p. 479)** *He roamed the United States just looking and dreaming.*

Write to Learn In your Learner's Notebook, write a sentence for each vocabulary word. Be sure to use the words correctly.

English Language Coach

EL

Dialect and Word Choice A **dialect** is a form of language spoken by the people in a particular group. Dialect influences not only how a person pronounces words but also what words he or she uses. For example, in the northeastern part of the United States some people say that they sit on their front *stoop* in the summer. In the Midwest, however, most people would say that they sit on their front *porch.* Of course, not everyone in the same region of the United States speaks exactly the same dialect.

Many other factors go into a person's dialect and word choice. How old a person is, what kind of education the person has had, which social groups the person belongs to—all these factors and many others shape how a person talks and what words he or she uses. Authors are aware of differences in dialects and use those differences to help show what characters are like.

Partner Talk Do teens express themselves the same way as their parents? Do they use different words? With a classmate discuss some of these differences. Then write a short conversation between a teenager and a parent in which each person's choice of words reflects who he or she is. Here are some ideas for conversations:

- a talk in which a parent and a teenager describe the kind of music each of them likes best
- a chat between a parent and a teenager about the latest video games
- a discussion in which a parent and a teenager talk about their favorite movies

Additional Support

Author Search To expand students' appreciation of Otis Redding, have them access the Web site for additional information and resources.

Literature Focus Lesson

Chorus Otis Redding's song shows how songwriters use repetition to convey meaning. A chorus is a group of lines that are repeated after each verse. The chorus usually states the main idea of the song. Then the verses provide explanations or support for this main idea. By repeating the chorus, the songwriter is able to emphasize his or her point. Have students choose a favorite song and copy or print its lyrics from the Internet. Have students identify the chorus, its main idea, and the explanations included in the various verses. Tell students to use this technique to analyze the upcoming selection. **OL AL**

Skills Preview

Key Reading Skill: Evaluating

R1

Although you may not have thought of it, song lyrics are closely tied to poetry. How would you go about evaluating lyrics to a song?

On Your Own What do you think a good song should communicate to listeners? Write your ideas in your Learner's Notebook.

Literary Element: Lyrics

Lyrics are words set to music. In fact, the word *lyrics* is tied to music. The term comes from the ancient Greek word *lyra,* which refers to a musical instrument that is similar to a harp. Lyrics also have much in common with poetry. Like poetry, lyrics may have these elements:

- repeated lines
- rhyming words
- a set rhythm, or "beat"
- figurative language such as similes and metaphors

As you read the lyrics to "Sittin' on the Dock of the Bay," pay attention to the rhythm of the lines, and look to see which phrases and lines are repeated. Ask yourself, *What is the "beat"? Which lines are repeated and to what effect?*

Small Group Discussion With a small group of classmates, think of the lyrics to a song that everyone knows and that is appropriate to discuss in class. What "poetic" elements do the lyrics contain: Rhythm? Figurative language? Rhyme? Repetition? Make a list of elements, give an example from the lyrics of each element, and then discuss what the elements add to the lyrics.

Interactive Literary Elements Handbook
To review or learn more about the literary elements, go to www.glencoe.com.

Get Ready to Read

Connect to the Reading

R2

"I don't know what to do." Think about a time in your life when you felt that way. Did you get different advice from your family and friends? How did you decide which advice to follow? As you read "Sittin' on the Dock of the Bay," think about how it feels not to have a clear direction in life.

Write to Learn In your Learner's Notebook, jot down some notes about a time you couldn't figure out what to do. Explain what you finally decided to do and why.

Build Background

The song lyrics you are about to read tell about a man who travels from his home in Georgia to California. Traditionally, California is a place where people go to start over or make their fortunes.

- Otis Redding wrote the lyrics on a houseboat in Sausalito, California, a beautiful city located in the San Francisco Bay Area near the north end of the Golden Gate Bridge.
- Sausalito has one of the few ungated marinas in the Bay area, so people can feel free to relax there and enjoy the view.

Set Purposes for Reading

BIG Question Read the selection "Sittin' on the Dock of the Bay" to find out how it feels for someone who doesn't know what to do.

Set Your Own Purpose What else would you like to learn from this selection for help in answering the Big Question? Write your own purpose on the "Sittin' on the Dock of the Bay" page of Foldable 4.

Keep Moving

Use these skills as you read the following selection.

Teach

R1 Reading Skill

Evaluating Say: Write a list of the ways you evaluate poetry, such as examining the content, the form, and the literary devices. You can use the same criteria to evaluate song lyrics. In addition, you can also evaluate the music that accompanies the lyrics. Discuss how you might evaluate the music. *(Responses will vary.)* OL AL

R2 Reading Skill

Review Connecting Say: Recall a time in your life when you were tempted to just give up and stop trying because you thought nothing you did would make a difference. How were you convinced to hang in there and try to do your best? *(Responses will vary.)* AS

Interactive Literary Elements Handbook Have students access the Web site to improve their understanding of lyrics.

Differentiated Instruction

Rhyme and Rhythm Write the limerick below on the board. Read it aloud, emphasizing the stressed syllables as you read.

I once saw an elephant fly.
It soared straight up to the sky.
It got a huge itch,
And started to twitch,
And fell in a heap. My, oh, my!

Invite students to clap the rhythm as you read it again. Ask them to name the rhyming words. EL BL
Have students work in groups to write animal limericks, using the starter *I once saw. . . .* OL

Indiana English/Language Arts Academic Standards
SE: 8.3.1, 8.3.6
TWE: *Literature Focus Lesson* 8.3.1, *Differentiated Instruction* 8.3.1

Teach

Viewing the Photo

Say: This photo shows the San Francisco Bay with the Golden Gate Bridge in the background. Why might a spot near water like the one in the photo be a good place to think when you're not sure what to do? *(Possible response: Water is calming, quiet, and pretty.)* **Ask:** How does this photo illustrate the song lyrics? *(It shows the San Francisco Bay, the setting of the song.)* AS

READING WORKSHOP 2

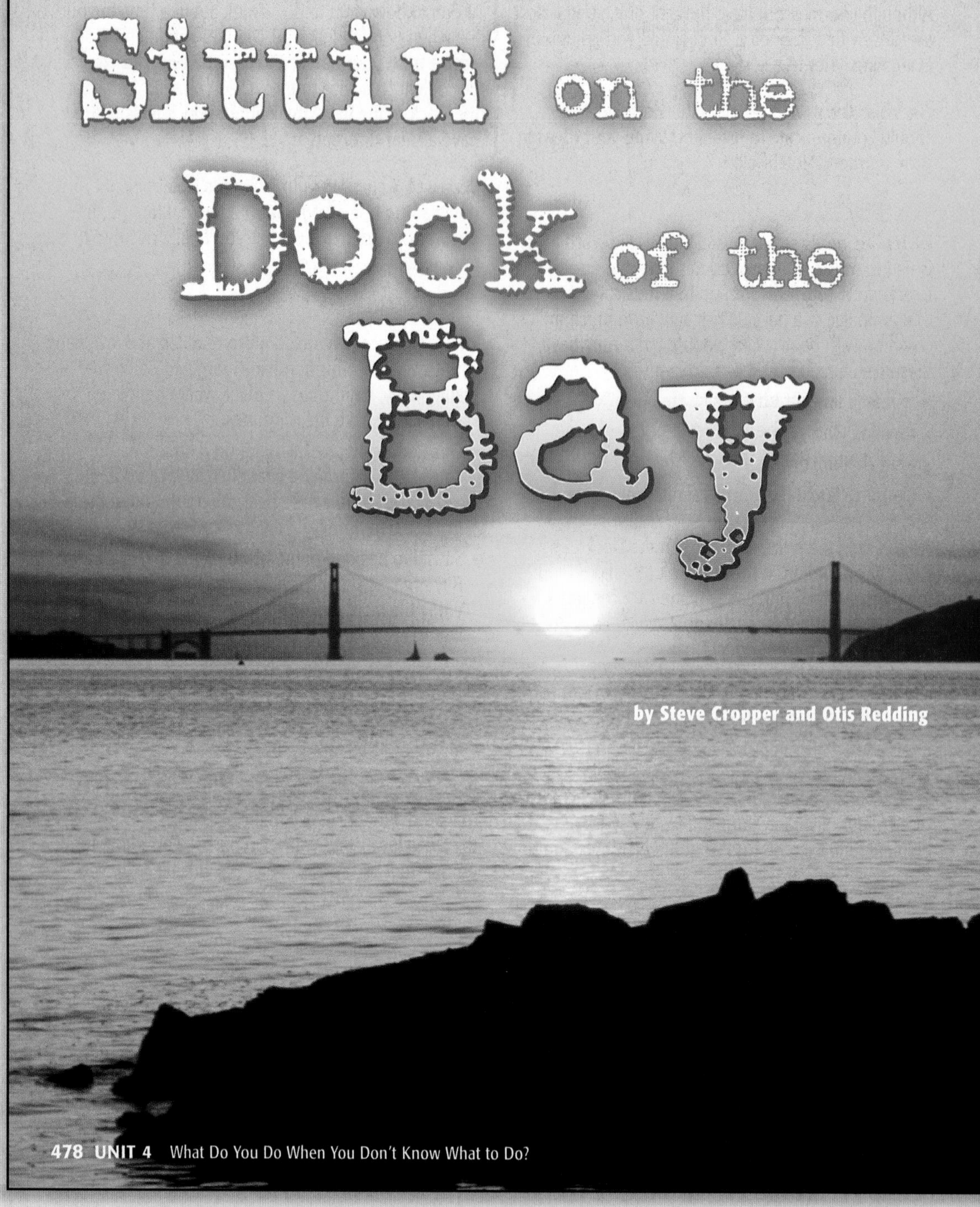

Sittin' on the Dock of the Bay

by Steve Cropper and Otis Redding

Additional Support

Reading in the Real World

Careers Students who enjoy music may be interested in learning more about the careers of songwriter and performer. Have student partners use the Internet to research job benefits (such as travel, fame, compensation), as well as skills, education, training, and other requirements for a musical career. Have students write a brief explanation of what it takes to succeed in a musical career, identifying all the skills needed. Invite students to share their research with the rest of the class. OL AL

Sittin' in the morning sun,
I'll be sittin' when the evening comes,
Watching the ships roll in.
Then I watch 'em roll away again, yeah.
I'm sittin' on the **dock** of the bay,
Watching that tide* roll in,
Just sittin' on the dock of the bay wastin'
time. **1**

I left my home in Georgia; **2**
Headed for the Frisco* Bay.
I had nothing to live for.
Looks like nothing's gonna come my way,
So I'm just sittin' on the dock of the bay,
Watching the tide roll in.
I'm sittin' on the dock of the bay
wastin' time. **3**

Looks like nothing's gonna change;
Everything still remains the same.
I can't do what ten people tell me to do,
So I guess I'll remain the same.
Just sittin' here resting my bones.
And this loneliness won't leave me alone;
This 2,000 miles I **roamed**, just to make this dock my home
Now I'm sittin' on the dock of the bay,
Watching the tide roll in. **4**
Sittin' on the dock of the bay wastin' time. **5** ❍

6 The ***tide*** is the rise and fall of the ocean that occurs about every twelve hours.
9 ***Frisco*** is short for San Francisco.

Vocabulary

dock (dok) *n.* a platform where boats land at the edge of a body of water

roamed (rohmd) *v.* wandered; went from place to place without purpose or direction

Practice the Skills

1 English Language Coach

Dialect and Word Choice This song is not written in dialect, but it spells out many elements of pronunciation that are found in American dialects. Make notes of some of them in your Learner's Notebook.

2 Reviewing Skills

Connecting Have you ever left a place you were familiar with to try something new? How did it feel? Explain.

3 Literary Element

Lyrics Which lines in the lyrics are repeated? What does the repetition add to the lyrics?

4 Key Reading Skill

Evaluating How successful is the song at getting a message across and creating a mood?

5 BIG Question

Think about how the speaker of these lyrics feels about his life. What do you think he would say about the importance of choosing a direction even if you don't exactly know what to do with your life? Write your answer on the "Sittin' on the Dock of the Bay" page of Foldable 4. Your response will help you complete the Unit Challenge later.

READING WORKSHOP 2

Teach

EL Language Coach

Dialect Say: Read line 11, containing the word *gonna.* What two words does this word combine? *(going to)* **Ask:** What other shortened words combine two words? *(Possible responses: wanna, hafta, dontcha)* **OL**

C Critical Thinking

Analysis Say: Reread the second stanza. How would you describe the speaker's life experiences? *(Possible response: He's lonely and few positive things have happened to him.)* **Ask:** Which lines support your answer? *(Possible response: I had nothing to live for./Looks like nothing's gonna come my way)* **OL AL**

Assess

Use the CheckPoint questions provided on Presentation Plus! to check for comprehension of the selection. These questions can be used with interactive response keypads for immediate student feedback.

Differentiated Instruction

Evaluating Music Have students consult their lists of criteria for evaluating music from page 477, if they participated in this activity. If not, have them complete this activity now to prepare for evaluating music. Then play a recording of "Sittin' on the Dock of the Bay" for students. You might play it two or three times so students get a good sense of the song and its performance. Finally, have students use their lists of criteria to evaluate the song. Have students consider how the music complements the tone of the lyrics. Also, suggest that students evaluate the voice of the singer and how well it fits the lyrics and the music. Allow students time to discuss their evaluations in class. **OL**

Indiana English/Language Arts Academic Standards
SE: 8.3, 8.3.6
TWE: *Reading in the Real World* 8.4.4, *Differentiated Instruction* 8.5.7

Assess

Resources for page 480

- Selection Quick Check, p. 34
- Selection and Unit Assessment, p. 40
- ExamView Assessment Suite
- Interactive Tutor: Self-Assessment

Students can respond to the *After You Read* items in their Learner's Notebooks or on a separate sheet of paper.

Answering the

1. Responses will vary.
2. the tide roll in and the ships roll in and out
3. lonely

Critical Thinking

4. Possible response: He felt his life in Georgia gave him nothing to live for.
5. Possible response: Just as tides keep the same pattern day after day, the speaker's life never changes.
6. Most students will respond that the speaker is dissatisfied because he's still lonely. Some, however, may point out that he seems to have accepted his fate and has found a measure of peace on the dock.

After You Read

Sittin' on the Dock of the Bay

Answering the

1. How do the lyrics to "Sittin' on the Dock of the Bay" help you think about the Big Question: What do you do when you don't know what to do?
2. **Recall** What does the speaker watch from the dock?
   TIP **Right There**
3. **Summarize** How has the speaker felt since he left home?
   TIP **Right There**

Critical Thinking

4. **Infer** Why do you think the speaker decided to travel so far from home? Explain.
   TIP **Author and Me**
5. **Compare** In what way is the speaker's life like the rolling tide that comes in and goes out again? Explain.
   TIP **On My Own**
6. **Infer** Do you think the speaker is satisfied with his decision to leave home? Why or why not?
   TIP **On My Own**

Write About Your Reading

Character Sketch Write a character sketch of the speaker of "Sittin' on the Dock of the Bay." Follow these steps.

Step 1: Your sketch should convey a main impression of the character. What one character trait stands out the most to you?

Step 2: Find specific details in the song lyrics to support the trait you wish to emphasize. How do the speaker's words, actions, thoughts, or feelings support the trait you have chosen to convey?

Step 3: Decide on the most effective order for presenting your details. Do you want to present your most important details first? Or do you want to start with the less important details and work your way up to the more important ones?

Step 4: Write your character sketch.

Step 5: Proofread your sketch for errors in grammar, usage, and mechanics. Fix any mistakes.

Indiana English/Language Arts Academic Standards (pp. 480–481)

8.3 Comprehension and Analysis of Literary Text Respond to grade-level-appropriate literature... **8.5.7** Write for different purposes... **8.3.1** Determine... purposes and characteristics of different forms of poetry... **8.3.6** Identify significant literary devices, such as... dialect... **8.6 English Language Conventions** Sentence structure

For a complete description of the standards, see p. IN 11.

Write About Your Reading

Possible response:

I think the speaker was searching for a better life because he had no family or friends. In the poem, he says he had "nothing to live for" in Georgia. Basically, he's lonely, trying to escape loneliness but not succeeding, even after traveling 2,000 miles to California. He seems confused, saying he can't do what ten people tell him to do. He's discouraged and directionless, almost acting like an old man as he talks about resting his bones while most young people would be full of energy. He's given up trying because his desperate cross-country trip didn't change his life.

Skills Review

Key Reading Skill: Evaluating

7. Think about how you would evaluate the lyrics. Would you recommend that other eighth-graders read them? Why or why not?

Literary Element: Lyrics

8. Reread the second verse of the lyrics (lines 8–14). Which words rhyme?
9. What is the effect of the rhymes?

Reviewing Skills: Connecting

10. Think of situations in which you wasted time because you weren't sure what to do next. How do your experiences compare to those of the speaker in the poem?

Vocabulary Check

Answer "true" if a statement is true or "false" if it is false. Rewrite any false statement to make it true.

11. If a boat is near a dock, it is near a shore.
12. If someone roamed away from home, he or she went directly to a preplanned destination.
13. **Academic Vocabulary** How did evaluating help you understand the song lyrics?
14. **English Language Coach** Do you think the speaker's pronunciation and word choice are appropriate to the kind of person he is? Explain.

Web Activities For eFlashcards, Selection Quick Checks, and other Web activities, go to www.glencoe.com.

Grammar Link: Agreement in Inverted Sentences

Usually the subject comes before the verb in a sentence. However, in some sentences all or part of the verb comes before the subject. These sentences are in inverted, or reverse, order. Two common types of inverted sentences are:

A. Questions In many questions all or part of the verb comes before the subject.

- Do you and your family have a car?
  helping verb / subject / main verb

To make it less tricky to find the subject and verb, turn the question into a statement.

- You and your family do have a car.

B. Sentences that Begin with *Here/There* The words *here* and *there* cannot be subjects. To find the subject of a sentence that begins with *here* or *there,* omit the word. Find the verb; then ask yourself, who or what ___?

Example: There is a new girl in our class.

Omit *there;* then find the verb.

~~There~~ is a new girl in our class.

Ask, who or what is? *Girl* is.

There is a new girl in our class.
verb subject

Grammar Practice

Copy each sentence on a separate sheet of paper. Underline the subject of each sentence once and the verb twice. If the subject and verb do not agree, fix the verb.

15. Is my brother and you going to the party?
16. Here is his jacket and his books.
17. Are you and Janice invited?
18. There is a few items missing from my locker!

Writing Application Review your character sketch. Look for questions and for sentences that begin with *here* or *there.* Make sure that the subjects and verbs in all these sentences agree.

Skills Review

Key Reading Skill: Evaluating

7. Responses will vary. Some students may feel that the lyrics are too depressing for people their age. Others may state that the lyrics reflect how they feel when they don't know what to do.

Literary Element: Lyrics

8. Bay and way rhyme.
9. Responses will vary.

Reviewing Skills: Connecting

10. Responses will vary.

Vocabulary Check

11. true
12. false: If someone roamed away from home, he or she wandered aimlessly.

Academic Vocabulary

13. Responses will vary.

English Language Coach

14. Most students will probably respond that the pronunciation and word choice are appropriate. They seem laid-back, lazy, and unhurried, just like the speaker, who is content to just sit and waste time watching the tides.

Close

Ask students what they learned from the song that helps them answer the Big Question.

Grammar Link: Agreement in Inverted Sentences

Grammar Practice

15. Are my brother and you going to the party?
16. Here are his jacket and his books.
17. Are you and Janice invited?
18. There are a few items missing from my locker!

Literature Online

Web Activities Have students access the Web site for interactive activities that will help them assess their understanding of the selection.

Indiana English/Language Arts Academic Standards
SE: 8.3, 8.3.1, 8.3.6, 8.5.7, 8.6

Interpreting

Teaching Students to Interpret

Why Is It Important?

- Every reader constructs meaning on the basis of what he or she understands about the world. Students will learn how to use their own understanding of the world to decide what the events or ideas in a selection mean.
- Finding meanings is all about interacting with the text. Interpreting text will allow students to become more active readers.
- Students will learn how to determine what a writer is really saying in his or her work.

How to Help Students Get It

- Have students think about what they already know about themselves and the world and how that knowledge relates to each selection.
- Tell students to ask themselves questions as they read such as, "What is the author really trying to say here? What larger idea might these events be about?"
- Remind students that interpreting is more than just remembering and understanding facts—it's creating meaning in text by using what they know about the world around them.

Reading to Answer the Big Question

To the Democratic National Convention by Jesse Jackson
In Jackson's speech, famous for its closing statement "Keep hope alive," Jackson tells his audience he understands them. He understands poverty and being looked down on and treated poorly. He encourages his listeners not to surrender. Even when the future looks bleak, one must keep striving.

Fable for When There's No Way Out by May Swenson
This poem presents a moral: When you've tried everything, try something else. It describes a chick's frustration in trying to hatch and its eventual success.

Workshop Resources

Pacing (Days) Standard	Block	Lesson	Student Materials	Teacher Resources
1	1/2	Key Skill Lesson: Interpreting	Key Reading Skills Practice, p. 21 English Language Coach Review, p. 41	Bellringer Options Transparencies – Daily Language Practice 37 Read Aloud, Think Aloud Transparencies – Key Reading Skills 14 Presentation Plus!
1	1	"To the Democratic National Convention"	Glencoe Online Unit Vocabulary Review, p. 39 Academic Vocabulary Review, p. 43 English Language Coach Active Reading Graphic Organizer, p. 22 Literary Analysis, p. 24 StudentWorks Plus™ Online Student Edition Literature Classics Selection and Unit Assessments, p. 41	Literary and Text Analysis Transparencies 42 Puzzlemaker Skill Level Up!™ A Language Arts Game BookLink 3 Assessment by Learning Objective (Diagnostic and Formative) Interactive Tutor: Self-Assessment TeacherWorks Plus™
1		"Fable for When There's No Way Out"	Glencoe Online Unit Vocabulary Review, p. 39 Academic Vocabulary Review, p. 43 English Language Coach Active Reading Graphic Organizer, p. 25 StudentWorks Plus™ Online Student Edition Literature Classics Selection and Unit Assessments, p. 42	Puzzlemaker Skill Level Up!™ A Language Arts Game BookLink 3 Assessment by Learning Objective (Diagnostic and Formative) Interactive Tutor: Self-Assessment TeacherWorks Plus™

Keys for Unit Resource

- Blackline Master
- Workbook
- Supplemental Text
- CD-ROM
- DVD
- Transparency
- Web-based
- Fast File

Level Appropriate Code

AS = Activities for all students
AL = Activities for students working above grade level
OL = Activities for students working at grade level
BL = Activities for students working below grade level
EL = Activities for English language learners

Focus

BELLRINGER Options

Daily Language Practice Transparency 37
Focus Activity Say: Recall the last time you felt discouraged or hopeless. Who gave you a pep talk about not giving up? *(Responses will vary.)* **AS**

Teach

Analyzing the Cartoon

Ask: How does the mother in the cartoon feel when the kids interpret her instructions incorrectly? *(Possible responses: angry, upset, frustrated, unhappy)*
Ask: When have you misinterpreted what a parent said? *(Responses will vary.)* **AS**

V Vocabulary

Academic Vocabulary Say: The verb *interpret* gives its meanings to other parts of speech. The noun *interpretation* refers to someone's explanation of the meaning of events and ideas. What noun uses *interpret* to describe a person who translates words from one language to another? *(interpreter)* **OL**

READING WORKSHOP 3

Skills Focus

You will practice these skills when you read the following selections:

- *from* "To the Democratic National Convention," p. 486
- "Fable for When There's No Way Out," p. 492

Reading

- Interpreting speeches and poems

Literature

- Identifying the sound devices alliteration and repetition and their effects

Vocabulary

- Understanding how word choice is affected by the author's purpose and audience
- Academic Vocabulary: *interpret*

Writing/Grammar

- Making verbs agree with indefinite pronoun subjects
- Making verbs agree with collective nouns

Skill Lesson

Interpreting

Learn It!

What Is It? When you **interpret** as you read, you use your own understanding of the world to decide what the events or ideas in a selection mean. For example, when you read the poem "The Road Not Taken" (page 447), you were asked to think about how you have made decisions when you didn't know what to do. You used what you know about making choices to understand how the speaker in the poem reached a decision. Now learn to interpret every time you read.

Analyzing Cartoons
The kids in this cartoon respond to the mother in their own creative way. How do they interpret—or misinterpret—the mother's order?

Indiana English/Language Arts Academic Standards (pp. 482–483)

8.3 Comprehension and Analysis of Literary Text Respond to grade-level-appropriate literature...

For a complete description of the standards, see p. IN 11.

Academic Vocabulary

interpret (in TUR prit) *v.* to find the meaning of events or ideas

Additional Support

English Language Coach

Nonstandard English In the cartoon, the words *play outside* were intended to mean *go outside and play a game suitable for outdoors, such as a sport.* Ask students to volunteer meanings of these slang expressions that could be easily misinterpreted: *cool it, break a leg, I'm outta here, kicking back,* and *pumped up.* Partner English language learners with students who have strong language skills. Have the pairs list three other slang terms or expressions that could be misunderstood and give their intended meanings. **EL** **OL**

Why Is It Important? When you interpret text, you increase your understanding by using what you have learned through experience. You make sense of the text by bringing your own knowledge and experience to it.

How Do I Do It? As you read, think about what you already know about **R** yourself and the world. To interpret the meaning of text, ask yourself, *What point is the author trying to make? Which details and examples make this point?* While you read, take notes to record your ideas. Here are notes a student took after reading part of the poem in this unit's Genre Focus.

Literature Online

Study Central Visit www.glencoe.com and click on Study Central to review interpreting.

from **The Road Not Taken**
I shall be telling this with a sigh
Somewhere ages and ages hence:
Two roads diverged in a wood, and I—
I took the one less traveled by,
And that has made all the difference.

When the speaker says that he took the less-traveled road, I think he's saying that he didn't follow the crowd and do what everyone else does. He doesn't seem sorry about the decision, so I interpret that to mean he thinks it's good to take the road less traveled by. After all, he ends the poem by saying, "That has made all the difference." To me, that means his decision changed his life.

Practice It!

Below are some lines and sentences from the selections you will read in this Workshop. How would you interpret each one? Jot down some thoughts in your Learner's Notebook.

- "Keep hope alive."
- "Character breeds faith."
- "Rage works if reason won't."

Use It!

As you read from "To the Democratic National Convention" and "Fable for When There's No Way Out," remember the notes you made to practice interpreting. When you find a detail that helps you discover meaning, add it to your notes.

READING WORKSHOP 3

Teach

Literature Online

Study Central Have students access the Web site to review interpreting and to complete a related activity.

R Reading Skill

Interpreting **Ask:** When might interpreting written language correctly be very important? *(Possible responses: when I am taking tests; when I am reading road directions or emergency directions)* **AS**
Ask: How does interpreting affect you when you write something others will read? *(Possible response: I need to make sure my writing is clear and easy to understand so that others will be able to correctly interpret my ideas.)* **OL** **AL**

Resources for page 483

Use Key Reading Skills Transparency 14 in *Read Aloud, Think Aloud* to help students practice interpreting.

Reading in the Real World

Citizenship Like Jesse Jackson, whose speech students are about to read, many people overcome obstacles in order to succeed. These people can be sources of inspiration for others. Brainstorm problems people face, such as poor health, and racism or other forms of prejudice. Have students identify a public figure who has overcome some obstacle and read a biography about that person. Have students give a brief report about the person's life and suggest advice the person might give to those who struggle. **AL**

Indiana English/Language Arts Academic Standards
SE: 8.3
TWE: *English Language Coach* 8.1.1, *Reading in the Real World* 8.5.1

Teach

More About the Author

As a student, Jackson participated in sit-ins to desegregate his local library. Later, he helped found the SCLC (Southern Christian Leadership Conference) and was appointed its director by Dr. Martin Luther King Jr. Jackson was a presidential candidate in 1984 and, again, in 1988. Although he wasn't elected, many feel Jackson was a success because he inspired millions to register to vote and helped African Americans get elected to state and local offices.

EL Language Coach

Word Choice and Audience

Ask: How does your intended audience affect your word choice? *(Possible responses: If the audience is a teacher or another adult, the writing will likely be formal, whereas an e-mail to a friend is informal.)*

Say: Think about your audience before you write. Choose your words accordingly. AS

Before You Read

from To the Democratic National Convention

Jesse Jackson

Meet the Author

Jesse Jackson was born in 1941, a time when the United States did not recognize equality among the races. During the 1960s, Jackson became involved in the Civil Rights movement. In 1968 he was ordained as a Baptist minister. Jackson has also played an important role in American politics, founding the Rainbow Coalition and traveling around the world on peace-making missions.

Author Search For more about Jesse Jackson, go to www.glencoe.com.

Indiana English/Language Arts Academic Standards (pp. 484–487)

8.1 Vocabulary Development Use...growing knowledge of English... to determine the meaning of words... **8.3 Comprehension and Analysis of Literary Text** Respond to grade-level-appropriate literature... **8.3.6** Identify significant literary devices...

For a complete description of the standards, see p. IN 11.

Vocabulary Preview

abandonment (uh BAN dun munt) *n.* the state of being deserted or left alone without help **(p. 486)** *Antoine's sense of abandonment when his father left was overwhelming.*

nomination (nah mih NAY shun) *n.* the act of proposing a candidate for an office or honor **(p. 487)** *She placed Rodriguez in nomination for governor of her state.*

surrender (suh REN dur) *v.* to give up **(p. 487)** *When the fight gets tough, you may want to surrender.*

Write to Learn Write a one-paragraph story that uses all three vocabulary words. With the whole class, take turns reading your stories aloud. Discuss how these vocabulary words affected each story and added to its meaning.

English Language Coach

EL

Word Choice and Audience Good writers and speakers tailor their word choice to their audiences. Jackson is a well-educated man with a very large vocabulary. But in the speech you're about to read, he uses simple, informal language because he wants to reach out to people who may not have had the opportunity to get a good education. He uses simple language for many reasons:

- so his audience will understand his message
- so his audience will see that he is one of them
- so his audience will share his feelings

The words on the left come from Jackson's speech. The words on the right are words he might have used to appeal to a different audience.

Informal Diction	Formal Diction
mama	mother
the projects	low-income housing
make it	be successful

Partner Talk With a partner, read the sentences below. Rewrite them to appeal to a more formal audience (of parents or teachers).

1. That movie was so cool.
2. I was like, "Why'd you do that?"
3. Ryan's excuse was way lame.

Additional Support

Author Search To expand students' knowledge of Jesse Jackson, have them access the Web site for additional information and resources.

Literature Focus Lesson

Persuasive Speech Speeches, such as the one Jesse Jackson delivered at the Democratic Convention, are written with the purpose of persuading an audience to take action. Ask students to use the following criteria to evaluate the writing techniques Jesse Jackson uses:

- Clear, logical progression of ideas
- Provides examples and statistics that support statements
- Connects to the audience through word choice and tone
- Appeals to logic and/or emotions of the audience
- Presents a convincing argument AS

Skills Preview

Key Reading Skill: Interpreting

In "To the Democratic National Convention," Jesse Jackson says, "Wherever you are tonight you can make it. Hold your head high, stick your chest out. You can make it. It gets dark sometimes, but the morning comes."

R

What do you think the last sentence means?

Partner Talk Discuss the statement with a classmate. Together, interpret what it means. Put your interpretation in your own words.

Literary Element: Repetition

Repetition is the repeating of sounds, words, phrases, or whole sentences for emphasis. Repetition can also give a sense of unity and continuity to writing. Repetition is especially effective in spoken forms like speeches. Jackson uses repetition several times in the speech that you are about to read.

As you read, use these tips to learn about repetition.

- Look for words and phrases the writer uses again and again. Try reading aloud to find them.
  Which words and phrases does the writer repeat?
- Consider why Jackson chose these particular words and phrases to repeat.
  What is the effect of the repeated words or phrases?

Write to Learn Read the second paragraph of Jackson's speech (on page 486). What words are repeated? Why do you think Jackson repeats them? Jot down your thoughts in your Learner's Notebook.

Interactive Literary Elements Handbook
To review or learn more about the literary elements, go to www.glencoe.com.

Get Ready to Read

Connect to the Reading

Think about a time when you felt that you would never reach an important goal or see a dream come true. Why did this goal mean so much to you? Did you find a way to reach it? As you read Jackson's speech, notice how he explains how he helped himself when his path was not clear. What might you have done in his place?

Small Group Discussion With a small group of classmates, talk about the kinds of problems that are hard to solve. Brainstorm some ways that people can make decisions and act when they are not sure what to do. What powers within you might help at such a time? Where else could you turn for help?

Build Background

The speech you are about to read was made by Jesse Jackson at the Democratic National Convention in August 1988.

- A *convention* is a formal meeting of members of a group, such as a political group.
- The *Democratic National Convention* is the official meeting of the Democratic Party every four years for the purpose of nominating, or choosing, someone in the party to run for president of the United States.

Set Purposes for Reading

BIG Question Read this excerpt from "To the Democratic National Convention" to learn how Jesse Jackson's upbringing prepared him to help others find solutions to their problems.

Set Your Own Purpose What else would you like to learn from the speech to help you answer the Big Question? Write your own purpose on the "To the Democratic National Convention" page of Foldable 4.

Keep Moving

Use these skills as you read the following selection.

Teach

R Reading Skill

Interpreting **Ask:** How did Jesse Jackson want people to feel when he asked them to hold their heads high and stick out their chests? *(Possible responses: proud, self-confident)* **Say:** You might say that Jesse Jackson's speech was a "pep talk" to encourage those who are poor or disadvantaged to keep going. In what ways do you think Jackson's speech might have been encouraging? *(Responses will vary.)* AS

Interactive Literary Elements Handbook Have students access the Web site to improve their understanding of repetition.

English Language Coach

Word Choice One of the main goals of writing is to be clear and concise. Explain to students that if their writing is clear, then their audience will be able to understand what they are saying. Write on the board: *I failed to comprehend the set of instructions that accompanied the stereo, which caused it to malfunction and me to become quite perturbed.* Have students rewrite the sentence, making it clearer and more concise. *(Possible response: I was upset because my stereo didn't work. I couldn't understand the instructions for putting it together.)* EL BL

Indiana English/Language Arts Academic Standards
SE: 8.1, 8.3, 8.3.6
TWE: *Literature Focus Lesson* 8.3.6, *English Language Coach* 8.5.6

Teach

R Reading Skill

Interpreting **Say:** At the end of the second paragraph, Jackson says, "I understand when nobody knows your name. I understand when you have no name." What does "having no name" symbolize? *(Possible response: It symbolizes having no power or position within society.)* AL

EL Language Coach

Word Choice and Audience
Ask: What details does Jackson use to describe his home? *(three-room, outdoor bathroom, no running water, wallpaper to reduce drafts)* BL **Ask:** What can you conclude from the description? *(His family was poor.)* **Ask:** What effect might this fact have on his audience? *(Possible response: He is probably addressing people with the same background as his. Therefore, the audience can connect to him.)* OL

Readability Scores
Dale-Chall: 4.0
DRP: 48
Lexile: 620

READING WORKSHOP 3

from To the Democratic National Convention

by Jesse Jackson

I have a story. I wasn't always on television. Writers were not always outside my door. When I was born late one afternoon, October 8th, in Greenville, South Carolina, no writers asked my mother her name. Nobody chose to write down our address. My mama was not supposed to make it. And I was not supposed to make it. You see, I was born to a teen-age mother who was born to a teen-age mother. 1

I understand. I know **abandonment** and people being mean to you, and saying you're nothing and nobody, and can never be anything. I understand. Jesse Jackson is my third name. I'm adopted. When I had no name, my grandmother gave me her name. My name was Jesse Burns until I was twelve. So I wouldn't have a blank space, she gave me a name to hold me over. I understand when nobody knows your name. I understand when you have no name. I understand. R

I wasn't born in the hospital. Mama didn't have insurance. I was born in the bed at home. I really do understand. Born in a three-room-house, bathroom in the backyard,[1] slop jar by the bed, no hot and cold running water. I understand. Wallpaper used for decoration? No. For a windbreaker. I understand. I'm a working person's person, that's why I understand you whether you're black or white. 2 3 EL

I understand work. I was not born with a silver spoon in my mouth. I had a shovel programmed for my hand. My mother, a working woman. So many days she went to work early with runs in her stockings. She knew better, but she

1. ***Bathroom in the backyard*** means an outhouse without water or electricity.

Vocabulary

abandonment (uh BAN dun munt) *n.* the state of being deserted or left alone without help

Practice the Skills

1 English Language Coach

Word Choice and Audience Think about Jackson's choice of words in this paragraph. How does he tailor his word choice to fit the needs of the audience he most wants to reach?

2 Literary Element

Repetition What words does Jackson repeat in this paragraph? What is the effect of that repetition?

3 Key Reading Skill

Interpreting How do you interpret what Jackson has said so far? Write a sentence in your Learner's Notebook that sums up what you think he says in the first three paragraphs.

Additional Support

Reading Fluency

Build Fluency Some students may benefit from reading along silently as they listen to an audiotape of this speech. Ask students to list four words and phrases Jackson emphasizes—with increased volume, changed rate of speed, pauses, and other speaking techniques. When they are finished, ask students to take turns reading the speech aloud to a partner or small group. AS wore runs in her stockings so that my brother and I could have matching socks and not be laughed at at school.

Visual Vocabulary ***Cranberries*** are bright red berries that have a sour taste.

I understand. At 3 o'clock on Thanksgiving Day we couldn't eat turkey because mama was preparing someone else's turkey at 3 o'clock. We had to play football to entertain ourselves and then around 6 o'clock she would get off the Alta Vista bus; then we would bring up the leftovers and eat our turkey—leftovers, the carcass, the cranberries around 8 o'clock at night. I really do understand.

Every one of these funny labels they put on you, those of you who are watching this broadcast tonight in the projects, on the corners, I understand. Call you outcast, low down, you can't make it, you're nothing, you're from nobody, subclass, underclass—when you see Jesse Jackson, when my name goes in **nomination**, your name goes in nomination. 4

I was born in the slum, but the slum was not born in me. 5 And it wasn't born in you, and you can make it. Wherever you are tonight you can make it. Hold your head high, stick your chest out. You can make it. It gets dark sometimes, but the morning comes. Don't you **surrender.** Suffering breeds character. Character breeds faith. In the end faith will not disappoint.

You must not surrender. You may or may not get there, but just know that you're qualified and you hold on and hold out. We must never surrender. America will get better and better. Keep hope alive. Keep hope alive. Keep hope alive. On tomorrow night and beyond, keep hope alive. 6

I love you very much. I love you very much. ○

Vocabulary

nomination (nah mih NAY shun) *n.* the act of proposing a candidate for an office or honor

surrender (suh REN dur) *v.* to give up

Practice the Skills

4 English Language Coach

Word Choice and Audience How would you describe Jackson's word choice in this sentence? Which members of his audience do you think he's trying to reach?

5 Key Reading Skill

Interpreting What does Jackson mean when he says, "the slum was not born in me"?

Analyzing the Photo The Rev. Jesse Jackson hugs his mother, Helen Burns, at a 1988 Atlanta speech. What does Jackson say to connect with his audience?

6 BIG Question

What is Jackson saying to people who feel confused and hopeless? Write your answer on the "To the Democratic National Convention" page of Foldable 4. Your response will help you complete the Unit Challenge later.

READING WORKSHOP 3

Teach

L Literary Element

Repetition Say: Read the paragraph that starts "I was born in the slum." Why do you think Jackson repeats "You can make it"? *(Possible response: to convince or inspire the audience members)* OL

EL Language Coach

Word Choice and Audience

Say: Jackson says in the next to last paragraph, "You may or may not get there . . . and you hold on and hold out." What is the difference between *hold on* and *hold out*? *(Possible response:* Hold on *means not to give up.* Hold out *means to resist the demands of others.)* OL

Assess

CheckPoint

Use the CheckPoint questions provided on Presentation Plus! to check for comprehension of the selection. These questions can be used with interactive response keypads for immediate student feedback.

Reading in the Real World

Career Some students may be interested in careers as elected officials. Have students research one of the following federal government careers: congressperson, senator, president. Have them focus on the requirements and duties of the job and how someone in that role can help American citizens. Invite students to share the information they gather with the rest of the class. AL

Indiana English/Language Arts Academic Standards

SE: 8.1, 8.3, 8.3.6

TWE: *Reading Fluency* 8.7, *Reading in the Real World* 8.4.4

Assess

Resources for page 488

- Selection Quick Check, p. 35
- Selection and Unit Assessment, p. 39
- ExamView Assessment Suite
- Interactive Tutor: Self-Assessment

Students can respond to the *After You Read* items in their Learner's Notebooks or on a separate sheet of paper.

Answering the BIG Question

1. Responses will vary.
2. His mother was poor and had no insurance.
3. Responses will vary but should include three of the following: poverty, discrimination, single-parent home, mother and grandmother who became parents as teens, poor living conditions, no insurance.

Critical Thinking

4. Possible response: Jackson's mother was a cook, maid, or housekeeper in another person's home. She brought home leftovers from her employer's house for Thanksgiving dinner.
5. Possible response: Jackson hoped that discrimination would end. He had worked for years to desegregate public facilities and to improve opportunities for victims of poverty and discrimination.
6. Responses will vary.

After You Read

from To the Democratic National Convention

Answering the 

1. What advice does Jesse Jackson's speech give about what to do when you don't know what to do?
2. **Recall** What reason does Jackson give for being born at home instead of in a hospital?
   TIP Right There
3. **List** What are some of the obstacles Jackson had to overcome to be successful? List at least three.
   TIP Think and Search

Critical Thinking

4. **Infer** What do you think Jackson's mother did for a living when he was a child? Give details from the speech to support your answer.
   TIP Think and Search
5. **Infer** Near the end of his speech, Jackson says, "We must never surrender. America will get better and better." In what way or ways do you think Jackson hopes America will improve? Explain your reasoning.
   TIP Author and Me
6. **Evaluate** How powerful do you think Jackson's speech is? Do you think it affected listeners? Explain your answer.
   TIP On My Own

Talk About Your Reading

Oral Response Imagine yourself as a member of the audience at the convention where Jesse Jackson delivered his speech. Prepare a response to it. You can write it out word for word or just take notes, whichever you prefer. Tell Jackson how you felt about what he said. Could you identify or connect with his story? Mention any points in the speech that you agree or disagree with, and tell how his speech affected you. Rehearse your response and deliver your speech to the class.

Indiana English/Language Arts Academic Standards (pp. 488–489)

8.3 Comprehension and Analysis of Literary Text Respond to grade-level-appropriate literature... **8.2.9** Make reasonable statements and draw conclusions... **8.7.11** Deliver oral responses to literature... **8.3.6** Identify significant literary devices...
8.6 English Language Conventions
For a complete description of the standards, see p. IN 11.

Talk About Your Reading

Possible Response:
Reverend Jackson, you've given me hope when I was about to give up. I haven't been able to find a job. Even though I'm qualified, it seems like no one wants to hire me. My parents each worked two jobs so I could go to college. Now, here I am with a college degree, and no one will let me use it. I will hold on, though, as you said. Somewhere, someone will see a qualified, intelligent human being. Thanks for your understanding and encouragement!

Skills Review

Key Reading Skill: Interpreting

7. At the beginning of his speech, Jackson says, "I have a story. I wasn't always on television. Writers were not always outside my door." What is Jackson saying about himself in these sentences? Interpret what he means. Put your interpretation in your own words.

Literary Element: Repetition

8. When Jackson repeats the sentence "I understand," what is he saying he understands? How can you tell?
9. If you were giving this speech, how would you say "Keep hope alive"? Would it sound the same each time you said it? Explain.

Vocabulary Check

Read each word in column A. On a separate sheet of paper, write the letter of the correct definition from column B.

Column A	Column B
10. nomination	a. to give up control
11. surrender	b. state of being deserted or left alone
12. abandonment	c. act of proposing a candidate for office

13. **Academic Vocabulary** What do you do when you interpret a piece of literature?
14. **English Language Coach** Find three words and phrases from the selection that you think are especially well chosen for the audience. Write these words and phrases in your Learner's Notebook. Then explain why you think they are good examples.

Grammar Link: Agreement with Indefinite Pronouns

Indefinite pronouns are noun substitutes that do not refer to a particular person, place, or thing. Certain indefinite pronouns are always singular, or equal to *he, she,* or *it.* Study the list below.

anybody	everybody	no one
anyone	everyone	nothing
anything	everything	somebody
each	neither	someone
either	nobody	something

See if you can make the subject and verb agree in the sentences below. (Use the list above for help.)

- No one (is, are) to blame for the accident.

If you chose *is*, you're right. *No one* is singular, or equal to *he, she,* or *it.* So the right verb form is *is.*

- Neither of the cars (has, have) bad brakes.

If you chose *has,* you're right. The subject is *neither,* which is singular. (If you thought *cars* was the subject, remember that prepositional phrases do not contain subjects and verbs. *Cars* is in the phrase *of the cars,* so it can't be the subject.)

Grammar Practice

Write the correct verb form for each sentence.

15. Each of the CDs (sounds, sound) good.
16. There (is, are) nothing wrong with any of them.
17. Everyone (wants, want) a copy of that new CD.
18. Someone (needs, need) to see how good they are.
19. Neither of the musicians (is, are) nominated for an award.

Web Activities For eFlashcards, Selection Quick Checks, and other Web activities, go to www.glencoe.com.

Skills Review

Key Reading Skill: Interpreting

7. Possible response: I wasn't always famous. At one time, I was an unknown, poor African American like many of you.

Literary Element: Repetition

8. Responses will vary.
9. Responses will vary.

Vocabulary Check

10. c
11. a
12. b

Academic Vocabulary

13. Possible response: You use your reading skills to determine the meaning of words, phrases, or an entire piece of literature.

English Language Coach

14. Responses will vary.

Close

Ask students what they learned from Jackson's speech about how to keep going when times are difficult.

Grammar Link: Agreement with Indefinite Pronouns

Grammar Practice

15. sounds
16. is
17. wants
18. needs
19. is

Literature Online

Web Activities Have students access the Web site for interactive activities that will help them assess their understanding of the selection.

Indiana English/Language Arts Academic Standards
SE: 8.2.9, 8.3, 8.3.6, 8.6, 8.7.11

Teach

More About the Author

Part of a big family, May Swenson helped with cooking, laundry, cleaning, canning, and ironing. At age twelve, Swenson began a diary, using the books of blank pages her father had made. She was known as a storyteller by her siblings. Her older cousin was surprised to discover that Swenson's diaries were actually filled with poetry.

V Vocabulary

Use Vocabulary Say: Write a story about a time when you didn't know what to do. Use each of the vocabulary words in your story. When you finish, share your story with your classmates. *(Responses will vary.)* AS

Before You Read

Fable for When There's No Way Out

May Swenson

Meet the Author

Many people consider May Swenson (1913–1989) one of the best American poets of the 20th century. Swenson once said her poetry came from "a craving to get through the curtains of things as they *appear*, to things as they *are*, and then into the larger, wilder space of things as they *are becoming*." See page R7 of the Author Files at the back of the book for more on May Swenson.

Author Search For more about May Swenson, go to www.glencoe.com.

Indiana English/Language Arts Academic Standards (pp. 490–493)

8.3 Comprehension and Analysis of Literary Text Respond to grade-level-appropriate literature... **8.3.6** Identify significant literary devices...

For a complete description of the standards, see p. IN 11.

Vocabulary Preview

instinct (IN stinkt) *n.* unlearned knowledge that a person or an animal is born with **(p. 492)** *A mother hen knows by instinct how to care for her chicks.*

V **ambition** (am BISH un) *n.* a strong drive or desire to succeed **(p. 492)** *Meg's ambition is to be an astronaut.*

despair (dih SPAIR) *n.* a complete loss of hope **(p. 493)** *Despair overcame Susan when she realized her cat was gone forever.*

rage (rayj) *n.* a feeling of great anger or fury **(p. 493)** *Jen's rage when her brother stepped on her artwork was overwhelming.*

Write to Learn For each of the above vocabulary words, write a sentence that shows what the word means.

English Language Coach

Word Choice, Purpose, and Audience Writers choose words that further their purpose and communicate best with their readers. For example:

- If a friend who doesn't know much about technology asks you to explain what instant messaging is, you might say, "With instant messaging, you communicate in real time. You send the message and the person gets it and answers you right away, almost as if you're having a phone conversation. But with e-mail, you may not get the message right away."
- An article in a magazine for technology experts might explain the same idea in very different words, like these: "Virtual communication in cyberspace may be characterized as either synchronous or asynchronous. In synchronous communication like IM, conversations happen in real time; in asynchronous communication, there's often a time lag."

Which explanation is better? It depends on the author's purpose and audience. If an author's purpose is to explain something to an audience that's probably unfamiliar with her subject, she'll use simple, informal words. But if the purpose is to communicate with specialists in a field, she'll use the technical language they understand.

On Your Own Rewrite the sentence below by replacing the big words with shorter, simpler ones. Use a dictionary.

- Music is aesthetically pleasing vocal or instrumental sounds having some degree of melody, harmony, or rhythm.

Additional Support

Author Search To expand students' appreciation of May Swenson, have them access the Web site for additional information and resources.

Reading in the Real World

College Discuss with students that when they get to college, they will be required to write essays about literary works. These essays will be their own interpretations of the texts they read. Sometimes they will be required to find other interpretations to include in their essays, but often they will just explain their own interpretations without outside support. Have students choose a poem from the library or Internet to interpret. Have them read the poem at least two times and then write a one-page essay on their interpretation of the poem. Have them answer the questions: What does the poem mean? How does the author present the theme? AL

Skills Preview

Key Reading Skill: Interpreting

Sometimes a poem seems to be only about something in nature. But when you think about it, you realize you can interpret it differently. You can see how that animal or bird is like you. You can look at that storm or earthquake or process of nature and see how it's like your life. When you interpret that way, poetry comes alive! R

Write to Learn As you read "Fable for When There's No Way Out," try to interpret the poem in two ways–as the story of a chick breaking out of an egg and as a story about life. Write your conclusions in your Learner's Notebook.

Key Literary Element: Alliteration

Poetry was originally a way for important stories and lessons to be passed from person to person. Poetic techniques like **alliteration** were used to make the poems easier to remember. Poets and audiences realized that the sounds of poems were also beautiful, like music in words.

Alliteration was the main sound device in the oldest of English poetry, even more important than rhyme. It is the repetition of sounds at the beginnings of words. Most often, the repeated sounds are consonants. Here is a famous example of alliteration from the poet Alexander Pope. (A zephyr is a "breeze.") L

Soft is the strain when Zephyr gently blows,
And the smooth stream in smoother numbers flows.

Very smooth. But alliteration isn't always smooth. This is from a poem by Vachel Lindsay:

Beat an empty barrel with the handle of a broom,
Hard as they were able,/ Boom, boom, BOOM.

Small Group Discussion Together with some classmates, make up some riddles using alliteration. Here's a sample: What do you call a short novel? A brief book.

Get Ready to Read

Connect to the Reading

Have you ever worked really hard at something but still felt you were getting nowhere? If so, remember that feeling as you read this poem.

Partner Talk Talk with a classmate about what it means to give up. Are there situations where that's okay? Are there situations where giving up is not possible?

Build Background

You are going to read a poem about a chick's struggle to break through its shell and hatch.

- It takes a chick about 21 days to hatch. By Day 16, the chick turns around so that its head is close to the air cell at the larger end of the egg.
- Around Day 17, the chick uses its beak to break the inner membrane of the eggshell.
- The chick uses its sharp egg tooth to cut away at the shell. After it makes a hole in the shell, the chick must rest for three to eight hours before it succeeds in cracking the shell by pushing and pecking at it. The chick is then very tired.

Set Purposes for Reading

Read "Fable for When There's No Way Out" to explore what happens when the will to live is tested against a life-or-death situation.

Set Your Own Purpose What else would you like to learn from the poem that will help you answer the Big Question? Write your own purpose on the "Fable for When There's No Way Out" page of Foldable 4.

Literature Online

Interactive Literary Elements Handbook
To review or learn more about the literary elements, go to www.glencoe.com.

Keep Moving

Use these skills as you read the following selection.

Teach

R Reading Skill

Interpreting **Say:** The following poem ends "When locked up, bear down." Which words in the statement suggest people sometimes should do the opposite of what they're tempted to do in problem situations? *(up, down)* OL

L Literary Element

Alliteration **Say:** Advertisers often use alliteration to name or promote products. What product or slogan that uses alliteration can you think of? *(Responses will vary.)* AS

Interactive Literary Elements Handbook Have students access the Web site to improve their understanding of alliteration.

Literature Focus Lesson

Fables Draw the organizer to the right on the board. Then read a short fable aloud. Have students work with a partner to complete the organizer with information from the fable. BL

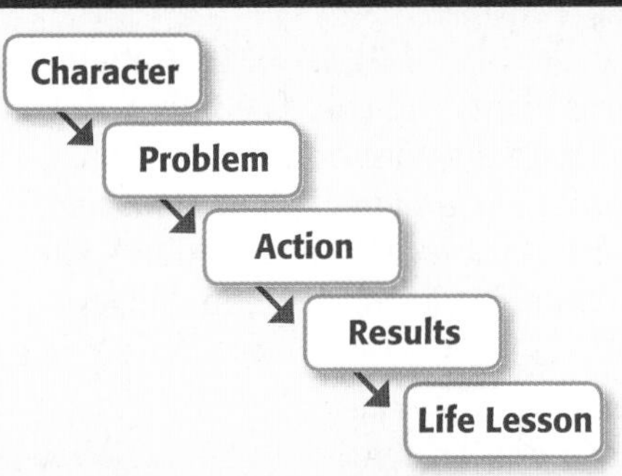

Indiana English/Language Arts Academic Standards
SE: 8.3, 8.3.6
TWE: *Reading in the Real World* 8.5.2, *Literature Focus Lesson* 8.2

Teach

R Reading Skill

Interpreting **Ask:** What is the poet describing in the first twelve lines of the poem? *(a baby chick's struggle to crack its way out of the egg)* AS **Ask:** What feeling does the poet try to suggest? *(Possible response: pity; worry; wanting the chick to succeed)* OL **Ask:** How can the image of a chick breaking out of a shell be related to the human experience? *(Possible response: It could symbolize people breaking through a fear.)* AL

Viewing the Art

Ask: What part of the poem does the art depict? *(A bird attempting to hatch out of an egg.)* **Say:** Although the creatures in the egg looked trapped, they seem to be celebrating or moving with excitement and determination. What might they be celebrating? *(Possible response: birth)* OL

Fable for When There's No Way Out

by May Swenson

In The Interior of Sight. Max Ernst (1891-1976). Oil on canvas. Musee National d'Art Moderne, Centre Georges Pompidou, Paris.

Grown too big for his skin,
and it grown hard,

without a sea and atmosphere— **1**
he's drunk it all up—

his strength's inside him now,
but there's no room to stretch.

He pecks at the top
but his beak's too soft;

though **instinct** and **ambition** shoves,
he can't get through.

Barely old enough to bleed
and already bruised! **2**

R

Vocabulary

instinct (IN stinkt) *n.* unlearned knowledge that a person or an animal is born with

ambition (am BISH un) *n.* a strong drive or desire to succeed

Practice the Skills

1 Key Reading Skill

Interpreting What does the phrase "without a sea and atmosphere" mean? Think about what it's like inside an egg once a chick is ready to hatch.

2 Key Literary Element

Alliteration What alliteration do you see in this stanza of the poem?

Additional Support

Differentiated Instruction

Using Graphic Organizers To help students clarify the chick's conflict, draw a web diagram on the board. In the center circle write, "What obstacles does the chick face?" Help students fill in the outer circles of the web diagram. You might discuss the poem stanza by stanza to identify the obstacles. *(Possible responses: grown too big for its skin; soft beak; hard shell; no air to breathe; bruised; no room to stretch)* BL

In a case this tough
what's the use

if you break your head
instead of the lid? **R**

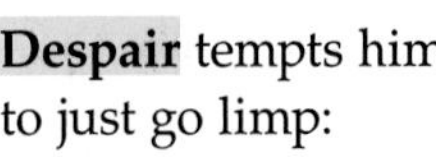

Despair tempts him
to just go limp:

Maybe the cell's
already a tomb,* **3**

and beginning end
in this round room.

Still, stupidly he pecks
and pecks, as if from under 

his own skull—
yet makes no crack . . .

No crack until
he finally cracks,

and kicks and stomps. **4**
What a thrill

and shock to feel
his little gaff* poke

through the floor!
A way he hadn't known or meant.

Rage works if reason won't. **5**
When locked up, bear down. **6** ❍

---

20 A ***tomb*** is a room or chamber where a dead body is placed.

32 A ***gaff*** is a sharp metal spur on the leg of a fighting bird.

Vocabulary

despair (dih SPAIR) *n.* a complete loss of hope

rage (rayj) *n.* a feeling of great anger or fury

Practice the Skills

3 Key Reading Skill

Interpreting What does the speaker compare to a cell and a tomb? What do you think this comparison means?

4 English Language Coach

Word Choice, Purpose, and Audience Do you get a chuckle out of the double meaning of *crack*? Picture the tiny chick going nuts, kicking and stomping and finally cracking through the shell. How does the poet achieve this effect?

5 Key Literary Element

Alliteration What words in this line begin with the same sound?

6 BIG Question

What do you think the poet wants you to learn from the chick's struggle? Write your answer on the "Fable for When There's No Way Out" page of Foldable 4. Your response will help you complete the Unit Challenge later.

READING WORKSHOP 3

Teach

R Reading Skill

Interpreting **Say:** Reread the first three stanzas on this page. What comment is the author making about humanity? *(Possible response: Everyone has been tempted to give up in the face of what seems to be overwhelming adversity.)* **OL** **AL**

EL Language Coach

Word Choice, Purpose, and Audience **Ask:** Why do you think the poet uses the word *stupidly* in line 23? Do you believe she really thinks the chick is stupid for trying? *(Possible response: She doesn't think he is stupid for trying. In fact, she seems to be impressed at his determination. She is making a comment about how overwhelming and seemingly impossible the task is.)* **EL** **BL**

Assess

Use the CheckPoint questions provided on Presentation Plus! to check for comprehension of the selection. These questions can be used with interactive response keypads for immediate student feedback.

Reading Fluency

Reading Aloud Explain to students that poets use punctuation to let readers know where ideas begin and end. In this poem, the poet uses a period to end each idea. Read the poem aloud as students read along silently. Stop after each period. Ask students to volunteer the idea presented by the sentence. When you've finished, ask students to take turns reading the poem with a partner, pausing at each period. **EL** **BL**

Indiana English/Language Arts Academic Standards

SE: 8.3, 8.3.6

TWE: *Differentiated Instruction* 8.2, *Reading Fluency* 8.7.14

Assess

Resources for page 494

- Selection Quick Check, p. 36
- Selection and Unit Assessment, p. 42
- ExamView Assessment Suite
- Interactive Tutor: Self-Assessment

Students can respond to the *After You Read* items in their Learner's Notebooks or on a separate sheet of paper.

Answering the BIG Question

1. Possible response: Although the chick isn't sure what will work, he keeps trying and gives an all-out effort to finding a solution to his problem.
2. The chick pecks at the hard shell with his soft beak.
3. The chick kicks and stomps and finally cracks the shell with his gaff.

Critical Thinking

4. Responses will vary but should include support from the text.
5. Possible response: The poet hints that some people may think the chick is stupid for continuing to try when his efforts aren't working.
6. Responses will vary but should include support from the text.

After You Read

Fable for When There's No Way Out

Answering the BIG Question

1. What does the chick's behavior in the poem teach you about what to do when you don't know what to do?
2. **Summarize** In lines 7–25, what does the chick do to try to hatch?
   TIP **Think and Search**
3. **Recall** How does the chick finally succeed in breaking the shell?
   TIP **Right There**

Critical Thinking

4. **Infer** Do you think the chick knows it must break the shell in order to survive? Why or why not?
   TIP **Author and Me**
5. **Analyze** Why do you think the poet uses the word "stupidly" in line 23 instead of "blindly," "instinctively," or a synonym?
   TIP **On My Own**
6. **Evaluate** How well does the poem help you imagine what it's like to be a hatching chick? Explain.
   TIP **On My Own**

Talk About Your Reading

Class Discussion Like many poems, "Fable for When There's No Way Out" has two different interpretations. One is a description of a chick pecking its way out of an egg. Another is about life and how to live it. As a class, discuss the second interpretation of the poem. First, several different students should give their view of the poem. Then everyone should talk about what message Swenson may be trying to get across. Try to think of situations in which that message might be helpful.

Indiana English/Language Arts Academic Standards (pp. 494–495)

8.3 Comprehension and Analysis of Literary Text Respond to grade-level-appropriate literature... **8.5.7** Write for different purposes... **8.3.6** Identify significant literary devices...
8.6 English Language Conventions
For a complete description of the standards, see p. IN 11.

Talk About Your Reading

Responses will vary. Students should relate their responses to the poem.

Skills Review

Key Reading Skill: Interpreting

7. The last two lines of the poem suggest that there's a lesson to be learned from the chick's experience. In your own words, how would you explain that lesson?

Key Literary Element: Alliteration

8. Which words are alliterative in lines 5–6?
9. What does alliteration add to the last lines of the poem?

Vocabulary Check

Choose the best word from the list to answer each question below.

instinct ambition despair rage

10. What kind of knowledge are you born with?
11. What is a strong feeling of anger?
12. What helps a person do well and succeed?
13. What does a person feel who has no more hope?
14. **Academic Vocabulary** Write the academic vocabulary word that means "to figure out the meaning of what you read."
15. **English Language Coach** Review the discussion of word choice and author's purpose on page 490. Then choose a sentence from the poem and rewrite it in your Learner's Notebook using more formal diction, as if for an audience of scientists.

Web Activities For eFlashcards, Selection Quick Checks, and other Web activities, go to www.glencoe.com.

Grammar Link: Subject-Verb Agreement with Collective Nouns

Collective nouns name a group made up of a number of people or things.

Common Collective Nouns

audience	committee	family	swarm
class	crowd	flock	team

Collective nouns present special subject-verb agreement problems because they can have either a singular or a plural meaning.

If you are speaking about a group as a unit, then the noun has a singular meaning.

- The jury is refusing to speak to the press.

If you are referring to the individual members of the group, then the noun has a plural meaning.

- The jury are arguing about the case.

Grammar Practice

Rewrite each sentence below, using the correct verb from the pair in parentheses.

16. The audience (is, are) not all in their seats yet.
17. The herd (spend, spends) every summer in the far pasture.
18. The class (take, takes) their lunch at different periods.
19. The team (is, are) taking showers and getting dressed.
20. Every spring the whole family (takes, take) a vacation together.

Skills Review

Key Reading Skill: Interpreting

7. Possible response: Although I may not be sure that I'm on the right track, I'll keep trying until I find something that works.

Key Literary Element: Alliteration

8. strength's and stretch, now and no
9. Responses will vary.

Vocabulary Check

10. instinct
11. rage
12. ambition
13. despair

Academic Vocabulary

14. interpret

English Language Coach

15. Responses will vary.

Close

Ask students how the poem helps them answer the Big Question.

Web Activities Have students access the Web site for interactive activities that will help them assess their understanding of the selection.

Grammar Link: Subject-Verb Agreement with Collective Nouns

Grammar Practice

16. The audience are not all in their seats yet.
17. The herd spends every summer in the far pasture.
18. The class take their lunch at different periods.
19. The team is taking showers and getting dressed.
20. Every spring the whole family takes a vacation together.

Indiana English/Language Arts Academic Standards
SE: 8.3, 8.3.6, 8.5.7, 8.6

Focus

BELLRINGER Options

Daily Language Practice Transparency 38

Focus Activity Say: It's time to reread your poem. Is the language clear and precise? Can readers picture what you do when you don't know what to do? You will have a chance to revise your poem in this workshop. AS

Teach

W Writing

Word Choice Say: In paragraph 1, the process of improving your draft is described as *polishing.* How can you relate that image to your revised poem? *(Possible response: If the poem is "polished," it will be in really good shape and ready to read.)* OL

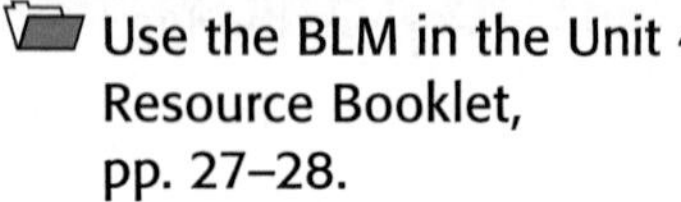

Resources for page 496

Use the BLM in the Unit 4 Resource Booklet, pp. 27–28.

Use the Grammar and Writing Workshop Transparencies 23–24.

WRITING WORKSHOP PART 2

Poem

Revising, Editing, and Presenting

ASSIGNMENT Write a poem

Purpose: To express your thoughts and feelings about what you do when you don't know what to do

Audience: Your teacher and possibly your classmates or family

In Writing Workshop Part 1, you gathered ideas and details and developed a draft. Now you'll revise and edit your draft to improve your poem. When you've finished polishing your poem, you'll share it with classmates and possibly friends or family members. Remember to keep a copy of it in your writing portfolio so that you and your teacher can evaluate your writing progress.

Revising

Make It Better

Skilled writers know that revising their work makes it better. Some even think it's the most important step in the writing process. Revising can take your poem from *blah* to *okay* to *fantastic.* Let's begin.

Improve Your Poem

Read the draft of your poem, looking especially for words that are boring, unclear, or too general. Now's your chance to replace them with more colorful and specific words. Use these tips to help you revise your poem.

Your poem should have . . .	Tip
action verbs	Read the verbs in your poem. Are they the most descriptive ones? Replace a few with words that *sound* like the idea you're describing (zoom, buzz, crackle).
adjectives and adverbs	Add to the word picture by telling exactly what things look like: Leon *proudly* placed the *blue wool* cap on his head.
specific nouns	Replace general nouns (like *music*) with ones that paint a more detailed picture (like *reggae*).
words that appeal to the senses	As you read your poem, do your senses come alive? Add words that help readers smell, taste, touch, hear, or see your poem.
figurative language, such as similes and metaphors	Read your poem as if you were someone else. Are your ideas easy to picture? If not, add similes or metaphors to compare them to things readers can easily picture. Example: Their laughter beat against my brain like a million fists.

Revising Rubric

Your revised poem should

- describe a situation clearly
- use lively, specific words
- use literary devices such as figurative language and sound patterns
- make subjects and verbs agree in number

See page 498 for a model of a poem.

Indiana English/Language Arts Academic Standards (pp. 496–499)

8.4.7 Review, evaluate, and revise writing for meaning and clarity. **8.4.8** Edit and proofread...writing... **8.4.9** Revise writing for word choice... **8.7.14** Recite poems...using voice modulation, tone, and gestures expressively to enhance meaning.

For a complete description of the standards, see p. IN 11.

Additional Support

English Language Coach

Slang Although slang and idioms help some readers connect to a poem, they may confuse other readers, especially those whose first language is not English. Write this poem on the board:

I'm so confused, I do not know
A world with *dude* and *chill.*
So, back off, man. Don't have a cow.
I'll get it. Yes, I will!

Have students copy the poem and underline the slang terms. Pair native English speakers with English language learners and have them work to determine replacements that are part of Standard English. EL OL

What else in your poem might you need to revise or strengthen?

Title

Think of a title as an invitation that makes people want to read the poem.

1. Read your poem aloud and ask yourself
   - *Does my title grab a reader's attention?*
   - *Does it suggest the feelings and ideas that I want?*
   - *Does it give a hint without giving away all the surprises?*
2. Keep editing your title until it sounds right.

Original title:	Funny Poem
Alternate titles:	Bad Day

Writing Tip

Title Trick If you have trouble thinking up a title for your poem, try taking the central word or phrase from your cluster web (page 465) and using alliteration.

How Does Your Poem Sound?

Good poets often use sound devices to make their poems memorable.

- **Rhyme** is the repetition of vowel sounds and succeeding sounds. For example, *game* rhymes with *fame* and *lame.*
- **Rhythm** is the pattern of sound created by stressed and unstressed syllables.
- **Repetition** of words, phrases, or lines can emphasize important ideas and give a sense of unity to a poem.
- **Alliteration** is the repetition of sounds at the beginnings of words. Example: "The siren split the silence of the night."

Writing Tip

Repetition Choose a favorite line from your poem and repeat it, maybe just once or twice, or maybe as the last line of every stanza.

Editing

Finish It Up

Use the Editing Checklist as you read your poem one last time.

Proofreading Checklist

☑ Words are spelled correctly.
☑ Punctuation is correctly used.
☑ Subjects and verbs agree.

Writing Models For models and other writing activities, go to www.glencoe.com.

Presenting

Show It Off

If you handwrite your poem, write legibly. If you type it, consider using a presentation program and illustrating it with clip art or magazine photos. Add your poem to your classmates' to create a class computer presentation.

Teach

W Writing

Word Choice **Ask:** Why is precise, powerful wording especially important in a title? *(Possible response: With few words, the poet must grab the reader's attention and communicate what the poem's about.)* OL AL

L Literary Element

Rhyme **Say:** When you reread your poem, you may find that some of the rhyming words you used really don't fit the poem. Did you choose some words just to fit the rhyme pattern? Underline the rhyming words in your poem. Does each connect to or describe the main idea? *(Responses will vary.)* **Say:** For those that don't, make a list of other rhyming words you might use instead. AS

Literature Online

Writing Models Have students access the Web site for an additional and interactive Writing Workshop-based student model.

Differentiated Instruction

Title Tips Some students may benefit from practicing different title techniques. Copy the chart below on the board. Discuss how each title models a technique. Ask students to use the chart to write three possible titles for their poem, using each of the three techniques. EL BL

Alliteration	Rhyme	Punctuation
Silly Sam Speaks	The Lone Tone	Why Me?
Perfectly Peachy Poem	Frogs and Dogs	Oh, No, You Don't!

Indiana English/Language Arts Academic Standards

SE: 8.4.7, 8.4.8, 8.4.9
TWE: *English Language Coach* 8.1.1, *Differentiated Instruction* 8.5.7

Teach

L Literary Element

Figurative Language—Metaphor and Simile

Say: Reread your poem. Are you sure readers can picture the ideas from your descriptions? With a partner, use similes and metaphors to put some *zing* into this poem. Then do the same with your own poem. When you've finished revising your draft, your poem should contain at least one simile or metaphor. *(Responses will vary. Students should demonstrate an understanding of how to use similes and/or metaphors.)* OL AL

Assess

Divide students into small groups to give mini-poetry readings. Each student should take a turn reading his or her poem and receiving feedback.

WRITING WORKSHOP PART 2

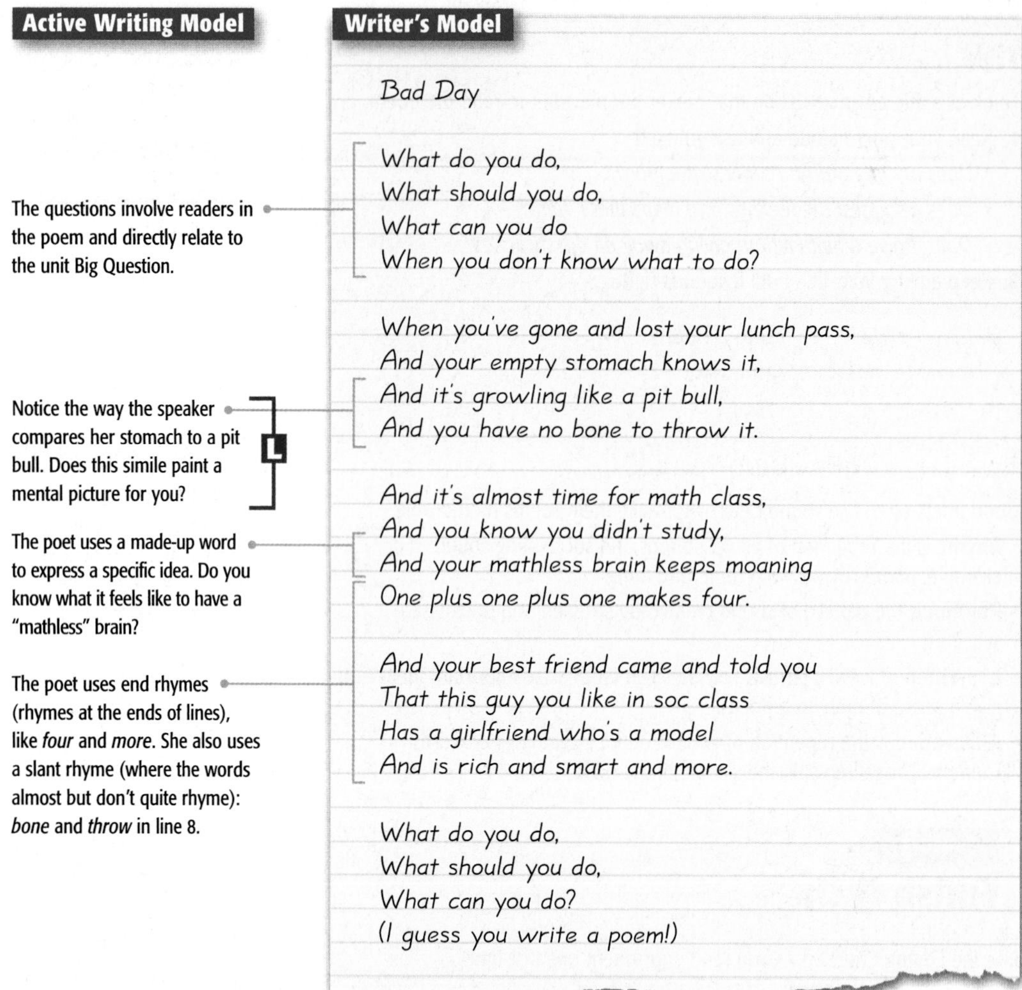

Active Writing Model

The questions involve readers in the poem and directly relate to the unit Big Question.

Notice the way the speaker compares her stomach to a pit bull. Does this simile paint a mental picture for you? L

The poet uses a made-up word to express a specific idea. Do you know what it feels like to have a "mathless" brain?

The poet uses end rhymes (rhymes at the ends of lines), like *four* and *more*. She also uses a slant rhyme (where the words almost but don't quite rhyme): *bone* and *throw* in line 8.

Writer's Model

Bad Day

What do you do,
What should you do,
What can you do
When you don't know what to do?

When you've gone and lost your lunch pass,
And your empty stomach knows it,
And it's growling like a pit bull,
And you have no bone to throw it.

And it's almost time for math class,
And you know you didn't study,
And your mathless brain keeps moaning
One plus one plus one makes four.

And your best friend came and told you
That this guy you like in soc class
Has a girlfriend who's a model
And is rich and smart and more.

What do you do,
What should you do,
What can you do?
(I guess you write a poem!)

Additional Support

Literature Focus Lesson

Poetry The poet of "Bad Day" may be a teenage girl. If not, the poet is definitely someone who understands bad days in teenagers' lives. Good poems connect to the lives and emotions of their audience. Have students work with partners to identify another problem that leads to a bad day. Ask them to write an additional stanza about the problem they selected. Invite students to share their additions. Then have students review their own poems for insights that help audiences connect. OL

Listening, Speaking, and Viewing

Reading Poetry Aloud

What Is It?

Poems are meant to be read aloud. They began as a form of spoken entertainment thousands of years ago. Rhyme and repetition made them easier to remember. We read and listen to poetry differently from other genres of literature.

Why Is It Important?

Reading poems aloud and listening to others read them helps you understand and appreciate the poets' craft. Good reading and listening skills make poems come alive.

How Do I Do It?

Use these tips as you get ready to read aloud.

- First read the poem to yourself. Do you understand it? Are there words you don't know or can't pronounce? Look them up or ask for help.
- Reread the poem to yourself, this time focusing on the feelings and mental pictures the poet creates. At different points in the poem, stop to close your eyes and "feel" each image.
- Practice reading the poem aloud to yourself. Look for punctuation. Pause at the ends of sentences, *not* at the end of every line. Pauses help listeners make sense of words. They also encourage your audience to think about what you've read and what will come next.
- Use your voice well. Don't read too fast, and don't use the same tone of voice the whole way through. Speak louder during important moments. Speak faster as you read action scenes. Use a higher voice for some characters and a lower one for others.
- Make eye contact with listeners. Make them feel as if *you* are the poet, sharing *yourself* as you read. Like any performer, gauge how you are doing by your audience's reaction.

Listening to Poetry

Follow these tips when you listen to poetry.

- What words or lines jumped out at you? Think about why they caught your attention. Did you connect them to experiences or feelings you've had? Could you feel what the poet felt?
- What word pictures did the descriptive details paint? What did you see in your mind?
- Which senses could you use as you listened to the poem? Did the poet make you almost taste or smell or touch something?
- Can you connect the message of the poem to your life? Even when you don't agree with the message, you can often find something in it that relates to your own life.
- Which words *sounded* just right? Did the author make the poem more fun with alliteration and other sound devices?

LSV

Perform In a small group, take turns reading poems aloud. You can read the poem you wrote or you can find another poem to read. Either way, practice reading the poem several times so you can perform it smoothly and easily for your audience.

"LORETTA, LORETTA, LORETTA
MY LOVE, YOUR SKIN IS AS
SOFT AS A NEW BASEBALL GLOVE.
YOUR EYES ARE LIKE MARBLES,
YOUR HAIR LIKE SPAGHETTI.
WHEN I LOOK AT YOU, MY
PALMS GET ALL SWEATY."
.... GEE. YOU SURE KNOW
HOW TO MAKE A GIRL
FEEL SPECIAL.
THANKS. I
WROTE IT
MYSELF.
NO
KIDDING.

Maybe making your own greeting cards isn't such a hot idea.

Analyzing Cartoons

Loretta doesn't find this poem very romantic. Why not? What feelings is her husband trying to express? Does he succeed or fail?

Differentiated Instruction

Listening and Evaluating Some poets and authors read their own work on stage, radio, or television. Others give book or poetry readings at bookstores, libraries, colleges, or universities. Play a tape of Garrison Keillor's radio show *A Prairie Home Companion* or another work of an author reading his or her writing. Before the reading, help students create a list of criteria they will use to evaluate both the literature and the reading style. After the reading, have students discuss their evaluations in small groups. AL

Teach

LSV Listening, Speaking, and Viewing

Listening to Poetry **Say:** Have you ever heard someone read a poem and thought, *I sure wish I could read like that*? A good reader uses voice techniques to make poetry come to life. I'm going to read the same paragraph two ways. How does the way I read give you very different interpretations of the author's message? What techniques do I use to help you interpret the same words differently? *(Responses will vary.)* AS

As you read the following paragraph to students, first assume the speaker is an adolescent who resents staying with Grandma. Roll your eyes, huff, sigh, and show your disdain for the "Grandma experience." Then assume you're a young child who wants to stay with Grandma. Read with smiles, excitement, and enthusiasm.

I'm going to Grandma's this weekend. My parents are flying to Cleveland for Dad's boss's wedding. No kids are invited. At Grandma's, we'll probably do chores first thing in the morning. Then we'll walk downtown where you can watch cheese being made. The dairy also sells homemade ice cream. Grandma always buys us each a cone.

Indiana English/Language Arts Academic Standards

SE: 8.7.14

TWE: *Literature Focus Lesson* 8.5.7, *Differentiated Instruction* 8.7.7

Monitoring Comprehension

Teaching Students to Monitor Comprehension

Why Is It Important?

- The whole point of reading is to understand a piece of text.
- By monitoring their comprehension of a selection, students will learn to think about whether they understand what they're reading.
- Asking questions while reading helps build overall reading skills.

How to Help Students Get It

- Tell students to keep asking themselves questions about main ideas, characters, and events as they read.
- Remind students that to monitor something is to pay attention to it and that comprehension is understanding.
- When they can't answer a question about what they've read, have them review, read more slowly, or ask someone to help them.

Reading to Answer the Big Question

O Captain! My Captain! by Walt Whitman
Profoundly affected by Lincoln's assassination, Whitman could not share in the celebration at the end of the American Civil War. In the extended metaphor of this classic poem, a ship (the United States) returns safely to port, thanks to the efforts of its now-dead captain (Lincoln).

Scorched! How to Handle Different Types of Burns by Stephen Fraser
This informational article describes physical characteristics of first-, second-, and third-degree burns, as well as what actions to take if you are burned.

Workshop Resources

Pacing (days) Standard	Block	Lesson	Student Materials	Teacher Resources
1	1/2	Key Skill Lesson: Monitoring Comprehension: Re-reading	Key Reading Skills Practice, p. 29 English Language Coach Review, p. 41	Bellringer Options Transparencies – Daily Language Practice 39 – Selection Focus 10 Read Aloud, Think Aloud Transparencies – Key Reading Skills 15 – Read Aloud, Think Aloud 35–36 Presentation Plus!
1	1	"O Captain! My Captain!"	Glencoe Online Unit Vocabulary Review, p. 39 Academic Vocabulary Review, p. 43 English Language Coach Active Reading Graphic Organizer, p. 31 Literary Analysis, p. 30 StudentWorks Plus™ Online Student Edition Literature Classics Selection and Unit Assessments, p. 43	Literary and Text Analysis Transparencies 43 Puzzlemaker Skill Level Up!™ A Language Arts Game BookLink 3 Assessment by Learning Objective (Diagnostic and Formative) Interactive Tutor: Self-Assessment TeacherWorks Plus™
1		"Scorched! How to Handle Different Types of Burns"	Glencoe Online Unit Vocabulary Review, p. 39 Academic Vocabulary Review, p. 43 English Language Coach Active Reading Graphic Organizer, p. 33 StudentWorks Plus™ Online Student Edition Literature Classics Selection and Unit Assessments, p. 44	Literary and Text Analysis Transparencies 26 Puzzlemaker Skill Level Up!™ A Language Arts Game BookLink 3 Assessment by Learning Objective (Diagnostic and Formative) Interactive Tutor: Self-Assessment TeacherWorks Plus™

Keys for Unit Resource

- Blackline Master
- Workbook
- Supplemental Text
- CD-ROM
- DVD
- Transparency
- Web-based
- Fast File

Level Appropriate Code

AS = Activities for all students
AL = Activities for students working above grade level
OL = Activities for students working at grade level
BL = Activities for students working below grade level
EL = Activities for English language learners

Focus

BELLRINGER Options

Selection Focus Transparency 10

Daily Language Practice Transparency 39

Focus Activity Ask: Have you ever lost someone or something that is precious to you? How did you feel? Journal write for several minutes about your experience. You will not share your writing with the class, so express your feelings freely. *(Responses will vary.)* AS

Teach

Analyzing the Cartoon

Ask: How does Jeremy's idea of reading a book differ from his mother's? *(Responses will vary.)* **Ask:** Which kind of reading will help him most in school? Why? *(Responses will vary.)* AS

V Vocabulary

Academic Vocabulary
Read aloud the definition of *comprehension*. Give students the synonyms *understanding, grasp,* and *knowledge*, with which they may be more familiar. Tell students that "monitoring comprehension" simply means checking to make sure they understand what they have read. AS

READING WORKSHOP 4

Skills Focus

You will practice using these skills when you read these selections:

- "O Captain! My Captain!" p. 504
- "Scorched! How to Handle Different Types of Burns," p. 510

Reading

- Monitoring comprehension of text

Literature

- Identifying types of rhyme and their effects
- Following instructions

Vocabulary

- Explaining how purpose, audience, and occasion influence word choice
- Academic Vocabulary: *comprehension*

Writing/Grammar

- Using correct subject-verb agreement

Indiana English/Language Arts Academic Standards (pp. 500–501)

8.2 Comprehension and Analysis (Focus on Informational Text) Develop [reading] strategies...

For a complete description of the standards, see p. IN 11.

Skill Lesson

Monitoring Comprehension

Learn It!

What Is It? You finish reading several pages of a book. You look up, and suddenly it dawns on you. You've gotten almost nothing out of what you read. In fact, you can hardly remember it. Sound familiar?

Reading is more than moving your eyes over print. It's making sense of what the print says. To make sure you "get" what you read, you need to monitor, or keep track of, your **comprehension**.

- Check to make sure you understand what you're reading *while you're reading it.*
- If you don't understand something, stop and strategize.

Analyzing Cartoons
Is Jeremy going to remember *David Copperfield* later? If not, why? Why is it important to think carefully about what you read?

V Academic Vocabulary

comprehension (kom prih HEN shun) *n.* the fact or power of understanding

Additional Support

Literature Focus Lesson

Allusion The cartoonist alludes to *David Copperfield*, a novel written by well-known nineteenth-century British author Charles Dickens. It is praised for its well-developed characters and sensitive portrayal of young David's journey from a difficult childhood into adulthood. Dickens himself wrote shortly before his death, "Of all my books, I like this [*David Copperfield*] the best." It often appears on suggested reading lists for high school students. The book is about nine hundred pages long. Ask students why they think it would be impossible for Jeremy to read the book so quickly and understand it. Discuss with them what about this allusion makes the cartoon funny. AS

Why Is It Important? When you monitor your comprehension, you make reading more meaningful. You become a more effective reader because you understand and remember more of what you read.

How Do I Do It? Recognize when your understanding breaks down. Pause from time to time to ask yourself, *Does this make sense to me? Could I explain it to somebody else?* If your answers are *no,* use one or more of the following strategies:

- Carefully reread what you've already read. Look for clues.
- Read on to see if your questions are answered later.
- Ask your teacher or a classmate for help.
- Paraphrase the hard parts by putting them in your own words.

Read on to see how a student applied some of the strategies to monitor her comprehension of a poem.

Literature Online

Study Central Visit www.glencoe.com and click on Study Central to review monitoring comprehension.

The Eagle

He clasps the crag with crooked hands;
Close to the sun in lonely lands,
Ring'd with the azure world, he stands. **R**
The wrinkled sea beneath him crawls;
He watches from his mountain walls,
And like a thunderbolt, he falls. **L**

Who's "he" in line 1? I'll reread the title to see if it gives clues. Hmmm. The title is "The Eagle." So I guess "he" may be a bird. I'll read on to see. I know that clasps means "hold tightly." Birds hold onto their perches tightly. And I know that crags are stony cliffs. I saw on a TV nature show that eagles sometimes nest on cliffs. So "he" probably is an eagle.

Practice It!

Discuss "The Eagle" with a small group of classmates. Then put the poem in your own words. Write your paraphrase in your Learner's Notebook.

Use It!

As you read "O Captain! My Captain!" and "Scorched! How to Handle Different Types of Burns," monitor your comprehension. Use at least two of the strategies above.

Teach

Study Central Have students access the Web site to review monitoring comprehension and to complete a related activity.

R Reading Skill

Monitoring Comprehension
Ask: Where is the eagle? *(He is perched atop a crag surrounded by water.)* **Ask:** What is he doing? *(He is watching the sea.)* **Ask:** What is happening when "he falls"? *(He is diving toward the water to grab a fish.)* **AS**

L Literary Element

Figurative Language—Metaphor and Simile **Ask:** What simile does the poet use to describe the eagle's fall? *(He says it is like a thunderbolt.)* **Ask:** What do you visualize from this simile? *(Possible response: a sudden drop or swoop)* **OL**

Resources for page 501

- Use Key Reading Skills Transparency 15 in *Read Aloud, Think Aloud* to help students practice monitoring comprehension.

English Language Coach

Word Choice Careful word choice is especially important in poetry, where ideas must be conveyed with few words. The poet on this page didn't settle for the word *blue*; instead, the poet used *azure* to describe the sky. Help English learners expand their vocabularies by suggesting precise words for each of the following: *walk, eat, smile, happy, sad, angry,* and *yellow.* Encourage several suggestions for each word. Allow students to consult a thesaurus if necessary. Write all responses on the board. **EL**

Indiana English/Language Arts Academic Standards
SE: 8.2
TWE: *Literature Focus Lesson* 8.3, *English Language Coach* 8.1

Teach

More About the Author

Walt Whitman loved his country. His work as poet, novelist, journalist, and lecturer reflected his devotion to the United States. *Memoranda During the War* urged Americans, both North and South and black and white, to bond together after the Civil War. Whitman wrote "When Lilacs Last in the Dooryard Bloom'd," an elegy for Abraham Lincoln, at his mother's home, where he found comfort after hearing of Lincoln's death.

EL Language Coach

Word Choice and Occasion

Ask: When might you use more formal words in your speaking? *(Possible responses: when I'm talking to a teacher or another adult; when I'm giving a presentation)* **Ask:** When might you choose more formal words in your writing? *(Possible response: when I write something for schoolwork)* **Ask:** When do you use informal language in your writing? *(Possible response: when I e-mail or instant message friends)* AS

Before You Read O Captain! My Captain!

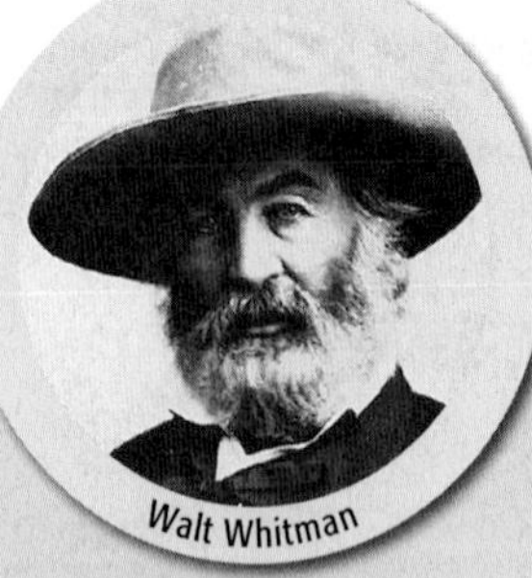

Meet the Author

Walt Whitman (1819–1892) brought a fresh voice to American poetry. His most famous book of poems, *Leaves of Grass,* is an American classic. Whitman is best known for his free verse, in which he writes in the rhythms of spoken language. However, some of his most popular poems are in a more traditional style. See page R7 of the Author Files in the back of the book for more on Walt Whitman.

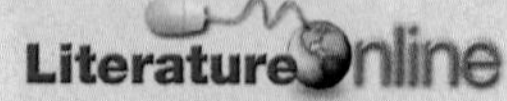

Author Search For more about Walt Whitman, go to www.glencoe.com.

Indiana English/Language Arts Academic Standards (pp. 502–505)

8.3 Comprehension and Analysis of Literary Text Respond to grade-level-appropriate literature...
8.2 Comprehension and Analysis (Focus on Informational Text) Develop [reading] strategies...
8.3.1 Determine...purposes and characteristics of different forms of poetry...

For a complete description of the standards, see p. IN 11.

Vocabulary Preview

grim (grim) *adj.* gloomy; somber **(p. 504)** *The team looked grim after losing the game.*

victor (VIK tor) *adj.* concerning a winner; concerning one who defeats an opponent **(p. 505)** *Al gets the victor prize money because he finished first.*

mournful (MORN ful) *adj.* filled with sadness or grief **(p. 505)** *We were mournful after our dog ran away.*

Think-Pair-Share Think about the words and definitions above. What do you think a poem that has these words in it might be about? Discuss your thoughts with a classmate.

English Language Coach

EL **Word Choice and Occasion** What clothes would you wear to watch a baseball game? Would you wear the same clothes to a wedding? If you're like most people, you dress to fit the occasion, or event. Just as you match your clothing style to the occasion, so authors and public speakers match their choice of words to the event. For formal occasions, authors and speakers might "dress up" their language and use formal words. For everyday events, they might choose informal words. Compare:

Formal Occasion	Informal Occasion
automobile	car
children	kids
dine	eat
father	dad

Write to Learn Below is part of a speech a student has written for graduation. The language he used is too informal for the occasion. In your Learner's Notebook, rewrite the speech. Make the words fit the occasion.

- Hey, I'm here this p.m. to say "Congrats!" to y'all 'cause you're almost outta here!

Additional Support

Author Search To expand students' appreciation of Walt Whitman, have them access the Web site for additional information and resources.

Literature Focus Lesson

Speaker The speaker of a poem is like the narrator of a story. The speaker's voice presents the poem. A common mistake is to assume the speaker is the poet, which is not always the case. Explain to students that to identify the speaker, they can ask themselves the following questions: *Who is the speaker? What kind of person is he or she? Why did the poet choose to present the poem through this voice? How might a different voice change the poem?* Have students work in small groups to answer these questions and discuss the selection. AS

Skills Preview

Key Reading Skill: Monitoring Comprehension

R1 Poems pack a lot of meaning in very few words. You can't skip over too many hard parts in a poem, or you'll get lost. That's why it's especially important to monitor your comprehension when you read poetry.

On Your Own As you read "O Captain! My Captain!" stop after every stanza, or set of lines, and ask yourself whether you "get" what it says. To be sure that you do, sum up the stanza in your own words.

Key Literary Element: Rhyme

The rhymes that you are most familiar with are those that repeat the vowel and consonant sounds (like *moon* and *loon,* or *happy* and *sappy*) at the end of the line. In most poetry, the rhyming words appear at the ends of the lines

Hickory-dickory dock, / the mouse ran up the clock.

But there are other kinds of rhymes. One is called **slant rhyme** or **near rhyme.** In a slant rhyme, the vowel sounds are repeated or the consonant sounds are repeated, but not both.

feet* and *seen ***mine* and *sight***

ball* and *fill ***tick* and *tock***

In a slant rhyme, the effect is like an end-of-a-line rhyme but not quite as strong. Many poets use slant rhymes to make their poetry musical without the sing-song quality that rhymed poetry can have.

Partner Talk Together with a classmate, choose a nursery rhyme and change the rhymes to slant rhymes. Talk about how the slant rhymes change the verse.

Interactive Literary Elements Handbook
To review or learn more about the literary elements, go to www.glencoe.com.

Get Ready to Read

Connect to the Reading

Think of a time when your feelings were different from those of the people around you. For example, you may have felt sad at a time when it seemed as if the whole world was happy. Or you may have been upbeat when everyone else was down.

Write to Learn In your Learner's Notebook, jot down what you were feeling and why.

Building Background

- "O Captain! My Captain!" is an **elegy** (EL uh jee)—a poem written to honor someone who has died. As you might expect, elegies are usually solemn and sad. They praise the person who has died, and they express a sense of loss over the person's death.
- R2 Whitman's elegy honors President Abraham Lincoln. Like most Americans, Whitman was shocked and saddened by Lincoln's death. After leading the United States through the long, dark days of the Civil War, Lincoln was shot and killed by John Wilkes Booth, a Southern sympathizer. Lincoln's greatest hope—that the nation would reunite—was realized when the war drew to a close and the South rejoined the Union. Soon after, Lincoln was killed.
- Have you ever heard someone refer to a nation or its government as a "ship of state"? Whitman uses this metaphor in "O Captain, My Captain." Throughout the poem, he compares post-war America to a ship returning from a difficult journey.

Set Purposes for Reading

BIG Question Read "O Captain! My Captain!" to see how a poet honored a fallen leader.

Set Your Own Purpose What else would you like to learn from the selection to help you answer the Big Question? Write your own purpose on the "O Captain! My Captain!" page of Foldable 4.

Keep Moving

Use these skills as you read the following selection.

Reading in the Real World

Citizenship At the time of the Civil War, slavery was legal according to the U.S. Constitution. Strong disagreements between Northern and Southern states on this issue played a big part in the South's decision to leave the Union. Discuss as a class why slavery was such a volatile issue, touching upon the belief in the equality of all human beings and the necessity for slave labor in order to keep the Southern plantation system afloat. As a class, discuss why people may or may not agree with Whitman's elevated view of Lincoln. OL AL

Teach

R1 Reading Skill

Monitoring Comprehension
Say: You can monitor your comprehension in a variety of ways. One way is to stop and summarize. Also, clarify difficult passages by paraphrasing, asking and answering questions about the passages, or rereading them. Which of these techniques would you find most helpful and why? *(Responses will vary.)* AS

R2 Reading Skill

Review Connecting Ask: What would you do to make yourself feel better after losing someone important in your life? *(Responses will vary.)* AS

Interactive Literary Elements Handbook Have students access the Web site to improve their understanding of rhyme.

Indiana English/Language Arts Academic Standards
SE: 8.2, 8.3, 8.3.1
TWE: *Literature Focus Lesson* 8.3, *Reading in the Real World* 8.3.7

Teach

R1 Reading Skill

Monitoring Comprehension
Say: In line 2 the poet uses the metaphor "the prize we sought is won." What is the "prize" he refers to? *(The Union was preserved.)* **AL**

L Literary Element

Rhyme **Ask:** What kind of rhyme does the poet use in lines 6 and 8? *(repeating vowel sounds)* **OL**

R2 Reading Skill

Monitoring Comprehension
Ask: Does the speaker actually expect his "Captain" to rise from the dead, as he demands in line 9? *(no)* **AS** **Say:** Describe what is happening in lines 9–11. *(Possible response: The speaker is celebrating the dead man, namely Lincoln, by explaining the ways that the crowd is honoring his memory.)* **OL** **AL**

READING WORKSHOP 4

O Captain! My Captain!

by Walt Whitman

O Captain! my Captain! our fearful trip is done;
The ship has weather'd every rack,* the prize we sought
is won; **1**
The port is near, the bells I hear, the people all exulting,*
While follow eyes the steady keel,* the vessel **grim** and
daring:
But O heart! heart! heart!
O the bleeding drops of red,
Where on the deck my Captain lies,
Fallen cold and dead. **2**

O Captain! my Captain! rise up and hear the bells;
Rise up—for you the flag is flung—for you the bugle
trills; **3**
For you bouquets and ribbon'd wreaths—for you the shores
a-crowding;

2 Here, ***rack*** means "storm" or "jolt."

3 People who are ***exulting*** are filled with joy.

4 The keel is the main timber that runs along the bottom of a boat. So a ***steady keel*** is a straight, even course.

Vocabulary

grim (grim) *adj.* gloomy; somber

Practice the Skills

1 Reviewing Skills

Symbol In this poem, the ship is a symbol for the country, the United States of America. Who would the captain of the ship be?

2 Key Reading Skill

Monitoring Comprehension Stop and think about the first stanza. Could you explain it in your own words? If not, reread it and discuss it with someone.

3 Key Literary Element

Rhyme Reread lines 9–10. What word does each line end with? What type of rhyme do these two words create?

Additional Support

Reading Fluency

Reading Aloud Tell students that reading poetry aloud is a good way for them to build reading fluency. Read the poem aloud for students, or have them listen to an audio recording, as they follow along in their textbooks. Then have students take turns reading stanzas aloud. You might divide students into groups of three and have each group member read a stanza. After students have had time to practice reading aloud, allow them to perform a reading for the rest of the class. Remind students to pay attention to punctuation marks and line breaks as they read. **AS**

For you they call, the swaying mass, their eager faces
  turning:
  Here, Captain! dear father!
    This arm beneath your head;
      It is some dream that on the deck,
        You've fallen cold and dead. 4

My Captain does not answer, his lips are pale and still;
My father does not feel my arm, he has no pulse nor will;
The ship is anchor'd safe and sound, its voyage closed
  and done;
From fearful trip, the **victor** ship comes in with object won:
  Exult, O shores, and ring, O bells!
    But I, with **mournful** tread,
      Walk the deck my Captain lies,
        Fallen cold and dead. 5

R

Practice the Skills

4 **English Language Coach**

Word Choice and Occasion Whitman uses formal language in the poem. Why is that type of language fitting for an elegy?

5 **BIG Question**

What does the speaker do to cope with the "captain's" death? Write your answer on the "O Captain! My Captain!" page of Foldable 4. Your response will help you complete the Unit Challenge later.

Flying Cloud, 1852. Currier and Ives. Private collection.

Vocabulary

victor (VIK tor) *adj.* concerning a winner; concerning one who defeats an opponent

mournful (MORN ful) *adj.* filled with sadness or grief

READING WORKSHOP 4

Teach

R Reading Skill

Monitoring Comprehension

Say: The poet calls Lincoln "Captain." What is the significance of this title? *(Possible response: A captain is responsible for a ship's safety and operation, and Lincoln was responsible for restoring the country to wholeness and safety.)* **Ask:** Why does he also call Lincoln "father"? *(Possible response: The poet feels affection for Lincoln.)* OL

Viewing the Art

Ask: In what ways does this art relate to the poem? *(Possible response: It shows a ship with an American flag, possibly like the one described in the first stanza.)* OL **Ask:** Do you think this artwork fits well with the poem? Explain. *(Responses will vary.)* AL

Assess

CheckPoint

Use the CheckPoint questions provided on Presentation Plus! to check for comprehension of the selection. These questions can be used with interactive response keypads for immediate student feedback.

English Language Coach

Word Choice Many poems have both rhyme and meter. To create both, poets sometimes invert word order within sentences and phrases. For example, Whitman writes "For you they call" instead of "They call for you." Have students rewrite this poem, arranging words in the order in which people normally say them (subject-verb-object). Ask students to evaluate which poem is more effective—Whitman's original or their rewritten versions. Ask them to explain their reasoning. OL

Indiana English/Language Arts Academic Standards

SE: 8.2, 8.3, 8.3.1

TWE: *Reading Fluency* 8.7.14, *English Language Coach* 8.3

Assess

Resources for page 506

- Selection Quick Check, p. 37
- Selection and Unit Assessment, p. 43
- ExamView Assessment Suite
- Interactive Tutor: Self-Assessment

Students can respond to the *After You Read* items in their Learner's Notebooks or on a separate sheet of paper.

Answering the BIG Question

1. Possible response: Sometimes writing about your feelings helps you deal with a difficult situation.
2. to the port
3. at the port or shoreline

Critical Thinking

4. Possible response: The Civil War is the "fearful trip" that has ended. The war threatened the existence of the nation and took the lives of hundreds of thousands of people.
5. Possible response: Lincoln has succeeded in preserving the Union.
6. Responses will vary.

After You Read

O Captain! My Captain!

Answering the BIG Question

1. After reading "O Captain! My Captain!" what are your thoughts about what to do when you don't know what to do?
2. **Recall** Where is the ship headed at the beginning of the poem?
   TIP **Right There**
3. **Recall** Where are the people who are waiting for the ship to return?
   TIP **Think and Search**

Critical Thinking

4. **Interpret** In line 1, what "fearful trip" has the "ship of state" completed? What made the trip so fearful?
   TIP **Author and Me**
5. **Interpret** In line 2, what "prize" has the "captain" won?
   TIP **Author and Me**
6. **Evaluate** In your opinion, is the comparison between post-war America and a ship returning home an effective one? Explain.
   TIP **On My Own**

Talk About Your Reading

Literature Groups With a small group of classmates, compare and contrast the speaker's feelings with those of the other people in the poem.

- *In what ways are his feelings the same as theirs?*
- *In what ways are his feelings different?*
- *Why are his feelings different?*

Back up your ideas with specific details from the poem. Keep track of your ideas on a Venn diagram like the one pictured below.

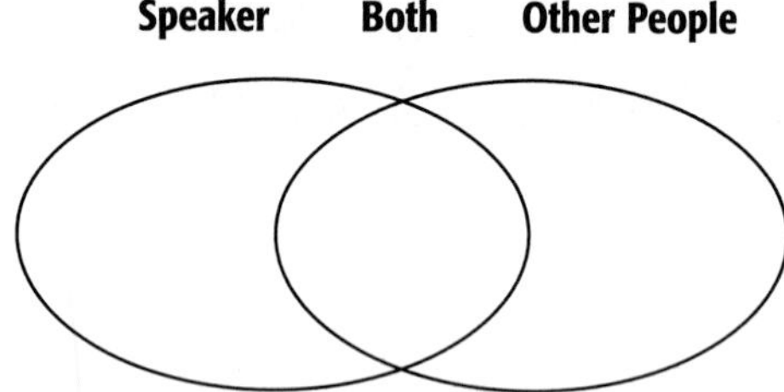

Indiana English/Language Arts Academic Standards (pp. 506–507)

8.3 Comprehension and Analysis of Literary Text Respond to grade-level-appropriate literature... **8.7.11** Deliver oral responses to literature...
8.2 Comprehension and Analysis (Focus on Informational Text) Develop [reading] strategies...
8.3.1 Determine...purposes and characteristics of different forms of poetry...
8.6 English Language Conventions
For a complete description of the standards, see p. IN 11.

Talk About Your Reading

Possible response:
The speaker shares the pleasure of Lincoln's success with the crowds he describes. It seems that the crowd is focused on celebrating the victory and the preservation of the Union, while the speaker's focus is on the loss of Lincoln, the Captain, and the speaker is mourning that loss.

Skills Review

Key Reading Skill: Monitoring Comprehension

7. a. What strategies did you use to monitor your comprehension as you read the poem?

b. Will you use these strategies when you read poetry again? Why or why not?

Key Literary Element: Rhyme

8. What end rhymes can you find in the third stanza? List them in pairs, like this: still/will

9. What is the slant rhyme in the third stanza? Fill in the blanks: ___ / ___

10. a. How does rhyme help unify the ideas in the poem?

b. How does rhyme add to the "music" of the poem?

Vocabulary Check

Choose the best word from the list to complete each sentence below. Rewrite each completed sentence on a separate sheet of paper.

grim victor mournful

11. If you're filled with sadness and grief, you're ___.

12. If you've won a game or contest, you are the ___.

13. If a situation is very serious, it is ___.

14. Academic Vocabulary Define *comprehension* in your own words.

15. English Language Coach Change the language below to make the phrases sound less formal.

- "the prize we sought is won"
- "the people [are] all exulting"
- "the vessel [is] grim and daring"

16. English Language Coach If your word changes were put in the first stanza of the poem, how would the poem change? Do you think the changed poem would still fit the occasion? Explain.

Grammar Link: Agreement in Relative Clauses

Relative pronouns refer to nouns. The five relative pronouns are *that, which, who, whom,* and *whose.*

A **relative clause** is a group of words that begins with a relative pronoun followed by a noun and a verb or a verb only.

- The bike that Collin wants is expensive. (The relative pronoun *that* refers to the noun *bike.* The relative clause begins with *that* followed by the noun *Collin* and the verb *wants.*)
- This bike, which is on sale, costs a lot less. (The relative clause begins with the relative pronoun *which* followed by the verb *is.*)

Be careful to choose the correct verb form for relative clauses. A relative pronoun may be singular or plural, depending on the noun it refers to.

- The boy who runs the bike club owns a racer. (The relative pronoun *who* refers to the noun *boy.* Because boy is singular, or equal to *he,* the present tense verbs that go with *boy* must end in *-s.* Both *runs* and *owns* end in *-s,* so they are correct.)
- Two boys who race for the club win awards. (The relative pronoun *who* refers to the noun *boys.* Because *boys* is plural, or equal to *they,* the present tense verbs that go with *boys* should not end in *-s.* Neither *race* nor *win* ends in *-s,* so both verbs are correct.)

Grammar Practice

Underline the relative clause in each sentence. Then choose the correct verb form.

17. The girl who (wants, want) a bike (is, are) here.

18. The model that we (sells, sell) (is, are) the best.

Web Activities For eFlashcards, Selection Quick Checks, and other Web activities, go to www.glencoe.com.

Skills Review

Key Reading Skill: Monitoring Comprehension

7. Responses will vary.

Key Literary Element: Rhyme

8. still/will; done/won; tread/dead

9. lips/still

10. a. Possible response: End rhymes help readers know which lines are part of the same thought. **b.** Possible response: End rhymes help readers predict the next line, similar to the way listeners can guess what the next song line will be.

Vocabulary Check

11. mournful

12. victor

13. grim

Academic Vocabulary

14. Possible response: *Comprehension* is your understanding of what you read or hear.

English Language Coach

15. Possible responses:

- We won the prize we were after.
- Everyone is celebrating.
- The ship is dark and frightening.

16. Responses will vary.

Grammar Link: Agreement in Relative Clauses

Grammar Practice

17. The girl who wants a bike is here.

18. The model that we sell is the best.

Close

Ask students to discuss how Abraham Lincoln responded to a situation in which he did not know what to do. Also, discuss Walt Whitman's writing the poem as a way to do something in a difficult situation.

Indiana English/Language Arts Academic Standards
SE: 8.2, 8.3, 8.3.1, 8.6, 8.7.11

Teach

More About Sunburns

Sunburn occurs when the skin is overexposed to the sun's ultraviolet radiation. Exposure to the sun is the number one cause of skin cancer. Today the risk of getting skin cancer is one in eighty-seven. To avoid sunburn:

- Apply sunscreen thirty to forty-five minutes before sun exposure.
- Use the right SPF sunscreen for your skin type. A sunscreen with 30 SPF will block about 97 percent of all radiation.
- Reapply sunscreen every two hours, or sooner if swimming or sweating.

V Vocabulary

Synonyms Have students review the sentences they wrote for the Vocabulary Preview. Then have them substitute synonyms for each of the vocabulary words in their sentences. Provide access to a thesaurus. *(Possible responses: hobbled/limped; severity/seriousness; minor/small, unimportant; sterile/clean)* AS

Before You Read

Scorched! How to Handle Different Types of Burns

Did You Know?

Every year, about a million Americans go to hospitals to get treatment for burns. The burns range from mild (a slightly blistered finger) to extremely serious (burns over 20 percent or more of the body). Yet most burn accidents are preventable. How many of the following safety steps have you and your family taken?

- Keep home water heaters set at 120 degrees F or below.
- Turn pot handles toward the back of the stove.
- Never put hot foods or liquids near the edges of tables or counter tops.
- Check the cords on your electrical appliances to ensure they're in good shape.
- Make sure you have smoke alarms near sleeping areas in your home.
- Keep matches, lighters, and all other fire-starting materials away from children.

Indiana English/Language Arts Academic Standards (pp. 508–513)

8.1 Word Recognition, Fluency, and Vocabulary Development Use... context clues...to determine the meaning of words... **8.2 Comprehension and Analysis (Focus on Informational Text)** Develop [reading] strategies...

For a complete description of the standards, see p. IN 11.

Vocabulary Preview

hobbled (HOB uld) *v.* walked with difficulty; limped; form of the verb *hobble* **(p. 510)** *Xavier hobbled to school on his sprained ankle.*

severity (suh VAIR ih tee) *n.* state of being very dangerous or harmful **(p. 510)** *Because of the severity of her injury, we called for an ambulance to rush her to the hospital.*

minor (MY nur) *adj.* of little importance; not serious **(p. 511)** *Minor injuries can be treated at home.*

sterile (STAIR ul) *adj.* free from germs; very clean **(p. 512)** *Cover the cut with a sterile bandage.*

V **Write to Learn** For each of the above vocabulary words, write a sentence that shows what the word means.

English Language Coach

Word Choice and Subject To write about some subjects, authors must use specialized terms—words that are specific to the particular subjects. For example, authors writing about cooking might use the specialized terms *sauté, blanch*, and *fricassee,* while authors writing about football might use the terms *down, snap,* and *sack.* Authors do not define specialized terms if they are writing for readers who already know their subjects. When writing for general audiences who may not know the terms, the authors explain what the words mean. Specialized terms are useful because they allow people to communicate about a subject clearly and precisely.

Whole Class Discussion Which of the above specialized terms can class members define? As a class, write a definition for each term. Your definition should explain the terms clearly to people who know nothing about cooking or football. Copy the chart below into your Learner's Notebook. Fill in the right column with the definitions you write.

Subject	Specialized Term	Definition
cooking	sauté	
	blanch	
	fricasee	
football	down	
	snap	
	sack	

Additional Support

Differentiated Instruction

Making Posters Posters give instructions on all kinds of topics—from building a fence to giving an infant CPR. Because many posters deal with life-and-death situations, instructions on them must be accurate, complete, and clear. Have students work with partners to choose and research a topic for which an educational poster would be helpful. Students should decide on the best presentation techniques, such as bulleted or numbered steps, diagrams, or illustrations. Display finished posters in the classroom. OL

Skills Preview

Key Reading Skill: Monitoring Comprehension

When you monitor your comprehension, pause from time to time to make sure you understand what you are reading. If you don't understand, strategize.

Whole Class Discussion As a class, list and discuss strategies that can help readers improve their comprehension. Review the strategies on page 501, and add strategies of your own.

Text Element: Instructions

Instructions are explanations of how to perform a process. Recipes that explain how to cook something, on-screen commands that tell how to program a DVD player, and a teacher's directions on how to do homework are all examples of instructions. Instructions are usually written in **chronological order,** or time order, so that the first step in the process is presented first, the next step is presented second, and so on. When you read instructions, follow these tips: R

- Quickly read through all the instructions before you begin to follow them. Get an overview.
- Remember that numbered, step-by-step instructions are usually the easiest to read and follow. If instructions are not in that format, take notes. In your notes, break the process into steps and number each step.
- As you read, picture yourself doing each step. Visualizing will help you understand and follow the instructions successfully.

Partner Work With a partner, jot down instructions on how to perform a simple process, such as brushing your teeth or washing a car. Then give your instructions to another pair of students for evaluation.

Interactive Literary Elements Handbook To review or learn more about the literary elements, go to www.glencoe.com.

Get Ready to Read

Connect to the Reading

As you read "Scorched! How to Handle Different Types of Burns," try to remember everything you know about taking care of a burn.

Small Group Discussion What do you know about taking care of skin after a burn? When might you be able to take care of a burn by yourself? When would you need to call a doctor right away? See how much your class already knows about first aid for this kind of injury.

Build Background

The selection you are about to read tells you how to begin to treat a burn.

- C The most common types of burns come from fire, boiling water, or too much time in the sun.
- Chemicals can also cause burns and should be handled carefully.

Set Purposes for Reading

BIG Question Read the selection "Scorched! How to Handle Different Types of Burns" to find out about how to deal with burns—from mild to serious.

Set Your Own Purpose What else would you like to learn from the selection to help you answer the Big Question? Write your own purpose on the "Scorched!" page of Foldable 4.

Keep Moving

Use these skills as you read the following selection.

Teach

R Reading Skill

Review Interpreting Say: Many buildings have posters with instructions for emergencies. Do you think these are necessary? Explain. *(Responses will vary.)* **Ask:** Why are posters used, rather than pamphlets? *(Possible response: Posters can be read in a hurry and contain just the important information.)* AS

C Critical Thinking

Analysis Say: What effect do the statistics presented in the Build Background section have? *(Possible response: They convince readers that burns are serious and can happen to them.)* AS

Interactive Literary Elements Handbook Have students access the Web site to improve their understanding of instructions.

Reading in the Real World

Citizenship Explain to students that the text they are about to read tells them how to handle different types of burns. However, it does not address how to avoid burns. First, have students read the Build Background section on the student page to learn more about the causes of common burns. Then have them work in small groups to write manuals on how to avoid burns in the first place. Suggest that they make pamphlets, fliers, or small booklets to give instructions on how to avoid burns. Remind them to make sure to use catchy titles and include illustrations. Have volunteers share their manuals with the rest of the class. OL

Indiana English/Language Arts Academic Standards
SE: 8.1, 8.2
TWE: *Differentiated Instruction* 8.5.7, *Reading in the Real World* 8.5.7

Teach

R Reading Skill

Monitoring Comprehension
Ask: Which words in the first paragraph help you picture a fuse? *(gas trail leading away from the stump)* **Ask:** In this case, what is the purpose of a fuse? *(to start a fire)* OL

EL Language Coach

Word Choice and Subject
Say: Read the first sentence of the third paragraph. Which word is used as specialized medical terminology? *(sustaining)* **Ask:** What does the word mean in this context? *(It means he experienced or suffered burns.)* EL

C Critical Thinking

Analysis **Ask:** What is the author's purpose for introducing the selection with this anecdote? *(Possible response: It is interesting and frightening, showing readers that the same thing could happen to them. It draws readers in so that they will pay attention to the instructions that follow.)* AL

Readability Scores
Dale-Chall: 5.7
DRP: 58
Lexile: 850

READING WORKSHOP 4

INFORMATIONAL TEXT
MAGAZINE
Current Health

SCORCHED!

How to Handle Different Types of Burns

by Stephen Fraser

Bryant Rice, 14, of Ravenna, Neb., was home alone one day when he decided to burn a stump in the yard. First he tried lighting the stump with a match. When that failed, he poured gasoline onto it and made a gas trail leading away from the stump, thinking the trail would act as a fuse. R

Suddenly, the gasoline caught fire. Bryant's clothing went up in flames. Fortunately, he remembered a technique from a fire-safety class in school, namely, stop-drop-roll. He did just that: He dropped to the ground and rolled on the grass, which put out the flames. 1 C

After sustaining burns on 20 percent of his body, he **hobbled** indoors, drew a cool bath, and sat in it while he called his mom. When Bryant's mother arrived home, she took one look at her peeling son and called 911. EL

Burns are classified according to the degree of **severity** of skin damage as follows: first degree, second degree, and third degree. That day, Bryant messed with fire and experienced the worst kind of burn—third degree. If you were in Bryant's shoes, would you know what to do? Get the burn basics. 2

If your clothes catch fire, don't run! Stop where you are, drop to the ground, cover your face with your hands, and roll over and over to smother the flames.

Practice the Skills

1 Text Element

Instructions The author gives simple instructions here. What are the three steps in the process?

2 English Language Coach

Word Choice and Subject "Third-degree burn" is a specialized term. Here, the author defines it very simply. Later, he will define it in detail.

Vocabulary

hobbled (HOB uld) *v.* walked with difficulty; limped

severity (suh VAIR ih tee) *n.* state of being very dangerous or harmful

Additional Support

Literature Focus Lesson

Organization Have students skim through the selection, noting the boldfaced heads. Ask students to explain what purpose the heads serve. Then discuss with students how the author has organized the text. Students should note that he has divided his instructions into three categories: first-degree, second-degree, and third-degree burns. He tells what each is, how serious each is, and what to do in each instance. Ask students why they think he has organized the text this way. OL
Then ask them to explain whether or not they think this method of organization is an effective way to present the information. AL

What It Is: First-degree burn

What It Looks Like Only the top layer of skin is damaged, resulting in redness, swelling, and pain. For example, most sunburns are first-degree burns. The healing time for a first-degree burn is about three to six days. R1

How Serious Is It?

If the burn is large or involves the face, feet, groin, or buttocks, see a doctor. If not, the burn should be treated as minor. See treatment for **minor** burns, below. R2

What to Do

Cool it! Hold the burned area under cool (not cold) running water for about 15 minutes, or apply a cold compress[1] to it. Cooling reduces swelling by conducting heat away from the skin. *Never* put ice on a burn; frostbite could result.

Visual Vocabulary ***Aloe vera*** is a plant whose leaves contain a jellylike material which is often used to make lotions that soothe the skin.

Moisturize. To prevent drying, apply an aloe vera lotion, an antibiotic ointment,[2] or a moisturizer. Avoid home remedies, such as butter or olive oil. Those can do harm by mixing with bacteria on the skin and causing infection. 3 EL

1. A ***compress*** is a pad or cloth that can be used to apply cold, heat, or medicine.
2. ***Ointment*** is an oily substance put on the skin to heal or protect it.

Vocabulary

minor (MY nur) *adj.* of little importance; not serious

Practice the Skills

3 Key Reading Skill

Monitoring Comprehension Do you understand now what to do for a minor burn? If not, reread this section.

English Language Coach

Specialized Words Sometimes special dictionaries or glossaries are written to help people understand words in specific career fields, such as medicine. Have students work with partners to identify ten words in the selection that qualify as specialized medical vocabulary. Ask students to create a glossary, arranging the terms alphabetically, providing definitions, and including illustrations where helpful. EL BL OL

Teach

R1 Reading Skill

Monitoring Comprehension
Ask: Is a minor burn extremely serious according to the text? *(not usually)* **Ask:** Which information helped you decide? *(Possible response: You don't need to see a doctor for a minor burn unless it is large or on the face, feet, groin, or buttocks. Also, the definition of* minor *is "unimportant" or "small.")* AS

R2 Reading Skill

Review Connecting **Ask:** Have you ever had a minor burn? How did you treat the burn? *(Responses will vary.)* AS

EL Language Coach

Word Choice and Subject
Say: Reread the last paragraph on this page. Based on context clues, what is a common word for remedies? *(Possible responses: cures; medicines)* EL

Indiana English/Language Arts Academic Standards
SE: 8.1, 8.2
TWE: *Literature Focus Lesson* 8.2.6, 8.2.7; *English Language Coach* 8.1

Teach

R1 Reading Skill

Monitoring Comprehension
Ask: When would a second-degree burn on the arm need a doctor's attention? *(if it is more than two inches wide)* AS

E Text Element

Instructions Ask: Under which heading does the author include instructions? *("What to Do")* **Ask:** Where else can you find instructions? *(Under the heading "How Serious Is It?")* OL

R2 Reading Skill

Monitoring Comprehension
Ask: Why might someone with third-degree burns not realize how bad the burns are? *(Possible response: Third-degree burns can be painless due to nerve damage.)* OL

READING WORKSHOP 4

Cover the burn with a **sterile** gauze[3] bandage. The bandage, placed loosely over the burn, will reduce pain and prevent blistering.

What It Is: Second-degree burn

What It Looks Like The top layer of skin is burned through, and the second layer is damaged. The skin takes on a red, blotchy look, and blisters form. 4 Severe pain and swelling may occur, and healing can take weeks.

How Serious Is It?

If the burn involves the face, feet, groin, or buttocks, or is more than 2 inches wide, see a doctor. Otherwise, treat the burn as minor. You may need to add the steps listed below. R1

What to Do

Take an over-the-counter pain reliever. Watch for signs of infection—increased pain, redness, fever, swelling, or oozing. If any of those signs appear, seek medical help. E

Don't pierce blisters; they protect against infection. If a blister accidentally breaks, wash the area with soap and water, then apply an antibiotic ointment and a gauze bandage.

What It Is: Third-degree burn

What It Looks Like All layers of skin and the underlying tissue are permanently damaged. The burned area may be dry and leathery or charred with black or white patches. R2 Because nerve damage may occur, a third-degree burn can be painless. Healing is slow, and new skin has difficulty forming, except on the edges of the burn.

How Serious Is It?

Very serious. Seek immediate medical help. E

3. ***Gauze*** is a light-weight cloth used as a bandage for a wound.

Vocabulary

sterile (STAIR ul) *adj.* free from germs; very clean

Practice the Skills

4 English Language Coach

Word Choice and Subject
The author does not use specialized language in his description of second-degree burns. Why do you think he uses simple, everyday language?

Additional Support

Reading in the Real World

Career Students may be interested in finding out about careers as firefighters, paramedics, and emergency medical technicians. As a class, prepare interview questions about job duties, educational requirements, compensation, working conditions, and job opportunities. Invite a member of a burn treatment-related profession to visit the classroom. Allow the volunteer to explain his or her job, and then have a question-and-answer period. Finally, have students compose a one-page description of the job discussed. AS

What to Do

- Dial 911 for emergency medical assistance.
- Make sure the victim is not in contact with burning material or exposed to either heat or smoke.
- Make sure the victim is breathing, and perform cardiopulmonary resuscitation (CPR) if necessary.
- Don't remove burned clothing or apply ointments to the burn.
- Cover the burn with a cool, moist bandage or a clean cloth. 5 ❍

Practice the Skills

R1

R2

EL

5 BIG Question

Why do you think the writer of "Scorched!" gives readers such careful instructions for treating burns? Do you think most people could tell the difference between a mild burn and a more serious one? Do you think this article can help readers deal with burns in the future? Write your answers on the "Scorched!" page of Foldable 4. Your response will help you complete the Unit Challenge later.

Teach

R1 Reading Skill

Review Evaluating Ask: Are the steps in the "What to Do" section in logical order? Explain. *(Possible response: Yes, the steps make sense because they're organized in order of importance.)* AL

R2 Reading Skill

Monitoring Comprehension

Ask: Why is the second bulleted point necessary? *(so the victim isn't further hurt by burning material, heat, or smoke)* AS

EL Language Coach

Word Choice and Subject

Ask: What specialized word in the bulleted list describes a method of restoring someone's breathing? *(cardiopulmonary resuscitation, or CPR)* EL

Assess

Use the CheckPoint questions provided on Presentation Plus! to check for comprehension of the selection. These questions can be used with interactive response keypads for immediate student feedback.

Differentiated Instruction

Using Graphic Organizers Draw the following chart on the board and ask students to work in pairs to fill in information from the text. You might lead students through an example, completing the column for first-degree burns. Suggest students keep their charts as study aides. BL

Information	First-Degree Burn	Second-Degree Burn	Third-Degree Burn
How it Looks			
Damage Done			
What to Do			

Indiana English/Language Arts Academic Standards

SE: 8.1, 8.2

TWE: *Reading in the Real World* 8.4, *Differentiated Instruction* 8.2

Assess

Resources for page 514

- Selection Quick Check, p. 38
- Selection and Unit Assessment, p. 44
- ExamView Assessment Suite
- Interactive Tutor: Self-Assessment

Students can respond to the *After You Read* items in their Learner's Notebooks or on a separate sheet of paper.

Answering the

1. Responses will vary.
2. He stopped, dropped, and rolled.
3. Possible response: I can call 911 and make sure that I'm away from flames, smoke, and heat. I can cover my burn with a cool, moist bandage or clean cloth. If it's someone else, I can also perform CPR.

Critical Thinking

4. Possible response: This method keeps oxygen from feeding the flames.
5. Possible response: Burns to the face could keep someone from seeing or breathing. Burns on the feet could make it impossible for someone to walk.
6. Possible response: By knowing the degree of a burn

After You Read

Scorched! How to Handle Different Types of Burns

Answering the BIG Question

1. What are your thoughts about what you do when you don't know what to do after reading the selection "Scorched! How to Handle Different Types of Burns"?
2. **Recall** When Bryant realized that his clothing had caught fire, how did he save himself from further harm?
   TIP Right There
3. **Summarize** What can you do if you or someone around you is burned?
   TIP Think and Search

Critical Thinking

4. **Infer** Why do you think the stop-drop-roll method is a good one to use?
   TIP Author and Me
5. **Infer** Why do you suppose it is important to get medical treatment for a burn on the face or feet?
   TIP On My Own
6. **Evaluate** How important is it to recognize the degree of a burn injury?
   TIP On My Own

Write about Your Reading

Step-by-Step Instructions Apply what you learned from reading "Scorched! How to Handle Different Types of Burns." Write numbered, step-by-step instructions on how to recognize and treat a first-degree burn.

Follow these guidelines as you write your instructions.

- Think through what you would do to treat a first-degree burn. Refer to the article if you need a reminder of what to do.
- Clearly explain each step. These are important instructions. Readers must be able to understand them.
- Use chronological order to sequence the steps.
- Be sure to write your instructions in your own words.

Indiana English/Language Arts Academic Standards (pp. 514–515)

8.3 Comprehension and Analysis of Literary Text Respond to grade-level-appropriate literature...
8.5.7 Write for different purposes...
8.2 Comprehension and Analysis (Focus on Informational Text) Develop [reading] strategies
8.2.6 Evaluate the...structural patterns of text.
8.6 English Language Conventions
For a complete description of the standards, see p. IN 11.

Write About Your Reading

Possible Response:
How to Recognize and Treat a First-Degree Burn

1. Identify redness and swelling. Make sure there are no blisters, blotches, or severe swelling.
2. If the burn is large or involves the face, feet, groin, or buttocks, see a doctor.
3. If not, cool the area by holding it under cool water for 15 minutes or apply a cold compress.
4. Apply an aloe vera lotion, an antibiotic ointment, or a moisturizer.
5. Avoid using oils or butter because they can lead to infection.

Skills Review

Key Reading Skill: Monitoring Comprehension

7. As you read "Scorched!" how did you monitor your comprehension?
8. What reading strategies did you use to improve your comprehension as you read?

Text Element: Instructions

9. In your opinion which of the following text features in "Scorched!" was the most helpful aid to reading the instructions? Explain your choice.
   - the red subheads
   - the black subheads
   - the pictures of the stop-drop-roll process
   - the bulleted list

Vocabulary Check

Answer *true* or *false* to each statement.

10. Getting dirt in a burn or other wound helps to keep it sterile.
11. If someone hobbled to school, he or she walked gracefully.
12. A description of the severity of a burn would tell how serious the burn is.
13. A minor problem is small and easily solved.
14. **English Language Coach** How does using specialized terms, or words that are specific to a particular subject, help you communicate more clearly? List three specialized terms that you know, and the subjects to which they apply.

Web Activities For eFlashcards, Selection Quick Checks, and other Web activities, go to www.glencoe.com.

Grammar Link: Agreement with Special Singulars

Usually a noun that ends in *-s* is plural, or more than one in number. To make a verb agree with *-s* ending plural nouns, you must use the form that goes with plural subjects (which are equal to *they*).

- Three teachers are absent today.
- Two homes need new roofs.
- Those books include maps.

There are a few exceptions to the *-s* ending plural noun rule. Some nouns that always end in *-s* are singular in meaning. These nouns generally refer to specialized fields and diseases.

Always Singular

- mumps
- mathematics
- physics
- measles
- civics
- economics

- The mumps usually lasts only a few days.
- Mathematics is my favorite subject.

Look out! A few nouns that always end in *-s* are plural in number: *pants, trousers, scissors* are common examples.

- His pants have unusual cuffs.

Grammar Practice

Write the correct form of the verb in parentheses.

15. Physics (is, are) the study of matter and energy.
16. The measles sometimes (lingers, linger) for days.
17. Civics (is, are) an interesting subject,
18. The scissors (needs, need) sharpening.

Writing Application Look over the Write About Your Reading assignment you completed. Make sure you used the right verb form with all subjects.

Skills Review

Key Reading Skill: Monitoring Comprehension

7. Responses will vary.
8. Responses will vary.

Text Element: Instructions

9. Responses will vary, but students should support their opinions.

Vocabulary Check

10. false
11. false
12. true
13. true

English Language Coach

14. Responses will vary.

Close

Ask students what they learned from the selection and how they can apply that knowledge to the Big Question.

Literature Online

Web Activities Have students access the Web site for interactive activities that will help them assess their understanding of the selection.

Grammar Link: Agreement with Special Singulars

Grammar Practice

15. is
16. lingers
17. is
18. need

Indiana English/Language Arts Academic Standards

SE: 8.2, 8.2.6, 8.3, 8.5.7, 8.6

Reading Across Texts External and Internal Conflict

Teaching Students to Recognize External and Internal Conflict

Why Is It Important?

- Recognizing the different types of conflict and how they affect each other will help students identify aspects of plot and character.
- Students will benefit from connecting the external events in a story to the internal workings of its characters.
- Students who master the difference between external and internal conflict will be more skilled writers and better readers.

How to Help Students Get It

- Point out to students that many times in literature, external conflict provides an obstacle for a character to overcome; often, it also generates or reveals internal conflict.
- Ask: "What physical problems do the characters encounter?" Things you can see or hear or feel, things outside yourself, are external.
- Ask: "What mental difficulties do the characters go through?" When you disagree with yourself, or cannot choose between mutually exclusive goals or values, you are experiencing internal conflict.
- Clarify that conflict does not refer to small matters that can be resolved easily. In literature, conflict involves significant issues; either a character must change (internal), or the world must change around the character (external) to resolve the conflict.

Reading to Answer the Big Question

from *Thura's Diary* by Thura Al-Windawi
A young Iraqi girl keeps a diary during the war in 2003. The diary concludes with a message of optimism and hope: the narrator looks forward to a time when the war is over and she can visit other survivors in peace.

Escaping by Zdenko Slobodnik
Slobodnik's family tried more than once to leave communist Czechoslovakia. Their daring escape hiking across the Alps succeeds, and they are able to enter a refugee center in Austria. From there, they travel to America, where the family is able to further their careers.

Workshop Resources

Pacing (Days) Standard	Block	Lesson	Student Materials	Teacher Resources
1	1	Reading Across Texts: External and Internal Conflict	English Language Coach Review, p. 41	Bellringer Options Transparencies –Daily Language Practice 40 Presentation Plus!
1	1	from *Thura's Diary*	Glencoe Online Unit Vocabulary Review, p. 39 Academic Vocabulary Review, p. 43 English Language Coach Reading Across Texts Graphic Organizer, p. 34 StudentWorks Plus™ Online Student Edition Literature Classics	Literary and Text Analysis Transparencies Puzzlemaker Skill Level Up!™ A Language Arts Game BookLink 3 Assessment by Learning Objective (Diagnostic and Formative) Interactive Tutor: Self-Assessment TeacherWorks Plus™ ExamView Assessment Suite
1		"Escaping"	Glencoe Online Unit Vocabulary Review, p. 39 Academic Vocabulary Review, p. 43 English Language Coach Reading Across Texts Graphic Organizer, p. 34 StudentWorks Plus™ Online Student Edition Literature Classics	Puzzlemaker Skill Level Up!™ A Language Arts Game BookLink 3 Assessment by Learning Objective (Diagnostic and Formative) Interactive Tutor: Self-Assessment TeacherWorks Plus™ ExamView Assessment Suite

Keys for Unit Resource

- Blackline Master
- Workbook
- Supplemental Text
- CD-ROM
- DVD
- Transparency
- Web-based
- Fast File

Level Appropriate Code

AS = Activities for all students
AL = Activities for students working above grade level
OL = Activities for students working at grade level
BL = Activities for students working below grade level
EL = Activities for English language learners

Focus

BELLRINGER Options

Daily Language Practice Transparency 40

Focus Activity Write the following on the board: Recall two problems you tried to fix by taking a risk. Use this chart to compare what you did. OL

Problem	Action	Results

Teach

L Literary Element

Internal and External Conflict Read the following monologues to students.

- *Should I go to the dance? Last time the music was rotten and my friends ignored me.*
- *Luis! Why'd you tell Ms. Thorpe that I didn't give you the math assignment you missed when you were absent? You know I gave you that assignment.*

Say: Identify the internal and external conflict. How do you know? *(Possible respose: The first conflict is internal. The speaker is arguing with himself. The second is external. The speaker is angry with another student.)* OL

READING ACROSS TEXTS WORKSHOP

from Thura's Diary & Escaping

by Thura Al-Windawi

by Zdenko Slobodnik

Skill Focus

You will use these skills as you read and compare the following selections:

- from *Thura's Diary,* p. 519
- "Escaping," p. 526

Reading

- Making connections across texts
- Comparing/contrasting internal and external conflict in different texts

Literature

- Identifying and analyzing internal and external conflicts in nonfiction texts

Writing

- Writing to compare and contrast

Indiana English/ Language Arts Academic Standards (pp. 516–517)

8.3 Comprehension and Analysis of Literary Text Respond to grade-level-appropriate literature...identifying...plot...and making connections and comparisons across texts.

For a complete description of the standards, see p. IN 11.

L Have you ever fought with a friend, or wrestled with a tough decision? If so, you've experienced conflict. Conflict is struggle between opposing forces. Conflict can be internal (something you worry about on the inside), or external (a problem you have with other people or forces). However, most conflicts—even the small ones—are both.

Great stories are full of conflict. Characters who struggle with their feelings or beliefs face **internal conflict.** Characters who struggle with other people or forces—like nature or society—face **external conflict.**

How to Read Across Texts: Internal and External Conflict

As you look for conflict in this part of *Thura's Diary* and "Escaping," pay attention to the people you're reading about. What worries them? What keeps them from being healthy and happy? Are they forced to make any painful decisions? If so, what are the results? How do they solve—or try to solve—their problems?

Also, think about how internal conflicts cause external conflicts for the people in these selections. Pay attention to the way in which external conflicts lead to internal conflicts as well. Just remember that internal conflict and external conflict—in stories and real life—are a two-for-one special. Order one, and you'll probably get the other, too.

Additional Support

Literature Focus Lesson

Diaries Most diaries contain private thoughts that no one else will ever read. Often, "Dear Diary" takes the place of talking to a real person about a problem. Thura, however, wanted others to read about her situation, her feelings, and her hopes for the world. Have students choose personal conflicts they'd like to share. Ask them to write diary entries about the conflicts, their feelings, and how they tried to resolve the conflicts. Then have those who would like to share their entries read them to the class. AS

READING ACROSS TEXTS WORKSHOP

Get Ready to Compare

In your Learner's Notebook, copy a chart like the one below for both of the selections in this workshop. As you read, use these charts to keep track of conflict in the selection from *Thura's Diary* and "Escaping."

Selection Title (Example: from Thura's Diary)

Character	Problem, Obstacle, or Tough Decision	Conflict: Internal, External, or Both?	Resolution?

Use Your Comparison

The people in the selections you are about to read experienced similar forms of conflict. For example, people in both selections were forced to leave home as a result of war or political persecution. The details of their experiences differ, though. So do their internal conflicts.

As you read, look for specific similarities and differences between the characters' internal and external conflicts. Do the characters resolve all of their conflicts? If so, how? If not, why?

For help comparing and contrasting conflict in *Thura's Diary* and "Escaping," take detailed notes in the charts you just made.

R

Teach

R Reading Skill

Connecting Have students name conflicts they've seen in books, in films, and on TV. Write their responses on the board. Ask volunteers to identify each conflict as internal or external.

Ask: Which of these conflicts could happen in real life? *(Responses will vary.)* **Ask:** Why do writers often choose to write about real-life conflicts? *(Possible responses: to show how real problems can be solved; so that people will relate to their stories)* **Ask:** What is the value of nonrealistic conflicts? *(Possible response: to entertain; to make people happy that they'll never have to face those kinds of problems themselves)* OL

Assess/Close

Have students write a paragraph comparing and contrasting two of the conflicts you have written on the board. Remind them to interpret why the conflicts occurred and how they could have been prevented. *(Responses will vary.)* AS

Resources for page 517

Use the Reading Across Texts Graphic Organizer BLM in the Unit 4 Resource Booklet, p. 34.

Reading in the Real World

Careers Ask students to research the job duties of three career people, such as a judge, social worker, doctor, police officer, firefighter, veterinarian, or government official, who have to make difficult decisions. Have students use a chart such as the one in the *Get Ready to Compare* section to record possible conflicts that each person might experience on the job. As a class, discuss the possible conflicts. Then invite students to suggest why they think some people are willing to pursue such challenging careers. OL

Indiana English/Language Arts Academic Standards
SE: 8.3
TWE: *Literature Focus Lesson* 8.5.7

Teach

More About Diaries

The Diary of Anne Frank, written by a young Jewish girl during World War II, shows the horrors of the Holocaust. Explorers Lewis and Clark kept a journal of their journeys in the western frontier. Susie King Taylor, a nurse, kept a diary of her experiences during the Civil War. Diaries help readers learn not only facts but also the thoughts people had and the feelings they experienced during historical events.

V Vocabulary

Writing Sentences Say: Remember that a good way to recall the meaning of a new word is to write it in a sentence. In your Learner's Notebooks, write one sentence using each of the vocabulary words correctly. *(Responses will vary.)* AS

EL Language Coach

Diction Say: Most diaries are read only by the people who write them. What type of diction do you think is used in most diaries? *(informal)* AS

Before You Read from *Thura's Diary*

Thura Al-Windawi

Meet the Author

Thura Al-Windawi began keeping a diary to deal with her feelings about the war in Iraq, her home country. She says she found strength in writing about her family's experiences. Al-Windawi now attends college at the University of Pennsylvania, but hopes to return to Iraq someday. In the meantime, she hopes her diary spreads a message of peace.

Author Search For more about Thura Al-Windawi, go to www.glencoe.com.

Indiana English/Language Arts Academic Standards (pp. 518–524)

8.2 Comprehension and Analysis (Focus on Informational Text) Develop [reading] strategies...identifying and analyzing structure...and perspective...

For a complete description of the standards, see p. IN 11.

Vocabulary Preview

V

extinguished (ek STING gwisht) *adj.* put out **(p. 520)** *The extinguished candle filled the room with smoke.*

rations (RASH unz) *n.* portions of needed items **(p. 521)** *During wartime, many people survive on small rations of food, water, and other supplies.*

bombardment (bom BARD munt) *n.* an attack **(p. 522)** *Outside Thura's home, gunshots and explosions signaled the neighborhood's bombardment.*

English Language Coach

EL

Diction The writer's word choice is called **diction.** Diction can be formal or informal, depending on the writer's audience and purpose. Look at this sentence from *Thura's Diary:* "I'll get myself to America one day—not to take revenge, but to study and live and love like anyone else." Thura's diction is informal. Still, it sincerely conveys her hope for a better life.

Get Ready to Read

Connect to the Reading

The people in this selection faced fear and uncertainty when their country went to war. Think about a time when you felt uncertain about something. Did you also feel afraid? How did you resolve your feelings?

Build Background

In 2003 the United States invaded Iraq and removed its president, Saddam Hussein, from power. In Hussein's Iraq, people did not have the right to say negative things about the government in public. If they did, they could be jailed or killed. Thura wrote much of her diary while Hussein was still in power. The part of her diary you are about to read describes life in Baghdad, Iraq's capital, a few days after the invasion began. Thura and her family have been staying with her grandmother.

Set Purpose for Reading

BIG Question Read to find out what Thura Al-Windawi did when her way of life was in danger and she didn't know what to do.

Set Your Own Purpose What else would you like to learn about how Thura handled the conflicts in her life? Write your own purpose on the Reading Across Texts page of Foldable 4.

Additional Support

Author Search To expand students' appreciation of Thura Al-Windawi, have them access the Web site for additional information and resources.

Literature Focus Lesson

Conflict and Plot Conflict moves a story's plot along. Conflicts develop during the *rising action*, reach their peak at the *climax*, and are resolved in the *falling action*. Read the following paragraph. Have students identify the stages of conflict as they develop.

The storm was raging, but we couldn't let it stop us. Angry rain pelted our faces as we raced along the country road. Suddenly, a lightning bolt struck a nearby tree. Only a few more feet and we'd have been hit! At last, we made it to the sturdy park shelter. We were finally safe! OL

from Thura's Diary

by Thura Al-Windawi

Monday, 24 March 2003

Dear Diary,

Today I briefly went back home to get phone numbers of friends.[1] Lina and Wathika are in Adhamiya, where there is a lot of bombing. They said the bombing hit the Mukhabarat,[2] and that glass is everywhere. **C**

Another friend, Abir, called me. She said all our group of friends are gone—some went to suburbs outside Baghdad, some went to their relatives' houses.

We're worried about another friend in Mosul. I'm most worried about Abir—she lives near Saddam International Airport. **1**

Tuesday, 25 March 2003

Dear Diary,

At last we are back home. I am going to be in my bedroom again. It's so nice to be home sweet home. I think I'll be able to sleep, now that I've calmed down a bit. **R** Some of the young guys who live around here have volunteered to defend the neighbourhood, and they're taking it in turns to keep watch around the clock. They've put sandbag defences at the street corners, and the Baath Party has supplied them with Kalashnikovs.[3] But all the same, they won't be able to

1. Thura and her family have been staying with Thura's grandmother.
2. The equivalent of the CIA and the FBI rolled into one, the ***Mukhabarat*** was Iraq's main intelligence agency.
3. The ***Baath Party*** is a political party in Iraq and Syria. The ***Kalashnikov*** is an assault rifle designed by Russian military general M.T. Kalashnikov.

Practice the Skills

1 Reading Across Texts

Internal and External Conflict Thura is afraid for her friends. At the same time, she needs to go on with her life. Do you think her feelings are in conflict?

Teach

C Critical Thinking

Analysis Ask: Where have Thura and her family been staying? *(at her grandmother's home)* **BL** **Ask:** Why do you think Thura and her family have been staying with her grandmother? *(Possible response: They think her grandmother's home is safer; they want to protect her.)* **OL**

R Reading Skill

Review Connecting Say: Have you ever missed your home when you were away from it? If so, how did you feel when you finally got home? *(Responses will vary.)* **Ask:** Based on your feelings, how do you think Thura feels when she returns home? *(Responses will vary.)* **OL**

Readability Scores

Dale-Chall: 5.0
DRP: 51
Lexile: 910

Reading Fluency

Build Fluency To build reading fluency, have students find a quiet place to practice reading the selection aloud. Suggest that they reread it several times until they can smoothly read all sentences with expression and understanding. Encourage them to make their reading sound like natural speech. You may choose to have each student practice reading with a partner. **EL** **BL**

Indiana English/Language Arts Academic Standards

SE: 8.2, 8.3
TWE: *Literature Focus Lesson* 8.3.2, *Reading Fluency* 8.7

Teach

L Literary Element

Internal and External Conflict **Ask:** What are some of the external conflicts described on this page? *(the weather, the air, the burning of oil)* OL

R Reading Skill

Review Connecting **Say:** Have you ever had trouble breathing? If so, what caused you to have trouble breathing? What did you do? *(Responses will vary.)* BL **Say:** Now use your actions and feelings to connect to how Thura and her family are feeling because of the thick clouds of smoke in Baghdad. Write a short description detailing how you think Thura or one of her family members feels. *(Responses will vary.)* OL

READING ACROSS TEXTS WORKSHOP

do anything about the noise of the planes and the bombs. It has become like a weird, disturbing kind of music to me. 2

Wednesday, 26 March 2003

Dear Diary,

During the last few days there have been freak sandstorms here—it's as though Mother Nature's showing us how angry and hurt she is about the war. The weather's been chopping and changing, and the air has been so thick with red dust from the desert that you can only see a few metres in front of you. 3

What's made matters worse is that the government's been burning huge amounts of oil inside Baghdad itself, because they think that by sending up clouds of black smoke they can affect the aim of the American missiles. They did the same thing in 1991, except that then they burnt piles of used tyres [tires] instead. This time they've dug dozens of ditches in and around the city, then filled them with crude oil and set the oil alight. The air is covered with thick, black smoke. The smell reminds me of the smoke trail that comes off a freshly **extinguished** match. I can't stand the smell or the way it pollutes the air. At night, as the sun goes down, the sky turns a combination of shades, from deep purples to fire-engine red.

Breathing is so difficult. It feels like you are stuck in a burning building, choking on the fumes. There is no fresh air any more. The leaves on the trees start to wilt. How will we get rid of all this dust and black smoke? Even if it rains, it will rain black drops of water. And it will hurt the soil. Every single living cell will be harmed by this

On March 22, 2003, smoke rises from oil fires burning in trenches around Baghdad.

Analyzing the Photo How does this photo illustrate Thura's description of her environment?

Practice the Skills

2 Reading Across Texts

Conflict Thura feels a little safer with the sandbags and the neighborhood guys with guns. But she can't forget the war and her fears. How do you think this causes an internal conflict?

3 English Language Coach

Diction Look at the words Thura uses to describe the sights and smells of her surroundings. How does her diction convey meaning? What imagery does this diction create?

Vocabulary

extinguished (ek STING gwisht) *adj.* put out

Additional Support

Literature Focus Lesson

Personification Thura makes nature human by calling it "Mother Nature." Giving nonliving things human qualities is called *personification*. Authors use personification to make their writing more vivid and to describe things in a way that people can imagine and understand. Have students use personification to describe some of the situations Thura wrote about in her diary entry dated Wednesday, 26 March 2003. When students are finished, ask volunteers to share their responses with the class. You may also wish to have students illustrate their examples for a classroom display. OL weather. There are no sounds from the birds. Mother Nature is depressed and in pain.

This pollution is what causes lung cancer. I smell the dust and I go to the bathroom to wash my face, hoping maybe I will breathe fresh air. But it doesn't help. Poor Aula and Mum, they are sensitive to the dust. Every two minutes they must blow their noses with tissue. It looks like they are sick. They carry tissues with them wherever they walk. We are drowning in this polluted, black, dusty world. **4**

Mum has finished cleaning the living room that we watch TV in. She also cleaned the kitchen. She had to sponge everything down with a bucket of water to wipe away all the dust, and she had to clean the glasses by hand. We all helped. Each of us has a certain amount of water to use for cleaning. We have a three-gallon bucket each, filled halfway to the top. It came from our **rations** stored in the bathroom.

Sama was sitting and straightening up her Barbie dolls and teddy bears. We could not clean the whole house, only the ground floor and the bathrooms.

Friday, 28 March 2003

Dear Diary,

Today relatives and friends came to visit us. They are starting to visit a lot because they are worried about us and want to know if we are OK. The phone lines have been cut because the telephone exchange has been bombed. It is getting harder and harder to contact each other and find out exact news.

Saturday, 29 March 2003

Dear Diary,

My dad's friend Saad Al-Adamy and his wife and three children came to visit us. One of the children is only seven months old—just a baby. We tried to stop him being afraid of the noise from the bombs. We took him in our arms and comforted him. His sister Assal is twelve years old, but she is

Vocabulary

rations (RASH unz) *n.* portions of needed items

Practice the Skills

4 Reading Across Texts

Internal and External Conflict Sometimes people struggle against forces outside of themselves. What outside forces do Baghdad residents face here? Think about what is preventing them from leading healthy, happy lives. Write your answer in your chart.

READING ACROSS TEXTS WORKSHOP

Teach

L Literary Element

Internal and External Conflict **Say:** What is Thura's family doing to handle their external conflicts? *(Possible response: They are cleaning to get rid of the dust; Thura washes her face regularly; Aula and Mum are carrying tissues with them; they are conserving water from their rations.)* **OL**

C Critical Thinking

Comprehension **Ask:** How do Thura's relatives deal with the conflict of the telephone lines being cut? *(They stop by to visit Thura and her family to see if they are OK.)* **BL** **Ask:** Do you think this is a safe solution to the conflict? Explain. *(Possible response: No, it is probably not a good idea to be going from house to house when bombs are being dropped.)* **OL**

Differentiated Instruction

Drawing the Scene Drawing what they visualize from Thura's diary entries may help some students better comprehend the selection. Tell students to draw what is happening in the entry from March 26. Have them share their drawings with a partner. **EL** **BL** Then ask pairs to evaluate each other's drawings based on the information from the entry. **OL**

Indiana English/Language Arts Academic Standards
SE: 8.2
TWE: *Literature Focus Lesson* 8.5.7

READING ACROSS TEXTS WORKSHOP

Teach

C Critical Thinking

Comprehension Ask: According to Thura, why is it especially hard to take care of children during war? *(They want to go outside and play, but they can't; it's hard to control them at night.)* BL **Ask:** Do you agree with Thura's statements about taking care of children during war? Explain. *(Responses will vary.)* OL **Ask:** What do you think are other difficulties brought on by war? *(Possible responses: little money because many can't work; deaths; uncertainty)* AL

EL Language Coach

Word Choice Say: Look at the definition of the word *bombardment*. List three synonyms for the word. *(Possible responses: attack, onslaught, barrage, assault)* EL **Ask:** Do you think the author chose the best word to describe what is happening near Granny's apartment? *(Responses will vary.)* OL

just as scared. I don't want her to be afraid because the bombs are everywhere all the time. And it is getting worse. She is starting to understand that, and she is better than when I last spoke with her on the phone. Her older brother, Sayef, is sixteen and understands the whole situation. But they are still children. And it's difficult to take care of children during war. It's hard to control them at night, and during the day they like to go out; they like to play. Now they have to stay inside the house. They cannot play, they cannot see friends a lot—it's not easy. 5 C

Just as every other day, the dust is everywhere. It's as if we didn't do any cleaning yesterday. But today there is more. I feel sorry for Aula and Mum—they are still sneezing. We didn't clean the whole house today, just the living room, kitchen and sitting room. Mum said we would have to wait to get rid of all of it.

Although I took my shower yesterday, I feel the dust all over me, on my hair, on my body. And because water is so precious, it's important that I only use a little amount of it, just to wash over myself to get off this dust. I would usually have a good bath, but not now. I use a quarter of the water I would normally use. Mum has difficulty washing the dishes. There are so many guests and visitors coming to our house and she hardly has any water to wash up after them.

How I wish all this dust would stop. It's getting boring, so boring. I just hope that it will stop soon.

Granny came. She was very worried about us after she heard from my aunt that we still hadn't left Baghdad. The troops are getting closer all the time. Granny's face was full of panic. She and my uncle Haydar came as fast as they could to see how we were. They couldn't call because the phones aren't working. She was relieved that she had come and that we hadn't been harmed.

Because they were here, and because there was no water at their house, they had a bath. Granny told us it was a very good thing that we had left her apartment because the **bombardment** there was very heavy and very frightening. The Al-Alwiya Maternity Hospital, where I was born, was damaged; it must have been terrifying for the mothers and EL

Vocabulary

bombardment (bom BARD munt) *n.* an attack

Practice the Skills

5 Reading Across Texts

Internal and External Conflict Could fear be one of the forces the Iraqi children are struggling with? Does fear cause an external or internal conflict?

Additional Support

Reading in the Real World

Citizenship The author of this selection is a Muslim. Students may benefit from learning more about this major world religion. Ask students to research one aspect of this religion with a partner. Possible topics are Friday prayers, mosques, the Koran, Shi'ites and Sunnis, and world demographics of Islam. Have students present their findings to the class in posters, songs, poems, news reports, or computer presentation programs. AS babies inside. In some way, somehow, it is quieter here.

Dad decided we should go and see my uncle Khalil who lives in our neighbourhood in an area called Al-Shamisiya, which is one of the oldest parts of Baghdad. Our families are very close. Uncle Khalil and his family have decided that they're not leaving their house under any circumstances, even though they're in an incredibly dangerous position, because a lot of weapons have been hidden in nearby palm groves. C

Analyzing the Photo Smoke billows up in a Baghdad neighborhood. What conclusions can you draw from this photo about war's effect on a city?

My three cousins, Omar, Mounaf and Senan, are all teenagers but they were obviously terrified. Omar is older than me, and when I look at him I see a very strong man, but he and his brothers have in some way been affected by the storming bombardment near their house. Now, every time there is the slightest noise outside, they think it is a missile or a plane coming. The family all sleep in the dining room because it'll be the safest place if the windows get broken in an explosion. But Omar doesn't sleep, he lies awake waiting for the nightmare to begin; the coming of tons of missiles. But my uncle's not the sort to fuss about things like that, and he insists on sleeping in his own bedroom upstairs. The real problem is his wife, Afaaf; she gets into a complete panic if so much as a cockroach gets into the house. She was beside herself with worry[4] when the bombing started—because of the insects that might come into the house if the windows broke! Dad advised her to go to the shelter in her neighbours' basement, but her reply was hilarious. 'I can face the American missiles,' she said, 'but I couldn't sleep in that shelter if there was an insect in it.' 6 R

Uncle Khalil told Dad that their elder brother Kadhim, who's seventy years old now, has decided not to leave his house, even though the rest of his family have all gone to

4. The phrase ***beside herself with worry*** is a figure of speech. Thura means that her aunt is anxious and distracted.

Practice the Skills

6 Reading Across Texts

Internal and External Conflict What conflict does Afaaf experience? Is it internal or external? Explain.

Teach

C Critical Thinking

Synthesis **Ask:** Why might people like Thura's Uncle Khalil have decided not to leave their homes regardless of what might happen? *(Possible response: Some may have thought they would be safe; some may have been worried about getting burglarized; some may not want to be bullied.)* OL

R Reading Skill

Review Evaluating **Say:** Thura calls Afaaf's reply "hilarious." Why do you think Thura says this? *(because Afaaf seems more afraid of insects than missiles)* BL **Ask:** Do you think Thura's statement about Afaaf's reply is accurate? Explain. *(Responses will vary.)* OL

English Language Coach

Diction Discuss with students how *Thura's Diary* seems to be a mixture of formal and informal language. Ask students to work with a partner to first decide if each of the following words or phrases from the selection is formal or informal; then ask students to write alternate types of expressions for each: *Mum, Granny, home sweet home, check up on it, extinguished, depressed.* AS

Indiana English/Language Arts Academic Standards

SE: 8.2

TWE: *Reading in the Real World* 8.7.12, *English Language Coach* 8.1

Teach

R1 Reading Skill

Review Monitoring Comprehension **Ask:** Why hasn't Kadhim left his home? *(He thinks that no one will be able to get him out of the shelter.)* BL

R2 Reading Skill

Review Evaluating **Ask:** Do you think Kadhim's decision to stay in his house is a sound decision? Explain. *(Possible responses: No, he's more likely to get hit by a missile if he stays in his house. Several people could help him get out of the shelter if he wanted to.)* OL

BQ BIG Question

Ask: What would you do if you faced the problems Thura and her family face? *(Responses will vary.)* AS

Assess

Use the CheckPoint questions provided on Presentation Plus! to check for comprehension of the selection. These questions can be used with interactive response keypads for immediate student feedback.

Syria. The problem is that his house is only a stone's throw away from some palaces belonging to Saddam's family and his half-brother Barzan. If Kadhim really does stay in his house it's sure to be the end of him; the palace complex has already come under attack, and it's bound to again. Kadhim refuses to go to the shelter under his house because he's convinced there won't be anyone to get him out if he does. So, instead, he's decided to take shelter in his garden, under a roofed area made out of concrete. 'If you don't find me, you'll know I've died over in that corner,' he said to my uncle. So far he's all right, thank God. R1 R2

This evening we came back home again. Like my cousins, we were fed up with all the nationalistic[5] songs they keep repeating on Iraqi TV. The Iraqi army leaders only ever talk about their victories, but I don't believe a word of it—their propaganda's[6] just the same as it was during the first Gulf War, even though things are completely different now. This time it's a battle for the control of Iraq by the greatest power the world has ever known, with all the latest technology at its disposal. I keep wondering: *What will happen in the end?* 7

Analyzing the Photo Flanked by soldiers, a young Iraqi girl pauses in Baghdad. What does this photo tell you about her environment?

5. If something is ***nationalistic,*** it promotes a nation's independence and unity.

6. ***Propaganda*** is information, often false or one-sided, that is used to promote a cause.

Practice the Skills

7 **BIG Question**

What does Thura do when she doesn't know how to handle the problems she faces? How does she deal with the conflicts that define her life in Iraq? Write your answer on the *Thura's Diary* page of Foldable 4. BQ

Additional Support

Differentiated Instruction

Writing Poetry Remind students that writing poetry is often a way people deal with their emotions. Now that they have read the realistic and dramatic story about Thura and her family, your students may feel sad or even angry about war. Encourage them to write their feelings in a poem. OL

Have students plan a poetry slam where they share their poems with the class and perhaps the entire school. You may even want to invite war veterans or others affected by war to hear the poetry and share how they dealt with or are dealing with some of the emotions war evokes. AL

Before You Read Escaping

Meet the Author

Zdenko Slobodnik was born in communist Czechoslovakia. His family escaped to America when he was very young, and he wrote this account when he was eighteen. Slobodnik has a black belt in Tae Kwan Do. He also sings, acts, and plays guitar. He has dedicated his writing to his parents, for whose sacrifices he is very grateful.

Author Search For more about Zdenko Slobodnik, go to www.glencoe.com.

Vocabulary Preview

perseverance (pur suh VEER ens) *n.* steady determination **(p. 526)** *Perseverance is the key to success.*

glistened (GLIH sund) *v.* shone brightly; form of the verb *glisten* **(p. 527)** *The lights of the city glistened in the valley.*

indomitable (in DOM ih tuh bul) *adj.* unable to be conquered or overcome **(p. 527)** *Despite the harsh conditions, the refugees had indomitable hope.*

English Language Coach

Diction Writers choose their words carefully. Use the chart below to better understand the differences between formal and informal diction.

Formal: *Leaving Czechoslovakia at that point was very difficult, however.*
The writer's word choice tells readers that this is a serious subject.
Informal: *Getting out of there was tough, though.*
The casual diction doesn't effectively show that the writer is serious about the subject.

Get Ready to Read

Connect to the Reading

BQ The family in this selection left home to make a new home in America. What does home mean to you? Is it a place, a group of people, or both?

Build Background

Zdenko Slobodnik was born in the former Czechoslovakia, a communist country in central Europe. Under communism, economic conditions were poor and people had few rights. In 1993 Czechoslovakia split into two countries: the Czech Republic and Slovakia. Today, citizens of the Czech Republic are governed by a parliamentary democracy.

Set Purpose for Reading

BIG Question Read to find out how one family triumphed over conflict to build a better life.

Set Your Own Purpose What else would you like to learn about the selection to help you answer the Big Question. Write your purpose on the Reading Across Texts page of Foldable 4.

Indiana English/Language Arts Academic Standards (pp. 525–527)

8.2 Comprehension Develop [reading] strategies...identifying and analyzing structure...and perspective...

For a complete description of the standards, see p. IN 11.

Literature Focus Lesson

Personal Narrative Ask students what makes personal narratives so powerful. (They're written by *real* people about *real* events and with *real* emotions. They help readers connect with history by showing the personal or human side of events.) Draw this organizer on the board. Ask students to use it to connect events in the story to the narrator's emotions. AS

This happened.	The narrator feels . . .	I know because the text says . . .

Teach

More About Personal Narratives

Many people have written personal narratives of escaping from situations in which they were denied personal freedom. For example, *I Was Born a Slave* is a collection of narratives written by African American slaves. The book gives readers a glimpse of what it was like to be a slave, to dream of freedom, and to risk one's life to follow that dream. Ask students to share summaries of other personal narratives they have read.

BQ BIG Question

Say: Suppose you are in a situation that makes you desperately unhappy. After thinking of possible solutions, the one that stands out as the best solution is the one that requires the biggest risk. How might you feel as you consider taking this step? *(Possible responses: scared, nervous, uncertain, confused)* AS

Indiana English/Language Arts Academic Standards

SE: 8.2

TWE: *Reading in the Real World* 8.5.7, 8.7.14; *Literature Focus Lesson* 8.2

Teach

R1 Reading Skill

Review Monitoring Comprehension **Say:** Reread paragraph 1. How many siblings did the narrator have? *(one, a sister)* OL

EL Language Coach

Word Choice **Ask:** Why might the author have chosen the word *prisoners* to describe the people of Czechoslovakia under communist rule? *(Possible response: Because the Czechoslovakian people weren't free to come and go or do what they wanted to do, it was as if they were locked into a prison.)* OL AL

R2 Reading Skill

Review Interpreting **Ask:** What is the author saying about his parents with the comment that "Their spirits were crushed"? *(Possible response: They were discouraged.)* OL

Readability Scores
Dale-Chall: 6.2
DRP: 61
Lexile: 1060

by Zdenko Slobodnik

I learned about **perseverance** when my parents decided that they wanted a better life for their children, their three-year-old son and their six-year-old daughter. R1 We had been living in communist Czechoslovakia and were tired of the life we were living and the system.[1] At first they had doubts, as anyone might, but they would not let their children grow up as prisoners. EL 1

Leaving Czechoslovakia at that point was very difficult, however. They had to figure out a way to get to Austria, which was a free country. At first the plan was simple: They would claim I needed to see a doctor there for my ear infection. Their spirits were crushed when a border guard[2] gave their request a stern "No." R2 As we approached a second border crossing, they hoped for a different response. However, as we sat in our car, the guard reached in, yanked out the keys and ordered my parents to turn themselves in to the police. 2

Feeling hopeless, they decided to take one last chance, which would be difficult. We would hike across the Alps[3] into Austria, leaving behind everything we could not carry.

1. The ***system*** refers to all the rules, punishments, and hardships connected to living under communist rule.
2. A ***border guard*** is a soldier who prevents people from illegally crossing a country's border.
3. The ***Alps*** is a large mountain range in Europe. It stretches through many countries, including Austria, Italy, France, and Germany.

Vocabulary

perseverance (pur suh VEER ens) *n.* steady determination

Practice the Skills

1 Reading Across Texts

Internal and External Conflict What large external conflict do the Slobodniks face? Who or what stands between them and their happiness? Write your answer in your chart.

2 Reading Across Texts

Internal and External Conflict Sometimes people struggle against a general force, like nature or society. Sometimes they struggle against a specific person or situation. Is the Slobodniks' conflict general, specific, or both? Explain your answer in your chart.

Additional Support

Reading in the Real World

Citizenship Show students a political map and a physical map of central Europe before 1993. Point out the Soviet Union and explain the concept of *satellite nations* (countries politically controlled by another country). Have students research information on the Internet or in the library to learn more about life in the Soviet Union and read other stories of escape. You may wish to have students work in groups to construct salt maps showing the physical obstacles the Slobodniks faced in their escape. Encourage students to consult atlases to correctly scale their map features. AS

It was extremely dangerous, and getting caught meant prison or even death. Yet we marched on because the freedom of America **glistened** in our souls. As my parents saw the sign welcoming us to Austria, they knew they had succeeded. **3**

Once in Austria, they found a refugee center[4] and then a hotel. We lived in this overcrowded, infested, dirty hotel for over a year. They often wondered if they had made the right decision leaving their homeland. However, once their time came to go to America and begin new, free lives, their question was answered. **4**

Even in America, life was very hard at first. We lived in slums in Boston where my parents had to fight with the landlord to give us heat, and waking up every day was a hard realization. My parents' perseverance was strong, though, and within a few years my father had gained recertification[5] of his medical degree and my mother, foreign accent and all, finished first in her dental-assistant school.

Perseverance is a valuable law of life, imperative to reaching one's dreams. My parents had little when we lived under Communism, yet they were willing to live with nothing. Realizing that I cannot fully appreciate my parents' perseverance and **indomitable** spirit that brought us here, I remain thankful for the chance to live a wonderful life, in which I had boundless opportunities. In my parents' case, "Perseverance [made] the difference between success and defeat," and I am glad it did. **5** ❍

Practice the Skills

3 English Language Coach

Diction How does diction help you understand and connect to the Slobodniks' struggle?

4 Reading Across Texts

Internal and External Conflict What internal conflicts might the Slobodniks have faced about leaving their homeland? Think about the life they left behind, and the risks they took to reach their goal.

R1

5 BIG Question

After two failed attempts to leave Czechoslovakia, the Slobodniks probably felt like they didn't know what to do. What did they do then? What would you have done? Write your answer on the "Escaping" page of Foldable 4. Your response will help you complete the Unit Challenge later.

R2

Analyzing the Photo This sign, posted on the Austria–Czechoslovakia border, points the way for the refugees. What part of the writer's life does this image represent?

4. A ***refugee center*** offers people who have left or been forced to leave their homes a temporary place to stay.
5. Although the writer's father was a doctor in Czechoslovakia, he had to pass tests, or gain ***recertification,*** in the United States before he could work as a doctor here.

Vocabulary

glistened (GLIH sund) *v.* shone brightly

indomitable (in DOM ih tuh bul) *adj.* unable to be conquered or overcome

Differentiated Instruction

Pros and Cons To weigh a decision's advantages and disadvantages, students may find it helpful to use a chart like the one below. Draw the chart on the board. Have each student work with a partner to choose a decision kids their age might face. Have them analyze the decision by charting the pros and cons. **AS**

Decision	Advantages (Pros)	Disadvantages (Cons)
	1.	1.
	2.	2.
	3.	3.

Teach

R1 Reading Skill

Review Connecting Say: Think about a time when you were uncomfortable or miserable after making a decision. Did you stick with your decision or change your mind? Why? *(Responses will vary.)* **Ask:** Why might people question their decisions? *(Responses will vary.)* **OL**

R2 Reading Skill

Review Evaluating Ask: Did the author do a good job of helping you picture life in Czechoslovakia under communist rule? Explain. *(Responses will vary.)* **OL**

Assess

CheckPoint

Use the CheckPoint questions provided on Presentation Plus! to check for comprehension of the selection. These questions can be used with interactive response keypads for immediate students feedback.

Indiana English/Language Arts Academic Standards
SE: 8.2
TWE: *Reading in the Real World* 8.2

Assess

Resources for page 528

- Selection Quick Check, pp. 39–40
- ExamView Assessment Suite
- Interactive Tutor: Self-Assessment

Vocabulary Check

from **Thura's Diary**

1. Possible response: Blowing out the match, Andrew extinguished the flame.
2. Correct
3. Possible response: During the bombardment, the neighborhood was noisy and unsettled.

Escaping

4. Correct
5. Possible response: Because it was indomitable, Hector's spirit was unbroken.
6. Possible response: The runners showed true perseverance when they stayed in the race.

English Language Coach

7. Responses will vary. Students should demonstrate that they understand the difference between formal and informal diction.

After You Read

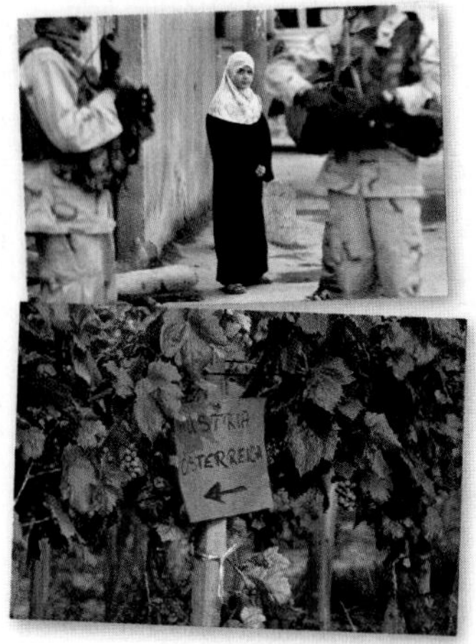

from Thura's Diary & ESCAPING

by Thura Al-Windawi

by Zdenko Slobodnik

Vocabulary Check

Copy the sentences below. If the boldfaced vocabulary word is used correctly, write *correct* next to the sentence. If not, rewrite the sentence to show the boldfaced word's true meaning.

Thura's Diary

extinguished rations bombardment

1. Lighting a match, Andre **extinguished** the flame.
2. When camping, people often take **rations** of food and water.
3. During the **bombardment,** the neighborhood was still and quiet.

ESCAPING

perseverance glistened indomitable

4. The wet pavement **glistened** in the streetlight.
5. Because it was **indomitable,** Hector's spirit had broken.
6. The runners showed true **perseverance** when they quit the race early.
7. **English Language Coach** Rewrite the sentence below using informal diction.

   Realizing that I cannot fully appreciate my parents' perseverance, I remain thankful for the chance to live a wonderful life.

Indiana English/Language Arts Academic Standards (pp. 528–529)

8.3 Comprehension and Analysis of Literary Text Respond to grade-level-appropriate literature...making connections and comparisons across texts.

8.5.2 Write responses to literature...

For a complete description of the standards, see p. IN 11.

Reading/Critical Thinking

On a separate sheet of paper, answer the following questions. Read the tips to find the information that you need.

Thura's Diary

8. **BIG Question** What does Thura do when she doesn't know what to do? How does she express her thoughts and feelings?
9. **Recall** What physical problems do Thura's mother and sister, Aula, deal with, and why?

   TIP Think and Search
10. **Analyze** Who or what are Thura and her family mainly in conflict with? Explain.

    TIP Author and Me

ESCAPING

11. **BIG Question** Despite the obstacles in their path, the Slobodniks made it to the United States. What did they do when they didn't know what to do? What does Zdenko believe is necessary for success?

    TIP Right There
12. **Recall** How did the Slobodniks finally escape Czechoslovakia?

    TIP Right There
13. **Summarize** In one sentence, summarize Zdenko's message to others whose goals seem impossible to reach.

    TIP Author and Me

Writing: Reading Across Texts

Use Your Notes

14. Follow these steps to compare internal and external conflict in *Thura's Diary* and "Escaping."

    Step 1: Look at the notes in the charts you just completed. Circle the external conflicts shared by people in both selections.

    Step 2: Did the people in both selections experience similar internal struggles? If so, underline those conflicts in your charts.

    Step 3: Now think about the differences between the selections. In your Learner's Notebook, list three differences between the external conflicts faced by the families in both selections. For help, use the notes in your charts.

    Step 4: Finally, think about the differences between internal conflicts in the selections you read. No two people's thoughts are ever *exactly* alike—so how were Thura's internal conflicts different from Zdenko's parents' internal conflicts? *Hint: The selections are told from different points of view. Do you know as much about the Slobodniks' inner thoughts as you do about Thura's? If not, why might this be?*

Get It on Paper

To show that you understand conflict in *Thura's Diary* and "Escaping," copy the following statements in your Learner's Notebook. Leave yourself plenty of room to write. Complete the statements with your own thoughts.

15. Thura's largest external conflict is with ___.
16. This conflict results in the following internal conflict(s): ___.
17. These conflicts are resolved/are not resolved/are resolved in part (circle one).
18. The Slobodnik family's largest external conflict is with ___.
19. This conflict results in the following internal conflict(s): ___.
20. These conflicts are resolved/are not resolved/are resolved in part (circle one).
21. Seeking ___, both families experienced ___.

BIG Question

22. In both selections, ordinary people take extraordinary risks in order to survive. How far would *you* go to reach a goal? What would you do if you didn't know what else to do?

READING ACROSS TEXTS WORKSHOP

Reading/Critical Thinking

from **Thura's Diary**

8. **BIG Question** Possible response: Thura writes in her diary.
9. They are sensitive to the dust, so they have to blow their noses often.
10. Responses will vary.

Escaping

11. **BIG Question** Possible response: The Slobodniks decided to take a big chance and escape from Czechoslovakia. Zdenko believes perseverance is imperative to success.
12. The Slobodniks hiked across the Alps into Austria.
13. Possible response: If you stick with it and persevere, you can accomplish goals.

Writing: Reading Across Texts

Use Your Notes

14. Students will vary in the way they mark and analyze their charts.

Get It on Paper

15. Possible response: Thura's largest external conflict is with the bombing of Baghdad.
16. Possible response: This conflict results in the following internal conflicts: fear for her safety and that of her loved ones.
17. Possible response: These conflicts are not resolved.
18. Possible response: The Slobodnik family's largest external conflict is with starting over in a new country without many things they left behind.
19. Possible response: This conflict results in the following internal conflicts: worries about finding a permanent place to live and jobs.
20. Possible response: These conflicts are resolved.
21. Possible response: Seeking safety, both families experienced hardship.

BIG Question

22. Responses will vary.

Indiana English/Language Arts Academic Standards
SE: 8.3, 8.5.2

The Unit Challenge

Focus

BELLRINGER Options

Daily Language Practice Transparency 41

Focus Activity Ask: After reading the selections in this unit, which author or character would you go to for advice if you didn't know what to do? Why? AS

The discussion will remind students of the selections they've read, which will help them begin the group activity or the solo activity.

Teach

Group Activity: Advice Column

- You may put students in groups or let them form their own. Each group should have between three and five members.
- Group members should agree on a name for the column and an identity for the advice columnist.
- Be sure students are ready to write letters seeking advice by midway through the class period so they have time to complete responses to the letters.
- Each student should prepare the final drafts of his or her letter and response.
- Make each student responsible for checking his or her work for errors.

UNIT 4 WRAP-UP

Answering The BIG Question What Do You Do When You Don't Know What to Do?

You've just read several selections and you have thought about what to do when you don't know what to do. Now use what you've learned to complete the Unit Challenge.

The Unit Challenge

Choose Activity A or Activity B and follow the directions for that activity.

A. Group Activity: Advice Column

Sometimes when you don't know what to do you could use a little advice to help point you in the right direction. Your group has been chosen to write an advice column called "What to Do When You Don't Know What to Do."

1. Discuss the Assignment

- Choose one group member to be the note-taker for the discussion.
- Review any notes that you wrote in your Learner's Notebook and your Foldable for the selections you read in the unit.
- Discuss some of the decisions that characters or speakers in the selections made. For example, the speaker in the poem "The Road Less Traveled" decided to take a path that differed from other people's paths. The speaker in the poem "Wishing Well" decides to wait to see if her wish will come true.

2. Ask for Advice

- Advice columnists need something to give advice about. So you and the members of your group will write letters seeking advice.
- You can write about a real or an imaginary problem that you just can't decide how to solve. Sign your letter with an amusing name, such as "Confused in Columbus."
- When each member is done writing, put the letters in a box or a bag.

3. Give Advice

- Have each member draw a letter from the box to answer.
- Imagine you are writing the answer to the problem as one of the speakers or characters from a selection you read. Write your advice from the perspective of that speaker or character.

4. Share the Letters When you're done, read aloud the letter asking for advice and your "character's" or "speaker's" response. Select the best ones, and consider publishing them in a school newspaper or newsletter.

Assess/Close

Group Activity

Ask: What have you learned from the process of seeking and giving advice that will help you the next time you don't know what to do? *(Suggest that students write responses in their Learner's Notebooks.)* AS

B. Solo Activity: Award for Best Supporting Role

In life, it's usually the main character that gets all the glory. Now is your chance to change all that by honoring someone in the best supporting role. Follow these steps to create your award.

1. **Create a List of Nominees**
   - List characters or speakers from the selections who played an important supporting role in helping someone solve a problem. Use the notes from your Foldables to help you.
   - Add to the list the name of someone you know who has helped other people.
   - Beside each name, jot down a few notes about the problem he or she helped solve. Now review your list, and choose the person or character you wish to honor.

2. **Designing Your Award** Design and create your award. Here are some suggestions:
   - Research award designs on the Internet or make up your own.
   - Include a photo, drawing, or painting of the honoree.
   - Get the correct spelling of the person's name.
   - Write the text that will appear on the award, such as:

     _______________ *is hereby honored with the* _______________ *Award for his/her supporting role in helping* _______________ *solve* _______________ *problem.*

   - Choose an unusual font or add a border to make your award look special.

3. **Call the Press!** No award is complete without a press release, or announcement to the public.
   - In your release include a headline at the top telling the name of the award and the person receiving it. Be sure to include the date and a person to contact for more information (you).
   - Include a brief paragraph explaining the meaning or significance of the award and the reason why this person is receiving it.

4. **And the Winner Is . . . .** Roll out the red carpet. It's Award Time. You've got a few options here:
   - If your award is going to a fictional character, consider getting a friend to play that role. You play the presenter, and you can interview the winner right after you present the award.
   - If your award is going to a real person, consider inviting him or her to the classroom to accept your award. Do everything to make the person feel comfortable and honored.
   - If you don't care to make a big scene, simply post your press release and award side-by-side in your classroom. You may wish to read them aloud to the class.

Literature Online

BIG Question Link to Web resources to further explore the Big Question at www.glencoe.com.

Teach

Solo Activity: Award for Best Supporting Role

- For this award, have students consider at least three characters from the selections and three real-life people they know.
- To help students think of real-life people who have helped them solve a problem, have them consider the different areas of their lives: school, family, friends, community.
- Encourage students to write their notes in their Learner's Notebooks.
- Make telephone books or the Internet accessible so that students can verify the spelling of their honorees' names.
- Allow students who do not have access to computer software to handprint their awards. Inform students that all awards must be neat, legible, accurately completed, and visually appealing.

Assess/Close

Solo Activity

Encourage students to use this experience to think about the importance of other people's help when they don't know what to do. Have students make small wallet cards with the names and phone numbers of people they can contact for advice. **AS**

Big Question Have students access the Web site for English and Spanish summaries and annotated links to related Web resources.

Focus

Build Background

This poem examines a speaker's feelings and fears about death. He finds some solace in the reading of a book.

- Fears of death are often expressed in poetry. For example, John Donne, who wrote in the sixteenth and seventeenth centuries, penned the poem "Death Be Not Proud," along with many other Holy Sonnets addressing the topic of death.
- During the twentieth century, Dylan Thomas wrote "Do Not Go Gentle into That Good Night," a poem encouraging his subject to fight death.

Teach

Viewing the Art

Say: The art shows light emanating from the book along with the shock on the reader's face that could be a result of the speaker's thoughts presented in the poem. What feeling do you get from viewing the art? *(Possible response: It looks like the person is enthralled by the reading. It gives a sense of surprise and engagement.)* **OL**

UNIT 4

Your Turn: Read and Apply Skills

David Ignatow

Meet the Author

David Ignatow is remembered as a poet who wrote popular verse about the common man and the issues that all people encounter in daily life. Before becoming a writer, Ignatow worked as a butcher, a hospital admitting-clerk, and a paper salesman. It was only later in his career that he received acclaim for his writing. Ignatow once said that he admired poetry "where you can feel the mind running like an electrical current through the muscles." See page R3 of the Author Files for more information about Ignatow.

Author Search For more about David Ignatow, go to www.glencoe.com.

Analyzing the Photo How does this image represent the poem's message?

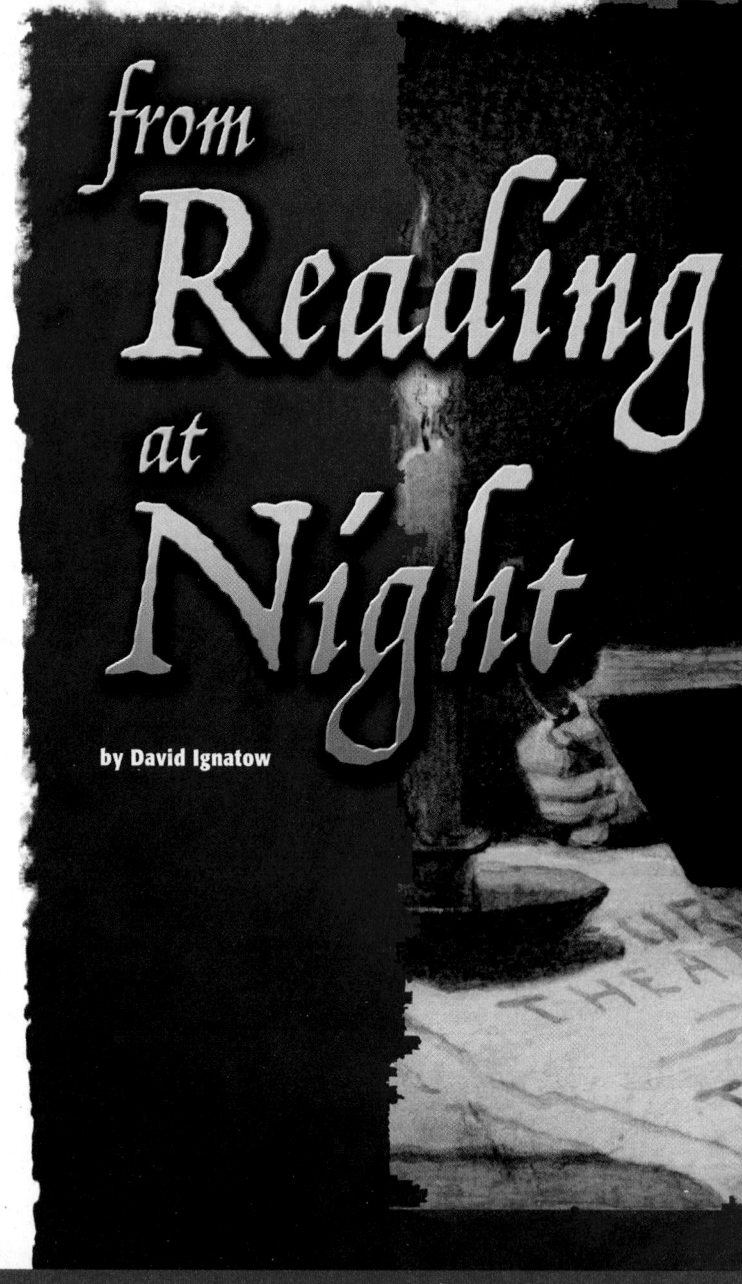

from Reading at Night

by David Ignatow

Additional Support

Author Search To expand students' appreciation of David Ignatow, have them access the Web site for additional information and resources.

Literature Focus Lesson

Free Verse Some free verse reflects the poet's thought process—somewhat disorganized, sometimes written in fragments, filled with questions and possible answers. As a class, write a poem about school that begins with a question. Ask students to share their own thoughts for this free verse poem. After you finish the class poem, ask students to work with partners to write free verse poems, using some questions about childhood and growing up. **OL** **AL**

The Ghost Story. Frederick Smallfield (1829-1915). Watercolor.

What have I learned that can keep me
from the simple fact of my dying?
None of the ideas I read stay
with me for long, I find the dark
closed in about me as I close
the book and I hurry to open it
again to let its light shine
on my face.

Teach

R1 Reading Skill

Interpreting Ask: How does the second sentence in the poem reinforce the idea that the speaker is very tired but refuses to go to sleep? *(Possible response: Having so many things connected in one sentence gives the impression of someone who's half asleep and rambling on.)* OL AL

R2 Reading Skill

Interpreting Say: The speaker in the poem reads to find the answer that will keep the fear of death away. What lines from the poem tell you that these efforts are wasted? *("None of the ideas I read stay with me for long.")* OL

L Literary Element

Alliteration Ask: What alliteration is used in the next to last line of the poem? *(the* l *in let and light)* AS

R3 Reading Skill

Connecting Ask: Have you ever been so afraid of something that you couldn't stop thinking about it? How did you try to get the frightening thoughts out of your head? *(Responses will vary.)* AS

Differentiated Instruction

Understanding Symbols The poet in this selection uses light and dark to represent life and death. To help students understand this symbolism, have them complete cluster charts, like the one to the right, with ideas they link to light and dark. For example, students might associate fear with the dark and joy or sunshine with the light. BL

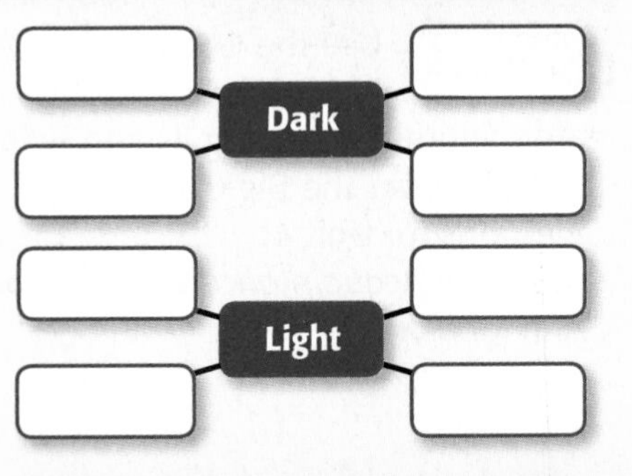

Indiana English/Language Arts Academic Standards

TWE: *Literature Focus Lesson* 8.5.7, *Differentiated Instruction* 8.3.6

Tips for Independent Reading

Stress the importance of reading different literary genres that deal with making decisions when you don't know what to do. Suggest the books listed here that are related to the Big Question.

Fiction

Explain to students how reading fictional stories of people who have faced difficult times and have struggled with internal and external conflicts will help students deal with similar issues in their own lives.

Ask students to tell about a fictional book they've read that shows what people have done when they didn't know what to do.

UNIT 4

Reading on Your Own

To read more about the Big Question, choose one of these books from your school or local library. Work on your reading skills by choosing books that are challenging to you.

Fiction

Over the Wall
by John H. Ritter

Thirteen-year-old Tyler is spending the summer with his aunt, uncle, and cousins in New York. This time away from his father, who has serious problems of his own, gives Tyler a chance to deal with his explosive temper and to begin to understand his family's past.

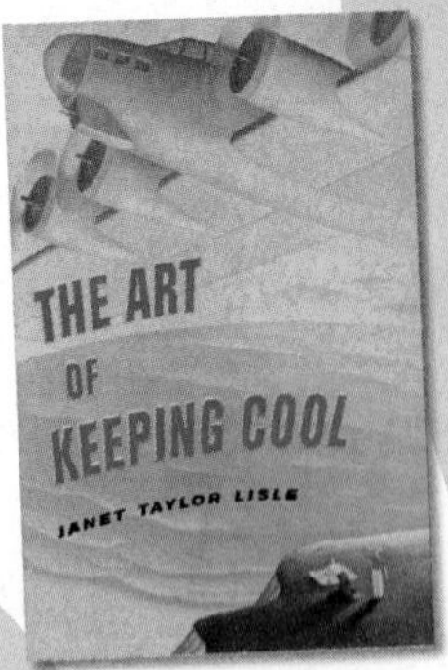

The Art of Keeping Cool
by Janet Taylor Lisle

During World War II, thirteen-year-old Robert discovers family secrets and his community's wartime fears. Themes of prejudice and loss emerge as Robert, his cousin, and their artist friend discover how destructive even a faraway war can be.

The Princess of Pop
by Cathy Hopkins

Squidge dares her friend Becca to enter the Prince and Princess of Pop competition, an *American Idol* type contest. Accepting the challenge forces Becca to face her fear of failure. The tension grows as she advances in the competition and struggles to find her true self.

Chu Ju's House
By Gloria Whelan

In China, where fourteen-year-old Chu Ju lives with her parents in a small village, families are allowed only two children, and girls are often considered inferior. When Chu Ju's mother gives birth to a second daughter, the parents decide to put the baby up for adoption so that they can try again to have a boy. To save her sister from this fate, Chu Ju decides to run away so that her family will have only one daughter.

Additional Support

Differentiated Instruction

Use the Glencoe BookLink CD-ROM to create customized reading lists to help students answer the Big Question. Suggestions for Unit 4:

Grade 4: *An Acquaintance with Darkness* by Ann Rinaldi
Grade 5: *Angels of the Swamp* by Dorothy Raymond Whittaker
Grade 6: *Audibles: My Life in Football* by Joe Montana
Grade 7: *African American Scientists* by Jetty St. John
Grade 8: *The Call of the Wild* by Jack London

Nonfiction

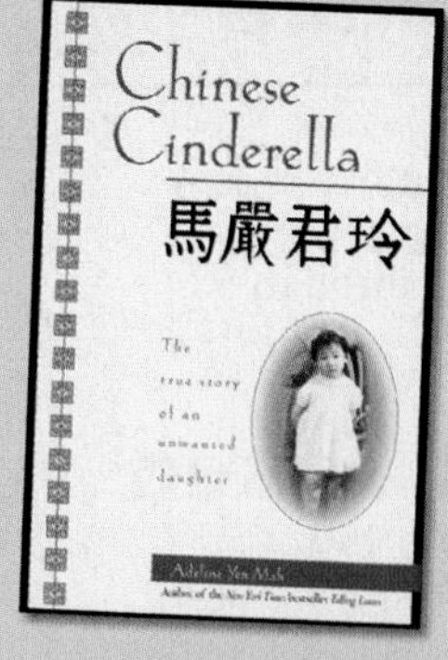

Chinese Cinderella
by Adeline Yen Mah

Adeline Yen Mah's autobiography, like the fairy-tale Cinderella, tells of a childhood dominated by a cruel stepmother. It is only when she wins a writing contest that her father finally notices Yen Mah and grants her wish to attend college. The book includes the legend of the original Chinese Cinderella.

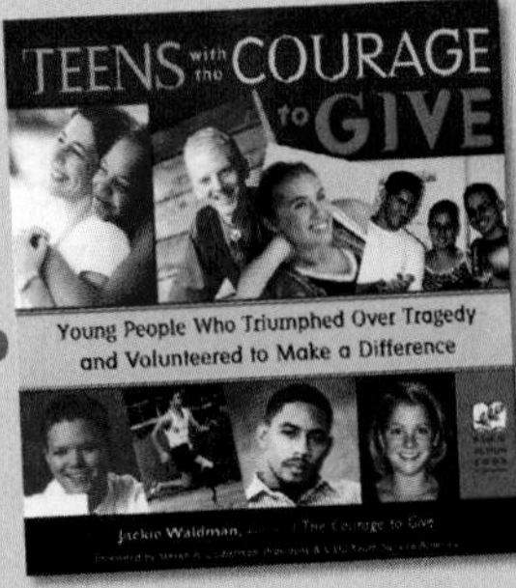

Teens with the Courage to Give: Young People Who Triumphed Over Tragedy and Volunteered to Make a Difference
by Jackie Waldman

This book profiles thirty young people who overcame great personal odds to reach out and help others. With their stories, these teens take us to the depths of their struggles and the heights of their newfound sense of purpose and peace.

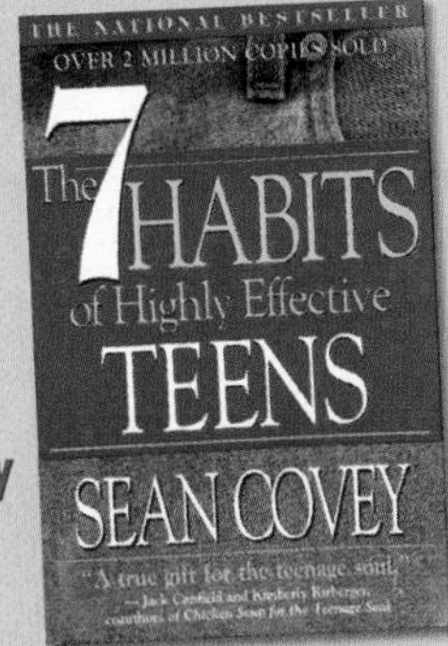

The 7 Habits of Highly Effective Teens
by Sean Covey

Here is a collection of stories about real teens from all over the world who have overcome obstacles to succeed. Covey includes cartoons, quotes, clever ideas, and step-by-step guides to help readers reach their full potential.

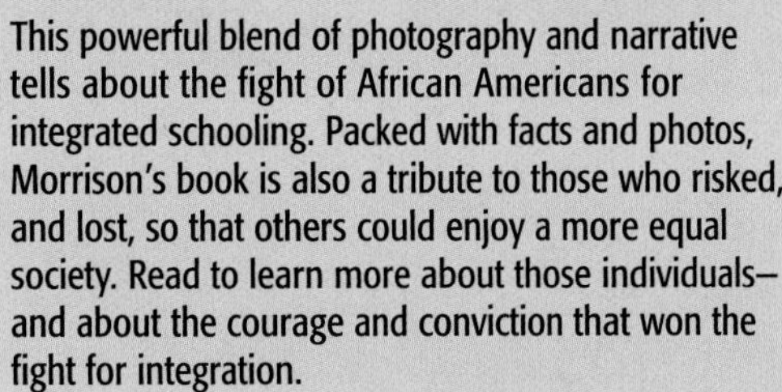

Remember: The Journey to School Integration
by Toni Morrison

This powerful blend of photography and narrative tells about the fight of African Americans for integrated schooling. Packed with facts and photos, Morrison's book is also a tribute to those who risked, and lost, so that others could enjoy a more equal society. Read to learn more about those individuals—and about the courage and conviction that won the fight for integration.

READING ON YOUR OWN

Nonfiction
Tell students that all the books on this page are nonfiction. The authors of the books tell about their lives or the lives of other real people and the decisions they made when they didn't know what to do.

Reading for Inspiration
Ask: Can you tell why reading one or more of these books might help you know what to do when you're not sure? *(The books are about real people with conflicts and uncertainties who made decisions when they weren't sure what to do. Students may identify with one or more of the real-life people in these books as they overcome uncertainty to solve their problems.)* **OL**

Test-Taking Tips

TIP For poetry-based questions, tell students that they should read the poem, read the questions, and then read the poem again before they answer the questions. Because poems are generally shorter than prose pieces, students will usually have time to read a poem at least twice during a test. Each time they read, they will likely see a new element they did not notice before.

ISTEP+ Test Practice

Directions

Read this poem carefully. Then, answer questions 1 through 5.

The Road Not Taken

by Robert Frost

Two roads diverged in a yellow wood,
And sorry I could not travel both
And be one traveler, long I stood
And looked down one as far as I could
To where it bent in the undergrowth;

Then took the other, as just as fair,
And having perhaps the better claim,
Because it was grassy and wanted wear;
Though as for that the passing there
Had worn them really about the same,

And both that morning equally lay
In leaves no step had trodden black.
Oh, I kept the first for another day!
Yet knowing how way leads on to way,
I doubted if I should ever come back.

I shall be telling this with a sigh
Somewhere ages and ages hence:
Two roads diverged in a wood, and I—
I took the one less traveled by,
And that has made all the difference.

1 Read the first stanza of the poem.

Two roads diverged in a yellow wood,
And sorry I could not travel both
And be one traveler, long I stood
And looked down one as far as I could
To where it bent in the undergrowth;

As it is used in the first line, *diverged* means

A disappeared
B went into the same place
C wandered
D went in different directions

2 What do the roads in the woods MOST LIKELY symbolize?

A ideas
B options
C mistakes
D actual places

3 Read these lines from the third stanza of the poem.

And both that morning equally lay
In leaves no step had trodden black.

In the poem, the word *trodden* MOST LIKELY means

A walked on
B avoided
C run through
D hidden

4 The tone of the poem is BEST described as

A enthusiastic
B accepting
C uncertain
D angry

Answers:

1. D
2. B
3. A
4. B

Resources for pages 536–541

Use these resources to review, assess, or reteach the chapter: Active Learning and Note-Taking Guide, ExamView Pro, and Differentiated Instruction Tool Software.

Answers:

5. C

6. B

7. A

8. D

5 Based on the poem, choose the idea with which Robert Frost would MOST LIKELY agree.

A Avoid situations that might be uncomfortable.
B When facing two paths, take the easy one.
C Wise people meet life head on and live with their choices.
D To avoid problems, learn from the mistakes you have made in the past.

Question 6 is based on your knowledge of the writing process.

6 You want to share with people some of the history of how Robert Frost wrote his poetry. The BEST form of writing for this purpose would be

A narrative
B informational
C persuasive
D poetic

Questions 7 and 8 are based on your knowledge of language conventions.

7 Which of the following sentences is an example of the CORRECT use of parallelism?

A Students wanting to memorize and needing to study poetry that features imagery from rural life should read Robert Frost.
B Students who want to memorize and who are needing to study poetry that features imagery from rural life should read Robert Frost.
C Students wanting to memorize and who need to study poetry that features imagery from rural life should read Robert Frost.
D Students who want to memorize and needing to study poetry that features imagery from rural life should read Robert Frost.

8 Which of the following sentences is an example of the CORRECT use of capitalization?

A Robert frost is a beloved american poet.
B Robert Frost is a Beloved American Poet.
C Robert Frost is a beloved American Poet.
D Robert Frost is a beloved American poet.

Directions

Read this poem carefully. Then, answer questions 9 through 13.

Fable for When There's No Way Out

by May Swenson

Grown too big for his skin,
and it grown hard,

without a sea and atmosphere—
he's drunk it all up—

his strength's inside him now,
but there's no room to stretch.

He pecks at the top
but his beak's too soft;

though instinct and ambition shoves,
he can't get through.

Barely old enough to bleed
and already bruised!

In a case this tough
what's the use

if you break your head
instead of the lid?

Despair temps him
to just go limp:

Maybe the cell's
already a tomb,

Test-Taking Tips

TIP Advise students to pay particular attention to any words or images that stand out or catch their attention while they are reading a poem. A poet may use these words as signals to draw the reader's attention to the meaning or message of the poem. If students are allowed to write on test papers, tell them to consider underlining significant words or images as they read.

Test-Taking Tips

TIP Remind students to fill in every answer on the test. When a student does not know the answer, the best method is to eliminate as many choices as possible, take his or her best guess, and move on to the next question. Students can go back to review any items they weren't sure of if they have time left at the end of the test.

and beginning end
in this round room.

Still, stupidly he pecks
and pecks, as if from under

his own skull—
yet makes no crack . . .

No crack until
he finally cracks,

and kicks and stomps.
What a thrill

and shock to feel
his little gaff poke

through the floor!
A way he hadn't known or meant.

Rage works if reason won't.
When locked up, bear down.

Questions 9 through 13 are based on "Fable for When There's No Way Out."

9 In the poem, the poet compares the shell to

A a floor
B the atmosphere
C the ocean
D a cell

10 How does the chick finally break through the shell?

A by pushing with his wings
B by pecking with his beak
C by kicking and stomping
D by stretching from side to side

11 Read these lines from the poem.

Still, stupidly he pecks
and pecks, as if from under

his own skull—
yet makes no crack . . .

No crack until
he finally cracks

As it is used in the sixth line, "he finally cracks" MOST LIKELY means that the chick

A makes a decision
B breaks the shell
C takes a break
D goes wild

12 The tone of the poem is BEST described as

A lively
B pessimistic
C confident
D wistful

13 A fable is a story with a moral, a lesson about life. What is the moral of this poem?

A Once you have broken free of difficulty, be optimistic about the future.
B When you're trapped, find the strength to push your way out.
C Always keep a cool head when you are in a difficult situation.
D Don't depend on other people to help you.

Answers:

9. D
10. C
11. D
12. A
13. B

UNIT 5
Skills Scope and Sequence

Readability Scores Key
Dale-Chall/**DRP**/**Lexile**

PACING (DAYS) STANDARD	BLOCK	INSTRUCTIONAL SEGMENT LITERATURE	READING SKILLS	LITERARY ELEMENTS
1	1	**Unit Warm-Up, pp. 542–557** Genre Focus: "Born Worker" by Gary Soto 5.5/**52**/**780**, SE p. 547	Fluency, TWE p. 543 Analyzing, SE pp. 546, 551, 554, 556 Questioning, SE pp. 546, 552, 553 Predicting, SE pp. 546, 548, 552, TWE p. 555 Making Inferences, SE pp. 546, 550, 551, 555, TWE pp. 548, 549, 557 Identifying Author's Purpose, TWE pp. 547, 557	Tone, TWE p. 550 Irony, TWE p. 552 Characterization, SE pp. 546, 547, 557, TWE pp. 549, 556 Plot, SE pp. 546, 548, 553, 555, TWE pp. 550, 556 Theme, SE pp. 546, 557 Setting, SE pp. 546, 549 Conflict, TWE p. 544
3	2	**Reading Workshop 1, pp. 558–579** "Cream Puff" by Linnea Due 4.3/**50**/**840**, SE p. 562 "The Question of Popularity" by Tamara Eberlain 5.7/**53**/**930**, SE p. 574	Analyzing, SE pp. 558, 559, 561, 562, 564, 565, 568, 573, 576, TWE pp. 563, 574, 575, 577 Monitoring Comprehension, SE p. 567, TWE p. 566 Connecting, TWE pp. 563, 573, 577 Predicting, TWE p. 568	Characterization, SE pp. 561, 563, 564, 566, 567, TWE pp. 562, 565 Direct Quotations, SE pp. 573, 575, 577 Conflict, TWE p. 565 Tone, TWE p. 569 Theme, TWE p. 576
1		**Writing Workshop, Part 1, pp. 580–583** Writing Product: Short Story	Fluency, TWE p. 582	Character, TWE p. 580 Plot, TWE p. 580 Conflict, TWE p. 581 Imagery, TWE p. 581
3	1	**Reading Workshop 2, pp. 584–603** "an african american" by Meri Nana-Ama Danquah SE p. 588 "One Throw" by W. C. Heinz 3.3/**44**/**670**, SE p. 596	Questioning, SE pp. 584, 585, 587, 588, 590, 595, 597, 599, 600, TWE pp. 589, 596, 598 Fluency, TWE p. 589 Interpreting, SE p. 598, TWE p. 599 Connecting, TWE p. 587, 589 Monitoring Comprehension, TWE 599, 601 Analyzing, TWE p. 591	Sensory Imagery, SE pp. 587, 589, 590, 591 Plot, SE pp. 595, 596, 598, 600, 601, TWE p. 599 Repetition, TWE p. 588 Symbols, TWE p. 588 Characterization, TWE pp. 597, 600

Unit 5 Big Question

The question **"How do you stay true to yourself?"** is designed to help students think about how their actions reflect who they are and what they believe.

Unit 5 Genre

Many of the selections in this unit are **short stories** that will help students answer the big question: "How do you stay true to yourself?" The stories will give students examples of how characters have struggled to remain true to themselves.

CRITICAL THINKING	VOCABULARY	WRITING AND GRAMMAR	LISTENING, SPEAKING, AND VIEWING
Comprehension, TWE p. 553		Verbs, TWE p. 556 Write a Report, TWE p. 557	
Comprehension, TWE pp. 562, 564, 567 Infer, SE pp. 570, 578 Evaluate, SE pp. 570, 578 Classify, SE p. 578	Multiple-Meaning Words, TWE p. 568 Word Analysis, SE pp. 560, 563, TWE pp. 561, 564 Word Families, SE pp. 572, 576	Write About Your Reading, SE p. 578 Clauses and Phrases, SE pp. 571, 579	Talk About Your Reading, SE p. 570
		Short Story: Prewriting and Drafting, SE pp. 580–582 Compound and Complex Sentences, SE p. 583 Dialogue, TWE p. 582 Suspense, TWE p. 582	
Interpret, SE pp. 592, 602 Analyze, SE pp. 592, 602, TWE pp. 590, 601 Evaluate, SE p. 592 Infer, SE p. 602 Comprehension, TWE pp. 596, 597	Academic Vocabulary, SE p. 584 Suffixes, SE pp. 586, 589, 591, 594, 596, 598, 599, TWE p. 601 Write to Learn, TWE p. 586 Verb Usage, TWE p. 594 Context Clues, TWE p. 600	Commas in Compound Sentences, SE p. 593 Write About Your Reading, SE p. 602 Commas in Complex Sentences, SE p. 603 Write a Poem, TWE p. 591	Talk About Your Reading, SE p. 592 Viewing the Art, TWE p. 598

UNIT 5

Skills Scope and Sequence *continued*

Readability Scores Key
Dale-Chall/**DRP**/Lexile

PACING (DAYS) STANDARD	BLOCK	INSTRUCTIONAL SEGMENT LITERATURE	READING SKILLS	LITERARY ELEMENTS
3	3	**Reading Workshop 3, pp. 604–627** "The Medicine Bag" by Virginia Driving Hawk Sneve 5.7/**52**/910, SE p. 608 "A Year of Living Bravely" by Emily Costello 4.7/**52**/580, SE p. 622	Questioning, TWE p. 616 Predicting, SE pp. 604, 605, 608, 609, 610, 611, 612, 614, 621 Connecting, TWE pp. 607, 613, 621 Identifying Main Idea and Supporting Details, TWE p. 611 Monitoring Comprehension, TWE pp. 615, 623	Sequence, TWE p. 612 Characterization, TWE pp. 608, 609, 610 Theme, SE pp. 607, 613, 617, TWE pp. 612, 622 Attention-Getting Device, SE pp. 621, 622
1		**Writing Workshop, Part 2, pp. 628–633** Writing Product: Short Story	Read Aloud, TWE p. 630 Identifying Main Idea and Supporting Details, TWE p. 655	
3	1	**Reading Workshop 4, pp. 634–661** *The Fire Pond* by Michael J. Rosen 4.2/**55**/1070, SE p. 638 from *Savion! My Life in Tap* by Savion Glover and Bruce Weber 4.9/**50**/790, SE p. 654	Making Inferences, SE pp. 634, 635, 637, 638, 639, 640, 641, 642, 646, 647, 648, 653, 656, TWE p. 655 Fluency, TWE p. 634 Interpreting, SE p. 643 Connecting, SE p. 646, TWE pp. 638 Predicting, SE p. 648, TWE p. 645	Symbols, TWE p. 649 Setting, SE pp. 637, 638, 641, 643, 644, 645 Tone, SE pp. 653, 654, 657, 658, TWE p. 645 Characterization, TWE pp. 639, 655
3	2	**Comparing Literature Workshop, pp. 662–685** "A Retrieved Reformation" by O. Henry 6.9/**54**/900, SE p. 665 An Adaption of "A Retrieved Reformation" by Gary Gianni, SE p. 675	Fluency, TWE p. 665 Activating Prior Knowledge, TWE p. 665 Making Inferences, TWE pp. 666, 667 Monitoring Comprehension, TWE p. 669	Characterization, SE pp. 662, 665, 675, 676, 677, 678, 679 Point of View, TWE p. 670 Irony, TWE p. 671 Foreshadowing, p. 671
4	2	**Unit Wrap-Up, pp. 686–707** "Thank You in Arabic" by Naomi Shihab Nye 6.1/**55**/950, SE p. 688	Reading Independently, SE pp. 700–701 Monitoring Comprehension, TWE pp. 691, 693	Fiction, TWE p. 700 Nonfiction, TWE p. 701

CRITICAL THINKING	VOCABULARY	WRITING AND GRAMMAR	LISTENING, SPEAKING, AND VIEWING
Synthesis, TWE pp. 610, 614, 617 Infer, SE p. 618 Interpret, SE pp. 618, 626 Analyze, SE pp. 618, 626, TWE pp. 605, 608, 610, 613, 615, 624 Evaluate, SE p. 626	Synonyms and Antonyms, TWE p. 620 Prefixes, SE pp. 606, 609, 612, 620, 624 Academic Vocabulary, SE p. 604 Using Vocabulary, TWE p. 606	Writing About Your Reading, SE p. 618 Combining Sentences, SE pp. 619, 627	Talk About Your Reading, SE p. 626 Viewing the Art, TWE p. 614 Viewing the Photo, TWE pp. 622, 624
		Conflict, TWE p. 632 Resolution, TWE p. 632 Characterization, TWE pp. 628, 631 Writing a Short Story: Revising, Editing, Presenting, SE pp. 628, 630 Plot, TWE p. 629 Dialogue, TWE p. 631 Spelling, TWE p. 630 Applying Good Writing Traits: Organization, SE p. 629, TWE p. 629	Group Discussion, SE p. 633 Presenting, TWE p. 630
Analyze, SE pp. 650, 660, TWE p. 642, 653, 656, 659 Evaluate, SE pp. 650, 660 Comprehension, TWE pp. 641, 646 Synthesis, TWE pp. 644, 648, 657	Academic Vocabulary, SE p. 634 Prefixes, SE pp. 636, 639 Context Clues, TWE pp. 638, 640, 648, 654, 659 Suffixes, SE pp. 652, 655 Vocabulary, TWE p. 652	Write About Your Reading, SE p. 650 Run-on Sentences, SE pp. 651, 661	Talk About Your Reading, SE p. 660
Evaluation, TWE p. 677 Analyze, SE p. 685, TWE pp. 668, 669, 670 Interpret, SE p. 685 Comprehension, TWE pp. 663, 683 Application, TWE p. 679	Multiple Affixes, SE pp. 664, 669, 674, 681 Context Clues, TWE pp. 665, 667	Writing: Compare the Literature, TWE p. 685	Viewing the Illustrations, TWE p. 675
Analysis, TWE pp. 691, 693, 694, 698	Analogies, TWE p. 696	Values Chart, SE p. 687	Videotape a Soap Opera, SE p. 686

UNIT 5

Unit Resources

Reading with Purpose offers a comprehensive package of tools to optimize student learning and the teaching experience. Each resource has been designed to assist students in specific areas and to offer instructional support for teachers. While all of these areas are covered in the core textbook, some students may need extra practice or additional help in specific areas. The resource package is designed so that you, the teacher, can choose which items will best assist your students. You may also use these resources as homework assignments and for assessment purposes. The following are resources recommended for use with Unit 5.

Keys for Unit Resources

- Blackline Master
- Workbook
- Supplemental Text
- CD-ROM
- DVD
- Transparency
- Web-based
- Fast File

Essential Instructional Support

FAST FILE UNIT 5 RESOURCES

Reading and Literature

- Academic Vocabulary Review
- Big Question: School to Home
- The Big Question Foldable
- Unit Challenge: Planner and Rubrics
- Comparing Literature Graphic Organizer
- Key Reading Skills
- Active Reading Graphic Organizers
- Literary Analysis
- Unit Vocabulary Review

Writing, Grammar, and Spelling

- Spelling and Handwriting Practice
- Grammar Practice
- Writing Workshop Graphic Organizer

Listening, Speaking, and Viewing

- Viewing and Representing
- Listening and Speaking

English Language Learners

- English Language Coach Review

DIFFERENTIATED INSTRUCTION

- Leveled Vocabulary Development
- Skills Level Up!™ A Language Arts Game
- Listening Library CD
- BookLink 3
- Literature Library Vocabulary Puzzlemaker
- Vocabulary Puzzlemaker

ASSESSMENT

GLENCOE'S ASSESSMENT ADVANTAGE

- Selection and Unit Assessments
- Selection Quick Checks
- Assessment by Learning Objectives
- Rubrics for Assessing Student Writing, Listening, and Speaking
- Glencoe Online Essay Grader
- Interactive Tutor: Self-Assessment
- ExamView Assessment Suite
- Literature Library ExamView Assessment Suite

Additional Instructional Support

WRITING, GRAMMAR, AND SPELLING

- Real Success in Writing: Research and Reports
- Writing Constructed Responses
- Spelling Power eWorkbook
- Grammar & Composition Handbook
- Grammar and Language Workbook
- Revising with Style eWorkbook

TRANSPARENCIES

- Read Aloud, Think Aloud Transparencies
- Literary and Text Analysis Transparencies
- Bellringer Options Transparencies
- Grammar and Writing Workshop Transparencies
- Fine Art Transparencies

ENGLISH LANGUAGE LEARNER

- English Language Coach
- Fluency Practice and Assessment
- inTime Magazines (Spanish)
- Spanish Listening Library CD

PROFESSIONAL DEVELOPMENT

- Professional Development Package

READING AND LITERATURE

- Active Learning and Note Taking Guide
- inTime Magazines
- Backpack Reader Volume 1
- Literature Library
- Literature Launchers Pre-Reading Videos DVD
- Literature Classics

TECHNOLOGY

- TeacherWorks Plus™
- StudentWorks Plus™
- BookLink 3
- Skill Level Up!™ A Language Arts Game
- ExamView Assessment Suite
- Interactive Tutor: Self-Assessment
- Listening Library CD
- Spanish Listening Library CD
- Literature Classics
- Literature Launchers Pre-Reading Videos DVD
- Literature Library ExamView Assessment Suite
- Vocabulary Puzzlemaker
- Literature Library Vocabulary Puzzlemaker
- glencoe.com
- Online Student Edition
- Presentation Plus!
- Glencoe Online Essay Grader

Additional Glencoe Resources

Dinah Zike's Foldables

Foldables are three-dimensional, interactive graphic organizers that help students practice basic writing skills, review key vocabulary terms, and answer Big Questions. Every unit contains a foldable activity. You can find the pattern and directions for the Unit 5 Foldable in the Unit 5 Resources Fast Files booklet. You can use the foldables as they are presented or modify them to suit the needs of your students. More information about foldables for Unit 5 can be found on pages R8–R9.

Glencoe Literature Library

This collection of hardcover books includes full-length novels, novellas, plays, and works of nonfiction. Each volume consists of at least one complete extended-length reading accompanied by several related readings from a broad range of genres. A separate Study Guide for each Glencoe Literature Library book provides teaching notes and reproducible activity pages for students.

Glencoe Literature Library titles that complement this unit include:

The Call of the Wild, by Jack London
Catherine, Called Birdy, by Karen Cushman
The Pigman, by Paul Zindel

For a wealth of online resources that support the instruction in Unit 5 of *Glencoe Literature: Reading with Purpose,* students and teachers can visit our Web site at www.glencoe.com. Students will find additional learning, practice, and assessment opportunities such as these, which are noted in the student text:

- **Big Question Overview**
- **Study Central**
- **Author Search**
- **Writing Models**
- **Interactive Literary Elements Handbook**
- **Web Activities**

Teachers will find planning and instructional tools that include the following:

- **Book Lesson Plans**
- **Teacher Forum**
- **Professional Development**
- **Web Activities Lesson Plans (with answers to student activities)**

Go to www.glencoe.com to see the entire selection of Reading with Purpose online resources.

Use the Glencoe **BookLink 3** CD-ROM, a database of more than 26,700 titles, to *create customized reading lists* for your students.

- Search for award-winning titles, (e.g., Newbery Award winners, Coretta Scott King Award winners, and Caldecott Medal winners) and for books on several state-recommended reading lists.
- Find Degrees of Reading Power™ (DRP) and Lexile™ readability scores for all selections.
- Organize reading lists by students' reading level, author, genre, theme, or area of interest.
- Get a brief summary of each selection.

You can find recommended leveled readings for this unit with Reading on Your Own (see page 700).

Glencoe's **Presentation Plus!**, a multimedia teaching tool, lets you present dynamic lessons that will engage your students. Using Microsoft PowerPoint,® you can customize the presentations to create your own personalized lessons. Use **CheckPoint** questions with interactive response keypads to get immediate student feedback during lessons, to increase student participation, and to assess student comprehension.

A lively collection of articles drawn from issues of the TIME family of magazines helps students develop the skills they need to interact with informational text in a meaningful way. Each of the news stories, feature articles, reviews, profiles, and essays in the magazine connect to an author, work, or theme in *Glencoe Literature: Reading with Purpose.* Articles for Unit 5 are found in Volume B. See the *inTIME* Teacher's Guide for specific connections to each unit and for reproducible student worksheets designed to develop students' reading and critical thinking skills.

Literature Launchers

Set the scene with Glencoe's Literature Launchers, engaging video segments that introduce each unit's genre focus. Each video brings the genre to life, relating it to your students' worlds.

Insert the Glencoe Literature Launchers Pre-Reading Videos DVD into your DVD player. Select the Unit 5 Launcher from the menu to introduce the genre and Big Question for this unit.

Online Essay Grader

Use Glencoe's **Online Essay Grader** to score your students' writing and to provide individualized feedback to each student automatically.

You and your students can visit www.glencoe.com to link to the essay grader. *Students* can enter their essays and receive feedback on demand. *You* can manage demographic data, assign tests and generate individual student and aggregated reports. The essay grader can help you

- Save time with automatic scoring and individualized feedback.
- Supplement in-class writing instruction using guided writing practice.
- Get reports for individual students or for special populations.
- Track student improvement over time.

REAL Success: Reading Excellence at All Levels

Glencoe now provides all of your students with the tools they need to become better, more enthusiastic readers. The REAL Success suite of reading and language arts products encourages reading excellence by meeting the needs of students at all levels. Glencoe products that can be used in conjunction with Unit 5 include the following:

- Jamestown Literature: An Adapted Reader
- Jamestown *Reading Fluency*
- Jamestown *Critical Reading Series, In the Line of Duty*
- *Vocabulary Builder*
- *The Glencoe Reader, Course 3*

To order these products, call Glencoe at 1-800-USA-READ.

Teacher Wraparound Edition Key

Level Appropriate Code

AS = Activities for all students

AL = Activities for students working above grade level

OL = Activities for students working at grade level

BL = Activities for students working below grade level

EL = Activities for English language learners

Teacher Wraparound Prompts

R **Reading Skill** These activities help you teach reading comprehension skills.

V **Vocabulary** These activities help students comprehend words and incorporate them into their reading and writing.

C **Critical Thinking** These strategies help students apply and extend what they have learned.

BQ **BIG Question** These activities and questions prompt students to prepare to answer the Big Question.

W **Writing** These activities provide writing opportunities to help students practice writing and comprehend text.

L **Literary Element** These activities and questions help students comprehend selections and learn more about each genre.

E **Text Element** These activities help students comprehend text elements.

LSV **Listening, Speaking, Viewing** These activities help students practice listening, speaking, and viewing skills.

EL **English Language Coach** These skills help English language learners as well as students who need additional reading support.

UNIT 5

Professional Development Center

Douglas Fisher

From an Author:

Preparing Students to Read Short Stories

Set a purpose. In Unit 1, students learned about the importance of setting a purpose for reading. In Unit 3, they learned about previewing. This unit, on the short story, provides an excellent opportunity to review these skills. Remind students that they should preview a text before reading it. For the short story, this means spending fewer than three minutes figuring out who the characters are and what might be happening in the plot. In previewing a short story, students should focus on the beginning and end of the story, as these are important parts in short stories. Illustrations can also give students clues to what the story is about. Finally, students should generate questions based on their previewing that they will answer during their reading.

Engage students with the text. Reading Workshop 3 in this unit teaches students about predicting. As students preview the short stories and other selections in this unit, you may help them learn to make simple predictions to pique their interest. Predictions also help students remain engaged with the text and comprehend the story. Start with the title. Ask students to speculate what the main idea of the short story will be based on the title the author gave to the piece. While predicting is important, and a skill that students can learn to use, it is even more important that students learn from their predictions. Returning to predictions, verifying the guesses, and looking for missed clues when predictions are not quite accurate are also skills that students must develop. These same skills will help them as they analyze, question, and make inferences, which are the other skills taught in this unit.

Teacher to Teacher

Claire C. Meitl
Howard County Public School
Ellicott City, Maryland

Answering the Big Question, "How do you stay true to yourself?" begins with analyzing the lives of the characters portrayed in short stories. Readers gain an understanding not only of the story itself but also of their own character as they react to the life portrayed. One of the best analysis tools anyone can apply to any situation is "Why?" Children instinctively ask this as they explore the world around them and learn to interact with others. Why did that character act the way he or she did? Why do I sometimes act the same way, or why do I act differently? When reading short stories, I ask my students to constantly ask and answer and reflect on "Why?"

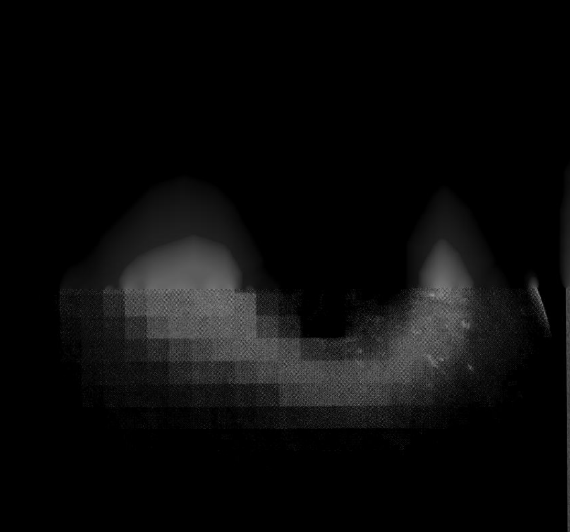

Using Short Stories

Why teach short stories?

Short stories often contain structural and character elements that are familiar to students. These can be used as guides to help students think about the actions, themes, and contexts of the plot. For students who are not familiar with "story grammar," short stories provide an excellent opportunity to develop or extend this knowledge base. Like longer pieces of fiction, short stories often contain characters, plot, setting, conflicts, imagery, and points of view. Each of these components can be analyzed in the short story so that students develop a stronger sense of these devices.

What are the teaching points for short stories?

As noted above, short stories can provide students and teachers an opportunity to develop an enhanced understanding of story grammar and literary devices. For example, students might focus on the role of characters while reading a particular short story and use the following questions to guide their reading:

- Which, if any, characters are flat or stereotypical?
- What makes characters behave as they do?
- How does the dialogue increase our understanding of the character?

In another short story, students might focus on point of view, using the following questions to guide their inquiry:

- Whose voice tells the story or provides the information readers need to understand what is happening?
- Does one character control the understanding of events, or do readers have an all-knowing narrator who provides facts and insights that the characters themselves do not have?
- How does the point of view shape our understanding of the events and actions of the characters?
- What might happen if another point of view took charge?

How can students be motivated to read short stories?

To motivate students, remind them that short stories are a way that writers convey life lessons quickly. Ask them what they'd like to learn about life and tell them that they might find an answer or insight in one of the short stories they'll read.

UNIT 5

The BIG Question: How Do You Stay True to Yourself?

> "Be who you are and say what you feel, because those who mind don't matter, and those who matter don't mind."
>
> —Dr. Seuss
> pen name of Theodor Geisel (1904–1991), author of *The Cat in the Hat*

Key Unit Objectives

- Answer the Big Question
- Analyze the literary elements of short stories
- Apply strategies for reading short stories
- Write a short story

Why Is It Important?

Dealing with this question will help students think about how their actions reflect who they are and what they believe.

Viewing the Image

Ask: What is the woman doing? *(She appears to be painting a solid color, but the sky and clouds are coming through.)* **Ask:** What do you think of when you look at this image? *(Responses will vary.)* **Ask:** Does the image remind you of staying true to yourself? Explain. *(Responses will vary.)* **Say:** Read the quote by Dr. Seuss. Restate the quote in your own words. *(Possible response: It's okay to be yourself and express your feelings. Anyone who holds it against you doesn't matter; the people in your life who really care about you like you for who you are, and how you express yourself.)* **AS**

Unit Skills

BIG Question How do you stay true to yourself?
Genre Focus: Short Story

Reading Skills

- Analyzing, p. 558
- Questioning, p. 584
- Predicting, p. 604
- Making Inferences, p. 634

Literary Elements

- Characterization, p. 561
- Plot, p. 595
- Theme, p. 607
- Setting, p. 637

Vocabulary

- Word Analysis, p. 560
- Suffixes, p. 586
- Word Families, p. 572
- Prefixes, p. 606

Writing Skills/Grammar

- Short Story, pp. 580, 628
- Organization, p. 629

LOOKING AHEAD

The skill lessons and readings in this unit will help you develop your own answer to the Big Question.

About the Reading

Each selection in this unit provides insights that can help students address the question, "How do you stay true to yourself?" The short stories and other selections in this unit revolve around the Big Question and provide various perspectives for students to consider.

About the Skills

The skills taught in this unit have been selected because they are particularly helpful when reading the featured genre—short story. Each reading selection provides students with opportunities to practice and develop these skills.

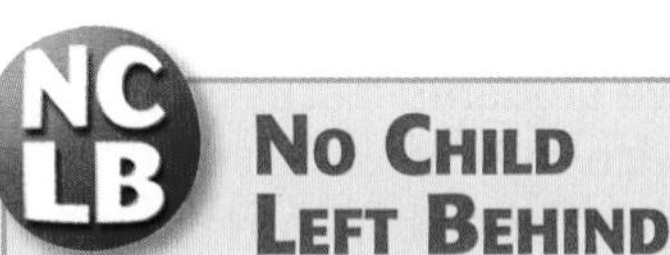

The Report of the National Reading Panel identifies five key skills for reading success. One of those key skills is the ability to understand and gain meaning from what is read. Teaching students the skills in this unit—analyzing, questioning, predicting, and making inferences—will help them understand and gain meaning from a variety of texts.

Reading Fluency

Partner Reading In order to develop fluency, students should hear good models, practice with properly leveled materials, and evaluate their own progress. One way to help students develop fluency is to pair them and have them read orally to one another from an appropriate text, such as portions of the short stories in this unit. The listener should keep a record of miscues and errors for the other person. They can repeat the activity until fluency improves. **OL**

Indiana English/Language Arts Academic Standards
TWE: *Reading Fluency* 8.1

Focus

BELLRINGER Options

Daily Language Practice Transparency 42

Focus Activity Say: Think about a time when you wanted to do what you knew was right, but your friends did not see it your way. Did you go with your gut instinct, or did you cave in to peer pressure? *(Responses will vary)* AS

BQ BIG Question

- Have students work in small groups to read the profiles and look at the pictures of Rashad and Sara.
- Have students discuss the advice they would give Rashad and Sara. AS

L Literary Element

Conflict Say: The conflict in a story is the central struggle between opposing forces. If this were a story about Sara, what would be the conflict? *(The conflict is whether or not Sara should go to the party.)* **Ask:** Who is the conflict between? *(Sara and herself.)* OL

UNIT 5 WARM-UP

Connecting to The BIG Question How Do You Stay True to Yourself?

To be true to yourself, you have to be true to your own values and beliefs. They affect what you do. Sometimes it's hard to figure out what you should do, but as you gain more experience, strong beliefs and values can help you make good choices. In this unit you'll explore how to stay true to yourself and to your values.

Real Kids and the Big Question

RASHAD was walking home from school when he found a wallet. He wants to return the wallet to the person who owns it, but his friends are trying to talk him into keeping the money. Rashad could use the money, but he doesn't feel it's right to keep it. What should Rashad do to be true to himself?

BQ

SARA has been invited to James's party. She finds out later that James's parents won't be home during the get-together. She wants to go, but she knows that her parents won't approve. What should Sara do to stay true to herself?

L

Warm-Up Activity

With a partner, make a list of different ways Rashad and Sara can solve their problems. Decide on a solution that best helps Rashad and Sara stay true to themselves.

Additional Support

Reading in the Real World

Citizenship Both Rashad and Sara have to decide what to do in order to stay true to themselves. Part of being a good citizen is making decisions that are good for you and your community. Have students work in groups to make a pamphlet titled "Being a Good Citizen." Their pamphlets should list different things that people can do to make their community a better place. Encourage students to include images in their pamphlets. To help students get started, hold a class discussion to generate ideas about improving communities. *(Possible responses: caring for the environment, looking out for others, helping your neighbors, watching out for crime, and staying safe)* OL

You and the Big Question

Reading about how other people stayed true to themselves will help you work out your own answer to the Big Question. 

Plan for the Unit Challenge

At the end of the unit, you'll use notes from all your reading to complete the Unit Challenge.

You'll choose one of the following activities:

A. Videotape a Soap Opera With a group you will role-play ways a teen can be true to herself, her friends, and her parents.

B. Values Chart Make a chart for help in ranking your own values.

- As you read the selections, think about the problems faced by the characters and people you read about. How did the problems challenge the people? How did they manage to stay true to themselves?
- In your Learner's Notebook, you'll write down what the characters and people did to stay true to themselves.
- You'll also comment on whether the people solved their problem, learned to live with it, or handled it in some other way.

Literature Online

BIG Question

Link to Web resources to further explore the Big Question at www.glencoe.com.

Keep Track of Your Ideas

As you read, you'll make notes about the Big Question. Later you'll use these notes to complete the Unit Challenge. See pages R8–R9 for help with making Foldable 5. The diagram below shows how it should look.

1. Use this Foldable for all the selections in this unit. On the front cover, write the unit number and the Big Question.
2. Turn the page. Across the top, write the selection title. To the left of the crease, write **My Purpose for Reading.** To the right of the crease, write **The Big Question.**
3. Repeat step 2 until you have all the titles in your Foldable. (See page 543 for the titles.)

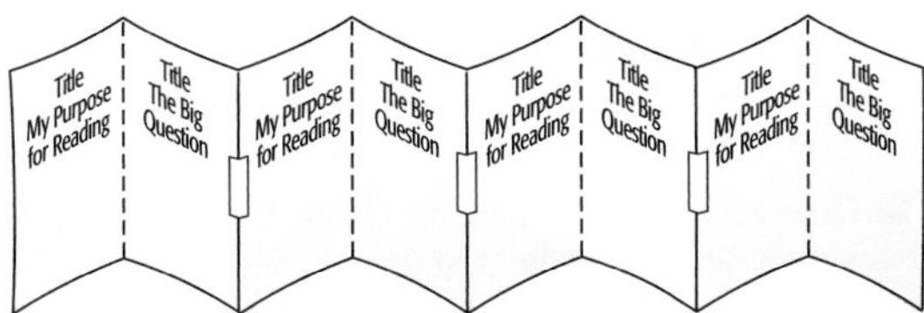

Differentiated Instruction

Musical Accompaniment In today's culture, most students relate to music or enjoy listening to music. Tell students that the lyrics of some songs give ideas about this Big Question. As students read the short stories and take notes about them in their Learner's Notebooks, they can try to think of any songs that relate to the ideas in the story, especially as they relate to the Big Question. Tell students to write the name of the song and the lyrics that relate to the Big Question in their Learner's Notebooks. OL

UNIT 5 WARM-UP

Teach

Big Question Have students access the Web site for English and Spanish summaries and annotated links to related Web resources.

BQ BIG Question

Have students write some of their initial ideas about what it means to "stay true to yourself" in their Learner's Notebooks. OL

For each selection they read, students will enter notes about how that selection applies to the Big Question. For details about using Dinah Zike's Foldables, see pages R8–R9.

Assess/Close

Have students discuss why they think it is important to stay true to themselves. AS

Resources for page 545

- Use the Unit Challenge Planner BLM in the Unit 5 Resource Booklet p. 35.
- Use the Foldable BLM in the Unit 5 Resource Booklet p. 7.

Indiana English/Language Arts Academic Standards
TWE: *Reading in the Real World* 8.5.7, *Differentiated Instruction* 8.3.5

Focus

BELLRINGER Options

Daily Language Practice Transparency 43

Focus Activity Say: Think of a time when someone else took credit for something you did. How did it make you feel? Did you make sure that other people knew you really did it, or did you let it go? Why? *(Responses will vary.)* AS

Teach

R Reading Skill

Questioning Say: Think about plot, characters, setting, and point of view. What are some questions you might ask about each of these story elements? *(Possible responses: **Plot:** What is going to happen next? When did this character first find out about that? **Characters:** Who is this person? What makes this person tick? **Setting:** Where and when is this story set? **Point of View:** Who is telling the story and why?)* OL

Have students try to think of a Who, What, Where, When, Why, and How question for each of the story elements. *(Responses will vary.)* AL

UNIT 5 GENRE FOCUS: SHORT STORY

A **short story** is a brief fictional, or made-up, narrative about people, places, and events. Unlike a **novel,** or book-length story, a short story usually focuses on one incident and its effects on one or a few characters.

Skills Focus

- Key skills for reading short stories
- Key literary elements of short stories

Skills Model

You will see how to use the key reading skills and literary elements as you read

- **"Born Worker,"** p. 547

Why Read Short Stories?

Short stories are entertaining. Some stories make you laugh, and others stretch your imagination. Stories make you think about the challenges people face and ways that people stay true to themselves. When you read short stories, you'll not only enjoy yourself but also discover things like these:

- how characters deal with problems similar to yours
- how characters find ways to stay true to themselves

How to Read Short Stories

Key Reading Skills

These reading skills are especially useful tools for reading and understanding short stories. You'll see these skills modeled in the Active Reading Model on pages 547–557, and you'll learn more about them later in this unit.

- **Analyzing** Looking at the separate parts of a selection to discover how they work together to express ideas. (See Reading Workshop 1.)
- R **Questioning** Asking yourself 5 Ws and an H questions about the plot, characters, setting, and the point of view of a story to make sure you understand it. (See Reading Workshop 2.)
- **Predicting** Making educated guesses about the characters and events in a story as you learn more about them. (See Reading Workshop 3.)
- **Making Inferences** Using clues and "reading between the lines" to figure out ideas that an author has not directly stated. (See Reading Workshop 4.)

Indiana English/Language Arts Academic Standards (pp. 546–557)

8.2 Comprehension and Analysis (Focus on Informational Text) Develop [reading] strategies...
8.3 Comprehension and Analysis of Literary Text Respond to grade-level-appropriate literature...identifying story elements such as character, theme, plot, and setting...**8.3.4** Analyze the importance of the setting to the mood, tone, and meaning of the text.

For a complete description of the standards, see p. IN 11.

Key Literary Elements

Recognizing and thinking about the following literary elements will help you understand more fully what the writer is telling you.

- **Characterization:** methods authors use to show what characters are like, such as describing what they think and do (See "Cream Puff.")
- **Plot:** the events in a story and the order in which they are arranged; main plot parts include exposition, rising action, climax, and falling action. (See "One Throw.")
- **Theme:** the lesson in life the characters learn through experience, such as "honesty is the best policy" (See "The Medicine Bag.")
- **Setting:** the time and place in which the events in a story happen, including the culture of that time and place (See "The Fire Pond.")

Additional Support

Literature Focus Lesson

Characterization Help students see that creating a character is much more than just telling how that person looks or feels. Ask students to think of a person they know and list at least eight different things about the person. If they need guidance, you can give students these examples: smart, athletic, shy, funny, tall, enjoys movies, looks out for her friends, and good student. Choose different volunteers to read one item from their list. Ask the class to think of different ways that a writer could *show* each item students list. For example, a writer might show that a character "looks out for her friends" by having the character actually do this in a story. OL

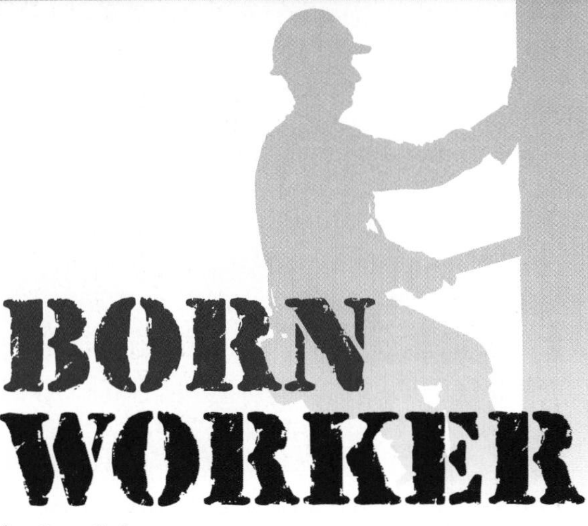

The notes in the side columns model how to use the reading skills and literary elements you read about on page 546.

Short Story

ACTIVE READING MODEL

BORN WORKER

by Gary Soto

They said that José was born with a ring of dirt around his neck, with grime under his fingernails, and skin calloused from the grainy twist of a shovel. They said his palms were already rough by the time he was three, and soon after he learned his primary colors, his squint was the squint of an aged laborer. They said he was a born worker. By seven he was drinking coffee slowly, his mouth pursed the way his mother sipped. He wore jeans, a shirt with sleeves rolled to his elbows. His eye could measure a length of board, and his knees genuflected[1] over flower beds and leafy gutters. **L**

They said lots of things about José, but almost nothing of his parents. His mother stitched at a machine all day, and his father, with a steady job at the telephone company, climbed splintered, sun-sucked poles, fixed wires and looked around the city at tree level. **1** **R**

"What do you see up there?" José once asked his father.

"Work," he answered. "I see years of work, *mi'jo*."[2]

José took this as a truth, and though he did well in school, he felt destined to labor. His arms would pump, his legs would bend, his arms would carry a world of earth. He believed in hard work, believed that his strength was as ancient as a rock's. **2**

1. To ***genuflect*** is to kneel respectfully, as in church.
2. The contraction ***mi'jo*** stands for the Spanish phrase *mi hijo,* which means "my son."

1 Key Reading Skill

Making Inferences *The author doesn't say it straight out, but I can guess that "they" are the people in the community. From my own experience in life I can also guess that they approve of Jose.*

2 Key Literary Element

Characterization *Early in the story I learned that José is a hard worker and acts grown-up for his age. I learned these things about José from the narrator.*

Teach

L Literary Element

Characterization **Ask:** How does Gary Soto describe José's appearance? *(He has dirty, calloused hands and he looks like a grownup when he drinks coffee.)* **OL** **Ask:** What do you think Soto wants the reader to think about José? *(Possible response: He may want to show that he believes in hard work. Or he may want to show that—even at an early age—José had a mindset beyond his years.)* **AL**

R Reading Skill

Review Identifying Author's Purpose **Ask:** After reading some descriptions of José and his parents, what do you think Soto's purpose is for giving us this background? *(Possible response: Soto's purpose is to help me understand where José comes from and why he is the person he is. All this background information will help me better understand José.)* **AL**

Readability Scores

Dale-Chall: 5.5
DRP: 52
Lexile: 780

Reading in the Real World

Career In this story, José's father works for the phone company by climbing telephone poles and repairing lines. However, there are many different careers in the telecommunications field. Have students work in groups to brainstorm a list of different careers. Then have them do some research by visiting the Web site of your local phone company, specifically looking for different career opportunities. Ask students to describe what they learned from their research. Were they surprised by the number and types of jobs they discovered? Which careers sounded most interesting to them? **OL**

Indiana English/Language Arts Academic Standards

SE: 8.2, 8.3, 8.3.4

TWE: *Literature Focus Lesson* 8.3, *Reading in the Real World* 8.4.4

Teach

R Reading Skill

Making Inferences **Ask:** What are some of the reasons that José does not like his cousin? *(Possible response: He thinks Arnie is lazy and spoiled.)* **Ask:** Based on this, how might the cousins treat each other? *(Possible response: Maybe Arnie acts as if he is better than José. Maybe José shows Arnie that he thinks he is a snob.)* **OL**

L Literary Element

Plot **Say:** The plot is made up of the exposition, rising action, climax, falling action, and resolution. In a short story, these can come very close together. At this point, we have read the exposition. This is when the writer introduces the characters, setting, and situation. **AS**

"Life is hard," his father repeated from the time José could first make out the meaning of words until he was stroking his fingers against the grain of his sandpaper beard.

His mother was an example to José. She would raise her hands, showing her fingers pierced from the sewing machines. She bled on her machine, bled because there was money to make, a child to raise, and a roof to stay under.

Analyzing the Photo Which character in the story might this woman be? Why do you say so?

One day when José returned home from junior high, his cousin Arnie was sitting on the lawn sucking on a stalk of grass. José knew that grass didn't come from his lawn. His was cut and pampered, clean.

"José!" Arnie shouted as he took off the earphones of his CD Walkman.

R "Hi, Arnie," José said without much enthusiasm. He didn't like his cousin. He thought he was lazy and, worse, spoiled by the trappings[3] of being middle class. His parents had good jobs in offices and showered him with clothes, shoes, CDs, vacations, almost anything he wanted. Arnie's family had never climbed a telephone pole to size up the future. 3

Arnie rose to his feet, and José saw that his cousin was wearing a new pair of high-tops. He didn't say anything.

"Got an idea," Arnie said cheerfully. "Something that'll make us money."

José looked at his cousin, not a muscle of curiosity twitching in his face.

Still, Arnie explained that since he himself was so clever with words, and his best cousin in the whole world was good at working with his hands, that maybe they might start a company. 4

"What would you do?" José asked.

3. The ***trappings*** of middle class are the things Arnie's family owns that show they have a comfortable life.

ACTIVE READING MODEL

3 Key Literary Element
Plot *During this first part of the plot, I learned about the setting, the characters, and possible conflicts. I can tell there might be a conflict between José and Arnie, because their lifestyles and values are so different.* L

4 Key Reading Skill
Predicting *Arnie is a fast talker. He could create a problem for José if they go into business together.*

Additional Support

Differentiated Instruction

Character Comparison This story presents two very different characters—José and his cousin Arnie. Have students take notes about the two characters in their Learner's Notebooks. **AS** Encourage students to use a Venn Diagram to record what they find. After students read the story, have them use their notes and diagrams to compare and contrast the two characters. **OL** Hold a class discussion on the two characters and have students describe the future they see for each character. **AL**

ACTIVE READING MODEL

"Me?" he said brightly. "Shoot, I'll round up all kinds of jobs for you. You won't have to do anything." He stopped, then started again. "Except—you know—do the work." R

"Get out of here," José said.

"Don't be that way," Arnie begged. "Let me tell you how it works."

The boys went inside the house, and while José stripped off his school clothes and put on his jeans and a T-shirt, Arnie told him that they could be rich.

"You ever hear of this guy named Bechtel?"[4] Arnie asked.

José shook his head.

"Man, he started just like us," Arnie said. "He started digging ditches and stuff, and the next thing you knew, he was sitting by his own swimming pool. You want to sit by your own pool, don't you?" Arnie smiled, waiting for José to speak up. 5

"Never heard of this guy Bechtel," José said after he rolled on two huge socks, worn at the heels. He opened up his chest of drawers and brought out a packet of Kleenex.

Arnie looked at the Kleenex.

"How come you don't use your sleeve?" Arnie joked.

José thought for a moment and said, "I'm not like you." He smiled at his retort.

"Listen, I'll find the work, and then we can split it fifty-fifty."

José knew fifty-fifty was a bad deal.

"How about sixty-forty?" Arnie suggested when he could see that José wasn't going for it. "I know a lot of people from my dad's job. They're waiting for us."

José sat on the edge of his bed and started to lace up his boots. He knew that there were agencies that would find you work, agencies that took a portion of your pay. They're cheats, he thought, people who sit in air-conditioned offices while others work.

"You really know a lot of people?" José asked.

"Boatloads," Arnie said. "My dad works with this millionaire—honest—who cooks a steak for his dog every day."

4. ***Bechtel*** is probably Stephen D. Bechtel (1900–1989), who was president of a large and famous construction and engineering company.

5 Key Literary Element

Characterization *You can tell what Arnie is like by thinking about what he says. From what he says here, Arnie is the kind of guy who wants to make a lot of money without working hard for it.*

UNIT 5 GENRE FOCUS

Teach

R Reading Skill

Making Inferences Ask: How can you tell that these boys have had trouble before? *(Possible responses: José immediately tells his cousin to go away. He does not even want to hear the idea. José assumes that Arnie is going to cause him harm or take advantage of him in some way.)* OL

L Literary Element

Characterization Guide students in a discussion about the kind of characters Arnie and José represent. Use these questions as prompts:

- Do you know people like Arnie?
- How do you react to their ideas?
- Do you know people like José?
- How do you react to them and their ideas? *(Responses will vary.)* OL

Ask: What do you learn about José from reading his thoughts? *(Possible response: José is smart and skeptical. He knows that Arnie is trying to take advantage of him.)* AL

English Language Coach

Figurative and Literal Language Point out Arnie's dialogue in which he says, "They're waiting for us." Help students understand that Arnie is using this in a figurative way. Either read this paragraph aloud for students or have a volunteer do so, enabling students to hear the tone that Arnie uses to say it. Ask students to explain what Arnie means, using more literal words. *(Possible responses: They are not using anyone else for the work. All we have to do is call them up, and they'll hire us.)* EL

Indiana English/Language Arts Academic Standards

SE: 8.2, 8.3

TWE: *Differentiated Instruction* 8.3, 8.4.1; *English Language Coach* 8.1.1

Teach

L1 Literary Element

Review Tone Give pairs of students a chance to read these lines of dialogue aloud for the class. Have the class decide who reads the dialogue with the most realistic tone. *(Students are likely to think that Arnie would speak with a proud or arrogant tone, and José would use a sarcastic tone.)* OL

L2 Literary Element

Plot Say: The rising action is the part of the plot that adds complications to the story. What makes this the beginning of the rising action? *(Possible responses: Arnie and José have been working together for two weeks, and Arnie has not done any actual work. José decides to ignore Arnie.)* OL

ACTIVE READING MODEL

He's a liar, José thought. No matter how he tried, he couldn't picture a dog grubbing[5] on steak. The world was too poor for that kind of silliness.

"Listen, I'll go eighty-twenty," José said.

"Aw, man," Arnie whined. "That ain't fair."

José laughed.

"I mean, half the work is finding the jobs," Arnie explained, his palms up as he begged José to be reasonable.

José knew this was true. He had had to go door-to-door, and he disliked asking for work. He assumed that it should automatically be his since he was a good worker, honest, and always on time. 6

"Where did you get this idea, anyhow?" José asked.

"I got a business mind," Arnie said proudly.

"Just like that Bechtel guy," José retorted.

"That's right."

José agreed to a seventy-thirty split, with the condition that Arnie had to help out. Arnie hollered, arguing that some people were meant to work and others to come up with brilliant ideas. He was one of the latter. Still, he agreed after José said it was that or nothing.

In the next two weeks, Arnie found an array of jobs. José peeled off shingles from a rickety garage roof, carried rocks down a path to where a pond would go, and spray-painted lawn furniture. And while Arnie accompanied him, most of the time he did nothing. He did help occasionally. He did shake the cans of spray paint and kick aside debris so that José didn't trip while going down the path carrying the rocks. He did stack the piles of shingles, but almost cried when a nail bit his thumb. But mostly he told José what he had missed or where the work could be improved. José was bothered because he and his work had never been criticized before.

But soon José learned to ignore his cousin, ignore his comments about his spray painting, or about the way he lugged rocks, two in each arm. He didn't say anything, either, when they got paid and Arnie rubbed his hands like a fly, muttering, "It's payday."

6 Key Reading Skill

Making Inferences *José doesn't like the way Arnie is trying to take advantage of him. But he knows that Arnie will save him the trouble of finding jobs, a kind of work he does not like to do.*

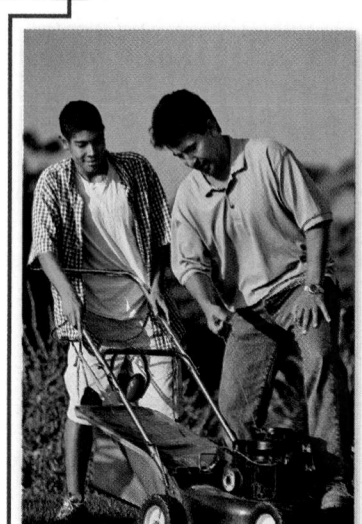

Analyzing the Photo Which characters do these people remind you of? Why?

5. *Grub* is slang for food, so ***grubbing*** is eating.

Additional Support

Differentiated Instruction

Role Playing José and Arnie do not have a great working relationship. In fact, you could say they are in conflict. Have students think about different ways that José could have handled the conflict with Arnie (other than just ignoring it, the way he does in the story). Allow several pairs of students to role-play the conflict resolution for the class. BL Remind students to consider how the boys' family relationship might affect the way they try to solve their conflict in this business relationship. Lead students in a discussion about the challenges (and benefits) of family members working together. OL

ACTIVE READING MODEL

Then Arnie found a job scrubbing a drained swimming pool. The two boys met early at José's house. Arnie brought his bike. José's own bike had a flat that grinned like a clown's face.

"I'll pedal," José suggested when Arnie said that he didn't have much leg strength. 7

With Arnie on the handlebars, José tore off, his pedaling so strong that tears of fear formed in Arnie's eyes.

"Slow down!" Arnie cried.

José ignored him and within minutes they were riding the bike up a gravel driveway. Arnie hopped off at first chance.

"You're scary," Arnie said, picking a gnat from his eye.

José chuckled. 8

When Arnie knocked on the door, an old man still in pajamas appeared in the window. He motioned for the boys to come around to the back.

R1 "Let me do the talking," Arnie suggested to his cousin. "He knows my dad real good. They're like this." He pressed two fingers together.

José didn't bother to say OK. He walked the bike into the backyard, which was lush with plants—roses in their last bloom, geraniums, hydrangeas, pansies with their skirts of bright colors. José could make out the splash of a fountain. Then he heard the hysterical yapping of a poodle. From all his noise, a person might have thought the dog was on fire. 9

"Hi, Mr. Clemens," Arnie said, extending his hand. "I'm Arnie Sanchez. It's nice to see you again."

José had never seen a kid actually greet someone like this. Mr. Clemens said, hiking up his pajama bottoms, "I only wanted one kid to work."

"Oh," Arnie stuttered. "Actually, my cousin José really does the work and I kind of, you know, supervise."

Mr. Clemens pinched up his wrinkled face. He seemed not to understand. He took out a pea-sized hearing aid, fiddled with its tiny dial, and fit it into his ear, which was surrounded with wiry gray hair.

R2 "I'm only paying for one boy," Mr. Clemens shouted. His poodle click-clicked and stood behind his legs. The dog bared its small crooked teeth.

7 Key Reading Skill

Analyzing *It's just like Arnie to say something to get out of doing the hard work of pedaling. That fits in with his other comments and actions. You can tell that he believes he shouldn't have to work hard.*

8 Key Reading Skill

Making Inferences *José rides fast because he's disgusted with Arnie for pretending that his legs don't have much strength. José laughs because he got back at Arnie.*

9 Key Literary Element

Setting *This part of the story is set at a home where the family is well off. You can tell because the back yard is "lush with plants" and has a fountain. Also, the owner of the house has a poodle. Poodles are sometimes seen as dogs for rich people.*

Teach

R1 Reading Skill

Making Inferences **Ask:** What do you think Arnie might be inferring when he tells José that his father and Mr. Clemens are close? *(Possible response: He might be inferring that his father has a better job than José's dad and that his family is better off, both financially and socially.)* AL

R2 Reading Skill

Predicting **Ask:** When Mr. Clemens says he'll only "pay for one boy," what do you think will happen next? *(Possible responses: Arnie might talk his way out of the situation, convincing Mr. Clemens to pay both boys; José might do all of the work, but Arnie will still try to collect the money.)* OL

Reading in the Real World

Citizenship José is surprised when he sees his young cousin shake hands with Mr. Clemens as he says hello. Have students work in groups to research different cultural customs for greeting people, especially across age differences. Then have each group give a class presentation with members of the group demonstrating the different customs. Create a class handbook on cultural customs for greeting people around the world. OL

Indiana English/Language Arts Academic Standards

SE: 8.2, 8.3.4

TWE: *Differentiated Instruction* 8.7, *Reading in the Real World* 8.7.12

Teach

L Literary Element

Review Irony Ask: What is ironic about the fact that Mr. Clemens thinks of Arnie's dad as "Mexican fella"? *(Possible response: Arnie thinks that he is better than his cousin José because his family has more money and his father has a better job. Mr. Clemens shows that he thinks of both boys as being the same—inferior and Mexican.)* OL

R Reading Skill

Questioning Say: As you read about José putting on gloves and gathering the bottles, you are likely to ask, "Why is he doing this?" What are some other questions you might ask yourself at this point in the story? *(Possible responses: What is going to happen next? How are things going to work out between Arnie and José? What is Mr. Clemens going to do when it is time to pay the boys—will he pay only José?)* OL

"That's right," Arnie said, smiling a strained smile. "We know that you're going to compensate[6] only one of us." 10

Mr. Clemens muttered under his breath. He combed his hair with his fingers. He showed José the pool, which was shaped as round as an elephant. It was filthy with grime. Near the bottom some grayish water shimmered and leaves floated as limp as cornflakes.

Analyzing the Photo What does this photograph of an empty pool suggest about the job José has to do?

"It's got to be real clean," Mr. Clemens said, "or it's not worth it."

"Oh, José's a great worker," Arnie said. He patted his cousin's shoulders and said that he could lift a mule.

Mr. Clemens sized up José and squeezed his shoulders, too.

"How do I know you, anyhow?" Mr. Clemens asked Arnie, who was aiming a smile at the poodle.

"You know my dad," Arnie answered, raising his smile to the old man. "He works at Interstate Insurance. You and he had some business deals."

Mr. Clemens thought for a moment, a hand on his mouth, head shaking. He could have been thinking about the meaning of life, his face was so dark.

"Mexican fella?" he inquired.

"That's him," Arnie said happily.

José felt like hitting his cousin for his cheerful attitude. 11 Instead, he walked over and picked up the white plastic bottle of bleach. Next to it were a wire brush, a pumice stone, and some rags. He set down the bottle and, like a surgeon, put on a pair of rubber gloves.

"You know what you're doing, boy?" Mr. Clemens asked.

José nodded as he walked into the pool. If it had been filled with water, his chest would have been wet. The new hair on his chest would have been floating like the legs of a jellyfish.

6. To ***compensate*** is to pay someone for his or her work.

ACTIVE READING MODEL

10 Key Reading Skill
Predicting *Arnie probably won't help José clean the pool. Arnie is very lazy, and all he does is talk. I'll keep reading to see if my prediction is right.*

11 Key Reading Skill
Questioning *Why is José so annoyed with Arnie's cheerful attitude? Maybe José thinks Arnie should be upset about Mr. Clemens's identifying Arnie's father as a "Mexican fella."*

Additional Support

Differentiated Instruction

Social Class This part of the story might be difficult for students to read because of the way that Mr. Clemens treats the boys and Arnie's response to him. Have students research the different social classes in the United States, particularly in the Southwest. Hold a class discussion on social class and why Mr. Clemens, Arnie, and José act the way that they do with each other. OL

Have students analyze the language and gestures each character uses to communicate their social position *(Possible responses: Arnie uses complicated words; Mr. Clemens uses words like "boy." They both squeeze José's shoulders. José gets to work.)* AL

ACTIVE READING MODEL

"Oh, yeah," Arnie chimed, speaking for his cousin. "José was born to work."

José would have drowned his cousin if there had been more water. Instead, he poured a bleach solution into a rag and swirled it over an area. He took the wire brush and scrubbed. The black algae[7] came up like a foamy monster. **12**

"We're a team," Arnie said to Mr. Clemens.

Arnie descended into the pool and took the bleach bottle from José. He held it for José and smiled up at Mr. Clemens, who, hands on hips, watched for a while, the poodle at his side. He cupped his ear, as if to pick up the sounds of José's scrubbing.

"Nice day, huh?" Arnie sang.

"What?" Mr. Clemens said.

"Nice day," Arnie repeated, this time louder. "So which ear can't you hear in?" Grinning, Arnie wiggled his ear to make sure that Mr. Clemens knew what he was asking.

Mr. Clemens ignored Arnie. He watched José, whose arms worked back and forth like he was sawing logs.

"We're not only a team," Arnie shouted, "but we're also cousins."

Mr. Clemens shook his head at Arnie. **13** When he left, the poodle leading the way, Arnie immediately climbed out of the pool and sat on the edge, legs dangling.

"It's going to be blazing," Arnie complained. He shaded his eyes with his hand and looked east, where the sun was rising over a sycamore, its leaves hanging like bats.

José scrubbed. He worked the wire brush over the black and green stains, the grime dripping like tears. He finished a large area. He hopped out of the pool and returned hauling a garden hose with an attached nozzle. He gave the cleaned area a blast. When the spray got too close, his cousin screamed, got up, and, searching for something to do, picked a loquat from a tree.

Visual Vocabulary
A ***loquat*** is a small, yellowish fruit that is juicy and tart. It grows in bunches.

12 Key Literary Element
Plot *The tension between José and Arnie is growing here. This must be the rising action of the plot.*

13 Key Reading Skill
Questioning *What is Mr. Clemens thinking about Arnie? Maybe he, too, is disgusted with Arnie's laziness.*

7. ***Algae*** are plants, such as pond scum, that grow in water.

Teach

C Critical Thinking

Comprehension Ask: Do you think Mr. Clemens believes that they are a team? *(Possible response: Probably not, because he tells them that he only wants one boy. And he still seems confused about why Arnie is there or why there are two boys.)* **OL**

R Reading Skill

Questioning Ask: What are some questions you hope the writer will answer as the story continues? *(Possible responses; Will Mr. Clemens actually pay both boys? Will Mr. Clemens get angry at Arnie for eating his fruit and make him leave? Is Arnie going to learn a lesson in this story? How will José finally get rid of his cousin?)* **OL**

Literature Focus Lesson

Setting Tell students that sometimes the clues about setting are in the small details. In this story, the reader knows it is somewhere warm enough to have an outdoor pool (at least in summer time). The reader also knows that there are roses (in their last bloom), hydrangeas, pansies, and loquat growing there. Interested students can research these plants to find out which climates (or regions) are hospitable to all of these plants. They can then use this information to figure out where this story might take place. **OL**

Indiana English/Language Arts Academic Standards
SE: 8.2, 8.3
TWE: *Differentiated Instruction* 8.3, 8.4.5; *Literature Focus Lesson* 8.3

Teach

L Literary Element

Review Description Ask: Which of the five senses does the writer appeal to in this description of Arnie eating the fruit? *(Possible responses: Sound: hearing Arnie curse himself; Taste and Touch: the juice dripping out of the fruit and the cheeks full; Sight: seeing the juice drip on the shoes)* **OL**

R Reading Skill

Analyzing Ask: Do you think Arnie knows his cousin is upset? *(Possible responses: Yes, because he keeps talking to him, trying to make light conversation. Maybe he is even trying to rub in the fact that he does not have to work; No, because he just keeps on talking and acting like nothing is wrong. He is so self-centered that he wouldn't notice if someone else was upset.)* **AL**

ACTIVE READING MODEL

"What's your favorite fruit?" Arnie asked.

José ignored him.

Arnie stuffed a bunch of loquats into his mouth, then cursed himself for splattering juice on his new high-tops. He returned to the pool, his cheeks fat with the seeds, and once again sat at the edge. **L** He started to tell José how he had first learned to swim. "We were on vacation in Mazatlán.[8] You been there, ain't you?"

José shook his head. He dabbed the bleach solution onto the sides of the pool with a rag and scrubbed a new area.

"Anyhow, my dad was on the beach and saw this drowned dead guy," Arnie continued. "And right there, my dad got scared and realized I couldn't swim."

Arnie rattled on about how his father had taught him in the hotel pool and later showed him where the drowned man's body had been.

"Be quiet," José said.

"What?"

"I can't concentrate," José said, stepping back to look at the cleaned area.

Arnie shut his mouth but opened it to lick loquat juice from his fingers. He kicked his legs against the swimming pool, bored. He looked around the backyard and spotted a lounge chair. He got up, dusting off the back of his pants, and threw himself into the cushions. He raised and lowered the back of the lounge. Sighing, he snuggled in. He stayed quiet for three minutes, during which time José scrubbed. His arms hurt but he kept working with long strokes. José knew that in an hour the sun would drench the pool with light. He hurried to get the job done. **14**

Arnie then asked, "You ever peel before?"

José looked at his cousin. His nose burned from the bleach. He scrunched up his face. **R**

"You know, like when you get sunburned."

"I'm too dark to peel," José said, his words echoing because he had advanced to the deep end. "Why don't you be quiet and let me work?"

Arnie babbled on that he had peeled when on vacation in Hawaii. He explained that he was really more French

14 Key Reading Skill

Analyzing *Here, the author shows the two cousins side by side, inviting readers to contrast Arnie with José. While Arnie lies around eating and talking, José works so hard his arms hurt.*

8. ***Mazatlán*** is a seaport in western Mexico. It is popular with tourists who like beaches and fishing.

Additional Support

Literature Focus Lesson

Imagery Have students write a poem or draw a picture that depicts one of the images or ideas on this page: the loquats, the hot sun, José's hard work, or learning how to swim. Ask volunteers to share their poems and images with the class. Discuss how the author makes the story come alive using details and descriptive language so readers can experience the story. **OL**

ACTIVE READING MODEL

than Mexican, and that's why his skin was sensitive. He said that when he lived in France, people thought that he could be Portuguese or maybe Armenian, never Mexican. 15

José felt like soaking his rag with bleach and pressing it over Arnie's mouth to make him be quiet.

Then Mr. Clemens appeared. He was dressed in white pants and a flowery shirt. His thin hair was combed so that his scalp, as pink as a crab, showed.

"I'm just taking a little rest," Arnie said.

Arnie leaped back into the pool. He took the bleach bottle and held it. He smiled at Mr. Clemens, who came to inspect their progress.

"José's doing a good job," Arnie said, then whistled a song.

Mr. Clemens peered into the pool, hands on knees, admiring the progress.

"Pretty good, huh?" Arnie asked.

Mr. Clemens nodded. Then his hearing aid fell out, and José turned in time to see it roll like a bottle cap toward the bottom of the pool. It leaped into the stagnant water with a plop. A single bubble went up, and it was gone.

"Dang," Mr. Clemens swore. He took shuffling steps toward the deep end. He steadied his gaze on where the hearing aid had sunk. He leaned over and suddenly, arms waving, one leg kicking out, he tumbled into the pool. He landed standing up, then his legs buckled, and he crumbled, his head striking against the bottom. He rolled once, and half of his body settled in the water. 16 R1

"Did you see that!" Arnie shouted, big-eyed.

José had already dropped his brushes on the side of the pool and hurried to the old man, who moaned, eyes closed, his false teeth jutting from his mouth. A ribbon of blood immediately began to flow from his scalp.

"We better get out of here!" Arnie suggested. "They're going to blame us!"

José knelt on both knees at the old man's side. He took the man's teeth from his mouth and placed them in his shirt pocket. The old man groaned and opened his eyes, which were shiny wet. He appeared startled, like a newborn. R2

15 Key Reading Skill

Making Inferences *It seems as if Arnie may be prejudiced against Mexicans, even though he himself has Mexican roots. He seems to think that having a skin tone lighter than José's somehow makes him special.*

16 Key Literary Element

Plot *A terrible thing has happened that José has to deal with. This must be the climax of the story because the action of the story has reached a high point.*

Reading in the Real World

Citizenship Every day someone makes a decision to save a stranger's life or to do something courageous. There are stories about these people in newspapers all over the country. Have students look through the different newspapers in your area from the last week (or month), looking for such stories. If possible, have different students report on different stories and the heroes they found. You may also have students go online to look for stories. OL

Teach

R1 Reading Skill

Making Inferences Ask: What do you think has happened to Mr. Clemens? *(Possible responses: He fell and is seriously hurt; he had a stroke or heart attack.)* OL

R2 Reading Skill

Predicting Ask: What do you think Arnie is going to do next? *(Possible response: He is going to go home as quickly as he can. He may even lie when asked about what happened, and say that he was never there.)* **Ask:** What do you think José will do next? *(Possible response: He will probably help Mr. Clemens, carry him out of the pool, or call an ambulance.)* OL

Indiana English/Language Arts Academic Standards

SE: 8.2, 8.3

TWE: *Literature Focus Lesson* 8.3, *Reading in the Real World* 8.7.12

Teach

L1 Literary Element

Characterization Ask: What do you learn about José from this story? *(Possible responses: He is a hard worker. He cares about people and is willing to help. He takes responsibility and does not just wait for others to act.)* OL

R Reading Skill

Analyzing Ask: Do you think José's behavior will change the way Mr. Clemens views him? *(Possible responses: No, Mr. Clemens seems stuck in his ways, and will always view José as just a kid who cleaned his pool. Yes, Mr. Clemens has an air of superiority, this experience might humble him.)* AL

L2 Literary Element

Plot Ask: What has happened in the story so far? How did José end up sitting in a pool holding Mr. Clemens? *(Responses will vary.)* BL

"Sir, you'll be all right," José cooed, then snapped at his cousin. "Arnie, get over here and help me!"

"I'm going home," Arnie whined.

"You punk!" José yelled. "Go inside and call 911."

Arnie said that they should leave him there.

"Why should we get involved?" he cried as he started for his bike. "It's his own fault."

José laid the man's head down and with giant steps leaped out of the pool, shoving his cousin as he passed. He went into the kitchen and punched in 911 on a telephone. He explained to the operator what had happened. When asked the address, José dropped the phone and went onto the front porch to look for it.

"It's 940 East Brown," José breathed. He hung up and looked wildly about the kitchen. He opened up the refrigerator and brought out a plastic tray of ice, which he twisted so that a few of the cubes popped out and slid across the floor. He wrapped some cubes in a dish towel. When he raced outside, Arnie was gone, the yapping poodle was doing laps around the edge of the pool, and Mr. Clemens was trying to stand up.

"No, sir," José said as he jumped into the pool, his own knees almost buckling. "Please, sit down."

Mr. Clemens staggered and collapsed. José caught him before he hit his head again. The towel of ice cubes dropped from his hands. With his legs spread to absorb the weight, José raised the man up in his arms, this fragile man. He picked him up and carefully stepped toward the shallow end, one slow elephant step at a time. 17

"You'll be all right," José said, more to himself than to Mr. Clemens, who moaned and struggled to be let free.

The sirens wailed in the distance. The poodle yapped, which started a dog barking in the neighbor's yard.

"You'll be OK," José repeated, and in the shallow end of the pool, he edged up the steps. He lay the old man in the lounge chair and raced back inside for more ice and

ACTIVE READING MODEL

17 Key Reading Skill
Analyzing *It's interesting that José lifts up the old man. José's actions show just how grown-up José really is. Here he's literally carrying a man's weight, even though he is not yet a man.*

Additional Support

English Language Coach

Verbs Have students identify at least six verbs from the story that they either found confusing or were new to them. Instruct students to write the verbs in their Learner's Notebooks. Choose different volunteers to use their own words to explain what the verb means and act it out if possible. Remind students that using synonyms for a word can be a great way to define it. EL

ACTIVE READING MODEL

another towel. He returned outside and placed the bundle of cubes on the man's head, where the blood flowed. Mr. Clemens was awake, looking about. When the old man felt his mouth, José reached into his shirt pocket and pulled out his false teeth. He fit the teeth into Mr. Clemens's mouth and a smile appeared, something bright at a difficult time. 18

"I hit my head," Mr. Clemens said after smacking his teeth so that the fit was right.

José looked up and his gaze floated to a telephone pole, one his father might have climbed. If he had been there, his father would have seen that José was more than just a good worker. He would have seen a good man. He held the towel to the old man's head. The poodle, now quiet, joined them on the lounge chair. R1

A fire truck pulled into the driveway and soon they were surrounded by firemen, one of whom brought out a first-aid kit. A fireman led José away and asked what had happened. He was starting to explain when his cousin reappeared, yapping like a poodle.

"I was scrubbing the pool," Arnie shouted, "and I said, 'Mr. Clemens, you shouldn't stand so close to the edge.' But did he listen? No, he leaned over and . . . Well, you can just imagine my horror."

José walked away from Arnie's jabbering. He walked away, and realized that there were people like his cousin, the liar, and people like himself, someone he was getting to know. 19 He walked away and in the midmorning heat boosted himself up a telephone pole. He climbed up and saw for himself what his father saw—miles and miles of trees and houses, and a future lost in the layers of yellowish haze. ❍ R2

18 Key Literary Element
Characterization *You can tell a lot about José from his actions. He calmly does what has to be done to help Mr. Clemens. José is a responsible, caring young man.*

19 Key Literary Element
Theme *It looks as if José has learned something from his experiences with Arnie and Mr. Clemens. José seems to think he did the right thing. So the theme of the story may be that it is more important to be responsible and caring than rich.*

Partner Talk With a partner, take turns retelling parts of the story. Choose a particular event and give all the important details.

Write to Learn Answer these questions in your Learner's Notebook: Why does José walk away and let Arnie tell lies to the firemen? How was José being true to himself?

Study Central Visit www.glencoe.com and click on Study Central to review short stories.

Teach

R1 Reading Skill

Making Inferences **Say:** José thinks about what his dad would have noticed if he had been watching. What does José think his dad would have seen? *(a good man)* BL **Ask:** What might this tell you about the things that José has learned from his dad? *(Possible response: José's father has probably taught him that it is important to be a good man, to care about other people, and to do what is right.)* AL

R2 Reading Skill

Review Identifying Author's Purpose **Ask:** Why do you think the author wrote this story? *(Possible response: to show the different kinds of people there are; to show that it is not important to be recognized for doing good things, but it is important to do them; to point out that to stay true to yourself you must first know yourself)* OL

Study Central Have students access the Web site to review short stories and to complete a related activity.

Differentiated Instruction

Write a Report Have students write their own report about what happened at Mr. Clemens's house as if they are news reporters. Direct half of the class to write the story with all the information they have from the story, including the facts about how José helped out. Direct the other half of the class to write their articles as if they arrived after José left and only heard Arnie's side of the story. OL Alternately, you may challenge students to write a letter to the editor as if they are Mr. Clemens and responding to either of the news reports described above. AL

Indiana English/Language Arts Academic Standards
SE: 8.2, 8.3
TWE: *English Language Coach* 8.1, *Differentiated Instruction* 8.5.7

Analyzing

Teaching Students to Analyze

Why Is It Important?

- Readers can better understand how a text works by analyzing the author's use of elements such as word choice and dialogue.
- Analytic skills are essential to critical reading, including the determination of an author's purpose for writing and how the author wants the reader to respond.
- Analysis of texts can help make readers better writers by helping them learn to organize and critique.

How to Help Students Get It

- Remind students that stories can mean different things to different readers. Help them develop an interest in exploring different perspectives on texts and learn that there is no one "right" meaning.
- Emphasize that the author and reader work together to make meaning and that analyzing the author's choices increases appreciation of the author's skills.
- Encourage students to read a text from different perspectives to show how beliefs can influence the meaning.
- Remind students that it is crucial to consider who the author is and why he or she wrote the text. This is especially important when reading information from sources such as blogs and other Internet sites that have not been filtered by editors or publishers.

Reading to Answer the Big Question

Cream Puff by Linnea Due
Jen has been accepted to an exclusive statewide basketball camp. She knows that she is a good player but runs into problems. The famous coach lives up to her reputation for being tough; Jen finds her father's advice not helpful; and a girl named Jinx seems determined to expose every weakness in Jen's game. Jen can't depend on any adult to help her out, so she turns to the one person she can rely on—herself.

The Question of Popularity by Tamara Eberlein
This article from TIME discusses the factors that contribute to being "popular." Middle schoolers are encouraged to prioritize close friendships over being one of the "cool kids," and to focus on being accepted for who they truly are.

Workshop Resources

Pacing (Days) Standard	Block	Lesson	Student Materials	Teacher Resources
1	1/2	Key Skill Lesson: Analyzing	Key Reading Skills Practice, p. 9 English Language Coach Review, p. 41	Bellringer Options Transparencies –Daily Language Practice 44 Read Aloud, Think Aloud Transparencies –Key Reading Skills 2 Presentation Plus!
1	1	"Cream Puff"	Glencoe Online Unit Vocabulary Review, p. 39 Academic Vocabulary Review, p. 42 English Language Coach Active Reading Graphic Organizer, p. 11 Literary Analysis, p. 10 StudentWorks Plus™ Online Student Edition Literature Classics Selection and Unit Assessments, p. 49	Literary and Text Analysis Transparencies 6 Puzzlemaker Skill Level Up!™ A Language Arts Game BookLink 3 Assessment by Learning Objective (Diagnostic and Formative) Interactive Tutor: Self-Assessment TeacherWorks Plus™
1		"The Question of Popularity"	Glencoe Online Unit Vocabulary Review, p. 39 Academic Vocabulary Review, p. 42 English Language Coach Active Reading Graphic Organizer, p. 13 StudentWorks Plus™ Online Student Edition Literature Classics Selection and Unit Assessments, p. 50	Literary and Text Analysis Transparencies 15 Puzzlemaker Skill Level Up!™ A Language Arts Game BookLink 3 Assessment by Learning Objective (Diagnostic and Formative) Interactive Tutor: Self-Assessment TeacherWorks Plus™

Keys for Unit Resource

- Blackline Master
- Workbook
- Supplemental Text
- CD-ROM
- DVD
- Transparency
- Web-based
- Fast File

Level Appropriate Code

AS = Activities for all students
AL = Activities for students working above grade level
OL = Activities for students working at grade level
BL = Activities for students working below grade level
EL = Activities for English language learners

Focus

BELLRINGER Options

Daily Language Practice Transparency 44

Focus Activity Write on the board: "It is more important to be happy with who you are than to make other people happy." Have the class discuss whether or not they agree with this statement. *(Responses will vary.)* AS

Teach

R Reading Skill

Analyzing Say: We analyze by looking at the different parts of something to figure out how they work as a whole. What are some of the different parts of a movie that you might analyze to better understand it? *(Possible response: the characters, the plot, the setting)* OL

READING WORKSHOP 1

Skills Focus

You will practice using these skills when you read the following selections:

- "Cream Puff," p. 562
- "The Question of Popularity," p. 574

Reading

- Analyzing fiction and informational text

Literature

- Identifying character traits
- Analyzing characters
- Identifying and analyzing attention-getting devices

Vocabulary

- Recognizing and using base words to infer meaning
- Academic Vocabulary: *significant*

Writing/Grammar

- Identifying clauses and phrases

Indiana English/ Language Arts Academic Standards (pp. 558–559)

8.2 Comprehension and Analysis (Focus on Informational Text) Develop [reading] strategies such as...analyzing structure, organization, perspective, and purpose.

For a complete description of the standards, see p. IN 11.

Skill Lesson

Analyzing

Learn It!

R **What Is It?** You might remember from Unit 2 that when you analyze you take a close look at the **significant** elements that make up a story or a work of nonfiction. For example, you might look at plot, characters, point of view, text structure, and supporting details. You then figure out how these elements contribute to the meaning of a selection.

Analyzing Cartoons
Did these kids analyze the characters or the look of the book?

Academic Vocabulary

significant (sig NIH fih kunt) *adj.* having meaning; having much importance

Additional Support

Differentiated Instruction

Media Analysis Explain to students that film critics often analyze a movie by looking at how the plot, characters, and point of view all work together. Have students write their own critical reviews of television commercials. Instruct students to choose a commercial and analyze two or three of the elements mentioned on page 558 (plot, characters, point of view, supporting details). If possible, have students videotape the commercial and play it for the class before reading their review aloud. OL Ask students to analyze what makes a successful commercial. AL

Why Is It Important? Analyzing helps you gain a deeper understanding of the selections you read and the ways that authors put the selections together.

Literature Online

Study Central Visit www.glencoe.com and click on Study Central to review analyzing.

How Do I Do It? To analyze fiction, determine which elements are significant and why. Some questions you can ask yourself are as follows:

- What is each character in the story like?
- How can you tell? Through dialogue? Action? The narrator's descriptions?
- What, if anything, do the characters learn from their experiences?
- Which characters, if any, change as a result of their experiences?

When analyzing nonfiction, pay attention to text structure and the details that support the writer's main idea.

- How does the organization of the text help make the writer's points clear?
- What kinds of details does the writer include?

Here's how a student analyzed a passage from a short story.

Tom and Maddy stared out the window of their log cabin. The blizzard had not let up for two days. Maddy shivered. A tear ran down her cheek. Tom looked grim. What if Maddy had their baby before the storm was over? His horse would never be able to make the ride to Dr. May's in deep snow.

You can tell from Maddy's actions that she is sad and worried. She shivers, and a tear runs down her cheek. Tom, on the other hand, is worried and grim. You can tell by the way he looks and also by the thoughts that are going through his head. The setting adds to Tom and Maddy's problem. The location of their cabin makes it hard to get a doctor.

Practice It!

Analyze the setting of the passage. When and where do you think the story takes place? What details make you think so?

Use It!

As you read "Cream Puff," analyze what the characters are like.

Teach

Literature Online

Study Central Have students access the Web site to review analyzing and to complete a related activity.

R Reading Skill

Analyzing Say: The characters live in a log cabin and have to get a doctor by riding a horse. Where is the woman planning to have the baby? *(in her home with the doctor there)* **Ask:** When do you think this story takes place? *(Possible responses: Possibly in the 1700s, 1800s, or even early 1900s—at a time when people did not typically deliver their babies in hospitals.)* OL

Resources for page 559

Use Key Reading Skills Transparency 2 in *Read Aloud, Think Aloud* to help students practice analyzing.

Reading in the Real World

Career Professional athletes are very popular. Create a diverse list of famous athletes. Assign small groups of students to research two of the athletes from the list. Have each group come up with questions they want to answer about their athletes before they begin their research. Ask groups to share their findings with the class. Hold a class discussion about the popularity of sports and the role professional athletes play in our culture. OL

Indiana English/Language Arts Academic Standards
SE: 8.2
TWE: *Differentiated Instruction* 8.5.7, *Reading in the Real World* 8.7.12

Teach

More about the Author

Linnea Due has been hailed for creating believable and dynamic characters in her writing. She says she likes it when her characters gain their own identities and take over the story. Her novel *High and Outside* was listed among the best books for young adults by the American Library Association. Due lives in California.

EL Language Coach

Word Analysis Divide the class into small groups and assign each group a different prefix, such as *un-*, *pre-*, *dis-*, and *in-*. Tell the groups to list as many words as they can that use their prefix. Have the groups figure out the meaning of the prefix for all the words on their lists. EL

Before You Read Cream Puff

Linnea Due

Meet the Author

Linnea Due is the author of many short stories, novels, and magazine articles. She began playing sports as a young child and quickly became a fan of basketball, baseball, and other sports. Her novel *High and Outside* is about a teen softball player. *See page R1 of The Author Files in the back of the book for more on Linnea Due.*

Author Search For more about Linnea Due, go to www.glencoe.com.

Indiana English/ Language Arts Academic Standards (pp. 560–569)

8.1 Word Recognition, Fluency, and Vocabulary Development Understand... word parts... **8.2 Comprehension and Analysis (Focus on Informational Text)** Develop [reading] strategies such as... analyzing structure, organization, perspective, and purpose. **8.3 Comprehension and Analysis of Literary Text** Respond to grade-level-appropriate literature... identifying... character...

For a complete description of the standards, see p. IN 11.

Vocabulary Preview

swaggered (SWAG urd) *v.* walked boldly or showed off; form of the verb *swagger* **(p. 568)** *It was clear that Jinx had plenty of confidence when she swaggered onto the basketball court.*

barreling (BAIR ul ing) *v.* running headlong; form of the verb *barrel* **(p. 568)** *Jen stepped aside when Jinx came barreling toward her.*

On Your Own In your Learner's Notebook, answer these questions.

1. If a boy swaggered past you, would you think he was shy or bold?
2. Which is more likely to go barreling across a field, a horse or a fly?

English Language Coach

EL

Word Analysis To understand the meaning of a word, it may help to look at its parts. For example, the word *unhappy* is formed by the prefix *un* and the word *happy*. Happy is called the **base word.** Letter combinations added to the front of a base word are called **prefixes.** Letter combinations added to the end of a base word are called **suffixes.** Sometimes there is a slight spelling change when a suffix is added.

You can sometimes figure out the meaning of an unfamiliar word by analyzing its parts. Look below at the word *unsinkable.*

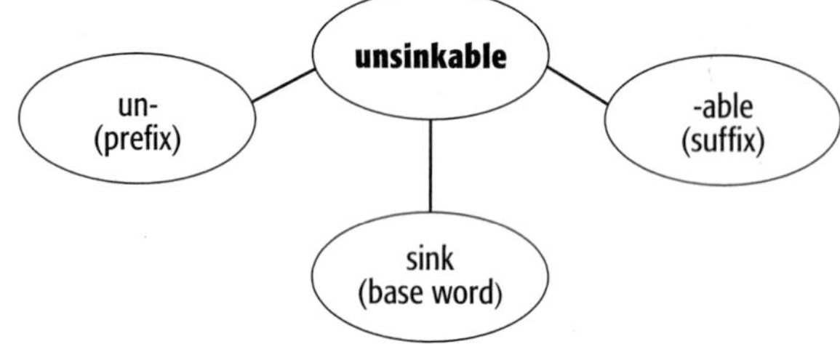

What does *unsinkable* mean? If you know that *un-* means "not" and *-able* means "can be done," you can guess *unsinkable* means "cannot be sunk."

Partner Work For each word below, make a word web like the one above.

- **disrespectful**
- **unbeatable**
- **preapproval**

Additional Support

Author Search To expand students' appreciation of Linnea Due, have them access the Web site for additional information and resources.

Literature Focus Lesson

Sports Magazines Have students examine several different sports magazines and make generalizations about this genre. Students should try to answer the following questions:

- Who is the target audience of the magazine?
- What types of articles are found in these magazines?
- Do the magazines mostly appeal to athletes or fans?
- What types of advertisements are found in these magazines? OL

Skills Preview

Key Reading Skill: Analyzing

As you read "Cream Puff," you'll be asked to analyze the conflicts that Jen, the main character, has. You've already learned that there can be **external conflict** between the main character and

- another person
- nature, in the form of animals or floods and so forth
- a person and society

There can also be **internal conflict,** a struggle of emotions going on within the character. As you're reading "Cream Puff," watch for signs of both kinds of conflict.

EL

Key Literary Element: Characterization

A **character** is an individual in a story or other literary work. The qualities that make up a character's personality are **character traits.** A character might be greedy or generous, cowardly or courageous, kind or mean, and so on. The author reveals these traits through **characterization.** Methods of characterization include describing what a character looks like, says, thinks, and does and what other characters say about the character.

- Characters with several sides to their personalities are **dynamic** (dye NAM ik) **characters.** They grow and change as a result of their experiences.
- Characters with only one or two traits are **static** (STAT ik) **characters.** They don't change during the course of the story.

The main character of a story is usually dynamic. Minor characters are usually static.

Small Group Discussion With a small group of classmates, make a list of main characters from recent movies or TV shows you've seen. Together, label each character on the list either "dynamic" or "static." Give reasons for each label you use.

Elements Handbook To review or learn more about the literary elements, go to www.glencoe.com.

Get Ready to Read

Connect to the Reading

Think of a time when you had a problem and turned to others for advice. Did their suggestions help or did you have to figure out a solution on your own?

Write to Learn In a few sentences in your Learner's Notebook, explain how you solved the problem.

Build Background

Women first played basketball at the college level in the 1890s. Both on the court and off, women wore long dresses because it was thought to be in bad taste for a woman to show more than her head, neck, and hands in public. Players sometimes tripped over the hems of their long skirts, hurting themselves. Uniforms changed in the late 1890s, when female players began wearing bloomers—baggy shorts gathered at the knee.

"Cream Puff" takes place at a fictional basketball camp for teens. At basketball camps, kids work to improve their playing skills.

The narrator in "Cream Puff" uses real basketball terms:

- *drove for the basket* (ran quickly and aggressively toward the basket)
- *pump-faked* (pretended to throw)
- *possession* (control of the ball)
- *turnover* (when one team loses the ball and the other team takes possession)

Set Purposes for Reading

BIG Question Read "Cream Puff" to find out how the main character stays true to herself.

Set Your Own Purpose What else would you like to learn from the selection to help you answer the Big Question? Write your own purpose on the "Cream Puff" page of Foldable 5.

Keep Moving

Use these skills as you read "Cream Puff."

Teach

EL Language Coach

Word Analysis Say: Using the prefixes for the words "internal" *(in-)* and "external" *(ex-)* can help you differentiate between the two types of conflict. What do each of these prefixes mean? *(in- means inside, and ex- means outside)* **Ask:** How does this help you understand the meaning of the two types of conflict? *(Possible responses: Internal conflicts are inside a person; they are personal conflicts; External conflicts are outside the person; they are conflicts people have with other people.)* EL BL

Literature Online

Interactive Literary Elements Handbook Have students access the Web site to improve their understanding of characterization.

Differentiated Instruction

Static or Dynamic Have students think about the different static and dynamic characters they named in their small-group discussion. Direct the groups to write statements from the perspective of each character that tell something about the character and what makes that character static or dynamic. Here are some examples you may give your students to help get them started.

- I do not show up on the show very often and have little to say.
- I am stubborn and my ideas do not change no matter what happens.
- I am a teenager, and I have many learning experiences on the show. OL

Indiana English/Language Arts Academic Standards

SE: 8.1, 8.2, 8.3

TWE: *Literature Focus Lesson* 8.2, *Differentiated Instruction* 8.3

Teach

L Literary Element

Characterization Say: Jen tells us what her dad would want her to do by quoting something he said to her in the past. What does this tell you about Jen's relationship with her father? *(Possible response: She thinks of his advice when she has a problem, so maybe they have a good relationship and she respects him. Or maybe she is just trying to find a way to please him.)* OL

C Critical Thinking

Comprehension Ask: According to the narrator, what was the main difference between playing with little kids and playing in the city league? *(The little kids do not play as rough as those in the city league.)* BL

Readability Scores
Dale-Chall: 4.3
DRP: 50
Lexile: 840

READING WORKSHOP 1

CREAM PUFF

by Linnea Due

Okay, I stepped aside. Wait a minute—*step* is too big a word. My big toe shifted a half inch to the left. Maybe my heel. I couldn't believe Coach Brandt could even notice, but she did, and she's been screaming at me ever since. *Wuss. Cream puff. Scared of your own shadow.* Things that make you laugh in real life or get up in someone's face just to show you can. In basketball, when the coach says those things, you're dead meat. The other kids stopped looking at me. I could smell the shame. **1**

That huge girl was caroming[1] down the court like a three-foot-wide brick wall on Rollerblades. Who wouldn't slide south? Only that's exactly what you can't do. You have to stand in there, take the hit. Dad's told me, over and over. "I'm small, Jen," he points out, and at six feet, he is, for basketball anyway. "These big guys'd come and bust me up. I had bruises up and down my arms, on my chest . . . even my neck! But you gotta take the hits if you're gonna play." **L**

He was mad 'cause I'd told him I'd had it with basketball. When I used to play with the little kids, we didn't bust each other up on purpose. Then I got into the city league when I was eight and learned how real kids play. Rough. They muscle you out of the way and they stomp on your foot and they jab you with their elbows. Mom wanted me to quit the first day. I might have if I'd thought of it first. Every time I **C**

Practice the Skills

1 Key Reading Skill

Analyzing Jen says that she is "dead meat" and that she could "smell the shame." From these descriptions, you can tell that she's having an internal conflict, or troubling feelings.

1. ***Caroming*** is hitting and bouncing off like a ball. The big girl was pushing off the other players on her way down the court.

Additional Support

English Language Coach

Italics Point out the words in italics in the first paragraph on page 562. Often a writer uses quotation marks to show what people are saying. However, in this story, the writer is not telling exactly what was said in a given moment. In other words, the coach may not have said, *Wuss. Cream puff. Scared of your own shadow.* in one sentence. The writer uses italics to show that these are words *spoken* by the coach, but the writer does not use quotation marks because the coach may not have said these exact words in this order. EL wanted to quit **afterward**, what came up in my head was a picture of Mom saying, "I told you so," or Dad with a really disappointed look on his face. **2** Four years after that first day at city league, I still don't like getting hit. R1

When the coach ran out of stuff to call me, I slunk off the court and sat on the bench. Nobody came near me; nobody wanted to catch what I had. I could see everybody on the floor tighten up and start popping each other good—it looked like the WWF[2] out there. Still, if you had to choose between getting smashed in the nose and having Coach Brandt call you a cream puff, what would you pick? There's no shame in a broken nose. L

Analyzing the Photo What does the photo add to your understanding of the relationship between Jen and her coach?

Keisha swung down next to me. "Whatcha scared of her for?" she asked. "She's just a big slow white girl." Then she giggled. "You're a big *fast* white girl, and that gives you the edge." **3**

Keisha was one of my roommates back in the dorm at San Francisco State. All of us had been chosen by our schools or city leagues to come to Bay Eagles coach Katherine Brandt's weeklong basketball camp. It was a huge honor, and now I was worried that Sharon Demming should have been picked instead of me. I felt like a pretend Rising Young Star, not a real one. R2 And I sure didn't like how that slow white girl—her name tag read JINX—kept catching my eye just so I wouldn't miss her sneering at me. She reminded me of my uncle Robert, who can always find something mean to say about anybody.

2. The ***WWF*** is the World Wrestling Federation.

Practice the Skills

2 **English Language Coach**

Word Analysis The word **afterward** has two parts: the base word *after* and the suffix *-ward,* which means "in the direction of." Other words that have this suffix are *toward, forward,* and *backward.*

3 **Key Literary Element**

Characterization From what Keisha says, you can tell two of her character traits. She is supportive of her friends, and she has a sense of humor.

Reading in the Real World

College Part of college life can be the dorm-room experience. This almost always includes a roommate. Have students pretend they are about to go to college. Instruct students to write a letter to a roommate introducing themselves and telling a little about what they hope will happen their first year of college. Students should tell the roommate about their likes, dislikes, study habits, and their goals for college. Tell students they can write real information about themselves, or they can make it up. Ask for volunteers to read their letters to the class. AL

Teach

R1 Reading Skill

Review Connecting **Ask:** Have you ever done something just so that someone could not say, "I told you so"? *(Responses will vary.)* AS

L Literary Element

Characterization **Say:** Notice the way Jen describes herself and the way that she feels others view her. Look at the last three lines of the second paragraph. What do you learn about Jen when you read these lines? *(Possible responses: She thinks it is better to be tough, and is more bothered by being called "cream puff" than she would be if she had a broken nose. She is concerned about her image as a tough girl and thinks it is being ruined.)* OL

R2 Reading Skill

Analyzing **Ask:** Who is Sharon Demming? *(Possible responses: She is a girl from Jen's school or city league who probably is a good basketball player but did not get chosen to go to this camp because Jen did.)* OL

Indiana English/Language Arts Academic Standards
SE: 8.1, 8.2, 8.3
TWE: *English Language Coach* 8.2, *Reading in the Real World* 8.5.7

Teach

C Critical Thinking

Comprehension **Ask:** What generalization did Jen make about coaches? *(She generalized that all coaches are really hard on people.)* **Ask:** How does learning about Evelyn's coach challenge this generalization? *(Possible response: It shows that it is not really true—some coaches are not hard on people.)* OL

EL Language Coach

Word Analysis Explain how the suffix *–ize* changes a noun to a verb. **Ask:** What is the root word of visualizing? *(visual)* EL

L Literary Element

Characterization **Ask:** What nickname does Keisha give Jen? *(Suburban)* **Ask:** What do you think Keisha means by this? *(Possible response: She probably means that Jen is from the suburbs and Keisha is from the city—their personalities or attitudes represent different ways of looking at life, which come from where they grew up.)* OL AL

By the time we got back to the dorm, my roommates had teased me so much, I felt better. Evelyn told me that Coach Brandt had a reputation for being really hard on people. I said I figured every coach has that reputation, but Evelyn said no, that her coach in Long Beach was really sweet and gave everybody candy. Keisha said she'd never heard of coaches giving out candy and was her coach a dirty old man? Evelyn laughed for a whole minute, and then Keisha turned to me and said, "That girl was *big*! I woulda got out of her way, too." C

But that night, when the others were asleep, I started worrying again. What if it turned out I was a fraidy-cat? What if being scared was something I couldn't make go away? I love basketball. I love it more than eating and TV and video games and even swimming, which is what I love second best. I'm already five-seven, and like Keisha says, I'm fast and I can jump, too. I've got a chart on my wall at home that lists the top teams—the Tennessee Lady Vols, LSU, UConn, the Georgia Bulldogs, and closer to home, Stanford and Cal. The chart measures my height, so I can look at it and see I've gained two inches this year alone. I think about how everything's coming together: my desire, my body, my ability. I can't be afraid! 4

To get to sleep, I pictured myself shooting baskets, keeping my wrist loose and letting the ball trail off my fingers like I'm caressing a baby. I run it through my head so often, I can make it happen for real—it's called visualizing. That doesn't mean I don't practice 24/7. I spend so much time shooting baskets that Mr. Ashton next door asked Mom to put up a sound wall. He was joking, I think. 5 EL

The next day, Jinx was waiting near the basket, a slight smile on her face. Even though we're the same height, she outweighs me by twenty pounds, and it was easy for her to muscle me aside. Keisha looked worried. "Stick it to her, Suburban. Make her back off." I tried to stay in front of her when she drove for the basket, but I was concentrating so much on sticking to my spot that I forgot to defend. Coach Brandt was on me in a heartbeat. "You're not in the game, Jennifer," she warned. "If you didn't come to play, you might as well get on the bus back to Sacramento." I could feel my face turning red and my eyes going black, which they always do when I'm mad. L

Practice the Skills

4 Key Reading Skill

Analyzing State the internal conflict that is bothering Jen. Think about these things:

- She doesn't want to disappoint her father.
- She doesn't like being hit.
- She says she loves basketball more than anything.
- She says she thought that everything was "coming together" for her.

5 Key Literary Element

Characterization Jen practices "24/7." What does this tell you about her personality?

Additional Support

Differentiated Instruction

Creating Scenes Have students work in small groups or with partners to list different generalizations adults make about kids their age. Instruct students to then write a skit or create a commercial that shows how one of the generalizations on their lists is wrong. Have students perform their skits or present their commercials to the class. Discuss how making generalizations about people can lead to inaccurate conclusions. OL

But a minute later I was back to chewing on my bottom lip. What *could* I do about Jinx? She was standing by the bench with a couple of other girls, and the three of them kept glancing over at me and rolling their eyes. Keisha stayed right on my shoulder, but I didn't want her fighting my fights. What would Dad do? He wouldn't let some big old player get up over his head every other minute, no matter how short he was. No answer came. Trying to figure out what my dad would do made me more nervous 'cause I didn't know, and that was even worse than not being able to handle Jinx in the first place. 6 L1

All that practice, I kept trying to show her up, but instead everything I did played into her hands. If I stood still, she went up over me. When she pump-faked, I jumped, and then she shot as I was coming down. Every mistake made me more upset, and the more upset I got, the more mistakes I made.

Practice the Skills

6 Key Reading Skill

Analyzing Jen's internal conflict is getting more complicated. Why does thinking about her dad make her even more nervous?

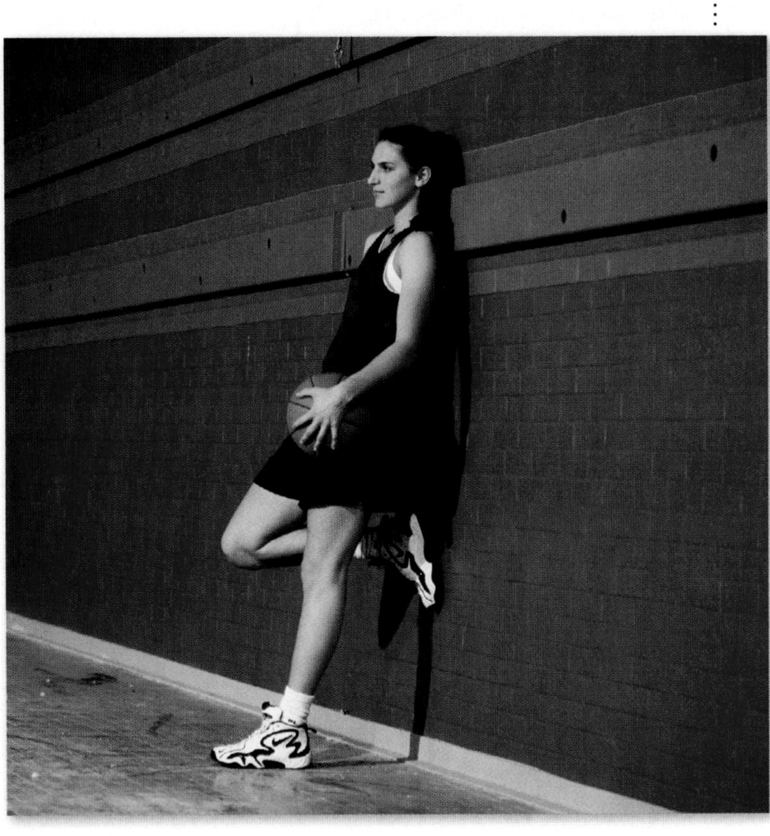

Analyzing the Photo What aspect of Jennifer's experience at basketball camp might this photo illustrate?

Teach

L1 Literary Element

Review Conflict **Ask:** What is the internal conflict here? *(Jen does not know what to do.)* **Ask:** What is the external conflict here? *(Jinx is playing very well against Jen and gets the ball no matter what Jen does.)* OL **Ask:** How does the internal conflict affect the external conflict? *(Possible response: Jen is frustrated and confused. This causes her to be indecisive and make even more mistakes, and she gets more frustrated.)* AL

L2 Literary Element

Characterization **Ask:** What are some of Jen's character traits, or qualities that make her who she is? *(Possible responses: She is self-conscious, sets high expectations for herself, is determined to improve, but isn't very aggressive.)* OL

Reading in the Real World

Citizenship Jen is faced with a problem that she needs to solve. She has tried several solutions, and none has worked so far. Have students write a list of problems they have faced and the solutions they found. Then have students find resources that teach skills for problem solving. As a class, design a bulletin board that highlights what students think of as the best skills when it comes to solving problems. Include skills that come from students' personal experiences as well as the resources they found. OL

Indiana English/Language Arts Academic Standards
SE: 8.2, 8.3
TWE: *Differentiated Instruction* 8.7.13, *Reading in the Real World* 8.2

Teach

L Literary Element

Characterization: Ask: Did you expect Jen to respond to her coach in this way? Explain. *(Responses will vary.)* AS **Ask:** What kind of teen would stand up to the coach in this way? *(Possible response: Someone who is frustrated, or who desperately needs advice and expects the coach to help.)* OL **Ask:** Does this help you to relate to Jennifer more or less? Does it make her seem more realistic? *(Possible responses: It is easier to relate to her because she stands up for herself. She does not seem as realistic because most kids would not say something like that to their coach, especially if the coach was as hard as this one.)* AL

R Reading Skill

Review Monitoring Comprehension Ask: Why did Jen call her mom that night? *(Possible responses: She was upset about what happened and wanted to vent; she needed some advice.)* **Ask:** What does Jen mean when she says, "Thanks Mom"? *(She is being sarcastic and is frustrated by her mom focusing on things like socks and hair in her eyes.)* OL

READING WORKSHOP 1

"She's rattled you," Evelyn said. She was the pretty one in our little group—her mother was Filipino and her dad African American. "Forget Keisha and her gang banging. Just play your own game."

But that was the problem—I didn't have one. I felt blank, like a window that opened onto nothing.

As we were leaving that afternoon, Coach Brandt called me over. "There will always be bullies, Jennifer," she said quietly. "At some point you'll have to learn to deal with them."

As she walked away, my eyes went black again, and this time I couldn't stop myself. "Wait a second," I called to her, knowing I was stepping over the line and not caring. "You have to say more than that. You're the coach!" **L**

She turned back with a laugh. "You want me to motivate you? Okay, here's the best advice I can give: Motivate yourself or get out. This game is too demanding to depend on a coach or your parents or your teammates to keep you in. You've got the ability to go all the way—and that's not something I say to many kids. But you need more than ability to make it. You even need more than wanting it so badly you can taste it." She could see the surprise cross my face, and she nodded as if it confirmed something she already knew. She took a deep breath and said, "You need *drive* to make it work. You can have the best engine on the face of this planet, and if you don't have a starter,[3] you'll never go an inch. That's what drive is, and it's what you're missing, Jennifer. I hope you find it." 8

That night I called my mother. "What's wrong?" she asked. She could always tell when I had a problem. I said, "I keep thinking about Dad. He never gave up, and he was so small."

She waited for me to go on, and when I didn't, I could hear her sigh. "Jen, I know you won't believe this, but basketball isn't very important to your father. It never was." **R**

"But that can't be true," I sputtered. "All he ever does is talk about it." I started to say more, but what was the point in arguing when I knew she was wrong? After a moment, she sighed again and asked me if I'd worn holes in any more socks and was my hair still in my eyes. Thanks, Mom.

3. The ***starter*** is the part of a car engine that turns it on.

Practice the Skills

8 Key Literary Skill

Characterization Coach Brandt has been giving Jen a hard time all week. Do you think what the coach says here shows more of the same or a different attitude toward Jen? Explain.

Additional Support

English Language Coach

Parts of Speech Point out the word "drive" in the middle of the fifth paragraph and explain that it is used as a noun. **Say:** You can see that it is a noun (and not a verb) because it is the object of the verb "need." *Drive* is what the coach tells Jen that she needs. Allow several volunteers to try to explain what the coach means by the word "drive." Encourage them to think of synonyms. EL

READING WORKSHOP 1

Analyzing the Photo Jennifer's coach tells her that she needs *drive* in order to succeed. How does the girl in this photo exhibit that quality?

But when I went back to the room, Evelyn started talking about how her dad always goes to the playground with her, and I suddenly felt like somebody had dumped a bucket of ice-cold water on my head. Dad was too busy to come to my games, much less play in the driveway with me. The couple of times I'd gotten him to play, I was surprised at how bad he was. He blustered about how he'd lost his edge and did a lot of shoving and jumping around, but now that I was looking close, I could see how maybe that edge had never been sharp. **9**

I didn't want to get out of bed the next morning. Here I was, at the statewide camp, finding out I'm a cream puff and my dad all talk and no help at all, and this girl Jinx was going to make me look even worse than I did yesterday, 'cause yesterday I had Dad to help and today I didn't. When I pulled the pillow over my head, Keisha told me she was going to jump on me, so I had to get up or risk broken ribs on top of a broken heart. How could my dad have pretended like that to me? **C**

While I warmed up, I pictured my dad scrimmaging[4] with the starters season after season, knowing he wouldn't get into the games. I knew the other guys liked him, 'cause they'd call when they came through Sacramento, and Dad would have them over to the house. Maybe what Dad really missed was being on a team. **10**

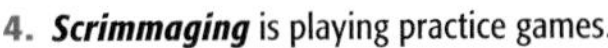

4. ***Scrimmaging*** is playing practice games.

Practice the Skills

9 **Reading Skill Review**

Monitoring Comprehension Jen realizes something important about her dad here. Do you "get" what it is? Make sure by putting it in your own words.

10 **Key Literary Element**

Characterization What character trait does Jen's thinking in this paragraph reveal about her? Think about how angry she was with her father and how she feels about him now.

Teach

C Critical Thinking

Comprehension **Ask:** Why doesn't Jen want to get out of bed in the morning? *(Possible responses: she is feeling sorry for herself; she is starting to believe she is just a "cream puff;" she's starting to see her dad in a different way and believes that he really cannot help her.)* **OL**

Differentiated Instruction

Research Have students research different sports, such as basketball, baseball, swimming, gymnastics, or soccer. Direct students to focus on how the team affects the individual players. Write these questions on the board to help students focus their research:

- How is the game played?
- Do individual players get the trophies or does the team win?
- How does team spirit affect players?

Discuss the differences between team sports and individual sports. **OL**

Indiana English/Language Arts Academic Standards

SE: 8.2, 8.3

TWE: *English Language Coach* 8.1, *Differentiated Instruction* 8.4

Teach

R1 Reading Skill

Analyzing **Say:** Jennifer mistook her dad's interest in the game as an effect of missing the game he loved. What was the real cause of his interest in the game? *(Possible response: He wants to connect with Jennifer because he loves her, especially because he is "too busy" to go to her games.)* OL

R2 Reading Skill

Review Predicting **Ask:** What do you think will happen in the story now that Jen has decided she doesn't have anyone's footsteps to walk in? *(Possible response: The story will probably show how Jen finds her own technique and manages to play well, even against Jinx.)* OL

EL Language Coach

Multiple-Meaning Words **Say:** Jen says she needs to find out where she lives to play her game. What is the meaning of *live* in this context? *(Possible response: Jen uses* live *as a metaphor to mean she needs to figure out who she is as a basketball player.)* OL

Visual Vocabulary
A ***comet*** is a bright heavenly body made mostly of ice and dust. It develops a cloudy tail when it orbits near the sun.

When Jinx came pounding down the court at me during the drills, I stood in there and took hit after hit. I felt so bad, I didn't care if I got hurt. But here's the terrible part: all my blocking didn't stop her making the shots. Oh, a couple of times I tipped away the ball, but I could tell I wasn't playing good, and I just didn't know what else to do. My Rising Young Star was blinking out like a dying comet. **11**

By the time Coach Brandt called lunch, I was so low, I could have crawled across the floor. Why was I even here? For Mom? She'd wanted me to quit the first day. For Dad? Mom was right; he really didn't care about basketball. He talked it all the time 'cause he wanted to connect with me, and he knew there was no better way to do that than talk basketball. Besides, now that I was seeing the awful truth, I realized that Dad couldn't have helped me much anyway—we were very different players. I was tall and he was short, I was fast and cagey, and he was more like a battering ram.[5] I didn't have anybody's footsteps to walk in, except maybe my own. And that's when it really hit me—basketball was *my* game, not Dad's, not Mom's, not even Keisha's or Evelyn's. When Evelyn told me to play my own game, she meant to burrow deep under the surface of what basketball looked like and find out where *I* lived. **12**

After lunch, when Jinx **swaggered** back onto the court for scrimmages, I was ready for her. On the first possession, when she came **barreling** toward me, I sidestepped her easily and snagged the ball as she came past. I could see Keisha's eyes widen—would Coach Brandt yell at me 'cause I'd moved aside? But she didn't say a word—she stood near the bench, her eyes narrowed in concentration. In the next five minutes, I trailed two shots over Jinx's shoulder, and the coach made a note on her clipboard. Why challenge Jinx head-to-head? She

5. In the Middle Ages, a ***battering ram*** was a big, heavy log used to break down the gates of a castle.

Vocabulary

swaggered (SWAG urd) *v.* walked boldly or showed off

barreling (BAIR ul ing) *v.* running headlong

Practice the Skills

11 Key Reading Skill

Analyzing Jen repeats the phrase "Rising Young Star." What part of her internal conflict does this represent?

12 Key Reading Skill

Analyzing What do you learn from the way Jen finally resolves her internal conflict?

Additional Support

Reading in the Real World

Citizenship Have students discuss the meaning of the phrase "walking in another person's footsteps." Ask students what it might mean for them if they walked in someone else's footsteps. *(Possible response: trying to be a musician like my dad or being good at math like my aunt.)* Ask them to share when it might be a good idea to walk in someone's footsteps and when it might not be a good idea. OL Have students write a statement on how to balance the pressures of walking in someone else's footsteps with the inspiration and lessons they can learn from following someone's footsteps. AL

Analyzing the Photo Going up for a rebound, these four girls compete for the win. What did Jennifer learn at basketball camp about competition? What does this photo show about competition?

was heavier and slower, and that made her easy to beat. She tried to run right over me a few times, and I avoided her like a matador[6] teases a bull. I could see the worry lines start in her forehead, and I felt sorry for her. A big smile was building on Evelyn's face, and Keisha had begun to laugh. **13**

L The third time I forced a turnover, Keisha shouted, "Go-o-o, Cream Puff!" I could tell the name was going to stick, and it has, even after me and Evelyn and Keisha came back this year for our second camp. The kids that go to the camp all know each other, and word travels fast.

I still don't like getting hit. Nobody does—it's just part of the game. But I love being called Cream Puff. It reminds me of that summer I figured out who was missing from the court: me. ❍

6. In bullfighting, the ***matador,*** or bullfighter, teases the bull by making it chase after his cape.

Practice the Skills

13 BIG Question

Jen has found a way to stay true to herself. What is it? Write your answer on the "Cream Puff" page of Foldable 5. Your response will help you complete the Unit Challenge later. **BQ**

READING WORKSHOP 1

Teach

L Literary Element

Review Tone **Say:** Think about the tone Keisha used when she yelled "Go-o-o, Cream Puff!" How has the tone of this nickname changed from the way it was used earlier in the story? *(Possible response: Now it is used in a positive, or affectionate, way.)* **OL**

BQ BIG Question

Ask: What has this short story taught you about staying true to yourself? *(Possible response: I can try to find my own way of doing things instead of trying to be like someone else.)* **AS**

Assess

CheckPoint

Use the CheckPoint questions provided on Presentation Plus! to check for comprehension of the selection. These questions can be used with interactive response keypads for immediate student feedback.

Differentiated Instruction

Plan and Conduct a Survey Have students plan and conduct a schoolwide survey about nicknames. The class should work together to come up with the survey questions they would like to ask and how they plan to gather and evaluate the data. Possible questions:

- Do you have a nickname? If yes, do you like the nickname? Did you get the nickname from a positive or negative experience?
- Do the people you know have nicknames?

Have students present the findings of their surveys to the class. Discuss the positives and negatives of nicknames. **OL**

Indiana English/Language Arts Academic Standards
SE: 8.2
TWE: *Reading in the Real World* 8.1.1, 8.5.2; *Differentiated Instruction* 8.4

Assess

Resources for page 570

- Selection Quick Check, p. 41
- Selection and Unit Assessment, p. 49
- ExamView Assessment Suite
- Interactive Tutor: Self-Assessment

Students can respond to the *After You Read* items in their Learner's Notebooks or on a separate sheet of paper.

Answering the BIG Question

1. Students are likely to say that Jen would not have been true to herself if she had quit basketball because she really liked the game.
2. Coach Brandt tells Jen to play her own game.
3. Possible response: Jen learns that basketball is important to her father only because it helps him get close to his daughter.

Critical Thinking

4. Possible response: Jen does not want Keisha to fight her fights because she wants to be able to stand up for herself.
5. Responses will vary. Students may feel that Coach Brandt was right to call Jen a "cream puff" because she could see what kind of person Jen was and predicted that it would motivate her. Other students may feel that a coach should motivate players by pointing out their strengths.

After You Read — Cream Puff

Answering the BIG Question

1. Do you think Jen would have stayed true to herself if she had quit basketball? Why or why not?
2. **Recall** What advice does Coach Brandt give Jen about how to succeed at basketball?
   TIP Right There
3. **Summarize** What does Jen learn about her dad from her mother? Sum it up in a sentence.
   TIP Right There

Critical Thinking

4. **Infer** Why doesn't Jen want Keisha to fight her fights?
   TIP Author and Me
5. **Evaluate** Do you think Coach Brandt is right to call Jen a "cream puff" in order to motivate her? Why or why not?
   TIP On My Own

Talk About Your Reading

Small Group Discussion What is Jen like? With a small group of classmates, discuss Jen's character traits. Each person should name a different character trait, then name the method of characterization the author uses to reveal the trait. Record your group's responses on a chart like the one pictured below. An example has been filled in to help you start.

Character Trait	Method(s) of Characterization
1. *insecure*	*what Jen says about feeling ashamed (p. 562) and what she thinks about late at night (p. 564)*
2.	
3.	

Indiana English/Language Arts Academic Standards (pp. 570–571)

8.3 Comprehension and Analysis of Literary Text Respond to grade-level-appropriate literature…identifying…character…**8.7.11** Deliver oral responses to literature…**8.2 Comprehension and Analysis (Focus on Informational Text)** Develop [reading] strategies such as…analyzing structure, organization, perspective, and purpose. **8.6 English Language Conventions**

For a complete description of the standards, see p. IN 11.

Talk About Your Reading

Charts will vary. Sample character traits and methods of characterization are given below.

Character Trait	Methods of Characterization
easily embarrassed	does not want to get out of bed when she thinks of other players calling her a "cream puff" and not knowing what to do about it (p. 567)
determined to succeed	refuses to quit basketball when she first starts in the city league (pp. 562–563)
is a worrier	she stays up late at night worrying about things (p. 564)

Skills Review

Key Reading Skill: Analyzing

6. Why does Jen fail several times before figuring out how to motivate herself? Support your answer with specific details from the story.
7. What do you think the story says about what it takes to succeed? Why do you say so? Use examples from the story to back up your answer.

Key Literary Element: Characterization

8. Which characters in the story are static? Which are dynamic? How can you tell? Using the list of characters that follows, label each character either "static" or "dynamic." Explain each choice.

   Jen • Keisha • Coach Brandt • Jinx

9. Did you learn more about Jen from what she said or from what she did? Explain.

Vocabulary Check

Copy the following sentences on a separate sheet of paper. Then fill in each blank correctly with either *swaggered* or *barreling.*

10. The cart got loose and went _____ down the path.
11. In his new leather jacket, Manny _____ into the room.

English Language Coach As you read "Cream Puff," you analyzed the words *afterward* and *quietly.* Use what you learned to define the words below.

12. seaward
13. skyward
14. secretly
15. thoughtfully
16. **Academic Vocabulary** Are **significant** details in a story the most or least important ones?

Grammar Link: Clauses and Phrases

A **clause** is a group of words that work together to express meaning and that contain a subject and a predicate. A **phrase** is a group of words that work together but do not contain a subject and predicate.

Earlier, you learned that an **independent clause** can stand alone as a simple sentence. That's because an independent clause expresses a complete thought. A **dependent clause** cannot stand alone as a complete sentence. It does not express a complete thought. It "depends on" an independent clause to make its meaning complete.

Dependent Clause: when she is happy

Independent Clause: Mom sings

Dependent Clause + Independent Clause: When she is happy, Mom sings.

A **phrase** does not express a complete thought. Types of phrases include (a) modifying phrases, (b) noun phrases, and (c) verb phrases.

(a) Early Tuesday morning, we will leave.

(b) My brother, sister, and I have packed.

(c) For two weeks we will be traveling.

Grammar Practice

On a separate sheet of paper, identify whether the underlined words are a *phrase* or a *clause.*

17. The drama teacher watched the rehearsal.
18. I'm going to the school dance with my friends.
19. When the movie ends, we can go shopping.
20. If I get a part in the school play, I will be happy.

Web Activities For eFlashcards, Selection Quick Checks, and other Web activities, go to www.glencoe.com.

Skills Review

Key Reading Skill: Analyzing

6. Possible response: At first, Jen tries to do what she thinks her dad would do. Then she tries to do what other players would do. Finally, she finds her "own" way.
7. Responses will vary.

Key Literary Element: Characterization

8. Possible response: Jen is dynamic because she learns something in the story and changes. Keisha might be static because she does not really change during the story. Coach Brandt is static because she, too, does not change during the story. Jinx is static, especially because she does not change her tactics even when Jen figures out how to handle her.
9. Responses will vary.

Close

Ask students to summarize how they answered the Big Question after reading "Cream Puff."

Web Activities Have students access the Web site for interactive activities that will help them assess their understanding of the selection.

Vocabulary Check

10. barreling **11.** swaggered

English Language Coach

Possible responses:

12. in the direction of the sea
13. up, or toward the sky
14. to be secretive
15. to be thoughtful

Academic Vocabulary

16. the most important ones

Grammar Link: Clauses and Phrases

Grammar Practice

17. clause **19.** phrase

18. phrase **20.** clause

Indiana English/Language Arts Academic Standards

SE: 8.2, 8.3, 8.6, 8.7.11

Teach

More about the Author

Tamara Eberlein is a free-lance writer who lives in Connecticut. One of her books on child development won an award from the American Society of Journalists and Authors.

EL Language Coach

Word Families **Ask:** Which two words on the web have suffixes that are opposite in meaning? *(useless and usable)* **Ask:** What are some other words with *use* as their base? *(abuse, unused)* OL

Before You Read

The Question of Popularity

Meet the Author

Tamara Eberlein has written many articles about mental and physical health as well as parenting. She is also the author of books on child development. Eberlein is the mother of twins.

Author Search For more about Tamara Eberlein, go to www.glencoe.com.

Vocabulary Preview

factor (FAK tur) *n.* something that produces or contributes to a certain result **(p. 574)** *The amount of time people spend studying is very frequently a factor in their grades.*

obnoxious (ub NOK shus) *adj.* very disagreeable or offensive **(p. 574)** *The boys in that "in" crowd are obnoxious and often put others down.*

majority (muh JOR ih tee) *n.* more than half; the greater part **(p. 575)** *The majority of people are nice; only a few cause problems.*

Think-Pair-Share Use the three vocabulary words in a paragraph. Leave blanks where the vocabulary words go. Then pair up with a classmate and trade paragraphs. Fill in the blanks in the paragraph.

English Language Coach

EL

Word Families A **word family** is a group of words that have the same base word. For example, all the words on the web below are in the same family because they all have *use* as their base word. In each case, either a prefix *(mis-, re-)* or a suffix *(-able, -less)* has been added to the base word to form a new word. Take a few minutes to study the chart.

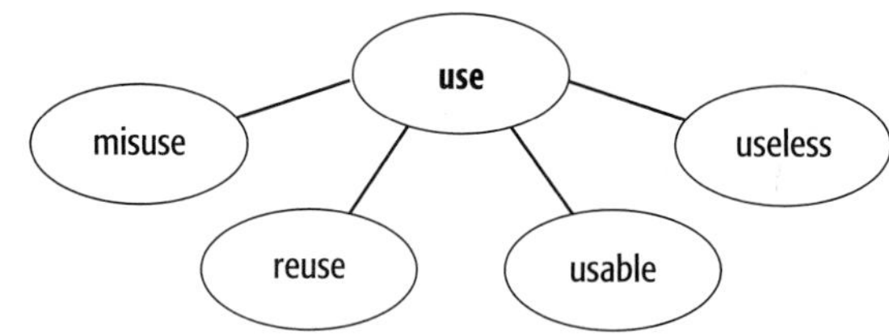

Whole Class Discussion Brainstorm a list of words in the same word family as *act.* Come up with at least two words created with prefixes and two words created with suffixes. Record your list on a web.

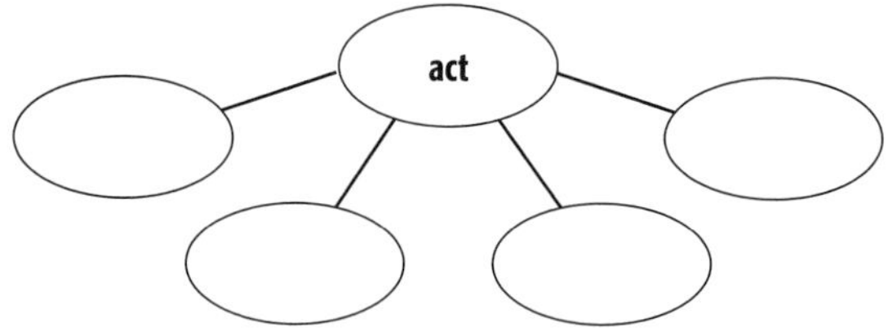

Indiana English/Language Arts Academic Standards (pp. 572–577)

8.1 Word Recognition, Fluency, and Vocabulary Development Understand. . . word parts and relationships. . . **8.2 Comprehension and Analysis (Focus on Informational Text)** Develop [reading] strategies. . . identifying and analyzing structure, organization, perspective, and purpose.

For a complete description of the standards, see p. IN 11.

Additional Support

Author Search To expand students' appreciation of Tamara Eberlein, have them access the Web site for additional information and resources.

Literature Focus Lesson

Magazine Articles While many magazine articles are nonfiction, they are not always pure fact. Show students examples of magazine articles that are more "advertisement" than article. For example, in many women's magazines, there are articles that deal with makeup, beauty, or skin care—these will often feature specific products with quotes from representatives of those companies. The same is true of home decorating magazines, only the articles will deal with home repair or decorating. AS Challenge students to write a one-page compare / contrast report on the differences and similarities between two factual and non-factual articles. AL

Skills Preview

Key Reading Skill: Analyzing

As you read "The Question of Popularity," you'll be asked to analyze the main idea and supporting details. To prepare for the analysis, look over the article.

Whole Class Discussion As a class, discuss which paragraphs on the first page of the article form the introduction and what you think the main idea of the article is. What details do you think the author might present to support that main idea?

Text Element: Direct Quotations

Direct quotations tell exactly what people said in their own words. Authors of nonfiction use direct quotations for many reasons:

- to develop a main idea
- to add vivid details to writing
- to analyze what someone said
- to persuade the reader to agree with them by quoting experts who share their opinion

E

As you read "The Question of Popularity," notice when the author quotes someone. Then ask yourself these questions:

- *Why does the author quote this person?*
- *What does this quotation add to the article?*

Partner Talk Interview a classmate in order to write a one-paragraph biography of him or her. To add vivid detail to the biography, directly quote the person at least once. Be sure to put quotation marks both before (") and after (") the quotation.

Interactive Literary Elements Handbook
To review or learn more about the literary elements, go to www.glencoe.com.

Get Ready to Read

Connect to the Reading

Think about the importance of popularity in your school. How much does popularity matter to you and your friends? To most kids at your school?

Write to Learn In your Learner's Notebook, list the advantages and disadvantages of being popular.

Build Background

People of all ages like to form social groups. Some groups are carefully organized; others are informal. Cliques are small, snobbish, informal associations. Clique members try to hang on to a special advantage—such as a leadership position—by refusing to let "non-members" join.

Studies show that most kids who make bad decisions are with their friends at the time. They're giving in to peer pressure—pressure from members of their social group to act certain ways in order to "fit in." Of course, peers can be good role models too. They can encourage good values, healthy behaviors, and teamwork—if kids choose the right peers to listen to.

Set Purposes for Reading

BIG Question Read "The Question of Popularity" to find out what other kids in middle school think about popularity.

Set Your Own Purpose What else would you like to learn from the selection to help you answer the Big Question? Write your own purpose on "The Question of Popularity" page of Foldable 5.

Keep Moving

Use these skills as you read "The Question of Popularity."

Teach

E Text Element

Direct Quotations Have students write two sentences, one in which they use a direct quotation and another in which they tell what the person said. *(Responses will vary.)* Allow volunteers to either read their two sentences aloud or write them on the board. Help the class recognize the difference between these two types of sentences. OL

R Reading Skill

Review Connecting Ask: How do cliques prevent "non-members" from joining? *(Possible responses: They do not treat the non-members nicely and do not include them in their activities.)* **Ask:** How do members in a clique feel? *(Possible responses: popular, included).* OL

Interactive Literary Elements Handbook Have students access the Web site to improve their understanding of direct quotations.

Reading in the Real World

Career Peer groups are a part of life wherever we go. They are even an important aspect on the job. People who do well in their job usually have respect from their peers and get along with them. Have students ask an adult in their life about the kinds of peer groups they deal with in their jobs. Ask volunteers to report to the class about what they learned. OL Alternately, challenge students to work in groups, come up with a list of questions, interview adults, and report their findings as a group. AL

Indiana English/Language Arts Academic Standards
SE: 8.1, 8.2
TWE: *Literature Focus Lesson* 8.2.3, *Reading in the Real World* 8.7.1

Teach

E Text Element

Review Titles and Heads
Ask: What is the subtitle of this article? *(How much does popularity matter?)* **Ask:** How does the subtitle help you know what the article will really be about? *(Possible response: It tells me that the article will discuss whether or not it is really important to be popular.)* OL

R1 Reading Skill

Analyzing **Say:** The writer contrasts what parents think it means to be "cool" with what it really means. What assumption do parents make that is not necessarily correct? *(Possible response: They assume cool kids are well-liked or admired.)* OL

R2 Reading Skill

Analyzing **Ask:** Do you think Emily Kaplan is part of the "in crowd?" Explain. *(Possible response: No, because she says negative things about the girls and boys in the "in crowd.")* OL

Readability Scores
Dale-Chall: 5.7
DRP: 53
Lexile: 930

READING WORKSHOP 1

TIME

The Question of Popularity

How much does popularity matter? E

By TAMARA EBERLEIN

Being popular isn't as important as having a few close friends who accept you for who you are.

Sean Murphy/Stone/Getty Images

Being popular means that other kids think you're cool. It doesn't mean (as many parents may think) that the cool kids are especially well liked or nice or admired for their smarts. Popular kids may be envied for their cool **factor,** but they may not have a lot of close friends. R1

If you're like most middle schoolers, you've probably thought about how much (or perhaps how little) popularity matters to you. It's not unusual to want to fit in. But it's more important to have a few close friends, accept yourself for who you are, and be comfortable with the people you do hang out with. 1

1 Key Reading Skill

Analyzing What opinion is the writer stating in the final sentence of this paragraph? Does that opinion give you a clue about the article's main idea? Explain.

The In Crowd

Kids know that in most schools there is an "in crowd" of kids who are the most popular. Emily Kaplan, a middle schooler in Larchmont, New York, describes her school's in crowd this way: "The girls are kind of snobby, the boys **obnoxious.** If R2

Vocabulary

factor (FAK tur) *n.* something that produces or contributes to a certain result

obnoxious (ub NOK shus) *adj.* very disagreeable or offensive

Additional Support

Differentiated Instruction

Act It Out Tamara Eberlein says that many parents have wrong ideas about what it means to be popular. Have students act out scenes in which they explain to their parents what it is really like to be (or not to be) popular. Challenge students to be realistic in their dramas and really use the tone and language that their parents might use. OL Have students take it a step further and actually write up a dialogue or script, and act out the scene for the class. AL you laugh at something, they just go, 'That's not funny.' [But] when you're alone together, the popular girls are really nice." Emily's friend Liana Diamond adds, "When they're with their other friends, they don't talk to you." **E**

Who is popular varies from place to place. And of course, not every popular kid is obnoxious or a snob or unfriendly. Believe it or not, for some kids who are popular, it's hard work to stay that way. Trying to stay on top can cause stress and insecurity because who's popular and who's not can change daily. **2**

The Middle Group

The **majority** of kids fall somewhere in between the top and the bottom—and many adults say that kids in the middle group may be happiest and best off. "These kids have several close friends and are also part of a larger group that explores their interests, like soccer or music. They aren't overly caught up in the popularity game," says Sandy Sheehy, who has written a book about friendships. "What's important is not [if you get] invited to the 'right' sleepovers. It's whether [you have] a few close friends."

Margaret Sagarese, coauthor of a book about cliques, has a tip for kids who are trying to figure out where they belong. She suggests that you keep a list of what you like about yourself. "Social acceptance and personal acceptance are two very different things. [You] need to see that liking [yourself] is more important than being part of the in crowd," she says. **3** If being a part of the in group means acting in ways that you wouldn't normally act or want to act, then stay true to yourself. Make decisions according to your own values. Don't be afraid to be you. **R**

2 Key Reading Skill

Analyzing How does this paragraph help support the main idea that "it's more important to have a few close friends . . . and be comfortable with the people you do hang out with"?

3 Text Element

Direct Quotations Explain how the quotations in this paragraph help support the idea that "it's more important to have a few close friends . . . and be comfortable with the people you do hang out with."

Michael Newman/PhotoEdit

Having several close friends and being part of a larger group may make kids happiest and best off.

Vocabulary

majority (muh JOR ih tee) *n.* more than half; the greater part

Teach

E Text Element

Direct Quotations **Ask:** Why do you think the author quotes middle school students in the article? *(Possible response: to show the opinions of real kids and not their parents, or another adult)* **OL**

R Reading Skill

Analyzing **Ask:** How can making a list of what you like about yourself help you? *(Possible response: it can remind me of what is good about me and help keep my focus away from trying to be popular or get in with the cool crowd)* **OL**

Differentiated Instruction

Intrapersonal List Have students make their own lists of what they like about themselves, such as the way they treat others, the kind of sportsmanship they show, the kind of friends they are, being smart or funny, and so on. Challenge students to write a poem or draw a picture titled "Why I Like Me." Ask for volunteers to share their lists, poems, and drawings. **EL** **BL**

Indiana English/Language Arts Academic Standards

SE: 8.2

TWE: *Differentiated Instruction* 8.7.2, *Differentiated Instruction* 8.5.7

Teach

R Reading Skill

Analyzing **Ask:** What is the difference between good friends and the "in crowd"? *(Possible response: Good friends last longer.)* **Ask:** Do you agree with the article? For instance, do you think students who are a part of the "in crowd" would be more or less likely to disagree? Explain. *(Responses will vary.)* OL

L Literary Element

Review Theme **Ask:** How do these quotes relate to the theme of the selection? *(Possible responses: Babyjohn's quote shows that he was not accepted by the in crowd at his old school. He now worries about being left out by his new "closest friends." This shows that he does not really believe the kids in the in crowd are true friends. Riverrunner actually says that she is happier with her few friends that are not in the popular group.)* OL

The Free Thinkers

What makes a kid less than popular? Sometimes it's the "wrong" clothes. Sometimes it's an embarrassing incident that a young person can't live down. And sometimes there's just no way of knowing.

"My friends and I are kind of the geeky group," says Zach McGraw,* a middle schooler in South Bend, Indiana. "I've wished I could be popular millions of times. But I've managed to find a good group to hang out with."

Kids like Zach might find a new friend or a group to hang out with outside of school—at church, synagogue,[1] martial arts classes, book clubs, or summer camps. Seeking out others with similar interests is often a good place to start trying to fit in and to develop relationships.

Having one good friend whom you can connect with makes a world of difference. When you like who that person is and can trust that person—then you have a true friendship that will last. Good friends build us up and help us feel confident about ourselves. They will most likely be around long after the in crowd is just a memory. **4** R

IN THEIR OWN WORDS:

Kids Talk About Popularity

Want to know what other teens really think about cliques, geeks, and being cool? Read on for the innermost thoughts of middle schoolers.

BABYJOHN: "At my old school I didn't have many friends. When I moved, I was suddenly accepted into the in crowd. But I have bad memories of being unpopular, and I sometimes worry that my closest friends will exclude me." L

RIVERRUNNER: "I had no real friends for about one-third of the year. When I finally thought I had found a true friend, she said to me that a different girl we hang out with was 'popular,' that she was '**semipopular**,' and that 'no offense, but you're a total geek.' **5** Now we just don't ever talk, and I am more happy with the not-so-popular group. And I have a few friends outside of school that I hang out with."

* Name and location have been changed to protect privacy.

1. A ***synagogue*** is a Jewish house of worship.

4 Key Reading Skill

Analyzing In these two paragraphs the writer is giving advice. How does that advice support the idea that "it's more important to have a few close friends . . . and be comfortable with the people you do hang out with"?

5 English Language Coach

Word Families The words *unpopular* and **semipopular** belong to the same word family. What is their base word?

Additional Support

Reading in the Real World

Citizenship Have students poll other students in your school. Direct the class to write a short paragraph that asks students to respond to the question of popularity. Then have the class create a "Question of Popularity" polling box with the paragraph attached. Put the box in the lunchroom or other place in the school. Students can then write their responses anonymously and put them in the box. After about a week, have the class read the various responses and discuss whether or not they are surprised by any of them. OL

CHERRY-COLA: "Lately, I have been feeling so unhip. I buy clothes and jewelry that make me seem more like everyone else. I feel as though I have to keep updating myself so that other people won't think I'm a loser. How you dress has everything to do with who you are."

TESTSCHIK182: "My best friend of five years was put in classes with all of the popular people. She'll do anything to be in the in crowd. I am definitely not a dork, but I'm not popular. [My best friend] has started to ignore me in the hall. How can I talk to her without feeling like an idiot? Her new friends aren't true friends at all."

MARISSA: "At the beginning of this year, the most popular guy in school liked me. I had tons of friends. But toward the middle of the year, Mr. Popular dumped me. Now I'm really lonely, I get made fun of a lot, and most kids don't like me."

HAPPY DUDE: "I get teased, hit, punched. I don't know if I should hit them back or just run away; I feel that rips apart my courage and self-confidence. I don't know what to do." 6

SHORTY11: "During the school year, I was rejected and not invited to parties, movies, etc. But once the summer began, I met new people who accepted me for who I was, not for the clothing I wore or for my looks. So my advice to other kids is to hang on to the friends you've got and make an effort to meet new people." 7

—Updated 2005, from *Family Life*, August 2001

6 **Text Element**

Direct Quotations Everybody quoted in this section is a kid. What makes the kids experts on this topic?

7 BIG Question

Why do some kids find it difficult to stay true to themselves when making friends? Write your answer on "The Question of Popularity" page of Foldable 5. Your response will help you complete the Unit Challenge later.

Teach

R1 Reading Skill

Review Connecting Have students write for five to ten minutes about the quote they connect with the most and why. Ask partners to share their writing with each other. *(Responses will vary.)* OL

R2 Reading Skill

Analyzing **Ask:** How do each of these quotes relate to the author's point that it is better to have a few close friends? *(Responses will vary.)* OL

BQ BIG Question

Ask: What does this article suggest will help you stay true to yourself? *(Possible response: finding a few close friends who like you for who you are, without making you feel the need to change)* AS

Assess

Use the CheckPoint questions provided on Presentation Plus! to check for comprehension of the selection. These questions can be used with interactive response keypads for immediate student feedback.

Differentiated Instruction

Advice Column Have students write an advice column that responds to one of the quotes on page 577. Give students copies of several different advice columns from newspapers and magazines. Instruct them to model their response after the style of one of these columns. Have students use computers to type in the quote and their response, making it look like a real column. Remind students to add the "Dear ___" line and "sign" the person's name at the end. Encourage students to be creative in thinking of a name for themselves as the advice giver. Display the different advice columns on a bulletin board. OL AL

Indiana English/Language Arts Academic Standards

SE: 8.1, 8.2

TWE: *Reading in the Real World* 8.3; *Differentiated Instruction* 8.4.6, 8.5.7

Assess

Resources for page 578

- Selection Quick Check, p. 42
- Selection and Unit Assessment, p. 50
- ExamView Assessment Suite
- Interactive Tutor: Self-Assessment

Students can respond to the *After You Read* items in their Learner's Notebooks or on a separate sheet of paper.

Answering the

1. Responses will vary.
2. The author describes the in crowd, the middle group, and free thinkers.
3. Possible response: The main idea of the article is that kids should look for a few good friends and not worry about being popular.

Critical Thinking

4. Possible response: The writer would say a good friend is someone who likes you just the way you are, has similar interests, and is someone you can trust.
5. Responses will vary. Students should include reasons for their responses.
6. Responses will vary.

After You Read

The Question of Popularity

Sean Murphy/Stone/Getty Images

Answering the 

1. In your opinion, is staying true to yourself more important than being popular? Why or why not?
2. **Recall** According to the writer of the article, what three groups do middle school students fall into?
   TIP **Think and Search**
3. **Summarize** Sum up the article's main idea and most important supporting details in a few sentences.
   TIP **Think and Search**

Critical Thinking

4. **Infer** What two or three qualities would the writer say make a good friend? Why?
   TIP **Author and Me**
5. **Connect** Review the quotations at the end of the article. Do they help you connect to the article? Give reasons for your answer.
   TIP **Author and Me**
6. **Evaluate** Did the writer succeed in convincing you of her opinion? Why or why not? Support your answer with details from the article.
   TIP **Author and Me**

Write About Your Reading

Essay Write a short essay to express your opinion about social groups in your school. Consider these questions before you begin to write.

- Are social groups important to most kids in middle school?
- Is there any advantage to belonging to a particular social group?
- What are the different social groups in your school?

Be sure to state your opinion clearly in your introduction. Give convincing supporting details to explain and elaborate on your opinion.

Indiana English/Language Arts Academic Standards (pp. 578–579)

8.5.7 Write for different purposes… **8.2 Comprehension and Analysis (Focus on Informational Text)** Develop [reading] strategies…identifying and analyzing structure, organization, perspective, and purpose. **8.1 Word Recognition, Fluency, and Vocabulary Development** Understand…word parts and relationships… **8.6 English Language Conventions 8.6.8** Identify…participles…and infinitives…

For a complete description of the standards, see p. IN 11.

Write About Your Reading

Sample essay:

My school has many social groups. Three of the groups are the jocks, the geeks, and the popular kids. In some ways it is good to belong to a group because then you have some friends and you have a place to "belong." Usually the groups are pretty closed, and they are mean to kids in other groups. I wish there were fewer cliques and we could get along better.

Skills Review

Key Reading Skill: Analyzing

7. When you analyzed the selection, what evidence did you find to support that main idea? Did your analysis make you think there should be more evidence? Explain your answer.

Text Element: Direct Quotations

8. What do the student quotations add to the article? Give examples from the article to support your answer.

Vocabulary Check

Answer each sentence *true* or *false.* Rewrite every false statement to make it true.

9. Watching too much TV can be a factor in the grades a student receives.
10. An obnoxious person is friendly and helpful.
11. A majority is always less than half of the total.
12. **English Language Coach** Find at least three words in the article that belong to the same word family as *friend.* Create a word web like the one below for this word family.

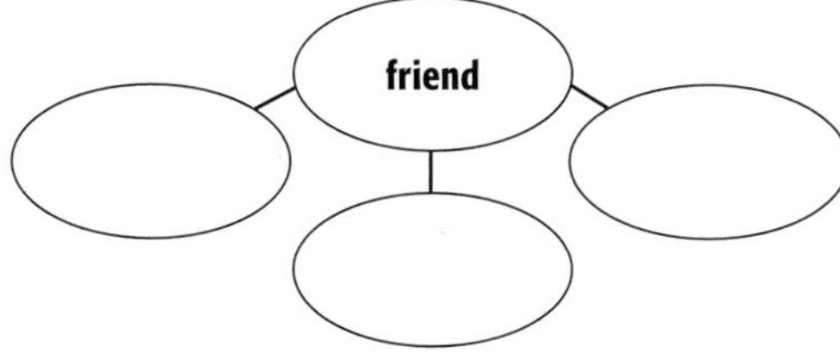

13. **Academic Vocabulary** Is the main idea of an article the most or least **significant** idea in the whole selection? Explain.

Literature Online

Web Activities For eFlashcards, Selection Quick Checks, and other Web activities, go to www.glencoe.com.

Grammar Link: Clauses and Phrases as Parts of Speech

A clause can take the place of a one-word part of speech in a sentence. A phrase also can take the place of a one-word part of speech.

Noun clauses take the place of nouns.

- Whoever scores the next point wins.

Adjective clauses take the place of adjectives.

- The ball, which he had hit hard, soared high.

Adverb clauses take the place of adverbs.

- When he hit it, the ball soared over our heads.

Prepositional phrases begin with a preposition and end with a noun or pronoun. They take the place of adjectives or adverbs.

- The chapter about the rescue was exciting.

(The prepositional phrase *about the rescue* functions as an adjective to describe the noun *chapter*.)

- The rescue team pulled the dog from the river.

(The prepositional phrase *from the river* functions as an adverb to describe the verb *pulled*.)

Verbal phrases act as nouns, adjectives, or adverbs.

As Noun: Bicycling in the mountains is hard work.

As Adjective: Staring outside, she saw rain.

As Adverb: We will hike to exercise.

Grammar Practice

Copy the underlined phrases on a separate sheet of paper. Write which part of speech each one is.

14. We built a feeder to feed wild birds.
15. However, squirrels climbed into the feeder.
16. They ate all the seeds that we placed there.
17. Stopping the squirrels was hard.

Writing Application Underline two clauses or phrases you used as parts of speech in your essay.

Skills Review

Key Reading Skill: Analyzing

7. Responses will vary.

Text Element: Direct Quotations

8. Possible response: The quotations make the article more believable. The author is not just giving her opinion about middle schoolers.

Vocabulary Check

9. true
10. false. An obnoxious person is not friendly and helpful.
11. false. A majority is always more than half of the total.

English Language Coach

12. Possible response: unfriendly, friendships, friends

Academic Vocabulary

13. The main idea of an article is the most significant idea in the whole selection.

Close

Ask students to tell how reading "The Question of Popularity" helps them answer the Big Question.

Grammar Link: Clauses and Phrases as Parts of Speech

Grammar Practice

14. adverb
15. adverb
16. adjective
17. noun

Literature Online

Web Activities Have students access the Web site for interactive activities that will help them assess their understanding of the selection.

Indiana English/Language Arts Academic Standards
SE: 8.1, 8.2, 8.5.7, 8.6, 8.6.8

Short Story

Teaching Students to Write a Short Story

Why Is It Important?

- Using imagination to create a short story will help students differentiate between fact and fiction.
- Writing a short story will help students recognize literary elements such as plot, character, setting, and dialogue in what they read.
- Becoming authors of short fiction will help students practice writing on non-academic subjects.
- Writing a fictional story is a way to share attitudes and feelings about life through made-up characters and events.
- Students will gain a deeper understanding of different organizational structures by practicing this form of narrative.

How to Help Students Get It

- The short story selections in this unit can serve as models for students. Remind students to notice elements and ideas that other authors use and borrow those structures for their own creations.
- To begin writing, students may need to review "Medicine Bag" or "Fire Pond" and pay attention to the structure of the plot. Both are written in sequential order, a good structure for beginning writers.
- Encourage students to think about what will happen first in their stories, what will happen to develop the conflict, and what will happen to resolve the conflict. They may want to use a graphic organizer to compile their thoughts.
- Contrast "short fictional story" with "autobiographical narrative." Remind students that while autobiography is about something that happened to the author, fiction is about made-up events.
- Fiction can be fun! Remind students that unlikely or impossible things can be part of the plot of a short story.
- Make sure students can identify the climax of their story and the actions that lead up to it.
- Discuss the different ways point of view can impact the telling of a story: Has the writer told the story from the most logical point of view?
- Encourage students to use details to draw their characters and move the story along.
- Highlight the importance of conflict and resolution. If nothing happens, there's no story. On the other hand, the reader will feel unsatisfied if the main problem goes unsolved.

Writing Trait	Student Checklist
Ideas	the message or the theme and the details that develop it
Unit Focus **Organization:** the arrangement of main points and supporting details	• Are the beginning, middle, and end clearly linked? • Is the order of ideas easy to follow? • Does the introduction capture readers' attention? • Do sentences and paragraphs flow from one to the next in a way that makes sense? • Does the conclusion wrap up the composition?
Voice	a writer's unique way of using tone and style
Word Choice	the vocabulary a writer uses to convey meaning
Sentence Fluency	the smooth rhythm and flow of sentences that vary in length and style
Conventions	correct spelling, grammar, usage, and mechanics
Presentation	the way words and design elements look on a page

Workshop Resources

Pacing (Days) Standard	Block	Lesson	Student Materials	Teacher Resources
1	1/2	Writing Workshop Part 1: Prewriting and Drafting	Writing Workshop Graphic Organizer, p. 14 Grammar Practice, p. 15 Spelling and Handwriting Practice, p. 44 Grammar and Composition Handbook, p. 194 Real Success in Writing: Research and Reports	TeacherWorks Plus™ Presentation Plus! Rubrics for Assessing Student Writing, Listening, and Speaking, p. 25 Grammar and Writing Workshop Transparencies 9–10
2	1	Writing Workshop Part 2: Editing, Revising, and Presenting	Interactive Grammar and Language Workbook Grammar and Composition Handbook, p. 194 Real Success in Writing: Research and Reports Listening and Speaking, p. 27 Viewing and Representing, p. 28	Grammar and Writing Workshop Transparencies 26–27 Interactive Grammar and Language Workbook Rubrics for Assessing Student Writing, Listening, and Speaking, p. 25

Focus

BELLRINGER Options

Daily Language Practice Transparency 45

Focus Activity Ask: What kinds of conflicts do students in middle school face today? Talk about how students struggle to stay true to themselves. *(Responses will vary.)* AS

Teach

L1 Literary Element

Character Ask: What might a reader want to know about the characters in a story? *(Responses will vary.)* OL

L2 Literary Element

Plot Ask: What are conflict and resolution? *(The conflict is the struggle; the resolution is the end of the struggle.)* BL

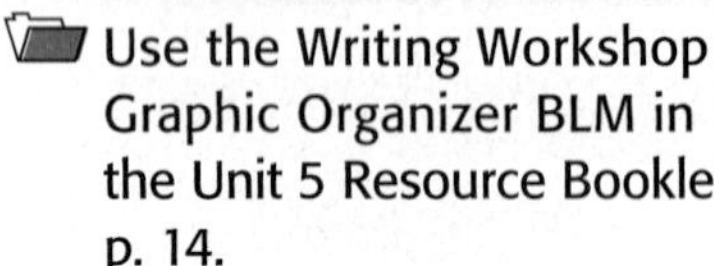

Resources for page 580

Use the Writing Workshop Graphic Organizer BLM in the Unit 5 Resource Booklet p. 14.

Use the Grammar and Writing Workshop Transparencies 9–10

WRITING WORKSHOP PART 1

Short Story

Prewriting and Drafting

ASSIGNMENT Write a short story

Purpose: To tell a story about a character who struggles to stay true to himself or herself

Audience: Your teacher and your classmates

Writing Rubric

As you write your short story, you should

- stay focused on the conflict in your story (how someone struggles to stay true to himself or herself)
- give readers details about the setting of the story
- create well-developed characters
- develop a plot with a clear beginning, conflict, and resolution
- use realistic dialogue

See pages 631–632 in Part 2 for a model of a short story.

Indiana English/ Language Arts Academic Standards (pp. 580–583)

8.5.1 Write…short stories… **8.4 Processes and Features** Prewriting and drafting. **8.6.1** Use correct and varied sentence types…to present a lively and effective personal style. **8.6 English Language Conventions**

For a complete description of the standards, see p. IN 11.

When you read a short story, you have the opportunity to connect to the characters, learn something about the world, and learn something about yourself. When you write a short story, you do the same thing, except *you* get to decide what happens in the story.

Writing about a character's personal struggle, or conflict, will help you think about the Unit 5 Big Question: How do you stay true to yourself? As you write your short story, refer to the **Writing Handbook,** pp. R17–R27.

Your story should have the basic elements you find in short stories.

- **Characters** are the actors in the story. They are *who* the story is about.
- **Conflict** is the struggle or problem your main character must solve. It's *what* the story is about. Conflict is developed through plot, which is the sequence of events that occurs in the story.
- **Setting** is the place and time in which the story happens. It's *where* and *when* the events take place, and it is usually conveyed through descriptive details.
- **Resolution** is the story's final outcome. It tells *how* the conflict is solved.
- **Dialogue** is conversation between characters. It helps readers understand what the characters are like and moves the plot forward.

Prewriting

Get Ready to Write

The following guidelines can help you plan and write your story, but you don't have to follow them word for word. Remember that you're in charge of your own writing process. You already know your story will be about a character's struggle to stay true to herself or himself, but you'll need to think about the character and the conflict before you start writing.

Gather Ideas

At this stage, start picturing whom and what you want to write about. Character and conflict affect each other. For example, if your main character is a thirteen-year-old boy, the conflict should be something that someone his age would be likely to experience.

Additional Support

Literature Focus Lesson

Short Stories Have students spend several minutes visualizing what their characters look like and what happens in their stories. As they picture it, students can jot down any key words that will help them remember what they visualized. Have students who like to draw create a storyboard that shows the different events and characters in their stories. OL Students can also try describing the characters or events in their stories to partners. Tell them to include as many details as possible in their descriptions. The partner will then describe what they heard. Students should listen to see if their descriptions are clear and memorable. AL

Characters Think about the people in your story, starting with the main character. Picture each character in detail. What does he or she look like? How does he or she act? What is important to him or her? Take notes in a format that you find helpful. For example, you might list each character's traits, write a paragraph about each one, or make a word web for each one.

My protagonist will be Marisol, a teenager with long black hair and gentle eyes. She is a great soccer player and plays for her school team. She is very close to her grandmother, who lives with the family.

Literature Online

Writing Models For models and other writing activities, go to www.glencoe.com.

Conflict List the events of your story in the order they'll happen. Or if you prefer, start by writing a scene that reveals the conflict.

- What causes the conflict?
- How will the main character stay true to himself or herself?
- How will the conflict be resolved?

If you don't know what to write about, think about your own experiences with trying to stay true to yourself. Or think about people you know and their struggles. Then use your imagination to add fictional details. For example, your main character might not want to go to an event with his family, or friends might be pressuring her to do something, or a brother or sister might ask him to help cover up a mistake they made. L1

Writing Tip

Sequence Most stories are told in chronological order: first this happened, then that happened, and then the next thing happened. That form of organization is usually easiest for readers to follow.

Marisol didn't know what to do. She didn't want to quit the soccer team, but she wanted to spend more time with her grandmother because she knew her grandmother wouldn't be around much longer.

Setting Describe where and when your story will take place. Use sensory imagery, such as descriptions of sights, smells, and sounds. L2

Part of the story will take place at Marisol's school, and part will take place at her house, which will smell like her abuela's wonderful cooking.

Writing Tip

Vivid Details Details that paint pictures in readers' minds include sensory imagery that appeals to the senses (the *sweet, crunchy tang* of honey chicken), vivid verbs (*ambled* instead of *walked*), specific nouns (*tulip,* not *flower*), and effective modifiers (*rusted-out* car with a *crumpled fender*).

Differentiated Instruction

Flow Chart Students may benefit from drawing a flow chart to map out the sequence of events in their story.

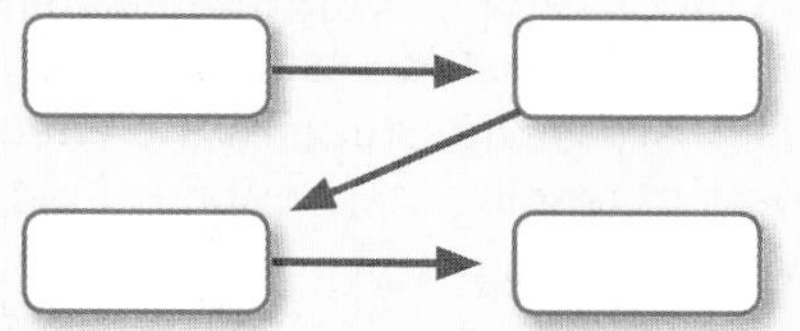

Write a list of transitional words on the board that indicate chronological order *(first, next, then, finally)*. Ask students to diagram their story using transitional words to show the sequence of events. Give students time to then use their diagram to write their story. Ask students what they found helpful about using a flow chart to write their stories. OL

Teach

Writing Models Have students access the Web site for an additional and interactive Writing Workshop-based student model.

L1 Literary Element

Conflict Ask: What kinds of conflicts would cause a character to struggle with staying true to himself or herself? *(Possible response: Conflicts that force a character to think about his or her values.)* Lead the class in a discussion of different ideas for conflicts in their stories. Guide students by offering ideas that you might use for a conflict in a story about a character who struggles to stay true to himself or herself. OL

L2 Literary Element

Imagery Say: Onomatopoeia is the use of words that sound like the object they refer to, such as "shhh" or "clip clop." One great way to appeal to the sense of hearing is to include onomatopoeia in your writing. OL

Ask students to think of other ways to use imagery that appeals to the senses in their stories. *(Responses will vary.)* AL

Indiana English/Language Arts Academic Standards

SE: 8.4, 8.5.1

TWE: *Literature Focus Lesson* 8.4.1; *Differentiated Instruction* 8.4.1, 8.4.10

Teach

W1 Writing

Dialogue Tell students they do not have to use the "he said, she said" model for all of their dialogue. When there is a lot of running dialogue, there may be no need to identify the speakers each time they speak. However, the writer will need to add identifiers to some quotes, so the reader does not get confused. Write examples of running dialogue on the board that do not identify the speakers every time they speak. Also write examples of dialogue that use verbs like "yelled" or "cried" to show students different ways to add variety to their dialogue. AS

W2 Writing

Suspense Use the following questions to help students build suspense in their stories:

- Does your story build suspense, or does it give the ending away too soon?
- Which clues or information can you take out in order to build more suspense?
- How else can you keep the interest of your readers?

Discuss ways for students to engage readers in their stories and keep their interest. *(Responses will vary.)* OL

Drafting

Start Writing!

Now that you have ideas about the basic elements of your story, it's time to start writing the first draft–your first version of your story.

Get It on Paper

To draft your short story, use the notes you made. Some of the decisions you made about your story may change as you write. That's OK. Just keep writing. If you're not sure how to begin your story, try these tips.

- Reread your prewriting. Underline words, phrases, or sentences you like.
- W1 Start with dialogue. Have two characters start talking, and see what they have to say. Dialogue can tell you a lot about the characters as well as the conflict. Writing dialogue is a good way to get ideas flowing.

Writing Tip

Getting Started Writing a short story should be fun. Don't make it into work. Relax and use your imagination. If your imagination runs dry, talk to friends or family members about your story.

Develop Your Draft

Writers do a lot of different things to make their writing exciting to read. Look at the writing you've done so far. Use these tips to develop your draft.

1. Use details and descriptions to *show* your readers the characters, setting, and events. Specific and vivid details help to bring readers into the story and create a clear picture in their minds.

Tears came into Marisol's eyes. Her grandmother looked so small and weak. Marisol pushed back her hair, pulled her jean jacket tighter, and ran to catch the bus.

2. W2 Short stories keep readers interested by building suspense–making the reader wonder what is going to happen next. Help readers understand the conflict so they are interested in how the conflict is resolved.

What was she going to do? She loved playing soccer, but she loved her grandmother more. If she didn't play, would she lose all her friends?

Writing Tip

Show; Don't Tell To make your writing more vivid, don't tell what characters feel. Show their reactions instead. Don't write "She felt angry." Write "She slammed her fist into her hand. Her face grew red."

Additional Support

Reading Fluency

Reading Aloud and Revising

Writing Have each student give a draft of his or her story to a partner. Ask students to read their partners' stories until they feel confident in their ability to read them fluently. Then have students read their partners' stories aloud to them. Ask students to listen as their stories are read for what they think is best about their stories and what they would change about them. After all of the stories have been read, have students revise their drafts. Discuss with students the effectiveness of reading their writing aloud as a revision strategy. OL

Grammar Link

You have learned that a **simple sentence** is an independent clause. **Compound** and **complex sentences** are made up of a combination of independent and dependent clauses.

What Are Compound and Complex Sentences?

A **compound sentence** contains two or more simple sentences (independent clauses) joined by a comma and a coordinating conjunction (*and, but, or, nor, for, so,* and *yet*). In the following compound sentence, the independent clauses are underlined.

- <u>The pears were ripe</u>, but <u>the plum was rotten</u>.

A **complex sentence** contains at least one independent clause and one dependent clause. In the following complex sentences, the independent clause is underlined.

- Though the pears were ripe, <u>the plum was rotten</u>.
- When I picked it up, <u>I could see</u> that the plum was rotten from sitting in the sun.

Why Are Compound and Complex Sentences Important?

Using a variety of sentence types makes your writing more interesting. A series of simple sentences can be choppy and awkward to read. Combining different types of sentences creates a more natural flow. Compare the following:

Simple sentences only: I had so much fun at the zoo last Saturday. The panda bears were very playful. Tonya and I watched them for over an hour. The cub climbed on his mother. She sent him tumbling to the ground.

Simple, compound, and complex: I had so much fun at the zoo last Saturday. The panda bears were very playful, and Tonya and I watched them for over an hour. When the cub climbed on his mother, she sent him tumbling to the ground.

How Do I Use Compound and Complex Sentences?

Use a **compound sentence** to combine two ideas that are equally important.

- *The music was great.* + *The cake was delicious.* = The music was great, and the cake was delicious.

Use a **complex sentence** to combine ideas when one idea "depends on" another to make sense. Put the main idea in the independent clause. Put the idea that "depends on" the main idea in the dependent clause. The independent clause is underlined.

- *I slept in.* + *My alarm didn't go off.* = Because my alarm didn't go off, <u>I slept in</u>.

Write to Learn Reread your draft. Add variety and make your short story flow more smoothly by combining sentences to form compound and complex sentences.

Looking Ahead

Keep the writing you did here, and in Part 2 you'll learn how to turn it into a short story that you'll be proud of.

WRITING WORKSHOP PART 1

Teach

W Writing

Compound and Complex Sentences Ask students to read the compound and complex sentences in their stories and make sure that each sentence has at least one independent clause. If students are not sure, write an independent clause on the board and diagram the components that make it an independent clause. Guide students as they look for the independent clauses in their stories and identify the compound and complex sentences. OL

Assess

Have students exchange their drafts with a partner and critique each other's work. Tell students to see if their partners have done a good job of showing more than they tell. They should also check to be sure the conflict is realistic for the characters in the story. After a few minutes, tell students to assess their partners' comments, make any needed revisions, and save their papers for later use. OL

English Language Coach

Compound and Complex Sentences Have students practice changing simple sentences into compound and complex sentences. Direct students to begin by writing a simple sentence. Then have students choose a conjunction *(but, and, nor, or, for, so, yet)* and add a dependent or an independent clause to the sentence. Challenge students to add another clause to the first one. For example, *I rode my bike to school today, but it rained in the afternoon so my mom had to pick me up after school.* EL Ask students to go through their short stories and experiment with adding more compound and complex sentences to their writing. OL

Indiana English/Language Arts Academic Standards
SE: 8.4, 8.5.1, 8.6, 8.6.1
TWE: *Reading Fluency* 8.4.7, *English Language Coach* 8.6.1

READING WORKSHOP 2

Questioning

UNIT 5

Teaching Students Questioning Strategies

Why Is It Important?

- Questioning strategies help students monitor their comprehension.
- Questioning strategies are fundamental to engaging in inquiry.
- Questioning strategies are central to peer-led discussion.
- Questioning strategies are essential for students to demonstrate what they have learned in a variety of assessment settings.

How to Help Students Get It

- Make sure that students understand the relationship between the question asked and the source(s) of information for answering the question.
- Tell students that information can be found in their own background knowledge and experiences as well as in the texts they read.
- Emphasize to students that different types of questions are asked before, during, and after reading.
- Teach students strategies that will align well with particular types of questions (e.g., skimming and scanning in response to questions that ask for text details; making inferences in response to questions that ask the reader to fill in gaps or read between the lines). Model these strategies for students.

Reading to Answer the Big Question

an african american by Meri Nana-Ama Danquah
This poem explores what it means to be an African American. The speaker identifies as strongly with her birth country, Ghana, as she does with her adopted country, the United States. Instead of choosing one over the other, she stays true to herself by choosing both.

One Throw by W.C. Heinz
The New York Yankees are scouting Pete Maneri, but Pete is almost ready to give up. He's a good baseball player, but it looks as if he'll be stuck in the minor leagues. When Eddie Brown, talent scout for the Yankees, makes a suggestion he says is sure to get Pete noticed by the team, Pete has an important decision to make. Will he deliberately mess up the game, or will he play to the best of his abilities, no matter what? Pete chooses to stay true to himself.

Workshop Resources

Pacing (Days) Standard	Block	Lesson	Student Materials	Teacher Resources
1	1/2	Key Skill Lesson: Questioning	Key Reading Skills Practice, p. 16 English Language Coach Review, p. 41	Bellringer Options Transparencies –Daily Language Practice 46 Read Aloud, Think Aloud Transparencies –Key Reading Skills 19 Presentation Plus!
1	1	"an african american"	Glencoe Online Unit Vocabulary Review, p. 39 Academic Vocabulary Review, p. 42 English Language Coach Active Reading Graphic Organizer, p. 17 StudentWorks Plus™ Online Student Edition Literature Classics Selection and Unit Assessments, p. 51	Literary and Text Analysis Transparencies 25 Puzzlemaker Skill Level Up!™ A Language Arts Game BookLink 3 Assessment by Learning Objective (Diagnostic and Formative) Interactive Tutor: Self-Assessment TeacherWorks Plus™
1		"One Throw"	Glencoe Online Unit Vocabulary Review, p. 39 Academic Vocabulary Review, p. 42 English Language Coach Active Reading Graphic Organizer, p. 20 Literary Analysis, p. 19 StudentWorks Plus™ Online Student Edition Literature Classics Selection and Unit Assessments, p. 52	Read Aloud, Think Aloud Transparencies –Read Aloud, Think Aloud 37–44 Literary and Text Analysis Transparencies 37 Puzzlemaker Skill Level Up!™ A Language Arts Game BookLink 3 Assessment by Learning Objective (Diagnostic and Formative) Interactive Tutor: Self-Assessment TeacherWorks Plus™

Keys for Unit Resource

- Blackline Master
- Workbook
- Supplemental Text
- CD-ROM
- DVD
- Transparency
- Web-based
- Fast File

Level Appropriate Code

AS = Activities for all students
AL = Activities for students working above grade level
OL = Activities for students working at grade level
BL = Activities for students working below grade level
EL = Activities for English language learners

Focus

BELLRINGER Options

Daily Language Practice Transparency 46

Focus Activity Say: Suppose you could only use one or two words to describe yourself. What word or words would they be and why? *(Responses will vary.)* AS

Teach

R Reading Skill

Questioning Walk students through the questioning process by having them discuss a story the class has recently read and is familiar with. Pause along the way to write down a question you might ask yourself as you are reading. Then model how finding the answer to that question leads to another question. BL

V Vocabulary

Academic Vocabulary

Say: Read the definition of the word *conversation* at the bottom of this page. Now write a short paragraph describing what Barry and his brother are doing in the cartoon. Include the word *conversation* in your description. *(Responses will vary.)* EL BL

READING WORKSHOP 2

Skills Focus

You will practice using these skills when you read the following selections:

- "an african american," p. 588
- "One Throw," p. 596

Reading

- Questioning in order to improve comprehension

Literature

- Interpreting the effects of literary devices
- Analyzing features and styles of poetry
- Identifying and analyzing the plot elements in a story
- Explaining how conflict is related to the plot

Vocabulary

- Using suffixes to determine meaning
- Academic Vocabulary: *conversation*

Writing/Grammar

- Using commas in compound and complex sentences

Indiana English/ Language Arts Academic Standards (pp. 584–585)

8.2 Comprehension and Analysis (Focus on Informational Text) Develop [reading] strategies such as asking questions…

For a complete description of the standards, see p. IN 11.

Skill Lesson

Questioning

Learn It!

R **What Is It? Questioning** is asking yourself questions about what you are reading. By asking and answering your own questions, you keep a **conversation** with yourself—a conversation that helps you better understand what you read. You might ask about people or characters in a selection. You might ask about the importance of what you're reading. Or you might ask about anything that puzzles you. Here are some sample questions.

- Who are the people or characters?
- How does one event relate to another?
- What is the main idea or theme?

Analyzing Cartoons

To find out about vultures, Barry questions his brother. To better understand the cartoon, you might ask yourself, *How does Barry's first question lead to his second question?*

V **Academic Vocabulary**

conversation (kon vur SAY shun) *n.* a talk between people

Additional Support

Differentiated Instruction

Research Questions Have students choose a topic they would like to learn more about by doing research. Discuss the process of coming up with good research questions before starting research. Have students write five research questions they have about their topic. Guide students to come up with questions that can be answered through research. OL Have students go to the library or use the Internet to answer their questions and report to the class about their research process and what they learned about their topic. AL

Why Is It Important? By asking questions, you make sure you understand what you are reading. As you answer your questions, you also keep track of important ideas and details.

How Do I Do It? As you read, stop from time to time and ask yourself questions. Many helpful questions begin with the 5Ws and an H: Who? What? When? Where? Why? How?

Literature Online

Study Central Visit www.glencoe.com and click on Study Central to review questioning.

Look at how a student used questions to understand the following passage.

Dad pedaled like mad, flapped his paper wings, and . . . nothing happened. Unless, of course, riding into the pond counts.

As I ran to help him, I heard Grandma shout, "You're going to break your fool head riding that contraption of yours, Sam McKenzie!"

She hates Dad's inventions. I love them—and Dad. When he finally manages to build the first successful flying machine, we'll be rich.

R

I can hardly wait for that day, because right now, to be perfectly honest, we're poor. We might not have a roof over our head if it weren't for Grandma.

Dad spends most of his time and money on his inventions. The old barn is filled with metal parts.

What is the father in the story riding? I think it must be some kind of bike, because it says he "pedaled like mad." But it also says he "flapped his paper wings." Hmmm. The narrator says they'll be rich when his dad invents a successful flying machine. So the "contraption" must be a kind of flying machine with wheels, pedals, and wings.

Practice It!

Who do you think is telling the story? When do you think it takes place? Write your answers in your Learner's Notebook.

Use It!

As you read the selections, ask yourself 5Ws and an H questions. Answer your questions in your Learner's Notebook.

Teach

Literature Online

Study Central Have students access the Web site to review questioning and to complete a related activity.

R Reading Skill

Questioning Guide students as they think of other questions the student might ask as he or she continues reading the story. *(Possible responses: Where is the dad going to fly the machine once he gets it working? Why does the family need money? How does Grandma support the family?)* OL

Resources for page 585

Use Key Reading Skills Transparency 19 in *Read Aloud, Think Aloud* to help students practice questioning.

Reading Fluency

Questioning Poetry Guide students as they write questions before they read "an african american." Write the title of the poem and the 5Ws and H questions on the board. Have each student write one question for "an african american." Model good pre-reading questions for students. Then have students share their questions with the class. Discuss questioning as a pre-reading strategy for students to use before they read any text. Tell students to keep track of the answers to their questions as they read the poem. OL Challenge students to develop new questions that use the 5Ws and H as they read the poem and learn more about its subject. AL

Indiana English/Language Arts Academic Standards
SE: 8.2
TWE: *Differentiated Instruction* 8.4.11, *Reading Fluency* 8.2

Teach

More About the Author

When Meri Nana-Ama Danquah first came to the United States, she lived with her mom who had come three years earlier. Her father joined them later. Her childhood home in Washington, D.C., was filled with African art. This poem is one of many works in which Danquah describes her life as a woman of two continents—Africa and North America.

V Vocabulary

Write to Learn Have students read aloud their paragraphs using the vocabulary words. Ask students to watch for these words as they read the poem. AS

EL Language Coach

Suffixes Have students think of other words for each of the suffixes listed in the chart. Write the new words on the board. *(Responses will vary.)* EL BL Have students write a short paragraph that includes at least six of the new words.*(Responses will vary.)* OL

Before You Read an african american

Meet the Author

Meri Nana-Ama Danquah was born in Ghana, West Africa, and raised in Washington, D.C. In addition to being an accomplished actress, poet, playwright, and performance artist, she is the author of a memoir, *Willow Weep for Me,* and the editor of two anthologies: *Becoming American* and *Shaking the Tree.* She divides her time between Los Angeles, California, and Accra, Ghana.

Author Search For more about Meri Nana-Ama Danquah, go to www.glencoe.com.

Indiana English/Language Arts Academic Standards (pp. 586–591)

8.1 Word Recognition, Fluency, and Vocabulary Development Understand… word parts… **8.2 Comprehension and Analysis (Focus on Informational Text)** Develop [reading] strategies such as asking questions… **8.3.6** Identify significant literary devices…

For a complete description of the standards, see p. IN 11.

Vocabulary Preview

mimicked (MIM ikt) *v.* copied; imitated; form of the verb *mimic* **(p. 589)** *Keesha mimicked the girls' laughter, hoping they would include her in their conversation.*

unison (YOO nih sun) *n.* one voice **(p. 590)** *The chorus sang in perfect unison at the school assembly.*

anthem (AN thum) *n.* the official song of a country, school, or group **(p. 590)** *The band plays its school's anthem before every game.*

V **Write to Learn** Write a paragraph using all the vocabulary words.

English Language Coach

Introduction to Suffixes A **suffix** is a word part that is added to the end of a root or base word. If you think about the meaning of the root or base and the suffix, you may be able to figure out the meaning of the word. Suppose, for example, that you see the word *flutist* in the following sentence: *Donna is an excellent flutist.* If you know that the suffix *-ist* means "person who," you can guess that a *flutist* is a person who plays the flute.

EL

A suffix may change more than a word's meaning. It may also change the word's part of speech. For example, adding the suffix *-er* to the verb *teach* makes the word *teacher,* which is a noun. Look at the suffixes listed on the chart below. You'll see some of them in "an african american." When any of these suffixes is added to a word, the word usually becomes a noun.

Suffix	Meaning	Word Example
-an, -ian	"person who"	musician
-ance,	"action or process of"	performance
-ence	"quality or state of"	existence
-ation, -ion	"action of or result of"	invention
-ist	"person who"	artist
-ness	"state, quality, or condition of"	sadness

Write to Learn Make each word below a noun by adding one of the suffixes above to it. Use a dictionary if you need help.

dark • reflect • assist • special

Additional Support

Author Search To expand students' appreciation of Meri Nana-Ama Danquah, have them access the Web site for additional information and resources.

Differentiated Instruction

Poetic License This term describes the fact that poets do not always follow the rules of grammar, punctuation, usage, and pronunciation. As students read "an african american," they will immediately notice the poem does not use capitalization. Have them try to identify any other rules the poet seems to ignore. *(For example, she does not use any punctuation except for possessive apostrophes.)* OL Challenge students to think of reasons the poet may have ignored these rules in this poem. *(Possible responses: She is writing about two different worlds and using the language of one of them to do it. Maybe by not following Standard English she is able to show that she is also African, not just American.)* AL

Skills Preview

Key Reading Skill: Questioning

The selection you are about to read is a poem. Think about the questions you might have as you read a poem. Here are some examples:

- Who is the speaker?
- What is the speaker describing?

Write to Learn In your Learner's Notebook, write three other questions you might ask about a poem.

Literary Element: Sensory Imagery

Artists use colors, shapes, and patterns to pull you into their paintings. One way that writers pull you into their work is by using **sensory imagery,** or descriptions that appeal to the five senses.

Sensory imagery helps readers imagine how something looks, sounds, feels, smells, and tastes. Poets use sensory imagery to make their poems come alive and help readers connect to people, places, events, and ideas. As you read poetry, use these tips to find and understand sensory imagery. L

- Notice descriptions of sights, sounds, textures, odors, and tastes. Ask yourself, *What do these details add to the selection?*
- Think about the speaker in the poem who makes the descriptions. Ask yourself, *What do the speaker's descriptions tell me about him or her?*

Partner Talk With a partner, discuss which senses the following sentences appeal to.

- When Ted bit into the shiny red apple, the fruit was so crisp that it snapped. With every crunchy bite he savored its sweetness.

Interactive Literary Elements Handbook
To review or learn more about the literary elements, go to www.glencoe.com.

Get Ready to Read

Connect to the Reading

R Have you ever moved to a new neighborhood, city, or country? Think of what it would be like to adjust to life in a new place. How would you try to fit in? Would you act differently, or would you try to stay the same?

Partner Talk With a partner, list some things you might have to get used to if you moved someplace new.

Build Background

In the poem, the speaker mentions places in Africa and places in the United States.

- Washington, D.C., the capital of the United States, is on the east coast between Maryland and Virginia. The initials *D.C.* stand for District of Columbia. According to the last government census, or "head count," more than 550,000 people live in Washington, D.C. More than half the population identify themselves as African American or black.
- Atlanta is the capital of Georgia, a southern U.S. state. States that border Georgia are North Carolina, South Carolina, Florida, Alabama, and Tennessee. About 400,000 people live in Atlanta. More than 60 percent of the population identify themselves as African American or black.

Set Purposes for Reading

BIG Question Read "an african american" to learn what values are important to the speaker in the poem and whether she is determined to stay true to herself.

Set Your Own Purpose What else would you like to learn from the poem to help you answer the Big Question? Write your own purpose on "an african american" page of Foldable 5.

Keep Moving

Use these skills as you read "an african american."

Teach

L Literary Element

Sensory Imagery **Ask:** What sensory imagery would you use to describe your home or neighborhood? Have students make a list of images for each of the five senses to describe either their home or their neighborhood. Ask for volunteers to read their list to the class. Have students comment on what they imagine from the list of images. *(Responses will vary.)* OL

R Reading Skill

Review Connecting Ask students who have moved from one city to another to tell what was most difficult to adjust to when they moved. *(Responses will vary.)* OL Discuss with students the skills necessary to adjust to a new place and a new culture. AS

Interactive Literary Elements Handbook Have students access the Web site to improve their understanding of sensory imagery.

Literature Focus Lesson

Imagery Before class, put a few items into several small brown bags, such as plastic fruit, a small toy car, and other small representatives of bigger items. Alternatively, you can put slips of paper into each bag with the names of things on them. Divide the class into small groups of three, giving each group one of the bags. Have the groups open their bags without showing the contents to any of the other groups. Ask students to write descriptions of each of the items, without naming them, using sensory imagery. Have them put the items back into the bags and then read their descriptions aloud to the class while other students guess what is being described. OL

Indiana English/Language Arts Academic Standards
SE: 8.1, 8.2, 8.3.6
TWE: *Differentiated Instruction* 8.3.1, *Literature Focus Lesson* 8.5.6

Teach

L1 Literary Element

Review Repetition **Ask:** What line is repeated in the first two stanzas of this poem? *(i wanna tell you a story)* BL Have students look for other lines that are repeated as they finish reading the poem. *(Possible responses: asante princess; african queen)* OL

L2 Literary Element

Review Symbols Remind students that poetry uses symbols even more than other works of literature. For example, in many works of literature, the word "black" may symbolize darkness, evil, or even death. This is not true of this poem. **Ask:** What does the poet mean when she describes the soil as black and the nation as black? *(Possible response: She is referring to the fact that most of the people living there are black.)* OL Tell students that if they don't see it already, as they read on, they will see that in this poem black is a positive symbol. AS

READING WORKSHOP 2

an african american

by Meri Nana-Ama Danquah

i wanna tell you a story
of washington, dc
of atlanta, georgia
of addis abbaba
of tangier, soweto and lagos*

i wanna shed some light
on the dark continent*
i wanna tell you a story
of me **1** L1

i stand before you
dark and proud
asante princess
african queen
born and bred
on black soil
in a black nation
they call ghana L2

i spoke the language
of my ancestors
i ate the food
planted by our mothers' hand
i danced the drumbeats
of our animist* gods

---

5 ***Addis Abbaba*** is the capital of Ethiopia in East Africa. ***Tangier*** is a city in Morocco in North Africa. ***Soweto*** is a group of townships in the country of South Africa. ***Lagos*** is a city in Nigeria in West Africa.

7 Europeans called Africa the ***dark continent*** in the nineteenth century because parts of it were so difficult for them to explore that they didn't know a lot about it.

23 An ***animist*** believes that all things in nature have a spirit or soul within them.

Practice the Skills

1 Key Reading Skill

Questioning Ask yourself these questions after reading the first few lines of the poem:

- *What is the title of the poem?*
- *How does the title relate to the places mentioned in the first nine lines? To the speaker?*

Then answer the questions.

Additional Support

Reading in the Real World

Citizenship Give students a map of Africa and have them locate the places that are named in the poem. Have them notice the distance between these cities and townships, especially how far some of them are from Ghana. Ask students to write for 5–10 minutes about why they think the poet included all of these other places in her poem when she is an immigrant from Ghana. OL Challenge students to research some of these places and find out about their similarities and differences in culture, climate, language, food, and ethnic groups. Create a bulletin board that displays all of the information students gathered about each place in Africa. AL

an asante princess
an african queen
who crossed the middle passage*
arrived in america
speaking very little english
with thick lips
and thick accent

unable to pronounce my name
people called me
the foreigner
the african girl
i went to school
with your daughters and sons
your cousins and friends
mimicked their speech
dressed their style
seemingly became one of them **2**

i wove my **blackness**
my **africanness** **3**
chameleon-like*
into the red, the white and the blue
which is the fabric of this nation
wanting desperately to belong

when i sleep
i snore with the lions and tigers
in the safari land
i snore with the sounds
of the noontime traffic on georgia avenue
in the district of columbia

R1

Analyzing the Photo How does the teenager in this photo illustrate one important aspect of the speaker's identity?

Practice the Skills

2 Literary Element

Sensory Imagery Which descriptions in lines 24–40 appeal to the sense of sight?

3 English Language Coach

EL

Suffixes Adding the suffix *-ness* to the adjectives *black* and *african* changes them into nouns. Review the meaning of *-ness;* then define the two nouns.

26. The ***Middle Passage*** was the journey that many slave ships took from West Africa across the Atlantic Ocean to the Americas.

43. A ***chameleon*** is a type of lizard that changes the color of its skin to fit in with its surroundings.

Vocabulary

mimicked (MIM ikt) *v.* copied; imitated

Reading Fluency

Reading Poetry Have students choose partners. Ask them to meet in a quiet place and take turns reading lines from "an african american." Have them practice reading until they feel confident that they can read the poem fluently with expression. Then ask partners to read the poem together to the class. EL BL

Encourage students to be creative while they read to the class by using props to perform the lines of the poem. For example, they could use a globe for lines 2–5 or an American flag for lines 44–45. Discuss what students enjoy about reading the poem and what they find difficult. OL

READING WORKSHOP 2

Teach

R1 Reading Skill

Review Connecting **Ask:** Have you had a similar experience with people not being able to pronounce your name or having trouble pronouncing someone else's name? How did you feel when someone pronounced your name wrong or when you were unable to pronounce another person's name? *(Responses will vary.)* AS **Ask:** Based on your experiences, how do you think the speaker felt when people could not pronounce her name? *(Responses will vary.)* OL

EL Language Coach

Suffixes Have students think of other words that have *-ness* as a suffix. Challenge students to use each word in a sentence. *(Responses will vary.)* EL

R2 Reading Skill

Questioning Have students ask questions in response to each stanza of the poem. *(Possible response: How did you weave your blackness into the red, white, and blue?)* OL Challenge students to use their questions in a call-and-response reading of a portion of the poem. Ask volunteers to read their questions after you read the lines of the poem. *(Responses will vary.)* AL

Indiana English/Language Arts Academic Standards
SE: 8.1, 8.2, 8.3.6
TWE: *Reading in the Real World* 8.3, *Reading Fluency* 8.7.14

Teach

L Literary Element

Sensory Imagery **Ask:** What do you think the speaker means when she says that the Mississippi River "croons" and the Nile "screams" to her? *(Possible response: She is using the Mississippi River as a symbol of the United States and the Nile River as a symbol of Africa, and saying that both of these worlds are part of who she is. She is reminded by the crooning and screaming of these "rivers" to be true to what it means to be American and what it means to be African.)* AL

C Critical Thinking

Analysis **Say:** The author includes two quotations at this point in the poem: "lift every voice and sing" and "africa, oh africa, cry freedom for all your children." What sources could you read to find out who she is quoting? *(Possible responses: a book of famous quotations; websites on quotations)* OL Challenge students to find the source of each quotation and report back to the class. AL

when i dream
the voices of jomo kenyatta, patrice lumumba
and dr. martin luther king, jr.*
speak to me in **unison**
when i cry
rain falls on the sahara
and the potomac river overflows* 4
i sway to alpha blondy*
as easily as i do stevie wonder

open your ears
my children
and listen to this griot*
talk of history
being made
i wanna tell you this story
of my life

the blood which flows
through the left side of my body
is the mississippi river
every day i wake it croons
"lift every voice and sing"
the **anthem** of the american negro

the blood which flows
through the right side of my body
is the nile river
every day i rise it screams out loud
"africa, oh africa, cry freedom
for all your children" 5

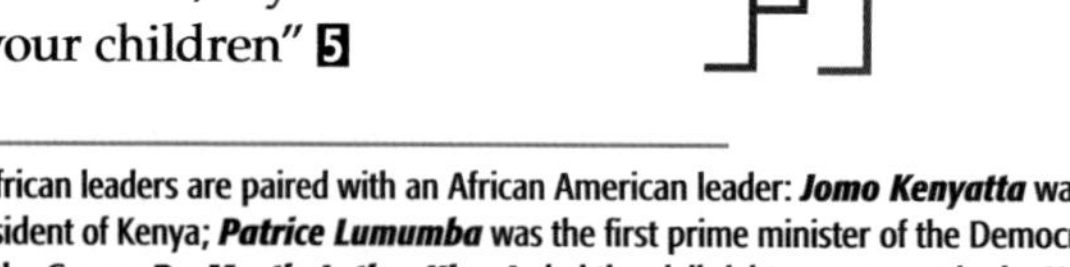

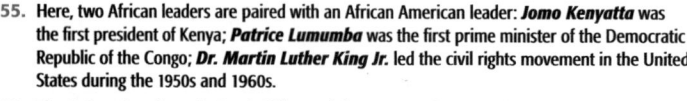

55. Here, two African leaders are paired with an African American leader: ***Jomo Kenyatta*** was the first president of Kenya; ***Patrice Lumumba*** was the first prime minister of the Democratic Republic of the Congo; ***Dr. Martin Luther King Jr.*** led the civil rights movement in the United States during the 1950s and 1960s.

59. The ***Sahara*** is a desert in North Africa, and the ***Potomac*** is a river that runs through Washington, D.C.

60. ***Alpha Blondy*** is a popular reggae musician from Ivory Coast in Africa.

64. A ***griot*** is a West African storyteller and musician who shares the history of his or her people.

Vocabulary

unison (YOO nih sun) *n.* one voice

anthem (AN thum) *n.* the official song of a country, school, or group

Analyzing the Photo In 1960 Patrice Lumumba became the first prime minister of the Democratic Republic of the Congo. He was assassinated in 1961. What do you learn about him in this photo?

Practice the Skills

4 Literary Element

Sensory Imagery A person crying doesn't really create rain in the desert or make a river overflow. What idea is the author trying to get across here?

5 Key Reading Skill

Questioning To what does the speaker compare the blood flowing through her body? Reread lines 69–80 to help yourself answer this question.

Additional Support

Differentiated Instruction

Build Background Most students are familiar with Dr. Martin Luther King, Jr. and his work in the Civil Rights Movement. As such, they should know that he was not an elected official or a government leader in the way that Jomo Kenyatta and Patrice Lumumba were. Lead students in a discussion about why the poet would list these three men together. Assign small groups of students to research one of the men. Ask them to create a timeline for the life of each man, which includes all important events. Have students display their timelines in the class. Discuss how each man impacted the world. OL

don't think me confused
because i don't know
where home is anymore
i just know
that the veins
in the body from the right and the left
flow to the heart
and become one love

if i die on african soil
bury me in jeans and sneakers
let my tombstone read in english
"native **washingtonian**"
and sing an old negro spiritual for me please **6**

if i die on american soil
pour libation* on the ground
lay a flag of red, green and gold
with a black star*
on my coffin
let the talking drums spread the news
let the words on my tombstone
be multi-lingual and let them scream
asante princess
african queen **7**

let no one question my origin
let me live and die in peace
as who i am
because you see
i have broken all barriers
of love and unity
i am
in the truest sense of the word
an african american **8** ❍

R

95. To ***pour libation*** is to pour wine or oil on the ground as an offering to the gods in a religious ceremony.

97. The flag of Ghana has ***red, green, and gold bands with a black star.***

Practice the Skills

6 English Language Coach

Suffixes Washington is a place. How does adding the suffix *-ian* change the meaning? What is a **Washingtonian**?

7 Literary Element

Sensory Imagery What sound imagery is in lines 100–104?

8 BIG Question

BQ In this poem, the speaker defines who she is. How does she stay true to herself? Write your answer on "an african american" page of Foldable 5. Your response will help you complete the Unit Challenge later.

READING WORKSHOP 2

Teach

R Reading Skill

Review Analyzing **Ask:** What does the speaker want people to do for her depending upon where she dies? *(If she dies in Africa, she wants to be buried in American clothing with her tombstone written in English. If she dies in America, she wants a traditional African funeral with the flag of Ghana draped over her coffin and her tombstone written in more than one language.)* **Ask:** How does this help show her as an African American? *(Possible response: She wants to be remembered as both.)* **OL**

BQ BIG Question

Ask: What advice do you think Meri Nana-Ama Danquah would give you about staying true to yourself? *(Possible response: She would tell me not only to remember what my roots are, but also to remember what culture or other influences are part of my life today.)* **OL**

CheckPoint

Use the CheckPoint questions provided on Presentation Plus! to check for comprehension of the selection. These questions can be used with interactive response keypads for immediate student feedback.

Differentiated Instruction

Write a Poem Challenge students to write their own poems about their identities. Instruct students to begin the writing process by thinking about what aspects of their identities are important to them. Have students brainstorm the following ideas:

- words you use to identify yourself
- family traditions that help define you
- activities you do that help define you

Have students read their completed poems or create a bulletin board on identity and post student poems there. **OL** **AL**

Indiana English/Language Arts Academic Standards

SE: 8.1, 8.2, 8.3.6

TWE: *Differentiated Instruction* 8.3, 8.5.3; *Differentiated Instruction* 8.5.7

Assess

Resources for page 592

- Selection Quick Check, p. 43
- Selection and Unit Assessment, p. 51
- ExamView Assessment Suite
- Interactive Tutor: Self-Assessment

Students can respond to the *After You Read* items in their Learner's Notebooks or on a separate sheet of paper.

Answering the BIG Question

1. Responses will vary.
2. The speaker is from Ghana.
3. Students should explain that she would want traditional African rituals performed.

Critical Thinking

4. She compares her journey across the Atlantic Ocean to the passage African slaves made hundreds of years before her.
5. Responses will vary. Students may feel that she is like a chameleon because she fits into both the American and African worlds and changes to fit her surroundings.
6. Responses will vary.

After You Read

an african american

Answering the BIG Question

1. How does the speaker of this poem remain true to herself?
2. **Recall** What part of Africa is the speaker from?
   TIP **Right There**
3. **Recall** What does the speaker want if she dies on African soil?
   TIP **Right There**

Critical Thinking

4. **Interpret** To what does the speaker compare her journey to America, and how is that important?
   TIP **Author and Me**
5. **Analyze** In lines 41–44 the speaker compares herself to a chameleon, saying, "i wove my blackness / my africanness / chameleon-like / into the red, the white and the blue." In what way or ways do you think that the speaker is like a chameleon?
   TIP **Author and Me**
6. **Evaluate** In your opinion, is the title "an african american" a good one for the poem? Back up your opinion with details from the poem.
   TIP **On My Own**

Talk About Your Reading

Whole Class Discussion Throughout the poem, the speaker describes the "African side" of her and the "American side" of her. As a class, reread the poem to find all the examples she gives of her "Africanness" and all the examples she give of her "Americanness." Record your findings on a chart like the one pictured below. Then discuss how identifying the examples helps you understand the poem.

African Side	American Side

Indiana English/Language Arts Academic Standards (pp. 592–593)

8.3 Comprehension and Analysis of Literary Text Respond to grade-level-appropriate literature... **8.7.11** Deliver oral responses to literature... **8.2 Comprehension and Analysis (Focus on Informational Text)** Develop [reading] strategies such as asking questions... **8.3.6** Identify significant literary devices... **8.6 English Language Conventions**

For a complete description of the standards, see p. IN 11.

Talk About Your Reading

Possible responses:

African Side	American Side
addis ababa tangier, soweto and lagos dark and proud, asante princess, african queen, black soil, black nation, ghana spoke the language of ancestors danced the drumbeats of animist gods thick lips, thick accent snore with the lions and tigers jomo kenyatta, patrice lumumba nile river	washington, dc atlanta, georgia went to school with your daughters and sons, mimicked their speech, dressed their style snore with the sounds of noontime traffic on georgia avenue in the district of Columbia dr. martin luther king, jr. potomac river mississippi river

Skills Review

Key Reading Skill: Questioning

7. How did questioning help you understand the speaker and the poem? Write two questions that you wrote in your Learner's Notebook and explain how they helped you.

Literary Element: Sensory Imagery

8. The poem contains a lot of imagery that appeals to the senses of sight and sound. List at least five examples of each. Include a line number for each image you list.

Vocabulary Check

Fill in each blank with the word that makes sense in the sentence.

mimicked • unison • anthem

9. The dancers performed in ______ and won first prize at the competition.
10. When the apes ______ human expressions, the people were amazed.
11. Many countries have their own national ______.
12. **Academic Vocabulary** If you are having a **conversation,** what are you doing?

English Language Coach For each noun below, write its base word and the suffix that makes it a noun.

13. flirtation
14. fairness
15. European
16. clearance

Web Activities For eFlashcards, Selection Quick Checks, and other Web activities, go to www.glencoe.com.

Grammar Link: Commas in Compound Sentences

The most basic kind of **compound sentence** contains two or more simple sentences (independent clauses) joined by a comma and a coordinating conjunction (*and, but, for, nor, or* and sometimes *so* and *yet).*

- Uma couldn't come to our get-together, and Joanne missed it, too.

  (The first simple sentence is "Uma couldn't come to our get-together." The second simple sentence is "Joanne missed it, too." The comma and conjunction *and* join the simple sentences.)

- I like watching martial arts like karate, but I do not want to learn them myself.

  (The first simple sentence is "I like watching martial arts like karate." The second simple sentence is "I do not want to learn them myself." The comma and conjunction *but* join the simple sentences.)

Look Out! If both simple sentences in a compound sentence are short—five words or less—you can omit the comma. In all other compound sentences, put a comma before the coordinating conjunction.

- Uma performs well and she enjoys learning.

  (Both simple sentences are three words long. Because they are short, the comma can be omitted.)

- Uma performs well in her karate class, and she enjoys learning new moves.

  (The comma is needed because the first simple sentence is more than five words long.)

Grammar Practice

Add a comma to each compound sentence that needs one.

17. I like to fly kites and I like to skateboard.
18. Ellie has had the chicken pox but she has never had the measles.
19. I finished cutting the grass so now I can go out.

Grammar Link: Commas in Compound Sentences

Grammar Practice

17. (no comma needed)
18. Ellie has had the chicken pox, but she has never had the measles.
19. (no comma needed)

Close

Ask students to summarize how they would answer the Big Question after reading "an african american."

Skills Review

Lesson Skill: Questioning

7. Answers will vary.

Literary Element: Sensory Imagery

8. Answers will vary. Possible response: **Sight:** stand before you dark and proud (lines 10–11), danced the drumbeats (line 22), thick lips (line 29), bury me in jeans and sneakers (line 90), lay a flag of red, green and gold with a black star on my coffin (lines 96–98) **Sound:** spoke the language of my ancestors (lines 18–19); the drumbeats (line 22), thick accent (line 30) the sounds of traffic on georgia avenue (line 51), the voices of jomo kenyatta, patrice lumumba and dr. martin luther king, jr. (lines 54–55)

Vocabulary Check

9. unison
10. mimicked
11. anthem

Academic Vocabulary

12. Possible response: I am talking with someone else.

English Language Coach

13. flirt, ation
14. fair, ness
15. Europe, an
16. clear, ance

Indiana English/Language Arts Academic Standards
SE: 8.2, 8.3, 8.3.6, 8.6, 8.7.11

Teach

More About the Author

W. C. Heinz began his writing career as a sports editor for his college newspaper at Middlebury College in Vermont. He then went to work for the *New York Sun.* During World War II, he worked as a reporter in Europe. After the war, he came back to the United States and worked again for the *Sun*. He wrote his own column titled "The Sport Scene" for several years. Heinz wrote about many sports but seemed to have a particular interest in boxing. In fact, he won four awards for boxing stories.

V Vocabulary

Verb Usage Point out to students that the verb "egging" is generally used with "on." Write the example sentence given at the top of page 594 on the board. Underline the word "egging" and the word "on." Have students use "egging" in a sentence. *(Responses will vary.)* BL EL

Before You Read

One Throw

W. C. Heinz

Meet the Author

W. C. Heinz worked as a reporter in Europe during World War II and afterward became a sports editor. Besides articles he has written fiction and nonfiction books about sports. He is also the coauthor of the novel *MASH,* which inspired a movie and a TV series. *See page R2 of The Author Files in the back of the book for more on W. C. Heinz.*

Author Search For more about W. C. Heinz, go to www.glencoe.com.

Indiana English/Language Arts Academic Standards (pp. 594–601)

8.1 Word Recognition, Fluency, and Vocabulary Development Understand...word parts...**8.2 Comprehension and Analysis (Focus on Informational Text)** Develop [reading] strategies such as asking questions...**8.3 Comprehension and Analysis of Literary Text** Respond to grade-level-appropriate literature...identifying...plot...

For a complete description of the standards, see p. IN 11.

Vocabulary Preview

egging (EG ing) *v.* urging; encouraging to take action; form of the verb *egg* **(p. 600)** *The boys said, "Do it!" egging their brother on until he finally took the dare.*

needle (NEE dul) *v.* cause to take action by repeated stinging comments **(p. 601)** *Your teasing remarks will not needle me into doing anything.*

English Language Coach

Other Common Suffixes You've already learned that adding a suffix to a word can change the word's meaning and part of speech. Remember that learning what common suffixes mean can help you unlock the meaning of unfamiliar words—especially in conjunction with context.

Study the common suffixes and their meanings below. You'll see some of these suffixes in the selection you are about to read, "One Throw."

Suffix	Meaning	Word Example
-er, -or	"that which" or "person who"	baker, sailor
-hood	"state, condition, or quality of"	neighborhood
-ment	"action or process of" or "result of"	arrangement
-ship	"state, condition, or quality of"	friendship

Partner Talk Which suffixes from the chart above could be added to the words below? With a classmate, find the suffix that goes with each word. Use a dictionary if necessary. Discuss how adding the suffix changes the word's meaning.

1. enjoy
2. child
3. speak
4. citizen

Additional Support

Author Search To expand students' appreciation of W.C. Heinz, have them access the Web site for additional information and resources.

Literature Focus Lesson

Surprise Endings "One Throw" has a surprise ending. Discuss why authors will sometimes write endings that surprise readers. To familiarize students with surprise endings, bring in a book of short stories or poems. Read a poem or story to the class and leave out the ending. Have students write their own ending to the text you read. Then have them read their endings to the class. OL Read another poem or story and challenge students to write an ending that surprises readers. AL

Skills Preview

Key Reading Skill: Questioning

Before you read "One Throw," think about questions you might ask yourself to understand the plot, characters, and theme of the short story. Here are some sample questions you might ask:

R
- *Who are the main characters?*
- *What causes a character to act a certain way?*
- *How does one event lead to another?*

Partner Talk With a partner, add questions to the list that you could ask yourself as you read. Write your questions in your Learner's Notebook. Refer to them as you read the story, and jot down answers to them.

Key Literary Element: Plot

L

Plot is the sequence of events in a fictional story in which a problem is explored and then solved. Plot is created through **conflict**—a struggle within or between people or forces. A plot has these parts:

1. **exposition**—the beginning that introduces the characters, setting, and conflict
2. **rising action**—the complications that arise as the protagonist faces the conflict
3. **climax**—the most emotional or suspenseful point in the story
4. **falling action**—the events that show how the conflict will probably work out
5. **resolution**—the outcome of the conflict

Whole Class Discussion "One Throw" is about a young baseball player who plays in the minor leagues. From this situation, what conflicts do you think you might find in the story? Make a list. Then read the story to see whether you guessed right.

Interactive Literary Elements Handbook
To review or learn more about the literary elements, go to www.glencoe.com.

Get Ready to Read

Connect to the Reading

Recall a time when a friend gave you advice that you thought was bad. Did you follow the advice?

Write to Learn In your Learner's Notebook, jot down a few sentences describing what the advice was, whether you followed it, and why.

Build Background

To understand "One Throw," you need to know a little about baseball's minor leagues and major leagues. Here is some background on those subjects.

- A *league* is a group of teams that play each other.
- The different minor leagues have groups of teams that play at different levels. Players who have good skills and who show promise are often moved up to a higher-level minor-league team.
- The best minor-league players are asked to join major-league teams. There, the players are the most skilled, and the competition is tough.
- These are the highest levels of the minor leagues:
  - –Class AAA, sometimes called the "parking lot" because so many good players are "parked," or held on reserve, there
  - –Class AA, home to many experienced players hoping to enter U.S. baseball from foreign leagues
  - –Class A, where many promising young players work on improving their skills

Set Purposes for Reading

BIG Question Read "One Throw" to discover how a ballplayer stays true to himself.

Set Your Own Purpose What else would you like to learn from the story to help you answer the Big Question? Write your own purpose on the "One Throw" page of Foldable 5.

Keep Moving

Use these skills as you read "One Throw."

Teach

R Reading Skill

Questioning Have students read aloud the questions they wrote in their Learner's Notebooks for *Partner Talk*.
Ask: How do you think writing down these questions will help you as you read the story? *(Responses will vary.)* OL

L Literary Element

Plot Have students use the elements of plot to make up their own story about something that happened in your school. Have students identify the exposition, rising action, climax, falling action, and resolution of the story. Ask for volunteers to map or diagram their stories on the board. AL

Interactive Library Elements Handbook Have students access the Web site to improve their understanding of plot.

Differentiated Instruction

Mapping Activity Have students research the world of professional baseball. Ask them to find out which minor league teams are affiliated with each major league team and where these minor league teams play. Students can make a map showing the different major and minor league teams using a color-coded system or legend to identify each league. *(For example, blue for major leagues, red for Class A minor leagues, and yellow for Class AA minor leagues.)* Challenge students to find out how much an average player in each league earns. Have students present their maps and findings to the class. OL

Indiana English/Language Arts Academic Standards
SE: 8.1, 8.2, 8.3
TWE: *Literature Focus Lesson* 8.5.2, *Differentiated Instruction* 8.7.12

Teach

C Critical Thinking

Comprehension **Say:** The hotel worker says that Maneri is "down." What does he think is the cause of this? *(Possible response: He thinks it is because Maneri wants to be playing for the Yankees, but he is stuck playing ball in a small town.)* OL

L Literary Element

Plot **Say:** In the beginning of this story, the author gives us a lot of information. Where does this story take place? *(a small town)* **Ask:** Who are the characters so far? *(the narrator, the guy at the hotel desk, and Maneri)* **Ask:** What do you imagine the conflict in this story will be? *(Possible response: something to do with Maneri wanting to play for the Yankees)* OL

R Reading Skill

Questioning **Ask:** What questions could you ask about this story after reading the first page? *(Responses will vary.)* Have students make a list of their questions to answer as they read the story. OL

Baseball at Night, 1934. Morris Kantor. Oil on linen. Smithsonian American Art Museum.

One Throw

by W. C. Heinz

I checked into a hotel called the Olympia, which is right on the main street and the only hotel in the town. After lunch I was hanging around the lobby, and I got to talking to the guy at the desk. I asked him if this wasn't the town where that kid named Maneri played ball.

"That's right," the guy said. "He's a pretty good **ballplayer**." 1

"He should be," I said. "I read that he was the new Phil Rizzuto."[1]

"That's what they said," the guy said.

"What's the matter with him?" I said. "I mean if he's such a good ballplayer what's he doing in this league?"

"I don't know," the guy said. "I guess the Yankees[2] know what they're doing."

"He's a nice kid," the guy said. "He plays good ball, but I feel sorry for him. He thought he'd be playing for the Yankees soon, C and here he is in this town. You can see it's got him down." 2

1. ***Phil Rizzuto*** was the star shortstop for the New York Yankees in the 1940s.
2. The ***Yankees*** were the dominant baseball team in the major leagues in the 1940s and 1950s.

Practice the Skills

1 English Language Coach

More Common Suffixes A **ballplayer** is someone who plays ball. Look at how the word *ballplayer* is formed: ball (noun) + play (verb) + er (suffix).

2 Key Literary Element

Plot In this beginning part of the plot, called *exposition*, you learn a little about the setting, the characters, and a possible conflict to come. L

Additional Support

Readability Scores
Dale-Chall: 3.3
DRP: 44
Lexile: 670

Reading in the Real World

Career Professional athletes are idolized in American culture. The media often represents them as living an easy life while making a great deal of money. Have students research the work that goes into being a professional athlete. Use the library and Internet sources to have students read about the pros and cons of a career as a professional athlete. OL Hold a debate about whether professional athletes earn their salaries or whether they live easy lives and are overpaid. AL

"He lives here in this hotel?"

"That's right," the guy said. "Most of the older ballplayers stay in rooming houses,[3] but Pete and a couple other kids live here."

He was leaning on the desk, talking to me and looking across the hotel lobby. He nodded his head. "This is a funny thing," he said. "Here he comes now."

The kid had come through the door from the street. He had on a light gray sport shirt and a pair of gray flannel slacks.

I could see why, when he showed up with the Yankees in spring training,[4] he made them all think of Rizzuto. He isn't any bigger than Rizzuto, and he looks just like him.

"Hello, Nick," he said to the guy at the desk.

"Hello, Pete," the guy at the desk said. "How goes it today?"

"All right," the kid said but you could see he was exaggerating.

"I'm sorry, Pete," the guy at the desk said, "but no mail today." 3

"That's all right, Nick," the kid said. "I'm used to it."

"Excuse me," I said, "but you're Pete Maneri?"

"That's right," the kid said, turning and looking at me.

"Excuse me," the guy at the desk said, introducing us. "Pete, this is Mr. Franklin."

"Harry Franklin," I said.

"I'm glad to know you," the kid said, shaking my hand.

"I recognize you from your pictures," I said.

"Pete's a good ballplayer," the guy at the desk said.

"Not very," the kid said.

"Don't take his word for it, Mr. Franklin," the guy said.

"I'm a great ball fan," I said to the kid. "Do you people play tonight?"

"We play two games," the kid said.

"The first game's at six o'clock," the guy at the desk said. "They play pretty good ball."

"I'll be there," I said. "I used to play a little ball myself."

"You did?" the kid said.

"With Columbus," I said. "That's twenty years ago."

"Is that right?" the kid said. . . .

C

L

3. ***Rooming houses*** are private houses where the owners rent out rooms.

4. ***Spring training*** is a period in late winter and early spring when baseball players prepare for the regular playing season.

Practice the Skills

3 Key Reading Skill

Questioning What do you think Pete is hoping will come in the mail? Why do you think so?

Differentiated Instruction

Act It Out Have pairs of students act out the scene in the hotel lobby. Before students start acting, have them think about how each character will sound. Encourage students to be creative while portraying the characters in a way that is consistent with the story. Have students play the roles of Mr. Franklin, Pete, and the guy at the hotel desk. You may also have students play the roles of other hotel guests. These guests might interrupt Pete and Mr. Franklin in order to say hello or ask questions about the game that night. OL

Teach

L Literary Element

Review Characterization
Ask: How does Pete Maneri respond when Nick compliments his playing? *(He says he's not really that good of a ballplayer.)* BL **Ask:** What might this tell you about Pete? *(Possible response: He is modest and does not like to brag, or he really doesn't think he's that good.)* OL

C Critical Thinking

Comprehension Say: This part of the story is almost all dialogue. Sometimes a writer will use dialogue to give readers important information in a story. What do you learn from this dialogue? *(Responses will vary.)* Have students summarize this page of dialogue in three or four sentences. Ask students to read their summaries to a partner. AL

R Reading Skill

Questioning Ask: Why do you think Mr. Franklin is so interested in Pete Maneri? *(Responses will vary.)*
Ask: What other questions do you have about the story? Have students write their questions in their Learner's Notebooks. *(Responses will vary.)* OL

Indiana English/Language Arts Academic Standards
SE: 8.1, 8.2, 8.3
TWE: *Reading in the Real World* 8.7.13, *Differentiated Instruction* 8.7

Teach

Viewing the Art

Ask: How can you tell that this picture is from a time very different from our own? *(Possible responses: The fans are dressed more formally; the men are wearing hats and suits. No one is wearing jeans or baseball caps. The stands are old.)* **Ask:** How would a picture of today's baseball stands look different? *(Responses will vary.)* **OL**

R Reading Skill

Questioning **Ask:** What kind of stories do you think Mr. Franklin told? *(Possible response: He told stories about the days when he used to play baseball.)* **Ask:** Why do you think Pete was a "real good listener"? *(Responses will vary.)* **OL** **Ask:** What other questions do you have about the story? *(Responses will vary.)* **AS**

EL Language Coach

Suffixes Put a list of verbs on the board *(play, enjoy, dance)*. Ask students to add suffixes to them to change them into other words. Have students define each word they make with a suffix. *(Responses will vary.)* **EL**

READING WORKSHOP 2

#71 Minor League, 1946. Clyde Singer. Oil on canvas. Butler Museum of American Art, Youngstown, OH.

Analyzing the Painting How does this picture capture the "feel" of a minor-league baseball game?

That's the way I got to talking with the kid. They had one of those pine-paneled taprooms[5] in the basement of the hotel, and we went down there. I had a couple and the kid had a Coke, and I told him a few stories and he turned out to be a real good **listener.** **4** **R**

"But what do you do now, Mr. Franklin?" he said after a while.

"I sell hardware,"[6] I said. "I can think of some things I'd like better, but I was going to ask you how you like playing in this league." **EL**

"Well," the kid said, "I suppose it's all right. I guess I've got no kick coming." **5**

"Oh, I don't know," I said. "I understand you're too good for this league. What are they trying to do to you?"

"I don't know," the kid said. "I can't understand it."

"What's the trouble?"

"Well," the kid said, "I don't get along very well here. I mean there's nothing wrong with my playing. I'm hitting .365 right now. I lead the league in stolen bases. There's nobody can field with me, but who cares?" **6**

"Who manages this ball club?"

"Al Dall," the kid said. "You remember, he played in the outfield for the Yankees for about four years."

5. A ***pine-paneled taproom*** is a bar with pinewood paneling on the walls.

6. In this context, ***hardware*** is tools and equipment made from metal.

Practice the Skills

4 English Language Coach

Suffixes *Listen* is a verb. What happens when you add the suffix *-er* to this verb? Define **listener.**

5 Skill Review

Making Inferences What do you think Pete means when he says, "I guess I've got no kick coming"? Write your answer in your Learner's Notebook.

6 Key Literary Element

Plot Pete seems to be experiencing an inner conflict. What do you think that conflict is?

Additional Support

Reading in the Real World

Career Tell students that one of the most important skills in most careers is knowing how to work well with others. Lead the class in a discussion about the advantages and disadvantages of working in a group or on a team. Ask students to consider such questions as:

- Who makes the decisions?
- How many people are there to do the work?
- Who gets the credit?
- What is hardest about working with a team?
- What do you like best about working with a team? **AS**

"I remember."

"Maybe he is all right," the kid said, "but I don't get along with him. He's on my neck all the time."

"Well," I said, "that's the way they are in the minors sometimes. You have to remember the guy is looking out for himself and his ball club first. He's not worried about you." R2

"I know that," the kid said. "If I get the big hit or make the play he never says anything. The other night I tried to take second on a loose ball and I got caught in the run-down. He bawls me out in front of everybody. There's nothing I can do." R1

"Oh, I don't know," I said. "This is probably a guy who knows he's got a good thing in you, and he's looking to keep you around. You people lead the league, and that makes him look good. He doesn't want to lose you to Kansas City or the Yankees." 7

"That's what I mean," the kid said. "When the Yankees sent me down here they said, 'Don't worry. We'll keep an eye on you.' So Dall never sends a good report on me. Nobody ever comes down to look me over. What chance is there for a guy like Eddie Brown or somebody like that coming down to see me in this town?"

"You have to remember that Eddie Brown's the big shot," I said, "the great Yankee scout."[7]

"Sure," the kid said. "I never even saw him, and I'll never see him in this place. I have an idea that if they ever ask Dall about me he keeps knocking me down."

"Why don't you go after Dall?" I said. "I had trouble like that once myself, but I figured out a way to get attention."

"You did?" the kid said.

"I threw a couple of balls over the first baseman's head," I said. "I threw a couple of games away, and that really got the **manager** sore. 8 I was lousing up his ball club and his record. So what does he do? He blows the whistle[8] on me, and what happens? That gets the brass[9] curious, and they send down to see what's wrong." L

"Is that so?" the kid said. "What happened?"

"Two weeks later," I said, "I was up with Columbus."

"Is that right?" the kid said.

7. A ***scout*** is someone who looks for new, talented sports players.

8. To ***blow the whistle*** is to give information about wrongdoing to someone in charge.

9. Here, ***brass*** means people in high positions.

Practice the Skills

7 Key Reading Skill

Questioning Why does the narrator takes an interest in Pete?

8 English Language Coach

Suffixes The suffix *-er* changes the verb *manage* into a noun. Notice that the base word ends in an *e*, so you add only the *r* of the suffix.

READING WORKSHOP 2

Teach

R1 Reading Skill

Review Interpreting Ask: What does Pete mean when he says that Al Dall is on his neck all the time? *(He means that Al is always criticizing him.)*
Ask: Why do you think Al Dall criticizes Pete all the time? *(Possible response: He wants Pete to be the best player he can be.)* OL

R2 Reading Skill

Review Monitoring Comprehension Ask: Why does Mr. Franklin say that the manager is not worried about Pete? *(Possible response: He means that the manager has to think about the team and his own reputation and career. He cannot worry about the players or each player's feelings.)* OL

L Literary Element

Plot Say: The author is building the plot here and giving you information about the characters and the conflict of the story. How is the author keeping your attention? *(Responses will vary.)* **Ask:** What do you think is going to happen next in the plot? *(Responses will vary.)* OL

English Language Coach

Jargon Define *jargon* for students and discuss how baseball jargon helps make this story seem more real. Have students make a list of baseball words from this story. *(manager, player, scout, second-baseman, brass)* BL Then have students try to think of other words that have to do with baseball and add them to the list. *(pitcher, catcher, fan, umpire)* Finally, have students write their own simple definition or explanation for each word. OL Challenge students to come up with jargon that someone would need to know to understand the life of a student in middle school. AL

Indiana English/Language Arts Academic Standards
SE: 8.1, 8.2, 8.3
TWE: *Reading in the Real World* 8.3, *English Language Coach* 8.1

Teach

L1 Literary Element

Review Characterization **Ask:** What do you learn about these two characters from this conversation? *(Possible response: Mr. Franklin says he is "egging him on," so I learned that he is the kind of person who tries to get someone to do something or to be upset. Pete shows that he really does think he is a good player and is upset with his manager.)* OL

EL Language Coach

Context Clues **Ask:** What is a hard chance? *(a difficult play)* Have students explain how they used the context of the story to figure out the meaning of *hard chance.* OL

L2 Literary Element

Plot **Say:** At this point in the story, the writer begins to set up the conflict that will lead to the climax. What do you think the conflict will be? *(Possible response: whether or not Pete will try out Mr. Franklin's idea, and what will happen if he does try it out.)* **Ask:** What do you want Pete to do and why? *(Responses will vary.)* OL

"Sure," I said, **egging** him on. "What have you got to lose?"

"Nothing," the kid said. "I haven't got anything to lose." **9**

"I'd try it," I said.

"I might try it," the kid said. "I might try it tonight if the spot comes up."

I could see from the way he said it that he was madder than he'd said. Maybe you think this is mean to steam a kid up like this, but I do some strange things.

"Take over," I said. "Don't let this guy ruin your career."

"I'll try it," the kid said. **10** "Are you coming out to the park tonight?"

"I wouldn't miss it," I said. "This will be better than making out route sheets and sales orders."

It's not much ballpark in this town—old wooden bleachers and an old wooden fence and about four hundred people in the stands. The first game wasn't much either, with the home club winning something like 8 to 1.

The kid didn't have any hard chances, but I could see he was a ballplayer, with a double and a couple of walks and a lot of speed.

The second game was different, though. The other club got a couple of runs and then the home club picked up three runs in one, and they were in the top of the ninth with a 3–2 lead and two outs when the pitching began to fall apart and they loaded the bases.

I was trying to wish the ball down to the kid, just to see what he'd do with it, when the batter drives one on one big bounce to the kid's right.

Visual Vocabulary
A ***backhand*** catch is very difficult because the player's arm is twisted and the body is turned away from the ball.

The kid was off for it when the ball started. He made a backhand stab and grabbed it. He was deep now, and he turned in the air and fired. If it goes over the first baseman's head, it's two runs in and a panic—but it's the prettiest throw you'd want to see. It's right on a line, and the runner is out by a step, and it's the ball game. **11**

Vocabulary

egging (EG ing) *v.* urging; encouraging to take action

Practice the Skills

9 Key Reading Skill
Questioning What does Pete actually have to lose?

10 Key Reading Skill
Questioning What is the "it" that Pete says he will try?

11 Key Literary Element
Plot This is the climax, or moment of highest tension, when Pete makes an important decision. Did he decide to follow the narrator's advice? Explain.

Additional Support

Differentiated Instruction

Write a Baseball Glossary The writer uses a lot of baseball terms that will be familiar to some students and completely foreign to others. Write these phrases and words on the board and ask volunteers to explain what they mean.

- top of the ninth
- loaded the bases
- the batter drives one

Have students make a glossary of words that a reader would need to know to understand this story. BL OL Ask students who speak other languages to translate the glossary. Call attention to words that have no translation. EL

I walked back to the hotel, thinking about the kid. I sat around the lobby until I saw him come in, and then I walked toward the elevator like I was going to my room, but so I'd meet him. And I could see he didn't want to talk. EL

"How about a Coke?" I said.

"No," he said. "Thanks, but I'm going to bed."

"Look," I said. "Forget it. You did the right thing. Have a Coke."

We were sitting in the taproom again. The kid wasn't saying anything.

"Why didn't you throw that ball away?" I said.

"I don't know," the kid said. "I had it in my mind before he hit it, but I couldn't." **12**

"Why?"

"I don't know why."

"I know why," I said.

The kid didn't say anything. He just sat looking down.

"Do you know why you couldn't throw that ball away?" I said.

"No," the kid said.

"You couldn't throw that ball away," I said, "because you're going to be a major-league ballplayer someday."

The kid just looked at me. He had that same sore expression.

"Do you know why you're going to be a major-league ballplayer?" I said. C

The kid was just looking down again, shaking his head. I never got more of a kick out of anything in my life.

"You're going to be a major-league ballplayer," I said, "because you couldn't throw that ball away, and because I'm not a hardware salesman and my name's not Harry Franklin."

"What do you mean?" the kid said.

"I mean," I explained to him, "that I tried to **needle** you into throwing that ball away because I'm Eddie Brown." **13** R

Practice the Skills

12 **Key Literary Element**

Plot This is the falling action of the plot, when you begin to see how the resolution to the conflict will probably work out. The resolution is that Pete couldn't throw the ball away. Why couldn't Pete do it?

13 **BIG Question**

What do Pete's actions tell you about how he stays true to himself? Write your answer on the "One Throw" page of Foldable 5. Your response will help you complete the Unit Challenge later.

Vocabulary

needle (NEE dul) *v.* cause to take action by repeated stinging comments

READING WORKSHOP 2

Teach

EL Language Coach

Suffixes **Ask:** What is the base word and suffix of "elevator"? *(The base word is* elevate *and the suffix is* -or.*)* **Ask:** What does the word mean? *(Something that elevates or lifts up people or objects.)* BL

C Critical Thinking

Analysis **Ask:** Why does Mr. Franklin think that Pete's actions show him to be a great ballplayer? *(He cared more about the game than about his own personal gain.)* OL **Ask:** Why do you think Pete is confused about his own actions? *(Possible response: He's still trying to figure out why he did the right thing.)* AL

R Reading Skill

Review Monitoring Comprehension **Ask:** Who is Eddie Brown? *(He is a scout for the Yankees.)* **Ask:** What does it mean to Pete that Mr. Franklin is actually Eddie Brown? *(Possible response: It means that since Mr. Franklin is really the scout, Pete is most likely going to play for the Yankees.)* OL

Reading in the Real World

College There are many careers that involve working with athletes. Most of them require a college degree. Have students research the different fields that relate to athletics, like sports medicine and sports management. Break students into small groups and have each group answer the following questions about one field:

- What are the college degree requirements?
- What schools offer these degrees?
- How long do you have to study?
- What subjects do you have to study?

Have each group report back to the class on what they learned about the field they researched. OL

Indiana English/Language Arts Academic Standards

SE: 8.2, 8.3

TWE: *Differentiated Instruction* 8.1, *Reading in the Real World* 8.7.12

Assess

Resources for page 602

- Selection Quick Check, p. 44
- Selection and Unit Assessment, p. 52
- ExamView Assessment Suite
- Interactive Tutor: Self-Assessment

Students can respond to the *After You Read* items in their Learner's Notebooks or on a separate sheet of paper.

Answering the BIG Question

1. Pete stays true to himself by playing his best and not throwing the game.
2. He pretends to be a hardware salesman named Mr. Franklin.
3. His real name is Eddie Brown, and he's a recruiter for the Yankees.

Critical Thinking

4. Possible response: The narrator wants to see what Pete will do in the situation.
5. Possible response: He wants to know if Pete really cares about the game before he recruits him.
6. Possible response: One meaning of the phrase is that one throw, or one play, determined Pete's future. The other meaning of the phrase is that Pete was asked to "throw" the game just one time.
7. Responses will vary.

After You Read

One Throw

Answering the BIG Question

1. How did Pete stay true to himself?
2. **Recall** Whom does the narrator pretend to be?
   TIP **Right There**
3. **Recall** What is the narrator's real name and job?
   TIP **Right There**

Critical Thinking

4. **Infer** Why does the narrator keep his real identity a secret until his last conversation with Pete?
   TIP **Author and Me**
5. **Infer** Why does the narrator try to get Pete to throw a game?
   TIP **Author and Me**
6. **Interpret** The title "One Throw" has a double meaning. What are the two meanings of "throw" in this context?
   TIP **Author and Me**
7. **Analyze** Think about how Pete resolves his conflict and what happens to him at the end of the story. What theme, or message, do you think the story is trying to get across?
   TIP **Author and Me**

Write About Your Reading

Press Release Imagine that you work in the New York Yankees publicity office. You want to announce that Pete Maneri has just been signed by the team. In a small group, discuss how you would introduce the new player.

- Identify who Pete is. Include his age, the position he plays, and other personal information. Use facts from the story and your imagination.
- Describe his experience. Mention where he played before, what his statistics are as a player, and what his abilities are.
- Explain what the team's expectations are for his future.

When you are finished, write your press release and share it with the class.

Indiana English/Language Arts Academic Standards
(pp. 602–603)

8.3 Comprehension and Analysis of Literary Text Respond to grade-level-appropriate literature…identifying…plot…**8.5.7** Write for different purposes…**8.2 Comprehension and Analysis (Focus on Informational Text)** Develop [reading] strategies such as asking questions…**8.1 Word Recognition, Fluency, and Vocabulary Development** Understand…word parts…**8.6 English Language Conventions**

For a complete description of the standards, see p. IN 11.

Write About Your Reading

A sample press release is given.

The Yankee ball club is proud to announce that Pete Maneri has been added to our team roster. He will play his first game this Saturday against the Boston Red Sox. Maneri has shown his great talent while playing in the minor leagues in Olympia. He is from Minnesota and is very excited to be here in New York. His batting average is .365 and he leads the minors in stolen bases. At just 21 years of age, he has many years of great promise, and we look forward to what he will bring to this clubhouse.

Skills Review

Key Reading Skill: Questioning

8. Think back to the questions that you asked yourself while you were reading "One Throw." Did any of them prepare you for the surprise ending? Explain your answer.

Key Literary Element: Plot

9. What happens in each part of the plot of "One Throw"? Copy the graphic organizer below. Under each heading, list the events from the story that make up that part.

exposition	rising action	climax	falling action	resolution

Vocabulary Check

10. The verbs *egg* and *needle* are similar in meaning as slang words. Write a sentence using one of them. Then replace it with the other. Did you have to change anything else in the sentence?

English Language Coach Find the noun in each sentence below that was made by adding a suffix to a base word. On a separate sheet of paper, write the base word and the suffix for each sentence.

11. Joe hired a builder to make the kitchen larger.
12. The U.S. government has three main branches.
13. Part of a team's success depends on its leadership.
14. Juan was my favorite actor in the school play.

Grammar Link: Commas in Complex Sentences

A **complex sentence** contains at least one independent clause and one dependent clause. The clauses are joined by a subordinating conjunction, such as *after, although, because, before, if, since, unless, until, when,* and *while.*

When a complex sentence begins with an *independent* clause, it does not need a comma.

- We will have dinner when Curtis arrives.
  independent / dependent

When a complex sentence begins with a *dependent* clause, put a comma **after** the dependent clause.

- When Curtis arrives, we will have dinner.
  dependent / independent

Look Out! Do not put a comma after a subordinating conjunction. Put the comma after the whole dependent clause.

Wrong: Although, I studied I didn't do well on the quiz.
Right: Although I studied, I didn't do well on the quiz.

Grammar Practice

On a separate sheet of paper, copy the complex sentences below. Add commas where needed.

15. Eduardo has loved camping since he was a child.
16. When he was little he always pretended to camp out.
17. Once he is older he will save to buy a camper.

Web Activities For eFlashcards, Selection Quick Checks, and other Web activities, go to www.glencoe.com.

Skills Review

Key Reading Skill: Questioning

8. Responses will vary.

Key Literary Element: Plot

9. **Exposition:** A man meets Pete Maneri and introduces himself as Mr. Franklin; **Rising Action:** The man tells Pete that he should throw the game; **Climax:** Pete has to decide if he will throw the game or not. He chooses to play his best; **Falling Action:** Pete and Mr. Franklin talk after the game; **Resolution:** Mr. Franklin is really Eddie Brown and is going to recruit Pete.

Vocabulary Check

10. Responses will vary.

English Language Coach

11. build/er
12. govern/ment
13. leader/ship
14. act/or

Close

Ask students what they learned from reading "One Throw" to answer the Big Question.

Grammar Link: Commas in Complex Sentences

Grammar Practice

15. (no change)
16. When he was little, he always pretended to camp out.
17. Once he is older, he will save to buy a computer.

Literature Online

Web Activities Have students access the Web site for interactive activities that will help them assess their understanding of the selection.

Indiana English/Language Arts Academic Standards
SE: 8.1, 8.2, 8.3, 8.5.7, 8.6

Predicting

Teaching Students to Predict

Why Is It Important?

- Predicting helps readers monitor comprehension when they compare what they had expected to read to what they have actually read.
- Predicting engages students more actively with the texts they read.
- Predicting is a familiar skill that can serve as a good example of how using reading strategies enhances comprehension.

How to Help Students Get It

- Point out that reading is an interactive process involving both the reader and the author.
- Emphasize that using background knowledge (including what they have already read in the text) to make a prediction is one way to become more engaged with what they read.
- Predicting is one way to make inferences. To make a prediction, readers have to think about what they have already read, recall what they know about the relevant events or information, and compose an idea of what will happen next.

Reading to Answer the Big Question

The Medicine Bag by Virginia Driving Hawk Sneve
Grandpa Joe Iron Shell leaves the Sioux reservation for the first time to visit his family and to give an important gift to his great-grandson. Martin is embarrassed at first; he fears that his friends will laugh at his grandpa, who is so different from Indians on TV. But Martin soon realizes that his grandpa's wisdom is valuable and that the medicine bag is more than just a "dirty leather pouch." As Martin accepts the gift, he accepts himself as part of a larger tradition, and learns more about who he truly is.

A Year of Living Bravely by Emily Costello
Thirteen-year-old surfer Bethany Hamilton was attacked by a shark and lost her left arm just below the shoulder. Within the following year, she co-wrote a book, won an award from the ESPN sports network, and participated in a major surfing competition. This article tells the true story of her amazing recovery, and how her belief in herself got her back on the board.

Workshop Resources

Pacing (Days) Standard	Pacing (Days) Block	Lesson	Student Materials	Teacher Resources
1	1/2	Key Skill Lesson: Predicting	Key Reading Skills Practice, p. 22 English Language Coach Review, p. 41	Bellringer Options Transparencies –Daily Language Practice 47 Selection Focus 11 Read Aloud, Think Aloud Transparencies –Key Reading Skills 17 Presentation Plus!
1	1	"The Medicine Bag"	Glencoe Online Unit Vocabulary Review, p. 39 Academic Vocabulary Review, p. 42 English Language Coach Active Reading Graphic Organizer, p. 24 Literary Analysis, p. 23 StudentWorks Plus™ Online Student Edition Literature Classics Selection and Unit Assessments, p. 53	Literary and Text Analysis Transparencies 54 Puzzlemaker Skill Level Up!™ A Language Arts Game BookLink 3 Assessment by Learning Objective (Diagnostic and Formative) Interactive Tutor: Self-Assessment TeacherWorks Plus™
1		"A Year of Living Bravely"	Glencoe Online Unit Vocabulary Review, p. 39 Academic Vocabulary Review, p. 42 English Language Coach Active Reading Graphic Organizer, p. 26 StudentWorks Plus™ Online Student Edition Literature Classics Selection and Unit Assessments, p. 54	Puzzlemaker Skill Level Up!™ A Language Arts Game BookLink 3 Assessment by Learning Objective (Diagnostic and Formative) Interactive Tutor: Self-Assessment TeacherWorks Plus™

Keys for Unit Resource

- Blackline Master
- Workbook
- Supplemental Text
- CD-ROM
- DVD
- Transparency
- Web-based
- Fast File

Level Appropriate Code

AS = Activities for all students
AL = Activities for students working above grade level
OL = Activities for students working at grade level
BL = Activities for students working below grade level
EL = Activities for English language learners

Focus

BELLRINGER Options

- **Selection Focus Transparency 11**
- **Daily Language Practice Transparency 47**

Focus Activity Write the word "tradition" on the board. Ask students to talk about the different traditions they practice. **Ask:** Do you think traditions are important? Why or why not? *(Responses will vary.)* AS

Teach

R Reading Skill

Predicting **Ask:** How do you make predictions in your daily life? *(Responses will vary.)* OL Give examples from your own experience to help students think about how they use predicting as a life skill. AS

V Vocabulary

Academic Vocabulary **Say:** Read the definition of *relevant* at the bottom of page 604. What is relevant information? *(Possible response: information that is important to the subject)* OL

READING WORKSHOP 3

Skills Focus

You will practice using these skills when you read the following selections:

- "The Medicine Bag," p. 608
- "A Year of Living Bravely," p. 622

Reading

- Predicting future events and behaviors in a story
- Predicting the content of a nonfiction selection

Literature

- Identifying and interpreting theme
- Identifying attention-getting devices

Vocabulary

- Using prefixes to determine meaning
- Academic Vocabulary: *relevant*

Writing/Grammar

- Combining sentences

Indiana English/Language Arts Academic Standards (pp. 604–605)

8.2 Comprehension and Analysis (Focus on Informational Text) Develop [reading] strategies such as...making predictions...

For a complete description of the standards, see p. IN 11.

Skill Lesson

Predicting

Learn It!

R **Predicting** is making an educated guess about what will happen in a story or what a nonfiction text will be about. Use your knowledge, your experience, and **relevant** information in a selection to predict things like these:

- what events will happen next in a story
- how characters will behave
- how conflicts will be resolved
- what you will find in a nonfiction text

Analyzing Cartoons

Hobbes makes a prediction based on what he knows he is going to do to Calvin. Do you think he is going go push Calvin into the mud? Your answer will be a prediction.

V **Academic Vocabulary**

relevant (REH luh vunt) *adj.* important to the subject at hand; significant; pertinent

Additional Support

Literature Focus Lesson

Foreshadowing Point out to students that writers use different techniques to help readers follow the story and predict what will happen next. One of these techniques is called foreshadowing. Foreshadowing is the planting of clues to prepare readers for events that will happen later. For example, a writer might describe how a person feels about another person, with a line stating "I hoped never to see Manny again." This may be a clue that the two characters will meet later in the story or perhaps something tragic will happen where they would never see each other again. As students read "The Medicine Bag," have them pay attention to clues that might help them predict what will happen. OL

Why Is It Important? Making predictions keeps you involved in a selection because it's fun to guess and see whether your guesses are right. Predicting also helps you think critically about the selection. As you predict, you are actually analyzing the events, the characters, and the content.

Study Central Visit www.glencoe.com and click on Study Central to review predicting.

How Do I Do It? Combine your knowledge of people and the world with the information in the story to predict what will happen. Make guesses that fit the characters' personalities, their situation, and their surroundings. Don't worry if a prediction is wrong. Analyze where you went wrong. (For example, did you misunderstand why a character was acting a particular way?) Then read on and revise your predictions to fit new information. Here's what a student predicted while reading a story about a family that has a dog and gets a new kitten.

> Holding the kitten in her arms, Josie knelt down in front of the big brown dog. "Rover, this is Andy," she said. Rover sniffed Andy and began to growl.

I don't think Rover will welcome the new kitten. In fact, I think he's seconds away from biting Andy. Most dogs I know don't growl when they are being friendly.

Practice It!

In your Learner's Notebook, write your own prediction about what Andy will do. Then read the next paragraph of the story:

> Andy began licking the dog's head. Rover looked surprised and stopped growling. Soon he was licking back. It looked as if the two were becoming friends.

Was your prediction right? Why or why not? Do you think the author was trying to surprise you?

Use It!

As you read the selections in this workshop—"The Medicine Bag" and "A Year of Living Bravely"—make predictions about how the main characters will handle the problems they face.

Teach

R Reading Skill

Predicting Ask: Why is predicting important as you read? Write a list of student answers to this question on the board. **Ask:** What are some ways that you can make predictions as you read? *(Responses will vary.)* OL

C Critical Thinking

Analysis Say: The student made his prediction based on what he knew about dogs. However, he did not think about how the new kitten might act. How did the kitten's actions change the outcome? *(Possible response: The kitten licked the dog's head. This made the dog decide to be friendly, too.)* Emphasize that predictions are not always right, but students should continue to guess what will happen next based on what they already know. OL

Resources for page 605

Use Key Reading Skills Transparency 17 in *Read Aloud, Think Aloud* to help students practice predicting.

Reading in the Real World

Career Tell students that many businesses use analysts who make predictions in a variety of areas. Emphasize that these predictions have to be based on information. Encourage students to list the types of things businesses would need analysts to predict. Then have students choose one of the topics and find out what tools analysts use to make their predictions in the particular area. OL Have students research the skills analysts need to do their jobs well. Then have them create a job description for a business analyst. AL

Indiana English/Language Arts Academic Standards
SE: 8.2
TWE: *Literature Focus Lesson* 8.3, *Reading in the Real World* 8.4

Teach

More About the Author

Virginia Driving Hawk Sneve has written over twenty books. Several of them are about Sioux Indians. Her overall life message, in her teaching and her writing, has been about accepting and understanding cultural diversity. In particular, Driving Hawk Sneve has tried to present Native Americans in a more realistic and balanced way than she felt many other books presented them. In fact, she did not write children's books until she saw that her children were reading books that depicted stereotypical Native Americans. She wanted children to read more complete stories about Native Americans, so Driving Hawk Sneve started writing them.

V Vocabulary

Using Vocabulary Challenge students to use all of the vocabulary words in a short paragraph about their family. Have volunteers share their paragraphs with the class. *(Responses will vary.)* OL

Before You Read: The Medicine Bag

Meet the Author

Virginia Driving Hawk Sneve grew up on the Rosebud Reservation in South Dakota. She is a teacher, school counselor, and editor. Sneve has written many books about the history and culture of Native American peoples. She says her grandmothers gave her a love of Indian traditions and storytelling. *See page R6 of The Author Files in the back of the book for more on Virginia Driving Hawk Sneve.*

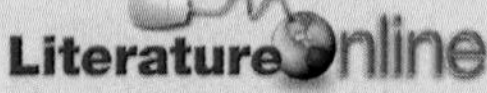

Author Search For more about Virginia Driving Hawk Sneve, go to www.glencoe.com.

Indiana English/Language Arts Academic Standards (pp. 606–617)
8.1 Word Recognition, Fluency, and Vocabulary Development Understand…word parts and patterns… **8.2 Comprehension and Analysis (Focus on Informational Text)** Making predictions… **8.3 Comprehension and Analysis of Literary Text** Identify… theme…
For a complete description of the standards, see p. IN 11.

Vocabulary Preview

V

authentic (aw THEN tik) *adj.* real; genuine **(p. 608)** *Martin and his sister got authentic Sioux gifts from their great-grandfather.*

stately (STAYT lee) *adj.* grand; impressive; dignified **(p. 608)** *The banquet was held at a stately mansion.*

commotion (kuh MOH shun) *n.* noisy, confused activity **(p. 609)** *There was so much commotion in the lunchroom she couldn't hear herself think.*

descendants (dih SEN dunts) *n.* blood relatives of an earlier generation **(p. 611)** *Martin and his sister are the descendants of their grandfather.*

sacred (SAY krid) *adj.* holy; having to do with religion **(p. 615)** *Sage is part of a sacred ritual.*

Partner Talk With a classmate, talk about the vocabulary words and their definitions. Based on them, what do you think might happen in the story?

English Language Coach

Prefixes That Mean "Not" Breaking a word down into its parts can help you understand its meaning. A **prefix** is a syllable added to the beginning of a base word or root word. Just like suffixes, prefixes change or add to the meaning of the base word or root word. Here are some common prefixes that turn words into their opposites. You will see several of the prefixes in "The Medicine Bag." Look for them as you read.

Prefix	Word Examples	Meaning
dis-	disbelieve	"not believe"
il-	illegal	"not legal"
im-	imperfect	"not perfect"
in-	invisible	"not visible"
ir-	irregular	"not regular"
un-	unhappy	"not happy"

On Your Own Write a sentence using each of these words from the chart.

1. disbelieve
2. imperfect
3. invisible
4. unhappy

Additional Support

Author Search To expand students' appreciation of Virginia Driving Hawk Sneve, have them access the Web site for additional information and resources.

Literature Focus Lesson

Coming of Age Stories A coming of age story centers around a young person, who is often around middle school age, and who experiences a turning point in life. In these stories, the main character will change something about his or her personality or learn something that changes the way he or she views the world. Have students think of other stories they have read about young people who come of age. Discuss the characteristics these stories have in common. Challenge students to write an outline for their own coming of age story.

- Who would their characters be?
- What would the conflict be?
- How would they resolve the conflict? OL

Skills Preview

Key Reading Skill: Predicting

When you read fiction, start making predictions early in the story. Look at the following elements:

- title
- Meet the Author and Build Background
- illustrations and captions
- first paragraph

Whole Class Discussion Before you read "The Medicine Bag," look at all the elements listed above. Then make these predictions:

- who the main characters will be
- what the subject of the story will be
- what the title means

Key Literary Element: Theme

The main message of a short story or other work of fiction is its **theme.** Themes are usually lessons in life about right (or wrong) ways to solve problems, such as "Violence only brings more violence." Themes may also be comments about human nature, such as "Everybody makes mistakes."

The theme of the "The Medicine Bag" is **implied,** which means it is not directly stated. You have to figure out what it is. To do so, think about the conflicts in the story. As you read, ask yourself:

- *What internal and external conflicts do the characters experience?*
- *How are the conflicts resolved?*
- *What life lesson does the main character learn from his experiences?*

Write to Learn Think about a conflict you and a friend resolved in the past. How did you resolve the conflict? What did you learn from it? If you wrote a story about your experience, what would the theme be? Answer in your Learner's Notebook.

Get Ready to Read

Connect to the Reading

In this selection, Martin's great-grandfather gives Martin a family treasure. Think of an object you would like to pass down to your children someday. Pick something that you think represents your family.

Write to Learn In your Learner's Notebook, write a few sentences about the family treasure you would pick. Explain its history and why it is important to your family. How does it represent who you are?

Build Background

In this selection Martin, the narrator, calls his great-grandfather "Grandpa." Grandpa is Sioux, a Native American who belongs to a group made up of seven tribes of the Great Plains. The plains are prairie land that covers the area from North Dakota to Wisconsin, south through Iowa and Missouri, and west into Wyoming.

Grandpa lives on a reservation—a limited area which the U.S. government set aside for Native Americans to live on after they were forced from their land.

Set Purposes for Reading

Read "The Medicine Bag" to find out how Martin learns to appreciate the values of the Sioux side of his family and bring them into his suburban life.

Set Your Own Purpose What else would you like to learn from the story to help you answer the Big Question? Write your own purpose on "The Medicine Bag" page of Foldable 5.

Literature Online

Interactive Literary Elements Handbook
To review or learn more about symbols, go to www.glencoe.com.

Keep Moving

Use these skills as you read "The Medicine Bag."

Teach

L Literary Element

Theme Say: Think about the theme of your favorite story in this unit. Is the theme stated directly in the story or is it implied? *(Responses will vary.)* OL **Ask:** If the theme is implied, how did you come up with the theme? *(Possible response: I thought about the main conflict in the story and how it was resolved.)* AL

R Reading Skill

Review Connecting Allow several volunteers to tell what object they would like to pass down and why. *(Responses will vary.)* If students have difficulty thinking of an object, challenge them to think of something they would like their parents or grandparents to pass down to them. BL OL

Literature Online

Interactive Literary Elements Handbook Have students access the Web site to improve their understanding of theme.

Differentiated Instruction

Research It Have students work in groups to create reports about the Sioux Indians. Each member of the group should have a clear responsibility. For example, groups may have a different person look into each of these topics: the history, the culture, the family structure, and the area where they lived. Groups should decide how they will report back to the class. They can create diagrams and maps. They can produce a short video clip. They might want to have students role-play as Sioux Indians and perform a skit. Encourage students to be creative in their reports. OL AL

Indiana English/Language Arts Academic Standards
SE: 8.1, 8.2, 8.3
TWE: *Literature Focus Lesson* 8.3.5, *Differentiated Instruction* 8.7.12

Teach

L Literary Element

Review Characterization
Ask: What do you learn about the narrator and Cheryl? *(Possible responses: They are Sioux; they have friends in the city and a grandfather who lives on a reservation. They like to brag to their friends about their grandfather.)* BL

C Critical Thinking

Analysis **Say:** The narrator explains why he never showed his friends his grandfather's picture. What does the narrator's explanation tell you about him? *(Possible responses: It shows that he cares a lot about what his friends think. It also shows that he wants his friends to think highly of his grandfather.)* OL

R Reading Skill

Predicting **Ask:** Based on the title and the first page of this selection, what do you predict will happen in this story? *(Possible response: Grandpa will give a medicine bag to someone.)* OL

Readability Scores
Dale-Chall: 5.7
DRP: 52
Lexile: 910

THE Medicine Bag

by Virginia Driving Hawk Sneve

My kid sister Cheryl and I always bragged about our Sioux grandpa, Joe Iron Shell. Our friends, who had always lived in the city and only knew about Indians from movies and TV, were impressed by our stories. Maybe we exaggerated and made Grandpa and the reservation sound glamorous, but when we'd return home to Iowa after our yearly summer visit to Grandpa we always had some exciting tale to tell. L

We always had some **authentic** Sioux article to show our listeners. One year Cheryl had new moccasins that Grandpa had made. On another visit he gave me a small, round, flat, rawhide drum which was decorated with a painting of a warrior riding a horse. He taught me a real Sioux chant[1] to sing while I beat the drum with a leather-covered stick that had a feather on the end. Man, that really made an impression. 1

C We never showed our friends Grandpa's picture. Not that we were ashamed of him, but because we knew that the glamorous tales we told didn't go with the real thing. Our friends would have laughed at the picture, because Grandpa wasn't tall and **stately** like TV Indians. His hair wasn't in braids, but hung in stringy, gray strands on his neck and he

1. A ***chant*** is a simple song that has several syllables or words sung to the same note.

Vocabulary

authentic (aw THEN tik) *adj.* real; genuine

stately (STAYT lee) *adj.* grand; impressive; dignified

Practice the Skills

1 Key Reading Skill

Predicting The narrator spends a lot of time describing his Sioux roots. From this, you might predict that his Sioux heritage will be important to the story.

Additional Support

Leveled Reading An adapted version of this selection (4th grade readability) is available on page 112 of **Jamestown Adapted Literature** for Grade 8.

English Language Coach

Verbs Work with the class to list all of the verbs from page 608. Write the words on the board. Point out those verbs that are not physical action words, although they are things a person does *(bragged, exaggerated)*. Also point out those that are state-of-being verbs *(impressed)*. Have students choose four or five of the verbs that are most difficult for them. Direct students to write these verbs in their Learner's Notebooks, along with a definition and one sentence using the word. EL

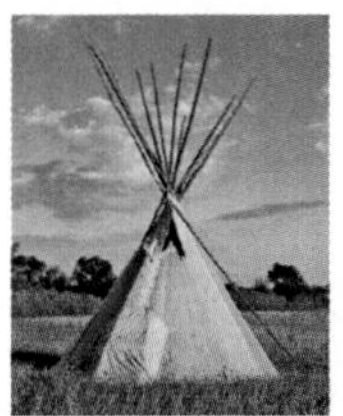

Visual Vocabulary
A ***tipi*** is made of animal skins—usually buffalo—and supported by poles.

was old. He was our great-grandfather, and he didn't live in a tipi, but all by himself in a part log, part tar-paper shack on the Rosebud Reservation in South Dakota. So when Grandpa came to visit us, I was so ashamed and embarrassed I could've died.

There are a lot of yippy poodles and other fancy little dogs in our neighborhood, but they usually barked singly at the mailman from the safety of their own yards. Now it sounded as if a whole pack of mutts were barking together in one place. L1

I got up and walked to the curb to see what the **commotion** was. About a block away I saw a crowd of little kids yelling, with the dogs yipping and growling around someone who was walking down the middle of the street. **2**

I watched the group as it slowly came closer and saw that in the center of the strange procession was a man wearing a tall black hat. He'd pause now and then to peer at something in his hand and then at the houses on either side of the street. I felt cold and hot at the same time as I recognized the man. "Oh, no!" I whispered. "It's Grandpa!"

I stood on the curb, **unable** to move even though I wanted to run and hide. **3** Then I got mad when I saw how the yippy dogs were growling and nipping at the old man's baggy pant legs and how wearily he poked them away with his cane. "Stupid mutts," I said as I ran to rescue Grandpa. L2

When I kicked and hollered at the dogs to get away, they put their tails between their legs and scattered. The kids ran to the curb where they watched me and the old man.

"Grandpa," I said and felt pretty dumb when my voice cracked. I reached for his beat-up old tin suitcase, which was tied shut with a rope. But he set it down right in the street and shook my hand.

"*Hau, Takoza,* Grandchild," he greeted me formally in Sioux.

All I could do was stand there with the whole neighborhood watching and shake the hand of the leather-brown old man. I saw how his gray hair straggled from under his big

Vocabulary

commotion (kum OH shun) *n.* noisy, confused activity

Practice the Skills

2 Key Reading Skill

Predicting This is a good point in the story to guess what will happen next. Think about what you've learned so far. Who do you think is walking down the street?

3 English Language Coach

Prefixes That Mean "Not" Break the word **unable** into its parts. The prefix *un-* means "not." The base word *able* means "can do." From this, you can see *unable* means "cannot do."

READING WORKSHOP 3

Teach

L1 Literary Element

Review Sensory Imagery

Ask: To what sense does the description of the yipping dogs appeal? *(sense of hearing)* **BL** **Ask:** What words does the author use to further describe the dogs? *(barked singly, whole pack of mutts, growling)* **OL** **Ask:** How does this help create the setting? *(Possible response: It helps the reader better understand what the narrator is seeing and hearing.)* **AL**

L2 Literary Element

Review Characterization

Say: At this point in the story, the narrator shows that he has conflicting feelings about his grandfather. What are those conflicting feelings? *(Possible response: He loves his grandfather and wants to help him—he gets angry when he sees the dogs barking at his grandfather and yipping at his feet. At the same time, he is embarrassed by his grandfather.)* **OL**

Differentiated Instruction

Create a Glossary Have students create a glossary of the different Sioux phrases and expressions used in this story. If students need help finding these phrases and expressions, explain that they appear in italics in the story because they are in a different language. Have students write each phrase and expression and what they think it means based on the context of the story. Then have students look online or do research in the library to find out what each phrase literally means and write it below their predicted translation. **OL** Challenge students to learn how to correctly pronounce the Sioux words in this story. **AL**

Indiana English/Language Arts Academic Standards
SE: 8.1, 8.2
TWE: *English Language Coach* 8.1, *Differentiated Instruction* 8.1.3

Teach

C Critical Thinking

Synthesis **Ask:** Why doesn't Martin's mom hug her father? What does it mean that Martin's sister is "still young enough to be hugged"? *(Possible response: In Sioux culture adult men and women do not show affection.)* AL

L Literary Element

Review Characterization
Ask: How did Martin feel when he saw how his sister acted? *(ashamed)* BL **Ask:** How does the writer use the sister's actions to help develop Martin's character? *(Possible response: The writer shows how other children would react in the same situation. The writer also uses this to show how Martin thinks he should feel.)* OL

R Reading Skill

Predicting **Ask:** How did you come up with your prediction about why Grandpa came to visit? *(Responses will vary.)* AS

READING WORKSHOP 3

black hat, which had a drooping feather in its crown. His rumpled black suit hung like a sack over his stooped frame. As he shook my hand, his coat fell open to expose a bright-red, satin shirt with a beaded bolo tie under the collar. His getup wasn't out of place on the reservation, but it sure was here, and I wanted to sink right through the pavement.

"Hi," I muttered with my head down. I tried to pull my hand away when I felt his bony hand trembling, and looked up to see fatigue in his face. I felt like crying. I couldn't think of anything to say so I picked up Grandpa's suitcase, took his arm, and guided him up the driveway to our house.

Mom was standing on the steps. I don't know how long she'd been watching, but her hand was over her mouth and she looked as if she couldn't believe what she saw. Then she ran to us.

"Grandpa," she gasped. "How in the world did you get here?"

She checked her move to embrace Grandpa and I remembered that such a display of affection is unseemly to the Sioux and would embarrass him.

"*Hau*, Marie," he said as he shook Mom's hand. She smiled and took his other arm.

As we supported him up the steps the door banged open and Cheryl came bursting out of the house. She was all smiles and was so obviously glad to see Grandpa that I was ashamed of how I felt.

"Grandpa!" she yelled happily. "You came to see us!"

Grandpa smiled and Mom and I let go of him as he stretched out his arms to my ten-year-old sister, who was still young enough to be hugged. 4

"*Wicincala*, little girl," he greeted her and then collapsed.

He had fainted. Mom and I carried him into her sewing room, where we had a spare bed.

After we had Grandpa on the bed Mom stood there helplessly patting his shoulder.

"Shouldn't we call the doctor, Mom?" I suggested, since she didn't seem to know what to do.

"Yes," she agreed with a sigh. "You make Grandpa comfortable, Martin."

I reluctantly moved to the bed. I knew Grandpa wouldn't want to have Mom undress him, but I didn't want to, either.

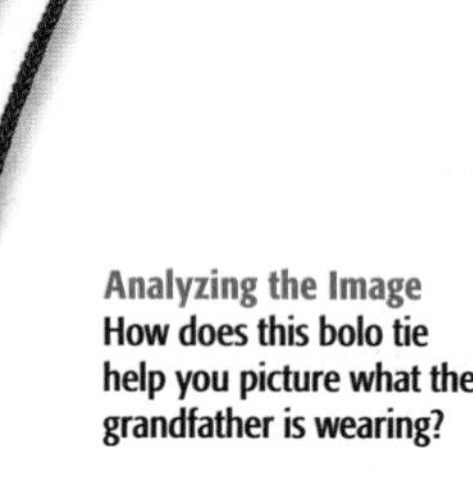

Analyzing the Image How does this bolo tie help you picture what the grandfather is wearing?

C Practice the Skills

4 Key Reading Skill

Predicting Why do you think Grandpa has come to visit? R

Additional Support

English Language Coach

Idioms Remind students that an idiom is a word or phrase that has a meaning other than its dictionary (or literal) meaning. Point out the phrase, "sink right through the pavement." Tell students that Martin was very embarrassed and wished he could just disappear. Divide the class into small groups and have them think of other idioms with similar meanings. *(Possible response: I was so embarrassed I could have died.)* Then have students list idioms that they have heard or use in their everyday language. EL Discuss why authors use idioms in their writing and why people use idioms when they speak. AS

He was so skinny and frail that his coat slipped off easily. When I loosened his tie and opened his shirt collar, I felt a small leather pouch that hung from a thong[2] around his neck. I left it alone and moved to remove his boots. The scuffed old cowboy boots were tight and he moaned as I put pressure on his legs to jerk them off.

I put the boots on the floor and saw why they fit so tight. Each one was stuffed with money. I looked at the bills that lined the boots and started to ask about them, but Grandpa's eyes were closed again. **5**

Mom came back with a basin of water. "The doctor thinks Grandpa is suffering from heat exhaustion,"[3] she explained as she bathed Grandpa's face. Mom gave a big sigh, *"Oh hinh,* Martin. How do you suppose he got here?"

We found out after the doctor's visit. Grandpa was angrily sitting up in bed while Mom tried to feed him some soup.

"Tonight you let Marie feed you, Grandpa," spoke my dad, who had gotten home from work just as the doctor was leaving. "You're not really sick," he said as he gently pushed Grandpa back against the pillows. "The doctor said you just got too tired and hot after your long trip."

Grandpa relaxed, and between sips of soup he told us of his journey. Soon after our visit to him Grandpa decided that he would like to see where his only living **descendants** lived and what our home was like. Besides, he admitted sheepishly, he was lonesome after we left.

I knew everybody felt as guilty as I did—especially Mom. Mom was all Grandpa had left. So even after she married my dad, who's a white man and teaches in the college in our city, and after Cheryl and I were born, Mom made sure that every summer we spent a week with Grandpa.

I never thought that Grandpa would be lonely after our visits, and none of us noticed how old and weak he had become. But Grandpa knew and so he came to us. He had ridden on buses for two and a half days. When he arrived

2. A ***thong*** is a narrow strap of leather or similar material.

3. ***Heat exhaustion*** is dizziness and faintness from being in the sun too long.

Vocabulary

descendants (dih SEN dunts) *n.* blood relatives of an earlier generation

Practice the Skills

5 Key Reading Skill

Predicting Why do you think Grandpa has stuffed his boots with money?

Teach

R1 Reading Skill

Review Identifying Main Idea and Supporting Details Have students carefully read page 611. **Ask:** What is the main idea? *(Grandpa is old and tired and has come to his family because he is lonely.)* Ask students to list the supporting details that helped them figure out the main idea *(Possible responses: He is skinny and frail; The doctor says he has heat exhaustion; Grandpa says he was lonely.)* **OL**

R2 Reading Skill

Predicting Say: At this point in the story, the writer has given a lot of background information and developed the characters, but he has not revealed the conflict. Based on what you have learned, what do you think the conflict of this story will be? *(Possible response: The conflict will be between Martin and his grandfather.)* **OL**

Reading in the Real World

Career There are many different careers in the field of elder care. Brainstorm with students some of the possible careers, such as nurses, doctors, physical and occupational therapists, pharmacists, home healthcare providers, and running a nursing home or assisted living facility. Have a person who works in this field visit the class and talk about how the field has changed over the years and what some of the future needs may be in elder care. Ask students to prepare questions for the visitor about elder care. **OL** Some students may have experience caring for an elder. Ask for volunteers to share their experience with caring for elders. **AS**

Indiana English/Language Arts Academic Standards
SE: 8.2
TWE: *English Language Coach* 8.1.1, *Reading in the Real World* 8.7.1

Teach

L1 Literary Element

Review Sequence **Ask:** How did Grandpa get to Martin's house? *(He rode on a bus for two days. Then he decided to walk to his daughter's house. He rested on the steps of a building downtown. A police officer took him to the bus stop and made sure he got on. Grandpa took the bus to Bell View Drive and then started walking again. This time the kids and dogs followed him. Eventually, Martin came out and helped him in.)* Have students draw a sequence chart to show the steps of Grandpa's trip. **OL**

L2 Literary Element

Theme **Say:** Martin's father tells Grandpa that he will never be a burden to them. He also apologizes for not bringing him to their home sooner. The writer seems to be hinting at a theme of the importance of family. Based on the information in the story thus far, what do you think the author might be saying about family? Put this theme of the story in your own words. *(Responses will vary.)* **AL**

in the city, tired and stiff from sitting for so long, he set out, walking, to find us.

He had stopped to rest on the steps of some building downtown and a policeman found him. The cop, according to Grandpa, was a good man who took him to the bus stop and waited until the bus came and told the driver to let Grandpa out at Bell View Drive. After Grandpa got off the bus, he started walking again. But he couldn't see the house numbers on the other side when he walked on the sidewalk so he walked in the middle of the street. That's when all the little kids and dogs followed him.

I knew everybody felt as bad as I did. Yet I was proud of this 86-year-old man, who had never been away from the reservation, having the courage to travel so far alone.

"You found the money in my boots?" he asked Mom.

"Martin did," she answered, and roused herself to scold. "Grandpa, you shouldn't have carried so much money. What if someone had stolen it from you?"

Grandpa laughed. "I would've known if anyone tried to take the boots off my feet. The money is what I've saved for a long time—a hundred dollars—for my funeral. But you take it now to buy groceries so that I won't be a burden to you while I am here." **6**

"That won't be necessary, Grandpa," Dad said. "We are honored to have you with us and you will never be a burden. I am only sorry that we never thought to bring you home with us this summer and spare you the **discomfort** of a long trip." **7**

Grandpa was pleased. "Thank you," he answered. "But do not feel bad that you didn't bring me with you for I would not have come then. It was not time." He said this in such a way that no one could argue with him. To Grandpa and the Sioux, he once told me, a thing would be done when it was the right time to do it and that's the way it was.

"Also," Grandpa went on, looking at me, "I have come because it is soon time for Martin to have the medicine bag."

We all knew what that meant. Grandpa thought he was going to die and he had to follow the tradition of his family to pass the medicine bag, along with its history, to the oldest male child.

Practice the Skills

6 Key Reading Skill

Predicting Was your prediction about the money in Grandpa's boots correct?

7 English Language Coach

Prefixes That Mean "Not" Divide the word **discomfort** into its two parts–its prefix and its base word. What does *discomfort* mean?

Additional Support

Differentiated Instruction

Writing About the Text Students may improve their comprehension of this selection by writing about the text. Have students find a quiet place to read the story. Then ask them to write in their Learner's Notebooks about the story. Have them answer the following questions:

- What do you like most about the story and why?
- What do you like least about the story and why?
- What image stays with you the most from the story?
- What questions do you have about the story? **OL**

"Even though the boy," he said still looking at me, "bears a white man's name, the medicine bag will be his."

I didn't know what to say. I had the same hot and cold feeling that I had when I first saw Grandpa in the street. The medicine bag was the dirty leather pouch I had found around his neck. "I could never wear such a thing," I almost said aloud. I thought of having my friends see it in gym class, at the swimming pool, and could imagine the smart things they R would say. But I just swallowed hard and took a step toward the bed. I knew I would have to take it.

But Grandpa was tired. "Not now, Martin," he said, waving his hand in dismissal, "it is not time. Now I will sleep."

So that's how Grandpa came to be with us for two months. My friends kept asking to come see the old man, but I put them off. I told myself that I didn't want them laughing at Grandpa. But even as I made excuses I knew it wasn't Grandpa that I was afraid they'd laugh at. 8

Nothing bothered Cheryl about bringing her friends to see Grandpa. Every day after school started there'd be a crew of giggling little girls or round-eyed little boys crowded around the old man on the patio, where he'd gotten in the habit of sitting every afternoon.

Grandpa would smile in his gentle way and patiently answer their questions, or he'd tell them stories of brave warriors, ghosts, animals, and the kids listened in awed silence. Those little guys thought Grandpa was great.

Finally, one day after school, my friends came home with me because nothing I said stopped them. "We're going to see the great Indian of Bell View Drive," said Hank, who C was supposed to be my best friend. "My brother has seen him three times so he oughta be well enough to see us."

When we got to my house Grandpa was sitting on the patio. He had on his red shirt, but today he also wore a fringed leather vest that was decorated with beads. Instead of his usual cowboy boots he had solidly beaded moccasins on his feet that stuck out of his black trousers. Of course, he had his old black

Practice the Skills

8 Key Literary Element

Theme To understand the theme of this story, think about the conflicts in it.

- Martin is afraid of being embarrassed by his grandfather and the medicine bag. L
- Martin doesn't want to hurt his grandfather's feelings.
- Martin has mixed feelings about his grandfather and his Sioux heritage.

A Singing Indian. W. Ufer. Oil on canvas, 30 x 25¼ in.

Analyzing the Painting What items in this painting reflect the man's Native American heritage? What details about Grandpa reveal his identity as a Sioux?

Teach

R Reading Skill

Review Connecting
Ask: Have you ever felt like Martin—afraid that your friends would laugh at you if they knew something about you or your family? Describe how you felt and how Martin may be feeling in the story. *(Responses will vary.)* OL

L Literary Element

Theme List the conflicts in the story on the board. **Ask:** How do the conflicts in a story relate to the theme? *(Possible response: The way an author resolves the conflicts shows what the theme of the story is.)* **Ask:** Based on Martin's conflicts, what do you think the theme of the story will be? *(Responses will vary.)* OL

C Critical Thinking

Analysis **Ask:** Why do you think Martin describes Hank as the boy "who was supposed to be my best friend"? *(Possible response: Martin is upset because Hank insists on visiting Grandpa; Martin thinks Hank is joking about Grandpa.)* AL

Differentiated Instruction

Compare and Contrast Have students make a Venn diagram to compare the Sioux world and Grandpa's values to the modern American world and Martin's values. Tell students to include objects of importance to each person, as well as the kinds of things that they say and do. OL Discuss whether students think Grandpa and his world have something to teach Martin. Have students talk about the conflicts they experience between old ways and new ways. Encourage students to use specific examples as they discuss these conflicts. AL

Indiana English/Language Arts Academic Standards
SE: 8.1, 8.2, 8.3
TWE: *Differentiated Instruction* 8.2, *Differentiated Instruction* 8.3

Teach

C Critical Thinking

Synthesis **Say:** Martin drew a conclusion about his grandfather when he saw the expression on his face. What was that conclusion? *(That his grandfather had known all along about Martin being embarrassed to bring his friends to see him.)* **OL** **Ask:** How do you think Martin felt when he made that discovery? *(Possible response: He may have felt sorry that he had hurt Grandpa's feelings.)* **AL**

Viewing the Art

Ask: How does the picture of this vest help you see what Martin meant when he said his Grandpa's clothes were out of place? *(Possible response: It is not typical dress for people in Martin's neighborhood or in current American culture.)* **OL**

R Reading Skill

Predicting **Ask:** What do you think will happen later in the story? *(Grandpa is probably going to get sick and die.)* **OL** **Ask:** What information in the story helped you to make this prediction? *(Possible response: that Grandpa's strength hasn't returned; that he is going to give Martin the medicine bag tomorrow)* **AL**

hat on—he was seldom without it. But it had been brushed and the feather in the beaded headband was proudly erect, its tip a brighter white. His hair lay in silver strands over the red shirt collar.

I stared just as my friends did and I heard one of them murmur, "Wow!" **9**

Grandpa looked up and when his eyes met mine they twinkled as if he were laughing inside. He nodded to me and my face got all hot. I could tell that he had known all along I was afraid he'd embarrass me in front of my friends. **C**

"Hau, hoksilas, boys," he greeted and held out his hand.

My buddies passed in a single file and shook his hand as I introduced them. They were so polite I almost laughed. "How, there, Grandpa," and even a "How-do-you-do, sir."

"You look fine, Grandpa," I said as the guys sat on the lawn chairs or on the patio floor.

"Hanh, yes," he agreed. "When I woke up this morning it seemed the right time to dress in the good clothes. I knew that my grandson would be bringing his friends."

"You guys want some lemonade or something?" I offered. No one answered. They were listening to Grandpa as he started telling how he'd killed the deer from which his vest was made.

Grandpa did most of the talking while my friends were there. I was so proud of him and amazed at how respectfully quiet my buddies were. **10** Mom had to chase them home at supper time. As they left they shook Grandpa's hand again and said to me:

"Martin, he's really great!"

"Yeah, man! Don't blame you for keeping him to yourself."

"Can we come back?"

But after they left, Mom said, "No more visitors for a while, Martin. Grandpa won't admit it, but his strength hasn't returned. He likes having company, but it tires him." **R**

That evening Grandpa called me to his room before he went to sleep. "Tomorrow," he said, "when you come home, it will be time to give you the medicine bag."

Sioux vest, Plains Indian. British Museum, London.

Analyzing the Photo How is the vest in this photograph like the one Martin describes?

Practice the Skills

9 Key Reading Skill

Predicting Do you think Martin will be embarrassed in front of his friends by his grandfather? Why or why not?

10 Key Reading Skill

Predicting Did you correctly predict how Martin's friends would react to his grandfather? If not, why not?

Additional Support

Reading in the Real World

Career Clothing is an important part of any culture. The fashion industry has many career opportunities. Brainstorm with students a list of jobs in the fashion industry. **AS** Then have students find out what the requirements are for at least one of the jobs listed. They should also find out which cities around the world offer the most opportunities for the job they have chosen. **OL** Students may also want to conduct further research on Sioux clothing and its importance to Sioux culture. **AL**

I felt a hard squeeze from where my heart is supposed to be and was scared, but I answered, "OK, Grandpa." C1

All night I had weird dreams about thunder and lightning on a high hill. From a distance I heard the slow beat of a drum. When I woke up in the morning I felt as if I hadn't slept at all. At school it seemed as if the day would never end and, when it finally did, I ran home. 11

Grandpa was in his room, sitting on the bed. The shades were down and the place was dim and cool. I sat on the floor in front of Grandpa, but he didn't even look at me. After what seemed a long time he spoke.

"I sent your mother and sister away. What you will hear today is only for a man's ears. What you will receive is only for a man's hands." He fell silent and I felt shivers down my back.

"My father in his early manhood," Grandpa began, "made a vision quest[4] to find a spirit guide for his life. You cannot understand how it was in that time, when the great Teton Sioux[5] were first made to stay on the reservation. There was a strong need for guidance from *Wakantanka*, the Great Spirit. R But too many of the young men were filled with despair and hatred. They thought it was hopeless to search for a vision when the glorious life was gone and only the hated confines of a reservation lay ahead. But my father held to the old ways.

Visual Vocabulary
A ***butte*** (byoot) is a steep, flat-topped hill that stands alone.

"He carefully prepared for his quest with a purifying sweat bath and then he went alone to a high butte top to fast and pray. After three days he received his **sacred** dream—in which he found, after long searching, the white man's iron. He did not understand his vision of finding something belonging to the white people, for in that time they were the enemy. When he came down from the butte to cleanse himself at the stream below, he found the remains of a campfire and the broken shell of an iron kettle. This was a sign which C2

4. A ***vision quest*** was a special trip made by young Sioux men to receive a dream that gave them a song or an object that protected and guided them in life.

5. The ***Teton Sioux*** are the largest Sioux tribe. They were traditionally buffalo hunters.

Vocabulary

sacred (SAY krid) *adj.* holy; having to do with religion

Practice the Skills

11 Key Reading Skill

Predicting How do you think Martin will react when Grandpa gives him the medicine bag? Why do you think so?

Teach

C1 Critical Thinking

Analysis **Ask:** Why do you think Martin is scared? *(Possible responses: He doesn't know much about the medicine bag; he's afraid his grandfather will die when he passes on the medicine bag.)* OL

R Reading Skill

Review Monitoring Comprehension **Ask:** Why didn't the young Sioux men want to go on a vision quest? *(Possible response: They were so filled with despair and hatred about being forced to live on a reservation that they thought a vision quest was meaningless.)* OL

C2 Critical Thinking

Analysis **Ask:** Why do you think Grandpa is telling Martin this story? *(Possible response: He wants Martin to understand his heritage.)* OL

Differentiated Instruction

Gender Roles Some students, particularly the girls, may find it difficult to understand, relate to, or even accept the fact that Grandpa tells Martin his words are "only for a man's ears." Other students will say that there are things in their culture that are special just for males and just for females. Have students write about the cultural practices that they know of that are different for males and females. Ask volunteers to read their writings. Hold a class discussion on gender roles and how students feel about them. OL

Indiana English/Language Arts Academic Standards
SE: 8.2
TWE: *Reading in the Real World* 8.4, *Differentiated Instruction* 8.3

Teach

R Reading Skill

Review Questioning Pause at this point in reading the story to allow several volunteers to ask their own questions about Iron Shell and his medicine bag. You may need to begin by modeling a question of your own. *(Possible responses: What is so important about the iron? How will Iron Shell learn about his medicine? Why did he take the iron if he did not understand its meaning?)* OL

BQ

Ask: How does Grandpa stay true to his self? *(Possible responses: he carries the medicine bag his father gave him and wants to continue the tradition of passing it on; he remembers his father's stories and honors his traditions.)* OL

READING WORKSHOP 3

reinforced his dream. He took a piece of the iron for his medicine bag, which he had made of elk[6] skin years before, to prepare for his quest.

"He returned to his village, where he told his dream to the wise old men of the tribe. They gave him the name *Iron Shell,* but neither did they understand the meaning of the dream. This first Iron Shell kept the piece of iron with him at all times and believed it gave him protection from the evils of those unhappy days. R

"Then a terrible thing happened to Iron Shell. He and several other young men were taken from their homes by the soldiers and sent far away to a white man's boarding school.[7] He was angry and lonesome for his parents and the young girl he had wed before he was taken away. At first Iron Shell resisted the teachers' attempts to change him and he did not try to learn. One day it was his turn to work in the school's blacksmith[8] shop. As he walked into the place he knew that his medicine had brought him there to learn and work with the white man's iron.

"Iron Shell became a blacksmith and worked at the trade when he returned to the reservation. All of his life he treasured the medicine bag. When he was old, and I was a man, he gave it to me, for no one made the vision quest any more." 12

Grandpa quit talking and I stared in disbelief as he covered his face with his hands. His shoulders were shaking with quiet sobs and I looked away until he began to speak again.

"I kept the bag until my son, your mother's father, was a man and had to leave us to fight in the war across the ocean. I gave him the bag, for I believed it would protect him in battle, but he did not take it with him. He was afraid that he would lose it. He died in a faraway place."

Again Grandpa was still and I felt his grief around me. BQ

"My son," he went on after clearing his throat, "had only a daughter and it is not proper for her to know of these things."

He unbuttoned his shirt, pulled out the leather pouch, and lifted it over his head. He held it in his hand, turning it over and over as if memorizing how it looked.

6. An ***elk*** is a very large type of deer with broad antlers.
7. A ***boarding school*** is a school where students live together as well as go to school.
8. A ***blacksmith*** makes iron objects, such as horseshoes, kettles, and door hinges.

Practice the Skills

12 BIG Question
How might the story of the vision quest help Martin understand his true self?

Additional Support

Literature Focus Lesson

Symbolism Tell students that authors often use objects and symbols to represent other things. The medicine bag is one such symbol. Now that students know the story behind the medicine bag, have them discuss what the medicine bag symbolizes for Iron Shell, Grandpa, and now Martin. Tell students to think about:

- how the medicine bag was created
- why the medicine bag was created
- what is inside the medicine bag
- how each recipient of the medicine bag responds to it OL

"In the bag," he said as he opened it and removed two objects, "is the broken shell of the iron kettle, a pebble from the butte, and a piece of the sacred sage."[9] He held the pouch upside down and dust drifted down.

"After the bag is yours you must put a piece of prairie sage within and never open it again until you pass it on to your son." He replaced the pebble and the piece of iron, and tied the bag.

I stood up, somehow knowing I should. Grandpa slowly rose from the bed and stood upright in front of me holding the bag before my face. I closed my eyes and waited for him to slip it over my head. But he spoke.

"No, you need not wear it." He placed the soft leather bag in my right hand and closed my other hand over it. "It would not be right to wear it in this time and place where no one will understand. Put it safely away until you are again on the reservation. Wear it then, when you replace the sacred sage."

Grandpa turned and sat again on the bed. Wearily he leaned his head against the pillow. "Go," he said, "I will sleep now."

"Thank you, Grandpa," I said softly and left with the bag in my hands. **13**

That night Mom and Dad took Grandpa to the hospital. Two weeks later I stood alone on the lonely prairie of the reservation and put the sacred sage in my medicine bag. **14** C

Boy on Edge of Chasm, 1993 (detail). Kam Mak. Oil on panels, 14 x 10½ in. Collection of the artist.

Analyzing the Painting How does this painting capture the seriousness of the moment when Martin receives the medicine bag?

9. ***Sage*** is a sweet-smelling plant. Different varieties are used as medicine or spice.

Practice the Skills

13 Key Literary Element

Theme Martin's internal conflict about his grandfather is resolved. What did Martin learn from the experience? The answer to that question is the theme of the story.

14 BIG Question

BQ How does accepting the medicine bag help Martin stay true to himself? Write your answer on "The Medicine Bag" page of Foldable 5. Your response will help you complete the Unit Challenge later.

Teach

C Critical Thinking

Synthesis Ask: Why do you think Martin decides to accept the medicine bag and place the sacred sage inside it? *(Possible response: He decided to embrace his heritage and his meaningful legacy.)* **Ask:** Now that Martin has placed the sage inside the bag, what must he do? *(He must never open the bag again until he passes it on to his son.)* **OL**

BQ BIG Question

Ask: What does this story say about family, culture, and heritage? *(Possible response: It says that our family, our culture, and our heritage are an important part of who we are, and we cannot just ignore them. We also should not be afraid of or embarrassed by them.)* **OL**

Assess

Use the CheckPoint questions provided on Presentation Plus! to check for comprehension of the selection. These questions can be used with interactive response keypads for immediate student feedback.

Reading in the Real World

Citizenship Now that students have read about the journey of Iron Shell and the legacy he left, have them find out about the journeys of their own ancestors. Ask students to interview one of the oldest living members of their families. Have students write questions before the interview. Tell students to also ask their elder for advice on how to stay true to themselves. **OL** Students should write short stories similar to "The Medicine Bag" based on their interviews. Encourage volunteers to share their ancestors' advice on staying true to yourself. **AL**

Indiana English/Language Arts Academic Standards
SE: 8.3
TWE: *Literature Focus Lesson* 8.3.6; *Reading in the Real World* 8.5.1, 8.7.1

Assess

Resources for page 618

- Selection Quick Check, p. 45
- Selection and Unit Assessment, p. 53
- ExamView Assessment Suite
- Interactive Tutor: Self-Assessment

Students can respond to the *After You Read* items in their Learner's Notebooks or on a separate sheet of paper.

Answering the BIG Question

1. Students are likely to say that Martin is his true self with both his friends and his family. Some students may say that Martin is learning who his true self is as he grows up.
2. At the beginning of the story, Martin is embarrassed by his Sioux background.
3. Grandpa has come to visit his family because he is dying and wants to give his medicine bag to Martin. He also wants to see his family before he dies.

Critical Thinking

4. Responses will vary.
5. Possible response: The medicine bag symbolizes Iron Shell's journey to discover himself and his life's work. It may also symbolize what is left of the Sioux culture.
6. Responses will vary.

After You Read

The Medicine Bag

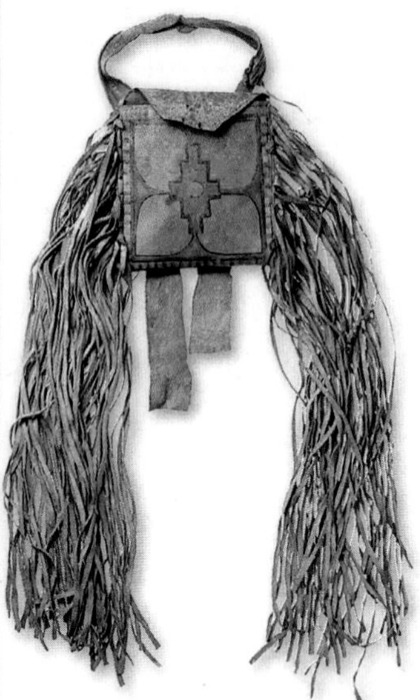

Answering the BIG Question

1. What do you think is Martin's true self, the way he is with his friends or with his family—or both? Explain.
2. **Recall** How does Martin feel about his Sioux background at the start of the story, when his grandfather first comes to visit?
   TIP **Right There**
3. **Summarize** In a sentence or two, sum up the reasons that Grandpa has come to visit Martin and his family.
   TIP **Think and Search**

Critical Thinking

4. **Infer** Why do you think Grandpa cries after he tells Martin how Iron Shell gave him the medicine bag?
   TIP **Author and Me**
5. **Interpret** A symbol is a person, place, or thing that stands for something more than what it is. For example, a red rose can represent, or symbolize, love. What do you think the medicine bag symbolizes in the story? Give details from the story to support your answer.
   TIP **Author and Me**
6. **Analyze** The story is told in the first-person from Martin's point of view. How might your feelings toward Martin change if the story were told in the third-person by an outsider watching what happens?
   TIP **On My Own**

Indiana English/ Language Arts Academic Standards (pp. 618–619)

8.3 Comprehension and Analysis of Literary Text Respond to grade-level-appropriate literature...identifying...theme...**8.5.7** Write for different purposes...**8.2 Comprehension and Analysis (Focus on Informational Text)** Develop [reading] strategies such as...making predictions...**8.1 Word Recognition, Fluency, and Vocabulary Development** Understand...word parts and patterns...**8.6 English Language Conventions**

For a complete description of the standards, see p. IN 11.

Write About Your Reading

Diary Entry Imagine that you are Martin. Write a diary entry about the day Grandpa gave you the medicine bag. Be sure to include the following ideas:

- your feelings about the history of the medicine bag
- your feelings about owning the medicine bag
- how owning the medicine bag has changed you

Write About Your Reading

A sample diary entry is given below.

Dear Diary,

Grandpa gave me his medicine bag a few weeks ago. We went to his funeral today. I miss him a lot, but I have his medicine bag. It is like a little piece of him. It is also a little piece of my mom's dad-grandfather, and my great-great-grandpa, too. I like to think about him going on that vision quest. I wonder how he felt when he found the broken kettle piece. It must have been so cool when he ended up working as a blacksmith. When Grandpa first said he was going to give me the bag, I was afraid of wearing it and being embarrassed. Now I am proud of having it.

Skills Review

Key Reading Skill: Predicting

7. Explain how making predictions as you read helped you understand the story. Discuss the predictions you made about the characters and the plot.

Key Literary Element: Theme

8. In a sentence or two, state the theme of "The Medicine Bag."
9. How did understanding the conflicts in the story help you figure out the theme?

Vocabulary Check

Write *T* for each true statement and *F* for each false one.

10. An **authentic** medicine bag is made of plastic.
11. A group of government officials on their way to an important meeting would probably walk in a **stately** fashion.
12. A quiet, orderly exit from school is a **commotion.**
13. Your children will be your **descendants.**
14. A **sacred** object is likely to be holy to people.
15. **Academic Vocabulary** Why is an understanding of Martin's Sioux heritage **relevant** to a discussion of "The Medicine Bag"?

English Language Coach On a separate sheet of paper, write the prefix and the base word that make up the listed word. Then write a definition of the word. If you need help, use a dictionary.

16. disappear
17. unclean
18. immaterial
19. disbelieve
20. disinfect
21. unafraid

Grammar Link: Combining Sentences

Too many short, simple sentences can make writing sound choppy. Vary the lengths and kinds of sentences you use by combining simple sentences.

Method A: Compound Sentences Combine two simple sentences (independent clauses) to form a compound sentence. Form it with a comma and a coordinating conjunction (*and, but, nor, or, for, so, yet*).

- The sky darkened. It started to rain big drops.
- The sky darkened, **and** it started to rain big drops.

Method B: Complex Sentences Combine two simple sentences (independent clauses) to form a complex sentence. Add a subordinating conjunction to one of the independent clauses to make it a dependent clause.
Common subordinating conjunctions include *after, although, as, because, before, if, since, though, unless, until, when, whether,* and *while.*

- **After** the sky darkened, it started to rain big drops.

Grammar Practice

Combine sentences to vary the sentence patterns in the paragraph below. Include at least one compound sentence and one complex sentence. (There's more than one right way to revise the paragraph.)

Spring is here. The weather is warm. The beach will reopen soon. Baseball is back. You and your family will visit. We can catch up on old times.

Writing Application Review the diary entry you wrote for the Write About Your Reading activity. Make sure it contains at least one compound sentence and one complex sentence.

Web Activities For eFlashcards, Selection Quick Checks, and other Web activities, go to www.glencoe.com.

Skills Review

Key Reading Skill: Predicting

7. Students are likely to say that making predictions helped them understand the story because they had a better sense of what was going to happen next and why.

Key Literary Element: Theme

8. Possible response: The theme of "The Medicine Bag" is that our family and our culture are important, and they help make us who we are.
9. Possible response: Martin's embarrassing feelings toward his grandfather's traditions helped me understand that part of the theme was about being proud of your heritage.

Vocabulary Check

10. F
11. T
12. F
13. T
14. T

Academic Vocabulary

15. Possible response: because you need to understand Martin's Sioux heritage to understand why a medicine bag is important

Enlish Language Coach
Definitions will vary.

16. dis; appear
17. un; clean
18. im; material
19. dis; believe
20. dis; infect
21. un; afraid

Grammar Link: Combining Sentences

Grammar Practice

Possible response:
Spring is here, and the weather is warm. The beach will reopen soon and baseball is back. When you and your family visit, we can catch up on old times.

Indiana English/Language Arts Academic Standards
SE: 8.1, 8.2, 8.3, 8.5.7, 8.6

Teach

More About the Author

Students may be familiar with some of Emily Costello's fiction books from the *Nancy Drew, Sweet Valley Twins,* and *Sweet Valley Kids* series. Costello lives in Boston with her family and continues writing nonfiction and fiction.

V Vocabulary

Synonyms and Antonyms Have students write a sentence for each synonym and antonym they wrote for the vocabulary words. Ask students to read their sentences to a partner. *(Responses will vary.)* OL

EL Language Coach

Prefixes That Show Relationships Review with students the meaning of the prefixes *co-*, *pre-*, and *post-*. Have students read aloud the best sentences they wrote in their Learner's Notebooks for the *English Language Coach* exercise. *(Responses will vary.)* EL

Before You Read A Year of Living Bravely

Emily Costello

Meet the Author

Emily Costello was born in 1966. She has written many books and articles for young adults, including fiction and biography, and articles on science topics. Costello tells young people who want to write, "Keep a diary. Record what's happening in your life and practice explaining how you're feeling each day."

Author Search For more about Emily Costello, go to www.glencoe.com.

Vocabulary Preview

confesses (kun FES ses) *v.* tells a truth that one rarely talks about; form of the verb *confess* **(p. 623)** *Bethany confesses to being afraid sometimes.*

exotic (eg ZOT ik) *adj.* strangely beautiful and foreign **(p. 624)** *Bethany goes to exotic places to surf with her family and friends.*

hardships (HARD ships) *n.* things that cause pain or suffering; misfortunes **(p. 625)** *In spite of the hardships the fire caused, the family was happy because no one was hurt.*

V **Partner Talk** With a partner, look over the vocabulary words. Then write down a synonym and an antonym for each word. (Remember that synonyms share almost the same meaning; antonyms have opposite meanings.)

English Language Coach

EL **Prefixes That Show Relationships** A prefix is a syllable added to the beginning of a word to change the word's meaning. If you know the meaning of common prefixes, you can unlock the meaning of words that begin with prefixes. The chart below lists prefixes that show relationships.

Prefix	Word Example	Meaning
co- means "with," "together," or "partner"	coworker	"one who works with another person"
	coexist	"to exist together"
	coauthor	"an author who writes as a partner of another"
pre- means "before"	preseason	"before the regular season"
post- means "after"	postseason	"after the regular season"

Think-Pair-Share Use a dictionary to find three words that begin with the prefixes *co-*, *pre-*, or *post-*. Make a two-column chart in your Learner's Notebook, and write the words in the first column. In the second column, write a sentence using the word. Challenge a classmate to guess the meanings of the words by using word analysis and context clues.

Indiana English/Language Arts Academic Standards (pp. 620–625)

8.1 Word Recognition, Fluency, and Vocabulary Development Understand...word parts and relationships... **8.2 Comprehension and Analysis (Focus on Informational Text)** Develop [reading] strategies such as...making predictions, and identifying and analyzing structure and organization...

For a complete description of the standards, see p. IN 11.

Additional Support

Author Search To expand students' appreciation of Emily Costello, have them access the Web site for additional information and resources.

Literature Focus Lesson

Informational Text Most of what students have read in this unit has been fiction. The next selection is an informational article. Prepare students to read this article by talking about the differences between fiction and nonfiction. Put a chart on the board with two columns, one for each genre. Have students list the characteristics of each genre and then compare and contrast them. Ask students how an informational article can help them answer the big question differently than a work of fiction. Suggest a trip to the library or the computer lab to look for other informational articles on what it means to live bravely. OL

Skills Preview

Key Reading Skill: Predicting

"A Year of Living Bravely" is about Bethany Hamilton, a teenaged surfer who was badly hurt in a shark attack in 2003. From this information and the title of the article, predict what the article will say about Bethany.

Whole Class Discussion As a class, guess what kinds of facts and details you will find in the article. To get started, think about the 5Ws and an H.

Text Element: Attention-Getting Device

Many nonfiction writers begin their articles with a statement intended to capture readers' attention and make them want to read on. This kind of beginning is an **attention-getting device.** Types of attention-getting devices include the following:

- a statement that presents interesting information
  Example: Bees have been producing honey for more than 100 million years.
- a **rhetorical** (reh TOR ih kul) **question**—a question that readers are not expected to answer
  Example: Did you know that bees have been producing honey for more than 100 million years?
- a surprising fact
  Example: A single bee colony has a lot of worker bees—in fact, more than 50,000!

Partner Talk With a classmate, read the first paragraph of a magazine or newspaper feature article. What type of attention-getting device does the writer use? Discuss whether it makes you want to read on.

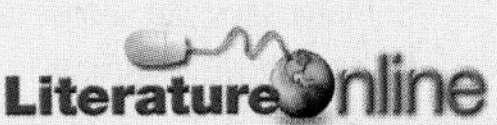

Interactive Literary Elements Handbook To review or learn more about author's purpose, go to www.glencoe.com.

Get Ready to Read

Connect to the Reading

Bethany Hamilton loves to surf. Being a surfer is a big part of who she is. What is your favorite activity or hobby? What would you do if an injury stopped you from doing it? Would you substitute a different activity?

Write to Learn In your Learner's Notebook, jot down a few sentences describing what your hobby is. Tell what you think you might do if you couldn't enjoy it anymore and why you think you would do that.

Build Background

Surfing dates back to prehistoric times. It is believed to have originated in the South Pacific among Polynesian sailors. During the 1800s, missionaries banned surfing in the South Pacific. Hawaiian Duke Kahanamoku revived the sport of surfing in the early 1900s. He started Waikiki's first surf club and introduced surfing to Australia. Today surfing is a popular sport in many parts of the world.

- The surfboards of the early 1900s were made of wood. They were eight to ten feet long. They were also heavy, weighing in at 100 pounds.
- Modern boards are made of plastic and are only about six feet long. They weigh five or six pounds and have fins on the bottom so the rider can steer.

Set Purposes for Reading

BIG Question Read "A Year of Living Bravely" to learn how Bethany stays true to herself in spite of her injury.

Set Your Own Purpose What would you like to learn from the selection to help you answer the Big Question? Write your own purpose on the "A Year of Living Bravely" page of Foldable 5.

Keep Moving

Use these skills as you read "A Year of Living Bravely."

Teach

E Text Element

Attention-Getting Device

Say: Read the three examples of attention-getting devices. Which type of attention-getting device would make you most likely want to read the story about bees? Why? *(Responses will vary.)* AS

R Reading Skill

Review Connecting Say: List five emotions you would experience if you could no longer participate in your favorite activity. Use these emotions to connect to how Bethany Hamilton probably felt in "A Year of Living Bravely." OL

Interactive Literary Elements Handbook Have students access the Web site to improve their understanding of predicting.

Reading in the Real World

College Most students will write autobiographical essays for their college applications. They may have already written this type of essay for a class or competition. Challenge students to write three or four attention-getting sentences that they could use in a nonfiction essay about themselves. Instruct students to look at the examples under *Text Element: Attention-Getting Device* and model their sentences after these examples. Have students share their opening sentences with a partner. Then ask students to think of a title for their autobiographical essays. Have students vote on the most interesting title. OL

Indiana English/Language Arts Academic Standards

SE: 8.1, 8.2

TWE: *Literature Focus Lesson* 8.2, *Reading in the Real World* 8.4

Teach

Viewing the Photo

Say: Describe this picture of Bethany surfing. What do you learn about her from this picture? *(Possible response: She is determined; she is a really talented surfer to be able to surf with one arm; she looks really strong.)* **OL**

E Text Element

Attention-Getting Device Have students rewrite the first paragraph using another attention-getting device. Ask volunteers to read their rewrites aloud to the class. *(Responses will vary.)* **AL**

L Literary Element

Review Theme Say: Bethany says that "desire" is the reason she recovered. What do you think will be the theme of this article? *(Possible response: Having a goal or a strong desire to get better helps people deal with tragedies.)* **OL**

Readability Scores
Dale-Chall: 4.7
DRP: 52
Lexile: 580

A Year of Living Bravely

by Emily Costello

Bethany Hamilton had a horrifying experience last Halloween. A tiger shark attacked her while she was surfing off the coast of Hawaii. The shark chewed off Bethany's left arm just below the shoulder. By the time she reached the hospital, she'd lost half the blood in her body. She was near death. Bethany had two surgeries to close the wound. She spent eight days in the hospital. **1** **E**

Nobody would have blamed Bethany if she'd never surfed again. Instead, she recovered with surprising speed. Less than a month after the attack, she was surfing again. On January 10, she entered a major competition. She took fifth place out of 24.

What helped Bethany recover so quickly? She loves to surf, and she wanted to start again. "Desire is the answer," she says, "and I had that." **2** **L**

Practice the Skills

1 Text Element

Attention-Getting Device By opening with interesting statements, the author tries to interest you in reading the rest of the article. Do the facts make you want to read on? Explain.

2 Key Reading Skill

Predicting To predict what the article will say about Bethany, think about these facts:

- The title of the selection is "A Year of Living Bravely."
- Bethany says she recovered fast to return to surfing.

From these facts, you can guess that the article will tell in more detail what Bethany did during the year after the shark attack.

Additional Support

Reading in the Real World

Career It is likely that Bethany's care after the accident began with an emergency medical crew and an ambulance ride. Some ambulances are run by volunteers; others are staffed by paid people. Either way, they require special training. Have students find out about the emergency medical technicians (EMTs) in your area. Are they volunteers? What training do they have? What types of emergencies are they most likely to deal with in your area? Have students who are interested in a career as EMTs do further research to find out what they would need to do to become an EMT in your area. **OL**

Cool Accessories

Bethany isn't self-conscious about her missing arm. She calls what's left of her left arm "Stumpy." She rarely covers Stumpy with long-sleeved shirts. Instead, she wears what she's always liked to wear—tank tops and bathing suits.

Her new arm, which is made of plastic and metal, has a nickname too. She calls it "Haole Girl." Haole (HOWLee) means "white." It's a word Hawaiians use for non-natives. The name fits. Originally the arm was much paler than Bethany's own skin. It was recently dyed darker. **R**

The arm was a gift from the manufacturer. It cost $45,000 to make! Still, the arm is mostly for looks. Bethany has to move it with her good arm. She **confesses** that she rarely takes it out of the closet.

"I'm complete without it," Bethany says. "I can paddle and balance on a surfboard. I can cut an orange by holding it between my feet. And I like my new look." **L**

Suddenly Famous 3

Bethany has adjusted to a one-armed life without much trouble. But other parts of her new life have been challenging. "I'm learning how to balance my life—schooling, surfing, and my career," Bethany says.

Bethany is in the eighth grade. She's home-schooled[1]—although "on-the-road-schooled" might be more accurate.

During the past year, Bethany has had little time at home. She appeared on the TV news-magazine show *20/20*. She was on the cover of

1. Someone who is ***home-schooled*** is taught school subjects outside of school by a parent or a tutor rather than in school by a teacher.

Vocabulary

confesses (kun FES ses) *v.* tells a truth that one rarely talks about

Practice the Skills

3 Key Reading Skill

Predicting What do you think this section will be about? Think about these things:

- what you've learned so far about Bethany
- what the subtitle, or subhead, "Suddenly Famous" tells you.

Analyzing the Photo Hamilton smiles on arriving for the 2004 premier of the film *Open Water*. How does this photograph convey her confidence?

READING WORKSHOP 3

Teach

R Reading Skill

Review Monitoring Comprehension

Ask: Why did Bethany name her arm "Haole Girl"? *(Possible response: Because her arm was very white and paler than her own skin. Her arm is non-native to her body.)* **OL**

L Literary Element

Review Characterization

Say: Think about what Bethany says about her arm and how she is "complete without it." What kind of person do you think Bethany is? *(Possible response: She is self-confident and a positive person. She does not feel sorry for herself in any way.)* **OL**

Differentiated Instruction

Self-Esteem Letters Most eighth-graders are very conscious of their appearance, even without missing an arm. Bethany says "I like my new look." Using Bethany as an example, have students write a letter telling other eighth-graders how to feel good about themselves and appreciate who they are and what they have. Have students create a bulletin board on self-confidence and body image. Assign groups of students to find other resources on self-confidence and body image to contribute to the bulletin board. Use student letters as part of the display. Ask students to come up with a theme for the bulletin board. **OL**

Indiana English/Language Arts Academic Standards

SE: 8.2

TWE: *Reading in the Real World* 8.4, *Differentiated Instruction* 8.5.7

Teach

Viewing the Photo

Ask: How does this photo show that teens are interested in hearing Bethany Hamilton's story? *(The picture shows people who are very interested in hearing from Bethany and who are excited about being there.)* **BL** **Ask:** Why do you think Bethany agrees to go on these shows? *(Responses will vary.)* **OL**

C Critical Thinking

Analysis: Ask: Why do you think the author chose to put in all these details about what Bethany does? *(Possible response: These details show that Bethany has a very active life and losing her arm has not slowed her down at all.)* **OL**

L Literary Element

Review Characterization

Ask: What do you learn about Bethany from this page of the article, including the photograph and the text? *(Possible response: She has her own style; she is confident in her appearance; she gets to travel all over the world surfing.)* Have students summarize Bethany as a person based on what they have learned from this article. *(Responses will vary.)* **OL**

READING WORKSHOP 3

Analyzing the Photo Hamilton appears with Damien Fahey, veejay of MTV's *Total Request Live,* in 2003. How might Hamilton's story encourage other teens who face setbacks?

People and *Teen Vogue*. She **co-wrote** a book called *Soul Surfer*. **4** She has a movie in the works. The ESPN sports network gave her an Espy Award. She made an appearance at the Teen Choice Awards. She threw out the first pitch at the Oakland A's season opener. She has done hundreds of interviews for magazines. **C**

Of course, being famous isn't all hard work. For Bethany, one of the perks[2] is going to **exotic** places to surf. Bethany traveled to Nicaragua and Portugal earlier this year, and loved it. "She wakes me up at 5 a.m. and screams, 'Let's go

2. ***Perks*** is short for *perquisites,* which are special privileges.

Vocabulary

exotic (eg ZOT ik) *adj.* strangely beautiful and foreign

Practice the Skills

4 English Language Coach

Prefixes That Show Relationships The prefix *co-* means "with," "together," or "partner." What does **co-wrote** mean?

Additional Support

Differentiated Instruction

Create an Award Tell students they are going to create their own award for a student in middle school. Guide students as they make these decisions about their award:

- What type of heroism will it honor?
- What will the award be called?
- How will you choose a winner?
- Where and when will you give the award?

Once students have completed this process, assign different students to make posters about the award, to design the actual award (a sculpture, a plaque, or something else), and to write an explanation of the award for people who want to nominate others. Hold a contest in your classroom or in the school for the award. **OL** surfing!'" her best friend, Alana Blanchard, told *USA Today.* "She just always wants to surf."

The Hard Part

Bethany is always training to become a better surfer. She plans to surf for the rest of her life.

But she admits that sometimes being in the ocean feels weird. She gets a little scared. When that happens, she calls to friends surfing nearby. Or she sings a song to herself.

"I have nightmares," Bethany confesses. When the nightmares come, she says it helps to think about other people's problems. This summer, Bethany hopes to raise $50,000 for disabled kids through a charity called World Vision.

Bethany notes that there are 120 million disabled kids worldwide. Landmines[3] injured many of them. In poor countries, few disabled kids get to go to school. Some poor families abandon disabled kids. Thinking about such **hardships,** Bethany knows how lucky she really is.

"Why shouldn't I be happy?" she asks. "I'm surfing and traveling and really doing all I ever wanted." 5 ❍

3. ***Landmines*** are explosive devices that are placed on or beneath the ground.

Vocabulary

hardships (HARD ships) *n.* things that cause pain or suffering; misfortunes

Practice the Skills

E

5 **BIG Question**

Do you think it was important for Bethany to surf after her accident? Explain why or why not. Write your answer on the "A Year of Living Bravely" page of Foldable 5. Your response will help you complete the Unit Challenge later. BQ

Teach

E Text Element

Review Titles and Subheads

Say: This article used subheads throughout the text. **Ask:** How did these subheads help you read and understand the article? *(Possible response: They helped me to know what each section was going to be about so I could follow the article easily.)* EL BL

BQ BIG Question

Ask: How did Bethany stay true to herself? *(Possible response: Bethany stayed with her passion, surfing, even after most people would have been afraid to get in the water. She also tried to do something good with all of the fame she has—she is using it to raise money for disabled children around the world.)* OL

Assess

CheckPoint

Use the CheckPoint questions provided on Presentation Plus! to check for comprehension of the selection. These questions can be used with interactive response keypads for immediate student feedback.

Reading in the Real World

Citizenship Have students work individually, with partners, or with groups to plan their own fundraising effort to help disabled children. Students can look into World Vision and decide if they want to raise money to be part of Bethany's effort. Or they may choose another charity that helps children. Guide students as they decide how they will raise money and how they will get their message out. Challenge students to make posters, have their event (if they are having one) advertised in the school and local newspapers, and maybe even make a short video clip. Have students make their first presentation at a class or school event. OL AL

Indiana English/Language Arts Academic Standards

SE: 8.1

TWE: *Differentiated Instruction* 8.5, *Reading in the Real World* 8.5.7

Assess

Resources for page 626

- Selection Quick Check, p. 46
- Selection and Unit Assessment, p. 54
- ExamView Assessment Suite
- Interactive Tutor: Self-Assessment

Students can respond to the *After You Read* items in their Learner's Notebooks or on a separate sheet of paper.

Answering the

1. Responses will vary.
2. Bethany lost her left arm in a shark attack.
3. Bethany gets over her nightmares by thinking about people who have problems much worse than hers.

Critical Thinking

4. Possible response: She is comfortable with herself just the way she is without her plastic arm.
5. Possible response: The main idea is that people can survive tragedies by staying focused and by helping others. Some facts that show this are: Bethany saying she had "desire"; Bethany going back to surfing as soon as she could; Bethany appearing on different TV shows and magazines; Bethany trying to raise money for charity.
6. Responses will vary.

After You Read

A Year of Living Bravely

Answering the BIG Question

1. From reading "A Year of Living Bravely," what have you learned about how someone stays true to himself or herself?
2. **Recall** How did Bethany lose her left arm?
   TIP **Right There**
3. **Recall** What does Bethany say she does to get over her nightmares?
   TIP **Right There**

Critical Thinking

4. **Interpret** What does Bethany mean when she says, "I am complete without [the plastic arm]"?
   TIP **Author and Me**
5. **Analyze** What is the main idea of the article? Write it in your own words. Then explain which facts, details, and other clues in the article helped you find the main idea.
   TIP **Author and Me**
6. **Evaluate** Would you recommend this article to other eighth-graders? Why or why not? Use details from the article to support your answer.
   TIP **On My Own**

Talk About Your Reading

Whole Class Discussion Bethany Hamilton has been in the news a lot. She has been interviewed by TV, magazine, and newspaper reporters. She has won awards. She has written a book, and she is working on a movie about her life. As a class, discuss why Bethany has gotten so much publicity, or news coverage, and what more you'd like to know about her.

- Why do you think people are interested in her story?
- Why do you think she wants to tell others her story?
- If you could meet Bethany, what would you like to ask her? Why?

Indiana English/Language Arts Academic Standards (pp. 626–627)

8.2 Comprehension and Analysis (Focus on Informational Text) Develop [reading] strategies such as…making predictions, and identifying and analyzing structure and organization… **8.7 Listening and Speaking** Careful listening and evaluation of content. Speaking skills…are developed…and applied…**8.6 English Language Conventions**

For a complete description of the standards, see p. IN 11.

Talk About Your Reading

Sample responses:

People like reading about other people who have overcome difficulties.
People are inspired by the things that Bethany does and says.
Bethany may want to tell others her story to help raise money for charity.
She may also want to tell her story so that people who have bad things happen to them can be inspired to overcome their situations.
Students may want to ask Bethany why she likes surfing so much.
Students may want to ask Bethany what it's like to live without an arm.
Students may want to ask Bethany what she wants to do for a career.

Skills Review

Key Reading Skill: Predicting

7. Look back at the predictions you made before you read "A Year of Living Bravely" and while you read it. Which of your predictions were correct? Did anything in the story surprise you? Explain.

Text Element: Attention-Getting Device

8. The author begins her article with interesting statements about Bethany's accident. Use a different attention-getting device, such as a rhetorical question or surprising facts, to write a new first paragraph for the selection. Then tell which introduction you think is better and why.

Vocabulary Check

Answer *true* or *false* to each statement. If a statement is false, rewrite it to make it true.

9. Someone who **confesses** to a crime admits to doing an illegal act.
10. An **exotic** place is a familiar location.
11. **Hardships** often cause unhappiness.
12. **Academic Vocabulary** If your teacher tells you to pick **relevant** details, what kind of details will you look for as you read?

English Language Coach On a separate sheet of paper, write the prefix and the base word that make up each of the words below. Then write a definition of the word. If you need help, use a dictionary.

13. cohost
14. preview
15. copilot
16. postgame
17. prerecorded

Web Activities For eFlashcards, Selection Quick Checks, and other Web activities, go to www.glencoe.com.

Grammar Link: More Sentence Combining

Combining sentences is a useful way to avoid repeating ideas. Notice the repetition in the following paragraph. Repeated words and ideas are underlined.

- I often have to babysit <u>my twin brothers</u>. <u>My twin brothers</u> are Sam and Danny. They never sit still. <u>They like</u> to run around the house. <u>They like</u> to chase the dog. <u>They like</u> to throw baseballs at each other.

To fix repeated words and phrases, try combining sentences by using one or more of the following methods.

Method A: Explanatory Phrase Make the repeated idea into an explanatory phrase.

- Repetitious: I often have to babysit <u>my twin brothers</u>. <u>My twin brothers</u> are Sam and Danny.
- Better: I often have to babysit my twin brothers, <u>Sam and Danny</u>.

Method B: Series of Items Combine the repeated ideas in a series.

- Repetitious: <u>They like</u> to run around the house. <u>They like</u> to chase the dog. <u>They like</u> to throw baseballs at each other.
- Better: <u>They like</u> to run around the house, chase the dog, and throw baseballs at each other.

Grammar Practice

Use a method described above to combine each pair of repetitious sentences below. Write your sentences on a separate sheet of paper.

18. We like to visit Middletown Ocean View. Middletown Ocean View is a beautiful aquarium.
19. On our vacation we went swimming. We went boating. We also went hiking.
20. My little brother borrowed my favorite book. My favorite book is *Tuck Everlasting.*
21. The Tucks are the family described in the book. The Tucks have found the secret of eternal life.
22. They go into the forest. They drink water from a magic fountain. They never grow old.

Skills Review

Key Reading Skill: Predicting

7. Students should clearly identify those predictions that were accurate and what may have been surprising.

Text Element: Attention-Getting Device

8. Responses will vary.

Vocabulary Check

9. T
10. False; An exotic place is a beautiful place that is unfamiliar or foreign.
11. T

Academic Vocabulary

12. Possible response: I will look for details that are important to the topic.

English Language Coach

13. co; host
14. pre; view
15. co; pilot
16. post; game
17. pre; recorded

Close

Ask students what they learned from reading "A Year of Living Bravely" to answer the Big Question.

Grammar Link: More Sentence Combining

Grammar Practice

Possible responses:

18. We like to visit Middletown Ocean View, a beautiful aquarium.
19. On our vacation we went swimming, boating, and hiking.
20. My little brother borrowed my favorite book, *Tuck Everlasting.*
21. The Tucks, the family described in the book, have found the secret of eternal life.
22. They go into the forest, drink water from a magic fountain, and never grow old.

Indiana English/Language Arts Academic Standards
SE: 8.2, 8.6, 8.7

Focus

BELLRINGER Options

Daily Language Practice Transparency 48

Focus Activity Go around the room and ask students what part of this writing assignment was most difficult for them. Then ask what part they enjoyed the most. Ask for volunteers to read their favorite part of their story to the class. *(Responses will vary.)* AS

Teach

W Writing

Characterization Ask: How do you feel when you read a book or see a movie with an unrealistic character? *(Possible response: I feel frustrated because I spend my time thinking about how a person wouldn't really do or say those things.)* OL

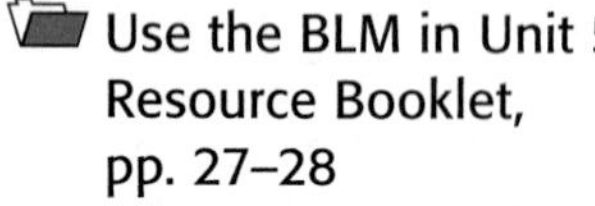

Resources for page 628

- Use the BLM in Unit 5 Resource Booklet, pp. 27–28
- Use the Grammar and Writing Workshop Transparencies 25–26.

WRITING WORKSHOP PART 2

Short Story

Revising, Editing, and Presenting

ASSIGNMENT Write a short story

Purpose: To tell a story about a character who struggles to stay true to himself or herself

Audience: Your teacher and your classmates

Revising Rubric

Your revised short story should have

- a clear focus and effective organization
- well-developed characters
- a plot with a clear beginning, conflict, and resolution
- a setting that fits your plot
- realistic dialogue

Indiana English/Language Arts Academic Standards (pp. 628–633)

8.5.1 Write…short stories… **8.4.7** Review, evaluate, and revise writing for meaning and clarity. **8.4.8** Edit and proofread…writing… **8.4.9** Revise writing for…appropriate organization… **8.4.10** Create an organizational structure… **8.7 Listening and Speaking** Careful listening and evaluation of content. Speaking skills…are developed…and applied…

For a complete description of the standards, see p. IN 11.

In Writing Workshop Part 1 you wrote a draft of your short story. Now it's time to improve it. Keep a copy of your story in your writing portfolio so that you and your teacher can evaluate your writing progress over time.

Revising

Make It Better

Take a fresh look at your draft. This is your chance to improve it.

1. Read your draft quickly and put it aside. Then think about the general impression you get from your story. Ask yourself these questions.
   - *Does my writing tell the story I want to tell? Does everything in it contribute to one overall effect without wandering away from the point?*
   - *Are there any parts that are awkward or confusing?*
   - *Do my characters seem like real people?* (See the next section for help in developing your characters.)
   - *Is the conflict understandable?*
   - *Is the resolution satisfying?*
   - *Do I describe the setting well enough that readers can picture it?*
   - *Does my story have a consistent point of view? Is everything seen through the same character's eyes?*
2. Reread the draft slowly. Mark places where you want to rewrite.

Develop Believable Characters

W Good characters are lifelike people your readers can care about. Characterization is how you bring them to life. You can develop characters by describing how they look, how they talk, how they act, and how they feel. You can also reveal what other characters say about them. Dialogue is another good way to develop your characters. Reread your story, looking for opportunities to further develop your characters.

Additional Support

Literature Focus Lesson

Characterization Have students write the names of their characters on a separate sheet of paper. Ask students to answer these two sets of questions about each character:

- What does your character look like? What color hair does he or she have? How tall, big, or small is he or she? Is there anything unusual about how he or she looks?
- How does your character talk? Does he or she speak a dialect or have a unique voice in any way?

Once students answer each of the questions about their characters, have them revise their stories to add details about each character. OL

Applying Good Writing Traits

Organization

Good short stories are well organized and focused. They have a point. They move clearly from the beginning to the middle to the end. The writing is smooth, and the conclusion makes sense.

What Is Organization?

Organization is the inner structure of a piece of writing–the order in which the ideas are arranged. The organization of a story guides readers through a sequence of events.

Why Is Organization Important in My Writing?

W1

- Organizing your ideas can help you get them down on paper more quickly and easily.
- Clear organization guides readers through your ideas and makes your writing easier to follow.
- Strong organization gives readers a sense of direction while they read.

How Do I Organize My Writing?

Different types of writing are organized in different ways. The following guidelines will help you strengthen the organization of narratives, or stories.

- Organize the events of your story in a logical order. Set up the conflict clearly before you try to resolve it. Use transition words (*then, next, finally*) to link ideas and events.
- Write a satisfying end to your story. Show how the conflict is resolved and what the main character learns. Don't leave readers feeling as if you got up to answer the door and forgot to come back. Also avoid overused endings such as "and then I woke up" or "we lived happily ever after."

Organization Practice Check the organization of your story by making a story map like this one. Do the three stages of your story do their jobs?

W2

Beginning
Introduce characters, conflict, setting.

Middle
Develop characters and conflict.

End
Resolve conflict. Tell what protagonist learned.

Analyzing Cartoons
This boy could sure use some help getting organized! If you wrote to a friend about your opinion of this cartoon, how would you organize your writing?

Teach

W1 Writing

Organization Say: It is important to organize any piece of writing that you do. Each type of writing benefits from organization for different reasons. For example, an informational text needs to be organized so readers can understand all of the information it provides. Why do you think it might be important to organize short stories? *(Possible response: It will help readers follow the plot development.)* OL

W2 Writing

Plot Direct attention to the story map on page 629. Talk about the fact that the end of the story should *not* develop new characters or add new conflicts. The end should only resolve conflicts and show what the characters learned. Have several students write their story maps on the board and discuss the choices they made about characters, conflict, and resolution. *(Responses will vary.)* OL

Differentiated Instruction

Rewriting Point of View Have students identify the point of view of their stories. Then have students choose one part of their story to rewrite from a different point of view. Have students break into small groups. Have each student read the two versions of the part they rewrote: the first version from the original point of view and the second from the new point of view. Ask the other members of the group to comment on which point of view they like better and why. Discuss how changing the point of view changes the story. Encourage students who like the change in point of view to revise their stories so they are told from the new point of view. OL

Indiana English/Language Arts Academic Standards
SE: 8.4.7, 8.4.9, 8.4.10, 8.5.1
TWE: *Literature Focus Lesson* 8.4; *Differentiated Instruction* 8.3.8, 8.5.1

Teach

W Writing

Spelling **Say:** One problem people have with the spell check on a computer is that the computer does not know if you misspell a homonym. Write these three common sets of homonyms that people mix up or misspell on the board:

- their/they're/there
- its/it's
- to/too/two

Have students give you definitions for each word. Then have students check their drafts for these words to make sure they used them correctly. AS

LSV Listening, Speaking, and Viewing

Presenting While all of the short stories students wrote are about the same theme, some of them may also have other common threads. Have students get into small groups and read each other's stories. Ask each group to report back to the class about the commonalities they found among their stories. **Ask:** Do they have similar characters? Are there similar conflicts among the stories? Did they resolve their conflicts in similar ways? *(Responses will vary.)* OL

Editing

Finish It Up

Writing Tip

Spelling If you are using a computer, you can use the Spell Check feature, but the only way to be 100 percent sure of a word's spelling is to look it up in a dictionary. W

When you are satisfied with your story, look carefully to see whether there are any errors in grammar, usage, and mechanics.

Use the Editing Checklist to spot and correct errors. Get rid of any words that aren't needed. If you have trouble recognizing your mistakes, try reading your story aloud. Hearing the words may help you catch mistakes that you miss when you only see the words on the page.

Editing Checklist

- ☑ Pronouns agree with their antecedents.
- ☑ The writing is free of sentence fragments and run-ons.
- ☑ All verbs agree with their subjects.
- ☑ Punctuation is correct.
- ☑ Spelling and capitalization are correct.

Take one last quick look through your short story before you hand it in. Ask yourself, *Is this as good as I can make it? Did I miss anything?*

Presenting

Show It Off

Writing Tip

Read Aloud Another way to present your story is to read it to your class. You can act out scenes, use different voices for different characters—whatever you feel like doing. Have fun performing!

Stories are meant to be read! With your classmates, make a book of short stories that you can share with other classes. Your character's struggle to stay true may help readers handle something they are going through.

1. Neatly copy your story or, if possible, use a word-processing program to enter and print out a final copy of your story.
2. If you want to, add pictures to your story to help readers visualize a character, setting, or mood (the general feeling of your story). You can draw an illustration, find a picture in a magazine or newspaper, or search the Internet for an image you can use. Be sure that the image you choose captures an event or mood from your story.
3. Put all of the stories and pictures together in a binder. Now you have a collection of short stories about many different characters and situations but about the same theme (staying true to oneself in a difficult situation).
4. Finally, work together as a class to brainstorm possible titles for your collection. Vote to choose one of them.

Additional Support

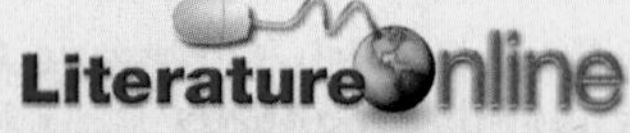

Writing Models Have students access the Web site for an additional and interactive Writing Workshop-based student model.

Reading Fluency

Reading Aloud Have students listen to various recordings of short stories **Ask:** What did you like about listening to the stories? How is listening to a story different from reading a story? *(Responses will vary.)* OL Have students record themselves reading their own stories aloud. Tell them to model what they liked about what they heard on the recordings as they read their stories aloud. Encourage students to work in groups so that different students can read the parts of different characters. AL

Writer's Model

Being There for Abuela

Marisol finished getting ready for school. She went into the kitchen and grabbed her lunch, tuna fish and wheat bread, from the counter. She walked into the living room, where her grandmother sat on the couch knitting a blue sweater. "Abuela, how are you feeling today?"

"I am feeling better, Marisol. Are you leaving for school?" her grandmother asked.

"Yes, I have a math test. I will see you after school."

"Good, I will make us some asopao for dinner. I know it's your favorite."

Marisol walked out of the house into the cold morning. The tears came into her eyes. Her grandmother looked so small and weak. Marisol pushed back her hair and pulled her jean jacket more tightly together. She ran to catch the bus.

All day in school she thought about her grandmother. They had all moved so far to get to the United States. Her mom, dad, and brother were doing great. But her grandmother was dying. She was really old, and she did less and less every day. Marisol loved her so much. The thought of losing her broke Marisol's heart. She tried to finish writing her essay in English class, the last period of the day, but she couldn't concentrate. Finally, the bell rang, and she was free to go home.

Marisol went to her locker to get her books for homework. Her three best friends were there waiting for her. Julie, Tracy, and Sam had been there for Marisol since she moved to the new school. They were all on the soccer team and hung out together.

"Hey, Marisol, you ready for practice?" Julie yelled down the hallway.

"I can't go today," Marisol yelled back as she ran to her locker. "I have to get home and see my grandmother. She's not doing so well."

Active Writing Model

- The beginning of the story introduces you to Marisol and her grandmother.
- Dialogue and description show you what the main character acts like and looks like.
- The writer uses third-person point of view ("she," "her") here and throughout the story. The words "I" and "my" appear only in dialogue.
- Dialogue shows you the relationship between characters and gives you information about the conflict.

Literature Focus Lesson

Setting This model has a couple of settings: the high school and the kitchen. Have students work in small groups to write detailed descriptions of how they imagine each of these settings. Ask each group to read its descriptions aloud to the class. Talk about the similarities and differences between the descriptions. Once students finish the detailed descriptions for this story, have them work on adding details to their own stories to help readers better picture what they had in mind when they wrote their stories. OL

Teach

W1 Writing

Dialogue Say: Notice that the grandmother says she is "feeling better." What does this tell you about what may have happened before the story began? *(Her grandmother was probably sick.)* OL

C Critical Thinking

Analysis Ask: What details does the writer use to describe the characters and the setting? *(Possible responses: use of Spanish words like* abuela *and* asopao, *tuna fish and wheat bread, blue sweater, math test, they moved to the U.S. as a family)* **Ask:** What do these details tell you about the characters in this story? *(Possible responses: they live in an extended family; they are immigrants; they are Latinos.)* OL

W2 Writing

Characterization Ask: What do you learn about Marisol's grandmother at this point in the story? *(She is getting older and weaker)* **Ask:** What do you learn about Marisol from her actions at school? *(Possible response: She is very connected to her grandmother and cares deeply for her family.)* OL

Indiana English/Language Arts Academic Standards

SE: 8.4.8, 8.5.1

TWE: *Reading Fluency* 8.7, *Literature Focus Lesson* 8.3

Teach

W1 Writing

Conflict **Ask:** What details does the writer use to show the conflict? *(Marisol closes her locker door. She walks down the hall one way and her friends go down the hall toward the soccer field.)* OL **Ask:** Does Marisol have an internal or an external conflict? *(internal)* BL

W2 Writing

Resolution **Ask:** What made Marisol's decision difficult for her? *(the fact that she might lose her friends and that she might not be able to go to college if she does not play soccer)* **Ask:** What made the decision easier? *(thinking about the fact that her grandmother would not be with her forever)* OL

Active Writing Model

"Coach isn't going to like it. That's three practices you've missed, and we have a game tomorrow," said Sam.

W1

"I know, but I can't help it." Marisol got her books and shut her locker door. "See you later," she said to her friends. They all looked at her.

Tracy smiled. "Tell your grandma we hope she feels better. See you tomorrow." The three of them turned and walked away toward the soccer field. Marisol walked down the other hall.

When she got home, she could smell the garlic from the asopao. She ran into the kitchen to see her grandmother, who stood at the stove. Her grandmother turned and smiled at her. Marisol knew then that not going to soccer practice was the right decision.

The writer moves the story's setting to the kitchen to give readers a better sense of the relationship between Marisol and her grandmother. Concrete details help readers imagine sights and sounds.

"Just in time," said her grandmother as she ladled the meat and vegetables into a bowl and placed it on the table. "Sit and eat."

Marisol sat down and put her books on the floor. Her grandmother sat across from her, straightening her red dress around her as she got comfortable. "Tell me about your day," she said, and Marisol began to talk. They sat there for hours as the sun went down and the rest of the family came home from work and school.

After dinner, Marisol went into her room. She sat on her bed and spread her books out. What should she do? She loved playing soccer, but she loved her grandmother more. If she didn't play, would she lose all her friends? What about college? Without a soccer scholarship, she didn't think she would be able to go. Marisol sat in her room and thought about her grandmother dying. How long did she have? Marisol knew it wasn't long.

This paragraph focuses on the main conflict: Marisol's decision about whether to stay on the soccer team or spend time with her dying grandmother.

W2

As Marisol started her homework, she made her decision. She would quit the soccer team this year. She could always play next year, but her grandmother might not be here then. With her decision made, Marisol finished her homework with no problem. Her mom came in to say good night. Marisol went to bed and slept better than ever.

The resolution of the story shows Marisol making her decision and being true to herself when she realizes that soccer will always be there, but her grandmother will not.

Additional Support

Differentiated Instruction

Chart It Have students make a chart of the pros and cons for Marisol, showing the advantages and disadvantages of quitting the soccer team. When students have finished working individually on their charts, have them compare their charts with partners. **Ask:** What would have been the consequences if Marisol had stayed on the soccer team? What would have been the benefits? What did Marisol gain by quitting the team? Do you agree or disagree with her decision? Why or why not? OL

Listening, Speaking, and Viewing

Group Discussion

Do you enjoy a good talk with your friends? In a group discussion you can try to persuade classmates to share your opinions.

What Is Group Discussion?

A group discussion is a gathering of three or more students to talk about a piece of writing. You might discuss one specific question (for example, What is the main conflict? Is the protagonist's behavior believable?), or you might cover several elements of a story. It's usually a good idea to take notes on the group's ideas so you can share them with the entire class.

Why Is Group Discussion Important?

In a group discussion students help each other learn. You voice and support your own opinions and listen to other people's. You develop skills in listening, dealing with conflict, and making decisions. When you share information and debate its meaning, you can learn new ideas and teach them. You also get a chance to see things from other people's perspectives and appreciate their different ways of communicating.

How Do I Take Part in Group Discussion?

Use the tips that follow to participate effectively in group discussion.

- Think before you speak, but then speak up. Volunteer your ideas and opinions.
- Use the skills of inferring and drawing conclusions in your discussion. Bring your own prior knowledge and experience to the conversation.
- Listen to what others have to say. Give everyone a chance to talk. Be encouraging.
- If you don't understand the point someone is making, ask for more information.
- It's okay to disagree with a classmate, but be polite. You might say, "But have you considered . . ." not "That doesn't make any sense."
- Build on other group members' comments.
- Help the group summarize its progress. Stop every few minutes and say, "This is what we've figured out so far. What else do we need to know or figure out?"
- Identify missing information in the group's answer. Help the other members fill in blanks.

Try It Out Use the guidelines on conducting a group discussion when you discuss these questions: **(1)** Did Marisol do the right thing to resolve her conflict? **(2)** Is there some way she could have handled it better? Be prepared to support your opinions with examples from the text and from life.

Analyzing Cartoons
Would Calvin have found Tommy's story funny if he had read it in a book?

Teach

LSV1 Listening, Speaking, and Viewing

Group Discussion Remind students that a group discussion involves both sharing and listening. In almost every group there will be people who are eager to speak, and there will be people who seem quiet or may even be shy. The people who are quick to speak have to make sure to give others time to speak up. Quiet people have to learn how to speak in a group setting. Tell students to go around the group and give each person a minimum of two minutes to speak. AS

LSV2 Listening, Speaking, and Viewing

Group Discussion Before students break into groups, help them brainstorm a list of questions or expressions to use when they are confused or disagree. Write these examples on the board:

- I'm not sure I understand what you mean.
- What I think you said was . . .
- I never thought of it that way before. AS

Reading in the Real World

Citizenship Part of being a good citizen is knowing how to listen and how to express yourself. After students finish their group discussions, ask them to write a critique of their process. Have students evaluate their discussions by answering the following questions:

- Did everyone get a chance to speak?
- Did everyone listen to what others had to say?
- What did individuals learn from other group members?
- What would you change about your group process?

Have each group report back to the class about their group discussions. OL

Indiana English/Language Arts Academic Standards
SE: 8.7
TWE: *Differentiated Instruction* 8.3, *Reading in the Real World* 8.7

Making Inferences

Teaching Students to Make Inferences

Why Is It Important?

- Inferences depend on seeing connections that are not articulated.
- Most writers do not tell everything a character thinks; readers need to make inferences to fully comprehend what is being communicated.
- Students who make inferences successfully are better able to understand characters and to identify themes.

How to Help Students Get It

- Tell students to always pay attention to everything a writer tells them through a character's actions as well as words.
- Help students notice descriptions, dialogue, events, and relationships.
- Encourage students to ask themselves: "Why does the author tell me this? What does this mean about this character or situation?"
- To build their confidence in making inferences while reading, remind students that they already make many inferences in everyday life.

Reading to Answer the Big Question

The Fire Pond by Michael Rosen
A fire pond is intended to be used only as a water source in case of fire, but the narrator's grandpa stocks his with rainbow trout. A flood kills the fish and devastates the farm, but Grandpa stocks the pond again. A fire, barely a year later, empties the pond completely and kills the fish. When contemplating restocking the pond, Grandpa gives the narrator some advice on how to be true to yourself: "You stock your life with what all makes you happy."

from *Savion!: My Life in Tap* by Savion Glover
Savion Glover adopts a conversational tone and addresses the reader directly, engaging such subjects as learning theater, conducting oneself as a performer, and working with greats like Lon Chaney and Gregory Hines. He talks about the advice he received as a young man, how it helped him become a better dancer, and how it helped him become who he is.

Workshop Resources

<table>
<tr><th colspan="2">Pacing (Days)</th><th rowspan="2">Lesson</th><th rowspan="2">Student Materials</th><th rowspan="2">Teacher Resources</th></tr>
<tr><th>Standard</th><th>Block</th></tr>
<tr><td>1</td><td>1/2</td><td>Key Skill Lesson: Making Inferences</td><td>Key Reading Skills Practice, p. 29
English Language Coach Review, p. 41</td><td>Bellringer Options Transparencies –Daily Language Practice 49
Read Aloud, Think Aloud Transparencies –Key Reading Skills 15
Presentation Plus!</td></tr>
<tr><td>1</td><td rowspan="2">1</td><td>"The Fire Pond"</td><td>Glencoe Online
Unit Vocabulary Review, p. 39
Academic Vocabulary Review, p. 42
English Language Coach
Active Reading Graphic Organizer, p. 31
Literary Analysis, p. 30
StudentWorks Plus™
Online Student Edition
Literature Classics
Selection and Unit Assessments, p. 55</td><td>Literary and Text Analysis Transparencies 45
Puzzlemaker
Skill Level Up!™ A Language Arts Game
BookLink 3
Assessment by Learning Objective (Diagnostic and Formative)
Interactive Tutor: Self-Assessment
TeacherWorks Plus™</td></tr>
<tr><td>1</td><td>from Savion!: My Life in Tap</td><td>Glencoe Online
Unit Vocabulary Review, p. 39
Academic Vocabulary Review, p. 42
English Language Coach
Active Reading Graphic Organizer, p. 33
StudentWorks Plus™
Online Student Edition
Literature Classics
Selection and Unit Assessments, p. 56</td><td>Literary and Text Analysis Transparencies 56
Puzzlemaker
Skill Level Up!™ A Language Arts Game
BookLink 3
Assessment by Learning Objective (Diagnostic and Formative)
Interactive Tutor: Self-Assessment
TeacherWorks Plus™</td></tr>
</table>

Keys for Unit Resource

- Blackline Master
- Workbook
- Supplemental Text
- CD-ROM
- DVD
- Transparency
- Web-based
- Fast File

Level Appropriate Code

AS = Activities for all students
AL = Activities for students working above grade level
OL = Activities for students working at grade level
BL = Activities for students working below grade level
EL = Activities for English language learners

Focus

BELLRINGER Options

Daily Language Practice Transparency 49

Focus Activity Ask: What hobbies do you have? What do you enjoy about them? Guide students in a discussion about why hobbies are so important to some people.

Teach

R Reading Skill

Making Inferences Ask: What does a detective do? *(solves crimes by looking for clues)* BL **Say:** A good detective will notice clues that other people do not. When you make inferences, you need to pay close attention to the text and look for the clues that help you understand what is happening in the story. AS

Analyzing the Cartoon

Ask: What can you infer from the cartoon about how each character feels? *(The adults feel frustrated. Jeremy is confused.)* **Ask:** What clues did you use to make your inferences? *(The man yells and makes a sarcastic comment; Jeremy asks a question that seems obvious to the adults.)* OL

READING WORKSHOP 4

Skills Focus

You will practice using these skills when you read the following selections:

- "The Fire Pond," p. 638
- from *Savion!: My Life in Tap,* p. 654

Reading

- Inferring unstated ideas in text

Literature

- Analyzing the setting of a story
- Recognizing how setting affects characters and conflicts
- Analyzing tone

Vocabulary

- Using prefixes to infer word meaning
- Academic Vocabulary: *imply*

Writing/Grammar

- Avoiding run-on sentences

Skill Lesson

Making Inferences

Learn It!

What Is It? Inferring is like being a detective. It's using your knowledge and information you gather from a text to make a good guess. Writers often **imply,** or hint at, an idea without stating it outright. To make inferences, you "read between the lines" and use what you know to figure out what the hints mean. For instance, while reading fiction you might make inferences about the following:

- why a character does something
- what a character is feeling
- how setting affects conflicts and characters

Analyzing Cartoons
What clue tells Jeremy's dad that the phone call was for Jeremy?

Indiana English/Language Arts Academic Standards (pp. 634–635)

8.2 Comprehension and Analysis (Focus on Informational Text) Develop [reading] strategies…

For a complete description of the standards, see p. IN 11.

Additional Support

Reading Fluency

Build Fluency The first selection in this workshop is a short story that has some level of complexity. Encourage students to find a quiet place to read the story silently. Instruct them to take notes as they read. Assign reading partners and have them take turns reading the story to each other. Ask each pair to come up with a list of questions they have about the text. Hold a class discussion on the story and have students ask their questions. Ask students which part of the text they enjoyed reading the most and why. OL

Why Is It Important? In life you often do not have complete information about people or situations. You must use the information you *do* have to make inferences. Likewise, texts you read may not spell out every idea for you. You must use the information authors *do* give you.

How Do I Do It? As you read, pay attention to details. They are clues that will help you make inferences. Combine the clues with your own knowledge and experience. Then make inferences to figure out implied ideas. Read the following passage from a story. Then read to see how a student inferred what a character was like.

R

Study Central Visit www.glencoe.com and click on Study Central to review making inferences.

My brother is eight years older than I am. But he seems to be twenty years wiser. Though I wouldn't say I'm jealous of him, exactly, I do sort of feel as if I live in the shadow of a giant. He seems to have it all—brains, looks, a great sense of humor, kindness. He's quarterback of his college football team, and girls are continually e-mailing and calling him. My aunt calls him Mr. Amourica because *amour* means "love" in French. I'll never get that kind of attention.

I think the narrator has mixed feelings about his brother. On the one hand, he seems to admire "Mr. Amourica," because he talks about all his great qualities. On the other hand, the narrator seems to want to be his own person. He may feel pressured to be like his brother. I've seen situations like that. I have a friend whose older sister did well in everything—school, sports, work, you name it. My friend had trouble in school. She hated being compared to her sister. She just wanted to be liked for who she was.

Practice It!

Do you agree with the student's inferences? List positive things the narrator says about his brother. Then jot down notes about anything negative about their relationship. Think about similar brother or sister relationships you've seen or experienced. Write a few sentences describing the relationship between the narrator and his brother.

Use It!

As you read "The Fire Pond" and from *Savion!: My Life in Tap,* make inferences based on details and descriptions in the texts.

Teach

Study Central Have students access the Web site to review making inferences and to complete a related activity.

R Reading Skill

Making Inferences **Say:** It may seem that inferring is similar to connecting. However, when you infer, you take "connecting" one step further. You use your understanding from your life experiences to help you make an educated guess and fill in the blanks about what is happening in the story. BL

Resources for page 635

Use Key Reading Skills Transparency 15 in *Read Aloud, Think Aloud* to help students practice making inferences.

English Language Coach

Multiple-Meaning Words Have students make a list of the words that describe emotions from the passage on page 635. *(kindness, jealousy, love)* Tell students to write each word in their Learner's Notebooks, along with a translation of that word into their first language. Then ask students to write a sentence using each word. Lead the class in a discussion, or have partners discuss, the many different meanings of the word *love* in English. *(For example: I love chocolate; I love that show; I love my parents; My mom loves my dad.)* EL

Indiana English/Language Arts Academic Standards
SE: 8.2
TWE: *Reading Fluency* 8.3, *English Language Coach* 8.1

Teach

More About the Author

Every summer during Michael J. Rosen's childhood, he went to a summer camp in the country. When Rosen got older, he went to college. He then got a master's degree in poetry from Columbia University. Rosen lives out in the country near that very summer camp he used to attend. Not only does Rosen write and illustrate books, but he is also very involved in charity and humanitarian efforts. He has written several books to raise money for Share Our Strength, an organization that helps local food pantries.

EL Language Coach

Prefixes That Show Position Instruct students to study the words listed in the chart on page 636. Go around the room and ask each student to say a word that uses one of the prefixes and to use that word in a sentence. *(Responses will vary.)* EL BL

Before You Read The Fire Pond

Meet the Author

Michael J. Rosen writes, edits, and illustrates books. He lives in the country and loves nature. He works hard for the humane treatment of dogs. Rosen believes that to succeed at any task takes persistent effort. He says, "Inspiration's overrated. Strike until the iron is hot."

Author Search For more about Michael J. Rosen, go to www.glencoe.com.

Indiana English/ Language Arts Academic Standards (pp. 636–649)

8.1 Word Recognition, Fluency, and Vocabulary Development Understand…word parts… **8.2 Comprehension and Analysis (Focus on Informational Text)** Develop [reading] strategies… **8.3.4** Analyze the importance of the setting to the mood, tone, and meaning of the text. **8.3.9** Analyze the relevance of setting…

For a complete description of the standards, see p. IN 11.

Vocabulary Preview

fortune (FOR chun) *n.* luck; riches **(p. 639)** *When he won the lottery, the old man could not believe his good fortune.*

recedes (ree SEEDS) *v.* moves or pulls back; form of the verb *recede* **(p. 641)** *Whenever we have hot, dry weather for several days, the water in the pond recedes.*

salvaged (SAL vujd) *v.* saved from ruin; rescued; form of the verb *salvage* **(p. 641)** *We salvaged a few pieces of furniture and some pictures from our home after the flood.*

calculating (KAL kyoo lay ting) *v.* using math or logic to figure out something; form of the verb *calculate* **(p. 646)** *My sister is calculating how long it will take her to save for a new bicycle.*

On Your Own In your Learner's Notebook, write a sentence for each of the vocabulary words. Be sure to use each word correctly.

English Language Coach

EL

Prefixes That Show Position Knowing what common prefixes mean will help you unlock the meaning of many words. Look at the chart below. All the prefixes on the chart show position. As you read "The Fire Pond," look for words that begin with these and other prefixes that show position.

Prefix	Meaning	Word Examples
out-	"outside" or "beyond"	outfield, outbuilding
sub-	"beneath"	submarine, subway
under-	"less than" or "below"	underpay, underground
over-	"on top of" or "too much"	overcoat, overshoot

Partner Work For each prefix, write a word that begins with the prefix. (Do not repeat the words on the chart.) Then use the word in a sentence. Work with a classmate, and use a dictionary if you need to.

Additional Support

Author Search To expand students' appreciation of Michael J. Rosen, have them access the Web site for additional information and resources.

Differentiated Instruction

Idiomatic Expressions Point out the last two sentences in *Meet the Author* and tell students that Rosen is referring to two expressions: 1) success is 99 percent perspiration and 1 percent inspiration; and 2) strike while the iron is hot. The first expression refers to the idea that to be successful, a person has to work hard despite the quality of his or her idea. The second expression refers to blacksmithing. You must heat the iron and then strike it when it is hot because that is when it can be shaped. It means you should take advantage of opportunities when they come your way. AS

Skills Preview

Key Reading Skill: Making Inferences

Authors rarely say exactly what a character values or believes. But you can usually infer what a character values. While you are reading "The Fire Pond," make inferences about the characters' values. Pay special attention to these points:

- what or whom the characters respect
- what the characters do
- how the characters treat each other

Whole Class Discussion How can you tell what a person values? List ideas.

R

Key Literary Element: Setting

Setting is the time and the place in which the events of a story occur. Setting includes the ideas, customs, values, and beliefs of the people who live in a particular time and place. For example, suppose that a story takes place now, in your neighborhood. The values and beliefs of the characters may be different from those of people in a story set in ancient Greece.

Setting may also influence the conflicts developed in a story. For example, if a story is set in a place often hit by tornadoes, then an external conflict—people against a force of nature—may arise from that setting.

To understand the setting and its effects on "The Fire Pond," ask yourself questions like these as you read: *When and where does the action take place? What is the relationship between the characters and their setting? Does conflict arise from the setting? If so, how does that affect the characters?*

L

Small Group Discussion "The Fire Pond" is set in the country. Before you read the story, get together with a small group of classmates and discuss possible similarities and differences between country life and city life. Take notes on a Venn diagram.

Get Ready to Read

Connect to the Reading

What makes you happy? Your idea of happiness may be different from that of your parents, your classmates, or your friends.

Write to Learn In a few sentences describe what makes you happy and why. Then briefly describe how you act when you're happy.

Build Background

People who live in the country may not have access to public water pipes and fire hydrants as people in cities do. So how do farm people find water to put out a fire?

- Many farms have ponds that can supply the thousands of gallons of water needed to put out a fire. Rural fire departments have special pumps that move the water from a pond into the hoses.
- Many rural fire departments are staffed by volunteer firefighters. They train together but do not stay at the fire station. When a fire is reported, the firefighters must rush to the fire station from their homes or jobs to pick up the equipment and fire trucks before they can get to the fire to extinguish it.

Set Purposes for Reading

BIG Question Read "The Fire Pond" to discover how the narrator of the story learns by example to stay true to himself.

Set Your Own Purpose What else would you like to learn from the story to help you answer the Big Question? Write your purpose on "The Fire Pond" page of Foldable 5.

Literature Online

Interactive Literary Elements Handbook To review or learn more about the literary elements, go to www.glencoe.com.

Keep Moving

Use these skills as you read "The Fire Pond."

Teach

R Reading Skill

Making Inferences Have students discuss the list they made of how you can tell what a person values. Talk about the differences among student lists and why people value different things. *(Responses will vary.)* OL

L Literary Element

Setting Have students discuss what would be unique about a story set in their city or community at the present time. *(Responses will vary.)* Ask students to make a list of details they would use to describe a story set in their neighborhood. OL

Literature Online

Interactive Literary Elements Handbook Have students access the Web site to improve their understanding of setting.

Literature Focus Lesson

Setting One way for students to understand the importance of setting is to consider how the story would change if the setting changed. Have the class brainstorm a list of movies or books that they are familiar with and that are dependent upon their settings. BL Divide the class into groups of three or four students. Assign each group a different movie or book. Instruct the groups to choose a new setting for the story and then describe what they would have to change in order to make the story fit its new setting. Groups can then describe their new stories to the class. You may also have students try this exercise with one or more of the selections in this unit. OL

Indiana English/Language Arts Academic Standards

SE: 8.1, 8.2, 8.3.4, 8.3.9

TWE: *Differentiated Instruction* 8.1.1; *Literature Focus Lesson* 8.3.4, 8.3.9

Teach

R1 Reading Skill

Making Inferences **Say:** The story starts with a lot of detail and description. What can you infer about the fire pond? *(Possible response: The pond is going to play a big role in this story.)* **Ask:** What can you infer about the deer? *(The deer eat a lot of the crops and damage them.)* **Ask:** What can you infer about the rainbows? *(Possible response: They are fish that the narrator and his grandfather catch for sport, and they are also going to be important to the story.)* OL

R2 Reading Skill

Review Connecting **Say:** The narrator describes the fire pond as a very special place that has been in his life for as long as he can remember. Are there any places in your life that are like this? *(Responses will vary.)* OL

Readability Scores
Dale-Chall: 4.2
DRP: 55
Lexile: 1070

READING WORKSHOP 4

The Fire Pond

by Michael J. Rosen

We stock the fire pond with rainbows. "Fire pond's" a thing I've said for fourteen years and never once thinking what it means besides this lake that Grandpa and friends dug behind the barn before I was born—before Dad was born. It's perfect for swimming, if you're not afraid of snakes (which you shouldn't be since snakes are more scared of you), and it's clear, so you can see your legs treading water[1] underneath. The pond's large enough to row around in a boat, and good for skating, too, unless you're hotdogging and **R1** trying those Olympic-medal spins. It's a place the cows and horses will drink—deer, too, though we'd rather they hang out at another farm and leave our crops alone. **1**

The rainbows are Grandpa's. A few times a summer, we fish out half a dozen for supper. **2** Sometimes we'll catch them on these hooks that don't have barbs, so we can measure the trout and release them again. But the rainbows aren't really for eating, just like the pond's not really for raising fish.

On the ride back from school, I stop and pick up loaves of two-day-old bread that Angela at the bakery holds for Grandpa (her mom was Grandpa's girlfriend before he met Grandma) and, every now and then, a piece of lung the butcher saves. Then Grandpa chops it all up and showers

1. ***Treading water*** is staying upright in the water by moving the feet up and down, as if walking.

Practice the Skills

1 Key Literary Element

Setting The following details in the story tell you that it takes place in the country.

- There's a lake behind a barn.
- There are snakes.
- Cows, horses, and deer drink from the lake.
- There's a farm and crops.

2 Key Reading Skill

Making Inferences What are rainbows in the context of the story? The narrator says several things about them. Here are some clues:

- "We stock the pond with rainbows."
- "We fish out half a dozen for supper."

Additional Support

English Language Coach

Context Clues Have students make a list of any words they don't understand that relate to the context of this story *(rainbows, treading, row, skating, hot-dogging, hooks, barbs, release)*. Assign partners to define each of the words using dictionaries and the context of the story. As a class, make a chart of the words and their definitions. Have students add to this chart as they read. Discuss the context of the story, and guide students as they encounter words that have unfamiliar meanings due to the context. OL handfuls around the dock so the rainbows surface, blurring Grandpa's reflection until it's gone and, looking down, the fish are all you can see.

He talks to the fish whether I'm there or not. Tells them stuff the way I guess I talk to the cats when they follow me around the barn.

"I do all the talking," Grandpa says. "I'm not expecting them to answer."

We have two farm cats—and also this Lab-shepherd mix that's owned by Mrs. Collins, except he spends all day across the road at our place following whoever of us is on the tractor. Grandpa never takes much notice of them. The rainbows are what he's got instead of pets—instead of lots of things. He walks the edge of the fire pond every day, just looking, just admiring what he's got there. It's like the story about the king—or was it the thief?—who has to count his riches every day because, well, I guess he can't believe his **fortune** or his luck. Not that Grandpa's really lucky or fortunate. Not that a bunch of fish swimming around a fire pond is something you count on. **3**

"That one's big as a railroad tie!"[2] he'll shout to me, if I'm walking with him, which I do, especially since Grandma died. **R**

"At least," I answer.

"I don't go in for exaggerating and you know that. Don't need to when they're this beautiful big. But you're my witness, just in case someone doubts."

Analyzing the Photo The narrator's grandpa spends a lot of time at the pond. Why might this be? What is it about the pond that he seems to love most?

2. A ***railroad tie*** is a piece of wood that joins the two rails on which trains run and holds them in place.

Vocabulary

fortune (FOR chun) *n.* luck; riches

Practice the Skills

3 Key Reading Skill

Making Inferences What do you think the fish mean to Grandpa? Think about these clues:

- He talks to them.
- He has them instead of pets or other interests.
- He admires them every day.

Reading Fluency

Read with Expression The author of this selection used dialectic speech to bring the characters alive for readers. Have students find a quiet place to read the story until they can understand it and read it with expression. Then have volunteers read parts of the story aloud while trying to capture the speech patterns of the characters. **OL** Assign students to read the parts of the narrator and Grandpa and act out the dialogue in the beginning of the story. **AL**

READING WORKSHOP 4

Teach

R Reading Skill

Making Inferences **Ask:** Why do you think the narrator walks with Grandpa more now that Grandma has died? *(Possible responses: Maybe Grandma used to walk with Grandpa. Perhaps walking with Grandpa helps the narrator when he is missing his grandmother.)* **OL**

L Literary Element

Review Characterization
Ask: Using the details the narrator gives about Grandpa, how would you describe him as a character? *(Possible responses: He seems lonely and sad. It seems like he has lost a lot and finds hope in the rainbows.)* **OL**
Ask: What have you learned about the narrator from the way he describes his grandfather? *(Possible response: He cares a lot about his grandfather and their relationship is very important to him.)* **AL**

Indiana English/Language Arts Academic Standards
SE: 8.1, 8.2, 8.3.4
TWE: *English Language Coach* 8.1.3, *Reading Fluency* 8.7.14

Teach

EL Language Coach

Context Clues **Say:** The narrator lists a lot of different fish in the first paragraph *(rainbow, tuna, perch, bluefish)*. **Say:** Look up the definition of each kind of fish. What are the differences among the fish? *(Possible responses: Rainbows are freshwater fish, and tuna fish is a saltwater fish. Each fish has a different kind of meat and a different taste.)* OL

R Reading Skill

Making Inferences **Say:** The narrator says that he likes what the fish mean to Grandpa more than what the fish mean to him. What do you think he means by this? *(Possible responses: For the narrator, the fish are just fun to look at and watch in the water. For Grandpa, the fish seem to be everything. The narrator likes that they mean so much to Grandpa.)* AL

READING WORKSHOP 4

Analyzing the Photo How does this picture illustrate the changed landscape that the narrator describes?

Rainbow's the only fish that Grandpa will eat. "No other fish worth catching, neither," he says. Me, I like tuna fish better. (Only fish Mom and Dad love is the perch on those all-you-can-eat nights at the lodge.) I like trawling[3] for bluefish, too, which I've done twice, on visits with Mom's family in Maryland. So I think I like what all the fish mean to Grandpa more than what the fish mean to me. Mainly, it's cool to watch their shiny bodies darting like the sun's shine on the water, only under. **4**

The day the Allegheny[4] floods, all hell breaks loose. That's how Grandpa calls it: "See, even that devil creature is loose." And he means the rattlers, which take to moving from the riverbanks toward higher ground near Salamanca. They're hanging from the elderberries[5] along the road. Who even knew snakes could drown. **5**

Practice the Skills

4 Reviewing Elements

Sensory Imagery Have you ever seen the sun shining on a lake or pond? The slightest bit of wind causes the water to ripple and the sun's reflection to break up. Use that image to help you see what the rainbows looked like just under the surface of the water.

5 Key Literary Element

Setting How has the setting become part of the plot?

3. ***Trawling*** is fishing from the side of a boat by using a bag-shaped net.
4. The ***Allegheny*** is a large river in western New York and Pennsylvania.
5. ***Elderberries*** are large shrubs that have white flowers and purple berries used in cooking.

Additional Support

Literature Focus Lesson

Metaphors and Similes Write a definition of metaphor and simile on the board. Have partners look for metaphors and similes on page 640. *(Metaphor: Grandpa describes the rattlers as the devil creature, "even that devil creature is loose"; Similes: fish "bodies dart like sun's shine," "our place looks like another country, like seeing islands in an ocean")* Direct the partners to choose one of these examples of figurative language, to explain what it means, and to talk about how it helped to make the story more vivid and interesting to read. EL BL OL

Every house I visit is filled with rainwater to the doors—inside and outside. Creek water. Pond water. Lots of farms are worse than ours, but to see our place, it looks like another country, like you're looking down from an airplane and seeing these islands in an ocean—like Hawaii—except it's all just our two hundred acres. Our whole farm is all pond except for the stables across the road, and the highest spots in the meadow, and the animal buildings, which were built on higher ground just for a time like now that was never supposed to happen. The fire pond connects with the creeks, and it's deep enough for powerboats, and there are some, too, trying to save the washed-away things—ours, and stuff from nearby houses—that float or bob to the surface. So much lost and stranded livestock,[6] too, that take weeks to return to their farms. And drowned ones, too. **6** **C**

Over and over Mom says things like, "No matter what we lost, we're still blessed." **7**

As for the rainbows, they're spilled like oil spots down the highway.

It's hard to know if any are left in our pond when the water **recedes**—when the banks of the fire pond are where I remember them, when the rain stops long enough to pump the water from the buildings. We start two lists: what's been ruined or lost, and what can be **salvaged.** It's months, really, before the house feels dry, and then the winter cold seeps in, freezing all that extra water into frost and ice—at least, that's how it feels. **R**

It's more months before the check arrives from the insurance people, which doesn't pay for hardly anything, and the check from the state and federal governments on account of our being declared a disaster area. Almost every day I remember some little thing I used to have and didn't realize the flood had swept it away. But our damages are minor compared with some people we meet, compared with families in Knapp Creek, or nearer the Allegheny.

6. ***Livestock*** are farm animals, such as cows and sheep, which farmers raise for profit.

Vocabulary

recedes (ree SEEDS) *v.* moves or pulls back

salvaged (SAL vujd) *v.* saved from ruin; rescued

Practice the Skills

6 Key Literary Element

Setting At the beginning of the story, the fire pond was a very peaceful place. How does the flood cause problems for the characters living in this setting?

7 Key Reading Skill

Making Inferences After the problems the flood causes, why might the mother think the family is still blessed?

Teach

C Critical Thinking

Comprehension Ask: What is the effect of the Allegheny River flooding? *(Possible responses: The snakes move closer to where people live, people's homes are flooded, a lot of property is lost or damaged, and livestock is killed.)* **Ask:** What does the flooding do to the fire pond and the rainbows? *(The pond overflows, and the rainbows are washed all over the place; many of them die.)* **OL**

R Reading Skill

Making Inferences Say: The writer does not tell what time of year it was when the Allegheny flooded. Now the narrator gives some clues about this. What time of year do you think it was? *(Possible response: spring or summer)* **Ask:** Why do you think this? *(Possible response: He says it took months for the house to feel dry, but then winter set in. This means the flood must have happened many months before winter.)* **OL**

Differentiated Instruction

Mapping The narrator mentions several different geographical locations in the story. Have students use a map of western New York to locate the many places he mentions. Ask students to first find the Allegheny and chart its course. Then direct them to use symbols for the different locations and to use a scale of miles to tell how far the different places are apart from each other. **OL** Have students use their maps to describe the important places and events in the story. Challenge students to learn if there are still farms in this area and how many people live there today. **AL**

Indiana English/Language Arts Academic Standards
SE: 8.2, 8.3.4
TWE: *Literature Focus Lesson* 8.1.1, *Differentiated Instruction* 8.3

Teach

C Critical Thinking

Analysis **Say:** Grandpa adds fingerlings to the pond, but Dad thinks he should leave it alone. Why do you think Grandpa insists on putting new fingerlings in the pond? *(Possible response: Grandpa really enjoys watching the rainbow fish, and they are all gone. He wants to be able to enjoy watching the rainbows again. He is not ready to give up that part of his life.)* OL

R Reading Skill

Review Connecting Have students talk about any experiences they have had with an aging grandparent or authority figure. Discuss what it's like as a young person to watch someone you care about age. *(Responses will vary.)* AS

READING WORKSHOP 4

With the start of winter, the fire pond's dark gets lighter and lighter as ice heals over the surface like a scar. No one goes there much. We just stare at the pond and it stares back—that is, when it isn't covered with fresh snow. I hardly skate at all. A few times at my friend Troy's pond. But it's like I've lost my appetite for skating or for the pond, but I don't know if that's possible. As for Grandpa, he has no reason to trudge through the drifts and walk to the pond. He heads to North Carolina for a month to visit his sister. And he spends two weeks in Atlanta, staying with Uncle Miles and his family. And the other thing is, Grandpa comes back tired, though vacations are supposed to be for rest. 8

Around about Mother's Day, it's finally warm enough for Grandpa to stock the pond again, even though Dad tries to suggest in a nice way that maybe the pond's better left on its own. Grandpa won't hear of that. A truck arrives with fingerlings[7] I can't believe will grow as large as the rainbows we lost. Same day, Grandpa calls Angela and the butcher to start saving up treats for his fish. C And that night, after dinner, out of the clear blue, Grandpa reaches into his shirt pocket as he leaves the table, and places his driver's license beside the centerpiece[8] like he's presenting us with the check. "I'm done driving," he says, and then he points to me: "You'll need a car soon anyway."

He's already out of the room when Mom and Dad are saying things like, don't be silly, and why on earth, and Pop, come back in here.

Come to find out from Uncle Miles, Grandpa's had an accident—just a fender bender—in Atlanta. Afterward, he insisted on going to an optometrist or ophthalmologist[9]—whatever—who told him he had the eyes of a teenager. He did suggest glasses to help reduce the glare at night. But as soon as he got home, Grandpa decided he wasn't going out on the road. "First and last accident in my life," he said, when we tried to talk some sense into him, which is something

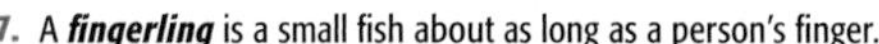

7. A ***fingerling*** is a small fish about as long as a person's finger.
8. A ***centerpiece*** is a decoration that goes in the center of the dinner table.
9. An ***optometrist*** examines the eyes and prescribes glasses to correct eyesight problems. An ***ophthalmologist*** treats diseases of the eyes.

Practice the Skills

8 Key Reading Skill

Making Inferences What do you think is making Grandpa feel so tired? (Hint: What is missing from his life?)

Additional Support

Literature Focus Lesson

Theme Grandpa came back different after his trips to North Carolina and Atlanta. Have students role play a scene between the narrator and his parents in which they discuss the changes they have noticed. (Remind students that Grandpa is Dad's father.) Encourage students to be creative but stay true to the characters and events in the story. After students have a chance to role play, lead the class in a discussion about their experiences. Here are some questions you might ask:

- What do you think worried Mom and Dad when Grandpa came back?
- What was the most dramatic change in Grandpa?
- How do you think the narrator felt about all of it? OL

only Grandma could do—and once in a blue moon, she could actually succeed. It's a year before I can get my license.

Early summer's one of the driest on record, but the pond's its normal size. Except for sleeping later than six o'clock, which is when I get up for morning chores during school, I do what work everyone else does: putting in the crops, mowing, moving the animals out to pasture and back in, repairing the grain auger[10] and the tractors with Dad. Most of my school friends do the same at their farms, and after supper, we meet at the quarry to swim or bike over to DeWitt's for ice cream. 9

In no time flat it's halfway through summer vacation, August first. Grandpa is reading after the rest of us are in bed. He reads more than he sleeps at night. "Don't much like closing my eyes," he says. "At my age, seeing's a kind of being proud." So Grandpa goes to make some tea, and he sees smoke rising near the barn. If he'd been asleep—if it hadn't been a clear night with an almost full moon—I don't see how any one of us would be alive now. 10

R Grandpa shouts as he runs up the stairs. He pounds on our bedroom doors. He's the one who phones the head firefighter from Hinsdale—they're the closest, still about twelve minutes away—and they start the chain of calls to rally the volunteers and summon Mr. Tyler at the general store to sound the siren, which we can't hear from here, but I know is blaring from when I bike near town.

L2 Until they come, there's just the four of us, and Mrs. Collins and her son, Dean, who live across the road. We all know what to do though, as if we've had fire drills every month, like at school. We start moving the animals, and then the machines. It's like a parade marching out into the middle of the field, but jumbled and scattered and in the dark. The cows and pigs are so frightened, they'd trample a person without even knowing it.

When the volunteers from Hinsdale arrive, it's no one but Grandpa who drags the fire truck's pump hose to the pond and lowers it, hand over hand, like an anchor. Even these

10. A ***grain auger*** is a farm machine with a long tube that lifts grain from a truck to the top of a tall storage building.

Practice the Skills

9 Key Literary Element

Setting How does having to do chores on a farm bring the family closer together?

10 Reviewing Skills

Interpreting What do you think Grandpa means when he says that "seeing's a kind of being proud"?

Teach

R Reading Skill

Review Connecting **Say:** The narrator describes how circumstances worked to save his family–his grandfather's being awake and its being a clear night with an almost full moon. Ask volunteers to share a time when they or someone they know was saved from disaster by miraculous circumstances. **Ask:** How did you explain what happened? Was it coincidence, fate, luck, or something more? *(Responses will vary.)* OL

L1 Literary Element

Setting **Ask:** How does the setting of a farm affect the way that the characters react to a fire? *(Since they live on a farm, they have to do what they can to get their animals out of the barn and away from the fire.)* **Ask:** How would you and your family react differently because of where you live? *(Responses will vary.)* OL

L2 Literary Element

Review Sequence Have students create a chart that shows the sequence of events for the fire. Start the chart with Grandpa seeing smoke rising near the barn. Ask a volunteer to write his or her chart on the board to use as an example. OL

Reading in the Real World

Career Most students will be probably unfamiliar with the life of a career farmer. If you have students who are familiar with farms, ask them to share their experience. Then ask students to conduct research on farms and farming in the United States. Have them answer the following questions:

- How many working farms are there in the U.S.? What do they farm? Where are they located?
- What does a career farmer do for work each day?

If there are farms in your area, invite a farmer to come to the class to talk about what it's like to be a farmer in the U.S. today. Or schedule a field trip to a local farm. OL

Indiana English/Language Arts Academic Standards

SE: 8.2, 8.3.4, 8.3.9

TWE: *Literature Focus Lesson* 8.7, *Reading in the Real World* 8.7

Teach

C Critical Thinking

Synthesis Say: Grandpa puts the hose into the fire pond to get water to put out the fire. What will be the consequences of this? *(The hose will drain the pond and all of the new fish will die without water.)* OL

R Reading Skill

Review Monitoring Comprehension Ask: Why does Grandpa tell them to let the barn burn? *(No barn is going to stand on a half-burnt frame.)* **Ask:** Why does Grandpa want them to move the horses? *(The wind is moving in the direction of the stables, and the fire will go with it.)* OL

READING WORKSHOP 4

new fish have learned the sound of his boots on the dock, the scattering of food on the water that follows. From faraway as the front yard, I can see how the glassy surface of the moonlight shatters into ripples by the dock where the rainbows are chomping at the empty air.

I help strap the Indian fire pumps on a few of the volunteers, and they join the truck at the barn to do what they can. The fire's already spread to the corn crib, where Grandpa's stationed himself.

Now, after a whole year, Grandpa will laugh if someone makes a joke about the fire. "If only we'd have grown *popping* corn, the fire would have popped enough corn to serve all the whole crowd! It looked like a drive-in movie with all those cars." But that night, the dried field-corn burns so fast and hot that the sweat steams beneath Grandpa's rubber coat—but he won't turn away except until he passes out from the heat, and the smoke, too. **11**

A man I don't know carries Grandpa to the house, where he checks his breathing, his eyes, and his pulse. (All the volunteers—Dad's one, too—take first-aid courses.)

"Your grandpa's fine. Long as he stays inside and rests," he tells me, and *I* believe him, though Grandpa won't: He is going to catch his breath and head back out. I learn the man's name is Hawkins when he phones to tell some doctor that he's needed here.

Mom makes me stay with Grandpa. Her voice is so serious, I think even Grandpa might listen for once.

"Tell them to let the barn burn!" he orders Hawkins before he leaves the house. "No barn's going to stand on a half-burnt frame. And move the horses."

"But the stables are across the road . . ." I start to say, and then answer my own question. The twelve horses have got to be spooked. And even if they're safe for now, they'll get to panicking and kick through their stalls, break a bone or tear themselves up on the wire. **R**

Grandpa gives me a reason I hadn't thought of. "Look out there. Too much wind."

Even though the fire's around the other side, from the back door that faces the stables and the corral, I see them **outlined** like by moonlight, only it's orange because of the flames. **12** I see Mom shove the gates free. She slides open the stable's door,

Practice the Skills

11 Reviewing Skills

Clarifying Notice that the sequence, or order, of events shifts during this part of the story. How much time has passed since the fire occurred? Reread the paragraph if you're not sure.

12 English Language Coach

Prefixes The word **outlined** contains the prefix *out-*, which means "outside" or "beyond." It means "to make a line around the outside" of something. Does that make sense in this sentence?

Additional Support

Differentiated Instruction

Picture It This story has many vivid descriptions and lots of imagery. Have students draw, paint a watercolor, or use another medium to illustrate something from this story. Give less artistic students the option of looking through art books to find an illustration that depicts the mood of a certain event in the story. They can go to the library, look through different books, and make a copy of the picture. Have students write about their picture on a note card and explain why they chose it, or what they have drawn or painted. Display student pictures along with their note cards on a bulletin board about this story. AS

READING WORKSHOP 4

jumping clear since the horses charge out instantly and all at once. The horses are pitch-black, but the fire's light gives them even darker shadows, however that's possible. A few horses bolt along the fence to the entrance of the meadow, and some of them leap the rails as though it weren't the fence at all that kept them here every day, but something else. We've lost a horse before, accidentally, but never all of them at once, and never in a panicking herd. But now isn't the time for asking how we'll find them. We will. People around here know us even if we are spread out far from one another. **13**

Then there's a new sound, louder, closer than the fire. Before I can turn to ask Grandpa the question, he tells me, "It's all right," which suddenly makes me think it's not. A spray of water bursts on the picture window. The jet runs across the wall and back, back and forth, across and back, as though it were erasing something.

"That means the house's caught fire?" I ask.

"No, no. Just preventing it," he says, but his voice is too faint; it's a whisper like a part of the farm already gone up in smoke.

Which makes me say and ask at the same time (that has to be possible): "Grandpa, we're going to be okay."

His nodding means yes and at the same time I don't know. **L**

The one hose pounds the roof and wall and doesn't stop. It's like our own storm: one thunderbolt rumbling right against the house, but more like heat lightning since it's bright in all the windows. Water pours down the panes in sheets, and the view is blurred and wobbly, like looking through the sheer curtains when the window's cracked open in Grandpa's room. But even so, I know what's out there: I watch the embers float, slower than pennies in a wishing well, from the barn to the stables, to the milk house, to the grain elevator that's thirty-six feet tall—the tallest thing for miles—and over to one and then the other silo.

Behind me, from the couch where Grandpa's supposed to be lying still, I hear him talking like he's talking to the rainbows, or like he's giving directions and he's still out there fighting the flames. I can see the fire outside in his eyes, which must mean it's reflected in my eyes, too, if Grandpa looks up to see it.

Practice the Skills

13 Key Literary Element

Setting The narrator and his family don't stop to look for the horses because they believe the animals will be returned to them. What does that tell you about the community where the story takes place?

Teach

L Literary Element

Review Tone **Ask:** What tone does the narrator use when he says, "Grandpa, we're going to be okay"? *(He uses a questioning or scared tone while trying to sound sure of himself.)*
Ask: What tone does the story have during this part of the narrative? *(Possible response: The tone is suspenseful.)* **OL**
Ask: How does the author set the tone? *(Possible response: By describing in detail what is happening with the fire and the thoughts in the narrator's head.)* **AL**

R Reading Skill

Review Predicting **Ask:** What do you think is going to happen next in the story? What will be the outcome of the fire? *(Responses will vary.)* **AS**

English Language Coach

Descriptive Language One of the strongest aspects of this story is its descriptive language. The author uses strong verbs and detailed descriptions to really bring the story alive for readers. Some students may be unfamiliar with the verbs and adjectives the author uses. Have students make a list of the verbs used on page 645. Then have them make a list of the adjectives. Ask students to define each of the words and to use a dictionary if they need help with the definitions. Discuss how using a variety of verbs and descriptive adjectives can help readers get a better sense of the events in a story. Encourage students to use this technique in their own writing. **EL**

Indiana English/Language Arts Academic Standards
SE: 8.2, 8.3.4, 8.3.9
TWE: *Differentiated Instruction* 8.3, *English Language Coach* 8.1

Teach

R1 Reading Skill

Making Inferences Ask: What does the narrator wish he could be doing? *(helping outside where the fire is)*
Ask: Why does he need to stay inside with his grandfather? *(He has to stay inside so his grandfather will stay inside and not risk his health.)* OL

C Critical Thinking

Comprehension Say: The narrator says that the fire burned up "whatever it is inside a person that's supposed to make us want to eat or want to wake up." What does he mean by this? *(Possible response: The fire made the narrator and his family so sad that they didn't want to get up each day.)* OL

R2 Reading Skill

Review Connecting Have students share the real-life examples that they came up with for how disasters can bring out the best in people. AS
Ask: What do you think makes people want to help each other when disaster strikes? *(Possible responses: human kindness, a sense of community)* OL

"The pond's not deep enough," Grandpa tells me, as if he'd just remembered how deep they'd dug it. I bring him some juice from the fridge. I don't know why I can't be doing something more than watching Grandpa—though if I weren't here, he wouldn't be either. **14**

There's so much light, I keep forgetting it's night. Besides the flames, there's the white flash of cameras: someone from the insurance company and a photographer for the *Journal*. And probably people just wanting to shoot some cool pictures. And then, even at the farther-away dark edges, there are yellower lights, and red ones—new ones: headlights and taillights of cars pulling in. (The *Journal*, which only comes out once a week, will say that two thousand people attended the fire—drove from nearby towns like we were some kind of county fair that opened after midnight. There should have been another story to say how people kept coming for days—not thousands, but more than just people we know by name—strangers coming to drop off things they had extra of, like a milking machine or a bridle, and, of course, things to eat, as though the fire had burned the kitchen, too, but it didn't—only whatever it is inside a person that's supposed to make us want to eat or want to wake up.) **15**

When I crack the front door just to see something clearly, a burst of smoke slips in before my eyes can really make out much.

"Seems like maybe there's even more firemen now, Grandpa," I tell him, and he nods, as though he'd been **calculating** how long it'd take the volunteers from each of the neighboring villages to make their way here.

"Probably. Probably be at least three fire trucks by now." And then, after too long a pause, he finishes. "Look at it go. Fire's just like trout heading upstream: slow and certain of where it's going."

That's when Mom comes in again with one of the cats, bringing not only the smell but also the heat of the fire in her clothes and hair. She confirms what Grandpa guessed: "There's three trucks pumping water now. And so many other people wanting to help, they've got two men just

Vocabulary

calculating (KAL kyoo lay ting) *v.* using math or logic to figure out something

Practice the Skills

14 Key Reading Skill

Making Inferences Grandpa says that the pond "isn't deep enough." What isn't it deep enough for?

15 Reviewing Skills

Connecting Sometimes disasters bring out the best in people. Strangers go out of their way to help others in need. What real-life examples of this can you give?

Additional Support

Reading in the Real World

Citizenship Have students imagine that they work for a newspaper that reports on the deeds of good citizens. As reporters, they have heard about the fire at the farm and have gone to investigate two days later. Ask students to write a newspaper article about the events of the fire and what happened after the fire. What damage did the fire do? How did the citizens respond during and after the fire? Encourage students to include direct quotations from characters in the story, firefighters, and citizens of the community. Ask volunteers to read their story to the class as if they were reporting the news. OL

READING WORKSHOP 4

keeping the crowd back." Her eyes leak tears down her cheek—maybe it's just from the smoke—her talk has more important things to do than sob. We fill bottles and jugs of water at the sink to take to the firefighters.

The seven thousand hay bales blaze all night, glowing right alongside the dawn, when all that's left of the barn is an arch that frames the sunrise. It's quiet, then, suddenly, like an alarm clock went off, but one that wakes you with silence since the night was so loud. The firemen coil their hoses half-filled with pond sludge, and the last of the crowds drive home to Portville, Ischua, and Knapp Creek. **16**

Friends in Olean, and farther south than Hinsdale, smell the smoke at sunup, the dead fish at dusk. The phone is always ringing. One call is from the Luthers, who have managed to pen the four horses that escaped. They'll hold them as long as we need them to.

It's three days before the coals lose heat, before Mom and Dad are done meeting the insurance people and the county agents. Grandpa and I comb the property after supper. **R** The machines are still clustered in the pasture like cows, as though the only job they had was to wait. Since nothing else stands but the house and the woods—and the stables across the road, which were unharmed, after all—we watch the ground as if something were left here and we had to come to look. Instead of grass or dirt it's ashes, wet wherever we step. Across the meadow where the fire pond was, there's a mud valley now that's like a mirage of water, shimmering the way a highway in the summer heat looks wet until you get closer and see it's not. The pond shimmers, but closer up, it's the silt rippling where the tails are flaring beneath.

Practice the Skills

16 **Key Reading Skill**

Making Inferences How do you think Grandpa feels about having all the water drained from the pond? Why do you think so?

Analyzing the Photo How does this picture illustrate changes in the pond?

Teach

R Reading Skill

Making Inferences **Say:** The narrator says that he and his grandfather comb, or search, the property. Why do you think they are combing the property? What are they looking for? *(They are looking for anything that might have survived the fire.)* **OL**

L1 Literary Element

Review Figurative Language **Say:** We've talked about how the author uses figurative language in this story. What figurative language do you notice on this page? *(quiet like an alarm clock; machines clustered in the pasture like cows; mud valley like a mirage of water)* **OL**

L2 Literary Element

Setting **Say:** The story begins with the pond as the main setting. It is also the most important place in the narrator's world. What has happened to that setting? *(Possible response: The setting of the story has gone from being full of life to being dead.)* **OL**

Ask: How do you think the changes in the setting will change the characters in the story? *(Possible response: The characters have been deadened by what happened to the pond.)* **AL**

Literature Focus Lesson

Short Story Remind students of the plot elements for short stories: exposition, rising action, climax, falling action, and resolution. Have individual students or partners map this story and identify each of the elements. The conflicts in this story are more complex than students may be used to when reading short stories. Ask students to define the conflicts in this story and the resolutions for each of them. Discuss Grandpa, his conflict, and resolution. And then discuss the narrator, his conflict, and resolution. Model your thinking as students work to identify the conflicts and resolutions. **OL**

Indiana English/Language Arts Academic Standards

SE: 8.2, 8.2.9

TWE: *Reading Skill* 8.2.9, *Literary Element* 8.3.9, *Reading in the Real World* 8.5.7, *Literature Focus Lesson* 8.3.2

Teach

R Reading Skill

Making Inferences **Say:** Both Grandpa and the narrator know they cannot save the fish. Why do they go to the pond? *(Possible responses: They want to see the fish one last time; Grandpa wants his grandson to understand about not giving up.)* OL

EL Language Coach

Context Clues **Say:** The narrator says that the last few fish that move have drowned in the air. What does the verb *drown* mean? *(to die by suffocation in water)* **Ask:** What does it mean to drown in the air? *(Since fish breathe water, breathing air will suffocate them.)* OL

C Critical Thinking

Synthesis **Ask:** Why is it a bad thing to stock the fire pond with fish? *(Possible response: The fish will die if there ever is a fire.)* **Ask:** Why do you think Grandpa stocks the pond anyway? *(Possible response: What he gets from the fish is much greater than the risk of losing them if there is a fire)* AL

When Grandpa takes off his shoes and socks, I take off mine. We set them on the dock and climb down to the muck of the bottom. Forty years ago, I think to myself, Grandpa stood on the bottom like this.

We start off walking, our feet sinking into the clay, then popping free with a suction sound.

"It's raining," Grandpa announces to me, or maybe he's just used to talking to himself at the pond. He's smiling, even though no amount of water—not from clouds, not from our springs or our well, not from tanker trucks with nothing better to do than to cart water here—nothing will save the rainbows. The ones at the shallow end are dead. These last few that move have already drowned in the air.

Grandpa says, "I already hear them talking."

"Who, Grandpa?" I ask. I know he doesn't mean the fish.

"Just people. I hear them. 'You'd think that old fool'd have learnt that first time never to stock a fire pond.'" 17

"No, they're not, Grandpa," I answer him, "they won't," though this is just another thing I don't know. I don't know if Grandpa's thinking about restocking the pond, or if I should plead with him not to if only so he'll slap me hard enough to let me cry. I don't know even why I think this, because he'd never do that. 18

Practice the Skills

17 Key Reading Skill

Making Inferences Do you think Grandpa cares whether other people think he's a fool? Why or why not?

18 Reviewing Skills

Predicting Do you think Grandpa will restock the pond with rainbows? Explain.

Additional Support

Reading Fluency

Partner Reading The last scene of the story is very important to understanding the plot. Have students get into pairs and practice reading pages 648–649. Have one student read the part of the narrator and one student read the part of Grandpa. Ask each pair to read these pages aloud to the class once they have practiced and can read fluently with expression. Discuss the importance of this scene to the story. OL

"I'm going to tell you something," he says, "and I don't care if you're old enough to think you should start ignoring advice."

I do know I should tell him I'm not, that I'm listening, to go ahead, to keep walking—*something*. So I take a step forward. Grandpa's planted there like he's a boot that just slipped off your foot and stuck there. So I have to step back.

"You stock your life with what all makes you happy, you hear me? You put rainbows anyplace you like, not excepting your young heart." BQ

And then it's Grandpa who turns, ready to complete our tour, if that's what we're doing, drawing a circle with footstep dashes around the fire pond like it's something you could cut out. But before I can say anything like I'm sorry or I believe you, he adds: "I'm not expecting you to answer."

Grandpa's footprints are the size of mine (the size of the fingerlings—grown a lot, of course, since May): They're little ponds the coming rain will fill, then flood, then wash away. 19 ❍

Practice the Skills

19 **BIG Question**

How does Grandpa stay true to himself? Write your answer on "The Fire Pond" page of Foldable 5. Your response will help you answer the Unit Challenge later.

Analyzing the Photo Look closely at the water. How does the photo help you picture what the rainbows in the fire pond look like?

Teach

L Literary Element

Review Symbols Ask: What do the rainbows symbolize for Grandpa? *(They symbolize the things that make a person happy, a person's hopes and dreams.)* **Ask:** What do you think they symbolize for the narrator? *(Possible responses: his grandfather, his childhood, the farm)* AL

BQ BIG Question

Ask: What does Grandpa tell the narrator about staying true to himself? *(Possible response: Do not worry about what other people think you should do, just follow your dreams and do what you think is right. Just because it does not always work out does not mean you should not have done it, and you should still try again if you believe in it.)* OL

Assess

Use the Checkpoint questions provided on Presentation Plus! to check for comprehension of the selection. These questions can be used with interactive response keypads for immediate student feedback.

Literature Focus Lesson

Theme Grandpa tells the narrator to put rainbows anyplace he likes, even his young heart. Create a class display of the rainbows students have put or would like to put someplace. First have students define the metaphor of rainbows. Then have students write for 15–20 minutes about the rainbows they have put someplace or would like to put someplace in their future. Using markers, paint, and other colorful materials, have students create a symbol for each of the rainbows they would like to share with the class. Ask students to label each rainbow with what it is and where it has been or will be placed. Have students share their rainbows with the class as they place them on the bulletin board. OL

Indiana English/Language Arts Academic Standards
SE: 8.2
TWE: *Reading Fluency* 8.7.14, *Literature Focus Lesson* 8.5.7

Assess

Resources for page 650

- Selection Quick Check, p. 47
- Selection and Unit Assessment, p. 55
- ExamView Assessment Suite
- Interactive Tutor: Self-Assessment

Students can respond to the *After You Read* items in their Learner's Notebooks or on separate sheets of paper.

Answering the BIG Question

1. Responses will vary.
2. The first natural disaster is when the Allegheny floods.
3. The fire pond floods at the beginning of the story. Later on, the pond is emptied out as it is used to put out a fire on the farm.

Critical Thinking

4. Possible response: The narrator wants to learn from his grandfather, he seems to respect him and wants to be like him. Some evidence from the story is the way that the narrator wants to tell his grandfather he is listening, and the fact that he notices Grandpa's footprints are the same size as his.
5. Responses will vary.
6. Responses will vary.

After You Read

The Fire Pond

Answering the BIG Question

1. What did you learn about staying true to yourself from reading the story?
2. **Recall** What is the first natural disaster in the story?
   TIP Right There
3. **Summarize** In two or three sentences, sum up what happens to the fire pond during the course of the story.
   TIP Think and Search

Critical Thinking

4. **Analyze** How does the narrator feel about Grandpa at the end of the story? Give evidence from the story to back up your answer.
   TIP Author and Me
5. **Analyze** What do you think the narrator learns from his experiences? Support your answer with evidence from the story.
   TIP Author and Me
6. **Evaluate** Do you think Grandpa would be foolish to restock the pond with rainbows? Explain why or why not.
   TIP On My Own

Write About Your Reading

Letter What do you think happens next? Write a letter from the narrator to a friend telling what happens during the year after the story ends. Use your imagination to "fill in the blanks," but make the characters behave in ways that are consistent with the story. Use the questions below to get started.

- What does the family do about the farm?
- What happens to Grandpa? Does he restock the pond?
- What happens to the narrator? Does he change? If so, how?

Indiana English/Language Arts Academic Standards (pp. 650–651)

8.3 Comprehension and Analysis of Literary Text Respond to grade-level-appropriate literature... **8.5.2** Write responses to literature... **8.2 Comprehension and Analysis (Focus on Informational Text)** Develop [reading] strategies... **8.2.9** Draw conclusions... **8.3.4** Analyze...mood, tone, and meaning... **8.3.9** Analyze the relevance of setting... **8.1 Word Recognition, Fluency, and Vocabulary Development** Understand word parts... **8.6 English Language Conventions**

For a complete description of the standards, see p. IN 11.

Write About Your Reading

Possible response:

Dear Tom,

Spring came again. Once again people came from all around to help us. This time, they came to help us rebuild. They also came to help us refill our fire pond. Dad and Mom told Grandpa not to restock the pond. I told my parents to let him be. I said it's really important to Grandpa. He needs to do what makes him happy. It's summer now, and Grandpa and I go out to feed the rainbows each day.

Sincerely,

Your Friend

Skills Review

Key Reading Skill: Making Inferences

7. At the beginning of the story, Grandpa says he talks to the trout even though he doesn't expect them to answer. When he talks to the narrator at the end of the story, why doesn't Grandpa expect the narrator to answer him either?

Key Literary Element: Setting

8. Grandpa dug the fire pond years before the story begins. How else has he influenced the setting?
9. How might the story change if it were set in a big city? Identify at least two events that would turn out differently, and explain the differences.

Reviewing Skills: Connecting

10. What part of the story could you most easily relate to, or connect with? Why?
11. How did making the connection help you better understand or enjoy the story?

Reviewing Skills: Interpreting

12. What does Grandpa mean when he says, "You put rainbows anyplace you like, not excepting your young heart"? Support your answer with details from the story.

Vocabulary Check

Match each word with the word or phrase that means the opposite.

13. salvaged **a.** destroyed
14. recedes **b.** using instincts
15. fortune **c.** advances
16. calculating **d.** poverty

17. **English Language Coach** Copy the following words on another sheet of paper. Circle the prefix on each word. Then define the word. Check your definitions in a dictionary.

outpatient • subtitle • undersea • overreach

18. **Academic Vocabulary** If a theme is **implied,** is it directly stated? Explain why or why not.

Grammar Link: Run-on Sentences

A **run-on sentence** is two or more independent clauses run together without correct punctuation or conjunctions. Run-on sentences are mistakes that make it hard for readers to understand where one thought ends and the next begins.

Run-On: Estela loves to play the piano it relaxes her.

To fix a run-on sentence, put a period between the two independent clauses, or simple sentences. The period shows readers where one thought ends and the next begins.

Correct: Estela loves to play the piano. It relaxes her.

Another way to fix a run-on sentence is to separate the independent clauses with a comma and a coordinating conjunction.

Correct: Estela loves to play the piano, and it relaxes her.

You can also correct a run-on sentence by adding a subordinating conjunction to one of the clauses.

Correct: Estela loves to play the piano because it relaxes her.

Grammar Practice

On another sheet of paper, copy and fix the following run-on sentences, using each of the ways listed above.

19. She practices every day she doesn't mind.
20. She wants to be a music teacher someday she must learn to play different instruments.

Writing Application Review your Write About Your Reading activity. Find and fix any run-on sentences.

Web Activities For eFlashcards, Selection Quick Checks, and other Web activities, go to www.glencoe.com.

Skills Review

Key Reading Skill: Making Inferences

7. Responses will vary.

Key Literary Element: Setting

8. Possible response: He has built the farm and influenced all of the decisions that went into building it.
9. Responses will vary.

Reviewing Skills: Connecting

10. Responses will vary.
11. Responses will vary.

Reviewing Skills: Interpreting

12. Responses will vary.

Vocabulary Check

13. a **15.** d
14. c **16.** b

17. **Outpatient:** out-; a patient who does not stay overnight in a hospital **Subtitle:** sub-; a title that appears under the main title **Undersea:** under-; below the surface of the sea **Overreach:** over-; to reach too far
18. It is not directly stated because implied means something is not stated directly.

Close

Ask students to summarize how they answered the Big Question after reading "The Fire Pond."

Grammar Link: Run-on Sentences

Grammar Practice

19. She practices every day. She doesn't mind; She practices every day, for she doesn't mind; She practices every day because she doesn't mind.
20. She wants to be a music teacher someday. She needs to learn to play different musical instruments; She wants to be a music teacher someday, so she needs to learn to play different musical instruments; She needs to learn to play different musical instruments because she wants to be a music teacher someday.

Indiana English/Language Arts Academic Standards
SE: 8.1, 8.2, 8.2.9, 8.3, 8.3.4, 8.3.9, 8.5.2, 8.6

Teach

More About the Author

Savion Glover has been dancing professionally since he was fourteen years old. He won the Tony Award for his dancing and his choreography in *Bring in 'Da Noise, Bring in 'Da Funk.* Glover teaches dance at the Broadway Dance Center in New York City.

V Vocabulary

Vocabulary Have students share the clues they wrote for their partners for the *Partner Talk* activity. Ask them to talk about which clues worked best and why. *(Responses will vary.)* AS

EL Language Coach

Adjective and Adverb Suffixes Remind students that an adverb describes a verb, or tells "how" something is done. An adjective describes a noun. Write examples of adverbs and adjectives on the board and model how they are used in sentences. Ask students to read the new adverbs and adjectives they formed to complete the activity for *Partner Work.* EL

Before You Read from *Savion!: My Life in Tap*

Meet the Authors

Savion Glover was born in 1973. He is an award-winning dancer and actor who has performed on stage and in the movies. He also choreographs, or works out dance moves, for other dancers. He says, "My class . . . is an opportunity to pick up some of the knowledge and experience that I learned from the people who taught me."

Bruce Weber reports on culture and the arts for *The New York Times.* He also writes for many magazines.

Author Search For more about Savion Glover and Bruce Weber, go to www.glencoe.com.

Indiana English/Language Arts Academic Standards (pp. 652–659)

8.1 Word Recognition, Fluency, and Vocabulary Development Understand...word parts...
8.2 Comprehension and Analysis (Focus on Informational Text) Develop [reading] strategies... **8.3** Respond to grade-level-appropriate literature... identifying story elements...

For a complete description of the standards, see p. IN 11.

Vocabulary Preview

askew (uh SKYOO) *adv.* turned or twisted to one side **(p. 654)** *He wore his baseball cap askew as a fashion statement.*

hygiene (HY jeen) *n.* cleanliness; habits that lead to good health **(p. 655)** *To maintain good personal hygiene, he takes a shower every day.*

translates (TRANZ laytz) *v.* changes successfully into another form or language; form of the verb *translate* **(p. 658)** *Savion feels his dancing translates into life lessons.*

V **Partner Talk** Without saying the definitions, give clues to help your partner guess what each vocabulary word is. Give ideas and activities associated with the words. Then switch and have your partner give you clues.

English Language Coach

Adjective and Adverb Suffixes Knowing what common suffixes mean can help you figure out the meaning of many unfamiliar words. Recall that a **suffix** is a combination of letters added to the end of a word. Adding a suffix may change the word's meaning and part of speech. For example, adding the suffix *-ous* to the noun *glamor* makes the adjective *glamorous.* Look at the suffixes on the chart below.

Suffix	Part of Speech	Word Example
-ly	adverb	quickly
-ic	adjective	poetic
-ive	adjective	selective
-ful	adjective	playful
-ous	adjective	marvelous

EL **Partner Work** With a classmate, look at each word below and decide what part of speech it is. Then separate the word into its base word and suffix. Decide what part of speech the base word is. Then use both the word and suffix in a sentence.

- gruffly
- heroic
- protective
- sorrowful

Additional Support

Author Search To expand students' appreciation of Savion Glover and Bruce Weber, have them access the Web site for additional resources.

Literature Focus Lesson

Memoir A memoir is a narrative or story that tells about a person's experiences during a certain time period or event. Memoirs are typically autobiographical; the narrator is the person who is having the experiences. Memoirs are also nonfiction. Remind students of this before they begin reading this selection as they have read mostly fictional pieces in this unit. Discuss the differences between a short story and a memoir. Ask students how other selections in this unit might have been different if they had been told as memoirs; for example, how would "The Fire Pond" be different? AS

Skills Preview

Key Reading Skill: Making Inferences

In *Savion!: My Life in Tap,* Savion Glover talks about his experiences as a youngster and an adult working on stage. What inferences can you make about the content of the article? What do you think he might talk about in the article?

Whole Class Discussion As a class, discuss what kinds of information you think you might find.

Literary Element: Tone

Tone is an author's attitude toward a subject as shown in the language he or she uses. The tone of a selection may be admiring, sarcastic, angry, joyous, funny, ironic, neutral–any word that you can use to describe an attitude can be used to describe tone. To identify the tone of *Savion!: My Life in Tap,* ask yourself the following questions: L

- *How does Savion feel about the person, place, or thing he is describing? How can I tell?*
- *If I were reading this aloud with expression, what feelings would I try to show in my voice? Why?*

Partner Talk Read the following passage from *Savion!: My Life in Tap.* With a classmate, identify the tone. Give reasons for your ideas.

> "[J]ust a few years ago, in *Tap,* I was hangin' with Sammy Davis, Jr., and he was on the set drinking Kool-Aid and wearing a do-rag. It was red Kool-Aid, I remember, and he drank it in a big mug. Like regular folks. Sammy Davis, man!
>
> And then I was on *Sesame Street,* which was also cool, a nice vibe. That's when people started recognizing me on the street . . ."

Interactive Literary Elements Handbook
To review or learn more about the literary elements, go to www.glencoe.com.

Get Ready to Read

Connect to the Reading

Savion Glover talks about older people whom he admired as he was growing up. Are there people in your life you feel that way about? It could be your parents, teachers, or coaches. Perhaps it's a neighbor. Think about how you feel when that person pays attention to you and helps you.

Partner Talk With a partner, discuss someone you admire.

Build Background

- Tap dancing developed in the nineteenth century. It mixed steps from jigs and reels danced by Irish and Scottish immigrants with African steps danced by African Americans. Irish dancers contributed the use of shoes with wooden soles that increased the sound. African Americans contributed the stress on rhythm, contrasting beats, and improvisation.
- By the 1920s, metal taps under the heels and toes began replacing wooden soles.
- Challenges are contests between dancers during jam sessions. Each dancer tries to outdo the previous one by using trickier or faster steps.

Set Purposes for Reading

BIG Question Read the selection from *Savion!: My Life in Tap* to find out how Savion learned to be true to himself as a dancer and as a human being.

Set Your Own Purpose What else would you like to learn from the selection to help you answer the Big Question? Write your purpose on the *Savion!: My Life in Tap* page of Foldable 5.

Keep Moving

Use these skills as you read from *Savion!: My Life in Tap.*

Teach

L Literary Element

Tone Have students think about different tones that an author might take when writing a memoir. **Ask:** How do you think each of these tones would affect the story being told? How would a memoir read if the tone was funny? How about sarcastic? *(Responses will vary.)* OL

Literature Online

Interactive Literary Elements Handbook Have students access the Web site to improve their understanding of tone.

Reading in the Real World

Career Invite a tap dancer to perform for your class. If one of your students taps, allow him or her to be the performer or to dance with the performer. Ask the dancer to come prepared to tell the class a little about his or her dance experience. Guide students to prepare a list of questions for the dancer. Try to give the dancer this list of questions ahead of time, so that he or she will know what your students are interested in learning. OL Have students who are interested do further research on careers in dance and report their findings to the class. AL

Indiana English/Language Arts Academic Standards
SE: 8.1, 8.2, 8.3
TWE: *Literature Focus Lesson* 8.3, *Reading in the Real World* 8.7.1

Teach

R Reading Skill

Making Inferences **Ask:** Why is Savion so excited about working with Sammy Davis, Jr.? *(Sammy Davis was a famous dancer, and Savion was a kid when he got to work with him for the first time.)* OL AL

EL Language Coach

Context Clues **Say:** The author uses a lot of slang in this piece. What is a *do-rag*? *(a piece of cloth worn around the head)* **Ask:** What is a *nice vibe*? *(a good feeling)* EL

L Literary Element

Tone **Ask:** What effect does using slang have on the tone of the story? *(Possible response: It sets a very informal tone.)* **Ask:** Do you like the informal tone? Why or why not? *(Answers will vary.)* OL

Readability Scores
Dale-Chall: 4.9
DRP: 50
Lexile: 790

READING WORKSHOP 4

from Savion!: My Life in Tap

by Savion Glover and Bruce Weber

I look back on it now, and it seems like everything happened so fast. It's hard to believe all that has happened since I was twelve years old and getting ready to go onstage for the first time in *Tap Dance Kid*. I mean, just a few years ago, in *Tap*, I was hangin' with Sammy Davis, Jr.,[1] and he was on the set drinking Kool-Aid and wearing a do-rag. It was red Kool-Aid, I remember, and he drank it in a big mug. Like regular folks. Sammy Davis, man! EL R

And then I was on *Sesame Street*, which was also cool, a nice vibe. That's when people started recognizing me on the street. Kids. And I noticed a lot of them were wearing their hats **askew,** like I did on the show. I liked Elmo; he was my favorite, so innocent even when he was doing wrong stuff. 1

Anyway, looking back to *Tap Dance Kid*, I can see I knew nothing, nothing. I went through all the rehearsals, all the

1. ***Sammy Davis Jr.*** became a big star in the 1950s. He was an all-around performer, working in theater, movies, and television as a singer, dancer, and actor.

Vocabulary

askew (uh SKYOO) *adv.* turned or twisted to one side

Practice the Skills

1 Literary Element

Tone Remember that tone is the attitude a writer takes toward a subject. Savion's tone is enthusiastic. Look at the details he mentions:

- He hung out with celebrities when he was a kid.
- He was on *Sesame Street*.
- People started recognizing him on the street.

Additional Support

English Language Coach

Build Background Give students some background about *Sesame Street*. This show began in 1969 and uses Muppets, a type of puppet. The show has helped countless preschool aged children learn basic pre-reading and early math skills. Jim Henson invented the Muppets and was the voice of two main characters on the show, Kermit the Frog and Ernie, until he died in 1990. Elmo was added to the show in the 1980s. Bring pictures of the characters into class and ask students to share any experiences they might have with *Sesame Street*. EL understudy's rehearsals, and what did I know about scripts and scenes and blocking and upstaging and cues[2] and exit lines and all that? I had no idea how to change clothes between scenes in time to get back on. Someone's going to change me? Whoa! Hinton Battle,[3] the star, he was always on us kids about warming up, getting ready. And other stuff too, like **hygiene.** I can remember him pulling me aside and saying, "Yo, man, I don't know if you're using any deodorant, but you better get some." And he was right. I *was* funky that day. **L**

My opening night I was **nervous,** out of my mind nervous. **2** Butterflies in my stomach and everywhere else. I'm not that great a singer to begin with, but that night my voice was shaky as milk. The only thing that saved me was my family. There was a scene in the show on the Roosevelt Island tram, and I rode across the stage on this tram, and while I was riding it, I saw my mom for the first time, and this relaxing feeling came over me. I saw her face, and it was, like, relief. I was comfortable from then on. **R1**

What I learned from *The Tap Dance Kid* was the basics, really the basics. The basic basics. Familiarity with the stage. How to position myself. How to prepare. How to listen. How to react to the audience. I took it on myself to learn the theater, walked around it as if I were working there, went up on the catwalks[4] to see what the guys do up there, backstage, all that. It was, like, I'm here to perform, but I'm also interested in what's behind the secret door. I guess I was ready for it to be real, not so magical anymore. You know, I was part of it. The magician has to know what the explanation for his magic is. **R2**

Anyway, that was why *Tap Dance Kid* was important for me. As for my performance, I didn't really feel like I was

2. An ***understudy*** is an actor who knows another performer's part and can substitute if needed. ***Blocking*** is working out the places on stage where the actors should stand during the different scenes. ***Upstaging*** is drawing attention to oneself and taking it away from another actor. A ***cue*** is the action or line that tells an actor to enter the stage or give a speech.
3. ***Hinton Battle*** won a Tony award for Best Actor for *Tap Dance Kid.* He learned to tap to play the role and has been known as a dancer ever since.
4. A ***catwalk*** is a narrow bridge above a stage from where the stage crew works the sets and lights.

Vocabulary

hygiene (HY jeen) *n.* cleanliness; habits that lead to good health

Practice the Skills

2 **English Language Coach**

Adjective and Adverb Suffixes What is the base word of **nervous?** How does adding the suffix change the part of speech?

Reading in the Real World

College Savion Glover writes that he learned the "basics" when he worked on *Tap Dance Kid.* Students will need to know a lot of "basics" before they go to college. These basics can include much more than reading and math, just like Glover's basics included listening and positioning himself. Have students interview different people they know who have graduated from college and ask them to name some of the basic things they wish they had known before going to college. Ask students to write a summary of what they learned from each person they interviewed. Hold a class discussion on how students plan to use what they learned from their interviews to help them prepare for college. OL

Teach

L Literary Element

Review Characterization
Say: Think about how Savion Glover reacts to Hinton Battle telling him to wear deodorant. What does this tell you about Savion? *(Possible response: He was willing to learn. He did not take things too personally and made changes when he needed to.)* OL

R1 Reading Skill

Making Inferences **Ask:** What can you infer about Savion Glover's relationship with his mother? *(Possible response: They were close; his mother was supportive of him and made him feel confident—he was not worried about letting her down, so her presence did not make him nervous.)* OL

R2 Reading Skill

Review Identifying Main Idea and Supporting Details **Say:** Look at the last sentence on page 655. This tells you that the paragraph before this sentence summarizes the main idea about why *Tap Dance Kid* was important. Why was *Tap Dance Kid* so important to Savion? *(Possible response: It taught him that the magician has to know what the explanation for his magic is.)* OL

Indiana English/Language Arts Academic Standards
SE: 8.1, 8.3
TWE: *Reading Skill* 8.2.9, *Reading in the Real World* 8.7.1

Teach

R1 Reading Skill

Review Monitoring Comprehension **Ask:** Who is Willie? *(Willie is the star of* Tap Dance Kid *and the character played by Savion Glover.)* BL **Ask:** Why does Savion feel like the audience is clapping for Willie and not him? *(Because he felt like he was Willie when he was on stage and not Savion.)* OL

C Critical Thinking

Analysis **Say:** Lon Chaney and Jimmy Slyde are two famous tap dancers known for their skill and expertise. What important lesson did they teach Savion? *(That dancing is about expressing yourself, not about pleasing the audience.)* **Ask:** How did they teach him this lesson? *(They taught him this lesson by example, by dancing to express themselves in* Black and Blue*.)* AL

Analyzing the Photo A tap sensation, Savion dances opposite Gregory Hines in the Broadway musical *Jelly's Last Jam.* What does Savion learn about performing from his fellow dancers?

performing. That was *my* life up there, and being onstage was just like sitting around the kitchen table telling a story about what happened to me that day. And every night, when we'd take our solo bow, I felt like: These people aren't clapping for me, for Savion; they're clapping for Willie, the Tap Dance Kid. I never felt like Savion was taking that bow. R

It was after I got started on *Black and Blue* that I began to understand it didn't have to be that way. During the show I'd go out and do double times,[5] big steps, trying to please the audience, and then afterward I was hanging out with Slyde and Chaney, and just by watching them, I saw it wasn't about pleasing the audience; it was about expressing yourself. 3 It didn't happen right away. You don't just wake up and find your voice, your style. It has to develop. But during *Black and* C

5. Dancing ***double time*** is dancing very fast by doing twice the number of steps that the beat calls for.

Practice the Skills

3 **Key Reading Skill**

Making Inferences What do you think the difference is between pleasing the audience and expressing oneself?

Additional Support

Reading Fluency

Partner Reading Have students find a partner and practice reading this memoir. When students feel comfortable reading in pairs, ask for volunteers to read the story to the class. OL You can also ask students to perform the text as though it were a play, with Savion as the main character telling the story of his life. AL

Blue was when I started realizing I could create my own kind of dance. Up to that point all I was doing was dancing.

It wasn't anything they told me, not really. It was just being there every day. During rehearsals in New York I'd just be looking—at Slyde, at Chaney,[6] at Chuck, even at the women, like Dianne[7]—and I'd be watching them, saying to myself: This is nothing like what I was taught in dance class. The sounds, their bodies, the way they handled themselves. Once **R** we got over to Paris, I'm in the wings watching them, I'm in Chaney's back pocket when he comes offstage. I was like that with all of them. I just wanted to follow them around. I don't know why; they were interesting, is all. This was a club I wanted to join.

I was learning how to hang out, to enjoy. People think I hung out with them and only learned dance. But remember, I had no father image in my life. And these cats were men, and they were accepting me, and I was just this little kid running around, and they let me hang out with them everywhere. We went out. We went to clubs. You ask what they taught me? Everything. About life. About being a man. **C** About how to be. The point is I still spend time conversating with myself about these men. It doesn't matter where I am, something one of them said'll hit me, mad things, like footnotes—"Make sure you put the right foot first, even if it's the left one," or "If you can't flow with it, don't go with it"—and I'll have to ask myself: Are you talking about the dance or life? **4**

Slyde would drop info on me. He's such a wise man. Through the dance he'd tell me, "Swing a little, sing the song." I would always come out and do double time, all the time fast, fast, and Slyde told me, "You should try swinging." And the first time I tried it, I danced for seven minutes, and my breathing was different. I was relaxed, not tense, not holding my breath. I felt like I was singing what I was dancing. So that was something he told me that helped my dancing. But he was always telling me, "Stay comfortable." Now is that about just dancing?

6. Jimmy ***Slyde*** has been a tap dancer since the 1940s. His stage name comes from his style of dancing that makes him appear to slide across the stage. Lon ***Chaney*** is part of Slyde's generation of tap dancers and has influenced many younger artists.

7. ***Chuck Green*** began dancing as a child in the 1920s. Audiences loved him for his graceful style. ***Dianne Walker*** is known as an elegant dancer. Her dance students call her "Aunt Dianne."

Practice the Skills

4 Literary Element

Tone What is Savion's attitude toward the men who helped him learn about dancing and life? Does that attitude come across clearly in the tone of this paragraph?

Teach

R Reading Skill

Review Connecting Ask: What does Savion Glover mean when he says, "This was a club I wanted to join?" *(He means that he wanted to be like these dancers. He wanted to fit in with them.)* **OL** **Ask:** How have you had similar experiences to this? *(Students are likely to describe wanting to be part of a certain group of kids or to belong to a certain crowd.)* **Ask:** How is Savion Glover's experience different from yours? *(Possible response: The only way to join this club is to be a good dancer with your own style. You cannot join by conforming.)* **AL**

C Critical Thinking

Synthesis List the things that Savion learned from the men he danced with on the board. **Ask:** Do you agree with these words of advice? Why or why not? *(Responses will vary.)* Ask students to come up with three pieces of advice they would give to a young person. *(Responses will vary.)* **OL** Challenge students to word their advice as if they were Savion. **AL**

Differentiated Instruction

Write It Out Have students write their own short memoirs or poems titled "Stay Comfortable." Tell them to think about what they read in this excerpt from *Savion! My Life in Tap* and how they think the idea of staying comfortable can help them in their lives. Students who have a particular hobby, sport, or interest may want to write their memoirs or poems specifically for that hobby, sport, or interest. However, all students can write about what it might mean to stay comfortable while living life. **OL**

Indiana English/Language Arts Academic Standards
SE: 8.2, 8.2.9, 8.3
TWE: *Reading Fluency* 8.7, *Differentiated Instruction* 8.5.7

Teach

R Reading Skill

Review Monitoring Comprehension Say: Savion describes *Jelly's* as a turning point. What is a turning point? *(a time in a person's life when something important changes)* **Ask:** How do things change for Savion during *Jelly's*? *(He starts feeling like himself on the stage; he starts getting to know Gregory.)* OL

L Literary Element

Tone Ask: How is Gregory different from the other mentors Savion has had? *(Possible response: He is more of a father figure and more of a friend.)* **Ask:** What is the tone that Savion uses when he describes Gregory? *(It is an affectionate tone; Savion is describing someone who has become part of his family.)* OL

READING WORKSHOP 4

And Chaney would tell me, "Hit it! Put it *down*, young man!" and I understand that as a dancer and as a man. I can take that information about the dance and use it in my everyday life. It **translates.** You see what I'm saying? And I remember Chuck telling me, "Keep on the cardboard." What does that mean? I have no idea. "Keep on the cardboard." But I remember it, and I know, like twenty years from now, it'll come to me. That's what Chuck meant!

When we came back to Broadway, I was really trying to find myself as a tap dancer. My performance began to change, and even my mom noticed. I wasn't smiling as much, not trying to *please* so much. It wasn't, like, Hey, I'm here, it's show time! anymore. It was more, like, Hey, let's go out and dance! Forget what *they* think they want to see. Chaney, Slyde, those cats—they saw my progress. It was real. I was finally asking, Why am I performing?

R And then came *Jelly's*,[8] which was really the turning point, the first time I ever performed in a show and felt like it was me. Savion, up there, getting the applause and not the character I was pretending to be. But mostly *Jelly's* was important to me because of Gregory.[9] He took me under his wing after *Tap*, and it was Gregory who made sure I got cast in *Jelly's*.

L He wasn't like Slyde, who's more a grandfather type, with all the mysterious wisdom he lays on me. For me, knowing Gregory is like knowing you have a pops but not meeting him until you're twenty years old, and it turns out he's been very cool all this time. We met in Paris when he came to see *Black and Blue*, and little did I know he was setting up this audition for *Tap*. Right away he was calling me Save, which only my brothers call me. After that we just started hanging out. We'd go to Knicks games; he'd come over to family barbecues. 5

8. The full name of the musical is ***Jelly's Last Jam.***

9. ***Gregory Hines*** began dancing as a child in the 1950s. He was also an actor, and many of his movies included dancing.

Vocabulary

translates (TRANZ laytz) *v.* changes successfully into another form or language

Practice the Skills

5 Literary Element

Tone Describe Savion's tone. What words and sentences does he use to describe Slyde and Gregory Hines?

Additional Support

Differentiated Instruction

Visual/Audio Representation

Savion describes his dance moves and the shows he has performed on throughout his career. Bring in videos of some of his performances or the performances of some of the other people mentioned in this memoir (Sammy Davis, Jr., Hinton Battle, Jimmy Slyde, Lon Chaney, Chuck Green, Dianne Walker, Gregory Hines). Or bring in the sound tracks from some of the shows mentioned *(Tap Dance Kid, Black and Blue, Jelly's Last Jam)*. Play video clips or audio tracks for your students. Discuss the performances and what it's like for students to see and/or hear what they read about in this memoir. AS

Savion rehearses his steps at New York's Joyce Theater in January 2005.

Analyzing the Photo How does this photo capture Savion's love of dance?

Anyway, that relationship made it easy for me to, like, complete my education as a tap dancer, putting the finishing touches on all the stuff that Slyde and them had begun to teach me. And in *Jelly's*, I was playing the kid and he was playing the adult, and it seemed perfect to me that we were just there being two sides of the same person. And that number in the second act, Jelly's Isolation Dance, that was the highlight. I would do everything he did, right away, right away, keep spitting back to him what he was handing me, and we'd really be laying it down some nights. It was supposed to be a five-minute number, but it went on longer and longer and longer, we'd go on and on, jamming, and some nights people would just gather in the wings and watch. It was six, seven, eight minutes of joy every performance. And yeah, it felt like he was passing the torch down to me every night. 6

It was humbling. Still is. ❍

Practice the Skills

6 **BIG Question**

How does Savion stay true to himself? Write your answer on the *Savion!: My Life in Tap* page of Foldable 5. Your response will help you answer the Unit Challenge later.

Reading in the Real World

Citizenship Pose this question for students: Do you think the audience benefited when Savion Glover decided not to dance for them but to dance for himself? Why or why not? Have students discuss this in small groups. OL Then ask students what happens when people do things for themselves and not to please others in their schools and communities. Challenge small groups of students to find a way to rephrase the theme of this selection so it works as a community motto. Ask each group to share their motto with the class. AL

Teach

C Critical Thinking

Analysis Ask: What does Savion mean when he says "people would just gather in the wings and watch"? *(People would stand on the sides of the stage and watch them perform.)* **Ask:** Why do you think people were gathering in the wings to watch? *(Possible response: Because Savion and Gregory pushed each other to their limits.)* OL

EL Language Coach

Context Clues Say: *Passing the torch* means "to hand over responsibility". What does Savion mean when he says that it felt like Gregory was passing the torch to him? *(He was handing him the responsibility of being a great dancer.)* AL

BQ BIG Question

Ask: What might Savion tell you about how to stay true to yourself? *(Responses will vary.)* OL

Assess

Use the CheckPoint questions provided on Presentation Plus! to check for comprehension of the selection. These questions can be used with interactive response keypads for immediate student feedback.

Indiana English/Language Arts Academic Standards
SE: 8.3
TWE: *Differentiated Instruction* 8.7, *Reading in the Real World* 8.3

Assess

Resources for page 660

- Selection Quick Check, p. 48
- Selection and Unit Assessment, p. 45
- ExamView Assessment Suite
- Interactive Tutor: Self-Assessment

Students can respond to the *After You Read* items in their Learner's Notebooks or on a separate sheet of paper.

Answering the BIG Question

1. Savion learned that dancing is about expressing yourself and not about pleasing the audience.
2. Savion started performing when he was still a child and spent a lot of time on the road with the adults he danced with on stage.
3. Savion needed mentors because he was not home a lot and his father was not part of his life.

Critical Thinking

4. Possible response: Yes, from the very beginning, he wanted to learn everything about the stage and the performance. He also wanted to become the best dancer he could be. He did this by learning from his role models.
5. Possible response: They taught him about hygiene, having fun and ignoring the audience, and how to dance well.
6. Responses will vary.

After You Read

from *Savion!: My Life in Tap*

Answering the  BIG Question

1. What did Savion learn from his mentors about dance?
2. **Summarize** What was Savion's life like as a child?
   TIP Think and Search
3. **Recall** Why did Savion need mentors to help him figure out how to dance and live?
   TIP Right There

Critical Thinking

4. **Evaluate** Do you think Savion had the right attitude and work ethic to become successful as a tap dancer?
   TIP Author and Me
5. **Analyze** In what ways did Savion's role models set positive examples for him? Give details from the article to support your answer.
   TIP Author and Me
6. **Analyze** Savion says that when he watched older performers he thought, "This is nothing like what I was taught in dance class." Do you think Savion feels his classes were not useful? How is what he learned from the performers different from what he learned in his classes?
   TIP On My Own

Talk About Your Reading

Small Group Discussion Savion uses a lot of **slang,** or informal language that is specific to a particular group of people. With a small group of classmates, find and list at least ten examples of slang in the selection. You may include single words or whole expressions. Then discuss how the slang affects your understanding of Savion and the selection. Use the following questions to guide your discussion.

- What does Savion's use of slang tell you about him?
- How would the selection change if the author had translated Savion's slang into standard English?
- Is the slang Savion uses still in fashion? Explain.

Indiana English/Language Arts Academic Standards (pp. 660–661)

8.3 Comprehension and Analysis of Literary Text Respond to grade-level-appropriate literature... identifying story elements... **8.5.1** Write... autobiographies... **8.2 Comprehension and Analysis (Focus on Informational Text)** Develop [reading] strategies... **8.2.9** Make reasonable statements and draw conclusions... **8.1 Word Recognition, Fluency, and Vocabulary Development** Understand... word parts... **8.6 English Language Conventions**

For a complete description of the standards, see p. IN 11.

Talk About Your Reading

Examples of slang expressions students may list will vary.

Possible responses to the questions: Savion's slang tells me he is African American and very comfortable with who he is because he doesn't feel the need to conform to Standard English. If his slang had been translated, the selection would have become more formal, and it would have sounded less like Savion. Some of the slang is still used, but most of it is outdated.

Skills Review

Key Reading Skill: Making Inferences

7. We know what Savion thought about working with the men who were his role models, but what do you think these men thought about him? What makes you say so?

Literary Element: Tone

8. How would you describe the overall tone of the article? Why? Quote specific words or phrases that illustrate the tone.

Vocabulary Check

Copy the sentences below on another sheet of paper. Then fill in the blank in each sentence with the correct vocabulary word from the list below.

askew • hygiene • translates

9. To avoid infecting patients, the doctors and nurses practiced good ______.
10. After the toddler slept on the rug, he left it lying ______ on the floor.
11. Studying hard often ______ into good grades.

English Language Coach Use one of the suffixes below to make each word listed either an adjective or an adverb. You may use a dictionary if you need to.

-ly • -ic • -ive • -ful • -ous

12. Change the verb *thank* into an adjective.
13. Change the verb *ponder* into an adjective.
14. Change the noun *electron* into an adjective.
15. Change the adjective *sincere* into an adverb.
16. Change the verb *obsess* into an adjective.

Web Activities For eFlashcards, Selection Quick Checks, and other Web activities, go to www.glencoe.com.

Grammar Link: More Run-on Sentences

In the last Grammar Link you saw one kind of run-on sentence—two independent clauses that run together.

Run-on: I like soccer I like hockey even more.

A second kind of run-on sentence occurs when two independent clauses are separated by just a comma.

Run-on: I like soccer, I like hockey even more.

A comma alone is not strong enough to separate independent clauses, or simple sentences. Fix this type of run-on, which is sometimes called a **comma splice,** by using any of these methods:

A. Separate the sentences with a period.
- I like soccer. I like hockey even more.

B. Put a comma and a coordinating conjunction between the independent clauses.
- I like soccer, but I like hockey even more.

C. Add a subordinating conjunction to one of the clauses to make it a dependent clause.
- Though I like soccer, I like hockey even more.

Grammar Practice

Copy the following paragraph on another sheet of paper. Then find and fix the three run-on sentences. Use any of the methods shown above.

Last fall my family and I went to the beach. I had never seen the ocean before, it was quite an experience. At first my little brother was a little nervous about getting in the water the waves were big and noisy. Everyone else was having fun, so he finally decided to try going in. He went in the water up to his knees, a wave knocked him over. Instead of being afraid, he started laughing. After that, we had so much fun! I can hardly wait to go back to the beach.

Grammar Link: More Run-on Sentences

Grammar Practice

Sample changes to the paragraph: Last fall my family and I went to the beach. **I had never seen the ocean before. It was quite an experience. At first my little brother was a little nervous about getting in the water because the waves were so big and noisy.** Everyone else was having fun, so he finally decided to try going in. **He went in the water up to his knees, and a wave knocked him over.** Instead of being afraid, he started laughing. After that, we had so much fun! I can hardly wait to go back to the beach.

Skills Review

Key Reading Skill: Making Inferences

7. Answers will vary. Students are likely to say that the men liked Savion and his work. They continued spending time with him, and Gregory even worked to get Savion the part for *Jelly's Last Jam*.

Literary Element: Tone

8. Possible response: The overall tone of the article is enthusiastic and respectful. Savion clearly loves to dance, and he has a great deal of respect for all of his mentors. Examples of specific words or phrases will vary.

Vocabulary Check

9. hygiene
10. askew
11. translates

English Language Coach

12. thankful
13. ponderous
14. electronic
15. sincerely
16. obsessive

Close

Ask students to tell how the Big Question helped them as they read from *Savion! My Life in Tap.*

Indiana English/Language Arts Academic Standards
SE: 8.1, 8.2, 8.2.9, 8.3, 8.5.1, 8.6

Comparing Literature: Characterization

Teaching Students to Compare Characterization Across Texts

Why Is It Important?

- Understanding characterization is integral to understanding stories. Students who understand the methods of characterization that authors use will be prepared to interpret and understand characters.
- Recognizing characterization allows readers to more deeply consider the characters in a story and to relate the characters to themselves.
- Different authors will not use characterization in exactly the same way or use only one method of characterization throughout their texts.

How to Help Students Get It

- Model identifying and comparing characterization in texts by doing a Think Aloud with your students. Choose two selections. As you read the first selection, comment on significant descriptions, actions, thoughts, words, interactions, and responses to a character. As you progress, shift the responsibility for identifying characterization to the students. When you read the second selection, compare the methods of characterization to those in the first selection.
- Remind students that most authors use a combination of methods to reveal character traits: describing a character's appearance, displaying or relating actions, describing thoughts, describing what the character says and does, and describing the reactions of others to the character. Divide students into five groups. Assign each group one of the forms of characterization and ask them to find an example of that form in a story, a play, a poem, a biography, or an article.

Reading to Answer the Big Question

A Retrieved Reformation by O. Henry
Safecracker Jimmy Valentine is the best at what he does. Immediately upon his release from prison, he resumes his lucrative career as a thief. However, falling in love changes him completely. When policeman Ben Price tracks him down, Jimmy has assumed a new identity, the successful and legitimate businessman Ralph Spencer. When he has to break into a "burglar-proof" safe to save the life of a child, Jimmy thinks his life as Ralph Spencer is over. Ben Price, having seen who Jimmy really is, disagrees.

A Retrieved Reformation adapted by Gary Gianni
Gianni's illustrated adaptation of the O. Henry tale uses text sampled directly from the story.

Workshop Resources

Pacing (Days) Standard	Pacing (Days) Block	Lesson	Student Materials	Teacher Resources
1	1	Comparing Literature: Characterization	English Language Coach Review, p. 41	Bellringer Options Transparencies –Daily Language Practice 50 Presentation Plus!
1	1	"A Retrieved Reformation" (graphic)	Glencoe Online Unit Vocabulary Review, p. 39 Academic Vocabulary Review, p. 42 English Language Coach Comparing Literature Graphic Organizer, p. 34 StudentWorks Plus™ Online Student Edition Literature Classics	Puzzlemaker Skill Level Up!™ A Language Arts Game BookLink 3 Assessment by Learning Objective (Diagnostic and Formative) Interactive Tutor: Self-Assessment TeacherWorks Plus™ ExamView Assessment Suite
1		"A Retrieved Reformation" (short story)	Glencoe Online Unit Vocabulary Review, p. 39 Academic Vocabulary Review, p. 42 English Language Coach Comparing Literature Graphic Organizer, p. 34 StudentWorks Plus™ Online Student Edition Literature Classics	Puzzlemaker Skill Level Up!™ A Language Arts Game BookLink 3 Assessment by Learning Objective (Diagnostic and Formative) Interactive Tutor: Self-Assessment TeacherWorks Plus™ ExamView Assessment Suite

Keys for Unit Resource

- Blackline Master
- Workbook
- Supplemental Text
- CD-ROM
- DVD
- Transparency
- Web-based
- Fast File

Level Appropriate Code

AS = Activities for all students
AL = Activities for students working above grade level
OL = Activities for students working at grade level
BL = Activities for students working below grade level
EL = Activities for English language learners

Focus

BELLRINGER Options

Daily Language Practice Transparency 50

Focus Activity Write "A leopard cannot change its spots" on the board. Explain that this expression means that people don't ever really change. Ask students to discuss whether or not they agree with this statement.

Teach

L Literary Element

Characterization Say: In this workshop, you are going to be comparing a graphic story to a short story. Let's think about how these two types of stories can show the same thing differently. For instance, a graphic story can use a picture to show a character's anger by depicting his or her expression; whereas, a short story can describe a character's angry feelings and actions through words. For example, The man stomped his feet and yelled loudly, "What do you mean?!" Graphic stories use pictures to show the emotions and events of a story, while short stories use words to do this. AS

A RETRIEVED REFORMATION

by O. Henry

&

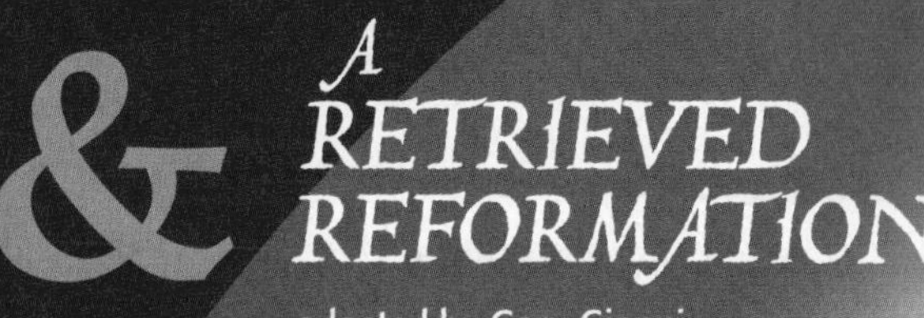

adapted by Gary Gianni

Skills Focus

You will use these skills as you read and compare the following selections:

- "A Retrieved Reformation," p. 665
- Adaptation of "A Retrieved Reformation," p. 675

Reading

- Comparing and contrasting literary elements in texts

Literature

- Comparing and contrasting characterization in stories

Vocabulary

- Using word analysis
- Academic Vocabulary: *reveal*

Have you ever watched a movie that was based on a book? If so, you've seen an adaptation. The word *adapt* means "change." An **adaptation** is a changed, or new, version of an existing literary work.

Adaptations tell the same story in different ways. In this workshop, you will read a short story and its illustrated, graphic story adaptation. As you read, pay attention to the similarities and differences between the two versions of the story. Notice what things you are told in words in the print version of the story and what things you are told in pictures in the graphic story version.

How to Compare Literature: Characterization

L **Characterization** refers to the methods that an author uses to show what characters are like. An author may **reveal** what a character does, says, and thinks as well as what other characters or the narrator says. In print stories authors often reveal character through descriptions of actions and thoughts. In graphic stories authors often reveal character through dialogue and pictures.

As you read, think about how the author reveals character in each selection. What does O. Henry tell you about the main character? What does Gary Gianni show you?

Academic Vocabulary

reveal (rih VEEL) *v.* show

Indiana English/ Language Arts Academic Standards (pp. 662–663)

8.3 Comprehension and Analysis of Literary Text Respond to grade-level-appropriate literature... identifying... character... and making connections and comparisons across texts.

For a complete description of the standards, see p. IN 11.

Additional Support

Literature Focus Lesson

Adaptations The two selections in this workshop are a short story and its adaptation into a graphic story. Explain what an adaptation is to students *(when a text has been changed into another form)*. Have students think about how each of these things might be different (or the same) in an adaptation from short story to graphic story:

- plot
- setting
- descriptions
- characters
- dialogue

Have students keep track of the differences between the short story and its graphic adaptation as they read the selections in this workshop. OL

Get Ready to Compare

In your Learner's Notebook, make a chart like the one below. Use your chart to record details that characterize—tell you about—Jimmy Valentine. Pay attention to the differences between the two versions. When you're finished reading, you will use your chart to compare Jimmy's characterization in the original story and in the graphic story adaptation.

Jimmy Valentine's character is revealed through . . .	Examples from the original story	Examples from the graphic story
his speech		
his actions		
his thoughts		
his appearance		
other characters' reactions to him		

R

Use Your Comparison

Who are the characters in your life? Perhaps you have a cousin who is just as funny as your best friend, or a teacher who has a lot of the same caring qualities as a favorite aunt. Choose two people you know or that you've read about and tell about each of them in a few paragraphs. Discuss how each person is alike and different.

You also may decide to illustrate a storyboard about the characters you've chosen. (A storyboard is a panel of drawings that shows a story's action.) For example, one frame may show the mother from a story you've read talking with her child, and the other may show your mother talking with you. Keep it brief—use four to six frames.

C

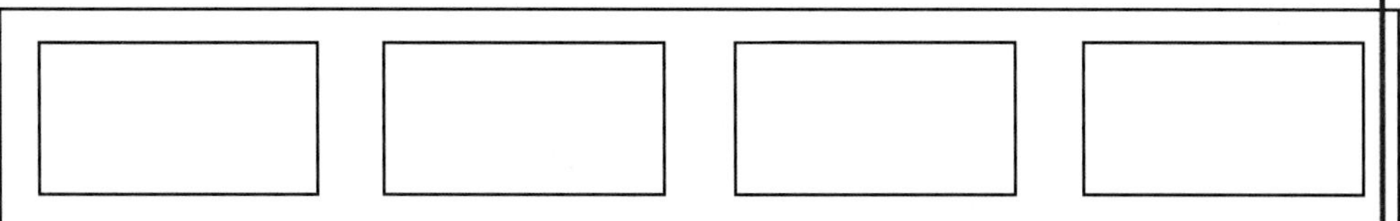

Teach

R Reading Skill

Review Setting a Purpose for Reading **Ask:** How can the chart on page 663 help you set a purpose for reading? *(Possible response: The chart shows different ways that a character is revealed in each story.)* BL

C Critical Thinking

Comprehension After students finish their storyboards, have them get into small groups and compare the boards they created. Discuss which details they included from the story and which details they left out. AS

Ask: How will your storyboard help you compare a short story to a graphic story? *(Possible response: Seeing "Kamau's Finish" as a storyboard helps me understand what a short story would look like as a graphic story.)* AL

Assess/Close

Resources for page 663

Use the Comparing Literature Graphic Organizer BLM in the Unit 5 Resource Booklet p. 34.

Differentiated Instruction

Picture It Before class, cut out several different magazine ads with people in them. Give one or more ads to pairs of students. Instruct students to examine the picture(s) and describe the character(s) based on these pictures *(angry, friendly, funny, happy, sick)*. Then have students look at one picture at a time and write a few sentences about each picture as if they were writing a short story about the image. Ask several volunteers to show their ads to the class and read their short story versions. OL Alternately, you may do this activity with the whole class. Show one picture at a time to the class, and discuss it together. Choose a volunteer to give a short story version of it aloud. BL

Indiana English/Language Arts Academic Standards
SE: 8.3
TWE: *Literature Focus Lesson* 8.3, *Differentiated Instruction* 8.5.1

Teach

More About the Author

William Sydney Porter was born in Greensboro, North Carolina. He moved to Texas as a teen and lived there for many years. Porter was sent to jail in Ohio and served three years of his sentence. Like the character in this selection, Porter changed his name when he got out of jail. He wrote over 600 short stories, and he is most known for his surprise endings.

E Text Element

Review Titles and Subheads Have students use dictionaries to define the words in the title "A Retrieved Reformation." **Ask:** What does the word *retrieved* mean? *(got back; rescued or saved)* **Ask:** What does the word *reformation* mean? *(a change for the better)* **OL** **Ask:** What is a *retrieved reformation*? *(Possible response: a change for the better that was saved from being lost)* **AL**

Readability Scores
Dale-Chall: 6.9
DRP: 54
Lexile: 900

Before You Read E A Retrieved Reformation by O. Henry

O. Henry

Meet the Author

O. Henry's real name was William Sydney Porter. He was born in 1862. He began writing stories while serving a short prison sentence for stealing money from a bank where he had worked. When he left prison in 1901, Porter began writing under the pen name O. Henry, partly to hide his past. Porter lived in New York City until his death in 1910.

Author Search For more about O. Henry, go to www.glencoe.com.

Indiana English/Language Arts Academic Standards
(pp. 664–673)

8.1 Word Recognition, Fluency, and Vocabulary Development Understand...word parts... **8.3 Comprehension and Analysis of Literary Text** Respond to grade-level-appropriate literature...identifying...character and plot...and making connections and comparisons across texts.

For a complete description of the standards, see p. IN 11.

Vocabulary Preview

compulsory (kum PUL suh ree) *adj.* required **(p. 666)** *The final exam was compulsory for everyone in the course.*

retribution (re trih BYOO shun) *n.* punishment for past deeds **(p. 668)** *The judge believed that all crimes deserved stiff retribution.*

simultaneously (sy mul TAY nee us lee) *adv.* at the same time **(p. 671)** *Both doors slammed simultaneously, creating a loud noise.*

English Language Coach

Multiple Affixes Did you know that more than one prefix and suffix can be added to the same base word? Look at the words *villainously* and *immovable* on the chart below. Then complete the chart by jotting down, in the last column, what you think the words mean. Use the chart to understand some of the prefixes and suffixes in "A Retrieved Reformation."

Word	Base Word	Prefixes or Suffixes	Meaning
villainously	*villain* = an evil person	*-ous* = full of *-ly* = in a particular way	
immovable	*move* = to change places	*im-* = not *-able* = capable	

Get Ready to Read

Connect to the Reading

Think of a time when you did the wrong thing. How did you feel afterward?

Build Background

O. Henry is known for his plots–and plot twists. A **plot twist** is an unexpected turn of events in a story.

Set Purposes for Reading

BIG Question Read to find out what Jimmy Valentine, the main character of "A Retrieved Reformation," risks to stay true to himself.

Set Your Own Purpose What else would you like to learn from the selection to help you answer the Big Question? Write your own purpose on the "A Retrieved Reformation" page of Foldable 5.

Additional Support

Author Search To expand students' appreciation of O. Henry, have them access the Web site for additional information and resources.

English Language Coach

Affixes Ask students to keep track of the prefixes and suffixes used in this story. Have them create a chart similar to the chart on page 664 for each page of the story and record the affixes used and their definitions. Explain to students that breaking down words into their roots and affixes will help them to better understand what they read, especially if the text has a difficult vocabulary. At the end of the story, have students share their charts and discuss what affixes were used in the story. **EL** Ask students to analyze what they learned by charting the affixes as they read. **AL**

A RETRIEVED REFORMATION

by O. Henry

A guard came to the prison shoe shop, where Jimmy Valentine was assiduously stitching uppers,[1] and escorted him to the front office. There the warden handed Jimmy his pardon, which had been signed that morning by the governor. Jimmy took it in a tired kind of way. He had served nearly ten months of a four-year sentence. He had expected to stay only about three months, at the longest. When a man with as many friends on the outside as Jimmy Valentine had is received in the "stir"[2] it is hardly worthwhile to cut his hair. **1**

"Now, Valentine," said the warden, "you'll go out in the morning. Brace up, and make a man of yourself. You're not a bad fellow at heart. Stop cracking safes, and live straight."

"Me?" said Jimmy, in surprise. "Why, I never cracked a safe in my life."

"Oh, no," laughed the warden. "Of course not. Let's see, now. How was it you happened to get sent up on that Springfield job? Was it because you wouldn't prove an alibi for fear of compromising somebody in extremely high-toned society? Or was it simply a case of a mean old jury that had it in for you? It's always one or the other with you innocent victims." **2**

"Me?" said Jimmy, still blankly virtuous. "Why, warden, I never was in Springfield in my life!"

1. If you do something ***assiduously,*** you do it steadily and with care. Jimmy was busy sewing the ***uppers***—the top part of shoes—onto the soles.
2. The ***"stir"*** is another name for prison.

Practice the Skills

1 Comparing Literature

Characterization The narrator means that Jimmy has a lot of important friends—friends who will make sure that Jimmy doesn't stay in prison for very long.

2 Comparing Literature

Characterization Does the warden believe that Jimmy is telling the truth? Think about the warden's

- words
- tone
- facial expressions and gestures

Teach

R Reading Skill

Review Activating Prior Knowledge Say: Think about other stories you have read or movies you have seen about prison. Why is Jimmy at the prison shoe shop? *(Many prisoners have jobs, although today they would not be sewing shoes.)* **Ask:** What is a pardon? *(a written document that allows a criminal to go free from prison)* **OL**

L Literary Element

Characterization Ask: What do you learn about Jimmy from the warden's speech? *(why he was in jail in the first place)* **OL** **Ask:** Does the writer make you think Jimmy is guilty or innocent? Explain. *(Most students will say the writer makes him seem guilty because the story begins by telling how he had many friends on the outside, and he only "expected to stay a few months." These are typical attitudes for guilty prisoners in books and movies.)* **AL**

EL Language Coach

Context Clues Ask: What does it mean to be blankly virtuous? *(to look unknowing and innocent)* **OL**

Reading Fluency

Read Aloud The first paragraph of the story is told by an omniscient narrator. Define omniscient narrator for students *(a narrator that sees and knows everything about the characters and events in a story)*. Have students practice reading the first paragraph aloud as if they are the narrator who speaks at the beginning of a play. Explain that this does not mean they should add a lot of emotion to their reading. It means they should read the paragraph clearly and at a pace that enables listeners to get a sense of the setting. **OL**

Indiana English/Language Arts Academic Standards
SE: 8.1, 8.3
TWE: *English Language Coach* 8.1, *Reading Fluency* 8.7.2

Teach

L Literary Element

Characterization **Ask:** What do you learn about Mike from this dialogue? *(Mike was one of the friends who helped get Jimmy out of jail.)* OL

R Reading Skill

Review Making Inferences
Ask: What does Mike mean by a "protest from Springfield to buck against"? *(Possible response: There must have been people in Springfield who did not want Jimmy to get out of jail or to be pardoned. They may have been political leaders or just ordinary citizens who protested.)* AL

"Take him back, Cronin," smiled the warden, "and fix him up with outgoing clothes. Unlock him at seven in the morning, and let him come to the bull-pen. Better think over my advice, Valentine."

At a quarter past seven on the next morning Jimmy stood in the warden's outer office. He had on a suit of the villainously fitting, ready-made clothes and a pair of stiff, squeaky shoes that the state furnishes to its discharged **compulsory** guests.

The clerk handed him a railroad ticket and the five-dollar bill with which the law expected him to rehabilitate himself into good citizenship and prosperity. The warden gave him a cigar, and shook hands. Valentine, 9762, was chronicled on the books "Pardoned by Governor," and Mr. James Valentine walked out into the sunshine.

Disregarding the song of the birds, the waving green trees, and the smell of the flowers, Jimmy headed straight for a restaurant. There he tasted the first sweet joys of liberty in the shape of a broiled chicken and a bottle of white wine—followed by a cigar a grade better than the one the warden had given him. From there he proceeded leisurely to the depot. He tossed a quarter into the hat of a blind man sitting by the door, and boarded his train. Three hours set him down in a little town near the state line. He went to the café of one Mike Dolan and shook hands with Mike, who was alone behind the bar. 3

"Sorry we couldn't make it sooner, Jimmy, me boy," said Mike. "But we had that protest from Springfield to buck against, and the governor nearly balked. Feeling all right?"

"Fine," said Jimmy. "Got my key?"

He got his key and went upstairs, unlocking the door of a room at the rear. Everything was just as he had left it. There on the floor was still Ben Price's collar-button that had been torn from that eminent detective's shirt-band when they had overpowered Jimmy to arrest him. 4

Pulling out from the wall a folding-bed, Jimmy slid back a panel in the wall and dragged out a dust-covered suitcase. He opened this and gazed fondly at the finest set of burglar's

Vocabulary

compulsory (kum PUL suh ree) *adj.* required

Practice the Skills

3 Comparing Literature

Characterization What does Jimmy's behavior reveal about his character? Keep in mind the time of the story. With only five dollars, Jimmy was able to buy a broiled chicken, a bottle of wine, and a good cigar. But he wouldn't have much more left than the quarter he gave the blind man.

4 Comparing Literature

Characterization In this one sentence, the author introduces a new character. How much does that sentence tell you about Ben Price?

Additional Support

Differentiated Instruction

Descriptive Language The author of this selection used descriptive language to create the setting and the character of Jimmy. Have students make a list of all the words or phrases on page 666 that seem most descriptive to them *(seven in the morning; villainously fitting; ready-made clothes; stiff; squeaky shoes; waving green trees; dust-covered suitcase)*. Discuss how these words work together to create a vivid setting and a realistic protagonist. Ask students to summarize or draw pictures of the setting and Jimmy's character. Have volunteers share what they wrote or drew with the class. OL tools in the East. It was a complete set, made of specially tempered steel, the latest designs in drills, punches, braces and bits, jimmies, clamps, and augers, with two or three novelties invented by Jimmy himself, in which he took pride. Over nine hundred dollars they had cost him to have made at ______, a place where they make such things for the profession.

In half an hour Jimmy went downstairs and through the café. He was now dressed in tasteful and well-fitting clothes, and carried his dusted and cleaned suitcase in his hand. **5**

"Got anything on?" asked Mike Dolan, genially.

"Me?" said Jimmy, in a puzzled tone. "I don't understand. I'm representing the New York Amalgamated Short Snap Biscuit Cracker and Frazzled Wheat Company."

This statement delighted Mike to such an extent that Jimmy had to take a seltzer-and-milk on the spot. He never touched "hard" drinks.

A week after the release of Valentine, 9762, there was a neat job of safe-burglary done in Richmond, Indiana, with no clue to the author. A scant eight hundred dollars was all that was secured. Two weeks after that a patented, improved, burglar-proof safe in Logansport was opened like a cheese to the tune of fifteen hundred dollars, currency; securities and silver[3] untouched. That began to interest the rogue catchers. Then an old-fashioned bank safe in Jefferson City became active and threw out of its crater an eruption of banknotes amounting to five thousand dollars. The losses were now high enough to bring the matter up into Ben Price's class of work. By comparing notes, a remarkable similarity in the methods of the burglaries was noticed. Ben Price investigated the scenes of the robberies, and was heard to remark: "That's Dandy Jim Valentine's autograph. He's resumed business. Look at that combination knob—jerked out as easy as pulling up a radish in wet weather. He's got the only clamps that can do it. And look how clean those tumblers were punched out! Jimmy never has to drill but one hole. Yes, I guess I want Mr. Valentine. He'll do his bit next time without any short-time or clemency foolishness." **R**

3. ***Currency*** is paper money, ***securities*** are stocks and bonds, and ***silver*** is silver coins. Valentine is careful not to steal securities that could be difficult to sell or silver that could be heavy and attention-getting. He doesn't want to get caught.

Practice the Skills

5 Comparing Literature

Characterization How do the author's descriptions help you picture Jimmy? Make notes on your chart about the way O. Henry describes Jimmy's appearance.

Teach

EL Language Coach

Context Clues **Say:** There are a lot of words on this page that depend on their context for meaning. Ask students to make a list of the words and phrases on page 667 that have to do with robbing safes *(tempered steel, drills, punches, braces and bits, jimmies, clamps, augers, patented, currency, securities, combination knob, tumblers, punched out)*. Have small groups of students define each of the words. Create a class glossary for this selection and have students add to it as they read. AS

R Reading Skill

Review Making Inferences
Ask: Who is Ben Price? *(a police detective)* **Ask:** What makes Ben Price think that Valentine committed these burglaries? *(The crimes are committed in the same way that Valentine's other crimes were done.)* **Ask:** What skills and tools does Jimmy have that make him unique as a bank robber? *(special clamps, some tools he invented on his own, he usually only drills one hole)* **Ask:** What is clemency? *(mercy or kindness)* OL

Reading in the Real World

Career Valentine makes up the company name of "New York Amalgamated Short Snap Biscuit Cracker and Frazzled Wheat Company." Have students create an advertisement for this company and a product they might sell. BL You may also wish to challenge students to make up their own company name and an ad for something it makes. For either of the projects, students who are more musically inclined can write a jingle instead of making an ad. OL Discuss careers available in advertising. Have interested students do further research on this and report their findings back to the class. AL

Indiana English/Language Arts Academic Standards
SE: 8.3
TWE: *Reading Skill* 8.2.9, *Differentiated Instruction* 8.3.6; *Reading in the Real World* 8.4, 8.5.4

Teach

L Literary Element

Characterization **Ask:** What did you learn about Jimmy as a thief from this page? *(Possible response: I learned about his habits: long jumps, quick get-aways, no confederates, and a taste for good society)* OL **Ask:** What else did you learn about him? *(Possible response: He is attractive and seems interested in the young woman.)* AL

C Critical Thinking

Analysis **Say:** The author says that Jimmy looked into the young woman's eyes, "forgot what he was, and became another man." What does this mean? *(Possible response: He fell in love at first sight, and it changed him.)* **Ask:** Do you think this will change Jimmy's character? *(Responses will vary.)* AL

Ben Price knew Jimmy's habits. He had learned them while working up the Springfield case. Long jumps, quick get-aways, no confederates,[4] and a taste for good society—these ways had helped Mr. Valentine to become noted as a successful dodger of **retribution.** It was given out that Ben Price had taken up the trail of the elusive cracksman, and other people with burglar-proof safes felt more at ease. 6

One afternoon Jimmy Valentine and his suitcase climbed out of the mailhack[5] in Elmore, a little town five miles off the railroad down in the blackjack country of Arkansas. Jimmy, looking like an athletic young senior just home from college, went down the board sidewalk toward the hotel.

A young lady crossed the street, passed him at the corner, and entered a door over which was the sign "The Elmore Bank." Jimmy Valentine looked into her eyes, forgot what he was, and became another man. She lowered her eyes and colored slightly. Young men of Jimmy's style and looks were scarce in Elmore. 7

Jimmy collared a boy that was loafing on the steps of the bank as if he were one of the stockholders, and began to ask him questions about the town, feeding him dimes at intervals. By and by the young lady came out, looking royally unconscious of the young man with the suitcase, and went her way.

"Isn't that young lady Miss Polly Simpson?" asked Jimmy, with specious guile.[6]

"Naw," said the boy. "She's Annabel Adams. Her pa owns this bank. What'd you come to Elmore for? Is that a gold watch-chain? I'm going to get a bulldog. Got any more dimes?"

Jimmy went to the Planters' Hotel, registered as Ralph D. Spencer, and engaged a room. He leaned on the desk and declared his platform to the clerk. He said he had come to

4. ***Confederates,*** here, are friends or accomplices.
5. The ***mailhack*** was a horse-drawn carriage that delivered mail and carried passengers.
6. ***Guile*** is deceit. If something is ***specious,*** it seems true but isn't. Jimmy wants to look as if he's asking an innocent question, even though he's not.

Vocabulary

retribution (re trih BYOO shun) *n.* punishment for past deeds

Practice the Skills

6 Comparing Literature

Characterization Make notes on your chart about Jimmy's characteristics as a thief.

7 Comparing Literature

Characterization Based on what you know about Jimmy so far, do you think he can change and become a good person? Why or why not?

Additional Support

Literature Focus Lesson

Dialect No matter where you go, you will find people who speak their own variation of language. A dialect is a variation of a language that is spoken by a specific group of people within a geographic region. By definition, a dialect will not follow the standard rules of the language; this may include grammar, structure, pronunciation, or form. A writer uses dialects to help create setting and develop characters. Dialects show how characters actually speak and sound. They also give clues about where characters are from, and a dialect may help differentiate one character from others in a story. Have students discuss the different dialects they have encountered in the selections in this unit. AS

Elmore to look for a location to go into business. How was the shoe business, now, in the town? He had thought of the shoe business. Was there an opening?

The clerk was impressed by the clothes and manner of Jimmy. He, himself, was something of a pattern of fashion to the thinly gilded youth of Elmore, but he now perceived his shortcomings. While trying to figure out Jimmy's manner of tying his four-in-hand[7] he cordially gave information. 8

Yes, there ought to be a good opening in the shoe line. There wasn't an exclusive shoe store in the place. The dry-goods and general stores handled them. Business in all lines was fairly good. Hoped Mr. Spencer would decide to locate in Elmore. He would find it a pleasant town to live in, and the people very sociable.

Analyzing the Image These are the kinds of shoes men and women wore in Jimmy Valentine's day. How do they differ from the shoes people wear today?

Mr. Spencer thought he would stop over in the town a few days and look over the situation. No, the clerk needn't call the boy. He would carry up his suitcase, himself; it was rather heavy.

Mr. Ralph Spencer, the phoenix that arose from Jimmy Valentine's ashes—ashes left by the flame of a sudden and alterative attack of love—remained in Elmore, and prospered. He opened a shoe store and secured a good run of trade. 9 C R

Socially he was also a success and made many friends. And he accomplished the wish of his heart. He met Miss Annabel Adams, and became more and more captivated by her charms.

At the end of a year the situation of Mr. Ralph Spencer was this: he had won the respect of the community, his shoe store was flourishing, and he and Annabel were engaged to be married in two weeks. Mr. Adams, the typical, plodding, country banker, approved of Spencer. Annabel's pride in him almost equaled her affection. He was as much at home in the family of Mr. Adams and that of Annabel's married sister as if he were already a member.

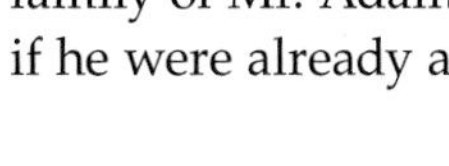

7. A ***four-in-hand*** is a necktie.

Practice the Skills

8 Comparing Literature

Characterization Do most people respond positively or negatively to Jimmy? How can you tell? Write your answer on your chart.

9 English Language Coach

Multiple Affixes If you alter something, you change it. The suffix *-ive* means "having the quality of." What do you think the word **alterative** means?

Differentiated Instruction

Then and Now It was much easier for Jimmy to change his name in the early 1900s than it is today. Very few people had cars, so no one had driver's licenses. There was also no other photo identification system. This meant you were whoever you said you were. Challenge students to think of other differences they have noticed between the time when the story was written and now. What advantages do they see to modern life? What disadvantages? Have students discuss their ideas in small groups. OL

Teach

R Reading Skill

Review Monitoring Comprehension **Ask:** How is the new Mr. Spencer earning his living in Elmore? *(He runs a successful shoe store.)* **Ask:** Where did Jimmy learn to work on shoes? *(in prison)* BL

C Critical Thinking

Analysis Have students look up the myth of the phoenix to understand this analogy. **Ask:** What is a phoenix? *(A phoenix is a mythological bird that was consumed by fire and later rose from its own ashes.)* **Ask:** What does the writer mean when he says "Mr. Ralph Spencer, the phoenix that arose from Jimmy Valentine's ashes"? *(Possible response: He means that Mr. Spencer is a renewed Jimmy.)* **Ask:** What is the fire that consumed him? *(love)* AL

Indiana English/Language Arts Academic Standards
SE: 8.1, 8.3
TWE: *Literature Focus Lesson* 8.3.6, *Differentiated Instruction* 8.3

Teach

L Literary Element

Review Point of View **Say:** The narrator is a limited third person. This means the narrator does not know everything and cannot tell the reader what Jimmy is thinking or why he does certain things. What purpose does the letter from Jimmy have in this story? *(It tells readers what Jimmy is thinking and what his intentions are for the future.)* AL

C Critical Thinking

Analysis **Ask:** How long has Jimmy been living in Elmore? *(about one year)* **Say:** According to his letter, he has not been stealing anything during that time. Why do you think that Ben Price has come to Elmore looking for Jimmy? *(Ben Price was investigating the burglaries that happened before Jimmy moved to Elmore. He has been searching for Jimmy and has finally found him.)* OL

One day Jimmy sat down in his room and wrote this letter, which he mailed to the safe address of one of his old friends in St. Louis:

DEAR OLD PAL:

I want you to be at Sullivan's place, in Little Rock, next Wednesday night, at nine o'clock. I want you to wind up some little matters for me. And, also, I want to make you a present of my kit of tools. I know you'll be glad to get them—you couldn't duplicate the lot for a thousand dollars. Say, Billy, I've quit the old business—a year ago. I've got a nice store. I'm making an honest living, and I'm going to marry the finest girl on earth two weeks from now. It's the only life, Billy—the straight one. I wouldn't touch a dollar of another man's money now for a million. After I get married I'm going to sell out and go West, where there won't be so much danger of having old scores brought up against me. I tell you, Billy, she's an angel. She believes in me; and I wouldn't do another crooked thing for the whole world. Be sure to be at Sally's, for I must see you. I'll bring along the tools with me.

Your old friend,

JIMMY 10

Visual Vocabulary
A ***livery buggy*** is a hired horse-drawn carriage.

On the Monday night after Jimmy wrote this letter, Ben Price jogged unobtrusively into Elmore in a livery buggy. He lounged about town in his quiet way until he found out what he wanted to know. From the drugstore across the street from Spencer's shoe store he got a good look at Ralph D. Spencer.

"Going to marry the banker's daughter are you, Jimmy?" said Ben to himself, softly. "Well, I don't know!"

The next morning Jimmy took breakfast at the Adamses. He was going to Little Rock that day to order his wedding suit and buy something nice for Annabel. That would be the first time he had left town since he came to Elmore. It had been more than a year now since those last professional "jobs," and he thought he could safely venture out.

After breakfast quite a family party went down together—Mr. Adams, Annabel, Jimmy, and Annabel's married sister with her two little girls, aged five and nine. They came by the

Practice the Skills

10 Comparing Literature

Characterization You've learned a lot about Jimmy from narrative description. This letter, however, contains Jimmy's own words. What does the letter reveal about Jimmy's personality? How do you picture Jimmy now?

Additional Support

Reading in the Real World

Career The wedding industry is a big business. Have students make lists of the different businesses and professionals who are part of this industry *(photographers, caterers, dress manufacturers, tuxedo rental companies, limousine drivers, travel agencies).* Direct students to make a chart of the different businesses and list some of the types of jobs that might be found in each of these businesses. OL Finally, challenge students to choose one job and find out more specifics about it: the training or education required, its main responsibilities, the growth potential, and general pay scale. AL hotel where Jimmy still boarded, and he ran up to his room and brought along his suitcase. Then they went on to the bank. There stood Jimmy's horse and buggy and Dolph Gibson, who was going to drive him over to the railroad station.

All went well inside the high, carved oak railings into the banking room—Jimmy included, for Mr. Adams's future son-in-law was welcome anywhere. The clerks were pleased to be greeted by the good-looking, agreeable young man who was going to marry Miss Annabel. Jimmy set his suitcase down. Annabel, whose heart was bubbling with happiness and lively youth, put on Jimmy's hat and picked up the suitcase. "Wouldn't I make a nice drummer?" said Annabel. "My! Ralph, how heavy it is. Feels like it was full of gold bricks." L1

Analyzing the Photo This bank vault is from the same time period as the story. How does the photo help you understand the actions that occur on this page?

"Lot of nickel-plated shoehorns in there," said Jimmy, coolly, "that I'm going to return. Thought I'd save express charges by taking them up. I'm getting awfully economical."

The Elmore Bank had just put in a new safe and vault. Mr. Adams was very proud of it, and insisted on an inspection by everyone. The vault was a small one, but it had a new patented door. It fastened with three solid steel bolts thrown **simultaneously** with a single handle, and had a time lock. Mr. Adams beamingly explained its workings to Mr. Spencer, who showed a courteous but not too intelligent interest. The two children, May and Agatha, were delighted by the shining metal and funny clock and knobs. 11 L3

Practice the Skills

11 Comparing Literature

Characterization Why does Jimmy show little interest in the vault? Do you believe that he has really changed?

Vocabulary

simultaneously (sy mul TAY nee us lee) *adv.* at the same time

Differentiated Instruction

Compare and Contrast Have students write a paragraph comparing and contrasting Jimmy to "Ralph Spencer." Students can begin by using a Venn diagram to gather information for their paragraphs. OL Students should compare their occupations, attitudes about life, and any other character traits they notice. Ask: Which character is more honest about who he is and what he does? Which character do you like more and why? *(Responses will vary.)* OL Ask students to write a theme about the change in Jimmy's character. AL

Teach

L1 Literary Element

Characterization **Ask:** How do Annabel's actions show that she enjoys being with Jimmy? *(She plays around by putting on his hat and picking up his suitcase.)* BL **Ask:** What do her actions show you about their relationship? *(Possible response: That they are comfortable with each other, and she has no idea what's in the suitcase, which means she knows nothing about his past.)* AL

L2 Literary Element

Review Irony **Say:** O. Henry used irony in this story to give it a humorous twist. Can you give one example of irony in this story? *(Possible response: Jimmy marrying the daughter of a bank owner; the bank owner showing Jimmy the vault)* OL

L3 Literary Element

Review Foreshadowing Write a definition of *foreshadowing* on the board. **Ask:** Why do you think the author keeps mentioning the new high-security safe? *(Possible response: Something might happen involving the safe.)* AL

Indiana English/Language Arts Academic Standards
SE: 8.3
TWE: *Literary Element* 8.3.8, *Reading in the Real World* 8.4, *Differentiated Instruction* 8.5.2

Teach

L1 Literary Element

Characterization **Say:** Think about the way that Mr. Adams talks to Spencer and asks him for an idea. What does this show about the relationship between the two men? *(It shows that Mr. Adams thinks of Spencer as an equal.)* OL

L2 Literary Element

Review Symbolism **Ask:** If someone gives you roses, what might that mean? *(That person loves you.)* OL **Ask:** If a rose symbolizes love, why do you think Jimmy asked Annabel to give him her rose? *(Taking action by cracking the safe will give away his identity, and possibly end their relationship.)* AL

C Critical Thinking

Analysis Have students carefully read page 672. **Ask:** How would you describe the roles men and women play in this story? *(the women rely on the men to take care of things; the men take charge.)* **Ask:** Do you think the roles would be different if the story were written today? *(Responses will vary.)* AL

While they were thus engaged Ben Price sauntered in and leaned on his elbow, looking casually inside between the railings. He told the teller that he didn't want anything; he was just waiting for a man he knew.

Suddenly there was a scream or two from the women, and a commotion. Unperceived by the elders, May, the nine-year-old girl, in a spirit of play, had shut Agatha in the vault. She had then shot the bolts and turned the knob of the combination as she had seen Mr. Adams do.

The old banker sprang to the handle and tugged at it for a moment. "The door can't be opened," he groaned. "The clock hasn't been wound nor the combination set."

Agatha's mother screamed again, hysterically.

"Hush!" said Mr. Adams, raising his trembling hand. "All be quiet for a moment. Agatha!" he called as loudly as he could. "Listen to me." During the following silence they could just hear the faint sound of the child wildly shrieking in the dark vault in a panic of terror.

"My precious darling!" wailed the mother. "She will die of fright! Open the door! Oh, break it open! Can't you men do something?"

"There isn't a man nearer than Little Rock who can open that door," said Mr. Adams, in a shaky voice. "My God! Spencer, what shall we do? That child—she can't stand it long in there. There isn't enough air, and, besides, she'll go into convulsions from fright." L1

Agatha's mother, frantic now, beat the door of the vault with her hands. Somebody wildly suggested dynamite. Annabel turned to Jimmy, her large eyes full of anguish, but not yet despairing. To a woman nothing seems quite impossible to the powers of the man she worships.

"Can't you do something, Ralph—try, won't you?"

He looked at her with a queer, soft smile on his lips and in his keen eyes. 12

"Annabel," he said, "give me that rose you are wearing, will you?" L2

Hardly believing that she had heard him aright, she unpinned the bud from the bosom of her dress, and placed it in his hand. Jimmy stuffed it into his vest pocket, threw off his coat and pulled up his shirt sleeves. With that act

Practice the Skills

12 Comparing Literature

Characterization Why does Jimmy give a strange smile when Annabel asks him to do something?

Additional Support

English Language Coach

Sequence Have students make a diagram or sequence chart showing the sequence of events described on page 672. Point out that the narrative uses past-tense verbs. Ask students to retell the story using present-tense verbs. EL Have small groups of students act out the last two pages of the story. Assign each student in a group the role of a character. Have them practice their lines and then perform for the class. OL Challenge students to come up with different endings for the story and have them act those out. AL

Ralph D. Spencer passed away and Jimmy Valentine took his place.

"Get away from the door, all of you," he commanded, shortly.

He set his suitcase on the table, and opened it out flat. From that time on he seemed to be unconscious of the presence of anyone else. He laid out the shining, queer implements swiftly and orderly, whistling softly to himself as he always did when at work. In a deep silence and immovable, the others watched him as if under a spell.

In a minute Jimmy's pet drill was biting smoothly into the steel door. In ten minutes—breaking his own burglarious record—he threw back the bolts and opened the door. 13

Agatha, almost collapsed, but safe, was gathered into her mother's arms.

Jimmy Valentine put on his coat, and walked outside the railings toward the front door. As he went he thought he heard a faraway voice that he once knew call "Ralph!" But he never hesitated. At the door a big man stood somewhat in his way.

"Hello, Ben!" said Jimmy, still with his strange smile. "Got around at last, have you? Well, let's go. I don't know that it makes much difference, now."

And then Ben Price acted rather strangely.

"Guess you're mistaken, Mr. Spencer," he said. "Don't believe I recognize you. Your buggy's waiting for you, ain't it?"

And Ben Price turned and strolled down the street. 14 ❍

This postcard image shows a typical main street around the year 1900.

Analyzing the Image In what ways is the town shown here similar to the town in the story?

Practice the Skills

13 Comparing Literature

Characterization Are you surprised that Jimmy is willing to "burglarize" the safe to save Agatha? Why or why not?

14 BIG Question

Jimmy risks losing his new life when he decides to crack the safe. Do you think he stays true to himself by making that decision? Explain. Write your answer on the first "A Retrieved Reformation" page of Foldable 5. Your response will help you complete the Unit Challenge later.

BQ L

Teach

L Literary Element

Characterization Ask: Why does Ben Price tell "Mr. Spencer" to take his buggy? *(Possible response: He is letting Jimmy go, and he is telling Jimmy he will not reveal his secret past.)* **Ask:** What do you learn about Ben Price from this? *(Ben Price is a forgiving person. He saw that Jimmy was willing to give up everything to save a child; Jimmy truly has changed.)* OL

BQ BIG Question

Say: Imagine that you could ask Jimmy about how to be true to yourself. What do you think he would say? *(Responses will vary.)* OL

Assess

Use the CheckPoint questions provided on Presentation Plus! to check for comprehension of the selection. These questions can be used with interactive response keypads for immediate student feedback.

Differentiated Instruction

News Reports Have students write a news report about what happened at the bank. Tell them to decide if their report will include information about Ralph Spencer's identity. Some other things students may want to include are:

- reactions from Agatha
- reactions from Agatha's mother and sister
- reactions from Mr. Adams

Ask volunteers to read their news report to the class. OL

Indiana English/Language Arts Academic Standards
SE: 8.3
TWE: *English Language Coach* 8.3.2, *Differentiated Instruction* 8.5.7

Teach

More About the Author

Gary Gianni studied art at The Chicago Academy of Fine Art. He has worked as a newspaper illustrator and a courtroom sketch artist. Since then, Gianni has gone on to illustrate several stories and books. The selection in this unit is just one of many stories that Gianni has adapted into a graphic version. He adapted several other O. Henry stories as well as the novel, *20,000 Leagues Under the Sea* by Jules Verne.

L Literary Element

Characterization **Say:** Think of other books you have read or movies you have seen in which a character changes who he or she is for some reason. Was the character *really* able to change, or was he or she too drawn to the past? *(Responses will vary.)* Guide students in a discussion about what it takes for a person to change. Have them think about both external and internal factors, like the death of a loved one, falling in love, and personal desire. OL

Before You Read

A Retrieved Reformation
adapted by Gary Gianni

Gary Gianni

Meet the Author

Gary Gianni spends months—and sometimes years—creating all the pen and ink drawings and oil paintings needed to illustrate a book. The work is often painstaking. In addition to his two graphic novel adaptations, Gianni has written and drawn for Dark Horse Comics. Gary Gianni is also the creator of *The Monstermen Mysteries.*

Author Search For more about Gary Gianni, go to www.glencoe.com.

Indiana English/ Language Arts Academic Standards (pp. 674–683)

8.1 Word Recognition, Fluency, and Vocabulary Development Understand... word parts... **8.3 Comprehension and Analysis of Literary Text** Respond to grade-level-appropriate literature... making connections and comparisons across texts.

For a complete description of the standards, see p. IN 11.

Vocabulary Preview

eminent (EM uh nunt) *adj.* of outstanding rank or quality **(p. 676)** *In an effort to fully understand her condition, the patient consulted several eminent physicians.*

flourishing (FLUR ish ing) *v.* thriving; doing extremely well; form of the verb *flourish* **(p. 680)** *The flowers Sharma planted were flourishing in the summer sun.*

sauntered (SAWN turd) *v.* walked leisurely; form of the verb *saunter* **(p. 682)** *Looking cool and relaxed, Julio sauntered into the library.*

English Language Coach

Multiple Affixes Some words have both prefixes and suffixes. Study the chart below. Look for words in "A Retrieved Reformation" that follow a pattern similar to the word *unperceived.*

Word	Base Word	Prefix	Suffix
unperceived	*perceive* = to see	*un-* = not	*-ed* = past tense

Get Ready to Read

Connect to the Reading

Jimmy Valentine's life changed for the better when he fell in love with Annabel. What other forces can change people's lives in a positive way? Think of the people and things that influence you.

Set Purposes for Reading

BIG Question Read Gary Gianni's version to help you think further about what Jimmy Valentine risked to stay true to himself.

Set Your Own Purpose What would you like to learn from the selection to help you answer the Big Question? Write your own purpose on the "A Retrieved Reformation" page of Foldable 5.

Additional Support

Author Search To expand students' appreciation of Gary Gianni, have them access the Web site for additional information and resources.

Reading in the Real World

College In college, students will read many textbooks with new and technical vocabulary words. Students can get into the habit of writing these new words in a Vocabulary Notebook. For each word, students should write the definition and a sentence that helps them understand the word. Familiarize students with reputable dictionaries and their locations in the library as well as online. Discuss the importance and power of having a developed vocabulary as speakers, readers, and writers. AS

L 1

Practice the Skills

1 Comparing Literature

Characterization Notice Jimmy's facial expressions and posture in the first nine frames. Look at the warden's gestures toward Jimmy. Make notes on your chart about your impression of Jimmy in this story so far. Did you have the same impression of him at the beginning of the print version? Why or why not?

COMPARING LITERATURE

Teach

R Reading Skill

Review Questioning Say: Suppose you had not read the original version of this story. What are some questions you might have at this point in the text? *(Possible responses: Who is the jailed man? Is he guilty or innocent?)* **OL**

L Literary Element

Review Tone Ask: What tone do you think the Warden uses in the eighth frame? *(He is being sarcastic. He believes that the man really committed the crimes and is trying to show how ridiculous it is for him to claim he did not do it.)* **Ask:** What tone do you think Jimmy uses in the seventh and ninth frames? *(He is trying to sound innocent and disbelieving.)* **OL** Have students read the frames using different tones of voice. **AL**

Viewing the Illustration

Ask: How does seeing the pictures change your reading of the story? *(Responses will vary.)* **Ask:** Is this how you pictured Jimmy? *(Responses will vary.)* **OL**

Differentiated Instruction

Thought Bubbles Have students discuss what the characters might be thinking in each of the frames on the first page, especially the last three frames. Instruct students to write their own thought bubbles for those frames, writing what they imagine the characters are thinking for each frame. Ask several volunteers to share their work with the class. Discuss the different ideas with the class. **Ask:** How does leaving a character's thoughts out make a story more open-ended? *(It lets the reader try to figure out what the character is thinking.)* **OL**

Indiana English/Language Arts Academic Standards
SE: 8.1, 8.3
TWE: *Reading in the Real World* 8.1, *Differentiated Instruction* 8.3

Teach

L Literary Element

Review Sequence **Ask:** How does the cartoon show the sequence of events that happen after Jimmy gets out of jail? *(Possible responses: The writer puts each event in a separate text box. The one that happened first is at the top of the frame. The next two are at the bottom of the frame, with the second event above the third event.)* OL

R Reading Skill

Review Making Inferences **Ask:** Who is the "we" Mike Dolan is referring to? *(Mike is probably referring to other friends of theirs.)* **Ask:** What couldn't they do sooner? *(get him out of jail)* **Ask:** What do you think they were protesting in Springfield? *(Jimmy's release from prison)* OL

Practice the Skills

2 Comparing Literature

Characterization What do you think Jimmy feels when he looks at the button?

3 Comparing Literature

Characterization How does this picture make Jimmy—and his profession—seem more menacing?

Vocabulary

eminent (EM uh nunt) *adj.* of outstanding rank or quality

Additional Support

Differentiated Instruction

On the Outside The first thing that Jimmy does when he gets out of jail is go to a restaurant. Ask students what they would do first if they had spent a long time cooped up inside or a long time away from home. Have students discuss what they most enjoy about their lives and would miss if they didn't have the freedom that they do. Ask them to write a poem or a paragraph about what they would do if they were Jimmy when he first got out of jail and why. Encourage students to illustrate their poems or paragraphs. Have small groups of students share their poems and paragraphs. OL

In half an hour, Jimmy went downstairs.

4

GOT ANYTHING ON?

ME? I'M REPRESENTING THE NEW YORK AMALGAMATED SHORT SNAP BISCUIT CRACKER AND FRAZZELED WHEAT COMPANY.

A week after the release of Valentine, there was a neat job of safeburglary done in Richmond, Indiana, with no clue to the author.

Two weeks after that, a patented, improved, burglar-proof safe in Logansport was opened like a cheese.

Then a bank in Jefferson City threw out of its crater an eruption of bank-notes amounting to five thousand dollars.

The losses were now high enough to bring the matter up to Ben Price's class of work.

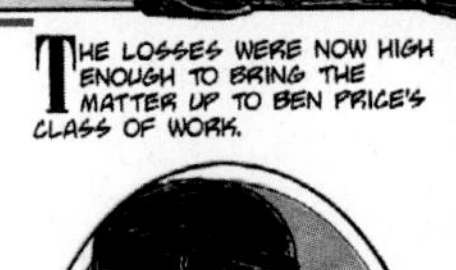

R

It had been given out that he had taken up the trail of the elusive cracksman, and people with burglar-proof safes felt more at ease.

5

1. ***Clemency*** is mercy or forgiveness for wrongdoing.

Practice the Skills

4 Comparing Literature

Characterization Notice Jimmy's height and size compared to Mike Dolan's. Who appears to be the more powerful person? How does this drawing add to or change your perception of Jimmy Valentine?

5 Comparing Literature

Characterization In your opinion, does this illustrated version of the story leave out important parts of the original? Do you think this version is true to O. Henry's descriptions? Explain your answers on your chart.

Teach

L Literary Element

Characterization Say: A graphic version of a story shows you how a writer visualizes characters. Now that you can see pictures of Jimmy and Ben, how would you describe their characters? *(Responses will vary.)* **OL Ask:** Did Gianni draw them differently than you would have? Explain. *(Responses will vary.)* **AL**

C Critical Thinking

Evaluation Ask: Is it easier to read a graphic version of a story than a version that only has words? Explain. *(Responses will vary.)* **Ask:** What do the pictures add to or detract from the story? *(Responses will vary.)* **AL**

R Reading Skill

Review Monitoring Comprehension Ask: Why did the police wait to call in Ben Price? *(He only gets called into cases where the amount stolen is very high.)* **AS Ask:** What does he mean when he says the safe has Jim's autograph? *(Jim left his mark on the safe because of the way it was robbed—in his own style.)* **OL**

Reading Fluency

Read Aloud with a Partner Students who are unfamiliar with graphic stories may have a difficult time following the frames of this story. Have pairs of students work together to read this version of the story. Ask pairs of students to take turns reading frames to each other. Or have students choose characters to play and read the parts of their characters throughout the frames of the story. Ask for volunteers to read pages of the story to the class. **AS**

Indiana English/Language Arts Academic Standards
SE: 8.3
TWE: *Reading Skill* 8.2.9, *Differentiated Instruction* 8.5.7, *Reading Fluency* 8.7

Teach

L1 Literary Element

Review Setting **Ask:** How do the pictures help you better understand the setting of the story? *(Possible responses: I can better see the town, the transportation, and the landscape.)* **OL** **Ask:** What details does this version of the story add that the original did not have? *(Possible responses: This version of the story tells the state where Elmore is located—Arkansas. It also describes Elmore as "black-jack country.")* **AL**

L2 Literary Element

Characterization **Ask:** How does the author use the picture of Annabel to help create her character? *(Possible response: He shows that she is well dressed, very pale, and has long hair.)* **OL**

C Critical Thinking

Analysis **Say:** The author depicts Jimmy falling in love with two doves touching beaks, Cupid, and a ring of flowers. What do you think of this image of love? *(Responses will vary.)* **OL** **Ask:** How would you draw a frame to show Jimmy falling in love and becoming another man? *(Responses will vary.)* **AL**

ONE AFTERNOON, JIMMY VALENTINE AND HIS SUITCASE CLIMBED OUT OF A MAIL-HACK IN ELMORE IN THE BLACK-JACK COUNTRY OF ARKANSAS. JIMMY, LOOKING LIKE AN ATHLETIC YOUNG SENIOR JUST HOME FROM COLLEGE, WENT DOWN THE SIDEWALK TOWARD THE HOTEL.

DRUG STORE

L1

L2

6

7

Practice the Skills

6 Comparing Literature

Characterization How does Gianni illustrate Jimmy's change? On your chart, list the items in this frame that stand for feelings of peace and love. **C**

7 Comparing Literature

Characterization On your chart describe Jimmy's posture. Does he seem confident or uncertain? Serious or relaxed? How does this picture affect what you know or think about Jimmy?

Additional Support

Literature Focus Lesson

Graphic Novels The graphic novel has become a popular genre. Have students learn more about them. Choose several graphic novels to bring into class and share with students. Assign small groups of students to go to the library or go online to look for graphic novels that have been written as adaptations of written texts. Discuss graphic novels as a new genre. **Ask:** Why do you think graphic novels have become so popular? What do you like about them? Would you rather read a graphic novel than a novel that only has words? Why or why not? **OL**

JIMMY WENT TO A HOTEL.
GUEST REGISTRY
NAME: Ralph Spencer
OCCUPATION: Shoe Business
I THOUGHT I'D STOP IN ELMORE FOR A FEW DAYS. I'M LOOKING FOR A LOCATION TO GO INTO BUSINESS.
THERE OUGHT TO BE A GOOD OPENING IN THE SHOE LINE, MISTER SPENCER.
SUCCESS
MISTER RALPH SPENCER, THE PHOENIX THAT AROSE FROM JIMMY VALENTINE'S ASHES--ASHES LEFT BY THE FLAME OF A SUDDEN ATTACK OF LOVE--REMAINED IN ELMORE, AND PROSPERED. HE OPENED A SHOE STORE AND SECURED A GOOD RUN OF TRADE.
RESPECT
LOVE
SOCIALLY, HE WAS ALSO A SUCCESS, AND MADE MANY FRIENDS, AND HE ACCOMPLISHED THE WISH OF HIS HEART. HE MET MISS ANNABEL ADAMS, AND BECAME MORE AND MORE CAPTIVATED BY HER CHARMS.

2. A ***phoenix*** is a bird in Greek mythology that burns up when it dies and is reborn from its own ashes.

Practice the Skills

8 Comparing Literature

Characterization In these two frames Gianni leaves out several sentences from the original story. He also changes Jimmy's dialogue with the hotel clerk. How might this shortened scene affect your understanding of Jimmy's character? What is gained or lost in this adaptation? Make notes on your chart about the way Gianni reveals Jimmy's character here.

9 Comparing Literature

Characterization Notice Jimmy's facial expression and gesture. How does this Jimmy Valentine seem different from the one who arrived in Elmore? How do the other drawings in this frame show other people's views of Jimmy?

Teach

L Literary Element

Review Symbols Ask: What are some symbols in this last frame and what do they mean? *(Possible responses: The American flags are symbols of freedom and good citizenship. They show that Jimmy achieved the American dream by becoming an honest man and working hard. The shoes pictured are symbols of his business.)* **OL** **Ask:** Do you think that respect and love equal success? Explain. *(Responses will vary.)* **AL**

C1 Critical Thinking

Application Ask: What caused Jimmy to become a new man? *(falling in love with Annabel Adams)* **BL** **Ask:** Do you think that falling in love can change a person so much? Why or why not? *(Responses will vary.)* **OL**

C2 Critical Thinking

Evaluation Have students share what they think about Gianni changing this part of the short story. **Ask:** Do you think important information was lost in this adaptation? Why or why not? Explain. *(Responses will vary.)* **AL**

English Language Coach

Connotation This graphic story uses the words *success, respect,* and *love* to describe the new Jimmy Valentine, or Ralph Spencer. These are abstract nouns. The story also relies on the connotations of the words to get its message across. Have students work with partners to think of sentences that describe each of these concepts. The sentences should not be direct explanations of the terms but rather examples of the terms. *(Possible response: Success: doing well at a business, making a lot of money, and enjoying your work.)* **EL** Challenge students to draw pictures that show their meanings for each of these concepts. **AL**

Indiana English/Language Arts Academic Standards
SE: 8.3
TWE: *Literature Focus Lesson* 8.3, *English Language Coach* 8.1

Teach

C Critical Thinking

Analysis Have students look at each frame on the top of page 680. Ask each student to write two to three sentences for each frame describing what they see in the picture. Have students share their descriptions and discuss how a picture communicates ideas without using words. OL

R Reading Skill

Review Making Inferences
Ask: What can you infer about the friend to whom this letter is addressed? *(Possible responses: Jimmy has truly reformed; his friend has not. Jimmy and this man used to work together; they have not seen each other in quite a while; Jimmy and he were close–Jimmy is going to give him his tool kit.)* OL

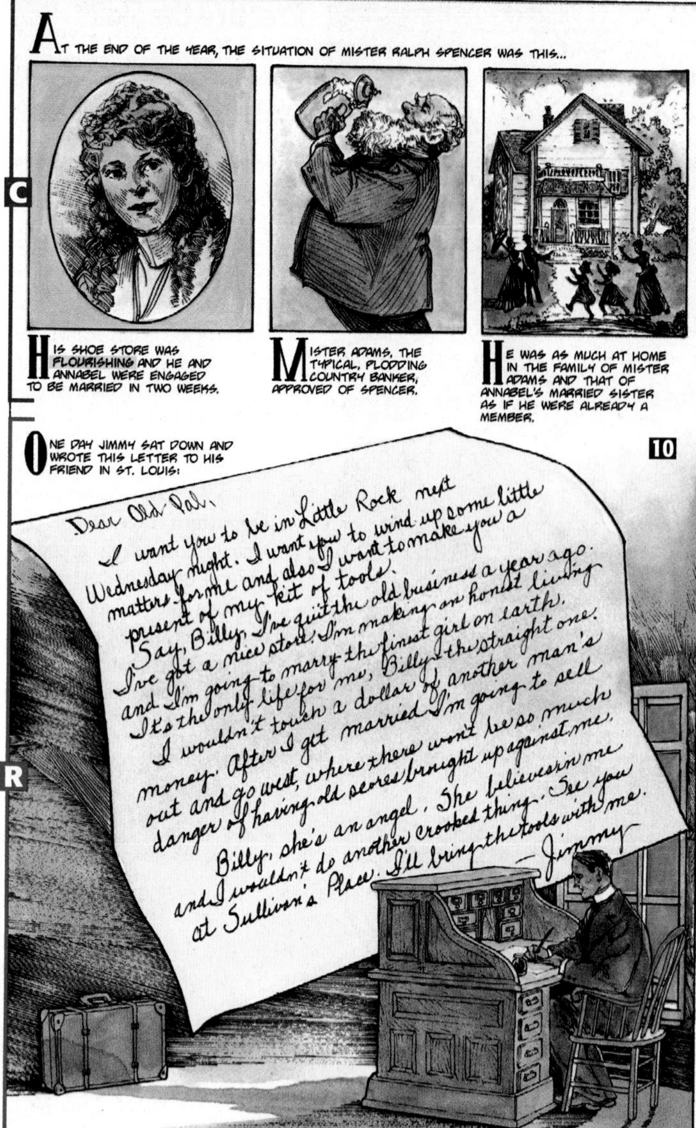

AT THE END OF THE YEAR, THE SITUATION OF MISTER RALPH SPENCER WAS THIS...
HIS SHOE STORE WAS FLOURISHING AND HE AND ANNABEL WERE ENGAGED TO BE MARRIED IN TWO WEEKS.
MISTER ADAMS, THE TYPICAL, PLODDING COUNTRY BANKER, APPROVED OF SPENCER.
HE WAS AS MUCH AT HOME IN THE FAMILY OF MISTER ADAMS AND THAT OF ANNABEL'S MARRIED SISTER AS IF HE WERE ALREADY A MEMBER.
ONE DAY JIMMY SAT DOWN AND WROTE THIS LETTER TO HIS FRIEND IN ST. LOUIS:
Dear Old Pal,
I want you to be in Little Rock next Wednesday night. I want you to wind up some little matters for me and also I want to make you a present of my kit of tools.
Say, Billy, I've quit the old business a year ago. I've got a nice store. I'm making an honest living and I'm going to marry the finest girl on earth. It's the only life for me, Billy—the straight one.
I wouldn't touch a dollar of another man's money. After I get married I'm going to sell out and go west, where there won't be so much danger of having old scores brought up against me.
Billy, she's an angel. She believes in me and I wouldn't do another crooked thing. See you at Sullivan's Place. I'll bring the tools with me.
—Jimmy

10

Practice the Skills

10 Comparing Literature

Characterization Imagine that this page of the story did not include words. From the sketches in this frame, what would you say Jimmy values most now?

Vocabulary

flourishing (FLUR ish ing) *adj.* thriving; doing extremely well

Additional Support

Reading in the Real World

College One skill students need for college is the ability to formulate an argument. Have students consider the ethics of this issue and debate it in class: If Jimmy is really serious about living the straight life, should he tell Annabel the truth about his past before they get married? You may allow students to choose which side they would like to be on for the debate. Or you may assign students to different sides. In this way, students will learn to identify the arguments for something, even if they are against it. Have students use their own beliefs and experiences, or other sources, to back up their arguments. AL

ONE MONDAY NIGHT AFTER JIMMY WROTE THIS LETTER, BEN PRICE JOGGED UNOBTRUSIVELY INTO ELMORE.
11

HE LOUNGED ABOUT THE TOWN IN HIS QUIET WAY UNTIL HE FOUND OUT WHAT HE WANTED TO KNOW.

GOING TO MARRY THE BANKER'S DAUGHTER ARE YOU, JIMMY? WELL, I DON'T KNOW.

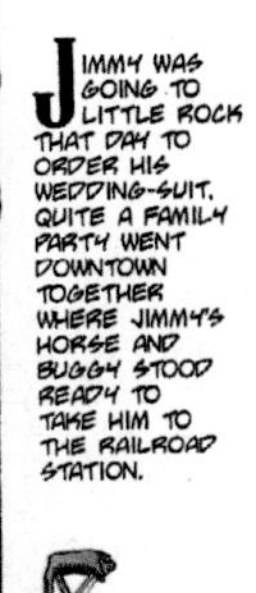
JIMMY WAS GOING TO LITTLE ROCK THAT DAY TO ORDER HIS WEDDING-SUIT. QUITE A FAMILY PARTY WENT DOWNTOWN TOGETHER WHERE JIMMY'S HORSE AND BUGGY STOOD READY TO TAKE HIM TO THE RAILROAD STATION.

ALL WENT INSIDE THE BANK-- MISTER ADAMS, ANNABEL AND ANNABEL'S MARRIED SISTER WITH HER TWO LITTLE GIRLS. JIMMY WAS INCLUDED, FOR MISTER ADAMS' FUTURE SON-IN-LAW WAS WELCOME ANYWHERE.
C

MY! RALPH, HOW HEAVY THIS SUITCASE IS.
LOTS OF NICKEL-PLATED SHOE-HORNS IN THERE.

THE BANK HAD JUST PUT IN A NEW SAFE. MISTER ADAMS WAS VERY PROUD OF IT, AND INSISTED ON AN INSPECTION BY EVERYONE.
THIS VAULT IS A SMALL ONE, BUT IT HAS A NEW PATENTED DOOR. IT FASTENS WITH THREE SOLID STEEL BOLTS...
...AND IT HAS A TIME-LOCK.
12
R

Practice the Skills

11 English Language Coach

Multiple Affixes The word **unobtrusively** contains one prefix and two suffixes. The prefix *-un* means "not." The suffix *-ive* changes words into adjectives. The suffix *-ly* means "in the manner of." If something obtrudes, it becomes noticeable. Ben Price jogged into Elmore *unobtrusively*, or in a way that was not noticeable.

12 Comparing Literature

Characterization Does this version of the story show that Jimmy is trying to look uninterested in the safe? Do the sketches create a strong sense of danger about the vault? If so, how? Write your answers in your chart.

Teach

C Critical Thinking

Analysis Ask: How does the author show the relationship between Annabel and Jimmy? *(Possible response: He shows them holding hands, standing close to each other. He shows her lifting Jimmy's suitcase and commenting on its contents.)* **Ask:** After looking at the pictures, how would you describe their relationship? *(They seem to like each other and are comfortable with each other in public. They also still have secrets.)* **OL**

R Reading Skill

Review Predicting Ask: What does the last frame on this page make the reader think the girls are about to do? *(It makes it look like the girls are going to run into the vault.)* **AL**

Differentiated Instruction

Act It Out Have students imagine they are Ben Price. They have been trying to find and catch Jimmy for over a year. Now they have finally found him. Today is going to be the day. Have students write down what they imagine Ben is thinking. Then have them write an internal monologue in bubbles as though they were writing captions for the graphic story. **OL** Challenge students to act out a dramatic monologue showing Ben's thoughts. Have students practice a few times before reading aloud for the class. Encourage students who like to draw to create their own pictures to go with the internal monologue they wrote. **AL**

Indiana English/Language Arts Academic Standards

SE: 8.1, 8.3

TWE: *Reading in the Real World* 8.7.13; *Differentiated Instruction* 8.3, 8.7

Teach

C Critical Thinking

Analysis Have students study the middle frame. **Ask:** What does this frame show? *(Possible responses: It shows the confusion and excitement in the room. Everyone was probably talking at once, and no one knew what to do.)* **OL** **Ask:** How is Jimmy positioned in this frame? *(Possible response: The people seem to lean in towards him for guidance, but he is pulling away from everyone.)* **Ask:** What does his position communicate? *(Possible response: It communicates that he is undecided about how involved to be in rescuing Agatha from the vault.)* **AL**

EL Language Coach

Context Clues **Say:** Read the definition of *sauntered* at the bottom of page 682. When does a person *saunter*? *(Possible response: when he or she is relaxed)* Ask for volunteers to demonstrate sauntering. **OL** **Ask:** What does it show about Ben's character that he sauntered into the bank? *(Possible response: It shows he is confident in his ability to catch Jimmy.)* **AL**

Vocabulary

sauntered (SAWN turd) *v.* walked leisurely

EL

Practice the Skills

13 Comparing Literature

Characterization How does Gianni show Jimmy's transformation? Look at Jimmy's posture, gestures, and facial expression. Also, pay attention to the shape of Jimmy's face. Does it seem harder or more angular than in previous frames? Why might this be? Make notes in your chart.

Additional Support

Reading in the Real World

Career Gary Gianni has made a career as an illustrator and as a writer. Have students research different illustrators and writers who have been able to make careers out of words and images. Assign students to learn about the education needed for these careers as well as how someone gets started in these fields. **OL** If there are any well-known illustrators or writers in your community, invite them to the class to talk about their careers. Have students prepare questions to ask them when they come to visit. **AS**

Practice the Skills

14 Comparing Literature

Characterization Jimmy hangs his head in shame or sorrow in this version, but not in the original. Why might Gianni have added this gesture? How could it affect your impression of Jimmy?

15 BIG Question

BQ What did Jimmy have to do to stay true to himself? What did he risk? Do you think he's glad that he stayed true to himself? Write your answer on the second "A Retrieved Reformation" page of Foldable 5. Your response will help you complete the Unit Challenge later.

Teach

C Critical Thinking

Comprehension Ask: Why does Jimmy say, "I don't know that it makes much difference now"? *(Possible response: Jimmy feels that he has lost his true love. Nothing else matters to him. He does not even care about going to jail.)* OL **Ask:** Why does Ben Price tell Jimmy he is mistaken? *(Because he has decided not to arrest Jimmy and expose his past.)* OL

BQ 

Ask: Do you think that Jimmy will continue to be true to himself? Why? *(It seems that he will because he was even willing to turn himself in to Ben Price.)* OL

Assess

CheckPoint

Use the CheckPoint questions provided on Presentation Plus! to check for comprehension of the selection. These questions can be used with interactive response keypads for immediate student feedback.

Differentiated Instruction

Role Playing The story does not tell what Annabel was thinking when she watched Ralph open his suitcase and open the vault. Have students act out the scene in the bank just after Ralph walked outside. Students can role-play Annabel, Mr. Adams, Agatha's mother, and a few bank employees. After one group of students improvises the scene, choose an entirely new group of students. Direct this group to improvise a different scenario. (For example, if the first group shows Annabel as still trusting Ralph, the second group may show her as feeling betrayed and angry.) OL

Indiana English/Language Arts Academic Standards
SE: 8.3
TWE: *Reading in the Real World* 8.4, 8.7.1; *Differentiated Instruction* 8.7

Assess

Resources for page 684

- Selection Quick Check, pp. 49–50
- ExamView Assessment Suite
- Interactive Tutor: Self-Assessment

Students can respond to the *After You Read* items in their Learner's Notebooks or on a separate sheet of paper.

Vocabulary Check

O. Henry's A Retrieved Reformation

1. Possible response: Going to school is compulsory until you are eighteen.
2. Being grounded might be a form of retribution because it is a payment for doing something wrong, or a punishment.
3. a

Gary Gianni's A Retrieved Reformation

4. eminent
5. sauntered
6. flourishing

English Language Coach

7. Burglarious means full of thieving.

Academic Vocabulary

8. show

After You Read

A Retrieved Reformation
adapted by Gary Gianni

Indiana English/Language Arts Academic Standards (pp. 684–685)

8.3 Comprehension and Analysis of Literary Text Respond to grade-level-appropriate literature…identifying…character…and making connections and comparisons across texts. **8.5.2** Write responses to literature…

For a complete description of the standards, see p. IN 11.

Vocabulary Check

In your Learner's Notebook, answer questions 1–3 below.

O. Henry's A RETRIEVED REFORMATION

1. Give an example of something that is **compulsory.**
2. How might being grounded be a form of **retribution?**
3. If two things happen **simultaneously,** do they happen **a)** at the same time, **b)** at different times, or **c)** in the same way?

Copy the sentences below. Draw a line through the italicized word or phrase; then replace it with the vocabulary word that fits.

Gary Gianni's *A RETRIEVED REFORMATION*

eminent flourishing sauntered

4. The reception honored a group of *distinguished* scientists.
5. Mel *strolled* in ten minutes late.
6. Students were *doing well* under the new teacher's instruction.
7. **English Language Coach** What does the word *burglarious* mean? Use what you have learned to fill in the chart below.

Word	Base Word	Suffix	Meaning
burglarious	*burgle* = to thieve	*-ous* = full of	

8. **Academic Vocabulary** Which of the following comes closest to the meaning of **reveal?**
   - complain
   - show
   - listen

15. Sample Chart

	"Me? Why, warden, I never was in Springfield in my life!"	"Me? I'm representing the New York Amalgamated Short Snap Biscuit Cracker and Frazzled Wheat Company"
	He tossed the quarter into the hat of a blind man sitting by the door	he was a success and made many friends and he accomplished the wish of his heart
	he gazed fondly, looked into her eyes, forgot what he was, and became another man	I wouldn't touch a dollar of another man's money; I wouldn't do another crooked thing

Reading/Critical Thinking

On a separate sheet of paper, answer the following questions.

O. Henry's A RETRIEVED REFORMATION

9. BIG Question How does Jimmy stay true to himself by saving Agatha?

TIP **Author and Me**

10. Recall How does Ben Price know that Jimmy has "resumed business"?

TIP **Right There**

11. List Jimmy gained several things when he moved to Elmore. List three of them.

TIP **Right There**

Gary Gianni's *A RETRIEVED REFORMATION*

12. Analyze When Agatha gets locked in the vault, Jimmy must make a choice. Explain that choice and its possible consequences.

TIP **Author and Me**

13. Interpret Look at the picture of a keyhole on the first page of the graphic story. What could it symbolize, or mean?

TIP **Think and Search**

14. Evaluate How does Jimmy change by the end of the story?

TIP **Author and Me**

Writing: Compare the Literature

Use Your Notes

15. Follow these steps to compare Jimmy Valentine's characterization in the original and graphic versions of "A Retrieved Reformation."

Step 1: Look at the first column of your Comparison Chart. Underline examples of O. Henry's narrative description.

Step 2: Look at the second column of your chart. When does Gianni choose to draw, or show, details that O. Henry describes, or tells? Underline examples.

Step 3: Compare both columns of your chart. What important dialogue or description (from O. Henry's version) does Gianni change or leave out? Underline these differences.

Step 4: Circle the stories' similarities that you noted on your chart. Think about why Gianni left original dialogue and description in some parts, but did not choose to leave them in others.

Get It On Paper

Answer these questions on a separate sheet of paper. Use examples from the chart and the notes you just made to explain your answers.

16. After reading O. Henry's story, how did you picture Jimmy Valentine in your mind?

17. Did your mental picture of Jimmy change after you read Gianni's version? If so, how?

18. Do you think Gianni's version of Jimmy is accurate? Would you have drawn Jimmy the same way? Why or why not?

19. Which version is more descriptive? Which version is more interesting? Did you learn more about Jimmy Valentine from O. Henry's description or Gianni's drawings?

20. Why might someone read a graphic story instead of a text story? What did O. Henry's story gain in graphic form? Lose in graphic form?

BIG Question

21. Jimmy stays true to himself by helping someone else. What does this tell you about the "self" to whom he stays true? Think about the change Jimmy undergoes in Elmore.

Web Activities For eFlashcards, Selection Quick Checks, and other Web activities, go to www.glencoe.com.

15. Sample Chart continued from p. 684

	dressed in tasteful and well-fitting clothes, young men of Jimmy's style and looks were scarce in Elmore, gold watch-chain	looking like an athletic young senior just home from college
	impressed by the clothes and manner of Jimmy	Mr. Adams approved of Spencer; Mr. Adams's future son-in-law was welcome anywhere

Close

Ask students to summarize what they learned from reading both versions of "A Retrieved Reformation" to answer the Big Question.

Reading/Critical Thinking

O. Henry's A Retrieved Reformation

9. Possible response: Jimmy loves Annabel and all of her family. Since he loves them, he has to save Agatha anyway that he can, even if it means he will not be able to marry Annabel.

10. Ben Price knows that Jimmy has started stealing again when he sees the different burglaries that are done with his style.

11. Three things Jimmy gained are a family, a business, and self-respect.

Gary Gianni's A Retrieved Reformation

12. Jimmy has to decide if he will show everyone what is in his bag, risk losing his true love, and save Agatha. If he does not save Agatha, he will have to live with her death.

13. Responses will vary.

14. Responses will vary.

Writing: Compare the Literature

15. Completed charts will differ.

Get It On Paper

16.–20. Responses will vary.

BQ 

21. Responses will vary.

Indiana English/Language Arts Academic Standards
SE: 8.3, 8.5.2

The Unit Challenge

Focus

BELLRINGER Options

Daily Language Practice Transparency 51

Focus Activity Say: Think about how the different characters in this unit stayed true to themselves. Which character did you admire the most? Why? *(Responses will vary.)* AS

The discussion will remind students of the selections they've read, which will help them begin the group activity or the solo activity.

Teach

Group Activity: Videotape a Soap Opera

- Encourage students to take turns role-playing different characters. This way, the group can decide who plays each role the best.
- Students can work together to write the script. They can work as a large group and write the entire dialogue from beginning to end. Or they can split into pairs and have the different partners write sections of the dialogue. Have students make sure that everyone has some input into the final dialogue of the script.
- The camera person may also need a director to help move people around and keep the show going.

UNIT 5 WRAP-UP

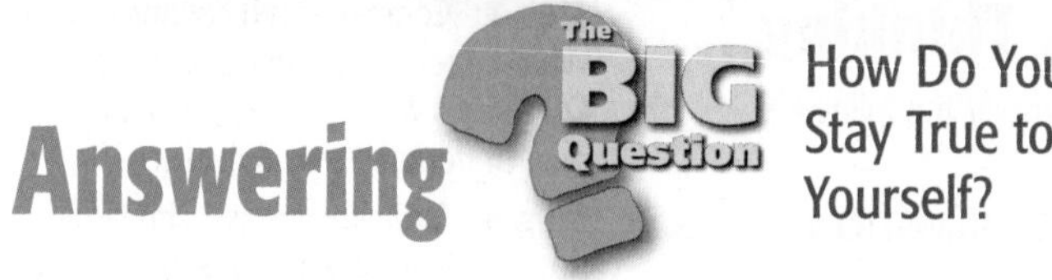

Answering The BIG Question: How Do You Stay True to Yourself?

You have read about people who worked to figure out how to stay true to themselves. Now use what you learned to do the Unit Challenge.

The Unit Challenge

Choose Activity A or Activity B and follow the directions for that activity.

A. Group Activity: Videotape a Soap Opera

With a group of students, read the following situation. Prepare to turn it into a TV show.

It's Friday, and Chris has a big test on Monday in English. English is the hardest subject for her. Chris started studying on Wednesday but still doesn't feel ready to take the test. Chris will need to study all weekend if she wants to do well on the test, which she needs to do to pass English this year. Late Friday afternoon, Chris learns that one of her friends, Steve, is having a party Saturday night. Steve really wants Chris to come to his party. Chris should stay home and study, but she really wants to go to the party too. Chris's parents have left it up to her to decide about Saturday night. What should Chris do?

1. **Role Play the Situation** Have group members take the parts of Chris, Chris's friends, and Chris's parents. Act out the situation several times, making sure everyone has a turn. Each time the group role plays, come up with a different way of handling the situation. Look at your Foldable for ideas about how characters in similar situations stayed true to themselves.
2. **Discuss the Different Role Plays** As a group, talk about which parts of the different role plays worked best. Decide which of Chris's values are being challenged in each situation. Figure out how Chris can deal with her dilemma in a way that (1) does not upset her parents, or (2) jeopardize her future, yet (3) allows Chris to be true to herself.
3. **Write a Script** Use your role plays to write a script for your soap opera. End your script with the best solution you came up with for Chris. Show why this course of action is best.
4. **Videotape and Present Your Soap** Have each group member, except the camera person, take a role and rehearse. Then videotape your show. Afterward, show your soap to the class.

Assess/Close

Group Activity

When students show their soap opera to the class, have them describe some of the possible endings the group considered and explain why they chose the ending they did. AS

B. Solo Activity: Values Chart

It's important to think clearly when making major decisions. Sometimes it's helpful to put things on paper to clarify your thoughts. Make a chart like this one to figure out the things you need to keep in mind to stay true to yourself.

Very Important	Less Important	Rank

1. **Determine Your Values** On the chart list the things that are very important to you and those that are less important. You might include such things as having time alone, respecting your parents' opinions, and figuring out solutions to problems for yourself.
   - Look over your notes in your Foldable and your Learner's Notebook to get ideas for your chart. Think about what was important to each main character.

2. **Consider Your Values** After you fill in your values, review them. Think about why you listed the different items in each column. You may want to make changes.

3. **Rank Your Values** Rank your values. Put a number next to each value in the "very important" column. Make number 1 the most important. You may want to give the same number to more than one value. Then do the same for the "less important" column.

4. **Write a Reflection** Think about what your values say about you. Write a paper describing yourself and your values. Consider the following questions:
   - What do your values show about you?
   - What do you value most and why?
   - What do you value least and why?
   - Where do you think your values come from? Parents? Family? Friends?
   - Are there values you would change? Are there values you would like to have that you don't right now?

   Finish your paper by discussing how you think your values will shape the way you live.

5. **Revise and Present Your Values** Review your chart and your paper. Make sure there are no mistakes in grammar, usage, or mechanics. Then share your work with a partner. Do you have values that are the same? What values do you have that are different? When you are done sharing, hand in your chart and reflection paper.

Big Question Link to Web resources to further explore the Big Question at www.glencoe.com.

Teach

Solo Activity: Values Chart

- Have students look back at the things that the characters valued in the stories to help them get ideas for what to list in their chart. Thinking about the selections and what other people value may help spark ideas for students as they fill in their charts.
- Direct students to think of the things their families value—students may choose to write some of these on their charts.
- Students can take strips of paper and write a separate value on each one. Instruct students to arrange the strips of paper in order of importance to them. Once students are satisfied with the order, they can write numbers on the paper strips and then put those numbers in their charts.
- As students write their reflections, they should use information from their values chart. Students may also want to give an example of something they value or how their families passed the value on to them.

Assess/Close

Solo Activity

Have each student report to the class on his or her partner's paper and chart. In particular, students should report what they learned about their partners and how they and their partners are alike and different. AS

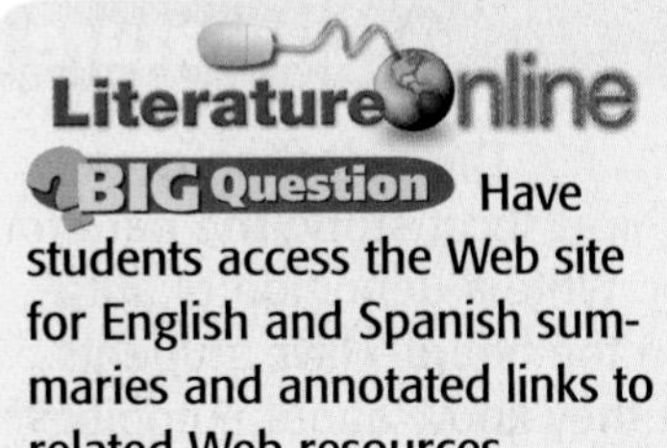

Have students access the Web site for English and Spanish summaries and annotated links to related Web resources.

Focus

Vocabulary Preview
List the following words on the board:
- notoriety
- lilt
- insolence
- valiant
- sprawled
- brocade

Have students look up the words in a dictionary and write their definitions in their Learner's Notebooks.

Build Background
- Millions of people in the world speak Arabic as their first language.
- Israel became a nation in 1948.

Teach

L Literary Element
Review Characterization
Ask: What do you learn about the narrator on the first page of the story? *(Possible response: She is her brother's companion in mischief; she likes that he hid his vitamin C and got caught.)* OL

Readability Scores
Dale-Chall: 6.1
DRP: 55
Lexile: 950

Your Turn: Read and Apply Skills

Naomi Shihab Nye

Meet the Author
Naomi Shihab Nye is an Arab American. Her father is Palestinian, and her mother is American. She has published many books of poetry as well as a novel called *Habibi.* When she was a child, books were her escape. As an adult, she feels words help people discover the things that are important in their lives. Nye writes poems about little things that are an important part of people's lives. She says, "Familiar sights, sounds, smells have always been my necessities." See page R4 of the Author Files for more on Naomi Shihab Nye.

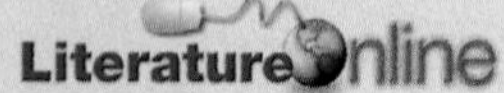

Author Search For more about Naomi Shihab Nye, go to www.glencoe.com.

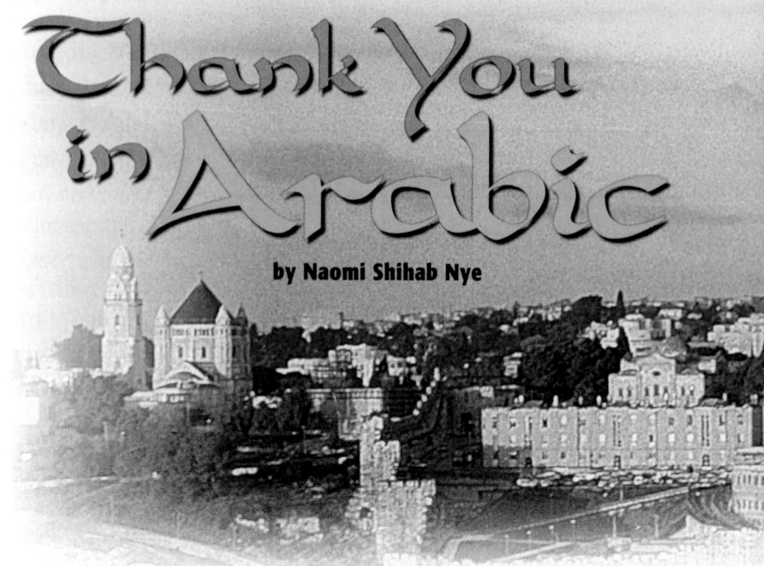

Thank You in Arabic

by Naomi Shihab Nye

Shortly after my mother discovered my brother had been pitching his vitamin C tablets behind the stove for years, we left the country. Her sharp alert, "Now the truth be known!" startled us at the breakfast table as she poked into the dim crevice with the nozzle of her vacuum. We could hear the pills go click, click, up the long tube.

My brother, an obedient child, a bright-eyed, dark-skinned charmer who scored high on all his tests and trilled a boy's sweet soprano, stared down at his oatmeal. Four years younger than I, he was also the youngest and smallest in his class. Somehow he maintained an intelligence and dignity more notable than those of his older, larger companions, and the pills episode was really a pleasant surprise to me.

Companions in mischief are not to be underestimated, especially when everything else in your life is about to change.

Additional Support

Author Search To expand students' appreciation of Naomi Shihab Nye, have them access the Web site for additional information and resources.

Literature Focus Lesson

Autobiography This selection is an autobiographical short story. The narrator is the author. Write a definition of autobiography on the board. Have students review what they know about autobiography. Emphasize that this is a work of nonfiction told by the person who lived the experiences described in the story.

Discuss other autobiographies students have read and what students enjoy and find challenging about reading autobi ographies. OL Bring in a copy of the novel *Habibi*, or the collection of poetry *19 Varieties of Gazelle*, both by Nye, to share with students who are interested in reading more of the author's work. AL

We sold everything we had and left the country. The move had been brewing for months. We took a few suitcases each. My **R1** mother cried when the piano went. I wished we could have saved it. My brother and I had sung so many classics over its keyboard—"Look for the Silver Lining" and "Angels We Have Heard on High"— that it would have been nice to return to a **R2** year later, when we came straggling back. I sold my life-size doll and my toy sewing machine. I begged my mother to save her red stove for me, so I could have it when I grew up—no one else we knew had a red stove. So my mother asked some friends to save it for me in their barn.

Our parents had closed their imported-gifts stores. Our mother ran a little shop in our neighborhood in St. Louis and our father ran a bigger one in a Sheraton Hotel downtown. For years my brother and I had been sitting with them behind the counters after school, guessing if people who walked through the door would buy something or only browse. We curled up with our library books on Moroccan hassocks[1] and Egyptian camel saddles. I loved the stacks of waiting white paper bags as they lay together, and the reams of new tissue. I'd crease the folds as our smooth father in dark suit and daily

1. ***Moroccan hassocks*** are large, tightly stuffed cushions made in Morocco, an Arab country in North Africa.

Teach

R1 Reading Skill

Review Monitoring Comprehension **Ask:** Why is the piano so special to the narrator? *(She has many memories of singing while playing music on it.)* **Ask:** Why does she want to keep the red stove? *(Because no one else has one like it, and she wanted to have it when she grew up.)* **OL**

R2 Reading Skill

Review Questioning **Say:** The narrator says that her family came "straggling back" a year later. What questions does this raise for you as a reader? *(Possible response: Why do they end up coming back? Why are they straggling?)* **OL**

L Literary Element

Review Description **Say:** One of the author's strengths as a writer is the amount of detail and description she includes in her story. List the details you notice on page 689. What senses does the author appeal to with her descriptions? *(sight, sound, smell, touch)* **Ask:** How does this affect you as a reader? *(Possible response: I feel like I am there with her as she is packing and in the store.)* **OL**

Differentiated Instruction

Connecting with Music Most cultures have their own forms of music. Have students list songs that are meaningful to them and make a chart with each song listed in one column and an explanation of why it is special in the other column. Have students choose appropriate music from their chart to share with the class. Ask students (whose music contains lyrics) to bring in a copy of the lyrics to share with their classmates. Discuss why music is so important to most people and to most cultures. **OL** Have interested students research the origins of different kinds of music and report their findings to the class. **AL**

Indiana English/Language Arts Academic Standards

TWE: *Literature Focus Lesson* 8.3; *Differentiated Instruction* 8.3, 8.7.12

Teach

R1 Reading Skill

Review Making Inferences
Ask: How would you describe the religious beliefs of the narrator and her family? *(Possible response: They seem to draw from many beliefs.)* AL

R2 Reading Skill

Review Analyzing Ask: Why do you think the girls were giggling when the narrator gave her "show" about how her father immigrated to the United States? *(Possible responses: They may have thought it was funny to see Jimmy wrapped in a keffiyah.)* OL

L Literary Element

Review Characterization
Ask: What do you learn about the narrator in this part of the story? *(She likes being the center of attention; she likes telling stories; her past is important to her.)* OL

drench of cologne counted change. Our mother rearranged shelves and penned the perfect tags with calligrapher's ink. My brother and I helped unpack the crates: nested Russian dolls, glossy mother-of-pearl earrings from Bethlehem, a family of sandalwood[2] fans nestled in shredded packaging. Something wonderful was always on its way.

But there were problems too. Sometimes whole days passed and nobody came in. It seemed so strange to wait for people to give you money for what you had. But that's what stores did everywhere. Then the stockroom filled with pre-Christmas inventory caught on fire and burned up, right when our father was between insurance policies. We could hear our parents in the living room, worrying and debating after we went to bed at night. Finally they had to give the business up. What seemed like such a good idea in the beginning—presents from around the world—turned into the sad sound of a broom sweeping out an empty space.

Our father had also been attending the Unity School for Christianity for a few years, but decided not to become a minister after all. We were relieved, having felt like imposters the whole time he was enrolled. He wasn't even a Christian, to begin with, but a gently nonpracticing Muslim. He didn't do anything like fasting or getting down on his knees five times a day. Our mother had given up the stern glare of her Lutheran ancestors, raising my brother and me in the Vedanta Society of St. Louis. When anyone asked what we were, I said, "Hindu." We had a swami,[3] and sandalwood incense. It was over our heads, but we liked it and didn't feel very attracted to the idea of churches and collection baskets and chatty parish good will.

Now and then, just to keep things balanced, we attended the Unity Sunday School. My teacher said I was lucky my father came from the same place Jesus came from. It was a passport to notoriety. She invited me to bring artifacts for Show and Tell. I wrapped a red and white *keffiyah*[4] around my friend Jimmy's curly blond head while the girls in lacy socks giggled behind their hands. I told about my father coming to America from Palestine on the boat and throwing his old country clothes overboard before docking at Ellis Island.[5] I felt relieved he'd kept a few things, like the *keffiyah* and its black braided band. Secretly it made me mad to have lost the blue pants from Jericho with the wide cuffs he told us about.

I liked standing in front of the group, talking about my father's homeland. Stories felt like elastic bands that could stretch and stretch. Big fans purred inside their metal shells. I held up a string of olivewood[6] camels. I didn't tell our teacher about the Vedanta Society. We were growing up ecumenical, though I wouldn't know that word till a long time later in college. One night I heard my father say to my mother in the next room, "Do you think they'll be confused when they grow up?" and knew he was talking about us. My mother, bless

2. ***Sandalwood*** is the wood of several trees that grow in Asia. It has a sweet, perfumed smell.

3. ***Vedanta*** is a branch of the Hindu religion that studies several holy books called the Vedas. A Hindu teacher is called a ***swami.***

4. A ***keffiyah*** is a cloth headdress for a man that is held in place by a rope.

5. ***Ellis Island*** in New York City was the station where immigrants entered the United States on the East Coast from 1892 until the mid-twentieth century.

6. ***Olivewood*** is the wood of the olive tree.

Additional Support

Literature Focus Lesson

Similes The narrator says that stories feel "like elastic bands that could stretch and stretch." Define this simile on the board. Have students write for 10–15 minutes about whether or not they agree with this comparison. Students should try to give examples from stories they know to support their arguments. Then ask students to write about how they would describe stories. Ask each student to come up with a simile or a metaphor for stories. OL Challenge students to write a poem or draw a picture depicting their ideas about stories. AL Ask for volunteers to share their poems and pictures.

her, knew we wouldn't be. She said, "At least we're giving them a choice." I didn't know then that more clearly than all the stories of Jesus, I'd remember the way our Hindu swami said a single word three times, "*Shantih, shantih, shantih*"—peace, peace, peace. R

Our father was an excellent speaker—he stood behind pulpits and podiums[7] easily, delivering gracious lectures on "The Holy Land" and "The Palestinian Question." He was much in demand during the Christmas season. I think that's how he had fallen into the ministerial swoon.[8] While he spoke, my brother and I moved toward the backs of gathering halls, hovering over and eyeing the tables of canapes and tiny tarts, slipping a few into our mouths or pockets.

What next? Our lives were entering a new chapter, but I didn't know its title yet.

We had never met our Palestinian grandmother, Sitti[9] Khadra, or seen Jerusalem, where our father had grown up, or followed the rocky, narrow alleyways of the Via Dolorosa,[10] or eaten an olive in its own neighborhood. Our mother hadn't either. The Arabic customs we knew had been filtered through the fine net of folktales. We did not speak Arabic, though the lilt of the language was familiar to us—our father's endearments, his musical blessings before meals. But that language had never lived in our mouths.

And that's where we were going, to Jerusalem. We shipped our car, a wide golden Impala, over on a boat. We would meet up with it later.

The first plane flight of my whole life was the night flight out of New York City across the ocean. I was fourteen years old. Every glittering light in every skyscraper looked like a period at the end of the sentence. Good-bye, our lives.

We stopped in Portugal for a few weeks. We were making a gradual transition. We stopped in Spain and Italy and Egypt, where the pyramids shocked me by sitting right on the edge of the giant city of Cairo,[11] not way out in the desert as I had imagined them. While we waited for our baggage to clear customs, I stared at six tall African men in brilliantly patterned dashikis[12] negotiating with an Egyptian customs agent and realized I did not even know how to say "thank you" in Arabic. How was this possible? The most elemental and important of human phrases in my father's own tongue had evaded me till now. I tugged on his sleeve, but he was busy with visas and passports. "Daddy," I said. "Daddy, I have to know. Daddy, tell me. Daddy, why didn't we ever *learn*?" An African man adjusted his turban. Always thereafter, the word *shookrun*, so simple, with a little roll in the middle, would conjure up the vast African baggage, the brown boxes looped and looped in African twine. L

We stayed one or two nights at the old Shepheard's Hotel downtown but couldn't sleep due to the heat and honking traffic beneath our windows. So our father moved

7. A ***pulpit*** is the stand inside a church from which a preacher delivers a sermon. A ***podium*** is a raised platform used by a speaker or music conductor.

8. To ***fall into the ministerial swoon*** is to get enthusiastic about becoming a minister.

9. ***Sitti*** means grandmother.

10. The ***Via Dolorosa*** is the Way of Sorrow, the streets Jesus walked on the way to his death.

11. ***Cairo*** is the capital of Egypt.

12. A ***dashiki*** is a loose-fitting, colorful African shirt.

Teach

R Reading Skill

Review Monitoring Comprehension **Ask:** What religious idea seems most important to the narrator? *(the concept of peace as described by her Hindu swami as "shantih, shantih, shantih")* OL

L Literary Element

Review Characterization **Ask:** What phrase does the narrator's vocabulary lack? *(thank you)* **Ask:** How does she feel about not being able to speak or understand her father's language? *(She wonders why she never learned the language.)* BL

C Critical Thinking

Analysis **Say:** Think about how the narrator feels, being incapable of understanding her father's native language. How is language a part of your identity, or who you are? *(Possible response: With language comes a connection to the people, traditions, culture, the land and its history, and who you are as a person.)* AL

Reading in the Real World

Citizenship Assign small groups of students to research The Holy Land and The Palestinian Question. Discuss the issues that surround these ideas and their implications for students. Show students a map of the Middle East, including Israel. You may also want to draw a timeline on the board that shows the series of events that led up to the current conflict in Israel. If there is an expert on these issues in your school or community, invite them to the class to talk about The Holy Land and The Palestinian Question. AL

Indiana English/Language Arts Academic Standards
TWE: *Literature Focus Lesson* 8.5.7

Teach

L Literary Element

Review Setting **Ask:** What are some unique features of the setting of this part of the story? *(Possible responses: pyramids near the city, riding camels)* **Ask:** How is this setting different from their lives in St. Louis? *(Possible response: St. Louis did not have any of these things.)* BL

R Reading Skill

Review Making Inferences **Ask:** Why will it be a long time before the narrator eats spaghetti again? *(Possible response: She associates spaghetti with being sick.)* BL **Ask:** Why do you think the narrator and her brother got so sick? *(Possible response: They ate or drank something in Egypt that made them sick; food poisoning.)* OL

Guests of Egypt's Mena House Hotel get a bird's-eye view of the Great Pyramid of Khufu.
Analyzing the Photo How does this photo help you better understand Nye's overseas experience?

us to the famous Mena House Hotel next to the pyramids. We rode camels for the first time, and our mother received a dozen blood-red roses at her hotel room from a rug vendor who apparently liked her pale brown ponytail. The belly dancer at the hotel restaurant twined a gauzy pink scarf around my brother's astonished ten-year-old head as he tapped his knee in time to her music. L

Back in our rooms, we laughed until we fell asleep. Later that night, my brother and I both awakened burning with fever and deeply nauseated, though nobody ever threw up. We were so sick that a doctor hung a Quarantine sign in Arabic and English on our hotel room door the next day. Did he know something we didn't know? I kept waiting to hear that we had malaria or typhoid,[13] but no dramatic disease was ever mentioned. We lay in bed for a week. The aged doctor tripped over my suitcase every time he entered to take our temperatures. We smothered our laughter. "*Shookrun*," I would say. But as soon as he left, to my brother, "I feel bad. How do you feel?" R

"I feel really, really bad."

"I think I'm dying."

"I think I'm already dead." R

At night we heard the sound and lights show[14] from the pyramids drifting across the desert air to our windows. We felt our lives stretching out across a thousand miles. The pharaohs stomped noisily through my head and churning belly. We had eaten spaghetti in the restaurant. I would not be able to eat spaghetti again for years.

Finally, finally, we appeared in the restaurant, thin and weakly smiling, and ordered the famous Mena House *shorraba*,

13. To ***quarantine*** is to separate people from everyone else to keep them from spreading diseases. ***Malaria*** is a disease that causes fever and chills. ***Typhoid*** causes intestinal problems.

14. A ***sound and lights show*** is a narrated presentation that uses sound effects and lighting effects.

Additional Support

Reading Fluency

Read Aloud with a Partner The author of this selection has a lyrical and poetic writing style. Model for students how to read this story with intonation and expression. Have pairs of students choose their favorite images from the story. Then have them practice reading the parts of the story that contain the images. Once students get comfortable reading in pairs, have them read their favorite part of the story to the class. OL lentil soup, as my brother nervously scanned the room for the belly dancer. Maybe she wouldn't recognize him now.

In those days Jerusalem, which was then a divided city, had an operating airport on the Jordanian side. My brother and I remember flying in upside down, or in a plane dramatically tipped, but it may have been the effect of our medicine. The land reminded us of a dropped canvas, graceful brown hillocks and green patches. Small and provincial, the airport had just two runways, and the first thing I observed as we climbed down slowly from the stuffy plane was all my underwear strewn across one of them. There were my flowered cotton briefs and my pink panties and my slightly embarrassing raggedy ones and my extra training bra, alive and visible in the breeze. Somehow my suitcase had popped open in the hold and dropped its contents the minute the men pried open the cargo door. So the first thing I did on the home soil of my father was re-collect my underwear, down on my knees, the posture of prayer over that ancient holy land.

Our relatives came to see us at a hotel. Our grandmother was very short. She wore a long, thickly embroidered Palestinian dress, had a musical, high-pitched voice and a low, guttural[15] laugh. She kept touching our heads and faces as if she couldn't believe we were there. I had not yet fallen in love with her. Sometimes you don't fall in love with people immediately, even if they're your own grandmother. Everyone seemed to think we were all too thin.

We moved into a second-story flat in a stone house eight miles north of the city, among fields and white stones and wandering sheep. My brother was enrolled in the Friends Girls School and I was enrolled in the Friends Boys School in the town of Ramallah[16] a few miles farther north—it all was a little confused. But the Girls School offered grades one through eight in English and high school continued at the Boys School. Most local girls went to Arabic-speaking schools after eighth grade.

R

I was a freshman, one of seven girl students among two hundred boys, which would cause me problems a month later. I was called in from the schoolyard at lunchtime, to the office of our counselor who wore shoes so pointed and tight her feet bulged out pinkly on top.

"You will not be talking to them anymore," she said. She rapped on the desk with a pencil for emphasis.

"To whom?"

"All the boy students at this institution. It is inappropriate behavior. From now on, you will speak only with the girls."

"But there are only six other girls! And I like only one of them!" My friend was Anna, from Italy, whose father ran a small factory that made matches. I'd visited it once with her. It felt risky to walk the aisles among a million filled matchboxes. Later we visited the factory that made olive oil soaps and stacked them in giant pyramids to dry.

"No, thank you," I said. "It's ridiculous to say that girls should only talk to girls. Did I say anything bad to a boy? Did anyone say anything bad to me? They're my friends. They're like my brothers. I won't do it, that's all."

L

15. A ***guttural*** laugh is a throaty laugh.

16. ***Ramallah*** is a town north of Jerusalem. The majority of the population is Christian.

R Reading Skill

Review Monitoring Comprehension **Say:** In this part of the story, the narrator returns to Israel with her family. Where do they decide to live? *(in a flat in a stone house north of Jerusalem)* **Ask:** Where does the narrator's brother go to school? *(Friends Girls School)* **Ask:** Where does the narrator go to school? *(Friends Boys School)* **Ask:** Why does the narrator have to go to the school for boys? *(It was the only high school that taught in English.)* **OL**

L Literary Element

Review Characterization
Ask: Were you surprised by the way that the narrator spoke to the counselor? Do you think she was right to do this? *(Responses will vary.)* **OL**

C Critical Thinking

Analysis **Ask:** How does the conflict at the boys' school show the conflict between the narrator's culture and the Israeli culture she is living in? *(Possible response: The narrator comes from a culture in which girls and boys talk to each other; however, she is living in a culture that considers this inappropriate. The narrator points out that she and the boys said nothing bad to each other, and she cannot see what the problem is.)* **AL**

English Language Coach

Building Background While the nation of Israel considers Jerusalem its capital, most other nations in the world (including the United States) do not. In fact, only two countries have their embassies in Jerusalem. The rest have them in Tel Aviv. The city of Jerusalem is part of the dispute between the Palestinians and Israelis. Israel maintains that all of Jerusalem is theirs. The Palestinians want to have part of Jerusalem as the capital of a Palestinian state. This is because Jerusalem holds not only the sacred Jewish Temple Mount (and other holy places) but also the Dome of the Rock, which is a holy place for Islam. **AS**

Indiana English/Language Arts Academic Standards
TWE: *Reading Fluency* 8.7.14

Teach

C Critical Thinking

Analysis **Say:** The narrator says that her brother is too young to know or imagine the troubles of the world. What troubles of the world do you think the narrator is referring to? *(Possible responses: her parents' struggle with money, the conflict in Israel between the Palestinians and Jews, cultural gender expectations)* **OL**

R Reading Skill

Review Making Inferences **Ask:** Why do you think the narrator and her brother set the chickens free? *(Possible response: Setting them free makes the narrator and her brother feel like they are doing a good thing, which makes them happy.)* **OL**

L Literary Element

Review Theme **Say:** There are many different themes in this story. What themes have you noticed so far? *(Possible response: freedom is important; equality is important; learning is important; all religions have value; peace is important)* **AL**

The counselor conferred with the headmaster and they called a taxi. I was sent home with a little paper requesting that I transfer to a different school. The charge: insolence. My mother, startled to see me home early and on my own, stared out the window when I told her.

C My brother came home from his school as usual, full of whistling and notebooks. "Did anyone tell you not to talk to girls?" I asked him. He looked at me as if I'd gone goofy. He was too young to know the troubles of the world. He couldn't even imagine them.

"You know what I've been thinking about?" he said. "A piece of cake. That puffy white layered cake with icing like they have at birthday parties in the United States. Wouldn't that taste good right now?" Our mother said she was thinking about mayonnaise. You couldn't get it in Jerusalem. She'd tried to make it and it didn't work. I felt too gloomy to talk about food.

Old City, Jerusalem.

Analyzing the Photo What can you learn about Jerusalem's climate and architecture from this photo?

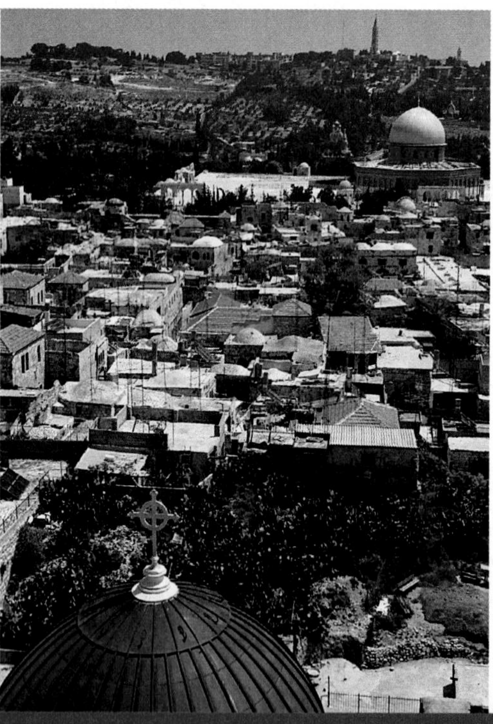

My brother said, "Let's go let Abu Miriam's chickens out." That's what we always did when we felt sad. We let our fussy landlord's red-and-white chickens loose to flap around the yard happily, puffing their wings. Even when Abu Miriam shouted and waggled his cane and his wife waved a dishtowel, we knew the chickens were thanking us. R

My father went with me to the St. Tarkmanchatz Armenian[17] School, a solemnly ancient stone school tucked deep into the Armenian Quarter of the Old City of Jerusalem. It was another world in there. He had already called the school officials on the telephone and tried to enroll me, though they didn't want to. Their school was for Armenian students only, kindergarten through twelfth grade. Classes were taught in three languages: Armenian, Arabic and English, which was why I needed to go there. Although most Arab students at other schools were learning English, I needed a school where classes were actually taught in English—otherwise I would have been staring out the windows triple the usual amount.

The head priest wore a long robe and a tall cone-shaped hat. He said, "Excuse me, please, but your daughter, she is not an Armenian, even a small amount?"

17. ***Armenia*** is a Christian country north of Turkey and Iran. The Armenian community in Jerusalem is very old. The Armenian Apostolic Church first set up churches there in the sixth century.

Additional Support

Differentiated Instruction

Food Memories Food is an important aspect of culture. In this story, the brother misses birthday cake, and the mother misses mayonnaise. Have students survey their parents, grandparents, or other adults in their lives about what food most reminds them of their childhood or what food they miss that is no longer available to them. Guide students as they compile the results of their surveys and put them on a Food Memories bulletin board. Discuss the findings with the class. Ask students what they can infer about each adult based on the foods he or she spoke about during the survey. **OL**

"Not at all," said my father. "But in case you didn't know, there is a stipulation in the educational code books of this city that says no student may be rejected solely on the basis of ethnic background, and if you don't accept her, we will alert the proper authorities." **L1**

They took me. But the principal wasn't happy about it. The students, however, seemed glad to have a new face to look at. Everyone's name ended in *-ian*, the beautiful, musical Armenian ending—Boghossian, Minassian, Kevorkian, Rostomian. My new classmates started calling me Shihabian. We wore uniforms, navy blue pleated skirts for the girls, white shirts, and navy sweaters. I waited during the lessons for the English to come around, as if it were a channel on television. While other students were on the other channels, I scribbled poems in the margins of my pages, read library books, and wrote a lot of letters filled with exclamation points. All the other students knew all three languages with three entirely different alphabets. How could they carry so much in their heads? I felt humbled by my ignorance. One day I felt so frustrated in our physics class—still another language—that I pitched my book out the open window. The professor made me go collect it. All the pages had let loose at the seams and were flapping free into the gutters along with the white wrappers of sandwiches.

Every week the girls had a hands-and-fingernails check. We had to keep our nails clean and trim, and couldn't wear any rings. Some of my new friends would invite me home for lunch with them, since we had an hour-and-a-half break and I lived too far to go to my own house.

Their houses were a thousand years old, clustered bee-hive-fashion behind ancient walls, stacked and curled and tilting and dark, filled with pictures of unsmiling relatives and small white cloths dangling crocheted edges. We ate spinach pies and white cheese. We dipped our bread in olive oil, as the Arabs did. We ate small sesame cakes, our mouths full of crumbles. They taught me to say "I love you" in Armenian, which sounded like *yes-kay-see-goo-see-rem*. I felt I had left my old life entirely.

Every afternoon I went down to the basement of the school where the kindergarten class was having an Arabic lesson. Their desks were pint-sized, their full white smocks tied around their necks. I stuffed my fourteen-year-old self in beside them. They had rosy cheeks and shy smiles. They must have thought I was a very slow learner.

More than any of the lessons, I remember the way the teacher rapped the backs of their hands with his ruler when they made a mistake. Their little faces puffed up with quiet tears. This pained me so terribly I forgot all my words. When it was my turn to go to the blackboard and write in Arabic, my hand shook. The kindergarten students whispered hints to me from the front row, but I couldn't understand them. We learned horribly useless phrases: "Please hand me the bellows[18] for my fire." I wanted words simple as tools, simple as *food* and *yesterday* and *dreams*. The teacher never rapped my hand, especially after I wrote a letter to the city newspaper, which my father edited,

18. A ***bellows*** is an accordion-like tool that pumps air through a tube. It is used to blow oxygen into a fire to make it burn hotter.

Reading in the Real World

Citizenship The narrator writes a letter to the editor expressing her anger over the way the teachers treated the kindergarten children in her school. Have students discuss these questions as it relates to that action and their own ideas about citizenship:

- Should the narrator have written a letter to the editor?
- Should she have been more direct and spoken to the teacher about what was upsetting her?
- What else could she have done?
- What would you do in a similar situation? **OL**

Teach

L1 Literary Element

Review Characterization
Say: Think about how the father treats the school officials. Think about how his daughter spoke to the counselor at the previous school. How do the father and daughter handle conflict in similar ways? *(They both tend to be very assertive and ask for what they want and believe is right.)* **OL**

R Reading Skill

Review Making Inferences
Ask: Does the narrator like her new school? *(Possible response: The narrator likes some things about her school, but there is a lot about the school that is difficult for her.)* **OL** **Say:** List the things that the narrator likes and dislikes about her new school. *(Responses will vary.)* **BL**

L2 Literary Element

Review Tone **Say:** The narrator is trying to be funny while expressing serious concerns. Give an example of something funny. *("They must have thought I was a slow learner" and "Please hand me the bellows for my fire.")* **Ask:** What is an example of something serious? *(her concerns about the way the teachers rapped the backs of the children's hands)* **OL**

Indiana English/Language Arts Academic Standards
TWE: *Differentiated Instruction* 8.7.1, *Reading in the Real World* 8.7

Teach

R Reading Skill

Review Identifying Author's Purpose **Ask:** Why do you think the author includes the conversation between her and her friends in the story? *(Possible response: to show that nonviolent people respond similarly to violence—no matter what culture they are from)* **OL** **Ask:** How might this hint at the author's purpose for writing the story? *(Possible response: The author may be writing the story to remind us that people mistreat each other everywhere—not just in war zones—and that those who are mistreated share a common bond.)* **AL**

L Literary Element

Review Characterization **Say:** Compare the narrator and her response to conflict with Sylvie and her response to conflict. How do their separate cultures and upbringing affect their actions? *(Possible response: The narrator does not back down to people in authority, even if it means getting kicked out of school. Sylvie obeys authority figures, even if it means marrying a fifty-year-old man.)* **OL**

protesting such harsh treatment of young learners. I wish I had known how to talk to those little ones, but they were just beginning their English studies and didn't speak much yet. They were at the same place in their English that I was in my Arabic.

From the high windows of St. Tarkmanchatz, we could look out over the Old City, the roofs and flapping laundry and television antennas, the pilgrims and churches and mosques, the olivewood prayer beads and fragrant *falafel*[19] lunch stands, the intricate interweaving of cultures and prayers and songs and holidays. We saw the barbed wire separating Jordan from Israel then, the bleak, uninhabited strip of no-man's land reminding me how little education saved us after all. People who had differing ideas still came to blows, imagining fighting could solve things. Staring out over the quiet roofs of afternoon, I thought it so foolish. I asked my friends what they thought about it and they shrugged.

R "It doesn't matter what we think about it. It just keeps happening. It happened in Armenia too, you know. Really, really bad in Armenia. And who talks about it in the world news now? It happens everywhere. It happens in your country one by one, yes? Murders and guns. What can we do?"

Sometimes after school, my brother and I walked up the road that led past the crowded refugee camp of Palestinians who owned even less than our modest relatives did in the village. The little kids were stacking stones in empty tin cans and shaking them. We waved our hands and they covered their mouths and laughed.

We wore our beat-up American tennis shoes and our old sweatshirts and talked about everything we wanted to do and everywhere else we wished we could go.

"I want to go back to Egypt," my brother said. "I sort of feel like I missed it. Spending all that time in bed instead of exploring—what a waste."

"I want to go to Greece," I said. "I want to play a violin in a symphony orchestra in Austria." We made up things. I wanted to go back to the United States most of all. Suddenly I felt like a patriotic citizen. One of my friends, Sylvie Markarian, had just been shipped off to Damascus, Syria, to marry a man who was fifty years old, a widower. Sylvie was exactly my age—we had turned fifteen two days apart. She had never met her future husband before. I thought this was the most revolting thing I had ever heard of. "Tell your parents no thank you," I urged her. "Tell them you *refuse*."

Sylvie's eyes were liquid, swirling brown. **L** I could not see clearly to the bottom of them.

"You don't understand," she told me. "In United States you say no. We don't say no. We have to follow someone's wishes. This is the wish of my father. Me, I am scared. I never slept away from my mother before. But I have no choice. I am going because they tell me to go." She was sobbing, sobbing on my shoulder. And I was stroking her long, soft hair. After that, I carried two fists inside, one for Sylvie and one for me.

Most weekends my family went to the village to sit with the relatives. We sat and sat and sat. We sat in big rooms and little rooms, in circles, on chairs or on woven mats or brightly covered mattresses piled on the floor. People came in and out to

19. ***Falafel*** are fried chickpea patties.

Additional Support

English Language Coach

Analogies The narrator describes an "intricate interweaving of cultures and prayers and songs and holidays." Remind students of the analogies people use to describe the mixture of cultures in the United States: melting pot and salad bowl. Write a definition for each of these on the board. Challenge students to consider all three ideas and tell which idea best describes the Israeli situation and why. **OL** Ask students which analogy best describes the United States and why. If students don't think any of these analogies best describes the United States, ask them to come up with their own analogies and share them with the class. **AL**

greet my family. Sometimes even donkeys and chickens came in and out. We were like movie stars or dignitaries. They never seemed to get tired of us.

My father translated the more interesting tidbits of conversation, the funny stories my grandmother told. She talked about angels and food and money and people and politics and gossip and old memories from my father's childhood, before he emigrated[20] away from her. She wanted to make sure we were going to stick around forever, which made me feel very nervous. We ate from mountains of rice and eggplant on large silver trays—they gave us little plates of our own since it was not our custom to eat from the same plate as other people. We ripped the giant wheels of bread into triangles. Shepherds passed through town with their flocks of sheep and goats, their long canes and cloaks, straight out of the Bible. My brother and I trailed them to the edge of the village, past the lentil fields to the green meadows studded with stones, while the shepherds pretended we weren't there. I think they liked to be alone, unnoticed. The sheep had differently colored dyed bottoms, so shepherds could tell their flocks apart. **L1**

During these long, slow, smoke-stained weekends—the men still smoked cigarettes a lot in those days, and the old *taboon*, my family's mounded bread-oven, puffed billowy clouds outside the door—my crying jags began. I cried without any warning, even in the middle of a meal. My crying was usually noiseless but dramatically wet—streams of tears pouring down my cheeks, onto my collar or the back of my hand.

20. To ***emigrate*** is to leave one's country to go live somewhere else.

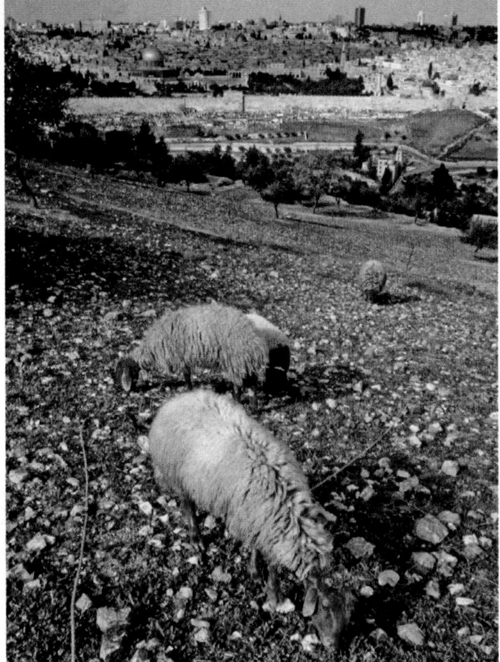

Analyzing the Photo Sheep graze on a hillside near Jerusalem's Old City. How does Jerusalem seem similar to or different from the cities you know?

Everything grew quiet.

Someone always asked in Arabic, "What is wrong? Are you sick? Do you wish to lie down?"

L2 My father made valiant excuses in the beginning. "She's overtired," he said. "She has a headache. She is missing her friend who moved to Syria. She is homesick just now."

My brother stared at me as if I had just landed from Planet X.

Worst of all was our drive to school every morning, when our car came over the rise in the highway and all Jerusalem lay sprawled before us in its golden, stony splendor pockmarked with olive trees and automobiles. Even the air above the city had a thick, religious texture, as if it were a shining brocade filled with broody incense. I cried hardest then. All those hours tied up

Teach

L1 Literary Element

Review Description **Ask:** What parts of this description are most vivid to you? *(Responses will vary.)* **Ask:** Which senses do these descriptions appeal to? *(sight, sound, taste, touch, smell)* **OL** Discuss descriptive writing as a technique for students to use in their own writing. Ask students to talk about the effect of the descriptive writing on them as readers. *(Responses will vary.)* **AS**

R Reading Skill

Review Questioning Have students write down any questions they have at this point in the story. **Ask:** What questions come to mind as you read this page? *(Possible responses: Why is she crying? How will her family help her? How will she stop crying?)* **Ask:** What other questions do you have? *(Responses will vary.)* **OL**

L2 Literary Element

Review Characterization
Ask: Why do you think the narrator's father makes excuses for her crying? *(Possible responses: He does not want people to worry about his daughter; He does not know what else to say; He is trying to protect his daughter.)* **OL**

Differentiated Instruction

Picture It Have students imagine they are working as illustrators for this story. Ask students to create art specs requesting illustrations to go with the text. Their specs should be as specific as possible and tell the artist or photographer exactly what should go on each page students want to illustrate. Remind students that illustrations should add to the text and provide readers with visuals that enhance their reading. Have students think of illustrations they like from other texts they have read to use as models. **OL** Ask students to share their specs with the class. Have interested students draw their own illustrations. **AL**

Indiana English/Language Arts Academic Standards
TWE: *English Language Coach* 8.3, *Differentiated Instruction* 8.3

Teach

R Reading Skill

Review Interpreting **Ask:** What does the narrator mean when she says, "it weighs too much"? *(Possible responses: It is too hard for me here; the problems are too great here with the Arab and Israeli conflict.)* **Ask:** Why do you think she hits the boys who stare at her on the street? *(Possible response: She feels threatened; she is insulted.)* OL

L Literary Element

Review Tone **Say:** Again the narrator adds humor to the piece. How do you know she is being funny? *(Nobody would use shoes as vases or drawers.)* **Ask:** How would you describe her sense of humor? *(Possible responses: slightly sarcastic; witty; unique)* OL

C Critical Thinking

Analysis **Say:** Notice how the writer just jumps right into the sudden move her family makes. There is no transition from the paragraph before it. Why do you think she does this? *(Possible response: This shows exactly how it happened. The narrator had no warning or time to prepare herself for the change.)* OL

in school lay just ahead. My father pulled over and talked to me. He sighed. He kept his hands on the steering wheel even when the car was stopped and said, "Someday, I promise you, you will look back on this period in your life and have no idea what made you so unhappy here."

R "I want to go home." It became my anthem. "This place depresses me. It weighs too much. I hate all these old stones that everybody keeps kissing. I'm sick of pilgrims. They act so pious and pure. And I hate the way people stare at me here." Already I'd been involved in two street skirmishes[21] with boys who stared a little too hard and long. I'd socked one in the jaw and he socked me back. I hit the other one straight in the face with my purse.

"You could be happy here if you tried just a little harder," my father said. "Don't compare it to the United States all the time. Don't pretend the United States is perfect. And look at your brother—he's not having any problems!"

"My brother is eleven years old."

I had crossed the boundary from uncomplicated childhood when happiness was a good ball and a hoard of candy-coated Jordan almonds.

One problem was that I had fallen in love with four different boys who all played in the same band. Two of them were even twins. I never quite described it to my parents, but I wrote reams and reams of notes about it on loose-leaf paper that I kept under my sweaters in my closet.

Such new energy made me feel reckless. I gave things away. I gave away my necklace and a whole box of shortbread cookies that my mother had been saving. I gave my extra shoes away to the gypsies. One night when the gypsies camped in a field down the road from our house, I thought about their mounds of white goat cheese lined up on skins in front of their tents, and the wild *oud*[22] music they played deep into the black belly of the night, and I wanted to go sit around their fire. Maybe they could use some shoes.

L I packed a sack of old loafers that I rarely wore and walked with my family down the road. The gypsy mothers stared into my shoes curiously. They took them into their tent. Maybe they would use them as vases or drawers. We sat with small glasses of hot, sweet tea until a girl bellowed from deep in her throat, threw back her head, and began dancing. A long bow thrummed across the strings. The girl circled the fire, tapping and clicking, trilling a long musical wail from deep in her throat. My brother looked nervous. He was remembering the belly dancer in Egypt, and her scarf. I felt invisible. I was pretending to be a gypsy. My father stared at me. Didn't I recognize the exquisite oddity of my own life when I sat right in the middle of it? Didn't I feel lucky to be here? Well, yes I did. But sometimes it was hard to be lucky.

C When we left Jerusalem, we left quickly. Left our beds in our rooms and our car in the driveway. Left in a plane, not sure where we were going. The rumbles of fighting with Israel had been growing louder and louder. In the barbed-wire no-man's land visible from the windows of our house, guns cracked loudly in the middle of the night. We lived right near the edge. My father heard disturbing rumors at the

21. In war, a ***skirmish*** is a short fight.

22. An ***oud*** is a stringed instrument that is plucked like a guitar.

Additional Support

Reading in the Real World

Career Belly dancing is one form of dancing that is common in the Middle East. Have students list different types of dancing on the board. Make sure to include types of dancing from different cultures. Assign small groups of students to find out what is unique about each kind of dance. Have a dancing instructor come to class and talk about some of the different forms of dance and how they are alike and different. Encourage students who know different kinds of dance to demonstrate the steps that go with the dances that they know. OL newspaper that would soon grow into the infamous Six Day War[23] of 1967. We were in England by then, drinking tea from thin china cups and scanning the newspapers. Bombs were blowing up in Jerusalem. We worried about the village. We worried about my grandmother's dreams, which had been getting worse and worse, she'd told us. We worried about the house we'd left, and the chickens, and the children at the refugee camp. But there was nothing we could do except keep talking about it all.

My parents didn't want to go back to Missouri because they'd already said goodbye to everyone there. They thought we might try a different part of the country. They weighed the virtues of different states. Texas was big and warm. After a chilly year crowded around the small gas heaters we used in Jerusalem, a warm place sounded appealing. In roomy Texas, my parents bought the first house they looked at. My father walked into the city newspaper and said, "Any jobs open around here?"

I burst out crying when I entered a grocery store—so many different kinds of bread.

A letter on thin blue airmail paper reached me months later, written by my classmate, the bass player in my favorite Jerusalem band. "Since you left," he said, "your empty desk reminds me of a snake ready to strike. I am afraid to look at it. I hope you are having a better time than we are."

Of course I was, and I wasn't. *Home* had grown different forever. *Home* had doubled. Back *home* again in my own country, it seemed impossible to forget the place we had just left: the piercing call of the *muezzin*[24] from the mosque at prayer time, the dusky green tint of the olive groves, the sharp, cold air that smelled as deep and old as my grandmother's white sheets flapping from the line on her roof. What story hadn't she finished?

Our father used to tell us that when he was little, the sky over Jerusalem crackled with meteors and shooting stars[25] almost every night. They streaked and flashed, igniting the dark. Some had long golden tails. For a few seconds, you could see their whole swooping trail lit up. Our father and his brothers slept on the roof to watch the sky. "There were so many of them, we didn't even call out every time we saw one."

During our year in Jerusalem, my brother and I kept our eyes cast upwards whenever we were outside at night, but the stars were different since our father was a boy. Now the sky seemed too orderly, stuck in place. The stars had learned where they belonged. Only people on the ground kept changing. ❍

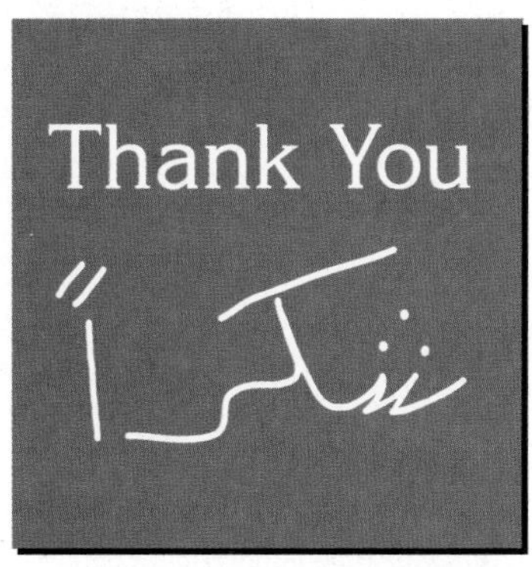

23. The ***Six Day War*** was fought in June 1967 between Israel on one side and Egypt, Syria, and Jordan on the other. Israel won and took control of the Old City of Jerusalem as well as territory from the other three countries.

24. The ***muezzin*** calls Muslims to prayer five times a day.

25. ***Meteors*** and ***shooting stars*** are the same thing: small heavenly bodies that burn up as they enter the earth's atmosphere from outer space.

Differentiated Instruction

Name the Stars Have students find out about the stars that are typically overhead in your area. Challenge them to make a picture or diagram showing what is in the sky at different times of the year. Ask students to learn the name of the constellations visible from your location. Also ask them to find out more about what shooting stars are and what makes them occur. If there is a planetarium in the area, plan a field trip to visit it or encourage students to gather information from there. Ask students to report their findings to the class. **OL** Discuss why the stars we see are dependent on the time of the year and our location in the world. **AS**

Teach

L Literary Element

Review Theme Ask: How has the narrator been changed by her time in Israel? What is the theme of the story? *(Possible responses: The theme of the story may be that "home" is a place we carry inside of us more than it is a country or location, and that "home" is part of your identity; no matter where it is.)* **OL**

BQ BIG Question

Ask: How does the Arabic "thank you" at the end of the story show how the narrator stays true to herself? *(Possible responses: At the beginning, she wanted to know how to say "thank you" in Arabic to show respect to other people. In the end, she finds that she wants to use the language to communicate her feelings. "Thank You" is written in both Arabic and English; like the narrator, it is a phrase that shares more than one culture.)* **OL**

Assess

CheckPoint

Use the CheckPoint questions provided on Presentation Plus! to check for comprehension of the selection. These questions can be used with interactive response keypads for immediate student feedback.

Indiana English/Language Arts Academic Standards
TWE: *Differentiated Instruction* 8.7.12

Tips for Independent Reading

Suggest that students set a goal for themselves, such as trying to read a chapter a day or a book a month. They can try reading some of the books shown here, related to the Big Question, or look for others in the local library that interest them.

Fiction

As students read about these fictional characters, they can learn about other ways that people, especially young people, deal with challenges and try to stay true to themselves.

Reading *A House for Mr. Biswas* may give students a different perspective on dealing with being different from the people all around them.

Students can find out how people who do not believe in war under any circumstances can remain true to themselves, even during a war, by reading *Slap Your Sides.*

In *The Glory Field*, students can read an historical fiction account of an enslaved family. Students are sure to encounter many different ideas about staying true to oneself as they read about different generations in the family and their unique struggles.

UNIT 5

Reading on Your Own

To read more about the Big Question, choose one of these books from your school or local library. Work on your reading skills by choosing books that are challenging to you.

Fiction

A House for Mr. Biswas
by V. S. Naipaul

A Hindu man tries to find a house of his own in the British colony of Trinidad in the Caribbean. In this humorous story he is forced to overcome people's prejudices against his culture to discover who he is inside and stick up for himself.

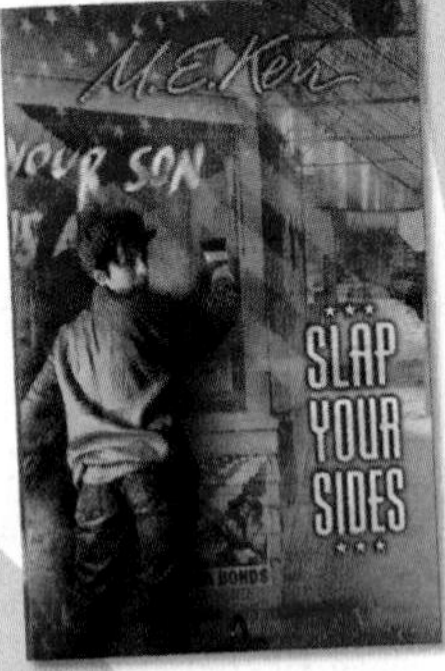

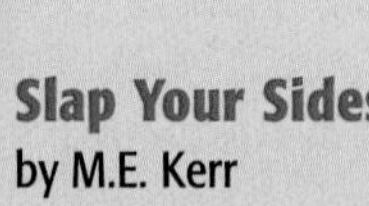

Slap Your Sides
by M.E. Kerr

This World War II-era story deals with issues of aggression and pacifism in the thirteen-year-old Jubal Shoemaker's Pennsylvania Quaker community. Are there times when it is wrong to fight? Are there times when it is wrong not to? Read this piece of fiction and then decide.

Of Sound Mind
by Jean Ferris

The only member of his family who can hear, Theo is frustrated by the silence in his household and by the individual demands of his high-maintenance relatives. Read this book to find out about the special friendship that helps Theo cope with the stress he has at home.

The Glory Field
by Walter Dean Myers

This novel traces the lives of an African American family, beginning with the capture and enslavement of the first member in 1753. Each generation struggles against poverty and racism. But their love for one another and for their land keeps the members of the Lewis family strong.

Additional Support

Differentiated Instruction

Use the Glencoe BookLink CD-ROM to create customized reading lists to help students answer the Big Question. Suggestions for Unit 5:

Grade 4: *Grasshopper Summer* by Ann Turner
Grade 5: *Freedom Songs* by Yvette Moore
Grade 6: *Yo, Alejandro* by Alejandro Gac-Artigas
Grade 7: *Freya on the Wall* by T. Degens
Grade 8: *The Call of the Wild* by Jack London

Nonfiction

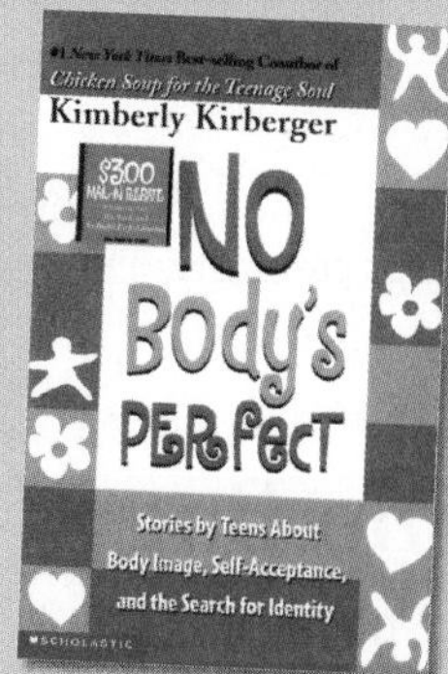

No Body's Perfect
by Kimberly Kirberger

A collection of poems, essays, and stories written by teenagers that look at the issues surrounding body image, food, and self-esteem. The author offers insight as well as hope and helps young people think about how to stay true to themselves.

The Rose That Grew from Concrete
by Tupac Shakur

Written by Tupac when he was 19 and not yet a star, these poems bring passion to the experience of staying true to yourself.

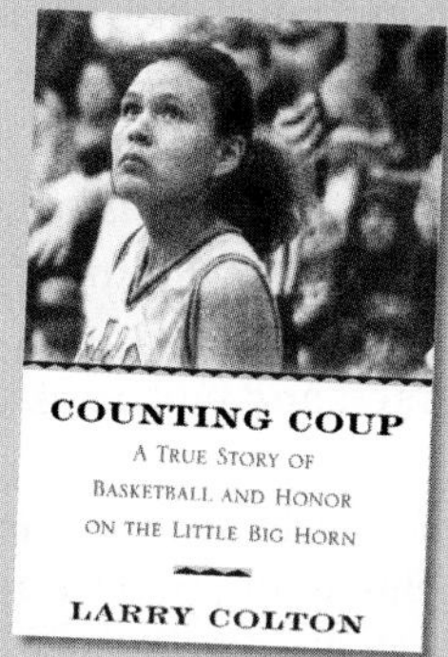

Counting Coup: A True Story of Basketball and Honor on the Little Big Horn
by Larry Colton

Battling racism, alcoholism, and domestic violence, the girls on the Hardin High School basketball team learn how to be winners on and off the court.

And Still We Rise: The Trials and Triumphs of Twelve Gifted Inner-City High School Students
by Miles Corwin

Twelve seniors from an Advanced Placement English class in Los Angeles dream of going to college. This book deals with the hard realities of their lives and their struggle to achieve their dreams.

Nonfiction

These nonfiction books deal with issues that teens face when thinking about who they really are and how they can be true to themselves.

The poems in *No Body's Perfect* will expose students to different voices and ideas about issues that teens deal with in their daily lives.

Readers who are interested in sports in general, and basketball in particular, may enjoy reading *Counting Coup: A True Story of Basketball and Honor on the Little Big Horn.*

Students can learn more about how other people stayed true to themselves by reading Tupac Shakur's poetry or Miles Corwin's narrative *And Still We Rise: The Trials and Triumphs of Twelve Gifted Inner-City High School Students.*

About the Subjects

Invite students to share information they know about the subjects of the books listed in *Reading on Your Own*. What do students know about these books or their authors?

Test-Taking Tips

TIP Tell students to make sure they read the test directions carefully. The directions often give valuable clues about the purpose and main idea of the passage.

TIP Remind students that, in most stories, the theme or main idea is not stated directly. It is revealed gradually through the plot and characters. To find the theme, students should read the passage carefully, then try to figure out what idea or message is most important in the story.

ISTEP+ Test Practice

Directions:

In this excerpt from a story about a boy's Sioux heritage, the boy confronts his mixed feelings about his grandfather. Read the excerpt carefully. Then, answer questions 1 through 7.

from The Medicine Bag

By Virginia Driving Hawk Sneve

We always had some authentic Sioux article to show our listeners. One year Cheryl had new moccasins that Grandpa had made. On another visit he gave me a small, round, flat, rawhide drum which was decorated with a painting of a warrior riding a horse. He taught me a real Sioux chant[1] to sing while I beat the drum with a leather-covered stick that had a feather on the end. Man, that really made an impression.

We never showed our friends Grandpa's picture. Not that we were ashamed of him, but because we knew that the glamorous tales we told didn't go with the real thing. Our friends would have laughed at the picture, because Grandpa wasn't tall and stately like TV Indians. His hair wasn't in braids, but hung in stringy, gray strands on his neck and he was old. He was our great-grandfather, and he didn't live in a tipi,[2] but all by himself in a part log, part tar-paper shack on the Rosebud Reservation in South Dakota. So when Grandpa came to visit us, I was so ashamed and embarrassed I could've died.

There are a lot of yippy poodles and other fancy little dogs in our neighborhood, but they usually barked singly at the mailman from the safety of their own yards. Now it sounded as if a whole pack of mutts were barking together in one place.

I got up and walked to the curb to see what the commotion was. About a block away I saw a crowd of little kids yelling, with the dogs yipping and growling around someone who was walking down the middle of the street.

I watched the group as it slowly came closer and saw that in the center of the strange procession was a man wearing a tall black hat. He'd pause now and then to peer at something in his hand and then at the houses on either side of the street. I felt cold and hot at the same time as I recognized the man.

[1] **chant:** a short, simple melody in which a number of syllables or words are sung to the same note.

[2] **tipi:** a cone-shaped tent, usually of animal skins, used especially by the Plains Indians. In the Sioux language, *tipi* is a combination of *ti*, "to dwell," and *pi*, "for use."

"Oh, no!" I whispered. "It's Grandpa!"

I stood on the curb, unable to move even though I wanted to run and hide. Then I got mad when I saw how the yippy dogs were growling and nipping at the old man's baggy pant legs and how wearily he poked them away with his cane. "Stupid mutts," I said as I ran to rescue Grandpa.

When I kicked and hollered at the dogs to get away, they put their tails between their legs and scattered. The kids ran to the curb where they watched me and the old man.

"Grandpa," I said and felt pretty dumb when my voice cracked. I reached for his beat-up old tin suitcase, which was tied shut with a rope. But he set it down right in the street and shook my hand.

"*Hau, Takoza,* Grandchild," he greeted me formally in Sioux.

All I could do was stand there with the whole neighborhood watching and shake the hand of the leather-brown old man. I saw how his gray hair straggled from under his big black hat, which had a drooping feather in its crown. His rumpled black suit hung like a sack over his stooped frame. As he shook my hand, his coat fell open to expose a bright-red, satin shirt with a beaded bolo tie[3] under the collar. His getup wasn't out of place on the reservation, but it sure was here, and I wanted to sink right through the pavement.

[3] **bolo tie:** a piece of cord (often leather) fastened at the neck with an ornamental bar or clasp.

Questions 1 through 7 are based on the excerpt from "The Medicine Bag."

1 The narrator and his sister haven't shown other kids their grandpa's picture because

A he has asked them not to
B he doesn't look the way they have described him
C they don't have a picture of him
D the picture doesn't look like him

2 Based on the excerpt, choose the theme of the story.

A showing affection
B avoiding danger
C being proud of your heritage
D accepting gifts

UNIT 5 ASSESSMENT

Answers:

1. B
2. C

Resources for pages 702–707

Use these resources to review, assess, or reteach the chapter: Active Learning and Note-Taking Guide, ExamView Pro, and Differentiated Instruction Tool Software.

Answers:

3. C

4. B

5. C

6 A

7. Student responses will vary. A typical correct response will include one example from each of the following lists. Students may paraphrase or describe the examples rather than quoting from the passage.

Feeling: ashamed or embarrassed
Example:
- "I stood on the curb, unable to move even though I wanted to run and hide."
- "His getup wasn't out of place on the reservation, but it sure was here, and I wanted to sink right through the pavement."
- other relevant text-based response

Feeling: proud
Example:
- "My kid sister Cheryl and I always bragged about our Sioux grandpa, Joe Iron Shell."
- ". . . when we'd return home to Iowa after our yearly summer visit to Grandpa we always had some exciting tales to tell."
- other relevant text-based response

3 What alerts the narrator to Grandpa's arrival?

A He gets a phone call.
B He sees someone in the street.
C He hears dogs barking.
D His sister tells him to look outside.

4 Unlike "TV Indians," the narrator's grandpa

A tells exciting stories
B lives in a shack
C speaks the Sioux language
D is tall and stately

Read the following sentence from the selection and answer questions 5 and 6.

5 *His rumpled black suit hung like a sack over his stooped frame.*
In this sentence, the phrase "like a sack" MOST LIKELY means

A tight
B heavily
C loosely
D stretched

6 In the same sentence, the words "stooped frame" MOST LIKELY mean

A hunched body
B wrinkled skin
C straight shoulders
D brittle bones

7 The narrator has mixed feelings about his grandpa. On a separate piece of paper, copy the following chart and give an example of each from the story.

Feeling	Example
Ashamed or embarrassed	
Proud	

Directions:

Read this story carefully. Then, answer questions 8 through 15.

Salvador Late or Early

By Sandra Cisneros

Salvador with eyes the color of caterpillar, Salvador of the crooked hair and crooked teeth, Salvador whose name the teacher cannot remember, is a boy who is no one's friend, runs along somewhere in that vague direction where homes are the color of bad weather, lives behind a raw wood doorway, shakes the sleepy brothers awake, ties their shoes, combs their hair with water, feeds them milk and corn flakes from a tin cup in the dim dark of the morning.

Salvador, late or early, sooner or later arrives with the string of younger brothers ready. Helps his mama, who is busy with the business of the baby. Tugs the arms of Cecilio, Arturito, makes them hurry, because today, like yesterday, Arturito has dropped the cigar box of crayons, has let go the hundred little fingers of red, green, yellow, blue, and nub of black sticks that tumble and spill over and beyond the asphalt puddles until the crossing-guard lady holds back the blur of traffic for Salvador to collect them again.

Salvador inside that wrinkled shirt, inside the throat that must clear itself and apologize each time it speaks, inside that forty-pound body of boy with its geography of scars, its history of hurt, limbs stuffed with feathers and rags, in what part of the eyes, in what part of the heart, in that cage of the chest where something throbs with both fists and knows only what Salvador knows, inside that body too small to contain the hundred balloons of happiness, the single guitar of grief, is a boy like any other disappearing out the door, beside the schoolyard gate, where he has told his brothers they must wait. Collects the hands of Cecilio and Arturito, scuttles off dodging the many schoolyard colors, the elbows and wrists crisscrossing, the several shoes running. Grows small and smaller to the eye, dissolves into the bright horizon, flutters in the air before disappearing like a memory of kites.

UNIT 5 ASSESSMENT

Test-Taking Tips

TIP Remind students to analyze each question and its answer choices. Sometimes a single word in a question or an answer choice may relate to a key word in the passage.

TIP Occasionally students will encounter questions that seem extremely difficult. When this happens, they should eliminate obvious wrong answers, guess, and then move on. If a student isn't able to eliminate any of the answer choices, it's still to his or her advantage to guess.

Answers:

8. C
9. A
10. B
11. D

Questions 8 through 15 are based on "Salvador Late or Early."

8 Unlike his brothers, Salvador

A goes to school every day
B is too young to take care of himself
C has many adult responsibilities
D gets extra attention from their mother

9 Read the following statement from the story.

Salvador whose name the teacher cannot remember, is a boy who is no one's friend, runs along somewhere in that vague direction where homes are the color of bad weather, lives behind a raw wood doorway . . .

What do the phrases "homes are the color of bad weather" and "raw wood doorway" tell you about the setting of the story?

A Salvador's neighborhood is run-down and poor.
B The houses in Salvador's neighborhood are painted dark colors.
C The story takes place during bad weather.
D Salvador's school and home are both on the outskirts of town.

10 What is the tone of this story?

A mocking
B compassionate
C cheerful
D distressing

11 Read the following sentence from the story.

Collects the hands of Cecilio and Arturito, scuttles off dodging the many schoolyard colors, the elbows and wrists crisscrossing, the several shoes running.

As it is used in the passage, "scuttles off" MOST LIKELY means that Salvador is

A strutting proudly to school
B walking slowly to school with his younger brothers
C trying to hurry his younger brothers to school
D skipping to school with his younger brothers

12 Read the following sentence from the story.

Grows small and smaller to the eye, dissolves into the bright horizon, flutters in the air before disappearing like a memory of kites.

This description is used to show that Salvador is

A faster than his brothers
B concerned only with himself
C barely noticed and easily forgotten
D always in a hurry to go home

13 Give **two** examples from the story to show that Salvador takes good care of his brothers.

Answer questions 14 and 15 based on your knowledge of language conventions.

14 Which sentence is written correctly?

A Salvador, Cecilio, and Arturito had to pick up the crayon's that Arturito dropped.
B Salvador, Cecilio, and Arturito had to pick up the crayons that Arturito dropped.
C Salvador Cecilio, and Arturito had to pick up the crayons that Arturito dropped.
D Salvador, Cecilio, and Arturito, had to pick up the crayons that Arturito dropped.

15 What is the BEST way to combine these two sentences?

Many students find trying to make friends difficult. Many students get frustrated trying to make friends.

A Many students find it difficult and frustrated trying to make friends.
B Many students find trying to make friends frustrated and difficult.
C Many frustrated students find it difficult trying to make friends.
D Many students trying to make friends find it difficult and get frustrated.

Answers:

12. C

13. Student responses will vary. A typical correct response will include two examples from the following list.
- He wakes his brothers.
- He dresses his brothers.
- He feeds his brothers.
- He takes his brothers to school.
- other relevant text-based response

14. B

15. D

UNIT 6

Skills Scope and Sequence

Readability Scores Key
Dale-Chall/**DRP**/**Lexile**

PACING (DAYS) STANDARD	BLOCK	INSTRUCTIONAL SEGMENT LITERATURE	READING SKILLS	LITERARY ELEMENTS
1	1	**Unit Warm-Up, pp. 708–731** Genre Focus: Drama The Diary of Anne Frank, Act 1, Scenes 1–2 by Frances Goodrich and Albert Hackett **4.0**/**NA**/**NA**, SE p. 713	Drawing Conclusions, SE pp. 712, 716, 721, 722, 723, 727, 729, 730, TWE pp. 724, 725, 726, 728 Interpreting, SE pp. 712, 715, 724, 725, 726, 728, TWE pp. 716, 720, 721, 727, 731 Paraphrasing and Summarizing, SE pp. 712, 717 How to Read Drama, TWE p. 712, 733	Dialogue and Monologue, SE pp. 712, 715, 723, TWE p. 717 Stage Directions, SE pp. 712, 714, 715, 717, 718, 731, TWE pp. 719, 722, 723, 726
3	2	**Reading Workshop 1, pp. 732–789** The Diary of Anne Frank, Act 1, Scenes 3–5 by Frances Goodrich and Albert Hackett **4.0**/**NA**/**NA**, SE p. 736	Drawing Conclusions, SE pp. 732, 735, 738, 739, 741, 742, 744, 747, 751, 753, 755, 757, 758, 759, 765, 766, 768, 769, 772, 773, 774, 776, 777, 778, 779, 780, 782, 785, TWE pp. 737, 740, 745, 752, 754, 756, 760, 783 Fluency, TWE pp. 739, 744, 754, 782	Act and Scene, SE pp. 735, 736, 752, 761 Dialogue and Monologue, SE pp. 765, 770, 772, 774, 776, TWE pp. 771, 785
1		**Writing Workshop, Part 1, pp. 790–793** Writing Product: Dramatic Scene		Characters, SE p. 791 Setting, SE pp. 791, 792 Stage directions, SE pp. 791, 792 Dialogue, SE pp. 791, 792
3	1	**Reading Workshop 2, pp. 794–845** The Diary of Anne Frank, Act 2 by Frances Goodrich and Albert Hackett **4.0**/**NA**/**NA**, SE p. 798	Interpreting, SE pp. 794, 795, 797, 800, 801, 802, 803, 805, 806, 809, 812, 814, 815, 816, 817, 818, 819, 820, 825, 827, 829, 830, 833, 834, 837, 840, 841, 843, TWE pp. 798, 811, 836, 839 Fluency, TWE pp. 800, 808, 820, 830 Drawing Conclusions, TWE pp. 799, 800, 815, 817, 826, 829, 833, 834 Analyzing, TWE pp. 801, 805, 828, 843	Stage Directions, SE pp. 797, 798, 802, 803, 808, 812, 817, 818, 821, TWE pp. 810, 813, 828, 831, 832, 840, 841 Irony, SE pp. 804, 835 Mood, SE pp. 825, 831, 832, 835, 836, 837, 842, TWE pp. 838, 843

Unit 6 Big Question

The question **"How do you keep from giving up when bad things happen?"** speaks to a concern we all have felt. Working to answer the question helps students learn how to persist in the face of adversity.

Unit 6 Genre

The majority of this unit is **dramatic text.** Reading this play will familiarize your students with drama, as well as help your students think about their inner reserves and the ways they keep from giving up in the face of adversity.

CRITICAL THINKING	VOCABULARY	WRITING AND GRAMMAR	LISTENING, SPEAKING, AND VIEWING
Comprehension, TWE pp. 715, 719, 724	Ellipsis Points in Dialogue, TWE p. 719 Multiple Meaning Words, Old Words, TWE p. 720 Figurative Language, TWE p. 729	Beginning an Essay, TWE p. 726 Developing an Essay, TWE p. 727 Diary Entry, TWE p. 731	Analyzing the Photo, SE pp. 718, 721, 727 Viewing the Photo, TWE pp. 708, 713, 718
Infer, SE pp. 762, 788 Predict, SE p. 762 Evaluation, SE pp. 762, 788, TWE pp. 738, 741 Interpret, SE p. 788 Comprehension, TWE pp. 749, 751, 757, 758, 759, 766	Word Parts, SE pp. 734, 737, 740, 743, 748, 752, 761, TWE p. 757 Historical Influences on English, SE pp. 764, 769, 779, 781, 783, 786, TWE pp. 768, 777, 778	Commas in a Series, SE p. 763 Write About Your Reading, SE p. 788 Commas with Direct Quotations, SE p. 789	Analyzing the Photo, SE pp. 745, 787, Viewing the Photo, TWE pp. 750, 767, 784 Talk About Your Reading, SE p. 762
	Writing Good Dialogue, TWE p. 790	Commas with Introductory Words, Phrases, and Clauses, SE p. 793 Choosing a Story Scene, TWE p. 790 Adapting a Scene, TWE p. 791 Writing the Script, TWE p. 791 Stage Directions, TWE p. 792	
Interpret, SE pp. 822, 844 Evaluation, SE pp. 822, 844, TWE p. 827 Analyze, SE p. 844, TWE p. 806 Comprehension, TWE pp. 801, 829, 836, 842, 843 Synthesis, TWE pp. 830, 835	Anglo-Saxon Roots, SE pp. 796, 804, 809, 813, 824, 826, 830, 838 Vocabulary Questions, TWE p. 796 Word Parts, TWE p. 824	Write About Your Reading, SE pp. 822, 844 Commas with Interrupting Words, SE p. 823 Commas with Appositives, SE p. 845	Analyzing the Photo, SE pp. 799, 811, 818, 827 Viewing the Photo, TWE pp. 818, 835, 841

UNIT 6

Skills Scope and Sequence *continued*

Readability Scores Key
Dale-Chall/**DRP**/Lexile

PACING (DAYS) STANDARD	BLOCK	INSTRUCTIONAL SEGMENT LITERATURE	READING SKILLS	LITERARY ELEMENTS
3	3	**Reading Workshop 3, pp. 846–867** "Bouncing Back" by Jan Farrington 5.1/**57**/910, SE p. 850 "Another Mountain" by Abiodun Oyewole SE p. 856 "Standing Tall" by Michael Dolan 9.3/**68**/1230, SE p. 862	Paraphrasing and Summarizing, SE pp. 846, 847, 849, 850, 853, 855, 857, 862, TWE pp. 851, 861, 865 Fluency, TWE p. 855 Connecting, TWE p. 849 Analyzing, TWE p. 854	Literal and Figurative Language, SE pp. 849, 850, 851, 857, TWE p. 853 Expository Writing, SE pp. 861, 863, TWE pp. 862, 864, 865
1		**Writing Workshop, Part 2, pp. 868–871** Writing Product: Dramatic Scene	Fluency, TWE p. 871	Mood, TWE p. 870
3	1	**Reading Workshop 4, pp. 872–889** "and sometimes i hear this song in my head" by Harriet Jacobs SE p. 876 from Sky by Hanneke Ippisch 5.9/**57**/950, SE p. 882	Visualizing, SE pp. 872, 873, 875, 876, 877, 881, 882, 883, 884, 885, 886 Analyzing, TWE p. 885 Interpreting, TWE p. 876 Connecting, TWE p. 881 Drawing Conclusions, TWE pp. 882, 886	Sound Devices, SE pp. 875, 877 Setting, SE pp. 881, 883, 885, 887, TWE p. 882 Reviewing Literal and Figurative Language, SE p. 882
3	2	**Comparing Literature Workshop, pp. 890–909** "Welcome" by Ouida Sebestyen 4.7/**48**/690, SE p. 893 "Alone" by Maya Angelou SE p. 906	Paraphrasing and Summarizing, TWE p. 893 Drawing Conclusions, TWE pp. 899, 902, 903, 904 Fluency, TWE p. 903 Visualizing, TWE p. 893	Figurative Language, SE pp. 890, 893, 894, 895, 896, 897, 898, 899, 901, 902, 903, 906, 907, TWE pp. 891, 900
4	2	**Unit Wrap-Up, pp. 910–921** Your Turn: "Flinn, on the Bus" by Naomi Shahib Nye SE p. 912	Interpreting, TWE pp. 912, 913 Paraphrasing and Summarizing, TWE p. 912 Drawing Conclusions, TWE p. 913	Dialogue and Monologue, TWE p. 912 Fiction, TWE p. 914 Nonfiction, TWE p. 915

CRITICAL THINKING	VOCABULARY	WRITING AND GRAMMAR	LISTENING, SPEAKING, AND VIEWING
:valuate, SE pp. 858, 866 :xplain, SE p. 858 nalysis, SE p. 858, TWE p. 856 nfer, SE p. 866 redict, SE p. 866 :omprehension, TWE p. 855	Greek Roots, SE pp. 848, 851, TWE p. 852 Content-Area Words, SE pp. 860, 862, 864	Write About Your Reading, SE pp. 858, 866 Commas with Relative Clauses, SE p. 859 Commas with Direct Address, SE p. 867	Analyzing the Photo, SE p. 852 Viewing the Photo, TWE pp. 856, 863
	Using Exact Words, TWE p. 869	Applying Goood Writing Traits: Voice, SE p. 869 Dialogue, TWE p. 868 Characterization, TWE p. 870	Dramatizing Literature-Performance, SE p. 871
nterpret, SE p. 878 nalyze, SE p. 878)raw Conclusions, SE p. 878 nfer, SE p. 888 :xplain, SE p. 888 :valuate, SE p. 888, TWE p. 899 :omprehension, TWE pp. 883, 884, 887	Latin Roots, SE pp. 874, 877, 880, 883 Suffixes, TWE p. 880	Write About Your Reading, SE p. 878 Commas to Prevent Misreading or Confusion, SE p. 879 Commas with Dates and Addresses, SE p. 889	Analyzing the Photo, SE pp. 886, 898 Talk About Your Reading, SE p. 888 Viewing the Photo, TWE p. 886
:omprehension, TWE pp. 895, 896, 904 nfer, SE p. 909 Evaluate, SE p. 909	Historical Influences on English, SE pp. 892, 894, 898, 899, 900, 905, 906 Writing Sentences, TWE p. 892	Writing: Compare the Literature, SE p. 909	Analyzing the Photo, SE p. 904 Analyzing the Painting, SE p. 907
		Create a Newspaper Ad, SE p. 910 Write a Poem, SE p. 911	

UNIT 6
Unit Resources

Reading with Purpose offers a comprehensive package of tools to optimize student learning and the teaching experience. Each resource has been designed to assist students in specific areas and to offer instructional support for teachers. While all of these areas are covered in the core textbook, some students may need extra practice or additional help in specific areas. The resource package is designed so that you, the teacher, can choose which items will best assist your students. You may also use these resources as homework assignments and for assessment purposes. The following are resources recommended for use with Unit 6.

Keys for Unit Resources

- Blackline Master
- Workbook
- Supplemental Text
- CD-ROM
- DVD
- Transparency
- Web-based
- Fast File

Essential Instructional Support

FAST FILE UNIT 6 RESOURCES

Reading and Literature

- Academic Vocabulary Review
- Big Question: School to Home
- The Big Question Foldable
- Unit Challenge: Planner and Rubrics
- Comparing Literature Graphic Organizer
- Key Reading Skills
- Active Reading Graphic Organizers
- Literary Analysis
- Unit Vocabulary Review

Writing, Grammar, and Spelling

- Spelling and Handwriting Practice
- Grammar Practice
- Writing Workshop Graphic Organizer

Listening, Speaking, and Viewing

- Viewing and Representing
- Listening and Speaking

English Language Learners

- English Language Coach Review

DIFFERENTIATED INSTRUCTION

- Leveled Vocabulary Development
- Skill Level Up!™ A Language Arts Game
- Listening Library CD
- BookLink 3
- Literature Library Vocabulary Puzzlemaker
- Vocabulary Puzzlemaker

ASSESSMENT

- Selection and Unit Assessments
- Selection Quick Checks
- Assessment by Learning Objectives
- Rubrics for Assessing Student Writing, Listening, and Speaking
- Glencoe Online Essay Grader
- Interactive Tutor: Self-Assessment
- ExamView Assessment Suite
- Literature Library ExamView Assessment Suite

Additional Instructional Support

WRITING, GRAMMAR, AND SPELLING

- Real Success in Writing: Research and Reports
- Writing Constructed Responses
- Spelling Power eWorkbook
- Grammar & Composition Handbook
- Grammar and Language Workbook
- Revising with Style eWorkbook

READING AND LITERATURE

- Active Learning and Note Taking Guide
- inTime Magazines
- Backpack Reader Volume 1
- Literature Library
- Literature Launchers Pre-Reading Videos DVD
- Literature Classics

TRANSPARENCIES

- Read Aloud, Think Aloud Transparencies
- Literary and Text Analysis Transparencies
- Bellringer Options Transparencies
- Grammar and Writing Workshop Transparencies
- Fine Art Transparencies

ENGLISH LANGUAGE LEARNER

- English Language Coach
- Fluency Practice and Assessment
- inTime Magazines (Spanish)
- Spanish Listening Library CD

PROFESSIONAL DEVELOPMENT

- Professional Development Package

TECHNOLOGY

- TeacherWorks Plus™
- StudentWorks Plus™
- BookLink 3
- Skill Level Up!™ A Language Arts Game
- ExamView Assessment Suite
- Interactive Tutor: Self-Assessment
- Listening Library CD
- Spanish Listening Library CD
- Literature Classics
- Literature Launchers Pre-Reading Videos DVD
- Literature Library ExamView Assessment Suite
- Vocabulary Puzzlemaker
- Literature Library Vocabulary Puzzlemaker
- glencoe.com
- Online Student Edition
- Presentation Plus!
- Glencoe Online Essay Grader

Additional Glencoe Resources

Dinah Zike's Foldables

Foldables are three-dimensional, interactive graphic organizers that help students practice basic writing skills, review key vocabulary terms, and answer Big Questions. Every unit contains a foldable activity. You can find the pattern and directions for the Unit 6 Foldable in the Unit 6 Resources Fast Files booklet. You can use the foldables as they are presented or modify them to suit the needs of your students. More information about foldables for Unit 6 can be found on pages R8–R9.

Glencoe Literature Library

This collection of hardcover books includes full-length novels, novellas, plays and works of nonfiction. Each volume consists of at least one complete extended-length reading accompanied by several related readings from a broad range of genres. A separate Study Guide for each Glencoe Literature Library book provides teaching notes and reproducible activity pages for students.

Glencoe Literature Library titles that complement this unit include:

Anne Frank Remembered, by Miep Gies with Alison Leslie Gold
Bridge to Terabithia, by Katherine Paterson
Little Women, by Louisa May Alcott

For a wealth of online resources that support the instruction in Unit 6 of *Glencoe Literature: Reading with Purpose,* students and teachers can visit our Web site at www.glencoe.com. Students will find additional learning, practice, and assessment opportunities such as these, which are noted in the student text:

- **Big Question Overview**
- **Study Central**
- **Author Search**
- **Writing Models**
- **Interactive Literary Elements Handbook**
- **Web Activities**

Teachers will find planning and instructional tools that include the following:

- **Book Lesson Plans**
- **Teacher Forum**
- **Professional Development**
- **Web Activities Lesson Plans (with answers to student activities)**

Go to www.glencoe.com to see the entire selection of Reading with Purpose online resources.

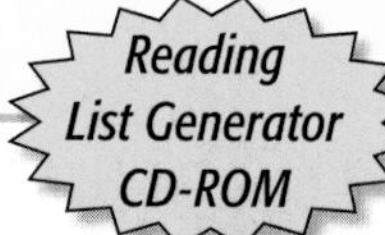

GLENCOE **BOOKLINK**

Use the Glencoe **BookLink 3** CD-ROM, a database of more than 26,700 titles, to *create customized reading lists* for your students.

- Search for award-winning titles, (e.g., Newbery Award winners, Coretta Scott King Award winners, and Caldecott Medal winners) and for books on several state-recommended reading lists.
- Find Degrees of Reading Power™ (DRP) and Lexile™ readability scores for all selections.
- Organize reading lists by students' reading level, author, genre, theme, or area of interest.
- Get a brief summary of each selection.

You can find recommended leveled readings for this unit with Reading on Your Own (see page 914).

Glencoe's **Presentation Plus!**, a multimedia teaching tool, lets you present dynamic lessons that will engage your students. Using Microsoft PowerPoint,® you can customize the presentations to create your own personalized lessons. Use **CheckPoint** questions with interactive response keypads to get immediate student feedback during lessons, to increase student participation, and to assess student comprehension.

A lively collection of articles drawn from issues of the TIME family of magazines helps students develop the skills they need to interact with informational text in a meaningful way. Each of the news stories, feature articles, reviews, profiles, and essays in the magazine connect to an author, work, or theme in *Glencoe Literature: Reading with Purpose.* Articles for Unit 6 are found in Volume B. See the *inTIME* Teacher's Guide for specific connections to each unit and for reproducible student worksheets designed to develop students' reading and critical thinking skills.

Literature Launchers

Set the scene with Glencoe's Literature Launchers, engaging video segments that introduce each unit's genre focus. Each video brings the genre to life, relating it to your students' worlds.

Insert the Glencoe Literature Launchers Pre-Reading Videos DVD into your DVD player. Select the Unit 6 Launcher from the menu to introduce the genre and Big Question for this unit.

Online Essay Grader

Use Glencoe's Online Essay Grader to score your students' writing and to provide individualized feedback to each student automatically.

You and your students can visit www.glencoe.com to link to the essay grader. *Students* can enter their essays and receive feedback on demand. *You* can manage demographic data, assign tests and generate individual student and aggregated reports. The essay grader can help you

- Save time with automatic scoring and individualized feedback.
- Supplement in-class writing instruction using guided writing practice.
- Get reports for individual students or for special populations.
- Track student improvement over time.

REAL Success: Reading Excellence at All Levels

Glencoe now provides all of your students with the tools they need to become better, more enthusiastic readers. The REAL Success suite of reading and language arts products encourages reading excellence by meeting the needs of students at all levels. Glencoe products that can be used in conjunction with Unit 6 include the following:

- Jamestown Literature: An Adapted Reader
- Jamestown *Reading Fluency*
- Jamestown *Critical Reading Series, In the Line of Duty*
- *Vocabulary Builder*
- *The Glencoe Reader, Course 3*

To order these products, call Glencoe at 1-800-USA-READ.

Teacher Wraparound Edition Key

Level Appropriate Code

AS = Activities for all students

AL = Activities for students working above grade level

OL = Activities for students working at grade level

BL = Activities for students working below grade level

EL = Activities for English language learners

Teacher Wraparound Prompts

R **Reading Skill** These activities help you teach reading comprehension skills .

V **Vocabulary** These activities help students comprehend words and incorporate them into their reading and writing.

C **Critical Thinking** These strategies help students apply and extend what they have learned.

BQ **BIG Question** These activities and questions prompt students to prepare to answer the Big Question.

W **Writing** These activities provide writing opportunities to help students practice writing and comprehend text.

L **Literary Element** These activities and questions help students comprehend selections and learn more about each genre.

E **Text Element** These activities help students comprehend text elements.

LSV **Listening, Speaking, Viewing** These activities help students practice listening, speaking, and viewing skills.

EL **English Language Coach** These skills help English language learners as well as students who need additional reading support.

Professional Development Center

From an Author:

Jeffrey Wilhelm

Preparing Students to Read Drama

Review conventions. There are several conventional features of scripts that should be reviewed before reading which can help students activate the correct expectations and infer tones, moods, intentions, purposes, and the like. These are:

Pre-reading/Framing Systems

- Titles (topics)
- Media (TV, stage, cinema, etc.)
- Cast (order, names, titles, class designations, physical descriptions)
- Genre tips (adventure, horror, documentary, etc.)

Setting Descriptions

- Settings (where the action takes place, the constraints that the setting and situation place on characters)
- Types of people living in this environment
- Social and historical situation and perspectives
- Cues of emotional mood and tone
- Descriptions embedded in dialogue

Technical Stage Directions

- Aural and visual cues: sounds, lighting, properties
- Description and movement of properties
- Cues for mood, tone, expectations, symbolic meanings

Character Cues from Dialogue

- Characters portrayed through dialogue (own and that of others)
- Character cues from tone, style, word choice, and voice
- Cues from subtext, purpose, and effect of language

Stage Directions/Descriptions of Characters

- Character portrayal from appearance
- Character portrayal from movements, gestures, body language, reactions of other characters
- Character portrayal from symbolic implications

Watch Performances. Dramatic scripts are not written to be read—except by producers, directors, and actors. They are written to be performed and experienced. Therefore it is important to watch versions of a script. You don't have to watch a whole performance, but you can select important and powerful scenes that can help students experience the script or consider important issues or ideas.

Teacher to Teacher

Sheila Blankenship
Schoarbar Middle School
Ketchikan, Alaska

I do in-depth historical lessons as well as literature lessons when teaching this unit. I use audiotapes of music from the 1930s and 1940s, and I show excerpts from *Schindler's List* and from videos that show the Jewish experience. At other times I have brought in speakers from the Jewish community or shown clips of Hitler giving speeches. I also show World War II footage and bring in *Life* magazine photographs, newspaper clippings, or posters. I want students to see many aspects of World War II and to see the power of courage, faith, and strength. Students are required to conduct a library and Internet search on World War II and how World War I contributed to World War II.

We discuss the move of the Frank family, then read the play. As a special project, students build a scale-model of the house where the Frank family hid from the Nazis.

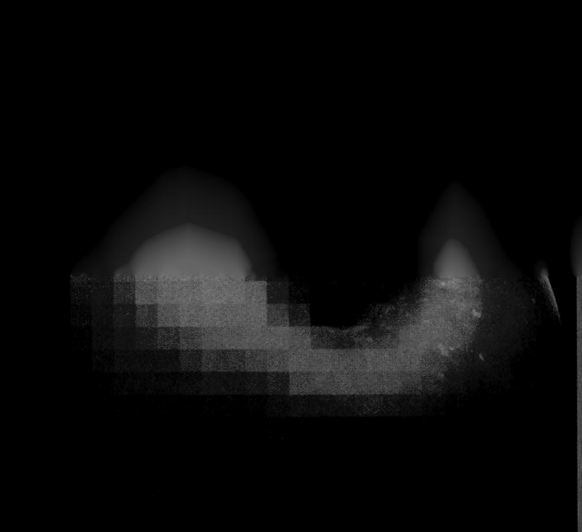

Using Dramatic Scripts

How can I help students learn to imagine a staged performance in their head as they read?

As always, the most important time to teach is before students undertake a challenge. One frontloading activity I use is designed to help students understand how the conventions of scripts help readers stage a play in their mind. Before reading a play, I have students translate cartoons into scripts for another group to perform. They quickly learn that many things that are obvious in a visual text must be described through various kinds of stage directions in a script. Through such activities, I can fairly quickly help students identify, read, and write the five cuing systems of scripts identified on the previous page.

I also have students watch performances. When I teach plays, I always watch video segments of one or even multiple versions of performances with my students. I also always watch major scenes in a play before we read the scene, since this provides background knowledge and frontloading that assists in the reading. After reading the scene, we can discuss how the director used or ignored particular stage directions and cues in the script.

How can putting on a production help students?

It is powerful to place students in the position of being producers, directors, actors, or critics. This gets them into the flow and makes them active participants using scripts. Get them to interpret, adapt, and perform scenes; make videos of scenes, ads, or promotions for a play; review and critique scripts and various professional interpretations. I especially like to bring in scripts of TV shows or popular movies (these are widely available on the Internet) to help students explore how their favorite shows or movies are scripted.

Students can also be asked to perform their own version of a scene or event. The performance could be set in their own school, or in another historical situation or setting. These can be contrasted with the video versions already viewed. Students can also be helped to compose and perform their own super-short plays or scenes that explore a major theme or issue from the reading in their own way or through their own experience.

Key Unit Objectives

- Answer the Big Question
- Identify and apply reading skills for drama
- Identify and apply the literary elements of drama
- Write a dramatic scene

BIG Question

Why Is It Important?
Addressing this big question helps students learn how to persist in the face of adversity.

Viewing the Photo
Lance Armstrong is one of the greatest cyclists of all time. He was diagnosed with cancer in 1996 but made a full recovery after surgery and other treatment. In 1997 he founded the Lance Armstrong Foundation, known for its yellow "Livestrong" bracelets. Armstrong returned to cycling in 1998 and in 1999 won the Tour de France, a 2,274-mile race that he eventually won six more times.
Ask: If you could ask Lance three questions, what would they be? *(Responses will vary.)* AS

UNIT 6

The BIG Question: How Do You Keep from Giving Up When Bad Things Happen?

"Even if I knew that tomorrow the world would go to pieces, I would still plant my apple tree."

—Martin Luther King Jr.
Baptist minister and Civil Rights leader
(1929–1968)

Unit Skills

BIG Question How do you keep from giving up when bad things happen?
Genre Focus: Drama

Reading Skills
- Drawing Conclusions, p. 732
- Interpreting, p. 794
- Paraphrasing and Summarizing, p. 846
- Visualizing, p. 872

Vocabulary
- Word Parts, p. 734
- Historical influences on English, p. 764
- Anglo Saxon Roots, p. 796
- Greek Roots, p. 848
- Content-Area Words, p. 860
- Latin Roots, p. 874

Literary Elements
- Act and Scene, p. 735
- Dialogue and Monologue, p. 765
- Mood, p. 825
- Stage Directions, p. 797

Writing Skills/Grammar
- Dramatic Scene, pp. 790, 868
- Voice, p. 869
- Commas with Introductory Words, Phrases, and Clauses, p. 793

LOOKING AHEAD

The skill lessons and readings in this unit will help you develop your own answer to the Big Question.

About the Reading

Each selection in this unit helps students address the question "How do you keep from giving up when bad things happen?" Students read about people who endure hardships but persevere with optimism and determination.

About the Skills

The skills taught in this unit have been selected because they are particularly helpful when reading the featured genre—drama. Each reading selection provides students with opportunities to practice and develop these skills.

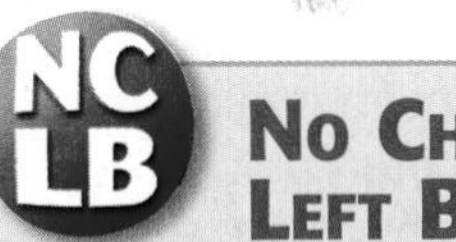

No Child Left Behind

Under No Child Left Behind, "English language learners will be assessed annually to measure how well they are learning English, so parents and teachers will know how well they are progressing." English Language Coach instruction and activities throughout the book are designed to help these students master English.

Differentiated Instruction

Respectful Listeners Because many of the selections in this unit are about tragedy or hardship, some students may wish to share personal stories that relate to the topics. Be sure to review with your students the boundaries about what is appropriate to discuss in a public forum. Remind students about the fundamentals of being a good, respectful listener, and establish an environment in which students feel comfortable sharing information that is suitable to the classroom setting. Be mindful that some students may be sensitive about some of the issues dealt with in the selections. Encourage students to share their thoughts and concerns with a trusted friend, relative, or counselor. AS

Indiana English/Language Arts Academic Standards
TWE: *Differentiated Instruction* 8.7

Focus

BELLRINGER Options

- **Literature Launcher**
- **Daily Language Practice Transparency 52**

Focus Activity Ask: How do you usually react when something bad happens to another person? *(Responses will vary.)* AS

Teach

R Reading Skill

Review Connecting To help students connect to the Big Question, ask them to write about helping someone who was going through a hard time. Provide these prompts:

- What did you do?
- What did you say?
- How did you help the person remain hopeful? OL

BQ BIG Question

- Have students look at the photos and read the profiles of Naomi and Chris and then write their journal entries.
- Have students tell what advice they would give Naomi and Chris. Ask them if writing the entry helped them come up with advice. OL

UNIT 6 WARM-UP

Connecting to The BIG Question

How Do You Keep from Giving Up When Bad Things Happen?

No matter how much we prepare for the future, we can't predict what will actually happen next. Unexpected events can often cause damage and hurt. But there are things we can do to help one another when we face hard times. In this unit, you'll read about how people remain hopeful when bad things happen. R

Real Kids and the Big Question

NAOMI has a very close family. They've always been together on holidays, but last year Naomi's brother Kyle went away to war. This year he's still away, and Naomi is upset by the things she sees on television. She feels scared and alone. What advice would you give her?

BQ

CHRIS lives in a neighborhood with many families. A few days ago, a storm destroyed some of the houses on his block. Chris's house is still in good shape, but several families have no home or food. What can Chris and his family do to help the people on his block?

Warm-Up Activity

On your own, write a journal entry from the point of view of Naomi or Chris. Explain how you feel and why.

Additional Support

Reading in the Real World

Citizenship Numerous organizations on both local and national levels support families of soldiers who are away at war, as well as the soldiers themselves. In addition, numerous organizations help victims of natural disasters such as hurricanes or earthquakes. Have students form small groups and conduct research on one organization that either Naomi or Chris could contact for support. Have students tell what the organization is and how it can help. Have them share their findings with the class. OL

You and the Big Question

Reading about how other people remain hopeful during difficult times will give you ideas that will help you answer this question. BQ

BIG Question Link to Web resources to further explore the Big Question at www.glencoe.com.

Plan for the Unit Challenge

At the end of the unit, you'll use notes from all your reading to complete the Unit Challenge, which will explore your answer to the Big Question.

You will choose one of the following activities:

A. Create a Newspaper Ad You'll work with classmates to write and design a newspaper ad in which you offer ways to help people in need.

B. Write a Poem Write a poem that is addressed to a person or people who have faced hard times.

- Start thinking about which activity you'd like to do so that you can focus your thoughts as you go through the unit.
- In your Learner's Notebook, write your ideas about the activity you'd like to do. Why did you choose that activity? Have you or a person you know ever gone through a difficult time?
- As you read each selection, take notes on how people act when they are faced with problems. In each case, think about what help or advice you would offer them.

Keep Track of Your Ideas

As you read, you'll make notes about the Big Question. Later, you'll use these notes to complete the Unit Challenge. See pages R8–R9 for help with making each Unit 6 Foldable. This diagram shows how each should look.

1. Make one Foldable for each workshop. Keep all of your Foldables for the unit in your Foldables folder.
2. On the bottom fold of your Foldable, write the workshop number and the Big Question.
3. Write the titles of the selections in the workshop on the front of the flaps—one title on each flap. For *Anne Frank,* add the act and scene numbers. (See page 709 for the titles.)
4. Open the flaps. At the very top of each flap, write **My Purpose for Reading.** Below each crease, write **The Big Question.**

Anne Frank
Act 2, Scenes 1–2

Anne Frank
Act 2, Scenes 3–5

Reading Workshop 2
How Do You Keep...

Teach

BQ 

Have students write about how their answer to the Big Question might change depending on the circumstances. AS

Have students use their Foldables to help them organize their thinking about the Big Question. For details about using Dinah Zike's Foldables, see pages R8–R9.

Assess/Close

Ask students to share their thoughts about why looking for an answer to the Big Question might be important.

Resources for page 711

- Use the Unit Challenge Planner BLM in the Unit 6 Resource Booklet, p. 36.
- Use the Foldable BLM in the Unit 6 Resource Booklet, p. 7.

Literature Focus Lesson

Tragedy Ask students to name and summarize poems, plays, short stories, or books about tragedy that they have read. Have them tell how the characters in the stories coped with the tragedy. OL Encourage students to consider which genres are appropriate to the topic of tragedy and perseverance. For example, prompt students to explain which is more powerful, reading a book about a tragedy or watching a movie about the same topic. AL

Indiana English/Language Arts Academic Standards
TWE: *Reading in the Real World* 8.2.5, *Literature Focus Lesson* 8.3

Focus

BELLRINGER Options

- **Selection Focus Transparency 13**
- **Daily Language Practice Transparency 53**

Focus Activity Ask: What do people mean when they say that their lives are full of *drama*? What does *drama* mean in this context? *(Possible response: In this context,* drama *means that the people have had many crises, conflicts, or intense emotions.)* OL

Teach

R Reading Skill

How to Read Drama

Ask: How might each of the reading skills be useful in reading drama? *(Possible responses: **Drawing Conclusions:** Making generalizations about what you read helps you understand the drama more fully. **Interpreting:** Figuring out what the author is really saying helps you understand the overall message. **Paraphrasing and Summarizing:** These skills help you understand and remember what you read. **Visualizing:** Picturing the characters, places, and events in your mind makes a play come alive.)* OL

UNIT 6 GENRE FOCUS: DRAMA

A **drama** is any story performed for an audience. The word *drama* is used two ways. It can refer to (a) a serious play or (b) any kind of play—comedy or tragedy; musical or not; stage, TV, film, or Internet; long or short.

Skills Focus

- Key skills for reading a drama
- Key literary elements of dramas

Skills Model

You will see how to use the key reading skills and literary elements as you read the first two scenes of

- ***The Diary of Anne Frank,*** p. 713

Why Read Drama?

When you see a play performed, the characters and their actions are right in front of you. The director, actors, and designers have already made many decisions that affect your understanding and enjoyment of the drama. Reading a play is different from seeing one. For the most part, you must "hear" it through the characters' speeches and use imagination to "see" the action. As a result, you make your own judgments.

Reading plays can help you make inferences, draw conclusions, and see how and why people grow and change. Some dramas, like *The Diary of Anne Frank,* also give you insight into historical periods and events.

How to Read Drama

Key Reading Skills

R

These reading skills are especially useful tools for reading and understanding drama. You'll learn more about these later in this unit.

- **Drawing Conclusions** As you read, use details about characters, ideas, and events to form general ideas. (See Reading Workshop 1.)
- **Interpreting** Using what you already know about yourself and the world, ask what the author is really saying. (See Reading Workshop 2.)
- **Paraphrasing and Summarizing** To make sure that you understand what you read, retell the main points about characters, ideas, and events in logical order and in your own words. (See Reading Workshop 3.)
- **Visualizing** Picture the characters, ideas, and events in your mind. (See Reading Workshop 4.)

Key Literary Elements

Recognizing and thinking about the following literary elements will help you understand more fully what a playwright is telling you. To learn more about them, see *The Diary of Anne Frank.*

- **Act and scene:** the major divisions of a play (See act 1, scene 3.)
- **Dialogue and monologue:** the words that the characters say to one another (See act 1, scenes 4–5.)
- **Stage directions:** descriptions of the settings, characters, sounds, and actions in a play script (See act 2, scenes 1–2.)
- **Mood:** the emotional effect a drama has on its audience (See act 2, scenes 3–5.)

Indiana English/Language Arts Academic Standards (pp. 700–731)

8.2 Comprehension and Analysis (Focus on Informational Text) Develop [reading] strategies... **8.3 Comprehension and Analysis of Literary Text** Respond to grade-level-appropriate literature... **8.3.2** Evaluate the structural elements of plot... **8.3.6** Identify significant literary devices...

For a complete description of the standards, see p. IN 11.

Additional Support

Literature Focus Lesson

Play Point out that plays have their own special format. Generally, all the characters in the play will be listed at the beginning under "Characters." Often, a description of the scene, and perhaps of the actors, will follow. Each character's name will often appear in caps, followed by a period and his or her dialogue. This allows actors to easily see their lines when practicing for a play. Have students scan *The Diary of Anne Frank* to see whether these play elements are included. BL

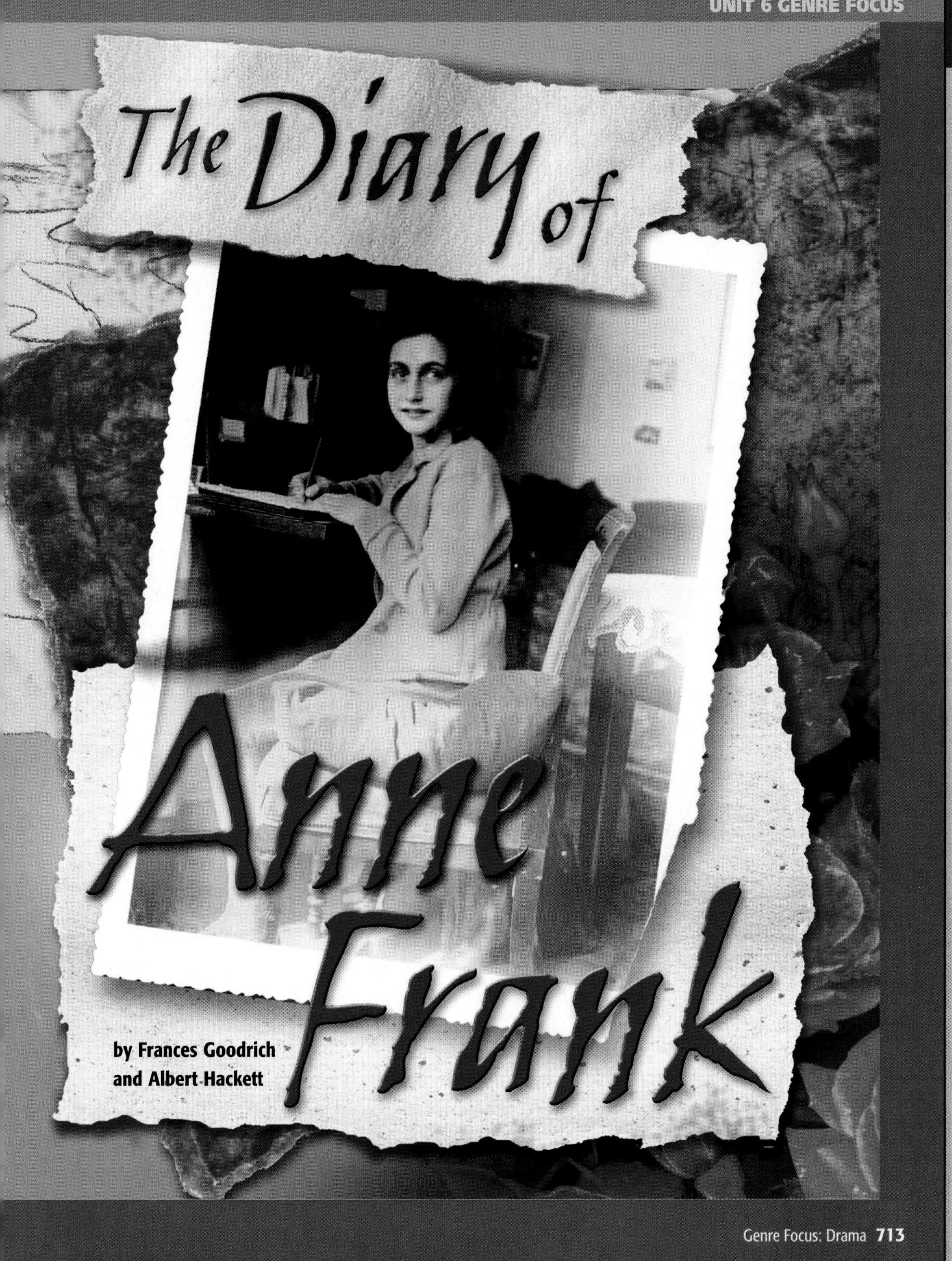

Teach

Viewing the Photo

Ask: How old do you think Anne Frank looks in the photograph? *(Responses will vary. Students may guess that she is between twelve and fifteen years old.)* **AS** **Ask:** How is this artwork arranged? *(Possible responses: It is a collage; it looks as if pieces of scrap paper and a photograph have been cut out and glued together.)* **OL** **Ask:** Considering that the title has the word "Diary" in it, why might the artwork look like a tattered collage of scraps and a photograph? *(Possible response: Anne Frank appears to be writing; maybe she wrote her diary on scrap paper, and perhaps it was torn, damaged, or survived destruction.)* **AL**

Differentiated Instruction

Collage Have students use the art shown here to design and make cover illustrations for their own diaries. Instruct them to include a personal photograph with their cover, and provide them with magazines to cut out additional images that reflect their personalities. Simply have students cut out photographs and other scraps to form the title "The Diary of [Insert Name]" and glue them onto construction paper. If students do not have access to personal photographs, encourage them to cut out other pictures from magazines or newspapers about sports, hobbies, or other activities that interest them. **AS**

Indiana English/Language Arts Academic Standards

SE: 8.2, 8.3, 8.3.2, 8.3.6
TWE: *Literature Focus Lesson* 8.3, *Differentiated Instruction* 8.7.9

Teach

L1 Literary Element

Stage Directions **Say:** In your own words, describe the scene. *(Possible response: The scene is three rooms and a tiny attic on the top floor of a warehouse. There is a bathroom, a few pieces of furniture, a sink, a gas ring for cooking, and a stove for warmth. The door to the rest of the building has been hidden by a bookcase.)* OL

Ask: Which details tell you the scene is a hideout? *(The windows are painted over or covered with curtains; the door has been concealed.)* AL

L2 Literary Element

Stage Directions **Ask:** To whom does the word *we* refer in this part of the stage directions: "When the door is opened we see that it has been concealed . . ."? *(Possible response: The word* we *refers to the audience or to readers.)* OL

Readability Scores
Dale-Chall: 4.0
DRP: N/A
Lexile: N/A

CHARACTERS

Mr. Frank	Peter Van Daan	Anne Frank
Miep	Mrs. Frank	Mr. Kraler
Mrs. Van Daan	Margot Frank	Mr. Dussel
Mr. Van Daan		

The notes in the side columns model how to use the skills and elements you read about on page 712.

Drama

ACTIVE READING MODEL

ACT 1 — SCENE 1

[The scene remains the same throughout the play. It is the top floor of a warehouse and office building in Amsterdam, Holland. The sharply peaked roof of the building is outlined against a sea of other rooftops, stretching away into the distance. Nearby is the belfry of a church tower, the Westertoren, whose carillon[1] *rings out the hours. Occasionally faint sounds float up from below: the voices of children playing in the street, the tramp of marching feet, a boat whistle from the canal.* 1

The three rooms of the top floor and a small attic space above are exposed to our view. The largest of the rooms is in the center, with two small rooms, slightly raised, on either side. On the right is a bathroom, out of sight. A narrow steep flight of stairs at the back leads up to the attic. The rooms are sparsely furnished with a few chairs, cots, a table or two. The windows are painted over, or covered with makeshift blackout curtains.[2] *In the main room there is a sink, a gas ring for cooking and a wood-burning stove for warmth.*

The room on the left is hardly more than a closet. There is a skylight in the sloping ceiling. Directly under this room is a small steep stairwell, with steps leading down to a door. This is the only entrance from the building below. When the door is opened we see that it has been concealed on the outer side by a bookcase attached to it.

The curtain rises on an empty stage. It is late afternoon, November, 1945.

The rooms are dusty, the curtains in rags. Chairs and tables are overturned.

The door at the foot of the small stairwell swings open. MR. FRANK *comes up the steps into view. He is a gentle, cultured*

1 Key Literary Element
Stage Directions *It's "scene 1," so there are other scenes, but the directions say "the scene remains the same." I guess that must mean that the same set is used for the whole play.*

1. A ***belfry*** is the tower of a church or other building in which a bell is hung. A ***carillon*** (KAIR uh lawn) is a set of bells sounded by machinery, rather than rung manually.
2. ***Blackout curtains*** were used to hide room lights from enemy bombers.

Additional Support

Literature Focus Lesson

Frame Story A frame story is one in which a story is told within a story. Tell students that this play begins and ends in 1945, with Mr. Frank, a Jewish businessman, visiting the attic in Amsterdam where he, his family, and four others spent twenty-five months hiding from the Nazis. The story of this visit "frames" the story of the actual stay in the attic, which occurred from 1942–1944. Point out that one of the purposes of the frame story is to show how Anne's diary is found. Have students note how the playwrights use portions of Anne's diary to transition from scene to scene. OL

ACTIVE READING MODEL

European in his middle years. There is still a trace of a German accent in his speech.

He stands looking slowly around, making a supreme effort at self-control. He is weak, ill. His clothes are threadbare.[3]

After a second he drops his rucksack on the couch and moves slowly about. He opens the door to one of the smaller rooms, and then abruptly closes it again, turning away. He goes to the window at the back, looking off at the Westertoren as its carillon strikes the hour of six, then he moves restlessly on. From the street below we hear the sound of a barrel organ and children's voices at play. There is a many-colored scarf hanging from a nail. MR. FRANK *takes it, putting it around his neck. As he starts back for his rucksack, his eye is caught by something lying on the floor. It is a woman's white glove. He holds it in his hand and suddenly all of his self-control is gone. He breaks down, crying.*

We hear footsteps on the stairs. MIEP GIES[4] *comes up, looking for* MR. FRANK. MIEP *is a Dutch girl of about twenty-two. She wears a coat and hat, ready to go home. She is pregnant. Her attitude toward* MR. FRANK *is protective, compassionate.*] 2 3

MIEP. Are you all right, Mr. Frank?

MR. FRANK. [*Quickly controlling himself.*] Yes, Miep, yes.

MIEP. Everyone in the office has gone home . . . It's after six. [*Then pleading.*] Don't stay up here, Mr. Frank. What's the use of torturing yourself like this?

MR. FRANK. I've come to say good-bye . . . I'm leaving here, Miep. 4

MIEP. What do you mean? Where are you going? Where?

MR. FRANK. I don't know yet. I haven't decided.

MIEP. Mr. Frank, you can't leave here! This is your home! Amsterdam is your home. Your business is here, waiting for you . . . You're needed here . . . Now that the war is over, there are things that . . .

2 Key Reading Skill
Interpreting *Mr. Frank is really upset by this place and by the glove. Maybe it belongs to his wife or to Anne, but why does it make him sad?*

3 Key Literary Element
Stage Directions *The whole section in italics is stage directions. They give really good descriptions, especially of the rooms and Mr. Frank. I didn't know stage directions would be so detailed, even about sounds.*

4 Key Literary Element
Dialogue and Monologue *I see. Dialogue is like conversation in a short story, but the speeches don't have quotation marks. It's clear who's speaking because the speaker is identified at the beginning of each speech.*

3. Clothes that are ***threadbare*** are so old or worn that the threads can be seen.
4. ***Miep Gies*** (meep gees)

Teach

R Reading Skill

Interpreting **Ask:** Why might Mr. Frank "[open] the door to one of the smaller rooms, and then abruptly [close] it again, turning away"? *(Possible response: The room may remind Mr. Frank of something painful.)* OL

C Critical Thinking

Comprehension To help students understand the context of the play, have them read the "Build Background" information on page 735. **Ask:** Why does Mr. Frank return to the place where his family hid? *(He says he returns to say goodbye.)* BL

L Literary Element

Dialogue and Monologue **Ask:** What do you learn about Miep and Mr. Frank from their dialogue? *(Possible responses: They know each other well; Mr. Frank is leaving but doesn't know where he's going; Miep wants Mr. Frank to stay; the war is over.)* OL

Literature Focus Lesson

Stage Directions Plays frequently begin with lengthy stage directions. Explain to students that these opening stage directions often "set the scene" in the same way that films introduce the audience to the setting during the opening sequence. Ask students, "In addition to the actual setting of the play, what else do these stage directions describe?" *(They describe Mr. Frank's appearance and actions and Miep Gies's appearance.)* OL Instruct students to write their own "stage directions" for the opening scene of their favorite movie. AL

Indiana English/Language Arts Academic Standards
SE: 8.2, 8.3.6
TWE: *Literature Focus Lesson* 8.3.2, *Literature Focus Lesson* 8.3

Teach

R1 Reading Skill

Drawing Conclusions
Say: Mr. Frank has just asked Miep to burn the papers. Why would he want to burn them without looking at them? *(Possible response: The papers might remind him of a painful past, or difficult memories.)* OL

R2 Reading Skill

Interpreting **Ask:** What does Mr. Frank mean when he asks, "Is it possible, Miep?" *(Possible responses: He might be surprised to see that the diary survived whatever chaos befell the room. Mr. Frank cannot believe that Anne's first diary entry was written only three years ago; it seems as though more time has passed since the Franks went into hiding.)* OL

ACTIVE READING MODEL

MR. FRANK. I can't stay in Amsterdam, Miep. It has too many memories for me. Everywhere there's something . . . the house we lived in . . . the school . . . that street organ playing out there . . . I'm not the person you used to know, Miep. I'm a bitter old man. [*Breaking off.*] Forgive me. I shouldn't speak to you like this . . . after all that you did for us . . . the suffering . . .

MIEP. No. No. It wasn't suffering. You can't say we suffered.

[*As she speaks, she straightens a chair which is overturned.*]

MR. FRANK. I know what you went through, you and Mr. Kraler.[5] I'll remember it as long as I live. [*He gives one last look around.*] Come, Miep.

[*He starts for the steps, then remembers his rucksack, going back to get it.*]

MIEP. [*Hurrying up to a cupboard.*] Mr. Frank, did you see? There are some of your papers here. [*She brings a bundle of papers to him.*] We found them in a heap of rubbish on the floor after . . . after you left. R1

MR. FRANK. Burn them. 5

[*He opens his rucksack to put the glove in it.*]

MIEP. But, Mr. Frank, there are letters, notes . . .

MR. FRANK. Burn them. All of them.

MIEP. Burn this?

[*She hands him a paperbound notebook.*]

MR. FRANK. [*Quietly.*] Anne's diary. [*He opens the diary and begins to read.*] "Monday, the sixth of July, nineteen forty-two." [*To* MIEP.] Nineteen forty-two. Is it possible, Miep? . . . Only three years ago. [*As he continues his reading, he sits down on the couch.*] "Dear Diary, since you and I are going to be great friends, I will start by telling you about myself. My name is Anne Frank. I am thirteen years old. I R2

5 Key Reading Skill
Drawing Conclusions
The war is over, and Mr. Frank is upset by memories that have to do with this place.

5. ***Kraler*** (KRAW lur)

Additional Support

Reading in the Real World

Career The process of writing a play can be quite different from that of writing a short story or novel. Playwrights often begin with a very rough draft of dialogue that is "workshopped," or read aloud by actors. The playwright will take notes and then use feedback from the workshop to revise and rewrite. Have students tell why a playwright might "workshop" a script. *(Possible response: Because plays are generally performed, not read, it might be helpful for a writer to hear actors reading his or her draft aloud.)* OL

ACTIVE READING MODEL

was born in Germany the twelfth of June, nineteen twenty-nine. As my family is Jewish, we emigrated to Holland when Hitler came to power.[6]"

[As MR. FRANK *reads on, another voice joins his, as if coming from the air. It is* ANNE'S VOICE.]

MR. FRANK AND ANNE. "My father started a business, importing spice and herbs. Things went well for us until nineteen forty. Then the war came, and the Dutch capitulation, followed by the arrival of the Germans.[7] Then things got very bad for the Jews."

[MR. FRANK'S *voice dies out.* ANNE'S VOICE *continues alone. The lights dim slowly to darkness. The curtain falls on the scene.*] 6

ANNE'S VOICE. You could not do this and you could not do that. They forced Father out of his business. We had to wear yellow stars.[8] I had to turn in my bike. I couldn't go to a Dutch school any more. I couldn't go to the movies, or ride in an automobile, or even on a streetcar, and a million other things. But somehow we children still managed to have fun. Yesterday Father told me we were going into hiding. Where, he wouldn't say. At five o'clock this morning Mother woke me and told me to hurry and get dressed. I was to put on as many clothes as I could. It would look too suspicious if we walked along carrying suitcases. It wasn't until we were on our way that I learned where we were going. Our hiding place was to be upstairs in the building where Father used to have his business. Three other people were coming in with us . . . the Van Daans and their son Peter . . . Father knew the Van Daans but we had never met them . . . L

[During the last lines the curtain rises on the scene. The lights dim on. ANNE'S VOICE *fades out.*] 7

6 **Key Literary Elements**

Stage Directions; Act and Scene There are three reasons for having Anne's voice heard in darkness. First, it gives the actors and crew time to prepare the new scene. Second, a "blackout" often signals a time change, just as in a movie. Third, the blackout forces the audience to focus on Anne's words.

7 **Key Reading Skill**

Paraphrasing and Summarizing *Let's see if I can summarize this scene. Mr. Frank is in the place where his family hid during the war. The Franks are Jews who moved to Holland because of Hitler. When Hitler took over Holland too, things got worse. Mr. Frank's friend Miep finds a notebook. It's the diary that Mr. Frank's daughter Anne started when the family came here three years ago.* R

6. Thousands of German Jews left the country after Adolf ***Hitler*** became the head of government in 1933.

7. Germany began its invasion of the Netherlands on May 10, 1940, and, within a few days, forced the Dutch army's surrender, or ***capitulation*** (kuh pich uh LAY shun).

8. The Nazis ordered Jews to wear ***yellow stars*** at all times for easy identification. The six-pointed Star of David is a religious symbol of the Jewish people.

UNIT 6 GENRE FOCUS

Teach

L Literary Element

Dialogue and Monologue

Ask: What important information do you learn during Anne's monologue? *(Possible response: You learn that life for Jews in Holland after the Germans arrived was very restricted and scary and that Anne's family had to go into hiding. You also learn that the Van Daans and their son Peter had to go into hiding with the Franks.)* OL

R Reading Skill

Paraphrasing and Summarizing

Ask: Why might it be helpful to summarize the information in the play at this point? *(Possible response: To keep the characters straight and review what has happened.)* BL **Say:** Summarize, or restate the play in your own words up to this point. *(Responses will vary.)* OL **Say:** Paraphrase life for the Franks before 1940. *(Possible response: The Franks lived in Germany, but, being Jewish, they emigrated to Holland when Hitler came to power. Mr. Frank had a successful business importing spices and herbs—the family seemed to be doing well until 1940.)* AL

Differentiated Instruction

Star of David Draw these popular symbols on the board and ask students to identify them: ℞ *(pharmacy)*, ☠ *(poison—or piracy)*, ☯ *(Taoist yin-yang—equilibrium in the universe)*. Now draw on the board: ✡. Explain that *The Magen David,* or "Star of David," appears on synagogues, Jewish tombstones, and the flag of the state of Israel. In antiquity, the symbol was used by many people, not just Jews, as a decoration. During the middle ages, Jews began using the sign more frequently, but it wasn't until the 17th century that it became a symbol of Judaism. Discuss with students both the positive and negative effects of identifying a group of people with a symbol—religious or not. OL

Indiana English/Language Arts Academic Standards

SE: 8.3, 8.3.6

TWE: *Reading in the Real World* 8.4

Teach

Viewing the Photo

Say: Reread the translation of Anne's handwritten note. What does it show about her personality? *(Responses will vary. Some students may say that Anne must have been an energetic, ambitious, outgoing person to have wanted to go to Hollywood. Others may say that she was typical of others her age.)* **OL**

L1 Literary Element

Act and Scene **Ask:** How do you know that this is a new scene? *(The new scene is labeled "Scene 2." There is also a time shift from 1945 to 1942. Though the scenes take place in the same rooms, in Scene 1 they are dusty and messy, and in Scene 2 they are clean and orderly.)* **BL**

L2 Literary Element

Stage Directions **Ask:** What do you learn about the Van Daans at the beginning of this scene? *(Mr. Van Daan is nervous, and he is wearing expensive clothing. Mrs. Van Daan is pretty and is also wearing expensive clothing. Peter is 16 years old. He is shy and awkward.)* **OL**

Anne Frank, 1942.

Analyzing the Photo In her handwritten note, Anne mentions her desire to go to Hollywood. As you read, think about how Anne's dreams are similar to or different from your own.

ACTIVE READING MODEL

SCENE 2

L1

[It is early morning, July, 1942. The rooms are bare, as before, but they are now clean and orderly.

MR. VAN DAAN, a tall, portly man in his late forties, is in the main room, pacing up and down, nervously smoking a cigarette. His clothes and overcoat are expensive and well cut.

MRS. VAN DAAN sits on the couch, clutching her possessions, a hatbox, bags, etc. She is a pretty woman in her early forties. She wears a fur coat over her other clothes.

PETER VAN DAAN is standing at the window of the room on the right, looking down at the street below. He is a shy, awkward boy of sixteen. He wears a cap, a raincoat, and long Dutch trousers, like "plus fours."[9] *At his feet is a black case, a carrier for his cat.* 8

8 **Key Literary Element**
Stage Directions *So we went back in time from November 1945 to July 1942. And there are new characters.* L2

9. ***Dutch trousers*** and ***plus fours*** are pants that end at or a few inches below the knees.

Additional Support

Reading Fluency

Build Fluency Have students use the descriptive stage directions on this page to practice reading aloud. Although stage directions are not meant to be read aloud, these sentences contain many commas and provide good practice in pausing appropriately. Explain that a short pause is required when a comma separates two modifying adjectives (as in the phrase "a tall, portly man"). Such a pause is shorter than the pause following end punctuation. Read the stage directions aloud once so that students can hear the rhythm and flow of the sentences. Have students read individually to build fluency. **EL** **BL**

ACTIVE READING MODEL

The yellow Star of David is conspicuous[10] *on all of their clothes.*]

MRS. VAN DAAN. [*Rising, nervous, excited.*] Something's happened to them! I know it!

MR. VAN DAAN. Now, Kerli!

MRS. VAN DAAN. Mr. Frank said they'd be here at seven o'clock. He said . . .

MR. VAN DAAN. They have two miles to walk. You can't expect . . .

MRS. VAN DAAN. They've been picked up. That's what's happened. They've been taken . . . 9

[*MR. VAN DAAN indicates that he hears someone coming.*]

MR. VAN DAAN. You see?

[*PETER takes up his carrier and his schoolbag, etc., and goes into the main room as MR. FRANK comes up the stairwell from below. MR. FRANK looks much younger now. His movements are brisk, his manner confident. He wears an overcoat and carries his hat and a small cardboard box. He crosses to the VAN DAANS, shaking hands with each of them.*]

MR. FRANK. Mrs. Van Daan, Mr. Van Daan, Peter. [*Then, in explanation of their lateness.*] There were too many of the Green Police[11] on the streets . . . we had to take the long way around.

[*Up the steps come MARGOT FRANK, MRS. FRANK, MIEP (not pregnant now), and MR. KRALER. All of them carry bags, packages, and so forth. The Star of David is conspicuous on all of the FRANKS' clothing. MARGOT is eighteen, beautiful, quiet, shy. MRS. FRANK is a young mother, gently bred, reserved. She, like MR. FRANK, has a slight German accent. MR. KRALER is a Dutchman, dependable, kindly. As MR. KRALER and MIEP go upstage*[12] *to put down their parcels, MRS. FRANK turns back to call ANNE.*]

C

L

9 Key Literary Element
Mood *It's hard to get the mood of this scene yet, but the Van Daans make me nervous for some reason.*

10. Something that is ***conspicuous*** (kun SPIK yoo us) stands out in an obvious way.
11. One branch of the Nazi police force was called the ***Green Police*** because its members wore green uniforms.
12. ***Upstage*** is toward the back of the stage; ***downstage*** is the front, near the audience.

Teach

C Critical Thinking

Comprehension Ask: What are Mrs. and Mr. Van Daan doing in this scene? *(waiting for the Franks)* **BL** **Ask:** Why is Mrs. Van Daan nervous? *(Possible responses: She fears the Franks will not arrive. She's afraid they've been picked up by the Germans.)* **OL**

L Literary Element

Stage Directions Ask: What information do these stage directions give? *(Possible response: They explain how the characters are supposed to move on the stage, and they also give details about how the characters are supposed to look and act.)* **OL**

English Language Coach

Ellipsis Points in Dialogue
Three periods, known as ellipsis points, indicate that one or more words have been omitted. Ellipses used in dialogue, indicate that a character is pausing or trailing off, usually because he or she is troubled, distracted, or anxious. Examine the use of ellipses on this page and instruct students in how to use ellipses properly. Remind students that although ellipses are used informally as "filler" (as in e-mail and online chat), they should be used sparingly in formal writing. **OL** Have students write three sentences in which they use ellipses correctly. **AL**

Indiana English/Language Arts Academic Standards
SE: 8.3.6
TWE: *Reading Fluency* 8.7, *English Language Coach* 8.6.5

Teach

L Literary Element

Mood **Ask:** What do you notice about how the Franks act, despite the tense mood? *(Possible response: The Franks make an effort to show good manners. Mr. Frank introduces his wife and children courteously, and Anne gives a polite curtsy when she meets Mr. Van Daan.)* **Ask:** How does Mrs. Van Daan add to the tension? *(Possible response: She worries that they'll be caught because the ration books will have their names on them. She is very nervous.)* OL

R Reading Skill

Interpreting **Ask:** What does Mr. Frank mean when he says that the group will have plenty of leisure to arrange everything? *(Possible response: He means that the families will be in the attic for a long time with nothing to do.)* OL

ACTIVE READING MODEL

MRS. FRANK. Anne?

[*ANNE comes running up the stairs. She is thirteen, quick in her movements, interested in everything, mercurial*[13] *in her emotions. She wears a cape, long wool socks and carries a schoolbag.*]

MR. FRANK. [*Introducing them.*] My wife, Edith. Mr. and Mrs. Van Daan [*MRS. FRANK hurries over, shaking hands with them.*] . . . their son, Peter . . . my daughters, Margot and Anne.

[*ANNE gives a polite little curtsy as she shakes MR. VAN DAAN's hand. Then she immediately starts off on a tour of investigation of her new home, going upstairs to the attic room. MIEP and MR. KRALER are putting the various things they have brought on the shelves.*]

MR. KRALER. I'm sorry there is still so much confusion. 10

MR. FRANK. Please. Don't think of it. After all, we'll have plenty of leisure to arrange everything ourselves.

MIEP. [*To MRS. FRANK.*] We put the stores of food you sent in here. Your drugs are here . . . soap, linen here.

MRS. FRANK. Thank you, Miep.

MIEP. I made up the beds . . . the way Mr. Frank and Mr. Kraler said. [*She starts out.*] Forgive me. I have to hurry. I've got to go to the other side of town to get some ration books[14] for you.

MRS. VAN DAAN. Ration books? If they see our names on ration books, they'll know we're here.

MR. KRALER. There isn't anything . . .

MIEP. Don't worry. Your names won't be on them. [*As she hurries out.*] I'll be up later.

MR. FRANK. Thank you, Miep.

10 Key Literary Element
Mood *The mood is still pretty confused too, but I guess that's natural with everyone coming and going and unpacking.*

13. Anne is described as ***mercurial*** (mur KYUR ee ul) because her emotions change quickly and unpredictably, like the mercury in a thermometer.

14. ***Ration books*** contain coupons that people use to buy a limited amount of food and supplies.

Additional Support

English Language Coach

Old Words Because several words on this page are no longer commonly used, they may be unfamiliar to English language students. Point out and define these words:

- **Cape:** a long cloak, a sleeveless coat
- **Curtsy:** an action in which someone (usually a girl) bends her knees as an act of respect
- **Stores of food:** supplies of food

As they read the play, have students compile and define a class list of other terms that are no longer commonly used. EL BL OL

ACTIVE READING MODEL

R1

MRS. FRANK. [*To* MR. KRALER.] It's illegal, then, the ration books? We've never done anything illegal.

MR. FRANK. We won't be living here exactly according to regulations.

[*As* MR. KRALER *reassures* MRS. FRANK, *he takes various small things, such as matches, soap, etc., from his pockets, handing them to her.*]

R2

MR. KRALER. This isn't the black market, Mrs. Frank. This is what we call the white market[15] . . . helping all of the hundreds and hundreds who are hiding out in Amsterdam. **11**

11 Key Reading Skill
Drawing Conclusions *Who is helping the hundreds of others in hiding? Miep and Mr. Kraler can't look out for them all, but they must know some of the other helpers.*

[*The carillon is heard playing the quarter-hour before eight.* MR. KRALER *looks at his watch.* ANNE *stops at the window as she comes down the stairs.*]

ANNE. It's the Westertoren!

MR. KRALER. I must go. I must be out of here and downstairs in the office before the workmen get here. [*He starts for the stairs leading out.*] Miep or I, or both of us, will be up each day to bring you food and news and find out what your needs are. Tomorrow I'll get you a better bolt for the door at the foot of the stairs. It needs a bolt that you can throw yourself and open only at our signal. [*To* MR. FRANK.] Oh . . . You'll tell them about the noise?

MR. FRANK. I'll tell them.

MR. KRALER. Good-bye then for the moment. I'll come up again, after the workmen leave.

Miep Gies, 1931.

Analyzing the Photo This is Miep eleven years before she helped the Franks hide. What can you tell about her from this portrait?

15. In the ***black market,*** goods were sold illegally, usually at very high prices. In the ***white market,*** which also violated Nazi laws, goods were donated by people who wanted to help the Jews.

Teach

R1 Reading Skill

Drawing Conclusions **Ask:** On the basis of Mrs. Frank's question and comment about the ration books, what is one conclusion that you can draw about her? *(Possible response: She is a law-abiding person who thinks that following the rules is important.)* **BL** **OL**

R2 Reading Skill

Interpreting **Ask:** Why must Miep and Mr. Kraler bring food and news to the Franks and the Van Daans? *(They are now in hiding. They cannot be seen in public, so Miep and Mr. Kraler must bring them everything they need.)* **OL** **Ask:** Why does Mr. Kraler refer to providing these goods through the "white market," as opposed to the "black market?" *(Possible response: Sometimes, but not always, black is considered a symbolic color of evil and white is considered a symbol color of good. In this case, the black market is illegal, and possibly considered of a darker nature, whereas the white market signifies a good cause.)* **AL**

Differentiated Instruction

Group Research Organize the class into several groups and assign each group one of these research topics: The Nazi regime; victims of the Holocaust; life in Holocaust ghettos; Holocaust liberators and rescuers. Allow students to conduct research during class time and encourage them to finish their research after school in a library or at home. Have students create a poster of their information including photographs and visual aids to present to the class. **OL** Encourage students to create a handout to accompany their presentations. **AL**

Indiana English/Language Arts Academic Standards
SE: 8.2, 8.3.6
TWE: *English Language Coach* 8.1.3, *Differentiated Instruction* 8.7.12, *Reading Skill* 8.2.9

Teach

R Reading Skill

Drawing Conclusions **Ask:** What can you conclude about Mr. Frank from Mr. Kraler's comment about him having to go into hiding? *(Possible response: You can conclude he is a good man who is well-respected.)* OL

L Literary Element

Stage Directions **Ask:** Why do you think the playwrights repeatedly call attention to the yellow Star of David on the Franks' clothing? *(Responses will vary. Students may suggest that the playwrights want to emphasize the Star of David because it is a symbol of how Jewish people were singled out by the Nazis.)* AL

ACTIVE READING MODEL

MR. FRANK. Good-bye, Mr. Kraler.

MRS. FRANK. [*Shaking his hand.*] How can we thank you?

[*The others murmur their good-byes.*]

MR. KRALER. I never thought I'd live to see the day when a man like Mr. Frank would have to go into hiding. When you think— 12

[*He breaks off, going out.* MR. FRANK *follows him down the steps, bolting the door after him. In the interval before he returns,* PETER *goes over to* MARGOT*, shaking hands with her. As* MR. FRANK *comes back up the steps,* MRS. FRANK *questions him anxiously.*]

MRS. FRANK. What did he mean, about the noise?

MR. FRANK. First let us take off some of these clothes.

[*They all start to take off garment after garment. On each of their coats, sweaters, blouses, suits, dresses, is another yellow Star of David.* MR. *and* MRS. FRANK *are underdressed quite simply. The others wear several things, sweaters, extra dresses, bathrobes, aprons, nightgowns, etc.*] L

MR. VAN DAAN. It's a wonder we weren't arrested, walking along the streets . . . Petronella with a fur coat in July . . . and that cat of Peter's crying all the way.

ANNE. [*As she is removing a pair of panties.*] A cat?

MRS. FRANK. [*Shocked.*] Anne, please!

ANNE. It's all right. I've got on three more.

[*She pulls off two more. Finally, as they have all removed their surplus clothes, they look to* MR. FRANK*, waiting for him to speak.*]

MR. FRANK. Now. About the noise. While the men are in the building below, we must have complete quiet. Every sound can be heard down there, not only in the workrooms, but in the offices too. The men come at about eight-thirty, and leave at about five-thirty. So, to be perfectly safe, from eight in the morning until six in the

12 Key Reading Skill

Drawing Conclusions

Mr. Kraler has a very good opinion of Mr. Frank. I think Mr. Kraler must be a good man to take the risk of hiding these people. R

Additional Support

Differentiated Instruction

Comparing Texts Although known for his children's literature, Dr. Seuss often wrote about social issues. To help students understand labeling in Nazi Germany (yellow stars on clothes), bring in a copy of Dr. Seuss's book "The Sneetches." (This is a story of a society with two classes: haves and have-nots. Access to good things in life is determined by whether or not a Sneetch has a star on its belly.) Read the story aloud to the class, and discuss how they would explain the complicated issue of labeling a type of person (for gender, race, or religion) to a child who was reading "The Sneetches." AS

ACTIVE READING MODEL

evening we must move only when it is necessary, and then in stockinged feet. We must not speak above a whisper. We must not run any water. We cannot use the sink, or even, forgive me, the w.c.[16] The pipes go down through the workrooms. It would be heard. No trash . . . [MR. FRANK *stops abruptly as he hears the sound of marching feet from the street below. Everyone is motionless, paralyzed with fear.* MR. FRANK *goes quietly into the room on the right to look down out of the window.* ANNE *runs after him, peering out with him. The tramping feet pass without stopping. The tension is relieved.* MR. FRANK, *followed by* ANNE, *returns to the main room and resumes his instructions to the group.*] . . . No trash must ever be thrown out which might reveal that someone is living up here . . . not even a potato paring. We must burn everything in the stove at night. This is the way we must live until it is over, if we are to survive. **13** **14**

[*There is silence for a second.*]

MRS. FRANK. Until it is over.

MR. FRANK. [*Reassuringly.*] After six we can move about . . . we can talk and laugh and have our supper and read and play games . . . just as we would at home. [*He looks at his watch.*] And now I think it would be wise if we all went to our rooms, and were settled before eight o'clock. Mrs. Van Daan, you and your husband will be upstairs. I regret that there's no place up there for Peter. But he will be here, near us. This will be our common room, where we'll meet to talk and eat and read, like one family. **15**

MR. VAN DAAN. And where do you and Mrs. Frank sleep?

MR. FRANK. This room is also our bedroom.

MRS. VAN DAAN. That isn't right. We'll sleep here and you take the room upstairs.

MR. VAN DAAN. It's your place.

[*Together*]

16. Short for "water closet," the ***w.c.*** is a bathroom.

13 Key Literary Element
Dialogue and Monologue Dialogue consists of the back-and-forth speeches between two or more people. One long speech by one character is a monologue, even when it's part of a dialogue. **L1**

L2 **14 Key Reading Skill**
Drawing Conclusions *If they have to be this quiet and careful, it means there's a big risk that a worker downstairs would report them to the Nazis. I guess not all Dutch people wanted to help like Miep and Mr. Kraler.*

15 Key Literary Element
Mood *The mood lightens a little from Mr. Frank's previous, very serious speech. He makes it sound like they'll all be one happy family.*

UNIT 6 GENRE FOCUS

Teach

L1 Literary Element

Dialogue and Monologue
Ask: What is the purpose of Mr. Frank's monologue? *(Possible response: to explain the seriousness of the situation and the importance of keeping the group's presence hidden)* **OL** **AL**

L2 Literary Element

Stage Directions **Say:** Notice that the playwrights indicate a moment of silence after Mr. Frank's monologue. What does the silence suggest about how the other characters feel? *(Possible responses: They are feeling shocked by their situation. They are absorbing the seriousness of their situation and the new rules for their new lives.)* **OL** **Ask:** Why might silence be more effective than speech in conveying the characters' reactions? *(Possible response: The silence emphasizes the people's shock. It also allows the audience to focus on the situation without distraction.)* **AL**

Reading in the Real World

Citizenship The need for absolute silence during the day indicates the possibility that workers in the building might report the group to the Nazis. Hold a discussion about following the orders of a government in power, such as the Nazi regime. Tell students that citizens ruled by the Nazis complied with the evils committed because they were merely "following orders." This caused people to behave in ways that they may have found morally unacceptable under normal conditions. Discuss the following: Why might people have followed orders despite knowing they were morally wrong? Can students think of any examples of this happening today? How would they have behaved in this situation? **AL**

Indiana English/Language Arts Academic Standards
SE: 8.2, 8.3.6
TWE: *Differentiated Instruction* 8.3, *Reading in the Real World* 8.2

Teach

C Critical Thinking

Comprehension **Ask:** Why is Mr. Frank grateful to Mr. Van Daan? *(Mr. Van Daan helped out Mr. Frank when he first came to Holland and was unable to speak the language.)* BL

R Reading Skill

Drawing Conclusions
Ask: On the basis of Anne's behavior so far, and on the ease with which she slept the night before, what can you conclude about her character? *(Possible response: Anne is optimistic, curious, confident, unafraid, and childlike even in such circumstances.)* OL

UNIT 6 GENRE FOCUS

ACTIVE READING MODEL

MR. FRANK. Please. I've thought this out for weeks. It's the best arrangement. The only arrangement.

MRS. VAN DAAN. [*To* MR. FRANK.] Never, never can we thank you. [*Then to* MRS. FRANK.] I don't know what would have happened to us, if it hadn't been for Mr. Frank.

MR. FRANK. You don't know how your husband helped me when I came to this country . . . knowing no one . . . not able to speak the language. I can never repay him for that. [*Going to* VAN DAAN.] May I help you with your things? C

MR. VAN DAAN. No. No. [*To* MRS. VAN DAAN.] Come along, *liefje*.[17]

MRS. VAN DAAN. You'll be all right, Peter? You're not afraid?

PETER. [*Embarrassed.*] Please, Mother.

[*They start up the stairs to the attic room above.* MR. FRANK *turns to* MRS. FRANK.] 16

MR. FRANK. You too must have some rest, Edith. You didn't close your eyes last night. Nor you, Margot.

ANNE. I slept, Father. Wasn't that funny? I knew it was the last night in my own bed, and yet I slept soundly. R

MR. FRANK. I'm glad, Anne. Now you'll be able to help me straighten things in here. [*To* MRS. FRANK *and* MARGOT.] Come with me . . . You and Margot rest in this room for the time being.

[*He picks up their clothes, starting for the room on the right.*]

MRS. FRANK. You're sure . . . ? I could help . . . And Anne hasn't had her milk . . .

MR. FRANK. I'll give it to her. [*To* ANNE *and* PETER.] Anne, Peter . . . it's best that you take off your shoes now, before you forget.

[*He leads the way to the room, followed by* MARGOT.]

16 Key Literary Element
Stage Directions *If I read all the stage directions, I can imagine how the people move around the apartment.*

17. ***Liefje*** (LEEF yuh) is Dutch for "darling."

Additional Support

Literature Focus Lesson

Characterization Remind students that authors can use a character's words and actions, as well as the words and actions of other characters, to help readers learn about a character. Have students choose one character from the play and write a brief description of him or her based on what they've read thus far. Students should note what actions or words tell the most about him or her. Have students share their descriptions with the class. Encourage them to add details as they continue reading. OL

ACTIVE READING MODEL

MRS. FRANK. You're sure you're not tired, Anne?

ANNE. I feel fine. I'm going to help Father.

MRS. FRANK. Peter, I'm glad you are to be with us.

PETER. Yes, Mrs. Frank.

[*MRS. FRANK goes to join MR. FRANK and MARGOT.*

During the following scene MR. FRANK helps MARGOT and MRS. FRANK to hang up their clothes. Then he persuades them both to lie down and rest. The VAN DAANS in their room above settle themselves. In the main room ANNE and PETER remove their shoes. PETER takes his cat out of the carrier.]

ANNE. What's your cat's name?

PETER. Mouschi.[18]

ANNE. Mouschi! Mouschi! Mouschi! [*She picks up the cat, walking away with it. To PETER.*] I love cats. I have one . . . a darling little cat. But they made me leave her behind. I left some food and a note for the neighbors to take care of her . . . I'm going to miss her terribly. What is yours? A him or a her? 17

PETER. He's a tom. He doesn't like strangers.

[*He takes the cat from her, putting it back in its carrier.*] 18

ANNE. [*Unabashed.*[19]] Then I'll have to stop being a stranger, won't I? Is he fixed?

PETER. [*Startled.*] Huh?

ANNE. Did you have him fixed?

PETER. No.

ANNE. Oh, you ought to have him fixed—to keep him from—you know, fighting. Where did you go to school?

PETER. Jewish Secondary.

R1

17 Key Reading Skill
Visualizing *The stage directions and dialogue make it easy to imagine Anne and Peter handling his cat. I can even see her as she leaves her own cat at home.*

18 Key Reading Skill
Interpreting *Ouch! Maybe it's Peter who doesn't like strangers! He's not being very nice to Anne.*

R2

18. ***Mouschi*** (MOOS kee)
19. ***Unabashed*** means "not ashamed; bold."

UNIT 6 GENRE FOCUS

Teach

R1 Reading Skill

Drawing Conclusions
Ask: What can you tell about Anne from her conversation with Peter? *(Possible responses: She is friendly and open. She is not shy, and she isn't put off by others' rudeness.)* AL

R2 Reading Skill

Interpreting **Ask:** Why might Peter be behaving so unkindly? *(Responses will vary. Some students may believe it is because he is trying to show he is older than Anne. Others may suggest he is nervous about living with new people.)* OL AL

Reading Fluency

Using Voice to Convey Tone Have students use the text on this page to practice building fluency and reading aloud. Put students in pairs and allow them to read this page of dialogue to one another. Explain to them that stage directions serve as clues for delivering lines effectively. For example, point out the words *unabashed* and *startled* as stage directions indicating behaviors for Anne and Peter. After students have worked in pairs, invite pairs to read their dialogue to the class. Encourage students to consider with what emotion and tone each line they read is meant to be delivered. EL BL

Indiana English/Language Arts Academic Standards
SE: 8.2, 8.3
TWE: *Reading Skill* 8.2.9, *Literature Focus Lesson* 8.3, *Reading Fluency* 8.7.2

Teach

R Reading Skill

Drawing Conclusions
Ask: Do you think that Anne and Peter would have become friends if they had been introduced at school? Explain. *(Possible response: The two might not have become friends because Peter is shy and Anne is outgoing.)* OL

L Literary Element

Stage Directions **Ask:** What purpose do the stage directions serve here? Explain. *(Possible response: The stage directions tell the actors playing Peter and Anne what to do while they are delivering their lines. Specifically, they tell Peter to throw the knife on the table, and they tell Anne to use the knife to start removing her star.)* OL

ACTIVE READING MODEL

ANNE. But that's where Margot and I go! I never saw you around.

PETER. I used to see you . . . sometimes . . .

ANNE. You did?

PETER. . . . in the school yard. You were always in the middle of a bunch of kids. R

[He takes a penknife from his pocket.]

ANNE. Why didn't you ever come over?

PETER. I'm sort of a lone wolf.

[He starts to rip off his Star of David.]

ANNE. What are you doing?

PETER. Taking it off. L

ANNE. But you can't do that. They'll arrest you if you go out without your star.

[He tosses his knife on the table.]

PETER. Who's going out?

ANNE. Why, of course! You're right! Of course we don't need them any more. *[She picks up his knife and starts to take her star off.]* I wonder what our friends will think when we don't show up today? 19

19 Key Reading Skill
Interpreting I know that the Star of David is a symbol of the Jewish religion. I think it's very important that Anne takes off the star. I'm not sure why she takes it off, so I'll think about it as I read.

PETER. I didn't have any dates with anyone.

ANNE. Oh, I did. I had a date with Jopie to go and play ping-pong at her house. Do you know Jopie de Waal?

PETER. No.

ANNE. Jopie's my best friend. I wonder what she'll think when she telephones and there's no answer? . . . Probably she'll go over to the house . . . I wonder what she'll think . . . we left everything as if we'd suddenly been called away . . . breakfast dishes in the sink . . . beds not made . . .

Additional Support

Differentiated Instruction

Beginning an Essay Discuss how going into hiding will affect Anne and Peter differently, given their contrasting personalities. Ask students to decide who will have the harder time. Some students may believe Anne's adjustment will be more difficult because she is used to socializing with friends. Others may think Peter will have more difficulty because he will be forced to be more sociable. Have students list reasons for their choice and then have them complete the thesis statement "The adjustment will be more difficult for ____ because ____." Finally, have each student use the thesis statement to write an introductory paragraph for an essay on this topic. AL

ACTIVE READING MODEL

[*As she pulls off her star, the cloth underneath shows clearly the color and form of the star.*] Look! It's still there! [PETER *goes over to the stove with his star.*] What're you going to do with yours?

PETER. Burn it.

ANNE. [*She starts to throw hers in, and cannot.*] It's funny, I can't throw mine away. I don't know why.

PETER. You can't throw . . . ? Something they branded you with . . . ? That they made you wear so they could spit on you?

ANNE. I know. I know. But after all, it is the Star of David, isn't it? 20

[*In the bedroom, right,* MARGOT *and* MRS. FRANK *are lying down.* MR. FRANK *starts quietly out.*]

PETER. Maybe it's different for a girl.

[MR. FRANK *comes into the main room.*]

R2 MR. FRANK. Forgive me, Peter. Now let me see. We must find a bed for your cat. [*He goes to a cupboard.*] I'm glad you brought your cat. Anne was feeling so badly about hers. [*Getting a used small washtub.*] Here we are. Will it be comfortable in that?

PETER. [*Gathering up his things.*] Thanks.

20 Key Reading Skill

R1 **Drawing Conclusions** The Nazis forced Jews to wear the Star of David to identify them as Jews. Peter is eager to burn the star as a symbol of evil, but Anne sees it as a symbol of Judaism as well. How important is his Jewish heritage to Peter? How important is her Jewish heritage to Anne?

Margot, Otto, Anne, and Edith Frank (left to right), 1941.

Analyzing the Photo How would you describe the family here? Are they happy? relaxed? upset?

Teach

R1 Reading Skill

Drawing Conclusions

Say: Anne can't seem to throw away her Star of David. She says, "It is the Star of David, isn't it?" On the basis of her response, what can you conclude about Anne's feelings toward the Star of David? *(Possible response: The Star of David has no negative associations for Anne. She has respect for it as a religious symbol.)* OL AL

R2 Reading Skill

Interpreting **Say:** Mr. Frank made Anne leave her cat behind, yet he tells Peter he's glad he brought his cat. Why might he have said this to Peter? *(Possible responses: He is being kind and respectful to make Peter feel welcome. He wants to make the best of a bad situation and doesn't want Peter to feel bad about bringing his cat.)* AL

Differentiated Instruction

Developing an Essay Have students use what they learn about Anne and Peter on this page to continue writing essays about how the two characters will adjust to their new situation. Suggest that students add Anne's and Peter's reactions to the Star of David to the list of reasons explaining why the adjustment will be difficult for each character. If necessary, students should revise the original thesis to reflect this new information. Students should use the list of reasons to develop three significant ideas that will form the body of an essay. Have students write a first draft of their essay. AL

Indiana English/Language Arts Academic Standards

SE: 8.3

TWE: *Reading Skill* 8.2.9, *Differentiated Instruction* 8.4, *Differentiated Instruction* 8.4.3

Teach

R1 Reading Skill

Drawing Conclusions
Say: Mr. Frank assures Anne she will like Peter. From his statement, what can you conclude about Mr. Frank and how he looks at the world? *(Possible response: He tries to look on the bright side of things.)* OL

R2 Reading Skill

Interpreting **Ask:** Does Anne seem as though she will make the best of her situation? Explain. *(Responses will vary. Some students may already have noted Anne's optimism. Others may say that it is too early to tell or that Anne doesn't seem to be making the best of her situation because she is already complaining.)* OL AL

ACTIVE READING MODEL

MR. FRANK. [*Opening the door of the room on the left.*] And here is your room. But I warn you, Peter, you can't grow any more. Not an inch, or you'll have to sleep with your feet out of the skylight. Are you hungry?

PETER. No.

MR. FRANK. We have some bread and butter.

PETER. No, thank you.

MR. FRANK. You can have it for luncheon then. And tonight we will have a real supper . . . our first supper together.

PETER. Thanks. Thanks.

[*He goes into his room. During the following scene he arranges his possessions in his new room.*]

MR. FRANK. That's a nice boy, Peter.

ANNE. He's awfully shy, isn't he?

MR. FRANK. You'll like him, I know. R1

ANNE. I certainly hope so, since he's the only boy I'm likely to see for months and months. 21

[*MR. FRANK sits down, taking off his shoes.*]

MR. FRANK. Annele,[20] there's a box there. Will you open it?

[*He indicates a carton on the couch.* ANNE *brings it to the center table. In the street below there is the sound of children playing.*]

ANNE. [*As she opens the carton.*] You know the way I'm going to think of it here? I'm going to think of it as a boarding house.[21] A very peculiar summer boarding house, like the one that we—[*She breaks off as she pulls out*

21 Key Reading Skill
Interpreting *Anne doesn't sound too thrilled. She's used to having lots of friends around. I'd have a hard time too if I had only one person near my age to talk to.* R2

20. Both ***Annele*** (AWN uh luh) and ***Anneke,*** which is used later, are affectionate nicknames.

21. A ***boarding house*** is like a small hotel in a private home. The owner provides rooms and meals to people who pay a weekly or monthly rent.

Additional Support

Reading in the Real World

Citizenship The United States Holocaust Memorial Museum, located in Washington, D.C., is an excellent resource for information about the Holocaust, including details about the life of the Frank family. Have students visit the museum's Web site to find more information about Holocaust history and to read ongoing discussions about the topic. Students may also take part in online interactive lessons that are based on the museum's exhibitions. Suggest that your school investigate participating in one of the museum's programs, workshops, or long-term partnerships. AS

ACTIVE READING MODEL

some photographs.] Father! My movie stars! I was wondering where they were! I was looking for them this morning . . . and Queen Wilhelmina![22] How wonderful!

MR. FRANK. There's something more. Go on. Look further.

[*He goes over to the sink, pouring a glass of milk from a thermos bottle.*]

ANNE. [*Pulling out a pasteboard-bound book.*] A diary! [*She throws her arms around her father.*] I've never had a diary. And I've always longed for one. [*She looks around the room.*] Pencil, pencil, pencil, pencil. [*She starts down the stairs.*] I'm going down to the office to get a pencil.

MR. FRANK. Anne! No!

[*He goes after her, catching her by the arm and pulling her back.*]

ANNE. [*Startled.*] But there's no one in the building now.

L

MR. FRANK. It doesn't matter. I don't want you ever to go beyond that door.

ANNE. [*Sobered.*] Never . . . ? Not even at nighttime, when everyone is gone? Or on Sundays? Can't I go down to listen to the radio?

MR. FRANK. Never. I am sorry, Anneke. It isn't safe. No, you must never go beyond that door.

[*For the first time* ANNE *realizes what "going into hiding" means.*] 22

ANNE. I see.

MR. FRANK. It'll be hard, I know. But always remember this, Anneke. There are no walls, there are no bolts, no locks that anyone can put on your mind. Miep will bring us books. We will read history, poetry, mythology. [*He gives her the glass of milk.*] Here's your milk. [*With his arm about her, they go over to the couch, sitting down side by side.*]

22 Key Reading Skill

Drawing Conclusions

It seems to me that Anne jumps into action without thinking about the possible results.

22. ***Wilhelmina*** (wil hel MEE nuh) was queen of the Netherlands from 1890 to 1948. She and her family escaped to England and then Canada at the time of the German invasion.

Teach

L Literary Element

Mood **Ask:** How would you describe the mood in this part of the scene? How does it change when Anne tries to go downstairs? *(Possible response: The mood is happy at first when Anne finds the diary. However, the mood becomes somber when she starts to go downstairs to get a pencil because she realizes she cannot go beyond the door.)* **OL**

R Reading Skill

Visualizing **Ask:** How do you visualize the stage at this point in the play? *(Responses will vary.)* **AS** **Ask:** How do you visualize the stage now compared to the beginning of the play when the same space seemed in disarray? *(Possible response: The stage seems less chaotic, no chairs are toppled over, and no garments are tossed on the floor—everyone has just moved in and their belongings have been neatly put away—there are more signs of life, and fewer signs of sad memories.)* **Ask:** What parts of the play help you to visualize the set? *(Possible response: Stage directions.)* **OL**

English Language Coach

Figurative Language Students who have limited proficiency in English may have difficulty understanding what Mr. Frank means when he says that "there are no walls, there are no bolts, no locks that anyone can put on your mind." Review the concepts of enclosure and locking, and list (using pictures, if necessary) some items that can be enclosed or locked. When students are familiar with this concept, help students see that our thoughts and imaginations cannot be locked. If possible, translate the phrase "freedom of thought" to reinforce the concept. **EL**

Indiana English/Language Arts Academic Standards

SE: 8.2, 8.3

TWE: *Reading in the Real World* 8.4.4, *English Language Coach* 8.3.6

Teach

R Reading Skill

Drawing Conclusions
Ask: On the basis of their exchange, what can you conclude about Anne's relationship with her father? *(Possible response: Anne and her father appear to be very close. It seems that Anne is more likely to argue with her mother, and that Mr. Frank is good at calming Anne.)* OL

L Literary Element

Mood Ask: What is the mood in your home in the morning? How does it compare with the mood in this part of the scene? *(Responses will vary. Some students may say that their homes are noisy and busy in the morning, whereas it is silent and motionless in the Franks' hiding place.)* AS

UNIT 6 GENRE FOCUS

ACTIVE READING MODEL

As a matter of fact, between us, Anne, being here has certain advantages for you. For instance, you remember the battle you had with your mother the other day on the subject of overshoes? You said you'd rather die than wear overshoes? But in the end you had to wear them? Well now, you see, for as long as we are here you will never have to wear overshoes! Isn't that good? And the coat that you inherited from Margot, you won't have to wear that any more. And the piano! You won't have to practice on the piano. I tell you, this is going to be a fine life for you! 23 R

[ANNE's panic is gone. PETER appears in the doorway of his room, with a saucer in his hand. He is carrying his cat.]

PETER. I . . . I . . . I thought I'd better get some water for Mouschi before . . .

MR. FRANK. Of course.

[As he starts toward the sink the carillon begins to chime the hour of eight. He tiptoes to the window at the back and looks down at the street below. He turns to PETER, indicating in pantomime[23] that it is too late. PETER starts back for his room. He steps on a creaking board. The three of them are frozen for a minute in fear. As PETER starts away again, ANNE tiptoes over to him and pours some of the milk from her glass into the saucer for the cat. PETER squats on the floor, putting the milk before the cat. MR. FRANK gives ANNE his fountain pen, and then goes into the room at the right. For a second ANNE watches the cat, then she goes over to the center table, and opens her diary. L

In the room at the right, MRS. FRANK has sat up quickly at the sound of the carillon. MR. FRANK comes in and sits down beside her on the settee, his arm comfortingly around her.

Upstairs, in the attic room, MR. and MRS. VAN DAAN have hung their clothes in the closet and are now seated on the iron bed. MRS. VAN DAAN leans back exhausted. MR. VAN DAAN fans her with a newspaper.

ANNE starts to write in her diary. The lights dim out, the curtain falls.

23 Key Reading Skill
Drawing Conclusions *Anne's father emphasizes positive things about their situation, but she's going to have a tough time ahead. She's too young and lively to be happy living like an animal in a cage.*

23. Here, ***in pantomime*** (PANT uh mym) means in silent gestures instead of in words.

Additional Support

Differentiated Instruction

Acting Out the Scene The stage directions on this page give detailed instructions about how the actors should move on stage (including pantomiming). Have students work in groups to act out this part of the scene. Read the stage directions aloud while students perform the actions. Encourage students to interpret the stage directions that explain mood in addition to those that dictate physical movement. Have students practice using facial expressions and body language to accompany the following direction: "the three of them are frozen for a minute in fear." AS

ACTIVE READING MODEL

In the darkness ANNE'S VOICE *comes to us again, faintly at first, and then with growing strength.*] 24 25

ANNE'S VOICE. I expect I should be describing what it feels like to go into hiding. But I really don't know yet myself. I only know it's funny never to be able to go outdoors . . . never to breathe fresh air . . . never to run and shout and jump. It's the silence in the nights that frightens me most. Every time I hear a creak in the house, or a step on the street outside, I'm sure they're coming for us. The days aren't so bad. At least we know that Miep and Mr. Kraler are down there below us in the office. Our protectors, we call them. I asked Father what would happen to them if the Nazis found out they were hiding us. Pim[24] said that they would suffer the same fate that we would . . . Imagine! They know this, and yet when they come up here, they're always cheerful and gay as if there were nothing in the world to bother them . . . Friday, the twenty-first of August, nineteen forty-two. Today I'm going to tell you our general news. Mother is unbearable. She insists on treating me like a baby, which I loathe.[25] Otherwise things are going better. The weather is . . .

[*As* ANNE'S VOICE *is fading out, the curtain rises on the scene.*]

24 Key Literary Element

Stage Directions Often, the stage directions in a published script are a record of what happened in the play's first production. In their original script, Goodrich and Hackett probably did not give such detailed descriptions of characters' actions.

25 Key Literary Element

Mood *It's almost as if it's nighttime, and everyone is getting ready for bed. Anne's diary isn't exactly a bedtime story, but the mood here is like that—calm and kind of ordinary.*

24. ***Pim*** is Anne's nickname for her father.
25. To ***loathe*** (lohth) is to regard with extreme disgust or hatred.

Write to Learn Anne decides to think of her time in hiding as if it were nothing more than an odd vacation. Think of a time when you used your imagination to make it easier to get through a difficult time. In your Learner's Notebook, write about what you did and whether or not it helped.

Study Central Visit www.glencoe.com and click on Study Central to review drama.

UNIT 6 GENRE FOCUS

Teach

R Reading Skill

Interpreting Ask: What does Anne mean when she says that it is "funny" to be unable to go outdoors or breathe fresh air? Explain. *(Possible response: Anne means that her situation is strange, something that she has never experienced before.)* BL OL

L Literary Element

Act and Scene Ask: Is the reading from Anne's diary an effective way to end this scene? Explain your answer. *(Possible response: Yes, Anne's diary entry summarizes what has been happening with her family while the actors get ready for the next scene.)* OL

Study Central Have students access the Web site to review drama and to complete a related activity.

Differentiated Instruction

Diary Entry The first two scenes reveal a lot about Mr. Frank and how he chooses to deal with the circumstances. Have students use Anne's diary entry as a model to write an entry from Mr. Frank's perspective. Students should write about the events that have taken place in the first two scenes. Encourage students to search through the first two scenes for any remarks or reactions from Mr. Frank that reveal elements of his personality. Invite volunteers to read their entries aloud for the class. OL AL

Indiana English/Language Arts Academic Standards
SE: 8.2, 8.3.6
TWE: *Differentiated Instruction* 8.7.2, *Differentiated Instruction* 8.4

Drawing Conclusions

Teaching Students to Draw Conclusions

Why Is It Important?

- Frequently in literature, conclusions are left to the reader. Authors are often not explicit, preferring to let the reader draw his or her own conclusions.
- Drawing conclusions allows students to consider the author's point of view and how that relates to their understanding and background knowledge.
- Students can create new meaning by applying sound reasoning.

How to Help Students Get It

- Introduce the *if . . . then* concept. Ask students to consider different ideas that can be added, such as "If I get up too late, then I could miss my bus." Ask them how they knew what to add to the "then" part. Tell students that these are conclusions—something known or assumed based on the available information.
- In preparation for teaching students about drawing conclusions, prepare several questions that can be used to guide their thinking. These questions should allow students to think about the information without giving them the information. The following sample questions might be helpful: What conclusions can be made based on the details and facts? Do the facts add up? How do you know the facts are accurate? What evidence does the author provide? What details and facts support the author's conclusions? What clues led to your conclusion?
- To cement students' knowledge of drawing conclusions, they should regularly be asked to identify the evidence from the text that they used to draw the conclusion. The key to drawing conclusions is to use what the author provided, not to simply make up information or ideas.

Reading to Answer the Big Question

The Diary of Anne Frank by Frances Goodrich and Albert Hackett
This two-act play is based on the journal of a Jewish girl from Amsterdam whose family is forced into hiding during the Nazi occupation of the Netherlands during World War II. Staying sequestered in a small space with seven other people for more than two years is very difficult for the young teen. Anne Frank's journal has become a famous document, inspiring hope and endurance during fearful and violent times.

Workshop Resources

Pacing (Days) Standard	Block	Lesson	Student Materials	Teacher Resources
1	1/2	Key Skill Lesson: Drawing Conclusions	Key Reading Skills Practice, p. 9 English Language Coach Review, p. 42	Bellringer Options Transparencies – Selection Focus 13 – Daily Language Practice 54 Read Aloud, Think Aloud Transparencies – Key Reading Skills 8 Presentation Plus!
1	1	*The Diary of Anne Frank* Act 1, Scene 3	Glencoe Online Unit Vocabulary Review, p. 40 Academic Vocabulary Review, p. 43 English Language Coach Active Reading Graphic Organizer, p. 11 Literary Analysis, p. 10 StudentWorks Plus™ Online Student Edition Literature Classics Selection and Unit Assessments, p. 61	Literary and Text Analysis Transparencies 1 Puzzlemaker Skill Level Up!™ A Language Arts Game BookLink 3 Assessment by Learning Objective (Diagnostic and Formative) Interactive Tutor:Self-Assessment TeacherWorks Plus™
1		*The Diary of Anne Frank* Act 1, Scenes 4–5	Glencoe Online Unit Vocabulary Review, p. 40 Academic Vocabulary Review, p. 43 English Language Coach Active Reading Graphic Organizer, p 11 Literary Analysis, p. 13 StudentWorks Plus™ Online Student Edition Literature Classics Selection and Unit Assessments, p. 62	Read Aloud, Think Aloud Transparencies, – Read Aloud, Think Aloud 45–54 Literary and Text Analysis Transparencies 13, 30 Puzzlemaker Skill Level Up!™ A Language Arts Game BookLink 3 Assessment by Learning Objective (Diagnostic and Formative) Interactive Tutor: Self-Assessment TeacherWorks Plus™

Keys for Unit Resource

- Blackline Master
- Workbook
- Supplemental Text
- CD-ROM
- DVD
- Transparency
- Web-based
- Fast File

Level Appropriate Code

AS = Activities for all students
AL = Activities for students working above grade level
OL = Activities for students working at grade level
BL = Activities for students working below grade level
EL = Activities for English language learners

Focus

BELLRINGER Options

- **Selection Focus Transparencies 13**
- **Daily Language Practice Transparency 54**

Focus Activity Say: Consider what you've learned about the Franks and the Van Daans. Which characters do you think will have the most trouble with living in hiding, and which do you think will have the least? Why? *(Responses will vary.)* **OL**

Teach

R Reading Skill

Drawing Conclusions

Say: You draw conclusions every day. For example, if you looked outside and saw a flag waving and trees swaying, you'd probably draw the conclusion that it's windy outside. Think of a conclusion you drew this week. Explain to a partner how you put together different pieces of information to reach your conclusion. *(Responses will vary. Students should give examples that demonstrate an understanding of the concept.)* **AS**

READING WORKSHOP 1

Skills Focus

You will practice using these skills when you read the following selections:

- *The Diary of Anne Frank,* Act 1, Scene 3, p. 736
- *The Diary of Anne Frank,* Act 1, Scenes 4–5, p. 766

Reading

- Drawing conclusions

Literature

- Understanding act and scene
- Understanding dialogue and monologue

Vocabulary

- Understanding historical influences on English
- Recognizing word parts

Writing/Grammar

- Using commas in series and with direct address and direct quotations

Skill Lesson

Drawing Conclusions

Learn It!

What Is It? A **conclusion** is a judgment you've made. **Drawing conclusions** means using a number of pieces of information to form a general idea of or make a general statement about people, places, ideas, or events.

Suppose, for example, that you notice that your dog has a slight limp and doesn't have much interest in eating or playing. You might—and should—draw the conclusion that your dog is sick or hurt and needs to see the vet.

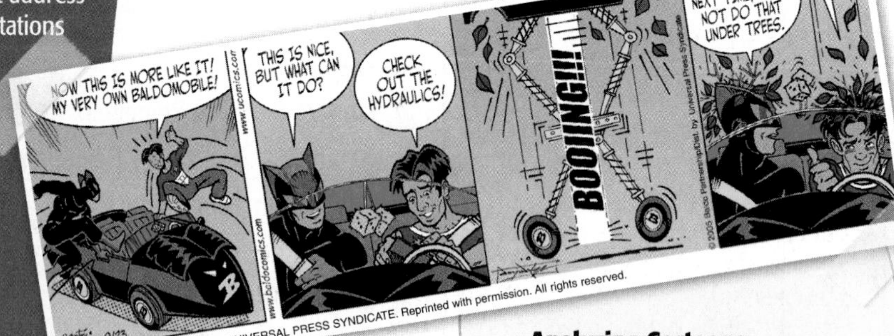

Analyzing Cartoons
Baldo is daydreaming a Batman-and-Robin adventure. "Batman" quickly draws the conclusion that using the hydraulics under a tree is a bad idea.

Indiana English/Language Arts Academic Standards (pp. 732–733)

8.3 Comprehension and Analysis of Literary Text Respond to grade-level-appropriate literature... **8.2.9** Make reasonable statements and draw conclusions...

For a complete description of the standards, see p. IN 11.

Additional Support

English Language Coach

Word Parts Explain that affixes are word parts, such as prefixes and suffixes, added to a word or root to change its meaning or part of speech. Challenge students to use affixes to generate as many words as they can that have the root *cycle,* which means "circle." Advise students to use a chart like the one shown to keep track of words. **EL** **BL**

Word Root	Affix(es)	New Word	Meaning
cycle	-ic	cyclic	Occurring or repeated in series or phases

Why Is It Important? By drawing conclusions, you make connections between ideas and events that help you see the "big picture." Noticing details is important in itself, but drawing conclusions helps you *do* something with those details.

Study Central Visit www.glencoe.com and click on Study Central to review drawing conclusions.

How Do I Do It? As you read, observe details about characters, ideas, and events. If there are illustrations or photos, check them for clues. Then make a general statement on the basis of these details. Be careful, though! Make sure you have enough information to draw a reasonable and proper conclusion. Here's how one student used details from *Harriet Tubman: Conductor on the Underground Railroad* to draw conclusions.

> The masters kept hearing whispers about the man named Moses. At first they did not believe in his existence. The stories about him were fantastic, unbelievable. Yet they watched for him. They offered rewards for his capture.
>
> They never saw him. Now and then they heard whispered rumors to the effect that he was in the neighborhood. The woods were searched. The roads were watched. But there was never anything to indicate his whereabouts.

Everyone hears amazing stories about this "Moses," but no one ever sees him. There are rewards for anyone who captures him, and people try. I conclude that Moses is either very clever or very lucky.

Practice It!

Use clues from the paragraph below and your own knowledge and experience to draw all the conclusions you can.

> Manuel walked quickly but quietly. If only he could find it before anyone else got there! He didn't bother to check behind the pictures on the wall. He went directly to the dresser. He ignored the little jewelry box and the two small drawers, instead opening the large top drawer first.

Use It!

Remember to practice drawing conclusions as you continue to read *The Diary of Anne Frank.*

Teach

Study Central Have students access the Web site to review drawing conclusions and to complete a related activity.

R Reading Skill

Drawing Conclusions

Say: Drawing conclusions is like putting together the pieces of a puzzle to see the full picture. To draw conclusions while you're reading, combine story details with your own knowledge or experience.

Draw this diagram on the board to help students visualize the process of drawing conclusions.

Story Details + What I Know → Conclusion

Suggest students use the diagram to help them complete the "Practice It!" activity. OL

Resources for page 733

- Use Key Reading Skills Transparency 8 in *Read Aloud, Think Aloud* to help students practice drawing conclusions.

Reading in the Real World

Citizenship Remind students that responsible citizens stay informed about issues. They also draw conclusions about issues based on information gathered from various sources. Ask students to name some important issues or events in the news. List these issues or events on the board. Have each student choose an item from the list and find and read a newspaper or magazine article about it. Have students use what they have read to draw one or two conclusions about the issues. Allow time for students to discuss their conclusions as a class. AL

Indiana English/Language Arts Academic Standards

SE: 8.2.9, 8.3

TWE: *English Language Coach* 8.1, *Reading in the Real World* 8.2

Teach

More About the Author

Frances Goodrich and Albert Hackett performed together in various plays on Broadway before moving to Hollywood, where they became a successful writing team. The couple wrote many screenplays in the 1930s and 1940s, including *The Thin Man* and *It's a Wonderful Life.* They often acted out the scenes they wrote. Afterward, Goodrich and Hackett would each write a draft, exchange drafts, and critique each other's work. They were both passionate about their work, so the critiques sometimes turned into screaming matches. The results were some of the best-loved plays and screenplays of the twentieth century.

V Vocabulary

Word Parts **Say:** Find another example for each of the roots listed in the chart. Join the roots with different prefixes and suffixes to make new words. *(creditable, photograph, pedestrian, repopulate)* EL OL

Before You Read

The Diary of Anne Frank, Act 1, Scene 3

Meet the Authors

Frances Goodrich and her husband, Albert Hackett, spent two years writing their play, inspired by *Anne Frank: The Diary of a Young Girl*. They met with Anne's father and visited the building in which the Franks had hidden. The finished play won the Pulitzer Prize and many other awards after it was first presented in 1955. See page R2 of the Author Files for more on these playwrights.

Author Search For more about Goodrich and Hackett, go to www.glencoe.com.

Indiana English/Language Arts Academic Standards (pp. 734–761)

8.1 Word Recognition, Fluency, and Vocabulary Development Understanding...word parts...
8.3 Comprehension and Analysis of Literary Text Respond to grade-level-appropriate literature... **8.3.2** Evaluate the structural elements of the plot...

For a complete description of the standards, see p. IN 11.

Vocabulary Preview

self-conscious (self KON shus) *adj.* too aware of one's own appearance and actions **(p. 737)** *Peter blushes and becomes self-conscious as a result of Anne's teasing.*

absurd (ub SURD) *adj.* not making sense; very silly **(p. 741)** *Mrs. Frank's fear might have been absurd in ordinary times, but now it made sense.*

vile (vyl) *adj.* very bad; extremely unpleasant **(p. 742)** *Anne had a very low opinion of math; she thought it was vile.*

mimics (MIM iks) *v.* makes fun of by imitating or copying; form of the verb *mimic* **(p. 743)** *Mr. Van Daan mimics his wife, showing that he's heard her tell the story many times before.*

aggravating (AG ruh vay ting) *adj.* irritating; annoying **(p. 748)** *Mr. Van Daan sees Anne as aggravating and spoiled.*

bickering (BIK ur ing) *n.* a quarrel or argument, especially about minor details **(p. 751)** *The Van Daans' endless bickering over every little thing begins to get on Mrs. Frank's nerves.*

meticulous (muh TIK yuh lus) *adj.* careful about small details **(p. 755)** *Dussel is meticulous about his appearance and his habits.*

Partner Talk With a partner, choose one of the vocabulary words and talk about all the situations you can think of in which you could use it.

English Language Coach

Word Parts In the last unit you learned about base words, roots, prefixes, and suffixes. Together, these word parts shape the meanings of many different words in the English language. For example, add a prefix to a root word, and you'll get a word that means something slightly different from the root. Look at the roots and their meanings in the following chart.

V

Root	Meaning	Word Example
cred	believe	incredible
graph	write	autograph
port	carry	portable
fort	strong	fortress

Partner Talk Review the word examples above. With a partner, discuss how adding prefixes and suffixes changes the meaning of the roots.

Additional Support

Author Search To expand students' appreciation of Frances Goodrich and Albert Hackett, have them access the Web site for additional information and resources.

English Language Coach

Word Families Exposure to word families can help students analyze new words and expand their vocabularies. Have students choose one of the roots listed in the chart above and identify three to five additional words that contain the root. Tell students to write the words on index cards, one word per card, with the definition on the reverse. Group members can use the cards to quiz one another on the new words and their meanings. Have groups exchange card sets for further vocabulary building. EL BL

Skills Preview

Key Reading Skill: Drawing Conclusions

Drawing conclusions is similar to making inferences. You combine clues from the writing with your own knowledge and experience to figure out what the writer is saying. One meaning of *conclusion* is "the final part of something." When you draw a conclusion, you make a "final" statement that you can explain logically and with supporting details.

Try not to draw a conclusion until you have solid facts and details to support it. And don't be afraid to change a conclusion when new information comes in.

Write to Learn What conclusion(s) can you draw about Mr. Frank, based on what you've read so far? Write your answer in your Learner's Notebook.

Key Literary Element: Act and Scene

An **act** is a division of a play, which may be divided into two or more acts. An act may be divided into two or more **scenes.** *The Diary of Anne Frank* has two acts, with five scenes in each. Act 1, scene 1 introduces the setting, situation, and two characters. The remaining characters appear in scene 2.

As you read, use these tips to understand how acts and scenes work:

- Each scene usually presents action in one time and place or in one situation. The setting may change from scene to scene or stay the same throughout an entire play.
- Plays are meant to be performed. Try to imagine how an act or scene break might affect you if you were in an audience watching the play. Between scenes, you and other audience members would stay seated. At the intermission, between acts, you could get up and move around.

Interactive Literary Elements Handbook To review or learn more about the literary elements, go to www.glencoe.com.

Get Ready to Read

Connect to Reading

Have you ever had to share a very small space with several people? What was that like? For more than two years, Anne Frank, her parents, her sister, and four other people lived together in a few small rooms.

Partner Talk With a partner, list what you'd have to give up if you shared a tiny house or apartment with others and had to be quiet most of the time.

Build Background

During World War II, many Jews in Europe were forced into hiding to avoid German labor and death camps. Most hideouts were tiny and uncomfortable—a barn, an attic, a basement, even the space under a floor.

- Anne Frank was born in 1929. She was a young girl when she and her family moved to the Netherlands after the Nazis gained power in Germany.
- When the Germans invaded the Netherlands, the Franks and four other Jews hid in the attic of an office building for 25 months. Sympathetic non-Jews brought them food, news, and other necessities.
- Anne "disguised" the identities of people in her diary. Those she called Van Daan were, in real life, named Herman, Auguste, and Peter van Pels. The man she calls Dr. Albert Dussel (who appears in scene 3 of the play) was actually Fritz Pfeffer.

Set Purposes for Reading

BIG Question Read the rest of act 1 to find out how Anne and the others find ways to go on despite enormous pressures and difficulties.

Set Your Own Purpose What would you like to learn from the play to help you answer the Big Question? Write your own purpose on the Workshop 1 Foldable for Unit 6.

Keep Moving

Use these skills as you read the following selection.

Teach

L Literary Element

Act and Scene Ask: What happens in act 1, scene 1? *(After World War II, Anne Frank's father returns to the attic in Amsterdam where his family and others hid during the Nazi occupation of the Netherlands. He finds Anne's diary and begins to read it.)* **Ask:** What is the setting of scene 2? *(Scene 2 takes place in July 1942 in the attic where the Frank family and others hid.)* BL OL

R Reading Skill

Review Connecting Ask: What difficulties might people face when living together in a small space? *(Responses will vary.)* **Ask:** What made the living situation for Anne and the others unusually difficult? *(Possible response: Many people had to live very close together in just a couple of rooms, and they couldn't go outside.)* OL

Literature Online

Interactive Literary Elements Handbook Have students access the Web site to improve their understanding of act and scene.

Literature Focus Lesson

Drama Point out that acts and scenes are dramatic conventions that signal transition. A shift in lighting or the lowering of a curtain indicates the end of a scene or an act. Often, shifts in time and setting occur between scenes and acts.

Ask students what other devices could be used to show the passage of time in plays such as *The Diary of Anne Frank.* *(Possible response: Dates might be given in a voiceover or stated in dialogue.)* OL

Indiana English/Language Arts Academic Standards

SE: 8.1, 8.3, 8.3.2

TWE: *English Language Coach* 8.1, *Literature Focus Lesson* 8.2

Teach

L Literary Element

Act and Scene Say: Compare the characters' actions and attitudes at the end of scene 2 to their actions and attitudes at the start of scene 3. *(At the end of scene 2, the characters are silent and they are tense as they begin their first day in hiding. At the start of scene 3, the characters are allowed to speak and move after a day of silence. The characters are relieved to be able to make noise. Anne shouts "WHEE!" to release her energy.)* OL

BQ BIG Question

Ask: How have the children been spending their days? *(They have been studying and doing schoolwork.)* BL Why might a daily routine be comforting for people in times of stress? *(Possible response: a routine is predictable and helps people achieve a sense of stability.)* OL

Readability Scores

Dale-Chall: 4.0
DRP: N/A
Lexile: N/A

READING WORKSHOP 1

SCENE 3

[It is a little after six o'clock in the evening, two months later. **1** *MARGOT is in the bedroom at the right, studying. MR. VAN DAAN is lying down in the attic room above.*

The rest of the "family" is in the main room. ANNE and PETER sit opposite each other at the center table, where they have been doing their lessons. MRS. FRANK is on the couch. MRS. VAN DAAN is seated with her fur coat, on which she has been sewing, in her lap. None of them are wearing their shoes.

Their eyes are on MR. FRANK, waiting for him to give them the signal which will release them from their day-long quiet. MR. FRANK, his shoes in his hand, stands looking down out of the window at the back, watching to be sure that all of the workmen have left the building below.

After a few seconds of motionless silence, MR. FRANK turns from the window.]

MR. FRANK. [*Quietly, to the group.*] It's safe now. The last workman has left.

[*There is an immediate stir of relief.*]

ANNE. [*Her pent-up energy explodes.*] WHEE!

MRS. FRANK. [*Startled, amused.*] Anne!

MRS. VAN DAAN. I'm first for the w.c.

[*She hurries off to the bathroom. MRS. FRANK puts on her shoes and starts up to the sink to prepare supper. ANNE sneaks PETER's shoes from under the table and hides them behind her back. MR. FRANK goes into MARGOT's room.*]

MR. FRANK. [*To MARGOT.*] Six o'clock. School's over. **2**

[*MARGOT gets up, stretching. MR. FRANK sits down to put on his shoes. In the main room PETER tries to find his.*]

PETER. [*To ANNE.*] Have you seen my shoes?

ANNE. [*Innocently.*] Your shoes?

PETER. You've taken them, haven't you?

ANNE. I don't know what you're talking about.

Practice the Skills

1 Key Literary Element

Act and Scene A new scene often signals the passage of time or a change in setting. Is there a change at the beginning of scene 3? If so, what is it?

2 BIG Question

What do Anne and the others do to make life seem more normal? Do these efforts help them keep from giving up? Explain your answers on the Workshop 1 Foldable for Unit 6. BQ

Additional Support

English Language Coach

Directional Words English language learners may have difficulty understanding the spatial relationships signaled by the directional words used to describe a setting. Review the terms *in front of, behind, next to, beside, above,* and *below.* Also explain that the directions *left* and *right*, when they appear in a script, are from the point of view of the actors, not the audience. Bring in a picture of a room from a magazine. Have students use each of the terms above to describe the location of various objects in the room. EL

PETER. You're going to be sorry!

ANNE. Am I?

[PETER goes after her. ANNE, with his shoes in her hand, runs from him, dodging behind her mother.]

MRS. FRANK. *[Protesting.]* Anne, dear!

PETER. Wait till I get you!

ANNE. I'm waiting! *[PETER makes a lunge for her. They both fall to the floor. PETER pins her down, wrestling with her to get the shoes.]* Don't! Don't! Peter, stop it. Ouch!

MRS. FRANK. Anne! . . . Peter!

[Suddenly PETER becomes **self-conscious**. *He grabs his shoes roughly and starts for his room.]*

ANNE. *[Following him.]* Peter, where are you going? Come dance with me.

PETER. I tell you I don't know how.

ANNE. I'll teach you.

PETER. I'm going to give Mouschi his dinner.

ANNE. Can I watch?

PETER. He doesn't like people around while he eats.

ANNE. Peter, please.

PETER. No!

[He goes into his room. ANNE slams his door after him.] **B**

R2 MRS. FRANK. Anne, dear, I think you shouldn't play like that with Peter. It's not dignified.[1]

1. ***Dignified*** (DIG nuh fyd) means "behaving in a calm, proper way."

Analyzing the Photo It's hard to tell what Peter is doing, but what can you learn about him from this photo?

Practice the Skills

B Reviewing Skills

Activating Prior Knowledge
In your experience, what does it mean when a teenage girl teases a teenage boy?

Vocabulary

self-conscious (self KON shus) *adj.* too aware of one's own appearance and actions

Teach

R1 Reading Skill

Drawing Conclusions Ask: What conclusion can you draw about the relationship between Peter and Anne from their actions in this scene? *(Possible response: They enjoy each other's company, but Peter can be self-conscious and standoffish. Anne is more outgoing, and Peter sometimes finds her behavior embarrassing.)* **OL**

R2 Reading Skill

Drawing Conclusions Ask: What conclusion can you draw about Mrs. Frank? What details support your conclusion? *(Possible response: You can conclude that she has strong ideas about what is appropriate behavior. She disapproves of, or is concerned about, Anne's behavior with Peter; she calls out to Anne in protest.)* **AL**

English Language Coach

Word Parts The stage directions say that Peter becomes self-conscious. Explain that the adjective *conscious* means "aware of." *Self-* refers to one's own person, appearance, and actions. When Peter roughhouses with Anne, he becomes self-conscious, or uncomfortably aware of his own behavior and appearance. *Self-* also means "to, with, or toward oneself," as in *self-centered*. Observe that the prefix *auto-* is similar in meaning to *self-*. *Auto-* means "same one; self; self-acting." As a class, generate lists of words that begin with each prefix. **BL**

Indiana English/Language Arts Academic Standards
SE: 8.1, 8.3.2
TWE: *English Language Coach* (p. 736) 8.1, *English Language Coach* (p. 737) 8.1, *Reading Skill* 8.2.9

Teach

C Critical Thinking

Evaluation **Ask:** What point does Mrs. Frank make about Anne's desire to be treated like a grown-up? *(She says that Anne wants to be treated like a grown-up but acts like a child.)* **BL** **Ask:** Does Mrs. Frank make a good point? Is Anne behaving like a grown-up? *(Possible response: Mrs. Frank does make a good point. Anne does not behave like a grown-up. After being quiet and still all day, she would rather make noise, run around, and act like a child.)* **OL**

R Reading Skill

Drawing Conclusions **Ask:** Why do you think remembering how to dance is important to Anne? What does her statement reveal about her character? *(Possible response: Remembering how to dance is important to Anne because she values activities that are enjoyable and artistic. Anne's statement shows that she will not let the effects of the war dampen her spirit.)* **AL**

ANNE. Who cares if it's dignified? I don't want to be dignified.

[MR. FRANK and MARGOT come from the room on the right. MARGOT goes to help her mother. MR. FRANK starts for the center table to correct MARGOT's school papers.]

MRS. FRANK. *[To ANNE.]* You complain that I don't treat you like a grown-up. But when I do, you resent it.

ANNE. I only want some fun . . . someone to laugh and clown with . . . After you've sat still all day and hardly moved, you've got to have some fun. I don't know what's the matter with that boy. **C**

MR. FRANK. He isn't used to girls. Give him a little time.

ANNE. Time? Isn't two months time? I could cry. *[Catching hold of MARGOT.]* Come on, Margot . . . dance with me. Come on, please.

MARGOT. I have to help with supper.

ANNE. You know we're going to forget how to dance . . . When we get out we won't remember a thing.

[She starts to sing and dance by herself. MR. FRANK takes her in his arms, waltzing with her. MRS. VAN DAAN comes in from the bathroom.] **4** **R**

MRS. VAN DAAN. Next? *[She looks around as she starts putting on her shoes.]* Where's Peter?

ANNE. *[As they are dancing.]* Where would he be!

MRS. VAN DAAN. He hasn't finished his lessons, has he? His father'll kill him if he catches him in there with that cat and his work not done. *[MR. FRANK and ANNE finish their dance. They bow to each other with extravagant formality.[2]]* Anne, get him out of there, will you?

ANNE. *[At PETER's door.]* Peter? Peter?

PETER. *[Opening the door a crack.]* What is it?

ANNE. Your mother says to come out.

2. In showing ***extravagant formality,*** Anne and her father make deep, formal bows, exaggerating the custom of bowing to one's partner at the end of a dance.

Practice the Skills

4 Key Reading Skill

Drawing Conclusions Why does Mr. Frank dance with Anne?

Additional Support

Literature Focus Lesson

Drama Explain to students that background music is often used in drama productions to help set the mood. The music used in a theatrical production or a movie is called a *score*. The sound that occurs onstage as part of the world of the play is called *actual sound*. Have students identify the points in scenes to which they would add music. Ask them to describe the type of music they would select and how it would help set the mood. As they read, alert students to examples of actual sound, such as when Peter steps on a creaky floorboard in scene 2. **OL**

PETER. I'm giving Mouschi his dinner.

MRS. VAN DAAN. You know what your father says.

[She sits on the couch, sewing on the lining of her fur coat.]

PETER. For heaven's sake, I haven't even looked at him since lunch.

MRS. VAN DAAN. I'm just telling you, that's all.

ANNE. I'll feed him.

PETER. I don't want you in there.

MRS. VAN DAAN. Peter!

PETER. [*To ANNE.*] Then give him his dinner and come right out, you hear?

[He comes back to the table. ANNE shuts the door of PETER's room after her and disappears behind the curtain covering his closet.]

R1

MRS. VAN DAAN. [*To PETER.*] Now is that any way to talk to your little girlfriend?

PETER. Mother . . . for heaven's sake . . . will you please stop saying that?

MRS. VAN DAAN. Look at him blush! Look at him!

PETER. Please! I'm not . . . anyway . . . let me alone, will you?

MRS. VAN DAAN. He acts like it was something to be ashamed of. It's nothing to be ashamed of, to have a little girlfriend. **5**

PETER. You're crazy. She's only thirteen.

MRS. VAN DAAN. So what? And you're sixteen. Just perfect. Your father's ten years older than I am. [*To MR. FRANK.*] I warn you, Mr. Frank, if this war lasts much longer, we're going to be related and then . . .

MR. FRANK. *Mazeltov!*[3]

R2

MRS. FRANK. [*Deliberately changing the conversation.*] I wonder where Miep is. She's usually so prompt. **6**

3. ***Mazeltov*** (MAW zul tawv) means "congratulations" or "best wishes" in Hebrew.

Practice the Skills

5 **Reviewing Skills**

Analyzing Using what you've read so far in the play, describe the relationship between Peter and his mother.

6 **Key Reading Skill**

Drawing Conclusions Why does Mrs. Frank change the subject?

Teach

R1 Reading Skill

Review Analyzing **Say:** Consider the interactions between Peter and his mother. Are you sympathetic to Peter? Explain. *(Responses will vary, but most students will sympathize with Peter because of his mother's teasing.)* **AS**

R2 Reading Skill

Drawing Conclusions **Ask:** What does Mrs. Frank think of the idea of Peter being Anne's boyfriend? *(Possible response: Mrs. Frank appears to be uncomfortable with the idea that Anne might have a boyfriend.)* **OL**

Reading Fluency

Active Listening Point out to students that listening to or watching a drama makes demands on an audience. Audiences must listen actively and remember events so that they can follow the story. Explain that one active listening technique is to think of questions about what is being said. Invite volunteers to take parts and read a page of dialogue from the play. Advise the remaining students to close their books and focus on listening. Ask students to think of two questions about the dialogue as they listen. When the page has been read, students should write their questions and use them later in a class discussion. **EL** **BL**

Indiana English/Language Arts Academic Standards

SE: 8.3

TWE: *Literature Focus Lesson* 8.2, *Reading Fluency* 8.7

Teach

R Reading Skill

Drawing Conclusions
Ask: What conclusion can you draw about the relationship between Peter and Anne based on their interaction here? *(Possible response: They tease each other like brother and sister. You can conclude they feel comfortable around each other, even if they are annoyed by each other)* AL

EL Language Coach

Word Parts **Say:** The prefix *un-* is similar in meaning to the prefix *in-*. Can you think of other words beginning with *un-* that are similar in meaning to *intolerable* and *insufferable*? *(Possible responses: unendurable, unbearable, unacceptable)* **OL** **Ask:** What other prefixes can mean "not"? *(Possible responses: non-, a-, an-, dis-)* AL

READING WORKSHOP 1

[Suddenly everything else is forgotten as they hear the sound of an automobile coming to a screeching stop in the street below. They are tense, motionless in their terror. The car starts away. A wave of relief sweeps over them. They pick up their occupations again. ANNE *flings open the door of* PETER*'s room, making a dramatic entrance. She is dressed in* PETER*'s clothes.* PETER *looks at her in fury. The others are amused.]*

ANNE. Good evening, everyone. Forgive me if I don't stay. [*She jumps up on a chair.*] I have a friend waiting for me in there. My friend Tom. Tom Cat. Some people say that we look alike. But Tom has the most beautiful whiskers, and I have only a little fuzz. I am hoping . . . in time . . .

PETER. All right, Mrs. Quack Quack!

ANNE. [*Outraged—jumping down.*] Peter!

PETER. I heard about you . . . How you talked so much in class they called you Mrs. Quack Quack. How Mr. Smitter made you write a composition . . . " 'Quack, quack,' said Mrs. Quack Quack." R

ANNE. Well, go on. Tell them the rest. How it was so good he read it out loud to the class and then read it to all his other classes!

PETER. Quack! Quack! Quack . . . Quack . . . Quack . . .

[ANNE *pulls off the coat and trousers.*]

ANNE. You are the most **intolerable**, **insufferable**[4] boy I've ever met! 7

[*She throws the clothes down the stairwell.* PETER *goes down after them.*]

PETER. Quack, quack, quack!

MRS. VAN DAAN. [*To* ANNE.] That's right, Anneke! Give it to him!

ANNE. With all the boys in the world . . . Why I had to get locked up with one like you! . . .

4. Both ***intolerable*** and ***insufferable*** mean "unbearable."

Practice the Skills

7 English Language Coach

Word Parts The base words *tolerate* and *suffer* mean "to put up with (something unpleasant)." Here, *in-* means "not," and *-able* means "worthy of." If you put these exact meanings together in order, they make no sense: "not to put up with worthy of." So you juggle them a little: "not worth putting up with." And that's a good definition for both **intolerable** and **insufferable**. EL

Additional Support

Differentiated Instruction

Building Background The conditions under which the Franks and Van Daans were living would likely cause them to be in poor physical and emotional health. People who are isolated indoors under stressful conditions with a poor diet can suffer serious health consequences. The human body takes some nutrients that it needs to stay healthy, such as vitamin D, from sunshine. In addition, people benefit from eating a wide variety of foods, especially fresh fruits and vegetables. Have students discuss how the families' emotional health might be affected by living in such close quarters. AL

R PETER. Quack, quack, quack, and from now on stay out of my room! 8

[As PETER passes her, ANNE puts out her foot, tripping him. He picks himself up, and goes on into his room.]

MRS. FRANK. *[Quietly.]* Anne, dear . . . your hair. *[She feels ANNE'S forehead.]* You're warm. Are you feeling all right?

ANNE. Please, Mother.

[She goes over to the center table, slipping into her shoes.]

MRS. FRANK. *[Following her.]* You haven't a fever, have you?

ANNE. *[Pulling away.]* No. No.

MRS. FRANK. You know we can't call a doctor here, ever. There's only one thing to do . . . watch carefully. Prevent an illness before it comes. Let me see your tongue.

ANNE. Mother, this is perfectly **absurd.**

C MRS. FRANK. Anne, dear, don't be such a baby. Let me see your tongue. *[As ANNE refuses, MRS. FRANK appeals to MR. FRANK.]* Otto . . . ?

MR. FRANK. You hear your mother, Anne.

[ANNE flicks out her tongue for a second, then turns away.]

MRS. FRANK. Come on—open up! *[As ANNE opens her mouth very wide.]* You seem all right . . . but perhaps an aspirin . . .

MRS. VAN DAAN. For heaven's sake, don't give that child any pills. I waited for fifteen minutes this morning for her to come out of the w.c.

ANNE. I was washing my hair!

MR. FRANK. I think there's nothing the matter with our Anne that a ride on her bike, or a visit with her friend Jopie de Waal wouldn't cure. Isn't that so, Anne? 9

Practice the Skills

8 Reviewing Skills

Connecting In anger, Peter tries to mock and embarrass Anne. Have you ever done such a thing? What good did it do?

9 Key Reading Skill

Drawing Conclusions Why is Mrs. Frank so concerned? Why is it so important to prevent illness? What does Mr. Frank think is wrong with Anne?

Vocabulary

absurd (ub SURD) *adj.* not making sense; very silly

Teach

R Reading Skill

Review Connecting
Ask: How would you feel if you were in Peter's place and Anne put on your clothes? *(Possible responses: annoyed, amused)* BL **Ask:** Do you think Peter's response is reasonable? Why or why not? *(Possible response: His response is reasonable because Anne invades Peter's privacy by going into his room and putting on his clothes.)* OL

C Critical Thinking

Evaluation Ask: Do you think that Mrs. Frank's fears about illness are justified? Why? *(Possible response: Her fears are justified because the families in hiding cannot call a doctor if someone gets sick.)* OL **Ask:** Do you think that Mr. Frank is correct in his guess about what is bothering Anne? Explain. *(Possible response: Mr. Frank is probably right because Anne seems to be an outgoing, friendly girl. Being trapped indoors with no friends would be difficult for her.)* AL

Literature Focus Lesson

Comparing Genres Remind students that the play was adapted from Anne's diary. Details were also added from the playwrights' discussions with Mr. Frank. Have students obtain Anne's diary from the library. Encourage them to find diary entries that correspond to some of the scenes in the play. Ask them to compare the playwrights' version of events with the diary entries. How is it different learning about the details from Anne's perspective? Have students make a chart in their Learner's Notebooks comparing elements of the diary and the play. AL

Indiana English/Language Arts Academic Standards
SE: 8.1, 8.3
TWE: *Differentiated Instruction* 8.2, *Literature Focus Lesson* 8.3

Teach

R1 Reading Skill

Drawing Conclusions

Ask: Why is Miep's arrival of greater concern than the passing of the bombers overhead? *(Possible response: Miep's arrival is of more immediate concern to the families because she brings them food and news of the outside world.)* **OL**

R2 Reading Skill

Drawing Conclusions

Ask: What can you tell about Mr. Van Daan and Anne from their different reaction to the news that they'll be eating yet more beans? Explain. *(Possible response: Mr. Van Daan's complaining shows he is tired of doing without. Anne's joking shows she is more adaptable and positive.)* **AL**

READING WORKSHOP 1

[*MR. VAN DAAN comes down into the room. From outside we hear faint sounds of bombers going over and a burst of ack-ack.*[5]] **10**

MR. VAN DAAN. Miep not come yet?

MRS. VAN DAAN. The workmen just left, a little while ago.

MR. VAN DAAN. What's for dinner tonight?

MRS. VAN DAAN. Beans.

MR. VAN DAAN. Not again!

MRS. VAN DAAN. Poor Putti! I know. But what can we do? That's all that Miep brought us.

[*MR. VAN DAAN starts to pace, his hands behind his back.* ANNE *follows behind him, imitating him.*]

ANNE. We are now in what is known as the "bean cycle." Beans boiled, beans *en casserole,* beans with strings, beans without strings . . . **11**

[*PETER has come out of his room. He slides into his place at the table, becoming immediately absorbed in his studies.*]

MR. VAN DAAN. [*To* PETER.] I saw you . . . in there, playing with your cat.

MRS. VAN DAAN. He just went in for a second, putting his coat away. He's been out here all the time, doing his lessons.

MR. FRANK. [*Looking up from the papers.*] Anne, you got an excellent in your history paper today . . . and very good in Latin.

ANNE. [*Sitting beside him.*] How about algebra?

MR. FRANK. I'll have to make a confession. Up until now I've managed to stay ahead of you in algebra. Today you caught up with me. We'll leave it to Margot to correct.

ANNE. Isn't algebra **vile,** Pim!

5. ***Ack-ack*** was the slang name for antiaircraft gunfire. It was the Allies who were bombing Nazi-controlled Netherlands.

Vocabulary

vile (vyl) *adj.* very bad; extremely unpleasant

Practice the Skills

10 Key Reading Skill

Drawing Conclusions Earlier in the scene, everyone stopped in fear when he or she heard a car. Here, no one pays much attention to the bombers and antiaircraft fire. What accounts for the different reactions? Explain.

11 Reviewing Skills

Connecting There's probably some kind of food that you get tired of eating, meal after meal. How do you express your feelings about it?

Additional Support

Literature Focus Lesson

Theme Writers use characters, dialogue, and events to convey themes, or general messages about life. Themes are very rarely stated directly, especially in plays. Instead, readers must infer them. Have students tell one possible theme that has been conveyed in the play thus far. Share these possible themes:

- Having a sense of humor can help people through hard times.
- Keeping up regular activities during extraordinary circumstances can make life easier.
- Terrible things can happen to good people. **OL**

MR. FRANK. Vile!

MARGOT. [*To* MR. FRANK.] How did I do?

ANNE. [*Getting up.*] Excellent, excellent, excellent, excellent!

MR. FRANK. [*To* MARGOT.] You should have used the subjunctive[6] here . . .

MARGOT. Should I? . . . I thought . . . look here . . . I didn't use it here . . .

[*The two become absorbed in the papers.*]

ANNE. Mrs. Van Daan, may I try on your coat?

MRS. FRANK. No, Anne.

MRS. VAN DAAN. [*Giving it to* ANNE.] It's all right . . . but careful with it. [ANNE *puts it on and struts with it.*] My father gave me that the year before he died. He always bought the best that money could buy.

ANNE. Mrs. Van Daan, did you have a lot of boyfriends before you were married? **12**

MRS. FRANK. Anne, that's a personal question. It's not courteous to ask personal questions.

MRS. VAN DAAN. Oh I don't mind. [*To* ANNE.] Our house was always swarming with boys. When I was a girl we had . . .

MR. VAN DAAN. Oh, God. Not again!

MRS. VAN DAAN. [*Good-humored.*] Shut up! [*Without a pause, to* ANNE. MR. VAN DAAN **mimics** MRS. VAN DAAN, *speaking the first few words in unison with her.*] One summer we had a big house in Hilversum. The boys came buzzing round like bees around a jam pot. And when I was sixteen! . . . We were wearing our skirts very short those days and I had good-looking legs. [*She pulls up her skirt, going to* MR. FRANK.] I still have 'em. I may not

6. The ***subjunctive*** (sub JUNK tiv) is the verb form used to express wishes, possibilities, or things that are opposed to fact. In the sentence, "If I were you, I wouldn't go," *were* is the subjunctive form of *to be.*

Vocabulary

mimics (MIM iks) *v.* makes fun of by imitating or copying

Practice the Skills

12 Key Reading Skill

Drawing Conclusions Anne jokes about beans and algebra and asks Mrs.Van Daan about boyfriends she had before she was married. What conclusions can you draw about Anne from these comments?

Teach

EL Language Coach

Word Parts Say: Mrs. Van Daan tells Anne to be careful with the fur coat. The base word of *careful* is *care*. List as many words as you can that share this base word. ***(carefree, caregiver, careless, caretaker, careworn, caring, uncaring.)*** **Ask:** What do the meanings of these words have in common? ***(All of these words relate to worry, concern, or responsibility.)*** **EL BL**

R Reading Skill

Review Comparing and Contrasting Ask: How do the personalities of Mrs. Frank and Mrs. Van Daan differ? ***(Possible response: Mrs. Van Daan is excitable and melodramatic and draws attention to herself. Mrs. Frank is more reserved, dignified, and concerned with polite, respectful behavior.)*** **OL**

Literature Focus Lesson

Figurative Language Read aloud Mrs. Van Daan's description of what life was like at her house when she was a girl. Focus on the sentences that describe the boys who came to visit. Point out that the statements "our house was always swarming with boys" and "the boys came buzzing round like bees around a jam pot" are examples of figurative language. These descriptions have a different meaning than the literal meanings of the words. Discuss what these images suggest about the young Mrs. Van Daan. Ask students to identify the ways in which the boys were like bees. **EL OL**

Indiana English/Language Arts Academic Standards

SE: 8.1, 8.2.9, 8.3

TWE: *Literature Focus Lesson* 8.3; *Literature Focus Lesson* 8.1.1, 8.3.6

Teach

R Reading Skill

Drawing Conclusions
Ask: Why is Peter embarrassed? *(Possible response: Peter may be embarrassed that his mother is flirting with Mr. Frank.)* BL **Ask:** Why do you think Mrs. Van Daan acts the way she does? *(Possible responses: Mrs. Van Daan probably wants attention. She may also be bored with her confinement.)* OL

L Literary Element

Review Irony **Say:** Remember that verbal irony occurs when a person says one thing but means another. Why does Peter agree with his father's statement that Peter should be ashamed of himself? *(Possible response: His father's comment has embarrassed and maybe even hurt him. Peter may be trying to lighten the mood by repeating and exaggerating his father's point.)* AL

be as pretty as I used to be, but I still have my legs. How about it, Mr. Frank? 13

MR. VAN DAAN. All right. All right. We see them.

MRS. VAN DAAN. I'm not asking you. I'm asking Mr. Frank.

PETER. Mother, for heaven's sake.

MRS. VAN DAAN. Oh, I embarrass you, do I? Well, I just hope the girl you marry has as good. [*Then to* ANNE.] My father used to worry about me, with so many boys hanging round. He told me, if any of them gets fresh, you say to him . . . "Remember, Mr. So-and-So, remember I'm a lady."

ANNE. "Remember, Mr. So-and-So, remember I'm a lady." 14

[*She gives* MRS. VAN DAAN *her coat.*]

MR. VAN DAAN. Look at you, talking that way in front of her! Don't you know she puts it all down in that diary?

MRS. VAN DAAN. So, if she does? I'm only telling the truth!

[ANNE *stretches out, putting her ear to the floor, listening to what is going on below. The sound of the bombers fades away.*]

MRS. FRANK. [*Setting the table.*] Would you mind, Peter, if I moved you over to the couch?

ANNE. [*Listening.*] Miep must have the radio on.

[PETER *picks up his papers, going over to the couch beside* MRS. VAN DAAN.]

MR. VAN DAAN. [*Accusingly, to* PETER.] Haven't you finished yet?

PETER. No.

MR. VAN DAAN. You ought to be ashamed of yourself.

PETER. All right. All right. I'm a dunce. I'm a hopeless case. Why do I go on?

MRS. VAN DAAN. You're not hopeless. Don't talk that way. It's just that you haven't anyone to help you, like the girls have. [*To* MR. FRANK.] Maybe you could help him, Mr. Frank?

Practice the Skills

13 Key Reading Skill

Drawing Conclusions What does Mrs. Van Daan want the others—especially Mr. Frank—to get from her story? What do her story and her behavior tell you about her?

14 Key Reading Skill

Drawing Conclusions Why does Anne repeat these words? (Hint: See Mr. Van Daan's next speech.)

Additional Support

Reading Fluency

Oral Reading The actors, with the help of the director, determine how to deliver lines in a play to best fit the mood and action of a scene. Have students work in small groups to rehearse and perform some of the dialogue on this page and the next. Suggest that students speak in different ways—quickly, slowly, sharply, angrily, or calmly—to capture the emotion of the dialogue. Remind students to read as though they are the characters rather than themselves. If time allows, offer students feedback and direction, and have them perform their readings again. AS

MR. FRANK. I'm sure that his father . . . ?

MR. VAN DAAN. Not me. I can't do anything with him. He won't listen to me. You go ahead . . . if you want.

MR. FRANK. [*Going to* PETER.] What about it, Peter? Shall we make our school coeducational?[7]

MRS. VAN DAAN. [*Kissing* MR. FRANK.] You're an angel, Mr. Frank. An angel. I don't know why I didn't meet you before I met that one there. Here, sit down, Mr. Frank . . . [*She forces him down on the couch beside* PETER.] Now, Peter, you listen to Mr. Frank. **15**

MR. FRANK. It might be better for us to go into Peter's room. **R**

[PETER *jumps up eagerly, leading the way.*]

MRS. VAN DAAN. That's right. You go in there, Peter. You listen to Mr. Frank. Mr. Frank is a highly educated man.

[*As* MR. FRANK *is about to follow* PETER *into his room,* MRS. FRANK *stops him and wipes the lipstick from his lips. Then she closes the door after them.*]

15 Key Reading Skill

Drawing Conclusions What conclusions can you draw about Mrs. Van Daan, Peter, and Mr. Frank from this dialogue? Explain.

Auguste and Herman van Pels (Van Daan), around 1940.

Analyzing the Photo
Two years before going into hiding, the van Pels enjoy a walk outdoors. In real life, the van Pels and Franks were long-time friends.

7. A ***coeducational*** school has both male and female students.

Teach

R Reading Skill

Drawing Conclusions

Ask: When Mr. Frank suggests that he and Peter study in Peter's room, why is Peter so eager to go? ***(He wants to escape the uncomfortable situation with his mother and father in the living room.)*** **OL** **Ask:** Do you think Mr. Frank and Peter would be able to get work done in the living room? Why or why not? ***(Possible response: They would probably not be able to get much work done with Mrs. Van Daan and Anne distracting them.)*** **AL**

Viewing the Photo

Ask: How does the photo of the Van Pels, who are referred to as the Van Daans in the play, add to your understanding of the living situation in the attic? *(Responses will vary. Students may say that the photo gives them a better idea of everything that the Van Pels and Franks had to give up when they went into hiding, such as walks outside and social time with friends.)* **OL**

English Language Coach

Word Parts Write the word *coeducational* on the board, and draw a slash between the prefix *co-* and the rest of the word: *co/educational.* Tell students that co- means "with" or "together." *Coeducation* is the education of girls and boys together in the same classes or school. Explain that many words in English contain the prefix *co-*. Have students brainstorm as many words as possible that include the prefix *co-* or one of its variants *(co-chair, coauthor, cooperate, copilot)*. List the words on the board. Ask students to share words and definitions. **EL** **BL**

Indiana English/Language Arts Academic Standards
SE: 8.2.9, 8.3
TWE: *Reading Skill* 8.2.9, *Reading Fluency* 8.7.2, *English Language Coach* 8.1

Teach

R1 Reading Skill

Review Comparing and Contrasting **Ask:** How does the bickering between Mr. and Mrs. Van Daan here differ from their bickering earlier in the scene? *(The bickering on the previous pages was light-hearted, but here it is more serious and hurtful.)* OL
Ask: Why do you think Mr. Van Daan becomes angry when he sees Anne staring? *(Possible responses: Mr. Van Daan does not want Anne to write in her diary about his fight with Mrs. Van Daan. He is upset that they have no privacy to argue.)* AL

R2 Reading Skill

Review Analyzing Have students consider Mrs. Frank's words and actions here and elsewhere in the scene.
Ask: What does Mrs. Frank seem to see as her role in the group? *(Possible responses: to create order and a sense of a "normal" life; to keep peace among the others)* OL

READING WORKSHOP 1

ANNE. [*On the floor, listening.*] Shh! I can hear a man's voice talking.

MR. VAN DAAN. [*To* ANNE.] Isn't it bad enough here without your sprawling all over the place?

[ANNE *sits up.*]

MRS. VAN DAAN. [*To* MR. VAN DAAN.] If you didn't smoke so much, you wouldn't be so bad-tempered.

MR. VAN DAAN. Am I smoking? Do you see me smoking?

MRS. VAN DAAN. Don't tell me you've used up all those cigarettes.

MR. VAN DAAN. One package. Miep only brought me one package.

MRS. VAN DAAN. It's a filthy habit anyway. It's a good time to break yourself. R1

MR. VAN DAAN. Oh, stop it, please.

MRS. VAN DAAN. You're smoking up all our money. You know that, don't you?

MR. VAN DAAN. Will you shut up? [*During this,* MRS. FRANK *and* MARGOT *have studiously kept their eyes down. But* ANNE, *seated on the floor, has been following the discussion interestedly.* MR. VAN DAAN *turns to see her staring up at him.*] And what are you staring at? 16

ANNE. I never heard grown-ups quarrel before. I thought only children quarreled.

MR. VAN DAAN. This isn't a quarrel! It's a discussion. And I never heard children so rude before.

ANNE. [*Rising, indignantly.*[8]] I, rude!

MR. VAN DAAN. Yes!

MRS. FRANK. [*Quickly.*] Anne, will you get me my knitting? [ANNE *goes to get it.*] I must remember, when Miep comes, to ask her to bring me some more wool. 17 R2

8. ***Indignantly*** (in DIG nunt lee) means "with anger in response to an insult or injustice."

Practice the Skills

16 Reviewing Skills

Predicting Which character seems to be having the most trouble being cooped up? Could you predict anything about this character?

17 Reviewing Skills

Analyzing Mrs. Frank steps in again to change the subject. Why does she do that?

Additional Support

Differentiated Instruction

Making a Venn Diagram Many of the characters in *The Diary of Anne Frank* have contrasting personalities. These contrasts help the audience appreciate how conflicts develop among the people in hiding. Tell students to select two characters to compare and contrast in a Venn diagram. Have students include both similarities and differences. BL
Finally, tell students to use their diagrams to write a paragraph explaining how differences between the characters have lead, or could lead, to conflict. OL

MARGOT. [*Going to her room.*] I need some hairpins and some soap. I made a list.

[*She goes into her bedroom to get the list.*]

MRS. FRANK. [*To* ANNE.] Have you some library books for Miep when she comes?

ANNE. It's a wonder that Miep has a life of her own, the way we make her run errands for us. Please, Miep, get me some starch. Please take my hair out and have it cut. Tell me all the latest news, Miep. [*She goes over, kneeling on the couch beside* MRS. VAN DAAN.] Did you know she was engaged? His name is Dirk, and Miep's afraid the Nazis will ship him off to Germany to work in one of their war plants. That's what they're doing with some of the young Dutchmen . . . they pick them up off the streets—

MR. VAN DAAN. [*Interrupting.*] Don't you ever get tired of talking? Suppose you try keeping still for five minutes. Just five minutes. **18**

[*He starts to pace again. Again* ANNE *follows him, mimicking him.* MRS. FRANK *jumps up and takes her by the arm up to the sink, and gives her a glass of milk.*]

MRS. FRANK. Come here, Anne. It's time for your glass of milk.

MR. VAN DAAN. Talk, talk, talk. I never heard such a child. Where is my . . . ? Every evening it's the same, talk, talk, talk. [*He looks around.*] Where is my . . . ?

MRS. VAN DAAN. What're you looking for?

MR. VAN DAAN. My pipe. Have you seen my pipe?

MRS. VAN DAAN. What good's a pipe? You haven't got any tobacco.

MR. VAN DAAN. At least I'll have something to hold in my mouth! [*Opening* MARGOT'S *bedroom door.*] Margot, have you seen my pipe?

MARGOT. It was on the table last night.

[ANNE *puts her glass of milk on the table and picks up his pipe, hiding it behind her back.*]

Practice the Skills

18 Key Reading Skill

Drawing Conclusions Why does Mr. Van Daan become so irritated? Is it only Anne's talking, or is something else bothering him?

Literature Focus Lesson

Word Choice Explain to students that good descriptive writing includes not only colorful adjectives, but strong, specific verbs. Point out that in the stage directions, the authors use descriptive action verbs to convey a great deal of information in a few words. For example, the stage directions note that Anne is "mimicking" Mr. Van Daan. This verb tells readers not only that Anne imitates Mr. Van Daan, but also that she does so in a funny, mocking way. Ask students to identify other examples of strong action verbs that appear either in the stage directions or in the dialogue. **OL**

Teach

R Reading Skill

Drawing Conclusions
Ask: How does Mr. Van Daan's life now compare with his life before he went into hiding? *(Possible response: Mr. Van Daan used to be the head of his household and a businessperson with authority. Now Mr. Frank is in charge, and Mr. Van Daan has little power.)* **OL** **Ask:** Why do you think Mr. Van Daan snaps at Anne? *(Possible response: Anne is an easy target because she is young and mischievous. However, Mr. Van Daan is actually more annoyed at his circumstances than at anything Anne has done.)* **AL**

L Literary Element

Review Irony **Say:** Irony is a contrast between what is said or done and what is expected. What is ironic in Mr. Van Daan's challenging Anne to stay quiet for five minutes? *(Possible response: It is ironic because Anne, like the others, must stay absolutely silent throughout most of the day.)* **OL**

Indiana English/Language Arts Academic Standards
SE: 8.3
TWE: *Differentiated Instruction* 8.4.1, *Literature Focus Lesson* 8.1

Teach

EL Language Coach

Word Parts **Say:** The word *aggravate* is a verb meaning "to cause displeasure or anger." When Mr. Van Daan calls Anne "aggravating," however, he uses the word as an adjective. When the suffix *-ing* is added to some verbs, the word can be an adjective. List other adjectives formed by adding the *-ing* suffix to a verb. *(Possible responses: frustrating, moving, engaging)* EL BL

R Reading Skill

Review Comparing and Contrasting **Say:** Consider Mr. Van Daan's relationship with his wife. Does Mrs. Van Daan fit her husband's description of the perfect wife? Support your answer with details from the text. *(Possible response: Mrs. Van Daan doesn't fit her husband's description. Earlier she was showing off, and he was amused. Often, she does not listen to him, and she is not a quiet person.)* OL

MR. VAN DAAN. I know. I know. Anne, did you see my pipe? . . . Anne!

MRS. FRANK. Anne, Mr. Van Daan is speaking to you.

ANNE. Am I allowed to talk now?

MR. VAN DAAN. You're the most **aggravating** . . . The trouble with you is, you've been spoiled. What you need is a good old-fashioned spanking. EL

ANNE. [*Mimicking* MRS. VAN DAAN.] "Remember, Mr. So-and-So, remember I'm a lady."

[*She thrusts the pipe into his mouth, then picks up her glass of milk.*]

MR. VAN DAAN. [*Restraining himself with difficulty.*] Why aren't you nice and quiet like your sister Margot? Why do you have to show off all the time? Let me give you a little advice, young lady. Men don't like that kind of thing in a girl. You know that? A man likes a girl who'll listen to him once in a while . . . a domestic[9] girl, who'll keep her house shining for her husband . . . who loves to cook and sew and . . . R

ANNE. I'd cut my throat first! I'd open my veins! I'm going to be **remarkable**! I'm going to Paris . . . 19

MR. VAN DAAN. [*Scoffingly.*] Paris!

ANNE. . . . to study music and art.

MR. VAN DAAN. Yeah! Yeah!

ANNE. I'm going to be a famous dancer or singer . . . or something wonderful. 20

[*She makes a wide gesture, spilling the glass of milk on the fur coat in* MRS. VAN DAAN'*s lap.* MARGOT *rushes quickly over with a towel.* ANNE *tries to brush the milk off with her skirt.*]

9. To be ***domestic*** (duh MES tik) is to enjoy cooking, cleaning, and caring for the family.

Vocabulary

aggravating (AG ruh vay ting) *adj.* irritating; annoying

Practice the Skills

19 English Language Coach

Word Parts The root *mark* means "notice." What prefix and suffix are added to *mark* to make the word **remarkable**? What does *remarkable* mean?

20 Reviewing Skills

Comparing and Contrasting How does Mr. Van Daan's description of the type of girl "a man likes" differ from Anne's vision of herself?

Additional Support

Differentiated Instruction

Diary Entry Have students write a brief diary entry about Anne spilling milk on Mrs. Van Daan's coat. Ask half the class to write entries from Anne's point of view and half to write them from Mrs. Van Daan's perspective. Have students tell what happened and how they felt about it. Remind them to use the first-person pronoun *I*. Invite volunteers to read their diary entries aloud to the class. How is the event different when told from the two different points of view? AS

MRS. VAN DAAN. Now look what you've done . . . you clumsy little fool! My beautiful fur coat my father gave me . . .

ANNE. I'm so sorry.

MRS. VAN DAAN. What do you care? It isn't yours . . . So go on, ruin it! Do you know what that coat cost? Do you? And now look at it! Look at it!

ANNE. I'm very, very sorry.

MRS. VAN DAAN. I could kill you for this. I could just kill you!

[*MRS. VAN DAAN goes up the stairs, clutching the coat. MR. VAN DAAN starts after her.*]

MR. VAN DAAN. Petronella . . . *liefje! Liefje!* . . . Come back . . . the supper . . . come back!

MRS. FRANK. Anne, you must not behave in that way.

ANNE. It was an accident. Anyone can have an accident.

MRS. FRANK. I don't mean that. I mean the answering back. You must not answer back. They are our guests. We must always show the greatest courtesy to them. We're all living under terrible tension. [*She stops as MARGOT indicates that VAN DAAN can hear. When he is gone, she continues.*] That's why we must control ourselves . . . You don't hear Margot getting into arguments with them, do you? Watch Margot. She's always courteous with them. Never familiar. She keeps her distance. And they respect her for it. Try to be like Margot.

ANNE. And have them walk all over me, the way they do her? No, thanks!

MRS. FRANK. I'm not afraid that anyone is going to walk all over you, Anne. I'm afraid for other people, that you'll walk on them. I don't know what happens to you, Anne. You are wild, self-willed. If I had ever talked to my mother as you talk to me . . .

ANNE. Things have changed. People aren't like that any more. "Yes, Mother." "No, Mother." "Anything you say, Mother." I've got to fight things out for myself! Make something of myself! 21

Practice the Skills

21 **BIG Question**

How would you describe Anne's attitude? How is it related to her determination to survive? Write your answer on the Workshop 1 Foldable for Unit 6.

Teach

C1 Critical Thinking

Comprehension **Ask:** Why is the fur coat so important to Mrs. Van Daan? *(It was a special and costly gift from her father.)* **Ask:** What does the coat symbolize for her? *(It symbolizes a better time, when she could enjoy luxuries.)* OL

C2 Critical Thinking

Application **Ask:** How does Anne think things have changed since her mother was growing up? *(Anne thinks that adolescents are much more likely to question their parents and to draw their own conclusions about life.)* OL **Ask:** Do you ever feel as Anne does? *(Responses will vary.)* AS

BQ BIG Question

Ask: What aspects of Margot's personality might help her cope with the confinement? *(Possible response: Margot's quietness and maturity may help her accept her confinement.)* **Ask:** What aspects of Anne's personality might help her cope? *(Possible response: Anne's imagination provides a way for her to escape. Her optimism and energy keep her from feeling hopeless.)* AL

Literature Focus Lesson

Conflict Remind students that conflict is a struggle between two opposing forces. In addition to the main conflict, between the people in the attic and the Nazis who force them into hiding, many conflicts occur between the members of the two families. As a class, discuss some of the conflicts that have occurred so far:

- between Anne and Peter
- between Anne and Mrs. Van Daan
- between Mr. and Mrs. Van Daan
- between the families and the Nazi forces OL

Indiana English/Language Arts Academic Standards

SE: 8.1, 8.3

TWE: *Differentiated Instruction* 8.5.7, *Literature Focus Lesson* 8.3.2

Teach

Viewing the Photo
Ask: What does this photograph suggest that Anne might miss while in hiding? *(Possible responses: She probably misses seeing friends, being outdoors, and enjoying games. She misses having a normal life.)* BL OL

R Reading Skill
Review Connecting Ask: Have you ever been compared unfavorably with someone else, as Anne is here? How did that make you feel? Compare and contrast your reaction and Anne's. *(Responses will vary.)* AS

Anne (right) and a friend, playing near the Franks' apartment in Amsterdam, 1930s.

MRS. FRANK. It isn't necessary to fight to do it. Margot doesn't fight, and isn't she . . . ?

ANNE. [*Violently rebellious.*] Margot! Margot! Margot! That's all I hear from everyone . . . how wonderful Margot is . . . "Why aren't you like Margot?"

MARGOT. [*Protesting.*] Oh, come on, Anne, don't be so . . . R

ANNE. [*Paying no attention.*] Everything she does is right, and everything I do is wrong! I'm the goat[10] around here! . . . You're all against me! . . . And you worst of all! 22

[*She rushes off into her room and throws herself down on the settee, stifling*[11] *her sobs.* MRS. FRANK *sighs and starts toward the stove.*]

MRS. FRANK. [*To* MARGOT.] Let's put the soup on the stove . . . if there's anyone who cares to eat. Margot, will you take the

22 Key Reading Skill

Drawing Conclusions Review Anne's dialogue on pages 748–750. Can you draw any new conclusions about the type of person she is? Why or why not?

10. A ***goat*** (or scapegoat) is one who is blamed or punished for other people's mistakes.
11. ***Stifling*** means "smothering; holding back."

Additional Support

English Language Coach

Word Origins Point out that Anne's description of herself as "the goat" is a reference to being a scapegoat. Read the definition of *goat,* or *scapegoat,* provided in the footnote on this page. Explain that the term *scapegoat* and its meaning can be traced to a ceremony described in the Bible in which the sins of the Jewish people were symbolically transferred to a goat on the holy day of Yom Kippur, "The Day of Atonement." The term *scapegoat* has come to refer to an innocent person who takes the blame for others. Ask students whether they agree that Anne is a scapegoat in this situation. EL BL OL bread out? [*MARGOT gets the bread from the cupboard.*] I don't know how we can go on living this way . . . I can't say a word to Anne . . . she flies at me . . .

MARGOT. You know Anne. In half an hour she'll be out here, laughing and joking.

MRS. FRANK. And . . . [*She makes a motion upwards, indicating the VAN DAANS.*] . . . I told your father it wouldn't work . . . but no . . . no . . . he had to ask them, he said . . . he owed it to him, he said. Well, he knows now that I was right! These quarrels! . . . This **bickering!** 23

MARGOT. [*With a warning look.*] Shush. Shush.

[*The buzzer for the door sounds. MRS. FRANK gasps, startled.*]

MRS. FRANK. Every time I hear that sound, my heart stops! R

MARGOT. [*Starting for PETER'S door.*] It's Miep. [*She knocks at the door.*] Father?

[*MR. FRANK comes quickly from PETER'S room.*]

MR. FRANK. Thank you, Margot. [*As he goes down the steps to open the outer door.*] Has everyone his list?

MARGOT. I'll get my books. [*Giving her mother a list.*] Here's your list. [*MARGOT goes into her and ANNE'S bedroom on the right. ANNE sits up, hiding her tears, as MARGOT comes in.*] Miep's here.

[*MARGOT picks up her books and goes back. ANNE hurries over to the mirror, smoothing her hair.*]

MR. VAN DAAN. [*Coming down the stairs.*] Is it Miep?

MARGOT. Yes. Father's gone down to let her in.

MR. VAN DAAN. At last I'll have some cigarettes!

MRS. FRANK. [*To MR. VAN DAAN.*] I can't tell you how unhappy I am about Mrs. Van Daan's coat. Anne should never have touched it.

MR. VAN DAAN. She'll be all right.

Vocabulary

bickering (BIK ur ing) *n.* a quarrel or argument, especially about minor details

Practice the Skills

23 Key Reading Skill

Drawing Conclusions Both Mrs. Frank and Margot try to act as peacemaker at various times. Have they been successful in that role? Explain.

Teach

R Reading Skill

Drawing Conclusions Ask: Why does Mrs. Frank says her heart stops when she hears the buzzer? *(She is terrified that someone has found their hiding place.)* OL

C Critical Thinking

Comprehension Have students explain why Miep's visits are so important to those in hiding. Encourage students to refer to specific characters and details from the text to support their observations. *(Responses will vary.)* OL

Differentiated Instruction

Analyzing Poetry Share with students the following poem, which is credited to German pastor Martin Niemöller.

First they came for the Communists,
and I didn't speak up,
because I wasn't a Communist.
Then they came for the Jews,
and I didn't speak up,
because I wasn't a Jew.
Then they came for the Catholics,
and I didn't speak up,
because I was a Protestant.
Then they came for me,
and by that time there was no one
left to speak up for me.

Have students discuss the poem's meaning. AL

Indiana English/Language Arts Academic Standards

SE: 8.2.9, 8.3

TWE: *English Language Coach* 8.1, *Differentiated Instruction* 8.3.5

READING WORKSHOP 1

Teach

L Literary Element

Act and Scene **Ask:** How does the atmosphere change briefly when Mr. Kraler arrives? *(Possible response: Before Mr. Kraler mentions the reason for his visit, the Franks and the Van Daans are happy to see him because he usually brings good news.)* OL

R Reading Skill

Drawing Conclusions
Ask: Why do you think Mr. Kraler carries food in his briefcase rather than in a crate or box? *(Possible response: He wants to make sure that no one knows he is taking food to the attic. Any suspicious behavior could be reported to the Nazis.)* OL

MRS. FRANK. Is there anything I can do?

MR. VAN DAAN. Don't worry.

[He turns to meet MIEP. *But it is not* MIEP *who comes up the steps. It is* MR. KRALER, *followed by* MR. FRANK. *Their faces are grave.*[12] ANNE *comes from the bedroom.* PETER *comes from his room.]* 24

MRS. FRANK. Mr. Kraler!

MR. VAN DAAN. How are you, Mr. Kraler?

MARGOT. This is a surprise.

MRS. FRANK. When Mr. Kraler comes, the sun begins to shine.

MR. VAN DAAN. Miep is coming?

MR. KRALER. Not tonight.

*[*KRALER *goes to* MARGOT *and* MRS. FRANK *and* ANNE, *shaking hands with them.]*

MRS. FRANK. Wouldn't you like a cup of coffee? . . . Or, better still, will you have supper with us?

MR. FRANK. Mr. Kraler has something to talk over with us. Something has happened, he says, which demands an immediate decision.

MRS. FRANK. *[Fearful.]* What is it?

*[*MR. KRALER *sits down on the couch. As he talks he takes bread, cabbages, milk, etc., from his briefcase, giving them to* MARGOT *and* ANNE *to put away.]*

MR. KRALER. Usually, when I come up here, I try to bring you some bit of good news. What's the use of telling you the bad news when there's nothing that you can do about it? But today something has happened . . . Dirk . . . Miep's Dirk, you know, came to me just now. He tells me that he has a Jewish friend living near him. A dentist. He says he's in trouble. He begged me, could I do anything for this man? Could I find him a hiding place? . . . So I've come to you . . . I know it's a terrible thing to ask of you, living as you are, but would you take him in with you?

---

12. Their faces are very serious and concerned *(grave).*

Practice the Skills

24 Key Literary Element

Act and Scene There is no actual scene break here, but notice the change in the "atmosphere" when Mr. Kraler makes a surprise visit.

Additional Support

Reading in the Real World

Citizenship Explain to students that sometimes being a conscientious citizen means standing up and fighting against unjust laws. The European Resistance were non-Jewish people who worked against the Nazi regime by helping Jews escape. These people were seen as heroes by many after the war as a result of the sacrifices they made to resist Nazi persecution. Have students research the life of Miep Gies, or others who helped Jews during World War II. How did their experiences affect the rest of their lives? OL

MR. FRANK. Of course we will. **25**

MR. KRALER. [*Rising.*] It'll be just for a night or two . . . until I find some other place. This happened so suddenly that I didn't know where to turn.

MR. FRANK. Where is he?

MR. KRALER. Downstairs in the office.

MR. FRANK. Good. Bring him up.

MR. KRALER. His name is Dussel . . . Jan Dussel.[13]

MR. FRANK. Dussel . . . I think I know him.

MR. KRALER. I'll get him.

[*He goes quickly down the steps and out.* MR. FRANK *suddenly becomes conscious of the others.*]

R1

MR. FRANK. Forgive me. I spoke without consulting you. But I knew you'd feel as I do.

MR. VAN DAAN. There's no reason for you to consult anyone. This is your place. You have a right to do exactly as you please. The only thing I feel . . . there's so little food as it is . . . and to take in another person . . . **26**

R2

[PETER *turns away, ashamed of his father.*]

MR. FRANK. We can stretch the food a little. It's only for a few days.

MR. VAN DAAN. You want to make a bet?

MRS. FRANK. I think it's fine to have him. But, Otto, where are you going to put him? Where?

PETER. He can have my bed. I can sleep on the floor. I wouldn't mind.

MR. FRANK. That's good of you, Peter. But your room's too small . . . even for *you.*

13. ***Jan Dussel*** (yawn DOOS ul)

Practice the Skills

25 **Key Reading Skill**

Drawing Conclusions What does Mr. Frank's response show about his character?

26 **Key Reading Skill**

Drawing Conclusions What does Mr. Van Daan's response show about his character?

Teach

R1 Reading Skill

Review Comparing and Contrasting **Say:** Compare and contrast the ways Mr. Frank and Mr. Van Daan respond to having Mr. Dussel join them in hiding. What do their responses reveal about them? *(Possible response: Mr. Frank doesn't think twice about inviting Dr. Dussel in. He is generous and accommodating. Mr. Van Daan complains that there is too little food for another person. He is more focused on his own needs.)* **OL**

R2 Reading Skill

Drawing Conclusions
Ask: Why do you think Peter feels ashamed of his father? *(Possible response: Peter feels ashamed that his father would hesitate before offering help to Mr. Dussel. Mr. Van Daan's selfishness embarrasses Peter.)* **OL**

Differentiated Instruction

Role-Playing Ask students to imagine that Mr. Frank did consult the others before responding to Mr. Kraler's request and inviting Mr. Dussel to join them. Tell students to consider how each person in the attic might have reacted. Organize students in small groups, and have them each play the role of one of the characters. Tell them to role-play each character's reaction to Mr. Kraler's request. Tell students that their scenes should reflect what they have learned about each character to this point in the play. Have each group practice their scene and present it to the class. **AS**

Indiana English/Language Arts Academic Standards
SE: 8.2.9, 8.3, 8.3.2
TWE: *Reading Skill* 8.2.9, *Reading in the Real World* 8.2, *Differentiated Instruction* 8.7.2

Teach

R Reading Skill

Draw Conclusions **Ask:** What do you learn about Peter's room from Mr. Frank? *(Peter's cat, Mouschi, has caught some rats in Peter's room.)* BL

Say: Consider this information and Peter's earlier offer to give his bed to Mr. Dussel and sleep on the floor. What does Peter's offer say about his character? *(Possible response: He is a generous person who cares more about others than about himself and his own comfort.)* OL

BQ BIG Question

Say: To determine how the behavior of the Franks and Van Daans relates to the Big Question, think about how they react to the news that someone else will be joining them. *(Possible response: They react by figuring out where he will sleep. They keep from giving up by focusing on the practical aspects of life, such as sleep arrangements.)* OL

ANNE. I have a much better idea. I'll come in here with you and Mother, and Margot can take Peter's room and Peter can go in our room with Mr. Dussel.

MARGOT. That's right. We could do that.

MR. FRANK. No, Margot. You mustn't sleep in that room . . . neither you nor Anne. Mouschi has caught some rats in there. Peter's brave. He doesn't mind. **R**

ANNE. Then how about this? I'll come in here with you and Mother, and Mr. Dussel can have my bed.

MRS. FRANK. No. No. No! Margot will come in here with us and he can have her bed. It's the only way. Margot, bring your things in here. Help her, Anne.

[*MARGOT hurries into her room to get her things.*]

ANNE. [*To her mother.*] Why Margot? Why can't I come in here?

MRS. FRANK. Because it wouldn't be proper for Margot to sleep with a . . . Please, Anne. Don't argue. Please.

[*ANNE starts slowly away.*]

MR. FRANK. [*To ANNE.*] You don't mind sharing your room with Mr. Dussel, do you, Anne?

ANNE. No. No, of course not. **27**

MR. FRANK. Good. [*ANNE goes off into her bedroom, helping MARGOT. MR. FRANK starts to search in the cupboards.*] Where's the cognac?[14]

MRS. FRANK. It's there. But, Otto, I was saving it in case of illness.

MR. FRANK. I think we couldn't find a better time to use it. Peter, will you get five glasses for me?

[*PETER goes for the glasses. MARGOT comes out of her bedroom, carrying her possessions, which she hangs behind a curtain in the main room. MR. FRANK finds the cognac and pours it into the five*

14. ***Cognac*** (KOHN yak) is an alcoholic drink.

Practice the Skills

27 BIG Question

Think about the words and behavior of Peter and the four Franks in this part of the scene. How does their behavior relate to the Big Question? Write your answer on the Workshop 1 Foldable for Unit 6. **BQ**

Additional Support

Reading Fluency

Build Fluency Remind students that the lines in a play are meant to be read aloud. Point out that punctuation marks such as ellipsis points (. . .), question marks (?), exclamation points (!), and dashes (—) give the actors or readers an idea of how the lines should be read. Select students to take parts in a passage from a scene. Have each student scan the passage to find his or her character's lines and review the lines for punctuation that provides clues as to how the lines should sound. Then have students read the scene aloud. They should speak the lines according to the punctuation clues given. EL OL *glasses that* PETER *brings him.* MR. VAN DAAN *stands looking on sourly.* MRS. VAN DAAN *comes downstairs and looks around at all the bustle.*]

MRS. VAN DAAN. What's happening? What's going on?

MR. VAN DAAN. Someone's moving in with us.

MRS. VAN DAAN. In here? You're joking.

MARGOT. It's only for a night or two . . . until Mr. Kraler finds him another place.

MR. VAN DAAN. Yeah! Yeah!

[MR. FRANK *hurries over as* MR. KRALER *and* DUSSEL *come up.* DUSSEL *is a man in his late fifties,* **meticulous,** *finicky . . . bewildered*[15] *now. He wears a raincoat. He carries a briefcase, stuffed full, and a small medicine case.*] EL

MR. FRANK. Come in, Mr. Dussel.

MR. KRALER. This is Mr. Frank.

DUSSEL. Mr. Otto Frank?

MR. FRANK. Yes. Let me take your things. [*He takes the hat and briefcase, but* DUSSEL *clings to his medicine case.*] This is my wife Edith . . . Mr. and Mrs. Van Daan . . . their son, Peter . . . and my daughters, Margot and Anne. R

[DUSSEL *shakes hands with everyone.*]

MR. KRALER. Thank you, Mr. Frank. Thank you all. Mr. Dussel, I leave you in good hands. Oh . . . Dirk's coat.

[DUSSEL *hurriedly takes off the raincoat, giving it to* MR. KRALER. *Underneath is his white dentist's jacket, with a yellow Star of David on it.*] **28**

DUSSEL. [*To* MR. KRALER.] What can I say to thank you . . . ?

15. ***Bewildered*** (buh WIL durd) means "confused."

Vocabulary

meticulous (muh TIK yuh lus) *adj.* careful about small details

Practice the Skills

28 Key Reading Skill

Drawing Conclusions Why was Dussel wearing someone else's coat?

Differentiated Instruction

Planning Explain to students that before going into hiding, Mr. Frank and others had to plan carefully. They had to consider what supplies they would need, how to avoid being discovered, how to get to their hideout, and contingency plans in case anything went wrong.

Ask students to imagine they are going on a thirty-day hike through the woods alone. Have them plan what they will take with them. They should make a list and explain why each item is included. **BL**

READING WORKSHOP 1

Teach

EL Language Coach

Synonyms Say: Remember that synonyms are words that have similar meanings. *Meticulous* and *finicky* are synonyms. Other words with similar meanings are: *particular* and *fussy.* What might a meticulous or finicky person look like? *(Possible response: Such a person would be very well-groomed, and his or her clothing would be neat, unwrinkled, and clean.)* **OL**

R Reading Skill

Drawing Conclusions Say: Consider how you would react if you unexpectedly found yourself in hiding with strangers. What belongings might you cling to? *(Responses will vary.)* **BL Ask:** Why do you think Mr. Dussel clings to his medicine case? *(Responses will vary. Students may suggest that Mr. Dussel clings to his medicine case because it contains his most valuable possessions. The case may also represent stability and familiarity for Mr. Dussel.)* **OL**

Indiana English/Language Arts Academic Standards
SE: 8.3
TWE: *Reading Fluency* 8.7, *Differentiated Instruction* 8.3

Teach

R1 Reading Skill

Review Analyzing **Say:** Mr. Kraler claims that he and Miep are not heroic. Recall what Mr. Frank said earlier about what happened to Dutch people who were caught helping Jews. In what way are people like Mr. Kraler and Miep heroes? Explain. *(They are heroes because they risk their lives to help others.)* AS

R2 Reading Skill

Drawing Conclusions
Say: Although Mr. Kraler asks Peter to bolt the attic door when he leaves, Mr. Frank insists on doing it. Why do you think Mr. Frank wants to be the one to bolt the door? *(Possible responses: Mr. Frank wants to make certain that the bolt is closed properly. He may also want to speak privately with Mr. Kraler before he leaves.)* OL **Ask:** What do Mr. Frank's actions reveal about his role in the group? *(Possible response: Mr. Frank sees himself as the leader and protector of everyone in the attic. He is like a father to them all.)* AL

READING WORKSHOP 1

MRS. FRANK. [*To* DUSSEL.] Mr. Kraler and Miep . . . They're our life line. Without them we couldn't live.

MR. KRALER. Please. Please. You make us seem very heroic. It isn't that at all. We simply don't like the Nazis. [*To* MR. FRANK, *who offers him a drink.*] No, thanks. [*Then going on.*] We don't like their methods. We don't like . . . R1

MR. FRANK. [*Smiling.*] I know. I know. "No one's going to tell us Dutchmen what to do with our damn Jews!"

MR. KRALER. [*To* DUSSEL.] Pay no attention to Mr. Frank. I'll be up tomorrow to see that they're treating you right. [*To* MR. FRANK.] Don't trouble to come down again. Peter will bolt the door after me, won't you, Peter? 29 R2

PETER. Yes, sir.

MR. FRANK. Thank you, Peter. I'll do it.

MR. KRALER. Good night. Good night.

GROUP. Good night, Mr. Kraler.

We'll see you tomorrow, etc., etc.

[*MR. KRALER goes out with MR. FRANK. MRS. FRANK gives each one of the "grown-ups" a glass of cognac.*]

MRS. FRANK. Please, Mr. Dussel, sit down.

[*MR. DUSSEL sinks into a chair. MRS. FRANK gives him a glass of cognac.*]

DUSSEL. I'm dreaming. I know it. I can't believe my eyes. Mr. Otto Frank here! [*To* MRS. FRANK.] You're not in Switzerland then? A woman told me . . . She said she'd gone to your house . . . the door was open, everything was in disorder, dishes in the sink. She said she found a piece of paper in the wastebasket with an address scribbled on it . . . an address in Zurich.[16] She said you must have escaped to Zurich.

ANNE. Father put that there purposely . . . just so people would think that very thing!

DUSSEL. And you've been *here* all the time?

16. ***Zurich*** (ZOOR ik) is a city in Switzerland, a nation that remained neutral during the war.

Practice the Skills

29 Reviewing Skills

Analyzing Why does Mr. Frank make a joke at this point? How does Mr. Kraler respond to it? (Notice the remark about treating Dussel right. Is Mr. Kraler serious or making his own joke?)

Additional Support

Differentiated Instruction

Building Background Dussel mentions he thought the Franks had gone to Zurich, a city in Switzerland. Explain that going to Switzerland was not an option for the Franks. Between 1942 and 1943, the Swiss government turned away 24,000 mostly Jewish refugees. The government cited high costs and food shortages as reasons for its policy of not accepting refugees, but anti-Jewish and anti-foreign beliefs also played a role. Have students research why the United States did not act until 1944 to establish the War Refugee Board to help Jewish people escape Nazi persecution. AL

MRS. FRANK. All the time . . . ever since July.

[ANNE *speaks to her father as he comes back.*]

ANNE. It worked, Pim . . . the address you left! Mr. Dussel says that people believe we escaped to Switzerland.

MR. FRANK. I'm glad. . . . And now let's have a little drink to welcome Mr. Dussel. [*Before they can drink,* MR. DUSSEL *bolts his drink.* MR. FRANK *smiles and raises his glass.*] To Mr. Dussel. Welcome. We're very honored to have you with us.

MRS. FRANK. To Mr. Dussel, welcome.

[*The* VAN DAANS *murmur a welcome. The "grown-ups" drink.*]

MRS. VAN DAAN. Um. That was good.

R MR. VAN DAAN. Did Mr. Kraler warn you that you won't get much to eat here? You can imagine . . . three ration books among the seven of us . . . and now you make eight.

[PETER *walks away, humiliated.*[17] *Outside a street organ is heard dimly.*]

DUSSEL. [*Rising.*] Mr. Van Daan, you don't realize what is happening outside that you should warn me of a thing like that. You don't realize what's going on . . . [*As* MR. VAN DAAN *starts his characteristic pacing,* DUSSEL *turns to speak to the others.*] Right here in Amsterdam every day hundreds of Jews disappear . . . They surround a block and search house by house. Children come home from school to find their parents gone. Hundreds are being **deported** . . . people that you and I know . . . the Hallensteins . . . the Wessels . . . 30

MRS. FRANK. [*In tears.*] Oh, no. No!

DUSSEL. They get their call-up notice . . . come to the Jewish theater on such and such a day and hour . . . bring only what

17. Peter is greatly embarrassed and ashamed ***(humiliated)***.

Practice the Skills

Fritz Pfeffer (Albert Dussel), 1930s.

30 English Language Coach

Word Parts The word **deport** includes the root *port* and the prefix *de-*, meaning "away." What does it mean?

Literature Focus Lesson

Drama and Audience Mrs. Frank starts to cry as Dussel describes what is happening in Amsterdam. *The Diary of Anne Frank* was first presented in Amsterdam on November 27, 1956, eleven years after the war ended. During the play, people in the audience sobbed aloud. Audience members cried out at the play's climax as well. As a class, discuss possible reasons for audiences' passionate responses to this play. Ask students whether they think audiences today would respond with equal emotion. Encourage students to record in their Learner's Notebooks their own thoughts and feelings as they read the play. OL

Teach

R Reading Skill

Drawing Conclusions Ask: Why do the Van Daans only murmur a welcome to Mr. Dussel? *(They are not enthusiastic about his joining them.)* **Ask:** Why is Peter humiliated? *(He is embarrassed by his father's selfishness, particularly where food is concerned.)* OL

EL Language Coach

Word Parts Direct students' attention to the word *deported.* **Say:** The root *port* means "carry," and the prefix *de-* means "away." *Deport* has come to mean "send out of the country." Try using the word in a sentence of your own. *(Responses will vary.)* EL BL

C Critical Thinking

Comprehension Ask: How does Mr. Dussel react to Mr. Van Daan's warning about the food? *(He explains that what is happening in Amsterdam is so terrible that having little food is of no concern to him.)* OL

Indiana English/Language Arts Academic Standards
SE: 8.1, 8.3
TWE: *Reading Skill* 8.2.9, *Differentiated Instruction* 8.2, *Literature Focus Lesson* 8.2

Teach

R Reading Skill

Drawing Conclusions:
Ask: Do you think Mr. Dussel is glad to be in the attic? Support your conclusion with details from the text. *(Possible response: Mr. Dussel is probably glad to be in hiding. He says that things have become much worse for Jews in Amsterdam. Each day, hundreds are called up and sent to death camps.)* BL OL

C Critical Thinking

Comprehension Ask: Why does Mr. Dussel's news about the de Waals upset Anne? *(Jopie de Waal was Anne's best friend, and Mr. Dussel tells Anne that the de Waals were deported to a death camp.)* BL

you can carry in a rucksack. And if you refuse the call-up notice, then they come and drag you from your home and ship you off to Mauthausen.[18] The death camp! **31**

MRS. FRANK. We didn't know that things had got so much worse.

DUSSEL. Forgive me for speaking so.

ANNE. [*Coming to* DUSSEL.] Do you know the de Waals? . . . What's become of them? Their daughter Jopie and I are in the same class. Jopie's my best friend.

DUSSEL. They are gone.

ANNE. Gone?

DUSSEL. With all the others.

ANNE. Oh, no. Not Jopie!

[*She turns away, in tears.* MRS. FRANK *motions to* MARGOT *to comfort her.* MARGOT *goes to* ANNE, *putting her arms comfortingly around her.*]

C

MRS. VAN DAAN. There were some people called Wagner. They lived near us . . . ?

MR. FRANK. [*Interrupting, with a glance at* ANNE.] I think we should put this off until later. We all have many questions we want to ask . . . But I'm sure that Mr. Dussel would like to get settled before supper. **32**

DUSSEL. Thank you. I would. I brought very little with me.

MR. FRANK. [*Giving him his hat and briefcase.*] I'm sorry we can't give you a room alone. But I hope you won't be too uncomfortable. We've had to make strict rules here . . . a schedule of hours . . . We'll tell you after supper. Anne, would you like to take Mr. Dussel to his room?

ANNE. [*Controlling her tears.*] If you'll come with me, Mr. Dussel?

[*She starts for her room.*]

18. ***Mauthausen*** (MOWT how zun) was a Nazi camp in Austria.

Practice the Skills

31 Reviewing Skills

Comparing and Contrasting How do problems inside the attic compare with the problems Jews on the outside are facing?

32 Key Reading Skill

Drawing Conclusions This time it's Mr. Frank who changes the subject. Why does he want to end this conversation?

Additional Support

Literature Focus Lesson

Characterization Have students use the chart below to record details about one character in act 1, scene 3 of the play. OL

Character's Name	Character's Words and Actions	Words That Describe the Character

DUSSEL. [*Shaking hands with each in turn.*] Forgive me if I haven't really expressed my gratitude to all of you. This has been such a shock to me. I'd always thought of myself as Dutch. I was born in Holland. My father was born in Holland, and my grandfather. And now . . . after all these years . . . [*He breaks off.*] If you'll excuse me.

[*DUSSEL gives a little bow and hurries off after ANNE. MR. FRANK and the others are subdued.*]

ANNE. [*Turning on the light.*] Well, here we are.

[*DUSSEL looks around the room. In the main room MARGOT speaks to her mother.*]

MARGOT. The news sounds pretty bad, doesn't it? It's so different from what Mr. Kraler tells us. Mr. Kraler says things are improving.

MR. VAN DAAN. I like it better the way Kraler tells it.

[*They resume their occupations, quietly. PETER goes off into his room. In ANNE's room, ANNE turns to DUSSEL.*]

ANNE. You're going to share the room with me.

DUSSEL. I'm a man who's always lived alone. I haven't had to adjust myself to others. I hope you'll bear with me until I learn. 33

ANNE. Let me help you. [*She takes his briefcase.*] Do you always live all alone? Have you no family at all?

DUSSEL. No one.

[*He opens his medicine case and spreads his bottles on the dressing table.*]

ANNE. How dreadful. You must be terribly lonely.

DUSSEL. I'm used to it.

ANNE. I don't think I could ever get used to it. Didn't you even have a pet? A cat, or a dog?

DUSSEL. I have an allergy for fur-bearing animals. They give me asthma.

Practice the Skills

33 Key Reading Skill

Drawing Conclusions Will Dussel be a good roommate? Why or why not?

Reading in the Real World

Citizenship Tell students that at the end of World War II, many photographs were taken of the surviving prisoners in Nazi concentration camps and the environment in which they had lived. For people around the world, seeing these pictures brought a fuller realization of the horrors of the Holocaust. The photographs also conveyed the dignity of the prisoners in a way that words never could. Ask students why they think that, for many people, these images proved more powerful than words. Have students share examples of powerful images they've seen about current events. AS

READING WORKSHOP 1

Teach

C Critical Thinking

Comprehension **Ask:** What makes Mr. Dussel remark that he always thought of himself as Dutch? *(Mr. Dussel identifies himself primarily as Dutch rather than as Jewish.)* AL

R Reading Skill

Drawing Conclusions **Say:** When Anne shows Mr. Dussel to their room, she learns several things about him. How does Anne react to what she learns? *(Possible response: Anne is quite surprised to learn that Mr. Dussel lives alone and has no family. She imagines that such a life must be "dreadful.")* BL **Ask:** Given what you know about Anne, why would she find it difficult to live alone? *(Possible response: Anne loves to talk and joke with others, and she finds it difficult to be quiet. She enjoys being social too much to live alone. In the play, Anne often asks Peter to talk and roughhouse with her. She won't take no for an answer.)* OL

Indiana English/Language Arts Academic Standards

SE: 8.2.9, 8.3

TWE: *Reading Skill* 8.2.9, *Literature Focus Lesson* 8.3, *Reading in the Real World* 8.7.9

Teach

BQ BIG Question

Ask: What does Anne see from her window? How is what she sees meaningful to her? *(Anne has a view of a houseboat on the canal. A family lives on the houseboat, and their activities remind Anne that life goes on and give her hope that one day her life will be normal again.)* OL

R Reading Skill

Drawing Conclusions Ask: What details suggest Mr. Dussel will have a hard time adjusting to life in the attic? *(He is used to living alone, he worries about the cat, he worries about spending time "with all the people" when Anne is alone in the room.)* OL

READING WORKSHOP 1

ANNE. Oh, dear. Peter has a cat.

DUSSEL. Here? He has it here?

ANNE. Yes. But we hardly ever see it. He keeps it in his room all the time. I'm sure it will be all right.

DUSSEL. Let us hope so.

[*He takes some pills to* ***fortify*** *himself.*] 34

ANNE. That's Margot's bed, where you're going to sleep. I sleep on the sofa there. [*Indicating the clothes hooks on the wall.*] We cleared these off for your things. [*She goes over to the window.*] The best part about this room . . . you can look down and see a bit of the street and the canal. There's a houseboat . . . you can see the end of it . . . a bargeman lives there with his family . . . They have a baby and he's just beginning to walk and I'm so afraid he's going to fall into the canal some day. I watch him. . . . 35 BQ

DUSSEL. [*Interrupting.*] Your father spoke of a schedule.

ANNE. [*Coming away from the window.*] Oh, yes. It's mostly about the times we have to be quiet. And times for the w.c. You can use it now if you like.

DUSSEL. [*Stiffly.*] No, thank you.

ANNE. I suppose you think it's awful, my talking about a thing like that. But you don't know how important it can get to be, especially when you're frightened . . . About this room, the way Margot and I did . . . she had it to herself in the afternoons for studying, reading . . . lessons, you know . . . and I took the mornings. Would that be all right with you?

DUSSEL. I'm not at my best in the morning.

ANNE. You stay here in the mornings then. I'll take the room in the afternoons.

DUSSEL. Tell me, when you're in here, what happens to me? Where am I spending my time? In there, with all the people?

ANNE. Yes.

Practice the Skills

34 English Language Coach

Word Parts The suffix *–ify* means "to make or cause to be." Look at the chart of roots to see the meaning of *fort*.

35 BIG Question

What, for Anne, is the "best part" about the room? How does it help her? Write your answer on the Workshop 1 Foldable for Unit 6. Your response will help you complete the Unit Challenge later.

Additional Support

Differentiated Instruction

Character Map Have students review the dialogue from Mr. Dussel's entrance to the end of the scene. Ask students to identify at least four character traits of this new member of the attic "family." Tell students to record the traits in a graphic organizer such as the web shown below. EL BL

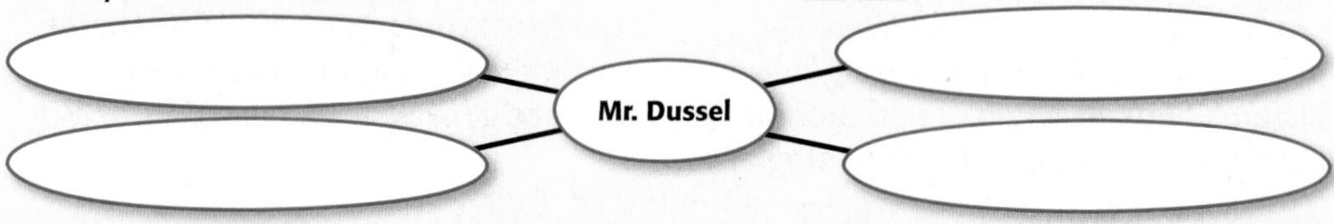

DUSSEL. I see. I see.

ANNE. We have supper at half past six.

DUSSEL. [*Going over to the sofa.*] Then, if you don't mind . . . I like to lie down quietly for ten minutes before eating. I find it helps the digestion.

ANNE. Of course. I hope I'm not going to be too much of a bother to you. I seem to be able to get everyone's back up.

[*DUSSEL lies down on the sofa, curled up, his back to her.*]

DUSSEL. I always get along very well with children. My patients all bring their children to me, because they know I get on well with them. So don't you worry about that. **36**

[*ANNE leans over him, taking his hand and shaking it gratefully.*]

ANNE. Thank you. Thank you, Mr. Dussel.

[*The lights dim to darkness. The curtain falls on the scene. ANNE'S VOICE comes to us faintly at first, and then with increasing power.*] **37**

ANNE'S VOICE. . . . And yesterday I finished Cissy Van Marxvelt's latest book. I think she is a first-class writer. I shall definitely let my children read her. Monday the twenty-first of September, nineteen forty-two. Mr. Dussel and I had another battle yesterday. Yes, Mr. Dussel! According to him, nothing, I repeat . . . nothing, is right about me . . . my appearance, my character, my manners. While he was going on at me I thought . . . sometime I'll give you such a smack that you'll fly right up to the ceiling! Why is it that every grown-up thinks he knows the way to bring up children? Particularly the grown-ups that never had any. I keep wishing that Peter was a girl instead of a boy. Then I would have someone to talk to. Margot's a darling, but she takes everything too seriously. To pause for a moment on the subject of Mrs. Van Daan. I must tell you that her attempts to flirt with father are getting her nowhere. Pim, thank goodness, won't play. **R**

[*As she is saying the last lines, the curtain rises on the darkened scene. ANNE'S VOICE fades out.*]

Practice the Skills

36 Reviewing Skills

Comparing and Contrasting Describe ways in which Anne and Dussel are different from one another. Do you see any similarities?

37 Key Literary Element

Act and Scene Each between-scenes reading provides helpful information. Sometimes, as in this one, there are details that don't relate to the action but tell us about Anne or another character. In each reading, Anne gives a date, which is the date of the next scene. Often, there's a summary of things that happened since the last scene. Why do the playwrights provide so much information in these readings? **L**

Teach

L Literary Element

Act and Scene Ask: What change in setting do you expect between scene 3 and scene 4? *(Possible responses: There will be a change in time; scene 4 will be some time later, but the location in the attic will probably not change.)* **AL**

R Reading Skill

Review Comparing and Contrasting Ask: According to Anne's diary entry, what does Mr. Dussel think of Anne? *(Mr. Dussel thinks that Anne can do nothing right.)* **BL**

Ask: How do the comments in Anne's diary contradict Mr. Dussel's statements about children? *(Mr. Dussel had assured Anne that he gets along well with children. According to Anne's diary, however, he and Anne are constantly fighting.)* **OL**

Assess

Use the CheckPoint questions provided on Presentation Plus! to check for comprehension of the selection. These questions can be used with interactive response keypads for immediate student feedback.

Differentiated Instruction

Summarizing When students read longer works, their comprehension improves if they pause to summarize what they have read. Point out to students that summarizing requires recalling and organizing and can be useful later for studying. Explain that a summary should be written in their own words and should include only main points.

Have students write a brief summary of scene 3. Ask them to review their summaries in a group to determine whether they have included the most important details.

Indiana English/Language Arts Academic Standards
SE: 8.1, 8.3
TWE: *Differentiated Instruction* 8.3, *Differentiated Instruction* 8.5

Assess

Resources for page 762

- Selection Quick Check, p. 51
- Selection and Unit Assessment, p. 61
- ExamView Assessment Suite
- Interactive Tutor: Self-Assessment

Students can respond to the *After You Read* items in their Learner's Notebooks or on a separate sheet of paper.

Answering the BIG Question

1. They must live in a small space with little food, and they cannot make noise during the day.
2. She talks a lot.
3. Anne accidentally spills milk on the coat and Mrs. Van Daan gets angry with her.

Critical Thinking

4. She writes in her diary, teases Peter, dances, and looks outside.
5. Mr. Frank helps Anne and Margot with their lessons. Mrs. Frank cooks. Margot and Peter study. Mr. Kraler brings good news.
6. Peter is ashamed of his father. Sometimes he becomes angry with his mother. Anne annoys him, but he also enjoys her company.
7. Answers will vary.
8. No, she is loud, shows off, and does not listen to Mr. Van Daan.
9. Answers will vary.

After You Read

The Diary of Anne Frank, Act 1, Scene 3

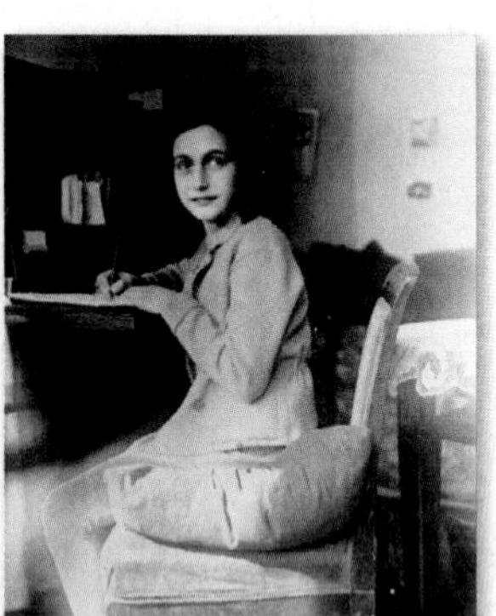

Answering the BIG Question

1. What problems, challenges, and dangers do the characters face?
2. **Recall** Why does Peter call Anne "Mrs. Quack Quack"?
   TIP Right There
3. **Describe** Tell what happened to Mrs. Van Daan's fur coat and how she reacted.
   TIP Think and Search

Critical Thinking

4. **Analyze** In addition to the problems that come with hiding, Anne has to grow up with no friends her own age. What are some of the things she does to keep herself going?
   TIP Think and Search
5. **Analyze** Identify one thing each of these characters does to keep from giving up: Mr. Frank, Mrs. Frank, Margot, Peter, and Mr. Kraler.
   TIP Think and Search
6. **Infer** How does Peter feel about his parents? How does he feel about Anne? Explain.
   TIP Author and Me
7. **Predict** Dussel describes terrible things going on in Amsterdam. How do you think this information will affect the Franks and the Van Daans?
   TIP Author and Me
8. **Analyze** Review Mr. Van Daan's ideas about the kind of girl men like (p. 748). Would you say that his wife fits this description? Explain.
9. **Evaluate** Do you think Mrs. Frank and Mr. Frank would like Anne to be more like Margot? Explain.
   TIP Author and Me

Talk About Your Reading

Literature Discussion Throughout the play so far, Anne shows more interest in the outside world than the other characters do. With a small group, find examples of this contrast between Anne and the other characters in the first three scenes. Then discuss possible reasons that Anne has for her interest and that the others have for not showing similar interest.

Indiana English/Language Arts Academic Standards (pp. 762–763)

8.3 Comprehension and Analysis of Literary Text Respond to grade-level-appropriate literature... **8.2.9** Make reasonable statements and draw conclusions... **8.7 Listening and Speaking** Speaking skills are developed... **8.3.2** Evaluate the structural elements of the plot... **8.1 Word Recognition, Fluency, and Vocabulary Development** Understanding...word parts... **8.6.5** Use correct punctuation

For a complete description of the standards, see p. IN 11.

Talk About Your Reading

Examples of Anne's interest in the outside world include putting the photographs on the wall, looking out the window, and talking about her travel and work plans for the future. Students may deduce the following reasons for Anne's interest in the outside world: she is younger and has less experience of the world than the others; she is curious and therefore interested in new people and things; she has a positive outlook and is fascinated by all aspects of life.

Skills Review

Key Reading Skill: Drawing Conclusions

10. By now, you should have drawn a lot of conclusions about the people living in the Annex, as well as the people who are helping them. Choose one of the characters and explain some things you have concluded about that character.

11. Do you think drawing conclusions about the people in the play helps you predict what will come next? Why or why not?

Key Literary Element: Act and Scene

12. Why do you think the play has two acts, instead of going nonstop from beginning to end?

13. In this play so far, what is the one thing that always changes when a scene changes? Explain.

Reviewing Skills: Analyzing; Comparing and Contrasting

14. Mr. Kraler's news of the "outside world" is somewhat different from Dussel's. What reasons would Mr. Kraler have for saying things are improving?

15. Compare the two sets of parents, noting at least one way they're alike as well as ways they're not.

Vocabulary Check

Match the vocabulary words with their best synonyms.

self-conscious absurd vile mimics aggravating bickering meticulous

16. nasty
17. arguing
18. ridiculous
19. fussy
20. annoying
21. imitates
22. uncomfortable

23. English Language Coach What is the root of the word *demand?* (You may look it up.) What's another English word from the same root?

Grammar Link: Commas in a Series

A comma is used to separate a series of three or more words, phrases, or clauses. Place commas between items in the series.

- Clams, shrimp, and crabs are types of shellfish.
- Cioppino is a stew made with fish, clams, crabs, scallops, and a flavorful tomato-based broth.
- We collected 11 boxes of crackers, 30 cans of vegetables, and 15 cans of soup for the shelter.
- I looked in the car, outside the house, and under the deck for my bat.
- Study your lines for the play when you're in study hall, while you walk home, and after you finish dinner.

The comma before the last item in a series may be left out unless it is necessary to make the meaning clear.

Unclear: I ate salad, grilled cheese and cake.

Clear: I ate salad, grilled cheese, and cake.

You do not need commas in a series when a coordinating conjunction is repeated between items.

- The deer and the birds and the rabbits all seemed to know that a storm was coming.

Grammar Practice

Copy the paragraph below, adding three commas in the appropriate places.

Our flight is booked the suitcases are packed and we're ready to leave for Florida. I want to taste fresh grapefruits oranges, and lemons. I love the sand and rolling waves and salt air.

Web Activities For eFlashcards, Selection Quick Checks, and other Web activities, go to www.glencoe.com.

Skills Review

Key Reading Skill: Drawing Conclusions

10. Responses will vary.
11. Responses will vary.

Key Literary Element: Act and Scene

12. to show how circumstances change
13. the passage of time

Reviewing Skills: Analyzing: Comparing and Contrasting

14. He doesn't want those in hiding to give up hope.
15. Both want their children to study. The Franks are more positive and consider the needs of others before their own.

Close

Ask students to answer the Big Question based on what they've read so far of *The Diary of Anne Frank*.

Web Activities Have students access the Web site for interactive activities that will help them assess their understanding of the selection.

Grammar Link: Commas in a Series

Grammar Practice

Our flight is booked, the suitcases are packed, and we're ready to leave for Florida. I want to taste fresh grapefruits, oranges, and lemons. I love the sand and rolling waves and salt air.

Vocabulary Check

16. vile
17. bickering
18. absurd
19. meticulous
20. aggravating
21. mimics
22. self-conscious

English Language Coach

23. root: mand; command

Indiana English/Language Arts Academic Standards
SE: 8.1, 8.2.9, 8.3, 8.3.2, 8.6.5, 8.7

Teach

V Vocabulary

Word Webs To expand their understanding of the vocabulary, have students create a word web for each vocabulary word.

- Tell students to write the word in the center circle of the web. Then ask students to write two synonyms for the word around the center circle.
- Students may use a dictionary or thesaurus as an aid.
- Have students compare their webs with a partner's.

(Responses will vary.)

EL BL OL

Before You Read

The Diary of Anne Frank, Act 1, Scenes 4–5

Vocabulary Preview

V

makeshift (MAYK shift) *adj.* used in place of the normal or proper thing **(p. 766)** *The couch in the main room served as a makeshift bed for Mr. and Mrs. Frank.*

wallow (WAH loh) *v.* to take selfish pleasure in comfort **(p. 772)** *Anne wanted to wallow in a tub full of warm, soapy water.*

sustenance (SUS tuh nuns) *n.* food and other necessities of life **(p. 773)** *Miep provided as much sustenance for the families as she could; she was their lifeline.*

jubilation (joo buh LAY shun) *n.* great joy and excitement **(p. 780)** *They all tried to show the usual holiday jubilation, despite their terrible situation.*

uncertainty (un SUR tun tee) *n.* the state of being unsure or not knowing **(p. 783)** *Even worse than being cut off from the outside world was their uncertainty about their future in that world.*

Write to Learn Use each vocabulary word correctly in a sentence about some part of your life. The sentences do not have to relate to one another.

English Language Coach

Historical Influences on English In the history of civilization, English is a fairly new language. As a new kid on the block, English has been influenced by many other languages.

Many English words have roots in Latin, Greek, and Anglo-Saxon. The following roots and their meanings can help you figure out the definitions of many words. (Sometimes the spellings of the roots change.)

Root	Origin	Meaning	Word Example
sanct	Latin	holy	sanctuary
cycle	Greek	circle	bicycle
knack	Anglo-Saxon	strike	knocking
logue	Greek	speech, word	dialogue

In literature, a dialogue (DY uh log) is a conversation between characters. The Greek prefix *dia-* means "through" or "across." A monologue (MON uh log) is a long, uninterrupted speech by one character. The Greek prefix *mono-* means "single" or "alone."

Partner Talk With a partner, talk about other word examples that come from the roots above.

Indiana English/Language Arts Academic Standards (pp. 764–787)

8.1.2 Understand the influence of historical events on...word meaning... **8.3 Comprehension and Analysis of Literary Text** Respond to grade-level-appropriate literature... **8.3.6** Identify significant literary devices...

For a complete description of the standards, see pp IN 11.

Additional Support

English Language Coach

Historical Influences on English In the fifth century, Germanic tribes settled in England. Known today as Anglo-Saxons, they spoke the earliest form of English. In the late 500s, Roman Christian missionaries came to England, introducing Latin. Many English words with Latin roots date from this period.

In 1066 French-speaking Normans conquered the Anglo-Saxons. In the centuries that followed, many French words entered the English language. Ask students to use dictionaries to find the origins of four English words and share their findings with the class. OL AL

Skills Preview

Key Reading Skill: Drawing Conclusions

One of the most important steps in drawing conclusions is to read carefully. Good readers train themselves to notice details in a story. Then they think about whether those details mean more than the author is telling them. As you read further in "The Diary of Anne Frank," use these questions to help you pay attention to the details you need to draw conclusions.

- What is important to each character?
- Is anyone hiding anything?
- Does the news from outside change?

Write to Learn Who would you say is having the hardest time adjusting to life in hiding? Write your answer in a paragraph in your Learner's Notebook. Use details from the play to support your choice.

Key Literary Element: Dialogue and Monologue

Dialogue is conversation between characters. **Monologue** is a long, uninterrupted speech by one character. Like conversation in a story, dialogue and monologue in a drama provide important information about characters, events, and ideas. In a story, each speaker's part of a dialogue is enclosed in quotation marks. Since all or most of a drama is conversation, quotation marks are not used in a play script. Instead, as you've seen, the speaker's name is always given before his or her speech.

You've already read quite a lot of dialogue, of course. You've also read a few monologues. In scene 2, for example, Mr. Frank goes on for a long time about the need to avoid making noise.

At the end of each scene, Anne's voice reads from her diary. These readings represent a different sort of monologue. In them, Anne expresses thoughts and feelings that she can't or won't tell other people in conversation. These speeches also give the audience (and readers) a flavor of Anne Frank's actual diary. L

Partner Work With a partner, locate every monologue spoken by a character in scene 3. (Not everyone has one in that scene.)

Get Ready to Read

Connect to the Reading

R Think about a time when you had to get along with difficult people. Was it a struggle? Did you want to give up? Anne Frank knew that her hope for the future depended on her ability to get along with the other people. As you read scenes 4 and 5, think about what you might have done in her place.

Write to Learn Briefly describe a time when you had trouble getting along with someone else. Explain how you acted and why.

Build Background

Anne Frank's diary shows the awful events of the day through the eyes of a teenager.

- The diary covers the period from June 12, 1942, to August 1, 1944.
- After the war the diary was translated into more than sixty languages, making Anne one of the most memorable figures to emerge from World War II.

Set Purposes for Reading

BIG Question Read act 1, scenes 4–5, of *The Diary of Anne Frank* to discover how Anne manages to keep from giving up during hard times.

Set Your Own Purpose What would you like to learn from the play to help you answer the Big Question? Write your own purpose on the Reading Workshop 1 Foldable for Unit 6.

Interactive Literary Elements Handbook
To review or learn more about the literary elements, go to www.glencoe.com.

Keep Moving

Use these skills as you read the following selection.

Teach

L Literary Element

Dialogue and Monologue

Ask: Which is more likely to be Anne Frank's actual words: the dialogue or the monologues? Which is more likely made up by the playwrights? *(The monologues—the readings from the diary entries—are Anne Frank's actual words. The dialogue is most likely made up by the playwrights.)* OL

R Reading Skill

Review Connecting Using their experiences as a guide, students should write two or three suggestions for Anne about how to get along with difficult people. Have students share their ideas with the class. Encourage students to read on to see how Anne gets along with the others in the attic. AS

Interactive Literary Elements Handbook Have students access the Web site to improve their understanding of dialogue and monologue.

Literature Focus Lesson

Dialogue Remind students that in a play, most of the information about characters and events must be conveyed through dialogue. Unlike novels or short stories, plays seldom contain narration. Challenge students to convert a passage from a favorite story into lines of dialogue for a play. Suggest students choose a fiction passage in which the characters engage in some dialogue. Ask students to convert information from narration to dialogue. Students should follow the conventions of a script, giving the speaker's name before his or her lines and including stage directions about movement and expression. AL

Indiana English/Language Arts Academic Standards
SE: 8.1.2, 8.3, 8.3.6
TWE: *English Language Coach* 8.1.2, *Literature Focus Lesson* 8.5

Teach

C Critical Thinking

Comprehension Ask: What does Mr. Van Daan do while everyone is sleeping? What details suggest that he is being secretive? *(He comes downstairs and goes to the food cupboard. He lights only two matches to find his way, and he moves quickly, suggesting he is being secretive.)* **BL Ask:** What do you know about Mr. Van Daan that might explain why he goes to the food cupboard? *(He is very concerned about the shortage of food.)* **OL**

R Reading Skill

Review Analyzing Say: A playwright can create a suspenseful mood by withholding information from the audience. What information is withheld at the start of scene 4? How? *(The audience does not know what Mr. Van Daan is doing or why. The audience may not understand why Anne is screaming. The darkness onstage and the lack of dialogue prevent the audience from knowing what is happening.)* **OL**

SCENE 4

[It is the middle of the night, several months later. The stage is dark except for a little light which comes through the skylight in PETER*'s room.*

Everyone is in bed. MR. *and* MRS. FRANK *lie on the couch in the main room, which has been pulled out to serve as a* **makeshift** *double bed.*

MARGOT *is sleeping on a mattress on the floor in the main room, behind a curtain stretched across for privacy. The others are all in their accustomed rooms.*

From outside we hear two drunken soldiers singing "Lili Marlene." A girl's high giggle is heard. The sound of running feet is heard coming closer and then fading in the distance. Throughout the scene there is the distant sound of airplanes passing overhead.

A match suddenly flares up in the attic. We dimly see MR. VAN DAAN. *He is getting his bearings.*[1] *He comes quickly down the stairs, and goes to the cupboard where the food is stored. Again the match flares up, and is as quickly blown out. The dim figure is seen to steal back up the stairs.* **1** **C**

There is quiet for a second or two, broken only by the sound of airplanes, and running feet on the street below.

Suddenly, out of the silence and the dark, we hear ANNE *scream.]*

ANNE. *[Screaming.]* No! No! Don't . . . don't take me!

[She moans, tossing and crying in her sleep. The other people wake, terrified. DUSSEL *sits up in bed, furious.]*

DUSSEL. Shush! Anne! Anne, for God's sake, shush!

ANNE. *[Still in her nightmare.]* Save me! Save me!

[She screams and screams. DUSSEL *gets out of bed, going over to her, trying to wake her.]*

Practice the Skills

1 Key Reading Skill

Drawing Conclusions There isn't enough solid information to draw a conclusion about what Mr. Van Daan is doing. For now, remember this part; it'll be useful in act 2. **R**

1. When Mr. Van Daan is ***getting his bearings,*** he's figuring out his position in the dimly lit room and deciding where to go.

Vocabulary

makeshift (MAYK shift) *adj.* used in place of the normal or proper thing

Additional Support

Differentiated Instruction

Anne Frank's Tree The British actress Emma Thompson has created a Web site named "Anne Frank's Tree," for the tree Anne saw through her window, includes quotes from Anne's diary and a place where people can enter information about how Anne has inspired them. Encourage students to create their own Anne Frank Tree. Draw or trace a large leaf, and make a copy for each student. Have students write sentences or words that describe Anne and her life on the leaf. Ask a student to draw the trunk and branches of the tree on large poster board, and have students glue their leaves to the tree. **OL**

READING WORKSHOP 1

Margot (left) and Anne, 1933.

DUSSEL. For God's sake! Quiet! Quiet! You want someone to hear? **2**

[In the main room MRS. FRANK *grabs a shawl and pulls it around her. She rushes in to* ANNE, *taking her in her arms.* MR. FRANK *hurriedly gets up, putting on his overcoat.* MARGOT *sits up, terrified.* PETER*'s light goes on in his room.]*

2 Key Reading Skill

Drawing Conclusions What does Dussel's reaction to Anne's cries tell you about him?

Teach

Viewing the Photo

Ask: How many years before the Franks went into hiding was this photograph of Anne and her sister taken? *(nine years)*

OL **Ask:** What do the many photographs of the Franks, such as this portrait of Anne and Margot, suggest about the family? *(Possible response: The many photographs suggest that the family was loving and shared good times together.)* **AL**

Differentiated Instruction

Anne's Dream Have students point out the purposes Anne's nightmare serves in the story. Supplement with these points:

- It indicates that despite her positive nature, Anne is deeply fearful of being caught.
- It shows that living in captivity is taking its toll on Anne.
- It allows the writers to show the characters' different personalities through their different reactions to her nightmare.
- It symbolizes the fears all the characters have of being caught. **OL** **AL**

Indiana English/Language Arts Academic Standards

SE: 8.3

TWE: *Differentiated Instruction* 8.5, *Differentiated Instruction* 8.2

Teach

EL Language Coach

Historical Influences on English **Say:** As she comforts Anne, Mrs. Frank tells her daughter to "hush." Use dictionaries to find the origins of the verb *hush*. *(This word comes from the Middle English* hussht *or* huissht, *a word used to ask for silence.)* OL AL

R Reading Skill

Drawing Conclusions **Say:** Dussel indicates that Anne is becoming more and more restless during her sleep. Why might this be the case? *(Possible response: Anne is very emotional, and as she spends more and more time in hiding, her fears become greater.)* OL

MRS. FRANK. [*To* ANNE, *in her room.*] Hush, darling, hush. It's all right. It's all right. [*Over her shoulder to* DUSSEL.] Will you be kind enough to turn on the light, Mr. Dussel? [*Back to* ANNE.] It's nothing, my darling. It was just a dream.

[*DUSSEL turns on the light in the bedroom. MRS. FRANK holds ANNE in her arms. Gradually ANNE comes out of her nightmare, still trembling with horror. MR. FRANK comes into the room, and goes quickly to the window, looking out to be sure that no one outside has heard ANNE's screams. MRS. FRANK holds ANNE, talking softly to her. In the main room MARGOT stands on a chair, turning on the center hanging lamp. A light goes on in the VAN DAANS' room overhead. PETER puts his robe on, coming out of his room.*]

DUSSEL. [*To* MRS. FRANK, *blowing his nose.*] Something must be done about that child, Mrs. Frank. Yelling like that! Who knows but there's somebody on the streets? She's endangering all our lives.

MRS. FRANK. Anne, darling.

DUSSEL. Every night she twists and turns. I don't sleep. I spend half my night shushing her. And now it's nightmares! 3

[*MARGOT comes to the door of ANNE's room, followed by PETER. MR. FRANK goes to them, indicating that everything is all right. PETER takes MARGOT back.*]

MRS. FRANK. [*To* ANNE.] You're here, safe, you see? Nothing has happened. [*To* DUSSEL.] Please, Mr. Dussel, go back to bed. She'll be herself in a minute or two. Won't you, Anne?

DUSSEL. [*Picking up a book and a pillow.*] Thank you, but I'm going to the w.c. The one place where there's peace!

[*He stalks out. MR. VAN DAAN, in underwear and trousers, comes down the stairs.*]

MR. VAN DAAN. [*To* DUSSEL.] What is it? What happened?

DUSSEL. A nightmare. She was having a nightmare!

EL Practice the Skills

3 Key Reading Skill

Drawing Conclusions Why is Anne having nightmares now? Do you think there's a specific cause, or is it the situation in general?

Additional Support

Differentiated Instruction

Group Psychology Students may be interested in exploring further the reasons that the people in the attic were having trouble getting along. Explain that studies show how a lack of sunlight and being housebound can affect people's moods. Have students use library resources to learn more abut the problems caused by the difficult conditions under which the group was living. Students may write a short paper or present an oral report to the class. AL

MR. VAN DAAN. I thought someone was murdering her.

DUSSEL. Unfortunately, no.

[*He goes into the bathroom.* MR. VAN DAAN *goes back up the stairs.* MR. FRANK, *in the main room, sends* PETER *back to his own bedroom.*]

MR. FRANK. Thank you, Peter. Go back to bed.

[PETER *goes back to his room.* MR. FRANK *follows him, turning out the light and looking out the window. Then he goes back to the main room, and gets up on a chair, turning out the center hanging lamp.*]

MRS. FRANK. [*To* ANNE.] Would you like some water? [ANNE *shakes her head.*] Was it a very bad dream? Perhaps if you told me . . . ?

ANNE. I'd rather not talk about it.

MRS. FRANK. Poor darling. Try to sleep then. I'll sit right here beside you until you fall asleep.

[*She brings a stool over, sitting there.*]

ANNE. You don't have to.

MRS. FRANK. But I'd like to stay with you . . . very much. Really.

ANNE. I'd rather you didn't.

MRS. FRANK. Good night, then. [*She leans down to kiss* ANNE. ANNE *throws her arm up over her face, turning away.* MRS. FRANK, *hiding her hurt, kisses* ANNE'S *arm.*] You'll be all right? There's nothing that you want?

ANNE. Will you please ask Father to come. 4

MRS. FRANK. [*After a second.*] Of course, Anne dear. [*She hurries out into the other room.* MR. FRANK *comes to her as she comes in.*] Sie verlangt nach Dir!

MR. FRANK. [*Sensing her hurt.*] Edith, Liebe, schau . . .

MRS. FRANK. Es macht nichts! Ich danke dem lieben Herrgott, dass sie sich wenigstens an Dich wendet, wenn sie Trost

Practice the Skills

4 Key Reading Skill

Drawing Conclusions Why does Anne respond to her mother as she does here? How do you suppose this makes Mrs. Frank feel?

Teach

L Literary Element

Review Irony **Ask:** Do you think Dussel's response to Mr. Van Daan is verbal irony? Why or why not? *(Responses will vary. Some students may think he doesn't really mean what he's saying and is just being cruel. Others may think he's fed up with Anne and wishes she were no longer in the attic.)* OL

R Reading Skill

Drawing Conclusions
Say: The stage directions say Mrs. Frank responds to Anne by "hiding her hurt." Why do you think she does this? *(Possible response: She doesn't like conflict. She probably does not want to quarrel with Anne.)* OL

Literature Focus Lesson

Characterization Have students explore the relationship Anne has with her parents by writing a diary entry from Anne's perspective. Encourage students to use their entries to compare and contrast Anne's relationship with her mother and her relationship with her father. Point out that in her diary entries, Anne recalls specific incidents. Guide students to cite specific interactions and conversations Anne has with her parents. Remind students to write in a style that matches Anne's. OL AL

Indiana English/Language Arts Academic Standards
SE: 8.2.9, 8.3
TWE: *Reading Skill* 8.2.9, *Differentiated Instruction* 8.2, *Literature Focus Lesson* 8.5

Teach

L Literary Element

Dialogue and Monologue
Say: What are some ways an actor portraying Mrs. Frank could convey to an English-speaking audience the sense of the lines written in German? *(She could use gestures, such as pointing towards Anne's room and touching Mr. Frank, to make it clear whom she is talking about and to. Her facial expressions and tone of voice could convey her emotions.)* AL

C Critical Thinking

Synthesis **Ask:** Who is Jopie? *(a friend of Anne's whose family was called up and sent away by the Nazis)* BL **Ask:** Who are the Green Police? *(Nazi police)* **Ask:** Does Anne's nightmare surprise you? Why or why not? *(Anne's nightmare is not surprising because she and the others in the attic live in constant fear of discovery by the Nazis.)* OL

braucht! Geh hinein, Otto, sie ist ganz hysterisch vor Angst. [*As* MR. FRANK *hesitates.*] Geh zu ihr.[2] [*He looks at her for a second and then goes to get a cup of water for* ANNE. MRS. FRANK *sinks down on the bed, her face in her hands, trying to keep from sobbing aloud.* MARGOT *comes over to her, putting her arms around her.*] She wants nothing of me. She pulled away when I leaned down to kiss her. 5 L

MARGOT. It's a phase . . . You heard Father . . . Most girls go through it . . . they turn to their fathers at this age . . . they give all their love to their fathers.

MRS. FRANK. You weren't like this. You didn't shut me out.

MARGOT. She'll get over it . . .

[*She smooths the bed for* MRS. FRANK *and sits beside her a moment as* MRS. FRANK *lies down. In* ANNE'S *room* MR. FRANK *comes in, sitting down by* ANNE. ANNE *flings her arms around him, clinging to him. In the distance we hear the sound of ack-ack.*]

ANNE. Oh, Pim. I dreamed that they came to get us! The Green Police! They broke down the door and grabbed me and started to drag me out the way they did Jopie. C

MR. FRANK. I want you to take this pill.

ANNE. What is it?

MR. FRANK. Something to quiet you.

[*She takes it and drinks the water. In the main room* MARGOT *turns out the light and goes back to her bed.*]

MR. FRANK. [*To* ANNE.] Do you want me to read to you for a while?

ANNE. No. Just sit with me for a minute. Was I awful? Did I yell terribly loud? Do you think anyone outside could have heard?

MR. FRANK. No. No. Lie quietly now. Try to sleep.

---

2. The Franks' conversation in German translates as follows: MRS. FRANK. "She wanted to see you!" MR. FRANK. "Edith, dear, look . . ." MRS. FRANK. "It's all right! Thank God that at least she turns to you when she is in need of comfort. Go in, Otto, she is hysterical with fear. Go to her."

Practice the Skills

5 Key Literary Element

Dialogue and Monologue
Why did the playwrights have Mr. and Mrs. Frank speak in German here? How could theatergoers who don't know German (and don't have a footnoted translation) get the ideas expressed in this conversation?

Additional Support

Reading in the Real World

Citizenship Most members of the Nazi police force were not subject to civil law. These officers could search homes, seize private property, and arrest anyone. Individuals targeted by the Nazi police had no rights under the law. Thousands of Jews, other "undesirables," and opponents of Nazism disappeared after being arrested. Share this information with students and ask them to describe how U.S. laws are designed to protect citizens from this treatment. *(For example, police must obtain warrants and have probable cause before searching someone's home or property; citizens have a right to a lawyer and a trial.)* OL AL

ANNE. I'm a terrible coward. I'm so disappointed in myself. I think I've conquered my fear . . . I think I'm really grown-up . . . and then something happens . . . and I run to you like a baby . . . I love you, Father. I don't love anyone but you. 6

MR. FRANK. [*Reproachfully.*] Annele!

ANNE. It's true. I've been thinking about it for a long time. You're the only one I love.

MR. FRANK. It's fine to hear you tell me that you love me. But I'd be happier if you said you loved your mother as well . . . She needs your help so much . . . your love . . .

ANNE. We have nothing in common. She doesn't understand me. Whenever I try to explain my views on life to her she asks me if I'm constipated. L1

MR. FRANK. You hurt her very much just now. She's crying. She's in there crying.

ANNE. I can't help it. I only told the truth. I didn't want her here . . . [*Then, with sudden change.*] Oh, Pim, I was horrible, wasn't I? And the worst of it is, I can stand off and look at myself doing it and know it's cruel and yet I can't stop doing it. What's the matter with me? Tell me. Don't say it's just a phase! Help me.

MR. FRANK. There is so little that we parents can do to help our children. We can only try to set a good example . . . point the way. The rest you must do yourself. You must build your own character.

ANNE. I'm trying. Really I am. Every night I think back over all of the things I did that day that were wrong . . . like putting the wet mop in Mr. Dussel's bed . . . and this thing now with Mother. I say to myself, that was wrong. I make up my mind, I'm never going to do that again. Never! Of course I may do something worse . . . but at least I'll never do *that* again! . . . I have a nicer side, Father . . . a sweeter, nicer side. But I'm scared to show it. I'm afraid that people are going to laugh at me if I'm serious. So the mean Anne comes to the outside and the good Anne stays on the inside, and I keep on trying to switch them around and have the good Anne

Practice the Skills

6 Reviewing Skills

Connecting It's been several months since Anne heard about her friend, but the nightmare suggests that she's more upset than she realized. Do you think that makes her a "terrible coward"? How would you react to similar news?

Teach

L1 Literary Element

Review Conflict **Ask:** According to Anne, what is the main cause of her conflict with her mother? *(They have nothing in common.)* **Ask:** How does Anne react to the news that she's hurt her mother's feelings? *(First, she defends her actions, saying she was just telling the truth; then, she realizes she's made a mistake and feels bad.)* BL **Ask:** Do you think Anne is fair to her mother? Why or why not? *(Possible response: Anne is not fair to her mother. Her mother is trying hard to understand and help Anne.)* OL

L2 Literary Element

Dialogue and Monologue **Say:** Anne shares information about her own character and self-image. Why do you think she shares these deeply personal feelings with her father? *(Possible response: Anne wants her father to understand the reasons that she sometimes does mean or selfish things. She wants him to know that she is trying to be a better person because she values his opinion.)* OL

Differentiated Instruction

Interview Mr. Frank says that all parents can do is set an example and that children "must build [their] own character." Encourage students to consider whether they agree with this statement. Have students interview an adult, such as a parent or caregiver, to get reactions to Mr. Frank's statement. Encourage students to ask three open questions, ones that require more than just a "yes" or "no" answer. Remind students to take notes during the interview so they can accurately recall the person's statements. Ask them to compare the person's response with their predictions. Students can present their findings to the class. AS

Indiana English/Language Arts Academic Standards

SE: 8.3, 8.3.6

TWE: *Reading in the Real World* 8.2, *Differentiated Instruction* 8.7.1

Teach

R Reading Skill

Drawing Conclusions
Say: Consider the characters' responses to Mr. Frank's question as well as what you have learned about each of their personalities. Tell how each character's response makes sense, given what you already know about him or her. Use examples from the play to support your response. *(Possible responses:* ***Mrs. Van Daan:*** *Her choice of being with her things makes sense because possessions are important to her. For example, she is attached to her fur coat.* ***Peter:*** *Peter's choice of a movie makes sense because he is a loner and he would want to do something on his own.* ***Mr. Dussel:*** *His choice makes sense because he kept his dentist bag close to him when he first arrived, indicating he feels most comfortable in his dentist role.* ***Anne:*** *Anne's desire to ride a bike, laugh, get new clothes, and have a hot bath all make sense given her outgoing personality and her love of life.)* OL AL

READING WORKSHOP 1

outside and the bad Anne inside and be what I'd like to be . . . and might be . . . if only . . . only . . . 7

[*She is asleep.* MR. FRANK *watches her for a moment and then turns off the light, and starts out. The lights dim out. The curtain falls on the scene.* ANNE'S VOICE *is heard dimly at first, and then with growing strength.*]

ANNE'S VOICE. . . . The air raids are getting worse. They come over day and night. The noise is terrifying. Pim says it should be music to our ears. The more planes, the sooner will come the end of the war. Mrs. Van Daan pretends to be a fatalist.[3] What will be, will be. But when the planes come over, who is the most frightened? No one else but Petronella! . . . 8 Monday, the ninth of November, nineteen forty-two. Wonderful news! The Allies have landed in Africa. Pim says that we can look for an early finish to the war. Just for fun he asked each of us what was the first thing we wanted to do when we got out of here. Mrs. Van Daan longs to be home with her own things, her needle-point chairs, the Beckstein piano her father gave her . . . the best that money could buy. Peter would like to go to a movie. Mr. Dussel wants to get back to his dentist's drill. R He's afraid he is losing his touch. For myself, there are so many things . . . to ride a bike again . . . to laugh till my belly aches . . . to have new clothes from the skin out . . . to have a hot tub filled to overflowing and **wallow** in it for hours . . . to be back in school with my friends . . . 9

[*As the last lines are being said, the curtain rises on the scene. The lights dim on as* ANNE'S VOICE *fades away.*]

3. A ***fatalist*** (FAY tul ist) is someone who believes that fate controls everything that happens.

Vocabulary

wallow (WAH loh) *v.* to take selfish pleasure in comfort

Practice the Skills

7 Key Literary Element

Dialogue and Monologue A monologue often reveals a great deal about the speaker. Why, do you think, is Anne so open and honest about herself here?

8 Key Reading Skill

Drawing Conclusions Judging from the first few lines of this speech, who is conducting these air raids–the Allies or Germany? Why does Mr. Frank say their noise should be "music to our ears"?

9 Key Reading Skill

Drawing Conclusions What do the responses to Mr. Frank's question tell you about these characters?

Additional Support

Differentiated Instruction

Perform a Scene To encourage teamwork and cooperation, have students work together in groups to perform a scene from the play. Discuss with students the elements involved in staging a drama, such as lights, props, sound effects, and costumes in addition to the presentation of the dialogue.

Have students select a scene and choose actors to play each role. Students who prefer not to act could direct or be in charge of props, costumes, music, lighting, or sound. Have the groups analyze and evaluate one another's performances. OL

SCENE 5

[*It is the first night of the Hanukkah celebration.* MR. FRANK *is standing at the head of the table on which is the Menorah. He lights the Shamos, or servant candle, and holds it as he says the blessing. Seated listening is all of the "family," dressed in their best. The men wear hats,* PETER *wears his cap.*[4]] R

MR. FRANK. [*Reading from a prayer book.*] "Praised be Thou, oh Lord our God, Ruler of the universe, who has **sanctified** us with Thy commandments and bidden us kindle the Hanukkah lights. **10** Praised be Thou, oh Lord our God, Ruler of the universe, who has wrought wondrous deliverances for our fathers in days of old. Praised be Thou, oh Lord our God, Ruler of the universe, that Thou has given us life and **sustenance** and brought us to this happy season." [MR. FRANK LIGHTS THE ONE CANDLE OF THE MENORAH AS HE CONTINUES.] "We kindle this Hanukkah light to celebrate the great and wonderful deeds wrought through the zeal with which God filled the hearts of the heroic Maccabees, two thousand years ago. They fought against indifference, against tyranny and oppression, and they restored our Temple to us.[5] May these lights remind us that we should ever look to God, whence cometh our help." Amen. [*Pronounced O-mayn.*] C

Visual Vocabulary
The ***Menorah*** (muh NOR uh) is a candlestick with nine branches.

ALL. Amen.

[MR. FRANK *hands* MRS. FRANK *the prayer book.*]

4. The eight-day Jewish holiday ***Hanukkah*** (HAW nuh kuh) is celebrated in December. It honors the Jews' victory over Syrian enemies in 165 B.C. One candle of the Menorah is called the ***Shamos*** (SHAW mus), or ***servant candle,*** because it's used to light the others. Jewish males wear some sort of hat during religious services and ceremonies. In the next few speeches, Mr. and Mrs. Frank read traditional Hanukkah blessings and prayers.
5. It was the ***Maccabees,*** a family of Jewish patriots, who led the Jews in their fight against the Syrians' cruel and unjust use of power ***(tyranny and oppression).***

Vocabulary

sustenance (SUS tuh nuns) *n.* food and other necessities of life

Practice the Skills

10 English Language Coach

Historical Influences Look at the word **sanctified**. It's a form of the verb *sanctify*. The suffix *-ify* can mean "to give a certain quality." Review the chart on page 764 to remember the meaning of the root *sanct*. What do you think *sanctify* means?

Teach

R Reading Skill

Drawing Conclusions
Ask: Why do you think the playwrights include this Hanukkah scene? *(Possible response: They want to show that the characters' faith and traditions are still important to them, even if they can practice these traditions only in hiding. The scene also shows that the group has not given up hope and that they find hope in one another.)* OL

C Critical Thinking

Synthesis **Ask:** What do the group in hiding and many other Jews in Europe have in common with the Maccabees? *(They are all victims of tyranny and oppression.)* OL

English Language Coach

Formal English Note that the language of traditional prayers and religious ceremonies and readings is more formal than everyday conversation and writing. Draw students' attention to the choice of words in the prayer read by Mr. Frank; the long, complex sentences; and the use of capital letters to begin words that refer to God (*Thou, Thy, Lord, Ruler,* and so on.). Organize students in five groups and assign each group a sentence from the reading. Ask the groups to rewrite their assigned sentences in less formal English. Students may use a dictionary to find the meanings of unfamiliar words. EL OL

Indiana English/Language Arts Academic Standards
SE: 8.2.9, 8.3, 8.3.6
TWE: *Differentiated Instruction* 8.7.2, *English Language Coach* 8.1

Teach

L Literary Element

Dialogue and Monologue
Say: Mrs. Frank's first set of lines on this page can be considered a monologue. Why? *(It is a long, uninterrupted speech by one character.)* OL

R Reading Skill

Drawing Conclusions
Ask: How can you tell that Mr. Dussel doesn't know much about Hanukkah? *(He thinks the celebration is over when Mrs. Frank finishes reading from the prayer book. He doesn't know that presents are exchanged during Hanukkah.)* BL **Ask:** From these details, what can you conclude about Mr. Dussel? *(Possible response: He is not a religious or practicing Jew.)* OL

MRS. FRANK. [*Reading.*] "I lift up mine eyes unto the mountains, from whence cometh my help. My help cometh from the Lord who made heaven and earth. He will not suffer thy foot to be moved. He that keepeth thee will not slumber. He that keepeth Israel doth neither slumber nor sleep. The Lord is thy keeper. The Lord is thy shade upon thy right hand. The sun shall not smite thee by day, nor the moon by night. The Lord shall keep thee from all evil. He shall keep thy soul. The Lord shall guard thy going out and thy coming in, from this time forth and forevermore." Amen. 11

ALL. Amen.

[*MRS. FRANK puts down the prayer book and goes to get the food and wine. MARGOT helps her. MR. FRANK takes the men's hats and puts them aside.*]

DUSSEL. [*Rising.*] That was very moving.

ANNE. [*Pulling him back.*] It isn't over yet!

MRS. VAN DAAN. Sit down! Sit down!

ANNE. There's a lot more, songs and presents.

DUSSEL. Presents?

MRS. FRANK. Not this year, unfortunately.

MRS. VAN DAAN. But always on Hanukkah everyone gives presents . . . everyone!

DUSSEL. Like our St. Nicholas' Day.[6]

[*There is a chorus of "no's" from the group.*]

MRS. VAN DAAN. No! Not like St. Nicholas! What kind of a Jew are you that you don't know Hanukkah? 12

MRS. FRANK. [*As she brings the food.*] I remember particularly the candles . . . First one, as we have tonight. Then the second night you light two candles, the next night three . . . and so on until you have eight candles burning. When there are eight candles it is truly beautiful.

6. In the Netherlands, Christian children receive gifts from ***St. Nicholas*** on December 6.

Practice the Skills

11 Reviewing Skills

Monitoring Comprehension After reading formal and difficult language, it's a good idea to monitor your comprehension. Ask yourself whether you understand what the prayers say.

12 Key Reading Skill

Drawing Conclusions What can you conclude from Dussel's questions and comments about his knowledge of Judaism?

Additional Support

English Language Coach

Building Background The lighting of the Menorah at Hanukkah is one of the most important aspects of the religious holiday. The eight candles lit on the Menorah are a celebration of the miracle of oil in the temple. When Judas Maccabeus entered a temple, he found only a small jar of consecrated (holy) oil, enough to last one day; however, the oil burned for eight days, until more consecrated oil was found. Have students read more online about this religious holiday. AS

MRS. VAN DAAN. And the potato pancakes.

MR. VAN DAAN. Don't talk about them!

MRS. VAN DAAN. I make the best *latkes*[7] you ever tasted!

MRS. FRANK. Invite us all next year . . . in your own home.

MR. FRANK. God willing!

MRS. VAN DAAN. God willing.

MARGOT. What I remember best is the presents we used to get when we were little . . . eight days of presents . . . and each day they got better and better.

MRS. FRANK. [*Sitting down.*] We are all here, alive. That is present enough. **13**

ANNE. No, it isn't. I've got something . . .

[*She rushes into her room, hurriedly puts on a little hat improvised from the lamp shade, grabs a satchel bulging with parcels and comes running back.*]

MRS. FRANK. What is it?

ANNE. Presents!

MRS. VAN DAAN. Presents!

DUSSEL. Look!

MR. VAN DAAN. What's she got on her head?

PETER. A lamp shade!

ANNE. [*She picks out one at random.*] This is for Margot. [*She hands it to* MARGOT, *pulling her to her feet.*] Read it out loud.

MARGOT. [*Reading.*]

"You have never lost your temper.
You never will, I fear,
You are so good.
But if you should,
Put all your cross words here." **14**

7. ***Latkes*** (LOT kuz) are potato pancakes.

Practice the Skills

13 BIG Question

BQ Do you think the characters should be celebrating Hanukkah despite their situation? What value do religion and tradition have in helping people through hard times? Write your thoughts on the Workshop 1 Foldable for Unit 6. Your response will help you complete the Unit Challenge later.

R

14 **Reviewing Skills**

Analyzing Anne's poem pokes fun at Margot's "perfect" behavior. What does it tell you about Anne?

Teach

BQ BIG Question

Before students respond to the Big Question note on this page, discuss as a class what religious holidays and traditions mean to people. Record students' thoughts and ideas on the board. Students may follow up by responding to the Big Question note in their **Workshop 1 Foldable.** **AS**

R Reading Skill

Review Predicting **Say:** Consider what you have already learned about Margot's character. How do you think she will react to Anne's teasing poem? Explain. *(Possible response: Margot will probably appreciate Anne's gesture and enjoy the humorous poem. Margot is calm and mature, so she is not likely to take offense.)* **OL**

Reading in the Real World

Citizenship Marge Kennedy and Janet Spencer King, two U.S. writers, have stated that a family is "what you make it. It is made strong . . . by the rituals you help family members create, by the memories you share, by the commitment of time, caring, and love you show to one another." Ask students whether the "family" in the attic fulfills the above description. Have students form small groups to discuss this question further and to formulate their own definitions of *family*. Ask each group to share its definition and thoughts with the rest of the class. **OL** **AL**

Indiana English/Language Arts Academic Standards

SE: 8.3, 8.3.6

TWE: *English Language Coach* 8.4.4, *Reading in the Real World* 8.2

Teach

R Reading Skill

Drawing Conclusions
Ask: How does Anne's gift-giving bring the "family" members together? *(Possible response: Anne's gift giving makes everyone feel included in the celebration of Hanukkah. It reminds them of celebrations they had when they were not in hiding.)* BL **Ask:** How do you think Anne's gifts make the others feel about her? *(Possible response: Anne's gifts make the others appreciate her positive attitude, her energy, her resourcefulness, and her thoughtfulness.)* OL

READING WORKSHOP 1

[*She tears open the package.*] A new crossword puzzle book! Where did you get it?

ANNE. It isn't new. It's one that you've done. But I rubbed it all out, and if you wait a little and forget, you can do it all over again.

MARGOT. [*Sitting.*] It's wonderful, Anne. Thank you. You'd never know it wasn't new.

[*From outside we hear the sound of a streetcar passing.*]

ANNE. [*With another gift.*] Mrs. Van Daan.

MRS. VAN DAAN. [*Taking it.*] This is awful . . . I haven't anything for anyone . . . I never thought . . .

MR. FRANK. This is all Anne's idea. 15

MRS. VAN DAAN. [*Holding up a bottle.*] What is it?

ANNE. It's hair shampoo. I took all the odds and ends of soap and mixed them with the last of my toilet water.[8]

MRS. VAN DAAN. Oh, Anneke!

ANNE. I wanted to write a poem for all of them, but I didn't have time. [*Offering a large box to* MR. VAN DAAN.] Yours, Mr. Van Daan, is really something . . . something you want more than anything. [*As she waits for him to open it.*] Look! Cigarettes!

MR. VAN DAAN. Cigarettes!

ANNE. Two of them! Pim found some old pipe tobacco in the pocket lining of his coat . . . and we made them . . . or rather, Pim did.

MRS. VAN DAAN. Let me see . . . Well, look at that! Light it, Putti! Light it.

[MR. VAN DAAN *hesitates.*]

ANNE. It's tobacco, really it is! There's a little fluff in it, but not much. 16

8. ***Toilet water*** is a lightly scented liquid used as a perfume.

Practice the Skills

15 Key Reading Skill

Drawing Conclusions Why does Mr. Frank make a point of saying this?

16 Key Literary Element

Dialogue and Monologue In good dialogue, the characters speak in ways that suit their personalities. For example, Anne talks often, at length, and with strong feeling. How do those things match her personality? As you read, notice how the other characters speak and imagine how they sound.

Additional Support

Literature Focus Lesson

Dialogue Point out that writing dialogue is different from other writing because people must be made to speak in a variety of ways for dialogue to be realistic. It must reflect the way each particular character would sound when speaking. For example, Anne speaks a great deal because she is outgoing, and she speaks quickly. Peter, who is shy, speaks less and in shorter sentences.

Have students write a dialogue that might occur between an elderly woman and a teenager. Encourage students to consider the words and manner of speech each character would use. OL AL

[*Everyone watches intently as* MR. VAN DAAN *cautiously lights it. The cigarette flares up. Everyone laughs.*]

PETER. It works!

MRS. VAN DAAN. Look at him.

MR. VAN DAAN. [*Spluttering.*] Thank you, Anne. Thank you.

[ANNE *rushes back to her satchel for another present.*]

ANNE. [*Handing her mother a piece of paper.*] For Mother, Hanukkah greeting.

[*She pulls her mother to her feet.*]

MRS. FRANK. [*She reads.*] "Here's an I.O.U. that I promise to pay. Ten hours of doing whatever you say. Signed, Anne Frank."

[MRS. FRANK, *touched, takes* ANNE *in her arms, holding her close.*]

DUSSEL. [*To* ANNE.] Ten hours of doing what you're told? Anything you're told?

R

ANNE. That's right.

DUSSEL. You wouldn't want to sell that, Mrs. Frank?

MRS. FRANK. Never! This is the most precious gift I've ever had! **17**

[*She sits, showing her present to the others.* ANNE *hurries back to the satchel and pulls out a scarf, the scarf that* MR. FRANK *found in the first scene.*]

EL

ANNE. [*Offering it to her father.*] For Pim.

MR. FRANK. Anneke . . . I wasn't supposed to have a present!

[*He takes it, unfolding it and showing it to the others.*]

ANNE. It's a muffler . . . to put round your neck . . . like an ascot, you know. I made it myself out of odds and ends . . . I knitted it in the dark each night, after I'd gone to bed. I'm afraid it looks better in the dark!

MR. FRANK. [*Putting it on.*] It's fine. It fits me perfectly. Thank you, Annele.

Practice the Skills

17 Key Reading Skill

Drawing Conclusions Why is Anne's gift to her mother particularly important and touching? Explain.

Reading in the Real World

Career Tell students that *statisticians* are people who collect and interpret numerical data. Students with logical and mathematical learning abilities may be interested in exploring statistics from the Holocaust. Point out that the Nazis ran many concentration camps and death camps where they sent not only Jews and other ethnic groups, but also people who violated their strict regulations—those who helped Jews, and those who spoke against the Nazis. Have students research information on the Nazi camps and make a map showing their locations. Students can include on the map statistics about each camp, such as how long it existed and how many prisoners it held. **AL**

READING WORKSHOP 1

Teach

R Reading Skill

Drawing Conclusions **Say:** Describe Anne's relationship with her mother. *(Their relationship is strained. Anne feels her mother doesn't understand her; she is sometimes cruel to her mother and disobeys her.)*
Ask: Why, then, is Anne's gift so precious to Mrs. Frank? *(Possible response: Anne's gift reassures Mrs. Frank that her daughter cares about and respects her.)* **OL**

EL Language Coach

Historical Influences on English **Say:** The word *satchel* can be traced back to a Latin word *saccus*, meaning "bag." A satchel is a bag like a knapsack. What other modern English word is spelled similarly to *saccus* and means "bag"? *(The modern word* sack *means "bag.")* **EL** **BL**

Indiana English/Language Arts Academic Standards
SE: 8.3, 8.3.6
TWE: *Reading Skill* 8.2.9, *Literature Focus Lesson* 8.5, *Reading in the Real World* 8.4

Teach

EL Language Coach

Historical Influences on English **Say:** The English word *mustache* comes from the French language, which adopted the word from Italian, which adopted it from Greek. Use a dictionary to find out what the original Greek word was and what it meant. *(moustaki, meaning "little upper lip")* OL

R Reading Skill

Review Analyzing **Say:** Recall Mr. Van Daan's comments about food supplies in the attic. How might his concerns influence his feelings about Mouschi? *(Possible response: Mr. Van Daan probably resents having to share the limited food supplies with an animal.)* OL

[ANNE *hands* PETER *a ball of paper, with a string attached to it.*]

ANNE. That's for Mouschi.

PETER. [*Rising to bow.*] On behalf of Mouschi, I thank you.

ANNE. [*Hesitant, handing him a gift.*] And . . . this is yours . . . from Mrs. Quack Quack. [*As he holds it gingerly*[9] *in his hands.*] Well . . . open it . . . Aren't you going to open it?

PETER. I'm scared to. I know something's going to jump out and hit me.

ANNE. No. It's nothing like that, really.

MRS. VAN DAAN. [*As he is opening it.*] What is it, Peter? Go on. Show it.

ANNE. [*Excitedly.*] It's a safety razor!

DUSSEL. A what?

ANNE. A razor!

MRS. VAN DAAN. [*Looking at it.*] You didn't make that out of odds and ends.

ANNE. [*To* PETER.] Miep got it for me. It's not new. It's second-hand. But you really do need a razor now.

DUSSEL. For what?

ANNE. Look on his upper lip . . . you can see the beginning of a mustache. 18 EL

DUSSEL. He wants to get rid of that? Put a little milk on it and let the cat lick it off.

PETER. [*Starting for his room.*] Think you're funny, don't you?

DUSSEL. Look! He can't wait! He's going in to try it!

PETER. I'm going to give Mouschi his present!

[*He goes into his room, slamming the door behind him.*]

MR. VAN DAAN. [*Disgustedly.*] Mouschi, Mouschi, Mouschi. 19

---

9. ***Gingerly*** (JIN jur lee) means "lightly; cautiously."

Practice the Skills

18 Key Reading Skill

Drawing Conclusions In scene 3, Anne made fun of Peter's "little fuzz." Why does she now give him a razor? Is she mocking him again?

19 Reviewing Skills

Analyzing Why do you think Mr. Van Daan is always so disgusted about Peter and his cat?

Additional Support

Differentiated Instruction

Recalling Important Events Some students may have difficulty reading and recalling the details of such a long text. Suggest students take notes on the main events in each scene. As a class, create a chart that shows the breakdown of the play into scenes. Record the important events and details of each scene thus far in the appropriate space on the chart. Help students add to the chart as they continue reading. EL BL

MR. VAN DAAN. [*Calling after him.*] I'm not doing it for you. That's all in your mind . . . all of it! [*He starts back to his place at the table.*] I'm doing it because I'm sick of seeing that cat eat all our food.

PETER. That's not true! I only give him bones . . . scraps . . .

MR. VAN DAAN. Don't tell me! He gets fatter every day! Damn cat looks better than any of us. Out he goes tonight!

PETER. No! No!

ANNE. Mr. Van Daan, you can't do that! That's Peter's cat. Peter loves that cat.

MRS. FRANK. [*Quietly.*] Anne.

PETER. [*To* MR. VAN DAAN.] If he goes, I go.

MR. VAN DAAN. Go! Go!

MRS. VAN DAAN. You're not going and the cat's not going! Now please . . . this is Hanukkah . . . Hanukkah . . . this is the time to celebrate . . . What's the matter with all of you? Come on, Anne. Let's have the song.

ANNE. [*Singing.*] "Oh, Hanukkah! Oh, Hanukkah! The sweet celebration."

MR. FRANK. [*Rising.*] I think we should first blow out the candle . . . then we'll have something for tomorrow night.

MARGOT. But, Father, you're supposed to let it burn itself out.

MR. FRANK. I'm sure that God understands shortages. [*Before blowing it out.*] "Praised be Thou, oh Lord our God, who hast sustained us and **permitted** us to celebrate this joyous festival." 23

[*He is about to blow out the candle when suddenly there is a crash of something falling below. They all freeze in horror, motionless. For a few seconds there is complete silence.* MR. FRANK *slips off his shoes. The others noiselessly follow his example.* MR. FRANK *turns out a light near him. He motions to* PETER *to turn off the center lamp.* PETER *tries to reach it, realizes he cannot and gets up on a chair. Just as he is touching the lamp he loses his balance. The chair goes out from under him. He falls. The iron lamp shade*

Practice the Skills

23 English Language Coach

Historical Influences The word **permitted** contains the Latin root *mit,* which means "send." What other words do we get from *mit*? (No, *mitt* and *mitten* are not from this root.)

Reading in the Real World

College Students who plan to attend college should be able to develop a convincing argument. Ask students to consider the disagreement Peter, Anne, Mr. Van Daan, and Mr. Dussel have about the cat. Divide the class into two groups: one to represent Mr. Van Daan and Mr. Dussel, and another to represent Peter and Anne. Tell students to develop an argument from the perspective of their characters about why the cat should or should not remain. Appoint a note-taker for each team. Then, have each team choose two representatives to present its reasons. Allow time for rebuttal. AS

Teach

L Literary Element

Review Conflict **Say:** Note that earlier in the scene, the mood was one of joy and sweetness, but now there is tension in the group. What causes the conflict in this part of the scene? *(Mr. Van Daan says that Peter's cat has to go.)* OL

R Reading Skill

Drawing Conclusions
Ask: Given what he says to Peter, what conclusions can you draw about Mr. Van Daan as a father? *(Possible response: Mr. Van Daan is, above all, selfish. Although he might not really sacrifice his son in order to have a little more to eat, his comment indicates that his main concerns focus on himself.)* OL

EL Language Coach

Historical Influences on English **Say:** The Latin root *mit* also appears as *mitt, mis,* or *miss.* What other English words contain this Latin root? *(Possible responses: transmit, missile, mission, commit, committee, admit)* EL BL OL

Indiana English/Language Arts Academic Standards
SE: 8.1.2, 8.3
TWE: *Reading Skill* 8.2.9, *Reading in the Real World* 8.5, *Reading in the Real World* 8.7

Teach

R1 Reading Skill

Review Analyzing **Ask:** What word in the stage directions describes the dog's barking? What does this word tell you about what might have prompted the barking? *(According to the stage directions, the dog barks "excitedly." This word indicates that the dog is barking in response to something.)* OL

R2 Reading Skill

Review Comparing and Contrasting **Say:** Mr. and Mrs. Frank and Mr. and Mrs. Van Daan react very differently to the events described here. Contrast the reactions of the two couples and tell what it reveals about them. *(Possible response: The Franks remain quiet, accepting that there is nothing they can do. This reveals that they are calm, logical people. The Van Daans assume the Green Police have found them and frantically demand that something be done. This reveals that they are less able to stay calm in difficult situations and are ruled by fear rather than logic.)* OL

crashes to the floor. There is a sound of feet below, running down the stairs.]

MR. VAN DAAN. [*Under his breath.*] God Almighty! [*The only light left comes from the Hanukkah candle.* DUSSEL *comes from his room.* MR. FRANK *creeps over to the stairwell and stands listening. The dog is heard barking excitedly.*] Do you hear anything? **24** R1

MR. FRANK. [*In a whisper.*] No. I think they've gone.

MRS. VAN DAAN. It's the Green Police. They've found us.

MR. FRANK. If they had, they wouldn't have left. They'd be up here by now.

MRS. VAN DAAN. I know it's the Green Police. They've gone to get help. That's all. They'll be back!

MR. VAN DAAN. Or it may have been the Gestapo,[11] looking for papers . . . R2

MR. FRANK. [*Interrupting.*] Or a thief, looking for money.

MRS. VAN DAAN. We've got to do something . . . Quick! Quick! Before they come back.

MR. VAN DAAN. There isn't anything to do. Just wait.

[MR. FRANK *holds up his hand for them to be quiet. He is listening intently. There is complete silence as they all strain to hear any sound from below. Suddenly* ANNE *begins to sway. With a low cry she falls to the floor in a faint.* MRS. FRANK *goes to her quickly, sitting beside her on the floor and taking her in her arms.*] **25**

MRS. FRANK. Get some water, please! Get some water!

[MARGOT *starts for the sink.*]

MR. VAN DAAN. [*Grabbing* MARGOT.] No! No! No one's going to run water!

MR. FRANK. If they've found us, they've found us. Get the water. [MARGOT *STARTS AGAIN FOR THE SINK.* MR. FRANK, *GETTING A FLASHLIGHT.*] I'm going down.

11. The ***Gestapo*** (guh STAH poh) were the Nazi secret police.

Practice the Skills

24 Reviewing Skills

Analyzing This is the second mention of the dog. (See the stage directions at the top of p. 779.) What might it mean to hear barking, silence, a crash on a floor below, then barking?

25 Key Reading Skill

Drawing Conclusions Why does Anne, of all people, faint? (Recall the beginning of scene 4.)

Additional Support

Reading Fluency

Building Fluency Have students practice reading aloud the characters' lines on page 782. Before students begin reading, tell them to imagine events from the perspective of the different characters. Encourage students to use their voices to show the characters' emotions. Have students reread the text several times until they can read with expression and without stumbling over words. Remind students to convey the emotional drama of the story through tone and expression. EL BL

[*MARGOT rushes to him, clinging to him. ANNE struggles to* ***consciousness***.] 26

MARGOT. No, Father, no! There may be someone there, waiting . . . It may be a trap!

MR. FRANK. This is Saturday. There is no way for us to know what has happened until Miep or Mr. Kraler comes on Monday morning. We cannot live with this **uncertainty.** R1

MARGOT. Don't go, Father!

MRS. FRANK. Hush, darling, hush. [*MR. FRANK slips quietly out, down the steps, and out through the door below.*] Margot! Stay close to me.

[*MARGOT goes to her mother.*]

MR. VAN DAAN. Shush! Shush!

[*MRS. FRANK whispers to MARGOT to get the water. MARGOT goes for it.*]

MRS. VAN DAAN. Putti, where's our money? Get our money. I hear you can buy the Green Police off, so much a head. Go upstairs quick! Get the money!

MR. VAN DAAN. Keep still!

MRS. VAN DAAN. [*Kneeling before him, pleading.*] Do you want to be dragged off to a concentration camp? Are you going to stand there and wait for them to come up and get you? Do something, I tell you!

MR. VAN DAAN. [*Pushing her aside.*] Will you keep still!

[*He goes over to the stairwell to listen. PETER goes to his mother, helping her up onto the sofa. There is a second of silence, then ANNE can stand it no longer.*]

ANNE. Someone go after Father! Make Father come back!

PETER. [*Starting for the door.*] I'll go.

MR. VAN DAAN. Haven't you done enough? R2

Vocabulary

uncertainty (un SUR tun tee) *n.* the state of being unsure or not knowing

Practice the Skills

26 English Language Coach

Historical Influences The Latin root *scientia* means "know." The words *science* and **consciousness** come from this root.

English Language Coach

Correct Word Usage Many students avoid using the word *fewer* and as a result misuse the word *less*. Review with students that *fewer* is the correct term to use when referring to individual items and *less* is correct when referring to concepts or categories of items. Use the following example: *Because they had less food, the Franks ate fewer meals.*

Have students identify the correct term to use with the following words: *trouble, children, money, dollars, sickness,* and *diseases*. Encourage them to suggest their own examples. EL BL

Teach

R1 Reading Skill

Drawing Conclusions

Ask: Why doesn't Mr. Frank want to wait until Miep and Mr. Kraler come on Monday to find out what happened downstairs? *(Possible response: He's concerned that everyone will become more fearful and that tension in the attic will increase.)* OL

R2 Reading Skill

Drawing Conclusions

Say: When Peter offers to go after Mr. Frank, Mr. Van Daan stops Peter, saying, "Haven't you done enough?" What does Mr. Van Daan mean by this? *(Possible response: Mr. Van Daan is referring to the noise Peter made in falling off the chair. He blames Peter for the possibility that someone has been alerted to their hiding place.)* BL **Ask:** What does Mr. Van Daan's comment reveal about his character? *(Possible response: This comment shows that Mr. Van Daan is uncaring and unforgiving. Peter probably already feels terrible about what he may have done.)* AL

Indiana English/Language Arts Academic Standards

SE: 8.1.2, 8.3

TWE: *Reading Fluency* 8.7.2, *English Language Coach* 8.1

Teach

Viewing the Photo

Ask: How does the scene in the photograph contrast with what is happening in the attic? *(Possible response: The photograph shows Anne, her father, and their friends in happier days, when they could enjoy going out. Their smiles show that they did not have the worries and fears about their safety that they have now.)* BL

R Reading Skill

Review Comparing and Contrasting **Ask:** Why does Mrs. Frank start to pray? *(She fears for her husband's safety and the safety of everyone in the attic.)* **Ask:** How does Mrs. Frank's response to what is happening differ from Anne's? What do their different responses indicate about their characters? *(Possible response: Mrs. Frank prays, while Anne encourages Mr. Van Daan to go look for her father. Anne does not like to wait during a crisis and would rather take action. Mrs. Frank prefers to wait and hope for the best.)* AL

READING WORKSHOP 1

Otto and Anne (both in light-colored coats) and friends, July 1941

[*He pushes* PETER *roughly away. In his anger against his father* PETER *grabs a chair as if to hit him with it, then puts it down, burying his face in his hands.* MRS. FRANK *begins to pray softly.*]

ANNE. Please, please, Mr. Van Daan. Get Father.

MR. VAN DAAN. Quiet! Quiet! 27

[ANNE *is shocked into silence.* MRS. FRANK *pulls her closer, holding her protectively in her arms.*]

MRS. FRANK. [*Softly, praying.*] "I lift up mine eyes unto the mountains, from whence cometh my help. My help cometh from the Lord who made heaven and earth. He will not suffer thy foot to be moved . . . He that keepeth thee will not slumber . . ." R

Practice the Skills

27 Reviewing Skills

Comparing and Contrasting Compare Peter and his father as they wait for Mr. Frank to return.

Additional Support

English Language Coach

Old Words and Phrases Explain that the prayer Mrs. Frank recites is Psalm 121 from the Bible. Note that some words and phrases in the prayer are archaic, not used in modern speech. Suggest that students "translate" these archaic words and phrases into modern English.

- mine eyes: my eyes
- from whence: from where
- cometh my help: comes my help
- thy: your
- keepeth: keeps (meaning "watches over")

Help students use their translations to restate the prayer in modern English. *(Note that here,* suffer *means "allow.")* EL BL

[She stops as she hears someone coming. They all watch the door tensely. MR. FRANK *comes quietly in.* ANNE *rushes to him, holding him tight.]*

MR. FRANK. It was a thief. That noise must have scared him away.

MRS. VAN DAAN. Thank God.

MR. FRANK. He took the cash box. And the radio. He ran away in such a hurry that he didn't stop to shut the street door. It was swinging wide open. [*A breath of relief sweeps over them.*] I think it would be good to have some light.

MARGOT. Are you sure it's all right?

MR. FRANK. The danger has passed. [MARGOT *goes to light the small lamp.*] Don't be so terrified, Anne. We're safe.

DUSSEL. Who says the danger has passed? Don't you realize we are in greater danger than ever? **28** R

MR. FRANK. Mr. Dussel, will you be still!

*[*MR. FRANK *takes* ANNE *back to the table, making her sit down with him, trying to calm her.]*

DUSSEL. [*Pointing to* PETER.] Thanks to this clumsy fool, there's someone now who knows we're up here! Someone now knows we're up here, hiding! L

MRS. VAN DAAN. [*Going to* DUSSEL.] Someone knows we're here, yes. But who is the someone? A thief! A thief! You think a thief is going to go to the Green Police and say . . . I was robbing a place the other night and I heard a noise up over my head? You think a thief is going to do that?

DUSSEL. Yes. I think he will.

MRS. VAN DAAN. [*Hysterically.*] You're crazy!

[She stumbles back to her seat at the table. PETER *follows protectively, pushing* DUSSEL *aside.]*

DUSSEL. I think some day he'll be caught and then he'll make a bargain with the Green Police . . . if they'll let him off, he'll tell them where some Jews are hiding!

Practice the Skills

28 Key Reading Skill

Drawing Conclusions Do you agree with Dussel? Explain.

Teach

R Reading Skill

Review Analyzing Ask: Do you agree with Mr. Dussel's assessment that the people in the attic "are in greater danger than ever"? Why? *(Possible response: I agree that they are in danger, but it is difficult to tell whether they are in "greater" danger. It depends on who was downstairs and whether the person realized someone was hiding upstairs.)* **OL**

L Literary Element

Dialogue and Monologue
Say: The dialogue here highlights the conflicts among the characters. How do the characters disagree at this point? *(Possible response: Mr. Frank says that the danger has passed, meaning that the thief has gone. However, Mr. Dussel thinks the thief will tell the Green Police they are hiding in the attic. Mrs. Van Daan does not think the thief will go to the police.)* **OL** **Ask:** Do you think Mr. Frank really believes that the danger has passed? Explain. *(Possible response: He is intelligent and not naïve, so he may say what he does to keep the others' spirits up and put their fears to rest.)* **AL**

Differentiated Instruction

Designing a Program Have students design a program, a booklet given to audience members that lists the actors and crew involved in a production and includes background information about the play. If possible, bring in a sample program for students to use as a model. Students should follow these steps:

- Cast famous actors in the main roles and create a cast of characters.
- Write a brief description of the historical background of the play.
- For illustrations, draw pictures or find photographs in magazines or online. **OL**

Indiana English/Language Arts Academic Standards
SE: 8.3
TWE: *English Language Coach* 8.1, *Differentiated Instruction* 8.5

Teach

 BIG Question

Ask: What reasons does Mr. Frank give the others for holding onto hope? *(They are still alive and safe even though a few minutes ago, they thought "it was the end.")* BL

R Reading Skill

Drawing Conclusions

Say: Earlier, Mr. Frank thought that singing the Hanukkah song would make everyone too enthusiastic. Why does he suggest singing the song now? *(Possible responses: He wants to raise everyone's spirits; he thinks they should celebrate because they were not discovered; he wants to distract everyone.)* OL

[He goes off into the bedroom. There is a second of appalled silence.]

MR. VAN DAAN. He's right.

ANNE. Father, let's get out of here! We can't stay here now . . . Let's go . . .

MR. VAN DAAN. Go! Where?

MRS. FRANK. *[Sinking into her chair at the table.]* Yes. Where?

MR. FRANK. *[Rising, to them all.]* Have we lost all faith? All courage? A moment ago we thought that they'd come for us. We were sure it was the end. But it wasn't the end. We're alive, safe. *[MR. VAN DAAN goes to the table and sits. MR. FRANK prays.]* "We thank Thee, oh Lord our God, that in Thy infinite mercy Thou hast again seen fit to spare us." *[He blows out the candle, then turns to ANNE.]* Come on, Anne. The song! Let's have the song! *[He starts to sing. ANNE finally starts falteringly to sing, as MR. FRANK urges her on. Her voice is hardly audible at first.]* 29 BQ R

ANNE. *[Singing.]*

"Oh, Hanukkah! Oh, Hanukkah!
The sweet . . . celebration . . ."

[As she goes on singing, the others gradually join in, their voices still shaking with fear. MRS. VAN DAAN sobs as she sings.]

GROUP. "Around the feast . . . we . . . gather
In complete . . . jubilation . . .
Happiest of sea . . . sons
Now is here.
Many are the reasons for good cheer."

[DUSSEL comes from the bedroom. He comes over to the table, standing beside MARGOT, listening to them as they sing.]

"Together
We'll weather
Whatever tomorrow may bring."

[As they sing on with growing courage, the lights start to dim.]

Practice the Skills

29 English Language Coach

Historical Influences The Latin root *aud* is the basis of many words, including *audio* and *auditorium*. What does *aud* mean? What word in this paragraph can help you figure out the root's meaning?

Additional Support

Differentiated Instruction

Debate Arguing a controversial point requires that students speak to persuade others and that they listen to understand opposing points of view. Have students debate the question of whether the families should leave the attic after the burglary. Organize students in two teams: one in favor of leaving and the other against it. To prepare for the debate, students on each team should discuss the points they will raise in their arguments. After the debate, evaluate the teams' performances and identify the team that made the stronger case. AL

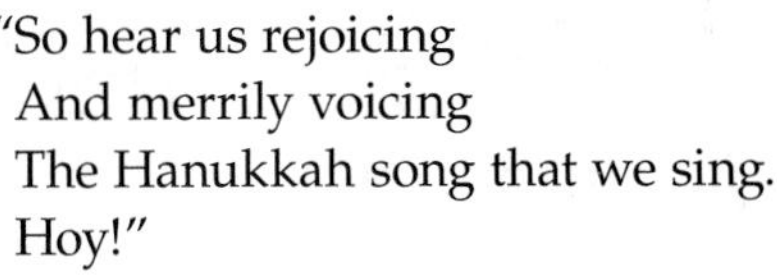

"So hear us rejoicing
And merrily voicing
The Hanukkah song that we sing.
Hoy!"

[*The lights are out. The curtain starts slowly to fall.*]

"Hear us rejoicing
And merrily voicing
The Hanukkah song that we sing." 30

[*They are still singing, as the curtain falls.*]

L

30 

How does Mr. Frank respond to the others' doubts and fears? Does it work? Write your answer on the Workshop 1 Foldable for Unit 6. Your response will help you complete the Unit Challenge later.

Anne in the Franks' Amsterdam apartment, 1941.

Analyzing the Photo At age twelve, Anne is still too small for the desk and sits on a cushion to write. Notice the picture's torn corner. Most of the photos of the Franks came from the family album or from Anne's own scrapbook.

READING WORKSHOP 1

Teach

L Literary Element

Review Irony Say: Note that the words of the Hanukkah song contribute to the irony in this play. Explain how the lines of the song are ironic. *(Possible response: The song says it is the "happiest of seasons," but the people in the attic are miserable, worried, and scared.)* BL **Ask:** What words in the song provide hope and encouragement? *(Together we'll weather whatever tomorrow may bring.)* OL

Assess

Use the CheckPoint questions provided on Presentation Plus! to check for comprehension of the selection. These questions can be used with interactive response keypads for immediate student feedback.

Differentiated Instruction

Readers' Theater Have students work in small groups to prepare a readers' theater presentation of a scene from act 1 of the play. Readers' theater does not require a stage set, props, or costumes; nor do students need to memorize their lines. Tell students to practice reading directly from the script, using the stage directions as a guide for saying their lines and making gestures. To present their scene, students can sit on chairs in a semicircle. BL OL

Indiana English/Language Arts Academic Standards
SE: 8.1.2
TWE: *Differentiated Instruction* 8.7.13, *Differentiated Instruction* 8.7

Assess

Resources for page 788

- Selection Quick Check, p. 52
- Selection and Unit Assessment, p. 62
- ExamView Assessment Suite
- Interactive Tutor: Self-Assessment

Students can respond to the *After You Read* items in their Learner's Notebooks or on a separate sheet of paper.

Answering the BIG Question

1. Possible response: No, celebrating Hanukkah gave them a feeling of hope and togetherness.
2. Anne dreams the Green Police have come to get them.
3. He says that it eats too much.
4. Paragraphs should mention Anne's nightmare, her gifts, her reaction to the break-in, and her fainting spell. Responses will vary.

Critical Thinking

5. Possible response: The Van Daans are frantic. The Franks are more calm. Dussel is cruel: he blames Peter.
6. Responses will vary.
7. Responses will vary.
8. Responses will vary.

After You Read

The Diary of Anne Frank, Act 1, Scenes 4–5

Answering the BIG Question

1. In scene 5, traditions and religious faith lift the characters' spirits—until things take a very bad turn. Would they be better off at the end of the scene if they had *not* celebrated Hanukkah?
2. **Recall** What happens in the nightmare that wakes Anne?
   TIP Right There
3. **Recall** Why does Mr. Van Daan say he wants to get rid of Peter's cat?
   TIP Right There
4. **Summarize** In a paragraph, tell what Anne goes through in scenes 4 and 5. Which one event or experience do you think affects her the most?
   TIP Think and Search

Critical Thinking

5. **Interpret** What do you learn about the characters from their reactions to the thief downstairs? Explain.
   TIP Think and Search
6. **Infer** Hanukkah is a celebration of freedom. How does the group's celebration of the holiday add to the meaning of the play?
   TIP Author and Me
7. **Evaluate** How do you think Anne affects the lives of the others?
   TIP Author and Me
8. **Interpret** From your experience, is Anne's conflict with her mother normal? Explain.
   TIP Author and Me

Indiana English/Language Arts Academic Standards (pp. 788–789)

8.3 Comprehension and Analysis of Literary Text Respond to grade-level-appropriate literature... **8.5.2** Write responses to literature... **8.3.6** Identify significant literary devices... **8.6.5** Use correct punctuation.

For a complete description of the standards, see p. IN 11.

Write About Your Reading

Written Response At the end of scene 4, Anne's voice says that Mr. Frank asked everyone "the first thing we wanted to do when we got out of here." She then lists four responses, but there are eight main characters. She does not tell what the other four wanted. Write a sentence or two answering Mr. Frank's question for each of the following:

- Mr. Van Daan
- Mr. Frank
- Mrs. Frank
- Margot

Write About Your Reading

Possible response:

Mr. Van Daan would want to go food shopping and have a big meal of his favorite foods.
Mr. Frank would want to gather his family again in their home.
Mrs. Frank would want to return to her home and make it cozy for her family.
Margot would want to return home and help her mother.

Skills Review

Key Reading Skill: Drawing Conclusions

9. Mrs. Van Daan asks Dussel "what kind of a Jew" he is. Based on the fact that he's in hiding, what can you conclude about the "kind of a Jew" the Nazis were sending to concentration camps?

Key Literary Element: Dialogue and Monologue

10. Describe one character, based on his or her part of the dialogue. Think about how often the character speaks, how much or little he or she says, and what vocabulary he or she uses.

11. Find two monologues in scene 5. For each, list the page number and identify the speaker. Then briefly tell one thing you learned about the speaker from this monologue.

Reviewing Skills: Analyzing

12. Scene 5 begins with good feelings and a sense of togetherness. What things occur during the scene to produce bad feelings in the group?

Vocabulary Check

Rewrite each sentence, filling in the blank with the best word from the list.

makeshift wallow sustenance jubilation uncertainty

13. Waiting to hear from the doctor after Jason's surgery was a time of terrible ___.

14. Many hungry and homeless people depend on food pantries for ___.

15. We love to ___ on the couch, watching the Sunday football games and eating pizza.

16. You've never seen such ___ as when we won the state championship.

17. Made from a torn-up shirt, the ___ bandages would have to do until they could reach a hospital.

18. **English Language Coach** Identify the roots in *recycling, reversible,* and *science.*

Grammar Link: Commas with Direct Quotations

Use a comma and quotation marks to set off a direct quotation. A **direct quotation** gives a speaker's exact words. If it *follows* the speaker's name, place the comma directly before the opening quotation mark.

- Tito replied, "Peru is in South America."

If the quotation comes *before* the speaker's name, place the comma after the last quoted word and before the closing quotation mark.

- "Peru is in South America," Tito replied.

If the speaker's name divides the quotation, place one comma after the first part and a second comma just before the next opening quotation mark.

- "Peru," Tito replied, "is in South America."

Grammar Practice

Rewrite the sentences below, inserting commas where they are needed.

19. "This is going to be fun" she said.

20. Martina yelled "Goodbye!"

21. "Don't forget" she said "that tomorrow is Sunday."

22. Ms. DeLonga said "Unfortunately, it's too rainy for us to go on the field trip to the nature reserve."

23. "The cardboard chewing gum was a great April Fool's trick" Salina and Janine said as they giggled.

24. "Digger," Ty yelled at his dog "stop digging up the yard! It's already full of your buried bones!"

Writing Application Review your Write About Your Reading activity. If you used any direct quotations, make sure that you used commas correctly.

Web Activities For eFlashcards, Selection Quick Checks, and other Web activities, go to www.glencoe.com.

Skills Review

Key Reading Skill: Drawing Conclusions

9. The Nazis were sending all Jews to concentration camps.

Key Literary Element: Dialogue and Monologue

10. Responses will vary.

11. Page 784: Mrs. Frank: She is a religious person. Page 786: Mr. Frank: He has great strength and faith.

Reviewing Skills: Analyzing

12. Peter plays a trick on Mr. Dussel, and someone breaks in downstairs.

Vocabulary Check

13. uncertainty

14. sustenance

15. wallow

16. jubilation

17. makeshift

English Language Coach

18. cycle; vers; scientia

Close

Ask students to summarize what they learned to answer the Big Question from reading Act 1, Scenes 4–5.

Grammar Link: Commas with Direct Quotations

Grammar Practice

19. "This is going to be fun," she said.

20. Martina yelled, "Goodbye!"

21. "Don't forget," she said, "that tomorrow is Sunday."

22. Ms. DeLonga said, "Unfortunately, it's too rainy for us to go on the field trip to the nature reserve."

23. "The cardboard chewing gum was a great April Fool's trick," Salina and Janine said as they giggled.

24. "Digger," Ty yelled at his dog, "stop digging up the yard! It's already full of your buried bones!"

Indiana English/Language Arts Academic Standards
SE: 8.3, 8.3.6, 8.5.2, 8.6.5

Dramatic Scene

Teaching Students to Write a Dramatic Scene

Why Is It Important?

- Identifying a scene in a story of the student's own choosing will clarify his or her understanding of conflict and character.
- Adapting a familiar text will provide support for less confident students to practice their writing and reading skills; more adventurous students will embrace the dramatic format.
- Writing in the play format will help students become better script readers and help them understand the differences between prose and drama.
- Describing characters who keep going when the going gets tough will help students think about answers to the Big Question: How do you keep from giving up when bad things happen?
- Performing their work for an audience will help students feel more invested in the written word and provide them a chance to experience the power of live theater.

How to Help Students Get It

- Review the definitions of scene, act, and script.
- Ask students to refer to *The Diary of Anne Frank* as a model for formatting their own scripts.
- Remind students that most of what they write should be dialogue and that stage directions should be used sparingly. This is in sharp contrast to most prose, which usually has less dialogue and more description.
- Remind students to choose their words with care. Attitude toward the subject matter makes a big difference in how a play is written.
- Talk about point of view. If the story being adapted has a third-person narrator, a student needs to find ways to provide the same information the story's narrator does. A play can have a narrator, but most dramatic characters and events are best revealed through actions and dialogue.
- Explain that a scene, even if it tells only part of a play's story, should include a beginning, middle, and end.
- As students' scenes progress, check in by asking questions such as "Why does he say this? Why does she do that? What do we learn about Jack here? Does Jill change during the scene?"

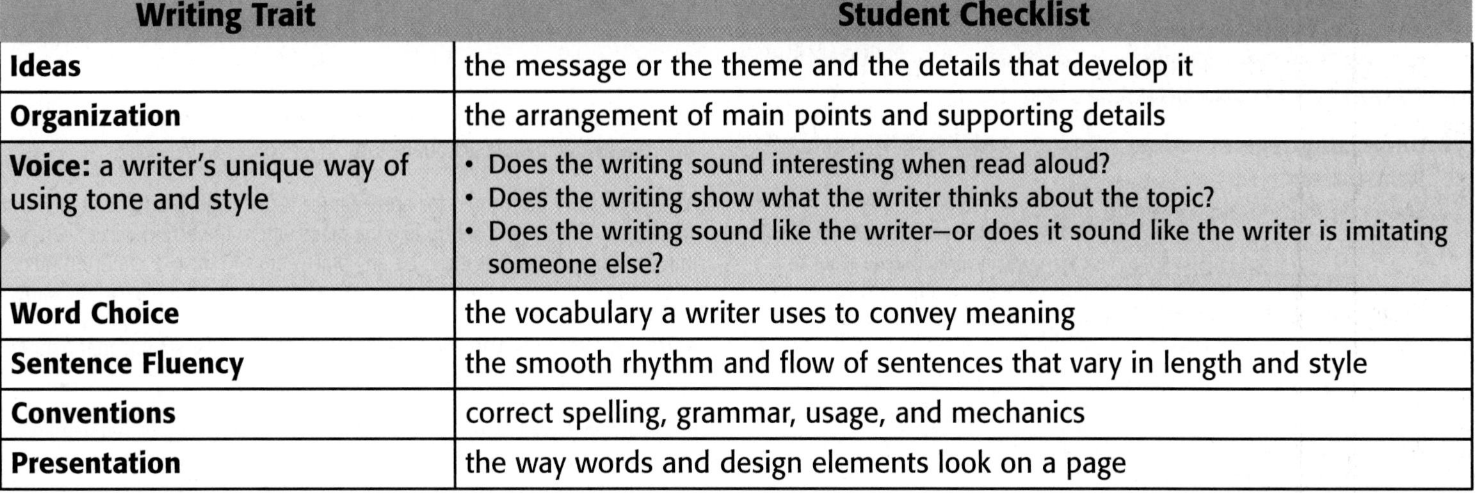

Writing Trait	Student Checklist
Ideas	the message or the theme and the details that develop it
Organization	the arrangement of main points and supporting details
Voice: a writer's unique way of using tone and style	• Does the writing sound interesting when read aloud? • Does the writing show what the writer thinks about the topic? • Does the writing sound like the writer—or does it sound like the writer is imitating someone else?
Word Choice	the vocabulary a writer uses to convey meaning
Sentence Fluency	the smooth rhythm and flow of sentences that vary in length and style
Conventions	correct spelling, grammar, usage, and mechanics
Presentation	the way words and design elements look on a page

Workshop Resources

Pacing (Days) Standard	Block	Lesson	Student Materials	Teacher Resources
1	1/2	Writing Workshop Part 1: Prewriting and Drafting	Writing Workshop Graphic Organizer, p. 14 Grammar Practice, p. 15 Spelling and Handwriting Practice, p. 45 Grammar and Composition Handbook, p. 263 Real Success in Writing: Research and Reports	TeacherWorks Plus™ Presentation Plus! Rubrics for Assessing Student Writing, Listening, and Speaking, p. 26 Grammar and Writing Workshop Transparencies 3–4
2	1	Writing Workshop Part 2: Editing, Revising and Presenting	Interactive Grammar and Language Workbook Grammar and Composition Handbook Real Success in Writing: Research and Reports, p. 263 Listening and Speaking, p. 28 Viewing and Representing, p. 29	Grammar and Writing Workshop Transparencies 27–28 Interactive Grammar and Language Workbook Rubrics for Assessing Student Writing, Listening, and Speaking, p. 26

Focus

BELLRINGER Options

Daily Language Practice Transparency 55
Focus Activity Say: Describe a movie, a TV show, or a play you have seen. Who was the main character? What conflict did he or she face? Did he or she give up or fight back? Explain. *(Responses will vary.)* AS

Teach

Writing

Choosing a Story Scene

Encourage students to choose a story scene that they can adapt into a dramatic scene that is two to three pages long. Remind them that the scene they choose should have a conflict that they can easily introduce. AS

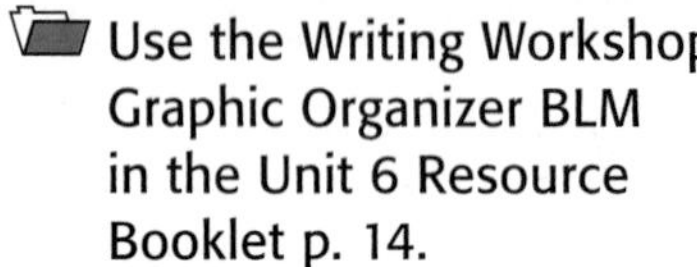

Resources for page 790

- Use the Writing Workshop Graphic Organizer BLM in the Unit 6 Resource Booklet p. 14.
- Use the Grammar and Writing Workshop Transparencies 3-4.

WRITING WORKSHOP PART 1

Dramatic Scene

Prewriting and Drafting

ASSIGNMENT Adapt a scene from a story and write it like a play

Purpose: To write an interesting scene about a person who doesn't give up when something bad happens

Audience: Your teacher and your classmates

Writing Rubric

As you write you should

- describe a setting
- create dialogue
- write stage directions
- develop characters

When you go to the movies, turn on a TV show, or see a play in a theater, you're watching people act out a story.

A play is a story performed for an audience. Actors take the roles of different characters. The stage is set up like the place where the action occurs. Often, that's a single room, but it can be any place—a farmhouse, a crater on Mars, or the Grand Canyon. And it can be as many places as the playwright wants.

A **dramatic scene** is a group of related actions or conversations that happen in a particular time and place.

In this Writing Workshop, you'll choose part of a story about what happens to someone when the going gets tough. You'll turn that story scene into a dramatic scene. You'll use the same elements you would use to write a whole play. However, you're adapting another writer's work. That means you need to try to be faithful to his or her original purpose and ideas.

Prewriting

Get Ready to Write

Choose a Story and Scene

Before you begin to write, you need to choose the story to use as the basis of your dramatic scene. Find a scene from one of the stories you've read in this book. Look for a character facing a big problem, because that's who and what your dramatic scene will be about. This checklist can help you choose. The more questions that you answer with a "yes," the better your choice will be.

Selection Checklist	Yes	No
Does the story contain a clear conflict?		
Can this conflict be acted out on a stage?		
Does the conflict occur in one particular place?		
Is it a problem that you feel strongly about?		
Is it a problem that will interest your audience?		
Does the story have characters you can use?		
Does the scene have fewer than six important characters?		
Does the story have dialogue, or can you write dialogue that will explain what is happening?		

Indiana English/Language Arts Academic Standards
(pp. 790–793)

8.4 Processes and Features
Prewriting and drafting. **8.4.1** Discuss ideas for writing... **8.5.7** Write for different purposes... **8.6.5** Use correct punctuation.

For a complete description of the standards, see p. IN 11.

Additional Support

English Language Coach

Dialogue Students should ensure the dialogue they write sounds like natural speech, but not include "ums," "ers," and everyday conversation such as "Hi, how are you?" and "I'm fine," which would be boring to audience members. Tell students that speakers often use

- contractions, such as *don't* rather than *do not*
- fragments, or incomplete sentences, such as "Better believe it!"

Have students write their dialogue, read it aloud, and have a partner help them revise anything that sounds formal or unnatural. AS

After deciding on a story scene, reread it and focus on the main conflict. Your dramatic scene can't include every detail from the story.

Literature Online

Writing Models For models and other writing activities, go to www.glencoe.com.

The Script

A play is written in a special form called a **script.** It includes these elements:

- **Characters** A script usually provides a simple list of characters in the order they first appear onstage. Some playwrights add short descriptions, including information such as age, occupation, or physical appearance. Minor characters don't necessarily need proper names but may be given descriptive titles such as "Nurse," "Man 1," "Man 2," or "Happy Woman."
- **Setting** A script often begins with a statement of the time and place. This can be simple ("The present. A room.") or detailed ("May 4, 1921, noon, the steps in front of the Virginia County Courthouse").
- **Stage directions** These describe what the sets, lights, sound effects, and music are like, as well as how characters look, move, and sound.
- **Dialogue** This will be *most* of a script. Right before each piece of dialogue is the name of the character who will say it. Like real-life conversation, well-written dialogue can tell the audience a great deal about a character's background, personality, and motives.

Drafting

Start Writing!

It's time to start writing! Think like a playwright. Imagine how each character looks, moves, and talks. The more details you can imagine, the easier it will be to write them. (You may decide to cut some of them out later.) Also, don't get carried away with stage directions; a good playwright leaves room for the actors, designers, and directors to make creative choices too.

First Draft

Every writer begins with a first draft. That means you shouldn't worry about how things look on the page right now. You can fix it all later on. Since you're adapting a story that already exists, do the easy parts first—the character list and setting. That will help you start thinking about the harder parts.

Characters

First list every character in the story scene. If that includes a "cast of thousands," you'll have to figure out whom to keep and whom to cut. Sometimes it's possible to combine two less important characters into one. If you were adapting a story about Harriet Tubman, your list might look like this:

Harriet Tubman
Harriet's brother
John, a slave
Ten other slaves

WRITING WORKSHOP PART 1

Teach

Writing Models Have students access the Web site for an additional and interactive Writing Workshop-based student model.

W1 Writing

Adapting a Scene Encourage students to make a copy of the story scene they'll be adapting. Have them highlight or circle the main characters and other important information to include in the script. AS

W2 Writing

Writing the Script Say: Sometimes, a drama will have a narrator. If you make use of a narrator, be sure to also spread out speaking parts with other characters. Try to develop information about the plot, the conflict, the characters, and the theme from dialogue and stage action as well. Before you begin drafting, take notes on key plot elements, conflict, characters, and theme. Place a checkmark next to each item in your notes as soon as you've included the information in the dialogue or stage directions. OL

Differentiated Instruction

Characterization Have students practice turning a narrative into a dialogue. Dictate the following paragraph and have students work in groups or pairs to adapt it. Have them share their scripts with the class.

Maria sleepily opened her front door the morning of her birthday. Standing on her porch was her friend Barry, and in his arms was a tiny chocolate Labrador puppy. Barry introduced Sam to Maria and explained that he was her birthday gift. Maria cried with joy. She thanked Barry over and over again and invited Sam in for a birthday breakfast of bacon strips. Barry and Maria laughed as Sam devoured his breakfast. EL BL

Indiana English/Language Arts Academic Standards

SE: 8.4, 8.4.1, 8.5.7

TWE: *English Language Coach* 8.5, *Differentiated Instruction* 8.3

Teach

W Writing

Stage Directions Say: Remember that stage directions are meant to give information to the actors and director. As you write, consider what information actors or a director might need to present the scene. For instance, consider any props you might want to add.
What important information does the writer provide about Harriet Tubman and her appearance? *(The writer tells what Harriet is wearing, dark clothing pulled close for warmth and ease of movement, and describes her facial expressions, alert and determined.)* OL

Assess

Have students exchange drafts with a partner and critique each other's work. Ask students to determine whether the partner included all the elements of a dramatic scene. After a few minutes, tell each student to assess his or her partner's feedback, make any needed revisions, and save the revised draft for later use.

Setting

Start by explaining the setting in the simplest, most general terms. Then add descriptive details for the benefit of the actors and director. In your final script, this information—and any other words that aren't dialogue—should be inside brackets. But now is not the time to worry about how the script looks. Now is the time to get ideas on paper. Here's a sample description:

[The 1850s. Maryland. It's a cold, dark night on the eastern shore. Except for an occasional owl, it's quiet.]

Writing Tip

Audience Plays are meant to be performed for an audience. Imagine that you are the audience and "watch" the play in your imagination.

Stage Directions: Character Descriptions

Briefly describe the characters who are onstage at the beginning. Give information to help the actors (and audience) understand why these characters are part of the scene. Putting characters' names in capital letters makes it easier for actors. Indenting the stage directions makes them look different from the dialogue.

W

[HARRIET TUBMAN appears from a cluster of trees. A few of the people she is helping escape can be seen looking from behind the trees. She is in dark clothing that she pulls close for warmth and to make it easier to travel through the thick brush. Her face is alert and filled with fierce determination. She is clearly in charge of the group.]

Use directions to describe characters' important movement and actions.

[TUBMAN peers ahead, then motions for the others to follow.]

Writing Tip

Conflict Discuss the scene with a friend. Ask whether the conflict is clear and, if not, what you could do to make it clearer.

Dialogue

At the beginning of each new speech, write the character's name in capital letters. This makes it easier to see and separates it from what the person says; but don't use all capitals for names in the speeches. Try to write dialogue that matches the character's personality.

TUBMAN. Follow me. Don't make any noise.

JOHN. Are we there yet? It'll be light soon, and we're getting tired. My wife can't keep walking much longer.

WIFE. [Quietly] I'm fine, John. Don't worry about me.

Writing Tip

Dialogue Write dialogue that explains the plot and action of the play. Listen to how people talk to one another to learn how to write better dialogue.

Stage Directions: Action

Add directions mainly when the characters should make important movements. This will help the actors understand what to do, especially if the dialogue doesn't suggest what's going on. Keep writing directions and dialogue until your scene does what you want it to.

[JOHN steps toward the trees. A sudden, sharp sound makes him stop suddenly. The others are frozen in shock.]

Additional Support

Literature Focus Lesson

Drama Provide students with a model for discussion before they begin writing. Reproduce pages 714 and 715, the first two pages of *The Diary of Anne Frank*, and give each student a copy. Have students highlight and label the character list, stage directions, and dialogue. BL
Then, lead students in a discussion about each element:

- How many characters are in the play?
- What is the setting? What details about the setting do the playwrights provide?
- What other information do the stage directions provide?
- How many characters are in this scene? Who are they? AS

Grammar Link

Commas with Introductory Words, Phrases, and Clauses

An **introductory word** introduces a sentence. It may be an interjection, an adverb, or a present participle (a verb that ends in *-ing).*

- Well, it certainly took you a long time to get here!
- Fortunately, I found the five dollars I dropped.
- Singing, she went about her chores.

An **introductory phrase** begins with a preposition or a participle and introduces the sentence.

- Under the maple tree, Sal dozed in the hammock. (prepositional phrase)
- Singing to herself, she went about her chores. (participial phrase)

An **introductory clause** is a dependent clause that answers the questions *How? When? Where?*

- Before the lesson began, the swimming instructor checked the chlorine levels in the pool.
- Whenever it thunders, my dog hides.

Why Are Commas Important?

Using a comma after an introductory word, phrase, or clause clarifies meaning and prevents misreading. The comma tells the reader where to pause before reading the rest of the sentence.

Wrong: Wherever you stop Joe will begin reading.

Right: Wherever you stop, Joe will begin reading.

How Do I Do It?

Use a comma after an introductory word to introduce a sentence. A *mild* interjection must be followed by a comma. Always use a comma after an introductory participle. Use a comma after an adverb to introduce a sentence unless the meaning is clear without it. Then you can omit the comma.

- Yes, I know the answer. (interjection)
- Giggling, Jose threw the fake frog at his sister. (participle)
- Clearly, the field won't dry in time for the game. (adverb)
- Today I will finish my project. (adverb)

Some introductory phrases, such as participial phrases, require commas.

- Wondering what to do, she raised her hand.

Always use a comma after two or more introductory prepositional phrases or after a single long prepositional phrase.

- By the end of the week, I will have run 25 miles.
- Throughout our great nation's history, people have counted on leadership.

You may leave out the comma after a single short prepositional phrase, but it's not wrong to use one.

- In 2001 my sister went to college in Maine.
- In 2001, my sister went to college in Maine.

Always use a comma after an introductory clause.

- Since it snowed so much, school was canceled.

Looking Ahead

Part 2 of this Writing Workshop is coming up. Keep the writing you did here, and in Part 2 you'll learn how to turn it into a really great play.

Teach

Grammar Link

Commas with Introductory Words, Phrases, and Clauses

Ask: What is the difference between a phrase and a clause? *(A phrase is a group of words without a subject and a verb; a clause is a group of words with both a subject and a verb.)* OL

Write the following sentences on the board (without the underscore or commas).

Ask: What is the introductory word, phrase, or clause in these sentences?

1. No, I didn't go to the meeting.
2. When I went to the meeting, I got bored.
3. To be honest, I'd rather go swimming.
4. Whenever I go swimming, I have a wonderful time.
5. Obviously, swimming is more fun than attending the meeting. EL BL OL

Say: Look at the draft of your dramatic scene. Underline any introductory words, phrases, or clauses. Make sure to add commas in the appropriate places. AS

Grammar Practice

Commas with Introductory Words, Phrases, and Clauses

Have students place appropriate commas in the following sentences.

1. Yes*(,)* I offered to take care of her canary this weekend.
2. Gently*(,)* I stroked my kitten's soft fur.
3. From where we sat*(,)* the stage seemed big.
4. Cautiously*(,)* he crossed the crumbling bridge.
5. Because I stayed up so late*(,)* I am sleepy this morning. OL

Indiana English/Language Arts Academic Standards

SE: 8.5.7, 8.6.5

TWE: *Literature Focus Lesson* 8.2, 8.4.1

Interpreting

Teaching Students to Interpret

Why Is It Important?

- Every reader constructs meaning on the basis of what he or she understands about the world. Students will learn how to use their own understanding of the world to decide what the events or ideas in a selection mean.
- Finding meaning is all about interacting with the text. Interpreting text will allow students to become more active readers.
- Students will learn how to determine what an author is really saying in his or her work.

How to Help Students Get It

- Have students think about what they already know about themselves and the world and how it relates to the topic of each selection.
- Tell students to ask themselves questions such as, "What is the author really trying to say here? What larger idea might these events be about?"
- Remind students that interpreting is more than just remembering and understanding facts—it's creating meaning in text by using what students know about the world around them.

Reading to Answer the Big Question

The Diary of Anne Frank by Frances Goodrich and Albert Hackett
This two-act play is based on the journal of a Jewish girl from Amsterdam whose family is forced into hiding during the Nazi occupation of the Netherlands during World War II. Staying sequestered in a small space with seven other people for more than two years is very difficult for the young teen. Anne Frank's journal has become a famous document, inspiring hope and endurance during fearful and violent times.

Workshop Resources

Pacing (Days) Standard	Block	Lesson	Student Materials	Teacher Resources
1	1/2	Key Skill Lesson: Interpreting	Key Reading Skills Practice, p. 16 English Language Coach Review, p. 42	Bellringer Options Transparencies – Selection Focus 13 – Daily Language Practice 56 Read Aloud, Think Aloud Transparencies – Key Reading Skills 14 Presentation Plus!
1	1	*The Diary of Anne Frank* Act 2, Scenes 1–2	Glencoe Online Unit Vocabulary Review, p. 40 Academic Vocabulary Review, p. 43 English Language Coach Active Reading Graphic Organizer, p. 18 Literary Analysis, p. 17 StudentWorks Plus™ Online Student Edition Literature Classics Selection and Unit Assessments, p. 63	Literary and Text Analysis Transparencies 49 Puzzlemaker Skill Level Up!™ A Language Arts Game BookLink 3 Assessment by Learning Objective (Diagnostic and Formative) Interactive Tutor: Self-Assessment TeacherWorks Plus™
1		*The Diary of Anne Frank* Act 2, Scenes 3–5	Glencoe Online Unit Vocabulary Review, p. 40 Academic Vocabulary Review, p. 43 English Language Coach Active Reading Graphic Organizer, p. 21 Literary Analysis, p. 20 StudentWorks Plus™ Online Student Edition Literature Classics Selection and Unit Assessments, p. 64	Literary and Text Analysis Transparencies 31 Puzzlemaker Skill Level Up!™ A Language Arts Game BookLink 3 Assessment by Learning Objective (Diagnostic and Formative) Interactive Tutor: Self-Assessment TeacherWorks Plus™

Keys for Unit Resource

- Blackline Master
- Workbook
- Supplemental Text
- CD-ROM
- DVD
- Transparency
- Web-based
- Fast File

Level Appropriate Code

AS = Activities for all students
AL = Activities for students working above grade level
OL = Activities for students working at grade level
BL = Activities for students working below grade level
EL = Activities for English language learners

Focus

BELLRINGER Options

Selection Focus Transparency 13

Daily Language Practice Transparency 56

Focus Activity Say: Anne Frank's story is tragic, yet many people believe good things came out of her diary. What good things might come out of a story like Anne's? *(Possible responses: People might learn to be more tolerant; people might have been inspired by Anne to write or to find other positive ways to deal with their own pain.)* OL

Teach

R Reading Skill

Interpreting In pairs, have students practice saying aloud the sentence "I'm glad you're my friend." Ask students to think about how the meaning of the sentence differs, depending on which word is emphasized. Invite volunteers to say the sentence aloud, placing the emphasis on a different word each time. Then have students discuss how their interpretation of the sentence changes. AS

READING WORKSHOP 2

Skills Focus

You will practice these skills when you read the following selections:

- *The Diary of Anne Frank,* Act 2, Scenes 1–2, p. 798
- *The Diary of Anne Frank,* Act 2, Scenes 3–5, p. 826

Reading

- Interpreting how and why events happen

Literature

- Understanding the importance of stage directions in a play
- Identifying and analyzing mood

Vocabulary

- Understanding Anglo-Saxon roots

Writing/Grammar

- Using commas with interrupting words and with appositives

Indiana English/Language Arts Academic Standards (pp. 794–795)

8.3 Comprehension and Analysis of Literary Text Respond to grade-level-appropriate literature...

For a complete description of the standards, see p. IN 11.

Skill Lesson

Interpreting

Learn It!

What Is It? Interpreting literature is using your own understanding of the world to decide the meanings of events and ideas in the work. You probably interpret people's words and actions every day. For example, your friend Joe says, "I'm glad you're here today." You could interpret this simple statement in many ways:

- R Joe is the *only* one who's glad I'm here.
- Joe is glad *I'm* here because he needs my help.
- Joe is glad I'm *here* and not at the mall.

To interpret Joe's statement, you use your knowledge of Joe and the situation as well as the specific words Joe uses. You must interpret what you read in a similar way to understand what the writer is really saying.

Cornered
by Mike Baldwin
YOU CAN MAKE A DIFFERENCE
NOT REALLY

Fortunately there was an interpreter for those who understood sign language.

Analyzing Cartoons
What is the speaker saying here? What is the woman's interpretation of his comment?

Additional Support

Reading in the Real World

Career Explain to students that interpreters translate words from one language into another (including American Sign Language). Interpreters work in many fields, including business and government. For the most part, interpreters deal strictly with direct translation, seeking to preserve the meaning of what is written or said as closely as possible. However, because words in some languages do not have corresponding words in other languages, interpreters must sometimes restate words in another language as best as they can. Unlike the situation depicted in the cartoon, interpreters rarely insert their own opinions. OL

Why Is It Important? Interpreting helps you connect to what you are reading. When you interpret, you use your understanding of the world around you to create a meaning that is special to you. Interpreting can help you get closer to the author's intended meaning. Examining how other people interpret the same ideas or events can also help broaden your views.

Study Central Visit www.glencoe.com and click on Study Central to review interpreting.

How Do I Do It? As you read, think about what you already know about yourself and the world. Ask yourself, "What is the writer really trying to say here? What larger idea might these events be about?" Here's how one student interpreted an early passage in *The Diary of Anne Frank.*

> MR. FRANK. There is so little that we parents can do to help our children. We can only try to set a good example . . . point the way. The rest you must do yourself. You must build your own character.

Mr. Frank is talking about how parents raise their children. Sometimes my mom and dad tell me why I shouldn't do something, but I don't always listen because sometimes I have to figure things out for myself. I think Mr. Frank is saying that all parents can do is act the way they want their kids to act and then trust them.

Practice It!

With a partner, study the sentence "I'm glad you're here today." Say the sentence aloud, stressing a different word each time. Find new ways to read the sentence. Then interpret what each reading means.

Use It!

As you read act 2 of *The Diary of Anne Frank,* use what you know about the world to interpret what the characters say and do. Ask yourself questions such as "What do the playwrights mean here?" and "What is this character really saying?"

Reading in the Real World

College Tell students that interpreting is an essential skill for college-level reading. In addition to comprehending what they read, students will also be responsible for thinking critically. The ability to demonstrate thought beyond mere comprehension is what will make students successful in their studies. Have students tell how they can use the process of interpreting in their other classes. For example, how are historical events open to interpretation? AL

Teach

Study Central Have students access the Web site to review interpreting and to complete a related activity.

R Reading Skill

Interpreting Draw this graphic organizer on the board.

Writer's Words

\+

What I Know

=

My Interpretation

Say: Write in the first box: "I'm glad you're here today." Write in the second box: "I know that yesterday, someone the speaker didn't like was here." Help students interpret the writer's words using the information from the second box. *(The writer means he or she is glad I'm here, not someone else.)* OL

Resources for page 795

Use Key Reading Skills Transparency 14 in *Read Aloud, Think Aloud* to help students practice interpreting.

Indiana English/Language Arts Academic Standards

SE: 8.3

TWE: *Reading in the Real World* (p. 794) 8.2, *Reading in the Real World* (p. 795) 8.2

Teach

V Vocabulary

Vocabulary Questions

After previewing the vocabulary, have students close their books and answer these questions about the vocabulary words. *(Correct responses are underlined.)*

1. If you have poise, are you frantic or calm?
2. Does apprehension mean fear or enjoyment?
3. Which is foreboding: a bad feeling or a calm reaction?
4. Which is more intimate: a conversation about a sports game or a conversation about your feelings?
5. Would you be disgruntled if you got a bad grade or a big allowance?
6. If you use your intuition, do you look things up or trust your knowledge? OL AL

Before You Read *The Diary of Anne Frank,* Act 2, Scenes 1–2

Indiana English/Language Arts Academic Standards (pp. 796–821)

8.1.2 Understand the influence of historical events on...word meaning... **8.3 Comprehension and Analysis of Literary Text** Respond to grade-level-appropriate literature... **8.3.6** Identify significant literary devices...

For a complete description of the standards, see p. IN 11.

Vocabulary Preview

disgruntled (dis GRUNT uld) *adj.* not pleased; in a bad mood **(p. 799)** *Anne's use of the room left Dussel disgruntled.*

foreboding (for BOH ding) *n.* a feeling that something bad has happened or will happen **(p. 804)** *Something in Mr. Kraler's words gives Margot a foreboding that there is bad news.*

apprehension (ap rih HEN shun) *n.* fear of what may happen **(p. 805)** *Apprehension increases after Mr. Kraler presents his bad news.*

intimate (IN tuh mit) *adj.* very close and personal; private **(p. 809)** *Anne feels she can't share intimate thoughts and feelings with anyone.*

intuition (in too ISH un) *n.* the ability to know things without having to reason them out **(p. 813)** *Anne trusts her intuition to help her through difficulties.*

poise (poyz) *n.* a calm, relaxed, and self-controlled manner **(p. 820)** *Even under great stress, Mrs. Frank shows poise.*

V

English Language Coach

Anglo-Saxon Roots Anglo-Saxon is the name of the language also known as Old English. It developed when the Angles and the Saxons came from what is now Germany to conquer England in the fifth century.

The Anglo-Saxons often spelled words the way they said them. For example, the word *knee* was *kuh NEE,* and *night* was *nikt.* Over the years, many pronunciations changed. Unfortunately, some of the spellings stayed the same. Fortunately, most Anglo-Saxon words that survive in modern English are fairly simple to say, spell, and use. They tend to be specific objects, actions, and relationships, like these:

bread	dinner	easy	love	old	sheep
child	earth	god	net	run	wife

Partner Talk 1 For each set of words, first guess which word comes from Anglo-Saxon. Then look up the origins of the word you chose.

1. acquaintance associate comrade friend
2. alluring beautiful pretty gorgeous
3. cut divide lacerate sever

Partner Talk 2 Using the pronunciation cues given above, say this sentence as an Anglo-Saxon might have: *The knight's knee hurts tonight.*

Additional Support

Literature Focus Lesson

Suspense Suspense is a state of nervous anticipation about how a story will be resolved. It is what keeps readers and audience members "on the edge of their seats." Even though many people know Anne's story, the playwrights still added elements of suspense to keep the audience asking, "What will happen next?" or "When will it happen?" Some techniques writers use to create suspense include

- withholding information that one or more characters knows
- foreshadowing (adding clues about what will happen next)

Have students look for ways the writers create suspense in the play. OL AL

Skills Preview

Key Reading Skill: Interpreting

The things people do are usually open to different interpretations. We make those interpretations every day. If a friend passes you in the hall without speaking, you may decide that person is angry with you. Or you may decide he or she is in a hurry and didn't see you. How you interpret actions often determines how **R** you feel and what you do next. The same is true when you're reading. If you interpret a character's words or actions one way, you will expect certain things to happen. If you interpret them another way, you will expect other things. And if you *don't* interpret them, you won't understand what's going on at all.

Key Literary Element: Stage Directions

A playwright's original **stage directions** are likely to be general tips to help the director, actors, and designers understand what the writer has in mind. The directions in a published script are usually a record of how the play was staged in its first production. Stage directions can help readers understand the play's **L** ideas and visualize the sets, characters, and action. Directions may give important information about:

- lighting, sets, costumes, sound effects, and music
- how characters look, sound, behave, move, and when they enter and exit
- action that takes place offstage

Small Group Work Choose eight to ten lines of dialogue from act 1 that do not have specific stage directions. Picture the scene in your head, and then write directions for the actors.

Interactive Literary Elements Handbook
To review or learn more about the literary elements, go to www.glencoe.com.

Get Ready to Read

Connect to the Reading

As the play goes on, Mr. and Mrs. Van Daan continue to argue. The others, who have nowhere to hide, must pretend not to listen. Have you ever been in the room when two people were arguing? How did you feel? As you read, think about how the others must feel when the Van Daans argue.

Partner Talk Imagine that you're a teenager growing up in a cramped living space without friends your own age. Only one other person can understand what you're going through—another teenager in the same situation. With a partner, think of one or two things that might be positive about your living arrangement.

Build Background

A year has passed since the end of act 1. In 1944 the war has begun to turn in favor of the Allies—primarily made up of the United States, Great Britain, and the Soviet Union.

- The Soviets have driven German forces out of the Soviet Union. American, British, and Canadian troops have forced the Germans out of North Africa and invaded Europe from the south.
- In June of 1944, the D-Day invasion will allow the Allies to enter Europe from the north and east. In the process, they will free much of the continent from Nazi rule.
- As act 2 begins, it is January 1, 1944, six long months before D-Day.

Set Purposes for Reading

BIG Question Read the next scenes to see how hope rises and falls for Anne and the others.

Set Your Own Purpose What would you like to learn from the story to help you answer the Big Question? Write your answer on the Workshop 2 Foldable for Unit 6.

Keep Moving

Use these skills as you read the following selection.

Teach

R Reading Skill

Interpreting **Ask:** Are the events in the play based on Anne Frank's writings or on Goodrich and Hackett's ideas? Explain. *(Responses will vary. Students may say that the events in the play are based on a combination of Anne's diary entries and the playwrights' creative interpretation.)* **OL**

L Literary Element

Stage Directions **Ask:** How might the roles of the director and the actors change, depending on the amount of stage direction the playwright includes? *(Possible response: A playwright who includes many stage directions leaves less room for the director and actor to interpret the play.)* **OL**

Interactive Literary Elements Handbook Have students access the Web site to improve their understanding of stage directions.

Differentiated Instruction

Time Line Have students create a class time line of the important events in the war, especially those that relate to Anne's story, such as the invasion of Holland, D-Day, and the end of the war. Divide the war into manageable time increments, and assign groups of students a time to study. Draw a line through several large poster boards and have groups enter their information on the appropriate space on the time line. Have volunteers add information about the Franks' life (their going into hiding, etc.). After students have finished reading the play, have them complete the time line. **OL** **AL**

Indiana English/Language Arts Academic Standards
SE: 8.1.2, 8.3
TWE: *Literature Focus Lesson* 8.3, *Differentiated Instruction* 8.2

Teach

R Reading Skill

Interpreting **Ask:** What do you think Anne means when she says "It seems that our life is at a standstill." *(Possible response: She means that their lives have not changed since they went into hiding, and she sees no end in sight.)* OL

L Literary Element

Stage Directions **Ask:** Why is everyone startled when they hear the buzzer? *(They do not know who is approaching. It might be the Green Police.)* **Ask:** What does this action show about the characters? *(It shows they are constantly in fear.)* **Ask:** How might the actors use body language to convey being startled? *(Possible response: They might jump suddenly, have a nervous facial expression, or gesture to one another.)* OL

ACT 2 — SCENE 1

[In the darkness we hear ANNE'S VOICE, *again reading from the diary.]*

ANNE'S VOICE. Saturday, the first of January, nineteen forty-four. Another new year has begun and we find ourselves still in our hiding place. We have been here now for one year, five months, and twenty-five days. It seems that our life is at a standstill. R

[The curtain rises on the scene. It is late afternoon. Everyone is bundled up against the cold. In the main room MRS. FRANK *is taking down the laundry which is hung across the back.* MR. FRANK *sits in the chair down left, reading.* MARGOT *is lying on the couch with a blanket over her and the many-colored knitted scarf around her throat.* ANNE *is seated at the center table, writing in her diary.* PETER, MR. *and* MRS. VAN DAAN, *and* DUSSEL *are all in their own rooms, reading or lying down.* 1

As the lights dim on, ANNE'S VOICE *continues, without a break.]*

ANNE'S VOICE. We are all a little thinner. The Van Daans' "discussions" are as violent as ever. Mother still does not understand me. But then I don't understand her either. There is one great change, however. A change in myself. I read somewhere that girls of my age don't feel quite certain of themselves. That they become quiet within and begin to think of the miracle that is taking place in their bodies. I think that what is happening to me is so wonderful . . . not only what can be seen, but what is taking place inside. Each time it has happened I have a feeling that I have a sweet secret. *[We hear the chimes and then a hymn being played on the carillon outside.]* And in spite of any pain, I long for the time when I shall feel that secret within me again.

[The buzzer of the door below suddenly sounds. Everyone is startled, MR. FRANK *tiptoes cautiously to the top of the steps and listens. Again the buzzer sounds, in* MIEP'S *V-for-Victory*[1] *signal.]* L

MR. FRANK. It's Miep!

1. The ***V-for-Victory signal*** was based on Morse Code for the letter *v*—three short buzzes followed by a long one.

Practice the Skills

1 Key Literary Element

Stage Directions Beginning with act 1, scene 2, all of the main characters are onstage almost all the time. The directions at the beginning of each scene tell where the characters are and what they're doing.

Additional Support

Reading in the Real World

Career Some historians have said that the World War II era saw the greatest collection of strong, charismatic, and powerful political and military leaders. Review with students that Winston Churchill, Franklin Roosevelt, Adolf Hitler, Benito Mussolini, Field Marshal Rommel, Field Marshal Montgomery, Joseph Stalin, and General Patton were important figures in World War II and they all had powerful leadership skills. Have students select one or two of these historic figures to study in more detail. Have them present their findings to the class, focusing on how the person(s) they have chosen interacted with the other leaders. AL

[*He goes quickly down the steps to unbolt the door.* MRS. FRANK *calls upstairs to the* VAN DAANS *and then to* PETER.]

MRS. FRANK. Wake up, everyone! Miep is here! [ANNE *quickly puts her diary away.* MARGOT *sits up, pulling the blanket around her shoulders.* MR. DUSSEL *sits on the edge of his bed, listening,* **disgruntled.** MIEP *comes up the steps, followed by* MR. KRALER. *They bring flowers, books, newspapers, etc.* ANNE *rushes to* MIEP, *throwing her arms affectionately around her.*] Miep . . . and Mr. Kraler . . . What a delightful surprise! R

MR. KRALER. We came to bring you New Year's greetings.

MRS. FRANK. You shouldn't . . . you should have at least one day to yourselves. 2

[*She goes quickly to the stove and brings down teacups and tea for all of them.*]

Anne's tenth birthday party, 1939.

Analyzing the Photo Can you tell which girl is Anne? What do you suppose her friends thought after Anne went into hiding?

Vocabulary

disgruntled (dis GRUNT uld) *adj.* not pleased; in a bad humor

Practice the Skills

2 Reviewing Skills

Drawing Conclusions Using Mrs. Frank's comment and what you know from act 1, what can you conclude about Mr. Kraler and Miep?

Teach

R Reading Skill

Review Drawing Conclusions

Ask: On the basis of how she speaks and acts, how do you think Mrs. Frank feels about Miep and Mr. Kraler? *(Possible response: By serving tea, Mrs. Frank shows that she considers Miep and Mr. Kraler to be honored guests to whom she owes a lot.)* OL

Viewing the Photo

Ask: What does this photograph suggest about Anne's life before going into hiding? *(Possible response: It suggests she had many friends and was a happy, outgoing child.)* OL

English Language Coach

Prepositions English language learners sometimes have difficulty selecting the appropriate preposition to accompany particular verbs. With practice, students can learn the correct English constructions. Use examples to demonstrate standard prepositional usage, such as "Anne is *seated at* the center table" (page 798), "He *goes* quickly *down* the steps," "Mr. Dussel *sits on* the edge of his bed," and "She *goes* quickly *to* the stove" (page 799). Explain the difference between *seated at* and *seated on* and *goes down* and *goes to.* Have students write one sentence using each of the constructions. EL

Indiana English/Language Arts Academic Standards

SE: 8.3

TWE: *Reading in the Real World* 8.7.12, *English Language Coach* 8.1

Teach

R1 Reading Skill

Review Drawing Conclusions
Ask: What conclusion can you draw about Anne from her smelling Miep's coat? *(Possible response: Anne misses being able to go outside.)* OL

R2 Reading Skill

Review Drawing Conclusions
Ask: What did Peter's father threaten about the cat in the last act? *(He threatened to get rid of the cat because it was eating too much food.)* OL
Ask: Do you think it's reasonable to conclude Peter's father got rid of the cat? Why or why not? *(Responses will vary. Some students may believe Peter's father would have gotten rid of the cat, citing his desperation about food. Others may note that Peter loved the cat so much that his father would not do such a thing.)* AL

ANNE. Don't say that, it's so wonderful to see them! [*Sniffing at* MIEP'S *coat.*] I can smell the wind and the cold on your clothes. 3

MIEP. [*Giving her the flowers.*] There you are. [*Then to* MARGOT, *feeling her forehead.*] How are you, Margot? . . . Feeling any better?

MARGOT. I'm all right.

ANNE. We filled her full of every kind of pill so she won't cough and make a noise.

[*She runs into her room to put the flowers in water.* MR. *and* MRS. VAN DAAN *come from upstairs. Outside there is the sound of a band playing.*]

MRS. VAN DAAN. Well, hello, Miep. Mr. Kraler.

MR. KRALER. [*Giving a bouquet of flowers to* MRS. VAN DAAN.] With my hope for peace in the New Year.

PETER. [*Anxiously.*] Miep, have you seen Mouschi? Have you seen him anywhere around? 4

MIEP. I'm sorry, Peter. I asked everyone in the neighborhood had they seen a gray cat. But they said no.

[MRS. FRANK *gives* MIEP *a cup of tea.* MR. FRANK *comes up the steps, carrying a small cake on a plate.*]

MR. FRANK. Look what Miep's brought for us!

MRS. FRANK. [*Taking it.*] A cake!

MR. VAN DAAN. A cake! [*He pinches* MIEP'S *cheeks gaily and hurries up to the cupboard.*] I'll get some plates.

[DUSSEL, *in his room, hastily puts a coat on and starts out to join the others.*]

MRS. FRANK. Thank you, Miepia. You shouldn't have done it. You must have used all of your sugar ration for weeks. [*Giving it to* MRS. VAN DAAN.] It's beautiful, isn't it?

MRS. VAN DAAN. It's been ages since I even saw a cake. Not since you brought us one last year. [*Without looking at the cake, to* MIEP.] Remember? Don't you remember, you gave us one on

Practice the Skills

R1

3 Key Reading Skill

Interpreting What does Anne mean in saying she can smell the wind and cold?

4 Key Reading Skill

R2

Interpreting What does Peter's question imply?

Additional Support

Reading Fluency

Read Fluently Suggest that students practice reading aloud the dialogue in the part of the scene in which Miep and Mr. Kraler arrive. Have students work with a partner, who can keep a record of miscues and errors for the other person. Students should repeat the activity until fluency improves. Encourage students with improved fluency to read with different voices for each character. EL BL

New Year's Day? Just this time last year? I'll never forget it because you had "Peace in nineteen forty-three" on it. [*She looks at the cake and reads.*] "Peace in nineteen forty-four!" R1

MIEP. Well, it has to come sometime, you know. [*As* DUSSEL *comes from his room.*] Hello, Mr. Dussel.

MR. KRALER. How are you?

MR. VAN DAAN. [*Bringing plates and a knife.*] Here's the knife, *liefje.* Now, how many of us are there?

MIEP. None for me, thank you.

MR. FRANK. Oh, please. You must.

MIEP. I couldn't.

MR. VAN DAAN. Good! That leaves one . . . two . . . three . . . seven of us.

DUSSEL. Eight! Eight! It's the same number as it always is!

MR. VAN DAAN. I left Margot out. I take it for granted Margot won't eat any. R2

ANNE. Why wouldn't she!

MRS. FRANK. I think it won't harm her.

MR. VAN DAAN. All right! All right! I just didn't want her to start coughing again, that's all.

DUSSEL. And please, Mrs. Frank should cut the cake.

MR. VAN DAAN. What's the difference?

MRS. VAN DAAN. It's not Mrs. Frank's cake, is it, Miep? It's for all of us.

DUSSEL. Mrs. Frank divides things better. 5 C

MRS. VAN DAAN. [*Going to* DUSSEL.] What are you trying to say?

MR. VAN DAAN. Oh, come on! Stop wasting time!

MRS. VAN DAAN. [*To* DUSSEL.] Don't I always give everybody exactly the same? Don't I?

Practice the Skills

5 Key Reading Skill

Interpreting How do you interpret Dussel's comments about cutting the cake?

Teach

R1 Reading Skill

Review Analyzing Ask: Why is the cake so important to the characters? *(Possible response: Having a celebration breaks up the monotony of the characters' days; they don't often get to eat anything sweet or enjoyable; it may remind them of better times.)* **OL**

R2 Reading Skill

Interpreting Say: Reread Mr. Van Daan's comment about Margot's cough. What does he say? *(He says he's worried she'll start coughing if she eats the cake.)* **BL** **Ask:** Do you think he means it? Why or why not? *(Possible response: He doesn't really mean it. He's more worried about getting a bigger piece of cake. He uses her coughing as an excuse to deny her some cake.)* **OL**

C Critical Thinking

Comprehension Ask: Why does Dussel insist that Mrs. Frank cut the cake? *(Possible response: He thinks Mrs. Frank is fairer than Mrs. Van Daan.)* **BL**

Literature Focus Lesson

Symbol Remind students that a symbol is an object, person, or place used to represent something else, usually an idea. Sometimes symbols have universal meaning. For example, the dove is a universal symbol of peace. Other times, a symbol has meaning in a specific context. Have students discuss what the cake might symbolize in this play:

- scarcity
- a growing lack of patience among the characters
- Mr. Van Daan's greed
- all that the characters have lost **OL**

Indiana English/Language Arts Academic Standards
SE: 8.3
TWE: *Reading Skill* 8.2.9, Reading Fluency 8.1, *Literature Focus Lesson* 8.3

Teach

R Reading Skill

Interpreting **Ask:** How does Mr. Frank try to lighten the mood? *(He makes a joke about the sugar cake going right to everyone's head.)* **BL** **Ask:** Does this action fit Mr. Frank's personality? Why or why not? *(Yes, it does because he's always trying to keep the peace so that everyone is comfortable in this living situation.)* **OL**

L Literary Element

Stage Directions **Ask:** How does the sound of the band outside contrast with the action on the stage? *(Possible responses: The music outside is a true celebration, whereas the celebration inside is tense and forced; the band outside is free to make noise, whereas the characters in hiding must keep quiet nearly all of the time.)* **Ask:** What is the effect of this contrast? *(Possible response: The contrast emphasizes how little the characters actually have to celebrate.)* **AL**

MR. VAN DAAN. Forget it, Kerli.

MRS. VAN DAAN. No. I want an answer! Don't I?

DUSSEL. Yes. Yes. Everybody gets exactly the same . . . except Mr. Van Daan always gets a little bit more.

[*VAN DAAN advances on DUSSEL, the knife still in his hand.*]

MR. VAN DAAN. That's a lie!

[*DUSSEL retreats before the onslaught of the VAN DAANS.*]

MR. FRANK. Please, please! [*Then to MIEP.*] You see what a little sugar cake does to us? It goes right to our heads! **6**

MR. VAN DAAN. [*Handing MRS. FRANK the knife.*] Here you are, Mrs. Frank.

MRS. FRANK. Thank you. [*Then to MIEP as she goes to the table to cut the cake.*] Are you sure you won't have some?

MIEP. [*Drinking her tea.*] No, really, I have to go in a minute.

[*The sound of the band fades out in the distance.*] **7**

PETER. [*To MIEP.*] Maybe Mouschi went back to our house . . . they say that cats . . . Do you ever get over there . . . ? I mean . . . do you suppose you could . . . ?

MIEP. I'll try, Peter. The first minute I get I'll try. But I'm afraid, with him gone a week . . .

DUSSEL. Make up your mind, already someone has had a nice big dinner from that cat!

[*PETER is furious, inarticulate.*[2] *He starts toward DUSSEL as if to hit him. MR. FRANK stops him. MRS. FRANK speaks quickly to ease the situation.*]

MRS. FRANK. [*To MIEP.*] This is delicious, Miep!

MRS. VAN DAAN. [*Eating hers.*] Delicious!

MR. VAN DAAN. [*Finishing it in one gulp.*] Dirk's in luck to get a girl who can bake like this!

2. Peter is so angry that he becomes unable to speak ***(inarticulate)***.

Practice the Skills

6 Key Reading Skill

Interpreting How do you interpret what has just happened? Is it all about the cake? 

7 Key Literary Element

Stage Directions The stage directions first mention the band just after Miep and Mr. Kraler arrive. What purpose could the playwrights have in including the sound of a band playing during this scene? L

Additional Support

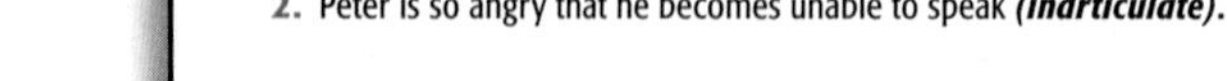

Differentiated Instruction

Celebrating Endurance Artists and writers have created many works that celebrate the spirit of Holocaust victims. Use online resources to find an inspiring work of art, such as *In Memory of the Holocaust* by Josef Elgurt, an artist who was imprisoned in Nazi ghettos during the war. Show the work to students, and lead them in a discussion about the importance of artistic creativity and self-expression as factors that might have kept Holocaust survivors from giving up. Have students show how the artwork expresses the suffering, the spirit, and the hope of Holocaust victims. **OL** **AL**

MIEP. [*Putting down her empty teacup.*] I have to run. Dirk's taking me to a party tonight.

ANNE. How heavenly! Remember now what everyone is wearing, and what you have to eat and everything, so you can tell us tomorrow. 8

MIEP. I'll give you a full report! Good-bye, everyone!

MR. VAN DAAN. [*To* MIEP.] Just a minute. There's something I'd like you to do for me.

[*He hurries off up the stairs to his room.*]

MRS. VAN DAAN. [*Sharply.*] Putti, where are you going? [*She rushes up the stairs after him, calling hysterically.*] What do you want? Putti, what are you going to do?

MIEP. [*To* PETER.] What's wrong?

PETER. [*His sympathy is with his mother.*] Father says he's going to sell her fur coat. She's crazy about that old fur coat. 9

DUSSEL. Is it possible? Is it possible that anyone is so silly as to worry about a fur coat in times like this?

R1 PETER. It's none of your darn business . . . and if you say one more thing . . . I'll, I'll take you and I'll . . . I mean it . . . I'll . . .

[*There is a piercing scream from* MRS. VAN DAAN *above. She grabs at the fur coat as* MR. VAN DAAN *is starting downstairs with it.*]

R2 MRS. VAN DAAN. No! No! No! Don't you dare take that! You hear? It's mine! [*Downstairs* PETER *turns away, embarrassed, miserable.*] My father gave me that! You didn't give it to me. You have no right. Let go of it . . . you hear?

L [MR. VAN DAAN *pulls the coat from her hands and hurries downstairs.* MRS. VAN DAAN *sinks to the floor, sobbing. As* MR. VAN DAAN *comes into the main room the others look away, embarrassed for him.*] 10

MR. VAN DAAN. [*To* MR. KRALER.] Just a little—discussion over the advisability[3] of selling this coat. As I have often reminded Mrs. Van Daan, it's very selfish of her to keep it when people

3. ***Advisability*** means "the quality of being wise, fitting, or proper."

Practice the Skills

8 Key Reading Skill

Interpreting How do you interpret Anne's wanting to know all about the party? Is it just curiosity?

9 Key Reading Skill

Interpreting How do you interpret Mrs. Van Daan's feelings about the coat? What do you think it means to her?

10 Key Literary Element

Stage Directions How do the stage directions in this section help to develop the Van Daans' characters?

READING WORKSHOP 2

Teach

R1 Reading Skill

Interpreting Ask: What do the ellipsis points in Peter's speech tell you about his mood at this time? *(Possible response: They tell you he's so furious he can barely get his words out. They may also indicate that he is angry but is too polite to actually threaten Mr. Dussel.)* AL

R2 Reading Skill

Interpreting Ask: What does the fur coat symbolize, or represent, for Mrs. Van Daan? *(Possible response: The coat symbolizes a connection to Mrs. Van Daan's life of comfort and luxury before the war.)* OL

L Literary Element

Stage Directions Ask: What do the stage directions reveal about Mr. Van Daan and his feelings towards his wife? *(Possible response: They show that Mr. Van Daan is a controlling person who has little respect for his wife's wishes.)* OL

English Language Coach

Multiple-Meaning Words Help English language learners select the appropriate definition of multiple-meaning words in this scene. For example, the stage directions note that Mrs. Van Daan is calling *hysterically.* Explain that *hysteria* can refer to any kind of emotional excitability and that a person who is *hysterical* may be laughing, crying, or extremely upset. In this case, Mrs. Van Daan is extremely upset. Also point out that when Peter says that his mother is *crazy* about her fur coat, he does not mean "mad or insane," but rather that she is "passionate" or "obsessed." EL BL

Indiana English/Language Arts Academic Standards
SE: 8.3
TWE: *Differentiated Instruction* 8.4.4, *English Language Coach* 8.1.3

Teach

L Literary Element

Review Irony **Ask:** Why is it ironic for Mr. Van Daan to call his wife selfish? *(It is ironic that he would accuse Mrs. Van Daan of being selfish when he wants to sell her coat and buy himself cigarettes.)* **OL** **Ask:** Do you think Mrs. Van Daan is being selfish here? Why or why not? *(Possible response: She is being selfish, but it is understandable. Her coat is her one last precious possession. Having it helps her survive her awful circumstances.)* **AS**

READING WORKSHOP 2

outside are in such desperate need of clothing . . . [*He gives the coat to* MIEP.] So if you will please to sell it for us? It should fetch a good price. And by the way, will you get me cigarettes. I don't care what kind they are . . . get all you can. **11**

MIEP. It's terribly difficult to get them, Mr. Van Daan. But I'll try. Good-bye.

[*She goes.* MR. FRANK *follows her down the steps to bolt the door after her.* MRS. FRANK *gives* MR. KRALER *a cup of tea.*]

MRS. FRANK. Are you sure you won't have some cake, Mr. Kraler?

MR. KRALER. I'd better not.

MR. VAN DAAN. You're still feeling badly? What does your doctor say?

MR. KRALER. I haven't been to him.

MRS. FRANK. Now, Mr. Kraler! . . .

MR. KRALER. [*Sitting at the table.*] Oh, I tried. But you can't get near a doctor these days . . . they're so busy. After weeks I finally managed to get one on the telephone. I told him I'd like an appointment . . . I wasn't feeling very well. You know what he answers . . . over the telephone . . . Stick out your tongue! [*They laugh. He turns to* MR. FRANK *as* MR. FRANK *comes back.*] I have some contracts here . . . I wonder if you'd look over them with me . . .

MR. FRANK. [*Putting out his hand.*] Of course.

MR. KRALER. [*He rises.*] If we could go downstairs . . . [MR. FRANK *starts ahead,* MR. KRALER *speaks to the others.*] Will you forgive us? I won't keep him but a minute.

[*He starts to follow* MR. FRANK *down the steps.*]

MARGOT. [*With sudden* **foreboding.**] What's happened? Something's happened! Hasn't it, Mr. Kraler?

Vocabulary

foreboding (for BOH ding) *n.* a feeling that something bad has happened or will happen

Practice the Skills

L

11 **BIG Question**

How does her fur coat help Mrs. Van Daan deal with their situation? How does Mr. Van Daan's reason for selling the coat help him deal with the situation? Write your answers on the Workshop 2 Foldable for Unit 6.

Additional Support

Literature Focus Lesson

Comic Relief Comic relief is a brief period of humor or lightheartedness that releases some of the built-up tension in a serious play. It often gives the audience a momentary release from the heaviness or tragic quality of a play, usually before the tension mounts again. Mr. Kraler's joke about the doctor on the phone asking him to stick out his tongue is an excellent example of comic relief. The laughter that ensues on stage—and probably in the audience—relieves some of the tension. Have students speculate about why Mr. Kraler might have told this joke. *(to lighten the mood; to detract attention from his illness; to hide the fact that he has bad news)* **OL**

[*MR. KRALER stops and comes back, trying to reassure MARGOT with a pretense of casualness.*]

MR. KRALER. No, really. I want your father's advice . . .

MARGOT. Something's gone wrong! I know it!

MR. FRANK. [*Coming back, to MR. KRALER.*] If it's something that concerns us here, it's better that we all hear it.

MR. KRALER. [*Turning to him, quietly.*] But . . . the children . . . ?

MR. FRANK. What they'd imagine would be worse than any reality. **12**

[*As MR. KRALER speaks, they all listen with intense* **apprehension**. *MRS. VAN DAAN comes down the stairs and sits on the bottom step.*]

MR. KRALER. It's a man in the storeroom . . . I don't know whether or not you remember him . . . Carl, about fifty, heavy-set, near-sighted . . . He came with us just before you left.

MR. FRANK. He was from Utrecht?[4]

MR. KRALER. That's the man. A couple of weeks ago, when I was in the storeroom, he closed the door and asked me . . . how's Mr. Frank? What do you hear from Mr. Frank? I told him I only knew there was a rumor that you were in Switzerland. He said he'd heard that rumor too, but he thought I might know something more. I didn't pay any attention to it . . . but then a thing happened yesterday . . . He'd brought some invoices to the office for me to sign. As I was going through them, I looked up. He was standing staring at the bookcase . . . your bookcase. He said he thought he remembered a door there . . . Wasn't there a door that used to go up to the loft? Then he told me he wanted more money. Twenty guilders[5] more a week.

4. ***Utrecht*** (YOO trekt) is a city in the central Netherlands.

5. The ***guilder*** (GIL dur) is the monetary unit of the Netherlands.

Vocabulary

apprehension (ap rih HEN shun) *n.* fear of what may happen

Practice the Skills

12 Key Reading Skill

Interpreting Do bad things seem better or worse when they're kept secret? Explain what Mr. Frank means here and tell whether you agree with him.

Differentiated Instruction

Distinguish Fact from Opinion

One of the conflicts among the characters is disagreement about how to interpret facts. Remind students that a fact is provable, while an opinion is a conclusion based on what one believes or feels. The fact that Peter's cat is missing, for example, is provable. The belief that the cat has been eaten, on the other hand, is an opinion. Have students review the exchange with Mr. Kraler and identify statements that are fact and those that are opinion. Encourage students to record facts and opinions in a two-column chart. **EL** **BL** **OL**

Teach

R Reading Skill

Review Analyzing **Ask:** Do you agree with Mr. Frank that Mr. Kraler should share the news with the whole group, no matter how bad it is? Explain. *(Responses will vary.)* **AS**

L Literary Element

Review Dialogue and Monologue **Ask:** What information is revealed in Mr. Kraler's monologue? *(A man is inquiring about Mr. Frank and his whereabouts. He believes Mr. Kraler knows where he is. He also knows that there is a door leading up to a loft where a bookcase now stands. And he wants more money from Mr. Kraler.)* **OL**

Indiana English/Language Arts Academic Standards

SE: 8.3, 8.3.6

TWE: *Literature Focus Lesson* 8.2, *Differentiated Instruction* 8.2

Teach

R Reading Skill

Interpreting Ask: What does Mr. Frank mean when he says that twenty guilders is "very modest blackmail"? How do you think Mr. Frank will suggest handling this situation? *(Possible response: He means the man from Utrecht could have asked for much more money. He might handle the situation by paying the man what he wants.)* **OL**

C Critical Thinking

Analysis Ask: Why is it important for the characters in hiding to know whether Mr. Kraler is really being blackmailed? *(Possible response: If Mr. Kraler pays the blackmail, then he is admitting to hiding Mr. Frank and the others. Doing so would risk his own safety and the safety of everyone in hiding.)* **AL**

READING WORKSHOP 2

MR. VAN DAAN. Blackmail! **13**

MR. FRANK. Twenty guilders? Very modest blackmail.

MR. VAN DAAN. That's just the beginning.

DUSSEL. [*Coming to* MR. FRANK.] You know what I think? He was the thief who was down there that night. That's how he knows we're here.

MR. FRANK. [*To* MR. KRALER.] How was it left? What did you tell him?

MR. KRALER. I said I had to think about it. What shall I do? Pay him the money? . . . Take a chance on firing him . . . or what? I don't know.

DUSSEL. [*Frantic.*] For God's sake don't fire him! Pay him what he asks . . . keep him here where you can have your eye on him.

MR. FRANK. Is it so much that he's asking? What are they paying nowadays?

MR. KRALER. He could get it in a war plant. But this isn't a war plant. Mind you, I don't know if he really knows . . . or if he doesn't know.

MR. FRANK. Offer him half. Then we'll soon find out if it's blackmail or not.

DUSSEL. And if it is? We've got to pay it, haven't we? Anything he asks we've got to pay!

MR. FRANK. Let's decide that when the time comes.

MR. KRALER. This may be all my imagination. You get to a point, these days, where you suspect everyone and everything. Again and again . . . on some simple look or word, I've found myself . . .

[*The telephone rings in the office below.*]

MRS. VAN DAAN. [*Hurrying to* MR. KRALER.] There's the telephone! What does that mean, the telephone ringing on a holiday?

Practice the Skills

R 13 Key Reading Skill

Interpreting Blackmail is money forced from a person in exchange for not revealing some secret. Mr. Van Daan interprets Carl's request as blackmail. Do you think it is?

Additional Support

English Language Coach

Word Origins The word *blackmail* has intriguing origins. Explain that *black* may refer either to "an evil practice," or to the use of goods as opposed to coin, or "white" money. The practice of blackmailing is believed to trace back to early Scottish farmers, who were forced to pay a fee to keep others from stealing their crops and cattle. **AS**

MR. KRALER. That's my wife. I told her I had to go over some papers in my office . . . to call me there when she got out of church. [*He starts out.*] I'll offer him half then. Good-bye . . . we'll hope for the best! **14**

[*The group call their good-bye's half-heartedly.* MR. FRANK *follows* MR. KRALER, *to bolt the door below. During the following scene,* MR. FRANK *comes back up and stands listening, disturbed.*]

DUSSEL. [*To* MR. VAN DAAN.] You can thank your son for this . . . smashing the light! I tell you, it's just a question of time now.

[*He goes to the window at the back and stands looking out.*]

MARGOT. Sometimes I wish the end would come . . . whatever it is. **15**

MRS. FRANK. [*Shocked.*] Margot!

[ANNE *goes to* MARGOT, *sitting beside her on the couch with her arms around her.*]

MARGOT. Then at least we'd know where we were.

MRS. FRANK. You should be ashamed of yourself! Talking that way! Think how lucky we are! Think of the thousands dying in the war, every day. Think of the people in concentration camps. **BQ1**

ANNE. [*Interrupting.*] What's the good of that? What's the good of thinking of misery when you're already miserable? That's stupid!

MRS. FRANK. Anne!

[*As* ANNE *goes on raging at her mother,* MRS. FRANK *tries to break in, in an effort to quiet her.*]

ANNE. We're young, Margot and Peter and I! You grown-ups have had your chance! But look at us . . . If we begin thinking of all the horror in the world, we're lost! We're trying to hold onto some kind of ideals . . . when everything . . . ideals, hopes . . . everything, are being destroyed! It isn't our fault that the world is in such a mess! We weren't around when all this started! So don't try to take it out on us! **16** **BQ2**

Practice the Skills

14 Reviewing Skills

Drawing Conclusions What conclusion can you draw from Mr. Kraler's lie to his wife?

15 BIG Question

Has Margot given up? What do Mrs. Frank's and Anne's next few speeches indicate about how they try to keep going? Write your answers on the Workshop 2 Foldable for Unit 6.

16 Reviewing Elements

Dialogue and Monologue Why does Anne pause several times during this monologue? Is she struggling to find the right words? Is she struggling with her emotions?

Teach

BQ1 BIG Question

Say: Reread the lines in which Mrs. Frank responds to Margot. Do you think that Mrs. Frank really considers herself lucky? Explain. *(Responses will vary. Some students may suggest that Mrs. Frank's optimism is forced or not genuine. Others may believe that she is truly as grateful and hopeful as she sounds.)* **AS**

BQ2 BIG Question

Ask: What does Anne suggest in her monologue about how she and other young people must think in order to keep from giving up during this terrible time? *(She says young people must hold on to ideals, even though they're being destroyed. She states that if they focus on the horror in the world, they will be lost.)* **OL**

Differentiated Instruction

Public Speaking One purpose of public speaking is to inform others. An example of this is broadcasting, which informs the listener or viewer of events. A good broadcasting report provides the audience with enough detail to understand the event. Have students prepare a news broadcast report based on information from act 2, scene 1. Suggest that the audience already knows that groups of people have been in hiding for some time. Reports might begin, "The government today admitted that their attempt to . . ." Ask volunteers to present their completed news reports to the class. **OL** **AL**

Indiana English/Language Arts Academic Standards
SE: 8.3, 8.3.6
TWE: *English Language Coach* 8.1.2, *Differentiated Instruction* 8.7

Teach

L1 Literary Element

Stage Directions **Ask:** Why might it be important for the audience to see what happens to the various pieces of cake? *(Responses will vary. Students should note that the celebration has disintegrated into conflict. The way in which each character handles his or her cake shows the impact of the conflict.)* AL

L2 Literary Element

Review Dialogue and Monologue Draw a Venn diagram on the board. Have students use it to compare and contrast Anne's monologue on page 807 and Peter's monologue on this page. *(Possible responses: **Anne:** eloquent; speaks for all young people; **Peter:** awkward; speaks only for himself; **Overlap:** frustrated; emotional)* OL

READING WORKSHOP 2

[*She rushes off to her room, slamming the door after her. She picks up a brush from the chest and hurls it to the floor. Then she sits on the settee, trying to control her anger.*]

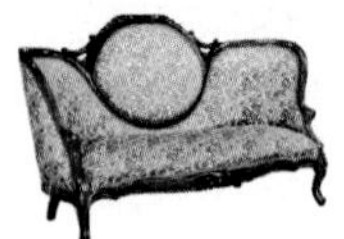

Visual Vocabulary
A ***settee*** (seh TEE) is a small sofa or a bench with a back.

MR. VAN DAAN. She talks as if we started the war! Did we start the war?

[*He spots* ANNE'S *cake. As he starts to take it,* PETER *anticipates him.*]

PETER. She left her cake. [*He starts for* ANNE'S *room with the cake. There is silence in the main room.* MRS. VAN DAAN *goes up to her room, followed by* MR. VAN DAAN. DUSSEL *stays looking out the window.* MR. FRANK *brings* MRS. FRANK *her cake. She eats it slowly, without relish.* MR. FRANK *takes his cake to* MARGOT *and sits quietly on the sofa beside her.* PETER *stands in the doorway of* ANNE'S *darkened room, looking at her, then makes a little movement to let her know he is there.* ANNE *sits up, quickly, trying to hide the signs of her tears.* PETER *holds out the cake to her.*] You left this. **17**

ANNE. [*Dully.*] Thanks.

[PETER *starts to go out, then comes back.*]

PETER. I thought you were fine just now. You know just how to talk to them. You know just how to say it. I'm no good . . . I never can think . . . especially when I'm mad . . . That Dussel . . . when he said that about Mouschi . . . someone eating him L2 . . . all I could think is . . . I wanted to hit him. I wanted to give him such a . . . a . . . that he'd . . . That's what I used to do when there was an argument at school . . . That's the way I . . . but here . . . And an old man like that . . . it wouldn't be so good. **18**

ANNE. You're making a big mistake about me. I do it all wrong. I say too much. I go too far. I hurt people's feelings . . . **19**

[DUSSEL *leaves the window, going to his room.*]

PETER. I think you're just fine . . . What I want to say . . . if it wasn't for you around here, I don't know. What I mean . . .

[PETER *is interrupted by* DUSSEL'S *turning on the light.* DUSSEL *stands in the doorway, startled to see* PETER. PETER *advances toward him forbiddingly.* DUSSEL *backs out of the room.* PETER *closes the door on him.*]

Practice the Skills

17 Key Literary Element

Stage Directions The details here can help you "see" the action and understand the characters' behavior.

18 Reviewing Elements

Dialogue and Monologue In Peter's first monologue of the play, what is he saying about the different ways he and Anne handle problems? Why does he keep trailing off and pausing? How is this monologue similar to and different from the one Anne just gave?

19 Reviewing Skills

Analyzing Do you think Anne is right about herself?

Additional Support

Reading Fluency

Build Fluency Some readers may become overwhelmed and stop reading when they encounter an unfamiliar word. They may pause to reread words. This habit interrupts the flow of reading and creates a barrier to understanding. Some of this can be avoided by prereading. Have students skim a page of the play to learn which characters are in the scene. Then ask them to read the page. Encourage students to continue reading when they reach an unfamiliar word and sound out the word, using their knowledge of sound-letter correspondences. Students may recognize the spoken word, or they may use context clues to identify and define the word. BL EL

ANNE. Do you mean it, Peter? Do you really mean it?

PETER. I said it, didn't I?

ANNE. Thank you, Peter!

[*In the main room* MR. *and* MRS. FRANK *collect the dishes and take them to the sink, washing them.* MARGOT *lies down again on the couch.* DUSSEL, *lost, wanders into* PETER'S *room and takes up a book, starting to read.*]

PETER. [*Looking at the photographs on the wall.*] You've got quite a collection.

ANNE. Wouldn't you like some in your room? I could give you some. Heaven knows you spend enough time in there . . . doing heaven knows what . . .

PETER. It's easier. A fight starts, or an argument . . . I duck in there.

ANNE. You're lucky, having a room to go to. His lordship is always here . . . I hardly ever get a minute alone. When they start in on me, I can't duck away. I have to stand there and take it. **20**

PETER. You gave some of it back just now.

ANNE. I get so mad. They've formed their opinions . . . about everything . . . but we . . . we're still trying to find out . . . We have problems here that no other people our age have ever had. And just as you think you've solved them, something comes along and bang! You have to start all over again. **R2**

PETER. At least you've got someone you can talk to.

ANNE. Not really. Mother . . . I never discuss anything serious with her. She doesn't understand. Father's all right. We can talk about everything . . . everything but one thing. Mother. He simply won't talk about her. I don't think you can be really **intimate** with anyone if he holds something back, do you? **21**

Vocabulary

intimate (IN tuh mit) *adj.* very close and personal; private

Practice the Skills

20 Key Reading Skill

Interpreting Who is "his lordship"? Why does Anne call him this?

21 Reviewing Skills

Connecting Have you ever felt the things Anne and Peter are talking about?

Differentiated Instruction

Family Relationships Anne experiences a moment of normalcy when she complains about her parents. Complaining about parents or guardians is something many teenagers do. Have students work in pairs to compose an imaginary dialogue between a modern teen and Anne. The subject of the dialogue should be the relationship between parents and teens. Tell students to include anecdotes or feelings about their own experience with parents or guardians. Have one student read the part of Anne and another read the part of the modern teen. **OL** **AL**

Teach

R1 Reading Skill

Review Comparing and Contrasting **Ask:** How did Anne and Peter treat each other in act 1? *(They treated each other like brother and sister; apart from bickering, they rarely spoke.)* **Ask:** How is Anne and Peter's relationship changing? *(Possible response: Peter is revealing that he likes Anne and that she helps him through hard times. Anne is appreciating his kindness and not teasing him. They are becoming more like good friends.)* **OL**

R2 Reading Skill

Interpreting **Say:** What does Anne means when she says "They've formed their opinions . . . we're still trying to find out"? *(She means that the adults have already decided how they feel about things, while she, Peter, and Margot are still trying to figure out how they feel about things.)* **OL** **Ask:** What makes growing up particularly challenging for Anne and the other teens? *(Possible responses: the war, being stuck in the attic, having few people their own age to talk to, being frightened all the time)* **AL**

Indiana English/Language Arts Academic Standards
SE: 8.3, 8.3.6
TWE: *Reading Fluency* 8.1, *Differentiated Instruction* 8.5

Teach

BQ 

Ask: How can Anne and Peter help keep each other from giving up? *(Possible response: They can enjoy each other's company. They can encourage each other to be strong.)* **OL**

L Literary Element

Stage Directions Ask: How do the stage directions symbolize the relationship among Dussel, Anne, and Peter? *(Possible response: Both Anne and Peter shut the doors to their rooms, leaving Dussel caught in the middle with nowhere to go. This is symbolic of how neither Peter nor Anne wants to let Dussel into his or her life.)* **AL**

READING WORKSHOP 2

PETER. I think your father's fine.

ANNE. Oh, he is, Peter! He is! He's the only one who's ever given me the feeling that I have any sense. But anyway, nothing can take the place of school and play and friends of your own age . . . or near your age . . . can it?

PETER. I suppose you miss your friends and all.

ANNE. It isn't just . . . [*She breaks off, staring up at him for a second.*] Isn't it funny, you and I? Here we've been seeing each other every minute for almost a year and a half, and this is the first time we've ever really talked. It helps a lot to have someone to talk to, don't you think? It helps you to let off steam.

PETER. [*Going to the door.*] Well, any time you want to let off steam, you can come into my room.

ANNE. [*Following him.*] I can get up an awful lot of steam. You'll have to be careful how you say that. **22**

PETER. It's all right with me.

ANNE. Do you mean it?

PETER. I said it, didn't I? **23**

[*He goes out.* ANNE *stands in her doorway looking after him. As* PETER *gets to his door he stands for a minute looking back at her. Then he goes into his room.* DUSSEL *rises as he comes in, and quickly passes him, going out. He starts across for his room.* ANNE *sees him coming, and pulls her door shut.* DUSSEL *turns back toward* PETER'S *room.* PETER *pulls his door shut.* DUSSEL *stands there, bewildered, forlorn.*

The scene slowly dims out. The curtain falls on the scene. ANNE'S VOICE *comes over in the darkness . . . faintly at first, and then with growing strength.*] **L**

ANNE'S VOICE. We've had bad news. The people from whom Miep got our ration books have been arrested. So we have had to cut down on our food. Our stomachs are so empty that they rumble and make strange noises, all in different keys. Mr. Van Daan's is deep and low, like a bass fiddle.

Practice the Skills

22 Reviewing Skills

Drawing Conclusions How has Anne changed since act 1? What has caused the difference? Explain.

23 Reviewing Skills

Predicting Did you predict that Anne and Peter would become friends? What do you predict will happen now?

Additional Support

English Language Coach

Idiomatic Expression Remind students that idioms are words or phrases that are used figuratively rather than literally. Point out the following idiomatic expressions and have students use context to guess their meaning:

- *To duck away* means "to get away."
- *To cut down on* means "to have less of."
- *To let off steam* means "to release anger or other emotions."

Have students use their knowledge of the idiom to tell what Anne means when she warns Peter she can "get up an awful lot of steam." *(She means she can bottle up a lot of anger or frustration.)* **EL**

Mine is high, whistling like a flute. As we all sit around waiting for supper, it's like an orchestra tuning up. It only needs Toscanini to raise his baton and we'd be off in the Ride of the Valkyries. Monday, the sixth of March, nineteen forty-four. Mr. Kraler is in the hospital. It seems he has ulcers.[6] Pim says we are his ulcers. Miep has to run the business and us too. The Americans have landed on the southern tip of Italy. Father looks for a quick finish to the war. Mr. Dussel is waiting every day for the warehouse man to demand more money. Have I been skipping too much from one subject to another? I can't help it. I feel that spring is coming. I feel it in my whole body and soul. I feel utterly confused. I am longing . . . so longing . . . for everything . . . for friends . . . for someone to talk to . . . someone who understands . . . someone young, who feels as I do . . . **24**

[*As these last lines are being said, the curtain rises on the scene. The lights dim on.* ANNE'S VOICE *fades out.*]

6. Arturo ***Toscanini*** (taw skuh NEE nee) was an Italian orchestra conductor. ***Ride of the Valkyries*** is a passage from an opera by Richard Wagner, a German composer. Mr. Kraler's ***ulcers*** are sores on the lining of his stomach.

Practice the Skills

R

L

24 **Reviewing Elements**

Dialogue and Monologue Anne's speech here is a mix of funny descriptions, important news, and confused emotions. At the end she keeps referring to "someone." In your opinion, is she referring to a particular, real person or to an ideal?

Analyzing the Photo Anne posted photos of movie stars and English princesses on her bedroom wall. In what ways do these photos reflect Anne's childhood interests? How might they show her hopes and goals as a young adult?

Teach

R Reading Skill

Interpreting **Ask:** What does Mr. Frank mean when he says that the Franks and the Van Daans are Mr. Kraler's ulcers? *(Possible response: Ulcers are painful and thought to result from stress. Mr. Frank is suggesting that having to hide and care for the Franks and the Van Daans has caused Mr. Kraler pain and stress.)* **AL**

L Literary Element

Review Dialogue and Monologue **Ask:** Why might Anne be skipping from one subject to another? *(Possible response: She is giddy about her growing relationship with Peter and excited about the possibility of the war ending.)* **OL**

Viewing the Photo

Ask: Why would it make sense that Anne would want photos of people on her wall? *(Possible response: Anne is very social and misses people. It makes sense she'd want to be surrounded by pictures of people.)* **AL**

Literature Focus Lesson

Similes Remind students that similes use the words *like* and *as* to compare two unlike things. Anne uses similes to describe the sound of the characters' empty stomachs. Have students point out the similes and tell what Anne compares the noises to *(instruments in an orchestra)*. Ask students to choose a sound, such as a crowded hallway or the school bell, and write a simile to describe it. Invite volunteers to read their similes for the class. **OL**

Indiana English/Language Arts Academic Standards
SE: 8.3, 8.3.6
TWE: *English Language Coach* 8.1.1, *Literature Focus Lesson* 8.1.1

Teach

L1 Literary Element

Stage Directions Say: The stage directions note that Mrs. Frank is mending and that Mrs. Van Daan is reading a fashion magazine. What do these directions indicate about the two women's interests? *(Possible response: Mrs. Frank is concerned with simple, practical matters, while Mrs. Van Daan is more interested in having nice possessions.)* OL

L2 Literary Element

Stage Directions Ask: Why is Peter smoothing his hair and putting on a tie? *(He is preparing to meet with Anne. The two have become very close.)* BL **Ask:** Are you surprised by this? Why or why not? *(Possible response: I am not surprised. In the last scene, their relationship grew more mature and serious.)* OL

SCENE 2

[It is evening, after supper. From outside we hear the sound of children playing. The "grown-ups," with the exception of MR. VAN DAAN, *are all in the main room.* MRS. FRANK *is doing some mending,* MRS. VAN DAAN *is reading a fashion magazine.* MR. FRANK *is going over business accounts.* DUSSEL, *in his dentist's jacket, is pacing up and down, impatient to get into his bedroom.* MR. VAN DAAN *is upstairs working on a piece of embroidery in an embroidery frame.*

In his room PETER *is sitting before the mirror, smoothing his hair. As the scene goes on, he puts on his tie, brushes his coat and puts it on, preparing himself meticulously for a visit from* ANNE. *On his wall are now hung some of* ANNE'S *motion picture stars.*

In her room ANNE *too is getting dressed. She stands before the mirror in her slip, trying various ways of dressing her hair.* MARGOT *is seated on the sofa, hemming a skirt for* ANNE *to wear.*

In the main room DUSSEL *can stand it no longer. He comes over, rapping sharply on the door of his and* ANNE'S *bedroom.]* **25**

ANNE. [*Calling to him.*] No, no, Mr. Dussel! I am not dressed yet. [DUSSEL *walks away, furious, sitting down and burying his head in his hands.* ANNE *turns to* MARGOT.] How is that? How does that look?

MARGOT. [*Glancing at her briefly.*] Fine.

ANNE. You didn't even look.

MARGOT. Of course I did. It's fine.

ANNE. Margot, tell me, am I terribly ugly?

MARGOT. Oh, stop fishing. **26**

ANNE. No. No. Tell me.

MARGOT. Of course you're not. You've got nice eyes . . . and a lot of animation,[7] and . . .

ANNE. A little vague, aren't you?

7. Here, ***animation*** means "liveliness."

Practice the Skills

25 Key Literary Element

Stage Directions How much time has passed since the end of scene 1? (Check the date in Anne's last monologue.) Based on the stage directions on this page, what event do you think is about to occur?

26 Key Reading Skill

Interpreting What does Margot mean? What does she suggest Anne is fishing for?

Additional Support

Literature Focus Lesson

Character Development The characters in this play are described as very real people. In addition to their good points, they all have flaws, and they all have conflicts with one another at one point or another. Have students discuss how this realistic portrayal of the characters affects the play:

- How might the play have been different if the playwrights had ignored the flaws of the people in the attic?
- Would their situation have seemed even more terrible if the characters were portrayed as flawless? Why or why not?

AL

[She reaches over and takes a brassière out of MARGOT*'s sewing basket. She holds it up to herself, studying the effect in the mirror. Outside,* MRS. FRANK*, feeling sorry for* DUSSEL*, comes over, knocking at the girls' door.]*

MRS. FRANK. *[Outside.]* May I come in?

MARGOT. Come in, Mother.

MRS. FRANK. *[Shutting the* **door** *behind her.]* Mr. Dussel's impatient to get in here.

ANNE. *[Still with the brassière.]* Heavens, he takes the **room** for himself the entire day. **27**

MRS. FRANK. *[Gently.]* Anne, dear, you're not going in again tonight to see Peter?

ANNE. *[Dignified.]* That is my intention.

MRS. FRANK. But you've already spent a great deal of time in there today.

ANNE. I was in there exactly twice. Once to get the dictionary, and then three-quarters of an hour before supper.

MRS. FRANK. Aren't you afraid you're disturbing him?

ANNE. Mother, I have some **intuition.**

MRS. FRANK. Then may I ask you this much, Anne. Please don't shut the door when you go in.

ANNE. You sound like Mrs. Van Daan!

[She throws the brassière back in MARGOT*'s sewing basket and picks up her blouse, putting it on.]*

MRS. FRANK. No. No. I don't mean to suggest anything wrong. I only wish that you wouldn't expose yourself to criticism . . . that you wouldn't give Mrs. Van Daan the opportunity to be unpleasant. **28**

Vocabulary

intuition (in too ISH un) *n.* the ability to know things without having to reason them out

Practice the Skills

27 English Language Coach

Anglo-Saxon Roots Both **door** and **room** were Anglo-Saxon words with the same meanings but slightly different spellings. Oddly, *room* goes back to the Latin word *rurrus,* or "open land."

28 Key Reading Skill

Interpreting How do you interpret this conversation between Anne and her mother? What does it suggest about Anne and Peter?

READING WORKSHOP 2

Teach

EL Language Coach

Anglo-Saxon Roots Ask: How are the meanings of the words *door* and *room* related? *(Possible response: A door provides a way to enter and leave a room.)* **BL** **Ask:** What other definition of *room* might be related to the concept of "open land"? *(Possible response: Room also means "space.")* **OL**

L Literary Element

Stage Directions Ask: How might an actor playing Anne use body language and voice to be dignified"? *(Possible response: She might hold her head up, turn her nose up, keep a very straight posture, and use a serious tone.)* **OL**

English Language Coach

Understanding Intuition Some students may be unfamiliar with the concept of intuition. Ask students whether they have ever encountered a person who never gets lost and always seems to know where he or she is headed. Explain that a sense of direction is a form of intuition; some people simply "know" which way to go without having to reason it out. Similarly, Anne says to her mother that she has some intuition about Peter. Anne essentially knows that Peter has feelings for her, even though they have not yet discussed their feelings about each other openly. **BL**

Indiana English/Language Arts Academic Standards

SE: 8.1.2, 8.3

TWE: *Literature Focus Lesson* 8.3, *English Language Coach* 8.1

Teach

R Reading Skill

Interpreting Ask: What are two possible things that could happen to Mr. Kraler that would put the characters in danger? *(Possible response: Mr. Kraler could be blackmailed by a man who knows about the hiding place, and the man could eventually tell the authorities; Mr. Kraler could become very ill and no longer be able to support the people in the attic.)* **OL**

L Literary Element

Review Dialogue and Monologue Ask: What does Anne learn from her dialogue with Margot? *(Possible response: Anne learns that although Margot is jealous that Anne has a reason to keep going, she is not jealous of Anne's relationship with Peter.)* **BL OL** **Ask:** What does Margot's response suggest about her? *(Possible response: She is generous in wanting Anne to be happy, but she would like to be happy herself, too.)* **AL**

READING WORKSHOP 2

ANNE. Mrs. Van Daan doesn't need an opportunity to be unpleasant!

MRS. FRANK. Everyone's on edge, worried about Mr. Kraler. This is one more thing . . . **29**

ANNE. I'm sorry, Mother. I'm going to Peter's room. I'm not going to let Petronella Van Daan spoil our friendship.

[*MRS. FRANK hesitates for a second, then goes out, closing the door after her. She gets a pack of playing cards and sits at the center table, playing solitaire. In ANNE's room MARGOT hands the finished skirt to ANNE. As ANNE is putting it on, MARGOT takes off her high-heeled shoes and stuffs paper in the toes so that ANNE can wear them.*]

MARGOT. [*To ANNE.*] Why don't you two talk in the main room? It'd save a lot of trouble. It's hard on Mother, having to listen to those remarks from Mrs. Van Daan and not say a word.

ANNE. Why doesn't she say a word? I think it's ridiculous to take it and take it.

MARGOT. You don't understand Mother at all, do you? She can't talk back. She's not like you. It's just not in her nature to fight back.

ANNE. Anyway . . . the only one I worry about is you. I feel awfully guilty about you.

[*She sits on the stool near MARGOT, putting on MARGOT's high-heeled shoes.*]

MARGOT. What about?

ANNE. I mean, every time I go into Peter's room, I have a feeling I may be hurting you. [*MARGOT shakes her head.*] I know if it were me, I'd be wild. I'd be desperately jealous, if it were me.

MARGOT. Well, I'm not.

ANNE. You don't feel badly? Really? Truly? You're not jealous?

MARGOT. Of course I'm jealous . . . jealous that you've got something to get up in the morning for . . . But jealous of you and Peter? No. **30**

Practice the Skills

29 Key Reading Skill

Interpreting Why are they nervous and upset ("on edge") about Mr. Kraler?

30 Key Reading Skill

Interpreting What does Margot mean when she says Anne has "something to get up in the morning for"?

Additional Support

Differentiated Instruction

Time Management Point out to students that the families in hiding had a great deal of time on their hands, so they would have needed to stay busy to prevent boredom. Ask each student to select one of the seven characters in hiding. Then tell students to write possible schedules for that character, describing how he or she would spend each hour of the day. Students should use information in the play as well as their own ideas to construct the schedules. Remind students to consider what activities are available to the characters, as well as the restrictions on noise that exist during most of the day. **AS**

[ANNE *goes back to the mirror.*]

ANNE. Maybe there's nothing to be jealous of. Maybe he doesn't really like me. Maybe I'm just taking the place of his cat . . . [*She picks up a pair of short white gloves, putting them on.*] Wouldn't you like to come in with us?

MARGOT. I have a book. **31**

[*The sound of the children playing outside fades out. In the main room* DUSSEL *can stand it no longer. He jumps up, going to the bedroom door and knocking sharply.*]

DUSSEL. Will you please let me in my room!

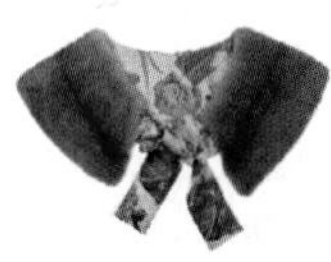

Visual Vocabulary
A ***stole*** is a long, wide scarf worn by women, usually across the shoulders.

ANNE. Just a minute, dear, dear Mr. Dussel. [*She picks up her Mother's pink stole and adjusts it elegantly over her shoulders, then gives a last look in the mirror.*] Well, here I go . . . to run the gauntlet.[8] **R1**

[*She starts out, followed by* MARGOT.]

DUSSEL. [*As she appears—sarcastic.*] Thank you so much. **32**

[DUSSEL *goes into his room.* ANNE *goes toward* PETER*'s room, passing* MRS. VAN DAAN *and her parents at the center table.*]

MRS. VAN DAAN. My God, look at her! [ANNE *pays no attention. She knocks at* PETER*'s door.*] I don't know what good it is to have a son. I never see him. He wouldn't care if I killed myself. [PETER *opens the door and stands aside for* ANNE *to come in.*] Just a minute, Anne. [*She goes to them at the door.*] I'd like to say a few words to my son. Do you mind? [PETER *and* ANNE *stand waiting.*] Peter, I don't want you staying up till all hours tonight. You've got to have your sleep. You're a growing boy. You hear? **R2**

MRS. FRANK. Anne won't stay late. She's going to bed promptly at nine. Aren't you, Anne?

ANNE. Yes, Mother . . . [*To* MRS. VAN DAAN.] May we go now?

8. To ***run the gauntlet*** is to endure opposition or difficulties.

Practice the Skills

31 **BIG Question**

Margot uses books as one way to escape bad times. Her conversation with Anne suggests she's developed another way as well. What is it? Write your answer on the Workshop 2 Foldable for Unit 6.

32 **Key Reading Skill**

Interpreting Sarcasm is related to irony. A sarcastic remark is a mocking statement that means the opposite of what it seems to mean. Examples are Anne's "dear, dear Mr. Dussel" (she doesn't think he's dear) and his "thank you" (he's annoyed, not grateful). Watch for several more instances of sarcasm in the next section.

Literature Focus Lesson

Sarcasm Sarcasm is usually easier to detect in speech, where facial expressions and tone can convey meaning, than in writing. Unless writers state that a character is being sarcastic, as in the stage directions for Dussel, readers must use context to detect sarcasm. Examine the example in which Anne says, "Just a minute, dear, dear Mr. Dussel." Ask students what details from the play tell them Anne is being sarcastic.

- She has said she doesn't like Dussel.
- She has complained about his using the room so much.
- He is bothering her to get into the room. **OL**

Teach

R1 Reading Skill

Interpreting Ask: Why are Anne and Dussel being sarcastic? *(They dislike each other and do not like having to share a room.)* **OL**

R2 Reading Skill

Review Drawing Conclusions Ask: Why does Mrs. Van Daan say, "My God, look at her!" in reference to Anne? *(Possible response: Anne is all dressed up and about to go on a "date" with Peter. Mrs. Van Daan may be annoyed she cannot spend time with her son. She also used to go on many dates herself. She may be jealous that it is Anne, not her, who gets to be distracted by a "date.")* **OL**

Indiana English/Language Arts Academic Standards
SE: 8.3
TWE: *Differentiated Instruction* 8.4.1, *Literature Focus Lesson* 8.3.6

Teach

R1 Reading Skill

Interpreting **Ask:** What makes Mrs. Van Daan suspicious of Anne's and Peter's behavior? *(Responses will vary. Some students may suggest that Mrs. Van Daan is suspicious because the door is closed and because Anne and Peter are young.)* OL

R2 Reading Skill

Review Comparing and Contrasting **Ask:** What have Anne and Peter as teenagers had to deal with that their parents did not? *(Possible response: Anne and Peter have had to deal with hardships, prejudice, loss of friends and possessions, and a lack of freedom. They have been exposed to great cruelty and fear that their parents may never have known as teenagers.)* BL OL

READING WORKSHOP 2

MRS. VAN DAAN. Are you asking me? I didn't know I had anything to say about it.

MRS. FRANK. Listen for the chimes, Anne dear.

[*The two young people go off into* PETER'S *room, shutting the door after them.*]

MRS. VAN DAAN. [*To* MRS. FRANK.] In my day it was the boys who called on the girls. Not the girls on the boys.

MRS. FRANK. You know how young people like to feel that they have secrets. Peter's room is the only place where they can talk.

MRS. VAN DAAN. Talk! That's not what they called it when I was young. 33

[MRS. VAN DAAN *goes off to the bathroom.* MARGOT *settles down to read her book.* MR. FRANK *puts his papers away and brings a chess game to the center table. He and* MRS. FRANK *start to play. In* PETER'S *room,* ANNE *speaks to* PETER, *indignant, humiliated.*]

ANNE. Aren't they awful? Aren't they impossible? Treating us as if we were still in the nursery.

[*She sits on the cot.* PETER *gets a bottle of pop and two glasses.*]

PETER. Don't let it bother you. It doesn't bother me.

ANNE. I suppose you can't really blame them . . . they think back to what they were like at our age. They don't realize how much more advanced we are . . . When you think what wonderful discussions we've had! . . . Oh, I forgot. I was going to bring you some more pictures. 34

PETER. Oh, these are fine, thanks.

ANNE. Don't you want some more? Miep just brought me some new ones.

PETER. Maybe later.

[*He gives her a glass of pop and, taking some for himself, sits down facing her.*]

ANNE. [*Looking up at one of the photographs.*] I remember when I got that . . . I won it. I bet Jopie that I could eat five ice-cream

Practice the Skills

33 Key Reading Skill

Interpreting What does Mrs. Van Daan mean here?

34 Reviewing Skills

Analyzing In what ways might Anne and Peter be "more advanced" than their parents were as teenagers, and why?

Additional Support

Differentiated Instruction

Interview Have students work in pairs to present an interview with one of the characters. Have the character tell how he or she deals with the difficulties of life in the attic, what lessons he or she has learned since going into hiding, and what suggestions he or she would give others for dealing with life's hardships. Encourage students to write a list of questions and responses from their chosen character's point of view. Ask pairs to present their interviews to the class. OL AL cones. We'd all been playing ping-pong . . . We used to have heavenly times . . . we'd finish up with ice cream at the Delphi, or the Oasis, where Jews were allowed . . . there'd always be a lot of boys . . . we'd laugh and joke . . . I'd like to go back to it for a few days or a week. But after that I know I'd be bored to death. I think more seriously about life now. I want to be a journalist . . . or something. I love to write. What do you want to do? **35**

PETER. I thought I might go off some place . . . work on a farm or something . . . some job that doesn't take much brains.

ANNE. You shouldn't talk that way. You've got the most awful inferiority complex. **36**

PETER. I know I'm not smart.

ANNE. That isn't true. You're much better than I am in dozens of things . . . arithmetic and algebra and . . . well, you're a million times better than I am in algebra. [*With sudden directness.*] You like Margot, don't you? Right from the start you liked her, liked her much better than me.

PETER. [*Uncomfortably.*] Oh, I don't know. **37**

[*In the main room* MRS. VAN DAAN *comes from the bathroom and goes over to the sink, polishing a coffee pot.*]

ANNE. It's all right. Everyone feels that way. Margot's so good. She's sweet and bright and beautiful and I'm not.

PETER. I wouldn't say that.

ANNE. Oh, no, I'm not. I know that. I know quite well that I'm not a beauty. I never have been and never shall be.

PETER. I don't agree at all. I think you're pretty.

ANNE. That's not true!

PETER. And another thing. You've changed . . . from at first, I mean.

ANNE. I have?

PETER. I used to think you were awful noisy.

Practice the Skills

35 Reviewing Elements

Character What do you learn about Anne from this speech? **R1**

36 Reviewing Skills

Clarifying Do you know what an inferiority complex is? If not, look it up. **R2**

37 Key Literary Element

Stage Directions Why does Peter answer "uncomfortably"? What does this stage direction suggest about his feelings for Margot and Anne?

Teach

R1 Reading Skill

Review Drawing Conclusions
Ask: Why might Anne now care more about a career than about eating ice cream with her friends? *(Possible responses: The war has stripped Anne's life of some of its carefree joy. Anne is growing up and thinking about her adult life rather than her life as a child.)* **OL** **AL**

R2 Reading Skill

Interpreting **Say:** What makes Anne suggest that Peter has an inferiority complex? *(Possible response: Peter says that he wants to find a job that doesn't take much brains.)*
Ask: Consider what you know about Peter's relationship with his parents. Where might his feelings of inferiority have come from? *(Possible response: from his father's criticism and unkindness)* **OL**

Literature Focus Lesson

Characterization Remind students that in a play, the audience can learn about a character by observing the character's behavior and by hearing what other characters say about him or her. Prompt a discussion about characterization with these questions:

- How do you learn about Margot on this page?
- Is Anne's description of Margot fair? Have students make a web with "Margot" in the center and adjectives that describe her personality in bubbles around it. Encourage students to determine whether each adjective describes Margot or reflects how Anne views her. **OL**

Indiana English/Language Arts Academic Standards
SE: 8.3
TWE: *Differentiated Instruction* 8.5, *Literature Focus Lesson* 8.3

Teach

Viewing the Photo

Say: Look at the size of the bathroom. How does the setting contribute to the conflict in the play? *(Possible response: The small size of the bathroom and other rooms makes the characters feel trapped and stuck with each other. Not having much time alone probably contributes to all the arguments that take place in the attic.)* **OL**

L Literary Element

Stage Directions **Ask:** Why do you think the playwrights chose to have the audience see what other characters are doing during Anne and Peter's date? *(Responses will vary. Students may say that the intrusion of the other characters reminds the audience that this is not a typical date.)* **AL**

READING WORKSHOP 2

A view of the bathroom in the attic of the warehouse building.

Analyzing the Photo This small bathroom was shared by eight people. Could you live with all the rules and restrictions that they did?

ANNE. And what do you think now, Peter? How have I changed?

PETER. Well . . . er . . . you're . . . quieter.

[*In his room* DUSSEL *takes his pajamas and toilet articles and goes into the bathroom to change.*] **38**

ANNE. I'm glad you don't just hate me.

PETER. I never said that.

ANNE. I bet when you get out of here you'll never think of me again.

PETER. That's crazy.

ANNE. When you get back with all of your friends, you're going to say . . . now what did I ever see in that Mrs. Quack Quack.

PETER. I haven't got any friends.

Practice the Skills

38 Key Literary Element

Stage Directions What is the purpose of stage directions like this and the earlier one about Mrs. Van Daan polishing a coffee pot? **L**

Additional Support

Literature Focus Lesson

Dynamic vs. Static Characters
Some characters in a literary work are static; they do not change significantly. Others go through a significant change; they are dynamic. Have students complete the following chart.

Students will likely note that Anne and Peter change more than the others. Point out that younger people often have personality changes and are also more likely to be affected by their environment. **OL**

Character	Dynamic or Static?	How character changed/stayed the same

ANNE. Oh, Peter, of course you have. Everyone has friends.

PETER. Not me. I don't want any. I get along all right without them.

R1

ANNE. Does that mean you can get along without me? I think of myself as your friend.

PETER. No. If they were all like you, it'd be different.

[He takes the glasses and the bottle and puts them away. There is a second's silence and then ANNE *speaks, hesitantly, shyly.]*

ANNE. Peter, did you ever kiss a girl?

PETER. Yes. Once.

ANNE. *[To cover her feelings.]* That picture's crooked. *[*PETER *goes over, straightening the photograph.]* Was she pretty?

PETER. Huh?

ANNE. The girl that you kissed.

PETER. I don't know. I was blindfolded. *[He comes back and sits down again.]* It was at a party. One of those kissing games.

R2

ANNE. *[Relieved.]* Oh. I don't suppose that really counts, does it? 39

PETER. It didn't with me.

ANNE. I've been kissed twice. Once a man I'd never seen before kissed me on the cheek when he picked me up off the ice and I was crying. And the other was Mr. Koophuis,[9] a friend of Father's who kissed my hand. You wouldn't say those counted, would you?

PETER. I wouldn't say so.

ANNE. I know almost for certain that Margot would never kiss anyone unless she was engaged to them. And I'm sure too that Mother never touched a man before Pim. But I don't know . . . things are so different now . . . What do you think? Do you think a girl shouldn't kiss anyone except if she's engaged or something? It's so hard to try to think what to do,

9. ***Koophuis*** (KOIP hus)

Practice the Skills

39 Key Reading Skill

Interpreting Why does Anne feel relieved?

Teach

R1 Reading Skill

Interpreting Say: At first, Peter says he doesn't want any friends, but then he says he wouldn't mind having friends if they were all like Anne. What does this suggest about Peter's desire for friends? *(Possible response: Peter really does want friends but he is shy and afraid.)* OL

R2 Reading Skill

Interpreting Ask: Why does Anne ask Peter so many questions about kissing? *(She wants Peter to kiss her.)* BL OL

English Language Coach

Contractions Point out that Anne and Peter frequently use contractions such as *it'd, don't, I'd, it's, she's,* and *wouldn't.* Tell students that contractions are common in informal speech and writing. Have students list the contractions on this page in a chart and write the words that are being contracted. Tell students to read several lines using complete words instead of contractions, and ask them to discuss which way sounds more natural. EL BL

Indiana English/Language Arts Academic Standards

SE: 8.3

TWE: *Literature Focus Lesson* 8.3, *English Language Coach* 8.1

Teach

R Reading Skill

Interpreting **Ask:** Does Peter want to express his feelings about Anne as badly as Anne does about him? Explain. *(Responses will vary. Some students may say that Anne is the one who wants to tell Peter how she really feels about him. Others may say that Peter, too, wants to express his feelings, but is limited by his shyness.)* OL

BQ BIG Question

Ask: How can this new relationship between Peter and Anne help them through their difficult situation? *(Possible response: It can distract them from their pain; it can give them something exciting to think about; it can give them hope for the future; it can provide them with a place to talk about their hopes and feelings.)* AS

READING WORKSHOP 2

when here we are with the whole world falling around our ears and you think . . . well . . . you don't know what's going to happen tomorrow and . . . What do you think? **40**

PETER. I suppose it'd depend on the girl. Some girls, anything they do's wrong. But others . . . well . . . it wouldn't necessarily be wrong with them. [*The carillon starts to strike nine o'clock.*] I've always thought that when two people . . .

ANNE. Nine o'clock. I have to go.

PETER. That's right.

ANNE. [*Without moving.*] Good night.

[*There is a second's pause, then* PETER *gets up and moves toward the door.*]

PETER. You won't let them stop you coming?

ANNE. No. [*She rises and starts for the door.*] Sometime I might bring my diary. There are so many things in it that I want to talk over with you. There's a lot about you.

PETER. What kind of things?

ANNE. I wouldn't want you to see some of it. I thought you were a nothing, just the way you thought about me.

PETER. Did you change your mind, the way I changed my mind about you?

ANNE. Well . . . You'll see . . . **41**

[*For a second* ANNE *stands looking up at* PETER, *longing for him to kiss her. As he makes no move she turns away. Then suddenly* PETER *grabs her awkwardly in his arms, kissing her on the cheek.* ANNE *walks out dazed. She stands for a minute, her back to the people in the main room. As she regains her* **poise** *she goes to her mother and father and* MARGOT, *silently kissing them. They murmur their good nights to her. As she is about to open her bedroom door, she catches sight of* MRS. VAN DAAN. *She goes*

Practice the Skills

40 **Reviewing Elements**

Dialogue and Monologue Why is Anne talking so much?

41 **Key Reading Skill**

Interpreting What is going on—or *not* going on—between Anne and Peter in this scene?

Vocabulary

poise (poyz) *n.* a calm, relaxed, and self-controlled manner

Additional Support

Reading Fluency

Build Fluency One way to have students build fluency is to have them follow along as another person reads aloud. Read aloud the dialogue between Anne and Peter, being sure to demonstrate how to pause for ellipsis points and alter your tone of voice for questions. Then invite volunteers to read parts of the dialogue aloud. Remind students to read only the dialogue, not the stage directions. EL BL *quickly to her, taking her face in her hands and kissing her first on one cheek and then on the other. Then she hurries off into her room.* MRS. VAN DAAN *looks after her, and then looks over at* PETER'S *room. Her suspicions are confirmed.*] **42**

MRS. VAN DAAN. [*She knows.*] Ah hah!

[*The lights dim out. The curtain falls on the scene. In the darkness* ANNE'S VOICE *comes faintly at first and then with growing strength.*]

ANNE'S VOICE. By this time we all know each other so well that if anyone starts to tell a story, the rest can finish it for him. We're having to cut down still further on our meals. What makes it worse, the rats have been at work again. They've carried off some of our precious food. Even Mr. Dussel wishes now that Mouschi was here. Thursday, the twentieth of April, nineteen forty-four. Invasion fever[10] is mounting every day. Miep tells us that people outside talk of nothing else. For myself, life has become much more pleasant. I often go to Peter's room after supper. Oh, don't think I'm in love, because I'm not. But it does make life more bearable to have someone with whom you can exchange views. No more tonight. P.S. . . . I must be honest. I must confess that I actually live for the next meeting. Is there anything lovelier than to sit under the skylight and feel the sun on your cheeks and have a darling boy in your arms? I admit now that I'm glad the Van Daans had a son and not a daughter. I've outgrown another dress. That's the third. I'm having to wear Margot's clothes after all. I'm working hard on my French and am now reading *La Belle Nivernaise.*[11] **43**

[*As she is saying the last lines—the curtain rises on the scene. The lights dim on, as* ANNE'S VOICE *fades out.*]

10. ***Invasion fever*** refers to the widely held belief that the Allies would soon invade and take control of areas occupied by German forces.

11. ***La Belle Nivernaise*** (law BEL NEE vur nayz) was a book by a nineteenth century French novelist.

Practice the Skills

42 Key Literary Element

L

Stage Directions What were Mrs. Van Daan's suspicions, and how were they shown to be correct?

43 BIG Question

What new thing does Anne have to help her keep from giving up? Explain. Write your answer on the Workshop 2 Foldable for Unit 6. Your response will help you complete the Unit Challenge later. BQ

Teach

L Literary Element

Stage Directions Say: The stage directions simply say, "She knows." How might an actor playing Mrs. Van Daan convey that she knows what just happened between her son and Anne while delivering the line? ***(Responses will vary. Students may suggest that the actor could cross her arms, point a finger, nod her head, or raise the volume of her voice.)*** AS

BQ BIG Question

Ask: Do Anne's strategies for not giving up seem realistic to you? Have you ever acted similarly to get through a difficult time? Explain. ***(Responses will vary.)*** AS

Assess

CheckPoint

Use the CheckPoint questions provided on Presentation Plus! to check for comprehension of the selection. These questions can be used with interactive response keypads for immediate student feedback.

Differentiated Instruction

Quotations Note that Anne says, "We all know each other so well now that if anyone starts to tell a story, the rest can finish it for him." Discuss with students whether, as the play progresses, readers also begin to feel that they know the characters well.

Have students list the names of all the characters in the play. Then have them select from the play one quotation from each character that illustrates his or her personality. Students should be prepared to explain what each quotation says about the character and why they chose it. OL

Indiana English/Language Arts Academic Standards

SE: 8.3.6

TWE: *Reading Fluency* 8.1, *Differentiated Instruction* 8.3

Assess

Resources for page 822

- Selection Quick Check, p. 53
- Selection and Unit Assessment, p. 63
- ExamView Assessment Suite
- Interactive Tutor: Self-Assessment

Students can respond to the *After You Read* items in their Learner's Notebooks or on a separate sheet of paper.

Answering the BIG Question

1. Possible response: The routines give them something to do to distract them from their fears.
2. a cake
3. She is getting ready for a date with Peter.

Critical Thinking

4. Possible response: Someone knowing they're in the attic threatens the group's safety.
5. Possible response: Anne refers to the Nazis terrorizing the Jewish people.
6. Possible response: Despite their bickering, the group is doing well. They are continuing with their lives as best they can.

After You Read

The Diary of Anne Frank, Act 2, Scenes 1–2

Answering the BIG Question

1. The characters in *The Diary of Anne Frank* develop routines of everyday life. How do these routines help them carry on through difficult times?
2. **Recall** What does Miep bring that causes an argument in the group?
   TIP Right There
3. **Explain** Why is Anne dressing up as scene 2 begins?
   TIP Right There

Critical Thinking

4. **Explain** Why is Mr. Kraler's news about the possible blackmail attempt so important to the group?
   TIP Author and Me
5. **Interpret** What does Anne mean when she says, "We have problems that no other people our age have ever had"? Use details from the play to support your answer.
   TIP Author and Me
6. **Evaluate** How do you think the characters are doing, given their living conditions? Are they dealing well with their situation?
   TIP Author and Me

Write About Your Reading

Letter In real life, Anne and Margot were like most sisters–laughing, loving, hurting, arguing, and sharing personal thoughts and feelings. While in hiding, they sometimes wrote letters to each other, saying things that they couldn't in person because of the crowded conditions and lack of privacy.

Imagine how Margot must have felt as she watched the relationship develop between her sister and Peter. Look again at the sisters' conversation in scene 2. Then put yourself in Margot's place. Write a letter to Anne about her friendship with Peter. Keep these things in mind:

- what kind of person Margot is
- how you think she feels, or felt, about Peter
- what she says to Anne in the play–what words she chooses, how she forms sentences, the tone she uses, and so on
- how you might feel in this situation or one like it

Indiana English/Language Arts Academic Standards (pp. 822–823)

8.3 Comprehension and Analysis of Literary Text Respond to grade-level-appropriate literature... **8.2.9** Make reasonable statements and draw conclusions... **8.5.7** Write for different purposes... **8.3.6** Identify significant literary devices... **8.6.5** Use correct punctuation.

For a complete description of the standards, see p. IN 11.

Write About Your Reading

Possible response:

Dear Anne,

It troubles me to think you worry I am jealous about your relationship with Peter. You are my sister. I love you, and I want you to be happy. I would never want you to go without any small joys you may find, especially now, with the threat of discovery filling our days. Love Peter and be happy. I wish only that I, too, may have love in my life one day.

Your sister,

Margot

Skills Review

Key Reading Skill: Interpreting

7. How do you interpret Anne's behavior toward Peter? Do you think she's falling in love? Does she just have a crush? Is it something in between? Give details from your experience and from the play to support your interpretation.

Key Literary Element: Stage Directions

8. Some information appears only in stage directions. Find one example in act 2, scenes 1-2. Briefly state the information and identify the page where it's given.

9. In the stage directions at the end of act 2, scene 2, Anne suddenly goes over to Mrs. Van Daan and kisses her cheeks. What do you think is the purpose of this stage direction?

Reviewing Skills: Drawing Conclusions

10. In act 2, scene 1, what reason does Mr. Van Daan state for wanting to sell his wife's fur coat? Do you believe him? If so, why? If not, what do you think was his real reason for selling the coat? Support your answer with details from the play.

Vocabulary Check

Match each vocabulary word with its definition.

disgruntled **foreboding** **apprehension**
intimate **intuition** **poise**

11. a calm, relaxed, and self-controlled manner

12. fear of what may happen

13. very close and personal; private

14. not pleased; in a bad mood

15. a feeling that something bad will happen

16. the ability to know things without having to reason them out

17. **English Language Coach** The Anglo-Saxon root *side* means "edge." Explain how this root relates to the meaning of *inside*.

Grammar Link: Commas with Interrupting Words

Some words or groups of words interrupt the flow of thought in a sentence. Place commas before and after interrupting words or phrases.

- Joshua, in my opinion, has no right to question us.
- The final score, I believe, was 25 to 18.
- Eating breakfast, in fact, improves your productivity.

Some Common Interrupting Words and Phrases		
after all	I believe	moreover
by the way	I suppose	nevertheless
for example	in addition	nonetheless
furthermore	in fact	of course
however	incidentally	therefore

Grammar Practice

Copy the following sentences, inserting commas to set off the interrupting words.

18. Anne you see was a typical teenage girl.

19. The cat if you ask me is getting fatter every day!

20. It's time I think to schedule a visit to the dentist.

21. The cost nonetheless is more than I want to pay.

22. Recycled plastic milk jugs incidentally are used to make plastic pipe, drainage tile, flower pots, and more.

23. Beyoncé Knowles I believe was born in Houston, Texas.

24. Jim Carrey not surprisingly would do comedy routines for his classmates when he was a child.

Writing Application Review the letter you wrote from Margot to Anne. If any words or phrases interrupt the flow of thought, set them off with commas.

Web Activities For eFlashcards, Selection Quick Checks, and other Web activities, go to www.glencoe.com.

Skills Review

Key Reading Skill: Interpreting

7. Responses will vary.

Key Literary Element: Stage Directions

8. Responses will vary.

9. Possible response: It shows that Anne is so happy she is willing to show compassion even for Mrs. Van Daan.

Reviewing Skills: Drawing Conclusions

10. He says it is selfish for her to keep it when so many people outside need a warm coat. Most students will not believe him. He really wants money to buy cigarettes and food.

Vocabulary Check

11. poise

12. apprehension

13. intimate

14. disgruntled

15. foreboding

16. intuition

English Language Coach

17. Edges are required to distinguish inside from outside.

Grammar Link: Commas with Interrupting Words

18. Anne, you see, was a typical teenage girl.

19. The cat, if you ask me, is getting fatter every day!

20. It's time, I think, to schedule a visit to the dentist.

21. The cost, nonetheless, is more than I want to pay.

22. Recycled plastic milk jugs, incidentally, are used to make plastic pipe, drainage tile, flower pots, and more.

23. Beyoncé Knowles, I believe, was born in Houston, Texas.

24. Jim Carrey, not surprisingly, would do comedy routines for his classmates when he was a child.

Close

Ask students to discuss how the play has changed the way they think about the Big Question.

Indiana English/Language Arts Academic Standards
SE: 8.2.9, 8.3, 8.3.6, 8.5.7, 8.6.5

Teach

V Vocabulary

Word Parts Say: Each vocabulary word in the "Vocabulary Preview" is made up of smaller word parts that can help you remember the definition. For example, the word *liberated* contains the Latin root *liber*, which means "free." Use a dictionary to help you identify the word parts in the remaining vocabulary words. EL BL

Before You Read *The Diary of Anne Frank,* Act 2, Scenes 3–5

Vocabulary Preview

V

stealthily (STEL thuh lee) *adv.* in a secret or sneaky manner **(p. 826)** *People in hiding had to move stealthily during the day to avoid being caught.*

pandemonium (pan duh MOH nee um) *n.* wild disorder and uproar **(p. 832)** *There was pandemonium outside; shots were being fired in all directions, and soldiers were running down the streets.*

liberated (LIB uh ray tid) *adj.* released; freed **(p. 833)** *The idea that they would soon be liberated lifted everyone's spirits.*

downcast (DOWN kast) *adj.* sad; depressed **(p. 835)** *The lack of good news made everyone downcast.*

English Language Coach

Anglo-Saxon Roots Anglo-Saxon, or Old English, was spoken and written in England for centuries. Old English was gradually replaced by Middle English, and Middle English was gradually replaced by Modern English.

Throughout those many years, words came into English from other languages, too. We study the roots of those words more than we study Old English roots because the words Old English gave us are so simple.

Most good dictionaries include a word's history. Here are some of the special symbols and abbreviations you're likely to see:

- Brackets enclose the word's history, which might be either at the beginning of the entry or at its end.
- **OE** means "Old English," **ME** means "Middle English," and **fr** stands for "from." (Check the dictionary's table of contents for a list of all abbreviations.)
- Earlier spellings of the word are printed in *italics*.

  knife *n* [ME *knif,* fr OE *cnif*]

  leap *vb* [ME *lepen,* fr OE *hleapan*]

Guess the Roots Guess which word in each pair came from Old English. Then check your guesses in a dictionary.

1. chicken / poultry
2. construct / build
3. break / fracture

Indiana English/Language Arts Academic Standards (pp. 824–843)

8.1.2 Understand the influence of historical events on...word meaning... **8.3 Comprehension and Analysis of Literary Text** Respond to grade-level-appropriate literature... **8.3.6** Identify significant literary devices...

For a complete description of the standards, see p. IN 11.

Additional Support

Literature Focus Lesson

Summary Act 2, Scenes 3–5
Miep arrives in the midst of a heated argument with news that the invasion has begun; the group is so happy that they forget their present situation. Weeks pass and the mood is tense once again. Three days go by without a visit from Miep. Everyone knows something is wrong. In the middle of a monologue in which Anne explains the importance of faith to Peter, the Green Police burst in, cutting off Anne's voice. In the final scene of the play, Mr. Frank finishes reading the diary and explains that Anne, Margot, and Mrs. Frank all died at Bergen-Belsen. OL

Skills Preview

Key Reading Skill: Interpreting

In this play, there is one thing you always need to keep in mind when you are interpreting behavior. These people hide in the Annex for more than two years. They don't see anyone else except Miep and Mr. Kraler. They don't get to go outside or listen to the radio. You can imagine how that would feel. Keep that feeling in mind as you read. It will be a very important part of your ability to interpret.

Group Discussion In a group, talk about situations where you were cut off from the outside world. They may include being grounded or sick or snowed in.

Key Literary Element: Mood

Mood is the emotional effect a piece of writing has on the reader. In most kinds of writing, the mood is created by the writer alone—and only through words. A playwright can set a mood in a script. However, when a play is performed, the mood is affected by lighting, sound effects, music, costumes, sets, direction, and acting. All of these things must work together to achieve the mood the playwright wants.

You can usually identify one general mood in a piece of writing, but each scene, chapter, or page may have a different emotional effect. The mood at the beginning of *The Diary of Anne Frank* might be described as sad and weary. That changes as characters are added and changes again as they interact.

Partner Talk Discuss act 1, scene 5, with a partner. In your Learner's Notebook, outline the important events of the scene in one column. Then, in a second column, write two or three words that describe the mood and how it changes (if it does) when each new event occurs.

Interactive Literary Elements Handbook
To review or learn more about the literary elements, go to www.glencoe.com.

Get Ready to Read

Connect to the Reading

Have you ever believed in something so much that you felt sure it would happen? In the next scene, the characters hear good news about the war and feel sure that they will soon be saved. As you read, imagine how you would react in their situation.

Group Talk In a small group, discuss a time when you really wanted something to happen. Describe your feelings as you waited. How did you react when your wish did—or did not—come true?

Build Background

Prisons are for convicted criminals. Prisoner-of-war camps are for captured soldiers. Concentration camps are for people who belong to the "wrong" ethnic groups or political parties. (*Concentration* refers to the process of gathering into one place.) The term "concentration camp" was first used in 1901.

- In the 1930s, the Nazis sent many Jews and other "enemies" and "undesirables" to camps in Germany and, later, in German-occupied countries.
- Beginning in 1942, entire communities of Jews were sent directly to extermination camps.
- It's estimated that some ten million people died in Nazi camps. Many were murdered outright. Others died of abuse, disease, and starvation.

Set Purposes for Reading

BIG Question Read the rest of *The Diary of Anne Frank* to see how people try to make the best of the most awful circumstances.

Set Your Own Purpose What would you like to learn from the play to help you answer the Big Question? Write your own purpose on the Workshop 2 Foldable for Unit 6.

Keep Moving

Use these skills as you read the following selection.

Teach

R Reading Skill

Interpreting Ask: Of all the characters, who do you think has the hardest time being cut off from the rest of the world? Why? *(Responses will vary.)* OL

L Literary Element

Mood Say: Use what you know about factors that can affect mood to describe the mood of your classroom at this moment. How might the mood change if:

- a famous athlete walked into the classroom?
- you announced a pop quiz?
- the principal announced a day off from school?
- someone made a rude or inappropriate comment?
- someone told a very funny joke? *(Responses will vary.)* AS

LiteratureOnline

Interactive Literary Elements Handbook Have students access the Web site to improve their understanding of mood.

Differentiated Instruction

Present Day Persecution Point out that dictatorships and the persecution of minorities did not end with World War II. Many news organizations have Web sites that provide in-depth reporting on worldwide events of this nature. Have students conduct research on world news Web sites to learn more about countries in which the government persecutes some minorities. Remind students that persecution may be in the form of violence rather than restrictions. Have them locate the country and identify its leader, the group being persecuted, and the form of persecution. OL

Indiana English/Language Arts Academic Standards
SE: 8.1.2, 8.3

Teach

R Reading Skill

Review Drawing Conclusions **Ask:** What conclusion can you draw about Mr. Van Daan and his priorities? *(Possible response: Mr. Van Daan cares more about his own welfare than the welfare of others.)* OL

L Literary Element

Review Monologue and Dialogue **Ask:** Why do you think the Franks speak German here? *(Possible responses: They are terrified and revert to their first language. The Franks do not want the other characters, who speak Dutch, to understand their conversation.)* OL

READING WORKSHOP 2

SCENE 3

[It is night, a few weeks later. Everyone is in bed. There is complete quiet. In the VAN DAANS' *room a match flares up for a moment and then is quickly put out.* MR. VAN DAAN, *in bare feet, dressed in underwear and trousers, is dimly seen coming* **stealthily** *down the stairs and into the main room, where* MR. *and* MRS. FRANK *and* MARGOT *are sleeping. He goes to the food safe and again lights a match. Then he cautiously opens the safe, taking out a half-loaf of bread. As he closes the safe, it creaks. He stands rigid.* MRS. FRANK *sits up in bed. She sees him.]* 1 2

MRS. FRANK. *[Screaming.]* Otto! Otto! Komme schnell!

[The rest of the people wake, hurriedly getting up.]

MR. FRANK. Was ist los? Was ist passiert?

*[*DUSSEL, *followed by* ANNE, *comes from his room.]*

MRS. FRANK. *[As she rushes over to* MR. VAN DAAN.*]* Er stiehlt das Essen![1]

DUSSEL. *[Grabbing* MR. VAN DAAN.*]* You! You! Give me that.

MRS. VAN DAAN. *[Coming down the stairs.]* Putti . . . Putti . . . what is it?

DUSSEL. *[His hands on* VAN DAAN'S *neck.]* You dirty thief . . . stealing food . . . you good-for-nothing . . .

MR. FRANK. Mr. Dussel! For God's sake! Help me, Peter!

*[*PETER *comes over, trying, with* MR. FRANK, *to separate the two struggling men.]*

PETER. Let him go! Let go!

*[*DUSSEL *drops* MR. VAN DAAN, *pushing him away. He shows them the end of a loaf of bread that he has taken from* VAN DAAN.*]*

1. The Franks' conversation in German translates as follows: Mrs. Frank. "Come quickly!" Mr. Frank. "What's the matter? What has happened?" Mrs. Frank. "He is stealing food!"

Vocabulary

stealthily (STEL thuh lee) *adv.* in a secret or sneaky manner

Practice the Skills

1 English Language Coach

Anglo-Saxon Roots The base work for **stealthily** is *stealth*. In Middle English it meant "the act of stealing." How do you think it came to mean "sneakiness"?

2 Reviewing Skills

Drawing Conclusions Reread the stage directions at the beginning of act 1, scene 4. Now what conclusions can you draw about Mr. Van Daan and his movements?

Additional Support

English Language Coach

Homophones English language learners may be confused by homophones. Point out to students that some words sound alike but have different spellings and different meanings. When a homophone word is used, the listener must determine which meaning and part of speech best fits the context. Read aloud the sentences in the opening stage directions containing the words *week, flares, bare, seen, stairs,* and *sees* and then write these words on the board. Have students define each word and then identify other spellings and meanings of words that sound the same as these. EL BL

DUSSEL. You greedy, selfish . . . !

[*MARGOT turns on the lights.*]

MRS. VAN DAAN. Putti . . . what is it?

[*All of MRS. FRANK's gentleness, her self-control, is gone. She is outraged, in a frenzy of indignation.*[2]] 3

MRS. FRANK. The bread! He was stealing the bread!

DUSSEL. It was you, and all the time we thought it was the rats!

MR. FRANK. Mr. Van Daan, how could you!

2. Mrs. Frank's ***frenzy of indignation*** is her state of great excitement and anger.

Practice the Skills

R

3 **Reviewing Skills**

Character Why do the directions make such a big deal of Mrs. Frank's behavior? Think about how she has behaved up to now.

A view of the front of the warehouse building.

Analyzing the Photo The attic windows had to be covered during daylight. Can you imagine Anne or Peter looking out the window into the night?

Teach

R Reading Skill

Interpreting Ask: How does Mrs. Frank's behavior now compare with her behavior up until this point in the play? *(Possible response: Up until this point in the play, Mrs. Frank has been able to maintain her gentleness and self-control. She loses both of these in this scene.)* OL **Ask:** Why does this particular event cause Mrs. Frank to lose control? *(Responses will vary. Students may say that Mr. Van Daan's actions threaten the well-being of Mrs. Frank's family.)* AL

C Critical Thinking

Evaluation Ask: Is this an effective way to begin the scene? Why or why not? *(Possible response: It is effective because its intensity and conflict captures the audience's attention.)* OL

Viewing the Photo

Ask: How many people live in the attic? *(eight)* BL **Ask:** How does this photo help you imagine their living situation? *(Possible response: The attic looks so small compared to the rest of the building. It helps me visualize the cramped quarters of the eight people.)* OL

English Language Coach

Cognates English, like Dutch and Danish, is a Germanic language. Many English words come from the same word origins as German words. Such words are called cognates. Point out to students the similarities between *komme* and the English translation *come*, *was ist* and the English translation *what is*, and *stiehlt* and the English translation *stealing*. Ask students to share any words in their home languages that sound similar to English words with the same meanings. EL

Indiana English/Language Arts Academic Standards
SE: 8.1.2, 8.3
TWE: *English Language Coach* 8.1.3, *English Language Coach* 8.1.2

Teach

L Literary Element

Review Stage Directions
Ask: Why does Mrs. Van Daan go to her husband protectively? Would you do the same thing in her place? Explain. *(Possible response: Mrs. Van Daan is probably used to protecting her husband from the accusations and anger of the others. Some students may say that they would do the same thing; others will say otherwise.)* OL

R Reading Skill

Review Analyzing **Ask:** Is Mrs. Frank overreacting by telling Mr. Van Daan to leave? Explain. *(Responses will vary. Some students may say that Mrs. Frank is not overreacting because she is acting in the best interests of her family. Others may say that she is overreacting because she is not thinking about the Van Daans' welfare.)* OL

MR. VAN DAAN. I'm hungry.

MRS. FRANK. We're all of us hungry! I see the children getting thinner and thinner. Your own son Peter . . . I've heard him moan in his sleep, he's so hungry. And you come in the night and steal food that should go to them . . . to the children!

MRS. VAN DAAN. [*Going to* MR. VAN DAAN *protectively.*] He needs more food than the rest of us. He's used to more. He's a big man. L

[*MR. VAN DAAN breaks away, going over and sitting on the couch.*]

MRS. FRANK. [*Turning on* MRS. VAN DAAN.] And you . . . you're worse than he is! You're a mother, and yet you sacrifice your child to this man . . . this . . . this . . .

MR. FRANK. Edith! Edith!

[*MARGOT picks up the pink woolen stole, putting it over her mother's shoulders.*]

MRS. FRANK. [*Paying no attention, going on to* MRS. VAN DAAN.] Don't think I haven't seen you! Always saving the choicest bits for him! I've watched you day after day and I've held my tongue. But not any longer! Not after this! Now I want him to go! I want him to get out of here! R

MR. FRANK. Edith!

MR. VAN DAAN. Get out of here?

MRS. VAN DAAN. What do you mean?

MRS. FRANK. Just that! Take your things and get out! 4

MR. FRANK. [*To* MRS. FRANK.] You're speaking in anger. You cannot mean what you are saying.

MRS. FRANK. I mean exactly that!

[*MRS. VAN DAAN takes a cover from the FRANKS' bed, pulling it about her.*]

MR. FRANK. For two long years we have lived here, side by side. We have respected each other's rights . . . we have managed to live in peace. Are we now going to throw it

Practice the Skills

4 BIG Question

Is Mrs. Frank just stressed out from hiding for so long? Is she right in trying to protect her family by telling Mr. Van Daan to leave? Is protecting her family one way she keeps going? Write your ideas on the Workshop 2 Foldable for Unit 6.

Additional Support

Differentiated Instruction

Tragedy In the 16th century and before, tragedies were mostly tales of members of royalty and others in high society who suffered some kind of downfall. Aristotle, the Greek playwright, believed that tragedies must involve a person from high society who suffers a great fall, often because of a tragic flaw. Have students contrast this tragedy to traditional tragedies:

- The characters have flaws, but they suffer primarily because of the deep flaws of others, not because of their own flaws.
- The characters are regular, everyday people, not kings and queens. OL

all away? I know this will never happen again, will it, Mr. Van Daan?

MR. VAN DAAN. No. No.

MRS. FRANK. He steals once! He'll steal again!

[*MR. VAN DAAN, holding his stomach, starts for the bathroom. ANNE puts her arms around him, helping him up the step.*]

MR. FRANK. Edith, please. Let us be calm. We'll all go to our rooms . . . and afterwards we'll sit down quietly and talk this out . . . we'll find some way . . .

MRS. FRANK. No! No! No more talk! I want them to leave!

MRS. VAN DAAN. You'd put us out, on the streets?

MRS. FRANK. There are other hiding places.

MRS. VAN DAAN. A cellar . . . a closet. I know. And we have no money left even to pay for that.

MRS. FRANK. I'll give you money. Out of my own pocket I'll give it gladly.

[*She gets her purse from a shelf and comes back with it.*]

MRS. VAN DAAN. Mr. Frank, you told Putti you'd never forget what he'd done for you when you came to Amsterdam. You said you could never repay him, that you . . . **C**

MRS. FRANK. [*Counting out money.*] If my husband had any obligation to you, he's paid it, over and over.

MR. FRANK. Edith, I've never seen you like this before. I don't know you.

MRS. FRANK. I should have spoken out long ago.

DUSSEL. You can't be nice to some people. **R1**

MRS. VAN DAAN. [*Turning on DUSSEL.*] There would have been plenty for all of us, if you hadn't come in here!

MR. FRANK. We don't need the Nazis to destroy us. We're destroying ourselves. **5**

Practice the Skills

5 Key Reading Skill

Interpreting Explain Mr. Frank's statement. Do you agree? **R2**

Teach

C Critical Thinking

Comprehension Ask: What does Mrs. Van Daan say to persuade the Franks to let them stay? Does it work? *(She reminds Mr. Frank of past favors Mr. Van Daan did for the Franks. Mrs. Frank says her husband's obligation has been paid.)* **OL**

R1 Reading Skill

Review Drawing Conclusions Ask: Do you think Mr. Dussel is acting in support of the Franks or out of personal greed? *(Possible response: He is probably acting out of personal greed. He has complained that Mr. Van Daan gets a greater portion of food than the others. He likely wants him to leave for his own benefit.)*

R2 Reading Skill

Interpreting Ask: How exactly are the characters "destroying" themselves? *(Possible response: The characters do not trust one another and bicker constantly. They have allowed their situation to make them angry and greedy.)* **OL**

Differentiated Instruction

Keeping Track of Time Some readers may have difficulty understanding lapses or shifts in time in a story. Previewing the text and keeping a chart can help these students understand the passage of time. Have students skim the opening stage directions for each scene of the play and create a list of acts and scenes. Next to each listing have them write important plot elements. When their lists are complete, ask students to review them and to write, between each entry, how much time has passed between the two scenes. **OL**

Indiana English/Language Arts Academic Standards

SE: 8.3

TWE: *Differentiated Instruction* 8.3, *Differentiated Instruction* 8.2

Teach

C Critical Thinking

Synthesis Ask: According to earlier scenes, how does Peter feel about his father? *(He seems to dislike him. He talks back to him and defends his mother when his parents argue. He is also embarrassed by his father's greed.)* **Ask:** Are you surprised by his loyalty? Explain. *(Possible responses: I am not surprised: Peter probably does not want to be far from his mother; I am surprised: Peter has become close to Anne and does not like his father.)* OL

R Reading Skill

Interpreting Ask: Is Anne acting selfishly when she tells the Van Daans not to leave? Explain. *(Responses will vary. Some students may say that Anne does not want any harm to come to anyone. Others may say that Anne wants the Van Daans to stay only because she likes Peter.)* AS

[He sits down, with his head in his hands. MRS. FRANK *goes to* MRS. VAN DAAN.*]*

MRS. FRANK. *[Giving* MRS. VAN DAAN *some money.]* Give this to Miep. She'll find you a place.

ANNE. Mother, you're not putting Peter out. Peter hasn't done anything.

MRS. FRANK. He'll stay, of course. When I say I must protect the children, I mean Peter too.

*[*PETER *rises from the steps where he has been sitting.]*

PETER. I'd have to go if Father goes. 6

*[*MR. VAN DAAN *comes from the bathroom.* MRS. VAN DAAN *hurries to him and takes him to the couch. Then she gets water from the sink to bathe his face.]* C

MRS. FRANK. *[While this is going on.]* He's no father to you . . . that man! He doesn't know what it is to be a father!

PETER. *[Starting for his room.]* I wouldn't feel right. I couldn't stay.

MRS. FRANK. Very well, then. I'm sorry.

ANNE. *[Rushing over to* PETER.*]* No, Peter! No! *[*PETER *goes into his room, closing the door after him.* ANNE *turns back to her mother, crying.]* I don't care about the food. They can have mine! I don't want it! Only don't send them away. It'll be daylight soon. They'll be caught . . . R

MARGOT. *[Putting her arms comfortingly around* ANNE.*]* Please, Mother!

MRS. FRANK. They're not going now. They'll stay here until Miep finds them a place. *[To* MRS. VAN DAAN.*]* But one thing I insist on! He must never come down here again! He must never come to this room where the food is stored! We'll divide what we have . . . an equal share for each! *[*DUSSEL *hurries over to get a sack of potatoes from the food safe.* MRS. FRANK *goes on, to* MRS. VAN DAAN.*]* You can cook it here and take it up to him. 7 8

*[*DUSSEL *brings the sack of potatoes back to the center table.]*

Practice the Skills

6 Reviewing Skills

Character So far in the play, Peter has not seemed to like or respect his father. Why do you think he says this?

7 Reviewing Elements

Conflict What things have contributed to this sudden conflict? How long has it been building?

8 Reviewing Skills

Predicting What do you think is going to happen? Will the Van Daans leave?

Additional Support

Reading Fluency

Build Fluency Hesitant oral reading usually occurs because the reader's eyes focus only on the word being read, and this practice slows the reader's pace. One way to improve reading aloud is to practice letting the eyes move forward to the next word or two while reading. If students are musically inclined, you may liken this process to sight-reading music. Have students work in small groups to improve oral reading skills. Taking turns, they should read aloud, concentrating on letting their eyes move ahead to the next word or two while they read. Encourage students to provide feedback to help one another improve their reading. EL BL

MARGOT. Oh, no. No. We haven't sunk so far that we're going to fight over a handful of rotten potatoes.

DUSSEL. [*Dividing the potatoes into piles.*] Mrs. Frank, Mr. Frank, Margot, Anne, Peter, Mrs. Van Daan, Mr. Van Daan, myself . . . Mrs. Frank . . .

[*The buzzer sounds in* MIEP'S *signal.*]

MR. FRANK. It's Miep!

[*He hurries over, getting his overcoat and putting it on.*]

MARGOT. At this hour?

MRS. FRANK. It is trouble.

MR. FRANK. [*As he starts down to unbolt the door.*] I beg you, don't let her see a thing like this!

MR. DUSSEL. [*Counting without stopping.*] . . . Anne, Peter, Mrs. Van Daan, Mr. Van Daan, myself . . .

MARGOT. [*To* DUSSEL.] Stop it! Stop it! 9

DUSSEL. . . . Mr. Frank, Margot, Anne, Peter, Mrs. Van Daan, Mr. Van Daan, myself, Mrs. Frank . . .

MRS. VAN DAAN. You're keeping the big ones for yourself! All the big ones . . . Look at the size of that! . . . And that! . . .

[DUSSEL *continues on with his dividing.* PETER, *with his shirt and trousers on, comes from his room.*]

MARGOT. Stop it! Stop it!

[*We hear* MIEP'S *excited voice speaking to* MR. FRANK *below.*]

MIEP. Mr. Frank . . . the most wonderful news! . . . The invasion has begun!

MR. FRANK. Go on, tell them! Tell them!

[MIEP *comes running up the steps, ahead of* MR. FRANK. *She has a man's raincoat on over her nightclothes and a bunch of orange-colored flowers in her hand.*]

MIEP. Did you hear that, everybody? Did you hear what I said? The invasion has begun! The invasion!

Practice the Skills

9 Key Literary Element

L1 **Mood** In a few words, describe the mood of the scene up to this point.

L2

Teach

L1 Literary Element

Mood Say: If you are uncertain how to describe the mood, consider how reading this part of the scene made you feel. What thoughts or feelings came to mind? *(Possible response: I felt tense and on edge. I was nervous and wanted the fighting to stop. I wanted to know what would happen.)* **BL** **Say:** Use your response to help you determine the mood of the scene. *(Possible response: The mood is serious, fearful, and suspenseful.)* **OL**

L2 Literary Element

Review Stage Directions
Say: Note the stage directions that have Mr. Dussel continue to count the potatoes while the characters talk, despite Mr. Frank's and Margot's pleas. What does this action contribute to the scene? *(Possible response: It emphasizes the desperation of the characters and their downfall into petty fighting.)* **AL**

Differentiated Instruction

Journal Writing Students may benefit from further reflection on the impact the events depicted in the play had on the characters.

Have students write a journal entry that any of the characters other than Anne might have written. Suggest that the journal entry be a description of what that character has learned from his or her experiences in hiding. Encourage students to consider what insights that character may have gained about himself or herself and about others. **OL**

Indiana English/Language Arts Academic Standards
SE: 8.3, 8.3.2, 8.3.6
TWE: *Reading Fluency* 8.7, *Differentiated Instruction* 8.5

Teach

L Literary Element

Review Stage Directions
Ask: Why does Mrs. Frank hug Mr. Van Daan? *(Possible response: The news of the invasion makes Mrs. Frank realize her grievances are unimportant.)* **OL**

R Reading Skill

Interpreting Ask: In addition to being angry at Mr. Van Daan for stealing the food, what else might have contributed to Mrs. Frank's outburst? *(Her frustration with being in hiding and her fear of what could happen to them made her angry at the Van Daans.)* **AL**

READING WORKSHOP 2

[*They all stare at* MIEP, *unable to grasp what she is telling them.* PETER *is the first to recover his wits.*]

PETER. Where?

MRS. VAN DAAN. When? When, Miep?

MIEP. It began early this morning . . .

[*As she talks on, the realization of what she has said begins to dawn on them. Everyone goes crazy. A wild demonstration takes place.* MRS. FRANK *hugs* MR. VAN DAAN.] **L**

MRS. FRANK. Oh, Mr. Van Daan, did you hear that?

[DUSSEL *embraces* MRS. VAN DAAN. PETER *grabs a frying pan and parades around the room, beating on it, singing the Dutch National Anthem.* ANNE *and* MARGOT *follow him, singing, weaving in and out among the excited grown-ups.* MARGOT *breaks away to take the flowers from* MIEP *and distribute them to everyone. While this* **pandemonium** *is going on* MRS. FRANK *tries to make herself heard above the excitement.*]

MRS. FRANK. [*To* MIEP.] How do you know?

MIEP. The radio . . . The B.B.C.! They said they landed on the coast of Normandy![3]

PETER. The British?

MIEP. British, Americans, French, Dutch, Poles, Norwegians . . . all of them! More than four thousand ships! Churchill spoke, and General Eisenhower![4] D-Day they call it!

MR. FRANK. Thank God, it's come!

MRS. VAN DAAN. At last! **10**

3. ***B.B.C.*** stands for British Broadcasting Corporation. ***Normandy*** is a region of France across the English Channel from the southern coast of England.

4. Winston ***Churchill*** was the prime minister of England, and Dwight D. ***Eisenhower*** commanded the Allied forces in Europe.

Vocabulary

pandemonium (pan duh MOH nee um) *n.* wild disorder and uproar

Practice the Skills

10 Key Literary Element

Mood Now describe the mood. Why does Miep's news cause the sudden change? How will the Allied invasion affect the characters?

Additional Support

Differentiated Instruction

Building Background D-Day, also called the Normandy Invasion, occurred on June 6, 1944. France had been taken over by Germany earlier in the war. Many countries—the U.S., England, France, and others—united in an effort to defend Europe against Germany. D-Day was a complicated, highly secret operation to liberate France from the Germans. Decoy plans about an invasion elsewhere were "leaked" to German military strategists to confuse them. On June 6, 150,000 U.S., British, and Canadian forces stormed five separate beaches at Normandy to begin the liberation of France. One of the bloodiest and most costly battles of the war, it was successful and ultimately led to the defeat of Germany. **AS**

MIEP. [*Starting out.*] I'm going to tell Mr. Kraler. This'll be better than any blood transfusion.[5]

MR. FRANK. [*Stopping her.*] What part of Normandy did they land, did they say?

MIEP. Normandy . . . that's all I know now . . . I'll be up the minute I hear some more!

[*She goes hurriedly out.*]

MR. FRANK. [*To* MRS. FRANK.] What did I tell you? What did I tell you?

[MRS. FRANK *indicates that he has forgotten to bolt the door after* MIEP. *He hurries down the steps.* MR. VAN DAAN, *sitting on the couch, suddenly breaks into a convulsive sob. Everybody looks at him, bewildered.*] **11**

MRS. VAN DAAN. [*Hurrying to him.*] Putti! Putti! What is it? What happened?

MR. VAN DAAN. Please. I'm so ashamed. R1

[MR. FRANK *comes back up the steps.*]

DUSSEL. Oh, for God's sake!

MRS. VAN DAAN. Don't, Putti.

MARGOT. It doesn't matter now! R2

MR. FRANK. [*Going to* MR. VAN DAAN.] Didn't you hear what Miep said? The invasion has come! We're going to be **liberated**! This is a time to celebrate!

[*He embraces* MRS. FRANK *and then hurries to the cupboard and gets the cognac and a glass.*]

MR. VAN DAAN. To steal bread from children!

5. A ***blood transfusion*** is the process of transferring blood from a healthy person to a sick person. Evidently, Mr. Kraler's ulcers have made him seriously ill.

Vocabulary

liberated (LIB uh ray tid) *adj.* released; freed

Practice the Skills

11 Key Reading Skill

Interpreting Why does Mr. Van Daan start crying at this particular point?

Literature Focus Lesson

Dramatic Irony When students have completed reading the play, return to this scene and point out its dramatic irony. Remind students that dramatic irony occurs when audience members know something characters onstage do not. In this case, audience members know that the celebration is premature because most of the characters will not survive in time to be liberated by Allied forces. Ask students how watching the characters naively celebrate might have added to the audience members' sadness. **AS**

Teach

R1 Reading Skill

Review Drawing Conclusions
Ask: Why do you think Mr. Van Daan cannot shift his attention to the celebration? *(Possible response: Now that he thinks he will survive and his hiding will end soon, he is very embarrassed by his behavior.)* **OL**

R2 Reading Skill

Interpreting Ask: What does Margot mean when she says that "it doesn't matter now"? *(She means that Mr. Van Daan's theft is no longer of any importance because the war is coming to an end and they are all going to be freed soon.)* **OL** **Ask:** Do you believe the events of the past can be erased? Explain. *(Possible response: They can't be erased, but the other characters can forgive Mr. Van Daan for his fear and greed.)* **AL**

Indiana English/Language Arts Academic Standards
SE: 8.3, 8.3.6
TWE: *Literature Focus Lesson* 8.3.6

Teach

R1 Reading Skill

Review Connecting

Ask: Have you ever admitted guilt or asked for forgiveness after something good happened? *(Responses will vary. Ask volunteers to share their experiences.)* EL BL

Ask: Why might good news cause people to act this way? *(Possible responses: Good things remind us that our behavior can sometimes be petty. Being in a better mood can allow us to see our flaws more clearly)* OL AL

R2 Reading Skill

Review Drawing Conclusions

Ask: What can you conclude about Dussel from his statement that the others are "spoiling the invasion"? *(Possible response: He doesn't really care about the relationships of the other characters. His primary concern is to get out of the attic.)* OL

MRS. FRANK. We've all done things that we're ashamed of.

ANNE. Look at me, the way I've treated Mother . . . so mean and horrid to her.

MRS. FRANK. No, Anneke, no.

[*ANNE runs to her mother, putting her arms around her.*]

ANNE. Oh, Mother, I was. I was awful.

MR. VAN DAAN. Not like me. No one is as bad as me!

DUSSEL. [*To MR. VAN DAAN.*] Stop it now! Let's be happy!

MR. FRANK. [*Giving MR. VAN DAAN a glass of cognac.*] Here! Here! Schnapps! *Locheim!*[6]

[*VAN DAAN takes the cognac. They all watch him. He gives them a feeble smile. ANNE puts up her fingers in a V-for-Victory sign. As VAN DAAN gives an answering V-sign, they are startled to hear a loud sob from behind them. It is MRS. FRANK, stricken with remorse. She is sitting on the other side of the room.*]

MRS. FRANK. [*Through her sobs.*] When I think of the terrible things I said . . .

[*MR. FRANK, ANNE and MARGOT hurry to her, trying to comfort her. MR. VAN DAAN brings her his glass of cognac.*]

MR. VAN DAAN. No! No! You were right!

MRS. FRANK. That I should speak that way to you! . . . Our friends! . . . Our guests!

[*She starts to cry again.*]

DUSSEL. Stop it, you're spoiling the whole invasion! 12 R2

[*As they are comforting her, the lights dim out. The curtain falls.*]

Practice the Skills

12 Key Reading Skill

Interpreting Dussel runs out of patience, but what does he mean here? How are the others "spoiling the invasion"?

6. ***Schnapps*** (shnawps) is a type of cognac, or liquor. ***Locheim!*** (luh KHY um) means "To life!"

Additional Support

Differentiated Instruction

Toasting After hearing the news of the invasion, Mr. Frank toasts "Locheim" (also "L'chaim"), which means "To life!" in Hebrew. Explain that unlike toasts such as "to your health," "Locheim" simply toasts to life itself, suggesting that those proposing the toast appreciate everything in life, including the bad things. The characters are toasting to a future in which life will be good, but they are also toasting to the lives that they have already led, which includes their time in hiding. Challenge students to write an extended toast from the perspective of one of the characters. OL AL

READING WORKSHOP 2

On June 6, 1944, Allied troops landed on the beaches of Normandy, France. The landing was the beginning of the Allied forces' sweep through Europe that eventually defeated Nazi Germany.

ANNE'S VOICE. [*Faintly at first and then with growing strength.*] We're all in much better spirits these days. There's still excellent news of the invasion. The best part about it is that I have a feeling that friends are coming. Who knows? Maybe I'll be back in school by fall. Ha, ha! The joke is on us! The warehouse man doesn't know a thing and we are paying him all that money! . . . Wednesday, the second of July, nineteen forty-four. The invasion seems temporarily to be bogged down. Mr. Kraler has to have an operation, which looks bad. The Gestapo have found the radio that was stolen. Mr. Dussel **C** says they'll trace it back and back to the thief, and then, it's just a matter of time till they get to us. Everyone is low. Even poor Pim can't raise their spirits. I have often been **downcast** myself . . . but never in despair. I can shake off everything if I write. But . . . and that is the great question . . . will I ever be able to write well? I want to so much. I want to go on living even after my death. Another birthday has gone by, so now I am fifteen. Already I know what I want. I have a goal, an opinion. **13** **14**

[*As this is being said—the curtain rises on the scene, the lights dim on, and* ANNE'S VOICE *fades out.*]

Vocabulary

downcast (DOWN kast) *adj.* sad; depressed

Practice the Skills

13 Reviewing Elements

Irony What is ironic—to a reader or theatergoer—about Anne's wondering whether she will ever be able to write well?

14 Key Literary Element

Mood In your own words, describe the mood of this monologue.

Teach

Viewing the Photo

Say: This is a photo of Allied troops landing on one of the beaches in Normandy, France, on D-Day, June 6, 1944. How would the people in the attic feel if they were to see this photo? *(Possible response: They would feel hopeful that they would soon be freed.)* **OL**

C Critical Thinking

Synthesis **Say:** Earlier in the play, Anne noted that, unlike the adults in the attic, she was still trying to develop her opinions. Anne is now only fifteen, but she says "I have a goal, an opinion." Why might Anne have developed goals and opinions so early in her life? *(Possible responses: She is more mature than most teens; she always knew she wanted to do something important; she has had a lot of spare time to consider what she wants.)* **OL**

Differentiated Instruction

Immortality Many writers have expressed the idea that writing can provide a kind of immortality, or life after death. Although writers may die, their thoughts and ideas live on in their words. Ask students to describe how Anne's diary has helped her "to go on living even after [her] death."

- Millions of people know about her life and thoughts.
- Her diary created interest in the attic, which is now a museum visited by thousands every year.
- The diary inspired the play, which has been read and seen by many people.

AL

Indiana English/Language Arts Academic Standards

SE: 8.3, 8.3.6

TWE: *Differentiated Instruction* 8.5, *Differentiated Instruction* 8.3

Teach

L Literary Element

Mood Ask: How does the telephone ringing contribute to the mood at the beginning of this scene? *(Possible response: No one can answer the phone for fear of being found out. The constant ringing adds to the tension.)* OL

R Reading Skill

Interpreting Ask: Why does the ringing of the telephone make the characters so anxious? *(Possible response: Usually someone working in the office below would answer the phone, but there is no one at work on this day. The characters are anxious because it's very odd that no one would be working on a Friday.)* OL

C Critical Thinking

Comprehension Ask: What does Mr. Dussel conclude? *(He concludes Mr. Kraler is dead.)* OL **Ask:** Why might he draw this conclusion? *(Possible responses: Everyone is nervous, Mr. Kraler has been ill, and Mr. Dussel often expects the worst.)* AL

SCENE 4

[It is an afternoon a few weeks later . . . Everyone but MARGOT *is in the main room. There is a sense of great tension. Both* MRS. FRANK *and* MR. VAN DAAN *are nervously pacing back and forth,* DUSSEL *is standing at the window, looking down fixedly at the street below.* PETER *is at the center table, trying to do his lessons.* ANNE *sits opposite him, writing in her diary.* MRS. VAN DAAN *is seated on the couch, her eyes on* MR. FRANK *as he sits reading. The sound of a telephone ringing comes from the office below. They all are rigid, listening tensely.* MR. DUSSEL *rushes down to* MR. FRANK.*]* 15

DUSSEL. There it goes again, the telephone! Mr. Frank, do you hear?

MR. FRANK. *[Quietly.]* Yes. I hear.

DUSSEL. *[Pleading, insistent.]* But this is the third time, Mr. Frank! The third time in quick succession! It's a signal! I tell you it's Miep, trying to get us! For some reason she can't come to us and she's trying to warn us of something!

MR. FRANK. Please. Please.

MR. VAN DAAN. *[To* DUSSEL.*]* You're wasting your breath.

DUSSEL. Something has happened, Mr. Frank. For three days now Miep hasn't been to see us! And today not a man has come to work. There hasn't been a sound in the building!

MRS. FRANK. Perhaps it's Sunday. We may have lost track of the days.

MR. VAN DAAN. *[To* ANNE.*]* You with the diary there. What day is it?

DUSSEL. *[Going to* MRS. FRANK.*]* I don't lose track of the days! I know exactly what day it is! It's Friday, the fourth of August. Friday, and not a man at work. *[He rushes back to* MR. FRANK, *pleading with him, almost in tears.]* I tell you Mr. Kraler's dead. That's the only explanation. He's dead and they've closed down the building, and Miep's trying to tell us!

Practice the Skills

15 Key Literary Element

Mood Even before anyone speaks, an audience would notice a sharp mood change. In reading these stage directions, what words and phrases tell you about the mood?

Additional Support

Literature Focus Lesson

Climax Remind students that the climax is the point of highest tension in a play or other narrative. Tell students that the climax occurs in this, the most emotional scene of the play. After reading scene 4, have students point out how the writers use suspense to build to the climax:

- The phone rings and no one answers it.
- The characters sit in terror wondering who has called.
- Miep hasn't come in three days, and Mr. Kraler hasn't gone to work in the office below.
- Pounding is heard and the door is forced open. This is the climax of the play. OL

MR. FRANK. She'd never telephone us.

DUSSEL. [*Frantic.*] Mr. Frank, answer that! I beg you, answer it!

MR. FRANK. No.

MR. VAN DAAN. Just pick it up and listen. You don't have to speak. Just listen and see if it's Miep.

DUSSEL. [*Speaking at the same time.*] For God's sake . . . I ask you. **16**

MR. FRANK. No. I've told you, no. I'll do nothing that might let anyone know we're in the building.

PETER. Mr. Frank's right.

MR. VAN DAAN. There's no need to tell us what side you're on.

MR. FRANK. If we wait patiently, quietly, I believe that help will come. **BQ**

[*There is silence for a minute as they all listen to the telephone ringing.*]

DUSSEL. I'm going down. [*He rushes down the steps.* MR. FRANK *tries ineffectually*[7] *to hold him.* DUSSEL *runs to the lower door, unbolting it. The telephone stops ringing.* DUSSEL *bolts the door and comes slowly back up the steps.*] Too late. [MR. FRANK *goes to* MARGOT *in* ANNE'S *bedroom.*]

MR. VAN DAAN. So we just wait here until we die.

MRS. VAN DAAN. [*Hysterically.*] I can't stand it! I'll kill myself! I'll kill myself! **L**

MR. VAN DAAN. For God's sake, stop it!

[*In the distance, a German military band is heard playing a Viennese waltz.*] **17**

MRS. VAN DAAN. I think you'd be glad if I did! I think you want me to die!

7. ***Ineffectually*** means "without effect; uselessly."

Practice the Skills

16 Reviewing Skills

Connecting Answering might give them away if the caller is not Miep. If it is Miep, she may have important information. What would you do? **R**

17 Key Literary Element

Mood Viennese waltzes are music for happy occasions. What do you think would be the effect on theatergoers of hearing a waltz in the background?

Teach

R Reading Skill

Interpreting Ask: What might be the effect of the ringing telephone on the audience? Why does it have this effect? *(Possible response: The ringing probably makes the audience feel anxious or on edge because they will want someone to answer it or at least stop the noise.)* **OL**

BQ BIG Question

Say: Mr. Frank states that the group should remain calm and that he believes "help will come." Think about what you know of Mr. Frank. How do you think he has managed to stay hopeful during all this time in the attic? *(Possible response: Mr. Frank is a calm, logical person. He probably uses his logic and his faith to stay hopeful.)* **AL**

L Literary Element

Mood Ask: What mood is created by the actions and words of Dussel and Mr. and Mrs. Van Daan? *(A desperate, terrifying mood is created.)* **AS**

Differentiated Instruction

Music and Mood Have students interested in music choose a song that they think best conveys the mood of this highly emotional and intense scene. Tell students that if the song has lyrics, they do not need to match the story's content or theme; however, they should be appropriate for a class setting. Ask students to play a portion of their song for the class. Have the class evaluate the choices. **EL BL OL**

Indiana English/Language Arts Academic Standards

SE: 8.3, 8.3.6

TWE: *Literature Focus Lesson* 8.3.2, *Differentiated Instruction* 8.2

Teach

L Literary Element

Mood **Say:** Contrast the mood as the Van Daans talk and the mood in Anne's monologue. *(The mood as the Van Daans talk is angry, accusatory, and mean. The mood in Anne's monologue is quieter and more celebratory.)* AL

BQ BIG Question

Ask: Do you think Anne is simply refusing to believe what is going on around her? Explain. *(Possible response: Anne is not in denial; she is choosing to focus on positive things to keep from giving up.)* OL

MR. VAN DAAN. Whose fault is it we're here? [*MRS. VAN DAAN starts for her room. He follows, talking at her.*] We could've been safe somewhere . . . in America or Switzerland. But no! No! You wouldn't leave when I wanted to. You couldn't leave your things. You couldn't leave your precious furniture. 18

MRS. VAN DAAN. Don't touch me!

[*She hurries up the stairs, followed by MR. VAN DAAN. PETER, unable to bear it, goes to his room. ANNE looks after him, deeply concerned. DUSSEL returns to his post at the window. MR. FRANK comes back into the main room and takes a book, trying to read. MRS. FRANK sits near the sink, starting to peel some potatoes. ANNE quietly goes to PETER's room, closing the door after her. PETER is lying face down on the cot. ANNE leans over him, holding him in her arms, trying to bring him out of his despair.*] L

ANNE. Look, Peter, the sky. [*She looks up through the skylight.*] What a lovely, lovely day! Aren't the clouds beautiful? You know what I do when it seems as if I couldn't stand being cooped up for one more minute? I think myself out. I think myself on a walk in the park where I used to go with Pim. Where the jonquils and the crocus and the violets grow down the slopes. You know the most wonderful part about thinking yourself out? You can have it any way you like. You can have roses and violets and chrysanthemums all blooming at the same time . . . It's funny . . . I used to take it all for granted . . . and now I've gone crazy about everything to do with nature. Haven't you? 19

PETER. I've just gone crazy. I think if something doesn't happen soon . . . if we don't get out of here . . . I can't stand much more of it!

ANNE. [*Softly.*] I wish you had a religion, Peter.

PETER. No, thanks! Not me!

ANNE. Oh, I don't mean you have to be Orthodox . . . or believe in heaven and hell and purgatory[8] and things . . . I just mean some religion . . . it doesn't matter what. Just to R

8. The ***Orthodox*** branch of Judaism is the most traditional, requiring strict obedience to ancient laws and customs. ***Purgatory*** is, some believe, a place of temporary punishment for the souls of the dead.

Practice the Skills

18 Reviewing Skills

Character What does Mr. Van Daan reveal about himself in the way he treats his wife?

19 BIG Question

What does Anne mean by "I think myself out"? In your own words, explain what she's doing to survive this extremely tense time. Write your answer on the Workshop 2 Foldable for Unit 6. BQ

Additional Support

Reading in the Real World

Citizenship Simon Wiesenthal was a Holocaust survivor who dedicated his life to documenting the crimes of the Holocaust and bringing Nazis to justice. In his book, *The Sunflower: On the Possibilities and Limits of Forgiveness,* he discusses that when he was in the concentration camp, a dying Nazi soldier asked him for forgiveness. Wiesenthal later asked many famous thinkers, including religious leaders and other Nazi victims, to tell what they would have done in this circumstance. Have students discuss how they might have responded to the soldier. What are the benefits of forgiveness? AL believe in something! When I think of all that's out there . . . the trees . . . and flowers . . . and seagulls . . . when I think of the dearness of you, Peter . . . and the goodness of the people we know . . . Mr. Kraler, Miep, Dirk, the vegetable man, all risking their lives for us every day . . . When I think of these good things, I'm not afraid any more . . . I find myself, and God, and I . . . **R**

[PETER *interrupts, getting up and walking away.*]

PETER. That's fine! But when I begin to think, I get mad! Look at us, hiding out for two years. Not able to move! Caught here like . . . waiting for them to come and get us . . . and all for what?

ANNE. We're not the only people that've had to suffer. There've always been people that've had to . . . sometimes one race . . . sometimes another . . . and yet . . .

PETER. That doesn't make me feel any better! **20**

ANNE. [*Going to him.*] I know it's terrible, trying to have any faith . . . when people are doing such horrible . . . But you know what I sometimes think? I think the world may be going through a phase, the way I was with Mother. It'll pass, maybe not for hundreds of years, but someday . . . I still believe, in spite of everything, that people are really good at heart. **21**

PETER. I want to see something now . . . Not a thousand years from now!

[*He goes over, sitting down again on the cot.*]

ANNE. But, Peter, if you'd only look at it as part of a great pattern . . . that we're just a little minute in the life . . . [*She breaks off.*] Listen to us, going at each other like a couple of stupid grown-ups! Look at the sky now. Isn't it lovely? [*She holds out her hand to him.* PETER *takes it and rises, standing with her at the window looking out, his arms around her.*] Someday, when we're outside again, I'm going to . . .

Practice the Skills

20 Reviewing Skills

Comparing and Contrasting Explain the difference in the views that Anne and Peter have been expressing.

21 BIG Question

Do you agree with Anne? How would this belief help her–or anyone–want to keep going despite terrible times? Write your answer on the Workshop 2 Foldable for Unit 6. **BQ**

Teach

R Reviewing Skill

Interpreting Ask: How would you describe Anne's definition of religion? *(Possible response: Anne describes religion as believing in something, or having faith in the world.)* **BL** **Ask:** What do you think she really wants for Peter? *(Possible response: She wants Peter to see the goodness of people, to be hopeful, and not to be afraid.)* **AL**

BQ BIG Question

Say: Suppose that you were one of the characters in hiding. Would you be able to believe that people are naturally good at heart? Explain. *(Responses will vary.)* **AS**

Differentiated Instruction

Designing Costumes Explain to students that making costumes for a drama is very important because clothes can reveal something about a character. In a play set in another time, costumes also contribute to the authenticity of the play's setting. Have students design costumes for two of the play's characters, using clues from the play and research about clothing at the time of the play's setting. The costumes should be consistent with each character, and students should explain why they chose the particular details of each costume. Students may wish to use photographs from film and theater adaptations for ideas. **OL**

Indiana English/Language Arts Academic Standards
SE: 8.3
TWE: *Reading in the Real World* 8.7, *Differentiated Instruction* 8.3

Teach

R Reading Skill

Interpreting **Ask:** How does Mr. Frank's statement that they can "live in hope" reflect his personality? *(Possible response: The statement reflects his calmness, his hopeful personality, and his refusal to give up.)* OL

L Literary Element

Review Stage Directions
Say: The first paragraph of the stage directions does not indicate how Anne reacts during this part of the scene. How do you imagine she would look and act? Why? *(Responses will vary. Some students may suggest that Anne would be calm and cooperative because she has peacefully accepted her situation. Others may suggest that she would be stricken with fear because she does not know what will happen to her family.)* AL

[She breaks off as she hears the sound of a car, its brakes squealing as it comes to a sudden stop. The people in the other rooms also become aware of the sound. They listen tensely. Another car roars up to a screeching stop. ANNE *and* PETER *come from* PETER*'s room.* MR. *and* MRS. VAN DAAN *creep down the stairs.* DUSSEL *comes out from his room. Everyone is listening, hardly breathing. A doorbell clangs again and again in the building below.* MR. FRANK *starts quietly down the steps to the door.* DUSSEL *and* PETER *follow him. The others stand rigid, waiting, terrified.*

In a few seconds DUSSEL *comes stumbling back up the steps. He shakes off* PETER*'s help and goes to his room.* MR. FRANK *bolts the door below, and comes slowly back up the steps. Their eyes are all on him as he stands there for a minute. They realize that what they feared has happened.* MRS. VAN DAAN *starts to whimper.* MR. VAN DAAN *puts her gently in a chair, and then hurries off up the stairs to their room to collect their things.* PETER *goes to comfort his mother. There is a sound of violent pounding on a door below.]*

MR. FRANK. [*Quietly.*] For the past two years we have lived in fear. Now we can live in hope. 22 R

[The pounding below becomes more insistent. There are muffled sounds of voices, shouting commands.]

MEN'S VOICES. Auf machen! Da drinnen! Auf machen! Schnell! Schnell! Schnell![9] etc., etc.

[The street door below is forced open. We hear the heavy tread of footsteps coming up. MR. FRANK *gets two school bags from the shelves, and gives one to* ANNE *and the other to* MARGOT. *He goes to get a bag for* MRS. FRANK. *The sound of feet coming up grows louder.* PETER *comes to* ANNE, *kissing her good-bye, then he goes to his room to collect his things. The buzzer of their door starts to ring.* MR. FRANK *brings* MRS. FRANK *a bag. They stand together, waiting. We hear the thud of gun butts on the door, trying to break it down.*

9. The voices are saying, in German: "Open up! Inside there! Open up! Quick! Quick! Quick!" The abbreviation *etc.* means "and so on." The actors are supposed to keep speaking until the curtain falls.

Practice the Skills

22 Key Reading Skill

Interpreting What do you think Mr. Frank means?

Additional Support

Reading in the Real World

Citizenship In many ways, Mr. Frank serves as the group's leader for the duration of the play. Have students brainstorm the qualities of a good leader and record their ideas on the board. Then, ask students to recall examples of things that Mr. Frank does as leader of the group in hiding. Have students evaluate Mr. Frank's leadership qualities, according to the list on the board. Is Mr. Frank a good leader? Why or why not? Discuss why Mr. Frank takes certain actions and what effect his decisions have on the other characters. OL

ANNE stands, holding her school satchel, looking over at her father and mother with a soft, reassuring smile. She is no longer a child, but a woman with courage to meet whatever lies ahead.

The lights dim out. The curtain falls on the scene. We hear a mighty crash as the door is shattered. After a second ANNE'S VOICE is heard.]

ANNE'S VOICE. And so it seems our stay here is over. They are waiting for us now. They've allowed us five minutes to get our things. We can each take a bag and whatever it will hold of clothing. Nothing else. So, dear Diary, that means I must leave you behind. Good-bye for a while. P.S. Please, please, Miep, or Mr. Kraler, or anyone else. If you should find this diary, will you please keep it safe for me, because some day I hope . . .

[*Her voice stops abruptly. There is silence. After a second the curtain rises.*] **23**

Practice the Skills

23 Key Reading Skill

Interpreting Why does her voice stop abruptly? What happened to Anne at this moment as she was writing?

This photograph shows the railway entrance to Auschwitz, one of the Nazi concentration camps.

Differentiated Instruction

Diary Entry Point out to students that Anne never has a chance to continue writing in her diary. Tell students to rewrite Anne's last entry, imagining that Anne knew these words would be the last she would write. What would she say? What advice would she offer? What memories of living in the attic would she recall? What are her hopes? Suggest that students use what they know about Anne and her writing style to complete the entry in Anne's voice. Invite volunteers to share their entries with the class. **OL**

READING WORKSHOP 2

Teach

L Literary Element

Review Stage Directions
Ask: What is the "mighty crash" that is heard? What might it symbolize? *(The crash comes from the shattering of the door to the building. Some students may suggest that it symbolizes the shattering of the characters' lives or of the Frank and Van Daan families.)* **OL** **AL**

R Reading Skill

Interpreting Ask: What does the abrupt ending show about when Anne wrote this entry? *(Anne wrote this last entry in the five minutes that she was given before being taken away.)* **OL**

Viewing the Photo

Remind students that mood is the emotional effect it has on the reader or viewer. **Ask:** How does this photograph make you feel and why? *(Possible response: The mood is eerie, dark, and cold. There is no life in this photo, only an empty railroad that was probably used for transporting prisoners to the camp, abandoned possessions that probably once belonged to the prisoners, and the intimidating, dark building of the camp where perhaps many prisoners were killed. I feel sad and helpless looking at this photo.)* **OL**

Indiana English/Language Arts Academic Standards
SE: 8.3
TWE: *Reading in the Real World* 8.3, *Differentiated Instruction* 8.5.7

Teach

L Literary Element

Mood **Say:** When the play first begins, Mr. Frank is very upset. How do you think he feels at this point, after he has read Anne's diary? *(Responses will vary. Some students may say that he feels sad, lost, or desolate. Others may say that he feels comforted.)* OL

C Critical Thinking

Comprehension **Ask:** What questions from the play are answered by Miep and Mr. Kraler? *(Where was Miep? How did the Nazi police find out the people were in the attic?)* BL

READING WORKSHOP 2

Analyzing the Photo Describe what you see in this photo. Do you think it does a good job of representing the play's ending?

SCENE 5

[*It is again the afternoon in November, 1945. The rooms are as we saw them in the first scene.* MR. KRALER *has joined* MIEP *and* MR. FRANK. *There are coffee cups on the table. We see a great change in* MR. FRANK. *He is calm now. His bitterness is gone. He slowly turns a few pages of the diary. They are blank.*] **24**

MR. FRANK. No more.

[*He closes the diary and puts it down on the couch beside him.*]

MIEP. I'd gone to the country to find food. When I got back the block was surrounded by police . . .

MR. KRALER. We made it our business to learn how they knew. It was the thief . . . the thief who told them.

[MIEP *goes up to the gas burner, bringing back a pot of coffee.*]

Practice the Skills

24 Key Literary Element

Mood This scene goes back to the time of act 1, scene 1. It is more than a year since the Germans took Anne and the others away. As you read, think about the mood, or emotional effect, of this scene and of the whole play.

Additional Support

Literature Focus Lesson

Theme Anne's belief that "people are really good at heart" is one of the main themes, or messages, of the play. Discuss with students which events and people in the play support this theme and which do not. OL For further discussion, have students state why Anne might have believed in people's goodness despite everything that happened to her. How would this belief help her carry on during the most difficult times? AL

MR. FRANK. [*After a pause.*] It seems strange to say this, that anyone could be happy in a concentration camp. But Anne was happy in the camp in Holland where they first took us. After two years of being shut up in these rooms, she could be out . . . out in the sunshine and the fresh air that she loved.

MIEP. [*Offering the coffee to* MR. FRANK.] A little more?

MR. FRANK. [*Holding out his cup to her.*] The news of the war was good. The British and Americans were sweeping through France. We felt sure that they would get to us in time. In September we were told that we were to be shipped to Poland . . . The men to one camp. The women to another. I was sent to Auschwitz. They went to Belsen. In January we were freed, the few of us who were left. The war wasn't yet over, so it took us a long time to get home. We'd be sent here and there behind the lines where we'd be safe. Each time our train would stop . . . at a siding, or a crossing . . . we'd all get out and go from group to group . . . Where were you? Were you at Belsen? At Buchenwald? At Mauthausen?[10] Is it possible that you knew my wife? Did you ever see my husband? My son? My daughter? That's how I found out about my wife's death . . . of Margot, the Van Daans . . . Dussel. But Anne . . . I still hoped . . . Yesterday I went to Rotterdam.[11] I'd heard of a woman there . . . She'd been in Belsen with Anne . . . I know now. **25**

[*He picks up the diary again, and turns the pages back to find a certain passage. As he finds it we hear* ANNE'S VOICE.]

ANNE'S VOICE. In spite of everything, I still believe that people are really good at heart.

[MR. FRANK *slowly closes the diary.*]

MR. FRANK. She puts me to shame.

[*They are silent.*]

THE CURTAIN FALLS ❍

10. ***Auschwitz*** (OWSH vitz), ***Belsen*** (BEL zun), ***Buchenwald*** (BOO kun vawlt), and ***Mauthausen*** were the sites of Nazi concentration camps in Poland, Austria, and Germany. These camps specialized in exterminating prisoners.

11. ***Rotterdam*** is a city in the southwestern Netherlands.

Practice the Skills

25 Key Reading Skill

Interpreting What does Mr. Frank "know now"?

Differentiated Instruction

Audience Tell students that *The Diary of Anne Frank* had its German opening in seven cities simultaneously on October 1, 1956. At the end of the play, the audiences sat in shocked silence without applauding. Shortly after, Germans began openly expressing remorse for the Holocaust. Since the end of the war, Germans had not publicly spoken about the Nazis' reign of terror. Lead students in a discussion about the effect of the play. Use the following questions to prompt students: Why were audiences silent? Why didn't Germans talk about the Holocaust immediately after the war? How did the play help people talk about the Holocaust? **AS**

Teach

C Critical Thinking

Comprehension Ask: How does Mr. Frank find out what happened to Anne? *(Mr. Frank hears the news of Anne's death from a woman who was in the camp with Anne.)* **BL**

R Reading Skill

Review Analyzing Ask: Why does Mr. Frank say that Anne puts him to shame? *(Possible response: Mr. Frank may have lost his faith in humanity and feels shame that his daughter maintained it to the very end.)* **OL**

L Literary Element

Mood Ask: How would you describe the mood at the end of the play? *(Responses will vary. Students may note that the mood is one of great sadness but also one of hope because of Anne's words.)* **OL**

Assess

Use the CheckPoint questions provided on Presentation Plus! to check for comprehension of the selection. These questions can be used with interactive response keypads for immediate student feedback.

Indiana English/Language Arts Academic Standards
SE: 8.3, 8.3.6
TWE: *Literature Focus Lesson* 8.3, *Differentiated Instruction* 8.7

Assess

Resources for page 844

- Selection Quick Check, p. 54
- Selection and Unit Assessment, p. 64
- ExamView Assessment Suite
- Interactive Tutor: Self-Assessment

Students can respond to the *After You Read* items in their Learner's Notebooks or on a separate sheet of paper.

Answering the BIG Question

1. Possible response: Although none of the characters gives up entirely, Anne is the only one who does not give in to moments of despair.
2. Miep brings orange flowers.
3. Mrs. Frank wants him to leave; Mr. Frank tries to calm his wife; Mrs. Van Daan excuses her husband; Peter is ashamed.

Critical Thinking

4. Possible response: Anne's views are based on her faith in life and in people. Peter's views are based on his fear of life and of people.
5. Possible response: Anne is open and outgoing. It makes sense she would focus on people's goodness.
6. Possible response: Anne's situation forced her to consider things other teens don't have to, making her grow up faster.
7. Responses will vary.

After You Read

The Diary of Anne Frank, Act 2, Scenes 3–5

Answering the BIG Question

1. Anne is a good example of someone who never gives up. How do the others hiding in the attic compare with her?
2. **Recall** What does Miep bring with her when she returns to announce that the invasion has begun?
   TIP **Right There**
3. **Summarize** How do the others react when they catch Mr. Van Daan stealing the bread?
   TIP **Think and Search**

Critical Thinking

4. **Analyze** What accounts for the difference between Peter's and Anne's view of their situation? Explain your answer with details from the play.
   TIP **Author and Me**
5. **Explain** Are you surprised by Anne's views on the war and about people in general? Explain.
   TIP **Author and Me**
6. **Evaluate** Do you think Anne would have grown up as fast as she does if she hadn't gone into hiding? Would she have learned the same lessons if she had had a normal childhood?
   TIP **Author and Me**
7. **Interpret** At the end of the play, Mr. Frank feels shamed by the part of Anne's diary that says, "I still believe that people are really good at heart." What does his comment suggest about his own belief in people's goodness? Do you think his belief changed over the three years since the family went into hiding? Explain your answers.
   TIP **Author and Me**

Indiana English/Language Arts Academic Standards (pp. 844–845)

8.3 Comprehension and Analysis of Literary Text Respond to grade-level-approriate literature... **8.5.2** Write response to literature... **8.3.6** Identify significant literary devices... **8.6.5** Use correct punctuation.

For a complete description of the standards, see p. IN 11.

Write About Your Reading

Monologue Imagine how this story would be different if it were told from Miep's point of view. Write a monologue from her perspective, similar to the excerpts from Anne's diary. Include these elements:

- how you feel about the actions of the Nazis
- what you think life must have been like for the Franks and the others
- why you decided to act the way you did
- how you feel about Anne and what happened to her

Write About Your Reading

Possible response:

What the Nazis did was wrong, and many German and Dutch people agreed. However, too many people were scared to defy the Nazis. I believed that it was my duty to act against them. I did not want to live in a world without people like Anne. If the Franks were brave enough to endure hiding like rats in an attic, then I could be brave enough to help them. What happened to Anne is tragic. She was a beautiful, young, vibrant girl, and she deserved to live in peace. I believe that there will be peace in the world—someday. I am sad Anne did not live to see it.

Skills Review

Key Reading Skill: Interpreting

8. "In spite of everything, I still believe that people are really good at heart." What does this famous sentence of Anne's mean to you?

Key Literary Element: Mood

9. In two or three words, describe the mood of the last scene of the play.

10. What overall mood for the entire play do you think the playwrights wanted to create for an audience of theatergoers? Explain.

Reviewing Skills: Drawing Conclusions

11. At the end of the play, Mr. Frank knows but doesn't directly say what became of Anne. What happened to her? How do you know?

Reviewing Elements: Stage Directions

12. The second-to-last line of the script is this stage direction: [*They are silent.*] What reason(s) might the playwrights have had for including this?

Vocabulary Check

Rewrite each sentence with the best word from the list.

stealthily **pandemonium** **liberated** **downcast**

13. ___ from the shed, the dog licked my face and then raced around the yard.

14. The robber entered ___, skillfully avoiding the guards posted at the main entrance.

15. "Don't be ___," the coach said. "Be proud that you did the very best you could."

16. There was ___ as police officers tried to control the angry protestors.

17. **English Language Coach** Below are the origins of two vocabulary words. Which word has Anglo-Saxon roots? Hint: Review the English Language Coach on page 824.

- **stealth** [ME *stelthe*, akin to OE *stelan* to steal]
- **pandemonium** [NL, fr Gk *pan-* all, every + *daimon* evil spirit]

Grammar Link: Commas with Appositives

Appositives are nouns or pronouns that rename, add more information about, or identify other nouns. Appositives can be either nonessential or essential. A nonessential appositive renames the noun or adds more information about it. The meaning of the sentence won't change if you read it without the appositive. Set off a nonessential appositive with commas.

- My sister, Maria, is the best singer. (Maria renames the noun sister. She is the speaker's only sister.)

An essential appositive identifies another noun or adds information that is necessary to the meaning of the sentence. DON'T set it off with commas.

- My sister Maria is the best singer. (Maria identifies this person as one of the speaker's sisters.)

Appositives can be phrases too. ALWAYS set off an appositive phrase with commas.

- Edison, inventor of the lightbulb, led an amazing life.

Grammar Practice

Rewrite the paragraph below. Find two nonessential appositives, and set them off with commas.

> Our civics teacher Mrs. Riccio loves to read to the class. She read parts of Joan Heilbroner's book *Meet George Washington* to us. She said that Washington our first president was a great statesman.

Writing Application Review the monologue you wrote. Check that you used commas correctly with appositives.

Web Activities For eFlashcards, Selection Quick Checks, and other Web activities, go to www.glencoe.com.

Skills Review

Key Reading Skill: Interpreting

8. Responses will vary.

Key Literary Element: Mood

9. Possible responses: *sad, empty, lonely,* or *regretful*

10. Responses will vary. Some students may say that the playwrights wanted audiences to feel sad or shocked. Some students will say the playwrights wanted the audience to recognize the beauty of life in the most tragic of situations.

Reviewing Skills: Drawing Conclusions

11. Mr. Frank finds out that Anne is dead. He knows because he met a woman who was at Belsen with her.

Reviewing Elements: Stage Directions

12. Responses will vary.

Close

Ask students to tell how learning about the tragedies suffered by people in the past can help them deal with their own hardships.

Vocabulary Check

13. Liberated

14. stealthily

15. downcast

16. pandemonium

English Language Coach

17. stealth

Grammar Link: Commas with Appositives

Grammar Practice

Our civics teacher, Mrs. Riccio, loves to read to the class. She read parts of Joan Heilbroner's book *Meet George Washington* to us. She said that Washington, our first president, was a great statesman.

Indiana English/Language Arts Academic Standards

SE: 8.3, 8.3.6, 8.5.2, 8.6.5

Paraphrasing and Summarizing

Teaching Paraphrasing and Summarizing

Why Is It Important?

- Research shows that summarizing is one of the most effective instructional approaches in fostering comprehension.
- The most effective form of summarizing involves paraphrasing and synthesizing an author's ideas.
- Paraphrasing is one of the processes that helps readers integrate critical reading to recall information, draw inferences, and reinforce comprehension.

How to Help Students Get It

- Emphasize the importance of putting an author's wording into one's own words to foster comprehension.
- Provide opportunities with guided practice in which you model, through think alouds, how you are actually summarizing as you go through a text; put up a transparency of the text that shows how you have located important information through underlining.
- Have students work in pairs to practice summarizing orally with shorter and then longer pieces of text.
- After guided practice on how summarizing works orally, have students jot down main ideas, list important words or phrases that support those ideas, and then rewrite the list into a short summary.

Reading to Answer the Big Question

Bouncing Back by Jan Farrington
This article on how to bounce back after getting knocked down includes stories of real-life resilient teens, tips for dealing with problems, and a mini-questionnaire to help readers measure their own resilience.

Another Mountain by Abiodun Oyewole
The speaker of this poem uses the image of climbing a mountain to represent coping with challenges and problems.

Standing Tall by Michael Dolan
This TIME article explains how architects and engineers are creating new designs and materials to make future skyscrapers that can stand in the face of fires, earthquakes, and even plane crashes.

Workshop Resources

Pacing (Days) Standard	Pacing (Days) Block	Lesson	Student Materials	Teacher Resources
1	1/2	Key Skill Lesson: Paraphrasing and Summarizing	Key Reading Skills Practice, p. 23 English Language Coach Review, p. 42	Bellringer Options Transparencies – Daily Language Practice 57 Read Aloud, Think Aloud Transparencies – Key Reading Skills 16 Presentation Plus!
1	1	"Bouncing Back" and "Another Mountain"	Glencoe Online Unit Vocabulary Review, p. 40 Academic Vocabulary Review, p. 43 English Language Coach Active Reading Graphic Organizer, pp. 24–25 StudentWorks Plus™ Online Student Edition Literature Classics Selection and Unit Assessments, p. 65	Puzzlemaker Skill Level Up!™ A Language Arts Game BookLink 3 Assessment by Learning Objective (Diagnostic and Formative) Interactive Tutor: Self-Assessment TeacherWorks Plus™
1		"Standing Tall"	Glencoe Online Unit Vocabulary Review, p. 40 Academic Vocabulary Review, p. 43 English Language Coach Active Reading Graphic Organizer, p. 27 StudentWorks Plus™ Online Student Edition Literature Classics Selection and Unit Assessments, p. 66	Literary and Text Analysis Transparencies 17 Puzzlemaker Skill Level Up!™ A Language Arts Game BookLink 3 Assessment by Learning Objective (Diagnostic and Formative) Interactive Tutor: Self-Assessment TeacherWorks Plus™

Keys for Unit Resource

- Blackline Master
- Workbook
- Supplemental Text
- CD-ROM
- DVD
- Transparency
- Web-based
- Fast File

Level Appropriate Code

AS = Activities for all students
AL = Activities for students working above grade level
OL = Activities for students working at grade level
BL = Activities for students working below grade level
EL = Activities for English language learners

Focus

BELLRINGER Options

Daily Language Practice Transparency 57

Focus Activity Say: Write a list of people you could talk to if you were having a hard time. Your list can include family, friends, neighbors, teachers, and counselors. Choose one person you think would be most helpful and write a sentence telling why. *(Responses will vary.)* **OL**

Teach

R Reading Skill

Paraphrasing and Summarizing Ask: Imagine a sixth grader wants to learn about dinosaurs but has a hard time reading some of the longer words in the encyclopedia article she is reading. How could you use the reading techniques on this page to help her learn about dinosaurs? *(Possible response: You could paraphrase the information, or tell it in simpler words that the sixth grader could understand.)* **OL**

READING WORKSHOP 3

Skills Focus

You will practice these skills when you read the following selections:

- Bouncing Back, p. 850
- Another Mountain, p. 856
- Standing Tall, p. 862

Reading

- Paraphrasing and summarizing

Literature

- Identifying and analyzing figurative language
- Understanding expository writing

Vocabulary

- Understanding Greek roots
- Understanding content-area words

Writing/Grammar

- Using commas with relative clauses
- Using commas with direct address

Skill Lesson

Paraphrasing and Summarizing

Learn It!

What Is It? Paraphrasing is restating something in your own words that you've read. If a friend asks you to help him understand something from class, you probably paraphrase the teacher's words.

R **Summarizing** is retelling the main events and ideas of a selection in your own words. You might summarize the first part of a movie for a friend who arrived late. When you summarize, it is important to put your ideas in a logical sequence. The order in which you summarize the main ideas or events should match the order in the selection.

Analyzing Cartoons
Why does Calvin want Hobbes to summarize the book? How would you summarize this cartoon if you were telling a friend about it?

Indiana English/Language Arts Academic Standards (pp. 846–847)

8.2 Comprehension and Analysis (Focus on Informational Text) Develop [reading] strategies...

For a complete description of the standards, see p. IN 11.

Additional Support

Literature Focus Lesson

Comic Strips Comic strips, like the one on this page, offer snapshots, or summaries, of the characters' adventures. Tell students to think about an event they experienced that involved them and one or two other people. Have students summarize the event in a three- or four-box comic strip. Remind students that comics convey information through illustrations and dialogue. Students should put dialogue in a bubble, as in the strip on this page. Explain that drawings do not have to be elaborate; stick figures will suffice. **BL** **OL**

R1 **Why Is It Important?** Paraphrasing and summarizing are helpful when you read long selections that contain lots of details. You can paraphrase to check whether you've understood an idea, and you can summarize to make sure that you've understood a paragraph, a selection, or even an entire book. Summarizing can also help you separate main ideas from supporting information and unnecessary details.

Study Central Visit www.glencoe.com and click on Study Central to review paraphrasing and summarizing.

How Do I Do It? To summarize, note major ideas and events as you read. When you come to the end of a section, ask yourself what it was about. Then put that information in an order that makes sense. To paraphrase, be on the lookout for passages that are complicated or hard to understand. When you read something that is difficult, try to restate it in your own words. Here's how one student paraphrased one of Anne's speeches in *The Diary of Anne Frank:* R2

> Oh, I don't mean you have to be Orthodox . . . or believe in heaven and hell and purgatory and things . . . I just mean some religion . . . it doesn't matter what. Just to believe in something! When I think of all that's out there . . . the trees . . . and flowers . . . and seagulls . . . when I think of the dearness of you, Peter . . . and the goodness of the people we know . . . Mr. Kraler, Miep, Dirk, the vegetable man, all risking their lives for us every day . . . When I think of these good things, I'm not afraid any more . . .

Anne is trying to explain how she keeps from giving up during difficult times. By focusing on the beauty of nature, the joy of relationships, and the goodness of people, she avoids being overcome with fear. She wants Peter to think this way too.

Practice It!

Choose a cartoon strip or an episode of a TV show that you remember well. Think about the main ideas and events and then write a summary in your Learner's Notebook. Remember to write the events in a logical sequence.

Use It!

As you read the selections in this workshop, use paraphrasing and summarizing to check whether you understand the more difficult parts.

Reading in the Real World

Career Critics often begin reviews of books, plays, and movies with short summaries. These summaries do not give away the climax or resolution. Instead, critics provide just enough information to catch readers' interest and to help them understand what a work is about. If possible, clip some reviews from a newspaper or magazine, and ask students to identify the summaries that appear in these reviews. **BL** Challenge students to write a short review of a movie or TV show they've seen recently. Students should include a brief summary and their opinion of the story. **OL**

Teach

Study Central Have students access the Web site to review paraphrasing and summarizing and to complete a related activity.

R1 Reading Skill

Paraphrasing and Summarizing **Ask:** Which details should you include in a summary? *(Possible response: details that are important to the main idea and that further explain or support the main idea)* **BL**

R2 Reading Skill

Paraphrasing and Summarizing **Ask:** What kinds of passages or sentences should you paraphrase? *(ones that are complicated or hard to understand)* **BL** **Ask:** What resources could you use to help you paraphrase? *(Possible responses: dictionary, thesaurus)* **OL**

Resources for page 847

- Use Key Reading Skills Transparency 16 in *Read Aloud, Think Aloud* to help students practice paraphrasing and summarizing.

Indiana English/Language Arts Academic Standards
SE: 8.2
TWE: *Literature Focus Lesson* 8.5, *Reading in the Real World* 8.5

Teach

More About the Author

Jan Farrington has written for *Current Health*, a periodical aimed at middle- and high-school students. Articles in *Current Health* address nutrition, fitness, mental health, and other health-related issues important to teens.

Abiodun Oyewole grew up in Queens, New York. He was inspired to write poetry by reading the poems of Langston Hughes and by listening to music. He is a member of a group of poets called the Last Poets. In strong, memorable voices, the Last Poets call for social change or, as in Oyewole's poem "Two Little Boys," for people to "come together to create."

Before You Read

Bouncing Back *and* Another Mountain

Meet the Authors

Jan Farrington is a freelance writer who contributes to *Current Health* and other publications.

Abiodun Oyewole's poetry often focuses on the damage done by racism and on the need to heal after being wounded. He once said, "We have to see how we can be the greatest part of us, which is the healing part of us. . . . I'd rather that folks learn how to save themselves." See page R5 of the Author Files for more on Oyewole.

Author Search For more about Abiodun Oyewole, go to www.glencoe.com.

Indiana English/Language Arts Academic Standards (pp. 848–857)

8.1.2 Understand the influence of historical events on English word meanings... **8.2 Comprehension and Analysis (Focus on Informational Text)** Develop [reading] strategies... **8.3.6** Identify significant literary devices...

For a complete description of the standards, see p. IN 11.

Vocabulary Preview

unfulfilling (un ful FIL ing) *adj.* not satisfying **(p. 850)** *We all want to be happy in our work; nobody grows up thinking, "Gee, I hope I'll be able to find an unfulfilling career!"*

resilient (rih ZIL yunt) *adj.* able to recover from or adjust easily to misfortune or change **(p. 850)** *Some people are resilient, while others can't seem to adjust well to challenges.*

strategies (STRAT uh jeez) *n.* plans for working through a problem or activity **(p. 851)** *Fortunately, there are several good strategies for dealing with the difficulties life may present.*

phase (fayz) *n.* a step in the development of a person or thing **(p. 853)** *Most teens go through a phase in which they question the "rules."*

destitute (DES tuh toot) *adj.* completely without money or possessions **(p. 853)** *For a destitute family, even macaroni and cheese can be a luxury.*

Partner Work With a partner, write four sentences about being a teenager. Use at least one vocabulary word in each sentence.

English Language Coach

Greek Roots and Combining Forms The Greek language gave English not only roots, prefixes, and suffixes, but word parts called **combining forms**. A combining form occurs only in combination with words, affixes, or other combining forms to form compounds such as *geophysics* and *geology*. In the first word, the combining form *geo-* is added to the word *physics*. In the second word, it's added to another combining form, *-logy*.

The Greek civilization was one of the earliest to form ideas about politics and education. As a result, many English words that have to do with government and learning come from the Greek roots and combining forms. Here are a few examples.

Root or combining form	Meaning	English word
arch	➡ govern, rule	➡ monarch
auto	➡ self	➡ automatic, automobile
bio	➡ life	➡ biology, biography
log, logy	➡ word, study, speech	➡ dialogue, biology

Additional Support

Author Search To expand students' appreciation of Jan Farrington and Abiodun Oyewole, have them access the Web site for additional information and resources.

English Language Coach

Greek Roots Challenge students to think of more words about government and learning that contain the roots listed below.

- *poli:* city *(police, political)*
- *sci:* know *(science, conscience)*
- *gnos:* know *(diagnose, prognosis)*
- *soph:* wise *(philosopher, sophisticated)*

AS

Skills Preview

Key Reading Skill: Paraphrasing and Summarizing

You probably paraphrase and summarize every day. When a friend asks about a homework assignment, you don't repeat the teacher's exact words. You paraphrase. When your parents ask what you learned in school, you don't list every single detail. You summarize.

Write to Learn Think of a story you know well. In your Learner's Notebook, summarize the story.

Literary Element: Literal and Figurative Language

Most of the time, people use words to state simple facts. When they do so, they use **literal language,** or language that uses words according to their exact definitions. "The sky at night is black with white stars" is an example of literal language.

People use **figurative language,** or language that has meaning beyond the literal definition of words, to be descriptive or imaginative. "The sky at night is a velvet blanket with sparkling diamonds" is an example of figurative language.

Three kinds of figurative language are:

- Similes and metaphors, which compare unlike things. Similes use *like* or *as*, while metaphors only imply the comparison.
- Symbolism, which uses one thing to stand for another because of a resemblance or association between the two things.
- Personification, which gives human qualities to an animal, object, or idea.

Write to Learn Use figurative language to describe an object in your classroom. Is a book a "window to the world"? Is the chalkboard "staring you down"? Perhaps the clock hands move slowly, "like students heading for class." Write two or three figurative descriptions of the object.

Get Ready to Read

Connect to the Reading

R The author of "Bouncing Back" offers advice about dealing with challenges. The speaker in "Another Mountain" keeps going despite difficulties. How do you deal with challenges and hardships?

Write to Learn Think about a time when you reacted poorly to a difficult situation. Write a few sentences about how you should have acted and what you can do the next time you face a similar situation.

Build Background

"Another Mountain" is, in part, about fighting racism.

- Oyewole's group, The Last Poets, was established in 1968 after the poets read their work at a memorial for Malcolm X.
- The Last Poets were African American activists influenced by radical groups such as the Black Panthers.
- The Last Poets are considered by many to be the founders of hip-hop.

Set Purposes for Reading

L Read "Bouncing Back" and "Another Mountain" to see how people face obstacles without losing their hope or their confidence.

Set Your Own Purpose What would you like to learn from the selections to help you answer the Big Question? Write your answer on the Workshop 3 Foldable for Unit 6.

Literature Online

Interactive Literary Elements Handbook
To review or learn more about the literary elements, go to www.glencoe.com.

Keep Moving

Use these skills as you read the following selections.

Literature Focus Lesson

Informational Texts Tell students that informational texts include main ideas, important concepts the writer wants to convey, and supporting details to explain those concepts. The magazine article "Bouncing Back" uses the stories of actual teens as supporting details for the main idea, "how to get on your feet when life knocks you down." Have students tell why stories about real people might be an effective way to support this main idea:

- Readers can learn how real people deal with hardships.
- Readers can learn that they, too, can deal with hard times. OL

Teach

L Literary Element

Literal and Figurative Language **Ask:** What topics and types of writing use mainly literal language? Why? *(Possible response: People writing scientific reports or about scientific subjects would use mainly literal language to be precise and accurate, leaving little to the reader's imagination.)* **Ask:** When might a writer choose to use figurative language rather than literal language? *(Possible response: to make a description more colorful for readers; to explain a difficult concept in a way people will understand)* OL

R Reading Skill

Review Connecting **Say:** Imagine that you are facing personal challenges. How might it help you to read about others who have coped with similar situations? *(Possible response: Reading about other people who have overcome obstacles can be encouraging and may offer useful strategies.)* OL

Literature Online

Intractive Literary Elements Handbook Have students access the Web site to improve their understanding of literal and figurative language.

Indiana English/Language Arts Academic Standards
SE: 8.1.2, 8.2, 8.3.6
TWE: *English Language Coach* 8.1, *Literature Focus Lesson* 8.3

Teach

R Reading Skill

Paraphrasing and Summarizing **Say:** When summarizing, you may find it helpful to make some quick notes about the main events, ideas, or details in a passage. List the most important details of the article's first three paragraphs. *(Possible responses: Beth's family had financial difficulties. Beth took a job and found ways to pay for college on her own. She is determined to make a good life for herself.)* OL

L Literary Element

Literal and Figurative Language **Say:** You can use context clues to help you guess the meaning of "life knocks you down." According to the author, who is good at "bouncing back" when knocked down? *(Beth)* BL **Ask:** What does this example suggest about the meaning of the phrase "life knocks you down"? *(Possible response: Beth has overcome obstacles, so this example suggests that "life knocks you down" refers to life's challenges and setbacks.)* OL

Readability Scores
Dale-Chall: 5.1
DRP: 57
Lexile: 910

INFORMATIONAL TEXT
MAGAZINE
Current Health

BOUNCING BACK

How to Get on Your Feet When Life Knocks You Down

by Jan Farrington

When Beth Driscoll of Denton, Texas, was in middle school, she dreamed of following her friends to a private high school. Her family didn't have the money, so she went to the local public high school. Beth made it work. But in her senior year, she got more bad news—her dad had lost his job. Her parents told her they couldn't help pay for college.

You can see where this story line might go: Beth gives up, takes an **unfulfilling** job, and maybe dives into drugs. But that didn't happen. Instead, she applied for student loans, took a part-time job, and rented a tiny room near campus, where she's now studying to be a special-education teacher. R

Beth's life isn't perfect. She works too many hours to spend as much time studying as she'd like to. But Beth, now 21, is determined to earn her degree and make a good life for herself. 1

Six Tips for Taking Charge

When life knocks you down, do you have trouble getting off the ground? Or are you a **resilient** teen with a gift for bouncing back, like Beth? 2 L

"Some kids come into this world and have an easier time being happy and dealing with stress," Robert Brooks of Harvard Medical School told *Current Health.* Brooks is a

Vocabulary

unfulfilling (un ful FIL ing) *adj.* not satisfying

resilient (rih ZIL yunt) *adj.* able to recover from or adjust easily to misfortune or change

Practice the Skills

1 **Key Reading Skill**

Paraphrasing and Summarizing When you summarize, you retell the main ideas or events of a passage in a logical order. Summarize the information in the first three paragraphs about Beth Driscoll.

2 **Literary Element**

Literal and Figurative Language The phrase "life knocks you down" is figurative. Its meaning goes beyond the literal definition of the words. Explain what this expression means.

Additional Support

Reading in the Real World

College Many students combine loans, grants, and part-time employment to pay college costs. Share the following terms with students:

- *loan:* money given on the condition that it will be repaid later
- *grant:* money given to fund artistic or educational endeavors or research
- *financial aid:* money given and/or loaned to meet education costs
- *need-blind admissions:* college policy of accepting students without considering their ability to pay the costs of attendance

Tell students that some of the top schools in the country practice need-blind admissions. Discuss the benefits of this policy to prospective college students. OL AL family **psychologist** and a coauthor of *The Power of Resilience: Achieving Balance, Confidence, and Personal Strength in Your Life.* But what if you don't handle stress well? Brooks says there are many things that teens can do to take charge of their own problems and build better coping skills. He suggests the **strategies** below. 3

1. **Surround yourself with people who make you stronger.** Having a few close friends can be a great source of strength, says Brooks. "But some teens with low self-esteem would rather have friends who make fun of them and get them in trouble than be ignored," he added. Bottom line: Don't put up with friends who put you down.
2. **Involve adults in your life.** "Resilient people almost always say there were one or two adults who really believed in them and stood by them" when they were teens, Brooks said. For many teens, parents fit the bill.[1] For other teens, those caring adults may be relatives, family friends, or youth group leaders.
3. **Discover something you're good at.** By focusing on your strengths and talents, you can develop a sense of pride and dignity that will help you overcome obstacles in other areas of your life.
4. **Let yourself experience success.** "Success builds on success," noted Brooks. Your long-term goal may be to go to college, despite financial woes.[2] But along the way, achieving smaller goals (making a speech in public, studying for 30 minutes longer each night) can give you a taste of success that will help you cope with bigger challenges ahead. 4 R
5. **Believe things will get better.** "Most of the problems that teens face are solvable," Brooks told *CH.* "But if [teens are] feeling down or incompetent,[3] it's easy for them to feel their whole life is going to be that way." Think about all the

1. Here, to ***fit the bill*** means "to be right for a situation."
2. ***Financial woes*** are problems related to money.
3. Someone who feels ***incompetent*** thinks that he or she is not able to do things correctly or successfully.

Vocabulary

strategies (STRAT uh jeez) *n.* plans for working through a problem or activity

Practice the Skills

3 English Language Coach

Greek Roots The Greek *psych* means "mind, soul, or spirit." Look at the chart on page 848 to see what the combining form *-logy* means. And then add the information that *-ist* means "one who has a special skill." What, then, does **psychologist** mean? EL

4 Literary Element

Literal and Figurative Language "A taste of success" is a metaphor. Explain what it means and what comparison the writer is making.

Teach

EL Language Coach

Greek Roots Say: Think about the meanings of the Greek roots and combining forms *psych, bio,* and *logy.* What do you think *psychobiology* means? (Psychobiology *probably means the study of how the mind and body, or mental and physical processes, work together.)* OL

R Reading Skill

Paraphrasing and Summarizing Say: In one sentence, paraphrase the information in Strategy 4. *(Possible response: Succeeding at small goals, such as making a public speech, can help you eventually succeed at bigger goals, such as going to college.)* OL **Ask:** Do you agree with this statement? Why or why not? *(Possible response: I do agree with this statement. I think that achieving small goals can give you the confidence and skills to succeed at bigger goals.)* AS

Differentiated Instruction

Role Playing Students who learn from interacting with others may benefit from acting out some of the strategies listed on pages 851–852. Organize students in small groups, assigning each group one of the six strategies. Ask students to brainstorm a problem or difficulty for which the strategy would be useful. Have them develop short skits to present their ideas. After each presentation, discuss the effectiveness of the suggestion. After all of the groups have presented, discuss which strategies seem to be the most effective overall. BL OL

Indiana English/Language Arts Academic Standards

SE: 8.1.2, 8.2, 8.3.6

TWE: *Reading in the Real World* 8.1, *Differentiated Instruction* 8.7.13

Teach

EL Language Coach

Greek Roots **Say:** The word *leukemia* comes from the Greek language. Look up the word in a dictionary that includes word histories. What two Greek roots make up the word *leukemia*? What do these roots mean? *(The combining form* leuko- *means "white." The suffix* -emia *comes from the Greek word* haima, *which means "blood.")* **Ask:** What does *leukemia* mean? *(*Leukemia *is a disease in which white blood cells multiply uncontrollably.)* OL

BQ BIG Question

Ask: What difficulties did Robin Regan and Patricia Calderon face? *(Regan's mother broke her neck. Calderon's sister died of leukemia.)* BL **Ask:** How did the girls cope similarly with their difficulties? *(Possible response: Both girls coped with their hard times by working hard to achieve goals and to meet the standards they set for themselves.)* OL

READING WORKSHOP 3

changes you've seen in your life, and you'll realize that a "rough patch" is only temporary.

6. **Put yourself out there.** Volunteer at a food bank, at a nursing home, or with the local Special Olympics program. "Teens who help others are less likely to feel depressed or angry," said Brooks. "Giving back to the community gives teens an opportunity to shine and to feel they're making a difference in the world." 5

Classroom Heroes

What does resilience look like? Sometimes it looks like the kid sitting next to you in math class.

Robin Regan, 18, and Patricia Calderon, 19, had shared a class at their Orange County, Calif., high school. But until both girls won the 2003 Julie Inman Courage Award, neither had discussed what the other was going through.

Regan's mother had broken her neck in an accident, and Regan was helping her mom learn to walk again. Calderon had an older sister who was dying of leukemia.[4] Both teens were taking care of younger siblings, tackling household chores, and keeping up with honors classes, school commitments, and volunteer projects. But that didn't stop the two girls from graduating from high school on time. Regan and Calderon are now thriving college students. EL BQ

How did they manage? "I'm not going to lie," Regan said. "After Mom's accident, I was really angry. I thought, *This isn't fair; why did it have to happen just when I need her so much?*" she said. "But my parents' dream for me always was that I go to college. So I couldn't throw away all their hard work."

Calderon says she owes her strength to her sister. "She always told me to try my hardest. She didn't get to finish [her life], so I want to succeed not just for me but for her too."

Analyzing the Photo Why is it important to choose good friends? How do you friends help you be the best you can be?

Practice the Skills

5 BIG Question

Which of these six tips for taking charge do you find most helpful? Have you ever used any of these strategies? Explain your answer on the Workshop 3 Foldable for Unit 6.

4. ***Leukemia*** (loo KEE mee uh) is a deadly disease that affects blood cells.

Additional Support

Reading in the Real World

Citizenship Have students fill out a short self-examination to determine what type of volunteer experience they would most enjoy. Include the following questions:

- Do you prefer to work indoors or outdoors?
- Do you prefer working with young children, peers, adults, or animals?
- Do you prefer mental work or physical work?

Guide students to find information about local volunteer opportunities that fit their preferences and values. As a class, discuss the various volunteer opportunities that students have researched. AS

As remarkable as their stories are, Regan and Calderon fit the profile of typical Inman award winners. The annual awards recognize teens who have earned their diplomas in spite of broken homes, illnesses, or other challenges. "Sometimes these kids are overlooked, and all we see are the athletes and scholars," said Julie Inman, the inspiration for the award. Inman herself knows a lot about resilience. After a skiing accident left her paralyzed at age 15, she went on to get a college degree with honors and has never abandoned her goal of someday walking again. R

School of Hard Knocks L

No one enjoys tough times. Still, there can be a surprising upside to life's downturns: They make you stronger. "I am not the same person I was before," Calderon told *CH.* "Before, I always had older sisters who looked after me. But then suddenly I had to pull myself together and take over."

"Little things don't bother me anymore," Regan added. "I had to grow up pretty quick, but in the long run, I think that will be good. When other tough things come up, I can tell myself that I've gotten through something tough before, and I can handle it." 6

Tough Times of the Rich and Famous

U.S. senator Barack Obama went through a rebellious **phase** after his father left the family. Obama went so far as to experiment with alcohol and drugs. In his autobiography, *Dreams From My Father,* he writes that his mother's love and the support of some wonderful teachers and mentors[5] "pulled me out of it."

Country singer, Shania Twain grew up in a **destitute** family in a Canadian mining town. She was just 21 when her mother and stepfather were killed in a car accident. Nonetheless,

5. A **mentor** is a guide, coach, or role model.

Vocabulary

phase (fayz) *n.* a step in the development of a person or thing

destitute (DES tuh toot) *adj.* completely without money or possessions

Practice the Skills

6 **Key Reading Skill**

Paraphrasing and Summarizing Paraphrase in one sentence what Regan says in this paragraph.

Teach

R Reading Skill

Paraphrasing and Summarizing Say: In your own words, write the characteristics of a typical Inman award winner. *(Possible response: An Inman award winner has graduated from high school while dealing with a difficult situation at home, a serious disease, or another obstacle.)* OL

L Literary Element

Literal and Figurative Language Ask: What do you think the figurative phrase "hard knocks" means? *("Hard knocks" refers to the difficulties that people face.)* **Say:** The term "school of hard knocks" is figurative language that refers to a process of learning to cope with life's hardships. How might a person learn at a "school of hard knocks"? *(A person might learn by experiencing serious challenges and learning how to be stronger.)* OL

Differentiated Instruction

Creating Resources Rodriguez mentions getting support from the Boys and Girls Club during hard times in his life. Have students form groups and use a phone book or the Internet to develop a list of local resources that help teens deal with difficulties. Students should create a poster that lists the following information for each resource:

- the name of the resource
- its purpose
- how it can help teens through a hard time
- its phone number and/or address EL

Indiana English/Language Arts Academic Standards

SE: 8.2

TWE: *Reading in the Real World* 8.2.5, *Differentiated Instruction* 8.2.5

Teach

BQ BIG Question

Ask: What do you think Alex Rodriguez would say to young people facing crises? *(Possible response: He would probably urge students to work hard at school and at home. He might also suggest getting involved in volunteer activities.)* OL

R Reading Skill

Review Analyzing **Say:** Read question 1 and the answer choices. Would the actions in the *a* and *b* answer choices change or improve the outcome of the game? Explain. *(Possible response: Choice* a *would not change the outcome of the game. It might make the officials angry and encourage them to suspend you from the game. Choice* b *would not improve the outcome because the game would already be over.)* OL

Twain took charge of raising her three younger siblings. "It was a difficult time," she told *Rolling Stone.* "But boy, oh boy, did I get strong."

Yankees star player Alex Rodriguez hit tough times at age 10, when his father left the family. "It was hard. I did my best to help out around the house and bring home good grades to make my mom proud," he told *Sports Illustrated for Kids.* His high school baseball coach became like a second father to him, and he found a lot of support at a Boys and Girls Club in Miami. He's now a national spokesman for the clubs. 7 BQ

Would You Survive . . . or Thrive?

When bad things happen, feeling upset can be a normal first response. But what's your second response? Do you move in a positive direction or in a negative one?

In the situations below, think honestly about how you'd react, and circle the letter for that response. We'll help you analyze the results.

1. **The referee doesn't call pass interference when an opposing player keeps you from connecting with a pass. You**
   a) rush the ref and yell in his or her face.
   b) spend the ride home talking to your teammates about the bad call.
   c) tell yourself to get back in the game and play even harder and smarter than before. R

2. **You think you did fine on your English exam, but the teacher hands it back with a grade of C minus. You**
   a) tell yourself that the test questions were confusing and blame your teacher.
   b) decide you won't study as hard for the next test, because it won't do any good.
   c) take a long walk and then ask the teacher for study suggestions.

Practice the Skills

7 BIG Question

Think about the personal stories in this article. What kinds of things kept these people from giving up? Have you or anyone you know ever experienced things like the people in the article? Write your answers on the Workshop 3 Foldable for Unit 6. Your response will help you complete the Unit Challenge later.

Additional Support

Differentiated Instruction

Discussion with an Adult Have students share the advice in this article with a parent, guardian, or other trusted adult. Encourage students to ask the adult to respond to the advice and discuss his or her own techniques for dealing with difficult situations. Questions for discussion might include:

- Who supports you during hard times?
- What suggestions do you have for kids having a hard time?
- What did you learn about yourself from coping with difficulties?

Have students present a brief summary of the conversation with the class.
EL BL OL

3. **You apply to three colleges but get into only your "safety" school. Your best friend gets into the one school both of you wanted to attend. You**
   a) decide not to attend college and look for a job instead.
   b) congratulate your friend but still feel jealous. You go off to college with a bad attitude.
   c) find out all you can about the college that accepted you. You ask an admissions officer to connect you with current students who can tell you what's happening on campus.

4. **Your parents divorced last year, and your dad practically disappeared from your life. Now he's e-mailed to ask if you'll have dinner with him. You've spent all year feeling hurt. You**
   a) ignore his e-mail but think a lot about what a jerk he is.
   b) send him a nasty e-mail, turning down the dinner invitation and writing things both of you will have a hard time forgetting.
   c) accept the invitation but let your dad know that he's hurt you and that it's something you need to talk about.

C

If you have a lot of *a* or *b* answers, you probably have a hard time letting go of negative feelings about yourself and your life. Having a lot of *c* answers means you're pretty resilient: When you hit a rough patch, you try to turn things in a more positive direction.

Do you need to work on resiliency skills? Try some of the suggestions in the article, and remember: One of the best ways to get rid of negative emotions is to get involved in something outside yourself. Do something that's worth doing—for your family, for a community group, for your school—and you'll be making yourself stronger too. 8 ○

Practice the Skills

8 **Key Reading Skill**

Paraphrasing and Summarizing Paraphrase the writer's point in the last paragraph.

R

Teach

C Critical Thinking

Comprehension **Ask:** What qualities do the *c* choices in questions 3 and 4 reflect? *(The c choices show people making the best of a difficult situation.)* **Ask:** Why might a person with mostly *a* or *b* responses have trouble dealing with difficulty? *(Possible response: This person might focus on the negative aspects of situations rather than taking positive actions.)* **OL**

R Reading Skill

Paraphrasing and Summarizing **Say:** If you're having a hard time paraphrasing the writer's point, answer these questions first. What advice does the writer give? *(Get involved in something outside yourself.)* **Ask:** Why does the writer give this advice? *(It will make you stronger and help you get rid of negative emotions.)* **BL** **Say:** Now try paraphrasing the writer's point. *(Possible response: If you do something worthwhile that isn't just for you, you'll become stronger and happier.)* **AS**

Reading Fluency

Building Fluency Read aloud the final paragraph. Clearly emphasize the changes in pace and intonation that should occur with the different types of punctuation. After you read, point out that you changed your tone to emphasize the reminder that follows the colon, and you paused at the dashes to emphasize the examples. Have partners take turns reading the paragraph aloud to each other. Ask the listener to identify points the reader could emphasize by changing his or her intonation, volume, or pace. **EL** **BL**

Indiana English/Language Arts Academic Standards
SE: 8.2
TWE: *Differentiated Instruction* 8.7.1, *Reading Fluency* 8.7.2

Teach

Viewing the Photo

Ask: How would you describe the mountains in the background of the photo? *(Possible response: The mountains look majestic, and the patches of snow show that they are tall.)* BL **Say:** Suppose you needed to climb these mountains. How might this challenge change your opinion of the mountains? *(Possible response: Climbing the mountains might cause me to think of them less as beautiful features of nature and more as difficult obstacles.)* OL

C Critical Thinking

Analysis Ask: Based on the photo and the title "Another Mountain," what do you think Oyewole's poem might be about? *(Possible response: The poem might be about climbing a real mountain or it could be about climbing figurative "mountains," as in facing challenges and overcoming obstacles.)* AL

READING WORKSHOP 3

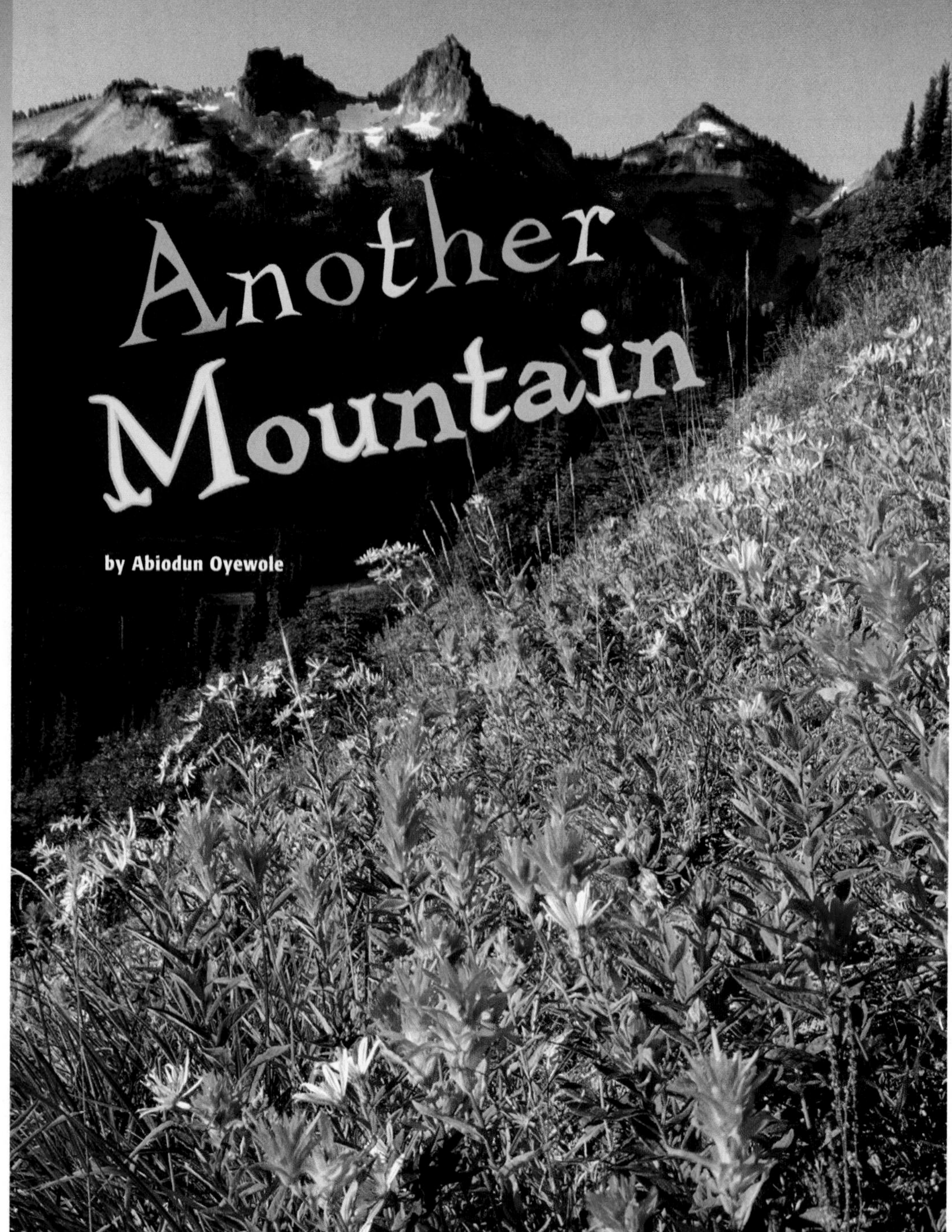

Another Mountain

by Abiodun Oyewole

Additional Support

Differentiated Instruction

Guided Reading Because this poem lacks punctuation, students may benefit from hearing it read aloud. Read the poem aloud for students, allowing students to get a sense of how the poem sounds. Encourage students to see that the lack of punctuation makes the poem seem like a stream of thought.

Next, read the poem aloud, and stop after every few lines to help students paraphrase the ideas in the poem. Encourage students to point out any words or phrases that confuse them. Finally, ask them to give a one- or two-sentence summary of the poem. EL BL

Sometimes there's a mountain
that I must climb [1]
even after I've climbed one already
But my legs are tired now
and my arms need a rest
my mind is too weary right now
But I must climb before the storm comes
before the earth rocks
and an avalanche of clouds buries me
and smothers my soul
And so I prepare myself for another climb
Another Mountain
and I tell myself it is nothing
it is just some more dirt and stone
and every now and then I should reach
another plateau* and enjoy the view
of the trees and the flowers below [2]
And I am young enough to climb
and strong enough to make it to any top
You see the wind has warned me
about settling too long
about peace without struggle
The wind has warned me
and taught me how to fly
But my wings only work
After I've climbed a mountain [3] ❍

16 A ***plateau*** is a large, flat area of land that is higher than the surrounding land on at least one side. Figuratively, it can mean "a level of achievement."

Practice the Skills

1 Literary Element

Literal and Figurative Language The poem's main image involves the metaphor of climbing a mountain. However, the poet also uses symbolism and personification. **L**

2 Key Reading Skill

Paraphrasing and Summarizing See the footnote about *plateau* and decide what the word means here. Then paraphrase lines 15-17.

3 BIG Question

These lines suggest that working wings, or the ability to fly, is the speaker's reward for climbing a mountain. Is there always a reward for getting through struggle and hardship? Explain your answer on the Workshop 3 Foldable for Unit 6. Your response will help you complete the Unit Challenge later.

READING WORKSHOP 3

Teach

L Literary Element

Literal and Figurative Language Say: An extended metaphor is a comparison that extends throughout an entire poem or literary work. What is the extended metaphor in this poem? What two things are being compared? *(The extended metaphor is a comparison between life's hardships and climbing mountains.)* **Ask:** How well does the extended metaphor express the speaker's thoughts? *(I think the metaphor is effective because dealing with a conflict can be exhausting and physically challenging, as climbing a mountain can be. Also, problems can sometimes seem enormous, like mountains looming in front of you.)* **OL**

CheckPoint

Use the CheckPoint questions provided on Presentation Plus! to check for comprehension of the selections. These questions can be used with interactive response keypads for immediate student feedback.

English Language Coach

Figurative Language Some students may find the poem's figurative language difficult. Review with students the list of phrases below. First have them identify the literal meanings of these phrases. Then explore their figurative meanings.

- the storm *(a great difficulty)*
- avalanche of clouds *(a host of problems or setbacks)*
- smothers my soul *(forces me to give up)*
- reach another plateau *(come to a place where I feel content and secure)*
- the wind has warned me about settling too long *(Experience has taught me that contentment can lead to smugness, self-satisfaction, and laziness.)* **EL BL**

Indiana English/Language Arts Academic Standards
SE: 8.2, 8.3.6
TWE: *Differentiated Instruction* 8.3.1, *English Language Coach* 8.1.1

Assess

Resources for page 858

- Selection Quick Check, p. 55
- Selection and Unit Assessment, p. 65
- ExamView Assessment Suite
- Interactive Tutor: Self-Assessment

Students can respond to the *After You Read items* in their Learner's Notebooks or on a separate sheet of paper.

Answering the BIG Question

1. The six tips are surrounding yourself with supportive people, involving adults in your life, discovering something you're good at, letting yourself experience success, believing things will improve, and getting involved in worthwhile activities.
2. All lost a parent through death or divorce.

Critical Thinking

3. Possible response: The speaker remembers the benefits of overcoming struggles.
4. Positive people will offer encouragement and help you see challenges as manageable. Negative people will reinforce fears and anxieties.
5. The speaker confirms that the mountain is only dirt and stone and that he or she is young and strong enough to climb.
6. Responses will vary.

After You Read

Bouncing Back *and* Another Mountain

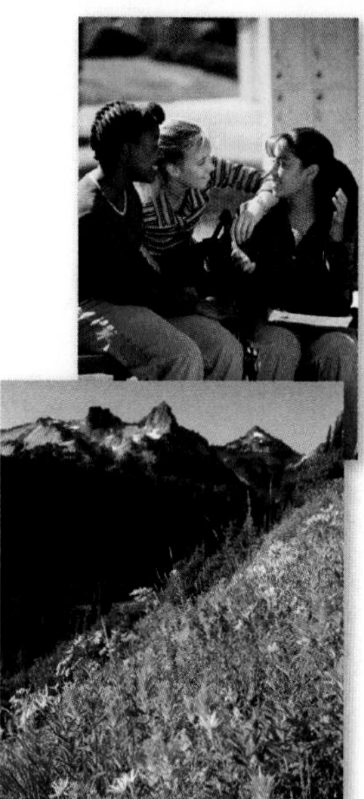

Answering the BIG Question

1. In "Bouncing Back," the writer gives six tips for handling stress. Without looking at the article, note as many tips as you can.
2. **Recall** What important, similar thing happened in the lives of Barack Obama, Shania Twain, and Alex Rodriguez?
   TIP **Right There**

Critical Thinking

3. **Evaluate** In your opinion, what keeps the speaker of "Another Mountain" from giving up?
   TIP **Author and Me**
4. **Explain** Why does it matter what kind of people you surround yourself with when there is trouble in your life?
   TIP **Think and Search**
5. **Analyze** How does the speaker in "Another Mountain" prepare mentally for the challenges to be faced?
   TIP **Author and Me**
6. **Evaluate** Which selection do you find more helpful or inspiring? Explain your answer.
   TIP **Author and Me**

Write About Your Reading

Written Response Review the six strategies for "taking charge" that are suggested in the article. Choose one strategy that has helped you deal with a problem in the past, or think of a different strategy that you've used.

Write three paragraphs about how you took charge of the situation. You don't need to give personal details or names. Just explain in general terms what the problem was and how you were able to deal with it.

- In the first paragraph, briefly describe the problem.
- In the second paragraph, identify the strategy you used and how it worked for you. (Again, try to give a clear explanation, but don't reveal details that you feel are too personal.)
- In the last paragraph, explain how the strategy you used might help other people deal with their problems and with stress.

Indiana English/Language Arts Academic Standards (pp. 858–859)

8.3 Comprehension and Analysis of Literary Text Respond to grade-level-appropriate literature... **8.5.7** Write for different purposes... **8.2 Comprehension and Analysis (Focus on Informational Text)** Develop [reading] strategies... **8.3.6** Identify significant literary devices... **8.6.5** Use correct punctuation.

For a complete description of the standards, see p. IN 11.

Write About Your Reading

Possible response:

I recently had to cope with my best friend moving to a new state. We'd been friends for ten years, and we spent a lot of time together talking and making crafts.

I coped by setting up an Internet account to instant message my friend, by taking a crafts class to meet new friends with similar interests, and by working out to release sadness and frustration.

Other people can benefit by keeping in touch with their friends and by making efforts to make new friends. They can also use exercise to release tension and clear their head.

Skills Review

Key Reading Skill: Paraphrasing and Summarizing

7. Write a brief summary of "Bouncing Back," listing the main ideas in a logical order. Then paraphrase two sentences from the selection that you believe are important to the overall idea or message.

Literary Element: Literal and Figurative Language

8. Is the title "Bouncing Back" meant to be taken literally? Explain.
9. Someone in the article says, "I had to pull myself together." Explain this figurative expression.
10. In the poem, what does the mountain (line 1) symbolize? What does Another Mountain (line 12) symbolize? Do they represent different things? Explain your answers.
11. Identify the thing that is personified in "Another Mountain," and give the line number(s) where the personification is found.

Vocabulary Check

Write the vocabulary word for each definition.

unfulfilling resilient strategies phase destitute

12. not satisfying
13. a step in the development of a thing
14. completely without money or possessions
15. plans for working through a problem or activity
16. able to recover from or adjust easily to misfortune or change
17. **English Language Coach** Add the Greek combining form *logy* to the word parts below, and write the definition of each word. (You may use a dictionary.)

zoo geo bio

Grammar Link: Commas with Relative Clauses

A **relative clause** begins with a relative pronoun like *that, who,* or *which*. If the clause is essential (necessary to make the meaning of the sentence clear) then it is not set off with commas. If the clause is nonessential (not necessary to make the meaning clear), then it is set off with commas.

Use the relative pronoun *that* or *who* to introduce an essential relative clause. Use the relative pronoun *which* or *who* to introduce a nonessential relative clause.

Essential: Jack London wrote a collection of short stories that was published in 1900.

Nonessential: Jack London's first book, which is a collection of short stories, was published in 1900.

Essential: Jack London is the author who wrote *The Call of the Wild*.

Nonessential: Jack London, who wrote *The Call of the Wild*, was the most popular novelist of his day.

Grammar Practice

Copy the following sentences and correctly add commas to set off the two relative clauses.

18. I will never forget the day that Mom brought home our first puppy.
19. The wind which was very strong brought down trees everywhere and caused a great deal of damage.
20. William Shakespeare who lived in the 1500s is the author who wrote *Romeo and Juliet*.

Writing Application Review your Write About Your Reading activity. Circle all relative pronouns. Make sure you used commas correctly with relative clauses.

Web Activities For eFlashcards, Selection Quick Checks, and other Web activities, go to www.glencoe.com.

Skills Review

Key Reading Skill: Paraphrasing and Summarizing

7. Responses will vary.

Literary Element: Literal and Figurative Language

8. No, to "bounce back" means to recover from a difficult situation.
9. To "pull yourself together" means to gather your strength and energy to deal with difficulties.
10. Possible response: The mountain represents an obstacle in a person's life. Another Mountain represents the next obstacle.
11. The wind is personified in lines 20 and 23.

Vocabulary Check

12. unfulfilling
13. phase
14. destitute
15. strategies
16. resilient

English Language Coach

17. zoology: the study of animals; geology: the study of the earth; biology: the study of all forms of life

Close

Ask students to list people and mottos that inspire them to work hard even when they are ready to quit.

Grammar Link: Commas with Relative Clauses

Grammar Practice

18. I will never forget the day that Mom brought home our first puppy.
19. The wind, which was very strong, brought down trees everywhere and caused a great deal of damage.
20. William Shakespeare, who lived in the 1500s, is the author who wrote *Romeo and Juliet*.

Indiana English/Language Arts Academic Standards

SE: 8.2, 8.3, 8.3.6, 8.5.7, 8.6.5

Teach

More About the Author

Michael Dolan has written about architecture from all parts of the world, including India, Africa, and the Caribbean. He has also written a book about the history and significance of porches in the United States. Dolan traces the origins of the porch to West Africa.

EL Language Coach

Content-Area Words

Help students answer the Partner Talk questions.
Say: Sentence one talks about two types of trees, old trees and saplings as well. What do contrast clues suggest *saplings* are? *(young trees)* **Ask:** What do guitarist's fingers generally move over? *(a part of a guitar)* **Say:** If you are on the top floor of a building, and you need to be safe, you will evacuate to a different place. What does this suggest *evacuate* means? *(leave)* EL BL

Before You Read | Standing Tall

Meet the Author

Michael Dolan is a reporter and feature writer for *Popular Science* magazine. He frequently takes complicated, technical subjects and makes them easy for people to understand.

Author Search For more about Michael Dolan, go to www.glencoe.com.

Indiana English/Language Arts Academic Standards (pp. 860–865)

8.1.3 Verify meaning of word in its context... **8.2 Comprehension and Analysis (Focus on Informational Text)** Develop [reading] strategies...identifying and analyzing structure...

For a complete description of the standards, see p. IN 11.

Vocabulary Preview

tribute (TRIB yoot) *n.* an action or a gift that shows respect, admiration, or thanks **(p. 862)** *The statue of Columbus was a tribute from members of the Italian American community.*

collapse (kuh LAPS) *v.* to fall apart, cave in, or break down **(p. 862)** *We knew the chimney needed repairs, but we didn't expect it to collapse.*

stable (STAY bul) *adj.* firm and steady; long-lasting **(p. 864)** *Abigail had to shift the ladder twice before it felt stable enough to climb.*

withstand (with STAND) *v.* to resist the effect of; stand up against **(p. 865)** *This coat is designed to withstand both rain and cold.*

Sentence Challenge Use each vocabulary word in a separate sentence. Then try to use all four words in one sentence that still makes sense.

English Language Coach

EL

Content-Area Words When you read about a certain subject, you may find words that are specific to that subject. These are called "content-area" words because they're used within a particular area, such as a job or a sport. Some words have different meanings in different content areas.

Word	Content areas	Meaning
baste	cooking, food science	to pour butter or fat over meat or fish while it's being cooked
	sewing, fashion design	to use large stitches to hold fabrics together for a short time
curveball	baseball	a particular type of pitch
extinct	environmental science	having died out completely

The structure and context of content-area words often give clues to their meanings. The next selection relates to building construction and uses the words *steel-mesh concrete*. You already know what concrete is, but what is "steel-mesh" concrete? Look for context clues to give some ideas.

Partner Talk With a partner, use clues in each sentence below to help find the meaning of the underlined word and identify the content area.

1. Mixed in with the old, fully grown trees were many **saplings**.
2. The guitarist's fingers moved over the **frets** quickly but accurately.
3. This could help people on the top floors **evacuate** to safety.

Additional Support

Author Search To expand students' appreciation of Michael Dolan, have them access the Web site for additional information and resources.

Literature Focus Lesson

Scientific and Technical Writing

Offer students these strategies for understanding texts about science and technology.

- Use side notes and footnotes for clues to unfamiliar vocabulary and concepts.
- Find context clues that restate complex ideas in different words.
- Examine visuals and their captions closely. Graphics may further explain concepts described in the text.
- If you are reading from a book, be sure to check the back of the book for glossaries and other resources that relate to what you're reading. EL BL

Skills Preview

Key Reading Skill: Paraphrasing and Summarizing

R "Standing Tall" discusses new methods and materials for making tall buildings stronger and safer. That was a one-sentence summary of the next selection. As you read the article, paraphrase and summarize difficult parts to help you understand the main ideas.

Partner Talk Explain to your partner something technical that you know how to do, such as creating a Web page. Or describe something you know from reading, such as a special effect in a movie. Explain the process clearly but briefly.

Text Element: Expository Writing

Descriptive writing describes a person, place, or thing. Narrative writing tells a story. Persuasive writing tries to change the reader's opinion. **Expository writing** informs and explains. An *exposition* is a detailed explanation. How-to books, newspaper and magazine articles, and instructions are some types of expository writing. Textbooks are also expository.

Most expository writing is organized using certain text structures. The following are most common. E

- **Description** may be needed to help readers understand a topic.
- **Time Order** shows the stages in which something happened or should happen.
- **Compare-Contrast** writing looks at how things are similar and different.
- **Cause-Effect** text shows the relationship between outcomes and their causes.
- **Problem-Solution** writing presents a problem and one or more solutions.

Interactive Literary Elements Handbook
To review or learn more about the literary elements, go to www.glencoe.com.

Get Ready to Read

Connect to the Reading

What's your favorite skyscraper? How tall is it? Where is it? Have you been inside? Have you been in a really tall building–one that has more than sixty stories?

The Empire State Building in New York City was the world's tallest building for more than forty years after its completion in 1931. In 1974 Chicago's Sears Tower took the record. In 2005 the tallest building in the world was the Taipei Financial Center in Taiwan. Is it still?

On Your Own Search online for "world's tallest buildings." Make a chart of the ten tallest buildings, showing how tall they are and where, when, and why they were built (for offices, homes, hotels, and so on).

Build Background

- The term *skyscraper* was first used in 1883.
- The development of elevators made it practical to have buildings more than four stories tall. In 1857 a New York City store had the first passenger elevator.
- The use of iron and steel in construction allowed buildings to be taller. In 1885 the ten-story Home Insurance Building in Chicago was the first "tall" building to have steel columns and beams.
- On September 11, 2001, the World Trade Center in New York was destroyed in a terrorist attack. All over the world, people wondered whether any skyscraper could ever be safe.

Set Purposes for Reading

BIG Question Read "Standing Tall" to learn how architects today are planning safer buildings.

Set Your Own Purpose What would you like to learn from the article to help you answer the Big Question? Write your own purpose on the Workshop 3 Foldable for Unit 6.

Keep Moving

Use these skills as you read the following selection.

Teach

R Reading Skill

Paraphrasing and Summarizing **Ask:** Why might an expert on a subject have to paraphrase difficult concepts? *(Possible response: An expert may have to paraphrase to make different audiences understand a difficult concept.)* OL

E Text Element

Expository Writing **Say:** You read examples of expository writing every time you read a science or social studies textbook. What are some characteristics that a science textbook and a social studies textbook share? *(Both textbooks contain many facts. Both attempt to explain concepts.)* BL **Ask:** Why must expository writing be precise? *(Possible response: To be useful, facts must be understandable and accurate.)* OL

Intractive Literary Elements Handbook Have students access the Web site to improve their understanding of expository writing.

Differentiated Instruction

Text Structures Have students identify which text structure would best suit the following types of expository writing:

- an essay on the major battles of World War II *(time order; description)*
- an essay telling the reasons why World War II occurred *(cause-effect)*
- an essay about the similarities and differences between World War I and World War II *(compare-contrast)*
- an essay on Hitler's regime and how it was conquered *(problem-solution)*
- an essay on the Japanese internment camps *(description)* EL BL OL

Indiana English/Language Arts Academic Standards
SE: 8.1.3, 8.2
TWE: *Differentiated Instruction* 8.5

Teach

R Reading Skill

Paraphrasing and Summarizing **Say:** Summarize the information in the first paragraph. *(Possible response: Skyscrapers can stand a quarter-mile high. These buildings symbolize people's needs to test a structure's limits and help solve such problems as overcrowding.)* **Ask:** What do you think builders do when they "test a structure's limits"? *(They see how tall they can safely construct a building.)* OL

E Text Element

Expository Writing **Ask:** What was an effect of the World Trade Center's collapsing after terrorists crashed a plane into its twin towers? *(Possible response: Skyscrapers around the world are now considered a target of terrorism.)* OL

Readability Scores
Dale-Chall: 9.3
DRP: 68
Lexile: 1230

READING WORKSHOP 3

TIME

Standing Tall

Architects and engineers are working with new designs and materials that can make future skyscrapers sturdier and safer.

By MICHAEL DOLAN

The idea of building a tower to touch the sky goes back thousands of years. And during the past century, concrete, steel, and other materials have made it possible for architects and engineers to design and build structures that stand a quarter-mile high. These buildings are a **tribute** to humankind's need to both test a structure's limits and solve problems such as overcrowding in cities. **1** R

But after September 11, 2001, **skyscrapers** are being seen in a whole new way. Terrorists hijacked[1] and crashed two planes into New York City's tallest buildings, causing the twin towers of the World Trade Center to **collapse.** Skyscrapers around the world suddenly gained a new label: target. **2** E

That new label has inspired builders to work on a new goal—creating the safest tall building in the world. The smartest minds in architecture and structural engineering are

1. When a plane is ***hijacked,*** one or more people take control of it by force.

1 Key Reading Skill

Paraphrasing and Summarizing The last sentence is complicated and contains two ideas. Put this sentence in your own words. What is it saying?

2 English Language Coach

Content-Area Words
Although **skyscrapers** can be considered a content-area word, we all understand and use it.

Vocabulary

tribute (TRIB yoot) *n.* an action or a gift that shows respect, admiration, or thanks

collapse (kuh LAPS) *v.* to fall apart, cave in, or break down

Additional Support

Reading in the Real World

Career Every job has its own set of content-area vocabulary. As a class, brainstorm a list of career fields that involve technical expertise, such as architecture and computer engineering. Organize students in small groups, assigning each group a career field. Ask groups to research their assigned professions and compile a list of three to five content-area words. Invite students to share the words and their definitions with the class. OL working together to figure out how to construct a building that could survive threats of terrorism[2] and natural disasters.

One material that could help architects and engineers is concrete. New types of concrete are being developed to help resist the force of bomb blasts and the 2,000°F temperatures of jet fuel fires. For example, one new type of concrete contains pieces of recycled stainless steel. The stainless steel increases the concrete's strength and its ability to stand up to a bomb blast or similar forces. **3**

A skyscraper made with steel-supported concrete wouldn't shatter as much when attacked. Instead its concrete would cling together in larger chunks, making it less likely to collapse. Steel-mesh concrete was originally used as a way to keep tall buildings safe in parts of the world where

3 Text Element

Expository Writing Based on these first few paragraphs, which text structure appears to be the main organization of this article? Explain. **E**

2. ***Terrorism*** is the use of violence, especially against civilian (non-military) targets, to try to make people or governments meet certain demands.

Farrell Grehan/Corbis

On September 11, 2001, terrorists crashed two planes into the twin towers of New York City's World Trade Center (two tallest buildings in center of photo), causing both to collapse.

Differentiated Iinstruction

Building Background Skyscrapers were first built in the United States in the late 1800s. These tall buildings differed substantially in their construction from shorter buildings. Buildings of up to about four stories are usually supported by their walls. However, skyscrapers are supported by skeletal frames generally made of steel. The walls are then hung from these frames, almost like curtains. This construction makes skyscrapers' great height possible. Ask students whether they think skyscrapers should continue to be built, considering they are now terrorist targets. **AS**

Teach

E Text Element

Expository Writing Say: The problem the writer presents is that skyscrapers have become terrorist targets. What do architects and engineers plan to do to solve this problem? *(They propose to strengthen and improve the structure of skyscrapers.)* **Ask:** What text structure does this suggest? *(problem-solution)* **OL** Explain that the text structure could also be cause and effect. The writer explains the effects of concrete building safety. **BL**

Viewing the Photo

Say: Many of the buildings in the Manhattan skyline are very tall. What does this reveal about the space available for building new ones? *(Possible response: So many tall buildings so close together indicates little available land for building. Building can only take place upward.)* **AL**

Indiana English/Language Arts Academic Standards

SE: 8.1.3, 8.2, 8.2.7

TWE: *Text Element* 8.2.7, *Reading in the Real World* 8.1.3, *Differentiated Instruction* 8.2

Teach

E Text Element

Expository Writing Say: Reread the last two paragraphs of the article. Why do you think the author ends the article with questions? *(Possible response: The author uses these questions to suggest the possible changes that might occur in skyscraper design and technology.)* AL

Ask: How might the destruction of one building influence an architect's or builder's work on future buildings? *(Possible response: Architects and builders will probably try to build future structures that are stronger or better able to withstand destructive forces.)* OL AL

READING WORKSHOP 3

earthquakes occur frequently. Now engineers are thinking of using this same material in all skyscrapers to protect against the force of airplane crashes and the fires they cause.

In addition to fire protection, various forms of concrete could make a skyscraper stronger and more **stable.** Whereas the World Trade Center towers got most of their support from steel columns around the outside of the buildings, many engineers now think every future skyscraper should have a **concrete core** that runs down the center of the building. 4

Just as your spine supports much of your body, a concrete core would serve as a building's spine and support its weight. It would also serve as a safety zone. Designers could place emergency escape routes and fireproof elevators and stairwells in the concrete core. These features could help more people escape if a disaster were to occur.

Builders are working hard to find answers to other questions that could make skyscrapers safer. Could a building's emergency staff use sensitive laser machines to find harmful chemical materials before they even reach the building? Is it possible to create a fireproof evacuation system[3] that could help people on the top floors find safety when the middle of the building is in flames?

There's still a lot of work to be done, but the answers to these questions and many others may be coming soon to a skyscraper near you. 5

—From *Popular Science*, July 2005

4 English Language Coach

Content-Area Words There are good context clues for **concrete core** here and in the next sentence.

5 BIG Question

How are the actions of builders and engineers an example of not giving up when bad things happen? Write your answer on the Workshop 3 Foldable for Unit 6. Your response will help you complete the Unit Challenge later. BQ

3. An ***evacuation system*** is a way to get people out of a building when there's an emergency. To evacuate is to clear out, or leave.

Vocabulary

stable (STAY bul) *adj.* firm and steady; long-lasting

Additional Support

Differentiated Instruction

Emergency Routes As a class, review the school's emergency evacuation plan. Ask students to identify primary evacuation routes, as well as alternative routes, from their classroom, cafeteria, and other areas of the building. If you live in a region vulnerable to flood or other natural disasters, have students review the policy for these emergencies as well. Carefully highlight any evacuation or response instructions that are particular to a specific type of emergency. Ask students why it is important to know evacuation routes even though it is unlikely they'll be needed. AS

Skyscraper Self-defense

Builders are exploring new ways to make office workers feel safe. Some ideas include steel-supported concrete, escape routes that could **withstand** bomb blasts, safety floors where people could wait out a fire, and laser machines that could identify dangerous chemicals. R

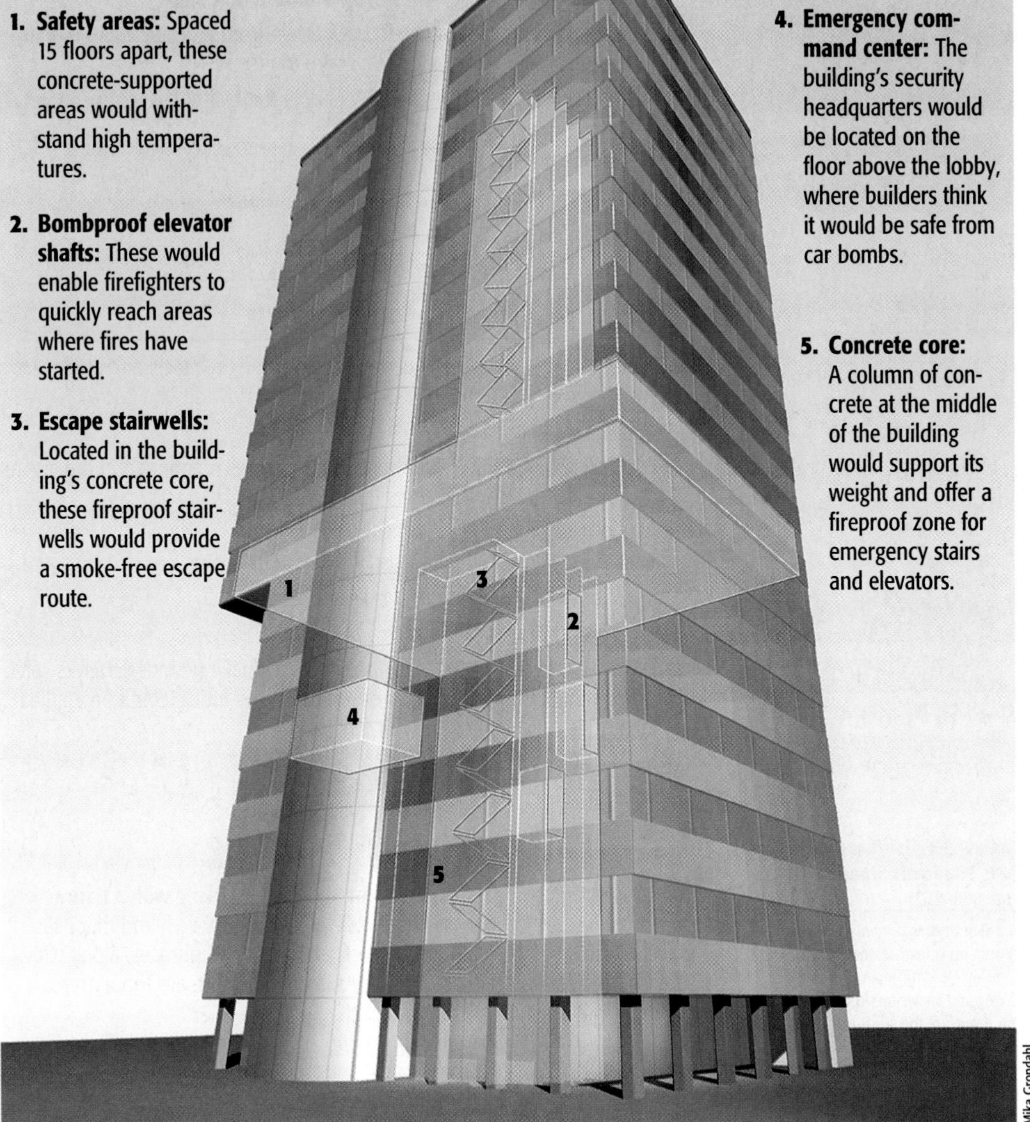

1. **Safety areas:** Spaced 15 floors apart, these concrete-supported areas would withstand high temperatures.
2. **Bombproof elevator shafts:** These would enable firefighters to quickly reach areas where fires have started.
3. **Escape stairwells:** Located in the building's concrete core, these fireproof stairwells would provide a smoke-free escape route.
4. **Emergency command center:** The building's security headquarters would be located on the floor above the lobby, where builders think it would be safe from car bombs.
5. **Concrete core:** A column of concrete at the middle of the building would support its weight and offer a fireproof zone for emergency stairs and elevators.
1
2
3
4
5

Mika Grondahl

Vocabulary

withstand (with STAND) *v.* to resist the effect of; stand up against

Reading in the Real World

Career Architects must have mathematical skills, design skills, and an eye for beauty. Have students research the qualifications and training necessary to become an architect and the different opportunities available. OL Challenge students to research and report on a famous design of a well-known architect, such as I.M. Pei, a male Chinese architect, or Zaha Hadid, a female architect from Iran. Student should include a photo or sketch of the architect's design in their report. AL

Teach

R Reading Skill

Paraphrasing and Summarizing **Say:** Paraphrase the new safety features listed in the paragraph at the top of this page. *(Possible response: Designers are developing stronger types of concrete, more secure evacuation passageways, fireproof safety spaces, and technology designed to detect harmful chemicals.)* OL

E Text Element

Expository Writing **Ask:** According to the newly designed skyscraper and accompanying description on this page, are builders more concerned with natural disasters or human attacks? *(Possible response: The skyscraper's design elements include "bombproof elevator shafts," and an "emergency command center" that is "safe from car bombs." These details suggest builders are more concerned with human attacks.)* OL AL

Assess

Use the CheckPoint questions provided on Presentation Plus! to check for comprehension of the selection. These questions can be used with interactive response keypads for immediate student feedback.

Indiana English/Language Arts Academic Standards
SE: 8.1.3
TWE: *Differentiated Instruction* 8.2, *Reading in the Real World* 8.5.3

Assess

Resources for page 866

- Selection Quick Check, p. 56
- Selection and Unit Assessment, p. 66
- ExamView Assessment Suite
- Interactive Tutor: Self-Assessment

Students can respond to the *After You Read* items in their Learner's Notebooks or on a separate sheet of paper.

Answering the

1. Possible response: Some people are strong willed and refuse to take no for an answer.
2. The terrorist attack of September 11, 2001, on the World Trade Center made people aware that skyscrapers are possible targets.
3. A concrete core can support weight and provide an escape route insulated from fire and smoke.

Critical Thinking

4. The writer admires the architects' and engineers' determination to build safer buildings. The positive descriptions of the new safety devices indicate the writer's attitude.
5. Possible response: If terrorists know a building is safe, they will likely not attack it.
6. Responses will vary.
7. Responses will vary.

After You Read

Standing Tall

Farrell Grehan/Corbis

Answering the BIG Question

1. Why do some people refuse to back down from a problem, no matter how much time and money it will take to face it?
2. **Recall** What event changed how people think about skyscraper safety?
   TIP **Right There**
3. **Summarize** What are the benefits of including a concrete core in a new skyscraper?
   TIP **Think and Search**

Critical Thinking

4. **Infer** What is the writer's attitude toward the architects and engineers who are working to build safer skyscrapers? How do you know?
   TIP **Think and Search**
5. **Predict** Do you think that the safety measures mentioned in the article could really make skyscrapers less of a target for attacks?
   TIP **Author and Me**
6. **Infer** How do you think people who work in skyscrapers feel about the new improvements in building design? Explain.
   TIP **Author and Me**
7. **Evaluate** "Standing Tall" discusses how to make new skyscrapers safer. Do you think the technologies described in the article could be applied to existing skyscrapers? Why or why not?
   TIP **Author and Me**

Indiana English/Language Arts Academic Standards (pp. 866–867)

8.2 Comprehension and Analysis (Focus on Informational Text) Develop [reading] strategies...identifying and analyzing structure... **8.2.7** Analyze the structure...of informational materials... **8.5.7** Write for different purposes... **8.6.5** Use correct punctuation.

For a complete description of the standards, see p. IN 11.

Write About Your Reading

Glossary Create a glossary for a content area. Working with a partner or in a small group, choose an area that you know fairly well and that uses specialized language. Then list at least ten words and phrases, along with their parts of speech and meanings. As examples, here are three areas, along with a few terms related to each.

- Baseball: *backstop, double play, fielder's choice, infield, home plate, out, outfielder, strike, umpire*
- Education: *auditorium, etymology, grade, No Child Left Behind, middle school, standardized test*
- Theater: *act, audition, box office, dialogue, director, intermission, opening night, sound effect*

Write About Your Reading

Responses will vary. Students' glossaries should feature words and definitions that are specific to their chosen subject areas.

Skills Review

Key Reading Skill: Paraphrasing and Summarizing

8. List three ways that concrete (or new types of concrete) could make tall buildings safer. Paraphrase and summarize what the writer says about this subject.

Text Element: Expository Writing

9. The text structure of this article could be identified as either problem-solution or cause-effect. Explain why it might be either one, using details from the article to support your answer.

Reviewing Skills: Comparing and Contrasting

10. The writer uses a comparison to explain the idea of a concrete core in a building. What two things are compared?

Vocabulary Check

Rewrite each sentence with the best vocabulary word from the list. Two words will be used twice.

tribute collapse stable withstand

11. There won't be a ___ peace if the two nations can't learn to live with one another.

12. Our roof cannot ___ the effects of one more winter snowstorm.

13. People meeting a king or queen are expected to bow as a ___.

14. Experts warn that the dam will ___ if it isn't strengthened before the rainy season begins.

15. Trust, patience, and work are required to build a ___ friendship.

16. It took me two weeks to build that bookcase but only a half-second for it to ___.

17. English Language Coach What makes **stainless steel** a good material for supporting concrete? (You may look it up.)

Grammar Link: Commas with Direct Address

A comma can be used to set off names used in **direct address.** Direct address is a name used in speaking directly to a person. It may also be a word or a phrase used in place of a name like *my dear*.

If the direct address appears at the beginning or the end of the sentence, place a comma between it and the rest of the sentence.

- Josh, did you get my message?
- Have you ever been skiing, Majid?

If the direct address is in the middle of the sentence, set it off with commas. If you remove the word between the commas, the sentence will still make sense.

- When you first came here from Greece, Mr. Pappas, was it difficult to learn English?
- I was wondering, pal, if you know today's date.
- Yes, Jane, I'll be glad to repeat it.
- Yes, I'll be glad to repeat it.

Grammar Practice

Rewrite the following letter, adding commas to punctuate the direct addresses correctly.

Dear Mr. Haslett:

You sir have an opportunity to own a musical pencil sharpener! Yes, my dear man imagine sharpening your pencil while listening to music in the comfort of your own office. It's yours for only $5.95 a month. Just sign the enclosed form Mr. Haslett and send it in by March 1.

Web Activities For eFlashcards, Selection Quick Checks, and other Web activities, go to www.glencoe.com.

Skills Review

Key Reading Skill: Paraphrasing and Summarizing

8. Concrete can resist bomb blasts and stand up to great amounts of heat. Skyscrapers made with concrete wouldn't shatter if attacked. Concrete would make the buildings stronger and allow for safer escape routes.

Text Element: Expository Writing

9. Problem-solution: The writer explains the problem, that skyscrapers are targets of terrorist attacks, and solutions, new safety features. Cause-effect: The writer explains the effects of the terrorist attacks and the effects of concrete for building safety.

Reviewing Skills: Comparing and Contrasting

10. The author compares a concrete core to the human spine. Both structures support weight from a central column.

Close

Ask students to think of examples of inventors, scientists, doctors, or engineers who have developed solutions to difficult problems after other people have given up.

Vocabulary Check

11. stable
12. withstand
13. tribute
14. collapse
15. stable
16. collapse

English Language Coach

17. Stainless steel mixed with concrete increases concrete's strength and makes it less likely to shatter when struck by a powerful impact.

Grammar Link: Commas with Direct Address

Grammar Practice

Dear Mr. Haslett:

You, sir, have an opportunity to own a musical pencil sharpener! Yes, that's right, my dear man, imagine sharpening your pencil while listening to music in the comfort of your own office. It's yours for only $5.95 a month. Just sign the enclosed form, Mr. Haslett, and send it in by March 1.

Indiana English/Language Arts Academic Standards
SE: 8.2, 8.2.7, 8.5.7, 8.6.5

Focus

BELLRINGER Options

Daily Language Practice Transparency 58

Focus Activity Say: When writers adapt a written work for the stage or screen, people often ask, "How close was it to the original?" How close is your dramatic scene to the narrative scene? What elements, if any, did you have to change to turn a narrative into a script? *(Responses will vary.)* OL

Teach

Writing

Dialogue Say: Label each line of dialogue according to its function with one or more of the following tags: *develops plot, shows character, relates to conflict,* or *creates mood.* OL

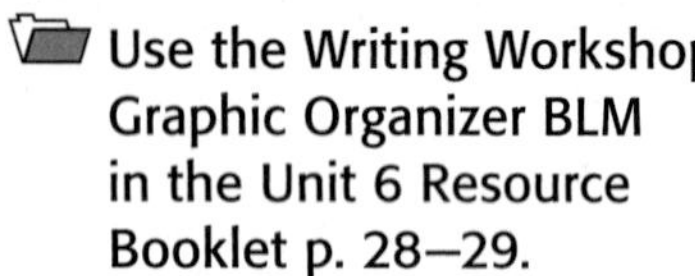

Resources for page 868

- Use the Writing Workshop Graphic Organizer BLM in the Unit 6 Resource Booklet p. 28–29.
- Use the Grammar and Writing Workshop Transparencies 27–28

WRITING WORKSHOP PART 2

Dramatic Scene

Revising, Editing, and Presenting

ASSIGNMENT Adapt a scene from a story and write it like a play

Purpose: To write an interesting scene about a person who doesn't give up when something bad happens

Audience: Your teacher and your classmates

Now it's time to improve your draft. You can change anything—characters, dialogue, or stage directions. Revise as much as you want. You're the editor as well as the writer. You'll keep a copy of it in a writing portfolio so that you and your teacher can evaluate your writing progress over time.

Revising

Make It Better

Reread your scene silently. In the margins, make notes about what sounds wrong. Then read the scene again, out loud this time. You may notice some dialogue that doesn't move the action along or a stage direction that isn't clear. Maybe a whole section is confusing. It's okay. Make it better.

Check the Revising Rubric to make sure your draft has all the parts you need. Ask yourself these questions, and then make any necessary changes.

- Does my scene have a clear conflict?
- Does the dialogue relate to the conflict?
- Are the characters developed through dialogue and action?
- Does the scene contain a character who doesn't give in when things go wrong?

Finally, think about making your scene even better by expanding it into a longer play. Adapt more of the original story to give the play a beginning, a middle, and an ending.

Revising Rubric

Your revised scene should have

- a clear conflict
- dialogue that relates to the conflict
- characters developed through dialogue and action
- characters who don't give up

Editing and Proofreading

Finish It Up

You've done a lot of work on your scene. Now do a final edit. Proofread your work carefully, using the symbols in the chart on page R19 to mark any needed corrections. Correct any grammar, spelling, or punctuation mistakes.

Make sure that you've done the special formatting used in scripts.

- Indent the stage directions, and put brackets around them.
- Capitalize character names at the beginning of lines of dialogue and inside the stage directions but not inside the dialogue itself.
- If you added, cut, or combined characters, change the character list.

Indiana English/Language Arts Academic Standards (pp. 868–871)

8.4.7 Review, evaluate, and revise writing... **8.4.8** Edit and proofread writing... **8.4.9** Revise writing for word choice... **8.7.14** Recite poems...speeches, or dramatic soliloquies using...[techniques] to enhance the meaning.

For a complete description of the standards, see p. IN 11.

Additional Support

Differentiated Instruction

Read Throughs Playwrights, such as the writers of *The Diary of Anne Frank,* often ask actors to read through their script as part of the drafting and revision process. Have students make six or seven copies of their play (enough for each character plus one for them). Tell students to form groups and take turns reading through each dramatic scene. Each group member should play the role of one of the characters, except the writer, who should listen and take notes. Have "actors" also note points where dialogue sounds unnatural, where voice could be further developed, or where the action is unclear. Actors should return their annotated scripts to the writers to use for revision. AS

Presenting

Show It Off

Now do something with your dramatic scene! You *could* just print a clean copy, put it in a binder, give it to your teacher, and not think about it again. The best thing, however, would be to perform it for an audience.

Literature Online

Writing Models For models and other writing activities, go to www.glencoe.com.

Applying Good Writing Traits

Word Choice

A great thing about a play is that you get to know a bunch of different people—or characters—as well as the playwright. You learn about the characters through what they do and say. You learn about the playwright from how he or she "talks" through the characters.

Analyzing Cartoons
Does Calvin's word choice show his personality? What does it tell you about him?

What Is Word Choice?

No two people sound exactly alike, choose exactly the same words, or put words together in exactly the same way. And no two people share exactly the same ideas and feelings.

It's important that each character sound like himself or herself. A character who is an English teacher probably won't say "ain't." A young person of today isn't going to say "gee whiz."

Why Is Word Choice Important in Dialogue?

Word choice is important in dialogue because that's where the audience gets most of its information. In a novel or short story, there can be descriptions of characters, telling you what they're like. In a play, everything has to come out in what the characters say and do. The writer of the play wants the audience to believe that the characters are real people, and that means making good word choices in dialogue.

How Do You Use Word Choice in Dialogue?

First, listen to the way people talk—in the lunchroom, in the halls, in the neighborhood. Just listen.

- Do people use complete sentences?
- Do people from different backgrounds use different words?
- What about slang? Who uses it and who doesn't?
- What about contractions?

Now read the dialogue in your play. Does it sound the way people talk? Read it aloud. Try to imagine that you are each character. Then ask, "Would I use those words?"

Partner Work When you feel that your scene is ready, have someone else read it and

- check that the voice is clear for each character.
- underline any dialogue that sounds unnatural.
- highlight any dialogue that's unclear or unrealistic.

Go over your scene one more time, and make all the appropriate changes.

English Language Coach

Using Exact Words Tell students that writers should say what they mean in as few words as possible. This rule applies to dialogue in a play, too. Characters who go on and on (not saying anything interesting or important or not using concise language) will bore audiences, just as they might bore you in a conversation.

When students revise their dramatic scenes, have them underline verbs and circle adjectives and adverbs. Are the verbs active? Are the adjectives and adverbs precise? Finally, have students look for wordiness; does a character use ten words when two or three would do? EL AS

Teach

Literature Online

Writing Models Have students access the Web site for an additional and interactive Writing Workshop-based student model.

W Writing

Voice Say: Think about the characters in your dramatic scene. Write one or two words to describe each character. Then, reread the lines of dialogue for each character. Ask yourself these questions:

- "Does the character have a distinct voice?" *(Responses will Vary.)*
- "Does the character's voice match his or her personality?" *(Responses will Vary.)*
- "What words or phrases might I add to give this character his or her own unique voice?" *(Possible response: They might be words from the original narrative or your own ideas.)* AS

Indiana English/Language Arts Academic Standards
SE: 8.4.7, 8.4.8, 8.4.9, 8.7.14
TWE: *Differentiated Instruction* 8.7, *English Language Coach* 8.4.9

Teach

W Writing

Characterization Ask: Based on the dialogue, how would you describe Tubman, Sarah, and John? *(Students may say that Tubman is determined, Sarah is self-sacrificing, and John is fearful.)* **OL**

L Literary Element

Mood Ask: What is the mood of the scene? *(fear or desperation)* **OL** **Ask:** How does the writer convey this mood? *(The writer conveys the mood through stage directions that indicate the characters are hesitant and desperate and word choices such as* beat *and* die.*)* **AL** **Say:** Return to your scene and determine its mood. If there is no distinct mood, what descriptions might you add to create one?*(Responses will Vary.)* **AS**

Active Writing Model

Writer's Model

The writer provides a brief statement of the time and place, followed by a more detailed description.

SETTING. The 1850s. Maryland. It's a cold, dark night along the wooded eastern shore. It's very quiet, except for the occasional cry of a hoot owl.

The characters in the scene are listed.

CHARACTERS: Harriet Tubman Sarah, John's wife
John, a slave four other slaves

The writer tells where the characters are as the scene begins. The stage directions are indented and character names capitalized for clarity.

[TUBMAN steps out from a cluster of trees. JOHN, SARAH, and the others can be seen looking out through the trees and bushes. TUBMAN pulls her dark clothing close for warmth and to make it easier to travel through the thick brush. Her face is full of fierce determination. She is clearly in charge. She motions for her fellow travelers to come.]

TUBMAN. [Quietly] Follow me. Don't make noise.

[The others move hesitantly out from the trees.]

JOHN. Are we there? My wife can't walk much longer.

SARAH. I'm fine. Don't worry none over me.

JOHN. We're all tired, and it'll be light soon.

Tubman's dialogue helps to establish her character.

TUBMAN. Brother, don't cause trouble. I've told you all to keep up. I won't say it again.

[The others take a few weary steps, except for JOHN.]

John's line shows he has reached the breaking point.

JOHN. No. Let me go back. . . . It's better to be a slave than to suffer like this and be free.

[Everyone stops, and TUBMAN turns to glare at JOHN.]

TUBMAN. You'll go with us.

JOHN. [Desperately] I can't. Not anymore. I'm tired. I'm hungry. I'm cold. Let me go. Let me go back. I'm going back.

The stage directions indicate necessary sounds, actions, and reactions.

[JOHN steps toward the trees. A sharp sound from the woods makes him stop suddenly. Everyone freezes. After a moment, TUBMAN moves to JOHN.]

The dialogue reveals Tubman's motivation.

TUBMAN. A deer. A bear. Or maybe "Master" come looking for you. [Pause] What's the first thing Master does if he gets hold of you? He beats you until you tell him who helped you. Who you stayed with. Who fed you. It won't be just you who loses the chance for freedom, but everyone else who might want to try. [To everyone] No one goes back. Freedom isn't bought with dust. We've got to go free or die. [To JOHN] Now you go with us, or you die right here.

The directions show that the conflict between Tubman and John is settled, at least for now.

[JOHN hesitates, and his body sags. SARAH touches his arm. TUBMAN watches, then turns and starts walking. JOHN, SARAH, and the others follow into the night.]

Additional Support

Literature Focus Lesson

Stage Directions Review with students the use of stage directions. Remind them that stage directions give information about setting, characters' appearance, and how characters should speak. Discuss where and why the writer includes each direction in the model. For example, the writer tells the actor playing Tubman to pause after the line "Master come looking for you," probably to heighten the sense of fear. Suggest that students return to their scenes to reconsider their use of stage directions. Have they included too many or too few? Tell students to revise their stage directions if necessary. **AS**

Listening, Speaking, and Viewing

Dramatizing Literature—Performance

What Is Performance?

Performance is bringing a play to life by acting it out in front of an audience. A performance can take place on the stage of a theater, on film or videotape, or even over the radio.

Why Is Performance Important?

Plays are meant to be performed. Books can be powerful, but staged performances can affect an audience in a different way. Why else are movies and TV shows so popular? Audiences enjoy seeing actors bring a story to life.

Analyzing Cartoons
Is the girl in the cartoon performing? Explain.

REAL LIFE ADVENTURES by Gary Wise and Lance Aldrich
WISE/ALDRICH
BUT MOMMMMEEEE, IF I CAN'T GO TO CHRISSI'S PARTY, I'LL JUST DIEEEEEEEE!
CLAP CLAP
BRAVO! BRAVO! IT WAS, PERHAPS, YOUR FINEST PERFORMANCE EVER. BUT NO.

Home theater.

How Do I Turn My Scene into a Performance?

Theater is a collaborative art. That means it takes a lot of people working together with the same goal. To perform your scene, you'll need some help. No matter what your dramatic scene is about, the following guidelines will help.

- You need a director to choose the actors and direct the action so that the scene is clear and interesting.
- For a full production, you need people to come up with a set, costumes, lights, and props. (Props are objects the actors use; for a meal scene, the props would include food, plates, forks, and so on.) You may also need music and sound effects. Just keep it all simple.
- For a readers' theater production, let the audience use their imaginations. Without the sets, costumes, lights, and props, the actors sit in a row and read their scripts aloud. A narrator can read stage directions to set the scene and describe the action.
- For either kind of production, with the director, choose actors to play the characters.
- Have the actors read the scene aloud together, sitting down. Ask the actors to memorize and practice their roles. The more they practice, the more natural the scene will look and feel.
- Practice in the space where the scene will be performed. Stand in the back of the room. Is it clear what is going on? Can you hear everyone?
- Be prepared, as a playwright, to make changes in the script. During rehearsal, you may hear things that don't work. Ask the actors and director for ideas. You don't have to do exactly what they say, but they may inspire something wonderful. Remember that successful playmaking requires people working together.

Present Your Scene Ask your teacher if you may perform your scene for the class. A series of scenes written and performed by you and your classmates would make an interesting class project. Perhaps the scenes can be videotaped and edited with titles and music added.

WRITING WORKSHOP PART 2

Teach

LSV Listening, Speaking, and Viewing

Performance Say: Choose between a full production and a readers' theater production. Decide if it will be live or videotaped. Then, make a plan:

- Form groups and choose one or two scenes.
- Choose a director, and assign roles.
- Directors should help actors learn their scripts by feeding lines when actors forget.
- Actors should practice using voice and body language to convey meaning. They should make adjustments based on constructive feedback from the director and other actors.
- Actors who are presenting onstage should exaggerate facial expressions and body language more than actors doing a readers' theater production in the classroom or videotaping the performance.
- Actors should do at least one final run-through before the actual performance. Any videotaping can be done by the director. AS

Assess

Lead students in a discussion of the effect of voice and movement on dramatic performance. How do these elements help actors communicate a message?

Reading Fluently

Dramatic Reading When students are reading their scenes aloud, monitor them for fluency. Encourage students who have difficulty reading their lines to take extra time to practice alone or with a partner. Be sure these students understand all the words in the scene and feel comfortable with pronunciation. If necessary, read the scene aloud with the student. You might model by reading the student's dialogue aloud and asking him or her to echo the reading back to you. EL BL

Indiana English/Language Arts Academic Standards
SE: 8.7.14
TWE: *Literature Focus Lesson* 8.4.7, *Reading Fluently* 8.7

Visualizing

Teaching Students to Visualize

Why Is It Important?

- Visualizing is picturing a writer's ideas or descriptions.
- Visualizing helps students better understand what the author saying.
- Visualizing helps students remember what they have read.

How to Help Students Get It

- Remind students to pay attention to each detail the writer uses to describe a character, the setting, etc.
- Tell students to constantly ask themselves as they read: "What would this look like? How would this work?"
- Some students may benefit from actually illustrating their visualizations. Encourage students to keep unlined paper nearby when they are reading selections in this unit. When they feel the need to see a description more vividly, invite them to draw what they visualize.

Reading to Answer the Big Question

and sometimes i hear this song in my head by Harriet Jacobs
This poem reflects on the significant role of music in helping African Americans maintain inner strength through difficult times.

from *Sky* by Hanneke Ippisch
In an excerpt from *Sky,* the author tells the true story of her life as a young girl in the German-occupied Netherlands during World War II. Ippisch writes about joining the Dutch Resistance to help save Jewish people from the Holocaust. She describes several experiences in which her courage and commitment are severely tested.

Workshop Resources

Pacing (Days) Standard	Block	Lesson	Student Materials	Teacher Resources
1	1/2	Key Skill Lesson: Visualizing	Key Reading Skills Practice, p. 30 English Language Coach Review, p. 42	Bellringer Options Transparencies – Daily Language Practice 59 Read Aloud, Think Aloud Transparencies – Key Reading Skills 30 Presentation Plus!
1	1	"and some-times i hear this song in my head"	Glencoe Online Unit Vocabulary Review, p. 40 Academic Vocabulary Review, p. 43 English Language Coach Active Reading Graphic Organizer, p. 31 StudentWorks Plus™ Online Student Edition Literature Classics Selection and Unit Assessments, p. 67	Literary and Text Analysis Transparencies 47 Puzzlemaker Skill Level Up!™ A Language Arts Game BookLink 3 Assessment by Learning Objective (Diagnostic and Formative) Interactive Tutor: Self-Assessment TeacherWorks Plus™
1		from *Sky*	Glencoe Online Unit Vocabulary Review, p. 40 Academic Vocabulary Review, p. 43 English Language Coach Active Reading Graphic Organizer, p. 33 StudentWorks Plus™ Online Student Edition Literature Classics Selection and Unit Assessments, p. 68	Literary and Text Analysis Transparencies 45 Puzzlemaker Skill Level Up!™ A Language Arts Game BookLink 3 Assessment by Learning Objective (Diagnostic and Formative) Interactive Tutor: Self-Assessment TeacherWorks Plus™

Keys for Unit Resource

- Blackline Master
- Workbook
- Supplemental Text
- CD-ROM
- DVD
- Transparency
- Web-based
- Fast File

Level Appropriate Code

AS = Activities for all students
AL = Activities for students working above grade level
OL = Activities for students working at grade level
BL = Activities for students working below grade level
EL = Activities for English language learners

Focus

BELLRINGER Options

Daily Language Practice Transparency 59

Focus Activity Ask: Have you ever known people you e-mailed, wrote letters to, or talked to on the phone before meeting? How did you picture them in your mind? How was your image of them different from how they looked when you met? *(Responses will vary.)* AS

Teach

R Reading Skill

Visualizing Say: Visualize the hallway after this class. Write what you see. *(Students might see students rushing to their lockers; lots of colorful clothes; people talking; books and back packs.)* OL **Ask:** Why might people visualize the same scene differently? *(Possible response: Everyone focuses on different things when visualizing, most likely on what he or she finds most important or interesting.)* AL

READING WORKSHOP 4

Skills Focus

You will practice these skills when you read the following selections:

- "and sometimes i hear this song in my head," p. 876
- from *Sky,* p. 882

Reading

- Visualizing text descriptions

Literature

- Understanding sound devices
- Analyzing setting

Vocabulary

- Recognizing and using Latin roots

Writing/Grammar

- Using commas to prevent confusion or misreading
- Using commas with dates and addresses

Skill Lesson

Visualizing

Learn It!

What Is It? Visualizing is creating pictures in your mind. And it's one of the easiest "skills" there is because everybody already visualizes a thousand times a day. Look, for example, at two events in a typical day for "Max."

R

- Max wakes up and smells bread toasting. *In his mind, he sees the shiny toaster in the kitchen. He sees the tops of two slices of bread, with a little bit of smoke rising around them.*
- While he's eating his lightly buttered toast, Max looks at the clock. *In his mind, he sees the school bus arrive at the end of his block. He sees himself run to catch it as the bus pulls away.*

Okay, you get the idea. With reading, visualizing works the same way except that you need to focus your imagination on the images presented by the writer.

Analyzing Cartoons
Is this character doing a good job of visualizing? Why or why not?

Indiana English/Language Arts Academic Standards (pp. 872–873)

8.3 Comprehension and Analysis of Literary Text Respond to grade-level-appropriate literature...

For a complete description of the standards, see p. IN 11.

Additional Support

English Language Coach

Building Background In the cartoon, a dolphin gives advice about how to visualize "flipping." The idea is that if the kid can "see" himself successfully flipping the burger, he'll be able to do it. Many people believe that visualizing something before it happens will help you make it happen. For example, if you "see" yourself scoring a winning touchdown or making the chess team, it will help make it come true. Have students discuss whether they agree with this belief and if so, what experiences they've had to confirm it. AS

Why Is It Important? Visualizing is a great way to understand and enjoy what you read. It can help you to recall the steps in a process and to imagine how characters, rooms, and objects look. If you can visualize what you read, selections will be sharper in your mind, and you'll recall them better later on.

Study Central Visit www.glencoe.com and click on Study Central to review visualizing.

How Do I Do It? Just pay attention to what the writer is telling you, and see it in your imagination. If you have a hard time with a particular part, try sketching it on paper. Here's how one student visualized a scene from "Kamau's Finish."

> My team is the Red House, and we're squashed between the Yellow and Blue House teams. Immediately across is the three-step winners' podium. I cross my eyes three times in its direction, shooting lucky *uganga* rays.

I'm picturing Kamau wearing a red uniform. I see his teammates are wearing red, too. To his left are runners dressed in yellow, and to his right are runners dressed in blue. Across from him is something that looks like the winners' platform at the Olympics. Kamau is doing some weird thing with his eyes to bring him good luck for the race.

Practice It!

Suppose someone is going to make a new movie version of *The Diary of Anne Frank.* (It was first filmed in 1959.) Look at the Hanukkah party in act 1. As you reread the scene, visualize the answers to the following questions:

- What actors do you see playing Anne and Peter? Who would play the other characters?
- How does the attic look? Is it decorated for the party?
- What kind of wrapping paper does Anne use for her gifts?
- How does Dussel look as he tries to remove the earplugs?

Use It!

As you read the selections in this workshop, notice the descriptive details the writers provide. Use them to visualize what's happening.

Teach

Study Central Have students access the Web site to review visualizing and to complete a related activity.

R Reading Skill

Visualizing Ask: Have you ever read a book that was made into a movie? How did the characters and setting in the movie differ from the way you visualized them when you read the book? *(Students may say that the movie actors did not match the description given in the book, so they were different from how students visualized them.)* OL **Say:** Think of a book you have read that gives descriptions of exotic scenery or an elaborate make-believe world. Would you rather see these details in a movie, or visualize them yourself? Explain. *(Responses will vary.)* AS

Resources for page 873

Use Key Reading Skills Transparency 30 in *Read Aloud, Think Aloud* to help students practice visualizing.

Literature Focus Lesson

Descriptive Language Tell students that writers often provide many descriptions to help readers visualize characters, settings, and events. In addition, writers may appeal to other senses to provide a more complete picture of a scene, including descriptions of smells, tastes, sounds, as well as descriptions of how objects might feel to the touch. Have students find a story, poem, or other work they've read so far this year and identify the descriptive language that lets them see, smell, taste, hear, and touch the elements of the work. OL

Indiana English/Language Arts Academic Standards
SE: 8.3
TWE: *Literature Focus Lesson* 8.3.6

Teach

Did You Know?

Spirit and Flame, the anthology in which Jacobs's poem appears, is a collection of over 200 poems by contemporary African American poets. The book's editor, Keith Gilyard, wanted to answer a question posed in an earlier anthology of African American writers: "What spirit will move the next African American poet?" Gilyard discovered in developing *Spirit and Flame* that African American poems today are "vibrant and diverse" and that "all kinds of spirits are moving African American poets at present."

EL Language Coach

Latin Roots Say: If you do not know the answers to the "Root to Learn" activity, scan a dictionary. EL BL Challenge advanced students to come up with three or more possible responses. AL *Possible responses follow.*

1. dictate, dictation, dictator, diction, dictionary
2. unicorn, unicycle, uniform, unify

Before You Read

and sometimes i hear this song in my head

Meet the Author

Harriet Jacobs lives in the Los Angeles area. She works in the financial services industry, writing poetry "on the side." Her works have appeared in several collections, including *Spirit & Flame: An Anthology of Contemporary African American Poetry,* in which "and sometimes i hear this song in my head" appears.

Author Search For more about Harriet Jacobs, go to www.glencoe.com.

Vocabulary Preview

English Language Coach

Latin Roots Many English words come from Latin words. Latin was spoken as early as the seventh century B.C. in villages of what is now central Italy. The word *Latin* comes from the name of one village, Latium. As Rome grew into a city and then an empire, the Latin language spread too.

Eventually the Roman Empire covered much of Europe and coastal areas of northern Africa. Most people under Roman rule continued to speak their own languages in daily life. But they used Latin for literature, education, religion, and, most importantly, business.

Even after the empire fell apart around A.D. 400, Latin remained a powerful influence throughout Europe. Latin is often called "the language of knowledge." Its influence can be seen in English words for law, war, art, literature, and architecture.

Below are some examples of Latin roots:

EL

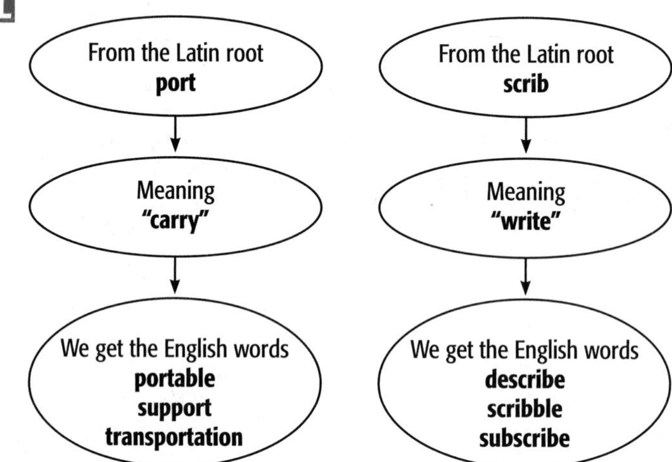

Root to Learn Fill in each blank with an English word that comes from the Latin root. (There's more than one correct answer for each blank.)

1. From the Latin root *dict,* meaning "say" or "speak," we get the English word ___.
2. From the Latin root *uni,* meaning "one," we get the English word ___.

Indiana English/Language Arts Academic Standards (pp. 874–877)

8.1.2 Understand the influence of historical events on...word meaning... **8.3 Comprehension and Analysis of Literary Text** Respond to grade-level-appropriate literature... **8.3.6** Identify significant literary devices...

For a complete description of the standards, see p. IN 11.

Additional Support

Author Search To expand students' appreciation of Harriet Jacobs, have them access the Web site for additional information and resources.

Literature Focus Lesson

Free Verse Harriet Jacobs's poem is written in free verse, a type of poetry that does not have a fixed meter (or rhythm scheme). Explain that free verse often sounds more like natural speech than poems with a fixed meter. Poems with free verse can still have rhythm and melody; they simply do not fit a set structure as some other poems do. Have students read the poem aloud and discuss its similarity to natural speech. OL

Skills Preview

Key Reading Skill: Visualizing

Words can give you the outlines and colors to paint pictures in your mind. If a writer says, "Light poured through the stained glass like streams of color," you have to pay attention to the words—"poured" and "streams." Then you have to try to remember when you saw water flowing in streams. When you picture it in your mind, you can see what the colored light looked like.

Write to Learn As you read "and sometimes i hear this song in my head," pay attention to the words and what they say or suggest that would help you form a picture in your mind. In your Learner's Notebook, describe at least one image that you visualize from words in the poem.

Literary Element: Sound Devices

You already know **alliteration** was the main sound device in the oldest English poetry. It is the repetition of sounds at the beginnings of words. Most often, the repeated sounds are consonants. You've also learned about **rhyme** and **rhythm**. All of these sound devices work together to provide the music of poetry. They also support the meaning of the words.

Onomatopoeia (AHN uh MAHT uh PEE uh) occurs when a word suggests the sound it describes, like *crack* and *buzz*. It's imagery that appeals to the sense of hearing. L

There are many other sound devices that poets use, even when there is no regular rhyme or rhythm. That's why it's so important to read poetry out loud.

Group Talk As a group, make a list of all the onomatopoetic words you can think of—such as *tweet* and *zip*, for example. Say them out loud and try to make them sound as much like what they describe as possible.

Get Ready to Read

Connect to the Reading

The first line in the poem is something that all readers can relate to; we all listen to music and we all hear certain songs in our minds. What songs might form a "soundtrack" to your life?

Partner Talk List the songs that would form your soundtrack, and then share them with a partner. Tell what your partner's list suggests to you about his or her life. Then listen to the ideas your partner gets from your list.

Build Background

- African American music has its roots in spirituals, which were sung by slaves.
- Spirituals gave birth to gospel and the blues. The blues formed the basis for jazz, which helped inspire most popular music that you hear today.

Set Purposes for Reading

BIG Question Read "and sometimes i hear this song in my head" to understand how music can play a positive role in difficult times.

Set Your Own Purpose What would you like to learn from the poem to help you answer the Big Question? Write your answer on the Workshop 4 Foldable for Unit 6.

Interactive Literary Elements Handbook
To review or learn more about the literary elements, go to www.glencoe.com.

Keep Moving

Use these skills as you read the following selection.

Literature Focus Lesson

Style Point out that Jacobs's style includes not capitalizing or punctuating her poem. The American poet e.e. cummings was famous for his lack of capitalization. Other poets have also chosen not to use punctuation. Have students note how their reading of the poem is influenced by Jacobs's style.

- Would it be easier to read the poem if Jacobs had used standard capitalization and punctuation? *(Responses will vary.)*
- What is the effect of her style? *(Possible response: It sounds like a person's everyday thoughts or speech, rather than a formal talk.)* OL AL

Teach

L Literary Element

Sound Devices **Say:** Listen to these sentences and tell which sound device they include.

- The troubled teen talked until her tears stopped. *(alliteration)*
- It was a heartbreaking tale of loving and longing. *(consonance)*
- The burning wood crackled in the fireplace. *(onomatopoeia)* OL
- Every energetic toddler eluded his exhausted mother. *(assonance)* OL

Interactive Literary Elements Handbook Have students access the Web site to improve their understanding of sound devices.

Indiana English/Language Arts Academic Standards
SE: 8.1.2, 8.3, 8.3.6
TWE: *Literature Focus Lesson* 8.3.1, *Literature Focus Lesson* 8.3

Teach

R1 Reading Skill

Review Interpreting **Ask:** What do you think the "clearing at the center of our selves" might be? *(Possible response: The place where we know who we are and aren't affected by our pain. The place where we have knowledge, such as the knowledge of the trees.)* AL

R2 Reading Skill

Visualizing **Ask:** What images come to mind as you read the first 16 lines of the poem? *(Possible response: I see people on boats singing, picking cotton, and crying "a jungle of tears.")* OL AL

and sometimes i hear this song in my head

by Harriet Jacobs

we have always heard music
found ways to smooth back the edges
of madness
stretched our voices
to the slap of oar against water **1**
heard blues in the snap of cotton breaking
from stem **2**
we always been a music
people
sometimes lost in a jungle of tears
but we keep finding our way back
to that
clearing
at the center
of our selves
where the trees still talk to us

R2 R1

Practice the Skills

1 Literary Element

Sound Devices What word in this line is an example of onomatopoeia?

2 Key Reading Skill

Visualizing Don't limit your visualizing to the sense of sight. In your mind, try to hear and feel lines 4–7 as well as see them.

Additional Support

Differentiated Instruction

Personification Remind students that personification is giving human qualities to objects, plants, or animals. Read aloud lines 10–16, pointing out that "the trees still talk to us" is an example of personification. BL Have students write two sentences that use personification. Ask volunteers to share their sentences with the class. OL AL

and our tongues keep **remembering** the rhythm 3
of the words we forgot
swaying on the backs of buses
and in hot kitchens
crooning
in pool halls and shared bathrooms 4
yeah/we carving a heartspace
and staring down the darkness some call our future
and they saying it be just dope and more dope
and no hope 5
and they don't even see we all the time
standing in the middle of the trees
and steady singing
you can't
you can't
you can't
touch this 6 ❍

Analyzing the Photo Can you imagine the "snap of cotton breaking" during a harvest?

Practice the Skills

3 English Language Coach

Latin Roots The word **remember** comes from the Latin *mem,* meaning "recall" or "keep in mind." What's another word with the same root?

4 Key Reading Skill

Visualizing What mental images do you get from lines 19-22? How are they different from the images in the earlier part of the poem?

5 Literary Element

Sound Devices The repetition and rhyme in lines 25-26 are there for a reason. What does the poet want to emphasize here?

6 BIG Question

In the last line, what does "this" refer to? How does "this" help "we" go on? Write your answer on the Workshop 4 Foldable for Unit 6. Your answer will help you complete the Unit Challenge later.

Teach

R Reading Skill

Visualizing Say: Visualize the images of "the backs of buses," "hot kitchens," "pool halls," and "shared bathrooms." Where do you think the people Jacobs describes are living? *(These people probably are living in a city.)* OL Are the images you form from this description positive or negative? Explain. *(Possible response: The images are negative because they describe crowded and uncomfortable places.)* BL

BQ BIG Question

Say: What does the phrase "steady singing" suggest to readers about how to go on during hard times? *(Possible response: It suggests that readers should be persistent and "steady" during struggles.)* OL

Assess

Use the CheckPoint questions provided on Presentation Plus! to check for comprehension of the selection. These questions can be used with interactive response keypads for immediate student feedback.

Literature Focus Lesson

Allusions Remind students that allusions are references to other literary works, events, or people. Point out the historical allusions Jacobs makes in her poem:

- Line 6 is an allusion to the work many enslaved African Americans did on Southern cotton plantations.
- Line 19 is an allusion to the pre-Civil Rights Southern U.S. laws requiring African Americans to sit at the back of buses and to give up their seats to white passengers.

Ask students if they see other allusions in the poem. What else is the poet alluding to? OL AL

Indiana English/Language Arts Academic Standards
SE: 8.1.2, 8.3, 8.3.6
TWE: *Differentiated Instruction* 8.3.6, *Literature Focus Lesson* 8.3

Assess

Resources for page 878

- Selection Quick Check, p. 57
- Selection and Unit Assessment, p. 67
- ExamView Assessment Suite
- Interactive Tutor: Self-Assessment

Students can respond to the *After You Read* items in their Learner's Notebooks or on a separate sheet of paper.

Answering the BIG Question

1. Possible response: Music allows people to express emotions. Music has power because it can affect our mood, uplifting us with positive messages, or helping us access our grief with sad lyrics.
2. Some say that their future is full of "darkness," "dope," and "no hope."

Critical Thinking

3. References to "blues," "cotton breaking," "the backs of buses," and "hot kitchens" all relate to the historical experience of African Americans.
4. Possible response: The poem's title refers to a song that gives the poet hope. Beginning the title with *and* might be a clue that the poem is part of an ongoing story.
5. Possible response: It is positive because music allows people to express themselves.
6. The poet paints a positive, unified picture of the future.

After You Read

and sometimes i hear this song in my head

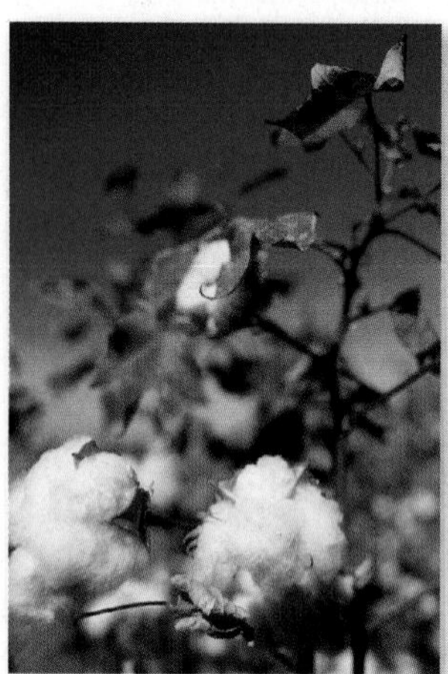

Answering the BIG Question

1. In what ways does music—any kind of music—help people to get through difficult times? Why do you think music has this sort of power?
2. **Recall** According to the poem's speaker, what do some people say about the future of African Americans?
   TIP Right There

Critical Thinking

3. **Interpret** This poem doesn't mention African Americans. What clues in the poem suggest that the speaker and the "we" of the poem are African American?
   TIP Think and Search
4. **Analyze** Explain the poem's title. Why do you think it begins with the word "and"? What effect does this have on how you read the poem?
   TIP Author and Me
5. **Interpret** The poem begins with "we have always heard music." Does the speaker view this as a positive or a negative thing? Explain.
   TIP Author and Me
6. **Draw Conclusions** What is the speaker's attitude toward the future of "we"? Support your answer with examples from the text.
   TIP Author and Me

Write About Your Reading

Chart Jacobs uses plenty of sensory imagery in her poem. Copy the chart below, but make the columns the length of your page. In the appropriate boxes, write words and phrases from the poem that appeal to the senses. (Some images may appeal to more than one sense.)

Sight	Sound	Touch	Smell	Taste

Indiana English/Language Arts Academic Standards (pp. 878–879)

8.3 Comprehension and Analysis of Literary Text Respond to grade-level-appropriate literature... **8.5.7** Write for different purposes... **8.3.6** Identify significant literary devices... **8.6.5** Use correct punctuation.

For a complete description of the standards, see p. IN 11.

Write About Your Reading

Student responses may include the following:
Sight: slap of oar, jungle of tears, swaying on the backs of buses
Sound: music, stretched our voices, slap of oar, snap of cotton breaking from stem, trees still talk to us, tongues remembering the rhythm
Touch: smooth back, hot kitchens

Skills Review

Key Reading Skill: Visualizing

7. This poem has plenty of visual details. Which image did you find easiest to visualize, or which did you like best? Identify the line number(s) and describe the mental picture you formed.

Literary Element: Sound Devices

8. The poet uses onomatopoeia in lines 5-6 with the words *slap* and *snap*. The effect is to call attention to the senses of hearing and touch. Why might Jacobs have done this? What do these words and senses have to do with music?
9. Identify the sound device the poet uses in these phrases:
   - remembering the rhythm
   - on the backs of buses
   - and steady singing
10. What is the effect of repeating the words "you can't" at the end of the poem? What point is the poet trying to make?
11. How might this poem benefit from being read aloud? Explain.

Reviewing Skills: Interpreting

12. In line 23, what does the speaker mean by "heartspace"? (Hint: See lines 10–15.)

Vocabulary

English Language Coach Rewrite each sentence, filling in the blank with the appropriate English word from the Latin root *scrib.*

13. In old times, a person whose job was to write or to copy writings was a ____.
14. A doctor's written order for medicine is a ____.
15. A copy of a play is a ____.
16. Certain religious writings are called ____.
17. A written or oral statement giving details of what someone or something is like is a ____.

Grammar Link: Commas to Prevent Misreading or Confusion

If the order of words in a sentence is confusing, the sentence may need a comma to prevent misunderstanding. You may even use an optional comma to make the meaning of a sentence more clear.

Unclear: Instead of writing Todd called his pen pal.

Clear: Instead of writing, Todd called his pen pal.

When a clause is introduced by the conjunction *for,* it is easy to misread *for* as a preposition. To prevent this, add a comma before the conjunction.

Unclear: She must like salad for she ate two bowls.

Clear: She must like salad, for she ate two bowls.

To prevent misreading a noun as part of the object of the preposition, add a comma after the prepositional phrase.

Unclear: Once aboard Ray put his suitcase down.

Clear: Once aboard, Ray put his suitcase down.

If a compound predicate is confusing, add a comma.

Unclear: I fell off the chair when it broke and cried.

Clear: I fell off the chair when it broke, and cried.

Grammar Practice

Rewrite the following sentences, adding commas to prevent misreading.

18. Although he saw two there were actually three cars.
19. If the window is open close it.
20. If you cut them onions will make your eyes water.

Web Activities For eFlashcards, Selection Quick Checks, and other Web activities, go to www.glencoe.com.

Skills Review

Key Reading Skill: Visualizing

7. Possible response: The slapping of the oars was easiest to visualize because I have rowed a boat before.

Literary Element: Sound Devices

8. These are sounds associated with slavery. People snap their fingers and slap their thighs to the beat of music.
9. All phrases use alliteration. "On the backs of buses" also uses consonance.
10. Repetition may sound rhythmic. The poet is suggesting no one can touch the strength and unity African Americans get from and express through music.
11. Responses will vary.

Reviewing Skills: Interpreting

12. *Heartspace* is a person's innermost self.

Close

Ask students what songs are important to them. How does music help them keep going during hard times?

Grammar Link: Commas to Prevent Misreading or Confusion

Grammar Practice

18. Although he saw two, there were actually three cars.
19. If the window is open, close it.
20. If you cut them, onions will make your eyes water.

Vocabulary

English Language Coach

13. scribe
14. prescription
15. script
16. scriptures
17. description

Indiana English/Language Arts Academic Standards
SE: 8.3, 8.3.6, 8.5.7, 8.6.5

Teach

More About the Author

Hanneke Ippisch served as the personal courier of Walraven van Hall, the leader of the Dutch resistance. Part of her job was to find safe places for the group to meet. While performing this task, Ippisch was caught by German soldiers and imprisoned until just before the end of the war, on May 5, 1945.

V Vocabulary

Suffixes Say: You can increase your vocabulary by adding suffixes and creating new words. The suffix *-tion* or *-ion*, when added to a verb, such as *anticipate*, creates a noun—*anticipation*. Similarly, you can add the suffix *-ant* to verbs to create adjectives. The verb *observe*, for example, becomes the adjective *observant*. Look for verbs in the reading that will accept the *-tion*, *-ion*, or *-ant* suffixes. *(introduce, adopt, transport, attend)* AS

Before You Read from *Sky*

Hanneke Ippisch

Meet the Author

Hanneke Ippisch was born in the Netherlands in 1925. As a teenager, she witnessed the Nazi occupation of her country in 1940. At the age of 17, she began to help Jews escape the Nazis. After the war, she moved to Montana, where she writes and speaks to young people about her experiences.

Author Search For more about Hanneke Ippisch, go to www.glencoe.com.

Indiana English/Language Arts Academic Standards (pp. 880–887)

8.1 Word Recognition, Fluency, and Vocabulary Development [Understand]...the basic features of words: word parts, patterns, relationships, and origins. **8.3 Comprehension and Analysis of Literary Text** Respond to grade-level-appropriate literature... **8.3.4** Analyze the importance of setting to the mood, tone, and meaning... **8.3.9** Analyze the relevance of setting...

For a complete description of the standards, see p. IN 11.

Vocabulary Preview

grave (grayv) *adj.* very serious; likely to produce harm or danger **(p. 882)** *The man was in grave condition for two days, and his doctors didn't know whether he would live or die.*

anticipation (an tis uh PAY shun) *n.* the act of looking forward to; expectation **(p. 883)** *My sister could barely contain her excitement in anticipation of her birthday.*

precautions (pruh KAW shunz) *n.* actions taken to prevent difficulty before it happens **(p. 884)** *Bug spray was one of the precautions Joan insisted on before she would agree to the camping trip.* V

observant (ub ZUR vunt) *adj.* quick to notice or observe; alert; watchful **(p. 884)** *An observant person would have seen the sign warning "Wet cement." Unfortunately, Mr. Edwards wasn't a very observant person.*

dreaded (DRED ud) *v.* feared greatly; form of the verb *dread* **(p. 886)** *I have always dreaded heights; bridges and skyscrapers terrify me.*

Write to Learn Describe your feelings about going to places where you've never been before. Use at least four of the vocabulary words.

English Language Coach

Latin Roots The Latin root *sist* ("to stand") and prefix *re-* ("against") give us *resist.* To resist is "to stand against or fight back." The next selection uses the noun form, but it's capitalized–*Resistance.* This was a group that worked in secret against the Germans during World War II. In the selection, the narrator hears a conversation between members of the Resistance. *Conversation* is built on the Latin root *vers,* meaning "a turn." Now, what does a turn have to do with a conversation? Easy! In a conversation, each person takes a turn at talking.

Partner Conversation Many English words come from *vers.* (The spelling sometimes changes to *vert.*) With your partner, find and explain the "turn" in each word listed below. (You may use a dictionary.)

advertise	
convertible	
versatile	
version	

Additional Support

Author Resources To expand students' appreciation of Hanneke Ippisch, have them access the Web site for additional information and resources.

Literature Focus Lesson

Memoir After World War II, many people wrote their memoirs, or recollections of the important events they had witnessed. Memoirs are a form of autobiography. They are generally told from the first-person *(I)* point of view. Unlike other historical records, they tell what happened from a personal perspective. Because writers may be relying on their memories of events that happened long ago, not all events depicted in memoirs happened exactly as they are described. Despite this, why might memoirs about World War II be important to read? *(They tell about the important events in the war from a personal perspective.)* OL

Skills Preview

Key Reading Skill: Visualizing

R1 Different writers help you visualize in different ways. The author of *Sky* gives you a lot of visual details. If you use your imagination, you'll find that there are dozens of pictures in this story. One way to help yourself see these pictures is to pretend that you are an illustrator. Then try to imagine what pictures you would draw to go with the story. Illustrate it for yourself–inside your mind.

Literary Element: Setting

The time and place in which events occur in a story is its **setting.** For the most part, setting is associated with fiction, drama, and biography, but it may be important in certain other writings too. Setting can be identified in general or specific terms. For example, we can say that *Anne Frank* is set in Europe during World War II. Or we can say it's set in the attic of an office building in Amsterdam, the Netherlands, between July 1942 and November 1945.

Understanding a story often depends on understanding its setting. To find meaning in *Anne Frank,* you don't have to know the economy of the Netherlands, but you should know the historical period–what was going on in Europe during World War II. Setting may also involve culture, religion, traditions, and spaces (rooms, buildings, landscapes, and so on).

Write to Learn Look over the fiction selections you've read so far in this book. In your Learner's Notebook, identify the settings of three stories. Remember to list both the time and place for each.

Interactive Literary Elements Handbook
To review or learn more about the literary elements, go to www.glencoe.com.

Get Ready to Read

Connect to the Reading

R2 Most of us know about spies only from movies and novels, and very few of those stories are about teenaged spies. In her autobiography, Hanneke Ippisch describes becoming a spy at the age of seventeen.

Write to Learn Could you be a good spy? What talents or skills do you have that a spy needs? Write your ideas in your Learner's Notebook.

Build Background

On May 12, 1940, Hanneke Ippisch learned that Germany was invading the Netherlands when she saw German planes flying high over her home. She joined the local Resistance group but was caught eventually and kept in prison until the end of the war in 1945.

- In German-occupied countries, people formed secret, illegal groups to oppose the Germans. These groups were the Resistance, or "underground."
- Resistance members included civilians working in secret as well as armed bands fighting military-style. They included Christians, Jews, and atheists, communists and non-communists, young and old.
- Resistance activities varied widely. Members passed information about enemy forces to the Allies. They destroyed supply trains and ambushed Nazi patrols. They helped airmen whose planes had been shot down. They hid Jews or smuggled them to safety.

Set Purposes for Reading

BIG Question Read the excerpt from *Sky* to see how the writer risked her life to save others.

Set Your Own Purpose What would you like to learn from the selection to help you answer the Big Question? Write your own purpose on the Workshop 4 Foldable for Unit 6.

Keep Moving

Use these skills as you read the following selection.

Differentiated Instruction

Reading Maps To help students understand the setting described in *Sky,* provide maps of wartime Europe, as well as a map of the Netherlands. Have students use the map of Europe to note the proximity of the Netherlands and Germany, tracing routes that the invading German army might have used. Students can use the map of the Netherlands to identify major bodies of water, such as canals, rivers, and bays. Have students discuss why bridges and ferries play such an important role in Ippisch's story. OL

Teach

R1 Reading Skill

Visualizing **Ask:** How can specific details help you visualize events that happened long ago? *(Possible response: If you are unfamiliar with a particular time or event in history, specific details about sight, sound, and touch can help you compare it to things you already know about.)* OL

R2 Reading Skill

Review Connecting **Say:** Hanneke Ippisch takes on an adult responsibility with adult consequences when she is only 17. Think of a time when you took on a big job. How did you feel when faced with a big responsibility? *(Possible response: I felt nervous but proud to be able to help.)* OL

Interactive Literary Elements Handbook Have students access the Web site to improve their understanding of setting.

Indiana English/Language Arts Academic Standards
SE: 8.1, 8.3, 8.3.4, 8.3.9
TWE: *Literature Focus Lesson* 8.3.7, *Differentiated Instruction* 8.2

Teach

L Literary Element

Setting Say: Describe the different settings in the first two paragraphs and what happens in each. *(The first setting is the house of Ippisch's father, where Ippisch overhears talking in the study. The next setting is the woman's house, where Ippisch introduces herself and says she wants to help.)* BL OL

R Reading Skill

Review Drawing Conclusions Ask: Why do you think the woman in the Resistance tells Ippisch to return to her studies? *(Possible response: She wants to make sure Ippisch has thought through her decisions and doesn't join the Resistance without understanding its possible dangers.)* AL

Readability Scores
Dale-Chall: 5.9
DRP: 57
Lexile: 950

from Sky

by Hanneke Ippisch

One night when I came home from Amsterdam during a break from my schooling, I once again overheard a conversation in my father's study, this one between him and an older woman. They were whispering, and I picked up the word "underground." Then I knew that my father was the kind of man who would be involved in the Resistance, and it made me feel very good. When the meeting ended and the woman left, I secretly followed her in the dark to her house. Maybe this was my chance to work against the enemy. 1 L

She lived across a bridge, on the other side of town, in a simple room behind a small vegetable store. I knocked on her door. When she opened it just a crack, I introduced myself, and she let me in. 2

I told her I wanted to join the underground forces. She looked at me and said, "I want you to go back to your studies and think about it for a long time. There is nothing adventurous or romantic about working against the enemy—it is incredibly hard work. Your life would not be yours anymore. Go back to your studies and maybe forget about it. You are very young." I left disappointed, her words resonating[1] in my mind, and returned to Amsterdam and my studies. R

The situation became more **grave** as the war continued. We students in Amsterdam heard stories about incidents

1. Here, ***resonating*** (REZ uh nayt ing) means "echoing; repeating."

Vocabulary

grave (grayv) *adj.* very serious; likely to produce harm or danger

Practice the Skills

1 Reviewing Elements

Literal and Figurative Language In this context, *underground* and *Resistance* are almost synonyms, but only one is literal language. Which word is used figuratively?

2 Key Reading Skill

Visualizing The story begins with an air of mystery. What words in the first paragraph help you visualize the scene?

Additional Support

English Language Coach

Build Background The people of the Netherlands are proud of their country's resistance to Germany's military occupation during World War II. The Netherlands has collected documents and artifacts from this period in the Dutch Resistance Museum ("Verzetsmuseum"), where visitors can stroll through street scenes and house interiors while learning about everyday life during wartime. Have students use library resources or the Internet to learn more about the Dutch Resistance. OL involving not only Jewish people, but also about students being taken to Germany against their will, and about the executions of political leaders in Holland.

About three months after my first conversation with the older woman in the vegetable store, I went back to her and told her that there was no doubt in my mind, I still wanted to join the underground.

"Very well," she said. "Tomorrow you will meet Piet in the square in front of the Protestant Church at exactly nine A.M. He will wear a brown wool hat and a gray raincoat. He will have a newspaper under his right arm and a shopping basket in his left hand. You will introduce yourself as Ellie. Good luck and be careful. Do not ever talk about what you are doing, including to your own family." **3**

After hearing those simple words, I left her. I did not sleep very well that night. I was repeating softly the things the old woman had told me: Nine A.M. in front of the Protestant Church, gray raincoat, brown hat, newspaper, shopping basket, Piet. Nine A.M. shopping basket, brown hat, Protestant Church, nine A.M. . . . Finally I fell asleep, but woke up early and paced the floor until it was time to go. I carried my books and my tennis racket with me, so my family would think I was going back to school. **4**

Full of **anticipation** and a little bit nervous, I headed for the square and spotted Piet immediately. He was indeed in the right place at the right time, wearing a gray raincoat, a brown hat, holding a newspaper under his right arm and a shopping basket in his left hand. He gave me my first assignment: I was to bring some identification papers and food coupons[2] to a Jewish family hidden in an old house in the town of Haarlem. He also handed me a falsified I.D.: My new name was Ellie Van Dyk. **C**

On that day my life changed completely. I rarely attended classes anymore. At night I was told where to meet my contact the next morning to receive new **instructions**, and which code words to use when approaching him or her. **5** **EL**

2. There were food shortages because the war limited production and imports. ***Food coupons*** were, in effect, permission slips for buying food.

Vocabulary

anticipation (an tis uh PAY shun) *n.* the act of looking forward to; expectation

Practice the Skills

3 Literary Element

Setting The old woman defines the setting where Ippisch's first assignment will begin. "Protestant Church" may sound vague to us, as readers, but Ippisch appears to understand it.

4 Key Reading Skill

Visualizing First visualize the narrator lying in bed repeating the old woman's words. Got it? Now visualize the church, Piet, and his shopping basket.

5 English Language Coach

Latin Roots The root of **instructions** is *struct,* meaning "build." How does the English word relate to the Latin root?

Teach

C Critical Thinking

Comprehension Ask: What does Ippisch learn when she meets Piet? *(She learns her assignment is to take food coupons and papers to a Jewish family in hiding. She also learns she has false papers and a new name: Ellie Van Dyke.)* **BL**

Ask: How would having fake names protect the Resistance workers should one of them be caught? *(Possible response: If any Resistance members were caught, they couldn't give away the identities of others because they wouldn't know their true names.)* **AL**

EL Language Coach

Latin Roots Ask: What are other words you can think of with the root *struct*? *(structure, construct, destruction)* **OL**

Ask: How do these words relate to building? *(Possible response: A structure is a building. To construct is to build. Destruction is destroying something that's been built.)* **AL**

Reading in the Real World

Citizenship The Dutch resisted German occupation in many ways. For example, dockworkers in Amsterdam halted the deportation of Dutch Jews to Germany by refusing to work. Have students find out more about *civil disobedience*, the refusal to obey the commands of a government. Ask students to find examples of civil disobedience in history, for example, Mohandas Gandhi's movement in India or the U.S. civil rights movement. Lead the class in a discussion of its obligations as citizens, and ask them to explain when they believe civil disobedience might be an appropriate response to a government's policy. **AL**

Indiana English/Language Arts Academic Standards

SE: 8.1, 8.3, 8.3.4

TWE: *English Language Coach* 8.4.4, *Reading in the Real World* 8.7

Teach

BQ BIG Question

Say: Farm families would have been at risk if German soldiers found Jewish children in their homes. Why do you think farm families accepted Jewish children anyway? *(Possible response: They thought saving children's lives was worth the risk of discovery.)* **BL**

Ask: What does the Resistance's network between cities and the countryside tell you about their determination? *(Possible response: People all over the Netherlands did not give up when bad things happened. They were willing to risk their lives to try to make a difference.)* **OL**

C Critical Thinking

Comprehension Ask: How did having to wear the Star of David on their coats affect the people who went into hiding? *(They could not get new coats, so they had to find ways to hide the unfaded star-shaped spots on their coats.)* **OL**

READING WORKSHOP 4

Analyzing the Photo Jews had to identify themselves by wearing a star with the label "Jew" in German. The Star of David is an ancient symbol of Judaism.

I was given a different assignment each day transporting Jewish people from one place to another, safer spot. Often we had to separate the children from their parents. I traveled with the children on trains and boats to the countryside, to the safer hiding places on farms, where the Germans rarely went. Quite a few of those children—unaware of **BQ** their families' fate—stayed in the countryside until the end of the war in 1945. Many farmers' families "adopted" the Jewish children and treated them as their own. They went to school with the other children in the villages. **6**

One problem was that clothing was getting scarce and the winter always seemed to get colder. Jewish people going into hiding ("underwater," as we called it) had to take the star off their coats. But cloth fades, and most old overcoats—which were so necessary during the cold winters—showed an obvious unfaded star-shaped spot. We always feared that star-shaped spot would be a dead giveaway and **C** just hoped that it would not be noticed. Some women ingeniously took material from the inside hem of the old coats and sewed pockets over the faded spot. Others wore wool scarves over their coats, while still others held a newspaper to hide the spot. **7** Then there were people who did not take any of these **precautions** and didn't get caught. Several times, however, while walking or traveling with us, Jews were arrested by some **observant** German. If that happened, we had to pretend we did not know the arrested person. Other Resistance workers told me about tragic

Vocabulary

precautions (pruh KAW shunz) *n.* actions taken to prevent difficulty before it happens

observant (ub ZUR vunt) *adj.* quick to notice or observe; alert; watchful

Practice the Skills

6 BIG Question

Many Jewish parents saved their children's lives by giving them over to the Resistance. Does what those parents did demonstrate an appropriate response to the Big Question? Write your thoughts on the Workshop 4 Foldable for Unit 6.

7 **Key Reading Skill**

Visualizing First imagine the yellow star sewn on a coat—on the left side of the chest. Then, in your mind, remove the star and see the unfaded "star-shaped spot." From there, it's easy to visualize the various ways people dealt with the problem.

Additional Support

Differentiated Instruction

Understanding Details Some students may benefit from listing ways in which people hid the evidence of the stars on their coats. First, tell students to write why people kept their coats after they tore off the stars. Then have students list the ways in which a person attempted to hide the star-shaped spot on his or her coat. **EL** **BL**

incidents,[3] but fortunately none of my Jewish traveling companions were ever caught.

Traveling to the Countryside, 1943 It was early in the morning and I dressed quickly and warmly. At seven A.M. I had to meet a Jewish couple, musicians who had played in the symphony in Amsterdam. I was to transport them to a village in the province of Friesland, where they were to be met and taken to a safe place on a farm. 8

When I arrived at the given address, I knocked three times hard and twice softly (a code knock) on the door. A smiling Dutch woman opened the door and let me in. "I will miss them," she said. "They have been good company for my husband and me, but there are too many German soldiers around lately walking the streets. It is better for our guests to move on." As she spoke I followed her up two flights of stairs, through a linen closet, which had a small door inside, and into a room, where the curtains in front of the windows were closed. A Jewish man and woman, both pale and nervous, were waiting. R1

"Hello," I said. "Are you ready to go?" They embraced their Dutch hostess and followed me through the linen closet, down the stairs, and out into the street. Each was carrying a small shopping basket in which they had packed all their belongings.

I walked ahead, pretending not to know them, and they followed. The wind was blowing hard, and the man's hat blew off. He had lots of grayish-black, curly, rather long hair, and the wind blew his hair high around his head. He ran after his hat, grabbed it, and put it firmly on his head, holding it with one hand so he wouldn't lose it again. 9

We rode a trolley car[4] to the Central Station, where I went to a ticket window and bought three round-trip tickets (the couple would only travel one way, but in case of a question they could say they were visiting a friend). I quickly handed their tickets to them, and we went to a platform where a train was waiting to take us to the northern part of the province of North Holland.

3. Ippisch is probably referring to times when Jews were caught and killed on the spot.

4. A ***trolley car*** runs along tracks laid in the street and is powered by electricity.

Practice the Skills

8 Literary Element

Setting As the subtitle and first paragraph suggest, the setting will change from city to country.

9 Key Reading Skill

Visualizing Use the narrator's descriptive details to visualize this man and his hat. R2

Teach

R1 Reading Skill

Review Analyzing Say: Notice the description of the hiding place for the Jewish couple. What does it reveal about the methods of the Dutch Resistance? *(Possible response: The approach through the linen closet is very well thought out, suggesting the Dutch Resistance was clever and well organized.)* OL **Say:** The narrator does not express surprise over the hidden entrance. What does her behavior reveal about the Netherlands during wartime? *(Possible response: Unusual hiding places were probably normal during wartime. As a member of the Resistance, she may be used to seeing such hidden rooms.)* AL

R2 Reading Skill

Visualizing Say: The author says that the man's hair is "grayish-black" and "rather long." What do these details tell you about him? *(Possible response: The gray in his hair is an indication of his age. The fact that his hair is rather long may indicate he has not had the time or opportunity to have it cut.)* OL

Differentiated Instruction

Modes of Transportation Ippisch and the Jewish couple use several types of transportation during their trip. Help students familiarize themselves with the following types of transportation, finding descriptions and pictures if possible.

- trolley car
- train compartment
- ferry boat
- horse-drawn farm cart EL BL

Indiana English/Language Arts Academic Standards

SE: 8.3, 8.3.4

TWE: *Differentiated Instruction* (p. 884) 8.2, *Differentiated Instruction* (p. 885) 8.2

Teach

R Reading Skill

Review Drawing Conclusions
Say: What can you conclude about why the German troops are on the train? *(The troops are looking for Jewish people trying to escape.)* **Ask:** Do you think the Jewish couple's I.D. cards are their own? Why or why not? *(Possible response: The I.D. cards had to be forged. If they showed identification revealing they were Jewish, the officer would have arrested them.)* **OL**

Viewing the Photo

Say: The caption says travelers were seated on a first-come, first-served basis. How could this possibly add to the danger of transporting Jewish people to safety? *(Possible response: The resistance couldn't plan where their agents and the Jews would sit, so they could end up sitting next to Germans or German supporters.)* **OL**

READING WORKSHOP 4

When we boarded the train we saw several compartments occupied by German officers. We walked through the corridors and finally found a compartment with only two older women sitting in it. The Jewish couple, immediately after sitting down, closed their eyes and pretended they were asleep. Suddenly a German officer opened the door of the compartment and hollered, "I.D. *bitte*." ("I.D. please.") All of us pulled out our I.D. cards, he looked at them and looked at us, and compared photos with faces, and looked again. Though shaky inside, I pretended to be calm. The Jewish couple, however, seemed visibly shaken. How could the officer not detect our fear? **10** **R**

After what seemed an eternity, the German handed our I.D. cards back to us and said with a smile, *"Danke schön und gute Reise."* ("Thank you very much and have a good trip.") Neither he nor the two older women in our compartment had noticed anything amiss.[5]

After about one hour the train stopped in the middle of some meadows. Passengers leaned out of the windows to see why the train had stopped. German soldiers were hollering and shouting commands. We heard that a small bridge had been slightly damaged, and the train could not safely cross it. We had to get out of the train and carefully walk, one after the other, over the damaged bridge. All three of us **dreaded**

This is a typical passenger train of the kind used throughout Europe in the early 1940s. Each train car was divided into small, semi-private rooms called *compartments.* Each room seated four to six passengers on a first-come, first-served basis.

Practice the Skills

10 Reading Skill

Visualizing Try to visualize this scene from the German officer's point of view. Why do you look at the I.D. cards? What do you see in this case?

5. ***Amiss*** means "wrong; not as it should be."

Vocabulary

dreaded (DRED ud) *v.* feared greatly

Additional Support

English Language Coach

Building Vocabulary Write the word *compartment* on the board, separating it into the following parts: *com-part-ment.* Tell students that the Latin root word *part* means "a portion of something that is divided." The prefix *com-* means "with," while the suffix *-ment* means "a product or thing." Have students use the word parts to define *compartment.* *(connected parts, or the sum of a group of connected parts)* **EL** **BL** **OL** Have students identify other words with the root *part.* *(partition, apartment, partnership)* **AL**

the watchful eyes of the German soldiers, but miraculously we crossed the bridge and boarded a waiting train on the other side without any problems.

We finally reached Enkhuizen, an ancient harbor town, where the brisk wind from the sea was blowing so hard that we had to hold on to hats, skirts, and scarves. We walked with farmers and their families to the ferry boat. The farmers were holding baskets full of chickens, purchased at the open-air market. **L** **11**

Many fishermen who made the trip across the inland sea to sell fish at the Enkhuizen market walked toward the boat, their baskets now filled with fresh produce to bring home.

We boarded the ferry boat and settled down rather close to each other, but not together. We ate some pieces of bread, bought some imitation coffee, then closed our eyes. The wind was blowing hard, and the ferry boat bounced on the waves. The Jewish woman began to look gray-green, but never spoke. The passage on the inland sea was uneventful, and after two hours we reached the northeast coast of Holland.

We stepped ashore, again under the watchful eyes of German officers, and went to a small waiting room. I wore a bright blue scarf and red mittens and was approached by a young man who wore a red scarf and blue wool gloves. The young man said, "Did you have a good trip? I am so happy to see you again. Come on, and we will have some coffee." **C**

I told him, "The trip was good, and I brought my aunt and uncle with me, so they can see a little bit of the countryside."

"Great!" he said. "You are very welcome."

After our coffee, the four of us left the small waiting room and climbed on a farm cart pulled by a horse. After about fifteen minutes of silent travel, the young man looked around. Nobody was in sight, and he stopped. He let me off the cart and then continued on with the Jewish couple.

I returned to the ferry boat on foot and started my long journey back to Amsterdam, very relieved that all had gone well that day. **12** ❍

Practice the Skills

11 Literary Element

Setting Notice the many details Ippisch provides to help you see each specific setting as she guides the couple to safety.

12 BIG Question

Ippisch really never mentions how or why she kept from giving up. Why do you think she is so dedicated to her cause? Write your answer on the Workshop 4 Foldable for Unit 6. Your answer will help you complete the Unit Challenge later.

Differentiated Instruction

Draw Scenes Students may benefit from using a visual method of documenting the events on page 887. Have these students identify at least four events or scenes from this page, and then use storyboards to sketch each scene in the order in which it happens. Students should provide captions that give a brief description of what is happening in each scene. **OL**

Teach

L Literary Element

Review Setting Ask: Does this "ancient harbor town" seem like a safe setting? Explain. *(Possible response: The presence of farmers and chickens makes it seem comforting. The wind, however, seems threatening.)* **OL**

C Critical Thinking

Comprehension Ask: Which details indicate that the narrator and the man she is meeting are using a code? *(Possible response: The narrator and the man wear scarves and mittens of opposite colors. She and the man must have identified themselves by the colors of their garments.)* **OL** **Ask:** What fictional story has the Resistance made up to explain why these people are taking this trip? *(A couple is traveling with their niece to see the Dutch countryside.)* **BL**

Assess

Use the CheckPoint questions provided on Presentation Plus! to check for comprehension of the selection. These questions can be used with interactive response keypads for immediate student feedback.

Indiana English/Language Arts Academic Standards

SE: 8.3, 8.3.4

TWE: *Literary Element* 8.3.4, 8.3.9; *English Language Coach* 8.1; *Differentiated Instruction* 8.7.9

Assess

Resources for page 888

- Selection Quick Check, p. 58
- Selection and Unit Assessment, p. 68
- ExamView Assessment Suite
- Interactive Tutor: Self-Assessment

Students can respond to the *After You Read* items in their Learner's Notebooks or on a separate sheet of paper.

Answering the BIG Question

1. Possible response: She chooses to put her own life in danger for the sake of others.
2. The woman tells the narrator that it is not "romantic" or "adventurous," and tries to persuade her not to join.
3. She is told where to meet her contact and which code words to use.

Critical Thinking

4. Possible responses: Her father inspired her; he was strongly opposed to the Nazis.
5. In rural areas, Jews were less likely to be noticed since there were fewer police officers watching them. In Amsterdam, Jews tended to live together, and they could be monitored more easily.
6. Responses will vary. Students may say that her father did not know because he would probably not approve of her doing something so dangerous at her age.

After You Read
from *Sky*

Answering the BIG Question

1. How is Hanneke Ippisch an example of someone who refuses to give up?
2. **Recall** How does the older woman respond when Ippisch goes to her house and asks to join the Resistance?
   TIP Right There
3. **Summarize** After joining the Resistance, how did Ippisch know which families to help and how to help them?
   TIP Think and Search

Critical Thinking

4. **Infer** Why do you think Ippisch decided to join the Resistance, in spite of warnings and knowing all that was at risk?
   TIP Author and Me
5. **Explain** Why was it important to get the Jews out of Amsterdam and moved to a more rural area?
   TIP Author and Me
6. **Evaluate** After the first paragraph, Ippisch never mentions her father. Do you think her father knew about her activities? If you were her father, would you approve of her joining the Resistance at such an early age? Explain your answer.
   TIP Author and Me

Talk About Your Reading

Debate Ippisch says that her life changed completely after she joined the Resistance. Looking at her life one way, you could say that she began to save people's lives. Looking at it another way, you could say that she began to tell lies, break laws, and risk lives. As a class, discuss whether it can be "right" to do "wrong." Begin by looking at the following questions.

- Apart from saving several lives, what good things came about as a result of Ippisch's choice?
- What risks were involved? Did her work for the Resistance endanger anyone other than Ippisch? If so, whom?
- When is it "right" to disobey a law? Does it matter who makes the law and why?

Indiana English/Language Arts Academic Standards (pp. 888–889)

8.3 Comprehension and Analysis of Literary Text Respond to grade-level-appropriate literature... **8.5.7** Write for different purposes... **8.3.4** Analyze the importance of setting to the mood, tone, and meaning... **8.3.9** Analyze the relevance of setting... **8.6.5** Use correct punctuation.

For a complete description of the standards, see p. IN 11.

Talk About Your Reading

Students should consider whether they can find justification for disobeying laws that they believe to be immoral. Students can discuss how to change rules or laws that they think are not fair.

Skills Review

Key Reading Skill: Visualizing

7. Choose a paragraph from the selection that you think is especially good for practicing visualizing. Identify three descriptive details and/or other information from the text to support your choice.

Literary Element: Setting

8. In general terms, identify the overall setting of this excerpt from *Sky*.

9. Which part of setting is most important in *Sky*? Which is least important? Explain your answers.

culture economy geography
spaces weather historical period

Reviewing Elements: Literal and Figurative Language

10. Explain the figurative meanings of *underground* and *underwater*, as used in this selection. Tell whom or what each term refers to.

Vocabulary Check

Rewrite each sentence, filling in the blank with the best vocabulary word from the list.

grave anticipation precautions observant dreaded

11. My sister always ___ the idea of walking home from the bus stop late at night.

12. "Stop, look, and listen" are ___ every child needs to learn about crossing the street.

13. Huge crowds gathered to wait in ___ of the annual fireworks display.

14. The worker who spotted the cracked beam was rewarded for being so ___.

15. The transit workers who went on strike created a ___ problem.

16. **English Language Coach** The Latin prefix *per-* means "through or throughout." What does the word *persist* mean? (For help, see the English Language Coach on page 880.)

Grammar Link: Commas with Dates and Addresses

Commas are used to set off items to prevent misreading. In a date, place a comma between the day and the year. If the date comes in the middle of a sentence, place another comma after the year. Don't use a comma if only the month and the year are given.

- The Last Poets performed at a memorial for Malcolm X on May 19, 1968.
- On May 19, 1968, the Last Poets performed at a memorial for Malcolm X.
- The Last Poets performed in May 1968.

Set off the name of a state or a country when it's used after the name of a city. Set off the name of a city when it's used after a street address. Don't use a comma after the state if it's followed by a ZIP code.

- Christian Sweerts lives in Liege, Belgium.
- Jon lived at 12 Bond Drive, Denton, Texas, for years.
- I'm moving to 229 Jamell Road, Ducks, PA 15609.

Grammar Practice

Copy each sentence, adding commas in the correct places.

17. My brother goes to college in Chicago Illinois.

18. My sister was born on February 20 1992.

19. My address is 500 Lee Avenue Boston MA 02121.

20. I was born at 2815 East Wilson Atlanta Georgia on March 14 1994 at 2:27 A.M.

Web Activities For eFlashcards, Selection Quick Checks, and other Web activities, go to www.glencoe.com.

Skills Review

Key Reading Skill: Visualizing

7. Possible response: The third full paragraph on page 887 includes images of the wind blowing, the boat on the waves, and a woman turning gray-green.

Literary Element: Setting

8. the Netherlands during World War II

9. Possible response: The historical period and culture are important, because the Netherlands is resisting the Nazi occupation. The weather is least important because the events do not depend on the weather.

Reviewing Elements: Literal and Figurative Language

10. *Underground* and *underwater* are used figuratively to describe hiding from the Nazis. Literally, something underground or underwater is not visible, and the Resistance operated out of sight of the Germans.

Vocabulary Check

11. dreaded

12. precautions

13. anticipation

14. observant

15. grave

English Language Coach

16. to continue or withstand

Grammar Link: Commas with Dates and Addresses

Grammar Practice

17. My brother goes to college in Chicago, Illinois.

18. My sister was born on February 20, 1992.

19. My address is 500 Lee Avenue, Boston, MA 02121.

20. I was born at 2815 East Wilson, Atlanta, Georgia, on March 14, 1994, at 2:27 A.M.

Close

Discuss with students why people were willing to continue their struggle against the Nazis.

Indiana English/Language Arts Academic Standards

SE: 8.3, 8.3.4, 8.3.9, 8.5.7, 8.6.5

Comparing Literature: Comparing Figurative Language

Teaching Students to Compare Figurative Language

Why Is It Important?

- Comparing figurative language helps students generate a better picture of the characters and events in a selection.
- Comparing figurative language also helps students pay more attention to specific details.
- Looking at the figurative language in selections from two different genres helps students make connections from text to text.

How to Help Students Get It

- Have students keep track of the figurative language as they read.
- Tell students to think about how the figurative language helps them better understand the similarities and differences between the characters, settings, and events in each selection.
- Remind students to look for similes, metaphors, and sensory images in the selections.

Reading to Answer the Big Question

Welcome by Ouida Sebsestyen
When Tina's parents separate, her mother takes Tina on a trip to visit her grandparents. On the way they spend some time with her father's family. His wise and loving Aunt Dessie is instrumental in helping Tina and her mother become ready to accept the radical change in their lives.

Alone by Maya Angelou
The speaker of this poem says that nobody can make it alone, whether the person is rich and successful or suffering through the storms of life.

Workshop Resources

Pacing (Days) Standard	Pacing (Days) Block	Lesson	Student Materials	Teacher Resources
1	1	Comparing Literature: Comparing Figurative Language	English Language Coach Review, p. 42	Bellringer Options Transparencies –Daily Language Practice 60 Presentation Plus!
1	1	"Welcome"	Glencoe Online Unit Vocabulary Review, p. 40 Academic Vocabulary Review, p. 43 English Language Coach Comparing Literature Graphic Organizer, p. 35 StudentWorks Plus™ Online Student Edition Literature Classics	Puzzlemaker Skill Level Up!™ A Language Arts Game BookLink 3 Assessment by Learning Objective (Diagnostic and Formative) Interactive Tutor: Self-Assessment TeacherWorks Plus™ ExamView Assessment Suite
1		"Alone"	Glencoe Online Unit Vocabulary Review, p. 40 Academic Vocabulary Review, p. 43 English Language Coach Comparing Literature Graphic Organizer, p. 35 StudentWorks Plus™ Online Student Edition Literature Classics	Puzzlemaker Skill Level Up!™ A Language Arts Game BookLink 3 Assessment by Learning Objective (Diagnostic and Formative) Interactive Tutor: Self-Assessment TeacherWorks Plus™ ExamView Assessment Suite

Keys for Unit Resource

- Blackline Master
- Workbook
- Supplemental Text
- CD-ROM
- DVD
- Transparency
- Web-based
- Fast File

Level Appropriate Code

AS = Activities for all students
AL = Activities for students working above grade level
OL = Activities for students working at grade level
BL = Activities for students working below grade level
EL = Activities for English language learners

Focus

BELLRINGER Options

Daily Language Practice Transparency 60
Focus Activity Ask: When you're having a hard time, do you generally choose to be alone or with others? What are the benefits of each choice? *(Responses will vary.)* AS

Teach

L Literary Element

Figurative Language Write the following sentences on the board. Ask students to identify the figurative language in each example:

- When my best friend Rosa said that she was moving to California, I felt as lost as a kitten in a storm. *(simile)*
- Rosa is a roller coaster. *(metaphor)*
- The wind whispered goodbye as Rosa's mother started the car. *(personification)*
- Rosa left me her jacket to remind me of the safety of our friendship. *(symbol)* OL

COMPARING LITERATURE WORKSHOP

Welcome

by Ouida Sebestyen

& Alone

by Maya Angelou

Skills Focus

You will use these skills as you read and compare the following selections:

- "Welcome," p. 893
- "Alone," p. 906

Reading

- Making connections from across texts

Literature

- Understanding literal and figurative language

Writing

- Writing to compare and contrast

Indiana English/Language Arts Academic Standards (pp. 890–891)

8.3.6 Identify significant literary devices, such as metaphor [or] symbolism...

For a complete description of the standards, see p. IN 11.

Figurative language is used for descriptive effect. Writers use figures of speech to connect two things that seem different or unrelated. The narrator of "Welcome" says that her aunt "unfolded out of the car like a carpenter's ruler." In this simile, the aunt's movement reminds the narrator of a ruler that folds up to fit in the carpenter's pocket. This can help you visualize the aunt more clearly.

How to Compare Literature: Figurative Language

Here's a review of some forms of figurative language:

- A **simile** compares two unlike things using the word *like* or *as.*
  Example: The baby's blanket was soft as a cloud.
- L A **metaphor** compares two unlike things without using *like* or *as.*
  Example: The baby's crib was a huge, colorful world.
- **Personification** gives a human quality to an animal, object, or idea.
  Example: Wind chimes sang the baby to sleep.
- A **symbol** is an object, person, place, or event that stands for something else.

As you read, watch for examples of figurative language. Look for

- words or phrases whose literal definitions don't make sense in their context
- objects that may represent larger ideas
- descriptions that involve comparisons

Additional Support

Literature Focus Lesson

Figurative Language Remind students that writers use similes and metaphors

- to encourage readers to think about familiar items in new ways
- to help readers visualize new or different places
- to help readers understand how a character is feeling
- to entertain readers with clever comparisons

Have students create their own simile or metaphor to describe

- a feeling, such as sadness or joy
- their favorite place
- a person they really like OL AL

Get Ready to Compare

Writers use figurative language to communicate specific shades of meaning, or to compare unlike things. Look at the simile below:

- The fresh snow glittered like diamonds.

Snow and diamonds don't share many characteristics. You would never confuse one with the other. However, the sentence above compares their one shared quality–their glitter–to help you create a mental picture.

In your Learner's Notebook, copy the sentences below. Tell whether each sentence is an example of simile, metaphor, or personification. Then tell what two things or ideas are being compared.

- The sun smiled on Diego as he walked down the street.
- Marco was a machine, scoring nearly thirty points a game.
- Selma's cast was as hard as a rock.

Use Your Comparison

As you read each selection, keep track of examples of figurative language by using a graphic organizer like the one below. Make an organizer for each selection. You will use these organizers to compare the selections later.

In column 1, list the page number. In column 2, note the figure of speech. In column 3, identify the kind of figurative language. In column 4, explain what you think it means.

"Welcome"			
page	Figure of Speech	Kind	Explanation
894	"Aunt Dessie unfolded out of the car like a carpenter's ruler."	simile	She's stiff and sore from the long ride and has to unbend slowly.

Teach

L Literary Element

Figurative Language **Say:** To help you organize your charts, consider color-coding them. For example, write similes in red, metaphors in blue, personification in green, and symbols in purple. This coding system will help you organize examples to use in your comparison at the end of the workshop on p. 909. **AS**

Assess/Close

Have each student write two sentences that include figurative language. Then have each student exchange papers with a partner and label the figurative language in their partner's sentences. **OL**

Resources for page 891

Use the Comparing Literature Graphic Organizer BLM in the Unit 6 Resource Booklet, p. 35.

Reading in the Real World

Career The selections in this workshop address the benefits of allowing others to help us through our pain. Tell students that many careers are available for people who wish to help others, from social workers and psychiatrists, who help people address their emotional pain, to doctors, nurses, emergency service technicians, and holistic practitioners, who help people address their physical pain. Have students discuss the benefits and challenges of these careers. **OL** Ask interested students to interview someone in a mental or physical health field about the pros and cons of the job and share responses with the class. **AL**

Indiana English/Language Arts Academic Standards
SE: 8.3.6
TWE: *Literature Focus Lesson* 8.3.6, *Reading in the Real World* 8.7.1

Teach

More About the Author

Ouida Sebestyen knows what it means to try different careers before landing on the one that's right. She held jobs cleaning houses and serving hamburgers. She ran her own child care center, and she worked as a civilian mechanic who repaired PT19's. Sebestyen said, "I wrote for thirty years before *Words by the Heart* became an instant success, and hope that my Cinderella story encourages other would-be writers to keep trying."

V Vocabulary

Writing Sentences **Say:** Write a sentence that uses each of the vocabulary words. Share your sentences with a partner to be sure you've used each word correctly. *(Responses will vary)* EL BL

Readability Scores
Dale-Chall: 4.7
DRP: 48
Lexile: 690

Before You Read | Welcome

Meet the Author

Ouida Sebestyen was born in Vernon, Texas in 1924. She began writing in high school, and tried to publish her first novel when she was twenty. It was not published, but she kept writing. Finally, in 1979, she published *Words by Heart,* which won several awards. Sebestyen hopes her story encourages other struggling writers to keep working on their craft. See page R6 of the Author Files for more on Sebestyen.

Author Search For more about Ouida Sebestyen, go to www.glencoe.com.

Indiana English/Language Arts Academic Standards (pp. 892–904)

8.1.2 Understand the influence of historical events on...word meaning... **8.3.6** Identify significant literary devices, such as metaphor [or] symbolism...

For a complete description of the standards, see p. IN 11.

Vocabulary Preview

V

dismal (DIZ mul) *adj.* gloomy or depressing **(p. 893)** *Rainy and cold, the day was dismal.*

ultimatum (ul tuh MAY tum) *n.* a final demand that, if unmet, carries harsh penalties **(p. 896)** *Pedro's mother gave him an ultimatum: if he didn't clean his room, he'd be grounded for a month.*

famished (FAM isht) *adj.* extremely hungry **(p. 900)** *After hiking for six hours, I was so famished I could have eaten a bear.*

pivoted (PIH vuh tid) *v.* turned around sharply; form of the verb *pivot* **(p. 902)** *Hurrying to prepare dinner, Jakob's father pivoted from the stove to the refrigerator.*

coaxed (kohkst) *v.* urged gently; form of the verb *coax* **(p. 903)** *Suzanne coaxed the rabbit from its hiding place beneath the house.*

English Language Coach

Historical Influences on English In this unit, you've learned that many English words came from other languages. A good example of that is the word *tripod* in "Welcome." The Romans took it from the Greek *tri-* ("three") and *pod-* or *pous* ("foot"). A tripod is a three-footed stool, table, or stand (for a camera or telescope). As you read the story, watch for words that contain these roots:

vers ➡ turn	punct ➡ point, dot

Get Ready to Read

Connect to the Reading

Think of a time when you faced change or uncertainty in your own life. Did you talk about your feelings with a friend? If so, what did you say? What did you do to keep from giving up?

Set Purposes for Reading

BIG Question Read to learn more about the welcome a girl and her mother receive when their travels take them off the beaten path.

Set Your Own Purpose What would you like to learn from the selection to help you answer the Big Question? Write your own purpose on the Comparing Literature Foldable for Unit 6.

Additional Support

LiteratureOnline

Author Search To expand students' appreciation of Ouida Sebestyen, have them access the Web site for additional information and resources

English Language Coach

Historical Influences Have students brainstorm other words that use the Greek *tri-*. Have each student draw a web diagram. In the center circle, students should write "Tri-." In the outer circles, students should write modern words that use *tri-*. Students can use a dictionary if they need help. After students have filled in the diagram, have them share their words with the class. Students may suggest words such as *triangle, tricycle, trio, triplet, triple,* or *triathlon.* EL BL

Welcome

by Ouida Sebestyen

My father's Aunt Dessie peered through the windshield at a road sign. "Slow up a little bit, Mary," she told my mother. "The last time I tried to find kinfolks I hadn't visited for a while, I got the house number and the street perfect, but I was in the wrong town." She turned to me in the back seat. "I ran across this yard yelling, 'Guess who's here, Annabelle,' and burst right in on a white lady. Perfect stranger." R1

I caught my mother's eyes in the rearview mirror and made a pretend smile for Aunt Dessie, thinking how I would describe her to my friend Sharon when I got home. *Picture this eighty-year-old drill sergeant? In drag? With this head of corn-row hair she must have made with a real hoe?* Sharon would double up. At least as far as she could double, now. R2

My mother slowed to a creep. Yesterday evening, bowling along through Texas on her way to see her parents, she had swerved off the interstate toward a **dismal** little town. 1 Before I could figure what in blazes she was doing, we were spending the night on Aunt Dessie's let-down couch between two whatnots crammed with spinster[1] junk. I had hissed, "What *is* this—I hate changes." But my mother just lay with her back

1. A ***let-down couch*** is a sofa that unfolds to become a bed. ***Whatnots*** are end tables. A ***spinster*** is an older, unmarried woman.

Vocabulary

dismal (DIZ mul) *adj.* gloomy or depressing

Practice the Skills

1 Comparing Literature

Figurative Language When the author says "bowling along through Texas," can you imagine the car as a bowling ball?

Teach

R1 Reading Skill

Review Paraphrasing and Summarizing Say: Paraphrase Aunt Dessie's story. Why is it funny? *(Possible response: Aunt Dessie was looking for relatives, and she had the address right, but she was in the wrong town. The story is funny because she ended up running across the yard, yelling, and bursting into the home of a complete stranger.)* OL AL

R2 Reading Skill

Review Visualizing Ask: What words in the narrator's description of Aunt Dessie tell you the narrator is not being very kind? *(drill sergeant, in drag, corn-row hair . . . made with a real hoe)* BL **Ask:** Does the narrator's description help you visualize Aunt Dessie? Why or why not? *(Possible response: Although the description isn't very nice, it does help me see an old, stern, and unattractive woman with cornrows.)* OL

Differentiated Instruction

Making Changes Tina, the narrator in the story, says she hates changes. Ask students whether they agree or disagree with her and why. As a class, brainstorm a list of changes they will have to make when they enter high school next year. Ask volunteers to assess whether they believe the changes will be good or bad. Tell students to read on to learn how Tina deals with a big change in her life. Have students determine the positive and negative aspects of this change. OL

Indiana English/Language Arts Academic Standards

SE: 8.1.2, 8.3.6

TWE: *English Language Coach* 8.1, *Differentiated Instruction* 8.3

Teach

L1 Literary Element

Figurative Language Ask: Why does the narrator call the tripod "unsteady"? *(There are problems in her family.)* OL AL

EL Language Coach

Historical Influences on English Say: In this context, what does *reverse* mean? *(It means "opposite.")* EL BL

L2 Literary Element

Figurative Language Ask: What does her mother's new, curly hair growth symbolize to the narrator? *(It symbolizes the end of her parents' love for each other.)* OL **Ask:** What might it symbolize for her mother? *(Possible responses: new freedom; not having to please her husband anymore; the end of her marriage)* AL

to me, pretending to be asleep, while strange summer things from the piney woods tapped against the screens.

Aunt Dessie said, "Noella's going to be as surprised as I was. I still can't believe I'm riding along beside you, Mary. After seventeen years."

"Is it that long?" my mother said.

Aunt Dessie turned back to me. "And to finally get to see you, pretty thing. The image of your daddy."

"Are you sure this is the road?" my mother said sharply. "We've really got to keep this visit brief."

"Then why don't you stop at that little place up there and let me ask. Some of this backwoods is hazy in my mind."

We stopped. Aunt Dessie unfolded out of the car like a carpenter's ruler, and yanked open the screen door of a little grocery that had been waiting for a customer since the Depression.[2]

I murmured, "Lordy mercy, as they say down here. Are we talking hazy or crazy?"

"That's enough smart lip," my mother warned me. "You be nice to her. She took us in like royalty. She didn't have to."

"If she tells me one more time I look like my daddy—"

"You do."

"I look like me." It mattered that I was my own special leg of the proud unsteady tripod my mother and father and I had always made. "I feel very guess-who's-here-Annabelle." **2**

"Me too, a little. But suddenly I just wanted to see her and your great-aunt Noella again. I've never forgotten how they took me into the family. No questions. No testing. Just welcome." She was silent, remembering. "I guess I needed their blessing, or something. But I can't tell if Dessie knows."

She lifted the hot hair off her coffee-and-cream neck. She had always worn her hair long and straightened, to please my father. **Reverse** perm after reverse perm. **3** But now the newest inch of it had its own natural crinkle, recording almost to the day, I guess, when they stopped loving each other. Old fears began to press me like fingers finding the deep secret acupressure[3] points of pain. "What do you mean, *if she knows?* What's to know? You're going to patch all this

2. The ***Depression*** ("the Great Depression") lasted from 1929 to 1939. The stock market crashed, banks and other businesses failed, and millions of people lost their jobs and savings.
3. ***Acupressure*** (AK yoo preh shur) is a type of massage used to relieve tension or pain.

Practice the Skills

2 Comparing Literature

Figurative Language If the narrator's family is a tripod, it has only three members. What does the rest of the metaphor suggest about the family? Make notes in your organizer. L1

3 English Language Coach

Historical Influences How does the Latin root *vers* give meaning to **reverse**? EL

Additional Support

Reading in the Real World

Career Explain to students that permanents are chemical solutions that make straight hair curly. Reverse permanents are also called relaxers. Relaxers make curly hair straight by breaking the bonds that give curly hair its strength. Because relaxers weaken hair and reduce natural scalp oils, it is important that relaxed hair be cared for properly. Students interested in careers as hair stylists may be interested in reading more about career training options as well as the processes used in styling hair for different ethnic groups. OL up. Like the other times, and everything's going to be fine again." 4

She put her hands on the wheel as if she needed to be driving.

"You are," I said.

"Tina, sometimes things—"

"No. You *are*."

Aunt Dessie came striding out, carrying a piece of paper in one hand and a bright canvas bag in the other.

"Lady in there makes these totes," she announced, handing it to me. "A souvenir."

I took it, surprised. "Thanks," I said, actually smiling in my confusion. Her old eyes studied me so long that I said too loudly, "Hey, I could embroider YUCK! on it and give it to Sharon for a diaper bag."

"Who's Sharon?" Aunt Dessie asked.

My mother started off with a jerk. "A bubble-headed little blonde Tina knows back home."

"Just my best friend," I said.

Aunt Dessie studied the scrap of paper someone had drawn a map on. "Ah," she nodded. "I see."

"Actually," my mother said, her voice accelerating with the car, "she's a strange little person who keeps trying to saddle Tina with all her problems. I hoped this trip would give them a vacation from each other."

Lie, I said to her back. *You'd rather run from that empty-feeling house than face up to your life.* C

Analyzing the Photo
What experience is this picture trying to suggest?

Practice the Skills

4 Comparing Literature

Figurative Language This paragraph begins with a metaphor describing the color of the mother's skin. A few sentences later, the narrator uses a simile to describe "old fears." Explain both figures of speech in your organizer. L

Teach

L Literary Element

Figurative Language Ask: How is it possible for fear to press like fingers? *(Responses will vary. Students may note that fear can cause physical reactions.)* OL

C Critical Thinking

Comprehension Call students' attention to the two lines at the bottom of page 895. **Ask:** What is different about these lines from the rest of the text? *(The lines are written in italics.)* **Ask:** Why are these lines in italics? *(Tina does not say this information aloud. These are her thoughts.)* OL

Differentiated Instruction

Word Portraits Say: The author has introduced four characters so far in this story. Create a "word portrait" of each person. First, make a list of details that you notice about each character. Use your own words and the words of the author. Then create a word portrait describing the character's appearance and actions. Add to your portraits as you learn more about these characters and are introduced to additional characters. At the end of the story, share your portraits with the class. EL BL OL

Indiana English/Language Arts Academic Standards
SE: 8.1.2, 8.3.6
TWE: *Reading in the Real World* 8.2, *Differentiated Instruction* 8.5

Teach

L Literary Element

Figurative Language Ask: What does Tina mean when she says that her mother "went off like a ton of dynamite?" *(Tina means that her mother got very angry.)* **OL** What actions do the three words the narrator uses after the simile emphasize about her mother's reaction? *(Possible response: They emphasize her mother's rage.)* **AL**

C Critical Thinking

Comprehension: Ask: What makes Tina's mother stop the car abruptly? *(She finds out that Tina gave Sharon keys to their house, and she's staying there while Tina and her mother are away.)* **OL**

"She didn't saddle me," I told Aunt Dessie. "Somebody has to look after Sharon, she's so casual, so inconceivably[4]—" I began to giggle crazily and couldn't stop. "I have to remind her what the doctor says to do, or she'll eat like she wants a French-fried baby with diet-cola blood."

"I think we can spare Aunt Dessie the details."

"Hey, all I did was ask if she could stay with us till the baby comes. And you went off like a ton of dynamite—rip, mangle, roar." My mother's eyes tried to grab mine in the mirror, but I wouldn't look. I wanted to give the details. Hadn't she driven miles out of her way to give her side of things to my father's aunts before he did? Okay, I wanted to tell about my friend who wasn't afraid to gulp down whole chunks of life I hadn't even dared to taste. **5**

She said, "The last thing I need is a tenth-grade dropout with a fatherless child on the way."

"There's always a father," I objected. "She just doesn't want him around." I tried to think what the slang had been in my mother's day. "He's a creep. She doesn't really like him."

"Turn left," Aunt Dessie said. My mother swerved.

"It's the baby that's important," I said. "Sharon's going to have something really truly her very own. She's glad about it."

"My God," my mother said. She bore through a tunnel of pines riddled with sunlight shafts. "But not in my house."

I braced myself carefully. "But she *is* in our house. I gave her the key before we left."

The car lurched to a stop. My mother swung around in her seat. "Tina! You knew perfectly well how I felt about that."

"Where else could she go?"

"Good heavens, she has parents."

"Oh, sure, her mother's in Florida with four stepchildren and her dad got an **ultimatum** from his girl friend. Who's she supposed to turn to besides us? I'm her friend. I thought you were, too, the way you were always nice to her and laughed when she did weird things—"

4. ***Inconceivably*** means "unbelievably."

Vocabulary

ultimatum (ul tuh MAY tum) *n.* a final demand that, if unmet, carries harsh penalties

Practice the Skills

5 Comparing Literature

Figurative Language You've noticed by now that Tina (the narrator) uses many figures of speech. In this paragraph alone, she uses three. Note each in your organizer, and explain what it tells you about Tina.

Additional Support

Literature Focus Lesson

Narrator and Mood Remind students that a story's mood, or atmosphere, is created by descriptions, events, and characters. Encourage students to see how the mood of the narrator affects the story's mood by answering the following questions:

- What is Tina's mood in the beginning of the story?
- How does her mood affect her descriptions of her aunt, her mother, and their trip?
- How do the descriptions affect the overall mood of the story? **AL**

Aunt Dessie said firmly, "Left again up there at that tree."

My mother started the car and drove past a field of sunflowers all staring at us with little happy faces. Slowly tears as hard as hailstones filled my throat. "I thought I could depend on you," I said, bumping along like the car. "To help her. But you slide out of things like a plate of noodles." **L1**

Aunt Dessie said, "I gather your daddy's away from home."

"He still travels, you know," my mother answered for me. "In his kind of work he has to, a great deal."

She slowed as the rutted road dipped for a creek. A little boy in overalls stood expectantly beside a mailbox. Suddenly I knew how my father had looked, growing up in those piney woods. Waiting for the mail carrier to come with something wonderful. I snapped my eyes shut to block him off. I didn't want to think about my father. I didn't even know how to think about him anymore. I just wanted everything to stand still, frozen like that little boy, so that nothing would ever have to arrive. **6** **L2**

"How long has he been dead?" I heard my mother say. I jerked to attention, but she added, "Noella's husband."

"I guess two years now," Aunt Dessie said. "Bless her heart, it must be hard for her." She turned around in the seat, raising her voice in case I had gone deaf. "Noella's husband was your Granddaddy Mayhew's brother, you see, and I'm from your grandmother's side, so Noella and I aren't anything like blood kin.[5]"

My mother said, "Why have you kept up with each other all these years?"

Aunt Dessie craned to read the name of a small wooden church we were passing. "I guess we just feel related." She turned back to me. "Your daddy stayed with me four years, so he could be close to a better school. I loved that boy."

I gazed at the crooked rows of her gray hair, wondering what age she had been when she stared into a mirror at her horse face and rawboned body and knew no man was ever going to love her. **7**

We passed a square unpainted house smothering under a trumpet vine. "Whoa!" Aunt Dessie commanded. "It says Mayhew on the mailbox."

5. Dessie and Noella are related by marriage only and are not blood relatives ***(blood kin)***.

Practice the Skills

6 Comparing Literature

Figurative Language What does Tina tell you about her father and their relationship? Remember to explain the figures of speech in your organizer.

7 Comparing Literature

Figurative Language Tina is saying that her aunt's features are horse-like. How does this comparison influence your mental picture of Aunt Dessie?

Teach

L1 Literary Element

Figurative Language **Ask:** What simile does Tina use to describe the tears in the throat? *(She says they are "as hard as hailstones.")* **OL** **Ask:** Why is Tina upset at her mother? *(She says she thought she could depend on her mother to help her friend. She is upset that her mother doesn't want to help out.)* **BL**

L2 Literary Element

Figurative Language **Ask:** Why does Tina want to freeze time? *(Tina thinks that if she can stop time, her father won't leave the family.)* **OL**

English Language Coach

Dialect A dialect is a way of speaking that is associated with a specific geographical area or a group of people. Authors use dialect to give their writing the flavor of a specific region and to reveal the economic or social class of a character. A dialect may have its own vocabulary, grammar, and system for pronunciation.

In the United States, the principal dialect is Standard English, but several regional dialects also exist. Encourage students to point out the dialect used by the older characters in this story:

- "Slow up a little bit" (page 893)
- "kinfolks" (page 893)
- "blood kin" (page 897) **AS**

Indiana English/Language Arts Academic Standards
SE: 8.3.6
TWE: *Literature Focus Lesson* 8.3, *English Language Coach* 8.1

Teach

L1 Literary Element

Figurative Language **Ask:** What does it feel like when you pull a plant out of the ground? *(Students may suggest that they can feel the roots cling to the dirt.)* AS **Ask:** What is Tina saying about Noella's arms? *(Responses will vary. Students may say that Noella's arms hold on like she's not going to let go, just as roots hold the earth.)* OL

L2 Literary Element

Figurative Language **Ask:** To what does Tina compare herself? *(a helpless rock)* BL **Ask:** What does this simile suggest about how Tina feels when Noella hugs her? *(Possible response: Tina feels trapped and doesn't want a long hug from Noella.)* OL

Analyzing the Photo Is this house similar to the one Tina describes?

"This is it?" My mother stopped and backed up. At the side of a barn two pigs lay in a juicy wallow.[6] Some little granny in **clodhopper** shoes just had to be around the corner, stewing the wash in a black pot. "Good heavens," she murmured. "I wouldn't live out here all alone for the world." 8

"Well, Noella's not alone, you remember. She's still got Arley with her." Aunt Dessie flipped her stiff old hand at a hill nearby. "And the old Mayhew cemetery's up there. There's family around."

We stopped in front of the house. The screen opened and a little dried-apple woman came to the edge of the porch. Aunt Dessie unfolded and strode up the steps into her arms.

"Who do you think I brought to see you, Noella?" she demanded. "Here's Jimmie's wife. Mary."

Jimmie? I thought. My father could never have been anyone but James. Cool upwardly mobile[7] James.

"Of course it's Mary," Noella said in a quavery voice as tender as cake. "You precious thing. I'm so thankful to see you again." She wound her arms around my mother like roots. 9

Aunt Dessie said, "And this is Jimmie's daughter. This is Tina." Then I was inside that root-hold, as helpless as a rock being broken by long gentle pressure. L2

"I would have known you," Noella said. I braced myself. "You have his face, your daddy's face. I always hoped I'd get to see you." She looked beyond me at the empty car.

My mother looked, too, as if she had just recalled the trips we used to take when my father would wake up in the back

6. Pigs lie in a ***wallow*** (a puddle of thick mud) to stay cool.

7. An ***upwardly mobile*** person can improve his or her social status.

Practice the Skills

8 English Language Coach

Historical Influences A *clod* (from Old English) is a lump of earth, and a **clodhopper** would logically be a farmer. However, the word has been used since the 1700s to make fun of farmers by suggesting that they're clumsy and crude. In the story, Tina may or may not be mocking "granny," but clodhopper shoes is a real term for heavy work boots.

9 Comparing Literature

Figurative Language What could it mean to say that someone's arms are like roots? Notice that Tina stretches this figure of speech into the next paragraph. L1

Additional Support

Differentiated Instruction

Character Description Point out to students that Tina describes Noella in terms of food. She calls her "a dried-apple woman" and says that her voice is as "tender as cake". Ask students what these descriptions suggest about Noella. Then ask each student to draw a picture of Noella and write an appropriate descriptive caption beneath the image. Make sure that students take Tina's descriptions into consideration. If some students would rather not draw, have them write a paragraph describing Noella's physical appearance. Invite volunteers to share their pictures or descriptions with the class. EL BL OL seat, yelling, "Hey, we've *arrived*—why didn't you tell me?" while we laughed. "James would have liked to come, I'm sure. But he's a busy man these days."

Noella took her arm. "Tell him I miss him."

"Yes," my mother said, glancing sharply at me to make sure I didn't blurt out, *How can she tell him when he moved out a month ago?*

We sat in Noella's cramped little living room while she slushed around in her slippers, bringing us iced tea. She and Aunt Dessie took big breaths and brought each other up-to-date on who had died since they last visited. They made me nervous, reminding me how life changes and the people we love fall away. **10** **R**

I stared out the window through a bouquet of plastic flowers that was never going to die. All at once I realized that a man's bearded face was staring at me.

I screamed, giving a start that filled my lap with iced tea.

Noella said calmly, "It's just Arley, precious. He wants to see who you are, but he's shy." The face scowled, punctured by a gaping mouth, and disappeared. She patted my skirt with everyone's pink paper napkins and sent me out into the sun to dry. **11** **L**

Aunt Dessie strolled out behind me. "Who's Arley?" I whispered, afraid I'd see that face again peeking through the beanpoles of the garden.

"Noella's son," Aunt Dessie said.

"But he's middle-aged." It sounded stupid, but I couldn't recall ever seeing a retarded adult. I guess I thought they stayed children.

"Of course he is. We grow, whether we're ready or not. We do the best we can." She picked a skinny red-pepper pod and bit off the end. "Mercy! Jalapeño.[8]" She fanned her tongue.

We walked along the garden rows while my skirt dried. Behind a hedge a bear-shaped shadow stayed even with us.

"Your mother seems very sad," Aunt Dessie said.

I shrugged. "Really?" Suddenly it would have been a relief to pour out the whole They've-split-again-and-it's-awful-and-I'm-scared story. **C**

"Trouble at home?"

8. The red ***jalapeño*** (haw luh PAY nyoh) pepper is indeed hot.

Practice the Skills

10 Comparing Literature

Figurative Language Of course, Tina doesn't mean that people physically fall. What does she mean? Who, in her own life, does Tina fear will "fall away"?

11 English Language Coach

Historical Influences Which word in this paragraph contains the root *punct*? Use the root's meaning to write a definition of this word.

Teach

R Reading Skill

Review Drawing Conclusions Ask: Based on Tina's earlier comment about hating change, why would the conversation between Noella and Dessie make Tina nervous? *(The two old woman are talking about people who have died. A discussion of this kind of change would make Tina nervous.)* **OL** **Ask:** What change in Tina's life is she probably reminded of while listening to their story? *(Tina's father is leaving the family.)* **AL**

L Literary Element

Figurative Language Ask: What does Tina mean when she describes Arley's face as punctured? *(Tina thinks that Arley's face looks as if someone has poked a hole in it and made a mouth.)* **OL**

C Critical Thinking

Evaluation Ask: At first, Tina seemed to dislike Aunt Dessie. What suggests she's changed her mind? *(Possible response: She wants to tell Aunt Dessie about the troubles in her family and her fear of things changing.)* **OL**

Differentiated Instruction

Family Tree Students may benefit from creating a family tree to show how all the characters in the story are related. Remind students that the aunts are related to Tina's father, not her mother. Show students a sample family tree from the Internet or a library book. Have students form groups to create their trees, and be sure they match the information in the story. If they choose, students might illustrate their trees with pictures of the characters. **EL** **BL** **OL**

Indiana English/Language Arts Academic Standards
SE: 8.1.2, 8.3.6
TWE: *Differentiated Instruction* (p. 898) 8.5, *Differentiated Instruction* (p. 899) 8.2

Teach

L Literary Element

Figurative Language **Say:** Aunt Dessie asks her gallbladder to forgive her. What type of figurative language is she using? *(personification)* OL **Ask:** Why is Aunt Dessie asking her gallbladder to forgive her? *(She is overeating.)* AL

Ask: What does Tina's mother lock out of her life? *(She locks out anything that scares her; for example, the reality that her husband has left her. She also locks out Sharon, Tina's friend.)* OL

I kept shrugging. "Not exactly. Well, maybe a little, but they'll work it out. They always do."

"Ah," Aunt Dessie said.

When we went into the kitchen, my mother was setting plates around a table that practically sagged under bowls of macaroni and cheese and sliced tomatoes and fried okra and chowchow[9] and peaches that perfumed the room. All at once I was **famished.**

Noella piled food on a tray and took it to the door, saying, "Arley wants to eat on the porch. It takes him a little while to get used to new people."

I stuffed myself. Aunt Dessie kept right up with me, begging her gall bladder to forgive and forget. My mother ate in silence, watching the two old faces opposite her like a play. L 12

Noella said, "The last time Dessie came for a visit she brought me the most beautiful crocheted[10] bedspread you ever set eyes on. I'll show it to you. Are you still doing bedspreads?"

"Can't afford the thread anymore," Aunt Dessie said. "Now it's bootees and little sacques[11] and caps. I sell some for baby showers and give the rest away to whoever's expecting."

Noella asked, "What kind of projects keep you busy, Mary?"

My mother opened her mouth and nothing came out. I waited with them, curious. *Tell them your hobby is collecting little keys that lock out the things in your life that scare you. And lock you in.* 13

A glass shattered out on the porch. We jumped again as something crashed against the wall. A blubbering growl rose and faded as footsteps pounded off the porch and away.

Noella took a broom and went out. We waited. My mother pressed a careful furrow in her food and we all studied it like a divination.[12] She asked, "Who will take care of him when she dies?"

9. ***Okra*** is a green vegetable, and ***chowchow*** is a pickle relish.
10. The ***crocheted*** (kroh SHAYD) bedspread was made with a kind of needlework similar to knitting.
11. A ***sacque*** (sak) is a baby's short jacket that fastens at the neck.
12. A ***divination*** (dih vuh NAY shun) is an object or event that is used to predict the future.

Vocabulary

famished (FAM isht) *adj.* extremely hungry

Practice the Skills

12 Comparing Literature

Figurative Language People with gall bladder problems are not supposed to eat rich foods or eat too much at one time. Here, the author personifies Aunt Dessie's gall bladder, giving it the qualities of a person. What words show the author personifying Aunt Dessie's gall bladder?

13 BIG Question BQ

Mary (Tina's mother) doesn't literally collect keys, of course. Tina uses this metaphor to describe how her mother deals with conflict. What exactly is she saying? Write your answer on the Comparing Foldable for Unit 6.

Additional Support

Differentiated Instruction

Writing to Sharon Have students write a letter from Tina to Sharon describing Tina's visit with Aunt Dessie and Noella. Students could describe one or more of the following in their letter:

- the people Tina met
- the setting
- the events
- how Tina feels about what happens

Encourage students to use figurative language, like Tina does, in their letters. OL

Aunt Dessie nodded, musing. "Yes. When he's alone. She worries terribly about that."

Unexpectedly my mother reached across the table and laid her hand on Aunt Dessie's. Aunt Dessie put her other hand on top of theirs and we all looked at the funny fragile layers of hands until Noella came back with the tray full of spilled food and broken glass.

In the hurting silence I found myself offering to do the dishes while they visited, but Noella shooed us out, saying she could do dishes when she didn't have us. I hung at the kitchen door, feeling somehow drawn to her, as she put up the food. "I'm sorry I screamed," I said. "I didn't know." **14**

"Of course you didn't, sugar." She took a dozen gorgeous peaches off the windowsill and put them in a sack. "When Arley was little and I finally knew he was never going to be right, I screamed too. Screamed and screamed." She put the sack into my hands. "Take these with you. Your mother said you're on your way to see her folks." **R1**

I wished she hadn't reminded me. "She never did this before." As if I had taken the bottom piece of fruit out of the pyramid at the market, everything began to tumble. "Left home, I mean. To go talk to her folks about it. Like this time it was—it was—" I felt silly tripping over a simple word like *serious.* **15** **R2**

"Bless your heart," Noella said.

When we went into the living room, Aunt Dessie asked us, "We do have time to go up to the cemetery a minute, don't we?"

My mother shook her head. "I'm afraid it's getting—"

"We have time," I said. I offered my arm to Noella and we went out past my mother's surprised face.

She and Aunt Dessie followed us up a shade-spattered road to the top of the hill. Noella opened a gate in a wire fence and let us into the little graveyard filled with dark cedars. "Used to be a church here, at the beginning," she said. I looked around, wondering why I had wanted so suddenly and urgently, back at the house, to stand up there with my kin.

Noella led us through the high weeds to a grave with a neat concrete cover. A jar with the stem of a rose in it stood beside the nameplate. Dried petals lay around it. "Arley comes," Noella said.

Practice the Skills

14 Comparing Literature

Figurative Language How might a "hurting" silence be different from an "awkward" or "angry" silence? Think about how a figure of speech can shade the meaning of a description.

15 Comparing Literature

Figurative Language What does Tina mean by *everything* here? What does the simile tell you about her feelings at this moment?

Teach

R1 Reading Skill

Review Making Inferences **Ask:** What does Noella do when she finds out her son is never going "to be right"? *(She screams.)* **BL** **Ask:** What does this suggest about how Noella copes with hard times? *(Possible response: She expresses her feelings in whatever way she can. She doesn't bottle them inside.)* **OL**

R2 Reading Skill

Review Analyzing **Ask:** How has Tina tried to protect herself from the truth of her father's leaving? *(By not giving voice to her fears, Tina has tried to protect herself from the truth.)* **OL** **Ask:** How can you tell she's opening up to Noella? *(She tells Noella her mother has never acted this way when her parents have fought before.)* **AL**

English Language Coach

Monitoring Comprehension One way to monitor comprehension is to ask and answer questions while reading. Active readers constantly ask themselves questions as they read because it helps with concentration and comprehension. A question about the passage on these pages, for example, is "Why is it important to Tina to honor Noella's wishes to visit the graveyard?"

Have students work in small groups to write questions for the last three pages. Compile a list of all the different questions. Then go around the room asking students to answer each one. **OL**

Indiana English/Language Arts Academic Standards

SE: 8.1.2, 8.3.6

TWE: *Differentiated Instruction* 8.5, *English Language Coach* 8.2

Teach

R1 Reading Skill

Review Inferring **Ask:** Why does the inscription on the gravestone make Tina's mother cry? *(It reminds her that her marriage is ending.)* **Ask:** What does Tina know that her aunts do not? *(Tina knows that her parents' marriage is over.)* OL

R2 Reading Skill

Review Drawing Conclusions **Ask:** What conclusion can you draw about Tina from her statement about her parents being adults? *(Possible response: You can conclude she thinks all adults should be able to fix their problems, no matter what.)* OL **Ask:** Do you think this is a reasonable expectation? Why or why not? *(Possible response: No, not all problems can be solved, even by responsible adults.)* AS

Analyzing the Photo In stories and movies, cemeteries are often scary places. What feelings do you get about this country graveyard?

Aunt Dessie pulled two weeds and brushed the nameplate with their leafy tops. "He was a good kind man, Noella." They looked down in silence. "You were fortunate."

"Oh, yes," Noella said, and put her thin arm through Aunt Dessie's bony one.

My mother walked slowly away toward a worn stone. Years of wind had scoured off all the inscription except one line. It said, *beloved wife of.*

She began to cry, with the loud surprised sound of an animal in pain. R1

"Oh, precious," Noella exclaimed. "Are you sick?"

My mother **pivoted** blindly into Aunt Dessie's arms. A sob broke through her fingers. They both caught her tight, not understanding. But I knew. 16

Fear froze me. My voice made a long arc. "Nooo—you can fix it, you can work it out, you're adults!" R2

My mother's head rocked back and forth, her long hair sliding.

"Oh, Mary," Aunt Dessie said. "No hope at all?"

"No hope," my mother sobbed.

"What?" Noella asked. "What?"

Practice the Skills

16 Comparing Literature

Figurative Language What might the graveyard and gravestone symbolize? What special meaning does the stone's inscription have for Tina and her mother?

Vocabulary

pivoted (PIH vuh tid) *v.* turned around sharply

Additional Support

Differentiated Instruction

Journal Entry Have students write a journal entry from the perspective of Tina's mother. Describe your experience in the graveyard. Offer answers to the following questions:

- Why were you shocked when Tina wanted to visit the cemetery?
- Why did you start crying after you looked at the worn stone?
- Why do you think there is no hope?

In your entry, include a description of the cemetery and mention who was with you. OL

"The marriage," Aunt Dessie said. "Over."

I whirled and ran. Before the fact could touch me. Over the humps of graves lost in the weeds. "No!" I insisted, with every gasp of breath.

But I knew the fact was right behind me, riding piggyback the way it always had, and there was no way I could ever run fast enough. My father had escaped. Oh, God, I knew it wasn't his fault that he had to keep growing. Out of the piney woods. Out of a marriage with somebody who was growing at a different speed. But I wished I could have hunted for that little boy he had been once, and **coaxed** him out, and made friends with him. **17** **R1**

The fence loomed up. I grabbed the rusty wire and hung over it, listening to myself gulping air as though nothing in me had died. **R2**

When I lifted my head, a hand was reaching toward me from behind a gravestone. I recoiled into the weeds before I saw that it was holding out a yellow flower.

Arley peeped out. "I'm nice," he whispered. "Don't cry." His soft wet mouth crumpled with anxiety. "I don't scare you." He pushed the flower closer.

I cringed away before I could stop myself. He did scare me. All the things I didn't understand scared me. Losing the people I had belonged to. Letting a special person change my life someday. Or mess it up, the way Sharon had let someone mess up hers. I had collected as many keys as my mother to lock the changes out. **18**

Carefully, Arley sniffed the flower to show me what he wanted me to do. He held it out again, smiling, with pollen on his nose.

"Don't cry," he begged. "I'm nice." He had my father's deep eyes. The family face. Mine.

"I know," I said shakily. I could see he was. A big, bearded man-child distressed to see me sad. "It's not you." A year's collection of tears tried to burst out, sweeping my breath away again. I pointed up the hill. "It's that."

He looked up and nodded solemnly, as if he knew all about divorces, and all about the key I'd given Sharon so she'd hang

Vocabulary

coaxed (kohkst) *v.* urged gently

Practice the Skills

17 Comparing Literature

Figurative Language Again, Tina stretches her figure of speech over two paragraphs, this time personifying "the fact."

18 Comparing Literature

Figurative Language Here, Tina returns to the "keys" figure of speech. What do the locks and keys symbolize for Tina?

COMPARING LITERATURE

Teach

R1 Reading Skill

Review Analyzing Ask: Why might Tina want to make friends with the little boy that was once her father? *(Possible response: She doesn't want to lose her father. She wants him to stay the way he was, instead of changing and moving on.)* **OL**

R2 Reading Skill

Review Drawing Conclusions Say: Tina implies that something in her has "died." What might have died inside Tina? *(Possible response: Her denial about her parents' breakup, or her innocent childhood, may have died.)* **OL**

Reading Fluency

Building Fluency Have each student choose a partner and read aloud a passage from the story, alternating paragraphs or other sections as appropriate. If the passage includes dialogue, have students choose parts. Tell partners to meet in a quiet place to practice reading the passage aloud several times until they can read it smoothly and with expression. Students should take cues from the description of the characters and other details in the text about how to deliver dialogue, if any. Partners who wish to volunteer might read aloud their passage for the whole class. **BL** **OL**

Indiana English/Language Arts Academic Standards
SE: 8.3.6
TWE: *Differentiated Instruction* 8.5, *Reading Fluency* 8.7

Teach

C Critical Thinking

Comprehension Ask: What does Tina mean when she says she is lucky? *(She means she doesn't have to cope with having a baby like her friend or with losing a husband like her mother.)* BL **Ask:** How has her attitude changed since the beginning of the story? *(At the beginning, she was angry and resentful. She was terrified of change and of losing her father. Now, she appreciates the good things in her life.)* OL

BQ 

Ask: How does Tina keep from giving up? *(Possible response: She finds strength by facing the truth, letting go of the past, and facing the future with her mother.)* OL

Assess

Use the CheckPoint questions provided on Presentation Plus! to check for comprehension of the selection. These questions can be used with interactive response keypads for immediate student feedback.

out at our house like always and teach me to be brave. He smiled as if he could explain why people kept rearranging themselves into families so they could take care of each other.

I looked up the slope. My mother was walking toward me, between Aunt Dessie and Noella. Her face was calm. She held their hands. She would cut her hair, I thought. She would let it go natural.

Slowly I reached out and took Arley's flower.

I wondered if he would nod if I suddenly said that, in spite of everything, I knew I was lucky. Lucky to be able to go on from this, without too much to handle like Sharon, or starting from scratch like my mother. C

Noella came to me and held me close in her root arms. She gave me a brisk pat. "I don't have a brain cell working. I forgot to show you Dessie's bedspread."

We went through the gate and down the road again. Behind me, my mother said, "Tina?" I felt the tips of her fingers brush my back. "If you're giving Sharon the diaper bag, maybe I could give her some bootees."

I stumbled around to look at her. My voice wiggled as I said, "Would you? It would mean a lot."

Aunt Dessie smiled. "What color shall they be, for this modern little mother? Purple, with orange ribbons?"

"Just a nice traditional white, I would think," my mother said. "Some things don't change." 19 ○

Practice the Skills

19 BIG Question

What are some of the things the four characters do to keep from giving up? In particular, how will Tina deal with her parents' breakup? Write your answers on the Comparing Foldable for Unit 6. Your answers will help you complete the Unit Challenge later. BQ

Analyzing the Photo
Does this picture reflect how Tina and her mother might feel now? Explain.

Additional Support

Literature Focus Lesson

Theme Remind students that the theme of a story is the important message about life the writer wants to convey. It is generally implied, rather than stated outright. In this story, the theme is related to change and the way it affects Tina and her family. Have students work in pairs to write a sentence stating the theme of the story. Tell students that stories may have several themes, but that they must be supported by elements of the text. Have students share their theme statements with the class. AL

Before You Read | Alone

Maya Angelou

Meet the Author

Maya Angelou is a writer, activist, and performer. Born in Missouri in 1928, Angelou spent much of her childhood with her grandmother in Arkansas. She writes about her experiences there in her autobiography, *I Know Why the Caged Bird Sings*. Angelou's work reflects her pride in her African American heritage and her religious faith. See page R1 of the Author Files for more on Angelou.

Author Search For more about Maya Angelou, go to www.glencoe.com.

Indiana English/Language Arts Academic Standards (pp. 905–907)

8.1.2 Understand the influence of historical events on...word meaning... **8.3.6** Identify significant literary devices, such as metaphor [or] symbolism...

For a complete description of the standards, see p. IN 11.

Vocabulary Preview

English Language Coach

Historical Influences on English Anglo-Saxon, Greek, and Latin are the three languages that have had the greatest influence in shaping the modern English language.

- Anglo-Saxon, or Old English, was spoken and written in England for hundreds of years. Most words that come from Old English are simple objects or actions, such as *bread, knife, sit,* and *say.*
- Many Greek roots and combining forms are related to government and learning. Examples are *biology, democracy,* and *cosmos.*
- Latin is remembered as the "language of knowledge," because ancient Rome influenced the development of many things: law, war, art, science, literature, architecture, and language. Examples of words from Latin are *construct, transport,* and *dictionary.*

Get Ready to Read

Connect to the Reading

Think of a time when you depended on someone—or someone depended on you—for friendship or support. Who helps you keep going when life gets you down?

Build Background

R Water is often a symbol of birth, and a raven may represent death. But a symbol's meaning is determined by the culture and experiences of both the writer and the reader. For example, an American is likely to see the bald eagle as a symbol of freedom, but a person from Egypt or Japan or Brazil might have other ideas. As you find symbols in "Alone," consider what they mean to you, what they might mean to other readers, and what they might have meant to the poet.

Set Purposes for Reading

BIG Question Read to find out why Angelou believes that people need each other.

Set Your Own Purpose What else would you like to learn from the selection to help you answer the Big Question? Write your own purpose on the Comparing Foldable for Unit 6.

Teach

More About the Author

Maya Angelou tried many careers before becoming a poet, teacher, and civil-rights activist. She held jobs as a streetcar conductor, a Creole cook, and a waitress. With regard to her writing, Angelou says, "I speak to the black experience, but I am always talking about the human condition—about what we can endure, dream, fail at, and still survive."

R Reading Skill

Review Connecting Say: Think of an object you own that is important to you. Tell what it symbolizes or represents. *(Possible response: My tennis trophy symbolizes all the hard work I spent practicing over the years and the good feeling I had when I won the championship.)* EL BL OL

Author Search To expand students' appreciation of Maya Angelou, have them access the Web site for additional information and resources

English Language Coach

Historical Influences Have students create a four-column chart in their Learner's Notebooks. Have students use a dictionary to complete the chart with five words from either "Welcome" or "Alone." EL BL

Word	Language It Came From	Original Meaning	Definition

Indiana English/Language Arts Academic Standards
SE: 8.1.2
TWE: *Literature Focus Lesson* 8.3, *English Language Coach* 8.1.2

Teach

L Literary Element

Figurative Language **Ask:** What is the speaker saying about her soul in this stanza? *(The soul finds life in being with others.)* OL

R Reading Skill

Review Interpreting **Say:** In lines 14–19, the speaker claims that there are some things that money cannot do. What is the speaker saying about the value of money? *(Money does not create connections among people, or make them or their families healthy or happy.)* BL

Alone

by Maya Angelou

Lying, thinking
Last **night**
How to find my soul a home
Where water is not thirsty
And bread loaf is not stone
I came up with one thing
And I don't believe I'm wrong
That nobody,
But nobody
Can make it out here alone. 1 2

L

Alone, all alone
Nobody, but nobody
Can make it out here alone.

There are some millionaires
With money they can't use
Their wives run round like banshees*
Their children sing the blues
They've got expensive doctors
To cure their hearts of stone.
But nobody
No nobody
Can make it out here alone. 3

R

16 In Irish folklore, a ***banshee*** was a female spirit whose mournful wail predicted death.

Practice the Skills

1 English Language Coach

Historical Influences Middle English gave us the word **night,** which came through Old English *(niht)*, Old High German *(naht)*, Latin *(nox)*, and Greek *(nyx)*.

2 Comparing Literature

Figurative Language What might water and bread symbolize here? Make notes about these symbols in your organizer.

3 Comparing Literature

Figurative Language The speaker uses a simile in line 16 and a metaphor in line 19 to comment on people with too much money. What does each figure of speech mean? What opinion is the speaker expressing in this stanza?

Additional Support

Differentiated Instruction

Poetry as Song Poems have rhythm, and many can be sung and accompanied by music. This poem has rhyme, rhythm, and repetition. Have musical students use Angelou's words as song lyrics and find or create music that matches the feelings created by this poem. Invite students to perform songs in class. OL

Alone, all alone
Nobody, but nobody
Can make it out here alone.

Now if you'll listen closely
I'll tell you what I know
Storm clouds are gathering
The wind is gonna blow
The race of man is suffering
And I can hear the moan,
Cause nobody,
But nobody
Can make it out here alone. **4**

Alone, all alone
Nobody, but nobody
Can make it out here alone. **5** ❍

BQ

Practice the Skills

4 **Comparing Literature**

Figurative Language What do the storm clouds represent to the speaker?

5 **BIG Question**

Think about the poem's three-line refrain. In what way is it a warning? Write your answer on the Comparing Foldable for Unit 6. Your response will help you complete the Unit Challenge later.

Cypress Maiden, 1995. Christian Pierre. Oil on canvas. Private Collection.

Analyzing the Painting Does this painting reflect the feeling you get from the poem? Why or why not?

Reading in the Real World

Citizenship The speaker in "Alone" says that people suffer from being alone. They may feel sad or unwanted. Have students brainstorm ways that they could help lonely people in their family, their community, or their city. Perhaps they could spend more time with a grand-parent or volunteer in a nursing home. Write students' ideas on the board. **AS**

Teach

R Reading Skill

Review Interpreting Ask: According to the speaker, why is the "race of man" suffering? *(People are isolated from one another.)* **OL**

BQ BIG Question

Ask: Do you agree with the speaker that "nobody, but nobody can make it out here alone?" Explain your response. *(Responses will vary.)* **OL**

Assess

CheckPoint

Use the CheckPoint questions provided on Presentation Plus! to check for comprehension of the selection. These questions can be used with interactive response keypads for immediate student feedback.

Indiana English/Language Arts Academic Standards
SE: 8.1.2, 8.3.6
TWE: *Differentiated Instruction* 8.3.1, *Reading in the Real World* 8.2

Assess

Resources for page 908

- Selection Quick Check, pp. 59–60
- ExamView Assessment Suite
- Interactive Tutor: Self-Assessment

Vocabulary Check

1. famished
2. ultimatum
3. pivoted
4. coaxed
5. ultimatum
6. dismal
7. famished
8. coaxed
9. pivoted
10. dismal

English Language Coach

11. bicycle
12. prescribed
13. pedestrian

After You Read

Welcome & Alone

by Ouida Sebestyen

by Maya Angelou

Vocabulary Check

Rewrite each sentence below, filling in the blank with the best word from the list. Each word will be used twice.

dismal ultimatum famished pivoted coaxed

1. If you're so ___, why don't *you* cook dinner?
2. The kidnapper's ___ included serious threats that the parents couldn't bear to think about.
3. I hoped that after I ___ my bed ninety degrees the morning sun wouldn't wake me up so early.
4. No matter how much we ___ or begged, the referee simply refused to change her ruling.
5. The principal gave everyone an ___; we would arrive on time for every class, or we'd be suspended.
6. That paint is horrible! The color is too ___ even for the basement of a funeral home!
7. The doctors were worried because some of the ___ survivors had become too weak to feed themselves.
8. It took a lot of time and effort, but the twins finally ___ the babysitter into giving the answer they wanted.
9. When the woman saw the security guard approaching, she ___ and rushed out of the store.
10. With no restaurants, shops, parks, or beaches, the little village was a ___ disappointment.

English Language Coach

Rewrite each sentence below, filling in the blank with a word that comes from the root shown in parentheses. The word should make sense in the sentence.

11. Since Helena lives far from school, she has to ride her ___. *(cycle)*
12. Pedro's dog was sick, so the veterinarian ___ medication. *(scrib)*
13. When crossing the street, the ___ always has the right of way. *(ped)*

Indiana English/Language Arts Academic Standards (pp. 908–909)

8.3 Comprehension and Analysis of Literary Text Respond to grade-level-appropriate literature... **8.3.6** Identify significant literary devices, such as metaphor [or] symbolism... **8.5.2** Write responses to literature...

For a complete description of the standards, see p. IN 11.

20. Sample Chart (sample chart continued on bottom of p. 909)

"Welcome"			
Page	**Figure of Speech**	**Kind**	**Explanation**
894	"She took us in like royalty."	simile	Aunt Dessie was very hospitable and welcomed them into her home.
896	"you went off like a ton of dynamite"	simile	Her mother got very angry, very quickly.
898	"a little dried-apple woman"	metaphor	Noella is old and looks shriveled.

Reading/Critical Thinking

Welcome

14. BIG Question How does Tina keep from giving up when she realizes her family is changing?
    TIP Think and Search
15. **Recall** What does Arley say and do to help Tina feel better?
    TIP Right There
16. **Summarize** Explain Tina's realization after she accepts Arley's flower.
    TIP Author and Me

Alone

17. **Infer** Why might the speaker believe that "the race of man is suffering"?
    TIP Author and Me
18. **Evaluate** Does the speaker make a good case against trying to survive alone? Why or why not?
    TIP Author and Me
19. **Infer** Why are the millionaires and their families in the third stanza so unhappy? What is the speaker saying about the relationship between wealth and happiness?
    TIP Author and Me

Writing: Compare the Literature

Use Your Notes

Writers use figurative language to communicate specific ideas and images. No two figures of speech are exactly alike, since their meaning always depends on their context. As you compare and contrast "Welcome" and "Alone," think about how figurative language added to or changed your understanding of the selections.

As you review the notes in your graphic organizers, ask yourself:

- What purpose does figurative language serve in the short story?
- What purpose does it serve in the poem?
- How are these purposes alike and/or different?

20. Follow these steps to compare the use of figurative language in "Welcome" and "Alone."

    Step 1: Look at the chart you completed for "Welcome." Circle a simile or metaphor that helped you visualize a character.

    Step 2: Underline a simile or metaphor that helped you visualize a place.

    Step 3: Draw a box around a simile or metaphor that helped you understand an idea or feeling.

    Step 4: Put a check mark beside the story's most important symbol.

    Step 5: Look at the chart you completed for "Alone." Repeat steps 1–4.

Get It on Paper

To show what you have learned about the use of figurative language in "Welcome" and "Alone," answer the questions below.

21. In "Welcome," how do similes and metaphors help you understand Tina, her mother, and her aunts? How does figurative language help you visualize these characters and their problems?
22. In "Alone," how do similes and metaphors help you understand the speaker and her concerns?
23. Were the similes and metaphors more descriptive in "Welcome" or "Alone"? Explain your answer.
24. Think about the symbols you checked above. Would the story still make sense without the symbol you chose? Would the poem? Compare the importance of the symbols you picked in "Welcome" and "Alone."

BIG Question

25. In both selections, the narrator and speaker feel alone, abandoned, or misunderstood. In "Welcome," how does Tina deal with these feelings? What does she do to make herself understood? In "Alone," what does the speaker say about surviving life alone?

Reading/Critical Thinking

Welcome

14. Tina lets go of the past and realizes she is lucky.
15. Arley offers Tina a flower and his friendship.
16. She sees she has people in her life who care for her.

Alone

17.–19. Responses will vary.

Writing: Compare the Literature

20. Charts will vary. See below.
21. They help you understand the characters' actions and feelings. They also provide vivid descriptions of the characters.
22. Responses will vary.
23. Those in "Welcome" are more descriptive because they create vivid images. The ones in "Alone" describe abstract concepts.
24. In "Welcome," the car symbolizes the main character's journey. She and her mother try to run from their problems, but return to rebuild their lives. In "Alone," the bread and water symbolize life. Neither the story nor the poem would make as much sense without the symbols.

BIG Question

25. Responses will vary.

20. Sample Chart (sample chart continued from bottom of p. 908)

"Alone"			
Page	**Figure of Speech**	**Kind**	**Explanation**
906	"find my soul a home"	personification	The speaker is saying her soul needs to be nurtured and have a place to grow.
906	"wives run round like banshees"	simile	The women are upset and crying.
906	"hearts of stone"	metaphor	The people are lonely and don't know what it's like to care for others.

Indiana English/Language Arts Academic Standards
SE: 8.3, 8.3.6, 8.5.2

The Unit Challenge

Focus

BELLRINGER Options

Daily Language Practice Transparency 61
Focus Activity Say: Think about all of the strategies the people in the unit used to keep from giving up when bad things happened. Which of these strategies could you use in your life? Explain.
The discussion will remind students of the coping strategies they've learned. They'll refer to one or more of these strategies in the unit challenge. **AS**

Teach

Group Activity: Create a Newspaper Ad

- Tell students that natural disasters might include earthquakes, tornadoes, or hurricanes.
- If students have access to the Internet, you might suggest they look at the Red Cross Web site for survival tips. Remind students to paraphrase ideas and to give the Red Cross credit for any information they use.
- Tell students they can find local resources, such as organizations, hotlines, and other services, by checking telephone books and local newspapers.
- If students are working on computers to create their ads, make sure they spend the majority of their time on the content and overall look of the ad. Minor design choices, such as font size, should be made when all research and writing is complete.

UNIT 6 WRAP-UP

Answering The BIG Question: How Do You Keep from Giving Up When Bad Things Happen?

You've just read about people who remained positive when they were faced with hardship. Now use what you've learned to complete the Unit Challenge.

The Unit Challenge

Choose Activity A or Activity B, and follow the directions for that activity.

A. Group Activity: Create a Newspaper Ad

With three other students, imagine that a natural disaster has occurred in a nearby community. Create a newspaper advertisement explaining how people in your community can help.

1. **Discuss the Assignment** Choose one group member to be the note-keeper for the discussion. Use your Foldables to review the hardships that people faced in the selections you read in this unit. Discuss ways that they dealt with hardships and which strategies were most effective.

2. **Fill in the Details** Decide on the imaginary disaster and the needs that your ad will be concerned with. Most natural disasters have three major effects:
   - death and physical injury of people and animals
   - psychological injury to survivors
   - damage to homes, businesses, roads, bridges, trees, power lines, and so on

   Brainstorm ideas about how your community can help. Ask questions such as these:
   - What kinds of help do people need?
   - What resources are available?
   - How can your community help?
   - How can you and your classmates organize the help efforts?

3. **Write the Ad** Identify specific ways people can help, such as by
   - donating food, clothes, and furniture
   - giving money
   - volunteering to work

   Tell people how to contact disaster-relief agencies—both government and private. List each organization's phone number and location. Look in local phone books for
   - emergency services
   - gas, water, electricity, and telephone companies
   - government offices
   - the Red Cross, Salvation Army, and other private aid organizations

4. **Design the Ad** Decide how large your ad will be (full page, half page, or quarter page). Have two group members choose the fonts and do the layout. Where appropriate, they can add hand-drawn illustrations or, on a computer, digital photographs.

5. **Publish It** Make sure the ad is clear, easy to read, and simple to understand. Have two or three group members proofread it. When you're confident that it's ready, display the ad in your classroom.

Assess/Close

Group Activity

Ask: How would your ad be helpful if a natural disaster struck? What other information might people need? *(Suggest that students write their answers in their Learner's Notebooks.)* **OL**

UNIT 6 WRAP-UP

B. Solo Activity: Write a Poem

Bad things can happen to people of all ages, races, nationalities, and religions. Write a poem addressed to a person or a group of people going through hard times. You may want to include advice or an encouraging message.

1. **Prepare to Write** Decide what the general idea of your poem will be and what form it will have. Ask yourself questions such as these:
   - What is the subject of the poem?
   - To whom are you addressing the poem?
   - What will the tone be?
   - How many stanzas will you write?
   - Will your poem rhyme?

2. **Create a Word Chart** Look over the notes on your Foldables. Then, brainstorm words and phrases to use in your poem. Start by choosing a word that has to do with hardship. Then write down another word that is somehow related to the first word. Continue the process, allowing your mind to wander.

Draw a blank chart based on the one below. Write your own words in the boxes as you think of them.

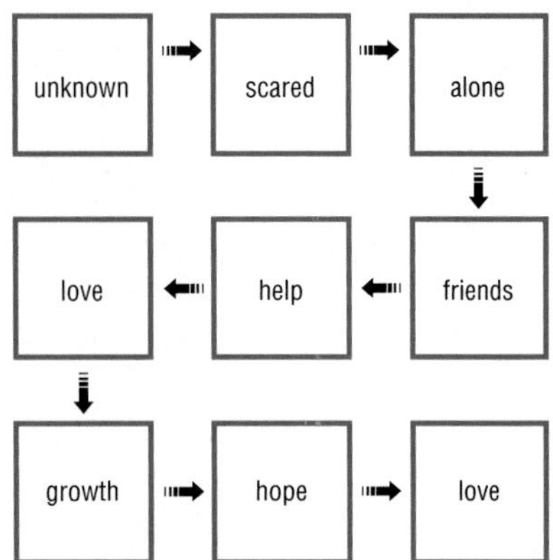

3. **Write the Poem** Use the words in your chart to write your poem. Write as if you were talking directly to someone. Use words and phrases that create mental pictures. Offer advice or sympathy to the person or people you are addressing.

4. **Present Your Poem** Read your poem aloud to yourself to make sure that it makes sense and has a clear message. Type or print it on a fresh piece of paper, and proofread it for errors. If you like, draw a picture to go along with it. Now you're ready to hand it in!

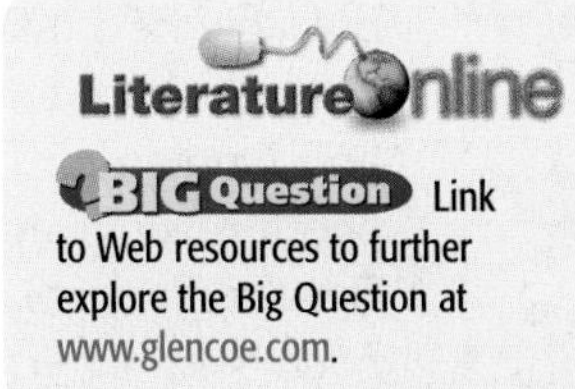

BIG Question Link to Web resources to further explore the Big Question at www.glencoe.com.

Teach

Solo Activity: Write a Poem

- Remind students that there are many different forms of poetry and that not all of them have a set rhyme scheme or meter. Encourage students to experiment with different forms of poetry to find one they like best.
- Encourage students to include at least one simile or metaphor in their poem.
- Before students begin writing, be sure they have answered all the questions in step 1.

Assess/Close

Solo Activity

Ask students to discuss how poetry and other forms of literature can inspire people during hard times. OL

Big Question Have students access the Web site for English and Spanish summaries and annotated links to related Web resources.

Focus

Build Background

- This poem takes place on September 11, 2001, the day terrorists hijacked four airplanes and attacked the World Trade Center in New York City and the Pentagon in Washington.
- "The buildings fell" is a reference to the World Trade Center towers, which both collapsed as a result of the attack.

R1 Reading Skill

Interpreting **Ask:** What do the words "You're my first hello" mean? *(Possible response: The speaker is the first person Flinn has spoken to since being released from prison.)* OL

L Literary Element

Dialogue and Monologue
Ask: Who is speaking the words written in italics? *(Flinn, the man who has just been freed from prison.)* BL

R2 Reading Skill

Paraphrasing and Summarizing **Say:** Paraphrase lines 15–18. *(Possible response: I'm not going to make the same mistakes that got me into prison in the first place.)* OL

UNIT 6

Your Turn: Read and Apply Skills

Meet the Author
Naomi Shihab Nye was born in 1952 to a Palestinian father and an American mother. She has lived in St. Louis, Missouri; Jerusalem, Israel; and San Antonio, Texas. She has won numerous awards for her poetry, essays, and novels. Nye often gets her inspiration from small things and everyday events. She once said, "Language can carry us to understanding and connect us to the things that matter in our lives." See page R4 of the Author Files for more on Naomi Shihab Nye.

Author Search For more about Naomi Shihab Nye, go to www.glencoe.com.

Flinn,
On the Bus
by Naomi Shihab Nye

Three hours after the buildings fell,
he took a seat beside me.
Fresh out of prison, after 24 months,
You're my first hello! R1
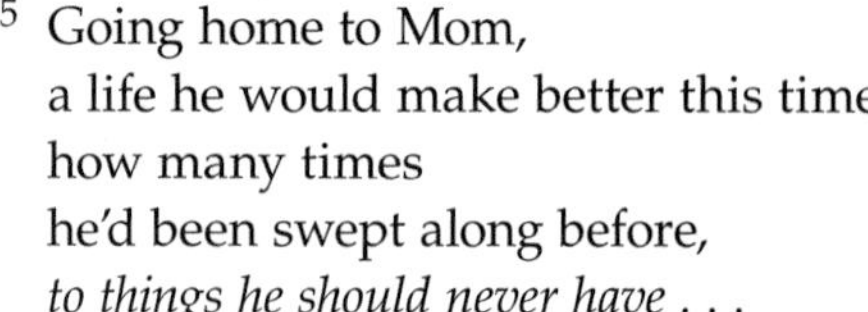
Going home to Mom,
a life he would make better this time,
how many times
he'd been swept along before,
to things he should never have . . .
drink and dope,
but now he'd take responsibility.
Lawyers had done him wrong
and women too. He thought
about revenge, now he was out.
But I'm in charge. I'll think
before I act. I don't ever
want to go there again.
Two wrongs don't make a right.

Additional Support

Author Search To expand students' appreciation of Naomi Shihab Nye, have them access the Web site for additional information and resources.

Literature Focus Lesson

Summary In this poem, a man named Flinn has been released after spending two years in prison. He boards a bus and takes a seat next to the narrator just three hours after the collapse of the World Trade Center towers. Unaware of the destruction that has occurred, Flinn confronts his lowly impulses and resolves not to make the same mistakes that put him in prison in the first place. The speaker considers telling Flinn about the terrorist attacks but doesn't, afraid to shatter his newfound optimism and convinced he will find out soon enough. OL

Somehow, in his mouth, that day,
it sounded new.
The light came through the window
on a gentle-eyed man in a
"Focus on the Game" T-shirt,
who had given up
assault with deadly weapons,*
no more, no good!
A man who had not seen TV in weeks,
secluding in his cell so colleagues*
wouldn't trip him up,
extend his stay.
Who had not heard the news.
We rolled through green Oklahoma,
the bus windows made all the trees look bent.
A trick of refraction*—
Flinn looked at his free hands
more than the fields,
turned them over in his lap,
no snap judgments, no quick angers,
I'll stand back, look at what happens,
think calmly what my next step should be.
It was not hard to nod,
to wish him well. But could I tell
what had happened in the world
on his long-awaited day,
what twists of rage greater
than we could ever guess
had savaged* skylines, thousands of lives?
I could not. He'd find out
soon enough. Flinn, take it easy.
Peace is rough. ❍

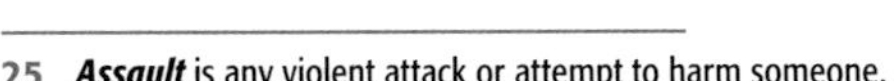

25 ***Assault*** is any violent attack or attempt to harm someone.

28 Here, ***secluding*** means "keeping (himself) separated from others." ***Colleagues*** (KAHL eegz) are fellow workers; here, it refers to Flinn's fellow inmates.

34 ***Refraction*** is the bending of light waves as they pass through, in this case, glass.

47 To ***savage*** (SAV ij) is to destroy in a fierce, cruel, uncivilized way.

Teach

R1 Reading Skill

Interpreting **Ask:** What does the speaker mean by, "Somehow, in his mouth, that day, it sounded new?" *(Possible response: The things Flinn says are clichés, or sayings used often, that have lost their meaning over time. However, since Flinn has just been released from prison and given a fresh start, the words sound "new.")* **AL**

R2 Reading Skill

Drawing Conclusions **Ask:** What conclusion does the speaker make about Flinn's knowledge of the day's events? Why? *(Possible response: The speaker concludes Flinn does not know about the terrorist attacks because he hasn't watched TV for weeks.)* **OL**

BQ BIG Question

Ask: What does the speaker decide not to do at the end of the poem? *(tell Flinn about the terrorist attack)* **BL** **Ask:** Why might the speaker have decided to do this? *(to allow Flinn to enjoy his freedom)* **OL** **Ask:** Do you think Flinn would have had a hard time coping with the information? Why or why not? (Possible response: He probably would have had a hard time because he could have felt plans to start a new life would be ruined.) **AL**

Differentiated Instruction

Group Discussion Have students form groups to discuss how they would have acted in the speaker's situation. Encourage students to list reasons for and against telling Flinn the truth. **OL** Encourage students to speculate about the meaning of the words "Peace is rough." **AL** Then have students take a vote to decide how most group members would have acted. Ask a volunteer from each group to share the main points of the discussion and the results of the vote with the class. **OL**

Tips for Independent Reading

Encourage a lifelong enjoyment of reading by suggesting students choose only those books that intrigue them. Have students read the blurbs accompanying each book and ask themselves, "What might I learn by reading this book?" or "How does this book apply to my life?" Students might use online resources to find out more about a book or its subject before making a selection.

Fiction

Tell students that reading fictional accounts of people who have endured tragedy will give them a chance to relate to characters and learn new ways to stay positive.

Ask students to discuss whether they think nonfiction accounts of tragedy are more or less powerful than fictional stories. Have them explain their responses.

UNIT 6

Reading on Your Own

To read more about the Big Question, choose one of these books from your school or local library. Work on your reading skills by choosing books that are challenging to you.

Fiction

Tree by Leaf
by Cynthia Voigt

Clothilde's father returns from World War I alive but disfigured and depressed. Read to find out how Clothilde's family deals with the challenges they must face.

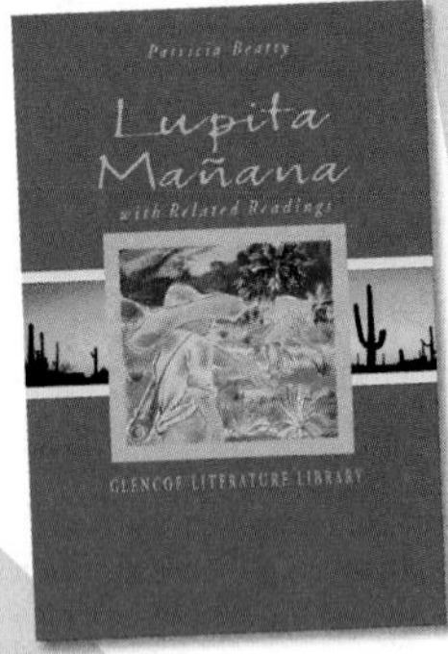

Lupita Mañana
by Patricia Beatty

Lupita Torres is thirteen when she and her older brother decide to go to the United States. They need jobs there to support their widowed mother and younger siblings. But are they prepared for the dangers and difficulties of crossing a border illegally?

Missing May
by Cynthia Rylant

Summer has had many homes, but when she joins her aunt and uncle, she is welcomed and deeply loved. Then Aunt May dies, and Summer and Uncle Ob must come to terms with their loss.

Kira-Kira
by Cynthia Kadohata

In the 1950s a Japanese American family moves to Georgia. The adjustment is difficult for everyone, and Katie turns to her sister Lynn for help and friendship. When Lynn becomes very ill, Katie's strength is tested in almost every way. Read to find out what *kira-kira* really means to Katie and her family.

Additional Support

Differentiated Instruction

Use the Glencoe BookLink CD-ROM to create customized reading lists to help students answer the Big Questions. Suggestions for Unit 6:

Grade 4: *The Clay Marble*
by Minfong Ho

Grade 5: *Mississippi Bridge*
by Mildred D. Taylor

Grade 6: *Beyond the Limits: A Woman's Triumph on Everest*
by Stacy Allison with Peter Carlin

Grade 7: *New Directions*
by Maya Angelou

Grade 8: *In the Heart of the Sea: The Tragedy of the Whaleship* Essex
by Nathaniel Philbrick

Nonfiction

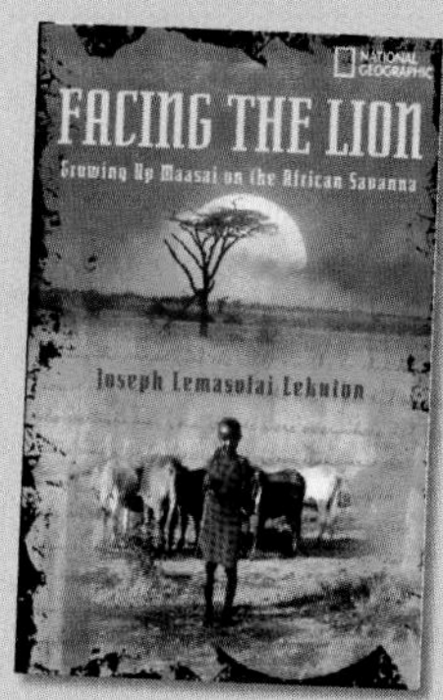

Facing the Lion: Growing Up Massai on the African Savanna
by Joseph Lemasolai-Lekuton

Joseph grew up in one of Kenya's poorest tribes. In this story of determination and courage, he describes his path from Kenya to the United States, as well as the ties that still bind him to the Africa he loves.

Jaime Escalante, Sensational Teacher
by Ann Byers

This fascinating biography discusses the challenges faced and overcome by a gifted and determined teacher. Escalante and his dedicated students proved to the world that hard work and desire can triumph over poverty and prejudice.

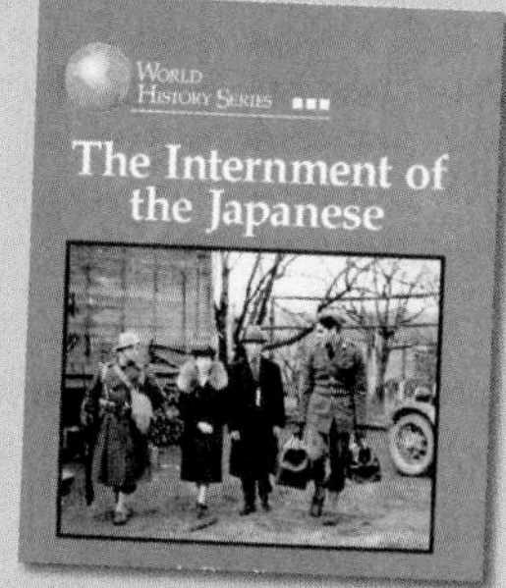

World History Series: The Internment of the Japanese
by Diane Yancey

This book explains how fear and hatred of Japanese Americans after the attack on Pearl Harbor led to their imprisonment in camps right here in the United States. Read about the unjust treatment of these citizens and how they managed to face racism with strength and dignity.

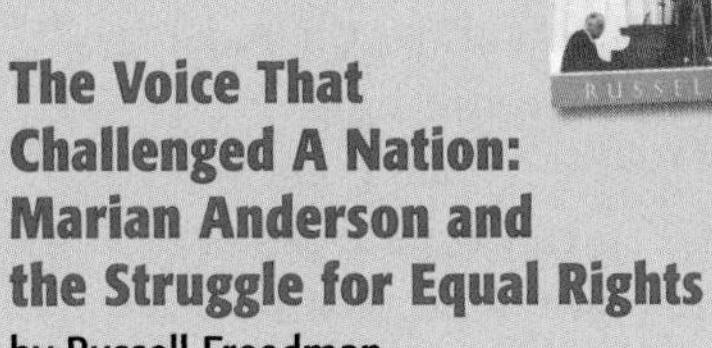

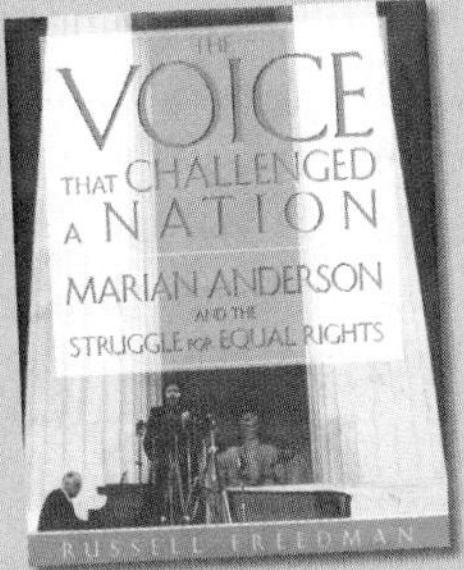

The Voice That Challenged A Nation: Marian Anderson and the Struggle for Equal Rights
by Russell Freedman

In the 1920s and 1930s, Marian Anderson became world famous for her singing voice. At home in the United States, this African American woman had to fight for the right to perform in concert halls that were restricted to whites.

READING ON YOUR OWN

Nonfiction

The books on this page are all true stories that give detailed accounts of real people, places, and events.

Case Studies: Minorities

Ask: What do the subjects of these books have in common? *(Possible responses: Every book is about a person or group of people who represents a minority. All of the books are about a person or people who endured some kind of struggle.)*

About the Subjects

Invite students to share information they know about the subjects on this page. To encourage students to pursue these books, discuss relevant background information and points of interest. For example, the story of math teacher Jaime Escalante has been made into a compelling film entitled *Stand and Deliver* (1988, rated PG). First lady Eleanor Roosevelt resigned from the Daughters of the American Revolution after they refused to allow Marian Anderson to sing in their hall.

Test-Taking Tips

TIP Take time to review the general strategy for answering multiple choice questions on high-stakes tests:

- First answer each question for which you know the answer.
- If you're not certain about the answer to a question, skip it for now.
- When you've answered all the questions you're sure about, return to the ones you're not sure about.
- For each of those, eliminate any answers that you know are wrong.
- If eliminating wrong answers reveals the right answer, fine. Move on.
- If eliminating wrong answers still leaves a choice, look back at the selection to find clues to the answer. Then make your best guess.

ISTEP+ Test Practice

from *The Diary of Anne Frank*, Act II, Scene 4

Directions

In this excerpt from a play about Jews hiding from the Nazis during World War II, Anne and Peter have a quiet conversation before their hiding place is discovered. Read the excerpt carefully. Then, answer questions 1 through 7.

[*ANNE quietly goes to PETER's room, closing the door after her. PETER is lying face down on the cot. ANNE leans over him, holding him in her arms, trying to bring him out of his despair.*]

ANNE. Look, Peter, the sky. [*She looks up through the skylight.*] What a lovely, lovely day! Aren't the clouds beautiful? You know what I do when it seems as if I couldn't stand being cooped up for one more minute? I think myself out. I think myself on a walk in the park where I used to go with Pim. Where the jonquils and the crocus and the violets grow down the slopes. You know the most wonderful part about thinking yourself out? You can have it any way you like. You can have roses and violets and chrysanthemums all blooming at the same time . . . It's funny . . . I used to take it all for granted . . . and now I've gone crazy about everything to do with nature. Haven't you?

PETER. I've just gone crazy. I think if something doesn't happen soon . . . if we don't get out of here . . . I can't stand much more of it!

ANNE. [*Softly.*] I wish you had a religion, Peter.

PETER. No, thanks! Not me!

ANNE. Oh, I don't mean you have to be Orthodox . . . or believe in heaven and hell and purgatory[1] and things . . . I just mean some religion . . . it doesn't matter what. Just to believe in something! When I think of all that's out there . . . the trees . . . and flowers . . . and seagulls . . . when I think of the dearness of you, Peter . . . and the goodness of the people we know . . . Mr. Kraler, Miep, Dirk, the vegetable man, all risking their lives for us

[1] The **Orthodox** branch of Judaism is the most traditional, requiring strict obedience to ancient laws and customs. **Purgatory** is, some believe, a place of temporary punishment for the souls of the dead.

every day . . . When I think of these good things, I'm not afraid any more . . . I find myself, and God, and I . . .

[PETER *interrupts, getting up and walking away.*]

PETER. That's fine! But when I begin to think, I get mad! Look at us, hiding out for two years. Not able to move! Caught here like . . . waiting for them to come and get us . . . and all for what?

ANNE. We're not the only people that've had to suffer. There've always been people that've had to . . . sometimes one race . . . sometimes another . . . and yet . . .

PETER. That doesn't make me feel any better!

ANNE. [*Going to him.*] I know it's terrible, trying to have any faith . . . when people are doing such horrible . . . But you know what I sometimes think? I think the world may be going through a phase, the way I was with Mother. It'll pass, maybe not for hundreds of years, but someday . . . I still believe, in spite of everything, that people are really good at heart.

PETER. I want to see something now . . . Not a thousand years from now!

[*He goes over, sitting down again on the cot.*]

ANNE. But, Peter, if you'd only look at it as part of a great pattern . . . that we're just a little minute in the life . . . [*She breaks off.*] Listen to us, going at each other like a couple of stupid grown-ups! Look at the sky now. Isn't it lovely? [*She holds out her hand to him.* PETER *takes it and rises, standing with her at the window looking out, his arms around her.*] Someday, when we're outside again, I'm going to . . .

Questions 1 through 6 are based on *The Diary of Anne Frank.*

1 In this scene, why does Anne go into Peter's room?

A to comfort him
B to scold him
C to ask for his help
D to explain why they are in hiding

2 Anne's attitude toward other people is BEST described as

A suspicious
B despairing
C indifferent
D optimistic

Test-Taking Tips

TIP Remind students that with longer or more complicated passages, it is usually a good idea to read the questions *before* they read the passages. They don't have to read the answer choices, but reading the questions will help them focus their reading on finding the answers they will have to give later.

Answers:

1. A

2. D

Resources for pages 916–921

Use these resources to review, assess, or reteach the chapter: Active Learning and Note-Taking Guide, ExamView Pro, and Differentiated Instruction Tool Software.

Answers:

3. A

4. B

5. D

6. A

3 In this scene, Peter is MOST upset about

A having to hide out for two years
B lacking religious belief
C not getting to go to the park with Anne
D fighting with his parents

4 Anne asks Peter if he is religious because

A she hopes he will join her religion
B she thinks religion might comfort him
C he comes from a religious family
D she hopes they can pray together

Read the following paragraph and then answer questions 5 and 6.

[1]Anne Frank and her family had to hide from German soldiers in 1942 in order to avoid being sent to prison camps. [2]German troops occupied the Netherlands, where the Franks lived, during World War II. [3]Jewish people were being deported from the Netherlands. [4]Jewish people were being forced to work in prison camps. [5]World War II was fought from 1939 to 1945. [6]The Frank family remained in hiding until 1944, when Nazi police officers discovered them.

5 Which sentence does NOT support the main idea of the paragraph?

A sentence 2
B sentence 3
C sentence 4
D sentence 5

6 What is the BEST way to combine sentences 3 and 4?

A Jewish people were being deported from the Netherlands and forced to work in prison camps.
B Jewish people from the Netherlands were being forced to work in prison camps and deported.
C Jewish people were being deported and forced to work in prison camps in the Netherlands.
D Jewish people from the Netherlands were forced to be deported and work in prison camps.

Directions

This passage is from a play about a girl, Helen Keller, who is deaf and blind, and the young woman, Annie Sullivan, who becomes her teacher. In the passage, Annie meets Helen's mother and brother for the first time. Read the excerpt carefully. Then answer questions 7 through 12.

from *The Miracle Worker,* Act I

by William Gibson

[*The railroad sounds off left have mounted in a crescendo to a climax typical of a depot at arrival time, the lights come up on stage left, and we see a suggestion of a station. Here* ANNIE *in her smoked glasses and disarrayed by travel is waiting with her suitcase, while* JAMES *walks to meet her; she has a battered paper-bound book, which is a Perkins report, under her arm.*]

JAMES. [*coolly*] Miss Sullivan?

ANNIE. [*cheerily*] Here! At last, I've been on trains so many days I thought they must be backing up every time I dozed off—

JAMES. I'm James Keller.

ANNIE. James?

[*The name stops her.*]

I had a brother Jimmie. Are you Helen's?

JAMES. I'm only half a brother. You're to be her governess?

ANNIE. [*lightly*] Well. Try!

JAMES. [*eying her*] You look like half a governess.

[KATE *enters,* ANNIE *stands moveless, while* JAMES *takes her suitcase.* KATE'S *gaze on her is doubtful, troubled.*]

Mrs. Keller, Miss Sullivan.

[KATE *takes her hand.*]

KATE. [*simply*] We've met every train for two days.

[ANNIE *looks at* KATE'S *face, and her good humor comes back.*]

ANNIE. I changed trains every time they stopped, the man who sold me that ticket ought to be tied to the tracks—...

You didn't bring Helen, I was hoping you would.

KATE. No, she's home... .

[*Now she voices part of her doubt, not as such, but* ANNIE *understands it.*]

I expected—a desiccated spinster. You're very young.

ANNIE. [*resolutely*] Oh, you should have seen me when I left Boston. I got much older on this trip.

Test-Taking Tips

TIP Advise students to adapt their reading to the passage. If it is a story or a play, they should try to predict what is going to happen as they read. If it is scientific or historical writing, students should look for facts. If it is a persuasive passage, students should try to figure out what the author is trying to convince the reader to think or do.

Test-Taking Tips

TIP Remind students to pay particular attention to text features when reading plays. Important information is often presented through stage directions rather than through dialogue.

TIP Remind students to analyze each question and its answer choices. Sometimes a single word in a question or an answer choice may relate to a key word in the passage that gives the answer.

KATE. I mean, to teach anyone as difficult as Helen.

ANNIE. *I* mean to try. They can't put you in jail for trying!

KATE. Is it possible, even? To teach a deaf-blind child *half* of what an ordinary child learns—has that ever been done?

ANNIE. Half?

KATE. A tenth.

ANNIE. [*reluctantly*] No.

[*KATE'S face loses its remaining hope, still appraising her youth.*]

Dr. Howe did wonders, but—an ordinary child? No, never. But then I thought when I was going over his reports—

[*She indicates the one in her hand*]

—he never treated them like ordinary children. More like—eggs everyone was afraid would break.

KATE. [*a pause*] May I ask how old you are?

ANNIE. Well, I'm not in me teens, you know! I'm twenty.

KATE. All of twenty.

[*ANNIE takes the bull by the horns, valiantly.*]

ANNIE. Mrs. Keller, don't lose heart just because I'm not on my last legs. I have three big advantages over Dr. Howe that money couldn't buy for you. One is his work behind me, I've read every word he wrote about it and he wasn't exactly what you'd call a man of few words. Another is to *be* young, why, I've got energy to do anything. The third *is*, I've been blind.

[*But it costs her something to say this.*]

KATE. [*quietly*] Advantages.

ANNIE. [*wry*] Well, some have the luck of the Irish, some do not.

[*KATE smiles; she likes her.*]

KATE. What will you try to teach her first?

ANNIE. First, last, and—in between, language.

KATE. Language.

ANNIE. Language is to the mind more than light is to the eye. Dr. Howe said that.

KATE. Language.

[*She shakes her head.*]

We can't get through to teach her to sit still. You *are* young, despite your years, to have such—confidence. Do you, inside?

[*ANNIE studies her face; she likes her, too.*]

ANNIE. No, to tell you the truth I'm as shaky inside as a baby's rattle!

[*They smile at each other, and KATE pats her hand.*]

KATE. Don't be.

[*JAMES returns to usher them off.*]

We'll do all we can to help, and to make you feel at home. Don't think of us as strangers, Miss Annie.

ANNIE. [*cheerily*] Oh, strangers aren't so strange to me. I've known them all my life!

[*KATE smiles again, ANNIE smiles back, and they precede JAMES offstage.*]

Questions 7 through 12 are based on *The Miracle Worker.*

7 Where does this scene take place?

A at the Kellers' home
B in Helen's room
C at a train station
D in a garden

8 What is the main thing Annie plans to teach Helen?

A writing
B language
C confidence
D manners

9 Annie's journey has been long, and she has experienced many hardships in her life. In general, her attitude is BEST described as

A nervous and afraid
B angry and hostile
C cheerful and determined
D quiet and gentile

10 When Annie says, "I'm not on my last legs," she MOST LIKELY means that

A her legs are strong
B she likes to travel
C she is not very old
D her legs have been healed

11 Read the following line from the play.

Language is to the mind more than light is to the eye....

The meaning of this line can BEST be stated as

A understanding language is more important than seeing
B language can help people see better with their eyes
C language and vision are equally important
D language is more important than light

12 Give TWO details from the selection that tell you what problems the Kellers are having with their daughter.

Answers:

7. C
8. B
9. C
10. C
11. A
12. Student responses will vary. A typical correct response will include two items from the following list. Answers do not have to be stated in complete sentences.

- The Kellers need a governess to teach, take care of, and control Helen.
- James thinks Annie is too small to control Helen.
- Mrs. Keller says Annie is very young "to teach anyone as difficult as Helen."
- Mrs. Keller doesn't know whether it's even possible to teach a child who can't see or hear anything. They haven't been able to teach Helen much.
- Mrs. Keller shakes her head when Helen says she'll teach Helen language.
- Mrs. Keller says they haven't been able to teach Helen to sit still.
- other relevant text-based response

UNIT 7
Skills Scope and Sequence

Readability Scores Key
Dale-Chall/**DRP**/Lexile

PACING (DAYS) STANDARD	BLOCK	INSTRUCTIONAL SEGMENT LITERATURE	READING SKILLS	LITERARY ELEMENTS
1	1	**Unit Warm-Up, pp. 922–929** Genre Focus: Persuasive Writing A Letter to Senator Edwards 8.0/**63**/1070, SE p. 927	Distinguishing Fact from Opinion, SE pp. 926, 927 Fluency, TWE p. 923 Questioning, SE pp. 926, 928 Reviewing, SE pp. 926, 927 Clarifying, SE pp. 926, 929	Persuasive Appeals, SE pp. 926, 928 Author's Bias, SE pp. 926, 929 Faulty Reasoning, SE pp. 926, 929
3	2	**Reading Workshop 1, pp. 930–951** "Saving Water: Why Save Something That Covers Two-thirds of the Earth?" by Marjorie Lamb 8.5/**57**/1040, SE p. 934 from *The Measure of Our Success* by Marian Wright Edelman 10.3/**58**/1000, SE p. 944	Distinguishing Fact from Opinion, SE pp. 930, 933, 934, 935, 939, 943, 946, 947, TWE pp. 936, 938, 945 Fluency, TWE p. 947 Paraphrasing and Summarizing, TWE p. 946 Analyzing, TWE p. 946 Making Inferences, TWE pp. 939, 947, 948	Persuasive Appeals, SE pp. 933, 936, 937, 938, TWE p. 935 Appeal to Ethics, SE pp. 943, 944, 945, 948
1		**Writing Workshop, Part 1, pp. 952–955** Writing Product: Persuasive Essay		Essay, TWE p. 952
3	1	**Reading Workshop 2, pp. 956–975** "All Together Now" by Barbara Jordan 5.9/**58**/890, SE p. 960 from *Through My Eyes* by Ruby Bridges 5.6/**56**/870, SE p. 968	Questioning, SE pp. 956, 959, 960, 961, 967, 969, 970, 971, 972, 973, TWE pp. 962, 968	Appeal to Emotions, SE pp. 959, 963, TWE pp. 961, 962 Point of View in Nonfiction, SE pp. 967, 968, 969, TWE pp. 970, 971, 972, 973

Unit 7 Big Question

The question **"What's worth fighting for? What's not?"** will help students think about their values. It will help them determine what is worth standing up for and what is not.

Unit 7 Genre

The majority of the selections in this unit are **persuasive texts.** Reading selections in this genre will expose students to various opinions on subjects. Students will read what some people value and be able to determine if they believe those values are worth fighting for.

CRITICAL THINKING	VOCABULARY	WRITING AND GRAMMAR	LISTENING, SPEAKING, AND VIEWING
			Viewing the Photo, TWE p. 922 Viewing the Art, TWE p. 928
Compare and Contrast, SE p. 940 Analyze, SE pp. 940, 950 Interpret, SE p. 950 Evaluate, SE p. 950 Comprehension, TWE pp. 931, 936, 944 Application, TWE p. 935 Synthesis, TWE p. 949	Denotations and Connotations, SE pp. 932, 935, TWE p. 948 Word Connotation in Persuasive Writing, SE pp. 942, 947 Using New Vocabulary, TWE p. 932 Word Parts, TWE p. 942	Write About Your Reading, SE p. 940 Colons to Introduce Items, SE p. 941 Colons to Separate Items, SE p. 951	Analyzing the Photo, SE pp. 945, 946, 949 Talk About Your Reading, SE p. 950 Viewing the Photo, TWE pp. 934, 944
		Supporting Reasons, SE p. 953 Organization, SE p. 953 Introduction, SE p. 954 Conclusion, SE p. 954 Apostrophes, SE p. 955	
Interpret, SE p. 964 Infer, SE pp. 964, 974 Evaluate, SE pp. 964, 974 Analyze, SE p. 974 Comprehension, TWE p. 967	Academic Vocabulary, SE p. 956 Extended Definition, SE pp. 958, 962, TWE p. 963 Denotation and Word Choice, SE pp. 966, 968, 969, TWE p. 973	Semicolons, SE p. 965 Write About Your Reading, SE p. 974 Semicolons wth Conjunctive Adverbs, SE p. 975	Analyzing the Photo, SE pp. 962, 970, 971 Talk About Your Reading, SE p. 964 Viewing the Photo, TWE pp. 960, 968, 970, 971

UNIT 7

Skills Scope and Sequence *continued*

Readability Scores Key
Dale-Chall/DRP/Lexile

PACING (DAYS) STANDARD	BLOCK	INSTRUCTIONAL SEGMENT LITERATURE	READING SKILLS	LITERARY ELEMENTS
3	3	**Reading Workshop 3, pp. 976–991** "The Trouble with Television" by Robert MacNeil 8.9/68/1160, SE p. 980 "Teen Curfews" by J. Todd Foster	Reviewing, SE pp. 976, 979, 980, 981, 983, 987, 988, TWE p. 977, 982, 989	Author's Bias, SE pp. 979, 981, 982, 987, 989, TWE pp. 983, 988 Persuasive Appeals, TWE p. 980
2		**Writing Workshop, Part 2, pp. 992–997** Writing Product: Persuasive Essay	Fluency, TWE p. 994	Persuasive Appeals, TWE p. 996
3	1	**Reading Workshop 4, pp. 998–1017** Rally for Better Food, student flyer and poster SE p. 1002 "Stop the Sun" by Gary Paulsen 54.0/48/730, SE p. 1008	Clarifying, SE pp. 998, 1001, 1003, 1007, 1008, 1009, 1012, 1013, 1014, TWE pp. 999, 1002, 1011 Predicting, SE pp. 1009, 1010, TWE p. 1012	Faulty Reasoning, SE pp. 1001, 1002 Climax, SE pp. 1007, 1011, 1015, TWE pp. 1010, 1013 Persuasive Appeals, TWE p. 1002 Conflict, TWE p. 1009
3	2	**Reading Across Texts Workshop, pp. 1018–1033** "Teens Tackle Pollution in Their Communities" by Sara Steindorf 10.1/63/1110, SE p. 1021 "A Change in Climate" by Emily Sohn 8.0/60/1040, SE p. 1027	Making Inferences, TWE p. 1022 Drawing Conclusions, TWE pp. 1024, 1028 Comparing and Contrasting, TWE p. 1027 Fluency, TWE p. 1029	Persuasive Appeals, SE pp. 1018, 1027 TWE pp. 1019, 1021, 1022, 1023, 1024, 1025, 1029, 1030, 1031 Appeal to Ethics, SE pp. 1021, 1023, 1024, 1029 Appeal to Reason, SE pp. 1022, 1024, 1025, 1027, 1028, 1029, 1031 Appeal to Emotions, SE pp. 1023, 1030, 1031
4	2	**Unit Wrap-Up, pp. 1034–1051** Your Turn: "The Treasure of Lemon Brown" by Walter Dean Myers 5.3/860/50, SE p. 1036	Distinguishing Fact and Opinion, TWE p. 1039 Reviewing, TWE p. 1038 Questioning, TWE p. 1039 Fluency, TWE p. 1043	Persuasive Appeals, TWE pp. 1039, 1040, 1043 Conflict, TWE p. 1037 Climax, TWE pp. 1037, 1043

CRITICAL THINKING	VOCABULARY	WRITING AND GRAMMAR	LISTENING, SPEAKING, AND VIEWING
Analyze, SE pp. 984, 990 Evaluate, SE pp. 984, 990 Interpret, SE p. 990,	Academic Vocabulary, SE p. 976 Semantic Slanting, SE pp. 978, 980, 986, 989, TWE pp. 981, 982, 983, 988 Suffixes, TWE p. 978 Multiple-Meaning Words, TWE p. 986	Quotation Marks, SE pp. 985, 991 Write About Your Reading, SE p. 990	Talk About Your Reading, SE p. 984 Viewing the Photo, TWE p. 980
	Word Choice, TWE p. 993	Proofread Backwards, SE p. 993 Applying Good Writing Traits: Revising, TWE p. 992 Fluency, SE p. 994	Understanding Persuasive Techniques, SE p. 995
Analyze, SE pp. 1004, 1016 Interpet, SE pp. 1004, 1016 Evaluate, SE pp. 1004, 1016, TWE pp. 1012, 1014	Academic Vocabulary, SE p. 998 Denotation and Slang, SE pp. 1000, 1003 Connotation and Denotation, SE pp. 1006, 1011, TWE pp. 1010, 1015	Write About Your Reading, SE p. 1004 Dashes, SE p. 1005 Parentheses, SE p. 1017	Analyzing the Image, SE p. 1013 Talk About Your Reading, SE p. 1016
Interpret, SE p. 1033 Analyze, SE p. 1033, TWE p. 1030 Comprehension, TWE p. 1028	Denotation and Connotation, SE pp. 1020, 1026, TWE pp. 1021, 1023, 1025, 1027, 1028, 1029 Connotation, SE pp. 1023, 1029	Writing: Reading Across Texts, SE p. 1033	Analyzing the Photo, SE p. 1028 Viewing the Photo, TWE p. 1021
Analysis, TWE pp. 1038, 1040, 1041 Synthesis, TWE p. 1043	Denotation and Connotation, TWE p. 1037 Extended Definition, TWE p. 1042	Propose a Change, SE p. 1035	Analyzing the Painting, SE p. 1039 Analyzing the Art, SE p. 1043

UNIT 7
Unit Resources

Reading with Purpose offers a comprehensive package of tools to optimize student learning and the teaching experience. Each resource has been designed to assist students in specific areas and to offer instructional support for teachers. While all of these areas are covered in the core textbook, some students may need extra practice or additional help in specific areas. The resource package is designed so that you, the teacher, can choose which items will best assist your students. You may also use these resources as homework assignments and for assessment purposes. The following are resources recommended for use with Unit 7.

Keys for Unit Resources

- Blackline Master
- Workbook
- Supplemental Text
- CD-ROM
- DVD
- Transparency
- Web-based
- Fast File

Essential Instructional Support

UNIT 7 RESOURCES

Reading and Literature
- Academic Vocabulary Review
- Big Question: School to Home
- The Big Question Foldable
- Unit Challenge: Planner and Rubrics
- Comparing Literature Graphic Organizer
- Key Reading Skills
- Active Reading Graphic Organizers
- Literary Analysis
- Unit Vocabulary Review

Writing, Grammar, and Spelling
- Spelling and Handwriting Practice
- Grammar Practice
- Writing Workshop Graphic Organizer

Listening, Speaking, and Viewing
- Viewing and Representing
- Listening and Speaking

English Language Learners
- English Language Coach Review

DIFFERENTIATED INSTRUCTION

- Leveled Vocabulary Development
- Skill Level Up!™ A Language Arts Game
- Listening Library CD
- BookLink 3
- Literature Library Vocabulary Puzzlemaker
- Vocabulary Puzzlemaker

ASSESSMENT

GLENCOE'S ASSESSMENT ADVANTAGE

- Selection and Unit Assessments
- Selection Quick Checks
- Assessment by Learning Objectives
- Rubrics for Assessing Student Writing, Listening, and Speaking
- Glencoe Online Essay Grader
- Interactive Tutor: Self-Assessment
- ExamView Assessment Suite
- Literature Library ExamView Assessment Suite

Additional Instructional Support

WRITING, GRAMMAR, AND SPELLING

- Real Success in Writing: Research and Reports
- Writing Constructed Responses
- Spelling Power eWorkbook
- Grammar & Composition Handbook
- Grammar and Language Workbook
- Revising with Style eWorkbook

TRANSPARENCIES

- Read Aloud, Think Aloud Transparencies
- Literary and Text Analysis Transparencies
- Bellringer Options Transparencies
- Grammar and Writing Workshop Transparencies
- Fine Art Transparencies

ENGLISH LANGUAGE LEARNER

- English Language Coach
- Fluency Practice and Assessment
- inTime Magazines (Spanish)
- Spanish Listening Library CD

PROFESSIONAL DEVELOPMENT

- Professional Development Package

READING AND LITERATURE

- Active Learning and Note Taking Guide
- inTime Magazines
- Backpack Reader Volume 2
- Literature Library
- Literature Launchers Pre-Reading Videos DVD
- Literature Classics

TECHNOLOGY

- TeacherWorks Plus™
- StudentWorks Plus™
- BookLink 3
- Skill Level Up!™ A Language Arts Game
- ExamView Assessment Suite
- Interactive Tutor: Self-Assessment
- Listening Library CD
- Spanish Listening Library CD
- Literature Classics
- Literature Launchers Pre-Reading Videos DVD
- Literature Library ExamView Assessment Suite
- Vocabulary Puzzlemaker
- Literature Library Vocabulary Puzzlemaker
- glencoe.com
- Online Student Edition
- Presentation Plus!
- Glencoe Online Essay Grader

- Skill Level Up!™ A Language Arts Game
- Interactive Tutor: Self-Assessment

Additional Glencoe Resources

Dinah Zike's Foldables

Foldables are three-dimensional, interactive graphic organizers that help students practice basic writing skills, review key vocabulary terms, and answer Big Questions. Every unit contains a foldable activity. You can find the pattern and directions for the Unit 7 Foldable in the Unit 7 Resources Fast Files booklet. You can use the foldables as they are presented or modify them to suit the needs of your students. More information about foldables for Unit 7 can be found on pages R8–R9.

Glencoe Literature Library

This collection of hardcover books includes full-length novels, novellas, plays, and works of nonfiction. Each volume consists of at least one complete extended-length reading accompanied by several related readings from a broad range of genres. A separate Study Guide for each Glencoe Literature Library book provides teaching notes and reproducible activity pages for students.

Glencoe Literature Library titles that complement this unit include:

Jacob Have I Loved by Katherine Paterson
Shabanu: Daughter of the Wind by Suzanne Fisher Staples
So Far from the Bamboo Grove by Yoko Kawashima Watkins

For a wealth of online resources that support the instruction in Unit 7 of *Glencoe Literature: Reading with Purpose,* students and teachers can visit our Web site at www.glencoe.com. Students will find additional learning, practice, and assessment opportunities such as these, which are noted in the student text:

- **Big Question Overview**
- **Study Central**
- **Author Search**
- **Writing Models**
- **Interactive Literary Elements Handbook**
- **Web Activities**

Teachers will find planning and instructional tools that include the following:

- **Book Lesson Plans**
- **Teacher Forum**
- **Professional Development**
- **Web Activities Lesson Plans (with answers to student activities)**

Go to www.glencoe.com to see the entire selection of Reading with Purpose online resources.

Use the Glencoe BookLink 3 CD-ROM, a database of more than 26,700 titles, to *create customized reading lists* for your students.

- Search for award-winning titles, (e.g., Newbery Award winners, Coretta Scott King Award winners, and Caldecott Medal winners) and for books on several state-recommended reading lists.
- Find Degrees of Reading Power™ (DRP) and Lexile™ readability scores for all selections.
- Organize reading lists by students' reading level, author, genre, theme, or area of interest.
- Get a brief summary of each selection.

You can find recommended leveled readings for this unit with Reading on Your Own (see page 1044).

Glencoe's **Presentation Plus!**, a multimedia teaching tool, lets you present dynamic lessons that will engage your students. Using Microsoft PowerPoint,® you can customize the presentations to create your own personalized lessons. Use **CheckPoint** questions with interactive response keypads to get immediate student feedback during lessons, to increase student participation, and to assess student comprehension.

A lively collection of articles drawn from issues of the TIME family of magazines helps students develop the skills they need to interact with informational text in a meaningful way. Each of the news stories, feature articles, reviews, profiles, and essays in the magazine connect to an author, work, or theme in *Glencoe Literature: Reading with Purpose.* Articles for Unit 7 are found in Volume B. See the *inTIME* Teacher's Guide for specific connections to each unit and for reproducible student worksheets designed to develop students' reading and critical thinking skills.

Literature Launchers

Set the scene with Glencoe's Literature Launchers, engaging video segments that introduce each unit's genre focus. Each video brings the genre to life, relating it to your students' worlds.

Insert the Glencoe Literature Launchers Pre-Reading Videos DVD into your DVD player. Select the Unit 7 Launcher from the menu to introduce the genre and Big Question for this unit.

Online Essay Grader

Use Glencoe's Online Essay Grader to score your students' writing and to provide individualized feedback to each student automatically.

You and your students can visit www.glencoe.com to link to the essay grader. *Students* can enter their essays and receive feedback on demand. *You* can manage demographic data, assign tests, and generate individual student and aggregated reports. The essay grader can help you:

- Save time with automatic scoring and individualized feedback.
- Supplement in-class writing instruction using guided writing practice.
- Get reports for individual students or for special populations.
- Track student improvement over time.

REAL Success: Reading Excellence at All Levels

Glencoe now provides all of your students with the tools they need to become better, more enthusiastic readers. The REAL Success suite of reading and language arts products encourages reading excellence by meeting the needs of students at all levels. Glencoe products that can be used in conjunction with Unit 7 include the following:

- Jamestown Literature: An Adapted Reader
- Jamestown *Reading Fluency*
- Jamestown *Critical Reading Series, In the Line of Duty*
- *Vocabulary Builder*
- *The Glencoe Reader, Course 3*

To order these products, call Glencoe at 1-800-USA-READ.

Teacher Wraparound Edition Key

Level Appropriate Code

AS = Activities for all students
AL = Activities for students working above grade level
OL = Activities for students working at grade level
BL = Activities for students working below grade level
EL = Activities for English language learners

Teacher Wraparound Prompts

R **Reading Skill** These activities help you teach reading comprehension skills.

V **Vocabulary** These activities help students comprehend words and incorporate them into their reading and writing.

C **Critical Thinking** These strategies help students apply and extend what they have learned.

BQ **BIG Question** These activities and questions prompt students to prepare to answer the Big Question.

W **Writing** These activities provide writing opportunities to help students practice writing and comprehend text.

L **Literary Element** These activities and questions help students comprehend selections and learn more about each genre.

E **Text Element** These activities help students comprehend text elements.

LSV **Listening, Speaking, Viewing** These activities help students practice listening, speaking, and viewing skills.

EL **English Language Coach** These skills help English language learners as well as students who need additional reading support.

UNIT 7
Professional Development Center

From an Author:

Preparing Students to Read Persuasive Text

Emphasize the importance of understanding persuasive text. Students are bombarded with persuasive messages in their everyday lives, and, at some point, these messages influence their actions, if they are persuasive enough. If students are to think critically about what they read, we need to ensure that the purposes for reading include making up one's mind. If students understand they have the ability to make up their own minds, they will be more likely to become engaged in assessing the messages they receive from television, radio, magazines, newspapers, the Internet, billboards, and so on.

Cynthia Shanahan

Explain how to analyze persuasive text. A first step is for students to think about what they currently believe about a topic. Then they must read with a critical eye. Readers who engage in critical reading of text read both inside and outside the text. That is, they read and evaluate the message itself, but they also evaluate the author's qualifications, pay attention to where the message appears (in an editorial or in a textbook, for example), when the message appears (in the 1950s or yesterday), and to whom the message was written. Wineburg (1991) calls these elements "sourcing" *(who wrote the message, where did it come from, what sources were used)* and "contextualization" *(when was it written and for whom; what about the context influenced the message).* In addition, Wineburg discusses "corroboration" (*comparing and contrasting the message with other messages on the same topic*). When a reader engages in sourcing, contextualization, and corroboration, he or she is evaluating the trustworthiness of the information. Using these elements also influences how he or she interprets the text. Reading both inside and outside the text helps readers make up their minds.

Teacher to Teacher

Fareeda J. Shabazz
Paul Revere Elementary School
Chicago, Illinois

When working with middle school students it is important to recognize that they can often be very opinionated individuals. Students need to know that their opinions and beliefs are valued. Persuasive writing has always been the most exciting and relevant writing genre for my students. When I begin the unit on persuasion, I remind students that the media is constantly trying to persuade them to think or act a certain way. Students quickly become passionate about what they believe and attempt to persuade others to analyze the situation from their point of view. Classroom discussions centered around various topics such as school lunches, uniforms, their favorite music groups, and even politics are great ways to help students evaluate why persuasion is so important. During these activities, students also obtain an understanding of why it is important to support your opinions and ideas with evidence when attempting to persuade others. On a more complex level, I invite students to discuss how famous world leaders, such as Dr. Martin Luther King, Jr. or Mahatma Gandhi used persuasion to ultimately transform the world that we live in today.

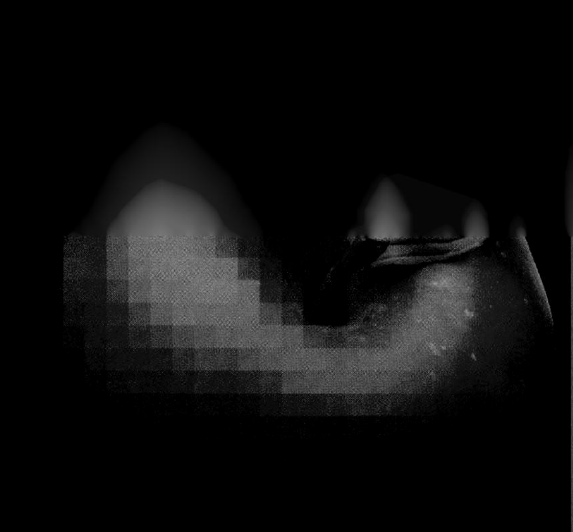

Teaching Students About Persuasive Text

How do I make persuasive text interesting to students?

Most students will be interested in persuasive text that deals with subjects they are interested in. Scan various media to find examples of persuasive texts or have students look for as many persuasive messages as they can find in one day. Then, as a class, discuss how these texts are persuasive, how the writers make their arguments, and how students are influenced by the texts.

What should I teach my students about persuasive text?

First, teach students how to read the text to find the persuasive message. We cover this in Reading Workshop 1 of this unit, where we show students how to understand persuasive techniques. Next, we recommend teaching students how to distinguish between fact and opinion. Students need to know when something is substantiated with evidence and proof and when something is simply someone's thoughts or ideas.

Questioning information and ideas is another skill that is useful when reading persuasive text. Encourage students to become engaged with what they read by considering what they would like to know about the issues presented in the text. Remind them of the basic inquiry questions *Who, What, When, Where, How* and *Why.* If they can't find answers to their questions in the text, direct them to other resources in the library and on the Internet.

To ensure that students have a clear understanding of a text, especially when complex ideas are presented, remind them to review and clarify as they read.

What can I do to help students understand the language that writers of persuasive text use?

Careful use of language is an important way for writers of persuasive text to convey their messages. Explain to students why identifying semantic slanting is important to evaluating a persuasive text. Share examples of semantic slanting that students encounter every day, such as in advertisements, news or magazine articles, and television commercials. Discuss how the semantic slanting leaves a positive or negative impression. Divide students into two groups and have each come up with language that uses semantic slanting to support opposite ideas.

UNIT 7

The BIG Question What's Worth Fighting For? What's Not?

"It is easier to fight for our principles than to live up to them."

—Alfred Adler (1870–1937), Austrian psychiatrist and author of *Understanding Human Nature*

Key Unit Objectives

- Answer the Big Question
- Analyze the literary elements of persuasive writing
- Apply strategies for reading persuasive writing
- Write a persuasive essay

Why Is It Important?

Addressing this big question helps students weigh what personal or societal causes are important to them and how they can act on those concerns.

Viewing the Photo

Ask: Do you think this image shows a time before or after the Civil Rights Act of 1964? *(before)* **Ask:** What details support your answer? *(possible responses: clothing, cars)* **Ask:** What do you think the people shown would have thought was worth fighting for? *(possible responses: right to vote, equal pay and education, an end to segregation and discrimination)* OL

Unit Skills

BIG Question What's worth fighting for? What's not?
Genre Focus: Persuasive essay

Reading Skills
- Distinguishing Fact from Opinion, p. 930
- Questioning, p. 956
- Reviewing, p. 976
- Clarifying, p. 998

Vocabulary
- Denotations and Connotations, p. 932

Literary Elements
- Persuasive Appeals, p. 933
- Author's Bias, p. 979
- Faulty Reasoning, p. 1001

Writing Skills/Grammar
- Persuasive Essay, pp. 952, 992
- Apostrophes, p. 955
- Fluency, p. 994

LOOKING AHEAD

The skill lessons and readings in this unit will help you develop your own answer to the Big Question.

About the Reading

Each selection in this unit encourages students to consider the question, "What's worth fighting for? What's not?" Students learn what other people find important, how they act on those values, and how they seek to persuade others.

About the Skills

The skills taught in this unit have been selected because they are particularly helpful when reading the featured genre—persuasive writing. Each reading selection provides students with opportunities to practice and develop these skills.

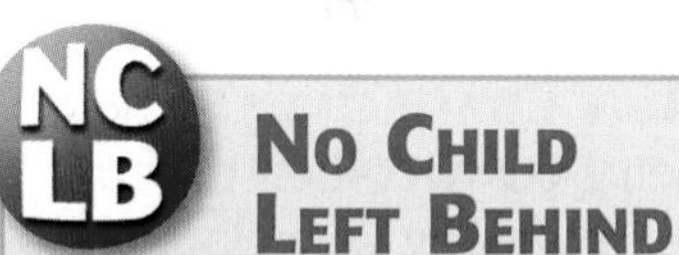

No Child Left Behind acknowledges the value of your direct instruction. You will help your students gain comprehension of persuasive writing as you explain and model reading strategies and help students practice and apply those skills.

Reading Fluency

Partner Reading For most of the selections in this unit, reading with fluency means reading with a persuasive tone. After students read "Saving Water: Why Save Something That Covers Two-thirds of the Earth?" or "All Together Now," for example, have each student choose one paragraph he or she especially likes. Then have students in pairs read their paragraphs to each other, with the goal of sounding smooth, natural, and persuasive. Listeners should make two specific suggestions for improvement, such as "Try emphasizing the phrase *a great deal*." Then the reader should read his or her paragraph a second time. OL

Indiana English/Language Arts Academic Standards
TWE: *Reading Fluency* 8.7

Focus

BELLRINGER Options

- **Literature Launcher**
- **Daily Language Practice Transparency 62**

Focus Activity Have students brainstorm for five minutes in their Learner's Notebooks about things they would like to change in their lives, families, communities, or even in the nation or world. *(Responses will vary.)* OL

Teach

R Reading Skill

Review Connecting To help students connect their experiences to the Big Question, ask them to write in their Learner's Notebooks about a time when they tried to accomplish something or change someone's mind. OL

BQ BIG Question

- Have students read the profiles and look at the pictures of Sajitha, Alejandro, and Pedro.
- Divide the class into groups and have the groups discuss the advice they would give Sajitha, Alejandro, and Pedro. OL

UNIT 7 WARM-UP

Connecting to The BIG Question What's Worth Fighting For? What's Not?

Sometimes you want things to change, but it's difficult to figure out how *you* can change them. So you learn to sort out what really matters to you and what doesn't. You learn what's worth fighting for and what's not. Then you decide how to act to make the change you want. R

Real Kids and the Big Question

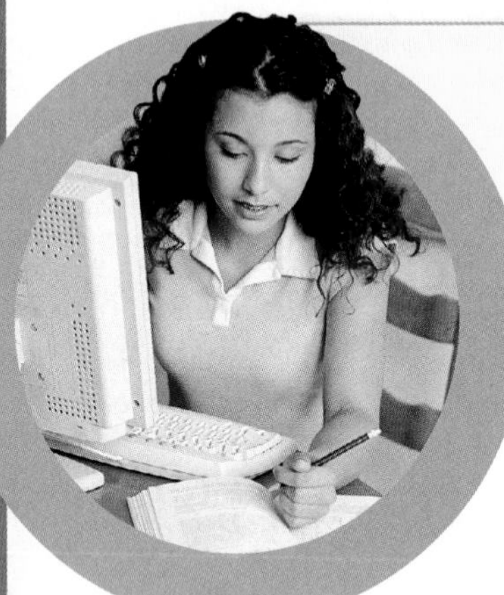

SAJITHA started a video games club at her school. There are a lot of games to choose from, but one game is everyone's favorite. A few of the older kids won't even let any of the younger kids play it. As a result, some of the younger kids have decided to leave the club. Sajitha is upset, but she is also a little afraid of the older kids. What advice would you give Sajitha? BQ

ALEJANDRO and his brother Pedro are planning to paint their room. Pedro insists that the room should be green. Alejandro wants to paint their room blue. Every time Alejandro brings it up, Pedro starts yelling, and their mother tells them to work it out. What would you say to Alejandro? What would you say to Pedro?

Warm-Up Activity

In small groups, talk about the advice you would give Sajitha, Alejandro, and Pedro. How and why might your advice help them?

Additional Support

Reading in the Real World

Career In some schools, students like Sajitha, Alejandro, and Pedro can go to peer mediators to help them solve their problems. Peer mediators are students who are trained to help others identify the cause of a conflict and work out a solution. If your school has a peer mediator program, invite a spokesperson to talk to the class. If not, have students research peer mediation programs. Some students may even want to propose a peer mediation program for your school. Point out that an interest in peer mediation can lead to a career in conflict resolution as a counselor or mediator in many fields, including education, business, and law. OL

You and the Big Question

Reading about what other people think is worth fighting for will help you work out your own answer to the Big Question.

Literature Online

BIG Question

Link to Web resources to further explore the Big Question at www.glencoe.com.

Plan for the Unit Challenge

At the end of the unit, you'll use notes from all your reading to complete the Unit Challenge.

You'll choose one of the following activities:

A. Make a Mural Make a poster-board mural honoring people who fought for what they believed in.

B. Propose a Change Write a proposal for a project that will help you make a change in your school or community.

- Start thinking about which activity you'd like to do, so you can focus your thoughts as you go through the unit.
- Do you want to learn about people who stood up for their beliefs? Start making a list of people and ideas.
- Is there a change you want to make in your school or community? Start thinking about how to persuade people that the change is needed.
- In your Learner's Notebook, write which activity you'd like to do.
- Each time you make notes about the Big Question, think about how your ideas will help you complete the Unit Challenge activity you chose.

Keep Track of Your Ideas

As you read, you'll make notes about the Big Question. Later, you'll use these notes to complete the Unit Challenge. See pages R8–R9 for help with making Foldable 7. This diagram shows how it should look.

1. Use this Foldable for all of the selections in this unit. On the top front flap, write the unit number and the Big Question. Label the bottom of each flap below with a title. (See page 923 for the titles.)
2. Open each flap. Near the top of each flap, write **My Purpose for Reading.**
3. Below each crease, write **the Big Question.**

Unit 7
What's Worth Fighting For? What's Not?

Title	Title
Title	Title
Title	Title
Title	Title
Title	Title

Teach

BQ 

Have students evaluate the list they brainstormed in the Bellringer activity and put check marks beside items they believe are worth fighting for. OL

For each selection they read, students will enter notes about how that selection applies to the Big Question. For details about using Dinah Zike's Foldables, see pages R8-R9.

Assess/Close

Ask students to share their thoughts about why looking for an answer to the Big Question might be important to them.

Resources for page 925

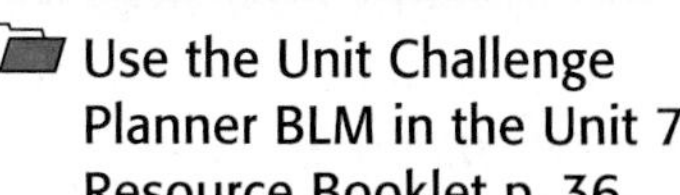
Use the Unit Challenge Planner BLM in the Unit 7 Resource Booklet p. 36.

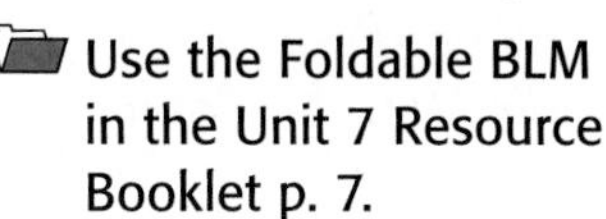
Use the Foldable BLM in the Unit 7 Resource Booklet p. 7.

Differentiated Instruction

Many Kinds of Notes Point out to students that the notes they take for the Unit Challenge need not all be written notes. They can also tape or clip other kinds of material into their Learner's Notebooks related to the project they have chosen. They could, for example, include pictures of people they admire, charts that provide background on something that needs changing, a tape of a song that supports their ideas, or physical objects related to their topics. Point out that these "notes" may help students develop their own ideas or become a part of their final product. OL

Indiana English/Language Arts Academic Standards
TWE: *Differentiated Instruction* 8.2

Focus

BELLRINGER Options

Daily Language Practice Transparency 63

Focus Activity Say: Name some of the people who try to persuade you to think a certain way or to do something they want you to do. *(Responses will vary but could include parents, friends, teachers, religious leaders, advertisers, and politicians.)* OL

Teach

E Text Element

How to Read Persuasive Writing Ask: Why do you think being able to recognize each text element is important to understanding persuasive writing? *(Possible responses: **Persuasive appeal:** Knowing how writers try to persuade us helps us evaluate the arguments. **Author's bias:** If we spot bias, we'll be more careful about accepting the author's arguments. The arguments might still be strong—but they also might be weak. **Faulty reasoning:** If we recognize faulty reasoning, we can reject it.)* OL

UNIT 7 GENRE FOCUS: PERSUASIVE WRITING

Skills Focus
- Key skills for reading persuasive writing
- Key literary elements of persuasive writing

Skills Model
You will learn how to use the key reading skills and literary elements as you read
- ***A Letter to Senator Edwards,*** p. 927

The goal of **persuasive writing** is to convince readers to agree with an opinion and, in some cases, act on it. Advertisements, critical reviews, speeches, and editorials are all examples of persuasive writing.

Why Read Persuasive Writing?

Reading persuasive writing lets you see what other people think about issues and ideas. When you read persuasive writing, you do the following things:

- learn what other people think about an issue
- think about how you feel about an issue
- learn to distinguish fact from opinion

How to Read Persuasive Writing

Key Reading Skills

These reading skills are useful tools for reading and understanding persuasive writing. You'll see these skills modeled in the Active Reading Model on pages 927–929, and you'll learn more about them later in this unit.

- **Distinguishing fact from opinion** To decide whether someone's arguments are trustworthy, you need to ask yourself, *Are these someone's personal beliefs, or can they be proved?* (See Reading Workshop 1.)
- **Questioning** To make sure you understand a selection, ask yourself questions while you read. (See Reading Workshop 2.)
- **Reviewing** Stop from time to time to go over what you've already read and to remember and organize important ideas. (See Reading Workshop 3.)
- **Clarifying** Reread confusing parts, look up words you don't know, and ask questions about what you don't understand. (See Reading Workshop 4.)

Key Text Elements

Recognizing and thinking about the following literary elements will help you understand more fully what writers are saying.

- **Persuasive appeals:** methods used to convince people to agree with a position. An author who appeals through the use of reason presents arguments based on facts and other kinds of evidence. An author who appeals through the use of ethics tries to show why he or she is trustworthy. An author who appeals through the use of emotion tries to spark strong feelings to get readers to care about an issue and take action. (See "Saving Water," *The Measure of Our Success,* and "All Together Now.")
- **Author's bias:** an inability or unwillingness to look at all sides of an issue (See "Teen Curfews.")
- **Faulty reasoning:** flawed thinking that leads to incorrect conclusions (See Rally for Better Food, student flyer and poster.)

E

Indiana English/ Language Arts Academic Standards (pp. 926–929)

8.2 Comprehension and Analysis (Focus on Informational Text) Develop [reading] strategies... asking questions, making predictions, identifying... perspective and purpose. **8.2.2** Analyze text that uses proposition (statement of argument) and support patterns.

For a complete description of the standards, see p. IN 11.

Additional Support

Literature Focus Lesson

Persuasive Writing Have students create a bulletin board display exploring the range of persuasive writing. Direct below-level students to find persuasive ads, both print and broadcast. (For broadcast ads have students sketch a visual and jot down notes on the verbal appeal.) BL Direct on-level students to find persuasive editorials, editorial cartoons, and letters to the editor. OL Instruct above-level students to find examples of persuasive speeches, critical reviews, and even stories (such as fables). AL As the class works through this unit, encourage students to keep their eyes open for additional examples. AS

A Letter to Senator Edwards

Dear Senator Edwards:

I am writing to you about proposed Bill 347.9. As a result of the accident rate for young drivers, our state is thinking of issuing restricted driver's licenses to young drivers who break the traffic laws. Under Bill 347.9, a driver under eighteen who is guilty of a moving violation (for example, speeding or running a red light) would get a restricted driver's license. The license holder could then drive only during daylight hours and with an adult licensed driver. These restrictions would remain in effect until the driver's eighteenth birthday. 1

R Safe roads are everyone's concern. I doubt that anyone would oppose reasonable measures to make streets safer. The reasoning behind Bill 347.9 is admirable. The bill's purposes are to keep offending[1] drivers off the roads, to provide supervision for less-experienced young drivers, and to make the roads safer for all travelers. However, as a young driver, I urge you to vote against this bill for two reasons. First, the bill unfairly targets one group for unusually harsh punishment. 2

The notes in the side columns model how to use the reading skills and text elements you read about on page 926.

Persuasive Writing

ACTIVE READING MODEL

1 Key Reading Skill
Reviewing *I need to reread the introductory paragraph, so I can really understand Bill 347.9. I know it affects young drivers, but I don't remember the details.*

2 Key Reading Skill
Distinguishing Fact from Opinion *It's a fact that the bill targets one group. It's an opinion that the bill is unfair.*

1. ***Offending*** drivers break the law.

Teach

R Reading Skill

Distinguishing Fact from Opinion **Ask:** Is the second sentence of the first paragraph a statement of fact or opinion? Why? *(Fact. It gives information that can be proved by reading the proposed law.)* **OL** **Ask:** What sentences in the second paragraph include opinions? *(first, second, third, and sixth)* **AL**

Resources for page 927

Use the Genre Study BLM in the Unit 7 Resource Booklet.

Readability Scores
Dale Chall: 8.0
DRP: 63
Lexile: 1070

Reading in the Real World

Citizenship For their Unit Challenge activity, students may want to contact public officials. Have students prepare a class chart listing these officials' names, titles, office and e-mail addresses, and phone numbers. Groups can identify local officials (the mayor, city council, or select board members), state officials (the governor or the school district's state representative), and national officials (the state's two senators and the district's representative). Point out that the same skills students use to find this information will help them identify other officials, such as the local animal control officer. **OL**

Indiana English/Language Arts Academic Standards
SE: 8.2, 8.2.2
TWE: *Literature Focus Lesson* 8.2.2

Teach

Viewing the Art

Ask: How does the image reinforce the writer's objections to the proposed restrictions on teenaged drivers? *(Possible responses: Signs like "no outlet" and "not a through street" suggest that the bill will make it difficult for teens to earn driving privileges; the jumbled arrangement suggests that teens will find many barriers to getting a driver's license.)* **OL**

R Reading Skill

Questioning Ask: What question might you ask yourself after reading this paragraph? *(Possible response: What is the key point the author is making here?)* **OL**

E Text Element

Persuasive Appeals Ask: What ethical appeal does the author make, even if indirectly? *(The author suggests that it would be unfair to limit the activities of hard-working and involved students.)* **OL**

ACTIVE READING MODEL

Second, the bill will make it difficult or even impossible for many students to hold part-time jobs and participate in after-school activities. **3**

Bill 347.9 discriminates against young drivers. Don't licensed drivers over the age of eighteen also commit moving violations? Yet no one is suggesting that they get restricted licenses. There is no evidence that speeding or running a red light is a greater safety danger when the driver is under eighteen. People can be safe or reckless drivers regardless of their age. They don't automatically become better drivers once they reach eighteen. The same rules should apply to drivers of all ages. **4** **R**

Another factor to consider about Bill 347.9 is the effect it will have on young people who depend on their driving privileges in order to work and participate in after-school activities. Many of my classmates hold part-time jobs. Some work to save money for college. Others work to **E**

3 Key Reading Skill
Questioning *Why will the bill make part-time jobs and after-school activities impossible?*

4 Key Text Element
Persuasive Appeals *Here, the writer appeals to readers' sense of reason by giving a logical argument in support of his opinion. He doesn't try to spark strong feelings or prove that he is a trustworthy expert on the subject.*

Additional Support

English Language Coach

Word Origins The origin of the word *bill* is the Latin word *bulla*, meaning "seal" or "document." Here it means the draft of a proposed law. Review with students (or have a student report on) the basic process by which a bill becomes a law on the state or national level: The bill is drafted and assigned a number, reviewed by legislative committees, voted on by the legislature, and if approved by the legislature and the executive, signed by the executive. (Review the definitions of *legislature* and *executive* with students as necessary.) People interested in the bill can urge acceptance or rejection at any stage. **EL** **OL**

ACTIVE READING MODEL

help out their parents. Anyone with a restricted license cannot hold a job unless he or she can walk to work, get a ride, or use public transportation. When these choices do not exist, or are not safe, many students will be forced to quit their jobs. Similar problems occur when students are unable to drive to and from after-school activities, such as music lessons, sport team practices, and games. If Bill 347.9 is passed, students will have to quit their after-school activities simply because they have had a single moving violation. 5

R Some people will argue that special rules and restrictions should apply to younger drivers, since they lack the experience and judgment of older drivers. But how will younger drivers ever gain the experience and judgment they need if they aren't allowed to drive by themselves? If Mom or Dad is always in the car, playing the role of "back-seat driver," how will a young person ever learn to drive independently out on the road? Laws already exist to restrict, suspend,[2] or take away the license of any driver who is truly reckless or a threat to public safety, regardless of age. Let's enforce the laws that already exist. Let's not pass new laws that discriminate against drivers under eighteen. 6

E In closing, I would like to thank you for considering my viewpoint. We young drivers of this state hope that we can count on you to watch out for our interests, as well as those of all citizens. In return, we will act responsibly both on and off the roads. 7 ❍

2. Here, ***suspend*** means "to force to give up something for a period of time."

5 Key Text Element
Faulty Reasoning *In the last sentence of this paragraph, the writer uses faulty "either/or" reasoning. If the bill passes, some students will still be able to get to and from activities by walking or taking public transportation.*

6 Key Reading Skill
Clarifying *I'm not sure about the difference between "suspend" and "take away." I'll read the footnote for help.*

7 Key Text Element
Author's Bias *I think the writer is a bit biased. He bases his opinion on personal experience. Since the writer is a young driver, he writes only about how the bill will affect people under eighteen.*

Partner Talk With a partner, discuss your opinion of Bill 347.9. Do you agree or disagree with the writer's opinion? Explain.

Study Central Visit www.glencoe.com and click on Study Central to review persuasive writing.

Teach

R Reading Skill

Clarifying **Say:** In your own words, restate the argument the author is making at the beginning of the second paragraph. *(Possible response: Young people will learn to be independent drivers only by driving independently.)* OL

E Text Element

Faulty Reasoning **Ask:** What either/or argument does the author make in the last paragraph? *(The author suggests that the senator has to agree with the author or be accused of not watching out for the interests of young people.)* OL
Ask: Why is this faulty reasoning? *(The supporters of the bill also believe they are working in the interests of young people.)* AL

Literature Online

Study Central Have students access the Web site to review persuasive writing and to complete a related activity.

Literature Focus Lesson

Persuasive Appeals Although students will likely support the letter writer's position, challenge them to come up with arguments against it. Write these arguments on the board. Now have students classify each as an appeal to reasoning, emotion, or ethics. Students might, for example, suggest "Let's compare how many moving violations young drivers and other groups commit" *(reasoning);* "Causing a serious accident could totally ruin a young person's life and maybe the lives of others" *(emotion);* and "Making laws that protect the majority of people is the right thing to do" *(ethics).* OL

Indiana English/Language Arts Academic Standards
SE: 8.2, 8.22
TWE: *English Language Coach* 8.2, *Literature Focus Lesson* 8.2.2

Distinguishing Fact from Opinion

Teaching Students to Distinguish Fact and Opinion

Why Is It Important?

- Students will learn that facts are statements that can be proven, while opinions are statements of belief that cannot be proven.
- While reading various texts, students will encounter writers who try to persuade them. If students can tell the difference between fact and opinion, they will be able to make up their own minds.
- As students learn how to recognize opinions, they'll be able to judge whether they should believe what they've heard or read. They will also learn that they can disagree with an opinion.

How to Help Students Get It

- Tell students to look at the title of the selection first. Sometimes the title expresses an opinion about a topic.
- As they read, remind students to think about which parts of the selection are convincing. Then ask them to try to determine if those parts are facts or opinions.
- Remind students that sometimes a good persuasive argument is a balance between a writer's opinions and the facts used to support those opinions.

Reading to Answer the Big Question

Saving Water: Why Save Something That Covers Two-Thirds of the Earth? by Marjorie Lamb
Students will learn interesting and important information about water. For instance, only 1% of Earth's water is available for our use, and it is the same water in which Moses floated thousands of years ago. The author explains why every person should fight to conserve this crucial resource and presents many simple ways to do it.

from *The Measure of Our Success* by Marian Wright Edelman
This text from a speech by Edelman offers seven lessons to help students learn to fight for their dreams. She discusses what's worth fighting for, offers practical ideas, and inspires students to never give up.

Workshop Resources

Pacing (Days) Standard	Pacing (Days) Block	Lesson	Student Materials	Teacher Resources
1	1/2	Key Skill Lesson: Distinguishing Fact from Opinion	Key Reading Skills Practice, p. 9 English Language Coach Review, p. 42	Bellringer Options Transparencies –Daily Language Practice 64 Read Aloud, Think Aloud Transparencies –Key Reading Skills 7 –Read Aloud, Think Aloud 55–62 Presentation Plus!
1	1	"Saving Water: Why Save Something That Covers Two-Thirds of the Earth?"	Glencoe Online Unit Vocabulary Review, p. 40 Academic Vocabulary Review, p. 43 English Language Coach Active Reading Graphic Organizer, p. 11 Literary Analysis, p. 10 StudentWorks Plus™ Online Student Edition Literature Classics Selection and Unit Assessments, p. 73	Literary and Text Analysis Transparencies 36 Puzzlemaker Skill Level Up!™ A Language Arts Game BookLink 3 Assessment by Learning Objective (Diagnostic and Formative) Interactive Tutor: Self-Assessment TeacherWorks Plus™
1		from *The Measure of Our Success*	Glencoe Online Unit Vocabulary Review, p. 40 Academic Vocabulary Review, p. 43 English Language Coach Active Reading Graphic Organizer, p. 13 Literary Analysis, p. 10 StudentWorks Plus™ Online Student Edition Literature Classics Selection and Unit Assessments, p. 74	Literary and Text Analysis Transparencies 36 Puzzlemaker Skill Level Up!™ A Language Arts Game BookLink 3 Assessment by Learning Objective (Diagnostic and Formative) Interactive Tutor: Self-Assessment TeacherWorks Plus™

Keys for Unit Resource

- Blackline Master
- Workbook
- Supplemental Text
- CD-ROM
- DVD
- Transparency
- Web-based
- Fast File

Level Appropriate Code

AS = Activities for all students
AL = Activities for students working above grade level
OL = Activities for students working at grade level
BL = Activities for students working below grade level
EL = Activities for English language learners

Focus

BELLRINGER Options

Daily Language Practice Transparency 64

Focus Activity Say: What are some things in your life you think are worth fighting for? They could be big or small. *(Possible responses: being safe and happy, not littering, recycling)* OL

Teach

R Reading Skill

Distinguishing Fact from Opinion Have students state which of the following are facts and which are opinions. Ask them to explain their responses, including telling which words indicate that a sentence is an opinion.

1. I think it's unfair that we have to clean our rooms. *(The words* think *and* unfair *indicate this is an opinion.)*
2. I went to the store on Saturday. *(This is a fact that can be verified.)*
3. I believe that's enough work for one week. *(The word* believe *indicates this is an opinion, and what is enough is a personal judgment.)* OL AL

READING WORKSHOP 1

Skills Focus

You will practice using these skills when you read the following selections:

- "Saving Water: Why Save Something That Covers Two-thirds of the Earth?" p. 934
- from *The Measure of Our Success,* p. 944

Reading

- Distinguishing fact from opinion

Informational Text

- Identifying persuasive appeals

Vocabulary

- Understanding connotation and denotation
- Academic Vocabulary: *ethical*

Writing/Grammar

- Using colons correctly

Skill Lesson

Distinguishing Fact from Opinion

Learn It!

What Is It? You can't always assume that what you read is true. It's up to you to decide whether to believe what a writer tells you. When you are deciding, distinguish facts from opinions.

R

- A **fact** is a piece of information that can be proved with supporting information.
- An **opinion** is a personal belief. Writers can support their opinions with facts, but an opinion cannot be proved.

Analyzing Cartoons
These three friends can't help but share their thoughts about their classmates. Are their comments facts or opinions?

Indiana English/ Language Arts Academic Standards (pp. 930–931)

8.2 Comprehension and Analysis (Focus on Informational Text) Develop [reading] strategies...

For a complete description of the standards, see p. IN 11.

Additional Support

Differentiated Instruction

Practicing Fact and Opinion Have each student choose one of these categories: storytelling, math, art, sports, music, or nature. Each student should write one statement of fact about his or her choice and one statement of opinion. For example, in the category of sports, a student might write these statements:

- Basketball is played on a court with a basket hung at each end. *(fact)*
- Basketball is an exciting sport. *(opinion)*

Divide students into small groups and ask them to share their statements for other group members to identify as fact or opinion. OL

Why Is It Important? Distinguishing fact from opinion helps you decide whether to trust information that you read. C

How Do I Do It? To distinguish fact from opinion, ask yourself these questions:

- *Are sources available to prove this information is correct?*
- *Does this sound like the author's view or belief?*
- *Is the writer an expert on this subject?*

Literature Online

Study Central Visit www.glencoe.com and click on Study Central to review distinguishing fact from opinion.

Below is part of a letter to the editor about improving schools. Read how one student distinguished fact from opinion in the passage.

I attend a school that is being run by state officials because of poor test scores. I think that a better way to improve my school, along with other American schools, is to imitate a successful school system, like Japan's. More than 99 percent of adults in Japan are able to read and write. In Japan, students go to classes five and one-half days per week, do more homework than American students, and wear school uniforms.

I can do research to verify how many Japanese adults can read and write. If the research proves that about 99 percent of Japanese adults are literate, that sentence is a fact. There is no way to prove whether American schools would be better if they imitated Japanese schools. That's the writer's opinion.

Practice It!

Identify each of the following statements as fact or opinion.

- Of all the water on Earth, 97 percent is salt water.
- The best way to relax is a hot bath.

Use It!

Use a two-column chart in your Learner's Notebook to distinguish facts from opinions. Label the left-hand column *Facts* and the right-hand column *Opinions.* As you read "Saving Water," write key pieces of information in the appropriate column.

READING WORKSHOP 1

Teach

R Reading Skill

Distinguishing Fact from Opinion **Say:** State a fact and an opinion about objects in the classroom. For the bulletin board, for example, you might say, "It shows examples of persuasive writing" *(fact)* and "It is well organized" *(opinion)*. OL

C Critical Thinking

Comprehension **Ask:** Why is it important to distinguish fact from opinion when you read? *(It is important because it helps you decide if information is trustworthy.)* BL **Ask:** What might you infer about a writer who uses a lot of opinions and not many facts? *(Possible response: He or she has a strong point of view based on emotion or experience rather than facts.)* OL AL

Resources for page 931

- Use Key Reading Skills Transparency 7 in *Read Aloud, Think Aloud* to help students practice distinguishing fact from opinion.

Reading in the Real World

Citizenship Explain that in a letter to the editor, a reader can comment on an event in the news or on how the newspaper has covered a subject. Have students find a letter to the editor in a community or school newspaper. Tell them to underline one fact and one opinion in the letter. Invite students who found interesting letters to read them aloud. Then discuss whether students find the facts believable and the opinions convincing. OL AL

Indiana English/Language Arts Academic Standards
SE: 8.2
TWE: *Differentiated Instruction* 8.2, *Reading in the Real World* 8.2

Teach

More About the Author

Marjorie Lamb says that her purpose in writing *2 Minutes a Day for a Greener Planet* is not to persuade people to go out and do big things but "to do something that takes very, very little time in their own home." She believes that such small activities can make a difference and that everyone can help make the world a better place. Lamb notes, "All the things that are wrong with the planet are things we have done as individuals. . . . I think it's individuals who can undo it."

V Vocabulary

Using New Vocabulary Challenge students to include all three vocabulary words in one sentence. *(Possible response: Contamination makes the distribution of water harder for municipal governments.)* AL

Before You Read

Saving Water: Why Save Something That Covers Two-thirds of the Earth?

Meet the Author

Marjorie Lamb's parents taught her that "you should always save things, you should always repair things, you should pass things on to the next person, and you should do your best to be kind to the planet in general." The following selection is from Lamb's book *2 Minutes a Day for a Greener Planet.*

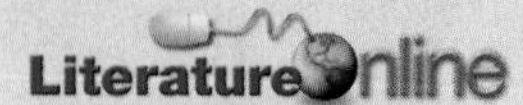

Author Search For more about Marjorie Lamb, go to www.glencoe.com.

Indiana English/Language Arts Academic Standards
(pp. 932–939)

8.1.3 Verify the meaning of a word in its context… **8.2 Comprehension and Analysis (Focus on Informational Text)** Develop [reading] strategies… **8.2.2** Analyze text that uses proposition (statement of argument) and support patterns.

For a complete description of the standards, see p. IN 11.

Vocabulary Preview

V

municipal (myoo NIS uh pul) *adj.* having to do with a city or town or its government **(p. 935)** *Water treatment is only one of many important municipal services that our local government oversees.*

distribution (dis truh BYOO shun) *n.* division into shares or portions **(p. 936)** *There would be fewer problems if the distribution of water were equal so that everyone had his or her fair share.*

contamination (kun tam uh NAY shun) *n.* pollution **(p. 936)** *Waste and contamination are two problems that we can fix.*

Partner Work In your Learner's Notebook, use each vocabulary word in a sentence. Find a partner and check each other's sentences to make sure each word is used correctly.

English Language Coach

Denotations and Connotations All words have **denotations** (dee noh TAY shunz), or dictionary definitions. But some words also have **connotations** (kon uh TAY shunz)—feelings, thoughts, and mental pictures that the words bring to mind. Take, for example, the words *thrifty* and *cheap.* Both words denote, or mean, "careful with money." Yet most people would rather be called "thrifty" than "cheap." That's because *thrifty* has positive connotations, while *cheap* has negative connotations.

Not all words have clear-cut connotations. A word like *the* does not have connotations, while a word like *thin* may have positive connotations for a successful dieter and negative connotations for someone trying to gain weight. Though connotations may differ, most are fairly clear. If you're not sure of a word's connotations, check an unabridged (complete) dictionary.

Partner Work Each of the following groups of words has about the same denotation but different connotations. With a classmate, classify the words in each group as positive, negative, or neutral. Write the words in a chart like the one shown. Use a dictionary if you need help.

- old, antique, decrepit
- spacious, big, overdone

Positive	Neutral	Negative
soft-spoken	quiet	secretive

Additional Support

Author Search To expand students' appreciation of Marjorie Lamb, have them access the Web site for additional information and resources.

English Language Coach

Denotation and Connotation To practice understanding the different connotations of words, have students answer these questions.

- Would you rather be called slim or skinny? Why?
- Is someone who is hanging around for no good reason waiting or loitering?
- Is it better to be aggressive or assertive? Why?
- What is the difference between being careless and happy-go-lucky?

EL BL OL

Skills Preview

Key Reading Skill: Distinguishing Fact from Opinion

As you read the article, ask yourself whether statements are facts or opinions. Remember that opinions are not necessarily wrong. An educated person's opinion may have the force of fact.

On Your Own Which of the following statements is an opinion? Why?

- George Washington was the first U.S. president. He was also the best president.

Key Text Element: Persuasive Appeals

Writers may use a variety of techniques to persuade readers to agree with their opinions or to take action. The three major techniques, or appeals, are as follows:

- **Appeal to reason:** appeal to the "head" rather than the "heart" through the use of logic, facts, or other types of hard evidence
- **Ethical appeal:** appeal to the reader's sense of right and wrong or to the writer's claim to be a good and moral person who can be trusted
- **Emotional appeal:** appeal to the reader's "heart," or emotions, in an effort to get the reader to care about a problem or an issue

E

Partner Talk Discuss the following statements. Decide which appeals to reason, which appeals to ethics, and which appeals to emotions.

Vote for Jon Doe for U.S. senator because . . .

- he is a good family man and a regular churchgoer.
- he is tough on law and order, so you and your family won't have to live in fear.
- he is an experienced legislator who has served two terms as a state senator.

Academic Vocabulary

ethical (ETH uh kul) *adj.* having to do with morals and standards of acceptable behavior

Get Ready to Read

Connect to the Reading

Think about all the water that you use in a day. Then think about where the water comes from and where it goes when you have finished using it.

Whole Class Discussion Suppose that every water source in your home had a meter. The meter would measure how much water your family used and show the total cost of using it. Would the meter change how your family uses water? Why or why not?

Build Background

Not everyone takes clean water for granted.

- Roughly one-sixth of the world's people do not have enough drinking water.
- In some African and Asian countries, people must walk nearly four miles to get water.

Set Purposes for Reading

Read "Saving Water: Why Save Something That Covers Two-thirds of the Earth?" to find out whether conserving fresh water is a cause worth fighting for.

Set Your Own Purpose What else would you like to learn from the article to help you answer the Big Question? Write your own purpose on the "Saving Water" flap of Foldable 7.

Literature Online

Interactive Literary Elements Handbook
To review or learn more about the literary elements, go to www.glencoe.com.

Keep Moving

Use these skills as you read the following selection.

Teach

E Text Element

Persuasive Appeals Say: You want to persuade your parents or guardians to let you get a part-time job babysitting or mowing lawns. Think of one of each of the three persuasive appeals you might make. *(Possible responses: Appeal to reason: "Having a part-time job will keep me out of trouble and allow me to earn money." Ethical: "It wouldn't be fair to require me to pay my own entertainment expenses without letting me earn the money to do so." Emotional: "Having a job will allow me to grow into the hardworking, honest young person you want me to be.")* AS

Interactive Literary Elements Handbook Have students access the Web site to improve their understanding of persuasive appeals.

Differentiated Instruction

Persuasive Appeals Assign small groups of students a topic, such as not littering or eating at Zizzi's Pizza Plaza. Each group should write one sentence that appeals to reason, one to ethics, and one to emotion. Have each group read their sentences aloud and ask the class to identify the appeals. As an example, you could use these sentences on cafeteria courtesy:

- Food tastes better when people are friendly. *(emotional)*
- Rudeness is wrong no matter where it happens. *(ethical)*
- More courtesy means fewer accidental spills. *(reasoning)* BL OL

Indiana English/Language Arts Academic Standards

SE: 8.1.3, 8.2, 8.2.2

TWE: *English Language Coach* 8.1.3, *Differentiated Instruction* 8.2.2

Teach

Viewing the Photo

Ask: Do you think watering the lawn is a waste of water? Why or why not? *(Responses will vary. Some students may think it's worth using the extra water to have a nice-looking lawn; others might think it's not necessary to water the lawn.)* OL **Ask:** Why might this photograph have been chosen to illustrate the article? *(Possible response: The photo shows water being used for a luxury, not a necessity.)* AL

 BIG Question

Ask: Does the author believe that saving water is something worth fighting for? Why? *(Possible response: Yes, because all life needs water and because there's only so much fresh water available.)* OL

Readability Scores
Dale-Chall: 8.5
DRP: 57
Lexile: 1040

READING WORKSHOP 1

Saving Water:
Why Save Something That Covers Two-thirds of the Earth?

by Majorie Lamb

All life on this planet is supported by a fixed quantity of water. We use the same water over and over again, the same water which our grandparents used for brickmaking, the same water in which Shakespeare washed his feet, the same water in which Moses floated in a basket through the bullrushes, the same water the ancient Romans transported through their aqueducts[1] to support life in their city. In fact, the water that you used to brush your teeth this morning is over four billion years old. So have a little respect.

Of all water on our planet Earth, 97% is salt water. Only 3% is fresh water, and most of that is frozen in the polar ice caps. Less than 1% of Earth's water is available for our use. 1

We can't make new water, any more than we can make new land. If we misuse the water we have, we can't send out for some fresh stuff. Water comes out of the tap in unlimited quantities whenever we want it. We generally assume that we have vast reserves of water available.

1. ***Aqueducts*** (AK wuh dukts) are canals, tunnels, or pipelines used to move water.

Practice the Skills

1 **Key Reading Skill**

Distinguishing Fact from Opinion Reread the boldface paragraph. You could prove the information is true by checking science books or encyclopedias. So the statements in this paragraph are facts.

Additional Support

Reading in the Real World

Career The job of a fact checker is to determine whether the facts included in a piece of writing are true. A person with a well-rounded education, rich in general knowledge, makes a good fact checker. Fact checkers should also know how to conduct research quickly. Daily newspapers generally don't have time to fact-check every article; they rely on journalists to be honest and thorough and editors to be alert for anything that looks suspicious. Magazines and book publishing houses, however, often employ many fact checkers. Have each student use another source to check one fact from this article. OL

And we generally assume that it's free, or almost free. But before clean water comes out of our taps, several things have to happen. We have to find a source of water, build machinery to pump it, piping to carry it, plants to treat it. Thanks to our treatment of water, chlorine[2] has become an acquired taste in millions of households. **2** We have to elect politicians who will run our **municipal** affairs, and look after our water treatment, and do the paperwork involved in supplying us with water. Once we get the water to our houses, we have to install pipes and valves and shut-offs and vents. We have to put in a separate line and a heater to heat some of the water.

E

Once we've got water, what do we do with it? We put it through our washing machines, toilets, sinks, dishwashers, car washes and pesticide-filled lawns. We use it to wash our windows, our sidewalks and streets. We spray it in the air for pretty fountains. We put out fires with it. We clean wounds with it. We make concrete with it. We use it in the production of plastics, steel and paper. We hose down chemical spills and industrial work sites with it. We clean paintbrushes in it. And we drink it.

What if we had water meters beside our kitchen sink? What if they read dollars and cents instead of gallons or liters?

C

Then we have to deal with getting rid of it. We need to build another whole network of drains to carry away our dirty water and sewage. We need to build treatment plants, and hire people to run them. And we need to elect politicians who will vow to "do something" to clean up the water that we've polluted.

The process costs billions of dollars worldwide, and still people suffer and die in many parts of the world for want of clean water, while we **blithely** open our taps and let our most precious resource pour down the drain. **3**

2. ***Chlorine*** (klor EEN), a green-yellow gas, is an element used to disinfect water.

Vocabulary

municipal (myoo NIS uh pul) *adj.* having to do with a city or town or its government

Practice the Skills

2 Key Reading Skill

Distinguishing Fact from Opinion It would be impossible to prove that "chlorine has become an acquired taste in millions of households." In fact, many people drink bottled water because they dislike the taste of tap water. Therefore, the author's statement is an opinion.

3 English Language Coach

Denotations and Connotations Here, the word **blithely** means "thoughtlessly." In this context *blithely* has negative connotations. It suggests we carelessly throw away something precious.

Reading in the Real World

Career Have the class act as junior hydrologists, scientists who study water supplies, such as rivers or lakes. Tell students to conduct research to find out the source of your community's water, as well as any existing or potential threats to the water supply. You could also ask students to research some of the key aquifers in the nation, such as the Great Lakes or the Ogallala Aquifer stretching from Texas to South Dakota. AL

Teach

E Text Element

Persuasive Appeals **Say:** The writer includes many facts about how water is processed and prepared to come through our taps. Do you think these facts are supposed to appeal to readers' reason, emotions, or ethics? *(They probably appeal to readers' reason.)* BL OL **Ask:** What might be the author's purpose in providing these facts? *(Possible response: to show that a complicated process is involved in getting clean water to our homes)* AL

C Critical Thinking

Application **Say:** When people buy gasoline, a meter on the pump shows how much they're spending. Does this affect their behavior? What do you think—would knowing the cost of each gallon of water as it's being used affect people's behavior? *(Responses will vary.)* OL

Indiana English/Language Arts Academic Standards

SE: 8.1.3, 8.2

TWE: *Reading in the Real World* 8.2, *Reading in the Real World* 8.4

Teach

C Critical Thinking

Comprehension Ask: What does the writer say readers cannot change? What does she think they can change? *(She thinks they cannot change the "unequal distribution of water in the world," but they can change other major problems, such as contamination and waste.)* **OL** **Ask:** What problem does the writer say she will address in the chapter you are reading? How do you think she will address it? *(Possible response: She says she'll address waste. She might give tips for how to prevent waste.)* **AL**

R Reading Skill

Distinguishing Fact from Opinion Say: Sometimes a writer uses one or more facts to support an opinion. What is the writer's opinion about bleach? What fact does she use to support her opinion? *(She expresses the opinion that bleach isn't terrific to have around and supports that opinion with the fact that bleach is a poison.)* **OL**

READING WORKSHOP 1

Analyzing the Photo How does this photograph relate to what the writer says about the cycle of water use in the United States? Explain.

There's not much we can do at home about the unequal **distribution** of water in the world. But the other major problems, **contamination** and waste, we can do something about. Although most of the advice in this chapter has to do with waste (we'll deal with contamination in other chapters), these two problems are connected in ways that might not be obvious. **C**

The more we process our water, the more chance it has to become contaminated. That's because we have one sewage system for all purposes. We put our drinking water, our toilet waste and commercially contaminated waters all down the same system. We do our best to clean it up, then we pour it all out into the same river, lake or stream, and then we drink it again. **4**

And of course, the more water we have to process, the more bleach we have to produce (which isn't a terrific thing to have around—it is, after all, a poison), and, naturally, the more we **R**

Practice the Skills

4 Key Text Element

Persuasive Appeals What kind of persuasive appeal is Lamb using in this paragraph? (Hint: She is using logic to counter, or argue against, the idea that water-processing plants have solved the problem of water pollution.)

Vocabulary

distribution (dis truh BYOO shun) *n.* division into shares or portions

contamination (kun tam uh NAY shun) *n.* pollution

Additional Support

Differentiated Instruction

Expanding the Concept Encourage students to use various media to explore the subject of fresh water:

- Have students with an interest in math and science find out average water use in several developed and developing countries and present their findings in a bar graph.
- Have students with an interest in music find a song or piece of music that celebrates fresh water. Suggest they explore New Age music, which sometimes combines the actual sound of water with the music.
- Have the artists in the class find or create an image that represents fresh water. **OL**

have to pay our governments for looking after all this stuff for us. So it's not so easy to keep cleaning our water.

E1 Yes, we could be drinking Shakespeare's bathwater, but more to the point, will our great grandchildren be able to drink the water we used to hose down the dog? Will there be any clean water left? 5

Does it make any sense for us to save water at home? Isn't our home usage just a drop in the bucket, compared to what agriculture and industry uses?

Household usage is about 5% to 10% of total fresh water used worldwide. Most of that is used in North America.

E2 On average each of us consumes nearly 53 gallons of water a day at home. Some citizens of water-poor countries survive on as little as 4 gallons a day. We've grown used to seeing water flow out of our taps and down the drains. What if we had an automatic shut-off on our household water that limited us to, say, 13 gallons of water a day?

What To Do

Turn the tap on briefly to wet your toothbrush, and turn it off until it's time to rinse.

In our house, the average toothbrushing time is about a minute and 20 seconds. If we turn on the tap at the beginning of that time and don't turn it off until we're finished, we will have put down the drain approximately 2 gallons of water. In our little household of three people, we could waste over 4000 gallons of water per year just in toothbrushing. 6

Take the test in your household. How long does it take you to brush your teeth? Multiply that by the number of times you brush your teeth each day, then multiply that by the number of people in your household, and you'll soon see that you could have a terrific amount of water rushing uselessly down the drains.

My sister, Elizabeth, spent a great deal of time traveling the earth's oceans on sailboats, where she learned to brush her teeth with ¼ cup of water. The captain brushed without any

Practice the Skills

5 Key Text Element

Persuasive Appeals On this page Lamb makes a strong statement in order to spark strong feelings. She points out that our grandchildren may not have clean water to drink. This statement is an emotional appeal.

6 Key Text Element

Persuasive Appeals Which persuasive appeal does Lamb use in this paragraph? Hint: She gives a lot of facts and figures:

- average toothbrushing time
- amount of water wasted in that time
- amount of water wasted in a year

English Language Coach

Idiomatic Expressions There are many idiomatic expressions involving water. Write these examples on the board and have students explain what they mean:

- drowning in debt
- being in hot water
- swimming against the tide
- treading water
- be like a fish out of water

Invite students to add to the list. EL

READING WORKSHOP 1

Teach

E1 Text Element

Persuasive Appeals Say: Explain how the argument that there may not be any clean water left for our great-grandchildren could also be called an ethical appeal. *(It could be called an ethical appeal because readers know robbing future generations of clean water is wrong.)* OL

E2 Text Element

Persuasive Appeals Say: What kind of argument is the writer using when she compares water usage in water-poor countries to water usage in the United States? Explain. *(Possible response: An appeal to reason. Readers can contrast the numbers to see that we use a lot more water than is truly needed.)* AL

Indiana English/Language Arts Academic Standards

SE: 8.2.2

TWE: *Differentiated Instruction* 8.4, *English Language Coach* 8.1.1

Teach

R1 Reading Skill

Distinguishing Fact from Opinion **Ask:** What reason does the author give to support her recommendation that people take showers instead of baths? *(Showers generally take less water.)* **Ask:** Is this reason a fact or an opinion? *(It is a fact.)* OL

R2 Reading Skill

Distinguishing Fact from Opinion **Say:** State one fact and one opinion the writer uses to support washing your hands in cold water. *(Possible response: fact: a lot of water ends up down the drain while you're waiting for the hot water; opinion: "I find it refreshing to start my day with a cold splash.")* OL

water at all. We don't need to go that far, but we could all use less water than we do.

Keep a bottle of water in the fridge.

We use bottled water—from the tap. Have you ever let the tap run for a minute to get an ice cold drink? About 15 years ago, I filled an empty soft drink bottle with tap water and stuck it in the fridge. That same bottle is still in our fridge today. Of course it has different water in it. 7

Our water bottle has its own spot, in one of those bottle hangers that goes under the fridge shelf (it's been in the same place for years, even when we've moved houses and changed fridges), so that we never have to run the tap for a drink of water. It's always cold and handy. If you're just starting this system, be sure to label the bottle "Drinking Water." Once, years ago, when my Dad was visiting, he took a big swig from the bottle in our fridge, only to discover that someone had put a bottle of white rum in to cool.

Take a five minute shower instead of bathing.

R1 Abandon the bathtub, and hit the showers. Sometimes it just feels great to soak in the tub, but that tub holds between nine and 33 gallons (40 to 150 liters) of water, depending on how full we fill it. We'd have to shower for 15 minutes before we used up the quantity of water it takes to fill the tub. When we were kids, we used to share a bath. We thought it was fun, but little did we know that our smart parents were saving on water heating. My daughter Caroline still enjoys a bath with her little cousin, Lisa.

Learn the cold water hand wash.

R2 If every time you wash your hands, you turn on the hot tap and wait for the water to get warm, you could run anywhere from a few cups to a gallon or more of water down the drain. There are two problems with that.

First, it's water that has gone through the entire system of our waterworks for nothing.

Practice the Skills

7 Key Text Element

Persuasive Appeals Here, Lamb shows that she practices what she preaches. This helps make her appear trustworthy. What kind of persuasive appeal is she using?

Additional Support

Reading in the Real World

College As students progress in their education, the ability to do independent research will become increasingly important. Ask students how they could find out how many miles of pipes their local water system has and how much energy it takes to process a gallon of drinking water. Brainstorm ways to find this information, such as interviewing someone from their local water utility or reading its annual reports, or visiting the Natural Resources Conservation Service Web site. AL

It's been pumped from the lake or river, using energy, it's been bleached, it's been pushed through miles of pipes, and then it just goes back down the drain to be processed all over again with our sewage, having done nothing.

Second, it's water that's already been heated in your home water heater, but has cooled before it gets to you. The energy that was used to heat it, which you pay for, has been wasted. R2

I even wash my face in cold water every morning and night. I'm trying to convince myself that cold water is kinder to my skin than hot, but frankly, I know of no studies that would back me up on this one. However, my partner, Barry, tells me he once read that Paul Newman soaks his face in ice water to stay young looking, so maybe I'm on to something here. Masochistic[3] as it may sound, I find it refreshing to start my day with a cold splash. I confess that so far I've made very few converts to this theory, but I still swear by it. 8

Do you get as clean with cold water as with warm? The answer is yes, although there are exceptions. If your hands are greasy or oily, warm water will help to dissolve the grease or oil more quickly than cold water. But for ordinary, garden-variety dirt or stickiness, cold water works just as well as warm.

What about germs? Ordinarily hand soap will take care of whatever germs are washable. If you wanted to be totally antiseptic, you would have to use boiling water, probably for several minutes. I think most of us would opt for just plain clean, thanks anyway.

Think of saving water this way: what if you had to carry home all the water you needed every day—in jars on your head? 9 R ○

3. Lamb is making a little joke here. If someone is ***masochistic*** (mass uh KISS tik), he or she doesn't mind pain or suffering.

Practice the Skills

8 **Key Reading Skill**

Distinguishing Fact from Opinion Lamb says that washing in cold water is "kinder to . . . skin." Is that statement a fact or an opinion? How can you tell?

9 **BIG Question**

BQ Do you agree that conserving the world's water is a cause worth fighting for? Explain. Write your answer on the "Saving Water" flap of Foldable 7. Your response will help you complete the Unit Challenge later.

Teach

R Reading Skill

Review Making Inferences

Ask: What does the writer probably believe would happen if people had to carry their water on their heads? *(Possible response: They would be more careful about how they used water.)* BL

BQ BIG Question

Say: The writer gives several suggestions about how ordinary people can save water. What ideas can you add to the list? *(Possible answers: taking shorter showers, buying water-saving washers and dishwashers, or not watering the lawn.)* OL

Use the CheckPoint questions provided on Presentation Plus! to check for comprehension of the selection. These questions can be used with interactive response keypads for immediate student feedback.

Differentiated Instruction

Public Service Announcement Have students write a public service announcement promoting water conservation. Ask them to think of public service announcements they have heard on the radio or seen on TV. Discuss what catches their attention. Before they begin writing (individually or in groups), share these tips:

- Focus on one main point.
- Choose words that create pictures.
- Use persuasive appeals to convince your listeners.
- Watch your timing. A 30-second spot should have about 60–70 words; a 60-second spot should have about 125–140 words.

Have students present their announcement to the class. OL

Indiana English/Language Arts Academic Standards

SE: 8.2, 8.2.2

TWE: *Reading in the Real World* 8.4, *Differentiated Instruction* 8.7.2

Assess

Resources for page 940

- Selection Quick Check, p. 61
- Selection and Unit Assessment, p. 73
- ExamView Assessment Suite
- Interactive Tutor: Self-Assessment

Students can respond to the *After You Read* items in their Learner's Notebooks or on a separate sheet of paper.

Answering the BIG Question

1. Possible response: Yes. I learned I can do small things to make the world better.
2. She is for it. Possible sentences: "If we misuse the water we have, we can't send out for some fresh stuff." ". . . we could all use less water than we do."
3. Possible response: Turn off the water while brushing teeth, keep a water bottle in the fridge, and take a five-minute shower.

Critical Thinking

4. We all drink water and clean with it. The U.S. uses a lot more water than water-poor countries.
5. Her placement shows the range of water uses and makes readers think about the way they clean and reuse water.
6. Possible response: She gives unusual statistics; e.g., the water used to brush our teeth is over four billion years old.

After You Read

Saving Water: Why Save Something That Covers Two-thirds of the Earth?

Answering the BIG Question

1. Has reading this article changed the way you think about what is worth fighting for? Explain your answer.
2. **Recall** What is Lamb's position, or stand, on the issue of water conservation: Is she for it or against it? Support your answer by quoting a sentence or two from the selection.
   TIP **Right There**
3. **List** What are some changes that Lamb thinks readers should make in the way they live? List at least three things that Lamb says people should do.
   TIP **Think and Search**

Critical Thinking

4. **Compare and Contrast** How is U.S. water use similar to that of "water-poor" countries? How is it different?
   TIP **Think and Search**
5. **Analyze** On page 935 Lamb says, "We clean paintbrushes in [water]. And we drink it." Why does she put these two uses of water next to each other? What is the effect of organizing the water uses this way?
   TIP **Author and Me**
6. **Analyze** Reread the first paragraph of the selection. What does Lamb say to capture readers' attention and make them want to read on?
   TIP **Author and Me**

Indiana English/Language Arts Academic Standards (pp. 940–941)

8.2 Comprehension and Analysis (Focus on Informational Text) Understand grade-level-appropriate material. Develop [reading] strategies... **8.5.7** Write for different purposes and to a specific audience... **8.2.2** Analyze text that uses proposition (statement of argument) and support patterns. **8.6 English Language Conventions**

For a complete description of the standards, see p. IN 11.

Write About Your Reading

Fact Sheet A **fact sheet** is a short, easy-to-read summary of key facts about a subject. Use information from the selection to write a fact sheet about water use–and waste–in the United States.

- Your readers: eighth-graders who have not read "Saving Water"
- Your purpose: to inform other students about people's use and abuse of water by giving them the most important facts. Do not include opinions.
- Your format: Make a list or lists of bulleted facts. Don't write in paragraphs.
- The length: one page

Write About Your Reading

Sample Response:
Save Water Now!

- Less than 1% of Earth's water is available for our use.
- Water processing costs billions of dollars worldwide.
- Household usage of water is about 5% to 10% of total fresh water used worldwide.
- The average American consumes nearly 53 gallons of water a day at home.
- Running water while you brush your teeth can waste up to 2 gallons of water each time.

Skills Review

Key Reading Skill: Distinguishing Fact from Opinion

7. Does Lamb rely mostly on facts or on opinions in her article? Explain.
8. Quote two facts and two opinions Lamb gives.

Key Text Element: Persuasive Appeals

9. Which kind of persuasive appeal does Lamb use most: reason, emotion, or ethics?

Vocabulary Check

Copy the sentences below on another sheet of paper. Fill in each blank with the right vocabulary word.

municipal • distribution • contamination

10. The Red Cross allotted the same amount of food to each flood victim so that the ______ of food would be fair and equal.
11. The U.S. president is a member of the federal government; the mayor of a city is a member of a ______ government.
12. The beach was closed because of the accidental ______ of lake water.
13. **English Language Coach** Explain why you must know the connotation of a word to understand its full meaning. Support your explanation with an example.
14. **Academic Vocabulary** If you say someone is **ethical,** what are you saying about the person?

Web Activities For eFlashcards, Selection Quick Checks, and other Web activities, go to www.glencoe.com.

Grammar Link: Colons to Introduce Items

A **colon (:)** is a punctuation mark used to introduce a list or series of items at the end of a complete thought. Sometimes the list or series is introduced by signal words such as *the following, these,* or *as follows.*

- Jamil packed these supplies for the trip: a tent, a lantern, sleeping bags, flashlights, clothes, and food.
- Bring the following items: a pen, paper, and your book.

Look out! Do not use a colon right after a verb or a preposition.

Wrong: The kids in my group are: Erin, Jim, and Andre.

Right: The kids in my group are Erin, Jim, and Andre.

Wrong: My family and I traveled to: Germany, France, and Austria.

Right: My family and I traveled to Germany, France, and Austria.

Grammar Practice

Copy the following sentences on a separate sheet of paper. Insert a colon in sentences that need one. (Some sentences don't need a colon.)

15. A variety of people traveled on the railroad the poor, the well-off, students, and more.
16. Recycle these materials glass, paper, and plastic.
17. Some of the important steps in my mother's life were the following enrolling at Alabama State University, joining CORE, and receiving a scholarship to Georgetown University.
18. The following students must report to the principal Diane Larson, Manny Greene, and Scott Freeman.
19. Many African Americans attended all-black colleges Tuskegee, Morehouse, and Spelman.
20. My favorite foods include apples, chicken, and corn.

Writing Application Review your Write About Your Reading activity. If you used colons in your fact sheet, make sure that you correctly used them.

Skills Review

Key Reading Skill: Distinguishing Fact from Opinion

7. Possible response: She uses a lot of facts to make her point about saving water.
8. Facts: Less than 1% of Earth's water is available for our use. Household usage of water is about 5% to 10% of total fresh water used worldwide. Opinions: Bleach isn't a terrific thing. Sometimes it feels great to soak in the tub.

Key Text Element: Persuasive Appeal

9. Lamb relies mostly on appeals to reason, although she also uses emotional and ethical arguments.

Vocabulary Check

10. distribution
11. municipal
12. contamination

English Language Coach

13. You must know the connotation of a word to understand whether a positive or negative attitude is being communicated. For example, calling someone "slender" is a compliment, while calling someone "bony" is not.

Academic Vocabulary

14. You are saying that they follow a set of moral principles.

Grammar Link: Colons

Grammar Practice

15. railroad:
16. materials:
17. following:
18. principal:
19. colleges:
20. no colon needed

Close

Ask students how this article affected their own thinking about water conservation. Were the writer's techniques convincing? Why or why not?

Indiana English/Language Arts Academic Standards

SE: 8.2, 8.2.2, 8.5.7, 8.6

Teach

More About the Author

Marian Wright Edelman was born in 1939 in Bennettsville, South Carolina, and grew up there with her parents and four siblings. As the founder of the Children's Defense Fund, Edelman speaks frequently for children's rights and lobbies Congress on behalf of children.

V Vocabulary

Word Parts Point out that the prefix *il-* on the word *illiterate* is actually the prefix *in-*, "not." Note that *in-* becomes *il-* when it is attached to words that begin with the letter *l*, so something that is *not legal* is *illegal*. **Ask:** What does the word *literate* mean? *(able to read and write)* OL

Before You Read from *The Measure of Our Success*

Meet the Author

In 1963 Marian Wright Edelman became the first female African American lawyer in Mississippi. By 1973 Edelman had relocated to Washington, D.C., and created the Children's Defense Fund, an organization that protects the interests of poor, socially disadvantaged children.

Author Search For more about Marian Wright Edelman, go to www.glencoe.com.

Indiana English/Language Arts Academic Standards
(pp. 942–949)

8.1.3 Verify the meaning of a word in its context... **8.2 Comprehension and Analysis (Focus on Informational Text)** Develop [reading] strategies... **8.2.2** Analyze text that uses proposition (statement of argument) and support patterns.

For a complete description of the standards, see p. IN 11.

Vocabulary Preview

persistence (pur SIS tuns) *n.* the act of refusing to give up **(p. 947)** *The whale watchers' persistence paid off when they saw a blue whale.*

corruption (kuh RUP shun) *n.* extreme immorality or wickedness **(p. 947)** *The government's corruption became well known after a newspaper ran a story about the scandal in city hall.*

racial (RAY shul) *adj.* characteristic of a race of people **(p. 948)** *Many people would argue that racial prejudice is one of the toughest problems the United States faces.*

V **illiterate** (ih LIT uh rit) *adj.* unable to read or write; uneducated **(p. 949)** *Although she was illiterate, Sojourner Truth spoke out powerfully in favor of women's rights and the abolition of slavery.*

Partner Talk Take turns using each vocabulary word in a sentence.

English Language Coach

Word Connotation in Persuasive Writing When an author's purpose is to persuade readers, he or she is careful to choose words with the right connotations, or emotions that come to mind. If the author wants readers to believe something is bad, he or she will choose words with negative connotations. If the author wants readers to believe that something is good, he or she will choose words with positive connotations.

Read the following ads for a car. Both describe the same car, but the words have different connotations. Which ad gives a positive description of the car?

> For sale: Vintage (1990) Arrow. The almost 100,000 miles on this slightly weathered dream mobile prove that it is truly "Old Reliable." A real bargain for the mechanically inclined!

> For sale: Aged (1990) Arrow. The almost 100,000 miles on this rusty lemon prove it is truly "Old Yeller." A real bargain if you don't count all the money it will take you to fix it!

Partner Talk With a classmate, compare and contrast the two ads. Which words have positive connotations? Negative ones?

Additional Support

Author Search To expand students' appreciation of Marian Wright Edelman, have them access the Web site for additional information and resources.

Literature Focus Lesson

Persuasive Speech Explain to students that a keynote speaker is a person invited to set the tone or explore a key idea of a gathering. Point out that the keynote speaker at a college graduation, as well as valedictorians who give speeches at high school graduations, often try to persuade students to believe or behave a certain way as they move forward into the next phase of their lives. Have students speculate on what kinds of appeals to reason, emotion, and ethics such speakers might use. If there is a videotape of a recent graduation in your community, play the valedictorian's speech for the class to see what kinds of persuasive appeals the speaker used. OL

Skills Preview

Key Reading Skill: Distinguishing Fact from Opinion

You will probably find more opinions than facts in the speech you are about to read. That's not necessarily a bad thing. Think about whether the writer establishes herself as an authority on the subject. On what does she base her opinions? Can you trust her opinions?

Write to Learn As you read, use a two-column chart to evaluate the writer's opinions. List opinions in the left-hand column. In the right-hand column, list her support for each opinion.

Key Text Element: Appeal to Ethics

People rarely listen to someone they don't trust. For this reason, authors of persuasive writing try to show that they are good, trustworthy people who know what they are talking about and have readers' best interests at heart. Together, these qualities make up an **appeal to ethics.** The ethical appeal is based on making readers trust the writer and believe that his or her position is the "right thing to do." Ethical appeals may include references to these things:

- community, family, home, parenthood
- religious or spiritual beliefs
- character, responsibility, or public service
- people whom audience members look up to

E

Whole Class Discussion What are some specific ways that an author can show that he or she is a good person? Well-informed? Concerned about readers' interests? As a class, discuss your ideas about ways authors make an appeal to ethics.

Interactive Literary Elements Handbook
To review or learn more about the literary elements, go to www.glencoe.com.

Get Ready to Read

Connect to the Reading

What are some of the most important lessons that your parents, family members, or guardians have taught you: To work hard? To treat others with respect? To value education? Think about what you've learned?

Write to Learn In your Learner's Notebook, write a paragraph about a person whose behavior and morals you admire. What important "life lessons" have you learned from this person?

Build Background

As founder and president of the Children's Defense League, Edelman is often asked to deliver commencement addresses (speeches for school graduations). The selection you are about to read is from a speech she made in 1992 in St. Louis, Missouri, for Washington University's spring graduation ceremony. The speech is based on her book *The Measure of Our Success: A Letter to My Children and Yours.* In the book and the speech, Edelman talks about her parents, her upbringing in a close-knit African American community, and the life lessons she learned. They are lessons she wants her children—and all children—to know.

Set Purposes for Reading

BIG Question Read the selection from *The Measure of Our Success* to find out what is worth fighting for and what is not.

Set Your Own Purpose What else would you like to learn from the speech to help you answer the Big Question? Write your own purpose on the *The Measure of Our Success* flap of Foldable 7. Your response will help you to complete the Unit Challenge later.

Keep Moving

Use these skills as you read the following selection.

Teach

E Text Element

Appeal to Ethics Point out to students that some speakers have moral authority by virtue of their position—as community or religious leaders, for example. Some people who have been immoral can gain moral authority—for example, a reformed gang member who now works to keep other young people out of gangs. **Ask:** Why might a community leader, a religious leader, and a former convict make ethical appeals? *(Community leader: to persuade citizens to act appropriately; religious leader: to persuade people to give money or to attend services; former convict: to convince young people that illegal behavior is wrong.)* OL

Literature Online

Interactive Literary Elements Handbook Have students access the Web site to improve their understanding of appeal to ethics.

Reading in the Real World

Citizenship Have students analyze the ethical appeals in these quotations from famous speakers. What does the speaker want his or her audience to think or do? What ethical appeal does he or she use?

- President John F. Kennedy: "Ask not what your country can do for you; ask what you can do for your country."
- Martin Luther King, Jr.: "Nonviolence is the answer to the crucial political and moral questions of our time."
- Maya Angelou: "I think it's important to remember how much we do, not so that we can stop, but so that we can be encouraged to do more." AL

Indiana English/Language Arts Academic Standards
SE: 8.1.3, 8.2, 8.2.2
TWE: *Literature Focus Lesson* 8.7.1, *Reading in the Real World* 8.2.2

READING WORKSHOP 1

Teach

Viewing the Photo

Ask: In the photograph, what evidence do you find that it was once legal to treat African Americans and white people differently? *(White people sit at the front, while African Americans sit at the back of the bus.)* **BL** **Ask:** What ethical appeal could be made based on this image? *(It is wrong to make laws that give different rights to different races.)* **OL**

C Critical Thinking

Comprehension Ask: What "message" from the external world did the writer not believe? *(She did not believe that she was not important.)* **Ask:** Who taught her to believe in herself? *(Her parents, teachers, and preachers taught her.)* **BL**

Readability Scores
Dale-Chall: 10.3
DRP: 58
Lexile: 1000

from THE MEASURE OF OUR SUCCESS

by Marian Wright Edelman

When I was growing up in my little rural Southern segregated[1] town, service was as essential a part of my upbringing as eating and sleeping. Caring black adults were buffers[2] against the external world that told me I, a black girl, was not important. But I did not believe it because my parents said it wasn't so. My teachers and preachers said it wasn't so. **C** So the childhood message I internalized was that as a child of God, no man or woman could look down on me and I could look down on no man or woman. **1**

1. If something is ***segregated*** (SEG ruh gay tid), it is separated according to race or skin color. Public facilities were segregated in the U.S. South until the Civil Rights Act was passed in 1964.
2. ***Buffers*** are people or objects that "soften the blow," or lessen the impact between colliding forces.

Practice the Skills

1 Key Text Element

Appeal to Ethics Edelman refers to parents, teachers, and preachers and calls herself a "child of God." These references help establish her as a good, trustworthy person. They are part of the ethical appeal.

Additional Support

Differentiated Instruction

Building Background Edelman discusses the segregation she faced as a child. Communities and businesses had totally separate schools, nursing homes, boarding houses, and drinking fountains for "whites" and "coloreds," as well as separate sections in theaters, waiting rooms, and prisons. African Americans often could not use white hotels, restaurants, and public parks, and laws defined areas where African Americans and whites could live. Have students discuss how these laws might have affected the writer differently if she had not come from such a strong community. **OL**

I could not play in segregated public playgrounds or sit at drugstore lunch counters, so Daddy, a Baptist minister, built a playground and canteen behind our church. Whenever he and my mother saw a need, they tried to respond. There were no black homes for the aged in my rural segregated town, so my parents began one across the street, and all of our family had to help out. I sure did not like it a whole lot at the time, but that is how I learned that it was my responsibility to take care of elderly family members and neighbors, and that everyone was my neighbor.

Black church and community members were my watchful extended parents. They applauded me when I did well and they reported on me when I did wrong. Doing well meant being helpful to others, achieving in school and reading. The only time Daddy would not give me a chore was when I was reading, so I read a lot. **R1**

Children were taught by example that nothing was too lowly[3] to do and that the work of our hands and of our heads were both important. **R2** Our families and community made us feel useful and important. And while life was often hard and resources scarce, we always knew who we were and that the measure of our worth was inside our heads and hearts, and not outside in personal possessions or ambitions. **2**

I was taught that the world had a lot of problems, that black folk had an extra lot of problems, but that I could struggle and change them; that intellectual and material gifts brought with them the privilege and responsibility of sharing with others less fortunate; and that service is the rent that each of us pays for living—the very purpose of life—and not something you do in your spare time or after you have achieved your personal goals. . . .

3. If something is ***lowly*** it is common or poor.

Practice the Skills

2 Key Text Element

Appeal to Ethics What references in this paragraph help develop a strong ethical appeal? Name at least two things.

Analyzing the Photo How does this photograph illustrate the writer's attitude toward community service?

READING WORKSHOP 1

Teach

R1 Reading Skill

Distinguishing Fact from Opinion **Ask:** How did Edelman's church and community define "doing well"? *(being helpful to others, achieving in school, and reading)* **BL** **Ask:** Is this definition a fact or their opinion? *(opinion)* **Ask:** How might other people define "doing well"? *(Possible responses: earning a lot of money, being healthy, being famous)* **OL**

R2 Reading Skill

Distinguishing Fact from Opinion **Ask:** Is the statement "the work of our hands and of our heads were both important" a fact or opinion? How do you know? *(It is an opinion. The word* important *tells you this is an opinion.)* **BL**

Reading in the Real World

Citizenship Discuss with students this excerpt from the 1954 Supreme Court ruling in *Brown* v. *Board of Education*, the decision that outlawed segregated schools: Today, education is perhaps the most important function of state and local governments. . . . It is the very foundation of good citizenship. . . . In these days, it is doubtful that any child may reasonably be expected to succeed in life if he is denied the opportunity of an education. Such an opportunity . . . is a right which must be made available to all on equal terms.

- What opinion is the excerpt expressing?
- What does the ruling suggest will happen to children who do not get an education? **AL**

Indiana English/Language Arts Academic Standards
SE: 8.2.2
TWE: *Differentiated Instruction* 8.3.7, *Reading in the Real World* 8.2

Teach

R1 Reading Skill

Review Paraphrasing and Summarizing **Ask:** In your own words, state the first lesson. *(Possible response: Nothing in life comes without a cost. You have to work hard for what you get.)* OL

R2 Reading Skill

Review Analyzing **Ask:** What does the writer mean when she says "Do not assume a door is closed; push on it"? *(Possible responses: Test your limits instead of assuming that something is impossible. Take responsibility for your life instead of making excuses.)* AL **Ask:** Who are some people you know or have heard of who have "pushed on doors"? *(Responses will vary. Encourage students to share examples of what these people have accomplished.)* OL

The standard for success for too many Americans has become personal greed rather than common good. The standard for striving and achievement has become getting by rather than making an extra effort or helping somebody else. . . . 3

. . . I also want to share a few lessons of life taken from a letter that I wrote my own three wonderful sons. Like them, I recognize that you can take or leave them, but you cannot say you were never told or reminded. Let me give you a few of them.

The first lesson is, there is no free lunch. Do not feel entitled to anything you do not sweat or struggle for. Help our nation understand that it is not entitled to world leadership based on the past or on what we say rather than how well we perform and meet changing world needs. . . .

R1 Remember not to be lazy. Do your homework. Pay attention to detail. Take care and pride in your work. Take the initiative[4] in creating your own opportunity and do not wait around for other people to discover you or do you a favor. Do not assume a door is closed; push on it. Do not assume if it was closed yesterday R2 that it is closed today. And do not ever stop learning and improving your mind, because if you do, you and America are going to be left behind.

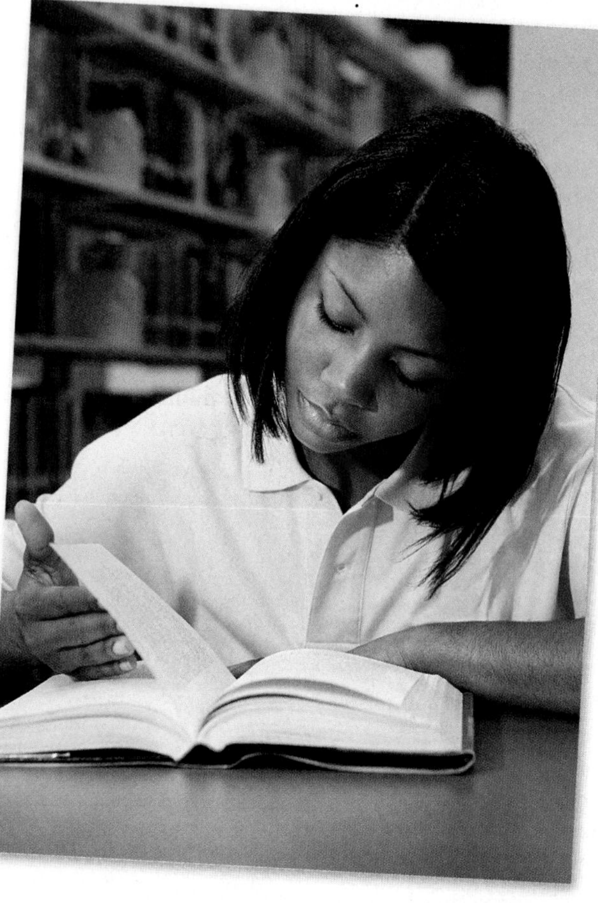

Analyzing the Photo How does this young woman illustrate Edelman's "first lesson"?

Practice the Skills

3 Key Reading Skill

Distinguishing Fact from Opinion In this paragraph Edelman states opinions. You may agree or disagree with her, but you can't *prove* that the "standard of success for too many Americans has become personal greed."

4. ***Initiative*** (ih NISH uh tiv) is the action of taking responsibility for something.

Additional Support

Differentiated Instruction

Using Your Skills Students with strong interpersonal and intrapersonal skills will likely be especially moved by this speech. If necessary, explain these terms to students: *interpersonal* refers to what happens between people, and *intrapersonal* refers to what happens within a person. Ask students to identify the writer's interpersonal advice—urging understanding, leadership, communication, and conflict resolution—and intrapersonal advice—urging self-awareness, self-improvement, and goal setting. OL

Lesson two is, assign yourself. Daddy used to ask us whether the teacher gave us any homework and if we said no, he said, well, assign yourself some. Do not wait around for somebody else to direct you to do what you are able to figure out and do for yourself. Do not do just as little as you can do to get by. R1

Do not be a political bystander or grumbler. Vote. Democracy is not a spectator sport. Run for political office. I especially want women to run for political office. We women certainly cannot do a worse job than the men in power now. **4** But when you do run and when you do win, don't begin to think that you or your reelection are the only point. If you see a need, do not ask why doesn't somebody do something, ask why don't I do something. Hard work and **persistence** and initiative are still the non-magic carpets to success for most of us.

Lesson three: Never work just for money. Money will not **save your soul** or **build a decent family** or help you sleep at night. We are the richest nation on earth with the highest incarceration[5] and one of the **highest drug addiction and child poverty rates** in the world. R2

Do not confuse wealth or fame with **character.** Do not tolerate or condone[6] **moral corruption** or **violence,** whether it is found in high or low places, whatever its color or class. It is not okay to push or to use drugs even if every person in America is doing it. It is not okay to **cheat** or to **lie** even if every public- and private-sector[7] official you know does. **Be honest** and demand that those who represent you be honest. . . . **5**

Lesson four: Do not be afraid of taking risks or being criticized. If you do not want to be criticized, do not do anything, do not say anything, and do not be anything. Do not be afraid of failing. It is the way you learn to do things right. It doesn't matter how many times you fall down. All

5. ***Incarceration*** (in car ser AY shun) is the state of being imprisoned.
6. To ***condone*** (kuhn DOHN) is to forgive, pardon, or overlook.
7. A ***sector*** (SEK ter)is a particular part of society.

Vocabulary

persistence (pur SIS tuns) *n.* the act of refusing to give up

corruption (kuh RUP shun) *n.* extreme immorality or wickedness

Practice the Skills

4 Key Reading Skill

Distinguishing Fact from Opinion Is this statement a fact or an opinion? (Hint: Can you prove that "women certainly cannot do a worse job than the men in power now"?)

5 English Language Coach

Word Connotation in Persuasive Writing Notice all the words with strong emotional associations. Which of them have positive connotations? Which have negative ones?

READING WORKSHOP 1

Teach

R1 Reading Skill

Review Making Inferences **Ask:** What character traits can you infer the writer values from the advice she gives in lesson two? Explain. *(Possible responses: She values hard work and initiative. She tells her audience to give themselves assignments and not to do "just as little as you can do to get by.")* **AL**

R2 Reading Skill

Distinguishing Fact from Opinion **Say:** Look at the third sentence of lesson three. Is this a fact or an opinion? *(It is a statement of fact.)* **BL** **Ask:** Why do you think the writer includes this statement? *(It supports her opinion that money does not create a good, moral life.)* **OL**

Reading Fluency

Build Fluency Because this selection was written and delivered as a speech, it is especially suited to building fluency. Assign one or two paragraphs to each student. Pair up students who have consecutive paragraphs and have them practice their portions of the speech. Encourage students to use the tone, rate, and volume of their voice to convey meaning. Then have the class read the speech aloud, each student staying alert to his or her cue, standing up quietly, reading that section, and sitting down quietly. **OL**

Indiana English/Language Arts Academic Standards
SE: 8.1.3, 8.2
TWE: *Differentiated Instruction* 8.2, *Reading Fluency* 8.7.14

Teach

EL Language Coach

Denotation and Connotation
Ask: What is the denotation of the word *snicker*? *(laugh)* **Ask:** What is its connotation? *(It is negative, meaning " to laugh in a mean way.")* OL

E Text Element

Appeal to Ethics **Ask:** Which words in lesson six indicate an ethical appeal? *(Possible responses: "fellowship," "more important," "democratic," "decent," and "fair.")* OL

R Reading Skill

Review Making Inferences
Ask: What do you think the "sound of the genuine in yourself" might be? *(Possible response: It might be your intuition or your knowledge of right and wrong.)* AL

that matters is how many times you get up. Do not wait for everybody to come along to get something done. It is always a few people who get things done and keep things going. . . .

Lesson five: Take parenting and family life seriously, and insist that those you work for and who represent you do so. . . .

I hope that you will stress family rituals and be moral examples for your children, because if you cut corners, they will, too. If you lie, they will, too. . . . If you tell **racial** or gender jokes or snicker at them, another generation will pass on the poison that our adult generation still does not have the courage to stop doing. EL

Lesson six is to please remember and help America remember that the fellowship of human beings is more important than the fellowship of race and class and gender in a democratic society. Be decent and fair and insist that others do so in your presence. . . . E

Lesson seven: Listen for "the sound of the genuine" within yourself. Einstein said, "Small is the number of them that see with their own eyes and feel with their own heart." Try to be one of them.

Howard Thurman, the great black theologian,[8] said, "There is in every one of us something that waits and listens for the sound of the genuine in ourselves, and it is the only true guide you'll ever have. And if you cannot hear it, you will all of your life spend your days on the ends of strings that somebody else pulls." 6

. . . I hope that you will learn to be quiet enough to hear the sound of the genuine within yourself so that you can then hear it in other people. R

Lesson eight: Never think life is not worth living or that you cannot make a difference. Never give up. I do not care how hard it gets; and it will get very hard sometimes. An old proverb[9] reminds us that when you get to your wit's end, remember that is where God lives. . . .

8. A ***theologian*** (thee uh LOH jun) is an expert in religious studies.
9. A ***proverb*** is a short, traditional saying that expresses some obvious truth.

Vocabulary

racial (RAY shul) *adj.* characteristic of a race of people

Practice the Skills

6 Key Text Element

Appeal to Ethics Notice Edelman's reference to Howard Thurman. Why does she mention Thurman? How does quoting Thurman strengthen Edelman's ethical appeal?

Additional Support

Differentiated Instruction

Collecting Quotations Edelman shares quotations from several people who have inspired her. Show students how to use a dictionary of quotations, whether in print or online. Ask students to find 3 to 5 quotations that provide an important "lesson of life." Have students choose one quotation to illustrate. Put the posters and pictures they create on display. OL

Analyzing the Photo What do Sojourner Truth's facial expression and posture in this photograph tell you about her? What might the writer have in common with Truth?

My role model was an **illiterate** slave woman, Sojourner Truth, who could not read or write, but she could not stand second-class treatment of women and she hated slavery. My favorite Sojourner story came one day when she was making a speech against slavery and she got heckled by a man who stood up in the audience and said, "Old slave woman, I don't care any more about your antislavery talk than for an old fleabite." And she snapped back and said, "That's all right. The Lord willing, I'm going to keep you scratching."

So often we think we have got to make a big difference and be a big dog. Let us just try to be little fleas biting. Enough fleas biting . . . can make very big dogs very uncomfortable. . . . 7 ❍

Vocabulary

illiterate (ih LIT uh rit) *adj.* unable to read or write; uneducated

Practice the Skills

7 **BIG Question**

For what cause did Sojourner Truth fight? How is Edelman's fight similar to Sojourner Truth's? Write your answers on the *Measure of Our Success* flap of the Foldable for Unit 7. Your responses will help you answer the Unit Challenge later.

READING WORKSHOP 1

Teach

C Critical Thinking

Synthesis Say: Name one piece of advice the writer gives that is an example of trying "to be little fleas biting." Explain your response. *(Possible response: The writer's advice not to laugh at or participate in offensive jokes is an example of being "a little flea biting." This is an action all people can take to make a difference in their lives and to influence others.)* AL

BQ BIG Question

Have students answer this question in their Learner's Notebooks: **Ask:** Which of Edelman's eight lessons do you think would help you personally to fight for what you believe in? Explain how it would help. *(Responses will vary.)* OL

Assess

CheckPoint

Use the CheckPoint questions provided on Presentation Plus! to check for comprehension of the selection. These questions can be used with interactive response keypads for immediate student feedback.

English Language Coach

Idiomatic Expressions Have students use slang or idiomatic dictionaries or the Internet to familiarize themselves with these idiomatic expressions from the selection:

- getting by
- take it or leave it
- a spectator sport
- a non-magic carpet
- second-class treatment

EL BL

Indiana English/Language Arts Academic Standards
SE: 8.2.2
TWE: *Differentiated Instruction* 8.3, *English Language Coach* 8.1.1

READING WORKSHOP 1

Assess

Resources for page 950

- Selection Quick Check, p. 62
- Selection and Unit Assessment, p. 74
- ExamView Assessment Suite
- Interactive Tutor: Self-Assessment

Students can respond to the *After You Read* items in their Learner's Notebooks or on a separate sheet of paper.

Answering the BIG Question

1. Possible responses: honest government, respect for the importance of family life, decency, fairness.
2. Responses will vary.
3. Possible response: 1. "There is no free lunch." 2. "Assign yourself." 3. "Never work just for money." 4. Take risks. 5. Be a good parent. 6. Our common humanity is more important than race, class, or gender. 7. Be genuine. 8. "Never give up."

Critical Thinking

4. Possible response: We have an obligation to help other people.
5. Possible response: to share lessons that will help graduates live productive lives
6. Responses will vary.

After You Read

from *The Measure of Our Success*

Answering the BIG Question

1. Now that you have read the speech, what are your ideas about causes that are worth fighting for?
2. **Quote** Copy an opinion with which Edelman wants you to agree.
   TIP **Right There**
3. **Recall** Identify the eight lessons Edelman wants to teach readers.
   TIP **Think and Search**

Critical Thinking

4. **Interpret** What does Edelman mean when she says that "service is the rent each of us pays for living"? Put the statement in your own words.
   TIP **Author and Me**
5. **Analyze** Think about the occasion for the speech–a university graduation ceremony. What do you think the purpose of Edelman's speech is?
   TIP **Author and Me**
6. **Evaluate** Do you think Edelman's lessons are still important and relevant today? Explain.
   TIP **On My Own**

Talk About Your Reading

Speech Write a short speech stating and describing two lessons that you think are important for living a good, moral life. Be sure to answer these questions in your speech:

- Why are these lessons important?
- How can people act on these lessons in their everyday lives?
- What sources support your opinions? Books? Articles? Real People?

Deliver your speech to a small group of classmates.

Indiana English/Language Arts Academic Standards (pp. 950–951)

8.2 Comprehension and Analysis (Focus on Informational Text) Understand grade-level-appropriate material. Develop [reading] strategies... **8.7.11** Deliver oral responses to literature... **8.2.2** Analyze text that uses proposition (statement of argument) and support patterns. **8.6 English Language Conventions**

For a complete description of the standards, see p. IN 11.

Talk About Your Reading

Possible response:

Work hard and be considerate of others. These are two lessons I think are important for living a moral life. We can act on them both at home and at school. We can help out at home, for example, and we can pay attention in class. We can also try to get along with our brothers, sisters, and classmates, and we can be kind to the younger kids here at school. This is not new advice. Our parents and teachers have been telling us for years that these things are important. Though we may disagree with parents and teachers sometimes, we have to admit that they're often right!

Skills Review

Key Reading Skill: Distinguishing Fact from Opinion

7. Does Edelman include more facts or more opinions in her speech? Why do you think that she makes this choice?

Key Text Element: Appeal to Ethics

8. What information and sources does Edelman mention to show readers that she is a good example of how to lead a moral life?

Vocabulary Check

Copy the following sentences on a separate sheet of paper. Write *T* if a sentence is true or *F* if it is false. Revise any false statement to make it true.

9. A person who gives up easily shows **persistence**.
10. **Corruption** is the opposite of goodness.
11. Someone who has **racial** pride is proud of his or her race, ethnicity, or cultural heritage.
12. A student who reads and writes well is **illiterate**.
13. **Academic Vocabulary** What are some of the **ethical** activities that Edelman's parents encouraged their children to do?
14. **English Language Coach** How does Edelman use words with positive connotations to support her opinions? Give at least two examples.

Web Activities For eFlashcards, Selection Quick Checks, and other Web activities, go to www.glencoe.com.

Grammar Link: Colons to Separate Items

The **colon** (:) is used in expressions of time. Separate the hour and the minutes with a colon when you use numerals to write the time of day.

- The movie starts at 11:15 a.m. and ends at 1:45 p.m.
- We have to be at the bus station at 3:45 p.m. today.
- At 12:00 noon, we will leave for the field trip.

Never use a colon when the time of day is written out.

- I didn't get home until one o'clock.

Also use a colon after the salutation of a business letter. (Use a comma after the salutation of a personal letter.)

- Dear Sir:
- Dear Sir or Madam:
- Dear Ms. Korsakov:
- Dear Grandma,

Grammar Practice

The following sentences make up two business letters. Copy the sentences on another sheet of paper. Add colons where needed.

15. Dear Ms. Kozar
16. I will not be able to bring snacks to the French Club meeting today at 400.
17. Mr. Fenton is tutoring me from 330 until 430.
18. Yours truly, Isabella
19. Dear Isabella
20. From 400 until 430 at today's meeting, a guest speaker will be talking about her travels to France.
21. Try to get there by 445.
22. We will serve snacks after the question-and-answer session.
23. Sincerely, Ms. Kozar

Skills Review

Key Reading Skill: Distinguishing Fact from Opinion

7. Opinions. Possible response: She believes her opinions are based on common sense and widely accepted values.

Key Text Element: Appeal to Ethics

8. She gives information about what her parents and community leaders taught her.

Vocabulary Check

9. F; possible correction: A person who refuses to give up shows persistence.
10. T
11. T
12. F; possible correction: An illiterate person cannot read or write.

Academic Vocabulary

13. Possible response: to help others and to share

English Language Coach

14. Responses will vary.

Close

Ask students to discuss how reading this speech affected their thinking about the Big Question.

Grammar Link: Colons

Grammar Practice

15. Kozar:
16. 4:00
17. 3:30, 4:30
18. no colon needed
19. Isabella:
20. 4:00, 4:30
21. 4:45
22. no colon needed
23. no colon needed

Indiana English/Language Arts Academic Standards
SE: 8.2, 8.2.2, 8.6, 8.7.11

Persuasive Essay

Teaching Students to Write a Persuasive Essay

Why Is It Important?

- The power to persuade is important in many kinds of writing. Practicing their ability to convince readers will help students become more lucid writers overall.
- Students will use facts to create supporting arguments for their essays. This will help them to master the distinction between fact and opinion and become more critical readers.
- In writing a persuasive essay, students will practice their ability to create a strong thesis and choose appropriate details to support it.
- Choosing a topic that is personally relevant will help students connect academic writing to their own lives and interests.
- Revising a first draft will help to clarify its focus and make the essay more persuasive.

How to Help Students Get It

- Remind students that strong feelings can lead to strong arguments; choosing a topic they're interested in will strengthen their papers, but using emotionally loaded terminology will not.
- Ask students to play devil's advocate: "Imagine that you felt exactly opposite to how you DO feel. What might you say then?"
- Some students may be most comfortable writing their two or three body paragraphs first and using that to determine the best way to phrase their thesis and conclusion.
- Refer students to the Writing Handbook at the end of the textbook. The Persuasive Writing Checklist will help them prepare the final draft for presentation.
- Peer editing may help many writers tighten up their theses and supporting arguments; classmates can point out unclear or sparse passages in first drafts.
- Before they begin writing, ask students to remember times they've been persuaded to, or not to, do something, believe something, or buy something. Ask "What made you change your mind? What persuasive techniques worked? What kind of persuasion did you see right through, or ignore?"
- Encourage writers to utilize the basic essay format discussed in Writing Workshop Part 1. The ready-made structure will allow advanced writers to lengthen and expand their writing while giving below-level writers the support they need to build skills.
- Ask students to think about selections from Unit 7 and how the authors did or did not succeed at persuading readers to agree with their positions.

Writing Trait	Student Checklist
Ideas	the message or the theme and the details that develop it
Organization	the arrangement of main points and supporting details
Voice	a writer's unique way of using tone and style
Word Choice	the vocabulary a writer uses to convey meaning
Unit Focus **Sentence Fluency:** the smooth rhythm and flow of sentences that vary in length and style	• Do sentences vary in length and structure? • Do transition words and phrases show connections between ideas and sentences? • Does parallelism help balance and unify related ideas?
Conventions	correct spelling, grammar, usage, and mechanics
Presentation	the way words and design elements look on a page

Workshop Resources

Pacing (Days) Standard	Block	Lesson	Student Materials	Teacher Resources
1	1/2	Writing Workshop Part 1: Prewriting and Drafting	Writing Workshop Graphic Organizer, p. 14 Grammar Practice, p. 15 Spelling and Handwriting Practice, p. 45 Grammar and Composition Handbook, p. 273 Real Success in Writing: Research and Reports	TeacherWorks Plus™ Presentation Plus! Rubrics for Assessing Student Writing, Listening, and Speaking, p. 16 Grammar and Writing Workshop Transparencies 9–10
2	1	Writing Workshop Part 2: Editing, Revising, and Presenting	Interactive Grammar and Language Workbook Grammar and Composition Handbook, p. 273 Real Success in Writing: Research and Reports Listening and Speaking, p. 28 Viewing and Representing, p. 29	Grammar and Writing Workshop Transparencies 29–30 Interactive Grammar and Language Workbook Rubrics for Assessing Student Writing, Listening, and Speaking, p. 16

Focus

BELLRINGER Options

Daily Language Practice Transparency 65

Focus Activity Say: Look back in your Learner's Notebook to the ideas you jotted down about what's worth fighting for. Choose one or two you think you might like to write about. OL

Teach

L Literary Element

Essay Say: Many people use the word *article* to name a short piece of nonfiction that is primarily factual and the word *essay* to name a piece that includes the author's opinion. Does that mean an essay will include few facts? *(Not necessarily. Writers use facts to support their opinions.)* OL

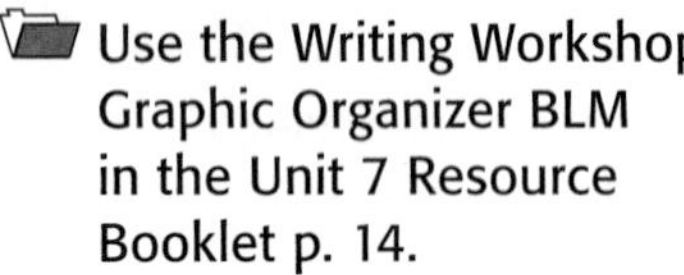

Resources for page 952

Use the Writing Workshop Graphic Organizer BLM in the Unit 7 Resource Booklet p. 14.

Use the Grammar and Writing Workshop Transparencies 9-10.

WRITING WORKSHOP PART 1

Persuasive Essay

Prewriting and Drafting

ASSIGNMENT Write a persuasive essay

Purpose: To make a case for something you think is worth fighting for

Audience: Your teacher, your classmates, and other people in your community

Writing Rubric

As you work through this writing assignment, you should

- write about something you feel strongly about
- write a clear position statement
- support your main idea with details and examples
- write a well-organized persuasive essay

See pages 996–997 in Part 2 for a model of a persuasive essay.

Indiana English/ Language Arts Academic Standards (pp. 952–955)

8.5.4 Write persuasive compositions that present…reasoning to support effective arguments and emotional appeals. **8.4 Processes and Features** Prewriting and drafting. **8.6 English Language Conventions**

For a complete description of the standards, see p. IN 11.

You probably already know what an essay is. It's a paper that tells a true story, explains a subject, or gives opinions. A persuasive essay also gives opinions, but the writer's goal is a little different. In a persuasive essay, the writer tries to convince readers to agree with his or her opinions. For example, if you believe that you and your classmates have too much homework, you might write a persuasive essay trying to convince teachers to agree with you. You might also go one step further and include a call to action, a statement asking readers to act on your opinions. You might, for example, ask teachers to give shorter daily assignments–ones that take no more than an hour to do.

For this workshop you may write either kind of persuasive essay. Writing a persuasive essay will help you think about the Unit 7 Big Question: What's worth fighting for? What's not?

Prewriting

Get Ready to Write

Your first step is to come up with a good topic. For this assignment you need to think of an issue that has two sides. Pick something that matters to you. The stronger your opinions, the easier it will be to write about them.

Gather Ideas

To come up with a good topic, ask yourself these questions:

- *What do I strongly believe in? Why do I think it is worth standing up for?*
- *What are some issues, ideas, or people that matter to me?*
- *What stories in the news have made me want to take a stand?*
- *What changes would I like to see made in my neighborhood or community?*

If you have trouble coming up with a topic, try looking through recent newspapers and magazines in the library or on the Internet. They often include articles about controversial issues–problems that have at least two sides to them. Or try freewriting for ten minutes about one of the issues that you think interests you. Remember that when you freewrite you jot down your thoughts quickly and freely. If you have trouble writing about the issue for ten minutes, you may want to change topics.

Additional Support

Literature Focus Lesson

Types of Essays Essays are sometimes classified by their writers' purposes. Review some of those purposes with students:

- A *descriptive essay* describes a person, a place, or a thing.
- A *narrative essay* tells a true story.
- An *expository essay* explains something. It might, for example, explain a process, explore causes and/or effects, compare and contrast things, or provide an extended definition.
- A *critical essay* analyzes someone else's work.
- A *persuasive essay* tries to persuade readers to think a certain way or to do something. OL

Generate Supporting Reasons

Once you have a topic in mind, write a position statement to be your main idea, or thesis. For your statement, write your opinion simply and clearly. For example, if you believe in protecting the environment, your position statement might be "I believe we must take steps to protect the environment." Then come up with a list of reasons why. A good way to do this is to discuss your ideas with classmates. W

Group Discussion Follow these steps with a small group of classmates.

1. Read your position statement aloud to the group. Ask group members whether your opinion is clear. If it isn't, rewrite your position statement together until it is clear.
2. Give at least two reasons why you believe your opinion is right. Discuss each reason with your classmates. Ask them to help you develop your reasons with facts, examples, or other types of details. Also ask group members to add reasons of their own. Classmates who agree with your opinion may have good reasons you have overlooked.
3. Take notes on your discussion. Be sure to include all the reasons you and your group generated.

It's important that we protect the environment because . . .
1. pollution threatens everyone's health
2. it's wrong to be wasteful
3. our children deserve a clean environment

Literature Online

Writing Models For models and other writing activities, go to www.glencoe.com.

Writing Tip

Supporting Reasons Remember that your purpose is to persuade your readers to agree with you. So keep your readers in mind when you list reasons why they should agree with your opinion. Your reasons must convince your readers, not just you.

Drafting

Start Writing!

Once you have a list of reasons, you're ready to start writing your essay. Don't worry if you don't have the whole essay worked out in your mind. Ideas will come to you as you write.

Writing Tip

Organization Think about the order in which you present your reasons. Don't just give them in the order you thought of them. Have a strategy. For example, you might give the least important reason first and the most important reason last. That way, your essay ends on a strong note.

Differentiated Instruction

Idea Webs Model how to create an idea web, or have the class brainstorm ideas while you record them on the board. For example, if the thesis is "Equal rights are worth fighting for," students might come up with these reasons and supporting examples: OL

Equal rights are worth fighting for.
Reason: People really are equal, so they should have equal rights.
Example: equal rights to education and jobs
Reason: This country was founded on the principle of equal rights.
Example: the Declaration of Independence

Teach

W Writing

Thesis Make sure students understand the difference between a topic and a thesis. The topic is the *what* of the essay—in this case, protecting the environment. The thesis is the *what about it*—in this case, that it's up to us to take steps to protect the environment.

Say: Suppose the topic is living on a budget. What are some possible positions you could take on this topic? *(Possible responses: Living on a budget makes good sense. Living on a budget doesn't mean you can never have fun. Learning to live on a budget should begin at a young age.)* OL

Literature Online

Writing Models Have students access the Web site for an additional and interactive Writing Workshop-based student model.

Indiana English/Language Arts Academic Standards
SE: 8.4, 8.5.4
TWE: *Literature Focus Lesson* 8.2, *Differentiated Instruction* 8.4.1

Teach

W1 Writing

The Writing Process **Say:** If you already have an idea for an attention-grabbing introduction, great! If you don't, don't worry about it. Instead, start with Step 2 and work on your reasons. Many writers find that writing the introduction is easier after they write the body of the essay. **OL**

W2 Writing

Thesis Statement **Say:** Review the three-part model. **Ask:** In this model, where does the main idea go? *(The thesis goes in the first paragraph, often at the end)* **Ask:** What happens in the middle section? *(The writer explains the thesis and gives reasons and examples to support it.)* **Ask:** What is the purpose of the last section? *(The conclusion summarizes what has been said and reminds readers why it matters; it may include suggestions for what people can do about a problem.)* Invite students to share their ideas about their thesis and the evidence they might use. **OL**

WRITING WORKSHOP PART 1

Develop Your Draft

To make your essay easier to write, break it down into parts. There should be three main parts to your essay: a beginning, a middle, and an end.

1. The beginning of your essay is the introduction—a paragraph that introduces your readers to your issue and your main idea, or thesis. Your introduction should also try to capture readers' attention and make readers care about your issue.

Writing Tip

Introduction Usually an introductory paragraph begins with an attention-getting statement and ends with a main idea, or thesis, statement. In this case, the thesis is the position statement.

W1

Imagine a world without trees, flowers, or animals. It could happen. Every day we pollute the air we breathe, the water we drink, and the ground we grow our food in. Slowly but surely we are ruining this planet. I believe we must take steps to protect the environment, and you should too.

2. The middle of your essay is the body. It is two or more paragraphs that explain the reasons why your readers should agree with you. Limit yourself to one reason in each paragraph. For each new reason, start a new paragraph.

W2

We need to start taking better care of the earth because it is a healthier way to live. The environment makes life possible. If we ruin the environment, we are ruining our own bodies. Anything harmful that we put into the earth eventually harms us. When we pollute the ground where we grow our food, the pollution gets into the food. When we eat the food, the pollution gets into our bodies.

Writing Tip

Conclusion Do not give new reasons in your conclusion. Your conclusion should sum up your position and the reasons you have already given.

3. The end of your essay is the conclusion. It is a paragraph in which you wrap up what you have said—and, if you wish, give a call to action.

It's not too late. We can still save our environment. I ask you to stop polluting, stop wasting resources, and save the planet for our children. You and future generations will be glad you did.

Additional Support

Literature Focus Lesson

The Writing Process Have a number and variety of magazines on hand. Divide students into small groups and have each group scan several magazines, looking just at the introductory paragraph of the articles or essays. Direct group members to talk about introductions they find especially effective and choose their favorite. Now have a spokesperson from each group read their choice aloud, and have the class orally identify what the author has done to capture readers' attention and make readers care about the topic. **OL**

Grammar Link

Apostrophes

What Is an Apostrophe?

An **apostrophe (')** is a punctuation mark used in possessive nouns, possessive indefinite pronouns, and contractions.

Why Are Apostrophes Important?

Apostrophes show when a noun is possessive.

- Bill's coat is on the bed.

(The apostrophe and *s* tell you that the noun *Bill* possesses, or owns, a coat.)

Apostrophes also tell when—and where—letters are missing from contractions, or shortened forms of words and numbers.

- it is = it's
- I will = I'll
- you are = you're
- is not = isn't
- 1998 = '98

How Do I Use Apostrophes?

To form the possessive of a singular noun, add an apostrophe and *-s ('s).*

- The girl's hat got lost on the bus.
- The dog's toy was stuck under the couch.

To form the possessive of a plural noun that does not end in *s,* use an apostrophe and *-s ('s).*

- The men's soccer game was canceled for the night.
- The mice's nest was under the haystack.

To form the possessive of a plural noun that ends in *s,* use an apostrophe after the final *s.*

- The boys' essays are displayed on the bulletin board.
- Both tables' legs were slightly bent.

W

To form the possessive of an indefinite pronoun, such as *everyone, everybody, anyone, no one,* or *nobody,* use an apostrophe and *-s ('s).*

- The park was everybody's to use on Saturday.

Look Out! Never use an apostrophe in the possessive personal pronouns *ours, yours, his, hers, its,* and *theirs.*

- The park was just ours on Monday.

Write to Learn Read over your draft. Check to make sure you have correctly used apostrophes. Circle any possessive nouns or possessive indefinite pronouns. Underline any contractions.

Looking Ahead

Part 2 of this Writing Workshop is coming up later. Keep the writing you did here. In Part 2 you'll learn how to turn it into an essay to be proud of.

WRITING WORKSHOP PART 1

Teach

W Writing

Using Apostrophes in Writing Write these phrases on the board and have students explain the apostrophe in each:

- the women's proposal *(possessive of plural noun not ending in* s*)*
- Mr. Montoya's class *(possessive singular noun)*
- doesn't matter a bit *(contraction)*
- four boys' answers *(possessive of plural noun ending in* s*)*
- back in the '90s *(omitted numbers)*
- the Smiths' house *(possessive of plural noun ending in* s*)*
- nobody's fault *(possessive indefinite pronoun)* OL

Assess

Encourage students to use questions as they look over the drafts of their essays: *Do I have an interesting introduction? Have I clearly stated my thesis? Have I provided reasons why readers should agree with me? Have I explained each reason or given examples or facts to support it? Have I effectively wrapped up my essay in the conclusion?* OL

Reading in the Real World

Career Provide several copies of telephone directories and have students work in small groups, browsing the yellow pages to find examples of business names or phrases from ads that include an apostrophe. Write a sampling of students' findings on the board and analyze them. Students may notice examples that include errors. Use these as the basis for discussion. Point out that sometimes an apostrophe can convey extra information. If a business is called Harris and Son's Auto Repair, for example, one son has joined the family business. If the name is Harris and Sons' Auto Repair, more than one son works there. OL

Indiana English/Language Arts Academic Standards

SE: 8.4, 8.5.4, 8.6

TWE: *Literature Focus Lesson* 8.3, *Reading in the Real World* 8.6

READING WORKSHOP 2

Questioning

UNIT 7

Teaching Students How to Question

Why Is It Important?

- Questioning strategies help students monitor their comprehension.
- Questioning strategies are fundamental to engaging in inquiry.
- Questioning strategies are central to peer-led discussion.
- Questioning strategies are essential for students to demonstrate what they have learned in a variety of assessment settings.

How to Help Students Get It

- Make sure that students understand the relationship between questions asked and the source(s) of information for answering the question.
- Tell students that information can be found in their own background knowledge and experiences as well as in the texts they read.
- Emphasize to students that different types of questions are asked before, during, and after reading.
- Teach students strategies that will align well with particular types of questions (e.g., skimming and scanning in response to questions that ask for important text details, making inferences in response to questions that ask them to fill in gaps or read between the lines.) Model these strategies for students.

Reading to Answer the Big Question

All Together Now by Barbara Jordan
Former congresswoman Barbara Jordan believed that better race relations were worth fighting for. In this article, she suggests that there will be peace and equality when individuals accept diversity in their homes, schools, and other areas of life.

from *Through My Eyes* by Ruby Bridges
This book excerpt chronicles Ruby Bridges's first days of school in 1960 as she bravely fights angry opposition to become the first African American student to attend the all-white William Frantz Public School in New Orleans, Louisiana. Surrounded by federal marshals in the midst of a screaming mob, the six-year-old child becomes a symbol of inspiration for integration.

Workshop Resources

Pacing (days) Standard	Block	Lesson	Student Materials	Teacher Resources
1	1/2	Key Skill Lesson: Questioning	Key Reading Skills Practice, p. 16 English Language Coach Review, p. 42	Bellringer Options Transparencies –Daily Language Practice 66 Read Aloud, Think Aloud Transparencies –Key Reading Skills 19 Presentation Plus!
1	1	"All Together Now"	Glencoe Online Unit Vocabulary Review, p. 40 Academic Vocabulary Review, p. 43 English Language Coach Active Reading Graphic Organizer, p. 17 StudentWorks Plus™ Online Student Edition Literature Classics Selection and Unit Assessments, p. 75	Literary and Text Analysis Transparencies 36 Puzzlemaker Skill Level Up!™ A Language Arts Game BookLink 3 Assessment by Learning Objective (Diagnostic and Formative) Interactive Tutor: Self-Assessment TeacherWorks Plus™
1		from *Through My Eyes*	Glencoe Online Unit Vocabulary Review, p. 40 Academic Vocabulary Review, p. 43 English Language Coach Active Reading Graphic Organizer, p. 20 Literary Analysis, p. 19 StudentWorks Plus™ Online Student Edition Literature Classics Selection and Unit Assessments, p. 76	Literary and Text Analysis Transparencies 39 Puzzlemaker Skill Level Up!™ A Language Arts Game BookLink 3 Assessment by Learning Objective (Diagnostic and Formative) Interactive Tutor: Self-Assessment TeacherWorks Plus™

Keys for Unit Resource

- Blackline Master
- Workbook
- Supplemental Text
- CD-ROM
- DVD
- Transparency
- Web-based
- Fast File

Level Appropriate Code

AS = Activities for all students
AL = Activities for students working above grade level
OL = Activities for students working at grade level
BL = Activities for students working below grade level
EL = Activities for English language learners

Focus

BELLRINGER Options

Daily Language Practice Transparency 66

Focus Activity Say: Sometimes the big issues of the day seem far away from our lives. A big trade agreement between nations, for example, isn't something we need to deal with on a daily basis. Can you think of some big issues that do touch our lives? *(Possible responses: civil rights, tolerance, violence in the streets, pollution)* OL

Teach

R Reading Skill

Questioning Say: We actually use this skill quite a bit, sometimes without even being aware of it. Right now, for example, what might you ask yourself to better understand what I'm saying? *(Possible responses: What does this have to do with the lesson? Is this important?)* OL

READING WORKSHOP 2

Skills Focus

You will practice using these skills when you read the following selections:

- "All Together Now," p. 960
- from *Through My Eyes*, p. 968

Reading

- Asking questions while reading

Literature

- Identifying persuasive appeals
- Understanding point of view

Vocabulary

- Understanding extended definitions
- Understanding denotation
- Academic Vocabulary: *valid*

Writing/Grammar

- Using semicolons correctly

Skill Lesson

Questioning

Learn It!

What Is It? Questioning is having a running conversation with yourself as you read. Just as you might ask yourself questions while watching a movie *(Why did he do that? What's the significance of that door they keep showing?)*, you should ask questions while R you read. By asking questions, you become involved in the selection and make sure that you understand it. Feel free to question anything! For example, you might ask yourself questions like these:

- *What just happened?*
- *Is this argument **valid**?*

Analyzing Cartoons
Here's a question to ask yourself to test your understanding of the cartoon: *What do the girls' questions show about their knowledge of jobs?*

Indiana English/Language Arts Academic Standards (pp. 956–957)

8.2 Comprehension and Analysis (Focus on Informational Text) Develop [reading] strategies such as asking questions...

For a complete description of the standards, see p. IN 11.

Academic Vocabulary

valid (VAL id) *adj.* based on correct information; logical; sound

Additional Support

Reading in the Real World

Career Journalists must be very good at questioning. Have students brainstorm other qualities young people interested in a career in journalism should have. Ideas could include the following:

- an interest in people and current events
- an ability to write clearly and accurately
- an ability to do research and to conduct interviews
- a willingness to work under pressure and to meet deadlines
- an ability to put aside one's own opinions in favor of the facts
- a desire to share information with people OL

Why Is It Important? Asking questions while you read is an important part of understanding a text. To make sure you understand, ask yourself "5Ws and an H" questions: *Who? What? Where? When? Why?* and *How?* R

How Do I Do It? Here are some sample questions you can ask yourself:

- *How does this event relate to other events in the text?*
- *What is this person doing and why?*
- *Why has the writer included this word, description, or piece of information?*

Below is a selection from *The Measure of Our Success.* Read how a student asked questions about the text.

Black church and community members were my watchful extended parents. They applauded me when I did well and they reported on me when I did wrong. Doing well meant being helpful to others, achieving in school and reading. The only time Daddy would not give me a chore was when I was reading, so I read a lot.

Children were taught by example that nothing was too lowly to do and that the work of our hands and of our heads were both important. Our families and our community made us feel useful and important. And while life was often hard and resources scarce, we always knew who we were and that the measure of our worth was inside our heads and hearts, and not outside in personal possessions or ambitions.

Why does the writer say that the church and community members were "extended parents"? They must have played a very important role in her childhood. Why does she mention that she read a lot? Reading may have something to do with the person she is today.

LiteratureOnline

Study Central Visit www.glencoe.com and click on Study Central to review questioning.

Practice It!

Reread the selection from *The Measure of Our Success* above. Then write down two additional questions that you could ask about the selection.

Use It!

As you read "All Together Now," ask yourself 5Ws and an H questions. Answer each question before going on.

READING WORKSHOP 2

Teach

Study Central Have students access the Web site to review questioning and to complete a related activity.

R Reading Skill

Questioning Ask: How can asking questions help us understand what we read? *(Possible responses: We become involved with the reading. It helps us focus on key ideas and details.)* OL

Resources for page 957

- Use Key Reading Skills Transparency 19 in *Read Aloud, Think Aloud* to help student practice questioning.

Differentiated Instruction

Appreciating Differences Write on the board, "It is important to appreciate differences in people because _______." Have students complete the sentence and then encourage them to work in groups to begin a rap song, a painting or collage, or a poem that celebrates differences in people and explains why it is important to do so. After students have read the selections in this workshop, have them return to the assignment and add references to the ideas shared by Barbara Jordan and Ruby Bridges. Ask volunteers to share their completed song, painting, collage, or poem with the class. EL OL

Indiana English/Language Arts Academic Standards
SE: 8.2
TWE: *Differentiated Instruction* 8.5.7

Teach

More About the Author

About the expression "We the people" that opens the Constitution of the United States, Barbara Jordan once said, "It is a very eloquent beginning. But when that document was completed . . . I was not included in that 'We, the people.'. . . .But through the process of amendment, interpretation and court decision, I have finally been included."

V Vocabulary

Word Parts Point out to students that two of the vocabulary words have the same prefix (*in-*, "not") and suffix (*-able*, "able"). Have students analyze the words using this information. *(not able to be dispensed, or done away, with; not able to be cured)* Also point out that the word used as an English Language Coach example, *tolerance*, has an antonym that uses the prefix *in-*, *intolerance*, and other forms that use the suffix *-able: tolerable* and *intolerable.* OL

Before You Read | All Together Now

Barbara Jordan

Meet the Author

Barbara Jordan was the first African American woman elected to the Texas Senate. When she was elected to the U.S. House of Representatives, she became the first African American woman to represent a former Confederate state in Congress. Jordan was also the first African American woman to give the keynote speech at a political convention.

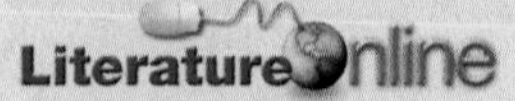
LiteratureOnline

Author Search For more about Barbara Jordan, go to www.glencoe.com.

Indiana English/Language Arts Academic Standards (pp. 958–963)

8.1.3 Verify the meaning of a word in its context… **8.2 Comprehension and Analysis (Focus on Informational Text)** Develop [reading] strategies such as asking questions… **8.2.2** Analyze text that uses proposition (statement of argument) and support patterns.

For a complete description of the standards, see p. IN 11.

Vocabulary Preview

V

harmonious (har MOH nee us) *adj.* getting along well together; friendly **(p. 960)** *We are all striving toward a more harmonious community.*

indispensable (in duh SPEN suh bul) *adj.* absolutely necessary **(p. 962)** *Tolerance and kindness are indispensable values.*

incurable (in KYOOR uh bul) *adj.* not likely to be changed or corrected **(p. 963)** *Racism is far from incurable; there are plenty of ways to stop it.*

optimist (OP tuh mist) *n.* a person who has a positive or cheerful outlook **(p. 963)** *If you are an optimist, those around you will think positively too.*

Write to Learn In your Learner's Notebook, write a short paragraph in which you correctly use each vocabulary word at least once.

English Language Coach

Extended Definition If you look up the word *tolerance* in the dictionary, you will find a definition similar to this one: "the willingness to let others hold opinions or follow practices that are different from one's own." This is the denotation of the word. In "All Together Now," Jordan gives her own definition of what tolerance means. Because she refers to civil rights and race relations to provide a longer, more specific definition of *tolerance,* you might say that she gives the word an **extended definition.**

Small Group Discussion With a small group of classmates, write an extended definition of *tolerance.* To begin, each group member should explain what he or she thinks *tolerance* means. The explanation could be a definition or an example. As each group member gives a definition or example, record it on a word web like the one pictured. Then use the word web to write a one- or two-paragraph extended definition of *tolerance.*

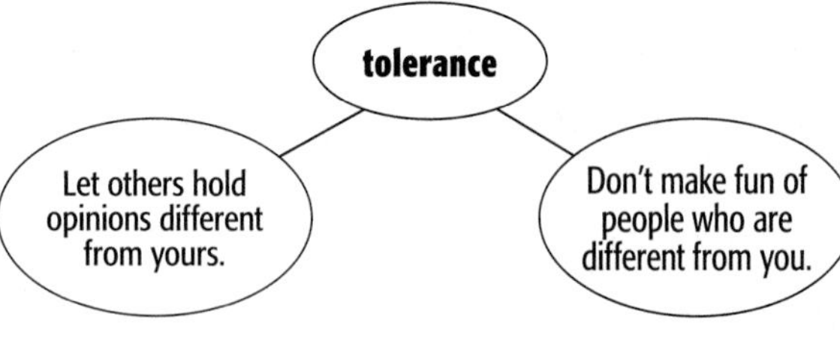
tolerance
Let others hold opinions different from yours.
Don't make fun of people who are different from you.

Additional Support

LiteratureOnline

Author Search To expand students' appreciation of Barbara Jordan, have them access the Web site for additional information and resources.

Reading Fluency

Build Fluency with Extended Definitions Extended definitions often end up in collections of quotations, like this one from Ralph Waldo Emerson: "Courage charms us, because it indicates that a man loves an idea better than all things in the world, that he is thinking neither of his bed, nor his dinner, nor his money, but will venture all to put in act the invisible thought of his mind." Have students find a meaningful quotation that defines a concept, such as beauty, friendship, or ambition. They should practice reading their choice aloud and deliver it to the class. AL

Skills Preview

Key Reading Skill: Questioning

"All Together Now" is a speech Jordan made in the 1990s. As you read the speech, ask yourself 5 Ws and an H questions to make sure you understand.

Partner Talk Jordan's speech is about the need for tolerance in the United States. What kinds of questions do you think you might ask yourself as you read the speech? Brainstorm a list with a classmate.

Key Text Element: Appeal to Emotions

Facts and figures can be very persuasive. If a writer wants to convince readers to agree with an opinion, presenting objective evidence is a good way to do so. But if the writer wants to move readers to take action, he or she may "put a human face" on facts and figures and appeal to readers' emotions.

Sometimes a writer relies only on an emotional appeal. That method is appropriate when the writer knows that readers agree with him or her but need to be persuaded to take action. Suppose, for example, that you belong to a school music club that sells candy to raise money. To move club members to sell as much as possible, you might try to inspire them with an emotional appeal. Usually, however, a writer uses all three appeals, giving facts (appeal to reason), showing why he or she is trustworthy (appeal to ethics), and trying to make readers care about the issue (appeal to emotions).

E

Whole Class Discussion Imagine that you want to persuade people to be more tolerant of others. As a class, think of emotional appeals you might make to move people into taking the right actions.

Interactive Literary Elements Handbook To review or learn more about the literary elements, go to www.glencoe.com.

Get Ready to Read

Connect to the Reading

How tolerant are you of other people's opinions? When you disagree with someone, are you able to "agree to disagree," or do you continue to try to convince the other person to adopt your position?

R

Partner Talk With a partner, find a topic about which you disagree, such as the best subject to study in school or which performer in a musical group is best. Take turns presenting your opinions on the topic. Monitor your feelings and behavior. Can you listen to your partner's opinion calmly, or do you find yourself wanting to jump in and argue your position? Explain.

Build Background

The 1960s were a busy time for the civil rights movement in the United States.

- In June of 1963, President John Kennedy proposed civil rights legislation, but Congress failed to act.
- In August of 1963, Dr. Martin Luther King, Jr., led a march on Washington, D.C., where he delivered his famous "I Have a Dream" speech.
- In July of 1964, at the urging of President Lyndon B. Johnson, Congress adopted the Civil Rights Act, which ended legalized segregation in the United States.

Set Purposes for Reading

BIG Question Read "All Together Now" to find out whether creating a society that is tolerant in action as well as in law is a cause worth fighting for.

Set Your Own Purpose What else would you like to learn from the article to help you answer the Big Question? Write your own purpose on the "All Together Now" flap of Foldable 7.

Keep Moving

Use these skills as you read the following selection.

Teach

E Text Element

Appeal to Emotions Say: After you brainstorm emotional appeals that could persuade people to be more tolerant, think of an appeal to reason and an ethical appeal that could support your argument. *(Possible response: Appeal to reason: Being tolerant of others allows us to expand our knowledge because we can learn about many different experiences. Ethical appeal: It is wrong to be intolerant of others.)* OL

R Reading Skill

Questioning Say: As you engage in Partner Talk, ask questions such as "Where did you get your information? When did you first think that? How do you know?" OL

Interactive Literary Elements Handbook Have students access the Web site to improve their understanding of persuasive appeals.

Literature Focus Lesson

Appeal to Emotions Advertisers frequently appeal to emotions when they try to persuade people to buy their product, patronize their business, or support their cause. Sometimes the appeal is just to associate a general feeling of happiness with the subject (scenes of happy people enjoying a soft drink, for example), but sometimes the appeal is to a specific emotion such as fear, pity, or vanity. Have students working in small groups collect examples of print ads that make emotional appeals and use them to create a collage. Choose some of the most intriguing images for class discussion. OL

Indiana English/Language Arts Academic Standards
SE: 8.1.3, 8.2, 8.2.2
TWE: *Reading Fluency* 8.7.2, *Literature Focus Lesson* 8.2.2

Teach

Viewing the Photo

Ask: What is happening in the photograph? *(President Johnson celebrates the signing of the Voting Rights Act of 1965.)* **BL** **Say:** This act was designed to do away with state barriers to minority voter registration, allowing all adult Americans the right to vote. Why might this photograph be an appropriate illustration for Jordan's article? *(Possible response: The title suggests that it will be about working together; the photograph shows two leaders, the president and a civil rights leader, who probably worked together to accomplish a goal.)* **AL**

R Reading Skill

Questioning **Ask:** What might you ask yourself as you look at the title of this article? *(Possible responses: How does the title fit the author's purpose? What does Jordan mean by "all together"?)* **OL**

Readability Scores
Dale-Chall: 5.9
DRP: 58
Lexile: 890

All Together Now R

by Barbara Jordan

On August 6, 1965, President Lyndon B. Johnson celebrated signing the Voting Rights Act into law with a group including (from left) Ralph Abernathy; Dr. Martin Luther King, Jr.; and Clarence Mitchell.

When I look at race relations today I can see that some positive changes have come about. But much remains to be done, and the answer does not lie in more legislation. We *have* the legislation we need; we have the laws. Frankly, I don't believe that the task of bringing us all together can be accomplished by government. What we need now is soul force—the efforts of people working on a small scale to build a truly tolerant, **harmonious** society. And parents can do a great deal to create that tolerant society. **1**

We all know that race relations in America have had a very rocky history. Think about the 1960s when Dr. Martin Luther King, Jr., was in his heyday and there were marches and protests against segregation and discrimination. The movement culminated[1] in 1963 with the March on Washington.

1. ***Culminated*** (KUL muh nay tid) means reached the highest point or climax.

Vocabulary

harmonious (har MOH nee us) *adj.* getting along well together; friendly

Practice the Skills

1 Key Reading Skill

Questioning A good question to ask yourself here is, *What is Jordan's main idea?*

Additional Support

Reading in the Real World

Citizenship Share with students these details about the key events Barbara Jordan mentions in her article:

- During the March on Washington, on August 28, 1963, more than 200,000 people gathered in a call for jobs and freedom.
- The Civil Rights Act of 1964 opened public places to African Americans.
- In effect, the Voting Rights Act of 1965 barred literacy tests and poll taxes and established a way to challenge unfair voting practices.

Have students imagine they are journalists in the 1960s and write a short news article telling about one of these incidents. **AL**

Following the enactment of the 1965 Voting Rights Act, African Americans in Alabama wait in line to vote.

Following that event, race relations reached an all-time peak. President Lyndon B. Johnson pushed through the Civil Rights Act of 1964, which remains the fundamental piece of civil rights legislation in this century. The Voting Rights Act of 1965 ensured that everyone in our country could vote. At last, black people and white people seemed ready to live together in peace.

But that is not what happened. By the 1990's the good feelings had diminished. Today the nation seems to be suffering from compassion[2] fatigue, and issues such as race relations and civil rights have never regained momentum.[3] **R**

Those issues, however, remain crucial. As our society becomes more diverse, people of all races and backgrounds will have to learn to live together. If we don't think this is important, all we have to do is look at the situation in Bosnia[4] today. **2** **E**

2. ***Compassion*** (kum PASH un) is sorrow for the sufferings or trouble of another.
3. ***Momentum*** is a strength or force that keeps growing.
4. In the early 1990s civil war erupted in ***Bosnia*** (BOZ nee uh) between the Serbs and the Croats. After a few months of fighting, the Serbs controlled most of the area. They attacked Sarajevo with the intent of killing all non-Serbs, a process known as *ethnic cleansing*.

Practice the Skills

2 Key Reading Skill

Questioning What situation is Jordan referring to? (See the note at the bottom of the page.)

READING WORKSHOP 2

Teach

R Reading Skill

Questioning **Say:** What question might you ask yourself about the second paragraph on this page? *(Possible response: Why does Jordan believe the good feelings of the 1960s have diminished?)* **OL**

E Text Element

Appeal to Emotions **Ask:** How might mentioning the war in Bosnia appeal to readers' emotions? *(Mentioning the war might appeal to people's fear and compassion.)* **Ask:** What idea is Jordan supporting by mentioning the war? *(the idea that people of all races and backgrounds must learn to live together)* **Ask:** What is she implying can happen if people don't learn to live together? *(They will end up fighting one another, as they did in Bosnia.)* **OL**

Literature Focus Lesson

Persuasive Writing Tell students that persuasive writers must grab their audience's attention from the start and use vivid language, examples, and descriptions to support their point of view. Have students evaluate Jordan's article:

- Does her opening grab your attention? If not, what might she have added to do so?
- Does she clearly state the purpose of her article? If so, what is it?
- What vivid language does she use to keep your attention?
- Does she use good examples and descriptions to support her point of view?
- What is her "call to action," or statement of what she wants her readers to do? **OL**

Indiana English/Language Arts Academic Standards

SE: 8.2

TWE: *Reading in the Real World* 8.5.7, *Literature Focus Lesson* 8.2.6

Teach

R Reading Skill

Questioning **Say:** You can use questions to review ideas. What might you ask yourself about Jordan's comment that she's "never seen a racist baby"? *(Possible response: How does Jordan believe children become prejudiced?)* **Ask:** How might you answer your question? *(Possible answer: She believes young children learn prejudice from adults.)* OL

E Text Element

Appeal to Emotions **Ask:** How does the "starting small" example appeal to our emotions? *(Possible responses: "Starting small" sounds doable instead of really hard; the mental image of small children playing happily makes us feel warm and good.)* OL

READING WORKSHOP 2

How do we create a harmonious society out of so many kinds of people? The key is **tolerance**—the one value that is **indispensable** in creating community.

If we are concerned about community, if it is important to us that people not feel excluded, then we have to do something. Each of us can decide to have one friend of a different race or background in our mix of friends. If we do this, we'll be working together to push things forward.

One thing is clear to me: We, as human beings, must be willing to accept people who are different from ourselves. I must be willing to accept people who don't look as I do and don't talk as I do. It is crucial that I am open to their feelings, their inner reality. 3

What can parents do? We can put our faith in young people as a positive force. I have yet to find a racist baby. Babies come into the world as blank as slates and, with their beautiful innocence, see others not as different but as enjoyable companions. Children learn ideas and attitudes from the adults who nurture them. I absolutely believe that children do not adopt prejudices unless they absorb them from their parents or teachers. R

The best way to get this country faithful to the American dream of tolerance and equality is to start small. Parents can actively encourage their children to be in the company of people who are of other racial and ethnic backgrounds. If a child thinks, "Well, that person's color is not the same as mine, but she must be okay because she likes to play with E

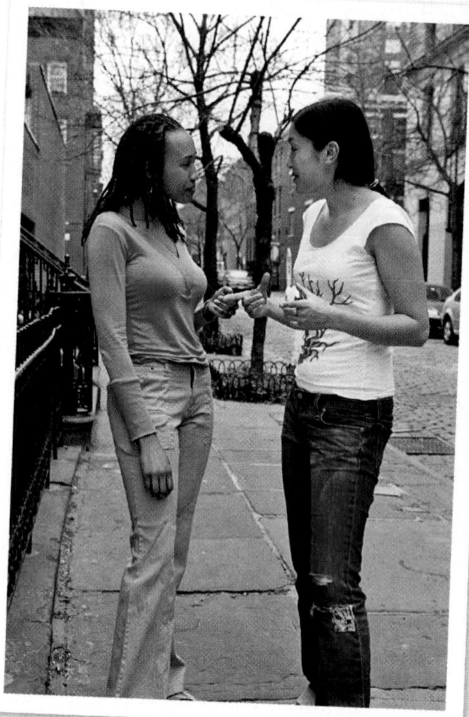

Analyzing the Photo How does this photograph illustrate Jordan's belief in the importance of cross-cultural friendships?

Practice the Skills

3 English Language Coach

Extended Definition In this paragraph and the one before, Jordan explains what she means by the word **tolerance.** Two parts of her extended definition are as follows:

- "[making] people not feel excluded"
- "decid[ing] to have one friend of a different race or back-ground"

How else does she define the word? Quote another part of her definition.

Vocabulary

indispensable (in duh SPEN suh bul) *adj.* absolutely necessary

Additional Support

Reading in the Real World

Career Many workplaces pay consultants to lead their employees in workshops on diversity training. These consultants teach employees about appropriate workplace behavior, including not telling inappropriate jokes and respecting and celebrating people's differences. Have students discuss skills that would be required of diversity training consultants:

- communication skills
- knowledge about diversity issues
- listening skills
- mediation skills AL

the same things I like to play with," that child will grow up with a broader view of humanity.

I am an **incurable** **optimist.** For the rest of the time that I have left on this planet I want to bring people together. You might think of this as a labor of love. Now, I know that love means different things to different people. But what *I* mean is this: I care about you because you are a fellow human being and I find it okay in my mind, in my heart, to simply say to you, I love you. And maybe that would encourage you to love me in return. **4**

It is possible for all of us to work on this—at home, in our schools, at our jobs. It is possible to work on human relationships in every area of our lives. **5** ❍

Practice the Skills

4 **Key Text Element**

Appeal to Emotions Notice that Jordan uses the word *love* four times. What feeling is she trying to spark in her audience? How will that help her fulfill her purpose?

5 **BIG Question**

Do you agree that a tolerant society is worth fighting for? Explain. Write your answer on the "All Together Now" flap of Foldable 7. Your response will help you answer the Unit Challenge later.

Vocabulary

incurable (in KYOOR uh bul) *adj.* not likely to be changed or corrected

optimist (OP tuh mist) *n.* a person who has a positive or cheerful outlook

READING WORKSHOP 2

Teach

EL Language Coach

Extended Definition **Ask:** How does Jordan define love? *(She defines it as caring about people simply because they are fellow human beings.)* EL BL **Ask:** How does this definition show her tolerance? *(Possible response: She loves everyone because they're people, not because they are like or unlike her.)* OL

BQ BIG Question

Ask: What is one thing you could do at home or in school to work on being more tolerant of others? Write your answer in your Learner's Notebook. *(Responses will vary.)* OL

CheckPoint

Use the CheckPoint questions provided on Presentation Plus! to check for comprehension of the selection. These questions can be used with interactive response keypads for immediate student feedback.

Differentiated Instruction

Enrichment Have students in small groups work on brief projects that will enrich their appreciation of this selection.

- Have musical students find and play for the class a number of songs associated with the civil rights movement or contemporary songs that celebrate tolerance.
- Have students interested in drama create a skit based on the playground scene Jordan describes.
- Have artistic students find and show the class pictures of fine art—painting, photography, or sculpture—that express tolerance. OL

Indiana English/Language Arts Academic Standards
SE: 8.1.3, 8.2.2
TWE: *Differentiated Instruction* 8.3

READING WORKSHOP 2

Assess

Resources for page 964

- Selection Quick Check, p. 63
- Selection and Unit Assessment, p. 75
- ExamView Assessment Suite
- Interactive Tutor: Self-Assessment

Students can respond to the *After You Read* items in their Learner's Notebooks or on a separate sheet of paper.

Answering the

1. Possible response: It is worth fighting for kindness, compassion, and tolerance as much as it's worth fighting for civil rights.
2. Parents. Laws can't bring us together, but parents can.
3. The Civil Rights Act of 1964 because it the "fundamental piece of civil rights legislation" of the twentieth century.

Critical Thinking

4. Possible response: People are tired of feeling sorry for other people's troubles.
5. Children are a positive force. She says babies are innocent and naturally tolerant.
6. Possible response: Yes. They are things every person can do by making changes in attitude and behavior.

After You Read

All Together Now

Answering the BIG Question

1. After reading Jordan's speech, what are your thoughts about what is worth fighting for and what is not?
2. **Recall** Which does Jordan think is a more important force for bringing about good race relations: the government or parents? Explain.
   TIP **Right There**
3. **Recall** According to Jordan, what is the most important civil rights law of the 20th century and why?
   TIP **Right There**

Critical Thinking

4. **Interpret** What does Jordan mean when she says that the U.S. has "compassion fatigue"? Explain in your own words.
   TIP **Author and Me**
5. **Infer** Why does Jordan think that people should put their faith in children? Support your answer with examples from the selection.
   TIP **Author and Me**
6. **Evaluate** Do you think Jordan's ideas about increasing tolerance are good ones? Explain why or why not.
   TIP **Author and Me**

Talk About Your Reading

Small Group Discussion Jordan says that parents can encourage their children to have friends from other ethnic or cultural backgrounds. What do you think students and schools should do to promote a tolerant society? With a small group of classmates, come up with at least three specific ways that the students in your school can support tolerance toward others. Remember that having special awareness days and visual displays are good tools for celebrating different cultures. But also think about what students can do to bring about long-term change that lasts and makes a real difference.

Indiana English/Language Arts Academic Standards (pp. 964–965)

8.2 Comprehension and Analysis (Focus on Informational Text) Understand grade-level-appropriate material...Develop [reading] strategies such as asking questions...**8.7 Listening and Speaking** Speaking skills are developed...**8.1.3** Verify the meaning of a word in its context...**8.2.2** Analyze text that uses proposition (statement of argument) and support patterns. **8.6 English Language Conventions**

For a complete description of the standards, see p. IN 11.

Talk About Your Reading

Encourage students to record their group's suggestions in their Learner's Notebooks. These ideas might be useful when students begin work on the Unit Challenge. Remind students that their ideas can include some special projects, such as awareness days, panel presentations, or displays. However, they should also include some everyday activities, such as avoiding offensive jokes.

Skills Review

Key Reading Skill: Questioning

7. Did you find it helpful to ask questions as you read? Explain your answer.

Key Text Element: Appeal to Emotions

8. Which persuasive appeal does Jordan use most often?

9. Was this type of persuasive appeal appropriate for the selection? Should Jordan have included other types of persuasive appeals? Explain.

Vocabulary Check

Match each vocabulary word on the left with its definition on the right.

10. harmonious	**a.** a person who has a positive or cheerful outlook
11. indispensable	**b.** not likely to be changed or corrected
12. incurable	**c.** getting along well together; friendly
13. optimist	**d.** absolutely necessary

14. Academic Vocabulary Are **valid** arguments logical or illogical? Explain.

English Language Coach

15. How does Jordan's extended definition of *tolerance* differ from the word's dictionary definition?

16. Write an extended (one- or two-paragraph) definition of one of these abstract words: *love, success, beauty.* Be sure to include specific examples in your definition of the word.

Web Activities For eFlashcards, Selection Quick Checks, and other Web activities, go to www.glencoe.com.

Grammar Link: Semicolons

You do not always have to use a coordinating conjuction to form a compound sentence. You can use a **semicolon** (;) to join two independent clauses or simple sentences to form a compound sentence.

Compound with conjunction: I like to play video games, and my brother likes to play music.

Compound with semicolon: I like to play video games; my brother likes to play music.

A semicolon alone works well in the example compound sentence above because the sentences are short and almost the same. When you join long or contrasting sentences, use a comma and a conjunction rather than a semicolon. A conjunction helps readers see the logical relationship between ideas.

Confusing: He takes my CDs without asking; I don't really mind. (You expect the speaker to mind, so you are surprised when he says that he doesn't.)

Better: He takes my CDs without asking, but I don't really mind. (The conjunction *but* warns you that the next idea will contrast with the first.)

Look out! Remember not to join two sentences with just a comma. You must use a semicolon or a comma and coordinating conjunction.

Grammar Practice

Copy the sentences below on another sheet of paper. Add semicolons or commas and conjunctions where they are needed.

17. We want to see a movie we can't find one we like.

18. I want to see a comedy I like to have a good laugh.

19. Renting videos is fun you can relax more at home.

20. Ogemageshig's father is Native American his mother is half white and half Latino.

Writing Application Using semicolons, combine two short, closely related sentences from the extended definition that you wrote for item 16.

Skills Review

Key Reading Skill: Questioning

7. Responses will vary.

Key Text Element: Appeal to Emotions

8. appeal to emotion

9. Responses will vary.

Vocabulary Check

10. c **11.** d **12.** b **13.** a

Academic Vocabulary

14. They are logical because being logical is part of what *valid* means.

English Language Coach

15. Possible response: She broadens it to include getting along, spending time with people who are different, and loving everyone.

16. Responses will vary.

Web Activities Have students access the Web site for interactive activities that will help them assess their understanding of the selection.

Grammar Link: Semicolons

Grammar Practice

Possible responses:

17. movie, but **19.** fun;

18. comedy; **20.** American;

Close

Ask students whether Jordan's article has made them more likely to stop a friend from telling an offensive joke. Why or why not?

Indiana English/Language Arts Academic Standards

SE: 8.1.3, 8.2, 8.2.2, 8.6, 8.7

Teach

More About the Author

Ruby Bridges said that her parents were divided at first about involving her in this historic event. Her mother believed she would get a better education in a new school and improve her chances of getting a good job as an adult. Her father disagreed. "Eventually my mother convinced my father that despite the risks, they had to take this step forward, not just for their own children, but for all black children."

EL Language Coach

Denotation and Word Choice Point out that the words *escort* and *drive* in the first example in the English Language Coach have a similar denotation, as do *accompany* and *stay with*. Ask students for examples of other words with similar denotations but different levels of difficulty. *(Possible responses:* exquisite *and* very pretty; frolicked *and* played*)* AL

Before You Read from *Through My Eyes*

Ruby Bridges

Meet the Author

In 1960 six-year-old Ruby Bridges became the first African American student to enroll in a white elementary school in New Orleans after segregation was outlawed there. Her attendance sparked large protests. Bridges says, however, that this experience taught her that "schools can be a place to bring people together—kids of all races and backgrounds."

Author Search For more about Ruby Bridges, go to www.glencoe.com.

Indiana English/Language Arts Academic Standards
(pp. 966–973)

8.1 Word Recognition, Fluency, and Vocabulary Development
8.2 Comprehension and Analysis (Focus on Informational Text) Develop [reading] strategies...
8.3 Comprehension and Analysis of Literary Text Respond to...literature... identifying story elements...
For a complete description of the standards, see p. IN 11.

Vocabulary Preview

taunts (tawnts) *n.* hurtful or mocking remarks **(p. 968)** *The taunts of the opposing team did not distract him as he took his free throw.*

barricades (BAIR uh kaydz) *n.* barriers put up to separate or to provide defense **(p. 969)** *The peaceful protesters did not try to tear down the barricades that surrounded the political meeting.*

integrated (IN tuh gray tid) *v.* ended the separation of racial and ethnic groups, form of the verb *integrate* **(p. 971)** *The Supreme Court decision* Brown v. Board of Education *integrated schools across the country.*

Think-Pair-Share In your Learner's Notebook, write a sentence for each of the vocabulary words. Use context clues in each sentence to help show what the word means. Trade sentences with a classmate. Check each other's work to see if it is right.

English Language Coach

Denotation and Word Choice Word choice can provide important information about a narrator or speaker. For example, a narrator who is a child might choose words with simple denotations, or definitions.

In the selection from *Through My Eyes,* the narrator describes an experience she had when she was six years old. Even though the author was an adult when she wrote this autobiography, she uses simple words with simple definitions to show that she saw things through a child's eyes.

Read the two sentences below. Think about which one sounds more like a description that a child might give.

EL
- "The U.S. federal marshals arrived to escort us to school and accompany us throughout the day."
- "They had come to drive us to school and stay with us all day."

The second sentence sounds like something a six-year-old would say. The narrator's word choice helps you understand what she is like.

Partner Talk With a partner, take turns reading aloud the first two paragraphs of the selection from *Through My Eyes.* After you have read the paragraphs, make a list with your partner of the words that help show that the narrator is looking back at an experience from her childhood.

Additional Support

Author Search To expand students' appreciation of Ruby Bridges, have them access the Web site for additional information and resources.

Literature Focus Lesson

Memoir Tell students that a memoir is a true account of a person's life told by that person. It is a form of autobiography. People often write memoirs about experiences many years after they occurred. Have students discuss how memoirs might be different from other forms of writing:

- They tell a story from one person's point of view.
- They tell what the person remembers, not necessarily everything that actually happened.

Tell students to think of one event from their childhood they might recount in a memoir. How might their recollection of the event be different from that of their parents or guardians or other adults present? OL AL

Skills Preview

Reading Skill: Questioning

Have you ever been listening to a speech or a talk and wished that you could stop the speaker to ask questions? When you read, you can ask all the questions you want.

- Basic questions such as *Who? What? When? Where? Why? How?* will help you follow what is happening.
- Asking yourself why an author includes certain information and whether a detail is important will make your reading more meaningful.

Write to Learn As you read, use a two-column chart to ask questions about the selection. In the left-hand column, write any questions that you have. Write the answer to each question in the right-hand column.

Literary Element: Point of View in Nonfiction

Point of view in nonfiction is the perspective from which a real-life story is told. In the **first-person point of view,** an author calls himself or herself "I" or "me" and describes real events that he or she took part in or observed. In the **third-person point of view,** the author does not refer to himself or herself. He or she is a nameless voice that tells what happened. To identify point of view in nonfiction, ask yourself this question:

- *Does the author refer to himself or herself as "I" or "me" (first person), or is the author a nameless voice (third person)?*

Whole Class Discussion *Through My Eyes* includes different points of view of the same story. It begins with a newspaper story about what happened. Then Ruby Bridges tells what happened from her point of view. Finally, Ruby's teacher tells what happened from her point of view. What differences might you expect to find between the newspaper version of the story and Ruby Bridges's? Between Ruby Bridges's and her teacher's?

Get Ready to Read

Connect to the Reading

Think about your first day of school. What were your feelings as you entered the building and found yourself surrounded by strangers? Was the classroom friendly?

Write to Learn In your Learner's Notebook, write about your first day of school or your first day in a new school. Include descriptions about how you felt.

Build Background

As you read the selection, you may wonder how Ruby Bridges was chosen to be the first African American student at a newly integrated school.

- African American kindergarteners in New Orleans were tested in the spring of 1960 to determine which students would go to integrated schools in the fall. From this testing, six children were chosen to go to integrated schools.
- Two of the children decided not to go, and three of the children were sent to another school. Ruby Bridges alone enrolled in William Frantz Public School.

Set Purposes for Reading

BIG Question Read the selection from *Through My Eyes* to discover other people's ideas about what is worth fighting for and what is not.

Set Your Own Purpose What else would you like to learn from the article to help you answer the Big Question? Write your own purpose on the *Through My Eyes* flap of Foldable 7.

Interactive Literary Elements Handbook
To review or learn more about the literary elements, go to www.glencoe.com.

Keep Moving

Use these skills as you read the following selection.

READING WORKSHOP 2

Teach

L Literary Element

Point of View in Nonfiction **Ask:** For telling about true events, what advantage might third-person point of view offer? *(Possible response: The author can be objective.)* **Ask:** What advantage might a first-person point of view offer? *(Possible response: The author can make readers feel as if they are there.)* AL

C Critical Thinking

Comprehension **Ask:** Do you think Ruby had an easier or harder time than the three children who went to another school? Why? *(Possible response: a harder time because no child shared her school days and experiences)* BL

Interactive Literary Elements Handbook Have students access the Web site to improve their understanding of point of view.

Literature Focus Lesson

Point of View Share with students these accounts of the first human being to walk on the moon in 1969 and have them identify the points of view.

American Neil Armstrong has become the first man to walk on the Moon. . . . As he put his left foot down first Armstrong declared: "That's one small step for man but one giant leap for mankind."
—BBC account *(third person)*

I was seven years old, we lived in a high-rise building in San Juan Puerto Rico. . . . I kept racing between the TV and the balcony and looking at the moon to see if I could see them on the moon.
—JR, of the United States *(first person)* OL

Indiana English/Language Arts Academic Standards
SE: 8.1, 8.2, 8.3
TWE: *Literature Focus Lesson* (p. 966) 8.3, *Literature Focus Lesson* (p. 967) 8.3

Teach

Viewing the Photo

Ask: Why do you think the photograph shows Ruby Bridges as a child? *(Possible responses: to reinforce the point of view; to help readers identify with a young child caught up in frightening events)*

R Reading Skill

Questioning **Ask:** What questions might you ask yourself as you read the newspaper account? *(Possible response: Why are so many police officers at the school? What are the housewives and teenagers doing at the school?)* BL

L Literary Element

Point of View in Nonfiction
Say: Rewrite the key ideas of the first sentence in the third paragraph from a first-person point of view. *(Possible response: I was with about 150 people, most of us housewives and teenagers. We were clustered. . . .)* OL

Readability Scores
Dale-Chall: 5.6
DRP: 56
Lexile: 870

from Through My Eyes

by Ruby Bridges

— The New York Times, November 15, 1960 *Today, hundreds of city policemen began to assemble in the mixed white and Negro residential districts of the two schools as the sun burned away the haze from the Mississippi River.*

Black squad cars cruised slowly through the narrow streets between modest white frame dwellings set among palms, oleanders, and crepe myrtle. Patrolmen in gold-striped uniforms, black boots, and white crash helmets dismounted from motorcycles to direct traffic. Police officials and detectives stationed themselves around the school buildings and inside the halls. Deputy federal marshals[1] *wearing yellow armbands made a final check and drove to the homes of the four pupils. . . .* **1** R

Some 150 whites, mostly housewives and teenage youths, clustered along the sidewalks across from the William Frantz School when pupils marched in at 8:40 a.m. One youth chanted, "Two, four, six, eight, we don't want to integrate; eight, six, four, two, we don't want a chigeroo." L

Forty minutes later, four deputy marshals arrived with a little Negro girl and her mother. They walked hurriedly up the steps and into the yellow brick building while onlookers jeered and shouted ***taunts***. **2**

1. The U.S. Department of Justice maintains a law enforcement agency made up of ***federal marshals*** (FED er ul MAR shulz). Among other tasks, the marshals are charged with putting into action federal and district court orders.

Vocabulary

taunts (tawnts) *n.* hurtful or mocking remarks

Practice the Skills

1 Literary Element

Point of View in Nonfiction
Like most newspaper stories, this story is told in the third-person point of view. You can tell because the narrator is a nameless voice describing what happened.

2 English Language Coach

Denotation and Word Choice
You can tell that an adult is describing what happened. Does he or she use simple words or sophisticated ones? Give examples.

Additional Support

Reading in the Real World

Citizenship Assign groups of students one of the following people involved in the Civil Rights movement. Have each group find five facts about the person. Post a photograph of each person on a large poster board. Then, have students write their facts under the person's name.

- Martin Luther King, Jr.
- Rosa Parks
- Malcolm X
- Linda Brown
- Medgar Evers
- Thurgood Marshall

EL BL OL

The girl, dressed in a stiffly starched white dress with a white ribbon in her hair, gripped her mother's hand tightly and glanced apprehensively toward the crowd. **3**

November 14, 1960

My mother took special care getting me ready for school. When somebody knocked on my door that morning, my mother expected to see people from the NAACP.[2] Instead, she saw four serious-looking white men, dressed in suits and wearing armbands. They were U.S. federal marshals. They had come to drive us to school and stay with us all day. I learned later they were carrying guns. **4** **R**

I remember climbing into the back seat of the marshals' car with my mother, but I don't remember feeling frightened. William Frantz Public School was only five blocks away, so one of the marshals in the front seat told my mother right away what we should do when we got there.

"Let us get out of the car first," the marshal said. "Then you'll get out, and the four of us will surround you and your daughter. We'll walk up to the door together. Just walk straight ahead, and don't look back." **5**

When we were near the school, my mother said, "Ruby, I want you to behave yourself today and do what the marshals say."

We drove down North Galvez Street to the point where it crosses Alvar. I remember looking out of the car as we pulled up to the Frantz school. There were **barricades** and people shouting and policemen everywhere. I thought maybe it was Mardi Gras,[3] the carnival that takes place in New Orleans every year. Mardi Gras was always noisy. **L**

As we walked through the crowd, I didn't see any faces. I guess that's because I wasn't very tall and I was surrounded by the marshals. People yelled and threw things. I could see the school building, and it looked bigger and nicer than my

2. The ***NAACP,*** or National Association for the Advancement of Colored People, began in 1909 with the goal of getting equal rights for African Americans.

3. ***Mardi Gras*** (MAR dee GRAH) is a French expression that means "Fat Tuesday." It is the name given to the celebration held the day before the fast that takes place during the Christian season of Lent.

Vocabulary

barricades (BAIR uh kaydz) *n.* barriers put up to separate or to provide defense

Practice the Skills

3 Key Reading Skill

Questioning Did you understand the newspaper story? To make sure, ask yourself 5Ws and an H questions. Answer these sample questions:

- *Who* is the little girl in the white dress?
- *What* is going on?
- *Where* is it happening?
- *When* is it happening?
- *Why* has a crowd gathered?
- *How* does the little girl feel?

4 Literary Element

Point of View in Nonfiction Who is speaking? What is the narrative point of view? Use these clues to answer:

- The narrator says her mother helped her get ready.
- The narrator calls herself "I."

5 English Language Coach

Denotation and Word Choice Reread the marshal's directions. Notice that he uses words with simple denotations. From his word choice, what do you think the marshall is like?

Teach

R Reading Skill

Questioning Say: Readers might ask, "Why does Ruby's mother take such special care this morning?" How would you answer this question? *(Possible responses: Her mother knows how important this day is. Her mother wants Ruby to make a good impression.)* **OL**

L Literary Element

Point of View in Nonfiction
Ask: Why does Ruby believe it is Mardi Gras? *(There are many people shouting, just like the noise during Mardi Gras.)* **BL** **Ask:** How does this comment show that she might be telling the story from the point of view of a child, not as an adult analyzing the event? *(A child would not understand what was happening and would try to compare it to something she knew. An adult would understand why the people were really making such a noise.)* **AL**

Differentiated Instruction

Art Ruby describes what it is like for her to walk into the school surrounded by police officers and protestors. Have students interested in art draw or paint a picture of the scene. Students can use the photographs in the textbook, as well as the details provided in the memoir and their own imaginations, to help them depict the scene. **OL**

Indiana English/Language Arts Academic Standards
SE: 8.1, 8.2, 8.3
TWE: *Reading in the Real World* 8.4, *Differentiated Instruction* 8.3

Teach

Viewing the Photo

Ask: How does the photograph emphasize how little and innocent Ruby is? *(The huge door and the large men contrast with Ruby's tiny figure.)* **AL**

L Literary Element

Point of View in Nonfiction
Ask: Why does Ruby think the place she is going to "must be college"? *(She thinks it must be an important place. College would seem important to a child.)* **OL** **Ask:** How does this statement show her innocence? *(She has no idea the policemen are there because of her.)* **AL**

READING WORKSHOP 2

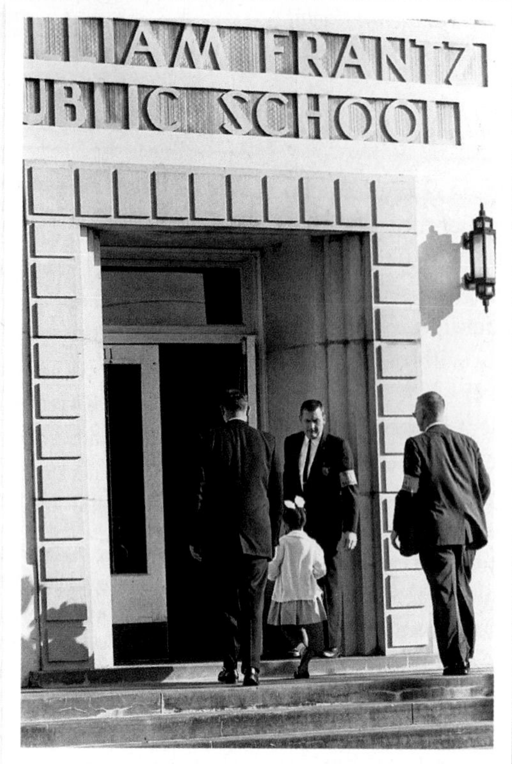

Escorted by three Deputy U.S. Marshals, Ruby Bridges enters her newly integrated public school.

Analyzing the Photo How does this photograph show the risks Ruby took to help integrate Frantz?

Practice the Skills

old school. **6** When we climbed the high steps to the front door, there were policemen in uniforms at the top. The policemen at the door and the crowd behind us made me think this was an important place. **L**

It must be college, I thought to myself.

6 Key Reading Skill

Questioning What does Ruby's description of the school tell you about the school system back in 1960?

The First Day at William Frantz

Once we were inside the building, the marshals walked us up a flight of stairs. The school office was at the top. My mother and I went in and were told to sit in the principal's office. The marshals sat outside. There were windows in the room where we waited. That meant everybody passing by could see us. I remember noticing everyone was white.

Additional Support

Literature Focus Lesson

Primary Sources Explain that the photograph on this page and Ruby's memoir are both primary sources, or first-hand accounts of what happened at the school. Have students compare the photograph to Ruby's memoir.

- What can you learn from the photograph that you do not learn from the memoir? *(Possible responses: what Ruby looked like, what she was wearing, how small she was, what the school looked like)*
- What information does the memoir supply that the photograph can't? *(Possible response: what Ruby was thinking and feeling)* **OL**

READING WORKSHOP 2

All day long, white parents rushed into the office. They were upset. They were arguing and pointing at us. When they took their children to school that morning, the parents hadn't been sure whether William Frantz would be **integrated** that day or not. After my mother and I arrived, they ran into classrooms and dragged their children out of the school. From behind the windows in the office, all I saw was confusion. I told myself that this must be the way it is in a big school. **7**

That whole first day, my mother and I just sat and waited. We didn't talk to anybody. I remember watching a big, round clock on the wall. When it was 3:00 and time to go home, I was glad. I had thought my new school would be hard, but the first day was easy. **L**

Going Home

When we left school that first day, the crowd outside was even bigger and louder than it had been in the morning. There were reporters and film cameras and people everywhere. I guess the police couldn't keep them behind the barricades. It seemed to take us a long time to get to the marshals' car.

Later on I learned there had been protestors in front of the two integrated schools the whole day. They wanted to be sure white parents would boycott[4] the school and not let their children attend. Groups of high school boys, joining the protestors, paraded

In this November 14, 1960, photo, a crowd protests Ruby's attendance at William Frantz Public School.

Analyzing the Photo How would you describe the people in this crowd? How would you feel about the crowd if you were Ruby?

4. To ***boycott*** means to protest against something, such as an organization or a company, by refusing to do business or interact with it.

Vocabulary

integrated (IN tuh gray tid) *v.* ended the separation of racial and ethnic groups

Practice the Skills

7 Key Reading Skill

Questioning How did Ruby explain away the confusion she saw?

Teach

L Literary Element

Point of View in Nonfiction

Say: Despite all the trouble outside and the fact that she and her mother had to sit in the office all day, Ruby says that her first day was easy. Why might a child have this opinion? *(Possible response: Children expect school to be hard work. Because Ruby didn't have to work hard, she thought the day was easy.)* **OL**

Viewing the Photo

Say: Compare the photograph to Ruby's version of her first day. Does the photograph support Ruby's memory of the day? Why or why not? *(Possible response: It does support her memory of the day; the details showing many people protesting agree with Ruby's memory of the event.)* **OL**

Differentiated Instruction

Building Background It wasn't just Ruby who was affected by her parents' decision to enroll her in the school. Mr. Bridges was eventually fired from his job because of the controversy over his child. Ruby's grandparents were forced to leave the farm where they lived and worked in Mississippi. Have students discuss the family's decision.

- Why was it important that Ruby go to the school, both for Ruby and for other children?
- Do you think the family believed it was worth the sacrifices they ended up making? Why or why not?
- Would you make similar sacrifices for equal rights? Why or why not? **OL**

Indiana English/Language Arts Academic Standards

SE: 8.2

TWE: *Literature Focus Lesson* 8.3, *Differentiated Instruction* 8.3

Teach

L1 Literary Element

Point of View in Nonfiction **Ask:** Why do you think seeing the doll in the coffin is more frightening to Ruby than all the yelling? *(Possible response: Children play with dolls. She would have understood this message even though she didn't really understand what was happening at the school.)* AL

L2 Literary Element

Point of View in Nonfiction **Ask:** How does Ruby's after-school play emphasize that the point of view is that of a child? *(Possible response: Ruby doesn't understand the chant. She probably just likes the rhythmic sound.)* OL

up and down the street and sang new verses to old hymns. Their favorite was "Battle Hymn of the Republic,"[5] in which they changed the chorus to "Glory, glory, segregation, the South will rise again." Many of the boys carried signs and said awful things, but most of all I remember seeing a black doll in a coffin, which frightened me more than anything else. L1 8

After the first day, I was glad to get home. I wanted to change my clothes and go outside to find my friends. My mother wasn't too worried about me because the police had set up barricades at each end of the block. Only local residents were allowed on our street. That afternoon, I taught a friend the chant I had learned: "Two, four, six, eight, we don't want to integrate." My friend and I didn't know what the words meant, but we would jump rope to it every day after school. L2 9

My father heard about the trouble at school. That night when he came home from work, he said I was his "brave little Ruby."

My First White Teacher

On the second day, my mother and I drove to school with the marshals. The crowd outside the building was ready. Racists spat at us and shouted things. One woman screamed at me, "I'm going to poison you. I'll find a way." She made the same threat every morning.

I tried not to pay attention. When we finally got into the building, my new teacher was there to meet us. Her name was Mrs. Henry. She was young and white. I had not spent time with a white person before, so I was uneasy at first. Mrs. Henry led us upstairs to the second floor. As we went up, we hardly saw anyone else in the building. The white students were not coming to class. The halls were so quiet, I could hear the noise the marshals' shoes made on the shiny hardwood floors.

Mrs. Henry took us into a classroom and said to have a seat. When I looked around, the room was empty. There were rows of desks, but no children. I thought we were too early, but Mrs. Henry said we were right on time. My mother sat

5. The ***"Battle Hymn of the Republic"*** was written by Julia Ward Howe after a visit to a Union army camp during the Civil War. Howe actively supported ending slavery.

Practice the Skills

8 Key Reading Skill

Questioning Why do you think Bridges describes the singing and chanting that she heard?

9 Key Reading Skill

Questioning Why do you think Ruby and her friend jump rope and chant these words?

Additional Support

Reading in the Real World

College Students aiming for college need to be able to do research in both primary and secondary sources. Challenge them to find both kinds of accounts of another significant event in school integration: the story of the enrollment of the Little Rock Nine at Central High School in Little Rock, Arkansas, in 1957. Like Ruby Bridges, the students—six girls and three boys—were faced with taunting crowds. Partly because the governor of Arkansas had ordered state troops to prevent the integration, these students were surrounded by more than 1,000 federal troops. Have students look for photographs to accompany their reports. AL down at the back of the room. I took a seat up front, and Mrs. Henry began to teach. **10**

I spent the whole first day with Mrs. Henry in the classroom. I wasn't allowed to have lunch in the cafeteria or go outside for recess, so we just stayed in our room. The marshals sat outside. If I had to go to the bathroom, the marshals walked me down the hall.

My mother sat in the classroom that day, but not the next. When the marshals came to the house on Wednesday morning, my mother said, "Ruby, I can't go to school with you today, but don't be afraid. The marshals will take care of you. Be good now, and don't cry." **11**

I started to cry anyway, but before I knew it, I was off to school by myself.

Ruby's Teacher's Comments

— Barbara Henry, Ruby's First-Grade Teacher *Leaving the school each day seemed even more frightening than arriving in the morning.*

I always drove to work and kept my car on the playground behind the school building. The police had turned the playground into a parking lot because it was the only area they could protect. **L**

On leaving school in the afternoon—even with a police escort— you were always fearful of how the people gathered along the sidewalks might choose to protest that day as you drove past them. The New Orleans police were supposed to be there to help us, but they very much disliked being the ones to enforce integration, so you never could be confident of their support and cooperation. ❍ **EL**

Practice the Skills

10 **Key Reading Skill**

Questioning Why is the classroom almost empty? Where are the other children?

11 **BIG Question**

Why is equality among races worth fighting for? How does society benefit by having equal treatment for all citizens? Write your answers on the *Through My Eyes* flap of Foldable 7. Your response will help you complete the Unit Challenge later.

Teach

L Literary Element

Point of View in Nonfiction **Ask:** What point of view is presented at the end of the story? *(the point of view of Ruby's first-grade teacher, Barbara Henry)* **OL** **Ask:** How does her account support Mr. Bridges's opinion that his daughter is "brave"? *(She talks about feeling afraid and receiving little support from the police.)* **AL**

EL Language Coach

Denotation and Word Choice **Ask:** Is the teacher's word choice and sentence structure more similar to the *New York Times* reporter's or to Ruby's? Why might this be the case? *(It is more similar to the reporter's; both are writing as adults for an adult audience.)* **OL**

Assess

Use the CheckPoint questions provided on Presentation Plus! to check for comprehension of the selection. These questions can be used with interactive response keypads for immediate student feedback.

Differentiated Instruction

Class Discussion Students may be interested to learn what happened after the events Ruby describes. For a long time, Ruby was the only student in William Frantz Elementary School, but eventually a few white parents brought their children back. By the next fall, the school was completely integrated. In 1999, Ruby Bridges founded the Ruby Bridges Foundation, the goal of which is to use education to change society. The foundation believes "racism is a grown-up disease, and we must stop using our children to spread it." Have students discuss this statement and discuss how adults might use children to spread racism. **AL**

Indiana English/Language Arts Academic Standards
SE: 8.2
TWE: *Reading in the Real World* 8.5.3, *English Language Coach* 8.3

Assess

Resources for page 974

- Selection Quick Check, p. 64
- Selection and Unit Assessment, p. 76
- ExamView Assessment Suite
- Interactive Tutor: Self-Assessment

Students can respond to the *After You Read* items in their Learner's Notebooks or on a separate sheet of paper.

Answering the

1. Possible response: a good education and racial equality
2. There was a large group of protestors outside the school.
3. Nothing. She didn't have class. She and her mother sat in the office.

Critical Thinking

4. Possible response: She did not see the danger. For example, the police and the crowd made her think first, that it was Mardi Gras, and second, that the school must be an important place, a college.
5. Possible response: She was nervous but determined to do her job. She describes the experience as frightening, but she went to work anyway.
6. Responses will vary.

After You Read

from *Through My Eyes*

Answering the BIG Question

1. After reading the selection, what are your thoughts about what is worth fighting for?
2. **Recall** Why did federal marshals accompany Ruby to school?
   TIP **Right There**
3. **Recall** What did Ruby do in class her first day of school?
   TIP **Right There**

Critical Thinking

4. **Analyze** How did Ruby's age and inexperience protect her from some of the bad things that happened? Support your answer with examples.
   TIP **Author and Me**
5. **Infer** How did Ruby's teacher feel about going to school during that difficult time? How can you tell?
   TIP **Author and Me**
6. **Evaluate** In your opinion, was it wise to ask a six-year-old child to take part in such a dangerous and historic event? Explain.
   TIP **On Your Own**

Write About Your Reading

Scene from a Play With a partner, choose one of the following scenes from Ruby's story and rewrite it as a script for a play.

- Ruby and her mother at home the morning of November 14, 1960, getting ready to go to William Frantz Public School for the first time.
- Ruby, her mother, and the federal marshals arriving at William Frantz Public School on the morning of November 14, 1960, and entering the building.
- Ruby, her mother, and the federal marshals leaving William Frantz Public School on the afternoon of November 14, 1960.

To write your script, use details from the newspaper story and Ruby's story. Use your imagination to write dialogue for the characters, but make the dialogue true to what the people say they thought, saw, and felt.

Indiana English/Language Arts Academic Standards (pp. 974–975)

8.2 Comprehension and Analysis (Focus on Informational Text) Understand grade-level-appropriate material. Develop [reading] strategies such as asking questions... **8.5.7** Write for different purposes... **8.3 Comprehension and Analysis of Literary Text** Respond to... literature...identifying story elements... **8.6 English Language Conventions**

For a complete description of the standards, see p. IN 11.

Write About Your Reading

Sample Script

Mother: Let's put on your good dress and shoes, sweetie. You look beautiful.
Ruby: Okay, Ma. Why do I have to wear church clothes to school?
Mother: Today's a very special day. You remember to be good today and to do what you're told.
Ruby: Of course, Ma. Do you think I'll meet some new friends?
Mother: I hope so, sweetie. It may take a while, but I hope so.

Skills Review

Key Reading Skill: Questioning

7. How did asking yourself questions as you read make the selection more meaningful for you?

Literary Element: Point of View in Nonfiction

8. Compare and contrast the newspaper version of events and Ruby's version. In what ways are they similar? Different? Put your ideas on a Venn diagram like the one pictured below.

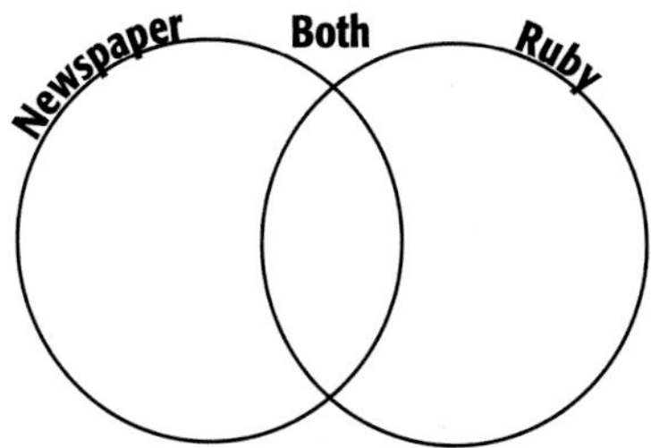

Vocabulary Check

Choose the vocabulary word that best completes each sentence.

taunts • barricades • integrated

9. She refused to let their _______ shake her self-confidence.
10. Public schools in New Orleans were not _______ until 1960.
11. The _______ did not keep the enemy's forces out of the castle for long.
12. **English Language Coach** How does the narrator's use of words with simple denotations help you better understand her character?

Web Activities For eFlashcards, Selection Quick Checks, and other Web activities, go to www.glencoe.com.

Grammar Link: Semicolons with Conjunctive Adverbs

When you join two independent clauses, or simple sentences, with a conjunctive adverb, put a **semicolon** (;) before the conjunctive adverb and a comma after it.

Conjunctive Adverbs	What They Express
therefore, thus, consequently	cause and effect, conclusion, result
however, otherwise, still	contrast, alternative
besides, furthermore, moreover	additional information

- Ina wrote the best essay in the contest; therefore, she deserves the first place award.
- I definitely need to study the science worksheet tonight; otherwise, I won't get a good grade.
- Alika is most qualified to be student council president; furthermore, she is well liked.

Grammar Practice

Copy each sentence on a separate sheet of paper. Insert one of these conjunctive adverbs in the blank: *consequently, besides, furthermore, however, still, therefore, thus.* Correctly punctuate the sentence.

13. The teacher gave us material from Chapter 4 on the test _______ it wasn't covered in class.
14. Terry upset his father _______ his father left the room.
15. Jorge found great artwork for the group project _______ he put it together in a colorful collage.
16. Businesses require people to have computer skills _______ schools teach them to students.
17. I want some fresh air, so I'm going to walk the dog instead of going shopping _______ shopping would be fun.

Writing Application Review your Write About Your Reading activity. Combine two sentences using a semicolon, a conjunctive adverb, and a comma.

Skills Review

Key Reading Skill: Questioning

7. Possible response: It made me feel part of the experience and it made me focus more closely on important points.

Literary Element: Point of View in Nonfiction

8. Check students' diagrams.

Vocabulary Check

9. taunts
10. integrated
11. barricades

English Language Coach

12. Possible response: They let me see how young and innocent Ruby was at this time.

Close

Discuss with students how reading about the courage of a small child has affected their thinking about the Big Question.

Literature Online

Web Activities Have students access the Web site for interactive activities that will help them assess their understanding of the selection.

Grammar Link: Semicolons with Conjunctive Adverbs

Grammar Practice

Possible responses:

13. test; however,
14. father; therefore,
15. project; furthermore,
16. skills; consequently,
17. shopping; however,

Indiana English/Language Arts Academic Standards
SE: 8.2, 8.3, 8.5.7, 8.6

Reviewing

Teaching Students to Review

Why Is It Important?

- Reviewing facilitates comprehension.
- Reviewing is a study habit that helps students succeed in all of their classes.
- Reviewing allows students to determine if they are addressing their purposes for reading.

How to Help Students Get It

- Discuss common ways that readers review what they have read, including rereading, skimming, and talking with others. Practice each of these with students.
- After reading a piece of text, ask students to create a graphic organizer of the information from the text. Discuss with students the fact that graphic organizers are one way that people can review the contents of a text without rereading the entire piece.
- Discuss the importance of note-taking as a way to review a text. Taking notes helps readers remember what they've read.
- Remind students that setting a purpose is an important skill in reading. We review as and after we read partly to determine whether we are staying true to our purpose and whether the text is meeting our needs.

Reading to Answer the Big Question

The Trouble with Television by Robert MacNeil
MacNeil argues persuasively that Americans must fight against the widespread negative influence of excessive television viewing. Its interference with concentration, complex thought, application of effort, and literacy are some of the issues addressed in this essay.

Teen Curfews by J. Todd Foster
When a town in West Virginia imposes a curfew on individuals under the age of eighteen, two teenagers decide that it is discriminatory and violates their constitutional rights. This article recounts the teens' fight to overturn the ordinance.

Workshop Resources

Pacing (Days) Standard	Block	Lesson	Student Materials	Teacher Resources
1	1/2	Key Skill Lesson: Reviewing	Key Reading Skills Practice, p. 22 English Language Coach Review, p. 42	Bellringer Options Transparencies –Daily Language Practice 67 Read Aloud, Think Aloud Transparencies –Key Reading Skills 21 –Read Aloud, Think Aloud 63–67 Presentation Plus!
1	1	"The Trouble with Television"	Glencoe Online Unit Vocabulary Review, p. 43 Academic Vocabulary Review, p. 43 English Language Coach Active Reading Graphic Organizer, p. 24 Literary Analysis, p. 23 StudentWorks Plus™ Online Student Edition Literature Classics Selection and Unit Assessments, p. 77	Literary and Text Analysis Transparencies 4 Puzzlemaker Skill Level Up!™ A Language Arts Game BookLink 3 Assessment by Learning Objective (Diagnostic and Formative) Interactive Tutor: Self-Assessment TeacherWorks Plus™
1		"Teen Curfews"	Glencoe Online Unit Vocabulary Review, p. 43 Academic Vocabulary Review, p. 43 English Language Coach Active Reading Graphic Organizer, p. 26 Literary Analysis, p. 23 StudentWorks Plus™ Online Student Edition Literature Classics Selection and Unit Assessments, p. 78	Literary and Text Analysis Transparencies 4 Puzzlemaker Skill Level Up!™ A Language Arts Game BookLink 3 Assessment by Learning Objective (Diagnostic and Formative) Interactive Tutor: Self-Assessment TeacherWorks Plus™

Keys for Unit Resource

- Blackline Master
- Workbook
- Supplemental Text
- CD-ROM
- DVD
- Transparency
- Web-based
- Fast File

Level Appropriate Code

AS = Activities for all students
AL = Activities for students working above grade level
OL = Activities for students working at grade level
BL = Activities for students working below grade level
EL = Activities for English language learners

Focus

BELLRINGER Options

Daily Language Practice Transparency 67

Focus Activity Write on the Board: Watching TV is a waste of time. Teens should be home and in bed by 10:00 every night. Ask volunteers to tell whether they agree or disagree with these statements and give one reason why. *(Responses will vary.)* OL

Teach

R Reading Skill

Reviewing Say: We use reviewing in school and in everyday life. What do you do when you review for a test in a subject area like science? *(Possible response: go back over the facts and ideas)* **Ask:** If you're running errands, for example, how might you use the skill of reviewing? *(Possible response: go over in your mind what you have to do)* OL

READING WORKSHOP 3

Skills Focus

You will practice using these skills when you read the following selections:

- "The Trouble with Television," p. 980
- "Teen Curfews," p. 988

Reading

- Reviewing what you read

Informational Text

- Recognizing bias

Vocabulary

- Understanding semantic slanting
- Academic Vocabulary: *concepts*

Writing/Grammar

- Using quotation marks with direct quotations

Skill Lesson

Reviewing

Learn It!

What Is It? If you've ever studied for a test, you've probably reviewed. **Reviewing** is going back over what you've already read to find important **concepts** and to organize ideas so you'll recall them later. You probably review various subjects in school every day. You review what you learned yesterday or last week so that you can remember important facts and ideas. Reviewing when you read helps you learn in the same way. R

WHY ARE YOU DOING HOME-WORK NOW?
I'M JUST REVIEWING!
I DON'T WANT TO FORGET EVERYTHING I LEARNED LAST YEAR!
ISN'T THAT WHAT SUMMER VACATION IS FOR?
BROWNE
7-20

Reprinted with permission of King Features Syndicate.

Analyzing Cartoons
The little girl knows that reviewing will help her remember important ideas and information. What do you need to review from the last Reading Workshop?

Indiana English/Language Arts Academic Standards (pp. 976–977)

8.2 Comprehension and Analysis (Focus on Informational Text) Develop [reading] strategies…

For a complete description of the standards, see p. IN 11.

Academic Vocabulary

concepts (KON septs) *n.* ideas; organized thoughts

Additional Support

Differentiated Instruction

Conduct a Survey Conduct a class survey by having students raise their hands in response to these questions. (Note answers on the board.)

- How many of you watch more than twenty hours of TV a week? Between ten and twenty? Less than ten?
- How many of you watch more TV during the school week than on the weekends?
- How many of you have family members who watch more TV than you?

Have students discuss whether they think they watch more or less TV than the average 8th grader and encourage them to consider some positive and negative consequences of watching TV. OL

Why Is It Important? Reviewing is especially helpful when you come across a lot of new information. When you review, you get the chance to find the most important ideas and organize your thoughts. Then you can think about those ideas and ask yourself, *What's this selection all about?*

Study Central Visit www.glencoe.com and click on Study Central to review reviewing.

How Do I Do It? As you read, pause every now and then to review. Ask yourself questions to make sure you understand what you've read. Take notes on the important points. Here's how a student reviewed the passage "November 14, 1960" from *Through My Eyes* on pages 969–970.

This selection is about Ruby's experience as one of the first African American children to attend an all-white school in the South, so it's important to remember the events and understand how she felt at the time. I'll use a graphic organizer to help me organize my notes.

R

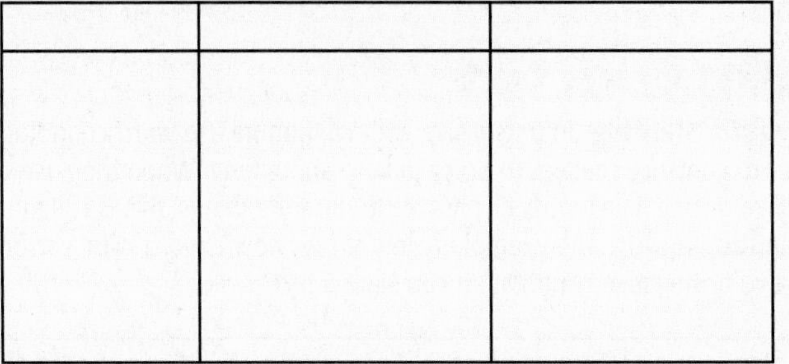

Practice It!

Make a chart like the one above. Then review the passage "The First Day at William Frantz" on pages 970–971. Fill in the chart using your own words.

Use It!

As you read "The Trouble with Television" and "Teen Curfews," stop every now and then to think about what you've read. Then review. Take notes on the important ideas.

Teach

Study Central Have students access the Web site to review reviewing and to complete a related activity.

R Reading Skill

Reviewing Help students complete the *Practice It!* activity by asking them the following questions:

- What does this portion of Ruby's memoir tell about? *(Ruby's first day at school, sitting in the office with her mother)*
- How does Ruby feel? *(She sees a lot of confusion and thinks it's because it's a big school. She doesn't say how she feels about this, but she does say she's glad to go home at 3:00.)*
- What is the main idea of the passage? *(On Ruby's first day, she is surrounded by confusion but is too young to understand it.)* EL BL

Resources for page 977

Use Key Reading Skills Transparency 21 in *Read Aloud, Think Aloud* to help students practice reviewing.

Reading in the Real World

College Point out that the ability to read, review, and take notes will be very important to students as they move into high school, college, and careers. Ask students to bring in their notebooks from another course, perhaps science or social studies. Have students discuss with a partner how they review in that class. Have students share techniques, such as rereading, asking questions, rewriting notes, underlining, or highlighting, with the class. AL

Indiana English/Language Arts Academic Standards

SE: 8.2

TWE: *Differentiated Instruction* 8.3, *Reading in the Real World* 8.2

Teach

More About the Author

Robert MacNeil has said that the best part of retirement from the news business is that he gets to choose the stories he concentrates on. He said in an interview after his retirement as a journalist that he enjoys life outside of the news world: "I never wanted to write op-ed pages or go on television and sound off about things or be a politician. I'm happy to have my own opinion and air it when I think it's necessary."

V Vocabulary

Suffixes **Say:** The suffix *–ly* often means "in a way that is." The word *passively* means "in a passive way," and the word *skeptically* means "in a skeptical way." What word would mean "in a perpetual way"? *(perpetually)* OL

Before You Read

The Trouble with Television

Meet the Author

Robert MacNeil was born and raised in Canada. His career in journalism began when he moved to London, England, after college to work for the Reuters News Agency. In 1975 he cofounded "The MacNeil/Lehrer NewsHour," a news program that discusses a single issue each night. In 1995, after twenty years as co-anchor of the show, MacNeil retired.

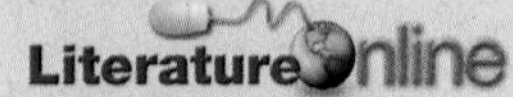

Author Search For more about Robert MacNeil, go to www.glencoe.com.

Indiana English/Language Arts Academic Standards
(pp. 978–983)

8.1.3 Verify the meaning of a word in its context... **8.2 Comprehension and Analysis (Focus on Informational Text)** Develop [reading] strategies... **8.2.2** Analyze text that uses proposition (statement of argument) and support patterns.

For a complete description of the standards, see p. IN 11.

Vocabulary Preview

V

perpetual (pur PEH choo ul) *adj.* continuing forever **(p. 981)** *Television is a perpetual display of moving images.*

passively (PAS iv lee) *adv.* not actively **(p. 981)** *Instead of passively watching television, you could exercise your brain by reading a book.*

strain (strayn) *v.* stretch to the limit; overwork **(p. 981)** *Television programmers do not want to strain your attention, so they keep programs short.*

virtually (VUR choo uh lee) *adv.* nearly **(p. 983)** *Virtually everyone, or almost the entire nation, watches television every day.*

skeptically (SKEP tik uh lee) *adv.* with doubt **(p. 983)** *The author looks at TV skeptically and questions its value to society.*

English Language Coach

Semantic Slanting In persuasive writing, authors use word connotation to try to convince readers to do or believe something. When they use very positive or negative words or phrases to describe things, this is called **semantic slanting.** The example below shows how a word with a strong positive or negative connotation can slant a text.

Sentence	Denotation of italicized word or phrase	Connotation of italicized word or phrase	Semantic Slanting
Nicole is *nosy* and likes to ask a lot of questions.	*nosy* = curious	*negative:* bothersome	suggests that Nicole is rude and does not have the right to ask questions

If you think that an author is using semantic slanting, try to paraphrase his or her words using words with neutral connotations.

Think-Pair-Share Find the negative word in each sentence. Share your results with a partner. Then discuss how the use of semantic slanting affects what you think of Andrea and "the driver of the other car."

1. Andrea likes to gossip about her neighbors.
2. As I was backing out, the driver of the other car smashed into my bumper.

Additional Support

Author Search To expand students' appreciation of Robert MacNeil, have them access the Web site for additional information and resources.

English Language Coach

Semantic Slanting Advertisers spend a lot of effort aiming for positive semantic slanting in slogans and advertisements. Have students collect print ads that use positive semantic slanting in descriptions of products, services, or political candidates. OL

Challenge students to find examples of ads with negative slanting, perhaps leveled against the competition. AL Have students exchange their finds with a partner and highlight the semantic slanting in each ad. AS

Skills Preview

Key Reading Skill: Reviewing

When you read persuasive writing, it's important to understand the main points of the writing. As you read "The Trouble with Television," stop to review the author's ideas and the information he gives to support them.

On Your Own Copy this chart and use it to take notes.

Main Point	Supporting Details

Key Text Element: Author's Bias

In persuasive writing, "one-sidedness" is known as **author's bias.** Having a firm opinion is not the same as being biased. The purpose of persuasive writing is to "take sides" and argue one position over another. Bias happens when writers close their minds to opinions or viewpoints different from their own. To identify bias, ask yourself these questions. If your answer to them is "yes," the writer may be biased.

- *Does the writer fail to admit that there are two sides to the story, or issue?*
- *Does the writer **overgeneralize,** or make broad statements without including exceptions to the rule?*
- *Does the writer work for or belong to a group that might make him or her biased?*

Whole Class Discussion It's almost election time. You have to decide who gets your vote for president—Joe Doe of Party A or Moe Doe of Party B. What resources would you look into to find unbiased information about each candidate?

E

Literature Online

Interactive Literary Elements Handbook To review or learn more about the literary elements, go to www.glencoe.com.

Get Ready to Read

Connect to the Reading

How often do you watch television? Take a moment to think about how many hours per week you sit in front of the TV. Do you spend as many hours doing more important activities, like homework?

On Your Own Make a list of your favorite activities. Calculate how much time you spent on each activity last week. What did you spend the most amount of time doing? What did you spend the least amount of time doing? Is there anything you would like to spend more time doing? If so, how will you find the time?

Build Background

In 1950 only 9 percent of U.S. households owned a TV. Today, over 98 percent of U.S. households have at least one TV. Viewers with cable or satellite TV may have access to more than 200 channels.

In the United States, one hour of network television usually contains between fifteen to twenty minutes of commercials advertising products and services.

Set Purposes for Reading

BIG Question Read "The Trouble with Television" to learn why the author thinks people should reduce the number of hours they spend watching television.

Set Your Own Purpose What would you like to learn from the selection to help you answer the Big Question? Write your own purpose on "The Trouble with Television" flap of Foldable 7.

Keep Moving

Use these skills as you read the following selection.

Teach

E Text Element

Author's Bias If students have a hard time thinking of resources for unbiased information about the political parties, have them evaluate these options. Encourage them to see that all sources have potential for bias.

- a news report
- a magazine published by a known supporter of Party A
- a political flyer published by Party B
- a flyer distributed by a non-profit group not affiliated with either party
- public records
- political ads AS

Interactive Literary Elements Handbook Have students access the Web site to improve their understanding of author's bias.

Literature Focus Lesson

Persuasive Essays Remind students that writers of persuasive essays present their opinion in a main idea, or thesis, usually in the first paragraph. Then, they present facts, expert opinions, statistics, examples, and anecdotes to support their main idea. Good persuasive writers use only reasons that support their main idea. Encourage students to set aside their personal opinions as they read "The Trouble with Television" and evaluate it based on the writer's reasons. Does he do a good job of supporting his point of view? Explain. OL AL

Indiana English/Language Arts Academic Standards

SE: 8.1.3, 8.2, 8.2.2

TWE: *English Language Coach* 8.1, *Literature Focus Lesson* 8.2.2

Teach

Viewing the Photo

Ask: What message do you think the photographer was trying to get across by showing many televisions with blank screens? *(Possible response: Televisions are everywhere but don't always provide much information.)* OL AL

E Text Element

Review Persuasive Appeals

Ask: What appeal to reason is MacNeil making with these statistics? *(Possible response: He is suggesting that people could be much more productive if they didn't watch so much television.)* **Ask:** How is this also an appeal to ethics? *(He suggests that it's wrong to waste so much time watching TV.)* OL

Readability Scores

Dale-Chall: 8.9
DRP: 68
Lexile: 1160

The Trouble with Television

by Robert MacNeil

It is difficult to **escape the influence** of television. If you fit the statistical averages,[1] by the age of 20 you will have been exposed to at least 20,000 hours of television. You can add 10,000 hours for each decade you have lived after the age of 20. The only things Americans do more than watch television are work and sleep. **1**

Calculate for a moment what could be done with even a part of those hours. Five thousand hours, I am told, are what a typical college undergraduate spends working on a bachelor's degree.[2] In 10,000 hours you could have learned enough to become an astronomer or engineer. You could have learned several languages fluently. If it appealed to you, you could be reading Homer in the original Greek or Dostoyevski[3] in Russian. If it didn't, you could have walked around the world and written a book about it. **E**

The trouble with television is that it discourages concentration. **2** Almost anything interesting and rewarding

1. ***Statistical averages*** tell you about a typical person's behavior.
2. ***Undergraduates*** are students at a college or university who do not yet have a degree. A ***bachelor's degree*** is awarded to undergraduates who complete a four-year program of study.
3. ***Homer*** was a Greek poet who is believed to have lived around 800 B.C. Fyodor ***Dostoyevski*** was a Russian novelist who lived from 1821–1881.

Practice the Skills

1 English Language Coach

Semantic Slanting The opening sentence could be paraphrased as follows: *It's hard not to be affected by television.* What is the author trying to persuade you of by using the phrase **escape the influence,** which has a negative connotation? Explain.

2 Key Reading Skill

Reviewing Here, MacNeil states his main idea, or position: "The trouble with television is that it discourages concentration." Write the main idea on your chart so you remember it.

Additional Support

Differentiated Instruction

Connect to the Text Have students imagine that all television programming has been taken off the air for an entire summer. Ask them to form groups and come up with alternatives to watching television. Have students describe how they would spend the time they usually spend watching TV. Encourage them to be creative and list multiple alternatives.

- What, besides using the Internet, will they do to entertain themselves?
- How will they learn what is going on in the world and in their community?

Have students share their alternatives with the class. Which alternatives sound like the most fun? OL in life requires some constructive, consistently applied effort. The dullest, the least gifted of us can achieve things that seem miraculous to those who never concentrate on anything. But television encourages us to apply no effort. It sells us instant gratification. It diverts[4] us only to divert, to make the time pass without pain. **3**

Television's variety becomes a narcotic, not a stimulus. Its serial, kaleidoscopic exposures[5] force us to follow its lead. The viewer is on a **perpetual** guided tour: thirty minutes at the museum, thirty at the cathedral, then back on the bus to the next attraction—except on television, typically, the spans allotted are on the order of minutes or seconds, and the chosen delights are more often car crashes and people killing one another. In short, a lot of television usurps[6] one of the most precious of all human gifts, the ability to focus your attention yourself, rather than just **passively** surrender it. **4**

Capturing your attention—and holding it—is the prime motive of most television programming and enhances its role as a profitable advertising vehicle.[7] Programmers live in constant fear of losing anyone's attention—anyone's. The surest way to avoid doing so is to keep everything brief, not to **strain** the attention of anyone but instead to provide constant stimulation through variety, novelty, action and movement. Quite simply, television operates on the appeal to the short attention span.

It is simply the easiest way out. But it has come to be regarded as a given, as inherent in the medium itself; as an imperative, as though General Sarnoff, or one of the other

4. ***Instant gratification*** is immediate satisfaction. ***Divert*** means "distract."
5. A ***narcotic*** is a substance that soothes. ***Serial kaleidoscopic exposures*** (SEER ee ul kul ide uh SKAHP ik ek SPOH zherz) are continuous and constantly changing images.
6. ***Usurps*** (yoo SERPS) means "takes by force or without right."
7. The author writes that the ***prime motive*** (goal) of television is to ***enhance*** (improve the value of) its role as a ***profitable advertising vehicle*** (a moneymaker for companies that broadcast advertisements).

Vocabulary

perpetual (pur PEH choo ul) *adj.* continuing forever

passively (PAS iv lee) *adv.* not actively

strain (strayn) *v.* stretch to the limit; overwork

Practice the Skills

3 Key Text Element

Author's Bias MacNeil overgeneralizes and shows bias when he says TV "diverts us only to divert, to make the time pass without pain." How about serious news programs such as the one he coanchored? Those shows aren't just entertainment, are they? What other exceptions can you think of?

4 Key Reading Skill

Reviewing Look back at what you have already read. What evidence does the author give to support his arguments? Write your answer on your chart.

Teach

EL Language Coach

Semantic Slanting Say: Explain how MacNeil is using semantic slanting when he compares television to a narcotic. *(The word* narcotic *has negative connotations, implying addiction, and he is hoping readers associate that negative feeling with television.)* **OL**

R Reading Skill

Reviewing Say: Review the paragraph that begins "Capturing your attention. . . ." What is the paragraph's main idea? *(The goal of programming is to keep viewers' attention.)* **Ask:** What two things does the writer say programmers do to keep viewers' attention? *(They keep things brief and they use constant stimulation.)* **Say:** Add these notes to your graphic organizer. **OL**

Reading in the Real World

Career Have interested students research one of the many careers in television:

- director
- producer
- advertiser
- actor
- writer
- journalist
- camera operator
- makeup artist

What training and experience is necessary? What qualities lead to success? Ask students to share their findings with the class. **OL**

Indiana English/Language Arts Academic Standards

SE: 8.1.3, 8.2, 8.2.2

TWE: *Differentiated Instruction* 8.7.11, *Reading in the Real World* 8.7

Teach

EL Language Coach

Semantic Slanting **Ask:** What negative words does the writer use to describe news shows? *(*boring *and* dismissible*)* BL **Say:** The fast pace of the TV news is supposed to keep the watcher's attention. According to the writer, what is the *true* effect of giving "fast ideas . . . to a fast moving, impatient public"? *(Possible response: The ideas end up being boring because they're so short no one can truly understand them.)* OL

R Reading Skill

Reviewing **Ask:** What does McNeil identify as the negative effects of television? *(inefficient communication, "decivilizing," and a decline in the ability to read and write)* OL

august pioneers of video, had bequeathed[8] to us tablets of stone commanding that nothing in television shall ever require more than a few moments' concentration.

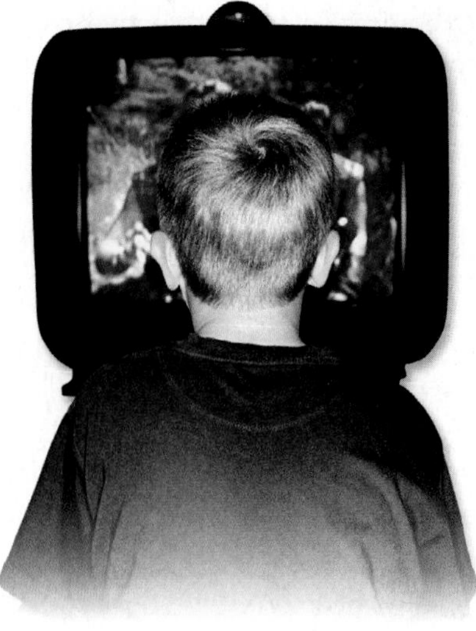

In its place that is fine. Who can quarrel with a medium that so brilliantly packages escapist entertainment as a mass-marketing tool? But I see its values now pervading[9] this nation and its life. It has become fashionable to think that, like fast food, fast ideas are the way to get to a fast-moving, impatient public.

In the case of news, this practice, in my view, results in inefficient communication. I question how much of television's nightly news effort is really absorbable and understandable. Much of it is what has been aptly described as "machine gunning with scraps." I think the technique fights coherence. I think it tends to make things ultimately boring and dismissible[10] (unless they are accompanied by horrifying pictures) because almost anything is boring and dismissible if you know almost nothing about it. 5 EL

I believe that TV's appeal to the short attention span is not only inefficient communication but decivilizing as well. Consider the casual assumptions that television tends to cultivate: that complexity must be avoided, that visual stimulation is a substitute for thought, that verbal precision is an anachronism.[11] It may be old-fashioned, but I was taught that thought is words, arranged in grammatically precise ways. R

There is a crisis of literacy in this country. One study estimates that some 30 million adult Americans are "functionally illiterate" and cannot read or write well enough to answer a want ad or understand the instructions on a medicine bottle.

Practice the Skills

5 Key Text Element

Author's Bias Remember that MacNeil was once an anchor on an hour-long news program that focused on only one issue. How might this background bias him?

8. Here, ***august*** (aw GUST) means "honored." ***Bequeathed*** (bih KWEETHD) means "handed down."
9. The author compares television to a ***mass-marketing tool,*** a device used to sell products to a large number of people. ***Pervading*** means "spreading through all parts of."
10. ***Aptly*** means "correctly and accurately." ***Coherence*** is the quality of fitting together in a way that makes sense. Something that is ***dismissible*** is easily put out of one's mind.
11. ***Decivilizing*** is getting rid of knowledge, good taste, and social skills. ***Assumptions*** are beliefs that have not been proven to be true. To ***cultivate*** something is to encourage it to grow. An ***anachronism*** is something that is out of place in the present time period.

Additional Support

Reading in the Real World

Citizenship Record a local news show and have students watch it to determine whether it fits MacNeil's description of television news. (Alternatively, ask students to watch a local news show at home.)

- Does it have continuous and constantly changing images?
- Does it offer constant variety and action?
- Is it trivial?
- How many commercials are there? How much of the thirty-minute show do they take up?
- How does the show attempt to capture viewers' attention? Does it succeed?
- Does it seem to "operate on the appeal to the short attention span"? If so, how? OL

Literacy may not be an inalienable human right, but it is one that the highly literate Founding Fathers might not have found unreasonable or even unattainable.[12] We are not only not attaining it as a nation, statistically speaking, but we are falling further and further short of attaining it. And, while I would not be so simplistic as to suggest that television is the cause, I believe it contributes and is an influence. **6**

Everything about this nation—the structure of the society, its forms of family organization, its economy, its place in the world—has become more complex, not less. Yet its dominating communications instrument, its principal form of national linkage, is one that sells neat resolutions[13] to human problems that usually have no neat resolutions. It is all symbolized in my mind by the hugely successful art form that television has made central to the culture, the thirty-second commercial: the tiny drama of the earnest housewife who finds happiness in choosing the right toothpaste.

When before in human history has so much humanity collectively surrendered so much of its leisure to one toy, one mass diversion? When before has **virtually** an entire nation surrendered itself wholesale[14] to a medium for selling? EL

Some years ago Yale University law professor Charles L. Black, Jr., wrote: ". . . forced feeding on trivial fare is not itself a trivial matter." I think this society is being force-fed with trivial fare, and I fear that the effects on our habits of mind, our language, our tolerance for effort, and our appetite for complexity are only dimly perceived. If I am wrong, we will have done no harm to look at the issue **skeptically** and critically, to consider how we should be resisting it. I hope you will join with me in doing so. **7** ❍ E

12. An ***inalienable human right*** is a basic right that cannot be taken away. ***Unattainable*** means "unable to be obtained."
13. ***Dominating*** means "commanding the most attention." ***Resolutions*** are answers or solutions.
14. In this paragraph, the author asks if there has been another time when ***humanity*** (the entire human race) has ***collectively*** (together as one) given up so much of its free time to one ***mass diversion*** (source of amusement), or ***surrendered itself wholesale***–given itself up completely to a medium for selling.

Vocabulary

virtually (VUR choo uh lee) *adv.* nearly

skeptically (SKEP tik uh lee) *adv.* with doubt

Practice the Skills

6 **Key Reading Skill**

Reviewing Review the last two paragraphs to make sure you understand what *literacy* and *illiteracy* mean. Then write the main point of these paragraphs on your chart.

7 **BIG Question**

What does the author ask you to join him in fighting for? Write your answer on "The Trouble with Television" flap of Foldable 7. Your response will help you complete the Unit Challenge later.

Teach

EL Language Coach

Semantic Slanting **Ask:** What words does the writer use to describe a TV in this paragraph? *(toy, mass diversion, medium for selling)* **Ask:** Do these words have a negative or positive connotation? Explain. *(They have a negative connotation. He is describing TV as a game meant to distract people from their lives and as a way to sell products.)* AL

E Text Element

Author's Bias **Say:** The writer says he thinks "this society is being force-fed with trivial fare." What possible bias does he show in this statement? *(Possible responses: He believes that people should not spend time doing trivial things. He may be biased against light forms of entertainment.)* OL

Assess

Use the CheckPoint questions provided on Presentation Plus! to check for comprehension of the selection. These questions can be used with interactive response keypads for immediate student feedback.

Differentiated Instruction

Challenge the Text Invite students to challenge MacNeil's judgment of the "trivial fare" offered on television. Have them use a programming guide to find a documentary they believe would make worthwhile viewing. Those interested in science, nature, or history will find many offerings. Students could also choose programs related to art and music. Those interested in practical matters can seek out a how-to program. Each student should create a small poster promoting his or her chosen show; use these to create a "Watch It!" display on the bulletin board. OL

Indiana English/Language Arts Academic Standards
SE: 8.2, 8.2.2
TWE: *Reading in the Real World* 8.7.9, *Differentiated Instruction* 8.5.4

Assess

Resources for page 984

- Selection Quick Check, p. 65
- Selection and Unit Assessment, p. 77
- ExamView Assessment Suite
- Interactive Tutor: Self-Assessment

Students can respond to the *After You Read* items in their Learner's Notebooks or on a separate sheet of paper.

Answering the BIG Question

1. Possible response: I agree that watching too much TV can be harmful, but watching a few hours per week doesn't seem that harmful.
2. 20,000
3. Possible response: It discourages concentration; it wastes our time.

Critical Thinking

4. Possible response: He wants to get readers' attention with startling statistics. He then shows how little value the thousands of hours spent watching TV offer.
5. Possible responses: to show that others believe as he does; to support his argument with expert opinion
6. Some students may say the article is thoughtful and well reasoned. Others may say MacNeil should include more research and examples.

After You Read

The Trouble with Television

Answering the BIG Question

1. Do you agree with the author that TV is harmful? Explain.
2. **Recall** By the age of twenty, how many hours of television has the average person watched?
   TIP **Right There**
3. **Recall** According to MacNeil, what are two negative effects of TV?
   TIP **Think and Search**

Critical Thinking

4. **Analyze** Why do you think MacNeil starts his article with statistics about the number of hours people spend watching TV? Use details from the selection to support your answer.
   TIP **Author and Me**
5. **Analyze** In the conclusion, MacNeil quotes Charles L. Black Jr. Why do you think he chose to quote Black?
   TIP **Author and Me**
6. **Evaluate** Do you think MacNeil argues his position well? Explain.
   TIP **Author and Me**

Talk About Your Reading

Small Group Discussion Get together with a small group of classmates and debate the pros and cons of TV. Guide your discussion with these questions:

- MacNeil says TV "discourages concentration." What examples does he give to back up his position? Is this evidence persuasive? Explain.
- MacNeil argues that TV is too simple a form of communication for today's complex world. Do you agree? Explain.
- Are there good things to be said for TV? If so, what are they?

Indiana English/Language Arts Academic Standards (pp. 984–985)

8.2 Comprehension and Analysis (Focus on Informational Text) Understand grade-level-appropriate material. Develop [reading] strategies... **8.7 Listening and Speaking** Speaking skills are developed... **8.2.2** Analyze text that uses proposition (statement of argument) and support patterns. **8.1.3** Verify the meaning of a word in its context... **8.6 English Language Conventions**

For a complete description of the standards, see p. IN 11.

Talk About Your Reading

In their discussion, students should address all of the issues raised:

- Does MacNeil prove that TV appeals to a short attention span? *(Students might note that MacNeil gives examples, such as keeping everything brief and providing variety, novelty, action, and movement.)*
- Is TV too simple for today's world? *(Students might note that people looking for more details about an issue might use another medium, such as a newspaper or the Internet.)*
- Are the effects of TV all bad, or does it have some benefits? *(Possible response: Some TV shows are positive because they depict people helping one another, or teach us about history and science, for example.)*

Skills Review

Key Reading Skill: Reviewing

7. How did reviewing help you understand this selection? Give examples.

Key Text Element: Author's Bias

8. Imagine that you're doing research to see whether television viewing harms people's ability to concentrate. To avoid bias, what other sources of information might you look into besides "The Trouble with Television?"

Vocabulary Check

Copy the following sentences on a separate sheet of paper. Fill in each blank with the correct word.

perpetual • passively • strain • virtually • skeptically

9. Turn on the light while you read so that you don't ______ your eyes.
10. After the party, ______ all the snacks were gone.
11. The doctor knew the little girl was pretending to be ill. ______, he examined her throat.
12. A person who is constantly on the go is in ______ motion.
13. Don't sit there ______ watching television; get out and do something productive!
14. **English Language Coach** Quote an example of semantic slanting from the selection. Does the word or phrase you quoted have positive connotations or negatives ones? Explain.
15. **Academic Vocabulary** List a few **concepts** you have recently studied in English class.

Web Activities For eFlashcards, Selection Quick Checks, and other Web activities, go to www.glencoe.com.

Grammar Link: Quotation Marks

Quotation marks (" ") are punctuation marks used to enclose the exact words of a speaker. When a speaker's words are not interrupted, **opening quotation marks** (") are placed before the quotation and **closing quotation marks** (") after it. The quotation may come at the end of a sentence or at the beginning.

- After they lost their lawsuit, the young women said, "We are still proud that we stood up for our beliefs."
- The reporter asked, "What will you do now?"
- "What will you do now?" asked the reporter.

A **direct quotation** states word for word what a speaker said. An **indirect quotation** does not repeat a person's exact words. It should NOT be enclosed in quotation marks.

Direct: Ms. Bosco said, "Mars has two moons."

Indirect: Ms. Bosco said that Mars has two moons.

Grammar Practice

Copy the following sentences on a separate sheet of paper. Add quotation marks where needed.

16. Please, Katelyn, would you wear white socks rather than black ones, her gym teacher said.
17. But all my socks are black, Katelyn complained.
18. The waiter apologized, We're all out of meatloaf.
19. One councilman growled, They are just taking up our precious time.
20. A student said that she thought they were brave.
21. Another student in the community said, We are grateful that the young women were willing to fight for our rights.
22. My sister said that she thinks the whole issue is ridiculous.
23. What is to be gained from all this fighting? she asked me.
24. The newspaper agrees with me that there is nothing to be gained.

Skills Review

Key Reading Skill: Reviewing

7. Possible response: Reviewing reminded me to stop from time to time to take notes on main ideas and important details.

Text Element: Author's Bias

8. Possible response: I might read many articles to get different perspectives. I might also read scientific studies about the effects of television.

Vocabulary Check

9. strain
10. virtually
11. Skeptically
12. perpetual
13. passively

English Language Coach

14. Possible response: The words *decivilizing, toy,* and *mass diversion* all have negative connotations.

Academic Vocabulary

15. Possible response: I have studied the concepts of bias and persuasive appeals.

Close

Ask students to comment on whether MacNeil's ideas have affected their answers to the Big Question.

Grammar Link: Quotation Marks

Grammar Practice

16. "Please, Katelyn, would you wear white socks rather than black ones," her gym teacher said.
17. "But all my socks are black," Katelyn complained.
18. The waiter apologized, "We're all out of meatloaf."
19. One councilman growled, "They are just taking up our precious time."
20. no quotation marks needed
21. Another student in the community said, "We are grateful that the young women were willing to fight for our rights."
22. no quotation marks needed
23. "What is to be gained from all this fighting?" she asked me.
24. no quotation marks needed

Indiana English/Language Arts Academic Standards
SE: 8.1.3, 8.2, 8.2.2, 8.6, 8.7

Teach

Did You Know?

It is not just cities that are enacting teen curfews. Many malls around the country have also enacted curfews, or "parental escort policies." Teenagers are often required to be accompanied by a parent or guardian over the age of 21. Malls cite large groups of teens congregating, harassment, theft, and rowdiness as reasons for the curfews. Teens counter by saying they are being punished for the actions of a few and worry that there are few other safe places for them to hang out.

V Vocabulary

Multiple-Meaning Words

Ask: What other definition does the word *convictions* have that is related to the word *violating?* *(instances of being found guilty of violating a law)* **Say:** Both senses of the word relate to the word *convince*: Your convictions are things you are convinced are right, and legal convictions result when the judge or jury is convinced of your guilt. OL AL

Before You Read | Teen Curfews

Meet the Author

J. Todd Foster began his journalism career in 1978 as a teenage sports editor in Winchester, Tennessee. Since then he has reported on medicine, the environment, politics, crime, and human-interest stories for various publications, including *People* magazine. In 2003 Foster became managing editor of *The News Virginian*, a newspaper based out of Waynesboro, Virginia, where he lives with his family.

Author Search For more about J. Todd Foster, go to www.glencoe.com.

Vocabulary Preview

V **convictions** (kun VIK shunz) *n.* strong beliefs or values **(p. 988)** *The young people were willing to take a risk because of their convictions.*

controversial (kon truh VUR shul) *adj.* causing disagreement **(p. 988)** *The new law was so controversial that the state's supreme court decided to hear the case and decide whether it was constitutional.*

violating (VY uh lay ting) *v.* breaking or disregarding a law or rule; form of the verb *violate* **(p. 988)** *The police arrested more than fifty kids who they suspected were violating the law.*

Write to Learn

1. List and briefly explain a few of your **convictions**.
2. Name a **controversial** topic you might examine in a persuasive essay for your English class.
3. What is an antonym for ***violating***?

English Language Coach

Semantic Slanting Remember that using words with strong positive or negative connotations can sway readers in one direction or another. The following two paragraphs argue for and against school uniforms. Notice the semantic slanting in each.

In favor of wearing school uniforms	*School uniforms free kids from being forced to choose a different outfit each day. Kids aren't pressured to think about whether their clothes meet the approval of their peers. They don't have to break the bank and fork out ridiculous amounts of money for expensive fads.*
Against wearing school uniforms	*School uniforms deny kids the right to make up their own minds about what they want to wear. Kids enjoy the challenge of creating outfits that earn the admiration of their peers. Trendy clothes help kids express their individuality.*

Small Group Work Form a group with a few other students. Identify the words and phrases in the paragraphs above that have strong positive or negative connotations. Discuss how they slant the texts.

Indiana English/Language Arts Academic Standards (pp. 986–989)

8.1.3 Verify the meaning of a word in its context... **8.2 Comprehension and Analysis (Focus on Informational Text)** Develop [reading] strategies... **8.2.2** Analyze text that uses proposition (statement of argument) and support patterns.

For a complete description of the standards, see p. IN 11.

Additional Support

Author Search To expand students' appreciation of J. Todd Foster, have them access the Web site for additional information and resources.

Differentiated Instruction

Anticipating Arguments Before students read "Teen Curfews," ask them to make a list of arguments for and against curfews. Invite students to share their arguments and note them on the board. Ask students to look for additional arguments as they read. Once students have finished the article, add any new arguments to the list. Then have them rank the arguments, with "1" being the most convincing. Explain that when they write persuasively, they should be prepared to counter the strongest argument on the other side. OL

Skills Preview

Key Reading Skill: Reviewing

As you read the selection, take time to pause and review. Check your understanding of information and reread to look for anything you've missed.

Write to Learn "Teen Curfews" is a news article about a series of events that takes place in Charleston, West Virginia. You probably already know that the important points to remember in a news article are *Who, What, When, Where, Why,* and *How.* Make a graphic organizer to keep track of this information.

Key Text Element: Author's Bias

Remember that an author who unfairly slants a story is guilty of **author's bias.** To evaluate an article for bias, it's important to consider whether the author favors one side of a story over others. Ask yourself:

- *Does the author have a special interest in putting someone in a positive or negative light?*
- *Is the author's evidence reliable?*
- *What are the author's sources?*
- *Does the author stereotype, generalize, or exaggerate?*
- *What information is the author leaving out? Why?*

E

Write to Learn Write a short news article describing an event that caused a disagreement between you and another person. For example, you could write about a time when you wanted something that you couldn't have or when a parent set a new rule in your home. Try to be completely neutral. Leave out your personal feelings and give a fair explanation of what happened. Switch papers with a partner and ask the person to check to see if your writing shows bias.

Interactive Literary Elements Handbook
To review or learn more about the literary elements, go to www.glencoe.com.

Get Ready to Read

Connect to the Reading

Do you think teenagers should be home by a certain time in the evening? Is it safe for teens to be out at late hours in your town?

Small Group Discussion Form a group with three other students. Discuss what teenagers in your town like to do in the evenings. Do you think they should be required to be home by a certain time at night?

Build Background

A curfew is an enforced time when people must be out of public places.

- Many parents give their teenagers curfews to ensure that their children will be home at a reasonable hour.
- Some cities have curfew laws for teenagers. These laws are intended to keep young people safe as well as to stop teens from committing crimes.
- Teens are not the only targets of curfews. Members of the armed forces have to obey curfews. Some colleges have curfews too—even for students over 18. During times of war and civil unrest, governments may enforce curfews to protect all citizens, regardless of age, during evening hours.

R

Set Purposes for Reading

BIG Question Read the article "Teen Curfews" to see how three teenagers responded to a law that limited when they could be out in public at nighttime.

Set Your Own Purpose What would you like to learn from the article to help you answer the Big Question? Write your own purpose on the "Teen Curfews" flap of Foldable 7.

Keep Moving

Use these skills as you read the following selection.

Teach

E Text Element

Author's Bias Ask: If you're uncertain about whether a writer is biased, how might you find out for sure? *(Possible responses: You could get more information or opinions on the subject by reading other articles. You could learn more about the writer or the magazine or newspaper where the article appeared.)* **OL**

R Reading Skill

Reviewing Say: Review the section labeled *Build Background.* What examples are listed of groups facing curfews? *(teenagers, soldiers, college students, citizens)* **OL**

Interactive Literary Elements Handbook Have students access the Web site to improve their understanding of author's bias.

Literature Focus Lesson

Author's Bias Appoint a committee of students to scan magazines targeted to teens to find a short persuasive or informative article on a topic of interest to classmates. Then have the committee conduct research in the library or on the Internet to find an article on the same or a similar topic but geared to general readers. Ask the committee to evaluate the articles for persuasive appeals, validity, and bias. Then have the committee hold a panel discussion for the class in which they first summarize the articles and then share their analyses, complete with examples from the articles. Finally, allow the class to ask questions of the panel. **AL**

Indiana English/Language Arts Academic Standards
SE: 8.1.3, 8.2, 8.2.2
TWE: *Differentiated Instruction* 8.2.2, *Literature Focus Lesson* 8.7.11

Teach

EL Language Coach

Semantic Slanting **Ask:** Is the writer describing Katelyn positively or negatively when he uses the word *precocious*? *(Possible response: The word has a positive connotation, so the writer is putting Katelyn in a positive light.)* AL

E1 Text Element

Author's Bias **Ask:** What factual information has the author *not* included among these facts about the ordinance? *(Possible responses: the reason it was passed, why the city council thought it was a good idea)* AL

E2 Text Element

Author's Bias **Ask:** Why do you think the author does not give his opinion about the curfew? *(Possible responses: He wants to be fair to both sides; his focus is on Katelyn's fight against the curfew rather than on whether curfews are legal or effective; he is reporting rather than writing an opinion piece.)* OL

Readability Scores
Dale-Chall: 7.9
DRP: 66
Lexile: 1290

READING WORKSHOP 3

TIME

Teen CURFEWS

Are teens unfairly targeted?

By J. TODD FOSTER

"Parents should bring up their kids," says Katelyn Kimmons, "not the establishment. I was brought up to stand up for myself."

When Katelyn Kimmons was 6 years old, the precocious youngster[1] announced to her family that she was "The Woman in Black" and that from then on she planned to wear nothing but black. Later, in high school, she aced chemistry but failed physical education for refusing to wear the required white socks. EL

With strong **convictions** like these, Katelyn surprised no one when, at 16, she took her city to court—and brought a **controversial** youth curfew program to a grinding halt for more than a year.

Katelyn was a junior at George Washington High School in Charleston, West Virginia, when the city council passed the Youth Protection Ordinance[2] in December 1997. The ordinance stated that individuals under 18 could not be in public places after 10 p.m. on weekdays or after midnight on weekends. Officially, there were exceptions, such as for emergencies and after-school jobs—but police officers could stop anyone they thought might be **violating** the ordinance. 1 E1

1 Key Reading Skill

Reviewing Review what you have read so far. Take notes on your graphic organizer.

Katelyn and classmates Anna Sale, then 18, and Lealah Pollock, then 15, agreed that the curfew violated their constitutional rights. With assistance from the West Virginia American Civil Liberties Union (ACLU), in March 1998 they

1. A ***precocious youngster*** is a child who acts like an adult.
2. An ***ordinance*** is a law.

Vocabulary

convictions (kun VIK shunz) *n.* strong beliefs or values

controversial (kon truh VUR shul) *adj.* causing disagreement

violating (VY uh lay ting) *v.* breaking or disregarding a law or rule

Additional Support

English Language Coach

Idiomatic Expressions This article includes a number of idiomatic expressions that may be new to some students. Invite pairs of students to use the SE, English dictionaries, bilingual dictionaries, or the Internet to familiarize themselves with these terms:

- She *aced* chemistry.
- It brought the program *to a grinding halt.*
- The girls *stood their ground.*

The word *curfew* has an interesting story behind it. Have students continue their research by looking up the history of this word. EL BL filed a lawsuit to overturn the city ordinance, claiming it **discriminates** against teenagers because of their age. "Kids are being unfairly targeted, scapegoated,"[3] says Lealah. "If someone commits a crime, then arrest them for that." 2

As the protest got under way, it churned up controversy in Charleston. Anna's parents got calls from friends and neighbors who complained about how much money the city was spending to defend itself against Anna's lawsuit. And many believed the curfew was necessary and important to make Charleston a better place by curbing delinquent behavior by juveniles.[4] "Parents tell me they can use this law to get their kids to come in at night," says Frederick Snuffer, the city council member who introduced the ordinance. R

However, Katelyn, Anna, and Lealah stood their ground, and the city of Charleston decided to put the curfew on hold until a judge could rule on it. On July 15, 1998, the three teenagers walked past a crowd of reporters, supporters, and protesters to testify before the county circuit court about their lawsuit and the discriminatory effect of the city curfew ordinance. Mike Carey, a lawyer on the opposing side, grilled each of them for several minutes. "I was fired up and excited," recalls Katelyn. "It bothers me when people in authority positions treat me as if I'm not worth as much because I'm younger." EL

But Katelyn's enthusiasm was short-lived: Less than a year later, the court ruled against the girls and upheld the curfew law. Since then, more than 50 Charleston kids have been arrested or were issued warnings and sent home to their parents. "Why does the city have the right to overrule parents?" asks Lealah.

The girls appealed to the West Virginia Supreme Court of Appeals. In July 2000, the West Virginia Supreme Court voted 4–1 to uphold the law.

"This [perspective] bothers me," Anna says. "There's this thinking that kids are predators,[5] that we are to be feared. Of course, I want to cure society's ills, but not by creating a law that says if you're under 18, then we don't trust you." 3 4

—Updated 2005, from *Teen People*, February 2004

3. To be ***scapegoated*** is to be blamed for what someone else has done.
4. ***Curbing delinquent behavior by juveniles*** means "limiting illegal behavior by teenagers." To ***curb*** is to hold back or control. ***Delinquent,*** as an adjective, refers to breaking the law or not following the rules. ***Juveniles,*** in its general meaning, refers to all children and young people. Most states define *juveniles* as being people under 18, but the age varies from state to state.
5. Among animals, a ***predator*** is one that kills and eats other animals. Among humans, a *predator* gets what he or she wants by stealing from or harming others.

2 English Language Coach

Semantic Slanting The word **discriminates** (*dis KRIM uh nayts*) means "shows preference for." It is often used to highlight unfair treatment and has a negative connotation.

3 Key Text Element

Author's Bias This article is from *Teen People,* a magazine whose audience is primarily teenagers. Do you think the writer had a special interest in putting one side of the story in a more positive light than the other? Explain.

4 BIG Question

What would Katelyn and her friends say is worth fighting for? Write your answer on your Foldable. Your response will help you complete the Unit Challenge later. BQ

Reading in the Real World

Citizenship The American Civil Liberties Union, founded in 1920, supports numerous legal cases that it believes support the rights granted Americans by the Bill of Rights (the first ten amendments to the Constitution), the post-Civil War amendments (the 13th, 14th, and 15th), and the amendment giving women the right to vote (the 19th). The ACLU's stances are sometimes controversial. Invite students to conduct an Internet search to find other examples of young people claiming civil rights violations. Ask students to evaluate whether these causes are worth fighting for or not. AL

Teach

R Reading Skill

Reviewing Say: Review the first full paragraph on this page to find reasons some residents support the ordinance. *(It limits teenage misbehavior; it helps parents control kids.)* OL

EL Language Coach

Semantic Slanting Ask: What does the word *grilled* mean here? *(questioned)* **Ask:** Why is this an example of semantic slanting? *(Possible response: The word* grilled *has a negative connotation and makes readers feel sympathy for the girls rather than for the lawyer on the opposing side.)* OL

BQ BIG Question

Ask: After what you've read about Katelyn, do you think she would have fought against the curfew even if she'd known she wouldn't win? Why or why not? *(Responses will vary.)* OL AL

Assess

CheckPoint

Use the CheckPoint questions provided on Presentation Plus! to check for comprehension of the selection. These questions can be used with interactive response keypads for immediate student feedback.

Indiana English/Language Arts Academic Standards

SE: 8.1.3, 8.2, 8.2.2

TWE: *English Language Coach* 8.1.1, *Reading in the Real World* 8.4

Assess

Resources for page 990

- Selection Quick Check, p. 66
- Selection and Unit Assessment, p. 78
- ExamView Assessment Suite
- Interactive Tutor: Self-Assessment

Students can respond to the *After You Read* items in their Learner's Notebooks or on a separate sheet of paper.

Answering the

1. Possible response: I would fight a teen curfew because I feel such curfews unfairly target one group.
2. She refused to wear white socks.
3. It violated their rights and unfairly discriminated against them.

Critical Thinking

4. Possible response: He describes an interesting, unusual young person.
5. Possible response: Parents, not the city, should set rules for their children.
6. Responses will vary. Some students will say all residents can fight for what they believe in. Others may say teenagers are too young to challenge the system or that residents shouldn't have to pay the costs of frivolous lawsuits involved in defending a city's laws.

After You Read

Teen Curfews

Tony Pearce

Answering the BIG Question

1. Would you fight a curfew for teens in your community? Why or why not?
2. **Recall** What made Katelyn stand out as an individual during her high school physical education class?
   TIP Right There
3. **Summarize** Sum up the teens' argument against the curfew.
   TIP Think and Search

Critical Thinking

4. **Analyze** What does the author do to capture readers' attention at the beginning of the selection?
   TIP Author and Me
5. **Interpret** What does Lealah mean when she says that the city shouldn't have the right to "overrule" parents?
   TIP Author and Me
6. **Evaluate** Do you think teenagers should have the right to sue their city if they disagree with its laws? Explain.
   TIP On My Own

Write About Your Reading

Letter to the Editor With a small group of classmates, discuss the possible pros and cons of the teen curfew law described in the selection. Take notes on what group members have to say. Decide where you stand on the issue of teen curfews–either for or against. Then, on your own, write a "letter to the editor" trying to persuade readers to agree with your position. Imagine that you're writing to the editor of your community newspaper and that your audience is grownups, not kids.

Indiana English/Language Arts Academic Standards (pp. 990–991)

8.2 Comprehension and Analysis (Focus on Informational Text) Understand grade-level-appropriate material. Develop [reading] strategies... **8.5.7** Write for different purposes and to a specific audience or person... **8.2.2** Analyze text that uses proposition (statement of argument) and support patterns. **8.6 English Language Conventions**

For a complete description of the standards, see p. IN 11.

Write About Your Reading

Possible response:

To the Editor:

I am writing to oppose the new curfew on teenagers. The surest way to make the streets safe at night would be to prevent anyone from being out after 10 P.M. However, the law doesn't try to do that because it is obviously impossible. Hospitals are open around the clock, and so are other businesses and places of entertainment. Yes, people, including teenagers, commit crimes after 10 P.M., and when they do, they should be arrested. It is simply not fair to create a law that targets one group of people.

Yours truly,

Marta Gonzalez

Skills Review

Key Reading Skill: Reviewing

7. Using your notes, summarize the article in a paragraph. Then review the selection to make sure you included all the important information.

Key Text Element: Author's Bias

8. The author tries to give a balanced view by including the opinions of people who disagree with Katelyn, Anna, and Lealah. What "opponent" of theirs does the author quote? What is this person's opinion?

Vocabulary Check

Answer *true* or *false* to the following statements.

9. A person with **convictions** doesn't know what he or she values.
10. A **controversial** topic causes people to disagree.
11. **Violating** the law could land you in jail.
12. **English Language Coach** The teens in the selection are sometimes guilty of semantic slanting. Scan the article and reread the parts that directly quote the teens. Find at least two examples of semantic slanting in the quotations. Write the examples on a chart like the one pictured. Then complete the chart by filling in the blanks.

Word or Phrase	Denotation (Meaning)	Connotation (Associations)

Web Activities For eFlashcards, Selection Quick Checks, and other Web activities, go to www.glencoe.com.

Grammar Link: More Quotation Marks

Put quotation marks around both parts of a split quotation. A **split quotation** occurs when an explanatory phrase divides a quotation.

- "Today," explained Mei, "is a busy day for me."

(The explanatory phrase "explained Mei" splits the quotation "Today is a busy day for me.")

If a quotation ends with a period, the period *always* goes *inside* the quotation marks. If a quotation ends with a question mark or an exclamation point, the end mark goes *inside* the quotation marks.

- Mei whined, "The bus broke down."
- Wanda said, "Couldn't you call?"
- Mei said, "I did call!"

If a quotation appears within a question or exclamation, the question mark or exclamation point goes *outside* the quotation marks.

- Are you sure that Mei said, "Meet me at 3 p.m."?

Also put quotation marks around the titles of short works, such as poems, stories, and articles. (The titles of longer works, such as plays and novels, are italicized. If the writer does not have access to italics, underlining is used instead.)

- Read the poem "One Day" in *Ten Poems.*

(The poem title is in quotation marks; the title of the book in which the poem appears is italicized.)

Grammar Practice

Put quotation marks where needed in each sentence.

13. I wonder, Lil said, if the ice has begun to melt.
14. Joe screamed, The ice is too thin for skating!
15. Did you read the article Teen Curfews?

Skills Review

Key Reading Skill: Reviewing

7. Possible response: Three young people in Charleston, West Virginia, believed a new youth curfew discriminated against teens. With the help of the ACLU, they sued the city. The city and some residents claimed the ordinance reduced youth crime and helped parents control their children. Although the first court and the West Virginia Supreme Court upheld the ordinance, the girls are still convinced they were right.

Key Text Element: Author's Bias

8. The author quotes city council member Frederick Snuffer, who believes the ordinance helps parents.

Vocabulary Check

9. false 10. true 11. true

English Language Coach

12. Check students' charts.

Close

Discuss with students whether it matters when those who fight for something lose their fight and how this consideration affects students' thoughts about the Big Question.

Grammar Link: More Quotation Marks

Grammar Practice

13. "I wonder," Lil said, "if the ice has begun to melt."
14. Joe screamed, "The ice is too thin for skating!"
15. Did you read the article "Teen Curfews"?

Web Activities Have students access the Web site for interactive activities that will help them assess their understanding of the selection.

Indiana English/Language Arts Academic Standards
SE: 8.2, 8.2.2, 8.5.7, 8.6

Focus

BELLRINGER Options

Daily Language Practice Transparency 68

Focus Activity Say: You've been reading examples of persuasive writing by professional authors—now it's your turn. You're going to take that draft you worked on earlier and make it shine. OL

Teach

W Writing

Revising Say: Remember: Nothing in your draft is cast in stone. You can change anything. You can cut out some sentences or paragraphs, and you can add new ones. Writing is a form of thinking. While you're looking at the body of your essay, for example, you may think of another good reason. Feel free to add a new paragraph! OL

Resources for page 992

- Use the Writing Workshop Graphic Organizer BLM in the Unit 7 Resource Booklet pp. 28-29.
- Use the Grammar and Writing Workshop Transparencies 29-30.

WRITING WORKSHOP PART 2

Persuasive Essay

Revising, Editing, and Presenting

ASSIGNMENT Write a persuasive essay

Purpose: To make a case for something you think is worth fighting for

Audience: Your teacher, your classmates, and other people in your community

Revising Rubric

Your revised essay should have these elements:

- a clear position statement
- a well-developed introduction, body, and conclusion
- clear reasons and supporting details and examples
- strong sentence fluency
- correct punctuation (including use of apostrophes), grammar, and spelling

Indiana English/Language Arts Academic Standards (pp. 992–997)

8.5.4 Write persuasive compositions that present...reasoning to support effective arguments and emotional appeals. **8.4 Processes and Features** Drafting, editing, and revising. **8.4.10** Create an organizational structure... **8.5.6** Write using precise word choices to make writing interesting and exact.

For a complete description of the standards, see p. IN 11.

In Writing Workshop Part 1, you developed your ideas and an early draft of your essay. Now it's time to head back to the workshop to finish your essay.

Revising

Make It Better

W Revising is an important step in the writing process. It's when you figure out how to make your draft better. You may spend more time revising than you did writing the first draft. That's normal! Your goal is to make your writing as clear and strong as you can.

Use the following checklist to revise your first draft. For every question you answer "No," revise until you can answer "Yes."

Revising Checklist

Yes	No	
		Introduction
❑	❑	**1.** Is the introduction at least one paragraph long?
❑	❑	**2.** Does it begin with an attention-grabber and end with a clear position statement?
		Body
❑	❑	**3.** Are there at least two paragraphs?
❑	❑	**4.** Does each paragraph clearly state a supporting reason and details?
❑	❑	**5.** Are the reasons and details likely to convince your readers?
		Conclusion
❑	❑	**6.** Is the conclusion at least one paragraph long?
❑	❑	**7.** Does the conclusion sum up main ideas?
❑	❑	**8.** Did you remember to include a call to action if you want readers to take action?

Additional Support

Differentiated Instruction

Reviewing Some students may benefit from applying the reading skill of reviewing to their own writing. Have them create a graphic organizer like the one on page 979. Students should take notes on the body paragraphs of their drafts and find the main point and supporting details. This may help them evaluate the content and the organization of their essays.

You've checked to make sure the organization of your essay is clear and all of the important details are in place. Now revise your essay to strengthen the language. Make changes like these:

- reorder the paragraphs to make the essay easier to follow
- add transitions such as *even though, in addition,* and *however* between sentences and paragraphs
- avoid repetition by deleting unneeded words or sentences
- substitute lively, precise words for dull, unclear ones

W1

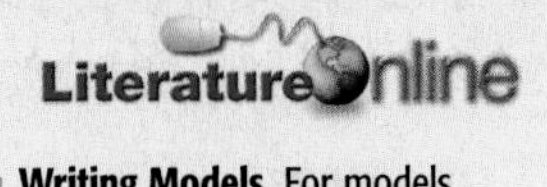

Writing Models For models and other writing activities, go to www.glencoe.com.

Editing

Finish It Up

Don't let mistakes take away from the persuasive power of your essay. Before you make your final copy, read your essay one sentence at a time and use the **Editing Checklist** to help you spot errors. Use the proofreading symbols on the inside back cover of this book to mark needed corrections.

Editing Checklist

- ❑ Sentences are complete. There are no fragments or run-ons.
- ❑ All words are correctly used.
- ❑ Spelling and capitalization are correct.
- ❑ Apostrophes and other punctuation are used correctly.

Many of us take too many things for granted, ~~Our~~ : our right to drive a big car that uses a lot of gas and our right to use as much water and power as we want. We think we don't have to be responsible for what we do. Soon we will have no clean air to ~~breath~~ breathe, no clean water to drink, and no clean soil to grow our food in.

W2

Writing Tip

Proofread Backwards If you are having trouble proofreading because you are so familiar with your essay, read it backwards, from the last paragraph to the first. That will help you focus on individual words rather than ideas.

Presenting

Show It Off

Once you have made your essay as good as you can, hand it in and share it with your audience. Be sure to keep a copy of your essay in your portfolio. That will help you and your teacher measure your progress.

WRITING WORKSHOP PART 2

Teach

W1 Writing

Editing Emphasize the focus on the big picture during editing. Assure students that of course they can make quick corrections if they spot an error, but their goal now is to make their case more convincing and their language more interesting. OL

W2 Writing

Proofreading Another good writing tip is "Partner Proofing." Have students in pairs make suggestions about how their partner's essays could be improved, explaining each suggested change. The original author should decide whether to accept the suggestions and to make the actual corrections. OL

Literature Online

Writing Models Have students access the Web site for an additional and interactive Writing Workshop-based student model.

English Language Coach

Word Choice Students have spent time in this unit analyzing the connotative power of words. Encourage students to use thesauruses as they edit for word choice, but remind them to consider connotation carefully as they weigh the possibilities. Use these questions as examples:

- What's a positive synonym for *happy—giddy* or *cheerful*? *(cheerful)*
- What's a negative synonym for *loosen up—relax* or *slack off*? *(slack off)*
- What's a positive synonym for *excited—wild* or *enthusiastic*? *(enthusiastic)*
- What's a negative synonym for *end—cut off* or *complete*? *(cut off)* OL

Indiana English/Language Arts Academic Standards

SE: 8.4, 8.4.10, 8.5.4

TWE: *Differentiated Instruction* 8.4.7, *English Language Coach* 8.5.6

Teach

W1 Writing

Fluency Write these sentences on the board and ask students how they could improve fluency by combining them: A cleaner environment is a healthier environment. It is also more pleasant. *(A cleaner environment is healthier and more pleasant.)* **OL**

W2 Writing

Fluency Write this sentence on the board and ask students how they could rewrite it in a different way: You have to do your part if you want a cleaner environment. *(If you want a cleaner environment, you have to do your part.)* **OL**

W3 Writing

Fluency Write these sentences on the board and ask students how they could improve fluency by using a transition: Some of these goals may seem difficult. They are crucial. *(Some of these goals may seem difficult. Nevertheless, they are crucial.)* **OL**

Applying Good Writing Traits

Fluency

You know what it feels like to read something that is choppy. It is confusing *and* boring. You probably also know how pleasant it is when writing moves smoothly from one sentence to the next.

W1

What Is Fluency?

Fluency describes how sentences "flow" in a piece of writing. One way to think about fluency is to think about how the writing *sounds.* Does it sound graceful, almost musical? That's fluency!

W2

Sentences are the main ingredient in fluency. In good writing, sentences have different lengths. They move from one idea to the next. They should be a pleasure to read!

W3

Why Is Fluency Important in My Writing?

Sentences that flow rhythmically interest readers and keep their attention. Choppy sentences can be confusing and distracting.

How Do I Do It?

- **Use different sentence lengths**—combine and divide sentences when needed.
- **Begin sentences in different ways**—try writing a sentence in several different ways before choosing the structure you want to use.
- **Use transitions to connect ideas and sentences**—include words such as *then, after, nevertheless, next* to move the reader smoothly.
- **Avoid too much repetition**—find other ways to emphasize ideas.

Write to Learn Look back at your persuasive essay. Read it aloud to yourself. Do the paragraphs hold together? How do the flow and rhythm sound? Are they choppy? If so, smooth out your writing by revising some of your sentences.

Analyzing Cartoons
When a sentence is fluent, it sounds smooth. How could you change the last sentence in the cartoon to be more fluent?

Additional Support

Reading Fluency

Use Verbal Fluency to Improve Written Fluency Explain to students that sometimes when we read our own work aloud, our eyes see what they expect to see, not necessarily what's on the page. One way around this difficulty is to listen as someone else reads our work—doing so lets us hear it with a fresh ear. Suggest that students in pairs read each other's essays aloud. The listener (the original writer) can take notes on spots that seem choppy or confusing and edit later for a smoother flow. Students can even repeat the exercise with the edited draft. **OL**

Listening, Speaking, and Viewing

Understanding Persuasive Techniques

You see or hear advertisements all the time—on TV or the radio, on Web pages, on billboards, and in magazines and newspapers. These ads were made to persuade you—the viewer or listener—to do something. Usually the ads try to persuade you to buy something, but they may try to make you think a certain way. For example, they may try to get you to vote for someone.

What Are Persuasive Techniques?

Persuasive techniques are the methods advertisers and others use to convince you to agree with their opinions and take the actions they want you to take.

Why Is It Important to Understand Persuasive Techniques?

Some persuasive techniques are based on facts. For example, an ad may list the standard features on a particular model of car. Other persuasive techniques bend the truth. If you can learn to figure out how those less-than-honest persuasive techniques work, you will make better decisions.

How Do I Recognize Them?

The best way to recognize questionable persuasive techniques is to become familiar with them. Here are several common techniques:

- **Appeal to emotions:** The ad tries to get an emotional response from people, such as fear, anger, or happiness, to move the people to do something. LSV1
- **Testimonial:** A famous or important person says that he or she uses a particular product, so viewers and listeners should too—regardless of whether the product is good. LSV2
- **Transfer:** The ad connects the product to ideas that make the audience feel good but that don't necessarily have much to do with the product.
- **Repetition:** The ad repeats an idea or phrase over and over so that it sticks in the viewer's or listener's head.
- **Exaggeration:** The ad overstates a point. LSV3
- **Bandwagon:** The ad talks about how many other people use a product or act a certain way, making the viewer want to be part of the "in crowd."

Activity Bring an ad from a magazine or newspaper to school. With a small group of classmates, analyze each group member's ad. Which persuasive techniques were used?

Analyzing Cartoons
What advice would you give Curtis to help him recognize questionable persuasive techniques?

Reprinted with permission of King Features Syndicate.

Differentiated Instruction

Persuasive Techniques Appoint a committee made up of one student from each group that participated in the activity that analyzed ads. The committee's task is to select the best suggested examples of each type of persuasive technique. If there are some techniques for which no examples were found, it is up to the committee to scout some out. Then have the committee arrange the examples on six posters for display in the classroom, one poster for each technique. Each poster should include the name of the technique in large, dark print. You can use these posters as a teaching tool for students who find these concepts difficult. AL

Teach

LSV1 Persuasive Techniques

Emotional Appeal Ask students for examples of someone in everyday life using an appeal to emotions to persuade someone else. *(Possible response: a parent who says, "If you clean up your room, you'll feel so good about yourself.")* OL

LSV2 Persuasive Techniques

Testimonial Ask students for examples of someone in everyday life using a testimonial to persuade someone else. *(Possible response: a friend who says, "The captain of the football team says Giovanni's Pizza is the best in town.")* OL

LSV3 Persuasive Techniques

Exaggeration Ask students for examples of someone in everyday life using exaggeration to persuade someone else. *(Possible response: a friend saying, "Come with me to the movie—it's supposed to be the best ever.")* OL

Indiana English/Language Arts Academic Standards
SE: 8.4, 8.5.6
TWE: *Reading Fluency* 8.4.9, *Differentiated Instruction* 8.2.2

Teach

W1 Writing

Introduction. Ask: Which sentence states the main idea of the essay? *(the last sentence)* **Ask:** Why didn't the author put that sentence first? *(Possible response: the author wanted to grab readers' attention with a dramatic image)* OL

E1 Text Element

Persuasive Appeals Ask: What kind of persuasive appeal is the author making in the third paragraph? *(appeal to reason with facts)* OL

E2 Text Element

Persuasive Appeals Ask: What kind of persuasive appeal is the author making in the fourth paragraph? *(appeal to ethics, to what is right)* OL

W2 Writing

Supporting Ideas Ask: How does the writer support the idea that we can all consider our own actions? *(with examples)* **Ask:** What is the effect of using a bulleted list instead of building each example into a sentence? *(Possible response: It is more dramatic to read and makes it easier for readers to make mental notes.)* OL

Active Writing Model

Writer's Model

Save Our Planet; Save Ourselves!

The essay begins with an attention-getter and ends with a clear position statement.

Imagine a world without trees, flowers, or animals. It could happen. Every day we pollute the air we breathe, the water we drink, and the ground we grow our food in. Slowly but surely we are ruining this planet. I believe we must take steps to protect the environment, and you should too.

This paragraph gives the first reason that supports the position statement.

Many of us take too many things for granted: our right to drive a big car that uses a lot of gas and our right to use as much water and power as we want. We think we don't have to be responsible for what we do. Soon we will have no clean air to breathe, no clean water to drink, and no healthy soil to grow our food in.

In this paragraph and throughout the essay, the writer gives details to support his point.

E1 We need to start taking better care of the earth because it is a healthier way to live. The environment makes life possible. If we ruin the environment, we are ruining our own bodies. Anything harmful that we put into the earth eventually harms us. When we pollute the ground where we grow our food, the pollution gets into the food. When we eat the food, the pollution gets into our bodies.

The writer uses an emotional appeal to persuade readers to care about the environment.

E2 We should also remember that the world does not belong just to us. It belongs to all people, even those not yet born. We should take care of the planet so that we can pass on a healthful environment to all future generations. Isn't that an important thing to provide for our children and grandchildren? And if we don't, there may not be any future generations.

I believe the environment is the most important thing we have as human beings. If we don't have a healthful environment, we don't have anything, because we need a healthy environment to survive. There is so much that can be done to save our environment. Each of us can consider his or her actions instead of being selfish. We can start by doing simple things like these:

Additional Support

Literature Focus Lesson

Titles Point out to students that a title may just state the topic in a straightforward way or it may seek to catch readers' attention and give a hint of what is to come. **Say:** Turn to p. 923 and evaluate the titles of the selections you have read so far. Which is the most straightforward? *(Possible response: "Teen Curfews")* **Ask:** Which starts out straightforward but adds something intriguing? *("Saving Water: Why Save Something that Covers Two-thirds of the Earth?")* **Ask:** Which is straightforward but startling? *("The Trouble with Television?")* Discuss the effect of the remaining three titles. Finally, ask students what they think of the title of the model essay. OL

Active Writing Model

- Recycling newspapers and glass, aluminum, and plastic containers we don't want anymore instead of just throwing them away in the garbage
- Buying products that are made of recycled materials, like paper towels made from recycled paper
- Using less water by taking shorter showers, turning off the tap while we brush our teeth, and not watering the lawn every day during warm months
- Buying smaller cars that use less gas
- Carpooling or using public transportation instead of driving large vehicles with only one or two passengers
- Turning off lights and appliances when we aren't using them

The writer gives readers specific examples of how they can help.

We can all make better choices in the way we live today to ensure a safe and healthy tomorrow. It's not too late. We can still save our environment. Please join me in doing so.

The conclusion sums up what was said before and ends with a call to action.

Reading in the Real World

Career To emphasize the importance of persuasive writing, have students brainstorm about situations when they might need to use this skill on the job. Start students off with these examples:

- A nurse might write a memo to his supervisor, trying to persuade her to change a procedure.
- A manager might write a proposal that his department should be run differently.
- A saleswoman might write to a potential customer, trying to persuade him to take a look at her product.
- A builder might write to city officials, urging that certain codes be changed. OL

Teach

W1 Writing

Finding Ideas **Say:** Notice that these examples are similar to ones a professional writer used in "Saving Water." Is that okay? *(Possible response: Of course. We should take into account things we have learned from many sources. The author of this essay did not use any direct quotations from "Saving Water.")* OL

W2 Writing

Evaluating Have students in small groups evaluate the model, using the checklist on page 992 and the Big Picture and Little Picture hints on page 993. Then have groups ask the Big Question: Has the author of the model made a persuasive case that this cause is worth fighting for? OL

Assess

Have students take a last look at their drafts, prepare clean copies, and add them to their portfolios.

Indiana English/Language Arts Academic Standards
TWE: *Literature Focus Lesson* 8.3

Clarifying

Teaching Students to Clarify

Why Is It Important?

- Clarifying helps students clear up difficult portions of text.
- Students often need to clarify one idea before they can grasp another idea in a selection.
- When students gain clarifying skills, they become better readers and have more confidence in reading new passages.

How to Help Students Get It

- Tell students to reread sections that are not clear.
- Advise them to stop to clarify ideas before they get too far into a confusing text.
- Encourage students to use dictionaries to look up unfamiliar words and to enter the definitions in their Learner's Notebook so they can review them.
- Emphasize the importance of context clues. What else is being said in the paragraph? Can this information help clarify the confusing part?
- Encourage students to practice several of the other reading strategies they have learned to clarify information. Questioning, responding, connecting, and activating prior knowledge can be particularly helpful when clarifying.

Reading to Answer the Big Question

Rally for Better Food
A flyer and a poster are designed to persuade students to rally to fight for fresher, healthier, better-tasting food in the school cafeteria.

Stop the Sun by Gary Paulsen
Terry Erickson's father is a Vietnam veteran who suffers from post-traumatic stress syndrome. Terry fights to understand his father's fears but realizes that he can never fully comprehend the horror of his experiences. He chooses to accept his father no matter how strangely he behaves.

Workshop Resources

Pacing (Days) Standard	Pacing (Days) Block	Lesson	Student Materials	Teacher Resources
1	1/2	Key Skill Lesson: Clarifying	Key Reading Skills Practice, p. 30 English Language Coach Review, p. 42	Bellringer Options Transparencies – Selection Focus Transparency 15 – Daily Language Practice 69 Read Aloud, Think Aloud Transparencies – Key Reading Skills 3 Presentation Plus!
1	1	"Rally for Better Food"	Glencoe Online Unit Vocabulary Review, p. 40 Academic Vocabulary Review, p. 43 English Language Coach Active Reading Graphic Organizer, p. 32 Literary Analysis, p. 31 StudentWorks Plus™ Online Student Edition Literature Classics Selection and Unit Assessments, p. 79	Literary and Text Analysis Transparencies 18 Puzzlemaker Skill Level Up!™ A Language Arts Game BookLink 3 Assessment by Learning Objective (Diagnostic and Formative) Interactive Tutor: Self-Assessment TeacherWorks Plus™
1		"Stop the Sun"	Glencoe Online Unit Vocabulary Review, p. 40 Academic Vocabulary Review, p. 43 English Language Coach Active Reading Graphic Organizer, p. 34 StudentWorks Plus™ Online Student Edition Literature Classics Selection and Unit Assessments, p. 80	Literary and Text Analysis Transparencies 7 Puzzlemaker Skill Level Up!™ A Language Arts Game BookLink 3 Assessment by Learning Objective (Diagnostic and Formative) Interactive Tutor: Self-Assessment TeacherWorks Plus™

Keys for Unit Resource

- Blackline Master
- Workbook
- Supplemental Text
- CD-ROM
- DVD
- Transparency
- Web-based
- Fast File

Level Appropriate Code

AS = Activities for all students
AL = Activities for students working above grade level
OL = Activities for students working at grade level
BL = Activities for students working below grade level
EL = Activities for English language learners

Focus

BELLRINGER Options

- **Selection Focus Transparency 15**
- **Daily Language Practice Transparency 69**

Focus Activity Say: You're reading directions for putting together a child's swing set when you come across a really confusing sentence. What could you do to help yourself understand what the sentence means? *(Possible response: You could ask a friend or family member if he or she understands the sentence, use a dictionary to look up new words, or call customer service for clarification.)* **OL**

Teach

R Reading Skill

Clarifying Ask: Why is it important to clarify as you read? *(Possible response: It prevents you from getting lost when you come across a confusing word, sentence, idea, or selection.)* **BL**

READING WORKSHOP 4

Skills Focus

You will practice using these skills when you read the following selections:

- "Rally for Better Food," student flyer and poster, p. 1002
- "Stop the Sun," p. 1008

Reading

- Clarifying ideas and text

Informational Text

- Recognizing faulty reasoning
- Identifying the story climax

Vocabulary

- Understanding connotation and denotation
- Academic Vocabulary: *clarify*

Writing/Grammar

- Using dashes and parentheses correctly

Skill Lesson

Clarifying

Learn It!

R **What Is It?** To **clarify** is to make something clear and understandable. To clarify as you read is to clear up confusing or difficult passages. Sometimes a word, a sentence, an idea, or even a whole selection of text can be confusing. When you don't understand something you're reading, you need to clarify what it means so that you don't get "lost."

Analyzing Cartoons
What is clarified for the mother in the cartoon?

Indiana English/Language Arts Academic Standards (pp. 998–999)

8.2 Comprehension and Analysis (Focus on Informational Text) Develop [reading] strategies…

For a complete description of the standards, see p. IN 11.

Academic Vocabulary

clarify (KLAIR uh fy) *v.* make clear

Additional Support

Reading Fluency

Improving Fluency Clarifying can help students build fluency. By taking the time to understand and paraphrase what they're reading, students can become adept at working through difficult texts rather than ceasing to read entirely whenever they come across a hard passage.

Encourage students to build fluency by stopping, clarifying difficult passages (and looking up the pronunciation of difficult words), and then going back and rereading the passages once they better understand their meaning. **EL** **BL**

Why Is It Important? Writers often build ideas on other ideas. If you don't clear up a confusing passage as you're reading, you may not understand main ideas or information that comes later.

How Do I Do It? First, figure out why you find the passage hard to understand. Then apply a strategy that will help you clear up the difficulty. Here are some ideas to get you started.

- **Unfamiliar words:** Find definitions in a dictionary or through context clues. Plug them in and reread the passage.
- **Long, complicated sentences:** Find the main ideas by looking for subjects and verbs. Put the ideas in your own words.
- **Too many unfamiliar concepts:** Find basic information by doing a quick Internet search. Or grab an encyclopedia to find basic information about the concepts.

R

Literature Online

Study Central Visit www.glencoe.com and click on Study Central to review clarifying.

Here's how a student clarified a difficult sentence in "The Trouble with Television" to better understand it.

> Capturing your attention—and holding it—is the prime motive of most television programming and enhances its role as a profitable advertising vehicle.

First, I reread the sentence. Then I looked up the word "vehicle," which refers to both a form of transportation and the means by which something is expressed. I realized that the author meant that television is a means by which advertising is expressed. Finally, I put the sentence in my own words: "Holding people's attention is important to TV programmers because TV makes money by getting people to watch commercials."

Practice It!

Clarify the following sentence from "The Trouble with Television" by putting the sentence in your own words: *"Forced feeding on trivial fare is not itself a trivial matter."*

Use It!

As you read the selections, note parts that need clarifying. Analyze why they are hard to understand; then strategize.

Teach

Study Central Have students access the Web site to review clarifying and to complete a related activity.

R Reading Skill

Clarifying Ask: What three techniques does your book recommend for clarifying difficult text? State them in your own words. *(1. Use a dictionary or context clues to define hard words. 2. Find the main ideas of long, complicated sentences and restate them in your own words. 3. Conduct research to find basic information.)* OL

Resources for page 999

Use Key Reading Skills Transparency 3 in *Read Aloud, Think Aloud* to help students practice clarifying.

Reading in the Real World

College Explain that clarifying is a listening skill, too, one that will be very important in lecture classes. Ask students how those listening to a lecture can clarify what they hear. Elicit ideas such as circling difficult words or concepts, including a question mark or even a brief question in their notes, asking questions if the lecturer provides a Q&A session, reviewing the lecture later with a fellow student, or checking for clarification in a textbook. AL Also point out that clarifying while listening is important in everyday life. Asking questions during conversations can prevent many misunderstandings. OL

Indiana English/Language Arts Academic Standards
SE: 8.2
TWE: *Reading Fluency* 8.2, *Reading in the Real World* 8.7.1

Teach

More about the Constitution

The First Amendment to the Constitution states the following: *Congress shall make no law respecting an establishment of religion, or prohibiting the free exercise thereof; or abridging the freedom of speech, or of the press; or the right of the people peaceably to assemble, and to petition the Government for a redress of grievances.*

EL Language Coach

Semantic Slanting Say: The vocabulary word *bogus* has a negative connotation. Can you think of a word with a similar denotation that seems more neutral? *(Possible responses: unreal, pretend)* **OL** **Ask:** Can you think of a word with a similar denotation but a more positive connotation? *(Possible response:* imaginary) **AL**

Before You Read

Rally for Better Food, student flyer and poster

Did You Know?

Freedom of speech and freedom of assembly are two of the five parts of the First Amendment to the United States Constitution. They are basic rights in a democracy.

- Freedom of speech gives people the right to express themselves freely.
- Freedom of assembly is the freedom to join with or organize any group, club, or organization.

You can see examples of these rights every day in the United States.

Vocabulary Preview

EL **bogus** (BOH gus) *adj.* bad; not real or genuine **(p. 1002)** *The bogus money is worthless, even though it looks real.*

nutritious (noo TRIH shus) *adj.* containing or giving nourishment **(p. 1003)** *The students wanted their cafeteria to serve more nutritious food.*

Write to Learn Write a sentence correctly using each vocabulary word.

English Language Coach

Denotation and Slang Some words have both formal and informal definitions. Take the word *bookmark.* Its formal denotation is "a marker for holding a place in a book." But it also has a slang meaning. If you say to someone that you'll "bookmark" him or her, you're saying you'll save the person's telephone number or email address.

Did you know the slang meaning of *bookmark?* If not, don't feel bad. The slang meaning may no longer be in use. Most slang words go in and out quickly. In fact, one of the points of using slang is to show you're "in"–up to date and in the know.

Writers are aware of slang's power and may use it to their advantage. If a writer wants readers to see him or her as part of their group, the writer might use slang terms the group uses. If a writer has a general audience, however, he or she usually avoids slang so as not to leave anyone out.

Partner Talk With a classmate, find the slang terms in the following ad. Together, identify what age group you think the writer is trying to reach and why.

Are You a Star?

Show them who you are. Be a star. Wear Star shoes.
They come in all of today's styles.
They're all that and a bag o' chips!

Indiana English/Language Arts Academic Standards
(pp. 1000–1003)

8.1.3 Verify the meaning of a word in its context… **8.2 Comprehension and Analysis (Focus on Informational Text)** Develop [reading] strategies… **8.2.2** Analyze text that uses proposition (statement of argument) and support patterns.

For a complete description of the standards, see p. IN 11.

Additional Support

Reading in the Real World

Citizenship Write the First Amendment to the Constitution on the board and have students read it silently. Then ask:

- How could a reader clarify the meaning of the word *abridging? (Use context clues, prior knowledge about our rights, and/or a dictionary.)*
- Is it enough to have the rights guaranteed by this Amendment, or do we need to *know* we have them? Why?
- Do you think the creators of the Constitution would approve or disapprove of modern American protests, marches, and rallies? Why? **OL**

Skills Preview

Key Reading Skill: Clarifying

Skim the student cafeteria flyer and poster to see if there are any words you don't know. List them in your Learner's Notebook. Then try to clarify their meanings by looking for context clues.

Write to Learn Jot down definitions for the words on your list. As you read, see if your definitions make sense.

Key Text Element: Faulty Reasoning

Faulty reasoning is flawed thinking, or thinking that has errors in it. You may find faulty reasoning in any form of persuasion such as commercials and ads, political speeches, and letters to the editor.

Though faulty reasoning may be accidental, advertisers and others may use it on purpose. That's why it's important to recognize errors in thinking. Here are some common examples:

Either/Or Fallacy: saying there are only two choices when there are actually more.

- *Example:* America–love it or leave it.

(Ask yourself, *Is there really no middle ground?*)

Faulty Cause and Effect: believing that because one event came before another, the first event caused the second event to happen

- *Example:* The last two games we won, I wore my favorite ring. That ring must be lucky.

(Ask yourself, *Did the ring actually cause the wins?*)

Bandwagon: thinking something's right because it's popular and "everybody's doing it."

- *Example:* Everybody's voting for Ed! Don't vote for Nancy. You'll just waste your vote.

(Ask yourself, *Is it true that everybody's doing it? And is something right just because it's popular?*)

E

Whole Class Discussion Brainstorm examples of each of the types of faulty reasoning. Are there other types you want to add to your list?

Get Ready to Read

Connect to the Reading

Have you ever felt so strongly about something that you wanted to convince others of your ideas?

Partner Talk Describe the cause of your feelings and any actions you took to persuade others.

Build Background

The student flyer and poster are examples that could have been written by eighth graders who wanted to fight for more healthful and nutritious food in their school cafeteria.

Nutrition has a major impact on your body and your mind. It can affect your health, your growth, and your ability to learn. Studies show that many school-aged children are not getting the nutrients they need. Their diets are high in sugar and fats, which can cause obesity. The number of overweight kids between the ages of six and seventeen has increased greatly in the United States in the last thirty years. This has become a serious issue because being overweight can increase the risk of illness.

Set Purposes for Reading

BIG Question Read the student flyer and poster to learn how some students might urge others to fight for more nutritious food in their school.

Set Your Own Purpose What would you like to learn from the student flyer and poster to help you answer the Big Question? Write your own purpose on the "Rally for Better Food" page of your Foldable 7.

Interactive Literary Elements Handbook
To review or learn more about the literary elements, go to www.glencoe.com.

Keep Moving

Use these skills as you read the following selection.

Teach

E Text Element

Faulty Reasoning Ask: What is faulty reasoning? *(It is thinking that has errors in it.)* **BL**
Ask: What might be a problem with using faulty reasoning in a persuasive essay or ad? *(Possible response: Your readers won't believe anything you say because they'll see that your thinking is flawed.)* **OL**
Ask: Why might someone use faulty reasoning on purpose? *(Possible responses: because they want to convince readers more than they want to tell the truth; because they think their readers won't notice)* **AL**

Interactive Literary Elements Handbook Have students access the Web site to improve their understanding of faulty reasoning.

Literature Focus Lesson

Faulty Reasoning Here are three examples of faulty reasoning. Read them to the class and have students identify which type of faulty reasoning is used in each.

- It rained because I lost my umbrella! *(faulty cause and effect)*
- If you don't join this club, you won't have any fun this year. *(either/or fallacy)*
- You'd better come to the game—everybody who's anybody is going to be there! *(bandwagon)* **OL**

Indiana English/Language Arts Academic Standards
SE: 8.1.3, 8.2, 8.2.2
TWE: *Literature Focus Lesson* 8.2.6

Teach

R Reading Skill

Clarifying **Say:** The flyer might puzzle you if you don't know what the word *boycott* means. Use the context to try to clarify the word. Does it likely mean something negative like "protest" or something positive like "enjoy"? *(something negative like "protest")* **Ask:** What does the word *boycott* mean? *(to protest by refusing to interact with)* OL

E Text Element

Review Persuasive Appeals **Ask:** Are the three "reasons to attend" appeals to emotion, ethics, or logic? Explain. *(They are appeals to emotion. They appeal to students' fear of suffering and desire to be happy and fit in.)* OL

FRIENDS DON'T LET FRIENDS EAT THE CAFETERIA FOOD!

We demand fresher, healthier, and better-tasting food! Come to a rally after school on March 15, 2006, outside the cafeteria to boycott the BOGUS grub we are being served! R

Reasons to attend:

- Either you protest NOW, or you suffer for the rest of your school days! 1
- Being healthy will make you happy, popular, and successful! E
- EVERYONE will be there! 2

REMEMBER, YOU ARE WHAT YOU EAT!

Practice the Skills

1 Key Text Element

Faulty Reasoning This is an example of "either/or thinking." Students want to persuade others to join the rally by claiming there are only two choices—joining the rally or suffering. Aren't there other courses of action? Explain your answer.

2 Key Text Element

Faulty Reasoning The writer of this flyer is trying to persuade others to join the rally by claiming, "Everyone will be there!" What type of faulty reasoning is this?

Vocabulary

bogus (BOH gus) *adj.* bad; not real or genuine

Additional Support

Literature Focus Lesson

Advertising Slogans The heading of this flyer is a variation of a well-known slogan: "Friends don't let friends drive drunk." Explain to students that a slogan is a short, memorable advertising statement, such as "Just Do It," or a highly condensed persuasive message, such as the Revolutionary-era slogan "One for all, and all for one." Advertisers frequently use slogans in ad campaigns. Have students provide other current examples. OL

FOOD FIGHT [3]

Junk the Junk & Come to a rally for more nutritious food

March 15, 2006
outside the cafeteria after school

NO MORE BOGUS GRUB! [4]

It's your life, and you're the only one who's going to live it! [5]

Practice the Skills

3 Key Reading Skill

R1 **Clarifying** This attention-grabbing phrase has two meanings in this context. Can you explain them both? If the answer is "no," reread the flyer to clarify the meaning.

R2

4 English Language Coach

Denotation and Slang What is the slang meaning of *bogus?* Of *grub?* What audience do these words appeal to?

5 BIG Question

Some of the students are unhappy with the food in their cafeteria. Do you think persuading others to participate in a rally is an effective way to get better food? Write your answer on the "Rally for Better Food" page of Foldable 7. Your response will help you answer the Unit Challenge later.

Vocabulary

nutritious (noo TRIH shus) *adj.* containing or giving nourishment

Differentiated Instruction

Reading Visual Messages If your school has a central bulletin board full of posters and flyers, take the class to see it. Discuss each in terms of these questions:

- Is its message clear and easy to understand?
- Is it strictly informational, or does it try to persuade viewers?
- If it is intended to be persuasive, what kinds of appeals does it make?
- Does it use faulty reasoning?
- Is it visually effective—eye-catching and attractive?
- If there are pictures, do they add to the message? OL

READING WORKSHOP 4

Teach

R1 Reading Skill

Clarifying **Say:** The term "food fight" has two meanings here. What do people normally mean when they refer to a food fight? *(They mean an event where people throw food at each other.)* BL **Ask:** What is going to take place at the rally? *(Students are going to request better food in the cafeteria.)* **Ask:** How is this a type of food fight? *(It is a "fight," or protest, about food.)* OL

R2 Reading Skill

Clarifying **Say:** Poster designers often use visuals to clarify meaning for viewers. How does this picture clarify the word *nutritious*? *(Nutritious foods include fruits and vegetables.)* BL **Ask:** How do viewers know the picture refers to nutritious food and not to junk food? *(Possible response: Junk is negative, and the picture is positive, showing fruits and vegetables in an appetizing way.)* OL

Assess

CheckPoint

Use the CheckPoint questions provided on Presentation Plus! to check for comprehension of the selections. These questions can be used with interactive response keypads for immediate student feedback.

Indiana English/Language Arts Academic Standards

SE: 8.1.3, 8.2, 8.2.2

TWE: *Literature Focus Lesson* 8.2; *Differentiated Instruction* 8.2, 8.7.9

Assess

Resources for page 1004

- Selection Quick Check, p. 67
- Selection and Unit Assessment, p. 79
- ExamView Assessment Suite
- Interactive Tutor: Self-Assessment

Students can respond to the *After You Read* items in their Learner's Notebooks or on a separate sheet of paper.

Answering the BIG Question

1. Possible response: Healthy food makes us feel and look better; therefore, I think it is worth fighting for.
2. Protest or suffer; eat healthy foods to be happy, popular, and successful; join the crowd.
3. Come to the rally and demand better cafeteria food.

Critical Thinking

4. They believe being healthy makes you happy, popular, and successful.
5. Get rid of food that isn't nutritious.
6. Possible response: The author's reasons related to health are strong; however, the author uses faulty reasoning that makes his/her argument weak.

After You Read

Rally for Better Food, student flyer and poster

Answering the BIG Question

1. Do you think fighting for healthier food in the cafeteria is a worthy cause? Why or why not?
2. **Recall** What reasons does the author of the flyer give to try to persuade the students to "protest now"?
   TIP **Right There**
3. **Summarize** In your own words, summarize the message of the student flyer and poster.
   TIP **Think and Search**

Critical Thinking

4. **Analyze** Why is being healthy important to the students who created the flyer?
   TIP **Author and Me**
5. **Interpret** What does "junk the junk" mean? Put it in your own words.
   TIP **Author and Me**
6. **Evaluate** Do you think the author's reasons to rally are strong or weak? Explain your answer.
   TIP **Author and Me**

Write About Your Reading

Persuasive Poster What issue do you feel strongly about? Take a stand and make a persuasive poster. Follow these guidelines:

- Make the issue–and your stand on it–clear.
- Use words and pictures to capture people's attention and make them care about the issue.
- Make every word count. Don't try to squeeze too many words onto your poster. People should be able to read it easily from several feet away.
- Avoid faulty reasoning.
- Avoid semantic slanting.

Indiana English/ Language Arts Academic Standards (pp. 1004–1005)

8.2 Comprehension and Analysis (Focus on Informational Text) Understand grade-level-appropriate material. Develop [reading] strategies... **8.5.7** Write for different purposes and to a specific audience or person... **8.2.2** Analyze text that uses proposition (statement of argument) and support patterns. **8.1.3** Verify the meaning of a word in its context... **8.6 English Language Conventions**

For a complete description of the standards, see p. IN 11.

Write About Your Reading

Possible response:

Don't Be a Litterbug!

→ Keep our classroom clean.
→ Keep our school healthy.
→ Keep our grounds beautiful.
→ Pitch in—for all of us!

Skills Review

Key Reading Skill: Clarifying

7. Clarify the expression "You are what you eat" by putting it in your own words.

Key Text Element: Faulty Reasoning

8. What form of faulty reasoning is used in this sentence: "Being healthy will make you happy, popular, and successful"?

9. What information could have been included in the flyer and poster to avoid faulty reasoning?

Vocabulary Check

Fill in each blank with a vocabulary word from the list.

bogus • nutritious

10. Fruits and vegetables are ______ food.

11. It was easy to tell that the money was ______ because it was printed on the wrong color paper.

12. English Language Coach What are some slang terms you and your friends use? How would you define the words? Make your own slang dictionary by choosing five slang terms and writing definitions for them. Use a chart like the one below.

Slang Word	Part of Speech	Definition

13. Academic Vocabulary Explain three ways that you can **clarify** the meaning of something you read.

Web Activities For eFlashcards, Selection Quick Checks, and other Web activities, go to www.glencoe.com.

Grammar Link: Dashes

A **dash** (–) is used in pairs to set off a long explanatory phrase or sudden break in thought.

- The books I read–*Great Aviators of the United States, What Happened to Amelia Earhart?* and *Famous Women of the 20th Century*–made me feel that Amelia Earhart was truly brave.
- I was confused–I had, after all, missed two days of school–so I asked my teacher for help.

In the first example the explanatory phrase that names the three books is set off with dashes because it is very long.

In the second example the clause *I had, after all, missed two days of school* is set off because it shows a sudden shift in thought.

Grammar Practice

Copy each of the following sentences on a separate sheet of paper. Add dashes wherever they are needed.

14. The rainforest a place I definitely hope to visit someday with my family is home to some amazing animals.

15. Flying frogs they glide through the air rather than fly, incidentally can be found in Africa.

16. There were only 30 seconds left in the game the team was down by one point when Jaquil took a jump shot and saved the day.

17. Your new shoes not the red denim sneakers but the blue leather ones are the most interesting I've ever seen!

Writing Application Look back at the persuasive poster you made. If you used dashes, make sure that you correctly used them. Also look for sentences that might need dashes.

Skills Review

Key Reading Skill: Clarifying

7. Possible responses: Food is what builds our bodies. Good food makes healthy bodies.

Key Text Element: Faulty Reasoning

8. Faulty cause and effect

9. Possible response: facts about why junk food is bad or what makes some foods nutritious

Vocabulary Check

10. nutritious

11. bogus

English Language Coach

12. Slang expressions will vary.

Academic Vocabulary

13. You can define a hard word, reread a sentence and say it in your own words, or conduct research to find out more about a concept.

Close

Ask students whether flyers and posters might be useful in promoting the causes they care about. Why or why not?

Grammar Link: Dashes

Grammar Practice

14. The rainforest–a place I definitely hope to visit someday with my family–is home to some amazing animals.

15. Flying frogs–they glide through the air rather than fly, incidentally–can be found in Africa.

16. There were only 30 seconds left in the game–the team was down by one point–when Jaquil took a jump shot and saved the day.

17. Your new shoes–not the red denim sneakers but the blue leather ones–are the most interesting I've ever seen!

Indiana English/Language Arts Academic Standards
SE: 8.1.3, 8.2, 8.2.2, 8.5.7, 8.6

Teach

More About the Author

Gary Paulsen is a former dog sledder who ran his dogs in the Iditarod race, rode a motorcycle to Alaska, and ate raw turtle eggs as research for a book. In addition to this short story, Paulsen has written *Soldier's Heart*, a novel about the Civil War that tells about the horrors of combat through the eyes of a fifteen-year-old.

EL Language Coach

Connotation and Denotation Students having a hard time completing the chart might need to use a dictionary or thesaurus for help. **Ask:** What do the words *unique* and *carefree* mean? *(Possible response: "one of a kind" and "relaxed")* **Ask:** What are negative words that mean almost the same as *unique* and *carefree*? *(Possible responses for* unique: peculiar, weird, abnormal, exclusive; *Possible responses for* carefree: uncaring, careless, irresponsible, unconcerned*)* EL BL

Before You Read: Stop the Sun

Gary Paulsen

Meet the Author

Gary Paulsen, a young adult novelist, writes survival stories. Paulsen credits his own survival in many ways to books. Never a dedicated student, Paulsen developed a passion for reading at an early age. As a young man he met a librarian, who changed his life. "When she handed me a library card, she handed me the world," he says. See page R5 of the Author Files for more on Paulsen.

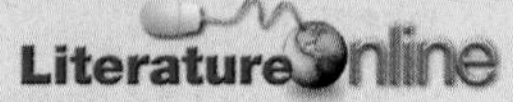

Author Search For more about Gary Paulsen, go to www.glencoe.com.

Indiana English/Language Arts Academic Standards (pp. 1006–1015)

8.1.3 Verify the meaning of a word in its context… **8.2 Comprehension and Analysis (Focus on Informational Text)** Develop [reading] strategies… **8.3.2** Evaluate the structural elements of the plot, such as…climax…

For a complete description of the standards, see p. IN 11.

Vocabulary Preview

syndrome (SIN drohm) *n.* a group of symptoms that point to a certain disease **(p. 1008)** *Terry's father was not the only one to suffer from the terrible effects of Vietnam syndrome.*

dry (dry) *adj.* dull or boring; not interesting **(p. 1009)** *The history books may have made a dry history of the war, but there was nothing boring about it to Terry's father.*

foundered (FOWN durd) *v.* broke down; collapsed; form of the verb *founder* **(p. 1012)** *Terry almost foundered when he saw how much his father did not want to discuss Vietnam.*

inert (in URT) *adj.* without power to move or act; lifeless **(p. 1013)** *The father's hands lay inert on the table as he told the horrible story.*

Write to Learn Create a crossword puzzle using the vocabulary. For clues write fill-in-the-blank sentences. Exchange puzzles with a classmate.

English Language Coach

Connotation and Denotation Denotation is the literal meaning of a word. Its connotations are the thoughts, feelings, and mental pictures that the word brings to mind.

What do you picture when you hear the word *clever?* Does that picture change when you hear the word *sly?* Both words have about the same denotation. Yet the connotations of *clever* and *sly* are very different. *Clever* has positive connotations, and *sly* has negative ones.

EL

On Your Own Copy the chart onto a separate sheet of paper. Then complete it using words with the opposite connotation. The first one has been done for you.

Positive Connotation	Negative Connotation
playful	silly
unique	
carefree	

Additional Support

Author Search To expand students' appreciation of Gary Paulsen, have them access the Web site for additional information and resources.

English Language Coach

Connotation and Denotation Explain that sometimes context determines whether a word has a positive or negative connotation. For example, in the sentence, "The cheerleaders were loud and excited, getting the crowd ready for the game" the word *loud* is positive. However, in the sentence "The loud teenagers caused trouble at the mall," *loud* takes on a negative connotation. Challenge students to write two sentences that use the word *rigid* or *unbending*, once in a way that makes it seem good (positive connotation) and once in a way that makes it seem bad (negative connotation). OL AL

Skills Preview

Key Reading Skill: Clarifying

Before you read the selection, make three columns in your Learner's Notebook, and fill them in as you read:

- one for new vocabulary
- one for phrases or ideas that you don't know
- one for questions you have as you read

Partner Talk With a partner, discuss what you know about the Vietnam War. Using resources like the Internet, find out why the war was fought.

Literary Element: Climax

L The **climax** of a story is the point of highest interest or suspense in the plot. It is the moment at which the central, or most important, conflict comes to a head. Often the climax is the moment when a main character makes an important realization or decision that affects how—or whether—the conflict is resolved. The ending of a story is dependent upon what happens during the climax.

To identify the climax of "Stop the Sun," ask yourself these questions:

- *Who is the most important character in the story?*
- *What conflict is the main character experiencing?*
- *At what point does the character make a decision or have a realization that affects the outcome of the conflict?*

Partner Talk With a partner, review a story you read in another unit of this book. Skim the story to refresh your memory of it. Discuss what you think the climax of the story is and why.

Interactive Literary Elements Handbook
To review or learn more about the literary elements, go to www.glencoe.com.

Get Ready to Read

Connect to the Reading

Have you ever had trouble communicating with a good friend or with a member of your family? How did you feel? Think of several words or phrases to describe that feeling. As you read "Stop the Sun," ask yourself whether Terry shares some of the feelings you had.

Whole Class Discussion As a group, list some of the reasons why family members might have trouble communicating at times.

Build Background

"Stop the Sun" takes place during the 1980s, but Terry's father cannot forget his experiences as a soldier during the Vietnam War.

- From 1965 to 1973, U.S. troops fought in Vietnam alongside the South Vietnamese against Communist North Vietnam.
- Many young Americans protested the war, believing it was a war that the U.S. had no business fighting.
- In 1973 all American troops were pulled out of Vietnam.
- Many soldiers returning from Vietnam suffered from physical or psychological problems as a result of their experiences during the war.

Set Purposes for Reading

BIG Question Read "Stop the Sun" to find out what a teenage boy and his father believe is worth fighting for.

Set Your Own Purpose What would you like to learn from the story to help you answer the Big Question? Write your own purpose on the "Stop the Sun" flap of Foldable 7.

Keep Moving

Use these skills as you read the following selection.

Teach

L Literary Element

Climax **Say:** To identify the climax of a story, you must know what the conflict is. What is the conflict in a story? *(It is the struggle between opposing forces.)* **OL** **Ask:** When does the climax occur? *(It occurs when the character makes an important realization or decision that affects the resolution of the conflict.)* **BL**

Interactive Literary Elements Handbook Have students access the Web site to improve their understanding of climax.

Literature Focus Lesson

Characterization Remind students that a writer can use many techniques to create characters in short stories, including:

- describing the character directly
- telling the character's thoughts and feelings
- telling the character's actions
- telling the character's words (dialogue)
- telling what other characters think of the character

Have students note which techniques the writer uses to develop the characters of Terry and his father. Ask them to tell what else about each character they'd like to know and how the writer could have shared this information. **OL** **AL**

Indiana English/Language Arts Academic Standards
SE: 8.1.3, 8.2, 8.3.2
TWE: *English Language Coach* 8.1.3, *Literature Focus Lesson* 8.3

Teach

R1 Reading Skill

Clarifying **Ask:** What does it mean to be "on the edge" in this context? *(It means "almost"; Terry is close to being a good athlete.)* OL

R2 Reading Skill

Clarifying **Ask:** What have you learned about Terry's father from reading this page? *(He is a Vietnam veteran who suffers from Vietnam syndrome.)* BL **Ask:** What is happening when his father's eyes go away? *(His father is, mentally, somewhere else; he may be thinking about or remembering another time and place.)* OL AL

Readability Scores
Dale-Chall: 4.0
DRP: 48
Lexile: 730

READING WORKSHOP 4

Stop the Sun

by Gary Paulsen

Con Thien Run, 1967. H. Avery Chenowith. Acrylic, 3½ x 2½ ft. United States Marine Corps Art Collection.

Terry Erickson was a tall boy, 13, starting to fill out with muscle but still a little awkward. He was on the edge of being a good athlete, which meant a lot to him. He felt it coming too slowly, though, and that bothered him. R1

But what bothered him even more was when his father's eyes went away.

Usually it happened when it didn't cause any particular trouble. Sometimes during a meal his father's fork would stop halfway to his mouth, just stop, and there would be a long pause while the eyes went away, far away. 1

After several minutes his mother would reach over and take the fork and put it gently down on his plate, and they would go back to eating—or try to go back to eating—normally. R2

They knew what caused it. When it first started, Terry had asked his mother in private what it was, what was causing the strange behavior.

"It's from the war," his mother had said. "The doctors at the veterans' hospital call it the Vietnam **syndrome**."[1]

1. ***Vietnam syndrome*** refers to physical and psychological problems that many Vietnam veterans have because of their experiences in the war. Symptoms of the psychological problems include anger, nervousness, and nightmares.

Vocabulary

syndrome (SIN drohm) *n.* a group of symptoms that point to a certain disease

Practice the Skills

1 Key Reading Skill

Clarifying What happens when the father's eyes "go away"? If you're not sure, read on.

Additional Support

Leveled Reading An adapted version of this selection (3rd grade readability) is available on page 16 of Jamestown Literature: An Adapted Reader for Grade 8.

Differentiated Instruction

Building Background War can take a terrible psychological toll on soldiers. Soldiers returning from war may suffer from Post-Traumatic Stress Disorder (PTSD), called "Soldier's Heart" during the Civil War, "battle fatigue" or "shell shock" during World Wars I and II, and "Vietnam syndrome" during the Vietnam War. Explain to students that, often, the strongest and healthiest soldiers end up suffering from PTSD because they see so much trauma during battle. Today, both psychologists and psychiatrists are included in medical units to help soldiers suffering from PTSD. Have students find out what psychologists and psychiatrists do and how they can help soldiers recover. OL

"Will it go away?"

"They don't know. Sometimes it goes away. Sometimes it doesn't. They are trying to help him."

"But what happened? What actually caused it?" **2**

"I told you. Vietnam."

"But there had to be something," Terry persisted. "Something made him like that. Not just Vietnam. Billy's father was there, and he doesn't act that way." **R1**

"That's enough questions," his mother said sternly. "He doesn't talk about it, and I don't ask. Neither will you. Do you understand?"

"But, Mom."

"That's enough."

And he stopped pushing it. But it bothered him whenever it happened. When something bothered him, he liked to stay with it until he understood it, and he understood no part of this.

Words. His father had trouble, and they gave him words like Vietnam syndrome. He knew almost nothing of the war, and when he tried to find out about it, he kept hitting walls. Once he went to the school library and asked for anything they might have that could help him understand the war and how it affected his father. They gave him a **dry** history that described French involvement, Communist involvement, American involvement. But it told him nothing of the war. It was all numbers, cold numbers, and nothing of what had *happened.* There just didn't seem to be anything that could help him. **3** **R2**

Another time he stayed after class and tried to talk to Mr. Carlson, who taught history. But some part of Terry was embarrassed. He didn't want to say why he wanted to know about Vietnam, so he couldn't be specific.

"What do you want to know about Vietnam, Terry?" Mr. Carlson had asked. "It was a big war."

Terry had looked at him, and something had started up in his mind, but he didn't let it out. He shrugged. "I just want to know what it was like. I know somebody who was in it."

"A friend?"

"Yessir. A good friend."

Vocabulary

dry (drī) *adj.* dull or boring; not interesting

Practice the Skills

2 Reviewing Skills

Predicting Do you think Terry's father's episodes will "go away" or get worse as the story progresses? Why?

3 Key Reading Skill

Clarifying Reread this paragraph to understand what kind of information Terry finds when he tries to research the effects of the war on veterans. Are there terms that you are unfamiliar with? Write them in your Learner's Notebook.

READING WORKSHOP 4

Teach

R1 Reading Skill

Clarifying Ask: What does this opening scene tell you about Terry? *(Possible response: He wants to understand what is going on around him, but he doesn't understand his father.)* **OL**

R2 Reading Skill

Clarifying Ask: What does Terry mean when he says he keeps "hitting walls" when he tries to find out what is wrong with his father? Give examples. *(He means he can't get any information. Dry history books don't explain his father's condition, and good books recommended by his teacher give some information but still don't help Terry understand his father.)* **OL**

L Literary Element

Review Conflict Ask: Is the conflict in this story an external one between Terry and his father or an internal one within Terry? Explain. *(Possible response: The conflict is internal. Terry seems to love and get along with his father, but the fact that he can't understand his father bothers him a lot.)* **OL**

Reading in the Real World

Career Explain that combat photographers first appeared during the Civil War. Before that, artists sketched scenes on site. War photographers are often in as much danger as the troops doing the fighting. Suggest that students research combat photography and learn more about those who do this work. Some students may prefer to do a review of combat photography over the years. Others may prefer to focus on a single conflict, such as World War II or the Iraq War. Have students share what they learn in either an oral or a written report that includes photographs. **OL**

Indiana English/Language Arts Academic Standards
SE: 8.2
TWE: *Differentiated Instruction* 8.4; *Reading in the Real World* 8.5.3, 8.7.12

Teach

L Literary Element

Climax **Ask:** What clues does the writer give that suggest the event at the shopping mall is important to the story? *(Terry says that something happened at the shopping mall that changed his life; he says it is "the most embarrassing thing that ever happened to him.")* OL

EL Language Coach

Denotation and Connotation
Say: Sometimes an author sets the mood of a scene by using words with a particular connotation. What words and phrases does Paulsen use in this scene to give a feeling of uneasiness? *(commotion, something wrong, suspicious, nervous laughs, made no sense)* OL AL

READING WORKSHOP 4

Mr. Carlson had studied him, looking into his eyes, but didn't ask any other questions. Instead he mentioned a couple of books Terry had not seen. They turned out to be pretty good. They told about how it felt to be in combat. Still, he couldn't make his father be one of the men he read about.

War & Peace, 1990. Tsing-Fang Chen. Acrylic on canvas, 66 x 96 in. Lucia Gallery, New York.

Analyzing the Painting How does the artist depict opposing ideas—war and peace—in this painting?

And it may have gone on and on like that, with Terry never really knowing any more about it except that his father's eyes started going away more and more often. It might have just gone the rest of his life that way except for the shopping mall. L

It was easily the most embarrassing thing that ever happened to him.

It started as a normal shopping trip. His father had to go to the hardware store, and he asked Terry to go along.

When they got to the mall they split up. His father went to the hardware store, Terry to a record store to look at albums.

Terry browsed so long that he was late meeting his father at the mall's front door. But his father wasn't there, and Terry looked out to the car to make sure it was still in the parking lot. It was, and he supposed his father had just gotten busy, so he waited.

Still his father didn't come, and he was about to go to the hardware store to find him when he noticed the commotion. Or not a commotion so much as a sudden movement of people. 4

Later, he thought of it and couldn't remember when the feeling first came to him that there was something wrong. The people were moving toward the hardware store and that might have been what made Terry suspicious.

There was a crowd blocking the entry to the store, and he couldn't see what they were looking at. Some of them were laughing small, nervous laughs that made no sense. EL

Terry squeezed through the crowd until he got near the front. At first he saw nothing unusual. There were still some

Practice the Skills

4 Reviewing Skills

Predicting What do you think the commotion is? Give reasons for your prediction.

Additional Support

Differentiated Instruction

The Vietnam Veterans Memorial
Have students interested in art conduct research on the Vietnam Veterans Memorial in Washington, DC, which includes the wall designed by Maya Ying Lin; *Three Servicemen*, a sculpture by Frederick Hart; and the Vietnam Women's Memorial. Ask students to show the pictures to the class and comment on the message of each. OL

people in front of him, so he pushed a crack between them. Then he saw it: His father was squirming along the floor on his stomach. He was crying, looking terrified, his breath coming in short, hot pants like some kind of hurt animal.

It burned into Terry's mind, the picture of his father down on the floor. It burned in and in, and he wanted to walk away, but something made his feet move forward. He knelt next to his father and helped the owner of the store get him up on his feet. His father didn't speak at all but continued to make little whimpering sounds, and they led him back into the owner's office and put him in a chair. Then Terry called his mother and she came in a taxi to take them home. Waiting, Terry sat in a chair next to his father, looking at the floor, wanting only for the earth to open and let him drop in a deep hole. He wanted to disappear. **5**

Words. They gave him words like Vietnam syndrome, and his father was crawling through a hardware store on his stomach. **6**

When the embarrassment became so bad that he would cross the street when he saw his father coming, when it ate into him as he went to sleep, Terry realized he had to do something. He had to know this thing, had to understand what was wrong with his father. **R**

When it came, it was simple enough at the start. It had taken some courage, more than Terry thought he could find. His father was sitting in the kitchen at the table and his mother had gone shopping. Terry wanted it that way; he wanted his father alone. His mother seemed to try to protect him, as if his father could break.

Terry got a soda out of the refrigerator and popped it open. As an afterthought, he handed it to his father and got another for himself. Then he sat at the table.

His father smiled. "You look serious."

"Well . . ."

It went nowhere for a moment, and Terry was just about to drop it altogether. It may be the wrong time, he thought, but there might never be a better one. He tightened his back, took a sip of pop. **L**

"I was wondering if we could talk about something, Dad," Terry said.

Practice the Skills

5 Literary Element

Climax The incident in the hardware store intensifies Terry's need to understand his father. This is the rising action leading to the climax.

6 English Language Coach

Connotation and Denotation An older term that means about the same as "Vietnam syndrome" is *shell shock*. Which of the two terms sounds more negative? Why?

Differentiated Instruction

The Music of War Have students interested in music seek out examples of martial music. Students might begin with military marches like those of John Philip Sousa and the anthems of the various branches of the armed services—the U.S. Marine Corps hymn "From the Halls of Montezuma" and the U.S. Air Force anthem "Into the Wild Blue Yonder," for example. Other students might scout out songs sung as protests during the Vietnam War, such as Pete Seeger's "Where Have All the Flowers Gone?" OL

Teach

R Reading Skill

Clarifying **Ask:** What does "ate into him" mean here? *(bothered him, filled his mind)* **Say:** Terry says two things started to happen to make him realize he had to do something. What are those two things? *(His embarrassment got so bad that he crossed the street to avoid his father, and the issue kept him awake at night.)* OL

L Literary Element

Climax **Say:** Notice that Terry senses a climax is coming. He has the choice of dropping his questions or continuing. What sentence tells you his choice even before he speaks? *("He tightened his back . . .")* OL

Indiana English/Language Arts Academic Standards

SE: 8.1.3, 8.2, 8.3.2

TWE: *Differentiated Instruction* 8.4

Teach

C Critical Thinking

Evaluation Ask: Do you think Terry does the right thing when he talks to his father about Vietnam? *(Responses will vary. Some may agree with Terry's mother that the subject is too painful for his father to discuss; others may agree with Terry that he needs to understand his father's pain so that he can have a good relationship with him.)* **OL**

R Reading Skill

Review Predicting Say: After Terry asks about Vietnam, he realizes he has "caused his [father's] eyes to go away." At this point in the story, how do you predict their conversation will end? *(Responses will vary. Students might believe the trauma Terry's father has suffered is too severe to allow for a happy ending. Some may think Terry's relationship with his father will improve.)* **OL**

His father shrugged. "We already did the bit about girls. Some time ago, as I remember it."

"No. Not that." It was a standing joke[2] between them. When his father finally got around to explaining things to him, they'd already covered it in school. "It's something else."

"Something pretty heavy, judging by your face."

"Yes."

"Well?"

I still can't do it, Terry thought. Things are bad, but maybe not as bad as they could get. I can still drop this thing.

"Vietnam," Terry blurted out. And he thought, there, it's out. It's out and gone.

"No!" his father said sharply. It was as if he had been struck a blow. A body blow. **C**

"But, Dad."

"No. That's another part of my life. A bad part. A rotten part. It was before I met your mother, long before you. It has nothing to do with this family, nothing. No."

So, Terry thought, so I tried. But it wasn't over yet. It wasn't started yet.

"It just seems to bother you so much," Terry said, "and I thought if I could help or maybe understand it better. . . ." His words ran until he **foundered**, until he could say no more. He looked at the table, then out the window. It was all wrong to bring it up, he thought. I blew it. I blew it all up. "I'm sorry." **7**

But now his father didn't hear him. Now his father's eyes were gone again, and a shaft of something horrible went through Terry's heart as he thought he had done this thing to his father, caused his eyes to go away. **R**

"You can't know," his father said after a time. "You can't know this thing."

Terry said nothing. He felt he had said too much.

"This thing that you want to know—there is so much of it that you cannot know it all, and to know only a part is . . . is too awful. I can't tell you. I can't tell anybody what it was really like."

2. A ***standing joke*** is one that continues to be told or shared over time.

Vocabulary

foundered (FOWN durd) *v.* broke down; collapsed

Practice the Skills

7 Key Reading Skill

Clarifying When Terry "foundered," what did he do? Clarify what he did and why by putting it in your own words.

Additional Support

Reading in the Real World

Citizenship The story does not say whether Terry's father enlisted or was drafted. Some protests against the Vietnam War had to do with the fact that so many young men were drafted to serve in it. After that war, the U.S. military became fully professional, depending on voluntary enlistment into all branches of the armed services. The military conducts advertising campaigns, operates recruiting centers, and sends representatives to high schools and colleges to talk about military service. Have students obtain some of these recruiting materials and analyze them. What does the modern military offer to recruits? What does it expect in return? **OL**

It was more than he'd ever said about Vietnam, and his voice was breaking. Terry hated himself and felt he would hate himself until he was an old man. In one second he had caused such ruin. And all because he had been embarrassed. **R** What difference did it make? Now he had done this, and he wanted to hide, to leave. But he sat, waiting, knowing that it wasn't done.

His father looked to him, through him, somewhere into and out of Terry. He wasn't in the kitchen anymore. He wasn't in the house. He was back in the green places, back in the hot places, the wet-hot places. **8**

"You think that because I act strange, that we can talk and it will be all right," his father said. "That we can talk and it will just go away. That's what you think, isn't it?"

Terry started to shake his head, but he knew it wasn't expected.

"That's what the shrinks say," his father continued. "The psychiatrists tell me that if I talk about it, the whole thing will go away. But they don't know. They weren't there. You weren't there. Nobody was there but me and some other dead people, and they can't talk because they couldn't stop the morning."

Terry pushed his soda can back and forth, looking down, frightened at what was happening. *The other dead people,* he'd said, as if he were dead as well. *Couldn't stop the morning.*

"I don't understand, Dad."

"No. You don't." His voice hardened, then softened again, and broke at the edges. "But see, see how it was. . . ." He trailed off, and Terry thought he was done. His father looked back down to the table, at the can of soda he hadn't touched, at the tablecloth, at his hands, which were folded, **inert** on the table.

"We were crossing a rice paddy in the dark," he said, and suddenly his voice flowed like a river breaking loose. "We

Practice the Skills

8 Key Reading Skill

Clarifying Where are the green places? How can you tell?

Analyzing the Image Here, farmers harvest rice in a Vietnamese paddy. What can you learn from this image about the place where Terry's father fought?

Vocabulary

inert (in URT) *adj.* without power to move or act; lifeless

Differentiated Instruction

Understanding Culture Ask students in small groups to conduct research and report to the class on what Vietnam is like today. Each group should choose an aspect of the country, such as the geography and climate, traditional art and music forms, the economy today, popular tourist destinations, or the effects of the Vietnam War. Encourage groups to bolster their reports with pictures. If some of your students are of Vietnamese or Cambodian heritage, they may want to volunteer for a particular topic or do an oral history project involving one of their relatives. **OL** **AL**

READING WORKSHOP 4

Teach

R Reading Skill

Clarifying Say: Clarify what Terry is thinking about. What "ruin" does he believe he has caused? *(Possible response: He fears he has caused his father pain by forcing him to remember Vietnam.)* **OL**

L Literary Element

Climax Ask: If Terry's inner conflict is his inability to understand his father, why might this conversation be the climax of the story? *(Possible response: The climax is the point in the story where the main character learns something that helps resolve the conflict. If Terry's father reveals information about why he suffers from Vietnam syndrome, he might help Terry understand him and help resolve Terry's conflict.)* **AL**

Indiana English/Language Arts Academic Standards

SE: 8.2

TWE: *Reading in the Real World* 8.2, *Differentiated Instruction* 8.7.12

Teach

R Reading Skill

Clarifying **Ask:** How does Terry's father's story explain the scene in the hardware store? *(Possible response: Something in the store made him return in his mind to Vietnam, where he had to crawl along the ground to avoid bullets.)* **OL**

C Critical Thinking

Evaluation **Ask:** How effective is the author's description of what it's like to be under fire? Explain. *(Responses will vary. Students who feel Paulsen's description is effective will probably note his use of images that appeal to various senses, his building of suspense with comments like "I didn't know there wouldn't be a Petey Kressler," and the compelling flow of the father's memories. Others may note that, like Terry, those who haven't been in combat can only partially understand it.)* **OL**

were crossing the paddy, and it was dark, still dark, so black you couldn't see the end of your nose. There was a light rain, a mist, and I was thinking that during the next break I would whisper and tell Petey Kressler how nice the rain felt, but of course I didn't know there wouldn't be a Petey Kressler."

He took a deep, ragged breath. At that moment Terry felt his brain swirl, a kind of whirlpool pulling, and he felt the darkness and the light rain because it was in his father's eyes, in his voice. **9**

"So we were crossing the paddy, and it was a straight sweep, and then we caught it. We began taking fire from three sides, automatic weapons, and everybody went down and tried to get low, but we couldn't. We couldn't get low enough. We could never get low enough, and you could hear the rounds hitting people. It was just a short time before they brought in the mortars[3] and we should have moved, should have run, but nobody got up, and after a time nobody *could* get up. The fire just kept coming and coming, and then incoming mortars, and I heard screams as they hit, but there was nothing to do. Nothing to do." **C**

"Dad?" Terry said. He thought, maybe I can stop him. Maybe I can stop him before . . . before it gets to be too much. Before he breaks.

"Mortars," his father went on, "I hated mortars. You just heard them *wump* as they fired, and you didn't know where they would hit, and you always felt like they would hit your back. They swept back and forth with the mortars, and the automatic weapons kept coming in, and there was no radio, no way to call for artillery. Just the dark to hide in. So I crawled to the side and found Jackson, only he wasn't there, just part of his body, the top part, and I hid under it and waited, and waited, and waited.

"Finally the firing quit. But see, see how it was in the dark with nobody alive but me? I yelled once, but that brought fire again, so I shut up and there was nothing, not even the screams."

His father cried, and Terry tried to understand, and he thought he could feel part of it. But it was so much, so much and so strange to him.

3. ***Mortars*** are small, portable cannons that fire explosive shells.

Practice the Skills

9 Key Reading Skill

Clarifying How can darkness and rain be in the father's eyes and voice? Explain in your own words what the author means.

Additional Support

Reading Fluency

Staging the Story Have student pairs practice reading aloud this climactic scene between Terry and his father, with one student playing each character. Tell them to read it as if they are on stage, reading just the direct quotations and using the rest of the text as cues for what they should do and how they should act and speak. As students read, circulate and give suggestions. Then have students reverse roles: the student who played Terry will now read the father, and vice versa. **OL**

"You cannot know this," his father repeated. It was almost a chant. "You cannot know the fear. It was almost dark, and I was the only one left alive out of 54 men, all dead but me, and I knew that the Vietcong were just waiting for light. When the dawn came, 'Charley'[4] would come out and finish everybody off, the way they always did. And I thought if I could stop the dawn, just stop the sun from coming up, I could make it." **10** **EL**

Terry felt the fear, and he also felt the tears coming down his cheeks. His hand went out across the table, and he took his father's hand and held it. It was shaking.

"I mean I actually thought that if I could stop the sun from coming up, I could live. I made my brain work on that because it was all I had. Through the rest of the night in the rain in the paddy, I thought I could do it. I could stop the dawn." He took a deep breath. "But you can't, you know. You can't stop it from coming, and when I saw the gray light, I knew I was dead. It would just be minutes, and the light would be full, and I just settled under Jackson's body, and hid."

He stopped, and his face came down into his hands. Terry stood and went around the table to stand in back of him, his hands on his shoulders, rubbing gently.

"They didn't shoot me. They came, one of them poked Jackson's body and went on and they left me. But I was dead. I'm still dead, don't you see? I died because I couldn't stop the sun. I died. Inside where I am—I died."

Terry was still in back of him, and he nodded, but he didn't see. Not that. He understood only that he didn't understand, and that he would probably never understand what had truly happened. And maybe his father would never be truly normal.

But Terry also knew that it didn't matter. He would try to understand, and the trying would have to be enough. He would try hard from now on, and he would not be embarrassed when his father's eyes went away. He would not be embarrassed no matter what his father did. Terry had knowledge now. Maybe not enough and maybe not all that he would need. **L**

But it was a start. **11** ❍

Practice the Skills

10 **Literary Element**

Climax During the climax of a story, a main character usually comes to an important realization. What does the father realize here?

11 **BIG Question**

Why does Terry believe it's so important to get his dad to talk about Vietnam? Write your answer on the "Stop the Sun" flap of your Foldable. Your response will help you complete the Unit Challenge later.

4. The ***Vietcong*** were the Communist forces. American soldiers often referred to them as ***Charley.***

Literature Focus Lesson

Short Story Remind students that a short story is a brief fictional narrative in prose. Elements of a short story include plot, character, setting, point of view, and theme. Challenge advanced students to analyze "Stop the Sun" in terms of some of these elements. One student might do a character study of Terry, one could chart the plot, one might speculate about how the story would change if it were told from the father's point of view, and one could explore the theme. Ask students to read their reports to the class and to be prepared to answer questions from other students. **AL**

Teach

EL Language Coach

Denotation and Connotation

Say: Sometimes connotation can be highly personal. To most people, for example, the word *cruise* has positive connotations, but to a person who gets seasick, the word may have highly negative connotations. What are the general connotations of the words *sun* and *dawn*? *(positive, suggesting light and warmth)* **BL** What connotations did they have in Terry's father's mind on this night in the rice paddy? *(negative, associated with death)* **OL**

L Literary Element

Climax **Ask:** What important realization does Terry come to after hearing his father's story? *(Terry realizes that though he will probably never completely understand his father, he will never again be embarrassed by him.)* **OL**

Assess

Use the CheckPoint questions provided on Presentation Plus! to check for comprehension of the selection. These questions can be used with interactive response keypads for immediate student feedback.

Indiana English/Language Arts Academic Standards

SE: 8.2, 8.3.2

TWE: *Reading Fluency* 8.7, *Literature Focus Lesson* 8.5.2

Assess

Resources for page 1016

- Selection Quick Check, p. 68
- Selection and Unit Assessment, p. 80
- ExamView Assessment Suite
- Interactive Tutor: Self-Assessment

Students can respond to the *After You Read* items in their Learner's Notebooks or on a separate sheet of paper.

Answering the BIG Question

1. Responses will vary.
2. He was his unit's only survivor in a bloody battle during the Vietnam War.
3. He asks his mother, he reads library books, and he talks to his history teacher.

Critical Thinking

4. Possible response: He married and had Terry after the war, and he wants to separate the war from his life now as much as possible. I disagree that Vietnam has nothing to do with this family. His current behavior, a result of the war, affects his family.
5. Possible response: Terry is a problem solver. He is willing to put effort into clarifying what he does not understand.
6. Responses will vary.

After You Read

Stop the Sun

Answering the BIG Question

1. Would you fight for a better relationship with a close family member? Why or why not?
2. **Recall** What event caused Terry's father's problems?
   TIP Right There
3. **List** List three ways Terry goes about trying to find the cause of his father's problems.
   TIP Think and Search

Critical Thinking

4. **Analyze** Why do you think Terry's father insists that Vietnam has "nothing to do with this family"? Do you agree? Explain.
   TIP Author and Me
5. **Interpret** What does the following sentence about Terry mean? "When something bothered him, he liked to stay with it until he understood it, and he understood no part of this."
   TIP Author and Me
6. **Evaluate** Is "Stop the Sun" a good title for this story? Why or why not? Explain your answer by giving details from the story.
   TIP Author and Me

Talk About Your Reading

Small Group Discussion Form a group of three or four students. Discuss the following questions. There is no right answer. Talk about the reasons behind your answers.

- How do Terry's feelings for his father change throughout the story?
- How might knowing about a family member's past affect how others feel about the person?
- What have you learned about the ways world events can affect ordinary families?

Indiana English/Language Arts Academic Standards
(pp. 1016–1017)

8.2 Comprehension and Analysis (Focus on Informational Text) Understand grade-level-appropriate material. Develop [reading] strategies... **8.7 Listening and Speaking** Speaking skills are developed... **8.3.2** Evaluate the structural elements of the plot, such as... climax... **8.6 English Language Conventions**

For a complete description of the standards, see p. IN 11.

Talk About Your Reading

After students have finished their discussion, ask them to summarize their answers to each of the three questions. Then have them choose a reporter to share their answers with the class. As students listen to the reports, encourage them to ask questions to clarify anything they don't understand.

Skills Review

Key Reading Skill: Clarifying

7. What skills did you use to clarify as you read? Which ones were most helpful and why? Which ones were least helpful and why?

Literary Element: Climax

8. What does Terry understand, and not understand, about his father after the climax occurs?
9. How does the action of the characters at the climax affect the outcome of the story?

Reviewing Skills: Predicting

10. How do you think Terry's experiences with his father will affect Terry as he grows up? What do you think he will learn from them? How do you think they will shape him as a person?

Vocabulary Check

Answer each question with the best word from the list. Some words will be used more than once.

syndrome • dry • foundered • inert

11. Which word suggests an activity that comes to a stop?
12. Which word relates to a medical condition?
13. Which word means "unable to move"?
14. Which word could you use to describe a topic that doesn't appeal to you at all?
15. Which TWO words could be antonyms for *lively?*
16. **English Language Coach** Explain why the term *Vietnam syndrome* is confusing to Terry.

Web Activities For eFlashcards, Selection Quick Checks, and other Web activities, go to www.glencoe.com.

Grammar Link: Parentheses

Parentheses ( ) are punctuation marks used to set off words that define or explain another word. You can replace commas with parentheses to separate words more clearly from the rest of the sentence. Use them to include a) extra information about a subject, b) a reflection, or c) an afterthought.

- Marian Wright Edelman, the founder of the Children's Defense Fund, has fought for the civil rights of young Americans for more than 30 years.
- Marian Wright Edelman (the founder of the Children's Defense Fund) has fought for the civil rights of young Americans for more than 30 years.
- Neil Armstrong took his first step on the moon (who could have imagined it was possible?) on July 20, 1969.
- Spinach helps prevent anemia (as do kidney beans) because it is an excellent source of iron.

Grammar Practice

Rewrite each sentence, adding parentheses where they are needed.

17. Edelman's father a Baptist minister taught his children the importance of taking care of others.
18. Edelman's essay originally a letter to her sons gives many important life lessons we can all adopt.
19. Soccer a national sport in the United Kingdom has gained popularity in this country.
20. Violets are very hardy and beautiful, for I've seen them growing out of a crack in the sidewalk.
21. It must have been exciting although a bit scary to have traveled with Columbus in 1492.
22. Neil Armstrong the first astronaut to walk on the moon said, "One small step for man, one giant leap for mankind."

Skills Review

Key Reading Skill: Clarifying

7. Responses will vary.

Literary Element: Climax

8. Terry understands why his father was so traumatized by his experience in Vietnam, but he doesn't understand why his father says he died and is still dead.
9. Terry's father shares his painful memories; Terry responds with acceptance and compassion. Their behavior toward each other provides some hopefulness and suggests that they may become closer.

Reviewing Skills: Predicting

10. Responses will vary.

Vocabulary Check

11. foundered
12. syndrome
13. inert
14. dry
15. dry, inert

English Language Coach

16. Terry cannot find out specifically what causes it or whether his father will ever recover from it.

Close

Ask students whether they were able to relate to Terry's struggle to find out more about his family. Why or why not?

Grammar Link: Parentheses

Grammar Practice

17. Edelman's father (a Baptist minister) taught his children the importance of taking care of others.
18. Edelman's essay (originally a letter to her sons) gives many important life lessons we can all adopt.
19. Soccer (a national sport in the United Kingdom) has gained popularity in this country.
20. Violets are very hardy (and beautiful), for I've seen them growing out of a crack in the sidewalk.
21. It must have been exciting (although a bit scary) to have traveled with Columbus in 1492.
22. Neil Armstrong (the first astronaut to walk on the moon) said, "One small step for man, one giant leap for mankind."

Indiana English/Language Arts Academic Standards
SE: 8.2, 8.3.2, 8.6, 8.7

Reading Across Texts: Persuasive Appeals

Teaching Students to Compare Persuasive Appeals

Why Is It Important?

- Students will learn how to compare different ways that writers try to persuade readers to share a certain point of view or take a particular action.
- Students will gain a better understanding of persuasive techniques as they compare the similarities and differences between two articles.
- By recognizing a variety of persuasive techniques in each text, students will learn how to form their own opinions about what each writer is trying to convey.

How to Help Students Get It

- Remind students that persuasive writing is usually a combination of *fact*—something that can be proven to be true—and *opinion*—something that expresses a personal feeling or judgment.
- Discuss the different propaganda techniques that utilize language that appeals to the emotions: glittering generalities, testimonial, and bandwagon.
- Help students create their comparison chart by reviewing different kinds of standards that they can use to compare the two selections.

Reading to Answer the Big Question

Teens Tackle Pollution in Their Communities by Sara Steindorf
This article spotlights three young people who fight to improve Earth's environment. They accomplish significant achievements in science, government, and business, proving that kids can effect change.

A Change in Climate by Emily Sohn
Global warming is the subject of this article which chronicles changes taking place in plant and animal life. The author argues that we must fight to reverse the effects of carbon dioxide and other "greenhouse" gases in the air or risk losing many precious plants and animals that cannot adapt to a rapidly warming climate.

Workshop Resources

Pacing (Days) Standard	Block	Lesson	Student Materials	Teacher Resources
1	2	Reading Across Texts: Persuasive Appeals	English Language Coach Review, p. 42	Bellringer Options Transparencies – Daily Language Practice 70 Presentation Plus!
2		"Teens Tackle Pollution in Their Communities"	Glencoe Online Unit Vocabulary Review, p. 40 Academic Vocabulary Review, p. 43 English Language Coach Reading Across Texts Graphic Organizer, p. 35 StudentWorks Plus™ Online Student Edition Literature Classics	Puzzlemaker Skill Level Up!™ A Language Arts Game BookLink 3 Assessment by Learning Objective (Diagnostic and Formative) Interactive Tutor: Self-Assessment TeacherWorks Plus™ ExamView Assessment Suite
2		"A Change in Climate"	Glencoe Online Unit Vocabulary Review, p. 40 Academic Vocabulary Review, p. 43 English Language Coach Reading Across Texts Graphic Organizer, p. 35 StudentWorks Plus™ Online Student Edition Literature Classics	Puzzlemaker Skill Level Up!™ A Language Arts Game BookLink 3 Assessment by Learning Objective (Diagnostic and Formative) Interactive Tutor: Self-Assessment TeacherWorks Plus™ ExamView Assessment Suite

Keys for Unit Resource

- Blackline Master
- Workbook
- Supplemental Text
- CD-ROM
- DVD
- Transparency
- Web-based
- Fast File

Level Appropriate Code

AS = Activities for all students
AL = Activities for students working above grade level
OL = Activities for students working at grade level
BL = Activities for students working below grade level
EL = Activities for English language learners

Focus

BELLRINGER Options

Daily Language Practice Transparency 70
Focus Activity Ask: What do you think of when you hear the word *environment*? *(Possible responses: air, water, pollution, plants, animals, etc.)* **Ask:** What do you think environmentalists might do? *(Possible responses: take care of the environment, fight for causes related to caring for the environment)* **OL**

Teach

E Text Element

Persuasive Appeals Write on the board: Please study for tomorrow's test. It will count as 10 percent of your grade, demonstrate how hard you've worked so far, and probably affect your mood for a week at least. **Ask:** What am I trying to persuade you to do? *(to study for a test)* **BL** **Ask:** What persuasive appeals am I using? *(all three kinds—logical, ethical, and emotional, in that order)* **OL**

READING ACROSS TEXTS WORKSHOP

Teens Tackle POLLUTION in Their Communities

by Sara Steindorf

& A CHANGE IN CLIMATE

by Emily Sohn

Skills Focus

You will use these skills as you read and compare the following selections:

- "Teens Tackle Pollution in Their Communities," p. 1021
- "A Change in Climate," p. 1027

Reading

- Comparing and contrasting elements in different texts

Informational Text

- Recognizing and analyzing persuasive appeals

Writing

- Writing to compare and contrast

Indiana English/Language Arts Academic Standards (pp. 1018–1019)

8.2 Comprehension and Analysis (Focus on Informational Text) Develop [reading] strategies…identifying and analyzing…perspective and purpose. **8.2.2** Analyze text that uses proposition (statement of argument) and support patterns.

For a complete description of the standards, see p. IN 11.

Writers often write with a single purpose: to convince their readers to think, feel, or act in a certain way. This type of writing is called persuasive writing. And it's everywhere—in advertisements, in letters to the editor, and in articles like some of the ones you've read in this unit.

How to Compare Literature: Persuasive Appeals

E As you read "Teens Tackle Pollution in Their Communities" and "A Change in Climate," ask yourself the questions in the chart below to help yourself recognize persuasive appeals.

Does the writer make . . .		
an appeal to **reason?**	an **emotional** appeal?	an **ethical** appeal?
Does the writer clearly state a thesis or main point?	Does the writer use words or images that make you feel strong emotions, such as anger, sadness, sympathy, or alarm?	Does the writer seem knowledgeable and trustworthy? Is he or she fair to opponents?
Does the writer support his or her main point with facts, examples, statistics, or quotations?	Does the writer appeal to your belief in certain ideas, such as freedom, love, patriotism, or justice?	Does the writer appeal to your values and beliefs? Does he or she appeal to your sense of right and wrong?
Do the writer's points make sense?	Does the writing make you feel strongly?	Is the writer trustworthy?

Additional Support

Literature Focus Lesson

Persuasive Appeals Many politicians try to address citizens' environmental concerns. Have students examine a political speech, interview, newsletter, or ad that relates to environmental issues and identify its persuasive appeals. **OL** Work with students to generate evaluation criteria: Are opinions supported by facts? Are any experts quoted really experts? Does the message use words with positive or negative connotations? What types of persuasive appeals does the politician make? **OL** **AL**

Get Ready to Compare

As you read, keep track of examples of the three persuasive appeals in a chart like the one below. You will use the notes in this chart to compare the selections later.

Persuasive Appeals Comparison Chart			
	Appeals to Reason	Appeals to Emotion	Appeals to Ethics
"Teens Tackle Pollution" Writer's Position:			
"A Change in Climate" Writer's Position:			

Use Your Comparison

Have you ever tried to avoid doing chores at home, or to convince your parents to buy you something? If so, you probably used basic principles of persuasion.

Look at the list below. Pick one statement with which you strongly agree or disagree. Write a paragraph that persuades a friend to think or feel the way you do about the topic you chose. Be creative! Use at least one appeal to reason and one appeal to emotion to make your case.

- Students should not use cell phones at school.
- Video games have educational value.
- People should be able to download music from the Internet for free.
- Schools should ban junk food from cafeteria vending machines.

E

When you're finished, use the checklist below to revise your paragraph.

- ☑ Did I state my opinion in a clear thesis statement?
- ☑ Did I support my position with facts and examples?
- ☑ Did I include opposing viewpoints to avoid bias?
- ☑ Did I conclude with a summary of my argument, a strong appeal, or a call to action?

Teach

E Text Element

Persuasive Appeals Suggest that pairs of students choose the same *Use Your Comparison* topic, though they do not necessarily have to have the same position on that topic. Have each student write his or her paragraph independently and then trade with the partner. The partner should take notes about the paragraph—the writer's position, what appeals were used, and what facts and examples back up those appeals. **OL**

Assess/Close

Ask: What persuasive appeals do you use when you want your parents to buy you something you saw advertised on television? *(Responses will vary.)* **AS** **Ask:** What persuasive appeals in those same advertisements are the most likely to draw you in? *(Responses will vary.)* **OL**

Resources for page 1019

Use the Reading Across Texts Graphic Organizer BLM in the Unit 7 Resource Booklet p. 35.

English Language Coach

Environmental Vocabulary

Encourage students to create a mini-dictionary in their Learner's Notebooks of words related to environmental issues and their definitions. Suggest students begin with the words below, but encourage them to add more as they proceed through this workshop. **AS**

- environment
- pollution
- climate
- recycle
- toxic
- contaminants
- habitat
- population
- extinct
- global warming
- ice age
- drought

Indiana English/Language Arts Academic Standards

SE: 8.2.2

TWE: *Literature Focus Lesson* 8.2.2, *English Language Coach* 8.1

Teach

Did You Know?

Rachel Carson (1907–1964) is considered the "mother of the environmental movement." Carson, a biologist, naturalist, and writer, wrote feature articles on science topics. Her famous book, *Silent Spring*, about the effects of pesticides, is considered by many to have started the modern environmental movement. "The more I learned about the use of pesticides," Carson recalled, "the more appalled I became and I realized that here was the material for a book. What I discovered was that everything which meant most to me as a naturalist was being threatened, and that nothing I could do would be more important."

READING ACROSS TEXTS WORKSHOP

Before You Read

Teens Tackle Pollution in Their Communities

Did You Know?

Did you know that nearly 1.5 billion people worldwide lack safe drinking water? That's 25 percent of the planet's population! Did you know that every year, more than 500 million people die of waterborne diseases? Do you think you can take fresh water for granted in this modern age? Unfortunately, you may have to think again.

Vocabulary Preview

emit (ee MIT) *v.* to give off **(p. 1023)** *Cars emit dangerous chemicals from their tailpipes.*

buoyed (BOO eed) *adj.* supported or uplifted **(p. 1023)** *Ruiz felt buoyed by his friends' good wishes.*

English Language Coach

Denotation and Connotation A word's **denotation** expresses its literal, or dictionary, definition. When a word has implied meanings or associations in addition to its dictionary meaning, it has a **connotation.** Writers often use words with connotative meanings to influence readers' attitudes.

Look at the examples of denotation and connotation in the chart below.

Word	Denotation	Connotation
yellowed	made yellow in color	old, worn
nestled	drawn close	safe, snug

Get Ready to Read

Connect to the Reading

Think of a time when you solved a problem to make a positive difference in your world. Who or what motivated you to take action?

Build Background

Check out the list below for tips on how to make your routine more green.

- Recycle! Buy recycled products and products with less packaging.
- Bring your lunch in reusable containers.
- Carpool with friends to get to and from school and practice.

Set Purposes for Reading

BIG Question Read to see how people are fighting for the environment.

Set Your Own Purpose What else would you like to learn from this selection to help you answer the Big Question? Write your own purpose on your Foldable 7.

Indiana English/Language Arts Academic Standards
(pp. 1020–1025)

8.1.3 Verify the meaning of a word in its context... **8.2 Comprehension and Analysis (Focus on Informational Text)** Develop [reading] strategies... identifying and analyzing... perspective and purpose. **8.2.2** Analyze text that uses proposition (statement of argument) and support patterns.

For a complete description of the standards, see p. IN 11.

Additional Support

Literature Focus Lesson

Visuals as Persuasive Appeals

Visuals can make a powerful persuasive appeal. Have students make a collection of images related to environmental issues of their choosing. Divide the class into two or three groups and put each group in charge of one section of the bulletin board or one poster. Hold a class discussion on the results. What kind of persuasive appeal does each display make overall? What individual images are most persuasive? EL BL OL

Teens Tackle POLLUTION in Their Communities EL

by Sara Steindorf

I bet you don't recycle your family's dryer lint. You probably don't reduce waste by reusing tuna cans as cookie cutters, either.

That's okay. The earth is packed full of plenty of areas that could stand a little improving. Take a look in your community—perhaps the pollution needs patrolling, or the sea turtles need saving. There's bound to be at least one environmental cause you find interesting and worthwhile. E

To celebrate this year's Earth Day,[1] we thought you might enjoy reading about some inspiring young environmentalists. Not only did they realize the powerful effects of a little perseverance and passion, but they also proved to the government, businesses, and even their own critics that kids must be seen and heard. **1**

Barbara: Putting used oil in its place

When Barbara Brown of Victoria, Texas, was 11, her friend Kate noticed her father pouring used motor oil on a fencepost to kill weeds.

"The weeds did die, but we wanted to know: What happened to the oil?" says Barbara, who is now 17.

What Barbara and her friends Kate Klinkerman and Lacy Jones found out was that the toxic oil seeped into the soil—and eventually into the water supply. "What we were doing

1. ***Earth Day*** is a day set aside each spring to celebrate the Earth and its resources. The first Earth Day was in 1970.

Practice the Skills

1 Reading Across Texts

Appeal to Ethics The powerful language in this sentence appeals to the readers' sense of right and wrong. To what values or beliefs does the writer appeal here?

Teach

Viewing the Photo

Ask: What do you think a school bus might have to do with pollution? *(Responses will vary.)* After students make their predictions, have them scan the subheadings to see if they were right. **Ask:** Can you think of other everyday sources of pollution that might be pictured here? *(Possible responses: factories, cars, cigarette smoke, used motor oil)* OL

EL Language Coach

Denotation and Connotation

Ask: What is the denotation of the word *tackle* in the title of this article? *(to try to solve)* **Ask:** What connotation does it have? *(a positive connotation, suggesting determination and admirable effort)* OL

E Text Element

Persuasive Appeals **Say:** Explain how the last sentence of the second paragraph represents an ethical appeal. *(It challenges readers to think of a worthwhile cause.)* OL

Readability Scores

Dale-Chall: 10.1
DRP: 63
Lexile: 1110

Reading in the Real World

Citizenship Have students browse local newspapers to identify environmental causes that are making news in their community or state. These causes can be large (saving the bay) or small (cleaning up a local park). Have students make a chart that includes each cause, the key goal of each cause, a brief description of ongoing efforts, the name of the group or groups supporting the goal, and if possible, information on a contact person. Post the chart in the classroom and invite the class to see how each issue is addressed in the coming weeks and months. OL AL

Indiana English/Language Arts Academic Standards

SE: 8.1.3, 8.2, 8.2.2

TWE: *Literature Focus Lesson* 8.7.9, *Reading in the Real World* 8.2

Teach

E Text Element

Persuasive Appeals **Say:** Notice the name the teenagers chose for their group—Don't Be Crude. How is this name a persuasive appeal? *(Possible response: It suggests that taking action means you're not a crude person; it also plays on the term "crude oil.")* OL **Say:** Explain how this is both an ethical and an emotional appeal. *(Possible response: It is an ethical appeal because it urges people to do the right thing; it is an emotional appeal because of the negative connotation of the word* crude. *People would feel bad if they thought they were acting crudely.)* AL

R Reading Skill

Review Making Inferences **Ask:** What can you infer about the girls' actions from the information in the third paragraph? *(Possible response: They put a lot of time and effort into their program.)* OL

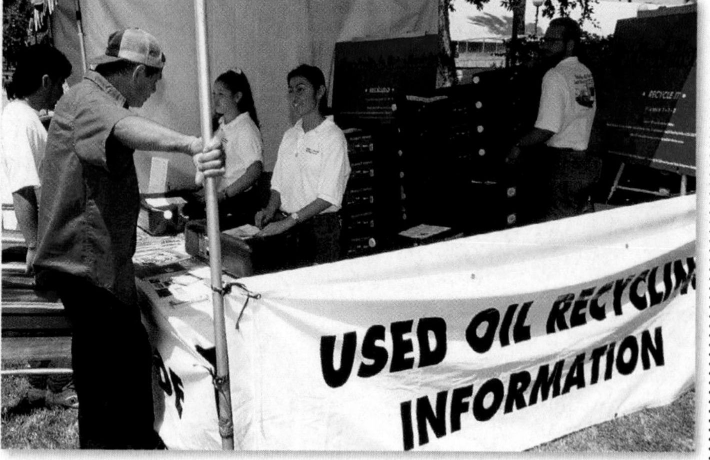

These teens hand out information–and recycling containers–at a used oil recycling booth. Why might efforts like this be especially important in farm communities?

on our land was possibly contaminating[2] our own water," Barbara says. 2

So the trio set out to clean up their own backyards—literally. "We knew that we were just sixth-graders, but that didn't stop us from doing what we believe is right," Barbara says.

In 1998, they formed the program Don't Be Crude, and began educating their community about the dangers of using motor fluids as weed and insect killers. (This is a common practice in rural areas like Victoria, especially since many folks live far from car-maintenance locations, which recycle used oil.) E

They also got support from the government and businesses to set up five do-it-yourself recycling units in Victoria County. R

Today, Don't Be Crude has 18 units in seven counties—and protects thousands of acres of groundwater from contamination through improper fluid disposal, says Barbara.

In addition, the girls speak to audiences across the nation (some as large as 1,500 people) to encourage young people to get involved in protecting the earth. 3

Sometimes, Barbara says, that involves getting rid of stereotypes.[3]

Practice the Skills

2 Reading Across Texts

Appeal to Reason A logical appeal uses facts, examples, or statistics to build a case. What fact about groundwater pollution do you learn here?

3 Reading Across Texts

Appeal to Reason Think about the writer's position on the topic of teen activism. How does she support her position that young environmentalists are proving that kids must be seen and heard? Take notes on your chart.

2. If something is ***contaminated,*** it has been poisoned or polluted.
3. A ***stereotype*** is an oversimplified or untrue notion about someone or something.

Additional Support

Differentiated Instruction

Build Background "People usually know about recycling," says one of the young people featured in this article. However, recycling is only one of the three R's: *Reduce, Reuse, Recycle.* The first action is *reduce*: buying fewer, longer-lasting products, for example. The second is *reuse*: refilling water bottles and donating magazines, for example. The last is *recycle*, which includes buying products made from recycled materials and composting organic wastes. Have students brainstorm how teenagers can use the three R's in their everyday lives to help improve the environment. OL

"In Texas, you're labeled a tree hugger if you do something to help the environment—but I think that's just because people aren't very educated about the environment," she says. 4

The team also tries to teach others that there's much more to protecting the planet than recycling cans. "People usually know about recycling," she says. "But they often simply don't realize how much more they could be doing."

Amir: Reducing school-bus pollution

In December 2001, Amir Nadav was in his junior year of high school when he decided he wanted to do something more to help the environment. So he wandered into a local Sierra Club[4] meeting. There, they were discussing new reports on the harmful effects of school-bus idling.

"I thought, this is really cool. I ride a school bus, I have friends who ride school buses, so this is an issue that clearly affects me," says the Eagan, Minn., teen. 5

School buses **emit** diesel exhaust, and when a driver stops the bus but leaves the engine on, it creates a lot of pollution that could be easily avoided, he says.

So Amir and two friends wrote a petition calling for reduced idling and increased maintenance inspections (a well-maintained vehicle pollutes less). Then they told fellow classmates about their petition—and to their surprise, they got 500 signatures on the first day. E

"I was a really shy person, and I didn't have the guts to just go up and approach people," Amir says. "But I felt really empowered because it was something I really believed in." 6 EL

Buoyed by their success, the petition writers and several Sierra Club members drafted a state bill calling for minimized idling of school buses.

Then they testified before the state legislature. When they ran into opposition, Amir and his co-leaders organized a rally of 150 students on the steps of the state capitol.

4. The ***Sierra Club*** is an environmental organization that works to protect both local communities and the planet as a whole.

Vocabulary

emit (ee MIT) *v.* to give off

buoyed (BOO eed) *adj.* supported or uplifted

Practice the Skills

4 English Language Coach

Connotation The term *tree hugger* refers to environmentalists. Do you think its connotations are positive or negative?

5 Reading Across Texts

Appeal to Ethics One way a writer establishes credibility is by citing knowledgeable sources. As you read about Amir Nadav, think about why the writer chose to tell his story.

6 Reading Across Texts

Appeal to Emotions What personal characteristic did Amir overcome to get the 500 signatures? Why do you think the writer chose to share this detail with readers?

Teach

E Text Element

Persuasive Appeals Ask: What kind of persuasive appeal did the young people use in their petition? *(A logical appeal; their main argument is a fact.)* OL

EL Language Coach

Denotation and Connotation
Ask: In Amir's description of how the petition drive made him feel, which word has a strong positive connotation? *(empowered)* OL **Ask:** What kind of power do you think Amir discovered? *(Possible response: He discovered he had the power to overcome his shyness, to influence people, and to help a cause he believes in.)* AL

Reading in the Real World

Citizenship Many organizations offer citizens opportunities to work for environmental change. Have students evaluate some of these organizations by visiting their Web sites and noting their goals and accomplishments. Students might visit the Sierra Club, the Nature Conservancy, the Audubon Society, as well as other official organizations supporting causes dear to their hearts—saving whales, for example, or cleaning up a river. Ask students to share their findings with the class. Which organization would they join? Why? OL AL

Indiana English/Language Arts Academic Standards
SE: 8.1.3, 8.2, 8.2.2
TWE: *Differentiated Instruction* 8.2, *Reading in the Real World* 8.2.5

Teach

R Reading Skill

Review Drawing Conclusions **Ask:** What conclusions might readers draw from Amir's story? *(Possible responses: If Amir can do this, so can they; their community needs a ban on idling; resistance can be overcome by organization and knowledge.)* OL

E1 Text Element

Persuasive Appeals **Say:** Many people did not take Amir seriously because of his age. How did he get the Senate Majority leader to listen? *(He presented 1,000 signatures on a petition, organized a rally that got media attention, and researched his topic so thoroughly that he was credible.)* OL

E2 Text Element

Persuasive Appeals **Ask:** What is the purpose of providing details about Gina's background? *(The details give her credibility because they tell us that she has knowledge in road building through her job and that she likes to invent things.)* OL

It was a success. They gained not only media attention, but key support from the Senate majority leader. He had walked down to check out the rally, and was impressed with the students' knowledge of the topic, along with the 1,000 signatures on the petition. E1

Last May, the bill finally became a law.

"If you had told me a few days before I attended that Sierra Club meeting what it would amount to, I would've laughed. It's unbelievable what can happen," he says.

Another lesson Amir learned is the importance of researching a cause he felt strongly about. "It's easy to go out and say, 'I want cleaner buses,'" he says. "But I had to know stuff like: retrofits are things you can do to engines to minimize pollution. Oxidation catalysts are parts you can add to buses to reduce pollution. . . . And diesel exhaust accounts for 75 percent of soot emitted from all vehicles," he says. 7

Such knowledge helped him feel empowered, especially in the beginning when people basically told him: "What you do won't matter—you don't even have the right to vote!" he says.

This year, the high school senior leads the Sierra Club's anti-idling campaign for students. In his free time, he travels the United States helping students get similar laws passed in their states (only about a dozen states already have bans on idling).

Gina: Paving roads with trash

Three years ago, Gina Gallant was driving with her family in Cash Creek, British Columbia—known locally as "Trash Creek" because of an overflowing landfill site nearby. Suddenly, inspiration struck: Why not use garbage to pave roads?

So the 13-year-old from Prince George, British Columbia, who has been inventing since first grade, took on the challenge. E2

Gina, now 15, already had some knowledge of road-building, thanks to a job at the asphalt division of Husky Oil. But she still needed to do a lot of research.

Practice the Skills

7 Reading Across Texts

Appeal to Ethics and Reason Amir shows here that he really "knows his stuff." How does this make him a credible source? What facts and statistics does he use to support *his* position on the need for cleaner buses? Make notes on your chart.

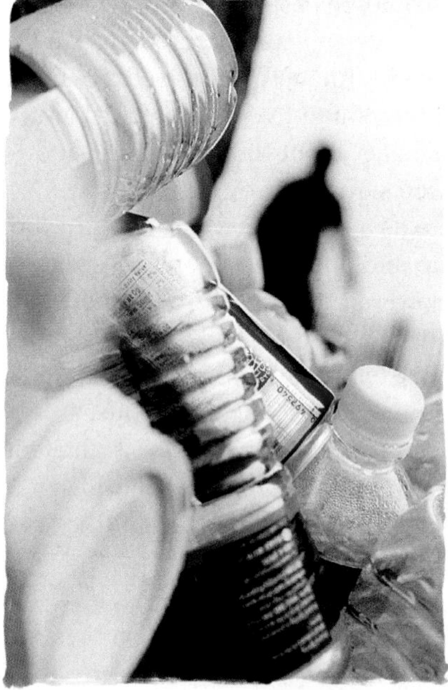

Consider the number of plastic bottles you use each week. Can you, like Gallant, think of any other uses for these landfill-bound containers?

Additional Support

Literature Focus Lesson

Anecdotes Rather than just providing dry data about the environment, the writer of this article focuses on anecdotes about teenagers who have made a difference. Anecdotes are brief stories or accounts of incidents. They give writing a more personal feel by including people's thoughts and ideas rather than just facts and statistics. Ask students to evaluate the use of anecdotes in this article. How might the article have been different if the writer had simply included information about the problems associated with used motor oil and talked about a new invention? How might the anecdotes encourage other teens to get involved with environmental causes? AL

Glass and rubber waste, Gina found, had already been tried in roads in the U.S. The materials hadn't worked well. So she turned to plastic—which takes up a whopping one-third of all landfill space around the world. (Just think of all the milk jugs, laundry-detergent containers, and water bottles that can pile up over time.) 8

"I thought that since both plastic and asphalt are petroleum-based,[5] they might be compatible," Gina says.

Bingo. EL

Gina's new paving material, dubbed PAR for PolyAggreRoad, mixes ground-up plastic bottles with stone material and liquid asphalt. To take the product out of the lab and onto the streets, she tracked down companies willing to grind the plastic to her specifications and mix up enough of the compound to pave an actual road.

"At first, some of [the companies] didn't take me seriously because they thought, you know, a 13-year-old can't do something like this," Gina says. "But they finally realized I knew what I was talking about." E

Finally, last October, the mayor allowed her to test PAR on a 160-foot strip of a local road. Now she's just waiting to see how her road holds up through freezes and thaws, and abuse from cars. Engineers already suspect the PAR will be able to withstand more movement without cracking than regular roads, Gina says.

"My ultimate goal is for a company to pick up my product," she says, "and to see it go all the way around the world to reduce garbage in landfill sites."

Her advice to others? "Believe in yourself and follow your heart, because if you can think of these ideas, you can do them." 9 ○

Analyzing the Photo A red maple sapling grows in recycled rubber chips. How might this image—and the possibilities it represents—symbolize hope for the future?

Practice the Skills

8 **Reading Across Texts**

Appeal to Reason Facts and examples strengthen any argument. What fact or example does the writer give here? How does it help you understand the pollution problem? Use your chart to take notes.

9 

How do the teens in this article demonstrate—and fight for—their beliefs? Would you fight for clean air and water the way these young people did? Why or why not? Write your answer on the "Teens Tackle" page of Foldable 7. Your response will help you complete the Unit Challenge later.

5. Petroleum is oil. If something is ***petroleum-based,*** its major component is oil.

Teach

EL Language Coach

Denotation and Connotation
Ask: What is the denotation of *bingo* in this context? *(Possible responses: "right on"; "that's it")* **Ask:** Where does this word come from? *(from the game of bingo, in which a player calls "bingo" when he or she completes a row and wins)* **Ask:** What is its connotation? *(positive; it suggests being on target or being a winner)* OL

E1 Text Element

Persuasive Appeals: **Say:** Gina says that, at first, the companies didn't take her seriously. How do you think she convinced them she knew what she was talking about? *(Possible response: She probably used logical appeals, providing facts and statistics to prove she was knowledgeable and that her product would work.)* AL

Assess

CheckPoint

Use the CheckPoint questions provided on Presentation Plus! to check for comprehension of the selection. These questions can be used with interactive response keypads for immediate student feedback.

Differentiated Instruction

Using Mottoes Gina Gallant's work with PolyAggreRoad won the gold medal at Canada's 2002 national science fair. Tests have shown that her paving material is more resistant to cracks than asphalt. It also reduces noise by five percent. Gina became an inventor in fifth grade when she found a way to keep the crackers in her soup from getting soggy. After her brother survived an accident because he was wearing his bicycle helmet, Gina developed lights that signal when a helmet is in the proper position. Write Gina's motto on the board: "Take something you don't like and fix it." Have students think of one thing they don't like and would like to fix. AS

Indiana English/Language Arts Academic Standards
SE: 8.2, 8.2.2
TWE: *Literature Focus Lesson* 8.2, *Differentiated Instruction* 8.4.1

Teach

More about the Author

Emily Sohn is a graduate of the Science Writing Program at the University of California, Santa Cruz. She began her career as a teacher. Then she became a science writer for *U.S. News and World Report.* In 2001, Sohn joined CNN's AmazonQuest team, which explored the Amazon River basin for five weeks.

Before You Read | A Change in Climate

Emily Sohn

Meet the Author

Emily Sohn is a writer for *Science News for Kids*, a Web site on science news for young people. She writes about a variety of science-related topics, including archaeology, anthropology, astronomy, animals, plants, environmentalism, and more.

Author Search For more about Emily Sohn, go to www.glencoe.com.

Indiana English/Language Arts Academic Standards
(pp. 1026–1031)

8.1.3 Verify the meaning of a word in its context... **8.2 Comprehension and Analysis (Focus on Informational Text)** Develop [reading] strategies... identifying and analyzing... perspective and purpose. **8.2.2** Analyze text that uses proposition (statement of argument) and support patterns.

For a complete description of the standards, see p. IN 11.

Vocabulary Preview

accumulate (uh KYOO myuh layt) *v.* gather or build up **(p. 1029)** *If you don't clean your house regularly, dust will accumulate on your tabletops.*

vulnerable (VUL nur uh bul) *adj.* exposed to danger **(p. 1030)** *Many species, large and small, are vulnerable to climate change.*

English Language Coach

Denotation and Connotation Context clues can help you understand a word's connotative meaning. In each sentence below, determine the boldface word's denotative and connotative meanings. Then use context clues to decide whether the connotations are positive or not.

- Some people like the **aroma** of freshly brewed coffee.
- The dry, wilted flowers produced a strange **aroma.**

Get Ready to Read

Connect to the Reading

Try to imagine what your community would be like if it were five degrees warmer every day. In what ways might the change in temperature affect the animals and plants in the area?

Build Background

The term *global warming* refers to an average increase in the earth's temperature. It is the result of human activities that cause pollution. For example, the earth has warmed by one degree Fahrenheit over the past 100 years. One degree doesn't sound like much, but it has already caused significant climate change in some places. Scientists fear the effects of global warming because a warmer Earth may lead to changes in rainfall patterns, a rise in sea level, and serious consequences for plants, wildlife, and people.

Set Purposes for Reading

BIG Question Read to find out how global warming is affecting plant and animal life around the world.

Set Your Own Purpose What else would you like to learn from this selection to help you answer the Big Question? Write your own purpose on your Foldable 7.

Additional Support

Author Search To expand students' appreciation of Emily Sohn, have them access the Web site for additional information and resources.

Literature Focus Lesson

Persuasive Appeals and Connotation

Many businesses and industries include "green" messages in their ads or build whole campaigns to persuade people they are environmentally responsible. Have students scan magazines for examples of such ads. Choose some of the students' findings for class discussion: What is the main message of each? What persuasive appeals are used? Is its "greenness" backed up by facts? Is it guilty of faulty reasoning? What words or phrases with strong connotations does it use? OL

by Emily Sohn

From one day to the next, weather can have a big effect on your life. When it rains, you have to stay indoors or carry an umbrella. When it's cold, you have to bundle up. R

Over the course of hundreds, thousands, and millions of years, weather trends affect life on Earth in more dramatic ways. Ice ages or long droughts, for example, can wipe out certain types of plants and animals. Although many species manage to survive such extreme, long-term climate shifts, their living conditions also change.

There's lots of evidence of drastic changes in climate occurring in the distant past. Earth today may again be in the midst of such a climate change. In the last 100 years, studies show, global temperatures have risen an average of 0.6 degrees C. EL

That might not sound so bad. After all, what difference does half a degree make?

A growing number of studies suggest, however, that such an increase could have a big impact on life. **1**

Biologists[1] and ecologists[1] are discovering, often by accident, that climate change is forcing some plants and animals into new habitats. Others are becoming extinct. Sometimes, scientists show up at a site they've studied for years, only to discover that the organisms they've been tracking are no longer there. What's more, it now looks like this redistribution of life on Earth is sometimes happening at an alarmingly fast pace. **2**

1. ***Biologists*** study plants and animals. ***Ecologists*** study living things and their environments.

Practice the Skills

1 Reading Across Texts

Persuasive Appeals Writers of persuasive pieces take a position on an issue and then support that position with evidence. What is the writer's position on the issue of climate change?

2 Reading Across Texts

Appeal to Reason The writer gives two examples of the effects of climate change on some animals and plants. Note these examples on your chart.

Teach

R Reading Skill

Review Comparing and Contrasting **Ask:** What comparison does the writer make in the first paragraph to help readers understand the effects of climate changes on Earth? *(She compares dramatic climate changes to day-to-day changes in the weather, which have an effect on readers' lives, making them stay indoors or carry an umbrella, for example.)* OL

EL Language Coach

Denotation and Connotation
Say: Many politicians now prefer the term *climate change* to *global warming* because some people think *climate change* sounds more like a natural process, or change. Why might *global warming* have a more negative connotation? *(Possible response: "Global warming" is a term people are more familiar with, and we associate that term negatively with pollution leading to holes in the ozone layer.)* OL

Readability Scores
Dale-Chall: 8.0
DRP: 60
Lexile: 1040

Differentiated Instruction

Responding to the Workshop Invite students to develop their own responses to this workshop. Here are some ideas:

- Students with interpersonal skills could interview a local environmental activist.
- Those interested in medical fields could investigate illnesses with an environmental component, such as asthma or mercury poisoning.
- Photographers might create a photo essay on a local environmental issue.
- Those interested in architecture could research green building techniques.
- Car buffs might find out about hybrid vehicles or alternative fuels. AS

Indiana English/Language Arts Academic Standards
SE: 8.1.3, 8.2, 8.2.2
TWE: *Literature Focus Lesson* 8.2.6, *Differentiated Instruction* 8.4

Teach

EL Language Coach

Denotation and Connotation
Say: Beever calls the information *warning signs*. What is the effect of the word *warning*? *(Possible response: The word* warning *has a negative connotation that implies the problem is serious; it turns the factual statement into an ethical appeal by implying that action needs to be taken.)* OL

R Reading Skill

Review Drawing Conclusions **Ask:** What conclusions might the writer want readers to draw from the account of shifting tree lines? *(It is a significant change caused by global warming.)* OL

C Critical Thinking

Comprehension **Ask:** What do many scientists believe is causing today's increased temperatures? *(Possible responses: human activities, such as burning coal, oil, and other fossil fuels)* BL

"These little pieces of information are all warning signs that stuff is going on," says Erik Beever. He's a research ecologist with the United States Geological Survey in Corvallis, Ore. "Our world is changing more rapidly than we have observed in the recent past," he says. EL

Tree line

One place to look for changes in plant and animal life that may be caused by a climate shift is in the mountains.

As the globe warms up, mountaintops get warmer, too. Trees start growing at higher altitudes than before. The tree line shifts upward.

In the Alps, a mountain range in Europe, records from the last 80 to 100 years show that plants have been working their way upward at a rate of about 4 meters[2] every decade. Researchers from the University of Vienna found this trend in two-thirds of the sites they checked. R

In one recent study in Nevada, Beever discovered that a type of tree called the Engleman spruce had moved its habitat upslope a dramatic 650 feet in just 9 years. "The site at the lowest elevation went from 41 individuals to just six," he says. At higher elevations, numbers increased. 3

"When I first saw the results," Beever says, "I had a really hard time believing it because it's just too fast."

Beever's analysis of the data suggests that global warming is mainly responsible for the shift. Studies in mountain ranges from New Zealand to Spain reveal similar trends.

Global warming

What's causing today's increased temperatures?

Many scientists say that human activities, such as burning coal, oil, and other fossil fuels,[3] are largely to blame. C These activities release heat-trapping gases, such as carbon dioxide, into the

2. ***Four meters*** is about 13 feet.
3. ***Fossil fuels*** are fuels that come from the remains of organisms preserved in rocks in the earth's crust.

Analyzing the Photo Smoke from a fossil-fuel refinery billows into the atmosphere. How do scientists explain the relationship between air pollution and global warming?

Practice the Skills

3 Reading Across Texts

Appeal to Reason What evidence does the writer give to support her assertion about the shifting tree line? Does it help build her case in a logical way? Make notes on your chart.

Additional Support

Differentiated Instruction

Responding to the Workshop
Here are some more ideas for student exploration:

- Naturalists in the class could do a botanical survey of the school grounds or a local park or conservation area.
- Budding politicians could investigate the Green Party in this country and in other countries.
- Swimmers and divers could investigate the effect of global warming on coral reefs.
- Students interested in zoology could investigate the effect of global warming on other animals besides pikas (which are dealt with later in the article), such as polar bears. AS

atmosphere. The more these gases **accumulate** in the atmosphere, the hotter things get on Earth. **4**

Some experts remain skeptical. They point out that natural causes may be playing an important role in today's global temperature increases. The same factors that caused ice ages, extreme heat waves, and massive droughts[4] in the past before human activities were important could still be at work now.

In the case of rising tree lines, they say, trees may still be recovering from an unusually cool period, known as the Little Ice Age,[5] which lasted from the 1300s into the middle of the 1800s. It's even possible that efforts to put out fires allow plants to move into new habitats. **5**

Mountain islands

Scientists predict that average temperatures may go up another 1.4 to 5.8 degrees in the next 100 years. If it occurs, such a rapid increase wouldn't give plants and animals much time to adapt to new conditions. **6**

Organisms that live on mountains may face the grimmest future. That's because mountaintops are, in many ways, like islands. They're isolated clearings that poke up above the tree line.

Although it's too cold for trees to grow at such heights, these alpine environments are ideal habitats for some animals, which have become highly specialized to live there.

"A lot of populations are just little **frostings** on peaks," says James Brown. Brown is a population ecologist at the University of New Mexico, who was recently quoted in the journal *Science*. **7**

Like animals on islands, these mountaintop creatures have no escape if conditions change.

4. A ***drought*** (drowt) is a shortage of water.
5. During the ***Ice Age***, glaciers covered a large part of the earth's surface.

Vocabulary

accumulate (uh KYOO myuh layt) *v.* gather or build up

Practice the Skills

4 Reading Across Texts

Appeal to Reason The writer explains the relationship between human activities and today's increased temperatures. How does this explanation provide support for her position?

5 Reading Across Texts

Appeal to Ethics Persuasive writers can make an ethical appeal by acknowledging opposing arguments in a fair and respectful way. Does the writer do this? Explain.

6 Reading Across Texts

Appeal to Reason How do the facts in this paragraph provide logical support for the writer's position? Make notes on your chart.

7 English Language Coach

Connotation What does the word **frosting** connote in this context?

Teach

E Text Element

Persuasive Appeals **Say:** The author provides two arguments made by skeptics to explain the shifting tree line. What are those arguments? *(that the world could still be recovering from the Little Ice Age or that putting out forest fires lets trees expand their habitat)* BL

EL Language Coach

Denotation and Connotation **Say:** There are degrees of connotation. The words *hardest* and *worst* could be substituted for *grimmest* in this sentence. Which of these three words has the least negative connotation? *(hardest)* Which has the most negative connotation? *(grimmest)* OL

Reading Fluency

Build Fluency Model fluency for students by reading aloud two paragraphs from the passage, using your tone of voice, volume, rate of speech, and pauses to help convey meaning. Then, ask students to form small reading groups to continue reading aloud, taking turns reading one paragraph at a time. If students stumble over a difficult word, encourage them to ask group members for help with pronunciation and to return to the beginning of the sentence when they continue reading. EL BL

Indiana English/Language Arts Academic Standards

SE: 8.1.3, 8.2, 8.2.2

TWE: *Differentiated Instruction* 8.4, *Reading Fluency* 8.7.2

Teach

E Text Element

Persuasive Appeals **Say:** Note 9 in your textbook asks how this paragraph *also* appeals to your emotions. What is the basic appeal here? *(to reason, stating a fact learned in an experiment)* OL

C Critical Thinking

Analysis **Ask:** Why does Beever think pikas are a good indicator of whether our climate is warming? *(Possible responses: Pikas are unusually sensitive to heat; if their habitat gets warmer, pikas typically don't move to cooler climates; their numbers are declining.)* OL

Scientists say that plants and animals that live on mountain tops like these are among the first affected by global warming. Why might this be?

Pick a pika

One of the most direct and dramatic demonstrations of the impact of global warming, Beever says, comes from a furry little creature called the pika.

Visual Vocabulary
A ***pika*** is a small gray mammal that lives in the mountains.

Hands down, pikas are among the most adorable animals you'll ever see in the wild. Though related to rabbits, they look like furry little gerbils. "Even as a male, I can say they're cute," Beever says. "They're pretty nifty little guys." 8

To see pikas, you have to go high up on a mountain because they can't survive warm weather. In a famous study in the 1970s, a scientist put pikas in cages at low elevations to see what would happen. Many of the animals died, even in the shade. It was just too hot for them. 9

Their habits make pikas particularly **vulnerable** to increased temperatures. "They don't move a lot," Beever

Vocabulary

vulnerable (VUL nur uh bul) *adj.* exposed to danger

Practice the Skills

8 Reading Across Texts

Appeal to Emotions
Emotional appeals can be serious or playful. What words here describe the pika? Does a description like this appeal to your head or your heart? Why?

9 Reading Across Texts

E **Appeal to Emotions** How might this paragraph also appeal to your emotions? How might it provoke sympathy for the pika and for the writer's position? Make notes on your chart.

Additional Support

Differentiated Instruction

Global Greens Charter In 2001, delegates from an international network of Green parties adopted the Global Greens Charter, a document that set out six guiding principles:

- ecological wisdom
- social justice
- participatory democracy
- nonviolence
- sustainability
- respect for diversity

Challenge advanced students to find out what these terms mean and how they are related to the goal of environmental health. Encourage students to create a poster or collage that illustrates these principles. AL says. "A 1-mile migration for a pika would be a huge, huge deal, and a pretty rare event, as far as we know." In other words, when conditions change, pikas can't do much about it. **10**

For more than 10 years, Beever has been surveying pika populations in the mountain states of the U.S. West. By the end of 1999, he had confirmed that seven out of 25 populations that he had originally surveyed were gone. More recently, Beever found that two more populations have disappeared. **11**

Early warning

Not all species are threatened by rising temperatures. Some plants and animals like it hot and dry. Others can move or adapt to get the cold or moisture they need to survive.

Pikas are different. "Pikas are an early warning sign," Beever says. "They are very clearly vulnerable to high temperatures."

So, the case of the disappearing pikas is reason enough to wake up and take notice, he says. Something in the weather *is* changing, and the trends look alarming. **E**

But, Beever says, there are things that you can do that may help. Choices you make every day—such as walking instead of going in a car—can add up. By reducing the levels of carbon dioxide and other "greenhouse" gases[6] in the air, we may be able to slow the warming trend.

If nothing else, do it for the pikas. The world could always use a little extra cuteness. **12** ❍ **BQ**

6. A ***"greenhouse" gas*** is an atmospheric gas, such as methane or carbon dioxide, which contributes to the greenhouse effect. The greenhouse effect occurs when Earth's atmosphere traps solar radiation.

Practice the Skills

10 Reading Across Texts

Appeal to Emotions
Innocent pikas, stranded on broiling mountaintops–how does this image appeal to the feelings you might have about cute, furry animals? Do you find this appeal effective?

11 Reading Across Texts

Appeal to Reason The writer makes a logical appeal when she cites Beever's work. Make notes about this appeal on your chart. Is this appeal more or less effective than her previous appeals to your emotions?

12 BIG Question

What does the writer fight for in "A Change in Climate"? What does she fight against? Write your answer on the "Change in Climate" page of Foldable 7. Your response will help you complete the Unit Challenge later.

Teach

E Text Element

Persuasive Appeals Ask: Is it the writer, Beever, or both making a persuasive appeal in the last section of the article? *(Both. Beever makes an appeal directly when he suggests things that people can do to slow global warming. The writer makes an indirect logical appeal by featuring Beever's opinion near the end of the article and a direct emotional appeal by asking readers to "do it for the pikas.")* **OL**

BQ BIG Question

Ask: Are environmental issues something you would personally fight for? Why or why not? Write your answer in your Learner's Notebook. *(Responses will vary.)* **OL**

Assess

CheckPoint

Use the CheckPoint questions provided on Presentation Plus! to check for comprehension of the selection. These questions can be used with interactive response keypads for immediate student feedback.

Differentiated Instruction

Evaluating Web Sites Remind students that anyone can post information on the Internet. Have students find two Web sites on global warming and evaluate each site, noting

- The name and address of the site
- Its author
- Examples of facts and opinions
- Bias (if any)
- Qualifications of experts cited
- Any spelling or grammar errors or "questionable" statements

OL AL

Indiana English/Language Arts Academic Standards
SE: 8.2, 8.2.2
TWE: *Differentiated Instruction* 8.5.3, *Differentiated Instruction* 8.2.3

Assess

Resources for page 1032

- Selection Quick Check, pp. 69-70
- ExamView Assessment Suite
- Interactive Tutor: Self-Assessment

Teens Tackle Pollution in Their Communities and A Change in Climate
Students can respond to the *After You Read* items in their Learner's Notebooks or on a separate sheet of paper.

Vocabulary Check

1. emit: take in
2. buoyed: held under
3. accumulate: lose
4. vulnerable: safe
5. emit
6. Vulnerable
7. buoyed
8. accumulate

English Language Coach

9. *Toxic* connotes danger.

After You Read

Teens Tackle POLLUTION in Their Communities

A CHANGE IN CLIMATE

Vocabulary Check

Copy the words below on a separate sheet of paper. Circle the word or phrase that most nearly means the opposite of the boldface word.

1. **emit**
   give off, reduce, take in
2. **buoyed**
   held under, supported, took away
3. **accumulate**
   build up, lose, set alongside
4. **vulnerable**
   safe, open to, excited

Now copy the sentences below. Fill in each blank with the correct vocabulary word.

emit buoyed accumulate vulnerable

5. A microwave can _______ powerful rays.
6. _______ to increasing temperatures, many plants and animals are forced to migrate.
7. Gino felt _______ by her family's kindness.
8. Don't let your homework _______, Salwa's teacher warned.

English Language Coach

9. What does the word *toxic* connote?

Indiana English/Language Arts Academic Standards
(pp. 1032–1033)

8.2 Comprehension Develop [reading] strategies…identifying and analyzing…perspective and purpose. **8.2.2** Analyze text that uses proposition (statement of argument) and support patterns. **8.5.7** Write for different purposes.

For a complete description of the standards, see p. IN 11.

16. Possible responses:

Persuasive Appeals Comparison Chart

Selection	Appeals to Reason	Appeals to Emotion	Appeals to Ethics
"Teens Tackle Pollution" Writer's Position: Young activists have proved that teenagers can help the environment.	Provides statistics and technical details; explains cause-and-effect relationships.	Counters stereotypes; uses humor (e.g., "Don't Be Crude); gathers supporters to show that people care about the environment; contains inspiring quotations from young activists.	Describes teens' efforts to establish their credibility and protect the earth by reducing contamination, pollution, and waste.
"A Change in Climate" Writer's Position: People should make choices that slow global warming.	Provides evidence for global warning and some possible effects; quotes expert.	Associates saving the environment with the cute, vulnerable pika; "warning signs" suggest we need to protect ourselves.	Says we should be aware of what's happening, make responsible choices, and protect the environment and defenseless wildlife.

Reading/Critical Thinking

Answer the following questions.

Teens Tackle POLLUTION in Their Communities

BIG Question

10. Why is a cleaner environment important to Barbara, Amir, and Gina? How do they stand up for their values and beliefs?
    TIP **Think and Search**
11. **Recall** Why does Amir Nadav decide to join the Sierra Club?
    TIP **Right There**
12. **List** List the three main sources of pollution discussed in the article.
    TIP **Think and Search**

A CHANGE IN CLIMATE

13. **Recall** In what two ways have mountains been affected by changes in global temperatures?
    TIP **Think and Search**
14. **Connect** How might global warming affect plants and animals in your community?
    TIP **On My Own**
15. **Interpret** What does Beever mean when he says that pikas are an "early warning sign"?
    TIP **Author and Me**

Writing: Reading Across Texts

Use Your Notes

As you prepare to write about "Teens Tackle Pollution in Their Communities" and "A Change in Climate," think about how the writer of each selection uses different persuasive techniques to convince you to think, feel, or act a certain way.

As you review the notes in your chart, ask yourself the following questions about each selection:

- *Did the writer state her position clearly?*
- *Did she back up her position with facts, statistics, examples, and quotations?*
- *Did she appeal to readers' emotions in an effective way?*
- *Did she address opposing viewpoints?*
- *Did she appeal to my values?*

16. Follow these steps to use the notes on your Comparison Chart to compare the appeals to reason, emotions, and ethics in "Teens Tackle Pollution in Their Communities" and "A Change in Climate."

    Step 1: Look at the notes you made for "Teens Tackle Pollution." Circle one appeal to reason that you found persuasive.

    Step 2: Underline one effective appeal to emotions.

    Step 3: Draw a box around one strong appeal to ethics. Does the example you chose rely on the writer's credibility, or does it appeal to your values?

    Step 4: Look at the notes you made for "A Change in Climate." Repeat steps 1–3.

Get It on Paper

To compare what you've learned about persuasive appeals in "Teens Tackle Pollution" and "A Change in Climate," answer the questions below.

17. Which article appealed most effectively to your sense of reason? Use examples from your chart to support your answer.
18. Which article contained more emotional appeals? Use examples from your chart to support your answer.
19. Which article contained more ethical appeals? Use examples from your chart to explain your answer.

BIG Question

20. How can you fight against pollution—and *for* clean air and water—in your community? Why is it so important to fight for the things you care about?

Reading/Critical Thinking

Teens Tackle Pollution in Their Communities

BQ BIG Question

10. Possible response: The teens know the dangers of pollution. Each adopts a specific cause and acts on his or her convictions.
11. He wants to help the environment.
12. Improper disposal of toxic wastes, diesel exhaust emissions, and disposal of plastics

A Change in Climate

13. The tree line has moved higher, and some animals have lost their habitat.
14. Responses will vary.
15. Possible responses: of global warming, of many plants and animals being threatened by global warming

Writing: Reading Across Texts

Use Your Notes

16. The comparison chart on the left-hand page shows some possible answers.

Get It on Paper

17. Responses will vary, but students will likely say "A Change in Climate" contains more appeals to logic.
18. Responses will vary, but students will likely say "A Change in Climate" contains more appeals to emotion.
19. Responses will vary, but students will likely say "Teens Tackle Pollution in Their Communities" contains more ethical appeals.

BIG Question

20. Responses will vary. Students should provide reasons for their responses, such as the example of the young people who worked to protect the environment.

Close

Ask students whether reading these two articles has affected what they believe they can accomplish in relation to the Big Question.

Indiana English/Language Arts Academic Standards
SE: 8.2, 8.2.2, 8.5.7

The Unit Challenge

Focus

BELLRINGER Options

- **Selection Focus Transparency 16**
- **Daily Language Practice Transparency 71**

Focus Activity Say: You've read about many characters and people who had to decide whether something was worth fighting for. Which character or person you read about is the best model of how to make that decision? *(Responses will vary.)*
The discussion will remind students of the selections they've read, which will help them begin the group activity or the solo activity. AS

Teach

Group Activity: Make a Mural

- Have at least one person take notes as the group discusses the questions in step 1.
- Make sure the group is on step 3 by midway through the class period to allow time to create the sketch.
- Schedule a time to work on the mural and have group members decide who is responsible for bringing each item needed to complete it.
- Help students find a place to display their mural in the classroom.

Answering The BIG Question What's Worth Fighting For? What's Not?

As you read the selections in this unit, you thought about what's worth fighting for and what's not. Now use what you've learned to complete the Unit Challenge.

The Unit Challenge

Choose Activity A or Activity B and follow the directions for that activity.

A. Group Activity: Make a Mural

With three classmates, design a mural that honors people who took a stand for what they believed in. You won't paint your mural on a wall, but you'll use poster board and other crafts to create something just as meaningful.

1. **Discuss the Assignment** Choose a group member to take notes about your discussion. Then talk about people who have stood up for what they thought was right. Discuss people who have fought against unfair treatment, ideas, or events. The notes you made on your Foldable will help you get started. For example, think about how Ruby Bridges and her mother stood up to segregation. Maybe you have a friend, parent, or neighbor who fought for what he or she believed by not giving in or giving up.

2. **Make a List** Write a list of the people you discussed. Then use textbooks, encyclopedias, and the Internet to add more people to your list. Your list might look like this one.

People Who Stood Up for Their Beliefs

Martin Luther King, Jr.	Susan B. Anthony
Cesar Chavez	Gandhi
George Washington	Sitting Bull
Rosa Parks	Uncle Frank

3. **Create Your Mural** Work together to make a mural that honors people on your list.
   - As a group, choose the people from your list that you want to include on your mural.
   - Create a sketch (a rough idea) of what your mural will look like. Decide how you want to represent the people and their beliefs—drawings or paintings, pictures from magazines or newspapers, names and descriptions, or a combination of these. Be creative!
   - Gather all the materials you'll need (poster board, paint and paint brushes, markers, etc.). When you all agree on an idea, divide the work among group members.

4. **Present Your Mural** Make sure all the people you want to honor are in your mural. Finish all the artwork. Then hang your mural in your classroom or school so other students can view it and learn from it.

Assess/Close

Group Activity

Ask: How does this mural express your ideas about what's worth fighting for?
Suggest that students write their answers in their Learner's Notebooks. *(Responses will vary.)* AS

B. Solo Activity: Propose a Change

Change starts with you! Write a proposal for a change you would like to see in your school or community. A proposal is a piece of writing that suggests an idea and explains to readers why that idea is important.

1. **Brainstorm Ideas** For 10 to 15 minutes, write about your school and community. What do you like about them? What would you like to be different? Your Unit 7 Foldable notes will help you think of ideas. Make a list of things you would like to change and reasons why you would like them to be different.

2. **Choose a Change** Once you have your list, choose one thing that is most important to you. Think about how *you* can help change it. Make a list of other people who can help you change it. Then think about any obstacles that you might face as you push for change.

3. **Organize Your Ideas** Make a brief outline of your ideas. Your outline should have three main sections:
   I. Introduce your idea for change
   II. Explain how the change can happen
   III. Describe how the change will help

4. **Write a Proposal** Using your outline and the ideas in your head, write about the change you think is important. Make sure your proposal answers the following questions:
   - What do you want to change?
   - Why is the issue important? Why is change necessary?
   - What steps can you and other people take to make the change happen?
   - Is there anything that will get in the way? How will you deal with any obstacles?
   - How will your school or community benefit from the change?

5. **Perfect and Present Your Proposal** Read and revise your proposal. Make sure that your ideas are clear. Correct any spelling or grammar mistakes. When your proposal is ready to present, read it to your class. With your classmates, discuss other ideas that may help you make the change. What is the next step?

Big Question Link to Web resources to further explore the Big Question at www.glencoe.com.

Teach

Solo Activity: Propose a Change

- Have students decide on what they want to change.
- If students have trouble thinking of a subject, have them review their Unit and Foldable notes or the editorial pages of the local paper.
- Remind students that they will need evidence that shows why a change is needed or how their idea will make things better.
- If students have trouble finding ways to deal with opposition, suggest that they review the way young activists handled it in "Teens Tackle Pollution in Their Communities."
- Have students write their outlines in their Learner's Notebooks. Review the outlines before students begin writing.

Assess/Close

Solo Activity

After students present their proposals, have a brief conference with them about how they could improve their proposals and what the next step might be. **OL**

Big Question Have students access the Web site for English and Spanish summaries and annotated links to related Web resources.

Focus

Vocabulary Preview

List the following words on the board:

- commence
- eerie
- gnarled
- impromptu
- intently
- ominous
- tentatively
- tremor

Have students learn the definitions of these words and quiz each other on their meaning. Ask students to use each word in a sentence before they begin the selection.

Build Background

The blues set the tone for this contemporary story set in Harlem.

- The blues are a highly rhythmic form of music that evolved from the experiences of African Americans over the last three centuries.
- The blues express sorrow and hardship. But the blues are more than a song or a tune; they are also a state of mind.
- The term *blues* comes from the phrase *blue devils*, a slang reference to the depression that accompanies withdrawal from alcohol addiction.

Readability Scores
Dale-Chall: 5.3
DRP: 50
Lexile: 860

UNIT 7

Your Turn: Read and Apply Skills

Meet the Author

Walter Dean Myers grew up in Harlem, a section of Manhattan in New York City. He had a speech problem as a young man, so one of his teachers encouraged him to write. Writing and reading gave Myers a whole new life. He says, "Books took me, not so much to foreign lands and fanciful adventures, but to a place within myself that I have been exploring ever since . . ." See page R4 of the Author Files for more on Walter Dean Myers.

Author Search For more about Walter Dean Myers, go to www.glencoe.com.

The Treasure of Lemon Brown

by
Walter Dean Myers

The dark sky, filled with angry swirling clouds, reflected Greg Ridley's mood as he sat on the stoop[1] of his building. His father's voice came to him again, first reading the letter the principal had sent to the house, then lecturing endlessly about his poor efforts in math.

"I had to leave school when I was 13," his father had said, "that's a year younger than you are now. If I'd had half the chances that you have, I'd. . . ."

Greg had sat in the small, pale green kitchen listening, knowing the lecture would end with his father saying he couldn't play ball with the Scorpions. He had asked his father the week before, and his father had said it depended on his next report card. It wasn't often the Scorpions took on new players, especially 14-year-olds, and this was a chance of a lifetime for Greg. He hadn't been allowed to play high school ball, which he had really wanted to do, but playing for the Community Center team was the next best thing. Report cards were due in a week, and Greg had been hoping for the best. But the principal had ended the suspense early when she sent that letter saying Greg would probably fail math if he didn't spend more time studying. L1

"And you want to play *basketball*?" His father's brows knitted over deep brown eyes. "That must be some kind of a joke. Now you just get into your room and hit those books."

1. A ***stoop*** is one or more steps at the entrance of a building that lead up to a raised platform or porch.

Additional Support

Leveled Reading An adapted version of this selection (3rd grade readability) is available on page 94 of Jamestown Literature: An Adapted Reader for Grade 8.

Literature Focus Lesson

Summary Greg Ridley's father has forbidden him to play basketball until his math grades improve. Greg leaves his Harlem house and seeks shelter in an abandoned tenement, where he meets a homeless vagrant, Lemon Brown. After Greg and Brown scare off three thugs who believe the old man has a treasure, Brown shows Greg his treasure—a battered harmonica wrapped in reviews of his days as a blues performer. Brown had given this treasure to his son, who died in a war, and when it was returned to him, Brown knew how much his son respected him. Through this experience, Greg gains more respect for his own father and comes to understand him better. OL

That had been two nights before. His father's words, like the distant thunder that now echoed through the streets of Harlem, still rumbled softly in his ears.

It was beginning to cool. Gusts of wind made bits of paper dance between the parked cars. There was a flash of nearby lightning, and soon large drops of rain splashed onto his jeans. He stood to go upstairs, thought of the lecture that probably awaited him if he did anything except shut himself in his room with his math book, and started walking down the street instead. Down the block there was an old tenement that had been abandoned for some months. Some of the guys had held an impromptu[2] checker tournament there the week before, and Greg had noticed that the door, once boarded over, had been slightly ajar.

Pulling his collar up as high as he could, he checked for traffic and made a dash across the street. He reached the house just as another flash of lightning changed the night to day for an instant, then returned the graffiti-scarred building to the grim shadows. He vaulted over the outer stairs and pushed tentatively[3] on the door. It was open, and he let himself in.

EL

The inside of the building was dark except for the dim light that filtered through the dirty windows from the streetlamps. There was a room a few feet from the door, and from where he stood at the entrance, Greg could see a squarish patch of light on the floor. He entered the room, frowning at the musty[4] smell. It was a large room that might have been someone's parlor at one time. Squinting, Greg could see an old table on its side against one wall, what looked like a pile of rags or a torn mattress in the corner, and a couch, with one side broken, in front of the window.

EL

He went to the couch. The side that wasn't broken was comfortable enough, though a little creaky. From this spot he could see the blinking neon sign over the bodega[5] on the corner. He sat awhile, watching the sign blink first green then red, allowing his mind to drift to the Scorpions, then to his father. His father had been a postal worker for all Greg's life, and was proud of it, often telling Greg how hard he had worked to pass the test. Greg had heard the story too many times to be interested now.

For a moment Greg thought he heard something that sounded like a scraping against the wall. He listened carefully, but it was gone.

Outside the wind had picked up, sending the rain against the window with a force that shook the glass in its frame. A car passed, its tires hissing over the wet street and its red tail lights glowing in the darkness.

Greg thought he heard the noise again. His stomach tightened as he held himself still and listened intently.[6] There weren't any more scraping noises, but he was sure he had heard something in the darkness—something breathing!

L2

He tried to figure out just where the breathing was coming from; he knew it

2. ***Impromptu*** (im PRAHM too) means "made or done on the spur of the moment, without preparation."

3. As used here, ***vaulted*** means "jumped." ***Tentatively*** (TEN tuh tiv lee) means "hesitantly or uncertainly."

4. A ***musty*** smell is stale or moldy.

5. The Spanish word ***bodega*** (boh DAY guh) can refer to a bar, a restaurant, a shop, or a pantry.

6. ***Intently*** means "with concentration."

Teach

L1 Literary Element

Review Climax **Ask:** What external and internal conflicts are hinted at in this opening scene and flashback? *(an external conflict between Greg and his father about Greg's grades and how he spends his time and an internal conflict about what he will do)* **AL** **Ask:** Which do you think will be more important in the story? *(Responses will vary.)* **OL**

EL Language Coach

Denotation and Connotation
Say: A writer often chooses words with a specific connotation to build a mood. What words does Myers use here to give a scary feeling to the scene? *(graffiti-scarred, grim, dark, dim, dirty, musty)* **OL**

L2 Literary Element

Review Conflict **Ask:** Might Greg be facing another external conflict here? *(Yes, he might be facing a dangerous person.)* **Ask:** What technique is the author using to move us toward the climax? *(suspense)* **OL**

Differentiated Instruction

Connect to the Story Put the sample web on the board and ask students to create one of their own, identifying objects they treasure most. You could then ask students in pairs to discuss one of their treasures with a partner or have students write a paragraph in their Learner's Notebooks. **BL** **EL**

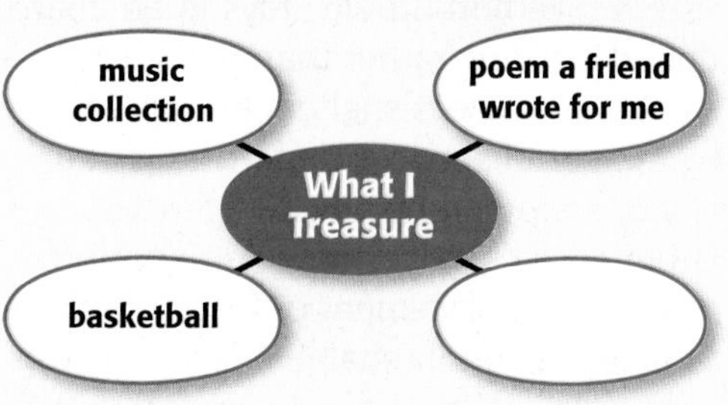

Indiana English/Language Arts Academic Standards
TWE: *Differentiated Instruction* 8.4.1

Teach

C Critical Thinking

Analysis **Say:** Lemon uses a double negative and drops some parts of words when he speaks to Greg. Why do you think the author decided to have Lemon speak in this way? *(Possible response: It shows a dialect sometimes spoken by some African Americans.)* **Ask:** How does Lemon's speech affect what you think of him as a character? *(Responses will vary.)* AL

R Reading Skill

Review Reviewing **Say:** Look back through this section. Why is Greg first frightened by Lemon Brown and then able to relax? *(Possible responses: He's frightened because it's a scary setting, and he's facing a grown man he doesn't know. He relaxes when he recognizes Lemon and decides that he poses little threat because he is old, small, and probably unarmed.)* OL

was in the room with him. Slowly he stood, tensing. As he turned, a flash of lightning lit up the room, frightening him with its sudden brilliance. He saw nothing, just the overturned table, the pile of rags and an old newspaper on the floor. Could he have been imagining the sounds? He continued listening, but heard nothing and thought that it might have just been rats. Still, he thought, as soon as the rain let up he would leave. He went to the window and was about to look out when he heard a voice behind him.

"Don't try nothin' 'cause I got a razor here sharp enough to cut a week into nine days!" C

Greg, except for an involuntary tremor[7] in his knees, stood stock still. The voice was high and brittle, like dry twigs being broken, surely not one he had ever heard before. There was a shuffling sound as the person who had been speaking moved a step closer. Greg turned, holding his breath, his eyes straining to see in the dark room.

R The upper part of the figure before him was still in darkness. The lower half was in the dim rectangle of light that fell unevenly from the window. There were two feet, in cracked, dirty shoes from which rose legs that were wrapped in rags.

"Who are you?" Greg hardly recognized his own voice.

"I'm Lemon Brown," came the answer. "Who're you?"

"Greg Ridley."

"What you doing here?" The figure shuffled forward again, and Greg took a small step backward.

"It's raining," Greg said.

"I can see that," the figure said.

The person who called himself Lemon Brown peered forward, and Greg could see him clearly. He was an old man. His black, heavily wrinkled face was surrounded by a halo of crinkly white hair and whiskers that seemed to separate his head from the layers of dirty coats piled on his smallish frame. R His pants were bagged to the knee, where they were met with rags that went down to the old shoes. The rags were held on with strings, and there was a rope around his middle. Greg relaxed. He had seen the man before, picking through the trash on the corner and pulling clothes out of a Salvation Army box. There was no sign of the razor that could "cut a week into nine days."

"What are you doing here?" Greg asked.

"This is where I'm staying," Lemon Brown said. "What you here for?"

"Told you it was raining out," Greg said, leaning against the back of the couch until he felt it give slightly.

"Ain't you got no home?"

"I got a home," Greg answered.

"You ain't one of them bad boys looking for my treasure, is you?" Lemon Brown cocked his head to one side and squinted one eye. "Because I told you I got me a razor."

"I'm not looking for your treasure," Greg answered, smiling. "*If* you have one."

"What you mean, *if* I have one," Lemon Brown said. "Every man got a treasure. You don't know that, you must be a fool!"

"Sure," Greg said as he sat on the sofa and put one leg over the back. "What do you have, gold coins?"

"Don't worry none about what I got," Lemon Brown said. "You know who I am?"

7. A shaking movement is called a ***tremor.***

Additional Support

Reading in the Real World

Career Lemon Brown stays in an abandoned building rather than going to a shelter. Homeless shelters are operated by the social services department of a city or state and by private agencies. Other social services include adoption services and placement of foster children, drug and alcohol rehabilitation programs, literacy classes, and visiting nurse programs. Divide the class into groups. Have two groups investigate the services offered by government and private agencies in your community. Have another find out what the job of a social worker entails and what training is recommended for this job. OL

"You told me your name was orange or lemon or something like that."

"Lemon Brown," the old man said, pulling back his shoulders as he did so, "they used to call me Sweet Lemon Brown."

"Sweet Lemon?" Greg asked.

"Yessir. Sweet Lemon Brown. They used to say I sung the blues so sweet that if I sang at a funeral, the dead would commence[8] to rocking with the beat. Used to travel all over Mississippi and as far as Monroe, Louisiana, and east on over to Macon, Georgia. You mean you ain't never heard of Sweet Lemon Brown?" R1

"Afraid not," Greg said. "What . . . what happened to you?"

"Hard times, boy. Hard times always after a poor man. One day I got tired, sat down to rest a spell and felt a tap on my shoulder. Hard times caught up with me."

"Sorry about that."

"What you doing here? How come you didn't go home when the rain come. Rain don't bother you young folks none."

"Just didn't," Greg looked away.

"I used to have a knotty-headed boy just like you." Lemon Brown had half walked, half shuffled back to the corner and sat down against the wall. "Had them big eyes like you got. I used to call them moon eyes. Look into them moon eyes and see anything you want." R2

"How come you gave up singing the blues?" Greg asked.

Music Lesson #1, 2000. Colin Bootman. Oil on canvas. Private Collection.

Analyzing the Painting What qualities might this man share with Lemon Brown?

L "Didn't give it up," Lemon Brown said. "You don't give up the blues; they give you up. After a while you do good for yourself, and it ain't nothing but foolishness singing about how hard you got it. Ain't that right?"

"I guess so."

"What's that noise?" Lemon Brown asked, suddenly sitting upright.

Greg listened, and he heard a noise outside. He looked at Lemon Brown and saw the old man was pointing toward the window.

Greg went to the window and saw three men, neighborhood thugs, on the stoop. One was carrying a length of pipe.

8. ***Commence*** (kuh MENS) means "to begin."

Teach

R1 Reading Skill

Review Distinguishing Fact and Opinion **Ask:** What fact and what opinion about himself does Lemon Brown share with Greg? *(Possible responses: Fact: He used to be a traveling musician. Opinion: He was a very good singer.)* OL

R2 Reading Skill

Review Questioning **Ask:** What does Lemon Brown mean when he talks about a knotty-headed boy? *(He might be referring to his son's curly hair, or he might be making a joke about his son having knots—odd notions—in his head.)* AL

L Literary Element

Review Persuasive Appeals **Say:** Lemon Brown is trying to persuade Greg that something is true of the blues. What is his point? *(that you can't sing the blues when things are going well for you)* **Ask:** What kind of persuasive appeal is this? *(logical)* **Ask:** Do you agree? *(Responses will vary. Some students may say that a singer is like an actor and can perform even without feeling what the song is expressing.)* OL

Literature Focus Lesson

Hyperbole Lemon Brown's language is colorful and rhythmic—he was, after all, a blues singer. Write his boast on the board: "I sung the blues so sweet that if I sang at a funeral, the dead would commence to rocking with the beat." Brown is using *hyperbole*—a figure of speech that uses exaggeration to express strong emotion, make a point, or create humor. Brown's kind of hyperbole is called a brag, and it has this structure: I [did what] so [how] that [exaggerated consequence]. Here's another example: I dance so gracefully that butterflies learn from me. Ask students to write brags about their own skills and to share their brags in a small group. OL

Indiana English/Language Arts Academic Standards
TWE: *Reading in the Real World* 8.4, *Literature Focus Lesson* 8.5.7

Teach

L Literary Element

Review Persuasive Appeals
Ask: Should Greg and Lemon Brown talk to the men and try to appeal to their ethics? *(Possible responses: No, that would be dangerous; "the voice was slurred" indicates that the men are probably under the influence of drugs or alcohol. It would also be useless, because Lemon is right when he says "They's bad men." The thugs have a weapon and say they are prepared to hurt Lemon if they "have to."* **OL**

C Critical Thinking

Analysis Ask: How are Greg and the three thugs similar in their view of treasure? *(Both assume that the word* treasure *must refer to money or something with monetary value.)* **OL**

Greg looked back toward Lemon Brown, who moved quietly across the room to the window. The old man looked out, then beckoned frantically for Greg to follow him. For a moment Greg couldn't move. Then he found himself following Lemon Brown into the hallway and up darkened stairs. Greg followed as closely as he could. They reached the top of the stairs, and Greg felt Lemon Brown's hand first lying on his shoulder, then probing down his arm until he finally took Greg's hand into his own as they crouched in the darkness.

"They's bad men," Lemon Brown whispered. His breath was warm against Greg's skin.

"Hey! Rag man!" A voice called. "We know you in here. What you got up under them rags? You got any money?"

Silence.

"We don't want to have to come in and hurt you, old man, but we don't mind if we have to."

Lemon Brown squeezed Greg's hand in his own hard, gnarled[9] fist.

There was a banging downstairs and a light as the men entered. They banged around noisily, calling for the rag man.

"We heard you talking about your treasure," the voice was slurred. "We just want to see it, that's all."

"You sure he's here?" One voice seemed to come from the room with the sofa.

"Yeah, he stays here every night."

"There's another room over there; I'm going to take a look. You got that flashlight?"

"Yeah, here, take the pipe too."

Greg opened his mouth to quiet the sound of his breath as he sucked it in uneasily. A beam of light hit the wall a few feet opposite him, then went out.

"Ain't nobody in that room," a voice said. "You think he's gone or something?"

"I don't know," came the answer. "All I know is that I heard him talking about some kind of treasure. You know they found that shopping bag lady with that money in her bags."

"Yeah. You think he's upstairs?"

"HEY, OLD MAN, ARE YOU UP THERE?"

Silence.

"Watch my back, I'm going up."

There was a footstep on the stairs, and the beam from the flashlight danced crazily along the peeling wallpaper. Greg held his breath. There was another step and a loud crashing noise as the man banged the pipe against the wooden banister. Greg could feel his temples throb as the man slowly neared them. Greg thought about the pipe, wondering what he would do when the man reached them—what he *could* do.

Then Lemon Brown released his hand and moved toward the top of the stairs.

9. Lemon Brown's fist is rough, twisted, and knotted (***gnarled***), like a tree branch.

Additional Support

Differentiated Instruction

The Generations of Music Suggest that students find a collection of Ray Billingsley's *Curtis* cartoons, which reflect classic generational music conflicts—Curtis is into rap; his dad loves jazz. Ask students to form small groups to discuss why music is such a powerful force in defining various generations. Which styles of music do they associate with which generations? How does liking the same music bring people together? How does music create difficulties between members of different generations? Are there kinds of music that appeal to all generations? **OL**

Greg looked around and saw stairs going up to the next floor. He tried waving to Lemon Brown, hoping the old man would see him in the dim light and follow him to the next floor. Maybe, Greg thought, the man wouldn't follow them up there. Suddenly, though, Lemon Brown stood at the top of the stairs, both arms raised high above his head. **C1**

"There he is!" A voice cried from below.

"Throw down your money, old man, so I won't have to bash your head in!"

Lemon Brown didn't move. Greg felt himself near panic. The steps came closer, and still Lemon Brown didn't move. He was an eerie[10] sight, a bundle of rags standing at the top of the stairs, his shadow on the wall looming over him. Maybe, the thought came to Greg, the scene could be even eerier.

Greg wet his lips, put his hands to his mouth and tried to make a sound. Nothing came out. He swallowed hard, wet his lips once more and howled as evenly as he could. **C2**

"What's that?"

As Greg howled, the light moved away from Lemon Brown, but not before Greg saw him hurl his body down the stairs at the men who had come to take his treasure. There was a crashing noise, and then footsteps. A rush of warm air came in as the downstairs door opened, then there was only an ominous[11] silence.

Greg stood on the landing. He listened, and after a while there was another sound on the staircase.

"Mr. Brown?" he called.

"Yeah, it's me," came the answer. "I got their flashlight."

Greg exhaled in relief as Lemon Brown made his way slowly back up the stairs.

"You O.K.?"

"Few bumps and bruises," Lemon Brown said.

"I think I'd better be going," Greg said, his breath returning to normal. "You'd better leave, too, before they come back."

"They may hang around outside for a while," Lemon Brown said, "but they ain't getting their nerve up to come in here again. Not with crazy old rag men and howling spooks. Best you stay awhile till the coast is clear. I'm heading out West tomorrow, out to east St. Louis."

"They were talking about treasures," Greg said. "You *really* have a treasure?"

"What I tell you? Didn't I tell you every man got a treasure?" Lemon Brown said. "You want to see mine?"

"If you want to show it to me," Greg shrugged.

"Let's look out the window first, see what them scoundrels be doing," Lemon Brown said.

They followed the oval beam of the flashlight into one of the rooms and looked out the window. They saw the men who had tried to take the treasure sitting on the curb near the corner. One of them had his pants leg up, looking at his knee.

"You sure you're not hurt?" Greg asked Lemon Brown.

"Nothing that ain't been hurt before," Lemon Brown said. "When you get as old as me all you say when something hurts is, 'Howdy, Mr. Pain, sees you back again.' Then when Mr. Pain see he can't worry you none, he go on mess with somebody else."

---

10. Something that is ***eerie*** (EER ee) is weird and frightening.
11. ***Ominous*** (AH muh nus) means "threatening harm or evil."

Teach

C1 Critical Thinking

Analysis Ask: Why do you think Lemon Brown comes out of hiding and stands at the top of the stairs? *(Possible responses: He intends to fight for his treasure. He wants to protect Greg by diverting the thugs' attention away from the boy.)* OL

C2 Critical Thinking

Analysis Ask: How do Greg and Lemon Brown together "persuade" the thugs to leave? *(Greg's howl and Lemon Brown's eerie appearance at the top of the stairs startle the men, and then Lemon Brown hurls himself into them and drives them away.)* OL

Differentiated Instruction

Singin' the Blues Ask some analytical students to research the blues: its origin and history and how it is doing today. Ask others to find out how Hurricane Katrina in 2005 affected the New Orleans blues scene and how blues singers responded to the storm.

Have students with strong empathic skills find blues lyrics that they believe reflect enduring human truths. Give musicians in class a choice: prepare an audio collage of older blues singers or an audio collage of current blues hits, sing or perform a blues number, write and perform their own blues number, or demonstrate how to play the harmonica. OL

Indiana English/Language Arts Academic Standards

TWE: *Differentiated Instruction* 8.3, *Differentiated Instruction* 8.7.12

Teach

EL Language Coach

Extended Definition **Say:** In effect, Lemon Brown has shared with Greg an extended personal definition of the word *treasure*. Summarize his definition. *(Possible responses: The harmonica and the clippings represent the work he did, the work he loved, the work that supported his son. They also symbolize his son's potential to accomplish something, just as Lemon has used his talents. His son's care for Lemon's treasure showed how much he respected his father and his legacy. That knowledge is precious to Lemon Brown and increases the value of his treasure.)* OL

BQ BIG Question

Say: Notice that Greg is asking the Big Question of our unit. We know what Lemon Brown's answer is—what is yours? Pause for thought but do not require responses. **Ask:** Did Lemon Brown do the right thing in risking his life for a harmonica? *(Responses will vary.)*

Greg smiled.

"Here, you hold this." Lemon Brown gave Greg the flashlight.

He sat on the floor near Greg and carefully untied the strings that held the rags on his right leg. When he took the rags away, Greg saw a piece of plastic. The old man carefully took off the plastic and unfolded it. He revealed some yellowed newspaper clippings and a battered harmonica.

"There it be," he said, nodding his head. "There it be."

Greg looked at the old man, saw the distant look in his eye, then turned to the clippings. They told of Sweet Lemon Brown, a blues singer and harmonica player who was appearing at different theaters in the South. One of the clippings said he had been the hit of the show, although not the headliner. All of the clippings were reviews of shows Lemon Brown had been in more than 50 years ago. Greg looked at the harmonica. It was dented badly on one side, with the reed holes on one end nearly closed.

"I used to travel around and make money for to feed my wife and Jesse—that's my boy's name. Used to feed them good, too. Then his mama died, and he stayed with his mama's sister. He growed up to be a man, and when the war come he saw fit to go off and fight in it. I didn't have nothing to give him except these things that told him who I was, and what he come from. If you know your pappy did something, you know you can do something too.

"Anyway, he went off to war, and I went off still playing and singing. 'Course by then I wasn't as much as I used to be, not without somebody to make it worth the while. You know what I mean?"

"Yeah," Greg nodded, not quite really knowing.

"I traveled around, and one time I come home, and there was this letter saying Jesse got killed in the war. Broke my heart, it truly did.

"They sent back what he had with him over there, and what it was is this old mouth fiddle and these clippings. Him carrying it around with him like that told me it meant something to him. That was my treasure, and when I give it to him he treated it just like that, a treasure. Ain't that something?"

"Yeah, I guess so," Greg said.

"You *guess* so?" Lemon Brown's voice rose an octave as he started to put his treasure back into the plastic. "Well, you got to guess 'cause you sure don't know nothing. Don't know enough to get home when it's raining."

"I guess . . . I mean, you're right."

"You O.K. for a youngster," the old man said as he tied the strings around his leg, "better than those scalawags what come here looking for my treasure. That's for sure."

BQ "You really think that treasure of yours was worth fighting for?" Greg asked. "Against a pipe?"

"What else a man got 'cepting what he can pass on to his son, or his daughter, if she be his oldest?" Lemon Brown said.

Additional Support

Literature Focus Lesson

Persuasion Remind students that reviews are a form of persuasive writing. The reviewer seeks to persuade readers that the music or the movie or the book or the restaurant is or is not worth seeking out. Ask students to choose a review of a current musical performer (they can check magazines or newspapers in the library or search the Web) and then listen to some of that artist's music (again, via the library or the Web). Have students in small groups play a short excerpt from their chosen performer and explain why they agree or disagree with the reviewer. OL

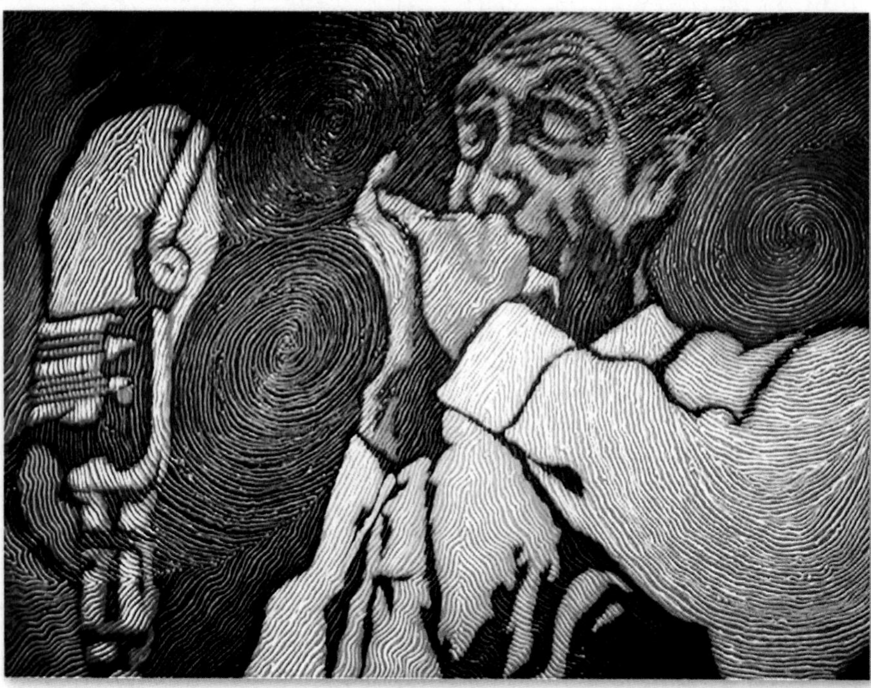

Analyzing the Art How does this picture capture the spirit of Lemon Brown's treasure?

"For a big-headed boy you sure do ask the foolishest questions."

Lemon Brown got up after patting his rags in place and looked out the window again.

"Looks like they're gone. You get on out of here and get yourself home. I'll be watching from the window so you'll be all right."

Lemon Brown went down the stairs behind Greg. When they reached the front door the old man looked out first, saw the street was clear and told Greg to scoot on home.

"You sure you'll be O.K.?" Greg asked.

"Now didn't I tell you I was going to east St. Louis in the morning?" Lemon Brown asked. "Don't that sound O.K. to you?

"Sure it does," Greg said. "Sure it does. And you take care of that treasure of yours."

"That I'll do," Lemon said, the wrinkles about his eyes suggesting a smile. "That I'll do."

The night had warmed and the rain had stopped, leaving puddles at the curbs. Greg didn't even want to think how late it was. He thought ahead of what his father would say and wondered if he should tell him about Lemon Brown. He thought about it until he reached his stoop, and decided against it. Lemon Brown would be O.K., Greg thought, with his memories and his treasure.

Greg pushed the button over the bell marked Ridley, thought of the lecture he knew his father would give him, and smiled. ❍

Teach

L1 Literary Element

Review Climax Ask: What is the climax of this story? What makes that the climax? *(The climax comes when Greg says, "Sure it does. And you take care of that treasure of yours." Greg is acknowledging that something other than money can be a treasure. If students suggest another climax, invite them to use evidence from the story to support their answer.)* OL

E Text Element

Review Persuasive Appeals Say: Without precisely trying to, Lemon Brown has persuaded Greg of something. What? *(the value of a father's concern for his son)* **Ask:** What kind of appeal has Brown made? *(appeal to emotions; he touched Greg's heart.)* OL

C Critical Thinking

Synthesis Say: Greg thinks he knows how his father will react to his late arrival. How do you think Greg will respond to his father's lecture? *(Possible response: His smile as he rings the doorbell suggests that he understands a little better why his father lectures him. He may see the lecture as an expression of his father's desire to protect his son and help him realize his potential.)* OL

Reading Fluency

Readin' the Blues This story lends itself to being read aloud, both because of the way language and pacing are used to build suspense and because of the musical quality of Lemon Brown's speech patterns. Have each student choose a section of the story to read, one about six inches long. Students should find a quiet place to practice reading their sections aloud. Recommend that students practice until they can read all the sentences smoothly with expression and understanding. Tell students to take special care with Greg and Lemon Brown's conversations and to try to pitch their voices slightly differently for each character. OL

Indiana English/Language Arts Academic Standards
TWE: *Literature Focus Lesson* 8.2.2, *Reading Fluency* 8.7.12

Tips for Independent Reading

Suggest that students choose the same book to read as one of their friends. The friends will enjoy sharing questions and reactions to their independent reading. In effect, they will have a private book club.

Fiction

Remind students that in this unit they have read two fictional accounts of people who have faced the Big Question—"Stop the Sun" and "The Treasure of Lemon Brown"—and they will gain still more insight and a great deal of pleasure from reading these longer works.

Ask students to share examples of other novels or short stories they have read in which the characters fight for something or are concerned about what's worth fighting for.

UNIT 7

Reading on Your Own

To read more about the Big Question, choose one of these books from your school or local library. Work on your reading skills by choosing books that are challenging to you.

Fiction

Animal Farm
by George Orwell

In *Animal Farm,* animals work to set up a free society, only to be oppressed by a select group of animals. Read to see how deception can make you confused about what is worth fighting for.

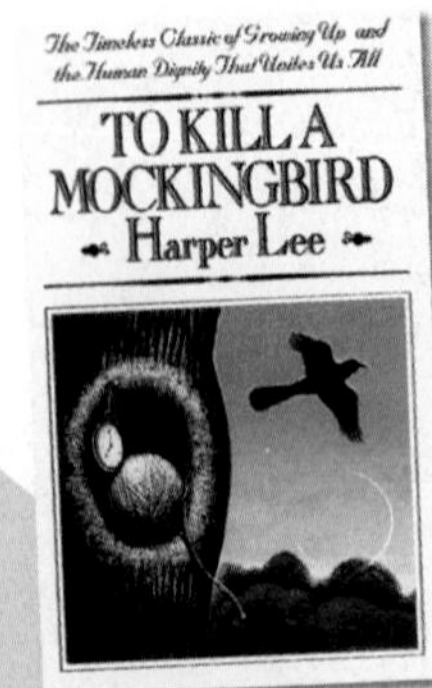

To Kill a Mockingbird
by Harper Lee

A young girl faces racism in her own town when her father—an attorney—defends an African American man who has been wrongfully accused of a crime. Scout, the young girl, learns what is worth fighting for in a deeply divided community.

Jump Ship to Freedom
by James Collier
and Christopher Collier

Daniel Arabus and his mother are slaves in the house of Captain Ivers during the Revolutionary War. Daniel's father, a soldier in the war, earns enough soldiers' notes to free his family, but his father dies and Mrs. Ivers takes the notes. Daniel must decide how to fight for freedom for himself and his mother.

Before We Were Free
by Julia Alvarez

After Anita de la Torres's aunts, uncles, and cousins suddenly leave the Dominican Republic for the United States, Anita becomes aware that her family is involved in the resistance against the Trujillo dictatorship. When Anita's father and uncle are arrested, she and her mother go into hiding.

Additional Support

Differentiated Instruction

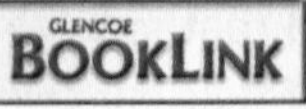

Use the Glencoe BookLink CD-ROM to create customized reading lists to help students answer the Big Question. Suggestions for Unit 7:

Grade 4: *Civil War on Sunday* by Mary Pope Osborne
Grade 5: *The Night Journey* by Kathryn Lasky
Grade 6: *His Majesty, Queen Hatshepsut* by Dorothy Sharp Carter
Grade 7: *The Good Fight: How World War II Was Won* by Stephen Ambrose
Grade 8: *Galileo and the Universe* by Steve Parker

Nonfiction

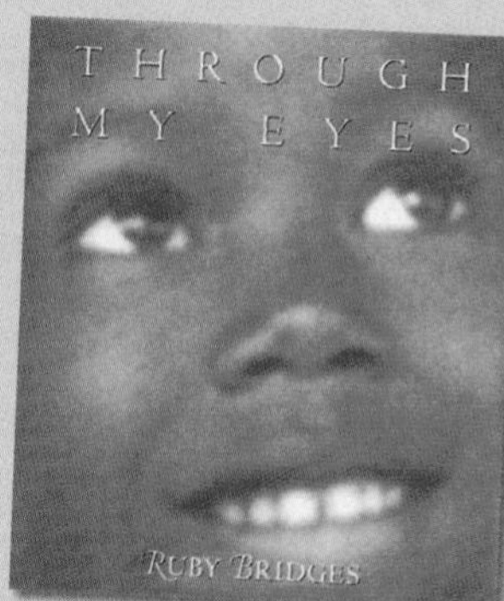

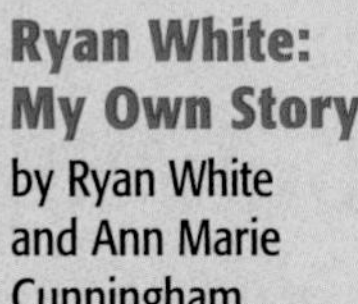

Through My Eyes
by Ruby Bridges

In 1960 Ruby Bridges was the first black student to attend an all-white New Orleans public elementary school. Nearly 40 years later, Bridges published her memoir about this historic and life-changing event. Read to find out more about the fight for civil rights.

Ryan White: My Own Story
by Ryan White and Ann Marie Cunningham

The young AIDS activist tells the story of his own life, including how he got AIDS and how he fought for the right to attend school. This moving book shares the voice of a young man who faced terrible circumstances and still stood up for tolerance.

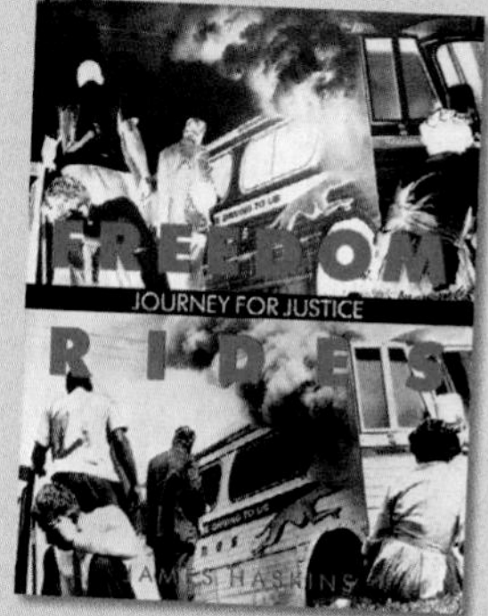

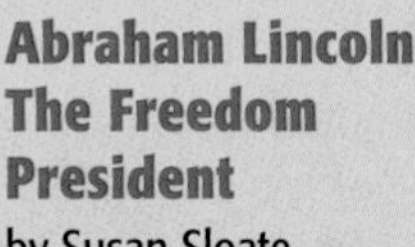

Freedom Rides
by James Haskins

In the 1960s, civil rights activists began standing up to racial segregation. The Freedom Riders were a group of individuals—some African American, some white—who fought segregation by riding buses together. In this fascinating book, one of the freedom riders describes his experiences.

Abraham Lincoln: The Freedom President
by Susan Sloate

Abraham Lincoln grew up in a poor family, but through hard work he eventually became the President of the United States. This book shows how this freedom-loving president believed in and stood up for equality.

Nonfiction

Remind students that nonfiction gives readers true stories. These recommendations are stories of real people who have fought for something.

Biography, Autobiography, and Memoir

Review with students the definitions of biography and autobiography. *(A biography is an account of a person's life written by someone else; in an autobiography, a person gives an account of his or her own life.)* Remind students that a memoir is a form of autobiographical writing. However, a memoir is focused on a particular period or event rather than the subject's whole life. Have students read the descriptions of the recommended books and identify the biography *(Abraham Lincoln: The Freedom President)*, the autobiography *(Ryan White: My Own Story)*, and the two memoirs *(Through My Eyes* and *Freedom Rides).*

About the Subjects

Remind students that they have already "met" Ruby Bridges, in an excerpt from her book in this unit. Ask which book is about another aspect of that same era and struggle. *(Freedom Rides)* Point out that the book *Ryan White: My Own Story* seems to be about a very different kind of struggle but that Ryan White also had to fight for his rights. Ask students to share what they know about Abraham Lincoln and how his story fits in with the Big Question.

Test-Taking Tips

TIP Remind students to read the directions carefully. Often the directions give important information about the passage. After students have read the questions, they may want to skim the passage, looking for key words that show the organization and main ideas of each paragraph.

TIP In a multiple choice test, sometimes the "best" answer is simply the "least bad" answer. Advise students that sometimes none of the answer choices will seem to be completely right. When that happens, students should try to eliminate the worst choices first. The choice they have left, the "least bad" choice, is the one they should pick.

ISTEP+ Test Practice

Directions:

The following speech was presented to a jury in court by George Vest, a lawyer whose client was suing a man who had shot his dog. The speech was the only statement Vest gave. It won the case. Read this speech. Then, answer questions 1 through 4.

A Tribute to the Dog

By George Graham Vest

GENTLEMEN OF THE JURY: The best friend a man has in the world may turn against him and become his enemy. His son or daughter that he has reared with loving care may prove ungrateful. Those who are nearest and dearest to us, those whom we trust with our happiness and our good name may become traitors to their faith. The money that a man has, he may lose. It flies away from him, perhaps when he needs it most. A man's reputation may be sacrificed in a moment of ill-considered action. The people who are prone[1] to fall on their knees to do us honor when success is with us, may be the first to throw the stone of malice[2] when failure settles its cloud upon our heads.

The one absolutely unselfish friend that man can have in this selfish world, the one that never deserts him, the one that never proves ungrateful or treacherous[3] is his dog. A man's dog stands by him in prosperity and in poverty, in health and in sickness. He will sleep on the cold ground, where the wintry winds blow and the snow drives fiercely, if only he may be near his master's side. He will kiss the hand that has no food to offer; he will lick the wounds and sores that come in encounter with the roughness of the world. He guards the sleep of his pauper[4] master as if he were a prince. When all other friends desert, he remains. When riches take wings, and reputation falls to pieces, he is as constant in his love as the sun in its journey through the heavens.

If fortune drives the master forth an outcast in the world, friendless and homeless, the faithful dog asks no higher privilege than that of accompanying him, to guard him against danger, to fight against his enemies. And when the last scene of all comes, and death takes his master in its embrace and his body

[1] **prone:** likely
[2] **malice:** meanness
[3] **treacherous:** unfaithful
[4] **pauper:** very poor

is laid away in the cold ground, no matter if all other friends pursue their way[5], there by the graveside will the noble dog be found, his head between his paws, his eyes sad, but open in alert watchfulness, faithful and true even in death.

[5] **pursue their way:** get on with their lives

Questions 1 through 4 are based on "A Tribute to the Dog."

1 Read this sentence from the passage.

A man's dog stands by him in prosperity and in poverty, in health and in sickness.

A contrast context clue in this sentence tells you that *prosperity* is

A wealth
B property
C disease
D unhappiness

2 Read this statement from the passage.

He is as constant in his love as the sun in its journey through the heavens.

The author uses this simile to emphasize a dog's

A good sense of direction
B willingness to travel
C purity
D consistency

3 The MAIN argument of this speech is that

A dogs are good at guarding your possessions
B dogs are better pets than other animals
C dogs will be faithful to you no matter what
D dogs won't bite you if you take care of them

4 The MAIN text structure used in this speech is

A cause-and-effect order
B chronological order
C comparison and contrast
D order of importance

Answers:

1. A
2. D
3. C
4. C

Resources for pages 1046–1051

Use these resources to review, assess, or reteach the chapter: Active Learning and Note-Taking Guide, ExamView Pro, and Differentiated Instruction Tool Software.

Test-Taking Tips

TIP Remind students that they will need to understand the author's ideas and how he or she presents those ideas in the passage to answer the questions. Suggest that students jot down a few quick notes while they read. Point out that in a real test situation, students should feel free to underline important ideas and make notes in the margins.

TIP Tell students that when they answer the questions, they should refer back to the passage and any notes they made to find clues to the correct answers. On standardized tests, passages either provide answers directly or they provide enough details for students to draw valid conclusions.

Directions:

This is the first civil rights speech delivered by Martin Luther King Jr. It followed the arrest of Rosa Parks, who had refused to give up her seat on a bus to a white man in Montgomery, Alabama. At the time of her arrest, African Americans in Montgomery and other places in the United States were forced to sit at the back of the bus and to give up their seats if asked by a white person. Read the speech, and then, answer questions 5 through 8.

from There Comes a Time When People Get Tired

By Martin Luther King Jr.

We are here this evening for serious business. We are here in a general sense because first and foremost we are American citizens and we are determined to apply our citizenship to the fullness of its meaning. We are here also because of our love for democracy, because of our deep-seated belief that democracy transformed from thin paper to thick action is the greatest form of government on earth.

But we are here in a specific sense, because of the bus situation in Montgomery. We are here because we are determined to get the situation corrected. This situation is not at all new. The problem has existed over endless years. For many years now, Negroes in Montgomery and so many other areas have been inflicted with the paralysis of crippling fears on buses in our community. . . . Just the other day, just last Thursday to be exact, one of the finest citizens in Montgomery—not one of the finest Negro citizens, but one of the finest citizens in Montgomery—was taken from a bus and carried to jail and arrested because she refused to get up and give her seat to a white person. . . . And just because she refused to get up, she was arrested.

And you know, my friends, there comes a time when people get tired of being trampled over by the iron feet of oppression. There comes a time, my friends, when people get tired of being plunged across the abyss[1] of humiliation[2], where they experience the bleakness of nagging despair. There comes a time when people get tired of being pushed out of the glittering sunlight of life's July and left standing amid the piercing chill of an alpine November. There comes a time.

We are here this evening because we're tired now. And I want to say that we are not here advocating violence. . . . My friends, don't let anybody make us

[1] **abyss:** deep hole
[2] **humiliation:** embarrassment

feel that we are to be compared in our actions with the Ku Klux Klan or with the White Citizens Council[3]. There will be no crosses burned[4] at any bus stops in Montgomery. There will be no white persons pulled out of their homes and taken out on some distant road and lynched for not cooperating. . . .

[3] **Ku Klux Klan White Citizens Council:** violent racist groups
[4] **crosses burned:** Klan members burned wooden crosses on or near the property of African Americans

Questions 5 through 8 are based on "There Comes a Time When People Get Tired."

5 Read this sentence from the passage. Then go back and read the entire paragraph in the passage.

And I want to say that we are not here advocating violence.

Context clues in the passage tell you that *advocating* means

A supporting
B denying
C enjoying
D stopping

6 This speech is titled "There Comes a Time When People Get Tired" because King wanted to emphasize that African Americans were ready to

A lose their temper
B refuse being arrested
C make changes
D give up

7 King mentions the actions of the Ku Klux Klan and the White Citizens Council MAINLY to

A tell people how not to act
B encourage people to get revenge
C make people afraid
D give evidence of racism in Montgomery

8 King MOST LIKELY uses phrases such as "paralysis of crippling fears" and "abyss of humiliation" to

A explain racist laws
B make his listeners angry
C show his talents as a speaker
D show the suffering caused by racism

Answers:

5. A
6. C
7. A
8. D

Test-Taking Tips

TIP Encourage students to use any time remaining after they've finished a test to review their answers. Tell them to make sure that each answer is marked clearly and that all written responses are legible.

Directions:

Read this portion of a speech by Barbara Jordan. Then, answer questions 9 through 13.

from All Together Now

By Barbara Jordan

When I look at race relations today I can see that some positive changes have come about. But much remains to be done, and the answer does not lie in more legislation. We *have* the legislation we need; we have the laws. Frankly, I don't believe that the task of bringing us altogether can be accomplished by government. What we need now is soul force—the efforts of people working on a small scale to build a truly tolerant, harmonious society. And parents can do a great deal to create that tolerant society.

We all know that race relations in America have had a very rocky history. Think about the 1960s when Dr. Martin Luther King Jr. was in his heyday and there were marches and protests against segregation and discrimination. The movement culminated in 1963 with the March on Washington.

Following that event, race relations reached an all-time peak. President Lyndon B. Johnson pushed through the Civil Rights Act of 1964, which remains the fundamental piece of civil rights legislation in this century. The Voting Rights Act of 1965 ensured that everyone in our country could vote. At last, black people and white people seemed ready to live together in peace.

But that is not what happened. By the 1990s the good feelings had diminished. Today the nation seems to be suffering from compassion fatigue, and issues such as race relations and civil rights have never regained momentum.

Those issues, however, remain crucial. As our society becomes more diverse, people of all races and backgrounds will have to learn to live together. If we don't think this is important, all we have to do is look at the situation in Bosnia today.

How do we create a harmonious society out of so many kinds of people? The key is tolerance—the one value that is indispensable in creating community.

If we are concerned about community, if it is important to us that people not feel excluded, then we have to do something. Each of us can decide to have one friend of a different race or background in our mix of friends. If we do this, we'll be working together to push things forward.

Questions 9 through 11 are based on "All Together Now."

9 The **main** idea of this passage is that

A civil rights are no longer an important issue
B everyone must play a role in improving our society
C life was much better in the 1960s than today
D no positive changes have been made in race relations

10 The speaker believes that the problem of race relations must be solved by

A the government
B the police
C schools
D individuals

11 Write TWO things that happened in the 1960s to help further the civil rights movement.

Use your knowledge of the writing process to answer questions 12 and 13.

12 Which sentence is written correctly?

A "How can I help" asked the curious child?
B "There's a lot to be done," said the mother to her child.
C "Susan, said her sister, it would be helpful if you did the dishes!"
D "What chore should I do, I asked."

13 Read the following sentences. If the sentences were written as a single paragraph, which sentence would be the MAIN IDEA?

A My Lab, Sal, likes to look for snacks in the trash can.
B I think I might try putting the pups in the garage.
C My collie, Wendy, loves to chew on my leather shoes.
D My puppies get into all kinds of mischief when I'm gone.

Answers:

9. B

10. D

11. Student responses will vary. A typical correct response will include two items from the following list:
- marches and protests against segregation and discrimination
- the March on Washington in 1963
- the Civil Rights Act of 1964
- the Voting Rights Act of 1965

12. B

13. D

UNIT 8
Skills Scope and Sequence

Readability Scores Key
Dale-Chall/**DRP**/**Lexile**

PACING (DAYS) STANDARD	BLOCK	INSTRUCTIONAL SEGMENT LITERATURE	READING SKILLS	LITERARY ELEMENTS
1	1	**Unit Warm-Up, pp. 1052–1063** Genre Focus: Historical Text "I Have a Dream" by Martin Luther King Jr. 902/**62**/**1130**, SE p. 1057	Identify Author's Purpose, SE p. 1058, TWE pp. 1059, 1061 Determining Main Idea, SE p. 1060 Understanding Cause and Effect, SE pp. 1060, 1063, TWE p. 1057 Analyzing, SE p. 1062, TWE pp. 1056, 1060, 1061 Fluency, TWE pp. 1053, 1063 Connecting, TWE p. 1054	Style; Metaphor, SE p. 1058 Metaphor, TWE p. 1058 Style; Cultural Reference, SE pp. 1058, 1062 Cultural Reference, TWE pp. 1057, 1062, 1063 Style, TWE pp. 1056, 1063 SE p. 1060
3	2	**Reading Workshop 1, pp. 1064–1081** "Volar" by Judith Ortiz Cofer 6.2/**57**/**1070**, SE p. 1068 from *The Century for Young People* 5.2/**54**/**950**, SE p. 1076	Analyzing, SE pp. 1064, 1067, 1069, 1075, 1076, 1079, TWE pp. 1068, 1070, 1077, 1078 Identifying Main Idea and Supporting Details, TWE pp. 1065, 1076 Fluency, TWE pp. 1067, 1077 Connecting, TWE p. 1078	Imagery, SE pp. 1067, 1068, 1070, TWE pp. 1065, 1069, 1071 Conflict, SE p. 1071 Chronological Order, SE pp. 1075, 1078, TWE p. 1076
1		**Writing Workshop, Part 1, pp. 1082–1085** Writing Product: Letter	Fluency, TWE p. 1084	
3	1	**Reading Workshop 2, pp. 1086–1101** "Lottery Winners Who Lost Their Millions" by Ellen Goodstein 7.3/**56**/**1010**, SE p. 1090 "The Gettysburg Address" by Abraham Lincoln 7.7/**62**/**1490**, SE p. 1098	Understanding Cause and Effect, SE pp. 1086, 1089–1091, 1097, 1099, TWE pp. 1087, 1092, 1093 Fluency, TWE pp. 1087, 1099 Identifying Main Idea and Supporting Details, TWE p. 1096 Paraphrasing and Summarizing, TWE p. 1097 Identifying Author's Purpose, TWE p. 1098	Theme and Topic, SE pp. 1089, 1093, TWE p. 1092 Style, SE pp. 1097, 1098 Figurative Language, TWE p. 1090 Style, TWE pp. 1097, 1098

Unit 8 Big Question

The question **"What Is the American Dream?"** speaks to the richness and diversity of America, and what America means. Answering it will help students gain understanding of America's past, present, and future.

Unit 8 Genre

Many of the selections in this unit are **historical texts,** which can include autobiographies, biographies, speeches, and stories. Reading these selections will help your students connect to the issues that people faced in the past, and answer the Big Question for themselves.

CRITICAL THINKING	VOCABULARY	WRITING AND GRAMMAR	LISTENING, SPEAKING, AND VIEWING
	Archaic Language, TWE p. 1057 Figurative Language, TWE pp. 1059, 1061	Write to Learn, SE p. 1063	Partner Talk, SE p. 1063 Viewing the Art, TWE p. 1059 Viewing the Photo, TWE pp. 1052, 1061
Contrast, SE p. 1072 Draw Conclusion, SE p. 1072 Analyze, SE p. 1072 Compare, SE p. 1080 Infer, SE p. 1080 Interpret, SE p. 1080 Comprehension, TWE pp. 1067, 1076 Evaluation, TWE pp. 1075, 1079	English as a Changing Language, SE pp. 1066, 1069, 1074, 1079 Vocabulary Flash Cards, TWE p. 1074	Write About Your Reading, SE pp. 1072, 1080 Misused Words, SE p. 1073 Confused Words, SE p. 1081	Viewing the Photo, TWE p. 1068 Analyzing the Photo, SE pp. 1069, 1070, 1077, 1078
Analysis, TWE p. 1082		Irregular Verbs, SE p. 1085 Business vs. Personal Letters, TWE p. 1083	Conducting an Interview, SE p. 1084 Interviewing Skills, TWE p. 1084 Interviewing Questions, TWE p. 1084
Explain, SE p. 1094 Evaluate, SE pp. 1094, 1100 Analyze, SE p. 1094 Interpret, SE p. 1100 Comprehension, TWE pp. 1087, 1091 Infer, SE p. 1100	English as a Changing Language, SE pp. 1088, 1090, 1091, 1096, 1098 Word Origins, TWE pp. 1091, 1099	Capitalization of Proper Nouns, SE p. 1095 Write About Your Reading, SE p. 1100 Capitalization of Places and Things, SE p. 1101	Talk About Your Reading, SE p. 1094 Analyzing the Photo, SE p. 1092 Analyzing the Painting, SE p. 1099

Skills Scope and Sequence *continued*

Readability Scores Key
Dale-Chall/ **DRP**/ Lexile

PACING (DAYS) STANDARD	BLOCK	INSTRUCTIONAL SEGMENT LITERATURE	READING SKILLS	LITERARY ELEMENTS
3	3	**Reading Workshop 3, pp. 1102–1127** "I Chose Schooling" by Jacqueling Nwaiwu 7.6/**55**/860, SE p. 1106 "The Electric Summer" by Richard Peck 5.1/**51**/800, SE p. 1114	Identifying Main Idea and Supporting Details, SE pp. 1102, 1105, 1106, 1107, 1111, 1113, 1117, 1118, 1119, 1122, 1124, TWE pp. 1116, 1125 Fluency, TWE pp. 1105, 1115 Analyzing, TWE p. 1122 Connecting, TWE p. 1123	Cultural Reference, SE pp. 1105, 1107, 1109, 1111, 1117, TWE pp. 1106, 1108, 1113, 1118 Dialogue, SE p. 1113, 1116, 1117, TWE pp. 1120, 1122, 1124, 1125
2		**Writing Workshop, Part 2, pp. 1128–1131** Writing Product: Letter	Fluency, TWE p. 1128	Style, TWE p. 1130
3	1	**Reading Workshop 4, pp. 1132–1151** "I, Too" by Langston Hughes SE p. 1136 from *Dandelion Wine* by Ray Bradbury 4.2/**52**/930, SE p. 1142	Identifying Author's Purpose, SE pp. 1132, 1135, 1137, 1141, 1143, TWE p. 1133 Analyzing, SE pp. 1144, 1146, TWE p. 1149 Understanding Cause and Effect, TWE pp. 1137, 1146, 1147	Metaphor, SE pp. 1135, 1137, TWE p. 1136 Hyperbole, SE pp. 1141, 1142, 1143, 1145, 1148, TWE p. 1147 Figurative Language, TWE pp. 1145, 1148
3	2	**Reading Across Texts Workshop, pp. 1152–1167** "Coming to America" by Joe McGowan, Marisa Wong, Vickie Bane, and Laurie Morice 9.0/**58**/840, SE p. 1155 "Coming to America" by Marianne Szegedy-Maszak 5.0/**55**/900, SE p. 1162	Reading Across Texts; Point of View, SE pp. 1155, 1157, 1158, 1160, 1163, 1164 Reading Across Texts; Evidence, SE pp. 1156, 1159, 1163, 1164 Reading Across Texts; Purpose, SE pp. 1156, 1160, 1162, 1165 Identifying Author's Purpose, TWE pp. 1152, 1157, 1160, 1162	Style, TWE p. 1155 Chronological Order, TWE pp. 1159, 1162 Cultural Reference, TWE p. 1164
4	2	**Unit Wrap-Up, pp. 1168–1181** Your Turn: "Business at Eleven" by Toshio Mori 3.6/**46**/620, SE p. 1170	Identifying Author's Purpose, TWE p. 1172 Identifying Cause and Effect, TWE p. 1173	Cultural Reference, TWE pp. 1170, 1172 Chronological Order, TWE p. 1171

CRITICAL THINKING	VOCABULARY	WRITING AND GRAMMAR	LISTENING, SPEAKING, AND VIEWING
Infer, SE pp. 1110, 1126 Conclude, SE pp. 1110, 1126 Analyze, SE p. 1110 Evaluate, SE pp. 1110, 1126, TWE p. 1109 Comprehension, TWE pp. 1102, 1115, 1119, 1120, 1121, 1123	English as Changing Language, SE pp. 1104, 1106, 1108, 1112, 1115, 1119, 1120, 1122, TWE pp. 1103, 1116 Reinforcing Vocabulary, TWE p. 1104 Reinforcing Meaning, TWE p. 1112	More Capitalization, SE p. 1111 Write About Your Reading, SE p. 1126 Capitalization of Sentences, SE p. 1127	Talk About Your Reading, SE p. 1110 Analyzing the Photo, SE pp. 1116, 1120, 1121, 1123, 1125 Analyzing the Painting, SE p. 1108
Style, TWE p. 1130	Transitions, TWE p. 1129	Establish Topic and Purpose, TWE p. 1128 Grammar, Usage, and Mechanics, TWE p. 1129 Paragraphs with Topic Sentences and Supporting Details, TWE p. 1130 Applying Good Writing Traits: Presentation, SE p. 1131	
Comprehension, TWE pp. 1142, 1144, 1148 Interpret, SE pp. 1138, 1150 Clarify, SE p. 1150 Evaluate, SE p. 1150 Explain, SE p. 1150	English as a Changing Language, SE pp. 1134, 1140, 1146, 1147 Etymology, TWE p. 1140	Verbals, SE p. 1139 Write About Your Reading, SE p. 1150 Homophones, SE p. 1151	Viewing the Art, TWE pp. 1136, 1144 Talk About Your Reading, SE p. 1138
Comprehension, TWE p. 1164 Recall, SE p. 1167 Infer, SE p. 1167 Evaluate, SE p. 1167 Interpret, SE p. 1167 Analyze, SE p. 1167	English as a Changing Language, SE pp. 1154, 1158, 1161, 1161, 1162 Word Origins, TWE pp. 1158, 1163, 1164, 1165	Writing: Reading Across Texts, SE p. 1167	Viewing the Photo, TWE pp. 1155, 1158
Comprehension, TWE p. 1171 Evaluation, TWE p. 1173	Word Origins, TWE p. 1173	Newsletter, SE pp. 1168–1169	Display and Presentation, SE p. 1169

UNIT 8 Unit Resources

Reading with Purpose offers a comprehensive package of tools to optimize student learning and the teaching experience. Each resource has been designed to assist students in specific areas and to offer instructional support for teachers. While all of these areas are covered in the core textbook, some students may need extra practice or additional help in specific areas. The resource package is designed so that you, the teacher, can choose which items will best assist your students. You may also use these resources as homework assignments and for assessment purposes. The following are resources recommended for use with Unit 8.

Keys for Unit Resources

- Blackline Master
- Workbook
- Supplemental Text
- CD-ROM
- DVD
- Transparency
- Web-based
- Fast File

Essential Instructional Support

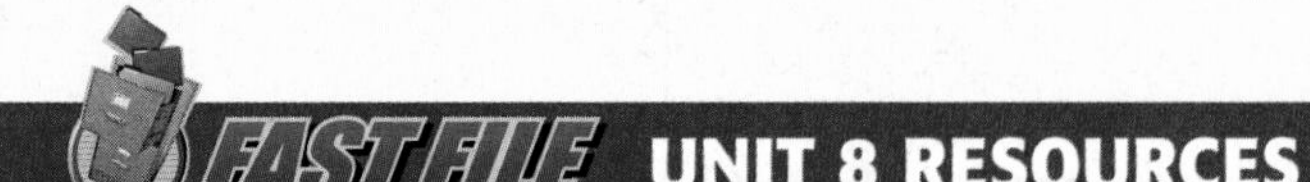

UNIT 8 RESOURCES

Reading and Literature

- Academic Vocabulary Review
- Big Question: School to Home
- The Big Question Foldable
- Unit Challenge: Planner and Rubrics
- Comparing Literature Graphic Organizer
- Key Reading Skills
- Active Reading Graphic Organizers
- Literary Analysis
- Unit Vocabulary Review

Writing, Grammar, and Spelling

- Spelling and Handwriting Practice
- Grammar Practice
- Writing Workshop Graphic Organizer

Listening, Speaking, and Viewing

- Viewing and Representing
- Listening and Speaking

English Language Learners

- English Language Coach Review

DIFFERENTIATED INSTRUCTION

- Leveled Vocabulary Development
- Skill Level Up!™ A Language Arts Game
- Listening Library CD
- BookLink 3
- Literature Library Vocabulary Puzzlemaker
- Vocabulary Puzzlemaker

ASSESSMENT

- Selection and Unit Assessments
- Selection Quick Checks
- Assessment by Learning Objectives
- Rubrics for Assessing Student Writing, Listening, and Speaking
- Glencoe Online Essay Grader
- Interactive Tutor: Self-Assessment
- ExamView Assessment Suite
- Literature Library ExamView Assessment Suite

Additional Instructional Support

WRITING, GRAMMAR, AND SPELLING

- Real Success in Writing: Research and Reports
- Writing Constructed Responses
- Spelling Power eWorkbook
- Grammar & Composition Handbook
- Grammar and Language Workbook
- Revising with Style eWorkbook

TRANSPARENCIES

- Read Aloud, Think Aloud, Transparencies
- Literary and Text Analysis Transparencies
- Bellringer Options Transparencies
- Grammar and Writing Workshop Transparencies
- Fine Art Transparencies

ENGLISH LANGUAGE LEARNER

- English Language Coach
- Fluency Practice and Assessment
- inTime Magazines (Spanish)
- Spanish Listening Library CD

PROFESSIONAL DEVELOPMENT

- Professional Development Package

READING AND LITERATURE

- Active Learning and Note Taking Guide
- inTime Magazines
- Backpack Reader Volume 1
- Literature Library
- Literature Launchers Pre-Reading Videos DVD
- Literature Classics

TECHNOLOGY

- TeacherWorks Plus™
- StudentWorks Plus™
- BookLink 3
- Skill Level Up!™ A Language Arts Game
- ExamView Assessment Suite
- Interactive Tutor Self-Assessment
- Listening Library CD
- Spanish Listening Library CD
- Literature Classics
- Literature Launchers Pre-Reading Videos DVD
- Literature Library ExamView Assessment Suite
- Vocabulary Puzzlemaker
- Literature Library Vocabulary Puzzlemaker
- glencoe.com
- Online Student Edition
- Presentation Plus!
- Glencoe Online Essay Grader

Additional Glencoe Resources

Dinah Zike's Foldables

Foldables are three-dimensional, interactive graphic organizers that help students practice basic writing skills, review key vocabulary terms, and answer Big Questions. Every unit contains a foldable activity. You can find the pattern and directions for the Unit 8 Foldable in the Unit 8 Resources Fast Files booklet. You can use the foldables as they are presented or modify them to suit the needs of your students. More information about foldables for Unit 8 can be found on pages R8–R9.

Glencoe Literature Library

This collection of hardcover books includes full-length novels, novellas, plays, and works of nonfiction. Each volume consists of at least one complete extended-length reading accompanied by several related readings from a broad range of genres. A separate Study Guide for each Glencoe Literature Library book provides teaching notes and reproducible activity pages for students.

Glencoe Literature Library titles that complement this unit include:

The House of Dies Drear by Virginia Hamilton
Johnny Tremain by Esther Forbes
Lupita Manana by Patricia Beatty

For a wealth of online resources that support the instruction in Unit 8 of *Glencoe Literature: Reading with Purpose,* students and teachers can visit our Web site at www.glencoe.com. Students will find additional learning, practice, and assessment opportunities such as these, which are noted in the student text:

- **Big Question Overview**
- **Study Central**
- **Author Search**
- **Writing Models**
- **Interactive Literary Elements Handbook**
- **Web Activities**

Teachers will find planning and instructional tools that include the following:

- **Book Lesson Plans**
- **Teacher Forum**
- **Professional Development**
- **Web Activities Lesson Plans (with answers to student activities)**

Go to www.glencoe.com to see the entire selection of Reading with Purpose online resources.

GLENCOE BOOKLINK

Use the Glencoe **BookLink 3** CD-ROM, a database of more than 26,700 titles, to *create customized reading lists* for your students.

- Search for award-winning titles, (e.g., Newbery Award winners, Coretta Scott King Award winners, and Caldecott Medal winners) and for books on several state-recommended reading lists.
- Find Degrees of Reading Power™ (DRP) and Lexile™ readability scores for all selections.
- Organize reading lists by students' reading level, author, genre, theme, or area of interest.
- Get a brief summary of each selection.

You can find recommended leveled readings for this unit with Reading on Your Own (see page 1174).

Glencoe's **Presentation Plus!**, a multimedia teaching tool, lets you present dynamic lessons that will engage your students. Using Microsoft PowerPoint®, you can customize the presentations to create your own personalized lessons. Use **CheckPoint** questions with interactive response keypads to get immediate student feedback during lessons, to increase student participation, and to assess student comprehension.

A lively collection of articles drawn from issues of the TIME family of magazines helps students develop the skills they need to interact with informational text in a meaningful way. Each of the news stories, feature articles, reviews, profiles, and essays in the magazine connect to an author, work, or theme in *Glencoe Literature: Reading with Purpose.* Articles for Unit 8 are found in Volume B. See the *inTIME* Teacher's Guide for specific connections to each unit and for reproducible student worksheets designed to develop students' reading and critical thinking skills.

Literature Launchers

Set the scene with Glencoe's Literature Launchers, engaging video segments that introduce each unit's genre focus. Each video brings the genre to life, relating it to your students' worlds.

Insert the Glencoe Literature Launchers Pre-Reading Videos DVD into your DVD player. Select the Unit 8 Launcher from the menu to introduce the genre and Big Question for this unit.

Online Essay Grader

Use Glencoe's Online Essay Grader to score your students' writing and to provide individualized feedback to each student automatically.

You and your students can visit www.glencoe.com to link to the essay grader. *Students* can enter their essays and receive feedback on demand. *You* can manage demographic data, assign tests and generate individual student and aggregated reports. The essay grader can help you

- Save time with automatic scoring and individualized feedback.
- Supplement in-class writing instruction using guided writing practice.
- Get reports for individual students or for special populations.
- Track student improvement over time.

REAL Success: Reading Excellence at All Levels

Glencoe now provides all of your students with the tools they need to become better, more enthusiastic readers. The REAL Success suite of reading and language arts products encourages reading excellence by meeting the needs of students at all levels. Glencoe products that can be used in conjunction with Unit 8 include the following:

- *Jamestown Literature: An Adapted Reader*
- Jamestown *Reading Fluency*
- Jamestown *Critical Reading Series, In the Line of Duty*
- *Vocabulary Builder*
- *The Glencoe Reader, Course 3*

To order these products, call Glencoe at 1-800-USA-READ.

Teacher Wraparound Edition Key

Level Appropriate Code

AS = Activities for all students
AL = Activities for students working above grade level
OL = Activities for students working at grade level
BL = Activities for students working below grade level
EL = Activities for English language learners

Teacher Wraparound Prompts

R Reading Skill These activities help you teach reading comprehension skills.

V Vocabulary These activities help students comprehend words and incorporate them into their reading and writing.

C Critical Thinking These strategies help students apply and extend what they have learned.

BQ BIG Question These activities and questions prompt students to prepare to answer the Big Question.

W Writing These activities provide writing opportunities to help students practice writing and comprehend text.

L Literary Element These activities and questions help students comprehend selections and learn more about each genre.

E Text Element These activities help students comprehend text elements.

LSV Listening, Speaking, Viewing These activities help students practice listening, speaking, and viewing skills.

EL English Language Coach These skills help English language learners as well as students who need additional reading support.

UNIT 8

Professional Development Center

From an Author:

Jeffrey Wilhelm

Preparing Students to Read Historical Texts

Discuss what a community is. In order to understand the relevance of historical texts, students need to comprehend what a community is and have background information about the community or culture they are reading about. Help students understand that a community is a group of people with some commonality. They can be members of a family, people who live in a certain neighborhood, people who share a cultural background, students who attend the same school, etc. Before you introduce the importance of historical texts, make sure students have a good grasp of the concept of community. This will be helpful when they answer the Big Question "What is the American dream?" as they recognize that a person's idea of community helps to shape his or her dream.

Define the genre. Help students understand how the writings they create could become historical texts. Do they send e-mails or letters? Do they keep diaries or journals? Have they ever clipped a photo or an article from a newspaper or magazine? Have students bring in one of these items and predict how a teenager in the year 2050 would respond to the content of their historical texts.

Once you think students have a clear understanding of the genre, you may proceed to share how you will study historical texts in this unit. Tell them they will read memoirs and news articles, all of which can be considered historical texts. They will also read other genres that address the Big Question. They will look at how historical texts can tell us about the different versions of the American dream that have existed at different periods in time.

Bonnie Mae Smith
Hettinger High School
Hettinger, North Dakota

Teacher to Teacher

On a large sheet of butcher paper, I write the words AMERICAN DREAM vertically. I use this vertical set of letters to create a poem horizontally. For each letter, students add a word that to them represents the question: What is the American dream? We end up with a poem the whole class wrote that expresses what the students feel it means to be American. In addition, we cut out words from newspapers and magazines that represent the theme "American dream." We then create a collage with the words and display it with the poem.

Teacher Chat Room

Using Historical Texts

How do I make historical texts interesting to students?

One key way to make students interested in historical texts is to point out to them the historical texts they are creating today. When students realize that historical texts were at one time functional documents that helped people live day to day or helped them communicate with others, students are less likely to think of the texts as "boring." Relating a document to a modern-day form of communication will help students understand its significance.

How do I help students learn from reading historical texts?

Help students see beyond the information so they can grasp the meaning behind the text. Have students ask themselves: "Why is this important? Why would someone write this in a letter or a journal entry? What is going on in the world or local community that could provoke the writer to respond in such a way? Why would someone need to use this document? How would it help a user?" Help students develop critical thinking skills while examining these texts.

Encourage students to read "historical" texts they create or use. Perhaps they can find a letter, report card, or other document that is at least one year old. Have them review the text and analyze its content. What was going on at the time? Why was the text created? What conclusions would someone reading this text in 50 years be able to make?

Discuss the reasons why historical texts survive. Why do individuals and governments preserve them? Why is it important for us to know what life was like decades or hundreds of years ago? Remind students that in addition to telling us details about the everyday life of people who lived in a certain time period, historical texts can teach us about their ideas and values.

Key Unit Objectives

- Answer the Big Question
- Analyze the literary elements of historical texts
- Apply strategies for reading historical texts
- Write letters

BIG Question

Why Is It Important?
Addressing this big question helps students consider the richness and multifaceted nature of the American dream. Explain that students will gain understanding by reading what the American dream has meant to different people in different times and places.

Viewing the Photo
Invite students to describe the photograph on this page. Ask them what it suggests and how it makes them feel. Talk about the power of the image of the Statue of Liberty for Americans and for people around the world. Ask students to explain how the quotation relates to the photograph. *(Possible response: The Statue of Liberty is a symbol of freedom, power, and the promise of a new life. The quotation explains how to attain that new life.)* OL

UNIT 8

The BIG Question: What Is the American Dream?

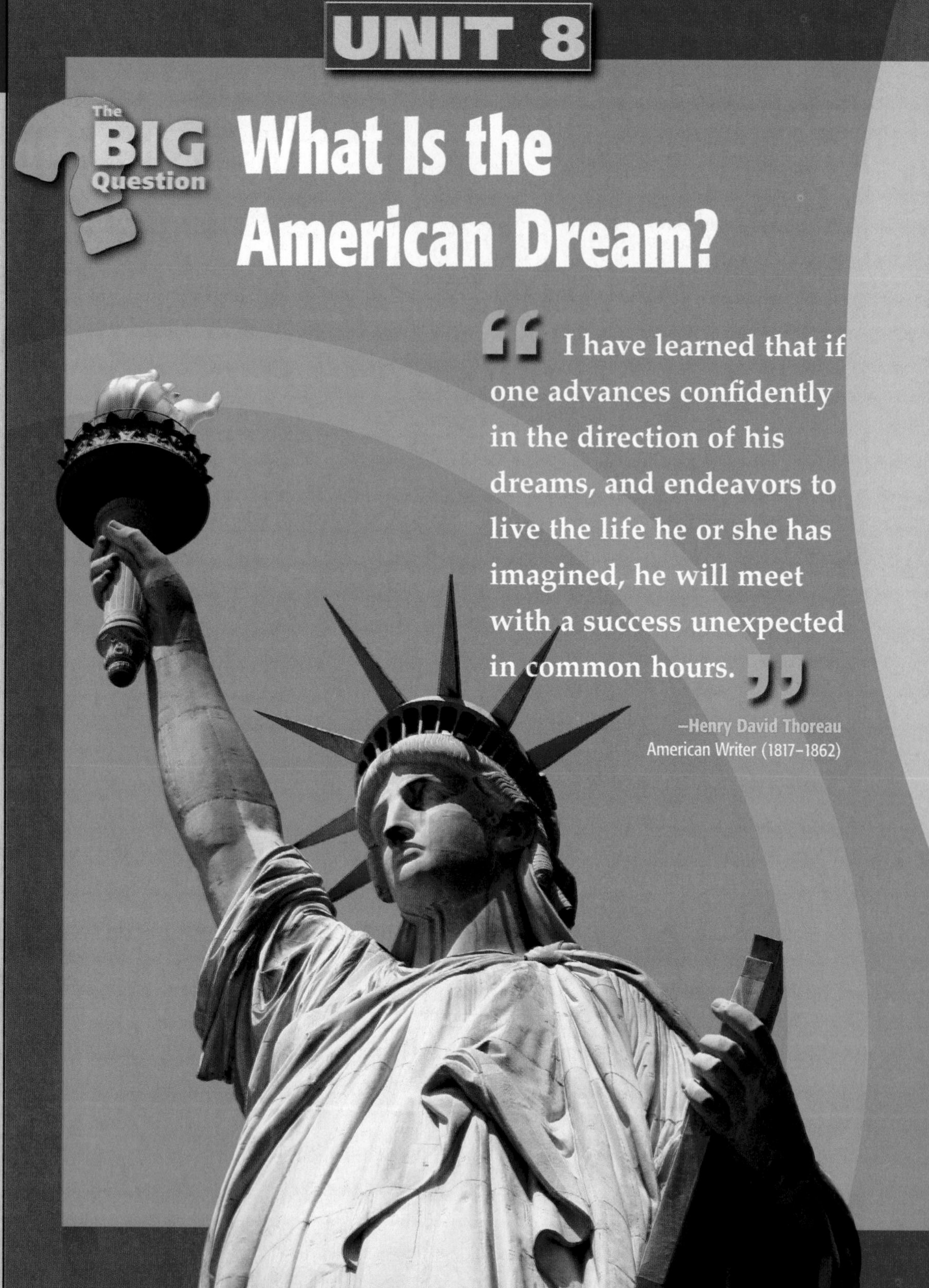

"I have learned that if one advances confidently in the direction of his dreams, and endeavors to live the life he or she has imagined, he will meet with a success unexpected in common hours."

—Henry David Thoreau
American Writer (1817–1862)

Unit Skills

BIG Question What is the American dream?
Genre Focus: Historical Text

Reading Skills
- Analyzing, p. 1064
- Understanding Cause and Effect, p. 1086.
- Identifying Main Idea and Supporting Details, p. 1102
- Identifying Author's Purpose, p. 1132

Vocabulary
- English as a Changing Language, p. 1066

Literary and Text Elements
- Chronological Order, p. 1075
- Style, p. 1097
- Cultural Reference, p. 1105
- Metaphor, p. 1135

Writing Skills/Grammar
- Letter, pp. 1082, 1128
- Irregular Verbs, p. 1085
- Presentation, p. 1131

LOOKING AHEAD

The skill lessons and readings in this unit will help you develop your own answer to the Big Question.

About the Reading

Each selection in this unit provides insights that can help students to address the question "What is the American dream?" Students consider what the American dream has meant to different people in different times and places and how the American dream is still being redefined and reinvented today.

About the Skills

The skills taught in this unit have been selected because they are particularly helpful when reading the featured genre—historical text. Each reading selection provides students with opportunities to practice and develop these skills.

NCLB places great emphasis on improving English fluency. Teaching the skills targeted in this unit and providing students with the opportunity to read aloud certain passages from this unit will help students achieve greater reading and English fluency.

Reading Fluency

Build Fluency To develop reading fluency with historical texts, provide students with a primary source from the eighteenth or nineteenth century, such as a letter or speech. Have students look up the meanings and pronunciations of any unfamiliar words. Then, invite them to find a quiet place to practice reading the passage aloud with partners. Explain that they should reread the passage several times until they can fluently read all the sentences with expression and understanding. Encourage them to try to make their reading sound like natural speech. Finally, allow students time to read their selections aloud for the class. BL

Indiana English/Language Arts Academic Standards
TWE: *Reading Fluency* 8.7.14

Focus

BELLRINGER Options

- **Literature Launcher**
- **Daily Language Practice Transparency 72**

Focus Activity Ask: What does the American dream mean to you? *(Responses will vary.)* Write responses on the board. **Ask:** Do you think the idea of the American dream meant something different to your parents? To your grandparents? Talk about how ideals can change over time. *(Responses will vary.)* AS

Teach

R Reading Skill

Review Connecting Ask: How does your idea of the American dream compare with those described in the first paragraph on this page? *(Responses will vary.)* AS

BQ BIG Question

- Have students read the profiles and look at the pictures of Yuri and Alexandra.
- Have partners discuss each situation and decide how they think each person would respond. AS

UNIT 8 WARM-UP

Connecting to The BIG Question What Is the American Dream?

The American dream means many things to many different people. One thing that many people agree on is that the American dream means that every person is free to achieve all that he or she is capable of. And every person should be recognized for who he or she is regardless of social class or ethnic background. In this unit, you'll read about different people and what the American dream means to them. R

Real Kids and the Big Question

YURI and his family moved here from a country outside the United States. His family had been displaced because of wars in their county. Now Yuri and his family live in an apartment near the school. Yuri and his sisters and brothers have made many new friends. They are learning all about American culture. If you asked Yuri what the American dream means to him, what do you think he would say?

BQ

ALEXANDRA was not at all sure that she wanted to attend the new magnet school. But she took the test and was admitted. She knows that getting a good education can help her achieve her goals. Her parents always tell her that if she stays in school, she can accomplish anything. If you ask Alexandra what the American dream means to her, what do you think she would say?

Warm-Up Activity

In a small group, discuss what you think the American dream means to you, Yuri, and Alexandra. Then discuss ways in which you hope to achieve your American dream.

Additional Support

Reading in the Real World

Career Yuri and his family are immigrants to this country. When people come here from a foreign country, they often need time to learn the language if English is not their first language. They also need to learn about American customs and traditions. Some students may be interested in careers that help immigrants. Have students work in small groups to research careers such as immigration lawyer or ELL teacher. Have students write reports covering aspects of a job of their choosing, including educational requirements, job opportunities, duties, and functions. OL AL

You and the Big Question

Reading about how other people define the American dream will help you think about how you would answer the Big Question. BQ

Literature Online

BIG Question Link to Web resources to further explore the Big Question at www.glencoe.com.

Plan for the Unit Challenge

At the end of the unit, you'll use notes from all your reading to complete the Unit Challenge, which will explore your answer to the Big Question.

You'll choose one of the following activities:

A. The American Dream Newsletter Work in groups to write, design, and produce a newsletter about people who achieve their American dreams.

B. An American Dream Spokesperson Write a short biography or speech, or create a poster to honor your American dream spokesperson.

- Start thinking about which activity you'd like to do so that you can focus your thinking as you go through the unit.
- In your Learner's Notebook, write your thoughts about which activity you'd like to do.
- Each time you make notes about the Big Question, think about how your ideas will help you with the Unit Challenge activity you chose.

Keep Track of Your Ideas

As you read, you'll make notes about the Big Question. Later, you'll use these notes to complete the Unit Challenge. See pages R8–R9 for help with making Foldable 8. This diagram shows how it should look.

1. Use this Foldable for all of the selections in this unit. Label the stapled edge with the unit number and the Big Question.
2. Label each flap with a title. (See page 1053 for the titles.)
3. Open each flap. Near the top of the page, write **My Purpose for Reading.** Below the crease, write **The Big Question.**

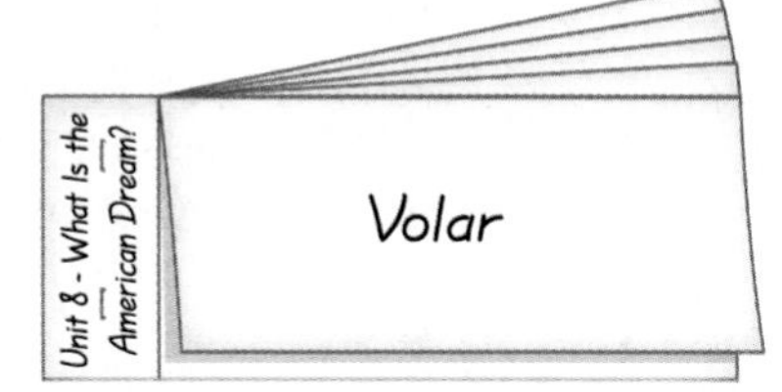

UNIT 8 WARM-UP

Teach

BQ 

Have students write three words that, for them, sum up the American dream. AS

Study Organizer For each selection they read, students will enter notes about how that selection applies to the Big Question. For details about using Dinah Zike's Foldables, see pages R8–R9.

Assess/Close

Ask students to share their thoughts on why reading about the Big Question might help them clarify their ideas about the American dream and its significance to them. Consider sharing some of your own thoughts about the American dream.

Resources for page 1055

 Use the Unit Challenge Planner BLM in the Unit 8 Resource Booklet p. 38.

 Use the Foldable BLM in the Unit 8 Resource Booklet p. 7.

Differentiated Instruction

Group Discussion Obtain copies of such songs as "America the Beautiful" and "My Country 'Tis of Thee" to play for students. Discuss how the songs depict America as a place and as a nation. You might also distribute copies of the songs' lyrics in order to better facilitate discussion. Divide students into small groups to discuss the lyrics. Then have students make textual connections between the songs and the Big Question. Ask students how the songs exemplify the American dream. When students finish their discussions, allow them to share the main points in the class as a whole. OL

Indiana English/Language Arts Academic Standards
TWE: *Reading in the Real World* 8.5.3, *Differentiated Instruction* 8.3

Focus

BELLRINGER Options

- **Selection Focus Transparency 17**
- **Daily Language Practice Transparency 73**

Focus Activity Ask: How do we know about the past? *(Possible responses: people tell us; oral histories; books; stories; documents; letters; newspapers)* **Say:** In this unit, you will read a variety of historical texts that tell the story of the past from many different perspectives. AS

Teach

R Reading Skill

Analyzing Ask: What does it mean to analyze text? *(Possible response: Analyzing is a way to think clearly and logically about a piece of writing.)* OL

L Literary Element

Style Ask: How might the style of a short story differ from that of a formal speech? *(Possible response: The style of a short story might be informal or friendly, whereas a formal speech would likely be more structured.)* OL AL

UNIT 8 GENRE FOCUS: HISTORICAL TEXT

Skills Focus

- Key skills for reading historical text
- Key literary elements of historical text

Skills Model

You will see how to use the key reading skills and literary elements as you read

- **"I Have a Dream,"** p. 1057

Have you ever imagined what it might have been like to live in North America before Europeans arrived, or during the Gold Rush in the West? These times and places can be explored through a variety of historical writings. **Historical text** can take many different forms including speeches, autobiographies, biographies, and stories. It can be nonfiction or fiction. Nonfiction historical text gives a factual account of past events, places, and people. Historical fiction combines fact and fiction in a story set in the past.

Why Read Historical Text?

Historical text allows you to understand the problems and issues that people faced in the past. Often this knowledge sheds light on the problems of our own time, and helps us better understand the choices we face.

How to Read Historical Text

Key Reading Skills

These key reading skills are especially useful tools for reading and understanding historical text. You'll learn more about these skills later in the unit.

R
- **Analyzing** As you read a selection, think about how its parts work together. Think about what the author is saying. Look at how the main ideas are organized. (See Reading Workshop 1.)
- **Understanding Cause and Effect** As you read, look for what makes something happen. (See Reading Workshop 2.)
- **Identifying Main Idea and Supporting Details** Find the most important idea in a paragraph or in a selection. Look for examples, reasons, or details that help you know it's the most important idea. (See Reading Workshop 3.)
- **Identifying Author's Purpose** As you figure out the author's purpose, you can evaluate his or her point of view. (See Reading Workshop 4.)

Key Literary and Text Elements

Recognizing and thinking about the following literary and text elements will help you understand historical texts more fully.

- **Chronological order:** the order in which events happen in time (See *The Century for Young People.*)
- L **Style:** an author's personal way of using language (See "The Gettysburg Address.")
- **Cultural reference:** the mention of a value, belief, tradition, or custom practiced in a certain culture (See "I Chose Schooling.")
- **Metaphor:** a figure of speech that compares two unlike things without using the words *like* and *as* (See "I, Too.")

Indiana English/ Language Arts Academic Standards (pp. 1056–1061)

8.2 Comprehension and Analysis (Focus on Informational Text) Develop [reading] strategies...identifying and analyzing structure, organization, perspective, and purpose. **8.3.6** Identify significant literary devices...which define a writer's style and use [them] to interpret a work.

For a complete description of the standards, see p. IN 11.

Additional Support

Reading in the Real World

College Explain to students that many historical texts are *primary sources,* or original records of events. Tell students that when they write research papers about a particular time period, they will need to consult primary sources, such as letters, newspaper articles, photographs, and other historical documents. Using primary sources adds credibility and interest to writing. Provide students with a primary source from the 1800s, such as a journal entry or letter from a soldier fighting in the Civil War, to read as a class. Lead a discussion about the differences in language use between then and now. AL

I Have a Dream

by Martin Luther King Jr.

Historical Text
ACTIVE READING MODEL

I am happy to join with you today in what will go down in history as the greatest demonstration for freedom in the history of our nation.[1]

Fivescore years ago, a great American, in whose symbolic shadow we stand today, signed the Emancipation Proclamation. This momentous[2] decree came as a great beacon light of hope to millions of Negro slaves who had been seared in the flames of withering injustice. It came as a joyous daybreak to end the long night of their captivity. **1** **R**

But one hundred years later, the Negro still is not free; one hundred years later, the life of the Negro is still sadly crippled by the manacles of segregation and the chains of discrimination;[3] one hundred years later, the Negro lives on a lonely island of poverty in the midst of a vast ocean of material prosperity; one hundred years later, the Negro is still languished[4] in the corners of American society and finds himself in exile in his own land. **2**

So we've come here today to dramatize a shameful condition. In a sense we've come to our nation's capital to

1 Key Text Element
L **Cultural Reference** *The references to Lincoln and the end of slavery would have had special significance to King's audience.*

2 Key Text Element
Chronological Order *To make the order very clear, King uses signal words—"fivescore years ago" in the previous paragraph and "one hundred years later" repeatedly here.*

1. King gave this speech at the March for Jobs and Freedom in Washington, D.C., on August 28, 1963. The crowd was estimated at between 250,000 and 400,000 people.
2. One score is twenty, so ***fivescore*** is one hundred. King is echoing Abraham Lincoln's Gettysburg Address, which begins with "fourscore and seven years ago." ***Momentous*** (moh MEN tus) means "extremely important."
3. ***Manacles*** (MAN uh kuls) are handcuffs. ***Segregation*** is the practice of separating people because of their race or skin color. ***Discrimination*** is unfair treatment, especially because of people's race or skin color.
4. King uses ***languished*** (LANG wishd) to mean something like "suffering from neglect."

Teach

R Reading Skill

Understanding Cause and Effect **Ask:** What words does King use to describe the effect of the Emancipation Proclamation? *(great beacon light of hope, a joyous daybreak to end the long night of their captivity)* **Ask:** What does King say about the reason for the march in Washington? *(to dramatize a shameful condition)* **OL** **AL**

L Literary Element

Cultural Reference **Ask:** Why do you think King's references to Lincoln (a great American) and the end of slavery (Emancipation Proclamation) would have had special significance to King's audience? *(Possible responses: As African Americans and other people fought against the injustices of segregation, they were reminded that Lincoln led the country during the Civil War, which included the struggle to end slavery.)* **AS**

Readability Scores
Dale-Chall: 9.2
DRP: 62
Lexile: 1130

English Language Coach

Archaic Language Martin Luther King Jr. used the archaic, or out-of-use, word *fivescore* in this speech, written in 1963. Abraham Lincoln made the expression "fourscore and seven years ago" famous when he used it in his "Gettysburg Address," which students will read later in this unit. Invite students to discuss why King might have used this old-fashioned expression in his speech. *(to remind listeners of the spirit of Lincoln and his "Gettysburg Address")* You might also point out that the use of the word *Negro* was preferred at the time of the speech, instead of *African American* or *black*. **EL** **OL**

Indiana English/Language Arts Academic Standards
SE: 8.2, 8.3.6
TWE: *English Language Coach* 8.3.6

Teach

L Literary Element

Metaphor **Ask:** How does using metaphor, or comparing two unlike things, add to the power of King's writing? *(Possible response: It helps clarify ideas such as injustice by comparing it to something concrete and familiar, like a bad check.)* AS

R Reading Skill

Identifying Author's Purpose Write the words *justice* and *equality* on the board. **Ask:** What do these words make you think of? *(Possible response:* Justice *makes me think of things that are "right" or considered "moral."* Equality *makes me think of everyone being treated the same or having the same amount of something.)* **Ask:** Why do you think King repeats the word *justice* throughout and contrasts it with injustice? *(Possible response: to make a point about the purpose of the assembly)* OL AL

ACTIVE READING MODEL

cash a check. When the architects of our republic wrote the magnificent words of the Constitution and the Declaration of Independence, they were signing a promissory note[5] to which every American was to fall heir. This note was the promise that all men, yes, black men as well as white men, would be guaranteed the unalienable[6] rights of life, liberty, and the pursuit of happiness. 3 4

It is obvious today that America has defaulted[7] on this promissory note in so far as her citizens of color are concerned. Instead of honoring this sacred obligation, America has given the Negro people a bad check; a check which has come back marked "insufficient funds." We refuse to believe that there are insufficient funds in the great vaults of opportunity of this nation. And so we've come to cash this check, a check that will give us upon demand the riches of freedom and the security of justice. L

We have also come to this hallowed spot[8] to remind America of the fierce urgency of now. This is no time to engage in the luxury of cooling off or to take the tranquilizing drug of gradualism.[9] Now is the time to make real the promises of democracy; now is the time to rise from the dark and desolate[10] valley of segregation to the sunlit path of racial justice; now is the time to lift our nation from the quicksands of racial injustice to the solid rock of brotherhood; now is the time to make justice a reality for all God's children. It would be fatal for the nation to overlook the urgency of the moment. This sweltering summer of the Negro's legitimate discontent will not pass until there is an invigorating[11] autumn of freedom and equality. 5 R

3 **Key Reading Skill**
Identify Author's Purpose *King makes his purpose clear when he says he's "come to dramatize a shameful condition"—America's failure to live up to its promise of equality for African Americans.*

4 **Key Literary Elements**
Style; Metaphor *Figurative language, including metaphors, are a part of King's style. Here he introduces the check and promissory note metaphors and then explains them in the final sentence and next paragraph.*

5 **Key Literary Elements**
Style; Cultural Reference *References to literature are another element of King's style. Here, "summer of . . . discontent" echoes the phrase "winter of our discontent" in* Richard III *by William Shakespeare.*

5. A ***promissory note*** is a written promise to pay a certain amount of money to someone at a future date.
6. ***Unalienable rights,*** according to the Declaration of Independence, are rights that may not be taken away.
7. ***Defaulted*** means "failed to do what was required."
8. King spoke from the steps of the Lincoln Memorial, a place many people consider holy ***(hallowed).***
9. ***Gradualism*** is the process of trying to bring about social change gradually, or slowly.
10. ***Desolate*** (DES uh lit) means "without comfort."
11. ***Sweltering*** means "very hot and humid," and ***invigorating*** means "bringing new life and energy." King is talking about more than just seasonal changes.

Additional Support

Literature Focus Lesson

Allusion Explain to students that an allusion is a reference to another text, person, or event from history or culture. Writers use allusions to add depth and interest to their work. King was a minister of a church. When he speaks of the "dark and desolate valley of segregation," many of his followers would hear echoes of Psalms 23, which says, "Yea, though I walk through the valley of the shadow of death. . . ." **Ask:** What other allusion does he make at the beginning of this page? *(He makes allusion to the Declaration of Independence.)* OL AL

King Mural, 1986. Don Miller. District of Columbia Public Library.

Nineteen sixty-three is not an end, but a beginning. And those who hope that the Negro needed to blow off steam and will now be content, will have a rude awakening if the nation returns to business as usual. There will be neither rest nor tranquility in America until the Negro is granted his citizenship rights. The whirlwinds of the revolt will continue to shake the foundations of our nation until the bright day of justice emerges. **R**

But there is something that I must say to my people, who stand on the warm threshold which leads into the

English Language Coach

Figurative Language Write this sentence on the board, underlining the phrases as shown. Then read the sentence aloud: The *whirlwind of the revolt* will continue to shake the *foundations of our nation* until the *bright day of justice* emerges. **Ask:** How is revolt like a whirlwind? *(Possible responses: chaotic, destructive)* **Say:** A building has a foundation made of concrete or stone. What kind of foundation does our nation have? *(Possible response: The Declaration of Independence or the Constitution)* **Ask:** When King says the "whirlwinds of revolt will . . . shake the foundations of our nation," what is he suggesting? *(That this period of unrest may upset the very founding principles of our nation.)* OL AL

Teach

Viewing the Art

Say: The mural depicted in the Student Edition is only a section of a much larger work that is displayed in the lobby of the Martin Luther King Jr. Memorial Library in Washington, D.C. It depicts events from 1955 to 1968. The artist, Don Miller, was born in Jamaica, raised in New Jersey, and has traveled the world searching for his African ancestry and its importance to his identity. How would you describe King based on this illustration? *(Possible response: serious, calm, assertive)* BL OL

R Reading Skill

Identifying Author's Purpose **Say:** King addresses himself to two distinct audiences. For each audience, he has a specific message. Who are these two audiences? *(1. the people who hope that the marches and civil unrest will soon be over and the nation will return to business as usual; 2. those fighting for equality)* **Ask:** What is King's message to the first audience? *(that peace will not return until justice is achieved)* **Ask:** What do you think his message will be to his people? *(Responses will vary.)* OL

Indiana English/Language Arts Academic Standards
SE: 8.2, 8.3.6
TWE: *Literature Focus Lesson* 8.3.6, *English Language Coach* 8.3.6

Teach

R1 Reading Skill

Analyzing **Say:** King talks about "meeting physical force with soul force." What does this mean to you? *(Possible response: Physical force refers to the police, dogs, and guns; soul force is conviction, commitment, and spirituality. He is saying that they should wage peaceful protests.)* AS

R2 Reading Skill

Indentifying Main Idea and Supporting Details
Ask: What is the main idea of the paragraph that begins, "There are those who . . ."? *(Possible response: We will be satisfied only when we have achieved our aim of justice.)*
Say: List details that support the main idea. *(These injustices must be addressed: police brutality, African Americans being barred from hotels and motels, African Americans' mobility limited to ghettos, their children robbed of dignity by segregation, their voting rights not respected or having nothing to vote for.)* OL AL

ACTIVE READING MODEL

palace of justice. In the process of gaining our rightful place, we must not be guilty of wrongful deeds. Let us not seek to satisfy our thirst for freedom by drinking from the cup of bitterness and hatred. We must forever conduct our struggle on the high plain of dignity and discipline. We must not allow our creative protest to generate into physical violence. Again and again we must rise to the majestic heights of meeting physical force with soul force; and the marvelous new militancy,[12] which has engulfed the Negro community, must not lead us to a distrust of all white people. For many of our white brothers, as evidenced by their presence here today, have come to realize that their destiny is tied up with our destiny. And they have come to realize that their freedom is inextricably[13] bound to our freedom. We cannot walk alone. And as we talk, we must make the pledge that we shall always march ahead. We cannot turn back. 6

There are those who are asking the devotees of Civil Rights, "When will you be satisfied?" We can never be satisfied as long as the Negro is the victim of the unspeakable horrors of police brutality; we can never be satisfied as long as our bodies, heavy with the fatigue of travel, cannot gain lodging in the motels of the highways and the hotels of the cities; we cannot be satisfied as long as the Negro's basic mobility is from a smaller ghetto to a larger one; we can never be satisfied as long as our children are stripped of their selfhood and robbed of their dignity by signs stating "For Whites Only"; we cannot be satisfied as long as the Negro in Mississippi cannot vote and a Negro in New York believes he has nothing for which to vote. No! no, we are not satisfied, and we will not be satisfied until "justice rolls down like waters and righteousness like a mighty stream.[14]" 7 8

I am not unmindful that some of you have come here out of great trials and tribulations.[15] Some of you have come fresh from narrow jail cells. Some of you have come

6 Key Reading Skill
Determining Main Idea *There are two main ideas in this paragraph. One is that African Americans must use peaceful methods to achieve freedom. The other is that white people who deny freedom to others are victims of their own ignorance and prejudice.*

7 Key Reading Skill
Identifying Cause and Effect *King states one effect (dissatisfaction) and ties it to a number of causes (police brutality and so on).*

8 Key Literary Element
Style *Another key part of King's style is repetition. The repetition gives the speech emotional power, just as it does in poems, song lyrics, and music.*

12. ***Militancy*** (MIH luh tun see) refers to being ready to fight for a cause.
13. ***Inextricably*** (ih nik STRIH kuh blee) means "in a way that cannot be separated."
14. This line is from the Old Testament's book of Amos.
15. ***Tribulation*** (trih byuh LAY shun) is a great misery or distress.

Additional Support

Differentiated Instruction

Analyzing Imagery and Allusion

Tell students that King's speeches reflect his theological background by alluding to or using biblical passages. Like sermons, King's speeches often draw on quotations from the Bible. The quotation at the end of the last full paragraph is drawn from Amos 5:23. Invite students to describe what kind of picture the quotation creates for them. *(Possible response: Waters in a mighty stream make me think of the rapids in the river outside the city. If justice is like those rapids, it is abundant and powerful.)* Ask students what literary device is used in this quotation. *(simile)* OL from areas where your quest for freedom left you battered by the storms of persecution and staggered by the winds of police brutality. You have been the veterans of creative **R1** suffering. Continue to work with the faith that unearned suffering is redemptive.[16] Go back to Mississippi. Go back to Alabama. Go back to South Carolina. Go back to Georgia. Go back to Louisiana. Go **R2** back to the slums and ghettos of our Northern cities, knowing that somehow this situation can and will be changed. Let us not wallow[17] in the valley of despair.

I say to you today, my friends, so even though we face the difficulties of today and tomorrow, I still have a dream. It is a dream deeply rooted in the American dream. I have a dream that one day this nation will rise up and live out the true meaning of its creed, "We hold these truths to be self-evident, that all men are created equal." I have a dream that one day on the red hills of Georgia, sons of former slaves and the sons of former slave owners will be able to sit down together at the table of brotherhood. I have a dream that one day even the state of Mississippi, a state sweltering with the heat of injustice, sweltering with the heat of oppression, will be transformed into an oasis of freedom and justice. I have a dream that my four little children will one day

At the Lincoln Memorial, the crowd listens as TV cameras capture King's speech.

16. If something is ***redemptive*** (rih DEMP tiv), it brings rescue or freedom.

17. In this context, to ***wallow*** is to become or remain helpless.

English Language Coach

Figurative Language Tell students that much of King's address is given in figurative language, including metaphors, similes, personification, and idioms. Direct students to the sentence on pages 1060–1061 that begins, "Some of you." Challenge students to find the implied metaphors in this sentence. *(storms of persecution, winds of police brutality)* Explain to students that King is comparing racism and prejudice to a violent storm. Have students identify parts of a storm, such as rain and wind. Lead students to see that King is comparing police brutality to wind, which is part of the storm. **EL** **OL**

Teach

R1 Reading Skill

Analyzing **Ask:** What do you think King means when he talks about "creative suffering"? *(Possible response: the many ways that people have found to torment and torture the sufferers)* **AL**

R2 Reading Skill

Identifying Author's Purpose
Ask: What is King's purpose in the first paragraph on this page? *(Possible response: to encourage people to return to the struggle with renewed energy)* **OL** **AL**

Viewing the Photo

Say: Martin Luther King Jr. delivered this speech in 1963 at the Lincoln Memorial. Over 200,000 civil-rights proponents attended that day. How do you think it would have felt to be in the crowd you see pictured here, listening to King's speech? *(Possible responses: inspiring, exciting, overwhelming)* **OL**

Indiana English/Language Arts Academic Standards
SE: 8.2, 8.3.6
TWE: *Differentiated Instruction* 8.3.6, *English Language Coach* 8.3.6

Teach

L Literary Element

Cultural Reference Direct students' attention to the reference to Alabama. Have students read the footnote about Governor George Wallace. Tell students that in June of 1963, Wallace prevented African American students from attending the University of Alabama. When he took office, he pledged, "Segregation Now, Segregation Tomorrow, Segregation Forever!" A month after King's speech, a black church in Birmingham, Alabama, was bombed, and four girls were killed as a result. **Say:** King's audience would be well aware of these incidents in Alabama. How do you think this reference affected his audience? *(Possible response: It solidified their belief that they needed to work toward change.)* OL

live in a nation where they will not be judged by the color of their skin, but by the content of their character. 9

I have a dream today!

I have a dream that one day down in Alabama—with its vicious racists, with its Governor having his lips dripping with the words of interposition and nullification[18]—one day right there in Alabama, little black boys and black girls will be able to join hands with little white boys and white girls as sisters and brothers. L

I have a dream today!

I have a dream that one day "every valley shall be exalted[19] and every hill and mountain shall be made low. The rough places will be made plain and the crooked places will be made straight, and the glory of the Lord shall be revealed, and all flesh shall see it together."[20]

This is our hope. This is the faith that I go back to the South with. With this faith we shall be able to transform the jangling discords[21] of our nation into a beautiful symphony of brotherhood. With this faith we will be able to work together, to pray together, to struggle together, to go to jail together, to stand up for freedom together, knowing that we will be free one day. And this will be the day. This will be the day when all of God's children will be able to sing with new meaning, "My country 'tis of thee, sweet land of liberty, of thee I sing. Land where my fathers died, land of the pilgrim's pride, from every mountain side, let freedom ring." And if America is to be a great nation, this must become true. 10

So let freedom ring from the prodigious[22] hilltops of New Hampshire; let freedom ring from the mighty mountains of New York; let freedom ring from the heightening Alleghenies of Pennsylvania; let freedom ring from the snowcapped Rockies of Colorado; let freedom ring from the curvaceous slopes of California.

ACTIVE READING MODEL

9 Key Reading Skill
Analyzing *At the climax, or high point, of his speech, King offers his dream for a better America.*

10 Key Literary Element
Cultural Reference *Earlier, King quoted from the King James Bible. Here, building up to a powerful conclusion, he quotes a patriotic song. Finally, at the end of the speech, he borrows from another song to connect with his audience.*

18. George Wallace, Alabama's then-governor, opposed all efforts to end official segregation in his state. ***Interposition*** and ***nullification*** are legal arguments regarding a state's right to reject or refuse to enforce federal laws.
19. Something that is ***exalted*** is raised in status, dignity, power, or glory.
20. This passage is taken from the Old Testament's book of Isaiah.
21. ***Discords*** are disagreements or conflicts.
22. Here, ***prodigious*** (pruh DIJ us) means "enormous."

Additional Support

Differentiated Instruction

Rhetoric Explain to students that speakers often use rhetorical devices in order to incite emotion in an audience and to add interest to their writing. Rhetorical devices can include rhetorical questions, allusions, repetition, parallelism, figurative language, and many other techniques. Have students work in small groups and read this page aloud. One student should read while the others listen and take notes. Students should identify any rhetorical devices they find, such as the repetition of "I have a dream" and the parallelism used in those sentences. AL

ACTIVE READING MODEL

But not only that. Let freedom ring from Stone Mountain of Georgia; let freedom ring from Lookout Mountain of Tennessee; let freedom ring from every hill and molehill of Mississippi. From every mountainside, let freedom ring.

And when this happens, and when we allow freedom to ring, when we let it ring from every village and every hamlet, from every state and every city; we will be able to speed up that day when all God's children, black men and white men, Jews and gentiles,[23] Protestants and Catholics, will be able to join hands and sing in the words of the old Negro spiritual: "Free at last. Free at last. Thank God Almighty, we are free at last." 11 ❍

11 Key Reading Skill
Identifying Cause and Effect *This is really a prediction of cause and effect. King says that if we achieve equality for African Americans, the effect will be that we are all free.*

23. People who are not Jews are known as ***gentiles*** (JEN tyls).

Write to Learn In your Learner's Notebook, jot down some of the images you thought were full of power. How do you think these images might have affected the people in the crowd when King spoke? Explain your answer.

Partner Talk With a partner, discuss whether King's dream for America has been fulfilled since he gave this speech. Work together to come to one conclusion and give reasons for it.

Study Central Visit www.glencoe.com and click on Study Central to review historical text.

Teach

L1 Literary Element

Style **Ask:** Was King's use of metaphor and repetition effective? Explain. *(Possible response: His repetition of "I have a dream" was inspirational because he passed his "dream" on to his audience. His use of metaphor and figurative language made the speech more interesting and colorful.)* AS

L2 Literary Element

Cultural Reference **Ask:** With what cultural reference does King conclude his speech? *(words from a Negro spiritual)* AS **Ask:** What effect does that cultural reference have? *(Possible response: It connects freedom from slavery with the need for freedom from segregation and other injustices.)* AL

BQ BIG Question

Ask: How do you think King would answer the Big Question? *(Possible response: The American dream is achieved when equality of all races and classes is realized.)* OL AL

Reading Fluency

Speech Reading Have students choose a passage from King's speech and look up any words whose meanings or pronunciations are unfamiliar. Then have students find a quiet place to practice reading the passage aloud with a partner. They should reread the passage several times until they can smoothly read all the sentences with expression and understanding. Ask students to take turns reading aloud and listening to their partner, stopping to self-correct as necessary. You might divide the speech into paragraphs or sections so that students can come together for a choral reading of the entire speech. AS

Indiana English/Language Arts Academic Standards
SE: 8.2, 8.3.6
TWE: *Differentiated Instruction* 8.3.6, *Reading Fluency* 8.7.14

Analyzing

Teaching Students to Analyze

Why Is It Important?

- Readers can better understand how a text works by analyzing the author's use of elements such as word choice and dialogue.
- Analytic skills are essential to critical reading, including the determination of an author's purpose for writing and how the author wants the reader to respond.
- Analyzing texts can make readers better writers by helping them learn to organize and critique.

How to Help Students Get It

- Remind students that stories can mean different things to different readers. Help them develop an interest in exploring different perspectives on texts and learn that there is no one "right" meaning.
- Emphasize that the author and reader work together to make meaning and that analyzing the author's choices increases appreciation of the writer's skills.
- Encourage students to read a text from different perspectives to show how beliefs can influence the meaning of a text.
- Remind students that it is crucial to consider who the author is and why they have written the text, and that this is especially important when reading information from sources such as blogs and other Internet sites that have not been filtered by editors or publishers.

Reading to Answer the Big Question

Volar by Judith Ortiz Cofer
A young girl growing up in the barrio dreams of being like Supergirl: beautiful, blonde, and able to fly. At the same time, her mother misses her family in Puerto Rico and also dreams of flying. Both dreams relate to the American dream of freedom and upward mobility.

from *The Century for Young People* by Alfred Levitt
This excerpt relates the experiences and impressions of a young immigrant to America in the early 1900s. The author's family left Russia, where Jews were segregated and persecuted. In New York City, Levitt was amazed by everything he saw but most especially by the diversity of people. In order to learn the language and culture more quickly, he transferred to a school with a diverse student population.

Workshop Resources

Pacing (days) Standard	Block	Lesson	Student Materials	Teacher Resources
1	1/2	Key Skill Lesson: Analyzing	Key Reading Skills Practice, p. 9 English Language Coach Review, p. 44	Bellringer Options Transparencies –Daily Language Practice 74 Read Aloud, Think Aloud Transparencies –Key Reading Skills 2 Presentation Plus!
1	1	"Volar"	Glencoe Online Unit Vocabulary Review, p. 42 Academic Vocabulary Review, p. 45 English Language Coach Active Reading Graphic Organizer, p. 10 StudentWorks Plus™ Online Student Edition Literature Classics Selection and Unit Assessments, p. 85	Literary and Text Analysis Transparencies 25 Puzzlemaker Skill Level Up!™ A Language Arts Game BookLink 3 Assessment by Learning Objective (Diagnostic and Formative) Interactive Tutor: Self-Assessment TeacherWorks Plus™
1		from *The Century for Young People*	Glencoe Online Unit Vocabulary Review, p. 42 Academic Vocabulary Review, p. 45 English Language Coach Active Reading Graphic Organizer, p. 13 Literary Analysis, p. 12 StudentWorks Plus™ Online Student Edition Literature Classics Selection and Unit Assessments, p. 86	Literary and Text Analysis Transparencies 44 Puzzlemaker Skill Level Up!™ A Language Arts Game BookLink 3 Assessment by Learning Objective (Diagnostic and Formative) Interactive Tutor: Self-Assessment TeacherWorks Plus™

Keys for Unit Resource

- Blackline Master
- Workbook
- Supplemental Text
- CD-ROM
- DVD
- Transparency
- Web-based
- Fast File

Level Appropriate Code

AS = Activities for all students
AL = Activities for students working above grade level
OL = Activities for students working at grade level
BL = Activities for students working below grade level
EL = Activities for English language learners

Focus

BELLRINGER Options

Daily Language Practice Transparency 74

Focus Activity Ask: Who are your favorite superheroes? *(Responses will vary.)* **Ask:** How do they represent the American Dream? *(Possible response: Superheroes can achieve anything they want, just as Americans have the opportunities for growth and success.)* AS

Teach

R Reading Skill

Analyzing Ask: When do you analyze something in daily life? *(Possible responses: the best route to get somewhere; the responses to test questions; the best strategy to take when you have a problem with a friend)* AS

Analyzing the Cartoon
Ask: After the men respond, "We lost," what question should Hagar ask to help his men analyze what went wrong? *(Possible response: Why did we lose?)* AS

READING WORKSHOP 1

Skills Focus

You will practice using these skills when you read the following selections:

- "Volar," p. 1068
- from *The Century for Young People*, p. 1076

Reading

- Analyzing

Informational Text

- Understanding imagery
- Understanding chronological order

Vocabulary

- Learning about English as a changing language

Writing/Grammar

- Using words correctly: misused and confused words

Skill Lesson

Analyzing

Learn It!

A police detective **analyzes** a crime scene, searching for clues. A medical researcher analyzes a cancer cell, looking for a cure. A football coach analyzes last week's game, wanting to help the team improve. A student analyzes a grammar assignment, intending to master the topic and get a good grade.

R When you analyze, you think critically. You think about the various elements of an object or situation in order to better understand the whole. What does that mean for reading? It means you question what you read. You break down a subject into separate parts to determine its meaning. You demonstrate awareness of a writer's technique and craft.

MEN, WE'RE NEVER GOING TO GET ANY BETTER UNTIL WE ANALYZE OUR BEHAVIOR DURING BATTLE...
NOW, WHAT DID WE DO WRONG TODAY ?
WE LOST ?
Uh... BESIDES THAT ?
CHRIS BROWNE
©2005 by King Features Syndicate, Inc. World rights reserved.

Reprinted with permission of King Features Syndicate.

Analyzing Cartoons
Hagar wants the guys to analyze their battle behavior so they can improve. What answer does one soldier give? Is his answer a good analysis? Why or why not?

Indiana English/Language Arts Academic Standards (pp. 1064–1065)

8.2 Comprehension and Analysis (Focus on Informational Text) Develop [reading] strategies such as asking questions...and identifying and analyzing structure, organization, perspective, and purpose.

For a complete description of the standards, see p. IN 11.

Additional Support

Reading in the Real World

Career Explain that there are many kinds of analysts in the professional world, including financial analysts, military analysts, sports analysts, and political analysts. Explain that analysts determine how things work together to produce a certain outcome. They pinpoint problems, and even suggest solutions. For example, a sports analyst may examine how a baseball team will be affected if their star pitcher is out with an injury. Invite students to choose one of these fields and find out more about what a professional analyst does. Have them write a short report to deliver to the class. AL

Why Is It Important? In today's world, we're offered loads of information about all sorts of subjects. To help make sense of it all, people need critical thinking skills so that they can make smart, informed decisions. Learning to analyze information is a good way to develop those critical thinking skills. Analyzing helps you look critically at a piece of writing to discover its theme or message. R

Literature Online

Study Central Visit www.glencoe.com and click on Study Central to review analyzing.

How Do I Do It? Start by thinking about the author's background, traditions, attitudes, and beliefs. To analyze fiction, think about what the author is saying through the characters, setting, and plot. For example, look at a character's words, actions, and purposes. Then use the knowledge you gain to better understand the character's behavior at other points of the story and the story as a whole.

To analyze nonfiction, look at the organization, main ideas, and supporting details. Here are some of the comments one student made in analyzing Martin Luther King's "I Have a Dream" speech.

It's important that King spoke at the Lincoln Memorial. It makes the point that Americans gave high honor to Lincoln but treated African Americans as second-class citizens. King says that right up front.

He creates images that just stick in your head. Freedom is a "beacon light of hope." Injustice is "searing flames." The promise of freedom is a "bad check." L

I also like his references to the Bible, Declaration of Independence, and even "My Country 'Tis of Thee." He makes me think about what the words really mean. He makes me want to make those words be true.

Practice It!

Below are some things to look for as you analyze the selections in this workshop. In your Learner's Notebook, jot down thoughts that occur to you as you read this list.

- the powers of super heroes
- the importance of family origins
- the importance of oral history
- what America means to immigrants

Use It!

As you analyze "Volar" and *The Century for Young People,* refer to your notes to help yourself focus on the important elements.

Teach

Study Central Have students access the Web site to review analyzing and to complete a related activity.

R Reading Skill

Review Identifying Main Idea and Supporting Details
Say: Read the section titled *Why Is It Important?* What is the main idea of the section? *(Analyzing is a useful and important critical thinking skill.)* AS **Ask:** What are some details that support the main idea? *(Possible response: Critical thinking skills help us make smart, informed decisions.)* OL

L Literary Element

Imagery **Say:** Reread the student's analysis of the imagery in King's speech. Do you agree with her? *(Responses will vary.)* BL **Ask:** What images from the speech stand out for you? *(Responses will vary.)* OL

Resources for page 1065

Use Key Reading Skills Transparency 2 in *Read Aloud, Think Aloud* to help students practice analyzing.

Differentiated Instruction

Class Debate Explain to students that, to a great extent, a democracy relies on citizens' ability to analyze complicated issues. Different groups try to persuade us that one decision or another is necessary. Informed citizens are able to analyze information on their own, understand the big picture, and make independent decisions. Challenge students to take a complex issue, such as the need to protect the environment versus the need to develop land for people. Have students research both sides of the argument and then have an in-class debate about the issue. AL

Indiana English/Language Arts Academic Standards
SE: 8.2
TWE: *Reading in the Real World* 8.7.12, *Differentiated Instruction* 8.7.13

Teach

More About the Author

An important aspect of Judith Ortiz Cofer's career as a writer is her commitment to community. She uses her writing to define her relationship with two cultures. She also writes fiction and poetry for young adults, including *The Meaning of Consuelo,* which was included on the New York Public Library's Books for the Teen Age 2004 List.

EL Language Coach

English as a Changing Language **Say:** Brainstorm a list of words that we use today to describe new technology. *(Possible responses: cell phone, Xerox, hi-tech.)* **Ask:** Are these words new uses of old words or completely new words? Check a dictionary for information. *(Possible responses:* Cell *is short for* cellular, *and* phone *is short for* telephone. *Xerox is a brand name but often used to mean "photocopy."* Hi-tech *is short for* high technology.*)* AS

Before You Read **Volar**

Judith Ortiz Cofer

Meet the Author

Judith Ortiz Cofer learned English only after her family moved to the U.S. mainland from the island of Puerto Rico. Her writing reflects the split between her two childhood homes. She has written, "The memories of [childhood and my parents] emerge in my poems and stories like time-travelers popping up with a message for me." See page R1 of the Author Files for more on Cofer.

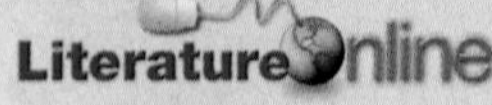

Author Search For more about Judith Ortiz Cofer, go to www.glencoe.com.

Indiana English/Language Arts Academic Standards (pp. 1066–1069)

8.1.2 Understand the influence of historical events on English word meaning and vocabulary expansion. **8.2 Comprehension and Analysis (Focus on Informational Text)** Develop [reading] strategies... **8.3.6** Identify significant literary devices...

For a complete description of the standards, see p. IN 11.

Vocabulary Preview

avid (AV id) *adj.* very eager or enthusiastic **(p. 1068)** *The ranger, an avid hiker himself, was happy to share trail information with park visitors.*

recurring (rih KUR ing) *adj.* happening or coming back again; repeating **(p. 1068)** *It's a recurring problem that must be solved once and for all.*

adolescence (ad uh LES uns) *n.* the period between childhood and adulthood **(p. 1070)** *In adolescence, people begin to develop their abilities.*

abruptly (uh BRUPT lee) *adv.* suddenly; unexpectedly **(p. 1071)** *Our discussion ended abruptly when the fire alarm went off.*

refuse (REF yooz) *n.* trash; rubbish **(p. 1071)** *During the garbage workers' strike, great bags of refuse piled up on the street.*

Partner Talk With a partner, use each vocabulary word in a separate sentence. Then write one sentence that uses all five words correctly.

English Language Coach

English as a Changing Language There are living languages and dead ones. Latin, the language of the Roman Empire, is dead. No one uses it now in everyday life. In contrast, English is a living language. To stay alive, a language drops words and meanings that are no longer needed or wanted. It borrows words from other languages, from slang, and from culture. A living language invents terms to deal with new technologies. As an example, see how the word *program* developed new meanings to keep up with culture and technology. EL

Program		
1	(1633)	*n.* a printed public notice or announcement
2		*n.* a printed outline of the order of a public performance
3	(1896)	*v.* to arrange or provide a program for a performance
4		*n.* the performance of a program, especially on radio or TV
5		*n.* a plan or system for action toward a goal
6	(1940s)	*n.* the coded instructions for a computer or other machine
7		*v.* to write the instructions for a computer or other machine
8		*v.* to control as if by a program

Group Program In a group, brainstorm words and meanings that you think are recent additions to English. Look closely at words related to technology *(computer)* and culture *(hip-hop)* or borrowed from other languages *(adios).*

Additional Support

Author Search To expand students' appreciation of Judith Ortiz Cofer, have them access the Web site for additional information and resources.

Literature Focus Lesson

Imagery Tell students that imagery comprises descriptive language and sensory details, which appeal to sight, hearing, smell, taste, and touch. For example, *The teacher walked down the hall* has few sensory details or descriptive language. Write that sentence on the board, and challenge students to add descriptive language and sensory details. BL Tell students to create their own vivid images using sensory details and include at least three vocabulary words from above. OL

Skills Preview

Key Reading Skill: Analyzing

Before you read the selection, reflect on what you know about

- the feeling of flying in a dream
- sacrifices parents make for their families

Write to Learn In your Learner's Notebook, describe some of your thoughts on the topics above.

Literary Element: Imagery

An image may be a picture or statue, a copy, something reflected in a mirror, or something seen in the mind. **Imagery** is language that appeals to any or all of the senses—not just sight. Imagery helps readers hear, feel, smell, and taste, as well as see, what is described in a written text.

Imagery isn't necessarily just a description. For example, the narrator of "Volar" wants to emphasize how much she loved comic books as a child and to tell how large her collection was. Using imagery, she says that she had a stack of comics "as tall as I."

As you read, use these tips to help you learn about imagery:

- Look for language that paints a picture you can see in your mind.

  Stop and see the picture; then reread the words that created that image for you.
- Look for language that activates your other senses—hearing, touching, smelling, and tasting.

  Reread the words and think about which specific words bring these senses to mind.

Interactive Literary Elements Handbook
To review or learn more about the literary elements, go to www.glencoe.com.

Get Ready to Read

Connect to the Reading

Imagine that you had long dreamed of coming to the United States for a better life. Then imagine that, after being here for a time, you find it's not what you had hoped for. Or you miss your homeland and want to go back. As you read "Volar," imagine why the narrator's parents brought the family to the United States and how they felt about being here.

Small Group Chat In a small group, talk about a time when you hoped or wished or dreamed for something and what happened when it came true. Was it the way you imagined it? Was it really what you were wishing for? Take turns sharing your experiences.

Build Background

"Volar" is from a collection of stories and poems called *The Year of Our Revolution.* This story is not necessarily about Judith Ortiz Cofer and her family, but it could be.

- In the 1960s, many Puerto Rican families came to the mainland in search of better opportunities.
- In 1964 when the author was twelve, her family moved to Paterson, New Jersey, an industrial town very different from Puerto Rico. Cofer's mother never adjusted well to American city life.
- Comic books were a cheap and popular form of entertainment for kids growing up in the 1960s.
- The Spanish verb *volar* means "to fly."

Set Purposes for Reading

BIG Question Read "Volar" to see how two members of the same family see the American dream.

Set Your Own Purpose What would you like to learn from the selection to help you answer the Big Question? Write your own purpose on the "Volar" page of Foldable 8.

Keep Moving

Use these skills as you read the following selection.

Reading Fluency

Build Fluency Invite students to choose one paragraph from the story that they particularly like. Have them find a quiet place to practice reading the paragraph aloud. Tell them to reread it several times until they can read with expression and understanding. They should try to make their reading sound like natural speech. Have English speakers ask Spanish speakers for correct pronunciations of Spanish words and expressions. BL After they have time to practice reading independently, allow students to pair up and read aloud to one another. EL OL

Teach

C Critical Thinking

Comprehension Ask: If you could have any superpower, what would it be? *(Responses will vary.)* **Say:** *Volar* means "to fly"; that's one thing many superheroes can do. What other meanings could that phrase have, besides to literally fly through the air? *(Possible response: to hide or escape)* **Say:** Imagine taking flight to another country. What reasons might people have for taking flight in that sense? *(Possible responses: freedom; religious persecution; better opportunities)* OL

Interactive Literary Elements Handbook Have students access the Web site to improve their understanding of imagery.

Indiana English/Language Arts Academic Standards
SE: 8.1.2, 8.2, 8.3.6
TWE: *Literature Focus Lesson* 8.5.6, *Reading Fluency* 8.7

Teach

Viewing the Photo

Ask: What does this photo show? *(a female superhero in mid-flight)* **Ask:** How does this picture relate to the story? *(The writer says she was an "avid consumer of comic books–Supergirl being my favorite.")* BL

R Reading Skill

Analyzing **Ask:** What is the narrator's dream? *(She dreams that she turns into a superhero.)* BL **Ask:** What does the dream say about her? *(Possible response: She wishes she looked more like the perfect superheroes that she reads about.)* OL

L Literary Element

Imagery **Say:** Look at the sentence "Supergirl had to be aerodynamic and sleek and hard as a supersonic missile." How does this simile add to the imagery of the selection? *(Possible response: It makes me see Supergirl as a powerful and speedy force.)* OL

Readability Scores
Dale-Chall: 6.2
DRP: 57
Lexile: 1070

READING WORKSHOP 1

by Judith Ortiz Cofer

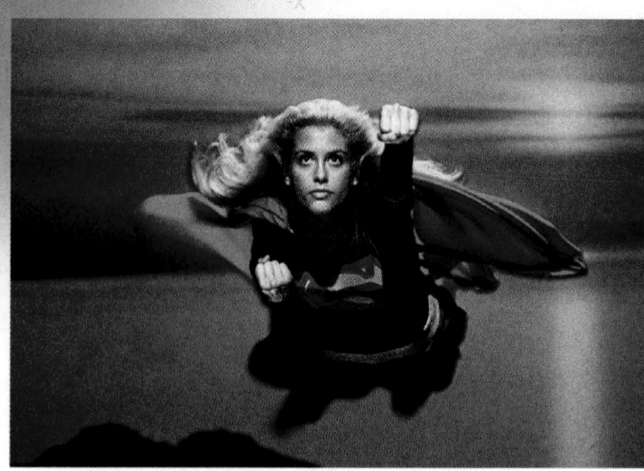

At twelve I was an **avid** consumer of comic books—*Supergirl* being my favorite. I spent my allowance of a quarter a day on two twelve-cent comic books or a double issue for twenty-five. I had a stack of *Legion of Super Heroes* and *Supergirl* comic books in my bedroom closet that was as tall as I. I had a **recurring** dream in those days: that I had long blonde hair and could fly. In my dream I climbed the stairs to the top of our apartment building as myself, but as I went up R each flight, changes would be taking place. Step by step I would fill out: my legs would grow long, my arms harden into steel, and my hair would magically go straight and turn a golden color. Of course, Supergirl had to be aerodynamic L and sleek and hard as a supersonic missile.[1] Once on the roof, my parents safely asleep in their beds, I would get on tip-toe, arms outstretched in the position for flight, and jump out of my fifth-story-high window into the black lake of the sky. 1 From up there, over the rooftops, I could see everything, even

1. To be ***aerodynamic*** (air oh dy NAM ik) is to be able to move through the air easily. To be ***supersonic*** is to be faster than the speed of sound.

Vocabulary

avid (AV id) *adj.* very eager or enthusiastic

recurring (rih KUR ing) *adj.* happening or coming back again; repeating

Practice the Skills

1 Literary Element

Imagery This paragraph has imagery that appeals to the senses of sight and touch (feeling). Here's a sampling:

- arms harden into steel
- hair turns golden
- sky described as black lake

Additional Support

Differentiated Instruction

Create a Hero Have students research the superheroes referred to in the story. Then ask students to imagine their own comic-book heroes and draw or write about them. Allow students to develop projects according to their individual interests and abilities. They might choose to (a) make charts detailing how their heroes look, what they fight for, and what superpowers they have; (b) write a brief short story about their heroes; or (c) illustrate their heroes in individual drawings, story-boards, or comic books. AS

Visual Vocabulary
The ***ermine*** is a small, furry animal of the weasel family. Its fur makes luxurious and expensive coats.

beyond the few blocks of our barrio;[2] with my x-ray vision I could look inside the homes of people who interested me. **R**

Once I saw our landlord, whom I knew my parents feared, sitting in a treasure-room dressed in an ermine coat and a large gold crown. He sat on the floor counting his dollar bills. I played a trick on him. Going up to his building's chimney, I blew a little puff of my super-breath into his fireplace, scattering his stacks of money so that he had to start counting all over again. **2** **L**

I could more or less **program** my Supergirl dreams in those days by focusing on the object of my current obsession.[3] **3**

2. In the United States, ***barrio*** refers to a city neighborhood in which most people are Hispanic.
3. An ***obsession*** is an idea or feeling, especially an unreasonable one, that takes over a person's thoughts.

Practice the Skills

2 Key Reading Skill

Analyzing Why do the narrator's parents fear the landlord?

3 English Language Coach

A Changing Language What does **program** mean here? (If you need help, review the table on page 1066.)

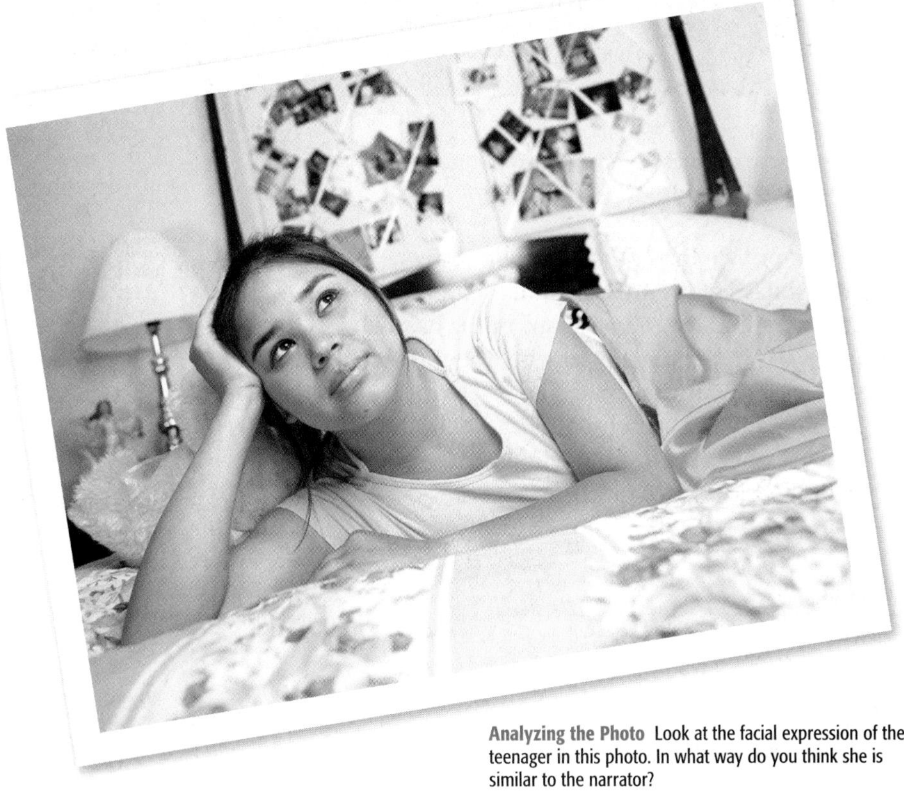

Analyzing the Photo Look at the facial expression of the teenager in this photo. In what way do you think she is similar to the narrator?

READING WORKSHOP 1

Teach

R Reading Skill

Analyzing **Ask:** What elements of the narrator's fantasy are common to most adolescents? *(Possible response: She imagines herself possessing extraordinary power, observing the lives of others and affecting those she doesn't like—things that adolescents and even adults might like to be able to do.)* **OL**

L Literary Element

Imagery **Ask:** If you were an artist, how would you draw the first paragraph, and how would you depict the landlord? *(Possible response: The landlord would have on a fur coat and gold crown. There would be an empty fireplace in the background and dollar bills would be flying all over the room. The landlord would be angrily clutching at the money.)* **AS** **Ask:** What makes the paragraph easy to envision? *(Possible responses: The author's use of imagery. There are many details, such as a gust of wind blowing the money around.)* **OL**

Literature Focus Lesson

Analyzing Fantasy vs. Reality Explain to students that the first three paragraphs of the text are made up mostly of the narrator's fantasy of being a superhero. However, these paragraphs give clues about the reality of her life. Have students record the main ideas and events of the narrator's fantasy on a Fantasy/Reality chart. Then have them reread the text to identify the reality of the girl's life. **AS** Students should use the information on their charts to write short compare-and-contrast essays. **OL** Additionally, encourage students to examine how the narrator's reality contributes to her fantasies of power and conventional American beauty. **AL**

Indiana English/Language Arts Academic Standards
SE: 8.1.2, 8.2, 8.3.6
TWE: *Literature Focus Lesson* 8.4.1, 8.5.2

Teach

Viewing the Photo

Ask: How could this picture represent the narrator's dream? *(Possible response: She dreams of flight, an ability adolescents often wish they had.)* **AL**

L Literary Element

Imagery **Ask:** Which words and phrases create a picture of the narrator's room? *(tiny, incongruous, white "princess" furniture)* **EL** **BL** **Ask:** Why is the word *princess* in quotation marks? *(Possible responses: to suggest that the furniture is what a princess might own; to suggest that the narrator doesn't like the furniture or for the idea of being a princess)* **OL** **AL**

R Reading Skill

Analyzing **Ask:** What does the narrator do in the morning? *(She stays in bed so as not to disturb her parents' time together.)* **AS** **Ask:** What does this say about her character? *(Possible response: It shows that she is considerate of her parents' need for time alone.)* **OL**

READING WORKSHOP 1

Supergirl, 1984. Tristar. Movie still.

Analyzing the Photo The narrator wants certain qualities. Which of those qualities are shown in this picture from the movie *Supergirl?*

This way I saw into the private lives of my neighbors, my teachers, and in the last days of my childish fantasy and the beginning of **adolescence**, into the secret rooms of the boys I liked. In the mornings I'd wake up in my tiny bedroom with its incongruous[4] —at least in our tiny apartment—white "princess" furniture my mother had chosen for me, and find myself back in my body; my tight curls still clinging to my head, my skinny arms and legs unchanged. **L** **4**

4. Something that's ***incongruous*** (in KAHN groo us) is out of place or not working in harmony with something else. Here, the narrator feels her fancy furniture is out of place.

Vocabulary

adolescence (ad uh LES uns) *n.* the period between childhood and adulthood

Practice the Skills

4 Literary Element

Imagery Notice how the narrator describes herself in the last clause. How does this picture of her compare with the image of her as Supergirl?

Additional Support

Reading in the Real World

Career The story uses both Spanish and English. Remind students that every time they see text in English with a translation near it, a professional translator was involved. Have students research jobs that require the ability to translate from one language to another. What level of education or experience is needed to be a professional translator? Instruct them to write a brief report on that profession and the role translating plays. **OL** Allow students who speak another language to translate a paragraph of the story into their language and read it to the class. **EL** **AL**

In the kitchen my mother and father would be talking softly over a *café con leche.*[5] She would come "wake me" exactly forty-five minutes after they had gotten up. It was their time together at the beginning of each day, and even at an early age I could feel their disappointment if I interrupted them by getting up too early. So I would stay in my bed recalling my dreams of flight, perhaps planning my next flight. In the kitchen they would be discussing events in the barrio. Actually, my father would be carrying that part of the conversation; when it was her turn to speak she would, more often than not, try shifting the topic toward her desire to see her *familia* on the Island: How about a vacation in Puerto Rico together this year, *querido?* We could rent a car, go to the beach. We could . . . And he would answer patiently, gently: *Mi amor,* do you know how much it would cost for all of us to fly there? It is not possible for me to take the time off . . . *Mi vida,*[6] please understand . . . And I knew that soon she would rise from the table. Not **abruptly.** She would look out the kitchen window. The view was of a dismal alley that was littered with **refuse** thrown from windows. The space was too narrow for anyone larger than a skinny child to enter safely, so it was never cleaned. My mother would check the time on the clock over her sink, the one with a prayer for patience and grace written in Spanish. A birthday gift. She would see that it was time to wake me. She'd sigh deeply and say the same thing the view from her kitchen window always inspired her to say: *"Ay, si yo pudiera volar.*[7]*"* 5 6 ❍

5. ***Café con leche*** (kuh FAY kohn LAY chay) is Spanish for "coffee with milk."
6. ***Familia*** (fah MEEL ee uh) is Spanish for "family," ***querido*** (kay REE doh) means "darling," ***mi amor*** (mee ah MOR) means "my love," and ***mi vida*** (mee VEE dah) means "my life." Here, *mi vida* is used the same way as "darling" and "my love."
7. The mother says "Oh, if I could fly."

Vocabulary

abruptly (uh BRUPT lee) *adv.* suddenly; unexpectedly

refuse (REF yooz) *n.* trash; rubbish

Practice the Skills

R

L

5 Reviewing Elements

Conflict What is the main conflict between the mother and father? What are some possible ways this conflict might be resolved?

BQ

6 BIG Question

How do the mother's wish and the daughter's dream reflect one another? Write your answer on the "Volar" page of Foldable 8. Your response will help you answer the Unit Challenge later.

Teach

L Literary Element

Imagery Ask: How does the description of the surroundings add to your feelings about the mother's predicament? *(Possible response: The description of the garbage, the lack of space, the clock, and the mother's sigh all add to my feelings of empathy for her.)* **Say:** The last sentence in the story has both a literal and a figurative meaning. What is the figurative meaning of the line? *(Possible response: She wishes she could rise above the life she lives.)* OL AL

BQ BIG Question

Ask: Why might the American dream be bittersweet for the narrator's mother? *(Possible response: She has traded the beauty and culture of her homeland for a place that presents opportunities but lacks the things she misses. She might not think the trade was equal.)* OL

Assess

Use the CheckPoint questions provided on Presentation Plus! to check for comprehension of the selection. These questions can be used with interactive response keypads for immediate student feedback.

English Language Coach

Spanish Translation and Pronunciation Invite students whose original language is Spanish to read aloud Spanish expressions from the text, such as *café con leche, familia, querido, mi amor, mi vida,* and the final line, *Ay, si yo pudiera volar.* Pair Spanish-speaking students with non-Spanish-speaking students and invite them to choose a passage containing Spanish expressions. Have them work together, helping each other read fluently and helping each other with unfamiliar pronunciations. Tell students to continue to reread the passage until they can read it fluently with expression. EL BL

Indiana English/Language Arts Academic Standards

SE: 8.3.6

TWE: *Reading in the Real World* 8.5.3, *English Language Coach* 8.7

Assess

Resources for page 1072

- Selection Quick Check, p. 71
- Selection and Unit Assessment, p. 85
- ExamView Assessment Suite
- Interactive Tutor: Self-Assessment

Students can respond to the *After You Read* items in their Learner's Notebooks or on a separate sheet of paper.

Answering the BIG Question

1. Possible response: For the narrator's mother, the American dream is a big disappointment.
2. Supergirl
3. For a holiday in her home country
4. Possible response: A small dark alley filled with garbage

Critical Thinking

5. Possible response: The father tells the mother they can't go to Puerto Rico for a holiday because he "can't take the time off." The mother wants to abandon the dream and return to her homeland.
6. Possible response: The narrator is growing up in America and probably speaks English at school and with her friends.
7. Responses will vary.

After You Read

Volar

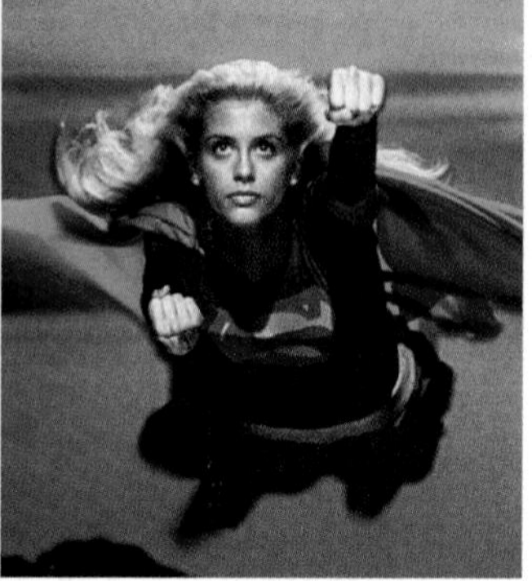

Answering the BIG Question

1. How do you think the narrator's mother would answer the question "What is the American dream?"
2. **Recall** Who was the narrator's favorite comic-book hero?
   TIP **Right There**
3. **Recall** According to the narrator, why does her mother want to fly to Puerto Rico?
   TIP **Right There**
4. **Describe** In your own words, describe the view from the kitchen window of the apartment.
   TIP **Think and Search**

Critical Thinking

5. **Contrast** What clues are there that the mother and father might have different attitudes toward their life in the United States? Support your answer with details from the story.
   TIP **Author and Me**
6. **Draw Conclusions** The title is a Spanish word, and the father and mother use Spanish words and phrases several times. Yet the narrator never uses Spanish to describe her own thoughts and dreams. What do you think accounts for the difference?
   TIP **Author and Me**
7. **Analyze** Each of the three characters expresses at least a thought about flying. What do you think flying represents to each person? Explain your answers, using details from the story to support your ideas.
   TIP **Author and Me**

Indiana English/Language Arts Academic Standards (pp. 1072–1073)

8.3 Comprehension and Analysis of Literary Text Respond to grade-level-appropriate literature... **8.5.7** Write for different purposes... **8.2 Comprehension and Analysis (Focus on Informational Text)** Develop [reading] strategies... **8.3.6** Identify significant literary devices... **8.6 English Language Conventions**

For a complete description of the standards, see p. IN 11.

Write About Your Reading

Descriptive Writing Imagine that you're a superhero in real life. What powers do you have, and what do you do with them? Write a few paragraphs describing

- your superhero self
- your most important superpowers
- how you use your powers

Write About Your Reading

Sample response:

I am a combination of Wonder Woman and the Bionic Woman. I can run faster than anyone, deflect bullets with my magic wrist cuffs, and fly through the air in my invisible jet. I am at the beck and call of the world's helpless and innocent. If a child is being bullied, I will protect him. If a war is being fought, I will deflect missiles from both sides. I work daily to bring peace and love to every community.

Skills Review

Key Reading Skill: Analyzing

8. Why does the narrator use one of her superpowers to "play a trick" on the landlord?

Literary Element: Imagery

9. List an image from the selection that appeals to each one of the five senses.
10. Explain this image from the first paragraph: "the black lake of the sky." How is the sky like a lake in the narrator's dream? Why is it black?

Reviewing Elements: Conflict

11. What is the narrator's main conflict in this story? Is it internal or external? Support your answer.

Vocabulary Check

Choose the best word from the list to complete each sentence below.

avid recurring adolescence abruptly refuse

12. She spent most of her ___ in Europe and didn't live in the United States until she was twenty.
13. Don't throw your litter on the highway! No one else wants your ___!
14. Before finishing her meal, she stood up and ___ left the room.
15. Nathan has every album the Beatles made; he's been an ___ fan for decades.
16. In this ___ nightmare, I'm always in bare feet, even in snow and freezing temperatures.
17. **English Language Coach** About when did people begin to use **program** as a verb? Find the answer in the chart on page 1066.

Web Activities For eFlashcards, Selection Quick Checks, and other Web activities, go to www.glencoe.com.

Grammar Link: Misused Words

English contains a number of confusing words, including the troublesome ones below. Some words are misused because they have *slightly* different meanings. Others are misused even though they have *very* different meanings.

between: used to talk about two people or things
- Choose **between** styles.

among: used to talk about groups of three or more
- Distribute the suits **among** the seven stores.

less: refers to a amount that you can't count
- There is **less** milk in that glass.

fewer: refers to an amount that can be counted
- I made **fewer** mistakes in this paragraph.

bring: to carry from a distant place to a closer one
- We **bring** goods into this country.

take: to carry from a closer place to a distant one
- They **take** goods to other countries.

leave: to go away
- I will **leave** on a camping trip.

let: to allow
- **Let** them bring a snack.

set: to place or to put
- They **set** our books on the desk.

sit: to place oneself in a seated position
- Let's **sit** here and talk about your problem.

Grammar Practice

Rewrite each sentence, filling in the correct word.

18. He evenly distributed the books (between, among) the four new students.
19. Rescue workers (bring, take) food to disaster sites.
20. The president will (leave, let) soon to visit Ohio.
21. The guests will (set, sit) on these chairs.
22. She has read (less, fewer) pages than I.

Writing Application Look back at your descriptive writing. If you used any of these troublesome words incorrectly, fix the mistakes.

Skills Review

Key Reading Skill: Analyzing

8. Possible response: The landlord is a person her parents fear. In reality they do not have the power to stand up to him, but in the narrator's fantasy she takes action on their behalf.

Literary Element: Imagery

9. Possible response: Sight: landlord dressed in an ermine coat and a large gold crown; Hearing: parents talking softly in next room in the morning; Smelling: café con leche; Tasting: café con leche; Touching: narrator's little superbreath that she sends down the landlord's chimney
10. Possible response: The sky is like a lake in that it stretches out wide and dark below, black because it is night.

Reviewing Elements: Conflict

11. Responses will vary. Students should support their answers with details from the story.

Close

Ask students to explain what they learned from the selection to help them answer the Big Question.

Vocabulary Check

12. adolescence
13. refuse
14. abruptly
15. avid
16. recurring

English Language Coach

17. When computers became popular (because they need to be programmed)

Grammar Link: Misused Words

Grammar Practice

18. among
19. take
20. leave
21. sit
22. fewer

Indiana English/Language Arts Academic Standards
SE: 8.2, 8.3, 8.3.6, 8.5.7, 8.6

Teach

More About the Author

When Alfred Levitt first arrived in America, he and his family lived in East Harlem. His family was too poor to pay for college, so Levitt spent his time at the New York Public library, teaching himself. Levitt became a famous painter with exhibits in the Whitney and Brooklyn museums. Later in life, Levitt became fascinated with the cave paintings in France, studied them in detail, and lectured widely on them.

V Vocabulary

Vocabulary Flash Cards Pass out four note cards. Have students write the word and its part of speech on one side of a note card. Instruct them to write the definition on the back. Have them work with a partner to take turns flashing one side of the card while the partner tells what's on the back. Students can flash either side of the card. AS

Before You Read from *The Century for Young People*

Alfred Levitt

Meet the Author

Alfred Levitt was born in 1894 in the Ukraine (then part of Russia). He was one of fourteen children. His family came to the United States to escape the Russian government's anti-Jewish campaigns. Here, Levitt became an artist. When he grew older, he gave this advice to a young artist: "Don't follow what other people tell you to do. [Your art] has to express who you are inside!"

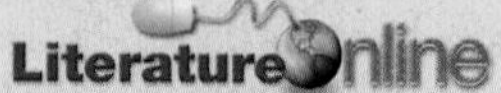

Author Search For more about Alfred Levitt, go to www.glencoe.com.

Indiana English/Language Arts Academic Standards (pp. 1074–1077)

8.1.2 Understand the influence of historical events on English word meaning and vocabulary expansion.
8.2 Comprehension and Analysis (Focus on Informational Text) Develop [reading] strategies...identifying and analyzing structure, organization, perspective, and purpose.

For a complete description of the standards, see p. IN 11.

Vocabulary Preview

V

literally (LIT ur uh lee) *adv.* actually; exactly **(p. 1076)** *The man couldn't even buy a pack of gum; he was literally penniless.*

accumulated (uh KYOO myuh lay tid) *v.* gathered or piled up, little by little; form of the verb *accumulate* **(p. 1077)** *The snow started slowly but soon accumulated into giant drifts that blocked the road.*

overwhelmed (oh vur WELMD) *v.* overpowered in thought or feeling; completely covered or flooded; form of the verb *overwhelm* **(p. 1077)** *We fell behind schedule because the work overwhelmed us.*

means (meenz) *n.* methods useful for achieving a particular purpose or goal; resources **(p. 1078)** *She watched her means of getting home on time disappear as the last bus of the night left without her.*

Culture Shock Imagine that you're an immigrant just arriving in the United States. Use the vocabulary words to write a short paragraph describing your first impressions.

English Language Coach

English as a Changing Language The 12th century inhabitants of a certain island were the Engles. Where they lived was "the Engles' land," which was later reduced to "England." This simple history shows another way English language changes–in place names. Of course, names often had more complex origins. **America** was based on a mistake; here's what happened:

1492	Christopher Columbus, the Italian explorer, lands in what he believes to be India.	**India**
1498	On a second voyage, he "discovers" South America.	▼
1499–1501	Amerigo Vespucci, also Italian, explores the coast of South America. Back home, he writes letters to friends, referring to these lands as the "New World."	**New World**
1507	Martin Waldseemueller, a German mapmaker, reads Vespucci's letters, thinks Vespucci discovered the continent, and suggests naming it in his honor. He prints a map with "America" across the southern continent, and the name sticks.	▼ **America**

Naming of Names Research the name of your family, city, state, or school. Write an encyclopedia-style entry explaining its origin.

Additional Support

Author Search To expand students' appreciation of Alfred Levitt, have them access the Web site for additional information and resources.

English Language Coach

Parts of Speech On the board, write *accumulated* and *overwhelmed* along with each word's part of speech as identified in Vocabulary Preview. Explain that these two words are used as those parts of speech in the text, but they can also function as other parts of speech in other texts. Write this sentence on the board: *The accumulated snow blocked the road.* Explain that in this sentence, *accumulated* is an adjective. Challenge students to use *overwhelmed* as the main verb of a sentence and share their sentences. EL

Skills Preview

Key Reading Skill: Analyzing

The selection you're about to read is an oral history. The words were spoken by one person and written down by someone else. As you read, consider its different parts to help you understand the whole selection. Think about what you already know about

- racism and religious discrimination
- what the Statue of Liberty represents
- how non-English-speaking immigrants learn English

Write to Learn In your Learner's Notebook, make a few notes about your knowledge of these topics.

Key Text Element: Chronological Order

Chronological order is a kind of sequence, a way of organizing events. The word *chronological* comes from the Greek word for *time,* and chronological order is the order in which events happen in time. In real life, events always take place in chronological order. These events are not directly related, but they're listed in the correct chronological order.

- Columbus discovers America.
- British colonies declare their independence.
- The Chicago White Sox win the 2005 World Series.

In reading, it's important to know the order of events. Time order is the clearest way to present travel directions, product instructions, and biographical narratives. Sometimes, however, writers present events in order of importance, trusting the reader to know—or figure out—the time order.

To keep track of the actual order of events, watch for signal words such as *before, first, next, then,* and *later.*

Interactive Literary Elements Handbook
To review or learn more about the literary elements, go to www.glencoe.com.

Get Ready to Read

Connect to the Reading

How would you feel if people shouted insults at you because you belonged to a particular ethnic group? How would you feel if you were not allowed to attend the same school as other students your age because of your religion? This is what happened to Alfred Levitt when he lived in Russia. As you read his selection, think about what you might have done in his place.

Partner Talk With a partner, talk about how it feels to have hurtful words used against you. Talk about how you act when you feel insulted, and explain why you act that way.

Build Background

Shortly after his 100th birthday, Alfred Levitt gave the interview that forms this oral history. As you'll see, his memories of life in Russia and his early years in America were still very clear.

- In Russia in the early 1900s, Jews were discriminated against, treated with violence, and often threatened with death. Many were killed.
- During this time, thousands of Jews and other immigrants from Europe who hoped to enter the United States came through New York City.
- Levitt's parents and their fourteen children all migrated to the United States by 1911. Levitt was then 14; he lived to the age of 105.

Set Purposes for Reading

Read the excerpt from *The Century for Young People* to think about what the American dream meant to Alfred Levitt.

Set Your Own Purpose What would you like to learn from the selection to help you answer the Big Question? Write your purpose on the "Century for Young People" page of Foldable 8.

Keep Moving

Use these skills as you read the following selection.

Teach

C Critical Thinking

Evaluation Ask: Do you think oral histories are important as historical documents? Why? *(Possible response: They are important because they are a way of preserving personal and historical information for the present and the future.)* **Ask:** If you were an oral historian, whose story would you like to record? *(Responses will vary.)* AS

Interactive Literary Elements Handbook Have students access the Web site to improve their understanding of chronological order.

Differentiated Instruction

Historical Report Inform students that this selection is an excerpt from a book called *The Century for Young People.* This selection is Alfred Levitt's oral history about the time his family left Russia to escape prejudice against Jews. Instruct students to research the conditions Jews lived in during the early 1900s in Russia. Allow them to use the library or the Internet to conduct research. Have students focus their research on a specific area of interest, such as what it was like to be a Jewish woman at the time. Have students compile brief reports on their topics. Then allow them to read their reports to the class. AL

Indiana English/Language Arts Academic Standards
SE: 8.1.2, 8.2
TWE: *English Language Coach* 8.1, *Differentiated Instruction* 8.7.12

Teach

R Reading Skill

Review Identifying Main Idea and Supporting Details
Say: Look at the first paragraph. What is the main idea? *(Levitt's family lives a hard life in a small Russian town.)* **Ask:** What details support this main idea? *(Possible response: the family is starving; they have no money)* AS

E Text Element

Chronological Order **Ask:** What clue indicates that this story will be told in chronological order? *(beginning with "I was born," then telling about Levitt's boyhood)* AS

C Critical Thinking

Comprehension **Ask:** What is Levitt's impression of America? *(Possible response: It's a wealthy country with jobs, where people are tolerant of Jews.)* BL **Ask:** How does that belief define Levitt's "American dream"? *(America is seen as a land of equality and opportunity.)* OL

Readability Scores
Dale-Chall: 5.2
DRP: 54
Lexile: 950

from The CENTURY for Young People

by Alfred Levitt

I was born in a small Russian town of about ten thousand people. We were a poor family. My father made the horse-drawn carriages that the bourgeoisie used on Sundays to promenade[1] down the street. It would take him about six months to build each carriage because he couldn't afford any tools and he had to build each one with his own ten fingers. E R

Visual Vocabulary ***Horse-drawn carriages*** are wheeled vehicles that are pulled by horses and carry people.

During the six months it took my father to finish a carriage, the family starved. We had no money, and the rich people wouldn't pay my father until he finished his carriage. It was a very hard life. 1

My family was part of a population of about two thousand Jews in our city. People yelled out "bad Jew" and "Christ-killer," and they said that we shouldn't be allowed to live. There was a pogrom[2] in 1905 where the Russians looted every store that was either owned or operated by a Jew. I remember my mother pulling me into a hiding place for fear that I would be hurt. It was this abuse against the Jews that made my two brothers decide to go to the United States. In Russia, everyone thought that America was such a rich country that you could **literally** find gold in the streets. At home there were no jobs C

1. ***Bourgeoisie*** (burzh wah ZEE) is a French word meaning "middle class." To ***promenade*** (prawm uh NAYD) is to go for a slow, relaxed drive or stroll.
2. A ***pogrom*** (POH gruhm) was an organized attack against Jews. A great many pogroms were carried out in eastern Europe up to the early 1900s. Often, all Jews in a certain area were murdered; less often, few were killed but their homes and businesses were destroyed.

Vocabulary

literally (LIT ur uh lee) *adv.* actually; exactly

Practice the Skills

1 Key Reading Skill

Analyzing In these first two paragraphs, Levitt describes the situation of his family and the Jews in Russia. Explain why the Levitts decided to go to America, and tell whether you think they made a wise decision.

Additional Support

Differentiated Instruction

Graphic Organizers Tell students that one way to visually organize chronological order is with a sequence of events chart. Draw such a chart on the board using boxes connected with arrows showing a sequence. Then, fill in the sequence of events chart with the class. Choose one student, and map the sequence of events in his or her day. Explain to students they can also use a time line to clarify the order of events; especially if a large expanse of time is covered. Have students make time lines of their lives from birth to present. They should divide it by years and record an important event from each year. BL for Jews, but in America surely my brothers would find work. They went to New York, worked hard as house painters, and **accumulated** enough money to buy passage[3] for the rest of the family. 2

I had never seen an ocean before we got on the boat for America. I looked out onto the sea and saw these huge waves crashing up against the rocks. It was a frightening experience. But then I saw the openness of the ocean, and that great body of water opened my mind to a world that I never knew existed. As we approached New York Harbor I saw the Statue of Liberty, and I was **overwhelmed** with a feeling of hope for a beautiful life in a new nation. Then we headed toward Ellis Island and I could see the big buildings of New York. It was R BQ

3. One meaning of ***passage*** is "a trip; a going across." Like most immigrants from Europe, the family crossed the Atlantic Ocean by ship.

Practice the Skills

2 **BIG Question**
How did Russians in the early 1900s picture America? Write your answer on the "Century for Young People" page of Foldable 8. Your response will help you complete the Unit Challenge later.

Vocabulary

accumulated (uh KYOO myuh lay tid) *v.* gathered or piled up, little by little

overwhelmed (oh vur WELMD) *v.* overpowered in thought or feeling; completely covered or flooded

Analyzing the Photo Immigrants at Ellis Island see the Statue of Liberty. How does this image suggest both hope and uncertainty?

READING WORKSHOP 1

Teach

BQ **BIG Question**

Say: Levitt describes his first sight of New York. Do you think this sight lived up to his idea of the American dream? Explain your answer. *(Possible response: yes, because he found the harbor and Statue of Liberty welcoming and promising hope)* AS

R Reading Skill

Analyzing Ask: How is the journey from a dangerously rocky shore into a welcoming harbor a metaphor for the life the narrator left behind to achieve his American dream? *(Possible response: Sailing through rough waters into in safe, open harbor is a metaphor for fleeing a difficult and dangerous life to get to a better life of promise and prosperity.)* AL

Reading Fluency

Reading Activity The Statue of Liberty is known around the world as a symbol of freedom. Copy and distribute the poem "The New Colossus" by Emma Lazarus. Explain that this poem is inscribed on the statue's pedestal. Instruct students to take turns reading the poem aloud to a partner. After they have read the poem with their partners, assign a few lines to students and conduct a round-robin group reading. As you discuss the poem, examine the power of a symbol to inspire people and give them courage. OL

Indiana English/Language Arts Academic Standards
SE: 8.2
TWE: *Differentiated Instruction* 8.2, *Reading Fluency* 8.7.14

Teach

R1 Reading Skill

Analyzing **Say:** This selection is taken from a book called *The Century for Young People.* What do you think the title means, and why do you think Levitt's oral history is included? *(Possible response: The title may refer to the twentieth century and its highlights. In that case, the book recaps the major events of the century through the stories of various American experiences. Levitt's piece is likely included because it is typical of the immigrant experience of that time.)* AS

R2 Reading Skill

Review Connecting **Ask:** Have you ever moved, transferred to a new school, or experienced a new place that was totally unfamiliar to you? What feelings did you have? *(Responses will vary.)* **Ask:** How does that experience help you to relate to the narrator's experience? *(Students might connect to the fear of the unknown and the joy of discovery.)* AS

an amazing sight. The city I came from only had little shacks made of wood and stone. Here everything was big and new. At Ellis Island[4] they looked in my eyes to see if I was healthy and they checked my hair for lice. When they determined that my family and I were not sick, they put us on another boat and we were finally admitted to the United States. 3

At first I was afraid to go in the subway. I didn't want to climb down into that dark hole. In Russia the only **means** of transportation that I knew about were horses and bicycles. When I did go in, I discovered a whole new world. There were advertisements that told me what to buy. And I saw people—blacks, yellows, all sorts of different facial looks and ethnic groups, people like I had never seen before. Most of all, R2

4. From 1892 to 1954, most European immigrants entered the United States at ***Ellis Island*** in New York Bay.

Vocabulary

means (meenz) *n.* methods useful for achieving a particular purpose or goal; resources

Analyzing the Photo What part of Levitt's experience does this photograph show?

Practice the Skills

3 Key Text Element

Chronological Order Notice the words in this paragraph—*before, then, as, then, when,* and *finally*—that signal time order.

Additional Support

Literature Focus Lesson

Chronological Order Some students may find it easier to understand chronological order if they work with a time line. Invite students to copy the list of events. As they read the selection, have them add the events to the time line in the order in which they occur. BL EL

- Levitt's brothers go to the United States. (3)
- Levitt travels by subway. (7)
- Levitt makes the voyage by sea to the U.S. (4)
- Levitt is born in small Russian town. (1)
- Levitt is checked at Ellis Island. (6)
- Levitt changes schools. (8)
- A pogrom occurs in 1905 in Levitt's town. (2)
- Levitt sees New York City for the first time. (5)

Analyzing the Photo Where do you think this picture was taken? What words would you use to describe this picture?

I was amazed that I could go anywhere for five cents. I was able to go all the way down to **Battery** Park, and then, if I chose, I could transfer and turn around and go all the way up to Yonkers[5] for the same nickel. 4

My first school was on 103rd Street near Third Avenue, but when I discovered that there were too many foreign boys in the same class, I left it, because I wasn't learning the American language fast enough. I wanted to learn the American language because I wanted to understand the American people, the American mind, and the American culture. I wanted to be completely American, and that couldn't happen in a school full of foreign boys. Mostly I wanted to get a good job somewhere, and I knew if I didn't speak English, I couldn't get a good job. So I walked down to another high school in Harlem on 116th Street and asked the supervisor to give me an audience.[6] I told him I wanted to learn the American language and I wasn't getting it on 103rd Street. He said, "I will give you two questions. If you pass them, you are admitted." He asked me to spell *accident* for him, and I did right away, with two *c*'s. Then he asked me what two-thirds of fifteen was, and I said, "Ten," so he admitted me to high school. In Russia, only a small percentage of Jewish children could go to school, and then it had to be a special Jewish school. In America, I could go to school with everyone else. 5 6 ○

5. ***Battery Park*** is a neighborhood at the southern edge of New York City, while ***Yonkers*** is a separate city about 25 miles north of Battery Park.

6. ***Harlem*** is a neighborhood of New York City. Here, ***audience*** means "a hearing; an interview."

Practice the Skills

4 English Language Coach

A Changing Language The early meaning of **battery** is "a beating." Later, a new meaning was added: a grouping of cannons in battle. *Battery Park* got its name from the second meaning.

5 Key Reading Skill

Analyzing Why did the man ask these two questions?

6 BIG Question

In what ways did the American dream become a reality for Levitt? Write your answer on the "Century for Young People" page of Foldable 8.

Teach

C Critical Thinking

Evaluation Ask: Why do you think the supervisor at the school on 116th Street gave Levitt a test? *(Possible response: to see if he'd be able to fit in with others in the school)* BL
Ask: Do you think the test he gave Levitt was a good indicator of Levitt's abilities? Explain. *(Responses will vary.)* OL

R Reading Skill

Analyzing Say: Reread the last two sentences of the selection. Levitt compares his life in Russia to his life in the United States. What does this comparison say about his views of America? *(Possible response: He is grateful to live in America and to be able to take advantage of the opportunities available here.)* OL

Assess

Use the CheckPoint questions provided on Presentation Plus! to check for comprehension of the selection. These questions can be used with interactive response keypads for immediate student feedback.

Differentiated Instruction

Oral History To help some students better understand the importance of Levitt's initiative in finding a new school for himself, invite students to tell their own oral histories. Have pairs of students tell each other about a time when they took initiative to get something or do something they wanted. Allow students time to think about their narratives before they begin. Students might make brief notes about their goals, the steps they took, and their accomplishments to keep their narratives on track. Students should end by explaining how they felt before, during, and after the event. EL OL

Indiana English/Language Arts Academic Standards
SE: 8.1.2, 8.2
TWE: *Literature Focus Lesson* 8.2, *Differentiated Instruction* 8.7.10

Assess

Resources for page 1080

- Selection Quick Check, p. 72
- Selection and Unit Assessment, p. 86
- ExamView Assessment Suite
- Interactive Tutor: Self-Assessment

Students can respond to the *After You Read* items in their Learner's Notebooks or on a separate sheet of paper.

Answering the BIG Question

1. Possible response: a chance to have more.
2. About six months
3. They were house painters.
4. Possible response: big and new; fascinated by people from different ethnic groups

Critical Thinking

5. Possible response: The Russian city had only little shacks of wood and stone; only transportation by horse and bicycle; only a small percentage of Jewish children could go to school. In New York, buildings were big, trains provided transportation, everyone got to go to school, and many nationalities were represented.
6. Possible response: Levitt probably would not have had as much opportunity.
7. Possible response: He wanted to absorb all the culture in America.

After You Read

from *The Century for Young People*

Answering the BIG Question

1. What did the American dream mean to Alfred Levitt?
2. **Recall** How long did it take Levitt's father to build one carriage?
   - TIP Right There
3. **Recall** What work did Levitt's brothers do after they came to New York?
   - TIP Right There
4. **Describe** Describe Levitt's impressions of his first experiences in America.
   - TIP Think and Search

Critical Thinking

5. **Compare** How was the Russian city Levitt was born in different from or similar to New York City? Give details from the oral history in your answer.
   - TIP Think and Search
6. **Infer** What do you think would have happened if Levitt hadn't decided to change schools? Explain your answer.
   - TIP Author and Me
7. **Interpret** In your own words, tell what Levitt means when he says he wanted to be "completely American."
   - TIP Author and Me

Write About Your Reading

Postcards Pretend that you are Levitt at age 17, soon after he arrives in New York City. You're going to send two picture postcards to friends back in Russia.

First, imagine the postcard scenes Levitt might have sent. Think of two different things that impressed him or two important experiences he had. Make a few notes about each scene and what it meant to Levitt.

Second, write the message for each postcard as Levitt might have written it. Tell each friend about the picture, what it represents to Levitt, and why he chose that image for his friend. Keep each message to four or five sentences.

Indiana English/Language Arts Academic Standards (pp. 1080–1081)

8.3 Comprehension and Analysis of Literary Text Respond to grade-level-appropriate literature...
8.5.7 Write for different purposes...
8.2 Comprehension and Analysis (Focus on Informational Text) Develop [reading] strategies...identifying and analyzing structure, organization, perspective, and purpose.
8.6 English Language Conventions

For a complete description of the standards, see p. IN 11.

Write About Your Reading

Possible response:

Dear Anna, this is the Statue of Liberty, the first thing I saw when in America. America truly is the land of freedom, where all kinds of people live and work side by side. Your friend, Alfred

Dear Nathan, these people are riding in a subway car under the ground! Riding the subway is fun because you can go all over the city for just a nickel. I've been exploring everywhere all by myself. This really is a New World, and I want to learn English and become a real American. Your friend, Alfred

Skills Review

Key Reading Skill: Analyzing

8. What things about New York City's subway system were especially impressive to Levitt? Why do you suppose those things affected him so much?

9. Write a sentence stating the main subject of each paragraph in the selection.

Key Text Element: Chronological Order

10. Put the following events from Levitt's life in the correct chronological order.
- His mother hides him during a pogrom.
- He is admitted to a new high school.
- He sees the ocean for the first time.
- He first sees the New York skyline.
- His brothers go to New York.
- He is born in Russia.

Vocabulary Check

For each vocabulary word, choose the word or phrase that means most nearly the same thing.

11. literally
really completely unbelievably

12. accumulated
spent saved up bought

13. overwhelmed
late undone overcome

14. means
ways purposes explanations

15. English Language Coach What is the connection between these meanings of *battery?*
(a) a beating (b) a grouping of cannons in battle

Web Activities For eFlashcards, Selection Quick Checks, and other Web activities, go to www.glencoe.com.

Grammar Link: Confused Words

These words are often confused because they sound alike. Learning the correct use of these words will help you as a speaker and as a writer.

accept: to receive
except: other than
- I **accept** your nomination.
- **Except** for Lois, we all came here as immigrants.

loose: not firmly attached
lose: to misplace or to fail to win
- These jeans are too **loose.**
- If you **lose** your way, call me on your cell phone.

then: at that time
than: introduces the second part of a comparison
- **Then** I asked him his name.
- My brother is a lot taller **than** I am.

who's: contraction of *who is*
whose: possessive form of *who*
- **Who's** going to the store this afternoon?
- **Whose** book is this?

it's: contraction of *it is*
its: possessive form of *it*
- **It's** almost time to go home.
- **Its** leaves had turned crimson and began to fall.

Grammar Practice

Rewrite each sentence, filling in the correct word.

16. Will you (accept, except) my apology?
17. We have to decide (who's, whose) going to go first.
18. Did you put the camera back in (it's, its) case?
19. Texas is bigger (than, then) some countries.

Writing Application Check the postcard messages you wrote. If you used any of these troublesome words incorrectly, fix the mistakes.

Vocabulary Check

11. really
12. saved up
13. overcome
14. ways

English Language Coach

15. Possible response: To *batter* something is to beat it. A group of cannons would certainly cause destruction, or "batter" something or somebody.

Grammar Link: Confused Words

Grammar Practice

16. accept
17. who's
18. its
19. than

Skills Review

Key Reading Skill: Analyzing

8. Possible response: There were people of different ethnic groups, advertisements, and the fact that you could travel easily around the city for just a nickel. In his Russian city, people were probably not so varied, and he may not have had the same mobility and freedom he did in America.

9. Responses will vary.

Key Text Element: Chronological Order

10.
- He is born in Russia.
- His mother hides him during a pogrom.
- His brothers go to New York.
- He sees the ocean for the first time.
- He first sees the New York skyline.
- He is admitted to a new high school.

Close

Ask students to compare their idea of the American dream to the narrator's.

Web Activities Have students access the Web site for interactive activities that will help them assess their understanding of the selection.

Indiana English/Language Arts Academic Standards
SE: 8.2, 8.3, 8.5.7, 8.6

Letter

UNIT 8

Teaching Students to Write a Letter

Why Is It Important?

- Writing a letter about how a sitcom portrays life experiences will help students distinguish between real life and TV life.
- Letter writing is one of the most common forms of written communication. It is important that students become familiar with the conventions of written correspondence.
- The subject is likely to be popular with most students. By thinking about something already part of their lives, students will build connections between academic writing and themselves.
- Analyzing the way the American dream is represented in the media will help writers think about answers to the Big Question: What is the American dream?
- Students will benefit from applying the principles of analysis to both televised entertainment and printed literature.

How to Help Students Get It

- Work with students to build or narrow their lists of TV shows, and be sure they know the difference between sitcoms and other types of show.
- Emphasize the real-world application of this letter. Many TV shows make contact information for certain individuals publicly available, and students can actually mail their letters. Any writing task is more engaging when the author can look forward to a response.
- During revision, make word processing software available, if possible. Many word processors have a built-in letter wizard that allows students to input the address and the body of the letter. Experimenting with this feature will help students become familiar with letter formats.
- Encourage students to be very specific in their interview questions; a too-broad topic may be discouraging or lead interviewees off course.
- Remind students that a letter shares many qualities of a well-written essay: organization, clearly stated position or thesis, support for argument, introduction, and conclusion.

Writing Trait	Student Checklist
Ideas	the message or the theme and the details that develop it
Organization	the arrangement of main points and supporting details
Voice	a writer's unique way of using tone and style
Word Choice	the vocabulary a writer uses to convey meaning
Sentence Fluency	the smooth rhythm and flow of sentences that vary in length and style
Conventions	correct spelling, grammar, usage, and mechanics
Unit Focus **Presentation:** the way words and design elements look on a page	Appearance matters, so encourage students to make their compositions inviting to read. Handwritten papers should be neat and legible. If a word processor is used, the text should be double spaced and the font should be readable. Encourage students to also use other design elements—such as boldfaced headings, bulleted lists, pictures, and charts—to make their papers attractive and inviting.

Workshop Resources

Pacing (Days) Standard	Block	Lesson	Student Materials	Teacher Resources
1	1/2	Writing Workshop Part 1: Prewriting and Drafting	Writing Workshop Graphic Organizer, p. 15 Grammar Practice, p. 18 Spelling and Handwriting Practice, p. 47 Grammar and Composition Handbook, p. 113 Real Success in Writing: Research and Reports	TeacherWorks Plus™ Presentation Plus! Rubrics for Assessing Student Writing, Listening, and Speaking, p. 17 Grammar and Writing Workshop Transparencies 15–16
2	1	Writing Workshop Part 2: Editing, Revising, and Presenting	Interactive Grammar and Language Workbook Grammar and Composition Handbook, p. 113 Real Success in Writing: Research and Reports Listening and Speaking, p. 16 Viewing and Representing, p. 17	Grammar and Writing Workshop Transparencies, 31–32 Interactive Grammar and Language Workbook Rubrics for Assessing Student Writing, Listening, and Speaking, p. 17

Focus

BELLRINGER Options

Daily Language Practice Transparency 75

Focus Activity Say: The word *sitcom* is short for *situation comedy.* Sitcoms find humor in everyday situations with a set group of characters. What is your favorite sitcom? Why? *(Responses will vary.)* AS You will write about a favorite sitcom in this Writing Workshop.

Teach

C Critical Thinking

Analysis Say: Sitcoms tell a lot about us as a people in a specific time. What problems and values do sitcoms show today? *(Possible responses: life in a diverse society; life in a changing suburb or crowded city; life with a quirky family)* AS

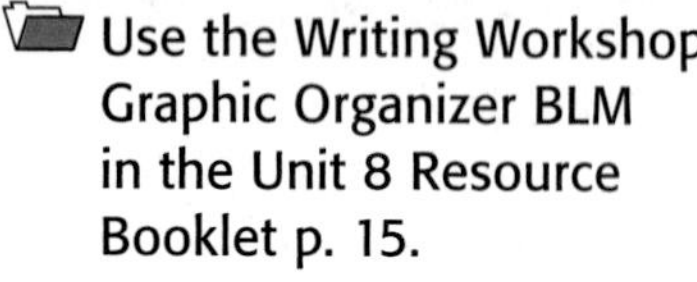

Resources for page 1082

- Use the Writing Workshop Graphic Organizer BLM in the Unit 8 Resource Booklet p. 15.
- Use the Grammar and Writing Workshop Transparencies 15-16.

WRITING WORKSHOP PART 1

Letter

Prewriting and Drafting

ASSIGNMENT Write a letter

Purpose: To evaluate and respond to the media

Audience: A TV producer or head of a media company

Writing Rubric

As you work through this writing assignment, you should follow these guidelines:

- clearly state your opinion
- develop and support your ideas with well-chosen details
- organize your ideas in a logical order
- interview a friend, classmate, or family member

See page 1130 in Part 2 for a model of a letter.

Indiana English/Language Arts Academic Standards (pp. 1082–1085)

8.5.7 Write for different purposes... **8.4 Processes and Features** Prewriting and drafting. **8.7 Listening and Speaking** Careful listening and evaluation of content... **8.6 English Language Conventions**

For a complete description of the standards, see p. IN 11.

C People watch more television than ever before. Most comedy series are sitcoms, short for "situation comedies." In each episode, the characters deal with a new situation, or a problem, in a humorous way.

You'll evaluate the way one comedy series presents Americans, their relationships, "ordinary" life in America, and the American dream. Then you'll write a letter to the producer of that series. Your evaluation will help you think about the Unit 8 Big Question: What is the American dream?

Prewriting

Get Ready to Write

Draw from your own experience as a TV viewer and from your knowledge of the elements of fiction. Sitcoms are like ongoing short stories with characters, conflicts, dialogue, settings, and themes.

Gather Ideas

Follow these steps to generate ideas for your letter.

- List the sitcoms that you enjoy watching, and choose one to write about.
- Identify the main characters, and write a few words describing each. What are their relationships? (Are they, for example, family members, coworkers, friends, or classmates?) What does each character do? (Teacher, garbage collector, student, or store clerk?)
- Describe the setting of the show. Is it urban, suburban, or rural? What city, state, or region of the country? When does it take place? Most sitcoms are set in the present. For an older show that's set in the past, give the decade—for example, the 1960s for *The Wonder Years*.
- Describe the sort of problem the characters face in a typical episode. Do they usually solve their problems? How?
- Decide whether the characters are realistic people or stereotypes. Stereotypes are characters with traits that are supposedly shared by all members of a particular group. For example, a stereotype of old people is that they're all grumpy and hard of hearing. A stereotype of teenagers is that they only want to have fun and don't care about serious issues.
- Consider what the sitcom says about America and Americans. What impressions do you think viewers in other countries would get from it?
- What advice do you have for the people who write or produce the show?

Additional Support

Reading in the Real World

Career Some students may be interested in careers as sitcom scriptwriters. Invite students to find writers of their favorite sitcoms by watching the credits or searching the Internet. Have them research the biographies of these people and report on their education and how they got into the television industry. OL Instruct them to compile a list of five questions they'd like to ask the scriptwriters about their careers and work. Have students write their questions in letters and send the letters to the show. AL

Organize Your Thoughts

Gather your notes. Then follow these steps.

1. Decide whom to write to. You'll need to do some research to find people who work behind the scenes. Check the Web site of the channel the show is on. For example, one student liked *The Simpsons* and decided to write to its creator, Matt Groening.
2. Write one sentence that clearly states your overall opinion about the show and how it presents American life.

   I think The Simpsons shows both our worst and best sides.

3. Give three or more reasons for your opinion. Later, you'll develop each reason into a paragraph.

   The mix of characters is true to life.
   Springfield's problems ring true for viewers.
   The main characters have their good points.

4. Write one or two sentences that sum up your message of praise, criticism, or a combination of both.

   Thanks for making us laugh at ourselves while encouraging us to solve our problems.

Literature Online

Writing Models For models and other writing activities, go to www.glencoe.com.

Writing Tip

Show Titles When you're typing the title of a TV series, you should use italics. When you're handwriting it, you can underline the title instead.

Writing Tip

Brainstorming If you need help getting started, try freewriting for three minutes without stopping. Write down anything that comes to mind about the show. After a break, read what you've written. You may find something to use as a starting point for your letter.

Drafting

Start Writing!

You have everything you need to get started: a topic, a clear position, some organized points, and a concluding statement.

Get It on Paper

These directions can help you get started on your first draft.

- Begin by explaining your purpose for writing and briefly stating your opinion of the show.
- Write a paragraph explaining each reason for your opinion. Back up your points with specific examples from the show. You might use a quotation from a classmate or family member to support one of your points.
- Write a conclusion that explains how well or how badly you think the show portrays America and Americans.
- Finish by complimenting or criticizing the show. If you're critical, make suggestions for how to improve it.

Writing Tip

Drafting Remember that this is only a first draft. When you go back to revise, you can add, delete, and move ideas.

WRITING WORKSHOP PART 1

Teach

W Writing

Business vs. Personal Letters **Ask:** What are some purposes for writing letters today? *(Possible responses: to request information, to complain, to state an opinion or persuade people to act in a certain way, to thank someone, to introduce yourself for a job)* Invite students to compare and contrast a business letter and a personal letter. You might want to provide examples for students before asking the questions. **Ask:** What similarities do personal and business letters share? *(Possible response: Both communicate information)* **Ask:** How do they differ? *(Possible responses: They use different kinds of language; writers use formal language in business letters and informal language in personal letters. They are written for different purposes. They have different formats on the page.)* **AS**

Literature Online

Writing Models Have students access the Web site for an additional and interactive Writing Workshop–based student model.

Differentiated Instruction

Following Examples Some students may find it easier to understand the purpose of a persuasive or critical letter if they read a letter to the editor. Invite students to read a letter to the editor from your local newspaper. Challenge them to explain the author's purpose for writing the letter. Have them complete the following sentences: In this letter to the editor, the writer's purpose is _______. The writer wants to (persuade/inform/thank/criticize). The writer does this by _______. Lead a class discussion about students' analyses of the letter to the editor. **AS**

Indiana English/Language Arts Academic Standards

SE: 8.4, 8.5.7

TWE: *Reading in the Real World* 8.4.4, *Differentiated Instruction* 8.2

Teach

LSV1 Listening, Speaking, and Viewing

Interview Skills **Say:** When you conduct an interview, the first thing you should do is ask the person's first and last name and get the correct spellings. Also, write down the person's profession or relationship to you. Note the time and date of the interview. At the end of the interview, take a moment to read over your questions and notes. A good way to close an interview is to ask, "Is there anything else you would like to add?" Be sure to thank the person you interviewed. If it is a business professional, you might consider mailing a note expressing your thanks for taking the time to help you. AS

LSV2 Listening, Speaking, and Viewing

Interview Questions **Say:** While it is very important to have a solid list of questions, it's okay to vary from that list once the interview begins. An interview can become like a conversation once you relax. Be sure to ask all of your questions, but remain open to other points of discussion. AS

Listening, Speaking, and Viewing

Conducting an Interview

As part of your evaluation, it's a good idea to ask other people what they think about the show. Interview at least two people.

Analyzing Cartoons
Is this a good interview? Why or why not?

What Is an Interview?

An interview is a conversation with the purpose of getting information about a particular topic. You hear, see, and read plenty of interviews, whether you realize it or not.

TV and radio shows, Web sites, newspapers, and magazines–they all make frequent use of interviews with all kinds of people, including

- government officials, crime victims, disaster survivors, and other people in the news
- movie stars, authors, coaches, athletes, and other celebrities
- sports fans, shoppers, and weather watchers

What Skills Do I Need, and Why Are They Important?

The same skills that help you talk to classmates, teachers, family members, and store clerks can help you interview them. You need to be organized and prepared. You need to be able to listen without interrupting. You need patience and understanding.

Listening to other people's ideas can reinforce or challenge your own opinions. Quoting other people can add spice to your writing.

How Do I Do an Interview?

Prepare by making a list of questions.

- Think about what supporting information you need and ask for opinions about those ideas. *Example:* If you believe the Simpson characters have their good points, you might ask, "What do you think of Bart? Why?"
- Don't ask leading questions. That is, don't phrase a question so that it suggests the answer you want. *Example:* Don't ask, "Do you agree that *The Simpsons* is biased against rural people?" Instead, ask, "Do you think the show portrays rural people in a fair way?"
- Phrase your questions so that the interviewee can't answer with a simple yes or no.

When you're ready to do an interview, don't rely on your memory. Write your questions down on note cards or paper. Record the conversation (only after asking permission), or take good notes.

- LSV1 Start with your prepared questions, but be ready to respond to what the interviewee says.
- Try not to show your own opinions. You want people to tell you what they really think, not what they think you want to hear.
- Be a good listener. Nodding and making eye contact show that you're paying attention. LSV2 Encourage people to keep talking by saying, "Go on" or "I see."
- If you don't understand something, ask the interviewee to clarify it. Paraphrase what the person said to check whether you understood correctly. *Example:* "When you said 'they,' did you mean the characters or the writers?"

Write to Learn Use your interviewees' responses in your letter. If you quote someone directly, use quotation marks and give the person's name. If you paraphrase, be sure you're presenting the interviewee's opinion accurately.

Additional Support

Reading Fluency

Peer Evaluation Some students may find it helpful to work with a partner to develop their list of interview questions. After they write a list of questions, pair students and allow them to practice asking their questions. Students will be able to hear how their questions sound as well as role-play possible answers. Instruct students to look for questions that are not clear, and questions that they think are missing. Allow students time to make corrections to their questions. AS

Grammar Link

Irregular Verbs

It is important to learn how to form verb tenses so you can use verbs correctly in a sentence. However, that is just the beginning. You also need to learn about irregular verbs that may be confusing.

What Are Irregular Verbs?

For regular verbs, you form the past tense and past participle by adding *-d* or *–ed* to the verb's base form.

- I want to live in Toledo, Ohio. (base form)
- I live**d** in Toledo, Ohio. (past tense)
- I have live**d** in Toledo, Ohio for a year. (past participle)

The past tense and past participle of irregular verbs are not formed this way.

- I am going to be in Toledo, Ohio. (base form)
- I went to Toledo, Ohio. (past tense)
- I have been to Toledo, Ohio. (past participle)

Several patterns are used to form irregular verbs. With time and practice, you'll remember them.

A. One vowel changes to form the past tense and the past participle. *(begin, began, have begun)*

B. The past tense and the past participle are the same. *(fight, fought, has fought)*

C. The base form and the past participle are the same. *(run, ran, had run)*

D. The past tense ends in *-ew,* and the past participle ends in *-wn. (draw, drew, have drawn)*

E. The past participle ends in *-en. (shake, shook, has shaken)*

F. The base form, the past tense, and the past participle are the same. *(cost, cost, have cost)*

G. The past tense and the past participle don't follow any pattern. *(be, was/were, had been)*

Why Are They Important?

When you use verbs incorrectly, it makes you sound less knowledgeable than you are. Also, you may confuse your readers if you use the wrong form or tense of a verb by treating an irregular verb as if it follows the regular pattern. For example, by using *falled* instead of *fell* or *have fell* instead of *have fallen,* you make it unclear when an action takes place.

Incorrect: I have fell out of a tree while climbing.
Correct: I have fallen out of a tree while climbing.

How Do I Use Irregular Verbs?

To express an action that happened at a fixed time in the past, use the past tense of the verb.

- The water froze in the pond.

To express an action that happened before another action in the past, use *had* before the past participle.

- The water had frozen in the pond by noon.

To express an action that will occur before a set time in the future, use *will have* before the past participle.

- The water will have frozen by the time we get home.

To express an action that occurred at an unspecified time in the past or an action that continues to happen into the present time, use *have* or *has* before the past participle.

- In the past, the water has frozen enough to allow ice skating.

Write to Learn Review your draft and fix any mistakes involving irregular verbs. If you need help, use a dictionary. The past tense and past participle of irregular verbs are usually included in the entry for the base form of the verb.

Looking Ahead

Keep the writing you've done so far. In Writing Workshop Part 2, you'll learn how to turn your writing into a strong and compelling letter.

English Language Coach

Irregular Verbs Tell English learners that mastering irregular verbs is one of the most difficult elements of learning English. Irregular verbs do not follow set rules, so learning the irregular forms is a matter of memorization. Draw a three-column chart on the board. Label the columns *Base Form, Past, Past Participle.* Then have students copy the chart in their Learner's Notebooks. Work with them to fill in each form for the irregular verbs used on this page. Tell students to continue to add to their charts as they progress through the unit. Explain that the chart will be a good reference for future use. EL

Teach

Grammar Link

Irregular Verbs Write the following sentences on the board. Have students copy the sentences in their Learner's Notebooks, circling the correct form of the irregular verbs.

1. I (be, was) on the corner at four o'clock, but you (was, were) not there.
2. He (gone, went) to Hawaii twice.
3. She (known, knew) the answer to the question.
4. The quarterback (fallen, fell) down in the middle of the pass.
5. The lake had (frozen, freezing) over by October.

Answers

1. was/were
2. went
3. knew
4. fell
5. frozen

Assess

Have students read to partners the first drafts of their letters. Ask partners to critique each other's writing. After a few minutes, have students assess their own letters, make any needed revisions, and save their revised letters for later use.

Indiana English/Language Arts Academic Standards
SE: 8.6, 8.6.8, 8.7
TWE: *Reading Fluency* 8.7.6, *English Language Coach* 8.6

Understanding Cause and Effect

Teaching Students to Understand Cause and Effect

Why Is It Important?

- Causal relationships are central to narrative and informational text.
- Students who understand cause and effect can understand that actions have consequences.
- Understanding cause and effect can provide a way to understand motivations and reactions in stories and in the real world.

How to Help Students Get It

- Emphasize that causal relationships are present at many levels in narratives: at the story level, in individual events, and in characters' behavior over time.
- Have students examine causal relationships within short stories, then apply the concept to a science experiment and a historical event.
- Use graphic organizers to help students map out causal relationships at each level.

Reading to Answer the Big Question

Lottery Winners Who Lost Their Millions by Ellen Goodstein
This article describes lottery winners who lost all their winnings and went into debt. It describes the emotional risks related to winning a large sum of money as well as common pitfalls lottery winners encounter. This article includes advice from financial planner Susan Bradley. One winner says "I won the American dream but I lost it, too."

The Gettysburg Address by Abraham Lincoln
Lincoln's eloquent speech honors the soldiers who died in battle and reminds his listeners to uphold the basic values on which the nation was founded—liberty and equality for all.

Workshop Resources

Pacing (Days) Standard	Pacing (Days) Block	Lesson	Student Materials	Teacher Resources
1	1/2	Key Skill Lesson: Cause and Effect	Key Reading Skills Practice, p. 19 English Language Coach Review, p. 44	Bellringer Options Transparencies –Daily Language Practice 76 Read Aloud, Think Aloud Transparencies –Key Reading Skills 26 Presentation Plus!
1	1	"Lottery Winners Who Lost Their Millions"	Glencoe Online Unit Vocabulary Review, p. 42 Academic Vocabulary Review, p. 45 English Language Coach Active Reading Graphic Organizer, p. 20 StudentWorks Plus™ Online Student Edition Literature Classics Selection and Unit Assessments, p. 87	Literary and Text Analysis Transparencies 54 Puzzlemaker Skill Level Up!™ A Language Arts Game BookLink 3 Assessment by Learning Objective (Diagnostic and Formative) Interactive Tutor: Self-Assessment TeacherWorks Plus™
1		"The Gettysburg Address"	Glencoe Online Unit Vocabulary Review, p. 42 Academic Vocabulary Review, p. 45 English Language Coach Active Reading Graphic Organizer, p. 23 StudentWorks Plus™ Online Student Edition Literature Classics Selection and Unit Assessments, p. 88	Read Aloud, Think Aloud Transparencies –Read Aloud, Think Aloud 68–69 Literary and Text Analysis Transparencies 50 Puzzlemaker Skill Level Up!™ A Language Arts Game BookLink 3 Assessment by Learning Objective (Diagnostic and Formative) Interactive Tutor: Self-Assessment TeacherWorks Plus™

Keys for Unit Resource

- Blackline Master
- Workbook
- Supplemental Text
- CD-ROM
- DVD
- Transparency
- Web-based
- Fast File

Level Appropriate Code

AS = Activities for all students
AL = Activities for students working above grade level
OL = Activities for students working at grade level
BL = Activities for students working below grade level
EL = Activities for English language learners

Focus

BELLRINGER Options

Daily Language Practice Transparency 76

Focus Activity Say: What if your biggest wish were suddenly granted? What would you do first? *(Responses will vary.)* AS

Teach

R Reading Skill

Understanding Cause and Effect Ask: Which comes first—a cause or an effect? *(a cause)* AS

Analyzing the Cartoon

Ask: What kind of growth is Jeremy (the blond boy) referring to? *(height; getting taller.)* **Ask:** What does Jeremy see as the cause of Hector's growth? *(eating sandwiches)* AS

READING WORKSHOP 2

Skills Focus

You will practice using these skills when you read the following selections:

- "Lottery Winners Who Lost Their Millions," p. 1090
- "The Gettysburg Address," p. 1098

Reading

- Understanding cause and effect

Informational Text

- Understanding theme and topic
- Identifying author's style

Vocabulary

- Learning about English as a changing language

Writing/Grammar

- Using capitalization with proper nouns, proper adjectives, and family relationships

Skill Lesson

Understanding Cause and Effect

Learn It!

What Is It? Cause and effect is a kind of text structure that writers can use to organize information.

- A **cause** is a condition or event that makes something happen.
- What happens as the result of that condition or event is an **effect.**

R For example, a person does something wrong (a cause), and a bad thing happens (an effect).

A cause-and-effect relationship can be difficult to identify exactly. Causes and effects can overlap. They may not seem directly linked. Not all events that seem to have a cause-and-effect relationship actually do.

Analyzing Cartoons
Jeremy thinks that eating sandwiches is making Hector grow taller. Do you agree with that cause-and-effect statement? Why?

Indiana English/Language Arts Academic Standards (pp. 1086–1094)

8.2 Comprehension and Analysis (Focus on Informational Text) Develop [reading] strategies...

For a complete description of the standards, see p. IN 11.

Additional Support

Differentiated Instruction

Cause and Effect Explain cause-and-effect sentence patterns to students: Cause brings about one or more effects. Effect occurs because of one or more causes. Write the following sentences on the board without the answers.
Say: Look for cause-and-effect patterns. Underline each cause and circle each effect. OL

- The storm created a huge power outage.
- Hunger, disease, and abuse are all products of poverty.
- His success is a result of hard work and determination.
- Car exhaust and aerosol cans are responsible for the depletion of the ozone layer.

Why Is It Important? When you understand cause-and-effect relationships, you have another tool to help you think critically as a reader. You can see why characters are in the situations they're in. You can recognize when events are connected and when they aren't. C

Study Central Visit www.glencoe.com and click on Study Central to review evaluating.

How Do I Do It? To identify cause-and-effect relationships in a selection, use your prior knowledge. Ask yourself what you know about the subject, what events may have caused it, and what events may have resulted from it. R

Here's how one student used his prior knowledge about Abraham Lincoln's Gettysburg Address.

I know this is one of Lincoln's most famous speeches. I know from history class that there was a huge Civil War battle at Gettysburg. And I think Lincoln spoke at a service honoring the soldiers who died there. So two effects of the battle were soldiers' deaths and Lincoln's speech.

Actually, there must be a whole chain of causes and effects related to this battle and the war. I wonder what effects the Gettysburg Address had.

Practice It!

Below are some things to look for as you analyze the selections in this workshop. Jot down a few notes in your Learner's Notebook about causes and effects related to the following topics:

- the dream of being rich
- winning millions of dollars
- the Civil War
- the idea that "all men are created equal"

Use It!

As you read "Lottery Winners Who Lost Their Millions" and "The Gettysburg Address," remember the notes you made. They'll help you focus on cause and effect as you read.

READING WORKSHOP 2

Teach

C Critical Thinking

Comprehension Ask: What might cause-and-effect relationships in texts tell readers about characters and events? *(Possible response: Cause-and-effect relationships may tell readers why characters are in the situations they're in, or whether and how events are connected.)* AS

R Reading Skill

Understanding Cause and Effect Say: Certain words signal cause-and-effect relationships. For example, *since, because, why, then, so, therefore,* and *as a result of* are all such words and phrases. When you encounter these within a text, look for the cause-and-effect relationship that follows. AS

Resources for page 1087

Use Key Reading Skills Transparency 26 in *Read Aloud, Think Aloud* to help students practice understanding cause and effect.

Reading Fluency

Build Fluency To help students build fluency reading prose, ask students to read along silently as they listen to you read the selection. When you've finished reading each person's account, stop to discuss the person's feelings and thoughts to help students understand the accounts. Then have them form groups and take turns reading aloud the accounts in the selection. Instruct them to continue reading aloud until they have finished the selection. EL BL

Indiana English/Language Arts Academic Standards
SE: 8.2
TWE: *Differentiated Instruction* 8.2, *Reading Fluency* 8.3

Teach

More About the Author

As a freelance writer, Goodstein has an opportunity to write articles on many different topics. In the past, she has used her writing talents to address such drastically different topics as reality show winners, funeral costs, and weight loss tips.

EL Language Coach

English as a Changing Language **Ask:** Which definition of *lot* would you use if you were buying a new home? *(a portion of land)* **Ask:** Which definition would you use to describe hours of homework? *(a large quantity or amount)* AS

Before You Read

Lottery Winners Who Lost Their Millions

Meet the Author

Ellen Goodstein is a freelance writer based in Florida. She contributes news stories and feature articles to both print and online publications.

Author Search For more about Ellen Goodstein, go to www.glencoe.com.

Indiana English/Language Arts Academic Standards (pp. 1088–1093)

8.1.2 Understand the influence of historical events on English word meaning and vocabulary expansion.
8.2 Comprehension and Analysis (Focus on Informational Text) Develop [reading] strategies...identifying and analyzing structure, organization, perspective, and purpose.

For a complete description of the standards, see p. IN 11.

Vocabulary Preview

siblings (SIB lingz) *n.* brothers and sisters **(p. 1091)** *My siblings and I gave our parents flowers for their anniversary.*

eventually (ih VEN choo ul lee) *adv.* happening at last; in the end **(p. 1091)** *Be patient; you'll eventually get to the front of the line.*

inevitable (in EV uh tuh bul) *adj.* sure to happen; unavoidable **(p. 1093)** *With its weak design and cheap materials, the car's failure to sell seemed inevitable.*

consequences (KON suh kwen suz) *n.* results or effects **(p. 1093)** *If you break the law, you will have to face the consequences.*

Write to Learn With a small group, choose a familiar board game or gameshow that involves making–and losing–money. Together, write a paragraph explaining how the game is played. Use each vocabulary word at least once.

English Language Coach

EL

English as a Changing Language Many English words have roots in ancient, long-dead languages. The base of *lottery* is *lot*, a word that goes back more than eight hundred years. (In Old English it was spelled *hlot*, but there isn't a hlot more to say about that.)

Originally, lots were pieces of shell, bone, or wood. They were used to help decide questions or issues, just as dice are used in many modern games. You threw the lots to the ground and "read" an answer to your question. Soon people started betting on how the lots would land. From there, it was a short leap to lotteries as we now know them. Over the centuries, the word *lot* took on additional meanings, including these:

lot
a share
a portion of land
an article or group of articles sold at auction
a large quantity or amount

Small Group Discussion With your group, look again at the paragraph you wrote about a board game or gameshow. Do any of the meanings of *lot* noted above relate to the game? Is any kind of lottery (or "throwing of lots") involved? How important is chance or luck in playing the game?

Additional Support

Author Search To expand students' appreciation of Ellen Goodstein, have them access the Web site for additional information and resources.

Literature Focus Lesson

Author's Purpose Writers create magazine articles for a number of reasons. Some entertain readers, others persuade, while still others inform or teach. Have students work with a partner to find articles that represent the three purposes and identify the author's purpose in each. Then have students swap articles with another set of students. Have them read the articles and identify them as persuasive, informative, or entertaining. As a class, discuss the elements of the texts that qualify the articles as persuasive, informative, or entertaining. OL AL

Skills Preview

Key Reading Skill: Understanding Cause and Effect

A fiction writer invents causes and effects to direct a story where he or she wants it to go. A nonfiction writer doesn't need to make them up; they're right there in real life. Nonfiction writing tries to present events so that the causes and effects are clear.

The next article you'll read tells what happened to a number of people who won millions of dollars. In each case, the cause can be described as winning money in a lottery. The article focuses on

- the effects that sudden wealth can cause
- the belief that money can fix anything
- strategies for dealing with unexpected wealth

Write to Learn In your Learner's Notebook, note ideas you have about causes and effects relating to money. What are possible effects of having no money? What are possible effects of having lots of money? Add to your notes as you read the selection.

Text Element: Theme and Topic

A story's **theme** is its central message. Sometimes the theme is stated directly; sometimes it's implied, and you must figure it out.

Don't confuse theme with topic. **Topic** is the broad subject that a story is about. It can be stated in a word or phrase. For example, both "Volar" and the selection from *The Century for Young People* are about the immigrant experience. However, the theme of "Volar" involves escaping what is unpleasant in life, and the theme of *Century* involves embracing what is new and exciting.

E

Interactive Literary Elements Handbook
To review or learn more about the literary elements, go to www.glencoe.com.

Get Ready to Read

Connect to the Reading

Imagine becoming a millionaire overnight. Would money solve your problems? What's the first thing you'd do? Buy things? Give money to charities? How would you deal with friends and relatives who would expect you to help them out? Who would you turn to for advice?

Money Talks With a partner, talk about the problems and solutions money can bring. Draw on your own experience and the experiences of people you know or have read about.

Build Background

As of 1999, thirty-seven U.S. states operated lotteries to raise money for public services. Canada, France, Great Britain, Japan, Mexico, and other countries run national lotteries. In a modern lottery, you pay a small sum of money for a chance to win a huge sum. Your chances and your prize depend on how many people enter the lottery.

A lottery can be very profitable for its sponsor because most participants don't win anything. Since ancient times, lotteries have been used to raise money for projects including the Great Wall of China; Jamestown (the first British colony in America); and Harvard, Yale, Princeton, and Columbia universities.

Set Purposes for Reading

BIG Question Read this article to study the role of money in the American dream.

Set Your Own Purpose What would you like to learn from the article to help you answer the Big Question? Write your purpose on the "Lottery Winners" page of Foldable 8.

Keep Moving

Use these skills as you read the following selection.

Teach

E Text Element

Theme and Topic Make sure students understand the difference between theme and topic. **Write on the board:** The migration of sea turtles / It is important to protect their environment. **Ask:** Which is the theme and which is the topic? *(Theme: It is important to protect their environment. Topic: The migration of sea turtles.)* BL OL

Interactive Literary Elements Handbook Have students access the Web site to improve their understanding of theme and topic.

English Language Coach

Multiple-Meaning Words Tell students that many words in English have multiple meanings. Explain that using context will help them determine which definition of a word is used. Have students use context to identify the definition of *lot* used in each sentence:

1. I placed a bid on a comic book lot. *(a group of articles sold at auction)*
2. The house sat on a small lot. *(a portion of land)*
3. I have to do a whole lot of chores this weekend. *(a large quantity)*
4. It was his responsibility to take care of his lot of work. *(share)* EL

Indiana English/Language Arts Academic Standards
SE: 8.1.2, 8.2, 8.3.5
TWE: *Literature Focus Lesson* 8.2, *English Language Coach* 8.1

Teach

L Literary Element

Review Figurative Language
Say: Read the first paragraph of the selection. Remember, similes are comparisons using *like* or *as*. What simile does the author use? *(She compares winning the lottery to a nightmare.)* OL

 BIG Question

Ask: According to the first sentence of the selection, what is the American dream? *(winning the lottery)* AS **Ask:** Do you think this is a realistic American dream? Why? *(Possible response: No, most Americans will never win the lottery. The American dream should be more than just winning a lottery. It should include success, acceptance, freedom, and happiness.)* OL AL

R Reading Skill

Understanding Cause and Effect **Ask:** What was the effect of Adams's gambling and bad choices? *(She lost all her money and lives in a trailer.)* AS

Readability Scores
Dale-Chall: 7.3
DRP: 56
Lexile: 1010

READING WORKSHOP 2

Lottery Winners Who LOST Their MILLIONS

by Ellen Goodstein

INFORMATIONAL TEXT
WEB ARTICLE
Bankrate.com

For a lot of people, winning the lottery is the American dream. But for many lottery winners, the reality is more like a **nightmare**. **1** BQ L

"Winning the lottery isn't always what it's cracked up to be," says Evelyn Adams, who won the New Jersey lottery not just once, but twice (1985, 1986), to the tune of $5.4 million. Today the money is all gone and Adams lives in a trailer. R

Visual Vocabulary A ***trailer*** is a vehicle that can be parked and serve as a home.

"I won the American dream but I lost it, too. It was a very hard fall. It's called rock bottom," says Adams. "Everybody wanted my money. Everybody had their hand out. I never learned one simple word in the English language—'No.' I wish I had the chance to do it all over again. I'd be much smarter about it now," says Adams, who also lost money at the slot machines in Atlantic City.[1] **2**

"I was a big-time gambler," admits Adams. "I didn't drop a million dollars, but it was a lot of money. I made mistakes, some I regret, some I don't. I'm human. I can't go back now so I just go forward, one step at a time."

Living on food stamps William "Bud" Post won $16.2 million in the Pennsylvania lottery in 1988 but now lives on his Social Security.[2]

"I wish it never happened. It was totally a nightmare," says Post.

1. ***Atlantic City,*** New Jersey, offers many forms of gambling.
2. The federal ***Social Security*** program works like a savings account for old age. A small portion of a worker's paycheck goes to the program, along with a matching amount paid by the employer. Upon retirement, the worker receives a monthly income from the program. Most U.S. employees participate in Social Security.

Practice the Skills

1 English Language Coach

A Changing Language In Old English, a *mere* was either a female horse or an evil being that brought bad dreams. In modern English, the spelling has changed, and we have different ideas about what causes a **nightmare**. A *mare* is still a horse, of course.

2 Key Reading Skill

Understanding Cause and Effect What does Adams say was the main cause of her problems after she won the lottery? What additional cause does she identify in the next paragraph?

Additional Support

English Language Coach

Idioms Identify the idioms *what it's cracked up to be* and *to the tune of* in the second paragraph. Point out that with many idiomatic expressions, knowing how to translate each word does not guarantee understanding. Ask students to infer the meanings of these idioms. *(what it's cracked up to be: "what was described, promised, or expected"; to the tune of: "for a total of")*
Have students work in groups to list several idiomatic expressions and their meanings. English language learners should include expressions from their first languages. Have each group share its list. EL BL

A former girlfriend successfully sued him for a share of his winnings. It wasn't his only lawsuit. A brother was arrested for hiring a hit man to kill him, hoping to inherit a share of the winnings. Other **siblings** pestered him until he agreed to invest in a car business and a restaurant in Sarasota, Fla.—two ventures[3] that brought no money back and further strained his relationship with his siblings. **C**

Post even spent time in jail for firing a gun over the head of a bill collector. Within a year, he was $1 million in debt.

Post admitted he was both careless and foolish, trying to please his family. He **eventually** declared **bankruptcy**.[4] Now he lives quietly on $450 a month and food stamps. **3** **R**

"I'm tired, I'm over 65 years old, and I just had a serious operation for a heart aneurysm.[5] Lotteries don't mean (anything) to me," says Post. **4**

Deeper in debt Suzanne Mullins won $4.2 million in the Virginia lottery in 1993. Now she's deeply in debt.

She borrowed $197,746.15, which she agreed to pay back with her yearly checks from the Virginia lottery through 2006. When the rules changed allowing her to collect her winnings in a lump sum, she cashed in the remaining amount. But she stopped making payments on the loan.

She blamed the debt on the lengthy illness of her uninsured son-in-law, who needed $1 million for medical bills. **EL**

Back to the basics Ken Proxmire was a machinist[6] when he won $1 million in the Michigan lottery. He moved to California and went into the car business with his brothers. Within five years, he had filed for bankruptcy.

"He was just a poor boy who got lucky and wanted to take care of everybody," explains Ken's son Rick. "It was a good ride for three or four years, but now he lives more simply.

3. ***Ventures*** (VEN churz) are risky business projects.
4. ***Bankruptcy*** is a legal status for people or businesses that are ruined financially and can't pay their debts.
5. An ***aneurysm*** (AN yuh rih zum) is a blocked blood vessel.
6. A ***machinist*** (muh SHEE nist) makes, assembles, or repairs machinery.

Vocabulary

siblings (SIB lingz) *n.* brothers and sisters

eventually (ih VEN choo ul lee) *adv.* happening at last; in the end

Practice the Skills

3 English Language Coach

A Changing Language The word **bankruptcy** comes from two Old Italian words–*banca,* "bank," and *rotta,* "broken."

4 Key Reading Skill

Understanding Cause and Effect What were some of the effects of Post's winning the lottery?

Teach

C Critical Thinking

Comprehension Ask: How do Post's friends and family react to his winning the lottery? *(A former girlfriend sued him, his brother hired a hit man to kill him, and other siblings pressured him into business ventures that didn't seem to work out.)* **OL**

R Reading Skill

Understanding Cause and Effect Ask: What does Post say caused him to be both careless and foolish? *(trying to please his family)* **AS**

EL Language Coach

Word Origins Say: The word *bill* comes from the Latin word *bulla,* meaning *"document"* or *"decree."* The Latin changed slightly to *billa,* which meant *"list."* How does this word history help you understand the meaning of *bill* in this article? *(Possible response: A bill is a document that lists what you owe to someone.)* **EL**

Differentiated Instruction

Cause-and-Effect Chart To help students track the cause-and-effect relationships that led people in the article from wealth to ruin, copy this organizer on the board. **Say:** Complete this organizer to visualize the relationship between events that caused Post to go bankrupt. **BL**

Cause	Effect/Cause	Effect/Cause	Effect
WINS LOTTERY			BANKRUPT

Indiana English/Language Arts Academic Standards
SE: 8.1.2, 8.2
TWE: *English Language Coach* 8.1.1, *Differentiated Instruction* 8.2

Teach

R Reading Skill

Understanding Cause and Effect Ask: What caused the Southeastern family to lose their winnings? *(purchasing a huge new house, cars, and gifts for relatives)* **Ask:** What effect did their actions on their lives? *(The couple is divorcing, they moved into smaller homes, and cashed in their life insurance.)* Point out to students that these are not simple cause-and-effect relationships. There are many causes and many effects that are all connected. AS

E Text Element

Theme and Topic Ask: What is the topic of this selection? *(lottery winners who have lost their money)* AS **Ask:** What message, or theme, does the author seem to be presenting at this point in the selection? *(Possible response: Money doesn't buy happiness.)* OL AL

Say: What cultural beliefs about money in the United States appear to cause problems for people? *(the belief that money solves problems and buys happiness)* AS

There's no more talk of owning a helicopter or riding in limos. We're just everyday folk. Dad's now back to work as a machinist," says his son.

Missourian Janite Lee won $18 million in 1993. Lee was generous to a variety of causes,[7] giving to politics, education and the community. But according to published reports, eight years after winning, Lee had filed for bankruptcy with only $700 left in two bank accounts and no cash on hand.

One Southeastern family won $4.2 million in the early '90s. They bought a huge house and gave in to repeated family requests for help in paying off debts.

The house, cars and relatives used up all their winnings. Eleven years later, the couple is divorcing, the house is sold and they have to split what is left of the lottery proceeds.[8] The wife got a very small house. The husband has moved in with the kids. Even the life insurance they bought ended up getting cashed in.

"It was not the pot of gold at the end of the rainbow," says their financial advisor.

Luck is fleeting These sad-but-true tales are not uncommon, say the experts.

"For many people, sudden money can cause disaster," says Susan Bradley, a certified financial planner in Palm Beach, Fla., and founder of the Sudden Money Institute, a resource center for people who have received large amounts of money and their advisors.

"In our culture, there is a widely held belief that money solves problems. People think if they had more money, their troubles would be over. When a family receives sudden money, they frequently learn that money can cause as many problems as it solves," she says. 5

Winning plays a game with your head Bradley, who authored "Sudden Money: Managing a Financial Windfall,"[9] says winners get into trouble because they fail to deal with the emotional connection to their unexpected wealth.

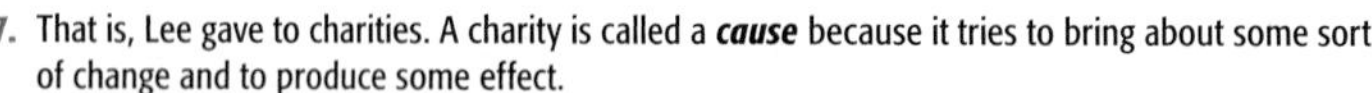

7. That is, Lee gave to charities. A charity is called a ***cause*** because it tries to bring about some sort of change and to produce some effect.
8. Here, ***proceeds*** (PROH seedz) refers to the money received.
9. A ***windfall*** is any unearned, unexpected, or sudden gain.

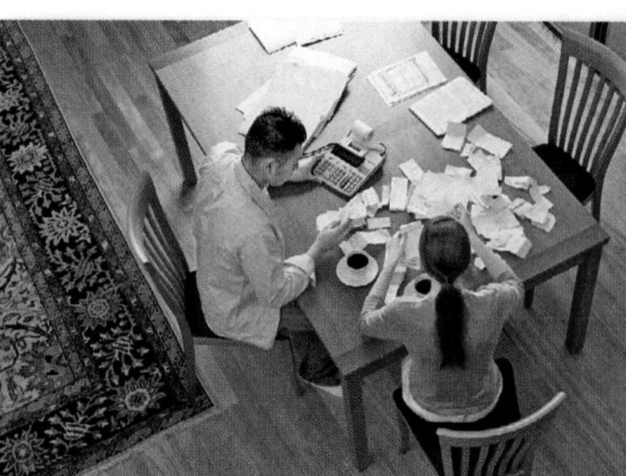

Analyzing the Photo How does this image illustrate the fact that money management takes work?

R

Practice the Skills

5 BIG Question

According to Bradley, what role does money play in the American dream? Write your answer on the "Lottery Winners" page of Foldable 8. Your response will help you complete the Unit Challenge later.

Additional Support

Reading in the Real World

Careers Students who are interested in finance may benefit from learning about the career of a financial planner. Have students work with a partner to research the job duties of and qualifications for this career. Have students write brief reports about their findings. Then allow students to discuss how a good financial planner could have helped the people in the article avoid costly mistakes. Have students share the advice they would give to the winners. OL AL

"Often they can keep the money and lose family and friends—or lose the money and keep the family and friends—or even lose the money and lose the family and friends," says Bradley.

Bill Pomeroy, a certified financial planner in Baton Rouge, La., has dealt with a number of lottery winners who went broke.

"Because the winners have a large sum of money, they make the mistake of thinking they know what they're doing. They are willing to plunk down large sums on investments they know nothing about or go in with a partner who may not know how to run a business." R

What if you get so (un)lucky? To avoid bad early decision-making and the **inevitable** requests of friends, relatives and strangers, Bradley recommends lottery winners start by setting up a DFZ or decision-free zone.

"Take time out from making any financial decisions," she says. "Do this right away. For some people, it's smart to do it before you even get your hands on the money.

"It's not a time to decide what stocks to buy or jump into a new house purchase or new business venture," she warns. "It's a time to think things through, sort things out and seek an advisory team to help make those important financial choices."

As an example, Bradley says that people who come into a windfall will usually put buying a house as No. 1 in list of 12 choices, whereas investing is No. 11.

"You really don't want to buy a new house before taking the time to think about what the **consequences** are. A lot of people who don't have money don't realize how much it costs to live in a big house—decorators, furniture, taxes, insurance, even utility costs are greater. People need a reality check before they sign the contract," she says.

Evelyn Adams, the N.J. lottery double-winner, learned these lessons the hard way. "There are a lot of people out there like me who don't know how to deal with money," says Adams. "Hey, some people went broke in six months. At least I held on for a few years." 6 ❍

Vocabulary

inevitable (in EV uh tuh bul) *adj.* sure to happen; unavoidable

consequences (KON suh kwen suz) *n.* results or effects

Practice the Skills

6 Text Element

Theme and Topic A stated theme usually appears near the beginning or ending of a work. Do you find a sentence that you think states the theme of this article?

Differentiated Instruction

Supporting Details Draw the following organizer on the board. **Say:** On this page, the writer describes how one decision—buying a new home—can have multiple effects. Complete this organizer to show the various effects of such a purchase. OL

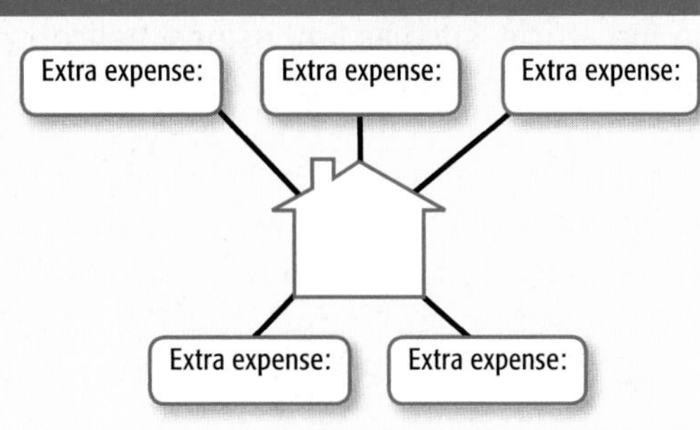

READING WORKSHOP 2

Teach

R Reading Skill

Understanding Cause and Effect **Ask:** What cause-and-effect relationship does Bill Pomeroy describe in the third paragraph? *(Cause: Winners have large sums of money. Effect: They think they know what they're doing.)* **Ask** What word in the sentence suggests this kind of relationship? *(Because)* AS **Ask** Do you think Pomeroy is right about this relationship? *(Possible response: Apparently many people fall into this category, given the information presented in this text.)* OL AL

E Text Element

Theme and Topic **Ask:** What is the theme of this article? *(Possible responses: Many people don't know how to deal with money. Sudden wealth can cause problems. Money can't buy happiness.)* AS

Assess

Use the CheckPoint questions provided on Presentation Plus! to check for comprehension of the selection. These questions can be used with interactive response keypads for immediate student feedback.

Indiana English/Language Arts Academic Standards
SE: 8.2, 8.3.5
TWE: *Reading in the Real World* 8.4, *Differentiated Instruction* 8.2

Assess

Resources for page 1094

- Selection Quick Check, p. 73
- Selection and Unit Assessment, p. 87
- ExamView Assessment Suite
- Interactive Tutor: Self-Assessment

Students can respond to the *After You Read* items in their Learner's Notebooks or on a separate sheet of paper.

Answering the BIG Question

1. Responses will vary.
2. her son-in-law's medical bills
3. Today, Ken Proxmire's life is no different than before he won the lottery.

Critical Thinking

4. Possible response: She won enough money to buy and do whatever she dreamed of, yet she lost it all through unwise decisions.
5. Possible responses: People ask lottery winners to give them money, go into business with them, or help them pay bills.
6. Possible response: When someone has an emotional connection to money, they experience excitement and thrill at the thought of having money.
7. Responses will vary.

After You Read

Lottery Winners Who Lost Their Millions

Answering the BIG Question

1. Financial advisor Susan Bradley says, "In our culture, there is a widely held belief that money solves problems." Do you agree with her? Explain your answer.
2. **Recall** According to Suzanne Mullins, what caused her to go into debt?
   TIP Right There
3. **Contrast** Contrast Ken Proxmire's life today with his life after he won $1 million in the Michigan lottery.
   TIP Think and Search

Critical Thinking

4. **Interpret** Evelyn Adams says in the article, "I won the American dream but I lost it, too." What does she mean?
   TIP Author and Me
5. **Explain** According to the article, what are some of the different ways that friends and family members of a lottery winner react?
   TIP Think and Search
6. **Evaluate** According to one expert, lottery winners need to deal with the emotional connection to their unexpected wealth. What is an "emotional connection" to money? Explain your answer.
   TIP On My Own
7. **Analyze** Susan Bradley recommends that lottery winners set up a "DFZ," or decision-free zone. How would this work? Could it be effective? Could the idea apply to other areas of life? Explain your answers.
   TIP Author and Me

Talk About Your Reading

Group Discussion Buying a house and investing were two of the top twelve choices that people made after they came into a lot of money. What were the other ten choices? In a small group, discuss the possibilities, and have one person write down your ideas. As a group, pick the other ten things that you think people did with their new wealth. Then, as a class, combine all the lists to create a single list of the Top Twelve Choices. What things did every group include? What surprising choices were listed?

Indiana English/Language Arts Academic Standards (pp. 1094–1095)

8.2 Comprehension and Analysis (Focus on Informational Text) Develop [reading] strategies...identifying and analyzing structure, organization, perspective, and purpose. **8.7 Listening and Speaking** Speaking skills...are developed... **8.1.2** Understand the influence of historical events on English word meaning and vocabulary expansion. **8.6 English Language Conventions**

For a complete description of the standards, see p. IN 11.

Talk About Your Reading

The combined group list will vary but could include other choices listed in the article, such as limousines, helicopters, business partnerships, gambling, vacations, and so on.

Skills Review

Key Reading Skill: Understanding Cause and Effect

8. Financial expert Bill Pomeroy says, "Because the winners have a large sum of money, they [think] they know what they're doing."
   - What does Pomeroy identify specifically as a cause?
   - What does he identify as an effect?
   - What one word indicates this cause-and-effect relationship?
9. What do you think leads people in our culture to believe that money can solve all their problems?

Text Element: Theme and Topic

10. What is the topic of this article?
11. Is the article's theme stated or implied? If stated, copy the sentence in which it's given. If implied, write the theme in your own words.
12. Tell why you think the statement below is or is not a good expression of this article's theme.

    "Money always causes problems."

Vocabulary Check

Rewrite each statement, filling in the blank with the best word from the list.

siblings eventually inevitable consequences

13. If you delay your homework, you do it ____.
14. If you don't tell the truth, there will be ____.
15. If you are an only child, you have no ____.
16. If you can't avoid something, it is ____.

English Language Coach

17. Five meanings of the word *lot* were given on page 1088. Which two meanings are related to the modern meaning of **lottery**?
18. The *rupt* part of **bankruptcy** means "broken." How does "bank-broken" (or "broken bank") make sense with the modern meaning of *bankruptcy?*

Grammar Link: Capitalization of Proper Nouns

A **common noun** is the general name of a person, place, thing, feeling, or idea. A **proper noun** names a *particular* person, place, or thing. Common nouns are not capitalized; proper nouns are. When proper nouns name people, capitalize all parts of their names and all initials that stand for their names.

- Roy J. Wilks called the manager into his office.

Capitalize a title or its abbreviation when it comes *before* a person's name. Do *not* capitalize a title that follows a person's name or is used as a common noun.

- It was Treasurer Sanchez who gave the first report.
- Janet Molloy was promoted to vice president.

Capitalize words that show family relationships when used as titles or substitutes for a person's name. Do *not* capitalize these words when they follow an article (*a, an,* or *the*) or a possessive noun or pronoun.

- In 2000 Father and Uncle Ray participated in a reenactment of the Battle of Gettysburg.
- My aunt Lisbeth wrote an article about the experience.

Grammar Practice

Rewrite the following sentences, correcting the six capitalization errors.

19. Joe stephenson played the role of a Villager from Gettysburg.
20. My dad played Brigadier-General james j. Pettigrew.
21. The Soldiers passed by my aunt Lila's house.
22. Looking up, uncle Ray yelled, "Don't be afraid!"

Web Activities For eFlashcards, Selection Quick Checks, and other Web activities, go to www.glencoe.com.

Skills Review

Key Reading Skill: Understanding Cause and Effect

8. Possible response: Pomeroy says that having a lot of money (cause) makes people feel they know what they are doing (effect). The word *because* indicates the cause-and-effect relationship.
9. Responses will vary.

Text Element: Theme and Topic

10. how lottery winners lose their winnings
11. Possible response: The theme, implied in the first paragraph, is that achieving the American dream isn't always what people expect it to be.
12. Responses will vary.

Vocabulary Check

13. eventually
14. consequences
15. siblings
16. inevitable

English Language Coach

17. a share and a large amount
18. Possible response: When a bank no longer has money, it can't function and could be considered "broken."

Grammar Link: Capitalization of Proper Nouns

Grammar Practice

19. Joe Stephenson played the role of a villager from Gettysburg.
20. My dad played Brigadier-General James J. Pettigrew.
21. The soldiers passed by my aunt Lila's house.
22. Looking up, Uncle Ray yelled, "Don't be afraid!"

Close

Ask students to summarize what they learned about the Big Question from reading the selection.

Indiana English/Language Arts Academic Standards
SE: 8.1.2, 8.2, 8.6, 8.7

Teach

More About the Author

Many people think Abraham Lincoln worked hard to achieve the American dream—for himself and for his country. From splitting fence rails on a farm to running a store to serving in the military to practicing law, Lincoln was always moving forward toward something bigger. His law partner once said of him, "His ambition was a little engine that knew no rest." Although his motives for signing the Emancipation Proclamation have been questioned, Lincoln remains one of America's most loved and respected presidents.

R Reading Skill

Review Identifying Main Idea and Supporting Details **Ask:** How does the writer support the idea that many words from the 1600s are archaic? *(by explaining the old-fashioned meaning of the word* score*)* OL

Before You Read The Gettysburg Address

Meet the Author

Abraham Lincoln, born in 1809, worked hard to educate himself and become a lawyer. While a member of the Illinois legislature, he lost a race for the U.S. Senate. Still, he earned a national reputation and, in 1860, was elected President. He is remembered as the president who saved the union.

Author Search For more about Abraham Lincoln, go to www.glencoe.com.

Indiana English/Language Arts Academic Standards (pp. 1096–1099)

8.1.2 Understand the influence of historical events on English word meaning and vocabulary expansion.
8.2 Comprehension and Analysis (Focus on Informational Text) Develop [reading] strategies...identifying and analyzing structure, organization, perspective, and purpose.
8.3.6 Identify significant literary devices... which define a writer's style...

For a complete description of the standards, see p. IN 11.

Vocabulary Preview

conceived (kun SEEVD) *v.* formed; imagined **(p. 1098)** *As conceived by Jim, the plan would solve several problems at once.*

proposition (prah puh ZIH shun) *n.* a plan or proposal **(p. 1098)** *Until the proposition is approved, we'll deal with things as we have in the past.*

endure (en DUR) *v.* to carry on; survive; last **(p. 1098)** *When we started out, no one thought the band would endure for three decades.*

detract (dih TRAKT) *v.* to take away from; reduce the value of **(p. 1098)** *One small flaw won't detract much from the final price.*

resolve (rih ZOLV) *v.* to decide firmly **(p. 1099)** *It's one thing to resolve to get up earlier and another thing to actually do it.*

perish (PAIR ish) *v.* to become ruined or destroyed; die **(p. 1099)** *My garden will perish if the weather doesn't warm up soon.*

Write to Learn Pretend you're writing a speech that includes a proposition for your audience to consider. Your suggested plan involves a way to make a better school, neighborhood, or world. Don't write the speech, but write a paragraph explaining your idea and using all the vocabulary words.

English Language Coach

English as a Changing Language In Abraham Lincoln's time, the most common translation of the Bible was the King James Version. England's King James I had published this "modern" English version in 1611. It had a strong influence on Lincoln's writing style, and it has a strong influence on how speakers of English use the language today.

R However, many words from the 1600s are archaic (ar KAY ik) in the twenty-first century; they're old-fashioned or out of use. For example, *score* used to be a number word, meaning "twenty," and was used like *decade* and *dozen.* If someone said "six score and five," the reader or listener had to do a bit of math (6 × 20, + 5). Now you have to do the sums. Write the numbers represented by these words:

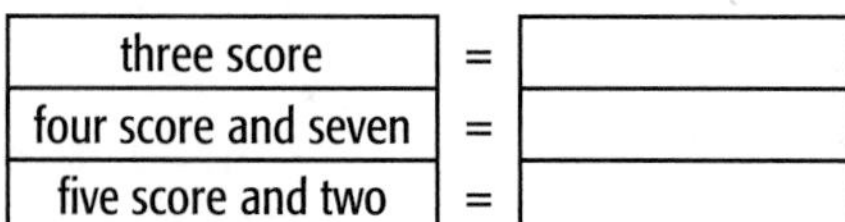

three score	=	
four score and seven	=	
five score and two	=	

What's the Score? With a partner, research the meanings of *score,* as a noun and a verb. Note whether each meaning is archaic or still in use.

Additional Support

Leveled Reading An adapted version of this selection (7th–8th grade readability) is available on page 236 of Jamestown Literature: An Adapted Reader.

English Language Coach

Archaic Meanings Point out that *score* is not an archaic word; it simply has one meaning that is archaic. Many words have meanings that are no longer used. Readers might need to find old meanings of words so that they can understand texts written long ago. A good dictionary will identify archaic meanings. Ask students to find an archaic meaning for the word *art.* Tell them to copy both one meaning that is no longer used and one meaning that is still commonly used. *(Archaic meanings: learning, scholarship; a skillful plan; the quality or state of being artful)* EL BL

Skills Preview

Key Reading Skill: Understanding Cause and Effect

Before you read the selection, reflect on what you know about

- the causes of the Civil War
- the effects of the Civil War

Write to Learn In your Learner's Notebook, jot down some of your thoughts on the topics above.

Key Literary Element: Style

Style is a writer's personal way of using language. It includes qualities that make one writer's work unlike the work of all other writers. These qualities include

- word choice
- use of imagery
- sentence lengths
- sentence patterns
- ways of moving from one idea to the next

L

As you read the Gettysburg Address, use these tips to learn about Lincoln's style:

- Look at Lincoln's word choice.
  Which words seem carefully chosen? Which words are particularly effective, and why are they so effective?
- Look at the way he arranged the words and sentences.
  Can you follow his thoughts easily? Does each sentence add to the power of what he said before, yet say something new?

Interactive Literary Elements Handbook
To review or learn more about the literary elements, go to www.glencoe.com.

Get Ready to Read

Connect to the Reading

For many of us, the American dream is about working to make a good life for our families. It's easy to forget that the American dream is rooted in American history, back to the founding of our nation. Lincoln refers to this in the Gettysburg Address.

Group Discussion People often say it is important to know history. But is it really true? If so, why? Does it change anything in the present? Can it influence the future? Do we learn from our mistakes? In small groups discuss these questions.

Build Background

Nowadays, presidents have speech writers. Lincoln himself wrote the Gettysburg Address for the dedication of a cemetery.

R

- A major battle of the Civil War was fought near the town of Gettysburg, Pennsylvania, July 1–3, 1863. Casualties (killed and wounded) were estimated at more than 40,000 soldiers.
- The people of Gettysburg had to bury the dead. The federal government bought the battleground for a cemetery, and it provided the coffins.
- At the cemetery dedication on November 19, 1863, the main speaker went on for two hours. Lincoln spoke for two minutes. His speech is considered one of the finest speeches of all time.

Set Purposes for Reading

BIG Question Read the Gettysburg Address to see the American dream in terms of our history.

Set Your Own Purpose What would you like to learn from the speech to help you answer the Big Question? Write your own purpose on the "Gettysburg Address" page of Foldable 8.

Keep Moving

Use these skills as you read the following selection.

Teach

L Literary Element

Style **Ask:** What elements contribute to an author's style? *(word choice, use of imagery, ways of moving from one idea to the next, sentence lengths, sentence patterns)* BL

R Reading Skill

Review Paraphrasing and Summarizing **Say:** Review and summarize the information in the Build Background section. *(Possible response: During the Civil War, a battle near Gettysburg killed or wounded 40,000. The federal government bought the battleground for a cemetery. President Abraham Lincoln gave a speech at the dedication of the cemetery.)* OL

Interactive Literary Elements Handbook Have students access the Web site to improve their understanding of style.

Reading in the Real World

Citizenship The American Civil War decided the fate of a nation. Lincoln felt strongly about preserving the union; however, both the North and the South felt they had valid reasons for engaging in the war. Have students work in groups to identify the issues over which American citizens fought. Students should construct a T-chart that shows how each side felt about an issue. After completing the chart, groups should write an opinion that agrees with the viewpoint of either the North or the South. Remind students to support their opinions with facts from their research. AL

Indiana English/Language Arts Academic Standards
SE: 8.1.2, 8.2, 8.3.6
TWE: *English Language Coach* 8.1; *Reading in the Real World* 8.4.1, 8.5.4

Teach

R Reading Skill

Review Identifying Author's Purpose **Ask:** Why do you think Lincoln begins his speech by talking about people 87 years in the past? *(Possible response: He wants people to connect the purpose of the war to the ideals on which the nation was founded 87 years before.)* OL AL **Ask:** To what highly debated topic of the war do these words refer? *(slavery)* AL

L Literary Element

Style **Ask:** What technique does Lincoln use in the first sentence of paragraph three? *(Repetition: he repeats the phrase "we can not.")* **Ask:** What is the effect of Lincoln's use of this technique? *(Possible response: It adds drama and emotion to his message.)* **Ask:** Can you think of another selection that has included this technique? *(Responses will vary, but could include Martin Luther King Jr.'s "I Have a Dream" speech when he repeats "one hundred years later" several times.)* OL AL

Readability Scores
Dale-Chall: 7.7
DRP: 62
Lexile: 1490

READING WORKSHOP 2

The Gettysburg Address

by Abraham Lincoln

Four score and seven years ago our fathers[1] brought forth on this continent a new nation, **conceived** in Liberty, and dedicated to the **proposition** that all men are created equal. R

Now we are engaged in a great civil war, testing whether that nation, or any nation so conceived and so dedicated, can long **endure.** We are met on a great battlefield of that war. We have come to dedicate a portion of that field, as a final resting place for those who here gave their lives that that nation might live. It is altogether fitting and proper that we should do this. 1

But, in a larger sense, we can not dedicate—we can not consecrate—we can not hallow[2]—this ground. 2 L The brave men, living and dead, who struggled here, have consecrated it, far above our poor power to add or **detract.** The world will

1. ***Four score and seven*** is 87. Lincoln refers to the "founding ***fathers,***" the men who wrote and adopted the Declaration of Independence and the U.S. Constitution.
2. In the first paragraph, ***dedicated*** meant "given completely." Here, ***dedicate*** means "set aside for a certain purpose." Similarly, both ***consecrate*** and ***hallow*** mean "make or honor as holy."

Vocabulary

conceived (kun SEEVD) *v.* formed; imagined

proposition (prah puh ZIH shun) *n.* a plan or proposal

endure (en DUR) *v.* to carry on; survive; last

detract (dih TRAKT) *v.* to take away from; reduce the value of

Practice the Skills

1 Key Literary Element

Style Pay close attention to Lincoln's word choices throughout the speech. What does he say in place of the word *cemetery?* How does he describe the dead? Does he talk about North and South?

2 English Language Coach

A Changing Language The word **hallow** is very nearly archaic. One place it is still used is in the name of a popular American holiday. Can you think of which one?

Additional Support

English Language Coach

English as a Changing Language English language learners may find nineteenth-century word choice and syntax difficult. Be sure students understand the reverence in Lincoln's words. Then, offer several simple paraphrases of the first sentence.

Work with students as a group to paraphrase Lincoln's address, using contemporary language and syntax. Call on students to identify subjects and predicates, to put sentences in subject-verb-object order, and to replace complex clauses. EL little note, nor long remember what we say here, but it can never forget what they did here. It is for us the living, rather, to be dedicated here to the unfinished work which they who fought here have thus far so nobly advanced. **3** It is rather for us to be here dedicated to the great task remaining before us—that from these honored dead we take increased devotion to that cause for which they gave the last full measure of devotion—that we here highly **resolve** that these dead shall not have died in vain[3]—that this nation, under God, shall have a new birth of freedom—and that government of the people, by the people, for the people, shall not **perish** from the earth. **4** ○

3. The phrase ***in vain*** means "for no good purpose; uselessly."

Vocabulary

resolve (rih ZOLV) *v.* to decide firmly

perish (PAIR ish) *v.* to become ruined or destroyed; die

Practice the Skills

3 **Key Reading Skill**

R **Understanding Cause and Effect** Lincoln is saying that the result of the Battle of Gettysburg should be–what? Rewrite this last sentence in your own words. **EL**

4 **BIG Question**

Lincoln suggests that more than the American dream is at stake. What is he talking about? Write your answers on the "Gettysburg Address" page of Foldable 8. Your response will help you complete the Unit Challenge later.

The Angle, Gettysburg, Pennsylvania, July 3, 1863, 1988. Mort Küntsler. Oil on canvas, 18 x 24 in. Collection of Mr. and Mrs. Robert L. Sharpe.

Analyzing the Painting What words or ideas in the Gettysburg Address does this painting illustrate?

READING WORKSHOP 2

Teach

R Reading Skill

Understanding Cause and Effect **Ask:** What does Lincoln suggest will be the effect if people do not remain dedicated to the war effort? *(The soldiers who died at Gettysburg will have died in vain, for nothing.)* **AS**

EL Language Coach

Word Origins **Say:** The English word *devotion* comes from the Latin *devovere,* which means "to *dedicate by a vow.*" How does the origin of this word suggest the action Lincoln calls for in his speech? *(Possible response: He wants listeners to vow, or promise, to continue fighting to save the union.)* **AS**

Assess

Use the CheckPoint questions provided on Presentation Plus! to check for comprehension of the selection. These questions can be used with interactive response keypads for immediate student feedback.

Reading Fluency

Build Fluency Speeches are great opportunities to build fluency because they are meant to be spoken. Therefore, more attention is often paid to the sound of the language than in ordinary prose. Before students begin practicing, read the speech aloud for them to demonstrate proper tone, expression, and pace. Or you might play the audiocassette or CD of the speech. After students have listened to a proficient example, have them practice building their own fluency. Divide students into pairs and have them work together to read Lincoln's speech fluently. Students should take turns reading the entire speech to each other. **EL** **BL**

Indiana English/Language Arts Academic Standards

SE: 8.1.2, 8.2, 8.3.6

TWE: *English Language Coach* 8.2, *Reading Fluency* 8.7.14

Assess

Resources for page 1100

- Selection Quick Check, p. 74
- Selection and Unit Assessment, p. 88
- ExamView Assessment Suite
- Interactive Tutor: Self-Assessment

Students can respond to the *After You Read* items in their Learner's Notebooks or on a separate sheet of paper.

Answering the BIG Question

1. Possible response: I think Lincoln would have said the American dream is one united country dedicated to the ideals of liberty and equality.
2. four score and seven, or eighty-seven

Critical Thinking

3. Possible response: Lincoln means that the brave sacrifices of the men who died on the battlefield make it a special place, not the mere words of people who arrived later.
4. Responses will vary.
5. Possible response: Lincoln wanted the people to remember why the soldiers had fought and died. He also was trying to persuade people to "hang in there" with the war, supporting the federal troops until they defeated the South and restored the union.

After You Read

The Gettysburg Address

Answering the BIG Question

1. After reading the Gettysburg Address, how do you think Lincoln would answer the question: What is the American dream?
2. **Recall** According to Lincoln, how many years ago did the forefathers of this nation establish the country?
   TIP **Right There**

Critical Thinking

3. **Interpret** Lincoln says that the people attending the cemetery dedication cannot make the battleground a holy place. He says that the men who "struggled" there have already made it holy. What does he mean?
   TIP **Think and Search**
4. **Evaluate** Lincoln was wrong when he said, "The world will little note, nor long remember what we say here." On the contrary, the world has long remembered what he said at Gettysburg. In your own words, explain why Lincoln's speech is so memorable.
   TIP **Author and Me**
5. **Infer** What was Lincoln's purpose in this speech? Was he trying to persuade the crowd to think or believe or do something? Explain.
   TIP **Author and Me**

Write About Your Reading

Eyewitness Report Suppose you were there at Gettysburg and heard Lincoln's speech. Describe the day.

Step 1: Decide on a point of view. You might write from the point of view of one of the following: a survivor of the Battle of Gettysburg; a family member who lost someone in the battle; a newspaper reporter observing the event.

Step 2: Jot down notes for sensory details (what that person might have seen, heard, smelled, tasted, and touched on that day).

Step 3: Jot down notes about your own (or the crowd's) feelings and mood before, during, and after Lincoln's speech. Write down how you feel about Lincoln's message, and if you agree or disagree with it.

Write to Learn Use your notes to create an "eyewitness" report of the Gettysburg Address.

Indiana English/Language Arts Academic Standards (pp. 1100–1101)

8.3 Comprehension and Analysis of Literary Text Respond to grade-level-appropriate literature...
8.5.7 Write for different purposes...
8.2 Comprehension and Analysis (Focus on Informational Text) Develop [reading] strategies...identifying and analyzing structure, organization, perspective, and purpose.
8.3.6 Identify significant literary devices...which define a writer's style...
8.6 English Language Conventions
For a complete description of the standards, see p. IN 11.

Write About Your Reading

Possible response:
I can't remember a day when I've experienced so many emotions. First, I was amazed to see the number of people gathered on the battlefield. Some were quietly crying, while others were craning their necks to get a better view. Then, I yawned my way through the first speaker's words. Two whole hours! I was about ready to pack up and go home when the President spoke. What he did in two minutes put the first speaker to shame! My toes tingled and tummy quivered when I heard his deep, quiet voice talking about the fallen soldiers. My tears mingled with pride in our country, its soldiers, and its president.

Skills Review

Key Reading Skill: Understanding Cause and Effect

6. Suppose the South had won the Civil War, and the United States did *not* survive as one nation. What do you think would have been some of the effects?

Key Literary Element: Style

7. Count the number of times Lincoln uses a form of the word *dedicate.* What does this suggest about his attitude and his purpose?
8. Compare and contrast Lincoln's style with that of Martin Luther King Jr. in his "I Have a Dream" speech. How are their styles similar? How are they different? Explain your answer.

Vocabulary Check

Write the vocabulary word that each clue describes.

conceived proposition endure detract resolve perish

9. make it through hard times
10. a suggestion for action
11. decide; settle
12. lessen; lower
13. die; decay
14. thought up
15. **English Language Coach** Research the word **hallow** and the origins of Halloween. How did the two originally relate to one another? What relation, if any, do they have today in common American custom?

Web Activities For eFlashcards, Selection Quick Checks, and other Web activities, go to www.glencoe.com.

Grammar Link: Capitalization of Places and Things

Capitalize the names of cities, counties, states, countries, continents, bodies of water, and geographic features.

- Milwaukee, Wisconsin, is a city on Lake Michigan.

Capitalize a compass-point name when it refers to a specific section of the country: *the West Coast, the North.* Do NOT capitalize a compass-point name if it refers to a general direction.

- I'm from the East, and I'm heading west to see the Rocky Mountains.

Capitalize the names of streets, highways, buildings, bridges, monuments, and celestial bodies.

- We live on Fifth Avenue, near the Empire State Building, on Planet Earth, in the Milky Way.

Capitalize the names of important historical events, periods of time, documents, and holidays.

- Battle of Yorktown
- Bill of Rights
- Bronze Age
- New Year's Eve

Capitalize the first word and the last word in titles. Also capitalize all other words except articles, conjunctions, or prepositions with fewer than five letters.

- *It's Not About Me*
- *Washington Post*
- "The Raven"
- *"On Top of the World"*

Grammar Practice

Rewrite these sentences, capitalizing words properly.

16. We spent thanksgiving day in columbus, ohio.
17. A southerly wind came in across the gulf coast.
18. I read about the middle ages in the *new york times.*
19. Have you read the poem "casey at the bat"?
20. The north won the american civil war.

Writing Application Make sure you capitalized proper nouns in your Gettysburg eyewitness account.

Skills Review

Key Reading Skill: Understanding Cause and Effect

6. Responses could include the idea that the United States today would be a much smaller, less powerful nation.

Key Literary Element: Style

7. Lincoln used forms of *dedicate* six times because he wanted listeners to stay committed to the ideals for which the Union was fighting.
8. Responses will vary.

Vocabulary Check

9. endure
10. proposition
11. resolve
12. detract
13. perish
14. conceived

English Language Coach

15. Possible response: *Hallow* means "holy" while the suffix *-een* is an abbreviated form of *evening. Halloween* started as the evening before All Saints Day, a religious holiday in many European countries. Some people believed that spirits of the dead rose on that evening. Today, many people dress like ghosts or scary creatures for Halloween.

Grammar Link: Capitalization of Places and Things

Grammar Practice

16. We spent Thanksgiving Day in Columbus, Ohio.
17. A southerly wind came in across the Gulf Coast.
18. I read about the Middle Ages in the *New York Times.*
19. Have you read the poem "Casey at the Bat"?
20. The North won the American Civil War.

Close

Have students discuss how Lincoln's speech helps them answer the Big Question.

Indiana English/Language Arts Academic Standards
SE: 8.2, 8.3, 8.3.6, 8.5.7, 8.6

READING WORKSHOP 3

Identifying Main Idea and Supporting Details

Teaching Students to Identify the Main Idea and Supporting Details

Why Is It Important?

- Understanding the main ideas in a selection helps students comprehend the material better.
- Supporting details help point readers to the main ideas.
- Readers can use the details they identify to visualize what is happening in the story, which will improve comprehension.
- When students can clearly distinguish main ideas from supporting details, they will also become better writers. They will better understand the need to add ideas that explain, confirm, and enhance their main ideas.

How to Help Students Get It

- Ask students where they think that they might find the key idea of a selection. The main idea is often presented as the topic sentence in informational text, but it's usually not included in a creative attention-getting introduction. It's also rare to have the main idea clearly stated in fiction.
- Ask students to review a text from a previous unit, focusing on the author's use of details. They should make a list of the words the author uses to convey his or her ideas. Remembering to notice details will help students to learn to incorporate them into their own writing.
- Discuss the types of details that an author can use, including facts, statistics, anecdotes, adjectives, dialogue, and rich descriptions.
- Ask students to use the details from a text to create visual images, which will help them determine main ideas.

Reading to Answer the Big Question

I Chose Schooling by Jacqueling Nwaiwu
Nwaiwu describes her first day of high school as a day of decision. She chose to follow the advice of her immigrant parents to pursue the American dream by studying hard. When she encounters students who scorn her academic values, Nwaiwu's faith in her decision is validated.

Electric Summer by Richard Peck
Geneva and her mother leave the farm to see the marvels at the 1904 world's fair in St. Louis. Their experiences help both mother and daughter realize that amazing times lie ahead for Geneva and for the nation.

Workshop Resources

Pacing (Days) Standard	Block	Lesson	Student Materials	Teacher Resources
1	1/2	Key Skill Lesson: Identifying Main Idea and Supporting Details	Key Reading Skills Practice, p. 25 English Language Coach Review, p. 44	Bellringer Options Transparencies –Daily Language Practice 77 Read Aloud, Think Aloud Transparencies –Key Reading Skills 6 Presentation Plus!
1	1	"I Chose Schooling"	Glencoe Online Unit Vocabulary Review, p. 42 Academic Vocabulary Review, p. 45 English Language Coach Active Reading Graphic Organizer, p. 27 Literary Analysis, p. 26 StudentWorks Plus™ Online Student Edition Literature Classics Selection and Unit Assessments, p. 89	Literary and Text Analysis Transparencies 10 Puzzlemaker Skill Level Up!™ A Language Arts Game BookLink 3 Assessment by Learning Objective (Diagnostic and Formative) Interactive Tutor: Self-Assessment TeacherWorks Plus™
1		"Electric Summer"	Glencoe Online Unit Vocabulary Review, p. 42 Academic Vocabulary Review, p. 45 English Language Coach Active Reading Graphic Organizer, p. 29 StudentWorks Plus™ Online Student Edition Literature Classics Selection and Unit Assessments, p. 90	Literary and Text Analysis Transparencies 13 Puzzlemaker Skill Level Up!™ A Language Arts Game BookLink 3 Assessment by Learning Objective (Diagnostic and Formative) Interactive Tutor: Self-Assessment TeacherWorks Plus™

Keys for Unit Resource

- Blackline Master
- Workbook
- Supplemental Text
- CD-ROM
- DVD
- Transparency
- Web-based
- Fast File

Level Appropriate Code

AS = Activities for all students
AL = Activities for students working above grade level
OL = Activities for students working at grade level
BL = Activities for students working below grade level
EL = Activities for English language learners

Focus

BELLRINGER Options

Daily Language Practice Transparency 77

Focus Activity Say: Think about your dream for the future. What do you need to do to make your dream come true? *(Possible responses: get an education, save money, learn a trade)* AS

Teach

C Critical Thinking

Comprehension Ask: What are two ways in which authors communicate main ideas? *(They directly state the main ideas, or they imply main ideas by presenting facts and supporting details.)* AS

Analyzing the Cartoon

Ask: What is apparent about the boy's motivation in questioning his mother? *(Possible response: He does not want to do his homework and is trying to manipulate her into doing it for him.)* AS

READING WORKSHOP 3

Skills Focus

You will practice using these skills when you read the following selections:

- "I Chose Schooling," p. 1106
- "The Electric Summer," p. 1114

Reading

- Identifying the main idea and supporting details

Literature

- Understanding cultural references
- Understanding the use of dialogue

Vocabulary

- Learning about English as a changing language

Writing/Grammar

- Using correct capitalization in writing

Indiana English/Language Arts Academic Standards
(pp. 1102–1103)

8.2 Comprehension and Analysis (Focus on Informational Text) Develop [reading] strategies...

For a complete description of the standards, see p. IN 11.

Skill Lesson

Identifying Main Idea and Supporting Details

Learn It!

C **What Is It?** The **main idea** is the most important idea in a paragraph or in a whole selection. It's the point, or message, the writer wants to communicate. Sometimes the writer directly states the main idea. Other times you have to figure out the main idea by looking at **supporting details**—facts that back up the author's ideas, or the actions of characters and the events in a story that support the message.

HEY, MOM, WHAT'S FOR DINNER?
SPAGHETTI.
WHAT'S THE WEATHER SUPPOSED TO BE LIKE TOMORROW?
COLD.
WHAT'S THE DOMINANT THEME OF "THE RED BADGE OF COURAGE," AND WHAT LITERARY DEVICES DOES THE AUTHOR EMPLOY TO CONVEY IT, CITING SPECIFIC PASSAGES FROM THE TEXT AND LIMITING YOUR ANSWER TO BETWEEN 500 AND 600 WORDS?
CAN'T BLAME ME FOR TRYING.
OH, YES I CAN.

Analyzing Cartoons
What's the main idea of this cartoon?

Additional Support

Literature Focus Lesson

Main Idea and Supporting Details

Say: Identifying main ideas and supporting details requires you to evaluate the information you read. You must ask yourself, "How important is this information?" To pick out the main idea, look at both the beginning and end of a paragraph. The main idea is often included in a topic sentence located in either position. If there is no topic sentence, you will have to synthesize the supporting details to determine the implied main idea.

Have students read a paragraph from another class's textbook. Have students identify the main idea and supporting details. EL BL

Why Is It Important? Finding the main idea helps you better understand the writer's message and reason for writing the selection. Finding details that support the idea helps you decide if that message is a good one.

How Do I Do It? Some writers directly state the main idea. When they don't and you have to figure it out, use these tips:

- In a work of nonfiction, ask yourself: *What is the writer saying about this topic?* In a short story or other work of fiction, ask: *What is the writer saying about the characters and situations?*
- To see if you've correctly identified the main idea, ask: *Do the important details explain or give evidence that supports this idea?*

Literature Online

Study Central Visit www.glencoe.com and click on Study Central to review evaluating.

One student used a diagram to figure out the main idea of this paragraph:

"Dad, do you believe it?" Musa exclaimed. "With this paycheck, I have enough money to buy that car at Sam's Used Cars I asked you to buy me! When you told me to get a job and save for it, I wasn't sure I could do it. Thanks, Dad." R

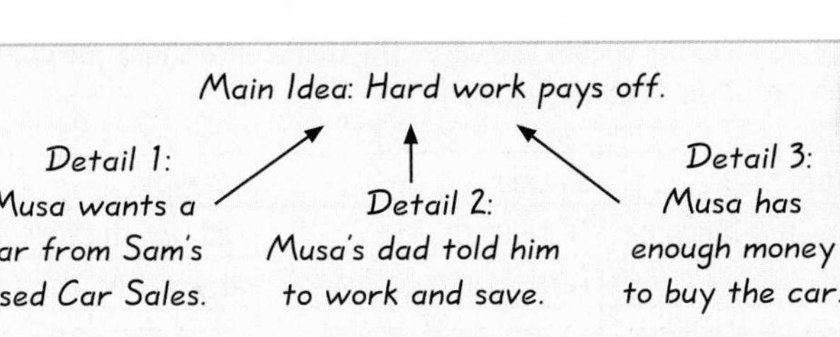
Main Idea: Hard work pays off.
Detail 1: Musa wants a car from Sam's Used Car Sales.
Detail 2: Musa's dad told him to work and save.
Detail 3: Musa has enough money to buy the car.

Practice It!

Draw your own diagram of the ideas in the paragraph below. It will help you get ready to write your response.

"You 'n me, Darren," Isaak said. "We've finally got a chance at Friday's game. Scouts from State will be there. If we look good, we can get full scholarships. Wouldn't that be awesome? A free college education for shootin' hoops!" EL

Use It!

As you read "I Chose Schooling" and "The Electric Summer," use a diagram to find the main idea and supporting details. Then you can decide if the writers made their points.

READING WORKSHOP 3

Teach

Study Central Have students access the Web site to review identifying main idea and supporting details and to complete a related activity.

R Reading Skill

Review Understanding Cause and Effect **Ask:** What effect did Musa's job have? *(It let him earn enough money to buy a car.)* AS

EL Language Coach

English as a Changing Language **Say:** The base word in *awesome* is *awe*, a word that first meant "fear or terror." How might the original meaning be part of today's usage of *awesome*? *(Possible response: When something is awesome, it can be so terrific it's scary.)* AL

Resources for page 1103

- Use Key Reading Skills Transparency 6 in *Read Aloud, Think Aloud* to help students practice identifying main idea and supporting details.

Reading in the Real World

Citizenship Explain to students that election campaign materials convey a candidate's main ideas on important topics. Voters need to be able to identify the main idea and decide how well the candidate supports the idea. In this way, voters select candidates who agree with them. Distribute copies of short campaign speeches to students. Have them work with partners to list the main idea of the speech, as well as the supporting details. Ask them to write a brief paragraph explaining why they agree or disagree with the candidate's view on the topic. OL

Indiana English/Language Arts Academic Standards

SE: 8.2

TWE: *Literature Focus Lesson* 8.2, *Reading in the Real World* 8.2.6

Teach

More About the Author

Jacqueling Nwaiwu's American dream was to work in the entertainment industry. Although she acted with a touring theater company as a teen, her parents urged her to go to college to prepare for a more dependable career. While in college, Nwaiwu realized she could still follow her dream. She majored in marketing and is enjoying the business end of entertainment.

V Vocabulary

Reinforcing Vocabulary

Say: Copy the vocabulary words in your Learner's Notebooks. Use each word in a sentence of your own. *(Responses will vary.)* AS

Before You Read I Chose Schooling

Meet the Author

Jacqueling Nwaiwu was born in Nigeria and came to the United States as a teenager. She is one of the "sisters" in *My Sisters' Voices,* a collection of writings by American teenage girls. The book was put together by 18-year-old Iris Jacob, who is biracial. In the introduction Jacob says: "We come from all different ethnic, cultural, and spiritual traditions. We are immigrants, some of us. We are beauties, inner and outer. We are heroines. . . . [W]e are the future!"

Author Search For more about Jacqueling Nwaiwu, go to www.glencoe.com.

Indiana English/Language Arts Academic Standards (pp. 1104–1109)

8.1.2 Understand the influence of historical events on English word meaning and vocabulary expansion. **8.2 Comprehension** Develop [reading] strategies... **8.3** Respond to grade-level-appropriate literature...

For a complete description of the standards, see p. IN 11.

Vocabulary Preview

V

prevailed (prih VAYLD) *v.* conquered; won; overcame; form of the verb *prevail* **(p. 1106)** *It was many years before peace finally prevailed.*

monumental (mon yuh MEN tul) *adj.* great and meaningful **(p. 1107)** *Climbing any mountain is a monumental accomplishment, if you ask me.*

attaining (uh TAY ning) *n.* the act of achieving, accomplishing, or succeeding **(p. 1107)** *Attaining a passing score will be impossible if I don't study.*

crucial (KROO shul) *adj.* extremely important **(p. 1107)** *A crucial part of every person's diet is some form of protein; it's necessary to live.*

agitated (AJ uh tay tud) *adj.* disturbed; upset **(p. 1108)** *The man wasn't harmed, but he was so agitated by the robbery that he couldn't speak.*

English Language Coach

English as a Changing Language Did you ever wonder how some words get into the English language? The chart below shows the origins of two words from "I Chose Schooling."

Word	*slacker*	*clammy*
Origin & Meaning	Old English *sleac*	Old English *claeman*
	careless in behavior	to smear or stick
Modern Meaning	someone who avoids work or responsibility	damp, soft, sticky, usually cool

There's nothing very unusual about the origins of these words, but another word in the selection—*geek*—has a more surprising history. Copy the chart below into your Learner's Notebook. Then look up *geek's* origin and meanings, and fill in the chart.

Word	geek
Origin & Meaning	
Modern Meanings	1
	2

Additional Support

Author Search To expand students' appreciation of Jacqueling Nwaiwu, have them access the Web site for additional information and resources.

Literature Focus Lesson

Personal Narrative Have students write a short personal narrative about a choice they made so they could follow a dream or meet a goal. Have students keep in mind these tips:

- Put the events in your narrative in chronological order.
- Use dialogue to make your narrative more interesting and realistic.
- Include sights, sounds, smells, and other sensory images you associate with the experience. Use them to convey how you felt. Share your narrative with a partner and discuss how your narratives differ. AL

Skills Preview

Key Reading Skill: Identifying Main Idea and Supporting Details

As you read "I Chose Schooling," pause to look for the main idea of a paragraph.

- What does the writer say is important to her?

  This could be a directly stated main idea.
- How do the details add to your understanding of the writer's ideas?

  Look for descriptions of her feelings, behavior, and actions.

To help identify the main idea of the entire selection, ask yourself these questions:

- What is the writer's most important idea or overall message?
- Which parts of the selection support this idea?

Write to Learn What was the main idea or message of a movie you've seen recently? List details (action, dialogue, and so on) that supported that idea.

Key Literary Element: Cultural Reference

Cultural references are mentions of objects, activities, products, forms of entertainment, and so on that are tied to a particular culture, place, and time. Slang is also a type of cultural reference. Notice the slang expressions as you read "I Chose Schooling." What does the slang tell you about the students' culture and time? **L**

Partner Work *Geek* started as carnival slang, then took a different (but related) meaning in American culture. With a partner, explore the slang word *bling-bling* (or *bling*). Explain its meaning, who invented it, and why. (Your best bet is to search online for "word definitions," "online dictionaries," or something similar.)

Interactive Literary Elements Handbook
To review or learn more about the literary elements, go to www.glencoe.com.

Get Ready to Read

Connect to the Reading

In most schools, students tend to divide up into groups according to their interests and goals. There are the athletes, the musicians, the kids who study a lot, the kids who don't, and so on. These kinds of groups are called cliques. Members of a clique share similar interests and leave out those who have different interests. In this essay, the writer describes her school's cliques and offers her opinions of them.

Build Background

This essay comes from the book *My Sisters' Voices: Teenage Girls of Color Speak Out.* Published in 2001, the collection features writings by girls from Hispanic, African American, Asian American, Native American, and biracial backgrounds. Some were native-born; some were immigrants.

U.S. Census Bureau statistics for the year 2000 reveal the following information:

• Total U.S. population		281.4 million
• Hispanic or non-white	21.0%	59.1 million
• Born in other countries	11.0%	30.9 million
• Ages 13–19	10.1%	28.4 million
• Girls, ages 13–19	4.9%	13.8 million
• Girls, ages 13–19, of color	1.0%	2.9 million

Set Purposes for Reading

BIG Question Read "I Chose Schooling" to see what a student born in another country thinks about education as part of the American dream.

Set Your Own Purpose What would you like to learn from the selection to help you answer the Big Question? Write your own purpose on the "I Chose Schooling" page of Foldable 8.

Keep Moving

Use these skills as you read the following selection.

Teach

L Literary Element

Cultural Reference Say: Everyone lives within a particular culture. Culture might be defined by ethnicity, social class, or even age. Discuss elements of the culture of your generation, such as popular songs, television shows, slang, current events, fashions, and so on. How does your culture compare to that of the generation before yours? Discuss this question in small groups. *(Responses will vary.)* **AS**

Literature Online

Interactive Literary Elements Handbook Have students access the Web site to improve their understanding of cultural reference.

Reading Fluency

Build Fluency Because cultural terms may not be understood by all students, pausing to decode the meanings of unfamiliar words and phrases may interfere with comprehension and reading flow. Before students read the selection, review aloud the pronunciations and meanings of culturally specific terms used in "I Chose Schooling." Then have students work with partners, taking turns reading paragraphs until they've completed the selection. **BL** **EL**

Indiana English/Language Arts Academic Standards
SE: 8.1.2, 8.2, 8.3
TWE: *Literature Focus Lesson* 8.5.1, *Reading Fluency* 8.7

Teach

BQ BIG Question

Ask: What goal did Nwaiwu have for her high school years? *(meeting new people and making new friends)* **AS**

L Literary Element

Cultural Reference Read the footnote to *Saved by the Bell.* Tell students that this is a perfect example of a cultural reference. It identifies the time period of Nwaiwu's culture. **Ask:** What television show about teenagers is part of your culture? *(Answers will vary.)* **AS**

Readability Scores
Dale-Chall: 7.6
DRP: 55
Lexile: 860

I Chose Schooling

by Jacqueling Nwaiwu

As I walked down the crowded halls of Central High on the first day of school, I was overcome with many emotions. I was physically tired because I was not accustomed to waking up so early, and I was also scared and nervous. It was my freshman year, and above all other emotions, nervousness **prevailed.** I was trembling; my hands were clammy and sweaty. Students were greeting each other. There were clusters of students by lockers chatting away, catching up on all the summer gossip. I continued to walk through the halls observing the madness. Kids were running through the halls playing tag and ramming into each other. Bewildered, I muttered, "So this is high school. It looks more like the circus. So much for thinking that high school is exactly like the **preppy,** well-mannered students in the weekly TV show *Saved by the Bell.*[1]" **1 2 3**

I managed to find my homeroom after walking around for fifteen minutes. When I went in, I noticed that over half of the students in my homeroom were students who attended the same junior high as me. I was annoyed with that fact because I wanted to meet new people and make new friends instead of interacting with the same old students from junior high. And with that, I quickly sat down next to a girl with spiky, blue hair, whom I did not know. **BQ** **L**

1. ***Saved by the Bell,*** which first aired in 1989, was a comedy focusing on six students at the fictional Bayside High School.

Vocabulary

prevailed (prih VAYLD) *v.* conquered; won; overcame

Practice the Skills

1 Key Reading Skill

Identifying Main Idea The main idea of this paragraph is directly stated. Nwaiwu says she is scared and nervous on her first day of school. Her description of her "clammy and sweaty" hands is a supporting detail that shows how she felt.

2 English Language Coach

A Changing Language As an adjective, **preppy** describes a style of clothing. In the 1960s, as a noun, it meant a student preparing for college at a preparatory (or "prep") school.

3 BIG Question

TV characters often have the lives real people dream of having. Name a character or show that, to you, represents the American dream (or part of it).

Additional Support

Differentiated Instruction

Identifying Feelings To help students identify the mixed feelings of the speaker on this page, draw the chart below on the board. Have them complete the remaining boxes. The first responses are provided. **BL**

Name of Feeling	Descriptive Details	Another Word for This Feeling
nervous	trembling; clammy, sweaty hands	jittery; anxious; tense
bewildered		
annoyed		

Right at that moment, my blond, skinny homeroom teacher, Ms. Larsen, shouted, "Welcome to high school!" She went on, saying, "These next four years will be **monumental.** These four years will define your character; you will either choose that path of excelling in school or you will decide that socializing with friends is more important. You have two paths to choose from. Today is the first day of school, choose your path wisely."

That statement remained with me for the whole day. I kept thinking to myself, This is the beginning of my high school career, I must do well in school. I must pick the right path.

Attaining a sound education has been my goal since before I could remember. Every day from the time I was in kindergarten to the present, my parents have always said, in their thick Nigerian[2] accents, "Read hard so that you may be successful." (To my parents, "reading hard" is synonymous with studying rigorously.) I have always endeavored to excel in school and a large portion of my motivation is because of that overused quote. Whenever stress mounts, and I feel that I never want to do another paper or another homework assignment, I always remember what my parents would tell me, "Read hard so that you may be successful." **4** **R1**

Schooling is **crucial** to me. I believe that the better one does in school, the more successful he or she becomes in the real world. I define a successful person as one who is happy, has a great family, and has a great-paying job. **R2**

Over the course of the year, every student in my homeroom chose either to take school seriously or to slack off. In homeroom, cliques started to form. The **slackers** sat on one side of the room, while the studious, grade-conscious students sat on the other side. **5** Students on the slacker side of the room constantly yelled and were rowdy, while the

2. ***Nigeria*** was governed by Great Britain from the early 1900s until 1964, and most *Nigerians* speak English.

Vocabulary

monumental (mon yuh MEN tul) *adj.* great and meaningful

attaining (uh TAY ning) *n.* the act of achieving, accomplishing, or succeeding

crucial (KROO shul) *adj.* extremely important

Practice the Skills

4 Key Reading Skill

Identifying Main Idea Again, Nwaiwu states the idea of the paragraph directly. What is that idea, and how does she support it?

5 Key Literary Element

Cultural Reference The **slackers** (a slang term) are one clique. Do you know of a slang term for the "grade-conscious" students?

Reading Fluency

Monitoring Comprehension One way to monitor comprehension is to ask and answer questions while reading. Active readers constantly ask themselves questions as they read because it helps with concentration and comprehension. A question about the passage on these pages, for example, is "How did Nwaiwu come to the conclusion that schooling is extremely important?"

Have students work in small groups to write questions about the passages on pages 1107–1108. Compile a list of all the different questions. Then go around the room asking individual students to answer. **OL**

Teach

R1 Reading Skill

Review Understanding Cause and Effect **Ask:** Why did Nwaiwu work to excel in school? *(Her parents taught her that studying was the way for her to succeed.)* **AS**

R2 Reading Skill

Identifying Main Idea and Supporting Details **Say:** Reread the fourth paragraph on this page. What is its main idea? *(Excelling in school leads to success in life.)* **OL** **Ask:** How does Nwaiwu define success? *(She says success is being happy, having a family, and having a high-paying job.)* **BL** **OL**

Indiana English/Language Arts Academic Standards

SE: 8.1.2, 8.2, 8.3

TWE: *Differentiated Instruction* 8.2, *Reading Fluency* 8.2

Teach

R Reading Skill

Review Visualizing Ask: What words help you imagine the "slackers" and their behavior in the first part of the paragraph? *(Possible responses: constantly yelled, rowdy)* **Ask:** What words and descriptions helped you imagine the other group of students? *(Possible responses: grade-conscious, busy, studying, doing homework)* **Ask:** What do you visualize when you read this paragraph? *(Possible response: a classroom full of students with half of them goofing off while the other half have their noses in books)* AS

L Literary Element

Cultural Reference Ask: What caused Nwaiwu to feel humiliated? *(The group of African American girls made fun of her.)* **Ask:** What cultural beliefs do these girls express? *(Possible response: that education is not important)* OL AL

Ask: Is Nwaiwu always sure that she's made the right choice about following her dream? *(Possible response: In the last paragraph, she regrets being different from other students, at least for a time.)* AS

READING WORKSHOP 3

students on the grade-conscious side of the room were busy trying to study or complete homework. R

One day, I came into homeroom and sat in my designated spot: the studious, grade-conscious side of the room. The morning announcements were blaring while I frantically tried to complete my homework. I was completing my math problems when suddenly the bell rang, indicating that it was time for first hour. I ignored it and continued to finish the problems due that hour. Before I knew it, the second bell rang and I was late for math class.

I quickly jammed my books in my bag and ran out of my fourth-floor homeroom. I ran down the hall and up the stairs to the fifth floor. When I got to the fifth floor, I was blocked by a group of African American girls. The five **rowdy** girls stood in the entrance of the stairwell. I was so **agitated.** I wanted to push the girls out of my way so I could get to class. But instead, I maneuvered[3] through the crowd. As I was doing that, one of the girls loudly said, "Who do she think she is anyway, huh?" The group of girls roared with laughter. Another girl said, "Ya'll leave her alone. She trying to get her an edgamacation." And with that, everyone laughed even more. I turned around and looked at them, but said nothing. I simply walked to my math class humiliated. 6 BQ L

Black Girl with Wings, 20th century. Laura James. Acrylic on canvas, 31.8 x 43.2 cm. Private Collection.

Analyzing the Painting In what ways does the girl in the painting reflect Nwaiwu's ideas about herself?

Practice the Skills

6 English Language Coach

A Changing Language The word **rowdy** means "loud, rude, and rough." It most likely comes from *row,* "a noisy disturbance." (With this meaning, *row* rhymes with *how.*)

3. When Nwaiwu ***maneuvered*** (muh NOO vurd) through the crowd, she changed directions several times to get where she wanted to be.

Vocabulary

agitated (AJ uh tay tud) *adj.* disturbed; upset

Additional Support

Literature Focus Lesson

Anecdote Tell students that an anecdote is a short account of a single incident. Explain that anecdotes are not the same as stories because they do not include a full plot or character description. Tell students that the paragraph that begins "One day . . ." is the start of an anecdote. Have students write their own anecdotes. Have them first brainstorm a list of events in their life, big and small. Then, have them list their experiences by category, such as *funniest, hardest, saddest, most mysterious, most surprising,* or *most rewarding.* Lastly, have them choose one event as their topic to write three paragraphs about. OL AL

At that moment, I strongly regretted running down the halls like some geek. I strongly regretted not saying something to them. I strongly regretted having the intense desire to go to my math class and do well in school. It was as if the girls were saying, "Who do she think she is, huh? A black girl trying to be white. An **oreo** black on the outside, but white on the inside. **7** Do she think she betta than us? She betta not, 'cause she ain't. School ain't that important for her to be running like that to some class. Some black girls don't know their race. Education ain't all that important. I'd rather clown wit my homies than run to class actin' like I'm white tryin' ta git an education." **L**

"Who she think she is anyway, huh?" I was furious. What exactly did she mean by that! I was only trying to get to class. Excuse me if school means a little more to me than "hangin' out wit da homies." I couldn't believe I gave those girls so much power that they were able to ruin my day.

The next day, I went to homeroom. I mentioned the story to Meg, the girl with the spiky, blue hair. **8** Meg said, "Forget them. School is more important than trying to fit into some popular clique. Look at me. I have blue hair. I try not to fit into groups who don't accept me for me. School is much more important. Don't waste your energy on ignorant people."

Right as she said that, everything was clear. I didn't have to waste my energy on them. I chose schooling over socializing. I chose to study for tests instead of "gossiping over someone's baby's mamma." I selected education over ignorance. I thought to myself, Maybe I am not "ghetto" and maybe I do choose to speak properly. I am not any less black; I am just being me. I preferred work over play, homework instead of fitting into a crowd where I don't belong. I chose schooling. **C**

When looking back at the experience I had with those girls, I thank God every day. That particular experience reaffirmed[5] my goal, which was to attain a sound education. I thank God for giving me the initiative to select the right path, despite all odds. **9** ❍

5. Nwaiwu's experience supported and strengthened ***(reaffirmed)*** her goal.

Practice the Skills

7 Key Literary Element

Cultural Reference The word **oreo** is a cultural reference in two ways. Capitalized, it's the brand name of a cookie. Here, it's a slang term that suggests certain values and beliefs.

8 Key Literary Element

Cultural Reference Even this girl provides a cultural reference, since no one would even have thought of having "spiky, blue hair" before a certain time.

9 BIG Question

How does Nwaiwu's idea of the American dream compare with yours? Write your answer on the "I Chose Schooling" page of Foldable 8. Your response will help you complete the Unit Challenge later.

Reading in the Real World

Career Focus on the advice that Meg gives Nwaiwu. Explain that giving such good advice is one aspect of a career as a guidance counselor. Not only do guidance counselors help you choose the right classes, they can also help you through personal issues by making suggestions, giving advice, and helping you figure out the best way to respond to a situation. Have students search the Internet or library for information on a career as a guidance counselor and identify the requirements for such a position, the duties of such a position, and the average salary. Have volunteers discuss their findings with the rest of the class. **AS**

Teach

L Literary Element

Cultural Reference Say: The author includes in her narrative dialogue of the girls who mocked her. She writes in *dialect,* or the speech patterns of a particular region or group. Do you think this dialect adds realness to the narrative? *(Responses will vary.)* **Ask:** Why do you think the author chose to include the dialect? *(Possible response: To emphasize the difference between herself and the attitudes and perspectives of those girls toward education)* **OL**

C Critical Thinking

Evaluation Say: Reread the next to last paragraph. Do you think that Nwaiwu's decision was a good one? Why or why not? *(Most students will say she made a good choice because she is obviously successful given that her writing appears in this book.)* **AS**

Assess

Use the CheckPoint questions provided on Presentation Plus! to check for comprehension of the selection. These questions can be used with interactive response keypads for immediate student feedback.

Indiana English/Language Arts Academic Standards

SE: 8.1.2, 8.3

TWE: *Literature Focus Lesson* 8.5.1

Assess

Resources for page 1110

- Selection Quick Check, p. 75
- Selection and Unit Assessment, p. 89
- ExamView Assessment Suite
- Interactive Tutor: Self-Assessment

Students can respond to the *After You Read* items in their Learner's Notebooks or on a separate sheet of paper.

Answering the BIG Question

1. Possible response: A good education helps in getting a job that is enjoyable and pays well.
2. She was nervous, bewildered, and annoyed.
3. A successful person is happy, has a great family, and has a well-paying job.

Critical Thinking

4. Possible response: to meet new people and make new friends
5. Possible response: Nwaiwu's parents knew their daughter would need an education to give her skills that would help her to live more easily than they had in their new country.
6. Possible response: Nwaiwu may not have had many friends since she spent a lot of time studying.
7. Possible response: They have similar goals.
8. Responses will vary.

After You Read

I Chose Schooling

Answering the BIG Question

1. How important is education for achieving the American dream?
2. **Recall** How did Nwaiwu feel on her first day at Central High?
   TIP Right There
3. **Give Examples** Give examples of what Nwaiwu considers a successful person to be.
   TIP Right There

Critical Thinking

4. **Infer** Why does Nwaiwu sit where she does in her homeroom?
   TIP Think and Search
5. **Infer** How and why might Nwaiwu's goals have been influenced by the fact that she was the daughter of immigrants?
   TIP Author and Me
6. **Conclude** How does working toward her dream affect Nwaiwu's life?
   TIP Author and Me
7. **Analyze** Explain how the blue-haired girl's comments show that Nwaiwu does "belong to a group."
   TIP Author and Me
8. **Evaluate** Is Nwaiwu's goal worth working for?
   TIP Author and Me

Indiana English/Language Arts Academic Standards
(pp. 1110–1111)

8.3 Comprehension and Analysis of Literary Text Respond to grade-level-appropriate literature... **8.7 Listening and Speaking** Speaking skills are developed... **8.2 Comprehension and Analysis (Focus on Informational Text)** Develop [reading] strategies... **8.1.2** Understand the influence of historical events on English word meaning and vocabulary expansion. **8.6 English Language Conventions**

For a complete description of the standards, see p. IN 11.

Talk About Your Reading

Literature Groups Different people have different ideas about the American dream. In a small group, compare the ideas of group members. Then discuss how your versions of the American dream compare to Nwaiwu's.

- What are your goals? How do you plan to reach them?
- What kind of life do you want for yourself ten years from now?
- How is your American dream similar to or different from Nwaiwu's dream? Why?
- How is your American dream similar to or different from the dreams of others in your group? Why?

Talk About Your Reading

Students' discussions should focus on the questions provided in the text. Make sure students not only answer the questions but also compare and contrast their dreams with their classmates' and Nwaiwu's.

Skills Review

Key Reading Skill: Identifying Main Idea and Supporting Details

9. What is the main idea of the selection? Is it directly stated? If so, give the page number and the first few words of the paragraph that contain the main idea. If it is not directly stated, explain how and where you identified it.
10. Name three supporting details for the main idea you identified.

Key Literary Element: Cultural Reference

11. One of the girls in Nwaiwu's class uses the slang *edgamacation* instead of the word *education.* What does her use of this term tell you about her and her values?
12. Nwaiwu mentions *Saved by the Bell.* TV shows often reflect the culture and times in which they are made. Name a show that you think reflects today's culture. Give examples that tie this show to current American culture.
13. Explain the slang expressions "hanging out with" and "homies."

Vocabulary Check

Label the following statements *true* or *false.*

14. **Attaining** an important goal means failing to meet the goal.
15. The team that **prevailed** on the soccer field won the game.
16. Finding a cure for cancer would be a **monumental** accomplishment.
17. When people are **agitated,** they're calm, cool, and confident.
18. A good diet is **crucial** to lasting good health.
19. **English Language Coach** Nwaiwu writes, "Attaining a sound education has been my goal since before I could remember." Look up the history of the word **sound** and explain how the word's origin relates to its meaning in Nwaiwu's statement.

Grammar Link: More Capitalization

Why do we capitalize the first letter of certain words? Capital letters are "look at me" flags! They tell readers that there's something special about these words.

Capitalize the first letter of a language name or a nationality. Capitalize the names of ethnic groups. In a multiple-word name, capitalize both words.

- Luc speaks English, but his first language is French.
- Eva's an American citizen; her origins are Mexican.
- Jose's Mexican American family lives on one side of us, and a Jewish family lives on the other side.

Capitalize the names of clubs, organizations, businesses, institutions, and political parties. Capitalize brand names but not the nouns following them.

- We have an International Club meeting tomorrow.
- The Data Corporation is expanding into Europe.
- We prefer Cruncho peanut butter.

Grammar Practice

For each of the following, choose the sentence that shows the correct use of capitalization.

20. A. I saw a film about native Americans.
    B. The Spanish weren't the first to settle the West.
21. A. One of the dialects in Louisiana is French Creole.
    B. I ate french food at a restaurant yesterday.
22. A. Jorge is proud to be a canadian.
    B. It will take work to preserve your Spanish heritage.

Writing Application Write a paragraph about someone you know who worked hard to achieve a dream.

Web Activities For eFlashcards, Selection Quick Checks, and other Web activities, go to www.glencoe.com.

Skills Review

Key Reading Skill: Identifying Main Idea and Supporting Details

9. Possible response: Education is important. It is stated on page 1107: "Schooling is crucial to me."
10. Possible responses include the description of Nwaiwu being part of the group who studies in homeroom, her rushing to math class, and Meg's advice.

Key Literary Element: Cultural Reference

11. Possible response: This girl purposely mispronounces *education* to show that she thinks education is unimportant.
12. Responses will vary.
13. Possible response: *Hanging out with* means "spending leisure time with." *Homies* are friends or people from your home neighborhood.

Vocabulary Check

14. false
15. true
16. true
17. false
18. true

English Language Coach

19. Possible response: The original meaning of *sound* is healthy, strong, uninjured, or safe. A *sound education* is a strong education.

Grammar Link: More Capitalization

20. B
21. A
22. B

Close

Have students discuss how they think the author would respond to the Big Question.

Indiana English/Language Arts Academic Standards
SE: 8.1.2, 8.2, 8.3, 8.6, 8.7

Teach

More About the Author

Richard Peck isn't an ordinary author. He uses an electric typewriter rather than a computer. Often, his characters are unique as well. In many his stories, a character leaves a group to become the person he or she is meant to be. A line from the dedication to his autobiography *Anonymously Yours* echoes Peck's view on life: "I read because one life isn't enough, and in the page of a book I can be anybody."

V Vocabulary

Reinforcing Meaning Review the vocabulary words with the class. Have students read the sentences aloud. Then have students write a paragraph in their Learner's Notebooks using the words. Paragraphs don't have to make total sense, but students must use the words in their proper context. *(Responses will vary.)* AS

Before You Read The Electric Summer

Richard Peck

Meet the Author

A former high school teacher, Richard Peck began writing novels for the same age group he taught. His books focus on the problems that teens face. Peck uses the characters in his books to show young people how others their age overcome problems as they take one step closer to adulthood. His novels include *Don't Look and It Won't Hurt, Are You in the House Alone?,* and *Father Figure*. See page R5 of the Author Files for more on Peck.

Author Search For more about Richard Peck, go to www.glencoe.

Indiana English/Language Arts Academic Standards (pp. 1112–1115)

8.1.2 Understand the influence of historical events on English word meaning and vocabulary expansion. **8.2 Comprehension and Analysis (Focus on Informational Text)** Develop [reading] strategies... **8.3.6** Identify significant literary devices, such as...dialect or quotations...

For a complete description of the standards, see p. IN 11.

Vocabulary Preview

V

novelty (NAH vul tee) *n.* anything new, strange, or unusual **(p. 1114)** *I grew up in the city, so seeing a cow face-to-face was a novelty.*

grandeur (GRAN jur) *n.* the state of being large and impressive; greatness **(p. 1121)** *I was deeply impressed by the grandeur of the mountains.*

hovering (HUV ur ing) *v.* remaining in or near one place in the air; form of the verb *hover* **(p. 1122)** *One eagle, hovering high above our heads, was the only living creature we saw as we hiked to the cabin.*

replica (REP lih kuh) *n.* a faithful copy **(p. 1123)** *The shop had row upon row of miniature buildings, each a replica of an original structure.*

rapture (RAP chur) *n.* a feeling of great joy **(p. 1124)** *The two felt that nothing could destroy the rapture of their wedding day.*

seasoned (SEE zund) *adj.* made fit by experience; adjusted to (something) because of experience **(p. 1125)** *A more seasoned player might have been able to predict what was coming next.*

English Language Coach

English as a Changing Language In "The Electric Summer," the main character is Geneva (juh NEE vuh), which is also the name of a city in Switzerland. Some people are named for places. Many places are named for people. Two places mentioned in the story were named for kings of France—Louis IX and Louis XIV. The French don't say the *-s* at the end of Louis, but Americans are more flexible. Read the words and pronunciations in the chart below.

St. **Louis,** Missouri	LOO ee *OR* LOO us
Louisville, Kentucky	LOO ih vil *OR* LOO ih vul
Louisiana	loo ee zee AN uh *OR* loo zee AN uh

Countless other U.S. place names come from foreign languages but have peculiarly American pronunciations. Here are three examples.

	Spanish	**"American"**
Los Angeles, California	lohs AHN hay lays	lahs AN juh lus
Madrid, Iowa	mah DREED	MAD rid
New Mexico	MEH hee koh	MEK sih koh

Additional Support

Author Search To expand students' appreciation of Richard Peck, have them access the Web site for additional information and resources.

Literature Focus Lesson

Tag Lines Authors sometimes use tag lines to help readers understand characters' emotions. Tag lines identify who is speaking and how, as in "Hooray!" *the crowd screamed.* Explain to students that they will encounter many different tag lines in the selection. Have students work with a partner to write a line of dialogue for each of the following tag lines and identify the emotion each one suggests. OL

- snapped
- moaned
- wheezed
- whined
- huffed
- comforted
- begged

Skills Preview

Key Reading Skill: Identifying Main Idea and Supporting Details

Most of the time, fiction authors don't directly state their main ideas. Instead, they provide details to help you figure them out. When you're reading fiction, use these questions to help identify the main idea:

- What points is the author trying to make about the characters' personalities and relationships?
- Which details support those points? Think about the characters' behavior and reactions to events.
- What is the main message of the story?
- What supporting details—such as events and their consequences—help the reader understand this message?

Literary Element: Dialogue

In literature, **dialogue** is the conversation between characters and it offers a great way to learn things about them. In "The Electric Summer," the dialogue gives readers a better understanding of the personalities of the major characters—Geneva, her mother, and her Aunt Elvera.

In a story with a first-person narrator, you need to be careful. It's easy to confuse what the narrator says with what the characters themselves reveal in the dialogue. Here, Geneva is the narrator, so she gives her ideas about characters and events, as well as her own thoughts and feelings. The other characters' dialogue reveals their own thoughts and feelings.

Use these tips as you read "The Electric Summer":

- What do you learn about each character's personality from what she says in the dialogue?
- What does the dialogue tell you about the events and situations?
- How does the dialogue help you understand what the characters experience in the story?

Partner Talk Have a dialogue with your partner. Choose a topic and discuss it for a couple of minutes. Then talk about your dialogue. What did you learn about your partner from what he or she said?

Get Ready to Read

Connect to the Reading

Do you recall the first time you saw a kangaroo or some other creature from a faraway place? How did you feel when you first flew in a plane or rode a roller coaster? In this story, a farm girl visits a big-city fair to see wonders from around the world.

Build Background

L

Long before TV and the Internet, world's fairs were held every few years in different cities around the world. Nations presented their food, art, and culture. Businesses showed off products and technologies. Visitors had the time of their lives!

At the 1904 world's fair in St. Louis, Missouri, the new products on display included everything from automatic egg boilers to pianos that played themselves. An automobile at one exhibit featured silk curtains, armchairs, a writing desk, an icebox, and a wash basin. (The car cost $18,000, a huge sum in 1904.)

Set Purposes for Reading

BQ

Read "The Electric Summer" to find out how a girl and her mother discover new ideas about the American dream.

Set Your Own Purpose What would you like to learn from the story to help you answer the Big Question? Write your own purpose on the "Electric Summer" page of Foldable 8.

Literature Online

Interactive Literary Elements Handbook
To review or learn more about the literary elements, go to www.glencoe.com.

Keep Moving

Use these skills as you read the following selection.

Reading in the Real World

Citizenship World's fairs and universal expositions have been held throughout the world since the mid-1800s. Ask students to work in groups to research a world fair or universal exposition other than the one described in the selection. Groups should use several media to inform other class members about the fair they selected. Some possibilities are computer presentations, posters, brochures, and music and dance. Have students include the following information in their presentations: date, location, theme, permanent structures still standing, and one noteworthy event or feature. OL AL

READING WORKSHOP 3

Teach

L Literary Element

Review Cultural Reference

Ask: Which detail in *Build Background* helps you to understand that 1904 American culture differs from current culture? *(Responses will vary, but should list either the description of the world's fair or one of the inventions.)* AS

BQ 

Ask: How do you think the American dream of 1904 differs from the dream of today? What similarities do you think they have? *(Responses will vary.)*
Say: Read the selection to find out more about the American dream. AS

Interactive Literary Elements Handbook Have students access the Web site to improve their understanding of dialogue.

Indiana English/Language Arts Academic Standards
SE: 8.1.2, 8.2, 8.3.6
TWE: *Literature Focus Lesson* 8.5.6, *Reading in the Real World* 8.7.12

Teach

Say: Do you think you could follow your dream if you lived where the narrator does? Explain. *(Responses will vary.)* **OL**

L Literary Element

Review Cultural Reference

Ask: What does the information on this page tell you about the setting of the selection? *(It is set in a rural area long ago.)* **Ask:** What details in particular support your answer? *(Possible response: the references to making preserves, picking berries, the garden, and the fact that only four cars existed in the town)* **AS**

Readability Scores
Dale-Chall: 5.1
DRP: 800
Lexile: 5.1

The Electric Summer

by Richard Peck

I was sitting out there on the old swing that used to hang on the back porch. We'd fed Dad and the boys. Now Mama and I were spelling each other to stir the preserves.[1] The screen door behind me was black with flies, and that smell of sugared strawberries cooking down filled all out-of-doors. A Maytime smell, promising summer.

Just turned fourteen, I was long-legged enough to push off the swing, then listen to the squeak of the chains. The swing was where I did my daytime dreaming. I sat there looking down past Mama's garden and the wind pump to the level line of long distance.[2] **1**

Like watching had made it happen, dust rose on the road from town. A black dot got bigger, scaring the sheep away from the fence line. It was an automobile. Nothing else churned the dust like that. Then by and by it was the Schumates' Oldsmobile, turning off the crown of the road and bouncing into our barn lot. There were only four automobiles in the town at that time, and only one of them driven by a woman—my aunt Elvera Schumate. She cut the motor off, but the Oldsmobile was still heaving. Climbing down, she put a gloved hand on a fender to calm it. **L**

As Dad often said, Aunt Elvera would have been a **novelty** even without the automobile. In the heat of the day she wore

1. In ***spelling*** each other, they were taking turns. Here, the ***preserves*** are strawberries being made into jam or jelly.
2. The ***level line of long distance*** refers to the horizon.

Vocabulary

novelty (NAH vul tee) *n.* anything new, strange, or unusual

Practice the Skills

1 Reviewing Skills

Visualizing Take a moment to form mental pictures of Geneva and the farm. Imagine, too, the smells and sounds she describes.

Additional Support

Literature Focus Lesson

Sensory Details On this page, the author connects the smell of summer with warm strawberry preserves. Remind students that sensory images appeal to the five senses: sight, touch, hearing, smell, and taste. With students, brainstorm sensory details they associate with school. Write student responses on the board. Then have students list five sensory details they connect with summer. Afterward, have students choose either school or summer as a topic and then write a paragraph using the sensory details they listed. **AS**

a wide-brimmed canvas hat secured with a motoring veil tied under her chin. Her duster was a voluminous poplin garment,[3] leather-bound at the hem.

My cousin Dorothy climbed down from the Olds, dressed similarly. They made a business of untangling themselves from their veils, propping their **goggles** up on their foreheads, and dusting themselves down the best they could. Aunt Elvera made for the house with Dorothy following. Dorothy always held back. **2**

Behind me Mama banged on the screen door to scare the flies, then stepped outside. She was ready for a breather even if it meant Aunt Elvera. I stood up from the swing as Aunt Elvera came through the gate to the yard, Dorothy trailing. Where their goggles had been were two circles of clean skin around their eyes. They looked like a pair of raccoons. Mama's mouth twitched in something of a smile. **C**

"Well, Mary." Aunt Elvera heaved herself up the porch steps and drew off her gauntlet gloves. "I can see you are having a busy day." Mama's hands were fire red from strawberry juice and the heat of the stove. Mine were scratched all over from picking every ripe berry in the patch.

"One day's like another on the farm," Mama remarked. **R**

"Then I will not mince[4] words," Aunt Elvera said, overlooking me. "I'd have rung you up if you were connected to the telephone system."

"What about, Elvera?" She and Mama weren't sisters. They were sisters-in-law.

"Why, the Fair, of course!" Aunt Elvera bristled[5] in an important way. "What else? The Louisiana Purchase Exposition in St. Louis. The world will be there. It puts St. Louis at the hub of the universe." Aunt Elvera's mouth worked wordlessly.

"Well, I do know about it," Mama said. "I take it you'll be going?"

3. Early cars were open, like horse carriages, and early roads were unpaved. To protect against dirt and bad weather, drivers and passengers wore ***dusters,*** long coats that were large ***(voluminous),*** to fit over their clothes, and made of a strong, woven fabric ***(poplin).*** A woman was likely to wear a hat with a ***motoring veil,*** a long, thin scarf that tied around her face. The next paragraphs mention more of a motorist's costume: ***gauntlet gloves,*** which extended over the wrists, and ***goggles,*** which protected the eyes.

4. Here, to ***mince*** is to speak in an unnaturally careful or dainty way.

5. Here, ***bristled*** (BRIH suld) means "showed anger or annoyance."

Practice the Skills

2 **English Language Coach**

A Changing Language The word **goggles** comes from the Middle English *gogolen,* which meant "to squint." Later, *goggle* came to mean "to stare at with wide eyes," which seems the opposite of its older meaning.

Teach

C Critical Thinking

Comprehension **Ask:** What was the narrator saying about her aunt when she said that Mama was ready for a breather "even if it meant Aunt Elvera"? *(Possible response: Aunt Elvera wasn't fun to talk to or be with, but her mother was so tired any break would be appreciated.)* AS

R Reading Skill

Review Making Inferences
Say: Mama says that "one day's like another on the farm." What was she saying about farm life? *(Every day was busy and full of work.)* BL OL **Ask:** How might this fact about farm life affect the narrator? *(Possible response: She may get tired of working on the farm and want to have new experiences.)* OL

Reading Fluency

Build Fluency Play an audiotape of this story or read part of this selection aloud as students read along silently. Ask students to pay special attention to how the dialogue moves back and forth between characters. Then have students form groups of four or five to read the selection. Remind students to change expression to mimic the attitudes of the characters as they speak. Allow groups time to practice until they can fluently read the entire selection. EL BL

Indiana English/Language Arts Academic Standards
SE: 8.1.2
TWE: *Literature Focus Lesson* 8.5.7, *Reading Fluency* 8.7

Teach

EL Language Coach

English as a Changing Language **Say:** The word *tight* has a Scandinavian origin meaning "of the same kind." Over time, the word has taken on many different meanings, such as "fitting very close," as in *tight pants,* or "stingy," as in *tight with money,* or "very firm or strict," as in *tight security.* Elvera says that her husband is as "tight as a new boot." What does she mean? *(He doesn't like to spend money.)* OL AL

R Reading Skill

Identifying Main Idea and Supporting Details **Ask:** Which supporting details does the narrator give to imply that Dorothy is not smart? *(She repeated fourth grade and moved her lips when she read silently.)* AS

Aunt Elvera waved her away. "My stars, yes. You know how Schumate can be. Tight as a new boot. But I put my foot down. Mary, this is the opportunity of a lifetime. We will not see such wonders again during our span.[6]" EL

"Ah," Mama said, and my mind wandered—took a giant leap and landed in St. Louis. We knew about the Fair. The calendar the peddler gave us at Christmas featured a different pictorial view of the Fair for every month. There were white palaces in gardens with gondolas[7] in waterways, everything electric-lit. Castles from Europe and paper houses from Japan. For the month of May the calendar featured the great floral clock on the fairgrounds. 3

"Send us a postal,[8]" Mama said.

"The thing is . . ." Aunt Elvera's eyes slid toward Dorothy. "We thought we'd invite Geneva to go with us."

My heart liked to lurch out of my apron. Me? They wanted to take me to the Fair?

"She'll be company for Dorothy."

Then I saw how it was. Dorothy was dim, but she could set her heels like a mule. She wanted somebody with her at the Fair so she wouldn't have to trail after her mother every minute. We were about the same age. We were in the same grade, but she was a year older, having repeated fourth grade. She could read, but her lips moved. And we were cousins, not friends. R

"It will be educational for them both," Aunt Elvera said. "All the progress of civilization as we know it will be on display. They say a visit to the Fair is tantamount[9] to a year of high school."

"Mercy," Mama said.

"We will take the Wabash Railroad directly to the gates of the Exposition," Aunt Elvera explained, "and we will be staying on the grounds themselves at the Inside Inn." She

6. A ***span*** is a period of time; here, it's a synonym for "lifetime."
7. ***Gondolas*** (GAHN duh luz) are long, narrow, high-ended boats such as are used on the canals of Venice, Italy.
8. This is short for ***postal*** card, which we now call a postcard.
9. ***Tantamount*** (TAN tuh mownt) means "equal in value, importance, or effect."

Analyzing the Photo
What aspect of the fair does this photo capture?

Practice the Skills

3 Literary Element

Dialogue Review the last few paragraphs of conversation between Mama and Aunt Elvera. What can you tell about Elvera's personality from this dialogue?

Additional Support

Reading in the Real World

Citizenship Ask students to volunteer the names of civic groups in your community. List these, as well as others with which you're familiar or that are listed in the phone directory. Explain that people form groups to accomplish goals that require the work and talents of many. Have students work in pairs to research one of the groups on the list or another group not represented locally. Students should prepare and present posters that inform the class of the group's purpose, membership requirements, and history. Display the posters in the classroom. Discuss with students which groups they'd consider joining and why. AS

READING WORKSHOP 3

leaned nearer Mama, and her voice fell. "I'm sorry to say that there will be stimulants for sale on the fairgrounds. You know how St. Louis is in the hands of the breweries." Aunt Elvera was sergeant-at-arms of the Women's Christian Temperance Union, and to her, strong drink[10] was a mocker. "But we will keep the girls away from that sort of thing." Her voice fell to a whisper. "And we naturally won't set foot on the Pike." 4

We knew what the Pike was. It was the midway of the Fair, like a giant carnival with all sorts of goings-on.

"Well, many thanks, but I don't think so," Mama said.

R1 My heart didn't exactly sink. It never dawned on me that I'd see the Fair. I was only a little cast down because I might never get another glimpse of the world.

"Now, you're not to think of the money," Aunt Elvera said. "Dismiss that from your mind. Schumate and I will be glad to cover all Geneva's expenses. She can sleep in the bed with Dorothy, and we are carrying a good deal of our eats. I know R2 these aren't flush[11] times for farmers, Mary, but do not let your pride stand in Geneva's way."

"Oh, no," Mama said mildly. "Pride cometh before a fall. But we may be running down to the Fair ourselves." 5

Aunt Elvera's eyes narrowed, and I didn't believe Mama, either. It was just her way of fending off[12] my aunt. Kept me from being in the same bed with Dorothy, too.

Aunt Elvera never liked taking no for an answer, but in time she and Dorothy made a disorderly retreat. We saw them off from the porch. Aunt Elvera had to crank the Olds to get it going while Dorothy sat up on the seat, adjusting the magneto[13] or whatever it was. We watched Aunt Elvera's rear elevation as she stooped to jerk the crank time after time. If the crank got away from you, it could break your arm, and we watched to see if it would. 6

10. Here, ***stimulants*** and ***strong drink*** refer to alcoholic beverages. In the early 1900s, St. Louis ***breweries*** (beer factories) produced a large portion of the nation's beer. The ***Women's Christian Temperance Union*** (WCTU) was founded in 1874 to improve moral life, especially by encouraging people not to drink alcohol. As ***sergeant-at-arms,*** Elvera was an officer who maintained order at WCTU meetings.

11. Here, ***flush*** means "prosperous; having extra money."

12. ***Fending off*** is defending against or fighting off.

13. To start the engine, one had to turn a ***crank*** and adjust various controls, such as the ***magneto.***

Practice the Skills

4 Reviewing Elements

Cultural Reference The WCTU still exists, but its period of greatest influence and activity was in the early 1900s. Watch for other cultural references as you continue reading.

5 Literary Element

Dialogue Judging from Mama's part of this long dialogue, what would you say is her opinion of Elvera?

6 Key Reading Skill

Identifying Main Idea The author wants to make it clear that the automobile was an imperfect invention at this time. What details support that idea?

Teach

R1 Reading Skill

Review Understanding Cause and Effect Ask: When Mama refuses Elvera's offer, what is the immediate effect on Geneva? *(She is disappointed because she thought she'd never get another glimpse of the world.)* AS

R2 Reading Skill

Identifying Main Idea and Supporting Details Ask: What details support the idea that "Aunt Elvera never liked taking no for an answer"? *(Even after Mama refuses the offer, Elvera continues to try to persuade Mama to let Geneva go to the fair.)* OL

Differentiated Instruction

Building an Argument Aunt Elvera works hard to persuade Mama to let Geneva go to the fair. Copy the following chart on the board, and have students identify the supporting details of Elvera's argument. BL

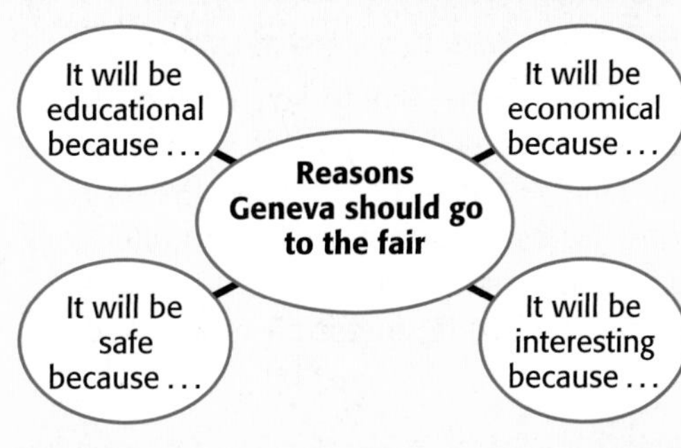
Reasons Geneva should go to the fair
It will be educational because . . .
It will be economical because . . .
It will be safe because . . .
It will be interesting because . . .

Indiana English/Language Arts Academic Standards

SE: 8.2, 8.3.6

TWE: *Reading in the Real World* 8.5.3, *Differentiated Instruction* 8.2

Teach

L1 Literary Element

Review Cultural Reference
Say: Geneva says she had to clean the lamp chimneys and trim the wicks. This cultural reference refers to a time when many houses didn't have electricity. What is another cultural reference in this same paragraph? *(Her brothers hitching Fanny to the trap refers to a time when people used horses and carriages for transportation.)* AS

E Text Element

Review Chronological Order **Ask:** What happened after supper at the farm? *(Geneva's brothers went into town, Geneva cleaned the lamp chimneys and trimmed the wicks, and Mama and Geneva sat on the porch swing.)* AS

L2 Literary Element

Review Figurative Language
Say: Geneva says the egg money is for "a rainy day." What does this idiomatic expression mean? *(A rainy day is an emergency or special need.)* BL OL

READING WORKSHOP 3

But at length the Olds coughed and sputtered to life. Aunt Elvera climbed aboard and circled the barn lot—she never had found the reverse gear. Then they were off back to town in a cloud of dust on the crown of the road.

I didn't want to mention the Fair, so I said, "Mama, would you ride in one of them things?"

Visual Vocabulary
A ***lamp chimney*** is the glass tube that surrounds the flame on an oil lamp.

"Not with Elvera running it," she said, and went back in the house.

I could tell you very little about the rest of that day. My mind was miles off. I know Mama wrung the neck off a fryer, and we had baking-powder biscuits to go with the warm jam. After supper my brothers hitched up Fanny to the trap[14] and went into town. I took a bottle brush to the lamp chimneys and trimmed the wicks. After that I was back out on the porch swing while there was some daylight left. The lightning bugs were coming out, so that reminded me of how the Fair was lit up at night with electricity, brighter than day.

Then Mama came out and settled in the swing beside me, which was unusual, since she never sat out until the nights got hotter than this. We swung together awhile. Then she said in a quiet voice, "I meant it. I want you to see the Fair." 7

Everything stopped then. I still didn't believe it, but my heart turned over.

"I spoke to your dad about it. He can't get away, and he can't spare the boys. But I want us to go to the Fair."

Oh, she was brave to say it, she who hadn't been anywhere in her life. Brave even to think it. "I've got some egg money put back," she said. We didn't keep enough chickens to sell the eggs, but anything you managed to save was called egg money.

"That's for a rainy day," I said, being practical.

"I know it," she said. "But I'd like to see that floral clock."

Mama was famous for her garden flowers. When her glads were up, every color, people drove by to see them. And there was nobody to touch her for zinnias.

Oh, Mama, I thought, *is this just a game we're playing?* "What'll we wear?" I asked, to test her.

"They'll be dressy down at the Fair, won't they?" she said.

14. A ***fryer*** is a young chicken. The ***trap*** is a light one-horse carriage.

Practice the Skills

7 Key Reading Skill

Identifying Main Idea What detail shows that Mama is serious about wanting Geneva to see the fair?

Additional Support

English Language Coach

End Punctuation and Quotation Marks "Mama, would you ride in one of them things?" "I mean it, I want to see the fair." "I know it," she said. Present these rules for end punctuation and quotation marks: Periods and commas always go inside; question marks and exclamation points go inside if they are part of the question or exclamation. Ask students to find five direct quotations from the story, copy each quotation, and explain how the end punctuation is handled. AS

"You know those artificial cornflowers I've got. I thought I'd trim my hat with them. And you're getting to be a big girl. Time you had a corset.[15]"

So then I knew she meant business.

That's how Mama and I went to the Louisiana Purchase Exposition in St. Louis that summer of 1904. We studied up on it, and Dad read the Fair literature along with us. **Hayseeds** we might be, but we meant to be informed hayseeds. They said the Fair covered twelve hundred acres, and we tried to see that in our minds, how many farms that would amount to. And all we learned about the Fair filled my heart to overflowing and struck me dumb with dread.[16] 8 C

Mama weakened some. She found out when the Schumates were going, and we planned to go at the same time, just so we'd know somebody there. But we didn't take the same train. 9

When the great day came, Dad drove us to town, where the Wabash Cannonball stopped on its way to St. Louis. If he'd turned the trap around and taken us back home, you wouldn't have heard a peep out of me. And I think Mama was the same. But then we were on the platform with the big locomotive thundering in, everything too quick now, and too loud.

We had to scramble for seats in the day coach, lugging one straw valise between us and a gallon jug of lemonade. And a vacuum flask of the kind the Spanish-American War[17] soldiers carried, with our own well water for brushing our teeth. We'd heard that St. Louis water came straight out of the Mississippi River, and there's enough silt in it to settle at the bottom of the glass. We'd go to their fair, but we weren't going to drink their water.

When the people sitting across from us went to the dining car, Mama and I spread checkered napkins over our knees and had our noon meal out of the valise. All the while, hot wind blew clinkers and soot in the window as we raced along like a crazed horse. Then a lady flounced up and R

15. A ***corset*** (KOR sut) is a long, tight, girdle-like undergarment for a grown woman.
16. She is temporarily unable to speak ***(dumb)*** because of great fear and worry ***(dread)***.
17. A ***valise*** (vuh LEES) is a suitcase. A ***vacuum flask*** (what we now call a "thermos") is used to keep liquids either hot or cold. The ***Spanish-American War*** was a brief conflict in 1898 between Spain and the United States over Spain's treatment of Cuba.

Practice the Skills

8 English Language Coach

A Changing Language Originally, **hayseeds** were bits of straw that clung to farmers' clothes. Later, city people began to use the word to refer to the farmers themselves.

9 Key Reading Skill

Identifying Main Idea In the next few paragraphs, notice the many details about the train trip. What idea(s) about train travel do you think the author wants to get across?

Teach

C Critical Thinking

Comprehension Ask: Why do Geneva and her parents want to be "informed hayseeds"? *(Possible response: They didn't want to be embarrassed by arriving at the fair unprepared or ignorant.)* **OL AL**

R Reading Skill

Identifying Main Idea and Supporting Details Ask: What detail on this page supports the idea that Geneva's family was not wealthy? *(Mama and Geneva ate a packed lunch, rather than going to the dining car.)* **AS**

Literature Focus Lesson

Setting Remind students that setting includes any elements in which the action occurs: time period; geographic region; season; weather; and spaces, such as buildings, rooms, and landscapes. The culture in which the characters develop is also part of the setting. Write the following chart on the board and tell students to copy it and write a brief description of the setting in this story in the second row. Students should continue filling in the chart as they read.

	Settings		
	Farm	Train	Fair
Description			

Indiana English/Language Arts Academic Standards
SE: 8.1.2, 8.2
TWE: *English Language Coach* 8.6.5, *Literature Focus Lesson* 8.3

Teach

L Literary Element

Dialogue Say: Reread Mama's response to the woman's question about the ladies' room. What does her response indicate? *(She does not understand what the woman is referring to.)* **Ask:** What does her response to Geneva's question about a privy demonstrate? *(Possible response: She is shocked by the thought of it.)* OL AL

C Critical Thinking

Comprehension Ask: What caused Mama and Geneva to search for the restroom? *(A woman asked them where it was.)* **Ask:** How does the sight of the water closet affect Mama and Geneva differently? *(Mama says she'd never use it, while Geneva wanted to know how it worked.)* BL

READING WORKSHOP 3

perched on the seat opposite. She had a full bird on the wing[18] sewed to the crown of her hat, and she was painted up like a circus pony, so we took her to be from Chicago. Leaning forward, she spoke, though we didn't know her from Adam. "Would you know where the ladies' rest room is?" she inquired.

We stared blankly back, but then Mama said politely, "No, but you're welcome to rest here till them other people come back." L

The woman blinked at us, then darted away, hurrying now. I chewed on[19] that a minute, along with my ham sandwich. Then I said, "Mama, do you suppose they have a **privy** on the train?" 10

"A *what*?" she said.

Finally, we had to know. Putting the valise on my seat and the hamper on hers, Mama and I went to explore. We walked through the swaying cars, from seat to seat, the cornflowers on Mama's hat aquiver. Sure enough, we came to a door at the end of a car with a sign reading LADIES. We crowded inside, and there it was. A water closet like you'd find in town[20] and a chain hanging down and a roll of paper. "Well, I've seen everything now," Mama said. "You wouldn't catch me sitting on that thing in a moving train. I'd fall off." C

But I wanted to know how it worked and reached for the handle on the chain. "Just give it a little jerk," Mama said.

We stared down as I did. The bottom of the pan was on a hinge. It dropped open, and there below were the ties of the Wabash tracks racing along beneath us.

We both jumped back and hit the door. And we made haste back to our seats. I guess we were lucky not to have found the lady with the bird on her hat in there, sitting down.

Then before I was ready, we were crossing the Mississippi River on a high trestle.[21] There was

18. ***Clinkers and soot***—cinders and fine ashes—were from the coal burned as fuel in the locomotive. The bird, whether real or artificial, was made to look as though it were flying ***(on the wing)***.
19. The expression ***chewed on*** means "thought over."
20. ***Water closet*** is another word for *toilet*. In the early 1900s few farms had indoor toilets.
21. A ***trestle*** (TREH sul) is a railroad bridge, especially a high one over a river or valley.

Practice the Skills

10 English Language Coach

A Changing Language The word **privy,** short for *private,* first appeared in the 14th century. But a toilet by any other name is still a toilet. And another one of those names appears in the next paragraph.

Covering nearly 16 acres, the Palace of Transportation exhibited 140 automobiles. Can you imagine Aunt Elvera in one of these cars?

Additional Support

Differentiated Instruction

Building Background To help students visualize mass transportation in the early 1900s, have them research passenger trains of the era. Suggest that they look for information on the following topics: dining cars, sleeping cars, day coaches, restrooms, train personnel, ticket costs, services, and passenger comfort. Have students use their notes to write letters home as if they were passengers describing their first train ride. Suggest that they include sensory details that help readers to visualize what train rides might have been like at the time. OL

READING WORKSHOP 3

nothing between us and the brown water. I put my hand over my eyes, but not before I glimpsed St. Louis on the far bank, sweeping away in the haze of heat as far as the eye could see.

We didn't stay at the Inside Inn. They wanted two dollars a night for a room, three if they fed you. We booked into a rooming house not far from the main gate, where we got a big square room upstairs with two beds for a dollar. It was run by a severe lady, Mrs. Wolfe, with a small, moon-faced son named Thomas clinging to her skirts. The place suited Mama, once she'd pulled down the bedclothes to check for bugs. It didn't matter where we laid our heads as long as it was clean. **C**

We walked to the Fair that afternoon, following the crowds, trying to act like everybody else. Once again I'd have turned back if Mama had said to. It wasn't the awful **grandeur** of the pavilions[22] rising white in the sun. It was all those people. I didn't know there were that many people in the world. They scared me at first, but then I couldn't see enough. My eyes began to drink deep. **11** **R**

We took the Intramural[23] electric railroad that ran around the Exposition grounds, making stops. The Fair passed before us, and it didn't take me long to see what I was looking for. It was hard to miss. At the Palace of Transportation stop, I told Mama this was where we got off.

There it rose before us, 250 feet high. It was the giant wheel, the invention of George Washington Gale Ferris. A great wheel[24] with thirty-six cars on it, each holding sixty people. It turned as we watched, and people were getting on and off like it was nothing to them.

"No power on earth would get me up in that thing," Mama murmured.

22. The ***pavilions*** (puh VIL yunz) are the fair's exhibit halls and other buildings.
23. The ***Intramural*** railroad ran only within the fairgrounds.
24. At the time, this was the only ***Ferris wheel*** in existence. Invented and built for the 1893 World's Columbian Exhibition in Chicago, it was moved to St. Louis in 1903. After the fair there, it was sold as scrap metal.

Vocabulary

grandeur (GRAN jur) *n.* the state of being large and impressive; greatness

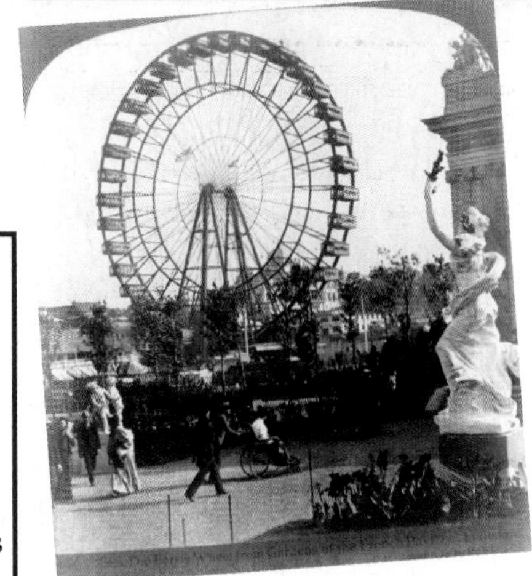

Analyzing the Photo How does the size of the Ferris wheel reflect the fair's grand scale?

Practice the Skills

11 Reviewing Elements

Figurative Language What does the last sentence mean? What kind of figurative language is used?

Teach

C Critical Thinking

Comprehension Ask: Where do Mama and Geneva stay, and why? *(Possible response: They stay in a rooming house not far from the main gate of the exposition grounds. They stay there because it is clean and less expensive than the inn.)* **BL**

R Reading Skill

Review Understanding Cause and Effect Ask: How did the crowds of people first affect Geneva? *(They scared her.)* **Ask:** Why did their effect on Geneva change? *(Possible response: She found the crowds interesting because she was seeing and learning new things.)* **OL**

Literature Focus Lesson

Character Traits Copy this organizer on the board. Explain that authors reveal what characters are like by what they say and do. Have students select one character from the story and use the organizer to identify three details about him or her from the story. Then have students explain what personality traits of the character these details suggest. **BL**

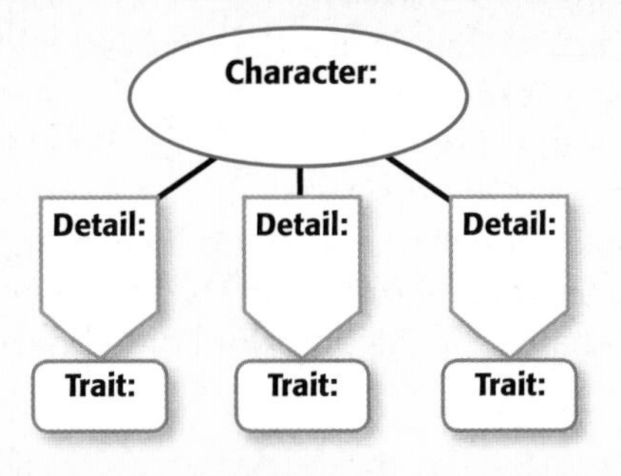

Indiana English/Language Arts Academic Standards
SE: 8.1.2, 8.3.6
TWE: *Differentiated Instruction* 8.5.7, *Literature Focus Lesson* 8.3

Teach

Ask: In what way might Mama be following a dream? *(Possible response: She's proving that she has the courage to try new things.)* OL AL

R Reading Skill

Review Analyzing Say: Mama thinks of the height of the Ferris wheel in terms of wind pumps. What does this say about her? *(Possible response: Mama relates new things to what she's used to on the farm in order to better understand them.)* OL AL

L Literary Element

Dialogue Say: Read the last bit of Mama's dialogue on the page. What can you conclude about Mama based on the dialogue? *(Possible response: She's proud she was brave enough to ride the Ferris wheel, and she is conscientious about money.)* OL AL

But I opened my hand and showed her the extra dollar Dad had slipped me to ride the wheel. "Dad said it would give us a good view of the Fair," I said in a wobbly voice.

"It would give me a stroke," Mama said. But then she set her jaw. "Your dad is putting me to the test. He thinks I won't do it." BQ

Gathering her skirts, she moved deliberately toward the line of people waiting to ride the wheel.

We wouldn't look up while we waited, but we heard the creaking of all that naked steel. "That is the sound of doom," Mama muttered. Then, too soon, they were ushering us into a car, and I began to **babble** out of sheer fear. 12

"A lady named Mrs. Nicholson rode standing on the roof of one of these cars when the wheel was up at the Chicago fair, eleven years ago."

Mama turned to me. "What in the world for?"

"She was a daredevil, I guess."

"She was out of her mind," Mama said.

Now we were inside, and people mobbed the windows as we swooped up. I meant to stand in the middle of our car and watch the floor, but I looked out. In a moment we were above the roofs and towers of the Fair, a white city unfolding. There was the Grand Basin with the gondolas drifting. There was the mighty Festival Hall. Mama chanced a look.

It was cooler up there. My unforgiving Warner's Rust-Proof Corset had held me in a death grip all day, but I could breathe easier that high. Then we paused, dangling at the top. Now we were one with the birds, like hawks **hovering** over the Fair. R

"How many wind pumps high are we?" Mama pondered. As we began to arch down again, we were both at a window, skinning our eyes to see the Jerusalem exhibit and the Philippine Village and, way off, the Plateau of States—a world of wonders.

Giddy when we got out, we staggered on solid ground and had to sit down on an ornamental bench. Now Mama was game for anything. "If they didn't want an arm and a leg for the fare," she said, "I'd ride that thing again. Keep the ticket stubs to show your dad we did it." 13 L

Vocabulary

hovering (HUV ur ing) *v.* remaining in or near one place in the air

Practice the Skills

12 English Language Coach

A Changing Language The word **babble** may come from a place name. In the Bible, the people of Babylon start to build a tower up to heaven—the Tower of Babel. They fail after God makes them "babble," or speak different languages, so that they can't communicate.

13 Key Reading Skill

Identifying Main Idea What is the main idea or message in this passage about the Ferris wheel ride? (Hint: What is the author saying about doing what you're afraid to do?)

Additional Support

Reading in the Real World

Career People like George Washington Gale Ferris create new things for several reasons. Some, like Ferris, are hired to invent. Others want to solve a problem or find a better way to do something. Have students work with a partner to research the life and work of an inventor they feel made a contribution to the world. Have them write a short biographical sketch of the person and include a drawing or description of the invention. Ask volunteers to present both to the class and explain why they think this person's contributions are important. AS

Braver than before, we walked down the Pike, as it was still broad daylight. It was lined with sidewalk cafes in front of all manner of attractions: the Streets of Cairo and the Palais du Costume, Hagenbeck's Circus and a **replica** of the Galveston[25] flood. Because we were parched, we found a table at a place where they served a new drink, tea with ice in it. "How do we know we're not drinking silt?" Mama wondered, but it cooled us off.

As quick as you'd sit down anywhere at the Fair, there'd be entertainment. In front of the French Village they had a supple young man named Will Rogers doing rope tricks. And music? Everywhere you turned, and all along the Pike, the song the world sang that summer was: "Meet me in St. Louis, Louis, meet me at the fair."[26]

We sat over our tea and watched the passing parade. Some of those people you wouldn't want to meet in a dark alley. Over by the water chutes a gang of rough men waited to glimpse the ankles of women getting out of the boats. But the only thing we saw on the Pike we shouldn't have was Uncle Schumate weaving out of the saloon bar of the Tyrolean[27] Alps.

I can't tell all we saw in our two days at the Fair. We tried to look at things the boys and Dad would want to hear about—the Hall of Mines and Metallurgy, and the livestock. We learned a good deal of history: the fourteen female statues to stand for the states of the Louisiana Purchase of 1803, and the log cabin that President U. S. Grant had been born in. But most of what we saw foretold the future: automobiles and airships and moving pictures.[28] **14**

25. In 1900, a terrible hurricane hit ***Galveston,*** Texas, killing 5,000 people and destroying much of the city.
26. In the song, a woman leaves a note telling her husband Louis (LOO ee) where to meet her in St. Louis (LOO ee).
27. ***Tyrolean*** (tuh ROH lee un) refers to a region, mostly in Austria, of the eastern Alps Mountains.
28. Cars, planes, and movies existed in 1904; they just weren't yet widely available or easily affordable.

Vocabulary

replica (REP lih kuh) *n.* a faithful copy

Practice the Skills

14 BIG Question

Geneva says that the things she saw at the fair "foretold the future." What does this tell you about the American dream in 1904? Write your answer on the "Electric Summer" page of Foldable 8.

Will Rogers (1879–1935) was one of the most popular entertainers of the time. In his live performances, he told jokes and performed rope tricks.

READING WORKSHOP 3

Teach

R Reading Skill

Review Connecting Say: Geneva seems to be in awe of the future—"automobiles and airships and moving pictures." What is in our future? If you were to go to an exposition highlighting modern advances in technology, what sort of technology would amaze you? *(Possible response: robots, space station, computerized objects)* **AS**

C Critical Thinking

Comprehension Ask: What are airships? *(Possible response: They are early versions of airplanes.)* **Ask:** What are moving pictures? *(They are movies.)* **OL**

Reading in the Real World

Career Will Rogers used his popularity as an entertainer to try many other careers. Have students research the life of Rogers and find at least three other jobs he did besides tell jokes and perform rope tricks. Then ask students to think about how the three careers relate to each other. What skills are needed to perform each successfully? What skills are needed to perform all three? **OL**

Indiana English/Language Arts Academic Standards
SE: 8.1.2, 8.2
TWE: *Reading in the Real World* (p. 1122) 8.7.12

Teach

E Text Element

Review Chronological Order **Ask:** What did Geneva and her mother see first: the bands or the floral clock? *(the bands)* AS **Ask:** Why might they have saved what they did for last? *(Possible response: They visited the floral clock last because of Mama's love of flowers. Saving it for last made it special.)* OL

R Reading Skill

Identifying Main Idea and Supporting Details **Ask:** Which details support the idea that the floral clock was huge? *(Its dial was 112 feet across; each hand weighed 2,500 pounds.)* AS

L Literary Element

Dialogue **Say:** Read Aunt Elvera's dialogue in the fourth paragraph. What does her dialogue indicate about her character? *(Possible response: She isn't a very nice person.)* AS

READING WORKSHOP 3

Our last night was the Fourth of July. Fifty bands played, some of them on horseback. John Philip Sousa, in gold braid and white, conducted his own marches. Lit in every color, the fountains played to this music and the thunder of the fireworks. And the cavalry from the Boer War[29] exhibit rode in formation, brandishing torches. 15

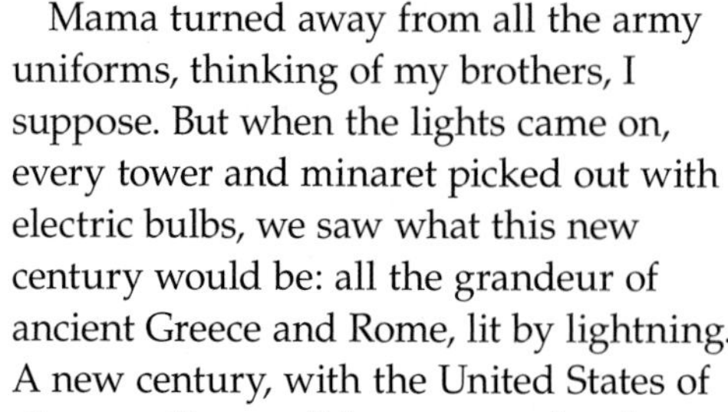

Visual Vocabulary
A ***minaret*** is a tall, slender tower on an Islamic temple.

Mama turned away from all the army uniforms, thinking of my brothers, I suppose. But when the lights came on, every tower and minaret picked out with electric bulbs, we saw what this new century would be: all the grandeur of ancient Greece and Rome, lit by lightning. A new century, with the United States of America showing the way. But you'd have to run hard not to be left behind. 16

We saved the floral clock for our last morning. It lay across a hillside next to the Agriculture Palace, and it was beyond anything we'd ever seen. The dial of it was 112 feet across, and each giant hand weighed 2,500 pounds. It was all made of flowers, even the numbers. Each Hour Garden had plants that opened at that time of day, beginning with morning glories. We stood in a **rapture**, waiting for it to strike the hour.

Then who appeared before us with her folding Kodak camera slung around her neck but Aunt Elvera Schumate. To demonstrate her worldliness, she merely nodded like we were all just coming out of church back home. "Well, Mary," she said to Mama, "I guess this clock shames your garden."

Mama dipped her head modestly to show the cornflowers on her hat. "Yes, Elvera," she said, "I am a humbler woman for this experience," and Aunt Elvera didn't quite know what to make of her reply. "Where's Dorothy?" Mama asked innocently.

"That child!" Aunt Elvera said. "I couldn't get her out of the bed at the Inside Inn! She complains of blistered feet. Wait till she has a woman's corns! I am a martyr to mine. I cannot get

29. ***Sousa*** (SOO zuh) was a popular composer and band leader. The ***cavalry*** (KAH vul ree) were soldiers on horseback. In the ***Boer War*** (1899–1902), Great Britain fought two of its former colonies in southern Africa.

Vocabulary

rapture (RAP chur) *n.* a feeling of great joy

Practice the Skills

15 Key Reading Skill

Identifying Main Idea Again, numerous details are given about the fair. What point is the author making?

16 BIG Question

What part does electricity play in the American dream of the early 1900s? Write your answer on the "Electric Summer" page of Foldable 8.

Additional Support

Literature Focus Lesson

Point of View Explain to students that this story is told in the first-person point of view. Geneva, a young farm girl, gives the reader her perspective of events. Point out clues in the text that show her bias. For example, in the next to last paragraph, Geneva explains, "Mama dipped her head modestly. . . ." The word *modestly* shows that Geneva believes her mother is not prideful, but humble. Have students look for other clues to see how Geneva's word choice affects how they understand the characters. Then have students write a short essay explaining how her perspective of events and characters affected their own. OL AL her interested in the Fair. She got as far as the bust of President Roosevelt sculpted in butter, but then she faded." Aunt Elvera cast me a baleful[30] look, as if this was all my fault. "Dorothy is going through a phase."

But there Aunt Elvera was wrong. Dorothy never was much better than that for the rest of her life. Mama didn't inquire into Uncle Schumate's whereabouts; we thought we knew.

On the train ride home we were **seasoned** travelers, Mama and I. When the candy butcher hawked his wares through our car, we knew to turn our faces away from his prices. We crossed the Mississippi River on that terrible trestle, and after Edwardsville[31] the land settled into flat fields. Looking out, Mama said, "Corn's knee high by the Fourth of July," because she was thinking ahead to home. "I'll sleep good tonight without those streetcars clanging outside the window." **R**

But they still clanged in my mind, and "The Stars and Stripes Forever" blended with "Meet Me in St. Louis, Louis."

"But Mama, how can we just go home after all we've seen?" **17**

Thinking that over, she said, "You won't have to, you and the boys. It's your century. It can take you wherever you want to go." Then she reached over and put her hand on mine, a thing she rarely did. "I'll keep you back if I can. But I'll let you go if I must." **L**

That thrilled me, and scared me. The great world seemed to swing wide like the gates of the Fair, and I didn't even have a plan. I hadn't even put up my hair yet. It seemed to me it was time for that, time to jerk that big bow off the braid hanging down my back and put up my hair in a woman's way.

"Maybe in the fall," said Mama, who was turning into a mind reader as we steamed through the July fields, heading for home. ❍

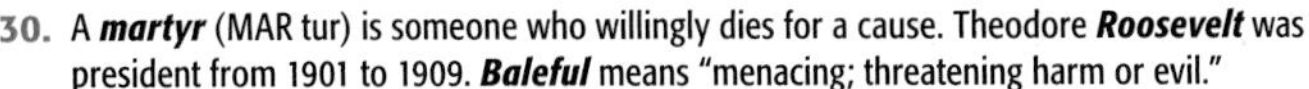

30. A ***martyr*** (MAR tur) is someone who willingly dies for a cause. Theodore ***Roosevelt*** was president from 1901 to 1909. ***Baleful*** means "menacing; threatening harm or evil."

31. ***Butcher*** is an old term for someone who sells ***(hawks)*** products ***(wares)***. ***Edwardsville,*** Illinois, is about 25 miles northeast of St. Louis.

Vocabulary

seasoned (SEE zund) *adj.* made fit by experience; adjusted to (something) because of experience

A daily guide helped visitors choose from among hundreds of exhibits and activities.

Practice the Skills

17 **BIG Question**

How has Geneva's idea of the American dream been affected by her visit to the fair? Write your answer on the "Electric Summer" page of Foldable 8. Your responses will help you complete the Unit Challenge later.

READING WORKSHOP 3

Teach

R Reading Skill

Identifying Main Idea and Supporting Details **Ask:** What is the main idea of the paragraph about the train ride home? *(Possible response: Mama and Geneva consider themselves "seasoned travelers" because they'd already ridden the train and had seen so many sights at the fair. However, home is still in their thoughts.)* **AS**

L Literary Element

Dialogue **Say:** Geneva asks, "But Mama, how can we just go home after all we've seen?" What does this indicate about Geneva? *(Possible response: She has been profoundly affected by her new and different experiences.)* **Ask:** What does Mama predict will happen? *(Possible response: Geneva will have the opportunity to move away from home and experience the world.)* **AS**

Assess

Use the CheckPoint questions provided on Presentation Plus! to check for comprehension of the selection. These questions can be used with interactive response keypads for immediate student feedback.

Differentiated Instruction

Time Lines To help students visualize the tremendous technological changes in the world during the twentieth century, ask them to research and locate the following events and inventions on a time line. Copy the list on the board without the years. **OL**

- first manned flight (1903)
- first jet planes (1930s)
- first TV transmission (1926)
- discovery of insulin (1921)
- development of penicillin (1940s)
- first people on the moon (1969)
- Panama Canal opens (1914)
- Ford Model T (1908)

Indiana English/Language Arts Academic Standards
SE: 8.2
TWE: *Literature Focus Lesson* 8.5.2, *Differentiated Instruction* 8.3.4

Assess

Resources for page 1126

- Selection Quick Check, p. 76
- Selection and Unit Assessment, p. 90
- ExamView Assessment Suite
- Interactive Tutor: Self-Assessment

Students can respond to the *After You Read* items in their Learner's Notebooks or on a separate sheet of paper.

Answering the BIG Question

1. Possible response: Technology gives people a chance to travel and learn more about the world.
2. ride the Ferris wheel
3. the floral clock

Critical Thinking

4. Possible response: I think the state is Illinois because Geneva and her mother cross the Mississippi River and then pass through Edwardsville, Illinois, to get back home from the fair, in Missouri.
5. Possible response: Now Geneva realizes how many new and different things are in the world and realizes how different her life will be from that of her parents.
6. Possible response: I think Mama wants Geneva to travel and learn about the world.

After You Read

The Electric Summer

Answering the BIG Question

1. How does technology fit into the American dream?
2. **Recall** What is the first thing that Geneva wants to do after she and Mama arrive on the fairgrounds?
   TIP Right There
3. **Recall** What is the exhibit that gives Geneva and Mama such joy on their second day at the fair?
   TIP Think and Search

Critical Thinking

4. **Draw Conclusions** Geneva lives on a farm, but the story doesn't say directly where the farm is located. Identify the state, and explain how you came to this conclusion.
   TIP Think and Search
5. **Evaluate** Before visiting the fair, Geneva got her ideas about the world mostly from what she had read. How does the fair change her?
   TIP Author and Me
6. **Infer** At the end of their visit, Mama tells Geneva that the century "can take you wherever you want to go." What do you think Mama wants for Geneva?
   TIP Author and Me

Write About Your Reading

Postcards Imagine that Geneva sent herself two postcards from the fair. (If she'd sent them to her dad and brothers, she probably would have been home before the mail arrived.) Describe the postcards you think she might have chosen, and write a brief message for each one. For each of the two postcards:

- Choose an image of something Geneva saw or did at the fair that she found especially enjoyable or impressive.
- Describe the image.
- Write the message. (Keep it to about 30 words.) Remember that you're pretending to be Geneva writing to herself. What would you say to remind yourself why you liked the thing pictured on the card?

Indiana English/Language Arts Academic Standards (pp. 1126–1127)

8.3 Comprehension and Analysis of Literary Text Respond to grade-level-appropriate literature... **8.5.7** Write for different purposes... **8.2 Comprehension and Analysis (Focus on Informational Text)** Develop [reading] strategies... **8.3.6** Identify significant literary devices, such as...dialect or quotations...**8.6 English Language Conventions**

For a complete description of the standards, see p. IN 11.

Write About Your Reading

Possible response:

(a postcard with a picture of the Ferris wheel)

The wheel took us higher than we've ever been. The wheel makes our wind pumps look short! I saw the whole fair from up there.

Skills Review

Key Reading Skill: Identifying Main Idea and Supporting Details

7. What is the main idea or message of this story?

8. It seems obvious that Geneva and Mama are not used to traveling by train. Note at least three details from the story that support this idea.

Literary Element: Dialogue

9. Choose two or more pieces of dialogue from the story that helped you understand Geneva's personality. Explain your choices.

10. How does the dialogue between Mama and Aunt Elvera show the differences in their personalities?

Reviewing Elements: Cultural Reference

11. Identify five cultural references in the story, with the page numbers where they're mentioned. List, for example, specific brand names or products, famous people, world events, or social movements that relate to the time of the story.

Vocabulary Check

Rewrite each sentence with the correct word.

novelty grandeur hovering
replica rapture seasoned

12. The ___ helicopter circled the air above the roof but didn't land.

13. The man couldn't resist buying a ___ of the Statue of Liberty in the gift shop.

14. Kria is a ___ soccer player. She's played in more than a hundred games this year.

15. Jesse was filled with ___ as he stood on the Olympic stand, a gold medal around his neck.

16. I enjoyed seeing Mount Rushmore, but I was more impressed by the ___ of South Dakota's Badlands.

17. That's a ___! I've never seen anything like it.

18. **English Language Coach** What does *Mississippi* mean in its original language?

Grammar Link: Capitalization of Sentences

You enter a house through a door. A capital letter is the door through which you enter a sentence. Always capitalize the first word of every sentence and the first word of every direct quotation.

- There were only four automobiles in the town.
- Looking out, Mama said, "Corn's knee high by the Fourth of July."

When a quoted sentence is interrupted by explanatory words, such as *he said,* do NOT begin the second part of the quotation with a capital letter.

- "I'd ride that thing again," she said, "if I could."

People often don't speak in complete sentences. Even if a quotation is just a single word or phrase, capitalize the first word.

- "That child!" Aunt Elvera said.

Grammar Practice

Rewrite the following paragraph, correcting the three capitalization errors.

"it will be a fun trip," Rena thought. her class was going to see an exhibit and eat at a French restaurant. "thanks," Rena told her teacher, "for planning this!"

Writing Application Review the postcards you wrote. Make sure you capitalized the first letter in each sentence and in any quotation.

Web Activities For eFlashcards, Selection Quick Checks, and other Web activities, go to www.glencoe.com.

Skills Review

Key Reading Skill: Identifying Main Idea and Supporting Details

7. Possible response: It is exciting to keep up with a changing world.

8. Responses could include that they thought the locomotive was too loud and quick, that they brought their own lunch rather than eating in the dining car, and that they didn't know the train had restrooms.

Literary Element: Dialogue

9. Responses will vary.

10. Possible response: Mama seems quiet, calm, and humble, while Aunt Elvera is hurried, forceful, and vain.

Reviewing Elements: Cultural References

11. Responses will vary.

Vocabulary Check

12. hovering

13. replica

14. seasoned

15. rapture

16. grandeur

17. novelty

English Language Coach

18. Possible response: The word is either an Objibwa (Chippewa) word for "great river" or "gathering of waters," or it is an Algonquin word for "big river."

Grammar Link: Capitalization of Sentences

Grammar Practice

"It will be a fun trip," Rena thought. Her class was going to see an exhibit and eat at a French restaurant. "Thanks," Rena told her teacher, "for planning this!"

Close

Ask students to summarize what they learned about the Big Question from this selection.

Indiana English/Language Arts Academic Standards

SE: 8.2, 8.3, 8.3.6, 8.5.7, 8.6

Focus

BELLRINGER Options

Daily Language Practice Transparency 78

Focus Activity Say: It's time to reread your letter. Is the language precise? Can readers follow your points? Is it clear how you think the sitcom addresses the American dream? *(Responses will vary.)* AS

Teach

W Writing Skill

Establish Topic and Purpose

Say: Read the first paragraph of your letter to make sure you identify yourself and clearly state your purpose. AS

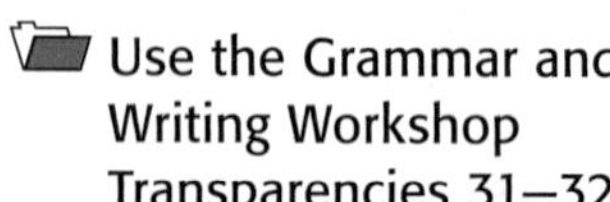

Resources for page 1128

- Use the Writing Workshop Graphic Organizer BLM in the Unit 8 Resource Booklet, p. 16–17
- Use the Grammar and Writing Workshop Transparencies 31–32.

WRITING WORKSHOP PART 2

Letter

Revising, Editing, and Presenting

ASSIGNMENT Write a letter

Purpose: To evaluate and respond to the media

Audience: A TV producer or head of a media company

Revising Rubric

Your revised letter should have

- a clear beginning, middle, and end
- a clearly-stated opinion supported by relevant details
- well-organized paragraphs
- correct forms of irregular verbs
- correct business letter presentation

See page 1130 for a model of a letter.

Indiana English/Language Arts Academic Standards (pp. 1128–1126)

8.5.7 Write for different purposes... **8.4.7** Review, evaluate, and revise writing for meaning and clarity. **8.4.8** Edit and proofread...writing... **8.4.9** Revise writing for...appropriate organization... **8.6.4** Edit written manuscripts to ensure that correct grammar is used.

For a complete description of the standards, see p. IN 11.

In Writing Workshop Part 1, you generated ideas for your letter and developed a first draft. In Part 2 you'll revise and edit your draft to make your letter even better. After you've finished your letter, you'll choose a method of publishing it. Remember to keep a copy in your writing portfolio so that you and your teacher can evaluate your writing progress over time.

Revising

Make It Better

Revising is all about improving your draft. But first you have to decide what improvements it needs. You must become your own editor, evaluating your writing and deciding what to fix.

Take a Fresh Look

As you read over the draft of your letter, ask yourself the questions below. You can either make changes now or write notes to yourself so you can go back and make the changes later.

- W Does the opening paragraph state your purpose for writing and your overall opinion?
- Does each paragraph in the body of your letter have a topic sentence that clearly states that paragraph's main idea?
- Does each paragraph in the body follow up the topic sentence with supporting details and specific examples from the show?
- Does your concluding paragraph provide closure by praising and/or criticizing the program and how it shows America and Americans? Do you offer suggestions to improve the show?
- Have you made your points clearly? You might want to swap letters with a partner to get a fresh perspective. Ask your partner if anything you wrote is confusing. Work together to phrase your comments in a way that's more understandable.
- Does your letter read smoothly? Read it out loud. If there are parts that you stumble over, find better ways to express them.

Additional Support

Reading Fluency

Build Fluency Invite students to build fluency by reading aloud their own letters. Advise them to find a quiet place to practice reading aloud. Have them read all the sentences and words with expression and understanding. Explain that this technique will also help them notice where they have left out words, used awkward expressions, or need to write another sentence or phrase to make their meaning clearer. AS

Editing

Finish It Up

Read the model on the next page. Look at the notes on the side to see how the writer revised and edited his letter about *The Simpsons*.

Then read your letter one sentence at a time and use the **Editing Checklist** below to help you spot errors. Use the proofreading symbols in the chart on page R19 to mark needed corrections.

W

If you're using a word processing program, you can use the grammar and spell-checking features to catch some kinds of mistakes. However, remember that a computer's spell-checker can't tell the difference between a misspelled word and its homophone. For example, if you meant to type "their" but accidentally typed "there," the computer won't alert you.

Editing Checklist

- ☑ Your letter is free of sentence fragments and run-on sentences.
- ☑ Verbs and subjects agree and all tenses are correct. You've used irregular verbs correctly.
- ☑ You've correctly spelled words that are easily confused, including homophones.
- ☑ You've used the proper letter format. You've correctly capitalized and punctuated direct quotations and the names of TV programs.

Revising Tip

Using Technology If you're writing on a computer, save your draft and make your revisions in a new file copy. By saving the original, you're free to experiment and make mistakes. If necessary, you can open up your original draft and try again.

Writing Models For models and other writing activities, go to www.glencoe.com.

Publishing

Show It Off

After you've made your final revisions and corrections, make a final copy of your letter. If your letter is written by hand, it must be neat and legible. Ask someone else to make sure your handwriting can be read.

Then figure out who should receive your letter and get it ready to send! To do that, be sure you have everything in the right format for a business letter. (Follow the guidelines on page 1131 and see page R25 of the Writing Handbook for extra help.)

The best place to send the letter is in care of ("c/o") the company that distributes the program or the TV network or local station that broadcasts it. Most TV and radio stations have Web sites that give their mailing addresses.

Revising Tip

Choosing Your Audience You could send your letter to the show's creator, director, producer, or writer. You could also write to the head of the network that runs the show or to the show's sponsors.

WRITING WORKSHOP PART 2

Teach

W Writing Skills

Grammar, Usage, and Mechanics Explain to students that business and formal writing needs to be free from mistakes in order to look professional. If a letter is filled with spelling or other errors, the validity and importance of the correspondence is questioned. Have students look over the editing checklist again. Tell students they should read through their letters several times, looking for one kind of error during each read. Allow students time to complete the editing process. **AS**

Literature Online

Writing Models Have students access the Web site for an additional and interactive Writing Workshop–based student model.

English Language Coach

Transitions Tell English learners that transitional words and phrases help define the relationships between events and ideas. The transitional words and phrases students use will depend on the organization of their letters. For example, if students are demonstrating cause-and-effect relationships, they will use words like *because, since, so, therefore,* and *why.* If they are describing a narrative in chronological order, they will use words like *first, next, last, then, after, before,* and so on. Have students review their letters for transitional words. **EL BL**

Indiana English/Language Arts Academic Standards

SE: 8.4.7, 8.4.8, 8.4.9, 8.5.7, 8.6.4

TWE: *Reading Fluency* 8.7.2; *English Language Coach* 8.4.9, 8.4.10

Teach

W Writing Skill

Paragraphs with Topic Sentences and Supporting Details **Say:** Reread paragraph 4 in the student model. What is the topic sentence? *(Finally,* The Simpsons *shows good things about Americans too.)* **Ask:** What details support the topic sentence? *(Possible responses: Homer and Marge are a loving couple; Lisa is the voice of reason; Bart is a creative problem solver; the community takes on tough problems; and people do their best to cope with a lot of change.)* OL

L Literary Element

Style **Say:** Transitional words help the reader follow your ideas from one sentence to the next or from one paragraph to the next. Which transitional words help the reader follow the writer's thoughts in this letter? *(First, Second, Finally, However)* **Say:** Check your own letter to see if you used transitional words between paragraphs. If not, add them to your letter to help make smooth transitions and connect important ideas. OL

Active Writing Model

Writer's Model

Dear Mr. Groening:

I am in eighth grade. My English class is evaluating how TV shows portray America. In my opinion, The Simpsons shows both the good and the bad.

The introduction states the writer's purpose and his opinion.

First, the mix of characters is fairly true to life. The show revolves around a white family, but there are also African Americans (Carl and Dr. Hibbert) and immigrants (Apu and his family). Every community contains people like Police Chief Wiggum, Mayor Joe Quimby, Moe, Marge's sisters, Principal Skinner, and even greedy power-plant owner Mr. Burns.

The writer's first reason for his opinion is stated in the topic sentence. He follows up with specific details from the show to support the topic sentence. Notice how paragraphs 2–5 all follow this pattern.

Second, like many American communities today, Springfield faces a range of problems, including natural disasters (Mt. Springfield erupts), corruption (the mayor takes bribes), and schoolyard bullies.

Finally, The Simpsons shows good things about Americans too. Homer and Marge are a loving couple with a lasting marriage. Lisa is the voice of reason. Even Bart is a creative problem solver. The community takes on tough problems. The Simpsons' America is going through a lot of change, but people do their best to cope with it.

However, I have one complaint. My classmates and I agree that you don't always show both sides of an issue. Sometimes you leave out the way we feel.

The writer expresses disagreement with the way the program shows the American dream.

My classmate Ken Aya, age 14, said, "I didn't like the episode that made Milhouse's dad and all the other divorced dads in his building look so pathetic. Many divorced men cope just fine. My dad lives in an apartment building, but he's not a loser."

Thanks, Mr. Groening, for making us laugh at ourselves while encouraging us to solve our problems. But please, don't always poke fun at the characters who share my outlook on life.

The writer closes by summarizing his message in the final paragraph. He thanks the show's creator but advises him on how to fix the show's flaw.

Additional Support

Differentiated Instruction

Closing Techniques Copy the chart below on the board. Discuss each closing technique and the example that goes with it. Ask students to use the chart to write three possible closings for their letters, one for each of the three techniques.

Closing Techniques

Technique	Example
End with a suggestion	I suggest you take on the issue of global warming next.
End with a question	What advice do you have for kids who are interested in a career in writing for television?
End with a powerful image	*The Simpsons* is one of the greatest achievements of today's culture.

Applying Good Writing Traits

Presentation

What Is Presentation?

A piece of writing is presented well if it's pleasing to the eye and easy to read. Its form should be right for the assignment.

Why Is Presentation Important?

No matter how hard you've worked on what you have to say, your letter will have little effect if it doesn't look good.

How Do I Use Presentation in My Writing?

Make sure your letter has the right format (the parts it contains and how they're laid out on the page). Business letters contain these elements: W

- **Heading and date:** your address and the date

  Raphael Thompson
  136 Matthews Street
  Binghamton, New York 13905
  March 30, 2007

- **Inside address:** the name and address of the person to whom you're writing (Note that this example is addressed "in care of" the local Fox TV station.)

  Mr. Matt Groening
  Creator of The Simpsons
  c/o FOX 40 WICZ-TV
  BINGHAMTON
  4600 Vestal Parkway East
  Vestal, NY 13850

- **Greeting or salutation:** begins with "Dear," then the name of the person to whom you are writing, followed by a colon

  Dear Mr. Groening:

- **Body of the letter:** all of the text (In the student model, the body is six paragraphs.)
- **Complimentary close:** "Sincerely," "Yours truly," or a similar closing, followed by a comma

  Yours truly,

- **Signature:** your signed name, followed by your name either typed or block-printed

Present Your Letter Add a copy of your letter to a binder for a class book. Give the book a title, such as *As Seen on TV: The American Dream.* Set up a book party to discuss the shows you and your classmates wrote about. To spark the conversation, read some of the letters.

Analyzing Cartoons
Jeremy's presentation of his skills probably won't lead to a job. What kind of business card would you design for yourself?

Teach

W Writing Skill

Presentation Say: One of the benefits of writing a letter on a computer is that you can choose your own font, or typeface. There are many different typefaces. Some are fancy and some are plain. You can give your letter a distinctive look when you choose your own font. On the other hand, if you choose a very fancy font, it can take your reader's attention away from what you are saying. The best choice is a font that is easy to read and not distracting. Look at the choice of fonts on a school or home computer. Try out different fonts for your letter. Consider how the presentation of your letter changes with each font. AS

Assess

Have students trade letters with a partner and give constructive feedback on how to improve the presentation of their letters.

Reading in the Real World

Citizenship Evaluating and responding to the media is an important role for citizens in a democracy. Discuss other aspects of the media and how they portray the American dream. For example, how is the American dream portrayed in ads and commercials? In music videos? In video games? On the nightly news? Hold an "Evaluate and Respond to the Media Day" in your classroom. Invite students to participate in a discussion. Have them discuss why evaluating and responding to the media is an important part of responsible citizenship. AS

Indiana English/Language Arts Academic Standards
SE: 8.4.9, 8.6.4
TWE: *Differentiated Instruction* 8.4, *Reading in the Real World* 8.7.13

Identifying Author's Purpose

Teaching Students to Identify Author's Purpose

Why Is It Important?

- Students will learn that an author's purpose for writing is affected by his or her perspective and experience.
- An author's purpose is not always clearly stated; identifying it will help students understand the point of the selection.
- Identifying an author's purpose will help students understand how the writer wants them to respond after they read the selection.

How to Help Students Get It

- Remind students that an author's purpose is his or her reason for writing about a topic.
- Tell students that they can look for clues in the text, such as the author's word choices and how he or she organized the writing, to help them identify the author's purpose.
- Students may also benefit from rereading the author's background to get a better sense of his or her purpose.

Reading to Answer the Big Question

I, Too, Sing America by Langston Hughes
Hughes uses the dinner table as a metaphor for the American dream and the bounty it promises. In this poem, the speaker promises that someday, he too will take a place at the table, unquestioned, and recognized as beautiful.

from *Dandelion Wine* by Ray Bradbury
When is the last time you wore a brand new pair of sneakers? Douglas knows that summer lives inside sneakers, and he's willing to work hard to get the ones he wants. The shoe-store owner accepts Douglas's offer to work off his debt for the shoes and is reminded of the limitless potential of a young nation, a young boy, or even a new pair of sneakers.

Workshop Resources

Pacing (Days) Standard	Block	Lesson	Student Materials	Teacher Resources
1	2	Key Skill Lesson: Identifying Author's Purpose	Key Reading Skills Practice, p. 31 English Language Coach Review, p. 44	Bellringer Options Transparencies –Daily Language Practice 79 Read Aloud, Think Aloud Transparencies –Key Reading Skills 10 Presentation Plus!
2		"I, Too, Sing America"	Glencoe Online Unit Vocabulary Review, p. 42 Academic Vocabulary Review, p. 45 English Language Coach Active Reading Graphic Organizer, p. 33 StudentWorks Plus™ Online Student Edition Literature Classics Selection and Unit Assessments, p. 91	Literary and Text Analysis Transparencies 46 Puzzlemaker Skill Level Up!™ A Language Arts Game BookLink 3 Assessment by Learning Objective (Diagnostic and Formative) Interactive Tutor: Self-Assessment TeacherWorks Plus™
2		from *Dandelion Wine*	Glencoe Online Unit Vocabulary Review, p. 42 Academic Vocabulary Review, p. 45 English Language Coach Active Reading Graphic Organizer, p. 35 StudentWorks Plus™ Online Student Edition Literature Classics Selection and Unit Assessments, p. 92	Read Aloud, Think Aloud Transparencies –Read Aloud, Think Aloud 70–78 Literary and Text Analysis Transparencies 23 Puzzlemaker Skill Level Up!™ A Language Arts Game BookLink 3 Assessment by Learning Objective (Diagnostic and Formative) Interactive Tutor: Self-Assessment TeacherWorks Plus™

Keys for Unit Resource

- Blackline Master
- Workbook
- Supplemental Text
- CD-ROM
- DVD
- Transparency
- Web-based
- Fast File

Level Appropriate Code

AS = Activities for all students
AL = Activities for students working above grade level
OL = Activities for students working at grade level
BL = Activities for students working below grade level
EL = Activities for English language learners

Focus

BELLRINGER Options

Daily Language Practice Transparency 79

Focus Activity Say: Have you ever announced a goal or a dream, only to have people laugh as if it were impossible? How did you feel? *(Possible responses: embarrassed, angry, upset)* AS

Teach

R Reading Skill

Identifying Author's Purpose Say: Reread the list of reasons authors write. What is the purpose of a newspaper editorial? *(to persuade)* OL

Analyzing the Cartoon

Ask: What does the light bulb symbolize? *(a bright idea)*
Ask: Why does the character hold the light bulb above her head? *(to get a bright idea about* Macbeth*)* AS

READING WORKSHOP 4

Skills Focus

You will practice using these skills when you read the following selections:

- "I, Too" p. 1136
- from *Dandelion Wine,* p. 1142

Reading

- Identifying author's purpose

Literature

- Identifying and understanding metaphor
- Recognizing hyperbole

Vocabulary

- Learning about English as a changing language

Writing/Grammar

- Understanding and using verbals
- Spelling and using homophones correctly

Indiana English/Language Arts Academic Standards (pp. 1132–1133)

8.2 Comprehension and Analysis (Focus on Informational Text) Develop [reading] strategies...identifying and analyzing... purpose.

For a complete description of the standards, see p. IN 11.

Skill Lesson

Identifying Author's Purpose

Learn It!

What Is It? Whether it's a novel or a poem, a newspaper article or a play, a cartoon or an ad, everything you read was written for a reason. Every author has some purpose in mind when he or she sits down to write. The most common purposes are

R
- to entertain
- to describe
- to inform or explain
- to persuade
- a combination of the above

Analyzing Cartoons
Paige needs a bright idea. A larger bulb *might* help, but it might be more helpful for her to think about her purpose. What do you think is her purpose for writing the essay?

Additional Support

Differentiated Instruction

Building Background William Shakespeare was an English playwright and poet born in 1564. *Macbeth* is a tragedy, or a story about the main character's downfall because of his or her weaknesses. Reading Shakespeare can be difficult. Some people have trouble understanding the Elizabethan English of his time. Instruct students to search the Internet or the library for a sample of Shakespeare's writing. Have them work with a partner to paraphrase the chosen sample in modern English and then share both the original version and the paraphrase with the rest of the class. EL BL OL

Why Is It Important? You read many different types of text each day. In the morning you read about prehistoric animals in your science book. Later you study a story for English. In the afternoon you do research on the Web. At home you check the directions before you microwave a snack. Before bed there's the newspaper sports section. Knowing why the authors wrote these texts can help you understand and evaluate what they say. R

Study Central Visit www.glencoe.com and click on Study Central to review evaluating.

How Do I Do It? Use these tips to help you identify an author's purpose.

- Consider the audience for whom a work is intended. Persuasive writing has a different target audience than poetry. Many nonfiction works are intended for experts, not casual readers.
- Examine the author's word choices. All writers select words for their suggested meanings as well as for their definitions. But a poet might want to suggest ideas indirectly while an editorial writer tries to be specific.
- Look at the text structure. Fiction is likely to be organized in time order, and cooking and assembly instructions had better be chronological. Other nonfiction is often organized as problem-solution or cause-effect. E

Here's how one student identified the author's purpose while reading the short story "The Electric Summer":

I think Mr. Peck was writing to entertain and inform. I think he wants people to see that it was exciting to live in the early 1900s. There were new things like electricity and cars and indoor plumbing. That's kind of a funny list, but only because we're so used to those things today.

Mr. Peck had a third purpose too, I think, and that was to say to keep your mind open to new ideas and experiences.

Practice It!

Look over the titles of the selections you read in Units 6 and 7. Choose five selections and, in your Learner's Notebook, briefly note what you think was the author's main purpose in each selection.

Use It!

As you read, look in the text for clues about the author's purpose. Then decide whether the author did a good job and achieved that purpose.

Teach

R Reading Skill

Identifying Author's Purpose

Ask: How can identifying the author's purpose help readers? *(It helps them understand and evaluate what they read.)* **Ask:** Do you think an author is more likely to have one purpose or multiple purposes for writing? *(Possible response: It depends on what the author is writing; a news article might be to inform and persuade, but a short story might be to entertain.)* AS

E Text Element

Review Chronological Order

Ask: Why is it important for cooking directions to be in chronological order? *(Possible response: If you don't add and prepare ingredients in the correct order, the dish you're preparing won't turn out properly.)* AS

Resources for page 1133

- Use Key Reading Skills Transparency 10 in *Read Aloud, Think Aloud* to help students practice identifying author's purpose.

Literature Focus Lesson

Identifying Author's Purpose Write the checklist below on the board. Point out that a checklist can help students identify the author's purpose.

- Are the characters in the story real people or make-believe?
- Does the writing contain facts?
- Do you find yourself reading it because it's fun?
- Do you learn how to do something from reading?
- Do you have a better understanding of a topic after reading?
- Have your feelings about a topic changed? BL

Indiana English/Language Arts Academic Standards

SE: 8.2

TWE: *Differentiated Instruction* 8.2, *Literature Focus Lesson* 8.2

Teach

More About the Author

To support his country during World War II, Langston Hughes wrote weekly columns in *The Chicago Defender.* He encouraged people to buy war bonds and support the Allied soldiers. A character he invented, Jesse B. Semple (later known as just *Simple*) urged African Americans to support the military, even though many resented its practice of segregation. Simple became a popular fictional character. Later, many of the Simple stories were collected into a book titled *Simple Speaks His Mind.*

E Text Element

Review Chronological Order **Ask:** Which was spoken first in England—a Germanic language or a Latin language? *(Germanic)* When was Old French introduced to the British Isles? *(1066)* AS

Before You Read I, Too

Meet the Author

Langston Hughes was one of the first African American writers to make a living as a writer and public speaker. He once said he wrote about people who are "up today and down tomorrow, working this week and fired the next, beaten and baffled, but determined not to be wholly beaten." See page R3 of the Author Files for more on Hughes.

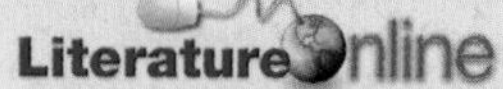

Author Search For more about Langston Hughes, go to www.glencoe.com.

Indiana English/Language Arts Academic Standards (pp. 1134–1137)

8.1.2 Understand the influence of historical events on English word meaning and vocabulary expansion. **8.2 Comprehension and Analysis (Focus on Informational Text)** Develop [reading] strategies...identifying and analyzing...purpose. **8.3.6** Identify significant literary devices, such as metaphor...

For a complete description of the standards, see p. IN 11.

Vocabulary Preview

English Language Coach

English as a Changing Language So what is all this stuff about "Old English" and "Middle French" and "Old High German"? It has to do with etymology (et uh MOL uh jee), the study of the origins and histories of languages. Each language has its own history, of course. Most grew out of another, older language. Some borrow from one another.

E Old English was a Germanic language, meaning it grew out of an early form of German. Then, in 1066, the Normans came over from the north of France and conquered England. The Normans spoke Old French, which was a Latin language (coming out of ancient Italy). With the Normans governing, the English adopted many French words relating to law and government. In most matters relating to daily life, however, people stuck to the language they knew. So, modern English is really the offspring of Old German crossed with Old French.

The neat thing about etymology is that it shows that bits and pieces of old languages survive in modern-day English. To see them, you need to be a detective, looking for and understanding root words and their origins and meanings.

Look at the example below. You'll see this word in the selection "I, Too."

Brackets contain information about a word's etymology.

Scholars sometimes have to make educated guesses about the origins of a word.

kitchen *n.* a room or an area equipped for preparing and cooking food [Middle English *kichene,* from Old English *cycene,* probably from Vulgar Latin *cocina,* from Late Latin *coquinus,* "of cooking," from *coquus,* "cook," from *coquere,* "to cook"]

Etymology usually begins with the most recent historical influence, and traces the word back in time to its earliest roots.

Scholars have given these names to different periods in time. Vulgar Latin refers to Latin the way it was spoken by ordinary people (as opposed to the "high" language of priests and kings).

Additional Support

Author Search To expand students' appreciation of Langston Hughes, have them access the Web site for additional information and resources.

Differentiated Instruction

Visualizing Theme Images often help readers understand ideas and themes in literature. For some learners, art provides the extra hint they need to understand the message a poet or author is trying to convey. Have students make a piece of art expressing their idea of the American dream. Prompt them to think about their dreams for the future or their idea of what the American dream is. The art can be in color or black and white; students should title their works and share them with the class. AS

Skills Preview

Key Reading Skill: Identifying Author's Purpose

You're about to read a poem by Langston Hughes. Poetry is a very focused kind of writing. A poem is intended to make you feel a certain feeling or think about a certain idea. "I, Too" is very brief and seemingly simple, but Hughes packs a lot into it.

As you read, think about who the speaker—the "I" of the poem's title—might be. Also, look closely at Hughes's word choices. Because most poems are short, poets are very careful to use words that mean and suggest exactly the right things. Finally, to help you understand what Hughes was writing about, recall what you know about him and the times he lived in.

Write to Learn Find out what you can about the "Harlem Renaissance." In your Learner's Notebook, make notes to answer the five basic questions—who, what, when, where, and why.

Key Literary Element: Metaphor

A metaphor is a figure of speech that compares seemingly unlike things without using words such as *like* and *as*. Here's an example that makes two comparisons: "When I first arrived in the city, I was a mouse in a maze." The writer or speaker is compared to a mouse and the city to a maze.

An **extended metaphor** is continued over a passage. In a poem, it might run throughout the entire piece. In a story or essay, it might run a few paragraphs or, in a short work, throughout the whole piece.

Hughes uses an extended metaphor in "I, Too" that's implied. In the earlier example, the comparison is directly stated: "I was a mouse." In "I, Too," the speaker mentions the "kitchen" and a "table" but leaves it to the reader to decide what they represent.

Class Discussion Hughes's poem "Mother to Son" (page 472) also uses an extended metaphor. Reread the poem and talk about the crystal staircase.

Get Ready to Read

Connect to the Reading

Imagine that, because of your hair color, you aren't allowed to eat in a certain restaurant. Or imagine that you're required to sit in the back corner of the theater because you're left-handed. Imagine that you're told to leave the room whenever visitors come.

Write to Learn Write a paragraph describing your feelings when you've been treated unfairly for reasons that you couldn't control or that made no sense.

Build Background

R

- In 1855 American poet Walt Whitman published a poem called "I Hear America Singing."
- In the 1920s Hughes wrote "I, Too." It includes lines that echo Whitman's. The United States was still a segregated nation in which African Americans and other minorities were treated unjustly.
- Poets express their own ideas and feelings in a poem, but readers should not assume that a poem's speaker is the poet. Think of the speaker as a poem's narrator or as a character.

Set Purposes for Reading

Read "I, Too" to see how someone who feels left out views the American dream.

L **Set Your Own Purpose** What would you like to learn from the selection to help you answer the Big Question? Write your purpose on the "I, Too" page of Foldable 8.

Literature Online

Interactive Literary Elements Handbook To review or learn more about the literary elements, go to www.glencoe.com.

Keep Moving

Use these skills as you read the following selection.

READING WORKSHOP 4

Teach

L Literary Element

Metaphor **Ask:** What do you think these metaphors describe? Max was a prince among thieves. *(Max kept bad company; he was a good guy compared to his friends.)* Her insults were water off a duck's back. *(Her insults were ignored or not very effective.)* OL

R Reading Skill

Identifying Author's Purpose **Ask:** From the information in Build Background, what do you think Hughes' purpose might be for writing "I, Too"? *(Possible response: to inform or persuade that minorities are Americans, too, and deserve equal rights)* AL

Literature Online

Interactive Literary Elements Handbook Have students access the Web site to improve their understanding of metaphor.

Literature Focus Lesson

Metaphor Present the students with a collection of photographs (all face down). Choose interesting images that allow for an underlying story (they could be mysterious, funny, or bizarre). Allow each student to pick one photograph and write a metaphor describing the situation in the image. OL

Have students write a brief summary or a poem (with at least two metaphors) of what they think is happening in the image. AL

Indiana English/Language Arts Academic Standards
SE: 8.1.2, 8.2, 8.3.6
TWE: *Differentiated Instruction* 8.3.5, *Literature Focus Lesson* 8.5.7

Teach

Viewing the Art

Say: This painting is a self-portrait, titled *Self Portrait.* Look at the background, the brushstrokes, colors, and expression on the artist's face. If you could give the painting a new title, what would it be? *(Responses will vary.)* **AS**

BIG Question

Ask: If you were going to make a painting titled *The American Dream,* what would you paint? *(Responses will vary.)* **AS**

L Literary Element

Metaphor Say: Create a metaphor comparing paintings and poems. *(Possible responses: Her poem was a painting made of words; a painting is a visual poem.)* **AL**

I, Too

by Langston Hughes

Additional Support

Differentiated Instruction

Poetry Comparison Group Work
Make copies of Walt Whitman's "I Hear America Singing," and distribute the poem to students. Have them work in groups to determine why they think Langston Hughes may have written "I, Too" as a response to Whitman's "I Hear America Singing." Instruct students to make comparisons and to examine why Hughes may have felt the need to respond to the poem with one of his own. Instruct them to consider the title, voice, theme, details, and especially author's purpose in each poem. Have each group present their findings to the class. **OL**

READING WORKSHOP 4

I, too, sing America.

I am the darker brother. **1**
They send me to eat in the kitchen
When company comes,
But I laugh,
And eat well,
And grow strong.

Tomorrow,
I'll be at the table
When company comes.
Nobody'll dare
Say to me,
"Eat in the kitchen,"
Then. **2**

Besides,
They'll see how beautiful I am
And be ashamed—

I, too, am America. **3**

Self Portrait, 1934. Malvin Gray Johnson. Smithsonian American Art Museum, Washington, D.C.

Practice the Skills

1 Key Literary Element

Metaphor The extended metaphor begins almost immediately. Who is the speaker?

2 Key Reading Skill

Identifying Author's Purpose What do you think Hughes wants his readers to understand? R1

3 BIG Question

What is the American dream to the speaker? Write your answer on the "I, Too" page of Foldable 8. Your response will help you complete the Unit Challenge later.

Reading Fluency

Build Fluency Read the poem aloud for students to hear it fluently. Have students work with partners to read the poem aloud. One student should read the first stanza and the partner should echo. Students should finish reading the poem in this manner and then reread it, switching roles so the first student echoes. Ask them to continue reading the poem aloud until they can read with fluency, expression, and comprehension. **EL BL**

Teach

R1 Reading Skill

Identifying Author's Purpose **Ask:** How does the poet view the future? *(Possible response: He believes African Americans will be treated equally.)* **OL**

R2 Reading Skill

Review Understanding Cause and Effect **Ask:** According to the speaker, what will cause people to be ashamed? *(Possible response: recognizing the beauty, or worth, of African Americans in contrast to the previous treatment of them)* **OL**

L Literary Element

Metaphor **Say:** Identify the metaphor in the last line of the poem. *(The speaker identifies himself as America.)* **AS** **Ask:** What does this metaphor mean? *(Possible response: The speaker feels that he is just as important as any other citizen, despite color differences.)* **AL**

Assess

Use the CheckPoint questions provided on Presentation Plus! to check for comprehension of the selection. These questions can be used with interactive response keypads for immediate student feedback.

Indiana English/Language Arts Academic Standards
SE: 8.2, 8.3.6
TWE: *Differentiated Instruction* 8.7.11, *Reading Fluency* 8.7.14

Assess

Resources for page 1138

- Selection Quick Check, p.77
- Selection and Unit Assessment, p. 91
- ExamView Assessment Suite
- Interactive Tutor: Self-Assessment

Students can respond to the *After You Read* items in their Learner's Notebooks or on a separate sheet of paper.

Answering the BIG Question

1. Possible response: Sometimes people have to work hard and wait a long time before their American dream comes true.
2. The speaker is treated as an outcast and inferior.
3. The speaker is determined to become strong.
4. Possible response: The speaker plans to dine with the guests.

Critical Thinking

5. Possible response: "Darker brother" refers to Americans of color. "They" are white Americans who denied people of color equal rights.
6. Possible response: equality
7. Possible response: The speaker reminds the reader that the speaker is, in every way, an equal citizen of the United States.

After You Read

I, Too

Answering the BIG Question

1. After reading "I, Too," what are your thoughts about the American dream? What are some of the restrictions people face in trying to achieve it?
2. **Recall** How is the speaker of the poem treated?
   TIP **Right There**
3. **Recall** How does the speaker respond to this treatment?
   TIP **Right There**
4. **Summarize** In one sentence, summarize what the speaker plans to do the next time there are guests.
   TIP **Right There**

Critical Thinking

5. **Interpret** How do you interpret "darker brother" (line 2) and "They" (line 3)? Who are they? What is their relationship? Explain.
   TIP **Author and Me**
6. **Analyze** What satisfaction does the speaker look forward to having "tomorrow"?
   TIP **Think and Search**
7. **Interpret** What does the speaker mean when he says, "I, too, sing America"? What does he mean by saying, "I, too, am America"? Why might he feel the need to say these things?
   TIP **Author and Me**

Talk About Your Reading

Discussion "You are what you eat," according to an old saying. It means that what you eat says things about you as a person. Change that saying to "You are *where* you eat," and discuss these questions:

- Each room in a home has one main purpose, even though it is likely used for many purposes. What is the difference between eating in a kitchen and eating in a dining room? How would you describe the sort of occasion when a meal is traditionally eaten in the dining room? What might it suggest when a meal is eaten in front of the living room TV? How does the event (not the food) of a restaurant meal differ from eating at home?

Now discuss this variation of the saying: "You are who you eat with."

Indiana English/Language Arts Academic Standards (pp. 1138–1139)

8.3 Comprehension and Analysis of Literary Text Respond to grade-level-appropriate literature... **8.7 Listening and Speaking** Speaking skills...are developed... **8.2 Comprehension and Analysis (Focus on Informational Text)** Develop [reading] strategies... identifying and analyzing...purpose. **8.3.6** Identify significant literary devices, such as metaphor...**8.6 English Language Conventions 8.6.8** Identify and use infinitives... and participles...

For a complete description of the standards, see p. IN 11.

Talk About Your Reading

Possible points of discussion could include the following:

- Dining rooms are used for special meals, including those to which guests are invited. Many families eat everyday meals in the kitchen. Meals eaten in front of the TV are casual, perhaps with only a few family members present.
- Fast food meals are often eaten by families "on the go." They aren't seen as "special" by most people, unlike "sit-down" restaurant meals, which are often reserved for special occasions.
- Who you eat with reflects the company you keep, and maybe even your status, or class.

Skills Review

Key Reading Skill: Identifying Author's Purpose

8. Why do you think Hughes chose *beautiful* for line 17? How would the meaning of this stanza (or the poem) be different if he had used another word, such as *powerful, angry,* or *happy*?

9. Walt Whitman's poem "I Hear America Singing" celebrates the courage, "stick-to-it" attitude, and unity of Americans. "I, Too" is a response to Whitman's work. What is that response? Does Hughes disagree about the qualities Americans possess? Is he adding something that Whitman might have overlooked? If so, what?

10. Do you think that, in this poem, Hughes is hopeful about the future? Explain.

Key Literary Element: Metaphor

11. Look at the word *brother* in line 2.

If it is used to mean "a male born of the same parents as another child," how does this word fit the metaphor? Who would be the speaker's other family members?

If it is used to mean "one who shares the same racial origin," would your interpretation of the metaphor change?

Which meaning of *brother* do you think makes the most sense, and why?

12. The table of line 9 is apparently in the dining room. Interpreting the metaphor, what might each of the two rooms–kitchen and dining room–represent?

13. Explain how the poem's extended metaphor shows the speaker's feelings about being an outsider in the house where he lives.

Vocabulary Check

14. English Language Coach The word *company* came from the Latin *com-* ("with; together") and *panis* ("bread; food"). Explain how these meanings make sense with the modern definition: "guests; visitors."

Grammar Link: Verbals

A verbal is a verb form that functions in a sentence as a noun, an adjective, or an adverb. There are three kinds of verbals: participles, gerunds, and infinitives.

A **participle** is a verb form that functions as an adjective. You form a present participle by adding *-ing* to a verb. You usually form a past participle by adding *-ed.*

- The soaring biplane flew 120 feet.
- The awed spectators watched in amazement.

A **gerund** is a verb form ending in *-ing* that is used as a noun. It can be used as the subject or the direct object of a sentence.

- Moving involves a lot of work. (subject)
- People enjoy traveling. (direct object)

An **infinitive** is made up of the word *to* and the base form of a verb. It may function as a noun and can be used as the subject or the direct object of a sentence.

- To skate is my ideal winter pastime. (subject)
- Many children like to skate. (direct object)

Grammar Practice

Copy each of the following sentences and underline the verbals. (There is only one verbal in each sentence.)

15. The girls gathered all the used containers and put them in the trash.

16. "Going home ten minutes ago will not be soon enough," the woman joked.

17. The cheering crowd rooted for the home team.

18. Drying the dishes became a sort of game.

19. To finish that novel will be an achievement.

Web Activities For eFlashcards, Selection Quick Checks, and other Web activities, go to www.glencoe.com.

Skills Review

Key Reading Skill: Identifying Author's Purpose

8. Responses will vary.

9. Responses will vary.

10. Responses will vary.

Key Literary Element: Metaphor

11. The "darker brother" fits into the metaphor of the "family" of America "dining" at the "table" of equality and opportunity.

12. Possible response: The kitchen represents the minimum amount of respect and rights, while the dining room represents full, equal rights and opportunity.

13. Possible response: The speaker is insulted that he's not accepted in all parts of the home, just as African Americans resented not being allowed to use the same facilities as white people, for example.

Vocabulary Check

English Language Coach

14. Possible response: It's common for people to serve food when guests visit.

Close

Encourage students to discuss how sometimes the American dream can be flawed.

Grammar Link: Verbals

Grammar Practice

15. The girls gathered all the used containers and put them in the trash.

16. "Going home ten minutes ago will not be soon enough," the woman joked.

17. The cheering crowd rooted for the home team.

18. Drying the dishes became a sort of game.

19. To finish that novel will be an achievement.

Indiana English/Language Arts Academic Standards

SE: 8.2, 8.3, 8.3.6, 8.6, 8.6.8, 8.7

READING WORKSHOP 4

Teach

More About the Author

Novelist, short story writer, playwright, poet, screenwriter, and essayist, Ray Bradbury sold newspapers on street corners to support himself while he spent his days at the typewriter and his nights at the public library. On his eightieth birthday, Bradbury commented, "The great fun in my life has been getting up every morning and rushing to the typewriter because some new idea has hit me. The feeling I have every day is very much the same as it was when I was twelve."

EL Language Coach

Etymology Say: Read all of the definitions you found for *pore* and *porous*. Which definitions relate best to "journey", the meaning of *poros*? *(Responses should include "passage" or "the ability to pass through.")* Remind students that the words may not have exactly the same meanings but should suggest similar ideas. Tell them to practice studying words with similar parts and their etymology to see how they relate. EL OL

Before You Read from *Dandelion Wine*

Ray Bradbury

Meet the Author

Ray Bradbury was born in 1920 in Waukegan, Illinois, where he discovered the pleasure of reading comic strips and science fiction. As an adult, he often wrote from the point of view of a kid growing up in small-town America. He has said, "It is nice to be in the twenty-first century. It is like a new challenge. It is really a good and threatening new century to create for!" See page R1 of the Author Files for more on Bradbury.

Author Search For more about Ray Bradbury, go to www.glencoe.com.

Indiana English/Language Arts Academic Standards (pp. 1140–1149)

8.1.2 Understand the influence of historical events on English word meaning and vocabulary expansion. **8.2 Comprehension and Analysis (Focus on Informational Text)** Develop [reading] strategies...identifying and analyzing...purpose. **8.3.6** Identify significant literary devices...

For a complete description of the standards, see p. IN 11.

Vocabulary Preview

capsize (KAP syz) *v.* to overturn or upset (especially a boat) **(p. 1142)** *He felt as if the whole place would capsize and sink beneath the ground.*

proprietor (pruh PRY uh tur) *n.* a person or firm that owns a property or a business **(p. 1145)** *The proprietor took pride in his shoe displays.*

rave (rayv) *v.* to speak about very favorably or with great enthusiasm **(p. 1146)** *How can you rave about a shoe you've never worn?*

alien (AY lee un) *adj.* strange; odd; peculiar **(p. 1147)** *The tennis shoes looked alien beneath the man's business suit.*

yielding (YEEL ding) *adj.* giving way to force or pressure **(p. 1148)** *The carpet was soft and yielding, like freshly turned soil.*

Write to Learn High-tops! Sandals! Loafers! Flip-flops! Why do some people have such strong feelings about footwear? What is it about shoes? Explain why certain people seem to have shoes "on their brains." Express your ideas in a few sentences using at least four vocabulary words.

English Language Coach

English as a Changing Language Etymology can be useful because, in learning about one word, you're actually learning about a family of words. When you come upon an unfamiliar word, you may be able to recognize the word family it belongs to. This chart shows a word from *Dandelion Wine.*

Word	*emporium*
Meaning	a retail store offering a variety of merchandise
Etymology	Latin, from Greek *emporion*, from *emporos* traveler, trader, from *em-* in + *poros* journey
Related Words	*pore, porous*

EL

Remember, though, that a word part may be spelled the same in different words but have different meanings. For example, *portfolio* and *transport* come from the Greek *poros.* However, *corporate* and *portray* have different roots, even though they include the word part *por.*

Write to Learn Look up *pore* and *porous.* How are their modern meanings related to the original meaning of the root *poros?*

Additional Support

Author Search To expand students' appreciation of Ray Bradbury, have them access the Web site for additional information and resources.

English Language Coach

Cognates Tell students that cognates are words that are the same or nearly the same in two or more languages. Ask Spanish-speaking students to say the Spanish word for *actor* and for *artist.* Point out that the pronunciation is slightly different, and an *a* is added to *artist,* but for the most part the words are the same. Have English learners work with native English speakers to come up with a list of cognates. Explain that sometimes the meaning is slightly different, so students should make notes about the meanings on their lists. Explain that studying cognates is a good way to increase vocabulary and comprehension. Have students share their lists with the rest of the class when they finish. EL OL

Skills Preview

Key Reading Skill: Identifying Author's Purpose

Short-story writers might have several purposes for writing. They usually want to entertain you, of course; and they usually want to make a point about life or about people. They may also want you to imagine events, people, and experiences you might not come across in your own life. To help you identify an author's purpose in a short story, think about

- word choices

  How do the author's word choices affect how you feel about the characters and events?
- intended audience

  Who is the author writing for? Which readers are most likely to make connections between the story and their own lives?
- main idea or theme

  What is the author's message?

R

Partner Work With a partner, identify the author's purpose in one of the short stories in this book.

Literary Element: Hyperbole

Hyperbole (hy PUR buh lee) is a figure of speech that uses exaggeration to express strong emotion, emphasize a point, or create humor. Most of us use hyperbole in ordinary conversation. (Have you ever said something "drove you crazy"?) Writers often use it too. For example, Langston Hughes says in a story that a woman carried "a large purse that had everything in it but hammer and nails."

L

Use these tips to help you learn about hyperbole.

- Look for any statement that may be hyperbole.

  Does the statement present a fact or an opinion? Is the exaggeration a really big one?
- Consider why the hyperbole is used.

  Does exaggeration add humor? Does it emphasize a point that's important to the speaker or writer? Does it express a strong emotion?

Get Ready to Read

Connect to the Reading

In this story, the main character spots a pair of tennis shoes in a store window—and he *has* to have them. He can't *explain* why he needs them, but he can *feel* why.

Write to Learn In your Learner's Notebook, write a paragraph or two about wanting something so badly that if you didn't get it, you'd just die. (This is the kind of situation where we all often use hyperbole.)

Build Background

This selection is an excerpt from *Dandelion Wine,* a novel first published in 1957.

- Bradbury's vision for this story is rooted in the past—his own and America's. The values he expresses are values he remembers from his childhood.
- Life in the 1950s was simple, in many ways. There were no cell phones, video games, or Internet. On TV, you probably got three channels. The only computers that existed were room-sized and belonged to the government.

Set Purposes for Reading

BIG Question Read *Dandelion Wine* to consider the American dream from the point of view of a boy growing up in a small Midwestern town.

Set Your Own Purpose What would you like to learn from the selection to help you answer the Big Question? Write your purpose on the "Dandelion Wine" page of Foldable 8.

Interactive Literary Elements Handbook To review or learn more about the literary elements, go to www.glencoe.com.

Keep Moving

Use these skills as you read the following selection.

Teach

R Reading Skill

Identifying Author's Purpose
Say: Ray Bradbury is famous for his science fiction stories. Why do you think he wrote them? *(Possible response: to entertain or spark people's imaginations about future possibilities)* OL

L Literary Element

Hyperbole **Ask:** What hyperbole might you use to describe how hungry you feel after school? *(Possible responses: "I could eat a horse!" "I'm starving!")* AS

Interactive Literary Elements Handbook Have students access the Web site to improve their understanding of hyperbole.

Differentiated Instruction

Building Background To help students better understand hyperbole, consider reading them an American legend, such as one of the Paul Bunyan or Pecos Bill stories. When you finish, have students form groups to list the hyperbole they heard in the story. Invite groups to share their lists with the class. EL Then ask groups to write their own American legends with original characters, making use of hyperbole to heighten reader interest and enjoyment. Suggest that the groups illustrate their stories and share both their stories and illustrations with the class. AS

Indiana English/Language Arts Academic Standards
SE: 8.1.2, 8.2, 8.3.6
TWE: *English Language Coach* 8.1, *Differentiated Instruction* 8.5.7

Teach

C1 Critical Thinking

Comprehension Say: This selection is an excerpt of a much longer novel. What details do you miss when you read an excerpt instead of the entire novel? *(Possible response: background information about characters and situations)*
Ask: Are there any benefits to reading an excerpt? *(Possible response: You might become curious enough about the story's outcome to want to read the entire book.)* AS

C2 Critical Thinking

Analysis Ask: What image is the author trying to create with the metaphor comparing the town to a boat? *(Possible response: a vision of spring and the life of nature that will overtake the town, like a body of water or a flood.)* AL

Readability Scores
Dale-Chall: 4.2
DRP: 52
Lexile: 930

READING WORKSHOP 4

from Dandelion Wine

by Ray Bradbury

Late that night, going home from the show with his mother and father and his brother Tom, Douglas saw the tennis shoes in the bright store window. He glanced quickly away, but his ankles were seized, his feet suspended, then rushed. The earth spun; the shop awnings slammed their canvas wings overhead with the thrust of his body running. His mother and father and brother walked quietly on both sides of him. Douglas walked backward, watching the tennis shoes in the midnight window left behind. **1** **C1**

Visual Vocabulary
An ***awning*** is a covering over the outside of a window or door for protection from the rain and sun.

"It was a nice movie," said Mother.

Douglas murmured, "It was . . ."

It was June and long past time for buying the special shoes that were quiet as a summer rain falling on the walks. June and the earth full of raw power and everything everywhere in motion. The grass was still pouring in from the country, surrounding the sidewalks, stranding the houses. Any moment the town would **capsize**, go down and leave not a stir in the clover and weeds. And here Douglas stood, trapped on the dead cement and the red-brick streets, hardly able to move. **C2**

Practice the Skills

1 Literary Element

Hyperbole As soon as Douglas sees the tennis shoes, what happens to him? Do you think this is actually happening, or is the author using hyperbole? Explain. Remember the reasons for using hyperbole.

Vocabulary

capsize (KAP syz) *v.* to overturn or upset (especially a boat)

Additional Support

Literature Focus Lesson

Precise Language Write the following paragraph on the board:

Mai walked into the house and put her books on the table. She looked for something, anything, to hit. She sat on the couch. "Life isn't fair!" Mai said to the living room walls. "One bad pitch and the coach pulls me out of the game!"

Then read the first paragraph of the story aloud. Point out that the action verbs in the story make the story exciting to read. Instruct students to copy the paragraph from the board and, with a partner, replace the underlined verbs with powerful action verbs. AS

"Dad!" He blurted it out. "Back there in that window, those Cream-Sponge Para Litefoot Shoes . . ."

His father didn't even turn. "Suppose you tell me why you need a new pair of sneakers. Can you do that?"

"Well . . ."

It was because they felt the way it feels every summer when you take off your shoes for the first time and run in the grass. They felt like it feels sticking your feet out of the hot covers in wintertime to let the cold wind from the open window blow on them suddenly and you let them stay out a long time until you pull them back in under the covers again to feel them, like packed snow. The tennis shoes felt like it always feels the first time every year wading in the slow waters of the creek and seeing your feet below, half an inch further downstream, with refraction,[1] than the real part of you above water. **2** R

"Dad," said Douglas, "it's hard to explain."

Somehow the people who made tennis shoes knew what boys needed and wanted. They put marshmallows and coiled springs in the soles and they wove the rest out of grasses bleached and fired in the wilderness. Somewhere deep in the soft loam of the shoes the thin hard sinews[2] of the buck deer were hidden. The people that made the shoes must have watched a lot of winds blow the trees and a lot of rivers going down to the lakes. Whatever it was, it was in the shoes, and it was summer.

Douglas tried to get all this in words.

"Yes," said Father, "but what's wrong with last year's sneakers? Why can't you dig *them* out of the closet?"

Well, he felt sorry for boys who lived in California where they wore tennis shoes all year and never knew what it was to get winter off your feet, peel off the iron leather shoes all full of snow and rain and run barefoot for a day and then lace on the first new tennis shoes of the season, which was better than barefoot. The magic was always in the new pair of shoes. The magic might die by the first of September, but now in late June there was still plenty of magic, and shoes like these could jump you over trees and rivers and houses. And if you wanted, they could jump you over fences and sidewalks and dogs. **3** L1 L2

1. ***Refraction*** is the bending of light rays as they travel through different substances. Light passing from air to water, for example, produces the effect the narrator describes here.
2. ***Loam*** is a rich, black soil. ***Sinews*** are tendons, the tissues that attach muscles to bones.

Practice the Skills

2 Key Reading Skill

Identifying Author's Purpose In this paragraph, what is the author's purpose? Bradbury chooses words that create strong images to help you get a feel for how Douglas feels about the tennis shoes.

3 Literary Element

Hyperbole Which parts of this paragraph would you say are hyperbole? Note those words and phrases in your Learner's Notebook.

Differentiated Instruction

Visualizing Draw the following organizer on the board. **Say:** In this story, the author uses sensory images to connect tennis shoes to the whole experience of summer. What do you connect with summer? Choose an item. Then use the organizer to help you understand why this item means summer.

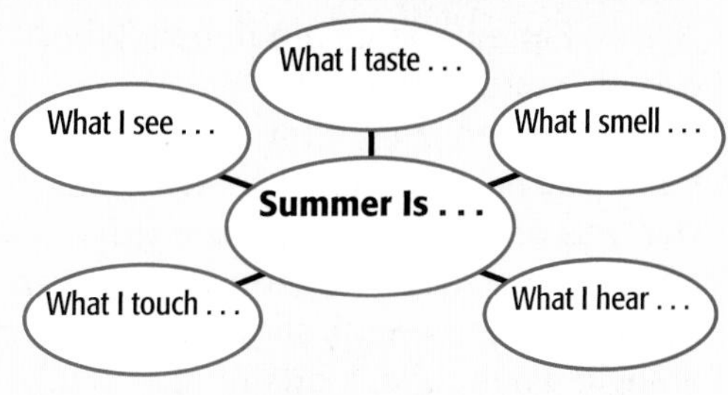

Teach

R Reading Skill

Identifying Author's Purpose **Say:** Bradbury contrasts Douglas's real conversation with his father and the thoughts that are going on in his mind. What do you think the author's purpose is in making this contrast between reality and imagination? *(Possible response: It shows what a vivid imagination the boy has while showing the limitations he has with communication.)* **AL**

L1 Literary Element

Hyperbole **Say:** Douglas uses the words *iron leather shoes* to describe his winter shoes. What contrast does this hyperbole make between winter shoes and tennis shoes? *(Possible response: Winter shoes are heavy, inflexible, and uncomfortable, while tennis shoes are lightweight, flexible, and comfortable.)* **OL**

L2 Literary Element

Hyperbole **Ask:** In the last paragraph, what magical effect does Douglas claim new shoes have? *(They allow people to jump over trees, rivers, houses, fences, sidewalks, and dogs.)* **Ask:** What effect does this hyperbole have on the reader? *(Possible response: It helps people understand the attachment the boy feels to the shoes.)* **AS**

Indiana English/Language Arts Academic Standards
SE: 8.2, 8.3.6
TWE: *Literature Focus Lesson* 8.5.6

Teach

Viewing the Art

Ask: Does this painting capture the essence of summer for you? *(Responses will vary.)* **Ask:** If you were going to draw a painting that captured the essence of summer, what would you paint? *(Responses will vary.)* AS

C Critical Thinking

Comprehension Ask: What is the author describing when he describes children "peeling like calendars each day to take more sun"? *(After "taking sun," the children are sunburned and their skin peels.)* OL

READING WORKSHOP 4

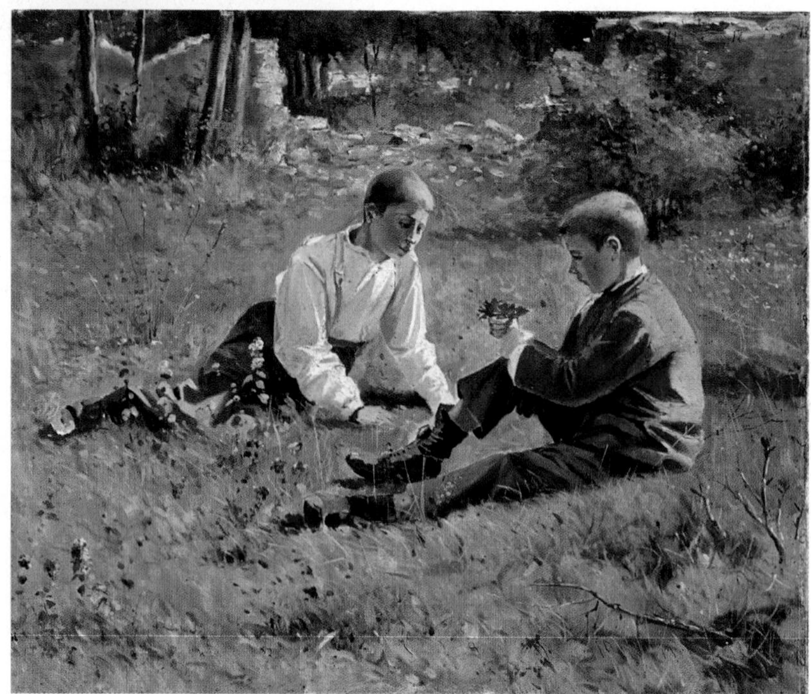

Children Playing, Grez-sur-Loing. Alexander Harrison. Oil on canvas, 50 x 61 cm.

"Don't you see?" said Douglas. "I just *can't* use last year's pair."

For last year's pair were dead inside. They had been fine when he started them out, last year. But by the end of summer, every year, you always found out, you always knew, you couldn't really jump over rivers and trees and houses in them, and they were dead. But this was a new year, and he felt that this time, with this new pair of shoes, he could do anything, anything at all. 4

They walked up on the steps to their house. "Save your money," said Dad. "In five or six weeks—"

"Summer'll be over!"

Lights out, with Tom asleep. Douglas lay watching his feet, far away down there at the end of the bed in the moonlight, free of the heavy iron shoes, the big chunks of winter fallen away from them.

"Reasons. I've got to think of reasons for the shoes."

Well, as anyone knew, the hills around town were wild with friends putting cows to riot, playing barometer to the C

Practice the Skills

4 Reviewing Skills

Analyzing How does the narration help you understand why Douglas wants the shoes so badly?

Additional Support

Reading in the Real World

Career Entrepreneurs are people who envision, start, and manage new businesses or enterprises. They definitely model Douglas's motto: *Whatever you want, you got to make your own way.* With a partner, have students research an American entrepreneur, such as Andrew Carnegie, Paul Cuffe, Madame C.J. Walker, or Jerry Yang, and make a time line of this person's life. Have students include events in their early lives that inspired them to become leaders, their major accomplishments, and any honors or recognition they received. Then ask volunteers to use their time line as a basis for an oral presentation. OL AL atmospheric changes, taking sun, peeling like calendars each day to take more sun. To catch those friends, you must run much faster than foxes or squirrels. As for the town, it steamed with enemies grown irritable with heat, so remembering every winter argument and insult. *Find friends, ditch enemies!* That was the Cream-Sponge Para Litefoot motto. *Does the world run too fast? Want to catch up? Want to be alert, stay alert? Litefoot, then! Litefoot!*

He held his coin bank up and heard the faint small tinkling, the airy weight of money there.

Whatever you want, he thought, you got to make your own way. During the night now, let's find that path through the forest. . . .

Downtown, the store lights went out, one by one. A wind blew in the window. It was like a river going downstream and his feet wanting to go with it.

In his dreams he heard a rabbit running running running in the deep warm grass.

Old Mr. Sanderson moved through his shoe store as the **proprietor** of a pet shop must move through his shop where are kenneled animals from everywhere in the world, touching each one briefly along the way. Mr. Sanderson brushed his hands over the shoes in the window, and some of them were like cats to him and some were like dogs; he touched each pair with concern, adjusting laces, fixing tongues. Then he stood in the exact center of the carpet and looked around, nodding.

There was a sound of growing thunder.

One moment, the door to Sanderson's Shoe Emporium[3] was empty. The next, Douglas Spaulding stood clumsily there, staring down at his leather shoes as if these heavy things could not be pulled up out of the cement. **5** The thunder had stopped when his shoes stopped. Now, with painful slowness, daring to look only at the money in his cupped hand, Douglas moved out of the bright sunlight of Saturday noon. He made careful stacks of nickels, dimes, and quarters on the counter, like

3. An ***emporium*** is a store.

Vocabulary

proprietor (pruh PRY uh tur) *n.* a person or firm that owns a property or a business

C **Practice the Skills**

5 **Literary Element**

Hyperbole Hyperbole emphasizes how heavy Douglas's shoes feel to him—as if they were stuck in cement.

Teach

L1 Literary Element

Review Cultural Reference
Say: American advertisers often come up with slogans, or mottos, like the one written to sell the tennis shoes in the story. What current advertising slogans do you know? Do you find them effective? *(Responses will vary.)* **AS**

L2 Literary Element

Review Figurative Language
Ask: What metaphor does Douglas use for coming up with a way to get the shoes? *(finding a path through the forest)*
Ask: What similes does Bradbury use on this page? *(He compares the wind blowing in the window to a river going downstream; the shoes to cats and dogs.)* **OL** **AL**

Literature Focus Lesson

Figurative Language On this page, the author uses a simile to describe how important his shoes are to Mr. Sanderson. The comparison between inanimate, or nonliving, shoes to live pets helps readers understand the affection Mr. Sanderson has for what he sells. Ask students to find a photo of any inanimate object that appeals to them and then write a short description of this object, comparing it to a pet animal. Have students give the object the qualities of pets, such as loyalty, a sense of humor, intelligence, love, and other emotions. Remind students to be innovative in their comparisons. Ask volunteers to share their description with the class. **AS**

Indiana English/Language Arts Academic Standards
SE: 8.2, 8.3.6
TWE: *Reading in the Real World* 8.7.10, *Literature Focus Lesson* 8.5.1

Teach

R1 Reading Skill

Review Drawing Conclusions
Ask: What does Mr. Sanderson conclude about Douglas before he even gets to speak? *(that Douglas wanted the tennis shoes and that he wanted to buy shoes on credit)* AS
Ask: Was Mr. Sanderson right or wrong? Explain. *(He was right about Douglas wanting the shoes. He was wrong about Douglas wanting credit.)*
Ask: Based on Douglas's plan, what can you conclude about his character? *(Possible response: He is innovative and determined.)* OL

R2 Reading Skill

Review Understanding Cause and Effect **Ask:** What did Douglas's excitement cause him to do? *(breathe hard, as if he'd run all night in his dreams)* OL

EL Language Coach

English as a Changing Language **Say:** The word *sneak* means "to creep or crawl silently". It is derived from the word *snake*. Why is *sneakers* an appropriate name for tennis shoes? *(Possible response: The soles muffle sound so that a person walks silently.)* EL

READING WORKSHOP 4

someone playing chess and worried if the next move carried him out into sun or deep into shadow.

"Don't say a word!" said Mr. Sanderson.

Douglas froze.

"First, I know just what you want to buy," said Mr. Sanderson. "Second, I see you every afternoon at my window; you think I don't see? You're wrong. Third, to give it its full name, you want the Royal Crown Cream-Sponge Para Litefoot Tennis Shoes: 'LIKE **MENTHOL**[4] ON YOUR FEET!' Fourth, you want credit." 6

"No!" cried Douglas, breathing hard, as if he'd run all night in his dreams. "I got something better than credit to offer!" he gasped. "Before I tell, Mr. Sanderson, you got to do me one small favor. Can you remember when was the last time you yourself wore a pair of Litefoot sneakers, sir?"

Mr. Sanderson's face darkened. "Oh, ten, twenty, say, thirty years ago. Why . . . ?"

"Mr. Sanderson, don't you think you owe it to your customers, sir, to at least try the tennis shoes you sell, for just one minute, so you know how they feel? People forget if they don't keep testing things. United Cigar Store man smokes cigars, don't he? Candy-store man samples his own stuff, I should think. So . . ."

"You may have noticed," said the old man, "I'm wearing shoes."

"But not sneakers, sir! How you going to sell sneakers unless you can **rave** about them and how you going to rave about them unless you know them?"

Mr. Sanderson backed off a little distance from the boy's fever, one hand to his chin. "Well . . ."

"Mr. Sanderson," said Douglas, "you sell me something and I'll sell you something just as valuable." 7

"Is it absolutely necessary to the sale that I put on a pair of the sneakers, boy?" said the old man.

"I sure wish you could, sir!"

4. ***Menthol*** is a chemical that has the odor and cooling effect of peppermint.

Vocabulary

rave (rayv) *v.* to speak about very favorably or with great enthusiasm

Practice the Skills

6 English Language Coach

A Changing Language The word **menthol** comes from German, which took it from the Latin word for *mint.*

7 Reviewing Skills

Analyzing What is Douglas doing in this conversation? What does he want to "sell" to Mr. Sanderson?

Additional Support

Literature Focus Lesson

Persuasive Writing **Say:** Have you ever wanted something that your parents thought was unnecessary or silly? How did you convince them that you needed that new sweater or concert ticket? Assume you're back in that situation. Write a letter to a parent, giving three reasons that you should have this item. Use hyperbole at least once to let your parent know how desperate you are. Make your description vivid with sensory details. OL Swap letters with a partner and evaluate how persuasive each other's letters are. AL

The old man sighed. A minute later, seated panting quietly, he laced the tennis shoes to his long narrow feet. They looked detached and **alien** down there next to the dark cuffs of his business suit. Mr. Sanderson stood up. 8

"How do they *feel?*" asked the boy.

"How do they feel, he asks; they feel fine." He started to sit down.

"Please!" Douglas held out his hand. "Mr. Sanderson, now could you kind of rock back and forth a little, sponge around, bounce kind of, while I tell you the rest? It's this: I give you my money, you give me the shoes, I owe you a dollar. But, Mr. Sanderson, *but*—soon as I get those shoes on, you know what *happens?*"

"What?"

"Bang! I deliver your packages, pick up packages, bring you coffee, burn your trash, run to the post office, telegraph office, library! You'll see twelve of me in and out, in and out, every minute. Feel those shoes, Mr. Sanderson, *feel* how fast they'd take me? All those springs inside? Feel all the running inside? Feel how they kind of grab hold and can't let you alone and don't like you just *standing* there? Feel how quick I'd be doing the things you'd rather not bother with? You stay in the nice and cool store while I'm jumping all around town! But it's not me really, it's the shoes. They're going like mad down alleys, cutting corners, and back! There they go!"

Mr. Sanderson stood amazed with the rush of words. When the words got going the flow carried him; he began to sink deep in the shoes, to flex his

Vocabulary

alien (AY lee un) *adj.* strange; odd; peculiar

EL Practice the Skills

8 English Language Coach

A Changing Language
The word **alien** hasn't changed much from the original Latin *alienus*. The word can also refer to a person of another family, race, nation, or planet.

Reading Fluency

Build Fluency To help students build fluency reading dialogue, have students meet with partners in a quiet place. Ask them to choose roles—Douglas and Mr. Sanderson. Have them read the dialogue between the two characters on pages 1146–1148. Ask them to reread the dialogue until they can read their parts with fluency, expression, and comprehension. Then have students switch roles, repeating the process until they are fluent readers of dialogue. EL BL

Teach

EL Language Coach

English as a Changing Language **Ask:** How does the definition of *alien* apply in this instance? *(It gives the sense that the sneakers do not belong with Mr. Sanderson's business suit.)* AS

R Reading Skill

Review Understanding Cause and Effect **Ask:** What, according to Douglas, will cause Mr. Sanderson to rave about sneakers? *(knowing them by wearing them)* AS

L Literary Element

Hyperbole **Ask:** What hyperbole describes the speed that Douglas can attain with the new tennis shoes? *("You'll see twelve of me... every minute.")* OL

Indiana English/Language Arts Academic Standards
SE: 8.2
TWE: *Literature Focus Lesson* 8.5.7, *Reading Fluency* 8.7

Teach

L Literary Element

Review Figurative Language **Ask:** How does the author talk about the store's setting? *(He describes it as if it were a jungle.)* **Ask:** Who experiences it as such? *(Mr. Sanderson)* AL

BQ 

Ask: What does Mr. Sanderson say about Douglas's American dream? *(Possible response: Douglas has the ability to make any dream he wants come true.)* AS **Ask:** Why does Mr. Sanderson believe this about Douglas? *(Possible response: because Douglas was such a good salesman, was dedicated to a purpose, and refused to give up)* OL

C Critical Thinking

Comprehension **Ask:** What will happen after Douglas finishes his errands for Mr. Sanderson? *(He will be fired.)* AS **Ask:** What does Mr. Sanderson mean by that? *(He means that Douglas won't owe him anything else for the sneakers.)* OL

READING WORKSHOP 4

toes, limber his arches, test[5] his ankles. He rocked softly, secretly, back and forth in a small breeze from the open door. The tennis shoes silently hushed themselves deep in the carpet, sank as in a jungle grass, in loam and resilient[6] clay. He gave one solemn bounce of his heels in the yeasty dough, in the **yielding** and welcoming earth. Emotions hurried over his face as if many colored lights had been switched on and off. His mouth hung slightly open. Slowly he gentled and rocked himself to a halt, and the boy's voice faded and they stood there looking at each other in a tremendous and natural silence. 9

A few people drifted by on the sidewalk outside, in the hot sun.

Still the man and boy stood there, the boy glowing, the man with revelation[7] in his face.

"Boy," said the old man at last, "in five years, how would you like a job selling shoes in this emporium?"

"Gosh, thanks, Mr. Sanderson, but I don't know what I'm going to be yet."

"Anything you want to be, son," said the old man, "you'll be. No one will ever stop you."

The old man walked lightly across the store to the wall of ten thousand boxes, came back with some shoes for the boy, and wrote up a list on some paper while the boy was lacing the shoes on his feet and then standing there, waiting.

The old man held out his list. "A dozen things you got to do for me this afternoon. Finish them, we're even Stephen, and you're fired."

"Thanks, Mr. Sanderson!" Douglas bounded away.

"Stop!" cried the old man.

Douglas pulled up and turned.

Mr. Sanderson leaned forward. "How do they *feel?*"

The boy looked down at his feet deep in the rivers, in the fields of wheat, in the wind that already was rushing him out

5. Here, ***flex, limber,*** and ***test*** all mean "to bend or loosen up."
6. Anything that's ***resilient*** (rih ZIL yunt) is capable of returning to its original size, shape, or position.
7. Generally, a ***revelation*** (rev uh LAY shun) is the act of revealing something, such as a truth.

Vocabulary

yielding (YEEL ding) *adj.* giving way to force or pressure

Practice the Skills

9 Literary Elementl

Hyperbole This paragraph includes figurative language, but is there any hyperbole? If so, what part(s)? If not, what kinds of figurative language are included?

Additional Support

Differentiated Instruction

Personal Response Mr. Sanderson experiences vivid memories when he dons the sneakers. Explain to students that Mr. Sanderson's feelings could be expressed in a number of ways: in writing, with music, through visual artwork. Have students work with partners to identify and illustrate one of Mr. Sanderson's responses to the sneakers. Have partners create poetry, songs, paintings, drawings, computer presentations, or other projects that interpret this scene and emotion. Have students share their creations with the class. OL

READING WORKSHOP 4

The antelope is a swift, graceful animal with long curved horns, and the gazelle is a type of small antelope. Although they look like deer, antelopes and gazelles are in the goat family. They live in Africa and Southwest Asia.

of the town. He looked up at the old man, his eyes burning, his mouth moving, but no sound came out. **10**

"Antelopes?" said the old man, looking from the boy's face to his shoes. "Gazelles?"

The boy thought about it, hesitated, and nodded a quick nod. Almost immediately he vanished. He just spun about with a whisper and went off. The door stood empty. The sound of the tennis shoes faded in the jungle heat.

Mr. Sanderson stood in the sun-blazed door, listening. From a long time ago, when he dreamed as a boy, he remembered the sound. Beautiful creatures leaping under the sky, gone through brush, under trees, away, and only the soft echo their running left behind.

"Antelopes," said Mr. Sanderson. "Gazelles."

R He bent to pick up the boy's abandoned winter shoes, heavy with forgotten rains and long-melted snows. Moving out of the blazing sun, walking softly, lightly, slowly, he headed back toward civilization. . . . **11** ❍

Practice the Skills

10 Literary Element

Hyperbole This paragraph has a series of metaphors. Individually, the metaphors just compare the shoes' "feel" to different parts of nature. Together, they become hyperbole.

11 BIG Question

What would you say is Douglas's idea of the American dream? Write your purpose on the "Dandelion Wine" page of Foldable 8. Your response will help you complete the Unit Challenge later.

Teach

R Reading Skill

Review Analyzing Say: Reread the last paragraph of the story. What does the last sentence mean? *(Possible response: Mr. Sanderson is leaving his daydream to return his focus to the shoe store and the present moment.)* **AL**

Assess

Use the CheckPoint questions provided on Presentation Plus! to check for comprehension of the selection. These questions can be used with interactive response keypads for immediate student feedback.

Literature Focus Lesson

Figurative Language Say: One of the main elements of this story is Douglas's use of his imagination. It is even contagious when he sells Mr. Sanderson on his plan. His imagination is sparked by a particular feeling he gets when he puts on new sneakers. Think about something that inspires your imagination. It can be an object, an event, or a place. What does it make you think about? How does it activate your imagination? Write a one-page story about the thing that inspires you. Use vivid language and sensory details to describe your imaginings over your topic. Share your completed stories in small groups. **OL**

Indiana English/Language Arts Academic Standards

SE: 8.2

TWE: *Differentiated Instruction* 8.3, *Literature Focus Lesson* 8.5.1

Assess

Resources for page 1150

- Selection Quick Check, p. 78
- Selection and Unit Assessment, p. 92
- ExamView Assessment Suite
- Interactive Tutor: Self-Assessment

Students can respond to the *After You Read* items in their Learner's Notebooks or on a separate sheet of paper.

Answering the BIG Question

1. Responses will vary.
2. To a pet shop owner
3. Possible response: Douglas needs new shoes filled with energy and zip to face the new, excitement-filled summer.

Critical Thinking

4. Possible response: Summer is a time in which children are on the go, running and playing endlessly.
5. Possible response: In exchange for the shoes, Douglas will help Mr. Sanderson feel the energy and vitality of his childhood again.
6. Responses will vary.
7. Possible response: Douglas was so effective at persuading Mr. Sanderson to try on shoes that he'd make an excellent salesperson.

After You Read

from *Dandelion Wine*

Answering the BIG Question

1. Do you think life in America has changed much since Bradbury wrote his novel in 1957? Do you think the American dream has changed? Explain.
2. **Recall** To what does the author compare Old Mr. Sanderson, the shoe store proprietor?
   TIP Right There
3. **Summarize** In your own words, tell why Douglas feels he needs a new pair of tennis shoes.
   TIP Think and Search

Critical Thinking

4. **Interpret** On page 1144, find the paragraph that begins "Well, as anyone knew . . ." Tell what you think the first two sentences mean.
   TIP Author and Me
5. **Clarify** What does Douglas mean when he says to Mr. Sanderson, "you sell me something and I'll sell you something just as valuable"?
   TIP Author and Me
6. **Evaluate** The narrator says, "Somehow the people who made tennis shoes knew what boys needed and wanted." Do you think this is true? Explain.
   TIP Author and Me
7. **Explain** Why does Mr. Sanderson ask Douglas if he would like a job selling shoes in five years?
   TIP Think and Search

Write About Your Reading

Journal Entry Put yourself in Douglas's shoes. Write the journal entry that he might have written after he got home with his new Royal Crown Cream-Sponge Para Litefoot Tennis Shoes. First, think what he might have to say about getting the shoes and about his plans for the rest of the summer. Then start writing. (Don't be afraid to use some hyperbole; it's what Douglas would do.)

Indiana English/Language Arts Academic Standards (pp. 1150–1151)

8.3 Comprehension and Analysis of Literary Text Respond to grade-level-appropriate literature...
8.5.7 Write for different purposes...
8.2 Comprehension and Analysis (Focus on Informational Text) Develop [reading] strategies... identifying and analyzing...purpose.
8.3.6 Identify significant literary devices...
8.6 English Language Conventions
For a complete description of the standards, see p. IN 11.

Write About Your Reading

Possible response:
Today is the best day of my entire life! I'm now the proud owner of a brand new, sparkling clean pair of Royal Crown Cream-Sponge Para Litefoot Tennis Shoes! Already I've put at least five miles on them. Dad said I didn't need them. I emptied my savings but was still a dollar short. No problem! When Mr. Sanderson had a chance to feel what these magical guys can do, he let me run errands for the extra dollar! I'm calling the guys tonight to plan our summer. I can't wait to zoom through tall grass, climb Bobby's apple tree, and race Zach down Water Tower Hill. It's going to be the best summer ever!

Skills Review

Key Reading Skill: Identifying Author's Purpose

8. Who would you say is Bradbury's intended audience for *Dandelion Wine?* Why do you think this?

9. Tell what purpose(s) you think Bradbury had in mind and whether he was successful. Use details from the selection to support your answers.

Literary Element: Hyperbole

10. Explain the hyperbole in saying that "shoes like these could jump you over trees and rivers and houses."

11. Douglas says that, once he's wearing the new tennis shoes, Mr. Sanderson will "see twelve of me, in and out, in and out, every minute." Is Douglas exaggerating to express strong emotion, to emphasize a point, to create humor, or for a combination of these reasons? Explain.

Vocabulary Check

Write the vocabulary word and the word or phrase in parentheses that is its synonym.

12. capsize (straighten, tip over)

13. proprietor (salesman, owner)

14. rave (praise, scold)

15. alien (ordinary, unusual)

16. yielding (flexible, resisting)

Copy each sentence, filling in the blank with one of the vocabulary words.

17. My neighbors are so weird that even Martians would think they're ___!

18. I don't mean to ___, but you've made me the happiest person in the history of the universe!

19. If this thing were to ___, we'd sink faster than you can say "Glub!"

20. English Language Coach What do *proper, property,* and *proprietor* have in common, besides their similar spellings?

Grammar Link: Homophones

Homophones are words that sound alike but have different spellings and different meanings.

- My brother is a musician; he plays the bass.
- My sister is a ballplayer; she plays first base.

Not recognizing a homophone could result in an embarrassing spelling error. Even a computer spell-checker can't fix your mistake if you wrote *lone* when you want a *loan*. Always check a dictionary if you're unsure about which homophone to use.

Some Common Homophones	
breaks, brakes	meat, meet
by, buy	prints, prince
for, four	there, their, they're
here, hear	to, too, two
lessen, lesson	weight, wait

Grammar Practice

Copy the following sentences and circle the homophone that correctly completes each sentence. If you need help, use a dictionary.

21. Angela couldn't (wait, weight) to see the sunrise.

22. I need to (by, buy) a necktie and a pair of shoes.

23. The boys will wait in (here, hear).

24. I got my (prints, prince) from the photo shop.

25. The truck's (breaks, brakes) screeched to a stop.

26. Let's (meet, meat) at the Aerosmith concert.

Web Activities For eFlashcards, Selection Quick Checks, and other Web activities, www.glencoe.com.

READING WORKSHOP 4

Skills Review

Key Reading Skill: Identifying Author's Purpose

8. Possible response: I think Bradbury is writing to grownups who've forgotten what it's like to zoom and race and feel magic.

9. Possible response: I believe Bradbury wanted to entertain his audience. His descriptions of how the sneakers feel make it easy for readers to connect with the experience and feelings.

Literary Element: Hyperbole

10. Possible response: No shoes could do this for anyone; Bradbury wants to emphasize the magical feeling the new shoes give Douglas.

11. Possible response: Douglas wants to express his determination, to emphasize how hard and fast he'll work, and to provoke a chuckle from Mr. Sanderson.

Close

Ask students if they think Douglas is a model example of the American dream, or not. Have them explain their answers.

Vocabulary Check

12. capsize/tip over

13. proprietor/owner

14. rave/praise

15. alien/unusual

16. yielding/flexible

17. alien

18. rave

19. capsize

English Language Coach

20. All words stem from the same word—*proprius,* which means "one's own" or "special".

Grammar Link: Homophones

Grammar Practice

21. wait **23.** here **25.** brakes

22. buy **24.** prints **26.** meet

Indiana English/Language Arts Academic Standards
SE: 8.2, 8.3, 8.3.6, 8.5.7, 8.6

Comparing Literature: Author's Purpose

Teaching Students to Compare Author's Purpose

Why Is It Important?

- Understanding the intention of the writer gives students a purpose for reading. Does the author want them to be persuaded, amused, informed, or entertained?
- Comparing authors' purposes helps students to read critically; they will look for satire, factual information, propaganda, irrational logic, symbolism, etc.
- Comparing authors' purposes from different genres, points of view, structures, and writing styles helps students make connections from text to text.
- People see things differently because of their own experiences, interests, and values. Students will learn that an author's purpose is affected by his or her perspective.
- Identifying an author's purpose will enable students to distinguish between the topic of the selection and the author's feelings about the topic.
- Identifying an author's purpose and perspective will also help students form their own opinions about a topic.

How to Help Students Get It

- Suggest that students ask the following questions as they read: "Does the title of the selection give any clues as to the author's purpose? Is the author's purpose clearly stated? Does the selection provide information, entertain, express the author's thoughts and feelings, or attempt to convince the reader of something?"
- Remind students to think about word choices. Authors select words according to their connotations and denotations.
- When comparing multiple selections, ask the students to consider each author's intended audience. A speech written for a pep rally would likely have a different purpose than one to be read to the state senate.
- Students may also benefit from rereading the author's background to get a better sense of his or her purpose and perspective.

Reading to Answer the Big Question

Coming to America
by Joe McGowan, Marisa Wong, Vickie Bane, and Laurie Morice
This TIME article introduces three young immigrants who describe their experiences and impressions of the U.S.

Coming to America by Marianne Szegedy-Maszak
This article describes the lives of two immigrant families in the U.S. The Osmanis came from Kosovo, and the Wilsons came from Liberia.

Workshop Resources

Pacing (Days) Standard	Block	Lesson	Student Materials	Teacher Resources
1	1	Comparing Literature: Author's Purpose	English Language Coach Review, p. 44	Bellringer Options Transparencies –Daily Language Practice 80 Presentation Plus!
1	1	"Coming to America"	Glencoe Online Unit Vocabulary Review, p. 42 Academic Vocabulary Review, p. 45 English Language Coach Reading Across Texts Graphic Organizer, p. 37 StudentWorks Plus™ Online Student Edition Literature Classics	Puzzlemaker Skill Level Up!™ A Language Arts Game BookLink 3 Assessment by Learning Objective (Diagnostic and Formative) Interactive Tutor: Self-Assessment TeacherWorks Plus™ ExamView Assessment Suite
1		"Coming to America"	Glencoe Online Unit Vocabulary Review, p. 42 Academic Vocabulary Review, p. 45 English Language Coach Reading Across Texts Graphic Organizer, p. 37 StudentWorks Plus™ Online Student Edition Literature Classics	Literary and Text Analysis Transparencies Puzzlemaker Skill Level Up!™ A Language Arts Game BookLink 3 Assessment by Learning Objective (Diagnostic and Formative) Interactive Tutor: Self-Assessment TeacherWorks Plus™ ExamView Assessment Suite

Keys for Unit Resource

- Blackline Master
- Workbook
- Supplemental Text
- CD-ROM
- DVD
- Transparency
- Web-based
- Fast File

Level Appropriate Code

AS = Activities for all students
AL = Activities for students working above grade level
OL = Activities for students working at grade level
BL = Activities for students working below grade level
EL = Activities for English language learners

Focus

BELLRINGER Options

Daily Language Practice Transparency 80

Focus Activity Write the following on the board and draw the chart below: From what country did your ancestors, friends, or other family members come? You can use this chart to compare their home culture to what they found in America. AS

Features	Homeland	United States
Language		
Food		
Jobs		

Teach

R Reading Skill

Identifying Author's Purpose **Say:** Think of a TV public service announcement and a commercial. Which of these was made to inform viewers? How can you tell? *(Possible response: A public service announcement informs viewers; it contains facts. A commercial hopes to persuade with opinions.)* AS

READING ACROSS TEXTS WORKSHOP

Coming to AMERICA & COMING to AMERICA

by Joe McGowan, Marisa Wong, Vickie Bane, and Laurie Morice

by Marianne Szegedy-Maszak

Skill Focus

You will use these skills as you read and compare the following selections:

- "Coming to America," p. 1155
- "Coming to America," p. 1162

Reading

- Reading and understanding informational texts
- Analyzing a writer's claims and conclusions

Writing

- Writing to compare and contrast

Writers help you form opinions all the time. How have the writers in this unit helped you form an opinion about the American dream?

As you read the selections in this workshop, think about how the writers view the American dream. How do their views influence yours?

How to Read Across Texts

R When you read two similar texts, it's important to compare and contrast the way different writers address the same subject. To do this, ask questions about the writers' purposes for writing, their credibility (how trustworthy they are), and the evidence they use to support their opinions. Also, pay attention to point of view. Thinking about how and why writers present information helps you decide whether to believe what you read.

The selections in this workshop deal with immigration. As you read, ask yourself the following questions:

- Why is the author writing about this subject? Is the purpose to inform, to entertain, to persuade, or something else?
- Is the author credible? What makes him or her qualified to write this story about this subject?
- Does the writer support his or her ideas by providing evidence, such as facts, examples, or interviews?
- What does the evidence in these selections say about the immigrant experience in America?

Indiana English/Language Arts Academic Standards (pp. 1152–1153)

8.2 Comprehension and Analysis (Focus on Informational Text) Develop [reading] strategies...identifying and analyzing...perspective and purpose.

For a complete description of the standards, see p. IN 11.

Additional Support

Literature Focus Lesson

Perspective Explain to students that point of view, or perspective, affects the message of a story. In the first selection, three different perspectives are given on what it's like to be an immigrant. These questions will help students compare perspectives. Instruct students to answer these questions as they read:

- Whose perspectives are expressed?
- What did I learn from each perspective?
- In what ways are the perspectives similar?
- Did any perspective change?
- How and why are the perspectives different? AS

Get Ready to Compare

In your Learner's Notebook, draw a graphic organizer like the one below. Use it to keep track of the details in the selections you are about to read. Your notes will help you better understand the subject and compare the selections. (By the way, *et al.* is the abbreviation of a Latin phrase that means "and others." It's used when it would be clumsy to repeat all the names in a list of people.)

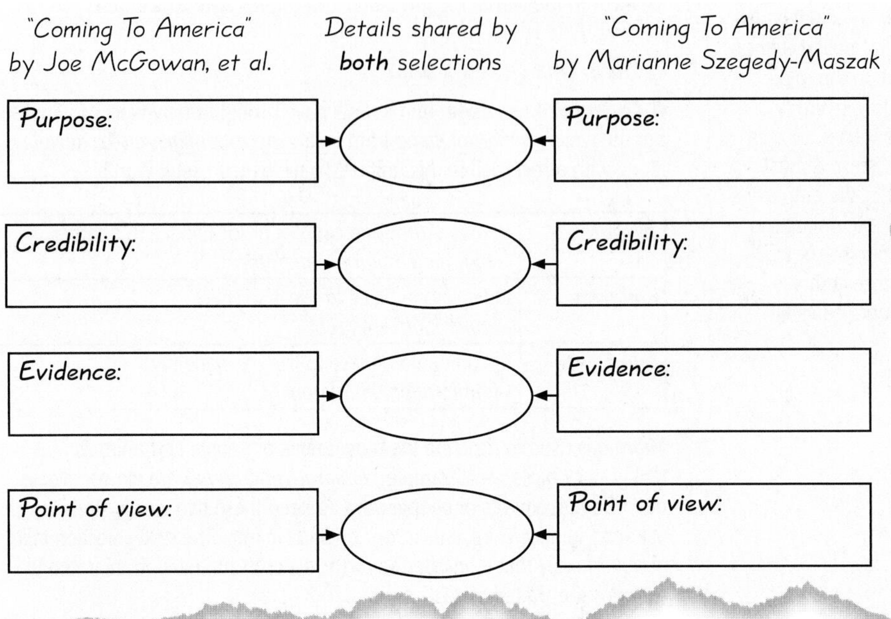

Use Your Comparison

Think of a time when a friend told you about something that happened to him or her. Now think of a time when a friend told you a story about something that happened to someone else. What details did you get from the first story that you didn't get from the second one? Do you trust a story told from a third-person point of view, or would you rather hear a first-person account?

The selections in this workshop deal with the same issue in different ways. Both articles are about immigration, but one relies heavily on first-person accounts. The other tells a story, but uses fewer direct quotations.

R As you read, use your graphic organizer to help you answer these questions about point of view:

- What do I learn about the immigrant experience from a story told in first-person point of view?
- What do I learn from a story told in third-person?
- Is one point of view more helpful than the other, or are both equally valuable?

Differentiated Instruction

Comparisons To help students draw comparisons, copy the organizer from the student page (without text) on the board. Title the left-hand column *Me,* the middle *What We Have in Common,* and the right-hand column *My Friend.* **Say:** How would you compare yourself to a friend? What factors would you choose? *(Responses will vary but could include appearance, character traits, and age.)* List points of comparison on the board and have students choose four categories for their comparison. Ask students to copy and complete the organizer with similarities and differences in these categories. **BL**

Teach

R Reading Skill

Review Understanding Cause and Effect The United States is a land of immigrants. Draw a box on the board with the head *Effect.* In the box write *People immigrated to the United States.* Draw several boxes to the left of the *Effect* box and connect them to it with arrows. Above these boxes write *Causes.* Have students brainstorm reasons that people come to America. Write their responses in the *Causes* boxes. Now draw several boxes labeled *Effects* to the right of the original *Effect* box. Draw lines connecting them to the original *Effect* box, and add *Cause* to the *Effect* head. **Ask:** What challenges do you think you'd face if you moved to a new, non-English-speaking country? List student responses in the boxes labeled *Effects.* **AS**

Assess/Close

Say: Write a paragraph comparing and contrasting your lifestyle in America with the one you'd experience in a third-world country. *(Responses will vary.)* **AS**

Resources for page 1153

Use the Comparing Literature Graphic Organizer BLM in the Unit 8 Resource Booklet p. 37

Indiana English/Language Arts Academic Standards

SE: 8.2

TWE: *Literature Focus Lesson* 8.2, *Differentiated Instruction* 8.2

Teach

More About Immigration

Although Ellis Island was the major port of entry during the peak years of immigration, other ports served the United States as well. Castle Garden served New York for thirty-five years before Ellis Island opened in 1892. San Francisco's Angel Island welcomed many Asian immigrants. Other ports in Boston, Baltimore, and Galveston also helped newcomers with their paperwork.

R Reading Skill

Review Connecting After students read the Connect to the Reading section, have them share times when they didn't know what to do or say. **Ask:** How did you feel? How did you deal with the situation? Would you change anything about the way you handled your situation? *(Responses will vary.)* AS

Before You Read

Coming to America

by Joe McGowan, Marisa Wong, Vickie Bane, and Laurie Morice

Did You Know?

Did you know that emigrating from China was once a very serious crime? In 1712 the Chinese emperor decreed that all Chinese emigrants should return to be beheaded. Of course, that policy eventually changed. In the mid-1800s, the Qing (chin) dynasty was forced to open China to the West. Almost 150 years after the emperor's threatening anti-emigration decree, the first major wave of Chinese immigrants arrived on American soil.

Vocabulary Preview

toiled (toyld) *v.* worked hard **(p. 1155)** *Many immigrants toiled in factories, hoping to build a good life in America.*

discriminates (dis KRIM uh nayts) *v.* treats unfairly **(p. 1160)** *In many places in the world, the law still discriminates against women.*

English Language Coach

A Changing Language Immigrants have brought many words to English, but the word *immigrant* came from Latin. The root *migrare* ("to move"), along with a few prefixes and suffixes, gave us ten useful words.

migrate	to move from one country or local place to another *–migration, migrant, migratory*
emigrate	to leave one place to live elsewhere *–emigration, emigrant*
immigrate	to come into a place to live permanently *–immigration, immigrant*

Migrate is used to describe the movements of people and animals ("migratory birds," for example). *Emigrate* and *immigrate* almost always describe movements of people only. To keep these two words straight, use their initials. Think *e* as in *exit* and *i* as in *into.* The next selection talks about a family that emigrated from (or *exited*) China and immigrated to (or *into*) the United States.

Get Ready to Read

Connect to the Reading

R Imagine that you had to move to a new place, adjust to a new way of life, and possibly learn a new language. That is the immigrant experience.

Set Purpose for Reading

BIG Question Read to find out about three school-age immigrants and their search for the American dream.

Set Your Own Purpose What would you like to learn from this selection to help you answer the Big Question? Write your own purpose on the "Coming to America" page of Foldable 8.

Indiana English/Language Arts Academic Standards (pp. 1154–1160)

8.1.2 Understand the influence of historical events on English word meaning and vocabulary expansion.
8.2 Comprehension and Analysis (Focus on Informational Text) Develop [reading] strategies...identifying and analyzing...perspective and purpose.

For a complete description of the standards, see p. IN 11.

Additional Support

Reading in the Real World

Citizenship Many magazines run human interest stories—stories that appeal to readers because they are about the lives of real people. Provide magazines in which students can look for human interest stories, or have students visit the library. To help them identify this type of article, brainstorm topics for human interest stories, such as life in war-torn countries, survivors of natural disasters, amazing accomplishments despite overwhelming odds, and so on. Have students write a brief summary of the story. Remind them to include only the main ideas in a summary. Have students share their summaries with the class. OL

Coming to AMERICA

PLEDGING ALLEGIANCE Proud, brand-new American citizens

The nation's newest immigrants share a time-honored dream with groups from the past.

By JOE MCGOWAN, MARISA WONG, VICKIE BANE, and LAURIE MORICE

The United States is a nation built by immigrants. From 1840 to 1870, the first wave of immigrants came from Ireland, England, Germany, and China to dig waterways and lay railroad tracks. From 1890 to 1924, a second wave crashed over Ellis Island,[1] the historic immigration station in New York Harbor, from countries such as Italy and Russia. These newcomers **toiled** in factories and built cities. **L**

Now, a new wave of immigrants is coming to America. Over 31 million immigrants live in the U.S. They make up about 11.5% of the population. Like those who came before, these immigrants are arriving in hopes of building their own version of the American Dream. **1** **R**

1 Reading Across Texts

Point of View What point of view do the writers use here? How do you know? Make notes in your organizer.

A New Era with New Challenges

Since the terrorist attacks of September 11, 2001, America has been rethinking its immigration policy. Some people want to

1. During these years, more than 20 million immigrants entered the United States through ***Ellis Island,*** a small island off the southern tip of Manhattan.

Vocabulary

toiled (toyld) *v.* worked hard

Teach

Viewing the Photo

Ask: Why are the newly sworn American citizens in the photo waving flags? *(Possible response: They've just promised to be loyal to the flag as a symbol of their new country.)* **AS**

L Literary Element

Review Style Say: Reread the first paragraph of the selection, looking for certain elements of the authors' style. How do the authors present their perspective, or point of view, of the immigrant experience through word choice? *(Possible response: They highlight the difficult work immigrants did in order to build the country of America, use words like* toiled, *and begin the paragraph with the idea that our country was built by immigrants.)* **OL**

R Reading Skill

Review Identifying Main Idea and Supporting Details Ask: What similarities do present-day immigrants share with those of the past? *(Possible response: They want to realize their own American dreams.)* **AS**

Readability Scores

Dale-Chall: 9.0
DRP: 58
Lexile: 840

Differentiated Instruction

Build Background At Ellis Island, early immigrants faced physical and mental health tests as soon as they landed in the United States. Because of the limitations Congress had set on Asian immigration in 1882, Asian newcomers were held on the island for up to two years before a decision was made. Locked up in crowded rooms with no privacy, they were asked hundreds of questions, in contrast to the twenty-nine questions asked of European immigrants at Ellis Island. Have students discuss how this likely affected Asian immigrants' ideas about America and their American dreams. **AS**

Indiana English/Language Arts Academic Standards

SE: 8.1.2, 8.2

TWE: *Reading in the Real World* 8.2, *Differentiated Instruction* 8.3.4

Teach

R1 Reading Skill

Review Understanding Cause and Effect **Ask:** According to the article, what is one effect of not graduating from high school? *(Possible response: low-paying jobs)* **Ask:** Why do more immigrant households now receive government assistance? *(Possible response: because non-government support groups aren't as strong as they once were)* AS

R2 Reading Skill

Identifying Main Idea and Supporting Details **Ask:** What details support the idea that many immigrants have one foot in the U.S. and one foot in their native land? *(Possible response: Cell phones and the Internet make it easy for people to stay in touch with their homelands.)* OL

limit the number of new immigrants to 300,000 a year. All foreign visitors face new delays, including high-tech screening and longer waiting periods. Still, more than 3.3 million new immigrants arrived between 2000 and 2004. On January 7, 2004, President George W. Bush proposed a plan to make it easier to track the 8 million illegal immigrants in the country. 2

Once here, immigrants need help. "Family is always the first resource," says Lily Woo, the principal of Public School 130, in New York City, where many Chinese newcomers attend school. Extended immigrant families help one another find housing and work. Other support groups, like churches and community centers, are not as strong as they once were. As a result, about 25% of immigrant households receive government assistance, typically for health care and school for their children. Some 30% of immigrants have not graduated high school, and many have low-paying jobs. R1

Early immigrants quickly took on all aspects of American culture. But, today, many immigrants have one foot in the U.S. and one foot in their native land. With cell phones and the Internet, it's now easier for newcomers to keep in touch with the country they left behind. R2

"I'm the luckiest kid in the world," says Prudence Simon, 10, who now lives in New York. "I have two homes, Trinidad and the U.S.A."

Only the future will reveal how the new immigrants will build their American Dream. But one thing is certain, they have a rich history on which to lay a foundation. 3

Immigrants Past and Present

They may come from different places, but immigrants share similar experiences. Starting over in a new country often takes time and can be hard. Here's a look at how three young immigrants dealt with their new American lives. 4

Corbis Bettmann

OPEN DOORS Immigrants arrive at Ellis Island, in New York Harbor, in 1920. Nearly 14 million foreign-born people were living in the U.S. that year.

2 Reading Across Texts

Evidence What do you learn about immigration from the facts presented here? Make notes in your organizer. How does the use of evidence build the writers' credibility?

3 Reading Across Texts

Purpose The writers say that new immigrants have a "rich history." What might their purpose be for writing about that history?

4 Reading Across Texts

Evidence Writers often use examples and direct quotations as evidence, or support, for their main idea. How does the use of examples help you find and understand the main idea in what you read? How does it build the writers' credibility?

Additional Support

Reading in the Real World

Citizenship Review with students the national security procedures and laws that were passed after the September 11 attacks. Ask students to decide how they feel about limiting immigration for security reasons. Have them write letters to their senators or representatives expressing their opinions. Remind them to support their opinions with sound evidence. OL Give students time to share their letters in small groups to get feedback on supporting arguments, style, organization, and tone. Encourage students to post their letters after their revisions. AS

Jin Hua Zhang

When she was 11 years old, Jin Hua's father brought his family to New York City. Although Jin Hua has made friends and is doing well in school, she still misses her home in China.

Erin Patrice O'Brien

Jin Hua shares this bedroom with her parents and older brother.

In my hometown of Ting Jiang, in southeastern China, people always said that America was very good, like some kind of wonderland. **R1** They said you could have a good life here. So when my mother, my brother, and I flew into New York City's LaGuardia Airport, I was so happy. It was night, and I thought, "This city is so good, so beautiful." I knew at that moment my life would be changing. I thought it would be great.

But then I came to my apartment. I was shocked. In China, my parents were bosses at a company that made bricks. We had a big house; it was very comfortable. Here, there were four of us squeezing into two small rooms [in Chinatown]. Everything is shared—I can't do anything in private. The next day, when I went down to the street, it was so noisy. And, oh, my gosh, so stinky! Starting school was hard too. In China, I'd been a good student—I completed every exam perfectly. Here, I didn't understand what the teacher was saying. It was the [toughest] time I've ever had. **5**

But the biggest difference between China and here was that I was lonely. Some Americans look at you differently [if you're an immigrant]; they look down on you. I had to make all new friends. In China, teenagers come together as a group and go out to play. Here, my parents didn't want me to hang out outside; they thought I could get lost or [might] hang out with bad people.

I know that my family decided to come here so my brother and I could get a better education. In China, they made money more easily, but they never felt like it was enough; **R2** they always wanted more. Now, they work all the time, every morning until midnight, [because they] want me to go to college [instead of] working in a factory like most Chinese

5 Reading Across Texts

Point of View The point of view has changed. What do you learn about Jin Hua and her move to New York from this first-person account? How does this paragraph show her personality?

Differentiated Instruction

Compare and Contrast Some students may benefit by using the chart below to compare and contrast Jin Hua's life in China with her new life in the United States. Have students complete the chart with four aspects of Jin Hua's life then and now. If students have difficulty thinking of aspects, possible suggestions are: food, language, work, education, living space, friendship. **AS**

Jin Hua's Life	China	United States
Aspect 1		
Aspect 2		
Aspect 3		
Aspect 4		

Teach

R1 Reading Skill

Identifying Author's Purpose **Ask:** Why do you think Jin Hua began her account as she did? *(Possible response: She wanted readers to understand what she'd been expecting, and how it differed from what she found.)* **OL**

R2 Reading Skill

Review Understanding Cause and Effect **Ask:** Why did Jin Hua's family move to the United States? *(so she and her brother could get a better education)* **Ask:** Do you think Jin Hua feels that her parents' goals are being accomplished? *(Possible response: I think she's questioning whether she'll get a good education because she's having a difficult time in school and at home.)* **AS**

Indiana English/Language Arts Academic Standards

SE: 8.2

TWE: *Reading in the Real World* 8.5.7, 8.7.6; *Differentiated Instruction* 8.3

Teach

EL Language Coach

Word Origins **Say:** The word *Hispanic* comes from the Latin word *Hispania,* which refers to the Iberian Peninsula, which includes Portugal and Spain. Why is this word appropriate for Mexican Americans? *(They come from Spanish ancestry.)* AS

R Reading Skill

Review Analyzing **Ask:** Why do you think kids laughed when Sonia read? *(Possible response: She may have mispronounced words.)* AS

Viewing the Photo

Ask: What additional information does the photo provide about Sonia? *(Possible response: She has at least one sibling.)* AS

immigrants [we know]. But I feel like I have less. I don't know if I consider myself an American. I feel like I'm really more Chinese. 6

Sonia Diaz

In 1994, Sonia's family moved to Asheboro, North Carolina, from the tiny town of San Francisco de Asis, Mexico. Caught between two worlds, she struggled to stay loyal to her Hispanic heritage while making the most of her new life in America. 7 EL

I wasn't ready for the racism I found when I started school here. In seventh grade, kids used to laugh at my accent when the teacher asked me to read in front of the class. By the time I was in ninth grade, my Mexican friends didn't like to talk to American people. They were scared of having people laugh. R So they didn't want to get involved in anything, no clubs, no sports. I wanted to, but I never could because no other Hispanics were.

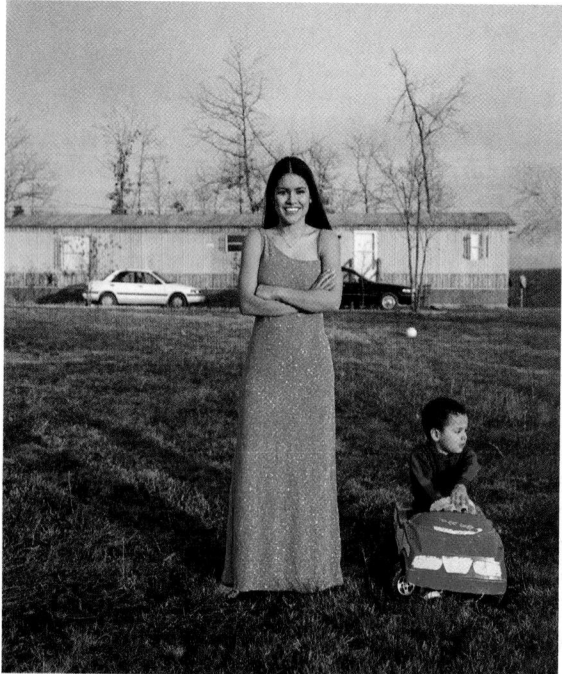

Jason Dewey

Sonia (with her little brother, Jose Luis) strikes a pose in front of her house in Asheboro, North Carolina.

6 Reading Across Texts

Point of View How does the point of view help you understand Jin Hua's experience? Are you surprised to learn that she feels more Chinese than American? Why or why not?

7 English Language Coach

A Changing Language The word **heritage** comes from Middle English, Old French, and Medieval Latin. Use a dictionary to find out more about its origins and meaning.

Additional Support

Differentiated Instruction

Research Project Have students form groups to research the immigration laws passed by Congress since the 1800s. Have each group read about and discuss a particular law and whether it was justified. Then write the inscription from the Statue of Liberty on the board: *Give me your tired, your poor, Your huddled masses yearning to breathe free, The wretched refuse of your teeming shore. Send these, the homeless, tempest-tost to me, I lift my lamp beside the golden door!* Have groups share what they learned from their research and discuss how it relates to the Emma Lazarus poem. AL

Then in 11th grade, I got put in mostly honors classes, because I had good grades. Back then, it was all Americans in those classes. So I needed to talk to them, and we made friends. My Hispanic friends would get mad—they'd say that I didn't know who I was. But after a while I was like, I'm going to talk to whomever I want to. And I did. I made American friends, and I had Mexican friends. I even have an American boyfriend. **E** **R1**

Things are different at my school now. There are lots more Mexican kids, and they're more involved, more open. The soccer team used to be mostly white; now it's mostly Hispanic. Looking back, I wish I could do high school over again. I'd take every honors class, join every club. I missed so many things because I didn't want people to make fun of me. I'm glad it's not like that anymore. **8** **R2**

8 Reading Across Texts

Evidence In your organizer, make notes about Sonia's experience. How is it similar to and different from Jin Hua's?

Peter Deng

Peter was one of Sudan's "Lost Boys," thousands of boys who were separated from their families by the ongoing civil war in their country, and then walked by themselves for months before finally finding safety at a refugee camp in Kenya. In March 2001, he was allowed to emigrate[2] to the United States, where he's building a brand-new life.

When I first came to Denver, [Colorado,] I had never slept in a bed. I had never seen television or snow. Even women in shorts—that's not so common in Africa.

I was born in the village of Jale, in the southern part of Sudan. Our homes were huts made out of long grasses. So the first week [that the Lost Boys were in Denver], we stayed inside, not coming out.

Peter stands tall at his school, the University of Colorado.

2. If you *emigrate*, you leave a country or region to live somewhere else.

Teach

E Text Element

Review Chronological Order Ask: At what point did Sonia begin to feel as if she were a part of her new country? *(when she reached eleventh grade)* **AS**

R1 Reading Skill

Review Understanding Cause and Effect Ask: What resulted from Sonia's being placed in honors classes? *(She made American friends.)* **Ask:** How did her Hispanic friends feel about it? *(They got mad at first and said she didn't remember who she was.)* **OL**

R2 Reading Skill

Review Identifying Main Idea and Supporting Details Ask: What is the main idea of paragraph 2 on this page? *(Possible responses: Sonia's school has more Mexican students and offers more opportunities for immigrants. Sonia now realizes that fear of being teased kept her from a lot of opportunities.)* **OL**

Reading in the Real World

Career Students who are interested in helping people like Peter Deng may enjoy researching a career as a relief agency worker. Have students work with a partner to select a national or international agency that helps people who are in danger or distress, such as the Red Cross or the Peace Corps. Ask them to find out job responsibilities, qualifications, and the geographic areas in which the agency works. Ask students to create a poster promoting their agency. **OL** Students should present their posters to the class and answer additional questions classmates may have about the agency. **AL**

Indiana English/Language Arts Academic Standards

SE: 8.1.2, 8.2

TWE: *Differentiated Instruction* 8.7.12; *Reading in the Real World* 8.5.7, 8.7

Teach

R Reading Skill

Identifying Author's Purpose **Ask:** Why did Peter Deng give details about his first paycheck? *(Possible response: He wanted to show how much he had to learn about his new way of life.)* OL

BQ BIG Question

Ask: What does the last paragraph say about Peter Deng's American dream? *(Possible response: He is living his dream and wants to share it with his brother.)* OL

Assess

Use the CheckPoint questions provided on Presentation Plus! to check for comprehension of the selection. These questions can be used with interactive response keypads for immediate student feedback.

There were eight of us sharing a house, two to a room. Ecumenical Refugee Services [who helped sponsor the Lost Boys] gave us a television. They also bought us clothes and groceries for the first two months and showed us how to cook. 9

There were so many things—the stove, the refrigerator—that we didn't know how to use. I was one of the first Lost Boys to get a job, as a warehouse clerk, processing customer orders. When I got my first paycheck, I didn't know what to do with it. I kept it under the bed for two weeks—until [somebody] told me I had to put it in the bank. R

Now I write checks. I've even bought a car. I love the United States. I like to watch basketball. I've started college, and I have friends—some African, some American. 10

Sometimes we get together for parties. People are so friendly and polite, and nobody **discriminates** or takes advantage of you. My mother died in 1998, but my younger brother is still in the camp in Kenya. I want to bring him here, to get the same opportunities as me. This is a very free life. It's very, very exciting. 11 BQ

—Updated 2005, from *TIME For Kids*, January 30, 2004, and *Teen People*, March 2003

9 Reading Across Texts

Point of View How is Peter's story different from Jin Hua's and Sonia's? What do the first-person accounts reveal about their likes, dislikes, and hopes for the future?

10 BIG Question

Are Jin Hua, Sonia, and Peter living the American dream? Why or why not?

11 Reading Across Texts

Purpose How would you describe the writers' purpose now? Make notes in your organizer.

Vocabulary

discriminates (dis KRIM uh nayts) *v.* treats unfairly

Additional Support

Differentiated Instruction

Sequencing Peter Deng's account shows his gradual transition from African to American culture. Have students create a step-by-step sequence line (like a time line, without the specific dates) showing how Deng "learned to be an American." Some points on the sequence line (in chronological order) should be: (1) Deng is born in Jale, Sudan. (2) March 2001—Deng emigrates to America. (3) Refugee Services gives him clothes, food, a television, and shows him how to cook. (4) Deng gets a job and paycheck. (5) He buys a car. (6) Deng goes to college. AS

Before You Read

Coming to America

Marianne Szegedy-Maszak

Meet the Author

Prize-winning journalist Marianne Szegedy-Maszak has worked for several major news sources, including *Newsweek,* ABC Radio, and National Public Radio. Currently, she is a senior editor at *U.S. News and World Report.* Szegedy-Maszak taught journalism at American University in Washington, D.C., and has lived in both the United States and Europe.

Author Search For more about Marianne Szegedy-Maszak, go to www.glencoe.com.

Indiana English/Language Arts Academic Standards (pp. 1161–1165)

8.1.2 Understand the influence of historical events on English word meaning and vocabulary expansion. **8.2 Comprehension** Develop [reading] strategies...identifying and analyzing...perspective and purpose.

For a complete description of the standards, see p. IN 11.

Vocabulary Preview

trivial (TRIV ee ul) *adj.* of very little value or importance **(p. 1163)** *His skates appeared trivial next to larger concerns.*

incongruous (in KONG groo us) *adj.* not in agreement **(p. 1164)** *The woman's dress seemed incongruous with her environment.*

immersed (ih MURSD) *v.* completely occupied mentally; form of the verb *immerse* **(p. 1165)** *He immersed himself in his studies.*

English Language Coach

EL

A Changing Language English is the official language of the United States because the country used to be British colonies. Britain was once a part of the Roman Empire. The Latin-speaking Romans were greatly influenced by the culture and language of Greece. So let's go straight back to Greek and Latin in the next selection. Watch for these words:

Word	Roots	Meaning
architect	Greek *archi* + Greek *tekton*	master + builder
television	Greek *tele* + Latin *visio*	far + seeing

Get Ready to Read

Connect to the Reading

What challenges do you face in your daily life? What sacrifices would you be willing to make for your dreams to become a reality?

Build Background

The families in this selection came to the United States as refugees. Refugees are people who flee their homelands to escape war, oppression, persecution, or natural disaster. What does the American dream mean to refugees? It often means freedom, opportunity, and sacrifices.

Set Purpose for Reading

BIG Question Read to find out about two refugee families and their search for the American dream.

Set Your Own Purpose What else would you like to learn from this selection to help you answer the Big Question? Write your own purpose on the "Coming to America" page of Foldable 8.

English Language Coach

Greek and Latin Roots Learning Greek and Latin roots and suffixes will help students expand their vocabulary. Have students work with a partner to determine the meaning and origin of the base word in each of these words that end in *-logy.* Use a dictionary if necessary. **Write on the board, with chart:**

The suffix -logy *comes from the Greek word for "science" or "study".* **AS**

Biology	Psychology
Numerology	Astrology
Sociology	Geology
Dermatology	Hematology

Teach

More About the Author

Winner of the Pulitzer traveling fellowship from Columbia University in 1986, Marianne Szegedy-Maszak lived in Hungary for a number of years. There, she covered the news of Central Europe. A journalist with a wide range of interests, Szegedy-Maszak has written articles on the illegal use of the Internet, mental health, differences between genders, conquering phobias, brainwashing as a criminal defense, and other assorted topics.

EL Language Coach

English as a Changing Language Ask: What other words do you know that begin with the Greek *tele,* meaning "far" or "distant"? *(Possible responses: telephone, telegraph, telecommute, telemarketer, telescope)* **OL AL**

Literature Online

Author Search To expand students' appreciation of Marianne Szegedy-Maszak, have them access the Web site for additional information and resources.

Indiana English/Language Arts Academic Standards

SE: 8.1.2, 8.2

TWE: *Differentiated Instruction* 8.2, *English Language Coach* 8.1

Teach

R1 Reading Skill

Identifying Author's Purpose **Ask:** Why might the author have mentioned the Winnie-the-Pooh T-shirt? *(Possible response: to show how the child is adapting to American culture)* OL

R2 Reading Skill

Review Understanding Cause and Effect **Ask:** What is the most common reason for immigration to the United States? *(to find a better life)* **Ask:** Why did the Osmanis come to the United States? *(They were fleeing civil war.)* AS

E Text Element

Review Chronological Order **Ask:** Did Kosovo refugees emigrate before or after those from Laos? *(after)* AS

Readability Scores
Dale-Chall: 5.0
DRP: 55
Lexile: 900

INFORMATIONAL TEXT
MAGAZINE
Good Housekeeping

COMING to AMERICA

by Marianne Szegedy-Maszak

"What day is today?" the teacher asks slowly, tossing a basketball to 11-year-old Dardan Osmani.

"Today is Monday," the boy answers with a slight accent. Then, passing the ball to a child in a Winnie-the-Pooh T-shirt, Dardan asks, "What day is tomorrow?" R1

"Tomorrow is **Wednesday**," the little boy starts to say, but the other children quickly interrupt with the correct answer. 1

There are 21 children learning English in this class at Marymount College in New York City—young survivors of the genocide in Kosovo.[1] Their parents are in another classroom down the hall. They are doctors, engineers, architects—highly educated professionals now trying to learn enough English to get jobs as dishwashers, maids, janitors.

Nearly 10 percent of the U.S. population—26.3 million—was born in other countries. Mostly they've come here for the reason immigrants usually leave their homes: hoping to find a better life for themselves and their children. But a small fraction, including Dardan Osmani's family, had no choice: They were fleeing civil wars or brutal governments. Last year our TV screens showed them leaving Kosovo. Before that, we saw them running from Bosnia, Rwanda, Laos, Cambodia. And then something remarkable happened. We began to see these same people not on our televisions but in the supermarket or at school. 2 E R2

1. ***Kosovo*** was one of the six provinces of Yugoslavia. In the 1990s the country fought a civil war and split apart. The leader of Serbia, another former province, ordered thousands of murders in Kosovo. He was later convicted of ***genocide*** (JEN uh syd), the organized destruction of a racial, political, or cultural group.

Practice the Skills

1 English Language Coach

A Changing Language The Romans had named the days of the week for their gods. Much later, the English chose new names to honor their own gods, one of whom was Woden. Woden's day eventually became **Wednesday**.

2 Reading Across Texts

Purpose Do you think the writer's purpose is to entertain, inform, or persuade? Explain your answer in your organizer.

Additional Support

Reading in the Real World

Citizenship Most states offer *literacy,* or reading, writing, and speaking, classes in English for immigrants. Some instructors are volunteers, while others are paid through community agencies and nonprofit organizations. Have students research literacy programs in their community. Ask students to write a newspaper article that informs local residents of the literacy services available in their community. AS

Which is, perhaps, the greatest gift America can offer: the gift of an ordinary life. 3

At the time that we're talking, the Osmanis have been in New York City just a month. But the father, Elez, 44, and his four oldest children—Dardan, his brother, Begatim, 15, and two sisters, Besarta, 14, and Dhurata, 6—move through the crowded streets like natives as they make their way from English class to an apartment in the Bronx. Nurije, a trim woman of forty, hugs her family as they enter, while baby Rrita, 13 months, wobbles happily among her sisters and brothers. 4

Speaking through an interpreter. Elez tells the family's story. On April 1, 1999, Serbian soldiers forced them to leave their apartment. They went to Macedonia.[2] "Waiting for the train was tough," Elez recalls. "It was raining. The children and old people were already scared. Meanwhile, the Serbian police, trying to create a panic, kept saying they would kill us all."

Conditions at the refugee camp were even rougher. Says Elez grimly, "There was mud everywhere, little food, no showers. And a lot of sickness—twenty-three people died that first week." 5

But the Osmanis were lucky. A week after they arrived, a friend invited the family to his home. Elez's uncle then contacted a cousin in America, who was willing to sponsor the family.

Since they left Kosovo, they've heard that their apartment has been looted. Nurije loses some of her calm self-control as she talks about the lost baby pictures. Dardan mentions his skates, then seems embarrassed that he's thinking about something so **trivial.** But Elez's encouragement keeps them all going. "I want to see my children working, learning," he says emphatically. "I want them to become citizens and not be threatened like their parents were once."

Now, that's beginning to happen. Last fall, the children started school. Elez, who was a magazine editor in Kosovo, found work as a maintenance worker. Nurije, a biology

2. ***Macedonia*** was another province of Yugoslavia.

Vocabulary

trivial (TRIV ee ul) *adj.* of very little value or importance

Practice the Skills

3 **BIG Question**
Why do you think "an ordinary life" is a part of the American dream?

4 **Reading Across Texts**
Point of View What point of view does the writer use here? Why might the writer use this point of view to tell about each member of the Osmani family?

5 **Reading Across Texts**
Evidence What information do you get from direct quotations? How do these direct quotations help you better understand the Osmanis' experience?

Teach

R Reading Skill

Review Identifying Main Idea and Supporting Details **Ask:** What detail in paragraph two supports the idea that the family is quickly adjusting to their new country? *(Elez and his children move through the crowds like natives after only a month.)* AS

EL Language Coach

Word Origins **Say:** The word *trivial* originates from the Latin word *trivialis,* which means "commonplace." How might you connect today's meaning with the Latin definition? *(Possible response: If something is common, it's ordinary. Often ordinary things are seen as unimportant, or trivial.)* AL

Literature Focus Lesson

Main Idea Authors use quotations to support ideas and to engage readers. Write the following paragraph on the board. Ask students to write out the main idea and two quotes from the paragraph that support the main idea: *The voyage was long, and the sea was rough. Many times, Yasha begged to return home. Reuben told her their home was gone. Their country was no longer safe. They thought about America, their new, wonderful home. They wondered if they would be happy there. They had such big plans for their children. Perhaps one would be a scientist and another, a teacher. Such was their dream.* OL

Indiana English/Language Arts Academic Standards
SE: 8.1.2, 8.2
TWE: *Reading in the Real World* 8.5.7, *Literature Focus Lesson* 8.2

Teach

R Reading Skill

Review Understanding Cause and Effect **Ask:** Why had Eva first become separated from her children? *(Civil war broke out in Liberia.)* AS

EL Language Coach

Word Origins **Say:** Two Greek words come together to form *asylos,* which means "impassable" or "dense." How does this word help you understand what asylum is for refugees? *(Possible answer: Asylum keeps harmful things away from people.)* AL

L Literary Element

Review Cultural Reference **Ask:** What cultural clue does the writer provide to let readers know that Eva hasn't forgotten her homeland? *(She's wearing a brightly colored African dress.)* AS

C Critical Thinking

Comprehension **Ask:** What do the Wilsons believe is the key to success in the United States? *(education)* AS

READING ACROSS TEXTS WORKSHOP

teacher, is at home.) He knew he'd have to take a job doing unskilled work, but it doesn't matter. All that counts, the parents agree is that this life "is better for the children." 6

The apartment in Silver Spring, Maryland, was small, and Eva Wilson shared it with a roommate. But on the day in 1996 when Eva welcomed her four children at Newark International Airport and brought them to live with her in that too-small space, only one thing mattered: They were together. "We didn't mind being crowded, all five of us in one room," says Eva, "because where we had been was worse." 7

"I want them to go to college, to learn all they can," says Eva Wilson of her daughters, Manny, Faith, and Peaches.

Where they'd been was Liberia, a country on Africa's west coast. A civil war had broken out there early in 1990, Eva's husband, Francis, had been killed, and she had been separated from her children—Franklin, then 12; Peaches, 8; Faith, 5; and her tiny daughter, Kimmy, only a month old. R

Unbelievably, it took three and a half years for them to be reunited. Even more unbelievably, Eva then had to leave her children again. Her visa[3] to the United States had finally come through. "I knew I had to go to the U.S. if I was going to provide any kind of stable life for my family," she says. "But it was tough, I will tell you. I had to tighten my heart and be strong." She was granted asylum[4] by the United States in 1995, and her children were permitted to join her a year later. 8 EL

Visual Vocabulary ***Town houses*** are houses that share walls with the houses around them.

Today, Eva, 43, is telling her story in her Gaithersburg, Maryland, home. It feels **incongruous,** this woman in a brightly printed African dress describing her ordeal amid town houses in a Washington, D.C. suburb. L The adjustment has been tough, but, like so many generations of immigrants before, the Wilsons know that education is the key. C Franklin, who had lost some time

3. A ***visa*** is a document that permits entry to or travel within a country.
4. Refugees who can't return to their home country can be granted ***asylum***, (uh SY lum), or permission to live, work, and eventually apply for citizenship in the United States.

Vocabulary

incongruous (in KONG groo us) *adj.* not in agreement

Practice the Skills

6 Reading Across Texts

Evidence What did you learn about the Osmanis? Think about how their story is similar to and different from the stories of Jin Hua, Sonia, and Peter from the first selection.

7 Reading Across Texts

Point of View and Evidence The writer uses third-person point of view. She supports her statements with direct quotations. What statement about the Wilsons does this quotation support?

8 Reading Across Texts

Point of View Do you get a better overview of events from a third-person account? Why might a writer choose this point of view to tell about several people, and the things that happen to them over time?

Additional Support

Differentiated Instruction

Comparison To help students organize details to compare the Wilsons and the Osmanis, copy the following chart on the board. Ask students to work with a partner to fill in the information. AS

Comparisons	Wilsons	Osmanis
Goals		
Employment		
Family		
Reasons for Emigrating		

Analyzing the Photo In this April 1999 photo, ethnic Albanian refugees wait at a checkpoint on the Kosovo-Macedonia border. How does this photo capture the frustration and uncertainty of the refugee experience?

in school, **immersed** himself in the eleventh grade and graduated on time, winning a scholarship to a college in Florida. The older girls, too, excel at their studies, and little Kimmy, who'd never had a normal life before coming here, is now studying hard. 9 R

For Eva, the challenge was work. She had a job at a school, but most days she had to be there from four in the afternoon until eight the next morning. Now, having just earned her certificate in early-childhood education, she is working at a day-care center. 10 EL

But the struggle has been worth it, says Eva. "Coming here was our only hope. Otherwise, we would have always been refugees." ❍

Practice the Skills

9 Reading Across Texts

Purpose How would you describe the writer's purpose now? Make notes in your organizer.

10 BIG Question

Do you think the American dream means the same thing to the Wilsons as it does to the Osmanis? Why or why not?

Vocabulary

immersed (ih MURSD) *v.* completely occupied mentally

Teach

R Reading Skill

Review Understanding Cause and Effect **Ask:** What do the opening lines on this page say about how immigration has affected the Wilson children? *(Possible response: Immigrating to America helped the children, who are doing well in school and leading normal lives.)* AS

EL Language Coach

Word Origins **Say:** The Latin word *certus* means "to make certain." A certificate "makes certain" that someone has accomplished or can do a certain task. What other English words have this Latin base word and meaning? *(Possible responses: certify, ascertain, certain, certification)* AL

Assess

CheckPoint

Use the CheckPoint questions provided on Presentation Plus! to check for comprehension of the selection. These questions can be used with interactive response keypads for immediate student feedback.

Literature Focus Lesson

Main Idea and Supporting Details
Each of the immigrants in this selection revealed events that took them from their homelands to life in America. They also revealed how they felt about their experiences, both in their native countries and in the United States. Have students work with partners to identify the major events in the lives of the Osmani and Wilson families. Then ask them to write a paragraph that supports this main idea: *Finding a new homeland takes courage and determination.* Allow students time to share their paragraphs with the rest of the class. OL

Indiana English/Language Arts Academic Standards
SE: 8.2
TWE: *Differentiated Instruction* 8.2, *Literature Focus Lesson* 8.4.3

Assess

Resources for page 1166

- Selection Quick Check, pp. 79–80
- ExamView Assessment Suite
- Interactive Tutor: Self-Assessment

Coming to America & Coming to America

Vocabulary Check

1. Possible response: oppresses
2. Possible response: out of place
3. Possible response: involved
4. Possible response: unimportant
5. Possible response: worked
6. Possible response: toil—building houses
7. Possible response: trivial—stamp collecting
8. Possible response: incongruous—green
9. Possible response: immerse—a school play
10. Possible response: discriminated—buildings with only stairs or with no ramps at entrances

English Language Coach

11. Italian
12. Spanish
13. Italian
14. Japanese
15. French
16. German
17. Russian
18. Chinese or Cantonese

After You Read

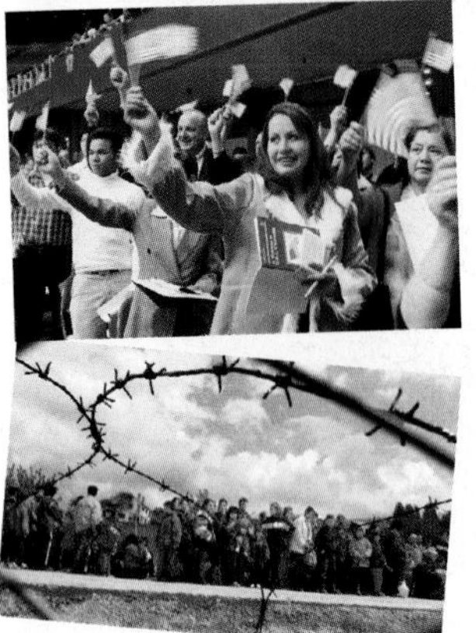

Indiana English/Language Arts Academic Standards (pp. 1166–1167)

8.2 Comprehension and Analysis (Focus on Informational Text) Develop [reading] strategies... identifying and analyzing... perspective and purpose.
8.5.7 Write for different purposes...

For a complete description of the standards, see p. IN 11.

Coming to AMERICA & COMING to AMERICA

Vocabulary Check

Each vocabulary word below is followed by a synonym. Copy each set, adding at least one synonym. (It can be a word or a phrase.) If you get stuck, use a thesaurus. Be sure to choose synonyms that are close to the meanings given on pages 1154 and 1161.

1. **discriminates:** shows prejudice
2. **incongruous:** mismatched
3. **immersed:** caught up in
4. **trivial:** insignificant
5. **toiled:** labored

Write each vocabulary word and an example of the thing described.

6. a job that requires people to **toil**
7. a hobby or activity that you find **trivial**
8. a color that you think is **incongruous** with purple
9. a recent project or activity you've had to **immerse** yourself in
10. a way that people in wheelchairs are sometimes **discriminated** against

English Language Coach

Each word below came into English from a modern foreign language with little or no change in spelling or pronunciation. Identify the original language (Spanish, for example, not the word's roots in Latin or Anglo-Saxon). If you're not sure, make a guess before you look up the word.

11. arcade
12. chili
13. confetti
14. karaoke
15. matinee
16. pretzel
17. tundra
18. wok

Reading/Critical Thinking

Coming to AMERICA

19. BIG Question What do Jin Hua, Sonia, and Peter want to achieve in America? How are their dreams alike and different?

TIP **Author and Me**

20. Recall What does Sonia wish that she could do over again?

TIP **Right There**

21. Infer Why do you think Jin Hua feels more Chinese than American?

TIP **Author and Me**

COMING to AMERICA

22. Interpret Eva uses a figure of speech when she says that she had to "tighten her heart." What does she mean?

TIP **Author and Me**

23. Interpret Why do you think that so many people choose to immigrate to the United States? What opportunities exist here that don't exist elsewhere?

TIP **On My Own**

24. Analyze Do the Osmanis and the Wilsons think their struggles have been worthwhile? Are they living their dreams?

TIP **Author and Me**

Writing: Reading Across Texts

Use Your Notes

What have you learned about the immigrant experience from these selections? As you review your chart and other notes, ask yourself these questions:

- *What facts and examples did I find in each selection?*
- *How did the selection's direct quotations and first-person accounts help me better understand the immigrant experience?*

25. Use the notes in your organizer to compare and contrast what you learned from the selections in this workshop.

Step 1: Look at your notes about purpose and credibility. Did you find similarities between the selections? Write them in the appropriate circle in your organizer. How did the writers' purposes differ? Underline the differences you noted.

Step 2: Write a paragraph comparing or contrasting the writers' purposes.

Step 3: Look at your notes about evidence and point of view. Record the similarities you found in the appropriate circle in your organizer. Underline the differences you noted.

Step 4: Write a paragraph comparing or contrasting the types of evidence used in these selections. Which selection contained the most information? From which selection did you learn the most?

Step 5: Write a paragraph comparing or contrasting point of view in both selections. Which point of view was most appealing? Did you learn more about the immigrant experience from a first- or third-person account?

Get It On Paper

To compare what you've learned from these selections, answer the questions below.

26. In the first selection, the writer's purpose was ___ .

27. In the second selection, the writers' purpose was ___ .

28. I learned ___ from the first selection that I didn't learn from the second selection.

29. I learned ___ from the second selection that I didn't learn from the first selection.

30. I found the (first, second) selection more interesting because I learned ___ from it.

BIG Question

31. You've read what the American dream means to people from other parts of the world. What does the American dream mean to you?

25. Check students' responses.

Get It on Paper

26. Possible response: to give different perspectives on the immigrant experience

27. Possible response: to show the courage and sacrifices made by immigrants who are forced to leave their homelands

28. Possible response: that some immigrants regret leaving their homeland

29. Possible response: that some people had no choice but to emigrate for their and their families' safety

30. Responses will vary.

BQ 

31. Responses will vary.

READING ACROSS TEXTS WORKSHOP

Reading/Critical Thinking

Coming to America

19. Possible response: All want to have better lives. Jin Hua sounds disappointed and frustrated with American life. At first, Sonia had difficulty adjusting, but now she enjoys life. Peter is grateful from the outset for the safety he finds here.

20. Go through high school

21. Possible response: She misses her large home, the clean streets, knowing the language, doing well in school, and time with her parents.

Coming to America

22. She had to be brave and strong.

23. Possible response: The United States is safe, has food, jobs, and free education. People have more freedom to choose careers, homes, and lifestyles than in some other countries.

24. Possible response: They both feel they are better off as immigrants than refugees. They know their dreams will take time, but they are trying to achieve them.

Close

Ask students to list other historical texts they have read about people who have pursued their dream in a new country.

Indiana English/Language Arts Academic Standards
SE: 8.2, 8.5.7

The Unit Challenge

Focus

BELLRINGER Options

Daily Language Practice Transparency 81

Focus Activity Ask: Of all the selections on the American dream that you read in this unit, which best represents your idea of the American dream? The discussion will remind students of the selections they've read, which will help them begin the group activity or the solo activity. AS

Teach

Group Activity: American Dream Newsletter

- As students brainstorm in groups, circulate to help them understand the "version" of the American dream each character or person represents. Students may need some help with this focus.
- As students begin to put together their chosen character or person with the *kind* of article they want to write, ask them to think about who their audience is, who would be interested in reading about this person or character, and why. Explain that answering these questions will help them in writing their articles.
- Be sure students clearly understand the type of article they choose to write and its purpose.
- Encourage students with interest in art or abilities with computer layout to assist in the final preparations of the newsletter.

UNIT 8 WRAP-UP

Answering The BIG Question What Is the American Dream?

You've just about read about the American dreams of real people and fictional characters. Now use what you've learned to do the Unit Challenge.

The Unit Challenge

Choose Activity A or Activity B and follow the directions for that activity.

A. Group Activity: American Dream Newsletter

Form a small group and create a newsletter that contains articles about people who obtain their American dreams.

1. **Talk about American Dreams** Choose one group member to be the note-keeper for the discussion. This person should make a chart with two columns labeled **Character/Person** and **American Dream/Values**. As a group, brainstorm a list of characters and real people from these Unit 8 selections whom you'd like to write about. Use your Foldable notes for ideas.
   - What versions of the American dream do the characters and people on your list have? What do they value in life?
   - What do they do or plan to do to accomplish their goals and achieve their dreams?

2. **Choose an Article** Group members can choose to write a newsletter article about a character or person from a selection or about a real person who isn't in the reading—a famous person, a friend, or a relative, for example. You can also choose to write about your version of the American dream in an opinion piece or in a persuasive essay.

   First, decide on the type of article you'd like to write. Here are some ideas:
   - a news article about a specific event in the person's life that helps him or her get closer to achieving the American dream
   - a feature article presenting a brief biography, including what the person has done to obtain the American dream
   - a feature article about the person's values and how they relate to the American dream
   - an article about the people and events that have influenced the person's ideas of the American dream
   - an opinion piece in which you present your idea of the American dream and why it's important to you
   - an essay that tries to persuade readers of the best ways to achieve the American dream

Assess/Close

Group Activity

Ask: Why has the American dream been so important to people living and writing in America? *(Suggest that students write responses in their Learner's Notebooks.)* AS

3. **Write Your Article** Sit down and write.
   - Decide what facts to include.
   - Decide on a main idea and back it up with supporting details.
   - Choose a text structure to help you present your ideas clearly.
   - Open with an attention-getter–something that will make your readers want to keep reading.
   - Create a title for your article.

4. **Create the Newsletter** Get together with your group again, and put the newsletter together.
   - Decide on a name, and have someone design it for the top of the newsletter.
   - Draw a rough draft of the layout, including ideas for photos and other text features.
   - Exchange articles with another group member for proofreading. If you have questions, ask the writer to clarify.
   - Type up or print out all the articles and cut and paste them into your newsletter. Add photos or other illustrations. Then make copies for your classmates.

B. Solo Activity: American Dream Spokesperson

You've read how people in different times and places have interpreted the American dream. Now choose someone to be an "American Dream Spokesperson."

1. **Make the Call** Review your Foldable notes, and then list the people and characters from the selections.
   - Add to the list people you know personally who have in some way lived, or worked toward, the American dream.
   - Choose a person or character from your list to be a spokesperson for the American dream.

2. **Speaking for Your Spokesperson** Decide how you want to honor your spokesperson. Here are some ideas:
   - Write a biography. You may need to research the details of a real person's life. If you chose a fictional character, you can write his or her biography based on details you know from the selection as well as from your imagination.
   - Write a speech. Have your spokesperson describe and explain his or her American dream. Be as specific as possible.
   - Create a poster. Include images and words that help show your spokesperson's idea of the American Dream.

3. **Go Public!** Take your American Dream Spokesperson public. Publish your biography, speech, or poster. Display it in the classroom, read it aloud, present it to the class, or put it on your class's Web site (if you have one).

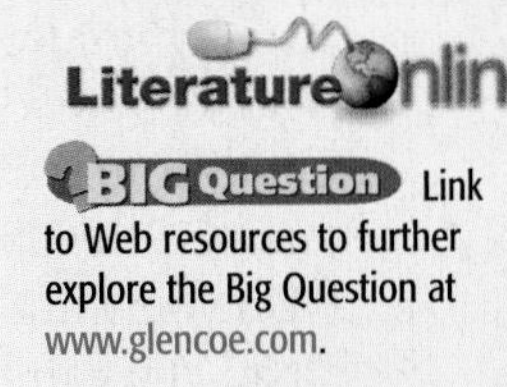

Link to Web resources to further explore the Big Question at www.glencoe.com.

UNIT 8 WRAP-UP

Teach

Solo Activity: American Dream Spokesperson

- Have students thoroughly review their Foldable notes for possible characters or people to be their American dream spokesperson. Suggest they write down specific ideas they noticed as they did the reading.
- Encourage students to think of people they know to add to the list. Even if they do not make them the spokesperson, it's a good exercise to join everyday people with heroes of history and literature.
- Remind students that their biographies or speeches do not have to be long. Rather, their written work needs to make a powerful point about why a person or character represents the American dream.
- Help students to find the right venue for publishing their work. Allow a place on the bulletin board or have a class "speak-a-thon" in which each student presents a candidate for American dream spokesperson.
- Ask students to carefully check their biographies, speeches, or posters for grammatical and spelling errors.

Assess/Close

Solo Activity

Encourage students to use this activity to think about what the American dream means to them. Have them write a summary in their Learner's Notebooks of what they would like to contribute to the American dream as they grow up. **AS**

Literature Online

Big Question Have students access the Web site for English and Spanish summaries and annotated links to related Web resources.

Focus

Build Background

Magazines were popular in the United States even before the American Revolution.

- Benjamin Franklin's *General Magazine and Historical Chronicle* circulated in Philadelphia in 1741.
- Soon after the war, the number of magazines increased to more than seventy.
- Weekly magazines became popular as early as the 1850s.

L Literary Element

Cultural Reference Say: Read the first paragraph of the story. What cultural reference is included in it? *(The Saturday Evening Post)* **Ask:** What does this tell you about the setting? *(It takes place in the early to middle part of the twentieth century.)* If necessary, have students check the library or Internet for information about this magazine. AS

Readability Scores
Dale-Chall: 3.6
DRP: 46
Lexile: 620

UNIT 8

Your Turn: Read and Apply Skills

Toshio Mori

Meet the Author

Toshio Mori was born in Oakland, California, in 1910. He knew at an early age that he would become a writer. But just before his first book was published, Japan attacked the U.S. Navy base at Pearl Harbor, Hawaii. The United States entered World War II and sent 110,000 Japanese-American citizens to specially built camps. Mori's family wound up in Utah. After the war, his book was published, and Mori was recognized as an important new writer.

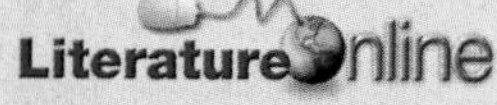

Author Search For more about Toshio Mori, go to www.glencoe.com.

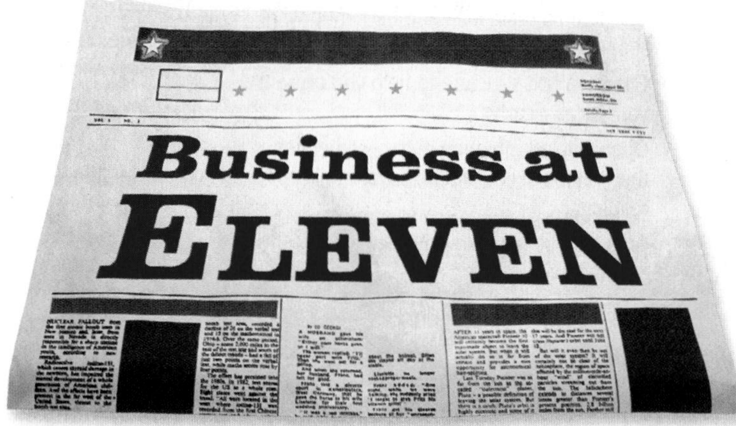

Business at Eleven

by Toshio Mori

When he came to our house one day and knocked on the door and immediately sold me a copy of *The Saturday Evening Post,* it was the beginning of our friendship and also the beginning of our business relationship.

His name is John. I call him Johnny and he is eleven. It is the age when he should be crazy about baseball or football or fishing. But he isn't. Instead he came again to our door and made a business proposition.

"I think you have many old magazines here," he said.

"Yes," I said, "I have magazines of all kinds in the basement."

"Will you let me see them?" he said.

"Sure," I said.

I took him down to the basement where the stacks of magazines stood in the corner. Immediately this little boy went over to the piles and lifted a number of magazines and examined the dates of each number and the names.

"Do you want to keep these?" he said.

"No. You can have them," I said.

"No. I don't want them for nothing," he said. "How much do you want for them?"

"You can have them for nothing," I said.

"No, I want to buy them," he said. "How much do you

Additional Support

Author Search To expand students' appreciation of Toshio Mori, have them access the Web site for additional information and resources.

Literature Focus Lesson

Summary In this story, the speaker develops a relationship with eleven-year-old John, whose mother died the previous year. John's unemployed father has five other children. John buys back copies of magazines from the narrator and sells them to customers who also buy current magazines from him. He uses his profits to buy clothing for his father and gifts for his clients as a sound business practice. At the end, the narrator learns that John must move with his newly remarried father to Los Angeles. John plans to continue his magazine sales to accomplish his dream: owning the largest bookstore in the Bay Region. AS want for them?"

This was a boy of eleven, all seriousness and purpose.

"What are you going to do with the old magazines?"

"I am going to sell them to people," he said.

We arranged the financial matters satisfactorily. We agreed he was to pay three cents for each copy he took home. On the first day he took home an *Esquire*, a couple of *Saturday Evening Posts*, a *Scribner's*, an *Atlantic Monthly*, and a *Collier's*. He said he would be back soon to buy more magazines.[1]

E When he came back several days later, I learned his name was John so I began calling him Johnny.

"How did you make out, Johnny?" I said.

"I sold them all," he said. "I made seventy cents altogether."

"Good for you," I said. "How do you manage to get seventy cents for old magazines?"

C Johnny said as he made the rounds selling *The Saturday Evening Post*, he also asked the folks if there were any back numbers[2] they particularly wanted. Sometimes, he said, people will pay unbelievable prices for copies they had missed and wanted very much to see some particular articles or pictures, or their favorite writers' stories.

"You are a smart boy," I said.

"Papa says, if I want to be a salesman, be a good salesman," Johnny said. "I'm going to be a good salesman."

"That's the way to talk," I said. "And what does your father do?"

"Dad doesn't do anything. He stays at home," Johnny said.

"Is he sick or something?" I said.

"No, he isn't sick," he said. "He's all right. There's nothing wrong with him."

R "How long have you been selling *The Saturday Evening Post?*" I asked.

"Five years," he said. "I began at six."

"Your father is lucky to have a smart boy like you for a son," I said.

That day he took home a dozen or so of the old magazines. He said he had five standing orders, an *Esquire* issue of June 1937, *Atlantic Monthly* February 1938 number, a copy of December 11, 1937 issue of *The New Yorker*, *Story Magazine* of February 1934, and a *Collier's* of April 2, 1938. The others, he said, he was taking a chance at.

"I can sell them," Johnny said.

Several days later I saw Johnny again at the door.

"Hello, Johnny," I said. "Did you sell them already?"

"Not all," he said. "I have two left. But I want some more."

"All right," I said. "You must have good business."

"Yes," he said, "I am doing pretty good these days. I broke my own record selling *The Saturday Evening Post* this week."

"How much is that?" I said.

"I sold 167 copies this week," he said. "Most boys feel lucky if they sell seventy-five or one hundred copies. But not for me."

"How many are there in your family, Johnny?" I said.

"Six counting myself," he said. "There is my father, three smaller brothers, and two small sisters."

1. All the magazines named in this story are or were known for printing new works by top American writers. As of 2006, only three of the magazines were still being published: *Atlantic Monthly* (which began in 1857), *The New Yorker*, and *Esquire*.

2. ***Back numbers*** refers to old issues.

Teach

E Text Element

Chronological Order Ask: When did the narrator first learn the boy's name? *(several days after he had agreed to sell his old magazines)* AS

C Critical Thinking

Comprehension Ask: How does Johnny sell old magazines, and why are people interested in buying them? *(As he's selling* The Saturday Evening Post, *he asks people if they want any back issues. Many people are interested in buying them because they missed an article or a story by their favorite writer.)* AS

R Reading Skill

Identifying Main Idea and Supporting Details Ask: What detail supports the idea that Johnny's father is lucky to have Johnny for a son? *(Possible response: Johnny has worked since he was six years old.)* OL

Differentiated Instruction

Historical Perspective To help students understand Johnny's determination, explain that the setting of the story is the 1940s. Have students work in groups to research wages and prices of common items during this time period, such as food, magazines, homes, and clothing. Ask students to calculate Johnny's weekly earnings from details in the story. Have students discuss how this information gives them a better understanding of Johnny's desire to achieve his American dream. AL

Indiana English/Language Arts Academic Standards
TWE: *Differentiated Instruction* 8.3.4

Teach

R Reading Skill

Identifying Author's Purpose **Ask:** Why does the author include information about Johnny's family? *(Possible response: to help readers understand why Johnny needs to work)* AS

L Literary Element

Cultural References **Ask:** Even if you don't know exactly when the American writers listed in the last paragraph lived, why can they be considered cultural references? *(Possible response: magazines from the early and middle 1900s included these author's stories, so they must have been current at that time.)* OL

"Where's your mother?" I said.

"Mother died a year ago," Johnny said.

He stayed in the basement a good one hour sorting out the magazines he wished. I stood by and talked to him as he lifted each copy and inspected it thoroughly. When I asked him if he had made a good sale with the old magazines recently, he said yes. He sold the *Scribner's* Fiftieth Anniversary Issue for sixty cents. Then he said he made several good sales with *Esquire* and a *Vanity Fair* this week.

"You have a smart head, Johnny," I said. "You have found a new way to make money."

Johnny smiled and said nothing. Then he gathered up the fourteen copies he picked out and said he must be going now.

THE SATURDAY EVENING POST
An Illustrated Weekly
Founded A.D. 1728 by Benj. Franklin
DECEMBER 19, 1925
5cts. THE COPY

"Johnny," I said, "hereafter you pay two cents a copy. That will be enough."

Johnny looked at me.

"No," he said. "Three cents is all right. You must make a profit, too."

An eleven-year-old boy—I watched him go out with his short business-like stride.

Next day he was back early in the morning. "Back so soon?" I said.

"Yesterday's were all orders," he said. "I want some more today."

"You certainly have a good trade," I said.

"The people know me pretty good. And I know them pretty good," he said. And about ten minutes later he picked out seven copies and said that was all he was taking today.

"I am taking Dad shopping," he said. "I am going to buy a new hat and shoes for him today."

"He must be tickled," I said.

"You bet he is," Johnny said. "He told me to be sure and come home early."

So he said he was taking these seven copies to the customers who ordered them and then run home to get Dad.

Two days later Johnny wanted some more magazines. He said a Mr. Whitman who lived up a block wanted all the magazines with Theodore Dreiser's stories inside. Then he went on talking about other customers of his. Miss White, the schoolteacher, read Hemingway, and he said she would buy back copies with Hemingway stories anytime he brought them in. Some liked Sinclair Lewis, others Saroyan, Faulkner, Steinbeck, Mann, Faith Baldwin, Fannie Hurst, Thomas Wolfe.[3] So it went. It was amazing how an eleven-year-old boy could

3. The writers named here are among the best American short story writers. Some of them also wrote novels and nonfiction.

Additional Support

Reading in the Real World

Career Point out to students that Johnny makes a great salesman because he is creative, smart, dedicated, and honest. Remind students of the *Dandelion Wine* excerpt in which Douglas is a great salesman, too. Some students might be interested in learning more about sales. Have students choose a field that interests them, such as car sales, book sales, pharmaceutical sales, and so on. Then allow them time to research the career. Students should identify the job expectations, salaries, experience, and education needed for their chosen positions. Invite students to share their research with the class. AS remember the customers' preferences and not get mixed up.

One day I asked him what he wanted to do when he grew up. He said he wanted a book shop all his own. He said he would handle old books and magazines as well as the new ones and own the biggest bookstore around the Bay Region.[4]

"That is a good ambition," I said. "You can do it. Just keep up the good work and hold your customers."

On the same day, in the afternoon, he came around to the house holding several packages.

"This is for you," he said, handing over a package. "What is this?" I said.

Johnny laughed. "Open up and see for yourself," he said.

I opened it. It was a book rest, a simple affair but handy.

"I am giving these to all my customers," Johnny said.

"This is too expensive to give away, Johnny," I said. "You will lose all your profits."

"I picked them up cheap," he said. "I'm giving these away so the customers will remember me."

"That is right, too," I said. "You have good sense."

After that he came in about half a dozen times, each time taking with him ten or twelve copies of various magazines. He said he was doing swell. Also, he said he was now selling *Liberty* along with the *Saturday Evening Posts.*

Then for two straight weeks I did not see him once. I could not understand this. He had never missed coming to the house in two or three days. Something must be wrong, I thought. He must be sick, I thought.

One day I saw Johnny at the door. "Hello, Johnny," I said. "Where were you? Were you sick?"

"No. I wasn't sick," Johnny said.

"What's the matter? What happened?" I said.

"I'm moving away," Johnny said. "My father is moving to Los Angeles."

"Sit down, Johnny," I said. "Tell me all about it."

He sat down. He told me what had happened in two weeks. He said his dad went and got married to a woman he, Johnny, did not know. And now, his dad and this woman say they are moving to Los Angeles. And about all there was for him to do was to go along with them.

"I don't know what to say, Johnny," I said.

Johnny said nothing. We sat quietly and watched the time move.

"Too bad you will lose your good trade," I finally said.

"Yes, I know," he said. "But I can sell magazines in Los Angeles."

"Yes, that is true," I said.

Then he said he must be going. I wished him good luck. We shook hands. "I will come and see you again," he said.

"And when I visit Los Angeles some day," I said, "I will see you in the largest bookstore in the city."

Johnny smiled. As he walked away, up the street and out of sight, I saw the last of him walking like a good businessman, walking briskly, energetically, purposefully. ❍

4. The ***Bay Region*** is the area around San Francisco, California.

Teach

EL Language Coach

Word Origins **Say:** The word *ambition* comes from the Latin word *ambition*, which meant "to ask for votes". How does this word help you understand the meaning of the English word *ambition*? *(Possible response: A person who goes around seeking votes is willing to work toward a goal. He or she has ambition.)* OL

R Reading Skill

Identifying Cause and Effect **Ask:** What caused Johnny to have to move to Los Angeles? *(his father's remarriage)* **Ask:** What effect did the upcoming move have on Johnny? *(Possible response: He didn't seem pleased about moving but felt he had no choice. Although he hated giving up the business he had built, he was determined to start over in his new home.)* AS

C Critical Thinking

Evaluation **Ask:** Do you agree with the speaker's prediction about Johnny? Why or why not? *(Responses will vary.)* AS

Literature Focus Lesson

Characterization Authors develop characters by including details of both physical and personality traits. By the end of the story, Mori has painted a vivid picture of Johnny. Tell students to think about what Mori has written and write their own one-paragraph character sketches of Johnny. BL

Indiana English/Language Arts Academic Standards
TWE: *Literature Focus Lesson* 8.3

Tips for Independent Reading

Stress the importance of reading different types of historical text, both fiction and nonfiction, including magazine and newspaper articles, books, novels, poems, and plays. Suggest the books listed here that are related to the Big Question.

Fiction

Explain to students how reading fictional stories of people whose experiences and decisions have helped them achieve the American dream can inspire them to work toward a goal in their lives.

Ask students to tell about a fictional story, book, or play they've read that models how someone achieved his or her American dream.

UNIT 8

Reading on Your Own

To read more about the Big Question, choose one of these books from your school or local library. Work on your reading skills by choosing books that are challenging to you.

Fiction

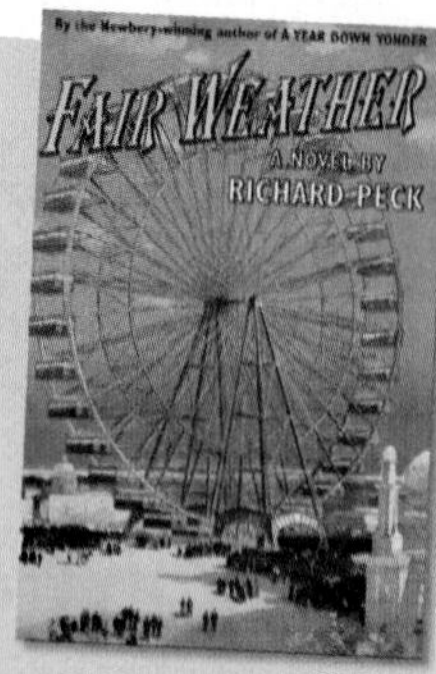

Fair Weather
by Richard Peck

In 1893 Rosie Beckett's farm life has few thrills. And then her aunt invites Rosie's family to stay at her house for a week so that they can visit the Columbian Exposition, or World Fair. Now Rosie's dreams of how her life might unfold are much more exciting.

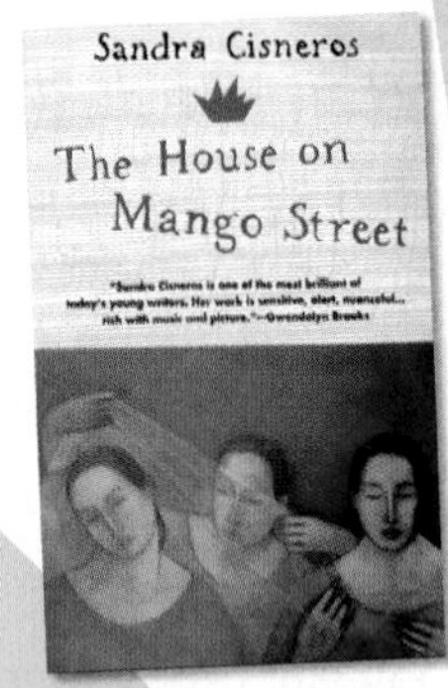

The House on Mango Street
by Sandra Cisneros

Esperanza Cordero is a young girl coming of age in a Hispanic neighborhood in Chicago. She uses poems and stories to express her feelings about growing up in an environment that she thinks is oppressive. Esperanza dreams of the house that she will own someday—a house that will not be on Mango Street.

House Made of Dawn
by N. Scott Momaday

This book tells the story of Abel, a young Native American, who journeys from a reservation and experiences the difficult environment of an American city.

Ellis Island: Land of Hope
by Joan Lowery Nixon

Rebekah Levinsky and her family are the main characters in this story of the American immigrant experience of the early 1900s. The book tells of the Levinsky family's voyage from Russia to America and their struggle to survive on New York's Lower East Side.

Additional Support

Differentiated Instruction

Use the Glencoe BookLink CD-ROM to create customized reading lists. Suggestions for Unit 8:

Grade 4: *One-Way to Ansonia*
by Judie Angell
Grade 5: *Drive: The Story of My Life*
by Larry Bird
Grade 6: *I Will Be a Doctor: The Story of America's First Woman Physician*
by Dorothy Clarke
Grade 7: *My Name is San Ho*
by Jane Pettit
Grade 8: *Children of the Dust Bowl: The True Story of the School at Weedpatch Camp*
by Jerry Stanley

Nonfiction

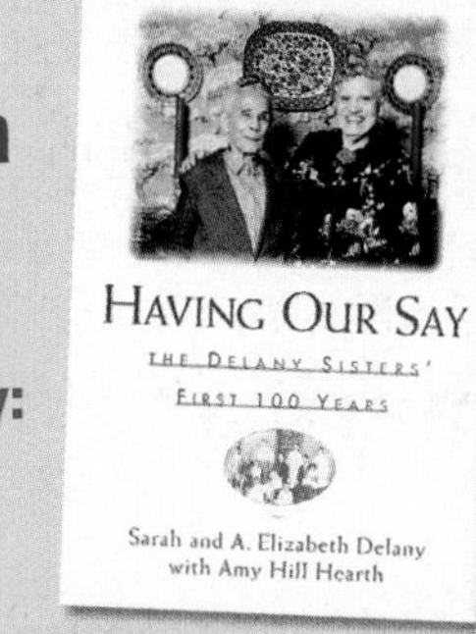

Having Our Say: The Delany Sisters' First 100 Years

by Sarah and A. Elizabeth Delany

Two feisty African American women who each lived to be more than a century old tell their life stories. They describe the social history of the twentieth century as they saw it, from the days of Jim Crow laws to the Harlem Renaissance, the Civil Rights movement, and beyond.

Manners and Customs

By Jim Barmeier

This book is from the series *Life in America 100 Years Ago,* which tells of the effects that immigration, technological advances, and the factory system had on daily life. It also paints a picture of the confusing American lifestyle that was the dream of many immigrants.

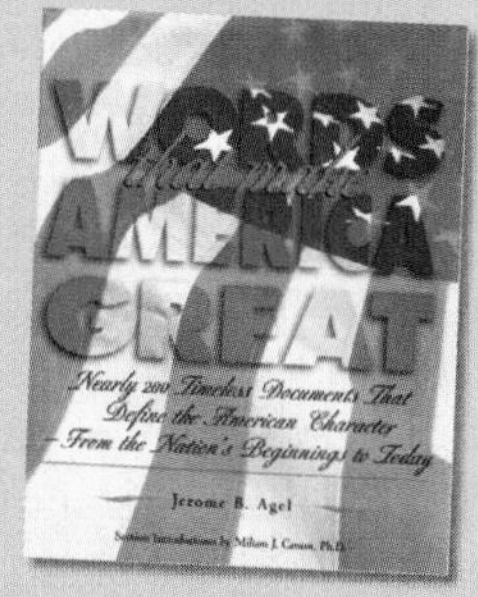

Words That Make America Great

Edited by Jerome Agel

This book presents 200 documents that have helped define America's character and ideals from its earliest days to the present. Included are many documents of the years 1750–1850, from the Declaration of Independence to the earliest rules of baseball. This is the basis of the American dream.

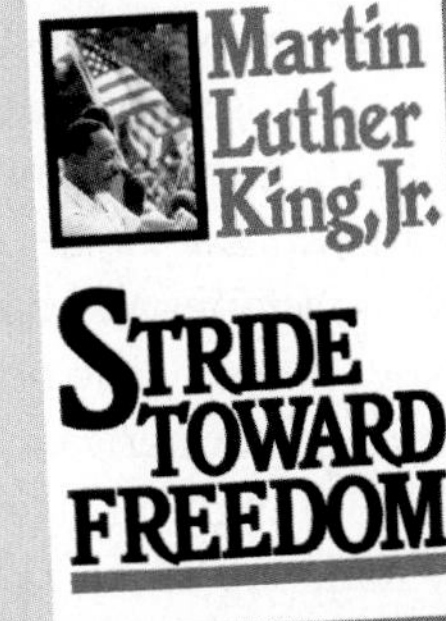

Stride Toward Freedom: The Montgomery Story

by Martin Luther King Jr.

Dr. King tells the story of the Montgomery bus boycott. He explains how it was conceived and organized. He describes the many violent threats on his life, and the obstacles that American society placed before those striving for their versions of the American dream.

READING ON YOUR OWN

Nonfiction

Tell students that all of the books on this page are nonfiction. The authors of the books tell about American history and how the American dream has evolved over the years.

Historical Text

Ask: Can you tell why reading nonfiction historical text might help you reach goals in your own life? Historical nonfiction describes real people who faced real challenges as they worked toward their goals. Students may identify with one or more of the authors as they relate how they or their subjects overcame challenges and adversities to accomplish their dreams. **OL**

About the subjects

Real-life sisters Sarah and A. Elizabeth Delaney and Dr. Martin Luther King Jr. model how dreams can survive despite challenges. The manners, customs, and documents of real-life Americans display how society and country foster the idea of an American dream for all citizens.

Test-Taking Tips

TIP Remind students that they do not have to answer test questions in the order in which they are presented. Students should answer the questions in the order that they feel most comfortable with. If a student is having trouble with the first question, he or she should skip it and come back to it later. Often a difficult question will be easy to answer after a student has completed the easier questions.

TIP Remind students to refer back to the passage to find evidence for their answers when they have to give a written response to a question.

ISTEP+ Test Practice

Directions

Read this article about the United States' newest immigrants. Then, answer questions 1 through 7.

from "Coming to America"

Time

by Joe McGowan, Marisa Wong, Vickie Bane, and Laurie Morice

The United States is a nation built by immigrants. From 1840 to 1870, the first wave of immigrants came from Ireland, England, Germany, and China to dig waterways and lay railroad tracks. From 1890 to 1924, a second wave crashed over Ellis Island, the historic immigration station in New York Harbor, from countries such as Italy and Russia. These newcomers toiled in factories and built cities.

Now, a new wave of immigrants is coming to America. Over 31 million immigrants live in the U.S. They make up about 11.5% of the population. Like those who came before, these immigrants are arriving in hopes of building their own version of the American Dream.

A New Era with New Challenges

Since the terrorist attacks of September 11, 2001, America has been rethinking its immigration policy. Some people want to limit the number of new immigrants to 300,000 a year. All foreign visitors face new delays, including high-tech screening and longer waiting periods. Still, more than 3.3 million new immigrants arrived between 2000 and 2004. On January 7, 2004, President George W. Bush proposed a plan to make it easier to track the 8 million illegal immigrants in the country.

Once here, immigrants need help. "Family is always the first resource," says Lily Woo, the principal of Public School 130, in New York City, where many Chinese newcomers attend school. Extended immigrant families help one another find housing and work. Other support groups, like churches and community centers, are not as strong as they once were. As a result, about 25% of immigrant households receive government assistance, typically for health care and school for their children. Some 30% of immigrants have not graduated high school, and many have low-paying jobs.

Early immigrants quickly took on all aspects of American culture. But, today, many immigrants have one foot in the U.S. and one foot in their native land. With cell phones and the Internet, it's now easier for newcomers to keep in touch with the country they left behind.

"I'm the luckiest kid in the world," said Prudence Simon, 10, who now lives in New York. "I have two homes, Trinidad and the U.S.A."

Only the future will reveal how the new immigrants will build their American Dream. But one thing is certain, they have a rich history on which to lay a foundation.

Questions 1 through 7 are based on "Coming to America."

1 Read this sentence from the article.

All foreign visitors face new delays, including high-tech screening and longer waiting periods.

What does the word *screening* mean in this context?

A harassment
B examination and evaluation
C assistance and protection
D rejection

2 According to the article, what event caused the United States to reevaluate its immigration policies?

A a second wave of immigrants
B the election of George W. Bush
C the terrorist attacks of September 11, 2001
D the invention of the cell phone

3 Which of the following sentences from the passage BEST serves as its topic sentence?

A Now, a new wave of immigrants is coming to America.
B Like those who came before, these immigrants are arriving in hopes of building their own version of the American Dream.
C Early immigrants quickly took on all aspects of American culture.
D "Family is always the first resource," says Lily Woo, the principal of Public School 130, in New York City, where many Chinese newcomers attend school.

UNIT 8 ASSESSMENT

Answers:

1. B
2. C
3. B

Resources for pages 1176–1181

Use these resources to review, assess, or reteach the chapter: Active Learning and Note-Taking Guide, ExamView Pro, and Differentiated Instruction Tool Software.

Answers:

4. A

5. D

6. D

7. Student responses will vary. A typical correct response will include two items from the following list. Answers do not have to be stated in complete sentences.
- Individuals face new delays and longer waiting periods to immigrate.
- New immigrants are subject to high-tech screenings.
- Sources of support for immigrants, such as churches and community centers, are not as strong as they used to be.
- Many immigrants have not graduated from high school and have low-paying jobs.
- other relevant text-based response

4 The writers wrote this article to

A inform people about immigrants in the United States
B convince people not to immigrate
C teach immigrants how to get help
D express themselves

5 Based on the article, what can you infer about new immigrants?

A They are wealthy.
B They reject American culture completely.
C They have no trouble finding high-paying jobs.
D They face new difficulties since the terrorist attacks of September 11, 2001.

6 Choose the sentence that is written correctly.

A "I love the United States and Mexico", said Yolanda.
B I love the United States and Mexico, said Yolanda.
C "I love the United States and Mexico." said Yolanda.
D "I love the United States and Mexico," said Yolanda.

7 Using information from the passage, give TWO examples of difficulties facing new immigrants in the United States.

Directions

Read this excerpt from a letter written by Martin Luther King Jr. Then, answer questions 8 through 15.

Letter from Birmingham Jail

by Martin Luther King Jr.

While confined here in the Birmingham city jail, I came across your recent statement calling my present activities "unwise and untimely." Seldom do I pause to answer criticism of my work and ideas.... But since I feel that you are men of genuine good will and that your criticisms are sincerely set forth, I want to try to answer your statements in what I hope will be patient and reasonable terms....

You deplore[1] the demonstrations taking place in Birmingham. But your statement, I am sorry to say, fails to express a similar concern for the conditions that brought about the demonstrations. I am sure that none of you would want to rest content with the superficial kind of social analysis that deals merely with effects and does not grapple[2] with underlying causes. It is unfortunate that demonstrations are taking place in Birmingham, but it is even more unfortunate that the city's white power structure left the Negro community with no alternative.

In any nonviolent campaign there are four basic steps: collection of the facts to determine whether injustices exist; negotiation; self-purification; and direct action. We have gone through all these steps in Birmingham. There can be no gainsaying[3] the fact that racial injustice engulfs this community. Birmingham is probably the most thoroughly segregated city in the United States. Its ugly record of brutality is widely known. Negroes have experienced grossly unjust treatment in the courts. There have been more unsolved bombings of Negro homes and churches in Birmingham than in any other city in the nation. These are the hard, brutal facts of the case. On the basis of these conditions, Negro leaders sought to negotiate with the city fathers. But the latter consistently refused to engage in good-faith negotiation....

We know through painful experience that freedom is never voluntarily given by the oppressor; it must be demanded by the oppressed.

[1] **deplore:** strongly disapprove of
[2] **grapple:** struggle
[3] **gainsaying:** denying

Test-Taking Tips

TIP Remind students that speeches, personal journals, letters, and historical documents often contain difficult language, punctuation, and spelling that aren't considered standard today. Students may need to skip over unfamiliar words until they understand the main idea of the passage. Then they can use context clues to figure out unfamiliar words and expressions.

TIP Remind students to read each question carefully and make sure they understand what the question is asking before looking for the answer.

Answers:

8. C
9. A
10. A

Frankly, I have yet to engage in a direct-action campaign that was "well timed" in the view of those who have not suffered unduly from the disease of segregation. For years now I have heard the word "Wait!" It rings in the ear of every Negro with piercing familiarity. This "Wait" has almost always meant "Never." We must come to see, with one of our distinguished jurists, that "justice too long delayed is justice denied."

Questions 8 through 15 are based on "Letter from Birmingham Jail."

8 Read this sentence from the letter.

> *We know through painful experience that freedom is never voluntarily given by the oppressor; it must be demanded by the oppressed.*

As used in this essay, *oppressor* is CLOSEST in meaning to which word?

A victim
B subordinate
C bully
D boss

9 Read this statement from the letter.

> *But since I feel that you are men of genuine good will and that your criticisms are sincerely set forth…*

In this statement, the phrase "set forth" MOST LIKELY means

A stated
B insulted
C taken
D misunderstood

10 Why was the author MOST LIKELY writing this letter?

A to answer questions about his involvement in demonstrations in Birmingham
B to secure his release from jail
C to protest demonstrations in Birmingham
D to pass the time

11 You can infer from the letter that

A leaders in Birmingham were open to negotiation
B there was no segregation in Birmingham
C the African American community in Birmingham was content
D conditions for African Americans in Birmingham were not acceptable

12 Give TWO examples from the letter of racial injustices in Birmingham.

13 According to the letter, what is the last step in a nonviolent campaign?

A determine whether injustices exist
B self-purification
C direct action
D negotiation

14 What does the author say is even MORE unfortunate than the demonstrations?

A the fact that the African American community had no other choice
B the fact that many were jailed
C the fact that violence occurred
D the fact that the African American community made no attempt to talk to city leaders

15 What does the phrase "justice too long delayed is justice denied" MOST LIKELY mean?

A People should not expect justice.
B Making people wait too long for justice is the same as refusing them justice.
C Justice is better late than never.
D If people are patient, they will eventually receive justice.

Answers:

11. D

12. Student responses will vary. A typical correct response will include two items from the following list. Answers do not have to be stated in complete sentences.
- segregation in Birmingham
- Birmingham's record of brutality
- unfair treatment of African Americans in the courts
- bombings of African American homes and churches
- city leaders' refusal to negotiate with African Americans seeking change

13. C

14. A

15. B

REFERENCE SECTION

AUTHOR FILES

Maya Angelou (1928–)

- was originally named Marguerite Johnson; Maya is the name her brother called her as a child
- at the age of three, was sent to live with her grandmother, who ran the only black-owned general store in the town of Stamps, Arkansas
- speaks French, Spanish, Italian, Arabic, and Fanti (a language of southern Ghana) fluently
- was the first African American woman to have a story adapted for a feature film

Ray Bradbury (1920–)

- does not like technology even though he writes about it; doesn't drive a car, use a computer, or fly in airplanes
- feels that much of his work is too fantastic to be considered science fiction, which he thinks has to be based on possibilities for the future
- has written short stories, novels, plays, screenplays, television scripts, and verse

Quote: *"The act of writing is, for me, like a fever—something I must do."*

Gwendolyn Brooks (1917–2000)

- born in Topeka, Kansas, but lived most of her life in Chicago
- in 1950 became the first African American woman to be awarded a Pulitzer Prize
- followed Carl Sandburg as poet laureate of Illinois in 1968; served until her death in 2000

Quote: *"I felt that I had to write. Even if I had never been published, I knew that I would go on writing, enjoying it, and experiencing the challenge."*

Judith Ortiz Cofer (1952–)

- grew up speaking Spanish at home, but learned English well enough to become a writer and college professor
- lives in Georgia on a farm that has been in her husband's family for generations
- believes that immigrants do not have to choose one identity over another and says she uses her art "as a bridge between my cultures . . . traveling back and forth without fear and confusion."

Meri Nana-Ama Danquah (1967–)

- was raised in the Washington, D.C., area
- has taught in schools and universities in Ghana and the United States
- appears regularly on National Public Radio to comment on a variety of issues, including the impressions Africans have about America

Quote: *"I am ever-changing, able to blend without detection into the colors and textures of my surroundings, a skill developed out of a need to belong, a longing to be claimed."*

Linnea Due (1948–)

- was born in Berkeley, California
- has worked as a graphic designer and typesetter
- locked herself in her study during a week off to write her first novel, the young adult book *High and Outside*

Quote: *"This is the joy of writing for me—when the characters assume their own identities and run away with the story, leaving my idea of the book behind."*

Nikki Giovanni (1943–)
- born Yolande Cornelia Giovanni, Jr.
- graduated early from high school and attended the historically black Fisk University
- is a University Distinguished Professor of writing and literature at Virginia Tech

Quote: *"Writers don't write from experience, though many are hesitant to admit that they don't. I want to be clear about this. If you wrote from experience, you'd get maybe one book, maybe three poems."*

Frances Goodrich (1890–1984)
- grew up in New Jersey and attended colleges in New York
- acted on Broadway before becoming a playwright
- won two Tony awards in 1956 for plays she co-wrote with her husband, Albert Hackett
- collaborated with her husband on screenplays for dozens of films, including the well-known classics *It's A Wonderful Life* and *Father of the Bride*

Albert Hackett (1900–1995)
- was the son of actors and had a brother, Raymond Hackett, who acted in silent films
- grew up in New York City
- first appeared onstage at age six, playing a girl
- acted in his first film at age twelve
- attended the Professional Children's School, a high school for young performing artists
- received four Academy Award nominations for screenplays he cowrote with his first wife, Frances Goodrich

Virginia Hamilton (1936–2002)
- was the granddaughter of a slave who escaped to rural Ohio on the Underground Railroad in the 1850s
- grew up on a farm near the homes of her large extended family
- began writing in grade school
- was influenced by her parents, who were gifted storytellers

Quote: *"I write books because I love chasing after a good story and seeing fantastic characters rising out of the mist of my imaginings."*

W. C. Heinz (1915–)
- edited the sports section of his college newspaper
- worked his way up from messenger boy to reporter at the *New York Sun*
- filed stories from Europe during World War II
- began writing about sports after the war and had a regular column about boxing
- Ernest Hemingway called Heinz's novel *The Professional* "the only good novel I've ever read about a fighter."

O. Henry (1862–1910)
- was raised by his grandmother when his mother died; his father spent all his time on an invention
- became a registered pharmacist
- fled to Honduras after being accused of stealing; came back home to Texas because his wife was dying
- published a newspaper called *Rolling Stone*
- wrote nearly 300 stories, 80 of them Westerns
- had millions of his books sold all over the world, but died poor and in debt

Langston Hughes (1902–1967)

- was elected class poet in the eighth and twelfth grades
- had lived in six different states and Mexico by the age of twelve
- worked as a truck farmer, cook, waiter, sailor, doorman and traveled extensively before the first of his books was published
- his first published poem, "The Negro Speaks of Rivers," is still one of his best known poems

Quote: *"Hughes's poems were meant to be read aloud, crooned, shouted, and sung."*

David Ignatow (1914–1997)

- was born in Brooklyn and lived most of his life in New York
- graduated from high school, but never went to college
- was known for writing in a direct and natural-sounding style
- won an award from the National Institute of Arts and Letters for "a lifetime of creative effort"

Quote: *"I want, as a poet, to speak the whole truth."*

Charlotte Foltz Jones (1945–)

- enjoyed sitting in her favorite rocking chair and coming up with story ideas when she was nine
- drew upon her experiences as an only child and the mother of an only child to write her first book, *Only Child: Clues for Coping*, which offers advice to children with no brothers and sisters
- enjoys papier-mache and sculpture

Quote: *"I write for myself–maybe for the part of me that never grew up, the part that still wonders and looks about in amazement."*

Daniel Keyes (1927–)

- joined the U.S. Maritime Service for a few years before entering college
- says he learned the craft of writing while working for a magazine publisher
- "Flowers for Algernon" was published first as a short story (1959) then as a novel (1966); it was filmed under the title "Charley" (1968).
- The short story won a Hugo Award, the novel won a Nebula Award, and the movie won a best actor Academy Award for Cliff Robertson.

Eric Kimmel (1946–)

- has wanted to be an author since kindergarten
- grew up in a neighborhood filled with Armenian, Italian, Chinese, Puerto Rican, Irish, and German families
- spoke Yiddish as a child
- draws inspiration from the stories his Ukrainian grandmother told him as a child
- is a professional storyteller
- loves bluegrass music and plays the banjo

Kathleen Krull (1952–)

- is the oldest of four children and has three younger brothers
- taught piano lessons as a teenager
- has worked in children's book publishing since the day after she graduated from college

Quote: *"I'm nosy about people . . . and [writing] the Lives of . . . series allows me to snoop behind the closed doors of some of my favorite groups of (really strange) people."*

Henry Wadsworth Longfellow (1807–1882)

- grew up in Portland, Maine
- began school at age three and showed an interest in writing at an early age
- loved music and played piano and flute
- entered Bowdoin College at fourteen
- was the most popular poet of the nineteenth century

Quote: *"You know I say just what I think, and nothing more and less. I cannot say one thing and mean another."*

Robert MacNeil (1931–)

- was born and raised in Canada; became an American citizen in 1997
- was an aspiring actor and playwright before becoming a journalist
- cofounded "The MacNeil/Lehrer News Hour," a news program on PBS
- won numerous awards for his work as a reporter and television news anchor
- retired in 1995, after twenty years as coanchor of the show

Edna St. Vincent Millay (1892–1950)

- was encouraged by her mother to be ambitious and to appreciate music and literature
- entered a poetry contest that helped her win a scholarship to Vassar College
- used modern ideas with traditional poetry styles
- was a very popular poet during her lifetime

Quote by author Thomas Hardy: *"America has two great attractions: the skyscraper and the poetry of Edna St. Vincent Millay."*

Toshio Mori (1910–1980)

- dreamed of being an artist, a Buddhist missionary, and a baseball player when he was young
- became interested in writing mostly through reading dime novels—popular fiction that sold for ten cents
- edited the literary journal *Trek* while interned in a camp during World War II
- was the first Japanese American writer to have his work published in the United States

Walter Dean Myers (1937–)

- went to live with foster parents in Harlem after his mother died when he was two
- had a speech impediment and at the suggestion of a teacher, began to write down his thoughts
- thought he could never go to college, but always kept writing, and after serving in the army was able to pay for college tuition with money from the G.I. Bill of Rights
- gets up by 5 A.M. and writes ten pages every day
- says rewriting is more fun for him than writing
- has won dozens of awards for his books

Naomi Shihab Nye (1952–)

- published her first poem at age seven
- lived in Jerusalem for a year when she was fourteen
- began keeping a journal as a child because she "wanted to remember everything"

Quote: *"In books, I hope that my characters are brave and strong. I want them to use their voices. I want young people to be reminded, always, that voices are the best tools we have."*

Dwight Okita (1958–)

- born and continues to live in Chicago
- has written poetry, plays, film scripts, and a novel
- started writing poems in first grade because he had difficulty writing stories
- earned a creative writing degree at University of Illinois at Chicago

Quote: *"I am lucky to have a diverse circle of friends–some of whom are in the arts and some who are not. I love them all equally."*

Abiodun Oyewole (1948–)

- born Charles Davis, he grew up in Queens, New York; was given the name Abiodun Oyewole by a Yoruba priest at age fifteen
- was influenced by jazz and gospel music and the poems of Langston Hughes while growing up
- cofounded The Last Poets, a musical group that is credited with being the originators of hip-hop music
- appeared with The Last Poets in the film "Poetic Justice" in 1993

Gary Paulsen (1939–)

- traveled with a carnival when he was a teenager
- has worked as a soldier, engineer, construction worker, ranch hand, truck driver, and sailor
- completed the 1,180-mile Alaskan sled dog race, the Iditarod, in 1983 and 1985
- wrote his first novel while living in a cabin in northern Minnesota
- one of the most popular writers of young adult fiction, he has written more than 175 books and even more short stories and articles

Josephine Preston Peabody (1874–1922)

- grew up in Brooklyn, New York, and Dorchester, Massachusetts
- was encouraged by her parents to paint, write, and read poetry, novels, and plays
- was one of the first women writers to achieve success as a playwright in America

Quote: *"One never learns by success. Success is the plateau that one rests upon to take breath and look down from upon the straight and difficult path, but one does not climb upon a plateau."*

Richard Peck (1934–)

- went to college in Indiana and England, was a U.S. soldier stationed in Germany, and taught English to teenagers before becoming a full-time writer for young adults
- seeks inspiration for his books by visiting schools to meet young people, teachers, and librarians

Quote: *"I want to write novels that ask honest questions about serious issues. A novel is never an answer; it's always a question."*

Ann Petry (1909–1997)

- born and grew up in a middle-class African American family that lived in a mainly white community in Connecticut
- enjoyed acting out scenes from her favorite books when she was a child
- wrote short stories while working as a pharmacist in her family's drugstore
- began her writing career after moving to New York City with her husband, mystery writer George Petry

Marge Piercy (1936–)

- was raised Jewish and has the Hebrew name Marah
- began writing when she was fifteen and had her own room for the first time
- credits her mother with making her a poet

Quote: *"As a would-be poet or fiction writer or playwright or writer of scripts, you must know what has been written in the past and what is being written right now. You have to read all the time and read a lot."*

Edgar Allan Poe (1809–1849)

- lost his parents, who were professional actors, when he was three years old
- struggled with poverty all of his life
- started writing poetry when he was a teenager
- joined the army and attended West Point
- worked as an editor of magazines
- helped develop detective mystery, science fiction, treasure hunt, and horror story formats
- has been a major influence on writers in Europe and Latin America as well as the United States

Graham Salisbury (1944–)

- grew up on the islands of Oahu and Hawaii with friends from many backgrounds, including Japanese, Chinese, Filipino, and Portuguese
- didn't wear shoes until he was in sixth grade
- saw snow for the first time at age nineteen
- is in a rock-n-roll band named *The Millennium,* which had a number-one hit in the Philippines
- says that writing is, "Magic . . . From the universe . . . A window, open to the Great Unknown."

Ouida Sebestyen (1924–)

- was an only child and had a close relationship with her father
- hated school because she had trouble making friends, but always loved to read and learn
- worked as a mechanic and repaired PT-19s (a type of airplane), cleaned houses, and owned a day-care business before becoming a writer
- writes primarily about the American West, which she calls "bleak and harsh but also beautiful, dramatic, and inspiring"

Virginia Driving Hawk Sneve (1933–)

- was the daughter of a minister
- grew up during the 1930s Great Depression
- became inspired to write when she discovered that realistic literature about Native American culture was scarce
- writes about the experiences of today's Lakota teenagers

Quote: *"In my books, I always try to write about something from the past that still affects us today and will in the future."*

Gary Soto (1952–)

- is a third-generation Mexican American
- has edited story collections and written poetry, essays, young adult and children's books and has made movies
- taught English and Chicano Studies at the University of California, Berkeley
- enjoys theater, tennis, basketball, traveling, and working in the garden

Quote: *"I discovered that reading builds a life inside the mind."*

Jerry Spinelli (1941–)

- wanted to be a cowboy until age ten
- was sixteen when he wrote a poem that was published in his hometown newspaper
- wrote several unpublished novels before his first young adult book was published
- has found material for his books from the experiences of his six kids

Quote: *"I think a person's life is a mixture of happy, sad and funny. So I try to make my books that way, too."*

May Swenson (1919–1989)

- was born and raised in Logan, Utah
- moved to New York City after earning a bachelor's degree at the University of Utah
- was a critic, playwright, translator, and editor as well as a poet
- once said her experience of poetry was "based in a craving to get through the curtains of things as they appear, to things as they are, and then into the larger, wilder space of things as they are becoming."

Yoshiko Uchida (1921–1992)

- encouraged by her parents, became interested in books and writing at an early age
- wrote stories on pages cut from brown wrapping paper during the Depression
- started off sending stories to magazines, and, after many rejections, switched to writing for young people
- traveled to Japan in 1952 to collect folktales, which she retold in her first book, *The Dancing Kettle and Other Japanese Folktales*

Walt Whitman (1819–1892)

- worked as a printer, an editor, a newspaper reporter, and at other jobs while writing forgettable poems and novels before 1855
- published nine different editions of *Leaves of Grass* between 1855 and 1892, revising and adding new poems with each edition
- worked as a volunteer aide in hospitals, caring for sick and wounded soldiers during the Civil War
- became a strong influence on many later poets who imitated his usually rhymeless free verse

FOLDABLES™

by Dinah Zike, M.Ed., Creator of Foldables™

Reading and Thinking with Foldables™

As you read the selections in each unit, the following Foldables will help you keep track of your ideas about the Big Questions. Follow these directions to make your Foldable, and then use the directions in the Unit Warm-Up for labeling your unit Foldable.

Foldable 1 and Foldable 5—For Units 1 and 5

Step 1 Fold five sheets of paper into ***hamburgers***.

Step 2 Cut the sheets of paper in half along the fold lines.

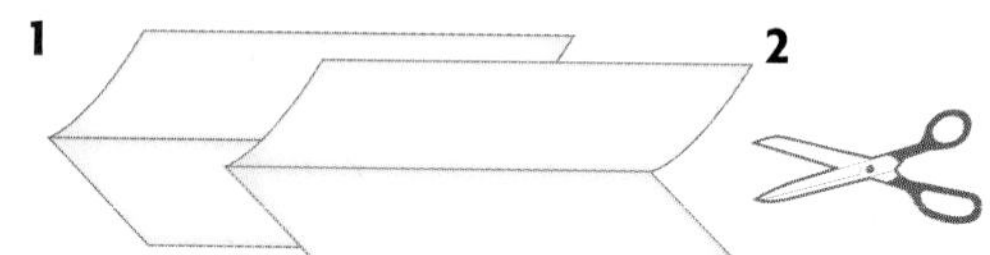

Step 3 Fold each section of paper into ***hamburgers***. However, fold one side one-half inch shorter than the other side. This will form a tab that is one-half inch long.

Step 4 Fold this tab forward over the shorter side, and then fold it back the opposite way.

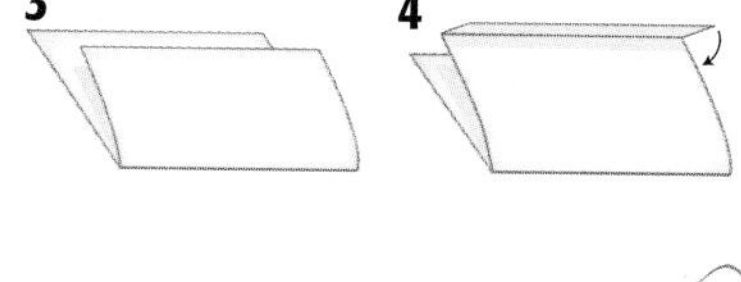

Step 5 Glue together to form an ***accordion*** by gluing a straight edge of one section into the ***valley*** of another section.

Step 6 On the front cover, write the unit number and the Big Question. Turn the page. Across the top, write the selection title. To the left of the crease, write **My Purpose for Reading**. To the right of the crease, write **The Big Question**. Repeat until you have all the titles from the Reading Workshops and the Comparing Literature Workshop in your Foldable.

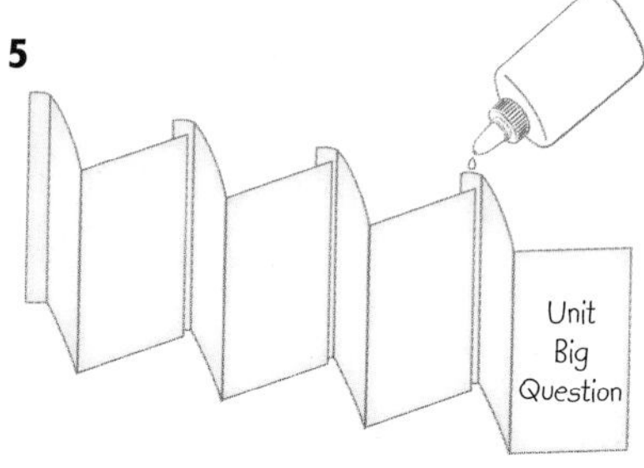

Foldable 2 and Foldable 7—For Units 2 and 7

Step 1 Stack three sheets of paper so that the bottom of each sheet is one inch higher than the sheet behind it.

Step 2 Fold down the tops of the paper to form six tabs. Align the edges so that all of the layers are about an inch apart.

Step 3 Crease the paper to hold the layers in place and then staple them together. Cut the bottom five layers up to the crease. Do not cut the top flap.

Step 4 On the top front flap, write the unit number and the Big Question. Write a selection title on the bottom of each flap. Then open each flap. Write **My Purpose for Reading** at the top of the flap and write **The Big Question** below the crease.

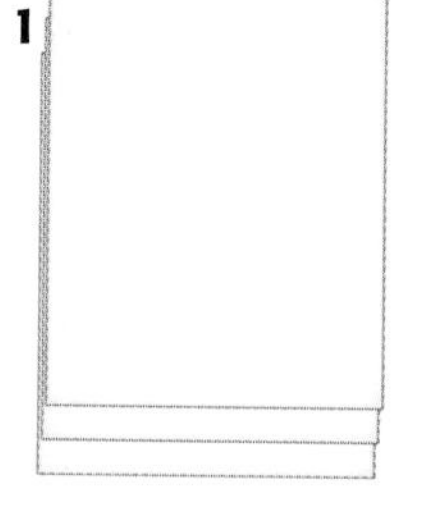

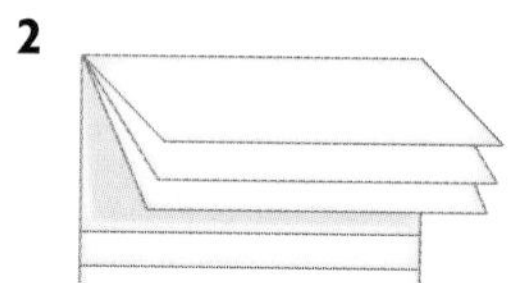

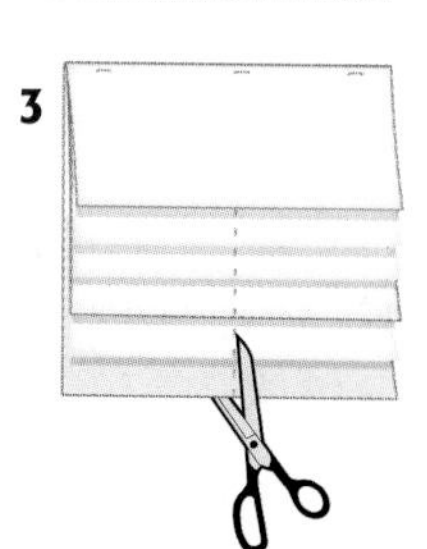

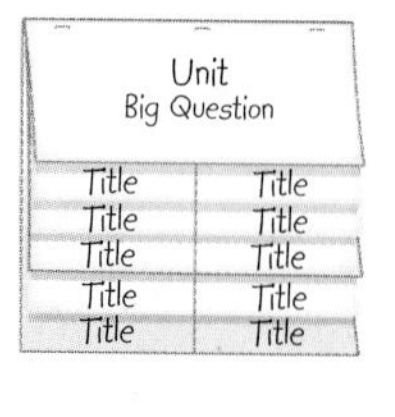

Foldable 3 and Foldable 6—For Units 3 and 6

Step 1 Fold a sheet of paper in half so that one side is one inch longer than the other side. Fold the one-inch tab over the short side to form a fold. On the fold, write the workshop number and the Big Question.

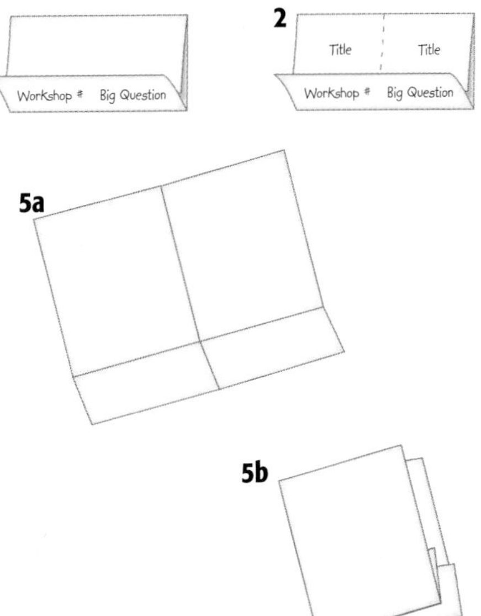

Step 2 Cut the front flap in half toward the top crease to create two flaps. Write the title of the first selection in Reading Workshop 1 on the left flap and the title of the second selection on the right flap.

Step 3 Open the flaps. At the very top of each flap, write **My Purpose for Reading**. Below each crease, write **The Big Question**.

Step 4 Repeat these steps for each remaining Reading Workshop and the Reading Across Texts or Comparing Literature Workshop.

Step 5 Fold a 11 x 17 sheet of paper in half. Open the paper and fold up one of the long sides two inches to form a pocket. Glue the outer edges of the pocket. Refold the paper so that the pockets are on the inside. Keep your Foldables for the unit inside.

Foldable 4 and Foldable 8—For Units 4 and 8

Step 1 Fold ten sheets of paper in half from top to bottom.

Step 2 On the top flap of each folded paper, make a cut one inch from the left side (top flap only).

Step 3 Stack the folded papers on top of one another. Staple the ten sections together. Write the unit number and Big Question on the stapled edge.

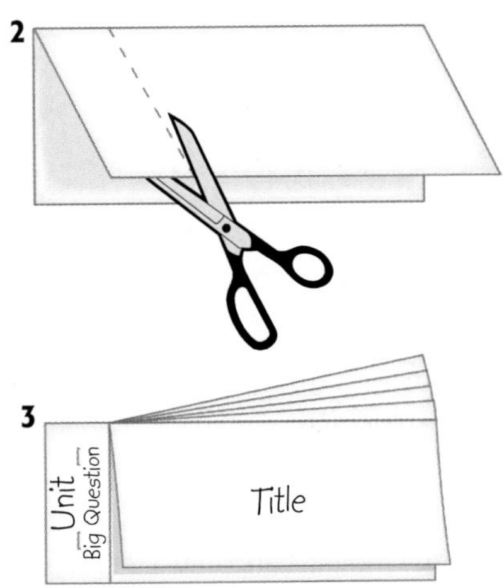

Step 4 On the top flap, write the first selection title from Reading Workshop 1. Open the flap. Near the top of the page, write **My Purpose for Reading**. Below the crease, write **The Big Question**.

Step 5 Repeat these steps for each remaining selection in the Reading Workshops and the Reading Across Texts Workshop.

LITERARY TERMS HANDBOOK

A

Act A major unit of a drama. A play may be subdivided into several acts. Many modern plays have two or three acts. A short play can be composed of one or more scenes but only one act.

See also SCENE.

Alliteration The repitition of consonant sounds, usually at the beginnings of words or syllables. Alliteration gives emphasis to words. For example,

Over the cobbles he clattered and clashed

Allusion A reference in a work of literature to a well-known character, place, or situation in history, politics, or science or from another work of literature, music, or art.

Analogy A comparison between two things, based on one or more elements that they share. Analogies can help the reader visualize an idea. In informational text, analogies are often used to explain something unfamiliar in terms of something known. For example, a science book might compare the flow of electricity to water moving through a hose. In literature, most analogies are expressed in metaphors or similes.

See also METAPHOR, SIMILE.

Anecdote A brief, entertaining story based on a single interesting or humorous incident or event. Anecdotes are frequently biographical and reveal some aspect of a person's character.

Antagonist A person or force that opposes the protagonist, or central character, in a story or a drama. The reader is generally meant not to sympathize with the antagonist.

See also CONFLICT, PROTAGONIST.

Anthropomorphism Representing animals as if they had human emotions and intelligence. Fables and fairy tales often contain anthropomorphism.

Aside In a play, a comment made by a character that is heard by the audience but not by the other characters onstage. The speaker turns to one side, or "aside," away from the other characters onstage. Asides are common in older plays–you will find many in Shakespeare's plays–but are infrequent in modern drama.

Assonance The repetition of vowel sounds, especially in a line of poetry.

See also RHYME, SOUND DEVICES.

Author's purpose The intention of the writer. For example, the purpose of a story may be to entertain, to describe, to explain, to persuade, or a combination of these purposes.

Autobiography The story of a person's life written by that person. *I Know Why the Caged Bird Sings,* by Maya Angelou is an example of autobiography.

See also BIOGRAPHY, MEMOIR.

B

Ballad A short musical narrative song or poem. Folk ballads, which usually tell of an exciting or dramatic episode, were passed on by word of mouth for generations before being written down. Literary ballads are written in imitation of folk ballads.

See also NARRATIVE POETRY.

Biography The account of a person's life written by someone other than the subject. Biographies can be short or book-length.

See also AUTOBIOGRAPHY, MEMOIR.

C

Character A person in a literary work. (If a character is an animal, it displays human traits.) Characters who show varied and sometimes contradictory traits are called **round.** Characters who reveal only one personality trait are called **flat.** A **stereotype** is a flat character of a familiar and often-repeated type. A **dynamic** character changes during the story. A **static** character remains primarily the same throughout the story.

Characterization The methods a writer uses to develop the personality of the character. In **direct characterization,** the writer makes direct statements about a character's personality. In **indirect characterization,** the writer reveals a character's personality through the character's words and actions and through what other characters think and say about the character.

Climax The point of greatest emotional intensity, interest, or suspense in a narrative. Usually the climax comes at the turning point in a story or drama, the point at which the resolution of the conflict becomes clear. The climax in "Icarus and Daedelus" occurs when Icarus forgets his father's warnings and flies too high.

Comedy A type of drama that is humorous and has a happy ending. A heroic comedy focuses on the exploits of a larger-than-life hero. In American popular culture, comedy can take the form of a scripted performance involving one or more performers–either as a skit that is part of a variety show, as in vaudeville, or as a stand-up monologue.

See also HUMOR.

Conflict The central struggle between opposing forces in a story or drama. An **external conflict** exists when a character struggles against some outside force, such as nature, society, fate, or another person. An **internal conflict** exists within the mind of a character who is torn between opposing feelings or goals.

See also ANTAGONIST, PLOT, PROTAGONIST.

Consonance A pleasing combination of sounds, especially in poetry. Consonance usually refers to the repetition of consonant sounds in stressed syllables.

See also SOUND DEVICES.

Couplet Two successive lines of verse that form a unit and usually rhyme.

D

Description Writing that seeks to convey the impression of a setting, a person, an animal, an object, or an event by appealing to the senses. Almost all writing, fiction and nonfiction, contains elements of description.

Details Particular features of things used to make descriptions more accurate and vivid. Authors use details to help readers imagine the characters, scenes, and actions they describe.

Dialect A variation of language spoken by a particular group, often within a particular region. Dialects differ from standard language because they may contain different pronunciations, forms, and meanings.

Dialogue Conversation between characters in a literary work.

See also MONOLOGUE.

Drama A story intended to be performed by actors on a stage or before movie or TV cameras. Most dramas before the modern period can be divided into two basic types: tragedy and comedy. The script of a drama includes dialogue (the words the actors speak) and stage directions (descriptions of the action and scenery).

See also COMEDY, TRAGEDY.

E

Elegy A mournful or melancholy poem that honors someone who is dead. Some elegies are written in rhyming couplets that follow a strict metric pattern.

Epic A long narrative poem, written in a dignified style, that celebrates the adventures and achievements of one or more heroic figures of legend, history, or religion.

See also NARRATIVE POETRY.

Essay A short piece of nonfiction writing on a single topic. The purpose of the essay is to communicate an idea or opinion. A **formal essay** is serious and impersonal. A **informal essay** entertains while it informs, usually in a light conversational style.

Exposition The part of the plot of a short story, novel, novella, or play in which the characters, setting, and situation are introduced.

Extended metaphor An implied comparison that continues through an entire poem.

See also METAPHOR.

F

Fable A short, simple tale that teaches a moral. The characters in a fable are often animals who speak and act like people. The moral, or lesson, of the fable is usually stated outright.

Falling action In a play or story, the action that follows the climax.

See also PLOT.

Fantasy A form of literature that explores unreal worlds of the past, the present, or the future.

Fiction A prose narrative in which situations and characters are invented by the writer. Some aspects of a fictional work may be based on fact or experience. Fiction includes short stories, novellas, and novels.

See also NOVEL, NOVELLA, SHORT STORY.

Figurative language Language used for descriptive effect, often to imply ideas indirectly. Expressions of figurative language are not literally true but express some truth beyond the literal level. Although it appears in all kinds of writing, figurative language is especially prominent in poetry.

See also ANALOGY, FIGURE OF SPEECH, METAPHOR, PERSONIFICATION, SIMILE, SYMBOL.

Figure of speech Figurative language of a specific kind, such as **analogy, metaphor, simile,** or **personification.**

First-person narrative. *See POINT OF VIEW.*

Flashback An interruption in a chronological narrative that tells about something that happened before that point in the story or before the story began. A flashback gives readers information that helps to explain the main events of the story.

Folklore The traditional beliefs, customs, stories, songs, and dances of the ordinary people (the "folk") of a culture. Folklore is passed on by word of mouth and performance rather than in writing.

See also FOLKTALE, LEGEND, MYTH, ORAL TRADITION.

Folktale A traditional story passed down orally long before being written down. Generally the author of a folktale is anonymous. Folktales include animal stories, trickster stories, fairy tales, myths, legends, and tall tales.

See also LEGEND, MYTH, ORAL TRADITION, TALL TALE.

Foreshadowing The use of clues by an author to prepare readers for events that will happen in a story.

Free verse Poetry that has no fixed pattern of meter, rhyme, line length, or stanza arrangement.

See also RHYTHM.

G

Genre A literary or artistic category. The main literary genres are prose, poetry, and drama. Each of these is divided into smaller genres. For example: **Prose** includes fiction (such as novels, novellas, short stories, and folktales) and nonfiction (such as biography, autobiography, and essays). **Poetry** includes lyric poetry, dramatic poetry, and narrative poetry. **Drama** includes tragedy, comedy, historical drama, melodrama, and farce.

H

Haiku Originally a Japanese form of poetry that has three lines and seventeen syllables. The first and third lines have five syllables each; the middle line has seven syllables.

Hero A literary work's main character, usually one with admirable qualities. Although the word *hero* is applied only to males in traditional usage (the female form is *heroine*), the term now applies to both sexes.

See also LEGEND, MYTH, PROTAGONIST, TALL TALE.

Historical fiction A novel, novella, play, short story, or narrative poem that sets fictional characters against a historical backdrop and contains many details about the period in which it is set.

See also GENRE.

Humor The quality of a literary work that makes the characters and their situations seem funny, amusing, or ludicrous. Humorous writing can be as effective in nonfiction as in fiction.

See also COMEDY.

I

Idiom A figure of speech that belongs to a particular language, people, or region and whose meaning cannot be obtained, and might even appear ridiculous, by joining the meanings of the words composing it. You would be using an idiom if you said you *caught* a cold.

Imagery Language that emphasizes sensory impressions to help the reader of a literary work see, hear, feel, smell, and taste the scenes described in the work.

See also FIGURATIVE LANGUAGE.

Informational text One kind of nonfiction. This kind of writing conveys facts and information without introducing personal opinion.

Irony A form of expression in which the intended meaning of the words used is the opposite of their literal meaning. *Verbal irony* occurs when a person says one thing and means another–for example, saying "Nice guy!" about someone you dislike. *Situational irony* occurs when the outcome of a situation is the opposite of what was expected.

J

Journal An account of day-to-day events or a record of experiences, ideas, or thoughts. A journal may also be called a diary.

L

Legend A traditional story, based on history or an actual hero, that is passed down orally. A legend is usually exaggerated and gains elements of fantasy over the years. Stories about Daniel Boone and Davy Crockett are American legends.

Limerick A light humorous poem with a regular metrical scheme and a rhyme scheme of *aabba.*

See also HUMOR, RHYME SCHEME.

Local color The fictional portrayal of a region's features or peculiarities and its inhabitants' distinctive ways of talking and behaving, usually as a way of adding a realistic flavor to a story.

Lyric The words of a song, usually with a regular rhyme scheme.

See also RHYME SCHEME.

Lyric poetry Poems, usually short, that express strong personal feelings about a subject or an event.

M

Main idea The most important idea expressed in a paragraph or an essay. It may or may not be directly stated.

Memoir A biographical or autobiographical narrative emphasizing the narrator's personal experience during a period or at an event.

See also AUTOBIOGRAPHY, BIOGRAPHY.

Metaphor A figure of speech that compares or equates seemingly unlike things. In contrast to a simile, a metaphor implies the comparison instead of stating it directly; hence, there is no use of connectives such as *like* or *as.*

See also FIGURE OF SPEECH, IMAGERY, SIMILE.

Meter A regular pattern of stressed and unstressed syllables that gives a line of poetry a predictable rhythm.

See also RHYTHM.

Monologue A long speech by a single character in a play or a solo performance.

Mood The emotional quality or atmosphere of a story or poem.

See also SETTING.

Myth A traditional story of unknown authorship, often involving goddesses, gods, and heroes, that attempts to explain a natural phenomenon, a historic event, or the origin of a belief or custom.

N

Narration Writing or speech that tells a story. Narration is used in prose fiction and narrative poetry. Narration can also be an important element in biographies, autobiographies, and essays.

Narrative poetry Verse that tells a story.

Narrator The person who tells a story. In some cases the narrator is a character in the story.

See also POINT OF VIEW.

Nonfiction Factual prose writing. Nonfiction deals with real people and experiences. Among the categories of nonfiction are biographies, autobiographies, and essays.

See also AUTOBIOGRAPHY, BIOGRAPHY, ESSAY, FICTION.

Novel A book-length fictional prose narrative. The novel has more scope than a short story in its presentation of plot, character, setting, and theme. Because novels are not subject to any limits in their presentation of these elements, they encompass a wide range of narratives.

See also FICTION.

Novella A work of fiction shorter than a novel but longer than a short story. A novella usually has more characters, settings, and events and a more complex plot than a short story.

O

Ode A lyric poem, usually rhymed, often in the form of an address and usually dignified or lofty in subject.

See also LYRIC POETRY.

Onomatopoeia The use of a word or a phrase that actually imitates or suggests the sound of what it describes.

See also SOUND DEVICES.

Oral tradition Stories, knowledge, customs, and beliefs passed by word of mouth from one generation to the next.

See also FOLKLORE, FOLKTALE, LEGEND, MYTH.

P

Parallelism The use of a series of words, phrases, or sentences that have similar grammatical form. Parallelism emphasizes the items that are arranged in the similar structures.

See also REPETITION.

Personification A figure of speech in which an animal, object, or idea is given human form or characteristics.

See also FIGURATIVE LANGUAGE, FIGURE OF SPEECH, METAPHOR.

Plot The sequence of events in a story, novel, or play. The plot begins with **exposition,** which introduces the story's characters, setting, and situation. The plot catches the reader's attention with a **narrative hook.** The **rising action** adds complications to the story's conflict, or problem, leading to the **climax,** or point of highest emotional pitch. The **falling action** is the logical result of the climax, and the **resolution** presents the final outcome.

Plot twist An unexpected turn of events in a plot. A surprise ending is an example of a plot twist.

Poetry A form of literary expression that differs from prose in emphasizing the line as the unit of composition. Many other traditional characteristics of poetry—emotional, imaginative language; use of metaphor and simile; division into stanzas; rhyme; regular pattern of stress, or meter—apply to some poems.

Point of view The relationship of the narrator, or storyteller, to the story. In a story with **first-person point of view,** the story is told by one of the characters, referred to as "I." The reader generally sees everything through that character's eyes. In a story with a **limited third-person point of view,** the narrator reveals the thoughts of only one character, but refers to that character as "he" or "she." In a story with an **omniscient point of view,** the narrator reveals the thoughts of several characters.

Props Theater slang (a shortened form of *properties*) for objects and elements of the scenery of a stage play or movie set.

Propaganda Speech, writing, or other attempts to influence ideas or opinions, often through the use of stereotypes, faulty generalizations, logical fallacies, and/or emotional language.

Prose Writing that is similar to everyday speech and language, as opposed to poetry. Its form is based on sentences and paragraphs without the patterns of rhyme, controlled line length, or meter found in much poetry. Fiction and nonfiction are the major categories of prose. Most modern drama is also written in prose.

See also DRAMA, ESSAY, FICTION, NONFICTION.

Protagonist The central character in a story, drama, or dramatic poem. Usually the action revolves around the protagonist, who is involved in the main conflict.

See ANTAGONIST, CONFLICT.

Pun A humorous play on two or more meanings of the same word or on two words with the same sound. Today puns often appear in advertising headlines and slogans—for example, "Our hotel rooms give you suite feelings."

See also HUMOR.

R

Refrain A line or lines repeated regularly, usually in a poem or song.

Repetition The recurrence of sounds, words, phrases, lines, or stanzas in a speech or piece of writing. Repetition increases the feeling of unity in a work. When a line or stanza is repeated in a poem or song, it is called a refrain.

See also PARALLELISM, REFRAIN.

Resolution The part of a plot that concludes the falling action by revealing or suggesting the outcome of the conflict.

Rhyme The repetition of sounds at the ends of words that appear close to each other in a poem. **End rhyme** occurs at the ends of lines. **Internal rhyme** occurs within a single line. **Slant rhyme** occurs when words include sounds that are similar but not identical. Slant rhyme usually involves some variation of **consonance** (the repetition of consonant sounds) or **assonance** (the repetition of vowel sounds).

Rhyme scheme The pattern of rhyme formed by the end rhyme in a poem. The rhyme scheme is designated by the assignment of a different letter of the alphabet to each new rhyme. For example, one common rhyme scheme is *ababcb.*

Rhythm The pattern created by the arrangement of stressed and unstressed syllables, especially in poetry. Rhythm gives poetry a musical quality that helps convey its meaning. Rhythm can be regular (with a predictable pattern or meter) or irregular, (as in free verse).

See also METER.

Rising action The part of a plot that adds complications to the problems in the story and increases reader interest.

See also FALLING ACTION, PLOT.

S

Scene A subdivision of an act in a play. Each scene takes place in a specific setting and time. An act may have one or more scenes.

See also ACT.

Science fiction Fiction dealing with the impact of real science or imaginary superscience on human or alien societies of the past, present, or future. Although science fiction is mainly a product of the twentieth century, nineteenth-century authors such as Mary Shelley, Jules Verne, and Robert Louis Stevenson were pioneers of the genre.

Screenplay The script of a film, usually containing detailed instructions about camera shots and angles in addition to dialogue and stage directions. A screenplay for an original television show is called a teleplay.

See also DRAMA.

Sensory imagery Language that appeals to a reader's five senses: hearing, sight, touch, taste, and smell.

See also VISUAL IMAGERY.

Sequence of events The order in which the events in a story take place.

Setting The time and place in which the events of a short story, novel, novella, or play occur. The setting often helps create the atmosphere or mood of the story.

Short story A brief fictional narrative in prose. Elements of the short story include **plot, character, setting, point of view, theme,** and sometimes symbol and irony.

Simile A figure of speech using like or as to compare seemingly unlike things.

See also FIGURATIVE LANGUAGE, FIGURE OF SPEECH.

Sonnet A poem containing fourteen lines, usually written in iambic pentameter. Sonnets have strict patterns of rhyme and usually deal with a single theme, idea, or sentiment.

Sound devices Techniques used to create a sense of rhythm or to emphasize particular sounds in writing. For example, sound can be controlled through the use of **onomatopoeia, alliteration, consonance, assonance,** and **rhyme.**

See also RHYTHM.

Speaker The voice of a poem—sometimes that of the poet, sometimes that of a fictional person or even a thing. The speaker's words communicate a particular tone or attitude toward the subject of the poem.

Stage directions Instructions written by the dramatist to describe the appearance and actions of characters, as well as sets, costumes, and lighting.

Stanza A group of lines forming a unit in a poem. Stanzas are, in effect, the paragraphs of a poem.

Stereotype A character who is not developed as an individual but as a collection of traits and mannerisms supposedly shared by all members of a group.

Style The author's choice and arrangement of words and sentences in a literary work. Style can reveal an author's purpose in writing and attitude toward his or her subject and audience.

Suspense A feeling of curiosity, uncertainty, or even dread about what is going to happen next. Writers increase the level of suspense in a story by giving readers clues to what may happen.

See also FORESHADOWING, RISING ACTION.

Symbol Any object, person, place, or experience that means more than what it is. **Symbolism** is the use of images to represent internal realities.

T

Tall tale A wildly imaginative story, usually passed down orally, about the fantastic adventures or amazing feats of folk heroes in realistic local settings.

See also FOLKLORE, ORAL TRADITION.

Teleplay A play written or adapted for television.

Theme The main idea of a story, poem, novel, or play, usually expressed as a general statement. Some works have a **stated theme,** which is expressed directly. More frequently works have an **implied theme,** which is revealed gradually through other elements such as plot, character, setting, point of view, symbol, and irony.

Third-person narrative. *See POINT OF VIEW.*

Title The name of a literary work.

Tone The attitude of the narrator toward the subject, ideas, theme, or characters. A factual article would most likely have an objective tone, while an editorial on the same topic could be argumentative or satiric.

Tragedy A play in which the main character suffers a downfall. That character often is a person of dignified or heroic stature. The downfall may result from outside forces or from a weakness within the character, which is known as a tragic flaw.

V

Visual imagery Details that appeal to the sense of sight.

Voice An author's distinctive style or the particular speech patterns of a character in a story.

See also STYLE, TONE.

The Writing Process

The writing process consists of five stages: prewriting, drafting, revising, editing/proofreading, and publishing/presenting. By following the stages in order, you can turn your ideas into polished pieces of writing. Most writers take their writing through all five stages, and repeat stages when necessary.

The Writing Process

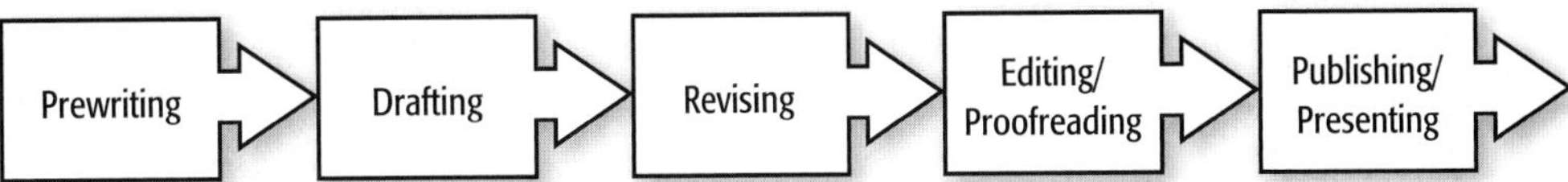

Prewriting

Prewriting is the process of gathering and organizing your ideas. It begins whenever you start to consider what you will write about or what will interest your readers. Try keeping a small notebook with you for several days and using it to jot down possible topics. Consult the chart below for tips on using the prewriting techniques known as listing, questioning, and clustering.

Listing, Questioning, and Clustering
LISTING List as many ideas as you can—whatever comes into your head on a particular subject. This is called brainstorming. Then go back over the list and circle the ideas you like best. Eventually you'll hit on an idea you can use.
QUESTIONING If your audience is your classmates, ask yourself questions such as the following: • *What do my friends like to learn about?* • *What do my friends like to read about?* • *What have I done that my friends might like to hear about?*
CLUSTERING Write your topic in the middle of a piece of paper. Organize related ideas around the topic in a cluster of circles, with lines showing how the ideas are related. Clustering can help you decide which part of a topic to write about.

When you have selected your topic, organize your ideas around the topic. Identify your main ideas and supporting ideas. Each main idea needs examples or facts to support it. Then write a plan for what you want to say. The plan might be an organized list or outline. It does not have to use complete sentences.

Drafting

Drafting is the stage that turns your list into sentences and paragraphs. Use your prewriting notes to remember what you want to say. Begin by writing an introduction that gets the reader's attention. Move ahead through the topic, paragraph by paragraph. Let your words flow. This is the time to express yourself or try out a new idea. Don't worry about mistakes in spelling and grammar; you can correct them later. If you get stuck, try one of the tricks below.

Tips for drafting

- Work on the easiest part first. You don't have to begin at the beginning.
- Make a diagram, sketch, or drawing of the topic.
- Focus on just one sentence or paragraph at a time.
- Freewrite your thoughts and images. You can organize them later.
- Pretend that you are writing to a friend.
- Ask more questions about your topic.
- Speak your ideas into a tape recorder.
- Take a break. Take a walk or listen to music. Return to your writing later.

Revising

The goal of revising is to make your writing clearer and more interesting. When you revise, look at the whole piece of writing. Ask whether the parts go together smoothly and whether anything should be added or deleted. You may decide to organize the draft in a different way. Some writers make several revisions before they are satisfied. Ask yourself these questions:

- ☑ Did I stick to my topic?
- ☑ Did I accomplish my purpose?
- ☑ Did I keep my audience in mind?
- ☑ Does my main idea come across clearly?
- ☑ Do all the details support the main idea?
- ☑ Did I give enough information? too much?
- ☑ Did I use transition words such as *first, then* and *next* to make my sentences flow smoothly?

Tips for revising

- Step back. If you have the time, set your draft aside for a while. When you look at it again, you may see it from a new point of view. You may notice that some information is missing or that part of the paper is disorganized.
- Read your paper aloud. Listen carefully as you read your paper aloud. How does it sound?
- Have a writing conference with a peer reviewer, one of your friends or classmates. A second opinion helps. Your reader can offer a fresh point of view.

Peer review

You can direct peer responses in one or more of the following ways.

- Ask readers to tell you what they have read in their own words. If you do not hear your ideas restated, revise your writing for clarity.
- Ask readers to tell you the part they liked best and why. You may want to expand those parts.
- Repeat what the readers have told you in your own words. Ask the readers if you have understood their suggestions.
- Discuss your writing with your readers. Listen to their suggestions carefully.

As you confer, make notes of your reviewers' comments. Then revise your draft, using your own judgment and including what is helpful from your reviewers' comments.

Editing/Proofreading

When you are satisfied with the changes you've made, edit your revised draft. Replace dull, vague words with lively verbs and precise adjectives. Vary the length of your sentences. Take time to correct errors in spelling, grammar, capitalization, and punctuation. Refer to the Proofreading Checklist on page R19 and on the inside back cover of this book.

Editing for style

Use the following checklist:

- ☑ Have I avoided clichés?
- ☑ Have I avoided wordiness?
- ☑ Is the tone of my writing appropriate to my purpose?
- ☑ Have I made clear connections between ideas?
- ☑ Do my sentences and paragraphs flow smoothly?

Publishing/Presenting

Now your writing is ready for an audience. Make a clean, neat copy, and add your name and date. Check that the paper has a title. If you wish, enclose the paper in a folder or binder to give it a professional look. Hand it in to your teacher, or share it in one of the ways described below. When the paper is returned, keep it in your writing portfolio.

Ideas for presenting

- **Illustrations** A photograph, diagram, or drawing can convey helpful information.
- **Oral presentation** Almost any writing can be shared aloud. Try including music, slides, or a group oral reading.
- **Class book** A collection of class writing is a nice contribution to the school library.
- **Newspaper** Some schools have a school newspaper. Local newspapers often publish student writing, especially if it is about local people and events.
- **Literary magazine** Magazines such as *Cricket* and *MidLink* publish student writing. Some schools have a literary magazine that publishes student writing once or twice a year.
- **Bulletin board** A rotating display of student writing is an effective way to see what your classmates have written. Illustrations and photographs add interest.

Some writing, such as journal writing, is private and not intended for an audience. However, even if you don't share your paper, don't throw it away. It might contain ideas that you can use later.

Proofreading Help

Use this proofreading checklist to help you check for errors in your writing, and use the proofreading symbols in the chart below to mark places that need corrections.

- ☑ Have I avoided run-on sentences and sentence fragments and punctuated sentences correctly?
- ☑ Have I used every word correctly, including plurals, possessives, and frequently confused words?
- ☑ Do verbs and subjects agree? Are verb tenses correct?
- ☑ Do pronouns refer clearly to their antecedents and agree with them in person, number, and gender?
- ☑ Have I used adverb and adjective forms and modifying phrases correctly?
- ☑ Have I spelled every word correctly, and checked the unfamiliar ones in a dictionary?

Proofreading Symbols		
⊙	Lieut Brown	Insert a period.
∧	No one came the party.	Insert a letter or a word.
≡	I enjoyed paris.	Capitalize a letter.
/	The Class ran a bake sale.	Make a capital letter lowercase.
⁀ ‿	The campers are home sick.	Close up a space.
(sp)	They visited N.Y.	Spell out.
∧ ;	Sue please come I need your help.	Insert a comma or a semicolon.
∿	He enjoyed feild day.	Transpose the position of letters or words.
#	alltogether	Insert a space.
ℓ	We went to to Boston.	Delete letters or words.
∨ ∨ ∨	She asked, Whos coming?	Insert quotation marks or an apostrophe.
/ = /	mid January	Insert a hyphen.
¶	"Where?" asked Karl. "Over there," said Ray.	Begin a new paragraph.

Writing Modes

There are four main types, or modes, of writing—expository, descriptive, narrative, and persuasive. Each mode has its own purpose and characteristics.

Expository Writing

Expository writing communicates knowledge. It provides and explains information; it may also give general directions or step-by-step instructions for an activity.

Use this checklist as you write.

- ☑ Is the opening paragraph interesting?
- ☑ Are my explanations accurate and complete? Is information clear and easy to read?
- ☑ Is information presented in a logical order?
- ☑ Does each paragraph have a main idea? Does all the information support the main idea?
- ☑ Does my essay have an introduction, a body, and a conclusion?
- ☑ Have I defined any unfamiliar terms?
- ☑ Are my comparisons clear and logical?

Kinds of expository writing

Expository writing covers a wide range of styles. The chart below describes some of the possibilities.

Descriptive Writing

Descriptive writing can make a person, place, or thing come to life. The scene described may be as unfamiliar and far away as the bottom of the sea or as familiar and close as the gym locker room. By presenting details that awaken the reader's senses, descriptive writing can help your readers see the world more clearly.

Use this checklist to help you revise your description.

- ☑ Does my introduction identify the person or place that will be described?
- ☑ Are my details vivid? Are nouns and adjectives precise?
- ☑ Do all the details contribute to the same impression?
- ☑ Is it clear why this place or person is special?
- ☑ Are transitions clear? Do the paragraphs follow a logical order?
- ☑ Does each paragraph contain a main idea?
- ☑ Have I communicated a definite impression or mood?

Kinds of Expository Writing	Examples
Instructional writing	Explain how to train for a cross-country race, how to arrange a surprise party, or how to avoid cleaning up your room.
Compare-and-contrast essay	Compare two athletes or two sports, two fictional characters, two books or movies, two places, or two kinds of vacations.
Step-by-step directions.	Give directions for building a model plane, making apple pie, or drawing on a computer screen.
Information and explanation	Explain what causes sunspots, how plants grow in the desert, or why camels have a hump.
Report or essay	Write a book report, a report on the Buddhist religion, or a report on a new wildlife center.

Narrative Writing

Narrative writing tells a story, either real or fictional. It answers the question *What happened?*

A well-written narrative holds the reader's attention by presenting interesting characters in a carefully ordered series of events.

This checklist will help you improve your narrative.

- ☑ Does my first sentence get the reader's attention?
- ☑ Are the characters and setting introduced with enough detail?
- ☑ Do the characters speak and behave realistically?
- ☑ Are the events narrated in an order clear enough for the reader to follow?
- ☑ Are there places where dialogue should be added?
- ☑ Is my ending satisfying to the reader?

Persuasive Writing

Persuasive writing presents an opinion. Its goal is to make readers feel or think a certain way about a situation or an idea. The writer includes facts and opinions often designed to urge readers to take action. Good persuasive writing can sometimes be hard to resist.

As you revise your persuasive writing, use this checklist as a guide.

- ☑ Is my main idea expressed in a clear statement?
- ☑ Have I presented good reasons to support my point of view?
- ☑ Have I supported my reasons with facts and opinions?
- ☑ Have I taken account of the opposing points of view?
- ☑ Have I addressed the interests of my audience?
- ☑ Have I ended with a strong closing statement?

Research Report Writing

When you write a research report, you explore a topic by gathering factual information from several different resources. Through your research, you develop a point of view or draw a conclusion. This point of view or conclusion becomes the main idea, or thesis, of your report.

Select a Topic

Because a research report usually takes time to prepare and write, your choice of topic is especially important. Follow these guidelines.

- Brainstorm a list of questions about a subject you would like to explore. Choose one that is neither too narrow nor too broad for the length of paper you will write. Use that question as your topic.
- Select a topic that genuinely interests you.
- Be sure you can find information on your topic from several different sources.

Do Research

Start by looking up your topic in an encyclopedia to find general information. Then find specific information in books, magazines, and newspapers, on CD-ROMs and the Internet, and from personal interviews when this seems appropriate. Use the computerized or card catalog in the library to locate books on your topic. Then search for up-to-date information in periodicals (magazines) or newspapers and from electronic sources, such as CD-ROMs or the Internet. If you need help in finding or using any of these resources, ask the librarian.

As you gather information, make sure each source you use relates closely to your topic. Also be sure that your source is reliable. Be extra careful if you are using information from the Internet. If you are not sure about the reliability of a source, consult the librarian or your teacher.

Make Source Cards

In a research report, you must document the source of your information. To keep track of your sources, write the author, title, publication information, and location of each source on a separate index card. Give each source card a number and write it in the upper right-hand corner. These cards will be useful for preparing a bibliography.

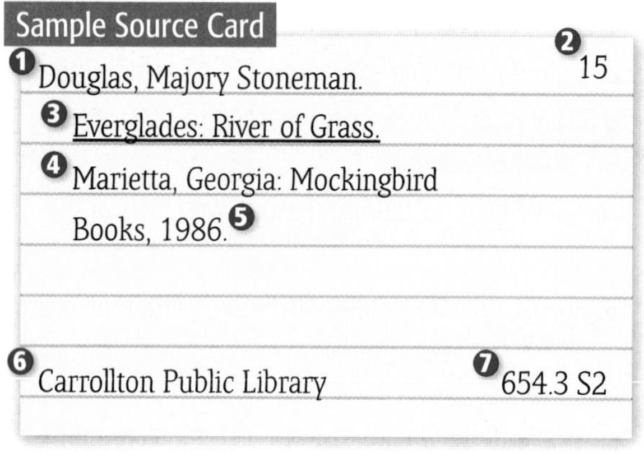
Sample Source Card

❶ Douglas, Majory Stoneman. ❷ 15
❸ Everglades: River of Grass.
❹ Marietta, Georgia: Mockingbird Books, 1986. ❺
❻ Carrollton Public Library ❼ 654.3 S2

❶ Author
❷ Source number
❸ Title
❹ City of publication/Publisher
❺ Date of publication
❻ Location of source
❼ Library call number

Take Notes

As you read, you encounter many new facts and ideas. Taking notes will help you keep track of information and focus on the topic. Here are some helpful suggestions:

- Use a new card for each important piece of information. Separate cards will help you to organize your notes.
- At the top of each card, write a key word or phrase that tells you about the information. Also, write the number of the source you used.
- Write only details and ideas that relate to your topic.
- Summarize information in your own words.
- Write down a phrase or a quote only when the words are especially interesting or come from an important source. Enclose all quotes in quotation marks to make clear that the ideas belong to someone else.

This sample note card shows information to include.

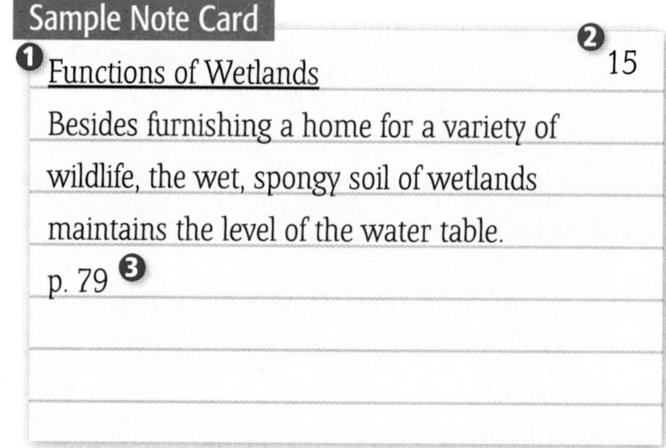
Sample Note Card

❶ Functions of Wetlands ❷ 15
Besides furnishing a home for a variety of wildlife, the wet, spongy soil of wetlands maintains the level of the water table.
p. 79 ❸

❶ Write a key word or phrase that tells you what the information is about.
❷ Write the source number from your source card.
❸ Write the number of the page or pages on which you found the information.

Develop Your Thesis

As you begin researching and learning about your topic, think about the overall point you want to make. Write one sentence, your *thesis statement,* that says exactly what you plan to report on.

Sample Thesis Statement

Everglades National Park is a beautiful but endangered animal habitat.

Keep your thesis in mind as you continue to do research and think about your topic. The thesis will help you determine what information is important. However, be prepared to change your thesis if the information you find does not support it.

Write an Outline

When you finish taking notes, organize the information in an outline. Write down the main ideas that you want to cover. Write your thesis statement at the beginning of your outline. Then list the supporting details. Follow an outline form like the one on the next page.

❶ Everglades National Park is a beautiful but endangered animal habitat.

I. Special aspects of the Everglades
   A. Characteristics of wetlands
   ❷ B. Endangered birds and animals

II. Pressures on the Everglades
   A. Florida agriculture
   B. Carelessness of visitors

III. How to protect the Everglades
   A. Change agricultural practices
   B. Educate park visitors
      1. Mandatory video on safety for individuals and environment ❸
      2. Instructional reminders posted throughout the park

❶ The thesis statement identifies your topic and the overall point you will make.

❷ If you have subtopics under a main topic, there must be at least two. They must relate directly to your main topic.

❸ If you wish to divide a subtopic, you must have at least two divisions. Each must relate to the subtopic above it.

Document Your Information

You must document, or credit, the sources of all the information you use in your report. There are two common ways to document information.

Footnotes

To document with footnotes, place a number at the end of the information you are documenting. Number your notes consecutively, beginning with number 1. These numbers should be slightly raised and should come after any punctuation. The documentation information itself goes at the bottom of the page, with a matching number.

In-text number for note:

The Declaration of Independence was read in public for the first time on July 6, 1776.[3]

Footnote at bottom of page:

[3] John Smith, The Declaration of Independence (New York: DI, 2001) 221.

Parenthetical Documentation

In this method, you give the source for your information in parentheses at the end of the sentence where the information appears. You do not need to give all the details of the source. Just provide enough information for your readers to identify it. Here are the basic rules to follow.

- Usually it is enough to give the author's last name and the number of the page where you found the information.

  The declaration was first read in public by militia colonel John Nixon (Smith 222).

- If you mention the author's name in the sentence, you do not need to repeat it in the parentheses.

  According to Smith, the reading was greeted with wild applause (224).

- If your source does not identify a particular author, as in a newspaper or encyclopedia article, give the first word or two of the title of the piece.

  The anniversary of the reading was commemorated by a parade and fireworks ("Reading Celebrated").

Full information on your sources goes in a list at the end of your paper.

Bibliography or Works Cited

At the end of your paper, list all the sources of information that you used in preparing your report. Arrange them alphabetically by the author's last name (or by the first word in the title if no author is mentioned) as shown below. Title this list *Works Cited.* (Use the term *bibliography* if all your sources are printed media, such as books, magazines, or newspapers.)

Works Cited (1)

(2) Bertram, Jeffrey. "African Bees: Fact or Myth?" *Orlando Sentinel* 18 Aug. 1999: D2.

(3) Gore, Rick. "Neanderthals." National Geographic. January 1996: 2–35. (8)

(4) Gould, Stephen J. The Panda's Thumb. New York: W. W. Norton & Co., 1982.

(5) "Governor Chiles Vetoes Anti-Everglades Bills–5/13/98." (9) Friends of the Everglades. May 1998. 26 Aug 1998 <http://www.everglades.org/pressrel_may28.htm>.

(6) "Neanderthal man." The Columbia Encyclopedia. 5th Edition. New York: Columbia University Press, 1993.

(7) Pabst, Laura (Curator of Natural History Museum), Interview. March 11, 1998.

(1) Indent all but the first line of each item.

(2) Newspaper article

(3) Magazine article

(4) Book with one author

(5) On-line article

(6) Encyclopedia

(7) Interview

(8) Include page numbers for a magazine article but not for a book, unless the book is a collection of essays by different authors.

(9) Include database (underlined), publication medium (online), computer service, and date of access.

Business Writing

Two standard formats for business letters are block style and modified block style. In block style all the parts of the letter begin at the left-hand margin.

Business Letter

The following business letter uses modified block style

❶ 10 Pullman Lane
Cromwell, CT 06416
January 16, 2006

❷ Mr. Philip Fornaro
Principal
Cromwell School
179 West Maple St.
Cromwell, CT 06416

❸ Dear Mr. Fornaro:

❹ My friends and I in the seventh grade at Brimmer Middle School feel that there is not enough to do in Cromwell during the winter vacation week. Some students can afford to go away for vacation. Many families, however, cannot afford to go away, or the parents have to work.

❺ I would like to suggest that you keep the Brimmer Middle School gym open during the vacation week. If the gym were open, the basketball teams could practice. The fencing club could meet. We could meet our friends there instead of going to the mall.

❻ Thanks for listening to my request. I hope you will think it over.

❼ Sincerely,
Kim Goodwin
Kim Goodwin

❶ In the heading, write your address and the date on separate lines.

❷ In the inside address, write the name and address of the person to whom you are sending the letter.

❸ Use a colon after the greeting.

❹ In your introduction, say who you are and why you are writing.

❺ In the body of your letter, provide details concerning your request.

❻ Conclude by restating your purpose and thanking the person you are writing to.

❼ In the closing, use *Sincerely, Sincerely yours,* or *Yours truly* followed by a comma. Include both your signature and your printed or typed name.

General guidelines

Follow these guidelines when writing a business letter.

- Use correct business-letter form. Whether you write by hand, or use a computer, use 8 1/2-by-11-inch white or off-white paper. Be sure your letter is neat and clean.
- Use Standard English. Check your spelling carefully.
- Be polite, even if you are making a complaint or expressing a negative opinion.
- Be brief and to the point. State your reason for writing within the first two or three sentences.
- Include all necessary information.
- If you are making a request, be specific. Make sure what you are asking is reasonable. Express your appreciation at the end of the letter.
- Be considerate. Request only information you cannot get another way.
- When expressing an opinion or a complaint, state your reasons clearly and logically. Avoid emotional language.
- When requesting an interview, make it easy for the interviewee to meet with you. Suggest a few dates.

Writing a Memo

A memo, or memorandum, is a brief, efficient way of communicating information to another person or group of people. It begins with a header that provides basic information. A memo does not have a formal closing.

TO: *Brimmer Banner* newspaper staff
FROM: Terry Glinski
SUBJECT: Winter issue
DATE: January 18, 2006

Articles for the winter issue of the *Brimmer Banner* are due by February 1. Please see Terry about your assignment as soon as possible! The following articles or features have not yet been assigned:

Cafeteria Mess: Who Is Responsible?
Teacher Profile: Mr. Jinks, Ms. Magee
Sports roundup

Using a Computer for Writing

Using a computer offers advantages at every stage of the writing process.

Prewriting

A computer can help you gather and organize ideas and information.

Brainstorming

While brainstorming for topics or details, you can dim the computer screen and do "invisible writing." Some writers find that this technique allows their ideas to flow more freely.

Researching

Use the Internet or a CD-ROM encyclopedia to find not only text and pictures, but also sound, animated cartoons or graphics, and live-action video clips.

Outlining

Some word-processing programs offer an outlining feature that automatically indents headings and uses different type styles for main headings and subheadings.

Drafting/Revising

Most word-processing programs make it easy to do the following.

- *insert* new text at any point in your document
- *delete* or *copy* text
- *move* text from one position to another
- *undo* a change you just made
- *save* each draft or revision of your document
- *print* copies of your work-in-progress for others to read

Editing/Proofreading

You can edit and proofread directly on the computer, or you can mark your changes on a printout, or hard copy, and then input the changes on screen. The following word-processing features are helpful.

- **Grammar checker** The computer finds possible errors in grammar and suggests revisions.
- **Spelling checker** The computer finds misspellings and suggests corrections.
- **Thesaurus** If you want to replace an inappropriate or overused word, you can highlight the word and the computer will suggest synonyms.
- **Search and replace** If you want to change or correct something that occurs several times in your document, the computer can quickly make the change throughout the document.

TIP

The grammar checker, spelling checker, and thesaurus cannot replace your own careful reading and judgment. Because English grammar is so complex, the suggestions that the grammar checker makes may not be appropriate. Also, the spelling checker will not tell you that you have typed *brake* when you meant *break,* for example, because both are valid words. The thesaurus may offer you several synonyms for a word, but you need to consider the connotations of each before deciding which, if any, fits your context.

Presenting

The computer allows you to enhance the readability, attractiveness, and visual interest of your document in many ways.

Formatting your text

The computer gives you a variety of options for the layout and appearance of your text. You can easily add or change the following elements.

- margin width
- number of columns
- type size and style
- page numbering
- header or footer (information such as a title that appears at the top or bottom of every page)

Visual aids

Some word-processing programs have graphic functions that allow you to create graphs, charts, and diagrams. Collections of *clip art,* pictures you can copy and paste into your document, are also available.

Troubleshooter

Use the Troubleshooter to recognize and correct common writing errors.

Sentence Fragment

A sentence fragment does not express a complete thought. It may lack a subject or verb or both.

- **Problem: Fragment that lacks a subject**

  The lion paced the floor of the cage. Looked hungry. *frag*

  Solution: Add a subject to the fragment to make a complete sentence.

  The lion paced the floor of the cage. He looked hungry.

- **Problem: Fragment that lacks a predicate**

  I'm painting my room. The walls yellow. *frag*

  Solution: Add a predicate to make the sentence complete.

  I'm painting my room. The walls are going to be yellow.

- **Problem: Fragment that lacks both a subject and a predicate**

  We walked around the reservoir. Near the parkway. *frag*

  Solution: Combine the fragment with another sentence.

  We walked around the reservoir near the parkway.

TIP

You can use fragments when talking with friends or writing personal letters. Some writers use fragments to produce a special effect. Use complete sentences, however, for school or business writing.

Run-on Sentence

A run-on sentence is two or more sentences written incorrectly as one sentence.

- **Problem: Two main clauses separated only by a comma**

  Roller coasters make me dizzy, I don't enjoy them. *run-on*

  Solution A: Replace the comma with a period or other end mark. Start the second sentence with a capital letter.

  Roller coasters make me dizzy. I don't enjoy them.

  Solution B: Replace the comma with a semicolon.

  Roller coasters make me dizzy; I don't enjoy them.

- **Problem: Two main clauses with no punctuation between them**

  Acid rain is a worldwide problem there are no solutions in sight. *run-on*

  Solution A: Separate the main clauses with a period or other end mark. Begin the second sentence with a capital letter.

  Acid rain is a worldwide problem. There are no solutions in sight.

  Solution B: Add a comma and a coordinating conjunction between the main clauses.

  Acid rain is a worldwide problem, but there are no solutions in sight.

- **Problem: Two main clauses with no comma before the coordinating conjunction**

  Our chorus has been practicing all month but we still need another rehearsal. *run-on*

Solution: Add a comma before the coordinating conjunction.

Our chorus has been practicing all month, but we still need another rehearsal.

Lack of Subject-Verb Agreement

A singular subject calls for a singular form of the verb. A plural subject calls for a plural form of the verb.

- **Problem: A subject that is separated from the verb by an intervening prepositional phrase**

  The two policemen at the construction site looks bored. *agr*

  The members of my baby-sitting club is saving money. *agr*

  Solution: Make sure that the verb agrees with the subject of the sentence, not with the object of the preposition. The object of a preposition is never the subject.

  The two policemen at the construction site look bored.

  The members of my baby-sitting club are saving money.

TIP

When subject and verb are separated by a prepositional phrase, check for agreement by reading the sentence without the prepositional phrase.

- **Problem: A sentence that begins with *here* or *there***

  Here come the last bus to Pelham Heights. *agr*

  There is my aunt and uncle. *agr*

  Solution: In sentences that begin with *here* or *there*, look for the subject after the verb. Make sure that the verb agrees with the subject.

  Here comes the last bus to Pelham Heights.

  There are my aunt and uncle.

- **Problem: An indefinite pronoun as the subject**

  Each of the candidates are qualified. *agr*

  All of the problems on the test was hard. *agr*

  Solution: Some indefinite pronouns are singular; some are plural; and some can be either singular or plural, depending on the noun they refer to. Determine whether the indefinite pronoun is singular or plural, and make sure the verb agrees with it.

  Each of the candidates is qualified.

  All of the problems on the test were hard.

- **Problem: A compound subject that is joined by *and***

  Fishing tackle and a life jacket was stowed in the boat. *agr*

  Peanut butter and jelly are delicious. *agr*

  Solution A: If the compound subjects refer to different people or things, use a plural verb.

  Fishing tackle and a life jacket were stowed in the boat.

  Solution B: If the parts of a compound subject name one unit or if they refer to the same person or thing, use a singular verb.

  Peanut butter and jelly is delicious.

- **Problem: A compound subject that is joined by *or* or *nor***

  Either my aunt or my parents plans to attend parents' night. *agr*

  Neither onions nor pepper improve the taste of this meatloaf. *agr*

  Solution: Make the verb agree with the subject that is closer to it.

  Either my aunt or my parents plan to attend parents' night.

  Neither onions nor pepper improves the taste of this meatloaf.

Incorrect Verb Tense or Form

Verbs have different tenses to show when the action takes place.

- **Problem: An incorrect or missing verb ending**

The Parks Department install a new water fountain last week. *tense*

They have also plant flowers in all the flower beds. *tense*

Solution: To form the past tense and the part participle, add *-ed* to a regular verb.

The Parks Department installed a new water fountain last week.

They have also planted flowers in all the flower beds.

- **Problem: An improperly formed irregular verb**

Wendell has standed in line for two hours. *tense*

I catched the fly ball and throwed it to first base. *tense*

Solution: Irregular verbs vary in their past and past participle forms. Look up the ones you are not sure of.

Wendell has stood in line for two hours.

I caught the fly ball and threw it to first base.

- **Problem: Confusion between the past form and the past participle**

The cast for *The Music Man* has began rehearsals. *tense*

Solution: Use the past participle form of an irregular verb, not its past form, when you use the auxiliary verb *have*.

The cast for *The Music Man* has begun rehearsals.

- **Problem: Improper use of the past participle**

Our seventh grade drawn a mural for the wall of the cafeteria. *tense*

Solution: Add the auxiliary verb *have* to the past participle of an irregular verb to form a complete verb.

Our seventh grade has drawn a mural for the wall of the cafeteria.

TIP

Because irregular verbs vary, it is useful to memorize the verbs that you use most often.

Incorrect Use of Pronouns

The noun that a pronoun refers to is called its antecedent. A pronoun must refer to its **antecedent** clearly. Subject pronouns refer to subjects in a sentence. Object pronouns refer to objects in a sentence.

- **Problem: A pronoun that could refer to more than one antecedent**

Gary and Mike are coming, but he doesn't know the other kids. *ant*

Solution: Substitute a noun for the pronoun to make your sentence clearer.

Gary and Mike are coming, but Gary doesn't know the other kids.

- **Problem: Personal pronouns as subjects**

Him and John were freezing after skating for three hours. *pro*

Lori and me decided not to audition for the musical. *pro*

Solution: Use a subject pronoun as the subject part of a sentence.

He and John were freezing after skating for three hours.

Lori and I decided not to audition for the musical.

- **Problem: Personal pronouns as objects**

Ms. Wang asked Reggie and I to enter the science fair *pro*

Ms. Wang helped he and I with the project. *pro*

Solution: Use an object pronoun as the object of a verb or a preposition.

Ms. Wang asked Reggie and me to enter the science fair.

Ms. Wang helped him and me with the project.

Incorrect Use of Adjectives

Some adjectives have irregular forms: comparative forms for comparing two things and superlative forms for comparing more than two things.

Problem: Incorrect use of *good, better, best*

Their team is more good at softball than ours. *adj*

They have more better equipment too. *adj*

Solution: The comparative and superlative forms of *good* are *better* and *best*. Do not use *more* or *most* before irregular forms of comparative and superlative adjectives.

Their team is better at softball than ours.

They have better equipment too.

Problem: Incorrect use of *bad, worse, worst*

The flooding on East Street was the baddest I've seen. *adj*

Mike's basement was in badder shape than his garage. *adj*

Solution: The comparative and superlative forms of *bad* are *worse* and *worst*. Do not use *more* or *most* or the endings *-er* or *-est* with *bad*.

The flooding on East Street was the worst I've seen.

Mike's basement was in worse shape than his garage.

Problem: Incorrect use of comparative and superlative adjectives

The Appalachian Mountains are more older than the Rockies. *adj*

Mount Washington is the most highest of the Appalachians. *adj*

Solution: Do not use both *-er* and *more* or *-est* and *most* at the same time.

The Appalachian Mountains are older than the Rockies.

Mount Washington is the highest of the Appalachians.

Incorrect Use of Commas

Commas signal a pause between parts of a sentence and help to clarify meaning.

Problem: Missing commas in a series of three or more items

Sergio put mustard catsup and bean sprouts on his hot dog. *com*

Solution: If there are three or more items in a series, use a comma after each one, including the item preceding the conjunction.

Sergio put mustard, catsup, and bean sprouts on his hot dog.

Problem: Missing commas with direct quotations

"A little cold water" the swim coach said "won't hurt you." *com*

Solution: The first part of an interrupted quotation ends with a comma followed by quotation marks. The interrupting words are also followed by a comma.

"A little cold water," the swim coach said, "won't hurt you."

Problem: Missing commas with nonessential appositives

My sneakers a new pair are covered with mud. *com*

Solution: Determine whether the appositive is important to the meaning of the sentence. If it is not essential, set off the appositive with commas.

My sneakers, a new pair, are covered with mud.

Incorrect Use of Apostrophes

An apostrophe shows possession. It can also indicate missing letters in a contraction.

Problem: Singular possessive nouns

A parrots toes are used for gripping. *poss*

The bus color was bright yellow. *poss*

Solution: Use an apostrophe and an *s* to form the possessive of a singular noun, even one that ends in *s*.

A parrot's toes are used for gripping.

The bus's color was bright yellow.

Problem: Plural possessive nouns ending in *-s*

The visitors center closes at five o'clock. *poss*

The guide put several tourists luggage in one compartment. *poss*

Solution: Use an apostrophe alone to form the possessive of a plural noun that ends in *s*.

The visitors' center closes at five o'clock.

The guide put several tourists' luggage in one compartment.

Problem: Plural possessive nouns not ending in *-s*

The peoples applause gave courage to the young gymnast. *poss*

Solution: Use an apostrophe and an *s* to form the possessive of a plural noun that does not end in *s*.

The people's applause gave courage to the young gymnast.

Problem: Possessive personal pronouns

Jenny found the locker that was her's; she waited while her friends found their's. *poss*

Solution: Do not use apostrophes with possessive personal pronouns.

Jenny found the locker that was hers; she waited while her friends found theirs.

Incorrect Capitalization

Proper nouns, proper adjectives, and the first words of sentences always begin with a capital letter.

Problem: Words referring to ethnic groups, nationalities, and languages

Many canadians in the province of quebec speak french. *cap*

Solution: Capitalize proper nouns and adjectives that refer to ethnic groups, nationalities, and languages.

Many Canadians in the province of Quebec speak French.

Problem: Words that refer to a family member

Yesterday aunt Doreen asked me to baby-sit. *cap*

Don't forget to give dad a call. *cap*

Solution: Capitalize words that are used as part of or in place of a family member's name.

Yesterday Aunt Doreen asked me to baby-sit.

Don't forget to give Dad a call.

TIP

Do not capitalize a word that identifies a family member when it is preceded by a possessive adjective: *My father bought a new car.*

Problem: The first word of a direct quotation

The judge declared, "the court is now in session." *cap*

Solution: Capitalize the first word in a direct quotation.

The judge declared, "The court is now in session."

If you have difficulty with a rule of usage, try rewriting the rule in your own words. Check with your teacher to be sure you understand the rule.

Troublesome Words

This section will help you choose between words and expressions that are often confusing or misused.

accept, except

Accept means "to receive." *Except* means "other than."

Phillip walked proudly to the stage to accept the award.

Everything fits in my suitcase except my sleeping bag.

affect, effect

Affect is a verb meaning "to cause a change in" or "to influence." *Effect* as a verb means "to bring about or accomplish." As a noun, *effect* means "result."

Bad weather will affect our plans for the weekend.

The new medicine effected an improvement in the patient's condition.

The gloomy weather had a bad effect on my mood.

ain't

Ain't is never used in formal speaking or writing unless you are quoting the exact words of a character or a real person. Instead of using *ain't,* say or write *am not, is not, are not;* or use contractions such as *I'm not, she isn't.*

The pizza is not going to arrive for another half hour.

The pizza isn't going to arrive for another half hour.

a lot

The expression *a lot* means "much" or "many" and should always be written as two words. Some authorities discourage its use in formal writing.

A lot of my friends are learning Spanish.

Many of my friends are learning Spanish.

all ready, already

All ready, written as two words, is a phrase that means "completely ready." *Already,* written as one word, is an adverb that means "before" or "by this time."

By the time the fireworks display was all ready, we had already arrived.

all right, alright

The expression *all right* should be written as two words. Some dictionaries do list the single word *alright* but usually not as a preferred spelling.

Tom hurt his ankle, but he will be all right.

all together, altogether

All together means "in a group." *Altogether* means "completely."

The Minutemen stood all together at the end of Lexington Green.

The rebel farmers were not altogether sure that they could fight the British soldiers.

among, between

Use *among* for three or more people, things, or groups. Use *between* for two people, things, or groups.

Mr. Kendall divided the jobs for the car wash among the team members.

Our soccer field lies between the gym and Main Street.

amount, number

Use *amount* with nouns that cannot be counted. Use *number* with nouns that can be counted.

This recipe calls for an unusual amount of pepper.

A record number of students attended last Saturday's book fair.

bad, badly

Bad is an adjective; it modifies a noun.
Badly is an adverb; it modifies a verb, an adjective, or another adverb.

The badly burnt cookies left a bad smell in the kitchen.

Joseph badly wants to be on the track team.

beside, besides

Beside means "next to." *Besides* means "in addition to."

The zebra is grazing beside a wildebeest.

Besides the zoo, I like to visit the aquarium.

bring, take

Bring means "to carry from a distant place to a closer one." *Take* means "to carry from a nearby place to a more distant one."

Please bring a bag lunch and subway money to school tomorrow.

Don't forget to take your art projects home this afternoon.

can, may

Can implies the ability to do something. *May* implies permission to do something.

You may take a later bus home if you can remember which bus to get on.

TIP

Although *can* is sometimes used in place of *may* in informal speech, a distinction should be made when speaking and writing formally.

choose, chose

Choose means "to select." *Chose,* the past tense of *choose,* means "selected."

Dad helped me choose a birthday card for my grandmother.

Dad chose a card with a funny joke inside.

doesn't, don't

The subject of the contraction **doesn't** *(does not)* is the third-person singular (*he* or *she*). The subject of the contraction **don't** *(do not)* is *I, you, we,* or *they.*

Tanya doesn't have any tickets for the concert.

We don't need tickets if we stand in the back row.

farther, further

Farther refers to physical distance. *Further* refers to time or degree.

Our new apartment is farther away from the school.

I will not continue this argument further.

fewer, less

Fewer is used to refer to things or qualities that can be counted. *Less* is used to refer to things or qualities that cannot be counted. In addition, *less* is used with figures that are regarded as single amounts.

Fewer people were waiting in line after lunch.

There is less fat in this kind of peanut butter.

Try to spend less than ten dollars on a present. [The money is treated as a single sum, not as individual dollars.]

good, well

Good is often used as an adjective meaning "pleasing" or "able." *Well* may be used as an adverb of manner telling how ably something is done or as an adjective meaning "in good health."

That is a good haircut.

Marco writes well.

Because Ms. Rodriguez had a headache, she was not well enough to correct our tests.

in, into

In means "inside." *Into* indicates a movement from outside toward the inside.

Refreshments will be sold in the lobby of the auditorium.

The doors opened, and the eager crowd rushed into the auditorium.

it's, its

Use an apostrophe to form the contraction of *it is.* The possessive of the personal pronoun *it* does not take an apostrophe.

It's hard to keep up with computer technology.

The computer industry seems to change its products daily.

lay, lie
Lay means "to place." *Lie* means "to recline."

I will lay my beach towel here on the warm sand.

Help! I don't want to lie next to a hill of red ants!

learn, teach
Learn means "to gain knowledge." *Teach* means "to give knowledge."

I don't learn very quickly.

My uncle is teaching me how to juggle.

leave, let
Leave means "to go away." *Let* means "to allow." With the word *alone,* you may use either *let* or *leave.*

Huang has to leave at eight o'clock.

Mr. Davio lets the band practice in his basement.

Leave me alone. Let me alone.

like, as
Use *like,* a preposition, to introduce a prepositional phrase. Use *as,* a subordinating conjunction, to introduce a subordinate clause. Many authorities believe that *like* should not be used before a clause in formal English.

Andy sometimes acts like a clown.

The detective looked carefully at the empty suitcase as she examined the room.

TIP

As can be a preposition in cases like the following: *Jack went to the costume party as a giant pumpkin.*

loose, lose
Loose means "not firmly attached." *Lose* means "to misplace" or "to fail to win."

If you keep wiggling that loose tooth, you might lose it.

raise, rise
Raise means to "cause to move up." *Rise* means "to move upward."

Farmers in this part of Florida raise sugarcane.

The hot air balloon began to rise slowly in the morning sky.

set, sit
Set means "to place" or "to put." *Sit* means "to place oneself in a seated position."

I set the tips of my running shoes against the starting line.

After running the fifty-yard dash, I had to sit down and catch my breath.

than, then
Than introduces the second part of a comparison. *Then* means "at that time" or "after that."

I'd rather go to Disney World in the winter than in the summer.

The park is too crowded and hot then.

their, they're
Their is the possessive form of they. *They're* is the contraction of *they are.*

They're visiting Plymouth Plantation during their vacation.

to, too, two
To means "in the direction of." *Too* means "also" or "to an excessive degree." *Two* is the number after one.

I bought two tickets to the concert.

The music was too loud.

It's my favorite group too.

who, whom
Who is a subject pronoun. *Whom* is an object pronoun.

Who has finished the test already?

Mr. Russo is the man to whom we owe our thanks.

who's, whose
Who's is the contraction of *who is. Whose* is the possessive form of *who.*

Who's going to wake me up in the morning?

The policeman discovered whose car alarm was making so much noise.

Mechanics

This section will help you use correct capitalization, punctuation, and abbreviations in your writing.

Capitalization

Capitalizing Sentences, Quotations, and Salutations

Rule: A capital letter appears at the beginning of a sentence.

Example: **A**nother gust of wind shook the house.

Rule: A capital letter marks the beginning of a direct quotation that is a complete sentence.

Example: Sabrina said, "**T**he lights might go out."

Rule: When a quoted sentence is interrupted by explanatory words, such as she said, do not begin the second part of the sentence with a capital letter.

Example: "There's a rainbow," exclaimed Jeffrey, "**o**ver the whole beach."

Rule: When the second part of a quotation is a new sentence, put a period after the explanatory words; begin the new part with a capital letter.

Example: "Please come inside," Justin said. "**W**ipe your feet."

Rule: Do not capitalize an indirect quotation.

Example: Jo said that **t**he storm was getting worse.

Rule: Capitalize the first word in the salutation and closing of a letter. Capitalize the title and name of the person addressed.

Example: **D**ear **D**r. **M**enino
Dear **E**ditor
Sincerely

Capitalizing Names and Titles of People

Rule: Capitalize the names of people and the initials that stand for their names.

Example: **M**alcolm **X** **J**. **F**. **K**.
Robert **E**. **L**ee **Q**ueen **E**lizabeth **I**

Rule: Capitalize a title or an abbreviation of a title when it comes before a person's name or when it is used in direct address.

Example: **D**r. **S**alinas
"Your patient, **D**octor, is waiting."

Rule: Do not capitalize a title that follows or is a substitute for a person's name.

Example: Marcia Salinas is a good **d**octor.
He asked to speak to the **d**octor.

Rule: Capitalize the names and abbreviations of academic degrees that follow a person's name. Capitalize Jr. and Sr.

Example: Marcia Salinas, **M.D.**
Raoul Tobias, **A**ttorney
Donald Bruns **S**r.
Ann Lee, **P**h.**D.**

Rule: Capitalize words that show family relationships when used as titles or as substitutes for a person's name.

Example: We saw **U**ncle Carlos.
She read a book about **M**other **T**eresa.

Rule: Do not capitalize words that show family relationships when they follow a possessive noun or pronoun.

Example: Your **b**rother will give us a ride.
I forgot my **m**other's phone number.

Rule: Always capitalize the pronoun I.

Example: After **I** clean my room, **I**'m going swimming.

Capitalizing Names of Places

Do not capitalize articles and prepositions in proper nouns: *the Rock of Gibraltar, the Statue of Liberty.*

Rule: Capitalize the names of cities, counties, states, countries, and continents.

Example: **S**t. **L**ouis, **M**issouri
Marin **C**ounty
Australia
South **A**merica

Rule: Capitalize the names of bodies of water and other geographical features.

Example: the **G**reat **L**akes   **C**ape **C**od
the **D**ust **B**owl

Rule: Capitalize the names of sections of a country and regions of the world.

Example: **E**ast **A**sia
New **E**ngland
the **P**acific **R**im
the **M**idwest

Rule: Capitalize compass points when they refer to a specific section of a country.

Example: the Northwest   the South

Rule: Do not capitalize compass points when they indicate direction.

Example: Canada is **n**orth of the United States.

Rule: Do not capitalize adjectives indicating direction.

Example: **w**estern Utah

Rule: Capitalize the names of streets and highways.

Example: **D**orchester **A**venue   **R**oute 22

Rule: Capitalize the names of buildings, bridges, monuments, and other structures.

Example: **E**mpire **S**tate **B**uilding
Chesapeake **B**ay **B**ridge

Capitalizing Other Proper Nouns and Adjectives

Rule: Capitalize the names of clubs, organizations, businesses, institutions, and political parties.

Example: **H**ouston **O**ilers
the **F**ood and **D**rug **A**dministration
Boys and **G**irls **C**lub

Rule: Capitalize brand names but not the nouns following them.

Example: **Z**ippo brand energy bar

Rule: Capitalize the names of days of the week, months, and holidays.

Example: **S**aturday   **J**une
Thanksgiving **D**ay

Rule: Do not capitalize the names of seasons.

Example: **w**inter, **s**pring, **s**ummer, **f**all

Rule: Capitalize the first word, the last word, and all important words in the title of a book, play, short story, poem, essay, article, film, television series, song, magazine, newspaper, and chapter of a book.

Example: ***N**ot **W**ithout **L**aughter*
***W**orld **B**ook **E**ncyclopedia*
"**J**ingle **B**ells"
Star **W**ars
Chapter 12

Rule: Capitalize the names of ethnic groups, nationalities, and languages.

Example: **L**atino   **J**apanese
European   **S**panish

Rule: Capitalize proper adjectives that are formed from the names of ethnic groups and nationalities.

Example: **S**hetland pony
Jewish holiday

LANGUAGE HANDBOOK

Punctuation

Using the Period and Other End Marks

Rule: Use a period at the end of a declarative sentence.

My great-grandfather fought in the Mexican Revolution.

Rule: Use a period at the end of an imperative sentence that does not express strong feeling.

Please set the table.

Rule: Use a question mark at the end of an interrogative sentence.

How did your sneakers get so muddy?

Rule: Use an exclamation point at the end of an exclamatory sentence or a strong imperative.

How exciting the play was!

Watch out!

Using Commas

Rule: Use commas to separate three or more items in a series.

The canary eats bird seed, fruit, and suet.

Rule: Use commas to show a pause after an introductory word and to set off names used in direct address.

Yes, I offered to take care of her canary this weekend.

Please, Stella, can I borrow your nail polish?

Rule: Use a comma after two or more introductory prepositional phrases or when the comma is needed to make the meaning clear. A comma is not needed after a single short prepositional phrase, but it is acceptable to use one.

From the back of the balcony, we had a lousy view of the stage.

After the movie we walked home. (no comma needed)

Rule: Use a comma after an introductory participle and an introductory participial phrase.

Whistling and moaning, the wind shook the little house.

Rule: Use commas to set off words that interrupt the flow of thought in a sentence.

Tomorrow, I think, our projects are due.

Rule: Use a comma after conjunctive adverbs such as *however, moreover, furthermore, nevertheless,* and *therefore.*

The skating rink is crowded on Saturday; however, it's the only time I can go.

Rule: Use commas to set off an appositive if it is not essential to the meaning of a sentence.

Ben Wagner, a resident of Pittsfield, won the first round in the golf tournament.

Rule: Use a comma before a conjunction (*and, or, but, nor, so, yet*) that joins main clauses.

We can buy our tickets now, or we can take a chance on buying them just before the show.

Rule: Use a comma after an introductory adverb clause.

Because I stayed up so late, I'm sleepy this morning.

Rule: In most cases, do not use a comma with an adverb clause that comes at the end of a sentence.

The picnic will be canceled unless the weather clears.

Rule: Use a comma or a pair of commas to set off an adjective clause that is not essential to the meaning of a sentence.

Tracy, who just moved here from Florida, has never seen snow before.

Rule: Do not use a comma or pair of commas to set off an essential clause from the rest of the sentence.

Anyone who signs up this month will get a discount.

Rule: Use commas before and after the year when it is used with both the month and the day. If only the month and the year are given, do not use a comma.

On January 2, 1985, my parents moved to Dallas, Texas.

I was born in May 1985.

Rule: Use commas before and after the name of a state or a country when it is used with the name of a city. Do not use a comma after the state if it is used with a ZIP code.

The area code for Concord, New Hampshire, is 603.

Please forward my mail to 6 Madison Lane, Topsham, ME 04086

Rule: Use commas or a pair of commas to set off an abbreviated title or degree following a person's name.

The infirmary was founded by Elizabeth Blackwell, M.D., the first woman in the United States to earn a medical degree.

Rule: Use a comma or commas to set off *too* when *too* means "also."

We, too, bought groceries, from the new online supermarket.

Rule: Use a comma or commas to set off a direct quotation.

"My nose," exclaimed Pinocchio, "is growing longer!"

Rule: Use a comma after the salutation of a friendly letter and after the closing of both a friendly letter and a business letter.

Dear Gary,

Sincerely,

Best regards,

Rule: Use a comma when necessary to prevent misreading of a sentence.

In math, solutions always elude me.

Using Semicolons and Colons

Rule: Use a semicolon to join the parts of a compound sentence when a coordinating conjunction, such as *and, or, nor,* or *but,* is not used.

Don't be late for the dress rehearsal; it begins at 7 o'clock sharp.

Rule: Use a semicolon to join parts of a compound sentence when the main clauses are long and are subdivided by commas. Use a semicolon even if these clauses are already joined by a coordinating conjunction.

In the gray light of early morning, on a remote airstrip in the desert, two pilots prepared to fly on a dangerous mission; but accompanying them were a television camera crew, three newspaper reporters, and a congressman from their home state of Nebraska.

Rule: Use a semicolon to separate main clauses joined by a conjunctive adverb. Be sure to use a comma after the conjunctive adverb.

We've been climbing all morning; therefore, we need a rest.

Rule: Use a colon to introduce a list of items that ends a sentence. Use words such as *these, the following,* or *as follows* to signal that a list is coming.

Remember to bring the following items: a backpack, a bag lunch, sunscreen, and insect repellent.

Rule: Do not use a colon to introduce a list preceded by a verb or preposition.

Remember to bring a backpack, a bag lunch, sunscreen, and insect repellent. (No colon is used after *bring.*)

Rule: Use a colon to separate the hour and the minutes when you write the time of day.

My Spanish class starts at 9:15.

Rule: Use a colon after the salutation of a business letter.

Dear Dr. Coulombe:
Director of the Personnel Dept.:

Using Quotation Marks and Italics

Rule: Use quotation marks before and after a direct quotation.

"Curiouser and curiouser," said Alice.

Rule: Use quotation marks with both parts of a divided quotation.

"This gymnastics trick," explained Amanda, "took me three months to learn."

Rule: Use a comma or commas to separate a phrase such as *she said* from the quotation itself. Place the comma that precedes the phrase inside the closing quotation marks.

"I will be late," said the cable technician, "for my appointment."

Rule: Place a period that ends a quotation inside the closing quotation marks.

Scott said, "Thanks for letting me borrow your camping tent."

Rule: Place a question mark or an exclamation point inside the quotation marks when it is part of the quotation.

"Why is the door of your snake's cage open?" asked my mother.

Rule: Place a question mark or an exclamation point outside the quotation marks when it is part of the entire sentence.

How I love "The Pit and the Pendulum"!

Rule: Use quotation marks for the title of a short story, essay, poem, song, magazine or newspaper article, or book chapter.

short story: "The Necklace"
poem: "The Fish"
article: "Fifty Things to Make from Bottlecaps"

Rule: Use italics or underlining for the title of a book, play, film, television series, magazine, newspaper, or work of art.

book: *To Kill a Mockingbird*
magazine: *The New Republic*
painting: *Sunflowers*

Rule: Use italics or underlining for the names of ships, trains, airplanes, and spacecraft.

ship: *Mayflower*
airplane: *Air Force One*

Using Apostrophes

Rule: Use an apostrophe and an *s ('s)* to form the possessive of a singular noun.

my brother's rock collection
Chris's hat

Rule: Use an apostrophe and an *s ('s)* to form the possessive of a plural noun that does not end in *s.*

the geese's feathers
the oxen's domestication

TIP

If a thing is owned jointly by two or more individuals, only the last name should show possession: *Mom and Dad's car.* If the ownership is not joint, each name should show possession: *Mom and Dad's parents are coming for Thanksgiving.*

Rule: Use an apostrophe alone to form the possessive of a plural noun that ends in *s.*

the animals' habitat
the instruments' sound

Rule: Use an apostrophe and an *s ('s)* to form the possessive of an indefinite pronoun.

everyone's homework
someone's homework

Rule: Do not use an apostrophe in a possessive pronoun.

The dog knocked over its dish.
Yours is the best entry in the contest.
One of these drawings must be hers.

Rule: Use an apostrophe to replace letters that have been omitted in a contraction.

it + is = it's
can + not = can't
I + have = I've

Rule: Use an apostrophe to form the plural of a letter, a figure, or a word that is used as itself.

Write three 7's.
The word is spelled with two m's.
The sentence contains three and's.

Rule: Use an apostrophe to show missing numbers in a year.

the class of '02

Using Hyphens, Dashes, and Parentheses

Rule: Use a hyphen to show the division of a word at the end of a line. Always divide the word between its syllables.

With the new recycling program, more residents are recycling
their trash.

TIP

One-letter divisions (for example, *e-lectric*) are not permissible. Avoid dividing personal names, if possible.

Rule: Use a hyphen in a number written as a compound word.

He sold forty-six ice creams in one hour.

Rule: Use a hyphen in a fraction.

We won the vote by a two-thirds majority.

Two-thirds of the votes have been counted.

Rule: Use a hyphen or hyphens in certain compound nouns.

great-grandmother

merry-go-round

Rule: Hyphenate a compound modifier only when it precedes the word it modifies.

A well-known musician visited our school.

The story was well written.

Rule: Use a hyphen after the prefixes *all-, ex-,* and *self-* when they are joined to any noun or adjective.

all-star

ex-president

self-conscious

Rule: Use a hyphen to separate any prefix from a word that begins with a capital letter.

un-American

mid-January

Rule: Use a dash or dashes to show a sudden break or change in thought or speech.

Daniel—he's kind of a pest—is my youngest cousin.

Rule: Use parentheses to set off words that define or helpfully explain a word in the sentence.

The transverse flute (*transverse* means "sideways") is a wind instrument.

Abbreviations

Rule: Abbreviate the titles *Mr., Mrs., Ms.,* and *Dr.* before a person's name. Also abbreviate any professional or academic degree that follows a name. The titles *Jr.* and *Sr.* are *not* preceded by a comma.

Dr. Stanley Livingston (doctor)

Luisa Mendez, M.A. (Master of Arts)

Martin Luther King Jr.

Rule: Use capital letters and no periods with abbreviations that are pronounced letter by letter or as words. Exceptions are *U.S.* and *Washington, D.C.,* which do use periods.

NAACP	National Association for the Advancement of Colored People
UFO	unidentified flying object
MADD	Mothers Against Driving Drunk

Rule: With exact times use A.M. (*ante meridiem,* "before noon") and P.M. (*post meridiem,* "after noon"). For years use B.C. (before Christ) and, sometimes, A.D. (*anno Domini,* "in the year of the lord," after Christ).

8:15 A.M.	6:55 P.M.
5000 B.C.	A.D. 235

Rule: Abbreviate days and months only in charts and lists.

School will be closed on

Mon., Sept. 3

Wed., Nov. 11

Thurs., Nov. 27

Rule: In scientific writing abbreviate units of measure. Use periods with English units but not with metric units.

inch(es) in.	yard(s) yd.
meter(s) m	milliliter(s) ml

LANGUAGE HANDBOOK

Rule: On envelopes only, abbreviate street names and state names. In general text, spell out street names and state names.

Ms. Karen Holmes

347 Grandville St.

Tilton, NH 03276

Karen lives on Grandville Street in Tilton, New Hampshire.

Writing Numbers

Rule: In charts and tables, always write numbers as numerals. Other rules apply to numbers not in charts or tables.

Student Test Scores

Student	Test 1	Test 2	Test 3
Lai, W.	82	89	94
Ostos, A.	78	90	86

Rule: Spell out a number that is expressed in one or two words.

We carried enough supplies for twenty-three days.

Rule: Use a numeral for a number of more than two words.

The tallest mountain in Mexico rises 17,520 feet.

Rule: Spell out a number that begins a sentence, or reword the sentence so that it does not begin with a number.

One hundred forty-three days later the baby elephant was born.

The baby elephant was born 143 days later.

Rule: Write a very large number as a numeral followed by the word *million* or *billion.*

There are 15 million people living in or near Mexico City.

Rule: Related numbers should be written in the same way. If one number must be written as a numeral, use numerals for all the numbers.

There are 365 days in the year, but only 52 weekends.

Rule: Spell out an ordinal number (*first, second*).

Welcome to our fifteenth annual convention.

Rule: Use words to express the time of day unless you are writing the exact time or using the abbreviation A.M. or P.M.

My guitar lesson is at five o'clock. It ends by 5:45 P.M.

Rule: Use numerals to express dates, house and street numbers, apartment and room numbers, telephone numbers, page numbers, amounts of money of more than two words, and percentages. Write out the word *percent.*

August 5, 1999

9 Davio Dr.

Apartment 9F

24 percent

Spelling

The following rules, examples, and exceptions can help you master the spelling of many words.

Spelling *ie* and *ei*

Put *i* before *e* except when both letters follow *c* or when both letters are pronounced together as an **a** sound.

believe	sieve	weight
receive	relieve	neighborhood

It is helpful to memorize exceptions to this rule. Exceptions include the following words: *species, science, weird, either, seize, leisure,* and *protein*.

Spelling unstressed vowels

Notice the vowel sound in the second syllable of the word *won-d_r-ful*. This is the unstressed vowel sound; dictionary respellings use the schwa symbol (ə) to indicate it. Because any of several vowels can be used to spell this sound, you might find yourself uncertain about which vowel to use. To spell words with unstressed vowels, try thinking of a related word in which the syllable containing the vowel sound is stressed.

Unknown Spelling	Related Word	Word Spelled Correctly
wond_rful	wonder	wonderful
fort_fications	fortify	fortifications
res_dent	reside	resident

Suffixes and the silent *e*

For most words with silent *e*, keep the e when adding a suffix. When you add the suffix *-ly* to a word that ends in *l* plus silent *e*, drop the *-le*. Also drop the silent *e* when you add a suffix beginning with a vowel or a *y*.

wise + ly = wisely
peaceful + ly = peacefully
skate + ing = skating
gentle + ly = gently

There are exceptions to the rule, including the following:

awe + ful = awful
judge + ment = judgment
true + ly = truly
noise + y = noisy
dye + ing = dyeing
mile + age = mileage

Suffixes and the final *y*

When you are adding a suffix to words ending with a vowel + *y*, keep the *y*. For words ending with a consonant + *y*, change the *y* to *i* unless the suffix begins with *i*. To avoid having two *i*'s together, keep the *y*.

enjoy + ment = enjoyment
merry + ment = merriment
display + ed = displayed
lazy + ness = laziness
play + ful = playful
worry + ing = worrying

Note: For some words, there are alternate spellings:

sly + er = slyer or slier
shy + est = shyest or shiest

Adding prefixes

When you add a prefix to a word, do not change the spelling of the word.

un + done = undone
re + schedule = reschedule
il + legible = illegible
semi + sweet = semisweet

Doubling the final consonant

Double the final consonant when a word ends with a single consonant following one vowel and the word is one syllable, or when the last syllable of the word is accented both before and after adding the suffix.

sit + ing = sitting
rub + ing = rubbing
commit + ed = committed
confer + ed = conferred

Do not double the final consonant if the suffix begins with a consonant, if the accent is not on the last syllable, or if the accent moves when the suffix is added.

cancel + ing = canceling
commit + ment = commitment
travel + ed = traveled
defer + ence = deference

Do not double the final consonant if the word ends in two consonants or if the suffix begins with a consonant.

climb + er = climber
nervous + ness = nervousness
import + ance = importance
star + dom = stardom

When adding *-ly* to a word that ends in *ll*, drop one *l*.

hill + ly = hilly full + ly = fully

Forming compound words

When forming compound words, keep the original spelling of both words.

home + work = homework
scare + crow = scarecrow
pea + nut = peanut

Forming Plurals

General Rules for Plurals

If the noun ends in	Rule	Example
s, ch, sh, x, or *z*	add *-es*	loss➛losses, latch➛latches, box➛boxes, bush➛bushes, quiz➛quizzes
a consonant + *y*	change *y* to *i* and add *-es*	ferry➛ferries, baby➛babies, worry➛worries
a vowel + *y*	add *-s*	chimney➛chimneys, monkey➛monkeys, toy➛toys
a vowel + *o*	add *-s*	cameo➛cameos, radio➛radios, rodeo➛rodeos
a consonant + *o*	add *-es* but sometimes add *-s*	potato➛potatoes, echo➛echoes photo➛photos, solo➛solos
f or *ff*	add *-s* but sometimes change *f* to *v* and add *-es*	proof➛proofs, bluff➛bluffs sheaf➛sheaves, thief➛thieves, hoof➛hooves
lf	change *f* to *v* and add *-es*	calf➛calves, half➛halves, loaf➛loaves
fe	change *f* to *v* and add *-s*	knife➛knives, life➛lives

Special Rules for Plurals

Rule	Example
To form the plural of most proper names and one-word compound nouns, follow the general rules for plurals.	Jones➛Joneses, Thomas➛Thomases, Hatch➛Hatches
To form the plural of hyphenated compound nouns or compound nouns of more than one word, make the most important word plural.	credit card➛credit cards mother-in-law➛mothers-in-law district attorney➛district attorneys
Some nouns have irregular plural forms and do not follow any rules.	man➛men, foot➛feet, tooth➛teeth
Some nouns have the same singular and plural forms	deer➛deer, species➛species, sheep➛sheep

LISTENING, SPEAKING, AND VIEWING HANDBOOK

Listening Effectively

A large part of the school day is spent either listening or speaking to others. By becoming a better listener and speaker, you will know more about what is expected of you, and understand more about your audience.

Listening to instructions in class

Some of the most important listening in the school day involves listening to instructions. Use the following tips to help you.

- First, make sure you understand what you are listening for. Are you receiving instructions for homework or for a test? What you listen for depends upon the type of instructions being given.
- Think about what you are hearing, and keep your eyes on the speaker. This will help you stay focused on the important points.
- Listen for keywords, or word clues. Examples of word clues are phrases such as *above all, most important,* or *the three basic parts.* These clues help you identify important points that you should remember.
- Take notes on what you hear. Write down only the most important parts of the instructions.
- If you don't understand something, ask questions. Then if you're still unsure about the instructions, repeat them aloud to your teacher to receive correction on any key points that you may have missed.

Interpreting nonverbal clues

Understanding nonverbal clues is part of effective listening. Nonverbal clues are everything you notice about a speaker *except* what the speaker says. As you listen, ask yourself these questions:

- Where and how is the speaker standing?
- Are some words spoken more loudly than others?
- Does the speaker make eye contact?
- Does he or she smile or look angry?
- What message is sent by the speaker's gestures and facial expression?

PRACTICE

Work with a partner to practice listening to instructions. Each of you should find a set of directions for using a simple device–for example, a mechanical tool, a telephone answering machine, or a VCR. Study the instructions carefully. If you can bring the device to class, ask your partner to try to use it by following your step-by-step instructions. If you cannot have the device in class, ask your partner to explain the directions back to you. Then change roles and listen as your partner gives you a set of directions.

Speaking Effectively

- Speak slowly, clearly, and in a normal tone of voice. Raise your voice a bit, or use gestures to stress important points.
- Pause a few seconds after making an important point.
- Use words that help your audience picture what you're talking about. Visual aids such as pictures, graphs, charts, and maps can also help make your information clear.
- Stay in contact with your audience. Make sure your eyes move from person to person in the group you're addressing.

Speaking informally

Most oral communication is informal. When you speak casually with your friends, family, and neighbors, you use informal speech. Human relationships depend on this form of communication.

- Be courteous. Listen until the other person has finished speaking.
- Speak in a relaxed and spontaneous manner.
- Make eye contact with your listeners.
- Do not monopolize a conversation.
- When telling a story, show enthusiasm.
- When giving an announcement or directions, speak clearly and slowly. Check that your listeners understand the information.

Presenting an oral report

The steps in preparing an oral report are similar to the steps in the writing process. Complete each step carefully and you can be confident of presenting an effective oral report.

Steps in Preparing an Oral Report	
Prewriting	Determine your purpose and audience. Decide on a topic and narrow it.
Drafting	Make an outline. Fill in the supporting details. Write the report.
Revising and editing	Review your draft. Check the organization of ideas and details. Reword unclear statements.
Practicing	Practice the report aloud in front of a family member. Time the report. Ask for and accept advice.
Presenting	Relax in front of your audience. Make eye contact with your audience. Speak slowly and clearly.

PRACTICE

Pretend that you have been invited to give an oral report to a group of fifth graders. Your report will tell them what to expect and how to adjust to new conditions when they enter middle school. As you plan your report, keep your purpose and your audience in mind. Include lively descriptions and examples to back up your suggestions and hold your audience's attention. As you practice giving your report, be sure to give attention to your body language as well as your vocal projection. Ask a partner to listen to your report to give you feedback on how to improve your performance. Do the same for your partner after listening to his or her report.

Viewing Effectively

Critical viewing means thinking about what you see while watching a TV program, newscast, film, or video. It requires paying attention to what you hear and see and deciding whether information is true, false, or exaggerated. If the information seems to be true, try to determine whether it is based on a fact or an opinion.

Fact versus opinion

A **fact** is something that can be proved. An opinion is what someone believes is true. **Opinions** are based on feelings and experiences and cannot be proved.

Television commercials, political speeches, and even the evening news contain both facts and opinions. They use emotional words and actions to persuade the viewer to agree with a particular point of view. They may also use faulty reasoning, such as linking an effect with the wrong cause. Think through what is being said. The speaker may seem sincere, but do his or her reasons make sense? Are the reasons based on facts or on unfair generalizations?

Commercials contain both obvious and hidden messages. Just as you need to discover the author's purpose when you read a writer's words, you must be aware of the purpose of nonverbal attempts to persuade you. What does the message sender want, and how is the sender trying to influence you?

For example, a magazine or TV ad picturing a group of happy teenagers playing volleyball on a sunny beach expresses a positive feeling. The advertiser hopes viewers will transfer that positive feeling to the product being advertised—perhaps a soft drink or a brand of beachwear. This technique, called **transfer,** is one of several propaganda techniques regularly used by advertisers to influence consumers.

Following are a few other common techniques.

Testimonial—Famous and admired people recommend or praise a product, a policy, or a course of action even though they probably have no professional knowledge or expertise to back up their opinion.

Bandwagon—People are urged to follow the crowd ("get on the bandwagon") by buying a product, voting for a candidate, or whatever else the advertiser wants them to do.

Glittering generalities—The advertiser uses positive, good-sounding words (for example, *all-American* or *medically proven*) to impress people.

PRACTICE

Think of a television commercial that you have seen often or watch a new one and take notes as you watch it. Then analyze the commercial.

- What is the purpose behind the ad?
- What is expressed in written or spoken words?
- What is expressed nonverbally (in music or sound effects as well as in pictures and actions)?
- What methods does the advertiser use to persuade viewers?
- What questions would you ask the advertiser if you could?
- How effective is the commercial? Why?

Working in Groups

Working in a group is an opportunity to learn from others. Whether you are planning a group project (such as a class trip) or solving a math problem, each person in a group brings specific strengths and interests to the task. When a task is large, such as planting a garden, a group provides the necessary energy and talent to get the job done.

Small groups vary in size according to the nature of the task. Three to five students is a good size for most small-group tasks. Your teacher may assign you to a group, or you may be asked to form your own group. Don't work with your best friend if you are likely to chat too much. Successful groups often have a mix of student abilities and interests.

Individual role assignments give everyone in a group something to do. One student, the group recorder, may take notes. Another may lead the discussion, and another report the results to the rest of the class.

Roles for a Small Group	
Reviewer	Reads or reviews the assignment and makes sure everyone understands it
Recorder 1 (of the process)	Takes notes on the discussion
Recorder 2 (of the results)	Takes notes on the final results
Reporter	Reports results to the rest of the class
Discussion leader	Asks questions to get the discussion going; keeps the group focused
Facilitator	Helps the group resolve disagreements and reach a compromise

For a small group of three or four students, some of these roles can be combined. Your teacher may assign a role to each student in your group. Or you may be asked to choose your own role.

Tips for working in groups

- Review the group assignment and goal. Be sure that everyone in the group understands the assignment.
- Review the amount of time allotted for the task. Decide how your group will organize its time.
- Check that all the group members understand their roles in the group.
- When a question arises, try to solve it as a group before asking a teacher for help.
- Listen to other points of view. Take turns during a discussion.
- When it is your turn to talk, address the subject and help the project move forward.

STUDY AND TEST-TAKING SKILLS HANDBOOK

Study Skills

Studying for school and doing your homework are like any other tasks—if you understand your assignment, set a goal, and make a plan, you'll save time and do great work. The tips that follow will teach you the skills you need to make schoolwork easier and more enjoyable.

Get Organized

- Keep an assignment notebook. Keep it up to date.
- Keep your notes for each course together in one place.
- Find a good place to study. Choose a place that has as few distractions as possible. Try to study in the same place each day.
- Try to study at the same time each day.
- Don't study one subject too long. If you haven't finished after thirty minutes, switch to another subject.
- Take notes on your reading. Keep your notes in one place.

Understand Your Purpose

The purpose is the reason you have been given a particular assignment. If you understand the purpose, you should be able to set a goal to work toward. With schoolwork, this means making sure you understand your assignment and you know how long you have to do it.

Set goals

These steps will help you set study goals for an assignment.

1. Listen as the teacher explains the assignment. Find out everything you need to do to finish the assignment.
2. Understand the quality of work your teacher expects from you. Are you supposed to turn in a finished paper or a rough draft?
3. Find out how much time you have. Ask: Is everything due on the same day, or are some parts due earlier?
4. In your assignment notebook, write down the assignment details and the dates when your work is due.

Homework Checklist

Goal: To understand and finish my homework assignment.

Plan: Follow these steps to reach my goal:

- ☑ Bring home the all the materials I need, including this textbook, and my notebook.
- ☑ Find a quiet space where I can concentrate. Also, make sure I have a table or other hard, flat surface to write on.
- ☑ Keep my notebook out and take notes as I read.
- ☑ Write down questions about the parts of the assignment that I don't understand. Ask my teacher or an adult at home to help me understand.
- ☑ Check this plan from time to time to make sure I stay on task.
- ☑ Take my completed homework back to school and hand it in.

Make a Plan

Making a plan is the best way to reach your goals. Try to make plans that include the work you have finish and the time you have until the assignment is due. Think about how you study best, when you might need help, and what gets in your way.

You can use a **task, obstacle, and solution chart** to show

1. what you need to do (task)
2. what might get in your way (obstacle)
3. how you can get around an obstacle (solution)

Karen's goal is to read a chapter of science before school tomorrow. Check out the chart she made, which includes **task, obstacle, and solution.**

1. (task)	I have to…	read chapter 4 tonight
2. (obstacle)	But…	after dinner I have basketball practice
3. (solution)	So I need to…	read before practice

Try it! In your **Learner's Notebook,** make your own **task, obstacle, and solution chart** for an assignment from this book. You can use Karen's plan as a model.

Take Notes

Writing notes about what you read or what you hear in a presentation will help you remember information you're expected to learn. The Cornell Note-Taking System is a way to organize the notes you take in class or the notes you take as you read. Use this system to organize your note-taking and make sense of the notes you take.

Cornell Notes

Divide the pages that you're using for notes into two sections or columns as shown below. As you read or listen, write notes in Section B. In Section A, write the highlights (main ideas and vocabulary) from Section B.

Section A [highlights]	Section B [notes]
Use this section SECOND. Review the notes you took in Section B and write in this section: • Vocabulary words to remember • Main idea statements • Questions and other hints that will help you remember the information	Use this section FIRST. As you read or listen, take notes in this section: • When you're taking notes on your reading, write down the subtitles that break the text into different section. In most cases, subtitles form an outline of the information in a chapter. • Write down the most important information: main ideas and concepts. Don't write every word or take time to write complete sentences. (Hint: if the teacher writes something on the board, it's probably important.) • Use abbreviations and shortened word forms to get the ideas on paper quickly. (For example, POV is a good abbreviation for Point of View.) • Define new terms and concepts in your own words so that you'll be able to understand them later.

Model These are some notes one student made as she read about biographies and autobiographies.

A.	B. Looking at the Genre: Biography
biography	What is it?
	real people, real life
autobiography	Autobiography is about yourself
	Why is it important?
	many reasons (interest, learn, entertain, etc.)
	What are the important elements?
Major elements of biography	Narrator: who tells the story
	Point of view: from who's telling the story
	Setting: time and place of a story

Try It! Divide a sheet of paper into two columns as shown above. Practice taking notes using the Cornell system as you read your homework assignment.

Test-Taking Skills

How well you perform on a test is not a matter of chance. Some specific strategies can help you answer test questions. This section of the handbook will show how to improve your test-taking skills.

Tips for preparing for tests

Here are some useful suggestions for preparing to take a test.

- Gather information about the test. When will it be given? How long will it take? Exactly what material will it cover?
- Review material from your textbook, class notes, homework, quizzes, and handouts. Review the study questions at the end of each section of a textbook. Try to define terms in boldface type.
- Make up some sample questions and answer them. As you skim selections, try to predict what may be asked.
- Draw charts and cluster or Venn diagrams to help you remember information and to picture how one piece of information relates to another.
- Give yourself plenty of time to study. Avoid cramming for a test. Several short review sessions are more effective than one long one.
- In addition to studying alone, study with a partner or small group. Quiz one another on topics you think the test will cover.

Plan your strategy

Try following these steps:

- Read all directions carefully. Understanding the directions can prevent mistakes.
- Ask for help if you have a question.
- Answer the easier items first. By skipping the hard items, you will have time to answer all the easy ones.
- In the time that is left, return to the items you skipped. Answer them as best you can. If you won't be penalized for doing so, guess at an answer.
- If possible, save some time at the end to check your answers.

Objective Tests

An objective test is a test of factual information. The questions are usually either right or wrong; there is no difference of opinion. On an objective test, you are asked to recall information, not to present your ideas. Objective test questions include true-or-false items, multiple-choice items, fill-in-the-blanks statements, short-answer items, and matching items. At the beginning of an objective test, scan the number of items. Then budget your time.

Multiple-choice items Multiple-choice questions ask you to answer a question or complete a sentence. They are the kind of question you will encounter most often on objective tests. Read all the choices before answering. Pick the best response.

What is a peninsula?

(a) a range of mountains

(b) a circle around the moon

(c) a body of land surrounded by water on three sides

Correct answer: (c)

- Read the question carefully. Be sure that you understand it.
- Read all the answers before selecting one. Reading all of the responses is especially important when one of the choices is "all of the above" or "none of the above."
- Eliminate responses that are clearly incorrect. Focus on the responses that might be correct.
- Look for absolute words, such as *never, always, all, none.* Most generalizations have exceptions. Absolute statements are often incorrect. (Note: This tip applies to true/false items also.)

Answering essay questions

Essay questions ask you to think about what you have learned and to write about it in one or more paragraphs. Some tests present a choice of essay questions. If a test has both an objective part and an essay part, answer the objective questions first, but leave yourself enough time to work on the essay.

Read the essay question carefully. What does it ask you to do? Discuss? Explain? Define? Summarize? Compare and contrast? These key words tell what kind of information you must give in your answer.

Key Verbs in Essay Questions	
Argue	Give your opinion and supporting reasons.
Compare and contrast	Discuss likenesses and differences.
Define	Give details that show exactly what something is like.
Demonstrate	Give examples to support a point.
Describe	Present a picture with words.
Discuss	Show detailed information on a particular subject.
Explain	Give reasons.
Identify	Give specific characteristics.
List (also outline, trace)	Give details, give steps in order, give a time sequence.
Summarize	Give a short overview of the most important ideas or events.

Tips for answering essay questions

You might wish to consider the following suggestions:

- Read the question or questions carefully. Determine the kind of information required by the question.
- Plan your time. Do not spend too much time on one part of the essay.
- Make a list of what you want to cover.
- If you have time, make revisions and proofreading corrections.

Taking standardized tests

Standardized tests are taken by students all over the country. Your performance on the test is compared with the performance of other students at your grade level. There are many different kinds of standardized tests. Some measure your progress in such subjects as English, math, and science, while others measure how well you think. Standardized tests can show how you learn and what you do best.

Preparing for standardized tests

There is no way to know exactly what information will be on a standardized test, or even what topics will be covered. The best preparation is to do the best you can in your daily schoolwork. However, you can learn the *kinds* of questions that will appear on a standardized test. Some general tips will also help.

Tips for taking standardized tests

You might find the following suggestions helpful.

- Get enough sleep the night before the test. Eat a healthful breakfast.
- Arrive early for the test. Try to relax.
- Listen carefully to all test directions. Ask questions if you don't understand the directions.
- Complete easy questions first. Leave harder items for the end.
- Be sure your answers are in the right place on the answer sheet.
- If points are not subtracted for wrong answers, guess at questions that you aren't sure of.

Analogies Analogy items test your understanding of the relationships between things or ideas. On standardized tests, analogies are written in an abbreviated format, as shown below.

man : woman :: buck : doe

The symbol : means "is to"; the symbol :: means "as."

This chart shows some word relationships you might find in analogy tests.

Relationship	Definition	Example
Synonyms	Two words have a similar meaning.	huge : gigantic :: scared : afraid
Antonyms	Two words have opposite meanings.	bright : dull :: far : near
Use	Words name a user and something used.	farmer : tractor :: writer : computer
Cause-Effect	Words name a cause and its effect.	tickle : laugh :: polish : shine
Category	Words name a category and an item in it.	fish : tuna :: building : house
Description	Words name an item and a characteristic of it.	knife : sharp :: joke : funny

GLOSSARY/GLOSARIO

Academic and Selection Vocabulary

English	Español
A	
abandonment (uh BAN dun munt) *n.* the state of being deserted or left alone without help **(p. 486)**	**abandono** *s.* estado de desolación o soledad sin poder contar con ayuda
abruptly (uh BRUPT lee) *adv.* suddenly; unexpectedly **(p. 1071)**	**abruptamente** *adv.* repentinamente; inesperadamente
absurd (ub SURD) *adj.* not making sense; very silly **(p. 741)**	**absurdo(a)** *adj.* sin sentido; disparatado
accumulate (uh KYOO myuh layt) *v.* gather or build up **(p. 1029); accumulated (p. 1077)**	**acumular** *v.* juntar y amontonar; acumularon
adolescence (ad uh LES uns) *n.* the period between childhood and adulthood **(p. 1070)**	**adolescencia** *s.* periodo entre la niñez y la edad adulta
aggravating (AG ruh vay ting) *adj.* irritating; annoying **(p. 748)**	**insoportable** *adj.* molesto y enfadoso
agitated (AJ uh tay tud) *adj.* disturbed; upset **(p. 1108)**	**inquieto(a)** *adj.* nervioso; agitado
alien (AY lee un) *adj.* strange; odd; peculiar **(p. 1147)**	**extraño(a)** *adj.* raro, de naturaleza distinta a la cosa de la que forma parte
ambition (am BISH un) *n.* a strong drive or desire to succeed **(p. 492)**	**ambición** *s.* deseo intenso de lograr o conseguir algo
analyzing (AN uh ly zing) *n.* examining by separating into parts and identifying relationships between the parts **(p. 160)**	**análisis** *s.* examen que se hace de las partes de un todo, qué las componen y cómo se relacionan entre ellas
anthem (AN thum) *n.* the official song of a country, school, or group **(p. 590)**	**himno** *s.* composición musical oficial de un país, escuela o grupo
anticipation (an tis uh PAY shun) *n.* the act of looking forward to; expectation **(p. 883)**	**expectativa** *s.* posibilidad de que algo suceda; anticipación
appealed (uh PEELD) *v.* made a serious request **(p. 119)**	**apelar** *v.* recurrir a alguien o algo con autoridad para resolver una situación
apprehension (ap rih HEN shun) *n.* fear of what may happen **(p. 805)**	**aprensión** *s.* miedo o figuración infundada
arc (ark) *n.* a curved line between two points **(p. 453)**	**arco** *s.* línea continua que forma una curva
askew (uh SKYOO) *adv.* turned or twisted to one side **(p. 654)**	**ladeado(a)** *adj.* oblicuo; inclinado; que no es recto
attaining (uh TAY ning) *n.* the act of achieving, accomplishing, or succeeding **(p. 1107)**	**logro** *s.* obtención con éxito de algo que se desea
audacity (aw DAS ih tee) *n.* reckless courage **(p. 50)**	**audacia** *s.* osadía; valor de hacer algo nuevo y arriesgado
authentic (aw THEN tik) *adj.* real; genuine **(p. 608)**	**auténtico(a)** *adj.* real, genuino
available (uh VAY luh bul) *adj.* at hand; easily obtained **(p. 296)**	**disponible** *adj.* algo que está libre para ser utilizado
avid (AV id) *adj.* very eager or enthusiastic **(p. 1068)**	**ávido(a)** *adj.* ansioso, con un deseo intenso

B

barreling (BAIR ul ing) *v.* running headlong **(p. 568)**

precipitándose *v.* arrojarse sin prudencia a hacer o decir algo; forma del verbo *precipitar*

barricades (BAIR uh kaydz) *n.* barriers put up to separate or to provide defense **(p. 969)**

barricadas *s.* obstáculo improvisado para separar o suministrar defensa

bewilderment (bih WIL dur munt) *n.* confusion **(p. 119)**

desconcierto *s.* confusión

bickering (BIK ur ing) *n.* a quarrel or argument, especially about minor details **(p. 751)**

riña *s.* discusión o pelea confusa

bogus (BOH gus) *adj.* bad; not real or genuine **(p. 1002)**

falso(a) *adj.* engañoso, que no es real

bombardment (bom BARD munt) *n.* an attack **(p. 522)**

bombardeo *s.* disparo de bombas contra un objetivo, generalmente desde un avión

buoyed (BOO eed) *adj.* supported or uplifted **(p. 1023)**

animado(a) *adj.* infundido de moral y alegría

C

cajoling (kuh JOHL ing) *v.* persuading, especially by using soothing words; coaxing **(p. 228)**

engatusar *v.* persuadir o ganar la voluntad de alguien a través de halagos

calculating (KAL kyoo lay ting) *v.* using math or logic to figure out something **(p. 646)**

calculando *v.* sacar cuentas a través de operaciones lógicas o matemáticas, forma del verbo *calcular*

capsize (KAP syz) *v.* to overturn or upset (especially a boat) **(p. 1142)**

volcaría *v.* torcer hacia un lado o de cabeza, forma del verbo *volcar*

clamor (KLAM ur) *v.* to demand something in a noisy or desperate way **(p. 326)**

clamar *v.* Exigir a voces y con vehemencia

clarify (KLAIR uh fy) *v.* make clear **(p. 998)**

aclarar *v.* explicar, despejar la confusión

coaxed (kohkst) *v.* urged gently **(p. 903)**

convenció *v.* consiguió que cambiara de opinión o comportamiento, lo persuadió; forma del verbo *convencer*

collapse (kuh LAPS) *v.* to fall apart, cave in, or break down **(p. 862)**

colapsar *v.* producir la destrucción brusca de un cuerpo

commotion (kuh MOH shun) *n.* noisy, confused activity **(p. 609)**

conmoción *s.* tumulto o perturbación violenta

compassion (kum PASH un) *n.* the feeling of sorrow or pity caused by someone else's misfortunes; sympathy **(p. 59)**

compasión *s.* sentimiento de pena y lástima por la desgracia ajena

compiled (kum PYLD) *v.* collected into a book or list **(p. 392)**

compilado *v.* partes de libros reunidos en una sola obra, forma del verbo *compilar*

comprehension (kom prih HEN shun) *n.* the fact or power of understanding **(p. 500)**

comprensión *s.* asimilación o entendimiento de algo

compulsory (kum PUL suh ree) *adj.* required **(p. 666)**

obligatorio(a) *adj.* que tiene que ser cumplido, obedecido

conceived (kun SEEVD) *v.* formed; imagined **(p. 1098)**

concebido *v.* idea o proyecto creada o imaginada; forma del verbo *concebir*

concepts (KON septs) *n.* ideas; organized thoughts **(p. 976)**

conceptos *s.* idea o representación de algo, pensamiento expresado en palabras

conclusive (kun KLOO siv) *adj.* definite; proven without doubt **(p. 327)**

confesses (kun FES ses) *v.* tells a truth that one rarely talks about **(p. 623)**

consciousness (KON shus nus) *n.* the state of being fully awake or alert **(p. 251)**

consequences (KON suh kwen suz) *n.* results or effects **(p. 1093)**

contamination (kun tam uh NAY shun) *n.* pollution **(p. 936)**

controversial (kon truh VUR shul) *adj.* causing disagreement **(p. 988)**

conversation (kon vur SAY shun) *n.* a talk between people **(p. 584)**

convictions (kun VIK shunz) *n.* strong beliefs or values **(p. 988)**

coordinate (koh OR duh nayt) *v.* to make (things) work together smoothly **(p. 103)**

corresponded (kor uh SPON did) *v.* wrote letters to one another **(p. 109)**

corruption (kuh RUP shun) *n.* extreme immorality or wickedness **(p. 947)**

cowered (KOW urd) *v.* moved away in fear **(p. 367)**

crucial (KROO shul) *adj.* extremely important **(p. 1107)**

D

deaden (DEH dun) *v.* to make weak or dull **(p. 251)**

decades (DEK aydz) *n.* periods of ten years **(p. 306)**

deferred (dih FURD) *adj.* set aside or put off until a later time **(p. 473)**

defiance (dih FY uns) *n.* the act of challenging authority **(p. 191)**

descendants (dih SEN dunts) *n.* blood relatives of an earlier generation **(p. 611)**

descent (dih SENT) *n.* lineage; ancestry **(p. 312)**

despair (dih SPAIR) *n.* a complete loss of hope **(p. 493)**

destiny (DES tuh nee) *n.* a person's fate or fortune **(p. 175)**

concluyente *adj.* que no se puede rebatir; no admite duda o discusión

confiesa *v.* expresar voluntariamente verdades que en el fondo no se quieren contar; forma del verbo *confesar*

conocimiento *s.* cada uno de los sentidos del ser humano en la medida en que están activos

consecuencias *s.* efecto; hecho o acontecimiento que resulta de otro

contaminación *s.* alteración dañina del estado puro y normal de algo

controvertido(a) *adj.* polémico, que provoca controversia o discusión dando lugar a opiniones contrapuestas

conversación *s.* comunicación mediante palabras

convicción *s.* ideas, creencias u opiniones firmes

coordinar *v.* organizar medios y esfuerzos para una acción común

mantenían correspondencia *frase v.* se escribían cartas entre sí, forma de la frase verbal *mantener correspondencia*

corrupción *s.* perversión o vicio que estropea la moral

(se) acobardó *v.* con miedo, forma del verbo *acobardar(se)*

crucial *adj.* momento o punto decisivo o importante en el desarrollo de algo

calmará *v.* aliviar o disminuir la intensidad de algo, forma del verbo *calmar*

décadas *s.* períodos de diez años, decenas del siglo

diferido(a) *adj.* aplazado, dejado para más tarde

desafío *s.* incitación a la lucha, rivalidad

descendientes *s.* generaciones sucesivas por línea directa de personas dentro de una familia

ascendencia *s.* conjunto de antepasado de una persona, ancestros

desesperación *s.* pérdida total de la esperanza

destino *s.* fortuna, fin, punto de llegada

destitute (DES tuh toot) *adj.* completely without money or possessions **(p. 853)**
indigente *adj.* persona que no tiene los medios para subsistir

detract (dih TRAKT) *v.* to take away from; reduce the value of **(p. 1098)**
detraerá *v.* restarle o reducirle valor, forma del verbo *detraer*

disclose (dis KLOHZ) *v.* to make known; reveal **(p. 227)**
revelar *v.* descubrir o anunciar algo ignorado o secreto

discriminates (dis KRIM uh nayts) *v.* treats unfairly **(p. 1160)**
discrimina *v.* selecciona excluyendo, con prejuicio, forma del verbo *discriminar*

disgruntled (dis GRUNT uld) *adj.* not pleased; in a bad humor **(p. 799)**
disgustado(a) *adj.* incomodado, descontento con algo o alguien

dismal (DIZ mul) *adj.* gloomy or depressing **(p. 893)**
lúgubre *adj.* deprimente, melancólico, sombrío

distinguished (dis TING gwisht) *adj.* well-known for excellence and honor **(p. 201)**
distinguido(a) *adj.* ilustre, que sobresale por alguna cualidad, noble

distracted (dih STRAK tid) *adj.* losing attention easily **(p. 261)**
distraído(a) *adj.* que no se da cuenta de lo que dice o hace, que no presta atención

distribution (dis truh BYOO shun) *n.* division into shares or portions **(p. 936)**
distribución *s.* reparto entre varios asignando a cada uno una parte

dock (dok) *n.* a platform where boats land at the edge of a body of water **(p. 479)**
muelle *s.* construcción realizada junto al agua que facilita el embarque y desembarque de embarcaciones

dormitory (DOR mih tor ee) *n.* a building with rooms for people to sleep in **(p. 70)**
dormitorio *s.* lugar destinado para dormir

downcast (DOWN kast) *adj.* sad; depressed **(p. 835)**
abatido(a) *adj.* persona desanimada, deprimida

dramatic (druh MA tik) *adj.* showing strong emotion **(p. 266)**
dramático(a) *adj.* que conmueve o interesa con intensidad

dreaded (DRED ud) *v.* feared greatly **(p. 886)**
temido *v.* tenerle pavor o miedo, forma del verbo *temer*

dry (dry) *adj.* dull or boring; not interesting **(p. 1009)**
árido(a) *adj.* que no es ameno, poco interesante

E

eclipsed (ee KLIPSD) *v.* made to seem unimportant **(p. 127)**
eclipsó *v.* oscureció, le quitó notoriedad; forma del verbo *eclipsar*

egging (EG ing) *v.* urging; encouraging to take action **(p. 600)**
incitar *v.* convencer o estimular a alguien para que haga algo

elegant (EL lih gunt) *adj.* beautiful and tasteful **(p. 198)**
elegante *adj.* que tiene gracia, distinción y nobleza

elite (eh LEET) *adj.* best or most talented **(p. 302)**
elitista *adj.* que pertenece a una minoría selecta destacada en un campo

eloquence (EL uh kwuns) *n.* the ability to speak expressively **(p. 227)**
elocuencia *s.* eficacia para expresarse con viveza, persuasión y de manera conmovedora

emerge (ih MURJ) *v.* to come out into view **(p. 191)**
emerger *v.* salir a la superficie, brotar

eminent (em uh nunt) *adj.* of outstanding rank or quality **(p. 676)**
eminente *adj.* que sobresale o destaca por algún mérito

emit (ee MIT) *v.* to give off **(p. 1023)**
emitir *v.* arrojar, expulsar, producir, echar hacia fuera

endure (en DUR) *v.* to carry on; survive; last **(p. 1098)**
perdurar *v.* durar mucho en un mismo estado y por un tiempo

ethical (ETH uh kul) *adj.* having to do with morals and standards of acceptable behavior **(p. 933)**

ético(a) *adj.* de acuerdo a las normas de conducta y de moral

evaluate (ih VAL yoo ayt) *v.* form an opinion or make a judgment **(p. 468)**

evaluar *v.* estimar el valor de algo

eventually (ih VEN choo ul lee) *adv.* happening at last; in the end **(p. 1091)**

finalmente *adv.* que sucede de último, al terminar, al fin y al cabo

exile (EG zyl) *n.* the state of living away from one's home country **(p. 172)**

exilio *s.* estado en el que la persona vive fuera de su patria

exotic (eg ZOT ik) *adj.* strangely beautiful and foreign **(p. 624)**

exótico(a) *adj.* extraño, desconocido, poco común

expectations (ek spek TAY shunz) *n.* outcomes considered likely to happen **(p. 301)**

expectativas *s.* tener la esperanza, ante la posibilidad razonable, de que algo suceda

expeditions (ek spuh DISH unz) *n.* groups that take trips for specific purposes **(p. 35)**

expediciones *s.* conjunto de personas que realizan un viaje o excursión con un fin determinado

extinguished (ek STING gwisht) *adj.* put out **(p. 520)**

extinguido(a) *adj.* se refiere a la llama o fuego cuando está apagado

F

factor (FAK tur) *n.* something that produces or contributes to a certain result **(p. 574)**

factor *s.* elemento que produce o afecta a un estado determinado

famished (FAM isht) *adj.* extremely hungry **(p. 900)**

hambriento(a) *adj.* que tiene mucha necesidad y ganas de comer

feat (feet) *n.* remarkable action **(p. 32)**

proeza *s.* hazaña o acción extraordinaria

fester (FES tur) *v.* to rot; to decay **(p. 473)**

(se) supure *v.* produce y echa pus, generalmente esto se debe a una infección; forma del verbo *supurar*

financial (fy NAN chul) *adj.* concerning money **(p. 261)**

financiero(a) *adj.* concerniente a la banca o los negocios mercantiles, relativo al dinero

flourishing (FLUR ish ing) *v.* thriving; doing extremely well **(p. 680)**

floreciendo *v.* prosperando, que hecha flor; forma del verbo *florecer*

foreboding (for BOH ding) *n.* a feeling that something bad has happened or will happen **(p. 804)**

presentimiento *s.* intuir un suceso del futuro gracias a señales o indicios

fortune (FOR chun) *n.* luck; riches **(p. 639)**

fortuna *s.* buena suerte, circunstancia o causa a la que se le atribuye un suceso bueno o malo

foundered (FOWN durd) *v.* broke down; collapsed **(p. 1012)**

colapsó *v.* se derrumbó, fracasó; forma del verbo *colapsar*

furnished (FUR nisht) *v.* supplied; given **(p. 270)**

abasteció *v.* proveer o suministrar alimentos u otras cosas necesarias; forma del verbo *abastecer*

G

glistened (GLIH sund) *v.* shone brightly **(p. 527)**

refulgían *v.* brillaban intensamente, forma del verbo *refulgir*

gory (GOR ee) *adj.* bloody; involving a lot of bloodshed **(p. 326)**

sangriento(a) *adj.* teñido de sangre, manchado de sangre

grandeur (GRAN jur) *n.* the state of being large and impressive; greatness **(p. 1121)**

grandeza *s.* de gran tamaño, majestad y poder

grave (grayv) *adj.* very serious; likely to produce harm or danger **(p. 882)**

grave *adj.* muy enfermo, de mucha importancia y seriedad

grim (grim) *adj.* gloomy; somber **(p. 504)**

ceñudo(a) *adj.* que arruga las cejas (el ceño) en señal de enfado

grimacing (GRIM us ing) *v.* making a face that shows discomfort or disgust **(p. 273)**

haciendo muecas *frase verbal.* gesticulando o contorsionando el rostro de manera burlesca; forma de la frase verbal, *hacer muecas*

H

hardships (HARD ships) *n.* things that cause pain or suffering; misfortunes **(p. 625)**

adversidades *s.* infortunios, situaciones desgraciadas o desfavorables

harmonious (har MOH nee us) *adj.* getting along well together; friendly **(p. 960)**

armonioso(a) *adj.* que tiene correspondencia entre sus parte

hilarious (hih LAR ee us) *adj.* very funny **(p. 251)**

divertidísimo(a) *adj.* que inspira muchísimas ganas de reír

hobbled (HOB uld) *v.* walked with difficulty; limped **(p. 510)**

cojeó *v.* caminó con dificultad, forma del verbo *cojear*

hovering (HUV ur ing) *v.* remaining in or near one place in the air **(p. 1122)**

planeando *v.* volando con las alas extendidas e inmóviles, suspendido en el aire

humiliated (hyoo MIL ee ayt ud) *adj.* embarrassed; ashamed **(p. 110)**

humillado(a) *adj.* con el orgullo abatido y el amor propio herido, cabizbajo

humiliation (hyoo mil ee AY shun) *n.* something that makes a person feel ashamed or foolish **(p. 459)**

humillación *s.* acción de humillar; efecto de avergonzar a alguien

hygiene (HY jeen) *n.* cleanliness; habits that lead to good health **(p. 655)**

higiene *s.* cuidado de la salud a través de la limpieza y el aseo

hypocritical (hip uh KRIT ih kul) *adj.* fake; pretending to be something one isn't **(p. 51)**

hipócrita *adj.* que finge cualidades o sentimientos

I

identify (eye DEN tuh fy) *v.* find; recognize **(p. 322)**

identificar *v.* reconocer si lo buscado ha sido encontrado o no

illiterate (ih LIT uh rit) *adj.* unable to read or write; uneducated **(p. 949)**

analfabeto(a) *adj.* persona que no sabe leer ni escribir, que no tiene cultura

illustrates (IL us trayts) *v.* shows clearly through examples **(p. 457)**

ilustrar *v.* aclarar un tema explicando con palabras, imágenes, ejemplos o cualquier otro modo

immersed (ih MURSD) *v.* completely occupied mentally **(p. 1165)**

ensimismado(a) *v.* inmerso, abstraído, concentrado en algo, forma del verbo *ensimismar*

implied (im PLYD) *adj.* expressed indirectly; suggested rather than said plainly **(p. 256)**

tácito(a) *adj.* que se sobrentiende, se infiere; algo que no está expresado porque se puede deducir

incompetence (in KOM puh tuns) *n.* lack of ability or skill **(p. 212)**

incompetencia *s.* falta de aptitud, de capacidad para hacer algo

incongruous (in KONG groo us) *adj.* not in agreement **(p. 1164)**

incongruente *adj.* falta de correspondencia, de relación y lógica, carente de sentido

incurable (in KYOOR uh bul) *adj.* not likely to be changed or corrected **(p. 963)**

incurable *adj.* que no se puede sanar o corregir, no tiene remedio

indelible (in DEL ih bul) *adj.* impossible to erase, remove, or blot out **(p. 391)**

indeleble *adj.* que no se puede borrar o remover

indispensable (in duh SPEN suh bul) *adj.* absolutely necessary **(p. 962)**

indispensable *adj.* absolutamente imprescindible y necesario

indomitable (in DOM ih tuh bul) *adj.* unable to be conquered or overcome **(p. 527)**

indomable *adj.* que no se deja amansar, someter o dominar

induce (in DOOS) *v.* convince to do something; influence **(p. 209)**

inducir *v.* provocar, persuadir de hacer algo

inert (in URT) *adj.* without power to move or act; lifeless **(p. 1013)**

inerte *adj.* sin vida, inactivo, sin capacidad de reacción

inevitable (in EV uh tuh bul) *adj.* sure to happen; unavoidable **(p. 1093)**

inevitable *adj.* que no puede impedirse, imposible de apartar

inferring (in FUR ing) *n.* using reason and experience to make an educated guess **(p. 182)**

inferencia *s.* algo que se deduce, que se concluye a través del razonamiento y de experiencia

instinct (in STINKT) *n.* unlearned knowledge that a person or an animal is born with **(p. 492)**

instinto *s.* conocimientos indoctos de una persona o animal

instinctively (in STINK tiv lee) *adv.* with a natural response **(p. 415)**

instintivamente *adv.* que se da través del sentimiento y el impulso, que no es obra de le reflexión o el juicio

integrated (IN tuh gray tid) *v.* ended the separation of racial and ethnic groups **(p. 971)**

integrado(a) *v.* alguien o algo pasó a formar parte de un todo; forma del verbo *integrar*

intercede (in tur SEED) *v.* to try to help settle differences between others **(p. 410)**

interceder *v.* tratar de mediar en favor de alguien para ayudarlo

interpret (in TUR prit) *v.* to find the meaning of events or ideas **(p. 482)**

interpretar *v.* explicar el sentido o significado de algo

intimate (IN tuh mit) *adj.* very close and personal; private **(p. 809)**

íntimo(a) *adj.* los interior, profundo o reservado

intuition (in too ISH un) *n.* the ability to know things without having to reason them out **(p. 813)**

intuición *s.* facultad de comprender o conocer algo rápidamente y sin necesidad de razonarlo

invariably (in VAIR ee ub lee) *adv.* constantly; always **(p. 367)**

invariablemente *adv.* que no sufre variación; constante; siempre el mismo

J

jubilation (joo buh LAY shun) *n.* great joy and excitement **(p. 780)**

júbilo *s.* viva alegría expresada

L

liberated (LIB uh ray tid) *adj.* released; freed **(p. 833)**

liberado(a) *adj.* eximido, puesto en libertad, sin ataduras

lingers (LING urz) *v.* waits or is slow in leaving **(p. 189)**

permanece *v.* quedarse o estar en un mismo sitio por un tiempo; forma del verbo *permanecer*

literally (LIT ur uh lee) *adv.* actually; exactly **(p. 1076)**

literalmente *adv.* conforme al sentido pleno de la palabra que lo acompaña; exactamente

lurching (LURCH ing) *v.* rolling or swaying in a jerky motion **(p. 199)**

sacudiendo *v.* movimientos bruscos, violentos; forma del verbo *sacudir*

M

majority (muh JOR ih tee) *n.* more than half; the greater part **(p. 575)**

mayoría *s.* parte mayor, más grande o de más número de un todo

makeshift (MAYK shift) *adj.* used in place of the normal or proper thing **(p. 766)**

improvisado(a) *adj.* algo hecho de pronto y con los medios que se dispone en el momento

maneuvers (muh NOO vurs) *n.* clever or skillful moves or actions **(p. 301)**

maniobra *s.* operación hecha con habilidad o astucia

means (meenz) *n.* methods useful for achieving a particular purpose or goal; resources **(p. 1078)**

medios *s.* elementos de los que se vale para alcanzar un fin

mesh (mesh) *n.* the weblike pattern of fibers in woven or knitted items **(p. 453)**

malla *s.* tejido en el que cuerdas e hilos se cruzan y anudan asemejando una red

meticulous (muh TIK yuh lus) *adj.* careful about small details **(p. 755)**

meticuloso(a) *adj.* que tiene cuidado y detalle

migrated (MY gray tud) *v.* moved from one place to another **(p. 391)**

migró *v.* desplazarse de un sitio de residencia a otro, forma del verbo *migrar*

mimicked (MIM ikt) *v.* copied; imitated **(p. 589); mimics (p. 743)**

imitó *v.* copió o hizo algo en semejanza a otra persona o cosa, forma del verbo *imitar*

minor (MY nur) *adj.* of little importance; not serious **(p. 511)**

menor *adj.* inferior o de menor importancia; pequeño

minority (muh NOR uh tee) *n.* a smaller group **(p. 18)**

minoría *s.* parte menor, más pequeña o de menor número de un todo

modified (MOD uh fyd) *adj.* changed; altered **(p. 327)**

modificado(a) *adj.* que está transformado o cambiado

monumental (mon yuh MEN tul) *adj.* great and meaningful **(p. 1107)**

monumental *adj.* grande, espectacular

mournful (MORN ful) *adj.* filled with sadness or grief **(p. 505)**

afligido(a) *adj.* con tristeza, apesadumbrado

municipal (myoo NIS uh pul) *adj.* having to do with a city or town or its government **(p. 935)**

municipal *adj.* que pertenece a un mismo término jurisdiccional, regido por el ayuntamiento o municipio; de carácter gubernamental

mutilated (MYOO tih lay tid) *adj.* damaged in a way that cannot be repaired **(p. 68)**

mutilado(a) *adj.* cortado, cercenado

N

needle (NEE dul) *v.* cause to take action by repeated stinging comments **(p. 601)**

provocará *v.* incitar, estimular o irritar a alguien con comentarios; forma del verbo *provocar*

neglected (nih GLEK tid) *adj.* given little attention or respect **(p. 458)**

descuidado(a) *adj.* desatendido, que no ha sido atendido con la diligencia que requería

nomination (nah mih NAY shun) *n.* the act of proposing a candidate for an office or honor **(p. 487)**

nominación *s.* propuesta o selección para la obtención de un honor

novelty (NAH vul tee) *n.* anything new, strange, or unusual **(p. 1114)**

novedad *s.* algo nuevo, reciente, nunca antes visto

nutritious (noo TRIH shus) *adj.* containing or giving nourishment **(p. 1003)**

nutritivo(a) *adj.* que aumenta la sustancia o la fuerza

O

oblivious (uh BLIV ee us) *adj.* not aware **(p. 21)**

ajeno(a) *adj.* que desconoce un asunto; carente de información

obnoxious (ub NOK shus) *adj.* very disagreeable or offensive **(p. 574)**

odioso(a) *adj.* desagradable, antipático

obscure (ub SKYOOR) *v.* to hide **(p. 371)**

oscurecer *v.* esconder, ocultar

observant (ub ZUR vunt) *adj.* quick to notice or observe; alert; watchful **(p. 884)**

observador(a) *adj.* que se fija en el detalle, que mira cuidadosamente

offensive (uh FEN siv) *adj.* unpleasant or disagreeable, causing anger **(p. 460)**

ofensivo(a) *adj.* que molesta y falta al respeto

oppressed (uh PRESD) *adj.* held down; held back; kept from making progress **(p. 56)**

oprimido(a) *adj.* sometido a la tiranía y humillación

optimist (OP tuh mist) *n.* a person who has a positive or cheerful outlook **(p. 963)**

optimista *s.* que tiende a juzgar las cosas, personas y situaciones de manera favorable

overwhelmed (oh vur WELMD) *v.* overpowered in thought or feeling; completely covered or flooded **(p. 1077)**

abrumado(a) *adj.* inundado con una sensación

P

pandemonium (pan duh MOH nee um) *n.* wild disorder and uproar **(p. 832)**

pandemónium *s.* lugar ruidoso y con mucha confusión

passively (PAS iv lee) *adv.* not actively **(p. 981)**

pasivamente *adv.* de manera inactiva, que deja transcurrir

perceives (pur SEEVZ) *v.* understands something in a particular way **(p. 333)**

percibe *v.* comprender o conocer algo a través de los sentidos, forma del verbo *percibir*

perish (PAIR ish) *v.* to become ruined or destroyed; die **(p. 1099)**

perecer *v.* fallecer, sufrir un gran daño, dejar de ser

perpetrated (PUR pih tray tid) *v.* was responsible for something harmful **(p. 416)**

perpetrado *v.* responsable por una falta grave o delito; formal del verbo *perpetrar*

perpetual (pur PEH choo ul) *adj.* continuing forever **(p. 981)**

perpetuo(a) *adj.* que dura para siempre

persecution (pur suh KYOO shun) *n.* constant cruel or harmful treatment **(p. 172)**

persecución *s.* continuo tratamiento cruel o dañino

perseverance (pur suh VEER ens) *n.* steady determination **(p. 526)**

perseverancia *s.* constancia en la ejecución de propósitos y resoluciones

persistence (pur SIS tuns) *n.* act of refusing to give up **(p. 947)**

persistencia *s.* firmeza, constancia e insistencia

petty (PEH tee) *adj.* having or displaying a mean, narrow-minded attitude **(p. 461)**

mezquino(a) *adj.* miserable, despreciable, ruin

phase (fayz) *n.* step in the development of a person or thing **(p. 853)**

fase *s.* cada uno de los estados sucesivos de un proceso en desarrollo o evolución

pivoted (PIH vuh tid) *v.* turned around sharply **(p. 902)**

giró *v.* dar vuelta sobre un mismo eje, forma del verbo *girar*

poise (poyz) *n.* a calm, relaxed, and self-controlled manner **(p. 820)**

aplomo *s.* circunspección, que muestra serenidad, seguridad

portray (por TRAY) *v.* to show or represent someone or something **(p. 327)**

retratar *v.* describir con cierta fidelidad

precautions (pruh KAW shunz) *n.* actions taken to prevent difficulty before it happens **(p. 884)**

precauciones *s.* cautela, medida que se toma para evitar o prevenir inconvenientes

predicting (pree DIKT ing) *n.* using clues to guess what will happen **(p. 204)**

predicción *s.* anuncio de algo que va a suceder en el futuro

premature (pree muh CHUR) *adj.* early; before the right time **(p. 57)**

prematuro(a) *adj.* que se da antes de tiempo

prevailed (prih VAYLD) *v.* conquered; won; overcame **(p. 1106)**

prevaleció *v.* sobresalió, venció sobre los demás, superioridad y ventaja; forma del verbo *prevalecer*

prior (PRY ur) *adj.* earlier; coming before **(p. 62)**

previo(a) *adj.* anterior; que viene primero

procedure (pro SEE jur) *n.* a series of steps taken to do something **(p. 124)**

procedimiento *s.* método, sistema, forma de ejecutar algo

procession (proh SEH shun) *n.* a group of individuals walking forward together in a ceremony **(p. 197)**

procesión *s.* grupo de personas que caminan de manera solemne y ordenada

promoter (pruh MOH tur) *n.* a person who organizes and pays the costs of a sporting event **(p. 271)**

promotor(a) *s.* persona que gestiona el logro de algo a través del impulso y la promoción

prone (prohn) *adj.* likely to act or be a certain way **(p. 78)**

propenso(a) *adj.* con tendencia, afición o inclinación hacia algo

proposition (prah puh ZIH shun) *n.* a plan or proposal **(p. 1098)**

proposición *s.* idea que se expresa o manifiesta para lograr un fin

proprietor (pruh PRY uh tur) *n.* a person or firm that owns a property or a business **(p. 1145)**

propietario(a) *s.* dueño, titular de algo; persona con derecho de propiedad sobre algo

prospect (PRAH spekt) *n.* that which is expected **(p. 250)**

perspectiva *s.* lo que se espera

publicized (PUB lih syzd) *v.* made the public aware of something **(p. 252)**

publicado(a) *v.* difundir, anunciar, dar a conocer una información; forma del verbo *publicar*

Q

quavered (KWAY vurd) *v.* spoke in a shaky or trembling voice **(p. 211)**

dijo con voz trémula *frase v.* habló con voz temblorosa, forma de la frase verbal *decir con voz trémula*

quench (kwench) *v.* to satisfy a need **(p. 244)**

saciar *v.* satisfacer un deseo o necesidad

R

racial (RAY shul) *adj.* characteristic of a race of people **(p. 948)**

racial *adj.* que se relaciona o pertenece la raza de un grupo de personas

rage (rayj) *n.* a feeling of great anger or fury **(p. 493)**

cólera *s.* ira, enojo exaltado y violento

rapture (RAP chur) *n.* a feeling of great joy **(p. 1124)**

éxtasis *s.* arrebatamiento, estado de extremo placer

rash (rash) *adj.* reckless; done without thought or concern **(p. 243)**

precipitado(a) *adj.* que está hecho con mucha prisa y sin haberlo reflexionado

rations (RASH unz) *n.* portions of needed items **(p. 521)**

raciones *s.* parte, porción o cantidad de algo

rave (rayv) *v.* to speak about very favorably or with great enthusiasm **(p. 1146)**

elogiar *v.* ensalzar, hablar sobre algo o alguien de manera favorable

recedes (ree SEEDS) *v.* moves or pulls back **(p. 641)**
(se) aleja *v.* se distancia, se pone lejos; forma del verbo *alejar*

recollections (rek uh LEK shunz) *n.* memories **(p. 125)**
recuerdos *s.* memoria o presencia en la mente que se tiene de algo que ya pasó

recurring (rih KUR ing) *adj.* happening or coming back again; repeating **(p. 1068)**
recurrente *adj.* que vuelve a pasar o aparecer de manera repetitiva

refuse (REF yooz) *n.* trash; rubbish **(p. 1071)**
desechos *s.* residuo, basura, lo que queda de algo que ya fue usado o utilizado

relentlessly (ruh LENT lis lee) *adv.* without pity or mercy **(p. 21)**
implacablemente *adv.* sin mostrar compasión o piedad

relevant (REH luh vunt) *adj.* important to the subject at hand; significant; pertinent **(p. 604)**
relevante *adj.* destacado, sobresaliente; significativo; pertinente

relish (REL ish) *n.* enjoyment or delight **(p. 109)**
deleite *s.* con entusiasmo, con gusto

reluctantly (ree LUK tunt lee) *adv.* against one's wishes **(p. 213)**
(a) regañadientes *adv.* de mala gana

replica (REP lih kuh) *n.* a faithful copy **(p. 1123)**
réplica *s.* copia exacta del original

residences (REH zuh den suz) *n.* places where one lives **(p. 79)**
residencias *s.* lugar donde se vive; vivienda

resilient (rih ZIL yunt) *adj.* able to recover from or adjust easily to misfortune or change **(p. 850)**
resistente *adj.* que es capaz de pervivir y mantenerse sin ceder

resolve (rih ZOLV) *v.* to decide firmly **(p. 1099)**
resolver *v.* tomar una determinación

restrictions (ree STRIK shunz) *n.* limits to things one can and can't do **(p. 332)**
restricción(ones) *s.* reducción de los límites de algo

retribution (re trih BYOO shun) *n.* punishment for past deeds **(p. 668)**
castigo *s.* pena impuesta por los actos del pasado

reveal (rih VEEL) *v.* show **(p. 662)**
revelar *v.* dar a conocer

ripened (RYP und) *v.* became ready to eat **(p. 313)**
maduraron *v.* alcanzaron el punto de desarrollo; forma del verbo *madurar*

roamed (rohmd) *v.* wandered; went from place to place without purpose or direction **(p. 479)**
deambuló *v.* recorrió; que anduvo de un lugar a otro sin rumbo fijo; forma del verbo *deambular*

S

sacred (SAY krid) *adj.* holy; having to do with religion **(p. 615)**
sagrado(a) *adj.* santo; relativo a la religión

salvaged (SAL vujd) *v.* saved from ruin; rescued **(p. 641)**
rescatamos *v.* salvamos de un peligro; recuperamos; forma del verbo *rescatar*

sauntered (SAWN turd) *v.* walked leisurely **(p. 682)**
anduvo (con aire despreocupado) *frase v.* entró o salió como si estuviera relajado; forma del verbo *andar*

scorned (skornd) *adj.* looked down upon by someone **(p. 164)**
desdeñado(a) *adj.* persona que es despreciada por otra

seasoned (SEE zund) *adj.* made fit by experience; adjusted to (something) because of experience **(p. 1125)**
avezado(a) *adj.* experimentado; acostumbrado o habituado a algo

self-conscious (self KON shus) *adj.* too aware of one's own appearance and actions **(p. 737)**
acomplejado(a) *adj.* que siente inhibición por tener demasiada conciencia de su aspecto físico y sus actos

self-esteem (self es TEEM) *n.* confidence and satisfaction in oneself **(p. 20)**

autoestima *s.* consideración y aprecio que se siente por uno mismo

sequence (SEE kwens) *n.* a regular order or arrangement in time, space, or importance **(p. 99)**

secuencia *s.* serie o sucesión ordenada de elementos que están relacionados entre sí

severity (suh VAIR ih tee) *n.* state of being very dangerous or harmful **(p. 510)**

gravedad *s.* seriedad o importancia de algo, esp. enfermedad

sheepishly (SHEEP ish lee) *adv.* with embarrassment **(p. 266)**

tímidamente *adv.* con vergüenza

siblings (SIB lingz) *n.* brothers and sisters **(p. 1091)**

hermanos *s. pl.* hermanos y hermanas

significant (sig NIH fih kunt) *adj.* having meaning; having much importance **(p. 558)**

significativo(a) *adj.* que da a entender algo; que tiene mucho valor

similar (SIM uh lur) *adj.* alike, but not exactly the same **(p. 238)**

similar *adj.* parecido o semejante, pero no igual

simultaneously (sy mul TAY nee us lee) *adv.* at the same time **(p. 671)**

simultáneamente *adv.* al mismo tiempo

skeptically (SKEP tik uh lee) *adv.* with doubt **(p. 983)**

(con) escepticismo *frase adv.* dudosamente

snarled (snarld) *v.* made tangled or knotted **(p. 166)**

enredó *v.* enmarañó o anudó; forma del verbo *enredar*

somber (SOM bur) *adj.* dark and gloomy **(p. 187)**

sombrío(a) *adj.* oscuro y melancólico

stable (STAY bul) *adj.* firm and steady; long-lasting **(p. 864)**

estable *adj.* firme y constante; duradero

stately (STAYT lee) *adj.* grand; impressive; dignified **(p. 608)**

señorial *adj.* majestuoso; grandioso; digno

stealthy (STEL thee) *adj.* slow and secretive to avoid being seen or heard **(p. 187); stealthily** *adv.* **(p. 826)**

furtivo(a) *adj.* hecho en secreto o a hurtadillas para no ser escuchado; **furtivamente** *adv.*

sterile (STAIR ul) *adj.* free from germs; very clean **(p. 512)**

estéril *adj.* libre de gérmenes; muy limpio

stifled (STY fuld) *adj.* held back; muffled **(p. 48)**

apagado(a) *adj.* contenido; sordo

stimulates (STIM yuh layts) *v.* makes active or more active **(p. 49)**

estimula *v.* activa o incita; forma del verbo *estimular*

stimulus (STIM yoo lus) *n.* something that causes a response **(p. 371)**

estímulo *s.* agente que provoca una reacción o respuesta

strain (strayn) *v.* stretch to the limit; overwork **(p. 981)**

esforzar *v.* someter a demasiada presión física o moral; trabajar demasiado

strategy (STRAT uh jee) *n.* a careful method or plan **(p. 43); strategies (p. 851)**

estrategia *s.* planificación o técnica para obtener algo; **estrategias**

structure (STRUK chur) *n.* the arrangement or organization of parts in a body or system **(p. 336)**

estructura *s.* distribución u orden de las partes de un cuerpo o cosa

surrender (suh REN dur) *v.* to give up **(p. 487)**

renunciar *v.* dejar o abandonar algo

sustenance (SUS tuh nuns) *n.* food and other necessities of life **(p. 773)**

sustento *s.* alimento y demás necesidades esenciales

swaggered (SWAG urd) *v.* walked boldly or showed off **(p. 568)**

pavoneó *v.* caminó con aire arrogante o haciendo ostentación; forma del verbo *pavonear*

syndrome (SIN drohm) *n.* a group of symptoms that point to a certain disease **(p. 1008)**

síndrome *s.* conjunto de síntomas que definen una enfermedad

T

tangible (TAN juh bul) *adj.* able to be seen, touched, or felt **(p. 364)**
tangible *adj.* que puede verse, tocarse o percibirse

taunts (tawnts) *n.* hurtful or mocking remarks **(p. 968)**
pullas *s.* bromas o burlas hirientes

texts (tekts) *n.* the words and forms of written or printed works **(p. 14)**
textos *s.* grupo de palabras forman un documento escrito

toiled (toyld) *v.* worked hard **(p. 1155)**
(se) afanó *v.* trabajó duro; forma del verbo *afanar(se)*

tolerance (TOL ur uns) *n.* the ability to recognize and respect different beliefs **(p. 410)**
tolerancia *s.* respeto y consideración por las opiniones ajenas

translates (TRANZ laytz) *v.* changes successfully into another form or language **(p. 658)**
(se) traduce *v.* se convierte o transforma en otra cosa; forma del verbo *traducir(se)*

treacherous (TRECH ur us) *adj.* dangerous; not reliable; not trustworthy **(p. 66)**
traicionero(a) *adj.* peligroso; astuto; que no es confiable

trekked (trekd) *v.* walked or hiked a long distance **(p. 35)**
caminaron *v.* recorrieron la distancia a pie o hicieron senderismo; forma del verbo *caminar*

tribute (TRIB yoot) *n.* an action or a gift that shows respect, admiration, or thanks **(p. 862)**
tributo *s.* acción de reconocimiento como muestra de respeto, admiración o agradecimiento

trivial (TRIV ee ul) *adj.* of very little value or importance **(p. 1163)**
trivial *adj.* de muy poco valor o importancia

U

ultimatum (ul tuh MAY tum) *n.* a final demand that, if unmet, carries harsh penalties **(p. 896)**
ultimátum *s.* propuesta definitiva acompañada de una amenaza

uncertainty (un SUR tun tee) *n.* the state of being unsure or not knowing **(p. 783)**
incertidumbre *s.* falta de seguridad o certeza

unfulfilling (un ful FIL ing) *adj.* not satisfying **(p. 850)**
insatisfecho(a) *adj.* que no está conforme

unison (YOO nih sun) *n.* one voice **(p. 590)**
unísono *s.* al mismo tiempo; con el mismo sonido

V

valid (VAL id) *adj.* based on correct information; logical; sound **(p. 956)**
válido(a) *adj.* que tiene valor porque es correcto; lógico; apropiado

valor (VAL or) *n.* courage **(p. 407)**
valentía *s.* coraje

veered (veerd) *v.* suddenly changed direction **(p. 242)**
viró *v.* cambió de dirección; forma del verbo *virar*

victor (VIK tor) *adj.* concerning a winner; concerning one who defeats an opponent **(p. 505)**
vencedor(a) *s.* ganador; que derrota al oponente

vile (vyl) *adj.* very bad; extremely unpleasant **(p. 742)**
repugnante *adj.* asqueroso; muy desagradable

violating (VY uh lay ting) *v.* breaking or disregarding a law or rule **(p. 988)**
violando *v.* quebrantando o desobedeciendo la ley; forma del verbo *violar*

virtually (VUR choo uh lee) *adv.* nearly **(p. 983)**
prácticamente *adv.* casi

visual (VIZH wul) *adj.* able to be viewed or seen **(p. 98)**
visual *adj.* que se puede ver

void (voyd) *n.* empty space **(p. 22)**
vacío *s.* sin contenido

vulnerable (VUL nur uh bul) *adj.* exposed to danger **(p. 1030)**

vulnerable *adj.* expuesto al peligro

W

wallow (WAH loh) *v.* to take selfish pleasure in comfort **(p. 772)**

regodear *v.* deleitarse y complacerse en un gusto

wavered (WAY vurd) *v.* swayed unsteadily **(p. 243)**

tambaleó *v.* perdió el equilibrio; forma del verbo *tambalear*

withstand (with STAND) *v.* to resist the effect of; stand up against **(p. 865)**

soportar *v.* que soporta el efecto de algo; mantenerse sin ceder

wretched (RECH id) *adj.* very unpleasant or uncomfortable; terrible **(p. 103)**

espantoso(a) *adj.* desagradable o miserable; horrible

Y

yielding (YEEL ding) *adj.* giving way to force or pressure **(p. 1148)**

blando(a) *adj.* suave y tierno, que cede al tacto

INDEX OF SKILLS

References beginning with R *refer to Handbook pages.*

References beginning with RH *refer to the Reading Handbook.*

Literary Concepts

Reading and Thinking

Grammar and Language

INDEX OF SKILLS

Vocabulary

Writing

Listening, Speaking, and Viewing

Research and Study Skills

INDEX OF AUTHORS AND TITLES

INDEX OF ART AND ARTISTS

ACKNOWLEDGMENTS

Unit 1

Excerpt from *I Know Why the Caged Bird Sings* by Maya Angelou, copyright © 1969 and renewed 1997 by Maya Angelou. Used by permission of Random House, Inc.

"Ice" by Graham Salisbury. From *Going Where I'm Coming From: Memoirs of American Youth* edited by Anne Mazer.

Excerpt from *The Book of Rock Stars* by Kathleen Krull. Text copyright © 2003 by Kathleen Krull.

Excerpt from *Mother Jones: Fierce Fighter for Workers' Rights* by Judith Pinkerton Josephson. Copyright © 1997 by Judith Pinkerton Josephson.

From *How to Get a Job If You're a Teenager,* by Cindy Pervola and Debby Hobgood. Copyright © 1998 by Cindy Pervola and Debby Hobgood. Reprinted by permission of Highsmith Press.

Excerpt from *Young Person's Occupational Outlook Handbook.* Copyright © 2005 by JIST Publishing, Inc.

Reprinted with the permission of Simon & Schuster Books for Young Readers, an imprint of Simon & Schuster Children's Publishing Division, from *The Invisible Thread* by Yoshiko Uchida. Copyright © 1991 by Yoshiko Uchida.

Reprinted with the permission of Scribner, an imprint of Simon & Schuster Adult Publishing Group, from *A Gift of Laughter* by Allan Sherman. Copyright © 1965 by Allan Sherman.

Excerpt from *Knots in My Yo-yo String: The Autobiography of a Kid* by Jerry Spinelli. Copyright © 1998 Jerry Spinelli.

"Knoxville, Tennessee" from *Black Feeling, Black Talk, Black Judgment* by Nikki Giovanni. Copyright © 1968, 1970 by Nikki Giovanni. Reprinted by permission of HarperCollins Publishers.

From *Dear Exile* by Hilary Liftin and Kate Montgomery, copyright © 1999 by Hilary Liftin and Kate Montgomery. Used by permission of Vintage Books, a division of Random House, Inc.

Unit 2

"Racing the Great Bear" from *Flying with the Eagle, Racing the Great Bear,* by Joseph Bruchac. Copyright © 1993 by Joseph Bruchac. Reprinted by permission of Barbara S. Kouts.

"The People Could Fly" from *The People Could Fly: American Black Folktales* by Virginia Hamilton, illustrated by Leo and Diane Dillon, copyright © 1985 by Virginia Hamilton. Illustrations copyright © 1985 by Leo and Diane Dillon. Used by permission of Alfred A. Knopf, an imprint of Random House Children's Books, a division of Random House, Inc.

"The Oxcart" from *Sword of the Samurai: Adventure Stories from Japan,* copyright © 1999 by Eric A. Kimmel, reprinted by permission of Harcourt, Inc.

"The Snake Chief" from *Tales from Africa* retold by Kathleen Arnott (OUP, 2000), copyright © Kathleen Arnott 1962, used by permission of Oxford University Press.

Excerpt from *Harriet Tubman: Conductor of the Underground Railroad* by Ann Petry. Reprinted by permission of Russell & Volkening as agents for the author. Copyright © 1955 by Ann Petry, renewed in 1983 by Ann Petry.

"A Dose of Medicine" from *Accidents May Happen* by Charlotte Foltz Jones, Illustrations by John O'Brien, copyright © 1996 by Charlotte Foltz Jones. Used by permission of Random House Children's Books, a division of Random House, Inc.

"Kamau's Finish" by Muthoni Muchemi, from *Memories of Sun: Stories of Africa and America*, copyright © 2004 by Jane Kurtz. Used by permission of HarperCollins Publishers.

"The Bunion Derby" by Leone Castell Anderson. Reprinted by permission of *Cricket* Magazine, May 2005, Vol. 32, No. 9, text © 2005 by Carus Publishing Company.

"The Best Coon-and-Possum Dog" by B. A. Botkin. From *A Treasury of Mississippi River Folklore* by B. A. Botkin. Copyright © 1955 by Ben A. Botkin.

Unit 3

From "Gymnasts in Pain: Out of Balance" by Scott M. Reid. *The Orange County Register,* December 19, 2004. Copyright © 2005 *The Orange County Register*. Reprinted by permission.

"In Response to Executive Order 9066," by Dwight Okita. Reprinted by permission of the author.

"The games kids play: are mature video games too violent for teens?" *Current Events*, February 7, 2003. Copyright © 2003 Weekly Reader Corporation. Reprinted by permission.

"Cruise Control: New Teen Driving Restrictions Put Parents in the Rear Window" by Kevin O'Leary, from *Teen People* © 2002. All rights reserved. Time Inc.

"Flowers for Algernon," by Daniel Keyes. Copyright © 1959, 1987 by Daniel Keyes. Reprinted by permission of the author. *Flowers for Algernon* and its companion book *Algernon, Charlie and I: A Writer's Journey* are available from Harcourt Inc.

"Tattoos: Fad, Fashion, or Folly?" by Linda Bickerstaff, from *ODYSSEY's* May 2005 issue: *The Skin You're In*, copyright © 2005, Carus Publishing Company, published by Cobblestone Publishing, 30 Grove Street, Suite C, Peterborough, NH 03458. All rights reserved. Used by permission of the publisher.

"We Real Cool" by Gwendolyn Brooks. Reprinted by consent of Brooks Permissions.

"The Market Economy" from *Circles on the Water* by Marge Piercy, copyright © 1982 by Marge Piercy. Used by permission of Alfred A. Knopf, a division of Random House, Inc.

"Wearing Hijab: Veil of Valor" by Emilia Askari from *Detroit Free Press.*

Prologue and excerpt from *Zoya's Story: An Afghan Woman's Struggle for Freedom,* by John Follain and Rita Cristofari. Copyright © 2002 by John Follain and Rita Cristofari. Reprinted by permission of HarperCollins Publishers.

"Potions from Poisons" by Andrea Dorfman. *Time*, January 15, 2001. © 2001 Time Inc. Reprinted by permission.

Unit 4

"Wishing Well" by Katherine Schmitt.

"Mother to Son" from *The Collected Poems of Langston Hughes* by Langston Hughes, copyright © 1994 by The Estate of Langston Hughes. Used by permission of Alfred A. Knopf, a division of Random House, Inc.

"Harlem" from *The Collected Poems of Langston Hughes* by Langston Hughes, copyright © 1994 by The Estate of Langston Hughes.

"Sittin' on the Dock of the Bay" by Otis Redding and Steve Cropper.

Excerpt from 1988 Democratic National Convention Address by Jesse Jackson.

"Fable for When There's No Way Out," by May Swenson. Used by permission of the Literary Estate of May Swenson.

"Scorched! How to Handle Different Types of Burns" by Stephen Fraser. *Current Health*, March 2005. Copyright © 2005 Weekly Reader Corporation. Reprinted by permission.

From *Thura's Diary* by Thura Al-Windawi, translated by Robin Bray, copyright © 2004 by Thura al-Windawi. Used by permission of Viking Children's Books, A Division of Penguin Young Readers Group, A Member of Penguin Group (USA) Inc., 345 Hudson Street, New York, NY 10014. All rights reserved.

"Escaping" by Zdenko Slobodnik, from *Teen Ink: What Matters,* © 2003 The Young Authors Foundation, Inc. Reprinted by permission of Teen Ink.

David Ignatow, "Reading at Night" from *David Ignatow: Poems 1934–1969,* copyright © by David Ignatow and reprinted by permission of Wesleyan University Press.

"Wheelchairs That Kneel Down Like Elephants," copyright © 1992 by Karen Fiser. Reprinted by permission of the author from *Words Like Fate and Pain*. Cambridge, MA: Zoland Books, 1992. Available from the author.

Unit 5

"Born Worker" from *Petty Crimes,* copyright © 1998 by Gary Soto, reprinted by permission of Harcourt, Inc.

"Cream Puff" by Linnea Due. From *Girls Got Game: Sports Stories and Poems* edited by Sue Macy.

"an african american," copyright © 1990 by Meri Nana-Ama Danquah. First published in *The Hollywood Review*. Reprinted by permission of Meri Nana-Ama Danquah.

"One Throw" by W.C. Heinz, copyright © 1950, renewed 1978 by W.C. Heinz. Reprinted by permission of William Morris Agency, LLC on behalf of the author.

"The Medicine Bag" by Virginia Driving Hawk Sneve. Reprinted by permission of the author.

From "A Year of Living Bravely" by Emily Costello, published in *Scholastic Action,* October 11, 2004 by Scholastic Inc. Copyright © 2004 by Scholastic Inc. All rights reserved. Used by permission.

"The Fire Pond" by Michael Rosen. Reprinted by permission of the author.

From *Savion!: My Life in Tap* by Savion Glover. Copyright © 1999 by Savion Glover. Used by permission of HarperCollins Publishers.

"Thank You in Arabic" from *Going Where I'm Coming From.* Copyright © 1995 by Naomi Shihab Nye. Reprinted by permission of the author.

From "A Safe Space" by Joyce Hansen, from *Lost and Found* by M. Jerry Weiss and Helen S. Weiss, copyright © 2000 by the author and reprinted by permission of St. Martin's Press, LLC and Tom Doherty Associates, LLC.

Unit 6

The Diary of Anne Frank (Play) by Frances Goodrich and Albert Hackett, copyright © 1956 by Albert Hackett, Frances Goodrich Hackett and Otto Frank. Used by permission of Random House, Inc.

"Bouncing Back" by Jan Farrington. *Current Health*, March 2005. Copyright © 2005 Weekly Reader Corporation. Reprinted by permission.

"Another Mountain" from *The Last Poets: On a Mission: Selected Poems and a History of the Last Poets* by Abiodun Oyewole and Umar Bin Hassan with Kim Green. Copyright © Abiodun Oyewole and Umar Bin Hassan. Reprinted by permission of Henry Holt and Company, LLC.

"and sometimes I hear this song in my head" from *Catalyst.* Copyright © 1991 by Harriet Jacobs.

Reprinted with the permission of Simon & Schuster Books for Young Readers, an imprint of Simon & Schuster Children's Publishing Division, from *Sky* by Hanneke Ippisch. Copyright © 1996 Hanneke Ippisch.

"Welcome" by Ouida Sebestyen, copyright © 1984 by Ouida Sebestyen, from *Sixteen: Short Stories*, Donald R. Gallo, ed. Used by permission of Random House Children's Books, a division of Random House, Inc.

"Alone" from *Oh Pray My Wings Are Gonna Fit Me Well* by Maya Angelou. Copyright © 1975 by Maya Angelou.

"Flinn, on the Bus" from *19 Varieties of Gazelle: Poems of the Middle East.* Copyright © 1994, 1995, 1998, 2002 by Naomi Shihab Nye. Reprinted by permission of the author.

From "Will-o'-the-Wisp" used with permission of Sterling Publishing Co., Inc., NY, NY, from *Whodunit – You Decide!* by Hy Conrad, copyright © 1996 by Hy Conrad.

"After Agatha Christie," copyright © 1975 by Linda Pastan, from *Carnival Evening: New and Selected Poems 1968–1998* by Linda Pastan. Used by permission of W.W. Norton & Company, Inc.

Unit 7

Excerpt from *2 Minutes a Day for a Greener Planet* by Marjorie Lamb. Copyright © 1990 by Marjorie Lamb. Reprinted by permission of the author.

From *The Measure of Our Success* by Marian Wright Edelman. Copyright © 1992 by Marian Wright Edelman. Reprinted by permission of Beacon Press, Boston.

"All Together Now" by Barbara Jordan. Originally printed in *Sesame Street Parents,* July/August 1994.

From *Through My Eyes* by Ruby Bridges. Published by Scholastic Inc./ Scholastic Press. Copyright © 1999 by Ruby Bridges. Reprinted by permission. All rights reserved.

"The Trouble with Television" by Robert MacNeil. (condensed from a speech delivered November 13, 1984, at the President's Leadership Forum, State University of New York at Purchase). Reprinted by permission of the author.

"Stop the Sun" copyright © 1986 by Gary Paulsen, from *Boys' Life,* January 1986.

"Teens Tackle Pollution in Their Communities" by Sara Steindorf. *Christian Science Monitor,* April 22, 2003. Copyright © 2003, The Christian Science Publishing Society. Reprinted by permission of Copyright Clearance Center.

"A Change in Climate" by Emily Sohn, from *Science News for Kids,* December 8, 2004. Reprinted with permission from *Science News for Kids,* copyright © 2004.

"The Treasure of Lemon Brown," reprinted by permission of Miriam Altshuler Literary Agency, on behalf of Walter Dean Myers. Copyright © 1983 by Walter Dean Myers.

"Baby Deer Do Need Your Help" by Nate Tripp. Reprinted by permission from the *New York State Conservationist,* April 1996.

"Take the Junk Out of Marketing Food to Kids" from *Detroit Free Press,* January 19, 2005. Copyright © 2005 by Detroit Free Press. Reprinted by permission.

Unit 8

"I Have a Dream" reprinted by arrangement with the Estate of Martin Luther King Jr., c/o Writers House as agent for the proprietor, New York, NY. Copyright 1963 Martin Luther King Jr., copyright renewed 1991 Coretta Scott King.

"Volar: To Fly" from *The Latin Deli: Prose and Poetry* by Judith Ortiz Cofer. Reprinted by permission of The University of Georgia Press.

From *The Century for Young People* by Peter Jennings and Todd Brewster, copyright © 1999 by ABC. Used by permission of Doubleday, a division of Random House, Inc.

"8 lottery winners who lost their millions" by Ellen Goodstein, Bankrate.com. Copyright: Bankrate.com, N. Palm Beach, FL 2006. Reprinted by permission.

"I Chose Schooling" by Jacqueling Nwaiwu from *My Sisters' Voices,* edited by Iris Jacob. © 2002 by Iris Jacob. Reprinted by permission of Henry Holt and company, LLC.

"The Electric Summer" by Richard Peck, copyright © 1999 by Richard Peck, from *Time Capsule: Short Stories About Teenagers Throughout the Twentieth Century* by Donald R. Gallo. Used by permission of Dell Publishing, a division of Random House, Inc.

"I, Too" from *The Collected Poems of Langston Hughes* by Langston Hughes, copyright © 1994 by The Estate of Langston Hughes. Used by permission of Alfred A. Knopf, a division of Random House, Inc.

Excerpt from *Dandelion Wine* by Ray Bradbury, reprinted by permission of Don Congdon Associates, Inc. Copyright © 1957, renewed 1985 by Ray Bradbury.

"Coming to America" by Marianne Szegedy-Maszak. From *Good Housekeeping,* January 2000. Copyright © Hearst Magazines January 2000.

"Business at Eleven," by Toshio Mori. Reprinted by permission of Caxton Press.

Reprinted with the permission of Atheneum Books for Young Readers, an imprint of Simon & Schuster Children's Publishing Division, from *Letters From a Slave Girl* by Mary E. Lyons. Copyright © 1992 by Mary E. Lyons.

Photography

Cover Hugh Gretschmer/Getty Images; IGetty Images; viii Images.com/CORBIS; x Buzz Pictures/SuperStock ; xii Kirk Aeder/Icon SMI; xiv Julie Nicholls/CORBIS; xvi Gandee Vason/Getty Images; xviii Tim de Waele/CORBIS; xx Colin Bootman/The Bridgeman Art Library; xxii Bill Ross/CORBIS; xxiv Getty Images; xxv (tr)Clay Bennett/The Christian Science Monitor, (others)Getty Images; xxvi xxvii Getty Images; xxx Jose Luis Pelaez/Corbis; xxxvi Dinah Mite Activities; xxxvii Getty Images; RH Getty Images; RH19 (l)Klee/Corbis, (r)Corbis; 0 Images.com/CORBIS; 2 (t)Jon Feingersch/CORBIS, (b)CORBIS; 5 Images.com/CORBIS; 7 Amanita Pictures; 8 Smithsonian American Art Museum, Washington DC/Art Resource, NY; 10 CORBIS; 12 John Kaprielian/Photo Researchers; 14 Lucky Cow/Mark Pett. Dist. By UNIVERSAL PRESS SYNDICATE; 15 John Evans; 16 Jeff Pfeffer/Random House Children's Books; 18 Tony Freeman/PhotoEdit; 19 CORBIS; 20 Kevin R. Morris/CORBIS; 21 AP/Wide World Photos; 25 David L. Moore/Alamy Images; 26 Stephanie Maze/CORBIS; 32 Time for Kids; 33 Royal Geographic Society; 34 (t)Royal Geographic Society, (b)BobBy Model; 35 BobBy Model; 36 Royal Geographic Society; 42 BALDO/Baldo Partnership. Dist. By UNIVERSAL PRESS SYNDICATE; 43 John Evans; 44 The Frank & Marie-Therese Wood Print Collection, Alexandria, VA; 46 The Image Bank/Getty Images; 49 Sausage International/CORBIS; 52 The Image Bank/Getty Images; 57 Topham Picturepoint/The Image Works; 58 Eric Robert/CORBIS; 59 C Squared Studios/Getty Images; 62 Zits Partnership, Reprinted with Permission of King Features Syndicate; 63 Laura Sifferlin; 64 Bob Bretell; 66 The Newberry Library/Stock Montage; 67 CORBIS; 69 The Newberry Library/Stock Montage; 71 72 Bettmann/CORBIS; 74 The Newberry Library/Stock Montage; 83 84 Michael Newman/PhotoEdit; 86 Richard Klune/CORBIS; 87 through 89 Getty Images; 94 Baldo/Baldo Partnership. Dist. By UNIVERSAL PRESS SYNDICATE; 96 Baldo/Baldo Partnership. Dist. By UNIVERSAL PRESS SYNDICATE; 97 File photo; 98 Mary Moylan; 100 through 104 SIRUIS Entertainment; 106 George Fry/Yoshiko Uchida photograph collection, #1986.059:269--PIC The Bancroft Library; 108 CORBIS; 110 Yoshiko Uchida photograph collection, The Bancroft Library; 111 Yoshiko Uchida photograph collection, The Bancroft Library; 112 Toru Hanai/Reuters/CORBIS; 113 ImageGap/Alamy Images; 114 CORBIS; 118 Everett Collection; 119 Chris Brown/Alamy Images; 120 Tom Rosenthal/SuperStock; 122 (t)SSPL/The Image Works, (b)Comstock Images/Alamy Images; 123 (t)Gettysburg College/Random House Children's Books, (b)Judie Burstein/Globe Photos; 124 SuperStock/Alamy Images; 125 Siede Preis/Getty Images; 126 Hulton Archive/Getty Images; 128 (t)Greg Stott/Masterfile, (b)The Bicycle Museum of America/New Bremen, OH; 129 SuperStock; 130 SuperStock/Alamy Images; 134 136 137 Courtesy Kate Montgomery; 138 139 Eclipse Studios; 146 Buzz Pictures/SuperStock; 148 (l)Charles Gullung/Photonica/Getty Images, (r)Photomondo/Getty Images; 151 Catherine Gehm; 152 (l)courtesy of the New York State Museum, Albany, NY, (r)Newberry Library, Chicago/SuperStock; 153 Werner Foreman/Topham/The Image Works; 154 155 157 Christie's Images; 158 blickwinkel/Alamy Images; 160 BIG TOP/Harrell. Dist. By UNIVERSAL PRESS SYNDICATE; 161 Raoul Minsart/Masterfile; 162 Ron Rovtar; 165 Courtesy Leo & Diana Dillon; 167 Courtesy the Wyeth Collection; 168 Courtesy Leo & Diana Dillon; 173 174 176 Manuel Bauer/Lookat; 182 Zits Partnership, Reprinted with Permission of King Features Syndicate; 183 Laura Sifferlin; 184 Bettman/CORBIS; 188 SuperStock; 190 Arthur Hoppock Hearn Fund - 1950 - The Metropolitan Museum of Art - NY (50.117) Estate of Grant Wood/Licensed By VAGA 192 SuperStock; 194 Eric Kimmel; 196 Erich Lessing/Art Resource, NY; 198 R.P. Kingston/Index Stock Imagery; 200 Brooklyn Museum of Art, NY. Frank L. Babbott Fund/Bridgeman Art Library; 201 Victoria and Albert Museum, London/AKG-Images; 202 Erich Lessing/Art Resource, NY; 204 Reprinted with permission of King Features Syndicate; 205 File photo; 208 Stapleton Collection/CORBIS; 209 Bridgeman Art Library; 210 David Else/Lonely Planet Images; 212 Inga Spence/Index Stock Imagery; 213 Ron Johnson/Index Stock Imagery; 215 Imagebroker/Alamy Images; 216 Stapleton Collection/CORBIS; 218 AP/Wide World Photos; 220 National Museum of American Art, Washington DC/Art Resource, NY; 221 R. & N. Bowers/VIREO; 222 Raymond Bial; 223 National Museum of American Art, Washington DC/Art Resource, NY; 225 Bettmann/CORBIS; 230 National Portrait Gallery, Smithsonian Institution/Art Resource, NY; 232 National Museum of American Art, Washington DC/Art Resource, NY; 238 BALDO/Baldo Partnership. Dist. By UNIVERSAL PRESS SYNDICATE; 239 File photo; 240 Radcliffe Archives, Radcliffe Institute, Harvard University; 242 Jason Hawkes/CORBIS; 244 Cindy Kassab/CORBIS; 245 Scala/Art Resource, NY; 246 Cindy Kassab/CORBIS; 248 Courtesy of Holiday House; 250 CORBIS; 251 Mary Evans Picture Library; 252 The Stapleton Collection/Bridgeman Art Library; 253 Bettmann/CORBIS; 254 CORBIS; 258 Wallace Garland/Muthoni Garland; 259 Hubertus Kanus/SuperStock; 260 Betty Press/Woodfin Camp; 262 Knut Mueller/africa-photo/Das Fotoarchiv; 264 Rubberball/Getty Images; 267 Leone Castell Anderson; 268 Melissa Farlow/Getty Images; 269 Bettmann/CORBIS; 270 VEER Thomas Francisco/Getty Images; 271 Bettmann/CORBIS; 272 Andreas Feininger/Time Life Pictures/Getty Images; 274 Melissa Farlow/Getty Images; 278 (l)Library of Congress/CORBIS, (r)Ace Stock Limited/Alamy Images; 280 281 Eclipse Studio; 288 Kirk Aeder/Icon SMI; 290 (t)BananaStock/SuperStock, (b)Brooke Fasani/CORBIS; 293 Timothy A. Clary/AFP/Getty Images; 294 Lou Cappozola/Sports Illustrated; 295 (t)David N. Seelig/Icon SMI, (b)Eric Miller/Reuters/CORBIS; 296 FOXTROT/Bill Amend of UNIVERSAL PRESS SYNDICATE; 297 John Evans; 298 Nick Koon/The Orange County Register; 300 303 AP/Wide World Photos; 304 Chris Trotman/NewSport/CORBIS; 305 CORBIS; 306 Mike Powell/Getty Images; 308 AP/Wide World Photos; 310 Dwight Okita; 322 FOXTROT/Bill Amend of UNIVERSAL PRESS SYNDICATE; 323 File photo; 326 328 David

Nicholls/CORBIS; 336 King Features Syndicate, Reprinted with special permission; 337 Paul Barton/CORBIS; 338 Courtesy of Daniel Keyes; 341 Spencer Grant/PhotoEdit; 343 PhotoFest; 344 Amanita Pictures; 345 Frithjof Hirdes/zefa/CORBIS; 347 Archive Pictures; 348 Erik Dreyer/Stone/Getty Images; 350 Archive Pictures; 352 Amanita Pictures; 356 Science Museum/SSPL/The Image Works; 358 Amanita Pictures; 359 Science Museum/SSPL/The Image Works; 361 Ramon Manent/Courtesy of Museum of Textil y de la indumentaria/CORBIS; 363 Amanita Pictures; 365 Movie Still Archives; 369 George Steinmetz/CORBIS; 371 Diana Ong/SuperStock; 372 Kodansha Ltd. 1986; 373 C Squared Studios/Getty Images; 377 Imagestopshop/Alamy Images; 378 Science Museum/SSPL/The Image Works; 386 Zits Partnership, Reprinted with Permission of King Features Syndicate; 387 RubberBall/SuperStock; 388 Courtesy of Linda Bickerstaff; 390 Marc Rosenthal/eStock Photo/Alamy Images; 391 Hulton Archive/Getty Images; 392 Charles & Josette Lenars/CORBIS; 394 (t)Dr. Kessel & Dr. Kardon/Tissues & Organs/Visuals Unlimited, (b)Chris McGrath/Getty Images; 396 Marc Rosenthal/eStock Photo/Alamy Images; 398 (t)Nancy Crampton, (b)Leapfrog Press; 406 Patricia Beck/Detroit Free Press. Image courtesy of Emilia Askari; 407 Peter Turnley/CORBIS; 409 Lon C. Diehl/PhotoEdit; 410 Ingo Jezierski/Getty Images; 411 David Sacks/The Image Bank/Getty Images; 412 Susan Van Etten/PhotoEdit; 414 AP/Wide World Photos; 415 Reuters/CORBIS; 418 AP/Wide World Photos; 422 (l)Bettmann/CORBIS, (r)Eureka Productions; 423 through 433 Eureka Productions; 434 435 Eclipse Studios; 442 Julie Nicholls/CORBIS; 444 (l)Peter Barrett/Masterfile, (r)Dann Tardif/CORBIS; 447 Patrick Kennedy/Natural Selection; 448 Reprinted with Permission of King Features Syndicate; 449 DK Stock/Getty Images; 450 Courtesy of Kate Schmitt; 452 through 454 CORBIS; 459 Steve Mason/Getty Images; 460 Malcolm Piers/Photographer's Choice/Getty Images; 461 Brand X/Punchstock; 462 Steve Mason/Getty Images; 466 468 King Features Syndicate Reprinted with special permission; 469 Rob Lewine/CORBIS; 470 Schomburg Center for Research in Black Culture; 472 Amistad Research Center, Tulane University; 473 National Portrait Gallery, Smithsonian Institution/Art Resource, NY; 474 (t)Amistad Research Center, Tulane University, (b)National Portrait Gallery, Smithsonian Institution/Art Resource, NY; 476 AP/Wide World Photos; 478 480 David Sanger; 482 FOXTROT/Bill Amend of UNIVERSAL PRESS SYNDICATE; 483 File photo; 484 Frank Trapper/CORBIS; 487 (t)Siede Preis/Getty Images, (b)James Keyser/Time Life Pictures/Getty Images; 488 James Keyser/Time Life Pictures/Getty Images; 490 Oscar White/CORBIS; 492 494 CNAC/MNAM/Reunion des Musees Nationaux/Art Resource, NY; 499 REAL LIFE ADVENTURES/GarLanco of UNIVERSAL PRESS SYNDICATE; 500 Zits Partnership, Reprinted with Permission of King Features Syndicate; 501 File photo; 502 FPG/Getty Images; 505 Art Resources; 506 Art Resources; 510 Jason Todd/Getty Images; 511 D. Hurst/Alamy Images; 513 514 Jason Todd/Getty Images; 518 Jeff Newton/Penguin Young Readers Group; 520 Mirrorpix/Getty Images; 523 Christophe Calais/In Visu/CORBIS; 524 Joe Raedle/Getty Images; 526 F. Damm/zefa/CORBIS; 527 Liba Taylor/CORBIS; 528 (t)Joe Raedle/Getty Images, (b)Liba Taylor/CORBIS; 532 Photo By Chris Conforti. Image courtesy of Yaedi Ignatow; 533 Christie's Images/CORBIS; 534 535 Eclipse Studios; 534 Ken Krull; 542 Gandee Vason/Getty Images; 544 (t)Noel Hendrickson/Getty Images, (b)Janeart/Getty Images; 548 Howard Grey/Getty Images; 550 CORBIS; 552 Under The Light/CORBIS; 553 Ottfried Schreiter/Imagebroker/Alamy Images; 556 Harry Bartlett/Taxi/Getty Images; 558 LUCKY COW/Mark Pett. Dist. By UNIVERSAL PRESS SYNDICATE; 559 WireImageStock/Masterfile; 560 Linnea Due; 562 Mike Powell/Allsport Concepts/Getty Images; 563 Jim Cummins/CORBIS; 567 Tim Pannell/CORBIS; 568 Digital Vision/Getty Images; 569 Mike Powell/Allsport Concepts/Getty Images; 570 Jim Cummins/CORBIS; 574 Sean Murphy/Stone/Getty Images; 575 Michael Newman/PhotoEdit; 578 Sean Murphy/Stone/Getty Images; 584 Reprinted with Permission of King Features Syndicate; 585 Rubberball/SuperStock; 588 Bob Burch/Index Stock Imagery; 589 Cleve Bryant/PhotoEdit; 590 Terrence Spencer/Time Life Pictures/Getty Images; 591 Vicky Kasala/Getty Images;
592 Bob Burch/Index Stock Imagery; 594 Gayl Heinz/William Morris Agency, LLC; 596 Smithsonian American Art Museum, Washington, DC/Art Resource, NY; 598 Butler Institute of American Art, Youngstown, OH/Gift of the Friends of American Art 1975/Bridgeman Art Library; 600 Jim Arbogast/Digital Vision/Getty Images; 602 Butler Institute of American Art, Youngstown, OH/Gift of the Friends of American Art 1975/Bridgeman Art Library; 604 CALVIN AND HOBBES/Bill Watterson. Dist. By UNIVERSAL PRESS SYNDICATE; 605 File photo; 608 David T. Vernon Collection of Native American Indian Center/Colter Bay Indian Arts Museum/Grand Teton National Park; 609 Tom Bean/CORBIS; 610 Doug Martin; 613 Christie's Images; 614 Werner Forman Archive/British Museum, London/Art Resource, NY; 615 A & L Sinibaldi/Stone/Getty Images; 617 Kam Mak/SIS; 618 David T. Vernon Collection of Native American Indian Center/Colter Bay Indian Arts Museum/Grand Teton National Park; 620 Courtesy of Emily Costello; 622 Kirk Aeder/Icon SMI/CORBIS; 623 Carlo Allegri/Getty Images; 624 Scott Gries/Getty Images; 625 CORBIS; 626 Kirk Aeder/Icon SMI/CORBIS; 629 Zits Partnership of King Features Syndicate; 633 CALVIN AND HOBBES/Bill Watterson. Dist. By UNIVERSAL PRESS SYNDICATE; 634 Zits Partnership of King Features Syndicate; 635 Brent Turner; 636 Will Shively; 638 Ric Ergenbright/CORBIS; 639 Masaaki Toyoura/Getty Images; 640 Getty Images; 642 Jeffrey Coolidge/The Images Bank; 647 Peter Johnson/CORBIS; 648 649 Wilfried Krecichwost/Getty Images; 650 Ric Ergenbright/CORBIS; 652 (t)Jamie Painter Young/CORBIS, (b)Getty Images; 654 Michael Daniel; 656 Martha Swope; 659 AP/Wide World Photos; 660 Michael Daniel; 664 Bettmann/CORBIS; 665 Douglas Grundy/Getty Images; 667 Ron Chapple/Thinkstock/JupiterImages/Comstock Images; 669 Mary Evans Picture Library; 670 MedioImages; 671 American Stock/Hulton Archive/Getty Images; 673 Mary Evans Picture Library; 674 Gary Gianni; 675 through 684 Eureka Productions; 688 American Stock Photography/Retrofile.com; 689 American Stock Photography/Retrofile.com; 692 Carl & Ann Purcell; 697 Richard T. Nowitz; 700 701 Eclipse Studios; 708 Tim de Waele/CORBIS; 710 (l)SuperStock, (r)SW Productions/Getty Images; 713 Handout/Reuters/CORBIS; 718 POPPERFOTO/Alamy Images; 721 Getty Images; 727 The Granger Collection, NY; 732 BALDO/Baldo Partnership. Dist. By UNIVERSAL PRESS SYNDICATE; 733 File photo; 734 UPI/Bettmann/CORBIS; 737 Getty Images; 745 Getty Images; 750 The Granger Collection, NY; 757 Getty Images; 762 Handout/Reuters/CORBIS; 764 AKG-images; 767 Reuters/CORBIS; 773 Michael Matisse/Getty Images; 784 AKG-images; 787 Handout/Reuters/CORBIS; 788 Reuters/CORBIS; 794 CORNERED/Mike Baldwin of UNIVERSAL PRESS SYNDICATE; 795 Rubberball/SuperStock; 796 Getty Images; 799 The Granger Collection, NY; 808 Ingram Publishing/Alamy Images; 811 The Granger Collection, NY; 815 Hugh Threlfall/Alamy Images; 818 Getty Images; 822 The Granger Collection, NY; 824 827 AKG-images; 835 Hulton-Deutsch Collection/CORBIS; 841 Bettmann/CORBIS; 842 Getty Images; 844 AKG-images; 846 CALVIN AND HOBBES/Bill Watterson. Dist. By UNIVERSAL PRESS SYNDICATE; 847 Laura Sifferlin; 848 Ray Tamarra/Getty Images; 852 Getty Images; 856 Brad Mitchell/Alamy Images; 858 (t)Getty Images, (b)Brad Mitchell/Alamy Images; 863 Farrell Grehan/CORBIS; 865 Mika Grondahl; 866 Farrell Grehan/CORBIS; 869 CALVIN AND HOBBES 1989 Bill Watterson. Dist. By UNIVERSAL PRESS SYNDICATE; 871 REAL LIFE ADVENTURES/GarLanco of UNIVERSAL PRESS SYNDICATE; 872 LUCKY COW/Mark Pett. Dist. By UNIVERSAL PRESS SYNDICATE; 873 Tim Thompson/CORBIS; 877 878 Gary Conner/Index Stock Imagery; 880 The Montana Standard/AP/Wide World Photos; 884 Bettmann/CORBIS; 886 Hulton-Deutsch Collection/CORBIS; 888 Bettmann/CORBIS; 892 Ouida Sebestyen; 893 Bob Daemmrich/The Image Works; 895 David H. Wells/CORBIS; 898 Yvonne Boyd/IPN Stock; 902 J. David Andrews/Masterfile; 904 Creatas/PhotoLibrary; 905 Yoham Kahana/Shooting Star; 907 Christian Pierre/SuperStock; 908 (t)Bob Daemmrich/The Image Works, (b)Christian Pierre/SuperStock; 911 Laura DeSantis/Getty Images; 912 (l)Matt Valentine/Valentine Photography, (r)Paul Edmondson/Getty Images; 914 915 Eclipse Studios; 922 Colin Bootman/Bridgeman Art Library; 924 CORBIS; 927 Plush Studios/Photographer's Choice/Getty Images; 928 Garry Gay/The Image Bank/Getty Images; 930 Zits Partnership of King Features Syndicate; 931 John Evans; 932 McClelland & Stewart; 934 John A Rizzo/Getty Images; 936 JW/Masterfile; 938 CORBIS; 940 John A Rizzo/Getty Images; 942 William F. Campbell/Time Life Pictures/Getty Images;

944 AP/Wide World Photos; 945 Jeff Greenberg/PhotoEdit; 946 CORBIS; 949 Hulton Archive/Getty Images; 950 AP/Wide World Photos; 956 STONE SOUP/Jan Eliot of UNIVERSAL PRESS SYNDICATE; 957 Kevin Peterson/Getty Images; 958 Wally McNamee/CORBIS; 960 CORBIS; 961 Flip Schulke/CORBIS; 962 Rosebud Pictures/Taxi/Getty Images; 963 Bryan F. Peterson; 964 CORBIS; 966 AP/Wide World Photos; 968 Bettmann/CORBIS; 970 AP/Wide World Photos; 971 974 Bettmann/CORBIS; 976 Reprinted with permission of King Features Syndicate; 977 Kevin Peterson; 978 Don Perdue/The NewsHour with Jim Lehrer and MacNeil Lehrer Productions; 980 ThinkStock LLC/Index Stock Imagery; 982 Robert Daly/Stone/Getty Images; 984 ThinkStock LLC/Index Stock Imagery; 988 990 Tony Pearce; 994 Zits Partnership of King Features Syndicate; 995 Reprinted with permission of King Features Syndicate; 998 FOXTROT/Bill Amend of UNIVERSAL PRESS SYNDICATE; 999 File photo; 1006 Ruth Wright Paulsen; 1008 Courtesy of H. Avery Chenowith and the United States Marine Corps Art Collection; 1010 Lucia Gallery, NY; 1013 Ernest Manewal/FPG; 1016 Courtesy of H. Avery Chenowith and the United States Marine Corps Art Collection; 1021 AP/Wide World Photos; 1022 Tony Freeman/PhotoEdit; 1024 H. Scheibe/zefa/CORBIS; 1025 Photographer's Choice/Getty Images; 1026 Courtesy of Emily Sohn; 1027 Miles/zefa/CORBIS; 1028 CORBIS; 1030 (t)CORBIS, (b)George D. Lepp/CORBIS; 1032 AP/Wide World Photos; 1036 Courtesy Harper Collins Publishers; 1039 Bridgeman Art Library; 1040 H. Scheibe/zefa/CORBIS; 1042 Christopher Cormack/CORBIS; 1043 Russell Leach; 1044 1045 Eclipse Studios; 1052 Bill Ross/CORBIS; 1054 (l)CORBIS, (r)Doug Martin; 1059 The King Mural By Don Miller District of Columbia Public Library; 1061 FPG; 1063 Bob Adelman/Magnum Photos; 1064 Reprinted with permission of King Features Syndicate; 1065 John Evans; 1066 Miriam Berkley; 1068 TRI-STAR/The Kobal Collection; 1069 (t)blickwinkel/Alamy Images, (b)Alyson Aliano/Getty Images; 1070 Content Mine International/Alamy Images; 1072 TRI-STAR/The Kobal Collection; 1074 Marian Goldman; 1077 Roger-Viollet/Topham/The Image Works; 1078 Bettmann/CORBIS; 1079 CORBIS; 1080 Roger-Viollet/Topham/The Image Works; 1084 Reprinted with permission of King Features Syndicate; 1086 Zits Partnership of King Features Syndicate; 1087 Laura Sifferlin; 1088 Bankrate.com, N. Palm Beach, FL 2006; 1090 (t)Getty Images, (b)CORBIS; 1092 Blend Images/SuperStock; 1094 Getty Images; 1096 Bettmann/CORBIS; 1099 From the original painting by Mort Kunstler, "The Angle." © 1988 Mort Kunstler, Inc.; 1100 Mort Kunstler, Collection of Mr. & Mrs. Robert L. Sharpe; 1102 FOXTROT/Bill Amend of UNIVERSAL PRESS SYNDICATE; 1103 File photo; 1104 Jacqueling Nwaiwu; 1106 Terry Vine/Getty Images; 1108 Bridgeman Art Library; 1110 Terry Vine/Getty Images; 1112 AP/Wide World Photos; 1114 SuperStock; 1116 Bettmann/CORBIS; 1118 Dagli Orti/Ara Collection Paris/The Art Archive; 1120 CORBIS; 1121 Library of Congress, Prints & Photographs Division #LC-USZ62-123456; 1123 Hulton Archive/Getty Images; 1124 L Hobbs/PhotoLink; 1125 AKG-images; 1126 SuperStock; 1131 Zits Partnership of King Features Syndicate; 1132 FOXTROT/Bill Amend of UNIVERSAL PRESS SYNDICATE; 1133 John Evans; 1134 Schomburg Center for Research in Black Culture; 1136 Smithsonian American Art Museum, Washington, DC/Art Resource, NY; 1138 Smithsonian American Art Museum, Washington, DC/Art Resource, NY; 1140 Satelight/Gamma Liaison/Getty Images; 1142 Owen Franken/CORBIS; 1144 Réunion des Musées Nationaux/Art Resource, NY; 1147 Marc Volk/Getty Images; 1149 Christophe Courteau/TMC/SuperStock; 1150 Marc Volk/Getty Images; 1155 AP/Wide World Photos; 1156 Bettmann/CORBIS; 1157 Erin Patrice O'Brien; 1158 Jason Dewey; 1159 Gerard Gaskin; 1161 Marianne Szegedy-Maszak; 1164 C. Borland/PhotoLink /Getty Images; 1165 Eric Draper/AP/Wide World Photos; 1166 (t)AP/Wide World Photos, (b)Eric Draper/AP/Wide World Photos; 1170 (l)courtesy of Caxton Press, (r)Masterfile; 1172 CORBIS; 1174 1175 Eclipse Studio.